Here's what people are saying about
THE SCRIBNER-BANTAM ENGLISH DICTIONARY

"Succinct, no-nonsense definitions . . . very useful."
—*Carlos Baker*

"It sets a new record for the most clear, precise definitions per cubic inch."
—*Herbert S. Bailey, Jr., Princeton University Press*

"Possesses the virtues of simplicity, easy pronunciation symbols, and a range of coverage from sachems to think-tanks, from cutthroats to cybernetics. The printing is remarkably readable."
—*Loren Eiseley*

"Commands an immediate advantage over its competitors by including the newest words and phrases . . . Best of all is the dictionary's layout. . . . The editors have gone out of their way to simplify definitions."
—*John Barkham Syndicate*

"The editors have done very well . . . A prefatory 'Guide to the Dictionary' is so thorough that it could almost serve as a miniature introduction to lexicography."
—*Library Journal*

"Straightforward definitions . . . readability . . . up-to-the-minute."
—*Herbert Mitgang, The New York Times*

"A monument to common sense in defining English words and in revealing their richness and variety."
—*Henry F. Graff, Columbia University*

Edwin B. Williams
General Editor

Christopher Stavrou
Associate General Editor

Sebastiano DiBlasi
Senior Editor

Associate Editors:

James E. Iannucci

Robert C. Melzi

Roger J. Steiner

John C. Traupman

Walter D. Glanze
Managing Editor

REVISED EDITION

THE SCRIBNER-BANTAM ENGLISH DICTIONARY

EDWIN B. WILLIAMS
GENERAL EDITOR

Revised Bantam edition / August 1979
1979
1980
1980

Published simultaneously in the United States and Canada

Hardcover edition published as
The Scribner-Bantam English Dictionary

United States paperback edition published as
The Scribner-Bantam English Dictionary

THE NEW BANTAM ENGLISH DICTIONARY
A Bantam Book

PRINTING HISTORY
Scribner edition originally published 1977
Revised Bantam edition/August 1979
2nd printing .... August 1979
3rd printing .... February 1980
4th printing .... June 1980

ISBN 0–553–14408–1

Published simultaneously in the United States and Canada

Bantam Books are published by Bantam Books, Inc. Its trademark, consisting of the words "Bantam Books" and the portrayal of a bantam, is Registered in U.S. Patent and Trademark Office and in other countries. Marca Registrada. Bantam Books, Inc., 666 Fifth Avenue, New York, New York 10019.

PRINTED IN THE UNITED STATES OF AMERICA

13 12 11 10 9 8 7 6 5 4

FOREWORD TO THE REVISED EDITION

THE SCRIBNER-BANTAM ENGLISH DICTIONARY is the latest addition to Bantam's series of original dictionaries. The editors, under the guidance of the renowned lexicographer Edwin B. Williams, wanted to create a different kind of dictionary, a dictionary that is not only precise and up to date but that is written in good English. A teaching dictionary. The editors seem to have succeeded: When the dictionary was published two years ago, as a Scribner hardcover book under Bantam's license, it was praised widely for the clarity and beauty of its language.

The revised edition includes, again, many words and phrases that have never before appeared in an English dictionary, ranging from *meltdown* and *hahnium* (atomic number 105) to *gas-guzzler* and *nerd*, from *videocassette recorder* and *spacefaring* to *Native American* and *Zimbabwe-Rhodesia*. Such new entries, with other improvements, will further contribute to making THE SCRIBNER-BANTAM ENGLISH DICTIONARY the most useful portable guide to the English language today.

MARCUS H. JAFFE, *1979*

FROM THE FOREWORD TO THE FIRST EDITION

The definitions in this dictionary stick in one's mind because one understands them on first reading. They flow like the spoken answer of a teacher or expert who is practiced in the art of removing the questioner's doubt or ignorance. Dip into the book at random and see for yourself the skill with which even subtle or complex ideas have been made clear....

THE SCRIBNER-BANTAM ENGLISH DICTIONARY contains numerous features which will enable the user to speak and write better. The style of the definitions is a writing lesson in itself, and it also demonstrates how American English at its best can combine lucidity and power. It is a joy to read—a claim that can rarely be made for a dictionary. One finds oneself browsing in its pages for the pleasure of good reading while acquiring knowledge of many kinds at the same time.

Charles Scribner's Sons has been publishing for more than 130 years the writings of American authors, as well as many books about the American experience. We are proud of our role in the nation's cultural life over that span of time and we are conscious now of making an important contribution to that life and to our tradition by associating ourselves with Bantam Books in publishing this remarkable new dictionary of our language.

CHARLES SCRIBNER, JR., *1977*

CONTENTS

Foreword	5a
Staff and Consultants	6a
A Guide to the Dictionary	8a
Pronunciation Key	33a
Abbreviations Used in This Dictionary	38a
ENGLISH DICTIONARY	1–1057
Principal Languages of the World	1058
Indo-European Languages	1060
Foreign Alphabets	1062
Proofreader's Marks	1064
Weights and Measures	
Equivalents	1066
Conversions	1071
Roman Numerals	1074
Forms of Address	1075

A GUIDE TO THE DICTIONARY

by Walter D. Glanze

THE SCRIBNER-BANTAM ENGLISH DICTIONARY is easy to use. All the important information is right there with the word the reader is looking up. He or she is not expected to study the rules to understand the elements of an entry and their order. The reader can rely on common sense and the Dictionary's consistency not only to see how a word is spelled, how it is pronounced, and what it means, but also to understand its hyphenation, its origin, its various forms, its use in phrases, its synonyms.

And yet this Dictionary can be used more effectively and can be more enjoyed by the reader who is thoroughly familiar with its many features and the editorial principles behind them. Studying this guide will be worth the effort.

This is not a lexicographical treatise. Some of the subjects are a little more technical than others, but the language remains simple and direct.

This guide is divided into the following sections and paragraphs.

1. BASIC RULES 1.1 Order 1.2 Main Entry 1.3 Pronunciation 1.4 Etymology 1.5 Part-of-Speech Labels 1.6 Irregular Inflections 1.7 Definitions 1.8 Run-On Entries 1.9 Synonyms 1.10 Truncation

2. SENSE DIVISION AND IDIOMS 2.1 Numbers and Letters 2.2 Position of Subject and Usage Labels 2.3 Order of Senses 2.4 Order of Idioms

3. THE MAIN ENTRY 3.1 Alphabetical Order 3.2 Forms of Main Entries 3.3 Homographs 3.4 Spaced and Hyphenated Compounds 3.5 Combining Forms 3.6 Entry Words That Have Meaning Only in a Phrase

4. SYLLABIFICATION 4.1 Syllable Markers 4.2 Syllabification and Pronunciation 4.3 End-of-Line Breaks 4.4 Attachment of Truncated Forms

5. PRONUNCIATION 5.1 Location 5.2 English Words 5.3 Foreign Words 5.4 Stress and Accent Marks 5.5 Syllable Breaks 5.6 Alternate Pronunciation 5.7 Truncated and Omitted Pronunciation 5.8 Pronunciation Treated in Other Sections

6. ETYMOLOGY 6.1 General 6.2 Symbols and Abbreviations 6.3 Types of Etymologies 6.4 Special Etymologies

7. PARTS OF SPEECH 7.1 Types of Labels 7.2 Position of Part-of-Speech Labels 7.3 Verb Labels 7.4 Changes in Part of Speech 7.5 Changes from Singular to Plural 7.6 Changes in Capitalization and Use of Article 7.7 Entries without Part-of-Speech Labels

8. INFLECTED FORMS 8.1 Regular and Irregular Inflections 8.2 Nouns 8.3 Verbs 8.4 Modal Auxiliaries 8.5 Adjectives 8.6 Pronouns

9. RUN-ON ENTRIES 9.1 General 9.2 Meaning 9.3 Pronunciation 9.4 Attributive Forms 9.5 Names of States of the U.S.

10. CROSS REFERENCES AND VARIANTS 10.1 Types of Cross References 10.2 Types of Variants 10.3 Homographs 10.4 Pronunciation 10.5 Etymology 10.6 Inflected Forms 10.7 Synonyms

11. USAGE INFORMATION 11.1 Types of Information 11.2 Subject Labels 11.3 Usage Labels 11.4 Other Qualifying Terms 11.5 Usage Notes in Definitions 11.6 Explanatory Examples 11.7 Objects and Subjects in Parentheses 11.8 Singular and Plural Labels

12. SYNONYMS, DISCRIMINATIONS, AND ANTONYMS 12.1 General 12.2 Parts of Speech 12.3 Discriminations 12.4 Cross References

13. SPECIAL ENTRIES 13.1 Elements 13.2 Chemicals 13.3 Animals and Plants 13.4 Geographical Names 13.5 Biographical Entries 13.6 Fictional Names

14. GENERAL

1. BASIC RULES

1.1 Order. The principal elements of an entry follow a strict order:

  main entry
  pronunciation
  etymology
  part-of-speech labels
  irregular inflections
  definitions
  run-on entries
  synonyms

Example:

  think /thiŋk′/ [OE *thencan*] *v* (**thought**) *vi* **1** to mediate, ponder; reason; **2** to have an opinion or judgment...|| *vt* **7** to form in the mind...**14 think up** to devise by thinking || **think′er** *n* || SYN conceive, meditate, believe...

1.2 Main Entry. The main entry and its spelling variants are set in boldface. Orthographic division is shown by raised dots or, if no complete pronunciation is given, by heavy and light accent marks. Homographs are followed by raised numbers. See section 3, page 11a.

1.3 Pronunciation. Pronunciation is shown between slant lines, with heavy and light accent marks. See section 5, page 14a.

1.4 Etymology. Etymology is given in brackets; the etymon is set in italics, the translation in roman type. Reference to other main entries for etymological information is made through words in boldface or italics. See section 6, page 17a.

1.5 Part-of-Speech Labels. Part-of-speech labels are set in italics. The first label comes after the etymology. Labels that mark changes in part of speech or changes in the function of verbs are preceded by parallels. See section 7, page 19a.

1.6 Irregular Inflections. Irregular inflections are shown in parentheses. Like main entries, they are set in boldface with orthographic division and

can be followed by pronunciation. See section 8, page 22a.

1.7 Definitions. For order, subdivision, and idioms, see section 2. For changes in part of speech, see section 7, page 19a. For cross references, see section 10, page 26a. For subject and usage labels and other information on usage, see section 11, page 28a.

1.8 Run-On Entries. Run-on entries (namely, undefined derivatives) are preceded by parallels. Like main entries, they are set in boldface with orthographic division and are followed by part-of-speech labels; also, they can be followed by pronunciation and irregular inflections (which, in turn, have boldface type, division, and sometimes pronunciation). See section 9, page 25a.

1.9 Synonyms. Synonyms, discrimination of synonyms, and antonyms are introduced by the abbreviations SYN, DISCR, and ANT in small capital letters, and each of these abbreviations is preceded by parallels. Part-of-speech labels can follow the abbreviations SYN and ANT. Main entries referred to under SYN and ANT are set in italics and in parentheses. See section 12, page 30a.

1.10 Truncation. Truncated (shortened) forms instead of the full forms are often used for irregular inflections, entry variants, pronunciation, and etymologies. In these cases the full form is evident from closely preceding information or from other entries where the full form or its component parts are listed:

  sim′pli·fy′...(**-fied**)...
  phy·lum /fil′əm/... (**-la** /-lə/)...
  ec·o·log·ic (**-i·cal**)...
  stat′u·esque′ /-esk′/...
  tear′drop′ /tir′-/...
  Hi·a·wath·a /hī′əwô∂′thə, -wä′-/...
  life /līf′/...(**lives** /-vz/)...
  sleight′ of hand′ /slīt′/...
  per·ma·nent...[L *permanens* (*-entis*)]...

2. SENSE DIVISION AND IDIOMS

2.1 Numbers and Letters. When an entry has more than one sense, the senses are numbered throughout the entry regardless of changes in part of speech and other variations. Numbered senses can be further divided by small letters. Numbers and letters are in boldface type, and the senses and subsenses they mark are separated by semicolons:

  crea·ture...*n* **1** anything created; **2** living being; **3** one who is the tool or agent of another

  ac·id...*adj* **3** sharp, biting, or sour in taste, manner, mood, or nature; **4 a** of, pert. to, or yielding acid; **b** containing an excessive amount of acid; **5** *geol* having much silica...

The subdividing letters are placed after an idiom, with a comma before a:

time...28 in time, a eventually; b not late; c in the correct tempo; 29 keep time, a to record the passing time, as a clock; b to fill waiting time with some activity...

2.1.1 The subdividing letters are occasionally placed within a sense:

or·a·cle...n 1 in ancient Greece, a reply, often ambiguous, of a god...; b agency transmitting such replies; c place where they were given...
an·nex...n 4 something annexed, as a an auxiliary building or b a section added to a document

2.1.2 Closely related meanings within a sense or subsense are separated by semicolons; and meanings that are almost synonymous are separated by commas:

tar·ry¹...vi 1 to stay in a place for a time; to delay, linger; 2 to wait

2.1.3 The most important sense dividers are the parallels, which indicate changes in part of speech and function of verb. See section 7.

As mentioned in 1.8 and 1.9, parallels also mark run-on entries, synonyms, discriminations of snyonyms, and antonyms. See sections 9 and 12.

2.1.4 Summary of sense dividers, in descending importance: Parallels; boldface numbers, boldface letters; semicolons, commas.

2.1.5 Reference from one entry to a numbered sense of another entry is explained in 10.1.6.

2.2 Position of Subject and Usage Labels. Subject and usage labels are set in italics (11.2, 11.3). Their position indicates which definitions they apply to.

(a) If the label stands before 1, it applies to all the senses of the entry:

Ju·dah...n Bib 1 a son of...; 2 one of the 12 tribes...; 3 Hebrew kingdom...
ain't...substandard 1 am not, is not, or are not; 2 have not or has not
Tri·as·sic...geol adj 1 designating or pert. to a period of the Mesozoic era...‖ n 2 the Triassic period

(b) If the label stands after a number, it applies to all that follows up to the next number (or parallels):

neu·ter...adj 1 gram pert. to the gender which is neither masculine nor feminine; 2 entom without

fully developed reproductive organs in adult life; 3 castrated; sterile; 4 bot sexless, having neither pistils nor stamens; 5 taking no sides; neutral...
crunch...n...3 colloq a financial stress and strain; b stress and strain of any kind ‖...

(c) If the label stands after a letter, it applies to all that follows up to the next letter or the next number (or parallels):

wrap...vt...5 wrap up, a to wrap something; b colloq to conclude, finish; c slang to damage by collision ‖...

2.2.1 The rules of (b) and (c) apply also to run-on entries. See section 9.

2.3 Order of Senses. In general, the senses are arranged according to the frequency of their use. Thus, any part of speech or function of verb can precede or follow the others, and each one begins with its most important sense.

2.3.1 Labeled senses can precede or follow nonlabeled senses, as in neuter in 2.2b.

2.3.2 Within each part of speech or function of verb, senses with changes in inflection or changes in capitalization and use of the article (7.5, 7.6), are generally placed after the other senses but always before the idioms (as before the idiom by the numbers, below). Senses with changes in inflection (as numbers) precede senses with changes in capitalization or use of the article (as the numbers):

num·ber...n...10 gram category of certain word classes (principally nouns in English) which indicates whether one or more than one are referred to; 11 numbers pl a considerable amount; b obs arithmetic; 12 the numbers numbers game; 13 by the numbers, a in unison to...‖ vt 16 to ascertain the number of...

2.4 Order of Idioms. Certain groups of words have a collective meaning that is not immediately clear because it is more than the sum of the meanings of the individual words, as give the shaft to in the sense of to betray or to sell out. There are other commonly used groups of words whose meaning is more obvious, as taste of and take off. In this guide both categories of phrases are referred to as idioms.

2.4.1 An idiom is generally listed under its most significant word. For example, give the shaft to appears under shaft, not under give. Some idioms are listed twice: with might and main appears under might and again under main.

2.4.2 Idioms are set in boldface. They are listed in alphabetical order within a part of speech or function of verb and are placed after the other senses, with continuing sense numbers:

do[1]...v...vt...8 to swindle; 9 to serve (a term of imprisonment); 10 **do in** slang a to kill; b to ruin; 11 **do out of** slang to cheat out of; 12 **do time** colloq to serve a prison term; 13 **do up** colloq a to wrap up; b to fix (the hair); c to clothe ‖ vi 14 to act, conduct oneself; 15 to fare; 16 to suffice; answer the purpose; 17 **do away with,** a to put an end to; b to kill; 18 **do or die** to extend oneself to the utmost; 19 **do with** to require, make use of; 20 **do without** to forgo: be able to dispense with; 21 **have to do with** to have a connection with; 22 **make do** to get along with whatever is available ‖ v aux...

An idiom can be a complete sentence:

size[2]...n...3 that's about the size of it colloq that is the actual fact of the matter...

2.4.3 An idiom is not given under the part of speech in which it would function as a unit in a sentence, but under the part of speech that the entry word has in the idiom. For example, the

head...n...18 **come to a head** to reach a crisis...‖ vt...35 **head off** to intercept, get in front of ‖ vi...

come to a head appears with nouns, not verbs, because **head** is used as a noun in this idiom, whereas **head off** appears with verbs because **head** is used as a verb in this idiom. (Both idioms have verb functions when used in a sentence.) In the example

know...v...vt...‖ vi...‖ n 8 **in the know** colloq having knowledge of a particular situation

in the know appears under n, not v, because **know** is used as a noun in this idiom.

2.4.4 A phrase like **taste of,** consisting of a verb plus a preposition, is used with an object ("This wine tastes of vinegar") and therefore this phrase as a whole is transitive; but the verb **taste** itself is intransitive here. (See also 7.3.2.) Consequently, such phrases are entered under intransitive verbs:

taste...vt...‖ vi...7 **taste of,** a to eat or drink a little of; b to smack of...

2.4.5 Phrases consisting of a verb plus an adverb (or a verb plus a preposition used as an adverb) can be transitive or intransitive. For example, the phrase **take off** is transitive in the sentence "She took off her gloves" because it has an object, "her gloves," but the same phrase is intransitive in the sentence "The airplane took off" because here it does not have an object. Accordingly, **take off** is listed twice, as is **make up** in the second example:

take...vt...49 **take off,** a to remove; b to deduct; c colloq to burlesque...‖ vi...59 **take off,** a colloq to depart; b to leave the ground, as an airplane...

make...vt...28 **make up,** a to put together; constitute; b to invent; c to arrange; d to repeat (a course one has failed in or an exam one has missed) ‖ vi...39 **make up,** a to become reconciled; b to dress in costume and put on make-up for a part in a play; c to apply make-up...

Therefore, if such a phrase or a particular sense of such a phrase cannot be found under one function of verb, the reader should look under another function of verb in the same entry.

2.4.6 Compound nouns, namely, combinations of two or more nouns or of an adjective and a noun, such as **sky marshal** or **absolute zero,** are listed as main entries, along with other types of spaced and hyphenated compounds. See 3.4.

3. THE MAIN ENTRY

3.1 Alphabetical Order. All main entries are in one alphabetical list: General vocabulary, parts of words, abbreviations, foreign words and phrases, proper names, etc.

3.1.1 All main entries are alphabetized letter by letter, without regard to the spaces between words, as in the position of ex libris:

ex·it...
ex li·bris...
ex·o-...
ex'o·bi·ol'o·gy...

o·paque...
op' art'...
op. cit....
OPEC...

3.1.2 Saints and entries derived from saints' names are placed as follows:

A·qui·nas..., Saint Thomas...
Je·rome, Saint...

Saint' Ber·nard'/...dog...
Saint' Pat'rick's Day'...

St.' Law'rence Riv'er...
St.' Paul'...capital of Minnesota...

3.2 Forms of Main Entries. The main entry and its spelling variants are set in boldface. Orthographic division is shown by raised dots or, if no complete pronunciation is given, by heavy and light accent marks. The main entry has one of the following shapes.

(a) It can be a word or a solid compound:

    stu·dent...
    ex′o·bi·ol′o·gy...
    count′down′...

(b) It can be a hyphenated or spaced compound (3.4):

    see′-through′...
    black′ hole′...
    no′-fault in·sur′ance...
    straight′ from the shoul′der...

(c) It can be a combining form (3.5):

    pre-...pref...
    -tion...n suf...
    ster-e-o-...comb form...
    -to-be...adj comb form...

(d) It can be an abbreviation (5.7.4, 7.7.3, 10.1.5):

    kHz...
    V A T...

3.2.1 For special entries, such as chemical elements and compounds, animals and plants, and proper names, see section 13.

3.2.2 For spelling variants of main entries and cross reference between main entries, see section 10.

3.3 Homographs. Homographs are words that are identical in spelling but different in origin, meaning, and/or pronunciation. They are listed as separate main entries and are followed by raised numbers:

    tear[1] /ter′/ [OE *teran*]...*vt* 1 to pull apart by force, rend...
    tear[2] /tir′/ [OE] *n* 1 small drop of watery liquid secreted by...

3.3.1 If homographs are also homophones, that is, if they are spelled and pronounced alike, the pronunciation is given for the first entry only:

    flag[1] /flag′/ [15th-cent. Eng perh imit of flapping sound] *n* 1 piece of light cloth, bearing a...
    flag[2] [prob < OF *flac* < L *flaccus* flabby]...*vi* 1 to hang loose; 2 to become languid...
    flag[3] [ME *flagge*] *n* any of various plants having...
    flag[4] [ON *flaga*] *n* flagstone

As the accentuation, too, is identical for these entries, no accent marks are given after the first entry:

    se·crete[1] /sikrēt′/ [< *secret*] *vt* to hide or conceal...
    se·crete[2] [L *secernere* (*secretus*) to discern] *vt* to separate or elaborate from blood or sap and make into a new substance...
    sa′vor·y[1] *adj* pleasing to taste or smell; palatable
    sa·vor·y[2] [ME *saverey*] *n* (-ies) fragrant herb...

3.3.2 Homographs are referred to from other main entries by their number:

    borne /bôrn′, bôrn′/ *pp* of bear[2]
    bear[2] [OE *beran*] *v* (bore; borne) *vt*...

If no number is shown, the reference applies to all homographs of the sequence:

    mould /mōld′/ *n*, *vt*, & *vi* var of mold
    mold[1] /mōld′/ [OE *molde* dust] *n* fine soft soil...
    mold[2] [< OF *modle* < L *modulus* measure] *n* 1 hollow form...|| *vt*...
    mold[3] [ME *mowlde*] *n* 1 any of many fungi which...|| *vt* 3 to cover with mold || *vi* 4 to become covered with mold

3.4 Spaced and Hyphenated Compounds. Spaced compounds (as street name) and hyphenated compounds (as air-to-air) are listed as main entries. Most of them consist of words that have a special meaning when used together:

    street′ name′ *n* stockbroker who holds a customer's securities in his own name...
    air′-to-air′ *adj* & *adv* from one aircraft in flight to another

3.4.1 When the individual words are listed elsewhere as main entries, compound entries are not given with pronunciation. But they are always syllabified by raised dots or accent marks (5.7).

3.4.2 All compound entries are followed by part-of-speech labels.

3.4.3 Compounds can be main entries or run-on entries, usually with different hyphenation (9.4):

    straight′ from the shoul′der *adv* directly, without evasion || straight′-from-the-shoul′der *adj*

3.5 Combining Forms. Many main entries begin or end with a hyphen. They are combining forms, used to form solid or hyphenated compounds.

3.5.1 Combining forms are either initial, as

up- *comb form* up, as *uplands*

pre- [L *prae-*] *pref* before in place, time, or standing

or final, as

-man /-mən, -man'/ *comb form* **1** member of a specified nation; **2** one doing a specified kind of work

-n't *comb form* not

-ard /-ərd/ also **-art** /-ərt/ [OF < Gmc] *suf* used to form nouns denoting one with an excess of a quality, usu. pejorative, as *drunkard, braggart*

Certain initial combining forms are labeled *pref* (prefix), and certain final combining forms are labeled *suf* (suffix). There are no objective criteria for making these distinctions. However, the labeling of certain combining forms as prefixes and suffixes is an established practice, which this Dictionary follows.

3.5.2 Many final combining forms, including most that are labeled *suf*, are given with part-of-speech labels. While these combining forms themselves are not parts of speech, the label indicates the part of speech of the compound word in which these forms can be used:

-gen /-jən, also -jen'/ [Gk *genes* born] *n comb form* producing, as *oxygen*

-a·tive /-ətiv/ [L *-ativus*] *adj suf* pert. to, as *decorative*

3.5.3 Combining forms can have most of the features of other entries, as syllabification, spelling variants, pronunciation, etymology, part-of-speech labels, subdivided senses, run-on entries:

-vore /-vôr', -vōr'/ [L *-vorus*] *n comb form* eating, as *carnivore* ‖ **-v·o·rous** /-v(ə)rəs/ *adj comb form,* as *carnivorous*

3.5.4 Compounds in which combining forms are used are either solid or hyphenated. The labels *pref* and *suf* indicate that these forms are added without a hyphen, as the prefix *re-* in *recall.* Whether a form labeled *comb form* is to be added with or without a hyphen can usually be seen (i) from the examples given in the entry itself, as in

-l·o·gy /-ləjē/ [Gk *-logia*] *comb form* **1** science, doctrine, theory, as *zoology;* **2** kind of speaking or writing, as *phraseology*

-sized' *comb form* having a specified size, as *large-sized*

or (ii) from the entries that follow and in which the form is used, as in these two successive entries:

bio- [Gk *bios*] *comb form* life

bi'o·chem'is·try /bī'ō-/ *n* chemistry of living organisms...

3.5.5 The main role of combining forms in this Dictionary is (i) to lead to the meaning of undefined words in which they appear elsewhere, mainly in run-on entries (9.2), (ii) to furnish the missing portions of phonetic transcriptions (1.10, 5.7), and (iii) to lead to the meaning of many words not listed in this Dictionary or, in many cases, in any other dictionary (3.5.6).

3.5.6 The common-sense use of combining forms makes it possible to understand thousands of words that are not in this Dictionary by recognizing their component parts. Such terms are usually of technical nature and often of very recent origin.

For example, it is not difficult to determine the meaning of *xylophagous* as "wood-eating," from the entries **xylo-**, "wood," and **-phagous,** "eating"; or the meaning of *otoscope* as an instrument for the inspection of the ear, from the entries **oto-**, "ear," and **-scope,** "instrument for observing." (There are obvious limits. The complex meaning of a chemical term like **xylose** cannot be fully understood from the meanings of its components, **xylo-,** "wood," and **-ose²,** "carbohydrate or sugar.")

3.5.7 This Dictionary does not include lists of undefined words beginning with such combining forms as **dis-, in-, multi-, non-, out-, over-, re-, un-,** and **under-,** and thereby saves valuable space for complete words and for combining forms that are defined.

3.6 Entry Words That Have Meaning Only in a Phrase. Certain main entries have meaning only in a phrase and are therefore defined in a phrase:

whit...[OE *wiht* thing, creature] *n* not a whit not the least bit

ca·boo·dle...*n* the whole caboodle *slang* the lot of them

smart'en *vt* smarten up, **1** to make stylish or spruce; **2** to make more knowledgeable; **3** to make brisker, as a pace ‖ also *vi*

3.6.1 The same treatment is given to main entries that do have a common meaning but that are entered in this Dictionary only because of their use in a phrase:

door'nail' *n* dead as a doornail dead beyond the shadow of a doubt

silver' spoon' *n* born with a silver spoon in one's mouth born into wealth

3.6.2 Also modal auxiliaries are entries that have meaning only in a phrase. For their treatment see 8.4.

4. SYLLABIFICATION

4.1 Syllable Markers. Main entries, run-on entries, and their spelling variants and irregular inflections are divided into orthographic syllables. The division is shown (i) by raised dots if the entry is followed by complete phonetic transcription, as in

po·lit·i·cal /pəlit′ikəl/ ...

or (ii) by light and heavy accent marks (and raised dots) if the phonetic transcription is not given or is given in truncated form (5.4.2), as in

hu′man·ize′ ...
land′scape′ /-skāp′/ ...

or (iii) by a hyphen at the end of a printed line.

The end-of-line hyphen replaces the raised dot or is put after the accent mark. See the entry **admire.**

4.1.1 When a word is repeated in an entry, syllabification is not shown again if it is unchanged; for example, in idioms (2.4), plurals of spaced compounds (8.2.21), senses with changes in inflection (7.5) or changes in capitalization and in use of the article (7.6):

clo·ver ... 3 in clover ...
pur·su′ant adj & adv pursuant to ...
ac·count′ pay′a·ble ... n (accounts payable) ...
lin·guis′tic ... adj ... ‖ n 3 linguistics sg ...
Eng·lish ... adj ... ‖ n 3 often english billiards ...
op′po·si′tion ... n ... 4 the opposition ...

4.2 Syllabification and Pronunciation. The orthographic division in this Dictionary follows the usual practice of American editors and printers, which is generally the practice adopted by English printers in the eighteenth century. While these principles are partly determined by speech, they have no scientific foundation. They are, however, a necessary and useful convention for breaking words at the end of lines.

In this Dictionary the breaks in the phonetic transcription do not follow this orthographic convention but are based on the realities of the spoken language. See 5.5.2.

4.3 End-of-Line Breaks. A raised dot or an accent mark shows where the writer or printer may put a hyphen at the end of a line. However, there are cases where a word should not be so divided although a syllable division may be shown in the dictionary for the sake of consistent syllabification:

4.3.1 A word should not be divided where a single initial letter or a single final letter would be put on a separate line. For example, a·live and cit·y should not be divided.

4.3.2 Common sense should prevent, where possible, any break that results in misleading grouping of letters or that is odd to the eye, as side·real and non-agenarian or nonage·narian. Better breaks for these examples are si·dereal, sidere·al; nona·genarian, nona·genar·ian, nonagenari·an.

4.3.3 The ending -ed must not be put on a separate line if the e of the ending is not pronounced, that is, if the ending is not preceded by d or t, as in matched or paged. The unpronounced ending is not a syllable and is therefore not set off by a raised dot or accent mark in this Dictionary. If the e is pronounced, -ed is shown as a syllable and may be separated, as in wait·ed. See 8.3.1.

4.4 Attachment of Truncated Forms. One of the functions of a raised dot or an accent mark is to indicate the point where the final syllable is to be detached so that the truncated syllable or syllables of variants and irregular inflections can be added (1.10):

ec·o·log·ic (-i·cal) ... adj ...
so·ci·e·ty ... n ... (-ties) ...
star·ry adj (-ri·er; -ri·est) ...

The hyphen can have the same function for final components:

ad′-lib′ v (-libbed; -lib·bing) vt & vi ...

5. PRONUNCIATION

5.1 Location. Phonetic transcription is shown between slant lines. It follows immediately the word that is transcribed. It can also occur by itself, after parallels, to indicate change in pronunciation for a new part of speech. See 7.4.1.

5.1.1 The symbols of the PRONUNCIATION KEY on page 33a apply only to the phonetic transcription. Where they occur as letters of the alphabet outside the slant lines, they are not meant to indicate pronunciation, as in the spelling of foreign words that may appear in boldface entries, etymologies, or definitions.

5.2 English Words. The phonetic symbols used in the transcription of English words are explained in section 1 of the PRONUNCIATION KEY.

5.2.1 The phonetic system of this Dictionary (developed by Dr. Stavrou) is simplified but precise. The common spellings of English sounds, more than 250, are rendered with only 42 symbols.

5.2.2 These symbols are phonemic, that is, each symbol stands for only one sound, and each sound is shown by only one symbol (with certain sound clusters treated as a single sound).

5.2.3 The symbols are easy to understand. Most are ordinary letters of the English alphabet with their ordinary sounds. Some are combinations of such letters: /ch/ as in much, /oi/ as in boy, /ŏŏ/ as in good, /ōō/ as in do, /ou/ as in sound, /sh/ as in shoe, /zh/ as in measure, and /th/ as in truth and /th/ as in this. Some are single letters that are slightly changed: /ă/ as in father, /ā/ as in say, /ī/ as in time, /ô/ as in warm, /ō/ as in know, /ē/ as in she, /ĕ/ as the y in shiny, and /i/ as the e in ragged. Only two symbols were taken from the International Phonetic Alphabet: /ə/ as the first e in perceive or the ou in curious, and /ŋ/ as the ng in king.

5.2.4 Each symbol is defined in the PRONUNCIATION KEY through a group of common words whose pronunciation is assumed to be known to the reader.

5.3 Foreign Words. Section 2 of the PRONUNCIATION KEY explains five symbols for foreign sounds: /kh/, /k̄h/, /œ/, /Y/, and /N/. These symbols are used in the approximate transcription of foreign words and phrases that are not fully Anglicized.

5.4 Stress and Accent Marks. Most English words have a heavy stress on one syllable and many have in addition one or more light stresses on other syllables. The heavy stress is shown by this accent mark ′, called primary, and the lighter stress is shown by this accent mark ′, called secondary.

5.4.1 The accent marks are placed after the stressed syllables.

5.4.2 They are given either in the phonetic transcription, as in

na·ture /nāch′ər/ . . .
as·tro·naut /as′trənôt′/ . . .

or in the spelling of an entry word if phonetic transcription is not shown or is shown incompletely, as in

Wa′ter·gate′ . . .
stat′u·esque′ /-esk′/ . . .
sleight′ of hand′ /slīt′/ . . .

5.4.3 A light stress is generally shown on full vowels (that is, all vowels except /ē/, /ə/, and, usually, /i/) if they are at least two syllables away from the primary accent, as in

ox′i·dize′ . . .
in′ter·state′ . . .
un′der·stand′ . . .
po·si′tion pa′per . . .
vid′e·o tape′ . . .

If a full vowel is adjacent to a primary accent, the light stress is not shown, as in

ox·ide /oks′īd/ . . .
in·tes·tate /intes′tāt/ . . .
fix·a′tion . . .
mal·prac′tice . . .
U·NES·CO /yōōnes′kō/ . . .

except that it is generally shown when it belongs to a separate word, as in

soft′ware′ . . .
north′east′ . . .
tape′ deck′ . . .
cloud′ seed′ing . . .
un·called′-for′ . . .

5.4.4 The heavy stress is generally shown for words of one syllable:

book /bŏŏk′/ . . .
smashed′ . . .

There are only a few words of one syllable that normally do not have any stress (but see homographs, 3.3.1):

and /and, ənd, ən/ . . .

5.5 Syllabic Breaks. The phonetic transcription in this Dictionary is not syllabified.

5.5.1 However, breaks are made throughout for purposes other than syllabification:

(a) To insert an accent mark (5.4).

(b) To insert a raised dot to show that two vowels are pronounced separately:

hi·a·tus /hī·āt′əs/ . . .

(c) To insert a raised dot to show that certain groups of consonants do not stand for a single sound:

ex·hale /eks·hāl′/ . . .

(d) To divide the transcription at the end of a printed line in places where it would not be broken by an accent mark or a raised dot, as in the entry encyclopedia.

(e) To follow, usually, the word spacing of spaced and hyphenated compounds:

San·ta Claus /sant′ə klôz′/ . . .
sa·voir-faire /sav′wär fer′/ . . .

At the end of a printed line the raised dot is replaced by a hyphen (4.1).

5.5.2 When the transcription has to be broken in any of the foregoing cases, this Dictionary makes an attempt at giving the breaks the way they occur in spoken English, not blindly following the convention of orthographic division (see 4.2):

cam·pus /kamp′əs/ (not /kam′-pəs/)
ban·tam /bant′əm/ (not /ban′təm/)
ran·som /rans′əm/ (not /ran′səm/)
fil·ter /filt′ər/ (not /fil′tər/)
ra·zor /rāz′ər/ (not /rā′zər/)
ca·ter /kāt′ər/ (not /kā′tər/)

(In the transcriptions in parentheses, /p/, /s/, /t/, and /z/ are on the wrong side of the phonological syllable.)

Many cases of phonetic transcription do agree with the orthographic division:

bail·iff /bāl′if/...

(The phonetic break is usually made after, not before, a consonant that is preceded by (i) a vowel marked with a macron, or long mark, as in bail·iff /bāl′if/, (ii) a diphthong, as in loi·ter /loit′ər/ or Boi·se /boiz′ē/, and (iii) certain consonant groups, as in bois·te·rous /boist′ərəs/, not /boi′stərəs/.)

In certain cases, as in words with double consonants, it is obvious that the phonetic transcription cannot agree with the orthographic division:

mar·riage /mar′ij/...

5.5.3 When no break is necessary for any of the purposes of 5.5.1, no syllabification is made in the phonetic transcription. See, for example, the first part of pronunciation and the last part of coordinate in 5.5.1b, or

ma·rine /mərēn′/...
se·date /sidāt′/...

5.6 Alternate Pronunciation. Transcription of alternate pronunciation can be (i) separated by commas, as in

source /sôrs′, sōrs′/...
bless·ed /bles′id, blest′/...
e·ra /ir′ə, ēr′ə, er′ə/...

or (ii) indicated by additions in parentheses, as in

sep·a·ra·ble /sep′(ə)rəbəl/...
ant·arc·tic /antär(k)′tik/...

or (iii) given for one of the words of an entry, as in

al·ma ma·ter /al′mə māt′ər, mät′-ər/...

The transcription is often truncated (see 5.7, 1.10):

as·per·sion /əspur′zhən, -shən/...
Hal′ti·an /-ē·ən, -shən/...

Alternate pronunciation often occurs with alternate stress, as in

as·say /əsā′, as′ā/...

and in some cases there is a change in stress only, as in

ai·grette /āgret′, āg′-/...

5.6.1 The order in which alternate pronunciation is given is not meant to correspond to any order of frequency or preference. However, restricted use can be indicated by a label or an explanation (section 11). The restriction can be (i) to a field or subject, as in

miz′zen·mast′ /-mast′, -mäst′, naut -mest/...

or (ii) to a region, as in

lab·o·ra·to·ry /lab′(ə)rətô′ē, -tor′-, or Brit ləbôr′ətrē/...

or (iii) to the position or use in a sentence or phrase, as in

the /thē′, thə (before a consonant), or thē (before a vowel)/...
a /ə; when stressed: ā/...

5.7 Truncated and Omitted Pronunciation. See 1.10 for explanation and examples of truncated phonetic transcription. Another example, with extreme truncation, is

an′o·dize′ /-ə-/...

for which the missing information can be found in the preceding entry

an·ode /an′ōd/...

and in the entry of the suffix

-ize /-īz′/...

5.7.1 The phonetic transcription is often omitted entirely. For these entries, too, the pronunciation can be determined from preceding entries or from the component parts. The pronunciation of the entry

Wa′ter·gate′...

is evident from the pronunciation of the words water and gate. The pronunciation of the entry

ex′o·bi·ol′o·gy...

is evident from the pronunciation of the combining form exo- and the word biology. The pronunciation of the entry

bi′o·feed′back...

is evident from the combining form bio- (whose pronunciation is shown with the first entry in which it is used, biochemistry) and the words feed and back. The pronunciation of the entry

su′per·con′duc·tiv′i·ty...

is evident from the pronunciation of the prefix super-, the word conduct, and the suffixes -ive and -ity. The pronunciation of the entry

bak′er...

is evident from the pronunciation of the word bake and the suffix -er[1].

5.7.2 Entries are given with accent marks whenever the phonetic transcription is truncated or omitted. See 5.4.2.

5.7.3 Words ending in -ism that have three or more syllables and are stressed on the third syllable from the end have a secondary stress on -ism. If they are followed by phonetic transcription, both accents are shown:

com·mu·nism /kom′yəniz′əm/...

If these words are not followed by phonetic transcription, only the primary accent is shown in the spelling of the word, but the secondary accent is understood. For example, the entry

con·sum′er·ism...

is pronounced /kəns(y)o͞om′əriz′əm/ according to the pronunciation of the word **consume** and the suffixes **-er** and **-ism** /iz′əm/.

5.7.4 Abbreviations are usually listed without pronunciation. Some are pronounced as though they were the full form they refer to; for example, **Hz** is commonly read with the pronunciation that is given for **hertz**, and **et seq.** can be read as it is given in the etymology, *et sequens, et sequentes,* or *et sequentia.* Some abbreviations, called letterwords, are read letter by letter, as **FBI** and **P.L.O.** Others, called acro-

nyms, are firmly established as full-fledged words and are listed with phonetic transcription (and part-of-speech label, see 7.7.3):

U·NES·CO /yo͞ones′ko/ *n* United Nations Educational, Scientific, and Cultural Organization
LI·FO /līf′ō/ [*last-in, first-out*] *adj...*
sna·fu /snaf′o͞o, snafo͞o′/ [*situation normal all fouled up*] *n...* ‖ *vt...*

5.8 Pronunciation Treated in Other Sections:

For the pronunciation of homographs, see 3.3.1.

For the pronunciation of changes in part of speech, see 7.4.1, 7.4.2.

For the pronunciation of plurals of nouns, see 8.2.1, 8.2.2j&k.

For the pronunciation of past tense and past participle, see 8.3.1, 8.3.2j.

For the pronunciation of the third person singular, see 8.3.3.

For the pronunciation of adjectives ending in **-ed,** see 8.5.3.

For the pronunciation of run-on entries, see 9.3.

6. ETYMOLOGY

6.1 General. Etymology deals with the origin and the history of words. It is given in brackets after the pronunciation or, if no pronunciation is shown, after the main entry:

a·mong... [OE *on gemonge* in a crowd] *prep...*
et·y·mon /et′imon′/ [Gk = true (meaning)] *n* (·mons or ·ma /-mə/) word or word root from which other words are derived

In rare cases, separate etymologies are given for separate senses of an entry:

al. 1 [L *alii*] other persons; 2 [L *alia*] other things

6.1.1 The etymon is set in italics; its translation is set in roman type. (Italics are also used for certain labels, as *pp,* and roman type is also used for language labels and other elements of etymologies.)

6.1.2 The translation of an etymon is not meant to be a definition of the main entry.

6.1.3 Cross reference to another main entry for etymological information is set in boldface:

et·y·mol·o·gy... [see **etymon**] *n...*
al·li·ance... [see **ally**] *n...*

al·ly... [OF *alier* < L *alligare* to bind] *v...*

Reference to other main entries for additional etymological information can be indicated through the etymon:

al·lied... [*pp* of **ally**] *adj...*
stress... [*abbr* of **distress**] *n...*
miss² [< **mistress**] *n...*
al·ways... [*all* + *way*] *adv...*

6.1.4 No etymology is given for many compound entries whose individual words are listed elsewhere with etymologies; for example, the etymology of **antepenult** can be found under **ante-** and **penult,** also **pen-.** For many entries the etymological information can be found in a preceding entry of the same family; for example, the etymology that is given for **silica** applies to the next six entries or to components of these entries, **silica gel, silicate, silicic acid, silicon, silicone, silicosis.**

For some entries, or for their components, the etymology is self-evident or evident from the definition, as for the component **Köchel** in

Kö′chel list′ing /kœkh′əl/ *n* catalogue of the authentic works (626 items) of Wolfgang Amadeus Mozart, published in 1862 by

Ludwig von Köchel (1800–1877) and revised in 1937 by Alfred Einstein

6.1.5 For etymologies given with homographs, see 3.3.

6.2 Symbols and Abbreviations. The following symbols are used in etymologies:

=   means

<   derived from (the language or the word that follows)

+   added to

?   (i) origin unknown or uncertain, (ii) perhaps, (iii) unverifiable form

*   hypothetical form

The many abbreviations of language labels and of other words used in etymologies are included in the list of abbreviations on page 38a.

6.2.1 Following are a few of the many language labels and the approximate dates they refer to:

OE (Old English = Anglo-Saxon) A.D. 450–1150
ME (Middle English) 1150–1500
OHG (Old High German) before 1100
OLG (Old Low German) before 1100
MHG (Middle High German) 1100–1500
MLG (Middle Low German) 1100–1500
LGk (Late Greek) 300–700
MGk (Middle Greek) 700–1500
LL (Late Latin) 200–600
ML (Middle Latin) 600–1500
NL (New Latin) since 1500
OF (Old French) before 1300
MF (Middle French) 1300–1600
OIr (Old Irish) before 1000
OIt (Old Italian) 900–1400
ON (Old Norse) 700–1300
OPers (Old Persian) before 300 B.C.
OSlav (Old Slavonic) 800–1000
OSp (Old Spanish) 1100–1600

6.3 Types of Etymologies. Etymologies can have one step, as given for **actor**, or several steps, as given for **apricot**, below. If an etymology begins with a language label that is not immediately followed by an etymon, the etymon is identical with the current English form, as the Latin and English word **actor** (and as the current **aye²**, which has the same form it had in Old Norse and Old English). Where necessary, the literal meaning is added, preceded by an equal sign, as for **acme**. If an

etymon has the same meaning as the entry, it is given without translation, as for **peyote, yak, aerie.** The following groups of examples show form and content of typical etymologies:

ac·tor . . . [L] *n* **1** theatrical performer; **2** doer; **3** participant
a·mok . . . [Malay] *n* . . .
ac·me . . . [Gk = point]   *n*   highest point, summit
a·da·gio . . . [It = at ease] *adj & adv* **1** *mus* slow ‖ *n* **2** musical piece or . . .
af·fi·da·vit . . . [L = he has pledged] *n* . . .
aye² also **ay** . . . [ON < OE ?] *adv* always, ever
-ard . . . also **-art** . . . [OF < Gmc] *suf* . . .
pe·yo·te . . . [Sp < Nahuatl *peyotl*] *n* . . .
yak . . . [Tibetan *gyag*] *n* . . .
aer·ie . . . [ML *aeria* < OF *aire* < L *area*] *n* . . .
ad·ven·ture . . . [OF *aventure* < L (res) *adventura* (thing) about to happen] *n* . . .
Ay·ma·ra . . . [< Sp < AmInd] *n* . . .
am·o·rous . . . [< L *amor* love] *adj* . . .
sir·loin . . . [< OF *sur* over + *longe* loin] *n* . . .
on·o·mat·o·poe·ia /on'əmat'əpē'ə/ [< Gk *onoma* (*-atos*) name + *poiein* to make] *n* **1** formation of words in imitation of natural sounds, as *hiss, bang*; **2** words so formed ‖ **on'o·mat'o·poe'ic** *adj*
a·pri·cot . . . [< Port *albricoque* < Ar *al-bir-qūq* < L *praecoquum* early-ripening] *n* . . .

ac·o·nite . . . also **ac'o·ni'tum** . . . [Gk *akoniton* wolfsbane via L] *n* . . .
ac·cul·tur·ate . . . [*ac-* + *culture* + *-ate*] *vt & vi* . . .
as·cer·tain . . . [< *a-⁵* + *certain*] *vt* . . .
zounds /zoundz/ [contr. of *God's wounds*] *interj archaic* . . .
zil·lion . . . [modeled on *million*] *n* . . .
an·cient . . . [MF *ancien* < VL *anteanus*] *adj* . . .
scut·tle /skut'əl/ [? < *scud*] *vi* . . .
tat·ter·de·mal·ion /tat'ərdimāl/yən, -mal'-/ [*tatter* + ?] *n* . . .
bam·boo·zle /bambōōz'əl/ [?] *vt* . . .

6.3.1 The etymologies are kept simple. Latin and Greek etyma themselves are usually not etymologized. For example, in the entry

as·cend . . . [L *ascendere*] *vt* . . .

ascend is shown as derived from the Latin word *ascendere;* but in this Dictionary this compound is not analyzed further as *ad-* + *scandere,* to climb.

The component parts are given, however, in the case of

    ar·rest...[MF *arester* < *ad-* + L *restare* to remain] *vt*...

because there is no Latin compound "arrestare."

Some etyma are accompanied by an inflected form that shows a closer relationship to the entry word, as in

    im·mi·grate...[L *immigrare* (*-atus*) to move in] *vi*...

    stu·dent...[L *studens* (*-entis*) studying] *n*...

6.4 Special Etymologies. There are etymologies that do not have to refer back to Old or Middle English or other languages. Most of these are in the following categories.

(a) Acronyms, as *laser*, and blends, as *shoran*:

    la·ser /lāz′ər/ [light *a*mplification by *s*timulated *e*mission of *r*adiation] *n*...

    zip′ code′ or **ZIP′ code′** [*z*one *i*mprovement *p*lan] *n*...

    Sea·bee′ [*C*onstruction *B*attalion] *n*...

    tar·na·tion /tärnāsh′ən/ [e*ternal* + *damnation*] *n*...|| *interj*...

    sho·ran /shō′ran, shō′-/ [*sho*rt *ra*nge *n*avigation] *n*...

    stag·fla·tion /stagflāsh′ən/ [*stag*nation + *in*flation] *n*...

(b) Onomatopoeic (sound-imitating) words:

    zing /ziŋ/ [imit] *n*...|| *vi*...||*vt*...

    hel·ter-skel·ter /helt′ərskelt′ər/ [imit] *adj* & *adv*...||*n*...

    whack /(h)wak′/ [prob imit] *n*...|| *vt*...

(c) Biographical, geographical, and other explanations (see also 13.5,1):

    Par′kin·son′s law′ [Cyril Northcote *Parkinson* (1909–   ) Eng historian] *n* observation that work expands as more time is made available for it

    as·tra·khan /as′trəkən/ [city in Russia] *n* skin of young lambs with...

    o′pen ses′a·me [phrase used by Ali Baba to gain entrance to the robbers' cave] *n* unfailing means of entrance or access

    dark′ horse′ [< former practice of disguising a fast horse with dark paint and entering it in a race with inferior horses to pull off a betting coup] *n* little-known entrant in a race or contest not given much chance of winning

(d) Trademarks. These are proprietary terms. See the definition of the entry **trademark.** Many trademarks have passed into wide general usage and are treated by most people like generic terms, as **Xerox, Levis, Sanforized,** or **Band-Aid.** However, trademarks are protected by law. A word that is believed to be a trademark is identified as such in the etymology; but the publishers of this Dictionary are not expressing an opinion on the legal status of any term by designating it as "trademark" or, in general, by entering or not entering any word in this Dictionary. Examples of trademarks:

    Xer·ox /zir′oks/ [trademark] *n* **1** process for...|| *vt* **2** to copy by this process

    Ping-Pong /piŋ′poŋ′/ [trademark] table tennis

    Tel′e·prompt′er [trademark] *n* device that enables a speaker or performer...

    LP [trademark < *L*ong *P*laying] *n* (LPs or LP's) long-playing record

    Au·re·o·my·cin /ôr′ē·əmīs′in/ [L *aureus* golden + Gk *mykes* fungus; trademark] *n* antibiotic...

7. PARTS OF SPEECH

7.1 Types of Labels. The eight traditional parts of speech are adjective, adverb, conjunction, interjection, noun, preposition, pronoun, and verb. They are indicated by labels which are abbreviated and set in italics:

    bi′o·de·grad′a·ble...*adj*...

    of·ten...*adv*...

    and...*conj*...

    wow¹...*interj*...

    vid′e·o·disk′ *n*...

    up·on...*prep*...

    we...*pron*...

    think...*v* (thought)*vt*...|| *vt*...

Verb labels are explained in 7.3.

7.1.1 Other functional labels are used in a similar way, mainly to indicate inflectional forms, for example, *sg* and *pl* for singular and plural, *ind* and *subj* for indicative and subjunctive, *comb form* for combining form and *art* for article. These labels, about forty, are included with the list of abbreviations on page 38a.

Whenever this guide mentions "part-of-speech labels" without further explanation (as in 1.1), this designation is meant to include other functional labels.

7.1.2 Often two or more part-of-speech and other functional labels are combined:

    un′der·neath′ *adv* & *prep*...

    am...*vi 1st pers sg pres ind* of **be**

They can also be combined or juxtaposed with subject or usage labels:

for·tis...*adj phonet*...
pease... *n archaic pl* of **pea**

For an explanation of subject labels, as *phonet* for phonetics, and usage labels, as *archaic*, see 11.2, 11.3, 2.2.

7.2 Position of Part-of-Speech Labels. Part-of-speech and other functional labels are given after the etymology or, if no etymology is shown, as close to the main entry as possible:

ep·ox·y /epok'sē/ [*ep-* + *-oxy*] *n*...
de·brief' /dē-/ *vt*...
fail'-safe' *adj*...

7.2.1 These labels are also given (i) after run-on entries (section 9) and (ii) after parallels, where they indicate a change in part of speech or function of verb (7.4).

7.2.2 These labels can be used in other contexts when needed, as *gen*, *pt*, and *vi* and *vt* in these examples:

Bo·ö·tes /bō-ō'tēz/ *n* (*gen -tis* /-tis/)...
could... *v* (*pt* of **can**) *modal aux*...
burn...[OE *byrnan vi* & *baernan vt*] *v*...

7.2.3 Part-of-speech labels can also be used after SYN and ANT. See 12.2.1.

7.3 Verb Labels. The functional labels used with verbs are *vt* (transitive verb), *vi* (intransitive verb), *v aux* (auxiliary verb), *v impers* (impersonal verb), *vt impv* and *vi impv* (imperative forms of a verb), and *modal aux* (modal auxiliary):

ac·cept...*vt*...
ab·stain...*vi*...
be'...‖ *v aux*...
me·thinks... *v* (me·thought) *v impers* archaic it seems to me
vi·de... [*impv* of L *video*] *vt impv* see (the page or place indicated)
stet...[*3rd pers sg pres subj* of L *stare* to stand]...‖ *vi impv* **2**... let it stand
must²...*modal aux*...

7.3.1 The part-of-speech label *v* is placed before irregular inflected forms, which are always followed by a functional verb label, as *v impers* in methinks above and as *vt*, *vi*, or both, or *modal aux* in these examples:

com·mit...*v* (-mit·ted; -mit·ting) *vt*...
come...*v* (came; come) *vi*...
find...*v* (found) *vt*...‖ *vi*...
pan'to·mime'...*vt* & *vi*...
can¹...*v* (could) *modal aux*...

The label *v* is used *only* with irregular inflected forms (except where it appears after SYN and ANT; see 12.2.1).

7.3.2 A verb is transitive when it needs an object to have a complete meaning, as in the example of **commit** above. A verb is intransitive when it has a complete meaning without an object, as in the example of **come** above. (See also 2.4.4, 2.4.5.) Many verbs are used in both functions, with the same or with different meanings, as in the examples of **find** and **pantomime** in 7.3.1.

The labels *vt* and *vi* do not really mean that a verb "is" transitive or intransitive, but that it has a transitive or intransitive function if it is used as defined in an entry or in one particular sense of an entry. Almost any verb can occasionally be used transitively or intransitively.

7.4 Changes in Part of Speech. Changes in part of speech or function of verb are marked by parallels and a label indicating the kind of change:

talk...*vt*...‖ *vt*...‖ *n*...
pho'to·graph' *n*...‖ *vt*...‖ *vt*...

7.4.1 When the new part of speech or function of verb has a different pronunciation or a different stress, this change is shown in one of the following ways.

(a) In most cases the change is shown by full or truncated phonetic transcription before the label:

es·say /es'ā/...*n*...‖ /esā'/ *vt*...
pred·i·cate /pred'ikāt'/...*vt*... ‖ /-kit/ *n*...
use /yōoz'/...*vt*...‖ /yōos'/ *n*...

Sometimes this transcription of the new part of speech adds alternate pronunciation or eliminates alternate pronunciation that was given earlier:

ad·dress /ədres'/...*vt*...‖ /ədres', ad'res/ *n*...
aer·i·al /er'ē-əl, ā·ir'ē-əl/ *adj*...‖ /er'ē-əl/ *n*...

(b) If the change in pronunciation and stress is accompanied by a change in syllabification, both the new form and the new phonetic transcription are shown:

pro·ject /prəjekt'/...*vt*...‖ **proj·ect** /proj'ekt/ *n*...

(c) If the change is in stress only, without change in pronunciation, the new form can be shown with different accent marks and without phonetic transcription. This kind of change occurs with certain prefixes, such as *inter-*, *over-*, and *under-*:

in'ter·change' *vt*...‖ **in'ter·change'** *n*...
o'ver·head' *adv*...‖ **o'ver·head'** *adj* ...‖ *n*...

7.4.2 When the new part of speech or function of verb has an irregular inflection that is different from the inflection of the main entry, the new inflection is given after the label:

sol·i·tar·y . . . *adj* . . . || *n* (-ies) . . .
try /trī'/ . . . *v* (**tried**) *vt* . . . || *vi* . . . || *n* (**tries**) . . .
stead·y /sted'ē/ *adj* (-**i·er**; -**i·est**) 1 firm . . . ; **9 go steady** to date one person exclusively || *n* (-ies) **10** *colloq* one with whom one goes steady || *v* (-**ied**) *vt* **11** to make or keep steady || *vi* **12** to become steady . . .

Sometimes the new inflection is accompanied by a change of pronunciation, as in

for·tis /fôrt'is/ *adj* . . . || *n* (-**tes** /-tēz/) . . .

or the pronunciation is given to show that there is no change, as in

arc /ärk'/ . . . *n* . . . || *v* (**arced** /ärkt'/; **arc·ing** /ärk'iŋ/) *vi* . . .

7.4.3 For entries that have different meanings with different inflections, the part-of-speech label is repeated. In the case of verbs the inflected form is again preceded by *v* and followed by *vt* and/or *vi*:

ox /oks'/ . . . *n* (**ox·en** /oks'ən/) 1 any bovine animal (genus *Bos*), including cattle; **2** castrated bull || *n* (**ox·es**) **3** clumsy oaf
cher·ub /cher'əb/ . . . *n* 1 beautiful, innocent child || *n* (**cher·u·bim** /cher'(y)əbim'/) **2** heavenly being (Ezek. 1:5–11) . . .
weave /wēv'/ . . . *v* (**wove**; **wo·ven** or **wove**) *vt* 1 to interlace, as threads . . . || *vi* 5 to work at weaving; make cloth . . . || *v* (**weaved**) *vt* 7 to make (one's way) by moving from side to side || *vi* 8 to wind in and out, as *the car weaved through the heavy traffic* || *n* . . .
pay /pā'/ . . . *v* (**paid**) *vt* 1 to satisfy the claims of . . . || *vi* 13 to make recompense; discharge a debt . . . || *v* (**payed** /pād'/) *vt* 16 pay out to pass out (a rope) by slackening || *n* . . .

7.4.4 The new part of speech or function of verb is not defined if its meaning is clear from the preceding definition (see also 9.2). It is then preceded by "also" and does not have a sense number:

run'-on' *n* 1 *pros* line that continues a preceding line without a syntactical break; **2** *typ* matter that is added or run on || also *adj*
air'drop' *n* delivery of supplies or personnel by parachute from flying aircraft || also *v* (-**dropped**; -**drop·ping**) *vt*

7.5 Changes from Singular to Plural. If a plural has a different meaning or

different use, the plural form is given after the sense number or the part-of-speech label, depending on which senses the plural applies to. The labels *sg* and/or *pl* indicate whether this form is used as singular or plural:

sta·tis·tic . . . *n* 1 numerical datum; **2 statistics**, a *pl* numerical facts . . . ; **b** *sg* science that deals with . . .
pol·i·tic . . . *adj* . . . || *n* **pol'i·tics** *sg* or *pl* **4** science or art of government; **5** political affairs . . .

The plural form can appear as one of the senses within the part of speech, as statistics, or represent a change from another part of speech to *n*, as **politics**.

See also 11.8 for the use of singular and plural labels with certain main entries.

7.5.1 Sometimes the labels *sg* or *pl* are accompanied by "often" or "usu."

sky . . . *n* (**skies**) 1 the heavens or upper atmosphere; **2** often **skies** *pl* climate or weather; **3** heaven . . .
quar·ter . . . *n* 1 one of the four . . . ; **12** usu. **quarters** *pl* lodgings, esp. military; **13** part of a . . .
stair . . . *n* 1 any of a set of steps connecting different levels; **2 stairs** usu. *pl* flight of steps

7.5.2 If the plural form is identical with the singular, this form, preceded by *pl*, is given in parentheses (see also 8.2.2d):

head . . . *n* 1 the part of the body . . . ; **17** (*pl* **head**) unit of counting, as *ten head of cattle;* **18** . . .

7.6 Changes in Capitalization and Use of Article. If a capitalized entry has a sense that is not capitalized or if, conversely, a noncapitalized entry has a sense that is capitalized, this change is shown by giving the other form:

Mo·roc·co . . . *n* 1 . . . kingdom . . . ; **2 morocco** fine grained leather . . .
in·dex . . . *n* . . . 1 forefinger . . . ; **7 Index** *R C Ch* list of books not to be read without special permission . . .
Eng·lish . . . *adj* . . . || *n* **3** often **english** *billiards* spinning motion . . .

7.6.1 If an entry has a specific sense in which it is used with the definite article, this use is shown by giving the entry with the article:

op·po·si·tion . . . *n* 1 act of opposing . . . ; **4 the opposition**, a the person, group, or . . . ; **b** the political party out of power . . .
rich . . . *adj* . . . || *n* **10 the rich** *pl* wealthy people collectively . . .
un·der·signed' *adj* . . . || *n* **2 the undersigned** *sg* or *pl* the person or

persons who sign a letter or document

south...*n* **1** one of the four cardinal points...; **2** often **South** region or territory lying in this direction; **3** the **South** the region of the U.S. south of...

A change in capitalization or in the use of the article can thus represent a change from another part of speech to *n*, as **english, the rich,** and **the undersigned,** or it can appear as one of the senses within the part of speech, as the other examples above.

7.7 Entries without Part-of-Speech Labels. Most entries, including proper names and spaced compounds, have one of the eight part-of-speech labels (7.1). There are exceptions that have other functional labels (as *pt* or *pref*), and there are exceptions that need no part-of-speech or other functional label at all.

7.7.1 Many entries that are variants or serve as cross references (section 10)

do not have part-of-speech labels, but some of these have other functional labels:

don't /dōnt'/ do not
ran /ran'/ *pt* of **run**

7.7.2 Prefixes and other initial combining forms as well as many final combining forms, including a few suffixes, do not have part-of-speech or other functional labels. See 3.5.1 for examples. However, many final combining forms, including most suffixes, do have a part-of-speech label in addition to *comb form* or *suf*. See 3.5.2 for explanation and examples.

7.7.3 Most abbreviations do not have a part-of-speech or other functional label (see also 10.1.5):

Per. Persia(n)
Os *chem* Osmium
P.M., p.m....

However, part-of-speech labels are given for abbreviations that are treated like words, as **UNESCO, LIFO,** and **snafu** in 5.7.4.

8. INFLECTED FORMS

8.1 Regular and Irregular Inflections. The inflected forms of nouns, verbs, adjectives, and adverbs can be regular or irregular. If they are regular according to the rules of this section, they are not given in this Dictionary.

8.1.1 Irregular inflected forms are shown in parentheses after the part-of-speech label of the entry. They are set in boldface, with orthographic division. They can be truncated (1.10), can be followed by pronunciation, can have variant forms, can be preceded by functional labels (7.1.1) or usage labels, and can appear in run-on entries.

8.1.2 Most irregular inflected forms are also listed as main entries. The entry with the base form is referred to in boldface, preceded by "of" in roman type:

wrote /rōt'/ *pt* of **write**
writ·ten /rit'ən/ *pp* of **write**
write /rit'/ [OE *writan* to inscribe, write] *v* (**wrote; writ·ten**) *vt*...

pease /pēz'/ *n archaic pl* of **pea**
pea...*n* (**peas** or *archaic* **pease**)...

8.1.3 For the joining of truncated inflected forms, see 4.4.

8.2 Nouns. To form the plural of regular nouns, (i) add **-s** to the singular, as **heart** (**hearts**), but (ii) add **-es** to singulars ending in *s, z, sh, ch, dz, tz,* or *x,* which have sibilant (hissing) sounds, as **match** (**matches**). Such regular plurals are not shown in this Dictionary.

8.2.1 The plural ending **-s** is pronounced /s/ (as the s in *student*) if it is preceded by the voiceless consonant sounds /f/, /k/, /p/, /t/, or /th/, as in **heart** (**hearts** /härts'/), **laugh** (**laughs** /lafs', läfs'/); but the same plural ending **-s** is pronounced /z/ (as the z in *zeal*) if it is preceded by the voiced consonant sounds /b/, /d/, /g/, /l/, /m/, /n/, /ŋ/, /r/, /v/, or /th/ or by a vowel sound, as in **guard** (**guards** gärdz'/), **bough** (**boughs** /bouz'/).

The plural ending **-es** that is added to sibilant sounds (that is, to /s/, /z/, /sh/, /ch/, /zh/, and /j/) is pronounced /iz/, as in **match** (**matches** /mach'iz/), **box** (**boxes** /boks'iz/).

Some nouns end in a consonant with a sibilant sound plus a silent e, as base; in these nouns, too, the e plus the **-s** of the plural are pronounced /iz/, as base (**bases** /bās'iz/).

8.2.2 Plural forms are shown in irregular or unfamiliar cases, as in the following examples.

(a) Nouns ending in **-y** that changes to **-ies:**

sky...*n* (**skies**)...
stud·y...*n* (**-ies**)...
ac'tu·al'i·ty...*n* (**-ties**)...
so·lil·o·quy...*n* (**-quies**)...

(But not for regular plurals such as **days** and **monkeys**.)

(b) Nouns ending in **-o**, if the plural is formed by adding **-es** or by adding **-es** or **-s**:

po·ta·to...*n* (-toes)...
in·nu·en·do...*n* (-does or -dos)...

(But not for regular plurals such as memos and radios.)

(c) Nouns with internal changes:

tooth...*n* (teeth)...
child...*n* (chil·dren /child'rən/)...
shelf...*n* (shelves /-vz/)...

(d) Nouns with identical plurals (see also 11.8 and head in 7.5.2):

swine...*n* (*pl* swine)...
craft...*n*... (*pl* craft)...
men·ha·den...*n* (*pl* -den)...
Ir·o·quois /ir'əkwoi(z)'/...*n* (*pl* -quois)...

(e) Nouns with alternate plurals, often with different use or meaning (see also 7.4.3):

scarf...*n* (scarfs or scarves /-vz/)...
off'spring' *n* (-spring or -springs)...
pen·ny...*n* (-nies or *Brit* pence denoting amount in value)...
doz·en...*n* (-ens; preceded by a number -en)...

(f) Nouns with foreign plurals:

syn·op·sis...*n* (-ses /-sēz/)...
ser·aph...*n* (-aphs or -a·phim /-əfim/)...
al·ga /al'gə/...*n* (-gae /-jē/)...

(g) Nouns with plurals that might be confused with plurals of other words:

mon·goose...*n* (-goos·es)...

(h) Compounds whose last component has an irregular plural or a plural that is "regular" but uncommon:

eye'tooth' *n* (-teeth)...
speak'-eas'y *n* (-ies)...
crow'foot' *n* (-foots)...
still' life' *n* (lifes)...
stand'-by' *n* (-bys)...
pass'er-by' *n* (passers-by)...

Also single words with "regular" but uncommon plurals:

zlo·ty...*n* (-tys)...

(i) Spaced compounds for which it may not be clear which components have the plural form:

ac·count' pay'a·ble...*n* (accounts payable)...
at·tor'ney gen'er·al *n* (attorney generals or attorneys general)...
nou·veau riche...*n* (nouveaux riches /.../)...

(j) Nouns with alternate or peculiar pronunciation of the plural:

path /path'/, päth'/...*n* (paths /-_thz_, -ths/)...

mouth /mouth'/...*n* (mouths /-_thz_/)...

(k) Solid compounds ending in **-house** are given with the pronunciation of the plural, and solid compounds ending in **-man** are given with the pronunciation of singular and plural:

store'house' *n* (-houses /-ziz/)...
space'man /-mən/ *n* (-men /-mən/)...
mus'cle·man' /-man'/ *n* (-men /-men'/)...
leg'man' /-man', -mən/ *n* (-men /-men', -mən/)...

8.2.3 No plural is given for irregular nouns that are generally not used in the plural:

chem'is·try *n*...

8.2.4 For nouns that are given as main entries in plural form only and are labeled *nsg*, *npl*, or *nsg & npl*, see 11.8. For changes from singular to plural form with different meaning or different use, see 7.5.

8.3 Verbs. To form the past tense and the past participle of regular verbs, add **-ed** to the infinitive, and to form the present participle of regular verbs, add **-ing** to the infinitive, after dropping the final **e** of infinitives that end in **e**, as in **call** (called; calling), **love** (loved; loving). If the infinitive ends in **ee**, both **e**'s are retained in the present participle, as in **agree** (agreed; agreeing). For such regular verbs no inflections of the principal parts are ordinarily shown in this Dictionary.

8.3.1 The **-ed** of the past tense and the past participle is pronounced /t/ if it is preceded by the voiceless consonant sounds /ch/, /f/, /k/, /p/, /s/, /sh/, or /th/, as in **matched** /macht'/; it is pronounced /d/ after the voiced consonant sounds /b/, /g/, /j/, /l/, /m/, /n/, /ŋ/, /r/, /v/, /z/, /zh/, or /_th_/ or after a vowel sound, as in **mailed** /mäld'/; and it is pronounced /id/ after the dental sounds /d/ and /t/, as in **waited** /wāt'id/. (PRONUNCIATION KEY, 3.1, p. 35a)

8.3.2 Past tense, past participle, and present participle, or only one or two of these principal parts, are shown for verbs that are irregular according to the foregoing rules. The order of these irregular inflected forms is past tense, past participle, present participle. When the first two are identical, the form is given only once. Inflected forms are shown in irregular or unfamiliar cases, as in the following examples.

(a) Verbs in which the final consonant is doubled:

star...*v* (starred; star·ring) *vt*...
con·trol...*v* (-trolled; -trol·ling) *vt*...

(b) Verbs that have an alternate form in which the final consonant is doubled:

> wed...*v* (wed·ded or wed; wed·ding) *vt*...
> bus...*v* (bussed or bused; bus·sing or bus·ing) *vt*...

(c) Verbs that have other types of alternate forms:

> spell[2]...*v* (spelled or spelt) *vt*...
> shear...*v* (*pp* sheared or shorn) *vt*...
> x...*v* (x·ed or x'd; x·ing or x'ing) *vt* 4 often x out to cross out, as...

If the use of a form is restricted, it is preceded by a usage label:

> stay[3]...*v* (stayed or *archaic* staid) *vi*...

(d) Verbs ending in y that changes to i before -ed is added (but having a regular present participle according to 8.3: drying):

> dry...*v* (dried) *vt*...
> syl·lab'i·fy'...*v* (-fied) *vt*...

(e) Verbs ending in ie that changes to y before -ing is added (but having a regular past tense and past participle according to 8.3: lied):

> lie[1]...*v* (ly·ing) *vi*...
> vie...*v* (vy·ing) *vi*...

(f) Verbs that do not drop the final e before -ing is added, usually to avoid confusion with other verbs (dying, singing):

> dye...*v* (dye·ing) *vt*...
> singe...*v* (singe·ing) *vt*...

(g) Verbs ending in c that add k before -ed or -ing is added:

> pan·ic...*v* (-icked; -ick·ing) *vt*...
> pic·nic...*v* (-nicked; -nick·ing) *vi*...

(h) Verbs with other, mainly internal, irregularities (so-called strong verbs):

> swim...*v* (swam; swum; swim·ming) *vi*...
> lie[2]...*v* (lay; lain; ly·ing) *vi*...
> write...*v* (wrote; writ·ten) *vt*...
> do[1]...*v* (did; done) *vt*...
> sit...*v* (sat; sit·ting) *vi*...
> think...*v* (thought) *vi*...
> burst...*v* (burst) *vi*...
> bite...*v* (bit; bit·ten or bit) *vt*...

(i) Verbs with different inflections for different meanings:

> hang...*v* (hung) *vt* 1 to attach to... || *vi* 8 to dangle...||*v* (hung or preferably hanged) *vt* 22 to suspend from the neck until dead... || *vi* 23 to die by hanging...

Also see **weave** (wove; woven or wove) vs. (weaved), and **pay** (paid) vs. (payed), in 7.4.3.

(j) Verbs with uncommon relationship between spelling and pronunciation:

> arc /ärk'/...*n*...|| *v* (arced /ärkt'/; arc·ing /ärk'iŋ/) *vi*...

(k) Most solid or hyphenated compound verbs whose last component has irregular inflections:

> o'ver·do' *v* (-did; -done) *vt*...
> ba'by-sit' *v* (-sat; sit·ting) *vi* . . .

8.3.3 To form the third person singular present of all regular verbs and of most irregular verbs, add -es or -s to the infinitive, using the same rules as for the plural of regular nouns (8.2, 8.2.1), as in bake (he, she, or it bakes /bāks'/), need (needs /nēdz'/), agree (agrees /əgrēz'/), watch (watches /woch'əz/); and write (writes /rīts'/), swim (swims 'swimz'/), blow (blows /blōz'/), choose (chooses /chōōz'iz/). The exception is verbs ending in a single o, which usually adds -es, as in go (goes /gōz'/), echo (echoes /ek'ōz/).

Such regular endings for the third person singular present are not shown in this Dictionary.

If these endings are formed irregularly or if they are pronounced irregularly, the forms are shown in the entry or listed as separate main entries:

> have...*v* (*3rd pers sg pres* has; *pt & pp* had) *vt*...|| *v aux*...
> say /sā'/...*v* (said; *3rd pers sg pres ind* says /sez'/) *vt*...
> does /duz'/ *3rd pers sg pres ind* of do[1]
> doesn't /duz'ənt/ does not

8.3.4 Occasionally other irregular forms are shown in an entry:

> be /bē'/...*v* (*pres* am, are, is; *pt* was, were; *pp* been) *vi*...|| *v aux*...

8.3.5 Certain archaic inflections are listed as main entries and labeled *archaic* (see also 8.3.2c):

> saith /seth'/ *archaic 3rd pers sg pres ind* of say
> dost /dust'/ *archaic 2nd pers sg pres ind* of do[1]
> me·thinks /mithiŋks'/ *v* (me·thought) *v impers archaic* it seems to me

8.4 Modal Auxiliaries. Modal auxiliaries are defective verbs that have only one or two forms, namely, for the present and the past tense: must, ought, can (could), may (might), will (would), shall (should). They (i) have no ending in the third person singular, (ii) have no participle, and therefore cannot form a compound tense, (iii) have no imperative, and (iv) have no infinitive form.

8.4.1 Also, they have no infinitive function. Therefore **can**, for example, cannot be defined as "to be able to" (as other dictionaries have it). Modal auxiliaries can be used only as part of verb phrases, and they are defined as part of verb phrases in this Dictionary (one of Dr. Stavrou's many innovations):

can¹...*v* (**could**) *modal aux* **1** am, are, or is able to; **2** know or knows how to; **3** have or has the right to; **4** have or has permission to...

may...*v* (**might**) *modal aux* **1** am, are, or is: **a** allowed to; **b** likely but not certain to; **c** able to; **2** expressing the earnest desire or wish of the speaker, as *may you enjoy good health*...

8.4.2 **Could, might, would,** and **should,** besides being past tenses, are also used as independent modal auxiliaries:

could...*v* (*pt* of **can**) *modal aux* used to express: **1** permission in the present, as *could I come in?;* **2** ability a in the past, as *I could not come yesterday;* **b** in the conditional, as *I could see you tomorrow*

8.5 Adjectives. To obtain the comparative of regular adjectives, add **-er** to the positive form, and to obtain the superlative of regular adjectives, add **-est** to the positive form, after dropping the final **e** of adjectives that end in **e**, as in slow (**slower; slowest**), fine (**finer; finest**). For such regular adjectives no comparative and superlative forms are shown in this Dictionary, except to indicate that the same rule applies to adjectives ending in **ee**: free (**freer; freest**).

8.5.1 Comparative and superlative are also not shown when they are formed with **more** and **most**, as **beautiful** (**more beautiful; most beautiful**), **stylish** (**more stylish; most stylish**), **amazing** (**more amazing; most amazing**).

8.5.2 Comparative and superlative are shown in the following irregular cases.

(a) Adjectives in which the final consonant is doubled:

big...*adj* (**big·ger; big·gest**)...
fit²...*adj* (**fit·ter; fit·test**)...

(b) Adjectives ending in **y** or **ey** that change to **i** before **-er** or **-est** or that have alternate forms:

dry...*adj* (**dri·er; dri·est**)...
stead·y...*adj* (**-i·er; -i·est**)...
home·y *adj* (**hom·i·er; hom·i·est**)...
shy¹...*adj* (**shi·er** or **shy·er; shi·est** or **shy·est**)...

(c) Adjectives that are entirely irregular or have entirely irregular variants:

well²...*adj* (**bet·ter; best**)...
ill...*adj* (**worse; worst**)...
old...*adj* (**old·er** or **eld·er; old·est** or **eld·est**)...

(d) Adjectives that change their pronunciation when **-er** or **-est** are added:

strong /strȯŋ′, stroŋ′/ ... *adj* (**strong·er** /strȯŋ′gər, stroŋ′gər/, **strong·est** /strȯŋ′gist, stroŋ′gist/)...

8.5.3 In past participles used as adjectives the ending **-ed** is pronounced /t/ or /d/ or /id/ according to 8.3.1 (and **PRONUNCIATION KEY** 3.1, p. 35a). By these rules the pronunciation of **-ed** is /id/ if the preceding consonant sound is /t/ or /d/, as in **mended** /mend′id/. Such regular pronunciations are not shown. However, there are past participles used as adjectives, and some other adjectives, in which **-ed** is pronounced /id/ although the preceding consonant sound is neither /t/ nor /d/. In these cases the pronunciation is given:

learn·ed /lurn′id/ *adj*...
crook′ed /-id/ *adj*...
rag·ged /rag′id/ *adj*...
bow′leg·ged /-leg′id, -legd′/ *adj*

8.6 Pronouns. Each pronoun and each inflected form of a pronoun is given as a separate main entry, as **I, my, mine,** and **me; who, whose,** and **whom:**

she /shē′/ [OE *sēo fem* of *dem pron se*] *pron* (*3rd pers sg fem nom*) **1**...

Inflected or derived forms are referred to the nominative form:

her /hur′, (h)ər/ [OE] *pron* **1** objective case of **she** ‖ *adj* **2** possessive of **she**: of or belonging to her

9. RUN-ON ENTRIES

9.1 General. Run-on entries are undefined derivatives of the main entry. They follow the last sense of the main entry and are preceded by parallels and followed by part-of-speech labels. Like main entries, they are set in boldface, show orthographic division through raised dots or heavy and light accent marks, can have variants, can be followed by pronunciation and, after the part-of-speech label, by irregular inflections (which, in turn, have boldface type, division, and sometimes pronunciation).

9.2 Meaning. The meaning of a run-on entry is obvious from the main entry and the addition or deletion of combining forms (3.5.5):

> sky′jack′ *vt* to hijack (an airplane) ‖ sky′jack′er *n* ‖ sky′jack′ing *n*
> ur·gent...*adj* 1 pressing,...; 2 insistent...‖ ur′gent·ly *adv* ‖ ur′gen·cy *n* (-cies)
> pho·net·ics...*nsg*... ‖ pho·net′ic *adj* ‖ pho·net′i·cal·ly *adv* ‖ pho·ne·ti·cian...*n*

9.2.1 Derived words that are hard to recognize, have a special meaning, or are used very frequently are listed and defined as main entries:

> man·age...*vt*...‖   man′age·a·ble *adj* ‖...
> man′age·ment *n*...
> man′ag·er *n*...‖ man′a·ge′ri·al... *adj*

9.3 Pronunciation. Changes from the main entry in pronunciation and stress are shown as needed:

> lex·i·cog·ra·phy   /lek′sikog′rəfē/ [Gk *lexikos* of words + -*graphy*] *n* the compiling of dictionaries ‖ lex′i·cog′ra·pher *n* ‖ lexi′co·graph′ic (-i·cal) /-kōgraf′-, -kəgraf′-/ *adj*
> Pe·trarch /pē′trärk/ *n* (1304–74) Italian poet and scholar ‖ Pe·trar′chan /pi-/ *adj*
> re·voke /rivōk′/...*vt*...‖ rev·o·ca·ble /rev′əkəbəl/ also re·vok′a·ble /rivōk′-/ *adj* ‖ rev·o·ca·tion /rev′əkāsh′ən/ *n*...
> a·lum·nus   /əlum′nəs/...*n* (-ni /-nī/) ...‖ a·lum′na /-nə/ *nfem* (-nae /-nē/)

9.3.1 Pronunciation as well as irregular inflections can be truncated, but the run-on entry words themselves are always spelled out.

9.4 Attributive Forms. Spaced compounds usually become hyphenated when they are used attributively, that is, when they function as adjectives. The attributive form is then given as a run-on entry (3.4.3):

sky′ blue′ *n* color of the clear sky ‖ sky′-blue′ *adj*
long′ dis′tance *n*...‖ long′-dis′tance *adj* & *adv*
Off′ Broad′way *n*...‖ Off′-Broad′way *adj*
straight′ from the shoul′der *adv*... ‖ straight′-from-the-shoul′der *adj*

9.4.1 Analogous to attributive compounds, there are other changes in part of speech that are accompanied by changes in hyphenation and that are given as run-on entries:

soft′ soap′ *colloq n*...‖ soft′-soap′ *vt*
skin′ div′ing *n*...‖ skin′-dive *vi* ‖ skin′-div′er *n*

9.4.2 Almost any noun, whether it is a compound or a single word, can occasionally function as an adjective. This function is not shown for nouns that do not change hyphenation, unless the use is very common. For the latter the attributive function is not indicated through a run-on entry but simply through a change in part of speech (see also 7.4.4):

life...*n*...‖ *adj* 17 of or pert. to life; animate; 18...
sat·el·lite...*n*...‖ also *adj*

9.5 Names of States of the U.S. Run-on derivatives of states of the United States are labeled nouns, not adjectives and nouns, for example,

Min·ne·so·ta...*n*...‖Min′ne·so′tan *n*
Tex·as...*n*...‖ Tex′an *n*

because it is generally the state name itself that has the adjectival function: "A Minnesotan hates the Minnesota weather," not the Minnesotan weather; "A Texan crosses the Texas state line," not the Texan state line. (This Dictionary is the only one to list these derivatives for all 50 states, and it is the only one to label them nouns, not adjectives and nouns.) The three exceptions for which the label is given as *adj* & *n* are the run-on entries Californian, Alaskan, and New Yorker because of their occasional use as adjectives.

10. CROSS REFERENCES AND VARIANTS

10.1 Types of cross references. Cross references are used extensively to give indispensable or additional information. They can be identified by "see," etc., or understood implicitly.

10.1.1 "See" usually refers from an undefined main entry to another main entry where the complete term is defined. The entry referred to is set in boldface, preceded by "see" in roman type:

Sal·va·dor /sal′vədôr′/ *n* see El Salvador ‖ Sal′va·dor′an *adj* & *n*
El Sal·va·dor /el sal′vədôr′/ *n* Spanish-speaking republic in Central America (3,037,000; 8,260 sq.mi; cap. San Salvador) ‖ Sal′va·dor′an *adj* & *n*

Pyth·i·as /pith′ē·əs/ *n* see Damon and Pythias
Da·mon and Pyth·i·as /dām′ən, pith′ē·əs/ *n class. myth.* devoted

friends, noted for their faithfulness unto death

For the use of "see" after synonyms and discriminations of synonyms, see 12.4.

10.1.2 "Var of" is used similarly, after undefined secondary variants:

moult /mōlt′/ *vi, vt, & n* var of **molt**

molt /mōlt′/...*vi*...‖ *vt*...‖ *n*...

-ise /-īz′/ var of **-ize**

-ize /-īz′/ [OF *-iser* < Gk *-izein*] *v suf* 1 to ...

10.1.3 "Cf." refers from a defined main entry to another main entry where related information can be found. The entry referred to is set in italics, preceded by "cf." in roman type. It is placed in parentheses, usually at the end of the definition:

ac·ro·nym /ak′rənim/ *n* word formed from the first letter or group of letters of the words in a set phrase...(cf. *letterword*)

let′ter·word′ *n* word in the form of an abbreviation which is pronounced by sounding the names of its letters...

For the use of "cf." after discriminations of synonyms, see 12.4.1.

10.1.4 "Opposite of" is used similarly as part of the definition, to refer to another main entry:

ag′o·ra·pho′bi·a . . . (opposite of *claustrophobia*)

10.1.5 Abbreviations and shortened forms are followed (i) by a full definition, as

PG designation of a film recommended for all ages, but with parental guidance suggested

we′ve /wēv′/ we have

or, more often (ii) by spelled-out words that serve as reference to the main entry where the full definition can be found:

SDR special drawing rights

spe′cial draw′ing rights′ *npl* reserve assets issued as a supplement or substitute for gold through the International Monetary Fund for adjusting the balance of payments among nations

Hz hertz

hertz...*n* (hertz or hertz·es) unit of frequency...

Au [< L *aurum*] *chem* gold

gold /gōld′/ [OE] *n* 1 precious yellow metal (Au; at.no. 79; at.wt. 196.967) remarkable for...

gy·ro /jī′rō/ *n* 1 gyrocompass; 2 gyroscope

gy′ro·com′pass...

gy′ro·scope′...

-n′t /-ənt/ *comb form* not

not /not′/...

Occasionally the main information is given with the abbreviation or the shortened form:

an·no Do·mi·ni /an′ō dom′inī′/ [L = in the year of the Lord] *adv*

A.D.

A.D. [L *anno Domini*] in the year of our Lord, since the birth of Christ

zo′o·log′i·cal gar′den *n* zoo

zoo /zōō′/ [zoological garden] *n* park or other...

10.1.6 If only one sense of another main entry is referred to, the sense number is shown in italics:

meg′a·hertz′ *n* (-hertz or -hertz·es) megacycle 2

meg′a·cy′cle *n* 1 one million cycles; 2 unit of radio frequency equal to one million cycles per second

print′er′s dev′il *n* devil 5

dev·il...5 printer's helper...

10.1.7 Many words that are part of a definition proper are also given as main entries where they can be consulted for more information:

trac′er bul′let *n* bullet containing a tracer

trac′er *n*...4 chemical added to ammunition to cause it to trail smoke and fire when fired, for the purpose of making its path visible...

10.1.8 Run-on entries, too, are a type of implicit cross reference. They refer both to their main entries and to other entries such as combining forms.

10.2 Types of Variants. Variants are preceded by an identifying word or given in parentheses.

10.2.1 Equal variants are identified through "or" and/or put in parentheses:

siz·able or size·able...

sweep′stake′ *n* or **sweep′stakes′** *nsg & npl*...

u′ni·ver′sal joint′ or **cou′pling**...

sub·or′di·nat′ing (or **sub·or′di·nate**) **con·junc′tion**...

be·half...*n* in or on behalf of...

ram′jet′ (en′gine)...

ma·ha·ra·ja(h)...

an·a·lyt·ic (-i·cal)...

10.2.2 Secondary variants are identified through "also":

as·phalt /as′fôlt/ also **as·phal′tum** /-əm/...

ac·com′pa·nist also **ac·com′pa·ny·ist**...

10.2.3 Other types of variants can have designations such as "often" and "usu.":

> mark′ing *n* often markings *pl*...
> snuff′er² *n* usu. snuffers *pl* 1...

10.2.4 Variants can be limited to only one sense of an entry (see also 7.5.1):

> quar·ter...*n* 1...; 12 usu. quarters *pl* lodgings, esp. military...
> short...*adj*...‖ *vt & vi* 29 often short out to short-circuit...
> raf·fle...*n*...‖ *vt* 2 also raffle off to dispose of by a raffle
> souf·flé...*n*...‖ *adj* 2 also suf·fléed′ light and fluffy...

See also the spelling variants in 7.6

10.2.5 Alternative proper names are given in parentheses after the part-of-speech label or are part of the definition proper:

El Gre·co /el grek′ō/ *n* (Domenikos Theotokopoulos) (1541–1614) Greek-born Spanish painter
Len′in·grad′ /-grad′/ *n* seaport in ...; formerly St. Petersburg (1703–1914) and Petrograd (1914–24)

10.3 Homographs. For cross reference to homographs, see 3.3.2.

10.4 Pronunciation. For alternate pronunciation, see 5.6.

10.5 Etymology. For cross reference between etymologies, see 6.1.3, 6.1.4.

10.6 Inflected Forms. For cross reference between inflected forms, see 8.1.2.

10.7 Synonyms. For cross reference between synonyms, discriminations of synonyms, and antonyms, see 12.4.

11. USAGE INFORMATION

11.1 Types of Information. There are many ways in which information on usage is given in this Dictionary. Sometimes it is given through restrictive labels and other means of direct guidance and sometimes through examples and other means of indirect guidance:

(a) Through subject labels. See 11.2.

(b) Through usage labels, that is, stylistic and regional labels. See 11.3.

(c) Through alternate spelling or alternate pronunciation, often with qualifying terms. See 11.4 and section 10.

(d) Through usage notes added in parentheses to definitions. See 11.5.

(e) Through explanatory examples added in italics to definitions. See 11.6.

(f) Through objects and subjects inserted in parentheses in definitions. See 11.7.

(g) Through the wording of the definitions proper, as in most entries of this Dictionary.

(h) Through the listing of synonyms and antonyms and through cross-referencing to synonyms in other main entries. See section 12.

(i) Through the narrative discrimination of synonyms under DISCR. See 12.3, 12.4.

(j) Through idioms and other phrases. See 2.4.

(k) As information on matters such as alternative proper names (10.2.5) or the singular and plural use of nouns (11.8, 7.5, 8.2) or their capitalization (7.6).

11.2 Subject Labels. In general, subject orientation is given through the definition itself, for example, through the mention of linguistics in

> as·ter·isk...*n* figure of a star * used as a reference, to indicate omission, or, in linguistics, a hypothetical or incorrect form

But in many cases a subject label is used to point out that a term belongs to a particular field of knowledge or activity or that it has a special meaning in that field.

11.2.1 Subject labels are set in italics and precede the definition or sense to which they apply. See 2.2 for examples of their position relative to the sense-dividing numbers and letters.

11.2.2 Over 150 subject labels are used in this Dictionary, ranging from *Buddhism* to *carnival slang*. Subject labels that occur frequently, about one half of the 150, are abbreviated and are included in the list of abbreviations on page 38a, as the labels for music, philosophy, chemistry, and bacteriology in these examples:

> weight...*n*...8 *statistics* relative importance of an object in relation to a set of objects to which it belongs...
> sig′na·ture...*n*...2 *mus* signs at the beginning of a staff showing the key and time...
> form...*n*...16 *philos* a essential nature; b idealized archetype; c that which determines the species or kind of something...
> mon·o·va·lent...*adj* 1 *chem* a having a valence of one; b having one valence; 2 *bacteriol* effective

against one pathological organism...

hit...*vt*...7 *baseball* to make (a base hit);...9 *underworld slang* to murder...‖ *n*...17 *baseball* base hit; 18 *underworld slang* planned murder...

snap'shot' *n* 1 instantaneous informal photograph; 2 *hunting* quick shot made without taking careful aim

Note that the label *photog* is not used for sense 1 of the last example because the subject or field is clear from the definition.

11.3 Usage Labels. Levels of usage are indicated by stylistic labels, as *substandard*. Geographic distribution of usage is indicated by regional labels, as *Australian*.

11.3.1 Like subject labels, usage labels are set in italics and precede the definition or sense to which they apply. See 2.2 for examples of their position relative to the sense-dividing numbers and letters.

11.3.2 Most of the stylistic labels (11.3.3) and the regional labels (11.3.4) are abbreviated and included in the list of abbreviations on page 38a.

11.3.3 Stylistic labels try to indicate commonly accepted levels of usage. This indication must be considered tentative and approximate. For example, it would be impossible to say objectively where *colloquial* usage ends and *slang* begins. Stylistic labels can be used together, as *poet. & literary*, or combined with regional labels, as *Brit vulgar*, or with other usage information, as: *often offensive* (11.4). Most of the stylistic labels used in this Dictionary appear in these examples:

dost...*archaic 2nd pers sg pres ind* of **do**[1]

yore...*n* of yore *poet. & literary* in old time; long ago

Ni-ag-a-ra...*n* 1 river...; 2 *fig* flood, torrent

who-ev'er *pron*...3 *emphatic* who

darn[2]...*vt, n, adv, interj euphem* damn

pret-ty...*adj*...3 *ironic* fine; 4 *colloq* considerable...

moon'light' *n*...‖ *vi* 2 *colloq* to work at another job after one's regular full-time work, esp. at night...

suck'er bet' *n slang* foolish bet which one has no chance of winning

snuck...*dial. pt & pp* of **sneak**

ain't...*substandard* 1 am not, is not, or are not; 2 have not or has not

youse...*pron illit* plural of **you**

grin-go...*n disparaging* (in Spanish-speaking countries of the Western Hemisphere) foreigner, esp. a citizen of the U.S.

11.3.4 Regional labels are given to indicate spelling, pronunciation, or meaning that is restricted to or typical of a country or a region.

(a) Words with variants of spelling or pronunciation, mainly in British usage:

gaol /jāl/ *n Brit* jail

lab-o-ra-to-ry /lab'(ə)rətôr'ȩ̄, -tōr'-, or *Brit* ləbôr'ətrē/...

(b) Words that are used differently outside the United States:

drap'er *n Brit* dealer in cloth, clothing, and dry goods

rip'ping *adj Brit slang* splendid

(c) Words that are used almost exclusively outside the United States:

bon-zer...*adj Australian* first-rate; wonderful

wig'ging *n Brit colloq* scolding

(d) Regional words or words with a particular regional meaning in the United States:

you-all /yōō-ôl', yôl'/ *pron S U.S.* used with plural meaning of *you*

sec-tion...*n*...5 *U.S. W of Ohio* subdivision of land one mile square, 1/36 of a township...

11.4 Other Qualifying Terms. Besides labels, which are used frequently, there are other terms that are used occasionally in qualifying roles in this Dictionary. Unlike labels, they are set in roman type. Some of them are abbreviated and are included in the list of abbreviations on page 38a.

11.4.1 Most of these qualifying terms occur in connection with cross references and variants, including the terms explained in section 10.

11.4.2 These qualifying terms (i) are used in conjunction with labels, as "chiefly" in "chiefly *Brit*," or (ii) precede directly the word they qualify, as "or preferably," or (iii) have other explanatory functions, as "usu. pejorative":

hang...*v* (**hung** or preferably **hanged**) *vt* 22 to suspend from the neck until dead...

-ard...also **-art**...*suf* used to form nouns...usu. pejorative, as *drunkard, braggart*

11.5 Usage Notes in Definitions. Many definitions are supplemented by usage notes, which are given in parentheses:

sic[1]...*adv* so, thus (often inserted in a quoted passage to indicate that it is quoted verbatim)

Ste. [F *Sainte*] Saint (referring to a woman)

11.6 Explanatory Examples. Many definitions are followed by examples that show the entry words in context. These examples are set in italics:

a·fraid...*adj* **1** frightened; **2** reluctant, as *afraid of work;* **3** regretful, as *I'm afraid I can't go...*

watch'er *n* **1** person who keeps watch or guard, as *car watcher;* **2** person who watches the passing scene out of curiosity or for some other motive, as *girl watcher;* **3** close observer of the internal conditions and the foreign policy of a foreign country, as *China watcher*

11.7 Objects and Subjects in Parentheses. Objects and subjects (and occasionally other words) are given in parentheses where needed. They indicate the context and the position of the entry word in a phrase or sentence, but are not themselves part of the meaning of the entry word:

nat'u·ral·ize' *vt* **1** to confer citizenship upon (an alien); **2** to adopt (a foreign word or custom); **3** to acclimatize (plants or animals)...

see'-through^ *adj* (garment) of transparent material, as mesh or net

11.8 Singular and Plural Labels. Certain main entries that are plural in form are labeled *nsg, npl,* or *nsg & npl* to show that they are (i) used as though they were singulars, or (ii) used as plurals only, or (iii) used as either singular or plural while retaining their plural form:

ge·net'ics *nsg...*
scis'sors...*npl...*
but'ter·fin'gers *nsg & npl...*
dram·a·tis per·so·nae...*npl.* **1** the characters in a play ‖ *nsg* **2** descriptive printed list of these characters

11.8.1 For nouns with identical forms in singular and plural, see 8.2.2d.

11.8.2 For singular nouns for which no plural form is given because they are not used in the plural, see 8.2.3.

11.8.3 For changes from singular to plural with different meaning or different use, see 7.5.

11.8.4 For different meanings with different plural forms, see 7.4.3.

12. SYNONYMS, DISCRIMINATIONS, AND ANTONYMS

12.1 General. Synonyms, discriminations of synonyms, and antonyms are given after all the other elements of an entry. They are introduced by the abbreviations SYN, DISCR, and ANT in small capital letters, and each of these abbreviations is preceded by parallels:

lib'er·ate'...*vt...*‖ **lib'er·a'tor** *n* ‖ **lib'er·a'tion** *n* ‖ SYN extricate, unfasten...‖ DISCR We *free* by setting at liberty that which...‖ ANT confine, restrain, hold

12.1.1 In addition to these groups, and in addition to cross references such as "opposite of" (10.1.4), there are many synonyms and antonyms that are discussed implicitly as part of the definitions.

12.2 Parts of Speech. A part-of-speech label follows SYN and ANT if the part of speech is different from the last part of speech of the main entry:

fit²...*adj...*‖ *v...vt...*‖ *vi...*‖ *n* ...‖ **fit'ly** *adv* ‖ **fit'ness** *n* ‖ SYN *adj* seemly...‖ DISCR To *fit* is to ...‖ ANT *adj* unsuitable...

12.2.1 Verbs are simply identified through *v.* This is the only instance where *v* is used in this Dictionary without irregular inflected forms and

where it is not followed by *vt* and/ or *vi* or *modal aux* (see 7.3.1):

a·ban·don...*vt...*‖ *n...*‖ **a·ban'don·ment** *n* ‖ SYN *v* leave...‖ DISCR...‖ ANT *v* keep...

Verbs following SYN and ANT are given without the "to" of the infinitive.

12.3 Discriminations. The discriminations of synonyms are usage notes. They are meant to be a feature that is both pleasant and useful, and for which this Dictionary is indebted to a defunct work, *The Winston (Senior) Dictionary.*

See, for example, the fine treatment of synonyms in the entry **ludicrous,** to which reference is made from the entries **comic, comical, droll, funny, laughable,** and **ridiculous.**

12.4 Cross References. Synonyms can refer to other main entries for related synonyms, discriminations, and antonyms. The entry referred to is set in italics, preceded by "see" in roman type, and put in parentheses. It appears at the end of the group of synonyms or, occasionally, instead of the synonyms:

plan...‖ SYN *n* project, purpose, sketch (see *design, scheme*)
grant...‖SYN *v* (see *give*); *n* (see *boon*¹)

12.4.1 A group of discriminated synonyms (DISCR) can refer to a group of related discriminated synonyms in another main entry. The entry referred to is set in italics, preceded by "see" or "cf." in roman type, and put in parentheses. This reference, which can be simple or reciprocal, appears at the end of the group labeled DISCR:

im·i·tate...‖ SYN...‖ DISCR To *imitate* is to...(see *follow*)

fol·low...‖ SYN...‖ DISCR *Follow*

is the general term. This verb has...

con·duct...‖ SYN...‖ DISCR *Conduct, direct,* and *manage* express ...(cf. *govern*)

gov·ern...‖ SYN...‖ DISCR To *command* is to...(cf. *conduct*)

12.4.2 See 10.1.4 for reference from the definition itself to the definition of another main entry that has an antonymous meaning ("opposite of").

13. SPECIAL ENTRIES

13.1 Elements. All chemical elements are listed. The definitions include symbol, atomic number, and atomic weight. These are shown in parentheses, and the symbol is set in boldface. The symbol, in addition, has its own entry if it has a different alphabetical position:

mer·cu·ry /murk′yərē/ [L *Mercurius*] *n* 1 heavy silvery metallic element (**Hg**; at.no. 80; at.wt. 200.59), liquid at...

Hg [L *hydrargyrum*] *chem* mercury

13.2 Chemicals. Chemical and pharmaceutical compounds are listed with formulae, which are set off by dashes:

so′di·um thi·o·sul′fate *n* white translucent powder —Na₂S₂O₃·5H₂O— used as a bleach and in photography...

as·pi·rin /asp′irin/ [acetyl + spiraeic acid] *n* drug —C₉H₈O₄— derived from salicylic acid, used as an analgesic for...

13.3 Animals and Plants. Animals and plants are listed with the Latin names of genus and species, which are set in italics and usually in parentheses, the genus beginning with a capital letter. Other biological divisions, such as family, order, class, and phylum, begin also with a capital letter, but are set in roman type:

aard·vark /ärd′värk′/ [Afrik = earth pig] *n* large ant-eating burrowing mammal of S Africa (*Orycteropus afer*) with long snout and slimy tongue

cat /kat′/ [OE *catt*, perh < L *cattus*] *n* 1 any of a family (Felidae) of carnivores, including the lion, tiger, and leopard; 2 small domesticated species (*Felis domestica*) often kept as a pet; 3...

ses·a·me /ses′əmē/ [Gk] *n* 1 tropical herb (*Sesamum indicum*) bearing edible seeds from which...

13.4 Geographical Names. Population, area, and capital are given for coun-

tries, the states of the United States, and provinces of Canada, etc.:

Guy·a·na /gī·an′ə, -än′ə/ *n* English-speaking nation in NE South America, formerly British Guiana (900,000; 83,000 sq.m.; cap. Georgetown)

Geor·gia /jôrj′ə/ *n* 1 state in SE United States (4,589,575; 58,876 sq.m.; cap. Atlanta); 2 constituent republic of the Soviet Union in Caucasia (4,000,000; 27,800 sq.m.; cap. Tiflis) ‖ **Geor′gian** *n*

Population is given for cities and towns, except very small ones:

Pe·king /pēk′iŋ′/ *n* capital of the People's Republic of China (8,000,000)

Get·tys·burg /get′izburg′/ *n* small town in S Pennsylvania, scene of crucial Civil War battle July 1–3, 1863

13.4.1 Geographical information can be hidden in the etymologies:

sher·ry /sher′ē/ [older *sheris* < *Xeres* (modern *Jerez*) town in Spain] *n* amber wine of varying sweetness...

13.5 Biographical Entries. Names of historical persons, past and present, are given as follows:

Ver·gil /vurj′il/ *n* (70–19 B.C.) Roman poet, author of the *Aeneid* ‖ **Ver·gil′i·an** *adj*

Rus·sell, Bert·rand /burt′rənd rus′əl/ *n* (Lord Russell) (1872–1970) British philosopher, mathematician, and social reformer; Nobel prize in literature 1950

Car·ter, Jim′my /kärt′ər/ *n* (1924–) 39th president of the U.S. 1977–

13.5.1 Much biographical information is hidden in the etymologies:

Or′ange·man /-mən/ [William of *Orange* (1650–1702), Protestant king of England 1689–1702, who defeated the Catholic James II in 1690] *n* (-men /-mən/) 1 member of an Irish secret society founded in 1795 to uphold Protestantism in Ireland; **2** Northern Irish Protestant

Also many *definitions* include biographical data, as **Köchel listing** (6.1.4).

13.5.2 For the alphabetical order of saints and entries derived from saints' names, see 3.1.2.

13.6 Fictional Names. Mythological, legendary, Biblical, and literary characters and entries are given as follows:

O·si·ris /ōsīr′is/ *n* chief Egyptian god of the underworld, brother and husband of Isis and father of Horus

E·ly′sian Fields′ *npl* *Gk myth.* abode of the blessed after death

Guin·e·vere /gwin′əvir′/ *n Arthurian legend* queen of King Arthur and mistress of Lancelot

Me·thu·se·lah /məthŏŏz′(ə)lə/ *n Bib* patriarch who is recorded to have lived 969 years (Gen. 5:27)

Bab·bitt /bab′it/ [protagonist of novel by Sinclair Lewis] *n* smug person who readily conforms to middle-class standards and conventions ‖ **Bab′bitt·ry** *n*

13.6.1 The information can be hidden in the etymologies:

si′mon-pure′ /sīm′ən/ [*Simon Pure* character in 18th-cent. play] *adj* real, genuine

14. GENERAL

14.1 This Dictionary is new in content and form. It is based on all the English dictionaries in print, on other printed and spoken sources, and on consultation with authorities in many fields.

14.2 This Dictionary is up to date. It includes a wealth of words, phrases, and meanings of current origin. Many of these terms are recorded for the first time in a dictionary.

14.3 Because of new space-saving techniques (too numerous to list here), this Dictionary contains more information than some dictionaries of much larger size.

14.4 The English of this Dictionary is American, but included are many words and meanings used in the United Kingdom, Canada, Australia, New Zealand, and other English-speaking countries.

14.5 A strong feature of this Dictionary is the amount of space given to the contemporary world of electronics, nuclear physics, ecology, surgery, space flight, etc., and the accuracy with which these entries are defined.

14.6 This Dictionary takes into account the advances in modern lexicography and is itself meant to make a contribution to lexicography through its methodological innovations.

14.7 Dictionaries are often classified as "prescriptive" (saying what is correct and what is wrong) on the one hand and "descriptive" (saying what is being said) on the other hand. Such a distinction may not be valid; but to the extent that it is made, this Dictionary leans toward being prescriptive. It is authoritative. When the average intelligent reader opens a dictionary, he or she wants to know the "correct" spelling or pronunciation or meaning of a word and is not interested in reading what the majority of speakers of the language tend to say.

However, THE SCRIBNER-BANTAM ENGLISH DICTIONARY acknowledges that language is alive, as can be seen from the many usage notes and the many examples that reflect *change* in the use of the language. It is obvious that all a dictionary can do is record the laws of language, it cannot make them. They are made by the user.

PRONUNCIATION KEY

*by Christopher Stavrou and
Edwin B. Williams*

1. English words are transcribed in this Dictionary with the following 42 symbols. Each symbol is defined here by examples of varied spellings and their phonetic transcriptions.

/a/

hat /hat′/, **plaid** /plad′/

/ä/

fa·ther /fä*th*′ər/, **calm** /käm′/, **hearth** /härth′/, **ser·geant** /sär′jənt/

/a, ä/

ask /ask′, äsk′/, **af·ter** /af′tər, äf′-/, **staff** /staf′, stäf′/, **class** /klas′, kläs′/, **graph** /graf′, gräf′/, **path** /path′, päth′/, **half** /haf′, häf′/, **calves** /kavz′, kävz′/, **sam·ple** /samp′əl, sämp′-/, **an·swer** /an′sər, än′-/, **dance** /dans′, däns′/, **branch** /branch′, bränch′/, **av·a·lanche** /av′əlanch′, -länch′/, **com·mand** /kəmand′, -mänd′/, **grant** /grant′, gränt′/

The letter a when accented and followed by s + stop, f + stop, ff, ss, ph, unvoiced th, lf /f/, lve /v/, mpl, ns, nc /ns/, nce, nch, nche, nd, or nt in about 150 words is pronounced /a/ in most parts of the United States; /ä/ in the south of England, in Boston, and in eastern Virginia; and with a sound intermediate between /a/ and /ä/ in the north of England, in Scotland, in Canada, and by some people in New England and New York City. In this Dictionary, when we show the pronunciation /a/ *and* /ä/ for a word, the intermediate sound is understood as an additional variant. Included among these words are **cas·tle** /kas′əl, käs′-/ although the t is silent, **rasp·ber·ry** /raz′ber′ē, räz′-/ although the p is silent, **rath·er** /ra*th*′ər, rä*th*′/ although the th is voiced, and three words with accented au instead of a, namely, **aunt** /ant′, änt′/, **draught** /draft′, dräft′/, and **laugh** /laf′, läf′/.

/ā/

fate /fāt′/, **aid** /ād′/, **say** /sā′/, **gaol** /jāl′/, **break** /brāk′/, **eight** /āt′/, **they** /*th*ā′/

/b/

bed /bed′/, **rob·ber** /rob′ər/

/ch/

cheep /chēp′/, **much** /much′/, **butch·er** /bŏŏch′ər/, **right·eous** /rīch′əs/, **na·ture** /nāch′ər/, **ques·tion** /kwes′chən/

/d/

day /dā′/, **rud·der** /rud′ər/

/e/

met /met′/, **man·y** /men′ē/, **said** /sed′/, **says** /sez′/, **feath·er** /fe*th*′ər/, **leop·ard** /lep′ərd/, **friend** /frend′/, **care** /ker′/, **chair** /cher′/, **prayer** /prer′/

/ē/

she /shē′/, **meet** /mēt′/, **beak** /bēk′/, **re·ceive** /risēv′/, **key** /kē′/, **peo·ple** /pēp′əl/, **ma·chine** /məshēn′/, **be·lieve** /bilēv′/, **ae·gis** /ē′jis/, **quay** /kē′/, **foe·tus** /fēt′əs/

/ē̗/

shin·y /shīn′ē̗/, **du·te·ous** /d(y)ŏŏt′ē̗-əs/, **lib·er·ty** /lib′ərtē̗/, **Mon·day** /mun′dē̗/, **mon·ey** /mun′ē̗/

This sound is similar to /ē/, but it is always unstressed and is shorter and laxer.

/ə/

or·phan /ôrf′ən/, **ma·chine** /məshēn′/, **moun·tain** /mount′ən/, **heav·en** /hev′ən/, **pen·cil** /pen′səl/, **par·don** /pärd′ən/, **po·ta·to** /pətāt′ō/, **bi·ol·o·gy** /bī·ol′əjē/, **au·gur** /ôg′ər/, **por·poise** /pôrp′əs/, **cu·ri·ous** /kyŏŏr′ē̗·əs/, **fa-**

33a

ther /fä*th*'ər/, per·ceive /pərsēv'/,
mar·tyr /mär'tər/

In this Dictionary the symbol /ə/
(called schwa) represents a sound that
is unstressed. When it is followed by
/r/, as in the last three examples above,
the two symbols together represent a
single sound, that of the so-called r-
colored vowel. The consonant sound
has disappeared, but its influence is
felt in the coloring of the vowel.

/f/

face /fās'/, muf·fin /muf'in/, phone
/fōn'/, tough /tuf'/

/g/

go /gō'/, give /giv'/, ag·grieve
/əgrēv'/, ex·act /igzakt'/

/h/

home /hōm'/, al·co·hol /al'kəhôl'/,
who /hōō'/

In this Dictionary /hw/ is taken to
represent two sounds, of which the /h/
is dropped by some speakers. It is,
therefore, shown thus /(h)w/; for example, when /(h)wen'/, white /(h)wīt'/

/i/

fit /fit'/, sieve /siv'/, se·ri·al /sir'ē·əl/,
been /bin'/, wom·en /wim'in/, bus·y
/biz'ē/, build /bild'/, hymn /him'/

/i/

rag·ged /rag'id/, serv·ice /surv'is/,
re·ceive /risēv'/

/i/ can act as an unstressed variant of
/ē/. It does not occur in final /ik/, for
example, eth·ic /eth'ik/; or in /iŋ/, for
example, fil·ings /fil'iŋz/

/ī/

time /tīm'/, night /nīt'/, tie /tī'/,
aisle /īl'/, height /hīt'/, eye /ī'/, buy
/bī'/, sky /skī'/, lye /lī'/

/j/

gem /jem'/, jeal·ous /jel'əs/, ver·dure
/vur'jər/, sol·dier /sōl'jər/, pledge
/plej'/, ex·ag·ger·ate /igzaj'ərāt'/, adjoin /əjoin'/

/k/

come /kum'/, ac·count /əkount'/,
back /bak'/, chord /kôrd'/, kick
/kik'/, ac·quit /əkwit'/, box /boks'/

/l/

late /lāt'/, al·low /əlou'/

/m/

man /man'/, sum·mer /sum'ər/

/n/

not /not'/, man·ner /man'ər/, know
/nō'/

/ŋ/

king /kiŋ'/, con·quer /koŋk'ər/, anx-
i·e·ty /aŋzī'itē/

/o/

hob·by /hob'ē/, prop·er /prop'ər/,
watch /woch'/

/ô/

north /nôrth'/, bought /bôt'/, warm
/wôrm'/, salt /sôlt'/, caught /kôt'/,
saw /sô'/

/o/ or /ô/

bor·row /bor'ō, bôr'ō/, sor·ry /sor'ē,
sôr'ē/, wash /wosh', wôsh'/, cof·fee
/kôf'ē, kof'ē/, gone /gôn', gon'/, song
/sôŋ', soŋ'/

The stressed o of many words is pronounced /o/ or /ô/, and this difference
is to some extent regional.

/ō/

nose /nōz'/, foam /fōm'/, foe /fō'/,
owe /ō'/, beau /bō'/, sew /sō'/,
though /*th*ō'/, know /nō'/, brooch
/brōch'/, yeo·man /yōm'ən/

/ô/ or /ō/

pork /pôrk', pōrk'/, more /môr',
mōr'/, glo·ry /glôr'ē, glōr'ē/, coarse
/kôrs', kōrs'/, door /dôr', dōr'/, court
/kôrt', kōrt'/

The letter o (also the digraphs oa, oo,
and ou) when stressed and followed by
r is also pronounced /ō/ in some
words.

/ô/ or /ä/

gaunt /gônt', gänt'/, saun·ter /sônt'ər,
sänt'-/, vaunt /vônt', vänt'/

The diagraph au when stressed and
followed by n is also pronounced /ä/.

/oi/

voice /vois'/, boy /boi'/, oys·ter
/oist'ər/

/ŏŏ/

wolf /wŏŏlf'/, good /gŏŏd'/, should
/shŏŏd'/, bush /bŏŏsh'/, pull /pŏŏl'/

/o͞o/

rude /ro͞od′/, move /mo͞ov′/, do /do͞o′/, lose /lo͞oz′/, tomb /to͞om′/, fool /fo͞ol′/, fruit /fro͞ot′/, ma·neu·ver /məno͞o′vər/, drew /dro͞o′/, group /gro͞op′/, two /to͞o′/

/ou/

bough /bou′/, sound /sound′/, cow /kou′/

/p/

pen /pen′/, sup·per /sup′ər/, stop /stop′/

/r/

rob /rob′/, art /ärt′/, car·ry /kar′ē/, far /fär′/, rhyme /rīm′/, ca·tarrh /kətär′/

The sounds of all the varieties of the letter r are shown in this Dictionary by /r/. The most common r in a large part of the United States and Canada and in many parts of England is a semivowel which is uttered with the point of the tongue turned up toward the hard palate and bent slightly back. In some positions it is very weak and can hardly be heard except when linked with the initial vowel of a following word. When r is preceded by /ə/ (above) or by /u/ (below), it disappears as a consonant sound, but gives a characteristic coloring to these vowel sounds.

/s/

sell /sel′/, es·say /es′ā/, hiss /his′/, schism /siz′əm/, cent /sent′/, fa·çade /fəsäd′/, box /boks′/, quartz /kwôrts′/

/sh/

shoe /sho͞o′/, schist /shist′/, o·cean /ōsh′ən/, ma·chine /məshēn′/, vi·cious /vish′əs/, man·sion /mansh′ən/, pas·sion /pash′ən/, is·sue /ish′o͞o/, na·tion /nāsh′ən/, con·science /konsh′əns/, sug·ar /sho͞og′ər/, anx·ious /aŋk′shəs/, push /po͞osh′/

/t/

ten /ten′/, bet·ter /bet′ər/, hat /hat′/

/th/

this·tle /this′əl/, e·ther /ēth′ər/, truth /tro͞oth′/

/th/

this /this′/, ei·ther /ēth′ər/, smooth /smo͞oth′/

/u/

cup /kup′/, love /luv′/, done /dun′/, does /duz′/, blood /blud′/, dou·ble /dub′əl/, burn /burn′/, bird /burd′/, jour·ney /jurn′ē/, myr·tle /murt′əl/

In this Dictionary this symbol represents a sound that is stressed. When it is followed by r, as in the last four examples above, the two symbols together represent a single sound, that of the so-called r-colored vowel. The consonant sound has disappeared, but its influence is felt in the coloring of the vowel.

/v/

vest /vest′/, riv·er /riv′ər/, of /uv′/, revved /revd′/

/w/

work /wurk′/, tweed /twēd′/, queen /kwēn′/, choir /kwī′(ə)r/

/y/

yes /yes′/, on·ion /un′yən/, feud /fyo͞od′/, few /fyo͞o′/, ewe /yo͞o′/, u·nit /yo͞on′it/

/z/

zeal /zēl′/, bus·y /biz′ē/, his /hiz′/, these /thēz′/

/zh/

az·ure /azh′ər/, gla·zier /glāzh′ər/, meas·ure /mezh′ər/, vi·sion /vizh′ən/, rouge /ro͞ozh′/

2. FOREIGN SOUNDS

(See paragraph 5.3 of the GUIDE TO THE DICTIONARY.)

/kh/

Scottish: loch /lokh′/; German: doch /dōkh′/, Johann Sebastian Bach /bäkh′/

/kh/

German: ich /ikh′/, nichts /nikhts′/, Kö′chel list′ing /kœkh′əl/

/œ/

French: feu /fœ′/, peu /pœ′/; German: schön /shœn′/, Goe·the /gœt′ə/

/Y/

French: tu /tY′/, dé·jà vu /dāzhä vY′/; German: grün /grYn′/, Walküre /välkY′rə/

/N/

This symbol is not a sound but indicates that the preceding symbol is a nasal. French: /aN/ and /äN/ in vin blanc /vaN′ bläN′/ and an·cien ré·gime /äNsyaN′ räzhēm′/, /ôN/ in bon /bôN/ and fait ac·com·pli /fa′-täkôNplē′/; Portuguese: /ouN/ in Saõ Pau·lo /souN pou′lo͞o/

3. PRONUNCIATION OF THE PAST TENSE

3.1 If a word ending in -ed (or -d after a mute e) is pronounced according to the following principles, its pronunciation is not shown in this Dictionary provided the pronunciation of the form without the ending is shown where it stands as a separate entry. The doubling of the final consonant after a simple stressed vowel does not alter the pronunciation of the ending -ed.

The ending -ed (or -d after a mute e) of the past tense, the past participle, and certain adjectives has three different pronunciations depending on the sound of the stem ending:

3.1.1 If the stem ends in a voiceless consonant sound except /t/, namely, /ch/, /f/, /k/, /p/, /s/, /sh/, or /th/, then -ed is pronounced /t/.

SOUND OF STEM ENDING	INFINITIVE	PAST TENSE AND PAST PARTICIPLE
/ch/	match /mach'/	matched /macht'/
/f/	loaf /lōf'/ knife /nīf'/	loafed /lōft'/ knifed /nīft'/
/k/	back /bak'/ bake /bāk'/	backed /bakt'/ baked /bākt'/
/p/	cap /kap'/ wipe /wīp'/	capped /kapt'/ wiped /wīpt'/
/s/	hiss /his'/ mix /miks'/	hissed /hist'/ mixed /mikst'/
/sh/	mash /mash'/ cache /kash'/	mashed /masht'/ cached /kasht'/
/th/	lath /lath'/	lathed /latht'/

3.1.2 If the stem ends in a voiced consonant sound except /d/, namely, /b/, /g/, /j/, /l/, /m/, /n/, /ŋ/, /r/, /th/, /v/, /z/, /zh/ or in a vowel sound, then -ed is pronounced /d/.

SOUND OF STEM ENDING	INFINITIVE	PAST TENSE AND PAST PARTICIPLE
/b/	ebb /eb'/ rob /rob'/ robe /rōb'/	ebbed /ebd'/ robbed /robd'/ robed /rōbd'/
/g/	egg /eg'/ sag /sag'/	egged /egd'/ sagged /sagd'/
/j/	page /pāj'/	paged /pājd'/
/l/	mail /māl'/ scale /skāl'/	mailed /māld'/ scaled /skāld'/
/m/	storm /stôrm'/ bomb /bom'/ name /nām'/	stormed /stôrmd'/ bombed /bomd'/ named /nāmd'/
/n/	tan /tan'/ sign /sīn'/	tanned /tand'/ signed /sīnd'/
/ŋ/	hang /haŋ'/	hanged /haŋd'/
/r/	fear /fir'/ care /ker'/	feared /fird'/ cared /kerd'/
/th/	smooth /smōōth'/ bathe /bāth'/	smoothed /smōōthd'/ bathed /bāthd'/
/v/	rev /rev'/ save /sāv'/	revved /revd'/ saved /sāvd'/

SOUND OF STEM ENDING	INFINITIVE	PAST TENSE AND PAST PARTICIPLE
/z/	buzz /buz′/ fuse /fyo͞oz′/	buzzed /buzd′/ fused /fyo͞ozd′/
/zh/	mas·sage /məsäzh′/	mas·saged /məsäzhd′/
vowel sound	key /kē′/ sigh /sī′/ paw /pô′/	keyed /kēd′/ sighed /sīd′/ pawed /pôd′/

3.1.3 If the stem ends in a dental sound, namely, /t/ or /d/, then **-ed** is pronounced /id/.

SOUND OF STEM ENDING	INFINITIVE	PAST TENSE AND PAST PARTICIPLE
/t/	wait /wāt′/ mate /māt′/	wait·ed /wāt′id/ mat·ed /māt′id/
/d/	mend /mend′/ wade /wād′/	mend·ed /mend′id/ wad·ed /wād′id/

THE PRONUNCIATION SYSTEM OF THIS DICTIONARY IS FURTHER EXPLAINED IN SECTION 5 OF THE GUIDE TO THE DICTIONARY.

ABBREVIATIONS USED IN THIS DICTIONARY

Common abbreviations such as **B.C.**, etc., **ft.**, **U.S.**, or chemical symbols are given as dictionary entries and are not included on this list.

Certain abbreviations on this list are used together, e.g., *Gk myth., phys geog, Prot Episc Ch,* or are combined with dictionary entries to form labels, e.g., *Norse myth., Scand folklore, archaic & poet.*

Most labels used in this Dictionary are not included on this list as they are taken entirely from dictionary entries, e.g., *tennis, Arthurian legend, western U.S.*

ab. about
abbr abbreviation
acc accusative
adj adjective
adv adverb
aeron aeronautics
AF Anglo-French
Afr African
Afrik Afrikaans
agr agriculture
Aleut Aleutian
alg algebra
alter. alteration
Am, Amer. American
AmInd American Indian
AmSp American Spanish
anat anatomy
anc ancient
ant antonym(s)
anthrop anthropology
approx. approximately
Ar Arabic
Aram Aramaic
arch. architecture
archaeol archaeology
arith arithmetic
art article; art
Assyr Assyrian
astrol astrology
astron astronomy
at.no. atomic number
at.wt. atomic weight
auto automobile
aux auxiliary
b. born
bacteriol bacteriology
Bib Bible

biochem biochemistry
biol biology
bot botany
Brit British
c., ca. circa (about)
Can Canadian
CanF Canadian French
cap. capital (of a country)
Carib Caribbean
carp carpentry
Cat Catalan
Celt Celtic
cent. century
cgs centimeter-gram-second
Ch Church
chem chemistry
Chin Chinese
class. classical
colloq colloquial(ism)
com commerce
comb form combining form
comp comparative
conj conjunction
Conn Connecticut
contr. contraction
d. died
D Dutch
dat dative
def definite
dem demonstrative
dial. dialect(al)
dim. diminutive
discr discrimination(s)
E East; eastern
eccl ecclesiastical
econ economics
educ education
Egypt. Egyptian
elec electricity
electron electronics
embryol embryology
Eng English; England
entom entomology
Episc Episcopal
esp. especially
euphem euphemism
F French
fem feminine
fig figurative
fin finance
Finn Finnish
Flem Flemish
G German
Gael Gaelic

38a

gen genitive
geog geography
geol geology
geom geometry
ger gerund
Gk Greek
Gmc Germanic
gov. governor
gram grammar
Heb Hebrew
heral heraldry
hist history; historical
horol horology
hort horticulture
Hung Hungarian
Icel Icelandic
illit illiterate
imit imitative
impers impersonal
impv imperative
ind indicative
Ind Indian
indef indefinite
interj interjection
Ir Irish
ISV International Scientific
    Vocabulary
It Italian
Jap Japanese
L Latin
LaF Louisiana French
LG Low German
LGk Late Greek
ling linguistics
LL Late Latin
mach machinery
masc masculine
math mathematics
Md Maryland
MD Middle Dutch
ME Middle English
mech mechanics
med medicine
meteor. meteorology
MexSp Mexican Spanish
MF Middle French
MFlem Middle Flemish
MGk Middle Greek
MHG Middle High German
mil military
mineral. mineralogy
mks meter-kilogram-second
ML Medieval Latin
MLG Middle Low German
mod modern
modal aux modal auxiliary
ModGk Modern Greek
ModHeb Modern Hebrew
mus music
myth. mythology
n noun
N North; northern
nat. native
naut nautical
nav naval; Navy
NE northeast(ern)
N Eng New England
neut neuter
nfem feminine noun
NL New Latin

nom nominative
Norw Norwegian
npl plural noun
nsg singular noun
num numeral
NW northwest(ern)
obs obsolete
ODa Old Danish
OE Old English
OF Old French
OHG Old High German
OIr Old Irish
OIt Old Italian
OLG Old Low German
ON Old Norse
ONF Old Norman French
OPers Old Persian
OProv Old Provençal
orig. originally
ornith ornithology
OSerbian Old Serbian
OSlav Old Slavic
OSp Old Spanish
Pa Pennsylvania
PaG Pennsylvania German
pathol pathology
perh perhaps
pers person
Pers Persian
pert. pertaining
pharm pharmacy
philol philology
philos philosophy
phonet phonetics
photog photography
phys physics; physical
physiol physiology
pl plural
poet. poetic
pol politics
Pol Polish
Port Portuguese
poss possessive
pp past participle
pref prefix
prep preposition
pres present
prob probably
pron pronoun
pros prosody
Prot Protestant
Prov Provençal
prp present participle
psychoanal psychoanalysis
psychol psychology
pt past tense
rad radio
R C Ch Roman Catholic
    Church
rhet rhetoric(al)
Rom Roman
Russ Russian
S South; southern
Sc Scottish
Scand Scandinavian
Scot Scotland; Scotch
SE southeast(ern)
Sem Semitic
sg singular
show bus. show business

Skt Sanskrit
Sp Spanish
SpAm Spanish America
spec. specifically
sq.m. square miles
subj subjunctive
suf suffix
superl superlative
surg surgery
Sw Swedish
SW southwest(ern)
SwissG Swiss German
syn synonym(s)
telg telegraphy
telv television
Teut Teutonic
theat theater
theol theology
trig trigonometry
Turk Turkish
typ typography, printing
UK United Kingdom
usu. usually
v verb
Va Virginia

var variant
v aux auxiliary verb
vi intransitive verb
v impers impersonal verb
VL Vulgar Latin
vt transitive verb
W West; western
WAfr West Africa
WInd West Indies
zool zoology

/pronunciation: between slant lines/

′   primary accent
‵   secondary accent

[etymology: in brackets]

=   means
<   derived from
+   added to
?   origin unknown; perhaps
*   hypothetical

THE
SCRIBNER-
BANTAM
ENGLISH
DICTIONARY

A

A, a /ā/ *n* (A's or As, a's or as) first letter of the English alphabet

A 1 *chem* argon; 2 first in order or in a series; 3 *mus* sixth tone in the scale of C major; 4 superior grade rating, as of bonds, credit risks, or student's work; 5 blood type; 6 something shaped like an A

a /ə; when stressed: ā/ [OE *ān* one] (used before singular nouns beginning with a consonant sound, as *a man, a union*) *indef art* 1 used before unspecified count nouns, as *I have a book*; 2 the same, as *birds of a feather*; 3 [by confusion with *a-¹*] per, as *once a week*

a-¹ [OE *an* on] *pref* 1 on, into, in, to, as *ashore*; 2 in the state of, as *asleep*; 3 in the act of, as *go a-hunting*

a-² [OE *ā, ar* up] *pref* up, out, away, as *arise*

a-³ [OE *of*] *pref* of, as *akin*

a-⁴ or **an-** [Gk] *pref* not, without, as *apathy, anarchy*

a-⁵ var of *ad-*

A. 1 America; 2 American; 3 angstrom unit; 4 April; 5 Academy; 6 Artillery

A., a. 1 acre(s); 2 [L *anno*] year; 3 [L *ante*] before

Å angstrom unit

A-1 *adj* excellent, first class

A.A. antiaircraft

aard·vark /ärd'värk'/ [Afrik = earth pig] *n* large ant-eating burrowing mammal of S Africa (*Orycteropus afer*) with long snout and slimy tongue

Aar·on /ar'ən, er'-/ *n* first high priest of the Hebrews, older brother of Moses (Ex. 28; 40:13-16)

A.A.U. Amateur Athletic Union

ab- [L = from] *pref* from, away, off, as *abduct, abdicate*

A.B. 1 [able-bodied] able seaman ‖ 2 [L *Artium Baccalaureus*] Bachelor of Arts

a·back /əbak'/ *adv* taken **aback** disconcerted

ab·a·cus /ab'əkəs/ [L < Gk *abax* counting tablet] *n* (-cus·es or -ci /-sī'/) 1 frame containing beads strung on wires, used for arithmetical calculations; 2 *arch.* flat layer of stone on top of the capital of a column

a·baft /əbaft', əbäft'/ [*a-¹* + ME *baft* aft] *naut prep* 1 behind ‖ *adv* 2 at, to, or toward the stern

ab·a·lo·ne /ab'əlōn'ē/ [AmSp *abulón*] *n* large edible sea mollusk (genus *Haliotis*), with an ear-shaped shell

a·ban·don /əban'dən/ [MF *abandoner*] *vt* 1 to give up entirely; 2 to desert; 3 to yield (oneself) without restraint,

as to an impulse ‖ *n* 4 freedom of manner, dash; 5 complete surrender to natural impulse ‖ **a·ban'don·ment** *n* ‖ SYN *v* leave, forsake, desert, renounce, relinquish, quit, forgo, surrender, resign, abdicate ‖ DISCR *Abandon, desert, forsake,* and *relinquish* are alike in the idea of leaving. To *abandon* is to leave entirely, either from necessity, as the crew *abandoned* the sinking ship; or from neglect or violation of duty, as the mother *abandoned* her child; or by a surrender of self-control, as he *abandoned* himself to dissipation. To *desert* is to leave by breaking the bonds of faithfulness or honor, as he *deserted* his aged father; the soldier *deserted* his post. To *forsake* is to leave by ceasing to seek or stay with, as he *forsook* all youthful companionship; my strength *forsakes* me in an emergency. To *relinquish* is to give up to another, as he *relinquished* his claim to the property. *Renounce* relates especially to giving up some abstract thing, as an idea, a belief, a friendship. To *forgo* is to give up something valued, for the sake of a greater good or for the benefit of another. *Resign* and *abdicate* both have to do with the giving up of a position; but an elected officer *resigns,* while a king *abdicates* his throne. *Surrender* suggests giving up under compulsion ‖ ANT *v* keep, cherish, retain, hold, attain, adopt, maintain

a·ban'doned *adj* 1 deserted; 2 unrestrained; 3 free from moral restraint, shameless

a·base /əbās'/ [MF *abaissier*] *vt* to humble, degrade ‖ **a·base'ment** *n* ‖ SYN humble, mortify, degrade, reduce, lower

a·bash /əbash'/ [AF *abair (-isse)* to astonish] *vt* to take away the self-possession of, disconcert ‖ **a·bashed'** *adj* ‖ SYN discomfit, humiliate, discompose (see *embarrass*)

a·bate /əbāt'/ [OF *abatre* to beat down] *vt* 1 to lessen in number, degree, force, or value; 2 *law* to end ‖ *vi* 3 to decrease, subside ‖ **a·bate'ment** *n* ‖ SYN lessen, moderate, mitigate (see *decrease*)

ab·a·tis /ab'ətis, -tē'/ [F] *n* (-tis·es or -tis /-tēz'/) defense of felled trees with branches pointing toward the direction of expected attack

A' bat·ter·y *n* battery of low voltage and high amperage for heating the filaments or cathode heaters of electron tubes for the purpose of causing the emission of electrons

ab·at·toir /ˈab/ətwär/ [F] *n* slaughter-house

ab·ba·cy /ˈab/əsē/ [LL *abbatia*] *n* (-cies) office, term, or tenure of an abbot

ab·bé /abā/, abˈā/ [F < L *abbas*] *n* 1 abbot; 2 title of respect of certain French priests

ab·bess /ˈab/is/ [OF *abaësse* < LL *abatissa*] *n* mother superior of a convent

ab·bey /ˈab/ē/ [OF *abaïe* < LL *abbatia*] *n* 1 monastery or convent; 2 abbey buildings; 3 abbey church

ab·bot /ˈab/ət/ [OE *abbod* < L *abbas* (-*atis*)] *n* head of a monastery

abbr. also **abbrev.** abbreviation

ab·bre·vi·ate /əˈbrēvˈē·āt/ [L *abbreviare* (-*atus*)] *vt* 1 to shorten; make shorter or briefer; 2 to shorten (a word) by omitting one or more initial or final syllables of it or by contracting it ‖ SYN reduce, contract, abridge, condense, curtail

ab·bre·vi·a/tion *n* 1 act or result of abbreviating; 2 shortened form of a word which can be pronounced and has all the grammatical characteristics of a part of speech, as *auto* for *automobile* and *phone* for *telephone;* 3 contracted form of a word which usu. cannot be pronounced and cannot be or is not used as an acronym or letterword, as *bldg.* for *building*

ABC /ˈā/bēˈsē/ *n* (**ABC's**, **ABCs**) 1 first steps or elementary facts of a subject; 2 **ABC's** *pl* the alphabet

ab·di·cate /ˈab/dikāt/ [L *abdicare* (-*atus*)] *vt* 1 to give up formally, as kingly power or rights; surrender, as power or duty ‖ *vi* 2 to give up sovereign power ‖ **ab/di·ca/tion** *n* ‖ **ab/di·ca/tor** *n* ‖ SYN relinquish, surrender, renounce (see *abandon*)

ab·do·men /ˈab/dōm/ən, abˈdōmən/ [L] 1 in higher vertebrates, the lower cavity of the body below the diaphragm; 2 in insects and crustaceans, the part of the body behind the thorax ‖ **ab·dom/i·nal** /-domˈinəl/ *adj*

ab·duct /abˈdukt/ [L *abducere* (-*ductus*)] 1 to carry off by force, kidnap; 2 *anat* to move away from the midline of the body ‖ **ab·duc/tion** *n* ‖ **ab·duc/tor** *n*

a·beam /əˈbēm/ *adv* & *adj* in a direction at right angles to the keel of a ship

a·bed /əˈbed/ *adv* in bed

A·bel /ˈā/bəl/ *n* second son of Adam and Eve, slain by his brother Cain (Gen. 4)

ab·er·rant /aˈber/ənt/ [< L *aberrare* to stray] *adj* 1 straying from the right or normal course; 2 atypical, abnormal ‖ *n* 3 aberrant person or thing ‖ **ab·er/rance** or **ab·er/ran·cy** *n*

ab·er·ra·tion /ˈab/ərāshən/ *n* 1 wandering from the right way; error; 2 deviation from the normal type; 3 partial derangement of the mind; 4 deviation from a true focus, as of light rays; 5 slight apparent shifting in position of a heavenly body

a·bet /əˈbet/ [OF *abeter* to bait] *v* (-bet·ted; -bet·ting) *vt* 1 to aid or encourage by upholding or supporting, usu. in criminal acts; 2 to aid, assist, or support ‖ **a·bet/ment** *n* ‖ **a·bet/ter** or **a·bet/tor** *n* ‖ SYN assist, countenance, sanction, instigate, incite

a·bey·ance /əˈbā/əns/ [AF < OF *abeance* expectation] *n* 1 holding or keeping inactive for a time, temporary inactivity; 2 *law* state of indeterminateness or expectancy

ab·hor /əbˈhôr/, ab-/ [L *abhorrere* to shrink back] *v* (-horred; -hor·ring) *vt* to regard with horror or disgust; to loathe ‖ SYN despise, detest, dislike, disdain, abominate

ab·hor/rence /-hôr/-, -hor/-/ *n* 1 feeling of detestation; loathing; 2 that which excites strong repugnance or is loathed

ab·hor/rent /-hôr/-, -hor/-/ *adj* 1 causing repugnance; 2 **abhorrent** to contrary to; in conflict with ‖ SYN offensive, loathsome, detestable (see *hateful*)

a·bide /əˈbīd/ [OE *ābīdan*] *v* (a·bode or a·bid·ed) *vt* 1 to await; 2 to submit to, tolerate ‖ *vi* 3 to reside; 4 to remain; 5 to continue, as in a state or condition; 6 **abide by, a** to remain steadfast to; **b** to conform to ‖ **a·bid/ance** *n* ‖ SYN accept, live, lodge, remain, dwell

a·bid/ing *adj* lasting, enduring

a·bil·i·ty /əˈbil/itē/ [MF *abilite* < L *habilitas* aptness] *n* (-ties) 1 sufficient physical or mental capacity to perform; 2 skill, talent ‖ SYN energy, force, capacity, talent, aptitude, skill, competency, efficiency, faculty, dexterity, power ‖ DISCR *Ability* is the general term for power, either physical or mental. *Ability* and *capacity*, when applied to persons, are alike in indicating mental power, but *capacity* signifies the native strength of the mind, developed or not; while *ability*, especially in the plural, signifies natural mental strength, plus training. Thus, *ability* includes natural *capacity*, as at thirty his *abilities* had placed him above men of greater natural *capacity*. *Talent* (cf. *genius*) is exceptional mental *ability*, as he is a man of *talent;* often it is a special mental gift, a particular power, as of play acting or performing on a musical instrument, capable of being developed through training, often expressed through perfection in technique. *Faculty* is a power of mind or body born in us, as the *faculty* of reasoning. *Competency* is power immediately equal to the demands made upon it; *efficiency* is the power to do quickly and well; *skill* and *dexterity* refer to an easy power to do or carry out some specific work; but *skill* refers to both hand and brain, while *dexterity* refers particularly to the use of the hands, as the *skill* of a bridge player or of a carpenter; the manual *dexterity* of a juggler || ANT incompetency, inefficiency, awkwardness, incapacity

-a·bil·i·ty *n suf* capacity to act or be acted on in a specified manner, as *vulnerability*

ab·ject /ab'jekt, abjekt'/ [L *abjectus* thrown down] *adj* 1 cringing, mean; 2 hopeless, wretched || **ab·ject'ly** *adv* ||**ab·ject'ness** *n* || **ab·jec'tion** *n* || SYN groveling, slavish, beggarly, servile, despicable

ab·jure /abjŏŏr'/ [L *abjurare* to deny on oath] *vt* 1 to renounce or give up under oath; 2 to repudiate, recant; 3 to abstain from || **ab·ju·ra'tion** *n* || **ab·jur'er** *n* || SYN repudiate, recant, retract, disavow, abandon, forswear || ANT maintain, uphold, retain, support, assert

ab·la·tion /ablāsh'ən/ [LL *ablatio* (-*onis*) < L *ablatus* carried away] *n* 1 removal of growths or parts of the body by surgery; 2 burning away of the nose cone of a rocket or space vehicle on reentry

ab·la·tive /ab'lətiv/ [< L *ablatus* carried away] *n* 1 grammatical case in Latin denoting chiefly separation, removal, or instrumentality; 2 noun in this case || also *adj*

ab·laut /ab'lout, äp'-/ [G = off-sound] *n* systematic alternation of the root vowel in different forms of the same word or related words, as *sing, sang, sung*

a·blaze /əblāz'/ *adj* 1 flaming; 2 gleaming; 3 eager, ardent

a·ble /āb'əl/ [MF < L *habilis* skillful] *adj* 1 possessed of sufficient power, fitness, or means; 2 competent; 3 well qualified mentally || *n* 4 Able communications code word for the letter A || **a·bly** /āb'lē/ *adv* || SYN capable, adequate, sufficient, qualified, sagacious, talented || ANT incapable, unable

-a·ble /-əbəl/ [MF < L -*abilis*] *adj suf* 1 able to, as *durable*; 2 capable of being, as *readable*; 3 fit to be, as *printable*; 4 characterized by, as *peaceable*

a'ble sea'man *n* deckhand on a merchant ship certified as able to perform certain routine duties

a·bloom /əblōōm'/ *adj* flowering

ab·lu·tion /əblōōsh'ən/ [L *ablutio* (-*onis*)] *n* 1 a washing of the body; b ceremonial washing done as a religious duty; 2 liquid used for washing

ab·ne·gate /ab'nigāt'/ [L *abnegare* (-*atus*)] *vt* 1 to deny, reject; 2 to give up or surrender || **ab'ne·ga'tion** *n*

ab·nor·mal /abnôr'məl/ [F *anormal* < ML *anormalis*] *adj* irregular, deformed, unnatural, not conforming to rule or type || **ab·nor'mal·ly** *adv* || **ab'nor·mal'i·ty** /-mal'-/ *n*

a·board /əbôrd', əbōrd'/ *adv* 1 on, into, or within a ship, train, plane, or bus || *prep* 2 on board of; on, in, or into (a conveyance)

a·bode¹ /əbōd'/ [ME *abood* stay] *n* 1 dwelling place, home; 2 stay

a·bode² *pt* & *pp* of **abide**

a·bol·ish /əbol'ish/ [MF *abolir* (-*lisse*)] *vt* to do away with, put an end to || SYN (see *cancel*) || ANT support, continue, renew

ab·o·li·tion /ab'əlish'ən/ *n* 1 act or state of abolishing; 2 political movement seeking to abolish slavery, esp. in the U.S. before the Civil War || **ab'o·li'tion·ism** *n* || **ab'o·li'tion·ist** *n*

A'-bomb' *n* atom bomb || also *vt*

a·bom·i·na·ble /əbom'inəbəl/ *adj* 1 odious, revolting, vile; 2 disagreeable, unpleasant; bad || **a·bom'i·na·bly** *adv* || SYN infamous, detestable, disgusting, loathsome

A·bom'i·na·ble Snow'man' *n* manlike or bearlike beast said to inhabit the Himalayas

a·bom'i·nate' /-nāt'/ [L *abominari* (-*atus*)] *vt* to regard with disgust or hatred, abhor || SYN abhor, loathe, detest, dislike, hate

a·bom'i·na'tion *n* 1 excessive hatred or disgust; loathing; 2 anything vile or hateful; anything that excites or deserves loathing || SYN nuisance, annoyance, offense, shame

ab·o·rig·i·nal /ab'ərij'inəl/ *adj* 1 a original, first, indigenous; b existing from the beginning; 2 pert. to the aborigines || *n* 3 aboriginal plant or animal

ab'o·rig'i·ne /-nē/ [L *ab origine* from the beginning] *n* 1 one of the first inhabitants of a region, esp. the primitive inhabitants of a country occupied by a technologically more advanced race; 2 **aborigines** *pl* native plants, animals, or people of a region

a·born·ing /əbôr'ning/ [a-¹ + dial. *borning* birth] *adv* 1 in birth; 2 coming into being

a·bort /əbôrt'/ [L *aboriri* (-*ortus*)] *vt* 1 to have a miscarriage; 2 to fail of development, remain rudimentary; 3 of a rocket or missile, to fail to complete a scheduled flight || *vt* 4 to end at a premature stage, as a pregnancy, disease, rocket or missile flight, plot, plan, uprising || *n* 5 abortive flight of an aircraft; 6 rocket or missile that has aborted

a·bor·tion /əbôr'shən/ *n* 1 spontaneous expulsion of a fetus during the first 12 weeks of pregnancy; **2** induced and sometimes illegal expulsion of nonviable fetus; **3** monstrosity; **4** failure of development, as of an embryo, disease, plan, etc.; **5** anything that fails to develop or mature

a•bor′tion•ist *n* person who performs illegal abortions

a•bor′tive /-tiv/ *adj* **1** born too soon; **2** imperfectly developed; **3** fruitless, unsuccessful ǁ **a•bor′tive•ly** *adv*

a•bound /əbound′/ [OF *abunder*] *vi* **1** to exist in plenty or abundance; **2** to have great plenty, teem

a•bout /əbout′/ [OE *abūtan* on the outside] *adv* **1** around; **2 a** approximately; **b** nearly, almost; **3** in a state of action, as *he was up and about;* **4 about to** on the point of ǁ *prep* **5** concerning; **6** somewhere around, as *he is about the house;* **7** all around, surrounding; **8** in the possession of, as *he kept his wits about him;* **9** over, throughout, as *rumors spread about the countryside;* **10** at about approximately at

a•bout′-face′ *n* reversal of position, direction, or attitude ǁ *also vt*

a•bove /əbuv′/ [OE *abufan*] *adv* **1** in a higher place, overhead; **2** of higher rank; **3** before or earlier, as in a book ǁ *prep* **4 a** higher than, over; **b** north of; **5** in excess of; **6** beyond ǁ *adj* **7** above-mentioned ǁ *n* **8** the **above** the previously mentioned persons or things

a•bove′board′ *adv & adj* without concealment or trickery

abr. 1 abridged; **2** abridgment

ab•ra•ca•dab•ra /ab′rəkədab′rə/ [LL] *n* **1** mystical word, the letters of which, arranged in a triangle, were supposed to possess magic powers; **2** spell; **3** jargon

a•brade /əbrād′/ [L *abradere* scrape off] *vt* **1** to wear or rub away, as by friction; **2** to break or injure, as the skin, by rubbing ǁ *also vi*

A•bra•ham /ā′brəham′/ *n* the first great patriarch of the Hebrews, founder of the race (Gen. 11–25)

a•bra•sion /əbrāzh′ən/ [< L *abrasus* scraped off] *n* **1** act of abrading; **2** abraded area, esp. of the skin

a•bra•sive /əbrās′iv, -ziv/ *adj* **1** causing abrasion ǁ *n* **2** substance used to abrade, as for polishing

a•breast /əbrest′/ *adv* **1** side by side; **2 abreast of** or **with, a** in a line with; **b** equal to in knowledge or progress; **c** informed of

a•bridge /əbrij′/ [L *abbreviare* via MF] *vt* **1** to shorten, using fewer words but retaining essential ideas; **2** to condense, curtail

a•bridg′ment or **a•bridge′ment** *n* **1** act of abridging or state of being abridged; **2** abridged form of a book ǁ **SYN** compendium, abbreviation, digest,

synopsis ǁ **ANT** expansion, elaboration, amplification

a•broad /əbrôd′/ *adv* **1** in or to foreign countries, esp. beyond N America; **2** out of doors, in the open; **3** widely, broadly, far and wide

ab•ro•gate /ab′rəgāt′/ [L *abrogare (-atus)*] *vt* to abolish or repeal by authority, as a privilege ǁ **ab′ro•ga′tion** *n* ǁ **SYN** revoke, suppress, rescind, repeal (see *cancel*)

ab•rupt /əbrupt′/ [L *abruptus* broken off] *adj* **1** rising or dropping at a sharp angle from a certain level; ending suddenly; **2** sudden; **3** unceremonious; **4** disconnected ǁ **ab•rupt′ly** *adv* ǁ **ab•rupt′ness** *n* ǁ **SYN** rough, sheer, steep, precipitous, perpendicular, rugged, sharp; hasty, unexpected; blunt, discourteous, brusque, curt; unconnected, broken ǁ **DISCR** *Abrupt, steep,* and *precipitous* are alike in describing irregularities of surface. *Abrupt* describes a sharp irregularity of surface and applies either to a rising or descending slope; *steep* suggests a very sharp ascent, as a *steep* hill; *precipitous* suggests a sheer, vertical drop. *Abrupt* and *rugged* are alike in expressing the idea of unevenness; the sharp drop of a canyon wall is *abrupt;* a wooded, rocky, *steep* road is *rugged. Rough* suggests an unevenness that is merely a lack of smoothness, as a floor of *rough* boards. *Abrupt* applied to words or acts implies bluntness; *rough* words are violent ǁ **ANT** level, unbroken, smooth, connected

abs- *pref* var of **ab-**

abs. 1 absent; **2** absolute; **3** abstract

Ab•sa•lom /ab′sələm/ *n* favorite son of David, slain while in rebellion against his father (2 Sam. 18)

ab•scess /ab′ses/ [L *abscessus* a going away] *n* collection of pus, of limited extent, in diseased tissues of the body ǁ **ab′scessed** *adj*

ab•scis•sa /absis′ə/ [L = cut off] *n* (-sas or -sae /-sē/) *math* horizontal coordinate of a point measured parallel to the x-axis

ab•scond /abskond′/ [L *abscondere* to hide away] *vi* to flee secretly and in haste; disappear, as to avoid arrest ǁ **ab•scond′er** *n*

ab•sence /ab′səns/ *n* **1** state or period of being away; **2** want, lack

ab′sence of mind′ *n* absent-mindedness

ab•sent /ab′sənt/ [MF < L *absens (-entis)*] *adj* **1** not present; **2** lacking, missing; **3** lost in thought, abstracted ǁ /absent′/ *vt* **4** to withdraw or keep (oneself) away ǁ **ab′sent•ly** *adv* ǁ **SYN** *adj* inattentive, listless, dreamy, musing, lost ǁ **ANT** *adj* present, intent, observant, alert, heedful

ab′sen•tee′ /-tē′/ *n* person who is absent or absents himself ǁ *also adj* ǁ **ab′sen•tee′ism** *n*

ab'sent-mind'ed *adj* forgetful; inattentive, abstracted ‖ **ab'sent-mind'ed·ly** *adv* ‖ **ab'sent-mind'ed·ness** *n*

ab·sinth or **ab·sinthe** /ab'sınth/ [F < Gk *apsinthion* wormwood] *n* 1 green, alcoholic, aromatic liquor, containing wormwood, anise, and other aromatic herbs; 2 the plant wormwood or its essence

ab·so·lute /ab'səlōōt'/ [L *absolutus* perfect, complete] *adj* 1 despotic, free from limitation; 2 perfect, complete; 3 unadulterated, pure; 4 positive, unquestionable; 5 independent of arbitrary or relative standards of measurement, as *absolute humidity;* 6 *gram* a standing outside the usual relations of syntax, as the *ablative absolute* in Latin; b (adjective) with the noun understood, as *give to the poor;* c (transitive verb) without an object ‖ *n* 7 that which is unrestricted or unlimited; 8 something perfect or complete ‖ SYN *adj* arbitrary, peremptory, unconditional

ab'so·lute'ly also **ab'so·lute'ly** *adv* in an absolute manner ‖ **ab'so·lute'ly** *interj* definitely!; of course!

ab'so·lute mag'ni·tude *n* magnitude a star would have to an observer at a distance of 10 parsecs

ab'so·lute ma·jor'i·ty *n* 1 number of votes representing more than half of the total cast; 2 number of voters representing more than half of those eligible to vote

ab'so·lute pitch' *n* 1 ability to match, by voice, any tone named, or to name correctly any tone heard; 2 pitch of a tone in terms of its vibration frequency

ab'so·lute tem'per·a·ture *n* temperature measured on the Kelvin scale, with zero corresponding to absolute zero

ab'so·lute ze'ro *n* coldest temperature possible, characterized by the complete absence of heat and equal to 0° K., −273.16° C., or −459.69° F.

ab'so·lu'tion *n* 1 act of absolving; 2 state of being absolved; 3 forgiveness, esp. the forgiveness of sins in the sacrament of penance

ab'so·lut'ism *n* 1 state of being without limitation; 2 principles underlying despotic government ‖ **ab'so·lut'ist** *adj & n*

ab·solve /əbzolv', -solv'/ [L *absolvere*] *vt* 1 to release, as from obligation or penalty; 2 to clear of crime, sin, or guilt ‖ SYN pardon, remit, discharge, forgive, excuse, justify, exonerate ‖ ANT accuse, condemn, bind

ab·sorb /əbsôrb', -zôrb'/ [L *absorbere*] *vt* 1 to drink in or suck in; 2 to engulf, swallow up, or incorporate; 3 to engross, as attention; 4 to pay for, as *to absorb the costs* ‖ **ab·sorb'a·bil'i·ty** /-bil'-/ *n* ‖ **ab·sorb'a·ble** *adj* ‖ **ab·sorb'ent** /-ənt/ *adj* 1 capable of ab-

sorbing ‖ *n* 2 anything that absorbs ‖ **ab·sorb'en·cy** *n*

ab·sorb'ing *adj* intensely interesting, engrossing

ab·sorp'tion /-sôrp'shən, -zôrp'-/ *n* 1 process or act of absorbing; 2 state of being engrossed ‖ **ab·sorp'tive** *adj*

ab·stain /əbstān'/ [MF *abstenir*] *vi* to refrain voluntarily (from an action) ‖ **ab·stain'er** *n* ‖ SYN fast, desist, refrain ‖ ANT indulge, gratify

ab·ste·mi·ous /əbstēm'ē·əs/ [L *abstemius*] *adj* moderate and sparing in the use of food and drink

ab·sten·tion /əbsten'shən/ [LL *abstentio (-onis)*] *n* act of abstaining ‖ **ab·sten'tious** *adj*

ab·sti·nence /ab'stinəns/ [OF < L *abstinentia*] *n* abstaining from the gratification of the appetite for food, liquor, or sexual congress ‖ **ab'sti·nent** *adj*

abstr. abstract(ed)

ab·stract /ab'strakt, abstrakt'/ [L *abstractus* drawn off] *adj* 1 perceptible to the mind rather than to the senses, not concrete; 2 theoretical; 3 denoting an idea or quality apart from particular circumstances, objects, or actions, as *goodness, beauty;* 4 *art* emphasizing intrinsic form rather than fidelity to the subject ‖ /ab'-/ *n* 5 summary, epitome; 6 abstract work of art; 7 **in the abstract** in theory ‖ /-strakt'/ *vt* 8 to take away, remove; 9 to derive or separate a general idea of, as a quality, from the object to which it belongs ‖ /ab'-/ *vt* 10 to summarize or abridge ‖ **ab·stract'ly** *adj* ‖ SYN *v* detach, remove, separate, withdraw, divert

ab·stract'ed *adj* lost in thought, absent-minded ‖ **ab·stract'ed·ly** *adv* ‖ SYN inattentive, preoccupied, musing, oblivious

ab·strac'tion *n* 1 act of abstracting or state of being abstracted; 2 a abstract idea or quality; b something imaginary or visionary; 3 absent-mindedness

ab'stract of ti'tle *n* abstract of the history of a real estate parcel, showing previous owners, encumbrances, etc.

ab·struse /əbstrōōs'/ [L *abstrusus* concealed] *adj* hard to understand ‖ **ab·struse'ly** *adj* ‖ **ab·struse'ness** *n* ‖ SYN obscure, recondite, difficult, deep, profound ‖ ANT shallow, manifest, obvious, plain

ab·surd /əbsurd', -zurd'/ [L *absurdus*] *adj* ridiculously unreasonable ‖ **ab·surd'ly** *adv* ‖ **ab·surd'ness** *n* ‖ SYN foolish, incongruous, inconsistent, senseless, wild, nonsensical ‖ ANT wise, consistent, sensible

ab·surd'i·ty *n* (-ties) 1 state of being absurd; 2 absurd thing

a·bun·dant /əbun'dənt/ [MF < L *abundans (-antis)* overflowing] *adj* ample,

plentiful ‖ **a·bun′dant·ly** *adv* ‖
a·bun′dance *n*

a·buse /əbyo͞oz′/ [MF *abuser* < L
abusus abused] *vt* 1 to use improperly; 2 to hurt, maltreat; 3 to rail at,
upbraid ‖ /əbyo͞os′/ *n* ‖ **a·bus′ive**
/-siv/ *adj* ‖ SYN vilify, reproach,
revile, defame, slander, malign, traduce, ill-use ‖ ANT commend, praise

a·but /əbut′/ [MF *abouter*] *v* (**a·but-
ted; a·but·ting**) *vt* 1 to border on, be
adjacent to ‖ *vi* 2 abut on, upon, or
against to border on, touch at one
end

a·but′ment *n* 1 act of abutting; 2 that
which abuts; 3 *arch.* supporting
structure or part, as for an arch,
bridge, or bridge pier

a·buzz /əbuz′/ *adj* bustling with activity

a·bys·mal /əbiz′məl/ *adj* 1 pert. to an
abyss; 2 immeasurably deep or great

a·byss /əbis′/ [Gk *abyssos* bottomless]
n 1 the original chaos; 2 a immeasurable depth; b bottomless gulf; c
deep chasm or pit

Abyss. 1 Abyssinia; 2 Abyssinian

a·byss′al *adj* 1 abysmal; 2 of or pert.
to the lowest depths of the ocean

Ab·ys·sin·i·a /ab′isin′ē·ə/ *n* former
name of Ethiopia ‖ **Ab′ys·sin′i·an**
adj & n

ac- *pref* var of **ad-**

-ac *adj suf* var of **-ic**

AC, A.C., ac, a.c. alternating current

Ac *chem* actinium

A/C or **a/c** 1 account; 2 account current

A.C. 1 [L *ante Christum*] before
Christ; 2 Army Corps

a·ca·cia /əkāsh′ə/ [Gk *akakia* a
thorny tree] *n* 1 any of many species
of a genus (*Acacia*) of flowering
trees or shrubs, commonly thorny,
growing in warm regions and producing tannin, medicines, and perfumes; 2 false acacia or common locust tree; 3 gum arabic

acad. 1 academic; 2 academy

ac·a·deme /ak′ədēm′/ [< *Academus*,
character in Gk myth.] *n* 1 academy
1; 2 college environment; 3 **Academe**
grove in Athens where Plato taught

ac′a·dem′ic /-dem′ik/ *adj* 1 pert. to a
school, college, academy, or the like,
or to higher learning; 2 pert. to liberal education as distinguished from
technical or professional education;
3 theoretical, not practical; 4 *art*
conforming to set rules or traditions;
conventional, formal ‖ *n* 5 teacher
or student at a college or university
‖ **ac′a·dem′i·cal** *adj* ‖ **ac′a·dem′i·**
cal·ly *adv*

ac′a·dem′i·cals *npl* or **ac′a·dem′ic cos′-**
tume *n* cap and gown

a·cad·e·mi·cian /əkad′imish′ən/ *n*
member of an academy *3*

a·cad·e·my /əkad′əmē/ [Gk *akadēmeia*
Plato's garden in Athens] (**-mies**) 1

secondary school, esp. private; 2
school or college for specialized
study, as a *military academy;* 3 association or society for the advancement of literature, science, or art; 4
the Academy, a the garden in Athens
where Plato taught; b his school of
philosophy or its adherents

A·ca·di·a /əkād′ē·ə/ *n* former French
colony in Canada, now known as
Nova Scotia, ceded to Great Britain
1713 ‖ **A·ca′di·an** *adj & n*

a·can·thus /əkan′thəs/ [Gk *akanthos*]
n (**-thus·es** & **-thi/-thī/**) 1 any of a
genus (*Acanthus*) of plants of
the Mediterranean region, having
prickly, spinous leaves; 2 *arch.* decoration shaped like the leaf of one
of these plants

a cap·pel·la /ä′ kəpel′ə/ [It = in chapel
style] *adj & adv* (choral singing) without instrumental accompaniment

A·ca·pul·co /ak′əpo͞ol′kō/ *n* seaport
and resort city in SW Mexico on the
Pacific (60,000)

acc. 1 accusative; 2 account; 3 accountant; 4 acceptance

ac·cede /aksēd′/ [L *accedere* to ap-
proach] *vi* 1 to agree or yield; 2 to
succeed, as to a throne; to enter
upon an office or position ‖ SYN
assent, consent, acquiesce, comply,
agree, accept, conform ‖ DISCR To
accede is to agree or yield, as to the
request or urgency of another, with
thoughtfulness rather than from impulse, and moved more by persuasion than compulsion, as George *ac-
ceded* to his brother's urgency and
joined the partnership. To *acquiesce*
is to yield or submit without contest-
ing the issue, either from compulsion
or indifference, as the defeated army
acquiesced in the demands of the
victor; John silently *acquiesced* when
his parents refused his request. To
assent is to express an agreement in
opinion, in cases where action may
or may not be called for. To *consent*
is to express willingness or compliance ‖ ANT protest, deny, dissent, disagree, object, differ

ac·cel·er·an·do /aksel′ərän′dō/ [It
= accelerating] *adj & adv mus* with
increasing speed

ac·cel·er·ate /aksel′ərāt′/ [L *accelerare*
(*-atus*)] *vt* 1 to hasten, increase the
speed of; 2 to cause to happen
sooner; 3 to increase the rate of
speed of ‖ *vi* 4 to go faster; 5 to
increase in rate of speed ‖ SYN
hurry, expedite, promote, drive, further ‖ ANT delay, hinder, retard, impede, clog

ac·cel·er·a′tion *n* 1 act of accelerating;
2 state of being accelerated; 3 time
rate of change in the velocity of a
body

ac·cel′er·a′tion of grav′i·ty *n* rate of increase of velocity toward the center

of the earth of a free-falling body under the influence of gravity, approx. 32 feet per second per second

ac·cel′er·a′tor /-/ *n* 1 one who or that which accelerates; 2 mechanical device, as a pedal in an automobile, by means of which the speed of an engine is increased; 3 substance that speeds up a chemical change; 4 electromagnetic or electrostatic device that imparts high velocities to charged particles and focuses them on a target

ac·cent /ak′sent/ [L *accentus*] *n* 1 stress laid by the voice on a particular syllable or syllables of a word or phrase; 2 a mark used in the alphabets of certain languages to show stress, vowel quality, or differences in meaning; b one of similar marks used in phonetic transcriptions to indicate stress and other features of pronunciation; 3 a mode of speech peculiar to a region or social class; b mode of speech of a person who has imperfectly learned the language of another country; 4 emphasis; 5 also **accents** varying or modulation of tone to express feeling; 6 regularly recurring stress in verse; 7 a *mus* emphasis placed upon certain notes in a bar of music; b mark indicating such emphasis; 8 symbol resembling an acute accent and used singly or doubly to indicate varying quantities and measurements, as prime and double prime, feet and inches, or minutes and seconds of arc || /ak′sent, aksent′/ *vt* 9 to stress (a syllable or word); 10 to mark with a written accent; 11 to emphasize || **ac·cen′tu·al** /-chōō-əl/ *adj*

ac·cen′tu·ate′ /-chōō-āt′/ *vt* 1 to emphasize; 2 to pronounce or mark with an accent || **ac·cen′tu·a′tion** *n*

ac·cept /aksept′/ [L *accipere* (-*ceptus*)] *vt* 1 to receive with approval; 2 to agree to; 3 to recognize as true; 4 to resign oneself to, as *to accept one's fate*; 5 to agree to pay; 6 to admit as a member; 7 to connect with, as *this socket accepts a standard plug* || **ac·cept′er** *n* || **ac·cept′a·bil′i·ty** /bil′-/ *n* || **ac·cept′a·ble** *adj* || **ac·cept′a·bly** *adv* || SYN assent, accede, bear, receive, assume, take

ac·cept′ance *n* 1 act of accepting; 2 approval; 3 state of being accepted or acceptable; 4 a agreement to pay a time draft or bill of exchange; b accepted draft or bill of exchange; 5 acceptation 2

ac′cep·ta′tion *n* 1 favorable acceptance; 2 generally accepted meaning of a word or phrase

ac·cept′ed *adj* generally approved; current, customary

ac·cep′tor /-ər/ *n* person who accepts a bill of exchange for payment

ac·cess /ak′ses/ [L *accessus* approach via MF] *n* 1 admittance or approach to a person or place; 2 means of approach or admission; 3 attack, as of disease; 4 accession

ac·ces′si·ble *adj* 1 easy of access; 2 obtainable || **ac·ces′si·bly** *adv* || **ac·ces′si·bil′i·ty** /-bil′-/ *n*

ac·ces′sion /-shən/ *n* 1 that which is added or joined; 2 increase; 3 coming to a throne, office, different condition, etc.; 4 assent; 5 onset, as of disease; 6 *law* addition to existing property by growth or improvement || SYN augmentation, increase, addition

ac·ces′so·ry /-ərē/ *adj* 1 aiding or assisting; 2 contributory; 3 subsidiary || *n* (-ries) 4 additional or subordinate thing, adjunct; 5 article not absolutely essential that adds to the attractiveness, convenience, effectiveness, or safety of something else; 6 one who, though not present, aids or abets in a crime either before its commission, as *an accessory before the fact*, or after, as *an accessory after the fact* || SYN abetter, ally, confederate, helper, assistant, accomplice, auxiliary

ac·ci·dence /ak′sidəns/ *n* 1 word inflections, as for number, case, or tense; 2 the part of grammar that deals with them

ac′ci·dent /-dənt/ [MF < L *accidens* (-*entis*) happening] *n* 1 unexpected happening; 2 unintentional event resulting in harm or loss; mishap; 3 chance; 4 incidental or nonessential feature; 5 surface irregularity || SYN chance, casualty, calamity, disaster, contingency, mishap, hazard

ac′ci·den′tal /-dent′əl/ *adj* 1 happening by chance || *n* 2 *mus* a sign, as sharp, flat, or natural, prefixed to a note and altering its pitch; b note so altered || **ac′ci·den′tal·ly** *adv* || SYN *adj* unexpected, fortuitous, haphazard, unpremeditated, unforeseen, unintended (see *fortuitous*) || ANT *adj* planned, certain, premeditated, designed

ac·claim /əklām′/ [L *acclamare*] *vt* 1 to hail by shouting or calling; applaud; 2 to proclaim by acclamation || *vi* 3 to shout applause || **ac·claim′er** *n*

ac·cla·ma·tion /ak′ləmāsh′ən/ *n* 1 vocal demonstration of hearty approval; 2 by **acclamation** by overwhelming voice vote || **ac·clam′a·to·ry** /əklam′ətôrē, -tôr′-/ *adj* || SYN cheering, cheers, plaudit, approbation, approval, praise || ANT derision, scorn, denunciation

ac·cli·mate /əklīm′it, ak′ləmāt′/ [F *acclimater*] *vt* 1 to accustom to a new climate or environment || *vi* 2 to become acclimated || **ac·cli·ma·tion** /ak′ləmāsh′ən/ *n*

ac·cli′ma·tize′ *vt & vi* to acclimate ‖ **ac·cli′ma·ti·za′tion** *n*

ac·cliv·i·ty /əkliv′itē/ [L *acclivitas* (*-atis*)] *n* (**-ties**) upward slope, ascent

ac·co·lade /ak′əlād′, -läd′, ak′əlād′, -läd′/ [F < It *accollata*] *n* 1 ceremonial sword tap on the shoulder signifying the conferring of knighthood; 2 award or laudatory mention; 3 *mus* brace joining several staffs

ac·com·mo·date /əkom′ədāt′/ [L *accommodare* (*-atus*)] *vt* 1 to adapt, make suitable; 2 to adjust, reconcile; 3 to furnish with something needed; 4 to render a service to; 5 **a** to find space for; lodge; **b** to have enough room for ‖ *vi* 6 to conform, adapt ‖ SYN suit, compose, arrange, furnish (see *fit²*)

ac·com′mo·dat′ing *adj* obliging, helpful ‖ **ac·com′mo·dat′ing·ly** *adv*

ac·com′mo·da′tion *n* 1 act of accommodating; 2 anything that helps, obliges, or supplies a need; 3 loan of money; 4 process by which the eye automatically focuses on objects at varying distances; 5 **accommodations** *pl* **a** lodgings; **b** place for a passenger on a ship, train, or plane

ac·com′mo·da′tion lad′der *n* portable stairway giving access between a ship's deck and a wharf or small boat

ac·com′mo·da′tion train′ *n* railroad train that stops at all stations to take on and discharge passengers and freight

ac·com·pa·ni·ment /əkump′(ə)nēmənt/ [see **accompany**] *n* 1 something added, as for ornament or symmetry; 2 concomitant occurrence; 3 *mus* supporting part that complements or provides background music for the principal part

ac·com′pa·nist also **ac·com′pa·ny·ist** /-nē·ist/ *n* one who plays an accompaniment

ac·com′pa·ny [MF *accompagnier*] *v* (**-nied**) *vt* 1 to go with; 2 to add to; 3 *mus* to perform an accompaniment for ‖ SYN attend, convoy, follow, conduct, escort

ac·com·plice /əkomp′lis/ [ME *a complice* (< MF) an accomplice] *n* helper in crime ‖ SYN confederate, partner, accessory (see *ally*)

ac·com·plish /əkomp′lish/ [MF *acomplir* (*-pliss-*)] *vt* 1 to fulfill, bring to pass; 2 to finish ‖ SYN execute, do, perform, consummate, realize, carry out, fulfill, achieve

ac·com′plished *adj* 1 completed, done; 2 expert, polished

ac·com′plish·ment *n* 1 act of accomplishing; 2 completion; 3 fulfillment; 4 **accomplishments** *pl* skill, grace, knowledge ‖ SYN *pl* qualifications, acquirements, attainments

ac·cord /əkôrd′/ [OF *acorder*] *vt* 1 to bring to agree; to adjust, reconcile; 2 to grant ‖ *vi* 3 to agree, har-

monize ‖ *n* 4 harmonious adjustment; 5 agreement; 6 of one's own **accord** voluntarily ‖ SYN *v* agree, harmonize, attune, assent, concede ‖ DISCR To *agree* is the general term expressing exact sameness of mind or feelings. To *accord* implies resemblance rather than identity, and carries with it the idea of harmonious relationship, as the sad atmosphere of the place *accorded* with my mournful feelings; his actions *accorded* with his beliefs ‖ ANT *v* conflict, differ, disagree, dissent, contradict, oppose, repudiate

ac·cord′ance /-əns/ 1 act of granting; 2 **in accordance with** in agreement with

ac·cord′ing as′ *conj* 1 just as, the same way as; 2 depending on whether, if

ac·cord′ing·ly *adv* 1 in agreement, conformably; 2 consequently, so

ac·cord′ing to *prep* 1 in agreement with; 2 on the strength or authority of; 3 depending on

ac·cor·di·on /əkôrd′ē·ən/ [< *accord*, by analogy with *clarion*] *n* 1 handheld wind instrument with keyboard and bellows ‖ *adj* 2 fluted or creased like an accordion, as *accordion pleats* ‖ **ac·cor′di·on·ist** *n*

ac·cost /əkôst′, -kost′/ [MF *acoster*] *vt* to approach and speak to, address

ac·couche·ment /əkŏōsh′mänt/ [F] *n* delivery in childbed, confinement

ac·count /əkount′/ [MF *aconter* < L *ad* to + *computare* to count] *vt* 1 to consider as, judge ‖ *vi* 2 **account for**, **a** to give an explanation for; **b** to cause; **c** to be responsible for bringing about, as *he accounted for two runs* ‖ *n* 3 explanatory statement; 4 narrative, description, report; 5 importance; 6 reason, consideration, as *on that account we can't do it;* 7 charge account; 8 bank account; 9 statement or summary of business transactions; 10 **a** business relation involving credit; **b** client; 11 **accounts** *pl* systematized and continuous record of business dealings; 12 **call to account** to ask for an explanation; 13 **on account of** because of; 14 **on no account** under no circumstances; 15 **on (a person's) account** for the sake of; 16 **take account of** or **take into account** to consider ‖ SYN *n* bill, charge; recital, chronicle, story

ac·count′a·ble *adj* 1 liable to be called to account, answerable; 2 explainable ‖ **ac·count′a·bly** *adv* ‖ **ac·count′a·bil·i·ty** /-bil′-/ *n*

ac·count′an·cy /-ənsē/ *n* profession or practice of an accountant

ac·count′ant /-ənt/ *n* person skilled in accounting

ac·count′ing *n* act or system of recording, stating, or auditing business transactions

ac·count′ pay′a·ble *n* (**accounts pay-**

able) liability to a creditor representing amount owed for goods or services

ac·count′ re·ceiv′a·ble *n* (accounts receivable) claim against a debtor representing amount due for goods or services

ac·cou·ter also **ac·cou·tre** /əkōōt′ər/ [F *accoutrer*] *vt* 1 to dress, equip; 2 to array in military dress, outfit (a soldier)

ac·cou′ter·ments *npl* 1 clothing, dress, outfit; 2 equipment of a soldier exclusive of arms and clothing

Ac·cra /əkrä′, ak′rə/ *n* seaport and capital of Ghana (600,200)

ac·cred·it /əkred′it/ [F *accréditer*] *vt* 1 to believe and accept as true; 2 to attribute; 3 to sanction, approve of officially; 4 to certify (an educational institution) as maintaining minimum standards; 5 to send (an envoy) with credentials ‖ **ac·cred′i·ta′tion** *n*

ac·crete /əkrēt′/ [L *accrescere* (*-cretus*)] *vi* 1 **a** to grow by addition of external material; **b** to be added to by natural growth; 2 to grow together or into one ‖ **ac·cre′tion** *n*

ac·cru·al /əkrōō′əl/ [see **accrue**] *n* 1 act or process of accruing; 2 that which accrues; amount by which anything accrues or grows by natural or inherent process

ac·cru′al ba′sis *n* method of recording transactions that includes income when earned and expenses when incurred

ac·crue /əkrōō′/ [< MF < L *accrescere*] *vi* 1 to grow, increase; 2 to come naturally, accumulate, be added; 3 *law* to be vested, become enforceable as a right

acct. account

ac·cul·tur·ate /əkul′chərāt′/ [*ac-* + *culture* + *-ate*] *vt* & *vi* to adapt to the culture of a more advanced race ‖ **ac·cul′tur·a′tion** *n*

ac·cu·mu·late /əkyōōm′yəlāt′/ [L *accumulare* (*-atus*)] *vt* 1 to collect or bring together by degrees, amass ‖ *vi* 2 to increase in size, number, or quantity ‖ **ac·cu′mu·la′tion** *n* ‖ **ac·cu′mu·la′tive** *adj* ‖ SYN gather, aggregate, assemble, hoard, amass ‖ ANT disperse, scatter, divide, waste

ac·cu′mu·la′tor *n* 1 person or thing that accumulates; 2 apparatus for collecting and storing energy; 3 *Brit* storage battery or cell

ac·cu·ra·cy /ak′yərəsē/ *n* (**-cies**) 1 state of being accurate; 2 precision

ac′cu·rate /-rit/ [L *accuratus*] *adj* 1 conforming exactly to truth or to some standard; 2 free from error, precise ‖ **ac′cu·rate·ly** *adv* ‖ **ac′cu·rate·ness** *n* ‖ SYN exact, true, precise (see *perfect, correct*)

ac·cursed /əkurst′, əkurs′id/ also **ac·curst** /əkurst′/ *adj* 1 lying under a

curse, doomed; 2 miserable, detestable ‖ **ac·curs′ed·ly** /-id-/ *adv* ‖ **ac·curs′ed·ness** /-id-/ *n*

ac·cu·sa·tion /ak′yəzāsh′ən/ [see **accuse**] *n* 1 act of accusing; 2 charge of wrongdoing, indictment

ac·cu·sa·tive /əkyōōz′ətiv/ *adj* 1 *gram* (case) of the direct object of a verb or of certain prepositions; 2 accusatory ‖ *n* 3 **a** accusative case; **b** word in this case ‖ **ac·cu′sa·tive·ly** *adv*

ac·cu′sa·to′ry /-tôr′ē, -tōr′-/ *adj* expressing an accusation

ac·cuse /əkyōōz′/ [OF *acuser* < L *cusare*] *vt* 1 to charge with wrongdoing, blame ‖ *vi* 2 to make an accusation ‖ **ac·cus′er** *n* ‖ **ac·cus′ing·ly** *adv* ‖ SYN censure, indict, arraign, blame, reproach

ac·cused′ *nsg* & *npl* the accused the defendant or defendants in a criminal case

ac·cus·tom /əkust′əm/ [MF *acostumer*] *vt* to make familiar by use, habituate ‖ **ac·cus′tomed** *adj*

ace /ās/ [OF *as* < L = unit, bronze coin] *n* 1 **a** single spot on a playing card or die; **b** card or die so marked; 2 in some games, an earned point; 3 aviator who shoots down a prescribed number of enemy planes; 4 person or thing of marked excellence; 5 *slang* one-dollar bill; 6 *golf* hole in one; 7 **within an ace** by a narrow margin ‖ *vt* 8 to score an ace against; 9 *golf* to make an ace on (a hole) ‖ *adj* 10 of marked excellence

ace′ in the hole′ [< the game of stud poker] *n* hidden resource revealed only at the opportune moment

-a·ceous /-āsh′əs/ [L *-aceus*] *suf* of the nature of, like, as *herbaceous*

a·cerb /əsurb′/ also **a·cer′bic** [L *acerbus*] *adj* acid or sour in taste, temper, disposition, or mood ‖ **a·cer′bi·ty** *n*

ac·er·bate /as′ərbāt′/ *v* 1 to sour, embitter; 2 to irritate, exasperate

acet- or **aceto-** [L *acetum* vinegar] *comb form* acetic, acetic acid

ac·et·an·i·lide /as′itan′əlid′, -lid/ or **-lid** /-lid/ [*acet-* + *aniline*] *n* white crystalline powder—$CH_3CONHC_6H_5$ —derived from aniline and acetic acid, used esp. to relieve pain or fever

ac·e·tate /as′itāt′/ *n* 1 salt or ester of acetic acid; 2 product made of cellulose acetate

a·ce·tic /əsēt′ik/ *adj* pert. to or producing vinegar or acetic acid

a·ce′tic ac′id *n* colorless pungent and extremely sour liquid—CH_3COOH— the essential constituent of vinegar

a·cet·i·fy /əset′ifī′/ *v* (**-fied**) *vt* & *vi* to turn into acetic acid or vinegar

ac·e·tone /as′itōn′/ [*acet-* + *-one*] *n* colorless inflammable liquid with etherlike odor—$(CH_3)_2CO$—used chiefly as a solvent and present in small quantities in blood and urine

a·cet'y·lene /əset'əlēn', -lin/ [acet-+-yl +-ene] n colorless gas with ether-like odor—HC ≡ CH—used as an illuminant and esp. in metal cutting and welding

A·chae·a /əkē'ə/ or **A·cha·ia** /əkā'ə/ n ancient district and modern department of Greece in N. Peloponnesus

A·chae'an or **A·cha'ian** n 1 native or inhabitant of Achaea; 2 Greek; 3 member of one of the four prehistoric Greek tribes believed to have settled Greece || also adj

ache /āk/ [OE acan] vi 1 to feel a continuous dull pain; 2 to feel compassion; 3 to yearn || n 4 constant dull pain || **ach'ing·ly** adv

a·chene /āken'/ [NL achaenium < a-ᵃ + GK chainein to gape] n bot hard, one-seeded, indehiscent fruit

a·chieve /əchēv'/ [MF achever to finish] vt 1 to perform, accomplish; 2 to bring to a successful end by effort || vi 3 to bring about a desired result || **a·chiev'a·ble** adj || **a·chiev'er** n || SYN earn, attain, accomplish (see get)

a·chieve'ment n 1 accomplishment, completion; 2 something achieved

A·chil·les /əkil'ēz/ n greatest Greek hero of the Trojan war, hero of Homer's Iliad, vulnerable only in the heel

A·chil'les' heel' n vulnerable point

A·chil'les' ten'don n sinew connecting the heel and the calf

ach·ro·mat·ic /ak'rəmat'ik/ adj 1 without color; 2 transmitting light without separating it into the spectral colors, as a lens; 3 not easily stained by dyes; 4 mus (scale) having no accidentals || **ach'ro·mat'i·cal·ly** adv || **a·chro·ma·tism** /ā'krōm'ətiz'əm/ n

ac·id /as'id/ [L acidus sour] n 1 sour substance, often liquid; 2 chem compound capable of reacting with a base to form a salt; it yields hydrogen ions in solution, its atom is able to take an unshared pair of electrons from a base, and its aqueous solution is sour and turns litmus paper red || adj 3 sharp, biting, or sour in taste, manner, mood, or nature; 4 a of, pert. to, or yielding acid; b containing an excessive amount of acid; 5 geol having much silica || **ac'id·ly** adv || **a·cid·ic** /əsid'ik/ adj || **a·cid'i·ty** n || SYN adj sour, tart, acetic, acidulated

ac'id-fast' adj resistant to decolorizing by acid

ac'id head' n habitual user of LSD

a·cid·i·fy /əsid'ifī'/ v (-fied) vt 1 to make acid; 2 to convert into an acid || vi 3 to become acid; 4 to be converted into an acid || **a·cid'i·fi·ca'tion** n || **a·cid'i·fi'er** n

ac'i·do'sis /-dōs'is/ n abnormal depletion of the alkali reserve of the body

ac'id test' n severe and crucial test

a·cid·u·late /əsij'əlāt'/ vt to make sour or slightly acid || **a·cid'u·la'tion** n

a·cid'u·lous [L acidulus somewhat sour] adj 1 somewhat sour or acid; 2 caustic in manner

-a·cious /-āsh'əs/ [L -ax (-acis) + -ous] adj suf characterized by, abounding in, as mendacious, fallacious

-ac·i·ty /-as'itē/ [L -acitas] n suf quality of, abounding in, as mendacity, veracity

ack. acknowledge(ment)

ack-ack /ak'ak'/ [Brit radio code for A.A., that is, antiaircraft] n 1 antiaircraft gun; 2 antiaircraft fire

ac·knowl·edge /aknol'ij/ [< OE ācnāwan to recognize] vt 1 to admit to be true; 2 to recognize, greet, as by a bow; 3 to admit the authority or claims of; 4 to assent in legal form to the genuineness or validity of; 5 to admit the receipt of, express thanks for || **ac·knowl'edg·ment** n || SYN grant, allow, concede, avow, assent, accept, certify, endorse || ANT disavow, deny, disclaim

A.C.L.U. American Civil Liberties Union

ac·me /ak'mē/ [Gk = point] n highest point, summit

ac·ne /ak'nē/ [Gk] n disease of the skin marked by an eruption of pimples

ac·o·lyte /ak'əlīt'/ [ML acolytus < Gk akolouthos] n 1 attendant, follower; 2 altar boy; 3 member of one of the minor orders of the Roman Catholic Church

A·con·ca·gua /äk'ənkäg'wə/ n mountain in the Andes in W Argentina (22,835 ft.), highest in the Western Hemisphere

ac·o·nite /ak'ənīt'/ also **ac'o·ni'tum** /-əm/ [Gk akoniton wolfsbane via L] n 1 any of a genus (Aconitum) of plants of the crowfoot family, with blue, white, or purple flowers; 2 medicine made from the common monkshood (A. napellus), used to slow the pulse and to check or allay fever

a·corn /ā'kôrn, āk'ərn/ [OE æcern] n seed of the oak, a small nut with its base held in a woody cup

a·cous·tic (-ti·cal) /əkōost'ik(əl)/ [< Gk akouein to hear] adj 1 pert. to the sense or organs of hearing; 2 pert. to the science of sound; 3 (material) designed to deaden sound || **a·cous'ti·cal·ly** adv

a·cous'tics nsg 1 science of sound || npl 2 qualities of a room, stadium, or auditorium with respect to the audibility and/or fidelity of sounds in it || **ac·ous·ti·cian** /ak'ōōstish'ən/ n

ac·quaint /əkwānt'/ [OF acointier < LL accognoscere to know perfectly] vt 1 to make aware or familiar; 2 to furnish information to

ac·quaint'ance n 1 personal knowledge,

gained through contact; **2** person whom one knows slightly || **ac·quaint'ance·ship'** *n* || SYN familiarity, intimacy, fellowship || DISCR *Acquaintance* denotes a slight knowledge of another, more than recognition but less than *familiarity*. *Familiarity* denotes a fuller knowledge based on continued *acquaintance;* it is of an informal character, and often suggests an offensive freedom, as in taking undue liberties, treating superiors as equals, etc. *Intimacy* is a close, confidential relationship, implying mutual affection and understanding. *Fellowship* denotes a sympathetic companionableness, as in a church or lodge

ac·qui·esce /ak'wē·es'/ [L *acquiescere* to rest] *vi* to agree by not objecting; yield or submit || **ac'qui·es'cence** *n* || **ac'qui·es'cent** *adj* || SYN accord, agree, assent, consent (see *accede*)

ac·quire /əkwīr'/ [MF *aquerre*] *vt* **1** to come into possession of; **2** to obtain by one's own physical or mental exertions, or through one's environment || **ac·quire'ment** *n* || SYN gain, procure, secure, obtain (see *get*)

ac·quired' char'ac·ter *n* character of an organism acquired from the environment and not by inheritance

ac·qui·si·tion /ak'wizish'ən/ [MF < L *acquisitio* (-*onis*)] *n* **1** act of acquiring; **2** thing acquired

ac·quis·i·tive /əkwiz'itiv/ *adj* strongly motivated to gain possession of material wealth || **ac·quis'i·tive·ness** *n*

ac·quit /əkwit'/ [OF *aquiter*] *v* (-**quit**ted; -**quit·ting**) *vt* **1** to declare not guilty, clear; **2** to bear or conduct (oneself), behave (oneself) || **ac·quit'tal** *n*

acr- or **acro-** [Gk *akros* topmost, outermost] *comb form* top, tip, extremity

a·cre /āk'ər/ [OE *æcer* tilled land] *n* **1** land measure containing 160 sq. rods, equal to 43,560 sq. ft. or 1/640 of a sq. mile; **2** acres *pl* **a** lands, estate; **b** large amount

A·cre /äk'ər, āk'-/ *n* seaport in NW Israel, captured by the Crusaders from the Saracens in 1191

a·cre·age /āk'ərij/ *n* **1** area in acres; **2** extent of land, usu. large

ac·rid /ak'rid/ [< L *acer* (*acris*) sharp] *adj* **1** sharp or bitter to the taste or smell; **2** irritating in manner

ac·ri·mo·ny /ak'rəmōn'ē/ [L *acrimonia*] *n* bitterness or biting severity of temper or speech || **ac'ri·mo'ni·ous** *adj* || **ac'ri·mo'ni·ous·ly** *adv* || SYN sharpness, tartness, acerbity, harshness, asperity, causticity || ANT gentleness, courtesy, blandness

ac·ro·bat /ak'rəbat'/ [Gk *akrobatos* going to the top] *n* **1** one who performs gymnastic feats at tumbling or on a tightrope, trapeze, or trampoline; **2** one adept at rapidly changing

his opinions || **ac'ro·bat'ic** *adj* || **ac'ro·bat'i·cal·ly** *adv*

ac'ro·bat'ics *nsg* **1** art or practice of acrobats || *npl* **2** performance of acrobats; **3** any performance marked by swift and agile reversals of mental or physical actions

ac·ro·nym /ak'rənim/ *n* word formed from the first letter or group of letters of the words in a set phrase, as *NASA* (National Aeronautics and Space Administration) or *radar* (radio detecting and ranging) (cf. *letterword*) || **ac'ro·nym'ic** or **a·cron'y·mous** /əkron'iməs/ *adj*

ac·ro·pho·bi·a /ak'rəfōb'ē·ə/ *n* abnormal fear of high places

a·crop·o·lis /əkrop'əlis/ [Gk] *n* **1** citadel of an ancient Greek city; **2 the** Acropolis the citadel of Athens, containing the Parthenon

a·cross /əkrôs', -krôs'/ *adv* **1** from side to side, crosswise; **2** from one side to another; **3** on the other side; **4** through to a person's understanding; **5** through to a successful conclusion; **6 come across** *slang* **a** to pay, contribute; **b** to do what is desired by someone else || *prep* **7** from side to side of; **8** on or to the other side of; **9** into an accidental meeting with

across'-the-board' *adj* **1** (bet on a horse) to finish first, second, or third; **2** covering all the categories involved

a·cros·tic /əkros'tik, -krôs'-/ [Gk *akrostichis*] *n* composition usu. in verse in which certain letters, as the first, middle, or final letter of each line respectively, taken in order, form a motto, phrase, name, or word || also *adj*

a·cryl'ic ac'id /əkril'ik/ [< L *acer* (-*cris*) pungent + -*yl*] *n* colorless liquid acid —CH$_2$ = CHCO$_2$H—used in the production of acrylic resin

a·cryl'ic res'in *n* transparent thermoplastic resin made by polymerizing acrylic acid or its derivatives

act /akt'/ [L *actus*] *n* **1** deed; that which is done; **2** process of doing; **3** law; **4** principal division of a play or opera; **5 a** separate and distinct part of a variety show or circus; **b** form of entertainment supplied in such part, as *a song and dance act;* **6** insincere conduct, pretense || *vt* **7** to perform or play the part of; **8 act one's age** to behave with the expected maturity; **9 act out** to play (a role) for illustrative purposes || *vi* **10** to do, perform special functions, serve, exert force; **11** to behave; **12** to have special effects; **13** to perform on the stage; **14 act up** *colloq* **a** of mechanical devices, to give signs of imminent breakdown; **b** of people, to behave badly

Ac·tae·on /aktē'ən/ *n Gk myth.* hunter who was turned into a stag and killed by his own hounds as punishment for having seen Diana bathing

ACTH /ā'sē'tē'āch'/ [adrenocorticotropic hormone] *n* 1 hormone produced by the pituitary gland; 2 this substance, extracted from animal pituitaries and used to treat rheumatic fever and certain forms of arthritis

actin- or **actino-** [Gk *aktis* (*-inos*) ray] *comb form* 1 actinic radiation; 2 *zool* having radial structure

act'ing *adj* 1 serving temporarily, esp. in another's absence ‖ *n* 2 art, profession, or activity of an actor

ac·tin·ic /aktin'ik/ [Gk *aktis* (*-inos*) ray] *adj* designating or pert. to the property possessed by radiation of producing photochemical effects

ac·tin'i·um /-ē·əm/ *n* radioactive trivalent metallic element (**Ac**; at.no. 89; at.wt. 227) found in pitchblende

ac'ti·nom'e·ter /-nom'itər/ *n* instrument that measures the intensity of luminous radiation, esp. of the sun

ac·ti·no·my·cete /ak'tənōmī'sēt/ [*actino-* + Gk *mykētes* fungi] *n* any of a group of rod-shaped microorganisms of the order Actinomycetales, which partake of the nature of bacteria and fungi

ac'ti·no·my'cin /-nōmī'sin/ *n* any of several antibiotics produced from certain soil bacteria

ac'ti·non' /-non'/ *n* heavy, inert, radioactive gaseous element (**An**; at.no. 86; at.wt. 219), isotopic with radon, a product of actinium decay

ac·tion /ak'shən/ [L *actio* (*-onis*)] *n* 1 state or process of acting or being active or in motion; 2 that which is done; deed; 3 mode of acting; behavior; 4 in a literary work, as a novel or drama, the sequence of important events on which the interest depends; 5 lawsuit; 6 effective or acting part of a mechanism, as in a piano or rifle; 7 battle, engagement; 8 **actions** *pl* conscious acts, directed by the will ‖ SYN motion, operation, act, achievement (see *battle*)

ac'tion·a·ble *adj* 1 giving ground for a lawsuit; 2 subject to a lawsuit

ac·ti·vate /ak'tivāt'/ *vt* 1 to rouse to activity, stimulate, make active; 2 to make ready for action; 3 to bring about radioactivity in; 4 to aerate (sewage) in order to speed up the action of microorganisms ‖ **ac'ti·va'·tion** *n* ‖ **ac'ti·va'tor** *n*

ac'tive /-tiv/ [MF *actif* (*-ve*) < L *activus*] *adj* 1 having the power of motion or force; 2 lively, brisk; 3 effective, busy, operating; not quiet or latent; 4 *gram* designating the voice or form of the verb which represents the subject as the doer of the action asserted by the verb ‖ *n* 5 active voice ‖ **ac'tive·ly** *adv* ‖ SYN *adj* sprightly, alert, agile, nimble, brisk, vigilant,

industrious, diligent, busy ‖ DISCR *Active* indicates quickness; *agile*, *brisk*, *alert*, and *vigilant* are alike in expressing quickness of motion. *Sprightly* and *brisk* add to the idea of quickness that of animation and liveliness; we speak of a *sprightly* old lady; of a *brisk* gait; *alert* and *vigilant* add keen watchfulness and readiness. *Nimble* motion is light, easy, swift, and gliding; *agile* motion is dexterous, vigorous, and easy with the ease of long practice. *Active*, *industrious*, and *diligent* share the idea of energetic faithfulness to the task in hand

ac'tiv·ist *n* believer in a policy of definite, energetic action, as for political ends ‖ **ac'tiv·ism** *n*

ac·tiv'i·ty *n* (*-ties*) 1 quality or state of being active; 2 liveliness; 3 organized group action, usu. for edification or entertainment

act' of God' *n* unpredictable accident, due to an uncontrollable natural force, for which no person can be held legally responsible

ac'tor /-tər/ [L] *n* 1 theatrical performer; 2 doer; 3 participant

ac'tress /-tris/ *n* female actor

Acts' or **Acts' of the A·pos'tles** *nsg* book of the New Testament

ac·tu·al /ak'chōō·əl/ [MF *actuel*] *adj* 1 existing, real; 2 present ‖ SYN positive, genuine, certain, sure, existent

ac'tu·al'i·ty /-al-/ *n* (*-ties*) 1 fact, reality; realism; 2 thing which is in full existence ‖ SYN truth, fact, realism (see *reality*)

ac'tu·al·ly *adv* 1 really, in truth; 2 as a matter of fact

ac'tu·ar'y /-er'ē/ [L *actuarius* stenographer] *n* (*-ies*) expert computer of insurance risks, premiums, etc. ‖ **ac'tu·ar'i·al** *adj*

ac'tu·ate' /-chōō·āt'/ [ML *actuare* (*-atus*)] *vt* 1 to move or incite to effort; 2 to put into motion ‖ **ac'tu·a'·tion** *n* ‖ **ac'tu·a'tor** *n*

a·cu·i·ty /əkyōō'itē/ [ML *acuitas*] *n* sharpness, as of vision

a·cu·men /əkyōōm'ən/ [L = sharpness] *n* quickness of mental perception ‖ SYN penetration, keenness, insight

ac·u·punc·ture /ak'yōōpuŋk'chər/ [L *acus* needle + *puncture*] *n* 1 Chinese art of inserting needles into various areas of the body to relieve pain during surgery and to cure disease; 2 puncture of the skin or tissue with a needle for vaccination or drawing off fluid

a·cute /əkyōōt'/ [L *acutus*] 1 sharppointed; 2 mentally keen; 3 sensitive, as *acute hearing*; 4 severe (pain or disease), coming quickly to a crisis; 5 critical, as *an acute shortage*; 6 high, shrill (sound); 7 *geom* **a** (angle) measuring less than 90 degrees; **b**

(triangle) containing only acute angles ‖ **a·cute′ly** *adj* ‖ **a·cute′ness** *n* ‖ SYN shrewd, intelligent, astute, poignant, discerning

a·cute′ ac′cent *n* diacritical mark ′, placed usu. over a vowel to indicate stress (as in Spanish) or vowel quality (as in French) or both (as in Portuguese and Italian)

-a·cy /-əsē/ [ML *-acia*] *n suf* quality, state, or office, as *accuracy, papacy*

ad /ad′/ *n* advertisement

ad- [L = to, toward] *pref* to, toward, in addition to, as *adhere, adjective*

-ad¹ /-ad′/ [Gk *-as (-ados)*] *n suf* forming: **1** collective numerals, as *triad*; **2** names of poems, as *Iliad*; **3** names of family groups with a common designation, as *dryad*; **4** names of some family plant groups

-ad² /-əd/ *n suf* var of **-ade¹**, as *ballad*

ad. 1 adverb; **2** advertisement

A.D. [L *anno Domini*] in the year of our Lord, since the birth of Christ

ad·age /ad′ij/ [MF] *n* proverb or pithy saying ‖ SYN saw, proverb, maxim (see *truism*)

a·da·gio /ədäj′(ē)ō/ [It = at ease] *adj & adv* **1** *mus* slow ‖ *n* **2** musical piece or movement in adagio tempo; **3** graceful dance emphasizing great technical skill

Ad·am /ad′əm/ *n* **1** the first man and progenitor of the human race (Gen. 2:7, 5:1–5); **2** the (old) **Adam** unredeemed human nature

Ad·am, James *n* (1730–94) and **Robert** *n* (1728–92) brothers, British architects and furniture designers

ad·a·mant /ad′əmənt, -mant′/ [Gk *adamas (-antos)* unconquerable] *n* **1** real or imaginary stone of great hardness; **2** any very hard and unyielding substance ‖ *adj* **3** extremely hard and unyielding; **4** immovable in attitude or opinion

Ad′ams, John *n* (1735–1826) 2nd president of the U.S. 1797–1801

Ad′ams, John Quin·cy /kwin′zē, -sē/ *n* (1767–1848) 6th president of the U.S. 1825–29, son of John Adams

Ad′ams, Samuel *n* (1722–1803) American statesman and a leader in the American Revolution

Ad′am's ap′ple *n* projecting cartilage on the larynx, conspicuous on the front of the human neck, esp. of men

a·dapt /ədapt′/ [L *adaptare*] *vt* **1** to make suitable, cause to conform, make fit by alteration ‖ *vi* **2** to become adapted ‖ **a·dapt′a·ble** *adj* ‖ **a·dapt′a·bil′i·ty** /-bil′-/ *n* ‖ **a·dap′tive** *adj*

ad·ap·ta·tion /ad′əptāsh′ən/ *n* **1** act of adapting; **2** state of being adapted; **3** that which is adapted

a·dapt′er also **a·dap′tor** /ədap′tər/ *n* **1** one who adapts; **2** device for fitting together noncompatible parts of an apparatus; **3** attachment that adapts

a machine, tool, or the like for a use for which it was not originally designed

add /ad′/ [L *addere*] *vt* **1** to join or unite into a whole, esp. to find the total of (a set of numbers); **2** to annex or bring (additional items) so as to increase the number, quantity, size, etc., as *to add stones to a pile*; **3** to affix; say further ‖ *vi* **4** to perform the operations of finding a sum; **5 add** to serve as an addition to; **6 add up** to make sense; **7 add up to** to indicate

ad·dend /ad′end, ədend′/ [L *addendum*] *n* number to be added

ad·den·dum /əden′dəm/ *n* (-da /-də/) thing added, as a note, remark, or appendix

ad·der /ad′ər/ [< ME *a naddre* an adder] *n* **1** any of several common American nonvenomous snakes of medium size; **2** the common European viper (*Vipera berus*)

ad·dict /ədikt′/ [L *addicere (-dictus)* to favor] *vt* **1** to habituate (oneself), as *he addicted himself to opium* ‖ /ad′ikt/ *n* **2** person who addicts himself, esp. to drugs ‖ **ad·dict′ed** *adj* ‖ **ad·dic′tion** *n*

ad·dic′tive *adj* habit-forming (narcotics)

Ad·dis A·ba·ba /ad′is ab′əbə/ *n* capital of Ethiopia (500,000)

Ad′di·son's dis·ease′ /ad′isənz/ [Thomas *Addison* (1793–1860) Eng physician] *n* disease caused by deficient secretion of the adrenal glands and causing weakness, low blood pressure, and brownish skin coloration

ad·di·tion /ədish′ən/ [L *additio (-onis)*] *n* **1** act, process, or result of combining numbers into a single sum; **2** act of adding, joining, or appending; **3** thing or amount added ‖ SYN increase, accession, enlargement, appendage

ad·di′tion·al *adj* added, extra, more ‖ **ad·di′tion·al·ly** *adv*

ad′di·tive *adj* **1** involving or produced by addition ‖ *n* **2** substance added to another to improve or preserve it

ad·dle /ad′əl/ [OE *adela* filth] *adj* **1** muddled, confused; **2** rotten (egg) ‖ *vt* **3** to muddle, confuse ‖ *vi* **4** to become confused; **5** to become rotten

ad·dress /ədres′/ [MF *adresser*] *vt* **1** to speak or write to; **2** to deliver a speech to; **3** to direct, as a letter; **4** to greet with the prescribed title; **5** to apply or direct (one's energy or skill) to a duty or task; **6** to pay court to; **7** to line up a golf club behind (the ball) preparatory to hitting it ‖ /ədres′, ad′res/ *n* **8** formal discourse; **9** place where a person or organization is located; **10** dexterity, adroitness; **11** bearing in conversation; **12** delivery in speaking or singing ‖ SYN v salute, greet, accost, court

ad·dress·ee /ˌadˈresēˊ, əd-/ n one to whom mail is addressed

ad·duce /əd(y)o͞osˊ/ [L *adducere* to lead to] vt to bring forward as a reason, cite as pertinent

-ade[1] [MF < LL *-ata* -ate] n *suf* 1 act or action, as *escapade;* 2 fruit drink, as *orangeade*

-ade[2] n *suf* var of **-ad**[1], as *decade*

Ad·e·laide /ˈadˌəlādˊ/ n capital of South Australia, Australia (590,000)

A·den /ˈädˈən, ädˊ-/ n 1 former British colony, now part of South Yemen; 2 seaport and capital of South Yemen (100,000)

aden- or **adeno-** [Gk *aden*] *comb form* gland, as *adenovirus*

A·de·nau·er /ˈadˈənouˌər, ˈädˈnouˌər/, **Konrad** n (1876–1967) chancellor of the West German Federal Republic 1949–63

ad·e·noids /ˈadˈənoidzˊ/ [< Gk *adenoeides* glandlike] npl mass of lymphoid tissue in the upper pharynx which obstructs breathing if enlarged ‖ **ad'e·noid'al** adj

a·dept /ˈadeptˊ/ [L *adeptus* one who has attained] adj 1 proficient, skilled ‖ /ˈadˈept, əˈdeptˊ/ n 2 one who is fully proficient; expert

ad·e·quate /ˈadˈəkwit/ [L *adaequatus* made equal] adj equal to the requirements, sufficient ‖ **ad'e·quate·ly** adv ‖ **ad'e·quate·ness** or **ad'e·qua·cy** /-kwəsēˊ/ n

ad·here /adhirˊ, əd-/ [L *adhaerere*] vi 1 to stick fast; 2 to become attached or devoted

ad·her·ence n 1 act or state of sticking fast; 2 unwavering attachment, fidelity, or devotion, as to a principle

ad·her·ent /-ənt/ adj 1 adhering ‖ n 2 one who adheres; follower, partisan ‖ SYN n ally, supporter, upholder, defender, backer

ad·he·sion /adˈhēzhˈən/ [L *adhaesio* (-*onis*)] n 1 state of adhering; 2 fidelity, attachment; 3 assent, concurrence; 4 that which adheres; 5 *phys* molecular attraction which holds together the surfaces of substances in contact; 6 *pathol* a sticking together of parts which do not normally adhere, as where a wound has healed; **b adhesions** pl fibers of accidental growth holding together inflamed tissues or parts

ad·he·sive /-sivˊ/ adj 1 holding fast, clinging; 2 gummed, sticky ‖ n 3 adhesive substance

ad·he·sive tape' n tape coated on one side with an adhesive, used to cover injuries and hold bandages in place

ad hoc /ˈadˈ hokˊ/ [L = for this] adj & adv for this special purpose

a·dieu /əd(y)o͞oˊ/ [F = to God] n **a·dieus, a·dieux** /-z/) 1 parting, farewell ‖ interj 2 good-by!, farewell!

ad in·fi·ni·tum /ˈadˈ inˈfinītˈəm/ [L] adv endlessly

ad in·te·rim /ˈadˈ intˈərim/ [L] adv 1 in the meantime ‖ adj 2 temporary

ad·i·os adˈē·ōsˊ/ [Sp = to God] *interj* good-by!, farewell!

ad·i·pose /ˈadˈəpōsˊ/ [< L *adeps* (-*dipis*) fat, suet] adj 1 fatty ‖ n 2 animal fat ‖ **ad'i·pos'i·ty** /-pos'-/ n

Ad'i·ron'dack' Moun'tains /ˈadˈironˊdak/ or **Adirondacks** npl mountain range in NE New York (highest elevation 5344 ft.)

ad·it /ˈadˈit/ [< L *aditus* approach] n 1 access; entrance; 2 *mining* nearly horizontal passage leading to a mine

adj. 1 adjourned; 2 adjective; 3 adjacent; 4 adjutant

ad·ja·cent /əˈjāsˈənt/ [L *adjacens* (-*entis*)] 1 close, contiguous; 2 (angles) having a common vertex and side ‖ **ad·ja'cence** or **ad·ja'cen·cy** n ‖ SYN bordering, neighboring, adjoining, contiguous

ad·jec·ti·val /ˌaj'iktīvˊəl/ adj 1 adjective; 2 using many adjectives ‖ **ad'·jec·ti'val·ly** adv

ad·jec·tive /ˈaj'iktīv/ [LL *adjectivus* via ME] n 1 word of a form class or part of speech used to modify a noun or a pronoun ‖ adj 2 pert. to or functioning as an adjective

ad·join /əˈjoinˊ/ [MF *adjoindre*] vi 1 to be contiguous ‖ vt 2 to be next to, abut on ‖ **ad·join'ing** adj

ad·journ /əˈjurnˊ/ [MF *ajourner*] vt 1 to suspend (a meeting or legislative session) until another time ‖ vi 2 to close or suspend a meeting or session; 3 to go (to another place) ‖ **ad·journ'ment** n ‖ SYN suspend, terminate, postpone, prorogue, dissolve ‖ DISCR To ad*journ* is to suspend, usually for a short period, the proceedings of a public body or of any meeting. To *prorogue* is also to adjourn. But as applied to the British parliament, it is to bring the session to a close, though the parliament still exists and is subject to the order of the sovereign to reassemble. To *dissolve* an assembly is to break it up entirely; thereafter the assembly as constituted ceases to exist, and new members must be elected

adjt. adjutant

ad·judge /əˈjujˊ/ [L *adjudicare* to decide via MF] vt 1 to decide judicially, decree; 2 to award or assign judicially; 3 to deem

ad·ju·di·cate /əˈjo͞odˈikātˊ/ [L *adjudicare* (-*atus*)] vt 1 to hear and decide judicially ‖ vi 2 to act as a judge ‖ **ad·ju'di·ca'tion** n ‖ **ad·ju'di·ca'tor** n

ad·junct /ˈaj'uŋkt/ [L *adjunctus* joined] n 1 something added to or connected with another thing in a subordinate or auxiliary capacity; 2 person or thing subordinately joined to another; 3 *gram* subordinate modifying word or phrase ‖ also adj ‖ SYN addition, appendage, attribute, auxiliary

ad·jure /əjŏŏr'/ [L *adjurare*] *vt* 1 to charge or command solemnly, as if under oath or pain of penalty; 2 to entreat earnestly ‖ **ad'ju·ra'tion** /aj'-/ *n* ‖ **ad·jur'a·to'ry** /-ətôr'ē̠, -ētôr'ē̠/ *adj* ‖ **ad·jur'er** or **ad·ju'ror** /-ər/ *n*

ad·just /əjust'/ [OF *ajuster* < LL *adjuxtare* to bring together] *vt* 1 to settle or bring into harmony; 2 to adapt or make correspond; 3 to regulate, make accurate; 4 to determine the amount of (an insurance claim) ‖ *vi* to become adapted ‖ **ad·just'a·ble** *adj* ‖ **ad·just'er** or **ad·jus'tor** /-ər/ *n* ‖ **ad·just'ment** *n* ‖ SYN regulate, accommodate, suit (see *fit⁴*)

ad·ju·tant /aj'ətənt/ [L *adjutans* (-*antis*) aiding] *n* 1 helper, aid; 2 adjutant stork; 3 *mil* staff officer who assists the commanding officer ‖ **ad'ju·tan·cy** *n*

ad'ju·tant gen'er·al *n* (**adjutants general**) *n* 1 chief administrative officer of a large army unit, as a corps or an army; 2 **Adjutant General** chief administrative officer of the U.S. Army

ad'ju·tant stork' *n* large Old World stork (*Leptoptilus dubius*)

Ad·ler /ad'lər/, **Alfred** *n* (1870–1937) Austrian psychiatrist, formulator of the theory that feelings of inferiority cause compensations that determine the behavior of individuals ‖ **Ad·ler·i·an** /adlir'ē̠·ən/ *adj*

ad lib /ad' lib'/ [< L *ad libitum*] *adv* 1 at will ‖ *n* 2 improvisation in speaking

ad'·lib' *v* (**-libbed; -lib·bing**) *vt* & *vi* to improvise, extemporize in speech or music

ad lib. *mus* ad libitum

ad lib·i·tum /ad'lib'itəm/ [L] *adv* at will

Adm. 1 Admiral; 2 Admiralty

ad'man' /-man'/ *n* (**-men** /-men'/) person in the advertising business

ad·min·is·ter /admin'istər/ [MF *administrer* < L *administrare*] *vt* 1 to manage or conduct; 2 to supply, dispense, as justice, the sacraments, or relief; 3 to give or apply, as medicine; 4 to cause to take, as an oath; 5 *law* to manage or settle, as an estate ‖ *vi* 6 **administer to** to minister to ‖ SYN conduct, execute, regulate, inflict

ad·min'is·trate' *vt* to administer ‖ **ad·min'is·tra·tive** /-strāt'īv, -strə-/ *adj*

ad·min'is·tra'tion *n* 1 act or process of administering; 2 **a** executive branch of governments that separate the executive from the legislative, as in the U.S.; **b** management of public affairs by the chief executive of such a government ‖ SYN execution, conduct, regulation, distribution

ad·min'is·tra'tor *n* 1 one who manages, governs, or directs affairs; 2

one appointed legally to manage or settle an estate ‖ **ad·min'is·tra'trix** /-triks/ *nfem* (**-tri·ces'** /-trisēz'/)

ad·mi·ral /ad'mirəl/ [MF *amiral* < Ar *amir-al-*(bahr) commander of the (sea)] *n* 1 2nd highest rank in the U.S. Navy, a four-star grade equivalent to full general in the Army; 2 any naval officer of flag rank (rear admiral and above)

ad'mi·ral·ty *n* (**-ties**) *n* 1 office and jurisdiction of an admiral; 2 court or law pert. to maritime questions or offenses

ad·mire /admī'ər/ [L *admirari* to wonder at] *vt* to regard with delighted approval and surprise ‖ **ad·mir'er** *n* ‖ **ad·mir'ing·ly** *adv* ‖ **ad'mi·ra·ble** /-mirəbəl/ *adj* ‖ **ad'mi·ra·bly** *adv* ‖ **ad'mi·ra'tion** /-mir-/ *n* ‖ SYN adore, approve, esteem, honor, respect, revere, venerate ‖ ANT abhor, scorn, disapprove, dislike

ad·mis·si·ble /admis'ibəl/ [F < ML *admissibilis*] *adj* 1 worthy of being allowed to enter; 2 allowable, permissible ‖ **ad·mis'si·bil'i·ty** /-bil'-/ *n*

ad·mis·sion /admish'ən/ *n* 1 power or permission to enter; entrance; 2 reception, acceptance; 3 acknowledgment, concession; 4 fact or point conceded; 5 price charged for the privilege of entrance ‖ SYN acknowledgment, acquiescence, concession, entrance, access, initiation (see *admittance*)

ad·mit /admit'/ [L *admittere*] *v* (**-mit·ted; -mit·ting**) *vt* 1 to permit to enter; 2 to have room for; 3 to concede as true; 4 to permit (persons) to have certain privileges, as *he was admitted to the bar* ‖ *vi* 5 **admit to** to acknowledge; 6 **admit of** to afford room for ‖ SYN grant, own, concede, acknowledge, confess

ad·mit'tance *n* 1 act of admitting; 2 permission to enter; 3 *elec* reciprocal of impedance ‖ SYN access, entrance, admission ‖ DISCR *Entrance* indicates the passing from the outside to the inside of a place, room, etc. *Admittance* refers to the permission or opportunity to enter a place, as *admittance* to the park; no *admittance* to children. *Admission* indicates that certain rights or privileges accompany the permission to enter, as *admission* to the theater; *admission* to membership in a club. Merely getting into a place constitutes *admittance*; *admission* depends on the consent of those admitting, the payment of a fee, or the satisfaction of requirements, such as those demanded of immigrants. *Entrance* is also used figuratively as indicating a setting out, or a joining, as *entrance* upon one's life work; *entrance* to college

ad·mit·ted·ly /admit'idlē̠/ *adv* confessedly, avowedly

ad·mix·ture /admiks′chər/ *n* **1** act or state of mixing; **2** that which is added by mixing; **3** mixture

ad·mon·ish /admon′ish/ [MF *amonester*] *vt* **1** to reprove gently, warn, esp. of an anticipated fault; **2** to exhort; **3** to remind ‖ **ad·mon′ish·er** *n* ‖ **ad·mon′ish·ment** or **ad′mo·ni′tion** /ad′mə-/ *n* ‖ **ad·mon′i·to′ry** /-tôr′-, -tōr′-/ *adj* ‖ SYN rebuke, instruct, censure, counsel (see *advise*)

ad nau·se·am /ad′nôz′ē·əm/ [L] *adv* to the point of nausea

a·do /ədo͞o′/ [ME dial. *at do* to do] *n* bustle, fuss

a·do·be /ədōb′ē/ [Sp < Ar *at-tōb* the brick] *n* **1** sun-dried brick; **2** heavy clay from which these bricks are made

ad·o·les·cent /ad′əles′ənt/ [L *adolescens* (*-entis*) growing up] *n* young person, esp. of the age between the onset of puberty and maturity ‖ also *adj* ‖ **ad′o·les′cence** *n*

A·do·nai /äd′ōnī′/ [Heb = my Lord] *n* Hebrew word used to refer to God, in place of the ineffable name Yahweh

A·do·nis /ədon′is, -dōn′-/ *n* **1** *Gk myth.* beautiful youth beloved of Aphrodite; **2** any very handsome man

a·dopt /ədopt′/ [L *adoptare* to choose] *vt* **1** to take as one's own (what is not naturally so, as a child); **2** to take or accept from someone else, as an opinion or course of action ‖ **a·dopt′a·ble** *adj* ‖ **a·dopt′a·bil′i·ty** /-bil′-/ *n* ‖ **a·dopt′er** *n* ‖ **a·dop′tion** *n*

a·dop′tive /-tiv/ *adj* **1** of or pert. to adoption; **2** related by adoption; **3** tending to adopt ‖ **a·dop′tive·ly** *adv*

a·dor·a·ble /ədôr′əbəl, -dōr′-/ *adj* **1** worthy of being adored; **2** delightfully charming ‖ **a·dor′a·ble·ness** or **a·dor′a·bil′i·ty** /-bil′-/ *n* ‖ **a·dor′a·bly** *adv*

a·dore /ədôr′, ədōr′/ [L *adorare* to worship] *vt* **1** to worship; **2** to love intensely; **3** to like (something or doing something) very much ‖ **ad′o·ra′tion** /ad′ə-/ *n* ‖ **a·dor′ing** *adj* ‖ **a·dor′ing·ly** *adv*

a·dorn /ədôrn′/ [MF *adorner* < L *adornare*] *vt* to beautify, ornament, decorate ‖ SYN decorate, embellish, bedeck, array, ornament

a·dorn′ment *n* **1** act of adorning; **2** ornament, decoration

ad·re·nal /ədrēn′əl/ [*ad-* + *renal*] *adj* **1** near the kidneys; **2** of or produced by the adrenal glands

ad·re′nal glands *npl* pair of ductless glands situated above the kidneys, that produce hormones and adrenaline

a·dren·a·line /ədren′əlin/ *n* epinephrine

A′dri·at′ic Sea′ /ā′drē·at′ik, ad′-/ *n* arm of the Mediterranean between Italy and Yugoslavia

a·drift /ədrift′/ *adv* & *adj* **1** floating at random, without anchor; **2** without purpose

a·droit /ədroit′/ [F] *adj* **1** dexterous, skillful; **2** quick-witted, tactfully clever ‖ **a·droit′ly** *adv* ‖ **a·droit′ness** *n* ‖ SYN expert, ready, deft, cunning, ingenious, apt, dexterous, skillful (see *clever*)

ad·sorb /adsôrb′, -zôrb′/ (*ad-* + *absorb*] *vt* to deposit molecules of (a gas, liquid, or solute) on the surface of a solid or liquid ‖ **ad·sorp′tion** *n* ‖ **ad·sorb′ent** & **ad·sorp′tive** *adj* & *n*

ad·u·late /aj′əlāt′/ [L *adulari* (*-atus*)] *vt* to flatter or praise extravagantly and servilely ‖ **ad′u·la′tion** *n* ‖ **ad′u·la′tor** *n* ‖ **ad′u·la·to′ry** /-lətôr′ē, -lətōr′ē/ *adj*

a·dult /ədult′, ad′ult/ [L *adultus* grown] *adj* **1** a fully grown; **b** of legal age ‖ *n* **2** one that is adult ‖ **a·dult′hood** *n* ‖ **a·dult′ness** *n*

a·dul·ter·ant /ədult′ərənt/ *n* adulterating substance ‖ also *adj*

a·dul′ter·ate′ /-āt′/ [L *adulterare* (*-atus*) to defile] *vt* to make inferior or impure by admixture of a poorer substance, but leaving the product with the appearance of genuineness ‖ **a·dul′ter·a′tor** *n*

a·dul·ter·a′tion *n* act, process, or result of adulterating

a·dul′ter·y [L *adulterium*] *n* (*-ies*) sexual relations between two persons either of whom is married to another ‖ **a·dul′ter·er** *n* ‖ **a·dul′ter·ess** /-(ə)ris/ *nfem* ‖ **a·dul′ter·ous** *adj* ‖ **a·dul′ter·ous·ly** *adv*

Adv. 1 Advent; **2** Advocate

adv. 1 ad valorem; **2** adversus; **3 a** adverb; **b** adverbial(ly); **4** advertisement

ad va·lo·rem /ad′ vəlôr′əm, -lōr′-/ (L = according to the value] *adj* (duty) proportionate to the value of imported goods ‖ also *adv*

ad·vance /ədvans′, -väns′/ [OF *avancer* < *ab-* + L *ante* before] *vt* **1** to move forward, cause to proceed; **2** to propose, as an opinion; **3** to further, as plans; **4** to promote, bring to a higher rank; **5** to make happen sooner; **6** to lend (money); **7** to give (part of one's remuneration) beforehand, as *the boss advanced him ten dollars on his salary;* **8** to raise, as price or rate ‖ *vt* **9** to move forward, proceed; **10** to rise, increase, as prices or rates; **11** to progress, develop; **12** to rise in rank or position ‖ *n* **13** forward movement; **14** progress, improvement; **15** money paid beforehand against expected remuneration, as *an advance on royalties;* **16** increase or rise in value or rate; **17** usu. advances *pl* approach, overture; **18 in advance** beforehand ‖ *adj* **19** occurring or being before in time or place ‖ **ad·vanced′** *adj* ‖

ad·vance'ment *n* || SYN *v* promote, exalt, expedite, improve, elevate

ad·vance' man' *n* person sent ahead by a traveling show or circus to the next town to make arrangements for publicity, lodging for the personnel, etc.

ad·van·tage /ədvant'ij, -vänt'-/ [MF *avantage*] *n* **1** any circumstance favoring an end; **2** superiority; power resulting from being master of a situation; **3** gain, profit; **4** *tennis* first point scored after deuce; **5 take advantage of, a** to make profitable use of (something); **b** to exploit the weakness of (someone); **6 to advantage to good effect** || *vt* **7** to favor, advance, profit

ad·van·ta·geous /ad'vəntāj'əs/ *adj* giving advantage; profitable, favorable || SYN gainful, beneficial, profitable, propitious

ad·vent /ad'vent/ [L *adventus* arrival] *n* **1** coming, arrival; **2 Advent,** a period of the church year including the four Sundays before Christmas; **b** first coming of Christ into the world; **c** second coming of Christ on Judgment Day

Ad·vent·ist /ad'ventist, advent'-/ *n* believer in the imminent Second Coming of Christ || **Ad'vent·ism** *n*

ad·ven·ti·tious /ad'vəntish'əs/ [L *adventicius* coming from abroad] *adj* **1** coming from an outside source; **2** accidental; **3** *pathol* acquired, not inherited; **4** *biol* appearing in an unusual location || **ad'ven·ti'tious·ly** *adv*

ad·ven·ture /adven'chər/ [OF *aventure* < L (res) *adventura* (thing) about to happen] *n* **1** bold or hazardous undertaking; **2** exciting or extraordinary experience; **3** business speculation || *vt* **4** to risk, dare || *vi* **5** to take a risk, venture || **ad·ven'ture·some** & **ad·ven'tur·ous** *adj*

ad·ven·tur·er *n* **1** one who seeks adventure; **2** soldier of fortune; **3** one who seeks personal fortune or glory by questionable means || **ad·ven'tur·ess** *nfem*

ad·verb /ad'vurb/ [MF *adverbe* < L *adverbium*] *n* word used to modify a verb, an adjective, another adverb, or an adverbial phrase or clause, by expressing circumstance, time, place, manner, or the like || **ad·ver'bi·al** /-bē-əl/ *adj* **ad·ver'bi·al·ly** *adv*

ad·ver·sary /ad'vərser'ē/ [L *adversarius*] *n* (-ies) **1** enemy, opponent; **2 the Adversary** Satan || SYN rival, foe, antagonist (see *enemy*)

ad·verse /advurs', ad'-/ [L *adversus* hostile] *adj* **1** hostile, unfavorable; **2** turned toward the axis, as a leaf || **ad·verse'ly** *adv* || **ad·verse'ness** *n*

ad·ver'si·ty *n* (-ties) *adj* **1** adverse state or condition; **2** calamity, disaster || SYN hardship, trouble, affliction, suffering, misery || ANT prosperity, wellbeing, happiness, blessing, joy

ad·vert /advurt'/ [L *advertere* to turn] *vi* **1** to turn the attention; **2** to refer casually

ad·vert'ent /-ənt/ *adj* attentive, heedful || **ad·vert'ent·ly** *adv* || **ad·vert'·ence** or **ad·vert'en·cy** *n*

ad·ver·tise /ad'vərtīz/ [MF *advertir* (-tiss-)] *vt* **1** to call the attention of the public to, usu. by means of billboards, printed notices, broadcasts, and/or insertions in newspapers or magazines; **2** to give public notice of, as by an insertion in a newspaper || *vi* **3** to make use of advertisements || **ad'ver·tis'er** *n*

ad·ver·tise·ment /ad'vərtīz'mənt, advurt'īzmənt/ *n* **1** act or process of advertising; **2** announcement, as of goods or services for sale, on radio, television, billboards, circulars, or in the press; **3** public notice, esp. in the press

ad'ver·tis'ing *n* **1** action or process of calling the public's attention to something for sale; **2** profession of preparing and placing advertisements; **3** advertisements

ad·vice /advīs'/ [OF *avis* opinion] *n* **1** opinion offered to influence another's course of action; **2** usu. **advices** *pl* informative communication from a distance || SYN suggestion, instruction, counsel, caution

ad·vis·a·ble /ədvīz'əbəl/ *adj* proper to be done, prudent, desirable || **ad·vis'a·bly** *adv* || **ad·vis'a·bil'i·ty** /-bil'-/ *n*

ad·vise /ədvīz'/ [OF *aviser*] *vt* **1** to counsel; **2** to recommend; **3** to notify, inform || *vi* **4** to consult, take counsel || **ad·vis'er** or **ad·vi'sor** /-zər/ *n* || SYN counsel, admonish, counsel. DISCR To *instruct* is to give clear and positive directions as to a future course of conduct. To *admonish* is gently to reprove errors and faults in order to prevent them in future; reproof of this nature refers to the moral conduct, and usually comes from one fitted by age or station to give it. To *advise* is to give wise suggestions as to future action, such suggestions being based on professional knowledge or wide experience, real or assumed. To *counsel* is to give a considered opinion on a serious matter from a fund of superior wisdom and knowledge of moral principles. An employer *instructs* an employee as to the nature of his duties; a mother *admonishes* her daughter as to the dangers of slovenliness; a doctor *advises* his patient; a clergyman *counsels* his flock

ad·vis·ed·ly /ədvīz'idlē/ *adv* after due consideration

ad·vise'ment *n* **under advisement** under consideration

ad·vi·so·ry /-zərē/ *adj* **1** having power to advise; **2** giving or containing advice || *n* **3** informative report

ad·vo·ca·cy /ad'vəkəsē/ *n* 1 act of advocating; 2 support

ad·vo·cate /ad'vəkit/ [MF *advocat* < L *advocatus*, pp of *advocare* to summon] *n* 1 one who pleads the cause of another; 2 one who defends some special cause; 3 legal counsel ‖ /-kāt'/ *vt* 4 to plead for, be in favor of ‖ **ad'vo·ca'tor** *n* /-tər/

adz or **adze** /adz'/ [OE *adesa* axe] *n* axe with a curved blade set at right angles to the handle, used in shaping and finishing timber

æ¹ Old English letter having the sound of *a* in *hat*, dropped from the English alphabet in the 13th century

æ² Latin digraph equivalent to Greek *ai* and originally having a sound like that of English *i*, replaced in the modern spelling of Latin and Latinized Greek words in English by *ae* or *e*

ae modern spelling of *æ²*, replaced in many words in English by *e*

AEC Atomic Energy Commission

a·e·des or **a·ë·des** /ā-ēd'ēz/ [Gk = unpleasant] *n* any of a genus (*Aedes*) of mosquitoes including the yellow-fever mosquito

ae·dile also **e·dile** /ē'dīl/ [L *aedilis*] *n* ancient Roman official who superintended public works, games, the grain supply, etc.

A.E.F. American Expeditionary Force

Ae·ge·an /ijē'ən/ *adj* 1 of or pert. to the Aegean Sea; 2 of or pert. to the pre-Hellenic civilization of the Aegean islands and nearby regions ‖ *n* 3 **the Aegean** the Aegean Sea

Ae·ge·an Sea' *n* arm of the Mediterranean between Greece and Turkey

ae·gis also **e·gis** /ēj'is/ [L < Gk *aigis*] *n* 1 *Gk myth.* shield or breastplate emblematic of the majesty of Zeus and Athena; 2 protection, sponsorship

Ae·ne·as /inē'əs/ *n class. myth.* Trojan prince, son of Anchises and Venus, the reputed ancestor of the Romans and hero of Vergil's *Aeneid*

ae·o·li·an /ē-ōl'ē·ən/ [< *Aeolus*] *adj* 1 pert. to, affected by, or due to the wind ‖ *n* 2 **Aeolian** member of one of the four tribes who conquered prehistoric Greece

ae·o'li·an harp' *n* instrument of several strings tuned in unison which gives out musical sounds when exposed to currents of air

Ae·o·lus /ē'ələs/ *n Gk myth.* god of the winds

ae·on also **e·on** /ē'ən, -on/ [Gk *aion*] *n* very long period of time, age

aer-, aeri-, or **aero-** [< Gk *aer* air] *comb form* air, aviation, as *aerate, aerodrome*

aer·ate /ā'ərāt', er'āt/ *vt* 1 to charge with gas, as with air or carbon dioxide; 2 to expose to the action of air; 3 to treat with oxygen, as the blood ‖ **aer·a'tion** *n*

aer'a·tor /-tər/ *n* device for aerating fluids or introducing air into a place for storing grain

aer·i·al /er'ē·əl, ā·ir'ē·əl/ *adj* 1 relating to, existing or happening in the air; 2 high, lofty; 3 like air, airy; 4 imaginary, lacking substance; 5 pert. to or used in connection with aircraft ‖ /er'ē·əl/ *n* 6 radio or television antenna; 7 *football* forward pass ‖ **aer'i·al·ly** *adv*

aer'i·al·ist *n* performer on a flying trapeze

aer'i·al lad'der *n* extendible ladder on a fire truck

aer'i·al tram' *n* carriage for carrying passengers up the side of a peak by means of overhead cables

aer·ie /er'ē, ā'ər·ē, ir'ē/ [ML *aeria* < OF *aire* < L *area*] *n* 1 nest of a bird of prey on a lofty crag or peak; 2 any high inaccessible dwelling

aero- *comb form* var of **aer-**

aer·o /er'ō/ *adj* of or pert. to aircraft or aeronautics

aer'o·bat'ics /-bat'iks/ [*aero* + *acrobatics*] *npl* 1 stunts performed with an airplane or glider ‖ *nsg* 2 art of stunt flying

aer'obe /-ōb/ [*aero-* + Gk *bios* life] *n* organism, as a bacterium, that requires oxygen to live ‖ **aer·o'bic** *adj*

aer·o·drome /er'ədrōm'/ *n Brit* airport

aer'o·dy·nam'ics *nsg* branch of dynamics dealing with the motion of air and gases in general and of the forces acting on solid bodies moving in such gases ‖ **aer'o·dy·nam'ic** *adj* ‖ **aer'o·dy·nam'i·cal·ly** *adv*

aer·om·e·ter /-om'itər/ [*aero-* + *-meter* via F] *n* instrument for measuring the weight and density of air and other gases ‖ **aer·om'e·try** *n* ‖ **aer'o·met'ric** /-əmet'rik/ *adj*

aer'o·naut' /-ənôt', -ənot'/ [*aero-* + Gk *nautes* sailor] *n* pilot or traveler in a lighter-than-air craft

aer'o·nau'tics *nsg* science or art of flight ‖ **aer'o·nau'tic** (**-ti·cal**) *adj*

aer'o·plane' *n Brit* airplane

aer'o·sol' /-sol', -sōl', -sôl'/ [*aero-* + hydro*sol*] *n* 1 suspension of fine particles of liquid or solid substances in pressurized air or gas, as mist, smoke, insecticide, disinfectant, paint; 2 spray can containing such a suspension

aer'o·space' *n* 1 the earth's atmosphere and the space beyond ‖ *adj* 2 pert. to objects, as vehicles and missiles, designed for use in aerospace

Aes·chy·lus /es'kələs/ *n* (525–456 B.C.) Greek dramatist ‖ **Aes·chy·le·an** /es'kəlē'ən/ *adj*

Aes'cu·la'pi·us /es'kyəlā'pē·əs/ *n class. myth.* god of medicine, the Greek *Asklepios* or *Asclepius* ‖ **Aes·cu·la'pi·an** *adj*

Ae·sop /ēs'op, ēs'əp/ *n* (c.620–c.560 B.C.) Greek fabulist ‖ **Ae·so·pi·an** /ēsōp'ē·ən/ or **Ae·sop·ic** /ēsop'ik/ *adj*

aes·thete also **es·thete** /es'thēt/ [Gk *aisthetes* one who perceives] *n* one who has or affects to have a cultivated taste for the beautiful in nature or art, one sensitive to beauty

aes·thet·ic also **es·thet·ic** /esthet'ik/ *adj* 1 pert. to beauty; 2 sensitive to the beautiful, possessing a cultivated, artistic taste

aes·thet·ics also **es·thet·ics** *nsg* branch of philosophy concerned with the beautiful in nature or art ‖ **aes·thet'i·cal** *adj* ‖ **aes·thet'i·cal·ly** *adv* ‖ **aes·the·ti·cian** /es'thitish'ən/ *n*

af- var of ad-

AF, A.F. 1 Air Force; 2 Anglo-French

A.F.A.M. or **A.F. & A.M.** Ancient Free and Accepted Masons

a·far /əfär'/ *adv* 1 at, to, or from a distance; 2 **from afar** from far away

AFB Air Force Base

af·fa·ble /af'əbəl/ [L *affabilis*] *adj* pleasant, courteous, easy to approach ‖ **af'fa·bly** *adv* ‖ **af·fa·bil'i·ty** /-bil'-/ *n* ‖ SYN amiable, genial, kindly, gracious, bland, benign (see *polite*) ‖ ANT brusque, curt, austere

af·fair /əfer'/ [MF *a faire* to do] *n* 1 that which is done or to be done; 2 matter, concern; 3 notorious incident, case; 4 amorous episode; 5 **affairs** *pl* a one's private interests; b matters of public concern

af·fair' of hon'or *n* duel

af·fect¹ /əfekt'/ [L *afficere* (*-fectus*)] *vt* 1 to produce a change in, influence; 2 to touch mentally or emotionally

af·fect² [MF *affecter* < L *affectare* to aim at, feign] *vt* 1 to pretend, feign; 2 to show a liking, preference, or affinity for

af·fec·ta·tion /af'ektāsh'ən/ *n* the assuming of a manner which is not one's own; pretense, display ‖ SYN artificiality, hypocrisy (see *mannerism*)

af·fect'ed¹ /-id/ [*affect¹*] *adj* 1 acted upon or influenced; 2 impaired, attacked, as by disease

af·fect'ed² [*affect²*] *adj* assumed, unnatural ‖ **af·fect'ed·ly** *adv* ‖ **af·fect'ed·ness** *n*

af·fect'ing *adj* moving, touching ‖ **af·fect'ing·ly** *adv*

af·fec'tion *n* 1 attachment, fondness; 2 disease; 3 **affections** *pl* feeling, sentiment ‖ SYN fondness, love, tenderness (see *attachment*)

af·fec'tion·ate /-nit/ *adj* having or expressing love; kind, fond ‖ **af·fec'tion·ate·ly** *adv*

af·fec'tive *adj* 1 emotional; 2 causing emotion ‖ **af'fec'tive·ly** *adv*

af·fer·ent /af'ərənt/ [< L *affere* to bring to] *adj physiol* carrying inward, as a nerve impulse to the brain or spinal column

af·fi·ance /əfī'əns/ [MF *afiancer*] *vt* to betroth

af·fi·ant /-ənt/ *n* person making an affidavit

af·fi·da·vit /af'idāv'it/ [L = he has pledged] *n* statement in writing to the truth of which an oath or affirmation is made before a properly authorized officer

af·fil·i·ate /əfil'ē·āt'/ [LL *affiliare* (*-atus*) to adopt as a son] *vt* 1 to receive as a member or branch; 2 to join as a member; 3 to fix the paternity of; 4 to trace the descent of, as a language ‖ *vi* 5 to be connected or associated ‖ /-ē·it/ *n* 6 affiliated person, business, or organization ‖ **af·fil'i·a'tion** *n*

af·fin·i·ty /əfin'itē/ [L *affinitas* connection by marriage] *n* (*-ties*) 1 nearness of kin; 2 relationship by marriage; 3 natural liking for a person; 4 physical or chemical attraction ‖ SYN kinship, relationship, likeness, similarity, resemblance, agreement, attraction ‖ ANT dislike, repulsion, antipathy, antagonism, aversion, dissimilarity

af·firm /əfurm'/ [MF *afermer* < L *affirmare* to assert] *vt* 1 to ratify; 2 to assert strongly; 3 *law* to declare solemnly but without taking oath ‖ *vi* 4 to assert something confidently; 5 to confirm the finding of a lower court ‖ **af·firm'ant** *n* ‖ **af'fir·ma'tion** *n* ‖ SYN maintain, declare, aver, allege, assert, state ‖ ANT contradict, deny, dispute, oppose, refute

af·firm'a·tive *n* 1 expression of affirmation or assent; 2 positive statement or proposition; 3 side of a debate that defends the stated proposition ‖ *adj* 4 positive; 5 (response) that assents or affirms, saying yes ‖ **af·firm'a·tive·ly** *adv*

af·fix /af'iks/ [L *affixus* fastened] *n* 1 bound form prefixed, infixed, or suffixed to a stem, producing derivative words or inflectional forms; 2 something attached or joined ‖ /əfiks'/ *vt* 3 to attach, fasten; 4 to add, append, as a signature; 5 to attribute, impute

af·fla·tus /əflāt'əs/ [L = blast of air] *n* state of spiritual exaltation; inspiration

af·flict /əflikt'/ [L *affligere* (*-flictus*)] *vt* 1 to cause pain or grief to, trouble grievously

af·flic'tion *n* condition or cause of continued pain and suffering ‖ **af·flic'tive** *adj* ‖ SYN tribulation, sorrow, calamity (see *grief*)

af·flu·ence /af'lōō·əns/ [MF < L *affluentia* abundance] *n* 1 great wealth; 2 profusion; 3 a flowing to or toward a point ‖ SYN abundance, plenty, richness, opulence ‖ ANT scarcity, want, poverty, penury, destitution

af'flu·ent /-ənt/ [< L *affluere* to flow to] *adj* 1 wealthy; 2 abundant; 3 freely flowing ‖ *n* 4 tributary stream

af·ford /əfôrd'-, -fôrd'/ [OE *geforthian*

to advance] *vt* **1** to supply, produce, yield; **2** to be able to bear the expense or sacrifice of

af·fray /əfrā'/ [AF *afray*] *n* noisy brawl

af·fri·cate /af'rikit/ [L *affricatus* rubbed together] *n phonet* unit phoneme consisting of a stop consonant released at once by a fricative, both elements belonging to the same syllable, as English *j* in *rejoice* and German *pf* in *empfangen*

af·fric·a·tive /əfrik'ətiv/ *n* **1** affricate ‖ *adj* **2** of or pert. to an affricate

af·front /əfrunt'/ [MF *afronter* to defy to one's face] *vt* **1** to face defiantly; **2** to insult intentionally ‖ *n* **3** deliberate insult ‖ SYN *v* annoy, displease, irritate, offend, provoke

af·ghan /af'gan, -gən/ *n* **1** crocheted or knitted wool blanket; **2 Afghan,** a native of Afghanistan; **b** language of Afghanistan ‖ also *adj*

Af'ghan hound' *n* tall hunting dog with long narrow head and silky coat, originating in the Near East

af·ghan·i /-gan'ē, -gä'nē/ *n* monetary unit of Afghanistan

Af·ghan·i·stan /afgan'istan'/ *n* republic in S central Asia (15,751,000; 250,000 sq.mi.; cap. Kabul)

a·fi·cio·na·do /əfish'ənäd'ō/ [Sp] *n* devotee; enthusiast ‖ **a·fi'cio·na'da** /-də/ *n fem*

a·field /əfēld'/ *adv* **1** to, in, or on the field; **2** astray; **3** away from home, abroad; **4** off the beaten path, as *far afield*

a·fire /əfīr'ər/ *adj* on fire

A.F.L. American Federation of Labor

a·flame /əflām'/ *adj* **1** on fire, ablaze

a·float /əflōt'/ *adv & adj* **1** floating on the water; **2** on shipboard; **3** awash; **4** adrift; **5** in circulation; **6** solvent

a·flut·ter /əflut'ər/ *adj* in a flutter

a·foot /əfŏŏt'/ *adv & adj* **1** on foot; **2** astir, about

a·fore /əfôr', -fōr'/ *adv, conj, & prep dial.* before

a·fore'men'tioned *adj* mentioned previously

a·fore'said' *adj* said or mentioned previously

a·fore'thought' *adj* premeditated, as *malice aforethought*

a for·ti·o·ri /ä' fôr'shē-ôr'ī/ [L = from the strongest] *adv* with the greater force, all the more (used in drawing a conclusion that is more compelling than a previous one)

a·foul /əfoul'/ *adj* **1** tangled, fouled ‖ *adv* **run afoul of** to become entangled with

Afr-, Afro- [L *Afer (Afris)*] *comb form* African

Afr. Africa(n)

a·fraid /əfrād'/ [*pp* of archaic *affray* to frighten] *adj* **1** frightened; **2** reluctant, as *afraid of work*; **3** regretful, as *I'm afraid I can't go* ‖ SYN

timid, timorous, fearful, frightened ‖ DISCR *Afraid* refers to a general state of fear, usually temporary and of a wide application; one may be *afraid* of anything from missing a train to death. *Timid, timorous,* and *fearful* refer to a lack of courage that is constitutional and is centered about self. A *timid* person fears to face a mouse, criticism, or a decision of his own mind, lest he be hurt by the consequences. One is *timorous* or *fearful* who is so easily alarmed that his imagination will serve as well as reality to frighten him: *fearful* of fraud; *fearful* of foul play. *Frightened* implies a sudden, intense, and usually temporary, attack of fear ‖ ANT bold, brave, courageous, self-controlled

a·fresh /əfresh'/ *adv* over again, anew

Af·ri·ca /af'rikə/ *n* continent S of Europe (250,000,000; 11,600,000 sq.m.) ‖ **Af'ri·can** *adj & n*

Af'ri·can vi'o·let *n* popular houseplant (*Saintpaulia ionantha*) with violet, pink, or white flowers

Af·ri·kaans /af'rikäns', -känz'/ [< D *Afrikaansch* African] *n* language developed from 17th-century Dutch, one of the official languages of the Republic of South Africa

Af·ri·ka·ner /af'rikän'ər/ also **Af'ri·kan'der** /-kan'dər/ *n* Afrikaans-speaking native of South Africa of European descent

Af'ro-A·mer'i·can /af'rō-/ also **Af'ra·mer'i·can** /af'rə-/ *n* American of African descent ‖ also *adj*

Af'ro-A'sian /af'rō-/ *adj* of or pert. to Africa and Asia

aft /aft/, **äft/** [OE *æftan* from behind] *adv & adj naut & aeron* at, to, or toward the stem or tail

af·ter /af'tər, äf'-/ [OE *æfter*] *adj* **1** next, subsequent, as *in after days*; **2** aft ‖ *adv* **3** behind, subsequently in time or place ‖ *prep* **4** behind in place; **5** in succession to; **6** later than; **7** in the manner of, as *a painting after Raphael*; **8** in pursuit of; **9** subsequent to; **10** concerning; **11** for the good of, as *look after the baby*; **12** with the name of, as *named after his father*; **13 after all** all things considered ‖ *conj* **14** subsequently to the time that

af'ter·birth' *n* placenta and fetal membranes expelled after birth

af'ter·brain' *n* posterior section of the hindbrain

af'ter·burn'er *n* **1** device that injects fuel into the exhaust gases of a jet engine to provide additional thrust; **2** device for burning the unconsumed fuel in the exhaust fumes of internal combustion engines in order to lower air pollution

af'ter·care' *n* care and treatment of convalescent patients

af′ter·deck′ n the part of the deck of a ship abaft the bridge

af′ter·glow′ n 1 radiance remaining after a bright light has gone; 2 warm remembrance of a pleasant experience

af′ter·im′age n image or sensation which persists after the stimulus has ceased

af′ter·life′ n 1 life after death; 2 later period of one's life

af′ter·math′ /-math′/ [after + obs math mowing] n result, consequence, often disastrous

af′ter·most adj naut farthest aft

af′ter·noon′ n 1 time between noon and evening; 2 late period, as of one's life

af′ter·noons′ adv during the afternoon regularly

af′ter·pains′ npl pain following childbirth, caused by the contraction of the uterus

af′ter·taste′ n taste or other sensation after the stimulus is gone

af′ter·thought′ n 1 thought occurring later; 2 thing added that was not included in the original design or plan

af′ter·ward /-wərd/ or **af′ter·wards** /-wərdz/ adv at a later time, subsequently

ag- var of ad-

Ag [L argentum] chem silver

a·gain /əgen′/ [OE ongēan opposite] adv 1 once more; 2 in return, back; 3 on the other hand; 4 again and again repeatedly

a·gainst /əgenst′/ [alter. of ME agaynes again] prep 1 in opposition to; 2 in contact with; 3 opposite to; 4 as protection from or in preparation for, as insurance against fire; 5 facing; in the direction of; 6 as an offset to, as payment against a loan; 7 contrasted with

Ag·a·mem·non /ag′əmem′nən/ n Gk myth. king of Mycenae and brother-in-law of Helen, Greek commander in chief at the siege of Troy

a·gape¹ /əgāp′/ adj & adv 1 with the mouth wide open; 2 wide open

ag·a·pe² /äg′əpā′/ [Gr = love] n love feast celebrated by the early Christians in connection with the Lord's Supper

a·gar /ä′gär, ag′-/ also **a′gar-a′gar** [Malay] n 1 gelatinous substance extracted from East Indian seaweeds, used as a substitute for gelatin and as a solidifying, thickening, or emulsifying agent; 2 culture medium with an agar base

ag·ate /ag′it/ [MF < Gk achates] n 1 variegated chalcedony with colors in stripes and clouds; 2 boy's playing marble, often made of agate; 3 5½-point type

ag′ate line′ n measure of advertising space, one column wide and ¹⁄₁₄ of an inch deep

a·gaze /əgāz′/ adj gazing

agcy. agency

age /āj/ [OF aage] n 1 particular period of time; 2 length of time already lived; 3 period of human or geological history; 4 one of the stages of life, as middle age; 5 advanced years; 6 a long time; 7 of age having full legal age; 8 over age too old for some specified task or duty; 9 under age below legal age ‖ v (ag·ing or age·ing) vi 10 to grow old; 11 to mature, mellow, as wine or cheese ‖ vt 12 to cause to become old, mature, or mellow

-age /ij/ [OF < L -aticum] n suf 1 collection, sum, as foliage, mileage; 2 act or process, as passage; 3 fees for or cost of, as cartage; 4 condition, rank, as peonage

ag·ed /ājd′/ adj 1 having (a specified number of) years; 2 having acquired maturity or mellowness with age ‖ /āj′id/ adj 3 grown old ‖ n 4 the aged /āj′id/ pl old people collectively

age·ism /āj′izm/ n discrimination on the basis of age, esp. against the middle-aged and elderly ‖ age′ist adj & n

age′less adj 1 never growing old; 2 timeless

age′long′ adj everlasting

a·gen·cy /āj′ənsē/ [ML agentia] n (-cies) 1 operation, action; 2 business of an agent; 3 relation between a principal and his agent; 4 instrumentality; 5 place where business is done for another person or firm; 6 government department or bureau

a·gen·da /əjen′də/ [L = things to be done] n list of things to be done, discussed, or voted on at a meeting; program

a·gent /āj′ənt/ [L agens (-entis) doing] n 1 one who acts for another; 2 one who acts for an official agency, as an FBI agent; 3 active power or cause; 4 instrument, means; 5 chem substance that causes a reaction ‖ a·gen·tial /ājen′shəl/ adj ‖ syn doer, factor, operator, performer, instrument

a·gent pro·vo·ca·teur /əzhän′ prōvok′-ətur′/ [F = inciting agent] n (agents provocateurs /same as sg/) secret agent employed to assist or induce suspected or disliked persons to commit some act which will make them liable to punishment

age′ of con·sent′ n age at which a female can legally give consent to sexual intercourse without the male incurring the penalties of statutory rape

age′-old′ adj ancient, traditional

ag·gior·na·men·to /əjôr′nəment/ō/ [It = coming of daylight] n bringing something up to date, spec., the modernization of the Roman Catholic Church

ag·glom·er·ate /əglŏm'ərāt'/ [L *agglomerare* (*-atus*) to wind on a ball] *vt & vi* 1 to gather into a cluster or heap ‖ /-it/ *adj* 2 agglomerated; 3 *bot* clustered together but not cohering ‖ *n* 4 haphazard collection of things; 5 mass of volcanic fragments of all sizes thrown together with no trace of stratification ‖ **ag·glom'er·a·tive** /-ətiv/ *adj* ‖ **ag·glom'er·a'tion** *n*

ag·glu'ti·nate' /əglōot'ənāt'/ [L *agglutinare* (*-atus*) to glue] *vt* 1 to unite, as by glue or adhesion; 2 *ling* to add (affixes) by agglutination ‖ *vi* 3 to unite, as by glue or adhesion

ag·glu'ti·na'tion *n* 1 act, process, or result of agglutinating; 2 *biol* coalescing of particles, as red blood cells or bacteria, into clumps through the action of an antibody; 3 *ling* formation of compound and derivative words by the affixing of forms which remain independent words or elements, as *hopeful* and *mankind* ‖ **ag·glu'ti·na'tive** *adj*

ag·glu'ti·nin /-nĭn/ [*agglutinate* + *-in*] *n biol* substance, as an antibody, causing agglutination

ag·gran·dize /ag'rəndīz'/ [F *agrandir* (*-diss-*)] *vt* 1 to make great or greater in power, rank, or riches; 2 to exalt in one's opinion ‖ **ag'gran·diz'er** *n* ‖ **ag·gran·dize·ment** /əgran'dĭzmənt/ *n*

ag·gra·vate /ag'rəvāt'/ [L *aggravare* (*-atus*) to make heavier] *vt* 1 to make worse or less bearable; 2 to annoy ‖ **ag'gra·vat'ing** *adj* ‖ **ag'gra·va'tion** *n* ‖ SYN heighten, increase, intensify, magnify, exasperate, irritate, provoke ‖ ANT alleviate, assuage, diminish, lessen, reduce, soften, palliate

ag·gre·gate /ag'rəgāt'/ [L *aggregare* (*-atus*) to add to] *vt* 1 to collect or bring together; 2 to amount to ‖ /-git/ *adj* 3 formed into a mass, total; 4 composed of mixed mineral substances, as granite; 5 *bot* formed into a dense cluster ‖ *n* 6 total; entire number; 7 mass formed of dissimilar particles; 8 hard material used in making concrete

ag'gre·ga'tion *n* collection gathered into one whole or mass

ag·gres·sion /əgresh'ən/ [< L *aggressus* attacked] *n* 1 attack or assault, esp. unprovoked; 2 *psychol* overt or suppressed feeling of hostility

ag·gres·sive /əgres'iv/ *adj* 1 combative; 2 hostile, menacing; 3 enterprising, full of initiative ‖ **ag·gres'sive·ly** *adv* ‖ **ag·gres'sive·ness** *n*

ag·gres'sor *n* one who attacks first; assailant

ag·grieve /əgrēv'/ [MF *agrever*] *vt* 1 to oppress, afflict; 2 to injure

ag·grieved' *adj* 1 wronged, offended; 2 troubled, distressed; 3 denied legal rights

a·ghast /əgast', əgäst'/ [ME *agast* frightened] *adj* struck with sudden surprise or horror

ag·ile /aj'əl/ [L *agilis*] *adj* 1 brisk, active, nimble; 2 quick-witted ‖ **a·gil·i·ty** /əjil'itē/ *n*

Ag·in·court /aj'ĭnkôrt'/ *n* village in N France near Calais, scene of a famous English victory over the French 1415

ag·i·tate /aj'ĭtāt'/ [L *agitare* (*-atus*)] *vt* 1 to move or shake violently; 2 to excite or disturb ‖ *vi* 3 to attempt to arouse public interest ‖ **ag'i·ta'tion** *n* ‖ SYN arouse, excite, kindle, provoke, disturb, quicken, ruffle, shake ‖ ANT soothe, allay, pacify

ag'i·ta'tor *n* 1 one who stirs up others in order to further his own designs; 2 device for mixing or shaking

ag·it·prop /aj'ĭtprop'/ [Russ = *agit*-(ation) + *prop*(aganda)] *n* 1 agitation and propaganda, esp. in the cause of communism; 2 individual or agency engaged in this activity ‖ also *adj*

a·gleam /əglēm'/ *adj* gleaming

ag·let /ag'lit/ also **aig·let** /āg'lit/ [MF *aiguillette* tag] *n* 1 metal sheath or tip at the end of a lace or ribbon to make it easier to put through an eyelet; 2 tagged point hanging from the shoulder of some uniforms

a·gley /əglē', əglī'/ [a-³ + Sc *gley* to squint] *adv* Scot dial. askew, wrong

a·glitter /əglit'ər/ *adj* glittering

a·glow /əglō'/ *adj* glowing

AGM air-to-ground missile

ag·nos·tic /agnos'tik/ [< Gk *agnostos* not known] *n* one who denies that man knows or can know God or the final nature of things ‖ also *adj* ‖ **ag·nos'ti·cism** *n* ‖ SYN disbeliever, unbeliever (see *skeptic*)

Ag·nus De·i /ag'nəs dē'ī/ or *R C Ch* än'yo͞os de'ē/ [L] *n* 1 Lamb of God, title applied to Jesus by John the Baptist (John 1:29); 2 emblem of Christ in the form of a lamb, often represented as bearing a banner marked with a cross; 3 a triple prayer used in the celebration of Mass, beginning with these words; **b** the accompanying music

a·go /əgō'/ [< OE *āgān* gone away] *adj* 1 gone, past, as *two days ago* ‖ *adv* 2 long ago a long time past

a·gog /əgog'/ [? MF *en gogues* in mirth] *adj & adv* in a state of eager excitement, astir

à go·go /ä gō'gō'/ [F] *adv* to one's heart's content (used in the U.S. chiefly as part of the names of night clubs and discothèques)

-a·gogue also **-a·gog** /-əgôg', -əgog'/ [Gk *-agogos* < *agein* to lead] *n suf* 1 leader, as *demagogue;* **2** *biol* withdrawing agent, as *emmenagogue*

ag·o·nize /ag′əniz′/ *vi* **1** to suffer extremely; **2** to make great effort of any kind ‖ *vt* **3** to cause to suffer greatly ‖ **ag′o·niz′ing** *adj*

ag·o·ny /ag′ənē/ [Gk *agonia* anguish] *n* (-nies) **1** intense suffering; **2** extreme mental or physical pain; **3** intense outburst, as of joy; **4** death struggle ‖ SYN anguish, torture, pang (see *distress*)

ag′o·ra·pho′bi·a /ag′ərəfōb′ē-ə/ [Gk *agora* marketplace + *phobia*] *n* morbid fear or dread of open spaces (opposite of *claustrophobia*)

agr. **1** agriculture; **2** agricultural

A·gra /äg′rə/ *n* city in Uttar Pradesh, N India (470,000); site of the Taj Mahal

ag·ra·pha /ag′rəfə/ [Gk = unwritten things] *npl* sayings of Jesus not contained in the Gospels

a·grar·i·an /əgrer′ē-ən/ [< L *agrarius* < *ager* field] **1** relating to land, esp. farm land or public land, or to its ownership; **2** pert. to farmers and their interests ‖ *n* **3** one who is in favor of an equal division of public lands ‖ **a·grar′i·an·ism** *n*

a·gree /əgrē′/ [MF *agreer* < *a gre* at pleasure] *vi* **1** to harmonize; be similar, match; **2** to yield assent, consent, accede; **3** to accord, come to one opinion; **4** to be suitable, as diet; **5** to be healthful, as *the climate agrees with me;* **6** *gram* to have an appropriate form or inflection, be alike in gender, number, case, or person ‖ SYN consent, assent, concur, coincide, accord, accede, comply, acquiesce, tally, harmonize, comport, fit ‖ DISCR *Agree* is the general term expressing sameness of mind or feelings. To *consent* is to agree by act of will or through the influence of the feelings. We *consent* to what we permit, or we *consent* to do a favor. To *assent* is to agree by act of the understanding; we *assent* to what we grant to be true, as, for instance, a religious doctrine. *Agree, concur,* and *coincide* are alike in expressing sameness of opinion; but to *concur* is to agree in opinion and often in consequent action, while *coincide* implies agreement in every particular with the opinion of another, without reference to action. To *comply* is to come into agreement by yielding to the wishes of another (see *accede, accord*)

a·gree′a·ble *adj* **1** pleasing to the mind or senses; **2** having pleasing manners; **3** in harmony or conformity; **4** willing, favorably inclined; **5** **agreeable to** or **with** in accordance with ‖ **a·gree′a·ble·ness** *n* ‖ **a·gree′a·bly** *adv* ‖ SYN pleasant, pleasing, amiable, acceptable

a·gree′ment *n* **1** harmony of opinions or feelings; **2** compact; mutual understanding; **3** *law* **a** contract; **b** its wording; **4** *gram* correspondence of one word with another in gender, number, case, or person ‖ SYN accord, concurrence; bargain (see *contract*)

ag′ri·busi′ness /ag′rə-/ *n* business of manufacturing farm equipment, developing acreage for raising and processing farm commodities, and distributing the output of these activities

ag·ri·cul·ture /ag′rəkul′chər/ [L *agricultura*] *n* farming; the science and art of cultivating fields and producing crops, livestock, or poultry ‖ **ag′ri·cul′tur·al** *adj* ‖ **ag′ri·cul′tur·ist** *n*

agro- [Gk *agros* tilled land] *comb form* soil, production of crops, as *agrology*

a·gron·o·my /əgron′əmē/ *n* scientific crop production; rural economy ‖ **ag·ro·nom·ic** (**-i·cal**) /ag′rənom′ik-(əl)/ *adj* ‖ **a·gron′o·mist** *n*

a·ground′ *adj* & *adv* **1** on the ground; **2** (ship) with keel on the bottom; stranded

agt. **1** agent; **2** agreement

a·gue /ā′gyōō/ [MF < LL (febris) *acuta* acute fever] *n* **1** malarial fever recurring at regular intervals with chills and sweating; **2** chill, or state of shaking, as with cold ‖ **a′gu·ish** *adj*

ah /ä′/ [ME] *interj* expressing sudden emotion, as mild wonder, contempt, or pity

a.h. ampere-hour

a·ha /ähä′/ [< *ah*] *interj* expressing triumph, surprise, or contempt

A·hab /ā′hab/ *n Bib* a wicked king of Israel, husband of Jezebel, slain in battle by the Syrians (1 Kings 16-22)

a·head′ *adv* **1** to or in the front; **2** forward; onward; **3** into or for the future; **4** at or to an earlier time; **5** **ahead of, a** in advance of; **b** in front of; **c** superior to

a·hem /əhem′/ [var of *hem*²] *interj* slight cough to attract attention

a·hold′ *n colloq* a hold, as *grab ahold of my hand*

a·hoy /əhoi′/ [var of *hoy*] *interj* term used in hailing a vessel, as *ship ahoy!*

aid /ād′/ [MF *aider* < L *adjutare*] *vt* **1** to assist, support ‖ *vi* **2** to give assistance ‖ *n* **3** help; **4** person, thing, or action that helps; **5** special tax paid by a feudal vassal to his lord ‖ SYN *v* relieve, succor, assist (see *help*)

A·i·da /ä·ēd′ə/ *n* in Verdi's opera, an Ethiopian princess enslaved in Egypt, who voluntarily dies with her entombed lover

aide /ād′/ [F = helper] *n* **1** aide-de-camp; **2** official assistant; **3** nurse's aide

aide-de-camp /ād′dəkamp′/ [F *aide de camp* camp assistant] *n* (**aides-de-**

camp) military officer who assists a superior

ai·grette /āgret′, ăg′-/ [F = tuft of feathers < OHG *heigir* heron] *n* plume or tuft, as of gems or esp. of feathers from egrets, worn on a headdress

ai·guil·lette /ā′gwĭlet′/ [F] *n mil* shoulder cord

ail /āl′/ [OE *eglan* to trouble] *vt* 1 to give or cause pain or discomfort to ‖ *vi* 2 to feel pain; be ill ‖ **ail′ing** *adj*

ai·lan·thus /ālan′thəs/ [Amboinese *ailanto* tree of heaven] *n* any of a genus (*Ailanthus*) of large, rapid-growing trees with long, compound leaves, imported from China, esp. *A. altissima*

ai·le·ron /āl′əron′/ [F, *dim.* of *aile* wing] *n* small hinged section of an airplane wing for controlling horizontal balance of the machine

ail′ment *n* disorder or disease of the body or mind; sickness ‖ SYN complaint, indisposition, illness (see *disease*)

aim /ām′/ [MF *aesmer* < L *aestimare* to estimate] *vi* 1 to endeavor; intend; 2 to point a weapon or the like, as at a mark ‖ *vt* 3 to point (a weapon) for the purpose of hitting; 4 to direct (a missile or remark) against someone or something ‖ *n* 5 purpose; endeavor; 6 target, goal; 7 pointing of a weapon; 8 direction in which a missile is pointed; 9 **take aim** to aim a weapon or missile ‖ SYN *n* goal, end, mark, target (see *design*)

aim′less *adj* without aim or purpose ‖ **aim′less·ly** *adv* ‖ **aim′less·ness** *n*

ain't /ānt′/ [prob contr. of *am not*] *substandard* 1 am not, is not, or are not; 2 have not or has not

Ai·nu /ī′nōō/ [Ainu = man] *n* (**Ainus** or **Ainu**) 1 one of an aboriginal Caucasoid people of the island of Hokkaido, Japan; 2 their language ‖ also *adj*

air /er′/ [OF < L *aēr* < Gk *aer*] *n* 1 that mixture of gases which comprises the atmosphere of the earth; 2 anything light and trifling; 3 light wind, breeze; 4 external manner, behavior; appearance; 5 publicity; 6 medium through which radio and television waves are popularly said to be transmitted, as *the program is on the air*; 7 empty space; 8 travel in aircraft, as *to go by air*; 9 ambience, as *a foreboding air*; 10 **airs** *pl* affected manners; 11 *mus* melody; 12 **get the air** *slang* to be rejected or dismissed; 13 **give the air** to *slang* to reject or dismiss; 14 **in the air** in circulation, as a rumor; 15 **into thin air** completely out of sight or touch; 16 **take the air, a** to go for an outing; **b** to leave hurriedly; 17 **walking on air** ecstatically happy; 18 **up in the air** unsettled ‖ *vt* 19 to expose to the air; dry; purify; ventilate; 20 to display, bring into public notice; 21 to broadcast or televise ‖ *vi* 22 to be exposed to the open air

air′ bag′ *n* large bag that is automatically inflated to keep automobile riders from hitting the windshield and other hard parts in case of a sudden stop

air′ base′ *n* station for military aircraft, their supplies and repair

air′borne′ *adj* 1 (aircraft) in flight; 2 carried or transported by air

air′ brake′ *n* 1 brake operated by compressed air; 2 device, as an aileron, for reducing the speed of an aircraft in flight

air′brush′ *n* atomizer for providing a fine spray, as of paint ‖ also *vt*

air′ com·mand′ *n* unit of the U.S. Air Force higher than an air force

air′-con·di′tion *vt* to provide (an interior) with desirable temperature and humidity by circulating treated air ‖ **air′-con·di′tioned** *adj* ‖ **air′ condi′tion·er** *n* ‖ **air′ con·di′tion·ing** *n*

air′-cooled′ *adj* 1 cooled by the circulation of air; 2 containing cooled air ‖ **air′-cool′** *vt*

air′craft′ *n* (-**craft**) any weight-carrying vehicle capable of navigating through the air

air′craft car′ri·er *n* warship designed to carry airplanes ready for flight and to serve as a navigable flying field

air′ cyl′in·der *n* cylinder in which compressed air is stored for various uses

air′ di·vi′sion *n* unit of the U.S. Air Force intermediate between a wing and an air force

air′drome′ *n* airport

air′drop′ *n* delivery of supplies or personnel by parachute from flying aircraft ‖ also *v* (-**dropped**; -**drop·ping**) *vt*

Aire·dale /er′dāl′/ [name of valley in Yorkshire] *n* terrier of a large rough-coated breed, tan and with dark-gray or grizzled back and sides

air′field′ *n* airport

air′flow′ *n* air motion caused by moving vehicles

air′foil′ *n* surface (as a wing or propeller) designed to lift and control aircraft in flight

air′ force′ *n* 1 that part of a nation's military organization devoted to air warfare; 2 unit of the U.S. Air Force intermediate between an air division and an air command; 3 **Air Force** the air force of the United States, established 1947

air′ gap′ *n* 1 air space between two magnetically related objects, as between the field and the armature of a dynamo; 2 space between the points of a spark plug

air′ gun′ *n* **1** gun from which the projectile is expelled by compressed air; **2** hand tool operated by compressed air

air′ hole′ *n* **1** local condition of the air which causes an airplane in flight to drop suddenly; **2** open spot in a sheet of ice, as on a lake; **3** hole for ventilation

air′ing *n* **1** walk or drive in the open air; **2** exposure to the air

air′ lane′ *n* route regularly traveled by aircraft; airway

air′lift′ *n* emergency airplane service transporting supplies and personnel ‖ also *vt*

air′ line′ *n* most direct route possible between two places on the earth's surface

air′line′ *n* **1** organized system of air transport operating on fixed routes and schedules, including its equipment and personnel; **2** tube or hose supplying air to a deep-sea diver or to a tool operated by compressed air

air′lin′er *n* passenger plane operated by an airline

air′ lock′ *n* **1** airtight antechamber in a caisson for regulating the air pressure; **2** *mach* malfunction caused by the presence of air impeding the flow of a liquid

air′ mail′ *n* **1** mail carried by aircraft; **2** system of so carrying it ‖ **air′-mail′** *adj, adv, & vt*

air′man /-mən/ *n* (**-men** /-mən/) **1** pilot; **2** enlisted man of one of the four lowest ranks of the U.S. Air Force, below that of staff sergeant

air′ mass′ *n* body of air covering a wide area exhibiting uniform conditions at any given level

Air′ Med′al *n* U.S. military decoration awarded for meritorious achievement while on aerial duty

air′ mile′ *n* mile used in air navigation equal to 6076.116 ft. or 1852 meters

air′ pi′ra·cy *n* hijacking of an airplane ‖ **air′ pi′rate** *n*

air′plane′ *n* [alter. of *aeroplane* < Gk *aeroplanos* wandering in the air] *n* heavier-than-air aircraft moving through the air by means of motor-driven propellers or jet engines, and kept aloft by the upward thrust of the air on its fixed wings

air′ pock′et *n* air hole *1*

air′port *n* tract of land or water equipped for the landing and take-off of aircraft and for receiving and discharging passengers and cargo, often with facilities for the repair and shelter of the planes that use it

air′ pow′er *n* military capability of a nation's air force

air′ pump′ *n* machine for exhausting, compressing, or transmitting air

air′ raid′ *n* military attack by aircraft ‖ **air′-raid′** *adj*

air′-raid shel′ter *n* shelter for protection against air raids

air′ re·sist′ance *n* resistance to forward motion in the air encountered by a solid body, as an airplane

air′ right′ *n* right-of-way of an aircraft to fly over the property of another; **2** right sold or leased to build above and over the property of another

air′ship′ *n* any mechanically propelled aircraft lighter than air

air′sick′ *adj* affected with nausea by the motion of an aircraft ‖ **air′sick′-ness** *n*

air′ sleeve′ also **air′ sock′** *n* windsock

air′ space′ or **air′space′** *n* portion of atmosphere lying above the earth over any given area

air′ speed′ *n* forward speed of an aircraft relative to the air

air′stream′ *n* airflow

air′strip′ *n* runway for the takeoff and landing of airplanes

air′tight′ *adj* **1** so closed that no air can enter; **2** impregnable

air′-to-air′ *adj & adv* from one aircraft in flight to another

air′ trap′ *n* trap *3*

air′ valve′ *n* device for removing the air from a pipe, tank, or radiator, as in a steam-heating system

air′waves′ *npl* so-called medium of radio and television transmission

air′way′ *n* **1** air route equipped with navigational aids; **2** ventilation passage in a mine; **3 airways** *pl* airline *1*

air′y *adj* (**-i·er; -i·est**) **1** exposed to the air; breezy; **2** unsubstantial; ethereal; **3** vivacious; **4** graceful, light in movement; **5** happening in the air; **6** lofty ‖ **air′i·ly** *adv* ‖ **air′i·ness** *n*

aisle /ī′(ə)l/ [MF *ele* < L *ala* wing, influenced by Eng *isle*] *n* **1** passageway between sections of seats in a church, auditorium, etc.; **2** in a cathedral, section on either side of the nave, separated from it by a row of pillars

a·jar¹ /əjär′/ [ME *on char* on the turn] *adj & adv* slightly opened, as a door

a·jar² [a⁻¹ + *jar* discord] *adj & adv* out of harmony, discordant(ly)

A·jax /ā′jaks/ [Gk *Aias*] *n* in Homer's *Iliad*, son of Telamon and, next to Achilles, the bravest of the Greeks

Ak·bar /ak′bär/ *n* (The Great) (1542–1605) Mogul emperor of India 1556–1605

a·kene /ākēn′/ *n* var of **achene**

a·kim·bo /əkim′bō/ [ME *in kene bowe* on a sharp bend] *adj & adv* with the hands on the hips and the elbows turned outward

a·kin /əkin′/ *adj* **1** of the same kin; **2** of similar nature

Ak·ka·di·an /əkād′ē·ən/ *n* **1** one of the Semitic people of Mesopotamia before 2000 B.C.; **2** their language ‖ also *adj*

Ak·kra /əkrä′, ak′rə/ *n* var of **Accra**

Ak·ron /ak′rən/ *n* city in NE Ohio (295,000)

al- *pref* var of **ad-**

-al¹ /-əl/ [OF < L -*alis*] *adj suf* of, like, pert. to, as *fatal, natural*

-al² [MF -*aille* < L -*alia*] *n suf* that which pertains to, as *recital, withdrawal*

-al³ /-al′, -ôl′, -əl/ [aldehyde] *n suf* *chem* containing an aldehyde group, as *butanal*

Al *chem* aluminum

al. 1 [L *alii*] other persons; 2 [L *alia*] other things

A.L. 1 American League; 2 American Legion

a la or **à la** /äl′ä, äl′ə, al′ə/ [F *à la* (*mode de*)] in the manner of, as *comedy a la Molière*

a·la /ā′lə/ (L (-lae /-lē/) *anat, bot, & zool* wing or winglike process or part

Ala. Alabama

Al·a·bam·a /al′əbam′ə/ *n* state in SE United States (3,444,000; 51,609 sq.m.; cap. Montgomery) ‖ **Al′a·bam′an** *n*

al·a·bas·ter /al′əbas′tər, -bäs′-/ [OF *alabastre* < L *alabaster* < Gk *alabastros*] *n* 1 white marblelike translucent mineral, a pure gypsum, found chiefly in Italy; 2 banded, translucent variety of calcite, used by the ancients for making perfume bottles and vases ‖ **al′a·bas′trine** /-trin/ *adj*

a la carte /äl′ əkärt′, al′-/ [F *à la carte* from the menu] *adj & adv* at a specified price for each item on the menu

a·lack /əlak′/ [ME] *interj* expressing blame, sorrow, or surprise

a·lac·ri·ty /əlak′ritē/ [L *alacritas* liveliness] *n* eager readiness; briskness

A·lad·din /əlad′ən/ *n* hero of a story in the *Arabian Nights' Entertainments*, the possessor of a magic lamp

al·a·me·da /al′əmēd′ə, -mād′-/ [Sp < *alamo*] *n* walk or promenade, esp. when shaded with alamos

al·a·mo /al′əmō′, äl′-/ [Sp = poplar] *n* 1 cottonwood or poplar tree; 2 **the Alamo** Franciscan mission in San Antonio, Texas, where a garrison was destroyed by Mexicans in 1836

a la mode /äl′ əmōd′, al′-/ [F *à la mode* in the fashion] *adj* 1 fashionable; 2 *cookery* a (dessert, as pie) topped with ice cream; b (beef) stewed with vegetables and served with brown gravy

al·a·nine /al′ənēn′/ [< *aldehyde*] *n* crystalline amino acid —CH₃CH-(NH₂)COOH— found in many proteins, and produced synthetically

a·lar /ā′lər/ [L *alaris* < *ala* wing] *adj* 1 pert. to or having wings; 2 winglike or wing-shaped

Al·a·ric /al′ərik/ *n* (ca. 370–410) king of the Visigoths, who captured Rome 410

a·larm /əlärm′/ [MF *alarme* < It *all'arme* to arms] *vt* 1 to arouse to a sense of danger; 2 to strike with fear of danger ‖ *n* 3 call to arms; 4 warning of danger; 5 fear of danger; 6 any device intended to give a signal or warning ‖ **a·larm′ing** *adj* ‖ **a·larm′ing·ly** *adv* ‖ SYN *v* startle, frighten, appall, terrify; *n* (see *horror*) ‖ ANT *v* cheer, encourage, reassure; *n* assurance, cheer, calmness, confidence, repose, security

a·larm′ clock *n* clock with a bell or buzzer which automatically rings at any time for which it is set

a·larm′ist *n* one who excites fear by exaggerating bad news or foretelling calamities ‖ also *adj* ‖ **a·larm′ism** *n*

a·las /əlas′, əläs′/ [OF *ha* ah + *las* wretched < L *lassus* weary] *interj* expressing unhappiness

Alas. Alaska

A·las·ka /əlas′kə/ *n* state of the U.S. in NW North America (302,000; 586,400 sq.m.; cap. Juneau) ‖ **A·las′kan** *adj & n*

alb /alb′/ [OE *albe* < L *albus* white] *n* close-sleeved white linen vestment worn by priests

Alb. 1 Albania(n); 2 Albany; 3 Alberta

al·ba·core /al′bəkôr′, -kōr′/ [Port *albacor* < Ar] *n* 1 long-finned tuna (*Thunnus germo*), the flesh of which is much used for canning; 2 any of various other tunas or tunalike fishes

Al·ba·ni·a /albān′ēə, -yə, ôl-/ *n* republic in SE Europe in the Balkans on the Adriatic (1,965,000; 11,100 sq.m.; cap. Tirana) ‖ **Al·ba′ni·an** *adj & n*

Al·ba·ny /ôl′bənē/ *n* capital of New York on the Hudson (130,000)

al·ba·tross /al′bətrôs′, -tros′/ [prob < Sp or Port *alcatraz* pelican] *n* any of several large web-footed seabirds (family Diomedeidae) of southern seas and the Pacific, having wings specially adapted for tireless flight

al·be·it /ôlbē′it/ [ME *al be it* although it be (that)] *conj.* even though; notwithstanding

Al·bert /al′bərt/ *n* Prince (1819–61) consort of Queen Victoria 1840–61

Al·bert·a /alburt′ə/ *n* province in W Canada (1,500,000; 255,285 sq.m.; cap. Edmonton)

Al·bi·gen·ses /al′bijen′sēz/ [LL < *Albi* town in southern France] *npl* members of a heretical sect in southern France in the 12th and 13th centuries, the extermination of which destroyed Provençal civilization ‖ **Al·bi·gen′si·an** /-sē·ən, -shən/ *adj*

al·bi·no /albī′nō/ [Port < L *albus* white] *n* 1 person who, on account of a congenital lack of skin pigment, has white skin and hair and pink eyes; **2** animal lacking pigment in the skin, hair, and iris ‖ **al′bin·ism** /-bĭn-/ *n*

Al·bi·on /al′bē·ən/ [< L *albus* white, in allusion to the white cliffs of Dover] *n poet.* England

al·bum /al′bəm/ [L = white tablet] *n* **1** blank book in which to insert photographs, autographs, stamps, or the like; **2 a** set of phonograph records with related selections, as of one composer, orchestra, or artist, or carrying a complete major work; **b** container for such a set of records

al·bu·men /albyōōm′ən/ [< L *albumen* (ovi) egg white] *n* **1** white of an egg; **2** nourishing substance about the embryo in a seed; **3** albumin

al·bu·min /albyōōm′ĭn/ *n* any class of water-soluble proteins occurring in blood, muscle, milk, eggs, and many animal and vegetable solids and fluids

al·bu′mi·nous *adj* pert. to or resembling albumin or albumen

Al·bu·quer·que /al′bəkurk′ē/ *n* city in central New Mexico (205,000)

al·ca·zar /alkaz′ər, al′kəzär′/ [Sp *alcázar* < Ar] *n* **1** Spanish fortress or palace; **2 Alcazar** royal palace of the Moors in Seville

al·che·my /al′kəmē/ [MF *alquimie* < LL *alchimia* < Ar *al-kīmiyā* < Gk *chemeia*] *n* **1** the chemistry of the Middle Ages, popularly associated with magic, and esp. devoted to the search for the elixir of life, the alkahest or universal solvent, and the means of transmuting baser metals into gold; **2** any mysterious change of substance or nature ‖ **al·chem′ic** (-i·cal) /-kem′-/ *adj* ‖ **al′che·mist** *n*

Al·ci·bi·a·des /al′sĭbī′ədēz′/ *n* (450?-404 B.C.) Athenian politician and general

al·co·hol /al′kəhôl′, -hol′/ [LL = powdered antimony < Ar *al-kuhul*] *n* **1** colorless volatile flammable watermiscible liquid —C₂H₅OH— a powerful solvent and antiseptic, the intoxicating element in all fermented and distilled liquors; **2** any liquid containing alcohol; **3** any of many substances having the hydroxyl group OH united with an organic radical, as *ethyl alcohol* and *methyl alcohol*

al′co·hol′ic /-hôl′ĭk, -hol′-/ *adj* **1** of, pert. to, caused by, or like alcohol; **2** containing alcohol; **3** addicted to alcoholic beverages ‖ *n* **4** one addicted to alcoholic beverages; **5** one suffering from alcoholism

al·co·hol·ism /al′kəhôliz′em, -hol-/ *n* diseased condition resulting from the excessive use of alcoholic beverages

al·cove /al′kōv/ [F *alcôve* < Sp *alcoba* < Ar] *n* **1** recess in a room, as

for a dining area, a bed, or bookcases; **2** retired spot, as in a garden

al·de·hyde /al′dəhīd′/ [< NL *alcohol dehydrogenatum* dehydrogenated alcohol] *n* any of a series of substances, generally liquid, containing the characteristic group -CHO, formed by the oxidation of an alcohol and having a sharp, suffocating odor

al·der /ôl′dər/ [OE *al(e)r*] *n* any of a genus (*Alnus*) of trees and shrubs, usu. growing in moist lands

al·der·man /ôl′dərmən/ [OE *ealdormann* < *ealdor* elder] *n* (-**men** /-mən/) **1** member of a municipal governing body; councilman; **2** *England* magistrate next in rank to the mayor; **3** *Eng hist* chief magistrate of a county or larger district

Al·der·ney /ôl′dərnē/ *n* **1** one of the Channel Islands; **2** one of a breed of small dairy cattle originating on Alderney

ale /āl′/ [OE *ealu*] *n* beverage similar to beer but more bitter and with a higher alcoholic content, made from malt, usu. with the addition of hops

a·lee /əlē′/ *adj & adv naut* on, to, or toward the lee

A·le·man·ni /al′əman′ī/ [L < Gmc] *npl* group of Germanic tribes that settled in S Germany and harassed the Roman Empire

A′le·man′nic *n* group of High German dialects spoken in Switzerland and SW Germany ‖ also *adj*

a·leph /äl′ef, äl′ĭf/ [Heb = ox] *n* first letter א of the Hebrew alphabet

A·lep·po /əlep′ō/ *n* city in NW Syria (450,000)

a·lert /əlurt′/ [It *all′erta* to the watchtower] *adj* **1** on the watch, vigilant; **2** active; ready ‖ *n* **3** warning call or signal of danger, as of a storm or an air raid; **4** period during which an alert is in effect; **5 on the alert** on guard against danger ‖ *vt* **6** to put on guard ‖ **a·lert′ly** *adv* ‖ **a·lert′ness** *n* ‖ SYN *adj* attentive, observant, prompt, wide-awake (see *active*) ‖ ANT *adj* drowsy, dull, inactive, slow

A·leut /əlōōt′, al′ē·ōōt′/ [Russ] *also* **A·leu·tian** /əlōōsh′ən/ *n* **1** member of either of two tribes related to the Eskimos, native in the Aleutian Islands; **2** their language ‖ also *adj*

A·leu′tian Is′lands or the **Aleutians** *npl* Alaskan islands extending in a great arc SW and W from the Alaska Peninsula

al·ex·an·der or **A·lex·an·der** /al′igzan′-dər, -zän′-/ *n* cocktail made from creme de cacao, cream, and brandy or gin

Al′ex·an′der the Great′ *n* (356-323 B.C.) king of Macedonia and one of the great conquerers of history, whose conquests extended from Greece and Egypt to Persia and India

Al′ex·an′dri·a /-drē·ə/ *n* seaport on

the Mediterranean in N Egypt (1,500,-000); ancient seat of Greek learning, founded by Alexander the Great 332 B.C. ‖ **Al′ex·an′dri·an** *adj & n*

al′ex·an′drine or **Al′ex·an′drine** /-drin/ [MF *alexandrin*, from 13th-cent. F poem on Alexander the Great, which first used the meter] *n* verse of six iambic feet with a pause after the third ‖ also *adj*

al·fal·fa /alfal′fə/ [Sp < Ar] *n* deep-rooted plant (*Medicago sativa*) of the pea family having cloverlike leaves and purple flowers; in the U.S. the staple hay and forage plant

Al′fred the Great′ /al′frəd/ *n* (849–899) king of the West Saxons 871–899; defeated the Danes

al·fres·co /alfres′kō/ [It *al fresco* in the cool (air)] *adj & adv* in the open air

alg- or **algo-** [Gk *algos*] *comb form* pain, as *algolagnia*

alg. algebra

Alg. 1 Algerian; 2 Algiers

al·ga /al′gə/ [L = seaweed] *n* (-gae /-jē/) any of a group of marine and fresh-water simple plants (phylum Thallophyta) ranging from one-celled organisms to very long plants, as seaweed and pond scums

al·ge·bra /al′jəbrə/ [ML < Ar *al-jebr* the reunion] *n* 1 branch of mathematics which treats of the properties and relations of quantities and which extends the field of arithmetic by using letters and other symbols to represent numbers and other values; 2 mathematical ring whose elements can be multiplied by real or complex numbers or by other elements of the ring; 3 logical or set calculus ‖ **al′ge·bra′ic** /-brā′ik/ *adj*

Al·ge·ri·a /aljir′ē·ə/ *n* Arabic-speaking republic in NW Africa (12,101,994; 919,597 sq.m.; cap. Algiers) ‖ **Al·ge′ri·an** *adj & n*

-al·gia /-al′j(ē)ə/ [Gk] *comb form* pain, as *neuralgia*

Al·giers /aljirz′/ *n* 1 seaport and capital of Algeria (943,142); 2 one of the former Barbary States, now Algeria

Al·gon·ki·an /algon′kē·ən/ [CanF *Algonquin*] *n* 1 Algonquian; 2 Proterozoic ‖ also *adj*

Al·gon′kin /-kin/ or **Al·gon′quin** /-kwin/ *n* (-kins or -kin; -quins or -quin) 1 member of a group of Indian tribes formerly of the Ottawa River valley in SE Canada; 2 their language; 3 Algonquian ‖ also *adj*

Al·gon′qui·an /-kwē·ən/ *n* 1 widespread American-Indian language family spoken from Labrador westward to the Rockies and southward to Illinois and North Carolina; 2 member of an Algonquian-speaking tribe ‖ also *adj*

Al·ham·bra /alham′brə/ [Sp < Ar *al-hamra′* the red house] *n* Moorish

royal palace in Granada, Spain, built in the 13th and 14th centuries

a·li·as /āl′ē·əs/ [L = at another time] *n* 1 assumed name ‖ *adv* 2 otherwise called, as *William Brown alias John Doe*

A·li Ba·ba /āl′ē bä′bə, al′ē bab′ə/ *n* youth in one of the stories of the *Arabian Nights′ Entertainments* who enters the cave of the Forty Thieves by uttering the words "Open sesame"

al·i·bi /al′ibī′/ [L = elsewhere] *n law* 1 plea of having been elsewhere at the time an offense was committed; 2 *colloq* excuse ‖ *vt* 3 *colloq* to offer an excuse ‖ *vt* 4 *colloq* to provide an alibi for

al·ien /āl′ē·ən, āl′yən/ [OF < L *alienus* belonging to another] *adj* 1 foreign; 2 strange; 3 living in a country not one's own without rights of citizenship; 4 belonging or pert. to non-citizens; 5 different; hostile ‖ *n* 6 foreigner; 7 person living in a country other than his own without rights of citizenship; 8 stranger; one estranged

al′ien·a·ble *adj law* transferable, as property, by sale or gift

al′ien·ate *vt* 1 to estrange or turn away, as the affections; 2 *law* to transfer to another, as property

al′ien·a′tion *n* 1 estrangement, as of feeling or the affections; 2 insanity; 3 *law* transfer of title to a property ‖ **syn** estrangement, derangement (see *insanity*)

a·light¹ /əlīt′/ [pp of obs *alight* to kindle] *adj* 1 lighted; kindled ‖ *adv* 2 in a flame

a·light² [OE *ālīhtan*] *vi* 1 to dismount; 2 to descend and settle

a·lign also **a·line** /əlīn′/ [F *aligner* < *ad-* + L *linea* line] *vt* 1 to place in a straight line; 2 to adjust to a line; 3 to array (oneself) with a party or cause ‖ *vi* 4 to fall into line; 5 to be in or come into correct adjustment ‖ **a·lign′ment** also **a·line′ment** *n*

a·like /əlīk′/ [< OE *gelīc* like and *anlīc* similar] *adj* 1 resembling each other, similar ‖ *adv* 2 in the same way ‖ **syn** similar, identical, synonymous ‖ **discr** *Alike* implies an actual sameness in definite respects between persons or things, as mother and daughter were *alike* in their fear of snakes. *Similar* is used to indicate merely a general likeness, and refers to circumstances, conditions, etc. *Identical* means the very same, as the signatures on the will and the letter were *identical*. *Synonymous* refers to words, and indicates a likeness of use in certain senses only, such as allows one word to be used for another within those senses ‖ **ant** dissimilar, different, unlike

al·i·ment /al′imənt/ [L *alimentum*] *n* food, nutriment

al·i·men·ta·ry /al'iment'ərē/ *adj* 1 pert. to food or nutrition; 2 nourishing

al'i·men'ta·ry ca·nal' *n* tract through which food is conveyed and in passage through which it is assimilated, extending from the mouth to the anus

al·i·mo·ny /al'imōn'ē/ [*L alimonia* nutriment] *n* 1 means of living; 2 *law* allowance made by court decree to a wife out of her husband's estate or income for her maintenance after separation or divorce, or pending an action for separation or divorce

a·live /əlīv'/ [OE *on līfe* in life] *adj* 1 having life; 2 in a state of action, sprightly; attentive; sensitive; 3 full of activity or living things; 4 alive to aware of; 5 alive with teeming with ‖ **SYN** live, living, animate, lively, active, brisk, quick

alk. alkali

al·ka·li /al'kəlī'/ [Ar *al-qalīy* the ashes of saltwort] *n* (-lis, -lies) 1 any of the hydroxides of the alkali metals and of ammonium that neutralize acids and turn litmus paper blue; 2 soluble mineral salt or salts found in the soils, esp. of arid regions, and detrimental to agriculture

al'ka·li met'al *n* any of the univalent metals whose hydroxides are alkalis: lithium, sodium, potassium, rubidium, cesium, and francium

al'ka·line' /-lin', -līn/ *adj* relating to, containing, or having the properties of an alkali ‖ **al'ka·lin'i·ty** /-lin'-/ *n*

al'ka·line' bat'ter·y *n* dry battery in which the positive pole is manganese dioxide, the negative pole zinc, and the electrolyte 30 to 40 per cent potassium hydroxide, and whose voltage is 1.5

al'ka·line' earth' *n* oxide of calcium, strontium, barium, and sometimes magnesium

al'ka·lin·ize' or **al'ka·lize'** *vt* to make alkaline

al'ka·loid *n* any of a class of basic nitrogenous organic compounds to which is due the active medicinal or toxic character of plants in which they occur, as morphine, nicotine, and quinine ‖ also *adj*

al·kyd /al'kid/ [*alkyl* + acid] or **al'kyd res'in** *n* any of a group of thermoplastic adhesive resins made synthetically from dicarboxylic acids and used chiefly in paints and adhesives

all /ôl'/ [OE (e)all] *adj* 1 the whole quantity, substance, duration, extent, amount, or degree of; 2 collectively, the whole amount or number of, as of individuals or particulars, or the whole number of parts of; 3 as much as possible, as *with all speed;* 4 every one of the, as *all kinds;* 5 any; every, as *beyond all doubt;* 6 nothing but, only, as *all*

work and no play; 7 having or using in excess, as *all legs, all ears;* 8 all the as much of (something) as, as *that's all the family he ever had;* 9 for all that in spite of everything ‖ *pron* 10 everybody; 11 everything; 12 every one (of a group of persons or things); 13 every part ‖ *n* 14 whole, entirety; 15 one's entire possessions; 16 above all beyond anything else; 17 after all nevertheless; 18 all in all everything considered; 19 at all, a in any way; b for any reason; 20 in all altogether; 21 once and for all finally ‖ *adv* 22 wholly, entirely, completely (often in composition with a hyphen), as *all-important, all-powerful;* 23 all but nearly, almost; 24 all in *colloq* exhausted; 25 all out with full effort; 26 all over everywhere; 27 all the better so much the better; 28 all the more so all the more reason for; 29 not all there *colloq* not in full possession of one's mental faculties, as *he's not all there;* 30 all told altogether; in all

all- *comb form* var of **allo-**

Al·lah /al'ə, äl'ə, älä'/ [Ar] *n* Islamic name for the Supreme Being

all'-A·mer'i·can *adj* 1 representing the entire United States; 2 *sports* selected as best in the United States; 3 composed exclusively of American elements ‖ also *n*

all'-a·round' *adj* 1 versatile; 2 having general usefulness

al·lay /əlā'/ [OE *ālecgan* to lay down] *vt* 1 to quiet or calm, assuage; 2 to abate or lessen; mitigate ‖ **SYN** alleviate, lighten, moderate, mollify, reduce, relieve, soothe, still, subdue (see *mitigate*) ‖ **ANT** agitate, arouse, excite, kindle, provoke, quicken

all' clear' *n* signal that danger (as of an air raid) has passed

al·le·ga·tion /al'əgāsh'ən/ [*L allegatio* (-*onis*) < *allegare* to allege] *n* 1 act of alleging; 2 that which is asserted or offered as a plea, excuse, or justification; 3 assertion made without proof; 4 *law* statement, by a party to a suit, of that which he is prepared to prove

al·lege /əlej'/ [AF *alegier* < L *allegare*] *vt* 1 to produce as argument, plea, or excuse; 2 to affirm, declare; 3 to assert without proof ‖ **SYN** advance, adduce, affirm, assert, aver, declare ‖ **ANT** contradict, deny, oppose

al·leged' *adj* 1 declared, asserted; 2 supposed; doubtful ‖ **al·leg'ed·ly** /-idlē/ *adv*

Al'le·ghe'ny Moun'tains /al'əgān'ē/ or **the Alleghenies** *npl* mountain range extending from Pennsylvania to Virginia and West Virginia, part of the Appalachians

al·le·giance /əlēj'əns/ [MF *ligeance*

< *lige* liege] *n* **1** tie or obligation of a person to his sovereign or government; **2** fidelity to a cause or person ‖ SYN faithfulness, homage, obedience, subjection ‖ ANT disaffection, disloyalty, rebellion, unfaithfulness

al·le·go·ry /al'igô'rē̆, -gôr'-/ [Gk *allegoria*] *n* (-ries) **1** representation in a story of abstract ideas by means of concrete images; **2** narrative in which a teaching is conveyed symbolically, as in *Pilgrim's Progress;* **3** emblem *1* ‖ **al'le·gor'i·cal** *adj* ‖ SYN parable, fable ‖ DISCR The *allegory* and the *parable* both present a truth under the guise of fictitious narrative or description. In other respects they are unlike. The *allegory* is not confined exclusively to religious subjects; it is developed to some length, and is adorned by such grace and beauty of style as is suitable. The *parable* is confined to religious and moral subjects; it is short and direct; and the emphasis lies on the lesson taught, rather than upon the manner of presentation. The *fable* is always short. It resembles *allegory* and *parable* in teaching a moral lesson, and in its use of concrete images for abstract ideas; but it differs in that its story is usually unreal, as of talking animals or plants, while the *parable* and the *allegory* portray persons

al·le·gret·to /äl'əgret'ō/ [It, dim. of *allegro*] *adj & adv mus* **1** somewhat fast or lively, between andante and allegro ‖ *n* **2** allegretto movement

al·le·gro /əleg'rō, əlāg'-/ [It= brisk, lively] *adj & adv mus* **1** fast, lively ‖ *n* **2** allegro movement

al·lele /əlēl'/ [< *allelomorph*] *n* genetics gene responsible for hereditary variation ‖ **al·lel'ic** *adj* ‖ **al·lel'ism** *n*

al·le·lu·ia /al'əlōō'yə/ [Gk *allelouia*] *interj & n* var of **hallelujah**

Al'len screw' /al'ən/ *n* setscrew tightened by means of an Allen wrench, which fits in a hexagonal depression in its head

Al'len·town' *n* city in E Pennsylvania (110,000)

Al'len wrench' *n* wrench for Allen screws, made from a hexagonal bar bent at a right angle

al·ler·gen /al'ərjən/ *n* substance which induces an allergy ‖ **al'ler·gen'ic** /-jen'-/ *adj*

al·ler·gic /əlur'jik/ *adj* **1** pert. to, inducing, or having an allergy; **2** excessively sensitive

al·ler·gist /al'ərjist/ *n* specialist in allergies

al·ler·gy /al'ərjē̆/ [*all-* + Gk *ergon* work, action] *n* (-gies) **1** hypersensitivity to certain things, as pollen, animals, heat, cold, certain foods, or antigens, characterized by skin rashes, sneezing, difficult breathing, and other reactions; **2** *colloq* antipathy

al·le·vi·ate /əlēv'ē̆·āt'/ [L *alleviare* (-*atus*)] *vt* to lighten, lessen, make easier, mitigate ‖ **al·le'vi·a'tion** *n* ‖ SYN allay, soften, assuage (see *mitigate*)

al·ley /al'ē̆/ [MF *alee* passage < *aller* to go] *n* **1** narrow passage, as from one part of a building to another; **2** narrow street in a city; **3** bowling alley; **4** lateral strip on a tennis court between singles sideline and doubles sideline; **5 up one's alley** *slang* to one's liking or abilities

al'ley·way' *n* narrow passageway, as between houses

all'-fired' *slang adj* **1** extreme ‖ *adv* **2** extremely

All' Fools'' Day' *n* April Fools' Day

all' fours' *npl* **1** all four limbs of man or animal; **2 on all fours, a** on an equal footing, consistent; **b** on one's hands and knees

All'hal'lows *nsg* All Saints' Day

al·li·ance /əlī'əns/ [see **ally**] *n* **1** act of allying or state of being allied; **2** union between nations or parties; **3** document or treaty embodying such a union; **4** nations or parties included in the union ‖ SYN confederacy, league, coalition, compact

al·lied /əlīd'/ [*pp* of *ally*] *adj* **1** joined by treaty; **2** related; **3 Allied** of or pert. to the Allies

Al·lies /al'īz, əlīz'/ [*pl* of *ally*] *npl* **1** *World War 1* nations allied against Germany and the Central Powers; **2** *World War II* nations allied against Germany and the Axis powers

al·li·ga·tor /al'əgāt'ər/ [Sp *el lagarto* the lizard] *n* **1** any of a genus (*Alligator*) of reptiles of SE United States and China, of the crocodile family, having a short blunt snout and frequenting marshes and river banks; **2** any crocodile; **3** alligator leather; **4** machine with powerful jaws for seizing and lifting

al'li·ga'tor pear' *n* avocado

al'li·ga'tor wrench' *n* wrench with toothed jaws for turning or holding pipes and other cylindrical and irregularly shaped pieces of metal

al·lit·er·a·tion /əlit'ərāsh'ən/ [< *ad-* + L *litera* letter] *n* repetition of the initial sound of a word in one or more closely following words, as in *over stock and stone* ‖ **al·lit'er·a'·tive** /-ā'·tiv, -ətiv/ *adj*

allo- [Gk *allos* other] *comb form* **1** other, different, as *allopatric;* **2** *ling* denoting a variant form or sound whose change of shape is usu. automatic, predictable, and in complementary distribution with the other variant or variants, as *allophone*

al·lo·cate /al'əkāt'/ [LL *allocare* (-*atus*) to allot] *vt* to assign or allot, apportion ‖ **al'lo·ca'tion** *n*

al'lo·morph' *n* **1** any of two or more

different forms of the same chemical compound; **2** *ling* one of two or more variant forms of a morpheme whose shape is usu. determined phonologically, as the three allomorphs of the regular plural in English are /s/ in *backs*, /z/ in *bags*, and /iz/ in *badges* ‖ **al'lo·mor'phic** *adj*

al'lo·path' *n* one who favors or practices allopathy

al·lop·a·thy /əlop'əthē/ *n* **1** method of treating disease by administering remedies to induce conditions or symptoms different from those accompanying the disease ‖ **al·lo·path·ic** /al'əpath'ik/ *adj* ‖ **al'lo·path'i·cal·ly** *adv*

al'lo·phone' *n* variant of a phoneme the phonetic realization of which depends on its environment and which is usu. in complementary distribution with the other variant or variants ‖ **al'lo·phon'ic** /-fon'ik/ *adj*

al·lot /əlot'/ [MF *aloter*] *v* (**-lot·ted;** **-lot·ting**) *vt* **1** to distribute or divide, as by lot; **2** to apportion, as shares; **3** to assign for a specific purpose ‖ **SYN** assign, apportion, destine, give, award

al·lot'ment *n* **1** act of allotting; distribution, as by lot; **2** that which is allotted; **3** money paid to a soldier's family for its support during his absence on active service

al·lo·trope /al'ətrōp/ [*allo-* + Gk *tropos* form] *n* one of the two or more different forms of an element, as diamond, lampblack, and graphite are allotropes of carbon ‖ **al'lo·trop'ic** /-trop'ik/ *adj* ‖ **al·lot'ro·py** /əlot'rəpē/ *n*

all'-out' *adj* & *adv* made with total effort

all'ov'er *adj* covering the entire surface

al·low /əlou'/ [MF *alouer* to place and MF *allouer* to approve] *vt* **1** to permit (a person) to do something, or (a thing) to happen; **2** to admit or accept as reasonable; acknowledge; grant, concede; **3** to take into account; to add or subtract in consideration of something; **4** to grant, allot, or yield; let one have, as a just share ‖ *vi* **5** to concede, admit; **6** **allow for** to make concession or provision for ‖ **SYN** allow, permit, suffer, tolerate ‖ **DISCR** *Allow*, *permit*, and *suffer* are alike in expressing the idea of consenting to or letting. *Permit* is more positive than the others; we *permit* when we state definitely that a certain thing may be done. We often *allow* passively, by merely not objecting; *permit* and *allow*, however, are sometimes used interchangeably. *Suffer* is like *allow*, but is less often used. *Tolerate* implies letting that go which we condemn, but cannot help, as people *tolerate* certain evils; it means in a narrower sense to endure something distasteful, as I can hardly *tolerate* his smugness

al·low'a·ble *adj* permissible; lawful; acceptable ‖ **al·low'a·bly** *adv*

al·low'ance /-əns/ *n* **1** act of allowing; **2** admission; concession; **3** definite sum or quantity granted; sum of money given, as for pocket money or specified expenses, as *allowance for depreciation*; **4** *mach* permissible difference in the dimensions of mating parts; **5** **make allowance(s) for** to excuse because of mitigating factors ‖ *vt* **6** to limit (provisions) to a fixed amount

al·loy /al'oi, əloi'/ [MF *aloier* < L *alligare* to combine] *n* **1** homogeneous substance made by fusing two or more metals or a nonmetal with a metal or metals; **2** baser metal used in mixture with a finer one; **3** admixture of evil with good; **4** something added which debases ‖ /əloi'/ *vt* **5** to melt together or otherwise mix (metals or metal with nonmetal) so as to form an alloy; **6** to reduce in quality by mixing; debase

al'loy steel' *n* steel containing certain other metals, as nickel, chromium, manganese, etc., to increase its strength or to give it certain special properties

all' right' *adj* **1** safe, well; **2** acceptable, satisfactory; **3** *colloq* good, honest, personable ‖ *adv* **4** very well, okay; **5** in an acceptable or satisfactory manner; **6** certainly

All' Saints' Day' *n* November 1, celebrated in honor of all the saints

All' Souls' Day' *n R C Ch* November 2, a day of commemoration, on which intercession is offered for all souls in purgatory

all'spice' *n* **1** West Indian tree (*Pimenta officinalis*) of the myrtle family; **2** its berry; **3** spice prepared from the berry, combining the flavors of cinnamon, nutmeg, and cloves

all'-star' *adj* **1** composed of star performers ‖ *n* **2** player on an all-star team

al·lude /əlōōd'/ [L *alludere* to play with] *vi* to refer indirectly

al·lure /əlŏŏr'/ [MF *alurer*] *vt* **1** to tempt by offering something really or apparently good; entice ‖ *n* **2** charm, attraction ‖ **al·lure'ment** *n* ‖ **SYN** *v* cajole, coax, decoy, draw, ensnare, entrap, inveigle, lure, seduce, entice, attract

al·lur'ing *adj* tempting; fascinating; charming ‖ **al·lur'ing·ly** *adv*

al·lu·sion /əlōōzh'ən/ [see **allude**] *n* casual, indirect reference; slight suggestion or mention of something ‖ **al·lu'sive** /-siv/ *adj*

al·lu·vi·al /əlōōv'ē·əl/ [< L *alluere* to wash] *adj* **1** of or pert. to alluvium ‖ *n* **2** alluvial soil

al·lu'vi·um /-əm/ *n* (-ums; -a /-ə/) 1 deposit of sand, clay, or the like, made by running water; 2 land so formed

al·ly /əlī'/ [OF *alier* < L *alligare* to bind] *v* (-lied) *vt* 1 to unite by marriage, treaty, league, or confederacy; 2 to bind or associate, as by ties of friendship || *vi* 3 to enter into an alliance || /al'ī, əlī'/ *n* (-lies) person, nation, or the like united or associated by such means || SYN *n* partner, colleague, associate, confederate, accomplice || DISCR *Partner* is used of an associate in business, in dancing, or on the same side in a game. *Colleague* is applied to one of a body of professional, ecclesiastical, or academic persons; it is not ordinarily applied to *partners* in a business. *Associates* work together in a business, profession, office, or the like. *Ally* is used of an associated party or state; it is especially applied to *associates* in war. *Confederate* and *accomplice* name those joined for a guilty purpose; but a *confederate* merely contributes to the commission of crime, whereas an *accomplice* may be any one of the group involved, from the leader down

al·ma·gest /al'məjest'/ [Ar *al-majisti* < Gk *megiste* greatest] *n* 1 famous second-century work on astronomy written by Ptolemy of Alexandria and first made known to medieval Europe through Arabic translations; 2 any of various medieval works on astrology, alchemy, etc.

al·ma ma·ter /al'mə mät'ər, mät'ər/ [L = fostering mother] *n* college or other school in which one has been educated

al·ma·nac /ôl'mənak'/ [ML *almanach* perh < Ar *al-manākh* the calendar] *n* 1 yearbook or calendar giving the days of the week and months, facts about the heavens, tide tables, etc.; 2 yearbook containing useful general information usu. in statistical or tabular form

al·might·y /ôlmīt'ē/ [OE *ealmihtig*] *adj* 1 possessing all power, of unlimited might; 2 *colloq* extreme || *n* 3 **the Almighty** God

al·mond /äm'ənd, am'-, al'mənd/ [OF *almande* < L *amygdala* < Gk] *n* 1 small tree (*Prunus amygdalus*) of the rose family similar to the peach; 2 nutlike kernel of its fruit

al·mon·er /al'mənər, äm'-/ [ME *aumoner* < LL *eleemosynarius* giver of alms] *n* 1 one who dispenses alms; 2 *Brit* social worker in a hospital

al·most /ôl'mōst, ôlmōst'/ [OE *ealmæst*] *adv* nearly, very nearly, all but

alms /ämz'/ [OE *ælmesse* < Gk *eleemosyne* pity] *nsg* or *npl* free gift to relieve the poor

alms'house' *n* (-hous·es /-ziz/) 1 *archaic* poorhouse; 2 *Brit* privately endowed home for the poor

al·ni·co /al'niko'/ [*aluminum* + *nickel* + *cobalt*] *n* strong permanent-magnet alloy containing principally aluminum, nickel, and cobalt

al·oe /al'ō/ [Gk *aloe*] *n* 1 any of a genus (*Aloe*) of plants of the lily family with thick spiny leaves clustered at the base, native in Old World warm climates; 2 century plant

al·oes *nsg* 1 bitter cathartic drug made from the juice of the leaves of some species of aloe; 2 fragrant resin or wood of an East Indian tree (*Aquilaria agallocha*)

a·loft /əlôft', -loft'/ [ON *ā lopt* to the sky] *adv* 1 on high; 2 in the air; 3 *naut* at the masthead or on the higher yards or rigging

a·lo·ha /əlō'ə, älō'hä/ [Hawaiian = love] *interj* 1 greetings!; 2 farewell! || also *n*

a·lone /əlōn'/ [ME *al one* all one] *adj* 1 without or apart from another; solitary; 2 only; 3 unique; 4 **let alone** not to mention || *adv* 5 solely; without or apart from others || SYN *adj* lonesome, companionless, unaccompanied, unattended, deserted, desolate, unique (see *lonely*)

a·long /əlôŋ', -loŋ'/ [OE *andlang*] *prep* 1 by the length of; lengthwise of; 2 in the course of; 3 in conformity with || *adv* 4 in a line parallel with the length; 5 onward, as *move along*; 6 with one, as *take along a book*; 7 from one to another, as *pass the order along*; 8 **all along** all the time; 9 **along with** together with

along'side' *adv* 1 by the side; side by side; 2 **alongside of** beside; compared with || *prep* 3 by the side of

a·loof /əloof'/ [*a*-¹ + perh D *loef* windward side] *adj* & *adv* at a distance; purposely apart or aside || **a·loof'ness** *n*

a·loud /əloud'/ *adv* 1 with raised voice, loudly; 2 audibly

alp /alp'/ [back formation < *Alps*] *n* lofty mountain

al·pac·a /alpak'ə/ [Sp < Aymara] *n* 1 animal of Peru (genus *Lama*) having long soft silky wool; 2 hair of the alpaca or cloth made from it

al'pen·glow' /al'pən-/ *n* reddish glow on snow-capped mountains at sunrise and sunset

al'pen·horn' *n* long wooden horn used by Alpine mountaineers

al'pen·stock' *n* strong staff, tipped with a spike, used by mountain climbers

al'pha /al'fə/ *n* 1 first letter of the Greek alphabet A, α; 2 beginning of anything; 3 **Alpha** brightest star in a constellation

al'pha and o·me'ga [the first and last

letters of the Gk alphabet] *n* the beginning and end (Rev. 1:8)

al'pha·bet' /-bet'/ [Gk *alphabetos* < *alpha* + *beta*] *n* **1** letters of a language in a conventional order; **2** system of characters or signs representing letters or sounds; **3** first rudiments ‖ **al'pha·bet'ic (-i·cal)** *adj* ‖ **al'pha·bet'i·cal·ly** *adv*

al'pha·bet·ize' /-bītīz'/ *vt* **1** to arrange in alphabetical order; **2** to supply with an alphabet ‖ **al'pha·bet'i·za'tion** *n*

Al'pha Cen·tau'ri /-rī/ *n* star in Centaurus, the closest star to the sun

al'pha·mer'ic (-i·cal) /-mer'ik(əl)/ *or* **al'pha·nu·mer'ic (-i·cal)** /-n(y)ŏŏ·mer'ik(əl)/ *adj* consisting of both letters and numbers, and also mathematical symbols, punctuation marks, and the like

al'pha par'ti·cle *n* positively charged nuclear particle consisting of two protons and two neutrons, emitted by radioactive substances or nuclear fission and identical to the nucleus of a helium atom

al'pha ray' *n* stream of alpha particles

al·pine /al'pīn/ [see **Alps**] *adj* **1** of, pert. to, or found on high mountains; **2** high, lofty; **3 Alpine, a** of or pert. to the Alps: **b** designating a hairy brachycephalic Caucasoid racial type of medium stature ‖ *n* **4** person of Alpine racial type

Alps /alps'/ [L *Alpes*] *npl* mountain range in S Europe extending from SW France through Switzerland, N Italy, Austria, and NW Yugoslavia

al·read·y /ôlred'ē/ [ME *al redy* all ready] *adv* **1** by or before a particular time, beforehand; **2** so soon

Al·sace /alsās', al'sas/ *n* region and former province of NE France on the Rhine

Al·sa·tian /alsāsh'ən/ *n* **1** native of Alsace; **2** German shepherd dog ‖ also *adj*

al·so /ôl'sō/ [OE *eallswā* all so] *adv* **1** likewise; **2** in addition; too; besides

al'so-ran' *n colloq* defeated contestant

alt. 1 alternate; **2** altitude; **3** alto

Alta. Alberta

Al·ta·ic /altā'ik/ *n* language family comprising the Turkic, Tungusic, and Mongolian subfamilies ‖ also *adj*

Al·ta·ir /altā'ir, -ter'/ [< Ar *al-tā'ir* the bird] *n* Alpha in the constellation Aquila

al·tar /ôl'tər/ [OE < L *altare*] **1** raised place or structure of earth or stone on which to offer sacrifice or burn incense as a religious rite; **2** table at which the communion is celebrated in ritualistic Christian churches

al'tar boy' *n* boy who assists the minister or priest at church services

al'tar·piece' *n* painted or carved screen or panel above or behind an altar

al'ter /ôl'tər/ [LL *alterare*] *vt* **1** to cause to change; modify; **2** to castrate or spay ‖ *vi* **3** to become different ‖ **al'ter·a·ble** *adj* ‖ **al'ter·a·bly** *adv* ‖ **al'ter·a·bil'i·ty** /-bil'-/ *n* ‖ SYN modify, change, qualify, shift, transform, convert ‖ ANT retain, abide, endure, keep, persist, stay

al'ter·a'tion *n* **1** act of altering or state of being altered; **2** change, modification

al'ter·ca'tion /-kāsh'ən/ [< L *altercari* (-atus) to dispute] *n* dispute; angry debate ‖ SYN controversy, contention, wrangle (see *quarrel*)

al·ter·nate /ôl'tərnāt, al'-/ [L *alternare* (-atus) to do by turns] *vt* **1** to cause to occur by turns ‖ *vi* **2** to take place or act by turns; **3** *elec* to reverse periodically in direction or sign ‖ /-nit/ *adj* **4** taking place by turns; **5** every other (one) ‖ *n* **6** one who takes the place of another ‖ **al'ter·nate·ly** *adv* ‖ **al'ter·na'tion** *n*

al'ter·nat·ing cur'rent *n* electric current that reverses direction constantly with rising and falling values, with a frequency of sixty cycles in ordinary house current in the U.S.

al·ter·na·tive /ôlturn'ətiv, al-/ *adj* **1** giving the choice of two or more things, only one of which may be taken, done, etc. ‖ *n* **2** choice of one of two or more things to be taken or done; **3** any of the things open to choice ‖ **al·ter'na·tive·ly** *adv* ‖ SYN *n* option, election, preference (see *choice*)

al'ter·na'tor *n* generator of alternating current

al·though also **al·tho** /ôlthō'/ *conj* though; even if; notwithstanding

alti- *or* **alto-** [L *altus*] *comb form* high, height, as *altimeter*

al·tim·e·ter /altim'itər, al'timēt'ər/ *n* instrument for measuring altitude

al·ti·tude /al'tit(y)ŏŏd'/ [L *altitudo* height] *n* **1** extent vertically; **2** height above sea level; **3** angular elevation of a heavenly body above the horizon; **4** perpendicular distance from the base of a geometric figure to the vertex, or between any two parallel faces of a solid ‖ **al'ti·tu'di·nal** *adj*

al·to /al'tō/ [It = high] *n* **1** lowest female singing voice; contralto; **2** person with such a voice; **3** second highest of a family of musical instruments, as the viola ‖ also *adj*

al'to·cu'mu·lus *n* (-li /-lī'/) high cloud of fleecy white or gray masses

al'to·geth'er /ôl'-/ *adv* **1** wholly, completely; **2** on the whole ‖ *n* **3 in the altogether** *colloq* in the nude

al·tru·ism /al'trŏŏ·iz'əm/ [F *altruisme* < It *altrui* for others] *n* unselfish regard for the interests of others ‖ **al'tru·ist** *n* ‖ **al'tru·is'tic** *adj*

al·um /al'əm/ [L *alumen*] *n* **1** any of a class of double sulfates, compounds of aluminum, iron, chromium, or manganese sulfate with sulfates of the alkali metals or ammonium: commonly potash alum, a double potassium aluminum sulfate; **2** aluminum sulfate —$Al_2(SO_4)_3$

a·lu·mi·na /əlōōm′inə/ *n* aluminum oxide —Al_2O_3— occurring in nature as corundum

a·lu·mi·num /-nəm/ or chiefly *Brit* **al·u·min·i·um** /al′yə-min′ē-əm/ *n* bluish-white, ductile, malleable metallic element (**Al;** at.no. 13; at.wt. 26.98), resistant to tarnishing and oxidizing when exposed to the air; the most plentiful of metallic substances, but never found in a pure state

a·lu′mi·num foil′ *n* aluminum in a thin sheet, used as a preservative wrapping

a·lum·nus /əlum′nəs/ [L = foster son] *n* (-ni /-nī/) male graduate of a school, college, or university ‖ **a·lum′·na** /-nə/ *nfem* (-nae /-nē/)

al·ve·o·lar /alvē′ələr/ *adj* **1** pert. to or containing alveoli; **2** *phonet* articulated with the tongue tip touching the teethridge

al·ve′o·lus /-ləs/ [L = small cavity] *n* (-li /-lī′/) **1** small cavity or cell, as in a honeycomb; **2** *anat* any small hollow or cell, as a tooth socket or an air cell in the lungs

al·ways /ôl′wăz, -wiz/ [*all* + *way*] *adv* at all times; continually

am /am′, əm/ [OE *eom*] *vi 1st pers sg pres ind of* **be**

AM amplitude modulation

Am *chem* americium

Am. America(n)

A.M., a.m. [(L *ante meridiem*) before noon] period from 12 midnight to 12 noon

A.M.A. American Medical Association

a·main /əmān′/ [< a⁻¹ + OE *mægn* force] *adv* with force, violence, or speed

a·mal·gam /əmal′gəm/ [MF *amalgame* < LL *amalgama*] *n* **1** any metallic mixture of which mercury is the chief ingredient; **2** mixture or compound

a·mal′ga·mate′ *vt* **1** to alloy or mix (a metal) with mercury; **2** to combine into one ‖ *vi* **3** to combine ‖ **a·mal′·ga·ma′tion** *n* ‖ SYN unite, blend, compound (see *combine*)

a·man·u·en·sis /əman′yōō-en′sis/ [L < *a* from + *manus* hand] *n* (-ses /-sēz/) one who writes for, or at the dictation of, another; secretary

am·a·ranth /am′əranth′/ [< Gk *amarantos* unfading] **1** imaginary never-fading flower; **2** any of several plants (genus *Amaranthus*) including several bright-colored garden flowers; **3** color mixture in which the chief ingredient is magenta ‖ **am′a·ran′·thine** /-thin, -thin′/ *adj*

am·a·ryl·lis /am′əril′is/ [L, name of a shepherdess] *n* any of a family (*Amaryllis*) of lilylike bulbous plants, chiefly tropical; esp. the belladonna lily, cultivated for its large brilliantly colored blossoms

a·mass /əmas′/ [MF *amasser*] *vt* to gather together in quantity, accumulate ‖ SYN collect, gather, hoard, store up, accumulate

am·a·teur /am′əchŏŏr′, -t(y)ŏŏr′/ [F < L *amator* lover] *n* **1** one who practices any art, study, or sport for pleasure and not for money; **2** one whose work lacks professional finish ‖ **am′a·teur·ism** *n* ‖ SYN dilettante ‖ DISCR An *amateur* chooses his art or sport for love of it, and, though not ranked as a professional, he may be expert and accomplished. The *dilettante* shares the *amateur's* love for his chosen field, but not his application; hence he is a dabbler, one who toys with his subject, a mere trifler

am′a·teur′ish *adj* crude, lacking in finish, as in athletic performance or technique in art ‖ **am′a·teur′ish·ly** *adv* ‖ **am′a·teur′ish·ness** *n*

A·ma·ti /ämät′ē/ [Nicolò *Amati* (1596–1684)] *n* violin made by one of the Amati family, which flourished at Cremona, Italy, from about 1550 to 1700

am·a·to·ry /am′ətôr′ē, -tōr′-/ [< L *amare* (-*atus*) to love] *adj* of or expressing love

a·maze /əmāz′/ [OE *āmasian* to confuse] *vt* to bewilder with wonder; astonish; perplex ‖ **a·maz′ing** *adj* ‖ **a·maz′ing·ly** *adv*

a·maze′ment *n* state of overwhelming surprise ‖ SYN awe, wonder, surprise, confusion, admiration

am·a·zon /am′əzon′, -zən/ [Gk] *n* **1** big, strong, or masculine woman; **2 Amazon** Gk *myth.* one of a warlike race of women from Asia Minor; **3 Amazon** river in N South America flowing 3900 miles east to the Atlantic, mostly in Brazil; largest river in the world ‖ **Am′a·zo′ni·an** /-zōn′-ē-ən/ *adj*

am·bas·sa·dor /ambas′ədər/ [MF *ambassadeur*] *n* government agent of the highest rank representing his country at a foreign capital or at international bodies, such as the U.N. ‖ **am·bas′sa·dress** *nfem* ‖ **am·bas′sa·do′ri·al** /-dôr′ē-əl, -dōr′-/ *adj*

am·ber /am′bər [ML *ambra* < Ar *'anbar* ambergris] *n* **1** yellowish fossilized translucent vegetable resin, capable of high polish and readily electrified by friction; **2** its color

am′ber·gris′ /-grēs′, -gris/ [MF *ambre* amber + *gris* gray] *n* waxy substance obtained from sperm whales and used in perfumery

ambi- [L] *comb form* both

am·bi·dex·trous /am′bidek′strəs/ *adj* **1** able to use both hands with equal skill; **2** skillful; **3** deceitful ‖ **am'bi-dex-ter'i-ty** /-ter'itẹ/ n

am-bi-ence /am'bẹ-əns/ n environment, pervading atmosphere

am'bi-ent [L *ambiens* (*-entis*) going around] *adj* surrounding, encompassing

am-bi-gu-i-ty /am'bigyōō'itẹ/ n (**-ties**) **1** vagueness, indefiniteness; uncertainty; **2** expression whose meaning can be taken in two or more ways

am-big-u-ous /ambig'yōō-əs/ [L *ambiguus* doubtful] *adj* **1** doubtful; not clear or definite; **2** having two or more possible meanings ‖ **am-big'u-ous-ly** *adv* ‖ SYN indeterminate, doubtful, uncertain, vague (see *equivocal, obscure*) ‖ ANT clear, definite, explicit, specific, decisive

am-bi-tion /ambish'ən/ [L *ambitio* (*-onis*) going about, in canvassing votes] n **1** eager or immoderate desire to obtain some object, as wealth or power; **2** object of such desire

am-bi'tious *adj* **1** full of ambition; **2** requiring great skill or effort for success ‖ **am-bi'tious-ly** *adv*

am-biv-a-lent /ambiv'ələnt/ [*ambi-* + L *valens* (*-entis*) worth] *adj* combining two impulses or tendencies usu. opposed to each other ‖ **am-biv'a-lence** n

am-ble /am'bəl/ [OF *ambler* < L *ambulare* to walk] *vi* **1** to go at an easy pace; **2** (of horses) to go at a pace in which the animal lifts the two feet on the same side together ‖ n **3** ambling gait of a horse; **4** any easy gait

am-bro-sia /ambrōzh'(ẹ)ə/ [Gk = food of the gods] n **1** *class. myth.* food of the gods; **2** anything exquisitely pleasing to taste or smell ‖ **am-bro'sial** *adj*

am-bu-lance /am'byələns/ [F = walking hospital < L *ambulare* to walk] n vehicle for carrying sick or wounded

am'bu-late' [L *ambulare* (*-atus*) to walk] *vi* to walk about ‖ **am'bu-lant** *adj*

am'bu-la-to'ry /-ətôr'ẹ, -ətōr'ẹ/ *adj* **1** pert. to walking; **2** able to walk

am-bus-cade /am'bəskād'/ [F *embuscade*] n ambush

am-bush /am'bŏŏsh/ [OF *embushier* < LL *imboscare* to set in ambush < LL *boscus* forest] n **1** concealed station where troops or others lie hidden to attack unexpectedly; **2** attackers so hidden; **3** act of lying in ambush ‖ *vt* **4** to attack from ambush; **5** to station in ambush

a-me-ba /əmēb'ə/ n var of **amoeba**

a-me-lio-rate /əmēl'yərāt'/ [*ad-* + L *meliorare* (*-atus*) to make better] *vt* **1** to make better ‖ *vi* **2** to improve, grow better ‖ **a-me'lio-ra'tion** n

a-men /ä'men', ā'men'/ [Heb = certainty] *interj* **1** verily, so be it! (used at the end of a prayer or in solemn assent) ‖ n **2** utterance of the word *amen*

a-me-na-ble /əmēn'əbəl, -men'-/ [< MF *amener* to lead up] *adj* **1** easy to lead, submissive; **2** liable or accountable ‖ **a-me'na-bly** *adv* ‖ **a-me'na-bil'i-ty** /-bil'-/ n

a-mend /əmend'/ [OF *amender* < L *emendare* to correct] *vt* **1** to change for the better; correct; **2** to change or alter formally or with authority, as a constitution ‖ SYN better, mend, improve, rectify, reform

a-mend'ment n **1** change for the better; correction; **2** alteration of a bill, motion, resolution, etc., by a deliberative body; **3** change in, or addition to, the constitution of a country, state, or society

a-mends /əmendz'/ *npl* compensation or satisfaction for loss or injury ‖ SYN reparation, satisfaction, restitution, recompense (see *redress*)

a-men-i-ty /əmen'itẹ, -mēn'/ [L *amoenitas* < *amoenus* pleasant] n (**-ties**) pleasantness, geniality; pleasing act or experience

A-men-Ra /äm'ənrä'/ n sun god of ancient Egypt

Amer. America(n)

A-mer-i-ca /əmer'ikə/ [*Americus* Vespucius, L form of Amerigo Vespucci] n **1** the United States; **2** North and/or South America; **3** also **the Americas** *pl* North and South America, the Western Hemisphere ‖ **A-mer'i-can** *adj* & n

A-mer'i-ca'na /-kan'ə, -kän'ə, -kän'ə/ *npl* **1** writings, records, objects, or the like, related or pert. to America and its culture; **2** collection of such materials

A-mer'i-can-ism n **1** phrase, word, trait, custom, or object peculiar to the United States; **2** spirit of loyalty to American ideals

A-mer'i-can-ist n **1** specialist in American studies; **2** specialist in the languages and cultures of the American Indians

A-mer'i-can-ize' *vt* & *vi* to assimilate to the language, customs, and institutions of the United States ‖ **A-mer'i-can-i-za'tion** n

A-mer'i-can plan' n hotel rate which includes room and meals

A-mer'i-can Sa-mo'a n the part of Samoa belonging to the United States (21,000; 76 sq.m.; cap. Pago Pago)

am-er-i-ci-um /am'ərish'ẹ-əm/ [< *America*] n radioactive metallic element (Am; at.no. 95) produced by bombarding uranium with high-energy helium nuclei

Am-er-ind /am'ərind'/ [*American* + *Indian*] n American Indian or Eskimo ‖ also *adj* ‖ **Am'er-in'di-an** *adj* & n ‖ **Am'er-ind'ic** *adj*

am-e-thyst /am'əthist/ [Gk *amethystos*

not drunken, the stone being considered a talisman against drunkenness] *n* 1 violet-purple variety of quartz; 2 purplish color

Am·har·ic /amhar'ik/ [< *Amhara* Ethiopian province] *n* official language of Ethiopia

a·mi·a·ble /ām'ē·əbəl/ [MF < L *amicabilis*] *n* friendly; lovable ‖ **a'mi·a·bly** *adv* ‖ **a'mi·a·bil'i·ty** /-bil'-/ *n*

am·i·ca·ble /am'ikəbəl/ [L *amicabilis*] *adj* friendly; peaceable ‖ **am'i·ca·bly** *adv* ‖ **am'i·ca·bil'i·ty** /-bil'-/ *n*

a·mi·cus cu·ri·ae /əmīk'əs kyŏŏr'ē·ē'/ [L = friend of the court] *n* (**a·mi·ci cu·ri·ae** /əmī'sī/) *n law* neutral bystander in a litigation who proffers advice or assistance to the court

a·mid /əmid'/ also **a·midst** /əmidst'/ [OE *on middan* in the middle] *prep* in the middle of; among ‖ SYN (see *between*)

a·mid'ships *adv* in the middle of a ship or aircraft

amin- or **amino-** [< *amine*] *comb form* containing the univalent group NH₂

a·mine /am'in, əmēn'/ [< *ammonia* +-*ine*] *n* any of a group of compounds derived from ammonia by replacing hydrogen with hydrocarbon radicals

a·mi·no /əmēn'ō, am'inō'/ *adj* containing or pert. to the group NH₂

a·mi'no ac'id *n* any of a group of organic acids containing the amino group NH₂, and which are the essential components of proteins

A·mish /äm'ish, am'-/ [< Jacob *Ammann* Swiss Mennonite of 17th cent.] *adj* 1 of or pert. to a sect of Mennonites which originated in 1620 ‖ *n* 2 the **Amish** *pl* members of this sect

a·miss /əmis'/ *adj* 1 wrong; faulty ‖ *adv* 2 wrongly; faultily; 3 astray; 4 **take amiss** to take offense at

am·i·ty /am'itē/ [MF *amitie* friendship] *n* (**-ties**) friendly or peaceful relations; friendship

Am·man /äm'män, ämmän'/ *n* capital of Jordan (330,000)

am·me·ter /am'mēt'ər/ [*ampere* + -*meter*] *n* instrument that measures electric current in amperes

am·mo /am'ō/ [<*ammunition*] *n colloq* ammunition

am·mo·nia /əmōn'yə/ [< *ammoniac*] *n* 1 clear pungent gas —NH₃— readily soluble in water and used in refrigeration and manufacturing; 2 also **ammonia water** solution of this gas in water

am·mo·ni·ac /əmōn'ē·ak'/ [Gk *ammoniakon* pert. to Ammon, Egypt. god] *adj* 1 pert. to ammonia ‖ *n* 2 also **gum ammoniac** resinous gum produced from a Persian shrub (*Dorema ammoniacum*) and used medicinally

am·mo'ni·um *n* univalent radical NH₄, which forms a group of compounds

similar to that of the alkaline metals; not found except in combination

am·mu·ni·tion /am'yənish'ən/ [*obs* F *l'amunition* < *la munition* < L *munitio* (-*onis*) fortification] *n* 1 missiles that explode or are propelled by explosive charges, as bullets, shells, bombs, grenades, rockets, etc.; 2 any material used to attack or defend

am·ne·sia /amnēzh'(ē)ə/ [Gk < *a-* + *mnes*, root of *mimneskein* to remind] *n* loss of memory

am·nes·ty /am'nistē/ [Gk *amnestia* forgetfulness] *n* (**-ties**) 1 general pardon, esp. for political offenses ‖ *v* (**-tied**) *vt* 2 to pardon

am·ni·o·cen·te·sis /am'nē·ō'sentē'sis/ [NL < *amnion* membrane containing the fetus + Gk *kentein* to puncture] *n* (**-ses** /-sēz/) extraction of amniotic fluid to determine diseases, genetic defects, and the sex of the fetus

am'ni·o'tic flu'id /am'nē·ot'ik/ [Gk *dim.* of *amnos* lamb] *n* fluid in the amniotic sac, in which the embryo is suspended

a·moe·ba /əmēb'ə/ [Gk *amoibe* change] *n* (**-bas** or **-bae** /-bē/) microscopic one-celled animal consisting of a mass of protoplasm constantly changing form ‖ **a·moe'bic** *adj*

a·mok /əmok', əmuk'/ [Malay] *n* 1 uncontrollable murderous frenzy ‖ *adv* 2 **run amok**, **a** to be possessed by a murderous frenzy; **b** to lose control of oneself

a·mong /əmuŋ'/ also **a·mongst** /əmuŋst'/ [OE *on gemonge* in a crowd] *prep* 1 in the midst of; surrounded by; in the group with; 2 by the combined action of; 3 by distribution to, as *divided among them* ‖ SYN (see *between*)

a·mor·al /āmôr'əl, -mor'-/ *adj* without moral standards: neither moral nor immoral ‖ **a'mo·ral'i·ty** /-əral'-/ *n*

am·o·rous /am'ərəs/ [< L *amor* love] *adj* 1 of or pert. to love; 2 erotic; fond of the opposite sex; 3 in love; loving ‖ **am'o·rous·ly** *adv*

a·mor·phous /əmôr'fəs/ *adj* 1 formless, of no determinate shape; 2 of no specified kind or character; not organized; 3 *chem* not crystalline

am·or·tize /am'ərtīz'/ [MF *amortir* (-*tiss*-) to deaden] *vt* to pay off (a debt) by means of periodic payments or a sinking fund ‖ **am·or'ti·za'tion** /əmôrt'-/ *n*

A·mos /ām'əs/ *n Bib* 1 Hebrew herdsman who became a prophet; 2 book of the Old Testament containing his prophecies

a·mount /əmount'/ [OF *amonter* < *amont* uphill] *vi* 1 to reach; be equal; 2 to add up or be equal ‖ *n* 3 sum total; 4 quantity; 5 full effect or value

a·mour /əmŏŏr'/ [OF] *n* love affair

a·mour-pro·pre /ämŏŏr′ prôp′rə/ [F] *n* self-respect, self-esteem

amp or **amp.** 1 ampere; 2 amperage

am·per·age /amp′ərij/ *n* strength of an electric current measured in amperes

am·pere /am′pir/ [André Marie *Ampère* (1775–1836) F physicist] *n* practical mks unit of measure of electric current, being the amount of current moved by one volt through a resistance of one ohm

am′pere-hour′ *n* unit of electricity, being the quantity of electricity conveyed by one ampere flowing for one hour

am′pere-turn′ *n* 1 one full turn of a coil through which one ampere passes; 2 magnetomotive force produced by one ampere passing through one full turn of a coil

am·per·sand /amp′ərsand′/ [< *and per se and* = "&" by itself makes "and"] *n* the sign & for the word *and*

am·phet·a·mine /amfet′əmēn′, -min/ [*al*pha + *meth*yl + *ph*enyl + *et*hyl + am*ine*] *n* drug —C₆H₅CH₂CH(NH₂)CH₃— used to relieve hay fever and head colds and in the form of its sulfates to combat depression and to control weight

amphi- [Gk = on both sides] *comb form* 1 on both sides; 2 of both kinds; 3 both

am·phib·i·an /amfib′ē·ən/ [*amphi-* + *bios* life] *n* 1 animal or plant living both on land and in water; 2 airplane designed to take off from or land on water or land ‖ *adj* 3 amphibious

am·phib′i·ous *adj* 1 able to live both on land and in water; 2 having two natures; 3 (military operation) by land and by sea

am·phi·the·a·ter /am′fi-/ *n* 1 elliptical or circular building with rows of seats sloping upward and backward around a central open space; 2 anything resembling such a structure, as a space out of doors partly surrounded by sloping ground, or a gallery in a theater

am·ple /amp′əl/ [MF < L *amplus*] *adj* 1 spacious; large; 2 abundant, sufficient for all needs ‖ **am′ply** *adv* ‖ SYN wide, copious, plentiful, plenteous, bountiful, liberal, adequate, rich, generous ‖ ANT small, scant, inadequate

am·pli·fi·er /amp′lifi′ər/ *n* 1 one who or that which amplifies; 2 *electron.* device or circuit that amplifies but does not change the form of a signal

am′pli·fy′ [MF *amplifier* < L *amplificare* to enlarge] *v* (-fied) *vt* 1 to make larger, stronger, or fuller ‖ *vi* 2 to add to what has been said or written ‖ **am′pli·fi·ca′tion** *n*

am′pli·tude′ /-t(y)ŏŏd′/ [L *amplitudo* largeness] *n* 1 extension in space, esp. in breadth and range; scope; 2 largeness of mind, breadth of thought; 3 *elec* maximum value of an alternating current; 4 *phys* maximum value of a periodically varying quantity

am′pli·tude′ mod′u·la′tion *n* 1 *electron.* modulation of a carrier wave by varying its amplitude; 2 *rad* broadcasting by means of such a carrier wave

am′pule /am′pyŏŏl/ or **am·poule** /am′pŏŏl/ [OF *ampoule* < L *ampulla* flask] *n* sealed glass container having a single dose of a hypodermic injection

am·pu·tate /amp′yətāt′/ [L *amputare* (-*atus*) to cut off around] *vt* to cut off, as a human limb ‖ **am′pu·ta′tion** *n*

am′pu·tee′ /-tē′/ *n* person who has had a limb or limbs amputated

Am·ster·dam /am′stərdam′/ *n* one of the two capitals of The Netherlands (862,488)

amt. amount

a·muck /əmuk′/ *n* & *adv* var of amok

am·u·let /am′yəlit/ [L *amuletum*] *n* charm worn to protect against evil

a·muse /əmyŏŏz′/ [MF *amuser* to cause to muse] *vt* 1 to entertain, divert; 2 to excite mirth in ‖ **a·mus′-ing** *adj* ‖ SYN enliven, interest, please, recreate, divert, entertain ‖ ANT annoy, bore, distract, disturb, tire, weary

a·muse′ment *n* 1 act of amusing or state of being amused; 2 that which entertains ‖ SYN diversion, recreation, entertainment, pastime ‖ DISCR *Amusement* is the general term signifying pleasure gained from occupying the mind agreeably and lightly. *Diversion, recreation, entertainment,* and *pastime* are forms of *amusement; diversion* distracts the mind from its ordinary course and often provokes mirth; *recreation* refreshes and relaxes after hard work; *entertainment* is usually secured by some definite means, such as a play or a novel, and has commonly an intellectual as well as a social appeal; *pastime* is any agreeable mode of enjoyment that passes the leisure hour

a·muse′ment park′ *n* park with devices for entertainment, as a roller coaster, merry-go-round, etc.

am·yl /am′il/ [Gk *amylon* starch] *n* any of several univalent isomeric groups with the formula C₅H₁₁, forming a fundamental part of many compounds, such as alcohol

amyl- or **amylo-** *comb form* starch

am·yl·ase /am′ilās′, -āz′/ *n* enzyme that helps change starch into sugar, present in blood and some plants

an /ən/ when stressed: an′/ [OE *ān* one] *indef art* (used before singular nouns and adjectives beginning with a vowel sound) var of **a**

an-[1] [L] var of **ad-**, used before *n*, as *announce*

an-[2] [Gk] var of **a-**[4], used before a vowel, as *anarchy*

an-[3] or **ana-** [Gk] *pref* up, back, anew; again, as *anode, anatomy*

-an /-ən/ [L *-anus*] *adj suf* **1** pert. to, as *American* ‖ *n suf* **2** one of, inhabitant of, as *a Chilean*

AN, A.N. Anglo-Norman

An *chem* actinon

an. [L *anno*] in the year

-a·na /an'ə, än'ə, än'ə/ or **i·a·na** /ē-/ [L] *npl suf* things pert. to, sayings or anecdotes of, information about, as *Americana, Shakespeariana*

An'a·bap'tist /an'ə-/ [<Gk *anabaptizein* to baptize again] *n* one of a sect of the 16th century, opposed to infant baptism

a·nab·a·sis /ənab'əsis/ [Gk] *n* (*-ses* /sēz'/) **1** military advance into a country; **2** *Anabasis* account by Xenophon of the march of the 10,000 Greeks to the Euphrates

a·nach·ro·nism /ənak'rəniz'əm/ [<*ana-* + Gk *chronos* time] *n* **1** error in the order of time; placing of something historically in the wrong time; **2** person or thing so placed; **3** obsolete person or thing

an·a·con·da /an'əkon'də/ [prob Sinhalese *henakandaya* type of snake] *n* **1** large South American boa (*Eunectes murinus*) that kills by crushing in its coils; **2** any large boa

a·nae·mi·a /ənēm'ē·ə/ *n* var of **ane·mia** ‖ **a·nae'mic** *adj*

an·aes·the·sia /an'isthēzh'ə/ *n* var of anesthesia

an'aes·thet'ic /-thet'ik/ *adj* & *n* var of anesthetic

an·a·gram /an'əgram'/ [*ana-* + Gk *gramma* letter] *n* word or sentence obtained by changing the order of the letters in another word or sentence

a·nal /ān'əl/ [see **anus**] *adj* pert. to the anus

anal. **1** analogous; **2** analogy; **3** analysis

an·al·ge·si·a /an'əljēs'ē·ə, -jēz'-/ [Gk = painlessness] *n* insensibility to pain

an'al·ge'sic *adj* **1** capable of dulling pain; **2** insensible to pain ‖ *n* **3** remedy that relieves pain

an·a·log /an'əlog', -lôg'/ *n* analogue

an'a·log com·put'er *n* computer that works on the principle of measuring, as distinguished from counting, as the simple slide rule

an'a·log'i·cal /-loj'-/ *adj* pert. to, or expressing analogy

a·nal·o·gous /ənal'əgəs/ *adj* **1** having resemblance; similar; corresponding in certain ways; **2** *biol* like in organic action but not in structure

an·a·logue /an'əlog', -lôg'/ *n* **1** that

which has some resemblance or correspondence to something else; **2** *biol* organ or part analogous to another

a·nal·o·gy /ənal'əjē/ [*ana-* + Gk *logos* ratio, proportion] *n* (*-gies*) **1** partial similarity between things that are somewhat different; **2** agreement, similarity; **3** *logic* form of reasoning which infers that things, conditions, processes, etc., which are alike in some ways, are alike in other ways; **4** *biol* likeness in purpose or action without likeness in structure; **5** *ling* process whereby the creation of new words and morphological changes follow existing patterns ‖ SYN similarity, relation, likeness, comparison

a·nal·y·sis /ənal'isis/ [Gk = breaking up] *n* (*-ses* /-sēz'/) **1** division or separation of a thing into the parts that compose it; **2** *chem* resolution of a compound into its parts; **3** psychoanalysis

an·a·lyst /an'əlist/ *n* **1** one who analyzes; **2** psychoanalyst

an·a·lyt·ic (**-i·cal**) /an'əlit'ik(əl)/ *adj* **1** separating into component parts; **2** skilled in analysis; **3** (language) showing many syntactical relationships by using function words rather than inflection; **4** *math* using the methods of algebra and calculus

an·a·lyze /an'əliz'/ *vt* **1** to separate into component parts; **2** to examine closely and critically

An·a·ni·as /an'əni'əs/ *n* follower of the Apostles, who was struck dead for lying (Acts 5:1–10)

an·a·pest /an'əpest'/ [Gk *anapaistos* reversed] *n* metrical foot consisting of two short syllables followed by a long one or of two unaccented syllables followed by an accented one

an·ar·chism /an'ərkiz'əm/ *n* **1** doctrine that all government is unnecessary and therefore evil; **2** advocacy of anarchy ‖ **an'ar·chist** *n*

an'ar·chy [*an-*[3] + *arche* government] *n* **1** absence or lack of government; **2** lawless condition of society; **3** terrorism; disorder; **4** theory of absolute individual liberty ‖ **an·ar·chic** (**-chi·cal**) /ənär'kik(əl)/ *adj*

an·as·tig·mat /ənas'tigmat', an'əstig'-/ [<*anastigmatic*] *n* compound lens through which rays are brought to a sharp focus in order to correct astigmatism

an'as·tig·mat'ic /an'əs-, anas'-/ [*an-*[3] + *astigmatic*] *adj* (lens) corrected for astigmatism

a·nath·e·ma /ənath'imə/ [Gk = accursed thing] *n* **1** person or thing thought to be accursed; **2** solemn curse of the church in excommunication; **3** curse, imprecation

a·nath'e·ma·tize' *vt* **1** to pronounce a curse upon ‖ *vi* **2** to utter denunciations, curse

An·a·to·li·a /anˈətōlˈẹ̇·ə/ n Asia Minor ‖ **An'a·to'li·an** adj & n

a·nat·o·my /ənatˈəmẹ̄/ [Gk anatome a cutting up] n (-mies) 1 science of dissection; 2 science that treats of the structure or parts of animals or plants; 3 a structure of an animal or plant; b description of such structure; 4 treatise on dissection; 5 analysis or examination ‖ **an'a·tom'ic (-i·cal)** /anˈətomˈ-/ adj ‖ **a·nat'o·mist** n

anc. ancient

-ance /-əns/ [OF < L -antia] n suf denoting action, process, quality, or state, as assistance, hindrance

an·ces·tor /anˈsestər/ [OF ancestre < L antecessor foregoer] n 1 person from whom one is descended, forebear; 2 progenitor from which later species are derived; 3 prototype, forerunner ‖ **an'ces·tress** nfem ‖ **ances'tral** adj

an'ces·try n (-tries) 1 line of descent traced from a more or less remote period; 2 lineage

an·chor /aŋkˈər/ [OE ancor < L ancora < Gk ankyra] n 1 heavy metal implement dropped to the bottom of the water to prevent a vessel from drifting, generally having flukes and connected to the vessel with a chain or cable; 2 any like device for holding fast a movable object; 3 that on which dependence is placed for security and stability; 4 any device for securing various parts of a structure; 5 at anchor anchored; 6 weigh anchor to raise the anchor ‖ vt 7 to hold fast with an anchor; 8 to fix firmly; 9 to be the anchor man of ‖ vi 10 to lie at anchor; 11 to take and hold a firm position

an'chor·age /-ij/ n 1 suitable place for anchoring; 2 act of anchoring or state of being anchored; 3 that to which anything is anchored

an·cho·rite /aŋkˈərit/ also **an·cho·ret** /aŋkˈəret/ [LL anachoreta < Gk anachoretes recluse] n 1 one who lives alone to devote his time to religion and philosophy; 2 recluse, hermit ‖ **an'cho·ress** nfem

an'chor man' n 1 key broadcaster who participates in and coordinates the work of several broadcasters; 2 sports strongest member of a team, who competes last

an·cho·vy /anchōvˈẹ̄, anˈchəvẹ̄/ [Sp anchova] n (-vies) small herringlike fish (family Engraulidae) common in the Mediterranean

an·cien ré·gime /äNsyaNˈräzhēmˈ/ [F = old regime] n 1 political system of France before the Revolution of 1789; 2 any governing group no longer in power

an·cient /ānˈshənt/ [MF ancien < VL *anteanus] adj 1 pert. to times long past, spec. to the time before the fall of Rome in 476; 2 very old, of great age ‖ n 3 one who lived in ancient times; 4 aged person ‖ **SYN** adj aged, antiquated, antique, immemorial, venerable, gray, timehonored, olden, hoary ‖ **ANT** adj new, recent, modern, novel, fresh

an·cil·lar·y /anˈsïlerˈẹ̄/ [< L ancilla maidservant] adj subordinate; auxiliary

-an·cy /-ənsẹ̄/ [L -antia] n suf denoting quality or state, as militancy

and /and, ənd, ən/ [OE] conj (connecting a word, phrase, clause, or sentence, with one of like kind) 1 together with, in addition to; 2 also, then again; 3 to, as try and get it

An·da·lu·sia /anˈdəloozhˈ(ẹ̄)ə/ n region of S Spain bordering on the Mediterranean and the Atlantic ‖ **An'da·lu'sian** adj & n

an·dan·te /andantˈẹ̄/ [It = walking] adj & adv mus moderately slow

An·der·sen /anˈdərsən/, Hans Christian n (1805–75) Danish author of fairy tales

An·des Moun'tains /anˈdēz/ npl mountain range extending along the whole length of South America near the Pacific Ocean

and·i·ron /andˈīˈərn/ [< OF andier] n one of two supports of metal for holding logs in a fireplace

and/or /andˈôrˈ/ conj either and or or

An·dor·ra /andôrˈə/ n Catalan-speaking republic in the E Pyrenees between Spain and France (14,366; 175 sq.m.; cap. Andorra) ‖ **An·dor'ran** adj & n

andr- or **andro-** [Gk aner (andros) man] comb form male, as androgen

An·drew /anˈdrōō/ n Bib one of the twelve apostles

An·dro·cles /anˈdrəklēzˈ/ n Roman slave of the first century who, sentenced to the arena, was spared by a lion because in the past he had drawn a thorn from its foot

an·dro·gen /anˈdrəjən/ n any substance that promotes masculine characteristics

an·drog·y·nous /androjˈinəs/ adj 1 having the characteristics of both male and female; 2 bot bearing at the same time both anthers and ovaries ‖ **an·drog'y·ny** n

An·drom·e·da /andromˈidə/ n (gen -dae /-dē'/) northern constellation

-an·drous /anˈdrəs/ [Gk aner (andros)] comb form male, as polyandrous

-ane¹ /-ān/ [L -anus] adj suf pertaining to, as urbane, humane

-ane² /-ān/ [by analogy with -ene, -ine, -one] n suf used in naming saturated hydrocarbons, as methane

an·ec·dote /anˈikdōtˈ/ [Gk anekdota things unpublished] n brief entertaining account of some incident ‖ **an'ec·dot'al** adj ‖ **SYN** story, tale ‖

DISCR *Anecdote, story,* and *tale* are alike in using incident as the base of narrative. *Anecdote* is the relation of a detached incident, short, often characteristic, sometimes witty. The *story* weaves a series of incidents into a narrative which moves to a definite climax through a well organized plot. The *tale* is a narrative in which the incidents that form its main source of interest are loosely held together; there may be but little plot; digression and speculation are admitted into its leisurely development, and it leaves an impression as a whole, rather than through any one acute point of interest

an·e·cho·ic /an'ekō'ik/ [*an-²* + *echo*] *adj* (recording studio, etc.) free of echoes and reverberations

a·ne·mi·a /ənēm'ē·ə/ [Gk *anaimia* lack of blood] *n* condition resulting from a deficiency of red corpuscles or of hemoglobin in the blood ‖ **a·ne'mic** *adj*

an·e·mom·e·ter /an'imom'itər/ [Gk *anemos* wind + *-meter*] *n* device for measuring the wind's velocity

a·nem·o·ne /ənem'ənē/ [Gk = *anemos* wind] *n* any of several plants of the crowfoot family (genera *Anemone* and *Anemonella*) without petals but with white or pinkish sepals

a·nent /ənent'/ [< OE *efen* beside] *prep* regarding, concerning

an·er·oid /an'əroid'/ [<*a-⁴* + Gk *neros* liquid] *adj* containing no liquid

an'er·oid ba·rom'e·ter *n* barometer whose pointer is controlled by the elastic lid of a box containing a partial vacuum

an·es·the·sia /an'isthēzh'ə/ [Gk *anaisthesia* lack of feeling] *n* loss of bodily feeling

an'es·thet'ic /-thet'ik/ *adj* **1** relating to or producing anesthesia ‖ *n* **2** substance that produces anesthesia

an·es·the·tist /ənes'thitist/ *n* person trained to administer anesthetics

an·es'the·tize' *vt* to render insensible to pain

an·eu·rysm also **an·eu·rism** /an'yəriz'əm/ [Gk *aneurysmos* dilation] *n* permanent dilation at some point in an artery caused by the pressure of blood on weakened tissues

a·new /ən(y)ōō'/ *adv* **1** afresh, over again; **2** in a new manner

an·gel /ān'jəl/ < Gk *angelos* messenger] *n* **1** messenger of God; **2** one of an order of spiritual beings having immortal life and forming a connection between the seen and the unseen worlds; **3** guiding, guarding, or controlling influence, as of a person; **4** person with great spiritual loveliness of character; **5** financial backer of a theatrical production ‖ **an·gel'ic (-i·cal)** /anjel'-/ *adj* ‖ **an·gel'i·cal·ly** *adv*

an'gel·fish' *n* any of several beautifully colored fishes (genera *Holacanthus* and *Pomacanthus*) with compressed bodies, found in warm seas

an'gel food' cake' *n* white sponge cake made with egg whites

An·ge·lus /an'jələs/ [first word of the prayer] *n* **1** devotion said morning, noon, and night in memory of the Annunciation; **2** church bell rung to announce such devotions

an·ger /aŋ'gər/ [ON *angr* grief] *n* **1** excessive emotion or passion aroused by a sense of injury or wrong; wrath ‖ *vt* **2** to make angry ‖ *vi* **3** to become angry ‖ SYN *n* anger, indignation, resentment, rage, wrath, ire, fury; also, temper, irritation, choler, hatred, animosity, passion ‖ DISCR The words of the first group express degrees of agitation aroused by offense and injury. *Anger* is a sudden, brief, violent displeasure. *Resentment* is a sullen, unyielding *anger* continued by brooding over the personal injury that caused it. *Wrath* is *anger* on a large scale, especially when felt by those in a superior position, as the *wrath* of the gods. *Ire* is a poetical term for *wrath*. *Indignation* is righteous *anger*, often impersonal and unselfish. *Rage* is a violence of angry feeling that sweeps one away from moderation and control; *fury* may go beyond control and render the furious person temporarily out of his mind

an·gi·na /anjin'ə/ [L = quinsy] *n* disease esp. of the pharynx or throat characterized by spasmodic suffocating attacks

an·gi'na pec'to·ris /pek'təris/ [L = angina of the chest] *n* painful muscular spasm of the chest, due to a diseased condition of a coronary artery

Angl. Anglican

an·gle¹ /aŋ'gəl/ [L *angulus*] *n* **1** figure formed near the intersection of two lines or planes, or three or more planes that meet in a point; **2** space included in such a figure; **3** amount of divergence between two lines or planes that are not parallel; **4** sharp edge or projection; **5** point of view ‖ *vi & vi* **6** to turn at an angle

an·gle² [OE *angel* fishhook] *vi* **1** to fish with hook and line; **2** to use artifice in accomplishing a purpose ‖ **an'gler** *n*

An·gle [< LL *Anglus* < Gmc] *n* member of a Germanic tribe which invaded Britain together with the Saxons and Jutes in the fifth century

an'gle i'ron *n* L-shaped piece of iron used to reinforce corners

an'gle·worm' *n* earthworm

An·gli·an /aŋ'glē·ən/ [< *Angle*] *n* **1** Angle; **2** one of the Old English dialects of central and N England ‖ also *adj*

An·gli·can /aŋ'glikən/ [LL *anglicanus* English] *n* member of the Church of England or of a church in communion with it ‖ also *adj*

An'gli·can Church' *n* Church of England

An'gli·cism /-siz'əm/ [< LL *Anglus* Englishman] *n* 1 English word, phrase, or idiom occurring in another language; 2 English trait, principle, or usage ‖ **An'gli·cize'** *vt*

An'glo- /-glō/ *comb form* England, English

An'glo·ma'ni·a *n* excessive respect for and imitation of that which is English

An'glo·phile' /-fīl'/ *n* one who admires the English

An'glo·pho'bi·a *n* intense dislike or fear of England ‖ **An'glo·phobe'** /-fōb'/ *n*

An'glo-Sax'on *n* 1 Englishman of the period from the fifth to the eleventh centuries; 2 Old English; 3 person of English descent ‖ also *adj*

An·go·la /aŋgōl'ə/ *n* republic in SW Africa (5,950,000; 481,350 sq.m.; cap. Luanda)

An·go·ra /aŋgôr'ə, -gōr'-/ [Gk *Ankyra* Ankara] *n* 1 cat prized for its long silky fur; 2 goat with long silky hair; 3 mohair

an·gry /aŋ'grē/ [<*anger*] *adj* (**-gri·er**; **-gri·est**) 1 feeling or exhibiting anger; 2 threatening; 3 red, inflamed (sore) ‖ **an'gri·ly** *adv*

an'gry young' man' *n* 1 British writer of the 1950's whose works express rebellion against the established political and social system; 2 person who is unhappy with his surroundings and the world in which he lives

ang'strom u'nit /aŋ'strəm/ [A. J. *Ångström* Sw physicist (1814–74)] *n* unit of wavelength equal to one ten millionth of a millimeter

an·guish /aŋ'gwish/ [OF *anguisse* < L *angustia* narrowness] *n* 1 intense mental or physical suffering ‖ *vt* 2 to cause to suffer anguish ‖ **an'guished** *adj* ‖ SYN *n* pain, misery, agony, torture (see *distress*)

an·gu·lar /aŋ'gyəlär/ [< L *angulus* angle] *adj* 1 having an angle or angles; 2 sharp-cornered; 3 pointed or full of points; 4 bony; 5 awkward; 6 measured by an angle, as *angular distance* ‖ **an'gu·lar'i·ty** /-lär'/ *n*

an·hy·dride /anhī'drīd/ [*an-*² + Gk *hydro* water] *n* compound formed by removing the water from another compound ‖ **an·hy'drous** *adj*

an·i·line /an'ilin, -līn'/ [< Ar *an-nīl* the indigo plant] *n* colorless oily liquid —C₆H₅NH₂— obtained from nitrobenzene and used in the synthesis of dyes

an·i·mad·ver·sion /an'imədvur'zhən/ *n* 1 censure, blame; 2 criticizing remark ‖ SYN reproach, reflection, aspersion (see *criticism*)

an'i·mad·vert' /-vurt'/ [< L *animus* mind + *ad-* + *vertere* to turn] *vi* to pass unfavorable comment; criticize

an·i·mal /an'iməl/ [L = living being] *n* 1 any living being that has feeling and the power of voluntary motion; 2 any one of the lower animals as distinguished from man; 3 mammal, as distinguished from a bird, insect, or fish; 4 brutish person ‖ *adj* 5 pert. to a living being rather than to a plant; 6 pert. to the physiological attributes of man held in common with the lower animals; 7 pert. to that part of man which is appealed to through the senses; carnal ‖ **an'i·mal'i·ty** /-mal'-/ *n* ‖ SYN *n* brute, beast ‖ DISCR *Animal* is applied to all living, moving, feeling beings; *brute* is applied to animals without the power of speech or reason, and limited in intelligence as compared to man; *beast* is applied to the larger quadrupeds, especially distinguishing them from reptiles, birds, etc. Applied to man, these are all terms of reproach, *animal* being associated in general with the lower nature, *brute* with cruelty, passion, or dulled perceptions, and *beast* with sensuality or filth

an'i·mal'cule /-mal'kyōōl/ [NL *animalculum* dim. of *animal*] *n* any minute or microscopic, usu. free-swimming form of life

an·i·mate /an'imāt'/ [L *animare* (-*atus*) to fill with breath] *vt* 1 to impart life to; 2 to inspire with energy, rouse ‖ /-mit/ *adj* 3 endowed with natural life; 4 moving; living; 5 full of vigor ‖ **an'i·mat'ed** *adj* ‖ **an'i·ma'tion** *n* ‖ SYN *v* exhilarate, invigorate, incite, stir, stimulate ‖ ANT *v* depress, dispirit, deaden, dull, enervate

an'i·mism [< L *anima* soul] *n* the belief that all natural objects, as trees and stones, possess an inherent spiritual being or soul ‖ **an'i·mist** *n* ‖ **an'i·mis'tic** *adj*

an·i·mos·i·ty /an'imos'itē/ [MF *animosite* < L *animositas* spirit, vehemence] *n* hostility, hatred, enmity

an·i·mus /an'iməs/ [L = mind, soul] *n* 1 moving spirit, purpose, or impulse; 2 hostile intention; malicious purpose

an·i·on /an'ī'ən/ [Gk = going up] *n* negative ion: atom that has gained one or more electrons and moves to the anode

an·ise /an'is/ [OF *anis* < L *anisum*] *n* 1 plant of the parsley family (*Pimpinella anisum*), native in the E Mediterranean region, yielding aniseed; 2 aniseed

an·i·seed /an'isēd'/ *n* aromatic seed of the anise plant

an·i·sette /an'iset', -zet'/ [F] *n* liqueur flavored with aniseed

An·ka·ra /aŋk'ərə/ *n* capital of Turkey (902,216)

an·kle /aŋk'əl/ [OE *anclēow*] *n* 1 joint connecting the foot with the leg; 2 leg between the foot and the calf

an·klet /aŋk'lit/ *n* 1 ornament worn around the ankle; 2 short sock

an·nals /an'əlz/ [< L *annales* (*libri*) yearly books] *npl* 1 record of events in the order of their happening, issued from year to year; 2 historical chronicles or records; 3 periodical recording the proceedings of an organization ‖ **an'nal·ist** *n* ‖ SYN record, register, chronicle (see *history*)

An·nap·o·lis /ənap'əlis/ *n* capital of Maryland (24,000), seat of the U. S. Naval Academy

an·neal /ənēl'/ [OE *anælan* to burn] *vt* 1 to heat so as to set colors in, as glass or earthenware; 2 to treat by heating and slow cooling, so as to make less brittle; 3 to temper, toughen

an·nex /əneks'/ [L *annexus* connection] *vt* 1 to add or attach, as a smaller or less important thing to a greater; 2 to take possession of; 3 to attach as a consequence, condition, or attribute ‖ /an'eks/ *n* 4 something annexed, as **a** an auxiliary building or **b** a section added to a document ‖ **an'nex·a'tion** /an'eks-/ *n*

an·ni·hi·late /ənī'əlāt'/ [L *annihilare* (*-atus*)] *vt* 1 to wipe out of existence; 2 to destroy utterly ‖ **an·ni'hi·la'tion** *n*

an·ni·ver·sa·ry /an'ivur'sərē/ [< L *annus* year + *vertere* (*versus*) to turn] *n* (*-ries*) 1 yearly return of the date of an event; 2 commemoration of such event

an·no Do·mi·ni /an'ō dom'inī'/ [L = in the year of the Lord] *adv* A.D.

an·no·tate /an'ōtāt'/ [L *annotare* (*-atus*) to write down] *vt* to provide with explanatory or critical notes ‖ **an'no·ta'tion** *n* ‖ **an'no·ta'tor** *n*

an·nounce /ənouns'/ [MF *anoncer* < L *annuntiare*] *vt* 1 to proclaim or make known publicly; 2 to make known the presence or arrival of; 3 to serve as an announcer of ‖ *vi* 4 to act as an announcer ‖ **an·nounce'·ment** *n* ‖ SYN proclaim, herald, reveal, publish (see *declare*)

an·nounc·er *n* 1 one who announces; 2 *rad & telv* person who announces the programs, reads advertisements, and identifies the station

an·noy /ənoi'/ [OF *enuier* to vex] *vt* to vex or bother, as by repeated irritating acts ‖ **an·noy'ing** *adj* ‖ SYN harass, vex, displease, exasperate, provoke, irritate ‖ DISCR To *harass* is to weary by persistent demands,

requests, etc.; to *annoy* is to disturb or trouble to the point of irritation; to *vex* is to irritate and displease to the point of offense. We are *harassed* by persistent reminders, *annoyed* by troublesome attentions, and *vexed* by the intentional slight of an acquaintance (see *irritate*) ‖ ANT ease, soothe, please, entertain

an·noy·ance *n* 1 act or instance of annoying; 2 one who or that which annoys ‖ SYN irritation, vexation, nuisance, trouble

an·nu·al /an'yōō·əl/ [< L *annus* year] *adj* 1 of or pert. to a year, yearly; 2 occurring or returning every year; 3 done, computed, or reckoned by the year; 4 *bot* lasting only a year or season ‖ *n* 5 publication appearing once a year; 6 plant living only one year or one season

an·nu·i·ty /ən(y)ōō'it̬ē/ [MF *annuite* < L *annuus* yearly] *n* (*-ties*) 1 sum of money payable yearly or at other regular intervals; 2 investment which produces a fixed yearly income

an·nul /ənul'/ [L *annulare* to bring to nothing] *v* (*-nulled; -nul·ling*) *vt* to make void, abolish, as a law, decree, or compact ‖ **an·nul'ment** *n* ‖ SYN nullify, revoke, expunge, invalidate (see *cancel*)

an·nu·lar /an'yələr/ [< L *anulus* ring] *adj* ring-shaped

an·nun·ci·a·tion /ənun'sē·āsh'ən, -shē-/ *n* 1 act of announcing; 2 **the Annunciation**, **a** the announcement by the angel Gabriel to Mary of the forthcoming birth of Jesus (Luke 1:28–38); **b** church festival commemorating this event

an·nun·ci·a·tor *n* electrical signaling apparatus for indicating on a panel the source of calls

an·ode /an'ōd/ [Gk *anodos* way up] *n* electrode that gains electrons through a vacuum or gas and loses them through the external circuit of a vacuum tube or of a primary or secondary cell, and attracts anions through an electrolyte. Internally it is conventionally called a positive electrode and externally a negative electrode or terminal

an'ode ray' *n* beam of positively charged particles emanating from a metallic anode in a discharge tube

an'o·dize' /-ə-/ *vt* to coat (a metal, esp. aluminum or magnesium) with a decorative or protective surface by making it the anode in an electrolytic solution

an·o·dyne /an'ədīn'/ [*an-²* + Gk *odyne* pain] *n* something that relieves pain ‖ *also adj*

a·noint /ənoint'/ [MF *enoint* anointed] *vt* 1 to pour oil or other liquid upon; 2 to consecrate by applying oil

a·nom·a·ly /ənom'əlē/ [< Gk *anomalos* irregular] *n* (*-lies*) 1 deviation from the natural order; **2** anything that is abnormal or irregular ‖ **a·nom′a·lous** adj

an·o·mie /an′əmē′/ [Gk *anomia* lawlessness] n **1** loss of social values, esp. among uprooted people; **2** disorientation and social isolation of an individual

a·non /ənon′/ [< OE *on ān* in one] adv *archaic* **1** right away; **2** soon; **3** at another time; **4 ever and anon** now and then

anon. anonymous

a·non·y·mous /ənon′iməs/ [< Gk *anonymos* nameless] adj **1** having no name; **2** without the author's name; **3** of unknown authorship ‖ **a·non′y·mous·ly** adv ‖ **an·o·nym·i·ty** /an′ənim′itē/ n

a·noph·e·les /ənof′ilēz′/ [Gk = useless, harmful] n mosquito of the genus *Anopheles*, certain species of which transmit malaria

an·oth·er /ənuth′ər/ [OE *ān* one + *ōther* other, second] pron **1** one more; **2** a different one; **3 one another** each other ‖ adj **4** an additional; **5** a different

an·swer /an′sər, än′-/ [OE *andswaru*] n **1** response to a summons, call, question, or argument; **2** solution, correct result ‖ vt **3** to reply to; **4** to correspond to; **5** to be sufficient for; **6** to solve ‖ vi **7** to reply; **8** to serve the purpose; **9** to be accountable

an′swer·a·ble adj **1** admitting of a reply; **2** accountable ‖ SYN accountable, liable (see *responsible*)

an′swer·ing serv′ice n agency whose business it is to answer telephone calls for its customers

ant /ant/ [OE *æmette*] n any of certain small insects constituting the family Formicidae and living in colonies, famed for their industry and complex social organization

ant- var of antero-

-ant /-ənt/ [< L -*ans* (-*antis*)] adj suf **1** equivalent of English -*ing*, as *regnant* (reigning), *defiant* (defying) ‖ n suf **2** doer, as *defendant, claimant*

ant·ac·id /ant·as′id/ n remedy that counteracts acidity ‖ also adj

An·tae·us /antē′əs/ n Gk myth. giant, unconquerable while touching the earth; conquered by Hercules, who lifted him into the air

an·tag·o·nism /antag′əniz′əm/ [< *anti-* + Gk *agon* conflict] n **1** active opposition of two opponents or opposing forces; **2** hostility, antipathy; **3** opposing force or principle ‖ **an·tag′·o·nist** n ‖ **an·tag′o·nis′tic** adj

an·tag′o·nize′ vt **1** to oppose; contend against; **2** to render hostile, provoke

ant·arc·tic /antär(k)′tik/ adj **1** relating to the region S of the Antarctic Circle and the South Pole ‖ n **2 the Antarctic** this region

Ant·arc′ti·ca n the continent surrounding the South Pole

Ant·arc′tic Cir′cle n parallel at 66°33′ south, separating the Antarctic Zone from the South Temperate Zone

Ant·arc′tic O′cean n ocean surrounding Antarctica

Ant·arc′tic Zone′ n region of the earth south of the Antarctic Circle

An·tar·es /anter′ēz/ [Gk = like Mars] n red star of the first magnitude, the brightest in the constellation Scorpio

an·te /ant′ē/ [< *ante-*] n **1** *poker* initial stake put up by each player; **2** any money put up in advance ‖ vi **ante up 3** to pay the ante in poker; **4** to pay one's share

ante- /ant′ē-, ant′ē-/ [L] pref before in time, place, or position, as *antedate, anteroom*

ant′eat′er n any of various mammals (order Edentata) that feed on ants

an′te·bel′lum /-bel′əm/ [L] adj before the war; spec., before the American Civil War

an′te·ced′ent /-sēd′ənt/ [< *ante-* + L *cedere* to go] adj **1** preceding, prior ‖ n **2** preceding event; **3** *gram* word to which a relative or other pronoun refers; **4** *math* **a** first term of a ratio; **b** first and third terms of a proportion; **5 antecedents** pl **a** ancestors; **b** previous events which affect a person's life ‖ **an′te·ced′·ence** n

an′te·cham′ber n room leading to another room and serving as a waiting room

an′te·date′ vt **1** to give an earlier date to; **2** to occur at an earlier time than

an′te·di·lu′vi·an /-dilōōv′ē-ən/ [< *ante-* + L *diluvium* deluge] adj **1** of or relating to the time before the Flood (Gen. 7,8); **2** antiquated, obsolete ‖ n **3** person who lived before the Flood; **4** old or old-fashioned person

an·te·lope /ant′əlōp′/ [LL *antalopus* < Gk *antholops* a legendary beast] n (-lope or -lopes) any of a large variety of mammals included in several subfamilies of the ox family (Bovidae), some deerlike and others oxlike in form

an·te·me·rid·i·an /ant′ēmərid′ē-ən/ [L] adj **1** of or pert. to the morning; **2** occurring before noon

an′te me·rid′i·em /-ē-əm/ [L] adj A.M., in the period between 12 midnight and noon

an·ten·na /antèn′ə/ [L = sailyard] n **1** wire or wires supported in the air to detect or transmit electromagnetic waves; **2** (-nae /-nē/) one of the hairlike or otherwise shaped feelers on the heads of insects and crustaceans

an′te·pe′nult n third syllable from the end in a word

an·te·ri·or /antir′ē-ər/ [L, *comp* of *ante*] adj **1** situated before or in front; **2** preceding, earlier in time

an·te·room /'/ *n* **1** room leading to another; **2** waiting room

an·them /anth′əm/ [OE *antefen* < L *antifona* antiphon] *n* **1** composition with parts sung alternately or responsively; **2** composition generally set to words from the Bible and used in church services; **3** song of praise or triumph

an·ther /anth′ər/ [Gk *antheros* blooming] *n* pollen-producing organ of a flower

an·thol·o·gy /anthol′əjē/ [<Gk *anthos* flower] *n* (-gies) collection of choice literary extracts either from one author or from several || **an·thol′o·gist** *n*

an·thra·cite /anth′rəsīt′/ [Gk *anthrakites* coal-like] *n* a hard coal, burning without smoke and giving intense heat

an·thrax /an′thraks/ [Gk = coal, carbuncle] *n* (-thra·ces /-thrəsēz′/) infectious disease of animals, transmissible to man, caused by *Bacillus anthracis*

anthrop- or **anthropo-** [Gk *anthropos*] *comb form* man, human, as *anthropology*

an·thro·poid /anth′rəpoid′/ *adj* **1** manlike (applied esp. to the large apes which most nearly resemble man) || *n* **2** anthropoid ape

an·thro·pol′o·gy /-pol′əjē/ *n* study of man as regards his origin, nature, races, customs, development, etc. || **an′thro·po·log′i·cal** /-pəloj′-/ *adj* || **an′thro·pol′o·gist** *n*

an′thro·po·mor′phic /-pəmôrf′ik/ *adj* pert. to the attribution of human form to God or of human characteristics to nonhuman things || **an′·thro·po·mor′phism** *n*

an·ti /ant′ī, ant′ē/ [< *anti-*] *n* one who is opposed

an·ti- [Gk *anti* against] *pref* **1** opposed to, as *antislavery;* **2** preventive of, as *antifreeze*

an·ti·bi·ot·ic /ant′ibī·ot′ik/ [< *anti-* + Gk *bios* life] *n* chemical substance produced by living microorganisms, used in the treatment of bacterial and other microorganic infections || also *adj*

an′ti·bod′y *n* (-ies) protein naturally existing in the blood or produced in response to an antigen, which counteracts the effect of an antigen

an·tic /ant′ik/ [< L *antiquus* ancient] *n* often **antics** *pl* grotesque caper; funny trick or action

an′ti·cath′ode *n* target plate, placed opposite the cathode in X-ray tubes, which gives forth X rays

An′ti·christ′ *n* **1** opponent of Christ; **2** great personal opponent, expected by many to be finally overthrown by Christ at his second coming (1 John 2:18, 22)

an·tic·i·pate /antis′ipāt′/ [< *ante-* + L *capere* to take] *vt* **1** to look forward to; **2** to be before (another) in doing something; **3** to foresee and carry out (as a command) beforehand; **4** to do, consider, or deal with before another or before the proper time; **5** to forestall || **an·tic′i·pa′tion** *n* || **an·tic′i·pa·to′ry** /-pətôr′ē, -tōr′-/ *adj* || SYN apprehend, expect, hope, foresee, forestall (see *prevent*)

an′ti·cli′max *n* **1** falling off, gradual or abrupt, in the importance or tone of ideas or statements; **2** ludicrous drop in thought and expression || **an′ti·cli·mac′tic** /-mak′-/ *adj*

an′ti·cy′clone *n* circulation of wind around a high-pressure region, clockwise in the Northern Hemisphere and counterclockwise in the Southern

an′ti·dote /-dōt′/ [*anti-* + Gk *dotos* given] *n* **1** substance that counteracts the effects of a poison; **2** that which counteracts or prevents misfortune

an′ti·freeze′ *n* substance, as alcohol, added to water in a radiator to prevent freezing

an′ti·fric′tion *adj* preventing or reducing friction

an′ti·gen /-jən/ [*anti*body + *-gen*] *n* any substance produced by the body or injected into it which stimulates the production of antibodies

an′ti·his′ta·mine *n* cold and allergy remedy that neutralizes the effects of histamine in the body

an′ti·knock′ *n* substance added to the fuel of internal-combustion engines to prevent knocking || also *adj*

An·til·les /antil′ēz/ *npl* the West Indies, not including the Bahama Islands

an′ti·ma·cas′sar /-məkas′ər/ [< *macassar* oil that was used as a hair dressing] *n* covering to protect the backs and arms of chairs and sofas from wear and soiling

an′ti·mat′ter *n* matter composed of the counterparts of ordinary matter, with electrical charges reversed

an′ti·mis′sile *adj* (missile) designed to intercept guided missiles of an enemy

an·ti·mo·ny /ant′imōn′ē/ [LL *antimonium*] *n* **1** white lustrous brittle crystalline metallic element (**Sb**; at.no. 51; at.wt. 121.75), used in various alloys and medicines; **2** stibnite

an′ti·ox′i·dant *n* **1** substance that prevents oxidation; **2** substance used as a preservative by inhibiting deterioration of soaps, oils, food products, rubber, and gasoline; **3** compound which hinders harmful chemical reactions in the body's individual cells

an·ti·pas·to /an′tipäs′tō/ [It] *n* assortment of appetizers, as olives, anchovies, etc.

an·tip·a·thy /antip′əthē/ *n* (-thies) **1**

strong aversion or dislike; **2** that which arouses aversion || **an'ti·pa·thet'ic** /-tipəthet'ik/ *adj* || **SYN** aversion, dislike, hatred, repugnance, disgust, malevolence || **DISCR** These terms express a turning away in feeling: they are opposed to sympathy and attraction. *Antipathy* is instinctive and irrational, and deeply ingrained, as there existed a deep *antipathy* between the brothers. *Aversion* is often constitutional, as some people are born with an *aversion* to snakes; but it is sometimes explainable, as deaf people have an *aversion* to crowds. *Dislike* is opposed to congeniality or attachment, and is milder than *hatred; dislike* is apt to be passive, but *hatred* is so intense that it is inclined to injure. *Repugnance* is antagonism with distaste as its chief element; *repugnance* carried a step further is *disgust*. *Malevolence* is *hatred* fired by the definite intent to injure || **ANT** affinity, attachment

an'ti·per'son·nel' *adj* (ammunition) to be used against enemy personnel

an'ti·phon' /-fon'/ *n* **1** psalm, hymn, or prayer, responsively chanted or sung; **2** musical composition for church use, made up of responsive singing or chanting || **an·tiph'o·nal** /-fənəl/ *adj*

an·tip·o·des /antip'ədēz'/ [*anti-* + Gk *podes* feet] *npl* **1** places on the earth's surface diametrically opposite to each other; **2** people living in these places || **an·tip'o·dal** /-dəl/ *adj*

an·ti·quar·i·an /ant'ikwer'ē·ən/ *adj* **1** relating to the study of antiquities || *n* **2** antiquary || **an'ti·quar'i·an·ism** *n*

an'ti·quar'y [L *antiquarius* pert. to antiquity] *n* (-ies) one who collects, studies, or deals in ancient objects

an'ti·quate' /-kwāt'/ [L *antiquare* (-*atus*) to restore to ancient condition] *vt* **1** to make old or obsolete; **2** to render antique || **an'ti·quat'ed** *adj*

an·tique /antēk'/ [MF < L *antiquus* ancient] *adj* **1** of or pert. to a former age; ancient || *n* **2** object of art, piece of furniture, or the like, of a former age or period, highly valued for its beauty, craftsmanship, or rarity || *vt* **3** to make (something) look antique

an·tiq·ui·ty /antik'witē/ *n* (-ties) **1** great age, ancientness; **2** ancient times, the early ages; **3** relic of ancient times

an'ti-Sem'ite *n* one who is opposed to the Jews || **an'ti-Sem'i·tism** /-sem'itiz'əm/ *n* || **an'ti-Se·mit'ic** /-sə-/ *adj*

an'ti·sep'tic *adj* **1** preventing the growth of disease germs || *n* **2** antiseptic substance || **an'ti·sep'sis** *n*

an'ti·so'cial *adj* **1** not sociable; **2** hostile or threatening to others; **3** opposed to the social order

an·tith·e·sis /antith'isis/ [< *anti-* + Gk *tithenai* to set] *n* (-ses /-sēz'/) **1** opposition; contrast; **2** direct opposite || **an'ti·thet'ic** (-i-cal) /-ithet'-/ *adj*

an'ti·tox'in *n* **1** substance formed in the tissues of a plant or animal by the action of a disease-germ poison and having the power to neutralize this poison; **2** substance taken from the blood of an infected animal and injected into the blood of a person to prevent or cure a disease by the same process of neutralization

ant·ler /ant'lər/ [MF *antoillier* < LL *antocularem* (ramum) (branch) in front of the eyes] *n* branched deciduous horn, as in the deer family

ant'li·on *n* any of a genus (*Myrmeleon*) of insects which, in the larval stage, make a pitfall, at the bottom of which they hide to capture insects, esp. ants

an·to·nym /ant'ənim/ [< *anti-* + Gk *onyma* name] *n* word which is directly opposite in meaning to another word

an·trum /ant'rəm/ [L < Gk *antron* cave] *n* (-trums; -tra /-trə/) anat natural cavity or sinus

Ant·werp /ant'wərp/ *n* seaport in N Belgium (305,000)

A·nu·bis /ən(y)ōōb'is/ *n* ancient Egyptian god with the head of a jackal, who guarded the tombs and conducted the spirits of the dead

an·u·ran /ən(y)ōōr'ən/ [< *an-²* + Gk *oura* tail] *n* any of an order (Anura) of amphibians, which contains the frogs and toads || also *adj*

a·nus /ān'əs/ [L = ring, anus] *n* posterior opening of the alimentary canal

an·vil /an'vil/ [OE anfilt(e)] *n* **1** block, generally of iron faced with steel, on which metals are hammered and shaped; **2** one of the three small bones in the middle ear

anx·i·e·ty /aŋzī'itē/ *n* (-ties) **1** mental uneasiness or distress arising from fear of what may happen; **2** eager desire for some purpose or object || **SYN** solicitude, concern, trouble (see *care*)

anx·ious /aŋk'shəs/ [L *anxius* troubled] *adj* **1** giving or accompanied by worry over an uncertainty; **2** deeply concerned or troubled; **3** solicitous; desirous || **anx'ious·ly** *adv*

an·y /en'ē/ [OE *ænig*] *adj* **1** of an indefinite number, quantity, or degree; **2** some; **3** every, as *any boy can do it* || *pron* **4** one individual, unit, or part out of a given number; anyone; anybody; anything || *adv* **5** to any extent, at all

an'y·bod'y /-bod'ē, -bud'ē/ *pron* **1** any person || *n* **2** someone of importance

an'y·how' *adv* **1** in any way whatever; **2** in any case; **3** haphazardly

an'y·one' *pron* any person, anybody

an'y one' *pron* any one of all of, one of

an·y·place′ *adv colloq* at or to any place; anywhere

an·y·thing′ *pron* 1 something or other, no matter what ‖ *n* 2 any kind of thing ‖ *adv* 3 to any extent; 4 **anything but** not in the least

an·y·way′ *adv* 1 anyhow; 2 nevertheless

an·y·where′ *adv* 1 in any place; 2 to any extent; 3 **not get anywhere** *colloq* to fail to achieve one's goal

an·y·wise′ *adv* in any way

An·zac /an′zak/ [Australia and New Zealand Army Corps] *n* soldier from Australia or New Zealand

a/o, A/O account of

A-O.K. /ā′ō′kā′/ *adj* perfect

A one, A-one, A 1, A-1 /ā′wun′/ *adj* 1 having the highest rating; 2 first-class

a·or·ta /ā-ôrt′ə/ [ML < Gk *aorte* that which is hung] *n* main artery of the body, starting from the left ventricle of the heart, which carries oxygenated blood to all parts of the body except the lungs ‖ **a·or′tic** *adj*

AP, A.P. 1 Associated Press; 2 Air Police

ap-¹ var of **ad-**

ap-² var of **apo-**

a·pace /əpās′/ [MF *a pas* at pace] *adv* quickly, rapidly

a·pache /əpash′/ [F < *Apache* (Indian)] *n* 1 Parisian gangster; 2 **A·pach·e** /əpach′ē/ [Sp] one of a tribe of American Indians inhabiting parts of Arizona, New Mexico, and Mexico

a·part /əpärt′/ [OF *a part* to the side] *adv* 1 separately in place or time; 2 aside; 3 separately in use or purpose; 4 asunder, in several parts; 5 **apart from** besides

a·part·heid /əpärt′hīt, -hāt/ [Afrik = separateness] *n* policy of strict segregation of the races as practiced in the Union of South Africa

a·part′ment *n* room or suite of rooms used as a dwelling

ap·a·thy /ap′əthē/ [< *a-*¹ + Gk *pathos* feeling] *n* (**-thies**) lack of feeling, want of passion or emotion, indifference ‖ **ap′a·thet′ic** /-thet′ik/ *adj* ‖ SYN (see *indifference*) ‖ ANT enthusiasm, desire

ape /āp/ [OE *apa*] *n* 1 monkey; 2 anthropoid ape; 3 mimic ‖ *vt* 4 to mimic, imitate

Ap·en·nines /ap′ənīnz′/ *npl* mountain range in Italy extending from north to south

a·pe·ri·tif /əper′itēf′/ [F = appetizer] *n* small alcoholic drink taken before meals

ap·er·ture /ap′ərchər/ [L *apertura*] *n* 1 opening, gap, hole, passage; 2 *optics* working diameter of a lens or mirror

a·pex /ā′peks/ [L = point] *n* (**a·pex·es** or **ap·i·ces** /ap′isēz′/) point, tip, or summit

a·pha·sia /əfāzh′ə/ [Gk = speechlessness] *n* loss or impairment of the power to use or understand words ‖ **a·pha′sic** /-zik, -sik/ *adj & n*

a·phe·li·on /əfēl′ē·ən, -yen/ [< *ap-²* + Gk *helios* sun] *n* point in the orbit of a planet or comet which is farthest from the sun

a·phid /āf′id, af′-/ [< NL *aphides* aphids] *n* plant louse (family Aphididae) parasitic on garden and house plants

aph·o·rism /af′əriz′əm/ [Gk *aphorismos* definition] *n* concise pithy statement of a truth or percept ‖ **aph′o·ris′tic** *adj* ‖ SYN proverb, adage, saw, saying (see *truism*)

aph·ro·dis·i·ac /af′rədiz′ē·ak′/ [< Gk *aphrodisios* of Aphrodite] *adj* 1 arousing sexual desire ‖ *n* 2 aphrodisiac substance or drug

Aph′ro·di′te /-dīt′ē/ *n* Gk *myth.* goddess of love and beauty; identified with the Roman Venus

a·pi·ar·y /āp′ē·er′ē/ [< L *apis* bee] *n* (**-ies**) place where bees are kept; group of beehives

ap·i·cal /ap′ikəl/ [< *apex* (*apicis*)] *adj* 1 at or pert. to an apex; 2 (sound) articulated with the tip of the tongue ‖ also *n*

a·piece′ /ə-/ *adv* to or for each person or thing

ap′ish /āp′ish/ *adj* 1 like an ape; 2 silly, affected; 3 imitative

a·plomb /əplom′/ [F = perpendicularly] *n* self-possession, assurance

apo- or **ap-** or **aph-** [Gk *apo* from] *pref* generally meaning from, off, away, as *apocope*

APO, A.P.O. Army Post Office

a·poc·a·lypse /əpok′əlips′/ [Gk *apokalypsis* uncovering] *n* 1 revelation, disclosure; 2 **Apocalypse** last book of the New Testament, the Revelation of St. John the Divine ‖ **a·poc′a·lyp′tic** *adj*

a·poc·o·pe /əpok′əpē/ [*apo-* + Gk *koptein* to cut] *n* omission of the last letter or syllable of a word

a·poc·ry·pha /əpok′rifə/ [*apo-* + Gk *kryptein* to hide] *n* 1 writings of doubtful authorship; 2 in the early church, writings uncertain as to origin and authority; 3 **Apocrypha** certain writings included as parts of the Old Testament in the Septuagint and in the Vulgate

a·poc′ry·phal *adj* 1 of doubtful authorship or authenticity; uncanonical; 2 false; invented; 3 **Apocryphal** of or pert. to the Apocrypha

a·pod·o·sis /əpod′əsis/ [Gk = giving back] *n* (**-ses** /-sēz′/) conclusion in a conditional sentence

ap·o·gee /ap′əjē′/ [*apo-* + Gk *ge* earth] *n* 1 point in the orbit of the moon or a satellite circling the earth which is most distant from the earth; 2 highest or most distant point; 3 climax, culmination

A·pol·lo /əpol′ō/ *n* 1 *class. myth.* one of the greatest and most typical of Greek and Roman divinities, god of the sun, music, poetry, eloquence, medicine, and the fine arts; 2 handsome young man; 3 one of a numbered series of manned spacecraft designed to travel to the moon and orbit around it while a lunar module is detached from it to land on the moon

a·pol·o·get·ic /əpol′əjet′ik/ *adj* 1 defending by words or argument; 2 making excuse or acknowledgment ‖ *n* 2 **apologetics** *sg* branch of theology that deals with the defense and proof of Christian doctrine ‖ **a·pol′o·get′i·cal·ly** *adv*

a·pol′o·gist *n* one who defends a person or cause by argument

a·pol′o·gize′ *vi* 1 to express regret; 2 to make an excuse

a·pol′o·gy [Gk *apologia* speech in defense] *n* (**-gies**) 1 something offered in defense or explanation; 2 expression of regret for an action; 3 poor makeshift ‖ SYN (see *excuse*) ‖ ANT censure, accusation

ap·o·plex·y /ap′əplek′sē/ [Gk *apoplexia*] *n* sudden loss of bodily function resulting from a broken or obstructed blood vessel in the brain ‖ **ap′o·plec′tic** *adj & n*

a·pos·ta·sy /əpos′təsē/ [< *apo-* + Gk *stasis* standing] *n* (**-sies**) abandonment of what one has professed or believed, as faith, principles, or party ‖ **a·pos′tate** /-tāt, -tit/ *adj & n* ‖ **a·pos′ta·tize′** *vi*

a pos·te·ri·o·ri /ä′postir′ē-ôr′ī/ [L = from the latter] *adj & adv* from effect to cause; based on actual observation

a·pos·tle /əpos′əl/ [OE *apostol* < Gk *apostolos* messenger] *n* 1 one of the twelve persons selected by Christ to teach his gospel (Luke 6:13); 2 first missionary who plants the Christian faith in any region; 3 pioneer of any great moral reform

ap·os·tol·ic /ap′əstol′ik/ *adj* 1 pert. to the twelve apostles of Christ; 2 handed down in due succession from the apostles; 3 papal

a·pos·tro·phe /əpos′trəfē/ [Gk = turning away] *n* 1 breaking off in a speech to address directly a person or persons who may or may not be present; 2 the sign ′ used to denote the omission of one or more letters from a word, the possessive case of nouns, or the plural of abbreviations and symbols, as *A.B.'s*, *x's*.

a·poth′e·car·ies′ meas′ure *n* system of liquid units of capacity used in pharmacy

a·poth′e·car·ies′ weight′ *n* system of units of weight used in pharmacy, based on the pound of 12 ounces

a·poth·e·car·y /əpoth′iker′ē/ [< ML *apotheca* shop, storehouse] *n* (**-ies**) pharmacist

ap·o·thegm /ap′əthem′/ [Gk *apophthegma*] *n* short, pithy, instructive saying

ap·o·the·o·sis /ap′əthē′əsis, əpoth′ē·ōs′is/ [< *apo-* + Gk *theos* god] *n* (**-ses** /-sēz′, -sēz/) 1 deification; 2 glorification, exaltation

Ap′pa·la′chi·an Moun′tains /ap′əlāch′(ē)ən, -lach′-/ also **Appalachians** *npl* mountain range in E North America extending from Quebec to Alabama

ap·pall or **ap·pal** /əpôl′/ [MF *apalir* to grow pale] *v* (**ap·palled; ap·pall·ing**) *vt* to frighten, depress, or discourage by fear; dismay ‖ **ap·pall′ing** *adj*

ap·pa·ra·tus /ap′ərat′əs, -rāt′-/ [L = equipment] *n* (**-tus; -tus·es**) 1 set of organized materials or equipment necessary for the accomplishment of any work; 2 any complex machinery or system designed for a particular function; 3 device or machine designed for a particular function; 4 *physiol* set of organs that have a specific function

ap·par·el /əpar′əl/ [OF *apareillier* to dress] *n* 1 dress, garb ‖ *v* (**-eled** or **-elled; -el·ing** or **-el·ling**) *vt* 2 to clothe, furnish, or fit out; equip

ap·par·ent /əpar′ənt, -per′-/ [L *apparens* (*-entis*) appearing] *adj* 1 visible; 2 obvious; 3 seeming ‖ **ap·par′ent·ly** *adv* ‖ SYN evident, obvious, manifest, clear, patent

ap·pa·ri·tion /ap′ərish′ən/ [LL *apparitio* (*-onis*) appearance] *n* 1 act of appearing; 2 appearance of something startling; 3 ghost, phantom

ap·peal /əpēl′/ [MF *apeler* < L *appellare* to address] *vt* 1 to refer (a case) to a higher court ‖ *vi* 2 to invoke aid, sympathy, or mercy; 3 to excite the interest; 4 to refer to a higher authority; 5 to refer to a higher court for decision ‖ *n* 6 call for aid or sympathy; 7 reference to another person or higher authority; 8 interest, attraction; 9 transfer of a case to a higher court ‖ **ap·peal′ing** *adj*

ap·pear /əpir′/ [OF *apareir* < L *apparere*] *vi* 1 to come in sight; become visible; 2 to seem; 3 to come before the public; 4 to come into court ‖ **ap·pear′ance** *n*

ap·pease /əpēz′/ [OF *apaisier* < a·⁵ + *pais* peace] *vt* to satisfy; pacify; placate ‖ **ap·pease′ment** *n*

ap·pel·lant /əpel′ənt/ [< L *appellare* to address] *n* one who appeals, esp. to a higher court

ap·pel·late /əpel′it/ *adj law* relating to or dealing with appeals, as a court

ap·pel·la·tion /ap′əlāsh′ən/ *n* 1 act of naming; 2 name, title, or designation ‖ SYN title, epithet, denomination, (see *name*)

ap·pend /əpend′/ [< L *appendere* to weigh] *vt* 1 to attach or hang; 2 to add as a supplement ‖ SYN attach, annex, affix, adjoin, add

ap·pend′age /-ij/ *n* something appended or attached, as an arm; 2 *biol* subordinate member, as a limb or antenna ‖ SYN accessory, adjunct, addition, attachment

ap·pen·dec·to·my /ap′əndek′təmē/ *n* (-mies) surgical removal of the vermiform appendix

ap·pen·di·ci·tis /əpen′disī′tis/ *n* inflammation of the vermiform appendix

ap·pen·dix /əpen′diks/ [L = appendage] *n* (-dix·es; -di·ces /-disēz′/) 1 supplementary material added at the end of a book; 2 vermiform appendix

ap·per·cep·tion /ap′ərsep′shən/ [*ad*— + L *percipere* (-*ceptus*) perceive] *n* 1 conscious perception; 2 conscious integration of new experience with background knowledge ‖ **ap′per·cep′tive** *adj*

ap·per·tain /ap′ərtān′/ [OF *apartenir*] *vi* 1 to belong by right, nature, or custom; 2 to pertain

ap·pe·tite /ap′ətīt′/ [OF *apetit* < L *appetere* (-*itus*) to desire] *n* 1 desire to satisfy a want or inclination; 2 desire for food or drink ‖ SYN craving, longing, passion (see *desire*)

ap′pe·tiz′er *n* 1 something that excites desire for anything; 2 bit of food or drink before a meal

Ap′pi·an Way′ /ap′ē·ən/ *n* ancient paved road running from Rome south to Brindisi, begun about 312 B.C.

ap·plaud /əplôd′/ [L *applaudere*] *vt* 1 to express approval of, esp. by clapping the hands; 2 to commend ‖ *vi* 3 to express applause or approval ‖ SYN extol, magnify, praise, acclaim, cheer, eulogize

ap·plause /əplôz′/ *n* public expression of approval, as by clapping

ap·ple /ap′əl/ [OE *æppel*] *n* 1 round fleshy edible fruit of any of a genus (*Malus*) of trees of the rose family; 2 the tree itself

ap′ple·jack′ *n* apple brandy

ap′ple of one's eye′ *n* anything especially loved or cherished

ap′ple pol′ish·er *n colloq* obsequious flatterer

ap′ple sauce′ *n* 1 apples sweetened and cooked to a pulp; 2 *slang* nonsense

ap·pli·ance /əplī′əns/ [see **apply**] *n* 1 act of applying; 2 device or apparatus, esp. electrical, for use in the home

ap·pli·ca·ble /ap′likəbəl/ *adj* 1 capable of being applied; 2 relevant, appropriate ‖ **ap′pli·ca·bil′i·ty** /-bil′-/ *n*

ap′pli·cant *n* one who applies; candidate

ap′pli·ca′tion *n* 1 act of applying or thing applied; 2 adaptation of a thing to a purpose; 3 practical dem-

onstration of a principle; 4 act of requesting; 5 request; 6 close attention; 7 persistent effort; 8 connection, relevancy

ap′pli·ca′tor /-tər/ *n* device for applying a substance, as glue

ap·plied /əplīd′/ *adj* made to serve; employed or used, as *applied mechanics*

ap·pli·qué /ap′likā′/ [F = applied] *adj* 1 laid on ‖ *n* 2 ornamentation, as for cloth, cut from one material and applied on another

ap·ply /əplī′/ [MF *aplier* < L *applicare*] *v* (-plied) *vt* 1 to bring into contact with something, put on; 2 to put into practice; 3 to devote to a particular purpose; 4 to activate, as *to apply the brakes* ‖ *vi* 5 to ask; 6 to be relevant

ap·point /əpoint′/ [MF *apointer* < *ad*- + L *punctum* point] *vt* 1 to assign; prescribe; establish by decree; 2 to fix, as the time or place for a meeting; 3 to name for an office or position; 4 to furnish or equip

ap·point′ive *adj* 1 (office) filled by appointment; 2 having the right to appoint

ap·point′ment *n* 1 act of appointing to an office or position; 2 position or office assigned; 3 engagement to meet someone; 4 **appointments** furniture or equipment

Ap·po·mat·tox /ap′əmat′əks/ *n* town in central Virginia, site of Lee's surrender to Grant (April 9, 1865)

ap·por·tion /əpôr′shən, -pōr′-/ [MF *apportionner*] *vt* to distribute or divide proportionately ‖ **ap·por′tion·ment** *n* ‖ SYN allot, assign, appoint, divide, distribute

ap·po·site /ap′əzit/ [L *appositus* placed near] *adj* appropriate, suitable; apt

ap′po·si′tion *n* 1 act of placing side by side, or state of being so placed; 2 *gram* relation between a noun or pronoun and a word or expression placed beside it, without connective, by way of explanation, as *Brown, the policeman, entered*

ap·prais·al /əpräz′əl/ *n* 1 act of appraising; 2 estimate, valuation

ap·praise′ [MF *apriser* < *ad*- + L *pretium* price] *vt* 1 to set a price upon; 2 to estimate the importance of ‖ **ap·prais′er** *n*

ap·pre·ci·a·ble /əprēsh′(ē)əbəl/ *adj* 1 capable of being valued or estimated; 2 perceptible; 3 considerable

ap·pre′ci·ate′ /-shē·āt′/ [L *appretiare* (-*atus*) to appraise] *vt* 1 to be aware of; 2 to value or esteem highly; 3 to be grateful for; 4 to raise the value of ‖ *vi* 5 to rise in value ‖ **ap·pre′ci·a·tive** /-sh(ē)ə-/ *adj*

ap·pre′ci·a′tion *n* 1 just valuation or recognition of worth; 2 sympathetic understanding; 3 rise in market value

ap·pre·hend /ap′rihend′/ [L *appre*-

hendere to lay hold of] *vt* **1** to seize, arrest; **2** to grasp the meaning of; **3** to anticipate with anxiety ‖ *vi* **4** to understand; **5** to look forward with anxiety ‖ SYN anticipate, perceive, conceive, capture, catch

ap·pre·hen·sion /-hen'shən/ *n* **1** act of seizure, arrest; **2** mental grasp; **3** sentiment, opinion; **4** anticipation of evil; anxiety ‖ SYN perception, capture, terror (see *horror*)

ap'pre·hen'sive *adj* anxious for the future; worried

ap·pren·tice /əprent'is/ [MF *aprentis* < *aprendre* to learn] *n* **1** person learning a trade by working under a skilled craftsman ‖ *vt* **2** to place as an apprentice ‖ **ap·pren'tice·ship'** *n*

ap·prise also **ap·prize** /əpriz'/ [F *appris pp* of *apprendre* to learn] *vt* to give notice to, inform

ap·proach /əprōch'/ [MF *aprochier* < *ad-* + L *propius* near] *vi* **1** to draw or be near ‖ *vt* **2** to come nearer to; **3** to come near to in quality, character, or condition; **4** to make overtures to ‖ *n* **5** act of approaching; **6** access; **7** method of solving a problem; **8** *golf* shot made with the intention of placing the ball on the green ‖ **ap·proach'a·ble** *adj*

ap·pro·ba·tion /ap'rəbāsh'ən/ [< L *approbare* (*-atus*) to approve] *n* approval, commendation

ap·pro·pri·ate /əprōp'rē̇·āt'/ [< *ad-* + L *proprius* one's own] *vt* **1** to take for oneself, as by right; **2** to set apart or assign to a particular use, as by a legislative act ‖ /-it/ *adj* **3** fitting, proper ‖ **ap·pro'pri·ate·ly** *adv* ‖ **ap·pro'pri·ate·ness** *n* ‖ SYN *adj* apt, becoming, fit, proper, suitable

ap·pro'pri·a'tion *n* **1** act of appropriating; **2** that which is appropriated, esp. grant of money by the government for a specific purpose

ap·prov·al /əprōōv'əl/ *n* **1** approbation, sanction, ratification; **2 on approval** subject to the satisfaction of the customer ‖ SYN acceptance, admiration, commendation

ap·prove /əprōōv'/ [OF *aprover* < L *approbare*] *vt* **1** to ratify, sanction formally; **2** to be pleased or satisfied with; commend ‖ *vi* **3** to express satisfaction ‖ **ap·prov'ing·ly** *adv*

ap·prox·i·mate /əprok'simāt'/ [L *approximare* (*-atus*)] *vi* **1** to come close to, be nearly the same as ‖ *vi* **2** to approach closely, be nearly equal ‖ /-mit/ *adj* **3** near in resemblance, fairly close; **4** almost equal; **5** fairly correct ‖ **ap·prox'i·ma'tion** *n*

ap·pur·te·nance /əpurt'(ə)nəns/ [< LL *appertinere* to belong to] *n* **1** that which belongs or relates to something else as an accessory; appendage; **2** incidental right of a property ‖ **ap·pur'te·nant** *adj & n*

Apr. April

a·pri·cot /āp'rikot', ap'-/ [< Port *albricoque* < Ar *al-bir-qūq* < L *praecoquum* early-ripening] *n* **1** round orange-colored fruit of a tree (*Prunus armeniaca*) allied to the plum and the peach; **2** the tree itself

A·pril /āp'rəl/ [L *Aprilis*] *n* fourth month of the year, having 30 days

A'pril fool' *n* **1** joke played on April Fools' Day; **2** butt of such joke

A'pril Fools'' Day' *n* April 1, traditionally dedicated to practical jokes

a pri·o·ri /ā'prī-ôr'ī/ [L = from the former] *adj & adv* from cause to effect; based on theory

a·pron /āp'rən/ [< ME *a napron* an apron < MF *naperon* tablecloth] *n* **1** garment worn over the front of the body as a protection for one's clothing; **2** anything like an apron in form or use; **3** paved area in front of a hangar

ap·ro·pos /ap'rəpō'/ [F = to the purpose] *adv* **1** appropriately, to the point; **2 apropos** of regarding ‖ *adj* **3** apt, appropriate ‖ SYN *adj* (see *relevant*)

apse /aps/ [L *apsis* round arch] *n* semicircular recess at the altar end of the chancel of a church

apt /apt/ [L *aptus* fastened] *adj* **1** suitable, appropriate; **2** likely, inclined; **3** quick of comprehension ‖ **apt'ly** *adv* ‖ **apt'ness** *n* ‖ SYN likely, liable ‖ DISCR *Apt* expresses an inherent tendency, as beauty without intelligence is *apt* to be vain. *Likely* suggests probability, as a selfish child is *likely* to have few friends. *Liable* indicates exposure to disadvantageous or unpleasant contingencies, such as accident, illness, or the like, as an insufficiently nourished child is especially *liable* to contagion

ap·ti·tude /ap'tit(y)ōōd'/ *n* **1** capacity for anything; **2** suitableness; **3** readiness to learn ‖ SYN ability, endowment (see *gift*)

aq·ua /ak'wə, āk'-/ [L] *n* **1** water; **2** aquamarine color

aq'ua·lung' /ak'wə-, āk'wə-/ *n* underwater breathing apparatus with air supplied from a cylinder on the swimmer's back

aq'ua·ma·rine' *n* **1** transparent, bluish-green variety of beryl; **2** bluish green

aq'ua·plane' *n* board towed by a swiftly moving boat on which one can stand as it is pulled along

aq'ua re'gi·a /rē'jē̇·ə/ *n* mixture of nitric acid and hydrochloric acid, used to dissolve gold and platinum

a·quar·i·um /əkwer'ē̇·əm/ [L = watering place for cattle] *n* (*-ums;* -a /-ə/) **1** tank or globe in which living fish and/or water plants are kept; **2** building in which they are kept and exhibited

A·quar'i·us /-əs/ [L = water bearer]

n 1 a southern zodiacal constellation, the Water Bearer; 2 eleventh sign of the zodiac

a·quat·ic /əkwät′ik, -kwät′-/ [L < *aqua*] *adj* relating to, growing or living in, or performed in water

aq′ua vi′tae /vīt′ē̵/ *n* 1 alcohol; 2 brandy, whiskey, or the like

aq·ue·duct /ak′widukt′/ [L *aquaeductus*] *n* 1 conduit or artificial canal for bringing water from a distant source; 2 structure for carrying this above ground

a·que·ous /ā̇k′wē̵·əs, ak′-/ *adj* of the nature of water; watery

a′que·ous hu′mor *n* watery fluid that fills the space between the cornea and the lens of the eye

aqui- also **aqua-** [< L *aqua* water] *comb form* water

aq·ui·fer /ak′wəfər/ [*aqui-* + *-fer*] *n* underground water-bearing strata that supply most of our well water ‖ **a·quif·er·ous** /əkwif′ərəs/ *adj*

Aq·ui·la /ak′wīlə/ [L = eagle] *n* northern constellation, the Eagle

aq·ui·line /ak′wīlīn′, -lin/ [< L *aquila* eagle] *adj* 1 relating to or resembling an eagle; 2 curved or hooked like an eagle's beak

A·qui·nas /əkwīn′əs/, **Saint Thomas** *n* (1225–74) Italian scholastic philosopher and Catholic theologian

Ar *chem* argon

-ar¹ /ər/ [L *-aris* alter. of *-alis* after the letter *l* in the preceding syllable] *adj suf* 1 like or pert. to, as *familiar* ‖ *n suf* 2 thing like or pert. to, as *exemplar*

-ar² *n suf* var of **-er¹** doer or agent, as *beggar*

Ar. 1 Arabic; 2 Aramaic

Ar·ab /ar′əb/ [L *Arabs* < Gk *Araps* (*Arabos*)] *n* 1 member of a Semitic race peopling Arabia and N Africa; 2 homeless street urchin; 3 horse of Arabian breed ‖ also *adj*

ar′a·besque′ /-besk′/ [It *arabesco* < *arabo* Arab] *n* 1 fanciful ornament consisting of fruits, flowers, foliage, etc., oddly combined or grouped; 2 fanciful short musical composition, esp. for piano ‖ also *adj*

A·ra·bi·a /ərāb′ē̵·ə/ *n* peninsula in SW Asia between the Red Sea and the Persian Gulf, homeland of the Arabs ‖ **A·ra′bi·an** *adj & n*

A·ra′bi·an Nights′′ En·ter·tain′ments *npl* collection of folktales of the East, chiefly Arabia, Persia, and India, dating from the 10th century

A·ra′bi·an Sea′ *n* arm of the Indian Ocean between India and Arabia

Ar·a·bic /ar′əbik/ *adj* 1 Arabian ‖ *n* 2 language of the Arabs

Ar′a·bic nu′mer·als *npl* the ten digits 0, 1, 2, 3, etc., borrowed by the Arabs from the Hindus and now in general use throughout the world

ar·a·ble /ar′əbəl/ [< L *arare* to plow] *adj* fit for the plow or for agricultural cultivation

a·rach·nid /ərak′nid/ [< Gk *arachne* spider] *n* arthropod of the class Arachnida, including the spiders and scorpions

Ar·a·gon /ar′əgon′/ *n* region and former kingdom of Spain, which was united with Castile in the 15th century

Ar·a·ma·ic /ar′əmā′ik/ *n* Semitic language spoken by the Jews in Palestine after the Babylonian captivity

A·rap·a·ho or **A·rap·a·hoe** /ərap′əhō′/ [native word = tattooed people] *n* (-ho or -hos; -hoe or hoes) member of a warlike Indian tribe now confined to Oklahoma and Wyoming; 2 their language ‖ also *adj*

ar·bi·ter /är′bitər/ [L] 1 umpire, judge, or arbitrator; 2 one who controls a result or outcome

ar·bi·trage /är′biträzh′/ [F] *n fin* traffic in a security with the purpose of deriving profit from the difference in price in different markets at the same time ‖ **ar′bi·trag′er** *n*

ar·bit·ra·ment /ärbit′rəmənt/ *n* 1 arbitration; 2 final decision, as of an arbiter

ar·bi·trar·y /är′bitrer′ē̵/ *adj* 1 capricious; unreasonable; 2 imperious; despotic ‖ **ar′bi·trar′i·ly** *adv* ‖ **ar′bi·trar′i·ness** *n* ‖ SYN dictatorial, absolute, imperious, peremptory

ar′bi·trate′ *vt* 1 to settle (a dispute) by arbitration; 2 to refer (a dispute) to arbitration ‖ *vi* 3 to employ arbitration

ar′bi·tra′tion *n* settlement of a dispute by an arbitrator

ar′bi·tra′tor *n* person chosen by the parties in a dispute to settle the differences between them

ar·bor /är′bər/ [< OF *herbier* green lawn < L *herba* grass] *n* bower or leafy roof formed by trees or vines overhead

ar·bo·re·al /ärbôr′ē̵·əl, -bōr′-/ [< L *arbor* tree] *adj* of, like, pert. to, or living in trees

ar′bo·re′tum /-ərēt′əm/ *n* (-tums; -ta /-tə/) place in which trees are grown for scientific and educational purposes

ar·bu·tus /ärbyōot′əs/ [L = wild strawberry tree] *n* 1 any of a genus (*Arbutus*) of evergreen trees; 2 creeping plant (*Epigaea repens*) of the heath family, with small flowers, often called *trailing arbutus*

arc /ärk/ [L *arcus* bow] *n* 1 any section of the circumference of a circle or of a curve; 2 curved band of light formed in the gap between two electrodes, caused by the passage of an electric current; 3 anything bowshaped ‖ *v* (**arced** /ärkt′/; **arc·ing** /ärk′iŋ/) *vi* 4 to form an electric arc (said of two electrodes or two adjacent wires, or of the current with which they are charged)

ar·cade /ärkād'/ [< It *arcata*] *n* **1** row of arches supported by pillars; **2** arched and roofed gallery

ar·cane /ärkān'/ [L *arcanus*] *adj* mysterious, obscure

arch[1] /ärch'/ [OF *arche* < L *arcus* bow] *n* **1** curved structure for spanning an open space, as in a doorway, or to support a bridge; **2** anything shaped like an arch || *vt* **3** to span with an arch; **4** to bend or curve || *vi* **5** to form an arch || **arched**/ *adj*

arch[2] [< *arch-*] *adj* **1** chief, outstanding; **2** coyly mischievous, roguish || **arch'ly** *adv* || **arch'ness** *n*

arch- [OE *arce-* < Gk *arch-*] *pref* chief, as *archbishop*

-arch /-ärk', -ərk/ [Gk *-arches, -archos*] *comb form* ruler, as *monarch*

arch. **1** archaic; **2** architect(ure); **3** archipelago

ar·chae·ol·o·gy or **ar·che·ol·o·gy** /ärk'ē·ol'ə·jē/ [< Gk *archaios* ancient + *-logy*] *n* study of ancient peoples through their material remains that have been revealed by excavation || **ar'chae·o·log'i·cal** /-əloj'ikəl/ *adj* || **ar'chae·ol'o·gist** *n*

ar·cha·ic /ärkā'ik/ [< Gk *archaios* ancient] *adj* **1** ancient; **2** old-fashioned; **3** (word) no longer in common use || **ar'cha·ism** /-kē-, -kā-/ *n*

arch'an'gel /ärk'-/ *n* angel of the highest rank

arch'bish'op /ärch'-/ *n* chief bishop of a church district or province

arch'dea'con /ärch'-/ *n* church dignitary ranking next below a bishop in the administration of a diocese

arch'di'o·cese /ärch'-/ *n* diocese under the jurisdiction of an archbishop

arch'duke' /ärch'-/ *n* **1** prince of the former imperial house of Austria; **2** any of several former sovereign princes in Europe || **arch'du'cal** *adj* || **arch'duch'ess** /-duch'is/ *nfem*

arch'en'e·my /ärch'-/ *n* (**-mies**) **1** chief enemy; **2** Satan

Ar·che·o·zo·ic or **Ar·chae·o·zo·ic** /ärk'ē·əzō'ik/ [< Gk *archaios* ancient + *zoe* life] *adj* designating or pert. to the earliest geological era, beyond 1,000,000,000 years ago

arch'er /ärch'ər/ [< *arch*[1]] *n* **1** one who shoots with a bow and arrow; **2** **the Archer** the zodiacal constellation Sagittarius

arch'er·y *n* art of an archer

ar'che·type' /ärk'ē-/ [Gk *archetypon*] *n* original pattern or model; prototype

Ar·chi·me·des /ärk'imēd'ēz/ *n* (287?–212 B.C.) Greek mathematician, physicist, and inventor || **Ar'chi·me'de·an** *adj*

ar·chi·pel·a·go /ärk'ipel'əgō'/ [*arch-*

+ Gk *pelagos* sea] *n* (**-goes; -gos**) **1** sea containing numerous islands; **2** island group

ar·chi·tect /ärk'itekt'/ [*arch-* + Gk *tekton* builder] *n* **1** one who professionally designs buildings and supervises their construction; **2** deviser, maker

ar'chi·tec'ture /-chər/ *n* **1** profession of designing and constructing buildings; **2** style of building; **3** construction; workmanship || **ar'chi·tec'tur·al** *adj*

ar'chi·trave' /-trāv'/ [It < *arch-* + L *trabs* beam] *n* **1** lowest division of an entablature; **2** molding above and on both sides of an opening, as a door

ar·chive /är'kīv/ [L *archivum*] *n* **1** record preserved as evidence; **2** **archives** *pl* **a** public documents or records of historical value; **b** place where such records are kept || **ar'chi·vist** /-ivist/ *n*

arch'way' /ärch'-/ *n* opening or passage under an arch

-ar·chy /-ärk'ē, -ərkē/ [Gk *-archia*] *comb form* rule, government, as *monarchy*

arc' lamp' or **arc' light'** *n* lamp whose source of light is the electric arc between two carbon rods

arc·tic /ärk')'tik/ [< Gk *arktos* bear] *adj* **1** frigid; **2** relating to the regions of the Arctic Circle and the North Pole || *n* **3** **the Arctic** this region; **4** **arctics** *pl* warmly lined waterproof overshoes

Arc'tic Cir'cle *n* parallel at 66°32' north, separating the Arctic Zone from the North Temperate Zone

Arc'tic O'cean *n* ocean around the North Pole

Arc'tic Zone' *n* region of the earth north of the Arctic Circle

Arc·tu·rus /ärkt(y)ŏŏr'əs/ [< Gk *arktos* bear + *ouros* keeper] *n* brightest star in the constellation Boötes

-ard /-ərd/ also **-art** /-ərt/ [OF < Gmc] *suf* used to form nouns denoting one with an excess of a quality, usu. pejorative, as *drunkard, braggart*

ar·dent /är'dənt/ [L *ardens* (*-entis*) burning] *adj* **1** passionate, eager, zealous || **ar'dent·ly** *adv* || **ar'den·cy** *n* || **SYN** fervent, spirited, passionate (see *sanguine*)

ar·dor /är'dər/ [L < *ardere* to burn] *n* warmth of affection or passion; eager desire, zeal

ar·du·ous /är'jōō·əs/ [L *arduus* steep] *adj* attended with great labor or exertion; difficult || **ar'du·ous·ly** *adv* || **SYN** troublesome, onerous, laborious (see *hard*)

are[1] /är', ər/ [OE *dial. aron*] *pl & 2d pers sg pres ind* of *be*

are[2] /er'/ [F < L *area* space] *n* metric measure of 100 sq. meters, or 119.6 sq. yards

ar·e·a /er′ē·ə/ [L = open space] *n* 1 any defined extent of land surface; 2 total flat surface measured in square units; 3 extent, range, scope ‖ *adj* local

ar·e·a code′ *n* three-digit code number which selects one of the large telephone areas into which a country is divided before calling the local number

a·re·na /ərēn′ə/ [L = sand] *n* 1 central space of a Roman amphitheater; 2 scene or field of combat or exertion of any kind, as for a contest

aren't /ärnt′/ are not

Ar·e·op·a·gus /ar′ē·op′əgəs/ [Gk = hill of Ares] *n* supreme tribunal of ancient Athens

Ar·es /er′ēz/ *n Gk myth.* god of War; identified with the Roman Mars

ar·gent /är′jənt/ [L *argentum* silver] *adj* made of or resembling silver; silvery-white

Ar·gen·ti·na /är′jəntēn′ə/ also **the Ar′gen·tine′** /-tēn′, -tīn′/ or **Ar′gen·tine′ Re·pub′lic** *n* Spanish-speaking republic in S South America (23,031,000; 1,072,075 sq.m.; cap. Buenos Aires) ‖ **Ar′gen·tine′** also **Ar′gen·tin′e·an** /-tin′ē·ən/ *adj & n*

Ar·go /är′gō/ *n Gk myth.* ship of Jason and the Argonauts

ar·gon /är′gən/ [Gk = idle] *n* odorless colorless inert gaseous element (A, Ar; at.no. 18; at.wt. 39.948) found in the atmosphere

Ar·go·naut /är′gənôt′/ [*Argo* + Gk *nautes* sailor] *n Gk myth.* one of the band of Greek heroes who sailed in quest of the Golden Fleece

ar·go·sy /är′gəsē/ [< earlier *ragusye* < It *ragusea* ship of Ragusa] *n* (-sies) *poet.* 1 large merchant vessel filled with costly goods; 2 fleet of such vessels

ar·got /är′gət, -gō/ [F] *n* conventional slang of a social group, as of the underworld, or of a profession or craft, as of lawyers ‖ SYN slang, jargon, lingo, cant (see *language*)

ar·gue /är′gyōō/ [L *arguere* to prove] *vi* 1 to offer reasons for or against something; 2 to contend in debate ‖ *vt* 3 to debate; 4 to prove; 5 to persuade by reasoning ‖ **ar′gu·a·ble** *adj* ‖ **ar′gu·er** *n* ‖ SYN dispute, reason, contest, wrangle, debate

ar′gu·ment /-gyə-/ *n* 1 presentation of reasons for or against something; 2 process of reasoning; 3 discussion or debate ‖ SYN disputation, debate, wrangling, discussion

ar′gu·men/ta·tive /-men′tətiv/ *adj* prone to argument

Ar·gus /är′gəs/ *n* 1 *Gk myth.* hundred-eyed giant; 2 sharp-eyed person ‖ **Ar′gus-eyed′** *adj*

Ar·gyle /är′gīl/ [*Argyll*, Sc county] *n* 1 diamond-shaped pattern used on socks and sweaters; 2 sock with this pattern ‖ also *adj*

a·ri·a /är′ē·ə, er′-/ [It = air] *n* melody or tune, esp. for a single voice in an opera

A·ri·an /er′ē·ən/ [< *Arius* 4th-cent. theologian of Alexandria] *n* follower of the doctrine that Christ was not of the same nature as God the Father ‖ also *adj* ‖ **Ar′i·an·ism** *n*

-ar·i·an /-er′ē·ən/ [< L *-arius* + Eng *-an*] *adj & n suf* expressing 1 occupation, as *veterinarian;* 2 habit of thought, as *utilitarian;* 3 age, as *nonagenarian*

ar·id /ar′id/ [L *aridus*] *adj* 1 dry, parched; 2 dull, uninteresting ‖ **a·rid′i·ty** /ərid′-/ *n*

Ar·ies /er′ēz, er′ē·ēz′/ [L = ram] *n* 1 a northern zodiacal constellation, the Ram; 2 first sign of the zodiac

a·right /ərīt′/ [OE *ariht*] *adv* correctly

a·rise /əriz′/ [OE *ārīsan*] *v* (**a·rose;** **a·ris·en**) *vi* 1 to get up; to change to a standing position from one of sitting, kneeling, or lying; 2 to come into view; 3 to spring up; proceed; originate ‖ SYN flow, proceed, spring, rise, issue, originate

a·ris·en /əriz′ən/ *pp* of **arise**

ar·is·toc·ra·cy /ar′istok′rəsē/ [< Gk *aristos* best + *-kratia* rule] *n* (-cies) 1 government by persons of the highest rank in the state; 2 state so governed; 3 nobility or chief persons in a state; 4 any group regarded as superior

a·ris·to·crat /əris′təkrat′/ *n* member or partisan of an aristocracy ‖ **a·ris′·to·crat′ic** *adj*

Ar·is·toph·a·nes /ar′istof′ənēz′/ *n* (448?–385? B.C.) Greek writer of comedies

Ar·is·tot·le /ar′istot′əl/ *n* (384–322 B.C.) Greek philosopher ‖ **Ar′is·to·te′li·an** /-tətēl′yən, -ē·ən/ *adj & n*

a·rith·me·tic /ərith′mətik/ [Gk *arithmetike* science of reckoning] *n* process of computation or reckoning by figures ‖ **ar·ith·met′ic** (*-i·cal*) /ar′ithmet′ik(əl)/ *adj* ‖ **a·rith′me·ti′cian** /-tish′ən/ *n*

ar′ith·met′ic pro·gres′sion *n math* sequence of numbers increasing or decreasing by a constant quantity, as 1, 4, 7, 10, 13

-ar·i·um /-er′ē·əm/ [< L *-arius*] *n suf* place where, as *aquarium*

Ariz. Arizona

Ar·i·zo·na /ar′izōn′ə/ *n* state in SW U.S. (1,772,000; 113,909 sq.m.; cap. Phoenix) ‖ **Ar′i·zo′n(i)an** *n*

ark /ärk/ [L *arca* chest] *n* 1 oblong box containing the Covenant, or tables of the Law, kept in the Holy of Holies in the Jewish Tabernacle, and later in the Temple of Solomon (Exod. 25; 1 Kings 8); 2 ship in which Noah and his family remained during the Deluge (Gen. 6)

Ark. Arkansas

Ar·kan·sas /ärk′ənsô′/ *n* state in S central U.S. (1,923,000; 53,103 sq.m.;

cap. Little Rock) || **Ar·kan·san** /ärkan'zən/ n

arm¹ /ärm/ [OE *earm*] n 1 limb of the human body which extends from the shoulder to the hand; 2 forelimb of any vertebrate; 3 any armlike part of a main body or machine, as the side piece of a chair, an inlet of the sea, etc.; 4 strength or power; 5 **at arm's length** not on friendly terms; 6 **with open arms** very cordially

arm² [L *arma* weapons] n 1 weapon; 2 branch of the military service; 3 **arms** pl weapons; 4 **under arms** armed and ready; 5 **up in arms**, a ready for battle; b indignant || vt 6 to furnish with weapons || vi 7 to fit oneself with arms || **armed'** adj

ar·ma·da /ärmäd'ə/ [Sp] n 1 fleet of warships; 2 any fleet of vehicles

ar·ma·dil·lo /är'mədil'ō/ [Sp, *dim.* of *armado* armed] n any of several South American burrowing mammals (order Edentata) with a carapace of horny plates, now found as far north as Texas

Ar·ma·ged·don /är'məged'ən/ n 1 Bib the great final battle to take place at the end of the world (Rev. 16:16); 2 any great and crucial conflict

ar·ma·ment /ärm'əmənt/ [< *arm²*] n 1 act of arming; 2 arms of a combat unit; 3 protective covering; 4 usu. **armaments** pl arms collectively

ar'ma·ture /-chər/ [L *armatura* armor] n 1 biol part used for offense and defense, as teeth or scales; 2 rotating part of a dynamo or motor; 3 vibrating part of buzzer or bell; 4 piece of iron or steel connecting the poles of a magnet or magnets

arm'chair' n 1 chair with side supports for the forearms || adj 2 not having any practical experience; not getting involved

Ar·me·ni·a /ärmēn'ē·ə, -yə/ n 1 ancient country of W Asia; 2 constituent republic of Soviet Russia (2,190,000; 11,500 sq.m.; cap. Yerevan) || **Ar·me'ni·an** adj & n

arm'ful n as much as the arms can hold

arm'hole' n opening for the arm in a garment

ar'mil·lar·y sphere' /är'miler'ē/ [< L *armilla* bracelet] n skeleton sphere consisting of rings which represent the principal circles of the celestial sphere such as the ecliptic, the equator, etc.

ar·mi·stice /ärm'istis/ [< L *arma* arms + *stitium* standing] n brief pause in a war by agreement of the opposing forces; truce

Ar'mi·stice Day' n original name of Veterans Day

arm'let /-lit/ [*dim.* of *arm¹*] n band worn around the upper arm

ar·mor /ärm'ər/ [OF *armeure* < L *armatura*] n 1 protective covering for the body in combat; 2 steel plat-

ing on a warship; 3 any protective covering, as fish scales || vt 4 to provide with armor || **ar'mored** adj

ar·mo'ri·al /-mŏr'ē·əl, -môr'-/ adj 1 relating to or bearing coats of arms || n 2 book of heraldic devices or coats of arms

ar'mor·y n (**-ies**) 1 place for storing weapons; 2 place for assembling soldiers for drilling; 3 factory for making weapons

arm/pit' n hollow beneath the arm at the shoulder

Arm'strong', Edwin Howard n (1890–1954) U.S. electrical engineer; developed frequency modulation

Arm'strong', Neil A. n (1930–) U.S. astronaut; first man to walk on the moon 1969

arm'-twist'ing n intense coercion, usu. to attain a political end

ar·my /är'mē/ [MF *armee* < L *armata* armed forces] n (**-mies**) 1 military land forces of a nation; 2 large unit of land forces, consisting of two or more corps; 3 body of persons engaged in furthering a cause, as of reform; 4 great number or multitude

ar'my corps' n part of an army made up of two or more divisions

ar'my group' n tactical military force made up of two or more armies

ar·ni·ca /är'nikə/ [?] 1 any of a genus (*Arnica*) of perennial herbs of the north temperate and arctic zones, one variety of which (*A. montana*) has medicinal value; 2 tincture of *A. montana*, used as a remedy for wounds and bruises

Ar·nold /är'nəld/, **Benedict** n (1741–1801) American Revolutionary War general who betrayed West Point to the British

Ar'nold, Matthew n (1822–88) English poet and essayist

a·ro·ma /ərōm'ə/ [Gk = spice] n 1 pleasant odor, fragrance; 2 characteristic quality

ar·o·mat·ic /ar'əmat'ik/ adj 1 having an aroma; sweet-smelling, fragrant || n 2 plant, herb, or drug yielding a fragrant smell || **syn** adj spicy, redolent, pungent (see *odorous*)

a·rose /ərōz'/ pt of arise

a·round /əround'/ adv 1 in a circle; 2 on every side; 3 roundabout; 4 in circumference; 5 in the opposite direction; 6 nearby || prep 7 encircling; 8 from one place to another in; 9 approximately; 10 in the vicinity of; 11 beyond the turn of, as *go around the corner*

a·rouse /ərouz'/ vt 1 to excite or stir to action; 2 to awaken || **a·rous'al** n || **syn** encourage, stir, goad, instigate, prompt

ar·peg·gio /ärpej'ō, -jē·ō'/ [It = harping] n rendering of the notes of a chord in rapid succession

ar·que·bus /är'kwibəs/ n var of **harquebus**

ar·raign /ərān′/ [OF *araisner*] *vt* 1 to call to account; accuse; 2 to summon (an accused person) into court ‖ **ar·raign′ment** *n* ‖ SYN accuse, charge, cite, impeach, indict, summon ‖ ANT acquit, condone, discharge, excuse, exonerate

ar·range /ərānj′/ [MF *arangier*] *vt* 1 to put in proper order or sequence; 2 to adjust or settle; 3 to prepare or plan; 4 *mus* to adapt (a composition) ‖ *vi* 5 to make preparations; 6 to come to an agreement ‖ SYN dispose, classify, adapt, adjust

ar·range′ment *n* 1 act of arranging; 2 that which is arranged; 3 method in which things are arranged; 4 adjustment or settlement; 5 **arrangements** *pl* preparations ‖ SYN preparation, disposition, adjustment, system

ar·rant /ar′ənt/ [var of *errant*] *adj* notorious, thorough, downright

ar·ray /ərā′/ [OF *areyer* < Gmc] *n* 1 orderly arrangement, as of troops, figures, facts, etc.; 2 attire ‖ *vt* 3 to place in order; marshal; 4 to deck or dress

ar·rears /ərirz′/ [< MF *arere* behind < *ad-* + L *retro* backward] *npl* 1 that which is undone, outstanding, or unpaid; 2 **in arrears** behind in payment

ar·rest /ərest′/ [MF *arester* < *ad-* + L *restare* to remain] *vt* 1 to stop or check; 2 to seize by legal authority ‖ *n* 3 act of arresting; 4 *mach* device for stopping motion; 5 **under arrest** in custody of the police ‖ SYN *v* capture, hold, detain, secure, stop, seize

ar·rest′ing *adj* striking, impressive

ar·riv·al /əriv′al/ *n* 1 act of arriving; 2 person or thing that arrives or has arrived

ar·rive /əriv′/ [OF *arriver* < *ad-* + L *ripa* shore] *vi* 1 to reach a destination; 2 to come; 3 to attain success; 4 **arrive at** to come to (a result or conclusion)

ar·ro·gant /ar′əgənt/ [L *arrogans* (*-antis*)] *adj* overbearingly haughty or contemptuous ‖ **ar·ro·gance** *n* ‖ SYN haughty, proud, presumptuous, disdainful, insolent, supercilious ‖ DISCR These words all describe those who claim undue importance for themselves. *Arrogant* describes one who is offensively overbearing; *haughty*, one so conscious of his high social station that he nourishes a lofty opinion of himself and a low one of others; *proud*, as here compared, one wrapped up in his own greatness, achievements, or the like; *presumptuous*, one who takes upon himself duties, privileges, or position which are not within his province; *disdainful*, one who entertains a scornful contempt for other poor mortals; *insolent*, one whose lack of consideration and whose sense of personal importance are grossly offensive; *supercilious*, one insolently superior

ar·ro·gate /ar′əgāt′/ [L *arrogare* (*-atus*) to assume] *vt* to take, assume, or demand unduly; claim without right ‖ SYN usurp, seize, appropriate, assume, claim

ar·row /ar′ō/ [OE *arwe*] *n* 1 slender pointed shaft, usu. feathered and barbed, intended to be shot from a bow; 2 arrow-shaped sign to indicate direction

ar′row·head′ *n* 1 head of an arrow; 2 any of a genus (*Sagittaria*) of aquatic plants, some species of which have leaves shaped like arrowheads

ar′row·root′ *n* 1 tropical American plant (*Maranta arundinacea*); 2 food starch obtained from its root

ar·roy·o /əroi′ō/ [Sp] 1 small stream or its dry bed; 2 deep dry channel

ar·se·nal /ärs′(ə)nəl/ [It *arsenale* < Ar *dār sinā′ah* house of industry] *n* 1 building for the storage or manufacture of weapons or munitions; 2 storehouse

ar·se·nic /ärs′(ə)nik/ [Gk *arsenikon* yellow arsenic] *n* grayish-white, lustrous, brittle, metallic element (**As**; at.no. 33; at.wt. 74.92), the compounds of which are used as poisons and in medicine ‖ **ar·sen·ic** /ärsen′ik/ *adj* designating compounds in which arsenic is pentavalent

ar·son /ärs′ən/ [OF < L *ardere* (*arsus*) to burn] *n* malicious or intentional burning of a building ‖ **ar′son·ist** *n*

art¹ /ärt′/ [OE *eart*] *archaic & poet.* 2nd *per sg pres ind* of **be**

art² [L *ars* (*artis*)] *n* 1 creative adaptation; 2 skill, knack; 3 application of skill to an end; 4 cunning or cleverness; 5 application of skill to the production of beautiful things, esp. in painting, sculpture, music, literature, architecture, and dancing; 6 any of these forms of production; 7 branch of learning, esp. in the fine arts or the humanities; 8 **arts** *pl* liberal arts

-art /-ərt/ var of **-ard**

art. 1 article; 2 artillery; 3 artificial; 4 artist

Ar·te·mis /ärt′imis/ *n* Gk *myth.* goddess of the moon, the hunt, and of maidenhood; identified with the Roman Diana

ar·te·ri·o·scle·ro·sis /ärtir′ē·ōsklrōs′is/ [*artery* + *sclerosis*] *n* thickening and hardening of the walls of the arteries

ar·ter·y /ärt′ərē/ [Gk *arteria*] *n* (**-ies**) 1 one of a system of tubes or vessels which carry the blood away from the heart; 2 main road or channel ‖ **ar·te·ri·al** /ärtir′ē·əl/ *adj*

ar·te′sian well /ärtēzh′ən/ [< OF *Arteis*, mod *Artois*, former F province] *n* 1 deep well in which water rises from internal pressure; 2 any deep-bored well

art′ful *adj* 1 cunning, crafty; 2 skillful, clever; 3 artificial ‖ **art′ful·ly** *adv* ‖ **art′ful·ness** *n* ‖ SYN sly, tricky, insincere, adroit, designing

ar·thri·tis /ärthrīt′is/ [< Gk *arthron* joint] *n* inflammation of a joint ‖ **ar·thrit′ic** /-thrit′-/ *adj & n*

ar·thro·pod /ärth′rəpod′/ [Gk *arthron* joint + -*pod*] *n* any of a phylum (Arthropoda) of invertebrates with jointed appendages, including the centipedes, insects, spiders, and crustaceans

Ar·thur /ärth′ər/ *n* legendary Celtic chieftain of Britain in the sixth century, the subject of many later romances ‖ **Ar·thu′ri·an** /-thŏŏr′ē·ən/ *adj*

Ar·thur, Chester A. *n* (1830–86) 21st president of the U.S. 1881–85

ar·ti·choke /ärt′ichōk′/ [It *articiocco* < Ar *al-khurshūf*] 1 thistlelike plant (*Cynara scolymus*) of the composite family; 2 its edible flower head

ar·ti·cle /ärt′ikəl/ [OF < L *articulus* joint] *n* 1 single section or clause of a formal document; 2 one item in a series of propositions or list of particulars; 3 prose composition in a newspaper, magazine, or reference work; 4 single member of a class, as *an article of clothing*; 5 commodity; 6 *gram* any of the words *a, an,* or *the,* used before a noun to define or limit its application

Ar′ti·cles of War′ *npl* ordinances for the government of military personnel, punishing as crimes acts which in civil life would be mere breaches of contract; replaced by the Uniform Code of Military Justice in 1951

ar·tic·u·late /ärtik′yəlt/ [L *articulatus* divided into joints] *adj* 1 jointed; 2 uttered distinctly; 3 able to speak; 4 systematically arranged ‖ /-lāt′/ *vt* 5 to unite by a joint; 6 to pronounce distinctly ‖ *vi* 7 to speak distinctly; 8 to become jointed ‖ **ar·tic′u·la′tion** *n*

ar·ti·fact /ärt′ifakt′/ [*art²* + L *factum* made] *n* product of human skill or workmanship, esp. a simple product of primitive art

ar·ti·fice /ärt′ifis/ [MF < L *artificium*] *n* 1 trickery; 2 ruse, trick ‖ SYN cunning, craft, device, deceit (see *subterfuge*)

ar·tif·i·cer /ärtif′isər/ *n* 1 skilled or artistic worker; 2 clever contriver ‖ SYN craftsman, mechanic, deviser (see *artisan*)

ar·ti·fi·cial /ärt′ifish′əl/ *adj* 1 not natural; 2 produced by human labor; 3 imitation; 4 feigned, assumed ‖ **ar′ti·fi′cial·ly** *adv* ‖ **ar′ti·fi′ci·al′i·ty** /-shē·al′itē/ *n* ‖ SYN fictitious, spurious, counterfeit ‖ DISCR These words alike describe that which is not real, natural, true, or genuine. *Artificial* may mean false as opposed to real, as *artificial* limbs, foliage, teeth; or

it may mean affected as opposed to sincere, as *artificial* ways, manners, conventions; or it may mean produced by manufacture rather than by natural growth, as *artificial* gas or flavorings. *Fictitious* describes that which is imagined by the mind, as a *fictitious* narrative or character. *Spurious* and *counterfeit* describe that which is deliberately deceitful; *spurious* claims are not what they seem to be; *spurious* signatures are false; *counterfeit* coins are imitations of the real ones

ar·til·ler·y /ärtil′ərē/ [MF *artillerie*] *n* 1 mounted cannon; ordnance; 2 troops or branch of an armed force handling such weapons ‖ **ar·til′ler·y·man** /-mən/ *n* (-men /-mən/)

ar·ti·san /ärt′izən/ [F < It *artigiano*] *n* skilled craftsman ‖ SYN artist, artificer, mechanic, craftsman, workman, laborer ‖ DISCR An *artist* is one who has creative ability in the field of fine art; the *artisan* is one who works in the lower plane of manual or mechanical art; the *artificer* is one who works with a measure of the *artist*'s ability, in the field of the *artisan*. A *mechanic* is one who repairs or adjusts machinery; a *craftsman,* one highly skilled in handicraft or a trade requiring manual expertness; *workman* is a broad term, and may or may not imply skill; a *laborer* is one whose work requires strength rather than skill or training

art′ist [< *art²*] *n* 1 person of especial talent in the fine or performing arts; 2 one especially skilled in his work

ar·tis′tic *adj* 1 pert. to art or artists; 2 done with or displaying skill in the fine arts; 3 exhibiting taste for the fine arts ‖ **ar·tis′ti·cal·ly** *adv*

art′ist·ry *n* artistic skill, quality, or technique

art′less *adj* 1 sincere, unaffected, ingenuous; 2 lacking skill; clumsy ‖ **art′less·ly** *adv* ‖ **art′less·ness** *n* ‖ SYN guileless, candid, ingenuous (see *open*)

art′y *adj* (-**i·er**; -**i·est**) *colloq* ostentatiously artistic ‖ **art′i·ness** *n*

-ar·y /-er′ē, -ərē/ [L *-arius*] *n suf* 1 denoting persons, places, or things, as *dictionary, library* ‖ *adj suf* 2 pert. to or characterized by, as *literary*

Ar·y·an /er′ē·ən, ar′ē·ən, är′yen/ [< Skt *arya* noble] *n* 1 member or descendant of prehistoric people who spoke Indo-European; 2 Indo-Iranian ‖ also *adj*

as /az′, əz/ [< OE *allswā* wholly so] *adv* 1 equally; 2 for example; 3 **as for** regarding; 4 **as if** or **though** as it would be if; 5 as yet till now ‖ *conj* 6 because; 7 that the result is; 8 while, when; 9 in the way in which; 10 though; 11 *colloq* that, as *I don't know as I can;* 12 as is without guarantee as to condition ‖ *prep* 13 in the role of

As *chem* arsenic

AS, A.S., A.-S. Anglo-Saxon

as·bes·tos also **as·bes·tus** /asbest′əs, az-/ [Gk = unquenchable] *n* fibrous incombustible mineral used in fire-proofing and insulation

as·cend /əsend′/ [L *ascendere*] *vt* 1 to go up, mount; 2 to succeed to ‖ *vi* 3 to rise, climb

as·cend′ant also **as·cend′ent** *adj* 1 rising; 2 superior, predominant; 3 above the horizon ‖ *n* 4 **in the ascendant** on the rise in power and prosperity ‖ **as·cend′an·cy, as·cend′en·cy** also **as·cend′ance, as·cend′ence** *n*

as·cen·sion /əsen′shən/ *n* 1 act of ascending; 2 **the Ascension** the ascent of Christ into heaven (Acts 1:9)

As·cen′sion Day′ *n* Holy Thursday, the fortieth day after Easter, commemorating the Ascension

as·cent /əsent′/ *n* 1 act of ascending; 2 upward slope

as·cer·tain /as′ərtān′/ [< *a-5* + *certain*] *vt* 1 to make certain; 2 to find out ‖ **as′cer·tain′ment** *n*

as·cet·ic /əset′ik/ [Gk *asketikos* hard-working] *n* 1 one who gives up the things of the world and devotes himself to religious exercises; 2 hermit, recluse ‖ also *adj* ‖ **as·cet′i·cism** *n*

As·cle·pi·us /əsklēp′ē-əs/ *n* Gk myth. god of medicine, the Roman Aesculapius

as·cor′bic ac′id /əskôrb′ik/ [< *a-5* + scorb*utic*] *n* scurvy-preventing vitamin C —C₆H₈O₆— present in citrus fruit and green leafy vegetables

as·cot /ask′ət/ [*Ascot* Heath, England] *n* tie with broad ends which are folded diagonally down from the knot

as·cribe /əskrīb′/ [< L *ascribere*] *vt* 1 to attribute or impute as to a cause; 2 to consider to belong ‖ **as·crip′tion** /-krip/shən/ *n*

-ase /-ās′, -āz′/ [< diast*ase*] *n suf* enzyme, as *oxidase*

a·sep·tic /əsep′tik, ā-/ *adj* free from disease-causing germs ‖ **a·sep′ti·cal·ly** *adv*

a·sex·u·al /āsek′shōō-əl/ *adj* 1 having no sex; 2 pert. to reproduction without sexual action ‖ **a·sex′u·al·ly** *adv*

ash¹ /ash′/ [OE *æsc*] *n* 1 any of a genus (*Fraxinus*) of common timber and shade trees with coarse bark and pinnate leaves; 2 its wood

ash² [OE *æsce*] *n* 1 grayish powdery residue remaining after something has burned; 2 gray color; 3 **ashes** *pl* a waste from burned substances; b remains of a dead human body when burned or reduced to dust by natural decay

a·shamed /əshāmd′/ [*pp* of *obs* **ashame** to be ashamed] *adj* feeling shame ‖ **a·sham′ed·ly** /-midlē/ *adv*

ash′en [< *ash²*] *adj* pale; ashy

Ash·ke·naz·i /ash′kfnäz′ē/ [Heb] *n* (-naz′im /-im/) Yiddish-speaking Jew from E Europe ‖ **Ash′ke·naz′ic** *adj*

ash·lar /ash′lər/ [< ME *ascheler* < MF *aisselier*] *n* 1 squared or hewn block of building stone; 2 such stones collectively

a·shore /əshôr′, -shôr′/ *adv* on shore; to shore; on land

ash·ram /äsh′rəm/ [Skt *aśrama*] *n* India religious meeting place

ash′tray′ *n* small receptacle for tobacco ashes

Ash′ Wednes′day *n* first day of Lent

ash′y *adj* (-i·er; -i·est) 1 pert. to or covered with ashes; 2 pale

A·sia /āzh′ə, āsh/ə/ *n* largest continent, extending from the Ural Mountains and the Aegean to the Pacific, and from the Arctic to the Indian Ocean (1,500,000,000; ab. 16,500,000 sq.m.) ‖ **A′sian** also **A·si·at·ic** /āzh′-ē-at′ik, -zē-, -shē-/ *adj* & *n*

A′sia Mi′nor *n* peninsula forming the westernmost part of Asia, between the Black and Mediterranean Seas

a·side /əsīd′/ *adv* 1 on or to one side; out of a given direction; 2 apart; away; 3 in reserve; 4 **aside from,** a apart from; b except for ‖ *n* 5 words spoken in a low tone and not intended to be heard generally

as·i·nine /as′inīn′/ [< L *asinus* ass] *adj* 1 pert. to or like an ass; 2 stupid; 3 obstinate ‖ **as′i·nin′i·ty** /-nin′itē/ *n*

-a·sis /-əsis/ [Gk *-asis*] *n suf* used for names of diseases, as *psoriasis*

ask /ask′, äsk′/ [OE *āscian*] *vt* 1 to request; petition or beg for; 2 to demand or require; 3 to inquire respecting; 4 to put a question to; inquire of; 5 to put a (question); 6 to set as a price; 7 to invite ‖ *vi* 8 to make a request; 9 to inquire ‖ SYN beg, claim, inquire (see *question*)

a·skance /əskans/ [?] *adv* 1 sideways, from the corner of the eye; 2 disdainfully; distrustfully

a·skew /əskyōō′/ *adv* 1 awry; obliquely; out of position ‖ *adj* 2 crooked, awry ‖ SYN *adj* crooked, distorted, awry

a·slant /əslant′, -slänt′/ *adv* 1 slanting obliquely ‖ *adj* 2 slanting, oblique ‖ *prep* slantwise across

a·sleep /əslēp′/ *adj* 1 sleeping; 2 dormant; 3 numb; 4 dead ‖ *adv* 5 in a state of slumber

a·so·cial /āsōsh′əl/ *adj* 1 withdrawn from society; 2 selfish, inconsiderate

asp /asp′/ [Gk *aspis*] *n* 1 small poisonous snake of Egypt; 2 common viper (*Vipera berus*) of Europe

as·par·a·gus /əspar′əgəs/ [Gk *asparagos*] *n* any of a large genus (*Asparagus*) of Old World perennial plants of the lily family, esp. *A. officinalis*, which has tender edible stalks

A.S.P.C.A. American Society for the Prevention of Cruelty to Animals

as·pect /as′pəkt/ [L *aspectus*] *n* 1 appearance to the eye or mind; 2 expression, mien; 3 side or part facing in any given direction; 4 phase, view; 5 *astrol* relative position of the planets at any time; 6 *gram* verb category in some languages referring to the completion or noncompletion of an action

as·pen /asp'ən/ [OE *æspen*] n 1 any of several species of poplar trees whose leaves tremble in the slightest breeze, as *Populus tremula* of Europe and *Populus tremuloides* of America ‖ *adj* 2 pert. to the aspen; 3 quivering, tremulous

as·per·i·ty /asper'itē/ [< L *asper* rough] n (-ties) 1 roughness of surface; unevenness; 2 roughness or harshness of tone, manner, or temper

as·per·sion /əspur'zhən, -shən/ [< L *aspergere* (*aspersus*) to sprinkle] n 1 derogatory remark, slander; 2 sprinkling

as·phalt /as'fôlt/ also **as·phal'tum** /-əm/ [Gk *asphalton*] n 1 brownish-black mixture of complex hydrocarbons, natural or artificial, used for paving, roofing, and cementing ‖ *vt* 2 to pave or cover with asphalt

as·pho·del /as'fədel'/ [Gk *asphodelos*] n 1 any of several European plants (genus *Asphodel*) of the lily family; 2 daffodil

as·phyx·i·a /asfik'sē·ə/ [Gk = stopping of the pulse] n suspension of breathing and animation due to failure of the supply of oxygen, as in suffocation ‖ **as·phyx'i·ate'** *vt* ‖ **as·phyx'i·a'·tion** n

as·pic /asp'ik/ [F] n clear meat jelly containing fowl, game, fish, etc.

as·pir·ant /əspīr'ənt, asp'irənt/ [see **aspire**] *adj* 1 aspiring ‖ n 2 one who aspires

as·pi·rate /asp'irāt'/ [L *aspirare* (-*atus*) to breathe upon] *vt* 1 to prefix or add the sound of *h* to (a word or sound) ‖ /-rit/ *adj* 2 aspirated ‖ n 3 aspirated sound or word

as·pi·ra'tion n 1 act of breathing; 2 ambition; 3 sound consisting of or combined with the sound of *h*; 4 *surg* use of the aspirator

as·pi·ra'tor n device for producing suction or removing fluids by suction, as from body cavities

as·pire /əspīr'/ [L *aspirare* to breathe] *vi* to seek or desire with longing

as·pi·rin /asp'irin/ [acetyl + spiraeic acid] n drug —C₉H₈O₄— derived from salicylic acid, used as an analgesic for headaches and body pains, and as a cold remedy

ass /as'/ [OE *assa*] n 1 donkey (*Equus asinus*); 2 silly fool

as·sail /əsāl'/ [OF *asaillir* < *ad-* + L *salire* to leap] *vt* 1 to fall upon or attack violently; 2 to attack with argument or abuse ‖ **as·sail'ant** n

as·sas·sin /əsas'in/ [Ar *hashshāshīn* hashish eaters] n murderer, esp. fa-

natical murderer of a prominent person

as·sas'si·nate' *vt* to kill by treacherous means ‖ **as·sas'si·na'tion** n ‖ SYN murder, butcher, slay (see *kill*)

as·sault /əsôlt'/ [< OF *asauter* < *ad-* + L *saltare* to leap] n 1 violent attack, onslaught, esp. by troops; 2 *law* attempt or offer to do bodily violence against the person of another; 3 rape ‖ *vt* 4 to make an assault on, attack ‖ **as·sault'er** n

as·sault' and bat'ter·y n *law* assault with actual violence committed on another

as·say /əsā', as'ā/ [MF *assai*] n 1 determination of the proportion of any one or more metals in a compound, ore, or alloy, esp. of precious metals; 2 substance tested; 3 result of such test ‖ /əsā'/ *vt* 4 to analyze for gold or silver content; 5 to test the value of ‖ **as·say'er** n

as·sem·blage /əsem'blij/ n 1 act of assembling or state of being assembled; 2 group or collection of persons or particular things ‖ SYN assembly, company, concourse, congregation

as·sem·ble /əsem'bəl/ [OF *assembler* < *ad-* + L *simul* together] *vt* 1 to collect or gather together into one place or body; 2 to fit together, as parts ‖ *vi* 3 to meet or come together

as·sem·bly n (-blies) 1 assemblage of persons gathered together for a common purpose; 2 bugle call to bring troops together; 3 putting together, as parts; 4 *mach* parts forming a self-contained unit; 5 lower house of a state legislature

as·sem'bly line n line in a factory, as a moving belt, where parts are added to incomplete units as they are conveyed along

as·sem'bly·man /-mən/ n (-men /-mən/) member of a state assembly

as·sent /əsent'/ [OF *asenter* < L *assentari*] *vi* 1 to agree, consent ‖ n 2 consent, concurrence ‖ SYN v accede, accord, acquiesce, accept, acknowledge, approve, concur (see *accede, agree*)

as·sert /əsurt'/ [L *asserere* (-*ertus*) to claim] *vt* 1 to declare positively; 2 to defend, as rights; 3 to thrust (oneself) forward ‖ **as·ser'tive** *adj* ‖ SYN claim, assert, affirm, allege, maintain, defend, vindicate ‖ DISCR To *assert* is to declare boldly, often controversially, our opinions, rights, etc. To *maintain* is to support these assertions; to *defend* is to uphold them in the face of opposition; to *affirm* is to declare their truth solemnly; to *vindicate* is to establish their merits successfully in the face of opposition or denial. To *allege* is to state without proving; an allegation is merely declarative and is open to question. To *claim* is to *assert* one's right or title to something. Thus, a man *claims* to be the owner of disputed goods, but he *asserts* or *maintains* that whatever is, is right

as·ser'tion *n* 1 act of asserting; 2 positive though unsupported statement

as·sess /əses'/ [LL *assessare* to impose a tax] 1 to determine the amount of (damages, a fine, etc.); 2 to value officially for the purpose of taxation; 3 to impose a charge on; 4 to evaluate ‖ **as·sess'ment** *n* ‖ **as·ses'sor** *n*

as·set /as'et/ [< OF *asez* enough] *n* 1 useful thing; 2 item of value; 3 assets *pl* all the property of value of a person or company

as·sev·er·ate /əsev'ərāt'/ [L *asseverare* (-*atus*) to speak earnestly] *vt* to declare positively ‖ **as·sev'er·a'tion** *n* ‖ SYN maintain, assert, aver, declare, affirm

as·sid·u·ous /əsij'ŏō-əs/ [L *assiduus* sitting down to] *adj* perseveringly diligent, unremitting ‖ **as·si·du·i·ty** /as'id(y)ŏō'ĭtē/ *n* ‖ SYN sedulous, industrious, diligent (see *busy*)

as·sign /əsīn'/ [OF *assigner* < L *assignare*] *vt* 1 to give out, allot; 2 to appoint; 3 to name, designate; 4 *law* to transfer to another ‖ SYN appoint, allot, specify, designate, fix, attribute, apportion, set, determine, mark

as·sig·na·tion /as'ignāsh'ən/ *n* appointment for a meeting, esp. of lovers

as·signed' risk' *n* poor insurance risk assigned by state law to a pool of insurers at high rates

as·sign'ment *n* 1 act of assigning; 2 thing assigned

as·sim·i·late /əsim'ĭlāt'/ [< L *assimilis* similar] *vt* 1 to bring to likeness or agreement with something else; 2 to absorb and incorporate; 3 to compare; liken; 4 to cause (a sound) to become similar to an adjacent sound ‖ *vi* 5 to become similar; harmonize; 6 to be absorbed and incorporated ‖ **as·sim'i·la'tion** *n*

as·sist /əsist'/ [L *assistere* to stand by] *vt* 1 to aid, help ‖ *n* 2 *baseball* play that helps put out an opponent ‖ **as·sis'tance** *n* ‖ SYN *v* aid, succor, relieve, back, support (see *help*)

as·sis'tant *adj* 1 helping, subordinate ‖ *n* 2 helper, subordinate

as·siz·es /əsīz'ĭz/ [< OF *asise* sitting] *npl* 1 sessions of court held at stated intervals in each county in England; 2 time or place for this court

as·so·ci·ate /əsōsh'ē·ĭt/ [*ad-* + L *sociare* (-*atus*) to join] *n* 1 companion; 2 confederate; 3 fellow member; 4 colleague; 5 one having partial membership ‖ /-āt'/ *vt* 6 to unite, join; 7 to make an associate of; 8 to connect in thought ‖ *vi* 9 to unite ‖ SYN *n* partner, colleague, companion (see *ally*)

as·so'ci·a'tion *n* 1 act of associating, or state of being associated; 2 body of persons organized for a common purpose; 3 connection of ideas

as·so·nance /as'ənəns/ [< L *assonare* to echo] *n* rhyme in which the vowel sounds, but not the consonants, of one word correspond with those of another, as in *foolish* and *crooning* ‖ **as'so·nant** *adj*

as·sort /əsôrt'/ [MF *assorter*] *vt* to separate into lots, classes, or kinds; classify

as·sort'ed *adj* of different kinds

as·sort'ment *n* mixed collection

asst. assistant

as·suage /əswāj'/ [OF *asouagier* < *ad-* + L *suavis* sweet] *vt* 1 to soften, soothe, lessen; 2 to appease, pacify ‖ **as·suage'ment** *n* ‖ SYN alleviate, lessen, relieve, pacify (see *mitigate*)

as·sume /əsōōm'/ [L *assumere* to take to] *vt* 1 to take upon oneself; 2 to suppose, take for granted; 3 to take on, adopt (a character or role); 4 to undertake; 5 to pretend to be or possess; 6 to enter into (an office, duties)

as·sump·tion /əsump'shən/ [< *assume*] *n* 1 act of assuming; 2 **Assumption** a bodily taking into heaven of the Virgin Mary; b feast that celebrates this, August 15 ‖ SYN arrogance, pretense, supposition, affectation

as·sur·ance /əshŏŏr'əns/ *n* 1 pledge, guaranty; 2 self-confidence; 3 sureness, confidence ‖ SYN confidence, impudence, boldness ‖ DISCR *Assurance* is a self-possession or a self-contained quality that produces *confidence*. Proper *confidence* is an admirable self-reliance. *Assurance* that escapes the bounds of control changes to *impudence*; shameless *assurance* becomes *boldness*; *confidence* bred by *impudence* or *boldness* begets aggressive self-sufficiency (see *trust*)

as·sure /əshŏŏr'/ [OF *aseurer* < *ad-* + L *securus* sure] *vt* 1 to make sure or certain; 2 to inspire confidence in; 3 to insure ‖ **as·sur'er** *n* ‖ SYN confirm, establish, prove, settle, substantiate

as·sured' *adj* 1 guaranteed, sure; 2 self-possessed, confident ‖ *n* 3 *insurance* a beneficiary; b insured person ‖ **as·sur'ed·ly** /-ĭdlē/ *adv*

As·syr·i·a /əsir'ē·ə/ *n* ancient empire in SW Asia of the seventh century B.C. ‖ **As·syr'i·an** *adj* & *n*

As·tar·te /əstärt'ē/ *n* Phoenician goddess of love and fertility, regarded by the Greeks as a moon goddess

as·ta·tine /as'tətēn'/ [< Gk *astatos* unstable] *n* radioactive halogen element (At; at. no. 85), produced by bombarding bismuth with alpha particles

as·ter /as'tər/ [Gk *aster* star] *n* 1 any of a large genus (*Aster*) of plants of the composite family, having flowers with variously colored rays about a yellow center; 2 China aster

as·ter·isk /ǎs'tərǐsk/ [Gk, dim. of *aster* star] *n* figure of a star * used as a reference, to indicate omission, or, in linguistics, a hypothetical or incorrect form

a·stern /əsturn'/ *adv naut* 1 at or toward the rear end of a ship; 2 backwards; 3 behind a ship

as·ter·oid /ǎs'tərȯid'/ [Gk *aster* + -*oid*] *n* one of a great number of small planets between Mars and Jupiter

asth·ma /ǎz'mə, ǎs'-/ [Gk = panting] *n* disease attended by coughing and difficult breathing, with frequent violent paroxysms caused by loss of breath ‖ **asth·mat'ic** /-mǎt'-/ *adj & n*

a·stig·ma·tism /əstǐg'mətǐz'əm/ [<*a-* + *stigma* (-*atos*) point] *n* defect of the eye or of a lens in which vertical lines and horizontal lines from the same object focus at different points ‖ **as·tig·mat·ic** /ǎs'tǐgmǎt'ǐk/ *adj & n*

a·stir /əstur'/ *adj & adv* on the move, in activity

as·ton·ish /əstŏn'ǐsh/ [prob < OF *estoner* to shock] *vt* to strike with sudden wonder, amaze ‖ **as·ton'ish·ing** *adj* ‖ **as·ton'ish·ment** *n* ‖ SYN astound, bewilder, dumfound, perplex

as·tound /əstound'/ [*pp* of obs verb *astone* to astonish] *vt* to astonish greatly ‖ **as·tound'ing** *adj*

astr- or **astro-** [Gk *astron* star] *comb form* star, as astronomy

a·strad·dle /əstrǎd'əl/ *adj & adv* astride

as·tra·khan /ǎs'trəkən/ [city in Russia] *n* skin of young lambs with curly furlike wool

as·tral /ǎs'trəl/ [< Gk *astron* star] *adj* relating to or proceeding from the stars

a·stray /əstrā'/ [< MF *estraier* to stray] *adj & adv* off the right way, lost

a·stride /əstrīd'/ *adj & adv* 1 with a leg on each side ‖ *prep* 2 with a leg on each side of

as·trin·gent /əstrǐn'jənt/ [< L *astringere* to tighten] *adj* 1 (substance) that contracts body tissues so as to check excessive discharges; styptic; 2 harsh, severe ‖ *n* 3 astringent substance ‖ **as·trin'gen·cy** *n*

as·tro·labe [ǎs'trəlāb'/ [< *astro-* + Gk *labein* to take] *n* instrument formerly used to measure the altitude of heavenly bodies

as·trol·o·gy /əstrǒl'əjē/ *n* prediction of events by the position and influence on human affairs of the sun, moon, and planets ‖ **as·trol'o·ger** *n* ‖ **as'tro·log'i·cal** /ǎs'trəlǒj'i-/ *adj*

as·tro·naut /ǎs'trənȯt'/ [*astro-* + Gk *nautes* sailor] *n* traveler in outer

space ‖ **as'tro·nau'tic** *adj* ‖ **as'tro·nau'tics** *nsg*

as·tro·nom·i·cal /ǎs'trənǒm'ikəl/ *adj* 1 pert. to astronomy; 2 enormous ‖ **as'tro·nom'i·cal·ly** *adv*

as·tro·nom'i·cal u'nit *n astron* unit of length equal to the mean radius of the earth's orbit, approx. 93,000,000 miles

as·tron·o·my /əstrǒn'əmē/ *n* science which treats of the heavenly bodies, their constitution, positions, motions, etc. ‖ **as·tron'o·mer** *n*

as'tro·phys'ics /ǎs'trō-/ *nsg* branch of astronomy which treats of the physical and chemical characteristics of the heavenly bodies ‖ **as'tro·phys'i·cal** *adj* ‖ **as'tro·phys'i·cist** *n*

as·tute /əst(y)oot'/ [L *astutus*] *adj* shrewd, keen, crafty

A·sun·ción /əsoon'sē-ōn'/ *n* capital of Paraguay (305,160)

a·sun·der /əsun'dər/ [OE *on sundran*] *adv* apart; separately; into parts

a·sy·lum /əsī'ləm/ [Gk *asylon* inviolate] *n* 1 place of refuge or security; 2 institution for the care of the aged, blind, orphans, or insane

a·sym·me·try /ǎsǐm'itrē/ *n* lack of symmetry ‖ **a'sym·met'ric** (-**ri·cal**) /-met'-/ *adj*

at /ǎt, ət/ [OE *æt*] *prep* 1 located in, on, or near in time or space, as *at noon, at the top;* 2 attending, as *at school;* 3 to or toward, as *at the target;* 4 by means of, as *enter at the door;* 5 because of, as *sad at his death;* 6 in the amount or rate of, as *at 40 cents a pound, at 20 miles an hour;* 7 in the state or condition of, as *at peace*

at- var of **ad-**

At *chem* astatine

At·a·brine /ǎt'əbrēn', -brǐn/ [trademark] *n* synthetic organic compound used in treating malaria

At·a·lan·ta /ǎt'əlǎnt'ə/ *n Gk myth.* princess who agreed to marry the suitor who could outrun her

at·a·vism /ǎt'əvǐz'əm/ [< L *atavus* ancestor] *n* 1 inheritance from a remote ancestor of a trait not possessed by nearer ancestors; 2 reversion to an earlier type ‖ **at'a·vis'tic** *adj*

ate /āt/ *pt* of eat

-ate /-āt, -ǐt, -āt'/ [L -*atus*] *suf* 1 occurring in adjectives derived from the Latin past participle, as *ornate;* 2 occurring in verbs derived from Latin, as *nominate;* 3 forming nouns denoting function, as *potentate;* 4 forming nouns naming persons or things, as *delegate, mandate;* 5 *chem* indicating that the word is the name of a salt and that the element to whose name in full or shortened form it is attached has a higher valence than in the corresponding salt with the suffix -*ite;* it corresponds to the suffix -*ic* in the adjective part of the name of an acid

a·te·lier /at'əlyā'/ [F = workshop] *n* studio, esp. that of a painter or sculptor

a tempo /ä temp'ō/ [It = in time] *adv mus* at the original tempo

a·the·ism /āth'ē·iz'əm/ [< Gk *atheos* godless] *n* disbelief in or denial of the existence of God ‖ **a'the·ist** *n*

A·the·na /əthēn'ə/ also **A·the'ne** /-nē/ *n Gk myth.* goddess of wisdom, the industrial arts, and war; identified with the Roman Minerva

ath·e·nae·um or **ath·e·ne·um** /ath'-inē'əm/ [< *Athena*] *n* 1 temple of Athena in Athens; 2 institution devoted to the study of literature and art; 3 library or reading room

Ath·ens /ath'inz/ *n* capital of Greece (1,900,000), leading center of learning in the ancient world ‖ **A·the·ni·an** /əthēn'ē·ən/ *adj & n*

ath·lete /ath'lēt/ [Gk *athletes*] *n* one trained to contend in feats of strength or agility

ath'lete's foot' *n* ringworm of the foot

ath·let'ic /-let'ik/ *adj* 1 pert. to athletes or their performance; 2 strong; muscular

ath·let'ics *nsg* 1 principles and practice of athletic training ‖ *npl* 2 athletic sports collectively

at-home' *n* informal afternoon reception at one's home

a·thwart /əthwôrt'/ *adv* 1 across, crosswise ‖ *prep* 2 across the course or direction of, as a ship; 3 from side to side of

a·tilt /ətilt'/ *adj & adv* in a tilted position or manner

a·tin·gle /ətiŋ'gəl/ *adj* tingling

-a·tion /-āsh'ən/ [L *-atio* (*-onis*)] *n suf* indicating: 1 act or process, as *creation*; 2 condition or state, as *starvation*; 3 something formed or made, as *plantation*

-a·tive /-ətiv/ [L *-ativus*] *adj suf* pert. to, as *decorative*

At·lan·ta /atlant'ə/ *n* capital of Georgia (496,973) and commercial metropolis of the Southeast ‖ **At·lan'tan** *n*

At·lan'tic Cit'y /atlant'ik/ *n* famous summer resort on the S New Jersey shore (60,000)

At·lan'tic O'cean or **the At·lan'tic** *n* the ocean separating Europe and Africa from North and South America

At·lan'tis /-tis/ *n* fabled island which was supposed by the ancients to exist west of Gibraltar and to have been submerged by an earthquake

at·las /at'ləs/ [Gk] *n* 1 book of maps; 2 (anat) highest vertebra of the neck, supporting the skull; 3 **Atlas, a** *Gk myth.* giant who bore the heavens on his shoulders; **b** U.S. intercontinental ballistic missile

At'las Moun'tains *npl* mountain range in NW Africa between the Sahara and the Mediterranean and extending through Morocco, Algeria, and Tunisia

at·mos·phere /at'məsfir'/ [< Gk *atmos* vapor + *sphere*] *n* 1 air which surrounds the earth; 2 envelope of gas around any heavenly body; 3 surrounding or pervading influence; 4 pressure of the atmosphere at sea level (14.7 lbs. per sq.in.) ‖ **at'mos·pher'ic** /-fer'ik/ *adj*

at. no. atomic number

a·toll /at'ôl, -ol/ [Maldivian *atolu*] *n* ring-shaped coral reef nearly or entirely surrounding a lagoon within

a·tom /at'əm/ [Gk *atomos* not divisible] *n* 1 smallest unit of an element that can be conceived to exist with characteristic individuation either separately or in combination with other elements; 2 smallest particle of an element in which a balance exists between protons and electrons; 3 minute quantity

at'om bomb' *n* highly destructive bomb utilizing the explosive force of nuclear fission ‖ **at'om-bomb'** *vt*

a·tom·ic /ətom'ik/ *adj* 1 pert. to an atom; 2 **a** pert. to or released by the energy of fission or fusion; **b** pert. to or released by the energy of fission, as in the atom bomb; 3 extremely minute

a·tom'ic age' *n* period in history beginning with the first use of the atom bomb 1945

a·tom'ic bomb' *n* atom bomb

a·tom'ic clock' *n* timepiece whose great accuracy is provided by the natural and invariable frequency of a beam of atoms of certain substances

a·tom'ic en'er·gy *n* energy released by the conversion of mass in nuclear reactions

a·tom'ic num'ber *n* number of protons in the nucleus of an atom and, accordingly, the number of electrons surrounding the nucleus (symbol: **Z**)

a·tom'ic weight' *n* average weight of an atom of an element based on a unit of 1/12 the weight of the carbon isotope that has the weight of 12

at'o·mize' *vt* 1 to reduce to atoms; 2 to destroy by bombing, esp. with an atom bomb; 3 **a** to reduce to fine particles or a spray; **b** to spray (a liquid)

at'om·iz'er *n* device that converts a liquid into a fine spray

at'om smash'er *n* accelerator 4

a·ton·al /ātōn'əl/ *adj mus* having no key ‖ **a'to·nal'i·ty** /-nal'-/ *n*

a·tone /ətōn'/ [< *at one* agreed] *vi* to make amends

A·tone'ment *n* Christ's redemptive sacrifice

a·top /ətop'/ *adv & adj* **1** on or at the top || *prep* **2** on top of

a·tro·cious /ətrōsh'əs/ [< L *atrox* (-*ocis*)] *adj* extremely wicked; cruel; horrible; outrageous || **a·tro'cious·ly** *adv* || SYN flagrant, monstrous, odious (see *heinous*)

a·troc·i·ty /ətros'itē/ *n* (-**ies**) **1** atrocious act or thing; **2** bad piece of work; ugly thing

at·ro·phy /at'rəfē/ [< Gk *atrophos* not fed] *n* **1** wasting away of the body or part of it on account of lack of nourishment; **2** degeneration from disuse || *v* (-**phied**) *vt* **3** to cause atrophy in || *vi* **4** to undergo atrophy

at·ro·pine /at'rəpēn', -pin/ [< Gk *atropa* deadly nightshade] *n* poisonous alkaloid —$C_{17}H_{23}NO_3$— found in plants of the nightshade family, used medicinally and to dilate the pupil of the eye

At·ro·pos /at'rəpos'/ *n class. myth.* that one of the three Fates who cut off the thread of life

at·tach /ətach'/ [OF *atachier*] *vt* **1** to fasten or affix, join; **2** to assign by authority, as to a military post; **3** to affix, as a signature; **4** to attribute, as *to attach importance to something;* **5** to unite by ties of affection; **6** *law* to seize by legal authority

at·ta·ché /at'əshā'/ [F] *n* one who is attached to an embassy, legation, or staff, as an aid or assistant

at·ta·ché' case *n* briefcase with a hinged cover

at·tach'ment *n* **1** act of attaching, or state of being attached; **2** affection; fidelity; **3** that which attaches, fastening; **4** something added, as an accessory for a home appliance; **5** *law* a legal seizure, as of goods; **b** writ effecting such seizure || SYN affection, love || DISCR *Attachment,* which can be felt for inanimate things as well as for people, indicates a strong liking. *Attachment* may be such a strong inclination that it approaches devotion, but it remains a weaker term than *affection,* which indicates a warm and tender state of the feelings, a kindly, calm, steady sentiment that is the basis of most of the tested ties between people. *Love* is far more powerful than *affection;* it is more ardent, more passionate, often less steady; it is far more selective and exclusive, though it can range from the potent feeling that exists between the sexes to that impersonal love for the race that prompts men to sacrifice their lives for its betterment and advancement || ANT antipathy, aversion, enmity, hostility, indifference

at·tack /ətak'/ [F *attaquer*] *vt* **1** to assault, set upon; **2** to assail violently by speech or writing; **3** to begin (an undertaking or job); **4** to set oneself vigorously to work upon; **5** to start to have an effect upon || *vi* **6** to make an assault or onset || *n* **7** act of attacking; **8** first step of an undertaking; **9** aggressive or offensive movement or operation; **10** seizure, as of indigestion || SYN *v* beset, besiege, encounter, set upon, combat, invade || ANT *v* defend, protect, befriend, shelter

at·tain /ətān'/ [OF *ataindre* < L *attingere* to touch upon] *vt* **1** to reach, as in time, space, motion, or experience; **2** to gain, achieve || *vi* **3** **attain to** arrive at, reach || **at·tain'a·ble** *adj* || SYN acquire (see *get*) || ANT abandon, fail, lose

at·tain'ment *n* **1** act of attaining as the result of effort; **2** something attained or achieved; **3** personal accomplishment; special ability || SYN accomplishment, acquisition, achievement

at·tar /at'ər/ [Pers *'atar*] *n* fragrant essential oil from the petals of flowers, esp. roses

at·tempt /ətempt'/ [L *attemptare*] *vt* **1** to make an effort to accomplish, try || *n* **2** effort, endeavor; **3** assault with intent to murder

at·tend /ətend'/ [OF *atendre* < L *attendere*] *vt* **1** to wait upon; look after; **2** to accompany, escort; **3** to be present at || *vi* **4** to pay heed; **5** to be present; **6** to look after or take charge of something || SYN serve, follow, visit, escort, accompany

at·tend'ance *n* **1** act of attending; **2** number of persons present

at·tend'ant *n* **1** one who attends; **2** that which accompanies or is consequent || *adj* **3** consequent, following upon

at·ten·tion /əten'shən/ *n* **1** act or faculty of applying the mind with concentration; **2** civility or courtesy; **3** consideration, care; **4** *mil* attitude of motionless erectness and readiness to obey orders; **5 attentions** *pl* courtesies rendered by a suitor || SYN industry, application, study, respect

at·ten'tive *adj* **1** heedful, observant; **2** courteous, regardful of others || **at·ten'tive·ly** *adv* || SYN thoughtful, considerate, intent, alert || ANT abstracted, careless, negligent

at·ten·u·ate /əten'yōo·āt'/ [L *attenuare* (-*atus*)] *vt* **1** to make thin; **2** to weaken; reduce in force or amount || *vi* **3** to become thin; **4** to lessen || **at·ten'u·a'tion** *n*

at·test /ətest'/ [L *attestari*] *vt* **1** to bear witness to, certify, esp. in an official capacity; **2** to give proof of; vouch for || *vi* **3** to bear witness || **at'tes·ta'tion** /at'-/ *n*

at·tic /at'ik/ [< *Attic*] *n* top part of a building directly beneath the roof

At'tic [< *Attica*] *adj* **1** of or pert. to

Attica or to Athens; **2** pure, refined, classic (style)

At'ti·ca n **1** region of ancient Greece of which Athens was the center; **2** division of modern Greece of which Athens is the capital (2,000,000)

At·ti·la /at'ilə/ n (406–53) king of the Huns, whose invasion of Europe was stopped in France in 451

at·tire /ətīr'/ [OF atirer to put in order] n **1** clothes; fine apparel ‖ vt **2** to dress, array, adorn

at·ti·tude /at'it(y)ōōd'/ [It attitudine aptitude] n **1** position of the body; **2** pose or position assumed to indicate feeling, opinion, or mood; **3** feeling or mental reaction in regard to a matter; **4** position of an aircraft as determined by the inclination of its axes to some frame of reference

at·tor·ney /əturn'ē/ [AF attourne turned] n **1** one legally qualified to act for another; **2** lawyer

at·tor·ney at law' n lawyer

at·tor·ney gen'er·al n (attorney generals or attorneys general) chief law officer of a state or nation

at·tract /ətrakt'/ [L attrahere (-tractus)] vt **1** to draw to or toward itself by physical force; **2** to draw to oneself by physical charm, moral influence, or the like ‖ SYN entice, draw, interest, charm, fascinate

at·trac'tion n **1** act or power of attracting; **2** quality of attracting; fascination, charm; **3** feature or characteristic that attracts; **4** public spectacle; **5** phys electric or magnetic force that acts between bodies and tends to draw them together and keep them from separating

at·trac'tive adj that attracts ‖ **at·trac'·tive·ly** adv ‖ **at·trac'tive·ness** n

attrib. attributive(ly)

at·trib·ute /ətrib'yŏōt/ [L attribuere (-butus)] vt **1** to ascribe as appropriate or belonging; impute, assign ‖ **at·tri·bute** /at'ribyŏōt/ n **2** characteristic, quality, essential property ‖ **at·trib'ut·a·ble** adj ‖ **at'tri·bu'tion** n ‖ SYN v ascribe, assign, charge, refer; n (see quality)

at·trib'u·tive adj **1** attributing; **2** (adjective) that precedes the noun it modifies ‖ n **3** attributive adjective or word which functions as an adjective

at·tri·tion /ətrish'ən/ [< L attritus rubbed away] n **1** abrasion, friction; **2** wearing away

at·tune /ət(y)ŏōn'/ [at- + tune] vt to bring into accordance or harmony with another; adjust

atty. attorney

ATVAE [phonological term, coined by Christopher Stavrou] American Television Announcer English

a·twit·ter /ətwit'ər/ adj twittering, aflutter

at. wt. atomic weight

a·typ·i·cal /ātip'ikəl/ adj not typical

Au [< L aurum] chem gold

au·ber·gine /ō'bərzhēn', -jēn'/ [F < Cat < Ar] n eggplant

au·burn /ôb'ərn/ [OF auborne < L alburnus whitish] n reddish-brown color ‖ also adj

Au'bus·son rug' /ō'bəsən/ n fine ornamental rug with a tapestry weave, made originally in the 16th century at Aubusson in central France

auc·tion /ôk'shən/ [L auctio (-onis) increase] n **1** public sale of property or goods to the highest bidder; **2** auction bridge ‖ vt **3** to sell by auction

auc'tion bridge' n variety of bridge in which tricks taken in excess of the contract are scored toward game

auc'tion·eer' n **1** person who conducts an auction sale ‖ vt **2** to auction

au·da·cious /ôdāsh'əs/ [L audax (-acis)] adj **1** bold, spirited; **2** insolent, impudent ‖ **au·dac'i·ty** /-das/-/ n ‖ SYN unabashed, fearless, shameless, bold, daring

au·di·ble /ôd'ibəl/ [< L audire to hear] adj capable of being heard ‖ **au'·di·bly** adv ‖ **au'di·bil'i·ty** /-bil'-/ n

au·di·ence /ôd'ē·əns/ n **1** group of persons assembled to listen or to see; **2** people reached by radio or television broadcasts; **3** formal interview granted by a high personage; **4** act of hearing

au·di·o /ôd'ē·ō'/ adj electron **1** pert. to audible frequencies ‖ n **2** audio part of television, as distinguished from video

au'di·o fre'quen·cy n frequency of audible sound and corresponding electric waves, between 15 and 20,000 cycles per second ‖ **au'di·o·fre'·quen·cy** adj

au'di·om'e·ter /-om'itər/ n instrument used to test and record the power and acuteness of hearing

au'di·o·vis'u·al adj **1** involving both hearing and seeing; **2** pert. to the presentation of information in both audible and visible form

au·dit /ôd'it/ [L auditus report] n **1** examination of accounts ‖ vt **2** to examine and adjust (accounts); **3** to attend (classes) as an auditor ‖ vi **4** to act as an auditor

au·di·tion /ôdish'ən/ n **1** sense or act of hearing; **2** trial hearing of a performer to test his competence ‖ vt **3** to give an audition to ‖ vi **4** to be given an audition

au'di·tor /-tər/ n **1** hearer or listener; **2** person who audits accounts; **3** college student permitted to take a course without credit and without having to take exams

au'di·to'ri·um /-tōr'ē·əm, -tôr'-/ n **1** space in a theater or other public building assigned to the audience; **2** large building for public gatherings

au'di·to'ry adj relating to hearing or to the sense or organs of hearing

Au·du·bon /ôd′əbon′, -bən/, **John** *n* (1785-1851) Haitian-born U.S. naturalist who painted and wrote about North American birds

auf Wie·der·seh·en /ouf vē′dərzän′/ [G] *interj* till we meet again!

Aug. August

Au·ge·an /ôjē′ən/ *adj* 1 *class. myth.* pert. to Augeas, king of Elis, or to his filthy stables, cleaned by Hercules; 2 extremely filthy

au·ger /ôg′ər/ [ME *a nauger* < OE *nafogār*] *n* tool for boring large holes

aught[1] /ôt′/ [OE *āwiht* ever a whit] *n* 1 anything, any part ‖ *adv* 2 in any way, at all

aught[2] [< *a naught*] *n* cipher, zero

aug·ment /ôgment′/ [< L *augere*] *vt* 1 to enlarge in size or extent ‖ *vi* 2 to grow larger ‖ /ôg′ment/ *n* vowel or syllable prefixed to a verb, or a lengthening of the initial vowel, to indicate past time, as in Greek ‖ **aug′men·ta′tion** *n*

aug·men·ta·tive /-tətiv/ *n* gram form of a word denoting increase in size ‖ also *adj*

au gra·tin /ō′grät′ən, -grat′-, ô′-/ [F] *adj* cooked with a crust of bread or cracker crumbs and cheese and browned in an oven

au·gur /ôg′ər/ [L] *n* 1 in ancient Rome, one who foretold events; 2 prophet ‖ *vi* 3 to be a sign; to bode ‖ *vt* 4 to predict ‖ SYN *v* divine, forebode, forecast, foretell, prognosticate, portend, predict, presage, prophesy

au·gu·ry /ôg′yərē/ *n* (-ries) 1 omen; 2 art or practice of an augur; 3 rite of an augur

au·gust /ôgust′/ [L *augustus*] *adj* 1 imposing, majestic, eminent ‖ SYN awful, grand, great, kingly, venerable, eminent

Au·gust /ôg′əst/ [< L Caesar *Augustus*] *n* eighth month of the year, having 31 days

Au·gus·ta /ôgust′ə/ *n* capital of Maine (22,000)

Au·gus·tine /ôg′əstēn′, ôgust′in/ *n* 1 **Saint** (354-430) Latin church father, bishop of Hippo in N Africa; 2 **Saint** (d. 604) missionary who converted the English, first archbishop of Canterbury 601-604

Au·gus·tin′i·an /-tin′ē-ən/ *adj* 1 pert. to St. Augustine of Hippo ‖ *n* 2 a R C Ch member of any of the orders named for St. Augustine of Hippo; **b** follower of St. Augustine of Hippo

Au·gus·tus /ôgust′əs/ *n* (63 B.C.-14 A.D.) nephew of Julius Caesar and first Roman emperor 27 B.C.-14 A.D. ‖ **Au·gus′tan** *adj*

au jus /ō′zhōōs′, -jōōs′, ô-/ [F] *adj* (meat) served in its natural juices

au na·tu·rel /ō nach′ərəl/ [F] *adj* 1 nude; 2 *cookery* **a** plain; **b** raw

aunt /ant′, änt′/ [OF *aunte* < L *amita*] *n* 1 sister of either parent; 2 an uncle's wife

au·ra /ôr′ə/ [Gk = breeze, breath] *n* distinctive air or atmosphere surrounding a person

au·ral /ôr′əl/ [< L *auris* ear] *adj* 1 pert. to the ear or the sense of hearing; 2 perceived or received by the ear

au·re·ole /ôr′ē-ōl′/ [L *aureola* golden] *n* 1 halo; 2 corona of the sun

Au·re·o·my·cin /ôr′ē-əmīs′in/ [L *aureus* golden + Gk *mykes* fungus; trademark] *n* antibiotic —C₂₂H₂₃N₂O₈Cl— used to treat infections

au re·voir /ō′rəvwär′/ [F] *n* good-by

au·ri·cle /ôr′ikəl/ [L *auriculus*] *n* 1 external ear; 2 one of the two upper cavities of the heart which receive the blood from the great blood vessels and transmit it to the ventricles

au·ric′u·lar /-yələr/ *adj* 1 relating to the ear or to the sense of hearing; 2 said into one's ear; 3 perceived by the ear; 4 ear-shaped; 5 pert. to an auricle of the heart

au·rif·er·ous /ôrif′ərəs/ [< L *aurifer*] *adj* gold-bearing

Au·ri·ga /ôrī′gə/ *n* (gen *-gae* /-jē/) northern constellation, the Charioteer

au·ro·ra /ôrôr′ə, -rōr′-/ [L] *n* 1 dawn; 2 radiant night lights of the polar regions; 3 **Aurora** Roman goddess of the dawn

au·ro′ra aus·tra′lis /ôsträl′is/ [L = southern aurora] *n* aurora of the southern latitudes, southern lights

au·ro′ra bo·re·al′is /bôr′ē-al′is/ [L = northern aurora] *n* aurora of the northern latitudes, northern lights

aus·pice /ôs′pis/ [L *auspicium* divination] *n* 1 omen, sign; 2 **auspices** *pl* patronage

aus·pi·cious /ôspish′əs/ *adj* 1 promising; favorable; 2 successful; prosperous ‖ SYN (see *propitious, happy*) ANT discouraging, hopeless, unfavorable, ill-omened, unpromising

Aus·sie /ôs′ē/ *n slang* Australian

aus·tere /ôstir′/ [Gk *austeros* harsh] *adj* 1 severe, strict; 2 grave, stern; 3 stripped of adornment; 4 sour, astringent ‖ **aus·ter′i·ty** /-ter′-/ *n* ‖ SYN severe, stern, strict, rigid, rigorous, harsh ‖ DISCR *Austere* as applied to persons describes one who is coldly aloof from the softnesses of life; as applied to things it denotes a severe formality, as an *austere* monk; an *austere* drawing-room. *Severe* as applied to persons indicates an unduly exacting quality; as applied to things, an unadorned simplicity, as a *severe* taskmaster; a *severe* style. *Stern* describes a person whose manner is as harsh as his exactions; it describes things or conditions as inflexibly unyielding, as a *stern* parent; *stern* necessity. *Strict* describes one who will not abate his requirements by a jot or a tittle; it describes conditions that must be met, as a *strict* teacher; *strict* rules. *Rigid* describes a severity that is as just as it is uncompromising; *rigorous* describes an unyielding severity that in extremes may cause hardship, as *rigorous* proofs or methods; a *rigorous* climate ‖ ANT affable, mild, gentle, soft, yielding, indulgent

Aus·tin /ôst'in/ *n* capital of Texas (190,000)

Aus·tral·ia /ôstrāl'yə/ *n* English-speaking continent and country SE of Asia (11,751,000; 2,967,909 sq.m.; cap. Canberra); member of the British Commonwealth of Nations ‖ **Aus·tral'ian** *adj & n*

Aus·tri·a /ôs'trē-ə/ *n* German-speaking republic in central Europe (7,100-000; 32,381 sq.m.; cap. Vienna) ‖ **Aus'tri·an** *adj & n*

Aus·tri·a-Hun·ga·ry *n* former monarchy in central Europe, consisting of the present countries of Austria, Hungary, and Czechoslovakia, plus parts of Poland, Romania, Yugoslavia, and Italy ‖ **Aus'tro-Hun·gar'i·an** /-trō-/ *adj & n*

aut- var of **auto-**

au·tar·chy /ôt'ärkē/ [Gk *autarchia* self-rule] *n* (**-chies**) despotism, absolute rule ‖ **au·tar'chic** *adj*

au·tar·ky /ôt'ärkē/ [Gk *autarkeia* self-sufficiency] *n* (**-kies**) national economic self-sufficiency ‖ **au·tar'kic** *adj*

au·then·tic /ôthent'ik/ [Gk *authentikos* original] *adj* 1 genuine; 2 certified as true or reliable; 3 *law* duly executed ‖ **au·then'ti·cal·ly** *adv* ‖ SYN genuine, attested, authorized, sure, true

au·then'ti·cate' *vt* 1 to give validity to; 2 to establish as genuine ‖ **au·then'ti·ca'tion** *n*

au·then·tic·i·ty /ôth'intis'itē/ *n* genuineness

au·thor /ôth'ər/ [OF *autor* < L *auctor* originator] *n* 1 beginner or originator; 2 one who writes a book, article, or other literary composition ‖ **au'thor·ess** *nfem*

au·thor·i·tar·i·an /ôthôr'iter'ē-ən, ôthor'-/ *n* one who favors the principle that individuals should obey an authority rather than exercise freedom ‖ also *adj* ‖ **au·thor'i·tar'i·an·ism** *n*

au·thor'i·ta'tive *adj* 1 having the power to demand or command; 2 coming from such a source as to ensure belief; 3 positive, peremptory

au·thor'i·ty [OF *autorite* < L *auctoritas*] *n* (**-ties**) 1 power or right to act or command; 2 power to act for another; 3 influence commanding respect; 4 expert; 5 quotation or opinion cited as proof; 6 agency or corporation established by a government to administer a public service and expected to be self-supporting; 7 the **authorities** government officials

au·thor·ize /ô'thərīz'/ *vt* 1 to give authority to, empower; 2 to give authority for ‖ **au'thor·i·za'tion** *n*

Au'thor·ized Ver'sion *n* King James Version of the Bible

au'thor·ship' *n* 1 occupation of a writer; 2 source of a written work

au·to /ôt'ō/ [*abbr* of *automobile*] *n* automobile

auto- [Gk *autos*] *comb form* self

au'to·bi·og'ra·phy *n* (**-phies**) story of one's life written by oneself ‖ **au'to·bi'o·graph'i·cal** *adj*

au·toch·tho·nous /ôtok'thənəs/ [Gk = of the land itself] *adj* native; indigenous

au·toc·ra·cy /ôtok'rəsē/ *n* (**-cies**) 1 government by one invested with uncontrolled power; 2 state having such a government

au·to·crat /ôt'əkrat'/ *n* 1 absolute ruler; 2 dictatorial or domineering person ‖ **au'to·crat'ic** *adj*

au'to·graph' *n* 1 one's own handwriting or signature; 2 manuscript written by the author himself ‖ *vt* 3 to write one's signature on or in

au'to·in·tox'i·ca'tion *n* poisoning from substances produced within one's own body

au'to·mat' /-mat'/ [< *automatic*] *n* restaurant in which orders of food are delivered from compartments when coins are inserted in appropriate slots

au'to·mate' *vt* to convert (machinery) to automatic operation ‖ also *vi*

au'to·mat'ic [< Gk *automatos* self-moving] *adj* 1 having the power of self-motion, self-regulation, or self-action; 2 done unconsciously, mechanically, or from force of habit ‖ *n* 3 automatic pistol ‖ **au'to·mat'i·cal·ly** *adv*

au'to·ma'tion *n* 1 act or process of automating or state of being automated; 2 the electronic or mechanical supervision and control of the operation of industrial machinery

au·tom·a·ton /ôtom'əton', -tən/ *n* (**-tons**; **-ta** /-tə/) 1 self-acting mechanism; 2 person whose actions are unthinking and mechanical

au·to·mo·bile /ôt'əməbēl', ôt'əmō'bēl/ [F] *n* self-propelled passenger vehicle powered usu. by an internal-combustion engine

au'to·mo'tive *adj* 1 pert. to automobiles; 2 self-propelled

au·ton·o·mous /ôton'əməs/ [*auto-* + Gk *nomos* law] *adj* self-governing, independent ‖ **au·ton'o·my** *n*

au·top·sy /ô'topsē, ôt'əp-/ [Gk *autopsia* seeing for oneself] *n* (**-sies**) examination of a dead body to determine the cause of death

au·tumn /ôt'əm/ [L *autumnus*] *n* season between summer and winter; from September 22 to December 21 in the Northern Hemisphere ‖ **au·tum·nal** /ôtum'nəl/ *adj*

au·tum'nal e'qui·nox' *n* equinox occurring in the fall, around September 22

aux. auxiliary

aux·il·ia·ry /ôgzil'(y)ərē/ [< L *auxilium* help] *adj* **1** helping; **2** subsidiary, reserve ‖ *n* (-ries) **3** helper or assistant; **4** subsidiary organization, as *the Ladies' Auxiliary* ‖ SYN *n* aid, ally, assistant, coadjutor, confederate, helper, promoter ‖ ANT *n* antagonist, hinderer

aux·il·ia·ry verb' *n* one of a class of verbs that precede nonfinite verbs and express certain distinctions of tense, mood, voice, or aspect

av. average

Av., Ave. Avenue

a·vail /əvāl'/ [< *a-²* + OF *valoir* to be worth] *vi* **1** to be of use, value, or service ‖ *vt* **2** to benefit or help; **3** **avail oneself of** to take advantage of ‖ *n* **4** use, benefit ‖ SYN *n* utility, service, benefit, advantage

a·vail'a·ble *adj* **1** usable; **2** at hand, accessible ‖ **a·vail'a·bil'i·ty** /-bil'-/ *n*

av·a·lanche /av'əlanch', -länch'/ [F] *n* **1** sudden sliding of a mass of snow, ice, rocks, earth, etc., down a mountain slope; **2** anything that overwhelms like an avalanche

Av·a·lon /av'əlon'/ [< Old Welsh] *n* island in the western seas, the earthly paradise of Celtic legend to which King Arthur was borne at death

a·vant-garde /ä'vän'gärd'/ [F] *n* vanguard, esp. in the arts ‖ also *adj*

av·a·rice /av'əris/ [< L *avarus* greedy] *n* insatiable desire for wealth

av'a·ri'cious /-rish'əs/ *adj* eager to possess and to keep riches; greedy for gain; grasping ‖ SYN covetous, close, miserly, niggardly, parsimonious, penurious, stingy ‖ DISCR The *avaricious* man is greedy for gold and other possessions; the *miserly* man is he whose avarice has become his ruling passion. The *miserly* man is as mean with himself as he is with others; the *avaricious* man occasionally indulges himself; but it is his wont to be frugal to excess if he is *parsimonious*, small to the last watched penny in his dealings if he is *niggardly*, sordidly saving if he is *penurious*, and reluctant to part with anything belonging to him, if he is *stingy*. One who desires the possessions of others is *covetous* ‖ ANT generous, prodigal

a·vast /əvast', əväst'/ [prob D *houd vast* hold fast] *interj naut* stop!, cease!

av·a·tar /av'ətär'/ [< Skt *avatāra* descent] *n* **1** *Hindu myth.* descent, as of a deity to earth in bodily form; **2** embodiment, manifestation

A·ve Ma·ri·a /ä'vā mərē'ə/ [L] *n* Hail Mary (the first words of a Roman Catholic prayer)

a·venge /əvenj'/ [OF *avengier* < ad-

+ L *vindicare*] *vt* **1** to take vengeance for (an act); **2** to take vengeance on behalf of (a person) ‖ *vi* **3** to take vengeance ‖ **a·veng'er** *n* ‖ SYN revenge, vindicate ‖ DISCR To *avenge* is to exact just punishment in behalf of wrongs or oppressions, from motives free from malice, often from a sense of duty to both the wrongdoer and the wronged; to *revenge* is to exact punishment from personal malice and resentment to gain the sense of vindictive triumph peculiar to revengeful people. To *vindicate* is to defend successfully in the face of opposition or against a charge

av·e·nue /av'ən(y)ōō'/ [F < L *advenire* to come to] *n* **1** way of approach or departure; **2** a wide roadway bordered by trees; **b** any street; **3** means of access or attainment

a·ver /əvur'/ [MF *averer* < LL *averare* to prove true] *v* (**a·verred**) *vt* to affirm positively, assert

av·er·age /av'(ə)rij/ [< MF *avarie* ship damage] *n* **1** generally accepted standard or rate; mean, norm; **2** result obtained by dividing the total of several quantities by the number of quantities; **3 on the average** usually ‖ *adj* **4** constituting an average; **5** ordinary, of everyday standard ‖ *vt* **6** to find the average of; **7** to do, take, or get on an average

a·verse /əvurs'/ [L *aversus* turned away] *adj* **1** unwilling, reluctant; **2** averse to having a repugnance to ‖ **a·verse'ly** *adv*

a·ver·sion /əvur'zhən/ *n* **1** repugnance, antipathy; **2** object of dislike or repugnance ‖ SYN dislike, repugnance, disgust (see *antipathy*)

a·vert /əvurt'/ [L *avertere*] *vt* **1** to turn aside or away; **2** to prevent ‖ SYN hinder, obstruct, preclude (see *prevent*)

A·ves·ta /əvest'ə/ [OPers] *n* ancient scriptures of Persia ‖ **A·ves'tan** *adj & n*

avi- [< *avis*] *comb form* bird

a·vi·an /ā'vē·ən/ *adj* of or pert. to birds

a·vi·ar·y /ā'vē·er'ē/ (-ies) *n* house, large cage, or enclosure for the keeping and rearing of birds

a·vi·a·tion /ā'vē·āsh'ən, av'-/ *n* **1** art or science of flying airplanes; **2** design, development, and manufacture of airplanes

a'vi·a'tor *n* operator of an airplane ‖ **a'vi·a'trix** /-triks/ *nfem*

av·id /av'id/ [L *avidus*] *adj* eager, greedy ‖ **av'id·ly** *adv* ‖ **a·vid'i·ty** /əvid'-/ *n*

a·vi·ta·min·o·sis /āvīt'əminōs'is/ *n* disease caused by lack of vitamins

av·o·ca·do /av'əkäd'ō, äv'-/ [< Sp *aguacate* < Nahuatl] *n* **1** West Indian tree (*Persea americana*); **2** its pearlike fruit

av·o·ca·tion /av'əkāsh'ən/ [L *avocare* (*-atus*) to call off] *n* occasional or minor occupation; hobby

A'vo·ga'dro's law' /ä'vəgä'drōz/ [Count Amadeo *Avogadro* (1776-1856) It chemist and physicist] *n* principle that equal volumes of gases at the same temperature and pressure contain the same number of molecules

a·void /əvoid'/ [< OF *esvuidier* to empty out] *vt* **1** to keep away from, shun; **2** *law* to make void, annul || **a·void'a·ble** *adj* || **a·void'ance** *n* || SYN shun, elude, escape, evade; void, cancel, annul

av·oir·du·pois /av'ərdəpoiz'/ [OF *avoir de pois* goods of weight] *n* **1** system of weights in the U.S. and Great Britain using the pound of sixteen ounces or 7,000 grains; **2** *colloq* excess weight

a·vouch /əvouch'/ [MF *avochier* to avow] *vt* **1** to affirm or acknowledge; **2** to guarantee

a·vow /əvou'/ [OF *avouer* < L *advocare*] *vt* to declare openly; admit || **a·vowed'** *adj* || **a·vow'ed·ly** /-idlḗ/ *adv* || **a·vow'al** *n* || SYN aver, admit, confess, affirm, declare

a·vun·cu·lar /əvuŋk'yələr/ [< L *avunculus* uncle] *adj* of or like an uncle

a·wait /əwāt'/ [OF *awaitier*] *vt* **1** to wait for, expect; **2** to be in store for

a·wake /əwāk'/ *v* (**a·woke** also **a·waked**) *vi* **1** to cease to sleep; **2** to arouse oneself, become alert || *vt* **3** to arouse from sleep; **4** to infuse new life into || *adj* **5** not sleeping; **6** in a state of vigilance or action

a·wak'en [OE *awæcnian*] *vt & vi* to rouse from sleep, awake

a·wak'en·ing *n* **1** act of waking; **2** revival; **3** new awareness

a·ward /əwôrd'/ [AF *awarder* < Gmc] *vt* **1** to grant after due consideration, as between contestants or by judicial decision || *n* **2** decision, as of judges; **3** prize; grant

a·ware /əwer'/ [OE *gewær* wary] *adj* **1** cognizant; **2** vigilant || **a·ware'ness** *n* || SYN informed, apprised (see *conscious*)

a·wash /əwosh', -wôsh'/ *adj & adv* **1** level with the surface of the water; **2** overflowing with water

a·way /əwā'/ [OE *on weg* on the way] *adv* **1** at or to a distance; off; **2** aside, in another direction; **3** out of one's possession, as *to give away;* **4** continuously, as *he worked away;* **5** into extinction, as *to die away;* **6** far; apart; **7** uninterruptedly, as *fire away;* **8** away with go or take away; **9** do away with to get rid of; **10** go away to leave || *adj* **11** absent; **12** distant, as *a mile away*

awe /ô'/ [ON *agi* fear] *n* **1** solemn

fear, reverence || *vt* **2** to inspire with awe || **awe'some** *adj* || **awe'strick'en** or **awe'struck'** *adj* || SYN *n* reverence, veneration, dread || DISCR *Awe* is a strong term. It expresses a feeling of respect tinged with fear and colored by solemnity; it is aroused by contemplating the sublime or sacred, and possesses crippling force, as *awe* held him motionless before this miracle of faith. *Reverence* is esteem, sometimes slightly mingled with fear; it is aroused by the noble and exalted, and causes us to bow before that which inspires it; it is a humbling sentiment. *Veneration* is an intensified *reverence,* chiefly with no touch of fear, often with a suggestion of personal affection or nearness; the *veneration* in which we hold a saint, for instance, is of this nature; we have *reverence* for the Scriptures. *Dread* is great and paralyzing fear, aroused by the terrible, as *dread* of disgrace or death

aw·ful /ôf'əl/ *adj* **1** awe-inspiring; **2** dreadful; **3** very bad || *adv* **4** *colloq* very || SYN alarming, august, dire, dreadful, grand, imposing, majestic, portentous, solemn, terrible || ANT base, beggarly, commonplace, contemptible, despicable

aw'ful·ly *adv* **1** terribly; **2** extremely

a·while /əw(h)īl'/ *adv* during or for a short time

awk·ward /ôk'wərd/ [< ON *afug* turned wrong + *-ward*] *adj* **1** unskillful, ungainly, clumsy; **2** difficult to deal with; dangerous; **3** embarrassing || **awk'ward·ly** *adv* || **awk'ward·ness** *n* || SYN clumsy || DISCR *Awkward* implies a lack of grace in motion. The *awkward* person is neither dexterous nor adroit; he manages his body ill, and hence has an *awkward* gait; he bungles in his social contacts, and so creates *awkward* situations. *Clumsy* actions result from a body ill-balanced, illformed, or stiff to the point of defect; a hippopotamus is *clumsy* from its build; a duck is *clumsy* on land. Figuratively, *clumsy* describes something unskillfully, heavily managed, as a *clumsy* lie || ANT adroit, polite, skillful

awl /ôl'/ [OE *æl*] *n* pointed tool for making small holes

awn·ing /ôn'iŋ/ [?] *n* rooflike covering, as of canvas, stretched upon a frame and used above or before any place as a shelter from rain or sun

a·woke /əwōk'/ *pt* of **awake**

A.W.O.L., a.w.o.l /often ā'wôl/ *adj* **1** absent without leave || *n* **2** soldier who is A.W.O.L.

a·wry /ərī'/ *adj & adv* **1** turned or twisted toward one side; **2** amiss

ax or **axe** /aks'/ [OE *æx*] *n* **1** tool with

a bladed head and a handle; **2 get the ax** to be dismissed; **3 have an axe to grind** to have an ulterior motive

ax·i·al /ak'sē-əl/ *adj* pert. to or applying to an axis

ax·il·la /aksil'ə/ [L] *n* (**-lae** /-lē/) armpit

ax·i·om /ak'sē-əm/ [Gk *axioma* worthy thing] *n* **1** self-evident truth; **2** accepted principle || **ax'i·o·mat'ic** /-mat'ik/ *adj* || **ax'i·o·mat'i·cal·ly** *adv* || SYN principle, proverb (see *truism*)

ax·is /ak'sis/ [L] *n* (**ax·es** /-sēz/) **1** straight line about which a body rotates; **2** central line, as of a body, plant, or part; **3** *geom* fixed straight line along which distances are measured or used for reference; **4** the Axis Germany, Italy, and Japan and their allies in World War II

ax·le /ak'səl/ [ON *öxul*] *n* **1** bar or spindle on which a wheel turns; **2** bar connecting two opposite wheels in a vehicle

aye¹ also **ay** /ī'/ [?] *adv* **1** yes || *n* **2** vote in the affirmative

aye² also **ay** /ā'/ [ON < OE?] *adv* always, ever

Ay·ma·ra /ī'märä'/ [< Sp < AmInd] *n* **1** member of an Indian people living in the mountains of Bolivia and Peru; **2** their language || **Ay'ma·ran'** *adj*

a·zal·ea /əzāl'yə/ [< Gk *azaleos* dry] *n* any of several species of shrubs of the heath family (genus *Rhododendron*), cultivated for its flowers

A·za·ni·a /əzä'nē-ə/ *n* (African name of the) *Republic of South Africa*

A·zer·bai·jan /ä'zərbī'jan, a'-/ *n* constituent republic of the Soviet Union, on the Caspian Sea (4,500,000; 33,000 sq.m.; cap. Baku)

az·i·muth /az'iməth/ [Ar *as-sumūt* the paths] *n* arc of the horizon measured clockwise between usu. the south point and the vertical plane which passes through any object, as a heavenly body, and the observer

A·zores /əzôrz', ā'zôrz/ *npl* Portuguese islands in the N Atlantic (315,000; 889 sq.m.)

Az·tec /az'tek/ [Sp *Azteca* < Nahuatl] *n* **1** member of the Nahuatl people whose highly developed empire was conquered by the Spaniards in 1519; **2** their language || also *adj* || **Az'tec·an** *adj*

az·ure /azh'ər, āzh'-/ [OF *azur* < Pers *lāzhuward* lapis lazuli *via* Ar] *n* sky blue || also *adj*

B

B, b /bē'/ *n* (**B's** or **Bs, b's** or **bs**) second letter of the English alphabet

B 1 *chem* boron; **2** second in order or in a series; **3** *mus* seventh tone in the scale of C major; **4 a** grade rating of good; **b** *movies* grade rating of mediocre; **5** blood type; **6** something shaped like a B; **7** *chess* bishop

B., b., 1 bass; **2** base; **3** born

Ba *chem* barium

B.A. [L *Baccalaureus Artium*] Bachelor of Arts

baa /bä'/ [imit] *vi* **1** to bleat, as a sheep || *n* **2** bleat of a sheep

Ba·al /bā'(ə)l/ [Heb *ba'al* lord] *n* (**Ba·als, Ba·al·im** /-im/) **1** one of numerous local gods among the ancient Phoenicians and Canaanites; **2** false god

Bab·bitt /bab'it/ [protagonist of novel by Sinclair Lewis] *n* smug person who readily conforms to middle-class standards and conventions || **Bab'bitt·ry** *n*

Bab'bitt met'al [Isaac *Babbitt* (1799-1862) Am inventor] *n* alloy of tin with small amounts of copper and antimony, used in bearings and around journals to minimize friction

bab·ble /bab'əl/ [ME *babelen*] *vi* **1** to utter indistinct or imperfect sounds; **2** to prattle; **3** to chatter continually; **4** to make a murmuring sound || *vt* **5** to utter indistinctly or imperfectly; **6** to tell, as secrets || *n* **7** foolish talk; **8** confused prattle; **9** continuous murmuring sound || **bab'bler** *n*

babe /bāb'/ [ME *baban*, prob imit] *n* **1** infant or young child; **2** naive person; **3** *slang* girl or woman

Ba·bel /bāb'əl, bab'-/ [perh Assyr *bab ilu* gate of god] *n* **1** city and tower described in Gen. 11, where the confusion of languages took place; **2 babel, a** confusion of voices and sounds; **b** tumult, confusion

ba·boon /baboon'/ [MF *babuin*] *n* any of several large monkeys (genus *Papio*) of Africa and Arabia, usu. short-tailed and with a doglike face

ba·bush·ka /bəboosh'kə/ [Russ = grandmother] *n* folded kerchief used as a woman's headcovering

ba·by /bāb'ē/ [dim. of *babe*] *n* (**-bies**) **1** child in arms, infant; **2** youngest member; **3** childish person; **4** *slang* **a** girl, woman; **b** sweetheart; **c** person or thing || *adj* **5** small or young, as a *baby bond, baby grand piano* || *v* (**-bied**) *vt* **6** to pamper, treat with care

ba·by car·riage *n* four-wheeled push carriage for a baby

ba·by farm' *n* place where small children are cared for and boarded for pay

Bab·y·lon /bab'ələn, -lon'/ *n* 1 ancient capital of Babylonia, noted for its splendor; 2 any rich and luxurious city noted for vice and wickedness

Bab·y·lo·ni·a /bab'əlōn'ē·ə/ *n* ancient empire of SW Asia of ab. 2800–1700 B.C. ‖ **Bab'y·lo'ni·an** *adj* & *n*

ba·by's-breath' also **ba'bies'-breath'** *n* 1 tall plant (*Gypsophila paniculata*) of the pink family, having small fragrant white or pink flowers; 2 any of several other plants with delicate scent, as the grape hyacinth

ba·by·sit' *v* (-sat; -sit·ting) *vi* to care for children while the parents are away for the evening ‖ **ba'by·sit'ter** *n*

bac·ca·lau·re·ate /bak'əlôr'ē·it/ [< LL *baccalaureus* alter. of *baccalarius* bachelor] *n* 1 the degree of bachelor; 2 a religious service for the graduating class; b sermon delivered at such service

bac·ca·rat /bak'ərä', bak'ərä'/ [F *baccara*] *n* French gambling game of cards

bac·cha·nal /bak'ənəl/ [< *Bacchus*] *adj* 1 bacchanalian ‖ /also bak'ənal', bak'ənəl'/ *n* 2 devotee of Bacchus; 3 drunken reveler; 4 riotous feast

Bac·cha·na·li·a /bak'ənāl'ē·ə/ *nsg* & *npl* 1 feast to Bacchus; 2 **bacchanalia** drunken revel ‖ **bac'cha·na'li·an** *adj*

Bac·chus /bak'əs/ *n* *class. myth.* Roman god of wine; identified with the Greek Dionysus

Bach /bäkh'/, **Johann Sebastian** *n* (1685–1750) German composer and organist, father of four other composers and organists

bach /bach'/ [< *bachelor*] *n* New Zealand week-end cottage in the mountains or by a stretch of water

bach·e·lor /bach'(ə)lər/ [OF *bacheler* young man < LL *baccalarius* farm laborer, student] 1 unmarried man; 2 one who has taken the first degree at a college or university; 3 young knight in the service of another

Bach'e·lor of Arts' *n* 1 bachelor's degree in the humanities or liberal arts; 2 holder of this degree

Bach'e·lor of Sci'ence *n* 1 bachelor's degree in the natural sciences or in pure science; 2 holder of this degree

ba·cil·lus /bəsil'əs/ [< L *bacillum* little rod] *n* (-li /-lī/) 1 any of several rod-shaped bacteria (genus *Bacillus*); 2 any straight rod-shaped bacterium; 3 any bacterium

back[1] /bak'/ [OE *bæc*] *n* 1 rear part of the body from the neck to the end of the backbone; 2 rear part of anything; 3 side or part of anything

away from the beholder; 4 vertical part of a chair or sofa for supporting people's backs; 5 *sports* a position behind the front lines; b player in such a position; 6 backbone; 7 **behind one's back** secretly; in one's absence; 8 **flat on one's back** helpless; 9 **get off someone's back** to stop annoying or finding fault with someone; 10 **turn one's back on** to forsake, abandon ‖ *vt* 11 to furnish with a back; 12 to second or support; 13 to bet on; 14 to cause to move backward; 15 **back water,** a to row backward; b to reverse the direction of the propellers in order to stop a ship or make it go backward; c to retreat from a position or stand ‖ *vi* 16 to move backward; 17 **back down** or **off** to abandon one's position; 18 **back out** to fail to keep a promise; 19 **back out of** to withdraw from; 20 **back up,** a (of water) to rise in a pipe because of some obstruction; b (of traffic) to stop moving ‖ *adj* 21 being behind or to the rear as to time, situation, or direction; 22 in arrears, overdue

back[2] [< OE *on bæc* aback] *adv* 1 to or toward the rear; 2 to or toward a former place, state, time, or condition; 3 in withdrawal, as *to take back hasty words*; 4 in retention or reserve; 5 in repayment or return; 6 **back and forth** from side to side; 7 **go back on,** a to back out of (one's promises); b to betray

back' bench' *n* *Brit* in the House of Commons, row of seats that may be occupied by any member ‖ **back'-bench'er** *n*

back'bite' *v* (-bit'; -bit·ten) *vt* 1 to slander (one who is not present) ‖ *vi* 2 to indulge in backbiting ‖ **back'-bit'er** *n*

back'bone' *n* 1 spinal column; 2 moral courage; 3 mainstay; 4 bound edge of a book; spine

back'down' *n* withdrawal from a previously held stand or position, often because of strong opposition

back'drop' *n* 1 curtain behind a stage setting; 2 background

back'er *n* one who aids or supports a person or cause

back'field' *n* football players positioned behind the line of scrimmage

back'fire' *n* 1 premature explosion of fuel in the intake manifold of an internal-combustion engine ‖ *vi* 2 to experience a backfire; 3 to have an effect opposite to that planned

back' for·ma'tion *n* 1 formation of a word by dropping an affix from an existing word; 2 word so formed, as *enthuse* from *enthusiasm*

back'gam'mon /-gam'ən/ [< ME *gamen* game] *n* game played on a board by two persons who move checkers in accordance with throws of dice

back′ground′ *n* **1** distant portion of the landscape; **2** surface upon which patterns or designs are executed; **3** retirement; obscurity; **4** individual's family, education, and culture; **5** antecedent circumstances which explain an event or situation; **6** intrusive noise that interferes with electronic signals

back′ground′er *n* news conference of a government official who talks freely but wishes to remain anonymous

back′ground mu′sic *n* **1** music, often recorded, played softly and unobtrusively in a public place; **2** music composed to accompany the dialogue or action of a visual production

back′hand′ *n* **1** handwriting which slopes upward to the left; **2** blow with the back of the hand; **3** *tennis* stroke made with the arm moving forward across the front of the body ‖ *adj* **4** made with the back of the hand or with the hand turned backward; **5** indirect; insincere ‖ *vt* **6** to hit with a backhand; **7** to catch backhanded

back′hand′ed *adj* **1** done with a backhand; **2** devious, insincere ‖ also *adv*

back′ing *n* **1** something placed behind to support or strengthen; **2** aid or support for a person or cause

back′lash′ *n* **1** *mach* play between loosely fitting parts; **2** snarled line on a fishing reel; **3** any strong reaction, as to a political movement

back′log′ *n* **1** reserve of stock, work, or unfilled orders ‖ *v* (-logged; -logging) *vt* **2** to accumulate a backlog of; **3** to hold in reserve

back′pack′ *n* **1** case in the form of a knapsack worn by hikers, students, astronauts, etc. to carry supplies and equipment ‖ *vt* **2** to carry in a backpack ‖ also *vi*

back′side′ *n* **1** hind part of anything; **2** buttocks

back′slap′per *n* person who displays loud and effusive good will

back′slide′ *v* (-slid) *vi* **1** to gradually turn away from one's religion; **2** to relapse into sinful ways ‖ **back′slid′er** *n*

back′stage′ *adj* relating to or occurring behind the stage of a theater ‖ also *adv*

back′stairs′ or **back′stair′** *adj* intriguing, underhand; secret

back′stop′ *n* **1** person or thing behind, serving to stop; **2** support or reinforcement ‖ *v* (-stopped; -stop·ping) *vt* **3** to serve as a backstop for; **4** to support

back′ talk′ *n* impudent, insolent reply ‖ **back′-talk′** *vi*

back′track′ *vi* **1** to retrace one's steps; **2** to reverse one's position

back′ward /-wərd/ *adj* **1** directed to the rear or past; **2** in a way opposite to normal; reversed; **3** retiring, bashful; **4** behind in learning or progress; dull ‖ also **back′wards** *adv* **5** toward the rear or past; **6** with the back coming foremost; **7** from better to worse; **8** in reverse direction ‖ **back′ward·ness** *n*

back′woods′ *npl* forests or partly cleared land on the outskirts of settled country

ba·con /bāk′ən/ [OF < OHG *bacho*] *n* **1** salted and dried or smoked flesh of the pig, esp. the back and sides; **2 bring home the bacon** *slang* **a** to earn a living; **b** to succeed in a set task; **3 save someone's bacon** to save a person from loss or defeat

Ba′con, Francis *n* (1561–1626) English essayist, statesman, and philosopher ‖ **Ba·co·ni·an** /bākōn′ē·ən/ *adj & n*

Ba′con, Roger *n* (ab. 1214–94) English philosopher and scientist

bac·te·ri·a /baktir′ē·ə/ [L < Gk *bakterion* little stick] *npl* widely distributed group of microscopic, one-celled vegetable organisms (class Schizomycetes), living on organic matter, dead or alive, and causing a great variety of processes and conditions affecting animal and vegetable life, as decay, fermentation, soil enrichment, and disease ‖ **bac·te′ri·al** *adj*

bac·te′ri·cide′ /-isīd′/ [*bacteri-* + *-cide*] *n* something that kills bacteria ‖ **bac·te′ri·cid′al** *adj*

bac·te·ri·ol·o·gy /baktir′ē·ol′əjē/ *n* science that deals with bacteria ‖ **bac·te′ri·ol′o·gist** *n* ‖ **bac·te·ri·o·log·ic** /-i·cal/ /baktir′ē·ələj′ik(əl)/ *adj*

bac·te′ri·um /-əm/ *sg* of **bacteria**

Bac′tri·an Cam′el /bak′trē·ən/ [< *Bactria* ancient country in W Asia] *n* Asian camel (*Camelus bactrianus*) with two humps on its back

bad /bad′/ [ME *badde* worthless < OE *bæddel* effeminate person] *adj* (**worse; worst**) **1** poor or unacceptable as to fit, manners, behavior, character, temper, mood, taste, accuracy, efficiency, adequacy, safety, workability, weather, legality, genuineness, validity, health, morals, reputation, honesty, accommodations, convenience, suitability, aesthetic effect, or beauty; **2** evil, wicked; **3** spoiled, rotten; **4** unpleasant, disagreeable; **5** severe, intense; **6** sorry, contrite ‖ *adv* **7** *colloq* badly ‖ *n* **8** that which is bad; **9 the bad** *pl* evil people collectively; **10 in bad** in trouble or disfavor ‖ **bad′ness** *n* ‖ SYN *adj* immoral, vicious, sinful, inferior, wrong, injurious, evil, wicked, naughty ‖ DISCR *Bad* is the opposite of *good*, and hence often implies merely the unsatisfactory nature, poor quality, or defective condition of the thing described, as *bad* manners; in *bad* form. When not so used, *bad* means harmful, or morally blamable, as a *bad* accident; *bad* conduct. *Evil* usually describes that which is morally *bad*, as *evil* thoughts or desires; but it may mean disastrous, as an *evil* day; or baleful, as an *evil* look. *Wicked* implies not only *evil* principles but *evil* practice. *Naughty* means perverse or disobedient, as a *naughty* child

bad′ blood′ *n* hostility, ill feeling

bade /bad′/ *pt* of **bid**

bad′ egg′ *n slang* evil, disreputable person

badge /baj′/ [ME *bage*] **1** distinctive mark, sign, or token to denote the occupation, association, or achievements of the person who wears it; **2** mark or token of anything

badg′er /baj′ər/ [perh < *badge*, from white mark on forehead] *n* **1** hairy, flesh-eating, nocturnal, burrowing mammal (genera *Meles & Taxidea*) with short legs and a flat body; **2** badger's fur; **3 Badger** nickname for a native or resident of Wisconsin || *vt* **4** to tease, annoy, worry

bad·i·nage /bad′inij, bad′inäzh′/ [F < *badiner* to jest] *n* **1** light or playful jesting || *vt* **2** to tease || SYN *n* chaff, raillery, persiflage, banter

Bad′ Lands′ *npl* barren and forsaken region of SW South Dakota and NW Nebraska

bad′ly *adv* **1** in a bad way; **2** *colloq* very much

bad·min·ton /bad′mint′ən/ [*Badminton* estate in England] *n* game similar to tennis in which a feathered cork called the shuttlecock is driven over a net with a light racket

Bae·de·ker /bād′əkər/ [Karl *Baedeker* (1801–59) G publisher] *n* **1** any of a series of guidebooks published by Baedeker; **2** any guidebook

baf·fle /baf′əl/ [?] *vt* **1** to confuse, bewilder; **2** to deflect, check, as gas, air, sound, or light || *n* **3** device for deflecting or checking the flow of gas, sound, or light || **baf′fle·ment** *n* || **baf′fler** *n* || **baf′fling** *adj* || SYN *v* balk, frustrate, thwart, confound, outwit

bag /bag′/ [ON *baggi*] *n* **1** sack, pouch; **2** valise; **3** amount contained in a bag; **4** game secured by a sportsman in one day; **5** purse; handbag; **6** baseball base; **7** *slang* slatternly woman; **8 hold the bag** to bear the blame; **9 in the bag** assured, certain || *v* (**bagged; bag·ging**) *vt* **10** to enclose in a bag; **11** to secure or capture, as game; **12** to cause to swell || *vi* **13** to swell; **14** to sag loosely

bag·a·telle /bag′ətel′/ [F < It *bagatella*] *n* trifle

ba·gel /bāg′əl/ [Yiddish *beygel* < Gmc] *n* hard doughnut-shaped roll

bag·gage /bag′ij/ [MF *bagage*] *n* **1** trunks, bags, and other containers used for travel; **2** saucy young woman

bag′gy *adj* (**-gi·er; -gi·est**) loose, hanging, or puffed out like a bag

Bagh·dad or **Bag·dad** /bag′dad/ *n* capital of Iraq, on the Tigris (1,745,328)

bag′man′ /-man′/ *n* (**-men** /-men′/) *colloq* collector of bribes and payoff money

bag′pipe′ *n* or **bag′pipes′** *npl* shrilltoned musical instrument consisting of a leather bag from which air is forced by the player's arm into pipes || **bag′pip′er** *n*

bah /bä/ *interj* expressing scorn, disgust, or disbelief

Ba·ha·i /bähä′ē, -hī′/ [Pers *baha'i* of glory] *n* member of a sect of Shiah Muslims originating in Persia in 1863 which emphasizes tolerance and the spiritual unity of men of all religions || **Ba·ha′ism** *n* || **Ba·ha′ist** *n*

Ba·ha·mas or **Ba·ha′ma Is′lands** /bəhäm′ə(z)/ *n* English-speaking nation consisting of a group of islands off the SE coast of Florida (144,000; 4404 sq.m.; cap. Nassau)

Bah·rein /bärän′/ *n* monarchy, consisting of a group of islands in the Persian Gulf (300,000; 256 sq.m.; cap. Manama)

baht /bät/ [Thai] *n* (**baht** or **bahts**) monetary unit of Thailand

bail¹ /bāl/ [OF *baillier* to take charge of] *vt law* **1** to deliver (an arrested person) to persons who become security for his appearance when summoned; **2** to procure security for the appearance of || *n* **3** temporary freedom given a defendant or prisoner when security is entered for his appearance; **4** security so given; **5** person giving such security; **6 go bail for** to put up bail for; **7 jump bail** to flee while free on bail; **8 on bail** released after having put up bail

bail² [MF *baille* bucket] *vt* **1** to empty of water by dipping; **2** to dip out, as water || *vi* **3** to dip out water; **4 bail out, a** to make a parachute jump; **b** *colloq* to rescue from a tight situation || *n* **5** vessel used in dipping water out of a boat

bail³ [ME *beyl* < ON] *n* **1** semicircular support, as for a wagon cover; **2** handle of a pail or the like; **3** bar with rollers for holding the paper in place in a typewriter or printing press

bail′ bond′ *n* security given by a prisoner, and by the person who guarantees his appearance, that he will appear in court when summoned

bail·iff /bāl′if/ [OF *baillif*] *n* **1** sheriff's officer or constable; **2** *Brit* agent in charge of an estate; **3** *Brit* chief magistrate in certain towns

bail·i·wick /bāl′-iwik/ [< ME *bailie* bailiff + OE *wīc* town] *n* **1** jurisdiction of a bailiff; **2** one's special area of competence or command

Bai·ly's beads/ /bāl'ēz/ [Francis *Baily* (1774–1884) Eng astronomer] *npl* bright beads of sunlight that appear around the edge of the moon a few seconds before and after an eclipse of the sun

bairn /bern'/ [Sc < OE *bearn*] *n* Scot child

bait /bāt'/ [ON *beita* food] *vt* **1** to set dogs on (an animal) for sport; **2** to torment, annoy persistently; **3** to put food on (a hook or trap); **4** to lure, entice || *n* **5** anything, as food, put on a hook or trap as a lure; **6** enticement

baize /bāz'/ [OF *baies* < *bai* bay-colored] *n* coarse woolen stuff of plain color, with a nap on one side, used esp. to cover billiard tables

bake /bāk'/ [OE *bacan*] *vt* **1** to cook (food) in an oven; **2** to harden by dry heat, as porcelain or bricks || *vi* **3** to bake food; **4** to be baked || *n* **5** process or result of baking; **6** social gathering featuring baked food

Ba·ke·lite /bāk'(ə)līt'/ [trademark] *n* synthetic resin produced from phenol and formaldehyde, used for molded plastic ware

bak'er *n* **1** one whose business it is to make and/or sell baked goods; **2** small movable oven; **3** *Baker* communications code word for the letter B

bak'er's doz'en *n* thirteen

bak·er·y /bāk'ərē/ *n* (-ies) place where baked goods are made or sold

bak'ing *n* the quantity of baked goods made at one time; batch

bak'ing pow'der *n* white powder containing an acid or acid salt and bicarbonate of soda, used to effect the quick rising of bread, cakes, etc.

bak'ing so'da *n* sodium bicarbonate

bak·sheesh /bak'shēsh/ [< Pers *bakhshīdan* to give] *n* (in the Near East) gratuity, tip

Ba·ku /bäkōō'/ *n* capital of Azerbaijan and port on the Caspian Sea (1,164,000)

bal. balance

ba·la·lai·ka /bal'əlīk'ə/ [Russ] *n* Russian musical instrument resembling a guitar

bal·ance /bal'əns/ [OF < L (libra) *bilanx* scale with two pans] *n* **1** apparatus for weighing, esp. one with a pivoted beam and pans at both ends; **2** equal poise of the two sides of a scale; **3** equal poise of any opposing forces; equilibrium or steadiness; **4** mental poise; **5 a** equality between the totals of two sides of an account; **b** excess shown on either side; **6** sum or weight necessary to make two unequal sums or weights equal; **7** act of weighing, as by mental comparison or estimate;

8 certain movement in dancing; **9** *horol* balance wheel; **10** amount remaining; **11 in the balance** not yet settled or decided; **12 on balance** when all sides are taken into consideration || *vt* **13** to weigh in a balance; **14** to weigh, compare, estimate; **15** to set off, as one thing against another; **16** to equal or make equal; **17 a** to find out the difference between the debits and credits of (an account); **b** to bring about an equality between; **18** to cause to be steady or in equilibrium || *vi* **19** to be of equal weight, force, or amount, as *the accounts balance;* **20** to keep one's equilibrium; **21** to waver || SYN *n* equipoise, equilibrium (see *remainder*)

bal'ance of pay'ments *n* difference between a nation's total payments to foreign countries and its total receipts from foreign countries in a given period

bal'ance of pow'er *n* equilibrium of military and economic power among nations

bal'ance of ter'ror *n* stand-off between the U.S. and the U.S.S.R. because of mutual fear of a nuclear holocaust

bal'ance of trade' *n* difference between the value of imports and exports of a country in a given period

bal'ance sheet' *n* statement of financial condition as of a given date

bal'ance wheel' *n* wheel, as in a watch, to regulate motion or rate of running

bal·bo·a /balbō'ə/ [*Balboa*] *n* coin and monetary unit of Panama

Bal·bo·a, Vas·co Nú·ñez de /bäs'kō nōōn'yeth de/ *n* (1475–1517) Spanish explorer, discoverer of the Pacific Ocean 1513

bal·brig·gan /balbrig'ən/ [*Balbriggan*, Ireland] *n* finely knitted cotton fabric for hosiery or underwear

bal·co·ny /bal'kənē/ [It *balcone* < *balco* scaffold] *n* (-nies) **1** platform or gallery built out from the wall of a building and enclosed by a balustrade or railing; **2** theater gallery

bald /bôld'/ [ME *balled* perh < obs *ball* white spot] *adj* **1** without hair on top of the head; **2** without natural covering, as of feathers, fur, leaves, etc.; **3** bare, unadorned; **4** without disguise; bold; **5** (bird) having a white patch on the head || **bald'ly** *adv* || **bald'ness** *n*

bald' ea'gle *n* large North American eagle (*Haliaetus leucocephalus*), the adult of which has a white head and neck

bal·der·dash /bôl'dərdash'/ [?] *n* nonsense

bald'pate' *n* baldheaded person

bal·dric /bôl'drik/ [OF *baudrei*] *n*

broad belt worn over the shoulder to support a sword or bugle

Bald·win /bôld′win/ [< OF] *n* variety of winter apple, bright red and moderately tart

bale /bāl′/ [OF < Gmc] *n* 1 large closely-pressed, bound package of merchandise, prepared for storage or transportation ‖ *vt* 2 to make into bales

Bal·e·ar′ic Is′lands /bal′ē-ar′ik/ *npl* group of islands in the W Mediterranean which constitute a province of Spain (440,000; 1936 sq.m.; cap. Palma)

bale·ful /bāl′fəl/ [< OF *balu* evil] of deadly intent; direful, destructive ‖ **bale′ful·ly** *adv* ‖ **bale′ful·ness** *n* SYN pernicious, baneful, noxious, bad, malign

Ba·li /bäl′ē/ *n* Indonesian island E of Java (1,800,000; 2147 sq.m.) ‖ **Ba·li·nese** /bä′linēz′, -nēs′/ *adj & n* (-nese)

balk /bôk′/ [OE *balca* ridge] *n* 1 barrier or check; disappointment; 2 *baseball* illegal motion made by the pitcher to deceive the opposing players as to the direction of the ball ‖ *vt* 3 to hinder, thwart ‖ *vi* 4 a to stop short and refuse to go; b to refuse to do something; 5 *baseball* to commit a balk

Bal·kan /bôlk′ən/ *adj* 1 pert. to the district in SE Europe between the Danube River and the Adriatic, Aegean, and Black Seas ‖ *n* the **Bal·kans** *pl* 2 the nations of this district: Yugoslavia, Rumania, Bulgaria, Albania, Greece, and the European part of Turkey

Bal′kan·ize′ *vt* to divide (a region) into small, dissenting, powerless states

balk′line′ /bôk′-/ *n* 1 straight line near and parallel to one end of a billiard table behind which cue balls are placed at the start of a game; 2 one of four lines parallel to the cushions of a billiard table

balk·y /bô′kē/ *adj* (-i·er; -i·est) stubborn, obstinate ‖ **balk′i·ness** *n*

ball[1] /bôl′/ [ON *böllr*] *n* 1 round or roundish body or mass; sphere; esp. solid or inflated and used in games; 2 bullet or other missile shot from firearms; 3 game played with a ball, as baseball; 4 any rounded and protuberant part; 5 *baseball* pitched ball, not struck at, which does not pass over the home plate between the levels of the batter's shoulders and knees; 6 **carry the ball** to do one's part; 7 **have a lot on the ball** to be talented or gifted; 8 **keep the ball rolling** keep things going; 9 **on the ball** on top of one's job; 10 **play ball** to cooperate ‖ *vt* 11 to make into a ball; 12 **ball up** *slang* to muddle, foul up ‖ *vi* 13 to form or gather into a ball

ball[2] [F *bal* < LL *ballare* to dance] *n* 1 large formal dance; 2 **have a ball** *colloq* to enjoy oneself thoroughly, have a gay time

bal·lad /bal′əd/ [OF *balade* < Prov *balada* dance song] *n* 1 simple song, often sentimental, usu. sung with a simple accompaniment; 2 short, popular narrative poem, suitable for reciting or singing

bal·lade /bəläd′/ *n* 1 old French form of poem consisting of several stanzas each ending with a refrain, and an extra stanza called the envoy; 2 short romantic composition for piano or orchestra

bal′lad·eer′ *n* singer of ballads

bal′lad·ry *n* 1 ballad poetry; 2 art of writing and singing ballads

ball′-and-sock′et joint′ *n* joint in which a ball moves within a spherical socket

bal·last /bal′əst/ [prob < LG] *n* 1 heavy material carried by a ship or balloon to balance or steady it; 2 small stones on the roadbed of a railway between and under the ties ‖ *vt* 3 to place ballast in or on

ball′ bear′ing *n* device for reducing friction by supporting a shaft upon balls of metal running in a groove and surrounding the shaft ‖ **ball′-bear′ing** *adj*

ball′ cock′ *n* valve operated by a float to maintain a liquid at a predetermined level

bal·le·ri·na /bal′ərēn′ə/ [It] *n* female ballet dancer

bal·let /bal′ā, balā′/ [F < It *balletto* dim. of *ballo* dance] *n* 1 artistic dance performed to music as part of a theatrical performance, often suggesting a story or an idea; 2 the dancers in such a dance

bal·lis·ta /bəlis′tə/ [L < Gk *ballein* to throw] *n* ancient war engine for hurling heavy missiles

bal·lis·tic /bəlis′tik/ *adj* 1 pert. to ballistics; 2 pert. to a body, as a missile, whose trajectory is determined by the laws of ballistics

bal·lis′tics *nsg* 1 science dealing with the trajectories of projectiles; 2 science dealing with the firing characteristics of firearms, bullets, and cartridges, usu. for identification

ball′ joint′ *n* ball-and-socket joint

bal·loon /bəlōōn′/ [It *ballone* large ball] *n* 1 large bag of silk or plastic which, when filled with a lighter-than-air gas or with heated air, ascends and floats in the air; 2 toy consisting of a brightly colored inflated rubber bag; 3 closed figure in comic strips enclosing the words of a speaker ‖ *vi* 4 to expand or swell out like a balloon

bal·lot /bal′ət/ [It *ballotta* little ball] *n* 1 ball, ticket, or paper by which a vote is cast; 2 act or system of voting; **3** round of voting, usu. one of a series; **4** total number of votes cast ‖ *vi* **5** to vote by ballot

ball′-point pen′ *n* fountain pen the point of which is a small rotating ball

ball′room′ *n* large room intended for dancing

ball′ valve′ *n* valve operated by the seating of a ball

bal·ly·hoo /bal′lĕhōō′/ [?] **1** *n* blatant and extravagant advertising or publicity ‖ *vt* **2** to promote by ballyhoo

balm /bäm′/ [OF *basme* < L *balsamum* balsam] *n* **1** fragrant resinous substance used for healing or soothing; **2** any healing ointment; **3** anything that soothes

balm′ of Gil′e·ad /gil′ĕ·əd, -ad′/ [anc district of Palestine noted for its balm (Jer. 8:22)] *n* **1** any of several plants of the genus *Commiphora;* **2** their fragrant oleoresin

balm′y *adj* (-i·er; -i·est) **1** soothing, mild; **2** *slang* daft, mildly insane

ba·lo·ney /bəlōn′ē/ [*bologna*] *n* **1** bologna; **2** *slang* nonsense

bal·sa /bôl′sə/ [Sp = raft] *n* **1** tropical American tree (*Ochroma lagopus*) having very light wood; **2** raft, spec. one made of two hollow cylinders of wood or metal

bal·sam /bôl′səm/ [L *balsamum*] *n* **1** oily fragrant resin obtained from certain trees and shrubs and used for medicine and in perfume; **2** anything soothing or healing; **3** any of several trees or shrubs yielding balsam, as the balsam fir; **4** flowering plant (*Impatiens*)

bal′sam fir′ *n* North American evergreen tree (*Abies balsamea*)

Balt /bôlt′/ *n* **1** German-speaking native of the Baltic states; **2** native or inhabitant of the Baltic States

Bal·ti /bul′tē/ *n* **1** member of a Tibetan people of N Kashmir; **2** their language

Bal·tic /bôlt′ik/ *adj* **1** of or pert. to the Baltic Sea; **2** of or pert. to the Baltic States; **3** of or pert. to a subgroup of the Balto-Slavic languages

Bal′tic Sea′ *n* sea in NE Europe east of Denmark

Bal′tic States′ *npl* the formerly sovereign states of Lithuania, Latvia, and Estonia

Bal·ti·more /bôlt′imôr′, -môr′/ *n* seaport in N Maryland on the Chesapeak Bay (905,759)

Bal′ti·more o′ri·ole [from the colors of Lord *Baltimore*'s coat of arms] *n* black and orange American oriole (*Icterus galbula*), which builds a hanging nest

Bal′to-Slav′ic /bôlt′ō-/ *n* group of Indo-European languages including the Baltic and Slavic subgroups ‖ also *adj*

bal·us·ter /bal′əstər/ [F *balustre* < It *balaustra*] *n* one of the pillars or posts supporting the handrail of a balustrade

bal·us·trade /bal′əstrād′/ *n* row of balusters supporting a handrail

bam·bi·no /bambēn′ō, bäm-/ [It] *n* **1** baby; **2** (**-ni** /-nē/) representation of the infant Jesus

bam·boo /bambōō′/ [Malay *bambu*] *n* **1** any of several treelike or woody plants of the grass family, as of the genera *Bambusa* and/or *Dendrocalamus,* mainly tropical, having a hard, hollow, jointed stem; **2** stem of this plant, used for furniture, poles, and canes

Bam·boo′ Cur′tain *n* political and military barrier preventing free intercourse between the Communist countries of Asia and much of the rest of the world

bam·boo·zle /bambōōz′əl/ [?] *vt* to mislead, deceive ‖ **bam·boo′zler** *n*

ban¹ /ban′/ [OF *ban* summons] *n* **1** public announcement; **2** decree of excommunication; **3** curse; **4** authoritative prohibition

ban² [OE *bannan* to summon + ON *banna* curse] *v* (**banned; ban·ning**) *vt* to prohibit

ba·nal /bənal′, bān′əl/ [MF = common to all] *adj* hackneyed, trite ‖ **ba·nal′i·ty** /-nal′-/ *n* (-ties)

ba·nan·a /bənan′ə/ [Port < nat. name in Guinea] *n* **1** tropical, treelike herb (genus *Musa*) bearing a long hanging cluster of sweet pulpy fruit; **2** its fruit

band¹ /band′/ [MF *bande* < Gmc] *n* **1** that which binds, fastens, or ties together; **2** thin strip used for binding; **3** narrow strip of material used on an article of dress for trimming or finishing; **4** stripe of contrasting color; **5** *rad* specific range of wavelengths ‖ *vt* **6** to tie or mark with a band

band² [MF *bande* company] *n* **1** group of persons, animals, or things of the same kind or united for some purpose; **2** company of musicians, esp. one that plays for marching or for dancing ‖ *vt* **3** to unite into a troop, confederacy, or the like ‖ *vi* **4** to unite, confederate

band·age /ban′dij/ [MF] *n* **1** strip of cotton or other material used for binding up wounds ‖ *vt* **2** to dress, cover, or bind with a bandage

Band′-Aid′ [trademark] *n* small adhesive bandage in which the adhesive is protected before use with a gauze pad

ban·dan·na or **ban·dan·a** /bandan′ə/ [Port < Hindi *bandhnu* method of dyeing spotted cloth] *n* large brightcolored handkerchief, usu. with a red or blue background having white or yellow spots or figures

band·box' n 1 light pasteboard box for holding hats; 2 any area or structure of substandard size

ban·deau /bandō', ban'-/ [F < OF *bandel* dim. of *bande* strip] n (-deaux /-dōz/) 1 brassiere; 2 narrow band or fillet worn above the forehead or around the hair

ban·dit /ban'dit/ [It *bandito* proscribed] n outlaw, brigand; highwayman

ban·do·lier or **ban·do·leer** /ban'dəlir'/ [MF *bandouliere*] n broad belt worn over the shoulder with loops for holding cartridges

band' saw' n endless saw on pulleys, usu. motor-driven

band' shell' n bandstand with shell-shaped backboard

band'stand' n raised platform on which a band or orchestra performs

band'wag'on n 1 wagon carrying the band, as in a circus parade; 2 seemingly irresistible party or movement

ban·dy[1] /ban'dē/ [?] v (-died) vt 1 to knock or toss to and fro, as a ball; 2 to give and take, exchange, as to *bandy words*

ban·dy[2] [obs *bandy* hockey stick] adj bent or bowed outward, as at the knees

bane /bān'/ [OE *bana* death] n 1 cause of ruin or destruction; woe; 2 poison (used only in compounds), as *ratsbane, henbane* || **bane'ful** adj

bang[1] /baŋ'/ [perh < ON *banga* to hammer] vt 1 to beat; thump; handle roughly; 2 to produce a loud sound by or from, as to *bang the door* || vi 3 to make a loud noise; 4 to thump violently || n 5 heavy blow, whack; 6 sound of a blow; 7 slang thrill || adv 8 all at once, abruptly; 9 directly, right

bang[2] [< *bangtail*] vt 1 to cut straight across, as the hair over the forehead || **bangs** npl 2 short fringe of hair over the forehead

Bang·kok /baŋ'kok/ n capital of Thailand (1,858,645)

Ban·gla·desh also **Ban·gla Desh** /baŋ'glədesh'/ n republic in SE Asia (50,850,000; 55,126 sq.m.; cap. Dacca)

ban·gle /baŋ'gəl/ [< Hindi *banglī* glass bracelet] n 1 ornamental ring worn on the wrists and ankles; 2 one of several slender bracelets worn together

bang'tail' [< *bang* = cut] n slang racehorse

bang'-up' adj colloq excellent

ban·ish /ban'ish/ [MF *banir* (-*iss*-)] vt 1 to exile by authoritative decree; 2 to expel or drive away || **ban'ish·ment** n || SYN exile, expatriate, transport, expel, oust, ostracize || DISCR These words agree in the idea of putting out either by civil authority or by moral compulsion. To be *banished* is to be put out of a country, not necessarily one's own, by formal authority, and, sometimes, under definite directions as to where to go. Figuratively, we *banish* fears or haunting thoughts. To be *exiled* is to be driven out of one's own country, by authoritative decree, either for a definite time or forever. Figuratively, we *exile* ourselves through any long absence occasioned as by pleasure or devotion to a cause. One may be *expatriated* only from his own country; he may be forced out, or he may *expatriate* himself by renouncing the citizenship of one country to take that of another. Convicts compelled to leave their own land for a designated colony are said to be *transported*. To *expel* is to cast out by force or dismiss by compulsion; the idea of disgrace accompanies expulsion. To *ostracize* is to put under a social ban; one *ostracized* is shunned and ignored

ban·is·ter also **ban·nis·ter** /ban'ister/ [var of *baluster*] n 1 baluster; 2 **banisters** pl balustrade of a staircase

ban·jo /ban'jō/ [perh var of obs *bandore* lute-like instrument] n (-jos, -joes) stringed musical instrument played by plucking, having a long neck and a body like a tambourine

bank[1] /baŋk'/ [< ON *bakki* river bank] n 1 heap, mound, or pile, as of earth, snow, or clouds; 2 steep slope; 3 land at the margin of a river or watercourse; 4 elevation or rising ground beneath the sea or at the mouth of a river; shoal; 5 lateral inclination of an airplane when turning || vt 6 to pile or heap up; 7 to cover (a fire) with ashes or packed coal to prevent rapid burning; 8 to incline (an airplane) laterally, as in turning; 9 to slope (a road) at a curve; 10 *billiards* to drive (a ball) to the cushion

bank[2] [OF *ban* bench] n row, tier, or set of similar objects, as of seats, lights, oars, organ keys, transformers, etc.

bank[3] [It *banca* money changer's bench or table] n 1 institution which deals in money and credit, where money may be deposited for safekeeping; 2 office or headquarters of such an institution; 3 *gambling* fund of the dealer || vt 4 to place (money) in a bank || vi 5 to have an account with a bank; 6 to conduct a banking business; 7 **bank on** to count on

bank' ac·count' n money held in a person's name by a bank, which may be withdrawn or against which checks may be drawn

bank'book' n depositor's passbook in which deposits and charges are recorded

bank′ draft′ *n* bill of exchange drawn by one bank on another bank

bank′er [<*bank*³] *n* **1** person or corporation engaged in banking; **2** *gambling* keeper of the funds

bank′ing *n* the business of a bank

bank′ note′ *n* promissory note issued by a legally authorized bank, payable to bearer on demand and acceptable as money

bank′ pa′per *n* **1** bankable drafts, bills, and acceptances; **2** bank notes

bank′ rate′ *n* discount rate set by a central bank

bank′roll′ *n colloq* **1** available funds ‖ *vt* **2** *colloq* to finance

bank·rupt /-rupt, -rəpt/ [It *banca* bank + *rotta* broken] *n* **1** one legally adjudged unable to pay his debts **2** a one unable to pay his debts; **b** one without money or credit ‖ *adj* **3** liable to, or under legal procedure for, insolvency; **4** unable to pay debts; **5** depleted; exhausted; **6** utterly deprived or bereft, as of hope ‖ *vt* **7** to make bankrupt ‖ **bank′rupt·cy** *n* (**-cies**)

ban·ner /bań′ər/ [OF *baniere* < LL *bandum* standard < Goth *bandwa* sign] *n* **1** cloth bearing a design, attached to a staff, and used as a standard by a person of rank; **2** any flag, ensign, or symbol; **3** banner line ‖ *adj* **4** leading, foremost

ban′ner line′ *n* headline that runs across the top of the front page of a newspaper

banns /banz/ [<*ban*¹] *npl* notice in church of a proposed marriage

ban·quet /bań′wit/ [F < It *banchetto* small bench] *n* **1** elaborate meal; **2** ceremonious public dinner ‖ *vt* **3** to feast or regale (someone) ‖ *vi* **4** to dine luxuriously

Ban·quo /bań′(w)ō/ *n* in Shakespeare's *Macbeth*, brave Scottish noble who haunts his slayer, Macbeth

ban·shee /bań′shē/ [Ir *bean sīdhe* fairy woman] *n* in Gaelic folklore, spirit whose wailing is believed to foretell death

ban·tam /bant′əm/ [*Bantam*, Java] *n* **1** domestic fowl of any of numerous small breeds; **2** small but combative person ‖ *adj* **3** diminutive

ban′tam·weight′ *n* boxer not over 118 pounds

ban·ter /bant′ər/ [?] **1** good-natured pleasantry or teasing ‖ *vt* **2** to make fun of good-humoredly ‖ *vi* **3** to use banter ‖ **ban′ter·ing·ly** *adv* ‖ SYN *n* badinage, persiflage, raillery, irony, derision

Ban·tu /bań′tōō/ *n* (**-tus, -tu**) **1** member of any of a large group of tribes of southern and central Africa; **2** one of many related languages of these people ‖ also *adj*

ban·yan /bań′yən/ [< Hindi *baniya*

trader] *n* Indian fig tree (*Ficus bengalensis*), the branches of which send out aerial roots that grow down to the ground and form new trunks

ban·zai /bän′zī/ [Jap = 10,000 years] *interj* Japanese battle cry and salutation

ba·o·bab /bā′əbab′, bou′-/ [nat. name] *n* African tree (genus *Adansonia*) with a very thick trunk, yielding a gourdlike fruit

bap·tism /bap′tizəm/ *n* **1** the sacrament of immersion in or sprinkling with water, symbolizing the washing away of sin and admission into membership of many Christian churches; **2** initial experience or ordeal that purifies or tests ‖ **bap·tis′mal** *adj*

Bap′tist *n* member of a Protestant denomination which believes that Christians should receive baptism only as adults after a public declaration of faith and by immersion ‖ also *adj*

bap·tis·ter·y /bap′tist(ə)rē/ (**-ies**) or **bap′tis·try** *n* (**-tries**) building or part of a church in which baptism is performed

bap·tize′ /also bap′-/ [Gk *baptizein*] *vt* **1** to sprinkle or pour water on or immerse in water, in the rite of baptism; **2** to purify; **3** to christen, name ‖ **bap·tiz′er** *n*

bar¹ /bär′/ [OF *barre*] *n* **1** rigid piece of solid matter, as wood or metal, long in proportion to its thickness; **2** rail, barrier; **3** obstacle; **4** a counter where liquor is served; **b** room containing such a counter; **c** tavern, saloon; **5** band, stripe; **6** *mus* a one of the upright lines drawn through the staff of a piece of music, dividing it into equal measures of time; **b** measure; **7** **the bar, a** the legal profession; lawyers collectively; **b** the division in a court between the judge's bench and the rest of the courtroom ‖ *prep* **8** but, except ‖ *v* (**barred; bar·ring**) *vt* **9** to fasten with a bar; **10** to prevent; **11** to exclude; **12** to close; prohibit; **13** to mark with bars

bar² [Gk *baros* weight] *n phys* cgs unit of pressure equal to 1,000,000 dynes per square centimeter

bar. 1 barometer; **2** barrister

Bar·ab·bas /bərab′əs/ *n Bib* robber who, at the trial of Jesus before Pilate, was freed instead of Jesus at the demand of the people (Matt. 27:16-21)

barb /bärb′/ [MF *barbe* < L *barba* beard] *n* **1** that which resembles a beard at the mouth of animals; **2** sharp point extending backward on an arrow, fishhook, etc.; **3** biting remark ‖ *vt* **4** to furnish with barbs

Bar·ba·dos /bärbā′dōz, -dōs/ *n* island in the E West Indies, former Brit colony, now independent (250,000; 165 sq.m.; cap. Bridgetown)

bar·bar·i·an /bärber′ē-ən/ [< Gk *barbaros* foreign] *n* 1 person in a rude, uncivilized state; 2 uncultured person ‖ also *adj* ‖ **bar·bar′i·an·ism** *n*

bar·bar′ic /-bar′ik/ *adj* 1 relating to or like barbarians; 2 crudely gorgeous or splendid, as *barbaric splendor*

bar′ba·rism /-bə-/ *n* 1 state or condition of being barbarous; 2 *gram* a misuse of a word or construction due to unfamiliarity with what is correct; b example of such misuse, as *between you and I*

bar·bar′i·ty /-bar′-/ *n* (-ties) 1 brutal or inhuman conduct; 2 violation of good taste

Bar·ba·ros′sa /bär′bəros′ə/ *n* Frederick I (1123–90) emperor of the Holy Roman Empire and king of Italy 1152–90

bar′ba·rous /-bərəs/ *adj* 1 pert. to or like a barbarian; 2 cruel, inhuman; 3 (language) unpolished, full of errors ‖ **bar′ba·rous·ly** *adv* ‖ SYN uncouth, brutal, savage, harsh (see *inhuman*)

Bar′ba·ry States′ /bär′bərē/ *n* formerly, Morocco, Algiers, Tunis, and Tripoli, noted for piracy

bar·be·cue /bär′bəkyoō′/ *n* [< Sp *barbacoa* framework of posts < Haitian] *n* 1 carcass of an ox, pig, etc., roasted whole; 2 outdoor feast featuring barbecued food ‖ *v* (-cued; -cu·ing) *vt* 3 to roast whole or in large pieces; 4 to cook in a highly seasoned sauce

barbed′ wire′ *n* twisted wire with sharp thornlike projections ‖ **barbed′-wire′** *adj*

bar′bell′ *n* bar with detachable disk-shaped weights on both ends, used in weight lifting

bar′ber [< L *barba* beard] *n* 1 one whose business is shaving, haircutting, and hairdressing ‖ *vt* 2 to shave; cut the hair or beard of

bar′ber·ry [LL *berberis*] *n* (-ries) 1 any of several prickly shrubs (genus *Berberis*) bearing berries which turn red in the fall, often used as a hedge; 2 its fruit

bar′ber's itch′ *n* ringworm of the face and neck

bar·bi·tal /bär′bitôl′, -tal′/ [*barbitu*ric acid + *veronal*] *n* addictive hypnotic —CO(HNCO)₂(C₂H₅)₂

bar·bi·tu·rate /-bich′ərit, -rāt′/ [G *Barbitu*rsäure barbituric acid] *n* any of a group of derivatives of barbituric acid, used as sedatives or as hypnotics

bar·bi·tu′ric ac′id /-bit(y)oŏ′rik/ *n* white crystalline acid —CO(NHCO)₂CH₂— used in making barbiturates

bar·ca·role or **bar·ca·rolle** /bär′kərōl′/ [It *barcarola* boat song < *barca* boat] *n* 1 simple, popular song sung by Venetian gondoliers; 2 any music imitating such songs

Bar·ce·lon·a /bär′səlōn′ə/ *n* seaport on the Mediterranean in NE Spain (1,696,765)

bard /bärd′/ [Gael = poet] *n* 1 ancient poet and singer; 2 any poet

bare /ber′/ [OE *bær*] 1 uncovered; undressed; naked; 2 unconcealed; 3 unadorned, plain; 4 unfurnished; 5 mere, scant ‖ *vt* 6 to lay bare; uncover; expose; ‖ **bare′ness** *n*

bare′back′ *adj* & *adv* on a horse without a saddle ‖ **bare′backed′** *adj*

bare′faced′ *adj* 1 without concealment, undisguised; 2 shameless

bare′foot or **bare′foot′ed** *adj* & *adv* with the feet bare

bare′head′ed *adj* & *adv* having the head uncovered

bare′ly *adv* 1 scarcely, just about; 2 nakedly; 3 openly

bar′fly′ *n* (-flies) *n colloq* drinker who spends all his time at bars, often cadging drinks

bar·gain /bär′gən/ [MF *bargaigne* < LL *barcaniare* to haggle] *n* 1 agreement on the terms of a transaction; 2 terms agreed upon; compact; 3 that which is acquired by bargaining; 4 advantageous purchase; 5 **in the bargain** in addition; 6 **strike a bargain** to agree to terms ‖ *vi* 7 to make an agreement; 8 to haggle ‖ *vt* 9 to part with or transfer for a consideration ‖ SYN *n* trade, deal, transaction (see *contract*)

barge /bärj′/ [OF < L *barca* boat] *n* 1 capacious flat-bottomed boat used in loading and unloading ships and for carrying freight on rivers and canals; 2 elegant boat used in pageants and celebrations; 3 *nav* large motorboat at the disposal of a flag officer ‖ *vt* 4 to transport by barge ‖ *vi* 5 **barge in** to intrude; 6 **barge into**, a barge in; b collide with

bar·i·tone /bar′itōn′/ [It *baritono* < Gk *barytonos* deep-sounding] *n mus* 1 male voice between tenor and bass; 2 person having such a voice; 3 large, valved band instrument ‖ also *adj*

bar·i·um /bar′ē·əm, ber′-/ [< Gk *barys* heavy] *n* soft silver-gray metallic element (**Ba**; at.no. 56; at.wt. 137.34) of the alkaline-earth group, occurring only in combination

bar′i·um sul′fate *n* white crystalline powder —BaSO₄— used chiefly as a pigment and filler and for X-ray diagnosis

bark¹ /bärk′/ [Scand = rind] *n* 1 outer covering of the trunk, branches, stems, etc., of trees and other woody plants ‖ *vt* 2 to strip the bark or similar covering from; 3 to scrape the skin from; 4 to enclose with or as with bark; encrust; **5** to tan by means of an infusion of bark

bark³ [OE *beorcan*] *n* **1** sound or cry made by a dog; **2** explosive sound, as of a gun; **3** brusque, peremptory tone of voice ‖ *vi* **4** to utter a bark; **5 bark up the wrong tree** to be misguided or misdirected

bark³ [F *barque* < L *barca* boat] *n* **1** three-masted vessel with foremast and mainmast square-rigged and mizzenmast fore-and-aft-rigged; **2** *poet.* any small boat

bar′keep′er or **bar′keep′** *n* one who owns or tends a bar

bark′en·tine′ /-əntēn′/ [*bark³* + brigantine] *n* three-masted vessel with the foremast square-rigged and the mainmast and mizzenmast fore-and-aft-rigged

bark′er *n* one who attracts patronage by crying loudly before a store or show

bar·ley /bär′lē/ [OE *bærlic*] *n* **1** grain used as food and in the manufacture of malt liquors; **2** plant (genus *Hordeum*) which yields the grain

bar′maid′ *n* female bartender

bar′man /-mən/ *n* (**-men** /-mən/) *n* bartender

Bar·me·cid·al /bär′mĭsĭd′əl/ or **Bar′me·cide′** [*Barmecide*, wealthy Persian in *The Arabian Nights* who gave a beggar a feast of imaginary food] *adj* sham, giving a false appearance of plenty

bar mitz·vah /bärmits′və/ [Heb] *n* **1** ceremony admitting a male who has attained the age of 13 into full membership in the Jewish community; **2** boy thus initiated

barn /bärn/ [OE *bern* < *bere* barley + *ærn* closed place] *n* farm building for housing produce, implements, or livestock

Bar·na·bas /bär′nəbəs/ *n* Bib Levite of Cyprus who accompanied Paul on his first missionary journey (Acts 4:36–37)

bar·na·cle /bär′nəkəl/ [ME *bernake*] *n* **1** any of several marine crustaceans (order Cirripedia) living in white shells and attaching themselves to rocks, logs, and ship hulls; **2** persistent follower or hanger-on; **3** barnacle goose

bar′na·cle goose′ *n* large European wild goose (*Branta leucopsis*) of the far north

barn′ owl′ *n* grayish-brown and white owl (*Tyto alba*) often living in barns

barn′storm′ *vi* **1** to tour throughout a region, usu. not staying longer than one day in any town, making political speeches or giving theatrical performances, sports exhibitions, exhibitions of stunt flying, or exhibitions of airplane racing ‖ *vt* **2** to tour (a region) barnstorming ‖ **barn′storm′er** *n*

barn′yard′ *n* **1** enclosure about or before a barn ‖ *adj* **2** of or like a barnyard; **3** bawdy, earthy

ba·rom·e·ter /bərom′itər/ [< Gk *baros* weight + *-meter*] *n* **1** instrument for measuring atmospheric pressure; **2** anything that indicates change ‖ **bar·o·met·ric** (**-ri·cal**) /bar′əmet′rik-(əl)/ *adj* ‖ **bar′o·met′ri·cal·ly** *adv* ‖ **ba·rom′e·try** *n*

bar·on /bar′ən/ [OF < LL *baro* (-*ronis*) man < Gmc] *n* **1** noble of the lowest rank; **2** man of great power in a specific business or industry, as *an oil baron* ‖ **bar′on·ess** *nfem*

bar′on·et /-ĭt/ *n* hereditary knight in England, ranking above the other orders of knighthood, but below a peer

bar′on·et·cy *n* (**-cies**) rank of a baron

bar′o·ny *n* (**-nies**) rank or domain of a baron ‖ **ba·ro′ni·al** /bərōn′ē·əl/ *adj*

ba·roque /bərōk′/ [F < Port *barroco* rough pearl] *adj* **1** of or like a style of art and architecture developed during the 17th century, characterized by extravagant ornamentation and complexity of form; **2** of or pert. to a style of musical composition that flourished up to about 1750, marked by elaborate ornamentation; **3** of a style of literary composition of the 17th and early 18th centuries, characterized by complexity, ingenious conceits, and intentional ambiguity; **4** flamboyant, ornate ‖ *n* **5** baroque style or work; **6** period of baroque style

ba·rouche /bərōōsh′/ [< G *Barutsche* < It *baroccio* < L *birotus* two-wheeled] *n* four-wheeled carriage with the driver's seat outside and two seats facing each other behind, with a collapsible top for the back seat

bar·racks /bar′əks/ [F *baraque* < Sp *barraca* hut] *npl* large structure or row of buildings for lodging soldiers

bar·ra·cu·da /bar′əkōōd′ə/ [AmSp] *n* (**-da** or **-das**) any of a genus (*Sphyraena*) of large, voracious, pikelike fishes of warm seas

bar·rage /bəräzh′, -räj′/ [F] *n* **1** dam in a stream or river; **2** barrier of artillery fire; **3** overwhelming amount or outpouring ‖ *vt* **4** to subject to a barrage

bar·ra·try /bar′ətrē/ [MF *baraterie* deception] *n* **1** fraud by a ship's captain or crew which victimizes the owners; **2** the offense of fomenting lawsuits and quarrels

barred /bärd′/ *adj* **1** provided with bars; **2** marked with alternate bands of different colors

bar·rel /bar′əl/ [OF *baril*] *n* **1** cylindrical, bulging cask or vessel having flat ends or heads; **2** standard capacity of a barrel 31½ gallons liquid;

3 anything barrel-shaped; drum, cylinder; **4** metal tube of a gun; **5** large quantity; **6** tubular part of a pen above the point; **7 over a barrel** in an embarrassing position ‖ *v* (**-reled** or **-relled; -rel·ing** or **-rel·ling**) *vt* **8** to put in barrels ‖ *vi* **9** *slang* to travel at high speed

bar′rel bolt′ *n* sliding bolt fastened to the edge of a door which it locks when fitted into a socket on the door-jamb

bar′rel·house′ [= disreputable saloon of New Orleans of ab. 1900] *n* vigorous jazz style with a heavy beat

bar′rel or′gan *n* crank-operated musical instrument

bar·ren /bar′ən/ [OF *baraine*] *adj* **1** sterile; **2** infertile; **3** unproductive, unprofitable; **4** dull, stupid ‖ **bar′rens** *npl* **5** sandy thinly wooded tract of land

bar·rette /bəret′/ *n* clasp for a woman's hair

bar·ri·cade /bar′ikād′/ [F] *n* **1** barrier hastily thrown up, as for defense; **2** any barrier or obstruction ‖ *vt* **3** to block with a barricade ‖ SYN *n* bulwark, barrier, fortification, rampart

bar·ri·er /bar′ē·ər/ [MF *barriere*] *n* anything that bars passage of persons, things, ideas, or social interactions, whether man-made, as a fence, natural, as a mountain, legislated, as a boundary or customs duty, cultural and traditional, as a caste system, or mental, as shyness ‖ SYN bar, hindrance, obstacle, obstruction, impediment ‖ ANT opening, access, aid, assistance

bar′ri·er reef′ *n* coral reef skirting a coast

bar·ring /bär′iŋ/ *prep* excepting

bar·ri·o /bär′ē·ō′/ [Sp] *n* in Spanish-speaking countries, section or ward of a city

bar·ris·ter /bar′istər/ *n* Brit lawyer who practices in the superior courts

bar′room′ *n* room in which liquors are sold over a counter

bar′row /bar′ō/ [OE *bearwe*] *n* **1** shallow boxlike receptacle with projecting handles for carrying goods; **2** wheelbarrow

bar′ sin′is·ter *n* condition of being of illegitimate birth

Bart. baronet

bar′tend′er *n* one who serves liquor at a bar

bar·ter /bärt′ər/ [perh < OF *barater* to cheat] *vt* **1** to exchange (goods); **2 barter away** to give away cheaply (what one prizes) ‖ *vi* **3** to engage in bartering ‖ *n* **4** act or practice of bartering ‖ SYN *v* traffic, exchange (see *trade*)

Bart·lett /bärt′lit/ [Enoch *Bartlett* first distributor of this fruit in America] *n* **1** variety of large juicy pear; **2** tree that bears this fruit

bas′al me·tab′o·lism /bās′əl/ [< *base¹*] *n physiol* energy used by a body at rest

ba·salt /bəsôlt′, bas′-/ [L *basaltes* dark marble] *n* dark, heavy rock of volcanic origin, often of columnar structure ‖ **ba·salt′ic** *adj*

base¹ /bās′/ [MF < Gk *basis* basis] *n* **1** the part of a thing on which it rests; **2** bottom part; **3** essential element; **4** line or point from which an operation starts, as in surveying; **5** *baseball* any one of the four corners of the infield; **6** *chem* compound capable of reacting with an acid to form a salt; it yields hydroxyl ions in solution, its atom is able to give up an unshared pair of electrons to an acid, and its aqueous solution is brackish and turns litmus paper blue; **7** *gram* word root to which affixes can be added; **8** *geom* line or surface on which a geometric figure is supposed to stand; **9** *math* number which serves as a starting point in a numbering system or logarithm; **10** *mil* supply depot and headquarters; **11 off base,** a *baseball* not touching the base sought; **b** badly mistaken; **c** unprepared ‖ *vt* **12** to justify, as a conclusion; **13** to lay a base for ‖ SYN *n* support, basis, foundation, groundwork

base² [MF *bas* low] *adj* **1** worthless; inferior; **2** alloyed (coin); **3** ignoble, morally low; **4** not precious (metal) ‖ **base′ly** *adv* ‖ **base′ness** *n* ‖ SYN vile, mean, servile, dishonorable, despicable

base′ball′ *n* ball game popular in the U.S. and adjoining regions of Latin America, played with bat and ball by nine players on a side, on a field with four bases at the corners of a diamond; **2** ball used in this game

base′board′ *n* wide molding at the base of the wall of a room

base′ hit′ *n* baseball fair hit which allows the batter to get safely to first base

base′less *adj* groundless, having no basis in fact

base′ment *n* lowest story of a building beneath the main floor

bash /bash/ [?] *vt* **1** *colloq* to strike forcibly ‖ *n* **2** *colloq* violent blow; **3** *slang* lively party; big celebration

bash′ful [< *abash*] *adj* shy, easily embarrassed, diffident ‖ **bash′ful·ly** *adv* ‖ **bash′ful·ness** *n* ‖ SYN timid, shy, retiring, sheepish (see *diffident*)

ba·sic /bās′ik/ *adj* **1** relating to a base; fundamental; **2** *chem* having the properties of a base; alkaline ‖ *n* **3** something basic or fundamental ‖ **ba′si·cal·ly** *adv*

bas·il /baz′əl/ [MF *basile* < Gk *basilikon* royal] *n* any of several plants (esp. *Ocimum basilicum*) of the mint family

ba·sil·i·ca /bəsil′ikə/ [L < Gk *basilikē* (oikia) royal (house)] *n* 1 in ancient Rome, oblong building used as a hall of justice and public meeting place; 2 earliest type of Christian church, with a nave and side aisles; 3 *R C Ch* church or cathedral accorded certain ceremonial privileges

bas·i·lisk /baz′ilisk, bas′-/ [Gk *basiliskos* little king] *n* 1 legendary lizard or dragon whose breath and look were fatal; 2 any of several tropical lizards (genus *Basiliscus*)

ba·sin /bās′ən/ [OF *bacin* < LL *bachinon*] *n* 1 round shallow vessel for holding liquids; 2 dock or other reservoir for water; 3 all the land drained by a river and its tributaries; 4 area surrounded by higher land

ba·sis /bās′is/ [Gk] *n* (*-ses* /-sēz/)] 1 base or foundation; 2 groundwork or first principle; 3 chief ingredient

bask /bask′, bäsk′/ [< ON *bathask* to bathe oneself] *vi* 1 to be exposed to pleasant heat; 2 to be at ease or thrive, as under kindly influences

bas·ket /bask′it, bäsk′-/ [ME] *n* 1 receptacle made of rushes, twigs, or other flexible material, plaited or interwoven; 2 *basketball* a basket-shaped net into which the players attempt to throw the ball; b scoring toss of the ball into it

bas′ket·ball′ *n* 1 game played by teams of five on each side, in which a ball must be thrown into elevated goals resembling baskets; 2 inflated spherical leather ball used in this game

Basque /bask′/ [< LL *Vasco* Gascon] *n* 1 member of a people living in Spain and France in the western Pyrenees; 2 their language || also *adj*

bas·re·lief /bä′rilēf′, bas′-/ [F < It *bassorilievo*] *n* sculpture in which the figures stand out very slightly from the background

bass¹ /bas′/ [OE *bærs*] *n* (**bass** or **basses**) any of various edible and game fishes of the families Serranidae and Centrarchidae, found in both fresh and salt water

bass² /bās′/ [< *base* + *ss* of It *basso* low] *n* 1 lowest part in music; 2 lowest male singing voice; 3 lowest-pitched musical instrument; 4 bass viol || also *adj*

bass′ drum′ /bās′/ *n* the largest of the drums, having two heads of membrane

bas′set hound′ /bas′it/ [F *dim.* of *bas* low] *n* short-legged hunting dog with drooping ears

bas·si·net /bas′inet′/ [F *dim.* of *bassin* basin] *n* basketlike cradle with a hood at one end

bas·so /bas′ō, bäs′ō/ [It = low] *n* bass singer or voice in opera

bas·soon /bəsoon′, ba-/ [F *basson* < It *bassone*] *n* deep-toned woodwind instrument having a long curved double-reed mouthpiece and a wooden tube || **bas·soon′ist** *n*

bass′ vi′ol /bās′/ *n* largest and lowest-toned instrument of the viol group, shaped like a violin

bass′wood′ /bas′/ *n* 1 linden tree, esp. *Tilia americana;* 2 soft wood of a linden tree

bas·tard /bast′ərd/ [< OF *bast* pack-saddle (used as a bed)] *n* 1 illegitimate offspring; 2 *slang* mean, despicable person || *adj* 3 born out of wedlock; 4 not genuine; 5 of special size or shape, not standard || **bas′tar·dy** *n*

baste¹ /bāst′/ [MF *bastir* to sew] *vt* to sew slightly, or fasten in position with long temporary stitches

baste² [?] *vt* to moisten (roasting meat) with melted fat, water, etc.

baste³ [?] *vt* 1 to beat, thrash; 2 to scold, upbraid

bas·tile or **bas·tile** /bastēl′/ [F] 1 jail; 2 **Bastille** castle in Paris used as a prison, destroyed in a popular uprising in 1789 heralding the French Revolution

bas·tion /bas′chən/ [MF] *n* 1 projecting part of a fortification; 2 any strong point of defense

bat¹ /bat′/ [OE *batt*] *n* 1 heavy stick or club, esp. one used in baseball; 2 *colloq* hard blow; 3 *slang* spree; 4 **at bat** *baseball* having one's turn batting; 5 **go to bat for** to intercede for; 6 **right off the bat** right away || *v* (**bat·ted; bat·ting**) *vt* 7 to hit or strike with, or as with, a bat || *vi* 8 *baseball* to use a bat

bat² [< ME *bakke* < Scand] *n* any of an order (Chiroptera) of nocturnal flying mammals with furry body and membranous wings

bat³ [var of *obs bate* to flutter] *v* (**bat·ted; bat·ting**) *vt* *colloq* to blink, as *he didn't bat an eye*

bat. 1 battery; 2 battalion

batch /bach′/ [< OE *bacan* to bake] *n* 1 quantity of bread baked at one time; 2 quantity or group of things produced at one time

bate /bāt′/ [abbr of *abate*] *vt* 1 to abate, moderate; 2 **with bated breath** with the breath held in suspense

ba·teau also **bat·teau** /batō′/ [F = boat] *n* flat-bottomed, double-ended river boat, used esp. in Canada and Louisiana

bath /bath′, bäth′/ [OE *bæth*] *n* (**-ths** /-ths, -thz/) 1 act of washing the body with water, or exposing it to a fluid or vapor; 2 bathtub; 3 bathroom; 4 bathhouse 1; 5 water or other liquid used in bathing

bathe /bāth′/ [OE *bathian*] *vt* 1 to put into water or other liquid; 2 to wash; wet; 3 to give a bath to; 4 to envelop or surround, as with a liquid, as *bathed in sunlight* || *vi* 5 to take a bath; **6** to envelop oneself as with a liquid || **bath′er** n

bath′house′ n (-hous·es /-ziz/) **1** building equipped for bathing; **2** house with dressing rooms for bathers

Bath·i·nette /bath′inet′/ [trademark] n portable folding bathtub for babies

ba·thos /bā′thos/ [Gk = depth] n **1** ridiculous descent from the lofty to the commonplace in writing or speech; **2** mawkishness || **ba·thet·ic** /bəthet′ik/ adj

bath′robe′ n loose-fitting robe worn to and from the bath and for lounging

bath′room′ n room containing a bathtub, washstand, and usu. a toilet bowl

bath′tub′ n tub, usu. in the form of a permanent porcelain fixture, for bathing

Bath·she·ba /bathshēb′ə/ n Bib woman whom David coveted and whom he married after sending her husband Uriah to death in battle; she became the mother of Solomon

bath·y·sphere /bath′isfir′/ [Gk bathy deep + sphere] n diving sphere for deep-sea observations

ba·tik /bətēk′, bat′ik/ [Javanese = painted] n **1** technique for dyeing fabrics in which the parts not to be dyed are covered with wax; **2** cloth dyed in this way

ba·tiste /bətēst′, ba-/ [F < Baptiste linen weaver of the 13th cent.] n fine cotton lawn or muslin

ba·ton /baton′, bə-/ [< bâton stick] n **1** staff used as a badge of office; **2** mus stick used by the conductor; **3** sports stick passed on to successive runners in a relay race

Bat′on Rouge′ /bat′ən rōōzh′/ n capital of Louisiana (155,000)

bats /bats/ [< batty] adj slang crazy

bat·tal·ion /bətal′yən/ [F bataillon] n **1** subdivision of a regiment consisting of at least two companies; **2** battalions pl **a** large organized force of soldiers; **b** large number of persons or things

bat·ten¹ /bat′ən/ [< baton] n **1** narrow strip of wood used to nail across two boards, to fasten a piece of canvas to something or to keep it taut, to cover a seam, etc. || vt **2** to fasten with battens

bat·ten² [ON batna to improve] vt **1** to fatten || vi **2** to grow fat; **3** to thrive at the expense of others

bat·ter¹ /bat′ər/ [ME bateren] vt **1** to strike with repeated heavy blows; **2** to damage by hard use || vi **3** to pound repeatedly || n **4** cookery thick beaten mixture, as of flour, eggs, milk, etc. || SYN v beat, pommel, pound, bruise, demolish

bat·ter² [< bat¹] n player using the bat in baseball

bat′ter·ing ram′ n large iron-headed beam formerly used to beat down the walls of besieged cities

bat·ter·y [MF battre to beat] n (-ies) **1** unlawful violence used against another; **2** mil number of guns forming a tactical unit; **3** nav guns of a warship; **4** elec cell or cells producing electric current; **5** group of related things or persons working together; **6** baseball the pitcher and catcher together

bat′ting [< bat¹] n wool or cotton prepared in sheets

bat·tle /bat′əl/ [OF bataille < L battualia gladiatorial exercises] n **1** fight between opposing forces; combat, contest || vt & vi **2** to fight || SYN n conflict, fight, skirmish, engagement, action || DISCR A battle is a combat between large bodies of organized forces, whether on land or sea. Conflict, literally a striking together, may name a long, bitter struggle which includes many battles, or a single sharp encounter between individuals. Engagement, another word for battle, has less force, though it may indicate an extensive operation. Skirmish and action name the minor acts of war, incident to scattered troops: scouting parties might meet in a skirmish; an ambush might cause an action. Action is sometimes used to name a single operation of fighting. Fight is a more general word, applying to a serious struggle, a short, fierce combat, or a brawl accompanied by fisticuffs

bat′tle-ax′ or **bat′tle-axe′** n **1** ax formerly used as a weapon; **2** slang domineering wife

bat′tle cruis′er n warship armed like a battleship, but speedier and with lighter armor

bat′tle·dore′ /-dôr′, -dōr′/ n light flat bat used in badminton

bat′tle·field′ or **bat′tle-ground′** n place where a battle is fought

bat′tle roy′al n violent fight engaged in by more than two persons

bat′tle·ship′ n warship of the largest size with the heaviest guns and armor

bat′tle wag′on n colloq battleship

bat′ty [< bat²] adj (-ti·er; -ti·est) slang out of one's mind

bau·ble /bôb′əl/ [ME babel] n **1** cheap ornament, trinket; **2** staff carried by a court jester

baux·ite /bôk′sīt′/ [< Les Baux, France] n hydrated aluminum oxide, principal ore of aluminum

Ba·va·ri·a /bəver′ē·ə/ n state in S Germany (10,000,000; 27,236 sq.m.; cap. Munich) || **Ba·va′ri·an** adj & n

bawd /bôd′/ [ME bawde] n prostitute

bawd′y adj (-i·er; -i·est) indecent, lewd || **bawd′i·ness** n

bawd′y·house′ n (-hous·es /-ziz/) brothel

bawl /bôl′/ [LL baulare to bark < Gmc] vi **1** to wail loudly || vt **2** to proclaim loudly; **3 bawl out** *colloq* to reprimand

bay¹ /bā′/ [MF *baie* < LL *baia*] *n* curve or recess in the shore of a sea or lake

bay² [MF *baee* opening] *n* **1** principal division in the arrangement of a structure; **2** alcove or recess; **3** the part of a window between two of the vertical bars of the frame; **4** bay window

bay³ [MF *baie* < L *baca* berry] *n* any of several trees and shrubs, mostly unrelated, including the European laurel

bay⁴ [< OF *abaier* to bark] *n* **1** deep-toned howl of a dog; **2 a** position of a person or animal forced to turn and face an enemy when no escape is possible, as *a stag at bay, a prisoner brought to bay;* **b** state of being held in check ‖ *vi* **3** to howl with a deep tone

bay⁵ [MF *bai* < L *badius*] *n* **1** reddish brown; **2** horse of this color ‖ also *adj*

Ba·yeux′ tap′es·try /bāyŏŏ′/ [city in Normandy, where it is kept] *n* strip of embroidered linen 231 feet long, depicting the Norman Conquest and dating from the 11th century

bay′ leaf′ *n* dried leaf of the bay tree (*Pimenta acris*) used in cookery and for making bay rum

bay·o·net /bā′ənit, -net′/ [< *Bayonne*, France] *n* **1** short sword attached to the muzzle of a rifle ‖ *v* (-**net·ed** *or* -**net·ted; -net·ing** *or* -**net·ting**) *vt* **2** to stab with a bayonet

bay′o·net mount′ *or* **sock′et** *n* socket with L-shaped slots in which knobs on the part to be joined lock into place

bay·ou /bī′ŏŏ/ [LaF < Choctaw *bayuk*] *n* in southern U.S., outlet of a lake or river

bay′ rum′ *n* fragrant toilet liquid distilled from bay leaves

bay′ win′dow *n* **1** window structure projecting from the outside wall of a building and forming a recess in the room within; **2** *slang* protruding belly

ba·zaar /bəzär′/ [Pers *bāzār*] *n* **1** Oriental market place; **2** sale of miscellaneous articles, usu. for charity

ba·zoo·ka /bəzŏŏk′ə/ [pipelike homemade musical instrument] *n* portable pipe-shaped rocket launcher

BB (**shot′**) /bē′bē′/ *n* size of shot (.18 in. in diameter) for use in an air rifle or BB gun

B′ bat′ter·y *n* battery used to provide a positive voltage to the plate of vacuum tubes

B.B.C. British Broadcasting Corporation

bbl. (bbls.) barrel

B.C. 1 before Christ; **2** British Columbia

bd. (bds.) board

be /bē/ [OE *bēon*] *v* (*pres* **am, are, is;** *pt* **was, were;** *pp* **been**) *vi* **1** to exist; **2** to take place; **3** to stay, remain, last, as *let it be;* **4** to mean, as *it is nothing to me;* **5** to be situated in place, time, or experience, as *she is in church; the meeting will be at three o'clock; he is in pain;* **6** to fit (a given description); **7** to coincide in identity with ‖ *v aux* used: **8** with the *prp* to make progressive forms; **9** with the *pp* to form the passive voice; **10** with the *inf* to express obligation or what is expected to happen, as *he is to arrive at six*

Be *chem* beryllium

be- [OE *be-, bi-*] *pref* **1** to cause to be, make (used to form transitive verbs from adjectives, nouns, and intransitive verbs), as *befoul;* **2** all over, completely, as *besmear;* **3** to surround or cover with; treat as; affect with (used to form transitive verbs from nouns), as *befriend;* **4** off, away, as *behead;* **5** adding a tone of depreciation to a participial adjective, as *bejeweled*

beach /bēch/ [?] *n* **1** smooth strip of sand or pebbles along the shore of a sea or lake ‖ *vt* **2** to run or haul onto a beach ‖ *vi* **3** to land on a beach; run aground

beach′ bug′gy *n* motor vehicle, with oversize tires, used for traveling around on beaches

beach′comb′er *n* **1** long curling wave rolling in from the ocean; **2** vagrant who lives on the seashore on the lookout for wreckage, plunder, or beach refuse

beach′head′ *n* area secured by invading troops on an enemy shore

bea·con /bēk′ən/ [OE *bēacen*] *n* **1** light or signal of warning or guidance on land, sea, or airways; **2** hill along the shore on which a fire or light is placed for guiding ships; **3** lighthouse; **4** any guiding light ‖ *vt* **5** to furnish with a beacon; **6** to give light to; **7** to guide; to warn ‖ *vi* **8** to shine as a beacon

bead /bēd/ [ME *bede* < OE *gebed* prayer] *n* **1** little ball of wood, glass, stone, etc., perforated and strung for use as a necklace or in a rosary, or in embroidery; **2** any small globe-shaped body; **3** drop or bubble; **4** front sight of a firearm; **5** narrow rounded molding; **6 count, say,** or **tell one's beads** to say prayers with a rosary; **7 draw a bead on** to aim at ‖ *vt* **8** to ornament with beads ‖ *vi* **9** to form beads; **10** to foam ‖ **bead′y** *adj*

bead′ed *adj* composed of or ornamented with beads

bea·dle /bēd′əl/ [< OE *bydel*] *n* Brit **1** lay officer who ushers and keeps order in church; **2** ecclesiastical and university bearer of the mace

bea·gle /bēg′əl/ [ME *begle*] *n* small

hound with drooping ears and short
legs

beak /bēk'/ [OF *bec*] *n* **1** bill of a bird;
2 long sharp mouth of some insects
and other animals; **3** *slang* nose

beak·er /bēk'ər/ [ME *biker* < Scand]
n **1** large goblet; **2** open-mouthed
glass vessel with projecting lip

beam /bēm'/ [OE = tree] *n* **1** long
piece of timber or iron; **2** extreme
breadth of a ship; **3** bar of a balance;
4 wave train of parallel rays emitted
by a radiating body; **5** set of radio
waves which are projected in parallel
lines in a given direction ‖ *vt* **6** to
send forth, as rays; **7** to direct (rays)
in a beam ‖ *vi* **8** to shine; **9** to smile
cheerfully ‖ **beam'ing** *adj*

bean /bēn'/ [OE] *n* **1** smooth kidney-
shaped seed of certain leguminous
plants; **2** plant bearing such seeds;
3 any of certain other seeds resembling beans; **4** *slang* head; **5 spill
the beans** *colloq* to disclose a secret
‖ *vt* **6** *slang* to hit on the head with
a missile such as a baseball

bean' ball' *n* *baseball* ball thrown intentionally at or near the batter's
head

beanie /bēn'ē/ *n* skullcap worn by
children and college freshmen

bear¹ /ber'/ [OE *bera*] *n* **1** any of an
extensive family (Ursidae) of large
quadrupeds having long shaggy fur
and a five-toed foot; **2** person with
rough or surly manners; **3** one who
attempts to lower stock prices for his
own advantage ‖ *adj* **4** characteristic
of or favoring declining stock-market
prices ‖ *vt* **5** to strive to lower prices
on (the stock market)

bear² [OE *beran*] *v* (**bore; borne**) *vt* **1**
to sustain or support; **2** to carry; **3**
to suffer or endure; **4** to keep, esp. in
the mind; **5** to admit of, as *it will not
bear examination;* **6** to show or exhibit, as testimony; **7** to bring forth
or produce; **8** to give birth to; **9** to
conduct (oneself); **10 bear out** to substantiate ‖ *vi* **11** to be fruitful; **12** to
tend; be in or have a given direction;
13 bear down to increase one's efforts; **14 bear down on, a** to weigh
down; **b** to approach; **15 bear on** to
be relevant to; **16 bear up** to endure; **17 bear with** to put up with ‖
bear'a·ble *adj* ‖ SYN endure, suffer,
undergo, support, stand, submit ‖
DISCR To *bear,* the general word of
this group, means to hold up a load
or burden that taxes the strength or
endurance. *Bear* may be used in connection with the merely trying or with
the serious, as she could not *bear* a
grating noise; she *bore* her misfortunes bravely. To *endure* is to *bear* by
bracing oneself against pain and suffering. One who *endures* may do it
grimly, with the teeth shut, or with
unwilling resignation, but he always

perseveres to the end. To *suffer* is to
put up with by refraining from objection; one who *suffers* insolence
may abstain from voicing his resentment. To *submit* is to *bear* by yielding, as to the inevitable. To *stand* is
to *bear* gamely, as he *stood* his punishment well; he *stands* ridicule well.
To *support* is to hold oneself up
under, as he *supports* opposition
gracefully

bear'cat' *n* *colloq* person, animal, or
thing that acts with unusual force or
violence

beard /bird'/ [OE] *n* **1** hair that grows
on the face of an adult man; **2** anything that resembles this ‖ *vt* **3** to
take by the beard; **4** to oppose face
to face, defy ‖ **beard'ed** *adj* ‖ **beard'-
less** *adj*

bear'er /ber'ər/ *n* **1** one who or that
which carries or sustains; **2** one who
presents a check or other order for
the payment of money

bear'ing *n* **1** manner of carrying or
comporting oneself; **2** meaning or
relevance; **3** the part of a machine
that supports a moving shaft; **4** also
bear·ings *pl* direction or relative position

bear'ish *adj* **1** rude; surly; **2 a** characterized by falling prices; **b** expecting a decline in prices

bear'skin' *n* **1** furry woolen material
used for making overcoats; **2** robe,
overcoat, rug, or other object made
of the skin of a bear; **3** high, black
military fur hat worn as part of the
dress uniform

beast /bēst'/ [OF *beste* < L *bestia*] *n*
1 any large four-footed animal; **2**
rude or coarse person; brute ‖ SYN
quadruped, brute (see *animal*)

beast'ly *adj* (**-li·er; -li·est**) **1** beastlike;
2 *colloq* unpleasant ‖ *adv* *colloq*
very, excessively

beast' of bur'den *n* domesticated animal used for carrying and hauling

beast' of prey' *n* predatory animal

beat /bēt'/ [OE *bēatan*] *v* (**beat; beat-
en**) *vt* **1** to strike repeatedly; **2** to
thrash or punish with blows; **3** to
dash or strike against; **4** to make (a
path) by repeated treading; **5** to
flutter (wings); **6** *cookery* to mix by
stirring; **7** *hunting* to range over, as
woods, in order to drive out game;
8 *mus* to mark (time); **9** *colloq* to
defeat; **10** *colloq* to baffle; **11** *slang*
to defraud; **12 beat back** to force
back; **13 beat down** to subdue; **14
beat it** *slang* to depart; **15 beat up** to
administer a beating to ‖ *vi* **16** to
strike repeatedly; **17** to throb ‖ *n* **18**
a stroke or blow; **b** sound made by a
stroke or blow; **19** stroke which is
made again and again; throb; **20**
round or course which is frequently
gone over, as by a policeman; **21**
mus **a** stroke marking a division of

time; **b** the division or stress so marked; **22** *phys* a periodic variation in the intensity of sound of two tones of different pitch sounded together, due to alternate reenforcement and interference of the sound waves; **b** similar variation in other wave motions; **23** *colloq* news item or feature which a source of information reports exclusively or before its rivals; **24** *slang* shiftless fellow, sponge; cheat ‖ *adj* **25** of or pert. to beatniks or the beat generation; **26** *colloq* exhausted ‖ SYN *v* strike, pommel, smite, bang, pound, batter, bruise, maul, punish; defeat, conquer

beat′en *adj* **1** shaped by hammering; **2** defeated; **3** worn by use; **4** exhausted

beat′er *n* **1** instrument used for beating, as *an egg beater;* **2** person who drives wild game from cover

beat′ gen·er·a′tion *n* generation which came of age in the late 1950's and affected unconventional dress and behavior

be·a·tif·ic /bē′ətif′ik/ *adj* blissful; saintly; blessed

be·at·i·fy /bē·at′ifī′/ [LL *beatificare* < L *beatus* blessed] *v* (*-fied*) *vt* **1** to make happy; **2** R C Ch to declare (a dead person) to have attained the rank of "the blessed" ‖ **be·at·i·fi·ca′·tion** /-fi-/ *n*

beat′ing *n* **1** act of one who or that which beats; **2** flogging; **3** defeat

be·at·i·tude /bē·at′it(y)ōod/ [L *beatitudo*] *n* **1** bliss; blessedness; **2** any of the declarations of blessedness made in the Sermon on the Mount (Matt. 5:3–12)

beat′nik /-nik/ [< *beat*] *n* one who rejects contemporary values and affects unconventional dress and behavior

beau /bō/ [F = beautiful] *n* (**beaus** or **beaux** /bōz′/) **1** male escort or frequent companion; **2** boyfriend; **3** fop, dandy

Beau′fort scale′ /bōf′ərt/ [Sir Francis *Beaufort* (1774–1857) Brit admiral] *n* scale of wind forces and velocities, ranging from force 0 (calm—one knot or less) to force 12 (hurricane —above 65 knots)

beau·te·ous /byōōt′ē·əs, -yəs/ *adj* beautiful; lovely

beau·ti·cian /-tish′ən/ worker in a beauty parlor

beau·ti·ful /byōōt′ifəl/ *adj* **1** possessing beauty; **2** excellent ‖ **beau′ti·ful·ly** *adv* ‖ SYN handsome, comely, lovely, fair, pretty ‖ DISCR *Beautiful* denotes the possession of such qualities as delight the eye, ear, mind, and soul. A *beautiful* object possesses such delicacy of outline, exquisite color, or harmony of proportion as arouses pleasurable emotions in the beholder; a *beautiful* person adds to

these outer graces the charm of spiritual loveliness. A noble thought, pleasing to the intellect, is *beautiful;* a holy act, pleasing to the moral sense, is *beautiful. Handsome* describes that which is symmetrical and well-proportioned; it does not necessarily include any idea of the *beautiful;* a *handsome* man might be a scoundrel, a *handsome* house merely impressive. That is *pretty* which is attractive to the eye, ear, or mind in a dainty and diminutive way; *pretty* lacks the spiritual dignity of *beautiful. Pretty* is used often of things not small to express merely the idea that they are pleasing to the senses, as a *pretty* room; a *pretty* cottage. *Fair* describes attractiveness based upon complexion and feature; that face is *fair* which is bright, smooth, and unblemished; hence, *fair* describes a superficial loveliness. *Comely* indicates an attractiveness in which a wholesome character and a rather full figure unite to produce a pleasing impression ‖ ANT ugly, repulsive, hideous, homely, unattractive, unlovely

beau′ti·ful peo′ple *npl* fashionable and sophisticated people much in the public eye

beau′ti·fy *v* (*-fied*) *vt* to make beautiful ‖ **beau′ti·fi·ca′tion** /-fi-/ *n* ‖ SYN decorate, embellish, adorn, bedeck, garnish

beau′ty [OF *beaute* < L *bellus* pretty] *n* (*-ties*) **1** that combination of qualities which is pleasing to the eye or ear; **2** particular grace or charm; **3** beautiful person or thing, esp. a lovely woman; **4** special advantage; **5** something excellent

beau′ty par′lor or **sa·lon′** or **shop′** *n* establishment dedicated to the beautification of women

beau′ty spot′ *n* **1** small black patch placed on the face to increase its charm; **2** mole, dark mark on skin; **3** place admired for its beauty

bea·ver /bēv′ər/ [OE *beofor*] **1** any of a genus (*Castor*) of amphibious rodents having a broad flat tail, strong teeth, and webbed hind feet, noted for dam building; **2** its fur; **3** *colloq* full beard

Bea′ver·board′ [trademark] *n* light fiber board used esp. for partitions

be·calm /bikäm′/ *vt* to render (a sailing ship) motionless from lack of wind

be·came /bikām′/ *pt* of **become**

be·cause /bikôz′/ [ME *bi cause* by cause] *conj* **1** for the reason that ‖ *adv* **2** because of on account of

beck /bek′/ [*abbr* of *beckon*] *n* at **one's beck and call** subject to one's slightest wish

beck·on /bek′ən/ [OE *bīecnan*] *vt & *

vi 1 to signal or summon by gesture; 2 to attract, entice

be·cloud /bĭkloud'/ *vt* to darken, obscure, as by a cloud

be·come /bĭkum'/ [OE *becuman* to happen] *v* (**-came; -come**) *vi* 1 to come or grow to be; 2 **become of** to happen to || *vt* 3 to befit; be suitable to

be·com'ing *adj* 1 appropriate; befitting; 2 enhancing one's appearance || SYN decent, seemly, suitable, decorous || DISCR That is *becoming* in conduct or bearing which, in the circumstances, is appropriate to the age, type, or general condition of the person in question. It is not *becoming* in a dabbler to scorn the opinions of experts. *Seemly* describes conduct that is conventionally proper, even sedately so; *suitable* emphasizes the fitness of conduct in reference to the existing circumstances. *Decent* describes behavior that fitly observes the fundamental proprieties. As applied to dress, *becoming* describes the pleasing effect of apparel well suited to the complexion, style, and bearing of the wearer. *Seemly* attire is modest, in good taste, and appropriate to the occasion. *Suitable* dress is that which accords with one's age, type, financial circumstances, and situation. *Decent* clothes do not offend against modesty or decorum || ANT indecent, unsuitable, awkward, ill-fitting

bed /bed'/ [OE] *n* 1 article of furniture upon which one lies to sleep; 2 anything in which something lies or is embedded; 3 portion of a garden prepared for plants; 4 bottom of a body of water; 5 any flat surface used as a foundation; 6 *geol* layer or seam || *v* (**bed·ded; bed·ding**) *vt* 7 to put to bed; 8 to lay flat; 9 to plant in a special place; 10 to embed || *vi* 11 to go to bed; 12 to form a compact layer

be·daz·zle /bĭdaz'əl/ *vt* to dazzle; bewilder, confuse

bed'bug' *n* bloodsucking wingless insect (*Cimex lectularius*) infesting beds

bed'clothes' *npl* sheets, blankets, etc. for a bed

bed'ding *n* 1 bedclothes and mattresses; 2 straw, litter, etc. to bed animals; 3 foundation

be·deck /bĭdek'/ *vt* to adorn; ornament || SYN beautify, adorn, deck, embellish

be·dev·il /bĭdev'əl/ *v* (**-iled** or **-illed; -il·ing** or **-il·ling**) *vt* to torment, plague || **be·dev'il·ment** *n*

bed'fel'low *n* 1 one who shares another's bed; 2 associate, collaborator

bed·lam /bed'ləm/ [< Hospital of St. Mary of *Bethlehem*, London asylum] *n* scene of uproar or confusion

Bed·ou·in /bed'ŏŏ·ĭn/ [Ar *badawin* desert dwellers] *n* (**-ins, -in**) 1 nomadic desert Arab of Arabia and N Africa; 2 any wanderer || also *adj*

bed'pan' *n* shallow chamber pot for the use of a person confined to bed

be·drag·gle /bĭdrag'əl/ *vt* to make wet and dirty by dragging in mud or rain || **be·drag'gled** *adj*

bed'rid'den *adj* confined to bed

bed'rock' *n* 1 solid rock underlying the upper crust; 2 any solid foundation

bed'room' *n* room with a bed; room for sleeping

bed'sore' *n* sore on the body of a bedridden person, caused by continual lying in bed

bed'spread' *n* outer covering of a bed, counterpane

bed'spring' *n* framework of springs in a bed supporting the mattress

bed'stead' *n* framework of a bed that supports the springs and mattress

bee /bē'/ [OE *bēo*] *n* 1 any of a large superfamily (Apoidea) of insects of the order Hymenoptera, some solitary and others living in colonies; 2 honeybee; 3 social meeting for work on behalf of a neighbor or charity, or for amusement

bee'bread' *n* brown-colored mixture of pollen and honey, stored by bees as food

beech /bēch'/ [OE *bece*] *n* 1 any species of a genus (*Fagus*) of trees of the temperate zone, having smooth gray bark and edible nuts; 2 its wood

beech'nut' *n* edible nut of the beech

beef /bēf'/ [OF *boef* ox, beef] *n* (**beeves**) 1 adult cow, steer, or bull raised for meat; 2 its flesh; 3 brawn, flesh || *n* (**beefs**) 4 *slang* complaint || *vi* 5 *slang* to complain

beef'steak' *n* slice of beef suitable for cooking

beef'y *adj* (**-i·er; -i·est**) brawny, thickset

bee'hive' *n* 1 shelter or home for a swarm of bees, either man-made or natural; 2 place full of activity

bee'line' *n* straight line or route from one point to another

Be·el·ze·bub /bē·el'zĭbub'/ *n* 1 *Bib* prince of devils; 2 devil

been /bĭn'/ *pp* of **be**

beep /bēp'/ [imit] *n* 1 short high-pitched tone, as of a horn || *vi* 2 to emit such a tone || *vt* 3 to sound (a horn)

beep'er *n* device that emits a beeping sound to indicate that a telephone conversation is being recorded

beer /bĭr'/ [OE *bēor*] *n* 1 fermented beverage made generally from malted barley with hops or other substances added; 2 carbonated soft drink flavored with roots, bark, etc.

bees'wax' *n* wax secreted by bees for honeycombs

beet /bēt'/ [OE *bēte* < L *beta*] *n* 1

plant (genus *Beta*) cultivated for its sweet edible root, used as a source of sugar; **2** its root

Beet·ho·ven, Lud·wig van /lŏōd'wig van bāt'ōvən/ *n* (1770–1827) German composer

bee·tle /bēt'əl/ [OE *bitela*] *n* member of the insect order Coleoptera having four wings, the horny outer pair serving to cover the inner membranous pair

bee·tle-browed' *adj* **1** having projecting brows; **2** sullen; scowling

beeves /bēvz/ *pl* of beef

be·fall /bifôl'/ [OE *befeallan* happen] *v* (-fell /-fel'/; -fall·en) *vt* **1** to happen to ‖ *vi* **2** to happen

be·fit /bifit'/ *v* (-fit·ted; -fit·ting) *vt* to be suitable or appropriate for ‖ **be·fit'ting** *adj*

be·fog /bifog', -fôg'/ *v* (-fogged; -fog·ging) *vt* **1** to envelop in a fog; **2** to mystify

be·fore /bifôr', -fōr'/ [OE *beforan*] *prep* **1** in front of; **2** preceding in space, time, rank, or preference; **3** in the presence, jurisdiction, or sight of; **4** sooner than ‖ *adv* **5** in front; **6** in advance; **7** previously; **8** sooner ‖ *conj* **9** earlier than the time when; **10** rather than

be·fore'hand' *adv* **1** in advance; **2** ahead of time

be·foul /bifoul'/ *vt* to soil, defile, sully

be·friend /bifrend'/ *vt* to be a friend to, aid ‖ SYN favor, stand by, succor, help, assist

be·fud·dle /bifud'əl/ *vt* **1** to confuse; **2** to stupefy, as with liquor

beg /beg/ [ME *beggen*] *v* (begged; beg·ging) *vt* **1** to ask in charity, as alms; **2** to ask earnestly; beseech; **3** to ask as a favor; **4 beg the question** to assume the truth of the matter in question ‖ *vi* **5** to ask alms or favors; **6 beg off** to ask to be excused; **7 go begging** to have no takers ‖ SYN implore, solicit, plead (see *pray*)

be·gan /bigan'/ *pt* of begin

be·get /biget'/ [OE *begitan* to get] *v* (-got or archaic -gat; -got or got·ten) *vt* **1** to become the father of; **2** to produce, cause

beg·gar /beg'ər/ *n* **1** one whose profession is begging; **2** scamp; **3** fellow ‖ *vt* **4** to impoverish; **5** to make words for (description or comparison) seem inadequate

beg·gar·ly *adj* **1** like a beggar; **2** wretchedly poor or small

be·gin /bigin'/ [OE *beginnan*] *v* (-gan /-gan'/; -gun /-gun'/; -gin·ning) *vi* **1** to come into existence; **2** to start ‖ *vt* **3** to originate; **4** to start ‖ **be·gin'ner** *n* ‖ SYN commence ‖ DISCR *Begin* and *commence* are identical in meaning, but *commence* is more formal than *begin*. *Commence* is often used to indicate the starting of some defi-

nite course of action, as to *commence a course of reading*; *begin* is used to indicate the starting point or first step of anything. *Begin* is often preferable to *commence* ‖ ANT delay, postpone, put off

be·gin·ning *n* **1** start; **2** origin; **3** first or early part

be·gone /bigôn', -gon'/ *interj* go away!

be·go·nia /bigōn'yə/ [Michel *Begon* (1638–1710) F botanist] *n* any of a large genus (*Begonia*) of tropical plants cultivated for their showy leaves and flowers

be·got /bigot'/ *pt* & *pp* of beget

be·got·ten *pp* of beget

be·grime /bigrīm'/ *vt* to make grimy

be·grudge /bigruj'/ *vt* **1** to envy (one) the possession of; **2** to give reluctantly ‖ **be·grudg'ing·ly** *adv*

be·guile /bigīl'/ *vt* **1** to mislead; **2** to pass (time) pleasantly; **3** to entertain ‖ **be·guile'ment** *n*

be·guine /bigēn'/ [F] *n* **1** South American dance; **2** music for it

be·gum /bēg'əm/ [Urdu *begam*] *n* Muslim princess of Pakistan or India

be·gun /bigun'/ *pp* of begin

be·half /bihaf', -häf'/ [ME *behalve* beside] *n* **in** or **on behalf of** **1** at the instance of; **2** as the representative of; **3** for the benefit of

be·have /bihāv'/ [be- + *have*] *vt* **1** to conduct (oneself) properly ‖ *vi* **2** to act or react; **3** to conduct oneself in a proper manner

be·hav·ior /-yər/ *n* **1** manner of behaving; **2** action or manner of a machine, substance, etc. ‖ **be·hav·ior·al** *adj* ‖ SYN demeanor, bearing, conduct, carriage, deportment, manner, manners, breeding, response, reaction ‖ DISCR These words all denote a mode of acting. *Behavior*, the most general word, applies to our action in the presence of others, and to our treatment of them. *Conduct* contains the idea of outward action, but names such action as proceeds from principle and one's idea of moral responsibility. *Deportment* is *behavior* which follows set rules; it is usually applied to the action of children. *Carriage* names simply the manner of holding the body; *bearing* is such a *carriage* as displays feeling or state of mind, as haughty *bearing*. *Demeanor* makes plain through bodily poses certain traits of character, as devout *demeanor*; demure *demeanor*

be·hav·ior·al sci·enc·es *npl* sciences concerned with the study of the behavior of living creatures, as sociology, anthropology, and psychology

be·hav·ior·ist *n* one whose approach to psychological study emphasizes the objective observation of behavior ‖ **be·hav·ior·ism** *n*

be·head /bĭhed'/ vt to cut off the head of

be·held /bĭheld'/ pt & pp of **behold**

be·he·moth /bĭhēm'əth, bē'im-/ [Heb] n 1 Bib enormous animal, prob the hippopotamus (Job 40:15–24); 2 any monstrous animal or thing

be·hest /bĭhest'/ [OE behæs] n command, order

be·hind /bĭhīnd'/ [OE behindan] prep 1 at the back of; 2 beyond; 3 remaining after; 4 inferior to; 5 supporting; 6 later than ‖ adv 7 at, to, or toward the back; 8 past in point of time; 9 in arrears ‖ n 10 slang buttocks

be·hind'hand' adj & adv 1 behind in time or in progress; 2 in arrears

be·hold /bĭhōld'/ [OE behealdan] v (-held) vt look at, observe ‖ be·hold'er n

be·hold'en adj indebted, under obligation

be·hoove /bĭhōōv'/ [OE behofian to need] vt 1 to be necessary or fit for, or becoming to, as it behooves me to go; 2 to be advantageous to

beige /bāzh'/ [F] n grayish tan ‖ also adj

be·ing /bē'iŋ/ [prp of be] n 1 life, existence; 2 one who or that which exists

Bei·rut /bāroot'/ n capital of Lebanon (700,000)

be·la·bor /bĭlāb'ər/ vt 1 to attack verbally; 2 **belabor the point** to make the same point over and over

be·lat·ed /bĭlāt'id/ adj delayed

be·lay /bĭlā'/ [OE belecgan] vt naut to fasten (a rope) by winding it around a pin

bel can·to /bel kän'tō/ [It] n style of operatic singing characterized by tonal lyricism and brilliant vocal facility

belch /belch'/ [OE bealcian] vi 1 to discharge gas from the stomach through the mouth; 2 to eject smoke, fire, lava, or the like ‖ vt 3 to eject, as smoke, etc. ‖ n 4 discharge of gas through the mouth

be·lea·guer /bĭlēg'ər/ [D belegeren to camp around] vt 1 to besiege, surround; 2 to beset

Bel·fast /bel'fast, -fäst/ n capital of Northern Ireland (450,000)

bel·fry /bel'frē/ [ME belfrei] n (-fries) tower or church steeple with a bell or bells

Belg. Belgium, Belgian

Bel·gium /bel'j(ē)əm/ n French- and Flemish-speaking kingdom in NW Europe on the North Sea (9,556,000; 11,779 sq.m.; cap. Brussels) ‖ **Bel'gian** adj & n

Bel·grade /bel'grād/ n capital of Yugoslavia (775,000)

Be·li·al /bēl'ē-əl, -yəl/ [Heb] n 1 personification of evil, Satan; 2 one of the fallen angels in Milton's Paradise Lost

be·lie /bĭlī'/ v (-ly·ing) vt 1 to show to be false; 2 to misrepresent; 3 to give the lie to

be·lief /bĭlēf'/ [< OE geleafa] n 1 acceptance of something as true; 2 religious faith; 3 opinion ‖ SYN faith, trust, conviction, persuasion, assurance, credence, credit ‖ DISCR Belief is an act of the mind—the mental assent to something as true. It may be based on reasoning, but it is often the fruit of authority and, not uncommonly, of ignorance or prejudice. It is a general term, variously applicable. We may express our belief in an unproved theory, the truthfulness of a story, or the outcome of a new venture. We believe in things, but we extend our trust to people. Trust is an assured reliance, often instinctive, upon the truthfulness, honesty, or uprightness of another. Faith is belief founded upon trust; faith is blindly sure of its object. It is applicable to both persons and things; we may have faith in the power of a physician, and in the virtue of the remedy he prescribes. Conviction is belief arrived at through reasoning confirmed by proof and evidence: consequently conviction is often a fixed belief not easily changed. Religiously, belief is assent to a given teaching, as, for instance, that there is a God. Trust goes further; trust not only believes, but, untroubled about the future, acts in the confidence that God will care for his children. Faith believes and trusts so fully that the outward conduct is governed by the inner light; the whole man is directed by his vision ‖ ANT disbelief, distrust, doubt, unbelief

be·lieve /bĭlēv'/ [< OE gelēfan] vt 1 to accept as true; 2 to place confidence in; 3 to think, suppose ‖ vi 4 to have faith ‖ **be·liev'a·ble** adj ‖ **be·liev'er** n

be·lit·tle /bĭlit'əl/ vt to speak slightingly of, disparage ‖ SYN decry, disparage, underrate, depreciate

Be·lize /belēz'/ n 1 British dependency in Central America (141,000; 8,867 sq.m.; cap. Belmopan); 2 seaport (48,500)

bell /bel'/ [OE belle] n 1 hollow cup-shaped metallic vessel which rings when struck; 2 anything shaped like a bell, as the flare at the mouth of a horn; 3 naut stroke on a bell to mark the time ‖ vt 4 to put a bell on ‖ vi 5 to become bell-shaped

Bell, Alexander Graham /grā'əm/ n (1847–1922) Scotch-born U.S. scientist, inventor of the telephone

bel·la·don·na /bel'ədon'ə/ [It bella donna fair lady] n perennial European herb (Atropa belladonna) of the nightshade family, yielding atropine, variously used in medicine, as to relieve pain and check spasms

bel·la·don·na lil′y /y n S African bulbous plant (*Amaryllis belladonna*) with white or rose-colored flowers

bell′boy′ also **bell′hop′** n hotel employee who carries guests' luggage and runs errands

belle /bel/ [F < L *bella* beautiful] n 1 beautiful woman; 2 popular young lady

belles-lettres /bel letr′/ [F = fine literature] nsg elegant literature; purely aesthetic writing ‖ **bel·le·tris·tic** /bel′ətrist′ik/ adj

bell′ ga′ble n upward extension of a gable which shelters a bell or bells

bel·li·cose /bel′ikōs′/ [L *bellicosus*] adj inclined to fight, quarrelsome ‖ **bel′li·cos′i·ty** /-kos′itē/ n

bel·lig·er·ent /bəlij′ərənt/ [< *bellum* war + *gerere* to wage] adj 1 relating to war; 2 waging war; 3 pugnacious ‖ n 4 country, party, or person carrying on war ‖ **bel·lig·er·ent·ly** adv ‖ **bel·lig′er·ence** n ‖ SYN adj bellicose, contentious, disputatious, pugnacious ‖ ANT adj peace-loving, conciliating, pacific

bell′jar′ n bell-shaped glass vessel used in laboratories

bel·low /bel′ō/ [OE *bylgian*] vi 1 to utter a full roaring sound, as a bull; 2 to roar, bawl ‖ vt 3 to utter loudly ‖ n 4 sound of bellowing ‖ SYN v roar, bawl, shout, clamor, proclaim

bel·lows /bel′ōz/ [see belly] nsg & npl 1 collapsible device, usu. of leather, for producing a current of air; 2 anything shaped like a bellows

bell′weth′er /-weth′ər/ [< OE *wether* castrated ram] n 1 ram wearing a bell that leads the flock; 2 one who or that which leads in ideas, movements, etc.

bel·ly /bel′ē/ [<OE *belg, belig* bag] n (**-lies**) 1 that part of the body between the breast and the thighs; abdomen; 2 stomach; 3 capacity for food; 4 the part of anything that bulges ‖ v (**-lied**) vt & vi 5 to bulge out

bel′ly·ache′ n 1 *colloq* abdominal pain ‖ vi 2 *slang* to complain

bel′ly·but′ton n *colloq* navel

bel′ly·ful′ n *slang* as much or more than one wants

bel′ly laugh′ n *colloq* hearty laugh

be·long /bilôŋ′, -loŋ′/ [*be-* + obs *long* to pertain] vi 1 to have a proper place, as *he belongs here*; 2 **belong to, a** to be the property of; **b** to be a part, member, or adjunct of

be·long′ings npl possessions

be·lov·ed /biluv′id, -luvd′/ n one who is greatly loved ‖ also adj

be·low /bilō′/ adv 1 in a low place; 2 of lower rank; 3 later, as in a book; 4 on earth; 5 in hell ‖ prep 6 a lower than, under; **b** south of; 7 unworthy of

Bel·shaz·zar /belshaz′ər/ [Heb] n *Bib* king of Babylon, warned by the handwriting on the wall (Dan. 5)

belt /belt′/ [OE < L *balteus*] n 1 band worn around the waist, often to hold up trousers; 2 any encircling band; 3 region that is distinctive as to products, vegetation, or climate; 4 *mach* endless band transmitting motion or conveying things; 5 **below the belt** unfair; 6 **tighten one's belt** to do with less ‖ vt 7 to gird with or fasten on a belt; 8 *slang* to strike

belt′ing n material from which belts are made

belt′line′ n waistline

belt′ line′ n railroad or other transportation system that runs around a city or port

be·lu·ga /bəlōog′ə/ [Russ] n great white sturgeon (*Acipenser huso*) of Europe, from the roe of which caviar is made

be·moan /bimōn′/ vt to lament ‖ SYN deplore, lament, mourn, bewail

be·muse /bimyōoz′/ vt to confuse, daze ‖ **be·mused′** adj

bench /bench′/ [OE *benc*] n 1 long seat; 2 worktable; 3 judge's seat in court; 4 office of a judge; 5 judges collectively, judiciary; 6 *sports* seat on which substitute players sit; 7 **on the bench,** a serving as judge; **b** *sports* (player) not playing ‖ vt 8 *sports* to take a player out of the game

bench′ mark′ n mark fixed in the ground and used as a reference point in leveling and surveying

bench′ war′rant n order issued by a court for the arrest of a person who has failed to appear when summoned

bend /bend′/ [OE *bendan* to draw tight] v (**bent**) vt 1 to curve or make crooked; 2 to turn, incline; 3 to direct to a certain point, as one's energies; 4 to cause to yield ‖ vi 5 to be or become curved or crooked; 6 to be turned toward or away from something; 7 to bow or stoop; 8 to submit; 9 **bend over backwards** to be extremely conciliatory in order to please or attain an end ‖ n 10 curve, turn; 11 act of bending or bowing; 12 **bends** pl caisson disease

ben·day /ben′dā′/ [*Benjamin Day* (1838–1916) American printer] n 1 process for producing shaded backgrounds on drawings and printing plates; 2 background so produced

bend′er n *slang* drunken spree

be·neath /binēth′/ [OE *beneothan*] prep 1 lower in place than; 2 under; 3 unworthy of ‖ adv 4 in or to a lower place; below, underneath

ben·e·dict /ben′ədikt/ [< *Benedick* in Shakespeare's *Much Ado About Nothing*] n newly married man, esp. one long a bachelor

Ben·e·dic·tine /ben′ədik′tin/ [< St. *Benedict* (ab. 480–ab. 543)] adj 1 of or pert. to St. Benedict or the monks of his order ‖ *n* **2** member of the order founded by St. Benedict; **3** **benedictine** sweet liqueur originally made by Benedictine monks

ben·e·dic·tion /ˈbenˈədikˈshən/ [< L *bene* well + *dicere* (*dictus*) to say] *n* **1** blessing; **2** short blessing pronounced at the close of public worship

ben'e·fac'tion /-fakˈshən/ [< L *bene* well + *facere* (*factus*) to do] *n* **1** act of conferring a benefit; **2** benefit conferred, esp. a charitable gift ‖ SYN. alms, charity, donation, bequest, gift, boon

ben'e·fac'tor /-fakˈtər/ *n* one who performs an act of kindness; patron ‖ **ben'e·fac'tress** *nfem*

ben'e·fice /-fis/ [MF] *n* **1** church office endowed with funds or property; **2** revenue from such property

be·nef·i·cent /bənefˈisənt/ *adj* doing or producing good; charitable ‖ **be·nef'i·cence** *n* ‖ SYN. magnanimous, bountiful, kind (see *generous*)

ben·e·fi·cial /ˈbenˈəfishˈəl/ *adj* helpful, advantageous ‖ **ben'e·fi'cial·ly** *adv* ‖ SYN. profitable, serviceable, advantageous, helpful

ben'e·fi'ci·ar·y /-fishˈərē, -fishˈēˌerˈē/ *n* (-ies) **1** one who receives a benefit; **2** person entitled to the income from a trust estate or to the proceeds of an insurance policy

ben'e·fit /-fit/ [AF *benfet*] *n* **1** act of kindness; favor; **2** whatever promotes happiness and well-being; **3** pecuniary advantage; **4** public performance for charity ‖ *v* (-fit·ed or -fit·ted; -fit·ing or fit·ting) *vt* **5** to do good to ‖ *vi* **6** to gain advantage; profit ‖ SYN *n* advantage, profit, use, avail, gain, favor

Ben·e·lux /ˈbenˈfluks/ [*Be*lgium + *Ne*therlands + *Lux*embourg] *n* economic association of Belgium, The Netherlands, and Luxembourg

be·nev·o·lence /bənevˈələns/ [L *benevolentia*] *n* **1** the desire to do good; charitableness; **2** act of kindness ‖ **be·nev'o·lent** *adj* ‖ SYN beneficence, charity, humanity, liberality, bounty, munificence, philanthropy, almsgiving ‖ DISCR *Benevolence*, which originally meant merely a wishing well, has come to mean both the wishing well and the doing well to others, and in this latter sense has, in ordinary usage, taken the place of *beneficence*. Charity is a form of *benevolence;* it now applies chiefly to almsgiving, though it may refer to tolerance or generous sympathy. *Humanity* marks us as men rather than brutes; *humanity* connotes kindness, the disposition to relieve suffering, compassion. *Philanthropy* has for its aim the betterment of mankind; it is based on *humanity,* and may include

charity, but it usually suggests large groups for the promotion of welfare, and is frequently accomplished through organizations

Ben·gal /benˈgôl', beŋ-/ *n* former province in NE India, now divided between India and Bangladesh ‖ **Ben·ga'li** /-lē/ *adj & n*

Ben·gal, Bay of *n* arm of the Indian Ocean between India and Burma

Ben·gha·zi /bengäˈzē/ *n* seaport and one of the two capitals of Libya (137,295)

be·night·ed /bə̄nītˈid/ *adj* dismally ignorant

be·nign /bənīn'/ [MF *benigne* < L *benignus*] *adj* **1** kindly, gentle; **2** favorable; **3** (disease or condition) that is not malignant ‖ **be·nign'ly** *adv*

be·nig·nant /bənigˈnənt/ *adj* **1** kind; condescendingly gracious; **2** helpful, salutary

be·nig'ni·ty *n* (-ties) **1** kindness; gentleness; **2** kindly act ‖ SYN kindness, propitiousness, graciousness

Be·nin /bänēn'/ *n* republic in W Africa, formerly Dahomey (3,400,000; 43,475 sq. mi.; cap. Porto-Novo)

ben·i·son /benˈizən, -sən/ [MF *beneison* < L *benedictio* (*-onis*)] *n* blessing; benediction

bent /bent'/ *pt & pp* of **bend** ‖ *adj* **1** curved, crooked; **2** determined, strongly inclined ‖ *n* **3** mental bias; tendency ‖ SYN *n* gift, inclination, prejudice, propensity, proneness ‖ ANT *n* ineptitude, aversion, disinclination

be·numb /bənum'/ [OE *benumen* deprived] *vt* **1** to make numb; **2** to stupefy

Ben·ze·drine /benˈzidrēn/ [trademark] *n* amphetamine

ben·zene /benˈzēn, benzēn'/ [see **benzoin**] *n* clear, colorless volatile liquid —C₆H₆— obtained from coal tar, and used in manufacturing chemicals and dyes and as a solvent

ben·zine [benˈzēn, benzēn'/ *n* mixture composed chiefly of saturated hydrocarbons, used chiefly as a solvent and in cleaning fluids

ben·zo·ate /benˈzō-ĭt, -āt'/ *n* salt or ester of benzoic acid

ben·zo'ic ac'id /-zo'ik/ *n* white crystalline powder —C₆H₅COOH— used chiefly as a germicide and preservative

ben·zo·in /benˈzō-ĭn, -zoin/ [MF *benjoin* < Ar *lubān jāwī* incense of Java] *n* fragrant resin from an aromatic tree (*Styrax benzoin*) of the East Indies, used in perfumery and medicine

Be·o·wulf /bāˈəwŏŏlf'/ *n* warlike hero of an Old English poem of the same name of the seventh or eighth century

be·queath /bikwēth', -th/ [OE *bec-·*

wethan/ vt 1 to give or leave by will; 2 to hand down, transmit

be·quest /bikwest′/ [ME] n 1 act of bequeathing; 2 legacy

be·rate /birāt′/ vt to scold, rebuke severely ‖ SYN rebuke, upbraid, chide, reprimand (see *scold*)

Ber·ber /bur′bər/ [Ar *barbar*] n 1 member of an indigenous N African race; 2 their language ‖ also *adj*

be·reave /birēv′/ [OE *berēafian*] v (-reaved or -reft /-reft′/) vt to deprive, as of something much prized or beloved ‖ **be·reave′ment** n

be·reft /bireft′/ adj deprived

be·ret /bərā′/ [F *béret*] n soft round rimless cap

berg /burg/ n iceberg

be·rib·boned /birib′ənd/ adj decorated with ribbons

ber·i·ber·i /ber′ēber′ē/ [Sinhalese *beri* weakness] n disease, chiefly of the Orient, caused by vitamin B₁ deficiency

Ber′ing Sea′ /ber′iŋ/ n arm of the Pacific north of the Aleutian Islands

Ber′ing Strait′ n strait between Alaska and Siberia

Berke·ley /burk′lē/ n city across the bay from San Francisco (112,000)

berke·li·um /burk′lē·əm, bərkēl′ē·əm/ n synthetic radioactive metallic element (Bk; at.no. 97)

Ber·lin /bərlin′/ n former capital of Germany, now divided into East Berlin, capital of East Germany, and West Berlin, part of West Germany (3,350,000) ‖ **Ber·lin′er** n

Ber·mu·da /bərmyōod′ə/ n group of British islands in the Atlantic 580 miles east of North Carolina (60,000; 19 sq.mi.; cap. Hamilton)

Ber·mu′da shorts′ npl knee-length shorts

Bern or **Berne** /burn/ n capital of Switzerland (165,000)

Ber·noul′li ef·fect′ /bərnōol′ē/ [Daniel *Bernoulli* (1700–82) Swiss mathematician and physicist] n decrease in fluid pressure with increase in velocity

ber·ry /ber′ē/ [OE *berie*] n (-ries) 1 any small pulpy fruit, as the strawberry; 2 dry seed of certain plants, as the coffee bean; 3 simple fruit with many seeds contained in a fleshy mass, as the tomato ‖ v (-ried) vi 4 to bear, produce, or gather berries

ber·serk /bərsurk′/ [ON *Berserkr* mythological Scand hero] adj & adv in a violent frenzy

berth /burth′/ [prob < *bear*³] n 1 bed or bunk on a ship or in a railroad car; 2 job, position; 3 ship's anchorage ‖ v vt 4 to furnish with or place in a berth ‖ vi 5 to occupy a berth

Ber′til·lon′ sys′tem /burt′ilon′/ [Alphonse *Bertillon* (1853–1914) F anthropologist] n system of identifying

persons, based upon measurements, scars, color of hair and eyes, etc.

ber·yl /ber′əl/ [OF *beril*] n stone of extreme hardness and varying color, of which the aquamarine and the emerald are gem varieties

be·ryl·li·um /bəril′ē·əm/ n rare metallic element (Be; at.no. 4; at.wt. 9.0122) used chiefly in copper alloys

be·seech /bisēch′/ [OE *besēcan*] v (-sought) vt 1 to entreat, implore; 2 to beg, plead for ‖ **be·seech′ing·ly** adv ‖ SYN beg, ask, supplicate, importune (see *pray*)

be·set /biset′/ v (-set; -set·ting) vt 1 to assail, harass; 2 to besiege, hem in ‖ **be·set′ting** adj ‖ SYN encompass, besiege, attack, invest, beleaguer

be·side /bisīd′/ [OE *be sīdan* by side] prep 1 at the side of; near; 2 in comparison with; 3 aside from, as *beside the point*; 4 in addition to; 5 **beside oneself** out of one's senses ‖ adv 6 along the side

be·sides′ adv 1 moreover, in addition ‖ prep 2 in addition to; 3 other than

be·siege /bisēj′/ vt 1 to lay siege to; 2 to assail; 3 to crowd in upon ‖ **be·sieg′er** n ‖ SYN invest, beleaguer, beset, attack, encompass

be·smirch /bismurch′/ vt 1 to soil; 2 to dishonor, sully

be·sot·ted /bisot′id/ [< *sot*] adj 1 stupefied with drink; 2 infatuated

be·sought /bisôt′/ pt & pp of beseech

be·spat·ter /bispat′ər/ vt 1 to soil or spot by spattering; 2 to slander

be·speak /bispēk′/ v (-spoke /-spōk′/; -spoke or -spo·ken) vt 1 to ask beforehand; 2 to show or give evidence of; 3 to reserve in advance

Bes′se·mer proc′ess /bes′əmər/ [Henry *Bessemer* (1813–1898) Brit engineer] n process for making steel in which air is blown through molten iron to remove the impurities

best /best′/ [OE *betst*] adj (superl of good) 1 having the highest degree of goodness or excellence; 2 most desirable, suitable, advantageous, etc.; 3 largest ‖ n 4 highest state of excellence; 5 utmost; 6 most excellent thing or person; 7 **all for the best** to the ultimate good; 8 **at best** at the most; 9 **get the best of,** a to defeat; b to outwit; 10 **make the best of** to do the best one can with (something) under the circumstances ‖ adv 11 in the highest degree; 12 in the most excellent manner; 13 **as best one can** the best way possible; 14 **had best** ought to ‖ vt 15 to get the better of, surpass

bes·tial /bes′chəl/ [MF < L *bestia* beast] adj 1 pert. to beasts; 2 sensual; 3 brutal ‖ **bes·ti·al·i·ty** /bes′chē·al′itē, -tē·al′-/ n

be·stir /bistur′/ v (-stirred; -stir·ring) vt to rouse (oneself) to vigor and action

best′ man′ *n* principal attendant of a bridegroom

be·stow /bistō′/ *vt* to present, give, or confer ‖ **be·stow′al** *n* ‖ SYN grant, present, impart, expend (see *give*)

be·strew /bistrō′/ *vt* to scatter over; litter

be·stride /bistrīd′/ *v* (**-strode** /-strōd′/; **-strid·den** /strid′ən/) *vt* 1 to stand or sit astride of; 2 to pass or step over

bet /bet′/ [?] *n* 1 wager; 2 that on which a wager is made ‖ *v* (**bet; bet·ting**) *vt* 3 to stake or wager (money) on the outcome of some contingent event; 4 to state in or as in a bet ‖ *vi* 5 to lay a wager

be·ta /bēt′ə, bāt′ə/ *n* second letter of the Greek alphabet B, β

be·take /bitāk′/ *v* (**-took; -tak·en** /-tāk′ən/) *vt* **betake oneself** to go

be′ta par′ti·cle *n* charged particle emitted from a nucleus in fission or radioactive decay

be′ta ray′ *n* stream of beta particles

be·ta·tron /bāt′ətron′/ *n* apparatus in which electrons are accelerated to high energies

Be·tel·geuse /bēt′əljooz′/ [F < Ar] *n* red giant star of the first magnitude in the constellation Orion

bête noire /bāt′nwär′/ [F = black beast] *n* something especially disliked; bugbear

Beth·le·hem /beth′lē·əm, -lîhem′/ *n* town SW of Jerusalem in which Jesus was born

be·tide /bitīd′/ *vt* 1 to happen to, befall ‖ *vi* 2 to happen

be·times /bitīmz′/ *adv* 1 early; 2 *archaic* soon

be·to·ken /bitōk′ən/ *vt* to serve as a sign of; indicate ‖ SYN indicate, foreshow, signify, portend, mark

be·took /bitŏōk′/ *pt of* **betake**

be·tray /bitrā′/ [*be-* + OF *traïr*] *vt* 1 to give over into the hands of an enemy by treachery; 2 to fail to be true to; 3 to disclose, as a secret; 4 to seduce and desert; 5 to reveal unintentionally, as an emotion ‖ **be·tray′er** *n* ‖ **be·tray′al** *n*

be·troth /bitrôth′, -trōth′/ *vt* to engage to give in marriage; affiance ‖ **be·troth′al** *n*

bet·ter[1] /bet′ər/ [OE *betera*] *adj* (*comp of* **good**) 1 having good qualities in a greater degree; 2 preferable as to value, rank, suitability, etc.; 3 improved in health; 4 more; larger ‖ *adv* 5 in a more excellent manner; 6 in a higher degree; 7 more; 8 **better off** in better circumstances; 9 **had better** ought to; 10 **think better of** to reconsider ‖ *vt* 11 to improve; 12 to surpass ‖ *n* 13 that which or one who is more excellent; 14 **betters** *pl* those superior in station, rank, intellect, etc.; 15 **get the better of** to prevail against ‖ **bet′ter·ment** *n* ‖ SYN *v* ameliorate, correct, reform, amend, surpass

bet·ter[2] *n* bettor

bet′ter half′ *n colloq* one's wife

bet′tor *n* one who bets

be·tween /bitwēn′/ [OE *betwēonum*] *prep* 1 in the space or time which separates; 2 from one to another of; 3 by the joint action of, as *we'll do it between us*; 4 in common, as *they only had a dollar between them*; 5 involving, as *a fight between two boys*; 6 by comparison of, as *a choice between two evils*; 7 **between ourselves** or **between you and me** confidentially ‖ *adv* 8 in an intermediate space or time ‖ SYN *prep* among, amid ‖ DISCR *Between* is used strictly of only two objects; *among* and *amid* are used of more than two. In cases where *among* does not convey the relation intended, *between* is used of more than two objects, as an agreement *between* the three brothers. The objects of *among* are usually individuals while the objects of *amid* belong to a group

be·twixt /bitwikst′/ [OE *betwix* between] *prep* 1 between ‖ *adv* 2 **betwixt and between** neither one nor the other

bev·el /bev′əl/ [MF] *v* (**-eled** or **-elled**; **-el·ing** or **-el·ling**) *vt* 1 to cut to an angle other than a right angle; 2 to give a sloping edge to ‖ *vi* 3 to slant or incline ‖ *n* 4 angle that one line or surface makes with another when not at right angles; 5 instrument for setting two surfaces at a fixed angle to each other ‖ *adj* also **bev′eled** aslant, oblique

bev·er·age /bev′ərij/ [MF *bevrage*] *n* drink of any kind except water

bev·y /bev′ē/ [ME *bevey*] *n* (**-ies**) 1 group esp. of women or girls; 2 flock esp. of quails or larks ‖ SYN flock, group, company (see *herd*)

be·wail /biwāl′/ *vt & vi* to mourn, lament ‖ SYN bemoan, complain, deplore, grieve, mourn

be·ware /biwer′/ [< *be ware* be careful] *vi* 1 to be on one's guard ‖ *vt* 2 to be wary of

be·wil·der /biwil′dər/ [*be-* + archaic *wilder* to bewilder] *vt* to confuse, puzzle, mystify

be·wil·der·ment *n* 1 state of being bewildered; 2 tangled or confused network ‖ SYN perplexity, confusion, distraction, mystification

be·witch /biwich′/ *vt* 1 to cast a spell over; 2 to fascinate, charm

bey /bā′/ [Turk = lord] *n* 1 governor of a province in Ottoman Turkey; 2 former Turkish title of respect

be·yond /biyond′/ [OE *begeondan*] *prep* 1 at or on the farther side of; 2 farther than, past; 3 out of the reach of; 4 above, surpassing ‖ *adv* 5 at a distance, yonder ‖ *n* **the (great) beyond** what follows death

bez·ant /bez′ənt, bizant′/ [MF *besant*

< Gk *Byzantion* anc name of Constantinople] *n* gold coin of the Byzantine Empire, in common use in Europe during the Middle Ages

bez·el /bez′əl/ [< perh OF, cf. F *biseau* bevel] *n* **1** slanting face on the edge of a chisel or similar tool; **2** grooved rim that holds a watch crystal; **3** oblique face of a cut gem

be·zique /bizēk′/ [F *besigue*] *n* card game similar to pinochle

B′-girl′ *n* woman hired to sit at a bar and induce men to buy her drinks

bhang /baŋ′/ [< Skt *bhangā* hemp] *n* **1** hemp; **2** its dried leaves and seed capsules used in India as a narcotic

bhp, b.h.p. brake horsepower

bi- [L = twice, two] *pref* **1** two, twice, doubly, as *biaxial*; **2** lasting two intervals of time, occurring every two intervals, as *biennial*; **3** coming or occurring twice, as *biweekly*; **4** *chem* having two parts of the substance named, as *bichloride*; **5** *biol* composed of similarly divided parts, as *bipinnate*

Bi *chem* bismuth

bi·an·nu·al /bī-/ *adj* occurring twice a year, semiannual || **bi·an′nu·al·ly** *adv*

bi·as /bī′əs/ [MF *biais* oblique] *n* **1** oblique or diagonal line, esp. one made diagonally across the threads of a dress material; **2** prejudice; **3** potential difference applied in a circuit; **4 on the bias** diagonally, slanting || *v* (-**ased** or -**assed**; -**as·ing** or -**as·sing**) *vt* **5** to influence, prejudice || SYN *n* bent, prejudice, inclination, propensity

bib /bib′/ [ME *bibben* to drink] *n* **1** cloth placed under a child's chin to protect the clothes; **2** that part of an apron above the waist

Bib. 1 Bible; **2** Biblical

Bi·ble /bīb′əl/ [OF < Gk *biblia* books] *n* **1** sacred book of Christianity (the Old and New Testaments); **2** sacred book of Judaism (the Old Testament); **3** book of the sacred writings of any people; **4 bible** any book regarded as an authority || **Bib′li·cal** /bib′-/ *adj*

biblio- [< Gk *biblion*] *comb form* book

bib·li·og·ra·phy /bib′lē̄-og′rəfē/ *n* (-**phies**) **1** history or description of books, their authorship, material, style of printing, dates, editions, etc.; **2** list of books relating to any given subject or author || **bib′li·og′·ra·pher** *n* || **bib′li·o·graph′i·cal** /-əgraf′ikəl/ *adj*

bib·li·o·phile′ /-əfīl′, -fil/ *n* lover of books

bib·u·lous /bib′yələs/ [< L *bibere* to drink] *adj* fond of drinking

bi·cam·er·al /bīkam′ərəl/ [*bi-* + *camera*] *adj* consisting of two legislative chambers

bi·car·bon·ate /bī-/ *n* salt of carbonic acid in which one of the two atoms

of hydrogen has been replaced by an atom of a metal

bi·car′bon·ate of so′da *n* sodium bicarbonate

bi′cen·ten′ni·al /bī′-/ *n* **1** 200th anniversary of an event || *adj* **2** occurring once in 200 years; **3** lasting 200 years; **4** pert. to a bicentennial

bi·ceps /bī′seps/ [< *bi-* + L *caput* head] *n* **1** muscle one end of which has two places of attachment; **2** large flexor muscle on the front of the upper arm

bi·chlo′ride of mer′cu·ry /bī-/ *n* deadly poison, HgCl₂, used as an antiseptic

bick·er /bik′ər/ [ME *biker*] *vi* **1** to engage in petty quarreling; wrangle || *n* **2** petty quarrel; wrangle || **bick′er·ing** *n*

bi·cus·pid /bīkus′pid/ [*bi-* + *cusp*] *adj* **1** having two points || *n* **2** in man, any of eight teeth having two-pointed crowns

bi·cy·cle /bīs′ikəl/ [F] *n* **1** vehicle having a metal frame, two wheels, and a saddle for the rider, propelled by means of treadles || *vi* **2** to ride on a bicycle || **bi′cy·clist** *n*

bid /bid′/ [combination of OE *bēodan* to offer & OE *biddan* to beg] *v* (**bade**; **bid·den** /bid′ən/ or **bid**; **bid·ding**) *vt* **1** to command; **2** to invite; **3** to express by words, as a welcome || *v* (**bid**; **bid·ding**) *vt* **4** a to propose as a price for; **b** *cards* to state the number of tricks one expects to take || *v* (**bid**; **bid·ding**) *vi* **5** to make a bid; **6 bid fair** to seem likely || *n* **7** offer of a price; **8** amount offered; **9** *cards* number of tricks one undertakes to win; **10** *colloq* invitation || **bid′der** *n* || SYN *v* direct, propose, charge, proffer, address

bid′ding *n* **1** command; **2** invitation

bid·dy /bid′ē/ [dim. of *Bridget*] *n* (-**dies**) *colloq* fussy old woman

bide /bīd′/ [OE *bīdan*] *v* (**bode** or **bid·ed**; **bid·ed**) *vt* **bide one's time** to wait patiently for an opportunity

bi·en·ni·al /bī·en′ē-əl/ [*bi-* + L *annus* year] *adj* **1** happening once in two years; **2** continuing or existing for two years || *n* **3** event which occurs once in two years; **4** plant which lives for two years || **bi·en′ni·al·ly** *adv*

bier /bir′/ [OE *bær*] *n* frame on which a corpse or coffin is placed

biff /bif′/ [prob imit] *slang n* **1** sharp blow, as with the fist || *vt* **2** to strike; whack

bi·fo′cals *npl* eyeglasses having lenses in two parts, one for near focus and the other for far focus

bi·fur·cate /bifurk′āt, bif′ərkāt′/ [L *bifurcare* (-*atus*)] *vi* **1** to divide in two branches || /-furk′it/ *adj* **2** divided into two branches, forked || **bi′fur·ca′tion** *n*

big /big′/ [?] *adj* (**big·ger**; **big·gest**) **1** large, of great size; **2** grown-up; **3**

important; **4** loud; **5** magnanimous ‖ *adv* **6** *colloq* **a** impressively; **b** boastfully ‖ **big′ness** *n* ‖ SYN great, large, massive, gross, puffed up, conceited ‖ ANT little, small, unimportant, petty

big·a·my /bĭg′əmē/ [<*bi*- + Gk *gamos* marriage] *n* willful contraction of a second marriage by a person already married ‖ **big′a·mist** *n* ‖ **big′a·mous** *adj*

big′ game′ *n* **1** large and dangerous game animals; **2** *colloq* important objective, sometimes involving considerable danger

big′ gun′ *n slang* important person

big′horn′ *n* (**-horns, -horn**) wild sheep of the Rocky Mountains (*Ovis canadensis*) with large spiral horns

big′ house′ *n slang* penitentiary

big·ot /bĭg′ət/ [F] *n* one blindly intolerant of the views of others, esp. in religion, politics, and race ‖ **big′ot·ed** *adj* ‖ **big′ot·ry** *n* (**-ries**) ‖ SYN intolerant, prejudiced, narrow-minded, biased ‖ ANT tolerant, liberal, broadminded, unbiased

big′ shot′ *n slang* **1** boss; **2** important person

big′ stick′ *n* great political or military strength

big′ time′ *n colloq* top rank in any line of endeavor, esp. in the performing arts ‖ **big′-time′** *adj*

big′ toe′ *n* largest and innermost toe

big′ top′ *n* **1** largest tent of a circus; **2** circus

big′ wheel′ also **big′wig′** *n colloq* important person

bike /bīk′/ [*bicycle*] *colloq n* **1** bicycle ‖ *vi* **2** to bicycle

bi·ki·ni /bĭkēn′ē/ [*Bikini* atoll in the Marshall Islands] *n* extremely brief two-piece bathing suit

bi·la′bi·al /bī-/ *n phon* sound formed by both lips ‖ also *adj*

bi·lat′er·al /bī-/ *adj* **1** relating to or having two sides; **2** affecting both sides equally

bile /bīl′/ [F < L *bilis*] *n* **1** bitter yellow or greenish fluid secreted by the liver; **2** ill humor, peevishness

bilge /bĭlj′/ [?] *n* **1** rounded part of a ship's bottom; **2** bilge water; **3** *slang* nonsense ‖ *vt* **4** to stave in the bottom of (a ship)

bilge′ wa′ter *n* water which gathers in a bilge

bi·lin′gual /bī-/ *adj* **1** spoken or written in two languages; **2** speaking two languages ‖ *n* **3** person fluent in two languages

bil′ious /bĭl′yəs/ *adj* **1** pert. to the bile; **2** caused by too much bile; **3** ill-tempered; peevish

bil·i·ru·bin /bĭl′irōōb′in, bī-/ [< L *bilis* bile + *ruber* red] *n* reddish-yellow organic pigment —$C_{33}H_{36}O_6N_4$— derived from hemoglobin and occurring in bile, blood, urine, and gallstones

-**bil·i·ty** /-bĭl′itē/ *n suf* var of **-ability**

bilk /bĭlk′/ [?] *vt* to defraud, cheat; deceive

bill¹ /bĭl′/ [ME *bille* < LL *bulla* sealed paper] *n* **1** draft of a proposed law; **2** account rendered of money owed, as for goods or services; **3** bank note, piece of paper money; **4** bill of exchange; **5** printed advertisement, poster; **6** theater program; **7** menu; **8** *law* written statement of complaint; **9** **fill the bill** to fulfill the requirements ‖ *vt* **10** to advertise by posters; **11** to enter on a program; **12** to make a list of; **13** to present with a statement of indebtedness

bill² [OE *bile*] *n* **1** bird's beak ‖ *vi* **2** **bill and coo** to whisper words of love; kiss and caress

bill′board′ *n* **1** display board for posters; **2** name of the sponsor and list of entertainers and features, shown at the beginning and sometimes at the end of a broadcast

bil·let /bĭl′it/ [MF *billette*] *n* **1** order providing lodging to military personnel; **2** quarters; **3** situation, job ‖ *vt* **4** to quarter or lodge

bil·let-doux /bĭl′ēdōō′/ [F = sweet note] *n* (**billets-doux** /bĭl′ēdōōz′/) love letter

bill′fold′ *n* wallet for paper money, with compartments for cards and other papers

bill′head′ *n* printed form with a business address at the top, for the issuing of a bill or statement of account

bil·liards /bĭl′yərdz/ [< F *billard* cue] *n* game played on a cloth-covered table with a resilient edge, by propelling ivory balls with a cue ‖ **bil′liard** *adj*

bil′lings·gate [*Billingsgate*, fishmarket in London] *n* coarse and abusive language

bil·lion /bĭl′yən/ [F < *bi*- + *million*] *n* **1** *U.S.* thousand million (1,000,000,000); **2** *Brit* million million (1,000,000,000,000) ‖ also *adj* ‖ **bil′lionth** *adj* & *n*

bil′lion·aire′ *n* person worth a billion dollars

bill′ of ex·change′ *n* written order to pay a sum of money to a specified person

bill′ of fare′ *n* menu

bill′ of goods′ *n* **sell someone a bill of goods** to put something over on someone

bill′ of lad′ing /lād′iŋ/ [<*obs lade* to load] *n* receipt issued by a carrier for goods accepted for shipping

Bill′ of Rights′ *n* first ten amendments to the Constitution of the U.S., guaranteeing civil rights

bill′ of sale′ *n* formal paper transferring to a buyer the title to personal property

bil·low /bĭl′ō/ [< ON *bylgja* to swell] *n* **1** great wave of the sea; **2** any surging mass ‖ *vi* 3 to surge or swell up ‖ **bil′low·y** *adj*

bill′post′er *n* one who sticks placards upon billboards

bil·ly /bil′ē/ [< OE *bill* sword] *n* (**-lies**) *colloq* truncheon

bil′ly goat′ *n* male goat

bi·month·ly /bī-/ *adj & adv* 1 once every two months; 2 semimonthly ‖ *n* (**-lies**) 3 magazine issued every two months

bin /bin′/ [OE *binn*] *n* box, crib, or compartment used for storage

bi·na·ry /bīn′ərē/ [LL *binarius*] *adj* 1 double; consisting of two things or parts; 2 *math* pert. to a nondecimal numerical system to the base 2 ‖ *n* (**-ries**) 3 something composed of two parts; 4 number of a binary system

bin·au·ral /binôr′əl, bī-, -nōr′-/ *adj* 1 of or pert. to sound reproduction from two signals and two directions; 2 pert. to perception of sounds by both ears

bind /bīnd′/ [OE *bindan*] *v* (**bound**) *vt* 1 to make fast with a cord or band; 2 to hold by physical force; 3 to unite by bonds of affection, loyalty, or duty; 4 to hinder or restrain; 5 to protect or strengthen by a band or tape; 6 to adorn, as by a band or border; 7 to bandage; 8 to obligate by a promise, law, duty, etc.; 9 to fasten together in a cover; 10 to constipate; 11 (of clothes) to chafe ‖ *vi* 12 to be obligatory; 13 to stick, be too tight ‖ *n* 14 *mus* tie; 15 **in a bind** *slang* in a tight predicament ‖ SYN *v* fasten, fetter, tie, secure, restrict, compel

bind′er *n* 1 one who or that which binds; 2 substance used to cause cohesion in a mass of loose pieces; 3 cover for loose papers

bind′er·y *n* (**-ies**) place where books are bound

bind′ing *n* 1 anything that binds; 2 outer cover of a book ‖ *adj* 3 obligatory, as an agreement

binge /binj′/ [Eng *dial.*] *n colloq* spree

bin·go /biŋ′gō/ [?] *n* gambling game played with cards containing numbered squares, the players covering the numbers as they are called out

bin·na·cle /bin′əkəl/ [alter. of *bittacle* < OSp *bitácula*] *n* case containing a ship's compass

bin·oc·u·lar /binok′yələr, bī-/ [< L *bini* double + *oculus* eye] *adj* 1 pert. to, or fitted for the use of both eyes; 2 using both eyes ‖ **bin·oc′u·lars** *npl* 3 field glasses

bi·no·mi·al /bīnōm′ē·əl/ [< *bi-* + L *nomen* name] *n* 1 *alg* expression consisting of two terms connected by a plus or minus sign; 2 *biol* name composed of two parts, one indicating the genus and the other the species ‖ *also adj*

bio- [Gk *bios*] *comb form* life

bi′o·chem′is·try /bī′ō-/ *n* chemistry of living organisms ‖ **bi′o·chem′ist** *n* ‖ **bi′o·chem′i·cal** *adj*

bi·o·cide /bī′əsīd/ [*bio-* + *-cide*] *n* preparation, such as an antibiotic or a pesticide, which kills living organisms

bi′o·de·grad′a·ble /-digrād′əbəl/ *adj* (substance, as a detergent or a container) that breaks down by organic action into its constituent elements or components when thrown out or disposed of

bi′o·feed′back′ *n* control by a patient of involuntary nervous-system functions, such as heartbeat and blood circulation, by the use of electronic monitoring devices

biog. 1 biographical; 2 biography

bi·og·ra·phy /bī·og′rəfē/ *n* (**-phies**) 1 written history of another person's life; 2 such writings in general ‖ **bi·og′ra·pher** *n* ‖ **bi·o·graph·ic** (**-i·cal**) /bī′əgraf′ik(əl)/ *adj*

biol. 1 biological; 2 biology

bi·o·log·i·cal /bī′əloj′ikəl/ *adj* 1 of or pert. to biology; 2 used in, or made by the methods of biology ‖ *n* 3 biological product, used esp. in the diagnosis, prevention, and treatment of disease

bi′o·log′i·cal clock′ *n* mechanism inherent in living creatures that determines certain cyclical phenomena in their behavior

bi′o·log′i·cal war′fare *n* germ warfare

bi·ol·o·gy /bī·ol′əjē/ *n* 1 science which deals with the origin, structure, functions, and life history of vegetable and animal organisms; 2 plant and animal life of an area ‖ **bi·ol′o·gist** *n*

bi·o·met·rics /bī′ōmet′riks/ *nsg* 1 measurement of the probable duration of human life; 2 branch of biology which makes a statistical study of the variation of those characteristics of living organisms which can be exactly measured and numbered

bi·o·phys·ics /bī′ōfiz′iks/ *nsg* study of the physics of living matter ‖ **bi′o·phys′i·cist** *n* ‖ **bi′o·phys′i·cal** *adj*

bi′o·rhythm′ *n* theoretical rhythm in certain biological and behavioral phenomena

bi′o·sphere′ *n* envelope made up of the earth's waters, land crust, and atmosphere, where all organisms can exist

bi′o·syn′the·sis *n* production of chemical compounds by living organisms by degradation or synthesis

bi·o·ta /bī·ōt′ə/ [Gk = life] *n* animal and plant life of a region or period

bi′o·te·lem′e·try *n* remote study of the habits and movements of humans and animals by the use of small electronic transmitters attached to them

bi·ot·ic /bī·ot′ik/ *adj* 1 of or pert. to life ‖ *n* 2 antibiotic

bi·o·tope /bī′ətōp′/ [*bio-* + Gk *topos* place] *n* ecologically balanced habitat

bip·a·rous /bip′ərəs/ [<*bi-* + L *parere* to produce] *adj zool* bringing forth two young at birth

bi·par·ti·san /bī-/ *adj* of or representing two parties ‖ **bi·par′ti·san·ship′** *n*

bi·par·tite /bīpärt′it/ [<*bi-* + L *partire* to divide] *adj* 1 divided into or having two corresponding parts; 2 involving two parties

bi·ped /bī′ped/ [< *bi-* + L *pes (pedis)* foot] *n* animal having two feet

bi′plane′ /bī′-/ *n* airplane with two sets of wings, one above the other

bi·pod /bī′pod/ [< *bi-* + Gk *pous (podos)* foot] *n* two-legged stand or support

bi·po·lar /bī-/ *adj* 1 having two poles; 2 ·pert. to both polar regions of the earth ‖ **bi′po·lar′i·ty** /-pəlar′itē/ *n*

bi·ra′cial /bī-/ *adj* made up of or representing two races

birch /burch′/ [OE *beorc*] *n* 1 any of several species of a genus (*Betula*) of northern forest trees, having close-grained wood and a smooth, layered outer bark; 2 its wood; 3 birch rod used for punishment ‖ *vt* 4 to whip

bird /burd′/ [OE *brid* young bird] *n* 1 any of a class (Aves) of warm-blooded, feathered, egg-laying vertebrates, generally having wings; 2 *slang* person, esp. if peculiar; 3 **bird in the hand** something securely in one's possession; 4 **birds of a feather** people who are very much alike; 5 **for the birds** *slang* of no use

bird′brain′ *n slang* weak-minded person

bird′ie *n golf* score of one under par for a hole

bird′s′-eye′ *adj* 1 seen from above; 2 marked with spots resembling a bird's eye, as *bird's-eye maple*

bird′ shot′ *n* small-size shot for shooting birds

bi·ret·ta /biret′ə/ [It *berretta*] *n* square cap worn by ecclesiastics

Bir·ming·ham /burm′iŋəm/ *n* 1 city in central England (1,105,000) ‖ /-ham′/ *n* 2 city in N Alabama (300-910)

birth /burth′/ [ON *byrthr*] *n* 1 fact of being born; 2 act of bringing forth offspring; 3 descent, lineage; 4 inherited disposition or bent; 5 origin; beginning; 6 **give birth to, a** to bear; **b** to originate

birth′day′ *n* 1 day when one is born; 2 any anniversary of it

birth′mark′ *n* mark on the skin at birth

birth′right′ *n* 1 any right, privilege, or possession to which a person is entitled by birth; 2 right of the first-born

birth′stone′ *n* one of twelve gems assigned to each sign of the zodiac, supposed to bring good luck

bis /bis′/ [L] *adv* 1 twice ‖ *interj* 2 encore!

bis·cuit /bis′kit/ [MF = twice cooked] *n* 1 small baked cake of raised bread dough; 2 *Brit* cracker; 3 unglazed pottery after one baking

bi·sect /bīsekt′/ [*bi-* + L *secare (sectus)* to cut] *vt* to cut or divide into two equal parts ‖ **bi·sec′tion** *n* ‖ **bi·sec′tor** *n*

bi·sex′u·al /bī-/ *adj* having both male and female reproductive organs

bish·op /bish′əp/ [OE *biscop* < Gk *episkopos* overseer] *n* 1 clergyman consecrated as head of a group of churches in a diocese; 2 chess piece which moves only diagonally on the board

bish′op·ric /-rik/ *n* office or see of a bishop

Bis·marck /biz′märk/ *n* capital of North Dakota (35,000)

Bis′marck, Prince Ot·to von /ot′ō von/ *n* (1815–98) German statesman, first chancellor of the German Empire 1871–90

bis·muth /biz′məth, bis′-/ [17th-cent. G] *n* heavy brittle metallic element (**Bi**; at.no. 83; at.wt. 208.980) similar to antimony; used in alloys and in medicine

bi·son /bīs′ən/ [L < Gmc] *n* (-son) wild ox-like animal of North America (*Bison americanus*) with a shaggy mane and a humped back, popularly called *buffalo*

bisque¹ /bisk′/ [of or from F province of *Biscaye*] *n* 1 thick soup made from meat, fish, or tomatoes; 2 ice cream containing crushed macaroons

bisque² [< *biscuit*] *n* unglazed pottery after one baking

bis·tro /bis′trō/ [F] *n* 1 small café; 2 night club

bi·sul′fate /bī-/ *n* an acid sulfate

bit¹ /bit′/ *pt & pp* of **bite**

bit² [< OE *bitan* to bite] *n* 1 removable drilling or boring tool used in a brace or drill; 2 metal mouthpiece of a bridle; 3 force which checks or restrains

bit³ [OE *bita*] *n* 1 small piece or fragment; 2 bit part; 3 eighth part of the Spanish duro or piece of eight, formerly current, esp. on the gulf coast; hence a, **two bits** 25 cents; **b, four bits** 50 cents; etc.; 4 **a bit,** a somewhat, a little; **b** a little while; 5 **bit by bit** gradually; 6 **do one's bit** to do one's share

bitch /bich′/ [OE *bicce*] *n* 1 female of the dog, wolf, and other canines; 2 *slang* **a** a viciously selfish woman; **b** anything unpleasantly difficult ‖ *vi* 3 *slang* to complain ‖ *vt* 4 *slang* to spoil or bungle

bitch′y *adj* (-i·er; -i·est) *slang* spiteful; malicious ‖ **bitch′i·ness** *n*

bite /bīt/ [OE *bītan*] *v* (bit; bit·ten or bit) *vt* 1 to seize, cut, or crush with the teeth; 2 to sting, as does an insect; 3 to cut into, as with a sword; 4 to cause smarting pain to; 5 to grip, take hold of; **6** to eat into, corrode; **7 bite someone's head off** to react with anger to someone's question or request; **8 bite the dust** to be killed in battle ‖ vi **9** to seize an object with the teeth; **10** to cause injury with the teeth; **11** to sting or smart; **12** to take a bait; **13** to take firm hold ‖ n **14** act of biting; **15** wound made by biting or stinging; **16** smarting sensation; **17** mouthful; **18** light repast; **19 put the bite on** to solicit money, as a gift or loan, from

bit'ing adj **1** sharp, stinging; **2** sarcastic

bit' part' n small role, with a few spoken lines, in a play or movie

bit·ten /bit'en/ pp of **bite**

bit·ter /bit'ər/ [OE biter] adj **1** having a sharp or harsh taste; **2** sharp to the feeling; **3** painful; grievous; **4** severe; relentless; **5** to **the bitter end** to the last extremity ‖ adv **6** very, extremely, as bitter cold ‖ **bit'ter·ly** adv ‖ **bit'ter·ness** n ‖ SYN adj acrid, biting, caustic, sour, sharp, stinging, acid, tart, keen ‖ DISCR Bitter describes a biting, sharp taste, as that of wormwood or quinine; sour and acid describe a vinegarish taste; tart, a slightly stinging sharpness of taste. Figuratively, bitter describes that which afflicts both mind and body painfully, as bitter grief; or one who is angered and resentful at misfortune or injustice. Used of words, bitter means stinging and severe. Sour is applied to one who is crabbed, morose, or habitually ill-humored. Acid speech is cutting and caustic, as acid criticism. Tart describes an asperity not always unpleasant, sometimes even tonic in its effect

bit'ter-end'er n one who is unwilling to compromise

bit·tern /bit'ərn/ [< MF butor] n any of several wading birds of the genera Botaurus and Ixobrychus, related to the herons

bit'ter pill' n something disagreeable or humiliating that must be accepted, often to avoid something worse

bit'ters npl liquor in which bitter herbs or roots have been steeped

bit'ter-sweet' adj **1** mingling sweetness and bitterness ‖ n **2** herbaceous vine (Solanum dulcamara) of the nightshade family, bearing poisonous, bright-red berries; **3** twining shrub (Celastrus scanders) with orange capsules opening to display scarlet-covered seeds

bi·tu·men /bit(y)ōōm'ən/ [L] n any native mixture of heavy hydrocarbons in viscid or solid form, as asphalt ‖ **bi·tu'mi·nous** /-mən-/ adj

bi·tu'mi·nous coal' n coal containing a large proportion of volatile hydrocarbons and burning with a smoky flame

bi·va·lent /bīvāl'ənt, biv'ə-/ [< bi- + L valens (-entis) worth] adj chem **1** having a valence of two; **2** having two valences ‖ **bi·va'lence** n

bi'valve' /bī-/ n mollusk having two shells hinged together, as the oyster

biv·ou·ac /biv'ōō·ak', -wak/ [F < LG biwake] n **1** encampment in the open ‖ v (-acked; -ack·ing) vi **2** to encamp in the open

bi·week'ly adj **1** occurring or appearing every two weeks; **2** semiweekly ‖ adv **3** once every two weeks ‖ n (-lies) **4** periodical issued every two weeks

bi·zarre /bizär'/ [F < Sp bizarro gallant < Basque bizar bearded] adj fantastic, grotesque, odd, unusual

Bk chem berkelium

bk (bks.) **1** bank; **2** book

b/l, B/L, b.l. bill of lading

B.L. [L baccalaureus legis] Bachelor of Laws

blab /blab'/ [ME blabbe] v (**blabbed; blab·bing**) vt **1** to reveal indiscreetly or thoughtlessly ‖ vi **2** to talk indiscreetly; **3** to gossip ‖ **blab'ber** n

black /blak'/ [OE blæc] adj **1** of the darkest color; spec. lacking all color: opposite of white; **2** without light; dark; **3** dark-skinned; **4** soiled, stained, dirty; **5** dismal, gloomy; **6** evil; **7** sullen; **8** reproving, as a black mark ‖ n **9** darkest color; opposite of white; **10** black pigment; **11** dark-skinned person; **12** mourning; **13** something black, as a horse or chess piece; **14 in the black** operating at a profit ‖ vt **15** to make black ‖ vi **16** to grow black; **17 black out** to lose consciousness ‖ **black'ness** n

black'-and-blue' adj **1** discolored (bruise); **2** bruised

black' and white' n **1** picture not in color; **2 in black and white** in print or in writing ‖ **black'-and-white'** adj

black'ball' n **1** negative vote ‖ vt **2** to vote against

black'ber'ry n (-ries) **1** fruit of any of several species of a large genus (Rubus) of brambles of the rose family; **2** the plant itself

black'bird' n **1** English songbird (Turdus merula) of the thrush family, the male of which is black; **2** any of several North American birds of the family Icteridae having black plumage

black'board' n panel of slate or of wood or other material, formerly black but now often colored, to be written or drawn upon with chalk

black' bod'y n phys hypothetical body that absorbs radiation at all frequencies without loss due to reflection

Black' Death' n epidemic of bubonic plague that struck Europe in the 14th century

black'en vi **1** to grow black or dark ‖ vt **2** to make black; **3** to speak evil of

black′ eye′ *n* **1** eye with a black iris; **2** discoloration of the skin around the eye caused by a blow; **3** discredit; bad reputation; **4** defect, setback, rebuff

black′-eyed Su′san /sⁿōⁿoz′ən/ *n* plant having flowers with a dark-brown center against a yellow background, esp. the yellow daisy *Rudbeckia hirta*

Black′foot′ *n* (**-feet, -foot**) **1** member of an Indian tribe of Montana and W Canada; **2** language of the Blackfeet

black′ gold′ *n* petroleum considered as the source of great riches

black-guard /blag′ärd, -ord/ [orig. = pot washer, kitchen menial] *n* scoundrel

black′head′ *n* black-tipped fatty mass in a pore of the skin

black′ hole′ *n* hypothetical star that is invisible because its gravitational pull is so intense that even light cannot escape from it

black′ing *n* black polish for shoes, stoves, etc.

black′jack′ *n* **1** small leather-covered club with a flexible handle; **2** card game, also called *twenty-one* ‖ *vt* **3** to strike with a blackjack

black′ light′ *n* invisible infrared or ultraviolet light

black′list′ *n* list of persons to be punished or excluded, as from employment ‖ also *vt*

black′ mag′ic *n* sorcery

black′mail′ [< ME *maille* tribute] *n* **1** payment of money under threat of public accusation or exposure of illegal or immoral acts; **2** threat of such accusation or exposure ‖ *vt* **3** to obtain or try to obtain by blackmail from; **4** to coerce by threat of blackmail ‖ **black′mail′er** *n*

Black′ Ma·ri′a /məri′ə/ *n* closed police truck used for conveying prisoners to and from jail

black′ mark′ *n* mark of censure or failure

black′ mar′ket *n* illicit trade in violation of government controls ‖ **black′ mar′ke·teer′** /-tir′/ *n*

black′out′ *n* **1** extinguishing or covering of all lights visible from the air; **2** extinguishing of all stage lights; **3** sudden unconsciousness; **4** stoppage of news

Black′ Sea′ *n* enclosed sea between Russia and Asia Minor

black′ sheep′ *n* person who disgraces his family or associates by his actions

black′smith′ *n* person who makes iron utensils and shoes horses

Black′stone′, Sir William *n* (1723–80) English jurist and legal authority

black′thorn′ *n* **1 a** Eurasian thorny shrub, the sloe (*Prunus spinosa*); **b** hard wood of this shrub; **c** walking stick made of it; **2** American shrub or tree (*Crataegus tomentosa*) with pear-shaped fruit

black′ tie′ *n* **1** black bow tie worn with dinner jacket; **2** semiformal men's evening clothes ‖ **black′-tie′** *adj*

black′top′ *n* asphalt paving ‖ also *vt*

black′ wid′ow *n* venomous jet-black North American spider (*Latrodectus mactans*)

blad-der /blad′ər/ [OE *blædre*] *n* **1** sac in animals in which fluid is collected, esp. the urinary bladder; **2** anything inflated

blade /blād/ [OE *blæd*] *n* **1** cutting edge of a knife, sword, or other instrument or tool; **2** any broad flat surface; **3** swordsman; **4** dashing young fellow; **5** leaf of a grass; **6** broad part of a leaf ‖ **blad′ed** *adj*

Blake, William /blāk′/ *n* (1757–1827) English poet, engraver, and painter

blame /blām/ [OF *blamer* < LL *blasphemare* to blaspheme] *n* **1** expression of disapproval; censure; fault; **2** responsibility for anything wrong ‖ *vt* **3** to find fault with, reproach; **4** to put the blame on; **5 be to blame** to be at fault ‖ **blam′less** *adj* ‖ SYN *v* condemn, chide, censure, reprove, reproach, rebuke, reprimand ‖ DISCR To have an adverse judgment against is the idea common to all these words. To *blame* is to find fault with, or to fix responsibility upon; either a person or a thing may be *blamed*. To *censure* is more positive than *blame*; it is used of more serious faults, and is severe. To *reprove* is to express adverse criticism directly, often severely, and usually with some authority, to a person. To *condemn*, legally, is to pronounce judicial sentence against; a court may *condemn* a person to punishment because of his guilt, or may *condemn* a schoolhouse to be torn down because unsafe

blame′wor′thy *adj* deserving blame ‖ SYN guilty, culpable, censurable

blanch /blanch′, blänch′/ [MF *blanchir*] *vt* **1** to bleach, make white; **2** *cookery* to scald quickly ‖ *vi* **3** to turn pale

bland /bland′/ [L *blandus*] *adj* **1** soft-spoken, suave; **2** mild, soothing ‖ **bland′ly** *adv* ‖ **bland′ness** *n* ‖ SYN gentle, tender, suave, gracious, complaisant

blan′dish /blan′dish/ [OF *blandir* (-*diss*-)] *vt* to flatter; coax, wheedle ‖ **blan′dish·ment** *n*

blank /blaŋk/ [MF *blanc* white < Gmc] *n* **1** empty space on a printed form to be filled in; **2** the form itself; **3** piece of metal prepared for stamping, as for a key or coin; **4** cartridge with powder but no bullet; **5** empty place; **6 draw a blank** *colloq* to be unsuccessful ‖ *adj* **7** free from writing or print; **8** empty, vacant; **9** utter, absolute ‖ *vt* **10** to cross out; **11** *sports* to keep (an opponent) from scoring ‖ **blank′ly** *adv*

|| **blank′ness** n || SYN adj unfilled, unmarked, unsigned (see *empty*)

blank′ check′ n 1 check with a signature but no stated amount; 2 free hand to do as one wills

blan·ket /blaŋk′it/ [OF] n 1 large rectangular cloth used for warmth, esp. as a bed covering; 2 any covering layer, as *a blanket of snow* || adj 3 all-inclusive, as *a blanket proposal* || vt 4 to cover as with a blanket

blank′ verse′ n unrhymed verse

blank′ wall′ n impenetrable barrier

blare /bler′/ [ME *bleren*] n 1 sound like a trumpet blast || vi 2 to give forth a loud brazen sound || vt 3 to trumpet forth

blar·ney /blär′nē/ [*Blarney* stone in Blarney, Ireland, the kissing of which bestows the gift of gab] n 1 flattery || vt 2 to soft-soap

bla·sé /bläzā′/ [F = cloyed] adj bored; surfeited; indifferent

blas·pheme /blasfēm′/ [LL *blasphemare*] vt 1 to speak irreverently or profanely of (God or sacred things) || vi 2 to utter blasphemy || **blas·phem′er** n

blas·phe·my /blas′fimē/ n (-mies) profanity or irreverence in speaking of God or sacred things || **blas′phe·mous** adj

blast /blast′, bläst′/ [OE *blæst*] n 1 strong gust of wind; 2 loud and sudden sound, as of a horn or whistle; 3 explosion; 4 (at) **full blast** at maximum speed or capacity || vt 5 to ruin, destroy; 6 to break open or shatter with an explosive; 7 *slang* to censure severely; 8 *slang* to shoot || vi 9 to make a blaring sound; 10 *slang* to discharge a firearm; 11 **blast off** to be launched into the atmosphere, as a rocket || **blast′er** n

blast′ed adj *colloq* confounded, damnable

blast′ fur′nace n smelting furnace in which the fuel is burned with the aid of high-pressure blasts of air

blast′-off n launching of a rocket

bla·tant /blāt′ənt/ [?] adj 1 blustering; noisy; 2 glaringly evident; 3 vulgarly obtrusive || **bla′tan·cy** n

blath·er /blath′ər/ [ME < ON *bladhra* to prattle] n 1 flow of nonsensical talk || vi 2 to talk nonsense

blath′er·skite′ /-skīt′/ [*blather* + *skate*[3]] n 1 person who talks much and noisily and to little purpose; 2 blustering, useless talk

blaze[1] /blāz′/ [OE *blæse* torch] n 1 burst of bright flame; 2 fire; 3 sudden outburst; 4 brilliant display || vi 5 to burst into flame; 6 to burn; 7 to glow brightly; 8 to show sudden emotion; 9 **blaze away** to keep steadily shooting firearms || SYN n conflagration, fire (see *light*)

blaze[2] [17th-cent. word < ON *blesi*] n 1 white spot on the face of a horse or other animal; 2 mark made on a tree by chipping off the bark || vt 3 to mark with blazes; 4 to discover or devise (a new path, method, etc.)

blaz′er [<*blaze*[1]] n brightly colored or striped sports jacket

bla′zon /blāz′ən/ [MF *blason*] n 1 coat of arms; 2 showy display || vt 3 to proclaim

bldg. (bldgs.) building

bleach /blēch′/ [OE *blæcean*] vt 1 to make white or colorless || vi 2 to become white || n 3 chemical for bleaching

bleach′ers npl uncovered seats for spectators at outdoor games

bleach′er·y n (-ies) establishment where bleaching is done

bleach′ing pow′der n chloride of lime

bleak /blēk′/ [OE *blāc*] adj 1 exposed to wind and cold; 2 cold; piercing; 3 cheerless || **bleak′ness** n || SYN waste, bare, windy, wind-swept, chill, cold, desolate || ANT warm, cheery, homelike, sunny

blear /blir′/ [ME *bleren*] adj 1 filmy or dim (eyes), as from tears || vt 2 to make (the eyes) dim or watery; 3 to blur || **blear′y** adj

bleat /blēt′/ [OE *blætan*] n 1 cry of a sheep, goat, or calf || vi 2 to utter a bleat

bleed /blēd′/ [OE *blēdan*] v (bled /bled′/) vi 1 to shed blood; 2 to exude sap or juice; 3 to be filled with sorrow or pity; 4 to run, as a dye or color || vt 5 to draw blood from; 6 to draw (sap or other concealed fluid); 7 *colloq* to extort money from

bleed′ing heart′ n 1 garden plant (*Dicentra spectabilis*) with red or pink heart-shaped blossoms; 2 *colloq* person who makes showy and hypocritical display of concern for others

blem·ish /blem′ish/ [MF *blemir* (-*miss*-) to wound] n 1 defect or imperfection || vt 2 to mar, deface || SYN n defect, flaw, taint || DISCR A *blemish* is a disfiguring mark or impairment which mars beauty; it is superficial, but it may range in seriousness from an ugly imperfection of countenance to a scratch on a table. A *defect* strikes deeper; it spoils completeness, for it is a want or lack of something essential, as a *defect* in the organs of speech. *Flaw* and *taint* are alike in that they name injury or fault in the very structure or tissues of an object; a bubble in glass is a *flaw*; decay in meat is *taint*. A break in a character otherwise admirable is, figuratively, a *flaw*; a streak of insanity, or of moral decay in a community, is a *taint*

blench[1] /blench′/ [OE *blencan* to deceive] vi to start or to shrink back; flinch

blench[2] vi to blanch; turn pale

blend /blend′/ [OE *blendan*] v (blend′ed or blent′) vt 1 to mix together || vi 2 to shade imperceptibly into each other, as colors; **3** to mix or mingle; **4** to harmonize ‖ *n* **5** smooth mixture or combination ‖ SYN *v* merge, fuse, commingle, combine (see *mix*)

bless /bles′/ [OE blētsian] *vt* **1** to make holy; **2** to call down God's favor upon; **3** to bestow happiness or well-being on; **4** to praise; adore, worship

bless·ed /bles′id, blest′/ *adj* **1** holy, hallowed; **2** favored with supreme happiness; **3** enjoying heavenly felicity; **4** beatified ‖ /blest′/ *adj* **5** endowed, as *blessed with keen vision* ‖ **bless′ed·ness** /bles′id–/ *n*

bless′ing *n* **1** bestowal or invocation of divine favor; **2** grace said before a meal; **3** anything which gives happiness; **4** approval ‖ SYN benediction, favor, boon, benefit, comfort ‖ ANT abomination, malediction, curse; disservice

blest /blest′/ *adj* var of **blessed**

blew /bloo′/ *pt* of **blow**

blight /blīt/ [?] *n* **1** diseased condition of plants resulting from insect pests or parasitic growth; **2** any of a number of fungi or insects causing blight; **3** any malign influence that destroys or frustrates ‖ *vt* **4** to cause growth to cease in; **5** to ruin; frustrate

blimp /blimp′/ [?] *n* small nonrigid dirigible balloon

blind /blīnd′/ [OE] *adj* **1** without the sense of sight; **2** lacking in judgment; **3** heedless; **4** without governing purpose; **5** concealed; obscure; **6** closed at one end, as *a blind alley;* **7** pertaining to those who are sightless; **8** *aeron* with instruments only ‖ *adv* **9** blindly ‖ *n* **10** anything which blocks vision or prevents the passage of light, as a window shade or screen; **11** means of concealment; **12** trick or subterfuge ‖ *vt* **13** to deprive of sight or judgment ‖ **blind′ly** *adv* ‖ **blind′ness** *n*

blind′ date′ *n slang* date with a stranger arranged through a third party

blind′ers *npl* leather flaps on a bridle to shut off a horse's side vision

blind′fold′ [ME *blindfelled* struck blind] *adj* **1** having the eyes covered; **2** heedless, reckless ‖ *vt* **3** to cover the eyes of ‖ *n* **4** something used to cover the eyes

blind′man's′ buff′ *n* game in which one who is blindfolded must catch and name one of the other players

blind′ spot′ *n* **1** small area on the retina of the eye which is not sensitive to light; **2** subject about which one is ignorant or lacking in judgment; **3** locality where radio reception is poor

blink /blingk′/ [ME *blinken*] *vt* **1** to wink rapidly, as the eyes; **2** to cause (a light) to flash repeatedly; **3** to shut one's eyes to ‖ *vi* **4** to wink quickly; **5** to twinkle; glimmer; **6** **blink at** to ignore ‖ *n* **7** **on the blink** *slang* out of order

blink′er *n* **1** blinking warning light; **2** device for blinking light signals; **3** **blinkers** *pl* **a** leather flaps on a bridle to shut off a horse's side vision; **b** goggles

blintz /blints′/ [< Yiddish < Russ] *n* pancake rolled around a filling and fried or baked

blip /blip′/ [imit] *n* **1** spot of light on a radarscope; **2** sharp, brief break in the sound of a telecast ‖ *v* (**blipped**) **blip·ping**) *vt* **3** to make a sudden cut in (the audio recording of a videotape) with consequent break in the sound of the telecast

bliss /blis′/ [OE] *n* **1** great happiness; **2** heavenly joy ‖ **bliss′ful** *adj* ‖ **bliss′ful·ly** *adv*

blis·ter /blist′ər/ [ON *blastr* swelling] *n* **1** bladderlike swelling on the skin, filled with watery matter, as from a burn or friction; **2** any blisterlike swelling ‖ *vt* **3** to produce a blister or blisters on; **4** to sail into angrily or scornfully ‖ *vi* **5** to become covered with blisters

blithe /blīth/, blīth′/ [OE] *adj* **1** gay, joyous; **2** carefree, heedless ‖ **blithe·ly** *adv* ‖ SYN merry, mirthful, glad, gay, joyous

blithe′some *adj* blithe

blitz /blits′/ [< *blitzkrieg*] *n* **1** blitzkrieg; **2** something that acts or happens quickly and violently ‖ *vt* **3** to overwhelm with a blitz

blitz′krieg′ /–krēg′/ [G = lightning war] *n* **1** war with a sudden overwhelming attack ‖ *vt* **2** to subject to a blitzkrieg

bliz·zard /bliz′ərd/ [?] *n* furious windstorm accompanied by snow and intense cold

blk. black

bloat /blōt′/ [ME *blout*] *vt & vi* **1** to swell, as with water or air; inflate; **2** to puff up with vanity

blob /blob′/ [?] *n* **1** drop; **2** small lump; **3** daub

bloc /blok′/ [F] *n* group of legislators, often of different parties, which votes as a unit for a definite objective

block /blok′/ [MF *bloc*] *n* **1** solid piece of inflexible material; **2** heavy table for chopping; **3** auctioneer's platform; **4** piece of wood supporting the neck of a person to be beheaded; **5** wooden form for molding and ironing hats; **6** piece of wood engraved for printing; **7** pulley in a frame; **8** connected row of buildings; **9** city square; **10** mass or division of something taken as a unit, as *a block of stock;* **11** obstruction or impediment; **12** **on the block** up for sale ‖ *vt* **13** to impede; obstruct; **14** to stop; **15** to mold or shape (a hat) on a block; **16 block up** to support by placing blocks underneath; **17 block out** to sketch roughly

block·ade' /-ād'/ n closing off an enemy port or coast by military or naval action, to prevent supplies from getting through ‖ also vt

block' and tack'le n system of blocks and ropes for lifting heavy objects

block'bust'er n 1 high-explosive bomb capable of blowing up an entire city block; 2 anything very successful or effective

block'bust'ing n the practice of driving people to sell their homes by threats of renting or selling a neighboring home to a member of a racial minority and thereby lowering real-estate values

block'head' n stupid fellow

block'house' n (-hous·es /-ziz/) fort of heavy timber with projecting upper story

block let'ters npl typ heavy letters without serifs

bloke /blōk'/ [?] n chiefly Brit fellow

blond /blond'/ [MF] n person, esp. a male, with light-colored hair and skin and blue or gray eyes ‖ also adj ‖ **blonde** nfem & adj

blood /blud'/ [OE blōd] n 1 red fluid which circulates in the arteries and veins of men and animals; 2 any vital fluid, as sap; 3 kinship; 4 lineage; 5 slaughter, murder; 6 mettle, temperament; 7 **the blood** noble or royal extraction, as a princess of the blood; 8 **in cold blood** without passion; 9 **make one's blood boil** to make one indignant; 10 **make one's blood run cold** to frighten

blood' bank' n reserve supply of blood or plasma for use in transfusion

blood' cell' n one of the red cells of the blood, which carry oxygen and carbon dioxide to and from the fixed cells of the body or one of the white cells of the blood, which are useful in destroying harmful bacteria

blood' count' n number of red and white corpuscles in a given volume of blood

blood'cur'dling adj extremely terrifying

blood'ed adj of the best stock or breed

blood' group' n blood type

blood'hound' n 1 one of a breed of large tracking dogs remarkable for their keen sense of smell; 2 colloq detective; spy

blood'line' n pedigree

blood' plas'ma n fluid portion of the blood

blood' poi'son·ing n toxic condition of the blood due to the presence of bacterial poisons

blood' pres'sure n pressure of the blood against the walls of the blood vessels

blood' re·la'tion n one related by birth

blood'shed' n spilling of blood; carnage

blood'shot' adj (eyes) red with suffused blood

blood'stream' n the blood circulating in the body

blood'suck'er n 1 animal that sucks blood, as a leech; 2 extortioner

blood'thirst'y adj murderous, eager to kill

blood' type' n one of four classes into which human blood is divided on the basis of its agglutinative characteristics

blood' ves'sel n artery, vein, or capillary

blood'y adj (-i·er; -i·est) 1 pert. to or like blood; 2 stained or running with blood; 3 attended by bloodshed; 4 murderous; cruel; 5 Brit vulgar confounded ‖ adv 6 Brit vulgar exceedingly ‖ v (-ied) vt 7 to stain with blood ‖ **blood'i·ly** adv ‖ **blood'i·ness** n

Blood'y Mar'y n alcoholic drink made with vodka and tomato juice

bloom /blōōm'/ [ON blōm] n 1 flower; 2 state of being in flower; 3 prime; freshness; 4 rosy youthful color; 5 waxy or powdery coating on certain fruits ‖ vi 6 to flower; 7 to glow with youth and freshness; 8 to flourish

bloom'ers [Amelia Bloomer (d. 1894) Am. feminist] npl 1 loose wide trousers gathered near the knee, worn by women in sports; 2 similar undergarment

bloom'ing adj 1 flowering; 2 flourishing; 3 Brit colloq darned

bloop /blōōp'/ [imit] n noise made by a splice in a film

bloop'er [< bloop] n 1 colloq blunder made in public; 2 baseball fly ball that goes just beyond the infield

blos·som /blos'əm/ [OE blōstm] n 1 flower of a plant; 2 **in blossom** flowering ‖ vi 3 to put forth flowers; 4 to flourish

blot /blot'/ [ME] n 1 spot or stain esp. of ink; 2 blemish, disgrace ‖ v (blot·ted; blot·ting) vt 3 to spot or stain; 4 to dry (ink) with a blotter; 5 **blot out, a** to obliterate or blur; **b** to destroy utterly; **c** to darken, obscure ‖ vi 6 to make a blot; 7 to become blotted ‖ SYN v expunge, efface, blur, sully, dishonor

blotch /bloch'/ [perh < blot + botch] n 1 large irregular stain; 2 coarse skin eruption ‖ vt 3 to mark with blotches ‖ **blotch'y** adj

blot'ter n 1 piece of blotting paper; 2 police record book

blot'ting pa'per n absorbent paper for drying wet ink

blouse /blous'/ [F] n 1 woman's or child's loose-fitting shirtwaist; 2 any similar garment, as that worn by sailors; 3 jacket of soldier's uniform

blo·vi·ate /blō′vē·āt′/ [blow?] *vi colloq* to talk with great windiness

blow[1] /blō/ [OE *blāwan*] *v* (**blew; blown**) *vt* 1 to move or impel by a current of air; 2 to sound; 3 to clear by forcing air through; 4 to shape with air currents, as glass or smoke rings; 5 to burst (a tire); 6 to burn out (a fuse); 7 *slang* to treat, as to a drink; 8 *slang* to squander; 9 *slang* to leave (a place) hurriedly; 10 *slang* to botch; 11 **blow out** to extinguish by blowing; 12 **blow up,** a to cause to explode; b to inflate; c *photog* to enlarge || *vi* 13 to move, as a current of air; 14 to eject air, steam, water, etc.; 15 to sound; 16 to pant; 17 to storm; 18 *colloq* to brag; 19 *colloq* to leave; 20 to burst or burn out, as a fuse, bulb, tire, etc.; 21 **blow hot and cold** to vacillate; 22 **blow off** to release pent-up emotion; 23 **blow out** to be extinguished by a current of air; 24 **blow over,** a to subside; b to be forgotten; 25 **blow up,** a to explode; b to lose one's temper || *n* 26 act of blowing; 27 strong wind

blow[2] [ME *blaw*] *n* 1 sudden hard stroke with the hand or a weapon; 2 calamity, misfortune || SYN buffet, cuff, stroke, impact, shock, knock, concussion, lash || DISCR A *blow* is a sudden violent striking, as by the clenched fist or a heavy object; a *stroke* is a long-drawn *blow*, given repeatedly, as the *strokes* of a whip; or it is a sweeping, recurrent motion given with force and precision, as the *stroke* of a swimmer, a piston, an oar. Figuratively, *blow* names a sudden calamity or unwelcome surprise. *Stroke* is applied to a sudden, prostrating attack; also, to any strikingly successful effort, as a *stroke* of luck (see *trouble*)

blow′er *n* device for producing a current of air

blow′fly′ *n* (-**flies**) *n* any of several flies (family Calliphoridae) which lay eggs in carrion and in wounds

blow′hole′ *n* 1 nostril of a whale; 2 air hole, as in the ice or in a tunnel

blown /blōn/ *pp* of **blow**

blow′out′ *n* 1 bursting of an automobile tire; 2 melting of an electric fuse; 3 flame-out; 4 uncontrollable eruption of an oil well; 5 *slang* lavish party

blow′torch′ *n* portable apparatus with an extremely hot gasoline flame directed and intensified by a blast of air

blow′up′ *n* 1 outburst of temper; 2 *photog* enlargement

blowz·y /blou′zē/ [< obs *blowze* wench] *adj* (-i·er; -i·est) 1 frowzy, slovenly; 2 of coarse, ruddy complexion

blub·ber /blub′ər/ [ME *bluber* bubble] *vi* 1 to weep noisily || *vt* 2 to utter sobbingly || *n* 3 act of blubbering; 4 whale fat || *adj* 5 swollen or protruding, as lips

blu·cher /blōōch′er, blōōk′-/ [Gebhart von *Blücher* (1742-1819) Prussian field marshal] *n* shoe in which the tongue and toe are made of one piece of leather, with the upper lapping over the tongue

bludg·eon /bluj′ən/ [?] *n* 1 short heavy-headed club || *vt* 2 to strike with a bludgeon; 3 to coerce

blue /blōō/ [OF *blou* < Gmc] *adj* 1 of the color of the clear sky; 2 lowspirited; 3 dismal; 4 puritanical, as *the blue laws;* 5 livid (skin); 6 *show bus.* risqué; 7 **blue in the face** worn out from vain effort || *n* 8 color of the clear sky; 9 blue pigment; 10 anything colored blue; 11 **out of the blue** unexpectedly; 12 **the blues** *pl* a melancholy, depression; b type of song of American Negro origin, with slow jazz rhythm and sad words || *v* (**blued; blu·ing** or **blue·ing**) *vt* 13 to make or dye blue; 14 to treat with bluing

blue′ ba′by *n* infant born with cyanosis caused by a congenital heart or lung defect

Blue′beard′ *n* 1 tyrannous husband of folklore, who murdered his first six wives; 2 wife killer

blue′bell′ *n* any of various plants bearing bell-shaped blue flowers

blue′ber′ry *n* (-ries) 1 any of several plants (genus *Vaccinium*) of the heath family, bearing round blue berries; 2 its fruit

blue′bird′ *n* any of several small North American songbirds (genus *Sialia*) with blue backs

blue′ blood′ *n* 1 aristocrat; 2 aristocratic descent

blue′bon′net *n* 1 cornflower (*Centaurea cyanus*); 2 blue-flowered lupine (*Lupinus subcarnosus*)

blue′ book′ *n* 1 social register; 2 blank notebook used in college examinations; 3 government report

blue′bot′tle *n* 1 cornflower (*Centaurea cyanus*); 2 blowfly with steel-blue body (*Calliphora erythrocephala*)

blue′ chip′ *n* 1 blue poker chip of high value; 2 high-priced common stock of great stability and safe dividend || **blue′-chip′** *adj*

blue′coat′ *n colloq* 1 policeman; 2 U.S. soldier before the twentieth century

blue′-col′lar *adj* of or pert. to wage earners who wear work clothes

blue′fish′ *n* (-fish or -fishes) widespread, highly prized food fish (*Pomatomus saltatrix*) of the western Atlantic

blue′grass′ *n* any grass of the genus *Poa* having bluish-green stems, as the Kentucky bluegrass

blue′jack′et *n colloq* sailor

blue′jay′ n noisy crested blue-backed bird (*Cyanocitta cristata*) of E North America

blue′ laws′ npl puritanical laws aimed esp. at preserving the sanctity of the Sabbath

Blue′ Nile′ n tributary of the Nile rising in Ethiopia and joining the Nile at Khartoum

blue′nose′ n puritanical person

blue′-pen′cil v (-ciled or -cilled; -ciling or -cil·ling) vt to edit, correct, or emend with or as with a blue pencil

blue′point′ n delicious small oyster, generally eaten raw, from a bed near Blue Point, Long Island

blue′print′ n 1 reproduction in white on blue paper usu. of architectural or mechanical drawings; 2 detailed plans || vt 3 to make a blueprint of

blue′ rib′bon n highest award in a contest; prized honor || **blue′-rib′bon** adj

blue′stock′ing n female highbrow

bluff¹ /bluf′/ [perh MD *blaf* smooth] adj 1 rising steeply or boldly; 2 rough and hearty || n 3 high, steep bank or cliff; 4 *Canadian* stand of trees || SYN adj curt, brusque, unceremonious, rude, gruff || ANT adj gentle, considerate, civil, polite, gracious

bluff² [D *bluffen* to bluster] vt & vi 1 to mislead by pretending to have more money, power, or high cards than one actually has || n 2 act or instance of bluffing; 3 **call one′s bluff** to challenge a person to make good his pretensions

blu·ing or **blue·ing** /bloo′ing/ n bluish preparation used in laundering to bring out the whiteness in fabrics

blu′ish or **blue′ish** adj somewhat blue

blun′der /blun′dər/ [ME *blondren*] n 1 stupid mistake || vi 2 to err stupidly; 3 to move or act clumsily || SYN n error, mistake, oversight, fault, omission || DISCR *Error*, the general term, is any departure from right or truth; we may commit *errors* of judgment, or make an *error* in a computation. *Mistake* and *blunder* are kinds of error. A *mistake* is an *error* of carelessness, inattention, or omission; it is not apt to be a grave matter, unless qualified by some such word as serious or grievous. A *blunder* is an *error* caused by stupidity, ignorance, conceit, or failure to understand. *Blunders* may be so serious as to bring punishment; sometimes they are ridiculous, and not infrequently pathetic

blun′der·buss′ /-bus′/ [< D *donderbus* thunder gun] n 1 short gun with a large bore and a flaring muzzle; 2 stupid, clumsy person

blunt /blunt′/ [ME] adj 1 having a thick or rounded edge or point; 2 dull, not discerning; 3 plain-spoken, abrupt || vt 4 to dull the edge or point of || **blunt′ly** adv || **blunt′ness** n || SYN adj thick, pointless, dull, stupid, obtuse || DISCR *Blunt*, as compared with *dull*, *stupid*, and *obtuse*, means slow of wit, insensitive to that which is presented to the understanding. Sometimes this condition is temporary, as a mind *blunt* from pain. *Dull* minds are sluggish, slow, heavy, lacking in that sort of wit that flashes or is intensely vivid. *Stupid* people are so closed to perception that they seem numb, lethargic. They are actually unable to grasp an idea, and are surpassed in this respect only by the *obtuse*. *Blunt* as the opposite of *keen* or *sharp* compares in this sense also with *dull*. *Dull* commonly describes an edge or tool no longer sharp; *blunt* describes a tool which, even when sharp, does not have a thin, tapering edge

blur /blur′/ [?] v (**blurred; blur·ring**) vt 1 to dim, make indistinct in outline; 2 to stain, smear || vi 3 to become indistinct in outline; 4 to be smeared or stained || n 5 smudge, smear; 6 indistinct appearance || **blur′ry** adj || SYN n spot, stain, obscuration, disfigurement

blurb /blurb′/ [coined by Gelett Burgess (1866–1951) Am writer] n short laudatory announcement or advertisement of a book

blurt /blurt′/ [imit] vt **blurt out** to say or divulge suddenly and thoughtlessly

blush /blush′/ [OE *blyscan*] vi 1 to redden, as from embarrassment or shame; 2 to feel shame || n 3 reddening, as of the face; 4 rosy tint; 5 **at first blush** at first glance

blus·ter /blust′ər/ [ME *blustren*] vi 1 to blow gustily, as the wind; 2 to talk in a noisy, threatening manner || vt 3 to utter or accomplish by blustering || n 4 blustering noise || **blus′ter·er** n || **blus′ter·y** adj || SYN n swaggering, commotion, bullying

blvd. boulevard

B.O. 1 box office; 2 *colloq* body odor

bo·a /bō′ə/ [L = water snake] n 1 any of various large nonpoisonous snakes (family Boidae) which kill by crushing; 2 long fur or feather neckpiece

bo′a con·stric′tor n large tropical American boa (*Constrictor constrictor*)

boar /bōr′, bôr′/ [OE *bār*] n 1 uncastrated male hog; 2 wild hog (*Sus scrofa*) of the Old World

board /bôrd′, bōrd′/ [OE *bord*] n 1 long flat piece of wood; 2 meals served for pay at stated times; 3 group of directors, officers, etc., organized to act as a body; 4 pasteboard; 5 flat piece of wood or pasteboard for some specific purpose, as a chessboard; 6 **boards** pl theater stage; **7 across the board, a** applying to everything and everybody proportionately; **b** (racing bet) placed to finish first, second, or third; **c** (radio or television program) scheduled at the same time on a sequence of days every week; **8 go by the board** to come to naught; **9 on board** aboard a vehicle or vessel || *vt* **10** to cover with boards; **11** to furnish with meals regularly for pay; **12** to put oneself on (a vehicle or vessel) || *vi* **13** to be regularly supplied with meals at a fixed charge

board/er *n* **1** one, esp. a lodger, who receives board; **2** one detailed to board an enemy ship

board/ foot/ *n* volume equal to that of a timber one foot by one foot by one inch

board/ing house/ *n* house where persons are regularly boarded

board/ing ramp/ *n* staircase that moves to the cabin door of an airplane for getting on and off

board/walk/ *n* promenade made of planks, as along a beach

boast /bōst/ [ME *bosten*] *vi* **1** to brag || *vt* **2** to brag of, glory in || *n* **3** proud speech; **4** cause or occasion of pride || **boast/er** *n* || **boast/ful** *adj* || SYN *v* swagger, crow, vaunt, brag

boat /bōt/ [OE *bāt*] *n* **1** small open watercraft; **3** serving dish resembling a boat; **4 in the same boat** in the same somewhat precarious situation

boat/er *n* **1** one who rows a boat; **2** stiff straw hat with a flat crown and straight brim

boat/ing *n* sailing or rowing

boat-swain /bōs′ən/ [OE *bātswegen* boat's lad] *n* ship's officer in charge of the rigging, anchors, and cables

boat/swain's chair/ *n* seat suspended from ropes, used for high exterior work

bob[1] /bob/ [ME *boben*] *v* (**bobbed; bob-bing**) *vt* **1** to give a short jerky motion to; **2** to cut short, as the hair || *vi* **3** to move up and down jerkily || *n* **4** jerking movement; **5** nod of the head; **6** *fishing* float; **7** weight, as on a pendulum or plumb line; **8** short haircut for women

bob[2] [?] *n* (*pl* **bob**) *Brit slang* shilling

bob-bin /bob′in/ [F *bobine*] *n* spool or reel for yarn or thread

bob-by /bob′ē/ [Sir *Robert* Peel (1788–1850) organizer of the London police] *n* (**-bies**) *Brit slang* policeman

bob/by pin/ [< use with bobbed hair] *n* flat pincerlike hairpin

bob/by-socks/ *npl* girls' ankle-length socks

bob/cat/ *n* American bay lynx (*Lynx rufus*)

bob-o-link /bob′əliŋk′/ [imit] *n* migratory American songbird (*Dolichonyx oryzivorus*) allied to the orioles

bob/sled/ *n* long, jointed racing sled

bob/tail/ *n* **1** short or docked tail; **2** animal with such a tail || **bob/-tailed/** *adj*

bob/white/ [imit] *n* common North American quail (*Colinus virginianus*)

Boc-cac-cio, Gio-van-ni /jōvän′ē bōkäch′ō, -chē-ō/ *n* (1313–75) Italian writer, author of *The Decameron*

bock/ (beer/) /bok′/ [G] *n* strong dark beer served in the spring

bode[1] /bōd/ *pt* of **bide**

bode[2] [OE *bodian*] *vt* to portend, presage

bod-ice /bod′is/ [< *bodies*] *n* **1** close-fitting waist or body of a woman's dress; **2** wide girdle, laced and tight-fitting from breast to waist

bod-i-ly /bod′ilē/ *adj* **1** material; **2** pert. to, in, or for the body || *adv* **3** in person; **4** entirely, completely || SYN *adj* corporeal, material (see *corporal*[1])

bod-kin /bod′kin/ [ME *badeken*] *n* **1** pointed instrument for piercing holes in cloth, leather, etc.; **2** blunt needle for drawing tape or ribbon through a hem or loop; **3** long pin to fasten up the hair

Bod-lei-an /bodlē′ən, bod′lē-/ [Sir Thomas *Bodley* (1545–1613) founder] *adj* pert. to the library of the University of Oxford, England || also *n*

bod-y /bod′ē/ [OE *bodig*] *n* (**-ies**) **1** form and substance of man or animal; **2** trunk of a man or animal; **3** main part of anything; **4** main passenger- or load-carrying structure of an automobile, airplane, or ship; **5** *colloq* person; **6** aggregate of persons or things, as *a legislative body, a body of facts;* **7** a distinct mass of matter, as *a heavenly body, a body of water;* **8** consistency, substance, as of wine; **9** *geom* solid || SYN corpse, carcass, remains || DISCR *Body* refers to the whole physical organism of a man or an animal, living or dead. Corpse is used only to refer to dead *bodies,* and is often avoided in favor of the word *remains. Carcass* refers to the *body* of an animal, usually to the body of a dead animal, though it is sometimes employed to refer to the bodies of very large living animals

bod/y-guard/ *n* **1** person or persons employed to protect someone; **2** retinue; escort

bod/y pol-i-tic *n* the people of a nation, state, or community regarded as a political unit

Boer /bōō′ər, bō′ər/ [D = farmer] *n* Afrikaans-speaking white South African || also *adj*

bog /bog′, bôg′/ [Gael = soft] *n* **1** tract of wet spongy ground; marsh || *v*

(bogged; bog·ging) *vt & vi* **2 bog down** to sink as in a bog ‖ **bog'gy** *adj* (**-gi·er; -gi·est**)

bo·gey¹ /bōg'ē/ [Colonel *Bogey* imaginary golfer] *n golf* one stroke over par on a hole

bo·gey² *n* var of **bogy**

bog·gle /bog'əl/ [?] *vt* **1** to startle, dumfound ‖ *vi* **2** to be startled, be dumfounded

Bo·go·tá /bōg'ətä'/ *n* capital of Colombia (1,697,311)

bo·gus /bōg'əs/ [?] *adj* counterfeit; not genuine

bo·gy /bōg'ē, bōōg'ē/ [< Sc *bogle*] *n* (**-gies**) hobgoblin, bugbear

Bo·he·mi·a /bōhēm'ē·ə/ *n* **1** province in W Czechoslovakia; **2** district or milieu of unconventional artists and writers ‖ **Bo·he'mi·an** *adj & n*

boil¹ /boil'/ [OF *boillir*] *vi* **1** to bubble and change to vapor through the action of heat; **2** to be cooked in boiling water; **3** to seethe with agitation like that of boiling; **4** to be excited by anger; **5 boil down** to to come down to, result in ‖ *vt* **6** to heat to the boiling point; **7** to cook by boiling ‖ *n* **8** act or state of boiling

boil² [OE *bȳl*] *n* inflamed festering sore on the skin enclosing a central core

boiled' shirt' *n slang* **1** man's formal dress shirt; **2** pompous fellow

boil'er /< *boil¹*/ *n* **1** strong metal vessel in which steam is produced for heating or for driving engines; **2** tank for storing hot water

boil'er·mak'er *n* **1** man who makes or repairs boilers; **2** *slang* whiskey with a beer chaser

boil'ing point' *n* **1** temperature at which a liquid boils or vaporizes; of water, 212°F, 100°C; **2** *colloq* point at which a person loses his temper

Boi·se /boiz'ē/ *n* capital of Idaho (35,000)

bois·ter·ous /boist'ərəs/ [ME *boistous* rough] *adj* violent; turbulent; noisy ‖ **bois'ter·ous·ly** *adv*

bold /bōld'/ [OE b(e)ald] *adj* **1** fearless; **2** daring; **3** steep, abrupt; **4** prominent, in high relief; **5** presuming, impudent; **6 make bold to** to venture to ‖ **bold'ly** *adv* ‖ **bold'ness** *n* ‖ SYN audacious, spirited, daring, confident, brazen ‖ ANT retiring, timid, faint-hearted, bashful, shy

bold'face' *n typ* heavy and conspicuous type, used for headings and for emphasis ‖ also *adj*

bold'faced' *adj* **1** brazen; **2** (type) that is heavy and conspicuous

bo·le·ro /bələr'ō/ [Sp] *n* **1** lively Spanish dance in three-four measure or the music for it; **2** woman's short open jacket

Bol·eyn, Anne /bōōl'in, bōlin'/ *n* (1507–36) second wife of Henry VIII

and mother of Queen Elizabeth I; beheaded

bol·i·var /bol'əvər/ *n* monetary unit of Venezuela

Bo·lí·var, Simón /sēmōn', bōlē'vär/ *n* (1783–1830) Venezuelan statesman, a leader in the South American revolt against Spain

Bo·liv·i·a /bəliv'ē·ə/ *n* Spanish-speaking inland republic in W central South America (3,801,000; 424,165 sq.m.; caps. La Paz and Sucre) ‖ **Bo·liv'i·an** *adj & n*

boll /bōl'/ [OE *bolla* bowl] *n* rounded seed pod of a plant, as of cotton or flax

boll' wee'vil /wēv'əl/ *n* beetle whose larvae infest cotton bolls

bo·lo·gna /bəlōn'yə, -lōn'ē/ [*Bologna*, Italy] *n* large seasoned sausage

Bol·she·vik /bōl'shəvik, bōl'-/ [Russ] *n* **1** member of the radical wing of the Russian Social Democrats, which ushered in the Revolution of 1917; **2** Communist ‖ also *adj* ‖ **Bol'she·vism** *n*

bol·ster /bōls'tər/ [OE] *n* **1** long cylindrical cushion or pillow; **2** any bolsterlike support ‖ *vt* **3** to support with or as with a bolster; **4** to abet, uphold

bolt /bōlt/ [OE] *n* **1** short thick arrow, shot from a crossbow; **2** flash of lightning; **3** metal pin or rod, threaded to take a nut, for fastening parts together; **4** sliding catch for a door; **5** that part of a lock which is drawn back by the key; **6** roll of cloth; **7** sudden dashing away; **8** desertion of a political party; **9 shoot one's bolt** to do one's best and be able to do no more ‖ *vt* **10** to blurt out unexpectedly; **11** to fasten (a door) with a bolt; **12** to fasten with bolts and nuts; **13** to swallow (food) without chewing; **14** to break away from (one's political party) ‖ *vi* **15** to dart away suddenly; **16** to break away from a political party ‖ *adv* **17 bolt upright** erect, straight up

bolt'-ac'tion *adj* (rifle) that seats the cartridge in the firing chamber by means of a manually operated sliding bolt

bomb /bom'/ [F *bombe*] *n* **1** device containing explosives, gas, smoke, napalm, etc., designed to be fired, thrown, dropped from a plane, or left in a locality to be activated by a timing device; **2** *theat* fiasco ‖ *vt* **3** to attack with bombs ‖ *vi* **4** to attack with bombs; **5** *theat* to flop, fail

bom·bard /bombärd'/ [MF *bombarde* cannon] *vt* **1** to attack with artillery or bombs; **2** to assail strongly, as with missiles or questions ‖ **bombard'ment** *n*

bom'bar·dier' /-bərdir'/ *n* airman who drops bombs from a bomber

bom'bast /-bast/ [MF *bombace*] *n*

pompous, inflated speech ‖ **bom·bas'-tic** *adj* ‖ **bom·bas'ti·cal·ly** *adv*

Bom·bay /bombā'/ *n* seaport in W India (4,250,000)

bomb' bay' *n* compartment in a bomber which contains the bombs

bomb·er /bom'ər/ *n* airplane used for bombing

bomb'shell' *n* **1** explosive missile or bomb; **2** someone or something that has an explosive effect

bomb'sight' *n* device for aiming bombs from an aircraft

bo·na fi·de /bōn'əfīd'ē/ [L = in good faith] *adj* without fraud, genuine

bo·nan·za /bənan'zə/ [Sp = fair weather, prosperity] *n* **1** rich vein of ore; **2** anything that yields unexpected wealth

Bo·na·parte /bōn'əpärt'/ *n* Corsican family, including Napoleon I and Napoleon III

bon·bon /bon'bon'/ [F = good-good] *n* piece of candy

bond /bond/ [ME var of *band*] *n* **1** that which fastens, ties, unites, or confines; **2** obligation or duty; **3** binding agreement; **4** bail; **5** obligation in writing; **6** obligation issued by a corporation or government to pay a principal sum on a certain date, with interest; **7** status of goods stored in a bonded warehouse until duties or taxes are paid; **8** surety against theft, embezzlement, etc.; **9** **bonds** *pl* fetters ‖ *vt* **10** to bind, join; **11** to place (employees, officials, goods) under bond ‖ *vi* **12** to stick, cohere

bond'age *n* serfdom, slavery ‖ SYN captivity, imprisonment, slavery, servitude

bond'ed ware'house' warehouse in which goods are stored under bond

bond'ed whis'key *s* 100-proof straight whiskey that has been aged in a bonded warehouse for at least four years before being bottled

bond' pa'per *n* high-quality watermarked paper for stationery

bonds'man /-mən/ *n* (-men /-mən/) **1** slave or serf; **2** one who becomes surety for another's debt, appearance for trial, etc.

bone /bōn/ [OE bān] *n* **1** one of the pieces forming the skeleton of a vertebrate; **2** any bonelike material or object; **3** subject of dispute or contention; **4** **bones** *pl* **a** the body; **b** mortal remains; **c** *slang* dice; **5** **make no bones about** to admit openly ‖ *vt* **6** to remove the bones from ‖ *vi* **7** **bone up** *slang* to study intensively ‖ **bone'less** *adj*

bone' ash' *n* powdery residue of burned bones, used as a fertilizer and in making ceramics

bone' chi'na *n* fine china made with bone ash

bone'-dry' *adj* **1** very dry; **2** opposed to or lacking intoxicating liquors

bone'head' *n* *slang* stupid person

bone' meal' *n* crushed bone used as a fertilizer and as feed

bon'er *n* *colloq* ludicrous blunder

bon·fire /bon'fī'ər/ [< *bone fire*] *n* large open-air fire

bon·ho·mie /bon'əmē/ [F] *n* genial good nature

bon mot /bon'mō'/ [F = good word] *n* (**bons mots** /bon'mōz'/) witty saying

Bonn /bon/ *n* capital of West Germany (140,789)

bon·net /bon'it/ [MF bonet] *n* **1** brimless hat tied under the chin; **2** *Brit* automobile hood

bon·ny also **bon·nie** /bon'ē/ [< OF bon good] *adj* (**-ni·er; -ni·est**) **1** comely, pretty; **2** cheerful, gay

bo·nus /bōn'əs/ [L = good] *n* anything given over and above the usual amount

bon vo·yage /bon'voiyäzh'/ [F = good voyage] *interj* have a good trip!

bon·y /bōn'ē/ *adj* (**-i·er; -i·est**) **1** of, like, or full of bones; **2** having conspicuous bones; **3** thin

bonze /bonz/ [< Jap *bonso*] *n* Buddhist monk, esp. of China or Japan

bon·zer /bon'zər/ [perh alter. of *bonanza*] *adj* *Australian* first-rate; wonderful

boo /bōō/ [ME *bo*] *interj* **1** made to express strong disapproval; **2** made to frighten ‖ *n* **3** instance of shouting "boo" ‖ *vi* **4** to shout "boo" ‖ *vt* **5** to shout "boo" at

boob /bōōb/ [prob < Sp *bobo*] *n* dunce, dull-witted fellow

boo'by *n* (**-bies**) boob

boo'by prize' *n* prize given to the worst scorer in a contest

boo'by trap' *n* disguised bomb or trap for the unsuspecting

boo·dle /bōōd'əl/ [D *boedel* goods] *n* *slang* **1** bribe money, graft; **2** loot, swag

boo·gey·man /bōōg'ēman'/ *n* (-men /-men'/) bogy

boo·gie-woo·gie /bōōg'ēwōōg'ē/ [?] *n* instrumental blues music with a repeated rhythmic bass

book /bōōk/ [OE bōc] *n* **1** collection of sheets of paper containing printed matter and bound together; **2** main division of a literary work; **3** volume of records or accounts; **4** libretto; **5** booklike packet containing a set of similar things, as tickets or matches; **6** **the Book** the Bible; **7** **books** *pl* business records; **8** **bring to book** to call to account; **9** **by the book** according to the rules; **10** **know like a book** to know intimately; **11** **make book** to accept bets; **12** **throw the book at** *colloq* to sentence (an offender) to the maximum penalty ‖ *vt* **13** to enter in a book or list; **14** to engage beforehand, as accommodations or performers; **15** to enter a charge against (an arrested person) in a police station

book'case' n set of shelves for books

book' end' n support for keeping a row of books upright

book'ie n colloq bookmaker

book'ish adj 1 fond of reading and studying; 2 pedantic

book'keep'er n one who keeps business records || **book'keep'ing** n

book' learn'ing n knowledge gained from books rather than from observation and experience

book'let n small book

book'mak'er n professional taker of bets

book'mark' n something placed between the leaves of a book to mark the place

book'plate' n label with the owner's name pasted on the inside of the front cover of a book

book' val'ue n value of anything as it appears on the account books of the owner, regardless of its market value

book'worm' n 1 any of various insects that feed on books; 2 very studious person

boom¹ /boom/ [D = beam] n 1 barrier extended across a river or harbor to stop traffic or to confine logs; 2 long pole or spar attached to a vertical mast, as on a ship or derrick; 3 **lower the boom on** slang to punish or discipline

boom² [imit] n 1 deep hollow sound, as of cannon; 2 period of great prosperity; 3 great increase in a candidate's popularity || vi 4 to make a booming sound; 5 to grow with a rush; 6 to be prosperous || vt 7 to give forth with a booming sound; 8 to cause to grow rapidly; 9 to push vigorously, as a candidate

boom'er·ang /-əraŋ/ [native Australian name] n 1 piece of flat curved wood which, when thrown, returns to the thrower; 2 action or plot which recoils upon the originator to his disadvantage || vi 3 to go awry, as a scheme, to the disadvantage of the perpetrator

boom' town' n town that is having a business boom

boon¹ /boon/ [ON bōn prayer] n benefit, blessing || SYN benefaction, bounty, bribe, bequest, gift, present, gratuity, grant, donation, largess, tip || DISCR A boon is an advantage or privilege craved; it may represent no more than is really the petitioner's due, but, being requested from one much higher in rank, bears the complexion of a favor; or it may be really a favor, as was the king's permission to Gareth to serve in the royal kitchen for a year ("Gareth and Lynette," in "Idylls of the King"). Gift denotes anything given without expectation of return; it can refer to the condescending bestowal of something by the rich on the poor, but it can also be used of a friendly token, as a birthday gift. Presents are exchanged between equals; sometimes, also, we give presents to superiors with a mollifying or conciliating intent. A gratuity is a present of money to reward an inferior for services; given to a public servant, as a waiter, or to one employed by some one other than the giver, a gratuity is called a tip. Largess is a term denoting bounteous bestowal, as by a person of rank upon many of his attendants. A donation is something given for public support, as of an institution. A grant is something, as lands, given by public concession

boon² [MF bon good] adj merry, convivial, as a boon companion

boon'docks' /-doks'/ [< Tagalog bundok mountain] npl slang backwoods; hinterland

boon'dog'gle /-dog'əl/ [coined word] n trivial work indulged in to make the doer look busy || also vi || **boon'dog'-gler** n

Boone, Dan·iel /boon'/ n (1734–1820) Am explorer who settled Kentucky

boor /boor'/ [LG būr farmer] n rude, ill-mannered person

boor'ish adj like a boor, having bad manners; ungainly; ignorant || **boor'-ish·ly** adv || SYN churlish, clownish, rude, ill-bred, rustic

boost /boost'/ [?] vt 1 to lift by pushing from behind or beneath; 2 to advance or promote; 3 to raise, increase || n 4 lift; 5 increase; 6 encouragement; praise

boost'er n 1 device for increasing the current in a circuit; 2 radio-frequency amplifier placed between the antenna and the receiving set; 3 a rocket that launches an aerospace vehicle; b auxiliary rocket; 4 also **booster shot** second injection of a vaccine to preserve immunity; 5 enthusiastic supporter

boost'er ca'ble n heavy electric cable used to connect an automobile battery to an outside power source for charging

boot¹ /boot'/ [MF bote] n 1 footwear that extends above the ankle; 2 Brit shoe; 3 kick; 4 navy or marine recruit; 5 **the boot** dismissal; 6 **lick the boots of** to fawn on || vt 7 to kick; 8 to dismiss; 9 to fumble

boot² [OE bōt advantage] n **to boot** in addition

boot'black' n one whose occupation is to polish shoes

boot'ee or **boot'ie** n baby's knitted boot

Bo·ö·tes /bō-ō'tēz/ n (gen **-tis** /-tis/) northern constellation, the Herdsman

booth /booth'/ [ME bothe hut] n (-ths /-thz, -ths/) 1 stall or stand for displaying or selling goods; 2 small structure for housing a public telephone; **3** enclosed compartment or structure for the use of one person, as for voting

boot'leg' [< hiding liquor in the leg of a boot] *adj* **1** made, sold, or transported illegally, as liquor or cigarets on which no tax has been paid ‖ *v* (**-legged; -leg·ging**) *vt & vi* **2** to sell or transport illegally ‖ **boot'leg'ger** *n*

boot'less [< boot²] *adj* without avail; useless ‖ **boot'less·ly** *adv*

boot'lick' *vt & vi* to flatter servilely ‖ **boot'lick'er** *n*

boo·ty /bo̅o̅'tē/ [MF *butin*] *n* (**-ties**) **1** supplies taken from an enemy; plunder; **2** any rich spoil ‖ syn plunder, pillage, loot, spoil

booze /boo̅z/ [ME *bousen*] *colloq vi* **1** to drink to excess ‖ *n* **2** liquor

bo·rax /bôr'aks, bōr'-/ [LL < Ar *būraq* < Pers] *n* white crystalline powder —Na₂B₄O₇·10H₂O— used as a flux and as an antiseptic and cleansing agent

Bor·deaux /bôrdō'/ *n* **1** seaport in SW France (260,000), noted for the export of wines; **2** any of the red or white wines produced in the region of Bordeaux

bor·del·lo /bôrdel'ō/ [It] *n* brothel

bor·der /bôrd'ər/ [MF *bordure*] *n* **1** edge, margin, rim; **2** boundary; **3** edging defining anything; **4** the **border, a** boundary between the U.S. and Mexico; **b** boundary between England and Scotland ‖ *vt* **5** to make a border about; **6** to lie next to ‖ *vi* **7** border on, **a** to be next to; **b** to verge on ‖ syn **n** boundary, confine, margin, verge, edge, rim, brink, brim, coast, shore, beach, strand, bank ‖ discr A *border* is that portion of a surface confined by a boundary line, or, more commonly, the limiting line itself, or the part of the surface adjacent to it. A *margin* is a definite *border*, as the blank space surrounding the printed part of a page, or a rather wide, level strip bordering a stream. A *verge* is an extreme *border;* figuratively, *verge* denotes the last possible limit of a condition, as on the *verge* of death. A *coast* is the bordering sea line of a country or continent; *shore* is the name for land bordering any body of water; *beach* denotes a level expanse, often of sand, on the *shore* of ocean, lake, or river bend. An *edge* is more definite than a *border;* it is a line, whether that terminating line ending a narrow surface, as of a knife blade, or the line where land and water meet. *Rim, brim,* and *brink* name kinds of *edge*. A *rim* is the *edge* of any vessel or opening, but commonly of a curved one; a *brim* is the outer, upper *edge* of a hollow vessel, as a bowl or cup; a *brink* is

the *edge* of a steep or deep place, as of a precipice or pool; figuratively, *brink* denotes the last step before something regarded as a fall, as the *brink* of disaster. *Bank* is the usual term for the *edge* of a watercourse

bor·der·land' *n* **1** land along a frontier; **2** indeterminate region, state, or conception

bor·der line' *n* **1** dividing line; **2** vague line between two qualities or conditions

bor·der·line' *adj* not clearly defined; typical but not definite

Bor'der States' *n* slave states which remained loyal to the Union in 1861: Delaware, Maryland, Kentucky, and Missouri; and also West Virginia, which seceded from Virginia in 1863

bore¹ /bôr', bōr'/ [OE *borian*] *vt* **1** to drill a hole in; **2** to form (a hole, tunnel, etc.) by, or as by, drilling ‖ *vi* **3** to make a hole, pierce ‖ *n* **4** hole made by boring; **5** hollow of a gun, pipe, or tube; **6** inside diameter of a drilled hole; caliber ‖ **bor'er** *n*

bore² [?] *vt* **1** to weary by dullness ‖ *n* **2** dull or tiresome person or thing ‖ **bore'dom** *n*

bore³ *pt* of **bear²**

bo'ric ac'ld /bôr'ik, bōr'-/ [< *borax*] *n* a white crystalline compound —H₃BO₃— used in manufacturing and as an antiseptic

born /bôrn'/ *adj* **1** brought forth by birth; **2** by nature, as *a born actor*

borne /bôrn', bōrn'/ *pp* of **bear²**

Bor·ne·o /bôr'nē·ō'/ *n* large island in the East Indies divided between Indonesia and the Federation of Malaysia

bo·ron /bôr'on, bōr'-/ [*borax* + carbon] *n* nonmetallic element (**B;** at.no. 5; at.wt. 10.811) occurring in nature only in combination and used in nucleonics and metallurgy

bor·ough /bur'ō/ [OE *burg* fortified town] *n* **1** incorporated municipality; **2** one of the five administrative districts of New York City; **3** one of the administrative districts which, with the cities of London and Westminster, comprise London

bor·row /bor'ō, bôr'-/ [OE *borgian*] *vt* **1** to obtain (something) with the promise of returning it; **2** to copy; adopt; appropriate ‖ *vi* **3** to borrow something ‖ **bor'row·er** *n*

bor'row·ing *n* **1** act of borrowing; **2** word taken from a foreign language

borsch /bôrsh'/ or **borscht** /bôrsht'/ [Russ *borshch*] *n* beet soup, usu. served with sour cream

bor·zoi /bôr'zoi/ [Russ = swift] *n* Russian wolfhound

bosh /bosh'/ [Turk = empty] *colloq n* nonsense, empty talk ‖ *interj* nonsense!

bos·om /booz'əm/ [OE *bōsm*] *n* **1** human breast; **2** the part of a garment which covers the breast; **3** midst, as *in the bosom of his family;* **4** breast as the seat of the emotions ‖ *adj* **5** intimate, as *a bosom friend*

Bos·po·rus /bos'pərəs/ *n* strait between the Black Sea and the Sea of Marmara, separating European from Asian Turkey

boss¹ /bôs, bos/ [OF *boce* swelling] *n* knob, stud, protruding ornament

boss² [D *baas*] *n* **1** superintendent, foreman; employer; **2** political chieftain; **3** *colloq* one in charge ‖ *adj* **4** chief ‖ *vt* **5** to be boss over ‖ *vi* **6** to be boss

boss'y *adj* (**-i·er; -i·est**) domineering ‖ **boss'i·ness** *n*

Bos·ton /bôst'ən, bost-/ *n* capital of Massachusetts (641,071) ‖ **Bos·to'ni·an** /-tōn'ē·ən/ *adj* & *n*

Bos·ton ter'ri·er also **Bos'ton bull'** *n* small, pug-faced, short-haired dog with a black or brown coat and white markings

bo·sun /bōs'ən/ *n* boatswain

Bos·well, James /boz'wel, -wəl/ *n* (1740–95) Scottish lawyer; biographer of Samuel Johnson

bot. 1 botany; **2** botanist; **3** botanical

bot·a·ny /bot'ənē/ [< Gk *botane* plant] *n* (**-nies**) science treating of plants, their forms, structure, classification, etc. ‖ **bot'a·nist** *n* ‖ **bo·tan·ic** (**-i·cal**) /bətan'ik(əl)/ *adj*

botch /boch/ [ME *bocchen* to repair] *n* **1** bungling work ‖ *vt* **2** to spoil; disfigure; bungle ‖ **botch'y** *adj* (**-i·er; -i·est**)

both /bōth/ [ON *bāthir*] *adj* & *pron* **1** the two, as *I saw both (men)* ‖ *conj* **2** both . . . and not only . . . but also

both·er /both'ər/ [18th-cent. Eng < ?] *vt* **1** to annoy, pester, worry ‖ *vi* **2** to take the trouble ‖ *n* **3** one who or that which gives trouble or annoyance ‖ **both'er·some** *adj*

Bot·swa·na /botswä'nä/ *n* republic in S Africa (800,000; 222,000 sq. mi.; cap. Gaborone)

bot·tle /bot'əl/ [MF *bouteille* < LL *butticula* small wine butt] *n* **1** narrow-necked usu. glass vessel for liquids; **2** its contents; **3** hit the bottle to drink liquor to excess ‖ *vt* **4** to put into bottles; **5** bottle up, **a** to entrap; **b** to repress (the emotions)

bot·tle·neck' *n* **1** narrow place in a passage or impediment in a process causing a slowdown ‖ *vi* **2** to slow down because of a bottleneck

bot·tom /bot'əm/ [OE *botm*] *n* **1** lowest part of anything; **2** underside; **3** foundation; **4** ground under a body of water; **5** seat of a chair; **6** buttocks; **7** low land; **8** part of a vessel below the water line; **9** *baseball* second half of an inning; **10 at bottom** fundamentally; **11 at the bottom of** responsible for ‖ *adj* **12** low-

est; **13** last (dollar) ‖ *vi* **14** to reach the bottom; **15 bottom out** to reach the lowest point possible, after which the only way to go is up ‖ **bot'tom·less** *adj*

bot·u·lism /boch'əliz'əm/ [< L *botulus* sausage] *n* bacterial disease caused by eating spoiled food

bou·doir /bōōd'wär/ [F = sulking place] *n* lady's private sitting room or bedroom

bough /bou/ [OE *bōg, bōh*] *n* main branch of a tree

bought /bôt/ *pt* & *pp* of **buy**

bouil·lon /bōōl'yon, -yen/ [F] *n* clear broth made from beef or other meat

boul·der /bōl'dər/ [< ME *bulderston* boulder stone] *n* large detached weatherworn rock

boul·e·vard /bōōl'əvärd'/ [F < MD *bolwerk* bulwark] *n* broad avenue, often lined with trees

bounce /bouns/ [ME *bounsen*] *vi* **1** to spring back, rebound; **2** to leap, spring; **3** *slang* to be rejected by a bank, as a check, for insufficient funds; **4 bounce back** to recover from adversity ‖ *vt* **5** to cause to bounce; **6** *slang* to eject (a person) ‖ *n* **7** act or instance of bouncing; **8 get the bounce** to be dismissed from a job

bounc'er *n* *slang* man hired to eject disorderly people

bounc'ing *adj* strapping, lusty, strong

bound¹ /bound/ [MF *bondir*] *vi* **1** to move in springy jumps; **2** to rebound, recoil ‖ *n* **3** rebound

bound² [OF *bonde, bodne* limit] *vt* **1** to set a limit to; **2** to form the limiting line to; **3** to name the countries or waters surrounding ‖ **bounds** *npl* **4** limits, boundaries; **5 out of bounds** beyond the permitted limits ‖ **bound'less** *adj* ‖ SYN *v* limit, circumscribe, terminate, restrict

bound³ 1 *pt* & *pp* of **bind** ‖ *adj* **2** tied; closely connected; **3** obliged; **4** made fast between covers, as a book; **5** determined; **6** certain

bound⁴ [ME *boun* < ON *būinn* ready] *adj* **bound for** going to, headed for

-bound¹ [< *bound³*] *comb form* bound in by, as *stormbound*

-bound² [< *bound⁴*] *comb form* headed toward, as *northbound*

bound'a·ry [< *bound²*] *n* (**-ries**) anything that limits or demarcates ‖ SYN barrier, confines, landmark, frontier, termination, line (see **border**)

bound'en [old form of *bound³*] *adj* **1** under obligation; **2** obligatory

bound'er [< *bound¹*] *n* *Brit slang* cad

bound' form' *n* linguistic form which never occurs by itself, as *un-* and *-ed* in *unwonted*

boun·te·ous /bount'ē·əs/ *adj* **1** giving freely; liberal; **2** freely bestowed ‖ **boun'te·ous·ly** *adv*

boun·ti·ful /bount'ifəl/ *adj* **1** liberal in

bestowing gifts or favors; **2** plentiful || **boun′ti·ful·ly** *adv* || SYN bounteous, munificent, beneficent, open-handed, abundant, ample, copious (see *generous*) || ANT stingy, close, miserly, avaricious, penurious, grasping

boun·ty /bount′ē/ [MF *bonte* < L *bonitas* goodness] *n* (**-ties**) **1** generosity in giving; **2** that which is freely given; **3** premium or reward || SYN benevolence, boon, grant, liberality, munificence

bou·quet /bōōkā′, bō-/ [F] *n* **1** bunch of flowers; **2** aroma, as of wine

bour·bon /bur′bən/ [*Bourbon* county, Ky.] *n* corn whisky

Bour·bon /bōōr′bən/ *n* **1** royal house which supplied kings of France, Spain, and Naples; **2** *politics* extreme conservative

bour·geois /bōōrzhwä′, bōōr′-/ [F] *n* (**-geois**) exponent or exemplar of middle-class morality, taste, political outlook, and values || also *adj*

bour′geoi·sie′ /-zē′/ *n* bourgeois collectively

bourn or **bourne** /bōrn′, bōōrn′/ [< OF *bodne* limit] *n* **1** boundary; **2** goal; **3** *poet.* realm

bout /bout′/ [ME *bought* bend] *n* **1** boxing session; **2** period or spell

bou·tique /bōōtēk′/ [F] *n* fashionable women's dress or specialty shop

bou·ton·nière /bōōt′ənir′/ [F = buttonhole] *n* flower worn on the lapel

bo·vine /bō′vīn, -vēn/ [L *bovinus* oxlike] *adj* **1** pert. or belonging to the genus (*Bos*) that includes cattle; **2** oxlike; dull || *n* **3** bovine animal

bow¹ /bou′/ [OE *būgan*] *vt* **1** to cause to bend, stoop, or incline; **2** to bend, as the head or body, in token of respect or submission; **3** to oppress, crush; **4** to usher in or out || *vi* **5** to bend the knee or head in respect or submission; **6** **bow and scrape** to be exceedingly obsequious || *n* **7** bending of the head or body; **8** **take a bow** to acknowledge applause

bow² /bō′/ [OE *boga*] *n* **1** something curved; **2** weapon of elastic wood, which drives an arrow by a taut string attached to both ends; **3** stick strung with horsehair for playing instruments of the violin class; **4** bowknot || *vt* & *vi* **5** to bend or curve like a bow; **6** *mus* to perform on a stringed instrument with a bow

bow³ /bou′/ [perh < D *boeg*] *n* front end of a vessel or airship

Bow′ bells′ /bō/ *npl* the bells of Bow church in the East End of London

bowd·ler·ize /boud′lərīz′/ [Thomas *Bowdler* (1754–1825) Eng expurgator of Shakespeare] *vt* to expurgate prudishly

bow·el /bou′əl/ [OF *boel* < *dim.* of LL *botulus* sausage] *n* **1** intestine; **2** **bowels** *pl* **a** intestines, entrails; **b** interior part of anything

bow·er /bou′ər/ [OE *būr* dwelling] *n* shelter made of boughs and twining plants; arbor

bow′ie knife′ /bō′ē, bōō′ē/ [James *Bowie* (1799–1836), its inventor] *n* strong hunting knife with curved point

bow′knot′ /bō′-/ *n* slipknot with a single or double loop, readily untied

bowl¹ /bōl/ [OE *bolla*] *n* **1** concave dish; **2** large drinking cup; **3** bowl-shaped thing or part; **4** stadium or amphitheater; **5** contents of a bowl

bowl² [MF *boule* < L *bulla* bubble] *n* **1** ball used in the games of bowls, ninepins, or tenpins; **2** turn at bowling; **3** **bowls** *pl* bowling game played on a bowling green || *vi* **4** to play with bowls or a bowling ball; **5** to move along smoothly || *vt* **6** to roll (a bowl or bowling ball); **7** **bowl over, a** to knock down with something rolled; **b** *colloq* to disconcert; to confuse; to astound

bow′leg′ /bō′-/ *n* leg bowed or curved outward || **bow′leg′ged** /-leg′id, -legd′/ *adj*

bowl′er /bō′-/ [<*bowl¹*] *n* derby hat

bowl′ing /bō′-/ [< *bowl²*] *n* game played by rolling a bowling ball on a bowling alley for the purpose of knocking down as many of the pins standing at the end as possible

bowl′ing al′ley *n* long narrow wooden lane for bowling

bowl′ing ball′ *n* large heavy ball used in bowling

bowl′ing green′ *n* smooth level lawn for the game of bowls

bow·sprit /bou′sprit′, bō′-/ [ME *bouspret*] *n* large spar projecting from the bow of a ship

bow′ tie′ /bō′-/ *n* necktie tied in a bow

box¹ /boks′/ [ME] *n* **1** blow with the hand or fist || *vt* & *vi* **2** to fight in a boxing match

box² [L *buxus*] *n* any of a genus (*Buxus*) of evergreen trees or shrubs much used for hedges

box³ [OE < LL *buxis* made of boxwood] *n* **1** case or container, usu. with a lid; **2** quantity contained in a box; **3** separate compartment with seats in a theater, stadium, etc.; **4** boxlike booth; **5** railed off space in court, as for the jury; **6** part of a page set off by a border of some kind; **7** *baseball* space where the batter stands || *vt* **8** to put in a box; **9** **box in** to shut in

box′car′ *n* enclosed railroad freight car

box·er /< box¹/ *n* **1** pugilist, prize fighter; **2** one of a breed of stocky short-haired dogs with tan coat and white markings

box′ing *n* art or profession of fighting with the fists

box′ing gloves′ *npl* padded mittens used in boxing matches

box′ of′fice *n* **1** ticket office, as of a

theater or sports stadium; **2** receipts of a performance; **3** appeal to an audience ‖ box**'**-of**'**fice *adj*

boy /boi**'**/ [perh < Frisian *boi*] *n* **1** male child; **2** *colloq* man; **3** male servant ‖ *interj* **4** expressing joy, wonder, or disgust ‖ **boy'hood'** *n* ‖ **boy'ish** *adj*

boy∙cott /boi**'**kot/ [Capt. *Boycott*, Irish land agent] *vt* **1** to refuse as a group to trade or deal with ‖ *n* **2** act of boycotting ‖ **boy'cot'ter** *n*

boy'friend' *n* favorite male companion

boy' scout' *n* member of the Boy Scouts, an organization for training boys in character by nonmilitary methods, as in camp life or civic service

boy∙sen∙ber∙ry /boiz**'**ən-/ [Rudolph *Boysen* U.S. botanist] *n* (-ries) bramble fruit resembling a large sweet raspberry or blackberry

Br *chem* bromine

Br. 1 Britain; **2** British

br. 1 branch; **2** brother; **3** brown

bra /brä**'**/ *n* brassiere

brace /brās**'**/ [MF] [L *bracchia* arms] *n* **1** that which supports anything or holds it firm; **2** clasp or clamp; **3** either of the signs { } connecting two or more lines or words; **4** pair, couple; **5** tool for holding and turning bits; **6** wire device for straightening the teeth; **7** appliance for supporting a weak body joint; **8** **braces** *pl* suspenders ‖ *vt* **9** to secure, strengthen, prop; **10** to furnish with a brace; **11** to prepare (oneself) for a shock or impact; **12** to stimulate ‖ *vi* **13** **brace up** to summon one's courage

brace' and bit' *n* boring tool consisting of a removable bit and a cranked handle that turns it

brace∙let /brās**'**lit/ [MF] *n* **1** ornamental band or chain for the wrist or arm; **2** *slang* handcuff

brac'er *n colloq* stimulant; drink of liquor

brach∙y∙ce∙phal∙ic /brak**'**ē̱-/ [< Gk *brachys* short] *adj* short-headed, having a breadth of head that is 80 per cent or more of the length from front to back

brac∙ing /brās**'**iŋ/ *adj* stimulating, tonic

brack∙en /brak**'**ən/ [ME] *n* large, tough fern (*Pteridium aquilinum*)

brack∙et /brak**'**it/ [MF *braguette* flap] *n* **1** angle-shaped supporting piece, as for a shelf, projecting from a wall; **2** either of two signs [ ] used to enclose words; **3** classification, as for income ‖ *vt* **4** to furnish with, connect by, or enclose within, brackets; **5** to group together

brack∙ish /brak**'**ish/ [< D *brak* briny] *adj* **1** salty; **2** distasteful, sickening

bract /brakt**'**/ [< L *bractea* plate of metal] *n* leaflike part growing at the base of a flower or flower cluster

brad /brad**'**/ [ON *broddr* spike] *n* nail having a thickened end instead of a head

brae /brā**'**, brē**'**/ [ON *brā* eyelash] *n Scot* hillside, sloping ground

brag /brag**'**/ [ME] *v* (**bragged; bragging**) *vi* **1** to talk about oneself and one's doings in a conceited manner ‖ *n* **2** boasting, boastfulness ‖ **brag'∙ger** *n*

brag∙ga∙do∙ci∙o /brag**'**ədōsh**'**ē̱-ō**'**/ [character in Spenser's *Faerie Queene*] *n* **1** empty boasting; **2** boaster, swaggerer

brag∙gart /brag**'**ərt/ [< *brag*] *n* one given to bragging

Brah∙ma /bräm**'**ə/ [< Skt *brahman* worship] *n* the Creator, or first member of the Hindu trinity

Brah∙man /bräm**'**ən/ *n* **1** Hindu of the highest, or priestly, class; **2** any of several breeds of humped cattle originating in India, popular in the American Gulf States for their resistance to heat

Brah'min /-min/ *n* **1** Brahman *1*; **2** superior and aloof intellectual, esp. of an old New England family

Brahms, Jo∙han∙nes /yōhän**'**əs brämz**'**/ *n* (1833–97) German composer

braid /brād**'**/ [OE *bregdan* to move to and fro] *vt* **1** to weave or intertwine; plait; **2** to arrange (the hair) by interweaving strands or with a band; **3** to trim or decorate with braid ‖ *n* **4** anything made or shaped by braiding; **5** band, as of tape or cloth, used for trimming or decorating clothing

Braille or **braille** /brāl**'**/ [Louis *Braille* (1809–52) F teacher] *n* system of writing for the blind, using raised tangible dots

brain /brān**'**/ [OE *brægen*] *n* **1** in vertebrates, the mass of nerve tissue filling the cranial cavity of the skull; **2** **brains** *pl* intelligence ‖ *vt* **3** to dash out the brains of

brain'child' *n* (-chil'dren) *n* creation of one's thoughts

brain' drain' *n slang* migration of persons of marked ability to another country because of more attractive opportunities

brain'less *adj* witless; senseless

brain'storm' *n colloq* **1** sudden inspiration; **2** sudden mental confusion or disturbance

brain' trust' *n* group of expert advisers

brain'wash' *vt* to effect a change in the beliefs and behavior of (a person) by thorough, coercive indoctrination ‖ **brain'wash'ing** *n*

brain' wave' *n* **1** *colloq* sudden impulse or inspiration; **2** **brain waves** *pl* rhythmic fluctuations of electricity between parts of the brain

brain'y adj (-i-er; -i-est) colloq clever, mentally acute ‖ **brain'i-ness** n

braise /brāz'/ [F braiser] vt to brown (meat or vegetables) and then simmer in a covered pan

brake[1] /brāk'/ [ME] n 1 device for checking the motion of a wheel, vehicle, etc. ‖ vt & vi 2 to slow down or stop, as by applying a brake

brake[2] [ME < MLG] n thicket

brake[3] [ME] n tall, coarse fern of the genus Pteridium

brake' drum' n cylinder fixed to a rotating shaft or wheel, against which the brake shoe presses in order to stop it

brake' horse'pow-er n horsepower of an engine over and above that necessary to drive the engine, measured with a dynamometer by means of a brake attached to the drive shaft

brake'man /-mən/ n (-men /-mən/) trainman who acts as an assistant to the conductor

brake' shoe' n metal plate which presses against the brake drum when the brake is applied

bram-ble /bram'bəl/ [OE bræmbel] n any rough prickly bush or shrub, esp. of the genus Rubus ‖ **bram'bly** adj (-bli-er; -bli-est)

bran /bran'/ [OF bren] n husks of wheat, rye, etc., separated from the flour by sifting

branch /branch', bränch'/ [OF branche] n 1 shoot or limb of a tree, shrub, or plant; 2 any offshoot, division, or constituent or divergent part; 3 tributary stream ‖ vi 4 to divide from the main body; diverge; 5 branch off to diverge, separate into branches; 6 branch out to extend one's activities or interests ‖ SYN n bough, limb, twig, offshoot; side issue, subhead

brand /brand'/ [OE = burning] n 1 burning or charred piece of wood; 2 mark burned with a hot iron to show ownership, as on cattle; 3 trademark; 4 make of a commodity; 5 stigma ‖ vt 6 to mark with, or as with, a brand; 7 to stigmatize ‖ **brand'er** n ‖ SYN v mark, sear, stigmatize (see burn)

bran-dish /bran'dish/ [MF brandir (-disse)] vt to wave or shake, as a sword ‖ SYN wave, parade, flaunt, flourish, shake, flutter

brand'-new' adj entirely new

bran-dy /bran'dē/ [D brandewijn distilled wine] n (-dies) liquor distilled from wine or fermented fruit juices

brash /brash'/ [?] adj 1 rash, impetuous; 2 bumptious, impudent ‖ n 3 sudden, passing illness

Bra-si-lia /brəzēl'yə/ n capital of Brazil since 1960 (250,000)

brass /bras', bräs'/ [OE bræs] n 1 yellow alloy of copper and zinc; 2 colloq effrontery; 3 the brass pl slang high-ranking officials; 4 brasses pl brass winds ‖ **brass'y** adj (-i-er; -i-est)

bras-sard /bras'ärd/ [F < bras arm] n badge worn on the upper arm

brass' hat' n slang high-ranking military official

brass'ie /-ē/ n golf club for hitting long, low drives

bras-siere /brəzir'/ [F brassière bodice] n woman's undergarment for supporting the breasts

brass' knuck'les nsg or npl metal finger guards worn over the fist as a weapon

brass' tacks' npl down to brass tacks down to essentials

brass' winds' npl mus wind instruments of the trumpet or horn family ‖ **brass'-wind'** adj

brat /brat'/ [?] n colloq unruly or impudent child ‖ **brat'ty** adj (-ti-er; -ti-est)

bra-va-do /brəväd'ō/ [OSp bravata boast] n (-does, -dos) 1 boastful pretense of courage; 2 bold front

brave /brāv'/ [OIt bravo] adj 1 courageous; 2 making a fine appearance ‖ vt 3 to face with courage; 4 to dare; defy ‖ n 5 American Indian warrior; 6 the brave pl brave people ‖ **brave'ly** adv ‖ SYN adj valiant, daring, resolute, courageous, venturesome, chivalrous, dauntless, intrepid

brav'er-y n (-ies) 1 valor, courage; 2 something fine or showy; exhibit ‖ SYN courage, gallantry, valor, chivalry, intrepidity, fortitude, heroism, prowess, pluck ‖ DISCR These words agree in that they express resistance to some opposing power. Courage, the noblest word, names a quality that is deep-seated in the character. It acts in time of danger, but not only then; it is available always, and meets a physical attack with no less steadfastness than a spiritual struggle or a period of trying illness. Courage is the product of reason and a marshaled force of resistance; it is a bigger quality than bravery, which is more a matter of instinct. Bravery is fiery, perhaps even spectacular; but it is a more common trait than courage, is apparent at the moment of need or danger only, and follows rather than leads. Gallantry is bravery with the luster of dash upon it; it surpasses bravery, for it connotes the power of leadership. Intrepidity is fearless and undaunted; it is a cool, admirable trait. Heroism is passionate courage; heroism forgets self, whether exhibited in actual fighting or in the calm control of one facing death for a cause or a faith. Fortitude is akin to this last-mentioned quiet courage; fortitude is a steely endurance under adversity or pain; it is determined, unfaltering, patient. *Valor* combines the heat of *bravery* with the ability of *courage* to lead and endure; *valor* fights with dash, but *prowess* may defeat *valor* by adding to its characteristics that measure of skill which the valiant one either lacks, or is too impatient to exercise. *Pluck* is a spirited, confident resolution, especially against odds

bra·vo /brä′vō/ [It] *interj* **1** well done! ‖ *n* **2** shout of bravo

bra·vu·ra /brəvyŏŏr′ə/ [It = bravery, spirit] *n* **1** show of daring or brilliance; **2** aggressive, self-confident manner; **3** *mus* brilliant or dashing display in performance; **4** *mus* passage requiring brilliant execution

brawl /brôl′/ [ME = bully] *n* **1** noisy quarrel ‖ *vi* **2** to quarrel or wrangle noisily ‖ **brawl′er** *n*

brawn /brôn′/ [OF *braon* flesh] *n* **1** firm muscle; **2** muscular strength ‖ **brawn′y** *adj* (-**i·er**; -**i·est**)

bray /brā′/ [OF *braire*] *n* **1** loud, harsh sound, as the cry of a donkey or the blast of a trumpet ‖ *vt* **2** to utter in a loud, harsh way ‖ *vi* **3** to give forth a bray

Braz. 1 Brazil; **2** Brazilian

braze /brāz′/ [F *braser*] *vt* to join with hard solder of brass and zinc

bra·zen /brāz′ən/ [OE *bræsen*] *adj* **1** of or like brass; **2** shameless ‖ *vt* **brazen out** or **through** to face shamelessly ‖ **bra′zen·ly** *adv* ‖ **bra′zen·ness** *n*

bra·zier¹ /brāzh′ər/ [F *brasier*] *n* open pan for holding burning charcoal

bra·zier² [< OE *brasian* to make of brass] *n* one who works in brass

Bra·zil /brəzil′/ *n* Portuguese-speaking republic in E South America (115,000,000; 3,286,488 sq.m.; cap. Brasília) ‖ **Bra·zil′ian** /-yən/ *adj & n*

Bra·zil′ nut′ *n* triangular edible seed of a tree (*Bertholletia excelsa*) of N Brazil

Braz·za·ville /braz′əvil′/ *n* capital of the Republic of Congo (136,200)

breach /brēch′/ [OE *bryce*] *n* **1** opening or gap made by breaking; **2** breaking of a law, promise, or contract; **3** rupture of friendly relations ‖ *vt* **4** to make a breach in

breach′ of prom′ise *n* failure to keep one's promise, esp. a promise to marry

bread /bred′/ [OE] *n* **1** baked food made from the flour or meal of grain; **2** food in general; **3** livelihood; **4** **break bread to eat** ‖ *vt* **5** to cover with bread crumbs before cooking ‖ **bread′ed** *adj*

bread′ and but′ter *n colloq* livelihood ‖ **bread′-and-but′ter** *adj*

bread′bas′ket *n* **1** agricultural region that supplies much grain; **2** *slang* stomach

breadth /bredth′/ [OE *brædu*] *n* **1** width; **2** freedom from narrowness

bread′win′ner *n* member of a family by whose labor it is supported

break /brāk′/ [OE *brecan*] *v* (**broke**; **bro·ken**) *vt* **1** to separate into pieces by a blow or strain; **2** to interrupt (a journey, silence, an electric circuit); **3** to destroy the arrangement of, as *to break ranks*; **4** to weaken the force of, as a fall; **5** to cut the surface of, as the skin; **6** to render inoperative; **7** to stop (a habit); **8** to bring (a strike) to an end; **9** to change (a banknote); **10** to violate, as a promise or a law; **11** to demote, degrade; **12** to disclose; **13** to tame, as a horse; **14** to dig up, as ground; **15** to make bankrupt; **16** to excel (a record); **17** to destroy the health or vitality of; **18** to solve (a case, a code); **19** to invalidate (a will); **20** **break ground** to begin excavation; **21** **break in,** a to train; b to begin to use in order to adjust; **22** **break up,** a to discontinue; b to scatter ‖ *vi* **23** to separate suddenly into pieces; burst; **24** to change abruptly, as a gait, tone, etc.; **25** to burst forth violently, as a storm; **26** to become inoperative; **27** to begin suddenly, as *he broke into a run;* **28** to come to public notice, as *a big story broke;* **29** **break down,** a to become inoperative; b to lose control of oneself; **30** **break even** to come out even; **31** **break in,** a to enter by force or stealth; b to interrupt; **32** **break off** to discontinue; **33** **break out,** a to begin abruptly; b to have a skin eruption; **34** **break up,** a to separate, scatter; b to dissolve a relationship; **35** **break with** to sever relations with ‖ *n* **36** act or instance of breaking; **37** broken place; **38** sudden dash; **39** suspension of friendly relations; **40** interruption of regularity; **41** abrupt change; **42** *colloq* a good luck; b opportunity; **43** rest period; **44** sharp fall in stock prices; **45** cessation, pause; **46** first appearance, as *the break of day;* **47** *colloq* blunder of speech or action ‖ **break′a·ble** *adj* ‖ SYN *v* crush, rend, tear, destroy, smash, crack, split, shiver, shatter, burst ‖ DISCR To *break* is to separate into two or more separate pieces; to *crack* is to cause a cleavage without complete separation of the parts. To *crush* is to *break* under such relatively severe external pressure that the object is destroyed. To *rack* is to injure with twisting, shaking, or other disabling violence. To *burst* is to blow to pieces from within, as a boiler, a shell, etc. To *bruise* is to injure by pressure, causing a contusion but not a break; fruits, soft parts of the body, tires on a stony road, are *bruised.* To *split* is to separate lengthwise, as wood with the grain. To *tear* or *rend* is to pull violently apart, as cloth. Figuratively, all these words can be used with a force not unlike that of their original meaning. To *break* a man by subjecting him to unbearable mental strain is not uncommon; we are *crushed* by grief, *torn* by dissension; our hearts are said to *burst* from pity, or *break* with compassion; we are *racked* by sympathies which are equally deserved by opposing parties

break·age /-ij/ *n* 1 act of breaking; 2 state of being broken; 3 things broken, or compensation for things broken

break·down' *n* 1 a breaking down; 2 failure of a machine to continue working; 3 failure of health; 4 analysis; 5 decomposition; 6 collapse of negotiations

break·er *n* 1 one who or that which breaks; 2 wave which dashes itself into foam

break·fast /brek'fəst/ *n* 1 first meal of the day || *vi* 2 to eat breakfast

break'-in' *n* 1 forcible entry into a home or office; 2 trial performance

break'neck' *adj* dangerously fast

break'through' *n* 1 *mil* piercing of the enemy's lines; 2 sudden significant advance in any field

break'up' *n* 1 dispersion; 2 collapse, disintegration; 3 dissolution, as of a marriage, association, etc.

break'wa'ter *n* structure built to break the force of the waves

breast /brest/ [OE *brēost*] *n* 1 front part of the body between the neck and the abdomen; 2 either of the milk-secreting glands on a woman's chest; 3 the part of a garment covering the chest; 4 seat of the affections; heart; 5 **make a clean breast of** to confess fully || *vt* 6 to face or oppose, as a storm or opposition

breast'-beat'ing *n* demonstrative lamentation

breast'bone' *n* sternum

breast' drill' *n* drill with a plate which is pressed by the chest for leverage

breast'plate' *n* piece of armor covering the chest

breast'stroke' *n* swimming stroke in which both arms move forward and sweep simultaneously to the rear in horizontal arcs

breast'work' *n* *mil* hastily constructed defensive wall or parapet of moderate height

breath /breth/ [OE *brǣth*] *n* 1 air drawn into or expelled from the lungs; 2 respiration; 3 power of breathing easily; 4 life; strength; 5 air charged with fragrance; 6 zephyr, breeze; 7 murmur, whisper; 8 condensed moisture produced by exhalation; 9 **save one's breath** to

avoid useless discussion; 10 **take one's breath away** to astonish, as by sheer size, splendor, etc.; 11 **under the** or **one's breath** in a whisper

breathe /brēth/ *vi* 1 to inhale and exhale; 2 to live; 3 to take time to respire; pause; 4 to exhale fragrance; 5 **breathe freely** to be free of anxiety || *vt* 6 to respire; 7 to utter softly; 8 to manifest, express; 9 to take in by inhaling, as fumes; 10 to instill, as *she breathed courage into the child;* 11 **breathe one's last** to die

breath·er /brĕth'ər/ *n* short pause or rest period

breath'less *adj* 1 unable to breathe; 2 lifeless; 3 paralyzed with fear, suspense, etc.; 4 exhausted; 5 excited; 6 windless || **breath'less·ly** *adv*

breath'tak'ing *adj* causing extreme awe or excitement

bred /bred/ *pt & pp* of **breed**

breech /brēch/ [OE *brēc* breeches] *n* 1 rear part of a firearm; 2 back part of anything

breech'cloth' *n* cloth worn about the loins

breech·es /brich'iz/ *npl* 1 trousers reaching to the knee; 2 *colloq* trousers

breech'es bu'oy /also brēch'iz/ *n* life-saving device consisting of a canvas sling suspended from a life preserver, in which persons can be hauled ashore or to another vessel from a wrecked vessel

breed /brēd/ [OE *brēdan* to nourish] *v* (**bred**) *vt* 1 to produce (offspring); 2 to cause, be the source of; 3 to bring up; train; 4 to raise, as cattle || *vi* 5 to bear young; 6 to be born; originate; 7 to propagate stock, etc. || *n* 8 stock, race; 9 sort, kind

breed'er *n* 1 person who breeds animals or plants; 2 person or animal that reproduces; 3 breeder reactor

breed'er re·ac'tor *n* apparatus in which a fissionable element is produced by bombarding a nonfissionable element with neutrons so that more fissionable material is produced than used

breed'ing *n* 1 propagation; 2 improvement or development of breeds of animals or plants; 3 behavior, good manners || SYN training, nurture, manners (see *education*)

breeze /brēz/ [OSp *briza*] *n* 1 fresh but gentle wind; 2 *slang* easy task; 3 **shoot the breeze** *slang* to chat || *vi* 4 *colloq* to move quickly and effortlessly

breeze'way' *n* roofed driveway or walk

breez·y *adj* (-i-er; -i-est) 1 airy; 2 animated, brisk || **breez'i·ly** *adv* || **breez'i·ness** *n*

Brem·en /brem'ən/ *n* seaport in N West Germany (580,000)

Bren'ner Pass' /bren'ər/ *n* Alpine pass between Austria and Italy

breth·ren /breth'rən/ [see **brother**]

npl brothers (used of lay members of a men's religious order and of male members of some churches)

Bret·on /bret'ən/ [LL *Britones* Britons] *n* 1 native of Brittany in NW France; 2 Celtic language of the Bretons || also *adj*

Bret'ton Woods' /bret'ən/ *n* site in New Hampshire of the international monetary conference in 1944 that established the International Monetary Fund and the World Bank

breve /brēv'/ [L = short] *n* mark ˘, as in e and ŏ, placed over a vowel to indicate that it is short

bre·vi·ar·y /brēv'ē·er'ē/ [L *breviarium* abridgment] *n* (**-ies**) book containing the services and prayers to be recited daily

brev·i·ty /brev'itē/ [< L *brevis* short] *n* 1 shortness; 2 conciseness

brew /broō'/ [OE *brēowan*] *vt* 1 to make (beer, ale, etc.) from malt, hops, and other materials by fermentation; 2 to make, as tea, by infusion; 3 to contrive; scheme || *vi* 4 to gather, grow, as a storm || *n* 5 beer or ale || **brew'er** *n*

brew'er·y *n* (**-ies**) place where beer or ale is made

bri·ar /brī'ər/ *n* var of **brier**

bribe /brīb'/ [MF = alms] *n* 1 anything given to a public official or any person in a position of trust to procure dishonest or illegal action || *vt* 2 to give a bribe to || **brib'er** *n* || **brib'er·y** *n* (**-ies**) || SYN emolument, gift, allurement, seduction

bric·a·brac /brik'əbrak'/ [F] *n* small objects of art or curiosity; knickknacks

brick /brik'/ [MF *brique* < MD] *n* 1 molded block of dried clay, used in building; 2 any bricklike object; 3 *colloq* fine fellow || *vt* 4 to build or wall in with bricks

brick'bat' *n* 1 piece of brick, esp. when used as a missile; 2 *colloq* criticism

brick'kiln' *n* furnace for baking or burning bricks

brick'lay'ing *n* art or occupation of laying bricks in construction || **brick'lay'er** *n*

brid·al /brīd'əl/ *n* 1 wedding || *adj* 2 pert. to a bride or wedding

bride /brīd'/ [OE *brȳd*] *n* woman newly married or about to be married

bride'groom' [< OE *guma* man] *n* man newly married or about to be married

brides'maid' *n* woman at a wedding who acts as an attendant of the bride

bridge¹ /brij'/ [OE *brycg*] *n* 1 structure built to carry a road across a river, valley, or other road; 2 anything resembling a bridge in form or use; 3 upper part of the nose; 4 fixed or removable frame for false teeth; 5 platform above the deck of a ship where the pilot is stationed; 6 piece of wood that raises the strings of a stringed instrument above the soundboard; 7 **burn one's bridges** to make one's course irrevocable || *vt* 8 to build a bridge over; span; 9 to get over, as a difficulty

bridge² [?] *n* any of several four-handed card games in which the bidder plays not only his own hand, but also that of his partner, who lays his cards face up on the table opposite the bidder

bridge'head' *n* 1 defensive position to protect the end of a bridge nearer the enemy; 2 position on the enemy side of a river used as a foothold for further advance; 3 commanding position

Bridge'port' *n* seaport in Connecticut (160,000)

bridge' ta'ble *n* portable card table with folding legs

Bridge'town' *n* capital of Barbados (11,250)

bridge'work' *n* dental bridge or bridges

bri'dle /brīd'əl/ [OE *brīdel*] *n* 1 horse's headgear with bit and reins; 2 check; restraint || *vt* 3 to put a bridle on; 4 to curb; control || *vi* 5 to toss one's head in pride, scorn, or anger

bri'dle path' *n* path for riding horses

brief /brēf'/ [OF *bref* < L *brevis* short] *adj* 1 short; curtailed; 2 concise || *n* 3 concise summary; 4 outline of an argument, as of a law case || *vt* 5 to summarize; 6 to give all the pertinent facts to || **brief'ing** *n* || **brief'ly** *adv*

brief'case' *n* flat leather case for carrying papers

bri·er¹ /brī'ər/ [OE *brēr*] *n* thorny plant or shrub, as the wild rose or blackberry

bri·er² [F *bruyère*] *n* 1 European white heath (*Erica arborea*); 2 tobacco pipe made from its root

brig /brig'/ [< *brigantine*] *n* 1 two-masted square-rigged vessel; 2 ship's prison

Brig. 1 brigade; 2 brigadier

bri·gade /brigād'/ [MF < OIt *brigata* company] *n* 1 subdivision of an army division, made up of regiments; 2 organized body acting under authority, as *a fire brigade* || *vt* 3 to form into a brigade

brig·a·dier /brig'ədir'/ *n* brigadier general in the British and some other armies

brig'a·dier' gen'er·al *n* army officer ranking between a colonel and a major general

brig·and /brig'ənd/ [MF < OIt *brigante* fighting man] *n* bandit, esp. one of a roving mounted band

brig·an·tine /brig'əntēn'/ [OIt *brigan-*

tino fighting ship] *n* vessel with a square-rigged foremast and a fore-and-aft rigged mainmast

bright /brīt/ [OE *beorht*] *adj* 1 showing light; luminous; 2 glorious, illustrious; 3 witty, mentally alert; 4 lively; gay; 5 auspicious, fortunate; 6 resplendent, striking; 7 glossy ‖ **bright′ly** *adv* ‖ **bright′ness** *n* ‖ SYN shining, radiant, refulgent, lustrous, luminous, brilliant, sunny, beaming, cheerful ‖ DISCR *Bright, shining,* and *radiant* are applied to bodies that are full of light. *Bright* describes that which sends forth or reflects light, as a *bright* star; a *bright* shield; applied to colors, *bright* means striking or vivid. *Shining* is applied to a source of steady or continuous light, as under the *shining* sun; figuratively, it describes the beaming effect of certain emotions, as his *shining* face betrayed his joy. *Radiant* describes a light sent forth in rays from a center; sunlight is *radiant*; figuratively, of beauty, it means dazzling; of the eyes or appearance, sending forth beams of joy or love. *Luminous* describes a body that is full of, or emits, light; the heavenly bodies are *luminous*; eyes that glisten with a soft radiance are *luminous*. *Lustrous* describes the rainbow sheen that appears on a polished surface shining with reflected light, as *lustrous* silk; *lustrous* pottery. *Brilliant* describes objects that glitter and flash with light, as diamonds

bright′en *vi* 1 to grow bright or brighter ‖ *vt* 2 to make bright or brighter

Bright′s dis·ease′ [Dr. Richard *Bright* (1789–1858) Eng physician] *n* disease marked by the persistent presence of albumin in the urine and high blood pressure

bril·liant /bril′yənt/ [F *brillant*] *adj* 1 sparkling, glittering; 2 shining brightly; 3 exceptionally talented or cultured; 4 very able or intelligent; 5 magnificent, splendid ‖ *n* 6 gem cut to show its sparkling quality ‖ **bril′liant·ly** *adv* ‖ **bril′liance** or **bril′lian·cy** *n* ‖ SYN *adj* sparkling, glorious, illustrious (see *bright*)

brim /brim/ [ME *brimme*] *n* 1 projecting edge, as of a hat; 2 rim or top, as of a glass or cup ‖ SYN rise, bank, verge (see *border*)

brim′ming *adj* full to the brim

brim′stone′ [OE *brinnan* to burn] *n* sulfur

brin·dle /brin′dəl/ [< ME *brended* brindled] *n* 1 gray or tawny color with dark streaks or spots; 2 animal so colored ‖ **brin′dled** *adj*

brine /brīn/ [OE *brȳne*] *n* 1 salt water; 2 sea water; 3 ocean ‖ **brin′y** *adj* (-i·er; -i·est)

bring /briŋ/ [OE *bringan*] *v* (**brought**)

vt 1 to convey or lead (a person or thing) with one; fetch; 2 to cause, as *the rain brought cool weather;* 3 to persuade, influence; 4 to sell for; 5 to conduct, convey; 6 *law* to institute; 7 **bring about** to cause; accomplish; 8 **bring down the house** to elicit tumultuous applause; 9 **bring forward, a** to introduce, as a proposal; **b** to carry forward, as a sum; 10 **bring home** to make vividly clear, prove conclusively; 11 **bring off** to accomplish; 12 **bring out, a** to reveal; **b** to present (to the public); **c** to introduce to society; 13 **bring round** or **over** to cause to change opinions, sides, etc.; 14 **bring to** to resuscitate, as from a faint; 15 **bring to bear** to cause to have influence; 16 **bring to book** to call to account; 17 **bring up, a** to rear, educate; **b** to stop short; **c** to introduce; **d** to vomit ‖ SYN bear, convey, carry, transport, fetch ‖ DISCR *Bring* suggests motion to the place where one is or resides; to *bring* a thing to me is to come with it to me. *Bring* also means to carry with oneself from the place where one is to the place where one is going, as when I come tomorrow, I will *bring* my transistor. *Fetching* is a kind of *bringing; fetch* is to go to a distance, get the thing designated, and *bring* it back to the speaker. To *carry* is often to take away; it indicates motion from the place where a thing is to where it is supposed to go, or where it is taken; to *carry* a message is to take it to its destination; to *carry* a parcel is to bear it to its addressee; to *carry* tales is to repeat them to others

brink /briŋk/ [ME] *n* 1 edge of a steep place; 2 verge ‖ SYN bank, shore, edge, verge (see *border*)

brink′man·ship′ *n* hazard of pushing the interests of one's country so far as to risk nuclear war

bri·quette /briket′/ [F] *n* pressed brick of coal dust or charcoal, used for fuel

Bris·bane /briz′bān, -bən/ *n* capital of Queensland, E Australia (575,000)

brisk /brisk′/ [MF *brusque*] *adj* 1 quick, energetic; 2 bracing, invigorating ‖ **brisk′ly** *adv* ‖ **brisk′ness** *n* ‖ SYN quick, sprightly, alert, spirited (see *active*)

bris·ket /bris′kit/ [ME *brusket*] *n* front part of the breast of an animal, or the meat from it

bris·tle /bris′əl/ [< OE *byrst*] *n* 1 any short stiff hair ‖ *vi* 2 to stand up like bristles; 3 to be covered as with bristles; 4 to come erect with sudden anger or defiance ‖ **bris′tly** *adj* (-tli·er; -tli·est)

Bris·tol /bris′təl/ *n* seaport in SW England (440,000)

Brit. 1 Britain; 2 British

Brit·ain /brit′ən/ *n* 1 Great Britain; 2

ancient Celtic-inhabited England, Scotland, and Wales

Bri·tan·ni·a /britan'ē-ə, -yə/ [L] *n poet.* Great Britain

Bri·tan'ni·a met'al *n* alloy of tin, antimony, and copper, and often with zinc, lead, and bismuth, used in making tableware and antifriction material

Bri·tan'nic *adj* British

britch'es *npl* var of **breeches**

Brit·i·cism /brit'isiz'əm/ also **Brit'ish·ism** *n* word, expression, or usage peculiar to the British

Brit·ish /brit'ish/ [OE *Bryttisc*] *adj* **1** of or pert. to Great Britain or its inhabitants; **2** relating to the ancient Britons || *n* **3** language of the ancient Britons; **4** **the British** *pl* the people of Britain || **Brit'ish·er** *n*

Brit'ish Co·lum'bi·a *n* Pacific-coast province of W Canada (1,873,674; 366,255 sq.m.: cap. Victoria)

Brit'ish Com'mon·wealth of Na'tions *n* group of independent nations, formerly part of the British Empire and ruled from London, now united by common allegiance to the British crown and often by tariff and monetary agreements

Brit'ish Gui·a'na *n* (former name of) *Guyana*

Brit'ish Hon·du'ras *n* (former name of) *Belize*

Brit'ish Isles' *n* group of islands in NW Europe, including Great Britain, Ireland, and many smaller islands

Brit'ish ther'mal u'nit *n* quantity of heat required to raise one pound of water one degree Fahrenheit

Brit·on /brit'ən/ [OF *Breton*] *n* **1** Celtic inhabitant of ancient Britain; **2** subject of Great Britain

Brit·ta·ny /brit'ənē/ *n* region and former province of NW France, lying between the English Channel and the Bay of Biscay

brit·tle /brit'əl/ [ME *britel*] *adj* **1** easily broken or shattered || *n* **2** hard brittle candy made with nuts || **brit'tle·ness** *n* || SYN fragile, delicate, frail, breakable, frangible || DISCR *Brittle* describes substances that break easily, especially as the result of a blow, shake, or jar, as glass or ice. *Fragile* is applied to objects which, because of delicate structure, cannot withstand the effects of time, or which, because of finely adjusted parts, are broken by the merest touch. Very fine china is both *brittle* and *fragile;* an extremely *delicate,* sensitive instrument is *fragile,* though not necessarily *brittle;* a bit of fine old lace is *fragile. Frail* indicates an inherent weakness; figuratively, *frail* implies moral weakness; a *frail* creature is one liable to be led into sin

bro. (bros.) brother

broach /brōch'/ [MF *broche* spit] *n* **1** tapered reamer || *vt* **2** to tap, as a keg of wine; **3** to begin a discussion of

broad /brôd'/ [OE *brād*] *adj* **1** wide; **2** spacious, vast; **3** liberal, openminded; **4** comprehensive; **5** open, clear, as *broad daylight;* **6** obvious, evident, as *a broad hint;* **7** generalized, touching only the main points; **8** outspoken, unreserved || *n* **9** *slang* woman || **broad'ly** *adv* || SYN *adj* wide, extensive, comprehensive, large, tolerant, liberal, catholic || ANT *adj* narrow, intolerant, prejudiced

broad'cast' *v* (-cast) *vt* **1** to scatter or spread in all directions || *v* (-cast or -cast·ed) *vt* & *vi* **2** to transmit by radio or television || *adj* **3** widely scattered; **4** of or pert. to broadcasting || *adv* **5** far and wide || *n* **6** that which is broadcast || **broad'cast'er** *n* || **broad'cast'ing** *n*

broad'cloth' *n* fine smooth fabric with a lustrous finish

broad'en *vt* & *vi* to widen

broad' jump' *n sports* jump for distance || **broad'-jump'** *vi*

broad'loom' (car'pet) *n* carpet woven on a wide loom

broad'-mind'ed *adj* liberal in opinions, tolerant

broad·side' *n* **1** side of a ship above the waterline; **2** simultaneous discharge of all the guns from one side of a warship; **3** large sheet printed on one side, as for advertising; **4** strong criticism || *adv* **5** with the side facing a given point

Broad·way' *n* **1** thoroughfare of New York City that extends the whole length of Manhattan; **2** the theater district of New York, the center and pinnacle of the theatrical profession in the U.S., located on Broadway || also *adj*

Brob·ding·nag /brob'diŋ·nag'/ *n* fabled country peopled by giants in Swift's *Gulliver's Travels* || **Brob'ding·nag'·i·an** *adj* & *n*

bro·cade /brōkād'/ [Sp *brocado*] *n* **1** fabric woven with raised designs || *vt* **2** to weave or decorate with a raised pattern

broc·a·tel /brok'ətel'/ [< It *broccatello*] *n* **1** brocade with a design in high relief; **2** ornamental marble, veined with white, gray, yellow, and red

broc·co·li /brok'əlē/ [It = cabbage tops] *n* variety of cauliflower (*Brassica oleracea botrytis*), the green tops and stalks of which are eaten as a vegetable

bro·chure /brōshŏŏr'/ [F < *brocher* to stitch] *n* pamphlet

brogue¹ /brōg'/ [Ir *brog* shoe] *n* man's heavy oxford shoe

brogue² [?] *n* Irish accent in speaking English

broil /broil'/ [MF *bruler* to burn] *vt* **1** to cook directly over a fire || *vi* **2** to be cooked by broiling; **3** to be intensely angered ‖ *n* **4** something broiled

broil·er *n* **1** device for broiling; **2** young chicken suitable for broiling

broke /brōk′/ **1** *pt* of **break** ‖ *adj* **2** *slang* without funds

bro·ken 1 *pp* of **break** ‖ *adj* **2** shattered, fractured; **3** not continuous, interrupted; **4** violated, as *a broken law*; **5** bankrupt; **6** crushed, subdued; **7** rendered infirm; **8** badly spoken; **9** tamed ‖ **bro′ken·ly** *adv*

bro′ken-down′ *adj* **1** in poor health; **2** ruined, no longer usable

bro·ken-heart′ed *adj* overcome by grief and misery

bro·ker /brōk′ər/ [ME *brocour* retailer < LL *broccator* barrel tapper] *n* agent who buys and sells for others on commission

bro′ker·age /-ij/ *n* **1** business of a broker; **2** broker's commission

bro·mide /brōm′īd, -id/ [< *bromine*] *n* **1** salt of bromine with a metal or a radical; **2** *colloq* a platitude, commonplace; **b** person who thinks and talks platitudes

bro·mine /brōm′ēn, brōm′in/ [< Gk *bromos* stench] *n* dark-reddish liquid halogen element (**Br**; at. no. 35; at. wt. 79.909) which emits a noxious vapor; used in making dyes, antiknock fuels, and drugs

bron·chi /broŋ′kī/ [Gk *bronchoi*] *npl* the two principal branches of the windpipe ‖ **bron′chi·al** /broŋk′ē·əl/ *adj*

bron′chi·al tubes′ *npl* the bronchi and their branches

bron·chi′tis /-kī′tis/ *n* inflammation of the mucous lining of the bronchial tubes

bron′cho·scope /-kə/ *n* instrument for inspecting the interior of the bronchi and for removing foreign bodies from them

bron·co /broŋ′kō/ [MexSp] *n* range pony of the W U.S., often untamed

bron′co·bust′er *n* tamer of broncos

bron·to·saur /bront′əsôr′/ also **bron′-to·sau′rus** [< Gk *bronte* thunder + *sauros* lizard] *n* extinct North American dinosaur (genus *Brontosaurus*)

Bronx, the /broŋks′/ *n* one of the constituent boroughs of New York City (1,500,000)

bronze /bronz′/ [F < It *bronzo*] *n* **1** alloy of copper and tin; **2** work of art cast or wrought in bronze; **3** reddish-brown color ‖ *vt* **4** to make the color of bronze; **5** to make (the skin) bronze by exposure to the sun

Bronze′ Age′ *n* period in the development of man, following the Stone Age and preceding the Iron Age, when bronze weapons and implements were made

brooch /brōch′, brooch′/ [see **broach**] *n* ornamental pin with a clasp

brood /brood′/ [OE *brōd*] *n* **1** all the birds hatched at one time; **2** all the young of one mother ‖ *vi* **3** to sit on eggs, as a hen; **4** to meditate long and moodily ‖ *vt* **5** to sit over, cover, cherish, as eggs, young; **6** to ponder

brood′er *n* **1** person lost in moody thought; **2** structure for raising chicks hatched in an incubator

brook¹ /brook′/ [OE *brōc*] *n* small natural stream

brook² [OE *brūcan* to use] *vt* to put up with (used mostly in the negative)

Brook·lyn /brook′lin/ *n* one of the constituent boroughs of New York City (2,700,000)

brook′ trout′ *n* speckled fish (*Salvelinus fontinalis*) of E North America

broom /broom′, broom′/ [OE *brōm*] *n* **1** any of a genus (*Cytisus*) of shrubs with slender branches and yellow, white, or purple flowers; **2** stiff long-handled brush for sweeping

bros. brothers

broth /brôth′, broth′/ [OE] *n* water in which meat, vegetables, or cereals have been boiled

broth·el /brôth′əl, broth′-/ [< OE *brēothan* to go to ruin] *n* house of prostitution

broth·er /bruth′ər/ [OE *brōthor*] *n* (-ers also **brethren** in senses 3 and 4) **1** male offspring of one's parents; **2** one closely united to others by a common race, creed, or interest; **3** lay member of a men's religious order; **4** male member of some churches; **5** brothers human beings in general

broth′er·hood′ *n* **1** quality or state of being a brother; **2** fellowship, community of feeling; **3** association of men for any purpose; fraternity

broth′er-in-law′ *n* (**brothers-in-law**) **1** husband's or wife's brother; **2** a sister's husband; **3** husband of the sister of one's husband or wife

broth′er·ly *adj* **1** like, or pert. to, a brother; **2** affectionate, kind ‖ **broth′-er·li·ness** *n*

brough·am /broo′əm, brō′əm, broom′/ [< H. B. *Brougham* (1778–1868) Sc jurist] *n* four-wheeled, closed carriage with the driver's seat outside

brought /brôt′/ *pt* & *pp* of **bring**

brou·ha·ha /broo′hä·hä′, broo′hähä′/ [F] *n* hubbub

brow /brou′/ [OE *brū*] *n* **1** forehead; **2** eyebrow; **3** edge of a steep place

brow′beat′ *v* (-**beat**; -**beat·en**) *vt* to intimidate by stern looks or words

brown /broun′/ [OE *brūn*] *adj* **1** of a dark shade of orange, the color of chocolate; **2** tanned ‖ *n* **3** brown color ‖ *vi* **4** to become brown ‖ *vt* **5** to make brown

Brown, John *n* (1800–59) U.S. abolitionist, hanged by the State of Virginia for leading a slave insurrection

Brown′i·an move′ment /-ē·ən/ [Robert

Brown (1773–1858) Eng botanist] *n* irregular motion of small particles suspended in a fluid

brown'ie *n* 1 good-natured helpful elf; 2 flat chocolate cake or cookie; 3 **Brownie** junior Girl Scout

Brown'ing, Elizabeth Bar·ret /bar'ıt/ *n* (1806–61) English poet, wife of Robert Browning

Brown'ing, Rob·ert *n* (1812–89) English poet

brown'-nose' *slang n* 1 obsequious flatterer ‖ *vt & vi* 2 to flatter obsequiously

brown'out' *n* 1 partial blackout, esp. in time of war; 2 reduction of electric power because of plant failure or a storm

brown'stone' *n* 1 brown sandstone used for building; 2 house with a brownstone front

brown' stud'y *n* deep thought

brown' sug'ar *n* unrefined sugar

browse /brouz'/ [16th-cent. Eng] *vi* 1 to graze; 2 to examine a book idly; to glance leisurely through art work or goods on display

bru·cine /brōō'sēn, -sın/ [< *J. Bruce* (1730–1794) Sc explorer in Africa] *n* white crystalline, poisonous alkaloid—$C_{23}H_{26}N_2O_4$—obtained from the seeds of nux vomica

bru·in /brōō'ın/ [D, name of the bear in *Reynard the Fox*] *n* bear

bruise /brōōz'/ [OE *brўsan* to crush] *vt* 1 to injure by a blow that does not cut the skin, leaving a bluish mark ‖ *vi* 2 to become bruised ‖ *n* 3 injury to the skin caused by bruising

bruis'er *n* strong tough man

bruit /brōōt'/ [MF = noise] *vt* to report, spread abroad

brunch /brunch'/ [breakfast + lunch] *n* 1 combination breakfast and lunch ‖ *vi* 2 to have brunch

bru·net' /brōōnet'/ [F] *n* person, esp. a male, with dark skin, hair, and eyes ‖ also *adj* ‖ **bru·nette'** *nfem & adj*

brunt /brunt'/ [ME] *n* main part of a shock, strain, or attack

brush /brush'/ [ME *brusshe*] *n* 1 implement made of bristles, hair, etc., fixed in a back or handle and used for cleaning, smoothing, painting, etc.; 2 act of using a brush; 3 light touch in passing; 4 brief encounter; 5 bushy tail, as of a fox; 6 brushwood; 7 thinly settled country; 8 part, usu. of carbon or copper, used to keep the rotor of a motor or generator in contact with the external circuit ‖ *vt* 9 to use a brush on, as for cleaning, smoothing, or painting; 10 to remove with a brush; 11 to touch lightly in passing; 12 **brush aside** to disregard; 13 **brush off** *slang* to rebuff ‖ *vi* 14 to move with haste; 15 to skim over with a light touch; 16 **brush up** to refresh one's memory; 17 **brush up on** to review (a subject)

brush'-off' *n slang* rebuff

brush'-up' *n* act of brushing up

brush'wood' *n* 1 thicket; 2 cut branches, as for firewood

brusque /brusk'/ [MF < It *brusco* sour] *adj* blunt, abrupt, curt ‖ **brusque'ly** *adv* ‖ SYN bluff, abrupt, curt, short, rude, offhand

Brus·sels /brus'əlz/ *n* capital of Belgium (1,075,000)

Brus'sels sprout' *n* 1 cabbagelike plant *Brassica oleracea gemmifera;* 2 **Brussels sprouts** *pl* small edible buds of this plant

bru·tal /brōōt'əl/ *adj* savage; cruel ‖ SYN barbarous, unfeeling, coarse, sensual, cruel

bru·tal·i·ty /brōōtal'ıtē/ *n* (-ties) 1 pitiless cruelty; 2 brutal act

bru'tal·ize' *vt* 1 to make brutal; 2 to treat brutally

brute /brōōt'/ [F *brut* rude < L *brutus* dull] *n* 1 beast, animal; 2 crude, insensitive, or cruel person ‖ *adj* 3 beastlike; 4 irrational, stupid; 5 cruel; 6 sensual ‖ SYN *n* creature, animal, beast ‖ DISCR An *animal* is a being with the power of sense perception and of voluntary motion, as distinguished from an inanimate object or a vegetal organism. A *brute* is an animal other than man; *brutes* are not gifted with reason or fine sensibility. A *beast* is one of the lower animals, commonly a quadruped. Man is properly classed as an *animal*, when regarded as an order of beings. Man additionally, classed as an *animal*, *brute*, or *beast*, is seriously reproached; as an *animal*, he fails to use that guiding reason and spiritual insight that should distinguish him above all living creatures; as a *brute*, he inclines overmuch to force, and is dull to that which is fine and noble; as a *beast*, he indulges appetites to excess, and is sottish, sensual, and often filthy

brut'ish *adj* 1 pert, to or like a brute; 2 savage; coarse; stupid ‖ SYN base, sensual, bestial, gross, irrational

B.S. Bachelor of Science

b.s., B/S bill of sale

B.T.U., BTU, B.t.u., Btu British thermal unit(s)

bu. bushel(s)

bub·ble /bub'əl/ [ME *bobel*] *n* 1 spherical film of liquid encasing a gas; 2 globule of air or gas inside a liquid or solid; 3 anything unreal or fanciful; delusion; 4 inflated speculation ‖ *vi* 5 to give forth bubbles; boil; 6 to make a gurgling sound ‖ **bub'bly** *adj*

bub'bler *n* device for a drinking fountain that shoots a stream of water into the mouth

bu·bo /byōō'bō/ [< Gk *boubon* groin] *n* (-boes) swelling of a lymphatic gland, esp. in the groin

bu·bon·ic plague /byōōbon′ik/ *n* fatal epidemic disease characterized by buboes

buc·ca·neer /buk′ənir′/ [F *boucanier*] *n* pirate

Bu·chan·an, James /byōōkan′ən/ *n* (1791–1868) 15th president of the U.S. 1857–61

Bu·cha·rest /b(y)ōōk′ərest′/ *n* capital of Rumania (1,250,000)

buck¹ /buk′/ [OE *bucca* he-goat] *n* 1 male of various animals, as the deer or rabbit; 2 dandy, young blade; 3 bucking of a horse; 4 *slang* dollar; 5 **pass the buck** *colloq* to shift responsibility to someone else || *vi* 6 to make a vertical leap in the air, as a horse; 7 *colloq* to resist obstinately; 8 **buck for** *slang* to work hard for (a promotion or raise); 9 **buck up** *colloq* to feel encouraged || *vt* 10 to butt; 11 to oppose; 12 **buck up** *colloq* to encourage, cheer up

buck² [ME *bouken*] *n* 1 mixture of soapsuds and lye || *vt* 2 to wash or soak in suds or lye

buck·et /buk′it/ [< OE *būc* pitcher] *n* 1 vessel suspended from a curved handle for holding or carrying water, sand, etc.; 2 bucketful; 3 anything like a bucket in form or function; 4 **drop in the bucket** infinitesimal amount; 5 **kick the bucket** *slang* to die

buck′et seat′ *n* low individual seat in a vehicle, with a rounded back

Buck′ing·ham Pal′ace /buk′iŋəm, -ham/ *n* London residence of the British sovereign

buck·le /buk′əl/ [ME *bocle*] *n* 1 metal clasp for fastening a belt or strap; 2 bulge, bend, or kink || *vt* 3 to close or fasten with a buckle; 4 to bend or warp || *vi* 5 to be closed or fastened with a buckle; 6 to bend, warp, collapse; 7 **buckle down** to apply oneself; 8 **buckle under** to yield, give in

buck·ler /buk′lər/ [MF *bocler*] *n* small round shield worn on the left arm

buck·ram /buk′rəm/ [OF *boquerant*] *n* coarse cloth of linen, cotton, or hemp, stiffened with glue

buck′saw′ *n* saw set in an upright frame and worked with both hands

buck′shot′ *n* large lead shot for shotguns

buck′skin′ *n* 1 soft grayish-yellow leather made from the skin of a deer or sheep; 2 **buckskins** *pl* clothes made of buckskin

buck′tooth′ *n* (-teeth) *n* projecting upper front tooth || **buck′toothed′** *adj*

buck′wheat′ [<obs *buck* beech] *n* dark flour made from the seeds of the buckwheat plant (*Fagopyrum esculentum*)

bu·col·ic /byōōkol′ik/ [< Gk *boukolos* herdsman] *adj* pastoral, rustic

bud /bud′/ [ME *budde*] 1 tip of a root,

stem, or branch which may develop into either root, stem leaves, or flowers; 2 **in the bud** at an immature stage; 3 **nip in the bud** to stop (something) at its inception || *v* (**bud·ded**; **bud·ding**) *vi* 4 to put forth buds; 5 to begin to develop || SYN *v* germinate, sprout, propagate

Bu·da·pest /bōōd′əpest′/ *n* capital of Hungary (1,944,000)

Bud·dha /bōōd′ə, bōōd′ə/ [Skt = awakened] *n* Gautama Siddhartha (d. ab. 480 B.C.), founder of Buddhism

Bud′dhism *n* a religion of India and Eastern Asia, which teaches self-denial, virtue, wisdom, and the attainment of a state of illumination through obedience and the denial of earthly passions || **Bud′dhist** *n* & *adj*

bud·dy /bud′ē/ [perh baby talk for *brother*] *n* (-dies) comrade, chum

budge /buj′/ [MF *bouger* to stir] *vt* & *vi* to move slightly, begin to move

budg·er·i·gar /buj′ərēgär′/ [< native Australian] *n* Australian pet parakeet (*Melopsittacus undulatus*) with green plumage

budg·et /buj′it/ [MF *bougette* small bag] *n* 1 estimate of probable income and expenses for a coming period; 2 money set aside for planned expenses || *vt* 3 to schedule the allotment of (money, time, etc.)

Bue·nos Ai·res /bwān′əs ir′iz/ *n* capital of Argentina (3,600,000)

buff /buf′/ [MF *buffle* buffalo] *n* 1 thick, light-yellow leather; 2 faded yellowish color; 3 stick or wheel covered with buff; 4 *colloq* bare skin; 5 *colloq* enthusiast or authority in some field or activity || *vt* 6 to polish with a buff or something like a buff

buf·fa·lo /buf′əlō′/ [It *bufalo*] *n* (-loes or -los) 1 any of various large Old World mammals of the ox family; 2 bison || *vt* *slang* 3 to intimidate; 4 to baffle; mystify

Buf·fa·lo *n* city in W New York on Lake Erie (535,000)

buf′fer¹ *n* device for buffing

buf′fer² [<obs *buff* to strike] *n* any device that serves to absorb shock, as of a collision

buf′fer state′ *n* small nation between two larger rival nations

buf·fet¹ /buf′it/ [OF, *dim.* of *buffe* blow] *n* 1 blow, esp. with the hand or fist || *vt* 2 to strike, slap, or hit against

buf·fet² /bəfā′/ [F] *n* 1 sideboard; 2 counter for refreshments; 3 meal laid out on a table from which guests serve themselves

buf·foon /bəfōōn′/ [MF *bouffon* < It *buffone*] *n* vulgar jester, clown || **buf·foon′er·y** *n* (-ies)

bug /bug′/ [ME *bugge* beetle] *n* 1 any of an order (Hemiptera) of insects which suck the blood of animals or the juice of plants; **2** any insect; **3** *colloq* germ or virus; **4** unforeseen defect in a new product; **5** *slang* hidden microphone; **6** *slang* enthusiast, fan; **7** *slang* obsession, craze || *v* (**bugged; bug·ging**) *vt* **8** *slang* to install a hidden listening device in; **9** *colloq* to pester

bug·a·boo /bug'əbōō'/ [?] *n* **1** imaginary terror; **2** source of concern or worry

bug'bear' [<*obs* bug goblin] *n* **1** bugaboo; **2** any object of dislike or dread

bug'-eyed' *adj slang* excited and with eyes bulging from surprise

bug·ger /bug'ər, bŏŏg'-/ [ME *bougre* < ML *Bulgarus* heretic] *slang n* **1** sodomite; **2** contemptible person; **3** fellow; lad || *vt* **4** to practice sodomy with; **5 bugger up** to botch || *vi* **6** to practice sodomy

bug·gy¹ /bug'ē/ [?] *n* (**-gies**) **1** light one-horse carriage for two persons; **2** small hand-pushed carriage for babies

bug'gy² *adj* (**-gi·er; -gi·est**) **1** infested with bugs; **2** *slang* crazy

bug'house' *slang n* (**-hous·es** /-ziz/) **1** insane asylum || *adj* **2** crazy

bu·gle /byōōg'əl/ [OF < young bull] *n* wind instrument similar to the trumpet, usu. without valves || **bu'gler** *n*

build /bild/ [OE *byldan*] *v* (**built**) *vt* **1** to make by putting together separate parts or materials; **2** to construct, erect, as a house; **3** to form, fashion, create; **4** to form slowly and establish, as an organization, business, or reputation; **5** to base, as hopes or plans; **6 build up, a** to increase, strengthen; **b** to urbanize; **c** *colloq* to build (someone's) reputation by publicity || *vt* **7** to construct buildings, bridges, etc.; **8 build on** or **upon** to depend or rely on || *n* **9** manner or style of construction; **10** figure, form || **build'er** *n*

build'ing *n* **1** act or business of erecting houses and other structures; **2** structure; anything erected with walls and a roof || SYN edifice, structure || DISCR *Building* is a term of wide range, covering anything with walls and a roof from a log cabin or a garage to a stately residence or an imposing cathedral. *Edifice* and *structure* suggest large, important, or magnificent *buildings*

build'ing and loan' as·so·ci·a'tion *n* society organized to enable its members to invest money to aid them with loans, usually for buying or improving real estate

build'ing trades' *npl* trades, such as carpentry, bricklaying, plastering, plumbing, etc., that are concerned with the construction of buildings

build'-up' *n* **1** strengthening, increase; **2** *colloq* favorable publicity

built /bilt/ *pt* & *pp* of **build**

built'-in' *adj* **1** forming an integral or permanent part of a structure; not detachable; **2** characteristic

built'-up' *adj* **1** enlarged by the addition of material; **2** urbanized

Bu·jum·bu·ra /bōō'jŏŏmbŏŏr'ə/ *n* capital of Burundi (71,000)

bulb /bulb/ [< Gk *bolbos* onion] *n* **1** underground bud formed by the overlapping of thick, fleshy leaves; **2** leaf bud which separates and becomes a new plant; **3** anything shaped like a bulb, as an incandescent lamp || **bulb'ous** *adj*

Bul·gar·i·a /bulger'ē·ə, bŏŏl-/ *n* republic in SE Europe in the Balkan peninsula (8,257,000; 42,823 sq.m.; cap. Sofia) || **Bul·gar'i·an** *n* & *adj* || **Bul'gar'** /-gär'/ *n*

bulge /bulj/ [OF < L *bulga* leather bag] *n* **1** rounded protuberance; a swelling outwards; **2 get the bulge on** *colloq* to gain an advantage over || *vt* & *vi* **3** to bend outward || **bulg'y** *adj*

bulk /bulk/ [ON *bûlki* cargo] *n* **1** magnitude in all directions; **2** main mass or body; **3** greater part or number; **4** food which when digested forms a bulky mass in the intestines, aiding in bowel movement; **5 in bulk** unpackaged || *vi* **6** to increase in volume; grow larger; **7** to loom up || **bulk'y** *adj* (**-i·er; -i·est**) || SYN *n* largeness, mass, magnitude, volume

bulk'head' *n* **1** strong wall or partition in a ship, dividing it into watertight compartments; **2** partition in a tunnel built to withstand the pressure of water, air, or earth; **3** face of a sea wall

bulk' mail' *n* printed matter mailed in quantity at less than first-class rates

bull¹ /bŏŏl/ [OE *bula*] *n* **1** male of any animal of the ox family; **2** male of various other large animals, as elephant, seal, etc.; **3** stock-market trader who expects stock prices to rise; **4** *slang* policeman; **5 take the bull by the horns** to face up to the situation || *adj* **6** characteristic of or favoring rising stock-market prices || *vt* **7** to shove, force; **8** to try to raise prices in (the stock market)

bull² [ML *bulla* seal] *n* formal papal document

bull³ [?] *n* **1** absurd blunder in language; **2** *slang* exaggerated nonsensical talk; **3 shoot** or **throw the bull** *slang* to boast or exaggerate wildly || *vt* **4** *slang* to fool by insincere talk

bull'dog' *n* **1** powerful medium-sized dog, short-haired and large-headed, with protruding lower jaw, remarkable for courage and tenacity of grip || *v* (**-dogged; -dog·ging**) *vt* **2** to throw (a steer) by twisting its head by the horns

bull'doze' [perh = to give a *dose* of the *bull*whip] *vt* **1** to bully or threaten into obedience or compliance; **2** to clear or grade with a bulldozer

bull′doz′er *n* tractor with a horizontal scraper used for grading and road building

bul·let /bŏŏl*ĭt*/ [MF *boulette* dim. of *boule* ball] *n* shaped piece of metal that is fitted in a cartridge and shot from a firearm

bul·le·tin /bŏŏl′ĭtĭn/ [F < It *bulletino*] *n* **1** brief account of the latest news; **2** periodic journal, as of an organization

bull′fight′ *n* in Spain and parts of Latin America, stylized slaughter of a bull in which the bull is baited and then dispatched with a sword in prescribed fashion ‖ **bull′fight′er** *n* ‖ **bull′fight′ing** *n*

bull′finch′ *n* any of several finches, esp. a handsome British songbird (*Pyrrhula pyrrhula*)

bull′frog′ *n* large frog (genus *Rana*) of North America remarkable for its loud bellowing croak

bull′head′ed *adj* excessively stubborn

bull′horn′ *n* electrically amplified megaphone

bul·lion /bŏŏl′yən/ [AF = mint] *n* **1** uncoined gold or silver, usu. in the shape of bars; **2** fringe of gold or silver thread, used for decorating uniforms

bull′ish *adj* **1** obstinate; stupid; **2** a characterized by rising prices; **b** expecting a rise in prices

bull·ock /bŏŏl′ək/ [OE *bulluc*] *n* castrated bull

bull′pen′ *n* **1** corral for bulls; **2** enclosure for prisoners; **3** *baseball* place where relief pitchers warm up

bull′ring′ *n* arena in which bullfights are held

bull′ ses′sion *n* *slang* informal group discussion

bull′s-eye′ *n* **1** center spot of a target; **2** shot that hits it; **3** round piece of thick glass in a floor or sidewalk to admit light

bull′whip′ *n* rawhide whip with short handle

bul·ly /bŏŏl′ē/ [< D *boel* lover] *n* (-lies) **1** one who intimidates others by threats ‖ *v* (-lied) *vt* **2** to act the bully toward ‖ *adj* **3** *colloq* excellent ‖ *interj* **4** *colloq* fine!, excellent!

bul′ly·boy′ *n* roughneck

bul·rush /bŏŏl′rush′/ [ME *bulrysche*] *n* any of various rushes growing along the banks of marshes or at the edges of ponds

bul·wark /bŏŏl′wərk/ [MD *bolwerk*] *n* **1** barrier or wall constructed for defense; rampart; **2** any person or thing that can be relied on in time of need or danger

bum /bum′/ [ME *bom* anus] *v* (**bummed; bum·ming**) *vi* **1** *colloq* to spend the time idly; live by sponging on others ‖ *vt* **2** *colloq* to cadge ‖ *n*

colloq **3** tramp; **4** dissolute, shiftless person; **5** *Brit slang* buttocks; **6** on **the bum** *slang* **a** broken down, not functioning; **b** living the life of a hobo ‖ *adj slang* **7** of poor quality; **8** false

bum′ble-bee′ /bum′bəl-/ [< ME *bumblen* to hum] *n* any of various species of large, hairy, social bees (genus *Bombus*)

bump /bump′/ [imit] *n* **1** shock from a blow; **2** collision; **3** swelling due to a knock or blow; **4** protuberance, as *a bump in the road;* **5** dance movement in which the pelvis is jerked forward ‖ *vt* **6** to bring violently together; **7** to strike against or collide with; **8 bump off** *slang* to murder ‖ *vi* **9** to collide or strike together; **10 bump into** *colloq* to meet by chance

bump′er *n* **1** one who or that which bumps; **2** horizontal metal bar at either end of a motor vehicle to absorb the shock of collisions ‖ *adj* **3** unusually large (crop)

bump′er stick′er *n* label stuck on the bumper of an automobile to show that the right or privilege of parking at a given place has been paid for or granted, to promote a candidate for election, to show the names of places visited, and for various other purposes

bump′kin /-kĭn/ [perh MD *boomekijn* cask] *n* clumsy rustic, yokel

bump′tious /-shəs/ [*bump* + *fractious*] *adj* self-assertive; forward

bump′y *adj* (-i·er; -i·est) **1** uneven (road); **2** rough (air); **3** (ride) full of jolts

bun /bun′/ [ME *bunne*] *n* **1** slightly sweetened roll; **2** hair worn in a roll on the head or neck

bunch /bunch′/ [ME *bunche*] *n* **1** cluster of things of the same kind grouped or fastened together; **2** *colloq* group of people ‖ *vt & vi* **3** to gather into a bunch

bun·co or **bun·ko** /buŋk′ō/ [perh < It *banco* bank] *n* swindle ‖ also *vt*

Bun·des·rat /bŏŏn′dəsrät′/ [G] *n* upper house of the legislature of West Germany

Bun·des·tag /bŏŏn′dəstäg′/ [G] *n* lower house of the legislature of West Germany

bun·dle /bun′dəl/ [ME *bundel* < MD] *n* **1** number of things bound together; **2** package; **3** group; collection; **4** *slang* a lot of money ‖ *vt* **5** to make into a bundle; **6 bundle off** to hustle off ‖ *vi* **7 bundle up** to dress warmly ‖ SYN *n* bunch, parcel, package, packet, pack ‖ DISCR *A bundle* is a group of things, as of clothes or odds and ends, loosely fastened together or rolled in a covering. A *bunch* is a cluster of flowers, grapes, etc., growing together, or a collection of like things fastened together, as a *bunch* of carrots. A *package* is something compactly wrapped for transportation or storing. A *parcel* is either a small *package* or a fairly large *bundle*

bung /buŋ′/ *n* stopper of a cask or barrel

bun·ga·low /buŋ′gəlō′/ [Port *bangalô* < Bengali *banglā* of Bengal] *n* one-story house or cottage

bung′hole′ *n* hole for filling or tapping a cask or barrel

bun·gle /buŋ′gəl/ [?] *vt* 1 to botch || *vi* 2 to work clumsily || *n* 3 clumsy performance; botch || **bun′gler** *n* || **bun′gling** *adj*

bun·ion /bun′yən/ [perh < It *bugnone* swelling] *n* swelling at a joint, usu. the first joint of the great toe

bunk[1] /buŋk′/ [prob < *bunker*] *n* 1 built-in shelflike bed, as on a ship || *vi* 2 to sleep in a bunk; 3 *colloq* to go to bed

bunk[2] [< *bunkum*] *n slang* nonsense, humbug

bunk′er [?] *n* 1 large bin or compartment; 2 *golf* sand trap or mound; 3 strongly built underground fortification || *vt* 4 to put (coal or oil) into a ship's bunker || also *vi*

bun·kum or **bun·combe** /buŋk′əm/ [*Buncombe* county, N.C.] *n colloq* bunk[3]

bun·ny /bun′ē/ [< Eng *dial.* *bun* squirrel] *n* (**-nies**) *colloq* rabbit

Bun′sen burn′er /buns′ən/ [R. W. *Bunsen* (1811–99) G chemist] *n* gas burner for laboratory use which produces an intense colorless or bluish flame

bunt /bunt′/ [ME *bunten*] *baseball vt* 1 to bat (the ball) lightly so that it lands close to home plate || *vi* 2 to bunt the ball || *n* 3 act or instance of bunting

bun′ting [?] *n* 1 loosely woven fabric used for flags; 2 flags; 3 festive decorations made of bunting, as streamers, esp. in the colors of the flag; 4 hooded baby's garment

buoy /boi′, bo͞o′ē/ [ME *boye*] *n* 1 anchored float used as a navigational guide; 2 life preserver || *vt* 3 to mark with buoys; 4 **buoy up**, a to keep afloat; b to encourage, hearten

buoy·an·cy /boi′ənsē, bo͞o′yənsē/ *n* 1 property of floating or rising in a liquid; 2 upward pressure exerted by a fluid on a body immersed in it; 3 gaiety of spirits || **buoy′ant** *adj*

bur[1] /bur′/ [ME *burre*] *n* 1 rough prickly seedcase of certain plants; 2 bur-bearing plant; 3 something that clings like a bur

bur[2] *n* var of **burr**

bur·den[1] /burd′ən/ [OE *byrthen*] *n* 1 something borne or carried; load; 2 load upon mind or spirit; 3 capacity

of a ship || *vt* 4 to load; 5 to oppress || **syn** *n* weight, load, impediment (see *encumbrance*)

bur·den[3] [MF *bourdon* humming] *n* 1 chorus or refrain; 2 something often repeated; 3 topic, gist

bur′den·some *adj* 1 hard to bear; onerous; 2 troublesome || **syn** cumbersome, onerous, heavy, weighty, troublesome, distressing

bur·dock /bur′dok/ [bur[1] + dock[4]] *n* plant of the genus *Arctium*, esp. *A. lappa*, with a burlike fruit and purplish flowers

bu·reau /byo͝or′ō/ [F = office, desk] *n* 1 chest of drawers for clothing, etc.; 2 government department; 3 office for special purposes, as *news bureau*, *travel bureau*

bu·reau·cra·cy /byo͝orok′rəsē/ *n* (**-cies**) 1 government by administrators and petty officials, following an unbending routine; 2 government officials collectively || **bu·reau·crat** /byo͝or′əkrat′/ *n* || **bu′reau·crat′ic** *adj*

burg /burg′/ [OE] *n colloq* town or city

bur·geon /bur′jən/ [OF *burjon* bud] *vi* to grow suddenly

burg·er /burg′ər/ [*hamburger*] *n colloq* a hamburger

bur·gess /bur′jis/ [OF *burgeis* citizen] *n* 1 *Eng* citizen of a borough; 2 *Pa* mayor of a borough; 3 *Conn* councilman; 4 *Md & Va* member of the lower house in the colonial legislature

burgh /burg′; Sc bur′ə/ [OE *burg*, *burh*] *n* in Scotland, corporate town, borough

burgh′er *n* citizen of a borough or town

bur·glar /burg′lər/ [AF *burgler*] *n* one who breaks into a building at night to commit a theft || **bur′glar·ize′** *vt* || **bur′gla·ry** *n* (**-ries**)

bur′go·mas′ter /burg′ə-/ [D *burgemeester*] *n* mayor of a town in Holland, Flanders, Austria, or Germany

Bur·gun·dy /burg′əndē/ *n* (**-dies**) 1 region in E France, formerly an independent duchy; 2 a wine made in this region; b wine of the same type made elsewhere || **Bur·gun′di·an** /-gun′-/ *adj & n*

bur·i·al /ber′ē·əl/ [see **bury**] *n* act of burying; funeral

burl /burl′/ [OF *bourle* knot of thread] *n* 1 small knot in thread or cloth; 2 a large knot on a tree trunk; b veneer made from such a knot

bur·lap /bur′lap/ [< earlier *borelap*] *n* coarse fabric made from jute or hemp

bur·lesque /bərlesk′/ [F < It *burlesco* ludicrous] *n* 1 ludicrous parody; 2 stage show featuring low comedy and female nudity || *vt* 3 to make ridiculous by caricatured representation ||

also *adj* ‖ SYN *n* travesty, extravaganza (see *parody*)

bur·ly /bur'lē/ [OE *būrlīc* handsome] *adj* (-li·er; -li·est) bulky, large; muscular of body

Bur·ma /bur'mə/ *n* republic in SE Asia adjoining India (25,246,000; 261,790 sq.m.; cap. Rangoon) ‖ **Bur·mese** /bərmēz', -mēs'/ *adj* & *n* (-mese)

burn /burn'/ [OE *byrnan vi* & *baernan vt*] *v* (**burned** or **burnt**) *vt* 1 to cause to undergo combustion; to reduce to ashes; 2 to destroy or injure by fire; 3 to inflame or tan (the skin); 4 to affect with a burning feeling; 5 to expose to fire or heat, as in manufacturing; 6 *chem* to combine with oxygen; 7 to use as fuel; 8 to overcook; 9 **burn down** to burn to the ground; 10 **burn oneself out** to use up all one's physical and mental powers; 11 **burn out, a** to cause to stop functioning; **b** to deprive of the use of a building because of destruction by fire; 12 **burn up, a** to consume by fire; **b** to make angry ‖ *vi* 13 to undergo combustion; oxidize; 14 to be on fire; 15 to suffer from or be injured by fire or heat; 16 to glow; 17 to give off heat; 18 to be inflamed by passion; 19 to feel heat; 20 to be overcooked; 21 *slang* to die in the electric chair; 22 **burn out** to stop functioning; 23 **burn up** to become very angry ‖ *n* 24 injury or other effect caused by fire; 25 firing or baking, as in making porcelain; 26 firing of the rocket of a spacecraft ‖ SYN *v* blaze, brand, consume, cremate, scorch, singe, char, incinerate ‖ DISCR *Burn* is the general word; the others are modes of burning. To *burn* is to change, injure, or utterly destroy by fire. To *blaze* is to *burn* with a bright flame; to *brand* is to *burn* with a hot iron, as marks on the hide of cattle. To *consume* is to *burn* up; anything *consumed* is destroyed, gone; to *consume* is often a gradual, thorough process. To *cremate* is to *burn* a dead body in extremely hot fire. *Scorch* and *singe* alike indicate surface burning; but to *scorch* is more serious than to *singe*; goods *scorched* are not only discolored by the heat but injured in texture. To *singe* is to burn slightly on the edge or surface

burn'er *n* the part of a lamp or gas fixture that emits the flame

bur·nish /bur'nish/ [OF *brunir* (-niss-)] *vt* 1 to polish by rubbing; 2 to make smooth and lustrous ‖ *n* 3 polish, brightness ‖ SYN *n* polish, luster, shine, glossiness

bur·noose /bərnōōs', bur'-/ [Ar *burnus*] *n* cloak and hood of wool combined in one piece, as worn by Arabs and Moors

Burns, Robert /burnz'/ *n* (1759–96) Scottish poet

burnt /burnt'/ 1 *pt* & *pp* of **burn** ‖ *adj* 2 (color) of a deeper shade

burnt' of·fer·ing *n* sacrifice burned upon an altar as an act of worship

burp /burp'/ [imit] *colloq n* 1 belch ‖ *vt* 2 to make (a baby) burp by patting its back ‖ *vi* 3 to belch

burr /bur'/ [?] *n* 1 rough edge left by a tool in cutting or drilling; 2 knob or growth on a tree; 3 dentist's drill; 4 whining noise; 5 guttural or trilled pronunciation of *r*; 6 Scotch accent

bur·ro /bur'ō, bŏŏr'ō/ [Sp] *n* donkey

bur·row /bur'ō/ [ME *borow*] *n* 1 hole in the ground dug by an animal; 2 any similar shelter ‖ *vi* 3 to dig a hole in or under something; 4 to live or hide as in a burrow ‖ *vt* 5 to make burrows in; 6 to build by burrowing

bur·sa /burs'ə/ [LL < Gk = leather pouch] *n* (**-sas** or **-sae** /-sē/) *anat* small sac or cavity, esp. between joints

bur·sar /burs'ər, burs'är/ [< *bursa*] *n* college treasurer

bur·si·tis /bərsīt'is/ *n* inflammation of a bursa

burst /burst'/ [OE *berstan*] *v* (**burst**) *vi* 1 to fly to pieces, explode; 2 to break suddenly into action, speech, or feeling, as *to burst into tears*; 3 to appear or enter suddenly ‖ *vt* 4 to cause to burst ‖ *n* 5 violent or sudden breaking forth, as *a burst of applause*; 6 explosion; 7 rush, spurt ‖ SYN *v* crack, destroy, split, shiver, shatter (see *break*)

Bu·run·di /bərun'dē, bŏŏrōōn'dē/ *n* kingdom in central Africa (3,210,090; 10,747 sq.m.; cap. Bujumbura)

bur·y /ber'ē/ [OE *byrgan*] *v* (**-ied**) *vt* 1 to place (a corpse) in a grave, tomb, or the sea, usu. with ceremony; 2 to cover, conceal; 3 to plunge in deeply, as a knife; 4 to cause to be forgotten, as a grievance; 5 to engross (oneself); 6 **bury the hatchet** to call off a feud, make peace ‖ SYN inter, entomb, conceal, hide, cover

bus /bus'/ [*omnibus*] *n* (**bus·ses** or **bus·es**) 1 large public motor coach carrying passengers usu. along a scheduled route; 2 *slang* automobile ‖ *v* (**bussed** or **bused**; **bus·sing** or **bus·ing**) *vt* 3 to convey by bus; 4 to clear (the dishes) from a table ‖ *vi* 5 to travel by bus; 6 to work as a busboy

bus'boy' *n* waiter's assistant who clears tables, fills water glasses, etc. ‖ **bus' girl'** *nfem*

bus·by /buz'bē/ [?] *n* (**-bies**) tall fur hat worn by certain regiments and by British guardsmen

bush /bŏŏsh'/ [ME] *n* 1 thickly branched low-growing plant, shrub; 2 anything resembling a bush; 3 uncleared land covered with trees and bushes; 4 *Australian* arid, uncleared, sparsely inhabited back country; 5

beat around the bush to fail to come to the point || **bush'y** *adj* (**-i•er; -i•est**)

bushed' *adj colloq* exhausted

bush•el /bōōsh'əl/ [MF *boissiel*] *n* 1 unit of dry measure containing 4 pecks or 32 quarts; 2 container holding this amount

bush'ing [< MD *busse* box] *n* 1 replaceable metal sleeve for reducing friction or decreasing the diameter; 2 insulated lining of a hole

bush' league' *n baseball* a second-rate minor league || **bush' lea'guer** *n*

bush'-league' *adj colloq* inferior, amateurish

bush'man /-mən/ *n* (**-men** /-mən/) 1 bush dweller; 2 **Bushman** one of a short nomadic people of southern Africa

bush'mas'ter *n* large venomous snake (*Lachesis mutus*) of tropical America

bush'whack' *vi* 1 to fight as a guerrilla or irregular soldier || *vt* 2 to ambush || **bush'whack'er** *n*

bus•i•ly /biz'ĭlē/ *adv* in a busy manner

busi•ness /biz'nĭs/ [see busy] *n* 1 occupation, profession, trade; 2 rightful concern; 3 affair, matter; 4 a commercial enterprise; 5 commercial pursuits in general; 6 volume of trade; 7 **mean business** to be in earnest || SYN trade, craft, commerce, profession, occupation, employment, pursuit, calling || DISCR *Business* is an interest, regularly pursued for pecuniary gain or to secure a livelihood. Collectively, *business* names those mercantile interests that require ability in the keeping of accounts, the management of finances, and the carrying on of money transactions. *Commerce* is *business* on a large scale. *Trade* designates the *business* of buying and selling goods, whether on a large or small basis; it may be applied to a much smaller unit than *commerce*. Thus we speak of interstate *commerce*, or world *trade*, but we may also speak of the *trade* of a hamlet. *Trade* in its special sense names a *business* carried on for gain; a *trade* is a *business* dependent on manual dexterity, and is distinguished from farming, *commerce*, the *professions*, the arts, and unskilled labor; a plumber or a carpenter has a *trade*. A *trade* highly specialized, and tending toward the artistic in its application of manual skill, becomes a *craft*; a worker in brass has a *craft*. Collectively, both *trade* and *craft* name all those skilled in a particular kind of work. An *occupation* is that at which one is busy or in which one is absorbed; it may be for any purpose, from a means of making a living to a method of passing the time. A *pursuit* is an *occupation* followed with eager interest. A *profession* requires scholarship and learning; it connotes frequently the

idea and the ideal of serving others, even though, like *business*, its primary aim is the earning of a livelihood. *Employment* has come to have a wide range of meaning; it can refer to one's regular *occupation* or *profession;* more commonly, it refers to work done for pay in the service of another. A *calling* is an *occupation* to which one is attracted by something within himself, as a sense of duty, or a love of the life involved. Loosely, *calling* is applied to any *occupation;* collectively, it names all those engaged in a particular *occupation*

busi'ness•like' *adj* efficient, systematic

busi'ness re•ply' card' *n* self-addressed post card marked with a notice that return postage will be paid by addressee and enclosed in a letter to facilitate an answer to a business proposal

busi'ness re•ply' en've•lope *n* envelope that is addressed and marked like a business reply card and has a similar purpose

busi'ness re•ply' mail' *n* business reply card or envelope

bus'ing or **bus'sing** *n* transportation of children to and from school, sometimes for the purpose of promoting racial integration

bus•kin /busk'ĭn/ [?] *n* 1 high, thick-soled laced shoe worn by ancient tragic actors; 2 tragic drama

buss /bus/ [?] *n* kiss || also *vt & vi*

bust¹ /bust'/ [F *buste* < It *busto*] *n* 1 woman's bosom; 2 sculpture of a person's head and shoulders

bust² [< *burst*] *slang vt* 1 to burst; 2 to ruin financially; 3 to demote; 4 to punch; 5 to arrest || *vi* 6 to burst; 7 to be ruined financially; 8 **bust out** to break out; 9 **bust up** to separate || *n* 10 failure; 11 spree; 12 punch

bus•tle¹ /bus'əl/ [perh < *obs buskle* to prepare] *n* 1 tumult, noisy activity || *vi* 2 to be noisily busy, make a fuss or stir || **bus'tling** *adj* || SYN *n* stir, haste, agitation, ado, fuss, commotion

bus•tle² [?] *n* pad formerly worn by women on the back below the waist to puff out the skirt

bus•y /biz'ē/ [OE *bisig*] *adj* (**-i•er; -i•est**) 1 actively at work; 2 occupied; 3 full of activities; 4 in use, as a telephone line; 5 meddlesome, prying || *v* (**-ied**) *vt* 6 to make or keep busy || SYN *adj* active, diligent, engaged, employed, sedulous, industrious, assiduous, persevering, occupied || DISCR *Busy* means keeping at what one has to do, often in a vigorously active fashion. It also describes one who has much to do, as he is a *busy* man. Sometimes it carries the sense of *occupied*, as the editor is too *busy* to see you. *Industrious* describes one who is habitually and zealously *busy*, usually to some productive end. *Busy* frequently relates to the active calls of everyday life; *industrious* applies to either the physical or the mental field. The *industrious* worker applies himself closely that he may waste no time; the *diligent* worker concentrates through love of his work. *Diligent* describes usually those following mental pursuits, but it is also applied to that whole-hearted adherence to principle made evident in works, whether good or bad, as he is a *diligent* Christian; she is a *diligent* collector of gossip. One *engaged* is *occupied*; he can start nothing new until he finishes what he is about. An *assiduous* person refuses to be exhausted till the end of his task. *Sedulous* also describes a persevering sort of application; a *sedulous* worker is absorbed until his stint is done ‖ ANT *adj* idle, inactive, indolent, lazy, procrastinating

bus'y·bod'y *n* (**-ies**) meddler

bus'y·ness *n* **1** state or quality of being busy; **2** brisk activity that accomplishes nothing

bus'y sig'nal *n* steady series of buzzes that indicates that the line dialed is busy

bus'y·work' *n* work that keeps one occupied but is not productive or useful

but /but′, bət/ [OE *būtan* outside, without] *adv* **1** only ‖ *prep* **2** except ‖ *conj* **3** still; however; yet, as *poor but honest;* **4** on the contrary, as *knowledge goes, but wisdom lingers;* **5** except, as *but for that I could go;* **6** that, as *I do not doubt but this is true;* **7** that not, as *who knows but he will succeed?*

bu·tane /byoo′tān/ [*butyl* + *-ane*] *n* gaseous hydrocarbon —C₄H₁₀— found in petroleum and natural gas, used as a fuel

butch·er /booch′ər/ [OF *bochier*] *n* **1** one who slaughters animals for food; **2** one who dresses or sells meats; **3** brutal murderer ‖ *vt* **4** to slaughter (animals); **5** to murder brutally; **6** to botch, ruin

butch'er·y *n* (**-ies**) **1** business of a butcher; **2** slaughterhouse; **3** horrible, cruel, and wanton murder ‖ SYN slaughter, massacre, bloodshed (see *carnage*)

but·ler /but′lər/ [OF *bouteillier*] *n* chief male servant in a household

butt¹ /but′/ [ME *bott* end] *n* **1** the blunt or thicker end of anything, as of a gun or whip; **2** stub, as of a cigar; **3** *slang* cigarette; **4** *slang* buttocks

butt² [OF *boter* to thrust] *n* **1** push or thrust with the head or horns ‖ *vt* **2** to strike with the lowered head ‖ *vi* **3** to strike objects with the head or horns; **4** to project; **5 butt in** *colloq* to intrude; **6 butt into** to collide with

butt³ [MF *but* goal] *n* **1** embankment back of a target to stop bullets; **2** object of ridicule and wit

butt⁴ [MF *botte*] *n* large cask, as for wine

butte /byoot′/ [F = mound] *n* steep and isolated hill or mountain rising in a plain

but·ter /but′ər/ [OE *butere* < Gk *boutyron*] *n* **1** fatty substance obtained from cream or milk by churning; **2** any of several substances having the consistency of butter ‖ *vt* **3** to spread with butter; **4 butter up** *colloq* to flatter

but'ter·cup' *n* any of several yellow cup-shaped wild flowers (genus *Ranunculus*) growing esp. in meadows

but'ter·fat' *n* natural fat of cow's milk

but'ter·fin'gers *nsg & npl* person who is always dropping things

but'ter·fly' *n* (**-flies**) **1** any of numerous diurnal insects (order Lepidoptera) with four brightly colored wings, a slender body, and knobbed antennae; **2** gay, frivolous idler

but'ter·milk' *n* sour liquid remaining when the butterfat has been removed from milk or cream

but'ter·nut' *n* North American white walnut (*Juglans cinerea*) or its edible fruit

but'ter·scotch' *n* **1** flavoring made with brown sugar and butter; **2** hard, brittle candy made with brown sugar and butter ‖ also *adj*

butt' joint' *n* joint made by uniting two pieces end to end without any part overlapping

but·tock /but′ək/ [OE *buttoc*] *n* either side of the rump of man or animal

but·ton /but′ən/ [MF *boton* bud] *n* **1** any small rounded object used for fastening or as an ornament; **2** anything resembling a button in size and shape; **3** small knob or disk pressed to operate an electric switch; **4** *slang* point of the jaw ‖ *vt* **5** to fasten with buttons

but'ton·hole'¹ *n* stitched hole for a button to pass through

but'ton·hole'² [< earlier *buttonhold*] *vt* to detain as if by grabbing the lapel and engage in conversation

but'ton·wood' *n* any plane tree, esp. the North American species (*Platanus occidentalis*), with rough buttonlike fruit

but·tress /but′ris/ [OF *boterez*] *n* **1** structure built against a wall for support; **2** any prop or support ‖ *vt* **3** to prop, support

butt' weld' *n* weld made as a butt joint ‖ **butt'-weld'** *vt*

bu·tyr'ic ac'id /byootir′ik/ [< Gk *boutyron* butter] *n* oily rancid liquid —C₃H₇COOH— occurring in spoiled butter

bux·om /buks′əm/ [ME *buxsom* pliant]

n robust, comely, plump (woman or girl)

buy /bī′/ [OE *bycgan*] *v* (**bought**) *vt* 1 to obtain by paying money; purchase; 2 to gain at a cost or sacrifice; 3 to bribe; 4 *slang* to accept; 5 **buy off** to appease, bribe ‖ *n* 6 purchase; 7 *colloq* bargain

buy′er *n* 1 purchaser; 2 purchasing agent

buzz /buz′/ [imit] *n* 1 humming noise, as of bees or conversation; 2 rumor; 3 *colloq* phone call ‖ *vi* 4 to make a humming sound; 5 to move busily about ‖ *vt* 6 to spread, as gossip; 7 to cause to give a buzzing sound; 8 to signal with a buzzer; 9 to fly a plane low over

buz·zard /buz′ərd/ [OF *busard*] *n* 1 any of several European hawks, as of the genus *Buteo*; 2 American turkey vulture (family Cathartidae)

buzz′er *n* electric signaling device making a buzzing sound

buzz′ saw′ *n* power-operated circular saw

BX or **BX cable** *n* electric wiring contained within flexible metal tubing

by /bī(′)/ [OE *bī*] *prep* 1 next or near to, as *a chair by the window;* 2 past, as *go by the park;* 3 not later than, as *finish by two o'clock;* 4 through the agency of, as *send word by messenger;* 5 through the action of, as *a poem by Shelley;* 6 because of, as *to succeed by industry;* 7 to the degree of, with a comparative, as *taller by two inches;* 8 with regard to, as *he dealt unfairly by me;* 9 with the witness of, as *swear by the Book;* 10 in the measure of, as *to sell by the pound;* 11 for a fixed time, as *by the month;* 12 in a different dimension, as *one by three feet;* 13 following, as *day by day;* 14 through, as *known by his walk;* 15 according to, as *by the rules;* 16 in or during, as *by night;* 17 by way of, as *go by Albany;* 18 through the medium of, as *by air, by train;* 19 *naut* one point in the direction of, as *north by east;* 20 by the way, **a** incidentally ‖ *adv* 21 near, beside, as *to stand by;* 22 aside, as *put some money by;* 23 past, as *he drove by;* 24 **by and by** after a while; 25 **by and large** speaking generally

by- /bī′-/ [< *by*] *pref* 1 secondary, as *byroad;* 2 near, as *bystander*

by′-blow′ *n* 1 accidental or incidental blow; 2 illegitimate offspring

bye-bye /bī′bī′/ [good-*by*] *interj colloq* good-by!

by′-e·lec′tion *n Brit* special election to fill a vacancy in Parliament

by′gone′ *adj* 1 past, gone by ‖ *n* 2 something in the past

by′law′ [< *by̆r town*] *n* rule adopted by a corporation, association, or the like, to supplement the constitution or other basic law

by′-line′ *n* line above a newspaper story giving the author's name

by′-pass′ *vt* 1 to detour around; 2 to avoid; 3 to ignore, go over the head of ‖ *n* 4 road that bypasses a city; 5 secondary pipe that conducts a fluid or gas parallel to the main pipe; 6 *elec* shunt

by′-path′ *n* (-**paths** /-ths, -thz/) *n* byway

by′play′ *n* action and speech incidental to the main action, as on the stage

by′-prod′uct *n* something produced incidentally while making something else

by′road′ *n* side road

By·ron, George Gordon /bīr′ən/ (Lord Byron) (1788–1824) English poet ‖ **By·ron′ic** /-ron′ic/ *adj*

by′stand′er *n* chance spectator, onlooker

by′way′ *n* private or secluded road or path

by′word′ *n* 1 proverb or saying, often satirical or scornful; 2 one at whom such a saying is directed; 3 nickname; epithet ‖ SYN adage, saw, precept, aphorism (see *truism*)

Byz·an·tine /biz′əntēn′, bizant′in/ [< Gk *Byzantion* anc name of Constantinople] *adj* 1 of or pert. to Byzantium or the Byzantine Empire; 2 designating a style of architecture developed in Byzantium, characterized by large domes, rounded arches, elaborate mosaics, and much color ‖ *n* 3 native or inhabitant of Byzantium

Byz′an·tine Em′pire *n* Eastern Roman Empire (330–1453); cap. Constantinople

By·zan·ti·um /bizan′shē·əm, -tē·əm/ *n* ancient Greek city, which became Constantinople and later Istanbul

C

C, c /sē′/ *n* (**C's** or **Cs, c's** or **cs**) third letter of the English alphabet

C 1 *chem* carbon; 2 Roman numeral 100; 3 *mus* first tone in the scale of C major; 4 grade rating of average; 5 central; 6 something shaped like a C; 7 third in order or in a series; 8 Centigrade

C., c. 1 cent(s); 2 centimeter; 3 century; 4 circa; 5 cubic

Ca *chem* calcium

C.A. Central America

cab /kab/ [*cabriolet*] *n* **1** taxicab; **2** horse-drawn vehicle for public hire; **3** enclosed part of a locomotive, truck, etc., where the operator sits

ca·bal /kəbal′/ [F *cabale* < Heb *qabbalah* traditional lore] *n* **1** small group of secret plotters; **2** secret scheme, intrigue ‖ SYN faction, conspiracy, coalition, gang

ca·ba·na /kəban′(y)ə/ [Sp *cabaña* hut] *n* cabinlike or tentlike beach shelter used as a bathhouse

cab·a·ret /kab′ərā′/ [F] *n* restaurant providing dancing and entertainment

cab·bage /kab′ij/ [OF *caboche*] *n* **1** plant (*Brassica oleracea*) of the mustard family with edible leaves formed into a compact head; **2** *slang* money

cab·by /kab′ē/ *n* (-bies) *colloq* cab-driver

cab·in /kab′in/ [MF *cabane*] *n* **1** small crude house or hut; **2** room on a ship; **3** enclosed space for passengers or the pilot in an airplane

cab′in class′ [euphemism for *second class*] *n* class of accommodations on passenger ships intermediate between first class and tourist class

cab·i·net /kab′init/ [F] *n* **1** piece of furniture with shelves and drawers to hold and display things; **2** piece of furniture containing radio, television, or a record-player; **3** built-in cupboard for dishes, medicine, etc.; **4** a body of advisers, called Secretaries in the government of the United States, appointed by and responsible to the president; **b** executive and policy-making group of ministers appointed by a prime minister and usu. responsible to a parliament ‖ *adj* **5** private; secret; **6** of or pert. to the cabinet of a government

cab′i·net-mak′er *n* maker of fine furniture ‖ **cab′i·net-mak′ing** *n*

ca·ble /kāb′əl/ [ME] *n* **1** large, strong rope or chain; **2** insulated bundle of electric wires; **3** cablegram ‖ *vt* **4** to send a cablegram to ‖ *vi* **5** to send a cablegram

ca′ble car′ *n* streetcar pulled by a moving cable

ca′ble-gram′ *n* message sent by submarine cable

ca′ble tel′e·vi·sion *n* community-antenna television

cab·o·chon /kab′əshon′/ [F] *n* convex, polished, precious stone, not cut in facets ‖ also *adv*

ca·boo·dle /kəbōōd′əl/ [?] *n* **the whole caboodle** *slang* the lot of them

ca·boose /kəbōōs′/ [D *kabuis* cook's cabin] *n* trainmen's car attached to the end of a freight train

cab·ri·o·let /kab′rēəlā′/ [< F *cabriole* goat's leap] *n* light two-wheeled one-horse carriage

ca·ca·o /kəkā′ō, kəkä′ō/ [Sp < Na-huatl] *n* **1** small evergreen tree (*Theobroma cacao*) of tropical America and the West Indies; **2** its seeds, used in making cocoa and chocolate

cache /kash/ [F] *n* **1** hiding place or that which is hidden in it ‖ *vt* **2** to hide away

cack·le /kak′əl/ [ME *cakelen*] *n* **1** cry of a hen; **2** chatter, idle talk ‖ *vi* **3** to utter a cackle

ca·coph·o·ny /kəkof′ənē/ [< Gk *kakos* bad + *phone* voice] *n* (-nies) harsh unpleasant sound; discord ‖ **ca·coph′o·nous** *adj*

cac·tus /kak′təs/ [Gk *kaktos* prickly plant] *n* (-tus·es or -ti /-tī/) any of a family (Cactaceae) of prickly or spiny desert plants, usu. having no true leaves

cad /kad/ [< *caddie*] *n* one whose behavior is not that of a gentleman

ca·dav·er /kədav′ər/ [L] *n* corpse

ca·dav′er·ous *adj* **1** like a corpse; **2** pale, gaunt

cad·die also **cad·dy¹** /kad′ē/ [Sc *cadee* < F *cadet*] *n* (-dies) **1** person who carries the clubs for a golf player ‖ *v* (-died; -dy·ing) *vi* **2** to act as a caddie

cad·dy² [Malay *kati* 1⅓ lb. weight] *n* (-dies) small box for tea

-cade /-kād′, -kād′/ [*cavalcade*] *comb form* procession, as *motorcade*

ca·dence /kād′əns/ [ME < It *cadenza* falling] *n* **1** fall of the voice in speaking; **2** rhythmic flow of sound; **3** uniform time and pace in marching

ca·den·za /kəden′zə/ [It] *n mus* brilliant passage for instrument or voice, usu. just before the close of a movement

ca·det /kədet′/ [F = younger brother] *n* **1** student in a military academy; **2** younger son ‖ **ca·det′ship** *n*

cadge /kaj/ [ME *caggen* to tie] *vt* **1** to get by begging ‖ *vi* **2** to sponge off others ‖ **cadg′er** *n*

cad·mi·um /kad′mē·əm/ [< Gk *kadmeia* Cadmean (earth)] *n* rare bluish-white metallic element [Cd; at.no. 48; at.wt. 112.41) used chiefly in alloys and in pigments

cad′mi·um cell′ *n* primary cell which gives a constant voltage of 1.0186 volts at room temperature and is used as a standard of electromotive force

cad′mi·um lamp′ *n* vapor lamp whose red light is used as a standard measuring unit of wave length

ca·dre /kad′rē/ [< It *quadro* square] *n* **1** framework; **2** nucleus of trained personnel, as in a military unit, which can be readily expanded to full strength

ca·du·ce·us /kəd(y)ōōs′ē·əs/ [L] *n* (-i /-ī′/) winged serpent-twined staff of Mercury, the symbol of the medical profession

cae·cum /sēk′əm/ *n var of* **cecum**

Cae·sar /sēz'ər/ n 1 **Julius** (100–44 B.C.) Roman general and statesman; 2 title of the early Roman emperors, later of their heirs; 3 dictator || **Cae'sar·ism** n

Cae·sar'e·an sec'tion /sizer'ē·ən/ [< *Caesar*, supposedly born thus] n delivery of a child by cutting through the walls of the abdomen and the uterus

cae·si·um /sēz'ē·əm/ n var of **cesium**

cae·su·ra /siz(y)ŏŏr'ə, -zhŏŏr'ə/ [L = cutting] n (-ras; -rae /-rē/) place in a line of verse where the sense permits a slight break or pause

ca·fé /kafā', kə-/ [F = coffee] n 1 restaurant; 2 barroom

ca·fé' au lait' /ō lā'/ [F] n 1 coffee with an equal portion of hot milk; 2 light-tan color

ca·fé so·ci'e·ty n fashionable people who frequent well-publicized night clubs

caf·e·te·ri·a /kaf'itir'ē·ə/ [Sp = coffee shop] n self-service restaurant

caf·feine /kafēn', kaf'ē·in/ [F *caféine*] n bitter, stimulating alkaloid —C₈H₁₀N₄O₂— found in coffee and tea

caf·tan /kaf'tən, käftän'/ [< Russ *kaftan* < Turk *qaftān*] n full-length undercoat with long sleeves and a sash, worn in the Near East

cage /kāj'/ [OF < L *cavea* cage] n 1 enclosure with bars for confining birds or animals; 2 anything that confines, as a prison; 3 any cagelike structure || vt 4 to confine in a cage

cag·ey also **cag·y** /kāj'ē/ [?] adj (cag·i·er; cag·i·est) colloq shrewd; wary || **cag'i·ly** adv || **cag'i·ness** n

ca·hoots /kəhŏŏts'/ [perh F *cahute* cabin] npl in **cahoots** slang in league

Cai·a·phas /kā'əfəs, kī-/ n Jewish high priest presiding at Jesus' trial (Matt. 26:57)

Cain /kān'/ n 1 first son of Adam and Eve, who killed his brother Abel (Gen. 4); 2 **raise Cain** slang to make a big commotion

cairn /kern'/ [Gael *carn*] n heap of stones erected as a monument or landmark

Cai·ro /kī'rō/ n capital of Egypt (4,196,998) || **Cai'rene** /-rēn/ adj & n

cais·son /kās'on, kās'ən/ [F] n 1 ammunition wagon or chest; 2 watertight compartment inside which construction work is carried on under water; 3 floating structure for raising sunken vessels

cais'son dis·ease' n disease caused by too sudden change to normal air pressure from the high pressure of deep underwater work

ca·jole /kəjōl'/ [F *cajoler*] vt & vi to coax, wheedle || **ca·jol'er·y** n (-ies)

Ca·jun /kāj'ən/ [< *Acadian*] n descendant of the French colonists of Acadia; expelled by the British in 1713, most of them settled in Louisiana

cake /kāk'/ [ON *kaka*] n 1 small mass of dough, sweetened and baked; 2 pancake; 3 small shaped fried ball, as a fishcake; 4 any shaped solid, as a cake of ice; 5 **take the cake** colloq to be extraordinary || vt & vi 6 to form into a hard mass

Cal. California

cal·a·bash /kal'əbash'/ [F *calebasse* < Sp *calabaza*] n 1 tree (*Crescentia cujete*) of tropical America, bearing a gourdlike fruit; 2 its fruit; 3 vessel or implement made from its dried shell

cal·a·boose /kal'əbŏŏs'/ [Sp *calabozo*] n slang jail

cal·a·mine /kal'əmīn', -min/ [LL *calamina*] n pink powder consisting mostly of zinc oxide, used chiefly as a skin ointment

ca·lam·i·ty /kəlam'itē/ [MF *calamite* < L *calamitas*] n (-ties) misfortune; disaster; affliction || **ca·lam'i·tous** adj || syn accident, disaster, affliction (see **trouble**)

cal·car·e·ous /kalker'ē·əs/ [L *calcarius*] adj like, or containing, calcium carbonate; chalky

cal·ci·fy /kal'sifī'/ [< *calcium* + -*fy*] v (-fied) vt & vi to harden by the addition of calcium salts

cal'ci·mine' /-mīn', min/ [< L *calx* (*calcis*) lime] n 1 white or tinted wash for walls or ceilings || vt 2 to cover with calcimine

cal'cite /-sīt/ n native calcium carbonate

cal'ci·um /-sē·əm/ n soft lustrous metallic element (Ca; at.no. 20; at.wt. 40.08), widely distributed in nature in combination, as in lime, marble, and chalk

cal'ci·um car'bide n compound of calcium and carbon —CaC₂— which when combined with water gives off acetylene gas

cal'ci·um car'bon·ate n white crystalline powder —CaCO₃— occurring as calcite, limestone, and chalk; used in polishes and in manufacturing

cal'ci·um chlo'ride n deliquescent salt —CaCl₂— used as a dehumidifying agent and to allay dust

cal·cu·late /kal'kyəlāt'/ [L *calculare* (-*atus*) to reckon with pebbles] vt 1 to compute by mathematics; 2 to determine by reasoning; estimate; 3 colloq to suppose; 4 **be calculated to** to be planned or intended to || vi 5 to make a computation; 6 **calculate on** to count on || **cal'cu·la·ble** adj || **cal'cu·la'tion** n || syn compute, number, estimate, rate || discr To *number* is to count an aggregate of things item by item, or one by one. To *calculate*, *estimate*, and *compute* are alike in the idea of arriving at a quantity or result by operations with figures or mathematical symbols according to certain principles. To *calculate* denotes operating in any way with numbers or symbols, but it specifically indicates the higher or more complicated mathematical processes, such as those used by astronomers. To *estimate* is to secure a quantity or sum by a comprehensive judgment of the values involved; since opinion or incomplete data are the bases of an *estimate*, the result is approximate, but it serves its purpose, as the contractor *estimated* the cost of a new Union Station. To *compute* is to make a numerical calculation; also, to reckon separately the items involved; *compute* is used of more accurate and certain operations than *estimate*, though one may also *compute* the probable or approximate. To *rate* is to fix a relative value by comparison, or by reasoning from a known quantity to an unknown, as judging from his expenditures, I would *rate* Mr. H. a rich man

cal·cu·lat·ed risk' *n* risk that is taken with full knowledge of the likelihood of failure

cal·cu·lat·ing *adj* **1** capable of performing calculations; **2** scheming; **3** shrewd

cal·cu·la·tor *n* **1** one who calculates; **2** calculating machine

cal·cu·lus /-ləs/ [L = pebble] *n* (-li /-lī'/ or -lus·es) **1** *math* any of several highly developed methods of treating problems, using a special system of algebraic notation; **2** abnormal stony formation within the body, as in the kidneys or gall bladder

Cal·cut·ta /kalkut'ə/ *n* seaport in NE India (3,000,000)

cal·dron /kôl'drən/ [AF *cauderon*] *n* large kettle or boiler

Cal·e·do·ni·a /kal'idōn'ē·ə/ *n* *poet.* Scotland || **Cal'e·do'ni·an** *adj & n*

cal·en·dar /kal'əndər/ [AF *calender* < L *calendarium* account book] *n* **1** method of reckoning the length and divisions of the year; **2** table showing the days, weeks, and months of the year; **3** schedule or agenda, as of court cases or legislative bills

cal·en·der /kal'əndər/ [MF *calandre* < L *cylindrus* cylinder] *n* **1** series of rollers between which paper or cloth is passed to give it a smooth, hard, and/or glossy finish || *vt* **2** to press in a calender

cal·ends /kal'əndz/ [L *kalendae*] *npl* first day of the month in ancient Rome

calf¹ /kaf', käf'/ [OE *cealf*] *n* (**calves** /-vz/) **1** young cow or bull; **2** young of other large mammals, as the whale or elephant; **3** calfskin

calf² [ON *kalfi*] *n* (**calves** /-vz/) fleshy

hind part of the human leg below the knee

Cal·i·ban /kal'iban'/ *n* savage and brutish slave of Prospero in Shakespeare's *Tempest*

cal·i·ber /kal'ibər/ [MF *calibre* < OIt *calibro*] *n* **1** diameter of the inside of a cylinder or tube; **2** diameter of a bullet or shell; **3** inside diameter of the barrel of a cannon or gun; **4** degree of ability, intellect, or merit

cal'i·brate' *vt* **1** to determine the caliber of (a tube or cylinder); **2** to determine, mark, or correct the graduations of (a measuring instrument) || **cal'i·bra'tion** *n*

cal·i·co /kal'ikō'/ [*Calicut,* India] *n* **1** kind of cotton cloth, usu. printed; **2** *Brit* plain white cotton cloth

Calif. California

Cal·i·for·nia /kal'ifôr'nyə, -nē·ə/ *n* Pacific coast state of the U.S. (19,953,000; 158,693 sq.m.; cap. Sacramento) || **Cal'i·for'nian** *n*

cal·i·for·ni·um /-əm/ *n* synthetic radioactive metallic element (Cf; at.no. 98)

cal·i·pers /kal'ipərz/ [< *caliber*] *npl* instrument with two adjustable legs, used in determining diameters or the like

ca·liph or **ca·lif** /kāl'if, kal'-/ [MF *caliphe* < Ar *khalīfah* successor to Mohammed] *n* temporal and spiritual ruler of a Muslim state || **cal'i·phate'** /-fāt', -fit/ *n*

cal·is·then·ics /kal'isthen'iks/ [< Gk *kalos* beautiful + *sthenos* strength] *npl* **1** light gymnastic exercise; **2** *nsg* art or practice of such exercise || **cal'is·then'ic** (-i·cal) *adj*

calk /kôk'/ *vt* var of **caulk**

call /kôl'/ [prob ON *kalla*] *vt* **1** to utter in a loud voice; **2** to summon or invite; **3** to awaken; **4** to choose for an office; **5** to give a name to; **6** to convoke or convene; **7** to characterize as being; **8** *poker* to compel (an opponent) to show his hand by equaling his bet; **9** to demand payment of, as a loan; **10** to telephone; **11** to cancel or stop, as a baseball game; **12** to direct (attention); **13** to require (bonds) to be turned in for redemption; **14** **call down** to rebuke; **15** **call in, a** to withdraw; **b** to ask as consultants; **16** **call off, a** to take away; **b** to cancel; **17** **call out** to summon into action; **18** **call up** to telephone || *vi* **19** to shout; **20** to telephone someone; **21** to visit; **22** *poker* to equal a bet; **23** to make a characteristic animal sound; **24** **call for, a** to pick up; **b** to demand, require; **25** **call on** or **upon, a** to ask; **b** to pay a visit to; **26** **call out** to shout || *n* **27** cry or shout; **28** summons; **29** impulse to some specific work, as *a call to the ministry;* **30** claim or demand; **31** short visit; **32** cry or note of an animal or bird; **33** *poker* demand for a show of hands; **34** demand for payment; **35** notice to holders to turn in their bonds for redemption; **36** occasion, as *there's no call for violence;* **37** lure, as *the call of the unknown;* **38** act or instance of telephoning; **39** option to buy stocks or commodities for an agreed price within a fixed period; **40 on call** readily available || **call/a-ble** *adj* || **call/er** *n* || SYN *v* convene, convoke, invite, summon; *n* shout, exclamation, invitation, summons, visit || DISCR To *call* is to attract, or try to attract, attention, either by lifting the voice in a name, words, etc., or by an inarticulate sound, as that made by an animal to its young. To *summon* is to *call* with authority, as a witness to give evidence at a trial. To *invite* is courteously to extend to someone your wish that he accompany or join you. The purpose of invitation is ordinarily pleasant, but one may also be *invited* to attend sad or formal ceremonies. To *call* is vocal, but its meaning has been extended to include the action of mechanical means of signaling, as we *call* a messenger by ringing a bell. To *summon* is to *call* by word of mouth or by a written and authoritative document. One may *invite* formally, by writing; or one may *invite* by a glance, a gesture, or a sign. One may *call* to people of any degree, in order to express a request or a demand; an invitation is commonly the expression of courteous good will between equals

cal·la also **cal/la lil'y** /kal'ə/ [L < Gk *kallaia* rooster's wattles] *n* familiar house plant (*Zantedeschia aethiopicum*) of the arum family, native to South Africa, cultivated for its showy white leaf around a yellow flower cluster

call/a·ble *adj* **1** (bond) subject to redemption at a specified price prior to maturity; **2** (money loaned) subject to payment on demand

call/boy' *n* **1** man or boy who calls actors to go on the stage; **2** bellboy

call/ girl' *n* high-priced prostitute who can be summoned by telephone

cal·lig·ra·phy /kəlig'rəfē/ [< Gk *kalos* beautiful + -*graphy*] *n* **1** beautiful handwriting; **2** art of producing it || **cal·lig'ra·pher** *n*

call/ing *n* **1** vocation; **2** summons, invitation || SYN trade, profession, occupation (see *business*)

cal·li·ope /kal'ē·ōp'/ [*Calliope*] *n* mechanical organ in which the notes are produced by steam whistles sounded from a keyboard

Cal·li·o·pe /kəli'əpē/ *n* Gk myth. Muse of epic poetry and eloquence

call/ let'ters *npl* identifying letters of

radio and television broadcasting stations

call/ loan' *n* loan repayable on demand

call/ num'ber *n* number assigned to and imprinted on the back of each book in a library whereby it may be located

cal·lous /kal'əs/ [L *callosus* thick-skinned] *adj* **1** hardened, as skin; **2** unfeeling || **cal/lous·ly** *adv* || **cal/lous·ness** *n* || SYN insensible, hardened, unsusceptible, obdurate

cal·low /kal'ō/ [OE *calu* bald] *adj* immature and inexperienced

cal·lus /kal'əs/ [L = hard skin] *n* thick hard place on the skin

calm /käm'/ [MF *calme* < Gk *kauma* heat] *n* **1** stillness, serenity || *adj* **2** quiet, still; **3** undisturbed, serene || *vt* **4** to make calm || *vi* **5 calm down** to become calm || **calm/ly** *adv* || **calm/ness** *n* || SYN *adj* —composed, cool, collected, placid, serene, dispassionate, self-possessed, tranquil, imperturbable, unruffled, peaceful || DISCR *Calm* describes a state free from noise, tumult, disturbance, or violent emotion. It can be applied to weather, to objects of the physical world, as the sea, to the mind of man, or to his spiritual condition. We speak of a *calm* night, a *calm* sea, of a victim *calm* in spite of his injuries. *Tranquil* suggests a quiet that lies more in the nature of the object or person than *calm;* applied to the physical, it suggests the presence of soothing, reposeful characteristics, as a *tranquil* scene; applied to people, it may describe those quiet merely between periods of agitation, but it is more apt to refer to one naturally unruffled. *Peaceful,* applied to persons, signifies undisturbed. *Serene* describes atmospheric conditions that are clear, bright, and tranquilizing; it describes a spirit that is poised, cheerful, often lofty. Serenity of soul may be an acquired blessing; placidity is an inherent trait. A *placid* mind is *peaceful* because it is content; a *placid* temper is unruffled; a *placid* sheet of water is a naturally still pool or lake. *Cool, composed,* and *collected* are alike in suggesting degrees of control in danger, risk, or trying circumstances. *Cool* suggests controlled alertness; the *cool* man neither underestimates his danger nor loses his power to combat it. *Composed* implies readiness to meet a situation by conquering agitation or excitement. *Collected* describes a person in complete command of all his faculties

cal·o·mel /kal'əməl, -mel'/ [< Gk *kalos* fair + *melas* black] *n* mercurous chloride —Hg$_2$Cl$_2$— used as a purgative and fungicide

ca·lor·ic /kəlôr'ik, -lor'-/ [< L *calor*

heat] *adj* 1 of or pert. to heat; 2 of or pert. to calories

cal·o·rie also **cal·o·ry** /kal'ərē/ [F *calorie* < L *calor* heat] *n* (-ries) 1 amount of heat required to raise one gram of water one degree centigrade, also called *small calorie*; 2 amount of heat required to raise one kilogram of water one degree centigrade, also called *large calorie* (= 1000 small calories or 3.968 BTU); 3 quantity of food capable of producing a large calorie of energy

calque /kalk/ [F] *n* loan translation

cal·u·met /kal'yəmet'/ [F *chalumeau* < L *calamus* reed] *n* long-stemmed tobacco pipe of North American Indians used for ceremonial purposes and as a symbol of peace

ca·lum·ni·ate /kəlum'nē·āt'/ *vt & vi* to slander ‖ **ca·lum'ni·a'tion** *n* ‖ SYN defame, slander, malign, detract, asperse ‖ DISCR To *calumniate* is to invent and circulate lies about another. To *slander* is to repeat and help to spread whatever lies or evil reports are already in circulation, especially behind the back of the person concerned. To *defame* is publicly to speak or write serious accusations against the character and reputation of another. To *asperse* is to cast reflections upon another's goodness or good name by insinuating things to his discredit. To *detract* is to speak so slightingly of another's virtues as to take away from them. To *malign* is to speak evil of, deliberately, falsely, and in a spirit of venomous rancor

cal·um·ny /kal'əmnē/ [L *calumnia*] *n* (-nies) false and malicious statement; slander

Cal·va·ry /kal'vərē/ [L *calvaria* skull; translation of Heb *Golgotha* place of the skull] *n* place where Jesus was crucified (Matt. 27:33)

calve /kav/, käv/ [see *calf*] *vi* 1 to give birth to a calf; 2 to throw off icebergs (said of glaciers)

calves /kavz/, kävz/ *pl* of **calf**

Cal·vin, John /kal'vin/ *n* (1509–64) French-Swiss theologian and reformer ‖ **Cal'vin·ism** *n* ‖ **Cal'vin·ist** *n* ‖ **Cal'vin·is'tic** *adj*

ca·lyp·so /kəlip'sō/ [< Afr *kai isu* go on!] *n* lively topical ballad and dance of the West Indies, often improvised

Ca·lyp·so *n Gk myth.* sea nymph who detained Ulysses on her island

ca·lyx /kā'liks, kal'iks/ [Gk = husk] *n* (-lyx·es, cal·y·ces /kal'isēz'/) circle of leaflike parts or sepals, below the petals of a flower

cam /kam/ [D or LG *kam* comb] *n mach* device for changing circular motion into straight-line or back-and-forth motion, as a disk rotating eccentrically on an axis

ca·ma·ra·de·rie /kam'ərad'ərē, käm'əräd'-/ [F] *n* comradeship, good fellowship

cam·ber /kam'bər/ [MF *cambre* bent] *n* 1 slight convexity of a surface ‖ *vt & vi* 2 to arch slightly in the center

cam·bi·um /kam'bē·əm/ [LL = exchange] *n* (-bi·ums, -bi·a /-bē·ə/) layer of growing tissue which lies between the sapwood and the bark of trees, and produces the layers of new wood and new bark

Cam·bo·di·a /kambōd'ē·ə/ *n* country in Indochina (5,728,771; 69,898 sq.m.; cap. Phnom Penh) ‖ **Cam·bo'di·an** *adj & n*

Cam·bri·a /kam'brē·ə/ [LL < Welsh *cymry* Welshmen] *n poet.* Wales

Cam'bri·an *adj* 1 of or pert. to Wales; 2 designating or pert. to strata of the earliest period of the Paleozoic era ‖ *n* 3 Welshman

cam·bric /kām'brik/ [*Kameryk*, Flem name of Cambrai, France] *n* fine linen or cotton fabric, usu. white

Cam·bridge /kām'brij/ *n* 1 city in E England (96,000), seat of Cambridge University; 2 city in Massachusetts (108,000) adjoining Boston, seat of Harvard University

came /kām/ *pt* of **come**

cam·el /kam'əl/ [Gk *kamelos* < Sem] *n* large ruminant (genus *Camelus*) with either one or two humps, domesticated for use in the deserts of Africa and Asia because of its ability to store water in its body

ca·mel·lia or **ca·me·lia** /kəmēl'yə/ [G J. *Kamel* (1661–1706) Jesuit missionary] *n* Asiatic evergreen shrub (*Camellia japonica*) cultivated for its double red and white flowers

Cam·e·lot /kam'əlot'/ *n* legendary site in SW England of King Arthur's palace and court

Cam'em·bert' (cheese') /kam'əmber'/ [*Camembert*, France] *n* soft cheese with a creamy center

cam·e·o /kam'ē·ō'/ [It] *n* gem or medallion on which small raised figures are carved

cam·er·a[1] /kam'(ə)rə/ [L = room] *n* **in camera** 1 privately; 2 in a judge's private chambers

cam·er·a[2] [< L *camera obscura* dark room] *n* 1 photographic apparatus, as a light-proof box, by means of which images can be admitted through the opening of a shutter and focused through a lens on light-sensitive film; 2 device that converts optical images into electrical impulses for transmission by television

Cam·e·roon /kam'ərōōn'/ *n* republic in W Africa (5,350,000; 183,570 sq. m.; cap. Yaoundé)

cam·i·sole /kam'isōl/ [F] *n* woman's fancy underwaist

cam·o·mile /kam'əmīl'/ [L *chamo-*

milla/ *n* any of a genus (*Anthemis*) of herbs, esp. *A. nobilis,* a strongly scented perennial used in medicine

cam·ou·flage /kam′əfläzh′/ [F < It *ca·muffare* to disguise] *n* **1** disguising of military works to deceive the enemy; **2** any disguise or deception ‖ *vt* **3** to conceal or hide by changing appearances ‖ *vi* **4** to practice camouflage

camp /kamp′/ [MF < L *campus* field] *n* **1** ground occupied by an army or other body of persons, with tents or huts put up for shelter; **2** tent or hut, or group of such structures, used by hunters, motorists, or vacationists; **3** persons in an encampment; **4** military life; **5** group favoring a particular cause; **6 break camp** to dismantle a camp ‖ *vi* **7** to set up a camp; **8** to live in a camp; **9** to settle oneself temporarily; **10 camp out** to go camping ‖ **camp′er** *n*

cam·paign /kampān′/ [F *campagne* country] *n* **1** military operations in a connected series for one special objective; **2** any similar series of operations, as *a political campaign* ‖ *vi* **3** to take part in a campaign ‖ **campaign′er** *n*

cam·pa·ni·le /kamp′ənēl′ē/ [It < *campana* bell] *n* (-les or -li /-lē/) bell tower

camp′ fol′low·er *n* **1** civilian who follows troops on a campaign, esp. a prostitute; **2** sympathizer or partisan

cam·phor /kam′fər/ [AF *caumfre* < LL *camphora* < Ar] *n* whitish translucent gum —$C_{10}H_{16}O$— with pungent odor, obtained chiefly from the camphor tree of E Asia; used in medicine and in making film, celluloid, plastics, lacquers, etc. ‖ **cam′phor·at′ed** *adj*

cam·pus /kamp′əs/ [L = field] *n* **1** grounds of a school or college; **2** college or university

cam′shaft′ *n* shaft of an engine that is fitted with one or more cams

can[1] /kan′, kən/ [< OE *cann, pres ind* of *cunnan* to know how] *v* (**could**) *modal aux* **1** am, are, or is able to; **2** know or knows how to; **3** have or has the right to; **4** have or has permission to ‖ SYN (see *may*)

can[2] /kan′/ [OE *canne*] *n* **1** hermetically sealed metal vessel, usu. cylindrical, for holding and preserving liquids and foods; **2** receptacle or container, as *ash can;* **3** *slang* toilet; **4** *slang* jail ‖ *v* (**canned; can·ning**) *vt* **5** to preserve by sealing in a jar or can; **6** *slang* to dismiss; **7** *slang* to stop

Can. **1** Canada; **2** Canadian

Ca·naan /kān′ən/ *n Bib* the *Promised Land,* promised by God to Abraham (Gen. 12:5–10); Palestine

Ca′naan·ite′ *n* one of an ancient Se-

mitic race dwelling in Palestine before its conquest by the Israelites

Can·a·da /kan′ədə/ *n* English- and French-speaking nation adjoining the U.S. on the north (20,441,000; 3,851,809 sq.m.; cap. Ottawa); member of the British Commonwealth of Nations ‖ **Ca·na·di·an** /kənā′dē·ən/ *adj & n*

ca·nal /kənal′/ [L *canalis* channel] *n* **1** artificial waterway for navigation or irrigation; **2** *anat* tube or passage

Ca·nal′ Zone′ *n* ten-mile-wide strip of land at the Isthmus of Panama containing the Panama Canal; leased by Panama to the U.S. (40,000; 553 sq.m.)

can·a·pé /kan′əpē′, -pā′/ [E] *n* appetizer consisting of bread or toast spread with anchovies, cheese, or the like

ca·nard /kənärd′/ [F = duck; hoax] *n* sensational rumor circulated as a hoax

ca·nar·y /kənər′ē/ [*Canary* Islands] *n* (-ies) **1** small yellow songbird (*Serinus canarius*); **2** light yellow color

Ca·nar′y Is′lands *npl* group of islands off NW Africa, constituting two provinces of Spain (920,000; 2850 sq.m.)

ca·nas·ta /kənas′tə/ [Sp = basket] *n* cards game of rummy played with two decks

Can·ber·ra /kan′bərə/ *n* capital of Australia (95,913)

can·can /kan′kan′/ [F] *n* rollicking dance characterized by high kicking

can·cel /kan′səl/ [ML *cancellare* to cross out] *v* (-celed or -celled; -celing or -cel·ling) *vt* **1** to revoke, make void; **2** to invalidate; **3** to balance, neutralize ‖ **can′cel·la′tion** *n* ‖ SYN annul, repeal, revoke, abolish, abrogate, nullify, obliterate, expunge, efface, annihilate ‖ DISCR The idea common to all these words is that of setting aside a law, obligation, custom, decision, etc., that has been in force. To *annul* is to make invalid or not binding; a marriage contract made by minors without the consent of their parents may be *annulled.* To *cancel* is a kind of *annulling;* deeds, bonds, agreements, private obligations, such as debt, are literally struck out when they are *canceled.* To *abolish* is to bring to a complete end either by direct action, as the legislature *abolished* child labor; or gradually and indirectly, as is necessary in the case of a custom or convention. To *abrogate, repeal, revoke,* and *nullify* apply especially to the setting aside of laws. To *abrogate* is to make void by act of a legislative body; a later law, by conflicting with it, may *abrogate* an earlier one. To *repeal* is to unmake a law; a law can be *repealed* only by the body that enacted it. To *revoke* is to take back a power or privilege once extended; a sovereign, or other individual in power, *revokes*. To *nullify* may be to deprive of force by inaction, or by a specific neutralizing act (see *erase*)

can·cer /kan′sər/ [L = crab] *n* **1** malignant tumor; **2 Cancer a** a northern zodiacal constellation, the Crab; **b** fourth sign of the zodiac; **c** tropic of Cancer ‖ **can′cer·ous** *adj*

can·de·la·brum /kan′dəlāb′rəm, -läb′-/ [L] *n* (**-bra** /-brə/; **-brums**) also **can′·de·la′bra** large branched candlestick

can·did /kan′did/ [L *candidus* white] *adj* **1** honest; frank; **2** unprejudiced; **3** unposed (photograph) ‖ **can′did·ly** *adv* ‖ **can′did·ness** *n* ‖ SYN artless, truthful, unreserved, blunt ‖ ANT crafty, close-mouthed, disingenuous, evasive, sham

can·di·date /kan′didāt′, -dit/ [L *candidatus* white-robed] *n* one who seeks or is proposed for an office, position, honor, or academic degree ‖ **can′di·da·cy** /-dəsē/ *n* (**-cies**)

can′did cam′er·a *n* camera with a fast lens for taking unposed pictures of unsuspecting people

can·died /kan′dēd/ *adj* **1** preserved with, or covered with, a coating of sugar; **2** cooked in sugar

can·dle /kan′dəl/ [OE *candel* < L *candela*] *n* **1** cylinder of tallow or wax surrounding a wick which gives light when burned; **2** unit of luminous intensity equal to ¹⁄₆₀ of the luminous intensity per sq. cm. of a black body operating at the temperature of solidification of platinum ‖ *vt* **3** to test (eggs) by holding to the light

can′dle·pow′er *n* intensity of light measured in candles

can′dle·stick′ *n* device with a cup or spike for holding a candle

can·dor /kan′dər/ [L = whiteness] *n* **1** frankness; **2** fairness ‖ SYN frankness, openness, ingenuousness, sincerity, impartiality, fairness, simplicity, unreserve ‖ DISCR These words are alike in that they are forms of outspokenness in speech. *Candor* is based upon the speaker's intention to be fair and truthful; it is impartial, without self-interest, and unreserved. *Candor* is usually appreciated; *frankness* frequently is not. *Frankness* consists in saying what one thinks; it is often the fruit of a warm-hearted impulse, and is not seldom a courageous form of truthtelling; but it is as apt to offend as to please. *Openness* is even freer in making disclosures than *frankness*; *frankness*, while free, may have reserves; *openness* reserves nothing; hence it is often indiscreet, if not actually offensive. *Ingenuousness* is a naïve disclosure of the whole matter involved, whether it be for or against the speaker so to declare himself; *ingenuousness* is artless, and appealingly without guile or pretense. *Sincerity* is the quality of meaning exactly what one says, whatever that may be; *sincerity* is convincing, and is more often valued than resented ‖ ANT reticence, reserve, hypocrisy

can·dy /kan′dē/ [MF *sucre candi* < Pers *qand* sugar cane] *n* (**-dies**) **1** confection of sugar, syrup, etc., often combined with other ingredients, as chocolate, nuts, or fruits ‖ *v* (**-died**) *vt* **2** to cook in syrup; **3** to encrust with crystallized sugar ‖ *vi* **4** to crystallize

cane /kān′/ [OF < L *canna*] *n* **1** long hollow jointed stem of certain palms and other plants; **2** plant with such a stem; **3** split rattan; **4** walking stick; **5** sugar cane ‖ *vt* **6** to beat with a cane; **7** to furnish or make with cane

cane′brake′ *n* thicket of canes

ca·nine /kā′nīn/ [< L *canis* dog] *adj* **1** pert. to the dog family; **2** doglike; **3** pert. to a canine tooth ‖ *n* **4** dog; **5** canine tooth

ca′nine tooth′ *n* one of the four sharp-pointed teeth between the incisors and the bicuspids

Ca·nis Ma′jor /kā′nis/ [L = larger dog] *n* southern constellation, containing the Dog Star, Sirius

Ca·nis Mi′nor [L = smaller dog] *n* small southern constellation, containing the bright star Procyon

can·is·ter /kan′istər/ [L *canistrum* wicker basket] *n* box usu. of metal for tea, coffee, etc.

can·ker /kaŋk′ər/ [OF *cancre* < L *cancer*] *n* **1** gangrenous ulcer, particularly in the mouth; **2** anything that corrupts or destroys ‖ **can′ker·ous** *adj*

canned /kand′/ *adj* **1** preserved in cans or jars; **2** *slang* recorded (music)

can′ner·y *n* (**-ies**) place where foods are canned

can·ni·bal /kan′ibəl/ [var of *caribal* Carib] **1** human being who eats human flesh; **2** animal that eats its own kind ‖ **can′ni·bal·ism** *n* ‖ **can′ni·bal·is′tic** *adj*

can′ni·bal·ize′ *vt* to take parts from (a wrecked or nonfunctioning mechanism) to repair another of the same kind

can·non /kan′ən/ [MF *canon* great tube] *n* (**-nons** or collectively **cannon**) mounted piece of artillery

can′non·ade′ *n* **1** continuous discharge of artillery ‖ *vt & vi* **2** to attack with artillery

can′non·ball′ *n* **1** round projectile discharged by cannon; **2** anything that moves with great speed

can′non fod′der *n* the men of a nation used up as soldiers in war

can·not /kan′ot, kanot′, kənot′/ can not

can·ny /kan'ē/ [< *can*[1]] *adj* (**-ni·er**; **-ni·est**) shrewd; cautious

ca·noe /kənōō'/ [F < Sp *canoa* < Arawak] *n* 1 light boat having a sharp prow at each end, propelled by paddles || *vi* 2 to paddle or sail in a canoe || **ca·noe'ist** *n*

can·on[1] /kan'ən/ [OE < Gk *kanon* rule] *n* 1 generally accepted law or rule; criterion; 2 *eccl* authoritative rule of discipline or doctrine; 3 authoritative books of the Bible; 4 *mus* round

can·on[2] [< OE *canonic* one under rule] *n* clergyman attached to a cathedral

ca·ñon /kan'yən/ *n* canyon

ca·non·i·cal /kənon'ikəl/ *adj* 1 pert. to, comprising, or conforming to, a law or rule, esp. an authoritative rule of the church; 2 accepted as a rule; 3 pert. to the books of the Bible accepted as authoritative || **ca·non'i·cals** *npl* 4 vestments prescribed to be worn by a clergyman officiating at services

can·on·ic'i·ty /-nis'itē/ *n* 1 genuineness; 2 right to inclusion in the Holy Scriptures

can'on·ize' *vt* 1 to pronounce (a deceased person) a saint; 2 to glorify || **can'on·i·za'tion** *n*

Ca·no·pus /kənōp'əs/ *n* second-brightest star in the heavens, in the constellation Carina

can·o·py /kan'əpē/ [ML *canopeum* < Gk *konopeton* mosquito net] *n* (**-pies**) 1 drapery or other covering suspended over a throne, bed, or seat as a shelter or mark of distinction; 2 any overhanging covering || *v* (**-pied**) *vt* 3 to cover, as with a canopy

cant[1] /kant'/ [L *cantus* song] *n* 1 thieves' slang; 2 jargon peculiar to a given trade, profession, or group; 3 pious but insincere talk || *vi* 4 to use cant || SYN *n* jargon, lingo, argot, affectation, hypocrisy

cant[2] [ME] *n* 1 sloping position; 2 beveled edge; 3 outside angle; 4 sudden movement resulting in a change of course or position || *vt & vi* 5 to tilt, slant

can't /kant', känt'/ cannot

Can·ta·brig·i·an /kant'əbrij'ē·ən/ [< ML *Cantabrigia* Cambridge] *adj* of or pert. to Cambridge (England or Mass.), Cambridge University, or Harvard University || also *n*

can·ta·loupe /kant'əlōp'/ [*Cantalupo*, Italy] *n* muskmelon (*Cucumis melo cantalupensis*) with a hard rind and sweet flesh

can·tan·ker·ous /kantaŋk'ərəs/ [perh < ME *contak* contention] *adj* ill-tempered, contentious || **can·tan'ker·ous·ly** *adv* || **can·tan'ker·ous·ness** *n*

can·ta·ta /kəntät'ə/ [It] *n* choral composition embodying a story but not acted

can·teen /kantēn'/ [F *cantine* < It *cantina* cellar] *n* 1 flask for carrying water; 2 shop in barracks or camp where personal necessities and refreshments are sold

can·ter /kant'ər/ [< *Canter*bury gallop] *n* 1 easy gallop || *vi & vt* 2 to ride at a canter

Can·ter·bur·y /kant'ərber'ē, -bərē, -brē/ *n* city and archdiocese in SE England, seat of the Anglican primate (33,500)

can·ti·cle /kant'ikəl/ [L *canticulum* dim. of *canticum* song] *n* 1 song; 2 passage of the Bible arranged for chanting in church services

can·ti·le·ver /kant'ilēv'ər, -lev'-/ [prob < *cant*[2] + *lever*] *n* 1 projecting beam or truss firmly secured at one end only; 2 structure projecting well beyond its support, used esp. in bridges

can·tle /kant'əl/ [ME *cantel*, dim. of LL *cantus* corner] *n* 1 part, segment, corner; 2 hind part of a saddle, usu. raised upward

can·to /kant'ō/ [It = song] *n* division of a long poem

can·ton /kan'ton, kanton'/ [MF = corner] *n* one of the states of Switzerland

Can·ton /kan'ton, kanton'/ *n* seaport in SE China (1,900,000) || **Can·ton·ese** /kan'tənēz', -nēs'/ *adj & n* (**-ese**)

can·ton·ment /kantōn'mənt, -ton'-/ *n* 1 large camp for troops in training; 2 place assigned to troops for quarters

can·tor /kant'ər/ [L = singer] *n* 1 principal singer in a church; 2 singer of liturgical solos in a synagogue

can·vas /kan'vəs/ [OF *canevas* < L *cannabis* hemp] *n* 1 coarse heavy cloth of hemp, flax, or cotton, used for tents, sails, etc., and as a surface for oil paintings; 2 article made of this cloth; 3 painting in oils; 4 **under canvas**, a with sails set; b in tents

can'vas·back' *n* North American wild duck (*Aythya valisineria*)

can·vass /kan'vəs/ [*obs canvas* to toss in a sheet of canvas] *vt* 1 to examine, discuss thoroughly; 2 to traverse (a district) for the purpose of securing votes, opinions, orders, etc. || *vi* 3 to solicit || *n* 4 close inspection or examination; 5 solicitation or survey || **can'vass·er** *n*

can·yon /kan'yən/ [Sp *cañón* long tube] *n* narrow gorge with steep sides

cap /kap/ [OE *cæppe* < LL *cappa* hooded cape] *n* 1 close-fitting head covering, brimless, with or without a visor; 2 anything resembling a cap in use, as a cover or top part; 3 percussion cap; 4 bit of explosive embedded in paper, used as a noisemaker in toy pistols || *v* (**capped**; **cap·ping**) *vt* 5 to cover with a cap; 6 to complete; 7 to match or surpass

cap. [L *capitulum*] 1 chapter; 2 capital

ca·pa·bil·i·ty /kāp'əbil'itē/ *n* (**-ties**)

1 quality of being capable; **2** mental power; mental attainment ‖ SYN power, faculty, capacity, competency (see *ability*)

ca·pa·ble /kāp′əbəl/ [LL *capabilis*] *adj* **1** having power, skill, or ability; **2** capable of, a having ability for; b susceptible of ‖ **ca·pa·bly** *adv* ‖ SYN able efficient, competent, skillful, gifted, susceptible ‖ ANT unfitted, incompetent, inefficient

ca·pa·cious /kəpāsh′əs/ [< L *capax* (-*acis*)] *adj* roomy; able to hold much ‖ **ca·pa′cious·ness** *n*

ca·pac·i·tance /kəpas′itəns/ [see ca·pacity] *n* **1** capacity or power to receive an electric charge; **2** ratio of the charge on one of the two surfaces of a capacitor to the potential difference between the surfaces

ca·pac′i·tate′ *vt* to enable, make fit

ca·pac′i·tor *n* device for accumulating and holding a charge of electricity; condenser

ca·pac·i·ty [L *capacitas*] *n* (-ties) **1** power of receiving or containing; **2** cubic content; amount that can be contained; **3** ability; **4** function, position; **5** measure of electric output in ampere-hours ‖ SYN power, faculty, talent, skill (see *ability*)

cap′ and gown′ *n* mortarboard and gown worn by graduates on receiving their degrees and by the faculty of a college or university in academic processions

ca·par·i·son /kəpar′isən/ [MF *caparaçon*] *n* **1** ornamental covering for a horse; **2** rich clothing ‖ *vt* **3** to cover with a caparison; **4** to adorn with rich dress

cape¹ /kāp′/ [ME, prob < Sp *capa*] *n* sleeveless outer garment fastened at the neck

cape² [MF *cap*] *n* piece of land projecting into a body of water

Cape′ Ca·nav′er·al /kənav′ərəl/ *n* cape on an island off the E coast of Florida, site of the U.S. missile test center

Cape′ Ken′ne·dy *n* name given formerly for a number of years to Cape Canaveral

ca·per¹ /kāp′ər/ [prob < *capriole* leap] *n* **1** playful leap; **2** prank; **3** *slang* robbery, burglary; **4** cut a caper or capers to play foolish tricks ‖ *vi* **5** to skip about playfully; frolic

ca·per² [ME *caperes* < Gk *kapparis*] *n* Mediterranean shrub (*Capparis spinosa*) the flower buds of which are pickled and used as a seasoning

Cape′ Town′ *n* legislative capital of South Africa (508,341)

cap·il·lar·i·ty /kap′ilar′itē/ [< L *capillus* hair] *n* surface tension which causes a liquid to rise or fall when it comes in contact with a solid

cap·il·lar·y /kap′ilər′ē/ *adj* **1** pert. to a hair or to a very thin tube; **2** pert. to capillarity ‖ *n* (-ies) **3** also capil-

lary tube very thin tube; **4** one of the minute blood vessels that connect the arteries with the veins

cap·i·tal¹ /kap′itəl/ [< L *caput* head] *adj* **1** chief, principal; **2** excellent, first-rate ‖ *n* **3** seat of government of a nation, state, or province; **4** capital letter; **5** wealth in money or property used in business; **6** accumulation of such wealth; **7** capitalists collectively ‖ **cap′i·tal·ly** *adv* ‖ SYN leading, cardinal, important, vital

cap′i·tal² [< L *capitellum* little head] *n* ornamental top of a column or pillar

cap′i·tal·ism *n* economic system based on private ownership of property and the conduct of business for private profit

cap′i·tal·ist *n* **1** person of large wealth that is available for promoting business enterprises; **2** believer in capitalism

cap′i·tal·ize′ *vt* **1** to convert into capital; **2** to supply capital for; **3** to write with capital letters ‖ *vi* **4** capitalize on to turn to account ‖ **cap′i·tal·i·za′tion** *n*

cap′i·tal let′ter *n* letter larger than, and mostly of different shape than, the corresponding small letter

cap′i·tal pun′ish·ment *n* death penalty

cap′i·tal struc′ture *n* the total holdings and obligations of a business in all their ramifications

cap·i·tol /kap′itəl/ [L *capitolium* < *caput* head] *n* **1** building in which the legislature of a state or of certain countries meets; **2** Capitol building in Washington in which the U.S. Congress meets

Cap′i·tol Hill′ *n* **1** hill in Washington, D.C. on which the Capitol stands; **2** U.S. Congress

ca·pit·u·late /kəpich′əlāt′/ [LL *capitulare* (-*atus*) to arrange under heads] *vi* to surrender to an enemy on terms agreed upon ‖ **ca·pit′u·la′tion** *n*

ca·pon /kāp′on, kāp′ən/ [OE *capun* < L *capo* (-*onis*)] *n* castrated rooster fattened for the table

ca·price /kəprēs′/ [F < It *capriccio*] *n* **1** sudden impulsive change of mind; whim; **2** tendency to sudden unreasoning change of purpose ‖ **ca·pri′cious** /-prish′əs/ *adj*

Cap·ri·corn /kap′rikôrn′/ [< L *caper* goat + *cornu* horn] *n* **1** a southern zodiacal constellation, the Goat; **2** tenth sign of the zodiac; **3** tropic of Capricorn

cap·si·cum /kap′sikəm/ [< L *capsa* box] *n* **1** any of a genus (*Capsicum*) of tropical plants of the nightshade family; **2** dried and powdered fruit of these plants, including cayenne and other peppers

cap·size /kap′sīz, kapsīz′/ [?] *vt & vi* to overturn, as a boat

cap·stan /kap′stən/ [ME] *n* upright drum for raising weights, as the anchor of a ship, by means of a rope or cable

cap'stone' *n* top stone of a structure

cap·sule /kap'səl/ [L *capsula* small box] *n* 1 small container of gelatin for holding a dose of oral medicine; 2 cap or seal to close the top of a bottle; 3 small sealed cabin for flight above the atmosphere

Capt. Captain

cap·tain /kap'tən/ [MF *capitaine* < L *caput* head] *n* 1 one in authority over others; 2 *sports* head of a team; 3 *army* commander of a company; 4 *navy* officer commanding a battleship (equal in rank to army colonel); 5 *naut* master of a ship || *vt* 6 to act as captain of, lead || **cap'tain·cy** *n* (-cies)

cap·tion /kap'shən/ [L *captio* (-*onis*) seizure] *n* 1 heading or title, as of an article or chapter; 2 legend of an illustration; 3 subtitle shown on a motion-picture screen || *vt* 4 to provide a caption for

cap'tious *adj* 1 fault-finding, hypercritical; 2 deceptive, tricky, insidious || **cap'tious·ly** *adv* || SYN petulant, caviling, carping, peevish, fretful

cap·ti·vate /kap'tivāt'/ [L *captivare* (-*atus*) to take prisoner] *vt* to charm, fascinate || **cap'ti·vat'ing** *adj* || SYN enchant, bewitch, charm || ANT estrange, repel

cap·tive /kap'tiv/ [ME < L *captivus*] *n* 1 prisoner || *adj* 2 made or held prisoner || **cap·tiv'i·ty** /-tiv'-/ *n* (-ties)

cap'tive au'di·ence *n* group of people who find themselves in a situation where they cannot escape a harangue, a broadcast, or the like in which they have no interest

cap'tor /-tər/ [L] *n* one who captures

cap·ture /-chər/ [MF < L *captura*] *vt* 1 to take or seize; 2 to make captive || *n* 3 act of capturing; 4 thing captured || SYN *v* arrest, apprehend, gain, seize, catch

car /kär/ [AF *carre* < LL *carra* wagon] *n* 1 vehicle running on tracks; 2 automobile; 3 passenger compartment of an elevator

Ca·ra·cas /kərak'əs/ *n* capital of Venezuela (1,764,274)

car·a·cul /kar'əkəl/ [*Kara Kul*, lake in USSR] *n* black fleece of young lambs of a certain central Asian breed

ca·rafe /kəraf', -räf'/ [F < It *caraffa* < Ar] *n* glass water bottle

car·a·mel /kar'əməl, -mel'/ [F < LL *caramellus* small reed] *n* 1 burnt sugar used for coloring or flavoring; 2 chewy caramel-colored candy

car·a·pace /kar'əpās'/ [F < Sp *carapacho*] *n* upper shell, as of a turtle or lobster

car·at /kar'ət/ [ML *carratus* < Ar *qirāt* weight of four grains] *n* 1 unit of weight for gems (= three grains); 2 karat

car·a·van /kar'əvan'/ [It *caravana* < Pers *kārwān*] *n* 1 group traveling together for safety, esp. across the desert; 2 any large group of persons or vehicles traveling together; 3 *Brit* house trailer

car·a·van·sa·ry /-sərē/ [Pers *kārwān* caravan + *sarāi* inn] *n* (-ries) 1 *Near East* inn for caravans; 2 large hotel

car·a·way /kar'əwā'/ [ME < Ar *karawyā*] *n* 1 plant (*Carum carvi*) bearing spicy seedlike fruits used for flavoring; 2 the seedlike fruits

carb- or **carbo-** [*carbon*] *comb form* carbon

car·bide /kär'bīd/ [< *carbon*] *n* 1 compound of carbon with a metal; 2 calcium carbide

car·bine /kär'bīn, -bēn/ [MF *carabine*] *n* short rifle

car'bo·hy'drate /kär'bō-, -bə-/ *n* compound, as sugar or starch, of carbon with hydrogen and oxygen

car·bol'ic ac'id /kärbol'ik/ [*carbon* + L *oleum* oil] *n* poisonous acid —C₆H₅OH— obtained from coal tar and used as a disinfectant and antiseptic

car·bon /kär'bən/ [F *carbone* < L *carbo* (-*onis*) charcoal] *n* 1 nonmetallic element (**C**; at.no. 6; at.wt. 12.011) occurring in nature as the diamond and as graphite, and found in combination in all organic compounds; 2 carbon copy; 3 carbon paper; 4 *elec* **a** one of two rods of hard carbon used as the terminals for the arc in an arc light; **b** rod or plate of carbon used as positive element of a battery

car'bon·ate' *n* 1 salt or ester of carbonic acid || *vt* 2 to charge with carbon dioxide || **car'bon·a'tion** *n*

car'bon cop'y *n* 1 copy of something written or typed made with carbon paper; 2 exact duplicate of something or someone

car'bon di·ox'ide *n* colorless, odorless, incombustible gas —CO₂— present in the atmosphere and exhaled from the lungs; used extensively in industry, in fire extinguishers, and in carbonated beverages

car'bon di·sul'fide *n* colorless, odorless, flammable liquid —CS₂— used to manufacture cellophane and viscose rayon and as a solvent for fats, resins, and rubber

car'bon 14 /kär'bən fôrtēn'/ *n* radioactive isotope of carbon with mass number 14, used as a tracer and in dating organic archeological materials

car·bon'ic ac'id /-bon'ik/ *n* acid —H₂CO₃— formed when carbon dioxide is dissolved in water

car'bon mon·ox'ide *n* colorless, odor-

less, poisonous combustible gas
—CO— produced by the incomplete
combustion of carbon and notably
present in auto exhaust

car′bon pa′per *n* paper coated on one side as with carbon, used between sheets of paper to reproduce what is written or typed on the top sheet

car′bon tet′ra·chlo′ride′ /tet′rə-/ *n* colorless, pungent, vaporous, toxic, nonflammable liquid —CCl₄— used in fire extinguishers and as a cleaning fluid and solvent

Car·bo·run·dum /kär′bərun′dəm/ [trademark] *n* hard abrasive made of carbon and silicon

car·boy /kär′boi/ [Pers *qarābah* flagon] *n* large glass bottle, usu. protected by basketwork, used esp, for acids

car·bun·cle /kär′bunkəl/ [MF < L *carbunculus* small coal] *n* 1 deep-red garnet cut without facets; 2 inflammation of the skin and deeper tissues, exuding pus

car·bu·re·tor /kär′bərāt′ər/ [< *obs carburet* carbide] *n* device for vaporizing gasoline and mixing it with air so as to produce an explosive mixture in the cylinders of an internal-combustion engine || **car′bu·re′tion** /-rāsh′-/ *n*

car·cass /kär′kəs/ [MF *carcasse*] *n* 1 dead body of an animal; 2 decaying remains of a bulky thing; 3 framework or skeleton || SYN corpse, remains, frame (see *body*)

car·cin·o·gen /kärsin′əjən/ [< Gk *karkinos* cancer] *n* cancer-producing substance || **car·cin·o·gen·ic** /kärs′-inojen′ik/ *adj*

car·ci·no·ma /kärs′inōm′ə/ [Gk *karkinoma*] *n* (-mas; -ma·ta /-mətə/) any of several varieties of epithelial cancer

car′ coat′ *n* hip-length topcoat

card /kärd′/ [MF *carte* < L *charta* paper] *n* 1 piece of thick stiff paper or pasteboard, printed or plain, used for various purposes, as *post card*, *greeting card*, *membership card*, etc.; 2 *sports* program; 3 *colloq* person who attracts attention; 4 playing card; 5 **cards** *pl* any of many games using playing cards; 6 **in the cards** probable; inevitable; 7 **put one's cards on the table** to be frank and open

card′board′ *n* thin pasteboard used for boxes, signs, etc.

card′-car′ry·ing *adj* being an acknowledged and fully committed member of a party, as *a card-carrying Communist*

car·di·ac /kärd′ē·ak′/ [< Gk *kardia* heart] *adj* 1 pert. to or situated near the heart || *n* 2 person suffering from heart disease; 3 heart remedy

Car·diff /kär′dif/ *n* seaport and the chief city of Wales (250,000)

car·di·gan /kärd′igən/ [7th Earl of *Cardigan* (1797–1868)] *n* knitted woolen jacket or waistcoat

car·di·nal /kärd′inəl/ [L *cardinalis*] *adj* 1 chief, fundamental || *n* 2 R C Ch highest-ranking prelate next to the pope; 3 rich deep red; 4 North American finch (*Richmondena cardinalis*) having brilliant red plumage

car′di·nal num′ber *n* any number expressing how many, as one, two, etc.

car′di·nal points′ *npl* north, south, east, and west

car·di·o- /kärd′ē·ə/ [< Gk *kardia*] *comb form* heart

car′di·o·gram′ *n* electrocardiogram

car′di·o·graph′ *n* electrocardiograph

card′sharp′ *n* professional cheater at cards

card′ ta′ble *n* light table at which four can sit for playing cards

care /ker′/ [OE *cearu* sorrow] *n* 1 worry, anxiety; 2 cause of worry; 3 object of concern; 4 watchfulness; heed; 5 charge; protection; 6 **care of** to the address of; 7 **take care** be careful; 8 **take care of, a** to attend to; **b** to watch over || *vi* 9 to be concerned; 10 to feel inclined; 11 **care for, a** to take care of; **b** to be fond of || SYN *n* attention, solicitude, heed, caution, worry, trouble, concern, anxiety, regard, forethought, prudence, watchfulness, vigilance || DISCR *Care* is a troubled uneasiness of mind resulting from responsibility, duty, overwork, etc., as worn by *care*. *Anxiety* is a state of mental distress or pain, felt toward some uncertain event; it is colored by hope rather than despair. *Solicitude* is a milder form of *anxiety*; it often names merely a tender hope for the welfare of another; it is warmly desirous for, and active in, securing benefits for those to be loved and protected. *Concern*, when applied to people, shares with *solicitude* an affectionate desire for their good; when applied to issues or objects, it connotes a sympathetic, often active, interest, as *concern* for another's safety. *Worry* names a futile, nervous agitation, often purposeless, always restless. *Heed* is an attentive watchfulness directed to the prevention of trouble; *caution* takes steps to avert what it fears. (see *wisdom* || ANT heedlessness, inattention, negligence

ca·reen /kərēn′/ [MF *carine* keel] *vi* 1 to tip to one side, as a ship or vehicle; 2 to dash along and swing in an uncontrolled fashion

ca·reer /kərir′/ [MF *carriere* race course < L (via) *carraria* carriage (road)] *n* 1 full speed; 2 progress through life; 3 occupation or profession || *vi* 4 to dash along || *adj* 5 following a profession as a career, as *a career diplomat*

ca·reer′ist *n* one who seeks to advance

his career, disregarding the moral, social, and political consequences of his actions ‖ **ca·reer′ism** n

care′free′ adj without cares or worries

care′ful adj 1 watchful, cautious; 2 painstaking ‖ **care′ful·ly** adv ‖ **care′-ful·ness** n ‖ SYN cautious, prudent, provident, foreseeing, circumspect, discreet, wary, heedful, vigilant ‖ DISCR *Careful* describes one who in every way tries to act responsibly and wisely. *Cautious* describes one who is actuated by fear or timidity to take steps against possible danger or loss. The *cautious* man so fears possible implications that he will never make a positive statement; he spends so gingerly that he appears stingy. *Prudent* describes one who takes the future into consideration in a sane, moderate way. *Discreet* applies to those whose words and actions are dictated by judgment rather than impulse. The *discreet* man speaks according to a shrewd appraisal of what the situation involves; he acts only when he has chosen the path best for him to follow. *Circumspect* describes one who looks before he leaps, both in speech and action. *Wary* describes one alertly watchful ‖ ANT heedless, careless, negligent, remiss

care′less adj 1 neglectful, heedless; 2 unstudied, easy; 3 without due consideration ‖ **care′less·ly** adv ‖ **care′-less·ness** n ‖ SYN indifferent, thoughtless, inattentive, reckless, rash ‖ ANT accurate, attentive, studied, thoughtful

ca·ress /kəres′/ [F *caresse* < It *carezza*] n 1 touch or gesture of affection; embrace ‖ vt 2 to touch with affection, fondle ‖ SYN v kiss, embrace, coddle, pet, fondle

car·et /kar′it/ [L = it lacks] n mark ⌄ indicating the place where something is to be added

care′tak′er n person who is in charge of a building or other property

care′tak·er gov′ern·ment n interim government which functions until a regular government can be set up

care′worn′ adj showing the marks of care, haggard

car·go /kär′gō/ [Sp = load] n (-goes, -gos) goods or merchandise conveyed in a vessel or an aircraft ‖ SYN freight ‖ DISCR *Cargo* refers to goods or merchandise taken by a vessel or aircraft for shipment; a ship's *cargo* is sometimes referred to as *freight*, but *freight* is ordinarily applied to loads shipped on public carriers on land

car′ hop′ n employee of a drive-in restaurant who serves patrons in their cars

Car′ib·be·an (Sea′) /-kar′ib̄ē′ən, kərib′ē-/ n sea bounded by Central

America, the West Indies, and South America

car·i·bou /kar′iboo̅′/ [CanF < Algonquian] n native reindeer of northern North America

car·i·ca·ture /kar′ikəchoor′/ [It *caricatura*] n 1 picture, description, or imitation of a person or thing in which the defects or peculiarities are ludicrously exaggerated ‖ vt 2 to represent in caricature ‖ **car′i·ca·tur′ist** n ‖ SYN n mimicry, burlesque, travesty (see *parody*)

ca·ries /ker′ēz, -ē·ēz′/ [L = decay] n tooth or bone decay

car·il·lon /kar′ilon′, -lən/ [F] n 1 set of bells chromatically tuned; 2 air played on such bells

car′load′ n load that will fill a freight car

car·mine /kär′min, -min/ [F *carmin* < L *carminus* < Ar] n purplish red

car·nage /kär′nij/ [It *carnaggio*] n slaughter, massacre ‖ SYN butchery, massacre, havoc, bloodshed, slaughter ‖ DISCR *Bloodshed* is the general term for the spilling of blood, for killing. *Massacre* names the promiscuous killing in great numbers of those who are defenseless or helpless to resist. *Slaughter* suggests the ruthless killing on a large scale of either men or animals. *Carnage* suggests the result of bloody and extensive *slaughter*, chiefly of men, and connotes heaps of corpses. *Slaughter* and *carnage* may be used of a fair struggle. *Butchery* is the savage taking of human life as if men were animals. *Havoc* is furious destruction of life or property, with panic and confusion, or of plans and hopes, as the war played *havoc* with his education

car·nal /kär′nəl/ [ME < L *carnalis*] adj 1 sensual; 2 worldly, not spiritual ‖ **car·nal′i·ty** /-nal′-/ n

car′nal a·buse′ n law lascivious touching of the sexual organs of a child by an adult

car·na·tion /kärnāsh′ən/ [L *carnatio* fleshiness] n 1 cultivated clove pink (*Dianthus caryophyllus*); 2 pink, light red ‖ adj 3 pink, light-red

Car·ne·gie, An·drew /kärnə·gē, kärn′ə-/ n (1835–1919) Scotch-born U.S. steel manufacturer and philanthropist

car·ni·val /kärn′ivəl/ [It *carnevale* Shrove Tuesday] n 1 season of rejoicing and feasting before Lent; 2 any feasting or revelry; 3 traveling amusement show

car·ni·vore /kärn′ivôr′, vôr′-/ [< L *caro* (*carnis*) flesh + *vorare* to eat] n animal that feeds on flesh ‖ **car·niv′o·rous** /-niv′ərəs/ adj

car·ol /kar′əl/ [OF *carole*] n 1 song of joy; 2 Christmas song ‖ v (-oled or -olled; -ol·ing or -ol·ling) vt & vi 3 to sing, warble ‖ **car′ol·er** or **car′ol·ler** n

Car·o·lin·gi·an /kar′əlin′jē·ən/ [LL

Carolingi family of Charles < *Charles* Martel (690?–741) king of the Franks] *n* member of the Frankish dynasty which ruled France 751–987 ‖ also *adj*

car·om /kar'əm/ [F *carambole* < Sp *carambola*] *n* 1 *billiards* shot in which the cue ball strikes two other balls; 2 rebound, as of a ball off a wall ‖ *vi* 3 to make a carom; 4 to rebound

car·o·tene /kar'ətēn'/ [< Gk *karoton* carrot] *n* orange hydrocarbon —C₄₀H₅₆— that acts as a plant pigment and is the source of vitamin A

ca·rot'id (ar'ter·y) /kərot'id/ [< Gk *karos* stupor] *n* either of the two chief arteries which convey the blood to the head

ca·rouse /kərouz'/ [< G *gar aus* (trinken) (to drink) right up] *n* 1 drunken revelry ‖ *vi* 2 to engage in a carouse ‖ **ca·rous'al** *n*

carp¹ /kärp'/ [ON *karpa* to brag] *vi* to find unreasonable fault; cavil

carp² [MF *carpe* < LL *carpa*] *n* (**carp** or **carps**) any of a family (Cyprinidae) of long-lived fresh-water fishes

car' park' *n* Brit parking lot

Car·pa'thi·an Moun'tains /kärpā'thē-ən/ *npl* mountain chain in central Europe which extends over Czechoslovakia, Hungary, and the Ukraine, and into Rumania

car·pel /kär'pəl/ [< Gk *karpos* fruit] *n* simple pistil, regarded as a modified leaf

car·pen·ter /kär'pəntər/ [ONF *carpentier* < LL *carpentarius* wagon maker] *n* one who works in timber and builds or repairs woodwork ‖ **car'pen·try** *n*

car·pet /kär'pit/ [MF *carpite*] *n* 1 thick fabric for covering floors; 2 anything like a carpet; 3 **on the carpet, a** being reprimanded; **b** under discussion ‖ *vt* 4 to cover with or as with a carpet

car'pet·bag'ger [< *carpetbag* traveling bag made from a piece of carpet] *n* 1 political adventurer from the North seeking profit in the South during Reconstruction; 2 any person moving into a new territory for political advancement

carpo- [Gk *karpos*] *comb form* fruit

car' pool' *n* 1 arrangement by which a number of people regularly going to the same place take turns providing and driving the automobile; 2 the group of people

car'port' *n* roofed area of a driveway next to an entrance to a building, used as a garage

-car·pous /-kärp'əs/ [Gk *karpos* fruit] *adj comb form* fruited

car·rel /kar'əl/ [ME *carole* ring] *n* small alcove in a library stack for individual study

car·riage /kar'ij/ [ONF *cariage*] *n* 1 four-wheeled horse-drawn passenger vehicle; 2 wheeled support, as of a cannon; 3 any part of a machine which carries another part, as on a typewriter; 4 bearing, posture ‖ SYN port, bearing, demeanor (see *behavior*)

car'riage trade' *n* wealthy patrons

car·ri·er /kar'ē·ər/ [see **carry**] *n* 1 one who or that which carries; 2 person or agency whose business is to transport goods; 3 aircraft carrier; 4 immune person who transmits disease germs

car'ri·er pig'eon *n* homing pigeon

car'ri·er wave' *n* radio-frequency wave used for the transmission of signals with or without wire by varying or modulating its amplitude, frequency, or phase

car·ri·on /kar'ē·ən/ [ONF *caronie*] *n* 1 dead or decaying flesh ‖ *adj* 2 of or like carrion; 3 feeding on carrion

car·rot /kar'ət/ [MF *carotte*] *n* 1 plant (*Daucus carota*) cultivated for its orange, tapering edible root; 2 its root; 3 red-haired person; 4 illusory reward or promise

car'rot-and-stick' *adj* characterized by a combination of enticement and compulsion

car·rou·sel /kar'əsel', -zel'/ [F < It *carosello*] *n* 1 merry-go-round; 2 circular conveyer which carries objects around until they are picked up by the person to whom they are destined

car·ry /kar'ē/ [ONF *carier*] *v* (**-ried**) *vt* 1 to convey from one point to another; 2 to take along; 3 to bear; 4 to transmit, as *air carries sound waves*; 5 to lead, conduct; 6 to transfer, as to a new ledger page; 7 to win, as an election, an audience; 8 to hold (oneself), behave (oneself); 9 to support the weight of; 10 to keep on hand, as merchandise; 11 to keep on one's account books; 12 to be pregnant with; 13 carry a tune to sing in key; 14 **carry away** to transport with emotion; 15 **carry on** to conduct or manage; 16 **carry out** to accomplish or execute; 17 **carry the day** to be the winner; 18 **carry too far** to exceed acceptable limits of conduct in ‖ *vi* 19 to perform the act of bearing or conveying; 20 to possess or exert propelling force, as a gun; 21 to have range, as a voice; 22 **carry on, a** to behave thoughtlessly or shamelessly; **b** to persevere in one's duty ‖ *n* (**-ries**) 23 distance covered by a ball or projectile ‖ SYN *v* convey, transport, bear, sustain (see *bring*)

car'ry·ing charge' *n* interest on an unpaid balance in a charge account

car'ry·o'ver *n* 1 something left over or kept for future use; 2 sum transferred to a new ledger page; 3 in a U.S. income-tax declaration, part of a loss or an unused credit that may be transferred from preceding taxable years

Car'son Cit'y /kär'sən/ *n* capital of Nevada (15,500)

cart /kärt/ [prob ON *kartr*] *n* 1 small wagon || *vt* 2 to convey in a wagon || **cart'er** *n*

cart'age /-ij/ *n* act or cost of carting or trucking

carte blanche /kärt' blansh', blänsh'/ [F = blank card] *n* full discretion

carte' du jour' /dəzhŏŏr'/ [F] *n* menu for the day

car·tel /kärtel'/ [MF < OIt *cartello* poster] *n* international monopoly

Car·ter, Jim'my /kär'tər/ *n* (1924–) 39th president of the U.S. 1977–

Car·te·sian /kärtēzh'ən/ [< ML *Cartesianus* < *Cartesius* L form of Descartes] *adj* of or pert. to Descartes or his method || also *adj* || **Car·te'sian·ism** *n*

Car·te'sian co·or'di·nates *npl math* system of coordinates for fixing the position of a point on a surface by its distance from each of two perpendicular intersecting lines or in space by its distance from any one of three planes perpendicular to each other and intersecting at a point

Car·thage /kärth'ij/ *n* ancient Phoenician city-state in N Africa near modern Tunis; rival of the Romans, who destroyed it 146 B.C. || **Car'tha·gin'i·an** /-əjin'ē-ən/ *adj* & *n*

Car·thu·sian /kärthōōzh'ən/ [< ML *Cartusianus* < *Catursiani* montes] *n* R C Ch monk or nun of an austere religious order founded in the mountains above Grenoble, France about 1084 by St. Bruno || also *adj*

car·ti·lage /kärt'līij/ [L *cartilago*] *n* tough, solid, elastic tissue; gristle || **car'ti·lag'i·nous** /-laj'inəs/ *adj*

car·tog·ra·phy /kärtog'rəfē/ [< F *carte* chart] *n* art of drawing maps or charts || **car·tog'ra·pher** *n*

car·ton /kärt'ən/ [F < It *cartone* pasteboard] *n* cardboard box

car·toon /kärtōōn'/ [It *cartone* pasteboard] *n* 1 caricature, usu. a line drawing, of a public person or event; 2 *movies* comic short subject consisting of line drawings || *vt* 3 to draw cartoons of || **car·toon'ist** *n* || SYN caricature, travesty (see *parody*)

car·tridge /kärt'rij/ [F *cartouche*] *n* 1 cylindrical case of metal or cardboard containing the powder and projectiles for a firearm; 2 container for daylight loading of a film in a camera; 3 disposable cartridgelike ink reservoir for a pen; 4 detachable case containing the stylus and pickup of a phonograph; 5 **a** large-type cassette; **b** cassette-type case with looped magnetic tape

carve /kärv'/ [OE *ceorfan*] *vt* 1 to form by cutting; 2 to cut or grave, as stone or wood; 3 to decorate by cutting; 4 to cut (meat) into slices or pieces || *vi* 5 to carve statues or figures; 6 to cut up meat

carv'ing *n* carved work or design

car' wash' *n* place for washing automobiles

car·y·at·id /kar'ē-at'id/ [Gk *karyatis* (-*idos*) priestess at Caryae] *n* (-**ids** or -**ides** /-idēz'/) supporting column having the shape of a woman

ca·sa·ba /kəsäb'ə/ [*Kassaba*, Turkey] *n* kind of large winter muskmelon with a yellow rind

Ca·sa·blan·ca /käs'äbläŋ'kə, kas'-əblaŋ'kə/ *n* Atlantic seaport in N Morocco (1,100,000)

Cas·a·no·va, Gio·van·ni /jōvän'ē kaz'-ənōv'ə/ *n* (1725–98) Italian writer and noted amorous adventurer

cas·cade /kaskād'/ [F < It *cascata*] *n* 1 small waterfall; 2 anything falling like or resembling a waterfall || *vi* 3 to fall in or as in a cascade

cas·car·a /kaskar'ə/ [Sp = bark] *n* Pacific coast buckthorn (*Rhamnus purshiana*), the bark of which is used as a laxative

case[1] /kās'/ [OF *cas* < L *casus* chance] *n* 1 instance or example, as *a case of poor training, a case of measles;* 2 state of affairs involving discussion or investigation; 3 lawsuit; 4 convincing argument; 5 special form of a substantive to show its relation to other words, as *man's, them;* 6 *colloq* peculiar person; 7 **in any case** anyhow; 8 **in case** if; 9 **in case of** in the event of; 10 **in no case** under no circumstances || SYN contingency, event, situation, plight, instance

case[2] [ONF *casse* < L *capsa* chest] *n* 1 container for enclosing, protecting, and/or carrying; 2 glass box for exhibiting wares; 3 frame or casing, as of a window || *vt* 4 to protect with or enclose in a case; 5 *slang* to survey carefully (a site), as for a burglary

case'hard'en *vt* 1 to harden the outer layer of (metal or a metal object); 2 to render insensible to feeling

case' his'to·ry *n* pertinent antecedents of an individual or group under study

ca·se·in /kās'ē-in, -sēn/ [< L *caseus* cheese] *n* protein precipitated from milk, forming the main part of cheese and certain plastics

case' law' *n* law based on selected judicial decisions

case'ment *n* window sash that swings open on hinges

case' stud'y *n* analysis of a case history

case'work' *n* sociological procedure based on case study with a view to eliminating maladjustments || **case'work'er** *n*

cash /kash′/ [MF *casse* cashbox] *n* 1 money in the form of bills and coins ‖ *vt* 2 to exchange for cash; 3 **cash in** to turn in for cash ‖ *vi* 4 **cash in** *slang* to die; 5 **cash in on** *colloq* to profit from

cash′ ba′sis *n* method of recording transactions that includes income when received in cash and expenses when paid in cash

cash·ew /kash′ōō/ [Port *caju*] *n* 1 tropical American tree (*Anacardium occidentale*); 2 its edible nut

cash·ier¹ /kashir′/ [MF *cassier*] *n* 1 employee who collects payments from customers; 2 officer in charge of the money transactions in a company or bank

cash·ier² [MD *kasseren* < MF *casser*] *vt* to dismiss in disgrace, esp. a military officer

cash·ier′s′ check′ *n* check drawn by a bank upon its own funds, signed by the cashier

cash·mere /kash′mir, kazh′-/ [*Kashmir*, India] *n* 1 fine downy hair of the Kashmir goat of India and Tibet; 2 wool made from this hair

cash′ reg′is·ter *n* machine with a money drawer which records and shows the amount of a sale

cas′ing *n* 1 covering; 2 outer shell of an automobile tire; 3 sausage skin; 4 framework around a door or window

ca·si·no /kəsēn′ō/ [It, *dim.* of *casa* house] *n* 1 public room or building for dancing, gambling, etc.; 2 also **cas·si·no** card game in which matching on the table are taken by matching with cards in the hand

cask /kask′, käsk′/ [MF *casque* < *casco*] *n* 1 large barrel, as for wine; 2 quantity it contains

cas·ket /kask′it, käsk′-/ [ME] *n* 1 small chest or box, as for jewels; 2 coffin

Cas′pi·an Sea′ /kas′pē·ən/ *n* large inland sea, between the Caucasus and Asia

Cas·san·dra /kəsan′drə/ *n* 1 *Gk myth.* one of Priam's daughters, who was endowed with the gift of prophecy but condemned never to be believed; 2 one who continually predicts misfortune

cas·sa·va /kəsäv′ə/ [Sp *cazabe*] *n* any of several tropical plants (genus *Manihot*) whose roots yield a starch from which tapioca is made

cas·se·role /kas′ərōl′/ [F = stewpan] *n* 1 covered baking dish; 2 food baked in it

cas·sette /kaset′, kə-/ [F *case* box] *n* 1 camera cartridge for daylight loading of film; 2 small cartridgelike case containing magnetic tape for automatic insertion into a recorder or player

Cas·si·o·pe·ia /kas′ē·əpē′ə/ [Gk] *n* constellation near the polestar

cas·sock /kas′ək/ [MF *casaque*] *n* long close-fitting garment worn by certain clergymen

cast /kast′, käst′/ [ON *kasta*] *v* (**cast**) *vt* 1 to throw, hurl; 2 to direct, as a glance; 3 to project, as a shadow; 4 to form or mold, as clay or molten metal; 5 to deposit (a ballot); 6 to select actors for (a play); 7 to assign (an actor) to a role; 8 to figure out (a horoscope); 9 **cast aside** to discard; 10 **cast off, a** to reject, discard; **b** to measure (a manuscript or galley proof) to determine the number of printed pages it will make ‖ *vi* 11 to throw the line in angling; 12 to receive shape in a mold; 13 to throw dice; 14 **cast about** to search; 15 **cast off** to let loose, as a ship from its moorings ‖ *n* 16 act of throwing; 17 thing thrown; 18 distance covered by a thing thrown; 19 throw of the dice; 20 slight squint of the eye; 21 shape, expression; 22 faint shade, tinge; 23 something formed by molding; 24 plaster form for immobilizing a limb; 25 throw of a fishing line; 26 group of actors playing all the roles in a particular play ‖ SYN *v* throw, hurl, fling, toss, pitch ‖ DISCR These terms express the idea of impelling one object from another. *Cast* has been displaced in familiar usage by the more vigorous *throw*, but *cast* appears in many idiomatic and special uses, as defined above. *Throw* implies more effort than *cast*; it means to impel with force intentionally expended, as to *throw* stones at a window; not infrequently, *throw* carries force intended offensively. The difference between *cast* and *throw* appears also in their figurative use; to *cast* aside a suggestion requires no more effort than to *cast* aside an unwanted object; to *throw* off bad associations, evil habits, etc., requires an actual exertion of the will. To *hurl* is to *throw* violently; often it suggests a large object, but it may merely indicate the force with which an object is impelled, as he *hurled* the missile at my head. To *fling* is to *throw* suddenly; it is used of small objects, like dice, or of a carelessly slung stone, but it may be backed by violence or anger, and send a missile, a spurned gift, or an insult, very directly to its destination. To *toss* is to *throw* lightly or carelessly with a slight motion of the upturned palm

cas·ta·nets /kast′ənets′/ [Sp *castañetas* < *castaña* chestnut] *npl* small spoon-shaped shells of wood or ivory, shaken with the fingers to beat time to Spanish dances

cast′a·way′ *n* 1 shipwrecked person; 2 person or thing cast off ‖ also *adj*

caste /kast′, käst′/ [Port *casta* lineage] *n* 1 one of the restricted hereditary divisions of society into which Hindus are separated; **2** any exclusive group or class; **3** class distinction based on birth, social position, or wealth; **4** social position ‖ SYN class, clan, order, rank, circle, coterie, club, clique, set, grade, degree ‖ DISCR Each of these words names a group of related persons or objects. *Class* is the general term for any group whose members possess common characteristics; it may designate a social group, as the leisure *class*; or it may be widely inclusive, as the voting *class*; membership in any particular *class* might vary greatly with time or conditions. On the other hand, *caste*, which involves hereditary and sacred distinctions, is the most rigid of the terms which name the divisions of society; membership in a *caste* is exclusive; people may drop out, but rarely, if at all, enter a *caste* unless born to it. Members of a *clan* are bound together by common lineage. Those who form a *circle* are united by common interests. A *coterie* is a select circle, often of a social nature. The members of a *club* have a definite organization and purpose. *Set* names a group of people with similar ideas and manners, usually less exclusive, because larger, than a *coterie*. *Clique* names a small group, usually within a larger one, and has an unfavorable connotation: a *clique* frequently works only for its own ends, and is apt to be snobbish as well as selfish. *Rank* is usually applied to hereditary or military *classes; order* is ordinarily applied to societies of churchmen, as an *order* of monks; or to honorary classes or societies founded by sovereigns, legislatures, etc., as the *Order* of the Knights of St. John. *Degree* is used specifically of academic distinctions. Loosely, *rank, order,* and *degree* may be used to refer to any group. *Grade* names any of several groups divided on the basis of a fixed standard of quality

caste′ mark′ *n* mark on a Hindu's forehead identifying his caste

cast′er *n* **1** small swiveled roller fastened under a piece of furniture so that it may be easily moved; **2 a** small container for holding salt, pepper, vinegar, or oil at table; **b** rack for holding these containers

cas·ti·gate /kast′igāt′/ [L *castigare* (*-atus*)] *vt* **1** to chastise; **2** to criticize severely ‖ **cas′ti·ga′tion** *n*

Cas·tile /kastēl′/ *n* region and former kingdom of Spain, which absorbed the other kingdoms in the 15th century

Cas·tile′ soap′ *n* soap made from olive oil

Cas·til·ian /kastil′yən/ *n* **1** native or inhabitant of Castile; **2** language of

Castile, now the standard form of the Spanish language as spoken in Spain ‖ also *adj*

cast′ing *n* metal object which has been cast in a mold

cast′ i′ron *n* pig iron made by casting

cast′-i′ron *adj* **1** made of cast iron; **2** unyielding, rigid; **3** strong, resistant

cas·tle /kas′əl, käs′-/ [OF *castel* < L *castellum*] *n* **1** fortified building or group of buildings, used as a residence by powerful nobles in feudal times; **2** imposing mansion; **3** *chess* rook ‖ *vi* **4** *chess* to move the king from its original position two squares left or right, and the rook to the square over which the king has passed

cas′tle in the air′ *n* impractical scheme, daydream

cast′off′ *adj* **1** thrown aside, discarded, as *a castoff garment* ‖ *n* **2** person or thing that has been cast off; **3** estimate of the number of printed pages a manuscript will occupy

cas·tor oil′ [< *castor*] *n* colorless viscid oil obtained from the castor-oil plant (*Ricinus communis*), used as a purgative and as a fine lubricant

cas·trate /kas′trāt/ [L *castrare* (*-atus*)] *vt* to emasculate by removing the testicles; geld ‖ **cas·tra′tion** *n*

cas·u·al /kazh′ōo̅·əl/ [MF *casuel* < LL *casualis*] *adj* **1** happening by chance; **2** offhand; **3** occasional; **4** nonchalant; **5** informal (clothes) ‖ **cas′u·al·ly** *adv*

cas·u·al·ty *n* (**-ties**) **1** accident resulting in bodily injury or death; **2** loss due to accident; **3** person injured or killed in an accident; **4** member of the armed forces killed, wounded, captured, or missing ‖ SYN accident, mishap, disaster, mischance

cas·u·ist·ry /kazh′ōo̅·istrē/ [< Sp *casuista* practitioner of casuistry] *n* (**-ries**) **1** application of general ethical principles to particular cases; **2** false reasoning as to moral conduct ‖ **cas′u·ist** *n*

ca·sus bel·li /kās′əs bel′ē/ [L] *n* hostile act that is bound to bring on a declaration of war

cat /kat′/ [OE *catt*, perh < L *cattus*] *n* **1** any of a family (Felidae) of carnivores, including the lion, tiger, and leopard; **2** small domesticated species (*Felis domestica*) often kept as a pet; **3** cat-o′-nine-tails; **4** spiteful woman; **5** *slang* person, fellow; **6 let the cat out of the bag** to reveal a secret

CAT *abbr* clear-air turbulence

cat·a·clysm /kat′əkliz′əm/ [Gk *kataklysmos*] *n* **1** physical, social, or political upheaval; **2** flood, deluge

cat·a·combs /kat′əkōmz′/ [MF *catacombes* < LL *Catacumbas*] *npl* underground burial place with niches hollowed out for the dead

cat·a·falque /kat′əfalk′, -fôk′/ [< F

< It *catafalco*] *n* draped structure on which the coffin rests during an imposing funeral

Cat·a·lan /kat'ələn'/ *adj* 1 of or pert. to Catalonia, its inhabitants, or their language || *n* 2 native or inhabitant of Catalonia; 3 language of Catalonia

cat·a·lep·sy /kat'ələp'sē/ [Gk *katalepsis* seizure] *n* sudden suspension of motion, feeling, and volition, with muscular stiffening || **cat'a·lep'tic** *adj*

cat·a·log or **cat·a·logue** /kat'əlog', -lôg'/ [Gk *katalogos*] *n* 1 systematic list, usu. alphabetical, of such items as names, book titles, articles in stock, etc. || *vt* 2 to enter in a catalog || *vi* 3 to make a catalog || SYN *n* inventory, tabulation, schedule, list

Cat·a·lo·ni·a /kat'əlōn'ē-ə, -yə-/ *n* region and former province of NE Spain

Cat·a·lo'ni·an *adj & n* var of **Catalan**

ca·tal·pa /kətal'pə/ [< Creek] *n* any of a genus (*Catalpa*) of rapidly growing trees, having large leaves, showy flower clusters, and winged seeds

ca·tal·y·sis /kətal'isis/ [Gk] *n* (-ses /-sēz'/) process of producing a reaction between other substances by means of a substance which itself remains unchanged || **cat·a·lyt·ic** /kat'əlit'ik/ *adj* || **cat'a·lyze'** *vt*

cat·a·lyst /kat'əlist/ *n* 1 substance that causes catalysis; 2 person or thing that precipitates a process or event without being involved

cat'a·lyt'ic con·vert'er *n* afterburner designed to cleanse automobile exhaust of carbon monoxide and hydrocarbons

cat·a·ma·ran /kat'əməran'/ [Tamil = wood tied together] *n* 1 any of various kinds of boats with two hulls or floats fastened together, sometimes with a space between them; 2 *colloq* scolding woman

cat·a·pult /kat'əpult'/ [L *catapulta*] *n* 1 ancient military machine for hurling missiles; 2 device for launching a plane from the deck of a ship || also *vt*

cat·a·ract /kat'ərakt'/ [L *cataracta*] *n* 1 large steep waterfall; 2 a abnormality of the eye in which the lens becomes opaque; b the opaque area

ca·tarrh /kətär'/ [Gk *katarrous* down flowing] *n* inflammation of the mucous membranes of the nose and throat || **ca·tarrh'al** *adj*

ca·tas·tro·phe /kətas'trəfē/ [Gk = overturn] *n* great disaster || **cat·a·stroph·ic** /kat'əstrof'ik/ *adj* || SYN misfortune, calamity, cataclysm (see *trouble*)

cat'bird' *n* dark-gray American songbird (*Dumetella carolinensis*) with a catlike call

cat'boat' *n* small boat with one sail near the bow

cat'call' *n* discordant sound expressing derision || also *vt & vi*

catch /kach/ [ONF *cachier* < L *captare*] *v* (**caught**) *vt* 1 to seize or grasp; 2 to overtake; get to in time; 3 to capture; 4 to entrap, as game; 5 to take with bait; 6 to perceive by the senses; 7 to understand; 8 to be infected with; 9 to surprise, detect; 10 to snag; 11 **catch it** *colloq* to be punished || *vi* 12 to take hold; 13 to become entangled; 14 to take fire; 15 *baseball* to act as catcher; 16 **catch at**, a to try to catch; b to seize eagerly; 17 **catch on** *colloq* a to understand; b to become popular; 18 **catch up** to come even with one's compeers; 19 **catch up with** to overtake || *n* 20 act or instance of catching; 21 anything that catches and holds, as a hook or latch; 22 choking sensation in the throat; 23 something caught; 24 good matrimonial prospect; 25 *colloq* concealed drawback

catch'all' *n* receptacle for holding odds and ends

catch'er *n baseball* player who stands behind the batter to catch the pitched balls the batter fails to hit

catch'ing *adj* 1 contagious; 2 fascinating

catch·up /kach'əp/ *n* ketchup

catch'word' *n* 1 popular word or phrase used for effect as for a political slogan; 2 guide word at the top of a column, as in a dictionary; 3 actor's cue

catch'y *adj* (-i·er -i·est) 1 pleasing and easily remembered; 2 tricky (question); 3 fitful (wind; breathing)

cat·e·chism /kat'əkiz'əm/ *n* 1 book of elementary instruction in the form of questions and answers, dealing with the principles of a particular religion; 2 any series of detailed direct questions

cat'e·chize' [Gk *katechizein* to make to hear] *vt* 1 to instruct by means of questions and answers; 2 to ask searching questions of

cat·e·gor·i·cal /kat'əgôr'ikəl, -gôr'-/ *adj* absolute, unconditional || **cat'e·gor'i·cal·ly** *adv*

cat'e·go'ry [Gk *kategoria* accusation] *n* (-ries) 1 division or class; 2 one of the classes into which all knowledge can be divided

cat·e·nar·y /kat'əner'ē/ [< L *catena* chain] *n* (-ies) 1 *math* curve assumed by the part of a cord or chain that hangs freely between two points; 2 cable hanging between two points || also *adj*

ca·ter /kāt'ər/ [AF *acatour* buyer] *vi* 1 to provide food and services, as for a banquet; 2 **cater to**, a to supply what is wanted to; b to pay special attention to || **ca'ter·er** *n*

cat'er·cor'nered /kat'ər-, kat'ē-/ [*obs*

cater four] *adj* 1 diagonal ‖ *adv* 2 diagonally

cat·er·pil·lar /kat'ə(r)-/ [prob < ONF *catepelose* hairy cat] *n* 1 wormlike larva of a butterfly or moth; 2 **Cat·erpillar** [trademark] tractor operating on an endless belt which turns like a moving track

cat·er·waul /kat'ərwôl'/ [ME *caterwawen*] *vi* 1 to wail like cats at night ‖ *n* 2 noisy wailing

cat'fish' *n* (**-fish** or **-fishes**) any of several scaleless fishes of a large family (Siluridae) having whiskerlike feelers around the mouth

cat'gut' *n* tough cord made from the intestines of animals, as sheep, used as strings for musical instruments, tennis rackets, surgical sutures, etc.

Cath. Catholic

ca·thar·sis /kəthär'sis/ [Gk] *n* 1 purging, as of the bowels; 2 relief of mental disorders by the removal of disturbing mental attitudes or complexes

ca·thar'tic /-tik/ *adj* & *n* purgative

Ca·thay /kathā'/ [ML *Cataya* < Turkic] *n archaic* & *poet.* China

ca·the·dral /kəthē'rəl/ [LL *cathedralis* containing the cathedra or bishop's throne] *n* 1 chief church of a diocese, containing the bishop's throne; 2 *nonepiscopal denominations* any imposing church

Cath'er·ine the Great' /kath'(ə)rin/ *n* (1729–96) empress of Russia 1762–96

cath·e·ter /kath'itər/ [Gk] *n* tube introduced into natural orifices of the body to withdraw fluids, esp. urine ‖ **cath'e·ter·ize'** *vt*

cath·ode /kath'ōd/ [Gk *kathodos* way down] *n* electrode that loses electrons through a vacuum or gas and gains them through the external circuit of a vacuum tube or of a primary or secondary cell, and attracts cations through an electrolyte. Internally it is conventionally called a negative electrode and externally a positive electrode or terminal

cath'ode ray' *n* beam of electrons emanating from the heated cathode of a vacuum tube

cath·o·lic /kath'əlik/ [Gk *katholikos* universal] *adj* 1 universal, general; 2 liberal, tolerant

Cath·o·lic *n* member of the Roman Catholic Church ‖ also *adj* ‖ **Ca·thol'i·cism** /kəthol'i-/ *n*

cath'o·lic'i·ty /-lis'itē/ *n* 1 universality; 2 tolerance; broad-mindedness; 3 **Catholicity** quality or character of being a Roman Catholic

cat·i·on /kat'ī'ən/ [Gk = going down] *n* positive ion: atom that has lost one or more electrons and moves to the cathode

cat·kin /kat'kin/ [< D *katteken* little cat] *n* downy, drooping spike of blossoms of the willow, pussy willow, birch, etc.

cat' nap' *n* short light sleep ‖ **cat'nap'** *v* (**-napped; -nap·ping**) *vi*

cat'nip' *n* common plant (*Nepeta cataria*) of the mint family, the odor of which is relished by cats

cat'-o'-nine'-tails' *nsg* whip with nine lashes of knotted cord

Cats'kill Moun'tains /kats'kil/ or **Cats'- kills** *npl* low mountain range in E New York

cat's'-paw' *n* dupe used to do someone's dirty work

cat·sup /kat'səp/ *n* ketchup

cat'tail' *n* tall marsh plant (*Typha latifolia*) with long narrow leaves, bearing furry cylindrical spikes of flowers

cat·tle /kat'əl/ [ONF *catel* property < ML *cap(i)tale* wealth] *npl* 1 livestock, esp. domesticated bovine animals; 2 *contemptuous* people

cat'ty *adj* (**-ti·er; -ti·est**) *colloq* slyly malicious; spiteful; gossipy ‖ **cat'ti·ness** *n*

cat'ty·cor'nered *adj* cater-cornered

CATV *abbr* community-antenna television

cat'walk' *n* narrow walk to provide access on foot in high places, as in an engine room, the top of a freight car, etc.

Cau·ca·sia /kôkāsh'ə, -kāzh'ə/ *n* region in the Soviet Union between the Black and Caspian Seas

Cau·ca'sian *n* 1 native of Caucasia; 2 member of the light-skinned subspecies of mankind inhabiting Europe and other parts of the world ‖ also *adj*

Cau'ca·sus /-kəsəs/ *n* 1 Caucasia; 2 mountain range in Caucasia

cau·cus /kôk'əs/ [prob Algonquian] *n* 1 meeting of a small group of politicians to decide upon candidates, policies, an agenda, etc. ‖ *v* (**-cused** or **-cussed; -cus·ing** or **-cus·sing**) *vt* 2 to hold a caucus

cau·dal /kôd'əl/ [< L *cauda* tail] *adj* 1 pert. to a tail; 2 taillike

caught /kôt/ *pt* & *pp* of catch

caul /kôl/ [MF *cale* small cap] *n* part of the fetal membrane which sometimes covers the head at birth

caul·dron /kôl'drən/ *n* caldron

cau'li·flow'er /kôl'i-, kol'-/ [It *cavolfiore* = cabbage flower] *n* variety of cabbage (*Brassica oleracea botrytis*) with a compact flowering head

cau'li·flow'er ear' *n* ear permanently thickened by repeated blows

caulk /kôk'/ [ME < L *calcare* to tramp] *vt* to make watertight by filling the crevices ‖ **caulk'er** *n*

caus·al /kôz'əl/ *adj* pert. to or expressing a cause ‖ **cau·sal'i·ty** /-zal'itē/ *n* (**-ties**)

cau·sa'tion *n* 1 act of causing or producing; 2 agency producing a result; 3 relation between cause and effect

caus'a·tive *adj* **1** effective as an agency; **2** *gram* expressing causation ‖ *n* **3** *gram* word, esp. a verb expressing causation, as the verb *have* in *John is having a new house built*

cause /kôz'/ [L *causa*] *n* **1** anything that produces a result; **2** circumstance, force, or condition from which an effect follows; **3** good reason, as *he was discharged without cause;* **4** subject which arouses interest and support; **5** lawsuit; **6** ground or subject matter of a lawsuit; **7 make common cause** to unite for a common end ‖ *vt* **8** to produce; bring about ‖ **cause'less** *adj* ‖ SYN *n* occasion, source, origin, reason, motive; *v* effect, create, occasion ‖ DISCR *Cause* is that which produces effect, and hence is the general term including in certain senses *motive*, *reason*, and *occasion*. *Cause* may be used of animate and inanimate things; whatever happens issues from a something that brought it about—a *cause*. A *reason* is the fact or argument offered by the mind of a rational being for an act, a conclusion, determination, etc.; loosely, a *reason* thus adduced is said to be the *cause* of the act or conclusion, though, technically, *reason* names a certain part or parts of a syllogistically expressed argument. Lack of capital may be the *reason*, or the *cause*, of failure in business. In "my *reason* for going does not concern you," however, *cause* could not be substituted for *reason*. A *motive* is an impulse of a rational being which, if allowed to run its course, results in action, as jealousy was the *motive* of the murderer; a *motive* may grow out of an external source as well, and become an incitement to, and hence a *cause* of, action, as the desire for fame was the *motive* of the explorer. An *occasion* is a juncture of circumstances that gives rise to, and hence causes, action, as he seized the *occasion* to retire; or it may present a definite *reason* for action, as the *occasion* demanded tact

cause'way' [ONF *caucie* < LL *calciata* paved] *n* raised road, as above shallow water or wet ground

caus·tic /kôs'tik/ [Gk *kaustikos* burning] *adj* **1** capable of burning or corroding living tissue by chemical action; **2** sarcastic, severely critical ‖ *n* **3** caustic substance ‖ **caus'ti·cal·ly** *adv*

caus'tic pot'ash *n* potassium hydroxide

caus'tic so'da *n* sodium hydroxide

cau·ter·ize /kôt'ərīz'/ [< Gk *kauterion* branding iron] *vt* to burn (a wound), as with a hot iron or a caustic, in order to destroy unwanted tissue and prevent infection ‖ **cau'ter·i·za'tion** *n*

cau·tion /kôsh'ən/ [L *cautio* (-*onis*)] *n* **1** heedfulness, care, wariness; **2** warning ‖ *vt* **3** to warn ‖ SYN *v* advise, warn, admonish, counsel, dissuade; *n* heed; advice, counsel (see *care*)

cau'tion·ar'y *adj* pert. to or conveying a warning

cau'tious *adj* exercising or characterized by caution ‖ **cau'tious·ly** *adv* ‖ **cau'tious·ness** *n* ‖ SYN watchful, wary, circumspect (see *careful*)

cav·al·cade /kav'əlkād/ [F < It *cavalcare* to ride] *n* procession, esp. of horses and carriages

cav·a·lier /kav'əlir'/ [MF = knight] *n* **1** horseman, knight; **2** gay adventurer; **3** lady's escort; **4 Cavalier** partisan of Charles I of England in his struggle with Parliament ‖ *adj* haughty, disdainful ‖ **cav'a·lier'ly** *adv*

cav·al·ry /kav'əlrē/ [It *cavalleria*] *n* (-ries) **1** mounted troops; **2** motorized armored units ‖ **cav'al·ry·man** /-mən, -man'/ *n* (-men /-mən, -men'/)

cave /kāv'/ [OF < LL *cava*] *n* **1** hollow place in the earth, den ‖ *vi* **2 cave in, a** to fall in, collapse; **b** *colloq* to give in

ca·ve·at /kāv'ē·at'/ [L = let him beware] *n* **1** warning; caution; **2** *law* notice given to a legal officer not to perform a certain act until the notifier is heard from

ca've·at' emp'tor /emp'tôr/ [L = let the buyer beware] *n* maxim of commercial law meaning that a buyer purchases at his own risk

cave'-in' *n* collapse, falling in, as of a hollow interior space

cave' man' *n* **1** Stone Age cave dweller; **2** *colloq* man who uses brute strength in a primitive way, esp. in his treatment of women

cav·ern /kav'ərn/ [MF *caverne*] *n* cave, esp. a large one

cav'ern·ous *adj* **1** like a cavern; **2** containing caverns; **3** hollow-sounding; deep

cav·i·ar or **cav·i·are** /kav'ē·är'/ [It *caviaro*] *n* sturgeon roe

cav·il /kav'əl/ [L *cavilla* mockery] *v* (-iled or -illed; -il·ing or -il·ling) **1** to find fault without good reason ‖ *n* **2** frivolous or captious objection

cav·i·ty /kav'itē/ [MF *cavité*] *n* (-ties) **1** hollow place; hole; **2** hollow place in a tooth caused by decay ‖ SYN gap, hole, opening, dent, excavation, hollow

ca·vort /kəvôrt'/ [?] *vi* to prance about; to caper, frolic

caw /kô/ [imit] *n* **1** cry of a crow ‖ *vi* **2** to utter a caw

cay /kā', kē/ [Sp *cayo*] *n* key²

cay·enne (**pep'per**) /kī·en'/ [earlier *cayan* < Tupi *kyinha*] *n* very hot red pepper made from the seeds or fruit of different species of capsicum

cay·use /kī'ōōs/ [*Cayuse* AmInd tribe] *n* Indian pony

Cb *chem* columbium

CB or **cit'i·zens band'** *n* shortwave radio frequencies for local and private two-way communication

C′ bat'ter·y *n* battery used to provide a voltage bias to the grid or other control electrode of a vacuum tube

cc or **cc.** or **c.c.** cubic centimeter(s)

Cd *chem* cadmium

Ce *chem* cerium

cease /sēs/ [OF *cesser* < L *cessare*] *vt & vi* to stop, discontinue ∥ **cease'-less** *adj* ∥ SYN terminate, desist, pause, refrain, quit

cease'-fire' *n* 1 suspension of hostilities; 2 order to suspend hostilities

ce·cum /sēk'əm/ [L (intestinum) *caecum* blind (gut)] *n* (**-ca** /-kə/) pouch-like upper end of the large intestine

ce·dar /sēd'ər/ [OF *cedre* < Gk *kedros*] *n* 1 any of several species (genus *Cedrus*) of Old World evergreen trees of the pine family having durable and fragrant wood; 2 any of several cone-bearing North American trees similar to the true cedar

cede /sēd'/ [L *cedere*] *vt* to give up; formally transfer title to ∥ SYN give, grant, yield, admit, transfer

ce·dil·la /sidil'ə/ [Sp = little z] *n* mark, placed under certain letters in some alphabets, as ç in French and Portuguese, to indicate a change in pronunciation

ceil·ing /sēl'ing/ [< ME *celen* to screen, line] *n* 1 overhead covering of a room; 2 upper limit; 3 highest sale price permitted; 4 a maximum altitude to which an airplane can ascend; b upper limit of visibility at a given time or place

cel·e·brant /sel'əbrənt/ *n* one who performs a public religious ceremony, as a priest at Mass

cel'e·brate' [L *celebrare* (-atus)] *vt* 1 to perform publicly with appropriate ceremonies; 2 to give honor and glory to; 3 to commemorate with suitable observances ∥ *vi* 4 to officiate at a religious ceremony; 5 to commemorate an event with festivities ∥ **cel'e·bra'tion** *n* ∥ SYN commemorate, keep, observe, solemnize ∥ DISCR To *celebrate* is to mark an event or occasion by suitable observance; we *celebrate* a happy occasion with joy, a grave occasion with dignity, a religious feast with fit ceremony. To *commemorate* is to signalize the memory of some person or event with appropriate formalities. To *observe* is to mark a day or occasion with prescribed conduct, as *observe* the Sabbath. *Keep* is applied chiefly to religious occasions;

it is less formal than *observe*, but implies a certain observance of procedure, as to *keep* the Passover. *Solemnize* is used of sacred rites, as to *solemnize* a marriage

cel'e·brat'ed *adj* renowned, famous ∥ SYN famed, famous, noted, glorious, eminent (see *distinguished*)

ce·leb·ri·ty /səleb'ritē/ *n* (**-ties**) *n* 1 renown; 2 person in the public eye

ce·ler·i·ty /səler'itē/ [MF *celerite* < L *celeritas*] *n* rapidity, swiftness ∥ SYN quickness, velocity, dispatch, rapidity, speed

cel·er·y /sel'ərē/ [F *céléri* < Gk *selinon*] *n* garden plant (*Apium graveolens*), the blanched stalks of which are used as food

ce·les·ta /səles'tə/ [< L *caelestis*] *n* keyboard instrument consisting of a series of steel plates struck by hammers and producing a bell-like tone

ce·les·tial /səles'chəl/ [< L *caelestis*] *adj* 1 pert. to the heavens or sky; 2 heavenly, divine ∥ SYN heavenly ∥ DISCR *Celestial* and *heavenly*, when used to designate the visible sky, are interchangeable, as *heavenly* bodies; the *celestial* blue. When not used in the physical sense, *celestial* describes what comes supposedly from heaven itself, as a *celestial* messenger; the *celestial* choir; *heavenly* is used more commonly in a spiritual sense, connoting the qualities of the divine

ce·les'tial e·qua'tor *n* projection of the equator upon the celestial sphere

ce·les'tial pole' *n* one of the points at which the axis of the earth, when extended, touches the celestial sphere and about which the stars seem to revolve

ce·les'tial sphere' *n* imaginary hollow hemisphere, forming the sky over an observer's head, on the surface of which the celestial bodies are seemingly attached

cel·i·ba·cy /sel'əbəsē/ *n* 1 state of being unmarried; 2 sexual continence

cel'i·bate /-bit/ [< L *caelebs* (-*libis*) unmarried] *n* 1 unmarried person; 2 sexually continent person ∥ also *adj*

cell /sel'/ [OF *celle* < L *cella* small room] *n* 1 small room, as in a monastery or jail; 2 minute mass of protoplasm, one of the units of structure of living matter; 3 small unit in a larger organization; 4 small cavity or compartment, as in a honeycomb or lung; 5 device for generating electricity by chemical action

cel·lar /sel'ər/ [AF *celer* < L *cellarium* pantry] *n* 1 room or rooms under a building, partly or wholly below ground; 2 *sports* lowest standing among a group of teams

cel·lar·et /sel'əret'/ [*dim.* of *cellar*] *n* cabinet for keeping bottles of wine

cell′ block′ *n* section of a prison containing cells

cel·lo /chel′ō/ [< It *violoncello*=small bass viol] *n* (-los or -li /-lē/) third largest member of the violin family, smaller and higher pitched than the bass viol || **cel′list** *n*

cel·lo·phane /sel′əfān′/ [< *cellulose* + Gk *phainein* to show] *n* thin transparent material made from cellulose, used for wrapping

cel·lu·lar /sel′yələr/ [< L *cellula* small room] *adj* pert. to, consisting of, or like cells

Cel·lu·loid /sel′yəloid′/ [trademark] *n* inflammable plastic made of camphor and guncotton

cel′lu·lose′ /-lōs′/ [< L *cellula* small room] *n* carbohydrate that is the chief substance of the cell walls of plants

cel′lu·lose ac′e·tate *n* any of a group of esters of cellulose, used in making artificial silks, lacquers, cigarette filters, photographic film, etc.

Cel·si·us /sel′sē·əs, -shəs/ [Anders *Celsius* (1701–44) Sw astronomer] *s* centigrade scale of temperature || also *adj*

Celt /selt′, kelt′/ [L *Celta*] *n* member of an Indo-European race comprising the Irish, Gaels, Welsh, Cornish, and Bretons || **Celt′ic** *adj* & *n*

ce·ment /siment′/ [OF *ciment* < L *caementum* stone chippings] *n* 1 calcined mixture of clay, limestone, and other materials which hardens when wet, used in construction; 2 any adhesive substance; 3 anything that binds or unites; 4 *dentistry* a bony substance that covers the roots of teeth; b plastic, made of zinc, copper, or silica, used to repair teeth || *vt* 5 to unite firmly, as with cement; 6 to cover or pave with cement || *vi* 7 to be cemented

ce·men′tum *n* dentistry bony substance that covers the roots of teeth

cem·e·ter·y /sem′iter′ē/ [Gk *koimeterion* sleeping place] *n* (-ies) burial ground, graveyard

cen·o·taph /sen′ətaf′, -täf′/ [< Gk *kenos* empty + *taphos* tomb] *n* sepulchral monument erected in memory of a person buried elsewhere

Ce·no·zo·ic /sēn′əzō′ik, sen′-/ [< Gk *kainos* recent + *zoe* life] *n* era of the rise of mammals, following the Mesozoic and preceding the Recent era || also *adj*

cen·ser /sens′ər/ [AF < ML *incensarium*] *n* vessel in which incense is burned

cen·sor /sens′ər/ [L = assessor] *n* 1 official who examines anything to be read, heard, or viewed, in order to suppress some objectionable feature on moral, political, or military grounds || *vt* 2 to act as censor of, expurgate || **cen′sor·ship′** *n* || **cen·so′ri·al** /-sôr′ē·əl, -sōr′-/ *adj*

cen·so′ri·ous /-sôr′ē·əs, -sōr′-/ *adj* critical, carping || SYN reproving, carping, condemnatory, blaming

cen·sure /sen′shər/ [L *censura*] *n* 1 strong expression of disapproval || *vt* 2 to find fault with, blame || **cen′sur·a·ble** *adj* || SYN *v* upbraid, chide, criticize, condemn (see *blame*) || ANT *v* praise, approve, commend, laud

cen·sus /sens′əs/ [L] *n* official count of persons, property, or things

cent /sent′/ [L *centum* 100] *n* 1 100th part of a dollar; 2 coin of this value, penny

cent. 1 centigrade; 2 central; 3 century

cen·taur /sent′ôr/ [Gk *kentauros*] *n* 1 *Gk myth.* one of a race of beings, half man and half horse; 2 **Centaur** *astron* Centaurus

Cen·tau′rus *n* (*gen* -ri /-rī/) southern constellation

cen·ta·vo /sentäv′ō/ [Sp & Port] *n* 100th part of the monetary units of the Portuguese and some Spanish-speaking countries

cen·te·nar·i·an /sent′ənər′ē·ən/ *n* person 100 years old or over || also *adj*

cen′te·nar′y /sent′əner′ē, [L *centenarius*] *n* (-ies) 1 100 years; 2 centennial || also *adj*

cen·ten·ni·al /senten′ē·əl/ [L *centum* 100 + *biennial*] *adj* 1 consisting of or enduring 100 years; 2 taking place once in 100 years || *n* 3 100th anniversary

cen·ter /sent′ər/ [Gk *kentron* center point] *n* 1 middle point, as within a circle or sphere, equidistant from all points on the circumference or surface; 2 middle point of anything; 3 pivot point; 4 focal point; 5 principal place of an activity, as *a financial center;* 6 *sports* player at the center of the line, floor, etc.; 7 **Center,** a members of a political party that follows policies midway between the Left and Right; b political moderates collectively || *vt* 8 to place on or at the center; 9 to gather to a point || *vi* 10 to be at or converge toward the center

cen′ter·board′ *n* extension keel that may be lowered vertically through the bottom of a boat to prevent lateral drift and leeway

cen′ter of grav′i·ty *n* point at which the weight of a body or system of bodies is equally balanced

cen′ter of mass′ *n* point in a body at which the entire mass of the body is considered concentrated

cen′ter·piece′ *n* ornament placed at the center of a table

cen′ter punch′ *n* tool for making slight dents in metal to mark the precise spot for drilling || **cen′ter·punch′** *vt*

cen·tes·i·mo /sentes′imō′/ [Sp & It] *n* 100th part of the monetary units of Italy and some Spanish-speaking countries

centi- [< L *centum*] *comb form* 1 hundred; 2 hundredth part of

cen'ti·grade' /sent'i-/ *adj* designating a temperature scale in which 0° is the freezing point and 100° the boiling point of water

cen'ti·gram' *n* 100th of a gram, or 0.15432 grain

cen'ti·li'ter *n* 100th part of a liter, or .6102 cubic inch

cen·time /sän'tēm/ [F] *n* 100th part of a franc

cen'ti·me'ter *n* 100th part of a meter, or ab. .3937 inch

cen'ti·me'ter-gram'-sec'ond *adj* of or pert. to the system of measurement in which the centimeter, gram, and second are the principal units of length, mass, and time

cén·ti·mo /sent'imō'/ [Sp] *n* 100th part of the monetary units of some Spanish-speaking countries

cen'ti·pede' /-pēd'/ [L *centipeda*] *n* any of a class (Chilopoda) of invertebrates with bodies of many segments, each segment bearing a pair of legs

cen·tral /sent'rəl/ [L *centralis*] *adj* 1 relating to, or situated in, the center; 2 chief, leading || *n* telephone exchange || **cen'tral·ly** *adv*

Cen'tral Af'ri·can Em'pire *n* country in central Africa (3,000,000; 241,305 sq.m.; cap. Bangui)

Cen'tral A·mer'i·ca *n* region of North America between Mexico and South America || **Cen'tral A·mer'i·can** *adj & n*

Cen'tral In·tel'li·gence A'gen·cy *n* agency of the executive branch of the U.S. Government that coordinates intelligence activities

cen'tral·ize *vt* 1 to draw or bring to the center; 2 to bring under one control || **cen'tral·i·za'tion** *n*

Cen'tral Pow'ers *npl* opponents of the Allies in World War I (Germany, Austria-Hungary, Bulgaria, and Turkey)

centri- [Gk *kentron*] *comb form* center

cen·trif·u·gal /sentrif'yəgəl/ [< *centri-* + L *fugere* to flee] *adj* 1 directed away from the center; 2 pert. to or operated by centrifugal force

cen'tri·fu'gal force' *n* force which impels a rotating body or objects on it away from the center of rotation

cen'tri·fuge' /-trifyōōj'/ *n* rotating apparatus which separates substances of different densities by centrifugal force

cen·trip·e·tal /-trip'itəl/ [< *centri-* + L *petere* to seek] *adj* 1 directed toward the center; 2 pert. to or operated by centripetal force

cen'trip'e·tal force' *n* force which impels a rotating body or objects on it toward the center of rotation

cen·tu·ri·on /sent(y)ŏŏr'ē·ən/ [see **century**] *n* ancient Roman commander of military unit of 100 men

cen·tu·ry /sench'ərē/ [L *centuria* division of 100] *n* (-ries) any period of

100 years, esp. one starting with a year ending in -01 (or the year 1) and ending in -00

cen'tu·ry plant *n* plant of the genus *Agave*, esp. *A. americana*, with long, fleshy, spiny leaves and a treelike flower stalk, mistakenly believed to bloom only once in 100 years

ce·phal·ic /səfal'ik/ [< Gk *kephale* head] *adj* of or pert. to the head

ce·phal'ic in'dex *n* ratio, multiplied by 100, of the breadth to the front-to-back length of the head

ceph·a·lo·pod /sef'ələpod'/ [< Gk *kephale* head + *pous* (*podos*) foot] *n* any mollusk of the class Cephalopoda, as the octopus, having tentacles attached to a central head

ce·ram·ic /səram'ik/ [< Gk *keramos* pottery] *adj* 1 of or pert. to objects made of clay and similar materials, as pottery, tiles, etc.; 2 pert. to ceramics

ce·ram·ics *nsg* 1 art and technology of making ceramic products || *npl* 2 ceramic products

Cer·ber·us /sur'bərəs/ *n class. myth.* three-headed dog which guarded the gates of Hades

ce·re·al /sir'ē·əl/ [< *Ceres*] *n* 1 any grass that yields a food grain; 2 any of these grains, as wheat and oats; 3 food made from grain || also *adj*

cer·e·bel·lum /ser'ibel'əm/ [L *dim.* of *cerebrum*] *n* (-lums; -la /-lə/) lobe at the back of the brain behind and below the cerebrum, which coordinates muscular movements

cer·e·bral /ser'əbrəl, sərēb'-/ *adj* 1 of or pert. to the brain or the cerebrum; 2 intellectual

cer'e·bral pal'sy *n* paralysis caused usu. by injury at birth, characterized by poor muscular control and spasms

cer·e·brum /ser'əbrəm, sərēb'-/ *n* (-brums; -bra /-brə/) [L = brain] larger part of the brain in front of and above the cerebellum and consisting of two hemispheres

cer·e·mo·ni·al /ser'əmōn'ē·əl/ *adj* 1 relating to or performed with ceremony; 2 formal || *n* 3 ritual; 4 proper observance of social formalities on a given occasion || **cer'e·mo'ni·al·ly** *adv*

cer·e·mo·ni·ous *adj* characterized by ceremony; formal || **cer'e·mo'ni·ous·ly** *adv* || SYN formal, conventional || DISCR These words are alike in indicating a devotion to form or ceremony. *Ceremonious* describes occasions or things characterized by fullness of rite or polite observance, as a *ceremonious* church service; a *ceremonious* visit. Carried to excess, *ceremonious* takes on an elaborateness that makes it pompous or even ridiculous. A *ceremonious* person is one who so fully observes every formality that he runs the risk of being too punctilious. *Formal* emphasizes a method of procedure; *formal* calls, *formal* intercourse between nations, *formal* parties, are carried out in an almost businesslike way; applied to the observance of social usages, *formal* suggests such a devotion to propriety that the result is oppressive. *Conventional* manners and people are those that are just what they are expected to be at all times

cer·e·mo·ny [MF *ceremonie* < L *caerimonia*] *n* (**-nies**) **1** sacred rite or observance; **2** prescribed and formal usages observed on a public occasion; **3** behavior regulated by strict etiquette; **4** empty formality ‖ SYN ceremonial, form, rite, observance ‖ DISCR *Form* emphasizes a customary or accepted mode of action; there is a certain *form* followed in conducting a church service; social behavior is governed by certain *forms*. *Formality* implies a strict adherence to *forms*, and frequently is no more than the routine execution of social or other duties, as the monotonous *formalities* of social life. *Ceremony* names an outward manifestation attending a religious or public occasion; *ceremony* is apt to be stately, rather elaborate, often beautiful and impressive, as the *ceremonies* dedicating the chapel were impressive. A *rite* is a solemn *observance* sanctioned by custom; it is applied to the stated ordinances of the church, or to the ceremonious acts comprising the ritual of a society

Ce·res /sir'ēz/ *n* Roman goddess of agriculture

ce·rise /sərēz'/ [F = cherry] *n* bright red ‖ also *adj*

ce·ri·um /sir'ē·əm/ [< *Ceres*] *n* hard brittle steel-gray metallic element (Ce; at.no. 58; at.wt. 140.12) of the rare-earth group

cer·tain /surt'ən/ [OF < L *certus*] *adj* **1** sure, positive; **2** fixed, settled; **3** destined, inevitable; **4** specific, but not named, as *a certain city;* **5** somewhat; **6 for certain** without a doubt ‖ SYN secure, positive, undeniable, confident, authentic ‖ ANT doubtful, equivocal, obscure, precarious

cer·tain·ly *adv* **1** surely, without fail; **2** gladly, of course

cer·tain·ty *n* (**-ties**) **1** established fact; **2** state of being certain; **3** something sure to happen ‖ SYN fact, certitude, confidence, assurance, proof, surety ‖ ANT doubt, uncertainty, misgiving, conjecture

cer·tif·i·cate /sərtif'ikit/ [ML *certificatum*] *n* **1** written statement serving as evidence of status, privileges, character, qualifications, etc. ‖ /-kāt'/ *vt* **2** to attest by a certificate; **3** to furnish with a certificate

cer'ti·fied pub'lic ac·count'ant *n* ac-

countant who holds an official certificate stating that he has met the requirements of his State

cer·ti·fy /surt'ifī'/ [< L *certus* certain + *-fy*] *v* (**-fied**) *vt* **1** to declare to be true, accurate, or valid, by formal statement; **2** to guarantee payment of (a check); **3** to issue a certificate of qualification to; **4** *Brit* to declare legally insane ‖ **cer'ti·fi'a·ble** *adj* ‖ **cer'ti·fi·ca'tion** *n*

cer·ti·o·ra·ri /sur'shē·ərer'ī/ [L = to be made more certain] *n law* writ requiring a lower court to furnish the records of a case to a higher court

cer·ti·tude /surt'it(y)ōōd'/ [L *certitudo*] *n* assurance, certainty

ce·ru·le·an /sərōōl'ē·ən/ [L *caeruleus*] *n* azure, sky blue ‖ also *adj*

Cer·van·tes, Mi·guel de /migel' dā sərvan'tēz/ *n* (1547–1616) Spain's most famous writer, author of *Don Quixote*

cer·vix /sur'viks/ [L = neck] *n* (**-vix·es** or **-vi·ces** /-visēz'/) *anat* **1** neck; **2** constricted part of an organ, as the lower end of the uterus ‖ **cer'vi·cal** *adj*

Cé·saire, Ai·mé /emā' sāzer'/ *n* (1913–) French poet, playwright, and politician, born in Martinique

ce·si·um /sēz'ē·əm/ [< L *caesius* bluish gray] *n* rare silvery metallic element (Cs; at.no. 55; at.wt. 132.905), used in photoelectric cells

ces·sa·tion /sesāsh'ən/ [< L *cessare* (*-atus*) to cease] *n* stopping, discontinuance ‖ SYN intermission, rest, respite, pause, end, close

ces·sion /sesh'ən/ [L *cessio* (*-onis*) surrender] *n* act of ceding

cess'pool' /ses'-/ [It *cesso* privy] *n* **1** deep hole in the ground to receive sewage; **2** filthy place; **3** place of moral filth

ces·tus /sest'əs/ [L *caestus*] *n* ancient Roman boxing glove consisting of leather thongs often loaded with lead or iron

ce·su·ra /siz(y)ōōr'ə, -zhōōr'ə/ *n* var of caesura

ce·ta·cean /sitāsh'ən/ [< L *cetus* whale] *n* any of an order (Cetacea) of sea mammals including the whale, dolphin, and porpoise

Cey·lon /sēlon'/ *n* former name of the island republic of Sri Lanka ‖ **Cey·lo·nese** /sē'lənēz', -nēs'/ *adj & n* (**-nese**)

Cf *chem* californium

cf. [L *confer*] compare

cg. centigram(s)

cgs also **c.g.s, CGS** centimeter-gram-second

ch. chapter

Ch., ch. church

Chab·lis /shablē'/ [town in France] *n* dry white French table wine, or one like it

cha-cha /chä'chä'/ *n* Latin American dance || also *vi*

Chad /chad'/ *n* republic in N central Africa, east of Lake Chad (3,360,000; 495,000 sq.m.; cap. N'djamena)

chafe /chāf'/ [MF *chaufer* to heat] *vt* 1 to warm by friction; 2 to abrade or make sore by rubbing; 3 to annoy, irritate || *vi* 4 to rub; 5 to be made sore by rubbing; 6 to be vexed; 7 **chafe at the bit** to become impatient || *n* 8 sore caused by friction or wear; 9 state of irritation || SYN *v* fret, gall, vex, pique, inflame, rub

chaff /chaf', chäf'/ [OE *ceaf*] *n* 1 husks of grain; 2 straw cut up for fodder; 3 anything worthless; 4 good-natured raillery || *vt & vi* to tease || SYN *n* badinage, banter, jesting, teasing, raillery

chaf·fer /chaf'ǝr/ [< ME *cheapfare* trade < OE *cēap* trade + *faru* journey] *vi* 1 to bargain, haggle; 2 to chat, chatter

chaf·finch /chaf'inch/ [< OE *ceaffinc*] *n* common European songbird (*Fringilla coelebs*)

chaf'ing dish' /chāf'iŋ/ *n* covered pan with a heating device for cooking at the table

cha·grin /shǝgrin'/ [F] *n* 1 vexation due to disappointment or mortification || *vt* 2 to excite vexation in, mortify || SYN *n* dismay, humiliation, shame, disappointment, vexation || DISCR *Mortification* is a painful feeling of *humiliation*, born of wounded pride or self-importance. *Vexation* is a compound of irritation and annoyance, often arising from dissatisfaction or disappointment. *Chagrin* combines the disagreeable elements of *mortification* and *vexation*, with a particularly large measure of *humiliation*; chagrin is keenly felt because the cause of it is usually unexpected. People who make a great show of poverty feel *mortification* when the fact that they have plenty of money is disclosed; *vexation* is natural when an always tardy friend causes us to miss the first act of a play; one who cherishes the belief that he is popular will experience *chagrin* when disillusioned. *Shame* brings a sense of guilt or culpable failure, and, often, of *humiliation*

chain /chān'/ [OF *chaeine* < L *catena*] *n* 1 series of links joined together; 2 any connected series, as a *chain of events*; 3 **chains** *pl* fetters; bondage || *vt* 4 to fasten with, or as with, a chain; 5 to fetter; restrain

chain' gang' *n* gang of convicts fastened together by a chain while at work

chain' let'ter *n* letter sent to a number of people, each of whom is supposed to make copies and send them to an equal number of people, as a means of spreading a message or collecting money

chain' re·ac'tion *n* 1 *chem* series of changes in which each successive change produces the causative factor to perpetuate the change throughout the available mass; 2 self-sustaining nuclear fission in which the number of neutrons produced is steadily equal to or greater than the number lost; 3 any series of events in which each event is the result of the one preceding and the cause of the one following

chain' smok'er *n* person who smokes one cigarette or cigar after another without letup

chain' store' *n* one of a number of stores under the same ownership

chair /cher'/ [MF *chaiere* < L *cathedra*] *n* 1 movable seat with a back; 2 office or position of honor, dignity, or authority; 3 chairman || *vt* 4 to preside over (a meeting)

chair' lift' *n* cable on which chairs carrying skiers are towed up the side of a slope

chair·man /-mǝn/ *n* (**-men** /-mǝn/) presiding officer of a meeting, committee, board, or college department || **chair'man·ship'** *n* || **chair'wom'an** *nfem*

chaise longue /shāz' lôŋ'/ [F = long chair] *n* (**chaise longues** /-ŋz/) couch with a long seat for the legs

chal·ced·o·ny /kalsed'ǝnē, kal'sǝdōn'ē/ [< *Chalcedon* city in Asia Minor] *n* (**-nies**) pale-blue or gray quartz, waxy in luster, including the onyx, agate, etc.

Chal·de·a /kaldē'ǝ/ *n* ancient country in Mesopotamia inhabited by a Semitic people who became the dominant group in Babylonia || **Chal·de'an** *adj & n*

cha·let /shalā'/ *n* wide-eaved cottage, common in the Swiss Alps

chal·ice /chal'is/ [MF < L *calix* (*-icis*)] *n* 1 goblet; 2 cup used in celebrating the Eucharist

chalk /chôk'/ [OE *cealc* < L *calx* (*calcis*) lime] *n* 1 soft white stone composed largely of calcium carbonate; 2 piece of this or a similar substance for writing on blackboards || *vt* 3 to write, mark, rub, or whiten with chalk; 4 **chalk up** to earn or score (points, runs, etc.) || **chalk'y** *adj* || **chalk'i·ness** *n*

chalk'board' *n* blackboard

chal·lenge /chal'inj/ [OF *challenge* < L *calumnia* calumny] *n* 1 call to engage in a contest or combat; 2 calling to question; 3 demand made upon someone; 4 demand for the countersign by a sentry; 5 objection to the seating of a juror || *vt* 6 to make a challenge to; 7 to call for, as inspection || **chal'leng·er** *n* || SYN *v* claim, summon, dispute, defy (see *question*)

cham'ber /chām'bər/ [MF *chambre* < L *camera* vault] *n* **1** room in a residence, esp. a bedroom; **2** a place where a legislative assembly meets; **b** the assembly itself; **3** enclosed space or compartment; **4** the part of a gun that holds the cartridge; **5** **chambers** *pl* office of a judge near the courtroom

cham'ber·lain /-lin/ [OF *chambrelenc*] *n* **1** official in charge of a sovereign's or nobleman's household; **2** treasurer, steward

cham'ber·maid *n* woman who cleans and takes care of bedrooms

cham'ber mu'sic *n* music suitable for a room or small hall and esp. for a small group of solo instruments

cham'ber of com'merce *n* association intended to further the business interests of a community

cham'ber pot' *n* portable vessel for urine, used in bedrooms

cha·me·le·on /kəmēl'ē·ən, -yən/ [MF *camelion* < Gk *chamaileon* ground lion] *n* **1** any of various European (family Chamaelontidae) or American (genus *Anolis*) lizards that have the power of changing color; **2** inconstant person

cham·ois /sham'ē/ [F] *n* **1** (-ois) goatlike antelope (*Rupicapra rupicapra*) found on high mountain peaks in Europe and western Asia; **2** soft thin leather originally made from chamois skin

champ[1] /champ'/ [prob imit] *vt* **1** to bite repeatedly and impatiently || *vi* **2** **champ at the bit** to show impatience at delay

champ[2] *n colloq* champion

cham·pagne /shampān'/ [*Champagne* F region] *n* light sparkling French wine or one like it

cham·pi·on /champ'ē·ən/ [OF < LL *campio* (-*onis*) fighter] *n* **1** winner in a competition; **2** person or thing superior to all others; **3** defender of a person or cause || *vt* **4** to defend or support || **cham'pi·on·ship'** *n*

chance /chans', chäns'/ [OF *cheance* < LL *cadentia* happening] *n* **1** luck, fortune; **2** possibility or probability; **3** opportunity; **4** risk; **5** unknown agency supposed to cause certain unexplained events; fate; **6** share in a lottery; **7** **chances** *pl* probability; **8** **by chance** without intent || *adj* **9** accidental || *vi* **10** to happen by chance; **11** **chance on** or **upon** to come upon by chance || *vt* **12** to risk || **SYN** *n* contingency, incident, accident, opportunity

chan·cel /chans'əl, chäns'-/ [MF = screened enclosure] *n* in certain churches, that part of the church surrounding the altar reserved for the clergy

chan'cel·ler·y /-ərē/ *n* (-ies) **1** office or position of a chancellor; **2** embassy or legation office

chan'cel·lor /-lər/ [OF *chancelier* < LL *cancellarius* usher in a law court] *n* **1** prime minister of certain countries; **2** president of certain universities; **3** secretary of a king, noble, or embassy; **4** judge of a court of chancery || **chan'cel·lor·ship'** *n*

Chan'cel·lor of the Ex·cheq'uer *n* British cabinet minister (= Secretary of the Treasury)

chan'cer·y /-sərē/ [*abbr* of *chancellery*] *n* (-ies) **1** court of equity in some states; **2** administrative office of a diocese; **3** **in chancery** *wrestling* with the opponent's head held under the arm

chan·cre /shaŋk'ər/ [MF < L *cancer*] *n* initial lesion of syphilis

chanc'y *adj* (-i·er; -i·est) risky, uncertain

chan·de·lier /shan'dəlir'/ [F = candlestick] *n* branched support for several lights hanging from a ceiling

change /chānj'/ [OF *changer* < LL *cambiare*] *vt* **1** to substitute something else for; **2** to exchange; **3** to alter; **4** to give or get smaller units of money for; **5** to replace the sheets of (a bed); **6** to replace the diapers on || *vi* **7** to undergo alteration, vary; **8** to pass from one place or phase to another; **9** to put on different clothes; **10** to make an exchange; **11** to change trains or buses, etc. || *n* **12** alteration; **13** variation; **14** substitution; **15** variableness, variety; **16** different set of clothes; **17** small coins collectively; **18** money returned with a purchase equal to the difference between the money paid and the purchase price; **19** **ring the changes,** **a** to ring a set of bells with all possible variations; **b** to repeat an act or statement with many variations || **chang'er** *n* || **change'a·ble** *adj* || **change'less** *adj* **SYN** *v* vary, transform, convert, substitute, alter, modify (see *qualify*) || **ANT** *v* continue, remain, keep

change'ling *n* child substituted for another

change' of life' *n* menopause

change' of ven'ue *n law* removal of a trial to another county

change'o'ver *n* conversion of one system of operation to another

chan·nel /chan'əl/ [OF *chanel* < L *canalis* water pipe] *n* **1** bed of a stream, river, etc.; **2** deepest part of a bay, harbor, etc., where ships may pass; **3** body of water joining two larger ones; **4** long groove or furrow; **5** way by which anything may be carried or communicated; **6** *electron.* frequency band for the transmission of signals; **7** **channels** *pl* official course of communication || *v* (-neled

or -nelled; -nel·ing or -nel·ling) vt 8
to cut a groove in; 9 to carry through
or as through a channel; 10 to direct into a particular course

Chan′nel Is′lands npl group of British
Islands in the English Channel off
the coast of France

chan·nel·ize′ vt 1 to channel; 2 to
widen, deepen, and straighten (a
waterway) to prevent flooding ||
chan·nel·i·za′tion n

chant /chant′, chänt′/ [MF *chanter* to
sing < L *cantare*] n 1 simple melody
in which a number of words are
sung to each note, used in church
services || vt & vi 2 to sing in a chant
|| **chant′er** n

chant·ey /shant′ē, ch-/ n song sung by
sailors while at work

chan·ti·cleer /shant′əklir′/ [OF *Chan-
tecler* rooster in *Reynard the Fox*] n
rooster

cha·os /kā′os/ [Gk] n 1 vacant formless space, as it was thought to have
been before the universe came into
existence; 2 utter confusion or dis-
order || **cha·ot′ic** /-ot′ik/ adj

chap¹ /chap′/ [ME *chappen*] v
(**chapped; chap·ping**) vt 1 to crack or
roughen (the skin) from cold || vi 2
to become chapped

chap² [abbr of Brit *chapman* peddler]
n fellow

chap. 1 chapter; 2 chaplain

chap·ar·ral /chap′əral′/ [< Sp *cha-
parro* evergreen oak] n dense thicket,
esp. of evergreen oaks

cha·peau /shapō′/ [F] (**-peaus, -peaux**
/-pōz′/) n hat

chap·el /chap′əl/ [OF *chapele* < LL
capella cloak] n 1 room or recess in
a cathedral containing an altar; 2
place of worship in a palace, school,
institution, etc.; 3 chapel service; 4
England church of a sect other than
Anglican or Catholic

chap·er·on or **chap·er·one** /shap′ərōn′/
[F = hood] n 1 older person who accompanies young unmarried women
in public || vt 2 to accompany as
chaperon

chap·lain /chap′lin/ [MF *chapelain* <
LL *capellanus*] n clergyman attached
to the armed forces, a public institu-
tion, a private household, etc. ||
chap′lain·cy n

chap·let /chap′lit/ [OF *chapelet*] n 1
garland for the head; 2 string of
beads, esp, prayer beads

chaps /chaps′/ [< Sp *chaparajos*] npl
cowboy's leather or fur overbreeches

chap·ter /chap′tər/ [OF *chapitre* < L
capitulum little head] n 1 main division of a book; 2 local branch of an
organization; 3 body of clergy attached to a cathedral

chap′ter and verse′ adv in full detail;
with great precision

char /chär′/ [< *charcoal*] v (**charred;
char·ring**) vt 1 to scorch; 2 to make

charcoal of || vi 3 to become charred

char·ac·ter /kar′iktər/ [Gk = stamp] n
1 letter or figure engraved or printed,
representing a sound, number, punctuation mark, mathematical symbol,
etc.; 2 distinctive quality or trait; 3
individuality or personality; 4 kind,
sort; 5 moral fiber; 6 status, position;
7 reputation; 8 person; 9 eccentric
person; 10 personage in a play or
novel; 11 structural or functional
trait of a plant or an animal || SYN
constitution, temper (see *disposition*)

char·ac·ter·is′tic adj 1 typical || n 2
distinguishing mark or quality; 3
math integral portion of a logarithm
|| **char·ac·ter·is′ti·cal·ly** adv || SYN n
peculiarity, mark, indication, linea-
ment, attribute, trait, feature, prop-
erty, quality || DISCR A *characteristic*
is a part of the nature of the person,
animal, thing, or group concerned; it
is a distinctive, typical mark, as
almond-shaped eyes are a *characteristic* of some Oriental peoples; charity is the outstanding *characteristic*
of the true Christian. A *feature* is
literally a salient part; it stands out
and arrests the attention, as to the
American, the striking *feature* of
British newspapers is the prosiness
of their news style. A *trait* is a *characteristic* that has the arresting quality of a *feature*; it is chiefly used of
people, since it names mental or
moral *characteristics*, as aggressiveness is an Anglo-Saxon *trait*

char·ac·ter·ize′ vt 1 to indicate the
character of, describe; 2 to mark or
distinguish || **char·ac·ter·i·za′tion** n

cha·rade /shərād′/ [F] n parlor game
in which words to be guessed are
acted out in pantomime

char′coal′ n 1 fuel made by partially
burning wood in the absence of air;
2 a drawing pencil made with it; b
drawing made with such a pencil

chard /chärd′/ [F *chardon* thistle] n
variety of beet (*Beta vulgaris cicla*)
with large edible leaves

charge /chärj′/ [OF *charger* < LL *car-
ricare* to load] vt 1 to provide with
the customary load, addition, or complement, as *to charge a storage battery*; 2 to command, instruct; 3 to
set as the price; 4 to record (an item)
as due; 5 to accuse, as *to charge with
a crime*; 6 to defer payment for (an
item purchased on a charge account);
7 to impose a duty or obligation
upon; 8 to rush upon, attack; 9 to
electrify; 10 *law* to instruct (a jury)
as to the law involved in a case || vi
11 to ask payment; 12 to make an at-
tack || n 13 quantity of material with
which an apparatus is loaded, as a
fire extinguisher or gun; 14 office,
trust, responsibility; 15 minister's
congregation; 16 command or direc-

tion; **17** price, cost; **18** accusation, imputation; **19** attack; **20 a** quantity of electricity that exists on the surface of an insulated electrified conductor; **b** process of charging a storage battery; **c** quantity of electricity in ampere-hours that a storage battery is capable of yielding; **21** *law* address of instruction to the jury; **22 in charge** in command ‖ SYN *v* impute, ascribe, censure, blame, accuse; *n* custody, management, care, cost

charge′ ac·count *n* account, as with a retail store, which enables a customer to buy goods and pay for them later

char·gé d′af·faires /shärzhā′ dəfer′/ [F = one in charge] *n* (**chargés d′af-faires**) diplomat in charge of an embassy or legation in the absence of the ambassador or minister

charg′er *n* **1** war horse; **2** device for charging storage batteries

char·i·ot /char′ē·ət/ [OF] *n* ancient two-wheeled horse-drawn car used in war, racing, and processions ‖ **char′i·ot·eer′** /-tir′/ *n*

cha·ris·ma /kəriz′mə/ [Gk] *n* (**-mata** /-mətə/) **1** gift or power conferred by God; **2** special gift or power possessed by certain leaders that inspires undying loyalty and devotion among their followers ‖ **charis-mat·ic** /kar′izmat′ik/ *adj*

char·i·ta·ble /char′itəbəl/ *adj* **1** liberal, generous; **2** forgiving, forbearing; **3** (institution, organization, etc.) providing for those in need ‖ **char′i·ta·bly** *adv* ‖ SYN benevolent, merciful, indulgent, generous, forgiving ‖ ANT stingy, hard-hearted, unforgiving

char·i·ty [OF *charite* < L *caritas* love] *n* (**-ties**) **1** leniency, tolerance; **2** generosity to the poor; **3** alms; **4** universal love and good will; **5** institution or fund for the poor ‖ SYN kindness, beneficence (see *benevolence*)

char·la·tan /shär′lətən/ [MF < It *ciarlatano* chatterer] *n* quack, impostor ‖**char′la·tan·ism** *n*

Char·le·magne /shär′ləmän′/ *n* (742–814) king of the Franks 768–814 and first emperor of the Holy Roman Empire 800–14

Charles I /chärlz′/ *n* **1** (1600–49) king of England and Scotland 1625–49; beheaded by Parliament; **2** (1500–58) king of Spain 1516–56 and, as Charles V, emperor of the Holy Roman Empire 1519–56

Charles II *n* (1630–85) king of England and Scotland 1660–85

Charles′ton /-tən/ *n* capital of West Virginia (86,000)

char′ley horse′ /chär′lē/ *n colloq* painful cramp in an arm or leg muscle from strain or a blow

Char·lotte /shär′lət/ *n* city in North Carolina (205,000)

Char′lotte A·ma′lie /əmäl′yə/ *n* capital of the U.S. Virgin Islands (13,000)

Char′lotte·town′ *n* capital of Prince Edward Island (19,000)

charm /chärm′/ [OF *charme* < L *carmen* song] *n* **1** words, action, or object thought to have magic power; **2** allure, fascination; **3** trinket worn on a bracelet, etc.; **4** *nuclear phys* indestructible property of certain particles that survives the changes occurring in a collision; **5 charms** *pl* attractiveness ‖ *vt* **6** to bewitch; **7** to fascinate, delight ‖ *vi* **8** to act as a charm; **9** to be delightful or attractive ‖ **charm′ing** *adj* ‖ **charm′er** *n* ‖ SYN *n* fascination, allurement; amulet, talisman; *v* captivate, enchant, fascinate, allure, bewitch, please

char′nel house′ /chärn′əl/ [MF = carnal] *n* place where bodies and bones are deposited

Char·on /ker′ən/ *n class. myth.* boatman who ferried souls across the river Styx to Hades

chart /chärt′/ [MF *carte* < L *charta* piece of paper] *n* **1** map, esp. one for navigation; **2** sheet giving information in tabular form or by graphic representation ‖ *vt* **3** to draw a chart of, map out ‖ SYN *n* map ‖ DISCR A *map* is a representation, as on paper, of all or a part of the earth's surface, or of the heavens. A *map* may show physical features, political divisions, distribution of population, etc. A *chart* is a particular *map* designed for the use of navigators, showing the position of shallows, channels, rocks, etc.

char·ter /chärt′ər/ [OF *chartre* < L *chartula* little paper] *n* **1** document issued by a government granting certain rights and privileges; **2** permission from a society to establish a local branch or chapter ‖ *vt* **3** to grant a charter to; **4** to hire for private use, as a ship or plane

char′ter mem′ber *n* founding member of an organization

char·treuse /shärtrooz′/ [< la Grande *Chartreuse,* F Carthusian monastery] *n* **1** pale green or yellow aromatic liqueur; **2** yellowish green

char′wom′an *n* (**-wom′en**) cleaning woman

char·y /cher′ē/ [OE *cearig* full of care] *adj* (**-i·er; -i·est**) **1** careful, wary; **2** shy; **3** fastidious; **4** economical ‖ **char′i·ly** *adv* ‖ **char′i·ness** *n* ‖ SYN frugal, economical, circumspect, careful

Cha·ryb·dis /kərib′dis/ *n class. myth.* voracious woman whom Jupiter transformed into a dangerous whirlpool between Sicily and Italy

chase¹ /chās′/ [MF *chasser* < VL *captiare*] *vt* **1** to pursue in order to catch; **2** to drive away; **3** to follow persistently ‖ *vi* **4** to pursue; **5** *colloq* to rush ‖ *n* **6** pursuit; **7** quarry; **8**

the chase the hunt ‖ SYN *v* expel, hunt, pursue (see *follow*)

chase² [< MF *enchasser* to engrave] *vt* to decorate, as a metal surface, by embossing or engraving

chas'er *n colloq* water or a mild beverage, as beer or ginger ale, taken after a drink of liquor

chasm /kaz'əm/ [Gk *chasma*] *n* 1 deep gap or cleft, as in the earth's surface; 2 void, break of continuity

chas·sis /shas'ē, ch-/ [F] *n* 1 frame that holds the body and motor of an automobile; 2 base and supporting framework, as of a radio or television set

chaste /chāst'/ [OF < L *castus* pure] *adj* 1 not guilty of unlawful sexual intercourse; 2 pure or simple in style ‖ **chaste'ly** *adv* ‖ **chas'ti·ty** /chast'-/ *n* ‖ SYN pure, unsullied, continent, undefiled, virtuous

chas·ten /chās'ən/ [see **chastise**] *vt* 1 to punish for the purpose of making better; 2 to subdue, curb ‖ SYN chastise, punish, castigate, correct, discipline ‖ DISCR It is often said that God *chastens* us by visiting us with affliction or trial to discipline us in obedience, meekness, purity, etc.; trouble and pain that subdue or temper us are also said to *chasten* us. To *chastise* is to try to correct or reform by inflicting physical suffering; criminals were formerly *chastised* by stripes or lashes of the whip; children are *chastised* to teach them not to repeat their faults. On the other hand, to *punish* may or may not be corporal; one may *punish* a child by a whipping, or by the denial of a privilege. *Chastise* and *punish* differ also in aim; to *punish* may have the effect of correcting, but punishment usually is of the nature of penalty for a past offense

chas·tise /chastīz'/ [OF *chastier* < L *castigare*] *vt* to discipline, esp. by beating ‖ **chas·tis'er** *n* ‖ **chas·tise'ment** *n* ‖ SYN castigate, discipline, correct (see *chasten*)

chat /chat/ [abbr of *chatter*] *v* (**chatted; chat·ting**) *vi* 1 to talk in an easy familiar manner ‖ *n* 2 familiar or informal talk; gossip ‖ SYN *v* chatter, prattle, gossip, prate

châ·teau /shatō'/ [F < L *castellum* fort] *n* (**-teaus, -teaux** /-tōz'/) 1 French castle; 2 large manor house

chat·e·laine /shat'əlān'/ [OF] *n* 1 lady of a château; 2 chain worn at the waist by women to hold keys, trinkets, a watch, etc.

Chat·ta·noo·ga /chat'ənoog'ə/ *n* city in SE Tennessee (130,000)

chat·tel /chat'əl/ [OF *chatel*] *n* moveable article of property

chat·ter /chat'ər/ [imit] *vi* 1 to utter sounds rapidly and indistinctly; 2 to rattle, as the teeth in shivering; 3 to

talk much and say little ‖ *n* 4 act or sound of chattering ‖ **chat'ter·er** *n*

chat'ter·box' *n* incessant talker

chat'ty *adj* (**-ti·er; -ti·est**) talkative, gossipy

Chau·cer, Geof·frey /jef'rē chôs'ər/ *n* (1340–1400) English poet, author of *Canterbury Tales*

chauf·feur /shōf'ər, shōfur'/ [F = stoker] *n* 1 person employed to drive someone else's car ‖ *vt* 2 to drive (a car) as a chauffeur; 3 to act as chauffeur for ‖ *vi* 4 to act as a chauffeur

chau·vin·ism /shōv'iniz'əm/ [N. *Chauvin* F superpatriot of Napoleon's time] *n* blind devotion; braggart patriotism ‖ **chau'vin·ist** *n* ‖ **chau'vin·is'tic** *adj*

cheap /chēp/ [OE *cēap* barter < L *caupo* tradesman] *adj* 1 low in price; 2 worth more than the price asked; 3 charging low prices; 4 of little value; 5 common, vulgar; 6 stingy ‖ *adv* 7 at small cost ‖ **cheap'ly** *adv* ‖ **cheap'ness** *n*

cheap'en *vt* 1 to make cheap ‖ *vi* 2 to become cheap

cheap'skate' *n slang* stingy person

cheat /chēt/ [OF *eschete* < LL *excadere* to fall] *n* 1 swindler ‖ *vt* 2 to deceive or defraud; 3 to elude, as *to cheat the gallows* ‖ *vi* 4 to act dishonestly; 5 **cheat on** *slang* to be sexually unfaithful to ‖ **cheat'er** *n* ‖ SYN *v* swindle, trick, hoodwink, hoax, dupe, deceive, defraud, gull, overreach

check /chek/ [OF *eschec* < Pers *shāh* king] *n* 1 *chess* position in which the king is under attack; 2 restraint; 3 obstruction; 4 bill for food and drink; 5 sudden stop; 6 means of securing accuracy or verification; 7 mark signifying verification; 8 ticket or counter for identification; 9 crack or chink; 10 written order to a bank to pay a specified sum of money; 11 pattern of squares; 12 **in check** under restraint ‖ *vt* 13 to restrain, stop; 14 to test, verify; 15 to mark as tested or verified; 16 to accept or deposit for safekeeping or transportation; 17 to menace (an opponent's king) ‖ *vi* 18 to prove to be right; 19 **check in** to register at a hotel; 20 **check out, a** to pay for lodging and depart; **b** to be verified; **c** *slang* to die; **check (up) on** to investigate ‖ *interj* 21 *colloq* okay!; 22 *chess* your king is now under attack ‖ SYN *v* tally, verify, restrain, curb, control, bridle, repress, rebuke ‖ ANT *v* unleash, release, arouse

check'book' *n* book containing blank bank checks

checked' *adj* having a pattern of squares

check'er *n* 1 **a** pattern of alternately colored squares; **b** one of the squares; 2 one of the red or black disks used in checkers; **3 checkers** *sg* game played by two people on a checkerboard

check′er·board′ *n* board divided into 64 squares of alternating colors, for checkers and chess

check′ered *adj* 1 marked with squares; 2 varied

check′mate′ [OF *eschec mat* < Ar *shāh māt* king is dead < Pers] *n* 1 *chess* check of an opponent's king from which it cannot escape, terminating the game; 2 complete frustration of one's plans || *vt* 3 to place in checkmate; 4 to frustrate utterly

check′off′ *n* compulsory deduction of union dues from wages

check′-out count′er *n* counter, as in a supermarket, where purchases are itemized and paid for

check′point′ *n* place where travelers are stopped for identification and inspection

check′up′ *n* examination to determine if anything is wrong

check′ valve′ *n* valve permitting free flow in one direction only

Ched·dar /ched′ər/ [village in England] *n* hard smooth-textured cheese

cheek /chēk/ [OE *cēace*] *n* 1 soft full part of the face below either eye; 2 *colloq* effrontery

cheek′bone′ *n* bone just below the eye

cheek′y *adj* (-**i·er**; -**i·est**) *colloq* impertinent, impudent

cheep /chēp/ [imit] *n & vi* peep, chirp

cheer /chēr/ [OF *chere* face < LL *cara*] *n* 1 temper or state of mind; 2 gladness, joy; 3 food, entertainment; 4 something that promotes a state of contentment; 5 shout of joy, approval, or encouragement; 6 **be of good cheer** be cheerful || *vt* 7 to make hopeful; 8 to gladden; 9 to encourage or incite, esp. with shouts; 10 to greet with shouts; 11 **cheer up** to make cheerful || *vi* 12 to applaud; shout cheers; 13 **cheer up** to become cheerful || **cheer′less** *adj* || SYN *v* comfort, gladden, encourage, refresh, enliven, exhilarate, reassure || ANT *v* discourage, dispirit

cheer′ful *adj* gay, full of cheer || **cheer′ful·ly** *adv* || **cheer′ful·ness** *n* || SYN cheering, cheery, sprightly, gay, merry, mirthful, gleeful, hilarious, joyful, jolly, sunny || DISCR *Cheerful* describes one whose whole being radiates contentment of the heart; the *cheerful* person is habitually unruffled of temper, equable in disposition, and free from gloom. *Cheery* people communicate their own good spirits to others; *cheery* words, *cheery* fires enliven and stimulate dull souls. A *sprightly* person has a buoyant spirit and a dancing body; a *sprightly* old lady is one who has retained the pleasing elasticity of youth. *Gay* people are sportive and merry; they love pleasure and take it, but since they

depend upon externals for it, it is transitory, and the *gay* mood goes with it. *Mirthful* describes one inclined to laughter; mirth is a jesting, jolly lifting of the spirits that is pleasurable but transient. *Hilarious* people are boisterously merry; their good time is accompanied by noise, if not tumult. *Gleeful* describes a lively type of good spirits that makes its delight manifest to others, as *gleeful* serenaders; the invalid children were as *gleeful* as elfin beings over their Christmas toys (see *sanguine*) || ANT disconsolate, depressed, sad, gloomy, pessimistic, blue, unhappy

cheer′y *adj* (-**i·er**; -**i·est**) 1 gay; full of good spirits; 2 promoting gladness or cheer || SYN (see *cheerful*) || ANT bleak, desolate

cheese /chēz/ [OE *cēse*] *n* 1 solid food made from pressed curds of milk; 2 **big cheese** *slang* big shot || *interj* 3 **cheese it!** *slang* a watch out!; b go away!

cheese′burg′er /-burg′ər/ *n* hamburger grilled with a slice of cheese

cheese′cake′ *n* 1 cake or one-crust pie made with cottage or cream cheese, eggs, milk, etc.; 2 *slang* publicity photographs featuring female legs and buttocks

cheese′cloth′ *n* thin netlike cloth

cheese′par′ing *adj* 1 stingy; parsimonious || *n* 2 something of little value; 3 stinginess; parsimoniousness

chees′y *adj* (-**i·er**; -**i·est**) 1 like cheese; 2 *slang* of very poor quality

chee·tah /chēt′ə/ [Hindu *chītā*] *n* leopardlike animal (*Acinonyx jubatus*) of Asia and Africa, often trained to hunt deer

chef /shef/ [F = chief] *n* cook, esp. a head male cook

Che·khov, An·ton /ant′ən chek′ôf/ *n* (1860–1904) Russian writer || **Che·khov·i·an** /-kŏv′ḡ·ən/ *adj*

chem. 1 chemical; 2 chemist; 3 chemistry

chem·i·cal /kem′ikəl/ [< Gk *chemeia* alchemy] *adj* 1 of, pert. to, produced by, or used in chemistry || *n* 2 substance produced by or used in a chemical process

chem′i·cal war′fare′ *n* warfare in which asphyxiating, poisonous, irritating, and debilitating gases and incendiaries are used to injure or destroy human beings, animals, or crops

che·mise /shəmēz′/ *n* woman's sleeveless undergarment

chem·ist /kem′ist/ [see **chemical**] *n* 1 one trained in chemistry; 2 *Brit* pharmacist

chem·is·try *n* science dealing with the nature and composition of substances and of the reactions which cause substances to break down or combine to form other substances

che·nille /shənēl′/ [F = caterpillar] *n* 1

tufted velvety cord of silk or worsted, used in trimmings and embroidery; **2** fabric made with chenille

cheque /chek'/ *n Brit* check

cher·ish /cher'ish/ [MF *cherir* (-*iss*-)] *vt* **1** to hold dear; **2** to treat with tenderness; **3** to nurse, cling to, as an idea or hope ‖ SYN nurse, nourish, nurture, foster, support, cultivate ‖ ANT cast off, neglect, disown, abandon

Cher·o·kee /cher'əkē'/ *n* (-**kees** or -**kee**) one of an Iroquoian tribe of American Indians originally inhabiting the southern Appalachians, now living chiefly in Oklahoma ‖ *also adj*

che·root /shəro͞ot'/ [Port *charuto* < Tamil] *n* cigar having both ends cut square

cher·ry /cher'ē/ [ONF *cherise*] *n* (-**ries**) **1** any of several trees (genus *Prunus*) bearing small fleshy fruit enclosing a stone or pit; **2** its fruit; **3** its wood; **4** bright red

cher·ry pick'er *n* tall crane used for working at elevated vertical or oblique positions

cher·ub /cher'əb/ [Heb *kerûbh*] *n* **1** beautiful, innocent child ‖ *n* (**cher·u·bim** /cher'(y)əbim'/) **2** heavenly being (Ezek. 1:5–11); **3** member of the second order of angels, usu. represented as a winged child ‖ **che·ru·bic** /chəro͞ob'ik/ *adj*

Ches'a·peake' Bay' /ches'əpēk'/ *n* 200-mile inlet of the Atlantic extending into Virginia and Maryland to the mouth of the Susquehanna River

chess /ches'/ [OF *esches* < Pers *shāh* king] *n* game played by two persons on a chessboard with 16 pieces to each side

chess'board' *n* board for playing chess, exactly like a checkerboard

chess'man /-mən/ *n* (-**men** /-mən/) any of the 32 pieces used in playing chess

chest /chest'/ [OE *cest* < Gk *kiste* box] *n* **1** strong box with a lid; **2** chest of drawers; **3** upper half of the body cavity, enclosed by the ribs

ches'ter·field /chest'ər-/ [Earl of *Chesterfield*] *n* overcoat with a fly front and velvet collar

chest·nut /ches'nət/ [OE *cysten* < L *castanea*] *n* **1** any of a genus (*Castanea*) of trees of the beech family; **2** its edible nut; **3** its wood; **4** reddish brown; **5** *colloq* stale joke or story

chest' of draw'ers *n* piece of bedroom furniture containing drawers

che·val' glass' /shəval'/ *n* framed full-length mirror swung between two uprights

chev·a·lier /shev'əlir'/ [MF = horseman] *n* **1** member of certain orders of honor, as of the French Legion of Honor; **2** chivalrous man; **3** *archaic* knight

chev·i·ot /shev'ē·ət/ [hills between

England and Scotland] *n* woolen cloth in a coarse twill weave

chev·ron /shev'rən/ [F = rafter] *n* V-shaped bar on the sleeves of a uniform to show rank

chew /cho͞o'/ [OE *cēowan*] *vt* **1** to crush and grind with the teeth; masticate; **2** **chew out** *slang* to reprimand; **3** **chew the fat** or **the rag** *slang* to chat ‖ *vi* **4** to perform the act of chewing; **5** **chew on** to ponder ‖ *n* **6** act of chewing; **7** that which can be chewed

chew'ing gum' *n* preparation, as of chicle, sweetened and flavored for chewing

chew'y *adj* (-**i·er**; -**i·est**) requiring much chewing

Chey·enne /shī·en'/ *n* capital of Wyoming (45,000)

chg. **1** change; **2** charge

chi /kī'/ [Gk] *n* twenty-second letter of the Greek alphabet X, χ

Chi·an·ti /kē·änt'ē/ [mountains in N Italy] *n* dry red Italian table wine or one like it

chi·a·ro·scu·ro /kē·är'əskyo͞or'ō/ [It = bright-dark] *n art* **1** use of contrasting light and shade in a picture; **2** picture in this style

chic /shēk', shik'/ [F] *n* **1** elegance in dress ‖ *adj* **2** elegantly stylish

Chi·ca·go /shikäg'ō/ *n* city in Illinois (3,366,957); metropolis of the Midwest and third largest city in the U.S.

chi·can·er·y /shikān'ərē/ [F *chicanerie*] *n* (-**ies**) **1** trickery, deception; **2** trick, subterfuge

chi·ca·no /chikän'ō/ [< Sp *chico* lad + *mejicano* Mexican] *n* American of Mexican descent

chick /chik'/ [< *chicken*] *n* **1** young chicken or other bird; **2** *slang* young woman or girl

chick'a·dee' /-ədē'/ [imit] *n* any of various American titmice

chick'en /-ən/ [OE *cicen*] *n* **1** common domestic fowl (*Gallus gallus*), esp. when young; **2** its flesh as food; **3** **no chicken** *colloq* not a young woman ‖ *adj* **4** *slang* cowardly ‖ *vi* **5** **chicken out** *slang* to lose one's nerve and fail to do something

chick'en feed' *n* *slang* insignificant amount of money

chick'en-heart'ed *adj* timorous, cowardly

chick'en pox' *n* mild, contagious disease, usu. of children, accompanied by skin eruptions

chick'en wire' *n* light large-meshed wire netting used for fencing

chick'pea' [F *chiche*] *n* **1** plant (*Cicer arietinum*) of the pea family, bearing edible seeds; **2** its seed

chic·le /chik'əl/ [Sp < Nahuatl] *n* gumlike substance obtained from certain tropical American trees, used as the base for chewing gum

chic·o·ry /chik'ərē/ [MF *chicoree*] *n*

(**-ries**) **1** plant (*Cichorium intybus*) the leaves of which are used for salad; **2** its root, ground and roasted, used to adulterate or substitute for coffee

chide /chīd′/ [OE *cīdan*] *v* (**chid·ed** or **chid** /chid′/) *vt* & *vi* to scold, reprove ‖ SYN blame, reprimand, censure (see *scold*)

chief /chēf′/ [OF < L *caput* head] *n* **1** person at the head of an organization, clan, tribe, group, etc.; **2** commander, leader, principal person; **3** principal or most valuable part ‖ *adj* **4** highest in office or authority; **5** principal, foremost ‖ SYN *n* chieftain, head, commander, captain, principal; *adj* foremost, leading, preeminent, paramount, principal, main ‖ DISCR *Chief* indicates rank, or precedence in title, as the *chief* justice; a *chief* clerk. *Principal* indicates importance, as the *principal* citizens; our *principal* motive. *Main* refers to preeminence in size, quantity, or extent, as the *main* building. Yet in other ways these words are interchangeable, as our *chief* interest lay in bonds; the *principal* signatures proved spurious; our *main* object was defeated

chief′ ex·ec′u·tive *n* head of the executive branch of a government, as the governor of a state, the president of the U.S., or a prime minister

chief′ jus′tice *n* presiding judge of a court consisting of several judges

chief′ly *adv* **1** principally; **2** for the most part

chief′ of state′ *n* titular head of a government, as the king of a limited monarchy or the president of a republic with a separate chief of the cabinet

chief′ pet′ty of′fi·cer *n* highest noncommissioned officer in the Navy or Coast Guard

chief′tain /-tin/ [OF *chevetaine* captain] *n* leader of a group, clan, tribe, etc.

chif·fon /shifon′/ [F < *chiffe* rag] *n* **1** soft, silky, thin gauze fabric; **2** chiffons *pl* feminine finery

chif·fo·nier /shif′ənir′/ *n* high chest of drawers, usu. with a mirror

chig·ger /chig′ər/ [?] *n* larva of a mite (family Trombiculidae) parasitic on man and animals, causing severe itching and spreading disease

chi·gnon /shēn′yon/ [F] *n* roll of hair worn by a woman at the back of the head

Chi·hua·hua /chiwä′wə/ [state in Mexico] *n* Mexican breed of small dogs with foxlike ears

chil·blains /chil′blānz′/ [*chill* + *blain* sore < OE *blegen*] *npl* inflammation of the hands and feet caused by exposure to cold

child /chī′(ə)ld/ [OE *cild*] *n* (**chil·dren**

/child′rən/) **1** offspring; **2** young boy or girl; **3** with child pregnant ‖ **child′hood** *n* ‖ **child′ish** *adj*

child′bed′ *n* state of a woman giving birth to a child

child′birth′ *n* act of giving birth to a child

chil·dren /child′rən/ *pl* of **child**

child′s′ play′ *n* something absurdly easy

Chil·e /chil′ē/ *n* Spanish-speaking republic along the Pacific coast in SW South America (8,690,000; 292,258 sq.m.; cap. Santiago) ‖ **Chil′e·an** *adj* & *n*

Chil′e salt·pe′ter *n* sodium nitrate in its natural state, used esp. as a fertilizer

chil·i or **chil·e** or **chil·li** /chil′ē/ [Sp *chile* < Nahuatl] *n* (**chil·ies**, **chil·es**, **chil·lies**) **1** very hot pod of red pepper; **2** chili con carne

chil′i con′ car′ne /kon′ kärn′ē/ [Sp = chili with meat] *n* dish of chilies, meat, beans, and spices originating in Texas

chil′i sauce′ *n* tomato sauce prepared with chilies and spices

chill /chil′/ [OE *ciele*] *n* **1** moderate coldness; **2** sudden coldness of the body accompanied by shivering; **3** discouragement; cold reception ‖ *adj* **4** uncomfortably cool; **5** unfriendly, not cordial ‖ *vt* **6** to cool; **7** to cause a chill in ‖ *vi* **8** to become or feel cold ‖ SYN *adj* bleak, raw, discouraging, formal, distant

chill′y *adj* (**-i·er; -i·est**) **1** unpleasantly cool; **2** cool in manner, unfriendly; **3** frightening ‖ **chill′i·ness** *n*

chime /chīm′/ [OF *chimbe* < L *cymbalum* cymbal] *vi* **1** to sound in harmony, as a set of bells; **2** to sound, as a gong; **3** to harmonize; **4** chime in, a to recite in cadence; b to intrude in a conversation, esp. for agreement ‖ *vt* **5** to give forth (music), as bells; **6** to announce (the time) by chiming; **7** to repeat in singsong ‖ *n* **8** chimes *pl* a set of tuned bells; b musical instrument containing chimes

Chi·me·ra or **Chi·mae·ra** /kimir′ə, kī-/ [Gk *chimaira* she-goat] *n* **1** *Gk myth.* fire-belching monster, with a lion's head, a goat's body, and a serpent's tail; **2** chimera, a frightful or foolish creature of the imagination; b wild fancy

chi·mer′i·cal *adj* **1** imaginary, visionary; **2** fantastic

chim·ney /chim′nē/ [MF *cheminee* < LL *caminata*] *n* **1** flue of a fireplace, furnace, etc., through which smoke and gases escape to the open air; **2** the part of a flue above a roof; **3** glass tube around the flame of a lamp or gas jet

chim′ney piece′ *n* mantelpiece

chim′ney pot′ *n* earthenware or metal pipe added to the top of a chimney to improve the draft and prevent smoking

chim'ney sweep' also **chim'ney sweep'-er** *n* person whose job it is to clean soot from chimneys

chim'ney swift' *n* American swift (*Chaetura pelagica*) which makes its nest in unused chimneys

chim-pan-zee /chimp'anzē', chimpan'-zē [nat. name] *n* anthropoid ape (*Pan troglodytes*) of central Africa, smaller and more arboreal than the gorilla

chin /chin'/ [OE *cinn*] *n* 1 the part of the face below the lower lip || *v* (**chinned; chin·ning**) *vt* 2 to pull (oneself) up, while hanging by the hands from a horizontal bar, until one's chin is level with the bar || *vt* 3 *slang* to talk; jabber

Chin. 1 China; 2 Chinese

chi-na /chīn'ə/ [*China*] *n* 1 fine porcelain originally from China; 2 any porcelain ware; 3 dishes collectively

Chi'na, Peo'ple's Re-pub'lic of *n* country in E Asia (1,000,000,000; 3,691,521 sq.m.; cap. Peking)

Chi'na as'ter *n* asterlike plant (*Callistephus chinensis*)

Chi'na Sea' *n* sea off the E and S coasts of China

chinch /chinch'/ [< Sp *chinche* < L *cimex* (-*icis*)] *n* bedbug

chinch' bug' *n* small bug (*Blissus leucopterus*) that is very destructive to grass and grain

chin-chil-la /chinchil'ə/ [Sp] *n* 1 small South American rodent (*Chinchilla lanigera*) with soft gray fur; 2 its fur

chin-cough /chin'kôf, -kof/ [< OE *cincung* guffaw + *cough*] *n* whooping cough

Chi-nese' /-nēz', -nēs'/ *n* (-**nese**) 1 native or inhabitant of China or a descendant of a native of China; 2 a official language of China; Mandarin; b any of the Sino-Tibetan languages || also *adj*

Chi'nese check'ers *nsg* checkerlike game played with marbles by from two to six players

Chi'nese puz'zle *n* anything extremely difficult to understand

chink[1] /chingk'/ [OE *cinu*] *n* 1 narrow crack || *vt* 2 to fill the chinks of

chink[2] [imit] *n* 1 sharp, metallic sound || *vt* 2 to cause (something) to make a chinking sound || *vi* 3 to make a chinking sound

chi-no /chēn'ō/ [?] *n* twilled cotton cloth used for uniforms, sports clothes, etc.

chintz /chints'/ [*obs chints pl* of Hindi *chint*] *n* cotton cloth, usu. glazed, printed in various colors

chip /chip'/ [ME] *v* (**chipped; chip-ping**) *vt* 1 to cut or break small pieces from || *vi* 2 to break off in small bits; 3 **chip in** *colloq* a to contribute; b to put chips or money in

the pot, as in card games || *n* 4 small piece of any hard substance cut or broken off; 5 place where a chip has broken off, as on a dish; 6 thin slice or piece of food; 7 piece of dried dung; 8 disk used in games as a counter; 9 **chip off the old block** person resembling his father in significant traits; 10 **chip on one's shoulder** inclination to quarrel; 11 **in the chips** *slang* wealthy

chip-munk /chip'mungk'/ [< earlier *chitmunk* < Algonquian] *n* any of a genus (*Tamias*) of small, striped, terrestrial rodents

chipped' beef' *n* smoked beef cut in very thin slices

Chip-pen-dale /chip'əndāl'/ *n* piece of furniture made by or in the style of Thomas Chippendale (1718?–79), English cabinetmaker, and influenced to some extent by Louis XV || also *adj*

chip-per /chip'ər/ [< *dial. kipper*] *adj colloq* lively, cheerful

chip-py /chip'ē/ [< *chipping* sparrow] *n* (-**pies**) 1 flirtatious, promiscuous woman; 2 prostitute

chiro- [Gk] *comb form* hand

chi-rop-o-dist /kīrop'ədist, ki-/ [< Gk *pous* (*podos*) foot] *n* one who treats minor foot ailments, as corns and bunions || **chi-rop'o-dy** *n*

chi-ro-prac-tic /kī'rəprak'tik/ [< Gk *praktikos* practical] *n* system or practice of treating bodily disorders by manipulating the bones of the spine || **chi'ro-prac'tor** *n*

chirp /churp'/ [imit] *n* 1 short, cheerful sound, as that of a bird or cricket || *vt* 2 to utter chirps || *vt* 3 to utter with chirps

chir-rup /chir'əp/ [form of *chirp*] *vt* 1 to chirp repeatedly || *vt* 2 to utter with a chirrup || *n* 3 sound of chirruping

chis-el /chiz'əl/ [ONF] *n* 1 tool consisting of a metal blade with a cutting end, for cutting and shaping; 2 *slang* fraud, swindle || *v* (-**eled** or -**elled; -el·ing** or -**el·ling**) *vt* 3 to cut or shape with a chisel; 4 *slang* a to swindle (someone); b to obtain by trickery || *vi* 5 to use a chisel; 6 *slang* to cheat, swindle || **chis'e·ler** or **chis'el·ler** *n*

chit /chit'/ [Hindi *chittī*] *n* voucher of money owed for food, drink, etc.

chit'chat' [reduplication of *chat*] *n* idle talk; prattle; gossip

chi-tin /kīt'ən/ [F *chitine* < Gk *chiton* tunic] *n* horny outer covering of insects, crustaceans, etc.

chiv-al-ry /shiv'əlrē/ [AF *chivalrie* knighthood] *n* 1 the system of medieval knighthood; 2 characteristics of the ideal knight, as bravery, nobleness, courtesy, respect for women, etc. || **chiv'al-rous** *adj*

chive /chīv'/ [AF] *n* perennial herb

(*Allium schoenoprasum*) closely related to the leek and onion

chlor- or **chloro-** [Gk *chloros*] *comb form* 1 green; 2 chlorine

chlo·ral /klôr′əl, klōr′-/ *n* colorless oily liquid —CCl₃CHO— formed by the action of chlorine on alcohol

chlo′ral hy′drate *n* white crystalline solid —CCl₃CH(OH)₂— used as a hypnotic

chlo′rate *n* salt of chloric acid

chlo′ric ac′id *n* strong oxidizing acid —HClO₃— which exists only in solution

chlo·ride /klôr′īd, klōr′-, -id/ *n* salt of chlorine with a metal or a radical

chlo′ride of lime′ *n* mixture of calcium chloride and calcium hypochlorite in the form of a powder, used as a bleach and disinfectant

chlo·rin·ate′ *vt* to combine or impregnate with chlorine or a chlorine compound ‖ **chlo′rin·a′tion** *n*

chlo′rine /-rēn, -rĭn/ *n* greenish-yellow, heavy, gaseous, poisonous halogen element (Cl; at.no. 17; at.wt. 35.453), possessing a characteristic odor and highly irritating to the throat; used as a bleach and for purifying water

chlo′rite /-rīt/ *n* 1 salt of chlorous acid; 2 any of a group of green hydrous silicates, closely allied with the micas

chlo·ro·form′ /-rə-/ *n* 1 colorless volatile liquid —CHCl₃— with a sweetish odor, used as an anesthetic and as a solvent ‖ *vt* 2 to anesthetize with chloroform; 3 to kill with chloroform

chlo′ro·phyll also **chlo′ro·phyl** /-əfil/ [< Gk *phyllon* leaf] *n* green coloring substance of plants, essential for photosynthesis

chlo′rous *adj* (chlorine compound) with a valence of three

chock /chok′/ [?] *n* 1 block or wedge to fill in a space so as to prevent motion, as beneath a wheel ‖ *vt* 2 to secure with chocks ‖ *adv* 3 as tight or as close as possible

chock′-full′ *adj* full to capacity

choc·o·late /chok′(ə)lĭt, chôk′-/ [Sp < Nahuatl] *n* 1 preparation made from the roasted seeds of the cacao; 2 beverage made from it; 3 candy made with chocolate; 4 dark brown ‖ also *adj*

choice /chois′/ [OF *chois*] *n* 1 act of selecting; 2 thing or person selected; 3 best part; 4 variety large enough to select from; 5 alternative ‖ *adj* 6 costly, select; 7 carefully chosen; 8 (beef) next in quality to prime ‖ SYN *adj* rare, cherished, dainty, costly (see *exquisite*); *n* preference, alternative, option ‖ DISCR These nouns agree in the idea of offering or affording a chance to choose. *Choice* is an act of the will; we make a *choice* on the merits of the thing chosen, according to the dictates of

our judgment. *Choice* names the act or power of choosing, as well as the thing chosen. *Alternative* is strictly a *choice* between two. Our *preference* is that to which desire leads us, even though judgment fails to strengthen inclination. Our *choice* contents us until we see something finer for which we have a *preference*. *Preference* may name the act or power of preferring, or the thing preferred. *Option* emphasizes the freedom or opportunity to choose, rather than the act or result

choir /kwī′(ə)r/ [OF *cuer* < L *chorus*] *n* 1 group of trained singers, esp. in a church; 2 the part of the church where they sing

choke /chōk′/ [OE *ācēocian*] *vt* 1 to strangle; 2 to stifle, check the growth of; 3 to clog; congest; 4 to partially close the air intake of the carburetor in (a gasoline engine) to enrich the mixture; 5 **choke back** to suppress, as the emotions ‖ *vi* 6 to become suffocated; 7 to become clogged; 8 **choke up** *colloq* to become speechless from emotion ‖ *n* 9 act or sound of choking; 10 carburetor valve which partially closes the air intake; 11 narrowest part of the muzzle of a chokebore; 12 choke coil

choke′bore′ *n* bore of a shotgun narrowed toward the muzzle to reduce the spread of the charge

choke′ coil′ *n* coil used to prevent the passage of excessive alternating currents

chol·er /kol′ər/ [MF *colere* < Gk *cholera* biliousness] *n* irritability; anger ‖ **chol′er·ic** /also kələr′ik/ *adj*

chol′er·a *n* highly infectious and usu. fatal disease caused by the microorganism *Vibrio comma* and originating in Asia, characterized by diarrhea and vomiting

cho·les·ter·ol /kəles′tərōl′, -rol′/ [< Gk *chole* bile + *stereos* solid] *n* crystalline alcohol —C₂₇H₄₅OH— occurring in animal fat, nerve tissue, blood, etc.

choose /chōōz′/ [OE *cēosan*] *n* (chose; cho·sen) *vt* 1 to pick, select; 2 to prefer; 3 to decide ‖ *vi* 4 to make a choice ‖ SYN decide, select, prefer (see *elect*)

choos′y *adj* (-i·er; -i·est) fussy, hard to please

chop /chop′/ [var of *chap¹*] *v* (**chopped; chop·ping**) *vt* 1 to cut with sharp blows, as with an ax or cleaver; 2 to cut into small pieces ‖ *vi* 3 to make a quick stroke or blow, as with an ax or the hand ‖ *n* 4 piece chopped off; 5 small piece of lamb, pork, etc., containing a rib or section of bone

chop′house′ *n* (-hous·es /-ziz/) restaurant specializing in chops and steaks

Cho·pin, Fréd·ér·ic /fred'ərik shō'pan/ *n* (1810–49) Polish composer and pianist

chop'per *n* 1 *colloq* helicopter; 2 *slang* submachine gun

chop'py *adj* (-pi·er; -pi·est) 1 (sea) full of short rough waves; 2 jerky (motion); 3 changeable (wind); 4 uneven (style)

chops [?] *npl* 1 jaw; 2 **lick one's chops** *colloq* look forward or wait with great pleasure

chop'sticks' [< pidgin Eng *chop* fast] *npl* two small sticks used in the Orient instead of a fork

chop' su'ey /sōō'ē/ [Cantonese *shap sui* odds and ends] *n* Chinese-style dish of stewed or fried chicken or pork, beans or bamboo sprouts, onions, etc.

cho·ral /kôr'əl, kōr'-/ [see **chorus**] *adj* 1 pert. to, written for, or sung by a choir or chorus ‖ /kəral'/ *n* 2 chorale

cho·rale /kəral'/ *n* 1 simple hymn tune to be sung in chorus either in unison or in parts; 2 group of singers of such music

chord[1] /kôrd'/ [Gk *chorde* musical string] *n* 1 straight line joining two points of an arc; 2 straight line between the trailing and leading edges of an airfoil

chord[2] [< *accord*] *n* combination of tones sounded simultaneously and in harmony

chor'date /kôr'dāt/ [< L *chorda* cord] *n* animal belonging to the phylum Chordata comprising the true vertebrates and animals having a notochord ‖ also *adj*

chore /chôr', chōr'/ [OE *cyrr*] *n* 1 small job; 2 difficult task; 3 **chores** *pl* routine household tasks

cho·re·og·ra·phy /kôrē·og'rəfē, kōr'-/ [< Gk *choreia* dance] *n* art of composing and arranging ballets and other stage dances ‖ **cho're·og'ra·pher** *n*

cho·rine /kôr'ēn, kōr'-/ *n slang* chorus girl

chor·tle /chôrt'əl/ [*chuckle* + *snort*] *vt* 1 to utter with a gleeful chuckle ‖ *vi* 2 to utter a gleeful chuckle ‖ *n* 3 gleeful chuckle

cho·rus /kôr'əs, kōr'-/ [L < Gk *choros* dance] *n* 1 body of dancers and singers who perform together; 2 number of persons singing or speaking together; 3 piece of music to be sung by voices in concert; 4 refrain recurring at the end of each stanza of a song; 5 **in chorus** in unison ‖ *vt & vi* 6 to sing or recite in chorus

cho'rus girl' *n* girl who sings and dances in the chorus of a musical production

chose /chōz'/ *pt* of **choose**

cho·sen /chōz'ən/ 1 *pp* of **choose** ‖ *adj* 2 selected

chow /chou'/ [Chin] *n* 1 one of a breed of Chinese dogs, similar to a small Eskimo dog; 2 *slang* food

chow·der /choud'ər/ [F *chaudière* kettle] *n* dish made by stewing fish, shellfish, and certain vegetables, and sometimes milk

chow mein /chou'mān'/ [Chin = fried dough] *n* Chinese-style steamed dish of meat, vegetables, and fried noodles

Chr. 1 Christ; 2 Christian

chres·tom·a·thy /krestom'əthē/ [< Gk *chrestos* useful + *manthanein* (math-) to learn] *n* (-thies) collection of choice extracts from literature, esp. of a foreign language

Christ /krīst'/ [Gk *christos* annointed] *n* 1 the Messiah, whose coming was foretold by the Jewish prophets; 2 title of Jesus as the fulfillment of this prophecy

chris·ten /kris'ən/ [OE *cristnian*] *vt* 1 to admit into a Christian church by baptizing; 2 to name at baptism; 3 to give a name to; 4 *colloq* to put to its first use ‖ **chris'ten·ing** *n*

Chris'ten·dom *n* 1 the Christian world; 2 Christians collectively

Chris·tian /kris'chən/ *n* 1 a believer in Christianity; b member of a Christian church; 2 person whose life and character conform to Christ's teaching ‖ also *adj* ‖ **Chris'tian·ize'** *vt*

Chris'tian e'ra *n* period of history dating from 1 A.D., the assumed year of Christ's birth

Chris·ti·an·i·ty /kris'chē·an'itē/ *n* 1 the religion taught by Christ and his apostles; 2 state of being a Christian; 3 Christian character or quality; 4 Christendom

Chris'tian name' *n* first name, given to Christians at baptism

Chris'tian Sci'ence *n* system of religious teaching and practice based on the Scriptures which is applicable to the preservation and recovery of health, without resort to medical treatment; founded in 1866 by Mary Baker Eddy

Christ·mas /kris'məs/ [OE *Cristes mæsse* Christ's mass] *n* annual festival (Dec. 25) which celebrates the birth of Christ

chrom- or **chromo-** [Gk *chroma* color] *comb form* 1 color, colored; 2 chromium

chro·mate /krō'māt/ *n* any of the salts of chromic acid, generally possessing brilliant colors and used as pigments and oxidizing agents

chro·mat·ic /krəmat'ik/ *adj* 1 of, having, or pert. to colors; 2 *mus* progressing in half tones to a tone having the same letter name ‖ **chro·mat'i·cal·ly** *adv*

chro·ma·tin /krōm'ətin/ *n* stainable substance of the cell nucleus, mainly composed of protein compounds and nucleic acid

chrome /krōm′/ [Gk *chroma* color] *n* **1** chromium, esp. as the source of brilliant colors; **2** *colloq* chromium-plated metal ‖ *vt* **3** to plate with chromium

-chrome /-krōm′/ *n & adj comb form* **1** color; **2** coloring agent

chro·mi·um /-ē·əm/ *n* hard, brittle, grayish-white metallic element (**Cr**; at.no. 24; at.wt. 51.996), used in making alloy steels and in plating other metals, and, in its salts, as a pigment

chro·mo·some /-əsōm′/ [< Gk *soma* body] *n* one of the minute chromatin bodies in the nucleus of a cell, which carry the genes

chron- or **chrono-** [Gk *chronos*] *comb form* time

chron·ic /kron′ik/ *adj* **1** deep-rooted, lingering (illness); **2** long-established, habitual

chron·i·cle *n* **1** chronological record of events ‖ *vt* **2** to register or enter as in a chronicle ‖ **chron′i·cler** *n* ‖ SYN *n* archives, annals, account (see *history*)

chron·o·graph′ *n* **1** instrument for registering very short intervals of time, as a stop watch; **2** instrument for recording graphically the time or duration of an occurrence

chron·o·log·i·cal /kron′əloj′ikəl/ *adj* arranged in the order of occurrence

chro·nol·o·gy /krənol′əjē/ *n* (**-gies**) **1** science that treats of events and arranges their dates in chronological order; **2** table of events in chronological order

chro·nom·e·ter /-nom′itər/ *n* highly accurate instrument for measuring time, designed to enable ships at sea to determine their longitude

chrys·a·lis /kris′əlis/ [Gk *chrysallis* golden thing] *n* (**-lis·es** or **chry·sal·i·des** /krisal′idēz′/) hard-shelled pupa of certain insects, as the butterfly or moth

chrys·an·the·mum /krisan′thəməm/ [< Gk *chrysos* gold + *anthemon* flower] *n* **1** any of a genus (*Chrysanthemum*) of plants of the composite family with large showy flowers; **2** flower of any such plant

chub /chub′/ [ME *chubbe*] *n* any of various carplike fresh-water fishes, esp. a common European carp (*Leuciscus cephalus*)

chub·by /< *chub*] *adj* (**-bi·er; -bi·est**) short and plump ‖ **chub′bi·ness** *n*

chuck[1] /chuk/ [?] *vt* **1** to pat playfully under the chin; **2** to throw, toss; **3** *colloq* to quit (one's job)

chuck[2] [var of *chock*] *n* **1** cut of beef between the neck and the shoulder blade; **2** device, as on a lathe or drill, for clamping work or a tool in place

chuck′-a-luck′ *n* gambling game with three dice

chuck′-full *adj* chock-full

chuck′hole′ [< wood*chuck*] *n* hole in a road

chuck·le /chuk′əl/ [?] *n* **1** quiet suppressed laugh ‖ *vi* **2** to utter a chuckle

chuck′le·head′ [< *obs. chuckle* hulking] *n* *colloq* blockhead ‖ **chuck′le·head′ed** *adj*

chuck′ wag′on *n* *western U.S.* cook-wagon for serving meals to outdoor workers

chuk·ker /chuk′ər/ [Hindi *chakkar* wheel] *n* one of the periods of a polo match

chum /chum′/ [?] *n* **1** intimate friend ‖ *v* (**chummed; chum·ming**) *vi* **2** to be intimately friendly; **3** to share a room, as at college ‖ **chum′my** *adj* (**-mi·er; -mi·est**)

chump /chump′/ [?] *n* *colloq* fool, dolt

chunk /chuŋk′/ [prob var of *chuck*[2]] *n* short, thick piece

chunk′y *adj* (**-i·er; -i·est**) stocky, thick-set

church /church′/ [OE *cirice* < Gk *kyriakon* the Lord's] *n* **1** building for public Christian worship; **2** entire body of Christian believers; **3** denomination or sect; **4** religious service; **5** clerical profession; **6** organized power of a religious body ‖ *adj* **7** of or pert. to a church; ecclesiastical

church′ fa′ther *n* any religious writer of the early Christian church accepted as authentic

church′go′er *n* person who attends church regularly

Church·ill, Sir Win·ston /wins′tən church′əl/ *n* (1874–1965) British statesman and author, prime minister 1940–45, 1951–55

church′man /-mən/ *n* (**-men** /-mən/) **1** clergyman; **2** member of a church

Church′ of Eng′land *n* national church of England and Wales, supported by the British government

church′ward′en *n* in Church of England and Protestant Episcopal parishes, lay officer who looks after church property

church′yard′ *n* grounds around a church, often used for burial

churl /churl′/ [OE *ceorl* freeman] *n* surly ill-bred person

churl′ish *adj* **1** ill-bred; **2** sordid, covetous, miserly; **3** hard to manage; stubborn ‖ **churl′ish·ly** *adv* ‖ **churl′ish·ness** *n* ‖ SYN boorish, sullen, surly, crabbed, loutish, cross-grained, niggardly ‖ ANT refined, cultivated, gentle

churn /churn′/ [OE *cyrin*] *n* **1** vessel in which milk or cream is made into butter by agitation ‖ *vt* **2** to make (butter) by stirring cream; **3** to stir (cream) to make butter; **4** to stir by violent motion ‖ *vi* **5** to stir cream in making butter; **6** to move in agitation

chute /shōōt'/ [F] *n* **1** inclined trough down which articles can slide; **2** smooth, rapid river fall; **3** toboggan slide; **4** *colloq* parachute ‖ *vt* **5** to send down a chute ‖ *vi* **6** to descend, as down a chute

chyme /kīm'/ [Gk *chymos* juice] *n* the mass of partly digested food before its passage from the stomach into the small intestine

CIA Central Intelligence Agency

ci·ca·da /sikãd'ə, -kãd'-/ [L] *n* (**-das** or **-dae** /-dē/) any of a family (Cicadidae) of large insects with four membranous wings, the males of which produce a shrill rhythmic sound

cic·a·trix /sik'ətriks, sikãt'riks/ [L] *n* (**-tri·ces** /-trī'sēz/) scar remaining after a wound has healed

Cic·e·ro /sis'ərō'/ *n* (106–43 B.C.) Roman statesman, writer, and orator ‖ **Cic'e·ro'ni·an** *adj & n*

Cid /sid'/ [Sp < Ar *sayyid* lord] *n* **El Cid** Rodrigo Diaz de Bivar (ab. 1040–99) Spanish chieftain in the wars against the Moors, hero of the great Spanish medieval epic and of numerous later ballads, dramas, and romances

C.I.D. Criminal Investigation Department of Scotland Yard

-cide /-sīd'/ [L *-cida*] *n comb form* killer

ci·der /sīd'ər/ [MF *sidre* < Gk *sikera* strong drink < Heb *shēkār*] *n* apple juice, used as a beverage or for making hard cider, vinegar, and applejack

C.I.F. cost, insurance, and freight

ci·gar /sigär'/ [Sp *cigarro*] *n* cylindrical roll of tobacco leaves, used for smoking

cig·a·rette also **cig·a·ret** /sig'əret'/ [F, *dim.* of *cigar*] *n* finely cut tobacco in a thin paper tube for smoking

cil·i·a /sil'ē·ə/ [L] *npl* **1** eyelashes; **2** *bot & zool* short hairlike processes

cinch /sinch'/ [Sp *cincha*] *n* **1** saddle girth, **2** *slang* something easy or certain ‖ *vt* **3** to fasten a cinch on; **4** *slang* to make sure of

cin·cho·na /siŋkōn'ə/ [< Countess of *Chinchón*] *n* **1** any of a genus (*Cinchona*) of South American evergreen trees; **2** the bark, a source of quinine

Cin·cin·nat·i /sin'sinat'ē, -nat'ə/ *n* city in S Ohio on the Ohio River (452,-524)

cin·der /sin'dər/ [OE *sinder*] *n* **1** burned or partially burned piece of coal or wood; **2 cinders** *pl* ashes

cin'der block' *n* concrete building block made with a cinder aggregate

Cin·der·el'la /-el'ə/ *n* **1** in an old fairy tale, maiden forced to work as a menial drudge until, aided by her

fairy godmother, she marries a prince; **2** any person who emerges from anonymity to great prominence

cin·e·ma /sin'əmə/ [Gk *kinema* movement] *n* **1** motion picture; **2** motion-picture theater; **3 the cinema** the art and profession of motion pictures ‖ **cin'e·mat'ic** /-mat'-/ *adj*

Cin'e·ma·Scope' [trademark] *n* motion-picture process that spreads the picture over a wide screen by the use of special lenses

Cin·e·ram·a /sin'əram'ə/ [trademark] *n* motion-picture process for achieving a three-dimensional effect by photographing a wide scene with three cameras

cin·na·mon /sin'əmən/ [Gk *kinnamon* < Heb *quinnāmōn*] *n* aromatic inner bark of any of several East Indian trees (genus *Cinnamomum*), used as a spice

C.I.O., CIO [*C*ongress of *I*ndustrial *O*rganizations] *n* affiliation of industrial labor unions

ci·pher /sīf'ər/ [ML *ciphra* < Ar *çifr* zero] *n* **1** zero, naught; **2** nonentity; **3** manner of secret writing; code ‖ *vi* **4** to work out arithmetical problems ‖ *vt* **5** to write in cipher; **6** to calculate or figure out

cir·ca /surk'ə/ [L] *prep & adv* about, approximately

Cir·ce /surs'ē/ *n* in Homer's *Odyssey*, enchantress who changed companions of Odysseus into swine

cir·cle /surk'əl/ [L *circulus* small ring] *n* **1** closed plane curve, all points of which are equidistant from the center; **2** plane surface enclosed by such a line; **3** anything resembling or arranged in a circle, **4** group united by a common bond: **5** completed series or course of operations: cycle; **6** area, scope, as of influence; **7** *logic* fallacy of proving a first proposition by a second which itself rests upon the first for proof ‖ *vt* **8** to surround, encircle; **9** to revolve around ‖ *vi* **10** to move around, revolve ‖ **SYN** *n* ring, circuit, orb, globe (see *caste*)

cir'cle/line /-līn'/ [*circle* + *line*] *n* fluorescent lamp in the shape of a hoop

cir·cuit /surk'it/ [L *circuitus* going around] *n* **1** act of going around something; **2** route passed over at regular intervals in one's work; **3** line surrounding any object or space; distance around anything; **4** chain of theaters; **5** *elec* **a** path of a current; **b** functional section of a circuit; **c** arrangement of the elements of a radio or television transmitter or receiver; **d** system of two-way communication by wire or wireless; **e** range of flow of magnetism, esp. through a section of iron or steel

cir'cuit break'er *n* device that automatically interrupts an electric circuit in case of an overload

cir·cu·i·tous /sərkyōō′itəs/ *adj* round-about, indirect ‖ **cir·cu′i·tous·ly** *adv*

cir′cuit·ry /surk′itrē/ *n* **1** complete layout of an electric circuit; **2** elements of an electric circuit

cir′cu·lar /-kyələr/ *adj* **1** of, pert. to, like, or moving in, a circle; **2** round-about, indirect ‖ *n* **3** letter or notice for general distribution ‖ **cir′cu·lar′i·ty** /-lar′itē/ *n*

cir′cu·lar·ize′ *vt* to send printed circulars to

cir′cu·late′ *vi* **1** to follow a circuit and return to the starting point, as blood; **2** to be distributed and sent, as a newspaper to its readers; **3** to pass from hand to hand, as money; **4** to become diffused or distributed, as air through a building ‖ *vt* **5** to cause to circulate ‖ SYN disseminate, spread, transmit, propagate

cir′cu·la′tion *n* **1** act of circulating; **2** distribution of a newspaper or periodical; **3** movement in a circle around to the starting point, as of the blood in the body or of forced air in a building

cir′cu·la·to·ry sys′tem /-ətōr′ē, -ətōr′ē/ *n* system of organs and vessels through which the blood and lymph circulate through the body

cir·cum- [L] *comb form* around, about, surrounding

cir·cum·cise /surk′əmsīz′/ [< L *caedere* (*cisus*) to cut] *vt* to cut off part or all of the foreskin of ‖ **cir′cum·ci′sion** /-sizh′ən/ *n*

cir·cum·fer·ence /sərkum′fərəns/ [< L *ferre* to carry] *n* **1** line that bounds a circle or any curved plane figure; **2** length of such a line

cir′cum·flex′ /-fleks′/ [< L *flectere* (*flexus*)] *n* mark ^, ˆ, or ˜, placed over a vowel in some alphabets to denote quality, stress, length, nasality, etc. ‖ also *adj*

cir′cum·lo·cu′tion *n* roundabout or overlong way of expressing oneself ‖ SYN periphrasis, diffuseness, wordiness, prolixity, redundancy, tautology, pleonasm, verbosity, verbiage ‖ DISCR These terms all denote a surplus of words, in some cases justifiable, and in others constituting a fault of style. *Circumlocution*, technically called *periphrasis*, consists of the use of many words where few would do; it is a defect when it results merely in indirect or round-about expression; it is justifiable when used for a purpose, a method of evasion. *Diffuseness* consists of a *wordiness* lacking all concentration of thought; it is the opposite of *conciseness*. Though *diffuseness* may not be desirable, it may yield substance enough to escape condemnation; but *prolixity* is always a fault. *Prolixity* presents a mass of trivial details, injudiciously selected and wearisome

in the extreme. *Redundancy* is a tiresome use of words in excess of what is required; *wordiness* likewise means excess, but it connotes a long-windedness and emptiness not necessarily implied by *redundancy*. *Tautology* consists in needlessly saying the same thing over in different words; it is seldom justifiable; but *pleonasm*, another form of repetition, may be a legitimate means of emphasis. *Pleonasm* consists in a use of words which, if omitted, would not affect the meaning. *Verbosity* is a hopeless maze of words containing very little thought; but *verbiage* is worse; it is an accumulation of mere words, with no thought at all

cir′cum·nav′i·gate′ *vt* to sail completely around, as the earth or an island ‖ **cir′cum·nav′i·ga′tion** *n*

cir′cum·scribe′ *vt* **1** to encircle with a line; **2** to restrict, limit ‖ **cir′cum·scrip′tion** /-skrip′shən/ *n* ‖ SYN confine, abridge, inclose, restrict, limit

cir′cum·spect′ /-əspekt′/ [< L *spicere* (*spectus*) to look] *adj* discreet, cautious ‖ SYN wary, watchful, guarded, discreet (see *careful*)

cir′cum·spec′tion *n* watchfulness; full attention to all the circumstances of a case ‖ SYN (see *wisdom*) ‖ ANT indiscretion, rashness

cir′cum·stance′ *n* **1** incident, occurrence, or fact accompanying, or relative to, another; **2** display, ceremony; **3 circumstances** *pl* **a** state of affairs surrounding an event; **b** material welfare; **4 under no circumstances** never; **5 under** or **in the circumstances** under these conditions ‖ SYN detail, fact, incident, item (see *event*)

cir′cum·stan′tial /-stansh′əl/ *adj* **1** pert. to or conditioned by circumstances; **2** detailed, precise

cir′cum·stan′tial ev′i·dence *n law* proof of attendant facts used to establish facts not provable by direct evidence

cir′cum·stan′ti·ate′ /-shē·āt′/ *vt* **1** to give proof of; **2** to describe in detail

cir′cum·vent′ /-vent′/ [< L *venire* (*ventus*) to come] *vt* **1** to gain an advantage over by stratagem; **2** to go round ‖ **cir′cum·ven′tion** *n* ‖ SYN thwart, frustrate, cheat, delude, overreach

cir·cus /surk′əs/ [L = ring] *n* **1** large traveling public spectacle presented usu. in a large tent, featuring acrobats, trained animals, clowns, etc.; **2** riotous entertainment; **3** *anc Rome* amphitheater for public games, chariot races, etc.; **4** *Brit* circular plaza

cir·rho·sis /sirōs′is/ [< Gk *kirrhos* tawny] *n* disease of the liver, resulting in an abnormal growth of hardened connective tissue

cir·ro·cu·mu·lus /sir′ōkyōōm′yələs/ *n* (-li /-lī′/) high-altitude cloud formation consisting of small, white, fleecy clouds

cir·ro·stra/tus /-strāt/-, -strat/-/ *n* (-ti /-tī/) high, fairly uniform, horizontal sheet of cloud, having the delicacy of the cirrus

cir·rus /sir/əs/ [L = curl] *n* (-ri /-rī/) light fleecy cloud spreading in filmy whisps at a great height

cis- [L] *pref* on this side of, as *cisalpine*

cis·tern /sis/tərn/ [ME < L *cisterna*] *n* reservoir or tank for storing water

cit·a·del /sit/ədəl/ [MF *citadelle* < It *cittadella*] *n* fortress, esp. one defending a city ‖ SYN refuge, stronghold, fortress, fort

cite /sīt/ [MF *citer* < L *citare*] *vt* 1 to quote by way of illustration; 2 to summon to appear in court; 3 *mil* to mention in orders for gallantry ‖ **ci·ta/tion** *n* ‖ SYN quote, adduce, allege ‖ DISCR To *quote* is, directly, to repeat the exact words of an author; indirectly, to give in substance what he has written. To *cite* is to mention a passage or an author as a reference, argument, or example; the underlying idea in *citing* is the summoning of authority, like a witness, to one's aid. To *adduce* is to bring up a passage, fact, etc., as evidence to sustain, invalidate, or illustrate something previously stated

cit·i·fied /sit/ifid/ [see city] *adj* having the manners, dress, etc., of a city dweller

cit·i·zen /sit/izən/ [AF *citesein*] *n* 1 native or naturalized member of a nation who owes his allegiance to it and enjoys full political rights and privileges; 2 generally, permanent resident of a city or state ‖ **cit/i·zen·ship/** *n*

cit/i·zen·ry *n* citizens collectively

cit/ric ac/id /sit/rik/ [< *citron*] *n* sharply sour acid occurring in many fruits, esp. lemons and limes; used mainly as a flavoring

cit·ron /sit/rən/ [It *citrone* < L *citrus*] *n* 1 fruit similar to the lemon but thick-skinned and larger, borne by the citron tree (*Citrus medica*); 2 its candied rind

cit/ron·el/la /-nel/ə/ [*dim.* of *citron*] *n* pungent oil distilled from a fragrant S Asiatic grass (*Cymbopogon nardus*); used as an insect repellant

cit/rus fruit/ /sit/rəs/ *n* any fruit of trees of the genus *Citrus*, as the citron, lemon, lime, and orange

cit·y /sit/ē/ [OF *cite* < L *civitas* commonwealth] *n* (-ies) 1 large important town; 2 incorporated municipality having local self-government; 3 inhabitants of a city collectively; 4 **the City** district of London, bailiwick of the Lord Mayor, now the financial center ‖ also *adj*

cit/y desk/ *n* newspaper department in charge of local news

cit/y hall/ *n* building housing a municipal government

cit/y-state/ *n* sovereign state consisting of a central city and the surrounding area, common in ancient Greece (Athens) and in Renaissance Italy (Florence)

civ·et /siv/it/ [MF *civette* < Ar *zabād*] *n* 1 any of various catlike animals (family Viverridae) of Asia and Africa; 2 thick yellowish substance of musklike odor secreted by the anal glands of the civet, used in perfumes

civ·ic /siv/ik/ [L *civicus*] *adj* pert. to, characteristic of, or befitting a city, citizen, or citizenship

civ/ics *nsg* study of city government or of good citizenship

civ·il /siv/əl/ [< L *civis* citizen] *adj* 1 pert. to or characteristic of citizens; 2 of or pert. to civilians; 3 not military or ecclesiastical; 4 formally polite; 5 civilized ‖ SYN obliging, well-bred, respectful (see *polite*)

civ/il dis/o·be/di·ence *n* refusal to obey certain laws because of disagreement with government policies

civ/il en/gi·neer/ *n* person in charge of designing, constructing, or maintaining large public works, as roads, bridges, and dams ‖ **civ/il en/gi·neer/-ing** *n*

ci·vil·ian /sivil/yən/ *n* person not a member of the armed forces ‖ also *adj*

ci·vil/i·ty *n* (-ties) 1 politeness; 2 act of courtesy ‖ SYN urbanity, politeness, affability, complaisance

civ/i·li·za/tion *n* 1 act or process of civilizing or becoming civilized; 2 state marked by a highly developed technology and culture; 3 collectively, those countries that have achieved such a state; 4 total culture of a given people or period

civ/i·lize/ *vt* 1 to bring out of a savage state; 2 to instruct in civility, refine ‖ **civ/i·lized/** *adj*

civ/il law/ *n* law dealing with private rights and matters, not crime

civ/il lib/er·ties *npl* full liberties of action, speech, and thought of an individual that do not infringe on similar liberties of others

civ/il mar/riage *n* marriage performed by a government official and not a clergyman

civ/il rights/ *npl* privileges, protection, and immunities guaranteed to all citizens by the Constitution ‖ **civ/il-rights/** *adj*

civ/il serv/ice *n* 1 government employees other than elected officials, the military, and the judiciary; 2 government employment or office secured by competitive examinations

civ/il war/ *n* 1 war between factions or regions within the same country; 2 **the Civil War** the war between the

North and the South in the U.S. 1861–65

Cl *chem* chlorine

clab·ber /klab'ər/ [Ir *clabar* mud] *vt & vi* 1 to curdle ‖ *n* 2 curdled milk

clad¹ /klad'/ *pt & pp* of **clothe**

clad² [clad¹] *v* (**clad; clad·ding**) *vt* to bond a metal to (another metal) for protection

claim /klām'/ [MF *claimer* < L *clamare* to shout] *vt* 1 to demand as a right or by authority; 2 to assert, maintain ‖ *n* 3 demand of a right; 4 assertion of a fact; 5 assertion of a right or title to anything; 6 thing claimed; 7 lay **claim to** to claim ‖ **claim'ant** *n* ‖ SYN *v* affirm, aver, maintain, state

clair·voy·ance /klervoi'əns/ [F] *n* 1 supposed power of seeing what is beyond the range of natural vision; 2 extraordinary insight or penetration ‖ **clair·voy'ant** *adj & n*

clam /klam'/ [< *clamshell* < *clampshell* shell that clamps] *n* 1 any of several varieties of edible bivalve mollusks; 2 *colloq* secretive or uncommunicative person; 3 *slang* dollar ‖ *v* (**clammed; clam·ming**) *vi* 4 to dig for clams; 5 **clam up** *slang* to refuse to talk

clam'bake' *n* 1 picnic at which clams are baked on hot stones, often with corn and other foods; 2 *colloq* any large social gathering

clam·ber /klam'bər, -ər/ [ME *clambren*] *vt & vi* to climb with difficulty, using hands and feet

clam'my [ME] *adj* (**-mi·er; -mi·est**) sticky, cold, and moist ‖ **clam'mi·ness** *n*

clam·or /klam'ər/ [L] *n* 1 loud and continued uproar; 2 noisy and persistent demand or complaint ‖ *vi* 3 to make a clamor ‖ SYN *n* uproar, vociferation, outcry, hubbub, racket (see *noise*) ‖ ANT *n* quiet, silence, peace

clam'or·ous *adj* 1 noisy; vociferous; 2 vigorous in making demands ‖ SYN uproarious, vociferous, obstreperous, riotous, noisy ‖ ANT quiet, silent, noiseless, peaceful

clamp /klamp'/ [prob MD *klampe*] *n* 1 device to hold or press two things together ‖ *vt* 2 to fasten or hold with a clamp ‖ *vi* 3 **clamp down (on)** to become more strict (with)

clam'shell' *n* 1 shell of a clam; 2 dredging bucket hinged like the shell of a clam

clan /klan'/ [Gael *clann* < L *planta* sprout] *n* 1 tribe or association of families claiming common ancestry; 2 group of persons descended from one ancestor; 3 set or clique ‖ **clans·man** /klanz'mən/ *n* (**-men** /-mən/) ‖ SYN tribe, set, clique (see *caste*)

clan·des·tine /klandes'tin/ [L *clandes·*

tinus] *adj* secret, concealed, surreptitious ‖ **clan·des'tine·ly** *adv* ‖ SYN hidden, stealthy, surreptitious, underhand, secret ‖ DISCR *Secret* acts, though often permissible, are those which are intentionally concealed; a *secret* thought remains untold; a *secret* vice is undiscovered. *Clandestine* carries the bad sense of *secret*, and adds to it the fact that what is *clandestinely* under way is not permitted, or is evil ‖ ANT open, aboveboard, honest

clang /klaŋ'/ [L *clangere*] *n* 1 loud, sharp, ringing metallic sound ‖ *vi* 2 to emit a clang ‖ *vt* 3 to cause to emit a clang

clan·gor /klaŋ'ər, -gər/ [L] *n* 1 continuous clanging; 2 noisy outcry

clank /klaŋk'/ [perh imit] *n* 1 sharp metallic sound ‖ *vi* 2 to emit a clank ‖ *vt* 3 to cause to emit a clank

clan·nish /klan'ish/ *adj* 1 of, pert. to, or characteristic of a clan; 2 exclusive; 3 prejudiced, narrow ‖ **clan'nish·ly** *adv*

clap /klap'/ [OE *clæppan*] *v* (**clapped; clap·ping**) *vt* 1 to strike together with a sharp noise; 2 to strike (one's hands) together to applaud; 3 to put, place, or move quickly, as *to clap someone into jail;* 4 to strike or slap lightly ‖ *vi* 5 to applaud by striking the hands together; 6 to come together with a sharp noise ‖ *n* 7 loud explosive noise; 8 blow delivered with suddenness; slap

clap'board' /also klab'ərd/ *n* long board used as siding for frame houses

clap'per *n* tongue of a bell

clap'trap' *n* 1 insincere empty language ‖ *adj* 2 cheaply showy

claque /klak'/ [F < *claquer* to applaud] *n* 1 group of people paid to applaud at a performance; 2 body of servile admirers

clar·et /klar'it/ [MF (vin) *claret* clear (wine)] *n* French red table wine, or one like it

clar·i·fy /klar'ifī/ [MF *clarifier*] *v* (**-fied**) *vt* 1 to make clear by removing impurities; 2 to explain, elucidate; 3 to enlighten ‖ *vi* 4 to become clear

clar·i·net /klar'inet'/ [F *clarinette*] *n* tubelike wood-wind instrument with a flaring mouth and a single-reed mouthpiece ‖ **clar'i·net'ist** *n*

clar·i·on /klar'ē·ən/ [ML *clario* (*-onis*)] *n* 1 ancient trumpet ‖ *adj* 2 loud and clear, rousing

clar·i·ty /klar'itē/ [L *claritas*] *n* clearness

clash /klash'/ [?] *vi* 1 to make a loud harsh noise; 2 to collide with a crashing sound; 3 to disagree; conflict ‖ *vt* 4 to strike noisily ‖ *n* 5 sound of clashing; **6** conflict, disagreement; battle

clasp /klasp/, kläsp/ [ME] *n* **1** fastening device; **2** grasp; **3** close embrace ‖ *vt* **4** to fasten with a clasp; **5** to grasp or grip; **6** to embrace ‖ SYN *v* hold, grasp, catch, embrace, clutch

clasp′ knife′ *n* knife with blades folding into the handle

class /klas/, kläs/ [F *classe* < L *classis*] *n* **1** set of persons or things having common characteristics; kind; **2** division or grading on the basis of quality; **3** group of students meeting together for instruction; **4** group of students graduated from an institution in the same year; **5** rank or order of persons of the same social status; **6** caste. rank; **7** *slang* elegance, polish; **8** *biol* great division of animals or plants comprising the group between phylum and order ‖ *vt* **9** to classify ‖ *vi* **10** to be classed ‖ SYN *n* rank, order, grade, division, kind (see *caste*)

class. **1** classic(al); **2** classification; **3** classified

clas·sic /klas′ik/ [L *classicus* of the first class] *adj* **1** of the highest rank or class; **2** of or pert. to ancient Greece and Rome; **3** imitating the styles of Greek and Roman antiquity; **4** of exemplary style or design; **5** most representative of a given style or period ‖ *n* **6** author or work of acclaimed excellence, esp. of ancient Greece and Rome; **7** artist or his work considered as standard; **8** something excellent of its kind; **9** the **classics** Greek and Latin literature

clas·si·cal *adj* **1** of or pert. to the Greek and Roman authors, artists, or their productions. **2** like or modeled after the work of these ancients: restrained, simple, and harmoniously proportioned; **3** pert. to or modeled on the architecture of ancient Greece and Rome well-proportioned and symmetrical; **4** pert. to, based on, or versed in, the classics; **5** *mus* conforming closely to the rules of composition and musical form ‖ **clas′si·cal·ly** *adv*

Clas′si·cal Lat′in *n* literary Latin used in the period from 80 B.C. to 200 A.D.

clas′si·cism *n* **1** agreement with or adherence to classical style; **2** principles of the classic style as representing dignity, elegance, proportion, and simplicity ‖ **clas′si·cist** *n*

clas′si·fied ad′ *n* short newspaper advertisement that offers jobs, services, sales, purchases, and the like

clas′si·fy′ *v* (**-fied**) *vt* **1** to arrange in classes according to a system; **2** to restrict the availability of (a government document) for security reasons ‖ **clas′si·fi·ca′tion** *n*

class·y /klas′ē/ *adj* (**-i·er; -i·est**) *slang* first class; stylish

clat·ter /klat′ər/ [ME *clatren*] *n* **1** rattling noise; **2** din, hubbub ‖ *vt* **3** to make a clatter ‖ *vt* **4** to cause to clatter

clause /klôz/ [ML *clausa*] *n* **1** division of a sentence containing a subject and predicate of its own; **2** distinct provision of a document, such as a contract, treaty, or law

claus′tro·pho′bi·a /klôs′trə-/ [< LL *claustrum* confined place] *n* morbid fear of enclosed places ‖ **claus′tro·phobe′** *n* ‖ **claus′tro·pho′bic** /-fōb′ik, -fob′ik/ *adj*

clav·i·chord /klav′ikôrd′/ [< L *clavis* key + *chorda* string] *n* stringed instrument with a keyboard, forerunner of the piano

clav·i·cle /klav′ikəl/ [L *clavicula* little key] *n* bone which connects the breastbone with the shoulder blade, collarbone

claw /klô/ [OE *clawu*] *n* **1** sharp hooked nail in the foot of an animal or bird; **2** pincer of a lobster, scorpion, etc.; **3** anything sharp and hooked like a claw ‖ *vt & vi* **4** to tear or scratch with or as with a claw

clay /klā/ [OE *clæg*] *n* **1** a common earth, plastic when wet, used in making pottery, bricks, etc.; **2** earth, mud; **3** earth as the material of the human body ‖ **clay′ey** *adj*

clay·more /klā′môr′, -mōr′/ [Gael *claidheamh môr* great sword] *n* heavy two-edged, two-handed sword, formerly used in battle by the Scottish Highlanders

clay′ pig′eon *n* **1** fragile disk thrown in the air as a target in trap shooting; **2** *slang* person who is an easy target for schemers

clean /klēn/ [OE *clæne*] *adj* **1** free from soil or dirt; **2** pure, unadulterated; **3** free from imperfections or defects; **4** morally pure, honorable; **5** clean by habit; cleanly; **6** complete, free of interference, as *a clean getaway*; **7** *slang* not wanted for a crime; **8** *slang* broke ‖ *adv* **9** completely, quite; **10** **come clean** *slang* to tell the truth, confess ‖ *vt* **11** to make clean; **12** to prepare (fish or fowl) for cooking by removing the entrails; **13** **clean house** to reorganize; **14** **clean out** to remove everything or everyone from; **15** **clean up** to tidy up ‖ *vi* **16** to undergo cleaning; **17** **clean up** *slang* to make a lot of money ‖ **clean′ness** *n* ‖ SYN *adj* **cleanly** ‖ DISCR *Clean* describes a condition free from dirt, soil, or defilement. *Cleanly* describes a person whose disposition or tendency is to keep *clean* and neat. *Clean* is also used in the moral sense, as a *clean heart*

clean'-cut' *adj* 1 sharply outlined; 2 neat and trim

clean'er *n* one whose occupation is cleaning clothes; dry cleaner

clean-ly /klen'lē/ *adj* (-li-er; -li-est) 1 clean by habit ‖ /klēn'lē/ *adv* 2 in a clean manner ‖ **clean'li-ness** /klen-/ *n*

cleanse /klenz/ [OE *clǣnsian*] *vt* to make clean or pure ‖ **cleans'er** *n*

clean'-shav'en *adj* with the face completely and smoothly shaved

clean'up' *n* 1 complete cleaning; 2 elimination of vice and crime; 3 *colloq* very large profit

clear /klir'/ [OF *cler* < L *clarus*] *adj* 1 easily visible; 2 bright; 3 transparent; 4 unclouded; undimmed; 5 unblemished; 6 audible, distinct; 7 easily understood, intelligible, plain; 8 perceptive, discerning; 9 certain, sure; 10 untroubled, serene; 11 free or rid of responsibility or entanglement; 12 unobstructed, as a view or way; 13 without further cost to be deducted, net; 14 unencumbered, free of debt; 15 free of accusation or blame ‖ *adv* 16 clearly; 17 quite, wholly; 18 apart, without contact, as *to fall clear* ‖ *vi* 19 to make clear; 20 to free from obstruction; 21 to empty, as a room; 22 to prove innocent; 23 to free from debt or encumbrance; 24 to jump over or pass by without touching; 25 to make beyond expenses; 26 to put through the clearing house, as a check; 27 to give clearance for (a ship to leave harbor; a person to have access to classified material); 28 **clear away** or **out** to remove in order to make room; 29 **clear up** to make clear ‖ *vi* 30 to become clear; 31 to settle accounts through a clearing house; 32 **clear away** to vanish, as mist; 33 **clear out** to leave; 34 **clear up** to become clear ‖ *n* 35 **in the clear** *colloq* guiltless ‖ **clear'ly** *adv* ‖ **clear'ness** *n* ‖ SYN *adj* vivid, lucid, apparent, obvious, transparent ‖ ANT *adj* dull, opaque, obscure, vague

clear'-air' tur'bu-lence *n* violent turbulence in a cloudless region of the sky that suddenly and unexpectedly buffets fast-moving aircraft

clear'ance *n* 1 act of clearing; 2 space between two passing objects; 3 space between the surface of a road and the underpart of a bridge overhead; 4 distance by which a moving part in a machine escapes touching another part; 5 exchange of checks, drafts, etc., through a clearing house; 6 governmental authorization to permit access to classified information

clear'ance sale' *n* sale of merchandise on hand at reduced prices to make room for new goods

clear'-cut' *adj* 1 having a well-defined outline; 2 self-evident

clear'ing *n* tract of land cleared of trees

clear'ing house' *n* institution through which banks exchange drafts and checks, settling in cash only the balances due

clear'sto'ry *n* (-ries) clerestory

cleat /klēt/ [OE *clēot*] *n* strip of wood or metal fastened across a board or gangway, against a wall, under a shelf, etc., to supply footing, give strength or support, or to hold something in position

cleav-age /klēv'ij/ [< *cleave*²] *n* 1 act of cleaving or state of being cleft; 2 cleft or fissure; 3 division in opinion and interest

cleave¹ /klēv'/ [OE *clifian*] *vi* to adhere, cling

cleave² [OE *clēofan*] *v* (cleft or cleaved or clove; cleft or clo-ven or cleaved) *vt* 1 to cut open, cut through; 2 to split; 3 to sever, chop off ‖ *vi* 4 to split, esp. along the grain or line of cleavage

cleav'er *n* butcher's chopper having a large heavy blade

clef /klef'/ [MF < L *clavis* key] *n mus* sign at the beginning of a staff indicating the pitch of the notes on each line and space of the staff

cleft¹ /kleft'/ [ME *clift*] *n* crack, fissure, split

cleft² 1 *pt & pp* of **cleave²** ‖ *adj* 2 split, divided

clem-a-tis /klem'ətis/ [Gk] *n* any of several plants (genus *Clematis*) of the crowfoot family, with white, yellow, or purple flowers

clem-en-cy /klem'ənsē/ [L *clementia*] *n* (-cies) 1 mercy, leniency; 2 mildness (of weather) ‖ **clem'ent** *adj* ‖ SYN mildness, indulgence, lenity (see *mercy*)

clench /klench'/ [ME *clenchen*] *vt* 1 to set closely together, as the teeth or fingers; 2 to grasp firmly

Cle-o-pa-tra /klē'əpat'rə, -pāt'-, -pät'-/ *n* (69–30 B.C.) queen of Egypt 51–30 B.C.

clere'sto'ry /klir'-/ [*clear* + *story*¹] *n* (-ries) 1 part of a cathedral wall, pierced with windows, between a lower roof over the aisle and the roof of the higher central part, which admits daylight; 2 similar part, as on the roof of a railroad car

cler-gy /klur'jē/ [OF *clergie*] *n* whole body of ordained persons in a religion, spec. ministers or priests

cler'gy-man /-mən/ *n* (-men /-mən/) member of the clergy

cler-ic /kler'ik/ [Gk *klerikos*] *n* clergyman

cler'i-cal *adj* 1 of or pert. to the clergy; 2 of or pert. to clerks or office workers ‖ *n* 3 person or party advocating clerical power; 4 cleric; 5 **clericals** *pl* garb of clergy

cler'i-cal-ism *n* undue influence of the clergy in government

cler·i·hew /ˈklerˈiˌhyo͞o/ [Edmund *Clerihew* Bentley (1875–1956), Eng writer who originated it] *n* humorous quatrain, rhyming *aabb*, about a person whose name supplies the rhyme in the first or second line for the first two lines

clerk /klurk/, *Brit* klärk/ [OE *clerc* < LL *clericus* priest] *n* 1 city or county official who keeps the records and conducts routine business; 2 employee in an office who keeps accounts, conducts correspondence, or assists generally; 3 salesclerk ‖ *vi* 4 to act as a clerk ‖ **clerk′ship** *n*

Cleve·land /ˈklēvˈlənd/ *n* city in NE Ohio on Lake Erie (750,903)

Cleve·land, Gro·ver /ˈgrōvˈər/ *n* (1837–1908) 22nd and 24th president of the U.S. 1885–89, 1893–97

clev·er /ˈklevˈər/ [ME *cliver*] *adj* 1 intelligent; 2 witty, facile; 3 dexterous, skillful; 4 ingenious ‖ **clev′er·ly** *adv* ‖ **clev′er·ness** *n* ‖ SYN keen, smart, adept, adroit, deft, dexterous, expert, skillful, skilled ‖ DISCR *Clever* describes a quick, neat power of motion or manual ability, as a *clever* manipulator, boxer, etc.; transferred to the mental field, it describes a ready and adaptable intelligence, perhaps not extraordinary, but operating effectively. *Dexterous* describes a ready, naturally efficient use of the hands; a *dexterous* workman is sure of touch and quick; mentally, *dexterous* describes readiness in inventing, as a *dexterous* expedient saved the situation; and also a certain ingenious ability, as *dexterous* in the art of managing men. *Adroit* connotes ability to handle a difficult or dangerous situation with cleverness or tact. One makes an *adroit* parry in fencing; an *adroit* and evasive reply to an overinquisitive and persistent person. *Skillful* implies proficiency: a *skillful* designer; a *skillful* device. To be *skillful* is often the result of practice and habit; it is not to such an extent born in one as dexterity. *Deft* describes persons or movements that are *dexterous*, neat, and practiced. *Expert* suggests practice, skill, experience, and often, specialization, as an *expert* radio operator ‖ ANT awkward, clumsy, bungling, slow, stupid, dull, thick-headed

clew /klo͞o/ [OE *cliewen* ball of yarn] *n* 1 var of **clue**; 2 *naut* a lower corner of a fore-and-aft sail; **b** one of the two lower corners of a square sail

clew′ rope′ *n naut* rope for hauling up the clews of spankers

cli·ché /klēshā′/ [F = stereotyped] *n* trite or hackneyed expression or idea

click /klik/ [prob imit] *n* 1 slight sharp sound, as that of a bolt in a lock ‖ *vi* 2 to make a click ‖ *vt* 3 to cause to click

cli·ent /ˈklīˈənt/ [L *cliens* (-*entis*)] *n* 1 one who engages the services of a lawyer, accountant, etc.; 2 customer, patron, 3 dependent

cli′en·tele/ /-telˈ/ [F] *n* customers, clients collectively

cliff /klif/ [OE *clif*] *n* high, steep face of rock; precipice

cliff′-hang′er *n* 1 serial in which each episode ends in suspense; 2 contest whose outcome remains unsettled until the very end

cli·mac·ter·ic /klīmakˈtərik, klīˈmakter′ik/ [< Gk *klimakter* ladder rung] *adj* 1 crucial ‖ *n* 2 crucial period in life; 3 menopause

cli·mate /ˈklīmˈit/ [Gk *klima* (-*atos*) region] *n* 1 generally prevailing weather conditions of a place; 2 region characterized by a certain climate ‖ **cli·mat′ic** /-matˈik/ *adj*

cli·max /ˈklīˈmaks/ [Gk = ladder] *n* 1 highest point in a series of events of ascending intensity; culmination; 2 orgasm ‖ *vt* 3 to bring to a climax ‖ *vi* 4 to reach a climax ‖ **cli·mac′·tic** /-makˈtik/ *adj* ‖ SYN *n* culmination, zenith, acme

climb /klīm/ [OE *climban*] *vt* 1 to ascend ‖ *vi* 2 to rise, ascend; 3 to slope upward ‖ *n* 4 ascent; 5 place to be climbed ‖ SYN *v* mount, ascend, scale, rise, slope

climb·er /klīmˈər/ *n* 1 climbing plant; 2 socially ambitious person

clime /klīm/ [Gk *klima* region] *n poet.* 1 place or region; 2 climate

clinch /klinch/ [var of *clench*] *vt* 1 to drive the point of (a nail) sideways after it has been hammered through something; 2 to settle decisively, as a sale or an argument ‖ *vi* 3 to seize a boxer tightly to prevent his using his fists; 4 to embrace ‖ *n* 5 act of clinching

clinch′er *n colloq* conclusive or decisive argument

cling /kliŋ/ [OE *clingan*] *v* (**clung**) *vt* 1 to adhere closely; 2 to embrace; 3 to remain close

cling′stone′ peach′ or **cling′ peach′** *n* peach whose pulp adheres closely to the stone

clin·ic /klinˈik/ [< Gk *kline* bed] *n* 1 treatment of patients in the presence of a class of students; 2 hospital department treating ambulatory patients; 3 place for group practice by medical specialists

clin′i·cal *adj* 1 pert. to materials used in medical treatment; 2 pert. to observation and treatment of disease rather than purely theoretical study

clink¹ /kliŋk/ [ME *clinken*] *n* 1 sharp tinkling sound ‖ *vi* 2 to give forth a clink ‖ *vt* 3 to cause to clink

clink² [*Clink* London jail] *n slang* jail

clink′er /n [D *klinker* glassy brick] *n* 1 stony residue from partly burned coal melted and hardened; 2 *slang* wrong note, as on the piano

Cli·o /klī′ō/ *n Gk myth.* Muse of history

clip[1] /klip′/ [OE *clyppan* to embrace] *v* (**clipped; clip·ping**) *vt* 1 to grip, fasten ‖ *n* 2 clasp, fastener

clip[2] [ON *klippa*] *v* (**clipped; clip·ping**) *vt* 1 to cut or trim with shears or scissors; 2 to cut short; 3 *colloq* to hit smartly; 4 *slang* to swindle ‖ *vi* 5 to move briskly ‖ *n* 6 smart blow; 7 pace, rate

clip′board′ *n* board with a clip on one end for holding papers

clip′ joint′ *n slang* café or restaurant that cheats its patrons by charging exorbitant prices for inferior food and drink

clip′per *n* 1 sailing ship designed and rigged for high speed; 2 also **clip·pers** *pl* tool for cutting, shearing, and trimming

clip′ping *n* piece cut out of a newspaper or periodical

clique /klēk′/ [F] *n* exclusive group, coterie ‖ **cli′quish** *adj* ‖ SYN circle, set, coterie (see *caste*)

clit·o·ris /klit′ōris, klīt′-/ [Gk *kleitoris*] *n* small, sensitive, erectile organ between the folds of the vulva in the female of most mammals

cloak /klōk′/ [ONF *cloke* < LL *cloca* bell-shaped cape] *n* 1 loose outer garment; 2 that which conceals ‖ *vt* 3 to cover with a cloak; 4 to conceal ‖ SYN *v* hide, secrete, disguise, mask (see *conceal*)

cloak′-and-dag′ger [perh var of *cloak-and-sword*, a loan translation of Sp (comedia) *de capa y espada* (drama) concerned with 17th-cent. knightly adventure and romance] *adj* dealing with undercover activities of all kinds and melodramatic intrigue

cloak′room′ *n* 1 room for leaving temporarily outer garments, umbrellas, etc, as in a school or restaurant; 2 *Brit* washroom

clob·ber /klob′ər/ [?] *vt* 1 to beat, batter; 2 to defeat, trounce

cloche /klōsh′/ [F = bell] *n* bell-shaped hat for women

clock[1] /klok′/ [MD *clocke* < LL *clocca* bell] *n* 1 device for measuring time, usu. mechanical and with hands to mark the time, and not made to be worn on the person; 2 **around the clock** day and night, ceaselessly ‖ *vt* 3 to time, as with a stopwatch ‖ *vi* 4 **clock in** to arrive for work (at a certain time)

clock[2] [?] *n* woven or embroidered ornament on the ankle of a stocking

clock′wise′ *adj & adv* in the same direction as the motion of the hands of a clock

clock′work′ *n* 1 mechanism of a clock; 2 any similar mechanism; 3 **like clockwork** with smooth precision

clod /klod′/ [ME *clodde*] *n* 1 lump of earth, turf, or clay; 2 stupid lout ‖ **clod′dish** *adj*

clod′hop′per *n* 1 country bumpkin; 2 strong heavy shoe

clog /klog′/ [ME *clogge* thick piece of wood] *n* 1 that which impedes, hindrance; 2 shoe with a wooden sole; 3 dance with clogs ‖ *v* (**clogged; clog·ging**) *vt* 4 to hinder; 5 to obstruct ‖ *vi* 6 to become blocked up

cloi·son·né /kloi′zənā′/ [F = partitioned] *n* colored enamelwork in which the colors are separated by wires embedded in the surface

clois·ter /kloist′ər/ [OF *cloistre* < L *claustrum* bolt] *n* 1 monastery or convent; 2 arched way or covered walk, often surrounding a courtyard ‖ *vt* 3 to confine in a convent or monastery; 4 to seclude from the world ‖ **clois′tered** *adj* ‖ SYN *n* abbey, hermitage

clone /klōn′/ also **clon** /klōn′, klon′/ [< Gk *klōn* twig] *n* 1 group of genetically identical cells that have descended from a single ancestor; 2 group of organisms that have descended from a single individual

close /klōz′/ [OF *clos* closed] *vt* 1 to shut; 2 to fill, stop up; 3 to make continuous by joining the parts, as an electric circuit; 4 to terminate, conclude; 5 **close down** or **up** to discontinue the operation of; 6 **close out** to dispose of (merchandise) by reducing the price ‖ *vi* 7 to become closed; 8 to grapple; 9 to end, finish; 10 to come close; 11 **close in** to approach from all sides 12 **close in on** to approach so as to capture ‖ *n* 13 conclusion, end ‖ /klōs′/ *adj* 14 narrow, shut in; 15 kept confined, guarded; 16 stuffy, humid; 17 secretive, reticent; 18 niggardly, stingy; 19 near in space, time, relationship, or intimacy; 20 dense, compact, as *close weaving*; 21 intimate; 22 almost equal, as *a close race*; 23 fitting snugly; 24 accurate, precise, as *close attention*; 25 almost like, as *a close resemblance*; 26 keenly observant, as *close scrutiny*; 27 very short, as *a close haircut*; 28 down to the skin, as *a close shave*; 29 *phonet* (vowel) articulated with the mouth relatively closed ‖ *adv* 30 near in space or time; 31 tightly; closely together ‖ **close′ly** *adv* ‖ **close′ness** *n* ‖ SYN *v* end, conclude, finish, complete, terminate, stop, expire ‖ DISCR To *end* is to bring or come to a final, often logical, issue, as the mischief *ended* when the perpetrators were caught; stories *end* well, badly. To *close* is to bring or come to an end by not continuing. We may *close* a letter hurriedly because of the arrival of a visitor, or a dispute because the differences concerning it prove irreconcilable. We also *close* that which is merely discontinued, as school for a vacation. To *conclude* is to bring to a suitable or a desired point. The letter hurriedly *closed* was not *concluded*. Orations, arguments, business, which have run a previously determined course, are *concluded*. What is *finished* has been done to its last touch; we *finish* what we plan; we *finish* a reading course, or a college course, and go on to other things; or we *finish* by perfecting, by polishing, as a work of art. To *complete* is to make a thing exactly what it should be, with no deficiencies. To *terminate* is to *end* because of the limitations of time or space, as life *terminates*; or to *end* because a fixed term has been set, as the dance *terminated* at twelve o'clock

close'-at-hand' /klōs'-/ *adj* 1 that will happen shortly; imminent; 2 that is not far away

close'-by' /klōs'-/ *adj* near, neighboring

close' call' /klōs'-/ *n colloq* narrow escape

closed'-cir'cuit tel'e·vi·sion /klōzd'-/ *n* television setup consisting of a transmitter which broadcasts usu. by cable to a limited number of receivers

closed' shop' /klōzd'/ *n* shop which hires only union members

close'fist'ed /klōs'-/ *adj* stingy

close'-fit'ting /klōs'-/ *adj* (garment) fitting closely to the body

close-mouthed /klōs'mouthd', -tht'/ *adj* uncommunicative, reticent

close' quar'ters /klōs'-/ *npl* 1 physical contact in a fight; 2 crowded space

close' shave' /klōs'-/ *n colloq* narrow escape

clos·et /kloz'it/ [MF < *clos* closed] *n* 1 small room or cabinet for storing, as clothes, kitchen utensils, etc.; 2 small private room. || *vt* 3 to shut up in a private room or office, as for a conference

close'-up' /klōs'-/ *n* photograph or movie shot taken at close range

clot /klot'/ [OE *clott* lump] *v* (clot·ted; clot·ting) *vt & vi* 1 to coagulate || *n* 2 semisolid mass, as of coagulated blood

cloth /klôth', kloth'/ [OE *clāth* garment] *n* (-ths/ -ths, -thz/) 1 woven fabric, as of wool, linen, cotton, etc.; 2 piece of such fabric used for a specific purpose, as a tablecloth or washcloth; 3 the **cloth** the clergy

clothe /klōth'/ [OE *clāthian*] *v* (clothed or clad) *vt* 1 to dress; 2 to cover with or as with a garment; 3 to provide with clothing

clothes /klōz', klōthz'/ *npl* 1 wearing apparel; 2 bedclothes

clothes'horse' *n* 1 woman who loves to display her fashionable clothes; 2 frame on which to hang clothes for drying

clothes' moth' *n* any of several moths

of the family Tineidae, whose larvae feed on wool and fur

clothes' pin' *n* clip of plastic or wood to hold clothes on a line

clothes' tree' *n* upright pole with hooks for hanging hats and coats

cloth·ier /klōth'yər/ *n* dealer in clothing or cloth

cloth·ing /klōth'iŋ/ *n* clothes, apparel, garments in general

Clo·tho /klō'thō/ *n class. myth.* youngest of the three Fates, who spins the thread of life

clo·ture /klōch'ər/ [F] *n* stoppage of parliamentary debate so that a vote may be taken

cloud /kloud'/ [OE *clūd* mass of rock] *n* 1 visible mass of water droplets or ice particles suspended in the air; 2 any similar mass, as of smoke or dust; 3 dimmed appearance or spot, as in marble; 4 that which obscures, threatens, or overshadows, as suspicion; 5 anything that moves in or like a mass, as many arrows or locusts in flight; 6 **in the clouds** lost in reverie; 7 **under a cloud, a** in disgrace; **b** under suspicion || *vt* 8 to overspread with or as with a cloud; 9 to render gloomy; darken; 10 to blacken or sully; 11 to cover with variegated spots || *vi* 12 to become clouded; 13 to become downcast || **cloud'y** *adj* (-i·er; -i·est)

cloud'burst' *n* sudden violent downpour of rain

cloud' nine' *n* **on cloud nine** *slang* in a state of bliss

cloud' seed'ing *n* stimulation of rainfall by infusing clouds with silver iodide or crystals of dry ice

clout /klout'/ [OE *clūt* patch] *colloq* *n* 1 rap, esp. with the hand; 2 influence, pull; 3 impact, wallop; 4 *baseball* long hit || *vt* 5 to strike, hit

clove[1] /klōv'/ [OE *clufu*] *n* one of the bulbs of a compound bulb, as of garlic

clove[2] [OF *clou* (de girofle) nail (of the gillyflower)] *n* 1 aromatic dried flower bud of a tropical evergreen tree, used as a spice; 2 the tree (*Eugenia aromatica*)

clove[3] *pt* of **cleave**[2]

clo·ven /klōv'ən/ *pp* of **cleave**[2]

clo'ven-foot'ed or **clo'ven-hoofed'** *adj* 1 having a cleft hoof, as cows; 2 satanic

clo·ver /klōv'ər/ [OE *clāfre*] *n* 1 any of a genus (*Trifolium*) of low-growing, usu. three-leaved leguminous plants found in temperate regions; 2 any of various other plants of the same family; 3 **in clover** enjoying comfort or wealth

clo'ver·leaf' *n* (-leaves) highway intersection resembling a four-leaf clover, in which one roadway crosses over the other, access being had from one to the other by means of curved ramps

clown /kloun'/ [perh ON *klunni* boor] *n* **1** clumsy boor; **2** professional jester || *vi* **3** to act as a clown

clown'ish *adj* like a clown; rude || **clown'ish·ly** *adv* || SYN ill-bred, awkward, rustic, loutish, boorish, rough || ANT gentle, polished, polite, urbane

cloy /kloi'/ [< MF *encloyer* to put a nail into < L *inclavare*] *vt* to fill to excess, surfeit, as with sweetness or pleasure || SYN satiate, glut, surfeit (see *satisfy*)

club /klub'/ [ON *klubba*] *n* **1** heavy stick, cudgel; **2** stick of various kinds used in games, as golf or polo; **3** a number of persons associated for a common purpose; **b** building or room where they meet; **4** playing card stamped with a black trefoil; **5** **clubs** *sg* or *pl* suit of cards so marked || *v* (**clubbed; club·bing**) *vt* **6** to beat with a club || *vi* **7** to form a club || SYN *n* organization, association, society (see *caste*)

club'foot' *n* (**-feet**) congenitally misshapen foot || **club'foot'ed** *adj*

club' so'da *n* soda water

cluck /kluk'/ [imit] *n* **1** call of a brooding hen to her chicks || *vi* **2** to make this sound

clue /kloo'/ [OE *cliewen* ball of yarn] *n* fact or hint forming a key to the solution of a problem

clump /klump'/ [?] *n* **1** cluster or group, as of trees, etc.; **2** lump, mass; **3** sound of heavy tramping || *vi* **4** to form into clumps; **5** to tread heavily || *vt* **6** to form clumps of

clum·sy /klum'zē/ [ME *clumsen* to be stiff with cold] *adj* (**-si·er; -si·est**) **1** awkward, lacking grace or tact; **2** unwiedy, badly made || **clum'si·ly** *adv* || **clum'si·ness** *n* || SYN (see *awkward*) || ANT skillful, adroit, dexterous

clung /klung'/ *pt & pp* of **cling**

clus·ter /klus'tər/ [OE *clyster*] *n* **1** number of persons or things grouped together; bunch || *vt & vi* **2** to gather in a cluster

clutch¹ /kluch'/ [ON *klekja* to hatch] *n* **1** brood of chicks; **2** nest of eggs

clutch² [OE *clyccan*] *vt* **1** to grasp tightly || *vi* **2** **clutch at** to try to clutch || *n* **3** grasp or grip; **4** device for gripping or holding; **5** device for engaging or disengaging a drive shaft; **6** control or pedal that operates a clutch; **7** crucial moment; **8** **clutches** *pl* control

clutch'bag' *n* small strapless handbag carried by women

clut·ter /klut'ər/ [ME *clotteren* to clot] *n* **1** disorder, litter, confusion || *vt* **2** to heap in disorder, litter

cm, *an.* centimeter(s)

Cm *chem* curium

Cmdr. Commander

C'-note' *n slang* hundred-dollar bill

CO, C.O. Commanding Officer

Co *chem* cobalt

co- /kō'-, kō-/ [< L *cum* with] *pref* **1** joint(ly), together, as *coheir*; **2** *math* complement, as *cosine*

Co. **1** Company; **2** County

c.o., c/o care of

coach /kōch'/ [MF *coche* < Hung *kocsi* of Kocs, place name] *n* **1** large closed four-wheeled carriage; **2** railroad passenger car, spec. day coach; **3** second-class airline accommodations; **4** one who trains and directs students, athletes, actors, and singers || *vt* **5** to transport in a coach; **6** to train or direct || *vi* **7** to act as a coach; **8** to be trained by a coach

coach'man /-mən/ *n* (**-men** /-mən/) man who drives a carriage

co·ad·ju·tor /kō·aj'oot'ər, kō·aj'ətər/ [L = helper] *n* assistant, spec. bishop who acts as assistant to another bishop

co·ag·u·lant /kō·ag'yələnt/ *n* substance that produces coagulation

co·ag'u·late' [L *coagulare* (-*atus*)] *vt & vi* to thicken, change from a liquid to a congealed mass || **co·ag'u·la'tion** *n*

coal /kōl'/ [OE *col*] *n* **1** black or brownish combustible mineral, formed by the decomposition of vegetable matter and used as a fuel; **2** ember || *vt* **3** to furnish with coal || *vi* **4** to take in coal

co·a·lesce /kō'ə·les'/ [L *coalescere*] *vi* to grow together, blend into one || **co'a·les'cence** || **co'a·les'cent** *adj* || SYN unite, fuse, combine, mingle (see *mix*)

co·a·li·tion /kō'ə·lish'ən/ [< *co-* + L *alere* (*alitus*) to nourish] *n* temporary alliance or combination

coal' oil' *n* kerosene

Coal'sack' *n* either of two dark regions in the Milky Way

coal' tar' *n* thick dark liquid obtained by distillation from soft coal, used for coatings and for the production of a large number of dyes, drugs, and other synthetic compounds || **coal'-tar'** *adj*

coarse /kôrs', kōrs'/ [ME *cors*] *adj* **1** of inferior quality; **2** large in texture, grain, or size; **3** not refined; crude and vulgar in manners and speech || **coarse'ly** *adv* || **coarse'ness** *n* || SYN common, rude, unpolished, vulgar, rough || ANT fine, polished, polite, delicate, dainty

coars'en *vt* **1** to make coarse || *vi* **2** to become coarse

coast /kōst'/ [MF *coste* < L *costa* side] *vi* **1** to sail along a shore; **2** to slide downhill on a sled; **3** to keep going on momentum || *n* **4** land along the sea; seashore; **5** slide downhill on a sled; **6** **the Coast** *colloq* the states along the Pacific Ocean || **coast'al** *adj* || SYN *n* margin, edge, bank, shore (see *border*)

coast'er *n* small dish or mat placed under a glass to protect the table

coast'er brake' *n* brake on the rear

wheel of a bicycle which is operated by pedaling backwards and which permits free coasting

Coast′ Guard′ *n* naval service under the Transportation Department in peacetime, which guards against smuggling, enforces maritime laws, and engages in rescue operations at sea

coast′ing trade′ *n* trade between ports along a coast

coast′wise′ *adj & adv* by way of or along the coast

coat /kōt′/ [OF *cote* < Gmc] *n* 1 sleeved outer garment; 2 any outside covering, as fur, skin, rind, paint, etc. ‖ *vt* 3 to cover with, or as with, a coat

co·a·ti /kō·ät′ē/ [Port < Tupi] *n* raccoonlike carnivorous mammal (genus *Nasua*) of tropical and subtropical America

coat′ing *n* thin layer or covering

coat′ of arms′ *n* 1 shield bearing the insignia of a family, school, organization, or place; 2 shield emblazoned with heraldic devices

coat′ of mail′ *n* garment made of small metal links, worn as protective armor

coax /kōks′/ [*obs cokes* fool] *vt* 1 to seek to persuade by soothing words or flattery; 2 to persuade by coaxing ‖ SYN flatter, entice, inveigle, allure, wheedle, blandish

co·ax·i·al /kō·ak′sē·əl/ [< *co-* + L *axis* pivot] *adj* 1 having a common axis; 2 (loudspeaker) with two or more cones of different frequencies mounted on the same axis

co·ax′i·al ca′ble *n* cable, consisting of an insulated conducting tube and an insulated conducting core running through it, used for transmitting high-frequency telephone, telegraph, or television signals

cob /kob′/ [ME *cobbe* leader] *n* 1 corncob; 2 small thickset horse; 3 male swan

co·balt /kō′bôlt/ [< G *Kobold* goblin] *n* steel-gray metallic element (Co; at.no. 27; at.wt. 58.933) used in heat-resisting and corrosion-resisting alloys

co′balt blue′ *n* deep blue

cob·bler /kob′lər/ [ME *cobelere*] *n* 1 one who mends shoes; 2 drink made of iced wine, lemon, etc.; 3 deep-dish fruit pie made with one crust

cob·ble·stone′ /kob′əl-/ [ME] *n* rounded stone formerly used for paving

co·bra /kō′brə/ [Port *cobra* (de capelo) (hooded) snake] *n* large venomous Old World snake (*Naja tripudians*), which when irritated dilates its neck like a hood

cob′web′ [< ME *coppe* spider] *n* 1 spider's web; 2 anything gauzy or entrapping

co·ca /kō′kə/ [Sp < Quechua] *n* 1 small shrub (*Erythroxyllum coca*)

of the Andes; 2 its dried leaves, which yield cocaine and are chewed as a stimulant

co·caine /kōkān′, kō′-/ [< *coca*] *n* bitter crystalline addictive alkaloid —C₁₇H₂₁NO₄— extracted from coca leaves, and used as an analgesic

coc·cus /kok′əs/ [Gk *kokkos* seed] *n* (**coc·ci** /kok′sī/) *n* spherical bacterium

coc·cyx /kok′siks/ [Gk = cuckoo] *n* (**coc·cy·ges** /koksī′jēz/) last bone of the spinal column

coch·i·neal /koch′inēl′/ [OSp *cochinilla*] *n* red dye obtained from the dried bodies of a tropical American insect, *Dactylopius coccus*

coch·le·a /kok′lē·ə/ [Gk = snail] *n* (-ae /-ē′/) spiral-shaped part of the inner ear which contains the auditory nerve endings

cock /kok′/ [OE *cocc*] *n* 1 rooster; 2 male of certain species of birds; 3 valve, faucet; 4 a hammer of a firearm; b its position when raised; 5 rakish tilt, as of a hat or eye ‖ *vt* 6 to turn up or set to one side; 7 to raise the hammer of (a gun)

cock·ade /kokād′/ [F *cocarde*] *n* rosette or badge worn on the hat

cock′-and-bull′ sto′ry *n* absurdly improbable story

cock′a·too′ /-ətoo′/ [Malay *kakatua*] *n* any of a subfamily (Cacatuinae) of crested white or brilliantly colored parrots of the East Indies and Australia

cock′crow′ *n* early morning

cocked′ hat′ *n* 1 three-cornered man's hat of the 18th century; 2 **knock into a cocked hat** *slang* to upset completely, as plans

cock′er·el /-ərəl/ [*dim.* of *cock*] *n* young rooster

cock′er span′iel [< (wood)*cock*] *n* small spaniel with a soft silky coat and drooping ears

cock′eyed′ *adj* 1 cross-eyed; 2 *slang* a awry; b absurd; c drunk

cock′fight′ *n* contest between gamecocks armed with spurs ‖ **cock′fight′ing** *n*

cock′horse′ [16th-cent. nursery term] *n* rocking horse

cock′le /-əl/ [MF *coquille* shell] *n* 1 any of various mollusks (genus *Cardium*) with heart-shaped fluted shells; 2 **cockles of one's heart** one's deepest feelings

cock′ney /-nē/ [ME *cokeney* cock's egg (i.e., malformed egg)] *n* 1 native of the East End of London, one born within sound of Bow bells and speaking a characteristic dialect; 2 this dialect ‖ also *adj*

cock′pit′ *n* 1 pit for cockfighting; 2 scene of constant wars; 3 a in small open airplanes, well in which the pilot sits; b in large airplanes, space occupied by the pilot and crew; 4

in small vessels, space aft, lower than the main deck

cock'roach' [Sp *cucaracha*] *n* any of several large insects (family Blattidae) with a flat body, chiefly nocturnal, which are household pests

cocks'comb' *n* **1** rooster's crest; **2** garden plant (genus *Celosia*) having a crest-shaped red or yellow blossom; **3** jester's cap with a red crest

cock'sure' *adj* **1** absolutely sure; **2** too decidedly positive

cock'tail' [?] *n* **1** mixed alcoholic drink, usu. chilled and often sweetened; **2** appetizer, usu. chilled seafood or fruit

cock'tail dress' *n* woman's dress designed for late-afternoon and early-evening wear

cock'tail lounge' *n* room or establishment serving cocktails and other alcoholic drinks

cock'tail shak'er *n* shaker 3

cock'y /kok'ē/ *adj* (-i·er; -i·est) arrogantly self-assertive; conceited

co·co /kō'kō/ [Port *coco* bogy] *n* **1** coconut palm; **2** coconut

co·coa /kō'kō/ [< *cacao*] *n* **1** powder made from the ground and roasted seeds of the cacao tree; **2** drink made from it; **3** reddish brown

co'co·nut' *n* **1** hard-shelled fruit of the coconut palm, with white edible meat and a milky liquid; **2** its shredded meat, used as a flavoring and topping

co'co·nut palm' *n* tall tropical palm (*Cocos nucifera*) yielding the coconut

co·coon /kəkoon'/ [F *cocon*] *n* **1** silky case spun by the larvae of many insects as a protective covering during the pupal stage; **2** any of various similar coverings, as of certain spiders; **3** plastic sprayed over inactive army and navy equipment to prevent rust

cod /kod/ [ME] *n* (**cod** or **cods**) large food fish (*Gadus callarias*) found in northern and temperate seas

C.O.D. cash on delivery

co·da /kō'də/ [It < L *cauda* tail] *n* *mus* independent passage added to the conclusion of a movement

cod·dle /kod'əl/ [ONF *caudel* warm drink] *vt* **1** to treat tenderly, pamper; **2** to cook in hot water below the boiling point

code /kōd/ [F < L *codex* wooden writing tablet] *n* **1** systematized body of laws, rules, or statutes; **2** any body of principles governing personal behavior; **3** any set of visual or aural signals for sending messages; **4 a** system of sending secret messages by means of symbols; **b** these symbols; **5** symbol or mark used for identification || *vt* **6** to encode

co·deine /kō'dēn, kōd'ē·in/ [Gk *kodeia* poppy head] *n* white crystalline alkaloid —C₁₈H₂₁NO₃H₂O— obtained from opium, and used as a sedative and analgesic

co·dex /kō'deks/ [L = wooden writing tablet] *n* (**-di·ces** /-disēz', kod'-/) ancient manuscript volume, as of the Bible or one of the classics

cod'fish' *n* (**-fish** or **-fishes**) cod

codg·er /koj'ər/ [perh var of *cadger*] *n* queer old fellow

cod·i·cil /kod'isəl/ [L *codicillus* dim. of *codex*] *n* addition to a will, modifying or revoking it

cod'i·fy' /kōd'-, kod'-/ *v* (**-fied**) *vt* to reduce to a system, as laws || **cod'i·fi·ca'tion** *n*

cod'-liv·er oil' *n* oil obtained from the liver of the cod and rich in vitamins A and D

co·ed or **co-ed** /kō'ed'/ [*coeducation*] *n* female student of a college or university attended by both sexes

co'ed·u·ca'tion *n* education of both sexes in the same institution

co'ef·fi'cient *adj* **1** working together || *n* **2** constant quantity or number placed as a multiplier before another quantity; **3** *phys* numerical multiplier that indicates the measure of some property of a substance, or of some change in a substance under certain conditions

co'ef·fi'cient of ex·pan'sion *n* change in length, volume, or area per unit of change in temperature of a substance at constant pressure

coe·len·ter·ate /silent'ərit, -rāt'/ [< Gk *koilos* hollow + *enteron* intestine] *n* any of a phylum (Coelenterata) of invertebrate sea animals consisting essentially of a sac open at one end and having the mouth surrounded by tentacles, including jellyfishes and sea anemones

co·erce /kōurs'/ [L *coercere* to restrain] *vt* **1** to compel or dominate by force or threat; **2** to effect or bring about by force or threat

co·er'cion *n* **1** act or process of coercing; **2** government by force || **co·er'cive** *adj* || SYN force, constraint, violence (see **compulsion**)

co·e·val /kō·ēv'əl/ [< LL *coaevus*] *adj* of the same age, date, or duration

co'ex·ist' *vi* to exist together in the same time or place, esp. peaceably || **co'ex·ist'ence** *n*

co'ex·ten'sive *adj* having the same limits or extent

cof·fee /kôf'ē, kof'ē/ [It *caffè* < Ar *qahwah*] *n* **1** tropical shrub (genus *Coffea*); **2** its seeds, ground and roasted; **3** beverage prepared from the seeds; **4** color of coffee with cream

cof'fee-and' *n* *slang* coffee and coffee ring, doughnuts, cake, pastry, or the like

cof'fee break' *n* short intermission from work for coffee-and

cof'fee klatsch' /klach'/ [G *Klatsch* noise] *n* informal social gathering for conversation and coffee

cof·fee·pot' *n* covered utensil with a spout or lip for making and serving coffee

cof·fee ring' *n* ring-shaped cake served with coffee

cof·fee shop' *n* eating place specializing in coffee, pastries, sandwiches, and simple meals

cof·fee ta'ble *n* low table, usu. placed before a sofa, for holding cups, glasses, ashtrays, etc.

cof·fer /kôf'ər, kof'-/ [OF *cofre* < Gk *kophinos* basket] *n* 1 chest for valuables; 2 **coffers** *pl* funds, treasury

cof'fer·dam' *n* watertight enclosure built under the water and pumped dry to allow men to work or make repairs

cof·fin /kôf'in, kof-/ [MF *cofin* chest] *n* case or chest in which a corpse is buried

cog /kog', kôg/ [ME *cogge* < Scand] *n* 1 gear tooth; 2 cogwheel

cogged' *adj* furnished with cogs

co·gent /kōj'ənt/ [L *cogens* (-*entis*) driving] *adj* having compelling force; convincing || **co'gen·cy** *n*

cog·i·tate /koj'itāt'/ [L *cogitare* (-*atus*)] *vi* 1 to ponder, meditate || *vt* 2 to meditate upon; plan || **cog'i·ta'tion** *n*

co·gnac /kōn'yak, kon'-/ [F] *n* 1 fine brandy from Cognac, France; 2 any fine brandy

cog·nate /kog'nāt/ [L *cognatus*] *adj* 1 related by blood; 2 of the same nature or quality; 3 related in origin, as words or languages || *n* 4 person, thing, or word that is akin to another by blood or derivation

cog·ni·tion /kognish'ən/ [L *cognitio* (-*onis*)] *n* 1 act or process of knowing or perceiving; 2 that which is known or perceived || **cog'ni·tive** *adj*

cog·ni·zance /kog'nizəns/ [MF *conoissance* < L *cognoscens* (-*entis*) knowing] *n* 1 knowledge, apprehension, notice; 2 right to exercise the legal or judicial power of a court || **cog'ni·zant** *adj*

cog·no·men /kognōm'ən/ [L < *co-* + *nomen* name] *n* (-**mens** or -**nom·i·na** /-nom'inə/) 1 ancient Rome third or family name, as *Caesar* in *Caius Julius Caesar*; 2 surname; 3 nickname

cog' rail'way' *n* railway in which locomotion is achieved by the engagement of a cogged wheel with a cogged track, used for ascending steep inclines

cog'wheel' *n* wheel with teeth or cogs in its rim

co·hab·it /kō-/ [LL *cohabitare*] *vi* to live together as husband and wife, even though not legally married || **co·hab'i·ta'tion** *n*

co·here /kōhir'/ [L *cohaerere*] *vi* 1 to stick together; 2 to be logically consistent or connected, as an argument || **co·her'ence** *n* || **co·her'ent** *adj*

co·he·sion /kōhēzh'ən/ *n* 1 act or state of cohering; 2 attractive force by which molecules of the same material are held together || **co·he'sive** /-siv/

co·hort /kō'hôrt/ [MF *cohorte* < L *cohors* (-*hortis*)] *n* 1 ancient Rome body of soldiers, the tenth part of a legion; 2 any body of soldiers; 3 band of persons; 4 associate

coif /koif'/ [< LL *cofea*] *n* hoodlike cap

coif·fure /kwäfyoŏr'/ [F] *n* 1 headdress; 2 hair style

coil /koil'/ [MF *coillir* to collect] *vt* 1 to wind or twist into spirals or rings || *n* 2 series of spirals or rings, as of a coiled rope; 3 single such ring; 4 *elec* copper wire or other conductor wound up in a coil

coin /koin'/ [MF = stamping die < L *cuneus* wedge] *n* 1 piece of metal legally stamped and authorized to be used as money; 2 metal money collectively || *vt* 3 to make (coins) by stamping pieces of metal; 4 to convert (metal) into coins; 5 to make up (a new word or phrase)

coin'age /-ij/ *n* 1 act or process of making coins; 2 that which is coined; 3 coins collectively; 4 anything invented, as a new word

co·in·cide /kō'insīd'/ [ML *coincidere*] *vi* 1 to correspond exactly, agree; 2 to occur at the same time; 3 to occupy the same place || *syn* concur, correspond (see *agree*)

co·in·ci·dence /kō·in'sidəns/ *n* 1 condition or state of coinciding; 2 instance of this; 3 notable falling together of events or circumstances, apparently accidental

co·in'ci·dent *adj* 1 coinciding in space or time; 2 in exact correspondence or agreement

co·in'ci·den'tal /-dent'əl/ *adj* characterized by coincidence

co·i·tus /kō'itəs/ [< L *coire* (-*itus*) to go together] *n* sexual intercourse

coke¹ /kōk'/ [*obs* *colk* core] *n* coal from which the volatile elements have been driven off by heating, used as an industrial fuel

coke² *n* *slang* cocaine

col- *pref* var of **com-**

Col. 1 Colonel; 2 Colorado

col·an·der /kul'əndər, kol'-/ [ME *colyndore*] *n* perforated pan used as a strainer

cold /kōld'/ [OE *cald*] *adj* 1 producing or experiencing the sensation of lowered temperature; 2 chilled or chilling; 3 indifferent, unresponsive; 4 not cordial; 5 depressing; 6 faint (scent or trail); 7 (color) tending toward blue; 8 *colloq* insensible || *n* 9 absence of heat; 10 sensation produced by heat loss from the body; 11 cold weather; 12 respiratory virus infection, often producing sneezing, coughing, etc.; 13 **catch cold** to get a cold; 14 **in the cold** ignored, neglected || *adv* 15 completely, as *he* *learned the lesson cold* || **cold′ly** *adv* || **cold′ness** *n* || SYN *adj* cool, frigid, wintry, unfeeling, unresponsive, stoical || ANT *adj* warm, balmy, cordial, genial

cold′-blood′ed *adj* 1 having blood the temperature of which changes to match that of the environment, said of reptiles; 2 callous, unfeeling

cold′ chis′el *n* steel chisel for cutting cold metals

cold′ cream′ *n* creamy preparation for soothing and cleansing the skin

cold′ cuts′ *npl* sliced meat served cold

cold′ feet′ *npl* loss of nerve or courage; backdown because of loss of confidence

cold′ shoul′der *n colloq* snub || **cold′-shoul′der** *vt*

cold′ sore′ *n* eruption of tiny blisters about the mouth, appearing during a cold or fever, and caused by the virus *Herpes simplex*

cold′ stor′age *n* storage of food, furs, etc. in an artificially refrigerated chamber

cold′ war′ *n* intense rivalry between nations stopping short of armed conflict

cold′ wave′ *n* 1 period, usu. prolonged, of intensely cold weather affecting a large area; 2 permanent wave set by a chemical preparation instead of heat

co·lec·to·my /kəlek′təmē/ [Gk *colon* + *-ectomy*] *n* (**-mies**) surgical removal of all or part of the colon

Cole·ridge, Samuel Taylor /kōl′rij/ *n* (1772–1834) English poet and critic

cole·slaw /kōl′slô′/ [D *koolsla* cabbage salad] *n* salad made of finely cut raw cabbage

col·ic /kol′ik/ [MB *colike* < Gk *kolikos* of the colon] *n* sharp spasmodic pain in the abdomen or bowels || **col′ick·y** *adj*

col′i·form ba·cil′lus /kol′-, kōl′-/ [< L *cŏlum* strainer] *n* microscopic one-celled organism (esp. of genera *Escherichia* and *Aerobacter*) which are always but not exclusively present in human intestines

col·i·se·um /kol′isē′əm/ [< *Colosseum*] *n* 1 large arena or stadium; 2 **Coliseum** Colosseum

co·li·tis /kəlīt′is/ [< Gk *kolon* colon] *n* inflammation of the colon

coll. 1 collect; 2 collection; 3 college

col·lab·o·rate /kəlab′ərāt′/ [< *co-* + L *laborare (-atus)* to work] *vi* 1 to work together; 2 to cooperate with an enemy occupying one's country || **col·lab′o·ra′tion** *n* || **col·lab′o·ra′tor** *n*

col·lab′o·ra′tion·ist *n* one who collaborates with the enemy

col·lage /kəläzh′/ [< F *coller* to glue] *n* 1 art composition made of paper, cloth, wood, metal, etc. glued on a flat surface and usu. framed like a picture; 2 heterogeneous assembly; 3 film showing a series of unconnected shots in rapid succession

col·lapse /kəlaps′/ [< *col-* + L *lapsus* fallen] *vi* 1 to cave in or break down suddenly; 2 to fail utterly; 3 to be compacted; 4 to break down physically || *vt* 5 to cause to collapse || *n* 6 sudden breakdown or caving in; 7 sudden and complete failure; 8 general physical prostration || **col·laps′i·ble** *adj*

col·lar /kol′ər/ [AF *coler* < L *collare*] *n* 1 the part of a garment that encircles the neck; 2 anything worn around the neck of man or animal; 3 ring or round flange around anything, as a pipe || *vt* 4 to seize by or as by the collar

col′lar-bone′ *n* clavicle

col·lard /kol′ərd/ [< *colewort* a plant] *n* variety of kale, *Brassica oleracea acephala*

col·late /kəlāt′/ [L *collatus* brought together] *vt* 1 to compare (texts) carefully; 2 to examine (the sheets of a book) before binding || **col·la′tor** *n*

col·lat·er·al /kəlat′ərəl/ [< *col-* + L *latus (-eris)* side] *adj* 1 at the side of; 2 parallel; 3 accompanying, supporting; 4 secondary; 5 related by descent from a common ancestor in a different line || *n* 6 security pledged for the repayment of a loan; 7 collateral relative

col·la′tion *n* 1 act of collating; 2 light meal

col·league /ko′lēg/ [MF *collegue*] *n* associate in one's work || SYN fellow member, associate (see *ally*)

col·lect /kəlekt′/ [L *colligere (-lectus)*] *vt* 1 to gather together; 2 to obtain payment of; 3 to make a collection of as a hobby; 4 to regain control of (oneself, one's scattered thoughts) || *vi* 5 to accumulate; 6 to assemble || *adj* & *adv* 7 to be paid by the recipient || /kol′ekt/ *n* 8 brief prayer used in certain church services || **col·lect′i·ble, col·lect′a·ble** *adj* || SYN *v* amass, accumulate, gather, assemble

col·lect′ed *adj* self-possessed, cool || SYN composed, undistracted, cool (see *calm*)

col·lec′tion *n* 1 act of collecting; 2 persons or things collected; 3 accumulation || SYN heap, pile, group, accumulation, mass

col·lec′tive *adj* 1 formed by collection; 2 pert. to a group taken together, combined || *n* 3 collective noun; 4 collective enterprise || **col·lec′tive·ly** *adv*

col·lec′tive bar′gain·ing *n* negotiation between labor and management regarding wages, hours, rules, and working conditions

col·lec′tive farm′ *n* farm managed and worked as a unit under government control

col·lec'tive noun' *n* noun, singular in form, denoting a group or collection, taking either a singular or plural verb

col·lec'tiv·ism *n* socialist doctrine of control by the state of all economic activity ‖ **col·lec'tiv·ize'** *vt*

col·lec'tor *n* 1 person employed to collect taxes, debts, etc.; 2 one who collects stamps, antiques, etc., esp. as a hobby; 3 *elec* device for providing contact between parts in relative motion; 4 *electron* output terminal of a transistor

col·lec'tor ring' *n* metal ring or rings mounted on the shaft of an alternating-current motor or dynamo to provide by means of brushes a flow of current between the rotating armature and the external circuit

col·leen /kolēn', kol'-/ [Ir *cailín*] *n* young Irish girl

col·lege /kol'ij/ [MF < L *collegium*] *n* 1 institution of higher learning granting the bachelor's degree; 2 constituent school of a university; 3 organized body having certain duties and rights, as *the electoral college, the College of Cardinals*

col·le·gian /kəlēj'(ē)ən/ *n* college student

col·le'giate /-j(ē)it/ *adj* of or pert. to a college or college student

col·lide /kəlīd'/ [L *collidere*] *vi* 1 to strike together with force; crash; 2 to conflict, clash

col·lie /kol'ē/ [*obs colly* black] *n* one of a breed of large dogs with long hair and snout, originally bred in Scotland as sheep dogs

col·lier /kol'yər/ *n* 1 coal miner; 2 vessel for carrying coal

col'lier·y *n* (-ies) coal mine and its surrounding buildings

col·li·sion /kolizh'ən/ *n* 1 act of colliding, of violently striking together; 2 conflict; clash of ideas; 3 *phys* brief encounter of two or more bodies, resulting in a change of energy or momentum in one or more of them ‖ SYN contact, conflict, impact, encounter, shock

col·li'sion course' *n* **on a collision course** (vehicles, persons, ideas, interests, etc.) headed precipitously for a collision

col·lo·di·on /kəlōd'ē·ən/ [< Gk *kollodes* < *kolla* glue] *n* inflammable solution of guncotton in ether and alcohol, used in coating wounds and in manufacturing photographic film

col·loid /kol'oid/ [< Gk *kolla* glue] *n* substance which when mixed in a liquid forms microscopic particles larger than the molecules of the liquid and which will not settle out and will not pass through a membrane ‖ **col·loid'al** *adj*

colloq. colloquial

col·lo·qui·al /kəlōk'wē·əl/ *adj* informal or familiar (speech or writing) ‖ **col·lo'qui·al·ly** *adv*

col·lo'qui·al·ism *n* 1 colloquial word or expression; 2 colloquial style

col·lo·quy /kol'əkwē/ [< L *colloqui* to speak together] *n* (-quies) discussion, conference ‖ SYN discussion, debate, conversation

col·lu·sion /kəlōōzh'ən/ [L *collusio* (-*onis*)] *n* secret agreement to obtain an unlawful object ‖ **col·lu'sive** *adj*

Colo. Colorado

co·logne /kəlōn'/ [F (eau de) *Cologne* (water of) Cologne] *n* perfumed toilet water

Co·logne /kəlōn'/ *n* city in W West Germany on the Rhine (857,380)

Co·lom·bi·a /kəlum'bē·ə/ *n* Spanish-speaking republic in NW South America adjoining the Isthmus of Panama (19,215,000; 439,516 sq.m.; cap. Bogotá) ‖ **Co·lom'bi·an** *adj & n*

Co·lom·bo /kəlum'bō/ *n* capital of Sri Lanka (650,000)

co·lon[1] /kōl'ən/ [Gk *kōlon* clause] *n* mark of punctuation : used before a quotation, summation, elaboration, enumeration, etc.

co·lon[2] [Gk] *n* (-lons or -la /-lə/) section of the large intestine between the cecum and the rectum

co·lon[3] /kəlōn'/ [Sp *Colón* Columbus] *n* monetary unit of Costa Rica and El Salvador

colo·nel /kurn'əl/ [MF *coronel* < It *colonello*] *n* regimental commander, ranking next to a brigadier general ‖ **colo·nel·cy** /kurn'əlsē/ *n* (-cies)

co·lo·ni·al /kəlōn'ē·əl/ [see *colony*] *adj* 1 of or pert. to a colony; 2 of or pert. to the British colonies in North America which became the United States ‖ *n* 3 inhabitant of a colony

co·lo'ni·al·ism *n* policy or practice of a nation's maintaining or seeking to maintain foreign territory as colonies

col·o·nist /kol'ənist/ *n* 1 settler of a colony; 2 colonial

col'o·nize' *vt* 1 to migrate to and settle in; 2 to establish a colony in ‖ *vi* 3 to establish a colony ‖ **col'o·ni·za'·tion** *n*

col·on·nade /kol'ənād'/ [F] *n* row or series of columns

col·o·ny /kol'ənē/ [L *colonia* < *colonus* farmer] *n* (-nies) 1 body of people who leave their native country and settle in another land, but remain subject to the mother country; 2 country thus settled; 3 group of people allied by race, common interests, etc., living close together as in a colony

col·o·phon /kol'əfon/ [Gk = summit] *n* 1 publisher's emblem on the title page of a book; 2 in old books, inscription or ornamental figure used as a tailpiece

col·or /kul'ər/ [AF < L] *n* 1 any one

of the hues of the spectrum or rainbow, loosely including black, white, and gray; **2** any tint or shade produced by the blending of the rainbow hues; **3** paint or pigment; **4** complexion; **5** ruddiness; **6** race other than white; **7** pretext; false show; **8** character; tone; **9** shade of mood, meaning, etc.; **10** colors *pl* a ribbon or dress worn as a badge, as *college colors:* **b** flag; **11** show one's (true) colors to reveal one's true nature; **12** with flying colors triumphantly ‖ *vt* **13** to impart a color to; tint, dye; **14** to give an exaggerated value or appearance to; misrepresent; **15** to give a distinctive quality to ‖ *vi* **16** to blush ‖ SYN *n* shade, tint, hue, tinge ‖ DISCR *Color* is the general term for that quality that makes the bands of the rainbow appear to the eye as violet, red, yellow, etc.; loosely, *color* also includes black and white. *Shade* refers to degree or intensity of a given *color*, as a bright *shade* of red. A pale *shade*, a delicate variety of *color*, is a *tint. Hue* suggests a variation or modification of a *color*, especially as a result of slight alteration in the predominant element, as green of a bluish *hue. Tinge* names a diffused coloring, sometimes faint and in light touches, sometimes deep and spreading

Col·o·rad·o /kol′ərād′ō, -rad′-/ *n* state in the W U.S. (2,207,000; 104,247 sq.m.; cap. Denver) ‖ **Col′o·rad′an** *n*

Col′o·rad′o Springs′ *n* city and resort in central Colorado; site of U.S. Air Force Academy (71,000)

col′or·a′tion /kul′-/ *n* appearance as regards color

col·o·ra·tu·ra /kul′ərət(y)ŏŏr′ə/ [It] *n* soprano adept at brilliant runs and trills

col′or-blind′ *adj* unable to perceive colors or to distinguish between certain colors ‖ **col′or blind′ness** *n*

col′ored *adj* **1** having color; **2** often *offensive* belonging to a dark-skinned race; **3** distorted

col′or·ful *adj* **1** full of color; **2** picturesque; **3** vivid

col′or·ing *n* **1** material producing color, pigment; **2** appearance as to color; **3** tone

col′or·less *adj* **1** having no color; **2** dull, uninteresting

col′or line′ *n* social, political, and economic restrictions based on skin pigmentation

col·os·se·um /kol′əse′əm/ [< L *colosseus* colossal] *n* **1** coliseum; **2** Colosseum large amphitheater in Rome built ab. 80 A.D.

co·los·sus /kəlos′əs/ [Gk *kolossos*] *n* (-sus·es or -si /-sī/) **1** statue of great size; **2** any very great person or object ‖ **co·los′sal** *adj*

co·los·to·my /kəlos′təmē/ [Gk *kolon*

colon + *stoma* mouth] *n* (-mies) surgical opening into the colon to act as an artificial anus

co·los·trum /kəlos′trəm/ [L] *n* first milk secreted by the mother after birth

colt /kōlt′/ [OE] *n* young male animal of the horse family

Co·lum·bi·a /kəlum′bē·ə/ *n* **1** *poet.* the United States of America; **2** river in SW Canada and NW U.S.; **3** capital of South Carolina (97,400)

col·um·bine /kol′əmbin′/ [< L *columba* dove] *n* any of a genus (*Aquilegia*) of spring plants of the crowfoot family, having flowers with five deeply spurred petals

Co·lum·bus /kəlum′bəs/ *n* capital of Ohio (539,677)

Co·lum·bus, Chris·to·pher /kris′təfer/ *n* (1446?–1506) Italian-born Spanish navigator and explorer, discoverer of America in 1492

Co·lum′bus Day′ *n* October 12, holiday commemorating the discovery of America by Columbus on October 12, 1492, now celebrated on the second Monday in October

col·umn /kol′əm/ [L *columna*] *n* **1** upright pillar supporting or adorning some part of a building or standing by itself, as for a monument; **2** anything suggestive of a column, as *the spinal column, a column of smoke;* **3** series of words, figures, etc., placed one above another in a vertical arrangement; **4** troops or ships arranged in deep formation and a narrow front; **5** vertical division of a book, newspaper, etc.; **6** regular by-lined department in a newspaper ‖ **co·lum·nar** /kəlum′nər/ *adj*

col′um·nist /-nist, -ist/ *n* author of a newspaper column

com- [< L *cum*] *pref* **1** together; **2** with; **3** completely

co·ma /kōm′ə/ [Gk] *n* profound and prolonged insensibility, caused by injury or disease

Co·man·che /kōman′chē/ [Sp < Shoshone] *n* member of a fierce predatory tribe of American Indians originally living in N Texas

com·a·tose /kom′ətōs′, kōm′-/ *adj* **1** relating to or in a coma; **2** drowsy, lethargic

comb /kōm′/ [OE *camb*] *n* **1** toothed strip of some hard substance, used to separate, smooth, or adjust the hair; **2** toothed ornament for the hair; **3** any comblike instrument; **4** cockscomb; **5** honeycomb ‖ *vt* **6** to arrange or clean with or as with a comb; **7** to search thoroughly

com·bat /kəmbat′, kom′bat/ [MF *combattre*] *v* (-bat·ed or bat·ted; -bat·ing or -bat·ting) *vt & vi* **1** to fight or oppose by force ‖ /kom′bat/ *n* **2** struggle; duel; fight ‖ SYN *n* contention, strife, contest, conflict, battle

com·bat·ant /kom′bətənt, kəmbat′ənt/
adj 1 disposed to fight; 2 bearing
arms; 3 fighting ‖ *n* 4 fighter
com·bat·ive /kəmbat′iv, kom′bətiv/ *adj*
pugnacious, disposed to fight
comb·er /kō′mər/ *n* steep curling wave
com·bi·na·tion /kom′bi̇nāsh′ən/ *n* 1 act
of combining or state of being combined; 2 union of separate parts; 3
association of persons or groups for
a common object; 4 a series of figures necessary for opening a combination lock; b mechanism that operates it; 5 *chem* a union of two or
more simple or compound substances
in definite proportions, resulting in
the formation of a more complicated
compound; b such a compound; 6 a
arrangement, as of objects, numbers,
or people, into a definite pattern or
grouping; b result of this arrangement; 7 one-piece garment for upper
and lower parts of body ‖ SYN alliance, league, confederacy (see *union*)
com′bi·na′tion lock′ *n* lock, as on a
safe, opening by turning a numbered
wheel a given number of times, stopping each time at a prescribed number in a prescribed order
com·bine /kəmbīn′/ [LL *combinare*] *vt*
1 to unite closely together
‖ *vi* 3 to unite ‖ *n* /kom′bīn/ 4 machine which harvests, threshes, and
cleans grain as it moves across a
field; 5 *colloq* combination of persons or groups for business or political ends ‖ SYN *v* join, unite, add,
consolidate, amalgamate, connect ‖
DISCR To *join* is to bring together into
any degree of closeness, as to *join*
hands; the buildings were *joined* by
a covered archway; it also indicates
such attachments as in marriage or
in allying oneself to clubs or similar
bodies. To *unite* is to *join* things hitherto separate and distinct, but capable of fusion, so that they merge into
a new body or whole; our forefathers
united the thirteen colonies into one
nation; people of accordant views
unite in expression or purpose. *Combine* is frequently used of widely dissimilar objects, as the different instruments *combined* to produce an
unexpected harmony; or it may be
used of things or people with similarity of purpose or aim; we *combine*
forces, qualities, flavors, materials,
etc. To *add* is to put another part of
what is already there, forming a unified whole; we can *add* millions to a
fortune, one five to another five, or
a porch to our house. To *consolidate*
is to join for resulting strength; we
consolidate two companies, increasing their ability to serve and reducing
their operating expenses. To *amalgamate* produces an even closer union,
in which the fused elements are indistinguishable, as to *amalgamate* so-

cieties, languages, races, etc. *Connect*
is used of an attachment secured by
some linking object or relationship
that ties together; it is, like *join*,
capable of expressing many degrees
of closeness
com·bin′ing form′ *n* word element used
only in combination with other words
or elements, as *proto-* in *protozoan*
com·bo /kom′bō/ [< *combination*] *n* 1
small dance or jazz band; 2 *colloq*
combination; 3 *Australian* white
man living among aborigines or with
an aboriginal woman
com·bus·ti·ble /kəmbust′əbəl/ *adj* 1
inflammable; 2 excitable; fiery ‖ *n* 3
combustible substance
com·bus·tion /kəmbus′chən/ [<L *com-
burere* (-*bustus*) to burn up] *n* 1 act
or process of burning; 2 *chem* oxidation, either rapid (accompanied by
heat and/or flame) or slow (no heat
or flame)
Comdr. Commander
come /kum/ [OE *cuman*] *v* (**came;
come**) *vi* 1 to move toward an objective point; 2 to draw near, approach; 3 to extend (to a given
point); 4 to become visible, audible,
perceptible, etc.; 5 to arrive; 6 to
issue from as a source; 7 to be descended; 8 to result; 9 to happen; 10
to occur in a certain order, as 3
comes after 2; 11 to be available; 12
to become; 13 **come about** to happen; 14 **come across,** a to find by
chance; b *slang* to do what someone wants; 15 **come around or round,**
a to revive; b to change one's opinion so as to agree with someone
else's; c to visit; 16 **come at** to attack; 17 **come back,** a to return; b
colloq to regain one's former eminence; 18 **come by** to obtain; 19 **come
down with** to contract (a disease); 20
come in, a to enter; b to be a winner; 21 **come into** to inherit; 22 **come
off,** a to be detached; b to result sat-
isfactorily; 23 **come on,** a to get
along well; b to begin; c also **come
upon** to encounter unexpectedly; 24
come out, a to be offered to the public; b to be disclosed; c to result; d
to be presented to society; 25 **come
over** to happen to; 26 **come through**
slang to be successful with a given
project; 27 **come′ to′** to amount to,
total; 28 **come′ to′** to recover consciousness; 29 **come under** to come
under the heading or responsibility
of; 30 **come up,** a to occur; b to be
brought up for discussion or action;
31 **come up to,** a to equal; b to come
abreast of; 32 **come up with,** a to
come abreast of; b to offer, supply
‖ *v impv* 33 pay attention!, behave!;
34 **come on!** hurry up!, let's go!
come′back′ *n* 1 *colloq* regaining of
former eminence; 2 *slang* witty retort
co·me·di·an /kəmēd′ē̇ən/ *n* 1 comic

actor; 2 professional teller of funny stories and jokes; 3 any amusing person

come'down' n colloq humiliating descent from eminence

com·e·dy /kom'ədē/ n (-dies) 1 play ending happily, usu. humorous or full of lively entertainment; 2 any humorous or ridiculous incident or series of incidents

come·ly /kum'lē/ [OE cȳmlic] adj (-li·er; -li·est) 1 attractive; 2 suitable, proper || **come'li·ness** n || SYN pleasant, wholesome, handsome (see beautiful)

come'-on' n slang inducement

com'er n colloq promising newcomer in any field

co·mes·ti·ble /kəmest'əbəl/ [LL comestibilis] adj 1 eatable || n 2 comestibles pl food

com·et /kom'it/ [Gk kometes longhaired] n heavenly body moving about the sun in an eccentric orbit, consisting of a bright head or nucleus and generally accompanied by a long luminous tail

come'up'pance /-up'əns/ n colloq just deserts

com·fort /kumf'ərt/ [OF conforter] n 1 state of physical and mental ease and well-being; 2 consolation; encouragement; 3 person or thing that brings consolation, well-being, etc., to another; 4 quilted cover for a bed || vt 5 to bring comfort to || SYN n ease, contentment, satisfaction, enjoyment || ANT n misery, wretchedness, discomfort

com'fort·a·ble adj 1 at ease; 2 enjoying contentment; 3 giving comfort; 4 sufficient, as a comfortable salary || n 5 padded quilt for a bed || **com'fort·a·bly** adv || SYN pleasant, snug, satisfied, contented || ANT cheerless, dreary, discontented, wretched

com'fort·er n 1 one who comforts; 2 long woolen scarf; 3 padded quilt for a bed; 4 **the Comforter** the Holy Spirit

com'fort sta'tion n public toilet

com·fy /kumf'ē/ adj (-fi·er; -fi·est) colloq comfortable

com·ic /kom'ik/ [< Gk komos revelry] adj 1 pert. to or characterized by comedy || n 2 comedian; 3 comics pl comic strips || SYN adj laughable, mirth-provoking, funny (see ludicrous)

com'i·cal adj funny, humorous || **com'i·cal·ly** adv || SYN laughable, diverting (see ludicrous)

com'ic book' n magazine containing comic strips

com'ic strip' n series of cartoons relating comic or adventure stories

com·ing /kum'iŋ/ adj 1 approaching, next; 2 promising success || n 3 approach, arrival

com'ing out' n 1 issuance of stocks or bonds; 2 debut in society

com·i·ty /kom'itē/ [L comitas] n (-ties) civility, politeness, esp. courtesy between nations in the recognition of one another's laws and customs

com·ma /kom'ə/ [Gk = clause] n punctuation mark, which indicates a slight separation in ideas or construction

com·mand /kəmand', -mänd'/ [OF comander] vt 1 to order, direct; 2 to control; exercise authority over; 3 to overlook, as from a height; 4 to exact, demand; 5 to have the use of, as a fortune || vi 6 to act as leader; give the orders || n 7 authority; 8 order; 9 dominating situation; 10 mastery, control; 11 military force under the command of one officer || SYN v bid, direct, instruct, enjoin, require, dominate (see govern); n (see order) || ANT v yield, submit

com·man·dant /kom'əndant', -dänt'/ [F] n officer in command of a fortified place or of a body of troops

com'man·deer' /-dir'/ [Afrik kommandeer] vt 1 to seize (private property) for official use; 2 to force into military service; 3 colloq to seize by force

com·mand·er /kəmand'ər, -mänd'-/ n 1 one who commands; leader; 2 one in command of a military unit; 3 nav officer next in rank below a captain

com·mand'er in chief' n (commanders in chief) supreme commander of all the military forces of a nation

com·mand'ing adj 1 impressive; 2 dominating, controlling; 3 in command || SYN dignified, imperious, imperative, authoritative

com·mand'ment n 1 mandate, precept; 2 any of the Ten Commandments || SYN law, edict, order, command

com·man'do /-dō/ [Afrik kommando military unit] n (-dos or -does) 1 small force of highly trained troops used for raids on special targets; 2 member of such a force

com·mem·o·rate /kəmem'ərāt'/ [L commemorare (-atus) to bring to mind] vt 1 to call to remembrance by a solemn ceremony; 2 to keep alive the remembrance of || **com·mem'o·ra'tion** n || **com·mem'o·ra'tive** /-rāt'iv, -rətiv/ adj || SYN observe, signalize, keep (see celebrate)

com·mence /kəmens'/ [MF comencer] vt & vi to begin, start || SYN (see begin)

com·mence'ment n 1 beginning; 2 ceremony of conferring academic degrees or diplomas

com·mend /kəmend'/ [L commendare] vt 1 to entrust; 2 to recommend; 3 to approve; praise || **com·mend'a·ble** adj || **com·mend'a·to'ry** adj || **com'men·da'tion** /kom'ən-/ n

com·men·su·ra·ble /kəmen'sərəbəl, -shər-/ [L commensurabilis] adj 1 capable of being exactly divided or measured by the same number or measure; **2** proportionate || **com·men′su·ra·bil·i·ty** /-bil′-/ *n*

com·men′su·rate /-rit/ *adj* **1** commensurable; **2** equal in size or measure; **3** corresponding in amount

com·ment /kom′ent/ [L *commentum* invention] *n* **1** remark; **2** talk; gossip; **3** note in explanation or criticism || *vi* **4** to make comments

com′men·tar′y /-mən-/ *n* (**-ies**) **1** explanation; **2** series of explanatory notes; an explanatory narrative

com′men·ta′tor *n* **1** one who makes commentaries; **2** person who discusses events on radio or television

com·merce /kom′ərs/ [L *commercium* < *merx* (*mercis*) merchandise] *n* **1** large-scale business intercourse; **2** personal relations

com·mer·cial /kəmursh′əl/ *adj* **1** engaged in or pert. to commerce; **2** prepared or done for private profit || *n* **3** *rad & telv* advertising presentation

com·mer′cial bank′ *n* bank that handles checking accounts and makes short-term loans

com·mer′cial·ize *vt* **1** to make commercial in character or spirit; **2** to emphasize the commercial aspect of || **com·mer′cial·ism** *n*

com·mer′cial pa′per *n* short-term negotiable paper, as drafts or bills of exchange, which may be used as security for bank loans

com·min·gle /kəming′əl/ *vt & vi* to mix, blend

com·mis·er·ate /kəmiz′ərāt′/ [L *commiserari* (*-atus*)] *vt* **1** to feel or express pity for || *vi* **2** commiserate **with** to condole with || **com·mis′er·a′tion** *n*

com·mis·sar /kom′isär′/ [Russ *kommissar*] *n* **1** formerly, head of a major government department in Russia, now called *minister;* **2** communist official in charge of political indoctrination

com′mis·sar′i·at /-ser′ē·ət/ *n* **1** army department furnishing provisions and supplies; **2** former name of a Russian government ministry

com′mis·sar′y *n* (**-ies**) **1** store that supplies food and equipment, as at an army post; **2** restaurant or cafeteria, as in a factory or studio

com·mis·sion /kəmish′ən/ [L *commissio* (*-onis*) beginning] *n* **1** act of committing, as a crime or error; **2** authority for a particular function or action; **3** entrusting of business to anyone; **4** trust, charge; **5** group of individuals entrusted with certain business or public duties; **6** in some cities, governing body; **7** compensation allowed an agent or broker for services rendered; **8** document conferring authority or rank, as on a military officer, notary public, etc.; **9 in commission** fit for use; **10 out of commission** out of order || *vt* **11**

to authorize; **12** *mil* to grant a commission to; **13** to put into service, as a warship

com·mis′sioned of′fi·cer *n* military officer holding rank by presidential commission, from second lieutenant and ensign up

com·mis′sion·er *n* **1** official in charge of some department of the public service; **2** member of a city commission

com·mit /kəmit′/ [L *committere* to entrust] *v* (**-mit·ted; -mit·ting**) *vt* **1** to give in charge or trust; **2** to consign to custody, as *to commit to prison or a mental hospital;* **3** to perform or perpetrate (a crime, sin, error, or the like); **4** to pledge, bind; **5** to consign for safekeeping, as by memorizing or writing down || **com·mit′tal** *n*

com·mit′ment *n* **1** act of committing, or state of being committed; **2** court order to commit a person; **3** pledge, promise

com·mit′tee *n* one or more persons selected to act on, consider, or report on any matter

com·mit′tee·man /-mən, -man′/ *n* (**-men** /-mən, -men′/) **1** member of a committee; **2** party leader of a political ward or precinct

com·mode /kəmōd′/ [F < L *commodus* convenient] *n* **1** chest of drawers; **2** covered washstand; **3** piece of furniture containing a chamber pot under a seat

com·mo′di·ous *adj* **1** roomy; spacious; **2** suitable or useful for the purpose || **SYN** spacious, suitable, adapted, roomy, convenient

com·mod′i·ty /-mod′-/ *n* (**-ties**) **1** something which is useful; **2** element of wealth; an economic good; **3** article that can be bought and sold to be delivered to a transportation company for forwarding, such as butter, sugar, coffee, meat, cotton

com·mo·dore /kom′ədôr′, -dōr′/ [alter. of *commander*] *n* **1** *nav* lowest grade of flag officer, below a rear admiral; **2** senior captain of a passenger-ship line; **3** head of a yacht club

com·mon /kom′ən/ [OF *comun* < L *communis*] *adj* **1** shared by everyone; **2** public; **3** widespread; **4** usual; frequent; **5** customary, trite; **6** ordinary; **7** having no rank or distinction; **8** vulgar, coarse; **9** (noun) referring to any member of a class || *n* **10** tract of open public land; **11 commons** *pl* **a** common people; **b** meals at a common table at a college; **c Commons** House of Commons || **com′mon·ness** *n* || **com′mon·ly** *adv* || **SYN** *adj* (see *general, mutual*) || **ANT** *adj* unusual, exceptional, singular, odd, extraordinary, uncommon

com′mon·al·ty /-əl-/ *n* (**-ties**) **1** common people; **2** general membership of a corporation

com′mon car′ri·er *n* person or company

engaged in transporting goods or persons for pay

com·mon de·nom·i·na·tor *n* 1 number that is the multiple of all the denominators in a set of fractions; 2 something shared by all the members of a group

com·mon·er *n* 1 one of the common people; 2 *UK* a any person not a peer; b member of the House of Commons

com·mon law· *n* law of custom or usage, not in the written statutes of a country || **com·mon-law·** *adj*

com·mon-law· mar·riage *n* relationship between individuals who live together as man and wife but have not been legally married

Com·mon Mar·ket *n* group of European nations (Belgium, Denmark, France, Great Britain, Ireland, Italy, Luxembourg, The Netherlands, West Germany) joined together to abolish all trade barriers among themselves and apply common tariffs to the outside world

com·mon·place *n* 1 ordinary or trite topic or remark; 2 anything ordinary || *adj* 3 uninteresting, common; dull, platitudinous || SYN *adj* everyday, ordinary, usual

com·mon pleas *npl* in some states of the U.S., court of civil jurisdiction

com·mon sense· *n* normal intelligence; sound practical judgment || **com·mon-sense·** *adj*

com·mon stock· *n* ordinary capital stock, not sharing the privileges of preferred stock

com·mon·weal· *n* public welfare, common good

com·mon·wealth· *n* 1 all the people of a nation; 2 democratic nation; 3 **Commonwealth** official designation of certain states, nations, and self-governing territories, as Virginia, Australia, and Puerto Rico

com·mo·tion /kəmōsh'ən/ [MF < L *commotio* (-*onis*)] *n* disorder, tumult, || SYN excitement, disturbance, riot, violence

com·mu·nal /kom'yənəl, kəmyōon'-əl/ *adj* 1 pert. to ownership in common; public; 2 pert. to a commune

com·mune¹ /kom'yōon/ [F < ML *communia*] *n* 1 smallest political division of certain European countries, as France; 2 local self-governing community

com·mune² /kəmyōon'/ [MF *comuner* to share < L *communicare*] *intr* 1 to converse together; take intimate counsel; 2 to partake of the Eucharist

com·mu·ni·ca·ble *adj* 1 capable of being communicated or transmitted, as a disease; 2 talkative

com·mu·ni·cant /-kənt/ *n* 1 partaker, esp. of the Eucharist; 2 one who communicates

com·mu·ni·cate [L *communicare* (-*atus*) to share] *vt* 1 to impart, transmit; 2 to make known, tell || *vi* 3 to be connected, as rooms; 4 to hold converse; impart ideas or information || **com·mu·ni·ca·tor** *n*

com·mu·ni·ca·tion *n* 1 act or process of communicating; 2 message; 3 also **communications** *pl* means of communicating || SYN correspondence, intelligence, message, news

com·mu·ni·ca·tive /-kətiv/ *adj* 1 ready to impart information; 2 unreserved, talkative; 3 of or pert. to communication

com·mun·ion /kəmyōon'yən/ [< L *communis* common] *n* 1 intercourse; fellowship; 2 common possession; 3 group of people having a common religious faith; 4 **Communion** sacrament of the Lord's Supper or the partaking of it; Eucharist

com·mu·ni·qué /kəmyōon'ikā'/ [F] *n* official bulletin

com·mu·nism /kom'yəniz'əm/ [< L *communis* common] *n* 1 theory or system whereby all property including industry is owned by all the people and controlled in their name by a totalitarian government through a single political party; 2 **Communism** political movement to bring this about || **com·mu·nist, Com·mu·nist** *adj* & *n* || **com·mu·nis·tic** *adj* || **com·mu·nize** *vt*

com·mu·ni·ty /kəmyōon'itē/ [MF *comunete* < L *communitas* fellowship] *n* (-ties) 1 social group with common interests living in the same locality and under the same laws; 2 group within a larger community having specialized interests of narrower scope, as *the business community*; 3 joint participation, sharing, or ownership; 4 likeness, common character; 5 the **community** the public in general

com·mu·ni·ty-an·ten·na tel·e·vi·sion *n* television transmitted from a single elevated antenna to subscribers by coaxial cable

com·mu·ni·ty col·lege *n* college administered by the local public school authorities

com·mu·tate /kom'yətāt'/ [see **commute**] *vt* 1 to reverse the direction of (an electric current); 2 to reverse every other cycle of (an alternating current) and thus produce a flow of direct current

com·mu·ta·tion *n* railroad ticket valid over a given route for a specified number of times within a specified period, sold at a reduced rate

com·mu·ta·tor *n* 1 switch for throwing an electric current in two or more ways or directions; 2 series of metal bars, insulated from each other, mounted around the shaft of a direct-current motor or generator, and connected directly with the coils of the armature and by means of brushes with the field; devised to provide a steady flow of direct current between the rotating armature, the field, and the external circuit and magnetization at the right time and place

com·mute /kəmyo͞ot'/ [L *commutare* to exchange] *vt* 1 to exchange, substitute; 2 to reduce the severity of, as a sentence ‖ *vi* 3 to travel regularly between home and work by means of public transportation, as on a suburban train

com·mut'er *n* person who travels regularly by train, bus, etc. between home and work

comp. 1 compare; 2 comparative; 3 compound

com·pact¹ /kom'pakt/ [L *compaciscī* (*-pactus*) to make a pact] *n* agreement, covenant

com·pact² /kəmpakt'/ [L *compactus* put together] *adj* 1 firmly packed, solid; 2 of small size, with no wasted space; 3 terse, condensed ‖ *vt* 4 to press or pack closely; make solid ‖ /kom'pakt/ *n* 5 small case containing face powder, a mirror, and a puff; 6 small economical automobile

com·pan·ion /kəmpan'yən/ [OF *compaignon* < *com-* + L *panis* bread] *n* 1 comrade or associate; 2 matching piece or part ‖ **com·pan'ion·ship'** *n* ‖ SYN fellow, friend, compeer, ally, chum

com·pan'ion·a·ble *adj* friendly, congenial

com·pan'ion·way' *n* stairway within or leading to a ship's hull

com·pa·ny /kump'ənē/ [OF *compaignie*] *n* (-nies) 1 society; 2 people one associates with; 3 group of people; 4 body of actors engaged in a specific play; 5 guest or guests; 6 fellowship, association; 7 business firm; 8 a small body of troops; b subdivision of a regiment or battalion, commanded by a captain; 9 ship's crew; 10 **keep company** *colloq* to go together as steady sweethearts; 11 **part company** to break off a relationship ‖ SYN assemblage, group, host, throng, concourse, party, clique, circle, association, assembly, troop, gang

com'pa·ny store' *n* retail store operated by a large manufacturer for the convenience of his employees

com'pa·ny town' *n* town most of whose labor force works for one employer

com'pa·ny un'ion *n* 1 labor union dominated by the employer; 2 labor union limited to the employees of a single firm

com·pa·ra·ble /komp'ərəbəl/ *adj* 1 capable of being compared; 2 more or less equal ‖ **com'pa·ra·bly** *adv*

com·par·a·tive /kəmpar'ətiv/ *adj* 1 pert. to or involving comparison; 2 relative; 3 designating the second degree in the comparison of adjectives and adverbs ‖ *n* 4 a comparative degree; b form in the comparative ‖ **com·par'a·tive·ly** *adv*

com·pare /kəmper'/ [L *comparare* (*-atus*) to match] *vt* 1 to liken; 2 to examine for similarity or dissimilarity; 3 to name in order the degrees in the comparison of (an adjective or adverb) ‖ *vi* 4 to be like or equal; 5 to be worthy of comparison ‖ *n* 6 **beyond compare** without equal

com·par·i·son /kəmpar'isən/ *n* 1 act of comparing or being compared; 2 resemblance, similarity; 3 change in form of adjectives and adverbs which shows a difference in degree ‖ SYN contrast ‖ DISCR *Comparison* is secured by observing the similarities between associated objects or qualities set side by side; the idea underlying *comparison* is resemblance. *Contrast* is obtained by observing the differences between associated objects or qualities; the idea underlying *contrast* is opposition

com·part·ment /kəmpärt'mənt/ [MF *compartiment*] *n* 1 division of a larger space, separated by a partition; 2 private bedroom on a train

com·pass /kump'əs/ [OF *compasser* to measure] *vt* 1 to encircle; 2 to go around; 3 to comprehend ‖ *n* 4 circumference or boundary of an area; 5 enclosed space; 6 extent, range, limits; 7 circular course, circuit; 8 any of various instruments designated to indicate the north; 9 often **compasses** *pl* instrument for drawing and dividing circles, transferring measurements, etc.

com'pass card' *n* movable circular dial on mariner's compass, divided into 32 equal divisions or points of the compass

com·pas·sion /kəmpash'ən/ [< *com-* + L *patī* (*passus*) to feel] *n* sorrow for the sufferings of others ‖ SYN pity, mercy, tenderness, kindness, sorrow (see *sympathy*)

com·pas'sion·ate /-it/ *adj* feeling or showing compassion ‖ SYN pitiful, sympathetic, merciful, tender, kind ‖ ANT cruel, harsh, pitiless, ferocious, savage

com·pa·ter·ni·ty /komp'əturn'itē/ [ML *compaternitas*] *n* relationship between the godparents and parents of a child

com·pat·i·ble /kəmpat'ibəl/ [*com-* + L *patī* to feel] *adj* harmonious; mutually suitable and agreeable ‖ **com·pat'i·bil'i·ty** /-bil'-/ *n* ‖ **com·pat'i·bly** *adv* ‖ SYN suitable, accordant, consistent, congruous

com·pa·tri·ot /kəmpāt'rē·ət/ [LL *com-*

patriota] *n* fellow countryman

com·peer /kəmpir′, kom′pir/ [MF *comper* < *com-* + L *par* equal] *n* 1 equal in rank; 2 companion

com·pel /kəmpel′/ [L *compellere* to force] *v* (**-pelled**; **-pel·ling**) *vt* 1 to urge irresistibly; 2 to oblige || SYN necessitate, coerce, constrain, make, drive, force

com·pen·di·um /kəmpen′dē·əm/ [L = saving] *n* (**-ums** or **-a** /-ə/) brief and condensed summing up of a book or subject || **com·pen′di·ous** *adj* || SYN epitome, abstract, brief, summary, abridgment

com′pen·sate /komp′ənsāt′/ [L *compensare* (*-atus*) to weigh together] *vt* 1 to offset, counterbalance; 2 to recompense || *vi* 3 to make amends || **com·pen·sa′tion** *n* || **com·pen·sa·to·ry** /kəmpen′sətôr′ē, -tôr′-/ *adj* || SYN repay, remunerate, counterbalance, pay

com·pete /kəmpēt′/ [L *competere* to coincide] *vi* to contend, vie

com·pe·tence /komp′itəns/ *n* 1 fitness, capability; 2 sufficient income, as *provided with a competence*

com′pe·ten·cy *n* 1 competence; 2 *law* eligibility of a witness to testify || SYN fitness, adequacy, efficiency (see *ability*)

com′pe·tent *adj* 1 able, qualified; 2 adequate; 3 legally qualified || **com·pe·tent·ly** *adv* || SYN capable, efficient, qualified, adequate, fit, able

com·pe·ti·tion *n* 1 rivalry; 2 contest || **com·pet′i·tor** *n* || SYN opposition, strife, rivalry (see *emulation*)

com·pet·i·tive /kəmpet′itiv/ *adj* 1 of or pert. to competition; 2 exhibiting competition; 3 able to compete; *that competes favorably*

com·pile /kəmpīl′/ [L *compilare* to plunder] *vt* 1 to bring together (documents, writings, etc.) from different sources; 2 to make or compose (a book, report, etc.) from such sources || **com·pil′er** *n* || **com·pi·la·tion** /komp′flāsh′ən/ *n*

com·pla·cence /kəmplās′əns/ or **com·pla′cen·cy** /-sē/ [< L *complacere* to please greatly] *n* 1 blind self-satisfaction; 2 contentment || **com·pla′cent** *adj*

com·plain /kəmplān′/ [MF *complaindre*] *vi* 1 to express pain, discontent, annoyance, or dissatisfaction; 2 to make an accusation || **com·plain′er** *n* || SYN lament, murmur, deplore, grumble, bewail, whine, repine, grieve || ANT rejoice, approve, commend

com·plain·ant /-ənt/ *n* one who makes a legal complaint

com·plaint′ *n* 1 expression of pain, discontent, or dissatisfaction; 2 illness; 3 *law* formal charge || SYN grievance, injury, malady, illness (see *disease*)

com·plai·sant /kəmplās′ənt, -plāz′-,

komp′ləzant′/ [F] *adj* obliging, inclined to please || **com·plai′sance** *n* || SYN civil, deferential, acquiescent (see *polite*)

com·ple·ment /komp′ləmənt/ [L *complementum*] *n* 1 full number or quantity; 2 that which completes; 3 one of two parts comprising a whole; 4 *gram* word or words added to complete a predicate; 5 amount by which a given angle or arc falls short of 90 degrees; 6 the full number of officers and crew needed to man a ship || /komp′ləment′/ *vt* 7 to make complete || **com·ple·men·ta·ry** *adj*

com·ple·men′ta·ry col′or *n* one of two colors opposite each other on a schematic chart, as red and green, which combine to form white

com·plete /kəmplēt′/ [L *complere* (*-pletus*) to fill up] *adj* 1 lacking nothing, entire, full; 2 absolute; 3 finished || *vt* 4 to make whole or perfect; 5 to finish || **com·plete′ly** *adv* || **com·plete′ness** *n* || **com·ple·tion** *n* || SYN *v* terminate, end, fulfill, achieve (see *close*)

com·plex /kom′pleks, kəmpleks′/ [L *complexus* embrace] *adj* 1 composed of various parts, not simple; 2 involved, complicated || /kom′pleks/ *n* 3 group of intricately interrelated parts; 4 group of repressed and partly unconscious ideas, memories, and impulses that strongly affect behavior; 5 fixed idea, obsession || **com·plex′i·ty** *n* (**-ties**) || SYN *adj* complicated, involved, intricate, entangled || DISCR *Complex* describes that which consists of many related or connected parts; a radio set is a *complex* piece of apparatus, in which the various parts interact to produce the result desired; a problem may be *complex*. *Complicated* describes that which is so *complex* and involved as to be difficult to understand. *Complicated* affairs sometimes defy untangling; no one can explain the *complicated* workings of the mind of man. One may sometimes apply both these words to the same thing; a clock is both a *complex* and *complicated* mechanism. A twisting maze is *intricate*; an *intricate* question is baffling; an *intricate* knot, perplexing

com·plex′ion [LL *complexio* (*-onis*) physical constitution] *n* 1 color of the skin, esp. of the face; 2 aspect, general appearance

com′plex sen′tence *n* sentence containing a main clause and one or more subordinate clauses

com·pli·ance /kəmpli′əns/ [see **comply**] *n* 1 act or state of yielding or consenting; submission; 2 accordance || **com·pli′ant** *adj* || SYN acquiescence, deference, obedience, agreement

com·pli·cate /komp/likāt/ [L *complicare* (*-atus*) to fold together] *vt* to make difficult, intricate, or involved ‖ **com/pli·cat/ed** *adj* ‖ **com/pli·ca/tion** *n*

com·plic·i·ty /kəmplis/itē/ [< LL *complex* (*-plicis*) confederate] *n* (**-ties**) partnership in wrongdoing or crime

com·pli·ment /komp/ləmənt/ [F < It *complimento* < Sp *cumplimiento*] *n* 1 formal act or expression of courtesy; 2 expression of approval or admiration; 3 **compliments** *pl* respects ‖ /komp/ləment/ *vt* 4 to pay compliments to ‖ **SYN** *n* flattery, adulation, praise, commendation ‖ **DISCR** A *compliment* is a gracious expression of admiration or approval; it may be sincere, or it may be a merely conventional expression used to be polite. *Flattery* is insincere praise bestowed directly upon its subject by one who loves so well that he sees no faults, or who has secret ends to be gained by hypocritical commendation. *Adulation* is a sickening sort of *flattery*, expressible in actions as well as words, characterized by subserviency and falseness, and motivated by base fear

com·pli·men·ta·ry /-ərē/ *adj* 1 expressing a compliment; 2 given free as a courtesy

com·ply /kəmplī/ [It *complire* < Sp *cumplir* to fulfill] *v* (**-plied**) *vi* to assent, agree, act as desired

com·po·nent /kəmpōn/ənt/ [L *componens* (*-entis*)] *n* 1 constituent, ingredient; 2 element into which a vector quantity may be resolved ‖ also *adj*

com·port /kəmpôrt/ [MF *comporter* to bear] *vt* 1 to conduct (oneself) ‖ *vi* 2 to agree, accord ‖ **com·port/ment** *n*

com·pose /kəmpōz/ [MF *composer*] *vt* 1 to constitute, make up; 2 to create (music, literature, etc.); 3 to calm, make tranquil; 4 to adjust, arrange in proper order; 5 to set (type) ‖ *vi* 6 to engage in composition, as of music

com·posed/ *adj* tranquil, serene ‖ **SYN** collected, undisturbed, unruffled (see *calm*)

com·pos·er *n* one who composes music

com·pos·ite /kəmpoz/it/ [L *compositus*] *adj* 1 made up of distinct parts or elements; 2 *bot* having small flowers arranged compactly in heads resembling a single flower, as in the daisy ‖ *n* 3 something composite

com·po·si·tion /komp/əzish/ən/ *n* 1 union of different parts to make a whole; 2 creation of a literary, musical, or other artistic work; 3 the work produced; 4 schoolroom exercise in writing; 5 make-up, as of a picture; 6 substance formed by mingling various materials

com·pos·i·tor /kəmpoz/itər/ *n* typesetter 1; person who sets type for printing

com/post /kom/pōst/ [MF = mixed dish] *n* mixture of decaying vegetation and manure, used as a fertilizer

com·po·sure /kəmpōzh/ər/ *n* serenity, self-possession ‖ **SYN** equanimity, equability, apathy, coolness, placidity, indifference, quietness, sedateness, calmness ‖ **DISCR** *Composure* is a calmness secured by the will; it presupposes not lack of agitation, but control of agitation. *Equanimity*, on the other hand, is an evenness of spirit that has its roots in the temperament

com·pote /kom/pōt/ [F] *n* 1 fruit stewed in syrup; 2 dish in which to serve fruit, dessert, etc.

com·pound¹ /kəmpound/ [MF *compondre*] *vt* 1 to mix or combine together; 2 to join or unite; 3 to form by mixing or joining; 4 to change by mixing with another element or part; 5 to add (interest) to the capital; 6 to settle (a debt) by compromise; 7 **compound a felony** to agree for a consideration not to prosecute a felony ‖ /kom/pound, kəmpound/ *adj* 8 composed of two or more elements, ingredients, or parts ‖ /kom/pound/ *n* 9 combination of two or more elements or parts; 10 *chem* substance formed by the union of two or more elements in definite proportions and often very different from any of them

com/pound² [Malay *kampong* village] *n* 1 *Orient* formerly, enclosure containing buildings used by Europeans; 2 any enclosure, as for prisoners

com/pound frac/tion *n* fraction in which the numerator or the denominator or both contain one or more fractions

com/pound frac/ture *n* fracture in which the broken bone projects through the skin

com/pound in/ter·est *n* interest paid on both the principal and the accrued interest

com/pound leaf/ *n* leaf composed of several leaf blades on a single stalk

com/pound num/ber *n* number having several units or denominations, as 6 ft. 10 in.

com/pound sen/tence *n* sentence in which there are two or more coordinate independent clauses

com·pre·hend /kom/prihend/ [L *comprehendere*] *vt* 1 to conceive, understand; 2 to include or comprise ‖ **com/pre·hen/si·ble** /-hen/sibəl/ *adj* ‖ **com/pre·hen/si·bil/i·ty** /-bil/-/ *n* ‖ **SYN** contain, embrace, include, comprise, grasp, embody, hold ‖ **DISCR** Both *contain* and *hold* mean to have something within as a part; *hold* also emphasizes capacity, though in actual usage the terms are interchangeable. A book *contains* a certain number of pages, or certain subject matter; a box may *hold* forty apples, but may actually *contain* only twenty. To *comprehend* is to *contain* within, usually, a definite limit, as this one book *comprehends* all that has been discovered on this subject. *Comprise,* derived from the same source as *comprehend,* is used similarly; his house *comprises* five rooms. *Embrace* suggests breadth of content; the peace program *embraces* all peoples. To *include* stresses the things that form the whole, as the gathering *included* every type

com'pre·hen'sion /-hensh/ən/ *n* act of comprehending; understanding

com'pre·hen'sive *adj* 1 all-inclusive, complete, full || *n* 2 comprehensive examination in a student's major field || SYN *adj* extensive, inclusive, full, synoptic, broad, compendious, wide, large || ANT *adj* narrow, abridged

com·press /kəmpres'/ [L *comprimere* (-*pressus*)] *vt* 1 to press together, compact; 2 to reduce the volume of (a gas) by pressure || /kom'pres/ *n* 3 soft pad used in surgery as a dressing or to maintain pressure || **com·press'i·ble** *adj* || SYN *v* condense, compact, abridge, concentrate, consolidate || ANT *v* expand, enlarge, expatiate

com·pres'sion *n* 1 act or effect of compressing; 2 increase in gas pressure in an internal-combustion engine just before ignition

com·pres'sion ra'tio *n* ratio of the volume of a cylinder of an internal-combustion engine at the beginning of the piston stroke to the volume at the end of the stroke

com·pres'sor *n* 1 anything that compresses; 2 machine for compressing air or gases

com·prise /kəmprīz'/ [MF *compris* comprised] *vt* 1 to contain, include; 2 to consist of || SYN embrace, imply (see *comprehend*)

com·pro·mise /komp'rəmīz'/ [MF *compromis* compromised] *n* 1 settlement of a dispute by mutual concessions; 2 result of such settlement; 3 something midway || *vt* 4 to settle by compromise; 5 to endanger the interests or reputation of || *vi* 6 to settle by compromise

Comp·tom·e·ter /komptom'itər/ [trademark] *n* office calculating machine

comp·trol·ler /kəntrōl'ər/ [< *controller*] *n* controller 2

com·pul·sion /kəmpul'shən/ [L *compulsio* (-*onis*)] *n* 1 act of compelling, or state of being compelled; 2 coercion, force; 3 irresistible impulse || SYN coercion, restraint, force, violence, constraint || DISCR *Force* sug-

gests physical power exerted on persons or things, as the only authority some people recognize is *force;* the study of physics comprises the workings of many *forces;* figuratively, that which has power to impress our minds has *force. Violence* is great *force* proceeding from intense feeling, most often anger. *Compulsion* and *coercion* are kinds of *force,* moral as well as physical, applied usually by persons to other persons who refuse to submit; *coercion* forces one who resists, as by punishment; *compulsion* drives its object to act contrary to his will. *Constraint* compels us to do what is not agreeable to us, or it restricts and binds us; lawless men know no *constraint;* modern children are free from much of the *constraint* of older times. *Restraint* keeps us from doing, even from feeling; we impose it upon ourselves, or conditions impress it upon us. *Constraint* usually refers to moral force; *restraint* may be so applied, but it refers to physical force or restriction as well, as the madman was placed under *restraint*

com·pul'sive *adj* 1 compelling; 2 *psychol* caused by some irresistible impulse || **com·pul'sive·ly** *adv*

com·pul'so·ry /-sərē/ *adj* required, obligatory

com·punc·tion /kəmpunk'shən/ [< L *compungere* (-*punctus*) to puncture] *n* mild remorse; uneasiness of conscience || SYN self-reproach, distress, regret (see *sorrow*)

com·pute /kəmpyōōt'/ [L *computare*] *vt* to figure, calculate || **com·pu·ta·tion** /komp'yətāsh'ən/ *n* || SYN figure, estimate, reckon, count (see *calculate*)

com·put'er *n* machine that performs highly complex mathematical calculations at very high speed

com·put'er·ize' *vt* 1 to perform (mathematical calculations) by means of a computer; 2 to convert (business operations, research calculations, etc.) to operation by computers

com·rade /kom'rad, -rid/ [MF *camarade* < Sp *camarada*] *n* 1 intimate friend, companion; 2 fellow member || **com'rade·ship'** *n*

con[1] /kon'/ [< L *contra*] *adv* 1 on the negative side; against || *n* 2 vote, voter, or argument against something

con[2] [*confidence*] *slang adj* 1 confidence, as *a con man* || *v* (**conned; con·ning**) *vt* 2 to swindle

con[3] *n slang* convict

con- *pref* var of **com-**

con·cat·e·nate /kənkat'ināt'/ [< *con-* + L *catena* chain] *vt* to link together, connect, as in a chain || **con·cat·e·na'tion** *n*

con·cave /kon′kāv/ [L *concavus*] *adj* hollow and curved, as the inner surface of a sphere ‖ **con·cav·i·ty** /kɔn-kav′itē/ *n* (-ties)

con′cave lens′ *n* lens one or both sides of which are concave

con·ceal /kǝnsēl′/ [AF *conceler*] *vt* to hide, keep secret ‖ **con·ceal′ment** *n* ‖ SYN dissemble, disguise, hide, secrete, cloak ‖ DISCR *Hide*, the general term, means to put under cover, to put intentionally out of sight. The act of hiding may result from a set purpose, an accident, or a limitation of nature; a factory may *hide* a lovely scene by merely obstructing the view; things are *hidden* in the course of nature from the blind, the obtuse, the unsympathetic. To *conceal*, when asserted of persons or living beings, is always the act of intention; it consists in so managing as to prevent facts, objects, purposes, from coming to the observation of others; it connotes design and artfulness. Pain may be *hidden*, feelings *concealed;* only objects may be *secreted*. To *secrete* is to place beyond the knowledge or observation of all but the person involved. Stolen goods are *secreted*. To *disguise, dissemble,* and *cloak* are attempts to *hide* by different means. We *disguise* by making a thing seem what it is not; we assume gaiety sometimes to *disguise* grief. We *dissemble* by false appearances, by pretense. We *cloak* when we attempt to *conceal* by covering, either literally or figuratively, the thing in question, as to *cloak* sins

con·cede /kǝnsēd′/ [L *concedere*] *vt* 1 to admit to be true; 2 to give or grant, as a right ‖ *vi* 3 to make a concession ‖ SYN acknowledge, accord, admit, allow

con·ceit /kǝnsēt′/ [see **conceive**] *n* 1 exaggerated opinion of oneself; vanity; 2 fanciful notion; 3 fanciful metaphor ‖ SYN self-esteem, vanity (see *egotism, pride*)

con·ceit′ed *adj* excessively vain ‖ SYN proud, overweening, opinionated, pompous ‖ ANT humble, modest, unassuming

con·ceiv·a·ble /kǝnsēv′ǝbǝl/ *adj* imaginable, capable of being imagined ‖ **con·ceiv′a·bly** *adv*

con·ceive′ [OF *conceivre*] *vt* 1 to become pregnant with; 2 to imagine, give form to in the mind; 3 to understand; 4 to put into words ‖ *vi* 5 to think; 6 to become pregnant ‖ SYN comprehend, imagine, fancy, grasp, realize

con·cen·trate /kon′sǝntrāt/ [L *concentrare* (*-atus*) to center] *vt* 1 to bring to one point or common center; focus; 2 to increase in strength or density by removing a diluting or

adulterating substance; **3** to fix, as the attention ‖ *vi* **4** to converge; **5** to focus one's attention ‖ *n* **6** concentrated substance ‖ **con′cen·tra′-tion** *n* ‖ SYN compress, compact, fix, focus, intensify

con·cen·tra′tion camp′ *n* place of confinement, esp. one set up by a totalitarian regime for political prisoners

con·cen′tric /kǝnsent′rik/ [ML *concentricus*] *adj* having a common center, as circles ‖ **con·cen′tri·cal·ly** *adv*

con·cept /kon′sept/ [L *conceptum*] *n* 1 mental impression of an object; 2 general idea ‖ **con·cep·tu·al** /kǝn-sep′chōō·ǝl *adj*

con·cep·tion /kǝnsep′shǝn/ *n* 1 act of becoming pregnant; 2 origin; beginning; 3 act or power of forming a mental image or impression; 4 impression so formed ‖ SYN image, thought, vision, comprehension

con·cern /kǝnsurn′/ [MF *concerner* < LL *concernere* to sift together] *vt* 1 to relate or belong to; 2 to interest or involve; 3 to make uneasy ‖ *n* 4 affair; 5 interest; 6 anxiety; 7 business firm ‖ SYN *n* solicitude, regard, matter, moment (see *care*)

con·cerned′ *adj* 1 involved; 2 worried, anxious

con·cern′ing *prep* relating to; regarding; about

con·cert /kon′sǝrt/ [F < It *concerto*] *n* 1 public musical performance, recital; 2 mutual agreement, accord; 3 **in concert** jointly ‖ /kǝnsurt′/ *vi* 4 to arrange by mutual understanding; 5 to plan, devise ‖ *vi* 6 to act together

con·cert·ed /kǝnsurt′id/ *adj* 1 mutually planned or agreed upon; 2 combined

con·cer·ti·na /kon′sǝrtēn′ǝ/ *n* small accordionlike musical instrument with hexagonal bellows

con′cert·mas′ter *n* leading first violinist of an orchestra

con·cer·to /kǝnchert′ō/ [It] *n mus* composition for one or more solo instruments and an orchestra

con·ces·sion /kǝnsesh′ǝn/ [L *concessio* (*-onis*)] *n* 1 act of conceding or yielding, as a point in dispute, a privilege, etc.; 2 thing conceded; 3 right granted by a government or company to conduct business on government or company property

con·ces′sion·aire′ /-ner′/ [F] *n* person holding a concession

conch /kɔŋk/, konch′/ [L *concha* < Gk *konche* mussel shell] *n* large spiral sea shell, often used as a horn

con·cierge /kon′sē·erzh′/ [F] *n* doorkeeper or janitor

con·cil·i·ate /kǝnsil′ē·āt′/ [L *conciliare* (*-atus*) to bring together] *vt* 1 to gain the affections or good will of, to placate; 2 to reconcile, make compatible || **con·cil′i·a·tor** *n* || **con·cil′-i·a′tion** *n* || **con·cil′i·a·to′ry** /-tôr′-, -tōr′-/ *adj* || SYN propitiate, placate, allay, adjust, pacify

con·cise /kənsīs′/ [L *concisus* cut off] *adj* terse; putting much in few words || **con·cise′ly** *adv* || **con·cise′ness** *n* || SYN laconic, pithy, brief, succinct (see *short*)

con·clave /kon′klāv, koŋ′-/ [L = locked room < *cum* with + *clavis* key] *n* **1** private meeting of cardinals to elect a new pope; **2** College of Cardinals; **3** private meeting; **4** assembly of influential leaders

con·clude /kənklōōd′/ [L *concludere*] *vt* **1** to finish; **2** to settle, determine; **3** to deduce, infer; **4** to resolve, decide || *vi* **5** to draw an inference; **6** to come to an end || SYN terminate, end, infer, decide (see *close*)

con·clu·sion /kənklōōzh′ən/ *n* **1** act of concluding; **2** end; **3** inference; judgment, decision; **4** summing up, as of a speech or debate; **5** main clause of a conditional sentence; **6** final determination, result || SYN consequence, termination, close, decision, inference, induction, deduction || DISCR A *conclusion* is a result arrived at by reasoning from previously admitted premises. That kind of reasoning known as *deduction* leads from the general to the particular; in this sort of reasoning, granting the truth of the general principle and its application to the particular case adduced, the *conclusion* arrived at is necessarily certain. That kind of reasoning known as *induction* proceeds from the particular to the general, reaching a probable *conclusion* by the examination of particular instances. An *inference* resembles an *induction* in that it is a *conclusion* drawn from evidence; it is unlike an *induction* in that it is sometimes hasty; an *induction* is the result of a careful and complete canvassing of facts

con·clu·sive /-siv/ *adj* decisive, final || **con·clu·sive·ly** *adv* || SYN ultimate, convincing, unanswerable (see *last*)

con·coct /kənkokt′/ [L *concoctus* cooked together] *vt* **1** to prepare, as food, by combining ingredients; **2** to devise, make up || **con·coc′tion** *n*

con·com·i·tant /kənkom′itənt/ [L *concomitans* (*-antis*)] *adj* **1** attendant, accompanying || *n* **2** that which accompanies something || SYN *adj* accessory, conjoined, coincident, attendant

con·cord /kon′kôrd, koŋ′-/ [L *concordia* agreement] *n* **1** harmony, agreement; **2** *gram* agreement **4**

Con·cord /koŋk′ərd/ *n* **1** capital of New Hampshire (29,000); **2** town in Massachusetts, home of Emerson,

Hawthorne, and Thoreau and scene of the second battle of the Revolutionary War

con·cord·ance /kənkôrd′əns/ *n* **1** agreement; **2** dictionary of the words and/or passages in a book, as the Bible, with references to the places where they occur

con·cor·dat /konkôrd′at/ *n* **1** official agreement; **2** agreement between the pope and a secular government concerning the regulation of church matters

Con′cord grape′ *n* large dark-blue grape grown in E U.S.

Con·cor·di·a /kənkôrd′ē·ə/ *n Rom myth.* goddess of peace

con·course /kon′kôrs, koŋ′-/ [MF *concours*] *n* **1** assembly or crowd; **2** large open space for the accommodation of crowds, as in a park or railroad station; **3** park driveway; **4** wide boulevard

con·crete /kon′krēt, konkrēt′/ [L *cretus* grown together] *adj* **1** pert. to actual events or things; material; **2** specific, not general || *n* **3** stonelike building material made of cement, gravel, sand, and water || /konkrēt′/ *vt* **4** to cover with concrete || **con·crete′ly** *adv* || **con·crete′ness** *n* || SYN individual, special, specific, particular, definite, actual || ANT abstract, general, indefinite

con·cre′tion *n* **1** act or process of solidifying; **2** hardened mass formed by cohesion or coalescence

con·cu·bine /koŋk′yəbīn′/ [L *concubina*] *n* **1** woman who cohabits with a man without being his wife; **2** in certain cultures, secondary wife of inferior status || **con·cu·bi·nage** /kənkyōōb′inij/ *n*

con·cu·pis·cent /konkyōōp′isənt/ [< L *concupiscere* to long for] *adj* lustful, sensual || **con·cu′pis·cence** *n*

con·cur /kənkur′/ [L *concurrere* to run together] *v* (**-curred;** **-cur·ring**) *vi* **1** to agree in action or opinion; **2** to happen at the same time || SYN assent, approve, combine, cooperate (see *agree*)

con·cur′rence *n* **1** act of concurring; agreement; **2** simultaneous occurrences; **3** *geom* point at which three or more lines meet

con·cur′rent *adj* **1** acting together; **2** joint and equal in authority; **3** in accord; agreeing; **4** happening at the same time || **con·cur′rent·ly** *adv*

con·cus·sion /kənkush′ən/ [L *concussio* (*-onis*)] *n* **1** shaking, shock, as from impact; **2** impaired condition, as of the brain, caused by a fall or violent blow on the head

con·demn /kəndem′/ [OF *condemner* < L *condemnare*] *vt* **1** to pronounce guilty; sentence; **2** to blame, censure; **3** to expropriate for public use; **4** to pronounce unfit for use ‖ **con'dem·na'tion** /kon'-/ ‖ SYN disapprove, upbraid, denounce, convict, sentence (see *blame*) ‖ ANT approve, justify, exonerate

con·den·sate /kon'dənsāt'/ *n* substance produced by condensation, as water from steam

con·dense /kəndens'/ [MF *condenser* < L *condensare*] *vt* **1** to make dense or denser; **2** to reduce to fewer words; **3** to reduce from a gas or vapor to a liquid or solid ‖ *vi* **4** to become dense; **5** to become liquid or solid, as a gas ‖ **con'den·sa'tion** /kon'-/ *n* ‖ SYN unite, compact, harden, boil down, contract, abridge, diminish, abbreviate ‖ ANT expand, enlarge

con·dens'er *n* **1** device for transforming gases or vapors into liquid or solid form; **2** lens for concentrating light rays; **3** device for accumulating an electric charge, consisting of two metallic plates separated by a dielectric

con·de·scend /kon'disend'/ [< con- + L *descendere* to go down] *vi* **1** to deal graciously with one's social inferiors; **2** to be patronizing ‖ **con'de·scend'ing** *adj* ‖ **con'de·scen'sion** *n*

con·di·ment /kon'dəmənt/ [MF < L *condimentum* spice] *n* seasoning for food; relish

con·di·tion /kəndish'ən/ [AF *condicioun* < L *condicio* (*-onis*) agreement] *n* **1** anything required as a prerequisite; **2** stipulation; **3** existing state, as of health or working order; **4** rank, social position; **5 in condition** in a healthy state; **6 on condition that** provided that ‖ *vt* **7** to make fit; **8** to stipulate; **9** to subject to a prerequisite; **10** to train (an individual) to react to a stimulus in a given way ‖ SYN *n* prerequisite, requirement, qualification

con·di'tion·al *adj* **1** pert. to or dependent upon certain conditions; **2** expressing or containing a condition ‖ **con·di'tion·al·ly** *adv*

con·di'tioned **re'flex** or **re·sponse'** *n* reaction to an unrelated stimulus by repeated association

con·dole /kəndōl'/ [LL *condolere*] *vi* to express sympathy ‖ **con·do'lence** *n*

con·dom /kon'dəm, kun'-/ [< Dr. *Condom*, 18th-cent. Eng physician, reputed inventor] *n* sheath to cover the penis for prophylactic or contraceptive purposes

con·do·min·i·um /kon'dəmin'ē·əm/ [NL] *n* **1** apartment house the units of which are individually owned, with right of sale, etc.; **2** apartment in such an apartment house; **3** joint sovereignty over a territory by more than one nation

con·done /kəndōn'/ [L *condonare* to present] *vt* to forgive or overlook (an offense or fault)

con·dor /kon'dər/ [Sp < Quechua *kuntur*] *n* either of two large vultures, *Vultur gryphus* of W South America, or *Gymnogyps californianus* of California, the largest flying birds in the world

con·dot·tie·re /kon'dətyer'ē/ [It] *n* (-**ri** /-rē/) **1** leader of a band of mercenary soldiers in Italy in the 14th and 15th centuries; **2** soldier of fortune

con·duce /kənd(y)ōōs'/ [< L *conducere* to lead] *vi* **conduce** to or toward to lead to; contribute to ‖ **con·du'cive** *adj*

con·duct /kon'dəkt/ [LL *conductus* escort] *n* **1** behavior; **2** management, direction; **3** guidance; escort ‖ /kəndukt'/ *vt* **4** to lead, guide; **5** to direct, manage; **6** to behave (oneself); **7** to serve as a medium or channel for (heat, electricity, or sound) ‖ *vi* **8** to direct, lead; **9** to act as a conductor ‖ SYN *n* bearing, demeanor, guidance, direction (see *behavior*); *v* govern, regulate, superintend, administer, manage, direct ‖ DISCR *Conduct, direct,* and *manage* express different ways of regulating affairs or guiding men. To *conduct* is to supervise by careful planning and arranging; to *conduct* a campaign requires knowledge and executive ability; to *conduct* a diplomatic correspondence requires wisdom as well; applied to people, *conduct* suggests personal leadership, as to *conduct* an orchestra; to *conduct* a sight-seeing tour. *Direct* is not used of such important affairs as require the use of *conduct*, but it stresses the authority involved, and frequently indicates less supervision of actual details than *conduct*. One who *directs* points out a course of action and orders others to follow it. A chief *directs* his subordinates at a fire; an engineer *directs* the construction of a bridge. To *manage* is to get into the thing involved and handle it to the last detail. The company which *conducts* a large department store defines its policy; they who *direct* such a company issue the orders that fulfill this policy; those who *manage* the several departments carry out this policy (cf. *govern*).

con·duct'ance *n* ability of a conductor to transmit an electric current, measured by the ratio of the current to the applied electromotive force

con·duc'tion *n* **1** act of conducting, as water through a pipe; **2** *phys* **a** transmission of heat from one part to another of a body, or from one body to another without the transfer of particles of matter; **b** transmission of electricity by the movement of electrons, ions, or rays from an anode or cathode through conducting media

con·duc′tive *adj* having the property of conducting heat, electricity, or sound ‖ **con′duc·tiv′i·ty** *n*

con·duc′tor *n* 1 one who conducts; 2 orchestra leader; 3 person in charge of a railroad train; 4 something that transmits heat, electricity, or sound

con·duit /kon′dit, -dōŏ·ĭt/ [OF = escort] *n* 1 pipe for carrying liquids; 2 tube for electric wires

cone /kōn′/ [Gk *konos*] *n* 1 body which tapers uniformly to a point from a circular base; 2 cone-shaped fruit of the fir, pine, etc.; 3 something shaped like a cone, as *an ice-cream cone, a paper cone*

con·fab /kon′fab/ [*abbr* of *confabulate* to talk together < L *confabulari* (-*atus*)] *n* 1 *colloq* informal discussion ‖ *v* (-**fabbed; -fab·bing**) *vi* 2 *colloq* to gossip or chat familiarly

con·fec·tion /kənfek′shən/ [< L *conficere* (-*fectus*) to prepare] *n* 1 process or result of making something; 2 something sweet, as candy, bonbons, or preserves

con·fec′tion·er *n* one who makes or sells candy

con·fec′tion·er′s sug′ar *n* extra-fine powdered sugar, used in making icings and confections

con·fec′tion·er′y *n* (-**ies**) 1 confectioner's shop; 2 confectioner's business; 3 candies, ice cream, cakes, preserves collectively

con·fed·er·a·cy /kənfed′ərəsē/ [< *con-* + L *foederare* (-*atus*) to form a league] *n* (-**cies**) 1 league or federation; 2 conspiracy, unlawful combination; 3 **the Confederacy** the Confederate States of America

con·fed′er·ate′ /-rāt′/ *vt & vi* 1 to unite in a league or alliance ‖ /-rit/ *n* 2 ally; 3 accomplice; 4 **Confederate** adherent of the Confederate States of America ‖ also *adj* ‖ SYN *n* accomplice, partner (see *ally*)

Con·fed′er·ate States′ of A·mer′i·ca *npl* the 11 southern states that seceded from the United States in 1860–61

con·fed′er·a′tion *n* 1 act of confederating; 2 alliance, federation; 3 **the Confederation** the union of the 13 original states in 1781–89, before the adoption of the Constitution

con·fer /kənfur′/ [L *conferre* to bring together] *v* (-**ferred; -fer·ring**) *vt* 1 to bestow ‖ *vi* 2 to have a conference ‖ SYN deliberate, counsel, advise (see *give*)

con·fer·ee /kon′fərē′/ *n* 1 one who takes part in a conference; 2 one upon whom something is conferred

con′fer·ence *n* 1 meeting for discussion or counsel; 2 athletic league of college teams; 3 association for common purposes, as of schools or churches

con′fer·ence call′ *n* conference held through a hookup of three or more telephones

con′fer·ence com·mit′tee *n* *U.S.* committee of members of the House and Senate whose function is to settle differences between bills passed by both bodies

con·fer′ral *n* act of bestowing

con·fess /kənfes′/ [MF *confesser* < LL *confessare*] *vt* 1 to acknowledge or disclose; 2 to admit as true; 3 to profess, as belief; 4 to hear a confession from; 5 to tell (one's sins) to a priest ‖ *vi* 6 to make acknowledgment or admission; 7 to disclose one's sins to a priest

con·fess′ed·ly /-idlē/ *adv* admittedly

con·fes′sion *n* 1 act of confessing; 2 that which is confessed; 3 profession of belief; 4 creed

con·fes′sion·al *n* place in a church where a priest hears confessions

con·fes′sor *n* 1 one who confesses; 2 priest who hears confessions; 3 Christian, esp. in spite of persecution

con·fet′ti /kənfet′ē/ [It = sweetmeats] *n* small pieces of colored paper tossed in the air by revelers at celebrations

con·fi·dant /kon′fidant′, -dänt′, kon′-/ *n* intimate friend to whom private affairs are imparted ‖ **con′fi·dante′** *nfem*

con·fide /kənfīd′/ [L *confidere*] *vt* 1 to entrust; 2 to tell confidentially ‖ *vi* 3 **confide in, a** to have faith in; **b** to impart secrets to

con·fi·dence /kon′fidəns/ *n* 1 reliance, trust; 2 assurance; 3 self-reliance; 4 secret not to be divulged; 5 **in confidence** as a secret ‖ SYN (see *assurance*) ‖ ANT distrust, uncertainty

con′fi·dence game′ *n* swindle based on the swindler's gaining the confidence of the victim

con′fi·dence man′ *n* practitioner of a confidence game

con·fi·dent *adj* 1 full of trust; 2 self-assured; 3 certain; 4 overbold ‖ *n* 5 confidant ‖ **con′fi·dent·ly** *adv* ‖ SYN hopeful, expectant, brave, self-reliant, certain (see *sanguine*) ‖ ANT uncertain, doubtful, timid

con′fi·den′tial /-den′shəl/ *adj* 1 not to be divulged; 2 trustworthy; trusted; 3 indicating confidence or intimacy ‖ **con′fi·den′tial·ly** *adv* ‖ **con′fi·den′ti·al′i·ty** /-shē·al′-/ *n* (-**ties**)

con·fid·ing /kənfīd′iŋ/ *adj* trustful, unsuspicious

con·fig·u·ra·tion /kənfig′yərāsh′ən/ [< L *configurare* (-*atus*) to shape] *n* 1 position of the parts of a thing relative to each other; 2 conformation

con·fine /kənfīn′/ [L *confinis* bordering upon] *vt* 1 to restrict within limits; 2 to imprison; secure; keep within doors; 3 **be confined** to be undergoing childbirth || /kon'fīn/ *n* 4 usu. confines *pl* boundary || SYN *v* restrain, restrict, bound, limit || ANT *v* release, liberate, relax, loose

con·fine'ment *n* 1 act of confining or state of being confined; 2 accouchement, childbirth

con·firm' /kənfûrm'/ [L *confirmare*] *vt* 1 to make firmer, strengthen; 2 to ratify, sanction; 3 to corroborate, verify; 4 to admit to full membership in a church, usu. at a special ceremony or rite || **con'fir·ma'tion** *n* || SYN corroborate, sustain, strengthen, verify, establish, attest, sanction (see *substantiate*) || ANT refute, overthrow, cancel, contradict, disprove

con·firmed' *adj* habitual, inveterate

con·fis·cate /kon'fĭskāt'/ [L *confiscare* (*-atus*)] *vt* 1 to seize as forfeited to the state; 2 to appropriate as by authority || **con'fis·ca'tion** *n* || **con·fis·ca·to·ry** /kənfĭs'kətôr'ē, -tōr-/ *adj*

con·fla·gra·tion /kon'fləgrāsh'ən/ [< L *conflagrare* (*-atus*) to burn up] *n* extensive and destructive fire

con·fla·tion /kənflāsh'ən/ [< L *conflare* to blow together] *n* 1 the combining of two variant texts into one reading; 2 the resultant reading

con·flict /kənflĭkt'/ [L *confligere* (*-flictus*)] *vi* 1 to come into or be in disagreement or opposition; clash; 2 to fight, contend || /kon'flĭkt/ *n* 3 incompatibility; interference; 4 fight, contention || SYN *n* (see *battle*) || ANT *n* accord, peace

con·flict'ing *adj* contradictory, incompatible

con·flu·ence /kon'flōō·əns/ [*con-* + L *fluens* (*-entts*) flowing] *n* 1 flowing or coming together, as of streams; 2 their place of meeting; 3 gathering or flocking together, assemblage

con·flu·ent /kon'flōō·ənt/ *adj* 1 flowing together || *n* 2 confluent stream

con·form /kənfôrm'/ [MF *conformer* < L *conformare*] *vt* 1 to make similar, bring into harmony || *vi* 2 to be in harmony; comply; 3 to be similar || **con·form'er** *n* || **con·form'ance** *n*

con·for·ma·tion /kon'fərmā'shən/ *n* 1 form, structure, shape; 2 symmetrical arrangement of parts

con·form·ist *n* one who conforms without question to the mores and practices of his group

con·form'i·ty *n* (*-ties*) 1 agreement, correspondence; 2 compliance with established forms

con·found /kənfound', kon-/ [OF *confondre*] *vt* 1 to throw into disorder or confusion; 2 to mix, confuse; 3 to amaze, perplex; 4 to refute, contradict; 5 *euphem* to damn || SYN baffle, dumbfound (see *perplex, embarrass*)

con·found'ed *adj euphem* damned

con'fra·ter'ni·ty /kon-'/ *n* (*-ties*) association or brotherhood, esp. one with a religious or professional purpose

con·frere /kon'frer/ [MF] *n* fellow member; colleague

con·front /kənfrunt'/ [< *con* < + L *frons* (*frontis*) face] *vt* 1 to face, esp. with defiance; 2 to bring face to face, as *to confront the prisoner with the evidence*

con·fron·ta·tion /kon'frəntā'shən/ *n* 1 act of confronting or state of being confronted; 2 a bringing face to face of hostile elements

Con·fu·cius /kənfyōōsh'əs/ *n* (551?–478? B.C.) Chinese philosopher, who taught the traditional Chinese principles of ethics, morals, and social obligations || **Con·fu'cian** *adj & n* || **Con·fu'cian·ism** *n*

con·fuse /kənfyōoz'/ [L *confundere* (*-fusus*)] *vt* 1 to bewilder, perplex; 2 to mix up, throw into disorder; 3 to mistake for another || **con·fus'ed·ly** /-ĭdlē/ *adv* || **con·fu'sion** *n* || SYN abash, disconcert, disarrange, distract, disturb, mystify, obscure (see *perplex, embarrass*)

con·fute /kənfyōot'/ [L *confutare*] *vt* to prove to be false or in error || **con'fu·ta'tion** /kon'fyōō-/ || SYN refute, disprove, controvert || DISCR To *disprove* is to offer evidence that shows the falseness or erroneousness of an assertion. To *controvert* is to oppose by vigorous denial, often without evidence or proof. To *refute* and to *confute* are to produce such conclusive evidence or proof that the question involved cannot again be raised

Cong. 1 Congress; 2 Congressional

con·ga /kong'gə/ [Sp] *n* Cuban dance performed by a group moving in a long, winding line || also *vi*

con' game' *n* confidence game

con·geal /kənjēl'/ [L *congelare*] *vt & vi* 1 to thicken, coagulate; 2 to freeze || **con·ge·la·tion** /kon'jəlāsh'ən/ *n*

con·ge·ner /kon'jənər/ [L] *n* one of the same genus or kind || **con'ge·ner'ic** /-ner'ĭk/ *adj*

con·gen·ial /kənjēn'yəl/ [*con-* + L *genius* guardian spirit] *adj* 1 of kindred spirit, compatible; 2 agreeable, friendly || **con·gen'ial·ly** *adv* || **con·ge'ni·al'i·ty** /-nē·al'ĭtē/ *n*

con·gen·i·tal /kənjen'ĭtəl/ [< L *congenitus* innate] *adj* existing at or from birth || **con·gen'i·tal·ly** *adv*

con·ger (eel') /kong'ər/ [OF *congre* < L *conger*] *n* large marine eel (*Conger conger*) used in Europe for food

con·ge·ries /kənjir'ēz, kon'jər-/ [L = heap] *nsg & npl* collection of individual objects in a mass; heap

con·gest /kənjest'/ [L *congerere* (*-gestus*) to heap] *vt* 1 to fill, overcrowd; **2** to cause the blood vessels of (a part of the body) to become too full ‖ also *vi* ‖ **con·ges'tion** /-chən/ *n*

con·glom·er·ate /kənglom'ərāt'/ [L *conglomerare* (*-atus*)] *vt* & *vi* **1** to gather into a round mass; **2** to cluster together ‖ /-it/ *adj* **3** clustered or massed together; **4** composed of miscellaneous matter adhering together ‖ *n* **5** conglomerate mass; **6** rock composed of pebbles or gravel; **7** company formed by merger with or acquisition of several companies in widely different industries

con·glom'er·a'tion *n* **1** act or result of conglomerating; **2** mixed collection, hodgepodge

Con·go /koŋg'ō/ *n* **1** river in central Africa flowing through the Democratic Republic of the Congo into the South Atlantic; **2** **Republic of Congo** republic in W central Africa (900,000; 132,046 sq.m.; cap. Brazzaville), formerly French Equatorial Africa; **3** **Zaire**, formerly Democratic Republic of the Congo, formerly the Belgian Congo ‖ **Con·go·lese** /koŋ'gəlēz', -lēs'/ *adj* & *n* **(-lese)**

con·grat·u·late /kəngrach'əlāt'/ [L *congratulari* (*-atus*)] *vt* to express pleasure to, on account of some happy event or good fortune ‖ **con·grat'u·la·to'ry** *adj* ‖ SYN felicitate ‖ DISCR *Felicitate* and *congratulate* agree in expressing joy and sympathy over good fortune. *Felicitate*, the more formal word, carries with it less of one's own sympathetic rejoicing than does *congratulate*, the warmer, more spontaneous word

con·grat'u·la'tion *n* **1** act of congratulating; **2** **congratulations** *pl* hearty expression of pleasure at another's good fortune

con·gre·gate /koŋ'grəgāt'/ [L *congregare* (*-atus*) to flock together] *vt* & *vi* **1** to collect into a crowd, assemble ‖ /-git/ *adj* **2** collective; formed by collecting; **3** gathered together; assembled

con'gre·ga'tion *n* **1** act or state of congregating; **2** assemblage; **3** worshipers at a church service; **4** organization of believers for joint religious activity

con'gre·ga'tion·al *adj* **1** pert. to a congregation; **2** designating a system of church organization in which each church is governed by its congregation; **3** **Congregational** designating a Protestant denomination with a congregational organization

con·gress /koŋg'ris/ [< L *congredi* (*-gressus*) to come together] *n* **1** coming together; meeting; intercourse; **2** conference, assembly; **3** national legislature of many Latin American countries; **4** **Congress**, a national leg-

islature of the United States, consisting of the Senate and the House of Representatives; **b** each two-year period of its existence between elections to the House of Representatives, as *the 80th Congress* ‖ **con·gres·sion·al**, **Congressional** /kəngresh'ənəl/ *adj* ‖ SYN council, parliament, convention, convocation

Con·gres'sion·al dis'trict *n* each of the electoral districts into which a State of the United States is divided and which elects one member of the House of Representatives

Con'gress·man /-mən/ *n* **(-men** /-mən/**)** member of the U.S. Congress, esp. the House of Representatives ‖ **Con'gress·wom'an** *n* fem

con·gru·ent /koŋ'grōō-ənt/ [L *congruens* (*-entis*)] *adj* **1** agreeing, accordant, congruous; **2** *geom* exactly alike ‖ **con'gru·ence** *n*

con·gru·ous /koŋ'grōō-əs/ *adj* **1** appropriate; **2** harmoniously grouped; **3** congruent ‖ **con·gru·i·ty** /kəngrōō'itē/ *n* **(-ties)**

con·ic /kon'ik/ [< *cone*] *adj* **1** conical ‖ *n* **2** conic section

con'i·cal *adj* shaped like a cone

con'ics *nsg* theory of conic sections

con'ic sec'tion *n* curve formed by the intersection of a plane with a right circular cone, as circles, ellipses, hyperbolas, and parabolas

co·ni·fer /kōn'ifər, kon'-/ [L = cone-bearer] *n* any of an order of evergreen trees having a cone for fruit, as the spruce, pine, etc. ‖ **co·nif'er·ous** /-nif'-/ *adj*

conj. **1** conjunction; **2** conjugation

con·jec·ture /kənjek'chər/ [L *conjectura*] *n* **1** opinion hazarded without sufficient evidence; guess ‖ *vt* & *vi* **2** to infer from insufficient grounds; guess ‖ **con·jec'tur·al** *adj*

con·join /kənjoin'/ [MF *conjoindre*] *vt* & *vi* to join together, unite ‖ **con·joint'** *adj*

con·ju·gal /kon'jəgəl/ [< con- + L *jugum* yoke] *adj* pert. to marriage or marital relations

con·ju·gate /kon'jəgāt/ [L *conjugare* (*-atus*) to yoke together] *vt* **1** to give the paradigm of (a verb) ‖ *vi* **2** to unite ‖ /-git/ *adj* **3** combined in pairs; coupled

con'ju·ga'tion *n* **1** act of conjugating; **2** verbal paradigm

con·junc·tion /kənjuŋk'shən/ [L *conjunctio* (*-onis*)] *n* **1** act of conjoining; **2** union, association; **3** combination, as of events; **4** coincidence; **5** word used to connect sentences, clauses, phrases, or words ‖ **con·junc'tive** *adj*

con·junc·ti·vi·tis /-tivīt'is/ *n* inflammation of the conjunctiva, or mucous membrane lining the eyelids and covering the front part of the eyeball

con·ju·ra·tion /kon'jərāsh'ən/ *n* **1**

magic spell; invocation; **2** practice of magic

con·jure /kon'jər/ [OF *conjurer* < L *conjurare* to swear] *vt* **1** to summon, as an evil spirit, by an invocation or spell; **2** to influence or affect as if by magic ‖ *vi* **3** to summon a spirit or devil by magic spells; **4** to practice magic ‖ /kənjŏŏr'/ *vt* **5** to appeal to solemnly, implore ‖ **con'jur·er, con·jur'er** *n* ‖ syn adjure, invoke, beseech, supplicate

conk /koŋk'/ [prob < *conch*] *slang vt* **1** to hit on the head ‖ *vi* **2 conk out** to go dead, as a motor or appliance

con' man' *n colloq* confidence man

Conn. Connecticut

con·nect /kənekt'/ [L *connectere*] *vt* **1** to bind or fasten together; unite; **2** to establish communication for; **3** to attach electrically; **4** to associate ‖ *vi* **5** to join; **6** to arrive at such time that passengers may transfer to another route ‖ **con·nect'er, con·nec'tor** *n* ‖ syn combine, unite, join, bind, fasten, link, associate ‖ ant detach, loosen, free, release

Con·nect·i·cut /kənet'əkət/ *n* state in New England (3,032,000; 5009 sq.m.; cap. Hartford) ‖ **Con·nect'i·cut·er** *n*

con·nect'ing rod' *n* rod which transforms reciprocating motion into circular motion or vice versa

con·nec'tion *n* **1** act of connecting or state of being connected; **2** means of connecting; **3** relationship, association; **4 connections** *pl* **a** transfer to another transportation line; **b** influential friends ‖ syn coherence, relation, association union, junction

con·nec'tive *adj* **1** serving to connect ‖ *n* **2** that which connects

conn'ing tow'er /kon'iŋ/ [< *conn* to steer < MF *conduire* to lead] *n* observation tower of a submarine

con·nip·tion /kənip'shən/ [?] *n colloq* fit, usu. of rage

con·nive /kəniv'/ [L *connivere* to shut the eyes] *vi* **1** to pretend not to see wrongdoing; **2** to cooperate secretly in wrongdoing ‖ **con·niv'ance** *n* ‖ **con·niv'er** *n* ‖ syn collude ‖ discr To *collude* is, with fraudulent or deceitful intent, to cooperate actively with another in some guilty plan or deed. To *connive* is to permit wrongdoing to go on while feigning ignorance of it; one who *connives* does not actively take part in the wrong act or deed, but he gives guilty assent to it

con·nois·seur /kon'əsur', -sŏŏr'/ [OF *connoiseor*] *n* person having competent judgment in art and other matters of taste

con·no·ta·tion /kon'ə-/ *n* **1** that which is suggested in addition to the primary meaning or denotation of a word; **2 a** implication or suggestion of something additional; **b** thing implied or suggested ‖ syn denotation ‖ discr *Denotation* is the actual meaning in question. *Connotation* adds to *denotation* all those ideas and emotions which human experience has attached to the original meaning. The *denotation* of the word "tiger" pictures a large beast of prey of the cat family, with characteristic black stripes. The *connotation* of the word "tiger" suggests the cunning, the lithesomeness, and the swiftness of the cat, combined with enormous strength and pitiless ferocity

con·note /kənōt'/ [*con-* + L *notare* to mark] *vt* **1** to mean in addition to the primary meaning; suggest; **2** to imply (something) in addition to that specifically stated ‖ **con'no·ta·tive** /also kənŏt'ətiv/ *adj*

con·nu·bi·al /kən(y)ŏŏb'ē·əl/ [L *connubialis*] *adj* pert. to marriage, conjugal

con·quer /koŋk'ər/ [OF *conquerre* < L *conquirere* to procure] *vt* **1** to gain by force; overcome, subdue ‖ *vi* **2** to be victorious ‖ **con'quer·or** *n* ‖ syn subjugate, defeat, surmount (see *vanquish*)

con·quest /kon'kwest, koŋ'-/ [MF *conqueste*] *n* **1** act of conquering; victory; **2** that which is conquered; **3 the Conquest** the Norman Conquest ‖ syn triumph, mastery, subjection (see *victory*)

con·quis·ta·dor /konkwist'ədôr'/ [Sp] *n* one of the Spanish conquerors of Mexico, Central America, and South America in the 16th century

con·san·guin·e·ous /kon'saŋgwin'ē·əs/ [L *consanguineus*] *adj* related by blood ‖ **con'san·guin'i·ty** *n*

con·science /konsh'əns/ [OF < L *conscientia*] *n* sense of right and wrong; that which urges to right conduct ‖ **con'science·less** *adj*

con·science-strick'en *adj* overcome by the knowledge of having done wrong

con·sci·en'tious /-shē·en'shəs/ *adj* influenced or governed by one's conscience; scrupulous; careful ‖ **con'sci·en'tious·ly** *adv* ‖ syn faithful, worthy, just, painstaking, exact, scrupulous

con·sci·en'tious ob·jec'tor *n* one who refuses to serve in the armed forces because of his conscience

con·scious /konsh'əs/ [L *conscius* knowing] *adj* **1** awake, in full possession of one's mental faculties; **2** aware (of something); **3** intentional; **4** known to oneself. **5** embarrassed, self-conscious ‖ **con'scious·ly** *adv* ‖ syn aware, sensible, certain, cognizant, advised, apprised, sure ‖ discr Generally speaking we are *conscious* of that which is felt or experienced within our own minds and being, as the speaker was *conscious* that he was losing his audience; we are *aware* of that which we perceive outside of ourselves. When, occasionally, *conscious* is applied to the external, it emphasizes the fact that something has penetrated the mind through sensation, as at last I became *conscious* that someone was standing behind me. If *aware* is applied to the sensations or workings of the inner self, it indicates a critical perception apart from sensation, as he was *aware* of his own defects

con·scious·ness *n* 1 state of being conscious; 2 sum total of all that one feels or thinks

con·script /kənskript'/ [L *conscribere* (-*scriptus*) to enroll] *vt* 1 to draft for military service || /kon'-/ *n* 2 draftee || **con·scrip'tion** *n*

con·se·crate /kon'sikrāt'/ [L *consecrare* (-*atus*)] *vt* 1 to set apart as sacred; 2 to hallow; 3 to devote || **con·se·cra'tion** *n*

con·sec·u·tive /kənsek'yətiv/ [con- + L *secutus* followed] *adj* 1 arranged in order without dislocation or omission; 2 successive || **con·sec'u·tive·ly** *adv*

con·sen·sus /kənsen'səs/ [L] *n* general agreement in opinion

con·sent /kənsent'/ [OF *consentir*] *vi* 1 to acquiesce; permit; agree || *n* 2 permission, assent; 3 agreement || *syn v* acquiesce, concur (see *accede, agree*)

con·se·quence /kon'səkwens', -kwəns/ [< L *consequens* (-*entis*) following] *n* 1 result; 2 importance; 3 **take the consequences** to accept the results of one's actions || *syn* issue, end, effect (see *result*)

con·se·quent /'-kwent', -kwənt/ *adj* following as a result; following logically

con·se·quen·tial /'-kwen'shəl/ *adj* 1 consequent; 2 self-important; 3 important

con·se·quent·ly *adv* as a result; therefore

con·ser·va·tion /kon'sərvāsh'ən/ [L *conservare* (-*atus*) to conserve] *n* 1 act of conserving; 2 official care and preservation of natural resources

con·ser·va·tion·ist *n* person who advocates and practices the care and preservation of natural resources

con·ser·va·tion of en'er·gy *n* principle that the amount of energy in an isolated system remains constant regardless of changes within the system

con·serv·a·tive /kənsur'vətiv/ *adj* 1 opposed to change in social and political institutions; 2 moderate, cautious; 3 traditional in style, décor, etc. || *n* 4 conservative person; 5 **Conservative** member of a conservative political party, as in Great Britain and Canada || **con·serv'a·tism** *n*

con·ser·va·to·ry /-tôr'ē, -tōr'ē/ *n* (-ries) 1 private greenhouse; 2 school of fine arts, esp. of music

con·serve' *vt* to preserve, keep from loss

con·sid·er /kənsid'ər/ [L *considerare*] *vt* 1 to contemplate, reflect on; 2 to treat with thoughtfulness; 3 to believe to be; 4 to make allowance for || *vi* 5 to deliberate || *syn* ponder, meditate, contemplate (see *muse*)

con·sid'er·a·ble *adj* large in size, extent, amount, etc. || **con·sid'er·a·bly** *adv*

con·sid'er·ate /-it/ *adj* having regard for others, thoughtful

con·sid·er·a'tion *n* 1 act of considering; 2 regard for others, thoughtfulness; 3 fee, remuneration; 4 something taken into account, reason; 5 *law* that which is accepted by one party, thus making a contract legally binding; 6 **take into consideration** to take into account; 7 **under consideration** being considered

con·sid'er·ing *prep* 1 allowing for; in view of || *adv* 2 *colloq* taking everything into account

con·sign /kənsīn'/ [L *consignare* to mark with a seal] *vt* 1 to deliver or hand over, commit; 2 to relegate, entrust; 3 to set apart, devote; 4 *com* to ship (goods) || **con·sign'or** *n*

con·sign·ee /kon'sīnē', -sīn-/ *n* one to whom goods are shipped

con·sign'ment *n* 1 act of consigning; 2 goods sent to an agent for sale or storage; 3 **on consignment** (goods) sent to an agent to be held until sold

con·sist /kənsist'/ [L *consistere* to exist] *vi* 1 **consist of** to be made up of; 2 **consist in** to have as a foundation, be based on; 3 **consist with** to be in accord with

con·sist'en·cy *n* (-cies) 1 density or firmness, as of thick liquids; 2 harmony, agreement; 3 unchanging adherence to principles and practice

con·sist'ent *adj* 1 dense, firm; 2 not self-contradictory; accordant, compatible; 3 unchanging in attitude and principles || **con·sist'ent·ly** *adv*

con·sis·to·ry /-tərē/ [L *consistorium* place of assembly] *n* (-ries) 1 church court; 2 church council; 3 papal senate; 4 meeting of such bodies

con·so·la·tion /kon'səlāsh'ən/ *n* 1 comfort, solace; 2 thing or person that consoles

con·sole¹ /kənsōl'/ [L *consolare*] *vt* to give comfort to, at a time of sorrow; cheer up || **con·sol'a·ble** *adj*

con·sole² /kon'sōl/ [F = bracket] *n* 1 desklike structure containing the keys and controls of an organ; 2 switchboard, panel; 3 **a** cabinet with doors, that stands on the floor; **b** such a cabinet for a radio, phonograph, or television set

con·sol·i·date /kənsol'idāt'/ [L *consolidare* (-*atus*) to make firm] *vt* & *vi* 1 to unite, combine into one; 2 to strengthen || **con·sol'i·da'tor** *n* || **con-**

sol'i·da'tion *n* ‖ SYN compress, solidify, join, merge (see *combine*)

con·som·mé /kon'səmā'/ [F] *n* strong clear soup made from meat

con·so·nance /kon'sənəns/ *n* agreement, harmony

con'so·nant [L *consonare* to sound together] *n* **1** speech sound made by occluding or obstructing the breath stream; **2** letter representing such sound ‖ *adj* harmonious, accordant; consistent ‖ **con'so·nan'tal** /-nant'əl/ *adj*

con·sort /kon'sôrt/ [L *consors* (*-sortis*) sharer] *n* **1** spouse, esp. of a reigning monarch; **2** ship that voyages in company with another ship ‖ /kənsôrt'/ *vt & vi* **3** to associate

con·sor·ti·um /kənsôrsh'(ē)əm/ [L] *n* (-ti·a /-sh(ē)ə/) **1** *law* partnership; **2** agreement among financial interests for united action in carrying out large financial dealings, esp. among nations

con·spic·u·ous /kənspik'yoo̅·əs/ [L *conspicuus*] *adj* **1** plainly visible; **2** outstanding, remarkable; **3** attracting attention because of some unusual characteristic, as *a conspicuous necktie, a conspicuous beauty* ‖ **con·spic'·u·ous·ly** *adv* ‖ SYN illustrious, prominent; showy, stunning (see *distinguished*)

con·spir·a·cy /kənspir'əsē/ [< L *conspiratio*] *n* (-cies) **1** act of conspiring; **2** unlawful plot; **3** group of conspirators; **4** *law* agreement between two or more persons for the performance of an unlawful act ‖ SYN confederacy, plot, cabal, intrigue, combination

con·spire /kənspīr'/ [MF *conspirer* < L *conspirare*] *vi* to plan together secretly for an unlawful purpose ‖ **con'spir'a·tor** /-spir'ətər/ *n* ‖ SYN scheme, plot, combine, concur, confederate

con·sta·ble /kon'stəbəl, kun'-/ [OF *conestable* < LL *comes stabuli* count of the stable] *n* **1** officer of the law, usu. with duties similar to those of a sheriff; **2** *Brit* policeman; **3** in the Middle Ages, high military or court official

con·stab·u·lar·y /kənstab'yəler'ē/ *n* (-ies) body of police organized along military lines

con·stan·cy /kon'stənsē/ *n* **1** quality of being true and faithful, as in love; **2** quality of remaining unchanging ‖ SYN fidelity, faithfulness, loyalty, steadiness, adherence, honesty, integrity, ardor ‖ DISCR *Faithfulness* consists in justifying by either acts or attitude the confidence which others have reposed in us. *Faithfulness* is rooted in the conviction that its object is trustworthy and is usually the mark of a warm or intimate personal relationship. *Fidelity* stresses the inclination or obligation to *faithful-ness*, as well as its fulfillment, and its use extends to duties, trusts, etc., as well as to people; it does not imply so warm an attachment as does *faithfulness*, but it observes the very letter of the law. Thus it often means exactness, as the model is copied with *fidelity. Constancy* names a *faithfulness* that never wavers

con·stant /kon'stənt/ [L *constans* (*-stantis*)] *adj* **1** true, faithful; **2** invariable, unchanging; **3** unremitting, persistent ‖ *n* **4** that which does not vary; **5** value that remains unchanged in a given context ‖ **con'stant·ly** *adv* ‖ SYN steadfast; invariable, unchanging (see *continual*)

Con·stan·tine /kon'stəntēn', -tīn'/ *n* (287?–337) Roman emperor 324–337; moved capital to Constantinople 330; first emperor to recognize Christianity

Con·stan·ti·no·ple /kon'stantinōp'əl/ *n* capital of the Eastern Roman Empire 330–1453; of the Ottoman Empire 1453–1922; now Istanbul

con·stel·la·tion /kon'stəlāsh'ən/ [L *constellatio* (*-onis*)] *n* **1** group of fixed stars having a special name; **2** group of distinguished persons

con·ster·na·tion /kon'stərnāsh'ən/ [< L *consternare* (*-atus*) to terrify] *n* great alarm, dismay ‖ SYN apprehension, fear, panic, dismay (see *horror*)

con·sti·pate /kon'stipat'/ [L *constipare* (*-atus*) to press together] *vt* to cause constipation in

con'sti·pa'tion *n* infrequent and difficult evacuation of the bowels

con·stit·u·en·cy /kənstich'oo̅·ənsē/ *n* (-cies) **1** electoral district; **2** its voters; **3** body of supporters

con·stit'u·ent *adj* **1** forming a necessary part, component; **2** having power to make or revise a constitution ‖ *n* **3** component; **4** voter

con·sti·tute /kon'stit(y)oo̅t'/ [L *constituere* (*-tutus*)] *vt* **1** to appoint, elect; **2** to set up, establish; **3** to compose or make up

con'sti·tu'tion *n* **1** act or process of constituting; **2** make-up or composition; **3** physical character in respect to vitality and health; **4** temperament, disposition; **5 a** principles of organization or basic law of a nation, state, or organization; **b** document embodying these principles; **6 Constitution** basic body of laws of the United States, drawn up in 1787 and put into effect March 4, 1789

con'sti·tu'tion·al *adj* **1** of, affecting, or inherent in the constitution of a person or thing; **2** pert. to or in accordance with the constitution of a nation, etc. ‖ *n* **3** walk for one's health

con'sti·tu'tion·al'i·ty /-al'itē/ *n* accordance with the constitution of a nation, etc.

con·strain /kənstrān'/ [MF *constreindre* < L *constringere*] *vt* 1 to restrain; 2 to compel; 3 to confine

con·straint' *n* 1 compulsion, force; 2 repression; 3 lack of naturalness; embarrassment; 4 confinement ‖ SYN necessity, unnaturalness (see *compulsion*)

con·strict /kənstrikt'/ [L *constringere* (-*strictus*)] *vt* to make narrower by squeezing; tighten ‖ **con·stric'tion** *n*

con·stric'tor *n* 1 that which constricts; 2 muscle that contracts part of the body; 3 serpent that crushes its prey in the coils of its body

con·struct /kənstrukt'/ [L *construere* (-*structus*)] *vt* 1 to build, form, devise, put together ‖ /kon'strəkt/ *n* 2 something constructed or synthesized

con·struc·tion /kənstruk'shən/ *n* 1 act of constructing; 2 manner in which something is constructed; 3 that which is built; structure; 4 interpretation; 5 arrangement of words or parts of a sentence

con·struc'tion·ist *n* one who interprets laws, statutes, decrees, etc. in a strict and rigid fashion

con·struc'tive *adj* positive and affirmative; tending to help rather than to hinder

con·strue /kənstroo'/ [L *construere* to construct] *vt* 1 to interpret, explain; analyze; 2 to explain the syntax of; arrange syntactically ‖ SYN parse, explain, infer, deduce (see *interpret*)

con'sul /kon'səl/ [L] *n* 1 official sent to a foreign city by a country to promote trade and to look after the interests of its citizens; 2 one of the two chief magistrates of the ancient Roman republic; 3 one of the three chief magistrates of the First Republic of France 1799–1804 ‖ **con'sul·ship'** *n* ‖ **con'su·lar** /-lər/ *adj*

con'su·late /-lit/ *n* office and residence of a consul

con'sul gen'er·al *n* (**consuls general**) consul of the highest rank, serving in an important city

con·sult /kənsult'/ [L *consulere* (-*sultus*)] *vt* 1 to ask advice of; 2 to refer to; 3 to have regard to or take into consideration ‖ *vi* 4 **consult with** to confer or take counsel with

con·sult'ant *n* 1 one who consults; 2 one who gives expert advice

con'sul·ta'tion /kon'səl-/ *n* 1 act of consulting; 2 conference, as of experts

con·sume /kəns(y)oom'/ [L *consumere*] *vt* 1 to destroy, as by fire or corrosion; 2 to eat or drink up; 3 to use up ‖ SYN expend, dissipate, devour, destroy, waste

con·sum'er *n* one who uses up goods and services

con·sum'er cred'it *n* credit provided by a bank, retail store, or other lender for the purchase of consumer goods

con·sum'er goods' *npl* goods rapidly worn out or used up, as clothing or food

con·sum'er·ism *n* 1 system of marketing which provides a wide choice to consumers; 2 movement of consumers demanding truth in advertising, fair value in purchases, government enforcement of honesty in packaging, etc.

con·sum·mate /kənsum'it/ [L *consummatus*] *adj* 1 perfect, complete; 2 superb ‖ /kon'səmāt'/ *vt* 3 to complete, bring to a finish; 4 to complete (a marriage) by sexual intercourse ‖ **con'sum·ma'tion** *n*

con·sump·tion /kənsump'shən/ [< L *consumptus* consumed] *n* 1 act of consuming; 2 amount consumed; 3 wasting disease, esp. pulmonary tuberculosis

con·sump'tive *n* one affected with tuberculosis of the lungs

cont. 1 containing; 2 contents; 3 continent(al); 4 continue(d)

con·tact /kon'takt/ [L *contactus*] *n* 1 a meeting or touching; close union; 2 personal connection; 3 *elec* joining point of two conductors through which a current may pass ‖ *vt* 4 to place in contact; 5 to get in touch with ‖ *vi* 6 to enter into or be in contact

con'tact lens' *n* small glass or plastic corrective lens placed directly over the pupil of the eye

con'tact print' *n photog* print the same size as the negative, made by placing the negative directly on the sensitized paper

con·ta·gion /kəntāj'ən/ [L *contagio* (-*onis*) contact] *n* 1 communication of disease by contact; 2 disease thus communicable; 3 pestilence; corruption; 4 communication of emotions, ideas, etc., from one mind to another ‖ SYN infection ‖ DISCR *Contagion* is transmission of disease by actual contact with the affected person, either directly by touch, or indirectly by objects used in common, or by the breath, etc. *Infection* names a far less definite means of disease transmission; general living conditions, such as those affecting air and water, are believed to foster a disease or susceptibility to it; for instance, in a swampy and badly drained country, *infection* by malarial germs is common. An infectious disease may be contagious as well

con·ta'gious *adj* 1 communicable by contact; 2 carrying infection; easily spread

con·tain /kəntān'/ [OF *contenir*] *vt* 1 to hold or include, as does a box or vessel; **2** to restrain or hold back; **3** *math* to be divisible by, without a remainder ‖ SYN include, comprise, cover (see *comprehend*)

con·tain′er *n* **1** anything made to hold or carry something, as a can, jar, box, carton, crate, etc.; **2** metal compartment, usu. sealed, in which freight is packaged for ready movement to or from a flatcar, ship, or the like

con·tain′er car′ *n* railroad car designed and used for carrying containers

con·tain′er·ize′ *vt* **1** to package (freight) in a container for shipment; **2** to ship (freight) in a container ‖ **con·tain′-er·i·za′tion** *n*

con·tain′er ship′ *n* ship designed and used for transporting containers

con·tam·i·nate /kəntam′ināt/ [L *contaminare* (-atus)] *vt* to pollute or make impure by contact ‖ **con·tam′-i·na′tion** *n* ‖ **con·tam′i·nant** *n*

con·temn /kəntem′/ [MF *contempner* < L *contemnare*] *vt* to scorn, treat with contempt

con·tem·plate /kont′əmplāt′/ [L *contemplare* (-atus)] *vt* **1** to look at] *vt* **1** to look at or consider with attention; **2** to intend ‖ *vi* **3** to meditate, muse ‖ **con′tem·pla′tion** *n* ‖ **con′tem·pla′-tive** *adj* ‖ SYN reflect upon, study, gaze at, behold, purpose, design, ponder, consider, meditate (see *muse*)

con·tem·po·ra·ne·ous /kəntemp′ərān′-ē-əs/ [L *contemporaneus*] *adj* contemporary ‖ SYN contemporary, synchronous, coeval, simultaneous, coincident ‖ DISCR *Contemporary* is used chiefly of persons, *contemporaneous*, of facts or events; the time implied by either is not necessarily exactly coincidental, but indefinite; *contemporary* writers exist in the same period, though their ages may be different or their lifetimes of different length. *Contemporaneous* events occur, or go on, in the same period

con·tem′po·rar′y /-rer′ē/ [*con-* + L *tempus* (*temporis*) time] *adj* **1** existing or occurring at the same time; **2** of the same age ‖ *n* (-ies) **3** person or thing existing at the same time as another ‖ SYN *adj* (see *contemporaneous*)

con·tempt /kəntempt′/ [L *contemptus*] *n* **1** feeling of scorn toward what one considers vile; **2** state of being despised; **3** *law* disobedience or disrespect to a court or legislative body

con·tempt′i·ble *adj* meriting contempt ‖ SYN vile, contemptuous, paltry, mean ‖ DISCR *Contemptible* describes that which deserves disdain and scorn; *contemptuous* describes that which expresses disdain and scorn, and also one who feels disdain and scorn; a *contemptible* trick will call forth *contemptuous* disapproval

con·temp′tu·ous /-chōo͞-əs/ *adj* show-

ing contempt ‖ **con·temp′tu·ous·ly** *adv* ‖ SYN arrogant, haughty, insolent (see *contemptible*)

con·tend /kəntend′/ [L *contendere*] *vi* **1** to strive in opposition or rivalry; **2** to dispute or debate ‖ *vt* **3** to maintain or assert ‖ **con·tend′er** *n* ‖ SYN contest, compete, oppose, struggle, combat

con·tent¹ /kon′tent/ [< L *continere* (-tentus) to contain] *n* **1** subject matter or meaning; **2** capacity, volume; **3 contents** *pl* **a** that which is contained; **b** subject matter

con·tent² /kəntent′/ [MF < L *contentus*] *adj* **1** satisfied with one's lot ‖ *vt* **2** to make content ‖ *n* **3** contentment

con·tent′ed *adj* full of contentment, satisfied ‖ **con·tent′ed·ly** *adv* ‖ **con·tent′ed·ness** *n* ‖ SYN happy, pleased, satisfied, resigned, willing

con·ten·tion /kəntensh′ən/ [see **con·tend**] *n* **1** struggle, strife; **2** argument, dispute; **3** point advanced in debate ‖ SYN struggle, conflict, dissension, debate, argument, rivalry, enmity, strife, controversy (see *quarrel*)

con·ten′tious *adj* **1** quarrelsome; **2** involving controversy ‖ SYN belligerent, wrangling, disputatious, perverse

con·tent′ment *n* state of being contented ‖ SYN pleasure, comfort, ease (see *happiness*)

con·test /kəntest′/ [MF *contester* < L *contestari* to call to witness] *vt* **1** to dispute, argue against; **2** to fight for ‖ *vi* **3** to contend, vie ‖ /kon′test/ *n* **4** competetive game; **5** fight, struggle; **6** dispute, controversy ‖ SYN *n* conflict, combat, battle, altercation, quarrel

con·test′ant *n* **1** one who contests; **2** one who takes part in a contest

con·text /kon′tekst/ [L *contextus* woven together] *n* those parts of a statement preceding or following a specific word or passage that determine its meaning ‖ **con·tex′tu·al** /-chōo͞-əl/ *adj*

con·tig·u·ous /kəntig′yōo͞-əs/ [L *contiguus* near] *adj* **1** touching; adjoining; **2** near ‖ **con·ti·gu·i·ty** /kon′tigyōo͞′itē/ *n* (-ties) ‖ SYN near, adjoining, touching, adjacent

con·ti·nence /kon′tinəns/ *n* **1** self-control; self-restraint; **2** abstention from sexual intercourse

con′ti·nent [L *continens* (-entis) containing] *n* **1** one of the great land masses of the earth; **2 the Continent** the mainland of Europe ‖ *adj* **3** exercising restraint with regard to carnal desires; **4** abstaining from sexual intercourse

con′ti·nen′tal *adj* **1** of or pert. to a continent; **2 Continental**, **a** pert. to the continent of Europe; **b** pert. to the American colonies at the time of the Revolution ‖ *n* **3** piece of paper money issued by the Continental Congress during the American Revolution; **4** something worthless; **5 Continental, a** soldier of the American army in the Revolution; **b** European

con'ti·nen'tal code' *n* variation of the Morse code in which spaces are eliminated, used outside the United States and esp. in radiotelegraphy

con'ti·nen'tal di·vide' *n* line of summits separating the river systems flowing to opposite sides of a continent

con'ti·nen'tal shelf' *n* shallow part of an ocean that rims the shores of a continent

con·tin·gen·cy /kəntin'jənsē/ *n* (-cies) **1** dependence on chance; uncertainty; **2** chance; accidental, or conditional event; **3** occurrence incidental to another occurrence || SYN possibility, chance, casualty (see *event*)

con·tin'gent [L *contingens* (-*entis*)] *adj* **1** possible; **2** occurring by chance; accidental; **3** conditional; depending on something uncertain or unsettled || *n* **4** something contingent; **5** proportionate part or share; **6** quota of troops; **7** group representing a specific area || SYN *adj* provisional, casual (see *fortuitous*)

con·tin·u·al /kəntin'yōō-əl/ [see *continue*] *adj* **1** frequently repeated; **2** continuous || **con·tin'u·al·ly** *adv* || SYN continuous, incessant, constant, steady, uninterrupted || DISCR *Continual* describes a succession or recurrence, or a condition that is suspended at intervals but starts up again as regularly as it stops, as *continual* recurrence of a situation. *Continual* emphasizes the idea of time; *continuous* applies to both time and space, and stresses the unbroken quality therein; a *continuous* piece of work is done without pause; a *continuous* stretch of water extends without break. *Incessant*, like *continual*, may admit of suspension and recurrence, as *incessant* pain. *Constant* connotes not only persistency of occurrence, but steadiness, especially of aim or affection, as *constant* noise, in the sense of *continuous* noise; *constant* service, friendship, ardor

con·tin'u·ance /-əns/ *n* **1** continuation; **2** unbroken succession; **3** *law* postponement

con·tin'u·a'tion *n* **1** act of continuing or being continued; **2** resumption; **3** sequel || SYN continuity || DISCR *Continuation* names the act of going on with or resuming, or the thing continued or resumed, as the *continuation* of a story. *Continuity* denotes an unbroken, connected coherence, as of a sequence of ideas or of a series of events. It is the quality that char-

acterizes procedure without interruption. *Continuity* names also the state of particles of physical matter held together by cohesion in a solid body

con·tin'ue /-yōō/ [L *continuare* to unite] *vt* **1** to go on with; **2** to resume; **3** to extend; **4** to let remain; retain; **5** *law* to grant a postponement of || *vi* **6** to stay; **7** to resume; **8** to keep on; extend; **9** to last; **10** to persist

con·ti·nu·i·ty /kon'tin(y)ōō'i-tē/ *n* (-ties) **1** continuous state; **2** uninterrupted succession; **3** unbroken whole; **4** motion picture scenario; **5** introductory and transitional parts of a radio script || SYN connection, union (see *continuation*)

con·tin'u·ous *adj* unbroken; uninterrupted || SYN unceasing, unbroken, constant (see *continual*)

con·tin'u·um /-əm/ [L] *n* (-a /-ə/) continuous or uninterrupted series or extent

con·tort /kəntôrt'/ [L *contorquere* (-*tortus*) to twist together] *vt* to bend or twist out of shape; distort || **con·tor'tion** *n*

con·tor'tion·ist *n* one who can twist his body into unnatural positions

con·tour /kon'tŏŏr/ [F] *n* outline of a figure or body, esp. when curved

con'tour farm'ing *n* system of plowing in furrows along contour lines to prevent erosion

con'tour line' *n* curved line connecting all points of a given elevation on a given part of the earth's surface

contr. contraction

con·tra /kon'trə/ [L] *prep* **1** against || *adv* **2** in opposition

con·tra- [L] *pref* **1** against; opposite to; **2** *mus* pitched an octave lower than, as *contrabassoon*

con'tra·band' /-band'/ [Sp *contrabanda* < It *contrabbando* against the law] *n* **1** smuggling; **2** smuggled goods || also *adj*

con'tra·band of war' *n* goods of a neutral nation subject to seizure by a belligerent

con'tra·cep'tion /-sep'shən/ [*contra-* + *conception*] *n* artificial prevention of conception

con'tra·cep'tive *adj* **1** preventing conception || *n* **2** contraceptive device

con·tract /kon'trakt/ [L *contractus* transaction] *n* **1 a** agreement, usu. written, enforceable by law; **b** document containing it || /kəntrakt'/ *vt* **2** to draw closer together, as a muscle; **3** to wrinkle (the brows); **4** to incur, as a debt; **5** to establish by formal agreement; **6** to shorten (a word) by omitting a part || *vi* **7** to shrink, become less; **8** to make or enter into a contract || SYN *n* bargain, agreement, arrangement, compact, stipulation, promise, covenant, bond || DISCR Of these terms, *agreement* is the most general. A *contract* is a binding *agreement;* it is, especially, a formal *agreement* duly executed before the law, naming the terms and obligations of a business transaction. A *compact* is a *contract* on a larger scale; it is of a more solemn nature, and refers to matters agreed upon under oath, to international affairs, treaties, and the like. *Stipulation,* though it may refer to the entire *agreement,* names specifically one of the provisions of a *contract* or *agreement. Bargain* refers primarily to *agreement* in matters of buying and selling

con′tract bridge′ *n* variety of bridge in which only so many tricks may be scored toward game as declarer contracts to take

con·trac′tion *n* 1 act of contracting or state of being contracted; 2 contracted word

con·tract·or /kon′traktər, kəntrak′-/ *n* 1 one who contracts to perform specified work, as construction, services, etc.; 2 something that contracts, as a muscle

con·trac′tu·al /-chōō-əl/ *adj* pert. to or secured by a contract

con·tra·dict /kon′trədikt′/ [L *contradicere* (-*dictus*)] *vt* 1 to assert the opposite of (a statement); 2 to deny the words of (another); 3 to be inconsistent with ‖ **con′tra·dic′tion** *n*

con′tra·dic′to·ry /-ərē̆/ *adj* 1 characterized by inconsistency or opposition, as *contradictory statements;* 2 given to asserting the contrary ‖ SYN inconsistent, opposed (see *opposite*)

con′tra·dis·tinc′tion *n* **in contradistinction to** as opposed to

con′trail /kon′-/ [*condensation + trail*] *n* visible condensation of water vapor in the wake of high-flying aircraft and missiles

con′tra·in′di·cate′ *vt med* to make (a remedy or procedure) inadvisable ‖ **con′tra·in′di·ca′tion** *n*

con·tral·to /kəntral′tō̆/ *n mus* 1 lowest female voice or part; 2 singer with a contralto voice ‖ also *adj*

con·trap·tion /kəntrap′shən/ [?] *n colloq* makeshift; contrivance, device

con′tra·pun′tal /-punt′əl/ [< It *contrappunto* counterpoint] *adj* pert. to or characterized by counterpoint

con·tra·ry /kon′trerē̆/ [MF *contrarie* < L *contrarius*] *adj* 1 opposed; contradictory; 2 in an opposite direction; 3 adverse; 4 /often kəntrer′ē̆/ perverse, obstinate ‖ *n* (-ries) 5 opposite; 6 one of two contrary things; 7 **on the contrary** in opposition to what has been said; 8 **to the contrary** to the opposite effect ‖ *adv* 9 in a contrary manner or direction ‖ **con′tra·ri·ly** *adv* ‖ **con′tra·ri·ness** *n* ‖ **con′tra·ri·wise′** *adv* ‖ SYN *adj* antagonistic, dissimilar, incongruous

con·trast /kəntrast′/ [MF *contraster* to

oppose] *vt* 1 to compare in order to note the difference ‖ *vi* 2 to exhibit difference upon comparison ‖ /kon′-trast/ *n* 3 act or state of contrasting or being contrasted; 4 striking difference of qualities as shown by comparison; 5 thing or quality showing such difference; 6 relative difference between the light and dark portions of a picture ‖ **con·tras′tive** *adj* ‖ SYN *v* compare, differentiate, discriminate, distinguish, oppose; *n* (see *comparison*)

con·trast′y *adj* (picture) exhibiting sharp gradations between light and dark areas

con·tra·vene /kont′rəvēn′/ [LL *contravenire*] *vt* 1 to act contrary to; oppose; 2 to infringe, violate ‖ **con′-tra·ven′tion** /-vensh′ən/ *n* ‖ SYN check, defy, nullify, resist, withstand, prevent, obstruct ‖ ANT aid, assist, uphold, support, abet

con·tre·temps /kŏN′trətäN′/ [F] *nsg & npl* awkward mishap

con·trib·ute /kəntrib′yŏŏt/ [L *contribuere* (-*utus*) to bring together] *vt* 1 to give to a common fund along with others; 2 to furnish, as a share; 3 to supply (a story, article, etc.) for publication ‖ also *vi* ‖ **con·trib′u·tor** *n* ‖ **con·trib′u·to′ry** /-tôr̆ĕ, -tôr′ĕ/ *adj*

con·tri·bu·tion /kon′trĭbyŏŏsh′ən/ *n* 1 act of contributing; 2 thing contributed

con·trite /kəntrīt′/ [L *contritus* bruised] *adj* remorseful, penitent ‖ **con·tri′tion** /-trish′ən/ *n*

con·triv·ance /kəntrīv′əns/ *n* 1 act of contriving; 2 something contrived, as a mechanical apparatus

con·trive /kəntrīv′/ [MF *controver* to find] *vt* 1 to devise cleverly; invent; 2 to work out; 3 to bring to pass, manage ‖ **con·triv′er** *n* ‖ SYN devise, invent, scheme, plot (see *discover*)

con·trol /kəntrōl′/ [< MF *contrerolle* audit copy] *n* 1 act or power of directing; authority; 2 check, restraint; 3 means of comparison, as for verifying; 4 person who checks or verifies; 5 **a** instrument for regulating a machine; **b** controls *pl* set of such instruments; 6 **out of control** (vehicle) beyond the power of the driver or pilot to direct ‖ *v* (**-trolled;** **-trol·ling**) *vt* 7 to restrain, check; 8 to direct, command; 9 to regulate; 10 to verify (a scientific experiment) by some outside standard ‖ SYN *v* regulate, check, manage, direct (see *govern*)

con·trol′ler *n* 1 one who or that which controls; 2 official who oversees and verifies accounts

con·trol′ tow′er *n* elevated structure from which the movements of aircraft taking off and landing at an airport can be controlled

con'tro·ver'sial /-vursh'əl/ *adj* **1** pert. to or subject to controversy; **2** given to controversy; contentious

con·tro·ver·sy /kont'rəvurs'ē/ *n* (-sies) dispute, argument; difference of opinion

con'tro·vert' /'-vurt', kon'trəvurt'/ [L *controvertere* to turn against] *vt* **1** to argue against; **2** to argue about || **con'tro·vert'i·ble** *adj* || SYN dispute, deny, counter, oppose (see *confute*)

con'tu·ma'cious /-măsh'əs/ *adj* insubordinate and scornful, esp. to lawful authority || **con'tu·ma'cious·ly** *adv* || SYN headstrong, perverse, rebellious, unruly

con·tu·ma·cy /kon't(y)ōōməsē/ [< L *contumax* (-*acis*) stubborn] *n* (-cies) obstinate and willful opposition to authority

con·tu·me·ly /kon't(y)ōōməlē/ [MF *contumelie* < L *contumelia*] *n* (-lies) **1** insolent, insulting language or abuse; **2** humiliating insult || **con'-tu·me'li·ous** /-mēl'ē-əs/ *adj*

con·tu·sion /kənt(y)ōōzh'ən/ [< L *contundere* (-*tusus*) to bruise] *n* bruise

co·nun·drum /kənun'drəm/ [?] *n* **1** riddle whose answer is a pun; **2** puzzle

con·ur·ba·tion /kon'urbăsh'ən/ *n* group of cities and towns not separated by rural areas

con·va·lesce /kon'vəles'/ [L *convalescere*] *vi* to recover strength and health after illness || **con'va·les'-cence** *n* || **con'va·les'cent** *adj & n*

con·vec·tion /kənvek'shən/ [< L *convehere* (-*vectus*) to collect] *n phys* transmission of heat by the movement of the heated parts of a gas or liquid

con·vene /kənvēn'/ [L *convenire* to come together] *vt & vi* to assemble, as for a meeting

con·ven·ience /-yəns/ *n* **1** quality of being convenient; **2** ease, accommodation; **3** that which adds to comfort, makes work easier, or offers material advantage

con·ven·ient *adj* **1** at hand, easy to get to or at; **2** affording accommodation; saving work or trouble || **con·ven'ient·ly** *adv* || SYN fitted, adapted, favorable, commodious, opportune, timely || ANT unhandy, awkward, unfitted

con·vent /kon'vənt, -vent/ [L *conventus* assembly] *n* **1** community or society of nuns; **2** their building || **con·ven·tu·al** /kənven'chŏō-əl/ *adj & n*

con·ven·tion /kənven'shən/ [see **convene**] *n* **1** assembly, as of delegates or representatives, met for some definite object; **2** international agreement; **3** general consent; usage, custom

con·ven·tion·al *adj* **1** following or sanctioned by established customs or fixed usage; **2** characterized by lack of originality or spontaneity; **3** nonnuclear (weapons; warfare) || **con·ven'tion·al·ly** *adv* || **con·ven'tion·al'·i·ty** /-al'itē/ *n* (-ties) || SYN customary, formal, usual (see *ceremonious*)

con·verge /kənvurj'/ [LL *convergere* to bend together] *vi* **1** to tend toward one point || *vt* **2** to cause to converge || **con·ver'gence** *n* || **con·ver'gent** *adj*

con·ver·sant /kon'vərsənt, kənvurs'-ənt/ *adj* **1** versed in; **2** well acquainted

con·ver·sa·tion /kon'vərsāsh'ən/ *n* **1** informal or familiar talk; **2** social intercourse; association || **con'ver·sa'tion·al** *adj* || SYN chat, parley, conference, talk, communication, discourse, colloquy, chatter, dialog || DISCR *Talk* consists of coherent speech, uttered presumably for the benefit of a listener. It may be purposeful and serious, or vapid and empty. *Conversation* is an interchange of sentiments or ideas between two or more persons, usually upon a subject worthy of attention. *Talk* is sometimes the endless *chatter* of one tiresome person; *conversation* requires that each person bear his part. A *chat* is a pleasant, familiar *talk;* it is not senseless, and neither is it serious. A *conference* is a formal *conversation,* held by appointment for the discussion of specific subjects, as the Peace *Conference.* A *parley* is a *conference* held to debate points under dispute

con·verse¹ /kənvurs'/ [L *conversari* to associate with] *vi* **1** to hold a conversation, talk familiarly || /kon'-vərs/ *n* **2** conversation

con·verse² /kənvurs', kon'vərs/ [L *conversus* turned around] *adj* **1** reversed in order or relationship, transposed || /kon'vərs/ *n* **2** opposite

con·ver·sion /kənvur'zhən/ [see **convert**] *n* act or instance of converting, or state of being converted

con·vert /kənvurt'/ [L *convertere* (-*versus*) to turn around] *vt* **1** to transform, change; **2** to change from one religion, faith, course, opinion, etc., to another; **3** to exchange, as a security, for something of equivalent value; **4** to assume ownership of, as another's property, unlawfully || *vi* **5** to become converted; **6** *football* to make a point after a touchdown by kicking, passing, or running the ball over the goal line || /kon'vərt/ *n* **7** converted person

con·vert'er *n* **1** one who converts; **2** device for converting, as iron to steel or direct current to alternating current and vice versa

con·vert'i·ble *adj* **1** capable of being

converted ‖ *n* **2** automobile with a folding top

con·vex /kon'veks, konveks', kən-/\ [L *convexus* arched] *adj* curved out like the outside of a sphere ‖ **con·vex'·i·ty** /kən-/ *n* (**-ties**)

con·vey /kənvā'/ [AF *conveier*] *vt* **1** to carry or transport from one place to another; **2** to transmit; **3** to impart, communicate; **4** *law* to transfer by deed to another ‖ SYN carry, transport, bear, bring, grant, transmit

con·vey'ance *n* **1** act of conveying; **2** means of conveying; vehicle; **3** *law* document of conveying

con·vey'or also **con·vey'or belt'** *n* moving endless belt or chain for conveying things

con·vict /kənvikt'/ [L *convincere* (*-victus*)] *vt* **1** to find guilty of a criminal offense ‖ /kon'vikt/ *n* **2** convicted person serving a prison sentence

con·vic'tion *n* **1** act of convicting or state of being convicted; **2** act of convincing or state of being convinced; **3** strong belief ‖ SYN persuasion, opinion (see *belief*)

con·vince /kənvins'/ *vt* to persuade by evidence or argument; cause to believe ‖ **con·vinc'ing·ly** *adv* ‖ SYN persuade ‖ DISCR To *convince* is to impress the understanding by satisfactory evidence, proof, or argument. *Persuade* occasionally has almost the same meaning, as I am *persuaded* that the man spoke the truth. More commonly, however, to *persuade* is to bring the will of another into accordance with one's own by appealing to his affections, influencing him through his weaknesses, or otherwise exerting personal power

con·viv·i·al /kənviv'ē·əl/ [L *convivium* feast] *adj* festive, gay, fond of merry company ‖ **con·viv'i·al'i·ty** /-al'itē/ *n*

con·vo·ca·tion /kon'vəkāsh'ən/ *n* **1** act of convoking or state of being convoked; **2** assembly, esp. of clergy or academics

con·voke /kənvōk'/ [L *convocare*] *vt* to call together, convene

con·vo·lu·tion /kon'vəlōōsh'ən/ [< L *convolvere* (*-volutus*) to roll up] *n* **1** a coiling or winding together; twisting; **2** coil or fold ‖ **con'vo·lut'ed** *adj*

con·voy /kənvoi'/ [MF *convoier*] *vt* **1** to accompany or escort for protection ‖ /kon'voi/ *n* **2** act of convoying; **3** convoying force; **4** ships or vehicles being convoyed

con·vulse /kənvuls'/ [L *convellere* (*-vulsus*)] to tear to pieces] *vt* **1** to agitate violently; **2** to affect with spasms, as of laughter

con·vul'sion *n* **1** any violent disturbance; **2** fit of laughter; **3** also **convulsions** *pl* violent twitching of the body because of involuntary contraction of muscles ‖ **con·vul'sive** *adj*

co·ny /kōn'ē/ [< OF *conis* pl of *conil* rabbit] also **co·ney** *n* (**-nies**) **1** rabbit fur, esp. when dyed; **2** rabbit

coo /kōō'/ [imit] *vi* **1** to cry like a dove or pigeon; **2** to converse amorously ‖ *vt* **3** to utter by cooing ‖ *n* **4** cooing sound

cook /kōōk'/ [OE *cōc* < L *coquus*] *n* **1** one who prepares food by cooking ‖ *vt* **2** to prepare for eating by the action of heat; **3** to subject to the action of heat; **4** **cook up** to concoct ‖ *vi* **5** to act as a cook; **6** to undergo cooking

cook'er *n* utensil or vessel for cooking

cook'ie or **cook'y** [D *koekje* little cake] *n* (**-ies**) **1** flat, sweet cake; **2** *slang* person, as *she's a smart cookie*

cook'ie sheet' *n* rectangular sheet of metal with rolled or turned-up edges on the back and sides, used for baking cookies and biscuits

cook'out' *n* backyard party featuring a meal cooked out of doors

cool /kōōl/ [OE *cōl*] *adj* **1** moderately cold; **2** giving a sense of coolness, as *cool clothes*; **3** calm, self-possessed; **4** lacking cordiality; **5** impudent, audacious; **6** *colloq* not exaggerated, as *he lost a cool million*; **7** *slang* very good, excellent ‖ *vt* **8** to make cool; **9** **cool it** *slang* to calm down ‖ *vi* **10** to become cool; **11** **cool off** *colloq* to calm down ‖ *n* **12** cool part, as *the cool of the evening* ‖ *adv* **13** *colloq* coolly ‖ **cool'ly** *adv* ‖ **cool'ness** *n*

cool'er *n* **1** device or container for keeping things cool; **2** *slang* jail; lockup

Cool·idge, Cal·vin /kōōl'ij/ *n* (1872–1933) 30th president of the U.S. 1923–29

coo·lie /kōōl'ē/ [Hindu *kūlī* day laborer] *n* unskilled Oriental laborer

cool'ing-off' *adj* (agreement or period) designed to allow contestants to negotiate before resorting to force

cool'ing tow'er *n* structure over which water is trickled in order to cool it by evaporation

coon /kōōn'/ *n colloq* raccoon

coop /kōōp'/ [ME *coupe* basket] *n* **1** enclosure for fowls, rabbits, etc.; pen ‖ *vt* **2** to confine in, or as in, a coop

co-op /kō'op, kō-op'/ *n* cooperative

coop'er /kōōp'ər/ [MD *cūper* < L *cupa* cask] *n* maker of barrels and casks ‖ **coop'er·age** /-ij/ *n*

co·op'er·ate' /kō-op'-/ *vi* **1** to act or work jointly for a common end; **2** to work together with others ‖ **co·op'er·a'tion** *n* ‖ **co·op'er·a'tor** *n*

co·op'er·a·tive /-ətiv, -rāt'iv/ *adj* **1** cooperating or willing to cooperate ‖ *n* **2** business, apartment, or organization owned jointly by consumers or dwellers who share in the profits or benefit from reduced costs

co·or·di·nate /kō·ôr′dinit/ [*co-* + L *ordinare* (*-atus*) to arrange] *adj* 1 equal in rank or importance; 2 pert. to coordination or coordinates ‖ *n* 3 coordinate person or thing; 4 *math* one of a set of magnitudes by which the position of a geometrical object is specified with respect to a fixed geometrical figure ‖ /-nāt′/ *vt* 5 to place in the same order or class; 6 to put, as parts, into proper relationship ‖ *vi* 7 to be coordinate; 8 to harmonize ‖ **co·or′di·na′tor** *n*

co·or′di·na′tion *n* 1 act or state of co-ordinating or being coordinated; 2 harmonious functioning; mutual adjustment

coot /kōōt/ [ME *cote*] *n* 1 short-winged aquatic bird of the genus *Fulica* of Europe and North America; 2 *colloq* codger

coot·ie /kōōt′ē/ [?] *n* body louse

cop /kop/ *slang n* 1 policeman ‖ *v* (**copped; cop·ping**) *vt* 2 to catch, nab; 3 to filch; 4 **cop a plea** to plead guilty to a lesser charge ‖ *vi* 5 **cop out** to quit before the end of a particular job or line of action, being satisfied with less than what might have been realized

cope[1] /kōp/ [MF *couper* to strike] *vi* **cope with** to handle with some degree of success

cope[2] [OE *cāp* < LL *capa* cap] *n* 1 priest's vestment consisting of a long semicircular mantle; 2 something resembling this in shape

Co·pen·ha·gen /kōp′ənhāg′ən/ *n* capital of Denmark (678,072)

Co·per·ni·cus, Nic·o·la·us /nik′əlā′əs kōpurn′ikəs/ *n* (1473–1543) Polish astronomer, formulator of the theory of the heliocentric solar system ‖ **Co·per′ni·can** *adj*

cop·i·er /kop′ē·ər/ *n* 1 person who copies; 2 imitator; 3 device for making instant copies of written and printed material

co′pi′lot *n* assistant pilot on an airplane

cop·ing /kōp′in/ [< *cope*[2]] *n* top masonry of a wall, often sloping so as to shed water

cop′ing saw′ *n* narrow saw held between the ends of a U-shaped frame for cutting curved patterns

co·pi·ous /kōp′ē·əs/ [< L *copia* plenty] *adj* plentiful, abundant ‖ **co′pi·ous·ly** *adv* ‖ syn bountiful, plentiful, overflowing, abundant, full, profuse, exuberant

cop·per[1] /kop′ər/ [OE *coper* < LL *cuprum* < (aes) *Cyprium* metal of Cyprus] *n* 1 common, reddish metallic element (**Cu;** at.no. 29; at.wt. 63.54), ductile and tenacious, an excellent conductor of heat and electricity; 2 copper color ‖ **cop′per·y** *adj*

cop·per[2] [< *cop*] *slang* policeman

cop′per·as /-əs/ [< L (aqua) *cuprosa* copper water] *n* ferrous sulfate —FeSO₄·7H₂O— a greenish crystalline salt used in making pigments and inks and in water purification

cop′per·head′ *n* 1 poisonous American snake (*Ancistrodon contortrix*), akin to the rattlesnake; 2 **Copperhead** Northerner who sympathized with the South during the Civil War

cop·ra /kop′rə/ [Port < Malayalam *koppara*] *n* dried coconut meat, the source of coconut oil

cops′ and rob′bers *n* children's game in which the players pretend they are policemen and thieves, the policemen chasing and capturing the thieves

copse /kops/ [MF *copeis* newly cut wood] *n* grove or thicket of small trees or bushes

Copt /kopt/ [Coptic *gyptios, kyptaios* Egyptian < Gk *Aigyptios*] *n* 1 descendant of the ancient Egyptians; 2 member of the ancient Christian Church of Egypt

Cop′tic *adj* 1 of or pert. to the Copts ‖ *n* 2 language of the Copts, used in the liturgy of the Coptic Church

cop·u·la /kop′yələ/ [L = link] *n* verb, as *be* or *seem*, that connects the subject with the predicate without involving action

cop′u·late′ /-lāt′/ *vi* to unite in sexual intercourse ‖ **cop′u·la′tion** *n*

cop′u·la·tive /-lətiv/ *adj* 1 serving to connect; 2 pert. to copulation; 3 *gram* pert. to copulas

cop·y /kop′ē/ [MF *copie* < L *copia* abundance] *n* (*-ies*) 1 imitation; 2 duplicate, reproduction; 3 manuscript or printed matter to be set up in type; 4 single one of a number of duplicates, as of a book ‖ *v* (*-ied*) *vt* 5 to make a copy of; 6 to imitate ‖ **cop′y·ist** *n* ‖ syn *n* (see *duplicate*); *v* follow, imitate, reproduce

cop′y·book′ *n* book containing specimens of handwriting for students to imitate

cop′y·boy′ *n* errand boy in a newspaper office

cop′y·cat′ *n* one who imitates another in work or action

cop′y desk′ *n* desk in a newspaper office at which copy is edited and headlines are written

cop′y·ed′it *vt* to prepare (a manuscript) for publication by checking spelling, punctuation, and grammar ‖ **cop′y ed′i·tor** *n*

cop′y·read′er *n* editor who corrects and prepares newspaper copy for the typesetter

cop′y·right′ *n* 1 exclusive right to the control, publication, and sale of a literary or artistic work for a certain number of years ‖ *vt* 2 to secure a copyright for ‖ **cop′y·right′ed** *adj*

cop′y·writ′er *n* writer of advertising copy

co·quet /kōket′/ [F *coqueter*] *v* (**-quetted; -quet·ting**) *vi* to flirt || **co·quet·ry** /kōk′itrē, kōket′-/ *n* (**-ries**)

co·quette /kōket′/ *n* female flirt || **coquet′tish** *adj*

cor- *pref* var of **com-**

cor·al /kôr′əl, kor′-/ [MF < Gk *korallion*] *n* **1** any of many species of higher coelenterates which secrete a hard calcareous skeleton; **2** these skeletons collectively, forming reefs and islands; **3** something made of coral; **4** pinkish-yellow color

cor′al snake′ *n* any of numerous venomous snakes (genus *Micrurus*) of the New World tropics, one species of which (*M. fulvius*) is found in the SE United States

cor·bel /kôr′bəl/ [< OF < ML *corvellus* little raven] *n* bracket of brick, stone, or other material, projecting from a wall and built as a support

cord /kôrd′/ [F *corde* < Gk *chorde* gut string] *n* **1** twisted string; thin rope; **2** rib on the surface of cloth; **3** ribbed cloth, esp. corduroy; **4** measure of cut wood, usu. a pile eight by four by four feet; **5** small electric cable, as for lamps and appliances; **6** any binding force; **7** *anat* cordlike structure || *vt* **8** to fasten with a cord; **9** to pile (wood) by the cord || **cord′ed** *adj*

cord·age /-ij/ *n* **1** ropes and cords collectively; **2** wood measured in cords

cor·date /kôr′dāt/ [< L *cor* (*cordis*) heart] *adj* heart-shaped

cord′ foot′ *n* quantity of wood four feet high, four feet wide, and one foot long

cor·dial /kôr′jəl/ [see **cordate**] *adj* **1** hearty, warm || *n* **2** sweet aromatic alcoholic beverage || **cor′dial·ly** *adv* || **cor·dial′i·ty** /-j(ē)al′-/ *n* (**-ties**) || SYN *adj* genial, friendly, sincere, real (see *hearty*)

cor·dil·le·ra /kôrd′əlyer′ə, kôrdil′ərə/ [Sp] *n* **1** chain of mountains, esp. the main system of parallel mountain ranges of a continent; **2 the Cordilleras** *pl* **a** the great parallel mountain ranges of W North America; **b** the Andes range in W South America

cord·ite /kôr′dīt/ [< *cord*] *n* smokeless gunpowder

cord′less *adj* powered by a battery and, therefore, having no electric cord for connection to an outlet

cor·do·ba /kôrd′əbə/ [Francisco Hernández de *Córdoba* (1475–1526) Sp explorer] *n* monetary unit of Nicaragua

cor·don /kôrd′ən/ [MF] *n* **1** cord or ribbon worn as a badge or decoration; **2** line or circle, as of police, soldiers, or ships, guarding or cutting off an area

cor·do·van /kôrd′əvən/ [< *Córdoba* Sp city] *n* fine leather of goatskin, pigskin, or split horsehide

cor·du·roy /kôrd′əroi′/ [?] *n* **1** ribbed or corded cotton cloth; **2** road made of logs laid transversely; **3 corduroys** *pl* trousers of corduroy || *vt* **4** to build (a road) of logs

core /kôr′/ [ME] *n* **1** heart or innermost part of anything; **2** central seed-bearing part of fruit like the apple and pear; **3** iron center of an electromagnet or an induction coil || *vt* **4** to extract the core from

co·re·li·gion·ist /kō′-/ *n* one having the same religious faith

co·re·spond·ent /kō′-/ *n* person jointly charged with the husband or wife against whom a divorce action is brought for adultery

Co·rin·thi·an /kərinth′ē·ən/ [< *Corinth*, Gk city noted in ancient times for its luxury] *adj* **1** pert. to Corinth; **2** luxurious, licentious; **3** pert. to or designating one of the orders of Greek architecture, with an ornamental bell-shaped capital topping a slender column || *n* **4** native of Corinth; **5 Corinthians** *sg* either of two books of the New Testament, written by Saint Paul

cork /kôrk′/ [ME < Ar *qurq* < L *quercus* oak] *n* **1** light elastic outer bark of the cork oak (*Quercus suber*), used for stoppers for bottles, floats, etc.; **2** something made of cork; **3** stopper for a bottle, as of cork or rubber || *vt* **4** to stop with or as with a cork

cork′age *n* fee charged in a restaurant for serving wine or liquor that was not bought on the premises

cork′er *n slang* **1** conclusive argument; **2** remarkable person or thing

cork′ing *adj colloq* excellent, fine

cork′screw′ *n* **1** spirally twisted steel instrument for drawing corks from bottles || *adj* **2** shaped like a corkscrew || *vt* & *vi* **3** to move in a spiral or zigzag course

cor·mo·rant /kôrm′ərənt/ [MF < L *corvus marinus* sea raven] *n* any of a genus (*Phalacrocorax*) of large sea birds having an extensible pouch beneath the bill for holding fish; used in the Far East for catching fish

corn¹ /kôrn′/ [OE = grain] *n* **1 a** tall cereal plant (*Zea mays*) bearing seeds on large ears; **b** the seeds; **2** *Eng* wheat; **3** *Scot* oats; **4** corn whiskey; **5** *colloq* trite or overly sentimental music, stories, or jokes || *vt* **6** to preserve in brine

corn² [MF *corne* < L *cornu* horn] *n* horny thickening of the skin esp. on the toe or foot, caused by friction or pressure

Corn′ Belt′ *n* region in the Midwest noted for raising feed corn

corn′cob′ *n* woody core of an ear of corn in which the kernels are set

corn′crib′ *n* small ventilated building for storing corn

cor·ne·a /kôrn′ē·ə/ [L = horny] *n* transparent front part of the outer coat of the eyeball, lying in front of the iris and pupil

cor·ner /kôrn′ər/ [AF < L *cornu* horn] *n* **1** angle; **2** point where two converging lines, sides, or edges meet; **3** recess, secluded place; **4** region, esp. a remote point; **5** awkward position, embarrassing situation; **6** monopoly; **7 cut corners** to reduce the time or expense required to achieve some end ‖ *vt* **8** to place in or drive into a corner; **9** to gain a monopoly of ‖ *vi* **10** to turn sharply at high speed, as an automobile

cor′ner·stone′ *n* stone at the corner of a building, esp. one with the date of construction carved on it, laid at public ceremonies

cor·net /kôrnet′/ [MF < *cornu* horn] *n* brass valve instrument of the trumpet family

corn′flow′er *n* plant (*Centaurea cyanus*) of the composite family, having showy blue, pink, or white flowers

cor·nice /kôrn′is/ [MF < It] *n* **1** ornamental molding on the wall of a room near the ceiling; **2** horizontal molded projection forming the top member of a wall, column, etc., as the part of an entablature above the frieze

Cor·nish /kôrn′ish/ [< *Cornwall*, Eng county and ancient region of SW Britain] *adj* **1** of or pert. to Cornwall ‖ *n* **2** extinct Celtic language of Cornwall

corn′ meal′ *n* coarsely ground corn ‖ **corn′meal′** *adj*

corn′ pone′ *n* cornmeal bread

corn′starch′ *n* starch in the form of flour made from corn, used in preparing foods

cor·nu·co·pi·a /kôrn′əkōp′ē·ə/ [L *cornu copiae* horn of plenty] *n* **1** *class. myth.* horn containing an endless supply of food; **2** plenty, abundance; **3** cone-shaped receptacle

Corn·wall /kôrn′wôl, -wəl/ *n* county in SW England (340,000; 1350 sq.m. county seat Bodmin)

Corn·wal·lis, Charles /kôrnwôl′is, -wol′-/ *n* (Lord Cornwallis) (1738–1805) British general whose surrender to Washington in 1781 at Yorktown, Va. signaled the end of the American Revolution

corn′ whis′key *n* whiskey made from fermented corn mash

corn′y *adj* (-i·er; -i·est) *colloq* trite, worn, commonplace; old-fashioned

co·rol·la /kərol′ə/ [L = little garland] *n* the petals of a flower collectively

cor·ol·lar·y /kor′əler′ē, kôr′-/ [LL *corollarium*] *n* (-ies) **1** obvious though incidental deduction; **2** inference; result; **3** *math* proposition readily deduced from a proof already established

co·ro·na /kərōn′ə/ [L = *crown*] *n* **1**

crownlike structure or part of the body, as the top of the skull; **2** halo surrounding a heavenly body, esp. the luminous halo around the sun seen during a total eclipse; **3** crownlike formation on the inner side of the corolla of a flower; **4** *elec* luminous discharge produced around terminals and wires of power lines

cor·o·nar·y /kôr′əner′ē, kor′-/ *adj* **1** pert. to or encircling like a crown; **2** pert. to the arteries that originate in the aorta and supply the heart ‖ *n* (-ies) **3** heart attack involving occlusion of a coronary artery

cor′o·na′tion *n* crowning of a king or queen

cor′o·ner [AF *corouner* officer of the crown] *n* official who investigates any death that is thought not due to natural causes

cor′o·net′ /-net′/ [MF *coronette*] *n* **1** small crown worn by various ranks of nobility; **2** ornamental band or wreath for the head

corp., corpl. corporal

corp., corpn. corporation

cor·po·ral¹ /kôrp′ərəl/ [MF, alter. of *caporal* < It *caporale*] *n* lowest-ranking noncommissioned officer in the army

cor·po·ral² [L *corporalis*] *adj* of the body; physical, bodily ‖ SYN corporeal, bodily, physical ‖ DISCR *Bodily,* opposed to mental, describes that centering in the body rather than in the mind, as *bodily* ills; or that which is a part or product of the body, as *bodily* endurance; *bodily* labor. *Physical* is often used interchangeably with *bodily,* as *physical* ills or discomforts, but *physical* has also a broader application relating to the natural or material world as opposed to the spiritual or imaginary, as *physical* phenomena; *physical* forces. *Corporeal* indicates the material substance or nature of the medium in which we have our being; it is opposed to spiritual: the body is the *corporeal* agent of the spirit. *Corporal* refers to something relating to the body rather than to the mind, as *corporal* punishment

cor′po·ral's guard′ *n* **1** small detachment of soldiers; **2** any small group of people

cor·po·rate /kôrp′(ə)rit/ [L *corporare* (-atus) to form into a body] *adj* **1** united, combined; **2** of or forming a corporation

cor′po·ra′tion /-pərāsh′ən/ *n* entity created by law consisting of a number of persons acting as one body for certain defined purposes, as the conducting of a business, the officers and stockholders of which are not individually liable for its acts

cor·po·re·al /kôrpôr′ē·əl/ [L *corporeus*] *adj* having a material body; tangible

‖ SYN material, physical, bodily (see *corporal*[2])

corps /kôr'/ [F = body] *n* (**corps** /kôrz'/) 1 army corps; 2 specialized branch of the armed forces; 3 body of persons associated in a common work

corpse /kôrps'/ [MF *corps* < L *corpus* body] *n* dead body ‖ SYN ashes, remains (see *body*)

cor·pu·lent /kôr'pyələnt/ [L *corpulentus*] *adj* fat, stout ‖ **cor'pu·lence** *n* ‖ SYN obese, stout, adipose, burly, pursy

cor·pus /kôrp'əs/ [L = body] *n* (**-po·ra** /-pərə/) *n* collection or body of writings, as on a specified subject

Cor'pus Chris'ti /krist'ē/ *n* seaport in S Texas (170,000)

cor·pus·cle /kôr'pusəl/ [L *corpusculum* little body] *n* 1 minute particle of matter; 2 blood cell ‖ **cor·pus'cu·lar** /-kyələr/ *adj*

cor'pus de·lic'ti /dĭlīk'tī/ [L = body of the transgression] *n law* fundamental facts of a crime, as in a murder the fact of the death of the victim

cor·ral /kəral'/ [Sp] *n* 1 enclosure for horses or cattle ‖ *v* (**-ralled; -ral·ling**) *vt* 2 to confine in or as in a corral; 3 to capture

cor·rect /kərekt'/ [L *correctus* made straight] *adj* 1 accurate, free from error, right; 2 measuring up to or meeting an accepted standard ‖ *vt* 3 to set or make right; 4 to mark errors in, emend; 5 to cure, as a fault; remedy; 6 to rebuke or punish; 7 to counteract, neutralize ‖ **cor·rect'ly** *adv* ‖ **cor·rect'ness** *n* ‖ SYN *v* (see *rectify*); *adj* accurate, exact, precise, definite, careful, right, true, truthful, proper, scrupulous, prim, decorous, perfect, punctilious ‖ DISCR *Correct*, *accurate*, *exact*, and *precise* agree in expressing conformity to a standard, rule, or prescription. *Correct* describes that which conforms without error, fault, or departure from truth; the care underlying correctness is negative, being rooted in the desire not to make a mistake. *Accurate* describes that which conforms through the exercise of a positive care, a devotion to the end of insuring rightness. A *correct* statement contains the truth; an *accurate* statement is not only truthful, but carefully complete. *Exact* describes a perfect conformity secured by fulfillment of every requirement and attention to every detail. *Exact* measurements conform perfectly with the actual dimensions of the thing measured; his *exact* words are his very words. *Exact* is applied to the scientific fields in a sense wherein *precise* is not used; but otherwise *exact* and *precise* are often interchangeable. *Pre-*

cise frequently connotes an overscrupulous fussiness

cor·rec'tion *n* 1 act of correcting; 2 that which is substituted for what was wrong, emendation ‖ **cor·rec'tion·al** *adj* ‖ SYN emendation, amendment, rectification, discipline, punishment, rebuke, reformation, improvement

cor·rec'tive *n* that which amends, makes right, true, proper, etc.; that which counteracts or neutralizes

cor·re·late /kôr'əlāt', kor'-/ [< *cor-* + L *relatus* related] *vi* 1 to have a mutual or reciprocal relation ‖ *vt* 2 to bring into such a relation ‖ *n* 3 either of two related things, esp. if one implies the other ‖ **cor're·la'tion** *n*

cor·rel·a·tive /kərel'ətĭv/ *adj* 1 having mutual or reciprocal relation; 2 corresponding; so related that one implies the other ‖ *n* 3 correlative thing or word

cor·re·spond /kôr'əspond', kor'-/ [ML *correspondere*] *vi* 1 to be similar, analogous, equal, in harmony, or in proportion; 2 to match, suit; 3 to communicate by letter; to keep up an exchange of letters ‖ **cor're·spond'ing** *adj*

cor're·spond'ence *n* 1 harmony; similarity; 2 communication by letters; 3 letters written and/or received

cor're·spond'ent *adj* 1 corresponding ‖ *n* 2 one with whom letters are exchanged; 3 person who writes for the press, esp. one covering a given area; 4 person or firm rendering services to another person or firm in another place

cor·ri·da /kərēd'ə/ [Sp] *n* bullfight

cor·ri·dor /kôr'idər, kor'-, -dôr'/ [MF < It *corridore*] *n* long hallway or passageway

cor·rob·o·rate /kərob'ərāt'/ [L *corroborare* (*-atus*) to strengthen] *vt* to confirm, make certain ‖ **cor·rob'o·ra'tion** *n* ‖ **cor·rob'o·ra'tive** /-rāt'ĭv, -rətĭv/ *adj* ‖ SYN confirm, establish, verify, ratify, strengthen

cor·rode /kərōd'/ [L *corrodere* to gnaw to pieces] *vt & vi* to eat away gradually; rust, consume ‖ **cor·ro'sion** /-zhən/ *n* ‖ **cor·ro'sive** /-sĭv/ *adj & n*

cor·ru·gate /kôr'əgāt', kor'-/ [L *corrugare* (*-atus*) to wrinkle] *vt & vi* to shape in alternate ridges and grooves; wrinkle ‖ **cor'ru·gat'ed** *adj* ‖ **cor'ru·ga'tion** *n*

cor·rupt /kərupt'/ [L *corruptus* destroyed] *adj* 1 putrid; 2 perverted; 3 (text) debased by errors or alterations; 4 crooked; open to bribery ‖ *vt* 5 to make corrupt ‖ *vi* 6 to become corrupt ‖ **cor·rupt'i·ble** *adj* ‖ **cor·rup'tion** *n* ‖ SYN *adj* adulterated, contaminated, vitiated, polluted, debased ‖ ANT *adj* pure, unspoiled, sound

cor·sage /kôrsäzh′/ [F] *n* small bouquet worn on a woman's dress

cor·sair /kôr′ser/ [MF *corsaire*] *n* 1 pirate; 2 pirate ship

cor·set /kôrs′it/ [OF] *n* 1 woman's undergarment laced to support or modify the shape of the figure ‖ *vt* 2 to enclose in a corset

Cor·si·ca /kôrs′ikə/ *n* island in the Mediterranean near Italy, a department of France (275,000; 3350 sq.m.; cap. Ajaccio) ‖ **Cor′si·can** *adj & n*

cor·tege /kôrtezh′/ [F < It *corteggio*] *n* 1 retinue; 2 ceremonial procession

Cor·tés also **Cor·tez,** **Her·nan·do** /ernän′dō kôrtez′/ *n* (1485–1547) Spanish conqueror of Mexico 1519

cor·tex /kôr′teks/ [L = bark] *n* (**-ti·ces** /-tisēz′/) 1 *bot* bark; rind; 2 *anat* a outer layers of an organ, as of the kidneys; **b** outer layer of gray matter of the brain, containing the higher nervous centers ‖ **cor′ti·cal** *adj*

cor·ti·sone /kôrt′isōn′, -zōn′/ [< *cortex*] *n* hormone —$C_{21}H_{28}O_5$— obtained from the adrenal glands of animals or made synthetically, used in the treatment of arthritis and rheumatic fever

co·run·dum /kərun′dəm/ [Tamil *kurundam*] *n* native aluminum oxide —Al_2O_3— noted for hardness, used as an abrasive, with transparent varieties occurring as gems

cor·us·cate /kôr′əskāt/, kor′-/ [L *coruscare (-atus)*] *vi* to sparkle, flash, gleam ‖ **cor′us·ca′tion** *n*

cor·vette /kôrvet′/ [MF < Sp *corbeta*] *n* small fast warship: **a** formerly, sailing ship with one tier of guns; **b** now, escort vessel smaller than a destroyer

cos cosine

cos. 1 companies; 2 counties

cosec cosecant

co·se·cant /kōsēk′ant, -sēk′ənt/ *n* *trig* ratio of the hypotenuse of a right triangle to the side opposite a given angle

co·sine /kō′sīn/ *n* *trig* ratio of the side adjacent to a given angle of a right triangle to the hypotenuse

cos·met·ic /kozmet′ik/ [Gk *kosmein* to adorn] *adj* 1 beautifying, esp. the face ‖ *n* 2 preparation designed to beautify

cos·mic /koz′mik/ [< Gk *kosmos* world] *adj* 1 of or pert. to the cosmos; 2 vast

cos′mic rays *npl* radiation of great penetrating power coming from outer space

cos·mog·o·ny /kozmog′ənē/ [Gk *kosmogonia* creation of the world] *n* (**-nies**) theory of the creation of the universe or world

cos·mo·line /koz′məlēn′/ [< *cosmetic*] *n* heavy grease used to protect weapons when stored

cos·mol·o·gy /-mol′əjē/ *n* theory or philosophy dealing with the structure and evolution of the universe

cos·mo·naut /koz′mənôt′/ [< Gk *kosmos* world + Gk *nautes* sailor] *n* astronaut, esp. a Russian one

cos·mo·pol·i·tan /-məpol′itən/ [< Gk *kosmos* world + *polites* citizen] *n* 1 one who or that which is equally at home everywhere in the world; 2 one free of parochialism ‖ also *adj*

cos·mop·o·lite /-mop′əlīt′/ *n* cosmopolitan person

cos·mos /koz′mos, -mōs, -məs/ [Gk = ordered universe] *n* 1 the universe as a manifestation of order; 2 any orderly whole developed from complex parts; 3 any of a genus (*Cosmos*) of plants of the composite family, with variously colored and showy flowers

Cos·sack /kos′ak, -ək/ [Russ *kazak* < Turk] *n* one of a tribe of S Russia, skilled as horsemen and often serving as cavalry

cost /kôst/, kost′/ [MF *coster* < L *constare* to tally] *vt* 1 to require the payment of; 2 to occasion the loss or expenditure of ‖ *n* 3 charge, price, 4 expenditure, outlay; 5 **costs** *pl* expenses of a lawsuit; 6 **at all costs** or **at any cost** regardless of cost

Cos·ta Ri·ca /kos′tə rēk′ə/ *n* Spanish-speaking republic in Central America (1,598,000; 19,600 sq.m.; cap. San José) ‖ **Cos′ta Ri′can** *adj & n*

cost′ly *adj* (**-li·er; -li·est**) expensive ‖ **cost′li·ness** *n* ‖ SYN valuable, expensive, gorgeous (see *dear*)

cost′-plus′ *n* method of arriving at the cost of government contracts based on the actual cost plus an agreed percentage of profit

cos·tume /kos′t(y)ōōm/ [F < It] *n* 1 dress of a given time, period, class, etc.; 2 complete set of garments, esp. those of a woman; ensemble; 3 historical dress, as worn in a play ‖ /kost(y)ōōm′/ *vt* 4 to provide with appropriate garments

cos′tume jew′el·ry *n* inexpensive jewelry made with nonprecious metals and imitation or semiprecious stones

co·sy /kōz′ē/ *adj & n* var of cozy

cot /kot′/ [Hindi *khāt* bedstead] *n* small portable bed, esp. one made of canvas

co·tan·gent /kōtan′jənt, kō′tan′-/ *n* *trig* in a right triangle, ratio of the side adjacent to a given angle to the side opposite that angle

cote /kōt′/ [OF] *n* shelter, as for sheep or pigeons

co·te·rie /kōt′ərē/ [MF = association of tenants] *n* clique; social set ‖ SYN club, clique, set, circle (see *caste*)

co·til·lion /kōtil′yən/ [F = petticoat] *n* 1 any of various lively French dances; quadrille; 2 formal ball for debs

cot·tage /kot′ij/ [ME *cotage*] *n* small

unpretentious house, usu. of one story

cot′tage cheese′ n soft white cheese made from the curds of sour milk

cot·ter /kot′ər/ [ME cotere] n Scot tenant farmer

cot′ter pin′ [?] n split pin kept in place by bending its ends outward

cot·ton /kot′ən/ [MF < OIt cotone < Ar qutun] n 1 soft, white, fibrous woollike substance surrounding the seeds of certain plants of the mallow family; 2 the plant (genus Gossypium); 3 thread or cloth made of cotton ‖ vi 4 **cotton to** colloq a to become fond of; b to agree with

cot′ton can′dy n cottony confection made of spun sugar

cot′ton gin′ n machine for separating cotton from the seeds

cot′ton·mouth′ n venomous snake (Ancistrodon piscivorus) found in the swamps of the SE United States

cot′ton-pick′in′ /-pik′ən/ adj slang damned, no-good

cot′ton·seed′ n seed of the cotton plant

cot′ton-seed oil′ n oil pressed from cottonseed, used in making soap, salad oil, lubricants, laxatives, and cosmetics

cot′ton·tail′ n any of several fluffy-tailed North American rabbits of the genus Sylvilagus

cot′ton·wood′ n any of several American poplars having a cottony tuft about the seeds

cot′ton wool′ n unprocessed raw cotton

cot′ton·y adj 1 like cotton; soft, fluffy; 2 covered with hair or nap; woolly

cot·y·le·don /kot′əlēd′ən/ [Gk = cupshaped] n rudimentary leaf of the embryo of seed plants

couch /kouch′/ [MF coucher to lie down] n 1 sofa ‖ vt 2 to lay as upon a couch; deposit; 3 to put into words

cou·gar /kōōg′ər/ [F couguar < Guarani cuguacu ara] n large tawny American cat (Felis concolor); puma, mountain lion

cough /kôf′, kof′/ [ME coghen] vi 1 to expel air violently from the lungs ‖ vt 2 **cough up,** a to expel by coughing; b slang to give reluctantly

could /kōōd′, kəd/ [< OE cūthe, pt of cunnan to know how] v (pt of **can**) modal aux used to express: 1 permission in the present, as could I come in?; 2 ability in the past, as I could not come yesterday; b in the conditional, as I could see you tomorrow

could·n't /kōōd′ənt/ could not

cou·lomb /kōō′lom, kōōlom′/ [Charles A. de Coulomb (1736–1806) F physicist] n mks unit of measurement of electricity, being the charge conveyed by one ampere in one second

coun·cil /kouns′əl/ [OF concile < L concilium assembly] n 1 assembly for consultation; 2 municipal or

other legislative body; 3 eccl assembly convened to consider important matters, as of doctrine

coun′cil·man /-mən/ n (-men /-mən/) n member of a city council

coun′cil of min′is·ters n cabinet of a prime minister

coun′cil·or or **coun′cil·lor** /-lər/ n member of a council

coun·sel /kouns′əl/ [OF conseil < L consilium advice] n 1 interchange of opinion; consultation; 2 advice; 3 purpose, plan; 4 **counsel** sg or pl one or more legal advisers, esp. in a particular case ‖ v (-seled or -selled; -sel·ing or -sel·ling) vt 5 to give advice to; 6 to recommend, as a course or plan ‖ vi 7 a to give advice; b to take advice ‖ SYN n admonition, warning, suggestion, caution; v instruct, caution, warn (see advise)

coun·se·lor or **coun·sel·lor** /-lər/ n 1 adviser; 2 supervisor at a children's camp; 3 lawyer; 4 embassy official

coun·se·lor-at-law n (counselors-at-law) lawyer, esp. trial lawyer

count¹ /kount′/ [MF conter < L computare] vt 1 to tell off (units) successively in order to find their number; sum up; enumerate; 2 to esteem, consider to be; 3 to include in an enumeration; 4 **count out** to declare (a boxer) defeated by counting ten seconds before he can get up from the floor ‖ vi 5 to tell off articles or numbers in order; 6 to be of worth or importance; 7 to have effect; 8 to be included in a counting; 9 **count off** to count aloud in rotation; 10 **count on** to rely on ‖ n 11 act of counting; 12 the total ascertained; 13 law statement of a separate cause of action; 14 **the count** ten-second period told off by a referee over a fallen boxer, signifying his defeat ‖ **count′a·ble** adj

count² [MF conte < L comes (-itis)] companion (of the king)] n nobleman of a rank equivalent to that of a British earl

count′down′ n audible descending count in constant units of time to zero, the precise time of firing a missile or explosive

coun·te·nance /kount′ənəns/ [OF contenance bearing] n 1 face or features; 2 facial expression; appearance; 3 support or approval; 4 composure ‖ vt 5 to tolerate, permit

count′er¹ [MF comptoir] n 1 that which keeps count, esp. a piece, as of metal, used to keep score in games; 2 table or display case for serving customers in a shop; 3 long narrow table in a restaurant, on one side of which are stools or chairs for patrons

coun·ter² [MF contre < L contra against] adj 1 contrary, opposite ‖ adv 2 in an opposite direction or manner ‖ *n* 3 opposite or contrary; 4 blow delivered in response to that of an opponent ‖ *vi* 5 to make a counter move; 6 to return a blow ‖ *vt* 7 to return (a blow) by another blow; 8 to combat, oppose, controvert

coun·ter- *comb form* counter²

coun'ter·act' *vt* to act in opposition to, neutralize ‖ **coun'ter·ac'tion** *n* ‖ SYN neutralize ‖ DISCR To *neutralize* is to render ineffective by opposite force or effect; to *counteract* is often to undo something already accomplished. In other words, by bringing together two things which *neutralize* each other, we prevent action. Thus, the addition of an alkali to an acid solution *neutralizes* the acid, and renders it inoperative. Or, a man who receives two successive opposite commands is brought to a standstill: one command has *neutralized* the other. To *counteract*, on the other hand, is to apply a contrary action to an effect which has already taken place

coun'ter·bal'ance *n* 1 opposed equal force; counterpoise ‖ **coun'ter·bal'ance** *vt* 2 to oppose by an equal force; offset

coun'ter·clock'wise' *adj & adv* in the direction opposite to the motion of the hands of a clock

coun'ter·cul'ture *n* movement hostile to the cultural norms of western civilization

coun'ter·feit /-fit/ [MF *contrefet* imitated] *vt* 1 to copy or imitate with intent to deceive or defraud, as money, virtues, etc. ‖ *vi* 2 to dissemble; 3 to make counterfeits, as of money ‖ *n* 4 imitation made with intent to deceive; forger ‖ also *adj* ‖ **coun'ter·feit'er** *n* ‖ SYN *adj* bogus, fictitious, false, sham (see *artificial*); *v* forge ‖ DISCR To *counterfeit* is to make imitations of coins, medals, bank bills, or the like, with intent to defraud. To *forge* is to change falsely a written or printed document, or to append a false signature to such a document, or to a check, note, etc.

coun'ter·foil' *n* part attached to a document, as a check, on which a memorandum of its contents may be retained; stub

coun'ter·ir'ri·tant *n med* agent used to inflame the surface in order to relieve a deep-seated inflammation

count'er·man' /-man/ *n* (-men /-men'/) man who serves food, sells automobile parts, etc., over a counter

coun'ter·mand' /-mand', -mänd/ [< L *mandare* to command] *vt* 1 to cancel (a command); 2 to reverse the orders of

coun'ter·pane' [alter. of ME *countrepointe* quilt] *n* bedspread

coun'ter·part' *n* 1 duplicate; 2 person or thing exactly or very nearly like another; 3 thing which forms the natural complement to another thing ‖ SYN facsimile, copy, complement (see *duplicate*)

coun'ter·point' [< LL *contrapunctum* pricked opposite (to original tune)] *n* 1 art of combining two or more melodies in a harmonic relationship; 2 art of writing part music

coun'ter·poise' *n* 1 counterbalancing force or weight; 2 condition of equilibrium or balance ‖ *vt* 3 to counterbalance; 4 to bring into equilibrium

Coun'ter Ref·or·ma'tion *n* reform movement within the Roman Catholic Church that followed the Protestant Reformation in the 16th century

coun'ter·rev'o·lu'tion *n* 1 political movement that resists revolutionary tendencies; 2 rebellion against a government itself established by a previous revolution ‖ **coun'ter·rev'o·lu'tion·ar'y** *adj & n* (-ies)

coun'ter·sign' *vt* 1 to confirm by signing (a document already signed by another) ‖ *n* 2 additional signature for authentication; 3 secret signal that must be given to enter a restricted area; 4 sign given in answer to another sign ‖ **coun'ter·sig'na·ture** *n*

coun'ter·sink *v* (-sunk) *vt* 1 to enlarge the top of (a hole) to receive the head of a screw or bolt so that it will lie flush with the surface; 2 to place (a screw or bolt) in such a hole ‖ *n* 3 tool for countersinking; 4 countersunk hole

count'ess *n* 1 wife or widow of an earl or count; 2 woman having the title of earl or count in her own right

count'less *adj* too many to count; innumerable

count' noun' *n gram* noun that typically refers to countable things and in English may take an indefinite article or a plural ending

coun·tri·fied also **coun·try·fied** /kunt'rifid/ *adj* rural; rustic in manners or appearance

coun·try /kunt're/ [OF *cuntree* < LL *contrata* land opposite] *n* (-tries) 1 tract of land; district, region; 2 rural parts, as opposed to cities and towns; 3 land of one's birth or citizenship; 4 territory of a nation; 5 people of a region or nation; public ‖ *adj* 6 pert to rural regions

coun'try club' *n* club with clubhouse and extensive grounds, featuring sports, esp. golf, and social activities

coun'try cous'in *n* naive person from the country

coun'try·man /-mən/ *n* (-men /-mən/) 1 one who lives in the country; 2 native or inhabitant of one's own country

coun·try·side /n 1 rural area; 2 its inhabitants

coun·ty /kount'ḗ/ [OF *conte* < LL *comitatus* office of a count] *n* (**-ties**) 1 administrative division of a state; 2 one of the chief administrative divisions of Great Britain and Ireland; 3 inhabitants of a county

coun'ty seat' *n* town where a county's government is centered

coup /kōō'/ [F = stroke] *n* (**coups** /kōōz'/) master stroke of strategy; brilliant accomplishment

coup' de grâce' /dǝgräs'/ [F = stroke of mercy] *n* (**coups de grâce** /same as *sg*/) 1 death blow or shot, spec. one delivered to end the suffering of a condemned person who has been shot but who is not yet dead; 2 any decisive stroke

coup' d'é·tat' /dätä'/ [F = stroke of state] *n* (**coups d'état** or **coup d'états** /-täz'/) sudden overthrow of a government by force

coupe /kōōp'/ also **cou·pé** /kōōpā'/ [F, *pp* of *couper* to cut] *n* two-door closed automobile with a body shorter than a sedan

cou·ple /kup'ǝl/ [OF *cople* < *copula* link] *n* 1 pair; 2 man and woman paired together as a married or engaged pair, partners in a dance, etc. 3 *mech* pair of equal forces acting in parallel but opposite directions, tending to produce rotation; 4, **a couple** *colloq* a small number (of items) || *vt* 5 to link or tie together || *vi* 6 to form in pairs

cou'plet /-lit/ [MF] *n* two successive lines of verse which rhyme

cou'pling *n* 1 device for joining parts, as drive shafts, lengths of pipe, hose, etc.; 2 device for hooking railroad cars together

cou·pon /k(y)ōō'pon/ [F = piece cut off] *n* 1 certificate, either separately printed or detachable, as from an advertisement, to be used to order something or entitling the holder to a discount or gift; 2 interest-bearing certificate on a bond

cour·age /kur'ij/ [OF *corage* < *cuer* heart] *n* bravery; quality of spirit which faces danger without flinching || SYN intrepidity, fortitude, valor (see *bravery*)

cou·ra·geous /kǝrāj'ǝs/ *adj* having or characterized by courage || **cou·ra'·geous·ly** *adv* || SYN daring, valiant, intrepid, gallant, fearless, dauntless || ANT afraid, timid, cowardly, spineless

cour·gette /kōōrzhet'/ [F] *n Brit* zucchini

cou·ri·er /kōōr'ē·ǝr, kur'-/ [OF *courrier* < Olt *correre*] *n* 1 messenger, esp one bearing urgent or confidential news or dispatches; 2 traveling attendant who arranges all the details of a journey

course /kôrs', kōrs'/ [OF *cours* < L *cursus*] *n* 1 onward movement; progress; 2 direction taken; 3 way, path; channel; 4 succession or series; 5 method of procedure; line of conduct; 6 the portion of a meal served at one time; 7 prescribed program of instruction in a given subject; 8 route followed by a vessel or aircraft; 9 golf course; 10 **in due course** in the usual order of events; 11 **of course, a** naturally; **b** certainly || *vi* 12 to run, race

cours'er *n poet.* swift horse

court /kôrt', kōrt'/ [OF < L *cohors* (-*hortis*) courtyard] *n* 1 open space surrounded by buildings and/or walls; 2 short street; 3 royal palace; 4 a sovereign and his ministers considered as a ruling power; 5 sovereign and his retinue; 6 official assembly held by a sovereign; 7 level space or playing area for certain games, as tennis; 8 place where accused persons are tried by law; 9 a judge or judges engaged in administering justice in a regular session of the tribunal; **b** the session itself; 10 attention paid to win favor, as of a woman || *vt* 11 to woo; 12 to flatter; 13 to solicit as favors; 14 to seek to attract; 15 to invite || *vi* 16 to woo

cour·te·ous /kurt'ē·ǝs/ [OF *corteis*] *adj* courtly, polite || **cour'te·ous·ly** *adv* || SYN civil, well-bred, kind, considerate (see *polite*)

cour·te·san /kôrt'izǝn, kurt'-/ [MF *courtisane* < It *cortigiana* lady of the court] *n* prostitute, esp. one having a clientele of noblemen or men of rank

cour·te·sy /kurt'isē/ [OF *corteisie] *n* (**-sies**) 1 courteous behavior; 2 courteous act or expression; 3 favor || SYN affability, urbanity, considerateness; civility

court'house' *n* (**-hous·es** /-ziz/) 1 building which houses courts of law, and often the administrative offices of a county; 2 county seat

court·i·er /kôrt'ē·ǝr, kōrt'-/ *n* 1 one who is attached to a royal court; 2 one who solicits favors; flatterer

court'ly *adj* (**-li·er; -li·est**) 1 of or pert. to a royal court; 2 polished, elegant, as of manners || **court'li·ness** *n* || SYN polite, elegant, polished, gracious, courteous

court'ly love' *n* code of stylized conduct in the love of married ladies and their knightly lovers, which yielded an important theme in medieval and Renaissance literature

court'-mar'tial *n* (**courts-martial**) 1 military court for the trial of offenses against military law; 2 trial by court-martial || *v* (**-tialed** or **-tialled; -tial·ing** or **-tial·ling**) *vt* 3 to try by court-martial

court′ of com′mon pleas′ *n* in some states, court of general jurisdiction

Court′ of St. James′′s [*St. James's Palace* in London] *n* British royal court, to which foreign diplomats are accredited

court′ship *n* act or period of courting a woman

court′yard′ *n* open space surrounded by a building or buildings

cous·in /kuz′in/ [OF *cosin* < L *consobrinus* maternal cousin] *n* child of one's uncle or aunt

cou·tu·ri·er /kŏotŏor′ē·ā′, -ē·ər/ [F] *n* man who designs and makes fashionable clothes for woman ‖ **cou·tu·ri·ère** /-tŏor′ē·er′/ *nfem*

co·va′lence /kō-/ *n* 1 number of electron pairs that an atom can share with other atoms; 2 bond thus formed

cove kōv′/ [OE *cofa* cave] *n* 1 inlet; 2 sheltered nook; 3 concave surface in the angle between wall and ceiling

cov·e·nant /kuv′ənənt/ [OF < *covenir* to agree] *n* 1 compact, agreement; 2 promises of God as conditioned and set forth in the Bible ‖ *vt* 3 to pledge by covenant ‖ *vi* 4 to bind oneself by a covenant

cov·er /kuv′ər/ [OF *covrir* < L *cooperire* to hide] *vt* 1 to put something, as a lid, upon; 2 to conceal, screen; 3 to overspread, extend over; 4 to deal with, include; 5 to pass over, as a distance; 6 to point a gun at; 7 *sports* to watch or guard; 8 to protect, shelter; 9 to match (a bet); 10 to make good (a loss); 11 to be responsible for, as a job; 12 to be sufficient for, as costs; 13 to insure against loss; 14 *journalism* to be present at (a newsworthy event); 15 **cover up** to conceal, as wrongdoing ‖ *vi* 16 to spread over a surface; 17 to act as substitute during someone's absence; 18 to conceal wrongdoing ‖ *n* 19 protection; shelter; 20 table setting for one person; 21 disguise, pretense; 22 anything that covers; 23 cover charge; 24 outside binding of a book; 25 front sheet of a magazine; 26 envelope or wrapper for mail; 27 **take cover** to seek shelter; 28 **under cover, a** secretly; **b** sealed in an envelope; **c** concealed ‖ SYN *v* hide, screen, shield, protect, disguise, cloak

cov′er·age /-ij/ *n* amount or extent covered, as of insurance, broadcasting, newspaper circulation, or news reporting

cov′er·all′ *n* often **coveralls** *pl* loose-fitting work garment worn over other clothing

cov′er charge′ *n* additional fee for entertainment in a restaurant, nightclub, etc.

cov′ered wag′on *n* large wagon with a canvas cover stretched over hoops, used by American pioneers in the 19th century

cov′er girl′ *n* beautiful model whose picture appears on magazine covers

cov′er·let /-lit/ [*cover* + OF *lit* bed] *n* bedspread

cov·ert /kuv′ərt, kŏv′-/ [OF = covered] *adj* 1 concealed; covered; disguised ‖ *n* 2 place that shelters; 3 thicket; shelter for game ‖ **cov′ert·ly** *adv*

cov′er-up′ *n* act or instance of covering up or concealing

cov·et /kuv′it/ [OF *cuveitier* < L *cupidus* desirous] *vt & vi* to desire eagerly and often guiltily

cov′et·ous *adj* 1 very desirous, esp. of another's property; 2 grasping, avaricious ‖ **cov′et·ous·ly** *adv* ‖ **cov′et·ous·ness** *n* ‖ SYN greedy, grasping, craving (see *avaricious*)

cov·ey /kuv′ē/ [OF *covee* < *cover* to hatch] *n* 1 brood or small flock of birds, as of partridges; 2 company or bevy ‖ SYN brood, flock, bevy, company (see *herd*)

cow¹ /kou/ [OE cū] *n* 1 mature female of the ox family, domesticated for its milk; 2 female of various other mammals, as the whale, elephant, and seal

cow² [ON *kuga* to frighten into submission] *vt* to intimidate, make fearful

cow·ard /-ərd/ [OF *coart*] *n* one without courage, one easily frightened ‖ **cow′ard·ly** *adj & adv* ‖ SYN dastardly, craven, fearful, fainthearted (see *recreant*) ‖ ANT courageous, heroic, intrepid

cow′ard·ice /-is/ *n* want of courage; dishonorable fear ‖ SYN pusillanimity, timidity, poltroonery, baseness ‖ ANT bravery, intrepidity, courage, valor

cow′bird′ *n* American blackbird (*Molothrus ater*), often found with cattle, that lays its eggs in the nests of smaller birds

cow′boy′ *n* 1 mounted employee of a ranch who herds and tends cattle; 2 *slang* reckless driver

cow′catch′er *n* wedge-shaped frame or bumper on the front of a locomotive or streetcar

cow·er /kou′ər/ [ME *couren* < Scand] *vi* to crouch down from fear or shame; quail

cow′ hand′ *n* cowboy 1

cow′herd′ *n* one who tends cattle at pasture

cow′hide′ *n* 1 skin of a cow; 2 braided leather whip ‖ *vt* 3 to whip with a cowhide

cowl /koul/ [OE *cugele* < L *cucullus* hood] *n* 1 **a** a monk's hood; **b** garment with such a hood attached; 2 hood-shaped covering; 3 the part of an automobile body just in front of the windshield; 4 cowling

cow′lick′ *n* tuft of hair, often above

the forehead, that is difficult to comb or control

cowl′ing *n* streamlined cover for an airplane engine

co′-work′er /kŏ′/ *n* fellow worker

cow′pox′ *n* contagious disease of cows, the virus of which is used in vaccination

cow′punch′er *n* cowboy 1

cow′slip′ [OE *cūslyppe* cow dung] *n* 1 English primrose (*Primula officinalis*); 2 marsh marigold

cox′comb′ /koks′-/ [< *cock's comb*] *n* fop; conceited, vain fellow

cox·swain /koks′in, -swān′/ [< *archaic cock* boat] *n* one who steers or has charge of a boat or of a racing shell

coy /koi′/ [MF coi < L *quietus* quiet] *adj* 1 shrinking from notice, shy; 2 simulating shyness ‖ **coy′ly** *adv* ‖ **coy′ness** *n* ‖ SYN modest, bashful, shrinking (see *diffident*)

coy·ote /ki′ōt, ki·ōt′ē/ [Sp < Nahuatl] *n* wolflike mammal (*Canis latrans*) of W North America

coy′pu /koi′pōō/ [Sp *coipú* < Araucan] *n* (-**pu** or -**pus**) large aquatic rodent (*Myocastor coypus*) of South America, yielding the fur nutria

coz·en /kuz′ín/ [?] *vt & vi* to beguile, cheat

co·zy /kōz′ē/ [prob < Scand] *adj* (-**zi·er; -zi·est**) 1 comfortable, snug ‖ *n* (-**zies**) 2 padded covering, as for a teapot that is to be kept warm ‖ **co′zi·ly** *adv* ‖ **co′zi·ness** *n*

C.P.A. Certified Public Accountant

Cpl. Corporal

C.P.O. Chief Petty Officer

CQ radio signal sent by a ham inviting others to reply

Cr *chem* chromium

crab /krab′/ [OE *crabba*] *n* 1 any of several crustaceans (suborder Brachyura) having a broad, flattened body, ten legs, and the abdomen curled under the body; 2 grouchy person; 3 crab louse; 4 **Crab** *astron* Cancer ‖ *v* (**crabbed; crab·bing**) *vi* 5 to fish for crabs; 6 to find fault, complain

crab′ ap′ple *n* 1 tree bearing small sour apples; 2 its fruit

crab·bed /krab′id/ *adj* 1 crabby; 2 cramped or difficult to read, as writing

crab′by *adj* (-**bi·er; -bi·est**) grouchy, peevish ‖ SYN churlish, ill-tempered, sour, cross-grained

crab′ grass′ *n* any of various coarse grasses that occur as weeds in lawns

crab′ louse′ *n* louse (*Phthirus pubis*) infesting the pubic hair

crack /krak′/ [OE *cracian* to resound] *vi* 1 to make a sharp snapping noise; 2 to break up short without dividing into parts; 3 to break with a rasping noise, as the voice; 4 to fail under pressure, as *he cracked under the strain;* 5 **crack down** *colloq* to take stern measures; 6 **crack down on** to

become strict with; 7 **crack up**, a *colloq* to crash, as in an automobile or airplane; b *slang* to break down emotionally or mentally; 8 **crack wise** *slang* to wisecrack; 9 **get cracking** *slang to* begin, get going ‖ *vt* 10 to cause to make a snapping sound; 11 to break without separating completely; 12 to burst, cause to split open, as a nut; 13 to open for drinking, as a bottle of wine; 14 to tell (a joke); 15 to utter or observe sententiously; 16 to decompose, as petroleum, by heat or pressure; 17 *colloq* to break open (a safe); 18 *colloq* to solve; 19 **crack a book** *slang* to open a book for study; 20 **crack a smile** *slang* to break into a smile; 21 **crack up** *colloq* a to wreck, as an automobile; b to extol, praise highly ‖ *n* 22 sudden snapping noise, report; 23 break, split; 24 crevice, chink; 25 sharp blow; 26 break in the voice; 27 *slang* try; 28 *slang* joke ‖ *adj* 29 *colloq* first-rate, excellent ‖ SYN *v* split, snap, burst, crush (see *break*)

crack′brained′ *adj* crazy, senseless

crack′down′ *n* act or instance of cracking down, of rigidly enforcing regulations

cracked′ *adj colloq* 1 eccentric; 2 insane

crack′er *n* 1 thin brittle biscuit; 2 firecracker; 3 *disparaging* ignorant and backward inhabitant of mountainous and rural areas of the Southeast

crack′er·jack′ *n colloq* person or thing exhibiting marked excellence

crack·le /krak′əl/ [< *crack*] *vi* 1 to make slight, repeated snapping noises, as a fire ‖ *n* 2 crackling noise; 3 lacework of fine cracklike lines, as in the glaze of certain kinds of porcelain

crack′pot′ *n colloq* extremely eccentric or fanatic person

crack′-up′ *n* 1 crash; 2 collapse; 3 *colloq* mental breakdown

-c·ra·cy /-krəsē/ [Gk -*kratia*] *comb form* rule, government

cra·dle /krād′əl/ [OE *cradol*] *n* 1 bed for an infant, usu. on rockers; 2 period or state of infancy; 3 birthplace; origin; 4 any of various cradlelike structures or frames in which things to be constructed or repaired are held in place; 5 part of telephone that holds the handset ‖ *vt* 6 to place or rock in or as in a cradle; 7 to nurse; shelter or protect; 8 to place in a cradle or frame

cra·dle·song′ *n* lullaby

craft /kraft′, kräft′/ [OE *cræft* strength] *n* 1 artistic manual skill; 2 cunning, guile; 3 occupation requiring manual skill; 4 members of a skilled trade or profession collectively ‖ *n* 5 (*pl* **craft**) ship, vessel;

aircraft || *vt* **6** to fashion with care || SYN art, dexterity, ingenuity, trade (see *business*)

crafts'man /-mən/ *n* (**-men** /-mən/) **1** artisan, skilled worker; **2** artist || **crafts'man·ship'** || SYN workman, artificer (see *artisan*)

craft' un'ion *n* labor union composed of workers in the same craft

craft'y *adj* (**-i·er; -i·est**) cunning, deceitful, tricky || **craft'i·ly** *adv* || **craft'i·ness** *n* || SYN cunning, shrewd, tricky, designing (see *wily*)

crag /krag/ [< Celt.] *n* steep projecting rock || **crag'gy** *adj* (**-gi·er; -gi·est**)

cram /kram/ [OE *crammian* to stuff] *v* (**crammed; cram·ming**) *vt* **1** to fill too full; force in, crowd in || *vi* **2** to study intensively, as for an exam

cramp /kramp/ [MF *crampe* < MD] *n* **1** painful spasmodic contraction of the muscles; **2** often **cramps** *pl* sharp abdominal pain || *vt* **3** to hinder in action or growth; confine, restrain

cran·ber·ry /kran'ber'ē, -b(ə)rē/ [LG *kraanbere*] *n* (**-ries**) **1** small red acid berry of certain shrubs (genus *Vaccinium*) of the heath family, growing in marshy land; **2** the shrub; **3** the North American species (*V. macrocarpon*)

crane /krān/ [OE *cran*] *n* **1** any of various tall wading birds (family Gruidae) with long necks, legs, and bills; **2** device for hoisting and carrying heavy weights by means of a swinging arm or a traveling horizontal beam || *vt* **3** to stretch (the neck) || *vi* **4** to stretch the neck

cra·ni·um /krān'ē·əm/ [ML < Gk *kranion*] *n* (**-ums** or **-a** /-ə/) skull, esp. the bones enclosing the brain || **cra'ni·al** *adj*

crank /krank/ [OE *cranc*] *n* **1** arm or lever connected to a shaft to impart rotation to it; **2** *colloq* **a** ill-tempered person; **b** eccentric person pursuing one idea or cause || *vt* **3** to wind up or turn with or as with a crank; **4** to start by cranking || *vi* to turn a crank

crank'case' *n* housing enclosing a crankshaft

crank'shaft' *n* shaft turning or turned by one or more cranks

crank'y *adj* (**-i·er; -i·est**) **1** grouchy, irritable; **2** eccentric

cran·ny /kran'ē/ [< MF *cran*] *n* (**-nies**) chink, crevice, fissure || **cran'nied** *adj*

crap[1] /krap/ [< *craps*] *n* **1** losing initial throw in craps || *vi* **2** **crap out** to lose the dice and the bet by rolling a seven

crap[2] [ME *crappe* chaff] *n* **1** nonsense; **2** rubbish; **3** *vulgar* excrement || *v* (**crapped; crap·ping**) *vi* **4** *vulgar* to defecate

crape /krāp/ [F *crêpe*] *n* **1** crepe; **2** band of black crepe used as a sign of mourning

craps /kraps/ [LaF < Eng *crabs* double-ace in a gambling game] *nsg* **1** gambling game played with two dice; **2** **shoot craps** to play craps || **crap'shoot'er** *n*

crap·u·lent /krap'yələnt/ [LL *crapulentus* drunk] *adj* sick from excessive drinking and eating || **crap'u·lence** *n* || **crap'u·lous** *adj*

crash[1] /krash/ [ME *crasche*] *vi* **1** to shatter noisily and violently; dash into pieces; **2** to attend uninvited or without paying || *vt* **3** to make a loud noise, as of thunder or breakage; **4** to break or fall with a crash; **5** to collide with a crash || *n* **6** a shattering; **7** collision or crashing; **8** sound caused by violent breakage, thunder, a burst of music, or the like; **9** sudden collapse, as of a business or prices on the stock market

crash[2] [Russ] *n* **1** coarse fabric used for towels, curtains, and dresses; **2** starched fabric used to reinforce bound books

crash' dive' *n* rapid emergency dive of a submarine to evade enemy action || **crash'-dive'** *vt* & *vi*

crash' hel'met *n* padded helmet worn to protect the head in crashes of vehicles

crash'-land' *vt* to land (an airplane) in an emergency under other than normal conditions, resulting in damage to the plane || also *vi* || **crash'-land'ing** *n*

crash' pro'gram *n* plan to carry out a project without regard to cost

crass /kras/ [L *crassus* thick] *adj* grossly stupid

-crat /-krat/ [< Gk *kratos* rule] *n comb form* **1** advocate of a particular form of rule; **2** member of a particular class || **-crat'ic** *adj comb form*

crate /krāt/ [L *cratis* wickerwork] *n* **1** box, usu. of slats, for containing and transporting goods; **2** old, decrepit car || *vt* **3** to pack in a crate

cra·ter /krāt'ər/ [Gk = mixing bowl] *n* **1** cup-shaped cavity forming the mouth of a volcano; **2** any similarly shaped opening in the ground, as those caused by the impact of meteorites, bombs, etc.

cra·vat /krəvat'/ [F *cravate* orig. *Croatian* (neckpiece)] *n* necktie

crave /krāv/ [OE *crafian* to ask] *vt* **1** to beg or ask for; **2** to long for

cra·ven /krāv'ən/ [ME *cravant*] *adj* **1** cowardly || *n* **2** abject coward || SYN *adj* spiritless, pusillanimous, dastardly, base (see *recreant*) || ANT *adj* brave, courageous, fearless

crav'ing [< *crave*] *n* intense longing or desire

craw /krô/ [ME *crawe*] *n* **1** crop of a bird or insect; **2** animal's stomach

craw'fish' *n* var of **crayfish**

crawl /krôl'/ [ON *krafla*] *vi* 1 to move by dragging the body along the ground; 2 to move on the hands and knees, creep; 3 to move very slowly; 4 to be, or feel as if, swarming with crawling things ‖ *n* 5 act or motion of crawling; 6 overhand swimming stroke

crawl' space' *n* area between floors or below a roof, with low overhead clearance, used for access or storage

cray'fish' /krǎ'-/ [< MF *crevice*] *n* (**-fish** or **-fishes**) 1 fresh-water crustacean (genera *Astacus* and *Cambarus*) resembling but smaller than a lobster; 2 similar marine crustacean with a spiny shell and no pincers

cray-on /krā'ən, -on/ [F < L *creta* chalk] *n* 1 stick or pencil of chalk, clay, or wax, used for drawing; 2 drawing made with crayons

craze /krāz'/ [ME *crasen* to break < Scand] *vt* 1 to drive insane ‖ *vi* 2 to become insane ‖ *n* 3 fad

cra·zy *adj* (**·zi·er, ·zi·est**) 1 insane; 2 unsound, senseless; 3 *colloq* **a** greatly desirous; **b** enthusiastic; 4 bizarre ‖ **cra'zi·ly** *adv* ‖ **cra'zi·ness** *n* ‖ SYN mad, raving, insane, cracked, distracted

cra'zy bone' *n* funny bone

cra'zy quilt' *n* 1 patchwork quilt with no regular pattern; 2 any irregular patchwork

creak /krēk'/ [ME *creken* to croak] *vi* 1 to make scraping, squeaking sounds ‖ *n* 2 creaking sound ‖ **creak'y** *adj* (**-i·er, -i·est**)

cream /krēm'/ [MF *creme* < Gk *chrisma* oil for anointing] *n* 1 rich, oily part of milk which gathers at the top; 2 best part of anything; 3 creamlike preparation used as a cosmetic; 4 soup made with cream or milk; 5 light-yellow color ‖ *vt* 6 to put cream into; 7 to beat together so as to form a smooth mixture; 8 to rub cosmetic cream on; 9 *slang* to defeat badly ‖ **cream'y** *adj* (**-i·er, -i·est**)

cream' cheese' *n* soft white cheese made of milk or cream

cream'er *n* small pitcher for cream

cream'er·y *n* (**-ies**) place where dairy products are produced

cream' of tar'tar *n* white crystalline powder —KHC₄H₄O₆— used in baking powder

cream' puff' *n* 1 hollow pastry shell filled with custard or whipped cream; 2 *slang* used car in very good condition

crease /krēs'/ [prob ME *creeste* crest] *n* 1 mark, line, or wrinkle left by a fold; 2 fold, wrinkle ‖ *vt* 3 to make a crease in ‖ *vi* 4 to become creased

cre·ate /krē·āt'/ [L *creare* (*-atus*)] *vt* 1 to bring into or cause to come into existence; make; originate; 2 to cause, give rise to; 3 to invest with a new rank or function

cre·a'tion *n* 1 act of creating; 2 that which has been created; 3 universe

cre·a'tive *adj* 1 having the power to create; 2 productive ‖ **cre'a·tiv'i·ty** *n*

cre·a'tor *n* one who creates; 2 **Creator** God

crea·ture /krēch'ər/ *n* 1 anything created; 2 living being; 3 one who is the tool or agent of another

crea'ture com'forts *npl* things, as food and warmth, that promote physical comfort

crèche /kresh', krāsh'/ [F = crib] *n* representation of the Nativity scene in the stable at Bethlehem

cre·dence /krēd'əns/ [ML *credentia*] *n* belief as to the truth of something

cre·den·tials /krɪdensh'əlz/ *npl* 1 that which bears testimony to one's claims or authority; 2 document proving one's right to authority or privileges

cre·den·za /krɪden'zə/ [It] *n* sideboard, esp. one without legs

cred'i·bil'i·ty /-bil'-/ *n* quality of being credible or believable

cred'i·bil'i·ty gap' *n* vast disparity between promise and performance

cred·i·ble /kred'ɪbəl/ *adj* believable; worthy of belief ‖ **cred'i·bly** *adv*

cred·it /kred'ɪt/ [MF < OIt *credito*] *n* 1 belief; trust; confidence; 2 trustworthiness; 3 character, good reputation; 4 commendation or praise; 5 source of commendation or honor; 6 acknowledgement of authorship or responsibility for something; 7 unit of school study; 8 trust in a person's ability to pay; 9 rating of a person or firm based on reputation for paying debts and financial resources; 10 time allowed a customer to pay; 11 sum at a person's disposal or in his favor; 12 entry in an account showing payment by or obligation to a customer ‖ *vt* 13 to believe, trust; 14 to ascribe; 15 to give credit to; 16 to enter (a sum) in a customer's favor

cred'it·a·ble *adj* praiseworthy, reflecting honor or credit ‖ **cred'it·a·bly** *adv*

cred'it card' *n* card entitling a person to charge purchases or services

cred'it line' *n* 1 line of copy acknowledging the source or origin of printed matter, film, videotape, etc.; 2 limit of credit that a customer is authorized to use

cred'i·tor *n* one to whom money is owing

cre·do /krē'dō/ [L = I believe] *n* 1 creed; 2 **Apostle's** or **Nicene Creed**

cre·du·li·ty /krɪd(y)ōol'ɪtē/ ‖ [L *credulitas*] *n* (**-ties**) readiness to believe anything

cred·u·lous /krej'ələs/ *adj* 1 apt to

believe without sufficient basis; **2** easily imposed upon

Cree /krē'/ *n* American Indian of one of the Algonquian tribes related to the Ojibwas, surviving in Manitoba

creed /krēd'/ [OE *crēda* < *credo*] *n* **1** formally phrased confession of faith; **2** informal summing up of religious belief; **3** formula of belief in any field ‖ SYN belief, doctrine, faith, confession, summary

creek /krēk'/ [ME *creke*] *n* stream between a brook and a river in size

Creek /krēk'/ *n* one of a tribe of American Indians originally in Alabama and Georgia, now largely confined to Oklahoma

creel /krēl'/ [ME *crele*] *n* **1** wicker basket for fish; **2** wickerwork fish or lobster trap

creep /krēp'/ [OE *crēopan*] *v* (crept) *vi* **1** to move with the body close to the ground; crawl; **2** to move stealthily or imperceptibly; **3** to move slowly; **4** to grow along the ground or a wall, as a plant ‖ *n* **5** *slang* weird or eccentric person; **6** the **creeps** *pl colloq* sensation of horror or repugnance ‖ **creep'er** *n*

creep'ing *adj* **1** (plant) that trails over the ground; **2** developing by small, imperceptible steps

creep'y *adj* (-i·er; -i·est) having or causing a sensation of repugnance, as of something crawling over one's body

cre·mate /krimāt', krē'māt/ [L *cremare* (-*atus*)] *vt* **1** to reduce (a corpse) to ashes; **2** to burn ‖ **cre·ma'tion** *n*

cre·ma·to·ri·um /krēm'ətôr'ē-əm, krem'ətôr'-/ *n* (-ums or -a -/ə/) or **cre'ma·to'ry** *n* (-ries) establishment or furnace for cremating

crème de ca·ca·o /krem'dəkō'kō, krēm'-/ *n* liqueur flavored with cocoa and vanilla

crème de menthe' /-dəmint', -menth/ *n* liqueur flavored with mint

Cre·ole /krē'ōl/ [F < Sp *criollo*] *n* **1** person descended from French or Spanish ancestors, but born and raised in the New World; **2** in Louisiana, person of French ancestry; **3** French patois spoken in Haiti, also in Louisiana; **4** creolized language ‖ *adj* **5** of or pert. to Creoles

cre'o·lized' *adj* (language) that was once a pidgin but that has become the native language of a group of speakers

cre·o·sote /krē'əsōt'/ [< Gk *kreas* flesh + *soter* preserver] *n* heavy, yellowish, oily liquid with a pungent odor, obtained from wood tar, and used as an antiseptic and as a wood preservative

crepe or **crêpe** /krāp'/ [F < L *crispa* curled] *n* **1** thin fabric with a crin-

kled or wavy surface; **2** crape used for mourning; **3** crepe paper

crepe' pa'per *n* thin crinkled paper used for napkins and decorations ‖ **crepe'-pa'per** *adj*

crêpe' su·zette' /sōōzet'/ [F] *n* dessert consisting of a pancake heated in orange-flavored liqueur and served flaming in burning brandy

crept /krept'/ *pt* & *pp* of **creep**

cre·scen·do /krishen'dō, -sen'dō/ [It = growing] *n* **1** gradual increase in loudness, force, or volume; **2** *mus* crescendo passage ‖ *adj* & *adv* **3** gradually increasing in loudness, force, or volume

cres·cent /kres'ənt/ [L *crescens* (-*entis*) growing] *adj* **1** increasing; growing; **2** shaped like a crescent ‖ *n* **3** figure of the moon between new moon and first quarter and also between last quarter and the next new moon; **4** any crescent-shaped object; **5** a the emblem of Turkey or of Islam; **b** the Crescent Turkish or Moslem power

cress /kres'/ [OE *cresse*] *n* any of several small green plants of the mustard family, having crisp peppery leaves

crest /krest'/ [MF *creste* < L *crista*] *n* **1** comb or tuft on the head of a bird; **2** ornament or emblem on the top of a knight's helmet; **3** heraldic device worn above the escutcheon of a coat of arms; **4** top of anything, as the summit of a ridge, the top line of a wave, or the highest point of a flood ‖ *vi* **5** to take the form of a crest or ridge; **6** (of a river in a flood) to reach the high level beyond which it will rise no further ‖ **crest'ed** *adj*

crest'fall'en *adj* dejected

Cre·ta·ceous /kritāsh'əs/ [< L *creta* chalk] *geol* designating or pert. to a period of the Mesozoic era, characterized by the disappearance of dinosaurs and the appearance of flowering plants and insects

Crete /krēt'/ *n* Greek island in the E Mediterranean SE of Greece ‖ **Cre'tan** *adj* & *n*

cre·tin /krēt'ən/ [MF < *chretien* Christian] *n* person suffering from deformity, dwarfism, and idiocy due to thyroid deficiency ‖ **cre'tin·ism** *n*

cre·tonne /kriton', krē'ton/ [< F *Creton* village in Normandy] *n* unglazed cotton fabric with printed patterns, used for draperies and slip covers

cre·vasse /krəvas'/ [F] *n* **1** deep fissure, as in glacial ice; **2** breach in a levee

crev·ice /krev'is/ [OF *crevace* < LL *crepatia*] *n* crack, fissure, chink

crew /krōō'/ [MF *creue* increase] *n* **1** the men manning a ship, esp. the common sailors; **2** any body or gang of men working together; **3** company, throng; **4** team that mans a racing shell; **5** sport of racing with a racing shell

crew′ cut′ *n* haircut with the hair cropped short

crew′ neck′ *n* collarless neckline, as on a sweater

crib /krib′/ [OE] *n* 1 manger for feeding cattle; 2 child's bed with high railed sides; 3 bin for storing grain; 4 *colloq* plagiarism; 5 *colloq* translation or set of answers used by students to cheat; 6 *New Zealand* bach ‖ *v* (**cribbed; crib·bing**) *vt* 7 to confine; 8 to furnish with a crib; 9 *colloq* to plagiarize; 10 *colloq* to steal ‖ *vi* 11 *colloq* to cheat by using a translation or key; 12 *colloq* to steal

crib·bage /krib′ij/ [<*crib*] *n* card game, usu. for two people, scored by inserting pegs in a small board

crick /krik′/ [ME *crikke*] *n* painful cramp in the muscles of the neck or back

crick·et¹ /krik′it/ [MF *criquet* goal post] *n* 1 English game played on a large field with wickets, bats, and a ball, by eleven players on each side; 2 fair play

crick·et² [MF *criquet*] *n* any of several black insects of the family Grillidae, the male of which makes a chirping sound by rubbing his outer wings together

cri·er /krī′ər/ *n* one who publicly cries or proclaims an announcement

crime /krīm′/ [OF < L *crimen*] *n* 1 serious offense against morality; sin; 2 commission of an act in violation of the law; 3 *colloq* foolish or shameful act ‖ SYN sin, vice, iniquity, wrong, offense, misdemeanor, abomination, wickedness ‖ ANT virtue, sinlessness

Cri·me·a /krīmē′ə/ *n* peninsula in S Russia jutting into the Black Sea ‖ **Cri·me′an** *adj*

crim·i·nal /krim′inəl/ *adj* 1 pert. to, involving, guilty of, or of the character of a crime ‖ *n* 2 one guilty of a crime ‖ **crim′i·nal·ly** *adv* ‖ **crim′i·nal′i·ty** /-al′itē/ *n* ‖ SYN *adj* culpable, guilty, immoral, nefarious, iniquitous, wrong, blameworthy; *n* culprit, felon, convict, malefactor ‖ ANT *adj* innocent, virtuous

crim·i·nol·o·gy /-ol′əjē/ *n* investigation and study of crime and criminals ‖ **crim′i·nol′o·gist** *n*

crimp /krimp′/ [ME *crympen*] *vt* 1 to fold or press into pleats, corrugations, or flutings; make wavy; 2 to hinder, slow down ‖ *n* 3 act of crimping; 4 that which is crimped; 5 **put a crimp** in *slang* to hinder

crim·ple /krimp′əl/ [ME *crymple*] *vt* 1 to cause to wrinkle ‖ *vi* 2 to become wrinkled ‖ *n* 3 wrinkle

crim·son /krim′zən/ [OSp *cremesin*] *n* 1 deep-purplish-red color ‖ *vt* 2 to make crimson ‖ *vi* 3 to become crimson; blush ‖ also *adj*

cringe /krinj′/ [OE *cringan* to yield] *vi* 1 to flinch; bend or crouch from fear or servility; 2 to fawn ‖ SYN truckle, stoop, cower, fawn, shrink, wince

crin·kle /kriŋk′əl/ [OE *crincan* to bend] *vt & vi* 1 to wrinkle, ripple; 2 to rustle ‖ *n* 3 wrinkle, ripple ‖ **crin′kly** *adj* (**-kli·er; -kli·est**)

crin·o·line /krin′əlin/ [F < It *crinolino*] *n* 1 coarse fabric used for stiffening garments; 2 hoop skirt

crip·ple /krip′əl/ [OE *crypel* creeper] *n* 1 one who is lame or maimed ‖ *vt* 2 to make a cripple of; 3 to disable, impair

cri·sis /krīs′is/ [Gk] *n* (**-ses** /-sēz/) 1 crucial or decisive moment; turning point; 2 critical time of great instability and strain ‖ SYN juncture, extremity, exigency (see *emergency*)

crisp /krisp′/ [OE < L *crispus* curled] *adj* 1 curly; 2 brittle; 3 decisive; terse; 4 sparkling, lively; 5 fresh and firm; 6 bracing, invigorating; 7 brisk, sharp ‖ **crisp′ly** *adv* ‖ **crisp′ness** *n*

criss·cross /kris′krôs′, -kros′/ [< *Christ's cross*] *adj* 1 having many crossing lines ‖ *adv* 2 in a crisscross manner ‖ *n* 3 mark or pattern of crosses or x's ‖ *vt* 4 to mark with crosses or x's; 5 to cause to move in a crisscross manner ‖ *vi* 6 to move in a crisscross manner

cri·te·ri·on /krītir′ē·ən/ [Gk] *n* (**-a** /-ə/) standard by which a correct judgment can be formed; measure, test ‖ SYN standard ‖ DISCR A *standard* is a definite or concrete measure to which everything of the same kind must conform; for instance, the value of monetary coins is fixed by a government *standard*. *Criterion* is a *standard* employed in matters of judgment, as of facts, principles, comparisons, or methods of conduct, and implies not so much the idea of conforming to as of meeting a test. A man's speech is a *criterion* by which we may judge his background and education; his conduct affords a *criterion* by which we may judge his principles

crit·ic /krit′ik/ [< Gk *krites* judge] *n* 1 person whose profession is to write opinions on the merits of literary or artistic works or of dramatic or musical performances; 2 faultfinder

crit·i·cal *adj* 1 inclined to find fault; 2 involving skilled judgment; 3 pert. to or characterized by a crisis; crucial; 4 of or pert. to critics or criticism; 5 *phys* designating or relating to a point at which a change in state or condition occurs ‖ **crit′i·cal·ly** *adv*

crit·i·cism *n* 1 act or instance of criticizing; 2 art, principles, and methods of critics; 3 scientific examination of the origin, history, etc., of literary documents; textual examination ‖ SYN comment, disapproval, animadversion, reflection, stricture ‖ DISCR

An *animadversion* is a censorious remark or statement, usually unreasonably faultfinding, and, because it is personal, often ill-natured and unjust. A *criticism* is an expression of judgment following careful examination; the judgment may be favorable or unfavorable, and it is made explicit by setting forth the virtues or blemishes which scrutiny has revealed. As here compared, *criticism* is usually unfavorable, as his carping *criticisms* robbed her of self-confidence. A *stricture* is an expression of severe *criticism*, either vehement and rancorous, as the railings of one political leader against another, ❖r judicious, as critical notes appended to an essay. A *reflection* is a casting of blame or censure, by aspersion, innuendo, implication, etc. A *comment* is an explanatory or critical remark, or series of remarks, as on some passage in a poem, or on some affair of ordinary experience. It involves judgment, not necessarily unfavorable, and is often the fruit of serious thought

crit·i·cize /krĭt′ĭ·cīze′/ *vt* 1 to judge and evaluate as a critic; 2 to find fault with || *vi* 3 to find fault

cri·tique /krĭtēk′/ [F] *n* critical evaluation or analysis

croak /krōk′/ [ME *croken*] *vi* 1 to make a hoarse, guttural sound like that of a frog; 2 *slang* to die || *vt* 3 to utter by croaking

Cro·at /krō′at/ *n* native or inhabitant of Croatia

Cro·a·tia /krō·āsh′ə/ *n* constituent republic of Yugoslavia

Cro·a′tian *n* 1 Croat; 2 language of Croatia || also *adj*

cro·chet /krōshā′/ [F *croche* hook] *n* 1 kind of knitting made with a single hooked needle || *v* (-cheted /-shād′/; -chet·ing /-shā′ĭŋ/) *vt & vi* 2 to knit with a single hooked needle

crock /krok′/ [OE *crocc*] *n* earthenware vessel

crocked′ *adj slang* drunk

crock′er·y *n* earthenware

croc·o·dile /krok′ədīl′/ [Gk *krokodeilos*] *n* any of several large lizardlike reptiles (genus *Crocodylus*) having a long pointed snout, and found in tropical streams and swamps

croc′o·dile tears′ *npl* insincere manifestation of grief

cro·cus /krōk′əs/ [Gk *krokos* saffron] *n* any of a genus (*Crocus*) of bulbous plants, having long leaves and bearing white, yellow, or purple flowers

Croe·sus /krēs′əs/ *n* 1 very wealthy king of ancient Lydia in Asia Minor, of the sixth century B.C.; 2 very rich man

Croix de Guerre /krwä′dəgər′/ [F = cross of war] *n* French medal awarded for bravery under fire

Cro·Mag·non /krōmag′nən/ [name of cave in France] *n* member of a race of men in Europe dating from the late glacial age, who used stone and bone implements

Crom·well, Ol·i·ver /krom′wəl, -wel/ *n* (1599–1658) English general and Puritan leader, Lord Protector of England after the execution of Charles I 1653–58

crone /krōn′/ [ME] *n* withered old woman

cro·ny /krōn′ē/ [?] *n* (-nies) friend, chum

crook /krook′/ [prob ON *krókr* hook] *n* 1 bend, curve; 2 hooked part; 3 hooked implement, as a shepherd's or bishop's staff; 4 *colloq* dishonest person, thief || *vt & vi* 5 to bend or curve

crook′ed /-ĭd/ *adj* 1 not straight; 2 dishonest || SYN twisted, wry, awry, askew, fraudulent, false

croon /kroon′/ [MD *kronen* to murmur] *vt & vi* 1 to sing softly or plaintively || *n* 2 sound of crooning || **croon′er** *n*

crop /krop′/ [OE = bird's crop] *n* 1 produce of cultivated plants; 2 season's total yield of a particular product; 3 anything likened to a harvest; 4 riding whip with a short stock and a loop; 5 hair cut short; 6 in birds, the enlargement of the alimentary canal into which the gullet discharges || *v* (cropped; crop·ping) *vt* 7 to cut or bite off the tops or ends of; 8 to cut short || *vi* 9 **crop up** to appear unexpectedly

crop′-dust′ing *n* spraying of crops with insecticides or fungicides from an airplane

crop′per *n* come a cropper, 1 to fall; 2 to fail

cro·quet /krōkā′/ [F dial. = hockey stick] *n* lawn game in which wooden balls are driven by mallets through a series of wire arches

cro·quette /krōket′/ [F < *croquer* to crunch] *n* ball of previously cooked food, as meat or fish, fried in deep fat

cro·sier /krōzh′ər/ [MF = crosier bearer] *n* hooked staff of a bishop or abbot

cross /krôs′, kros′/ [OE < OIr < L *crux*] *n* 1 upright timber bearing a transverse piece, upon which in ancient times criminals were executed; 2 the Cross, a cross upon which Jesus was crucified; b the Christian religion; 3 emblem of Christianity; 4 crucifix; 5 variously shaped device in the form of a cross, used in heraldry or as an ornament, decoration, etc.; 6 anything shaped like a cross; 7 suffering, affliction; 8 intermixture of breeds or varieties; 9 crossbreed || *vt* 10 to put or lay from one side to the other; 11 to draw a mark across; **12** to move or carry to the opposite side; **13** to go or travel to the opposite side of; **14** to meet and pass; **15** to intersect; **16** to make the sign of the cross upon; **17** to thwart, oppose; **18** to cause to interbreed, as plants or animals of different species or varieties; **19 cross off** or **out** to cancel by drawing a line through; **20 cross one's mind** to occur to someone; **21 cross up** *slang* to deceive, doublecross || *vi* **22** to go, move, or lie from one side to the other; **23** to meet and pass; **24** to interbreed || *adj* **25** transverse, not parallel; **26** opposed, counter; **27** peevish, ill-tempered; **28** crossbred; **29 cross at** *colloq* angry at

cross'bar' *n* transverse bar, line, or stripe

cross'bones' *npl* figure of two crossed bones, usu. under a skull, symbolizing death

cross'bow' /-bō'/ *n* medieval weapon having a bow across the stock which fired a bolt

cross'breed' *n* **1** hybrid || *v* (**-bred**) *vt* **2** to breed (hybrid offspring) || also *vi* || **cross'bred'** /-bred'/ *adj*

cross'-coun'try *adj* **1** over fields, fences, etc.; **2** from one end of the country to the other

cross'cut saw' *n* saw for cutting wood across the grain

cross'-ex·am'ine *vt* law to question (a witness for the other side) in order to discredit his testimony || **cross'-ex·am'i·na'tion** *n*

cross'-eyed' *adj* suffering from a condition in which the eyes turn inward toward the nose

cross'-grained' *adj* **1** having a fiber or grain running across or irregularly; **2** contrary, intractable

cross' hairs' *npl* fine hairs or wires crossing in the focal plane of an optical finder to aid in lining up the target

cross'hatch' *vt* to engrave or shade with intersecting sets of parallel lines

cross'ing *n* **1** a passing across; **2** place of intersection, as of two streets or a railway and a road; **3** place where streets, rivers, etc., may be crossed

cross'-pol'li·na'tion *n* transfer of pollen from one flower to the stigma of another, as by insects or wind || **cross'-pol'li·nate'** *vt*

cross'-pur'pose *n* **at cross purposes** with mutual frustration and misunderstanding

cross' ref'er·ence *n* reference or specific direction from one part of a book, list, or passage to another

cross'road' *n* **1** road that crosses a main road; **2 crossroads** *nsg* or *npl* road intersection; **3 at the crossroads** when and where a decision must be made

cross' sec'tion *n* **1** section made by a cut at right angles to the longest axis; **2** representation of this; **3** typical sample

cross'-stitch' *n* form of stitch in which one stitch crosses another forming an x || also *vt* & *vi*

cross'town' *adj* **1** situated at opposite ends of a town; **2** going across a town || also *adv*

cross'walk' *n* marked lane for use by pedestrians crossing a street

cross'wise' *adv* athwart, across

cross'word puz'zle *n* puzzle consisting of an arrangement of squares to be filled in with letters forming words, the definitions of which are given as clues

crotch /kroch'/ [prob < *crutch*] *n* **1** fork or forking; **2** point of separation into trunk and branch or into two branches; **3** division in the human body where the legs fork from the trunk

crotch·et /kroch'it/ [MF *crochet* little hook] *n* whim, fancy, eccentricity

crotch'et·y *adj* full of whims or fancies; cranky || **crotch'et·i·ness** *n* || SYN whimsical, fanciful, fickle, capricious, eccentric, grouchy, perverse

crouch /krouch'/ [ME *crouchen*] *vi* **1** to stoop or bend low || *n* **2** crouching posture

croup /krōōp'/ [*dial.* croup to croak] *n* disease characterized by laborious breathing and a harsh cough

crou·pi·er /krōōp'ē·ər, krōōp·ē·ā'/ [F] *n* employee of a gambling casino who collects bets and pays out winnings at a gaming table

crou·ton /krōō'ton, krōōton'/ [F = crust] *n* small cube of toasted bread used in soups

crow[1] /krō'/ [OE *crāwan*] *vi* **1** to utter the cry of a rooster; **2** to boast in triumph || *n* **3** cry of a rooster

crow[2] [OE *crāwe*] *n* **1** any of several large, shiny black, omnivorous, and intelligent birds of the genus *Corvus*; **2** any of several birds resembling crows; **3 as the crow flies** in a straight line; **4 eat crow** to retract in a humiliating manner

Crow *n* one of a tribe of American Indians now living in Montana

crow'bar' *n* steel bar flattened like a chisel at the working end, used as a lever

crowd /kroud'/ [OE *crūdan* to press] *vt* **1** to fill too full; **2** to press or cram; **3** to shove, push; **4** to urge or importune || *vi* **5** to collect in large numbers; throng; **6** to push forward, drive || *n* **7** large number of persons collected together; throng; **8** the common people, the masses; **9** group of persons, set || **crowd'ed** *adj* || SYN *n* multitude, populace, rabble (see *throng*)

crow'foot' *n* (**-foots**) any of a large widely distributed family (Ranunculaceae) of plants; esp., any plant of the typical genus *Ranunculus,* as the buttercup

crown /kroun'/ [OF *corone* < L *corona*] *n* **1** wreath worn as an emblem of victory; **2** royal head covering worn as a symbol of sovereignty; **3 a** regal power; **b** the sovereign himself; **4** article or ornament shaped like a crown; **5** anything likened to a crown, as the top of a hill, a hat, or the head; **6** the part of a tooth projecting from the gum; **7** artificial top or body of a tooth; **8** perfect state of anything; finishing touch; **9** British coin of the predecimal system, worth five shillings; **10** corona of a flower || *vt* **11** to put a crown on; **12** to invest with regal power; **13** to reward, honor; **14** to form or occupy the topmost part of; cap; **15** to add the finishing touch to; **16** to bring (efforts or exertion) to a fortunate outcome; **17** *slang* to hit on the top of the head

crown' glass' *n* optical glass having a high index of refraction

crown' prince' *n* heir apparent to a throne || **crown' prin'cess** *n fem*

crow's'-feet' *npl* wrinkles at the outer corners of the eyes

crow's' nest' *n naut* lookout's station on the top of a mast

cro·zier /krōzh'ər/ *n* var of **crosier**

cru·cial /krōōsh'əl/ [< L *crux* (*crucis*) cross] *adj* **1** decisive, critical; **2** severe, agonizing || **cru'cial·ly** *adv*

cru·ci·ble /krōōs'ibəl/ [ML *crucibulum*] *n* **1** vessel of heat-resistant material for melting ores, metals, etc.; **2** severe test

cru·ci·fix /krōōs'ifiks/ [L *crucifixus* the crucified] *n* cross bearing the sculptured figure of Christ

cru·ci·fix'ion /-fik'shən/ *n* **1** act of crucifying; **2 the Crucifixion** the crucifying of Christ

cru·ci·form' *adj* cross-shaped

cru·ci·fy' [OF *crucifier* < L *crucifigere*] *v* (-**fied**) *vt* **1** to put to death by fixing to a cross; **2** to torment, persecute

crude /krōōd'/ [L *crudus* raw] *adj* **1** in a raw or natural state, unrefined; **2** lacking in polish or refinement; **3** roughly constructed || **crude'ly** *adv* || **crude'ness** or **cru'di·ty** *n* (-**ties**) || SYN raw, unripe, inexperienced, crass, harsh, unfinished, unpolished, imperfect, superficial || ANT perfected, mature, polished, refined, elegant, delicate

cru·el /krōō'əl/ [L *crudelis*] *adj* **1** disposed to give pain and suffering to others without mercy; **2** painful, distressing; unrelenting || **cru'el·ly** *adv* || SYN brutal, ferocious, barbarous, implacable (see *inhuman*)

cru·el·ty *n* (-**ties**) **1** state of being cruel; **2** cruel act || SYN brutality, ferocity, savagery

cru·et /krōō'it/ [AF] *n* small glass bottle for vinegar or oil

cruise /krōōz'/ [D *kruisen* to traverse] *vi* **1** to move about from place to place without fixed destination, esp. at sea; **2** to travel in an airplane or automobile at a moderately fast speed || *vt* **3** to cruise over or about || *n* **4** cruising voyage

cruis'er *n* **1** one who or that which cruises; **2** warship smaller and faster than a battleship

crul·ler /krul'ər/ [D *krulle* twisted cake] *n* ring-shaped or twisted cake fried brown in deep fat

crumb /krum'/ [OE *cruma*] *n* **1** fragment broken off from bread, cake, etc.; **2** any small piece or amount || *vt* **3** to break into crumbs; **4** to cover with crumbs || *vi* **5** to break into crumbs

crum·ble /krum'bəl/ [< obs *crimble*] *vt & vi* to break into small pieces, disintegrate || **crum'bly** *adj* (-**bli·er**; -**bli·est**)

crum·my /krum'ē/ [?] *adj* (-**mi·er**; -**mi·est**) *slang* **1** shabby, run-down; **2** cheap, measly

crum·pet /krump'it/ [ME *crompid* curled] *n* cooked or toasted muffin

crum·ple /krump'əl/ [ME *crumpen* to curl] *vt* **1** to press into wrinkles, rumple || *vi* **2** to become rumpled; **3** to collapse

crunch /krunch'/ [perh imit] *vt & vi* **1** to crush or grind noisily, as with the teeth or under foot || *n* **2** act or noise of crunching; **3** *colloq* **a** financial stress and strain; **b** stress and strain of any kind || **crunch'y** *adj* (-**i·er**; -**i·est**)

cru·sade /krōōsād'/ [MF *croisade* & Sp *cruzada*] *n* **1** any of several military expeditions by the Christian nations during the 11th, 12th, and 13th centuries to recover the Holy Land from the Muslims; **2** any vigorous concerted action for the advancement or defense of some cause || *vi* **3** to engage in a crusade || **cru·sad'er** *n*

crush /krush'/ [MF *cruisir*] *vt* **1** to press out of shape; **2** to squeeze; **3** to break by pressure; **4** to bruise; mash; **5** to quell; overwhelm || *vi* **6** to become crushed || *n* **7** act of crushing or state of being crushed; **8** crowd; **9** *colloq* infatuation || **crush'er** *n* || SYN *v* vanquish, subjugate, press, mash (see *break*)

crush' hat' *n* hat that may be crushed or folded without damage

crust /krust'/ [L *crusta*] *n* **1** hard outside coating or rind; **2** hardened outer part of a loaf of bread; **3** piece of this, or of stale bread; **4** pastry casing of a pie; **5** *slang* insolence, gall || *vt* **6** to cover with, or form into, a crust || *vi* **7** to become covered with a crust

crus·ta·cean /krustāsh'ən/ [< L *crusta*

shell) *n* any of a class (Crustacea) of chiefly aquatic arthropods having a hard outer shell, including crabs, lobsters, and shrimps

crust'y *adj* (-i·er; -i·est) 1 resembling or having a crust; 2 cross; surly, snappish

crutch /kruch'/ [OE *crycc*] *n* 1 staff with a crosspiece to fit under the arm, used as a support in walking; 2 any support or prop

crux /kruks'/ [L = cross] *n* (**crux·es**; **cru·ces** /krōō'sēz/) *n* 1 hard point to settle; puzzle; 2 essential part of a question

cru·zei·ro /krōōzer'ō/ [Port = Southern Cross] *n* monetary unit of Brazil

cry /krī'/ [OF *crier* < L *quiritare* to cry for aid] *v* (**cried**) *vi* 1 to call aloud; complain or appeal loudly; 2 to shed tears; 3 to make the characteristic call, as animals ‖ *vt* 4 to utter loudly; 5 to announce, proclaim ‖ *n* (**cries**) 6 act or sound of crying; shout, call; 7 entreaty; 8 outcry, clamor; 9 characteristic call of an animal; 10 fit of weeping; 11 slogan or battle cry; 12 **a far cry** a great difference or distance; 13 **in full cry** in hot pursuit

cry'ba·by *n* (-**bies**) 1 one who cries readily; 2 one who complains too much when he loses

cry'ing *adj* demanding notice, flagrant

cryo- [Gk *kryos*] *comb form* cold

cry·o·gen /krī'əjen/ *n* substance used to attain very low temperatures

cry·o·gen·ics /krī'ōjen'iks/ *nsg* branch of physics that deals with low-temperature phenomena

crypt /kript'/ [Gk *krypte* hidden] *n* underground vault, esp. one below the main floor of a church, used as a burial place

crypt- or **crypto-** [Gk *kryptos* hidden] *comb form* hidden, secret

crypt'a·nal'y·sis *n* solving of secret codes

cryp'tic *adj* 1 hidden, secret; 2 puzzling; mysterious ‖ **cryp'ti·cal·ly** *adv*

cryp'to·gram' /krip'tə-/ *message* written in a secret code

cryp'to·graph' *n* 1 cryptogram; 2 secret code; 3 device for putting a clear message into code

cryp·tog·ra·phy /krip'tog'rəfē/ *n* science or act of devising, writing, deciphering, or solving messages in a secret code ‖ **cryp·tog'ra·pher** *n*

crys·tal /krist'əl/ [Gk *krystallos* ice] *n* 1 transparent quartz; 2 substance having a regular internal structure enclosed by symmetrically arranged plane surfaces; 3 glass of unusual brilliancy and clearness; 4 anything having the transparency and clearness of glass; 5 glass over the face of a watch

crys'tal ball' *n* ball of glass or crystal

in which supposedly one may see future events

crys'tal de·tec'tor *n rad* semiconducting crystal, such as galena, used with a fine contact wire to rectify incoming signals

crys'tal gaz'ing *n* practice of contemplating a crystal ball in order to foretell the future ‖ **crys'tal gaz'er** *n*

crys'tal·line /-lin/ *adj* 1 formed with or composed of crystals; 2 clear, transparent

crys'tal·line lens' *n* transparent convex body in the eye directly behind the pupil, which converges the light rays to a focus on the retina

crys'tal·lize *vt* 1 to form into crystals or cause to become crystalline; 2 to give permanent shape to ‖ *vi* 3 to form crystals or become crystalline; 4 to assume definite shape ‖ **crys'·tal·li·za'tion** *n* ‖ **crys'tal·liz'a·ble** *adj*

crys'tal·log'ra·phy *n* science that deals with the structure and classification of crystals ‖ **crys'tal·log'ra·pher** *n*

crys'tal·loid' *n usu.* crystallizable substance which when mixed in a liquid will pass through vegetable and animal membranes ‖ also *adj*

Cs *chem* cesium

cs. case(s)

C.S.A. Confederate States of America

CST, C.S.T. Central Standard Time

ct. 1 cent; 2 court

Cu [L *cuprum*] *chem* copper

cu. cubic

cub /kub'/ [?] *n* 1 the young of certain quadrupeds, as the fox, bear, wolf, lion, and tiger; 2 young and/or inexperienced person

Cu·ba /kyōōb'ə/ *n* Spanish-speaking island republic in the West Indies (8,033,000; 44,218 sq.m.; cap. Havana) ‖ **Cu'ban** *adj* & *n*

cub'by·hole' /kub'ē-/ [< *obs cub* pen] *n* small enclosed space

cube /kyōōb'/ [L *cubus*] *n* 1 solid body with six equal square sides; 2 product obtained by multiplying a quantity by its square; the third power ‖ *vt* 3 to raise to the third power; 4 to make cube-shaped; 5 to tenderize, as steak, by cutting the fibers in a checkered pattern

cu·beb /kyōōb'eb/ [< ML *cubeba* < Ar *kababah* < *kababah*] *n* 1 dried, unripe, spicy fruit of an East Indian climbing shrub (*Piper cubeba*), used medicinally and smoked in cigarettes; 2 cigarette containing cubeb

cube' root' *n* that factor of a number which, when raised to the third power, produces the number

cu'bic *adj* 1 having three dimensions, esp. as used in specifying the volume of a cube one edge of which is of the length of a given unit, as *a cubic yard*; 2 pert. to the measurement of volume; 3 *math* of the third degree; 4 cubical

cu·bi·cal *adj* having the form of a cube

cu·bi·cle [L *cubiculum* bedchamber] *n* small partitioned-off space

cub·ism *n* modern school of painting and sculpture, characterized by the use of geometrical figures to express the volume of the objects depicted || **cub·ist** *n*

cu·bit /kyōōb′it/ [OE < L *cubitum*] *n* ancient measure of 18 to 20 inches

cub′ report′er *n* beginning newspaper reporter

cub′ scout′ *n* member of the junior section of the Boy Scouts of America (ages 8 to 11)

cuck·old /kuk′əld/ [ME *cokewold*] *n* 1 husband of an adulterous wife || *vt* 2 to make a cuckold of || **cuck′-old·ry** *n*

cuck·oo /kōōk′ōō, kook′-/ [ME *cuccu*] *n* 1 any of several birds of the family Cuculidae, a European species (*Cuculus canorus*) being noted for its call and for laying eggs in other birds' nests; 2 its call; 3 crazy person, simpleton || *adj* 4 *slang* crazy

cuck′oo clock′ *n* clock which announces the hours by having a mechanical bird come out of a little door and make the sound of a cuckoo

cu·cum·ber /kyōō′kumbər/ [MF *cocombre*] *n* 1 creeping garden plant (*Cucumis sativus*) of the gourd family; 2 its long fleshy fruit, used as a salad or pickle

cud /kud′/ [OE *cwudu*] *n* food brought up from the first stomach of a ruminant into the mouth to be chewed over again

cud·dle /kud′əl/ [?] *vt* 1 to embrace tenderly || *vi* 2 to lie close and snug || *n* 3 act of cuddling || **cud′dly** *adj*

cudg·el /kuj′əl/ [OE *cycgel*] *n* 1 short thick club or stick || *v* (-**eled** or -**elled; -el·ing** or -**el·ling**) *vt* 2 to beat with a cudgel; 3 **cudgel one's brains** to think hard

cue¹ /kyōō′/ [F *queue* tail] *n* 1 long tapering rod used to propel billiard balls; 2 braid of hair hanging on back of head; 3 line of people waiting their turn

cue² [prob < *q* abbr of L *quando* when; used as a direction in 16th-cent. acting scripts] *n* 1 prearranged signal to an actor to begin a specific line or bit of action: 2 any signal or sign to a person to begin a specific course of action; 3 hint or suggestion || *v* (**cu·ing**) *vt* 4 to give a cue to; 5 **cue in,** **a** to direct (an actor) to come in; **b** to insert, as a song, a lighting effect, etc., into a continuing performance; **c** *colloq* to give information to

cue′ ball′ *n* ball struck with the cue in pool or billiards

cue′ card′ *n* large prompter's card, not seen by television viewers, with words or phrases to cue a speaker or performer

cuff¹ /kuf′/ [?] *n* 1 blow with the hand || *vt* 2 to strike, slap

cuff² [ME *cuffe* mitten] *n* 1 band to wear around the wrist; 2 fold on the lower part of a sleeve; 3 fold on the bottom of trousers; 4 wrist-covering part of a long glove; 5 handcuff; 6 **off the cuff** *slang* extemporaneously; 7 **on the cuff** *slang* on credit

cuff′ links′ *npl* pair of linked buttons or the like for fastening shirt cuffs

cui·rass /kwiras′/ [F *cuirasse*] *n* piece of armor covering the torso

cui·sine /kwizēn′/ [F = kitchen] *n* style or quality of cooking

cul-de-sac /kul′dəsak′/ [F = bottom of a bag] *n* (**culs-de-sac** /kulz′-/) blind alley

cu·li·nar·y /kyōōl′əner′ē/ [L *culinarius* < *culina* kitchen] *adj* pert. to the kitchen or cooking

cull /kul′/ [OF *cuillir* < L *colligere* to gather] *vt* 1 to pick out, gather || *n* 2 something picked out for rejection as inferior

cul·mi·nate /kul′mināt′/ [L *culminare* < *culmen* top] *vi* to reach the highest point or climax

cul′mi·na′tion *n* 1 highest point or degree; 2 attainment of highest point || SYN climax, summit, acme, crown, zenith

cu·lottes /k(y)ōō′lots/ [F = breeches] *npl* women's trousers cut very full so as to resemble a skirt

cul·pa·ble /kulp′əbəl/ [< L *culpare* to blame] *adj* deserving censure, blameworthy || **cul′pa·bly** *adv* || **cul′pa·bil′-i·ty** /-bil′-/ *n* || SYN guilty, wicked, wrong, censurable, reprehensible

cul·prit /kul′prit/ [< AF *culpable* + *prest* ready (to prove it)] *n* 1 one arraigned for an offense; 2 one guilty of a crime

cult /kult′/ [L *cultus* care] *n* 1 particular ritual or system of worship; 2 devotion to a person, thing, idea, or the like; 3 group bound together by some esoteric ideology

cul·ti·vate /kult′ivāt′/ [ML *cultivare* (-*atus*) to till] *vt* 1 to till, prepare (soil) for the growing of crops; 2 to improve or develop by care, labor, or study; refine; 3 to foster or promote the growth of; 4 to devote oneself to; 5 to seek the society or acquaintance of || **cul′ti·va′tion** *n* || SYN cherish, foster, improve, develop, work, till

cul·ti·va′tor *n* 1 one who or that which cultivates; 2 tool for loosening the ground around crops, destroying weeds, etc.

cul·tur·al an·thro·pol′o·gy *n* branch of anthropology concerned with human culture, its evolution, and its present status

cul·ture /kulch′ər/ [L *cultura*] *n* 1 cultivation of the soil; 2 care given to the rearing, growth, or development of animals, plants, or the like; 3 a growth of microorganisms for scientific study; **4** improvement or discipline by practice or training, as *physical culture*; **5** training of the mental or moral powers, or the result of such training; refinement; **6** particular type or stage of civilization, as of a people or period ‖ *vt* **7** to cultivate ‖ **cul'tur·al** *adj* ‖ SYN refinement, breeding (see *education*)

cul'tured *adj* **1** trained in good taste; **2** cultivated; **3** artificially grown, as *cultured pearls*

cul·vert /kul'vərt/ [?] *n* drain or channel under a road, street, sidewalk, etc.

cum·ber·some /kum'bərsəm/ [ME *cummyrsum*] *adj* **1** burdensome; bothersome; **2** unwieldy; hard to handle

cum lau·de /kum lôd'ē/ [L = with praise] *adj & adv* with academic distinction

cum·mer·bund /kum'ərbund'/ [Urdu *kamerband*] *n* wide sash worn around the waist under a man's dinner jacket

cum·quat /kum'kwot/ *n* var of kumquat

cu·mu·la·tive /kyōōm'yəlāt'iv, -lətiv/ [< L *cumulare (-atus)* to heap] *adj* **1** increasing or growing by successive additions; **2** accruing, as dividends or interest, so as to be added to future payments if not paid when due

cu·mu·lus /kyōōm'yələs/ [L = heap] *n* (-li /-lī'/) cloud having the appearance of heaped-up masses ‖ **cu'mu·lous** *adj*

cu·ne·i·form /kyōōnē'ifôrm', kyōōn'ē·i-/ [L *cuneus* wedge] *adj* **1** wedge-shaped ‖ *n* **2** cuneiform writing, as that of the ancient inscriptions of Assyria and Persia

cun·ning /kun'iŋ/ [< OE *cunnan* to know] *adj* **1** skillful, ingenious; **2** crafty, sly; **3** *colloq* cute, charming ‖ *n* **4** guile, craftiness ‖ SYN *adj* adroit, artful (see *wily*); *n* (see *subterfuge*)

cup /kup/ [OE *cuppe* < LL *cuppa*] *n* **1** small bowl-shaped drinking vessel, usu. with one handle; **2** anything shaped like a cup; **3** cupful; **4** ornamental vessel, as of gold, awarded as a prize in a contest; **5** chalice used in Communion or the wine taken at Communion; **6** one's fate or lot; **7** the hole in golf; **8 in one's cups** drunk ‖ *v* (**cupped; cup·ping**) *vt* **9** to shape like a cup

cup·board /kub'ərd/ *n* **1** closet fitted with shelves for holding cups, plates, etc.; **2** any small closet

cup'cake' *n* small round cake

cup'ful' *n* **1** as much as a cup will contain; **2** *cookery* half pint

Cu·pid /kyōōp'id/ [L *Cupido* < *cupere* to desire] **1** *Rom myth.* god of love; **2** cupid representation of Cupid as a small winged boy with a bow and arrow

cu·pid·i·ty /kyōōpid'itē/ [L *cupiditas*] *n* eager desire for possession; greed ‖ SYN appetite, avarice, covetousness (see *greed*)

cu·po·la /kyōōp'ələ/ [It < L *cupa* cask] *n* any small domelike structure on top of a roof

cupped' *adj* cup-shaped

cu·pric /k(y)ōōp'rik/ [< LL *cuprum* copper] *adj* pert. to or containing copper, esp. in the bivalent state

cu'pro·nick'el /k(y)ōōp'rə-/ [< LL *cuprum* copper] *n* alloy of copper and nickel

cu'prous *adj* containing copper in the univalent state

cur /kur/ [< ME *curdogge*] *n* **1** mongrel dog; **2** despicable person

Cu·ra·çao /k(y)ōōr'rəsou', -sō'/ *n* chief island of the Netherlands Antilles (133,000; 210 sq.m.)

cu·ra·re /kyōōrär'ē/ [Port & Sp < Carib *kurari*] *n* poisonous extract from tropical trees of the genus *Strychnus*, used by South American Indians for poisonous arrows, and in medicine

cu·rate /kyōōr'it/ [ML *curatus* < L *curare* to care for] *n* rector's or vicar's assistant ‖ **cu'ra·cy** /-rəsē/ *n* (-cies)

cur·a·tive /kyōōr'ətiv/ [see **cure**] *adj* **1** pert. to healing; **2** promoting cure ‖ *n* **3** remedy

cu·ra·tor /kyōōrāt'ər/ [< L *curare (-atus)* to take care of] *n* one having charge of a museum, art gallery, etc.

curb /kurb/ [MF *courbe* < L *curvus* bent] *vt* **1** to restrain, keep within bounds; control; **2** to furnish with a curb ‖ *n* **3** that which checks, restrains, or subdues; **4** stone or concrete rim or edge of a sidewalk next to the gutter; **5** market dealing in stocks and bonds not listed on a stock exchange ‖ SYN *v* check, restrain, control, subject, repress

curb'stone' *n* stone making up a curb

curd /kurd/ [ME *crud*] *n* the coagulated part of milk from which cheese is made ‖ *vt & vi* to curdle

cur·dle /kurd'əl/ [< *curd*] *vt & vi* **1** to form into curd; **2** to congeal

cure /kyōōr'/ [OF < L *cura* care] *n* **1** remedial treatment, as for disease; **2** restoration to health; **3** remedy; **4** method or course of treatment; **5** method of preserving, as pork, beef, etc. ‖ *vt* **6** to heal, restore to health; **7** to remedy, as an evil condition; **8** to preserve by salting, smoking, etc. ‖ *vi* **9** to cause a return to health; **10** to be preserved, as by salting

cure'-all' *n* remedy for all ills; panacea

cur·few /kur'fyōō/ [MF *cuevre-feu* cover the fire] *n* **1** formerly, ringing of a bell at a fixed hour in the evening as a warning that fires and lights were to be put out; **2** time in the evening established by the authorities after which no one, or no children under a certain age, may appear on the streets

Cu·ri·a /kyŏŏr′ē̇·ə/ [L = division of a tribe] *n* (-ri·ae /-rē̇·ē̇′/) **1** papal court at Rome; **2** its officials collectively ‖ **cu′ri·al** *adj*

cu·rie /kyŏŏr′ē̇, kyŏōrē′/ [Pierre (1859–1906) & Marie (1867–1934) Curie F chemists, discoverers of radium] *n* unit of radioactivity (3.7 × 10¹⁰ disintegrations per second)

cu·ri·o /kyŏŏr′ē̇·ō′/ [*abbr* of *curiosity*] *n* rare object of art, curiosity

cu·ri·os·i·ty /kyŏŏr′ē̇·os′it̄ē̇/ [L *curiositas*] *n* (-ties) **1** desire to know about something; **2** inquisitiveness; **3** something curious or odd

cu·ri·ous /kyŏŏr′ē̇·əs/ [L *curiosus*] *adj* **1** anxious to find out; inquisitive; **2** prying; **3** strange, odd ‖ **cu′ri·ous·ly** *adv* ‖ SYN novel, interesting, meddling, officious, prying

cu·ri·um /kyŏŏr′ē̇əm/ [< *curie*] *n* radioactive metallic element (**Cm**; at.no. 96) produced by bombarding plutonium with helium ions

curl /kurl′/ [< ME *crul* curly] *n* **1** ringlet of hair; **2** anything spiral-shaped; **3** act of curling or state of being curled ‖ *vt & vi* **4** to form into curls ‖ **curl′y** *adj* (-i·er; -i·est)

cur·lew /kur′lŏō/ [AF *curleu*] *n* any of a genus (*Numenius*) of long-legged shore birds with a long downward-curving bill

curl·i·cue also **curl·y·cue** /kurl′ikyŏō′/ [*curly* + *cue*] *n* fancy curve or flourish, as that made with a pen

curl′ing [?] *n* Scottish game in which flat stones are made to slide over smooth ice at a mark

cur·mudg·eon /kərmuj′ən/ [?] *n* irascible churlish fellow

cur·rant /kur′ənt/ [ME *rayson* of *Coraunte* raisin of Corinth (Gk port from which exported)] *n* **1** small acid berry of any of several garden shrubs of the genus *Ribes*; **2** any of these shrubs; **3** small seedless raisin, grown in the Levant and used in cookery

cur·ren·cy /kur′ənsē̇/ *n* (-cies) **1** circulation, as of words or coins; **2** state of being prevalent or accepted; **3** that which is in general use as a medium of exchange, money

cur·rent /kur′ənt/ [L *currens* (-*entis*) running] *adj* **1** in general use; **2** widely circulated; **3** of the present time ‖ *n* **4** flow, as of air or water; **5** body of air or water thus flowing; **6** speed of flow; **7** general course or tendency; **8** a movement of electricity, as along a wire; **b** time rate of such movement measured in amperes ‖ **cur′rent·ly** *adv*

cur·ric·u·lum /kərik′yələm/ [L = career] *n* (-lums or -la /-lə/) **1** courses of study offered by an educational institution; **2** particular course of study ‖ **cur·ric′u·lar** *adj*

cur·ric′u·lum vi′tae /vī′tē̇/ *n* brief résumé of one's career

cur·ry¹ /kur′ē̇/ [OF *correer* to prepare] *v* (-ried) *vt* **1** to rub down and clean (a horse); **2** to dress (leather) after tanning; **3 curry favor** to seek favor by flattery

cur·ry² [Tamil *kari* sauce] *n* (-ries) **1** highly spiced East Indian sauce; **2** stew seasoned with it

curse /kurs′/ [OE *curs*] *n* **1** profane oath; **2** expression of a wish that misfortune or injury should befall someone; **3** prayer or formula invoking such misfortune; **4** that which brings or causes evil or trouble; **5** calamity or evil invoked; **6** accursed object or person ‖ *v* (cursed or curst) *vt* **7** to wish or call down evil upon; **8** to blaspheme; **9** to swear at; **10** to torment, afflict; **11** to bring evil upon ‖ *vt* **12** to swear, blaspheme, utter curses ‖ SYN *n* execration, imprecation, anathema (see *malediction*) ‖ ANT *n* blessing, benediction

curs·ed /kurs′id, kurst′/ also **curst** /kurst′/ *adj* hateful, detestable

cur·sive /kurs′iv/ [ML *cursivus*] *adj* **1** flowing (said of characters or letters which are joined together); **2** pert. to or characterized by such letters ‖ *n* **3** cursive letter

cur·so·ry /kurs′ərē̇/ [< L *cursor* runner] *adj* hasty, superficial ‖ SYN desultory, fitful, careless, rapid, discursive ‖ DISCR *Cursory* describes that which is superficial because it is rapid; it connotes a running motion, as of the eye or mind, over a view, subject, etc. *Cursory* includes the idea of quickness, but not necessarily of carelessness; a *cursory* observation of something is the superficial, casual view of indifference; a *cursory* view of a subject may not be careless, but may be sufficient for the purpose in mind. *Desultory* differs from *cursory* in that it lacks the idea of coherence. *Cursory* conversation has some connection: *desultory* conversation leaps from one subject to another ‖ ANT thorough, critical, painstaking, methodical, comprehensive

curt /kurt′/ [L *curtus* short] *adj* concise; abrupt, brusque ‖ **curt′ly** *adv* ‖ **curt′ness** *n* ‖ SYN concise, brusque, uncivil, crusty (see *short*)

cur·tail /kərtāl′/ [ME *curtayle* to restrict] *vt* to cut short, lessen ‖ **cur·tail′ment** *n* ‖ SYN reduce, retrench, abbreviate, shorten, lessen

cur·tain /kurt′ən/ [OF *cortine* < L *cortina*] *n* **1** hanging covering which can be drawn up or aside, as on a window or stage; **2** anything that serves to conceal or screen; **3 curtains** *slang* death ‖ *vt* **4** to provide or shut off with or as with a curtain

cur'tain call' *n* summons to an actor to appear before the curtain at the end of a performance to acknowledge applause

cur'tain rais'er *n* **1** short piece given before the principal play; **2** first number of a program

curt-sy or **curt-sey** /kurt′sē/ [< *courtesy*] *n* (**-sies** or **-seys**) **1** bow made by a woman by bending the knees and lowering the body ‖ *v* (**-sied** or **-seyed**) *vi* **2** to make a curtsy

cur-va-ceous /kərvāsh′əs/ *adj colloq* (woman) having voluptuous curves

cur-va-ture /kur′vəchər/ *n* **1** act of curving or state of being curved; **2** curve

curve /kurv′/ [L *curvus* bent] *n* **1** line straight in no part; bend without angles; **2** *baseball* pitched ball that curves away from a straight path ‖ *vt & vi* **3** to bend or move in a curve

cur-vi-lin-e-ar /kur′vilin′ē-ər/ *adj* made up of or bounded by curved lines

cush-ion /kŏŏsh′ən/ [MF *coussin*] *n* **1** pillow or soft pad to sit, lie, or rest on; **2** elastic rim of a billiard table; **3** any device to dampen or reduce the shock of a jar or impact ‖ *vt* **4** to seat upon or furnish with a cushion; **5** to dampen, as shock; **6** to soften the effects of

cush-y /kŏŏsh′ē/ [Hindi *khrush* pleasant] *adj* (**-i-er**; **-i-est**) *slang* easy, soft (job or assignment)

cusp /kusp′/ [L *cuspis* point] *n* something shaped to a point, as the horns of the crescent moon or the prominences on the crown of a tooth ‖ **cusped'** *adj*

cus-pi-dor /kusp′idôr′/ [Port = spitter] *n* spittoon

cuss /kus′/ [var of *curse*] *colloq vt & vi* **1** to curse ‖ *n* **2** curse; **3** fellow ‖ **cuss'ed** /-id/ *adj*

cuss'ed-ness *n colloq* perverseness

cus-tard /kus′tərd/ [ME = kind of pie] *n* pudding or dessert made of eggs, milk, sugar, etc., baked or boiled

cus-to-di-an /kustōd′ē-ən/ *n* one who has custody; keeper, guardian ‖ **cus-to'di-an-ship'** *n*

cus-to-dy /kus′tədē/ [< L *custos* (-*odis*) guardian] *n* (**-dies**) **1** guardianship, care, charge; **2** restraint of liberty, imprisonment ‖ **cus-to-di-al** /kustōd′-ē-əl/ *adj*

cus-tom /kust′əm/ [OF *costume* < L *consuetudo*] *n* **1** habitual or usual course of action; **2** established or recognized usage; **3** patronage; **4 customs** *pl* duties on imported goods; **5 customs** *sg* department of government that collects duties ‖ SYN practice, wont, fashion, manner (see *habit*)

cus'tom-ar-y *adj* conforming to the usual or common practice ‖ SYN general, familiar, wonted, habitual, stated, usual

cus'tom-built' *adj* made to order; not mass-produced

cus'tom-er *n* **1** buyer, patron; **2** *colloq* unpleasant person with whom one has dealings

cus'tom-er's man' *n* employee of a brokerage firm who transmits orders to buy and sell stocks and bonds for customers of the firm

cus'tom-house' also **cus'toms-house'** *n* (**-hous-es** /-hou′ziz/) building for collecting customs and clearing vessels

cus'tom-made' *adj* made to order

cus'toms un'ion *n* union of independent nations for the purpose of removing tariff barriers between them

cut /kut′/ [ME *cutten*] *v* (**cut**; **cut-ting**) *vt* **1** to penetrate with an edged instrument; **2** to wound by cutting; **3** to hew, fell; **4** to sever, divide; **5** to cause (teeth) to break through the gums; **6** to make or shape by cutting, as a garment; **7** to shorten or reduce; trim, pare; **8** to snub; **9** to intersect, cross; **10** to dissolve, as grease; **11** to dilute, as wine; **12** to switch off, as an engine; **13** *colloq* to discontinue; **14** to divide (a deck of cards) into two or more parts; **15** to make a recording of; **16** to absent oneself from, as a class; **17 cut back** to curtail; **18 cut down, a** to lessen; **b** to disable, kill; **19 cut off, a** to sever; **b** to stop, disconnect; **c** to intercept; **d** to disinherit; **20 cut out, a** to excise; **b** *slang* to stop, discontinue; **21 cut up, a** to cut into pieces; **b** to lacerate ‖ *vi* **22** to do the work of a sharp-edged instrument, as *the knife cuts well;* **23** to pass or cross by a direct route, as *to cut across the lot;* **24** to take cutting, as *cheese cuts easily;* **25** to use a sharp-edged instrument; **26** to change direction (to the left or right); **27** *colloq* to depart hurriedly; **28 cut both ways** to have disadvantages as well as advantages; **29 cut down on** to decrease; **30 cut in, a** to interpose, interrupt; **b** *colloq* to stop a dancing couple and take the female as one's own partner; **31 cut up** *colloq* to clown, play pranks ‖ *n* **32** act of cutting; **33** result of cutting: incision, gash, channel, trench, etc.; **34** stroke or blow, as with a knife, bat, etc.; **35** piece cut off, slice; **36** fashion, style (of a garment); **37** cutting of a deck of cards; **38** reduction or curtailment; **39 a** act of shortening by excising a part; **b** the part cut out; **40** absence, as from a class; **41** snub; **42 a** engraved plate for printing; **b** printed picture; **43** *colloq* share; **44, a cut above** *colloq* somewhat better than

|| adj 45 that has been cut; 46 (gems or glass) with the surface cut, ground, and polished; 47 cut out for well fitted for

cut'-and-dried' adj 1 prearranged; 2 routine; boring

cu·ta·ne·ous /kyōōtān'ē-əs/ [< L cutis skin] adj pert. to or affecting the skin

cut'a·way' n 1 man's formal coat with the skirts cut back from the waist; 2 picture or example of an object with part of the outer surface or cover removed in order to reveal inner details || also adj

cut'back' n decrease or reduction in prices, production, expenses, etc.

cute /kyōōt/ [< acute] adj colloq 1 attractive, winning, bright; 2 shrewd, clever

cu·ti·cle /kyōōt'ikəl/ [L cuticula skin] n 1 outer layer of skin, epidermis; 2 hardened skin at the base and sides of the nails

cu'tis /kyōōt'is/ [L = skin] n the true skin which underlies the epidermis

cut·lass also cut·las /kut'ləs/ [MF coutelas] n short heavy sword with a wide curved blade

cut·ler /kut'lər/ n one who makes, sells, or repairs knives and other cutting instruments

cut'ler·y [MF coutelerie] n 1 cutting instruments collectively, esp. tableware; 2 trade of the cutler

cut·let /kut'lit/ [F côtelette] n 1 slice of meat cut from the ribs or leg for broiling or frying; 2 cake or croquette made from finely cut or ground meat

cut'off' n 1 road that provides a short cut; 2 shorter channel in a river cutting across a former bend; 3 device for stopping the flow of a fluid

cut'out' n 1 something cut out; 2 device by which an internal-combustion engine is made to exhaust directly into the air instead of through a muffler

cut' rate' n rate or charge below the usual one || cut'-rate' adj

cut'ter n 1 one who or that which cuts; 2 light sleigh for two persons; 3 any of various small swift boats, as those used by the Coast Guard

cut'throat' n murderous villain || also adj

cut'ting adj 1 deeply wounding the feelings; sarcastic; 2 piercing, chilling, as a cutting wind || n 3 piece cut from something; 4 slip or shoot of a plant for rooting; 5 Brit newspaper clipping

cut'tle·fish' /kut'əl-/ [OE cudele] n -fish or -fishes) any of a genus (Sepia) of marine carnivorous mollusks having ten tentacles, two large eyes, and a calcareous internal plate

cwt. hundredweight

-cy /-sē/ [OF -cie < L -tia & Gk -tia, teia] n suf 1 quality, state, as normalcy; 2 rank or office, as baronetcy

cy·an /sī'ən/ [Gk kyanos] n greenish dark blue

cy'a·nide' n salt of hydrocyanic acid, esp. potassium cyanide —KCN— a deadly poison

cy'a·no'sis /-nōs'is/ n purplish discoloration of the skin caused by a lack of oxygen in the blood

Cyb·e·le /sib'əlē/ n the great nature goddess of ancient Asia Minor

cy·ber·nate /sīb'ərnāt/ vt to control (a process or operation) by computers || cy'ber·na'tion n

cy·ber·net·ics /sīb'ərnet'iks/ [< Gk kybernetes helmsman] nsg comparative study of human and mechanical or electronic control systems || cy'ber·net'ic adj

cy·cle /sīk'əl/ [Gk kyklos circle] n 1 regularly recurring period of time, order of events, or series of phenomena; 2 complete series or round of actions, steps, or phenomena from starting point to starting point; 3 complete series, as of poems, dramas, or narrative prose, about a central figure or theme; 4 bicycle, tricycle, or similar machine; 5 one complete sequence of the periodically recurring values of an alternating current; 6 each of the strokes of an internal-combustion engine || vi 7 to revolve in or pass through cycles; 8 to ride a bicycle or similar machine || cy·clic (-cli·cal) /sīk'lik(əl), sik'-/ adj

cy'clist n one who rides a cycle

cyclo- comb form cyclic, circle, wheel

cy·clom·e·ter /sīklom'itər/ n instrument that measures the distance covered by a wheel

cy·clone /sī'klōn/ [Gk kyklon whirlwind] n storm caused by rotating winds which whirl inward toward a center of minimum pressure || cy·clon'ic /-klon'ik/ adj

Cy·clops /sī'klops/ [Gk = round eye] n (Cy·clo·pes /sīklōp'ēz/) class. myth. one of a race of one-eyed giants

cy'clo·ram'a /-ləram'ə, -räm'ə/ [cyclo- + Gk horama view] n 1 series of pictures arranged on a circular wall so as to appear in natural perspective to one standing in the center; 2 curved drop or curtain surrounding the rear of a stage

cy'clo·tron' /-ətron'/ [cyclo- + electron] n apparatus which accelerates particles in a spiral path until they attain very high energies

cyg·net /sig'nit/ [< L cygnus swan] n young swan

Cyg·nus /sig'nəs/ [L = swan] n the Swan, a northern constellation in the Milky Way

cyke /sīk/ n theat cyclorama 2

cyl·in·der /sil'indər/ [Gk kylindros] n

1 *geom* solid generated by a rectangle revolving about one of its sides as an axis; **2** any body having the form of a cylinder, as **a** the rotating part of a revolver; **b** the chamber of an engine or pump in which the piston slides; **c** the functioning part of certain locks into which the key is inserted ‖ cy·lin/dri·cal /sílin′-/ *adj*

cym·bal /sim′bəl/ [OE < Gk *kymbalon*] *n* concave circular metallic plate which emits a sharp ringing sound when struck

Cym·ric /kim′rik, sim′-/ [< Welsh *Cymry* Welshmen] *adj* **1** Welsh ‖ *n* **2** Welsh language

cyn·ic /sin′ik/ [Gk *kynikos* doglike] *n* **1** one who believes that all human actions are based on self-interest; **2** sneering pessimist ‖ cyn/i·cal *adj* ‖ cyn/i·cal·ly *adv*·‖ cyn/i·cism /-sizəm/ *n*

cy·no·sure /sin′əshŏŏr, sin′-/ [Gk *kynosoura* dog's tail] *n* **1** center of general attraction or attention; **2** something that serves as a guide

cy·press /sip′rəs/ [OE *cypresse* < LL *cypressus*] *n* **1** any of a genus (*Cupressus*) of cone-bearing trees of the pine family; **2** its wood

Cy·prus /sip′rəs/ *n* Greek- and Turkish-speaking island republic in the E Mediterranean (616,000; 3572 sq.m.; cap. Nicosia) ‖ Cyp·ri·an /sip′rē·ən/ also Cyp′ri·ot /-ət/ or Cyp′ri·ote′ /-ōt′/ *adj & n*

Cy·ril/lic al′pha·bet′ /siril′ik/ [< St. *Cyril* (827–69) Gk missionary to the Slavs] *n* alphabet derived from Greek, used for Old Church Slavonic, Russian, Serbian, and Bulgarian, and formerly for Rumanian

cyst /sist′/ [Gk *kystis* bladder] *n* **1** any sac, normal or abnormal, in an animal body, having gaseous, liquid, or semisolid content; **2** thickened outer layer of a unicellular organism, formed for protection

cyst/ic *adj* **1** pert. to a cyst; **2** pert. to the gall bladder or the urinary bladder

-cyte [< Gk *kytos* vessel] *comb form* cell

cy·tol·o·gy /sītol′əjē/ [< Gk *kytos* vessel] *n* study of the structure of cells and their activities

cy·to·plasm /sīt′əplaz′əm/ *n* protoplasmic substance of a cell exclusive of the nucleus

C.Z. Canal Zone

czar /zär′/ [Russ *tsar* < L *Caesar*] *n* **1** autocratic leader; **2 Czar** title of the former emperors of Russia ‖ cza·ri/na /-rēn′ə/ *nfem*

czar·das /chär′däsh/ [Hung *csárdás*] *n* Hungarian dance

czar/dom *n* **1** territory ruled by a Czar; **2** office or authority of a Czar

Czech /chek/ *n* **1** member of the most westerly branch of the Slavic peoples; **2** language of the Czechs

Czech·o·slo·va·ki·a /chek′əslōväk′ē·ə/ *n* republic in central Europe, revival of the medieval kingdom of Bohemia (14,305,000; 49,377 sq.m.; cap. Prague) ‖ Czech′o·slo·va/ki·an *adj & n*

D

D, d /dē/ *n* (**D's** or **Ds; d's** or **ds**) fourth letter of the English alphabet

D 1 *chem* deuterium; **2** Roman numeral 500; **3** *mus* second tone in the scale of C major; **4** grade rating of poor; **5** something shaped like· a D; **6** fourth in order or in a series; **7** Dutch

D. 1 December; **2** Democrat(ic); **3** Dutch

d. 1 date; **2** day; **3** died; **4** diameter; **5** [< L *denarius*] penny; pence

'd had, did, would, or should, as *I'd gone, I'd go*

D.A. District Attorney

dab /dab′/ [ME *dabben*] *v* (**dabbed; dab·bing**) *vt* **1** to touch or pat lightly; **2** to apply with light strokes ‖ *n* **3** soft blow or tap; **4** small moist lump, as of butter; **5** small amount

dab·ble /dab′əl/ [prob < *dab*] *vi* to do anything in a trifling manner

da ca·po /dä kä′pō/ [It] *adv mus* from the beginning

Dac·ca /dak′ə/ *n* capital of Bangladesh (830,000)

dachs·hund /däks′hŏŏnd′/ [G = badgerhound] *n* one of a breed of hounds with long body and short legs

Da·cron /dā′kron, -kron, dak′ron, -rən/ [trademark] *n* strong wrinkle-resistant synthetic fiber

dac·tyl /dak′təl/ [Gk *daktylos* finger] *n* **1** metrical foot consisting of a long syllable followed by two short ones or of an accented syllable followed by two unaccented ones; **2** finger or toe

dad /dad′/ [baby talk] *n* father

dad/dy *n* (**-dies**) dad

dad/dy-long′legs′ *nsg & npl* arachnid of the order Phalangida, having long slender legs

da·do /dā′dō/ [It = die or cube] *n* (**-does** or **-dos**) **1** lower part of the wall of a room when differently decorated from the upper part; **2**

face of a pedestal between base and cornice

Daed·a·lus /dĕd′ələs/ n Gk myth. Athenian architect exiled to Crete, where he built the Labyrinth and whence he escaped with his son Icarus by flight with wings attached with wax

daf·fo·dil /dăf′ədĭl/ [ME affodile < Gk asphodelos asphodel] n 1 narrow-leaved bulbous plant of the genus Narcissus, bearing large yellow flowers, esp. N. pseudo-narcissus; 2 flower of these plants

daff·y /dăf′ē/ [< obs daff fool] adj (-i·er; -i·est) colloq crazy, daft

daft /dăft/, däft′/ [OE gedæfte meek] adj 1 simple, foolish; 2 insane

dag·ger /dăg′ər/ [ME] n 1 short sharp-edged, pointed weapon for stabbing; 2 typ reference mark †; 3 **look daggers** at to look at with anger

da·guerre·o·type /dəger′ətīp′/ [< L. J. M. Daguerre (1789–1851) F inventor] n photograph made by an early method by which the pictures were taken on silver-coated plates

dahl·ia /dăl′yə, däl′-/ [< A. Dahl (d. 1789) Sw botanist] n 1 any of a genus (Dahlia) of tuberous-rooted Mexican plants of the composite family, widely cultivated as garden flowers; 2 bloom or tuber of any of these plants

Da·ho·mey /dəhōm′ē/ n (former name of) Benin

dai·ly /dāl′ē/ [OE dæglīc] adj 1 occurring or recurring each successive day || adv 2 on every day, day by day || n (-lies) 3 newspaper published every day || SYN adj diurnal || DISCR Daily, the opposite of nightly, is used properly of that which occurs in the daylight period of each twenty-four hours; loosely, however, it is used of any event that happens every twenty-four hours, even though this event occurs after nightfall, as some of the daily meals of an all-night worker. Diurnal is rarely employed in its ordinary sense of happening every day, except in poetry; scientifically, however, it is frequently used and is held strictly to its original exactness; a diurnal flower expands by day and closes by night; a diurnal bird flies only by day; here diurnal is the opposite of nocturnal. Astronomically, diurnal motion consumes an exact astronomical day

dai′ly dou′ble n bet at a race track in which the bettor must pick the winners of the first two races

dain·ty /dānt′ē/ [OF dainte < L dignitas worth] n (-ties) 1 something choice or delicious; tidbit || adj (-ti·er; -ti·est) 2 delicious; 3 elegant, tasteful; 4 sensitive, fastidious ||

dain′ti·ly adv || **dain′ti·ness** n || SYN adj elegant, fastidious (see exquisite)

dai·qui·ri /dīk′ərē, dak′-/ [Daiquiri town in Cuba] n cocktail made with rum, lemon or lime juice, and sugar

dair·y /der′ē/ [ME deierie] n (-ies) 1 place where milk is converted into butter and cheese; 2 farm for the production of milk, butter, and cheese; 3 shop where the products of a dairy are sold || **dair′y·man** /-mən/ n (-men /-mən/)

dair′y cat′tle n cows raised for their milk

da·is /dā′is/ [AF deis < L discus] n raised platform, as for a throne, table, or seats of honor

dai·sy /dāz′ē/ [OE dæges ēage day's eye] n (-sies) 1 any of various plants of the composite family bearing a yellow disk and white rays; 2 flower of one of these plants; 3 slang person or thing much admired

Dak. Dakota

Da·ko·ta /dəkōt′ə/ n 1 former U.S. territory, divided into the states of North Dakota and South Dakota; 2 Sioux Indian

Da·lai La·ma /dä′lī läm′ə/ [Tibetan = ocean priest] n high priest of Lamaism in Tibet

dale /dāl/ [OE dæl] n valley, glen

Dal·las /dăl′əs/ n city in NE Texas (844,401)

dal·ly /dăl′ē/ [AF dalier to chat] v (-lied) vi 1 to make sport, play, esp. amorously; 2 to trifle with a person's affections; 3 to waste time, loiter || vt 4 **dally away** to waste (time) || **dal′li·ance** n

Dal·ma·tian /dalmāsh′ən/ [< Dalmatia] adj 1 of or pert. to Dalmatia, the coastal region of Yugoslavia || n 2 native of Dalmatia; 3 one of a breed of short-haired dogs with white coats and black spots

dal·ton·ism /dôlt′əniz′əm/ [< John Dalton (1766–1844) Eng physicist] n color blindness, esp. inability to distinguish between red and green

dam¹ /dam′/ [ME] n 1 barrier built, as across a river, to hold back water; 2 any barrier acting like a dam || v (dammed; dam·ming) vt 3 to hold back or confine; 4 to provide with a dam

dam² [var of dame] n mother, usu. of an animal that is bred

dam·age /dam′ij/ [OF < dam < L damnum loss] n 1 injury or harm causing a loss; 2 **damages** pl a money compensation for a loss; b colloq price, cost || vt 3 to cause damage to || vi 4 to suffer damage || SYN n detriment, loss, evil, wrong, harm, hurt, impairment (see injury) || ANT n benefit, service, good

Da·mas·cus /dəmas′kəs/ n capital of Syria (599,669) || **Dam·a·scene** /dam′əsēn/ adj & n

dam·ask /dam′əsk/ [< *Damascus*] n 1 reversible fabric woven with elaborate patterns; 2 fine twilled table linen; 3 steel with a wavy pattern; 4 deep-pink color

dame /dām′/ [OF < L *domina* mistress] n 1 *slang* woman; 2 lady; 3 *Brit* title of a female member of the Order of the British Empire

damn /dam′/ [OF *damner* < L *damnare* to condemn] vt 1 to doom to eternal punishment; 2 to curse with the imprecation *damn;* 3 to condemn as bad or as a failure || vi 4 to swear, curse || n 5 curse; use of *damn* as an oath; 6 anything valueless; 7 **not give a damn** *colloq* to not be concerned at all || adj & adv 8 damned || interj 9 expression of anger or annoyance

dam·na·ble /dam′nəbəl/ adj 1 deserving damnation; 2 annoying, detestable || **dam′na·bly** adv

dam·na′tion n 1 act of damning or state of being damned; 2 eternal punishment; 3 condemnation || interj 4 expression of anger, disappointment, etc.

damned /damd′/ adj 1 condemned to eternal punishment; 2 outrageous; 3 detestable || adv 4 very, extremely

damned·est /dam′dist/ *colloq* adj 1 amazing || n 2 **one's damnedest** one's utmost

damn·ing /dam′iŋ, damn′-/ adj incriminating

Dam·o·cles /dam′əklēz′/ n courtier of the tyrant Dionysius of Syracuse who, because he envied his master for his wealth, was seated beneath a sword suspended by a single hair to make him realize the dangers of a monarch's life || **Dam′o·cle′an** /-klē′ən/ adj

Da·mon and Pyth·i·as /dām′ən, pith′-ē-əs/ n class. myth. devoted friends, noted for their faithfulness unto death

damp /damp′/ [MD = vapor] n 1 moisture in the air, humidity; 2 foul gas found in mines || adj 3 moist, humid; 4 depressed, discouraged || vt 5 to make damp; 6 to check, stifle; 7 to repeatedly diminish the amplitude of (waves or oscillations) || **damp′ness** n

damp′en vt 1 to make moist; 2 to depress or discourage; 3 to reduce, deaden || vi 4 to become damp

damp′er n 1 one who or that which damps; 2 moveable plate for regulating the draft in a stove or furnace; 3 device to check vibration in piano strings

dam·sel /dam′zəl/ [OF *dameisele*] n maiden; young unmarried woman

dam·son /dam′zən/ [ME < L (prunum) *damascenum* (plum) of Damascus] n 1 small oval purple plum

from a tree (*Prunus institia*) native to Asia Minor; 2 the tree

Dan. 1 Daniel; 2 Danish

dance /dans′, däns′/ [OF *dancier*] vi 1 to move the body and feet rhythmically to music; 2 to leap, skip about; 3 to move around, bob || vt 4 to cause to dance; 5 to perform (a dance) || n 6 regulated movement of the body and feet to a rhythmical musical accompaniment; 7 dancing party; 8 one round of dancing; 9 piece of music for dancing || **danc′er** n

dan·de·li·on /dan′dĭlī′ən/ [MF *dent de lion* lion's tooth] n common plant (*Taraxacum officinale*) of the composite family, having heads of yellow flowers, coarsely toothed leaves, and a tapering root

dan·der /dan′dər/ [< *dandruff*] n colloq temper, anger

dan·dle /dan′dəl/ [perh < It *dandola* doll] vt 1 to dance (an infant) up and down, as on the knee or in the arms; 2 to fondle, pet

dan·druff /dan′drəf/ [?] n dead skin on the scalp that comes off in scales

dan·dy /dan′dē/ [?] n (-dies) 1 man who gives much attention to his clothes, fop; 2 *colloq* something especially fine || adj (-di·er; -di·est) *colloq* excellent, fine

Dane /dān′/ [OE *Dene* Danes] n native or inhabitant of Denmark

Dane′law′ n 1 code of laws enforced by the Danes during their occupation of northeastern England in the ninth century; 2 territory governed by these laws

dan·ger /dān′jər/ [OF *dangier*] n 1 peril, risk; exposure to loss, injury, or death; 2 cause or instance of peril || SYN harm, insecurity, peril, hazard, risk, jeopardy || DISCR *Danger* is the generic term of these words, which share the idea of chance or uncertainty. *Danger* is exposure to prospective evil, as harm or injury; *danger* is positive, but contingent; for instance, the *dangers* of life are real enough, but under certain circumstances, they are escaped or escapable. A *peril* is an impending *danger*, not only about to happen, but of an extraordinary nature; our everyday life places us in some *danger* of death; an explorer in the jungle is in that extreme and imminent *danger* which is *peril;* tropical fevers, disease from improper nourishment, drought, and attack from wild beasts constantly place him in *peril* of death. *Jeopardy* is exposure to extreme *danger* with long chances against one, as the charge of first-degree murder placed him in *jeopardy* of his life. *Hazard* names the taking of long chances with some possibility of an even or fortunate break; it implies the possibility of good as well as evil, and herein differs from *risk*, which implies adverse conditions surrounding a voluntary undertaking or a mere contingency; we speak of the *risk* of loss, the *hazards* of losing or winning ‖ ANT security, safety, immunity

dan′ger·ous *adj* unsafe, perilous, full of danger ‖ **dan′ger·ous·ly** *adv*

dan·gle /dăng′gəl/ [< Scand] *vi* 1 to hang or swing loosely ‖ *vt* 2 to cause to dangle

Dan·iel /dăn′yəl/ *n Bib* 1 Hebrew prophet, captive at Babylon; 2 book of the Old Testament containing his history and prophecies

Dan·ish /dā′nĭsh/ *adj* 1 of or pert. to Denmark, its people, or its language ‖ *n* 2 language of Denmark; 3 *colloq* Danish pastry

Dan′ish pas′try *n* light pastry filled with fruit, cheese, or custard

dank /dăngk′/ [ME] *adj* unpleasantly damp ‖ **dank′ness** *n*

Da·no-Nor·we′gian /dăn′ō-/ *n* one of the two official written languages of Norway, essentially a modification of Danish

Dan·te A·li·ghie·ri /dänt′ē al′igyer′ē/ *n* (1265–1321) Italian poet, author of the *Divine Comedy* ‖ **Dan′te·an** *adj & n* ‖ **Dan·tesque** /däntesk′/ *adj*

Dan·ube /dăn′yōōb/ *n* river in central Europe, beginning in S Germany and flowing east to the Black Sea

dap·per /dăp′ər/ [MD = quick, strong] *adj* 1 trim and neat; 2 small and active

dap·ple /dăp′əl/ [ON *depill* spot] *adj* 1 spotted ‖ *n* 2 spotted animal; 3 spot or patch of color ‖ *vt* 4 to mark or cover with spots

D.A.R. Daughters of the American Revolution

Dar·da·nelles /där′dənelz′/ *npl* strait between Europe and Asia Minor, connecting the Sea of Marmara with the Aegean

dare /der′/ [OE *dear pres sg* stem of *durran*] *v* (*pt* **dared** or archaic **durst**) *vi* 1 to have courage; be bold enough ‖ *vt* 2 to venture upon, have the courage for; 3 to brave; 4 to challenge ‖ *n* 5 taunting defiance

dare′dev′il *n* recklessly daring person ‖ **dare′dev′il·try** *n*

dare′say′ *vt & vi* I daresay I venture to say, I assume

Dar es Sa·laam /där′es səläm′/ *n* capital of Tanzania (190,200)

dar′ing *n* 1 bravery, boldness ‖ *adj* 2 fearless, bold ‖ SYN *adj* adventurous, reckless, brave, heroic, courageous, audacious, rash, foolhardy, fearless, bold

dark /därk′/ [OE *deorc*] *adj* 1 without light; 2 not reflecting light; 3 approaching black in color, deep in shade; 4 of a brunette complexion;

5 gloomy, dismal; 6 secretive, secret; 7 little known; 8 ignorant, unenlightened; 9 evil, wicked ‖ *n* 10 absence of light, darkness; 11 night, nightfall; 12 **in the dark, a** in ignorance; **b** in secrecy or concealment ‖ SYN *adj* uncertain, dismal, dull, shadowy, somber, dim, obscure ‖ ANT *adj* bright, brilliant, light, gay

Dark′ Ag′es *npl* 1 period between the fall of the Western Roman Empire in A.D. 476 and the beginning of the 13th century; 2 whole of the Middle Ages

Dark′ Con′ti·nent, The [so called because it was little known until toward the end of the 19th century] *n* Africa

dark′en *vt* 1 to make dark or darker ‖ *vi* 2 to become dark

dark′ horse′ [< former practice of disguising a fast horse with dark paint and entering it in a race with inferior horses to pull off a betting coup] *n* little-known entrant in a race or contest not given much chance of winning

dark′ meat′ *n* poultry that is dark-colored when cooked

dark′room′ *n* room from which extraneous light is excluded, for developing pictures

dark′ star′ *n* star that emits no light, whose presence is revealed by the fact that a visible star revolves in an orbit around it and is sometimes eclipsed by it

dar·ling /där′lĭng/ [OE *dēorling*] *n* 1 one dearly loved or favored ‖ *adj* 2 dearly loved; 3 *colloq* charming, loveable

darn¹ /därn′/ [perh < OE *dernan* to hide] *vt & vi* 1 to mend with rows of stitches ‖ *n* 2 darned place

darn² [< *damn*] *vt, n, adj, adv, interj euphem* damn

darned′ *colloq adj* 1 confounded ‖ *adv* 2 very, extremely

dart /därt′/ [MF < Gmc] *n* 1 small pointed missile, to be thrown or shot; 2 anything like a dart, as an insect's stinger; 3 swift sudden movement; 4 **darts** *sg* game in which darts are thrown at a target ‖ *vt* 5 to throw or move suddenly and rapidly ‖ *vi* 6 to start suddenly and go quickly

dart′board′ *n* target in the game of darts

Dar·win, Charles /där′wĭn/ *n* (1809–82) English naturalist and author, propounder of the theory that the present forms of plants and animals have evolved from simpler forms by slight variations which have been transmitted, those forms tending to survive which are best fitted for their environment ‖ **Dar·win′i·an** /-wĭn′-/ *adj & n* ‖ **Dar′win·ism** *n*

dash /dăsh′/ [ME *dasshen*] *vt* 1 to throw violently; 2 to break by collision, shatter; 3 to splash, spatter;

4 to ruin, frustrate, impede; **5** to abash, put to shame; **6 dash off** to write or sketch hastily || *vi* **7** to rush or strike with violence; **8 dash off** to leave hurriedly || *n* **9** splash; **10** slight addition, touch; **11** decisiveness, animation, spirit; **12** punctuation mark — used to indicate an abrupt pause, separation, or parenthetical remark; **13** dashboard; **14** sudden rush; **15** short race; **16** *telg* signal longer than a dot and used with dots to represent letters

dash'board' *n* instrument panel in an automobile

dash·ing *adj* **1** spirited, bold; **2** showy, gay

das·tard /das'tərd/ [ME] *n* **1** base coward || *adj* **2** meanly shrinking from danger

das'tard·ly *adj* cowardly; slyly base and wicked || SYN *adj* craven, pusillanimous, base (see *recreant*)

dat. dative

da·ta /dāt'ə, dat'ə, dät'ə/ [L = things given; *pl* of *datum*] *nsg* or *npl* information or facts, used as a basis of inference or conclusion

da'ta proc'ess·ing *n* machine analysis and storing of information || **da'ta-proc'ess·ing** *adj*

date[1] /dāt'/ [MF < L *data* (Romae) given (at Rome)] *n* **1** time specified by year, month, and day, of an event; **2** period of time; age; **3** appointment for a fixed time; **4** a social engagement with a person of the opposite sex; **b** person of the opposite sex with whom one has a date; **5 out of date** out of use; out of fashion; **6 to date** up to now; **7 up to date,** a so as to include the latest data; **b** up to modern standards || *vt* **8** to put a date on; **9** to find the date of; **10** to show the age of; **11** to make a date with (a person of the opposite sex) || *vi* **12** to have a date; **13** to reckon time from a given time, era, event, or the like

date[2] [OF < Gk *daktylos* finger] *n* edible fruit of the date palm

dat'ed *adj* **1** carrying a date; **2** out-of-date

date' line' *n* international date line

date'line' *n* **1** line over a newspaper story giving the place of origin and date of the story || *vt* **2** to provide with a dateline

date' palm' *n* date-bearing palm tree (*Phoenix dactylifera*)

date' stamp' *n* device, as a rubber stamp, for stamping the date on mail or documents || **date'-stamp'** *vt*

da·tive /dāt'iv/ [L *dativus*] *n gram* case denoting the indirect object, as *him* in *give him the dollar* || also *adj*

da·tum /dāt'əm/ *n sg* of **data**

daub /dôb'/ [OF *dauber* to whiten] *vt* & *vi* **1** to cover or smear, as with mud or plaster; **2** to paint badly ||

n **3** cheap kind of plaster; **4** crude and inartistic painting; **5** smear, smudge || **daub'er** *n*

daugh·ter /dôt'ər/ [OE *dohtor*] *n* **1** female offspring of human parents; **2** female descendant

daugh'ter-in-law' *n* (**daughters-in-law**) wife of one's son

daunt /dônt', dänt'/ [OF *danter* < L *domitare* to tame] *vt* **1** to frighten; **2** to dishearten || SYN alarm, intimidate, subdue, check, cow, dispirit

daunt'less *adj* fearless, intrepid; undiscouraged

dau·phin /dôf'in/ [F < *Dauphiné* F province] *n* title given to the eldest son of the former kings of France

dau·phine /dôf'ēn/ *n* wife of a dauphin

dav·en·port /dav'ənpôrt'/ [?] *n* upholstered sofa, often convertible into a bed

Da·vid /dāv'id/ *n Bib* second king of Israel, father of Solomon (1 Sam. 16–31; 2 Sam.; 1 Kings 1, 2)

da Vin'ci, Le'o·nar'do *n* see Leonardo da Vinci

Da·vis, Jef·fer·son /dāv'is/ *n* (1808–89) president of the Confederate States of America 1861–65

dav·it /dav'it, dāv'-/ [?] *n* any of various cranelike devices on ships for lowering boats and anchors

Da'vy Jones's lock'er /dāv'ē/ *n* bottom of the sea; grave of those who have perished at sea

daw /dô/ [ME *dawe*] *n* **1** jackdaw; **2** *obs* fool, imbecile

daw·dle /dôd'el/ [?] *vi* **1** to waste time in a trifling manner || *vt* **2** to dawdle away to waste (time) in trifling || **daw'dler** *n* || SYN trifle, dally, delay, potter, loiter, linger

dawn /dôn'/ [OE *dagian*] *vi* **1** to begin to grow light in the morning; **2** to begin to develop or show promise; **3 dawn on** to begin to be evident or plain to || *n* **4** first appearance of daylight; **5** beginning or unfolding, as *the dawn of history*

day /dā'/ [OE *dæg*] *n* **1** period of light between sunrise and sunset; **2** period of twenty-four consecutive hours; **3** number of hours given to work, as *the eight-hour day*; **4** particular or recurring date, as *New Year's Day*; **5** day of conflict or contest, as *to gain the day*; **6, days** *pl* specified epoch or period, as *in days of old*; **7 call it a day** to stop working for the day; **8 day after day** every day

day' bed' *n* couch used also for sleeping

day'break' *n* first appearance of light in the morning

day' camp' *n* children's camp attended only during the day

day' coach' *n* ordinary railroad passenger car

day'dream' *n* **1** state of being lost in

thought; **2** visionary fancy ‖ *vi* **3** to indulge in daydreams

day′ la·bor·er *n* unskilled workman paid by the day

day′ let′ter *n* telegram with a minimum charge for 50 words, slower and cheaper than a regular telegram

day′light′ *n* **1** light of day; **2** time between dawn and dusk; **3 scare the daylights out** of *slang* to frighten to death; **4 see daylight** to approach the end of a difficult task

day′light-sav′ing time′ also **day′light time′** *n* time one hour ahead of standard time, used during the summer months to add one hour of daylight to the evening hours

day′long′ *adj* lasting all day

day′ nurs′er·y *n* place where babies and small children are cared for during the day, as while their mothers are working

day′ school′ *n* private school that does not lodge its students

days′ of grace′ *npl* number of days allowed for the payment of a bill, premium, or note, after it falls due

day′time′ *n* the hours of daylight

Day·ton /dātˊən/ *n* city in SW Ohio (265,000)

daze /dāz′/ [ME *dasen* < ON *dasask* to become weary] *vt* **1** to stun, stupefy, **2** to dazzle, bewilder ‖ *n* **3** dazed condition ‖ **daz·ed·ly** /dāzˊidlē/ *adv*

daz·zle /dazˊəl/ [< *daze*] *vt* **1** to overcome by a glare of light; **2** to bewilder by splendor ‖ *vi* **3** to shine in the light; **4** to be confused by excess of light; **5** to create surprise by brilliance or display ‖ *n* **6** act or instance of dazzling; **7** excess of light; brilliance

DC, D.C., ḋc, d.c. direct current

D.C. District of Columbia

D.D. Doctor of Divinity

D′-day′ *n* **1** day set for the beginning of a large-scale military operation; **2** June 6, 1944, the day of the invasion of German-occupied Europe by the Allies

D.D.S. Doctor of Dental Surgery

DDT [dichloro-diphenyl-trichloro-ethane] *n* white crystalline solid —(ClC₆H₄)₂CHCCl₃— used as an insecticide

de- [L *de* down, away from] *pref* **1** removal, as *defrost;* **2** reversal or negation, as *demobilize;* **3** down, as *depress;* **4** intensity, as *declaim;* **5** away from, as *debark*

dea·con /dēkˊən/ [OE *diacon* < Gk *diakonos*] *n* **1** member of a clerical order below that of priest; **2** layman appointed or elected to assist a minister; elder ‖ **dea′con·ess** *nfem*

dead /ded′/ [OE *dēad*] *adj* **1** no longer living; **2** without life, inanimate; **3** resembling death, as *a dead faint;* **4** inactive, showing no force, motion, or liveliness; **5** no longer operative; **6** obsolete, no longer used, as *a dead language;* **7** complete, utter, as *a dead loss;* **8** unerring, as *a dead shot;* **9** out of play, as *a dead ball;* **10** lacking fire, brilliance, or vivacity; **11** flat; **12** insensitive, unresponsive; **13** exhausted ‖ *n* **14** time of greatest darkness or cold, as *the dead of night;* **15 the dead** *pl* dead people ‖ *adv* **16** completely, as *dead sure;* **17** *naut* exactly, as *dead ahead* ‖ SYN *adj* lifeless, inanimate, spiritless, dull, defunct, deceased, departed, extinct, torpid ‖ DISCR *adj* Dead in literal use generally describes that which has had life, but from which life has departed. *Inanimate* describes that which never had life. *Lifeless* may describe either. We speak of a *dead* body, an *inanimate* block of stone; we may speak of the *lifeless* body of a *dead* person, or of the *lifeless* block of stone. *Lifeless* also describes that from which life has apparently gone, as the body of one under an anæsthetic appears to be *lifeless.* Figuratively, *lifeless* and *dead* (less frequently *inanimate*) imply dullness, spiritlessness, neutrality, a want of mental vitality, etc. *Dead* in this connection is stronger than *lifeless;* we speak of a *dead* issue; a *lifeless* party is dull and boresome ‖ ANT *adj* animate, alive, virile

dead′ a·head′ *adj* & *adv* directly ahead of a ship's course

dead′ a·stern′ *adj* & *adv* directly astern of a ship's course

dead′ beat′ *adj colloq* utterly exhausted

dead′beat′ *n colloq* **1** person who habitually and deliberately avoids paying for anything; **2** lazy loafer

dead′ cen′ter *n* **1** either of the two positions of a crank in which the connecting rod is in the same line as the crank and therefore cannot turn it if there is no flywheel momentum; **2** spindle of the tailstock of a lathe

dead′-drunk′ *adj* unconscious or incapable of moving from excessive drinking

dead′en *vt* **1** to lessen the intensity, activity, or velocity of; **2** to make numb ‖ **dead′en·er** *n*

dead′ end′ *n* **1** street, pipe, etc. closed at one end; **2** condition or position that offers no hope of change ‖ **dead′-end′** *adj*

dead′fall′ *n* trap which catches or kills animals by the fall of a heavy object

dead′head′ *n colloq* **1** person who has a free pass on a railway or to a place of amusement; **2** empty railroad car or train

dead′ heat′ *n* race in which two or more contestants finish in a tie

dead′ let′ter *n* **1** unclaimed letter; **2** law that is no longer enforced

dead/line/ *n* latest time by which something must be done, as filing a news story

dead/lock/ *n* 1 utter standstill, impasse || *vt* 2 to bring to a deadlock || *vi* 3 to come to a deadlock

dead/ly *adj* (-li·er; -li·est) 1 causing death, fatal; 2 relentless, implacable; 3 resembling death, as *a deadly pallor* || *adv* 4 like death; 5 relentlessly || **dead/li·ness** *n* || SYN mortal, implacable, destructive, fatal || DISCR *Deadly* describes that which causes, or can cause, death, as a *deadly disease*; a *deadly germ*; the poisonous nature of the *deadly nightshade*. *Mortal* also describes that which causes death, as a *mortal illness* or *wound*, but, unlike *deadly*, is not applied to that which has brought about the diseased or wounded condition; we do not speak of a *mortal germ* or the *mortal nightshade*. *Mortal* and *deadly* both describe that which is fought to the death, or is implacable, or merciless, as a *mortal battle*, *mortal enmity*; *deadly fighting*, *deadly hate*. *Mortal* also describes those subject to death; all creatures are *mortal*. *Fatal* describes that which is sure to kill, as a *fatal illness*

dead/march/ *n* piece of solemn funeral music

dead/pan/ *adj* & *adv* displaying no emotion on the face

dead/ reck/on·ing *n* calculation of one's position with no navigational aids other than compass and log

Dead/ Sea/ *n* large salt lake between Israel and Jordan, the lowest body of water in the world (1290 ft. below sea level)

dead/ set/ *adj* determined, resolved

dead/ sol/dier *n slang* bottle now empty that contained an alcoholic beverage

dead/ weight/ *n* 1 unyielding weight of any inert body; 2 weight of a vehicle distinguished from that of its load

dead/wood/ *n* anything useless and in the way

deaf /def/ [OE] *adj* 1 unable to hear; 2 unwilling to hear or pay regard || **deaf/ness** *n*

deaf/-and-dumb/ *adj* unable to hear or speak

deaf/en *vt* 1 to make deaf; 2 to stun with noise

deaf/-mute/ *n* one who is congenitally deaf and has not learned to speak || also *adj*

deal /dēl/ [OE *dǣl* part] *n* 1 act of dealing; 2 distribution of cards to the players; 3 *colloq* a business transaction; **b** bargain or secret agreement; 4 *colloq* treatment received from another person; 5 **a good deal** or **a great deal**, a large quantity or amount, as *he spent a good deal of money*; **b** very much, considerably,

as *he smokes a good deal*; 6 **make a great deal of** *colloq* to make a fuss about or over || *v* (**dealt**) *vt* 7 to apportion, distribute; 8 to distribute (playing cards) among the players; 9 to deliver, as a blow; 10 **deal** (someone) **in** *slang* to give (someone) a share or a chance to share || *vi* 11 a to do business, as *he deals with a New York firm; that company deals in coal*; **b** to be concerned, have to do, as *science deals with facts*; 12 to deal the cards; 13 to behave, comport oneself

deal/er *n* 1 person whose business is buying and selling without modification of the product; 2 player who deals the cards

deal/er·ship/ *n* authorization or franchise to sell a commodity

deal/ing *n* 1 conduct toward others; 2 **dealings** *pl* business transactions, relations

dealt /delt/ *pt* & *pp* of **deal**

dean /dēn/ [MF *deien* < L *decanus* chief of ten] *n* 1 head of a chapter in a cathedral; 2 a head of a college faculty; **b** head of a constituent school or college of a university; **c** supervisor of students in a college; 3 senior member of any group || **dean/ship** *n*

dear /dir/ [OE *dēore*] *adj* 1 beloved; 2 *in the salutation of letters* esteemed; 3 a expensive, costly; **b** charging high prices; 4 heartfelt, earnest || *n* 5 darling, favorite || *adv* 6 dearly, at a high rate || *interj* 7 expression of surprise, shock, pity, etc. || **dear/ly** *adv* || **dear/ness** *n* || SYN *adj* high-priced, costly, expensive, exorbitant, extravagant, excessive || DISCR *adj* That which is *dear* costs a great deal; the cost may be either actually great, as *dear* but ill-chosen furnishings; or it may be merely relatively great, as a scarcity of eggs makes them *dear*. *Expensive* implies that the article is priced for more than it is worth, or in excess of the purchaser's power to pay for it. *Costly* describes that which requires a great deal of money to pay for it; it implies gorgeousness, richness, or fine workmanship, as *costly robes*; *costly* curios. *Exorbitant* means priced beyond reason or right; tourists frequently pay *exorbitant* prices for souvenirs || ANT *adj* cheap, inexpensive, despised

Dear/ John/ *n slang* letter from a woman to her fiancé breaking off relations or from a wife to her husband asking for a divorce

dearth /durth/ [ME *derthe*] *n* scarcity, lack

death /deth/ [OE] *n* 1 act or instance of dying; 2 state of being dead; 3 destruction, extinction, end; 4 that which causes death; 5 **Death** personification of the agent of death; **6 at death's door** on the point of death; **7 do to death,** a to kill; b to repeat to the point of boredom; **8 to death** to a great degree || SYN departure, decease, demise, extinction

death'bed' n 1 bed in which one dies; 2 last hours of life

death'blow' n 1 something that causes death; 2 shock from which there is no recovery

death' house' n place in a prison for housing prisoners awaiting execution

death' knell' n 1 herald of death or extinction; 2 bell tolled to announce a death or a funeral

death'less adj immortal

death'ly adj 1 mortal, fatal; 2 resembling death || adv 3 very

death' mask' n cast taken of a dead person's face

death' rat'tle n sound of the breathing of a dying person

death' ray' n ray that is supposed to kill people at a distance

death' row' n row of cells housing prisoners awaiting execution

death's'-head' n human skull as the symbol of death

death'trap' n unsafe structure or situation

Death' Val'ley n very hot desert in SE California, lowest land in North America (280 ft. below sea level)

deb /deb'/ n colloq debutante

de·ba·cle /dɪbäk'əl, -bak'-/ [F débâcle] n complete rout, collapse

de·bar /dɪbär'/ [MF] v (-barred; -barring) vt 1 to shut out, exclude; 2 to hinder, stop || **de·bar'ment** n

de·bark /dɪbärk'/ vt & vi to disembark || **de'bar·ka'tion** /dē'-/ n

de·base /dɪbās'/ vt to reduce in quality or value || **de·base'ment** n

de·bat·a·ble /dɪbāt'əbəl/ adj questionable, doubtful

de·bate /dɪbāt'/ [MF debatre] vt 1 to discuss by presenting arguments for and against; 2 to dispute about; 3 to meditate upon, ponder || vi 4 to argue or discuss; 5 to engage in debate || n 6 controversy, discussion; 7 formal presentation of arguments on both sides of a question || **de·bat'er** n || SYN v deliberate, consider, argue, dispute, discuss; n contention, controversy, argument, discussion

de·bauch /dɪbôch'/ [F débaucher] vt 1 to corrupt in morals or principles; seduce, deprave || vi 2 to engage in debauchery || n 3 orgy

de·bauch'er·y n (-ies) intemperance, indulgence in sensual pleasures

de·ben·ture /dɪbench'ər/ [L debentur they are owing] n certificate of indebtedness, as an interest-bearing bond

de·bil·i·tate /dɪbil'itāt'/ vt to weaken, enfeeble

de·bil·i·ty /dɪbil'itē/ [MF debilite <

L debilitas] n (-ties) weakness, feebleness || SYN infirmity, weakness, feebleness, enervation, decrepitude, impotence || DISCR These words all name forms of physical deficiency. *Weakness,* the broadest term, names a general lack of strength; *weakness* may result from a natural cause, as a frail constitution; it may be permanent or temporary. *Feebleness* is a form of *weakness;* it is either a condition of age, as of infancy or senility, or such a state as resembles the shakiness or powerlessness of age. *Infirmity* names either a chronic disability, such as deafness, or that condition of deteriorated vitality characteristic of old age. *Debility* names a lack, usually of muscular power, due to overuse or increasing age, as senile *debility* caused his death

deb·it /deb'it/ [L debitum debt] n 1 entry of debt in an account; 2 bookkeeping left-hand page or column of an account, where such entries are made || vt 3 to enter (an amount) on the debit side; 4 to enter an amount to the debit of (a person or account)

deb·o·nair /deb'əner'/ [OF de bon aire of good disposition] adj 1 gay, light-hearted; 2 gracious, courteous

de·bouch /dɪbōōsh', -bouch'/ [F déboucher] vi to emerge or come out, as a river into a bay, a narrow pass into an open plain, or a body of troops into the open from a hidden place

de·brief' /dē-/ vt 1 to interrogate or question in order to gain information about a mission; 2 to instruct not to reveal classified information after release from employment

de·bris /dəbrē', dāb'rē/ [F débris] n fragments, rubbish

debt /det/ [OF dette < L debitum] n 1 that which is owed; **2 in debt** in a state of owing || **debt'or** n

de·bug /dɪbug'/ v (-bugged; -bug·ging) vt 1 to free of errors; to restore to normal operation; 2 to remove a hidden listening device from

de·bunk /dɪbuŋk'/ vt to strip of undeserved reputation, reveal in a true light; deflate

de·but /dɪbyōō', dāb'yōō/ [F début] n 1 first appearance, as of a performer before an audience or of a young girl in society; 2 any first attempt || vi 3 to make a debut

deb·u·tante /deb'yətänt', -tant'/ n young girl making a debut into society

Dec. December

dec·a· or **dec-** [Gk] comb form ten (used esp. in the metric system)

dec·ade /dek'ād/ [Gk dekas (-ados) group of ten] n 1 period of ten years; 2 group of ten

de·ca·dence /dikād'əns, dek'ədəns/ [MF < L decadere to fall away] n decay, decline, deterioration, as in morality, literature, and the arts ‖ **de'ca·dent** adj & n

dec·a·gon /dek'əgən/ n plane figure having ten sides

de·cal /dikal'/ dē'kal, dek'əl/ [< *decalcomania* < F *décalquer* to transfer a tracing + *-mania*] n design on special paper which is transferred to any smooth surface

de·cal·ci·fy dikal'sifī'/ v (-fied) vt to deprive of lime, as bones ‖ **de·cal'ci·fi·ca'tion** n

Dec·a·log or **Dec·a·logue** /dek'əlog/, -lôg'/ [*deca-* + Gk *logos* saying] n the Ten Commandments

De·cam·er·on /dikam'ərən/ [*deca-* + Gk *hemera* day] n work by Boccaccio containing 100 tales to be narrated in ten days

de·camp /dikamp'/ [F *décamper*] vi 1 to break up camp; 2 to depart suddenly or secretly ‖ SYN abscond, run away, escape, flee

de·cant /dikant'/ [ML *decanthare*] vt to pour gently without disturbing the sediment, as liquor from one bottle to another

de·cant'er n ornamental glass bottle for serving wine and liquor

de·cap·i·tate /dikap'itāt'/ [*de-* + L *caput* (-*itis*) head] vt to behead ‖ **de·cap'i·ta'tion** n

dec·a·pod /dek'əpod'/ [*deca-* + Gk *pous* (*podos*) foot] n any of an order (Decapoda) of the Crustacea, including shrimps, lobsters, and crabs, with five pairs of walking legs

de·cath·lon /dikath'lən, -lon/ [*deca-* + Gk *athlon* contest] n athletic contest consisting of ten different track-and-field events

de·cay /dikā'/ [ONF *decaïr* < *de-* + L *cadere* to fall] vi 1 to rot, putrefy; 2 to decline, deteriorate; 3 *phys* to change spontaneously into one or more different nuclei (said of a radioactive nucleus) ‖ vt 4 to cause to decay ‖ n 5 act, process, or instance of decaying ‖ SYN n impairment, decomposition, putrefaction, corruption ‖ ANT n growth, preservation, wholeness

de·cease /disēs'/ [OF *deces* < L *decedere* (-*cessus*) to depart] n 1 death ‖ vi 2 to die

de·ceased' adj 1 no longer living; dead ‖ n 2 **the deceased** dead person or persons

de·ce·dent /disēd'ənt/ n *law* one deceased

de·ceit /disēt'/ [OF *deceite*] n fraud, misrepresentation, deception, falsehood, double dealing ‖ **de·ceit'ful** adj ‖ **de·ceit'ful·ly** adv ‖ SYN imposition, imposture, artifice, treachery, sham, guile, duplicity, lying (see *deception*)

de·ceive /disēv'/ [OF *deceivre* < L *decipere* to take away] vt 1 to mislead or cause to err; delude ‖ vi 2 to use

deceit ‖ **de·ceiv'er** n ‖ SYN delude, gull, overreach, dupe, mislead, outwit, circumvent, hoodwink, ensnare, trick, betray, cheat

de·cel·er·ate /dēsel'ərāt'/ [*de-* + *accelerate*] vt & vi to slow down ‖ **de·cel'er·a'tion** n

De·cem·ber /disem'bər/ [L = tenth month (of Roman calendar)] n twelfth month of the year, having 31 days

de·cen·cy /dēs'ənsē/ [L *decentia*] n (-*cies*) 1 quality of being decent; 2 that which is decent; 3 propriety; modesty, respectability

de·cen·ni·al /disen'ē·əl/ [< LL *decennium* ten-year period] adj 1 consisting of ten years; 2 occurring at ten-year intervals ‖ n 3 decennial anniversary

de·cent /dēs'ənt/ [< L *decere* to be seemly] adj 1 becoming, suitable; 2 respectable; 3 free from obscenity; 4 passable, adequate; 5 kind, obliging ‖ **de'cent·ly** adv ‖ SYN proper, decorous, moderate (see *becoming*)

de·cen'tral·ize' /dē-/ vt 1 to transfer from a central point to outlying points; 2 to distribute, as governmental authority, to communities ‖ **de·cen'tral·i·za'tion** n

de·cep·tion /disep'shən/ [OF *decepcioun* < L *deceptus* deceived] n 1 act of deceiving; 2 state of being deceived; 3 that which deceives; fraud ‖ **de·cep'tive** adj ‖ SYN deceit, deceitfulness, falsehood, hypocrisy, dissimulation, guile, fraud, duplicity, delusion, untruth ‖ DISCR *Deceit* and *deception* both name the act of deceiving, but *deceit* always involves the intent to deceive; *deception*, though it may result from the intent to deceive, may also be unintentional. *Deceit* is practiced upon the understanding; *deception* may affect the senses as well. A mere false impression constitutes a *deception*; self-*deception* is common. *Deceitfulness* names the vice of, or tendency to, *deceit*. *Duplicity* is deliberate bad faith; it is accomplished by acting in one way while feeling, or intending to act, in another. *Guile*, as a characteristic, names a propensity to deceive that permeates the whole man; as an act, it denotes a *deception* accomplished by wiles or subtle artifice. An *untruth* is a false statement, spoken or written ‖ ANT frankness, veracity, honesty

dec·i- [< L *decimus* tenth] *comb form* tenth (used esp. in the metric system)

dec·i·bel /des'ībel'/ [*deci-* + *bel* < Alexander G. Bell (1847–1922) Scottish-born U.S. inventor of the telephone] n 1 unit for the measurement of the intensity of sound, one decibel representing the faintest sound that can be heard by the human ear; 2 unit which expresses the difference in power between two acoustic or electric signals, equal to one tenth the common logarithm of the ratio of the two levels

de·cide /dĭsīd'/ [MF *decider* < L *decidere* to cut off] *vt* 1 to settle, determine; bring to an issue or conclusion; 2 to cause (a person) to settle or determine something ‖ *vi* 3 to give a judgment or decision ‖ SYN settle, determine, judge, adjudge, arbitrate

de·cid'ed *adj* 1 definite, unquestionable; 2 determined, positive ‖ **de·cid'ed·ly** *adv*

de·cid·u·ous /dĭsij'ŏŏ-əs/ [< L *decidere* to fall down] *adj* 1 shedding the leaves annually; 2 shedding seasonally, as antlers; 3 shedding at a certain stage, as milk teeth

dec·i·mal /des'əməl/ [< L *decimus* tenth] *adj* 1 pert. to or based upon the number ten ‖ *n* 2 decimal fraction

dec'i·mal frac'tion *n* fraction having a power of ten as its denominator, indicated by a dot before the numerator

dec'i·mal point' *n* dot indicating that the number following is a decimal fraction

dec'i·mate' [L *decimare* (*-atus*) to take the tenth man] *vt* 1 to destroy a large part of; 2 to take a tenth of; 3 to select for execution every tenth man from ‖ **dec'i·ma'tion** *n*

dec'i·me'ter *n* metric measure of length equal to one tenth of a meter (3.937 in.)

de·ci·pher /dĭsīf'ər/ [*de-* + *cipher*] *vt* 1 to convert (secret or unknown characters) into understandable terms; decode; 2 to make out the meaning of, as something puzzling or hardly legible ‖ **de·ci'pher·a·ble** *adj*

de·ci·sion /dĭsizh'ən/ [see **decide**] *n* 1 act of deciding; 2 act of making up one's mind; 3 quality of being resolute and firm; determination; 4 judgment; legal settlement ‖ SYN conclusion, resolution, determination, resoluteness, stamina, firmness (see *determination*) ‖ ANT hesitation, irresolution, instability, vacillation

de·ci·sive /dĭsīs'iv/ *adj* 1 final, conclusive; 2 resolute, determined ‖ **de·ci'sive·ly** *adv* ‖ SYN conclusive, certain, final, decided, definite

deck /dek'/ [prob MD *dek* covering] *n* 1 a floor covering each level of a ship; b space between such floors; 2 pack of playing cards; 3 **clear the decks** prepare for combat or action; 4 **on deck** baseball (batter) next in line to bat ‖ *vt* 5 **deck out** to outfit, adorn ‖ SYN *v* decorate, embellish, ornament, array, garnish

deck' hand' *n* sailor who works on the deck of a ship

deck'le edge' /dek'əl/ *n* irregular untrimmed edge on handmade paper ‖ **deck'le-edged'** *adj*

de·claim /dĭklām'/ [L *declamare* to cry out] *vt & vi* to utter publicly in rhetorical style

dec·la·ma·tion /dek'ləmāsh'ən/ *n* 1 act or art of declaiming; 2 public speech made for oratorical effect ‖ **de·clam'a·to'ry** /dĭklam'ətôr'ē, -tōr'-/ *adj*

dec·la·ra·tion /dek'lərāsh'ən/ *n* 1 act of declaring; announcement; 2 that which is announced; 3 positive or formal statement ‖ SYN avowal, proclamation, profession, assertion

de·clar·a·tive /dĭklar'ətiv/ *adj* making a statement or declaration

de·clare /dĭklâr'/ [L *declarare* to make clear] *vt* 1 to make known publicly; 2 to proclaim formally; 3 to state emphatically; 4 to announce the payment of (a dividend); 5 *bridge* to make (a suit) trumps; 6 to make a statement of, as goods liable to duty or income liable to taxes ‖ *vi* 7 to proclaim an opinion, decision, etc. ‖ **de·clar'er** *n* ‖ SYN aver, avow, disclose, profess, announce, advertise, proclaim, publish, communicate, reveal, herald ‖ DISCR The idea common to all these words is that of making known. To *announce* is to tell that which is presumably not known, or not formally acknowledged, as to *announce* a prize contest, a candidacy, the arrival of a guest, or a marriage. To *declare* is to make a simple statement of fact or opinion, as he *declared* this interference to be an outrage; or to state explicitly, as to *declare* one's purpose or intentions; or to disclose where one stands on a question, or an action in consequence of one's situation; especially, thus to disclose formally, as to *declare* war. To *publish* is to make known through mediums that will reach everybody; it is commonly used of the medium of the press, though a gossiping woman can *publish* the news of a community quite as effectively as the printed page. To *proclaim* is literally to cry aloud; it is to make known some event of great consequence or merit in the way that will secure the greatest possible publicity, as to *proclaim* peace ‖ ANT suppress, conceal, withhold

de·clas·si·fy' /dē-/ *v* (**-fied**) *vt* to remove the secret classification from, as documents or information ‖ **de·clas'si·fi·ca'tion** *n*

de·clen·sion /dĭklen'shən/ [MF *de-clinaison* < L *declinare* to bend] *n* inflection of nouns, pronouns, and adjectives

dec·li·na·tion /dek'lĭnāsh'ən/ *n* 1 act or state of bending or moving downward; 2 angle between the direction of magnetic north and true north; 3

variation from some definite direction; 4 decline, decay; 5 refusal, non-acceptance; 6 angular distance of a heavenly body from the celestial equator

de-cline /diklīn′/ [L *declinare* to bend] *vi* 1 to deteriorate; 2 to draw to a close; 3 to refuse ‖ *vt* 4 to bend downward; 5 to refuse; 6 *gram* to inflect (noun, pronoun, or adjective) ‖ *n* 7 lessening, diminution; 8 decay, deterioration; 9 ending, final part ‖ SYN *v* repel, reject, rebuff, refuse, shun, bend, decay

de-cliv-i-ty /diklĭv′itē/ [< L *declivis* sloping down] *n* (-ties) downward slope

de-coct /dikŏkt′/ [L *decoctus* boiled down] *vt* to extract the essence of by boiling ‖ de-coc′tion *n*

de-code′ /dē′-/ *vt* to translate (a message in code) into intelligible language

dé-col-le-tage /dā′kŏltäzh′/ [F] *n* 1 neckline of a low-cut dress; 2 décolleté dress

dé-col-le-té /dā′kŏltā′/ [F=low-necked] *adj* 1 (dress) cut low in the neck; 2 wearing a low-necked dress

de-com-mis-sion /dē′-/ *vt* to retire from active service, as a warship

de-com-pose′ /dē′-/ *vt & vi* 1 to separate into its constituent parts; 2 to rot, putrefy ‖ de-com-po-si′tion *n*

de-con-tam-i-nate /dē′-/ *vt* to make free of contamination ‖ de-con-tam′-i-na′tion *n*

de-con-trol′ /dē′-/ *v* (-trolled; -trol-ling) *vt* to remove controls from ‖ also *n*

dé-cor /dākôr′/ [F] *n* 1 style of decoration, as of a room; 2 stage decoration; scenery

dec-o-rate /dek′ərāt′/ [L *decorare* (-*atus*)] *vt* 1 to ornament, adorn; 2 a to paint and refurbish, as a room; b to style in a particular fashion, as a room or interior; 3 to confer a badge of honor upon ‖ dec-o-ra-tive /dek′-ərətiv, -rāt′iv/ *adj* ‖ SYN embellish, deck, array, beautify, ornament

dec-o-ra′tion *n* 1 act of decorating; 2 ornament, trimming; 3 badge of honor, as a ribbon or medal

Dec′o-ra′tion Day′ *n* Memorial Day

dec-o-ra′tor *n* interior decorator

dec-o-rous /dek′ərəs, dikôr′əs, -kōr′-əs/ [see **decorum**] *adj* marked by propriety; decent; proper; polite ‖ dec′-o-rous-ly *adv* ‖ SYN seemly, fitting, staid, suitable, sedate, demure, becoming ‖ ANT unseemly, undignified, improper

de-co-rum /dikôr′əm, -kōr′-/ [L = that which is suitable] *n* 1 propriety of language, dress, and conduct; 2 suitableness; dignity

de-coy /dē′koi, dikoi′/ [D *de kooi* the cage] *n* 1 one who or that which entices into a trap; 2 artificial or

trained live animal used to lure other animals within gunshot ‖ /-dikoi′/ *vt* 3 to lure with or as if with a decoy ‖ *vi* 4 to be decoyed; be lured by a decoy ‖ SYN *v* entice, ensnare, entrap, inveigle, lure

de-crease /dikrēs′/ [OF *decreistre* < L *decrescere*] *vi* 1 to grow less, diminish, dwindle ‖ *vt* 2 to cause to decrease ‖ /dē′krēs/ *n* 3 abatement, reduction; 4 amount or degree of decreasing ‖ SYN *v* abate, lessen, reduce, decline, dwindle, diminish, slacken, mitigate, ebb, curtail, wane ‖ DISCR To *decrease* is to become less or fall off, especially by an inner or natural process, as winter days *decrease* in length until December 21. *Decrease* also has the meaning to make less, as the nurse *decreased* the dose. To *abate* is to grow less, especially in violence or vigor, as anger, the storm, a quarrel, *abates*; the waters *abated*; *abate* has also the meaning to bring down, as in degree, force, etc, as to *abate* unhappiness, pride; or, in legal language, to put an end to, as to *abate* a nuisance. *Lessen* (the more familiar term) and *diminish* mean to become less in size, number, or quantity, as his responsibilities *lessened* with age; the importance of royalty has *diminished*. Both these words also have the meaning to make less, as the cyclist *lessened* his speed; war *diminishes* the male population. To *dwindle* is to shrink or waste away, or to disappear gradually, as Rip Van Winkle's "estate had *dwindled* away under his management"

de-cree /dikrē′/ [OF *decre* < L *decretum* thing decided] *n* 1 ordinance or edict; 2 judicial decision ‖ *vt & vi* 3 to determine or decide by a decree ‖ SYN *v* dictate, command, enjoin, order, require

dec-re-ment /dek′rəmənt/ [see **decrease**] *n* 1 act of decreasing; waste; 2 amount by which something is decreased

de-crep-it /dikrep′it/ [L *decrepitus*] *adj* 1 feeble from age or infirmity; 2 worn out, broken down ‖ de-crep′i-tude′ /-t(y)ōōd′/ *n*

de-cry /dikrī′/ [F décrier] *v* (-cried) *vt* to blame, censure; disparage ‖ SYN belittle, depreciate, degrade, discredit (see *disparage*) ‖ ANT overrate, praise, extol

ded-i-cate /ded′ikāt′/ [L *dedicare* (-*atus*)] *vt* 1 to set apart by a solemn act or religious ceremony; 2 to devote, as one's life; 3 to inscribe, as a book ‖ ded′i-ca′tion *n* ‖ ded-i-ca-to-ry /ded′ikətôr′ē, -tōr′ē/ *adj* ‖ SYN devote, offer, consecrate, address

de-duce /did(y)ōōs′/ [L *deducere* to lead down] *vt* to derive (a truth or conclusion) from something known; infer || de•duc/i•ble *adj*

de-duct /didukt'/ [L *deductus* withdrawn] *vt* to take away, subtract || de•duct/i•ble *adj*

de-duc/tion *n* 1 act or process of deducting; 2 that which is deducted; 3 act or process of deducing; 4 something deduced; inference || de•duc/tive *adj* || SYN induction || DISCR *Deduction* names that form of reasoning which proceeds from the general to the particular. *Deduction* works from a general principle through a special case, adduced as an instance of the principle, to a conclusion. If the general principle is true, and if the instance cited actually does fall under this principle, the conclusion arrived at is true, as in a geometrical demonstration. *Induction* names that form of reasoning which proceeds from the particular to the general. It is the type employed in the formulation of general laws and principles. Many instances, critically examined, are observed to point through some common characteristic to a certain conclusion. If the instances are numerous enough, and the common characteristic is unfailing, the conclusion is probably true, though, as in the case of a natural law, it is impossible to assert that every instance in the universe has been adduced. As compared to a conclusion reached by *deduction*, therefore, a conclusion reached by *induction* is only probable (see *conclusion*)

deed /dēd'/ [OE *dæd*] *n* 1 that which is done; act; 2 great achievement, exploit; 3 legal document conveying or transferring title to land or other real property || *vt* 4 to convey by deed || SYN *n* action, feat, exploit, performance, document

deem /dēm'/ [OE *dēman*] *vt* to think, regard, believe

de-em'pha-size' /dē-/ *vt* to place less emphasis on, reduce in importance || de-em'pha-sis /-sis/ *n*

deep /dēp'/ [OE *dēop*] *adj* 1 extending or situated far down, in, or back; 2 sagacious; 3 profound, intense; 4 difficult to understand; 5 absorbed, engrossed; 6 low in pitch; 7 strongly colored; 8 earnest, heartfelt; 9 in depth, as *six feet deep* || *n* 10 deep part of an ocean; 11 vast extent; 12 culmination, middle, as *the deep of night*, 13 **the deep** *poet.* the ocean || *adv* 14 to or at a great depth; 15 **in deep** deeply involved || deep'ly *adv* || deep'ness *n*

deep'-dyed' *adj* unmitigated

deep'en *vt* 1 to make deep or deeper || *vi* 2 to become deep or deeper

deep'-freeze' *v* (-freezed or -froze; -freezed or -fro-zen) *vt* to quick-freeze

deep'-fry' *v* (-fried) *vt* to fry in fat deep enough to cover the food

deep'-laid' *adj* well arranged, carefully concealed, as a plot

deep'-sea' *adj* pert. to the open sea, or deeper parts of the ocean

deep'-seat'ed *adj* firmly implanted

Deep' South' *n* southern tier of states in the eastern U.S., ranging from Louisiana to South Carolina

deep' space' *n* outer space beyond the solar system

deer /dir'/ [OE *dēor* beast] *nsg & npl* any of several ruminants of the family Cervidae, the males of which bear deciduous antlers

de-es'ca-late' /dē-/ *vt & vi* to decrease in magnitude || de•es'ca•la'tion *n*

de-face /difās'/ [OF *desfacier*] *vt* to spoil or destroy the appearance of; disfigure || de•face'ment *n* || de•fac'er *n* || SYN deform, efface, injure, destroy, distort, ruin, mar

de facto /dēfak'tō/ [L] *adv* 1 actually, in reality || *adj* 2 actual though not necessarily legitimate, as *the rebels established a de facto government*

de-fal-ca-tion /dē'falkāsh'ən, -fôl-/ *n* 1 embezzlement of money held in trust; 2 sum embezzled

de-fame /difām'/ [OF *diffamer* < L *diffamare*] *vt* to injure or destroy the good reputation of, speak maliciously of || de•fam'er *n* || de•fam'a•to'ry /-famətôr'ē, -tōr'-/ *adj* || def'a•ma'tion /def'ə-, dēf'-/ *n* || SYN abuse, asperse, malign, slander (see *calumniate*)

de-fault /difôlt'/ [AF *defalte*] *n* 1 failure to act, or do what is required; 2 failure to make a payment when due; 3 absence; deficiency || *vi* 4 to commit default || *vt* 5 to fail to perform or pay; 6 *law* to declare to be in default; 7 *sports* to lose by default || de•fault'er *n* || SYN *n* lapse, forfeit, omission, neglect, absence

de-feat /difēt'/ [OF *desfeit* undone] *vt* 1 to win over, vanquish; 2 to frustrate, bring to naught || *n* 3 act or instance of defeating or state of being defeated || SYN *v* beat, conquer, subdue (see *vanquish*)

de-feat'ist *n* one who easily gives up hope of victory and thinks further struggle is futile || de•feat'ism *n*

def-e-cate /def'ikāt'/ [L *defaecare* (-*atus*) to cleanse] *vi* to pass excrement from the bowels || def'e•ca'tion *n*

de-fect /dē'fekt, difekt'/ [L *deficere* (-*fectus*) to fail] *n* 1 mental, moral, or physical imperfection; 2 fault, deficiency || /difekt'/ *vi* 3 to desert one's cause, party, or country in order to join the other side || SYN *n* deficiency, flaw, stigma, fault (see *blemish*)

de-fec'tion *n* 1 falling away from duty or allegiance; 2 failure

de·fec′tive *adj* 1 imperfect, faulty; 2 mentally deficient; 3 *gram* incomplete in inflection ‖ *n* 4 defective person

de·fec′tor *n* person who deserts his cause, party, or country to join the other side

de·fend /difend′/ [OF *defendre* < L *defendere* to ward off] *vt* 1 to guard or protect from harm or violence; 2 to maintain or uphold; 3 to contest (a lawsuit); 4 to represent (the accused) in court ‖ *vi* 5 *law* to make a defense ‖ **de·fend′er** *n* ‖ SYN protect, preserve, guard, keep, cover, shelter, screen, shield, vindicate, maintain, save, justify ‖ DISCR As here compared, to *defend* is ordinarily to drive away an enemy who is actually assaulting; to *guard* is to stand ready to fend off actual attack, to shield from threatened harm, or merely to keep in safety. Soldiers *defend* their country in time of war; they *guard* our coasts in time of peace; we *guard* against the spread of a contagious disease; we *guard* valuable possessions. To *protect* is to shield either from actual or possible harm; adults *protect* children; we *protect* ourselves from cold. To *preserve* is to keep from harm, as God *preserve* us from evil! We have *preserved* George Washington's Mount Vernon home; we *preserve* fruits for winter use. *Keep* in the sense of *defend* implies that the defense, as of a fortress, has been successful

de·fend′ant *n* one who is sued or accused

de·fense /difens′/ [OF *defens*] *n* 1 act of defending or state of being defended; protection; 2 person or thing that protects or defends; 3 that which justifies; vindication; 4 *law* a answer in court opposing or denying a charge or suit; b procedure used to contest a suit; c defendant and his counsel collectively ‖ **de·fense′less** *adj* ‖ **de·fen′si·ble** *adj* ‖ SYN rampart, bulwark, vindication, excuse, plea

de·fen′sive *adj* 1 serving to defend; 2 carried on for defense; 3 in a condition of making defense ‖ *n* 4 attitude or means of defense ‖ **de·fen′sive·ly** *adv*

de·fer¹ /difur′/ [MF *differer* < L *differre*] *v* (-ferred; -fer·ring) *vt & vi* 1 to delay, postpone; 2 to exempt temporarily from the draft ‖ **de·fer′ment** *n* ‖ SYN delay, postpone, procrastinate, retard, detain, hinder, prorogue, adjourn ‖ DISCR *Delay, procrastinate, defer,* and *postpone* agree in the idea of putting off. To *delay* is to put off beginning, to dally along without action, especially through laziness or indecision. To *procrastinate* is to put off doing that which really should be done—through inertia, neglect, or laziness. One who *delays* may act sometime; one who *procrastinates* is apt never to act. To *defer* and to *postpone* are to put off until another time—the time may or may not be specifically mentioned, but the intention to resume the matter in hand is always implied, *defer* being the more general in sense. Thus we *defer* making certain calls; we *postpone* discussions until the next meeting; a storm may cause us to *postpone* a trip

de·fer² [MF *deferer* < L *deferre* to bring down] *v* (-ferred; -fer·ring) *vi* 1 to yield in opinion or judgment ‖ *vt* 2 to refer; submit for decision

def·er·ence /def′ərəns/ *n* 1 a yielding to the opinions or wishes of another; 2 courteous submission, respect ‖ SYN respect, veneration, reverence, regard ‖ DISCR *Deference* is a courteous regard or submission to those whose age, position, or ability demands such recognition from us. *Deference* may not indicate agreement or preference on our part. *Respect* is a feeling of honor and genuine appreciation, with or without affection or agreement, tendered to a person or quality honestly deserving of it

def·er·en·tial /def′ərensh′əl/ *adj* expressing deference; respectful

de·fi·ance /difi′əns/ [see **defy**] *n* 1 scornful disregard; 2 challenge; 3 refusal to obey ‖ **de·fi′ant** *adj* ‖ **de·fi′ant·ly** *adv*

de·fi·cient /difish′ənt/ [L *deficiens* (-entis)] *adj* incomplete; defective ‖ **de·fi′cien·cy** *n* (-cies) ‖ SYN short, insufficient, inadequate, scanty, lacking

def·i·cit /def′isit/ [L = it is lacking] *n* shortage of money, as in an account, budget, etc.

de·file¹ /difil′/ [< OF *defouler* to trample on] *vt* 1 to make foul or impure; 2 to desecrate; 3 to sully ‖ **de·file′ment** *n* ‖ SYN soil, pollute, contaminate, violate

de·file² [F *défiler* to file off] *vi* 1 to march off in a line ‖ /defil′, difil′/ *n* 2 narrow pass

de·fine /difin′/ [OF *definer* to put an end to < L *definire*] *vt* 1 to fix the limits of; 2 to state the meaning of ‖ **de·fin′a·ble** *adj* ‖ SYN fix, settle, limit, prescribe, interpret, expound

def·i·nite /def′init/ *adj* 1 precise, exact; 2 positive; 3 having fixed or clear limits ‖ **def′i·nite·ly** *adv* ‖ SYN particular, certain, limited, clear, determinate

def′i·nite ar′ti·cle *n* article (in English, *the*) which makes definite the noun it modifies

def·i·ni′tion *n* 1 act of defining or making clear; 2 condition of being definite; 3 brief explanation of the exact meaning of a term; **4** sharpness of the image formed by a lens ‖ SYN description, exposition, interpretation, meaning, definitiveness, precision (see *explanation*)

de·fin·i·tive /difin′itiv/ *adj* **1** positive; final, fixed; **2** limiting; defining; **3** most reliable or complete, as a text or study

de·flate /diflāt′/ [L *deflare* (-*flatus*) to blow away] *vt* **1** to release air or gas from, as a tire; **2** to lessen or reduce (prices, size, importance, pride, etc.) or the price, size, importance, pride, etc. of

de·fla′tion *n* **1** act of deflating or state of being deflated; **2** process by which the volume of the medium of exchange decreases more rapidly than the volume of business done, as evidenced by a fall in prices

de·flect /diflekt′/ [L *deflectere*] *vt & vi* to bend or turn aside, swerve ‖ **de·flec′tion** *n* ‖ **de·flec′tor** *n*

def·lo·ra·tion /def′lərāsh′ən/ [< L *deflorare* to deflower] *n* act of deflowering

de·flow′er /di-/ *vt* **1** to deprive of flowers; **2** to despoil; **3** to deprive (a woman) of virginity

de·fo·li·ate /dēfōl′ē-āt′/ [*de-* + L *folium* leaf] *vt* **1** to strip or deprive of leaves; **2** to destroy (plant life) by use of chemical sprays or incendiary bombs ‖ **de·fo′li·a′tion** *n*

de·for·est /dē̆-/ *vt* to clear away the trees of ‖ **de·for′es·ta′tion** *n*

de·form /difôrm′/ [L *deformare*] *vt* **1** to render ugly or unshapely; disfigure; **2** to mar, deface; **3** *mech* to change the shape of ‖ **def′or·ma′·tion** /def′ər-, dē′fôr-/ *n*

de·form′i·ty *n* (-**ties**) **1** deformed part of the body; **2** state of being deformed

de·fraud /difrôd′/ [OF *defrauder* < L *defraudare*] *vt* to take or withhold something wrongfully from; cheat ‖ SYN cheat, swindle, trick, dupe, hoax

de·fray /difrā′/ [F *défrayer*] *vt* to pay (the costs or expenses) ‖ **de·fray′al** *n* ‖ SYN liquidate, discharge, satisfy, pay, settle

de·frost /di-/ *vt* **1** to remove the frost or ice from ‖ *vi* **2** to thaw

deft /deft′/ [ME] *adj* skillful, dexterous ‖ **deft′ly** *adv* ‖ SYN adroit, skillful, apt, handy (see *clever*)

de·funct /difuŋkt′/ [< L *defunctus* finished, dead] *adj* dead; extinct

de·fuze′, de·fuse′ /dē̆-/ *vt* **1** to remove the fuze from (a bomb, mine, etc.); **2** to make (a situation) safe by removing a dangerous or explosive element from it

de·fy /difī′/ [OF *desfier*] *v* (-**fied**) *vt* **1** to challenge or provoke to strife; dare; **2** to act in contempt of, resist openly; **3** to resist successfully

de Gaulle, Charles /dəgōl′/ *n* (1890–

1970) French general and statesman; president of France 1945–1946, 1959–1969

de·gauss /dēgous′/ [*de-* + *gauss*] *vt* to neutralize the magnetic field of (a ship, electric device, etc.) by means of electric coils

de·gen·er·ate /dijen′ərāt′/ [< L *degener* ignoble] *vi* **1** to decline physically, mentally, or morally, deteriorate; **2** *biol* to become of a lower type ‖ /-it/ *adj* **3** having degenerated ‖ *n* **4** degenerate person ‖ **de·gen′er·a·cy** /-əsē̆/ *n*

de·gen·er·a′tion *n* **1** state or process of degenerating; **2** *biol* a reversion to a simpler type; **b** decay or alteration of structure with loss or impairment of function ‖ SYN deterioration ‖ DISCR *Deterioration* names an impairment of what was, comparatively at least, sound; *deterioration* occurs in minds allowed to vegetate, in characters permitted to compromise, in monetary values which have declined, and, by natural processes, in fruits and other perishable products. *Degeneration*, like *deterioration*, contains the idea of becoming worse; applied to a race, it connotes reversion to a simpler type, often implying a falling off in standards

deg·ra·da·tion /deg′rə-/ *n* **1** act of degrading; **2** state of being degraded; **3** *chem* breakdown of a compound to a more simple compound; **4** *geol* lowering of the land surface by erosion ‖ SYN abasement, humiliation, dishonor, shame, disgrace, decline ‖ ANT honor, exaltation, elevation

de·grade /digrād′/ [*de-* + L *gradus* step] *vt* **1** to reduce in grade or rank; **2** to lower physically or morally; **3** to debase

de·grad′ing *adj* debasing; bringing disgrace or shame

de·gree /digrē′/ [OF *degree* < *de-* + L *gradus* step] *n* **1** step or grade in a series; **2** rank in society or life; **3** stage in progress; **4** step in a relationship; **5** title conferred by a college or university in recognition of academic work or special distinction; **6** relative amount, extent, or quality; **7** unit for measuring temperature; **8** 360th part of the circumference of a circle; **9** *gram* any of the three grades in the comparison of adjectives and adverbs; **10 by degrees** gradually; **11 to a degree, a** exceedingly; **b** somewhat

de·gree′-day′ *n* one degree of deviation of the daily mean temperature from some chosen standard, as 65° F, used to determine the amount of fuel consumed

de·hu·man·ize′ /dē-/ *vt* to strip of human characteristics, brutalize

de′hu·mid′i·fi·er /dē′-/ *n* device or substance for decreasing the amount of moisture in an interior or a container

de·hu·mid′i·fy /dē′-/ v (**-fied**) vt to remove moisture from

de·hy′drate /dē-/ vt 1 to extract the water from || vi 2 to lose water

de·ice /dē·īs′/ vt to remove the ice from, as the wings of an airplane

de·i·cide /dē′isīd′/ [< L deus god + -cide] n 1 slaying of a god; 2 slayer of a god

de·i·fy /dē′ifī′/ v (**-fied**) vt 1 to make a god of; 2 to worship as a god || **de′i·fi·ca′tion** n

deign /dān′/ [OF degnier < L dignare to deem worthy] vi 1 to condescend || vt 2 to condescend to give

de·ism /dē′izəm/ [< L deus god] n 1 belief in a personal God founded on reason rather than on the authority of a church; 2 belief that God created the world but has since been indifferent to it || **de′ist** n || **de·is′tic** (**-ti·cal**) adj

de′i·ty n (**-ties**) 1 god or goddess; 2 character, nature, or attributes of God; 3 **the Deity** God

dé·jà vu /dāzhä vY′/ [F] n sense of having witnessed scenes being lived through at the present time

de·ject /dijekt′/ [L dejicere (-jectus) to cast down] vt to dishearten, depress

de·ject′ed adj downcast; depressed; low-spirited || SYN cheerless, downhearted, despondent, blue

de·jec′tion n despondency, depression || SYN gloom, despondency, discouragement, sorrow, depression, melancholy, sadness || DISCR Depression, a state of low spirits or vitality, is usually occasioned by slight circumstances, and is often merely the expression of temporary downheartedness. Dejection is a deep depression; it is more lasting, and is caused by something serious or distressing. Sadness, a more inclusive term than either dejection or depression, may be a transient feeling, or one that is more enduring; it may be the sequel to a sorrowful event, the distress incident to an unhappy occasion, or the vague discontent resulting from unsatisfied desires. Melancholy is a constitutional or habitual tendency to sadness; if it reaches the stage of brooding or chronic despondency, it becomes pathological. Melancholy has, however, a lighter sense, in which it names a pensive sadness, in which it names a pensive sadness, a minor but pleasing note in moods or things || ANT elation, exaltation, happiness, glee

de ju·re /dējŏŏr′ē/ [L] adv & adj by right or lawful title

Del. Delaware

Del·a·ware /del′əwer′/ n state in E U.S. on Delaware Bay (548,000; 2057 sq.m.; cap. Dover) || **Del·a·war·e·an** /del′əwer′ē·ən/ n

de·lay /dilā′/ [OF delaier < L dilatare to defer] vt 1 to put off, postpone; 2 to make late, retard || vi 3 to act or proceed slowly, be tardy || n 4 act or instance of delaying || SYN v detain, stay, arrest, check, impede, retard (see defer¹) || ANT v impel, expedite, accelerate, begin

de·le /dē′lē/ [impv sg of L delere to erase] n 1 mark used to indicate matter in a manuscript or proof to be deleted || vt 2 to delete; 3 to mark with a dele

de·lec·ta·ble /dilek′təbəl/ [< L delectare to delight] adj 1 pleasant, delightful; 2 delicious

de·lec·ta′tion /dē′-/ n enjoyment, pleasure

del·e·gate /del′əgit/ [L delegatus] n 1 one sent to represent and act for others; representative; 2 member of a nominating convention; 3 member of the lower house of the legislatures of Maryland, Virginia, and West Virginia || /-gāt′/ vt 4 to assign authority to (another) to act as agent || SYN n agent, deputy, substitute, representative

del′e·ga′tion n 1 act of delegating; 2 body or group of delegates

de·lete /dilēt′/ [L delere (-etus) to blot out] vt to erase, take out (something written or printed) || **de·le′tion** n

del·e·te·ri·ous /del′itir′ē·əs/ [Gk deleterios noxious] adj harmful morally or physically; injurious || SYN pernicious, injurious, hurtful, noxious

Del·hi /del′ē/ √n city in N India (2,050,000), former capital

de·lib·er·ate /dilib′ərāt′/ [L deliberare to consider] vt & vi 1 to consider carefully || /-it/ adj 2 carefully considered; 3 intentional; 4 slow, unhurried || SYN v (see muse) adj slow, reflective, considered, well-advised || ANT adj rash, impetuous, hasty

de·lib′er·a′tion n 1 careful consideration; 2 discussion; 3 slowness in action or decision || **de·lib′er·a·tive** /-āt′iv, -ətiv/ adj

del·i·ca·cy /del′ikəsē/ n (**-cies**) 1 state or quality of being agreeable to the taste or other senses; 2 something dainty and pleasing, as food; 3 grace; 4 sensitivity, refinement; 5 fragility; 6 susceptibility to disease || SYN nicety, daintiness, refinement, tact

del·i·cate /del′ikit/ [L delicatus delightful] adj 1 fine in texture, construction, or workmanship; 2 subtle, refined; 3 requiring careful handling; 4 sensitive, fastidious; 5 fragile, easily damaged; 6 physically frail; 7 tactful; 8 sensitive to slight changes, as instruments || **del′i·cate·ly** adv || SYN elegant, sensitive (see exquisite, brittle)

del·i·ca·tes·sen /del′ikətes′ən/ [G < F délicatesse delicacy] n 1 prepared foods, as cooked meats, salads, and specialties; **2** place where these are sold

de·li·cious /dĭlĭsh′əs/ [< L *delicae* delight] *adj* highly pleasing to the mind or senses, particularly that of taste || **de·li′cious·ly** *adv* || **de·li′cious·ness** *n* || SYN palatable, luscious, savory, dainty, delightful || ANT nauseous, unpalatable, repulsive, unsavory

de·light /dĭlīt′/ [OF *delitier* < L *delectare*] *vt* **1** to gratify or please greatly || *vi* **2** to take pleasure (in doing something) || *n* **3** pleasure, joy; **4** that which causes pleasure || **de·light′ed** *adj* || **de·light′ful** *adj* || SYN *v* please, ravish, enchant, fascinate; *n* enjoyment, pleasure, gladness, bliss, rapture, transport, ecstasy, gratification (see *happiness*) || ANT *n* unhappiness, misery, annoyance, agony, abomination

De·li·lah /dĭlī′lə/ *n* Bib mistress and betrayer of Samson (Judges 16)

de·lim·it /dĭ-/ *vt* to mark out or fix the limits of || **de·lim′i·ta′tion** *n*

de·lin·e·ate /dĭlĭn′ē·āt′/ [L *delineare* (-*atus*)] *vt* **1** to sketch, draw; **2** to describe precisely in words || **de·lin′e·a′tion** *n* || **de·lin′e·a′tor** *n* || SYN trace, depict, outline, sketch, portray, set forth

de·lin·quent /dĭlĭnk′wənt/ [L *delinquens* (-*entis*) falling short] *adj* **1** neglectful of duty; **2** guilty of an offense; **3** past due; **4** in arrears in payment || *n* **5** one who is delinquent, esp. a youthful offender, as a *juvenile delinquent* || **de·lin′quen·cy** *n* (-cies) || SYN *adj* guilty, failing, faulty, defaulting, remiss

del·i·quesce /del′ĭkwes′/ [L *deliquescere*] *vi* **1** to melt; **2** to become liquid by absorption of moisture || **del′i·ques′cence** *n* || **del′i·ques′cent** *adj*

de·lir·i·ous /dĭlĭr′ē·əs/ *adj* **1** pert. to or caused by delirium; **2** wildly excited || SYN mad, crazed

de·lir·i·um /-əm/ [L = madness] *n* (-ums, -a /-ə/) **1** temporary mental disorder, often caused by fever, marked by wandering speech and hallucinations: **2** wild excitement || SYN frenzy, derangement, craziness (see *insanity*)

de·lir·i·um tre·mens /trēm′ənz/ [L = trembling madness] *n* form of acute insanity caused by excessive use of alcohol and characterized by terrifying delusions and trembling

de·liv·er /dĭlĭv′ər/ [OF *deliver* < de- + L *liberare* to free] *vt* **1** to set free; **2** to give, surrender; **3** to carry and hand over; **4** to send forth vigorously, as a blow or a ball; **5** to utter, as a speech; **6** to assist (a woman) in the birth of a child || *vi* **7** to produce what was promised or expected || SYN liberate, free, release, emancipate, rescue

de·liv·er·ance *n* **1** act of setting free;

rescue, release; **2** publicly expressed opinion

de·liv·er·y *n* (-ies) act, instance, or manner of delivering

dell /del′/ [OE] *n* small valley

Del·phic /delf′ĭk/ [< *Delphi* Greece, site of the oracle of Apollo, famous for giving ambiguous answers] *adj* **1** oracular; **2** obscure, ambiguous

del·phin·i·um /delfĭn′ē·əm/ [Gk *delphin* dolphin] *n* any of a genus (*Delphinium*) of plants, the larkspurs, cultivated for their spikes of showy flowers

del·ta /delt′ə/ *n* **1** fourth letter of the Greek alphabet Δ, δ; **2** fan-shaped deposit of sand or soil formed at the mouth of a river; **3** any triangular surface

del·toid /-toid/ *adj* **1** having the shape of a delta; triangular || *n* **2** triangular muscle in the shoulder, which raises the arm laterally

de·lude /dĭlood′/ [L *deludere* to play false] *vt* to deceive, mislead || SYN deceive, dupe, trick, betray

del·uge /del′yooj/ [OF < L *diluvium*] *n* **1** flood; **2** heavy downpour || *vt* **3** to flood; **4** to overwhelm

de·lu·sion /dĭloozh′ən/ *n* **1** act of deluding, or state of being deluded; **2** false belief, esp. one held persistently and abnormally || SYN fallacy, misconception, illusion, hallucination || DISCR *A delusion* is the result of a mental misconception or of faulty reasoning. In a pathological sense, it is a false impression or opinion symptomatic of mental disorder; for instance, a man who believes that he is a reincarnated John the Baptist is under a *delusion* of personality; the pauper who fancies himself rich, a *delusion* of grandeur. In a milder sense, *delusion* names either the state of one who has allowed himself to be foolishly deceived, or the act of one who has deceived him; the deceiver whose smooth tongue has persuaded the victim to entrust him with his savings practices the art of *delusion*. Both *illusion* and *hallucination* imply faulty or mistaken perception. In the motion picture, a series of still pictures produces an *illusion* of motion; a mirage is an optical *illusion*; unsweetened coffee is really smelled but seems to be tasted, by a gustatory *illusion*. In the case of *illusion* there is always some actual object or stimulus mistakenly perceived; a *hallucination* is a subjective experience with no external object or stimulus, a pure creation of the imagination. *Illusions* are common in normal mental experience; *hallucinations* are rarer and often pathological (cf. *deception*, *insanity*)

de·luxe /dĭlooks′, -luks′/ [F = luxurious] *adj* **1** sumptuous, luxurious ‖ *adv* **2** in a deluxe manner

delve /delv'/ [OE *delfan* to dig] *vi* to make earnest search for knowledge, information, etc.

Dem. Democrat(ic)

de·mag'net·ize' /dē-/ *vt* to deprive of magnetic force or properties ‖ **de·mag'net·i·za'tion** *n*

dem·a·gogue or **dem·a·gog** /dem'əgôg', -gog'/ [< Gk *demos* people + *agogos* leading] *n* political leader who appeals to the passions and prejudices of the people for his own advancement ‖ **dem'a·gog'ic** /-goj'ik, -gog'-/ *adj* ‖ **dem'a·gogu'er·y** /-gog'ərē/ or **dem·a·go'gy** /-goj'ē, -gog'ē/ *n*

de·mand /dimand', -mänd'/ [MF *demander* < *de-* + *mandare* to order] *vt* **1** to claim as due; **2** to ask for peremptorily; **3** to require, have need for ‖ *vi* **4** to make a demand ‖ *n* **5** act of demanding; **6** imperative request; **7** state of being sought after; **8** something demanded; **9** quantity of any commodity that will be required or sought in the market at any given price; **10 in demand** much sought after; **11 on demand** payable on presentation

de·mar·ca·tion also **de·mar·ka·tion** /dē'märkāsh'ən/ [Sp *demarcación*] *n* **1** act of defining or marking boundaries; **2** boundary

dé·marche /dāmärsh'/ [F] *n* **1** step, approach, plan; **2** diplomatic move

de·mean[1] /dimēn'/ [OF *demener*] *vt* to behave or conduct (oneself)

de·mean'[2] [< *mean*[2]] *vt* to debase or degrade

de·mean'or *n* behavior, bearing ‖ SYN conduct, deportment, carriage (see *behavior*)

de·ment·ed /diment'id/ [< *obs dement* to make mad] *adj* insane, out of one's mind

de·men·tia /dimensh'(ē)ə /[L] *n* loss or impairment of the intellect, will, or memory ‖ SYN madness, craziness, derangement (see *insanity*)

de·mer·it /dēmer'it/ [ML *demeritum*] *n* **1** fault, deficiency; **2** mark for failure or misconduct

de·mesne /dimān', -mēn'/ [OF *demeine* domain] *n* **1** *law* personal ownership of land; **2** manor house and the adjacent land; **3** domain

De·me·ter /dimēt'ər/ *n* Gk myth. goddess of agriculture, fruitfulness, and marriage; identified with the Roman Ceres

dem·i- /dem'ē-/ [MF < L *dimidium*] *comb form* **1** half; **2** lesser

dem'i·god' *n* **1** inferior god or one partly mortal; **2** deified mortal

dem'i·john' [F *dame-jeanne* Dame Jane] *n* large small-necked bottle usu. encased in wickerwork

de·mil'i·ta·rize' /dē-/ *vt* **1** to free from

military control; **2** to remove all troops and fortifications from

dem'i·mon·daine' /-mondān'/ *n* woman of ill repute

dem'i·monde' /-mond'/ [F = half-world] *n* women of ill repute collectively, and the circles in which they move

de·mise /dimīz'/ [OF *demis* displaced] *n* **1** death; **2** termination, end; **3** passing of a crown or of sovereign rights to a successor; **4** *law* conveyance of an estate by will or lease

dem'i·tasse' /-tas', -täs'/ [F = half cup] *n* **1** small cup of strong black coffee; **2** cup which contains it

demo- [< Gk *demos*] *comb form* people

de·mo'bi·lize' /dē-/ *vt* **1** to disband (troops); **2** to return to a peace footing ‖ also *vi* ‖ **de·mo'bi·li·za'tion** *n*

de·moc·ra·cy /dimok'rəsē/ *n* (-cies) **1** government by the people, usu. through elected representatives; **2** country so governed; **3** practical or social equality as opposed to aristocracy

dem·o·crat /dem'əkrat'/ *n* **1** advocate of democracy; **2** *Democrat* member of the Democratic party

dem'o·crat'ic *adj* **1** of, pert. to, characteristic of, or favoring a democracy; **2** believing in, or tending to, social equality; **3** *Democratic* pert. or belonging to the Democratic party

Dem'o·crat'ic par'ty *n* one of the two major political parties in the U.S., founded in 1828

de·mog·ra·phy /dimog'rəfē/ *n* statistical study of births, deaths, marriages, etc. of populations ‖ **de·mog'ra·pher** *n* ‖ **de·mo·graph·ic** /dem'əgraf'ik/ *adj*

de·mol·ish /dimol'ish/ [F *démolir* (-liss-)] *vt* to pull down, reduce to ruins, annihilate ‖ **dem·o·li·tion** /dem'əlish'ən/ *n* ‖ SYN ruin, raze, overthrow, devastate (see *destroy*)

de·mon /dēm'ən/ [Gk *daimon* deity] *n* **1** devil; malignant spirit; **2** cruel and evil person ‖ **de·mon·ic** /dimon'ik/ *adj*

de·mon·e·tize /dēmon'itīz', -mun'-/ [*de-* + L *moneta* money] *vt* **1** to deprive of monetary value, as money; **2** to withdraw from current use, as money ‖ **de·mon'e·ti·za'tion** *n*

de·mo·ni·ac /dimon'ē·ak'/ also **de·mo·ni·a·cal** /dēm'ənī'əkəl/ *adj* **1** pert. to, possessed by, or like, a demon; **2** frantic, raging

de·mon·stra·ble /dimon'strəbəl/ *adj* capable of being shown or proved ‖ **de·mon'stra·bly** *adv*

dem·on·strate /dem'ənstrāt'/ [L *demonstrare* (-atus)] *vt* **1** to prove by reasoned argument; **2** to teach by examples; **3** to exhibit the use and operation of; **4** to make manifest ‖ *vi* **5** to display feelings and opinions publicly on controversial issues, as by parading and carrying signs; **6** *mil* to make a show of force to de-ceive or impress the enemy ‖ SYN prove, exhibit, illustrate, evince, manifest

dem·on·stra′tion *n* **1** act of demonstrat-ing; **2** that which is demonstrated; **3** outward expression, as of feeling; **4** public show of sympathy or identity with some controversial political or social movement; **5** exhibition and description of specimens in teaching; **6** *math* process of proving certain conclusions from given premises; **7** *mil* show of force ‖ SYN certainty, evidence, proof ‖ ANT doubt, dis-proof

de·mon·stra·tive /dimon′strətiv/ *adj* **1** showing or proving; conclusive; **2** showing one's feelings, esp. of affec-tion, openly; **3** *gram* indicating or pointing out the thing referred to ‖ *n* **4** demonstrative word

dem′on·stra′tor *n* **1** one who or that which demonstrates; **2** one who takes part in a public demonstration; **3** one who teaches or aids another in teaching by showing specimens; **4** a one who exhibits and explains a product or a service to a prospective customer; **b** the product

de·mor·al·ize /di–/ *vt* **1** to lower or destroy the morale of; **2** to throw into confusion, disorganize ‖ **de·mor′al·i·za′tion** *n*

De·mos·the·nes /dimos′thənēz′/ *n* (384?–322 B.C.) Athenian orator and statesman

de·mote /dimōt′/ [*de-* + pro*mote*] *vt* to reduce in grade or rank ‖ **de·mo′tion** *n*

de·mount′a·ble /dē–/ *adj* capable of being taken down or removed

de·mur /dimur′/ [OF *demorer* < L *demorari* to delay] *v* (**-murred; -mur-ring**) *vi* **1** to raise objections; **2** *law* to enter an objection

de·mure /dimyōōr′/ [ME] *adj* **1** shy; modest, reserved; **2** affectedly coy or modest ‖ **de·mure′ly** *adv* ‖ SYN staid, modest, prim, sedate, coy, decorous, grave

de·mur′rage /-mur′ij/ *n* **1** undue delay of a ship or freight car in loading or unloading; **2** charge for such delay

de·mur′rer *n* **1** objection; exception; **2** *law* plea for the dismissal of a case by arguing insufficiency or legal de-fect while admitting the facts alleged

den /den/ [OE *denn*] *n* **1** lair of a wild beast; **2** haunt, as of thieves or gamblers; **3** cozy private room, as for study; **4** dirty little room

Den. Denmark

de·nat′u·ral·ize′ /dē–/ *vt* **1** to make un-natural; **2** to deprive of citizenship

de·na′ture /dē–/ *vt* **1** to deprive (some-thing) of its natural properties; **2** to render (alcohol) unfit to drink so

that it may be used for industrial purposes only

Den·eb /den′ib/ [Ar *dhanab* tail] *n* star of the first magnitude in the con-stellation Cygnus

de·ni·al /dini′əl/ [see **deny**] *n* **1** re-fusal to grant, believe, or admit; **2** assertion that a thing is untrue; **3** refusal to acknowledge a person or thing as having claims; **4** disavowal; **5** restraint, abstinence

de·nier /den′yər, dinir′/ [OF < L de-*narius* Roman silver coin] *n* unit of weight indicating the fineness of threads of silk, nylon, etc.

den·i·grate /den′igrāt′/ [L *denigrare* (*-atus*) to blacken] *vt* **1** to defame, villify; **2** to blacken ‖ **den′i·gra′tion** *n*

den·im /den′im/ [F (*serge*) *de Nîmes* (serge) of Nîmes] *n* coarse cotton material used for hangings, floor coverings, and work clothes

den·i·zen /den′tzən/ [AF *deinzein* one within (the city)] *n* **1** inhabitant, resi-dent; **2** naturalized plant or animal

Den·mark /den′märk/ *n* kingdom in N Europe (4,797,000; 16,629 sq.m.; cap. Copenhagen)

de·nom·i·nate′ /di–/ [L *denominare* (*-atus*)] *vt* to designate or give a name to

de·nom·i·na′tion *n* **1** act of denominat-ing; **2** name or designation; **3** class or division; **4** religious sect; **5** name for a certain class or unit in a series, as *coins of many denominations* ‖ SYN designation, title, appellation (see *name*)

de·nom·i·na′tion·al *adj* sponsored or controlled by a religious denomina-tion

de·nom′i·na′tor *n* term below the line in a fraction, that indicates the num-ber of equal parts into which a num-ber is divided

de·no·ta′tion /dē′–/ *n* **1** indication; name; **2** a plain marking out; **3** mean-ing, esp. the precise meaning ‖ SYN meaning, sign, designation (see *con-notation*)

de·note /dinōt′/ [F *dénoter* < *deno-tare*] *vt* **1** to signify or indicate; be-token; **2** to mark out plainly, as by a sign; **3** to refer to by name ‖ **de·no-ta·tive** /dē′nōtāt′iv, dinōt′ətiv/ *adj*

de·noue·ment /dānōōmän′/ [F = unty-ing] *n* **1** unraveling or solving of a mystery or plot; **2** thick; closing episode ‖ SYN outcome, event, catastrophe (see *trouble*)

de·nounce /dinouns′/ [OF *denoncier* to speak out] *vt* **1** to accuse publicly; censure; **2** to condemn; **3** to an-nounce the termination of (a treaty, etc.) ‖ **de·nounce′ment** *n*

dense /dens′/ [L *densus*] *adj* **1** having the parts crowded together; **2** thick; opaque; **3** stupid ‖ **dense′ly** *adv* ‖ **dense′ness** *n*

den·si·ty *n* (**-ties**) **1** closeness or compactness; **2** degree of opacity; **3** mass per unit volume; **4** stupidity

dent /dent/ [var of *dint*] *n* **1** small hollow or indentation, as from a blow || *vt* **2** to make a dent in || *vi* **3** to become dented

den·tal /dent′əl/ [< L *dens* (*dentis*) tooth] *adj* **1** pert. to or involving the teeth; **2** pert. to dentists or dentistry || *n* **3** dental consonant

den′tal floss′ *n* waxed thread for cleaning between the teeth

den·tate /den′tāt/ *adj bot & zool* toothed; having a notched edge

den·ti·frice /den′trifris/ [< L *dens* (*dentis*) tooth + *fricare* to rub] *n* preparation for cleaning the teeth

den·tin /den′tən/ also **den·tine** /den′tēn/ [< L *dens* (*dentis*) tooth] *n* the hard dense tissue under the enamel of a tooth

den·tist *n* one whose profession is the care, repair, and replacement of the teeth || **den′tist·ry** *n*

den·ture /dench′ər/ [F] *n* artificial tooth or set of artificial teeth

de·nude /din(y)ōōd′/ [L *denudare*] *vt* to strip, make bare

de·nun·ci·a·tion /dinun′sē-āsh′ən, -shē-/ [< L *denuntiare* to announce] *n* act or instance of denouncing || **de·nun′ci·a·to·ry** *adj*

Den·ver /den′vər/ *n* capital of Colorado (514,678)

de·ny /dinī′/ [OF *denier* < L *denegare*] *v* (**-nied**) *vt* **1** to refuse to believe or admit; **2** to refuse to give; **3** to repudiate, disown; **4** to refuse to accept as real; **5 deny oneself** to do without something greatly desired || *syn* gainsay, dispute, controvert, refute, refuse

de·o·dor·ant /dē-ōd′ərənt/ [*de-* + *odor*] *n* substance that destroys odors

de·o′dor·ize′ /dē-/ *vt* to rid of unpleasant odors || **de·o′dor·iz′er** *n*

de·ox·i·dize /dē-/ *vt* to free of oxygen

de·part /dipärt′/ [OF *departir*] *vi* **1** to leave; **2** to die; **3** to deviate || *syn* decamp, flee, quit, withdraw, abscond, vanish

de·part·ed *adj* **1** gone; past; **2** dead || *n* **3** the departed, **a** the dead person; **b** dead persons

de·part′ment *n* **1** separate division or branch, as in government organization, business, retail stores, or schools; **2** administrative unit of certain countries, as France || **de·part·men·tal** /dē′pärtmen′təl/ *adj*

de·part′ment store′ *n* large retail store selling a great variety of goods displayed in different departments

de·par·ture /dipär′chər/ *n* **1** act or instance of departing; **2** deviation, as from a standard, rule, etc.; **3** *archaic* death; **4** distance due east or west made by a boat or aircraft on its course

de·pend /dipend′/ [OF *dependre*] *vi* **1** to hang down, dangle; **2** to be pending; to be unsettled, as *that depends;* **3** depend on or upon, **a** to rely on; **b** to be contingent upon

de·pend′a·ble *adj* reliable, trustworthy; meriting trust || **de·pend′a·bly** *adv* || **de·pend′a·bil′i·ty** /-bil′-/ *n* || *syn* reliable, responsible, trustworthy, faithful

de·pend′ence also **de·pend′ance** *n* **1** state of being contingent on something; **2** subordination, subjection; **3** reliance, trust; **4** that on which one relies; **5** state of needing aid or support

de·pend′en·cy *n* (**-cies**) **1** dependence; **2** something dependent; **3** country under the control of another country

de·pend′ent also **de·pend′ant** *adj* **1** hanging down; **2** relying on someone or something else for support; **3** conditional; **4** subordinate || *n* **5** one who relies on another for support

de·pict /dipikt′/ [L *depingere* (*-pictus*)] *vt* **1** to portray; **2** to describe vividly || **de·pic′tion** *n*

de·pil·a·to·ry /dipil′ətôr′ē -tōr′-/ [< L *depilare* (*-atus*) to remove hair from] *n* (**-ries**) preparation for removing body hair || also *adj*

de·plane′ /dē-/ *vi* to disembark from an airplane

de·plete /diplēt′/ [L *deplere* (*-etus*)] *vt* to decrease or exhaust the supply of || **de·ple′tion** *n*

de·plor·a·ble /diplôr′əbəl, -plōr′-/ *adj* **1** sad, grievous; **2** meriting disapproval

de·plore /diplôr′, /-plōr′-/ [L *deplorare* to wail] *vt* **1** to lament, grieve for; **2** to express disapproval of || *syn* bewail, regret, bemoan, complain of, lament

de·ploy /diploi′/ [F *déployer*] *vt* **1** to spread out (troops) in line of battle; **2** to move strategically || *vi* **3** to extend the front line || **de·ploy′ment** *n*

de·po·lar·ize′ /dē-/ *vt* **1** to deprive of polarity; **2** to demagnetize; **3** to remove the deposit on the pole of (an electric battery)

de·po·nent /dipōn′ənt/ [L *deponens* (*-entis*) putting away] *adj* **1** designating verbs, as in Latin, which have passive forms but an active meaning || *n* **2** deponent verb; **3** one who testifies under oath or makes a sworn declaration in writing

de·pop′u·late′ /dē-/ *vt* to deprive of inhabitants || **de·pop′u·la′tion** *n*

de·port /dipôrt′, -pōrt′/ [L *deportare* to carry away] *vt* **1** to banish from a country; **2** to conduct (oneself) || **de′por·ta′tion** /dē′-/ *n*

de·por·tee /dē′pôrtē′, -pōr-/ *n* deported person

de·port′ment *n* conduct, behavior

de·pose /dipōz′/ [OF *deposer*] *vt* **1** to remove from high office; **2** to testify under oath ‖ *vi* **3** to testify under oath, as in a written statement

de·pos·it /dĭpŏz′ĭt/ [L *depositum* laid down] *vt* **1** to set down; **2** to put into a bank, as money; **3** to give as security or down payment; **4** to insert (a coin) in a slot; **5** to deliver and leave; **6** to cause or allow to settle ‖ also *n*

dep·o·si·tion /dĕp′əzĭsh′ən, dē-/ *n* **1** act of depositing; **2** removal from high office; **3** sworn testimony obtained out of court

de·pos′i·tor /-dĭ-/ *n* person with money in a bank

de·pos′i·to·ry /-tôr′-, -tōr′-/ *n* (**-ries**) place where something is placed for safekeeping

de·pot /dĕp′ō; *mil & Brit* dĕp′ō/ [F *dépôt*] *n* **1** railway station; **2** warehouse; **3** accumulation point for military supplies

de·prave /dĭprāv′/ [*de-* + L *pravus* crooked] *vt* to make morally bad; corrupt

de·praved′ *adj* morally debased; wicked, perverted ‖ **de·prav′i·ty** /-prăv′ĭtē/ *n* (**-ties**) ‖ SYN degenerate, corrupt, profligate ‖ ANT stainless, pure

dep·re·cate /dĕp′rəkāt′/ [L *deprecari* (-*atus*) to pray against] *vt* **1** to plead strongly against, express disapproval of; **2** to depreciate ‖ **dep′re·ca′tion** *n*

dep′re·ca·to·ry /-kətôr′ē, -tōr′-/ *adj* **1** apologetic; **2** protesting; disapproving

de·pre·ci·ate /dĭprēsh′ē-āt′/ [L *depretiare* (-*atus*) to undervalue] *vt* **1** to lower the value of; **2** to disparage ‖ *vi* **3** to fall in value ‖ **de·pre′ci·a′tion** *n* ‖ SYN (see *disparage*) ‖ ANT appreciate, praise

dep·re·da·tion /dĕp′rədāsh′ən/ [< L *depraedari* to plunder] *n* robbery, pillage

de·press /dĭpres′/ [OF *depresser* < L *depressus* pressed down] *vt* **1** to press down; **2** to sadden, dispirit; **3** to lower or cheapen; **4** to lower in force or activity, make dull ‖ SYN abase, discourage, cheapen, humble, degrade, dishearten ‖ ANT elevate, encourage, lift, inspire

de·pres′sant *n* sedative

de·pressed′ *adj* **1** downcast; gloomy, sad; **2** *bot, zool* flattened from above so as to be greater in width than in height ‖ SYN cheerless, dejected, dispirited, sad, humbled ‖ ANT cheerful, happy

de·pres′sion *n* **1** act of depressing or state of being depressed; **2** sunken area in a surface; **3** low spirits, dejection; **4** inactivity, dullness; **5** period of low business activity, with low profits and much unemployment ‖ SYN gloom, sorrow, melancholy (see *dejection*)

de·prive /dĭprīv′/ [OF *depriver* < L *deprivare*] *vt* to take something

from; withhold ‖ **dep·ri·va·tion** /dĕp′-rəvāsh′ən/ *n* ‖ SYN strip, bereave, despoil, rob, divest, debar

dept. department

depth /depth/ [ME *depthe*] *n* **1** state or quality of being deep; **2** distance below the surface or from the observer in any direction; **3** profoundness; **4** intensity; **5** that which is deep; **6** deepest or farthest part; **7** **in depth** very thorough(ly)

depth′ charge′ *n* explosive projectile for use esp. against submarines

depth′ of field′ *n* near and far distances from a point focused on by a lens within which objects produce sharp images

dep·u·ta·tion /dĕp′yətāsh′ən/ *n* **1** act of deputing; **2** person or persons so deputed

de·pute /dĭpyōōt′/ [OF *deputer* < LL *deputare* to select] *vt* **1** to appoint as an agent or deputy; **2** to give (authority) to a deputy ‖ SYN commission, charge, authorize, delegate, send

dep·u·tize /dĕp′yətīz′/ *vt* to appoint as deputy

dep′u·ty *n* (**-ties**) **1** one appointed to act for another; **2** assistant; **3** legislator ‖ SYN representative, substitute, legate, subordinate

de·rail′ /dē-/ *vt & vi* to run off the rails ‖ **de·rail′ment** *n*

de·range /dĭrānj′/ [F *déranger*] *vt* **1** to disorder, disarrange; **2** to make insane

de·ranged′ *adj* **1** out of order; **2** insane

de·range′ment *n* **1** act of deranging or state of being deranged or out of order; **2** insanity ‖ SYN confusion, disorder, madness (see *insanity*)

der·by /durb′ē, *Brit* därb′ē/ [Earl of *Derby*] *n* (**-bies**) **1** stiff felt hat with a dome-shaped crown and stiff rim; **2** **Derby,** a race for three-year-old horses, founded 1780, run annually at Epsom Downs, England; **3** any of certain other races, as *the Kentucky Derby*

der·e·lict /der′əlĭkt/ [L *derelictus* forsaken] *adj* **1** abandoned; adrift; **2** negligent ‖ *n* **3** anything left, forsaken, or cast away intentionally, as at sea; **4** abandoned person, bum

der·e·lic′tion *n* **1** deliberate neglect, as of duty; **2** abandonment

de·ride /dĭrīd′/ [L *deridere*] *vt* to mock, laugh at in scorn ‖ SYN scorn, laugh at, mock, scoff at, ridicule

de·ri·sion /dĭrĭzh′ən/ *n* **1** act of mocking; **2** ridicule, scorn, contempt; **3** that which is mocked or ridiculed ‖ SYN contumely, contempt, banter, mockery (see *ridicule*) ‖ ANT compliment, congratulation

de·ri·sive /dĭrīs′ĭv/ *adj* expressing ridicule ‖ **de·ri′sive·ly** *adv*

der·i·va·tion /der′ĭvāsh′ən/ *n* **1** act or process of deriving; **2** source from which something is derived; **3** something derived; **4** *gram* **a** etymology; **b** addition of affixes or change of stem to form derivatives || **der'i·va'·tion·al** *adj* || SYN origin, root, cause, extraction, source

de·riv·a·tive /dĭrĭv'ətĭv/ *adj* **1** derived; **2** secondary || *n* **3** something derived, as one word from another

de·rive /dĭrīv'/ [OF *deriver* < L *derivare* to draw off] *vt* **1** to draw from a specified source; **2** to deduce, infer; **3** to trace from or to a source || *vi* **4** to originate, be derived

der·ma·tol·o·gy /dûrm'ətol'əjē̱/ [Gk *derma* (-*atos*) skin + -*logy*] *n* science which treats of the skin and its diseases || **der'ma·tol'o·gist** *n*

dern /dûrn'/ *vt, adj, adv, interj dial.* **darn²**

der·o·gate /der'əgāt'/ [L *derogare* (-*atus*) to restrict] *vi* to detract || **der'o·ga'tion** *n*

de·rog·a·to·ry /dĭrog'ətôr'ē̱, -tōr'-/ *adj* tending to degrade; belittling, disparaging

der·rick /der'ik/ [*Derrick*, 17th-cent. hangman] *n* **1** framework with a long pivoted beam for hoisting heavy objects; **2** framework erected over a drill hole, as in an oil well

der·ri·ère /der'ē̱·er'/ [F] *n* buttocks

der·ring-do /der'iŋ dōō'/ [ME *dorryng don* daring to do] *n* heroic deeds

der·rin·ger /der'injər/ [Henry *Deringer* 19th-cent. U.S. gunsmith] *n* pocket pistol with a short barrel

der·vish /dûr'vĭsh/ [Pers *darvēsh* beggar] *n* mendicant Muslim friar of any of several orders whose characteristic ceremonies often include dancing, whirling, or howling

de·sal·i·nate /dē̱sal'ənāt'/, **de·sal·in·ize** /dē̱sal'əniz'/, or **de·salt** /dē̱sôlt'/ *vt* to remove salts and other minerals from (water, esp. sea water)

Des·cartes, René /rənā' dākärt'/ *n* (1596–1650) French philosopher and mathematician

de·scend /dĭsend'/ [OF *descendre* < L *descendere*] *vi* **1** to go or come from a higher to a lower position; **2** to pass from higher to lower in degree or rank or from earlier to later in time; **3** to be transmitted or inherited; **4 descend on** or **upon** to come suddenly to or in attack on; **5 be descended from** to be a descendant of || *vt* **6** to go down or along

de·scend'ant *n* offspring in any degree of removal

de·scent /dĭsent'/ *n* **1** act or instance of descending; **2** downward slope; **3** passage leading down; **4** sudden attack; **5** genealogical derivation from an ancestor; **6** decline || SYN declivity; origin, lineage, birth, extraction; deterioration, incursion, attack || ANT ascent, acclivity

de·scribe /dĭskrīb'/ [L *describere*] *vt* **1**

to tell or depict in speech or writing; **2** to trace (a specified course or path) by motion; **3** *geom* to draw or construct, as an arc || SYN portray, depict, characterize, picture, outline, relate, sketch, recount, delineate, set forth, express

de·scrip·tion /dĭskrĭp'shən/ *n* **1** act or method of describing; **2** statement or account that describes; **3** class, variety || SYN delineation, account, sketch, portrayal, relation, depiction; nature, kind, sort (see *explanation*)

de·scrip'tive *adj* serving to describe

de·scry /dĭskrī'/ [OF *descrier* to proclaim] *v* (-**scried**) *vt* **1** to discern (something distant or obscure); **2** to perceive, detect || SYN distinguish, perceive, espy, detect (see *discern*)

des·e·crate /des'ĭkrāt'/ [*de-* + *consecrate*] *vt* to profane; violate the sanctity of || **des'e·crat'er, des'e·cra'tor** *n* || **des'e·cra'tion** *n*

de·seg·re·gate /dē̱seg'-/ *vi* **1** to eliminate racial segregation || *vt* **2** to cause to desegregate || **de·seg're·ga'tion** *n*

de·sert¹ /dĭzûrt'/ [F *déserter* < LL *desertare*] *vt* **1** to forsake, abandon; **2** to run away from (one's unit in the armed forces), not intending to return || *vi* **3** to run away from or forsake one's duty or post || **de·sert'er** *n* || **de·ser'tion** *n* || SYN leave, forsake, fail, run from (see *abandon*)

des·ert² /dez'ərt/ [OF < LL *desertum*] *n* **1** arid, sandy waste; **2** any wasteland incapable of supporting life

de·serts' or **just' de·serts'** /dĭzurts'/ [< OF *deserte* deserved] *npl* deserved fate || SYN due, worth, worthiness, reward, merit, excellence

de·serve /dĭzûrv'/ [OF *deservir* < L *deservire* to serve zealously] *vt* **1** to be worthy of; to merit || *vi* **2** to be worthy or suitable, as for reward or punishment || **de·serv'ed·ly** /-ĭdlē̱/ *adv* || **de·serv'ing** *adj*

des·ic·cant /des'ĭkənt/ *n* substance which promotes dryness

des'ic·cate /des'ĭkāt'/ [L *desiccare* (-*atus*)] *vt & vi* to dry up completely || **des'ic·ca'tion** *n*

de·sid·er·a·tum /dĭsid'ərāt'əm/ [L = that which is desired] *n* (-**ta** /-tə/) something regarded as essential

de·sign /dĭzīn'/ [MF *designer* < L *designare* to mark] *vt* **1** to plan the form and construction of; **2** to intend for a special purpose; **3** to plan, intend || *vi* **4** to make plans, as for new models, constructions, etc. || *n* **5** outline, plan, or drawing, as for a new model or construction; **6** arrangement of parts or composition of a work of art; **7** artistic pattern; **8** scheme, plan; **9** purpose; **10 designs** *pl* hostile intentions || **de·sign'er** *n* || SYN *n* sketch, delineation, intent, purpose, plan, intention, end, aim, object ‖ DISCR A *design* is a preconceived notion of something to be done; it embraces not only the thing itself, but a method of accomplishing it with the means at hand; *designs* can be noble or artful, open or scheming. A *plan* is the detailed method by which a *design, purpose,* etc., is worked out. A *plan* should be practicable. A *purpose* is a thing resolutely and steadfastly proposed to the mind; it is usually definite, and depends for its accomplishment largely on the character of the proposer. An *intention* is also a thing proposed to the mind, but it may be vague as well as fixed, and its execution often turns upon circumstances as well as upon the character of the intender. *Intent,* though the equivalent of *intention,* is more formal, and is used chiefly as a legal, a poetical, or a philosophical term. To convict an accused man of first-degree murder, it must be proved that he had the *intent* to kill. An *end* is the *purpose* one has in view, regarded as the natural termination of the work involved. An *object* is the thing one is planning to get, or the consummation desired. An *aim* is that toward which our efforts are directed, regarded as a focusing point not to be lost sight of, like a target

des·ig·nate /dez′ignāt′/ *vt* 1 to indicate, point out; 2 to name; 3 to nominate or appoint ‖ **des′ig·na′tion** *n* ‖ SYN specify, show, entitle, denominate, particularize

de·sign·ed·ly /-īdlē/ *adv* intentionally, by plan

de·sign·ing *adj* 1 scheming, artful ‖ *n* 2 act or art of making designs

de·sir·a·ble /dizīr′əbəl/ *adj* pleasing, worth having ‖ **de·sir′a·bly** *adv* ‖ **de·sir′a·bil′i·ty** /-bil′-/ *n* ‖ SYN expedient, advisable, acceptable, proper, advantageous ‖ ANT inadvisable, injudicious, displeasing

de·sire /dizīr′/ [OF *desirer* < L *desiderare*] *vt* 1 to wish earnestly for, crave; 2 to ask for, request ‖ *n* 3 longing, craving; 4 that which is desired; 5 request; 6 passion, lust ‖ **de·sir′ous** *adj* ‖ SYN *n* appetite, inclination, aspiration, wish, longing, yearning, craving, coveting ‖ DISCR A *wish* is an eagerness to obtain or enjoy something; it is frequently directed toward the unattainable, or that which the wisher realizes to be beyond reason. Our tendency to indulge in vain *wishes* is epitomized in the proverb, "If *wishes* were horses, beggars might ride." *Desire* rises from a more vehement feeling than a *wish,* and has strength and intensity behind it; it is commonly directed toward that which by luck or effort can be obtained, but it often

names a vague and unsatisfied craving, as nothing could appease the man's *desire* for notoriety. *Longing* is ordinarily a stronger term than *desire;* it often emanates from the depths of one's nature, and has a touch of the imperious about it, as his *longing* to educate his children dominated his life. *Longing* is directed toward that which is far off, but will come sometime, as throughout the war-torn nations there spread a deep *longing* for peace. *Appetite* is used to express physical needs, as for food or drink, unless it is otherwise qualified, or used figuratively. *Inclination* expresses merely a tendency or a leaning; it does not connote either the definiteness or the warmth of the other words. *Coveting* is an improper *desire* directed toward that which belongs to another ‖ ANT *n* indifference, disinclination, apathy, antipathy

de·sist /dizist′/ [OF *desister* < L *desistere*] *vi* to cease, stop ‖ SYN cease, leave off, discontinue, quit, stop, abstain ‖ ANT continue, persist, persevere, keep on, carry on

desk /desk′/ [ML *desca* table] *n* 1 piece of furniture with a flat top and usu. drawers, for writing, drawing, keeping accounts, etc.; 2 the desk place in a hotel lobby where guests check in and out, pick up mail, and leave their keys

Des Moines /dəmoin(z)′/ *n* capital of Iowa (210,000)

des·o·late /des′əlit/ [< L *desolare* (-*atus*) to forsake] *adj* 1 uninhabited; 2 barren, devastated; 3 solitary, lonely; 4 miserable, forlorn ‖ /-lāt′/ *vt* 5 to make desolate ‖ SYN *adj* bereaved, forlorn, forsaken, solitary, uninhabited, waste, bleak (see *lonely*) ANT *adj* pleasant, happy, comfortable, cheerful, bright, glad

des·o·la·tion *n* 1 act of laying waste; 2 state of being laid waste; 3 solitude; ruin; destruction; 4 affliction; misery ‖ SYN havoc, devastation, waste, unhappiness, sadness ‖ ANT beauty, happiness, comfort, pleasure

de·spair /disper′/ [OF *desperer* < L *desperare*] *vi* 1 to abandon or be without hope ‖ *n* 2 loss of hope, hopelessness; 3 that which causes loss of hope ‖ **de·spair′ing** *adj* ‖ SYN *n* discouragement, desperation, despondency ‖ DISCR *Despair* is a feeling of utter hopelessness and *discouragement,* caused by frustration, repeated failure, lack of progress, etc. *Despondency* is a state of mind so spiritless and fallen that to it hope is impossible; *despondency,* often temporary, sometimes settles into a forlorn, chronic dejection. *Desperation* is *despair* roused to reckless action in a dare-devil "door-die" spirit. *Despair* checks effort; it overwhelms us with a sense of frustration. *Despondency* kills effort; it drowns us in a sense of futility. *Desperation* creates effort; it goads us to one more furious, self-forgetting trial

des·patch /dispach′/ *vt, vi, & n* var of **dispatch**

des·per·a·do /desp′ərä̐d′ō, -räd′ō/ [OSp < L *desperatus* desperate] *n* (-**does**, -**dos**) bold and reckless outlaw

des·per·ate /des′p(ə)rit/ [L *desperatus*] *adj* 1 without regard to danger; reckless; 2 proceeding from or denoting despair; frantic; 3 beyond hope or cure; extremely serious ‖ **des′per·ate·ly** *adv*

des′per·a′tion *n* 1 state of being desperate; 2 recklessness born of despair ‖ SYN hopelessness, recklessness (see *despair*)

des·pi·ca·ble /desp′ikəbəl/ [< L *despicari* to despise] *adj* contemptible, deserving to be despised

de·spise /dispiz′/ [OF *despire* (-*is*-) < L *despicere*] *vt* to scorn, loathe, regard with contempt ‖ SYN abhor, disregard, contemn, disdain, slight, spurn

de·spite /dispit′/ [OF *despit* < L *despectus* contempt] *prep* in spite of

de·spoil /dispoil′/ [OF *despoillier* < L *despoliare*] *vt* to plunder, rob ‖ **de·spo′li·a′tion** /-spōl′ē̆-/ *n*

de·spond·ent /dispon′dənt/ [< L *despondere* to give up] *adj* without hope, dejected, depressed ‖ **de·spond′en·cy** *n* ‖ SYN hopeless, dejected, discouraged, blue, melancholy

des·pot /desp′ət/ [Gk *despotes* master] *n* absolute ruler, tyrant ‖ **des′-pot·ism** *n* ‖ **des·pot·ic** /dispot′ik/ *adj*

des·sert /dizurt′/ [F] *n* something sweet served at the end of a meal

de·sta·lin·i·za·tion /dē′stäl′inizāsh′ən, -stal′-/ *n* deflation of Stalin, his record, and his cult

des·ti·na·tion /dest′nāsh′ən/ *n* 1 stated end of a journey; 2 purpose, object, goal

des·tine /dest′in/ [L *destinare* to settle] *vt* 1 to design, intend; 2 to decree the future of, as by fate; foreordain

des′tined *adj* destined for, a bound for; b intended for

des′ti·ny *n* (-**nies**) 1 fate; inevitable course of events; 2 lot, fortune ‖ SYN lot, fortune, portion, condition, fate, doom ‖ DISCR *Destiny, lot, fate,* and *doom* are alike in that they express the idea of a predetermined course of events. *Destiny* names a foreordained condition, conceived of as inescapable, which constitutes one's portion or fortune in life; it is regarded as marked out by an urgency beyond human control—in the case of Christians, by Divine Provi-

dence. *Destiny* is often used in the sense of fortune or luck, as though she loved the beautiful, it was her *destiny* to live in ugly and sordid surroundings. *Lot* names what one gets in the apportioning of *destiny;* it is our condition in life; one's *lot* may be happy or evil. In a general sense, *destiny* and *lot* are interchangeable. *Fate* adds to the ideas contained in *destiny* and *lot* that of fixedness, immutability. *Fate* is often used interchangeably with both *destiny* and *lot,* but it carries a tone of blind inexorableness which the other words lack. *Doom* is an evil, unhappy *destiny,* as *fate* steered even his childish footsteps toward his final *doom* of treason and betrayal

des·ti·tute /dest′it(y)ŏŏt/ [L *destitutus* forsaken] *adj* 1 without means; in extreme poverty; 2 destitute of lacking

des′ti·tu′tion *n* 1 extreme need; 2 complete want or lack ‖ SYN deficiency, indigence, penury (see *poverty*)

de·stroy /distroi′/ [OF *destruire* < L *destruere*] *vt* 1 to demolish completely, leave in ruins; 2 to kill; 3 to render void, neutralize ‖ SYN ruin, raze, demolish ‖ DISCR These words have in common the idea of breaking or tearing down that which has been built up. To *ruin* is to bring about a state of total loss or uselessness. To *destroy* is to bring to *ruin* that which functioned as a whole. To *demolish* is to tear down or knock down with such force that the mass loses its former shape and outline. To *raze* is to level to the ground. A building may be *ruined* by neglect, *destroyed* by fire even though not wholly consumed, *demolished* by artillery, *razed* by a wrecking company

de·stroy′er *n* 1 one who or that which destroys; 2 light fast warship, originally designed to destroy torpedo boats

de·struct /distrukt′/ [< *destruction*] *n* 1 act of intentional destruction of a rocket, missile, or spacecraft after launching ‖ *vt* 2 to destroy

de·struct′i·ble *adj* capable of being destroyed

de·struc′tion [< L *destructus* destroyed] *n* 1 act of destroying; 2 state of being destroyed; 3 agency of destruction or ruin ‖ SYN desolation, havoc, demolition, downfall, ruin

de·struc′tive *adj* 1 causing death or desolation; ruinous; 2 refuting without correcting; merely negative, as *destructive criticism* ‖ **de·struc′tive·ly** *adv* ‖ **de·struc′tive·ness** *n* ‖ SYN detrimental, hurtful, harmful, injurious, pernicious

de·struc′tive dis·til·la′tion *n chem* complete distillation of an organic substance, such as wood, coal, and oil shale, in a closed vessel to produce coke, oils, and gases

des·ue·tude /des′wit(y) o͞od/ [L *desuetudo*] *n* disuse

des·ul·to·ry /des′əltôr′ē̇, -tōr′-/ [< L *desultor* circus rider who leaps from horse to horse] *adj* 1 aimless, erratic; 2 disconnected, random || SYN rambling, unmethodical, fitful, loose, discursive (see *cursory*) || ANT thorough, coherent, methodical

de·tach /ditach′/ [F *détacher*] *vt* 1 to remove, disconnect; 2 to separate from the main body and detail for a special purpose, as troops || **de·tach′a·ble** *adj* || SYN sever, disengage, disjoin, withdraw, abstract, separate, disunite || ANT unite, connect, join

de·tached′ *adj* 1 separated; disconnected; 2 objective, impartial; 3 aloof, unconcerned

de·tach′ment *n* 1 act of detaching; 2 state of being detached; 3 troops or ships separated from the main body and employed for a special purpose

de·tail /dītāl′/ [F *détailler*] *vt* 1 to give full particulars of; 2 *mil* to assign to a special task || /also dē′tāl/ *n* 3 small part or item; 4 subordinate part; 5 minute account; 6 *mil* a small detachment for a special task; b this task; 7 in detail with full particulars

de·tain /dītān′/ [OF *detenir* < L *detinere*] *vt* 1 to hold back from departure; delay; 2 to place or keep in custody

de·tain′er *n* writ authorizing the continued detention of a person in custody

de·tect /dītekt′/ [L *detegere* (*-tectus*)] *vt* 1 to find out (something concealed); expose; 2 to separate (the audio-frequency signal) from the radio-frequency carrier wave || **de·tec′tion** *n*

de·tec′tive *n* policeman or private person who investigates crimes

de·tec′tor *n* 1 one who or that which detects; 2 device, as a vacuum tube, for rectifying the high-frequency alternating current in a radio receiver

de·tent /dītent′/ [F *détente*] *n* *mach* device for checking temporarily the movement of a part, released by the application of force

dé·tente /dātänt′/ [F] *n* easing or relaxing of international tension

de·ter /dītur′/ [L *deterrere*] *v* (-**terred**; -**ter·ring**) *vt* 1 to restrain from doing something, as by fear; 2 to check, prevent

de·ter·gent /dītur′jənt/ [L *detergere* to wipe off] *adj* 1 cleansing || *n* 2 synthetic cleaning agent containing no soap; 3 any cleaning agent

de·te·ri·o·rate /dītir′ē̇ərāt′/ [< L *deterior* worse] *vt* 1 to make worse, lower the quality or value of || *vi* 2 to become deteriorated || **de·te·ri·o·ra′·tion** *n*

de·ter·mi·na·tion /dīturm′ināsh′ən/ *n* 1 act of deciding; 2 state of being firm in decisions; purpose, resolution; 3 measurement, ascertainment; 4 finding, decision || SYN firmness, decision, resolution, resolve || DISCR As here compared, *determination* names a settling of one's purpose, a coming to a fixed intention; it is an act of the judgment, and is preceded by examination, weighing, and choice, as a *determination* to withdraw from politics. *Determination* also names that quality of character which resolutely carries out a purpose. *Decision* names either the habit of making up one's mind promptly when faced by the necessity of choice, or the result of so deciding, as the president made his *decisions* boldly; he was a man of *decision;* we approve his *decision* to drop the suit. A *resolve* is an act of the will; we make *resolves* to waste no time, etc. *Resolution* may mean the same as *resolve,* or may name that quality of character that boldly and firmly carries out its *resolves.* A *resolve* implies an act of will, *resolution* connotes sticking power and grit || ANT hesitation, vacillation

de·ter·mine /dīturm′in/ [OF *determiner* < L *determinare*] *vi* 1 to reach a decision || *vt* 2 to fix the bounds of; 3 to settle, as a dispute; 4 to decide, resolve; 5 to be the cause of; 6 to find out exactly || SYN settle, resolve, fix, bound, finish, influence

de·ter′mined *adj* 1 resolute; 2 decided

de·ter·rent /dītur′ənt/ *adj* 1 serving to deter || *n* 2 something that deters

de·test /dītest′/ [L *detestari* to call a god to witness against] *vt* to hate intensely, abhor || **de·tes·ta′tion** /dē′-/ *n*

de·test′a·ble *adj* deserving of being loathed; hateful || SYN odious, abominable, abhorred, loathsome (see *hateful*) || ANT likable, attractive, pleasing

de·throne /dē-/ *vt* to remove from a throne, depose || **de·throne′ment** *n*

det·o·nate /det′ənāt′/ [L *detonare* (*-atus*)] *vt & vi* to explode || **det′o·na′tion** *n*

det′o·na′tor *n* device that detonates an explosive charge

de·tour /dē′to͝or, dīto͝or′/ [F *détour*] *n* 1 roundabout way, esp. a way leading around an obstruction on a thoroughfare || *vi* 2 to follow a detour || *vt* 3 to route by a detour

de·tract /dītrakt′/ [L *detrahere* (*-tractus*) to pull down] *vt* 1 to draw away, divert || *vi* 2 detract from to take away something of value from || SYN defame, disparage, vilify, slander, malign (see *calumniate*) || ANT honor, praise, defend

de·trac′tion *n* belittlement or disparagement of the worth of a person or thing || **de·trac'tor** *n* || SYN censure, aspersion, disparagement, calumny

de·train' /dē-/ *vi* to get off a train

det·ri·ment /det'rimont/ [L *detrimentum*] *n* 1 that which causes damage or disadvantage; 2 injury, damage

det'ri·men'tal /-men'-/ *adj* injurious || SYN hurtful, prejudicial, disadvantageous, damaging

de·tri·tus /dĭtrīt'əs/ [L = that which is worn away] *n* 1 fragments of rock broken off or worn away by erosion; 2 waste, debris

De·troit /dĭtroit'/ *n* city in SE Michigan (1,511,482)

de trop /dətrō'/ [F] *adj* 1 too much; 2 unwelcome, in the way

deuce /d(y)ōōs'/ [MF *deus* two] *n* 1 cards, dice two; 2 tennis tie score after which one side must score twice in a row to win; 3 *slang* two dollars || *interj* 4 the deuce! the devil! (a mild oath)

deu·te·ri·um /dyōōtir'ē·əm/ [< Gk *deuteros* second] *n* isotope of hydrogen with twice the mass of ordinary hydrogen (D; at.no. 1; at.wt. 2.01)

Deu·ter·on·o·my /d(y)ōō'təron'əmē/ [< Gk *deuteros* second + *nomos* law] *n* fifth book of the Old Testament, in which the law of Moses is stated a second time

de·val·u·ate /dēval'yōō·āt'/ [< *de-* + *value*] *vt* to reduce the value of || **de·val'u·a'tion** *n*

de·val'ue /dē-/ *vt* to devaluate

dev·as·tate /dev'əstāt'/ [L *devastare* (*-atus*)] *vt* to lay waste, destroy utterly || **dev'as·ta'tion** *n*

de·vel·op /divel'əp/ [F *développer* < OF *desvoloper* to unwrap] *vt* 1 to cause to become better, more complete, or more advanced; 2 to elaborate, cause to grow; 3 to evolve, generate; 4 to render visible (the latent image on a film) by treating with chemicals || *vi* 5 to advance from one stage to another; 6 to become gradually apparent, become known || SYN grow, evolve, amplify, expand, promote

de·vel'op·er *n* 1 one who or that which develops; 2 *photog* chemical solution for developing

de·vel'op·ment *n* 1 act or process of developing; 2 state of being developed; 3 tract of new dwellings

de·vi·ate /dēv'ē·āt'/ [L *deviare* (*-atus*) to turn from the road] *vi* 1 to turn aside, diverge; 2 to digress || /-it/ *n* 3 person who deviates from accepted behavior; 4 pervert || SYN *v* digress, diverge, swerve, err (see *wander*)

de'vi·a'tion *n* 1 act of deviating; 2 departure from accepted behavior; 3 *naut* error of compass caused by the proximity of local magnetism; 4 *statistics* difference between a set of values and their mean

de'vi·a'tion·ism *n* departure from the

strict party line of the Communist party || **de'vi·a'tion·ist** *n*

de·vice /dĭvīs'/ [OF *devis* division] *n* 1 mechanical or electrical contrivance or apparatus; 2 scheme, plan; 3 trick, stratagem; 4 heraldic emblem; 5 **leave to one's own devices** to leave alone to do as one wishes || SYN artifice, trick, expedient, instrument, appliance

dev·il /dev'əl/ [OE *dēofol* < Gk *diabolos* slanderer] *n* 1 evil spirit, demon; 2 wicked person; 3 unfortunate person, as *the poor devil*; 4 daring or reckless person; 5 printer's helper; 6 the Devil Satan, the personification of evil; 7 **give the devil his due** to give credit to a person one dislikes; 8 **raise the devil** to create a commotion; 9 the devil! mild oath used to express annoyance; 10 **the devil to pay** great trouble || *v* (-lled or -illed; -il·ing or -il·ling) *vt* 11 to chop (cooked eggs, crab, etc.) fine and season hot; 12 *colloq* to annoy, pester, tease

dev'iled *adj* (food) prepared with hot seasoning after being chopped fine

dev'il·ish *adj* 1 like a devil; fiendish; 2 excessive, very great || *adv colloq* very; extremely

dev'il·ment *n* roguishness; mischief

dev'il's club' *n* handsome prickly shrub of W North America (*Oplopanax horridus*)

dev'il's food' cake' *n* rich chocolate cake

dev'il·try /-trē/ *n* (-tries) 1 mischief; 2 wickedness; 3 mischievous or wicked act

de·vi·ous /dēv'ē·əs/ [L *devius* out of the way] *adj* 1 indirect; circuitous; 2 crafty, tricky, using roundabout schemes || **de'vi·ous·ly** *adv* || **de'vi·ous·ness** *n*

de·vise /divīz'/ [OF *deviser* < L *divisus* divided] *vt* 1 to contrive, concoct; 2 to bequeath (real property) || *n* 3 gift of real property by will || SYN *v* imagine, plan, scheme, invent (see *discover*)

de·void /divoid'/ [OF *desvuider* to empty out] *adj* **devoid of** entirely without; empty of; lacking || SYN void, wanting, unendowed, empty, destitute

de·volve /divolv'/ [L *devolvere* to roll down] *vt* 1 to transfer, pass on, as a duty || *vi* 2 **devolve on** or **upon** to be passed on to

De·vo·ni·an /divōn'ē·ən [< *Devon* county in England] *adj* designating a period of the Paleozoic era more than 350,000,000 years ago

de·vote /divōt'/ [L *devovere* (*-votus*)] *vt* 1 **a** to give up wholly to some object; **b** apply (oneself) to some object; 2 to dedicate; consecrate

de·vot'ed *adj* 1 loyal, faithful; 2 dedicated || **de·vot'ed·ly** /-idlē/ *adv*

dev·o·tee /dev'ətē'/ *n* **1** one devoted to something; **2** enthusiast, fan

de·vo'tion *n* **1** act of devoting or state of being devoted; **2** strong affection; **3** **devotions** *pl* religious worship; piety; prayer ‖ **de·vo'tion·al** *adj*

de·vour /divour'/ [OF *devourer* < L *devorare*] *vt* **1** to swallow ravenously; **2** to consume or destroy rapidly; **3** to engulf; **4** to take in greedily with the eyes or ears

de·vout /divout'/ [OF *devot* < L *devotus*] *adj* **1** devoted to religion, pious; **2** expressing piety; **3** sincere, true ‖ **de·vout'ly** *adv*

dew /d(y)ŌŌ'/ [OE *dēaw*] *n* **1** atmospheric moisture condensed in small drops on cooled surfaces; **2** any moisture appearing in small drops or beads ‖ **dew'y** *adj* (**-i·er**; **-i·est**)

Dew'ar ves'sel d(y)ŌŌ'ər/ [Sir James *Dewar* (1842–1923) Sc scientist and inventor] *n* container which keeps its contents at a constant and generally low temperature by means of two external walls between which a vacuum is maintained

dew'drop *n* drop of dew

Dew·ey /dy ŌŌ'ē/, **George** *n* (1837–1917) U.S. admiral; destroyed the Spanish fleet in Manila Bay in 1898

dew'lap' *n* fold of skin that hangs from the neck of a bovine animal and some other animals

DEW' line' /d(y)ŌŌ'/ [*distant early warning*] *n* line of radar stations in North America north of the Arctic Circle to provide warning of approaching planes or missiles

dew' point' *n* the variable temperature at which water vapor condenses

dex·ter·i·ty /dekster'itē/ [< L *dexter* right hand] *n* **1** skill with the hands or body; agility; **2** mental adroitness, cleverness ‖ SYN expertness, aptitude (see *ability*)

dex·ter·ous /deks't(ə)rəs/ also **dex'·trous** *adj* skillful, quick mentally or physically; adroit, clever ‖ SYN deft, expert, skillful, handy (see *clever*)

dex·tran /deks'trən/ [L *dexter* right + *-an*] *n* heavy polymer —(C₆H₁₀O₅)ₙ— of glucose, used as a plasma substitute, an anticholesterol agent, a food additive, etc.

dex·trose /deks'trōs/ [L *dexter* right + *-ose*] *n* glucose present in plants and animals, obtained from starch by the action of mineral acids

dhow /dou'/ [Ar *dāwa*] *n* small lateen-rigged vessel used for coastwise trade in the Indian Ocean

di-¹ [Gk *dis* twice] *pref* two, twofold; double, as *digraph*

di-² *pref* var of **dis-**

di-a- also **di-³** [Gk = through, across] *pref* **1** through, across, as *diameter*; **2** apart, as *dialysis*; **3** thoroughly, as *diagnosis*

di·a·be·tes /dī'əbēt'ēz, -is/ [< *dia-* + Gk

bainein to go] *n* disease marked by excessive discharge of urine and by an excess of sugar in the blood and urine ‖ **di·a·bet'ic** /-bet'ik, -bēt'ik/ *adj* & *n*

di·a·bol·ic (**-i·cal**) /dī'əbol'ik(əl)/ [< Gk *diabolos* devil] *adj* **1** of or pert. to the devil; **2** wicked, devilish, fiendish ‖ **di·a·bol'i·cal·ly** *adv*

di·ab·o·lism /dī·ab'əliz'əm/ *n* **1** devil worship; **2** actions by or worthy of a devil

di·a·chron·ic /dī'əkron'ik/ *adj* *ling* **1** (phenomena) occurring or developing over a given period of time; **2** (study) of such phenomena

di·ac·o·nate /dī·ak'ənit, -nāt'/ [< Gk *diakonos* deacon] *n* **1** office of a deacon; **2** deacons collectively

di·a·crit·ic /dī'əkrit'ik/ [Gk *diakritikos* distinctive] *adj* **1** diacritical ‖ *n* **2** diacritical mark

di·a·crit'i·cal *adj* serving to distinguish

di·a·crit'i·cal mark' *n* mark used to show that a letter or symbol has a different pronunciation or stress from that of an unmarked letter or symbol

di·a·dem /dī'ədem'/ [OF *diademe* < Gk *diadema* band] *n* **1** crown, tiara; **2** ornamental headband

di·aer·e·sis /dī·er'isis/ *n* var of **dieresis**

di·ag·nose /dī'əgnōs', -nōz'/ [< *diagnosis*] *vt* **1** to identify or determine the cause of (a disease, malfunction, bad situation, or problem) ‖ *vi* **2** to make a diagnosis

di'ag·no'sis /-nōs'is/ [Gk = discernment] *n* (**-ses** /-sēz/) **1** process of determining the cause of a disease, malfunction, or problem; **2** the decision reached ‖ **di'ag·nos'tic** /-nos'tik/ *adj* ‖ **di'ag·nos·ti'cian** /-tish'ən/ *n*

di·ag·o·nal /dī·ag'ənəl/ [< *dia-* + Gk *gonia* angle] *adj* **1** *geom* extending from one vertex of a polygon to another not adjacent; **2** slanting, oblique; **3** having slanting or oblique lines ‖ *n* **4** diagonal line, plane, row, part, etc. ‖ **di·ag'o·nal·ly** *adv*

di·a·gram /dī'əgram'/ [Gk *diagramma* something marked out by lines] *n* **1** outline, drawing, or plan that explains the wiring, parts, or operation of something; **2** plan or chart ‖ *v* (**-gramed** or **-grammed**; **-gram·ing** or **-gram·ming**) *vt* **3** to make a diagram of; represent by a diagram ‖ **di'a·gram·mat'ic** /-grəmat'ik/ *adj*

di·al /dī'əl/ [ML *dialis* daily] *n* **1** face of a watch or clock; **2** graduated disk on a gauge or meter which registers measurements or amounts by means of a movable pointer; **3** rotatable disk for regulating electrical devices or tuning radio and television sets; **4** rotatable disk on a telephone for making calls automatically ‖ *v* (**-aled** or **-alled**; **-al·ing** or **-al·ling**) *vt* **5** to measure or indicate by a dial; **6** to regulate or tune in by means of a dial; **7 a** to reach (a telephone number) by rotating the dial; **b** to make a call to on a dial phone ‖ *vi* **8** to use a dial

dial. dialect(al)

di·a·lect /dīʹəlekt/ [Gk *dialektos* discourse] *n* **1** variety of a spoken language peculiar to a given region or social class; **2** variety of a language considered substandard ‖ **diʹa·lecʹtal** *adj* ‖ sᴠɴ tongue, speech (see *language*)

diʹa·lecʹtic *n* **1** art or practice of logical investigation; **2** logical argumentation; **3** dialectics ‖ *adj* **4** of or pert. to dialectic; **5** dialectal ‖ **diʹa·lecʹtical** *adj*

diʹa·lec·tiʹcian /-tishʹən/ *n* **1** one skilled in dialectic; **2** student of dialects

diʹa·lecʹtics *nsg* **1** logic and logical thought or reasoning; **2** any systematic reasoning or argument

di·a·log or **di·a·logue** /dīʹəlog′, -lôg′/ [OF *dialogue* < Gk *dialogos*] *n* **1** conversation between two or more persons; **2** conversation between characters in a play or story; **3** exchange of ideas between proponents of opposing views

diʹal telʹe·phone *n* telephone with a dial to actuate a selector which makes contact with the number sought

diʹal tone′ *n* low, steady hum in a telephone receiver which indicates that the line is not busy

di·al·y·sis /dīalʹisis/ [Gk = tearing apart] *n* (**-ses** /-sēzʹ/) separation of substances in solution by membranes on the basis of the relative rate of diffusion of their molecules, spec. separation of crystalloids from colloids in solution by diffusion of the crystalloids ‖ **di·a·lyt·ic** /dīʹəlitʹik/ *adj*

diam. diameter

di·am·e·ter /dīamʹitər/ [OF *diametre* < Gk *diametros*] *n* **1 a** straight line passing through the center of a circle or sphere from one side to the other; **b** its length; **2** width or thickness of any circular or cylindrical object

di·a·met·ric (**-ri·cal**) /dīʹəmetʹrik(əl)/ *adj* **1** pert. to or along a diameter; **2** complete, absolute ‖ **diʹa·metʹri·cal·ly** *adv*

dia·mond /dīʹ(ə)mənd/ [OF *diamant* < LL *diamas* (*-mantis*)] *n* **1** brilliant precious stone, usu. colorless, the hardest known substance, formed of nearly pure carbon in isometric crystals; **2** *baseball* **a** infield; **b** entire playing field; **3** *typ* 4½-point type; **4** plane figure with four equal straight sides and two acute and two obtuse angles; **5** playing card stamped with red figures of this shape; **6 diamonds** *sg* or *pl* suit of cards so marked

Di·an·a /dīanʹə/ *n* Rom myth. goddess

of the moon and of the hunt, the Greek Artemis

di·a·pa·son /dīʹəpāzʹən, -pāsʹ-/ [Gk *dia pason* (chordon) through all (strings)] *n* **1** entire range of a voice or instrument; **2** recognized standard of pitch; **3** either of two principal stops of a pipe organ

di·a·per /dīʹ(ə)pər/ [MF *diapre* ornamented cloth < Gk *diaspros* pure white] *n* **1** infant's breechcloth ‖ *vt* **2** to put a diaper on

di·aph·a·nous /dīafʹənəs/ [Gk *diaphanes*] *adj* gauzy, filmy, transparent

di·a·phragm /dīʹəfram′/ [Gk *diaphragma* midriff] *n* **1** muscular partition separating the thorax from the abdomen; **2** any thin sheet or film that separates; **3** vibrating disk in a telephone receiver and in a microphone; **4** device for regulating the amount of light that passes through a lens ‖ **di·a·phrag·mat·ic** /-fragmat′ik/ *adj*

di·ar·chy /dīʹärkē/ [*di-*1 + *-archy*] *n* (**-chies**) government in which the executive power is shared by two persons

di·ar·rhe·a or **di·ar·rhoe·a** /dīʹərēʹə/ [Gk *diarrhoia* flowing through] *n* abnormal frequency and liquidity of the bowel movements

di·a·ry /dīʹərē/ [L *diarium*] *n* (**-ries**) **1** record of daily events and experiences; **2** book for this ‖ **diʹa·rist** *n*

di·as·to·le /dīasʹtolē/ [Gk = difference] *n* normal rhythmic dilation of the heart ‖ **diʹas·tolʹic** /-əstol′-/ *adj*

di·a·ther·my /dīʹəthurmʹē/ [< *dia-* + Gk *thermos* hot] *n med* treatment by heating the body tissues with penetrating high-frequency electromagnetic oscillations ‖ **diʹa·ther′mic** *adj*

di·a·tom /dīʹətom′, -təm/ [Gk *diatomos* cut through] *n* any member of a large family (Diatomaceae) of microscopic algae having siliceous cell walls

diʹa·tomʹic *adj* **1** consisting of two atoms; **2** having two replaceable atoms

diʹa·tonʹic scale′ /-ton′ik/ [< Gk *diatonos* stretching] *n mus* scale consisting of five whole tones and two semitones

di·a·tribe /dīʹətrīb′/ [Gk = pastime] *n* bitter, abusive attack or denunciation

di·ba·sic /dī-/ [< *di-*1] *adj* **1** containing two replaceable or ionizable hydrogen atoms; **2** containing two univalent basic atoms of a metal

dice /dīs′/ [pl of *die*2] *npl* **1** small cubes marked on the faces with one to six spots, used in games such as craps; **2 no dice** *slang* nothing doing ‖ *vt* **3** to cut into small cubes

di·chot·o·my /dīkotʹəmē/ [Gk *dichotomia*] *n* (**-mies**) division into two parts, halves, or kinds ‖ **di·chotʹo·mous** *adj* ‖ **di·chotʹo·mize′** *vt*

dick /dik'/ *n slang* detective

dick·ens /dik'inz/ [< 16th-cent. *Dickon dim.* of *Richard*] *interj* the dickens! *euphem* the deuce!, the devil!

Dick·ens, Charles *n* (1812–70) English novelist ‖ **Dick·en·si·an** /diken'zē-ən/ *adj*

dicker /dik'ər/ [?] *vi* 1 to bargain ‖ *n* 2 petty bargain

dick·ey /dik'ē/ [< *Dicky dim.* of *Richard*] *n* 1 detachable collar or shirt front; 2 small bird

dict. 1 dictator; 2 dictionary

dic·ta /dik'tə/ *pl* of **dictum**

Dic·ta·phone /dik'tə-/ [trademark] *n* machine that records and reproduces dictation

dic·tate /dik'tāt, diktāt'/ [L *dictare* (-*atus*) to say] *vt* 1 to express orally for another to write down or for a machine to record; 2 to impose with authority ‖ *vi* 3 to say something to be taken down; 4 to give orders ‖ /dik'tāt/ *n* 5 injunction, command; 6 controlling principle ‖ **dic·ta'tion** *n* ‖ SYN *v* enjoin, order, command, suggest, prescribe, decree, impose ‖ ANT *v* accept, follow, submit, yield

dic·ta'tor /also dik'-/ *n* one possessing absolute power ‖ **dic·ta'tor·ship'** *n*

dic·ta·to·ri·al /dik'tətôr'ē-əl, -tôr'-/ *adj* 1 of or pert. to dictators or dictatorship; 2 overbearing, imperious ‖ SYN autocratic, domineering, peremptory, arbitrary

dic·tion /dik'shən/ [L *dictio* (-*onis*)] *n* manner of speaking or expression; choice of words; style ‖ SYN phraseology, expression, language, vocabulary, wording, style ‖ DISCR *Diction* is the term applied to that choice and use of words by which an author expresses his meaning. *Phraseology* stresses the effectiveness of words in groups and combinations. *Phraseology* names that distinctive touch in the arrangement of words which results in a characteristic mode of expression; such a mode may be highly literary, as that of Woodrow Wilson, or it may be stamped with the effect of isolation, as the *phraseology* of the backwoodsman; or it may be typical of a group or profession, as the technical *phraseology* of engineers. *Style* is the inclusive term which connotes all the characteristics of the writing of an author as opposed to the matter expressed—its *diction*, its *phraseology*, its effectiveness, its artistic merit, its individuality, even its method of securing these results. *Style* is also applied to the group characteristics of the authors of a certain period, as eighteenth-century *style*. *Vocabulary* names the store and range of words possessed by a writer or speaker (cf. *language*)

dic'tion·ar'y *n* (-ies) book listing alphabetically the words of a language,

giving their meanings and often information about their pronunciation, etymology, morphology, and usage, expressed either in the same or another language

dic·tum /dik'təm/ [L = thing said] *n* (-ta /-tə/, -tums) 1 positive opinion; authoritative assertion; 2 aphorism

did /did'/ *pt* of **do**

di·dac·tic (-ti·cal) /dīdak'tik(əl)/ [< Gk *didaskein* to teach] *adj* 1 instructive, explanatory; 2 inclined to lecture others; 3 teaching a moral lesson

did·dle /did'əl/ [?] *colloq vt* 1 to cheat ‖ *vi* 2 to waste time

did·n't /did'ənt/ did not

di·do /dīd'ō/ [?] *n* (-does, -dos) *colloq* caper, antic

Di·do /dīd'ō/ *n class. myth.* founder and queen of Carthage, who fell in love with Aeneas and killed herself when he left

die[1] /dī'/ [ME *dien* prob < ON *deyja*] *v* (died; dy·ing) *vi* 1 to cease to live; 2 to cease to exist; 3 to cease to function; 4 to faint, languish; 5 to suffer greatly, as *to die of boredom; 6 colloq* to be very anxious, desire greatly; 7 *colloq* to be convulsed, as with laughter; 8 *show bus.* to flop before an audience; 9 **die away** to cease gradually, as a sound; 10 **die down** to subside; 11 **die hard, a** to cling to life, a purpose, etc.; **b** to refuse to yield; yield reluctantly; 12 **die off** to die one by one ‖ SYN depart, decline, decrease, vanish, wane, decay ‖ ANT live, exist, flourish, increase, grow, bloom

die[2] [OF *de* < L *datum* thing given (by fate)] *n* 1 metal form for stamping coins or medals; 2 tool for cutting the threads of screws and bolts; 3 form or cutter, used in a press for shaping leather, sheet metal, etc.; 4 *sg* of **dice**; 5 **the die is cast** the decision is made and cannot be recalled

die'-hard' *n* stubborn defender of a lost cause or of outdated ideas ‖ also *adj*

di'e·lec'tric /dī'-/ *n* insulator or nonconductor ‖ also *adj*

di·er·e·sis /dī·er'isis/ [Gk *diairesis* division] *n* (-ses /-sēz'/) 1 the placing of two contiguous vowels within the same word into separate syllables; 2 mark placed over the second vowel to show this, as in *naïve*

die·sel /dēz'əl/ [Rudolf *Diesel* (1858–1913) G inventor] *adj* 1 of or pert. to a diesel engine; 2 equipped with a diesel engine ‖ *n* 3 diesel engine; 4 vehicle equipped with a diesel engine

die'sel-e·lec'tric *adj* driven by an electric motor that receives its power from a diesel-powered electric generator

die·sel en'gine *n* internal-combustion

engine burning oil ignited by very highly compressed air

die'stock' *n* frame for holding dies for cutting threads on screws and bolts

di·et¹ /dī'it/ [LL *dieta* assembly] *n* 1 parliamentary assembly; 2 international congress

di·et² [OF *diete* < Gk *diaita* way of life] *n* 1 usual food of a person or animal; 2 prescribed course of food taken for reasons of health or to lose weight ‖ *vi* 3 to follow a diet ‖ **di'et·er** *n* ‖ **di'e·tar'y** *adj* ‖ **di'e·tet'ic** /-tet'ik/ *adj*

di'e·tet'ics *nsg* science dealing with the planning and preparation of diets ‖ **di'e·ti'tian** or **di'e·ti'cian** /-tish'ən/ *n*

dif- *pref* var of **dis-**

diff. 1 difference; 2 different

dif·fer /dif'ər/ [MF *differer* to put off < L *differre*] *vi* 1 to be unlike; 2 to disagree

dif·fer·ence /dif'(ə)rəns/ *n* 1 state of being dissimilar; 2 instance of dissimilarity; 3 degree of dissimilarity; 4 controversy, quarrel; 5 discrimination; 6 amount by which one quantity is greater or less than another ‖ SYN diversity, unlikeness, inequality, estrangement, discord, distinction, contrast, disagreement, disparity, variation, variety, dissimilarity, discrepancy ‖ DISCR *Difference* names the state or quality of being unlike, or the degree of such unlikeness; it is opposed to similarity. *Distinction* names the mental recognition of such *difference;* it lies in the powers of perception, and is opposed to identity, for unless the things are perceived to be different, there can be no *distinction*

dif·fer·ence of po·ten'tial *n* condition determining the tendency of an electric charge to move or an electric current to flow from one point to another, measured in volts

dif'fer·ent *adj* 1 unlike; 2 distinct, not the same; 3 various; 4 unusual ‖ **dif'fer·ent·ly** *adv* ‖ SYN unlike, various, diverse, several, divers, sundry, contrary ‖ ANT uniform, same, alike, accordant

dif·fer·en'tial /-ən'shəl/ *adj* 1 pert. to, involving, or constituting a difference ‖ *n* 2 difference or the amount of difference; 3 differential gear; 4 *math* infinitesimal difference between two values of a variable quantity

dif'fer·en'tial cal'cu·lus *n* branch of mathematics dealing with the rate of change of functions with respect to their variables

dif'fer·en'tial gear' *n* arrangement of gears connecting two shafts, permitting them to turn at different speeds if necessary, as in the rear wheels of an automobile when turning

dif'fer·en'ti·ate' /-shē·āt'/ *vt* 1 to ob-

serve or state a difference between; 2 to mark out as unlike; 3 *biol* to modify in structure or function; 4 *math* to obtain the differential or the derivative of ‖ *vi* 5 to become differentiated; 6 to note a distinction ‖ **dif'fer·en'ti·a'tion** *n* ‖ SYN discriminate, distinguish, contrast

dif·fi·cult /dif'ikəlt, -kult'/ [< *difficulty*] *adj* 1 not easy; hard to do or understand; 2 not easily pleased; hard to manage ‖ SYN arduous, laborious, onerous, involved, intricate (see *obscure, hard*) ‖ ANT easy, pleasant, simple

dif'fi·cul'ty *n* (-ties) 1 state or condition of being difficult; 2 that which is difficult; 3 trouble, hindrance; 4 **difficulties** *pl* complication of affairs; embarrassment ‖ SYN impediment, obstacle (see *hindrance*)

dif·fi·dence /dif'idəns/ [< L *diffidere* to distrust] *n* lack of self-reliance; timidity; modest reserve; shyness ‖ SYN self-distrust, humility, hesitation ‖ ANT aggressiveness, forwardness, self-confidence

dif'fi·dent *adj* lacking self-confidence; shy, retiring ‖ SYN shy, bashful, coy, shrinking, demure, reserved, retiring, timid, modest ‖ DISCR *Diffident* people are those afflicted by such self-distrust as robs them of all self-reliance, and disqualifies them for the work which, in a proper state of mind, they could probably do. *Shy* people are uneasy in company, reserved, sometimes appearing ungracious or proud, and even stupid and blundering—an aspect often quite at variance with their actual characteristics. *Bashful* describes those whose shrinking from notice breeds that awkwardness and timidity oftenest observable in children; mature people who are *bashful* present to the world a shamefaced, sheepish behavior that is both incongruous and unbecoming. *Modest* behavior is always becoming; *modest* people have a proper, but never excessive, self-assurance and confidence; they are pleasantly at ease in the company of others, but never obtrusive. *Coy* behavior has not the sincerity of shyness; it is affectedly reticent, and often courts while it apparently evades attention

dif·fract /difrakt'/ [L *diffringere* (-*fractus*) to break up] *vt* to cause (a wave of light or sound) to be bent on passing the edge of an obstacle or in passing through a narrow slit ‖ **dif·frac'tion** *n*

dif·fuse /difyōoz'/ [L *diffundere* (-*fusus*) to pour forth] *vt* 1 to pour out and spread around; 2 to scatter, circulate ‖ *vi* 3 to spread or intermingle, as two contiguous liquids or gases ‖ /-fyōōs'/ *adj* 4 widely spread; **5** wordy, rambling ‖ **dif·fuse'ly** adv ‖ **dif·fu'sion** /-zhən/ n ‖ **dif·fu'sive** /-siv/ adj

dig /dig'/ [ME diggen] v (**dug; dig·ging**) vi **1** to work with a spade, excavate; **2 dig in** to make a stand, as by digging trenches; **3 dig into** colloq to apply oneself to ‖ vt **4** to loosen or break up (ground) with or as with a spade; **5** to make, as a hole, by casting out earth; **6** to thrust or force in, as to dig spurs into a horse's side; **7** slang **a** to appreciate; **b** to observe; **8 dig up, a** to obtain by digging; **b** colloq to come across (someone or something) ‖ n **9** poke or thrust; **10** cutting remark; **11** colloq archaeological excavation ‖ **dig'ger** n

di'gest /dijest'/, dī-/ [L digerere (-gestus) to distribute] vt **1** to arrange systematically; classify; **2** to condense, summarize; **3** to convert (food) in the alimentary canal for assimilation into the tissues of the body; **4** to assimilate mentally ‖ vi **5** to be digested, as food ‖ /dī'jest/ n **6** classified collection or summary, as of legal, scientific, or literary matter; **7** systematic compilation of laws or judicial decisions ‖ **di·gest'i·ble** adj

di·ges'tion /-jes'chən/ n **1** act or process of digesting food; **2** ability to digest food ‖ **di·ges'tive** adj

dig·it /dij'it/ [L digitus] n **1** thumb, finger, or toe; **2 a** any one of the nine numbers from one to nine; **b** any of the ten Arabic numeral symbols from 0 to 9

dig'i·tal clock' n clock that indicates the hour and minute with changing digits instead of hands

dig'i·tal com·put'er n computer that works on the principle of counting, as distinguished from measuring, as the simple abacus

dig'i·tal·is /-tal'is [L = digital] n **1** any plant of the genus Digitalis, as the foxglove; **2** dried leaves of the foxglove (D. purpurea), used as a heart stimulant

dig·ni·fied /dig'nifīd'/ adj characterized by dignity; noble, stately

dig'ni·fy' [OF dignifier < L dignus worthy] v (**-fied**) vt to exalt, confer honor upon ‖ SYN advance, honor ‖ ANT degrade, humble

dig'ni·tar'y n (**-ies**) one who holds high office or rank

dig'ni·ty [OF dignete < L dignitas worthiness] n (**-ties**) **1** noble conduct or bearing; **2** nobility of character; **3** degree of worth; **4** high rank

di'graph /dī'-/ [di-¹] n combination of two letters to represent one sound, as sh, th, oe

di·gress /digres'/, dī-/ [L digredi (-gressus)] vi to deviate from the main subject or argument ‖ **di·gres'sion** n ‖ **di·gres'sive** adj ‖ SYN diverge, swerve, deviate (see wander)

di·he·dral /dīhēd'rəl/ [di-¹ + Gk hedra base] adj **1** having or formed by two planes ‖ n **2** figure formed by two intersecting planes; **3** angle at which each side of the wing of an airplane is bent laterally up or down from the horizontal

dike /dīk'/ [OE dīc ditch] n **1** embankment thrown up to hold back the waters of a river or the sea; **2** earthen bank alongside a ditch; causeway

di·lap·i·dat·ed /dīlap'idāt'id/ [L dilapidare (-atus) to demolish] adj fallen into ruin or decay; broken down

di·late /dīlāt', dī-/ [L dilatare] vt **1** to enlarge or widen ‖ vi **2** to enlarge or widen; **3** dilate on or upon to speak or write at length on ‖ **di·la'tion** n

di·la'tor n **1** muscle that dilates some opening of the body; **2** instrument for dilating an orifice or canal in the body

dil·a·to·ry /dil'ətôr'ē, -tōr'-/ [< L dilator delayer] adj **1** causing delay; **2** slow, tardy ‖ SYN tardy, procrastinating, loitering, dawdling, late

di·lem·ma /dīlem'ə/- [di-¹ + lemma proposition] n **1** situation requiring a choice between two unpleasant alternatives; **2** any perplexing or awkward situation

dil·et·tan·te /dil'itant'(ē), -tänt'(ē)/ [It] n one who pursues the fine arts, literature, or science superficially and for amusement only ‖ SYN smatterer, dabbler, trifler (see amateur)

dil·i·gent /dil'ijənt/ [L diligens (-entis) careful] adj **1** industrious, hard-working, persevering; **2** performed with painstaking care ‖ **dil'i·gent·ly** adv ‖ **dil'i·gence** n ‖ SYN sedulous, persevering, industrious (see busy)

dill /dil'/ [OE dile] n European herb (Anethum graveolens) of the carrot family, with aromatic seeds used for flavoring pickles

dil·ly /dil'ē/ [obs slang = delightful] n (**-lies**) colloq something outstanding

dil'ly-dal'ly [reduplication of dally] v (**-lied**) vi **1** to loiter, trifle; **2** to waver

di·lute /dīlōōt', dī-/ [L diluere (-utus) to wash away] vt **1** to weaken, attenuate, or make more liquid by admixture, as with water or other fluid ‖ vi **2** to become diluted ‖ adj **3** diluted ‖ **di·lu'tion** n

dim /dim'/ [OE] adj (**dim·mer; dim·mest**) **1** not bright, obscure; **2** vague, faint; **3** ill-defined, not clearly seen; **4** lusterless; **5** not seeing or understanding clearly; **6 take a dim view of** to disapprove of ‖ v (**dimmed; dim·ming**) vt **7** to make dim ‖ vi **8** to become dim ‖ **dim'ly** adv ‖ **dim'ness** n

dim. 1 diminuendo; **2** diminutive

dime /dīm′/ [MF < *decima* tenth] *n* ten-cent coin

di·men·sion /dimensh′ən/ [MF < L *dimensio* (-*onis*) measurement] *n* **1** measure in any one direction, as length, etc.; **2 dimensions** *pl* **a** size or extent of a body in these measurements; **b** scope; importance ‖ **di·men′sion·al** *adj*

dime′ store′ *n* five-and-ten

di·min·ish /dimin′ish/ [ME] *vt* & *vi* **1** to lessen; **2** to weaken ‖ **dim·i·nu·tion** /dim′in(y)ŏŏsh′ən/ *n* ‖ **SYN** reduce, degrade, abase (see *decrease*)

di·min′ish·ing re·turns′ *npl* rate of profit or yield that, beyond a certain point, fails to increase proportionately with added effort or investment

di·min·u·en·do /dimin′yŏŏ·en′dō/ [It] *mus adj* **1** gradually growing softer in sound ‖ *n* **2** diminuendo passage

di·min·u·tive /-yətiv/ *adj* **1** small, tiny ‖ *n* **2** word formed from another by adding a suffix denoting smallness or endearment, as *Jackie* (from *Jack*) ‖ **SYN** *adj* small, slight, insignificant (see *little*)

dim·i·ty /dim′itē/ [< *di-*¹ + Gk *mitos* thread] *n* (-**ties**) thin cotton material with fine corded stripes or checks

dim′mer *n* **1** device for dimming electric lights; **2** device for lowering the beam of automobile headlights

dim′-out′ *n* partial blackout of the lights of a seacoast city, so that ships may not be silhouetted against them at night to become targets for enemy submarines

dim·ple /dimp′əl/ [ME *dimpel*] *n* **1** small natural hollow on the surface of the body, as on the cheek or chin; **2** dent ‖ *vi* **3** to form dimples ‖ *vt* **4** to mark with dimples

dim′wit′ *n colloq* slow-thinking person ‖ **dim′-wit′ted** *adj*

din /din′/ [OE *dyne*] *n* **1** insistent noise ‖ *v* (**dinned; din·ning**) *vt* **2** to repeat insistently; **3** to assail with din ‖ *vi* **4** to make a din

di·nar /dinär′/ [Ar < L *denarius* coin] *n* **1** any of various old Arabian gold coins; **2** monetary unit of Yugoslavia, Iraq, Jordan, Kuwait, and Tunisia

dine /dīn′/ [OF *diner* < *dis-* + L *jejunare* to fast] *vi* **1** to eat dinner ‖ *vt* **2** to give a dinner to

din′er /-ər/ *n* **1** one who dines; **2** dining car; **3** restaurant built like a dining car

di·nette /dīnet′/ *n* alcove serving as a dining room

ding /diŋ/ [imit] *vi* **1** to sound, as a bell, with a continuous monotonous tone ‖ *vt* **2** to impress by noisy repetition

ding′dong′ /-dôŋ′, -doŋ′/ [imit] *n* **1** sound of a bell; **2** monotonous repetition

din·ghy /diŋ′gē/ [Bengali *dingī*] *n* (-**ghies**) ship's small boat

din·go /diŋ′gō/ [< nat. Australian] *n* (-**goes**) wild dog of Australia (*Canis dingo*)

din·gy /din′jē/ [?] *adj* (-**gi·er; -gi·est**) grimy, dirty, faded ‖ **din′gi·ness** *n*

din′ing car′ /dīn′-/ *n* railroad car fitted out to cook and serve meals

din·ner /din′ər/ [OF *diner*] *n* **1** chief meal of the day, at noon or in the evening; **2** formal meal in honor of some person or event

din′ner clothes′ *npl* formal wear, as for a dinner

din′ner jack′et *n* tuxedo

di·no·saur /dīn′əsôr′/ [< Gk *deinos* terrible + *sauros* lizard] *n* any of a subclass (Dinosauria) of gigantic prehistoric reptiles

dint /dint′/ [OE *dynt* blow] *n* **by dint of** by the power of

di·o·cese /dī′əsis, -sēs′/ [Gk *dioikesis* administration] *n* jurisdiction of a bishop; bishopric ‖ **di·oc′e·san** /-os′isən/ *adj*

di·ode /dī′ōd/ [*di-*¹ + Gk *hodós* way] *n* **1** two-element electron tube allowing passage of current in only one direction; **2** crystal which functions similarly

Di·og·e·nes /dī·oj′inēz′/ *n* (412?–323 B.C.) Greek philosopher

Di·o·ny·sus /dī′ənis′əs/ *n Gk myth.* god of wine, the Roman Bacchus

di·op·ter /dī·op′tər/ [Gk *dioptra* optical instrument] *n* unit of measure of the refractive power of a lens equal to the reciprocal of the focal length in meters

di·ox′ide /dī-/ *n* oxide containing two atoms of oxygen per molecule

dip /dip′/ [OE *dyppan*] *v* (**dipped; dip·ping**) *vt* **1** to put temporarily into a liquid or powder; **2** to scoop up, as with a ladle or bucket; **3** to lower and raise, as a flag ‖ *vi* **4** to plunge temporarily into water or other liquid; **5** to enter slightly into anything; **6** to slope downward; **7** to sink down; **8** to lower the hand, a ladle, a dipper, or the like into a liquid or container in order to remove some of the contents ‖ *n* **9** act of dipping; **10** scoop of ice cream; **11** lowering or sinking; **12** short plunge; **13** liquid or cream in which something is dipped; **14** temporary descent; **15** *slang* pickpocket

diph·the·ri·a /difthir′ē·ə, dip-/ [< Gk *diphthera* leather] *n* acute infectious disease marked by the formation of a false membrane obstructing the air passages of the nose and throat

diph·thong /dif′thôŋ, -thoŋ, dip′-/ [Gk *diphthongos*] *n* combination of two vowel sounds in a single syllable, as in *noise, hound* ‖ **diph·thon′gal**

/-gəl/ *adj* || **diph′thong.ize′** /-gīz′/ *vt & vi*

di.plo.ma /diplōm′ə/ [L = official paper < Gk = paper folded double] *n* **1** certificate issued by an educational institution indicating that the recipient has graduated or has been granted a degree; **2** document conferring a privilege or honor; **3** historical or state document or charter

di.plo′ma.cy *n* (**-cies**) **1** conduct of international relations; **2** skill in conducting negotiations; tact

dip.lo.mat /dip′ləmat′/ *n* **1** person employed by a nation to represent it abroad and to conduct official negotiations with other countries; **2** tactful person

dip′lo.mat′ic [F *diplomatique* < L *diploma* official document] *adj* **1** of or pert. to diplomats and diplomacy; **2** tactful; **3** exactly reproducing an ancient text or document, as *a diplomatic edition* || **dip′lo.mat′i.cal.ly** *adv*

di.pole /dī′pōl′/ *n* **1** pair of equal electric or magnetic poles of opposite sign separated by a small distance; **2** also **di′pole an.ten′na** transmitting or receiving antenna that consists of two equal horizontal rods extending in opposite directions || **di′po.lar** *adj*

dip′per *n* **1** cup attached to a long handle, for dipping; **2 Dipper** either of two groups of stars in the northern sky shaped like a dipper, the **Big Dipper** in Ursa Major and the **Little Dipper** in Ursa Minor

dip.py [?] *adj* (**-pi.er; -pi.est**) *slang* foolish, silly, simple

dip.so /dip′sō/ *n slang* dipsomaniac

dip.so.ma.ni.a /dip′səmān′ē.ə/ [< Gk *dipsa* thirst] *n* uncontrollable craving for alcoholic drink || **dip′so.ma′ni.ac′** *n*

dire /dīr′/ [L *dirus* fearful] *adj* dreadful, terrible

di.rect /direkt′, dī-/ [L *directus*] *adj* **1** straight, not deviating or circuitous; **2** open, straightforward; **3** lineally related; **4** immediate; **5** exact, as *the direct opposite*; **6** with nothing intervening, as *direct elections*; **7** consequential, as *the direct result* || *vt* **8** to aim or point; **9** to guide or show; **10** to manage, conduct, run; **11** to control, regulate; **12** to give orders to; **13** to address, as a letter or remarks || *vi* **14** to act as a guide, conductor, or director || *adv* **15** directly || SYN *v* show, guide, regulate (see *conduct, govern*)

di.rect′ cur′rent *n* electric current of constant direction and substantially constant value

di.rect′ dis′course *n* exact quotation of a speaker's words

di.rec′tion *n* **1** act or instance of directing; **2** management, control; **3** line leading to a place or point; **4** point toward which anything faces

or moves; **5** address, as of a letter; **6** command, order; **7 directions** *pl* instructions, as for using or assembling || **di.rec′tion.al** *adj*

di.rec′tive *n* **1** authoritative statement of policy or plan to which a course of action must conform; **2** specific instruction or order

di.rect′ly *adv* **1** in a straight line; **2** immediately; **3** soon; **4** precisely; **5** with nothing intervening || SYN presently, straightway (see *immediately*)

di.rect′ ob′ject *n gram* word or words representing the immediate recipient of the action of a verb, as *Mary* in *John kissed Mary*

di.rec′tor *n* **1** one who directs; **2** member of a board running a corporation; **3** person in charge of putting on a show, as for the stage, motion pictures, etc. || **di.rec′tor.ship′** *n*

di.rec′to.rate /-rit/ *n* **1** office of a director; **2** body of directors

di.rec′to.ry *n* (**-ries**) **1** alphabetical list of names and addresses of the people of a city, locality, or particular group; **2** wall board listing the names and locations of the occupants of a building; **3** the **Directory** *F hist* the governing body of five during the years 1795–99

dire′ful *adj* dire

dirge /durj′/ [L *dirige* direct (first word of funeral hymn)] *n* **1** song or tune of grief or mourning; **2** *R C Ch* a office for the dead; **b** requiem mass

dir.ham /dərham′/ *n* monetary unit of Morocco

dir.i.gi.ble /dir′ijəbəl, dirij′-/ [see **direct**] *adj* **1** capable of being steered || *n* **2** cigar-shaped balloon driven by motors

dirk /durk′/ [?] *n* dagger

dirn.dl /durn′dəl/ [G = girl] *n* dress with full skirt, gathered at the waist

dirt /durt′/ [ON *drit* excrement] *n* **1** filth; foul substance; **2** earth; loose soil; **3** obscenity; **4** *colloq* gossip; **5 do someone dirt** *colloq* to act treacherously toward someone

dirt′-cheap′ *adj & adv* very cheap

dirt′ farm′er *n colloq* farmer who works the soil with his own hands

dirt′ poor′ *adj* poverty-stricken

dirt′ road′ *n* road made of soil or earth

dirt′y *adj* (**-i.er; -i.est**) **1** unclean; soiled; **2** contemptible; **3** obscene; **4** foul (weather); **5** unfortunate, as *a dirty shame*; **6** unsportsmanlike, unfair; **7** resentful, as *a dirty look* || *v* (**-ied**) *vt* **8** to make dirty || *vi* **9** to become dirty || **dirt′i.ness** *n*

dirt′y trick′ *n colloq* **1** wicked, underhanded act; **2** mean, underhanded act designed to hurt an opponent

dirt′y work′ *n colloq* **1** unpleasant, vexatious work; **2** wicked, underhanded activity

dis- /usu. dis- or dis′-/ [L] *pref* **1** removal, separation, as *disbar*; **2** negation, as *dissatisfy*; 3 reversal, as *dis-entangle*

dis·a·bil·i·ty /dis'əbil'itē/ *n* (-ties) 1 physical or mental weakness or incapacity; 2 state of being disabled; 3 lack of authority to act legally ‖ SYN inability, incapacity, weakness, impotence ‖ DISCR *Inability* is a lack of power or means, as of strength or age, innate and without remedy, that prevents a person from doing a certain thing. The *inability* of a chicken to swim is permanent; the *inability* of a newborn infant to walk is overcome only with increased age and growth. *Disability* is a want of ability under special circumstances, as one may suffer under a *disability* to act because of something requisite to the occasion or because of a legal disqualification

dis·a·ble /disāb'əl/ *vt* 1 to render unable; cripple, incapacitate; 2 to deprive of legal power or authority ‖ **dis·a'bled** *adj* ‖ **dis·a'ble·ment** *n*

dis·a·buse /dis'əbyōōz'/ *vt* to undeceive, set free from mistake

dis·ad·van'tage *n* 1 hindrance; 2 cause of loss or injury; 3 unfavorable position; 4 harm, detriment ‖ *vt* 5 to cause disadvantage to ‖ **dis'ad·van·ta'geous** *adj*

dis·af·fect' *vt* 1 to alienate the affection of; 2 to make discontented or disloyal ‖ **dis·af·fect'ed** *adj*

dis·af·fec'tion *n* 1 discontentment; disloyalty; ill will; 2 dislike; lack of affection ‖ SYN discontent, dislike, unfriendliness, estrangement, alienation ‖ ANT loyalty, harmony, allegiance

dis·af·firm' *vt* to disavow; deny; repudiate

dis·a·gree' *vi* 1 to differ in opinion; 2 to be unlike or unsuited; 3 to be unsuitable or harmful; 4 to quarrel

dis·a·gree'a·ble *adj* 1 unpleasant, repugnant; 2 unamiable, unfriendly ‖ **dis'a·gree'a·bly** *adv*

dis'a·gree'ment *n* 1 difference of opinion; 2 quarrel; 3 discrepancy ‖ SYN diversity, difference, dispute, dissension

dis·al·low' *vt* to refuse to allow; reject ‖ **dis·al·low'ance** *n*

dis·ap·pear' *vi* 1 to go out of sight, vanish; 2 to cease to exist ‖ **dis·ap·pear'ance** *n*

dis·ap·point' *vt* 1 to fail to fulfill the hope or expectation of; 2 to thwart or foil ‖ **dis·ap·point'ed** *adj*

dis·ap·point'ment *n* 1 defeat or failure of expectation; 2 state of depression caused by failure; 3 that which causes failure of expectation ‖ SYN frustration, humiliation, failure, defeat, chagrin, depression ‖ ANT fulfillment, pleasure, attainment

dis·ap·prove' *vt* 1 to hold an unfavorable opinion of; 2 to refuse to as-

sent to ‖ *vi* 3 to hold or express an adverse opinion ‖ **dis·ap·prov'al** *n* ‖ SYN blame, condemn, frown upon, deprecate

dis·arm /disärm'/ *vt* 1 to deprive of weapons; 2 to render harmless; 3 to make friendly ‖ *vi* 4 to lay down one's weapons ‖ **dis·ar'ma·ment** *n*

dis·arm'ing *adj* removing hostility; ingratiating

dis·ar·range' *vt* to put out of order, unsettle ‖ **dis·ar·range'ment** *n*

dis·ar·ray' *vt* 1 to throw into confusion or disorder; 2 to undress ‖ *n* 3 confusion, disorder; 4 disorderly clothing

dis·as·sem'ble *vt* to take apart

dis·as·so'ci·ate' *vt & vi* to dissociate

dis·as·ter /dizast'ər, -zäst'-/ [MF *desastre* < OIt *disastro*] *n* great calamity causing much harm ‖ **dis·as'trous** *adj* ‖ **dis·as'trous·ly** *adv* ‖ SYN calamity, misfortune, mishap, mischance, adversity, blow (see *trouble*)

dis·a·vow' *vt* 1 to deny, refuse to acknowledge; 2 to disown ‖ **dis'a·vow'al** *n* ‖ SYN disclaim, reject, renounce (see *repudiate*)

dis·band' *vt & vi* to break up or disperse ‖ **dis·band'ment** *n*

dis·bar' *v* (-barred; -bar·ring) *vt* to deprive (a lawyer) of the right to practice ‖ **dis·bar'ment** *n*

dis·be·lief' *n* 1 lack of belief or trust; 2 denial of a creed ‖ SYN unbelief, incredulity ‖ DISCR *Disbelief* is the state of mind in which one is convinced that a certain statement, tenet, principle, or assertion is not true. Hence, *disbelief* is positive. *Unbelief* may be negative and name merely an absence of all belief. In regard to religious creed or in Biblical use, however, *unbelief* names a positive lack of faith that amounts to *disbelief*. *Incredulity* is the state of mind of one inclined to be unbelieving, or even skeptical; in a popular sense, *incredulity* names the amazement evoked by something hard to believe, highly improbable, or extremely surprising, as the list of those involved in the government scandal was received with *incredulity*.

dis·be·lieve' *vt* 1 to refuse to believe or accept as true ‖ *vi* 2 **disbelieve in** to withhold belief in

dis·burse /dis·burs'/ [MF *desbourser* < *dis-* + L *bursa* purse] *vt* to expend, pay out ‖ **dis·burse'ment** *n*

disc /disk'/ *n* disk

dis·card' *vt* 1 to cast off or reject as without value; 2 **a** to throw off (a card or cards) from one's hand; **b** to play (a card not a trump, different from the suit led) ‖ *vi* 3 *cards* to make a discard ‖ **dis'card** *n* 4 act of discarding; 5 that which is discarded; 6 card or cards discarded ‖ SYN *v* reject, dismiss, discharge (see *repudiate*)

dis·cern /dĭzurn′, -surn′/ [L *discernere* to separate] *vt* to see or recognize clearly ‖ **dis·cern′i·ble** *adj* ‖ SYN perceive, descry, observe, detect, distinguish, discriminate ‖ DISCR To *perceive* is to lay hold of a thing by the mind or senses, as he *perceived* the meaning. To *discern* is to make out by effort of the eye or mind, as he *discerned* motionless figures in the darkness; whether the captain was friendly or hostile he could not *discern*. To *distinguish* is mentally to mark a difference between one object and another, usually by outward sign; a clergyman can be *distinguished* in a crowd by his clothing or his aspect. To *discriminate* is not only to note but to compare differences, arriving at an opinion accordingly, as a judge must *discriminate* between deliberate and accidental offenders. To *descry* is to succeed in making out with the eye or *discerning* with the mind, as the sailors turned shoreward, hoping to *descry* a port

dis·cern′ing *adj* perceptive; discriminating; having good judgment ‖ **dis·cern′ing·ly** *adv*

dis·cern′ment *n* 1 act of discerning; 2 clearness in judgment ‖ SYN penetration, sharpness, insight, astuteness, sagacity, acuteness, shrewdness (see *discrimination*)

dis·charge′ /dĭs-/ *vt* 1 to remove, as cargo or passengers; 2 to give forth, emit; 3 to shoot, as a gun; 4 to pay, as a debt; 5 to release or allow to leave; 6 to dismiss, as from employment; 7 to perform, as a duty; 8 to exhaust the charge in (an electric battery or condenser) ‖ *vi* 9 to get rid of any burden; 10 to emit fluid; 11 to fire a gun; 12 to discharge electricity ‖ also **dis′charge** *n* 13 act or instance of discharging; 14 that which is discharged; 15 emission, flowing ‖ SYN *v* accomplish, achieve, liberate, release, dismiss (see *effect*) ‖ ANT *v* fail, confine, burden

dis·ci·ple /dĭsĭp′əl/ [OE *discipul* < L *discipulus* pupil] *n* 1 pupil or follower of another's teaching; 2 early follower of Christ, esp. one of the twelve original followers

dis·ci·pli·nar·i·an /dĭs′ĭplĭner′ē·ən/ *n* one who believes in or enforces discipline

dis·ci·pline /dĭs′ĭplĭn/ [L *disciplina* training] *n* 1 strict and regular mental or moral training; 2 training through experience or adversity; 3 obedience; submission to control; 4 corrective measures, punishment; 5 system of rules governing the conduct of the members of a church or religious order; 6 branch of learning ‖ *vt* 7 to train to obedience or ef-

ficiency; 8 to punish ‖ **dis′ci·pli·nar′y** *adj* ‖ SYN *n* order, strictness, drill, correction, training

dis·claim′ /dĭs-/ *vt* 1 to disown, renounce; 2 to give up any claim to ‖ SYN renounce, deny, disavow, reject (see *repudiate*)

dis·claim′er *n* 1 disavowal, renunciation; 2 denial

dis·close /dĭsklōz′/ [OF *desclore* (-*clos*)] *vt* to uncover, reveal ‖ **dis·clo′sure** /-klōzh′ər/ *n* ‖ SYN uncover, tell, reveal, divulge, unveil ‖ DISCR To *disclose* is to remove the cover from, so as to expose what has hitherto been out of sight, as when the oyster was opened, a perfect pearl was *disclosed* within it. Figuratively, to *disclose* is to *uncover* that which was deeply hidden, as design or unsuspected motives. To *reveal* is to make known or show that which has been unknown or concealed, as the dawn *revealed* an upland country; the testimony *revealed* to us a stranger, not a friend. To *divulge* is to give out something to the general public which has been confided to one as a secret, or which has hitherto for other reasons been kept a secret, as to *divulge* a surprise, a plot

dis·col′or [OF *descolorer* < L *dicolor* of a different color] *vt* & *vi* to change in color; stain; fade ‖ **dis·col′or·a′tion** *n*

dis·com·fit /dĭskum′fĭt/ [OF *desconfit* < LL *disconfectus* undone] *vt* to frustrate, thwart, or disconcert ‖ **dis·com′fi·ture** /-chər/ *n* ‖ SYN balk, overthrow, embarrass, confuse, abash

dis·com′fort *n* 1 lack of comfort; unease; 2 that which causes discomfort ‖ *vt* 3 to cause discomfort to

dis·com·mode′ /-kəmōd′/ [MF *discommoder*] *vt* to disturb, inconvenience

dis·com·pose′ *vt* 1 to disarrange; 2 to disturb; ruffle ‖ **dis·com·po′sure** /-zhər/ *n*

dis·con·cert′ /-kənsurt′/ *vt* 1 to disturb the composure of, ruffle; 2 to confuse, disarrange; frustrate

dis·con·nect′ *vt* 1 to confuse, disarrange; 2 to break the connection between; separate, detach ‖ **dis·con·nec′tion** *n*

dis·con·nect′ed *adj* 1 disjointed, separate; 2 incoherent ‖ **dis′con·nect′ed·ly** *adv*

dis·con·so·late /dĭskon′səlĭt/ [*dis-* + *consolari* (-*atus*) to console] *adj* hopeless; sad, cheerless ‖ **dis·con′so·late·ly** *adv* ‖ SYN dejected, melancholy, forlorn, inconsolable, sorrowful ‖ ANT cheerful, optimistic, hopeful, gay

dis·con·tent′ /-kəntent′/ *n* 1 dissatisfaction with one's lot; restlessness ‖ *vt* 2 to displease, dissatisfy ‖ *adj* 3 not satisfied ‖ **dis′con·tent′ed** *adj* ‖ **dis′con·tent′ment** *n*

dis·con·tin′u·ance *n* 1 act or state of

discontinuing; 2 termination of a lawsuit by the action or failure to act of the plaintiff ‖ SYN interruption, intermission, cessation, end

dis·con·tin′ue [MF *discontinuer*] *vt & vi* to stop, cease; give up ‖ **dis′con·tin′u·a′tion** *n*

dis·con·tin′u·ous *adj* 1 not continuous; 2 intermittent, interrupted ‖ **dis′con·tin′u·ous·ly** *adv*

dis·cord /dis′kôrd/ [L *discordia*] *n* 1 lack of concord; disagreement; 2 harsh sound; 3 *mus* lack of harmony ‖ **dis·cord′ant** *adj* ‖ SYN variance, strife, difference, contention, clashing ‖ ANT peace, harmony, accord, agreement

dis·co·theque /disk′ōtek′/ [F] *n* place where people dance to recorded music

dis·count /diskount′, dis′kount/ [OF *desconter* < ML *discomputare*] *vt* 1 to deduct (a sum) from a bill or charge; 2 to make (a loan) with the interest deducted in advance; 3 to disregard; 4 to take into account and allow for ‖ /dis′kount/ *n* 5 act or instance of discounting; 6 deduction; 7 payment of interest in advance

dis′count rate′ *n* rate of interest charged by the Federal Reserve System to commercial banks

dis·cour′age *vt* 1 to deprive of courage; dishearten; 2 to dissuade; 3 to hinder, obstruct; 4 to advise against

dis·cour′age·ment *n* 1 act of discouraging; 2 lack of spirit or confidence; depression; 3 that which destroys courage ‖ SYN dejection, despair, hopelessness, opposition

dis·course /dis′kôrs, diskôrs′, -kôrs, -kôrs′/ [L *discursus* argument] *n* 1 connected expression of ideas; conversation; 2 formal written or spoken discussion as a lecture, treatise, or sermon ‖ /diskôrs′, -kôrs′/ *vi* 3 to talk or converse; 4 to give a formal speech or lecture

dis·cour′te·ous *adj* impolite, uncivil ‖ **dis·cour′te·ous·ly** *adv* ‖ SYN rude, unmannerly, inconsiderate, blunt

dis·cour′te·sy *n* (-sies) 1 rudeness, impoliteness; 2 discourteous act

dis·cov′er *vt* 1 to find out and make known the existence of (something previously unknown); 2 to learn of ‖ **dis·cov′er·er** *n* ‖ **dis·cov′er·y** *n* (-ies) ‖ SYN devise, invent, contrive, originate, ascertain, descry, detect ‖ DISCR As here compared, to *discover* is to find out that which we did not know as a certainty before, or that which we did not know existed at all. We *discover* new lands, new methods of treating or preventing disease, facts in general, new means of accomplishing old acts, unsuspected merits, hidden defects, etc. To *invent* is to *devise* new means for doing things previously done otherwise.

After the power of steam was *discovered*, the steam engine was *invented*. The possibility of communication by radio was first *discovered*; since then, scientists have worked to *invent* means of utilizing this method of communication. To *contrive* is to find a way to do a thing or accomplish a purpose by a clever use or adaptation of the means at hand; to *contrive* is to plan ingeniously in the face of difficulty. The Swiss Family Robinson *contrived* to use what raw material they could find

dis·cred′it *n* 1 lack of belief; distrust; 2 loss of reputation or esteem; 3 disgrace ‖ *vt* 4 to refuse to believe; 5 to dishonor; 6 to take away the reputation from or confidence in ‖ SYN *v* depreciate, decry, disgrace (see *disparage*)

dis·cred′it·a·ble *adj* bringing discredit; disgraceful

dis·creet /diskrēt′/ [OF *discret* < ML *discretus* separate] *adj* careful in speech and conduct; prudent ‖ **dis·creet′ly** *adv* ‖ SYN cautious, judicious, sagacious (see *careful*)

dis·crep·an·cy /diskrep′ənsē/ [< L *discrepans* out of tune] *n* (-cies) inconsistency, failure of agreement ‖ SYN difference, variance, contrariety, disparity

dis·crete /diskrēt′/ [L *discretus* separated] *adj* separate, detached, discontinuous

dis·cre·tion /diskresh′ən/ *n* 1 quality of being discreet; 2 freedom to act on one's own judgment and initiative ‖ **dis·cre′tion·ar′y** *adj*

dis·crim·i·nate /diskrim′ināt′/ [L *discrimen* distinction] *vt* 1 to observe or mark the difference between ‖ *vi* 2 to make or note a difference; 3 to show partiality because of racial, national, or class prejudice ‖ SYN differentiate, recognize, perceive (see *discern*)

dis·crim′i·nat′ing *adj* 1 noting nice distinctions; 2 having excellent taste

dis·crim′i·na′tion *n* 1 faculty of nice or exact judgment; discernment; 2 definition which marks a distinction between two synonyms; 3 unfavorable treatment of a person or group because of prejudice ‖ SYN acuteness, discernment, judgment, penetration, acumen, insight, distinction ‖ DISCR These words express degrees and modes of seeing with the mind. A *distinction* is a mental recognition of a difference marking one object or quality from another; *discrimination* is a higher degree of the same power, producing subtler, more precise, more carefully estimated results. One may make a *distinction* by noting obvious, outward signs; *discrimination* requires comparison, and weighs motives, character, qualities. In social intercourse, the *distinction* between the fluent and the labored conversationalist is easy to observe; a just *discrimination* as to the relative merit of the men who so express themselves is more difficult. *Discernment*, like *distinction*, sees and marks differences, but it is akin to *discrimination* in that it compares and estimates critically, though within a narrow range. It is sharply perceptive, however, and discovers characteristics, motives, realities, not patent to the dull or obtuse mind. Extraordinary *discernment* is *penetration*, which enters at lightning speed into the essence of a matter, uncovering that which is concealed. *Acuteness* is *penetration* exercised by an unusually sharp, capable, all-round intellect. *Acumen* names a high degree of intellectual capacity; it is penetrating, acute, and discerning. The business man of *acumen* has an intellect that is both pointed and comprehensive. *Insight* is *discernment* plus that intuitive sympathy that plumbs character at a glance. *Judgment* is a practical power of the mind which uses *discernment*, *discrimination*, *insight*, to arrive at conclusions as to the relations and values of things; it differs from all these other mental qualifications in that it creates independent decisions and courses of action based on what the others have previously discovered and compared ‖ ANT dullness, obtuseness, stupidity, slowness

dis·crim'i·na·to'ry /-tôr'-, -tōr'-/ *adj* exhibiting discrimination or bias

dis·cur·sive /diskurs'iv/ [< L *discurrere* (-*cursus*) to run about] *adj* wandering from one topic to another, rambling ‖ **dis·cur'sive·ly** *adv*

dis·cus /disk'ǝs/ [Gk *diskos*] *n* (-cus·es, -ci /-sī/) heavy disk, thrown in ancient and modern athletic contests

dis·cuss /diskus'/ [L *discutere* (-*cussus*)] *vt* to debate; give reasons for and against; discourse upon ‖ **dis·cus'sion** /-kush'ǝn/ *n*

dis·dain /disdān'/ [OF *desdeigner* < L *desdignare*] *vt* 1 to scorn, despise, look upon with contempt ‖ *n* 2 contempt, scorn

dis·dain'ful *adj* contemptuous; scornful; haughtily superior ‖ **dis·dain'ful·ly** *adv* ‖ SYN proud, supercilious, lofty (see *arrogant*)

dis·ease /dizēz'/ [OF *desaise*] *n* 1 any departure from a state of health; 2 disordered condition of mind or body marked by definite symptoms; malady, illness ‖ **dis·eased'** *adj* ‖ SYN ailment, complaint, infirmity, disorder, sickness, malady, illness, indisposition, morbidity ‖ DISCR In general, *disease* is any morbid state of the body; *sickness* is the state of

being affected with *disease; illness* names any form of physical disorder, as all her life she had been a prey to *illness*. Specifically, each word may name a particular morbid condition of the body, as pneumonia is often a fatal *disease;* grippe is a debilitating rather than a mortal *sickness;* and of what *illness* did he die? *Sickness* and *illness* are practically synonymous in general usage. An *ailment* is a troublesome, lingering, even if slight, *illness;* an *indisposition* is always slight. A *complaint* may be a deep-seated *malady*, or it may be merely an *indisposition* or an *ailment*

dis'em·bark' *vt* 1 to remove from a vessel; unload ‖ *vi* 2 to go ashore from a vessel ‖ **dis·em'bar·ka'tion** *n*

dis'em·bod'y *v* (-ied) *vt* to set free from the body, as a soul ‖ **dis'em·bod'i·ment** *n*

dis'em·bow'el *vt* 1 to remove the bowels from; 2 to wound so that the bowels protrude

dis'en·chant' *vt* to set free from enchantment or illusion ‖ **dis'en·chant'ment** *n*

dis'en·gage' *vt* 1 to release from a pledge, engagement, obligation, etc.; 2 to unfasten, disconnect; 3 *mil* to break off action with ‖ *vi* 4 to become disengaged ‖ **dis'en·gage'ment** *n* ‖ SYN disembarrass, disencumber, release, loose, clear

dis'en·tan'gle *vt* to rid of an entanglement; untangle, extricate ‖ **dis'en·tan'gle·ment** *n*

dis'es·tab'lish *vt* to withdraw state support from (an established church) ‖ **dis'es·tab'lish·ment** *n*

dis·fa'vor *n* 1 lack of esteem or favor; 2 state of being ill regarded ‖ *vt* 3 to slight, cease favoring

dis·fig'ure [OF *desfigurer*] *vt* to mar the appearance of, deform ‖ **dis·fig'ure·ment** *n*

dis·fran'chise *vt* to deprive of a political right, as the right to vote ‖ **dis·fran'chise·ment** /-chiz-/ *n*

dis·gorge' *vt* 1 to give up, as plunder; 2 to force out of the mouth or stomach ‖ *vi* 3 to eject, yield, or give up something; 4 to vomit

dis·grace' [MF < OIt *disgrazia* misfortune] *n* 1 ignominy, shame, dishonor; 2 cause of disgrace ‖ *vt* 3 to bring into disgrace ‖ **dis·grace'ful** *adj* ‖ SYN *n* disrepute, odium, reproach, opprobrium, infamy ‖ ANT *n* honor, fame, respect, favor

dis·grun'tle /disgrunt'ǝl/ [*dis-* + *obs* gruntle* to keep grunting] *vt* to make dissatisfied, cross, or ill-humored

dis·guise /disgīz'/ [OF *desguiser*] *vt* 1 to conceal or change the appearance or sound of; 2 to conceal the real nature of, misrepresent ‖ *n* 3 that which disguises; 4 act of disguising, or state off being disguised ‖ SYN *n* pretext, simulation, concealment; cloak; *v* (see *conceal*) ‖ ANT *n* reality, openness, candor

dis·gust /dɪsgust'/ [MF *desgouster* < *dis-* + L *gustare* to taste] *n* 1 repugnance, strong aversion ‖ *vt* 2 to cause distaste or loathing in; 3 to offend the taste or moral sense of ‖ **dis·gust'ed** *adj* ‖ **dis·gust'ing** *adj* ‖ SYN *n* abomination, abhorrence (see *antipathy*)

dish /dɪsh'/ [OE *disc* < L *discus*] *n* 1 more or less concave vessel used for serving food; 2 any container used at a meal; 3 food served in a dish; 4 particular kind of food; 5 *colloq* something one has a liking for or excels in, as *Latin is not his dish;* 6 *slang* attractive female ‖ *vt* 7 to put into a dish; 8 **dish it out** *colloq* **a** to scold noisily; **b** to praise effusively; 9 **dish out** *colloq* to distribute

dis·ha·bille /dɪs'əbēl'/ [< F *deshabiller* to undress] *n* state of being carelessly or informally dressed

dis·heart'en *vt* to depress, discourage ‖ SYN deject, dispirit, discourage, depress, abash

di·shev·el /dɪshev'əl/ [OF *descheveler* to dishevel the hair] *v* (-eled or -elled; -el·ing or -el·ling) *vt* to rumple or let hang in loose disorder, as the clothes or hair ‖ **di·shev'el·ment** *n*

dis·hon'est *adj* 1 not honest; 2 fraudulent ‖ **dis·hon'est·ly** *adv* ‖ **dis·hon'es·ty** *n*

dis·hon'or *vt* 1 to disgrace, bring shame on; 2 *com* to refuse or fail to pay, as a note when due ‖ *n* 3 disgrace, reproach, shame; 4 dishonest act; 5 lack or loss of honor ‖ **dis·hon'or·a·ble** *adj* ‖ SYN *v* degrade, humiliate, insult, disgrace, debauch

dish'wa'ter *n* water for washing dishes, or in which dishes have been washed

dis·il·lu'sion *n* 1 freedom from illusion; disenchantment ‖ *vt* 2 to free from illusion; disenchant ‖ **dis·il·lu'sion·ment** *n*

dis·in·cline' *vt* to make averse or unwilling ‖ **dis·in·clined'** *adj* ‖ **dis·in'cli·na'tion** /-klə-/ *n*

dis·in·fect' *vt* to cleanse from infection; purify of germs ‖ **dis·in·fect'ant** *adj & n*

dis·in·gen'u·ous *adj* not frank or candid; insincere

dis·in·her'it *vt* to deprive or cut off from inheritance

dis·in'te·grate' *vt & vi* to break up, separate into component parts ‖ **dis·in'te·gra'tion** *n*

dis·in·ter' *v* (-terred; -ter·ring) *vt* to dig up from or as from a grave; exhume ‖ **dis·in·ter'ment** *n*

dis·in'ter·est *n* lack of interest

dis·in'ter·est·ed *adj* 1 unbiased because of having no personal inter-

est; impartial; unprejudiced 2 not interested ‖ **dis·in'ter·est·ed·ly** *adv* ‖ **dis·in'ter·est·ed·ness** *n* ‖ SYN (see *uninterested*)

dis·joint'ed *adj* 1 dislocated; 2 incoherent, disconnected

disk /dɪsk'/ [Gk *diskos*] *n* 1 flat circular plate or object; 2 apparently flat surface of a heavenly body; 3 phonograph record

disk' jock'ey *n* announcer of a radio program devoted to recorded music

dis·like' *vt* 1 to regard with aversion or displeasure ‖ *n* 2 feeling of aversion or displeasure ‖ SYN *n* abhorrence, distaste, repugnance (see *antipathy*) ‖ ANT *n* affection, liking, affinity

dis·lo·cate /dɪs'lōkāt'/ [ML *dislocare* (-*atus*)] *vt* 1 to displace; 2 to disorder, upset; 3 to put out of joint, as a limb ‖ **dis'lo·ca'tion** *n*

dis·lodge' *vt* to remove or drive out from a particular place

dis·loy'al *adj* not loyal; false to duty, government, or friends ‖ **dis·loy'al·ty** *n* ‖ SYN traitorous, inconstant, untrue, treacherous, perfidious, disaffected ‖ ANT true, faithful, loyal

dis·mal /dɪz'məl/ [OF *dis mal* unlucky days < L *dies mali*] *adj* gloomy, depressing, dreary

dis·man·tle /dɪsmant'əl/ *vt* 1 to strip or deprive of, as equipment or means of defense; 2 to take apart

dis·may /dɪsmā'/ [ME *dismayen*] *vt* 1 to dispirit, discourage; 2 to terrify ‖ *n* 3 loss of courage; 4 bewildered terror ‖ SYN *n* consternation, fright, shock (see *horror*)

dis·mem'ber [OF *desmembrer*] *vt* 1 to cut or tear limb from limb; 2 to sever into parts; divide ‖ **dis·mem'ber·ment** *n*

dis·miss /dɪsmis'/ [*dis-* + L *mittere* (*missus*) to send] *vt* 1 to send away; permit to depart; 2 to discharge from employment; 3 to put away, lay aside; 4 *law* to discharge from court ‖ **dis·mis'sal** *n*

dis·mount' *vi* 1 to get off a horse, bicycle, or the like ‖ *vt* 2 to remove (something) from its mount; 3 to unhorse; 4 to dismantle (a machine)

dis·o·be·di·ent /dɪs'əbēd'ē·ənt/ *adj* refusing or failing to obey ‖ **dis·o·be'di·ence** *n*

dis·o·bey /dɪs'əbā'/ *vt & vi* to refuse or fail to obey

dis·or'der *n* 1 lack of order; confusion; 2 breach of public order; riot; 3 mental or physical disturbance; disease ‖ *vt* 4 to throw into disorder; 5 to derange in health of mind or body ‖ **dis·or'dered** *adj* ‖ SYN *n* disturbance, tumult, anarchy; clutter; ailment, disease ‖ ANT *n* order, method, regularity

dis·or'der·ly *adj* 1 untidy; lacking order; 2 turbulent, unruly; 3 violating law and order ‖ *adv* **4** in disorderly fashion

dis·or·der·ly con'duct *n law* conduct subversive of public order

dis·or·der·ly house' *n* **1** bawdyhouse; **2** house where the conduct becomes a nuisance to the neighborhood

dis·or'gan·ize' *vt* to destroy the regularity or systematic structure of; throw into confusion ‖ **dis·or'gan·i·za'tion** *n*

dis·own' *vt* to refuse to acknowledge as one's own; cast off responsibility for; renounce

dis·par·age /dispar'ij/ [OF *desparagier* to marry unequally] *vt* **1** to belittle; **2** to bring discredit upon ‖ **dis·par'age·ment** *n* ‖ SYN depreciate, undervalue, decry, discredit, belittle, lower, underrate ‖ DISCR To *depreciate* is to lessen in value, standing, esteem, or rank, as a centralized government tends to *depreciate* the power of the states; Russian currency was greatly *depreciated*. To *discredit* a person is to bring reproach upon him or his integrity; to *discredit* evidence, testimony, etc., is either to impugn it or to prove that it is unworthy of belief. To *disparage* a person, quality, or achievement is to *belittle* him or it, by implying a lack of merit. To *disparage* is also to speak directly and slightingly against a person or thing, to compare this person or thing disadvantageously with another, or to offer such perfunctory commendation that the effect of disapproval is produced. An unsuccessful man is apt to *disparage* the achievements of a thrifty and ambitious friend. To *decry* is to make an open clamor about, to cry down

dis·pa·rate /dis'pərit/ [L *disparatus* separated] *adj* totally different; not comparable

dis·par'i·ty /-par'itē/ *n* (**-ties**) inequality; lack of similarity; incongruity ‖ SYN dissimilarity, diversity, difference, inequality ‖ DISCR *Inequality*, as of size or amount, is a difference shown by comparison and may be of slight or great degree. *Disparity* commonly names a great difference, usually in kind, involving lack of harmony or adaptation

dis·pas'sion·ate /-nit/ *adj* free from passion; calm; impartial ‖ **dis·pas'sion·ate·ly** *adv*

dis·patch /dispach'/ [Sp *despachar* to ship] *vt* **1** to send off; **2** to dispose of quickly; **3** to put to death ‖ *vi* **4** to hurry, settle affairs quickly ‖ *n* **5** sending of a message or messenger; **6** act of putting to death; **7** speedy and satisfactory performance; **8** promptness; **9** message to be sent with speed; **10** official message; **11** news story sent to a newspaper or agency

dis·patch'er *n* **1** one who dispatches; **2** person who directs the departure of trains, planes, or buses

dis·pel /dispel'/ [L *dispellere*] *v* (**-pelled; -pel·ling**) *vt* to drive away, scatter, dissipate

dis·pen·sa·ble /dispen'səbəl/ *adj* **1** capable of being dispensed; **2** capable of being dispensed with

dis·pen'sa·ry /-sərē/ *n* (**-ries**) **1** place where medicines are dispensed; **2** institution which provides medical advice and medicines free or for a nominal fee

dis·pen·sa·tion /dis'pənsāsh'ən, -pen-/ *n* **1** act or instance of dispensing; **2** that which is dispensed; **3** that which is appointed or bestowed by a higher power; **4** suspension of a rule in some particular case; **5** a system of principles or rules, ascribed to divine inspiration, in operation during a specified period; **b** the period; **6** special arrangement by divine power, as *a dispensation of Providence*

dis·pense /dispens'/ [L *dispendere* (-*pensus*) to weigh out] *vt* **1** to deal out; distribute; **2** to carry out; administer; **3** to exempt; **4** to prepare and give out (medicine) ‖ *vi* **5** **dispense with, a** to do without; **b** to get rid of

dis·pens'er *n* container or package for dispensing small items one at a time

dis·perse /dispurs'/ [L *dispergere* (-*persus*)] *vt* **1** to scatter, spread; **2** to dissipate, dispel ‖ *vi* **3** to scatter ‖ **dis·per'sal** *n* ‖ **dis·per'sion** /-shən, -zhən/ *n*

dis·pir·it /dispir'it/ *vt* to depress the spirits of, dishearten

dis·pir'it·ed *adj* discouraged; dejected; melancholy ‖ SYN cheerless, downhearted, downcast, low-spirited, blue

dis·place' *vt* **1** to put out of place; **2** to replace ‖ SYN discharge, remove, depose, disturb, crowd out

dis·placed' per'son *n* person driven from his homeland by war or political upheaval

dis·place'ment *n* **1** act of displacing, or state of being displaced; **2** weight or volume of fluid displaced by a floating or submerged body; **3** volume displaced by the total travel of the piston in an engine

dis·play /displā'/ [AF *displeier* < LL *displicare* to unfold] *vt* **1** to spread out; unfold; **2** to exhibit, show ‖ *n* **3** something displayed; **4** show, ostentation

dis·play' ad' *n* advertisement in a publication meant to catch the eye, as with large type and illustrations; not a classified ad

dis·please' *vt* **1** to vex, annoy; offend ‖ *vi* **2** to cause dissatisfaction ‖ **dis·pleas'ure** /-plezh'ər/ *n*

dis·port /dispōrt', -pôrt/ [AF *desporter* < *dis-* + L *portare* to carry] *vt*

1 to amuse or divert (oneself) ‖ vi 2 to play, divert oneself

dis·pos·a·ble /dispōz′əbəl/ adj 1 available; 2 easily disposed of; designed to be disposed of after use; 3 (income) remaining after deduction of taxes

dis·pose /dispōz′/ [MF disposer] vt 1 to place, arrange; 2 to regulate or settle; 3 to incline or influence ‖ vi 4 **dispose of, a** to get rid of; **b** to settle; **c** to sell or give away ‖ **dis·pos′al** n ‖ SYN give, bestow, set, settle, regulate, arrange

dis·po·si·tion /dis′pəzish′ən/ [< L dispositus distributed] n 1 placing or arrangement; 2 final settlement or arranging; 3 inclination, temperament ‖ SYN bent, humor, nature, propensity, character, temper, temperament, inclination ‖ DISCR Disposition is that mental tendency or bias of the mind that is habitual or constitutional in an individual; it is the whole frame and make-up of the mind, showing itself in well-defined ways, as a disposition for merriment; a disposition to doubt; a bad disposition. Temper is disposition narrowed down to mean a certain, instead of the whole, frame of mind; it respects the state of the feelings, passions, affections, etc., and hence may vary at different times. Gifted politicians can perceive a change of temper among their constituents; a man may be of such temper that it is unsafe to deceive him. Temper, however, may name a certain habitual tendency to, or the state of, irritation and quick anger, as to show temper. Temperament is disposition as it is permanently influenced by one's physical and mental make-up, the effect showing in the manner of acting or thinking peculiar to the individual, as the artistic, the nervous, the placid temperament. Character comprehends all of that which makes us what we are; it is a word that connotes our mental and moral nature and our individual disposition, both as inherited and as changed by will and habit. Inclination is a mild turning of the mind toward a particular course of action, as an inclination to draw or to cry

dis′pos·sess′ vt to remove from ownership or occupation, esp. of land; eject ‖ **dis′pos·ses′sion** n

dis·proof′ n evidence that a statement is untrue

dis′pro·por′tion n 1 lack of proportion; 2 lack of proper relation in form, size, importance, etc. ‖ **dis′pro·por′tion·ate** /-nit/ adj

dis·prove′ vt to show to be false or wrong ‖ SYN refute (see confute)

dis·pu·ta·tion /dis′pyətāsh′ən/ n debate; verbal controversy

dis·pu·ta′tious adj inclined to argue

dis·pute /dispyŏot′/ [L disputare to discuss] vi 1 to debate, argue; 2 to quarrel ‖ vt 3 to argue about; 4 to argue against ‖ n 5 controversy, quarrel ‖ **dis·put′a·ble** /also dis-pyŏot′-/ adj ‖ **dis·pu′tant**/ also dis′-pyŏot-/ adj ‖ SYN v question, gainsay, impugn, wrangle, controvert ‖ ANT v accept, assent, affirm, concur, acquiesce, consent, agree

dis·qual′i·fy v (-fied) vt to make or declare ineligible, as for the exercise of a legal right or entry in an athletic contest ‖ **dis·qual·i·fi·ca′tion** n

dis·qui′et vt 1 to make uneasy; disturb, worry ‖ n 2 feeling of uneasiness; disturbance; anxiety ‖ **dis·qui′e·tude** n

dis·qui·si·tion /dis′kwizish′ən/ [L disquisitio (-onis) inquiry] n formal treatise or discussion

dis′re·gard′ vt 1 to fail to notice; ignore ‖ n 2 lack of attention; neglect

dis′re·pair′ n state of needing repair; dilapidation

dis′re·pute′ n lack of good reputation; discredit

dis′re·spect′ n lack of respect; rudeness ‖ **dis′re·spect′ful** adj

dis·robe′ vt & vi to undress

dis·rupt /disrupt′/ [< dis- + L rumpere (ruptus) to break] vt 1 to break up; 2 to break apart; 3 to interrupt (service) because of a breakdown ‖ **dis·rup′tion** n ‖ **dis·rup′tive** adj

dis·sat·is·fy v (-fied) vt to fail to satisfy, cause displeasure to ‖ **dis·sat′is·fac′tion** n

dis·sect /disekt′, dī-/ [L dissecare (-sectus) to cut up] vt 1 to cut apart (an animal body or a plant) in order to examine it; 2 to examine closely, analyze ‖ **dis·sec′tion** n

dis·sem·ble /disem′bəl/ [< MF dissimuler] vt 1 to hide (one's true feelings or motives) under a false appearance; 2 to pretend ‖ vi 3 to conceal one's true feelings or motives ‖ **dis·sem′bler** n ‖ **dis·sem′blance** n ‖ SYN feign, cover, hide, mask (see conceal)

dis·sem·i·nate /disem′ināt′/ [L disseminare (-atus)] vt to scatter about like seed; propagate; diffuse ‖ **dis·sem′i·na′tion** n ‖ SYN spread, circulate, promulgate, diffuse, disperse

dis·sen·sion /disensh′ən/ n discord; strife; angry disagreement ‖ SYN contention, discord, quarrel, wrangling, strife

dis·sent /disent′/ [L dissentire] vi 1 to disagree in opinion; 2 to reject the doctrines of an established church ‖ n 3 difference of opinion; disagreement; 4 religious nonconformity ‖ **dis·sent′er** n

dis·ser·ta·tion /dis′ərtāsh′ən/ [< L dissertare (-atus) to argue] n 1 formal discourse; learned treatise; 2 written thesis by a candidate for a doctorate

dis·serv·ice *n* harmful act; ill turn

dis·si·dence /dis'idəns/ [< L *dissidens* (-*entis*) disagreeing] *n* disagreement in opinion || **dis'si·dent** *adj & n*

dis·sim·i·lar *adj* unlike, different || **dis·sim'i·lar'i·ty** /-lar'-/ *n* (-ties)

dis·sim·i·late [*dis-* + *assimilate*] *vt* to cause (a sound) to become different from or less like an adjacent sound || **dis·sim'i·la'tion** *n*

dis·sim·u·late /dis'i'-/ *vt & vi* to dissemble || **dis·sim'u·la'tion** *n*

dis·si·pate /dis'ipāt/ [L *dissipare* (-*atus*) to scatter] *vt* 1 to scatter completely; 2 to squander || *vi* 3 to be scattered or dispelled; 4 to indulge in intemperate or dissolute pleasures || **dis'si·pat'ed** *adj* || **dis'si·pa'tion** *n*

dis·so·ci·ate /disōsh'ē·āt'/ [L *dissociare* (-*atus*)] *vt & vi* 1 to separate, disunite; 2 *chem* to break up into constituent parts || **dis·so'ci·a'tion** *n*

dis·sol·u·ble /disol'yəbəl/ *adj* capable of being dissolved || **dis·sol'u·bil'i·ty** /-bil'-/ *n*

dis·so·lute /dis'əlōōt'/ [L *dissolutus* dissolved] *adj* given to vice or dissipation || **dis'so·lute'ness** *n* || SYN wild, wanton, profligate, unbridled, licentious, abandoned || ANT restrained, controlled, moral

dis·so·lu'tion *n* 1 separation or breaking up into component parts; 2 termination and breaking up, as of a legislative assembly or a business partnership; 3 ending, disintegration, as of the body at death

dis·solve /dizolv'/ [L *dissolvere*] *vt* 1 to cause to pass into solution; 2 to cause to be absorbed by a liquid; 3 to separate into parts; disintegrate; 4 to break up or put an end to, as an assembly, marriage, partnership, or spell || *vi* 5 to become dissolved; 6 to melt; 7 to waste away, break up, or crumble; 8 to fade out of sight; 9 *motion pictures & telv* to fade out one scene while fading in another in its place || *n* 10 *motion pictures & telv* change of scenes made by dissolving

dis·so·nance /dis'ənəns/ [< *dis-* + L *sonare* to sound] *n* 1 discord; inharmonious mingling of sounds; 2 lack of agreement; incongruity || **dis'so·nant** *adj*

dis·suade /diswād'/ [L *dissuadere*] *vt* to divert (a person) from a plan or proposal by reasoning or persuasion || **dis·sua'sion** /-zhən/ *n*

dis·taff /dis'taf, -täf/ [OE *distæf*] *n* 1 staff from which flax or wool is drawn in spinning; 2 woman or her work

dis'taff side' *n* female side of a family

dis·tance /dist'əns/ [ME < L *distantia*] *n* 1 length of the straight line between two objects or points in space; 2 remoteness; 3 coldness or reserve of manner; 4 interval between two points; 5 distant place

dis'tant *adj* 1 so placed as to be (a stated distance) apart in time, space, or other relationship; 2 far off, remote; 3 reserved, cool; 4 widely separated || SYN remote, far, unapproachable, cold, aloof

dis·taste' *n* dislike, aversion || **dis·taste'ful** *adj*

dis·tem'per [*dis-* + L *temperare* to regulate] *n* 1 infectious viral disease of young dogs; 2 fatal viral disease of cats

dis·tend /distend'/ [L *distendere*] *vt & vi* to extend in all directions; expand, swell || **dis·ten'tion** *n*

dis·till also **dis·til** /distil'/ [LL *distillare* to drip] *v* (-tilled; -till·ing also -til·ling) *vt* 1 to subject to or obtain by distillation || *vi* 2 to undergo distillation

dis·til·late /dis'tilāt, -lit, distil'it/ *n* that which results from distillation

dis·til·la'tion /-shən/ *n* 1 process of vaporizing and then condensing a liquid in order to purify it or separate out the more volatile components; 2 substance so obtained || **dis·till'er** *n*

dis·till'er·y *n* (-ies) place where alcoholic liquors are produced by distillation

dis·tinct /distiŋkt'/ [L *distinctus*] *adj* 1 separate, marked off; 2 different; 3 clear, well-defined || **dis·tinct'ly** *adv* || **dis·tinct'ness** *n* || SYN individual, evident, unconfused, unlike, clear

dis·tinc'tion *n* 1 act of noting clearly or of marking off from others; 2 characteristic difference; 3 noting of such a difference; discrimination; 4 distinguishing quality; 5 eminence, superiority; 6 token of honor || SYN rank, eminence (see *difference, discrimination*)

dis·tinc'tive *adj* distinguishing, marking a difference

dis·tin·guish /distiŋ'gwish/ [< L *distinguere* to separate] *vt* 1 to mark off or perceive as distinct; 2 to discern clearly; 3 to make (oneself) prominent or famous; 4 to classify || *vi* 5 distinguish **between** to make a distinction between || **dis·tin'guish·a·ble** *adj* || SYN differentiate, characterize (see *discern*)

dis·tin'guished *adj* eminent, noted || SYN prominent, conspicuous, noted, eminent, glorious, illustrious, celebrated, famous || DISCR A *distinguished* person enjoys high standing in the community through rank, character, or the like, or through some achievement which has set him apart, as a company of *distinguished* gentlemen; he was *distinguished* for his foresight. An *eminent* man may stand out because he is of exalted station in life, or because his achievements surpass those of others, especially in his own particular field, as an *eminent* surgeon. An *illustrious* person is one whose deeds or character have a luster in the eyes of men; George Washington was an *illustrious* statesman. A *celebrated* man is one whose deeds have been made known through a considerable area; *celebrated*, however, represents a lesser degree of renown than *famous*. A *famous* man is known far and wide among all conditions of people. A *noted* person is well known; a *conspicuous* person stands out so as to be *distinguished* easily, as a *noted* welfare worker, *conspicuous* in public life. All these words may be applied to things or qualities; we may be a figure in a *distinguished* gathering, on a *conspicuous* errand; we may attend a *famous* university in a *noted* place; we may have an *illustrious* character, or show *eminent* devotion to a cause. These words are used for the most part (*illustrious* and *eminent* always) in a good sense; we may, however, mention a *distinguished* crook, a *famous* forger, a *celebrated* quack, a *conspicuous* fool, a *noted* gambler ‖ ANT unknown, obscure, ordinary

Dis·tin'guished Serv'ice Cross' *n* medal awarded to U.S. soldiers for extraordinary heroism

dis·tort /distôrt'/ [L *distorquere* (*-tortus*)] *vt* 1 to twist out of shape; 2 to pervert; misrepresent

dis·tor'tion *n* 1 act of distorting, or state of being distorted; 2 distorted image; 3 deformation of a modulated wave

dis·tract /distrakt'/ [L *distrahere* (*-tractus*)] *vt* 1 to turn away the attention of; divert; 2 to confuse, bewilder; 3 to derange ‖ **dis·tract'ed·ly** *adv* ‖ SYN confuse, puzzle, craze, madden (see *perplex*)

dis·trac'tion /-shən/ *n* 1 act of distracting or state of being distracted; 2 anything that distracts; diversion; 3 mental distress; 4 diversion, entertainment ‖ SYN bewilderment, distress, diversion, agitation, frenzy, madness ‖ ANT tranquility, poise, sanity

dis·traught /distrôt'/ [ME < L *distractus*] *adj* 1 bewildered, distracted; 2 agitated, deranged

dis·tress /distres'/ [OF *destresse*] *n* 1 physical or mental anguish; 2 misfortune, affliction; 3 state of extreme necessity or danger ‖ *vt* 4 to cause pain or anxiety to; grieve ‖ **dis·tress'ful** *adj* ‖ SYN *n* grief, pain, trouble, affliction, suffering, anguish, agony ‖ DISCR *Distress* names a painful degree of suffering, mental or physical, occasioned by the ordinary casualties and accidents of life. Unlike anxiety, *distress* is concerned over the present, not a future, evil, and its cause is always real, not imaginary. *Anguish* and *agony* name the extreme degrees of suffering to which humanity is liable; *anguish*, though sometimes used of physical suffering, denotes chiefly mental pangs, as the *anguish* of remorse. *Agony* is excruciating torture of mind and body, so great that the body writhes and twists with the force of it

dis·trib·ute /distrib'yŏŏt/ [L *distribuere* (*-utus*)] *vt* 1 to deal out or apportion; 2 to deliver, as goods or periodicals, to individual customers; 3 to classify; 4 to spread or scatter ‖ SYN share, dispense, deal, classify, assign, apportion, allot ‖ ANT collect, keep, retain

dis·tri·bu'tion *n* 1 act or process of distributing; 2 way a thing is distributed; 3 classification; 4 act of spreading or scattering; 5 *econ* a process of transporting commodities to the consumer from where they are produced; b apportionment of the total national output of commodities among the individuals and classes of individuals of the nation; c division of the total national money income in the form of shares to those who receive rent, wages, and profit respectively

dis·trib'u·tor *n* 1 one who or that which distributes; 2 person who distributes and markets goods throughout an area; 3 device for supplying the high voltage from the induction coil to the spark plugs of an internal-combustion engine in the proper sequence

dis·trict /dis'trikt/ [ML *districtus* jurisdiction] *n* 1 section of a city, county, state, etc., marked off for administrative reasons; 2 region ‖ *vt* 3 to mark off in districts

dis'trict at·tor'ney *n* chief prosecuting attorney of a county or other administrative district

Dis'trict of Co·lum'bi·a *n* federal district on the Potomac between Maryland and Virginia, coextensive with Washington, the national capital (756,500; 69 sq.m.)

dis·trust' *vt* 1 to lack trust in, doubt ‖ *n* 2 lack of trust, suspicion ‖ **dis·trust'ful** *adj* ‖ SYN *n* misgiving, suspicion (see *doubt*)

dis·turb /disturb'/ [L *disturbare* to demolish] *vt* 1 to break up the quiet or peace of; 2 to annoy, hamper; 3 to agitate, unsettle ‖ SYN rouse, annoy, trouble, interrupt, confuse, upset, vex, worry, derange ‖ ANT pacify, quiet, soothe

dis·turb'ance *n* 1 act of disturbing or state of being disturbed; 2 disorder; breach of the peace; 3 *meteor.* low-pressure area ‖ SYN commotion, tumult, uproar, turmoil

dis·turbed' *adj* 1 showing symptoms of mental illness; 2 agitated; disrupted

di·sul'fide /dī-/ *n* combination of two sulfur atoms with an element or a radical

dis·u·nite' *vt* 1 to divide, separate; 2 to set apart || **dis·u'ni·ty** *n* (-ties)

dis·use' /-yŏŏs'/ *n* cessation of use

di·syl·lab'ic /dī'-, dis'-/ *adj* consisting of or pert. to two syllables

ditch /dich'/ [OE *dīc*] *n* 1 trench or channel cut in the earth || *vt* 2 to drive (a vehicle) off the road and into a ditch; 3 to crash-land (a plane) on the water; 4 *slang* to get rid of || *vi* 5 to crash-land on water

dith·er /dith'ər/ [ME *didderen* to tremble] *n* flustered excitement

dith·y·ramb /dith'iram'/ [Gk *dithyrambos*] *n* song or poem in a wild exalted style || **dith'y·ram'bic** /-ram'bik/ *adj*

dit·to /dit'ō/ [It, var of *detto* said] *n* 1 the same as has been said above or before; 2 *colloq* duplicate || *adv* 3 as aforesaid; likewise || *vt* 4 to duplicate

dit'to mark' or **marks'** *n* two small marks " indicating the repetition of something appearing immediately above

dit·ty /dit'ē/ [OF *ditie* poem < L *dictata* things dictated] *n* (-ties) 1 little song; 2 short poem written to be sung

di·u·ret·ic /dī'yŏŏret'ik/ [Gk *diouretikos*] *adj* 1 promoting the secretion of urine || *n* 2 diuretic agent or medicine

di·ur·nal /dī-urn'əl/ [L *diurnalis*] *adj* 1 of or pert. to day or daylight; 2 daily

div. 1 divide(d); 2 dividend; 3 division; 4 divisor; 5 divine

di·va /dē'vo/ [It < L = goddess] *n* prima donna

di·va·lent /dīval'ənt/ [< *di-*¹ + *valence*] *adj* having a valence of two

di·van /dī'van/ [Pers *dīwān* tribunal] *n* couch, sofa

dive /dīv'/ [OE *dȳfan* to immerse] *v* (dived or dove; dived) *vi* 1 to plunge, usu. headforemost, into water; 2 to plunge or descend through the air; 3 to submerge; 4 to enter deeply and suddenly into a subject or activity; 5 to dart suddenly, as if to hide || *vt* 6 to cause to dive || *n* 7 act or instance of diving; 8 sudden and sharp drop, as in prices; 9 *colloq* cheap disreputable bar or nightclub; 10 take a dive *boxing* to deliberately lose a fight by a fake knockout

dive'-bomb' *vt* & *vi* to bomb with a dive bomber

dive' bomb'er *n* bombing plane which releases its bombs while diving

div'er *n* 1 one who or that which dives; 2 one whose business is diving, as for pearls or salvage; 3 bird of diving habits, such as the loon

di·verge /dīvurj'/, dī-/ [ML *divergere*] *vi* 1 to move or lie in different directions; branch off; 2 to differ from a norm, deviate || *vt* 3 to cause to diverge || **di·ver'gence** *n* || **di·ver'gent** *adj* || SYN (see *wander*)

di·vers /dī'vərz/ [OF < L *diversus* diverse] *adj* sundry; several

di·verse /dīvurs', dī-/ [L *diversus*] *adj* 1 dissimilar; 2 varied

di·ver'si·fy' *v* (-fied) *vt* 1 to make varied; give variety to; 2 to broaden the number and nature of (one's investments or manufactures) || **di·ver'si·fi·ca'tion** *n*

di·ver'sion /-zhən/ *n* 1 act of diverting or turning aside; 2 recreation or pastime; 3 act or instance of turning the attention of an enemy from the real point of attack; 4 *Brit* detour || SYN sport, game, recreation, fun (see *amusement*)

di·ver'si·ty *n* (-ties) 1 difference; unlikeness; 2 variety

di·vert /dīvurt', dī-/ [L *divertere*] *vt* 1 to turn aside from a course; 2 to entertain or amuse; 3 *Brit* to detour || SYN deflect, distract, entertain, amuse

di·ver·tisse·ment /dīvurt'ismənt/ [F = diversion] *n* 1 entertainment, amusement; 2 light piece of music

di·vest /dīvest', dī-/ [L *divestire*] *vt* 1 to strip or unclothe; 2 to despoil; 3 to deprive, as of rights or office || **di·vest'i·ture** /-chər/ *n*

di·vide /dīvīd'/ [L *dividere*] *vt* 1 to cut or separate into parts; 2 to part; 3 to cause to disagree; 4 to share or distribute; 5 to classify; 6 *math* to perform the process of division with (a number) || *vi* 7 to become divided; 8 to share; 9 *math* to perform the operation of division || *n* 10 ridge or height separating two drainage basins

di·vid'ed high'way *n* highway that has the lanes for opposing traffic separated by a median

div·i·dend /div'idend'/ *n* 1 number to be divided by the divisor; 2 a that part of the profits of a corporation paid out to the stockholders; b sum due to any one stockholder

di·vid'er *n* 1 that which divides into two areas, as a partition; 2 **dividers** *pl* compasses

div·i·na·tion /div'ināsh'ən/ *n* 1 act or process of foreseeing or foretelling the future or of guessing something hidden; 2 prophecy, augury

di·vine /divīn'/ [L *divinus* < *divus* god] *adj* 1 of or pert. to God or a god; 2 proceeding from God; 3 devoted to God; 4 sacred, holy; 5 superhumanly excellent; 6 *colloq* excellent; fashionable || *n* 7 theologian; 8 clergyman || *vt* & *vi* 9 to prophesy; 10 to guess, as by intuition; 11 to discover by means of a divining rod || **di·vine'ly** *adv* || **di·vin'er** *n* || SYN *adj* heavenly, superhuman, sacred

div'ing bell' *n* bell-shaped vessel in which to work under water, the water being kept out by the pressure of the air inside

di·vin'ing rod' *n* forked stick which is thought to reveal the presence of underground water or minerals by dipping toward the ground

di·vin·i·ty /-vin′-/ *n* (-ties) 1 state or quality of being divine; 2 god, deity; 3 theology; 4 the Divinity God

di·vis·i·ble /divíz′ibel/ [< L *divisus* divided] *adj* capable of being divided, esp. without a remainder ‖ **di·vis′i·bil′i·ty** /-bil′-/ *n*

di·vi·sion /divizh′ən/ *n* 1 act or state of being divided; 2 partition; 3 section; 4 dividing line; 5 disagreement; difference of opinion; 6 two or more brigades of an army under a single command, part of an army corps; 7 *math* operation of finding how many times one number or quantity is contained in another; 8 major administrative unit, as of a government, college, or corporation; 9 major classification or category ‖ **di·vi′sion·al** *adj* ‖ SYN portion, share, piece, severance (see *part*)

di·vi′sion sign′ *n* the symbol ÷, indicating division

di·vi·sive /divīs′iv/ *adj* creating disunity

di·vi·sor /diviz′ər/ *n* number or quantity by which the dividend is divided

di·vorce /divôrs′, -vōrs′/ [MF < L *divortium*] *n* 1 legal dissolution of a marriage; 2 separation, severance ‖ *vt* 3 to separate (a couple) by divorce; 4 to separate from (one's spouse) by divorce; 5 to sever, separate ‖ **di·vorce′ment** *n*

di·vor·cée /divôrsā′, -sē′, -vôr′sā, -sē/ [F] *n* divorced woman

div·ot /div′ət/ [?] *n* piece of turf torn from the fairway by a golf club

di·vulge /divulj′, dī-/ [L *divulgare*] *vt* to make known, disclose ‖ **di·vul′gence** *n* ‖ SYN impart, reveal, let out, tell (see *disclose*)

div·vy /div′ē/ [< *divide*] *v* (-vied) *slang vt & vi* 1 **divvy (up)** to share; divide ‖ *n* (-vies) 2 share, portion; sharing

Dix·ie /dik′sē/ [?] *n* 1 the southern states of the U.S.; 2 any of several Southern songs, esp. one composed in 1859 by D. D. Emmett

diz·zy /diz′ē/ [OE *dysig* foolish] *adj* (-zi·er; -zi·est) 1 affected by a swimming sensation in the head; giddy; 2 confused, bewildered; 3 producing dizziness; 4 *colloq* silly ‖ *v* (-zied) *vt* 5 to make dizzy ‖ **diz′zi·ly** *adv* ‖ **diz′zi·ness** *n*

D.J. *colloq* disk jockey

Dja·kar·ta /jəkärt′ə/ *n* capital of Indonesia (2,906,533)

Dji·bou·ti /jiboo̅′tē/ *n* republic in NE Africa (250,000; 8,900 sq.m.; cap. Djibouti)

D.Litt. [L *Doctor Litterarum*] Doctor of Letters

DNA [deoxyribo nucleic acid] *n* a nucleic acid found chiefly in cell nuclei, important in the transference of genetic characteristics and in synthesizing protein

do¹ /doo̅/ [OE *dōn*] *v* (**did**; **done**) *vt* 1 to carry out, perform; 2 to accomplish, finish; 3 to produce, make, work out; 4 to deal with; arrange; repair; 5 to render, bestow, give, as *to do one a service*; 6 to work at; 7 to suffice, be enough for; 8 to swindle; 9 to serve (a term of imprisonment); 10 **do in** *slang* to kill; **b** to ruin; 11 **do out of** *slang* to cheat out of; 12 **do time** *colloq* to serve a prison term; 13 **do up** *colloq* **a** to wrap up; **b** to fix (the hair); **c** to clothe ‖ *vi* 14 to act, conduct oneself; 15 to fare; 16 to suffice; answer the purpose; 17 **do away with, a** to put an end to; **b** to kill; 18 **do or die** to extend oneself to the utmost; 19 **do with** to require, make use of; 20 **do without** to forgo; be able to dispense with; 21 **have to do with** to have a connection with; 22 **make do** to get along with whatever is available ‖ *v aux* used 23 to form **a** an emphatic affirmative or imperative, as *I do try*; *do tell me*; **b** a negative, as *I don't know*; **c** an interrogative, as *does he know?*; 24 as a substitute verb, as *he eats as much as I do* ‖ SYN accomplish, fulfill, achieve, suffice

do² /dō/ [It] *n mus* first tone or keynote of the diatonic scale

dob·bin /dob′in [pet name for Robert] *n* farm or work horse

Do·ber·man pin·scher /dōb′ərmən pinsh′ər/ [G = Doberman terrier < L. *Dobermann* 19th-cent. G breeder] *n* one of a breed of short-haired medium-sized dogs with dark coats

doc·ile /dos′əl/ [L *docilis* teachable] *adj* tractable; easily managed ‖ SYN compliant, submissive, gentle

dock¹ /dok′/ [Flem *dok* cage] *n* place where the prisoner stays in court during trial

dock² [MD *docke*] *n* 1 artificial basin or waterway for ships; 2 wharf, pier ‖ *vt* 3 to bring to a dock and moor; 4 to couple (two or more spacecraft) in space ‖ *vi* 5 to arrive at a dock; 6 to become coupled in space

dock³ [ME *dok* solid part of a tail] *vt* 1 to cut off; cut off the tail of; 2 **a** to deduct from (wages); **b** to deduct from the wages of

dock⁴ [OE *docce* < MD *docke*] *n* any of several long-rooted weeds of the genus *Rumex*, with clusters of greenish or reddish flowers

dock′age /-ij/ *n* 1 docking of a vessel; 2 provision for docking; 3 charge for docking

dock′er [< *dock²*] *n* longshoreman, dock laborer

dock·et /dok′it/ [ME *dogget*] *n law* list or calendar of cases awaiting trial

dock′yard′ *n* shipyard with docks and appliances for building and repairing ships

doc·tor /dok′tər/ [L = teacher] *n* 1

licensed physician or surgeon; **2** holder of the doctor's degree, the highest degree granted by a university ‖ *vt* **3** to treat or prescribe for medically; **4** to mend, repair; **5** to tamper with ‖ *vi* **6** to take medicine; **7** to practice medicine

doc′tor·ate /-*it*/ *n* degree of doctor

Doc′tor of Phi·los′o·phy *n* **1** doctor's degee in the humanities or the sciences; **2** holder of this degree

doc′tor's de·gree′ *n* **1** earned university degree of the highest rank in humanistic, scientific, and professional subjects; **2** honorary degree of doctor

doc·tri·naire /dok′trīner′/ [F] *n* **1** one who has theoretical ideas and disregards practical considerations ‖ *adj* **2** visionary, impractical; **3** narrowly dogmatic

doc·trine /dok′trin/ [MF < L *doctrina* teaching] *n* **1** that which is taught or set forth for acceptance or belief; **2** principles or dogma of a church or party ‖ **doc′tri·nal** *adj* ‖ SYN tenet, creed, precept, opinion, article, maxim

doc·u·ment /dok′yəmənt/ [L *documentum* proof] *n* **1** legal or official paper attesting to something; **2** any written source of fact or information ‖ /-ment′/ *vt* **3** to furnish or support with documents ‖ **doc′u·men·ta′tion** /-mentāsh′ən/ *n*

doc′u·men′ta·ry *adj* **1** pert. to or based on documents ‖ *n* (**-ries**) **2** film of actual events presented in dramatic form

dod·der /dod′ər/ [ME *doderen*] *vi* to shake, tremble, totter ‖ **dod′der·ing** *adj*

dodeca- or **dodec-** [Gk] *comb form* twelve, as *dodecagon*

dodge /doj′/ [?] *vi* **1** to move aside or duck suddenly to avoid being hit; **2** to use evasive methods ‖ *vt* **3** to avoid or evade by dodging ‖ *n* **4** trick; action intended to deceive or cheat; **5** ingenious device or plan

dodg′er *n* one who evades a responsibility, as a *draft dodger*

do·do /dōd′ō/ [Port *doudo* madman] *n* (**-does** or **-dos**) **1** one of several extinct large, clumsy, flightless birds (genera *Raphus* and *Pezophaps*), formerly found on islands of the Indian Ocean; **2** *slang* dimwit, poke

doe /dō′/ [OE *dā*] *n* female of the deer, antelope, rabbit, and goat

do·er /dōō′ər/ *n* person who gets things accomplished

does /duz′/ *3rd pers sg pres ind* of **do**[1]

doe′skin′ *n* **1** leather from the skin of a doe; **2** fine woolen cloth with a velvety finish

does·n′t /duz′ənt/ does not

doff /dof′, dôf′/ [*do*[1] + *off*] *vt* to remove (clothing or a hat)

dog /dôg′, dog′/ [OE *docga*] *n* **1** any

of a great variety of domesticated carnivores (genus *Canis familiaris*); **2** male of the dog, fox, or wolf; **3** any of various mechanical devices for holding tight or fast; **4** contemptible fellow; **5** *slang* something worthless; **6** *slang* extremely ugly female; **7** dogs *pl slang* feet; **8 go to the dogs** *colloq* to go to ruin; **9 let sleeping dogs lie** to do nothing to disturb the situation; **10 put on the dog** *slang* to make a fine show in dress and manner ‖ *v* (**dogged; dog·ging**) *vt* **11** to track, hound

dog′ days′ *npl* hot period in July and August, formerly thought to be due to Sirius, the Dog Star

doge /dōj′/ [Venetian < L *dux* (*ducis*) leader] *n* chief magistrate in the former republics of Venice and Genoa

dog′-ear′ *n* turned-down corner of the page of a book ‖ **dog′-eared′** *adj*

dog′-eat′-dog′ *n* ruthless competition ‖ also *adj*

dog′face′ *n slang* infantryman

dog′fish′ *n* (**-fish** or **-fish·es**) any of several small ferocious sharks

dog′ged /-*id*/ *adj* stubborn, persistent ‖ **dog′ged·ly** *adv*

dog·ger·el /dôg′ərəl, dog′-/ [ME] *n* trivial, comic, or burlesque verse, often senseless and poorly constructed

dog·go /dôg′ō, dog′ō/ [< *dog*] *adv colloq* **lie doggo** to stay in hiding

dog′gone′ *colloq vt* **1** to damn ‖ *adj* also **dog′goned′** **2** darned, confounded

dog′gy *n* (**-gies**) **1** small dog ‖ *adj* (**-gi·er; -gi·est**) **2** of or pert. to dogs; **3** *colloq* showy; pretentious

dog′house′ *n* (**-hous·es** /-ziz/) **1** small shelter built for a dog; **2** any small structure resembling this, as on a deck or roof; **3 in the doghouse** *slang* in disfavor, in trouble

do·gie /dōg′ē/ [?] *n western U.S.* motherless calf

dog′leg′ *n* something with a sharp angle ‖ **dog′legged′** /-legd′, -leg′id/ *adj*

dog·ma /dôg′mə, dog′-/ [Gk = opinion] *n* (**-mas** also **-ma·ta** /-mətə/) **1** principle, doctrine, creed, or body of such principles, etc. accepted as authoritative; **2** asserted opinion; established belief

dog·mat′ic /-mat′ik/ *adj* **1** pert. to or of the nature of dogma; **2** arrogantly opinionated ‖ **dog·mat′i·cal·ly** *adv* ‖ SYN arrogant, imperious, dictatorial, autocratic (see *opinionated*) ‖ ANT unassertive, considerate, gentle

do′-good′er *n* earnest but ineffectual and misguided social reformer ‖ **do′good′ism** *n*

Dog′ Star′ *n* Sirius, the brightest star in the heavens, in the constellation Canis Major

dog′ tag′ *n* **1** identification attached to a dog's collar; **2** identification disk worn suspended from the neck by members of the armed forces

dog′-tired′ *adj colloq* exhausted

dog′tooth′ *n* (-teeth) canine tooth

dog′trot′ *n* slow, easy trot

dog′watch′ *n naut* either of two short watches: from four to six and from six to eight in the afternoon

dog′wood′ *n* **1** shrub or tree (genus *Cornus*) with hard, close-grained wood, some bearing small greenish-yellow flowers in clusters (*Cornus florida* of E North America), some with white flowers and bright-red twigs (*Cornus sanguinea* of Europe); **2** wood of any of these trees

doi·ly /dŏi′lē/ [*Doily*, 17th-cent. Eng draper] *n* (-lies) small embroidered lace or paper mat for placing under dishes

do·ings /dŏo′iŋz/ *npl* events; acts; conduct

do′-it-your·self′ /-ityər-, -ichər-/ *adj* designed for the person who wishes to do repair work or building around the house without employing professionals

dol·ce /dŏl′chā/ [It] *adj mus* soft and sweet

dol·drums /dŏl′drəmz, dol′-/ [?] *npl* **1** tropical zones of calms and variable winds; **2** dullness, inactivity, as in business or industry; **3** low spirits, depression

dole /dŏl′/ [OE *dāl* portion] *n* **1** anything dealt out sparingly; **2** charitable gift of money or food; **3** *UK* unemployment compensation ‖ *vt* **4 dole out** to deal out sparingly

dole′ful *adj* sorrowful, mournful ‖ **dole′ful·ly** *adv* ‖ SYN dolorous, mournful, woebegone, grievous, melancholy, rueful ‖ ANT joyous, glad, merry, gay

dol′i·cho·ce·phal′ic /-dol′ikō-/ [< Gk *dolichos* long] *adj* long-headed, having a breadth of head that is 33 per cent or less of the length from front to back

doll /dol′/ [nickname for *Dorothy*] *n* **1** child's toy resembling a baby or other human being; **2** *colloq* **a** beautiful female; **b** attractive male ‖ *vt & vi* **3 doll up** *slang* to dress stylishly and ostentatiously

dol·lar /dol′ər/ [G Joachims*thaler* (coin) of Joachimsthal, Bohemia] *n* **1** monetary unit of the U.S., Canada, and several other countries, equal to 100 cents; **2** *Brit slang* crown; five shillings

dol′lar gap′ *n* a country's shortage of dollars in its balance of payments with other countries

dol′lar mark′ or **dol′lar sign′** *n* symbol $ placed before a number to indicate dollar or dollars

dol·lop /dol′əp/ [?] *n* **1** lump or blob; **2** small helping or portion

doll′y [*dim.* of *doll*] *n* (-ies) **1** *baby talk* doll; **2** low-wheeled platform or frame for moving heavy objects; **3** *motion pictures & telv* four-wheeled platform for moving a camera about a set ‖ *v* (-ied) *vt* **4** to maneuver (a camera) on a dolly ‖ also *vi*

dol·man /dŏl′mən, dol′-/ [Turk *dolaman* long robe] *n* woman's mantle with capelike sleeves

do·lo·mite /dŏl′əmīt′, dōl′-/ [< *Dolomieu* (1750–1801) F geologist] *n* **1** calcium magnesium carbonate —CaMg(CO₃)₂—; **2** rock composed largely of this mineral; **3 Dolomites** *pl* E portion of the Alps, in NE Italy

do·lor·ous /dŏl′ərəs, dol′-/ [< L *dolor* sorrow] *adj* sorrowful; full of or causing sorrow or grief ‖ **do′lor·ous·ly** *adv* ‖ SYN mournful, doleful, dismal, distressing, pathetic

dol·phin /dolf′in/ [OF *dauphin* < Gk *delphin*] *n* **1** any of several sea mammals of the family Delphinidae, akin to the whales, with a fishlike body and a beaklike snout; **2** *naut* mooring bar or spar

dol′phin strik′er *n* spar extending downward from the bowsprit

dolt /dōlt′/ [?] *n* dunce, blockhead ‖ **dolt′ish** *adj*

-dom /-dəm/ [OE] *n suf* **1** rank, domain, as *dukedom;* **2** state, as *martyrdom;* **3** collection or group, as *officialdom*

do·main /dōmān′/ [MF *domaine* < L *dominium*] *n* **1** territory under one's rule or ownership; **2** province of thought; field of activity; range, scope

dome /dōm′/ [MF < It *duomo* cathedral < L *domus* house] *n* **1** large, rounded, usu. hemispherical vault; **2** roof or ceiling of this construction; **3** anything dome-shaped

domed′ *adj* **1** having a dome; **2** dome-shaped

do·mes·tic /dəmes′tik/ [L *domesticus* < *domus* house] *adj* **1** pert. to the home or to household affairs; **2** of or pert. to one's own country; **3** tame (animals), living with and depending on man ‖ *n* **4** household servant

do·mes′ti·cate′ *vt* **1** to make accustomed to home life; **2** to tame for domestic use ‖ **do·mes′ti·ca′tion** *n*

do·mes·tic·i·ty /dō′mestis′itē/ *n* (-ties) **1** domestic or home life; **2** home-loving character or nature; **3** household chore

dom·i·cile /dom′isil, -sīl′/ [MF < L *domicilium*] *n* **1** home, abode; **2** permanent legal residence ‖ *vt* **3** to settle in a domicile

dom·i·nant /dom′inənt/ [L *dominans* (-*antis*) ruling] *adj* **1** ruling, prevailing ‖ *n* **2** *mus* fifth tone of a scale; **3**

genetics characteristic which, if possessed by either of two parents, will appear in the offspring ‖ **dom/i-nance** *n* ‖ SYN *adj* governing, principal, preeminent, ruling

dom/i-nate/ *vt* 1 to govern or control; rule; 2 to tower above; 3 to guide, determine, characterize ‖ *vi* 4 to be dominant ‖ **dom/i-na/tion** *n*

dom/i-neer/ [D *domineren* < F *dominer* < L *dominari*] *vt & vi* to rule arbitrarily and tyrannically

dom/i-neer/ing *adj* overbearing; tyrannical ‖ SYN insolent, dogmatic, imperious, masterful, lordly, dictatorial ‖ ANT meek, unassertive, submissive

Dom-i-ni-ca /dom/ənē/kə, dəmin/əkə/ *n* island republic in the West Indies (80,000; 300 sq.m.; cap. Roseau)

Do-min-i-can /dəmin/ikən/ [< St. *Dominic* (1170–1221) Sp priest] *n* 1 member of a mendicant order founded by St. Dominic in 1215; 2 native or inhabitant of the Dominican Republic ‖ also *adj*

Do-min/i-can Re-pub/lic *n* Spanish-speaking republic occupying the eastern two thirds of the island of Hispaniola in the West Indies (3,889,000; 18,816 sq.m.; cap. Santo Domingo)

do-min-ion /dəmin/yən/ [MF < L *dominium*] *n* 1 authority or control; sovereignty; 2 territory under a single control; 3 one of the self-governing members of the British Commonwealth; 4 **the Dominion** Canada ‖ SYN jurisdiction, empire, power, authority, rule

dom-i-no /dom/inō/ [MF *domino* priest's hooded black cloak < ellipsis of L benedicamus *Domino* let us bless the Lord] *n* (-noes or -nos) 1 loose cloak or robe worn with a mask at masquerades; 2 small mask for the eyes; 3 person wearing such a cloak or mask; 4 small, rectangular, black piece of wood, bone, or ivory, the face of which is divided into halves, each half being blank or marked with from one to six dots; 5 **dominoes** *sg* game played with twenty-eight such pieces

dom/i-no the/o-ry *n* idea that, if one threatened country yields to an enemy, adjoining countries will automatically collapse one after the other like a lineup of dominoes

don¹ /don/ [*do¹* + *on*] *v* (donned; don-ning) *vt* to put on (clothes)

don² [Sp < L *dominus* lord] *n* 1 *Eng* college head or tutor; 2 **Don**, a *Spanish-speaking countries* Mr., Sir (prefixed to Christian names); **b** *Italy* title prefixed to a priest's Christian name

Don /don/ *n* river in S Russia flowing into the Black Sea

Do-ña /dōn/yə/ [Sp < L *domina* mistress] *n Spanish-speaking countries* Madam (prefixed to Christian names)

do-nate /dō/nāt, dōnāt/ [L *donare* (-*atus*) to give] *vt* 1 to make a donation of ‖ *vi* 2 to make a donation; contribute

do-na/tion *n* charitable gift; contribution ‖ SYN grant, offering, bestowal, gratuity (see *boon*)

done /dun/ 1 *pp* of **do¹** ‖ *adj* 2 completed, ended, finished 3 cooked enough; 4 **done for** *colloq* a finished, through; **b** dead or dying; 5 **done in** *colloq* exhausted

don-jon /dun/jən, don/jən/ [MF] *n* main tower and stronghold of an ancient castle, usually containing a prison

Don Juan /don/ wän/, don/jōō/ən/ *n* 1 legendary Spanish seducer and rake; 2 libertine

don-key /donk/ē, dunk/ē/ [?] *n* 1 small long-eared domesticated quadruped (*Equus asinus*) related to the horse; 2 stupid, obstinate person

don-nish /don/ish/ *adj* like a university don; pedantic

don/ny-brook/ /don/ē-/ [*Donnybrook*, Ireland, former site of fair] *n* wild free-for-all; brawl

do-nor /dōn/ər/ *n* 1 one who makes a donation; 2 one who gives blood for transfusion or other biological tissue

do/-noth/ing /dōō/-/ *adj* 1 lacking initiative; unproductive ‖ *n* 2 idler, loafer

Don Quix-ote /don kwik/sət, don/ kēhōt/ē/ *n* idealistic but hopelessly impractical hero of a satirical Spanish romance by Cervantes, written in 1605–15

don't /dōnt/ do not

doo-dle /dōōd/əl/ [?] *vt & vi* 1 to scribble or draw idly and aimlessly ‖ 2 aimless scribbling ‖ **doo/dler** *n*

doo-lie /dōōl/ē/ [?] *n* first-year cadet in the U.S. Air Force Academy

doom /dōōm/ [OE *dōm* decree] *n* 1 judgment; sentence; 2 destiny, fate; 3 destructive fate, ruin ‖ *vt* 4 to pronounce condemnation upon; 5 to sentence to punishment; 6 to pronounce as a penalty; decree ‖ SYN *n* fate, lot, ruin, death (see *destiny*)

dooms/day/ *n* 1 day of the Last Judgment; 2 any day of judgment

door /dôr/-, dōr/-/ [OE *duru*] *n* 1 movable barrier for opening and closing an entranceway; 2 doorway; 3 any means of access to something; 4 **out of doors** out in the open; 5 **show someone the door** to order someone to leave

door/ check/ *n* device that automatically closes an opened door without slamming

door/jamb/ *n* one of the vertical pieces of the frame surrounding a doorway

door/knob/ *n* knob which when turned releases the latch of a door

door/man/ /-man/, -mən/ *n* (-men /-men/, -mən/) uniformed employee who opens the door of a public building, hails taxicabs, etc.

door'mat' *n* 1 mat outside a doorway for wiping the shoes; 2 *colloq* person whom others easily take advantage of

door'nail' *n* **dead as a doornail** dead beyond the shadow of a doubt

door'post' *n* doorjamb

door' prize' *n* prize given a person attending a dance, banquet, etc., by drawing a number that matches the one on his admission ticket

door'stop' *n* 1 device for holding a door open; 2 bumper to keep a door from hitting a wall when it is swung open

door'way' *n* 1 opening in which a door is hung; 2 any means of access

dope /dōp/ [D *doop* sauce] *n* 1 thick liquid or grease for making machinery run more easily; 2 *aeron* kind of varnish applied to strengthen fabric surfaces; 3 *slang* narcotic; 4 *slang* information; 5 *Southern colloq* Coca-Cola; 6 *slang* stupid person || *vt* 7 *slang* to drug; 8 **dope out** *slang* to figure out, solve

dope'sheet' *n* *slang* sheet giving information on the horses in the day's races

Dopp'ler ef·fect' /dop'lər/ [C. J. Doppler (1803–53) Austrian physicist] *n* change of frequency to the frequency at which sound waves, light waves, or other electromagnetic waves reach an observer when the source of the waves or the observer is moving rapidly with respect to the other or both are moving rapidly with respect to each other, the frequency increasing when they approach each other and decreasing when they move apart

Do·ri·an /dôr'ē·ən, dōr'-/ [Gk *Dorios*] *n* member of the prehistoric Greek tribe which conquered the Peloponnesus in the 12th century B.C. || also *adj*

Dor·ic /dôr'ik, dor'-/ *adj* 1 Dorian; 2 pert. to or designating the oldest and simplest of the orders of Greek architecture, with a capital consisting of a ring topped by a square abacus || *n* 3 ancient Greek dialect spoken in the Peloponnesus, Crete, Sicily, Rhodes, and other islands and used by the poets Pindar and Theocritus

dorm /dôrm/ *n* *colloq* dormitory

dor·mant /dôrm'ənt/ [MF, *prp* of *dormir* to sleep] *adj* 1 sleeping; as if sleeping; torpid; 2 inactive, still; latent || **dor'man·cy** *n* || SYN latent, quiescent, unused, inactive, torpid

dor·mer /dôrm'ər/ [MF *dormoir* bedroom] *n* 1 projection built out from a sloping roof containing an upright window; 2 also **dor'mer win'dow** window in such a projection

dor·mi·to·ry /dôrm'itôr'ē, -tōr'-/ [L

(cubiculum) *dormitorium* sleeping (chamber)] *n* (-ries) 1 building, as at a college, containing living accommodations for many people; 2 room with beds for several people

dor'mouse' /dôr'-/ [<*dial.* dorm sleep <MF *dormir*] *n* (-mice) small hibernating rodent of the Old World (family Gliridae) resembling a squirrel

dor·sum /dôrs'əm/ [L] *n* (-sa /-sə/) 1 back of the body, esp. of an animal; 2 back or outer side of a part or organ || **dor'sal** *adj*

do·ry[1] /dôr'ē, dōr'ē/ [Central AmInd *dori* dugout] *n* (-ries) deep flat-bottomed boat with a sharp prow and a narrow square stern, used by fishermen

do·ry[2] /dôr'ē/ [<MF *doree* gilded] *n* (-ries) bright-colored, compressed marine fish of the family Zeidae, esp. *Zeus faber*

dos·age /dōs'ij/ *n* 1 administration of medicine in doses; 2 amount or size of a dose; 3 process of treating wine to add flavor, increase strength, and improve quality

dose /dōs/ [Gk *dosis* something given] *n* 1 quantity of medicine to be taken at one time; 2 *colloq* anything unpleasant to have to swallow or to have forced on one; 3 *phys* quantity of radiation absorbed by a given mass of material; 4 *slang* case of venereal disease, esp. gonorrhea || *vt* 5 to give a dose of medicine to; 6 to administer in doses

dos·si·er /dos'ē·ā', -ē·ər/ [F bundle of documents] *n* file of information on any one person or thing

dost /dust/ *archaic* 2d *pers sg pres ind* of **do**[1]

Dos·to·ev·ski, Feo·dor /fyô'dôr dos'-təyef'skē/ *n* (1821–81) Russian novelist

dot /dot/ [OE *dott* head of a boil] *n* 1 very small spot, point, or speck; 2 small round spot, as that over an *i*; 3 *math* a decimal point; b symbol of multiplication; 4 *mus* point placed after a note or rest to indicate that its length is to be increased by one half; 5 *telg* signal shorter than a dash and used with dashes to represent letters; 6 **on the dot** precisely on time || *v* (**dot·ted; dot·ting**) *vt* 7 to mark with a dot or dots; 8 to place a dot over; 9 to cover or adorn with dots or as with dots; 10 **dot one's i's and cross one's t's** to be extremely precise and correct || *vi* 11 to make a dot or dots

dot·age /dōt'ij/ *n* 1 senility; 2 foolish and extreme fondness

do·tard /dōt'ərd/ *n* person whose mind is impaired by age

dote /dōt/ [ME *doten*] *vi* 1 to show the feebleness of age; 2 **dote on** to be excessively fond of

doth /duth'/ *archaic 3d pers sg pres ind* of **do**[1]

dot'ted line' *n* 1 row of dots printed as a guide for cutting; 2 row of partial perforations made for easy detachment of part of a sheet of paper; 3 **sign on the dotted line** to sign unquestioningly or blindly

dot·tle /dot'əl/ [prob < **dot**] *n* plug of tobacco ash or half-burnt tobacco left in the bottom of a pipe after smoking

dot·ty /dot'ē/ [< ME *dotel*] *adj* (**-ti·er; -ti·est**) *colloq* 1 shaky; of feeble gait; 2 eccentric, crazy

Dou'ay Bi'ble /dōō'ā/ [*Douay* town in N France] *n* English translation of the Vulgate (Old Testament at Douai 1609–10, New Testament at Rheims 1582), the version commonly accepted by English-speaking Roman Catholics

dou·ble /dub'əl/ [OF < L *duplus*] *adj* 1 being or made twice as much, as many, as large, as high, or the like; 2 presenting two parts; paired; 3 folded over or up; 4 deceitful, insincere; 5 twofold; 6 (musical instrument) producing a tone an octave lower than that indicated by the notes || *adv* 7 twice; by twos || *n* 8 twice the value or quantity; twice as much; 9 duplicate or counterpart; 10 fold; 11 *motion pictures* substitute who performs hazardous feats in place of the star; 12 *baseball* two-base hit; 13 *bridge* doubling of an opponent's bid; 14 **doubles** *sg* match, as in tennis, with two players on each side; 15 **on the double** *colloq* a in double time; b as quickly as possible || *vt* 16 to make twice as large, as much, or as many; 17 to bend; turn over or back upon itself; 18 to exceed by an equal amount; be the double of; 19 to sail around, as a cape; 20 *bridge* to increase the value of tricks to be won or lost in (an opponent's bid); 21 *baseball* to put out (a player) as the second out of a double play || *vi* 22 to increase twofold; 23 *bridge* to double an opponent's bid; 24 *baseball* to make a two-base hit; 25 **double as** to serve in a second capacity as; 26 **double back** to turn back on a course, retrace one's steps; 27 **double in brass** *slang* to serve in two capacities; 28 **double up, a** to bend over, as from pain; b to share quarters with someone

dou·ble-ac'tion *adj* (revolver) cocked automatically when the trigger is pulled

dou'ble a'gent *n* 1 spy who is spying on the country by which he is employed to spy on another country; 2 spy simultaneously employed by two countries that are hostile to each other

dou'ble-bar'reled *adj* 1 (firearm) having two barrels; 2 having two parts or aspects; serving two purposes

dou'ble bass' /bās'/ *n* bass viol

dou'ble bed' *n* bed big enough for two adults

dou'ble boil'er *n* cooking vessel with one pot for the food fitting into another in which water is boiled

dou'ble-breast'ed *adj* 1 (coat) with overlapping front; 2 (suit) with such a coat

dou'ble cross' *n* betrayal, generally of one's colleague or one's accomplice || **dou'ble-cross'** *vt* || **dou'ble-cross'er** *n*

dou'ble date' *n colloq* date of two couples together || **dou'ble-date'** *vt & vi*

dou'ble-deal'ing *n* duplicity, treachery || also *adj* || **dou'ble-deal'er** *n*

dou'ble deck'er *n* 1 ship with two decks above the water line; 2 bus with two tiers for passengers; 3 two beds built as a unit with one bed above the other; 4 sandwich or cake made with two layers; 5 biplane

dou'ble dome' *n slang* egghead, intellectual

dou'ble-edged' *adj* 1 having two cutting edges; 2 acting against as well as for

dou·ble-en·ten·dre /dub'əl äntän'drə/ [*obs* F] *n* word or expression with two meanings, one of which is often risqué

dou'ble en'try *n* method of bookkeeping in which one debit and one credit entry are made in the ledger for each transaction

dou'ble ex·po'sure *n photog* two exposures on the same film or plate

dou'ble fea'ture *n* motion-picture program consisting of two main pictures

dou'ble-head'er *n* 1 two baseball games played one after the other between the same teams; 2 train drawn by two locomotives

dou'ble in·dem'ni·ty *n* payment to the beneficiary of twice the face value of a life insurance policy in case of accidental death

dou'ble jeop'ar·dy *n* subjection of a person acquitted of a crime to a second trial for the same offense

dou'ble-joint'ed *adj* having joints that permit the bending of the limbs at extreme angles

dou'ble neg'a·tive *n* use of two negative words in the same sentence to express negation, a use that is illiterate in modern English

dou'ble-park' *vt & vi* to park in the street next to a vehicle that is already parked parallel to the curb

dou'ble play' *n baseball* play resulting in two put-outs

dou'ble-reed' *adj* of or designating a wind instrument having two reeds, as the oboe

dou'ble room' *n* hotel room with a

double bed to be occupied by two persons

dou'ble-space' vt & vi to typewrite leaving a full space between lines

dou'ble stand'ard n unwritten moral code which permits more freedom of behavior to men than to women

dou'ble star' n star appearing single to the naked eye which, when seen through a telescope, is resolved into two stars either close together and revolving around a common center or one behind the other at a great distance

dou·blet /dub'lĭt/ [MF] n 1 one of a pair; 2 tight garment with or without sleeves, worn by men in Europe from the 15th to the 17th centuries; 3 two objects of the same kind; 4 one of two or more words in the same language developed from the same original, as *legal* and *loyal*, both from Latin *legalis*, but *loyal* coming through French

dou'ble take' n genuine or feigned startled reaction to the sudden realization, after a momentary delay, of the significance of an unusual or unexpected statement, situation, or turn of events

dou'ble-talk' n 1 speech consisting of normal sounds put together in meaningless syllables; 2 evasive and ambiguous language || also vi

dou'ble·think' n acceptance of two contradictory beliefs or opinions at the same time

dou'ble time' n 1 overtime rate of pay equal to twice the regular wage; 2 *mil* a rate of marching which amounts almost to running, 180 steps being taken per minute; b slow run of troops in step

dou·bloon /dəbloon'/ [Sp *doblón*] n former Spanish gold coin

dou'bly adv 1 in twice the quantity or degree; 2 in a double manner

doubt /dout'/ [OF *douter* < L *dubitare*] vi 1 to waver in opinion; be uncertain || vt 2 to suspect, distrust; 3 to hesitate to believe || n 4 uncertainty of mind; distrust; 5 uncertain state of affairs; **6 no doubt, a** probably; **b** certainly; **7 without doubt** unquestionably || **doubt'er** n || SYN n distrust, mistrust, hesitation, scruple, indecision, suspicion, question, uncertainty, misgiving, disbelief || DISCR *Doubt* is a condition of unsettled opinion, a feeling of uncertainty, an inclination to disbelieve. *Question* is active *doubt*, raised and expressed. We may silently entertain *doubts;* we speak our *question,* asking for proof, evidence, or source of information. A *suspicion* is an uneasy, partial conviction that something is wrong, someone is guilty, or some danger is afoot; it is partial because it is not confirmed by out-and-out evidence. *Suspicion* is hostile, and is

directed toward others, never toward oneself. *Distrust* is sometimes exactly synonymous with *suspicion*, though the two are arrived at in different ways; *distrust* ascribes nothing good to its object, while *suspicion* attributes actual evil to him. *Distrust*, unlike *suspicion*, can be felt toward oneself, naming a want of proper confidence or assurance

doubt'ful adj 1 uncertain; 2 causing doubt; 3 not settled in opinion; undecided || **doubt'ful·ly** adv || SYN wavering, distrustful, suspicious, dubious

doubt'less adj 1 free from doubt || adv 2 unquestionably; 3 probably || **doubt'less·ly** adv

douche /doosh'/ [F < It *doccia* pipe] n 1 jet of liquid applied to a body part or cavity; 2 syringe for douching || vt 3 to wash or cleanse by means of a douche

dough /dō'/ [OE *dāh*] n 1 soft paste of flour, water, etc., ready for baking; 2 any soft pasty mass; 3 *slang* money || **dough'y** adj (-i·er; -i·est)

dough'boy' n colloq U.S. infantry soldier in World War I

dough'nut' /also -nət/ n small usu. ring-shaped cake fried in deep fat

dough·ty /dout'ē/ [OE *dohtig* worthy] adj (-ti·er; -ti·est) brave; resolute

Doug'las fir' /dug'ləs/ [David *Douglas* (1798–1834) Sc botanist] n very tall coniferous tree (*Pseudotsuga taxifolia*) of W North America

dour /door', dou'(ə)r/ [< L *durus* hard] adj 1 hard, inflexible; 2 sullen, gloomy || **dour'ness** n

douse /dous'/ [?] vt 1 to plunge suddenly into a liquid; 2 to drench; 3 colloq to extinguish || **dous'er** n

dove¹ /duv'/ [OE *dūfe*] n 1 any of several birds of the family Columbidae, as the pigeons; 2 emblem of the Holy Ghost; 3 emblem of innocence, gentleness, and peace; 4 colloq person who takes a conciliatory stance

dove² /dōv'/ pt of **dive**

dove'cote' /duv'-/ n structure for housing pigeons

Do·ver /dōv'ər/ n 1 capital of Delaware (7,000); 2 seaport in SE England on Strait of Dover (36,000)

dove'tail' /duv'-/ n carp 1 joint with a tenon or tenons fitted into corresponding mortises || vt & vi 2 to fasten together by a dovetail; 3 to fit together harmoniously

dov·ish /duv'ish/ adj colloq conciliatory, favoring peace

dow·a·ger /dou'əjər/ [MF *douagere* < *douage* dowry] n 1 widow who has property or a title from her husband; 2 elderly woman of dignified appearance

dow·dy /doud'ē/ [< obs *dowd* slut] adj (-di·er; -di·est) slovenly; ill-dressed; shabby || **dow'di·ness** n

dow'el /dou'əl/ [ME *dowle*] **1** *n* peg or pin that connects two pieces of wood, metal, etc., by being sunk into each; **2** piece of wood driven into a wall to give nailing surface for other pieces ‖ *v* (-eled or -elled; -el-ing or -el-ling) *vt* **3** to fasten with dowels

dow-er /dou'ər/ [OF *douaire*] *n* **1** that part of a deceased husband's real estate which his widow enjoys during her lifetime; **2** dowry; **3** natural talents ‖ *vt* **4** to endow

Dow'-Jones' av'er-age /dou'-/ *n* index reflecting the average performance on any day of the common stocks of the 30 main industrial corporations listed on the New York Stock Exchange

down[1] /doun'/ [ON *dūn*] *n* **1** soft fine feathers of young birds; **2** undergrowth of soft fine feathers on adult birds; **3** any soft fine growth, as on the skin of some fruits ‖ **down'y** *adj* (-i-er; -i-est)

down[2] [OE *dūn* hill] *n Eng* turf-covered tract of rolling land used for pasture

down[3] [OE (*a*)*dūne* from the hill] *adv* **1** to, in, or at a lower position or degree; **2** to, in, or at a more southerly or central location, as *down in Florida, go down to City Hall;* **3** on the ground or floor; **4** in check, as *to hold the enemy down;* **5** from an earlier to a later time; **6** completely, as *down to the root of the trouble;* **7** seriously, earnestly, as *get down to work;* **8** in cash and at once; **9** to lesser activity, speed, or excitement, as *slow down;* **10** on paper, as *take this down;* **11** down with! away with!, overthrow! ‖ *adj* **12** descending, going down; **13** *sports* behind in points or games; **14** *football* (ball) not in play; **15** *baseball* out; **16** dejected; **17** **down and out** in abject condition with no hope of betterment; **18** **down in the mouth** downcast; **19** **down on** hostile to ‖ *prep* **20** along a descent of; from a higher to a lower point on; along the course of ‖ *vt* **21** to put, knock, throw, or shoot down; **22** to drink down ‖ *n* **23** descent; **24** *football* one of a series of four plays during which the team in possession of the ball must advance it at least ten yards

down'beat' *n* **1** *mus* down stroke of a conductor's baton, signaling the first beat of a measure ‖ *adj* **2** *colloq* gloomy, disheartening

down'cast' *adj* **1** directed downward; **2** melancholy, depressed ‖ SYN sad, downhearted, dispirited, dejected

Down' East' *adv* **1** in or to New England; **2** in or to the state of Maine ‖ also *adj*

down'fall' *n* **1** sudden drop from rank or power; ruin; **2** a cause of this; **3** heavy fall of rain or snow ‖ **down'-fall'en** *adj*

down'grade' *n* **1** downward slope; **2** **on the downgrade** declining, failing ‖ *vt* **3** to demote; **4** to minimize, denigrate ‖ also *adj & adv*

down'heart'ed *adj* depressed; discouraged ‖ **down'heart'ed-ly** *adv*

down'hill' *adv & adj* in a direction down a slope; downward

Down'ing Street' *n* **1** site in London of the official residence of the British Prime Minister, the foreign office, and of other government offices; **2** the British government

down' pay'ment *n* partial payment in cash made at the time of purchase

down'pour' *n* drenching rain

down'range' *adv* from a launching pad in the direction in which a missile is fired ‖ **down'range'** *adj*

down'right' *adj* **1** blunt; frank; **2** thorough, complete ‖ *adv* **3** thoroughly

down'stairs' *adv* **1** to or on a lower floor ‖ *adj* **2** on a lower floor

down'state' *adj* **1** of or from the southern part of a state ‖ *adv* **2** in or toward such a part

down'stream' *adv & adj* in the direction of the current of a stream or river

down'-the-line' *adj* unreserved; wholehearted ‖ also *adv*

down'-to-earth' *adj* realistic, practical

down'town' *n* **1** central business district of a city ‖ *adj & adv* **2** in, at, or to this district

down'trod'den *adj* oppressed, tyrannized

down'ward /-wərd/ *adj* **1** directed from higher to lower ‖ *adv* also **down'wards 2** toward a lower place, rank, or position

down'wind' /-wind'/ *adv & adj* **1** in the direction in which the wind is blowing; **2** to leeward

dow-ry /dou'rē/ [see *dower*] *n* (-ries) property a woman brings to a husband at marriage

douse[1] /dous'/ *vt* var of **douse**

dowse[2] /douz'/ [?] *vi* to try to locate the presence of underground water or minerals with a divining rod ‖ **dows'er** *n*

dox-ol-o-gy /doksol'əjē/ [Gk *doxologia* < *doxa* glory] *n* (-gies) hymn of praise to God

dox-y /dok'sē/ [< MD *docke* doll] *n* (-ies) *slang* disreputable woman; prostitute

doz. dozen(s)

doze /dōz'/ [< Scand] *vi* **1** to sleep lightly or fitfully; **2** **doze off** to fall asleep unintentionally ‖ *vt* **3** **doze away** to pass (time) in drowsiness ‖ *n* **4** light sleep, nap

doz-en /duz'ən/ [OF *dozaine*] *n* (-ens; preceded by a number -en) twelve things or persons of a kind ‖ **doz'-enth** *adj & n*

DP, D.P. displaced person

D.P.W. Department of Public Works

Dr. 1 Doctor; **2** Drive

drab /drab'/ [MF *drap* cloth] *adj* (**drab·ber; drab·best**) 1 dull, cheerless; washed out in appearance; 2 dull-brown, yellowish-gray

drach·ma /drak'mə/ [Gk *drachme*] *n* (**-mas** or **-mae** /-mē/) principal silver coin of ancient Greece and monetary unit of modern Greece

Dra·co·ni·an /drəkōn'ē-ən/ [< *Draco* Athenian statesman of the 7th cent. B.C. noted for his severe laws] *adj* oppressively severe

draft /draft', dräft'/ [AE *dragan* to draw] *n* 1 act of drawing; 2 preliminary sketch or outline, either in drawing or in words; 3 written order for the payment of money on account of the writer; bill of exchange; 4 drawing on any source of supply; claim; 5 recruiting of soldiers by conscription; 6 pulling of a load; 7 load; 8 depth of water from the surface to the keel of a floating ship; 9 current of air; 10 device for regulating the current of air, as in a stove; 11 drink, esp. one drawn from a barrel, as beer; 12 **on draft** (beer or ale) drawn from a barrel or keg || *vt* 13 to sketch, write, or draw in outline; 14 to compose (something) in writing; 15 to select for military service; 16 to draw off

draft' an'i·mal *n* animal used for hauling heavy loads

draft' beer' *n* beer in a barrel or keg from which it is drawn as needed

draft' board' *n* board of civilians who direct the selection of men for compulsory military service

draft dodg'er *n* one who avoids or tries to avoid military service

draft·ee' *n* man drafted into military service

drafts'man /-mən/ *n* (**-men** /-mən/) one who makes plans, maps, designs, mechanical drawings, etc.

draft' trea'ty *n* treaty drawn up in tentative or outline form

draft'y *adj* (**-i·er; -i·est**) exposed to or admitting drafts of air || **draft'i·ness** *n*

drag /drag'/ [OE *dragan*] *v* (**dragged; drag·ging**) *vt* 1 to pull by force or draw along slowly and heavily; 2 to search the bottom of (a body of water), as with a dragnet; 3 **drag in** to introduce irrelevantly; 4 **drag out** to stretch out tediously || *vi* 5 to trail along the ground, move heavily; 6 to lag behind; 7 to be protracted tediously; 8 to search with a grapnel or dragnet || *n* 9 act of dragging; 10 device for dragging a bottom; 11 anything towed by a ship to retard its progress; 12 resistance to forward movement of a body in water or air; 13 retardation or cause of it; 14 *slang* boring person or thing; 15 *colloq* puff on a cigarette, etc.; 16 *slang* transvestite clothing; 17 *slang* influence

drag' chute' *n* parachute for decelerating an aircraft or space capsule

drag' link' *n* 1 rod connecting the steering-gear lever to the steering knuckle; 2 link joining the cranks of two parallel shafts

drag'net' *n* 1 net for drawing along the bottom of a pond or stream or along the ground, to catch fish or small game; 2 police network for closing in on criminals

drag'on /drag'ən/ [OF < Gk *drakon*] *n* 1 fabulous monster represented as a winged serpent, often breathing fire; 2 fierce and severe person

drag'on·fly' *n* (**-flies**) any of an order (Odonata) of insects having a long slender body, large eyes, and four narrow, finely veined wings

dra·goon /drəgōōn'/ [F *dragon*] *n* 1 heavily-armed mounted soldier || *vt* 2 to coerce

drag' race' *n* short race between automobiles to determine the one with the fastest acceleration

drain /drān'/ [OE *drēahnian*] *vt* 1 to draw off (a liquid); 2 to empty or draw the liquid from; 3 to draw off completely, exhaust || *vi* 4 to become dry; 5 to flow off; 6 to leak out or away || *n* 7 act of draining; 8 channel, pipe, or trench for draining; 9 continual outflowing

drain'age /-ij/ *n* 1 act or process of draining; 2 system of pipes and sewers for removing waste water; 3 area drained; 4 that which is drained off

drake /drāk/ [ME] *n* male duck

dram /dram'/ [OF *dragme* < LL *drachma*] *n* 1 one eighth of an ounce in apothecary's weight; 2 one sixteenth of an ounce in avoirdupois weight; 3 small drink of liquor

dra·ma /dram'ə, dräm'ə/ [Gk] *n* 1 literary composition telling a story of conflicting interests in human life, usu. intended to be acted on the stage; 2 art of the drama; 3 series of events in real life having the interest of a drama || **dram'a·tist** *n* || **dra·mat·ic** /drəmat'ik/ *adj* || **dra·mat'i·cal·ly** *adv*

Dram·a·mine /dram'əmēn'/ [trademark] *n* synthetic antihistamine used in the treatment of allergies and as a preventive of airsickness and seasickness

dram·a·tis per·so·nae /dram'ətis pərsōn'ē, dräm'-/ [L] *npl* 1 the characters in a play || *nsg* 2 descriptive printed list of these characters

dram'a·tize' *vt* 1 to make or convert into a drama; 2 to express or represent in vivid, dramatic fashion

drank /draŋk/ *pt* of **drink**

drape /drāp'/ [MF *draper* < *drap* cloth] *vt* 1 to cover with cloth; adorn with hangings; 2 to arrange in graceful folds || *n* 3 curtain or hanging covering a wall, or on each side of a window, usu. capable of being drawn horizontally across it

drap'er *n Brit* dealer in cloth, clothing, and dry goods

drap'er·y *n* (**-ies**) **1** cloths or fabrics used for garments or hangings; **2 draperies** *pl* hangings or curtains of heavy fabric

dras·tic /dras'tik/ [Gk *drastikos* active] *adj* **1** acting with force and violence; **2** harsh, severe

drat /drat'/ [God *rot*] *interj colloq* darn!

drat'ted *adj colloq* darned

draught /draft', dräft'/ *n & vt chiefly Brit* **1** var of **draft** *1; 6–8; 9–14* ‖ *n* **2 draughts** *sg* checkers

Dra·vid·i·an /drəvid'ē·ən/ [< Skt *Drāvida* Tamil] *n* **1** member of the aboriginal people of S India; **2** family of languages spoken by the Dravidians ‖ *also adj*

draw /drô'/ [OE *dragan*] *v* (**drew; drawn**) *vt* **1** to pull or haul along; drag; **2** to pull out; haul up; **3** to infer, deduce (a conclusion); **4** to extend or increase in length; **5** to extract or bring out, as a sword, cork, revolver, or wine; **6** to choose by lot or at random; **7** to represent on paper; **8** to require (a specified number of feet) to float in; **9** to inhale; **10** to attract; **11** to receive or be issued, as pay, interest, money, cards, or supplies; **12** to finish (a contest) in a tie; **13** to pass (wire) through successively smaller holes down to the proper size; **14** to take or get from a source, as *to draw inspiration*; **15** to elicit (a reply); **16** to write (a check); **17 draw out, a** to pull out; **b** to withdraw; **c** to prolong; **d** to persuade (someone) to speak freely; **18 draw up, a** to arrange in line; **b** to halt (a car); **c** to draft (a document) ‖ *vi* **19** to act as a pulling force; entice; **20** to take, pull, or force something out; **21** to move or pass slowly, as *to draw near*; **22** to be pulled; **23** to practice the art of drawing pictures; **24** to allow a current of air to pass, as *the chimney draws well;* **25** to shrink; **26 draw on** to withdraw money from (a bank) ‖ *n* **27** act or result of drawing; **28** attraction; **29** choosing, lot; **30** tie contest; **31 beat to the draw, a** *Old West* to draw a gun faster than (one's opponent); **b** to outdo by superior enterprise ‖ SYN *v* drag, tug, haul, transport, attract

draw'back' *n* disadvantage; hindrance; objectionable feature

draw'bridge' *n* bridge which may be lifted up, let down, or drawn aside to prevent access or to allow boats to pass

draw·ee' *n* person on whom an order is drawn for the payment of money

draw·er /drô'ər/ *n* **1** one who or that

which draws; **2** person who draws an order for the payment of money ‖ **drawer** /drôr'/ *n* **3** boxlike compartment in a bureau or desk; **4 drawers** *pl* undergarment for the lower part of the body and the legs

draw'ing *n* **1** representation or picture; **2** lottery; **3** act of one who draws in a lottery

draw'ing ac·count' *n* account on which a partner or employee may draw to cover expenses

draw'ing board' *n* rectangular board to which paper is attached for making drawings and designs

draw'ing card' *n* person, performance, or thing that attracts many viewers or patrons

draw'ing room' [< *withdrawing room*] *n* **1** room for the reception and entertainment of guests; **2** private compartment on a railroad car

draw'knife' *n* (**-knives**) knife with a handle at both ends, used for shaving a surface

drawl /drôl'/ [?] *n* **1** slow manner of speech characterized by prolonging the vowels in a glide ‖ *vt & vi* **2** to utter with a drawl

drawn /drôn'/ **1** *pp* of **draw** ‖ *adj* **2** left undecided; **3** eviscerated; **4** tense, haggard

drawn' but'ter *n* **1** melted butter; **2** sauce of melted butter and other ingredients

draw' po'ker *n* poker game in which the players can discard some of their cards and draw others

draw'string' *n* string which, when both ends are pulled, closes the opening of a bag or article of clothing

dray /drā'/ [OE *dragan* to drawl] *n* **1** low cart with removable sides for heavy loads; **2** low sledge

dread /dred'/ [OE *drǣdan*] *vt* **1** to fear greatly; **2** to look forward to with fearful reluctance ‖ *vi* **3** to be in great fear ‖ *n* **4** apprehensive terror ‖ *adj* **5** inspiring fear; **6** awful, solemn ‖ SYN *n* dismay, terror, fright, alarm (see *awe, horror*) ‖ ANT *n* boldness, assurance, fearlessness

dread'ful *adj* **1** inspiring dread; **2** bad, awful ‖ SYN frightful, shocking, horrible, formidable

dread'nought' [Brit battleship *Dreadnought*, first of type, launched in 1906] *n* largest type of warship, with heavy armor and large-caliber guns in turrets

dream /drēm'/ [OE = joy] *n* **1** thoughts or images occurring during sleep; **2** something seen in the imagination; **3** fancy; hope or aspiration ‖ *v* (**dreamed** or **dreamt**) *vi* **4** to have a dream or dreams; **5** to daydream; **6 dream of** to dream about ‖ *vt* **7** to see in dreams; **8** to suppose, fancy; **9 dream up** *colloq* to devise fancifully ‖ **dream'er** *n* ‖ SYN *v* (see *muse*); *n* reverie ‖ DISCR A *dream* is a succession of pictures or, often, fantastic mental images perceived in sleep. A *reverie* is a waking *dream*; it is a conscious musing, an idle drifting in fancy

dream'boat' *n slang* someone or something highly desirable

dream'land' *n* lovely land seen in the imagination while sleeping or awake

dreamt /dremt'/ *pt & pp* of **dream**

dream'y *adj* (-i-er; -i-est) 1 pert. to or full of dreams; 2 imaginative, fanciful; 3 indistinct, vague; 4 soothing, languid; 5 *slang* wonderful ‖ **dream'i-ly** *adv* ‖ **dream'i-ness** *n* ‖ SYN pensive, musing, misty, fanciful, impractical

drear /drir'/ *adj poet.* dreary

drear'y [OE *dreorig* sad] *adj* (-i-er; -i-est) 1 gloomy, dismal; 2 boring ‖ **drear'i-ly** *adv* ‖ **drear'i-ness** *n*

dredge /drej'/ [ME *dreg*] *n* 1 apparatus for removing earth and mud, as from a river bottom ‖ *vt* 2 to clean out or deepen with a dredge ‖ *vi* 3 to use a dredge

dregs /dregz'/ [< Scand] *npl* 1 sediment of liquids; lees; 2 worthless part of anything

drench /drench'/ [OE *drencan*] *vt* to wet thoroughly; soak

Dres·den /drez'dən/ *n* 1 city in SE East Germany (500,000); 2 fine porcelain made in Dresden ‖ *also adj*

dress /dres'/ [MF *dresser* to arrange] *vt* 1 to put clothes on; 2 to deck out, adorn; 3 to arrange (the hair); 4 to finish or prepare, for table, market, use, etc., as to *dress meat*, to *dress stone*; 5 to align (soldiers) exactly; 6 to treat or bind up, as a wound; 7 **dress down** to rebuke; 8 **dress up** to dress in one's best clothes or in formal attire ‖ *vi* 9 to clothe oneself; 10 to put on formal clothes; 11 to form into a straight line ‖ *n* 12 woman's or child's gown; 13 woman's garment; 14 clothes, apparel ‖ SYN *n* apparel, costume, vesture, garb, raiment

dress' cir'cle *n* first balcony in an opera house

dress'er *n* 1 one who dresses; 2 chest of drawers with a mirror

dress'ing *n* 1 act of one who dresses; 2 bandages or applications for a wound; 3 stuffing for a fowl; 4 sauce, as for salads

dress'ing case' *n* small case for carrying toilet articles when traveling

dress'ing-down' *n* severe reprimand

dress'ing gown' *n* robe worn while dressing or lounging

dress'mak'er *n* 1 one who makes women's clothes ‖ *adj* 2 (women's clothes) not tailored or mannish ‖ **dress'mak'ing** *n*

dress' re·hears'al *n* final rehearsal, as of a play, with complete scenery and costumes

dress'y *adj* (-i-er; -i-est) 1 showy, ostentatious in dress; 2 formal in dress or style

drew /drōō'/ *pt* of **draw**

drib·ble /drib'əl/ [<*obs drib* drip] *vt* 1 to let fall in drops; 2 *soccer, hockey* to give slight kicks or shoves to (the ball or puck); 3 *basketball* to bounce (the ball) rapidly along the floor ‖ *vi* 4 to fall in small drops; trickle; 5 to drool; 6 to dribble a ball ‖ *n* 7 trickle

drib'let /-lit/ *n* small quantity; petty amount

dried'beef' /drīd'/ *n* beef preserved by being salted, dried, and smoked

dri·er /drī'ər/ *n* 1 one who or that which dries, 2 appliance for drying; 3 substance added to paint to accelerate drying

drift /drift'/ [OE *drīfan* to drive] *n* 1 state of being driven; 2 direction in which something is driven; 3 tendency; meaning, import; 4 driving force; controlling influence; 5 snow drift; 6 deviation from a set course, as of a ship, plane, or rocket; 7 loose rock and gravel carried along by a glacier; 8 direction of a current; 9 tapering tool for enlarging holes in metal ‖ *vt* 10 to drive along or heap up ‖ *vi* 11 to be carried along by a current or by circumstances; 12 to gather together in heaps ‖ SYN *n* purpose, meaning, scope, aim, tendency

drift'er *n* 1 one who drifts; 2 person who drifts from job to job; 3 hobo

drift'wood' *n* 1 floating wood cast ashore; 2 anything or anyone drifting aimlessly

drill[1] /dril'/ [D *dril*] *n* 1 tool for boring holes; 2 military exercises; 3 training by means of frequent repetition; 4 correct or accustomed procedure ‖ *vt* 5 to pierce with a drill; 6 to bore (holes); 7 to instruct thoroughly; train ‖ *vi* 8 to train by going through drills ‖ **drill'er** *n*

drill[2] [<G *Drillich* triple-twilled cloth] *n* durable twilled cotton or linen fabric

drill' press' *n* machine equipped with a vertical spindle for boring holes in metal

drink /dringk'/ [OE *drincan*] *v* (**drank**; **drunk**) *vi* 1 to swallow a liquid; 2 to indulge in alcoholic liquors habitually; 3 **drink to** to drink a toast to ‖ *vt* 4 to swallow; suck in; absorb; 5 to swallow the contents of; 6 **drink in** to take in through the senses ‖ *n* 7 any liquid swallowed; 8 single portion of a liquid, as *a drink of water*; 9 intoxicating liquor; 10 excessive taking of alcoholic liquors; 11 *slang* large body of water; ocean ‖ **drink'er** *n*

drip /drip′/ [OE *dryppan*] *v* (**dripped** or **dript; drip·ping**) *vi* **1** to fall in drops; **2** to shed ‖ *vt* **3** to let fall in drops ‖ *n* **4** act of dripping; **5** sound of dripping; **6** *slang* person with a negative personality

drip′ cof′fee *n* drink prepared by filtering boiling water through ground coffee into a receptacle below

drip′-dry′ *v* (**-dried**) *vi* to dry, as an article of clothing, without wrinkles, when left hanging and dripping ‖ also *adj*

drip′ pan′ *n* also **drip′ping pan′ 1** receptacle for catching oil or grease dripping from above; **2** pan to hold the fat that comes from roasting meat

drip′ping *n* **1** sound of something that drips; **2 drippings** *pl* fat or juice exuded from roasting meat ‖ *adv* **3 dripping wet** wet all over and through and through

drive /drīv′/ [OE *drīfan*] *v* (**drove; driv·en**) *vt* **1** to urge forward as by force; impel; **2** to urge and guide, as *to drive cattle*; **3** to control and steer, as an automobile; **4** to carry in a vehicle; **5** to carry through, as a bargain; **6** to hunt and pursue (game); **7** to urge to great or excessive exertion; **8** to set or keep in motion; **9** *sport* to hit or propel, as a ball; **10** *baseball* to advance (a runner) to a base or home by hitting the ball safely ‖ *vi* **11** to be moved forward with force; **12** to drive a vehicle; **13** to travel in a driven vehicle; **14** *golf* to strike the ball from a tee; **15 drive at** to allude to, mean ‖ *n* **16** act of driving; **17** road; **18** driveway; **19** trip in a vehicle; **20** driving along, as of cattle or game; **21** forward blow given to a ball; **22** inner urge; impelling need; **23** push, initiative; **24** vigorous onset toward a goal, as a military objective, civic campaign, or opponent's goal line; **25** method of application of force to achieve forward motion, as *four-wheel drive, chain drive* ‖ SYN *v* compel, impel, repel, press, thrust

drive′-in′ *n* place of business, as a motion-picture theater or snack bar, that accommodates patrons in their automobiles

driv·el /driv′əl/ [OE *dreflian*] *v* (**-eled** or **-elled; -el·ing** or **-el·ling**) *vi* **1** to drool, slobber; **2** to talk like an idiot ‖ *vt* **3** to utter idiotically ‖ *n* **4** saliva flowing from the mouth; **5** idle silly talk

driv·en /driv′ən/ *pp* of **drive**

driv·er /drīv′ər/ *n* **1** one who or that which drives, esp. a vehicle; **2** *golf* club for driving the ball from the tee

driv′er's seat′ *n* position of power or authority

drive′ shaft′ *n* shaft for imparting torque to machinery or wheels

drive′way′ *n* short road giving access to the street, as from a garage

drive′-your·self′ serv′ice *n* service or agency that rents out automobiles without providing drivers

driv′ing range′ *n* outdoor area for practicing golf drives

driz·zle /driz′əl/ [perh < OE *drēosan* to fall] *vi* **1** to rain gently in fine drops ‖ *n* **2** fine, misty rain ‖ **driz′-zly** *adj*

drogue /drōg′/ ‖< OE *dragan* to drag] *n* **1** small parachute used as a brake on a landing airplane or on a spacecraft or satellite in descent; **2** funnel-shaped device at the end of a hose, used for refueling in flight

droll /drōl′/ [MF *drolle* scamp < MD *drol*] *adj* **1** quaintly amusing, waggish ‖ *n* **2** funny fellow; jester ‖ **droll′er·y** *n* (**-ies**) ‖ SYN *adj* comical, queer, ridiculous, diverting, facetious, witty, laughable, funny, jocose (see *ludicrous*)

drom·e·dar·y /drom′ider′ē/ [LL *dromedārius* running] *n* (**-ies**) one-humped camel (*Camelus dromedarius*) of Arabia and Africa

drone /drōn′/ [OE *drān* bee] *n* **1** male of the honeybee, which does no work; **2** one who lives off others; parasite; **3** monotonous humming or buzzing; **4** pipe of bagpipe that produces a droning sound; **5** remote-controlled airplane used for reconnaissance or as a target ‖ *vi* **6** to make a monotonous tone or sound; **7** to speak in a drone ‖ *vt* **8** to utter or say in a drone; **9 drone away** to spend or pass idly or monotonously

drool /drōōl′/ [var of *drivel*] *vi* **1** to let saliva flow from the mouth, esp. in pleasurable anticipation; **2** to speak foolishly

droop /drōōp′/ [ON *drūpa*] *vi* **1** to sag, hang, or bend down; **2** to grow weak and faint or spiritless ‖ *vt* **3** to let droop ‖ *n* **4** act or result of drooping ‖ **droop′y** *adj* (**-i·er, -i·est**)

drop /drop′/ [OE *dropian*] *v* (**dropped** or **dropt; drop′ping**) *vi* **1** to fall in small spherical masses of liquid; **2** to sink to a lower position; **3** to fall, descend; **4** to lower in sound or pitch; **5** to fall wounded or dead; **6** to fall behind; **7** to cease, end; **8** to pass into a specified state, as *to drop asleep;* **9** to vanish, as *to drop out of sight;* **10** to die away, as the wind; **11 drop in** to visit informally; **12 drop off, a** to decline; **b** to fall asleep; **c** to die suddenly; **13 drop out** to stop being a student or a participant ‖ *vt* **14** to let fall; **15** to lower; **16** to let fall in small drops; **17** to have done with; **18** to utter casually, as a hint; **19** to mail (a note or letter); **20** to dismiss; **21** to leave off (a passenger); **22** to insert in a slot; **23** to give birth to (said of animals); **24** to omit, as a letter of the alphabet; **25** to fell with a blow or weapon; **26** *sports* to lose (a game) ‖ *n* **27** small spherical mass of liquid; **28** anything that hangs like or resembles a drop; **29** any very small quantity; **30** descent or fall; **31** distance through which something drops; **32** depository, as for mail; **33** mail slot; **34** lowering; **35** *theat* curtain; **36 get the drop on** *colloq* **a** to have one's gun aimed at (an antagonist); **b** to have at a disadvantage

drop′ ham′mer *n* large hammer used in forging and stamping, raised between vertical guides by mechanical power and allowed to fall by gravity

drop′ kick′ *n football* kick made by dropping the football and kicking it on the bounce ‖ **drop′-kick′** *vt & vi*

drop′ leaf′ *n* hinged extension on the edge of a table that can be folded down when not needed ‖ **drop′-leaf′** *adj*

drop′let /-lǐt/ *n* small drop

drop′light′ *n* light suspended from the ceiling that can be lowered and raised on a flexible cord

drop′-off′ *n* **1** steep or vertical descent; **2** decline in amount

drop′out′ *n* one who has dropped out, as from school

drop′per *n* small glass tube with a rubber bulb for expelling drops, as of medicine

drop′pings *npl* animal dung

drop′ ship′ment *n* shipment of goods from the manufacturer directly to the retailer, but billed by the distributor

drop·sy /drop′sē/ [OF *ydropisie* < L *hydropisis* < Gk *hydrops*] *n* abnormal accumulation of serous fluid in the cellular tissues or in a body cavity ‖ **drop′si·cal** *adj*

dro·soph·i·la /drəsof′ilə/ [< Gk *drosos* dew + *philos* loving] *n* any of a genus (*Drosophila*) of flies, esp. the fruit fly (*D. melanogaster*), much used for experiments in heredity

dross /drôs/, dros′/ [OE *drōs*] *n* **1** refuse skimmed from molten metal; **2** any worthless matter

drought /drout′/ or **drouth** /drouth′/ [OE *drūgath*] *n* **1** prolonged lack of rain; **2** continuing shortage

drove¹ /drōv′/ *pt* of **drive**

drove² [OE *drāf*] *n* **1** group of cattle or sheep driven in a body; **2** crowd of people ‖ SYN flock, shoal, crowd, multitude (see *herd*)

dro′ver *n* **1** one who drives cattle to market; **2** dealer in cattle

drown /droun′/ [ME *drounen*] *vi* **1** to die by suffocation in water or other liquid ‖ *vt* **2** to cause to drown; **3** to overwhelm; **4** to drench, flood; **5 drown out** to cover up (a sound or noise) ‖ SYN submerge, swamp, engulf, drench, overpower

drowse /drouz′/ [OE *drūsian* to droop]

vi **1** to be half asleep; doze ‖ *vt* **2** to make sleepy; **3** to spend (time) in drowsing ‖ *n* **4** light sleep; **5** sleepy state ‖ **drow′sy** *adj* (-si·er; -si·est)

drub /drub′/ [perh < Ar *daraba*] *v* (**drubbed; drub·bing**) *vt* **1** to beat soundly; thrash; **2** to defeat decisively ‖ **drub′bing** *n*

drudge /druj′/ [perh OE *drēogan* to endure] *vi* **1** to engage in drudgery ‖ *n* **2** one whose work is drudgery

drudg′er·y *n* (-ies) hard, disagreeable, or dull work ‖ SYN toil, work (see *labor*)

drug /drug′/ [MF *drogue*] *n* **1** substance used as a medicine; **2** narcotic; **3 drug on the market** article of commerce for which there is no demand ‖ *v* (**drugged; drug·ging**) *vt* **4** to put a harmful drug in (food or drink); **5** to poison or stupefy with a drug

drug′gist *n* **1** pharmacist; **2** dealer in drugs and medicines; **3** operator of a drugstore

drug′store′ *n* store selling drugs, medicines, and usu. a great variety of other commodities, and often containing a soda fountain and lunch counter

dru·id /drōo′id/ [L *druidae* < Gaulish *druides*] *n* priest of the ancient Celtic religion of Britain and Gaul ‖ **dru·id′ic** (-i·cal) /-id′ik(əl)/ *adj*

drum /drum′/ [prob D *trom*] *n* **1** percussion instrument consisting of a hollow cylinder with a taut membrane covering one or both ends, which produces a characteristic sound when struck, usu. with a drumstick; **2** sound of this instrument; **3** anything shaped like a drum, as a metal container or a windlass; **4 beat the drum** to advertise ‖ *v* (**drummed; drum·ming**) *vi* **5** to beat a drum; **6** to thump rapidly with the fingers; **7** to make a noise like that of a drum ‖ *vt* **8** to render on a drum or as if on a drum; **9 drum into** to drive, as an idea, into by constant repetition; **10 drum out** to dismiss in disgrace; **11 drum up** to solicit, as trade, by vigorous advertising

drum′beat′ *n* sound of a drum

drum′ corps′ *n* band of drum players

drum′fire′ *n* continuous gunfire

drum′head′ *n* membrane stretched over the end of a drum

drum′head′ court′-mar′tial *n* summary court-martial held while military operations are proceeding

drum′ ma′jor *n* leader of a band or drum corps

drum′ ma′jor·ette′ /-et′/ *n* girl who twirls a baton while marching at the head of a marching band or drum corps

drum′mer *n* **1** one who plays a drum; **2** *colloq* traveling salesman

drum′stick′ *n* **1** stick with which a

drum is beaten; **2** clublike segment of a fowl's leg

drunk /druŋk′/ **1** *pp* of **drink** ‖ *adj* **2** intoxicated; **3** overcome, as by emotion ‖ *n* **4** drunken person; **5** drunken spree

drunk·ard /-ərd/ *n* one frequently or habitually drunk

drunk′en *adj* intoxicated ‖ **drunk′en·ly** *adv* ‖ **drunk′en·ness** *n*

drupe /dro͞op′/ [L *drupa* overripe olive] *n* one of the characteristic types of fruit, consisting of a pulpy body enclosing a single hard-shelled stone with a kernel, as the peach ‖ **dru·pa′ceous** /-pāsh′əs/

dry /drī′/ [OE *drȳge*] *adj* (**dri·er**; **dri·est**) **1** free from moisture or wetness; **2** not yielding water, milk, or other liquid; **3** not under water, as *dry land*; **4** arid (climate); **5** lacking water, as a *dry lake*; **6** stale, as bread; **7** lacking interest; **8** matter-of-fact (wit); **9** not sweet, as *dry wine*; **10** thirsty; **11** prohibiting the general sale of intoxicants, as a *dry county* ‖ *v* (**dried**) *vt* **12** to make dry; **13 dry up** to make completely dry ‖ *vi* **14** to become dry; **15** to become completely dry; **b** *slang* to stop talking ‖ *n* (**drys**) **16** prohibitionist ‖ **dry′ly** *adv* ‖ **dry′ness** *n* ‖ SYN *adj* arid, parched, dull, insipid, uninteresting

dry·ad /drī′ad, -əd/ [Gk *dryas* (*-ados*)] *n class. myth.* wood nymph

dry′ bat′ter·y *n* dry cell or battery of dry cells

dry′ cell′ *n* primary electric cell from which the electrolyte cannot spill

dry′-clean′ *vt* to clean, as garments, with a liquid other than water ‖ **dry′ clean′er** *n* ‖ **dry′ clean′ing** *n*

dry′ dock′ *n* structure for the building and repair of ships, so made that the water can be pumped out and excluded after a ship has entered

dry′ farm′ing *n* method of farming practiced in arid regions based on special crops and methods of tillage to impede evaporation

dry′ goods′ *npl* woven fabrics and cloth products in general

dry′ ice′ *n* solidified carbon dioxide, that sublimes at −78.5°C and is used as a refrigerant

dry′ meas′ure *n* system of units of capacity used for dry commodities, as grain

dry′ nurse′ *n* woman who takes care of but does not suckle another's infant

dry′ rot′ *n* **1** decay of timber caused by certain fungi; **2** any of various fungous diseases affecting plants; **3** any concealed decay or corruption

dry′ run′ *n* **1** rehearsal or practice performance of an event; **2** firing practice without ammunition

dry′ wash′ *n* wash that has been dried but not ironed

D.S.C. Distinguished Service Cross

DST, D.S.T. Daylight Saving Time

d.t. *n* **the d.t.'s** *pl* delirium tremens

du·al /d(y)o͞o′əl/ [L *dualis*] *adj* **1** expressing, or composed of, two; double ‖ *n* **2** *gram.* dual number; **3** form in the dual ‖ **du·al′i·ty** /-al′-/ *n*

du′al car′riage·way′ *n* *Brit* divided highway

du′al high′way *n* divided highway

du′al·ism *n* **1** twofold condition; **2** doctrine of two separate natures in man, the spiritual and the bodily; **3** doctrine that there are two opposing principles in the universe, those of good and those of evil; **4** theory that the nature of the universe is dependent ultimately on two irreducible elements, matter and mind

dub¹ /dub′/ [OE *dubbian*] *v* (**dubbed**; **dub·bing**) *vt* **1** to bestow knighthood upon by tapping the shoulder with a sword; **2** to confer any rank, character, or name upon; **3** to rub or smooth, as leather; **4** *collog* to bungle ‖ *n* **5** *collog* awkward, bungling person

dub² [< *double*] *v* (**dubbed**; **dub·bing**) *vt* **1** to substitute a sound track on (a film) in order to change the language; **2 dub in** to add (speech, music, or sound effects) to a film or tape

du·bi·ous /d(y)o͞ob′ē·əs/ [< L *dubius*] *adj* **1** doubtful; **2** of questionable character or value ‖ **du′bi·ous·ly** *adv* ‖ SYN doubtful, unreliable, questionable, hesitating

Dub·lin /dub′lin/ *n* capital of Ireland (568,271)

du·cal /d(y)o͞ok′əl/ [LL *ducalis*] *adj* of or pert. to a duke or duchy

duc·at /duk′ət/ [MF < OIt *ducato*] *n* **1** former gold or silver European coin; **2** *slang* admission ticket

duch·ess /duch′is/ [MF *duchesse* *fem* of *duc* duke] *n* **1** wife or widow of a duke; **2** woman who holds title to a dukedom in her own right

duch′y [MF *duche* < LL *ducatus*] *n* (**-ies**) territory ruled by a duke or duchess

duck¹ /duk′/ [OE *dūce*] *n* **1** any of many flat-billed waterfowl (family Anatidae) with short legs and necks; **2** female duck

duck² [ME *douken*] *vt* **1** to plunge momentarily under water; **2** to lower suddenly, as the head or body; **3** to evade or dodge, as a blow, a task, or a responsibility ‖ *vi* **4** to bob or bend down suddenly; **5** to plunge the head or body suddenly under water; **6** to dodge or evade

duck³ [D *doeck* cloth] *n* **1** strong linen or cotton fabric; **2 ducks** *pl* slacks made of this material

duck′ hawk′ *n* an American falcon (*Falco peregrinus anatum*) akin to the Old World peregrine falcon

duck·ling *n* young duck

duck′pins′ *nsg* game resembling tenpins, played with smaller pins and balls

duck′ soup′ *n slang* something extremely easy

duck′y *adj* (**-i·er; -i·est**) *colloq* excellent; delightful

duct /dukt′/ [ML *ductus* < L = a conducting] *n* canal, pipe, or tube by which fluid or air is carried

duc·tile /duk′til, -til/ [L *ductilis*] *adj* 1 capable of being drawn out, as into threads or wire; 2 malleable, plastic ‖ **duc·til′i·ty** /-til′-/ *n*

duct′less gland′ *n* endocrine gland

dud /dud′/ [?] *n* 1 shell or bomb that has failed to explode; 2 failure

dude /d(y)ŌŌd′/ [?] *n* 1 dandy, fop; 2 city dweller, esp. one who vacations on a ranch

dude′ ranch′ *n* ranch for the entertainment of paying guests

dudg·eon /duj′ən/ [?] *n* 1 anger; resentment; 2 **in high dudgeon** angered; resentful

duds /dudz′/ [ME *dudde*] *npl colloq* clothes

due /d(y)ŌŌ′/ [MF *deu* pp of *devoir* to owe] *adj* 1 owed or owing; payable; 2 suitable, proper; 3 owing or attributable, as *loss due to leakage*; 4 expected to do something or to arrive at a certain time ‖ *n* 5 that which is due; 6 **give someone his due** to give a disliked person deserved credit; 7 **dues** *pl* membership fee ‖ *adv* 8 exactly, as *due east* ‖ SYN *adj* ascribable, just, fair, merited, appointed

du·el /d(y)ŌŌ′əl/ [ML *duellum* fight between two] *n* 1 prearranged fight between two persons with deadly weapons before witnesses; 2 any contest between two parties ‖ *v* (**-eled** or **-elled; -el·ing** or **-el·ling**) *vt & vi* 3 to fight in a duel ‖ **du′el·ist, du′el·list** *n*

du·en·na /d(y)ŌŌ·en′ə/ [OSp = mistress] *n* female chaperon

due′ proc′ess of law′ *n* constitutional doctrine that no one can be deprived of life, liberty, or property without proper legal proceedings

du·et /d(y)ŌŌ·et′/ [It *duetto*] *n* 1 composition for two performers; 2 the two performers or singers of such a composition

duff /duf′/ [var of *dough*] *n slang* buttocks

duf′fel bag′ /duf′əl/ [*Duffel* town in Belgium] *n* large canvas bag, as used by campers and soldiers

duff·er /duf′ər/ [?] *n* 1 *colloq* person inept at a particular sport or trade; 2 dull and ineffectual old man

dug[1] /dug′/ *pt & pp* of **dig**

dug[2] [< Scand] *n* teat or nipple

du·gong /dŌŌ′gȯŋ/ [Malay *duyong*] *n* sea cow; large plant-eating sea mammal (*Dugong*) of the Indian Ocean and adjacent seas, resembling the whale in form

dug′out′ *n* 1 canoe hollowed out from a log; 2 rough shelter dug in the side of a hill or bank; 3 *baseball* roofed structure occupied by a team when at bat

du·jour /dəzhŌŌr′/ [F = of the day] *adj* (food featured or prepared) for today, as *the soup du jour is chicken*

duke /d(y)ŌŌk′/ [OF *duc* < L *dux* (*ducis*) leader] *n* 1 sovereign ruler of a duchy or small state; 2 nobleman next in rank to a prince; 3 **dukes** *pl slang* fists ‖ **duke′dom** *n*

dul·cet /duls′it/ [MF *doucet* < L *dulcis* sweet] *adj* sweet or pleasant to the ear

dull /dul′/ [ME] *adj* 1 slow-witted; 2 without feeling or sensibility; 3 not bright or vivid; 4 blunt, not sharp; 5 not brisk or active; 6 wearisome, boring; 7 not clear, muffled; 8 not sharp or **acute**, as a *dull pain* ‖ *vt* 9 to make **dull** ‖ *vi* 10 to become dull ‖ **dul′ly** *adv* ‖ **dull′ness** *n* ‖ SYN *adj* depressing, sleepy, stupid, unintelligent, inanimate, commonplace, ordinary (see **dull**)

dull·ard /dul′ərd/ *n* stupid person

Du·luth /dəlŌŌth′/ *n* city in E Minnesota on Lake Superior (110,000)

du·ly /d(y)ŌŌl′ē/ [< *due*] *adv* in a fit manner; regularly

dumb /dum′/ [OE] *adj* 1 not able to speak; 2 silent; 3 *colloq* stupid ‖ **dumb′ly** *adv* ‖ **dumb′ness** *n* ‖ SYN mute, still, speechless, inarticulate, silent

dumb′bell′ *n* 1 device consisting of two weighted balls joined by a short bar, used for gymnastic exercise; 2 *slang* stupid person

dumb′wait′er *n* small elevator with shelves on which articles are moved from one floor to another

dum′dum bul′let /dum′dum/ [*Dum-Dum*, India] *n* soft-nosed bullet that expands on impact, inflicting a severe wound

dum′found′ or **dumb′found′** [*dumb* + con*found*] *vt* to amaze, make dumb with surprise

dum·my /dum′ē/ [< *dumb*] *n* (**-mies**) 1 representation of a human figure, used for displaying clothes, by ventriloquists, etc.; 2 *slang* one who is dumb or silent; 3 *colloq* stupid person; 4 sham, fake; 5 person who nominally occupies a position but does not perform its functions; 6 bound unprinted sheets of paper devised as the model of a book; 7 *cards* exposed hand played by a player in addition to his own ‖ *vi* 8 **dummy up** *thieves' slang* to remain silent

dump[1] /dump′/ [ME < Scand] *vt* 1 to unload or let fall in a heap without care; 2 to unload (a container) by tipping; 3 to get rid of; 4 to dismiss, drop from membership or employment; **5** *slang* to knock down; **6** *sports slang* to lose (a match) intentionally; **7** to flood the market with (goods) at a low price ‖ *n* **8** place for throwing rubbish; **9** place for storing military supplies; **10** *slang* dilapidated place

dump² [perh D *domp* haze] *n* **in the dumps** in a depressed state

dump′ing *n* the flooding of the market with a product below the market price in order to get rid of surplus or to beat competition, esp. in foreign trade

dump′ling [?] *n* **1** spoonful of dough boiled in meat stock; **2** shell of dough enclosing fruit or meat and baked or boiled; **3** *colloq* short fat person

dump′ truck′ *n* truck with a body that tilts for dumping

dump′y [?] *adj* (**-i·er; -i·est**) short and stout; stocky

dun¹ /dun′/ [OE *dunn*] *adj* dull grayish-brown ‖ also *n*

dun² [?] *n* **1** demand for payment ‖ *v* (**dunned; dun·ning**) *vt & vi* **2** to ask repeatedly and insistently for payment

dunce /duns′/ [John *Duns* Scotus, 13th-cent. Sc schoolman, ridiculed by the humanists] *n* **1** dull-witted, ignorant person; **2** backward, slow student

dunce′ cap′ *n* tall conical hat formerly worn in class by backward students

dun·der·head′ /dun′dər-/ [D *donder* thunder] *n* dunce, blockhead

dune /d(y)ōōn′/ [OF < OD *dūna*] *n* hill or ridge of drifted sand

dune′ bug′gy *n* covered jeeplike vehicle, with oversize tires, used for traveling over dunes and beaches

dung /duŋ′/ [OE] *n* animal excrement, manure

dun·ga·rees /duŋ′gərēz′/ [Hindi *dungrī* coarse] *npl* work clothes or trousers of blue denim

dun·geon /dun′jən/ [MF *donjon*] *n* **1** dark underground cell; **2** prison, esp. old and forbidding in appearance; **3** stronghold of an ancient castle, usually containing a prison

dung′hill′ *n* **1** heap of manure; **2** anything vile or ignoble

dunk /duŋk′/ [PaG *dunke* < G *tunken*] *vt* **1** to dip, as a doughnut, into coffee or the like before eating; **2** to immerse in a liquid

du·o /d(y)ōō′ō/ [It] *n* **1** *mus* duet; **2** any two persons appearing or working as a pair

duo- [L & Gk *duo*] *comb form* two

du·o·de·num /d(y)ōō′ədēn′əm/ [< L *duodeni* twelve parts; so called because about 12 fingerbreadths long] *n* (**-nums** or **-na** /-nə/) first section of the small intestine, immediately below the stomach ‖ **du′o·de′nal** *adj*

dup. duplicate

dupe¹ /d(y)ōōp′/ [MF *duppe* < tete

d′uppe head of a hoopoe, a stupid bird] *n* **1** one easily deceived; victim of deception ‖ *vt* **2** to deceive, trick ‖ SYN *v* trick, gull, mislead, impose upon, cheat

dupe² *colloq n* **1** duplicate ‖ *vt* **2** to duplicate

du·plex /d(y)ōō′pleks/ [L = twofold] *adj* **1** double; compound; twofold ‖ *n* **2** apartment with two floors; **3** two-family house

du·pli·cate /d(y)ōōp′likāt′/ [L *duplicare* (*atus*) to double] *vt* **1** to make an exact copy of; **2** to reproduce exactly ‖ /-kit/ *n* **3** exact copy; **4** counterpart; **5 in duplicate** with two copies ‖ *adj* **6** corresponding exactly ‖ **du′pli·ca′tion** *n* ‖ SYN *n* likeness, facsimile, replica, counterpart, copy, imitation, transcript ‖ DISCR The *duplicate* of an object is an exact reproduction of that object, which has the force, service, or use of the original, as well as its appearance, as he sent a *duplicate* of his diploma as evidence to the Board of Education. A *facsimile* is also an exact reproduction of an object, but only in appearance, as a *facsimile* of Lincoln's letter to the mother who lost five sons in the war has been hung in many college halls. The difference between *duplicate* and *facsimile* is thus seen to be the difference between substance and shadow. A signature produced in *facsimile* has only the force of a picture; a signature produced in *duplicate* has legal force. A *copy* is made from an original, and attempts to be exactly like it; a *copy* made by any reproducing machine, as a mimeograph, is necessarily exact. An *imitation* is a reproduction consciously essayed as a *copy;* it falls so far short of its model sometimes as to be obviously inferior, though there are *imitations* so clever as to deceive the initiated. A *counterpart* is a person or thing exactly like another; it may be a *facsimile*, as in a picture, or it may be an accidental conformity of feature and appearance

du′pli·cat′ing ma·chine′ *n* duplicator

du′pli·ca′tor *n* machine for making exact copies

du·plic·i·ty /d(y)ōōplis′itē/ *n* (**-ties**) deceitfulness in speech or action, double-dealing ‖ SYN fraud, deception, guile, bad faith

du·ra·ble /d(y)ōōr′əbəl/ [MF < L *durabilis*] *adj* enduring, lasting ‖ **du′ra·bil′i·ty** /-bil′-/ *n* ‖ SYN lasting, persistent, firm, stable (see *permanent*)

du′ra·ble goods′ *npl* manufactured goods not rapidly worn out or used up, as machinery

Du·ral·u·min /d(y)ōōral′(y)əmin/ [trademark] *n* alloy of aluminum with small proportions of copper, manganese, and magnesium; noted for lightness and great strength

dur·ance /d(y)ŏŏr'əns/ [MF = endur-ance] *n* imprisonment

du·ra'tion [< L durare (-atus) to last] *n* period during which a thing lasts

du·ress /d(y)ŏŏres'/ [MF duresse hard-ness] *n* **1** imprisonment; **2** compul-sion, coercion

dur·ing /d(y)ŏŏrĭŋ/ [prp of obs dure to last] *prep* **1** in the course of; **2** throughout the continuance of

durst /durst'/ archaic pt of **dare**

du·rum /d(y)ŏŏr'əm/ [< L durus hard] *n* a wheat (Triticum durum) used in making macaroni

dusk /dusk'/ [ME dosc dark < OE dox] *n* **1** dim light at the beginning and end of daylight; **2** darkness, dim-ness

dusk'y adj (-i·er; -i·est) **1** dim, shadowy; **2** dark, tending to blackness

dust /dust'/ [OE] *n* **1** fine, dry particles of earth or other matter; **2** cloud or film of such particles; **3** any fine powder; **4** low condition of life; **5 bite the dust** to fall in battle; **6 make the dust fly** to do something with speed and vigor; **7 throw dust in the eyes of** to mislead || *vt* **8** to remove the dust from; **9** to cover with a powder; **10** to sprinkle (a powder) on something || *vi* **11** to remove dust; **12** to apply a powder || **dust'y** adj (-i·er; -i·est)

dust'bin' *n* Brit can for ashes, trash, or garbage

dust' bowl' *n* area subject to dust storms, as the region in central U.S., afflicted with such storms in the 1930's

dust'er *n* **1** one who dusts; **2** cloth or brush for removing dust; **3** light over-garment to protect clothing from dust; **4** device for spraying dust or in-secticide on crops

dust' jack'et *n* detachable paper cover for a book

dust'pan' *n* shovellike pan into which dirt and dust can be swept

Dutch /duch'/ [MD Dutsch] *n* **1** lan-guage of The Netherlands; **2 the Dutch** *pl* **a** the people of The Nether-lands; **b** the Pennsylvania Dutch; **3 beat the Dutch** colloq to be beyond understanding; **4 in Dutch** slang in trouble or in disfavor || adj **5** of or pert. to The Netherlands or the Dutch; **6** of or pert. to the Pennsyl-vania Dutch; **7** slang German || adv **8 go Dutch** colloq to have each one pay his own way

Dutch' barn' *n* shelter closed only on the weather side and used for storing hay or tobacco

Dutch' cour'age *n* courage inspired by alcohol

Dutch' door' *n* door with upper and lower halves opening independently

Dutch' gold' *n* imitation gold leaf

Dutch'man /-mən/ *n* (-men /-mən/) na-tive or inhabitant of The Netherlands

Dutch' ov'en *n* heavy shallow kettle for roasting and baking, with a convex lid on which hot coals may be placed

Dutch' treat' *n* meal or entertainment in which each participant pays his own way

Dutch' un'cle *n* colloq one who sternly lectures and criticizes another for his good

du·te·ous /d(y)ŏŏt'ē·əs/ [< duty] adj obedient; dutiful

du·ti·a·ble /d(y)ŏŏt'ē·əbəl/ adj subject to payment of duty

du'ti·ful adj **1** obeying one's duty; **2** obedient, compliant, duteous, respectful, docile || **du'ti·ful·ly** adv || SYN obe-dient, compliant, duteous, respectful, docile

du'ty [AF duete that which is due] *n* (-ties) **1** moral or legal obligation to do what is right and expected; **2** assigned task, as on guard duty; **3** tax imposed on the import or export of goods; **4** fee imposed on certain goods and services; **5 duties** pl ac-tions required by one's occupation, as the duties of a policeman; **6 off duty** at liberty from one's post or work; **7 on duty** at one's post or work || SYN obligation, submission, requirement, obedience

dwarf /dwôrf'/ [OE dweorh] *n* **1** person of considerably less than normal size, esp. if having disproportionately short limbs; **2** plant or animal much smaller than the ordinary size; **3 dwarf star** || *vt* **4** to stunt the growth of; **5** to cause to look small by com-parison || *vi* **6** to become dwarfed || **dwarf'ish** adj || **dwarf'ism** *n*

dwarf' star' *n* star, like the sun, of fairly low luminosity, mass, and size

dwell /dwel'/ [OE dwellan to hinder, delay] *v* (dwelled or dwelt) *vi* **1** to reside, make one's home; **2 dwell on** to linger over, as a topic or thought || **dwell'er** *n* || SYN stay, abide, so-journ, tarry, inhabit, lodge, live

dwell'ing *n* house or place to live in; residence

dwelt /dwelt'/ pt & pp of **dwell**

dwin·dle /dwin'dəl/ [< OE dwīnan to waste away] *vi* to become gradually less; diminish, shrink || SYN fall away, waste away, decline (see de-crease)

Dy chem dysprosium

dye /dī'/ [OE dēag] *n* **1** liquid, stain, or other material used to give color to or change the color of paper, fab-rics, etc.; **2** color produced by dyeing || *v* (dye·ing) *vt* **3** to color or stain with a dye, or as with a dye || *vi* **4** to take on color by being dyed || **dy'er** *n*

dyed'-in-the-wool' adj through-and-through; intransigent

dye'stuff' *n* material that yields or is used as a dye

dy·ing /dī′iŋ/ 1 *prp* of **die**[1] ‖ *adj* 2 ceasing to live; 3 drawing to a close; 4 at the time of death, as *his dying words* ‖ *n* 5 act of ceasing to exist

dy·nam·ic /dīnam′ik/ [< Gk *dynamis* power] *adj* 1 forceful, energetic; 2 pert. to the forces that produce motion; 3 pert. to dynamics ‖ **dy·nam′·i·cal·ly** *adv*

dy·nam′ics *npl* 1 motivating forces in any field, physical or moral ‖ *nsg* 2 branch of mechanics that deals with the action of forces on systems

dy·na·mite /dīn′əmīt/ *n* 1 powerful explosive now made with ammonium nitrate mixed with an absorbing substance; 2 *slang* spectacular person or thing ‖ *vt* 3 to blow up with dynamite

dy′na·mo′ /-mō′/ [< *dynamo*electric] *n* 1 electric generator, esp. for direct current; 2 *colloq* dynamic person

dy′na·mo·e·lec′tric *adj* pert. to the conversion of mechanical to electrical energy or vice versa

dy′na·mom′e·ter /-mom′-/ *n* 1 device for measuring mechanical power; 2 device for measuring mechanical forces and torques

dy·nas·ty /dīn′əstē/ [< Gk *dynastes* ruler] *n* (-ties) succession of rulers of the same family ‖ **dy·nas′tic** /-nas′-/ *adj*

dyne /dīn′/ [< Gk *dynamis* power] *n* cgs unit of force, being the force which, acting on a mass of one gram, produces an acceleration of one centimeter per second per second

dys- [Gk] *pref* bad, ill, or difficult

dys·en·ter·y /dis′enter′ē/ [*dys-* + Gk *entera* bowels] *n* 1 infectious intestinal disease characterized by severe inflammation of the bowels and bloody diarrhea; 2 *colloq* diarrhea

dys·pep·si·a /dispep′sē·ə, -shə/ [*dys-* + Gk *pepsis* digestion] *n* indigestion ‖ **dys·pep′tic** *adj & n*

dys·pros·i·um /disprōs′ē·əm, -prōsh′-/ [< Gk *dysprositos* difficult of access] *n* rare-earth metallic element (**Dy**; at.no. 66; at.wt. 162.50)

E

E, e /ē′/ *n* (**E**'s or **Es**; **e**'s or **es**) fifth letter of the English alphabet

E 1 *mus* third tone in the scale of C major; 2 fifth in order or in a series; 3 something shaped like an E

E, E. 1 east(ern); 2 English; 3 excellent

e *math* constant equal to 2.718, used as the base of natural logarithms

e- *pref* var of **ex-**[1]

each /ēch′/ [OE *ǣlc*] *adj* 1 being one of two or more considered individually ‖ *pron* 2 each one ‖ *adv* 3 apiece

ea·ger /ēg′ər/ [OF *aigre* keen] *adj* 1 impatiently anxious; fervently desirous; 2 impetuous ‖ **ea′ger·ly** *adv* ‖ **ea′ger·ness** *n* ‖ SYN ardent, impetuous, fervent, impatient, spirited ‖ ANT indifferent, apathetic, unmoved, uninterested

ea′ger bea′ver *n colloq* overzealous person who volunteers for everything and offers to do more than his share

ea·gle /ēg′əl/ [OF *aigle* < L *aquila*] *n* 1 any of several large birds of prey akin to the hawks, noted for strength and keenness of vision; 2 emblem, seal, or insignia in the form of or bearing a representation of an eagle; 3 former U.S. ten-dollar gold coin; 4 *golf* score of two below par

ea′gle-eyed′ *adj* keen-sighted

ea′gle scout′ *n* boy scout with at least 21 merit badges

ear[1] /ir′/ [OE *ēare*] *n* 1 entire organ of hearing; 2 outer, visible part; 3 sense of hearing; 4 ability to discern delicate differences in sound; 5 sense of pitch; 6 attention, heed; 7 **be all ears** to give one's undivided attention; 8 **bend someone's ear** *slang* to bore someone with incessant talk; 9 **have** or **keep one's ear to the ground** to keep well-informed; 10 **pin someone's ear back** to trounce someone; 11 **play by ear**, **a** *mus* to play without written music; **b** to improvise as circumstances warrant; 12 **up to one's ears** deeply involved

ear[2] [OE *ēar*] *n* spike of a cereal plant containing the flowers or grains

ear′ache′ *n* pain in the ear

ear′drum′ *n* thin membrane that separates the outer ear from the cavity of the inner ear

earl /url′/ [OE *eorl*] *n* British nobleman next in rank below a marquis, equivalent to a count ‖ **earl′dom** *n*

ear·ly /ur′lē/ [OE *ǣrlīce*] *adv & adj* (**-li·er**; **-li·est**) 1 near the beginning; 2 before the expected time; 3 not long from now; 4 in the distant past

ear′ly warn′ing sys′tem *n* radar network for detecting hostile aircraft and missiles in time to launch counter measures

ear′mark′ *n* 1 identifying mark placed on the ear of an animal; 2 distinguishing mark or characteristic ‖ *vt* 3 to put an earmark on; 4 to set aside for a specific purpose

ear′muff′ *n* covering for the ear to protect it from the cold

earn /urn′/ [OE *earnian*] *vt* 1 to gain

or get for labor or services rendered; **2** to merit or deserve; **3** to gain as profit for the use of one's capital, as *to earn interest* ‖ *vi* **4** to receive remuneration or income ‖ SYN secure, win, acquire, achieve, attain (see *get*)

earned′ in′come *n* income earned for labor or services

ear·nest[1] /urn′ist/ [OE *eornost*] *adj* **1** serious, sincere, and determined in purpose or effort ‖ *n* **2 in earnest, a** serious, determined; **b** with seriousness and determination ‖ **ear′nest·ly** *adv* ‖ **ear′nest·ness** *n* ‖ SYN solemn, intent, fervent, sincere, hearty, sedate (see *serious*, *grave*[2]) ‖ ANT trifling, gay, lively, joking

ear·nest[2] [OF *erres* < Gk *arrhabon* pledge < Heb] *n* **1** partial advance payment to ensure the fulfillment of a bargain; **2** promise or indication of what will follow; pledge

earn′ings *npl* money earned; wages or profits

ear′ring *n* ornament worn on or hanging from the ear

ear′shot *n* distance within which the voice can be heard

earth /urth′/ [OE *eorthe*] *n* **1** the planet on which we live; **2** dry land; **3** ground or soil; **4** worldly things in contrast to those of the spirit; **5** this world as distinguished from heaven and hell; **6** all of the inhabitants of the globe; **7** any of certain stable mineral oxides, as alumina and strontia; **8 down to earth** practical; **9 move heaven and earth** to do everything possible; **10 on earth** in the world

earth′en *adj* **1** made of earth; **2** made of baked clay

earth′en·ware′ *n* vessels or other objects made of baked clay

earth′ling *n* dweller upon the earth; mortal

earth′ly *adj* **1** pert. to this world; secular, material; **2** conceivable ‖ SYN secular, temporal, mundane, worldly, carnal

earth′quake′ *n* vibration or trembling of the ground caused by volcanic action or by cracking and dislocation of the rock foundation

earth′ sci′enc·es *npl* sciences concerned with the study of the origin, history, composition, and characteristics of the earth, as geography, geology, geophysics, and mineralogy

earth′shak′ing *adj* drastic and unsettling (action or pronouncement)

earth′work′ *n* fortification made by piling up earth

earth′worm′ *n* slender worm of any of several genera found in moist earth

earth′y *adj* (-i·er; -i·est) **1** composed of, resembling, or pert. to the soil; **2** gross, coarse; **3** simple, unaffected

ease /ēz′/ [OF *aise*] *n* **1** freedom from pain, trouble, or mental anguish; **2** tranquility; comfort; **3** freedom from difficulty or effort; **4** financial security; **5** freedom from constraint in manners or behavior; **6 at ease** *mil* in a standing position of rest in which a soldier may relax and shift his weight but not speak or move his right foot ‖ *vt* **7** to comfort, free from care and anxiety; **8** to release from strain or pressure; **9** to lessen (pain); **10** to move with great care; **11** to facilitate ‖ *vi* **12** to lessen in severity, difficulty, pain, or discomfort ‖ SYN *n* content, enjoyment, comfort, naturalness, facility, expertness, readiness; *v* calm, pacify, disburden, alleviate, allay

ea·sel /ēz′əl/ [D *ezel* ass] *n* tripod or frame, as for holding a blackboard or picture

ease′ment *n* **1** that which gives ease; **2** *law* any of several rights which one may have over another's land, as that of free passage

eas′i·ly *adv* **1** with ease; **2** very likely; **3** by far

east /ēst′/ [OE] *n* **1** one of the four cardinal points of the compass, 90° to the right of north; the general direction of the rising sun; **2 the East, a** the countries of Asia; **b** the part of the U.S. bordering the Atlantic Ocean, esp. north of the Mason-Dixon line ‖ *adj* **3** situated in, directed toward, or facing the east; **4** (wind) blowing from the east ‖ *adv* **5** in or toward the east

East′ Ber·lin′ *n* eastern sector of Berlin, now the capital of East Germany (1,100,000)

east′bound′ *adj* headed east

East′ End′ *n* industrial and shipping section of E London, the home of the cockney

East′er [OE *ēastre*] *n* **1** festival of the Christian Church commemorating the resurrection of Jesus Christ; **2** day on which it falls, the Sunday following the full moon on or after the vernal equinox

east′er·ly *adj* & *adv* **1** in the direction of or moving toward the east; **2** (wind) from the east ‖ *n* (-lies) **3** east wind

east′ern *adj* **1** situated in, directed toward, or facing the east; **2 Eastern, a** of or pert. to the East; **b** Oriental ‖ **East′ern·er** *n*

East′ern Church′ *n* Eastern Orthodox Church

East′ern Hem′i·sphere′ *n* eastern part of the globe: the Old World, including Europe, Africa, Asia, and Australia

east′ern·most′ *adj* farthest east

East′ern Or′tho·dox Church′ *n* ancient Christian church of the Balkans, Russia, and the Near East, which separated from Rome in 1054

East′ern Ro′man Em′pire *n* that part of the later Roman Empire which had its capital at Constantinople

East′ Ger′ma·ny *n* country in central Europe created by the division of Germany in 1945 (18,000,000); 41,600 sq.m.; cap. East Berlin || **East′ Ger′man** *adj & n*

East′ In′dies *npl* the islands of SE Asia || **East′ In′di·an** *adj & n*

east·ward /-wərd/ *adj & adv* toward the east || **east′ward·ly** *adj & adv* || **east′wards** *adv*

eas·y /ē′ē/ [OF *aisie pp* of *aisier* to ease] *adj* (-i·er; -i·est) 1 not difficult; 2 free from constraint or self-consciousness; 3 free from pain, discomfort, trouble, or worry; 4 comfortable; 5 not burdensome; 6 moderate; 7 not exacting or oppressive; 8 *com* relatively abundant, as *easy credit* || **eas′i·ness** *n* || SYN untroubled, unconcerned, manageable, indulgent, mild, natural, unconstrained

eas′y chair′ *n* upholstered chair for lounging

eas′y·go′ing *adj* 1 calm; casual, relaxed; 2 not strict

eas′y mark′ *n* person easily taken advantage of

eas′y mon′ey *n* 1 money easy to earn; 2 money obtained fraudulently; 3 money available at low interest rates

eas′y street′ *n* on easy street *slang* affluent

eat /ēt/ [OE *etan*] *v* (ate; eaten) *vt* 1 to chew and swallow (food); 2 to devour; consume; 3 to corrode, wear away, as by rust; 4 to make by eating, as a hole || *vi* 5 to take food, have a meal || *n* 6 eats *pl slang* food || **eat′er** *n*

eat′a·ble *adj* 1 edible || *n* 2 eatables *pl* articles of food

eat·en /ēt′ən/ *pp* of eat

eaves /ēvz/ [OE *efes*] *npl* overhanging edge of a roof

eaves′drop′ *v* (-dropped; -drop·ping) *vi* to listen secretly to a private conversation || **eaves′drop′per** *n*

ebb /eb/ [OE *ebba*] *n* 1 flowing back of the tide; 2 decline; low condition || *vi* 3 to flow back, as the tide; 4 to decline; decay || SYN recede, retire, withdraw, decrease, subside

ebb′ tide′ *n* receding tide

eb·on·y /eb′ənē/ [ME *hebenuf* < Gk *ebenos*] *n* (-ies) 1 hard heavy black-colored wood; 2 tree that yields such wood (genus *Diospyros*); 3 deep black || also *adj*

e·bul·lient /ibul′yənt/ [L *ebulliens* (-entis) boiling up] *adj* 1 bubbling, boiling; 2 demonstrative, high-spirited || **e·bul′lience** *n*

ec- *pref* var of **ex-**¹

ec·ce ho·mo /ek′sē hōm′ō/ [L = behold the man, said by Pilate when he presented Christ to his accusers

(John 19:5)] *n* representation of Christ crowned with thorns

ec·cen·tric /eksent′rik/ [< Gk *ekkentros*] *adj* 1 out of center; 2 not having the same center, as two circles which partly coincide; 3 not perfectly circular, as an ellipse; 4 peculiar, erratic, odd || *n* 5 eccentric person; 6 disk mounted eccentrically on a shaft, which converts circular motion to back-and-forth motion || **ec·cen′tri·cal·ly** *adv* || **ec′cen·tric′i·ty** /-səntris′itē/ *n* (-ties) || SYN *adj* abnormal, peculiar, erratic, whimsical, strange, singular, odd, queer || DISCR *Eccentric* signifies off center, or aside from, a straight line. He is *eccentric* whose conduct deviates from the customary, whose actions are irregular; people living alone frequently fall into *eccentric* ways. *Erratic* is stronger than *eccentric*, and implies such a departure from the common course as to be unwise, if not blameworthy, as his conduct was so *erratic* that people questioned his sanity. *Strange* means unknown or unusual; a *strange* country is foreign or alien; a *strange* house is not one's own, or is unfamiliar; a *strange* explanation is an unexpected one, creating a vague distrust; *strange* actions are unaccountable, and savor somewhat of the mysterious, and, hence, the undesirable. *Odd* means unmatched, uneven; it differs from *eccentric* in suggesting failure to fit in rather than departing from a type. An *odd* person never wants to do what anyone else does; an *odd* number is uneven, an *odd* glove, one that has no mate, an *odd* idea is unfavorably out of the ordinary. *Singular* applies strictly to an only thing of its kind; used of a person, it marks him as having a distinguishing trait that separates him from others, as *singular* in his piety; *singular* in his dress. Applied to objects, customs, qualities, etc., it means unexampled, unconventional, unusual, as a *singular* course for a mother to take; a *singular* departure from etiquette; a *singular* place. *Queer* describes that which differs from the ordinary in an *odd* way; it sometimes connotes the abnormal and the creepy, and, not infrequently, the questionable, as a *queer* noise; a *queer*, dark street || ANT regular, ordinary, normal

Eccl. also **Eccles.** Ecclesiastes

Ec·cle·si·as·tes /eklēz′ē·as′tēz/ [Gk = assemblyman] *n* book of wisdom of the Old Testament

ec·cle·si·as·tic /-tik/ [< Gk *ekklesia* assembly] *adj* 1 pert. to the church or the clergy || *n* 2 person in holy orders; clergyman || **ec·cle′si·as′ti·cal** *adj*

ec·dys·i·ast /ekdiz′ē·ast′, -əst/ [coined

by H. L. Mencken from *ecdysis* shedding of an outer layer of skin < Gk *ekdysis* < Gk *ekdyo* strip off (clothing)] *n* stripteaser

ech·e·lon /esh'əlon'/ [F = ladder rung] *n* **1** *mil* arrangement, as of troops or ships, in the form of steps; **2** level of command or organization ‖ *vt &* *vi* **3** to form in an echelon

ech·o /ek'ō/ [Gk] *n* (-oes) **1** repetition of a sound caused by the reflection of its waves; **2** any repetition or imitation ‖ *vi* **3** to give forth an echo ‖ *vt* **4** to give forth an echo of; **5** to repeat the sound of

é·clair /ākler'/, ik-, ā'kler/ [F = lightning] *n* oblong frosted pastry shell filled usu. with custard

é·clat /āklä'/ [F] *n* **1** sensational, striking effect; **2** brilliant successs

ec·lec·tic /iklek'tik, ek-/ [< Gk *eklegein* to choose] *adj* **1** selecting or selected from various sources or systems according to taste or opinion ‖ *n* **2** one who follows an eclectic method ‖ **ec·lec'ti·cal·ly** *adv* ‖ **ec·lec'ti·cism** *n*

e·clipse /iklips'/ [< Gk *ekleipein* to fail to appear] *n* **1** total or partial darkening of a heavenly body, as the sun or moon, by the intervention of another body between it and the observer, or between it and the source of its illumination; **2** any overshadowing or loss of light, splendor, or fame ‖ *vt* **3** to cause an eclipse of; **4** to surpass, outshine

e·clip'tic *n* **1** great circle which is the apparent path of the sun among the stars ‖ *adj* **2** pert. to an eclipse or to the ecliptic

ec·logue /ek'log, -lôg/ [Gk *ekloga* selection] *n* short pastoral poem, usu. in dialogue form

ec'o·cide' /ek'ō-/ *n* substance which enters, permeates, and kills an entire ecosystem

e·col·o·gy /ikol'əjē/ [< G *Ökologie* < Gk *oikos* house + -*logy*] *n* **1** science dealing with the interactions of living organisms with each other and with their nonliving environment; **2** ecological condition at a given time or place ‖ **ec·o·log·ic** (-**i·cal**) /ek'əloj'ik(əl), ēk'ə-/ *adj* ‖ **e·col'o·gist** *n*

e·co·nom·ic /ēk'ənom'ik, ek'-/ [< Gk *oikonomia* household management] *adj* **1** pert. to the earning, distribution, and use of wealth and income; **2** pert. to economics; **3** pert. to the methods of providing for the needs of people

e'co·nom'i·cal *adj* **1** sparing in outlay; not wasteful; **2** economic ‖ **e'co·nom'i·cal·ly** *adv* ‖ SYN provident, chary, frugal, thrifty, sparing, saving, prudent ‖ DISCR *Economical* describes management that succeeds without waste; it indicates a purpose-

ful and practical regulation of one's affairs. *Economical* is sometimes, however, synonymous with *frugal*, connoting a disposition to save whether it is necessary or not; in this sense, *economical* and *frugal* indicate a grudging expenditure which excludes luxuries, but provides necessities, though never in excess; hence, a *frugal* meal might be sufficient, though not abundant. *Frugal* people incline to the uncomfortable ways of saving, but *thrifty* people live well, manage cleverly, save intelligently, and bank on their continued health and earnings as a source of surplus, rather than upon too strict deprivation. *Sparing* people are grudging, sometimes actually stingy; one may be *sparing* of food, words, sympathy, comforts, and the like. *Saving* people are adepts at cutting corners; they are both *frugal* and *economical*, and put themselves to much trouble to save small amounts. *Provident* people manage their affairs as well as the *economical*, better than the *frugal*, often as comfortably as the *thrifty*; provident people look toward the future and bend the present, as wisely as possible, to serve that end

e'co·nom'ics *nsg* **1** science dealing with the production, distribution, and consumption of wealth; **2** *npl* financial feasibility ‖ **e·con·o·mist** /ikon'-əmist/ *n*

e·con·o·mize /ikon'əmīz'/ *vt* **1** to use economically ‖ *vi* **2** to be economical ‖ **e·con'o·miz'er** *n*

e·con'o·my *n* (-mies) **1** economical management; **2** instance of thrift; saving; **3** economic system prevailing in a country

ec'o·sys'tem /ek'ō-/ *n* combination of all living organisms and their nonliving environment that exists and may be studied as a separate entity

ec·ru /ek'rōō/ [F = unbleached] *n* very light tan ‖ also *adj*

ec·sta·sy /ek'stəsē/ [OF *extasie* < Gk *ekstasis* trance] *n* (-sies) feeling of overpowering joy; rapture; exaltation ‖ **ec·stat'ic** /-stat'ik/ *adj* ‖ SYN joy, transport, exaltation (see *rapture*)

ecto- [Gk *ektos*] *comb form* outer, external

-ec·to·my /-ek'təmē/ [< Gk *ektemnein* to cut out] *comb form* surgical removal

ec·to·plasm /ek'təplaz'əm/ [< *ecto-* + Gk *plasma* thing formed] *n* **1** outer portion of a cell's cytoplasm; **2** spiritualism substance said to exude from the body of a medium

Ec·ua·dor /ek'wədôr'/ *n* Spanish-speaking republic in NW South America (5,508,000; 109,483 sq.m.;

cap. Quito) || **Ec'ua·do'ran** or **Ec'-ua·do're·an** *adj & n*

ec·u·men·i·cal /ek'yəmen'ikəl/ [< Gk *oikoumenikos*] *adj* 1 universal; 2 pert. to the whole Christian Church; 3 pert. to the movement for Christian unity

ec·u·me·nist /ek'yŏōmənist/ *n* one who supports the movement for Christian unity || **ec'u·me·nism** *n*

ec·ze·ma /igzēm'ə, ek'simə, eg'zi-/ [Gk] *n* inflammatory disease of the skin attended by scaling and itching

-ed¹ /-t *after a voiceless consonant sound; -id after t & d; -d after all other sounds*/ [OE -de, -ede, -ode, -ade] *suf* past tense ending of regular verbs, as *walked, wanted, weighed*

-ed² /*same as* -ed¹/ [OE -ed, -od, -ad] *suf* ending of the past participle of regular verbs

-ed³ /*same as* -ed¹/ or -id/ [< -ed²] *adj suf* having or characterized by, as *winged, four-footed*

E'dam (cheese') /ēd'əm, -dam/ [town in The Netherlands] *n* mild yellow cheese, shaped like a ball and coated with red wax

Ed.D. Doctor of Education

ed·dy /ed'ē/ [ME] *n* (-dies) 1 small whirlpool; 2 any similar rotary current, as of air || *v* (-died) *vt & vi* 3 to whirl in an eddy

e·del·weiss /ād'əlwīs', -vīs'/ [G = noble white] *n* small composite herb (*Leontopodium alpinum*) of the Alps, with white woolly leaves and flowers

e·de·ma /idēm'ə/ [Gk *oidema* swelling] *n* abnormal accumulation of serous fluid in the cellular tissues or in a body cavity || **e·dem'a·tous** /-dem'-/ *adj*

E·den /ēd'ən/ *n* 1 Bib first home of Adam and Eve; 2 any very delightful place or state; paradise

e·den·tate /iden'tāt/ [L *edentatus* toothless] *adj* 1 lacking teeth || *n* 2 any member of an order (Edentata) of mammals comprising certain anteaters, the sloths, and armadillos

edge /ej/ [OE *ecg* corner] *n* 1 sharp or cutting part of a blade; 2 extreme border of anything, or the part immediately next to it; 3 brink, margin; 4 keenness, sharpness; 5 *colloq* advantage; 6 **on edge** nervously tense; irritable || *vt* 7 to put a border on; 8 to make (one's way) along gradually || *vi* 9 to move gradually || SYN *n* rim, brim, margin, verge, bank (see *border*)

edge' tool' *n* tool with an edge for cutting

edge'wise' or **edge'ways'** *adv* with the edge foremost

edg'ing *n* border trimming

edg'y *adj* (-i·er; -i·est) on edge

ed·i·ble /ed'ibəl/ [< L *edere* to eat] *adj* fit to be eaten || **ed'i·bil'i·ty** /-bil'-/ *n*

e·dict /ē'dikt/ [L *edictum*] *n* proclamation or order issued by an official authority and having the force of law

ed·i·fice /ed'ifis/ [MF < L *aedificium*] *n* building, esp. one that is large and imposing || SYN structure (see *building*)

ed·i·fy /ed'ifī'/ [OF *edifier* < L *aedificare* to build] *v* (-fied) *vt* to instruct or benefit, esp. in religion or morals || **ed'i·fi·ca'tion** *n*

e·dile /ē'dīl/ *n* var of **aedile**

Ed·in·burgh /ed'ənbur'ŏ, -brə/ *n* capital of Scotland (475,000)

Ed·i·son, Thomas A. /ed'isən/ *n* (1847-1931) U.S. inventor

Ed'i·son bat'ter·y [trademark] *n* elec storage battery, used in mines and in railroad signaling, in which the active agents of the plates are nickel hydroxide and iron, the container nickel-plated iron, and the electrolyte potassium hydroxide

ed·it /ed'it/ [< *editor*] *vt* 1 to revise and prepare for publication; 2 to select and adapt for publication or viewing; 3 to direct the policies of; run, as a newspaper

e·di·tion /idish'ən/ *n* 1 published form of a literary work; 2 all printings from one set of type

ed·i·tor [< L *edere* (*editus*) to give out] *n* 1 one who edits; 2 conductor of a department of a newspaper or magazine, as *the sports editor;* 3 device for editing film

ed'i·to'ri·al /-tôr'ē·əl, -tōr'-/ *adj* 1 of or pert. to an editor or editing || *n* 2 article in a newspaper or magazine, or statement on radio or television, expressing the opinions of the editors or management

ed'i·to'ri·al·ize *vi* 1 to insert personal opinions in what purports to be a factual account; 2 to express an opinion in, or as if in, an editorial

ed'i·to'ri·al we' *n* the first person plural pronoun used by editors instead of *I* to avoid being personal

Ed·mon·ton /ed'məntən/ *n* capital of Alberta (290,000)

EDT Eastern Daylight Time

ed·u·cate /ej'əkāt'/ [L *educare* (-*atus*)] *vt* 1 to develop, improve, or train by instruction or schooling; 2 to send to school || **ed'u·ca·ble** *adj*

ed'u·cat'ed *adj* 1 trained by the process of education; 2 based on knowledge or experience

ed'u·ca'tion *n* 1 act or process of educating; 2 knowledge gained by being educated; 3 degree or level of instruction, as *a college education;* 4 science of teaching; pedagogy || **ed'u·ca'tion·al** *adj* || SYN instruction, breeding, training, culture, information, cultivation, knowledge, schooling || DISCR *Education* comprehends all that we assimilate from the beginning to the end of our lives in the development of the powers and faculties bestowed upon us at birth. It includes not only systematic schooling, but also that enlightenment and sense which an individual obtains through experience. *Instruction* is the knowledge and information given in a course of schooling or training. *Training* connotes not only the idea of knowledge received, but that of such knowledge digested through application, drill, and discipline. *Culture* is a state of advanced mental and moral development, accompanied by such fineness of feeling and taste, such social address and polished manners, as result from long contact with what is best. *Breeding* is the result of *training*, or the lack of it, in behavior and good manners. One well born and well trained, one schooled in the civilities of life has good *breeding;* one unused to social observances or unaccustomed to extending the little but significant courtesies of social life has bad *breeding. Culture* often bespeaks the heritage of generations who have had the advantages of wealth and leisure; *breeding* suggests the home from which one comes

ed·u·ca'tor *n* one who is professionally involved in education

e·duce /id(y)o͞os'/ [L *educere*] *vt* to draw out; infer; elicit || SYN elicit, evoke, evolve, develop, deduce

Ed·ward·i·an /edwôrd'ē·ən, -wärd'-/ *adj* pert. to or characteristic of the reign of Edward VII, King of Great Britain 1901-10

-ee /-ē', -ē'/ [MF *-e* < L *-atus* ending of *pp*] *n suf* one who receives or is affected by an action, as *payee*

eel /ēl'/ [OE *ǣl*] *n* (eel or eels) 1 any of an order (Apodes) of snakelike fishes; 2 any of various other snakelike fishes, as the lamprey

e'er /er'/ *adv poet.* ever

-eer /-ir'/ [MF *-ier* < L *-arius*] *n suf* 1 one who is concerned with, as *engineer* || *v suf* 2 to be concerned with or involved in, as *electioneer*

ee·rie also **ee·ry** /ir'ē/ [OE *earg* cowardly] *adj* (-ri·er; -ri·est) weird, awe-inspiring || **ee'ri·ly** *adv* || **ee'ri·ness** *n*

ef- *pref* var of **ex-¹**

ef·face /ifās'/ [F *effacer*] *vt* 1 to wipe out or erase; blot out; 2 to make (oneself) inconspicuous || **ef·face'ment** *n* || SYN obliterate, expunge, blot out, eclipse (see *erase*)

ef·fect /ifekt'/ [L *efficere (-fectus)*] *vt* 1 to bring about; accomplish; cause to happen || *n* 2 resulting state or condition; 3 impression made on someone; 4 influence, power to produce results; 5 state of being in force; 6 meaning, import; 7 effects *pl* personal property; 8 **in effect, a**

in fact; **b** virtually; **c** in force; **9 take effect, a** to become operative; **b** to produce the desired result || SYN *n* consequence, issue, event, product, intent, performance, impression; *v* produce, execute, perform, fulfill, discharge, accomplish, complete, administer || DISCR To *effect* is to make come to pass or bring to complete success a plan or purpose. Ordinarily we *effect* our own plans or designs. *Effect* commonly implies that the issue was brought about in spite of difficulties, and it stresses all that was done to that end, rather than the concluding or finishing act, as after long years, we *effected* the desired changes. To *execute* is to secure an actual and operating result by carrying a thing through, as to make a law is easier than to *execute* it. We ordinarily *execute* the biddings of others, and the actual completion rather than the whole operation of securing the result is stressed. Legally, *execute* means to make valid by following the procedure established by law, or to complete, as a document, by a required signature. *Perform* is the less familiar word for *do;* it often connotes a long-continued or regularly recurring action or duty. We *discharge* that which rests upon us as a responsibility or an obligation. We *accomplish* what we fulfill or finish, often after conquering obstacles

ef·fec'tive *adj* 1 producing a desired result; efficient; 2 impressive; 3 in operation; in effect || *n* 4 soldier fit for duty || **ef·fec'tive·ly** *adv* || **ef·fec'tive·ness** *n* || SYN *adj* operative, adequate, fruitful, competent, effectual, efficient, efficacious || DISCR That is *effective* which produces, or is adapted to produce, an effect; *effective* fire drills insure order in time of fire; *effective* laws are in operation; *effective* speeches produce the reactions which the speakers intended them to produce; speakers who achieve such results are themselves *effective*. That is *effectual* which answers its purpose; *effectual* carries the idea of final. *Effectual* measures taken to suppress a rebellion do suppress it; a nuisance against which *effectual* complaints have been made is abated. *Effectual* is not used of persons. *Efficient* describes a person or thing acting under inherent power or energy to the end of certain accomplishment; *efficient* is opposed to incompetent or incapable. An *efficient* executive creates a smoothly running organization; an *efficient* mechanical device does the work it was designed to do. That is *efficacious* which produces a desired result or effect, as an *efficacious* remedy; an *efficacious* method of teaching. *Efficacious* is not used of persons

ef·fec'tu·al /-chōō-əl/ *adj* producing or having the ability to produce a desired result || **ef·fec'tu·al·ly** *adv* || SYN (see *effective*) || ANT useless, powerless, vain

ef·fec'tu·ate' *vt* to effect

ef·fem·i·nate /ifem'init/ [< *ef-* + L *femina* woman] *adj* having the qualities or characteristics of a woman; delicate, unmanly || **ef·fem'i·na·cy** *n* (-cies) || SYN finical, soft, womanish, voluptuous

ef·fer·ent /ef'ərənt/ [L *efferens* (-*entis*) carrying away] *anat & physiol adj* 1 carrying away from an organ || *n* 2 efferent nerve or duct

ef·fer·vesce /ef'ərves'/ [<*ef-* + L *fervere* to be hot] *vi* 1 to give off gas in bubbles; hiss; 2 to be in exuberant spirits || **ef'fer·ves'scent** *adj* || **ef'fer·ves'cence** *n*

ef·fete /ifēt'/ [L *effetus* worn out by breeding] *adj* 1 no longer able to produce; sterile; 2 worn out; spent; infirm; useless

ef·fi·ca·cious /ef'ikāsh'əs/ [< L *efficax* (-*acis*) efficient] *adj* producing or capable of producing a desired result || **ef'fi·ca'cious·ly** *adv* || SYN powerful, sure, potent (see *effective*)

ef·fi·ca·cy /ef'ikəsē/ *n* power to produce desired results or effects || SYN power, potency, strength || ANT powerlessness, impotence, fruitlessness

ef·fi·cien·cy /ifish'ənsē/ [< L *efficiens* (-*entis*) effecting] *n* (-cies) 1 quality of producing the desired result or the maximum effect with the minimum effort or expense 2 extent or quality of effectiveness; 3 ratio of the useful work obtained from a machine to the energy supplied to it || SYN competency, capability, power (see *ability*)

ef·fi'cien·cy a·part'ment *n* one-room apartment with a kitchen alcove and bathroom

ef·fi'cient *adj* 1 producing desired results; 2 having the ability to accomplish a task with the least amount of waste || **ef·fi'cient·ly** *adv* || SYN capable, competent, operative (see *effective*)

ef·fi·gy /ef'ijē/ [L *effigies*] *n* (-gies) 1 image or portrait, as a head on a medal; 2 crude figure, as a dummy stuffed with straw, representing a public figure to be mocked, burned, or hanged in a public demonstration

ef·flu·ent /ef'lōō-ənt/ [L *effluens* (-*entis*)] *adj* 1 flowing out or issuing forth || *n* 2 outflow; 3 stream that flows out of a larger stream or lake; 4 discharge from an industrial smokestack, a sewer, a storage tank,

a nuclear power plant, etc. that may or may not carry pollutants || **ef'flu·ence** *n*

ef·flu·vi·um /iflōōv'ē-əm/ [L = a flowing out] *n* (-ums or -a /-ə/) vapor or exhalation, esp. a disagreeable odor

ef·fort /ef'ərt/ [MF] *n* 1 physical or mental exertion for a definite end; 2 attempt; 3 something produced by exertion; achievement || SYN attempt, trial, struggle, exertion, endeavor, essay, labor || DISCR *Effort* names the putting forth of power or strength, either physical or mental, in doing or struggling to do a certain definite thing. *Attempt* emphasizes the idea of trying to accomplish an end. The purpose under *effort* and *attempt* is the same, but *effort* looks toward success, while *attempt* admits the possibility of failure, since an *attempt* is an avowed experiment; hence, one definition of *attempt* is "an unsuccessful *effort*." Both *effort* and *attempt* name a single act; *endeavor* connotes a chain of activities; *endeavor* is a continuous *attempt*, directed as a rule toward that which is hard to conquer, renewed in spite of failure, and sustained by a firm purpose, as patient *endeavor* to be cheerful in affliction. *Exertion* is a vigorous, taxing, even violent, exercise of any power or faculty; it may or may not be directed toward a definite object

ef·fron·ter·y /ifrunt'ərē/ [F *effronterie*] *n* (-ies) shameless audacity || SYN audacity, presumption, assurance, brass, impudence || ANT diffidence, modesty, self-effacement

ef·ful'gent /iful'jənt/ [L *effulgens* (-*entis*)] *adj* shining brightly; radiant || **ef·ful'gence** *n*

ef·fuse /ifyōōz'/ [< *ef-* + *fundere* (*fusus*) to pour] *vt* 1 to pour or send forth || *vi* 2 to flow out; diffuse

ef·fu'sion /-zhən/ *n* 1 act of effusing; 2 unrestrained expression; 3 escape of a fluid from the vessel enclosing it

ef·fu'sive /-siv/ *adj* 1 pouring forth freely; 2 extremely demonstrative; gushing || **ef·fu'sive·ly** *adv* || **ef·fu'sive·ness** *n*

Eg. Egypt(ian)

e.g. [L *exempli gratia*] for example

e·gad /ēgad'/ [< *ah God*] *interj* used as a mild oath

e·gal·i·tar·i·an /igal'iter'ē·ən/ [< F *égalité* equality] *n* believer in the equality of all men || also *adj* || **e·gal'i·tar'i·an·ism** *n*

egg¹ /eg'/ [OE ǣg] *n* 1 female reproductive cell; 2 oval egg within a shell of any of certain animals, as birds and reptiles; 3 hen's egg or its contents, raw or cooked; 4 *slang* person; **5 lay an egg** *slang* to fail miserably

egg² [ON *eggja* to urge] *vt* **egg on** to urge or incite

egg′head′ *n colloq* intellectual

egg′nog′ *n* drink made of eggs, milk, sugar, and usu. spirits

egg′plant′ *n* cultivated herb (*Solanum melongena*) with edible purple or white fruit used as a vegetable

egg′ roll′ *n* Chinese and Chinese-American dish made of a roll of egg dough stuffed with minced vegetables and fried in deep fat

egg′ roll′ing *n* Eastertime race or contest of children in which eggs are rolled down a hill

eggs′ Ben′e·dict *n* poached eggs over fried ham on toast, topped with hollandaise sauce

e·gis /ēj′is/ *n* var of **aegis**

e·go /ēg′ō, eg′ō/ [L = I] *n* **1** the self; individual person or personality; **2** one's sense of importance; self-esteem; **3** *psychoanal* that part of the personality that mediates between the id and the outer world

e′go·cen′tric /-sen′trik/ *adj* **1** self-centered ‖ *n* **2** egocentric person

e′go·ism *n* **1** self-interest; **2** egotism; ‖ **e′go·ist** *n* ‖ **e′go·is′tic** (-ti·cal) *adj*

e′go·ma′ni·a *n* abnormal egotism ‖ **e′go·ma′ni·ac′** /-ak′/ *n* ‖ **e′go·ma′ni·a·cal** /-mənī′əkəl/ *adj*

e′go·tism *n* excessive conceit ‖ **e′go·tist** *n* ‖ **e′go·tis′tic** (-ti·cal) *adj* ‖ SYN egotism, self-esteem, vanity, conceit, self-consciousness, self-praise ‖ ⁀DISCR *Egoism* thinks of self; *egotism* talks of self. *Egoism* may be systematically selfish without being offensive; *egotism* is always offensive. The *egoist* is bent on his own ends and purposes; the *egotist* is merely in love with himself. *Self-esteem* has a very good opinion of self—often well-founded, but usually exaggerated. *Vanity* and *conceit* are cardinal weaknesses. *Vanity* is empty, offensive self-pride; *conceit* is overweening *self-esteem*, always offensive

e·gre·gious /igrēj′(ē)əs/ [L *egregius* outstanding] *adj* outstandingly bad; flagrant ‖ **e·gre′gious·ly** *adv*

e·gress /ēg′res/ [L *egressus*] *n* **1** departure; **2** means of exit

e·gret /ēg′rit/ [MF *egrete* < Gmc] *n* any of several herons bearing long white plumes in the breeding season

E·gypt /ēj′ipt/ *n* republic in NE Africa in the valley of the lower Nile, seat of an ancient civilization (28,000,000; 386,198 sq.m.; cap. Cairo) ‖ **E·gyp·tian** /ējip′shən/ *adj & n*

eh /ā′ e′/ [ME *ey*] *interj* what? (expressive of doubt, inquiry, or surprise)

ei·der /īd′ər/ [Icel *æthar*] *n* **1** also **ei′der duck′** any of several large

marine ducks (genus *Somateria*) of northern regions, valued for the feathers with which the female lines its nest; **2** also **ei′der·down′** soft breast feathers of the eider duck used in pillows, coverlets, etc.

eight /āt′/ [OE *eahta*] *n* **1** sum of seven and one (8; VIII); **2** set of eight persons or things; **3** card with eight spots ‖ also *adj & pron*

eight′ball′ *n* **1** billiard ball bearing the number 8; **2 behind the eightball** *slang* in a disadvantageous position

eight·een /ā′tēn′/ [OE *eahtatēne*] *n* sum of eight and ten (18; XVIII) ‖ also *adj & pron*

eight′eenth′ *n* **1** the one next in order after the seventeenth; **2** one of eighteen equal parts ‖ also *adj*

eight′fold′ *adj* **1** having eight times as much or as many ‖ *adv* **2** eight times as much or as many

eighth /ātth′/ [OE *eahtotha*] *n* **1** the one next in order after the seventh; **2** one of eight equal parts; **3** *mus* octave ‖ also *adj*

eight′i·eth *n* **1** the one next in order after the seventy-ninth; **2** one of eighty equal parts ‖ also *adj*

eight′y *n* (-ies) **1** eight times ten (80; LXXX); **2 the eighties** *pl* **a** the numbers from 80 to 89; **b** the years from 80 to 89 in a century or a lifetime ‖ also *adj & pron*

Ein·stein, Al′bert /īn′stīn/ *n* (1879–1955) German physicist (U.S. citizen in 1940), formulator of the theory of relativity

ein·stein′i·um /-ē-əm/ [Albert *Einstein*] *n* synthetic, radioactive element (E; at.no. 99)

Eir·e /er′ə/ *n* former name of the Republic of Ireland

Ei·sen·how·er, Dwight David /dwīt′ īz′ənhou′ər/ *n* (1890–1969) U.S. general, commander of the Allied forces in Europe 1942–45; Chief of Staff 1945–48; 34th president of the U.S. 1953–61

ei·ther /ēth′ər, īth′-/ [OE *æghther*] *adj* **1** one or the other . . . of two; **2** each . . . of two ‖ *pron* **3** one or the other ‖ *conj* **4** (used before two or more words or sentence elements connected by the correlative *or*, to indicate that they are coordinate alternatives): *either come in or go out* ‖ *adv* **5** (always used with a negative) **a** also, as well, as *she won't either;* **b** *colloq* no, as *I can catch you. You can't either*, that is, *No, you can't*

e·jac·u·late /ijak′yəlāt′/ [L *ejaculari* (-*atus*) to squirt] *vt* **1** to utter suddenly ‖ *vi* **2** to eject semen ‖ **e·jac′u·la′tion** *n*

e·ject /ijekt′/ [L *ejicio* (*ejectus*)] *vt* to drive or force out; expel ‖ **e·jec′tion** *n*

e·jec′tion seat′ *n* seat designed to catapult a flyer to a safe distance from the plane

eke /ēk'/ [OE *eacan* to increase] *vt* **eke out,** 1 to piece out, supplement; 2 to barely make (a living)

EKG electrocardiogram

el /el'/ *n colloq* elevated railroad

e·lab·o·rate /ilab'ərāt'/ [L *elaborare* (*-atus*) to work out] *vt* 1 to produce, develop, or improve in detail and with great care || *vi* 2 to add details || /-it/ *adj* 3 produced or developed with great detail; complicated || **e·lab'o·rate·ly** *adv* || **e·lab'o·rate·ness** *n* || **e·lab·o·ra'tion** *n*

é·lan /ālän', älan'/ [F = dash] *n* ardor, dash

e·land /ēl'ənd [D = elk] *n* large South African antelope (genus *Taurotragus*) with twisted horns

e·lapse /ilaps'/ [L *elabi* (*elapsus*) to glide away] *vi* to slip away or pass (said of time)

e·las·tic /ilas'tik/ [Gk *elastikos* propulsive] *adj* 1 able to return or spring back to its original size or form after an applied stress has been removed; 2 stretchable || *n* 3 elastic band or fabric || **e·las·tic'i·ty** /ē'-/ *n*

e·late /ilāt'/ [L *elatus* carried away] *vt* to raise the spirits of; make jubilant || **e·lat'ed** *adj* || **e·la'tion** *n*

El·ba /el'bə/ *n* Italian island between Italy and Corsica, scene of Napoleon's first exile 1814–15

el·bow /el'bō/ [OE *elnboga*] *n* 1 joint between the forearm and the upper arm; 2 anything containing a sharp bend; 3 **rub elbows with** to associate with || *vt & vi* 4 to jostle or push, as with the elbows

el'bow grease' *n colloq* hard work

el'bow·room' *n* plenty of space to move around in

eld·er[1] /el'dər/ [OE *eldra, comp* of *eald* old] *adj* 1 older, senior || *n* 2 one older or superior in age, rank, or station; 3 influential older member of a tribe, family, or organization; 4 governing officer in certain churches

el·der[2] [OE *ellærn*] *n* any of a genus (*Sambucus*) of the honeysuckle family, shrubs having large clusters of white or pink flowers and dark-purple or red berries

el'der·ber'ry *n* (**-ries**) 1 fruit of the elder, used for wine and jelly; 2 the shrub itself

eld'er·ly *adj* between middle and old age

eld'er states'man *n* retired person of high rank who remains influential

eld'est [OE *eldesta, superl* of *eald* old] *adj* oldest; first-born

El Do·ra·do /el'dəräd'ō/ [Sp = the gilded] *n* (**-does**) 1 fabulously wealthy legendary country sought by early Spanish explorers in South America, esp. Guyana; 2 any place full of money-making opportunities

e·lect /ilekt'/ [L *eligere* (*electus*) to choose] *vt* 1 to choose; 2 to select for an office by vote || *adj* 3 elected for office but not yet installed, as *the president elect* || *n* 4 **the elect** *sg & pl* person or persons chosen, as for divine preference || **e·lec'tion** *n* || SYN *v* cull, pick, prefer, choose, select || DISCR *Choose* is the general term. It means to take, by an act of the judgment and will, a thing or course from among those offered. We *choose* on the grounds of merit, convenience, service, or the like. *Prefer* means to feel an especial liking for one person, thing, or course, among several offered; we *prefer* what accords with our mode of life, or our tastes. Affections and inclinations sway preference; judgment determines choice. In buying a rug, we may *prefer* an Oriental, but if we cannot afford it, we *choose* a domestic. To *select* is to make a choice after carefully weighing and considering not only the merits of the objects, but also our own preferences concerning them. The government, when an investigation is necessary, will *select* men specially qualified to conduct it. *Pick* is used colloquially, as in the phrase *pick out*, in the sense of *select*. To *elect* is to *choose* by vote

e·lec'tion·eer' *vi* to canvass for votes; work to win an election

e·lec'tive *adj* 1 appointed or filled by election; 2 optional; 3 pert. to election || *n* 4 optional course of study

e·lec'tor *n* 1 one qualified to vote; 2 member of the electoral college; 3 one of the group of German princes and bishops who chose the emperor of the Holy Roman Empire || **e·lec'tor·al** *adj*

e·lec'tor·al col'lege *n* body of electors chosen by the voters of the individual states to elect the President and Vice President

e·lec'tor·ate /-rit/ *n* whole body of persons entitled to vote

electr- or **electro-** [Gk *elektron* amber] *comb form* electric(ity)

E·lec·tra /ilek'trə/ *n Gk myth.* daughter of Agamemnon who induced her brother Orestes to kill their mother

e·lec·tric /ilek'trik/ *adj* 1 relating to, containing, produced by, charged with, operated by, or capable of producing electricity; 2 stirring; full of excitement

e·lec'tri·cal *adj* 1 electric; 2 concerned with electricity, as *an electrical engineer* || **e·lec'tri·cal·ly** *adv*

e·lec'tric chair' *n* electrified chair used to execute condemned criminals

e·lec'tric eel' *n* large eellike South American fish (*Electrophorus electricus*) able to give a severe electric shock

e·lec'tric eye' *n* photoelectric cell

e·lec·tri·cian /ilektrish'ən, ē'lek-/ *n* one who installs, repairs, operates, or maintains electrical equipment

e·lec·tric·i·ty /ilektris'itē, ē'lek-/ *n* 1 fundamental physical agency composed of charged particles, producing light, heat, chemical decomposition, and other physical phenomena; 2 science dealing with it; 3 electric current; 4 electric excitement

e·lec'tri·fy' /-trəkyo͞ot/ [*electro-* + *execute*] *vt* 1 to kill by electricity; 2 to execute in the electric chair ‖ **e·lec'tro·cu'tion** *n*

electro- *se-* **electr-**

e·lec'tro·car'di·o·gram' /-trō-/ *n* tracing revealing heart abnormalities by showing the differences in electric potential produced by heart action

e·lec'tro·car'di·o·graph' *n* device that makes electrocardiograms

e·lec'tro·cute' /-trəko͞ot/ [*electro-* + *execute*] *vt* 1 to kill by electricity; 2 to execute in the electric chair ‖ **e·lec'tro·cu'tion** *n*

e·lec'trode /-trōd/ [*electr-* + *-ode*] *n* terminal conductor of an electric or electronic device through which current passes in or out

e·lec·trol·y·sis /ilektrol'isis, ē'lek-/ *n* 1 conversion by means of an electric current of a solution into an electrolyte with dissociation of its components and deposition of a metal at one electrode and liberation of gas at the other; 2 eradication of hair roots by an electric current

e·lec'tro·lyte' /-trəlīt/ *n* solution which becomes a conductor through the movement of ions when an electric current is passed through it and which undergoes chemical decomposition with liberation of its components at the electrodes ‖ **e·lec'tro·lyt'ic** /-lit'-/ *adj*

e·lec'tro·lyze' *vt* to subject to electrolysis; to decompose by electrolysis

e·lec'tro·mag'net /-trō-/ *n* core of magnetic substance, as soft iron, which is magnetized by the passage of an electric current through a coil of wire surrounding it ‖ **e·lec'tro·mag·net'ic** *adj*

e·lec'tro·mag·net'ic in·duc'tion *n* production of a magnetic field or of a flow of electric current by means of the variations in a neighboring magnetic field

e·lec'tro·mag·net'ic spec'trum *n* the whole range of radiation which extends in frequencies from 10²³ cycles per second to 0 cycles per second and in wavelengths from .001 angstrom to infinity, thus including gamma rays, X rays, ultraviolet, visible light, infrared, microwaves, radio waves, and alternating current

e·lec'tro·mag·net'ic wave' *n* wave propagated through space from an oscillating source consisting of a magnetic field and an electric field perpendicular to each other

e·lec'tro·mo'tive *adj* producing a flow of electricity

e·lec'tro·mo'tive force' *n* force which tends to cause a movement of electricity, expressed in volts

e·lec'tron /ilek'tron/ [Gk = amber] *n* elementary particle existing in or out of an atom and having a negative charge of about 1.602×10^{-19} coulomb and a mass of about 9.108×10^{-31} kilogram

e·lec·tron'ic /-tron'-/ *adj* 1 pert. to the electron; 2 pert. to electronics; 3 pert. to devices in which the action of electrons is applied

e·lec·tron'ics *nsg* branch of physical science dealing with the action of electrons in vacuums, gases, and semiconductors and with the construction and use of devices in which the action of electrons is applied

e·lec'tron mi'cro·scope' *n* high-power microscope that focuses electrons rather than rays of light on a fluorescent screen

e·lec'tro·plate' *vt* to cover with a thin coating of metal by electrolysis ‖ **e·lec'tro·plat'ing** *n*

e·lec'tro·scope' *n* apparatus, consisting of two pieces of gold leaf suspended in a glass chamber, for showing the presence, sign, and intensity of an electrostatic charge

e·lec'tro·shock' *n* shock therapy administered by inducing shock with electricity

e·lec'tro·stat'ic *adj* 1 of or pert. to static electricity; 2 produced by or using static electricity

e·lec'tro·stat'ic in·duc'tion *n* production of an electric charge by the proximity of another charge

e·lec'tro·type' *n typ* facsimile plate made by electroplating a mold of the original ‖ also *vt*

el·ee·mos·y·nar·y /el'imos'iner'ē/ [< Gk *eleemosyne* alms] *adj* of, for, derived from, or dependent on charity

el·e·gant /el'əgənt/ [L *elegans* (-*antis*)] *adj* 1 tasteful; luxurious; 2 graceful; refined; 3 excellent ‖ **el'e·gant·ly** *adv* ‖ **el'e·gance** *n* ‖ SYN dainty, tasteful, graceful (see *exquisite*)

el·e·gi·ac /el'iji'ak, ilēj'ē·ak'/ *adj* 1 like or pert. to an elegy; 2 mournful

el·e·gy /el'əjē/ [< Gk *elegos*] *n* (-gies) 1 mournful poem; 2 funeral song; 3 mournful musical composition

el·e·ment /el'əmənt/ [OF < L *elementum* first principle] *n* 1 component of a more complicated whole; ingredient; 2 natural environment; 3 *chem* any of a number of substances which are not decomposable by chemical analysis; 4 **elements** *pl* **a** rudiments; **b** forces of the atmosphere, as wind and rain

el'e·men'tal /-men'-/ *adj* 1 pert. to

first principles; primal; fundamental;
2 relating to, or characteristic of,
the physical world or the forces of
nature; 3 forming an essential part
of something; 4 *chem* pert. to the
elements

el·e·men·ta·ry *adj* 1 pert. to first principles; introductory; simple; 2 of or
pert. to an elementary school

el·e·men·ta·ry school' *n* school of the
first six or eight years

el·e·phant /el'əfənt/ [Gk *elephas*
(*-antos*)] *n* huge herbivorous mammal of India and Africa (family Ele-
phantidae), having thick wrinkled
skin, a long flexible snout or trunk,
and long curved ivory tusks

el·e·phan·ti·a·sis /-tī'əsis/ *n* chronic
skin disease in which the parts affected become hard, rough, and
greatly enlarged

el·e·phan·tine /el'əfant'īn, -tīn, -tēn/
adj 1 huge; unwieldy, clumsy; 2
pert. to or resembling an elephant

el·e·vate /el'əvāt'/ [L *elevare* (*-atus*)
to lift] *vt* 1 to raise to a higher level;
lift; 2 to raise to a higher rank; 3
to exalt intellectually, morally, or
spiritually ‖ SYN promote, exalt, dignify, cheer, erect, heighten

el'e·vat'ed (rail'road) *n* railroad operating on an elevated structure above
city streets

el'e·va'tion *n* 1 act of raising or state
of being raised; 2 raised place; 3
height above a specific level, esp.
sea level; altitude; 4 angular height
of a heavenly body above the horizon; 5 representation of the front,
one of the sides, or the rear of a
structure ‖ SYN height, altitude,
eminence, loftiness, exaltation

el'e·va'tor *n* 1 that which elevates; 2
cage or platform moving up and
down in a shaft to carry people or
goods from one level to another;
3 warehouse for the storage, lifting,
and distribution of grain; 4 movable
plane surface for controlling the altitude or inclination of an airplane

e·lev·en /ilev'ən/ [OE *endleofan*] *n* 1
one more than ten (11; XI);
2 team having eleven players ‖ also
adj & *pron*

e·lev'enth [OE *endlyfta*] *n* 1 the one
next in order after the tenth; 2 one
of eleven equal parts ‖ also *adj*

e·lev'enth hour' *n* last moment or opportunity for doing something

elf /elf/ [OE *ælf*] *n* (**elves** /-vz/)
fairy tales & folklore tiny mischievous sprite supposed to haunt hills
and wild places; fairy, pixie ‖ **elf'in**
or **elf'ish** *adj*

El Gre·co /el grek'ō/ *n* (Domenikos
Theotokopoulos) (1541-1614) Greek-
born Spanish painter

e·lic·it /ilis'it/ [L *elicere* (*elicitus*)] *vt*
to draw or bring out, as a response
‖ SYN educe, deduce, evoke, extract,
extort

e·lide /ilīd'/ [L *elidere* to strike out]
vt to leave out, omit, as a sound in
pronunciation

el·i·gi·ble /el'ijibəl/ [< L *eligere* to
choose] *adj* 1 fit to be chosen, qualified ‖ *n* 2 one who is eligible ‖
el'i·gi·bil'i·ty /-bil'-/ *n*

E·li·jah /ilīj'ə/ *n* Hebrew prophet of
the 9th century B.C., who was taken
to heaven in a chariot of fire (1 and
2 Kings)

e·lim·i·nate /ilim'ināt'/ [L *eliminare*
(*-atus*) to turn out of doors] *vt* 1 to
remove; 2 to leave out of consideration; 3 to excrete ‖ **e·lim'i·na'tion** *n*
‖ SYN expel, ignore, reject, exclude
‖ DISCR To *exclude* is to keep from
coming in that which has never been
in: the club *excluded* nonmembers
from the game. To *eliminate* is to get
rid of something that is already in
as a part, usually a constituent part;
in reducing expenses, we *eliminate*
unnecessary items

e·li·sion /ilizh'ən/ [see *elide*] *n* omission of the pronunciation of an initial or final unstressed vowel in
hiatus, often shown by a corresponding omission in spelling

e·lite /ilēt', ā-/ [F] *n* 1 best or choicest
part, as of society or a profession; 2
10-point type size, widely used in
typewriters ‖ also *adj*

e·lit·ism *n* 1 belief in the leadership of
an elite; 2 pride in belonging to the
elite ‖ **e·lit'ist** *adj* & *n*

e·lix·ir /ilik'sər/ [ML < Ar *al-iksīr*] *n*
1 aromatic sweetened alcohol solu-
tion containing medicine; 2 preparation sought by the medieval al-
chemists which was believed to prolong life indefinitely and to trans-
mute base metals into gold

E·liz·a·beth /iliz'əbəth/ *n* city in N
New Jersey (110,000)

Elizabeth I *n* (1533-1603) queen of
England 1558-1603

Elizabeth II *n* (1926-) queen of
Great Britain since 1952

E·liz'a·be'than /-bēth'ən, -beth'-/ *adj*
pert. to the times of Elizabeth I ‖
also *n*

elk /elk/ [ME] *n* (**elks** or **elk**) 1 large
old-world mammal (*Alces alces*) of
the deer family, closely akin to the
moose; 2 wapiti

ell¹ /el/ [OE *eln*] *n* former lineal
measure varying from 27 to 48 inches

ell² [< letter L] *n* 1 addition to a building at right angles with the main
structure; 2 right angle joint, as of
a pipe or tubing

el·lipse /ilips'/ [< *ellipsis*] *n* closed
noncircular and symmetrical curve
formed by a plane cutting a cone at
an oblique angle to its axis

el·lip·sis /ilip'sis/ [Gk *elleipsis* omis-
sion] *n* (**-ses** /-sēz/) 1 *gram* omission
of a word or words necessary to
make the grammatical construction

complete; **2** *typ* sign indicating an omission, as * * * or ...

el·lip'tic (-ti·cal) *adj* **1** relating to or formed like an ellipse; **2** pert. to or characterized by ellipsis

elm /elm'/ [OE] *n* any of a genus (*Ulmus*) of large and graceful shade trees having a hard, tough wood

el·o·cu·tion /el'əkyōōsh'ən/ [L *eloqui* (*elocutus*) to make a speech] *n* art of public speaking

e·lon·gate /ilôn'gāt, -loŋ'-/ [L *elongare* (*-atus*)] *vt* & *vi* to stretch, lengthen

e·lon·ga'tion /i-, ē'-/ *n* **1** act of elongating or state of being elongated; **2** angular distance of an interior planet from the sun

e·lope /ilōp'/ [AF *aloper*] *vi* **1** to run off secretly to get married; **2** to run away with a lover || **e·lope'ment** *n*

el·o·quent /el'əkwənt/ [see *elocution*] *adj* forceful, vivid, moving (speech or expression) || **el'o·quent·ly** *adv* || **el'o·quence** *n*

El Pas·o /el pas'ō/ *n* city in W Texas on the Rio Grande (322,261)

El Sal·va·dor /el sal'vədôr/ *n* Spanish-speaking republic in Central America (3,037,000; 8,260 sq.m.; cap. San Salvador) || **Sal'va·dor'an** *adj* & *n*

else /els'/ [OE *elles*] *adv* **1** differently; otherwise; **2** in a different place; **3 or else**, a if not, as *eat or else you'll get sick*; b or suffer the consequences, as **do it or else** || *adj* **4** other, different, as *somebody else*; **5** in addition, as *who else?*

else'where' *adv* in, at, or to some other place

e·lu·ci·date /iloōs'idāt'/ [L *elucidare* (*-atus*)] *vt* & *vi* to make clear, explain || **e·lu'ci·da'tion** *n* SYN illustrate, explain, expound (see *interpret*)

e·lude /ilōōd'/ [L *eludere*] *vt* to avoid or escape; evade ||

e·lu·sive /iloōs'iv/ *adj* **1** tending to elude; **2** hard to grasp mentally

elves /elvz'/ *pl* of **elf**

E·ly·sian /ilizh'ən, ilēzh'-/ *adj* **1** pert. to paradise; **2** full of the greatest bliss or happiness

E·ly'sian Fields' *npl* Gk myth. abode of the blessed after death

E·ly·si·um /ilizh'ē·əm, ilēzh'-, iliz'-, ilēz'-/ [L < Gk *ēlysion* (pedíon) Elysian plain] *n* **1** the Elysian Fields; **2** any place of bliss

em /em'/ [< letter *m*] *n* typ unit of measure of printed matter, equal to the square of the type size used

'em /əm/ [OE *hem*] *pron colloq* them

em- *pref* var of **en-**

e·ma·ci·ate /imāsh'ē·āt'/ [L *emaciare* (*-atus*)] *vt* to waste away the flesh of || **e·ma'ci·at'ed** *adj* || **e·ma'ci·a'tion** *n*

em·a·nate /em'ənāt'/ [L *emanare* (*-atus*) to flow out] *vi* to come forth or issue, as from a source

em'a·na'tion *n* **1** act of emanating; **2** something that emanates; **3** heavy gas produced by the disintegration of radium, thorium, and actinium

e·man·ci·pate /iman'sipāt'/ [L *emancipare* (*-tus*) to release] *vt* to free from bondage, restraint, or control || **e·man'ci·pa'tor** *n* || SYN release, deliver, manumit (see *liberate*)

e·man'ci·pa'tion *n* **1** act of emancipating; **2** state of being emancipated || SYN deliverance, enfranchisement (see *liberty*)

e·mas·cu·late /imas'kyəlāt'/ [L *emasculare* (*-atus*)] *vt* **1** to castrate; **2** to destroy the strength and vigor of by removing a vital part || **e·mas'cu·la'-tion** *n*

em·balm /embäm'/ [MF *embaumer*] *vt* to preserve (a dead body) with drugs and chemicals || **em·balm'er** *n*

em·bank·ment /embaŋk'mənt/ [< *bank¹*] *n* raised structure of stones or earth, to hold back water, carry a road, or for defense || SYN rampart, bulwark, defense, barrier, wall

em·bar·go /embär'gō/ [Sp] *n* (-goes) **1** government order forbidding commercial vessels to enter or leave a port or ports; **2** any legal restriction on commerce; **3** any restraint or prohibition, as against the publication of confidential information || *vt* **4** to lay an embargo on

em·bark /embärk'/ [MF *embarquer*] *vt* **1** to put on board ship || *vi* **2** to board a vessel; **3 embark on** to begin, as a journey or enterprise || **em'-bar·ka'tion** *n*

em·bar·rass /embar'əs/ [F *embarrasser* < Sp *embarazar*] *vt* **1** to abash, disconcert, mortify; **2** to put into financial difficulties; **3** to hinder, impede || **em·bar'rass·ment** *n* SYN entangle, hinder, trouble, abash, confound, confuse, mortify || DISCR To *embarrass* one is so to work upon his feelings in the presence of others as to rob him of composure; he is flustered, and cannot command himself as before. To *abash* one is to put him out of countenance suddenly and utterly, by making him feel ashamed, by belittling him, or by reproving him. A sense of social awkwardness *embarrasses* one; a sense of social inferiority *abashes* one. To *confuse* a person is to put his mental processes to rout; one may be *confused* by cross-examination on the witness stand, and contradict himself. To *confound* is to *confuse* so utterly as to overwhelm || ANT assist, assure, embolden, help, sustain

em·bas·sy /em'bəsē/ [MF *ambassee* < LL *ambactia* mission] *n* (-sies) **1** function, business, or residence of an ambassador; **2** ambassador and his suite

em·bat·tled /embat'əld/ [*em-* + *battle*] *adj* drawn up in fighting order; prepared for battle

em·bed /embed´/ v (-bed·ded; -bed·ding) vt to set in a surrounding mass

em·bel·lish /embel´ish/ [MF embelir (-liss-)] vt 1 to adorn, ornament; 2 to elaborate (a story) by fanciful additions ‖ **em·bel´lish·ment** n ‖ SYN adorn, decorate, bedeck, beautify, ornament

em·ber /em´bər/ [OE ǣmerge] n 1 glowing coal or piece of wood; 2 **embers** pl dying remains of a fire

Em´ber days´ [OE ymbrendǣg] npl period of three days (Wednesday, Friday, and Saturday) set apart for prayer and fasting in a certain week in each of the four seasons of the church year

em·bez·zle /embez´əl/ [AF embeseiller to destroy by fraud] vt to take by fraud (money or property) entrusted to one's care ‖ **em·bez´zler** n ‖ **em·bez´zle·ment** n

em·bit·ter /embit´ər/ vt to make (a person) bitter

em·bla·zon /emblāz´ən/ vt 1 to adorn with heraldic figures; 2 to decorate; display brilliantly; 3 to extol ‖ **em·bla´zon·ry** n

em·blem /em´bləm/ [Gk emblema insertion] n 1 symbol or representation of an idea; 2 badge or sign ‖ **em´-ble·mat´ic (-i·cal)** adj ‖ SYN symbol, sign, type, image, token ‖ DISCR An emblem is an object that stands for another object, or for an idea, by figurative, not direct, representation. A laurel wreath has long been an emblem of achievement; the dove is the emblem of peace; the flag is the emblem of the nation. A symbol stands for some object or idea; it is regarded by general consent as naturally representing this object or idea, and in this sense is synonymous with emblem, as black is the symbol of mourning; the cross is the symbol of Christianity. In another sense, symbol is not synonymous with emblem; a symbol can be a mark or character commonly agreed upon as a conventional representation of some idea or process, as algebraic symbols, or letters and figures employed as chemical symbols. A sign may be a trace or indication, furnishing proof or evidence, as a sign of spring; marks of blood were signs that the burglar was wounded. A sign, too, may be an arbitrary mark, used to designate an idea or thing, as the plus sign; the sign of the cross; a word sign in stenography. In this latter sense, sign comes close to symbol in meaning. A token is something given or done as a guarantee of authority, authenticity, or good faith, or as a pledge or memorial, as he sent his watch as a token that the message was authentic. Token in some cases is synonymous with sym-

bol and sign, as they flew a red flag from the tower as a token of defiance

em·bod·i·ment /embod´imənt/ n concrete expression; incarnation

em·bod´y v (-ied) vt 1 to give bodily form to; 2 to express in definite form; 3 to include in a united whole; incorporate ‖ SYN comprehend, include, comprise, clothe

em·bold·en /embōld´ən/ vt to make bold, encourage ‖ SYN encourage, hearten, assure, inspirit, animate

em·bo·lism /em´bəliz´əm/ [Gk embolismos] n obstruction of a blood vessel, as by a clot of blood

em·boss /embôs´, -bos´/ [< boss¹] vt 1 to ornament with raised work; 2 to raise in relief above the surface

em·bow·er /embou´ər/ vt to enclose or shelter in or as in a bower

em·brace /embrās´/ [OF embracer] vt 1 to clasp in the arms, hug; 2 to receive with willingness; 3 to adopt gladly; take up; 4 to include; 5 to enclose ‖ vi 6 to hug each other ‖ n 7 act of embracing, hug ‖ SYN v accept, comprise, clasp, encompass, encircle, enclose (see comprehend) ‖ ANT v repel, repulse

em·brac´er·y [< MF embraseor instigator] n (-ies) attempt to influence a jury by corrupt means

em·bra·sure /embrāzh´ər/ [F] n 1 opening in a parapet or wall, usu. widening toward the outside, from which guns may be fired; 2 beveled opening in a wall, widening toward the inside, as for a door or window

em·broi·der /embroid´ər/ [MF embroder] vt 1 to adorn with needlework; 2 to embellish or exaggerate, as a story ‖ vt 3 to do decorative needlework ‖ **em·broi´der·y** n (-ies)

em·broil /embroil´/ [MF embrouiller] vt 1 to involve in discord or contention; 2 to confuse; entangle ‖ **em·broil´ment** n ‖ SYN complicate, perplex, implicate, involve, trouble

em·bry·o /em´brē·ō/ [Gk embryon ingrowing] n 1 anything in an early undeveloped stage; 2 the young of an animal in the earliest stages of development, before birth or hatching; in mammals, the unborn young before life becomes apparent; 3 young plant partly formed in the seed ‖ **em´bry·on´ic** /-on´-/ adj

em·bry·ol·o·gy /-ol´ə·jē/ n study of the embryo, its formation and development ‖ **em´bry·ol´o·gist** n

em·cee /em´sē´/ [< M.C.] n 1 master of ceremonies ‖ vt 2 to act as master of ceremonies of ‖ also vi

e·mend /imend´/ [L emendare (-atus)] vt to alter or correct, as a literary text ‖ **e´men·da´tion** /ēm´ən-/ n

em·er·ald /em´(ə)rəld/ [MF esmeralde < Gk smaragdos] n 1 brilliant green gem, a double silicate of beryllium and aluminum; 2 rich green color

Em′er·ald Isle′ *n* the island of Ireland

e·merge /imurj′/ [L *emergere*] *vi* **1** to rise up, as from a fluid; **2** to come forth, become visible or apparent ‖ **e·mer′gence** *n* ‖ **e·mer′gent** *adj*

e·mer′gen·cy *n* (-cies) sudden or unexpected happening, demanding prompt action ‖ SYN exigency, crisis, necessity, pass, conjuncture ‖ DISCR These words agree in the idea of naming a pressing state of affairs. An *emergency* names such a condition as demands immediate action; it is sudden, unforeseen, and urgent. An *exigency*, too, is urgent, but it names a need rising out of a certain situation, rather than, like *emergency*, the situation itself. The *exigencies* of a journey require certain expenditures, adjustments, etc.; the loss, after one had started, of all the money one had provided for a journey in a strange land, would constitute an *emergency*. A *crisis* is such a turning point in one's affairs as to make a decision or decisive change necessary. Things that have come to a *crisis* can no longer go on; they must alter for better or for worse

e·mer′gen·cy brake′ *n* hand-set parking brake in an automobile

e·merg′ing na′tions *npl* underdeveloped nations that are beginning to realize their potential

e·mer·i·tus /imer′itəs/ [L = having served one's time] *adj* retired from active service but retaining honorary rank and title, as *professor emeritus* ‖ also *n* (-ti /-tī′/) ‖ **e·mer′i·ta** /-tə/ *adj & nfem* (-tae /-tē′/)

Em·er·son, Ralph Wal·do /ralf′ wôl′dō em′ərsən/ *n* (1803–82) U.S. essayist and poet ‖ **Em′er·so′ni·an** /-sōn′-ē-ən/ *adj*

em·er·y /em′ərē/ [MF *emeri* < Gk *smeris* polishing powder] *n* corundum in granular form mixed with oxides of iron and manganese, used for grinding and polishing

e·met·ic /imet′ik/ [Gk *emetikos*] *adj* **1** inducing vomiting ‖ *n* **2** emetic substance

emf, e.m.f., EMF, E.M.F. electromotive force

-e·mi·a /-ēm′ē-ə/ [< Gk *haima* blood] *n suf* (specified) condition of the blood, as *leukemia*

em·i·grate /em′igrāt′/ [L *emigrare* (-atus) to move away] *vi* to leave a country or region to settle in another ‖ **em′i·gra′tion** *n* ‖ **em′i·grant** /-grənt/ *adj & n*

é·mi·gré /em′igrā′/ [F] *n* emigrant, esp. a political refugee

em·i·nence /em′inəns/ *n* **1** high place; elevation or hill; **2** exalted rank, station, or repute; **3** Eminence title of honor given to cardinals

em·i·nent [L *eminens* (-entis)] *adj* **1** elevated; **2** high in merit, rank, or reputation; **3** conspicuous; noteworthy ‖ **em′i·nent·ly** *adv* ‖ SYN celebrated, illustrious (see *distinguished*)

em′i·nent do·main′ *n* right of the state to take private property for public use

e·mir /imir′/ [Ar *amīr* commander] *n* Arab prince or chieftain

e·mir′ate /-it, -āt/ *n* rank or domain of an emir

em·is·sar·y /em′iser′ē/ [see *emit*] *n* (-ies) agent sent on a specific mission

e·mis·sion /imish′ən/ *n* **1** act of emitting; **2** that which is emitted; discharge

e·mit /imit′/ [L *emittere* (*emissus*)] *v* (-mit·ted; -mit·ting) *vt* to send or give forth, as light, heat, sound, etc.

em·men·a·gogue /əmen′əgôg′, -gog′/ [< Gk *emmena* menses + -*agogue*] *n* medicine that promotes the menstrual flow

e·mol·lient /imol′yənt/ [L *emolliens* (-entis)] *adj* **1** softening or soothing to the skin or mucous membrane ‖ *n* **2** emollient substance

e·mol·u·ment /imol′yəmənt/ [< L *emoliri* to produce by exertion] *n* compensation or salary; remuneration

e·mo·tion /imōsh′ən/ [< L *emovere* (*emotus*) to move out] *n* **1** excited state of mind; **2** feeling of love, hate, joy, fear, or the like; **3** capacity for feeling; consciousness characterized by feeling ‖ SYN feeling, passion, sentiment, fervor (see *feeling*)

e·mo′tion·al *adj* **1** pert. to, caused by, or showing emotion; **2** easily affected by emotion; **3** appealing to the emotions ‖ **e·mo′tion·al·ly** *adv* ‖ **e·mo′tion·al·ism** *n*

e·mo′tive /imōt′iv/ *adj* pert. to or characterized by the emotions

em·pa·thize /em′pəthīz′/ *vi* to feel empathy

em·pa·thy /em′pəthē/ [Gk *empatheia* affection] *n* emotional or intellectual identification with another person

em·per·or /emp′ərər/ [OF *empereor* < L *imperator* commander] *n* sovereign or ruler of an empire

em·pha·sis /emf′əsis/ [Gk = outward appearance] *n* (-ses /-sēz′/) **1** importance, stress; **2** special stress of the voice calling attention to a particular word, phrase, or syllable; **3** forceful expression

em′pha·size′ *vt* to stress or give emphasis to

em·phat·ic /-fat′ik/ *adj* **1** done with emphasis; forceful; **2** striking ‖ **em·phat′i·cal·ly** *adv*

em·phy·se·ma /em′fisēm′ə/ [Gk = inflation] *n* condition in which the lungs lose their power to deflate and become distended with air

em·pire /em′pī(ə)r/ [OF < L *imperium*] *n* **1** group of nations, territories, and peoples under one rule; **2** any country, generally more extensive than a kingdom, ruled by an emperor or empress; **3** imperial power, domain, or government; **4** large holdings in a field or industry, as *a publishing empire* || *adj* **5 Empire** of or pert. to the first French Empire (1804–15); **6 Empire** of or pert. to a style of architecture, decoration, and furniture, characterized esp. by Egyptian motifs, which prevailed in France in the early decades of the 19th cent.

em·pir·ic (-i-cal) /empir'ik(ə)l/ [<Gk *empeirikos* experienced] *adj* based on or guided by experience or experiment || **em·pir'i·cal·ly** *adv* || **em·pir'i·cism** *n* || **em·pir'i·cist** *n*

em·place·ment /emplās'mənt/ *n* **1** placing; location; **2** platform or position of a heavy gun in a fortification

em·ploy /emploi'/ [MF *employer* < L *implicare* to fold in] *vt* **1** to engage the services of; **2** to use; **3** to keep busy || *n* **4** employment || **em·ploy'er** *n* || SYN *v* use, hire, occupy, busy || DISCR As applied to things, *employ* and *use* are interchangeable, though *employ* often carries the idea of making a special use of, as we *used* such methods of demonstrating as appealed to the eye; for this particular purpose we *employed* charts. In those cases, however, which naturally involve the destruction or consumption of the article *used*, *employ* cannot be substituted; we say that we *use*, not *employ*, five pounds of sugar per week. As applied to persons, *use* connotes degradation; one who lets himself be *used* for another's purpose deserves contempt. *Employ* and *hire* differ chiefly in a point of emphasis and consequent dignity; *employ* stresses the idea of the service rendered, and so is more dignified than *hire*, which frankly stresses the pay received

em·ploy·ee also **em·ploy·e** /emploi'ē, em'ploi·ē'/ *n* one who works for another for pay

em·ploy'ment *n* **1** act or state of being employed; **2** work, occupation || SYN engagement, trade, work, service (see *business*)

em·po·ri·um /empôr'ē·əm, -pōr'-/ [Gk *emporion* < *emporos* merchant] *n* (-ums or -a /-ə/) **1** commercial center or place of trade; **2** large department store

em·pow·er /empou'ər/ *vt* **1** to authorize; **2** to enable

em·press /emp'ris/ [OF *emperesse*] *n* **1** female ruler of an empire; **2** emperor's consort

emp·ty /em(p)'tē/ [OE *ǣmetig* at leisure] *adj* (-ti·er; -ti·est) **1** containing nothing; **2** vacant; unoccupied; **3** devoid of content or meaning; **4** *colloq* hungry || *n* (-ties) **5** *colloq* something empty, as a bottle or car-

ton || *v* (-tied) *vt* **6** to make empty; **7** to pour out, discharge || *vi* **8** to become empty || **emp'ti·ness** *n* || SYN *adj* vacant, blank, unfilled, inane, hollow, unoccupied, void || DISCR That is *empty* which has nothing in it; that is *vacant* which lacks what is supposed to fill or occupy it. An *empty* house is bare of furniture. A *vacant* house contains no inmates. A house, however, can be *empty* yet not *vacant*; and, on the other hand, a house to be let furnished can be *vacant* and not *empty*. Figuratively, *empty* and *vacant* have similar meanings; an *empty* honor leaves its recipient as well off as he was before; a *vacant* hour has nothing planned to fill it; a *vacant* stare is dull and idiotic. *Blank* describes that which is free from any writing or marks, as unused paper, or spaces, in printed matter, left to be filled in

emp'ty-hand'ed *adj* **1** with empty hands; **2** with nothing to show for one's efforts

em·py·e·ma /em'pī·ēm'ə/ [Gk = abscess] *n* accumulation of pus in a body cavity, esp. the pleural cavity

em·py·re·an /em'pərē'ən, -pī-/ [< Gk *empyrios* fiery] *n* **1** highest heaven, thought by the ancients to be composed of pure fire; **2** sky, heaven || also *adj*

e·mu /ē'myōō/ [< Port *ema* crane] *n* flightless ostrichlike bird (*Dromiceius novaehollandiae*) of Australia

em·u·late /em'yəlāt'/ [L *aemulari* (-*atus*)] *vt* **1** to try to equal or excel; **2** to equal or match || **em'u·la'tor** *n*

em·u·la'tion *n* **1** act of emulating; **2** imitation of another || SYN competition, opposition, rivalry, ambition, strife || DISCR *Competition* is a contest between those who are trying to gain the same object at the same time. *Emulation* is a striving to equal or surpass others; it is born of the contemplation of another's greatness, and the desire to outdo him; hence, it may be directed toward following the example of one who is dead. An author might strive in *competition* with living authors for a short-story prize, he might work in *emulation* of the smooth style of Stevenson. The result of *competition* is usually tangible; that of *emulation* may be one of feeling or attitude, as such industry as his either excites our *emulation*, or plunges us into apathetic despair. *Rivalry* exists between those striving against each other for favor in love or politics, for greatness, for influence, or the like. Those engaged in *rivalry* are often unfriendly, if not hostile; *competition* may be good-natured; *emulation* is honorable and commendable

e·mul·si·fy /imul'sifī'/ *v* (-fied) *vt* to

make or form into an emulsion ‖
e·mul′si·fi′er n ‖ e·mul′si·fi·ca′tion n

e·mul·sion /imul′shən/ [< L emulsus
milked out] n 1 suspension of one
liquid in another; 2 photog light-
sensitive coating consisting of silver
salts suspended in gelatine and
placed on film; 3 any milklike mixture or solution

en /en′/ [< letter n] n typ half the
width of an em

en- [OF < L in] v pref 1 in or into, as
ensnare; 2 on, as engrave; 3 to make,
as enfeeble

-en¹ /-ən/ [OE -nian] v suf to make,
as redden

-en² [OE] adj suf made of, as wooden

-en³ suf ending of the past participle of
many strong verbs, as eaten

en·a·ble /enāb′əl/ vt to render able;
furnish with means or power

en·act /enakt′/ vt 1 to decree, make
into law; 2 to carry to completion;
accomplish; 3 to act the part of; impersonate

en·act′ment n 1 process of enacting; 2
law or decree

e·nam·el /inam′əl/ [MF enamailler] n
1 opaque glassy substance fused on
metal, glass, or pottery for protection or decoration; 2 hard, glossy
varnish or paint; 3 hard glossy coating for the nails; 4 hard white outer
coating of the teeth ‖ v (-eled or
-elled; -el·ing or -el·ling) vt 5 to coat
with enamel

e·nam′el·ware′ n kitchen utensils made
of enameled metal

en·am·or /enam′ər/ [OF enamourer]
vt to inflame with love; captivate;
charm

en·camp /enkamp′/ vt & vi to lodge
or settle in a camp ‖ en·camp′ment
n

en·case /enkās′/ vt to enclose in or as
in a case

-ence /-əns/ [OF < L -entia] n suf act,
quality, state, or result, as divergence

en·ceinte /ensānt′/ [F] adj pregnant

en·ceph·a·li·tis /ensef′əlīt′is/ [< Gk en-
kephalon brain] n 1 inflammation of
the brain; 2 sleeping sickness ‖ en-
ceph′a·lit′ic /-lit′ik/ adj

en·chant /enchant′, -chänt′/ [MF en-
chanter < L incantare] vt 1 to cast
a spell over; 2 to charm, captivate
‖ en·chant′er n ‖ en·chant′ress nfem
‖ en·chant′ing adj ‖ en·chant′ment
n ‖ SYN captivate, allure, delight,
enrapture, fascinate

en·cir·cle /ensurk′əl/ vt to surround,
encompass; ring about ‖ en·cir′cle-
ment n

en·clave /en′klāv/ [F] n district of a
country entirely or almost entirely
surrounded by the territory of another

en·clit·ic /enklit′ik/ [Gk enklitikos] n
word joined to a preceding word and

pronounced without accent ‖ also
adj

en·close /-klōz′/ vt 1 to surround,
close in; 2 to insert in an envelope
or package

en·clo′sure /-zhər/ n 1 act of enclosing or state of being enclosed; 2
that which is enclosed; 3 paper or
document enclosed with a letter; 4
that which encloses, as a fence

en·code /enkōd′/ vt to convert into
code

en·co·mi·um /enkōm′ē·əm/ [Gk enko-
mion] n (-ums; -a /-ə-/) high praise;
eulogy ‖ SYN applause, praise, panegyric (see eulogy)

en·com·pass /enkump′əs/ vt 1 to surround, encircle; 2 to contain, include ‖ en·com′pass·ment n

en·core /än′kôr/ [F] interj 1 once
more!, again! ‖ n 2 repetition of a
performance in response to the call
or applause of the audience ‖ vt 3
to applaud for a the repetition of (a
performance) or b the reappearance
of (a performer)

en·coun·ter /enkount′ər/ [OF encon-
trer < L contra against] vt 1 to meet
in conflict; 2 to meet unexpectedly;
3 to come across ‖ vi 4 to meet in
conflict ‖ n 5 combat; 6 unexpected
meeting

en·cour·age /enkur′ij/ [MF encoragier]
vt 1 to hearten, inspire; 2 to help,
foster ‖ en·cour′age·ment n ‖ SYN
countenance, embolden, hearten, promote, urge, cheer ‖ ANT discourage,
dispirit, depress, dishearten

en·cour′ag·ing adj 1 inspiring, stimulating; giving confidence; 2 fostering
‖ SYN hopeful, opportune, fortunate,
promising, auspicious ‖ ANT hopeless, inauspicious, censorious

en·croach /enkrōch′/ [OF encrochier
to hook in] vi 1 to infringe or trespass on another's rights; 2 to advance gradually beyond due limits ‖
en·croach′ment n

en·crust /enkrust′/ vt & vi var of in-
crust

en·cum·ber /enkum′bər/ [MF encom-
brer] vt 1 to hamper or hinder; 2
to load down; burden ‖ SYN burden,
overload, hinder, impede, hamper,
obstruct, embarrass ‖ ANT relieve,
help, assist, ease

en·cum′brance n 1 that which encum-
bers; 2 law lien or claim on property
‖ SYN load, burden, pack, weight,
obstruction, impediment ‖ DISCR A
burden is a weight that bears one
down with the labor and difficulty
of sustaining it. A load is that which
is to be carried; a load may be light
or heavy. Burdens are commonly
borne by living beings, chiefly by
persons; loads may be carried by
people, animals, or conveyances. A
man may take a burden upon himself, or have it thrust upon him; a

load is usually laid on. Both *load* and *burden* apply to that which bears down upon the mind or spirit as well as upon the body. An *encumbrance* is such an additional *weight* as is burdensome, hindering, or retarding; debts, mortgages, lack of credit, are financial *encumbrances* (see *hindrance*)

-en·cy /-ənsē/ *n suf* equivalent of *-ence*

en·cyc·li·cal /ensik′likəl, -sīk′-/ [< Gk *enkyklios* circular] *n* letter from the pope to all the bishops of the church ‖ also *adj*

en·cy·clo·pe·di·a also **-pae-** /ensī′klə-pēd′ē-ə/ [< Gk *enkylios paideia* general education] *n* work in one or more volumes with articles in usu. alphabetical order on all branches of knowledge, or on all aspects of one branch

en·cy·clo·pe·dic also **-pae-** *adj* 1 pert. to encyclopedias; 2 comprehensive, as *an encyclopedic memory*

en·cyst /ensist′/ *biol vt* 1 to enclose in a cyst ‖ *vi* 2 to become enclosed in a cyst

end /end′/ [OE *ende*] *n* 1 termination or conclusion; 2 last part; 3 extreme limit or ultimate point; 4 extremity, tip; 5 death; 6 remnant; 7 object or purpose; 8 consequence or result; 9 *football* player stationed at either extremity of the line; **10 at loose ends** without definite plans or occupation; **11 at one's wit's end** not knowing what to do in a given situation; **12 end to end** in line with the ends touching each other; **13 keep** or **hold one's end up** to do one's full share; **14 make (both) ends meet** to live within one's income; **15 on end, a** upright; **b** continuously; **16 put an end to** to terminate ‖ *vt* 17 to finish, conclude ‖ *vi* 18 to come to an end; 19 to die; **20 end up, a** to finish; **b** to find oneself; **c** turn out to be ‖ SYN *n* (see *design*); *v* (see *close*)

end′-all′ *n* end of all things

en·dan·ger /endān′jər/ *vt* to expose to danger

en·dear /endir′/ *vt* to render beloved ‖ **en·dear′ing·ly** *adv*

en·dear′ment *n* 1 affection; 2 expression of affection

en·deav·or /endev′ər/ [ME *endeveren*] *vi* 1 to strive, try hard ‖ *n* 2 earnest attempt ‖ SYN *v* try, essay, aim, attempt; *n* (see *effort*)

en·dem·ic /endem′ik/ [< Gk *endemos*] *adj* 1 peculiar to a nation, people, or locality, as a disease ‖ *n* 2 endemic disease

end′ing *n* 1 conclusion, termination; 2 *gram* inflectional suffix

en·dive /en′dīv, än′dēv/ [MF] *n* herb (*Cichorium endivia*) of the composite family with curled leaves used as a salad

end′less *adj* 1 continuing forever, hav-

ing no end; 2 without ends, forming a closed loop, as *an endless chain* ‖ **end′less·ly** ‖ SYN continual, incessant (see *eternal*)

end′ man′ *n* one of the men on either end of the semicircle of a minstrel troupe who supply most of the humor

end′most′ *adj* farthest, most remote

en·do- [Gk] *comb form* within

en·do·car·di·um /en′dōkär′dē-əm/ [< *endo-* + Gk *kardia* heart] *n* serous membrane lining the heart

en·do·carp /en′dōkärp′/ [< *endo-* + Gk *karpos* fruit] *n* inner layer of a fruit having two covering layers, as that covering the seeds in an apple

en′do·crine /-krin, -krīn′, -krēn′/ [< *endo-* + Gk *krinein* to separate] *adj* secreting internally

en′do·crine gland′ *n* gland that secretes directly into the blood or lymph, instead of through a duct, as the thyroid or pituitary

en·dog·a·my /endog′əmē/ [< *endo-* + Gk *gamos* marriage] *n* marriage only within a tribe or social unit ‖ **en·dog′a·mous** *adj*

en·dorse /endôrs′/ [OF *endosser*] *vt* 1 to write a signature or the like on the back of (a check, paper, or other document); 2 to support, sanction ‖ **en·dorse′ment** *n*

en·do·ther·mic /en′dōthur′mik/ [< *endo-* + Gk *therme* heat] *adj* designating a chemical change in which heat is absorbed

en·dow /endou′/ [F *endouer* to provide with a dower] *vt* 1 to bequeath or give a permanent income or fund to; 2 to equip, furnish, as with natural gifts

en·dow′ment *n* 1 money or property settled upon a person or institution or devoted permanently to a cause; 2 act of making such a settlement; 3 **endowments** *pl* gifts of nature ‖ SYN aptitude, faculty, capacity, bent, talent, power (see *gift*) ‖ ANT incapacity, ineptitude, lack

end′ pa′per *n* folded sheet of paper with one half pasted down on the inside cover of a book and the other half pasted along the fold to the base of the first or last page

en·due /end(y)oo̅′/ [OF *enduire*] *vt* to invest, furnish, as with qualities, faculties, or gifts

en·dur·ance /end(y)oo̅r′əns/ *n* 1 power of enduring; 2 continuance, duration ‖ SYN fortitude, resignation, sufferance (see *patience*)

en·dure /end(y)oo̅r′/ [OF *endurer*] *vt* 1 to sustain or undergo without breaking or yielding; 2 to put up with, tolerate ‖ *vi* 3 to remain firm, as under adversity; 4 to last ‖ **en·dur′a·ble** ‖ SYN tolerate, abide, brook, stand (see *bear²*)

en·dur′ing *adj* lasting ‖ SYN fixed, unchanging, forbearing (see *permanent*)

end'ways' or **end'wise'** *adv* 1 on end; upright; 2 with the end forward or uppermost; 3 lengthwise

-ene /-ēn', -ēn/ [Gk *adj suf*] *n suf* unsaturated hydrocarbon, as *benzene*

en·e·ma /en'əmə/ [Gk] *n* 1 injection of a liquid into the rectum; 2 the injected liquid

en·e·my /en'əmē/ [OF *enemi* < L *inimicus* unfriendly] *n* (**-mies**) 1 hostile person, foe; 2 hostile nation or military force ‖ also *adj* ‖ SYN adversary, opponent, antagonist, foe, rival, competitor ‖ DISCR These words agree in naming an opposing agent. *Enemy*, as here compared, is the strongest term, connoting not only one who hates, but one who desires to injure the object of his hatred. An *enemy* is therefore personally hostile. *Foe*, in modern usage, is a literary or poetic equivalent for *enemy*, though it formerly indicated a more intense, because implacable, hatred. Since one cannot hate himself implacably, one can be his own worst *enemy*, but not his own *foe*. An *opponent* is one who upholds an opposite view, as in a debate, and can be quite without hostile or personal feeling. *Antagonist* names one who is engaged in an actual struggle and is influenced by animosity. *Adversary* names one hostilely and bitterly arrayed against another, with a feeling always personal. A *rival* is one who is striving to win the same goal at the same time as another, usually in the field of love, war, or politics ‖ ANT friend, ally, helper

en·er·get·ic /en'ərjet'ik/ *adj* 1 vigorous in action; forcible; 2 full of energy ‖ **en'er·get'i·cal·ly** *adv* ‖ SYN industrious, strenuous, potent, forceful, effective, vigorous ‖ ANT lazy, lax, languid, lifeless

en·er·gize' *vt* to activate; give energy to

en·er·gy [Gk *energeia* activity] *n* (**-gies**) 1 power or capacity for work; 2 strength, power, or spirit shown in words or action; 3 *phys* capacity to do work and to overcome resistance ‖ SYN power, force, vigor, strength, might ‖ DISCR *Power* is that principle which in all things moves, governs, changes, effects, accomplishes. The *power* of the mind to think, the *power* of a nation to enforce its laws, the *power* of an animal to move— these examples show how general is the application of the word. *Power* may be exerted or latent. *Energy, force, vigor,* and *strength* are particular forms of *power*. *Energy* has its root in the mind, and is the *power* of producing an effect, whether ex-

erted or not. A speech which galvanizes a sleepy audience into life is an example of *energy* actively at work. To predict that a man will act in a certain way under given conditions because of the *energy* of his character is to bank on a latent ability for efficient action. *Force* can mean *power* exerted on an object, it can mean mental and moral *strength*, or it can indicate constraint or coercion, as the *force* of a collision; the *force* of a stream of water or current of electricity; *force* of character; the *force* of an upright or unyielding attitude of mind; a promise obtained by *force*. *Strength* of mind connotes resolution; *strength* of soul, the *power* to endure or persevere in the face of temptation or heartache; *strength* of body implies a frame, a muscular system, and a constitution capable of standing up under severe physical strain. *Vigor* is that fresh quality of mind and body that has its roots in health ‖ ANT lifelessness, languor, lassitude

en'er·gy cri'sis *n* crisis in the availability of all sources of power, esp. fossil fuels

en·er·vate /en'ərvāt'/ [L *enervare* (*-atus*)] *vt* to deprive of nerve, force, or vigor ‖ **en'er·va'tion** *n*

en·fee·ble /enfēb'əl/ *vt* to weaken, make feeble

en·fi·lade /en'filād', en'filād'/ [F] *mil* *n* 1 raking fire from a line of troops or guns ‖ *vt* 2 to subject to an enfilade

en·fold /enfōld'/ *vt* 1 to wrap up, envelop; 2 to cover with folds; 3 to embrace

en·force /enfôrs', -fōrs'/ [OF *enforcier*] *vt* 1 to compel obedience to; 2 to impose (obedience); 3 to compel by force ‖ **en·force'a·ble** *adj* ‖ **en·force'ment** *n*

en·fran·chise /enfran'chīz/ [OF *enfranchir* (*-iss-*)] *vt* 1 to admit to the right to vote; 2 to free from slavery ‖ **en·fran'chise·ment** /-chīz-/ *n*

eng. engineer(ing)

Eng. 1 England; 2 English

en·gage /engāj'/ [MF *engager*] *vt* 1 to bind by oath or contract; 2 to betroth; 3 to hire; 4 *mil* to enter into conflict with; 5 *mach* to interlock with, mesh ‖ *vi* 6 to assume an obligation; 7 to occupy oneself; 8 *mil* to enter or open a conflict; 9 *mach* to mesh; interlock

en·ga·gé /äNgäzh䒒/ [F = engaged] *adj* involved, committed, not neutral or aloof

en·gaged' *adj* 1 busy; 2 affianced or betrothed; 3 embroiled in a conflict; 4 geared together; 5 *arch.* (column or pillar) partly attached to or built into another part ‖ SYN promised, bespoken (see *busy*)

en·gage′ment n 1 occupation; 2 betrothal; 3 appointment; 4 battle; 5 liability, commitment; 6 *mach* state of being in gear

en·gag′ing adj charming; attractive ‖ **en·gag′ing·ly** adv

en·gen·der /enjen′dər/ [OF *engendrer*] vt to beget, bring into being

en·gine /en′jin/ [OF *engin* < L *ingenium* skill] n 1 machine that converts heat energy into mechanical energy; 2 railway locomotive; 3 fire engine; 4 any mechanical contrivance

en·gi·neer′ n 1 one who practices engineering professionally; 2 one who operates an engine or locomotive; 3 one of a group trained in building bridges, roads, etc. for military use; 4 one who engineers ‖ vt 5 to plan, lay out, or direct

en·gi·neer′ing n science or art of planning, constructing, and using machinery, or of designing and constructing buildings, roads, bridges, plants, systems, etc.

Eng·land /iŋ′glənd/ n country in and part of Great Britain, a constituent of the United Kingdom (45,000,000; 50,874 sq.m.; cap. London) ‖ **Eng′land·er** n

Eng·lish /iŋ′glish/ [OE *englisc*] adj 1 of or pert. to England, its language, or its people ‖ n 2 language of England and of the British Isles, the British colonies, most of the British Commonwealth nations, and the U.S.; 3 often **english** *billiards* spinning motion imparted to a ball by striking it off center; 4 **the English** pl the people of England

Eng′lish Chan′nel n arm of the Atlantic - between England and France, connecting on the east with the North Sea

Eng′lish horn′ n large oboe, lower-pitched and with a richer tone, and having a pear-shaped bell

Eng′lish·man /-mən/ n (-men /-mən/) native or inhabitant of England ‖ **Eng′lish·wom′an** nfem (-wom′en)

Eng′lish muf′fin n muffin made from yeast dough and served toasted

Eng′lish sad′dle n saddle without a horn and with full side flaps and a padded seat

en·graft′ vt 1 to insert (a shoot) in a tree; graft; 2 to cause to take root, as an idea in the mind

en·grave /engrāv′/ [*en-* + *grave*[1]] vt 1 to cut or carve (letters or designs) on a hard surface; 2 to print from an engraved metal plate; 3 to impress deeply ‖ **en·grav′er** n

en·grav′ing n 1 act or art of an engraver; 2 engraved design; 3 engraved plate or block; 4 print made from such a plate

en·gross /engrōs′/ [AF *engrosser*] vt 1 to absorb; occupy wholly; 2 to write in a large distinct hand, as a public document ‖ syn absorb, swallow, engulf, occupy, engage

en·gross′ing adj absorbing; occupying the mind fully

en·gulf /en·gulf′/ vt to swallow up

en·hance /enhans′, -häns′/ [AF *enhauncer*] vt to intensify; augment ‖ **en·hance′ment** n

e·nig·ma /ənig′mə/ [Gk *ainigma*] n 1 riddle; 2 puzzling situation or person ‖ **e·nig·mat·ic** /en′igmat′ik, ēn′-/ adj ‖ syn conundrum, puzzle, problem, riddle

en·join /enjoin′/ [OF *enjoindre*] vt 1 to direct, command; 2 *law* to prohibit or restrain by judicial order ‖ syn prescribe, charge, admonish, order, require, bid, govern ‖ ant submit, yield, obey

en·joy /enjoi′/ [OF *enjoier* to give joy to] vt 1 to feel, sense, or perceive with pleasure; 2 to have the use or possession of; 3 **enjoy oneself** to have a pleasant time ‖ **en·joy′a·ble** adj

en·joy′ment n 1 act of enjoying; 2 that which provides satisfaction or joy ‖ syn satisfaction, delight, felicity, comfort, pleasure (see *happiness*) ‖ ant misery, wretchedness, discomfort

en·kin·dle vt 1 to set afire; to kindle; 2 to rouse; stir up, as a revolt or the passions

en·large /enlärj′/ [OF *enlargier*] vt 1 to make larger; increase; expand ‖ vi 2 to become larger; 3 **enlarge on** or **upon**, a to comment fully on; b to exaggerate ‖ **en·large′ment** n ‖ syn augment, broaden, expand, magnify ‖ ant diminish, reduce, abbreviate, decrease, curtail

en·light·en /enlīt′ən/ vt 1 to inform, instruct; 2 to endow with insight, free from ignorance ‖ **en·light′en·ment** n

en·list /enlist′/ vt 1 to enroll or engage for military or other public service ‖ vi 2 to engage oneself as for military service

en·list′ed man′ n member of the armed forces who is not a commissioned or warrant officer

en·list′ment n 1 act of enlisting; 2 period of time for which one enlists in the armed forces

en·liv·en /enlīv′ən/ vt 1 to make active; quicken; 2 to cheer, brighten up ‖ syn cheer, animate, inspire, rouse, exhilarate ‖ ant sadden, quiet, discourage, dampen

en masse /en mas′/ [F] adv collectively; all together

en·mesh /enmesh′/ vt to entangle in or as in a net

en·mi·ty /en′mitē/ [MF *enemite*] n (-ties) hostility; deep-seated ill will ‖ syn hostility, animosity, maliciousness, unfriendliness, bitterness, contention ‖ discr *Enmity* is a deep feeling of resentment or malice toward another. *Enmity* is personal, and may be latent; in the heart of one who awaits an opportunity to do evil, **enmity** may lie concealed, but nourished, for many years. If **enmity** is made manifest in action, it becomes **hostility**. **Hostility** is open and malicious. **Hostilities** between countries mean active fighting. **Animosity** is active **enmity** fired by a vindictive and passionate state of the feelings; it is so hot that it burns itself out, and hence is often a passing fever of ill will ‖ ANT friendliness, love, affection, good will, kindliness, sympathy

en·no·ble /enōb'əl/ [MF *ennoblir*] *vt* 1 to exalt, dignify; 2 to elevate to the nobility ‖ **en·no'ble·ment** *n*

en·nui /änwē'/ [F] *n* boredom; listlessness

e·nor·mi·ty /inôr'mitē/ *n* (-ties) 1 immensity; 2 atrociousness; 3 something outrageous ‖ SYN enormousness ‖ DISCR *Enormity* is used figuratively in reference to a great evil or crime; *enormousness* has literal application to great size or amount

e·nor·mous /inôr'məs/ [< MF *enorme* huge] *adj* very great; immense, vast ‖ **e·nor'mous·ly** *adv* ‖ SYN huge, immense, vast, colossal, prodigious, excessive, stupendous, gigantic ‖ DISCR That is *enormous* which far exceeds the ordinary size, number, or degree; *enormous* usually implies an excess that is out of proportion, or even abnormal. A man seven feet tall, an apple grown to three times the average size of its variety, the wickedness of Sodom, may all be termed *enormous*. *Huge* describes that which is very great or superlatively large in itself, usually referring to material bulk, as *huge* icebergs; it may, however, indicate extent; as, *huge* caverns; or, especially in recent usage, qualities, as a *huge* joker; but it is rarely applied to persons. *Vast*, which is usually applied to extent, means very great; *immense* means so great as to defy calculation or measurement. *Vast* distances separate the *immense* audiences reached by a powerful television hookup. *Colossal* describes a person or thing strikingly great or *gigantic*, as a man of *colossal* proportions; success attained by *colossal* leaps and bounds

e·nough /inuf'/ [OE *genōg*] *adj* 1 sufficient; equal to needs or requirements ‖ *n* 2 adequate amount or quantity ‖ *adv* 3 sufficiently; quite ‖ *interj* 4 stop!, no more!

e·now /inou', inō'/ *adj, n, & adv archaic & poet.* enough

en pas·sant /än' pasänt'/ [F = in passing] *adv chess* in the play in which a pawn in an initial two-square move is captured by the pawn commanding the square that it would have stopped in in a one-square move

en·plane /enplān'/ *vi* to get aboard an airplane

en·quire /enkwī'ər/ *vt & vi* var of **inquire**

en·rage /enrāj'/ [MF *enrager*] *vt* to make intensely angry, provoke to fury

en·rap·ture /enrap'chər/ *vt* to transport with delight ‖ SYN fascinate, bewitch, delight, enravish, charm

en·rich /enrich'/ [OF *enrichir*] *vt* 1 to increase the wealth of; 2 to improve the quality of, as soil; 3 to adorn; 4 to increase the ratio of radioactive isotopes in ‖ **en·rich'ment** *n*

en·roll /enrōl'/ [OF *enroller*] *vt* 1 to place on record in a list or register; 2 to enlist ‖ *vi* 3 to become a member ‖ **en·roll'ment** *n*

en route /en rōōt', än/ [F] *adv* on the way

en·sconce /enskons'/ [*en-* + D *schans* fort] *vt* 1 to fix securely or comfortably; 2 to shelter, hide

en·sem·ble /änsäm'bəl/ [F = together] *n* 1 general appearance; total effect; 2 entire costume of harmonious parts; 3 *mus* rendering of a composition by a full chorus or orchestra; 4 small choral or orchestral group

en·shrine /enshrīn'/ *vt* 1 to place in or as in a shrine; 2 to keep sacred

en·shroud /enshroud'/ *vt* to conceal, shroud

en·sign /en'sīn/ [OF *enseigne* < L *insignia*] *n* 1 flag or banner, esp. a military or naval standard ‖ /en'sin/ *n* 2 commissioned officer of the lowest grade in the U.S. Navy

en·si·lage /en'sĭlij/ [F < Sp *ensilar* to place in a silo] *n* preservation of green fodder in a silo ‖ also *vt*

en·slave /enslāv'/ *vt* 1 to make a slave of ‖ **en·slave'ment** *n*

en·snare /ensner'/ *vt* to entrap; inveigle

en·sue /ens(y)ōō'/ [OF *ensuivre*] *vi* to come afterward, follow as a consequence ‖ SYN result, succeed (see *follow*)

en·sure /enshŏŏr'/ [AF *enseurer*] *vt* to make sure, safe, or certain

-ent /-ənt/ [L *-ens* (-*entis*)] *adj & n suf* equivalent of *-ant*

en·tab·la·ture /entab'ləchər/ [MF] *n* in a structure supported by columns, the part between the columns and the eaves

en·tail /entāl'/ [MF *tailler* to cut] *vt* 1 to leave (landed property) to a specified succession of heirs so that no one of them can dispose of it to others; 2 to necessitate, involve ‖ *n* 3 entailed property ‖ **en·tail'ment** *n*

en·tan·gle /entaŋ'gəl/ *vt* 1 to involve in a tangle; 2 to ensnare; 3 to perplex, bewilder ‖ **en·tan'gle·ment** *n* ‖ SYN embarrass, embroil, twist, snarl, perplex, confuse

en·tente /äntänt'/ [F = understanding] *n* 1 agreement or understanding, esp. between countries; 2 alliance of the parties to an entente

en·ter /ent'ər/ [OF *entrer*] *vt* 1 to come or go into; 2 to penetrate; 3 to insert, put in; 4 to set down in writing; 5 to join or become a member of; 6 to begin or take up, as a business; 7 to place on record; 8 to gain admission for, as in a school ‖ *vi* 9 to go or come in; 10 **enter into,** a to take part in; b to be or become a part of; 11 **enter upon** to begin

en·ter·i·tis /ent'ərīt'is/ [< Gk *enteron* intestine] *n* inflammation of the intestines

en·ter·prise /ent'ərprīz'/ [MF *entrepris* pp of *entreprendre* to undertake] *n* 1 undertaking, esp. one of importance or risk; 2 energy; initiative ‖ SYN project, venture, essay; readiness, courage

en'ter·pris'ing *adj* ambitious; energetic; showing initiative

en·ter·tain /ent'ərtān'/ [MF *entretenir*] *vt* 1 to have as a guest; 2 to amuse, divert; 3 to harbor, as a grudge; 4 to take into consideration ‖ *vi* 5 to have guests

en'ter·tain'er *n* 1 one who entertains; 2 professional performer, as a singer, dancer, or comedian

en'ter·tain'ing *adj* diverting, amusing

en'ter·tain'ment *n* 1 act of entertaining or state of being entertained; 2 something, as a show, that gives amusement or diversion ‖ SYN feast, party, diversion (see *amusement*)

en·thrall or **en·thral** /enthrôl'/ *v* (**-thralled; -thral·ling**) *vt* 1 to enslave; 2 to charm, fascinate ‖ **en·thrall'ment** *n*

en·throne /enthrōn'/ *vt* 1 to place on or as on a throne; 2 to invest with authority; 3 to exalt ‖ **en·throne'ment** *n*

en·thuse /enthōōz'/ [< *enthusiasm*] *vi* 1 to be enthusiastic ‖ *vt* 2 to make enthusiastic

en·thu'si·asm [Gk *enthousiasmos* inspiration] *n* fervent zeal; intense interest, feeling, or emotion ‖ **en·thu'si·ast'** /-ast'/ *n* ‖ **en·thu'si·as'tic** *adj* ‖ **en·thu'si·as'ti·cal·ly** *adv* ‖ SYN zeal, devotion, ecstasy, ardor, earnestness, fervor, exaltation ‖ ANT apathy, indifference, coolness

en·tice /entīs'/ [OF *enticier* to incite] *vt* to allure or tempt by arousing hope or desire ‖ **en·tice'ment** *n* ‖ **en·tic'ing·ly** *adv* ‖ SYN decoy, invite, coax, seduce, inveigle

en·tire /entī'ər/ [OF *entier* < L *integer* whole] *adj* complete, whole, intact; lacking no parts ‖ **en·tire'ly** *adv* ‖ SYN perfect, unqualified, unreserved, unmixed

en·tire'ty *n* (**-ties**) 1 completeness; 2 a whole

en·ti·tle /entīt'əl/ [MF *entituler*] *vt* 1 to give a name to; 2 to give a right or claim to ‖ SYN designate, denominate, style, call, empower

en·ti·ty /ent'itē/ [ML *entitas*] *n* (**-ties**) 1 existence; 2 anything that has real existence

en·tomb /entōōm'/ *vt* 1 to place in a tomb; bury; 2 to serve as a tomb for ‖ **en·tomb'ment** *n*

en·to·mol·o·gy /ent'əmol'əjē/ [< Gk *entoma* insects] *n* branch of zoology dealing with insects ‖ **en'to·mol'o·gist** *n* ‖ **en'to·mo·log'i·cal** /-məloj'-ikəl/ *adj*

en·tou·rage /änt'ŏŏräzh'/ [F = surroundings] *n* retinue, attendants

en·trails /en'trālz, -trəlz/ [MF *entrailles*] *npl* intestines; viscera

en·train /entrān'/ *vt* 1 to put aboard a train ‖ *vi* 2 to go aboard a train

en·trance¹ /en'trəns/ [MF] *n* 1 act of entering; 2 place of entering; 3 permission or right to enter ‖ SYN ingress, access, accession, admission, entree, introduction, opening, portal, entry (see *admittance*)

en·trance² /entrans', -träns'/ *vt* 1 to put into a trance; 2 to charm, enrapture ‖ **en·tranc'ing** *adj*

en·trant /en'trənt/ *n* 1 one who enters; 2 competitor in a contest

en·trap /entrap'/ *v* (**-trapped; -trapping**) *vt* 1 to catch in or as in a trap; 2 to lure into a dangerous or compromising position ‖ **en·trap'ment** *n*

en·treat /entrēt'/ [MF *entraiter*] *vt* to solicit or ask earnestly ‖ SYN petition, importune, beseech (see *pray*)

en·treat'y *n* (**-ies**) earnest petition or request ‖ SYN supplication, solicitation, appeal, importunity

en·trée or **en·tree** /än'trā/ [F = entrance] *n* 1 act, privilege, or means of entering; 2 cookery a main course; b dish served between the chief courses

en·trench /entrench'/ *vt* 1 to surround or defend with trenches; 2 to establish solidly ‖ *vi* **entrench on** or **upon** to encroach or trespass on ‖ **en·trench'ment** *n*

en·tre·pre·neur /än'trəprənur'/ [F] *n* one who undertakes, organizes, and manages a business or enterprise, assuming the risks and taking the profits

en·tro·py /en'trəpē/ [< Gk *en* in + *trope* turn] *n* 1 *thermodynamics* a measure of the amount of energy unavailable for work during a natural process; b measure of disorder in a closed system; 2 tendency of matter and energy in the universe to reach a state of uniformity and inertia

en·trust /entrust'/ *vt* 1 to give in trust; 2 to confer a trust upon

en·try /en'trē/ [MF *entree*] *n* (-**tries**) 1 entrance; 2 a act of entering an item in a list, journal, or ledger; b item so entered; 3 a one entered in a contest; b more than one horse belonging to one owner and entered in the same race; 4 *law* a act of taking possession of land by setting foot on it; b act of entering a dwelling to commit a crime

en·twine /entwīn'/ *vt & vi* to wind or twist together

e·nu·mer·ate /in(y)ōōm'ərāt'/ [L *enumerare* (-*atus*)] *vt* 1 to reckon or name singly; 2 to count || **e·nu'mer·a'tion** *n* || SYN reckon, compute, estimate (see *calculate*)

e·nun·ci·ate /inun'sē·āt', -shē/ [L *enuntiare* (-*atus*)] *vt* 1 to declare or proclaim; 2 to pronounce (words) || **e·nun'ci·a'tion** *n*

en·vel·op /envel'əp/ [MF *enveloper* to wrap around] *vt* 1 to wrap up in or as in a covering; 2 to surround completely || **en·vel'op·ment** *n*

en·ve·lope /en'vəlōp', än'-/ *n* 1 flat paper container, usu. with a gummed flap, for letters and papers; 2 wrapper or surrounding cover

en·ven·om /enven'əm/ [OF *envenimer*] *vt* 1 to poison; 2 to embitter

en·vi·a·ble /en'vē·əbəl/ *adj* to be envied; desirable

en·vi·ous *adj* feeling or exhibiting envy || **en'vi·ous·ly** *adv*

en·vi·ron·ment /envīr'ənmənt/ [< MF *environ* around] *n* surroundings, influences, and circumstances affecting the development or existence of a person or organism || **en·vi'ron·men'tal** /-men'-/ *adj*

en·vi·ron·men·tal·ist *n* 1 one who studies environment and its influence on the life of the individual and of society; 2 one who considers environment as the overwhelming influence in the development of an individual or a group rather than heredity || also *adj*

en·vi·rons /envīr'ənz/ [F] *npl* outskirts or surrounding area of a city

en·vis·age /enviz'ij/ [F *envisager*] *vt* 1 to visualize; conceive; 2 to expect, plan

en·vi·sion /envizh'ən/ *vt* to have a mental picture of

en·voy /en'voi/ [F *envoyé*] *n* 1 representative or agent; 2 diplomat next in rank to an ambassador

en·vy /en'vē/ [OF *envie*] *n* (-**vies**) 1 jealousy and ill will engendered by another's good fortune; 2 object of such feeling || *v* (-**vied**) *vt* 3 to be envious of || SYN *n* covetousness, grudging (see *jealousy*)

en·zyme /en'zīm/ [< Gk *en* in + *zyme* leaven] *n* any of various complex organic substances, as pepsin, found in plants and animals, and capable of producing chemical transforma-

tions in other substances by catalytic action || **en'zy·mat'ic** /-mat'-/ *adj*

e·on /ē'ən, -on/ *n* var of **aeon**

E·os /ē'os/ *n Gk myth.* goddess of the dawn, the Roman Aurora

-e·ous /-ē·əs, -yəs/ [L -*eus*] *adj suf* having, resembling, as *beauteous*

ep- *pref* var of **epi-**

ep·au·let also **ep·au·lette** /ep'əlet'/ [F *épaulette*] *n* fringed shoulder strap on a dress uniform

é·pée /āpā'/ [F = sword] *n* three-sided rapier with a blunted tip used in fencing

e·pergne /ipurn', āpern'/ [perh < F *épargne* saving] *n* ornament for the center of a dining table, usu. of silver or glass

eph- *pref* var of **epi-**

e·phed·rine /ifed'rin/ [< Gk *ephedra* horsetail, a plant] *n* alkaloid —C₆H₅ CHOHCH(CH₃)NHCH₃— used in treating colds, hay fever, and asthma

e·phem·er·al /ifem'ərəl/ [< Gk *ephemeros*] *adj* 1 existing only for a day, as certain insects; 2 lasting a very short time || SYN short-lived, fleeting, transitory (see *transitory*)

e·phem·er·is /-is/ [Gk = daily calendar] *n* (**eph·e·mer·i·des** /ef'imer'idēz'/) collection of tables showing the daily positions of the heavenly bodies, used in celestial navigation

Eph·e·sus /ef'isəs/ *n* ancient Greek city in Asia Minor, S of Izmir

epi- [Gk *epi* upon, at] *pref* usu. meaning upon, above, or over, as *epidermis, epiglottis*

ep·ic /ep'ik/ [< Gk *epos* word, song] *n* 1 long narrative poem telling of the deeds of a hero or heroes, usu. drawing upon national traditions and written in a lofty style || *adj* 2 designating or pert. to such poetry; 3 heroic, imposing

ep·i·car·di·um /ep'ikär'dē·əm/ [*epi-* + Gk *kardia* heart] *n* (-a /-ə-/) innermost layer, next to the heart, of the pericardium

ep·i·cene /ep'isēn'/ [< *epi-* + Gk *koinos* common] *adj* 1 having qualities or characteristics of both sexes; 2 effeminate, weak || *n* 3 epicene person or thing

ep·i·cen·ter /ep'isen'tər/ *n* point on the earth's surface above the focus of an earthquake

ep·i·cure /ep'ikyōōr'/ [< *Epicurus* (342?–270 B.C.) Gk philosopher] *n* 1 person with a refined taste in food, liquor, and the arts; 2 person given to sensuous pleasures || **ep'i·cu·re'an** /-rē'-/ *adj*

ep·i·dem·ic /ep'idem'ik/ [*epi-* + Gk *demos* people] *adj* 1 widespread, generally prevalent, as a disease || *n* 2 epidemic disease; 3 widespread occurrence of anything

ep·i·de·mi·ol·o·gy /ep'idē'mē·ol'əjē/ *n*

branch of medicine dealing with the incidence and control of epidemics

ep·i·der·mis /ep′idur′mis/ [Gk] *n* outer layer of the skin ‖ **ep′i·der′mal** *adj*

ep·i·glot·tis /ep′iglot′is/ [Gk] *n* cartilaginous lid covering the entrance to the larynx during swallowing

ep·i·gram /ep′igram′/ [Gk *epigramma*] *n* short, witty, and pointed saying ‖ **ep′i·gram·mat′ic** /-grəmat′ik/ *adj*

ep·i·lep·sy /ep′ilep′sē/ [< Gk *epilepsis* seizure] *n* chronic functional disease characterized by attacks or fits in which there is generally loss of consciousness and sometimes convulsions ‖ **ep′i·lep′tic** *adj & n*

ep·i·log or **ep·i·logue** /ep′ilog′, -lôg′/ [Gk *epilogos* peroration] *n* 1 poem or speech at the end of a play; 2 conclusion added to the end of a book

ep·i·neph·rine /ep′inef′rin, -rēn/ (<Gk *nephros* kidney] *n* hormone —C₆H₃(OH)₂CHOHCH₂NHCH₃— produced by the adrenal glands, used as a heart stimulant

E·piph·a·ny /ipif′ənē/ [Gk *epiphaneia* apparition] *n* church festival observed on January 6, commemorating the manifestation of Christ to the Gentiles in the persons of the Magi

e·pis·co·pa·cy /ipis′kəpəsē/ *n* (-cies) 1 church government by bishops; 2 bishops collectively; 3 state or rank of a bishop

e·pis′co·pal /-pəl/ [< Gk *episkopos* overseer] *adj* 1 pert. to or governed by a bishop or bishops; 2 **Episcopal** of or pert. to the Protestant Episcopal or Anglican church

E·pis·co·pa′li·an /-pāl′ē·ən/ *n* member of the Episcopal Church ‖ *also adj* ‖ **E·pis′co·pa′li·an·ism** *n*

e·pis·co·pate /-pit, -pāt′/ *n* 1 position and authority of a bishop; 2 bishop's term of office; 3 bishops collectively

ep·i·sode /ep′isōd′/ [Gk *epeisodion*] *n* incident or action standing by itself but more or less connected with a series of events ‖ **ep′i·sod′ic** /-sod′-ik/ *adj*

e·pis·te·mol·o·gy /ipis′təmol′əjē/ [<Gk *episteme* knowledge] *n* theory or study of what constitutes the basis or essence of knowledge

e·pis·tle /ipis′əl/ [Gk *epistole* message] *n* 1 formal letter; 2 **Epistle** one of the letters written by the apostles in the New Testament; 3 in liturgical churches, an extract usu. from the Epistles read in the communion service ‖ **e·pis′to·lar′y** /-təler′ē/ *adj*

ep·i·taph /ep′itaf′, -täf′/ [Gk *epitaphion* on a tomb] *n* inscription on or suitable for a tomb

ep·i·the·li·um /ep′ithēl′ē·əm/ [< *epi-* + Gk *thele* nipple] *n* (**-ums** or **-a** /-ə/) cellular tissue covering the skin and mucous membranes ‖ **ep′i·the′li·al** *adj*

ep·i·thet /ep′ithet′/ [Gk *epitheton*] *n* 1 word or phrase denoting aptly some quality of the person or thing described; 2 abusive or contemptuous word or phrase ‖ syn appellation (see *name*)

e·pit·o·me /ipit′əmē/ [Gk = abridgment] *n* 1 summary or abstract; 2 part or representative that is typical of the whole ‖ syn summary, syllabus, compendium, analysis

e·pit′o·mize′ *vt* to make or be an epitome of

ep·i·zo·ot·ic /ep′izō·ot′ik/ [*epi-* + Gk *zoon* animal] *adj* 1 affecting many animals at once, as a disease ‖ *n* 2 epizootic disease

e plu·ri·bus u·num /ē′ ploŏr′ibəs yoŏn′-əm/ [L] one out of many (motto of the U.S.)

ep·och /ep′ək, ēp′ok/ [Gk *epoche*] *n* 1 point of time marked by an event or events of great importance; start of a new era; 2 period of time filled with unusual events; 3 subordinate division of geologic time ‖ **ep′och·al** *adj*

ep·o·nym /ep′ənim/ [Gk *eponymos* giving one's name] *n* historical or legendary person from whom a race, city, or institution takes its name, as *Romulus is the eponym of Rome* ‖ **ep·on′y·mous** /epon′-/ *adj*

ep·ox·y /epok′sē/ [*ep-* + *-oxy*] *n* (-**ies**) any of various resins derived by polymerization from chemicals containing an oxygen atom attached to two different atoms, usu. carbon atoms, already united in some other way; characterized by great adhesiveness, toughness, and corrosion resistance

ep·si·lon /ep′sīlon′, -lən/ *n* fifth letter of the Greek alphabet E, ε

Ep′som salts′ /ep′səm/ [*Epsom*, England] *npl* magnesium sulfate —MgSO₄·7H₂O— a white crystalline substance used as a cathartic or industrially in dyeing, finishing cotton goods, etc.

eq·ua·ble /ek′wəbəl, ēk′-/ *adj* 1 uniform, steady; 2 even and serene in temperament ‖ **eq′ua·bly** *adv* ‖ syn tranquil, regular, uniform, even, steady ‖ ant uneven, varying, unsteady, changing, unsettled

e·qual /ēk′wəl/ [L *aequalis*] *adj* 1 of the same extent, number, or magnitude; 2 adequate; 3 of the same rank, degree, or value; 4 evenly balanced ‖ *v* (**e·qualed** or **e·qualled**; **e·qual·ing** or **e·qual·ling**) *vt* 5 to be equal to; 6 to make or do something equal to ‖ *n* 7 one who or that which is equal ‖ **e′qual·ly** *adv* ‖ **e′qual·ize′** *vt* ‖ **e·qual·i·ty** /ikwäl′itē/ *n* ‖ syn alike, equable, commensurate, fair, impartial, equitable ‖ ant *adj* unlike, unequal, unjust

e·qual·i·tar·i·an /ikwäl′iter′ē·ən/ *n* believer in the doctrine of equality among men ‖ also *adj* ‖ **e·qual'i·tar'-i·an·ism** *n*

e'qual sign' *n math* symbol = indicating that the term coming before it is equal to the term following it

e·qua·nim·i·ty /ĕk'wənim'itē̆/ [L *aequanimitas*] *n* evenness of temper; calmness ‖ SYN tranquility, self-possession (see *composure*)

e·quate /ikwāt'/ [L *aequare* (*-atus*)] *vt* 1 to reduce to an average; 2 to regard, treat, or represent as equal

e·qua'tion /-zhən, -shən/ *n* 1 act of making equal or state of being equal; 2 symbolic representation of a chemical reaction showing the atomic and molecular result of a combination of elements and/or radicals; 3 *math* statement of equality between two expressions or quantities separated by the equal sign

e·qua·tor /ikwāt'ər/ [LL *aequator* equalizer] *n* 1 great circle of the earth, equidistant from both poles, the plane of which is perpendicular to the axis of rotation; 2 similar great circle of any rotating celestial body ‖ **e·qua·to·ri·al** /ēk'wətôr'ē̆·əl, ek'-, -tōr'-/ *adj*

eq·uer·ry /ek'wərē̆/ [< MF *escuirie* squires] *n* (**-ries**) officer who attends a prince or nobleman and has charge of his horses

e·ques·tri·an /ikwes'trē̆·ən/ [< L *equestris*] *adj* 1 pert. to horses or horsemanship; 2 mounted ‖ *n* 3 rider: skilled horseman ‖ **e·ques'tri·enne'** /-en'/ *nfem*

equi- [L *aequi-*] *comb form* equal or equally

e'qui·dis'tant /ēk'wi-/ *adj* separated by equal distances

e'qui·lat'er·al *adj* 1 having all the sides equal ‖ *n* 2 figure with equal sides; 3 side equal to the other sides

e'qui·lib'ri·um /-lib'rē̆·əm/ [< *equi-* + L *libra* balance] *n* (**-ums** or **-a** /-ə/) state of balance due to the equal action of opposing forces

e·quine /ēk'wīn/ [L *equinus* < *equus* horse] *adj* 1 of or like a horse ‖ *n* 2 horse

e·qui·nox /ēk'winoks', ek'-/ [*equi-* + L *nox* night] *n* either of the two times during the year when the sun crosses the celestial equator, making the day and night of equal length, occurring about March 21 and September 22 ‖ **e'qui·noc'tial** /-nok'-shəl/ *adj*

e·quip /ikwip'/ [MF *equiper*] *v* (**e·quipped**; **e·quip·ping**) *vt* 1 to furnish or fit out for any service or undertaking; 2 to dress, adorn, array

e·quip'ment *n* 1 anything used for equipping; 2 act of equipping or state of being equipped

e·qui·poise /ek'wipoiz', ēk'-/ *n* 1 equi-

librium or balance; 2 counterbalancing weight

eq·ui·ta·ble /ek'witəbəl/ *adj* just, fair ‖ SYN honest, right, reasonable, equal, upright, fair

eq·ui·ta·tion /ek'witāsh'ən/ [< L *equitare* (*-atus*) to ride] *n* act or art of riding a horse

eq·ui·ty /ek'witē̆/ [L *aequitas*] *n* (**-ties**) 1 justice, impartiality; 2 body of laws based on natural principles of justice, superseding or supplementing statute laws; 3 value of property, stock, or shares in a business, over and above any indebtedness ‖ SYN righteousness, impartiality (see *justice*)

e·quiv·a·lent /ikwiv'ələnt/ [L *aequivalens* (*-entis*)] *adj* 1 equal in value, force, measure, meaning, or effect ‖ *n* 2 equivalent thing ‖ **e·quiv'a·lence** *n*

e·quiv·o·cal /ikwiv'əkəl/ [< LL *equivocus* ambiguous] *adj* 1 doubtful; uncertain; 2 deliberately ambiguous; 3 open to suspicion ‖ **e·quiv'o·cal·ly** *adv* ‖ SYN obscure, dubious, indefinite, perplexing, suspicious, ambiguous ‖ DISCR An expression is *ambiguous* which leaves us entirely uncertain as to which of two possible meanings the writer or speaker intended to convey. An *equivocal* expression is one which is capable of a double interpretation, either because of the words used, or because of their possible application to two different things. *Equivocal* expressions are usually deliberately deceptive ‖ ANT certain, clear, definite, unquestionable

e·quiv'o·cate' /-kāt'/ *vi* to use deliberately ambiguous expressions ‖ **e·quiv'o·ca'tion** *n* ‖ **e·quiv'o·ca'tor** *n* ‖ SYN shuffle, quibble, evade, shift (see *prevaricate*)

-er¹ /-ər/ [OE *-ere* < *-arius*] *n suf* denoting 1 one who occupies himself with, as *lawyer*; 2 agent, as *lover*; 3 instrument, as *poker*; 4 one living in, as *New Englander*

-er² [OE *-ra*] *adj suf* forming the comparative degree of adjectives and adverbs, as *higher*

-er³ [OE *-r-*] *v suf* denoting repeated action, as *glimmer*

Er *chem* erbium

e·ra /ir'ə, ēr'ə, er'ə/ [L *aera*] *n* 1 period of time starting from a given date; 2 period with notable characteristics; 3 point of time from which a series of years is reckoned; 4 one of the five great divisions of geologic time

e·rad·i·cate /irad'ikāt'/ [L *eradicare* (*-atus*) < *radix* (*-dicis*) root] *vt* to destroy completely; erase, wipe out ‖ **e·rad'i·ca'tion** *n* ‖ SYN uproot, destroy, extirpate, exterminate ‖ DISCR Literally, *eradicate* means to get out by the root; *extirpate*, to get out the very stock of; **exterminate,** to put beyond the borders of existence, and so, all three, to destroy utterly. *Eradicate,* though still applied literally to plants removed in numbers, is now commonly employed in the figurative sense; we *eradicate* evils, faults, or offensive mannerisms. *Extirpate* is used of that which is so thoroughly rooted out that it can never reappear, as a species of animal, a nation, or weeds. Figuratively, *extirpate* means stamp out, as plagues, heresies, vice, etc. *Exterminate* is applied to those things that have life; tribes, races, or animals are *exterminated*

e·rase /irās′/ [L *eradere (erasus)*] *vt* to remove, as by rubbing; scrape off ‖ SYN delete, efface, obliterate, cancel, expunge ‖ DISCR These words refer, primarily, to the removal of written characters; they now have a figurative application as well, which is easily deduced from their literal use. To *erase* is to scrape or scratch out, usually in order to write something else in the space thus secured; to *erase* the chalk-made characters on a blackboard is simply to rub them out. To *efface* is to make illegible, sometimes by wiping or rubbing out, sometimes, as in the effect of weather upon inscriptions, by a gradual wearing process. To *obliterate* is utterly to remove, as a character or letter; time or accident may *obliterate*. To *cancel* is literally to cross out by a stroke or strokes made through the letters. To *expunge,* literally to take out by pricking with a sharp point, means now to blot out, as by ink spots, or to strike out, as by strokes with the pen. Figuratively, we *erase* a face from memory, *expunge* a passage from a book, *efface* a bad impression, *cancel* a social obligation, *obliterate* our identity

e·ras′er *n* device for rubbing out written marks, usu. of rubber for paper and of felt for blackboards

E·ras·mus, Des·i·de·ri·us /dez′idir′ē-əs iraz′məs/ *n* (1466–1536) Dutch scholar and theologian, a leader of the humanist movement ‖ **E·ras′mi·an** *adj*

e·ra·sure /irāsh′ər/ *n* 1 act or instance of erasing; 2 place where something has been erased

Er·a·to /er′ətō′/ *n Gk myth.* Muse of lyric and love poetry

er·bi·um /ur′bē-əm/ [< *Ytterby,* Sweden] *n chem* rare-earth metallic element (Er; at.no. 68; at.wt. 167.26)

ere /er′/ [OE *ær*] *conj & prep poet.* before

e·rect /irekt′/ [L *erigere (erectus)*] *vt* 1 to raise to an upright position; 2 to build, construct ‖ *vi* 3 to become distended and rigid, as erectile tissue ‖

adj 4 upright, vertical; 5 directed upward ‖ **e·rec′tor** *n* ‖ **e·rec′tion** *n*

e·rec′tile /-təl, -tīl/ *adj anat* (tissue) capable of becoming distended and rigid

er·e·mite /er′əmīt′/ [Gk *eremites* desert dweller] *n* recluse; religious hermit

erg /urg′/ [Gk *ergon* work] *n* cgs unit of work or energy, being the work expended in overcoming a resistance of one dyne over a distance of one centimeter

er·go /ur′gō/ [L] *conj & adv* therefore

E·rie /ir′ē/ *n* city in NW Pennsylvania on Lake Erie (140,000)

E′rie, Lake *n* one of the Great Lakes, bordered by New York, Pennsylvania, Ohio, Michigan, and Ontario

E′rie Ca·nal′ *n* canal in New York state, connecting the Hudson River at Albany with Lake Erie at Buffalo

Er·in /er′in/ *n poet.* Ireland

er·mine /ur′min/ [OF] *n* 1 Old World weasel (*Mustela erminea*) with a white winter coat; 2 the white fur; 3 emblem, dignity, or rank of a king, nobleman, or judge, whose robes are often trimmed with ermine

e·rode /irōd′/ [L *erodere* to eat away] *vt* 1 to eat or wear away, as soil or rocks by the action of water; 2 to form by wearing away, as a gully ‖ *vi* 3 to become eroded ‖ **e·ro′sive** *adj*

e·rog·e·nous /iroj′inəs/ [< Gk *eros* love] *adj* capable of producing sexual excitement or stimulation

E·ros /ir′os, er′-/ *n Gk myth.* god of love; identified with the Roman Cupid

e·ro·sion /irō′zhən/ *n* 1 act of eroding or being eroded; 2 action of water, wind, glaciers, etc. in wearing away and destroying the rock or soil of the surface of the earth

e·rot·ic /irot′ik/ [< *Eros*] *adj* 1 of or pert. to sexual love; 2 subject to or causing sexual desire ‖ **e·rot′i·cism** /-siz′əm/

err /ur′/ [OF *errer* < L *errare*] *vi* 1 to be incorrect or mistaken; 2 to go astray morally

er·rand /er′ənd/ [OE *ærende*] *n* 1 trip made to attend to some special business or to carry a message; 2 object or motive for which such trip is made

er·rant /er′ənt/ [OF *errant*] *adj* 1 wandering in search of adventure; 2 wayward, erring

er·rat·ic /irat′ik/ [L *erraticus*] *adj* 1 having no fixed course; wandering; 2 queer, eccentric ‖ SYN irregular, queer, odd (see *eccentric*)

er·ra·tum /erāt′əm/ [L] *n* (-ta /-tə/) error in printing or writing

er·ro·ne·ous /erōn′ē-əs/ [L *erroneus* straying] *adj* incorrect, mistaken ‖ **er·ro′ne·ous·ly** *adv*

er·ror /er′ər/ [L] *n* 1 false belief; 2 condition of believing what is untrue; **3** mistake; inaccuracy; **4** sin; **5** *baseball* misplay by a fielder ‖ SYN mistake, inaccuracy, unsoundness, offense; fault, sin, iniquity (see *blunder*)

er·satz /erzäts′, er′zäts/ [G = substitute] *n* substitute; synthetic substance ‖ also *adj*

Erse /urs/ [early var of *Irish*] *n* Scottish or Irish Gaelic

erst′while′ /urst′-/ [< OE *ærest* earliest] *adj* of old, former

er·u·dite /er′(y)o͞odīt′/ [< L *erudire* (-*itus*) to teach] *adj* learned, scholarly, well-read

er·u·di·tion /-dish′ən/ *n* book knowledge; learning in various abstruse fields ‖ SYN scholarship, lore (see *learning*)

e·rupt /irupt′/ [L *erumpere* (*eruptus*)] *vi* **1** to burst forth, as lava; **2** to eject volcanic matter; **3** to boil over, as anger; **4** to break out in a rash

e·rup′tion *n* **1** bursting forth, as of a volcano, war, or disease; **2** that which is ejected; **3** skin rash

-er·y /-ərē/ [OF -*erie*] *n suf* **1** place of business, as *bakery*; **2** qualities, conduct, practices, as *snobbery*; **3** class of goods, as *millinery*; **4** state, condition, as *slavery*

er·y·sip·e·las /er′isip′ələs, ir′-/ [Gk] *n* acute infectious bacterial disease marked by fever and local redness and swelling

er·y·the·ma /er′ithē′mə/ [Gk] *n* abnormal redness of the skin

e·ryth·ro- /irith′rə-/ [Gk *erythros* red] *comb form* red

e·ryth·ro·cyte /irith′rəsit′/ [*erythro-* + -*cyte*] *n* one of the disk-shaped cells which contain hemoglobin and give the blood its color and carry oxygen to the tissues and carbon dioxide back to the lungs

-es /-iz/ *suf* var of -s¹ and -s², as in *wishes*

E·sau /ē′sô/ *n Bib* son of Isaac and Rebekah, disinherited through the guile of his younger brother Jacob (Gen. 25: 25–34; 27: 1–40)

es·ca·late /es′kəlāt′/ [< *escalator*] *vt* & *vi* to increase in magnitude, as a war ‖ **es·ca·la′tion** *n*

es′ca·la·tor [< LL *scalare* to climb] *n* continuously moving stairway that works like an endless belt

es′ca·la·tor clause′ *n* clause in a contract between labor and management providing for an increase or decrease in wages as conditions change

es·cal·lop /eskol′əp, -kal′-/ *n* & *vt* var of *scallop*

es·ca·pade /es′kəpād′/ [F < Sp *escapada*] *n* **1** prank; reckless adventure; **2** breaking away from confinement or restraint

es·cape /eskāp′/ [ONF *escaper*] *vt* **1** to flee from; avoid, elude; **2** to slip from, as a sigh; **3** to elude the notice

or recollection of ‖ *vi* **4** to get free; **5** to get out of danger, avoid harm; **6** to leak out, as a fluid; **7** to slip away, as from memory ‖ *n* **8** act or instance of escaping; **9** means of escaping; **10** leakage; **11** release from reality

es·cape′ hatch′ *n* **1** emergency opening in an aircraft used for escape; **2** subterfuge; way out of a dilemma

es·cape′ment *n* toothed wheel with a pawl for securing regularity of movement, used in clocks, watches, typewriter carriages, etc.

es·cape′ ve·loc′i·ty *n* minimum speed that an object must attain in order to free itself from the gravity of a given body

es·cap′ism *n* avoidance of reality and responsibilities by occupying oneself with amusements and flights of the imagination ‖ **es·cap′ist** *n*

es·ca·role /es′kərōl′/ [F] *n* broadleafed chicory, used in salads

es·carp·ment /eskärp′mənt/ [F *escarpement*] *n* steep clifflike side of a hill

-esce /-es′/ [L -*escere*] *v suf* showing action just begun, as *convalesce*

-es·cent /-es′ənt/ [L *escens* (-*entis*)] *adj suf* being or becoming, as *quiescent* ‖ **-es′cence** *n suf*

es·cha·tol·o·gy /es′kətol′əjē/ [< Gk *eschatos* last] *n* body of teachings about last or final things, as death, resurrection, judgment, the millennium, etc.

es·cheat /es·chēt′/ [OF *eschete* < *escheoir* to fall to one's share] *law* *vt* **1** to take possession of (property to which there are no heirs) ‖ *vi* **2** to revert to the state because there is no legal heir ‖ *n* **3** the escheating of property; **4** escheated property

es·chew /es·cho͞o′/ [OF *eschiver*] *vt* to avoid, shun

es·cort /es′kôrt/ [F *escorte* < It *scorta*] *n* **1** one or more persons, vehicles, ships, or planes, accompanying others for protection, courtesy, or guidance; **2** man accompanying a woman in public ‖ /eskôrt′/ *vt* **3** to accompany as an escort

es·crow /es′krō/ [OF *escroue* scroll] *law* *n* **1** sealed instrument given to a third party for delivery upon stated conditions; **2** in escrow deposited with a third party pending fulfillment of the stated conditions

es·cu·do /esko͞od′ō/ [Sp & Port < L *scutum* shield] *n* **1** any of several gold and silver coins of Spanish-speaking countries; **2** monetary unit of Portugal and Chile

es·cutch·eon /eskuch′ən/ [ONF *escuchon* < L *scutum* shield] *n* **1** shield for displaying a coat of arms; **2** that part of a vessel's stern displaying the name; **3** plate around a keyhole, door handle, or light switch

-ese /-ēz′, -ēs′/ [OF -eis < L -ensis] *adj suf* pert. to a place or its language or inhabitants, as *Portuguese* || also *n suf*

Es·ki·mo /es′kəmō′/ [< name used of northern Indians by Algonquins] *n* (**-mos** or **-mo**) 1 one of a race of people inhabiting Labrador, Greenland, Alaska, and other arctic regions; 2 their language || also *adj*

Es′ki·mo dog′ *n* one of a breed of strong dogs of medium size used to pull sleds in arctic regions

e·soph·a·gus /isof′əgəs/ [Gk *oisophagos*] *n* (**-gi** /-jī′/) canal through which food and drink pass from the mouth to the stomach; gullet

es·o·ter·ic /es′əter′ik/ [Gk *esoterikos* inner] *adj* 1 understood by or meant for only a select few; 2 confidential, secret || **es′o·ter′i·cal·ly** *adv*

ESP extrasensory perception

esp. especially

es·pa·drille /es′pədril′/ [< F < Prov *espardilho*] *n* sandal with a canvas upper and a rope sole

es·pal·ier /espal′yər/ [< F < It *spalliera* back of chair] *n* 1 framework on which fruit trees or shrubs are trained to grow flat against a wall; 2 fruit tree or shrub so trained

es·par′to (**grass′**) /espärt′ō/ [Sp] *n* Spanish rush (*Stipa tenacissima*) used in weaving and in making paper

es·pe·cial /espesh′əl/ [MF < L *specialis* of a particular kind] *adj* 1 particular; special; 2 exceptional of its kind || **es·pe′cial·ly** *adv*

Es·pe·ran·to /esp′əränt′ō/ [Esperanto = one who hopes] *n* language invented in 1887 by L. L. Zamenhof (1859–1917), a Polish physician, as an international language

es·pi·o·nage /esp′ē·ənäzh′, -nij/ [F *espionnage*] *n* practice of spying, esp. by the agents of one country on another country

es·pla·nade /es′plənād′, -näd′/ [F < Sp *esplanada*] *n* open level space, esp. for public use in walking or driving

es·pouse /espouz′/ [MF *espouser*] *vt* 1 to wed; 2 to adopt, advocate, or defend, as a cause || **es·pous′al** *n*

es·pres·so /espres′ō/ [It = *pressed* (coffee)] *n* coffee made by forcing boiling water or live steam under pressure through ground coffee beans

es·prit /esprē′/ [F] *n* spirit, sprightly wit

es·prit′ de corps′ /dəkôr′/ [F] *n* sense of pride in one's organization, and a feeling of brotherhood toward its members

es·py /espī′/ [OF *espier*] *v* (**-pied**) *vt* to see at a distance, catch sight of

Esq. Esquire

-esque /-esk′/ [F < It -*esco*] *adj suf* 1 after the manner or style of, as *arabesque*; 2 like, as *statuesque*

es·quire /eskwī′ər, es′kwīr′ [MF *es-*

quier < L *scutarius* shield bearer] *n* 1 originally, armorbearer or attendant of a knight; 2 member of the English gentry ranking below a knight; 3 **Esquire** title of courtesy written after a man's name, esp. a lawyer's

-ess /-is, -es/ [OF -*esse* < Gk -*issa*] *n suf* forming feminines, as *prioress*

es·say /es′ā/ [MF *essai* attempt] *n* 1 short literary composition, esp. interpretive and analytical; 2 attempt, experiment || /esā′/ *vt* to try, test || **es′say·ist** *n* || SYN *n* treatise, dissertation, trial, effort, experiment

es·sence /es′əns/ [L *essentia* being] *n* 1 real character or indispensable quality of a thing; 2 spiritual entity; existence in the abstract; 3 concentrated substance having the characteristic properties of the original; 4 alcoholic solution of an essential oil; 5 perfume

Es·sene /esēn′/ *n* one of an ascetic Hebrew community formed in the second century B.C.

es·sen·tial /esen′shəl/ [see **essence**] *adj* 1 pert. to or being the essence of a thing; 2 indispensable, necessary || *n* 3 necessary, basic, or fundamental element || **es·sen′tial·ly** *adv* || SYN *adj* (see *inherent*, *necessary*); *n* (see *need*)

es·sen′tial oil′ *n* volatile oil in leaves, plants, and fruits, to which the characteristic flavor or odor is due

-est /-ist/ [OE -*st*, -*est*, -*ost*] *adj suf* forming the superlative degree of adjectives and adverbs, as *highest*

EST, E.S.T. Eastern Standard Time

es·tab·lish /estab′lish/ [MF *establir* (-*bliss*-)] *vt* 1 to place on a permanent basis, as a government, business, or profession; 2 to prove, substantiate; 3 to fix firmly; 4 to secure permanence or acceptance for; 5 to make a national institution of, as a church || SYN settle, found, verify (see *substantiate*)

es·tab′lish·ment *n* 1 act of establishing or state of being established; 2 something established and more or less permanently constituted, as a business, household, church, or army; 3 **the Establishment** the entrenched order that is running things; the holders of economic and political power

es·tate /estāt′/ [MF *estat* < L *status* standing] *n* 1 condition of life; rank or position; 2 distinct social and political class, as formerly in England and France; 3 piece of land with a residence, often imposing; 4 one's total property and possessions

es·teem /estēm′/ [MF *estimer* < L *aestimare* to value] *vt* 1 to value or regard highly; 2 to think, consider || *n* 3 favorable opinion; respect || SYN *n* (see *regard*); *v* favor, appreciate, honor, respect, regard, consider ||

DISCR To **esteem** a thing is to prize it, or to set a high mental valuation upon it; when applied to persons, *esteem* carries also the warmer interest of approval, cordiality, and affection. To *respect* is to yield deference to some one or something from a motive excited by the superiority of the subject; we *respect* age, or those who hold high office. To *regard* is to entertain a certain point of view concerning a person or thing, as to *regard* Shakespeare as a great poet

es·ter /est′ər/ [G < *essig* vinegar + *äther* ether] *n chem* compound, often fragrant, produced by the reaction of an acid and an alcohol with the elimination of water

Es·ther /est′ər/ *n Bib* 1 Jewish queen of Persia, who saved her people from slaughter; 2 book of the Old Testament

es·thete /es′thēt/ *n* var of **aesthete**

es·ti·ma·ble /est′iməbəl/ *adj* 1 deserving esteem; 2 capable of being estimated

es·ti·mate /est′imāt′/ [L *aestimare* (-*atus*)] *vt* 1 to form an opinion of; 2 to determine or calculate approximately the value, size, or cost of || *vi* 3 to make an estimate || /-mit/ *n* 4 judgment or opinion; 5 computed cost of work to be done || SYN *v* appraise, appreciate, rate (see *calculate*)

es·ti·ma·tion *n* 1 judgment or opinion; 2 respect, esteem

es·ti·vate /est′ivāt′/ [L *aestivare* (-*atus*) to spend the summer] *vi* to lie dormant in summer, as certain animals || **es′ti·va′tion** *n*

Es·to·ni·a /estōn′ē·ə/ *n* formerly independent nation in Europe on the Baltic, now a constituent republic of the Soviet Union (2,000,000; 16,955 sq.m.; *cap.* Tallinn) || **Es·to′ni·an** *adj* & *n*

es·trange /estrānj′/ [OF *estranger* < L *extraneare* to make foreign] *vt* 1 to cause to be strange; keep at a distance; 2 to alienate the affections of || **es·trange′ment** *n*

es·tro·gen /es′trəjən/ [Gk *oistros* frenzy] *n* any of several female sex hormones

es·tu·ar·y /es′choo̅·er′ē/ [L *aestuarium* < *aestus* tide] *n* (-**ies**) mouth of a river where its current meets the tide

-et /et′, it/ [OF] *n suf* small one, as *cigaret, islet*

e·ta /ēt′ə, āt′ə/ *n* seventh letter of the Greek alphabet H, η

et al. /et al′/ [L *et alii*] and others

etc. et cetera

et cet·er·a /et set′(ə)rə/ [L = and others] 1 and others; 2 and so forth

etch /ech′/ [D *etsen*] *vt* 1 to engrave by eating out a design on (metal, glass, or the like) with a corrosive, as an acid; 2 to make (a design or picture) by this method || *vi* 3 to practice etching || **etch′er** *n*

etch·ing *n* 1 art or process of producing etched plates or of making designs from etched plates; 2 design or drawing made from an etched plate

e·ter·nal /iturn′əl/ [< L *aeternus*] *adj* 1 without beginning or end, everlasting; 2 perpetual, unchangeable; 3 incessant || **e·ter′nal·ly** *adv* || SYN unceasing, unfailing, timeless, endless, everlasting, interminable, immortal, perpetual, ceaseless, uninterrupted, enduring || DISCR *Eternal* describes that which always has been and always shall be, as the *Eternal God*. That which is *everlasting* may not always have existed, but it reaches uninterruptedly and unceasingly into the future without end. *Eternal* and *everlasting* are often interchangeable, as *eternal* life, or life *everlasting;* even here, however, there is a slight distinction, for *eternal* stresses the nature, and *everlasting* the duration, of the thing described. *Endless* is partly synonymous with *everlasting*, but is used in many special senses, especially in mechanics, to mean continuous, as an *endless* band or belt. *Immortal* describes that which, living, is deathless, as the *immortal* soul; figuratively, *immortal* is interchangeable with *everlasting*, as *immortal* fame. *Interminable* stresses the never-ending or limitless quality of a thing, as the *interminable* stretches of the desert. *Perpetual* in its most extended sense means *eternal*, as light *perpetual;* in a lesser sense, it means never ceasing, as *perpetual* motion. Many of these words are used to connote boredom, wearisomeness, or monotony, as an *everlasting* nuisance. *Eternal*, too, is sometimes used of finite but very great duration, as *eternal* vigilance; the *eternal* snows

e·ter·ni·ty /iturn′itē/ [L *aeternitas* (-**ties**) 1 state of being eternal; 2 infinite time; 3 time or period that seems endless; 4 existence before earthly life or after death

-eth¹ /-*ith*/ [OE] *v suf archaic* ending of the *3rd pers sg pres ind*, as *singeth*

-eth³ [OE] *suf* var of **-th³**

eth·ane /eth′ān/ [< *eth*(yl) + -*ane²*] *n* colorless, odorless, flammable gas —CH₃CH₃— found in crude petroleum and natural gas

e·ther /ēth′ər/ [Gk *aither* upper air] *n* 1 compound in which a carbon atom of each of two hydrocarbon radicals is attached to an oxygen atom; 2 volatile, colorless liquid with aromatic odor —(C₂H₅)₂O— used as a solvent and as an anesthetic; 3 upper region of the sky; 4 hypothetical medium formerly assumed to fill all space and to form the means by which electromagnetic radiation is transmitted

e·the·re·al /ĭthir′ē·əl/ *adj* 1 light, delicate; 2 heavenly, spiritual

eth·ic /eth′ĭk/ [Gk *ethikos* ethical] *n* 1 system of ethics; 2 general character or ideals of character of a race or group of people

eth′i·cal *adj* 1 pert. to morality or ethics; 2 moral, conforming to morality; 3 conforming to the standards of conduct set by a profession; 4 (drugs) sold only on prescription ‖ **eth′i·cal·ly** *adv*

eth·ics *npl* 1 principles of right conduct; 2 *nsg* science that treats of morals and right conduct

E·thi·o·pi·a /ēth′ē·ōp′ē·ə/ *n* country in E Africa (23,000,000; 471,778; cap. Addis Ababa) ‖ **E′thi·o′pi·an** *adj & n*

eth·nic /eth′nĭk/ [< Gk *ethnos* nation] *adj* 1 pert. to races or peoples with special reference to their distinct ancestral, cultural, religious, or linguistic characteristics ‖ *n* 2 member of such a race or people

eth·no- [Gk] *comb form* race, people; culture

eth·no·cen·tric /eth′nōsent′rĭk/ *adj* believing in the superiority of one's own national culture ‖ **eth′no·cen′trism** *n*

eth·nog·ra·phy /ethnog′rəfē/ *n* scientific description of races and peoples ‖ **eth·nog′ra·pher** *n* ‖ **eth·no·graph·ic** /eth′nəgraf′ĭk/ *adj*

eth·nol·o·gy /ethnol′əjē/ *n* branch of anthropology that treats of races of men, their characteristics, origin, distribution, etc. ‖ **eth·nol′o·gist** *n* ‖ **eth·no·log·i·cal** /eth′nəloj′ĭkəl/ *adj*

e·thol·o·gy /ethol′əjē, ē-/ [see **ethos**] *n* scientific study of animal behavior

e·thos /ē′thos/ [Gk = custom, usage] *n* fundamental character and beliefs of a people or culture group

eth·yl /eth′əl/ [< *ether* + Gk *hyle* substance] *n* 1 monovalent hydrocarbon radical—C₂H₅; 2 tetraethyl lead, added to gasoline to reduce knocking

eth′yl al′co·hol *n* ordinary alcohol

e·ti·ol·o·gy /ēt′ē·ol′əjē/ [< Gk *aitia* cause] *n* study of causes and origins, esp. of diseases ‖ **e′ti·o·log′i·cal** /-əloj′ĭkəl/ *adj*

et·i·quette /et′ĭket′, -kit/ [F = ticket] *n* rules of conduct observed in polite society or in professional or official intercourse

Et·na, Mount /et′nə/ *n* active volcano in E Sicily (10,884 ft.)

E·tru·ri·a /ĭtrōō′rē·ə/ *n* ancient country in W Central Italy

E·trus·can /ĭtrus′kən/ also **E·tru′ri·an** *n* 1 inhabitant of Etruria; 2 its language ‖ also *adj*

et seq. [L *et sequens, et sequentes (pl),* or *et sequentia (neut pl)*] and the following

-ette /-et′/ [F, *fem* of *-et*] *n suf* 1 small one, as *statuette;* 2 female, as *usherette;* 3 imitation, as *leatherette;* 4 group, as *quartette*

é·tude /ā′t(y)ōōd/ [F = study] *n mus* composition affording practice on some point of technique, but which may also have artistic value

etym. 1 etymology; 2 etymological

et·y·mol·o·gy /et′imol′əjē/ [see **etymon**] *n* (-gies) 1 science treating of the origin and history of words; 2 origin and development of a word; 3 derivation of a word ‖ **et′y·mo·log′i·cal** /-məloj′ĭkəl/ *adj*

et·y·mon /et′imon′/ [Gk = true (meaning)] *n* (-mons or -ma /-mə/) word or word root from which other words are derived

Eu *chem* europium

eu- [Gk] *pref* well, good

eu·ca·lyp·tus /yōōk′əlip′təs/ [*eu-* + Gk *kalyptos* covered] *n* (-tus·es or -ti /-tī/) any of a genus (*Eucalyptus*) of aromatic trees of the myrtle family, which furnish timber and oil

Eu·cha·rist /yōōk′ərist/ [Gk *eucharistia* gratitude] *n* 1 Holy Communion; sacrament of the Lord's Supper; 2 consecrated elements, esp. the bread, used in that sacrament

eu·chre /yōōk′ər/ [?] *n* 1 card game ‖ *vt* 2 to prevent (the one who named trumps in the game) from scoring; 3 *colloq* to outwit

Eu·clid /yōōk′lĭd/ *n* 1 Greek mathematician of Alexandria of ab. 300 B.C.; 2 his treatise on geometry

Eu·clid′e·an ge·om′e·try /-klĭd′ē·ən/ *n* geometry of a space in which only one line can be drawn through a given point parallel to a given line

eu·lo·gy /yōōl′əjē/ [Gk *eulogia*] *n* (-gies) 1 praise; 2 formal statement in praise of another's life and character, esp. a funeral oration ‖ **eu′lo·gist** *n* ‖ **eu′lo·gize′** *vt* ‖ SYN praise, encomium, panegyric ‖ DISCR *Praise* is expressed approval of either a person or thing. *Eulogy, encomium,* and *panegyric* refer to modes of praising. A *eulogy* is a laudatory discourse addressed to an audience; it concerns persons rather than things, and, though usually formal and not infrequently extravagant in its commendation, it often possesses the merit of sincerity or truth. *Panegyric* also names a public address, usually about persons, but it differs from *eulogy* in being more elaborate, less judicious, and more apt to be based on servile rather than genuine admiration. An *encomium* may be delivered about either persons or things, but it usually concerns things; like the *eulogy* and the *panegyric,* it is formal, and often so high-flown as to be absurd

eu·nuch /yōōn′ək/ [Gk *eunouchos*

chamberlain] *n* castrated man, esp. an attendant of a harem

eu·phe·mism /yōōf′əmiz′əm/ [Gk *euphemismos*] *n* **1** substitution of a mild or inoffensive word or expression for one considered offensive or blunt; **2** word or expression so used ‖ **eu′phe·mis′tic** *adj* ‖ **eu′phe·mis′ti·cal·ly** *adv*

eu·pho·ny /yōōf′ənē̗/ [Gk *euphonia*] *n* (**-nies**) pleasantness of sound; harmonious combination of sounds ‖ **eu·pho′ni·ous** /-fōn′ē̗-əs/ *adj*

eu·pho·ri·a /yōōfôr′ē̗-ə, -fôr′-/ [Gk = well-being] *n* buoyant feeling of well-being ‖ **eu·phor′ic** *adj*

Eu·phra·tes /yōōfrā′tēz/ *n* river flowing through Turkey, Syria, and Iraq to join the Tigris and form the Shatt-al-Arab, which empties into the Persian Gulf

eu·phu·ism /yōōf′yoō·iz′əm/ [< *Euphues*, hero of Lyly's romance] *n* **1** affected style of writing, brought into fashion in England by John Lyly in the 16th century, marked by play on words, alliteration, elaborate simile, and antithesis; **2** affected or high-flown style of speech or writing ‖ **eu′phu·ist** *n* ‖ **eu′phu·is′tic** *adj*

Eur. 1 Europe; **2** European

Eur·a·sia /yōōrāzh′ə, -āsh′ə/ *n* Europe and Asia considered as a unit

Eur·a′sian *adj* **1** of or pert. to Eurasia; **2** of European and Asian descent ‖ also *n*

eu·re·ka /yōōrēk′ə/ [Gk *heureka* I have found] *interj* I've got it! (exclamation of triumph at a sudden discovery or solution of a problem)

Eu·rip·i·des /yōōrip′idēz′/ *n* (5th cent. B.C.) Greek dramatist ‖ **Eu·rip′i·de′an** /-dē′ən/ *adj*

Eu′ro·mar′ket or **Eu′ro·mart′** *n* Common Market

Eu·rope /yōōr′əp/ *n* continent W of Asia and N of Africa (570,000,000; 3,872,561 sq.m.) ‖ **Eu′ro·pe′an** /-pē′ən/ *adj & n*

Eu·ro·pe′an E·co·nom′ic Com·mu′ni·ty *n* Common Market

Eu·ro·pe′an plan′ *n* hotel rate by which guests are charged a fixed amount for rooms and pay extra for any meals they take

eu·ro·pi·um /yōōrōp′ē̗-əm/ [< *Europe*] *n* element of the rare-earth group (Eu; at.no. 63; at.wt. 151.96)

Eu·sta′chian tube′ /yōōstāk′ē̗-ən, -tāsh′ən/ [Bartolommeo *Eustachio* 16th-cent. It anatomist] *n* canal between the middle ear and the pharynx

Eu·ter·pe /yōōtur′pē̗/ *n* *Gk myth.* Muse of music and lyric poetry

eu·tha·na·si·a /yōōth′ənāzh′(ē̗)ə/ [Gk = easy death] *n* the putting to death painlessly of a person suffering from an incurable and painful disease

e·vac·u·ate /ivak′yōō·āt′/ [L *evacuare* (-*atus*) to empty out] *vt* **1** to empty;
2 to withdraw from; vacate; **3** to clear, as an area, of population; **4** to discharge, as excrement from the bowels ‖ **vi 5** to withdraw from an area or military position; **6** to defecate ‖ **e·vac′u·a′tion** *n*

e·vac′u·ee′ /-ē′/ *n* person evacuated from a place of danger

e·vade /ivād′/ [L *evadere* (-*asus*) to go away)] *vt* **1** to elude by cleverness or trickery; slip away from; **2** to avoid by trickery; **3** to avoid a direct answer to; **4** to elude, escape, baffle ‖ *vi* **5** to practice evasion; **6** to slip away ‖ SYN avoid, baffle, escape, elude (see *prevaricate*)

e·val·u·ate /ival′yōō·āt′/ [F *évaluer* to estimate] *vt* **1** to place a value on; **2** to find the amount of ‖ **e·val′u·a′tion** *n*

ev·a·nes·cent /ev′ənes′ənt/ [< L *evanescere* to vanish] *adj* disappearing gradually from sight; vanishing; fleeting ‖ **ev′a·nes′cence** *n* ‖ SYN ephemeral, disappearing (see *transitory*)

e·van·gel·i·cal /ē′vanjel′ikəl, ev′ən-/ [< Gk *euangelion* good news] *adj* **1** pert. to or consistent with the Gospels and their teachings; **2** maintaining the doctrine of some churches, based upon the Gospels, such as atonement by the death of Christ and justification by faith; **3** evangelistic ‖ *n* **4** believer in evangelical doctrines ‖ **e·van·gel′i·cal·ism** *n*

e·van·ge·list /ivan′jəlist/ *n* **1** preacher of the gospel; **2** revivalist; **3** ardent partisan of a cause; **4 Evangelist** any of the four writers of the Gospels ‖ **e·van′ge·lism** *n* ‖ **e·van′ge·lis′tic** *adj*

e·vap·o·rate /ivap′ərāt′/ [L *evaporare* (-*atus*)] *vi* **1** to become vapor; **2** to vanish; **3** to emit vapor ‖ *vt* **4** to convert into vapor; **5** to concentrate by removing moisture from, as milk ‖ **e·vap′o·ra′tor** *n* ‖ **e·vap′o·ra′tion** *n*

e·va·sion /ivāzh′ən/ [see **evade**] *n* **1** act or instance of evading; artful avoidance of questions, duty, responsibility, taxes, etc.; **2** excuse, subterfuge ‖ **e·va′sive** /-siv/ *adj* ‖ **e·va′sive·ly** *adv* ‖ **e·va′sive·ness** *n* ‖ SYN shift, equivocation, shuffling, dodge, excuse

eve /ēv′/ [< archaic *even* evening] *n* **1** day before a holiday; **2** period immediately before some event

Eve /ēv′/ *n* the first woman, wife of Adam (Gen. 3:20)

e·ven /ēv′ən/ [OE *efen*] *adj* **1** level, smooth; **2** equal in quantity, size, number, etc.; **3** uniform, constant; **4** on the same line or level; flush; **5** exactly divisible by two; **6** impartial, fair; **7** equally balanced; **8** calm, unruffled; **9** exact, as *an even mile*; **10** break even to neither gain nor lose; **11** get even to be revenged ‖ *vi* **12** to become even ‖ *vt* **13** to make even;

14 even up to balance, as accounts || *adv* **15** evenly; **16** still, as *even better;* **17** just, as *even as I spoke;* **18** so much as, as *I never even spoke;* **19** however improbable, as *it is clear even to a child* || e'ven·ly *adv* || e'ven·ness *n*

e'ven-hand'ed *adj* fair, impartial

eve·ning /ēv'ning/ [OE *æfnung*] *n* **1** close of day and beginning of the night; **2** declining period, as of life || also *adj*

eve'ning gown' *n* woman's formal gown for evening wear

eve'nings *adv* during the evening regularly

eve'ning star' *n* any of the brighter planets seen in the western sky just after sunset

e'ven mon'ey *n* equal odds in a bet

e·vent' /ivent'/ [L *eventus*] *n* **1** occurrence, incident; **2** result or outcome; **3** any single item in a sports program; **4 at all events** or **in any event** in any case; **5 in the event of** in case of || SYN occurrence, accident, adventure, issue, incident, contingency, circumstance || DISCR *Occurrence* is a general term for that which happens. An *event* is a happening of significance or note; history records the *events* of the past. An *incident* is a happening of minor importance, as the *incidents* of a journey. A *circumstance* is an *incident* occurring along with something else, as unforeseen *circumstances;* extenuating *circumstances.* A *contingency* is an *event* or *occurrence* considered as a possibility, depending on chance or on another *event* itself conditional or uncertain, as none of the expected *contingencies* happened (see *result*)

e·vent'ful *adj* **1** full of important events; **2** having important results || e·vent'ful·ly *adv*

e'ven·tide' *n poet. & archaic* evening

e·ven·tu·al /iven'chōō·əl/ *adj* **1** ultimate, final; **2** depending on events, contingent || e·ven'tu·al·ly *adv*

e·ven'tu·al'i·ty /-al'itē/ *n* (-ties) possible or contingent event or result

e·ven'tu·ate' *vi* to happen; turn out, result

ev·er /ev'ər/ [OE *æfre*] *adv* **1** always; **2** at any time, as *is he ever here?;* **3** at all, as *if he ever comes;* **4 ever so** exceedingly

Ev'er·est, Mount /ev'ərist/ *n* highest mountain in the world, in the Himalayas between Tibet and Nepal (29,141 ft.)

Ev'er·glades' *npl* large, swampy, and partly forested region of S Florida

ev'er·green' *adj* **1** having green leaves throughout the year || *n* **2** evergreen plant or tree; **3** evergreens *pl* branches or leaves of such plants or trees used for decorating, as at Christmas

ev·er·last'ing *adj* **1** perpetual; lasting forever; **2** incessant; **3** tiresome; tedious || SYN permanent, unfailing, immortal, undying, unceasing, interminable (see *eternal*)

ev'er·more' *adv* always, forever

eve·ry /ev'rē/ [OE *æfre ælc* ever each] *adj* **1** all, taken one at a time; each; **2** all inclusively; **3** all possible, as *every kindness;* **4 every bit** *colloq* in every respect; **5 every now and then** from time to time; **6 every other** every alternate

eve'ry·bod'y *pron* every person

eve'ry·day' *adj* **1** daily; **2** for ordinary weekdays; **3** usual, ordinary

eve'ry·one' *pron* everybody

eve'ry one' *pron* each person or thing (of a group), as *every one of these books is new*

eve'ry·thing' *pron* all things; all that is concerned in a given matter

eve'ry·where' *adv* in all places

e·vict /ivikt'/ [L *evincere (-victus)* to prevail over] *vt* to remove from property by force, dispossess, esp. a tenant || e·vic'tion *n*

ev·i·dence /ev'idəns/ *n* **1** proof or grounds for believing something; **2** sign or indication; **3** testimony or object presented in court to establish the true facts of a case || *vt* **4** to make evident, indicate || SYN indication, certainty, proof, demonstration

ev'i·dent [L *evidens (-entis)*] *adj* clear to the eyes or mind || ev'i·dent·ly *adv* || SYN apparent, visible, perceptible, conclusive, covert, hidden, indistinct

e·vil /ēv'əl/ [OE *yfel*] *adj* **1** morally bad; wicked; **2** injurious, harmful; **3** disastrous, calamitous; **4** of ill repute; **5 the evil one** Satan || *n* **6** conduct showing evil intention; **7** that which is evil || e'vil·ly *adv* || SYN *adj* wrong, depraved, corrupt, vicious (see *bad*)

e'vil·do'er *n* one who does evil || e'vil·do'ing *n*

e'vil eye' *n* power to do harm to or cast bad luck on a person; attributed to certain people

e·vince /ivins'/ [see *evict*] *vt* **1** to manifest or make evident; **2** to demonstrate, as a quality

e·vis·cer·ate /ivis'ərāt'/ [L *eviscerare*] *vt* **1** to disembowel; **2** to deprive of essential parts || e·vis'cer·a'tion *n*

e·voke /ivōk'/ [F *évoquer* < L *evocare*] *vt* to summon or call forth, elicit || e·vo·ca·tion /ev'əkāsh'ən/ *n* || e·voc'a·tive /ivok'-, ivōk'-/ *adj*

ev·o·lu·tion /ev'əlōōsh'ən/ [see *evolve*] *n* **1** act of unfolding or developing; growth; **2** something developed or involved; **3** prescribed movement, as of dancers or machines; **4** the gradual development of organisms and species to their present state || **ev'o-lu'tion-ar'y** /-ner'-/ adj || **ev'o-lu'-tion-ist** n

e-volve /ivolv'/ [L evolvere (evolutus) to unroll] vt & vi 1 to develop gradually; 2 to develop by evolution

ewe /yōō/ [OE eowu] n female sheep

ew-er /yōō'ər/ [AF < L aqua water] n large wide-mouthed pitcher

ex /eks'/ [see ex-¹] prep fin without, as ex dividend, ex rights

ex-¹ [L & Gk = out of] pref 1 out, as extract; 2 beyond, as excessive; 3 thoroughly, as exasperate; 4 former, as ex-president

ex-² var of exo-

ex. 1 example; 2 exception; 3 exchange Ex. Exodus

ex-ac-er-bate /igzas'ərbāt', iksas'-/ [L exacerbare] vt to make more sharp, virulent, or bitter, as feelings or symptoms; aggravate || **ex-ac'er-ba'-tion** n

ex-act /igzakt'/ [L exactus] adj 1 correct, precise; rigorous; 2 strict; particular || vt 3 to require, insist upon; 4 to force payment of || **ex-act'ly** adv || **ex-act'ness** n || SYN adj precise, punctual, accurate (see correct)

ex-act'ing adj 1 making rigid demands; 2 severe, arduous

ex-ac'tion n 1 act of exacting; 2 thing exacted

ex-act'i-tude' n quality of being exact

ex-ag-ger-ate /igzaj'ərat'/ [L exaggerare (-atus) to heap up] vt 1 to make (statements) beyond truth or reason; overstate; 2 to enlarge abnormally || vi 3 to use exaggerated expressions || **ex-ag'ger-a'tion** n || **ex-ag'ger-a'tor** n

ex-alt /igzôlt'/ [L exaltare] vt 1 to elevate in rank, station, or dignity; 2 to glorify or extol; 3 to raise the spirits of, elate || **ex'al-ta'tion** /eg'-zôl-, ek'sôl-/ n || SYN dignify, glorify, promote, raise, heighten

ex-am /igzam'/ n colloq examination

ex-am-i-na'tion n 1 act of examining or state of being examined; 2 test of knowledge, fitness, or ability; 3 law interrogation, as of a witness || SYN inspection, search, scrutiny, trial, test, analysis

ex-am-ine /-in/ [MF examiner < L examinare to weigh carefully] vt 1 to scrutinize or investigate carefully; 2 to test the knowledge and qualifications of, as a student or candidate; 3 law to interrogate, as a witness || **ex-am'in-er** n || SYN inspect, inquire into, explore (see question)

ex-am-ple /igzamp'əl, -zämp'-/ [MF < L exemplum] n 1 pattern, model; 2 parallel case; 3 sample, specimen; 4 instance that serves as a warning; 5 problem illustrating a method or rule, as in arithmetic || SYN standard, type, instance, precedent, prototype, exemplar, model, pattern (see specimen)

ex-as-per-ate /igzas'pərāt'/ [L exasperare (-atus)] vt to irritate exceedingly; to enrage || **ex-as'per-a'tion** n || SYN annoy, provoke, enrage, inflame (see irritate)

Ex-cal-i-bur /ekskal'ibər/ n King Arthur's sword

ex ca-the-dra /eks kəthēd'rə, kath'-idrə/ [L = from the chair] adv with authority (used esp. of papal pronouncements)

ex-ca-vate /eks'kəvāt'/ [L excavare to hollow out] vt 1 to dig or scoop out; 2 to form a hollow in; 3 to form by hollowing out; 4 to unearth; dig up || **ex'ca-va'tion** n || **ex'ca-va'tor** n

ex-ceed /iksēd'/ [L excedere] vt 1 to go beyond the limit or bounds of; 2 to surpass || SYN outdo, outstrip, over-do, overtax, exaggerate

ex-ceed'ing-ly adv very; extremely

ex-cel /iksel'/ [L excellere] v (-celled; -cel-ling) vi 1 to be superior; surpass others || vt 2 to surpass, be superior to || SYN outdo, eclipse, surpass, transcend, outstrip

ex-cel-lence /ek'sələns/ n 1 fact or state of excelling; superiority; 2 excellent quality; 3 **Excellence** Excellency || SYN superiority, goodness, greatness, distinction

Ex'cel-len-cy n (-cies) 1 title of honor of certain high officials, as ambassadors and governors; 2 R C Ch title of bishops and archbishops

ex'cel-lent adj of outstanding value, merit, or virtue; very good of its kind || **ex'cel-lent-ly** adv || SYN choice, select, superior, prime, valuable, fine

ex-cel-si-or /iksel'sē-ər/ [L = loftier] n fine wood shavings, used in packing

ex-cept /iksept'/ [L excipere (-ceptus) to take out] vt 1 to take out; exclude || prep 2 excluding; but || conj 3 a otherwise than; only; b unless; 4 except that with the exception that

ex-cept'ing prep not including; except

ex-cep'tion n 1 act of excepting; 2 that which is excluded, as not conforming to the general rule; 3 objection; 4 **take exception** to object || SYN objection, offense, complaint, cavil, exclusion

ex-cep'tion-a-ble adj objectionable; open to censure

ex-cep'tion-al adj unusual; extraordinary || **ex-cep'tion-al-ly** adv || SYN remarkable, signal, unusual, superior, rare

ex-cerpt /iksurpt'/ [L excerpere (-cerptus) to pluck out] vt 1 to take out or select, as a passage from a book; quote || /ek'sərpt/ n 2 excerpted passage

ex-cess /ikses'/ [L excessus] n 1 undue amount, superfluity or overabundance; 2 amount by which one thing is greater than another; surplus; 3 intemperance; 4 **in excess of** more than ‖ /ek′ses/ adj 5 over and above what is ordinary; extra ‖ SYN n indulgence, dissipation, waste, superabundance

ex·ces′sive adj extreme; too much; immoderate ‖ ex·ces′sive·ly adv ‖ ex·ces′sive·ness n ‖ SYN intemperate, immoderate, unrestrained, exorbitant, inordinate, extravagant, superabundant

ex·change /iks·chānj′/ [MF eschange < LL excambium] n 1 act of giving or taking one thing for another; barter; 2 reciprocal giving and taking; 3 act of substituting one thing for another; 4 system of settling accounts by the use of drafts, bills of exchange, etc.; 5 credit instruments, as bills of exchange; 6 act of exchanging currency of one country for that of another; 7 value of one currency in terms of another; 8 place where goods and services are exchanged; 9 stock exchange; 10 central office for the interconnection of telephone lines ‖ vt 11 to barter; 12 to interchange; 13 to part with in return for something else ‖ vi 14 to make an exchange; 15 to pass in exchange ‖ ex·change′a·ble adj

ex·cheq·uer /iks·chek′ər, eks′chekər/ [OF eschequier chessboard] n 1 national treasury; 2 cash or funds; 3 Exchequer British department of the treasury

ex′cise¹ (tax′) /ek′sīz/ [prob MD excijs] n tax on the manufacture, sale, or consumption of goods within a country

ex·cise² /iksīz′/ [L excidere (-cisus)] vt to cut off; cut out ‖ ex·ci′sion /-sizh′ən/ n

ex·cite /iksīt′/ [L excitare] vt 1 to animate; arouse; 2 to encourage, stimulate; 3 to arouse mentally or emotionally ‖ ex·cit′a·ble adj ‖ ex·cit′ed adj ‖ ex·cite′ment n ‖ SYN awaken, provoke, stir, animate, impel, instigate, spur, goad ‖ ANT lull, quiet, soothe, deaden

ex·cit′ing adj causing excitement; thrilling, stirring

ex·claim /iksklām′/ [L exclamare] vi 1 to cry out suddenly and vehemently ‖ vt 2 to utter loudly ‖ ex·clam·a·to·ry /iksklam′ətôr′ē, -tōr′ē/ adj

ex·cla·ma·tion /eks′kləmāsh′ən/ n 1 act of exclaiming; 2 interjection

ex′cla·ma′tion point′ n punctuation mark ! denoting strong emotion, surprise, etc.

ex·clude /iksklood′/ [L excludere (-clusus)] vt 1 to shut out; hinder from entrance; debar; 2 to force out; eject ‖ ex·clu′sion n ‖ SYN expel, thrust out, eject, reject (see eliminate)

ex·clu·sive /-siv/ adj 1 excluding all others; 2 sole, as exclusive rights; 3 restricted to a certain few; 4 exclusive of not including ‖ n 5 journalism exclusive news item ‖ ex·clu′sive·ly adv ‖ ex·clu′sive·ness n

ex′com·mu′ni·cate′ /eks′-/ [< ex¹ + L communicare (-atus) to communicate] vt to cut off from membership, esp. from the rites and sacraments of a church ‖ ex′com·mu′ni·ca′tion n

ex·co·ri·ate /ikskôr′ē·āt′, -kōr′-/ [L excoriare (-atus) to skin] vt 1 to skin; 2 to berate ‖ ex·co′ri·a′tion n

ex·cre·ment /eks′krimənt/ [L excrementum] n waste matter discharged from the bowels

ex·cres·cence /ikskres′əns/ [L excrescentia] n 1 abnormal outgrowth, as a wart; 2 normal outgrowth, as hair or horns

ex·crete /ikskrēt′/ [L excernere (-cretus) to sift out] vt to throw off (waste matter) from the body ‖ ex·cre′tion n

ex·cru·ci·at·ing /ikskrōōsh′ē·āt′iŋ/ [< L excruciare (-atus) to torment] adj unbearably painful

ex·cul·pate /eks′kəlpāt′, ikskul′pāt/ [L exculpare (-atus)] vt to free from blame ‖ ex′cul·pa′tion n ‖ ex·cul′pa·to·ry /-pətôr′ē, -tōr′ē/ adj ‖ SYN discharge, acquit, absolve, release, remit, clear, excuse, justify, vindicate, exonerate

ex·cur·sion /ikskur′zhən/ [< L excurrere (-cursus) to run forth] n 1 short trip for a special purpose; 2 day's outing; 3 round trip at a reduced rate; 4 digression ‖ ex·cur′sion·ist n ‖ SYN jaunt, ramble, expedition, trip

ex·cur′sive /-siv/ adj digressing

ex·cuse /ikskyōōz′/ [L excusare] vt 1 to make apology for; 2 to justify; 3 to pardon; overlook; 4 to release from obligation or duty; 5 to remit, as a claim or fine; 6 excuse oneself to ask for permission to leave ‖ /-kyōōs′/ n 7 explanation offered in extenuation; 8 pretext ‖ ex·cus′a·ble /-kyōōz′-/ adj ‖ SYN v pardon, condone (see forgive, palliate); n apology, extenuation, palliation ‖ DISCR An excuse implies an admitted fault and offers a partial explanation or justification, hoping to lessen the blame. One who makes an apology offers a regretful acknowledgment that he is in the wrong, or, if appearances are against him, offers assurance that no offense was intended. We make apologies for rudeness, incivility, or error. Extenuation and palliation are attempts to soften an admitted fault; extenuation seeks to lessen the greatness of the guilt or offense, as by a partial excuse; palliation seeks to cause the offense to appear less blameworthy than it is. Youth is often cited in extenuation of boyish pranks or escapades; the term "wild" instead of "bad" is often employed in charitable *pallia-tion* of the misconduct of young men

ex·e·cra·ble /ek'səkrəbəl/ *adj* 1 abominable; 2 very bad, of poor quality ‖ **ex'e·cra·bly** *adv*

ex'e·crate' /-krāt'/ [L *exsecrari* (*-atus*) to curse] *vt* 1 to curse; 2 to detest, abhor

ex'e·cra'tion *n* 1 act of cursing; 2 expression of detestation; 3 thing cursed ‖ SYN imprecation, anathema (see *malediction*)

ex·e·cute /ek'sikyŏŏt'/ [MF *executer*] *vt* 1 to carry out, accomplish; 2 to put to death under sentence of the law; 3 to perform, do; 4 to bring into being according to a design or plan; 5 *law* to complete, put into effect, or make valid ‖ **ex'e·cu'tion** *n* ‖ SYN enforce, manage, complete (see *kill, effect*)

ex'e·cu'tion·er *n* one who puts condemned criminals to death

ex·ec·u·tive /igzek'yətiv/ *n* 1 person or group in charge of administration, as of a company; 2 a branch of government charged with enforcing the laws and administering public affairs; **b** person in charge of this branch ‖ also *adj*

ex·ec'u·tive priv'i·lege *n* prerogative of the chief executive to keep sensitive information secret in the public interest

ex·ec'u·tive ses'sion *n* session, as of a legislative body, which is closed to all persons who are not accredited members

ex·ec'u·tor *n law* person appointed by a testator in his will to see that its terms are carried out ‖ **ex·ec'u·trix** *nfem* (**ex·ec·u·tri'ces** /-trī'sēz/ also **ex·ec·u·trix·es**)

ex·e·ge·sis /ek'sijēs'is/ [Gk = explanation] *n* (**-ses** /-sēz/) critical explanation or interpretation, esp. of Scripture

ex·em·plar /igzemp'lər/ [see **example**] *n* model to be copied; example or pattern ‖ SYN model, example, archetype, case, specimen

ex·em·pla·ry /igzem'plərē, eg'zəmpler'ē/ *adj* 1 commendable; serving as a model to be imitated; 2 serving as a warning; 3 serving as a sample or illustration

ex·em'pli·fy' [MF *exemplifier*] *v* (**-fied**) *vt* to show by example; illustrate ‖ **ex·em'pli·fi·ca'tion** *n*

ex·empt /igzempt'/ [L *eximere* (*exemptus*) to release] *adj* 1 free from duty, burden, or other limitation to which others are subject ‖ *vt* 2 to make exempt ‖ **ex·emp'tion** *n*

ex·er·cise /ek'sərsiz'/ [MF *exercice*] *vt* 1 to train by use; 2 to use; 3 to perform; carry out the duties of; 4 to employ actively, as muscles, mind, or the like; 5 to make anxious; worry ‖ *vi* 6 to undergo training; take exercise ‖ *n* 7 bodily or mental activity for health or development; 8 performance, as of a duty or an office; 9 active use, as of a mental faculty; 10 something done for practice and training; 11 **exercises** *pl* ceremony

ex·ert /igzurt'/ [L *exserere* (*-sertus*) to put forth] *vt* 1 to put forth, esp. with effort, as force or ability; 2 **exert oneself** to exercise one's energy or power

ex·er'tion *n* active use of any power; effort, as *the exertion of one's will* ‖ SYN exercise, work, trial, endeavor (see *effort*)

ex·hale /eks·hāl'/ [L *exhalare*] *vt* 1 to breathe out; emit ‖ *vi* 2 to breathe out ‖ **ex'ha·la'tion** /-hə-/ *n*

ex·haust /igzôst'/ [L *exhaurire* (*-haustus* to empty out] *vt* 1 to empty, drain; 2 to empty out or draw off; 3 to create a vacuum in; 4 to use up entirely; 5 to wear out, tire; 6 to treat thoroughly, as a topic ‖ *n* 7 escape of spent steam or gas from an engine; 8 the ejected gas; 9 pipe or part through which the gas is ejected; 10 ventilating fan ‖ **ex·haust'i·ble** *adj* ‖ **ex·haus'tion** /-ôs'chən/ *n*

ex·haus'tive *adj* 1 thorough, comprehensive; 2 tending to drain ‖ **ex·haus'tive·ly** *adv*

ex·hib·it /igzib'it/ [L *exhibere* (*-hibitus*) to hold out] *vt* 1 to present to view; display, show ‖ *vi* 2 to display a thing publicly ‖ *n* 3 object exhibited; 4 showing; 5 *law* article used as evidence ‖ **ex·hib'i·tor** *n*

ex·hi·bi·tion /ek'sibish'ən/ *n* 1 act of exhibiting; 2 public showing

ex'hi·bi'tion·ism *n* 1 tendency to call attention to oneself; 2 sexual deviation characterized by exposure of the genitals ‖ **ex'hi·bi'tion·ist** *n*

ex·hil·a·rate /igzil'ərat'/ [L *exhilarare* (*-atus*)] *vt* 1 to make merry; 2 to enliven; invigorate ‖ **ex·hil'a·ra'tion** *n* ‖ SYN animate, stimulate, enliven, cheer, rejoice

ex·hort /igzôrt'/ [L *exhortari* to encourage] *vt* to urge or advise earnestly ‖ **ex'hor·ta'tion** /eg'zôr-, ek's-/ *n*

ex·hume /igz(y)ŏŏm', eks·hyŏŏm'/ [< *ex-* + L *humare* to inter] *vt* to disinter or dig up (something that has been buried) ‖ **ex'hu·ma'tion** /eks'-hyŏŏ-/ *n*

ex·i·gen·cy /ek'sijənsē/ [< L *exigens* (*-entis*) demanding] *n* (**-cies**) 1 urgency; pressing necessity; 2 emergency; 3 **exigencies** *pl* demands or requirements inherent in a given situation ‖ **ex'i·gent** *adj* ‖ SYN need, pressure, necessity (see *emergency*)

ex·ig·u·ous /igzig'yŏŏ·əs, iks-/ [L *exiguus*] *adj* scanty, meager; diminutive

ex·ile /eg'zīl, ek's-/ [L *exsilium*] *n* 1

prolonged, often enforced residence in a foreign country; banishment; **2** exiled person ‖ *vt* **3** to banish, as from a native place ‖ SYN expel, expatriate, drive out (see *banish*)

ex·ist /igzist'/ [L *exsistere*] *vi* **1** to have actual being; live; be; **2** to persist or continue in being; to occur, be found

ex·ist'ence *n* **1** state of being; **2** life; **3** continued being; duration ‖ **ex·ist'ent** *adj*

ex·is·ten·tial·ism /eg'zistensh'əliz'əm/ *n* philosophical movement emphasizing personal freedom in an uncertain and purposeless world

ex·it /eg'zit, ek's-/ [L *exire* (-*itus*) to go out] *n* **1** act of going out, egress; **2** way out ‖ *vi* **3** to leave

ex li·bris /eks lĭb'ris/ .[L = from the books (of), used before the owner's name on a bookplate] *n* (*pl* -bris) bookplate

exo- /ek'sō-/ [Gk] *comb form* outside, outer

ex·o·bi·ol·o·gy *n* study of life on other planets ‖ **ex'o·bi·ol'o·gist** *n*

ex·o·dus /ek'sədəs/ [Gk] *n* **1** departure, going out; **2 Exodus** second book of the Old Testament; **3 the Exodus** the departure of the Jews from Egypt under Moses

ex of·fi·ci·o /eks'əfish'ē·ō/ [L = from the office] *adj & adv* by virtue of one's office

ex·og·a·my /eksog'əmē/ [*exo-* + Gk *gamos* marriage] *n* marriage outside a specific tribe or social unit ‖ **ex·og'a·mous** *adj*

ex·on·er·ate /igzon'ərāt'/ [L *exonerare* to unburden] *vt* **1** to clear of blame or guilt; **2** to relieve of an obligation ‖ **ex·on'er·a'tion** *n*

ex·or·bi·tant /igzôr'bitənt/ [< L *exorbitare* to go out of the wheel tracks] *adj* going beyond what is fair and reasonable; excessive ‖ **ex·or'bi·tance** *n* ‖ SYN excessive, immoderate, extravagant (see *dear*)

ex·or·cise /ek'sôrsīz'/ [Gk *exorkizein*] *vt* **1** to expel (an evil spirit) by prayers or magic words; **2** to deliver from evil spirits ‖ **ex'or·cism** *n*

ex·o·ter·ic /ek'səter'ik/ [Gk *exoterikos* outer] *adj* **1** understood by the general public; **2** open, undisguised ‖ **ex'o·ter'i·cal·ly** *adv*

ex·o·ther·mic /ek'sōthur'mik/ [*exo-* + Gk *therme* heat] *adj* designating a chemical change in which heat is liberated

ex·ot·ic /igzot'ik/ [Gk *exotikos* foreign] *adj* **1** foreign; strange; **2** glamorous, enticing

exp. **1** export(ed); **2** express

ex·pand /ikspand'/ [L *expandere* (-*pansus*) to spread out] *vt & vi* **1** to spread out, unfold; **2** to enlarge; increase in size or extent

ex·panse /ikspans'/ *n* wide extent; uninterrupted stretch or area

ex·pan·sion /-pan'shən/ *n* **1** act of expanding; **2** state of being expanded; **3** increase in size, extent, or volume; **4** *math* full development of some indicated operation ‖ SYN increase, dilatation, distension, enlargement, extent, immensity ‖ ANT abridgment, curtailment, condensation, decrease

ex·pan·sive *adj* **1** capable of expanding; **2** widely extended; large; **3** unrestrained, effusive ‖ **ex·pan'sive·ly** *adv*

ex par·te /eks pärt'ē/ [L = from a part] *adj* (judicial proceeding) with only one side present or represented

ex·pa·ti·ate /ikspāsh'ē·āt'/ [L *expatiari* to roam] *vi* to express oneself copiously ‖ **ex·pa'ti·a'tion** *n*

ex·pa·tri·ate /ikspāt'rē·āt'/ [< *ex-¹* *patria* native land] *vt* **1** to banish, exile; **2** to withdraw (oneself) from one's native country ‖ /-trē·it/ *n* **3** one who has expatriated himself or who has been exiled ‖ **ex·pa'tri·a'tion** *n* ‖ SYN *v* exile, drive out (see *banish*)

ex·pect /ikspekt'/ [L *exspectare* to await] *vt* **1** to look for as likely to occur or appear; **2** to look for as proper and justified; **3** to await the birth of (a baby); **4** *colloq* to suppose ‖ *vi* **5 be expecting** to be pregnant

ex·pect'an·cy *n* (-cies) **1** act or state of expecting; **2** state of being expected; **3** that which is expected; **4** statistically expected amount

ex·pect'ant *adj* expecting, awaiting ‖ **ex·pect'ant·ly** *adv*

ex·pec·ta·tion /eks'-/ *n* **1** act or state of expecting; **2** thing looked forward to; **3 expectations** *pl* good prospects for future gain or advancement ‖ SYN hope, anticipation, confidence, trust, presentiment, apprehension ‖ ANT realization, despair, doubt

ex·pec·to·rate /ikspek'tərāt'/ [L *expectorare*] *vt & vi* to spit ‖ **ex·pec'to·ra'tion** *n*

ex·pe·di·en·cy /ikspēd'ē·ənsē/ *n* (-cies) also **ex·pe'di·ence** **1** quality of being expedient; suitableness; **2** doing of what promises to be of use rather than what is right

ex·pe'di·ent [L *expediens* (-*entis*) settling] *adj* **1** fit or suitable for the purpose; **2** based on self-interest rather than right ‖ *n* **3** means to an end; **4** device ‖ SYN *adj* apt, practical, efficient, advantageous, wise, favorable, profitable, convenient (see *necessary*)

ex·pe·dite /eks'pidīt'/ [L *expedire* (-*ditus*) to free the feet] *vt* **1** to hasten, quicken; **2** to carry out quickly and efficiently ‖ **ex'pe·dit'er** *n*

ex'pe·di'tion /-dish'ən/ *n* **1** journey, march, or voyage, as by an army or group of persons, for some particular purpose; **2** persons in such an enterprise; **3** speed and efficiency in getting something done ‖ **ex'pe·di'tion·ar'y** /-ner'-/ *adj*

ex·pe·di'tious *adj* prompt and efficient ‖ SYN speedy, efficient, energetic, prompt, ready, quick, rapid, swift ‖ ANT slow, unready, inefficient

ex·pel /ikspel'/ [L *expellere* (*-pulsus*)] *v* (**-pelled; -pel·ling**) *vt* **1** to drive away; **2** to force out, eject; **3** to remove from membership ‖ SYN exile, eject, throw out, dismiss (see *banish*)

ex·pend /ikspend'/ [L *expendere* (*-pensus*) to weigh out] *vt* to spend, use up

ex·pend'a·ble *adj* **1** capable of being expended; **2** (men or equipment) that can be sacrificed to achieve a larger end

ex·pend'i·ture /-dichər/ *n* **1** consumption; spending; **2** expense

ex·pense /ikspens'/ *n* **1** paying out of money; **2** detriment or injury; **3** cost; money expended; **4** **expenses** *pl* charges incurred in one's work or business

ex·pen'sive *adj* costly, high-priced ‖ **ex·pen'sive·ly** *adv* ‖ SYN high-priced, exorbitant, costly (see *dear*)

ex·pe·ri·ence /ikspir'ē·əns/ [L *experientia*] *n* **1** personal trial, observation, or practice; **2** knowledge gained by practice, trial, or observation; **3** something lived through ‖ *vt* **4** to undergo ‖ **ex·pe'ri·enced** *adj* ‖ SYN *n* acquaintance, observation (see *knowledge*)

ex·per·i·ment /iksper'imənt/ [L *experimentum*] *n* **1** trial or operation to discover, test, or demonstrate something ‖ /iksper'iment'/ *vi* **2** to conduct an experiment ‖ **ex·per'i·men'tal** /-men'-/ *adj* ‖ SYN *n* test, proof (see *trial*)

ex·pert /ikspurt', ek'spərt/ [L *expertus* tried, tested] *adj* **1** skillful; proficient through practice or training ‖ /ek'-spərt/ *n* **2** person with special skill or knowledge in a particular field ‖ **ex·pert'ly** *adv* ‖ **ex·pert'ness** *n* ‖ SYN *adj* experienced, practiced, facile (see *clever*)

ex·per·tise /ek'spərtēz'/ [F = expert's report] *n* **1** expertness, skill; **2** expert opinion

ex·pi·ate /ek'spē·āt'/ [L *expiare* (*-atus*)] *vt* to atone or make amends for, as a sin ‖ **ex'pi·a'tion** *n*

ex·pire /ikspī'(ə)r/ [L *exspirare* to breathe out] *vt* **1** to exhale ‖ *vi* **2** to terminate, as a period of time; **3** to die ‖ **ex'pi·ra'tion** /ek'spi-/ *n*

ex·plain /iksplān'/ [L *explanare*] *vt* **1** to make intelligible or clear; **2** to account for ‖ *vi* **3** to give an explanation ‖ **ex·plan'a·to'ry** /-plan'-ətôr'ē̆, -tôr'ē̆/ *adj* ‖ SYN elucidate, define, decipher, expound, unfold (see *interpret*) ‖ ANT confuse, jumble, perplex, mix up

ex·pla·na'tion /ek'splənāsh'ən/ *n* **1** act of explaining; **2** that which explains; **3** meaning; interpretation; **4** clearing up a misunderstanding ‖ SYN explication, elucidation, exposition, interpretation, description, definition ‖ DISCR An *explanation* is a clearing up of that which is not understood, or is misunderstood or obscure. *Explanations* make meanings known, account for conduct, make motives intelligible, solve difficulties. An *exposition* is a full *explanation* of a text, passage, or the like, bringing out its whole sense, implication, and intent. The purchaser of a radio set gets an *explanation* of how to operate it; scientists write *expositions* of their theories; clergymen give *expositions* of Scriptural passages. *Interpretation* is the giving of the meaning of the language of one country or period in the language of another, or the expressing in familiar terms of that which is obscure, or the bringing out of the meaning of something either by artistic representation or by sympathetic understanding. An appreciative *interpretation* of a character on the stage is sympathetic and revealing. A *definition* is exact, precisely worded, comprehensive, exclusive; the nature of a thing or the meaning of a word should be unmistakably clear as the result of *definition*. A *description* is a verbal picture, chiefly concerned with those qualities of its subject which have pictorial value

ex·ple·tive /eks'plətiv/ [< L *expletus* filled up] *n* **1** word or phrase used to pad or fill out a sentence; **2** oath; exclamation

ex·pli·cate /eks'plikāt'/ [L *explicare* (*-atus*) to unfold] *vt* to explain, make clear ‖ **ex'pli·ca'tion** *n* ‖ **ex'pli·ca·ble** *adj*

ex·plic·it /iksplis'it/ [L *explicitus* unfolded] *adj* definite; clearly stated; unambiguous ‖ **ex·plic'it·ly** *adv* ‖ SYN open, unambiguous, plain, unequivocal, precise

ex·plode /iksplōd'/ [L *explodere* (*-plosus*) to hiss off the stage] *vi* **1** to burst with sudden noise and violence ‖ *vt* **2** to cause to explode; **3** to discredit, expose, as an idea

ex·ploit /eks'ploit/ [OF *esploite*] *n* **1** brilliant achievement or heroic deed ‖ /iksploit'/ *vt* **2** to make use of; **3** to promote, publicize; **4** to use selfishly for one's own purposes ‖ **ex·ploit'er** *n* ‖ **ex'ploi·ta'tion** *n* ‖ SYN *n* feat, deed, achievement, performance, act

ex·plore /iksplôr', -splōr'/ [L *explorare* to search out] *vt* **1** to search or examine thoroughly; **2** to travel through (a country) for discovery; **3** *med* to examine, as a wound ‖ **ex·plor'a·to'ry** /-tôr'-, -tōr'-/ *adj* ‖ **ex·plor'er** *n* ‖ **ex'plo·ra'tion** /eks'-/ *n*

ex·plo·sion /iksplōzh′ən/ [see **explode**] *n* 1 act or instance of exploding; 2 loud report; 3 sudden and noisy outbreak, as of laughter or anger; 4 great, sudden, and sustained increase, as *the population explosion*

ex·plo′sive /-siv/ *adj* 1 capable of exploding or likely to explode; 2 pert. to or like an explosion || *n* 3 explosive substance

ex·po·nent /ikspōn′ənt/ [L *exponens* (*-entis*) expounding] *n* 1 one who explains or interprets; 2 one who is regarded as a representative or symbol || *also* eks′pōnənt/ *n* 3 *math* symbol placed at the upper right of another to show the power to which the latter is raised, as x^3

ex·port /ikspôrt′, eks′pôrt, -pôrt′, -pôrt/ [L *exportare* to carry out] *vi* 1 to send (goods) to another country || /eks′pôrt, -pôrt/ *n* 2 act of exporting; 3 that which is exported || ex′por·ta′tion *n* || ex·port′er *n*

ex·pose /ikspōz′/ [MF *exposer*] *vt* 1 to lay open to danger or harm; 2 to bare to the elements; 3 to lay open to something specific, as books, influence, or ideas; 4 to disclose, reveal; 5 *photog* to subject (a film) to the action of light || SYN display, publish, exhibit, disclose, abandon

ex·po·sé /eks′pōzā′/ [F] *n* public disclosure of something scandalous

ex·po·si·tion /eks′pəzish′ən/ [< L *exponere* (*-positus*) to expose] *n* 1 detailed explanation or interpretation; 2 show or exhibition; 3 display, exposure || SYN definition, commentary, interpretation, exhibition, display, exposure (see *explanation*)

ex·pos·i·tor /ikspoz′itər/ *n* one who expounds || **ex·pos′i·to′ry** /-tôr′-, -tŏr′-/ *adj*

ex post fac·to /eks′pōst′fak′tō/ [L = from after the deed] *adv* after the fact; retroactively || *also adj*

ex·pos·tu·late /ikspos′chəlāt′/ [L *expostulare* (*-atus*) to demand] *vi* to reason earnestly, remonstrate || **ex·pos′tu·la′tion** *n* || SYN remonstrate, rebuke || DISCR *Expostulate* and *remonstrate* agree in the idea of reasoning with, or appealing to, a person to turn him from the course he is taking; one who *remonstrates* censures more than he appeals; one who *expostulates* entreats, earnestly or vehemently, more than he blames or rebukes

ex·po·sure /ikspōzh′ər/ [< *expose*] *n* 1 act of exposing; 2 situation, location, as *a southern exposure*; 3 *photog* a time a negative is exposed during the taking of a picture; b each section of film for taking a photograph

ex·po′sure me′ter *n photog* instrument for measuring the intensity of the light falling on a subject

ex·pound /ikspound′/ [OF *espondre* < L *exponere* to put forth] *vt* to set forth, explain, make clear

ex·press /ikspres′/ [MF *expres* < L *exprimere* (*-pressus*) to force out] *adj* 1 plainly stated; explicit; 2 special; 3 direct, fast, as a train or highway || *adv* 4 by express || *n* 5 express vehicle; 6 rapid method of conveyance for mail and goods || *vt* 7 to squeeze out, press; 8 to state, put into words; 9 to show, reveal; 10 to represent, as by a symbol; 11 to send express

ex·pres′sion *n* 1 act of putting into words; 2 particular word or phrase; 3 power of expressing in words; 4 wording; mode of speech; 5 aspect of countenance indicating feeling or emotion; 6 modulation or intonation of the voice; 7 *math* symbol or symbols representing a value or relationship || **ex·pres′sion·less** *adv* || SYN diction, language, utterance, aspect, looks

ex·pres′sion·ism *n* art style which seeks to depict the artist's subjective reaction and not objective reality

ex·pres′sive *adj* 1 full of expression; 2 serving to express

ex·press′ly *adv* 1 specially; 2 explicitly

ex·press′way′ *n* limited-access highway

ex·pro·pri·ate /eksprōp′rē·āt′/ [L *expropriare* (*-atus*) to deprive of ownership, as a person of land || **ex·pro′pri·a′tion** *n*

ex·pul·sion /ikspulsh′ən/ [see **expel**] *n* act of expelling or state of being expelled

ex·punge /ikspunj′/ [L *expungere*] *vt* to blot out, erase || SYN obliterate, cancel, blot out, destroy (see *erase*)

ex·pur·gate /eks′pərgāt′/ [L *expurgare* (*-atus*) to cleanse] *vt* to remove obscene or objectionable matter from (a book) || ex′pur·ga′tion *n*

ex·qui·site /ek′skwizit, ikskwiz′it/ [L *exquisitus* sought after] *adj* 1 delicately beautiful; appealing; refined, elegant; 2 intensely acute or keen || ex′qui·site·ly *adv* || SYN finished, fastidious, dainty, delicate, elegant, choice, rare, fine || DISCR *Fine*, as here compared, describes that which is beautifully finished, smooth, and of excellent quality, as *fine* linen; *fine* manners; *fine* feelings. That is *delicate* which is *fine*, slight, and shapely, as a *delicate* ear; the *delicate* wing of an insect. Skin is *delicate* which is soft, fine-grained, and clear; silk, which is fine and soft of texture; beauty, which is small, perfect, almost fragile-looking; colors, which are soft and faint. *Dainty* things possess a *delicate* beauty, are selected with exceptional taste, and radiate grace, cleanliness, and charm; *dainty* ways, carried to excess, become squeamish. *Elegant* movements are graceful; an *elegant* style is flowing and finished; *elegant* manners are polished and refined; *elegant* modes of life are tastefully luxurious. That is *exquisite* which possesses consummate excellence and beauty; *exquisite* implies that which is finely finished, *delicate* in outline and nature, *dainty* in coloring, as an *exquisite* design; *exquisite* tracery. Pleasure and pain can be so acute and fine-drawn as to be *exquisite*; extreme sensibility is *exquisite*; perception and discrimination can be so delicately nice as to be *exquisite*. That is *choice* which is of selected quality, as *choice* fruit; or which is carefully chosen, as *choice* poems. That is *rare* which is unusual and *fine*, as workmanship, a gem, etc. . .

ex·tant /ek'stənt, ikstant'/ [< L *exstare* to stand out] *adj* now existent; not destroyed or lost

ex·tem·po·ra·ne·ous /ikstemp'ərän'ḡ·əs/ [L *extemporaneus*] *adj* done or spoken without advance preparation; impromptu

ex·tem·po·re /ikstemp'ərē/ [L = out of the time] *adv & adj* without preparation; impromptu

ex·tem'po·rize' *vt & vi* 1 to speak or perform extempore; 2 to improvise

ex·tend /ikstend'/ [L *extendere* (-*tensus*) to stretch out] *vt* 1 to stretch out; lengthen or widen; 2 to enlarge in space, time, scope, power, or the like; 3 to straighten out at length, as *to extend an arm*; 4 to offer, accord; hold out || *vi* 5 to be extended; 6 to reach ¶ SYN lengthen, widen, prolong (see *increase*)

ex·ten'si·ble *adj* capable of being extended

ex·ten'sion *n* 1 act of extending or state of being extended; 2 additional part; annex; 3 extended or extensible part; 4 range, extent; 5 additional telephone on a line || *adj* 6 (courses) given off the campus or by correspondence; 7 (table, ladder, etc.) that can be extended to greater length

ex·ten'sive *adj* 1 wide, broad; 2 comprehensive, far-reaching || **ex·ten'·sive·ly** *adv* ¶ SYN capacious, comprehensive, broad, wide

ex·ten·sor /ikstens'ər/ *n* muscle that straightens or extends a part of the body

ex·tent /ikstent'/ [AF *extente*] *n* 1 space or degree to which a thing extends; 2 measure, limit; 3 extended space

ex·ten·u·ate /iksten'yōo͞-āt'/ [L *extenuare* (-*atus*) to thin] *vt* 1 to offer excuses for; 2 to lessen the seriousness of || SYN mitigate, lessen, soften (see *palliate*)

ex·te·ri·or /ikstir'ḡ·ər/ [L] *adj* 1 outer; on the outside; 2 coming from without; 3 for outside use || *n* 4 that which is outside; 5 outer surface; 6 outward appearance; aspect

ex·ter·mi·nate /iksturm'ināt'/ [L *exterminare* (-*atus*)] *vt* to get rid of completely; annihilate || **ex·ter'mi·na'tion** *n* || SYN root out, extirpate, destroy (see *eradicate*)

ex·ter'mi·na'tor *n* 1 one who exterminates; 2 one whose business is to exterminate household pests

ex·ter·nal /iksturn'əl/ [< L *externus*] *adj* 1 pert. to or coming from the outside; outer; 2 superficial; 3 visible; physical || *n* 4 outward part; 5 **externals** *pl* external features or parts || **ex·ter'nal·ly** *adv*

ex·tinct /ikstiŋkt'/ [L *exstinctus* quenched] *adj* 1 no longer existing; 2 (volcano) that has ceased erupting

ex·tinc·tion /ikstiŋk'shən/ *n* 1 act of extinguishing; 2 state of being extinguished or extinct; 3 destruction, annihilation

ex·tin·guish /ikstiŋ'gwish/ [L *exstinguere*] *vt* 1 to put out (a light or fire); 2 to suppress, destroy

ex·tin'guish·er *n* 1 one who or that which extinguishes; 2 device for putting out fires by chemical action

ex·tir·pate /ek'stərpāt', ikstur'-/ [L *exstirpare* (-*atus*) to pull out by the roots] *vt* to root out, exterminate || **ex'tir·pa'tion** *n* || SYN destroy (see *eradicate*)

ex·tol also **ex·toll** /ikstōl'/ [L *extollere* to raise] *v* (-**tolled**; -**tol·ling**) *vt* to praise highly, laud

ex·tort /ikstôrt'/ [L *extorquere* (-*tortus*) to wrest] *vt* to obtain by threats or violence

ex·tor'tion *n* 1 act of extorting; 2 that which is extorted; 3 oppressive or unjust exaction || **ex·tor'tion·er** or **ex·tor'tion·ist** *n*

ex·tra /ek'strə/ [< *extraordinary*] *adj* 1 over and above what is ordinary or required; additional; 2 better than usual || *n* 3 something extra; 4 special edition of a newspaper; 5 *movies, telv* person playing minor nonspeaking part || *adv* 6 exceptionally

ex·tra- [L] *pref* beyond, outside of

ex·tract /ikstrakt'/ [L *extrahere* (-*tractus*) to pull out] *vt* 1 to obtain by steeping, distilling, pressing, or the like; 2 to pull out; 3 to derive or deduce; 4 to extort; 5 to select, copy out, as a passage from a book; 6 *math* to calculate (the root of a number) || /ek'strakt/ *n* 7 excerpt; 8 concentrated solution or substance ¶ SYN *v* elicit, evoke, deduce, withdraw, quote

ex·trac·tion *n* 1 act of extracting, or state of being extracted. 2 lineage or descent; 3 that which is drawn or obtained from a substance; essence || SYN derivation, descent, lineage, birth; essence

ex·tra·cur·ric′u·lar /ek′strə-/ *adj* 1 apart from the regular curriculum; 2 pert. to school activities outside of the academic courses

ex′tra·dite′ /-dīt′/ [< *extradition*] *vt* 1 to surrender (a fugitive) to another state or nation for trial; 2 to secure the return of (a fugitive)

ex′tra·di′tion /-dish′/ [*ex-*¹ + L *traditio* (*-onis*) handing down] *n* surrender of a fugitive to another state or nation for trial

ex′tra·ga·lac′tic *adj* existing or originating outside or beyond the Milky Way

ex′tra·mar′i·tal *adj* adulterous; pert. to sexual relations with another than one's spouse

ex′tra·mu′ral *adj* 1 outside the walls of the city, fortress, school; 2 interscholastic; taking place between groups belonging to more than one school

ex·tra·ne·ous /ikstrān′ē-əs/ [L *extraneus* foreign] *adj* not belonging or proper; irrelevant ‖ **ex·tra′ne·ous·ly** *adv* ‖ SYN external, unessential, extrinsic, foreign

ex·tra·or·di·nar·y /ikstrôr′diner′ē ek′strə-ôr′-/ [L *extraordinarius*] *adj* 1 beyond the usual course; uncommon, unusual; 2 remarkable, noteworthy ‖ **ex·traor′di·nar′i·ly** *adv*

ex·trap·o·late /ikstrap′əlāt′/ [*extra-* + inter*polate*] *vt* 1 to infer from what is known; 2 to predict on the basis of past experience; 3 to estimate by extending known information ‖ also *vi* ‖ **ex·trap′o·la′tion** *n*

ex′tra·sen′so·ry /ek′strə-/ *adj* apart from or without using the ordinary senses

ex′tra·sys′to·le *n* premature contraction of the auricle or the ventricle of the heart or of both, that results in momentary interruption of the heart beat but does not disturb the normal rhythm

ex′tra·ter·res′tri·al *adj* outside the limits of the earth or its atmosphere

ex′tra·ter′ri·to′ri·al *adj* free from local jurisdiction ‖ **ex′tra·ter′ri·to′ri·al′i·ty** /-al′-/ *n*

ex·trav·a·gant /ikstrav′əgənt/ [< L *extravagari* to wander out] *adj* 1 exceeding reasonable limits; excessive; 2 wasteful, spending lavishly ‖ **ex·trav′a·gant·ly** *adv* ‖ **ex·trav′a·gance** *n* ‖ SYN profuse, prodigal, wasteful, unrestrained, wild, immoderate, excessive, exorbitant, dear, high

ex·trav′a·gan′za /-gan′zə/ [It] *n* lavish and spectacular stage show

ex′tra·ve·hic′u·lar *adj* performed outside a spacecraft during a flight in outer space

ex·tra·vert /ek′strəvurt′/ *n* var of *extrovert*

ex·treme /ikstrēm′/ [L *extremus*] *adj* 1 farthest removed from the normal; 2 farthest away; 3 last, final; 4 of the highest degree; 5 excessive; extravagant; 6 advanced, radical ‖ *n* 7 utmost degree; 8 excess; 9 either of two things as different or as remote as possible; 10 *math* first or last term of a proportion or series ‖ **ex·treme′ly** *adv*

ex·treme′ unc′tion *n R C Ch* sacrament administered to dying persons

ex·trem′ist *n* one who goes to extremes, esp. in political ideas

ex·trem·i·ty /ikstrem′itē/ *n* (**-ties**) 1 state of being extreme; 2 utmost degree; 3 end or edge; 4 condition of extreme distress or need; 5 extremities *pl* hands or feet

ex·tri·cate /ek′strikāt′/ [L *extricare*] *vt* to free from difficulties; disentangle ‖ **ex′tri·ca·ble** *adj* ‖ **ex′tri·ca′tion** *n* ‖ SYN release, disengage, relieve, free (see *liberate*)

ex·trin·sic /ikstrins′ik/ [L *extrinsecus* from without] *adj* 1 not inherent or essential; 2 external ‖ **ex·trin′si·cal·ly** *adv* ‖ SYN extraneous, unessential, outward, foreign

ex·tro·vert /ek′strəvurt′/ [< *extra-* + L *vertere* to turn] *n* person primarily interested in the people and things around him rather than in his inner thoughts ‖ **ex′tro·ver′sion** /-zhən or -shən/ *n*

ex·trude /ikstrōōd′/ [L *extrudere* to thrust out] *vt* 1 to force out; expel; 2 to form by forcing through a die, as metal ‖ *vi* 3 to protrude ‖ **ex·tru′sion** /-zhən/ *n*

ex·u·ber·ant /igzōōb′ərənt/ [< L *exuberare* to grow luxuriantly] *adj* 1 copious, abundant, overflowing; 2 abounding in good spirits; effusive ‖ **ex·u′ber·ance** *n* ‖ **ex·u′ber·ant·ly** ‖ SYN plentiful, prolific, fertile, rank (see *luxuriant*)

ex·ude /igzōōd′, iks-/ [L *exsudare* to sweat] *vt* & *vi* to discharge gradually, as through pores ‖ **ex′u·da′tion** /ek′sə-, eg′zə-, eks′yōō-/ *n*

ex·ult /igzult′/ [L *exsultare* to leap up] *vi* to rejoice above measure; be jubilant ‖ **ex·ult′ant** *adj* ‖ **ex′ul·ta′tion** /eg′zəl-, ek′səl-/ *n*

eye /ī′/ [OE *ēage*] *n* 1 organ of vision; 2 iris, as *blue eyes;* 3 region around the eye, as *a black eye;* 4 sight, vision; 5 power of observation, as *he has a good eye;* 6 appreciation, as *an eye for beauty;* 7 look, gaze; 8 anything which resembles an eye, as the hole in a needle or the bud in a potato; 9 eyes *pl* estimation, judgment, as *in the eyes of the world;* 10 catch one's eye to draw one's attention; 11 give someone the eye to ogle someone; 12 have an eye for to have discriminating taste for; 13 keep an eye on to watch closely; 14 lay eyes on to see; 15 make eyes at to look at amorously; 16 open one's eyes to realize the truth; **17 see eye to eye** to agree; **18 with an eye to** considering; **19 with one's eyes open** aware of all the facts || *v* (eye·ing or eye·ing) *vt* **20** to look at, observe || eye'less *adj*

eye'ball' *n* globe or ball of the eye

eye'bolt' *n* bolt with an eye at one end

eye'brow' *n* **1** bony ridge above either eye; **2** the hair on it

eye' catch'er *n* something that attracts the eye || eye'-catch'ing *adj*

eye'cup' *n* small cup with rim shaped to fit the eye, used in treating the eye with an eyewash

eye'ful' *n* something striking or startling to look at

eye'glass' *n* **1** lens for the eye; monocle; **2** eyepiece; **3** eyecup; **4** eyeglasses *pl* pair of lenses for the eyes set in a frame

eye'lash' *n* **1** fringe of hair on the edge of the eyelid; **2** one of the hairs

eye'let /-lit/ *n* **1** small hole to receive a lace or cord, or in embroidery; **2** small grommet; **3** peephole

eye'lid' *n* movable fold of skin that covers and uncovers the eye

eye'o'pen·er *n* **1** astonishing event or piece of news; **2** shot of liquor in the morning

eye'piece' *n* lens nearest the eye in an optical instrument

eye'-pop'per *n* something astonishing || eye'-pop'ping *adj*

eye'shade' *n* visor used to shield the eyes from an overhead light

eye' shad'ow *n* cosmetic coloring applied to the eyelids

eye'sight' *n* **1** sense of sight; **2** range of vision

eye'sore' *n* anything disagreeable to look at

eye'strain' *n* eye fatigue caused by excessive or incorrect use

eye'tooth' *n* (-teeth) one of the two pointed upper teeth on each side of the incisors

eye'wash' *n* **1** medicated water for bathing the eyes; **2** *slang* **a** nonsense; **b** flattery to deceive

eye'wit'ness *n* one who has actually seen an act or occurrence

ey·rie or ey·ry /er'ē̄, ir'ē̄/ *n* (-ries) var of aerie

E·ze·ki·el /izēk'ē-əl/ *n* Bib **1** one of the great Hebrew prophets during the Babylonian captivity; **2** book of the Old Testament

F

F, f /ef'/ *n* (F's or Fs, or f's or fs) sixth letter of the English alphabet

F 1 *chem* fluorine; **2** sixth in order or in a series; **3** *mus* fourth tone in the scale of C major; **4** failing grade for a student's work; **5** something shaped like an F

F, F. 1 Fahrenheit; **2** French

F. 1 Fellow; **2** February; **3** Friday

f. 1 fathom; **2** feminine; **3** foot; **4** franc; **5** *mus* forte

fa /fä'/ [It] *n mus* fourth tone of the diatonic scale

Fa·bi·an /fāb'ē-ən/ [< Quintus *Fabius Maximus*] *adj* **1** like the tactics of the Roman general, Fabius, who defeated Hannibal by delays and harassment rather than by open battle; **2** purposely dilatory || *n* **3** member or supporter of the Fabian Society

Fa·bi·an So·ci'e·ty *n* organization of English socialists founded in 1884 to bring about change by gradual development and education rather than by revolution

fa·ble /fāb'əl/ [L *fabula* story] *n* **1** fictitious story, particularly one which is intended to teach a moral lesson, in which animals talk; **2** myth or legend; **3** plot of a dramatic or epic poem; **4** false statement; **5** idle talk || **fa'bled** *adj* SYN story, fiction, tale, lie, gossip (see *allegory*)

fab·ric /fab'rik/ [L *fabrica* workshop] *n* **1** structure or framework; **2** quality of texture; **3** anything manufactured, esp. woven or knitted material, felt, or the like

fab·ri·cate /fab'rikāt'/ [L *fabricare* (-*atus*)] *vt* **1** to form or make; manufacture; **2** to invent, as a tale or lie || **fab'ri·ca'tor** *n* || SYN construct, frame, form, concoct, devise

fab·ri·ca'tion *n* **1** act of fabricating; manufacture; **2** fabricated article; **3** untruthful statement || SYN untruth, falsehood, fiction, invention (see *lie*[1])

fab·u·lous /fab'yələs/ [see *fable*] *adj* **1** legendary, mythical; **2** incredible, passing belief || SYN incredible, astonishing, fictitious, legendary || ANT real, true, unexaggerated

fa·çade /fəsäd'/ [F < It *facciata*] *n* **1** front or chief face of a building; **2** superficial appearance that may be false

face /fās'/ [F < L *facies*] *n* **1** fore part of the head; countenance; **2** principal side, as of a building, clock, card, etc.; **3** appearance, outward aspect; **4** reputation, as to *save* or *lose face*; **5** impudence; boldness; **6** operating surface of a tool or implement; **7**

printing surface of a type; **8** design or style of type; **9** surface, as of a solid or crystal; **10 face to face** confronting one another; **11 in the face of, a** in spite of; **b** confronted with; **12 make a face** to scowl, grimace; **13 on the face of it** seemingly; **14 set one's face against** to oppose; **15 to one's face** directly, in one's presence ‖ *vt* **16** to turn toward, confront; **17** to stand, be placed, or be situated opposite; **18** to confront with confidence or boldness; **19** to cover with an additional surface; **20** to line near the edge, as the hem of a skirt; **21** to cause to turn, as in a particular direction ‖ *vi* **22** to turn the face; stand or front in any given direction

face' card' *n* playing card that represents a king, queen, or jack

face'less *adj* **1** lacking a face; **2** lacking personal identity

face' lift'ing *n* **1** plastic surgery to remove signs of age from the face; **2** exterior modernization, as of a building

face' pow'der *n* cosmetic powder applied to the face to avoid shiny skin

face'-sav'ing *n* act of saving one's dignity or prestige ‖ also *adj*

fac·et /fas'it/ [F *facette* dim. of *face*] *n* **1** any of several small plane surfaces, esp. of a cut gem; **2** aspect, phase

fa·ce·tious /fəsēsh'əs/ [< L *facetia* jest] *adj* humorous, jocular ‖ SYN pleasant, jocose, droll, funny, witty, waggish, sportive ‖ ANT serious, grave, earnest

face' val'ue *n* **1** value printed on the face; **2** apparent value

fa·cial /fāsh'əl/ [< L *facies* face] *adj* **1** pert. to the face ‖ *n* **2** facial massage or similar treatment of the face

fac·ile /fas'il/ [L *facilis* easy] *adj* **1** easy to do; **2** expert; quick

fa·cil·i·tate /fəsil'itāt'/ *vt* to make less difficult; free from difficulty

fa·cil'i·ty *n* (-ties) **1** ease; freedom from difficulty; **2** skill; dexterity; aptitude; **3** ease or readiness of speech; fluency; **4 facilities** *pl* **a** devices or means by which something may be more easily done; **b** *colloq* toilet

fac·ing /fās'iŋ/ [see **face**] *n* **1** anything used to cover the front, as for decoration or protection; **2** lining near the edge of a garment

fac·sim·i·le /faksim'ilē/ [L = make the like] *n* **1** exact reproduction or copy ‖ *vt* **2** to make an exact copy of ‖ SYN copy, likeness, counterpart (see *duplicate*)

fact /fakt'/ [L *factum* (thing) done] *n* **1** *law* deed, act, as *before* (or *after*) *the fact*; **2** anything that actually happens in time or space; **3** quality of actuality, as *a matter of fact*; **4** statement certainly and strictly true; **5 in fact** indeed; really ‖ SYN detail,

item, particular, point, circumstance, certainty, truth, reality ‖ ANT fiction, falsehood

fac·tion /fak'shən/ [L *factio* (-*ōnis*)] *n* **1** group within an organization or political party, often with dissident aims; **2** dissension, discord ‖ **fac'·tion·al** *adj* ‖ **fac'tion·al·ism** *n* ‖ SYN cabal, gang, clique, combination, conspiracy

fac·tious /fak'shəs/ [L *factiosus*] *adj* **1** characterized by a tendency to oppose; **2** quarrelsome

fac·ti·tious /faktish'əs/ [L *facticius*] *adj* **1** artificial; **2** sham

fac·tor /fak'tər/ [L = maker, doer] *n* **1** one who transacts business for another; agent; **2** any one of the circumstances or elements which produce a result; **3** *math* one of the two or more quantities which, multiplied together, yield a given product; **4** company or person that buys, or lends money on accounts receivable; ‖ *vt* **5** *math* to resolve into factors

fac'to·ry [LL *factoria* treasury] *n* (-*ries*) place where goods are made

fac·to·tum /faktōt'əm/ [L = do all] *n* person employed for miscellaneous small jobs; handyman

fac'tu·al /-chŏŏ'əl/ [see **fact**] *adj* **1** pert. to, or containing, facts; **2** real, actual ‖ **fac'tu·al·ly** *adv*

fac'ul·ty /-əltē/ [MF *faculte* < L *facultas* skill] *n* (-ties) **1** power to act mentally or physically; **2** any one power of the mind, as the memory or imagination; **3** special aptitude in doing; skill; **4** any branch of learning or department of a university, as *the faculty of medicine*; **5** teachers collectively in an institution of learning ‖ SYN aptitude, dexterity, knack, capacity (see *ability, gift*) ‖ ANT incompetence, incapacity

fad /fad'/ [?] *n* passing notion, custom, or style followed enthusiastically for a while ‖ **fad'dist** *n*

fade /fād'/ [OF *fader* to grow dull] *vi* **1** to lose color, brightness, or distinctness of outline; **2** to disappear by degrees; **3** to lose freshness, as flowers; **4** to grow pale or weak; **5** *rad* to vary irregularly in intensity, said of signals ‖ *vt* **6** to cause to fade; **7 fade in** or **out** *motion pictures & telv* to cause (a scene) to become gradually clear on the screen, or to disappear ‖ **fad'ed** *adj*

fade'-in' *n* **1** gradual increase in visibility; **2** gradual increase in audibility

fade'-out' *n* **1** gradual decrease in visibility; **2** gradual decrease in audibility

fad'ing *n* **1** disappearance; decline; **2** irregular variation in the strength of received radio signals because of distance or disturbance in the intervening medium

fa·do /fä′dōō/ [Port = fate] n mournful, fatalistic Portuguese folk song

fae·ces /fēs′ēz/ npl var of **feces**

fa·e·na /fə-ä′nə/ [Sp = task] n final third of a bullfight consisting of a series of passes with the muleta before the kill

Faer′oe or **Far′oe Is′lands** /fer′ō/ npl Danish islands in the N Atlantic between Scotland and Iceland (38,000; 540 sq.m.; cap. Torshaven) ‖ **Faer′o·ese′** adj & n (**-ese**)

fag /fag′/ [ME fagge loose end] v (**fagged; fag·ging**) vt 1 to make work hard; exhaust ‖ n 2 slang male homosexual; 3 slang cigaret ‖ SYN v jade, tire, weary, fatigue, toil, drudge

fag′ end′ n 1 frayed end of a piece of cloth or rope; 2 meaner or more unprofitable part of anything; remnant

fag·got /fag′ət/ [?] n slang male homosexual

fag·ot or **fag·got** /fag′ət/ [MF] n bundle of sticks bound together for fuel

Fahr. Fahrenheit

Fahr·en·heit /far′ənhīt′/ [Gabriel D. Fahrenheit (1686–1736) G physicist] n thermometric scale having the freezing point of water at 32 degrees above zero and the boiling point at 212 degrees ‖ also adj

fa·ience /fā-äns′, fī-/ [F < It Faenza town where first made] n fine, glazed, brightly colored earthenware or porcelain

fail /fāl′/ [OF faillir < L fallere to deceive] vi 1 to fall short; be deficient, inadequate, or lacking; 2 to prove false or be found wanting; 3 not to succeed in some purpose; 4 to become bankrupt; 5 to grow weaker gradually; 6 to stop functioning ‖ vt 7 to be wanting or insufficient for; 8 to forsake, disappoint; 9 to omit to perform, as he failed to appear; 10 to assign the grade of failure to (a pupil) ‖ n 11 without fail certainly

fail′ing n 1 fault, weakness ‖ prep 2 in default of ‖ SYN n fault, foible, weakness, infirmity, peccadillo ‖ DISCR These terms name imperfections of character. A fault is a positive, though not a serious, defect; uncorrected faults may develop into vices. A failing is a shortcoming, usually good-naturedly admitted by its possessor. A foible is a special, slight weakness

faille /fīl′, fāl′/ [F] n soft, dull, light-grained silk, used for dresses or trimmings

fail′-safe′ adj 1 pert. to coded military controls designed to prevent bombers from advancing beyond a predetermined point except on direct orders from a designated authority ‖ n 2 fail-safe point

fail·ure /fāl′yər/ n 1 act of failing; lack of success; 2 deficiency; 3 nonattainment; 4 nonperformance; 5 bankruptcy; 6 loss of vigor or strength; 7 unsuccessful person, effort, or article; 8 pupil's grade below passing

fain /fān′/ [OE fægen glad] archaic adv 1 gladly, willingly ‖ adj 2 glad, willing; 3 desirous, eager

faint /fānt′/ [OF, pp of faindre to feign] adj 1 about to swoon or lose consciousness; 2 feeble, weak; 3 not bright or vivid in color or outline; 4 not loud or clear in sound ‖ n 5 swoon ‖ vi 6 to lose consciousness ‖ **faint′ly** adv ‖ **faint′ness** n ‖ SYN indistinct, pale, vague, giddy, languid

faint′heart′ed adj lacking courage, cowardly

fair¹ /fer′/ [OE fæger beautiful] adj 1 pleasing to the sight; handsome, beautiful; 2 not dark in color or complexion; blond; 3 without blemish; 4 not cloudy, fine (weather); 5 giving promise, favorable; 6 moderately satisfactory, pretty good; 7 not partial; just; 8 according to regulations; 9 allowing lawful pursuit, as fair game; 10 distinct, unobstructed, clear ‖ adv 11 favorably; 12 honestly, justly; 13 according to the rules; 14 directly, straight ‖ **fair′ly** adv ‖ **fair′ness** n ‖ SYN adj desirable, comely, blond, unblemished, middling, unprejudiced, unbiased (see beautiful)

fair² [OF feire < L feria holiday] n 1 gathering at a fixed time and place for the sale or exhibition of farm products, etc., and generally accompanied by entertainment, races, etc.; 2 sale of useful and fancy goods, as for charity

fair′ ball′ n batted baseball that settles within the foul lines in the infield, or that touches the ground within the foul lines in the outfield

fair′ground′ n often **fairgrounds** pl place where fairs, races, and exhibitions are held

fair′-haired′ boy′ n colloq man favored by his superiors

fair′ play′ n just conformance to honorable principles

fair′ sex′ n women collectively

fair′-trade′ vt 1 to sell (a product) at a minimum price fixed by the manufacturer ‖ adj 2 subject to fair-trading

fair′way′ n 1 the part of a river, harbor, or roadway which is open to navigation or traffic; 2 golf broad lane in which the grass is kept short, between a tee and its putting green

fair′-weath′er adj 1 for fair weather only; 2 loyal only during success

fair·y /fer′ē/ [OF faerie < fae fay] n (**-ies**) 1 imaginary being of graceful and tiny human form supposed to interfere in human affairs for good or evil; **2** *slang* male homosexual ‖ *adj* **3** of or pert. to fairies; **4** delicate, graceful

fair′y·land′ *n* **1** supposed home of the fairies; **2** enchanting and pleasant place

fair′y ring′ *n* small circle of grass greener than the surrounding turf, caused by an underground fungus but said to be caused by fairies in their dances

fair′y tale′ *n* **1** story concerning fairies; **2** unbelievable yarn; lie ‖ **fair′y-tale′** *adj*

fait ac·com·pli /fa′täkôⁿplē′/ [F = thing done] *n* something done, and so no longer worth opposing

faith /fāth/ [OF *feid* < L *fides*] *n* **1** belief; mental assent; conviction that a thing unproved by evidence is true; **2** trust, as in God or someone's purity of motive; **3** any organized system of belief, religious or political; creed; **4** promise or pledge, as *to keep faith;* **5** fidelity, honesty, as *good* or *bad faith;* **6** assent to the fundamental doctrines of one's religion and acceptance of its creeds ‖ SYN assent, conviction, trust, creed (see *belief*)

faith′ful *adj* **1** believing; **2** loyal; **3** trustworthy; **4** true, accurate ‖ **faith′-ful·ly** *adv* ‖ SYN accurate, constant, upright, trustworthy, loyal, dependable, devoted ‖ ANT faithless, treacherous

faith′ful·ness *n* quality of being faithful; loyalty; trustworthiness; accuracy ‖ SYN fidelity, dependability, steadiness, exactness (see *constancy*)

faith′less *adj* **1** not having belief; **2** disloyal ‖ **faith′less·ly** *adv* ‖ **faith′less·ness** *n* ‖ SYN treacherous, false, unstable, fickle, inconstant, shifting ‖ ANT faithful, loyal, dependable, true

fake /fāk/ [?] *vt* **1** to make (something) appear different from what it really is; falsify, fabricate; ‖ *vi* **2** to assume a deceptive appearance; deceive ‖ *n* **3** anything made to appear different from what it is; **4** fraudulent scheme; **5** person pretending to be what he is not ‖ *adj* **6** false; counterfeit ‖ **fak′er** *n* ‖ **fak′er·y** *n*

fa·kir /fəkir′, fāk′ər/ [Ar *faqīr* poor] *n* **1** member of any of the Mohammedan orders of monks who take vows of poverty and live either in monasteries or as wandering friars; **2** Mohammedan religious mendicant, often a wonder-worker

fal·con /fôl′kən, fôl′-, fôk′-/ [OF *faucon* < LL *falco* (*-onis*)] *n* any of various hawks or hawklike birds (subfamily Falconinae), esp. the Old World peregrine falcon (*Falco peregrinus*), trained for hunting

fal′con·er *n* one who breeds, trains, or hunts with falcons ‖ **fal′con·ry** *n*

fal·de·ral /fal′dəral′/ *n* var of **folderol**

Falk′land Is′lands /fôk′lənd/ *npl* British islands in S Atlantic (4,000; 4618 sq.m.; cap. Stanley); claimed by Argentina

fall /fôl/ [OE *feallan*] *v* (**fell, fall·en**) *vi* **1** to drop freely from a higher to a lower place; **2** to be dropped or uttered, as remarks; **3** to extend downward, depend, droop; **4** to drop to the ground from an erect position; collapse; **5** to be taken captive, as a besieged city; **6** to be deposed from power, as a leader; **7** to die; **8** to depart from moral behavior; be degraded; sin; **9** to decrease; abate; diminish in value; **10** to show dejection (said of the countenance); **11** to enter suddenly into a new condition, begin, as *he fell to cursing;* **12** to slope; sink; flow; **13** to come by chance or by inheritance; **14** to happen, befall; **15** to pass gradually into some state or condition, as to *fall in love;* **16** fall back on to have recourse to; **17** fall behind, a to allow others to get ahead of one; b to fail to make a payment on time; **18** fall down *colloq* to perform poorly; **19** fall flat to fail to produce the desired result; **20** fall for *slang* a to be deceived by (something); b to become infatuated with; **21** fall in, a to collapse; b *mil* to line up in the ranks; **22** fall off to decline, as business; **23** fall out, a to quarrel; b *mil* to dissolve the ranks; **24** fall through to come to nothing; **25** fall to to begin a task ‖ *n* **26** act or result of falling; **27** something which has fallen, as *a heavy fall of rain;* **28** dropping down or casting off, as of leaves; **29** autumn; **30** often falls *pl* cascade; **31** ruin; death; **32** overthrow of a city, country, etc.; **33** loss of power or position, as of a leader; **34** distance through which anything drops; difference of levels; **35** decrease in price or value; **36** slope; descent; **37** rope used in hoisting with a tackle; **38** *wrestling* throwing of one's antagonist; **39** spiritual downfall; **40** a opaque veil hanging from a woman's hat and down her back; b cascade of lace or ruffles hanging down from the collar; **41** the Fall loss of man's original innocence through Adam and Eve's eating of the forbidden fruit ‖ SYN *v* droop, sink, tumble, diminish, decrease, abate, subside, decline ‖ ANT *v* rise, ascend, mount, soar

fal·la·cious /fəlāsh′əs/ *adj* **1** deceptive; **2** erroneous ‖ **fal·la′cious·ly** *adv*

fal·la·cy /fal′əsē/ [L *fallacia* fraud] *n* (*-cies*) **1** that which deceives or misleads; **2** false reasonong; **3** mistaken idea

fall′en 1 *pp* of **fall** ‖ *adj* **2** prostrate;

3 immoral, degraded; **4** conquered, overthrown; **5** dead

fall′ guy′ *n slang* **1** person easily duped; **2** scapegoat

fal·li·ble /fal′ɪbəl/ [LL *fallibilis*] **1** liable to commit error; **2** liable to be deceived; **3** liable to be wrong ‖ **fal′li·bly** *adv* ‖ **fal′li·bil′i·ty** /-bil′-/ *n*

fall′ing-out′ *n* (fallings-out, falling-outs) quarrel

fall′ing sick′ness *n* epilepsy

fall′ing star′ *n* meteor visible in the night sky

fall′-off′ *n* decline, as in output

Fal·lo·pi·an tube /fəlōp′ē·ən/ [Gabriel *Fallopius* (d. 1562) It anatomist] *n* one of two tubes or oviducts which in female mammals convey the egg cells from the ovaries to the uterus

fall′out′ *n* **1** radioactive particles that slowly descend through the atmosphere as a result of a nuclear explosion; **2** incidental effect of some notable event

fal·low¹ /fal′ō/ [ME *falwe* plowed land] *adj* **1** plowed but not cultivated; **2** untilled; neglected; **3** unused; inactive

fal·low² [ME *falwe* sallow] *adj* of a pale-yellow or yellowish-brown color

fal′low deer′ *n* small Eurasian deer (*Dama dama*) of yellowish-brown color spotted with white, the antlers flattened and much branched near the ends

Fall′ Riv′er *n* seaport in SE Massachusetts (100,000)

false /fôls′/ [L *falsus* deceived] *adj* **1** not true; incorrect; **2** disloyal; **3** lying; **4** artificial; spurious; ‖ *adv* **5** wrongly, not truly ‖ **false′ly** *adv* ‖ **false′ness** *n* ‖ **SYN** *adj* faithless, perfidious, artificial, dishonest, lying ‖ **ANT** *adj* true, loyal, correct, genuine

false′ face′ *n* mask, often comical or grotesque

false′hood *n* misstatement with intention to deceive; lie ‖ **SYN** deception, untruth, misrepresentation (see *lie¹*)

false′ pre·tens′es *npl law* misrepresentation of facts in order to gain title to property rightfully belonging to another

false′ rib′ *n* one of the lower ribs not directly connected to the sternum

fal·set·to /fôlset′ō/ [It, *dim.* of *falso* false] *n* artificial register, esp. in some male voices, higher than the natural voice

false′work′ *n* temporary structure built to support work in process of construction or demolition

fals′ies *npl slang* padded brassieres

fal·si·fy [fôl′sifī′/ [MF *falsifier*] *v* (-fied) *vt* **1** to change by fraudulent means; **2** to counterfeit; forge; **3** to show to be false ‖ *vi* **4** to lie ‖ **fal′si·fi′er** *n* ‖ **fal′si·fi·ca′tion** *n*

fal·si·ty *n* (-ties) **1** quality of being false; **2** untruth

Fal·staff·i·an /fôlstaf′ē·ən/ [Sir John *Falstaff* Shakespearean character] *adj* pert. to or like Falstaff, esp. his bawdy, impudent, and brilliant wit and his good-natured rascality

fal·ter /fôlt′ər/ [ME *faltren*] *vi* **1** to walk unsteadily; stumble; **2** to show moral hesitancy, waver; **3** to speak with hesitation; stammer ‖ *vt* **4** to utter in a weak, trembling manner ‖ **fal′ter·ing·ly** *adv*

fame /fām′/ [L *fama* report] *n* **1** common report; rumor; **2** reputation; **3** renown ‖ **famed′** *adj* ‖ **SYN** reputation, renown, glory, honor, notoriety, celebrity, eminence, distinction, repute ‖ **DISCR** What is generally said or believed about one's character is one's *reputation*. Since *reputation* is usually the fruit of actual contact or direct observation, it is limited in range, but, for the same reasons, well founded, as a man may possess a *reputation* for integrity or for cheating. A *reputation* may be established by patient effort and ruined by an injudicious action. *Fame* is spread far and near and is based on report: usually it is taken in a good sense, though there is good *fame* and evil *fame*. *Renown* is *fame* in its best sense, and is usually the reward of distinguished achievement or merit: Roosevelt won *fame*; Lincoln won *renown*. Reno has won a dubious *fame*; Paris has won *renown* as a beautiful and cosmopolitan city. *Notoriety* is the quality of being unfavorably known, or the fact of being in ill repute. *Honor* is high respect, esteem, or tributes tendered to indicate such respect; "a prophet is not without *honor*, save in his own country, and in his own house" (Matt. 13:57); we pay military *honor* to the soldier dead. *Honor* is often the reward of virtue; *glory* is the reward of spectacular and extraordinary feats, as in war, distinguished statesmanship, or similar fields ‖ **ANT** discredit, disgrace, shame, dishonor, obscurity, oblivion

fa·mil·ial /fəmil′yəl/ [see *family*] *adj* of or pert. to a family

fa·mil·iar /fəmil′yər/ [see *family*] *adj* **1** intimate; well acquainted; **2** well-known; usual; **3** excessively free; bold, impertinent ‖ **fa·mil′iar·ly** *adv*

fa·mil′i·ar′i·ty /-ē·ar′itē/ *n* (-ties) **1** intimacy or close acquaintance; **2** freedom from ceremony; **3** remark or action offensively intimate; impertinence ‖ **SYN** intimacy, fellowship (see *acquaintance*)

fa·mil′iar·ize′ *vt* **1** to acquaint thoroughly; make accustomed, habituate; **2** to make known generally ‖ **fa·mil′iar·i·za′tion** *n*

fam·i·ly /fam′(ə)lē/ [L *familia* household] *n* (-lies) **1** group of persons made up of parents and their children; **2** the children alone of such a group; **3** group of persons under one roof, including parents, children, kin, servants, etc.; **4** group of persons connected by blood relationship; **5** descent, lineage; **6** group of things with some common characteristics; **7** *biol* classification of plants or animals larger than a genus but smaller than an order

fam′i·ly cir′cle *n* topmost gallery in an opera house, containing the cheapest seats

fam′i·ly man′ *n* **1** man with a family; **2** responsible man loyal to his wife and family

fam′i·ly name′ *n* name of one's family, name one inherits from one's family

fam′i·ly tree′ *n* **1** genealogy; **2** genealogical chart

fam′i·ly way′ *n* **in a** or **the family way** pregnant

fam·ine /fam′in/ [< L *fames*] *n* **1** extreme scarcity of food; **2** dearth of some specified article; **3** starvation

fam·ished /fam′isht/ *adj* very hungry; starving

fa·mous /fām′əs/ [see **fame**] *adj* **1** renowned; celebrated; **2** *colloq* excellent; delightful || **fa′mous·ly** *adv* || SYN eminent, illustrious, noted (see *distinguished*)

fan¹ /fan′/ [OE *fann* < L *vannus* winnowing basket] *n* **1** light, thin, flat, usu. sector-shaped object, intended to cool the face by stirring the air; **2** any device designed to excite a current of air; **3** anything shaped like a fan || *v* (**fanned; fan·ning**) *vt* **4** to drive a current of air upon; **5** to kindle (a flame); **6** to rouse, excite; **7** to spread like a fan; **8** *baseball* to strike out (a batter); **9** *slang* to spank || *vi* **10** to move or spread like a fan; **11** *baseball* to strike out by swinging and making the third strike

fan′² [perh < *fanatic*] *n* **1** enthusiast about a given sport; **2** enthusiastic admirer

fa·nat·ic /fənat′ik/ [< L *fanum* temple] *adj* **1** wildly extravagant in opinion or views, as of religion or politics || *n* **2** person with fanatic views || **fa·nat′i·cal** *adj* || **fa·nat′i·cal·ly** *adv* || **fa·nat′i·cism** *n*

fan·cied /fan′sēd/ [see **fancy**] *adj* imaginary

fan′ci·er /-sē-ər/ *n* one who takes particular interest in certain things, as one who breeds, buys, or sells animals

fan′ci·ful *adj* **1** possessing imagination; whimsical; **2** founded on imagination; unreal; **3** whimsically made or decorated || **fan′ci·ful·ly** *adv* || SYN fantastic, grotesque, visionary, chimerical, extravagant, imaginative || DISCR That is *fanciful* which is con-

ceived independently of fact or reason; it is out of the ordinary, whimsical, capricious, or odd, but pleasingly so; a *fanciful* costume is attractive and in good taste; a *fanciful* notion, though pleasantly novel, does not entirely lack judgment. *Fantastic* adds to *fanciful* the ideas of violent irregularity and extravagance; that which is *fantastic* is uncommon, peculiar, or displeasingly odd; eccentric people often have *fantastic* manners. *Grotesque* adds to *fantastic* the idea of the ridiculous or the unnatural; a *grotesque* decoration is ludicrous because it combines things jarringly out of keeping with one another. *Fantastic* and *grotesque* are applied to either persons or things, but *grotesque* when applied to persons describes only a distorted or unusual outward appearance. *Visionary*, like *fanciful*, describes that which is not founded on fact, or one who is given to seeing visions, especially impractical projects; unlike *fanciful*, *visionary* connotes practicality; a *visionary* scheme seems to the *visionary* man a miracle of easy doing || ANT real, congruous, literal, prosaic, commonplace

fan·cy /fan′sē/ [short for *fantasy*] *n* (**-cies**) **1** mental process of forming images of things not present to the eye, esp. if graceful, pleasing, or unusual; **2** mental image so formed; **3** fantastic notion; whim; delusion; **4** liking; capricious inclination; **5** fad; hobby || *adj* (**-ci·er; -ci·est**) **6** intended to strike the imagination; decorative; **7** founded on imagery rather than on fact; **8** fantastic; capricious; **9** beyond actual worth, as *fancy prices;* **10** of especially fine quality; choice || *v* (**-cied**) *vt* **11** to visualize; imagine; **12** to have a fondness for; **13** to suppose, guess || *interj* **14** used to express mild surprise or to call attention || SYN *n* caprice, conceit, idea (see *imagination*)

fan′cy-free′ *adj* **1** carefree; **2** not in love

fan′cy wom′an *n* **1** immoral woman; **2** prostitute

fan′cy-work′ *n* ornamental needlework, as embroidery

fan·dan·go /fandaŋ′gō/ [Sp] *n* **1** spirited Spanish dance or the tune for it; **2** lively dancing party or ball

fan·fare /fan′fer/ [F] *n* **1** flourish of trumpets; **2** ostentatious display; **3** publicity

fang /faŋ/ [OE = a taking < *fōn* to seize] *n* **1** one of the long sharp teeth with which an animal catches its prey; **2** any long sharp tooth, as a poison tooth of a serpent || **fanged′** *adj*

fan'jet' n 1 turbofan; 2 airplane with turbofan engines

fan' mail' n mail received by a public figure from his admirers

fan'tail' n 1 fan-shaped tail or end; 2 kind of pigeon having tail feathers spread out like a fan; 3 Australian or Oriental fly-catching bird having a fan-shaped tail; 4 stern or after overhang of a ship; 5 goldfish with double tail fins

fan·tan /fan'tan'/ [Chin *fan t'an* repeated divisions] n 1 Chinese gambling game played with coins or similar counters; 2 card game in which the winner is the player who first gets rid of his cards

fan·ta·si·a /fantäzh'(ē)ə, fant'əzē'ə/ [It = a fancy] n 1 instrumental composition not restricted by the usual laws of form, often improvised; 2 medley of familiar airs arranged with fancy variations

fan·tas·tic /fantas'tik/ [see **fantasy**] adj 1 imaginary, unreal; 2 whimsical; odd; grotesque ‖ **fan·tas'ti·cal·ly** adv ‖ SYN strange, absurd, grotesque (see *fanciful*)

fan·ta·sy /fan'təsē/ [Gk *phantasia* display] n (-sies) 1 faculty of making mental images, particularly of a fanciful kind; 2 mental image so produced; 3 whimsical contrivance or notion; 4 work of literature showing extravagant fancy in spirit and design

fan·tom /fant'əm/ n var of **phantom**

far /fär/ [OE *feor(r)*] adv (**far·ther; far·thest** or **fur·ther; fur·thest**) 1 distant in space, time, or degree; 2 to or from a remote distance, position, or time; 3 very much; 4 **as far as** to the degree that; 5 **by far** by a great deal; 6 **far and away** by far ‖ adj 7 situated distantly in time or space, as *a far country;* 8 more distant of the two, as *the far end of the room;* 9 reaching to great distances

far·ad /far'əd/ [Michael *Faraday* (1791–1867) Brit scientist] n unit of capacitance equal to the capacitance of a capacitor retaining a charge of one coulomb with a difference of potential of one volt

far·a·day /far'ədā'/ n unit of electricity used in electrolysis (= 96,500 coulombs)

far'a·way' adj 1 distant; 2 dreamy; absent-minded

farce /färs/ [F = stuffing] n 1 comedy in which humorous elements are broadly exaggerated; 2 ridiculously futile act or action ‖ **far'ci·cal** adj

fare /fer/ [OE *faran* to travel] vi 1 to journey; proceed; 2 to happen; work out; 3 to be in any condition or go through any experience; 4 to be entertained with food and drink ‖ n 5 sum paid for a journey; 6 person conveyed for hire in a vehicle; 7 food; provisions

Far' East' n that part of Asia comprising China, Japan, and neighboring nations

fare'-thee-well' n 1 state of perfection; 2 utmost degree

fare'well' *interj* 1 good-by! ‖ n 2 adieu; leave-taking ‖ also *adj*

far'-fetched' adj not easily deduced; strained, forced

far'-flung' adj widely spread

fa·ri·na /fərēn'ə/ [L = flour < *far* grain] n flour or meal obtained from the seeds of cereals, nuts, etc.

far·i·na·ceous /far'inäsh'əs/ adj 1 consisting of, made from, or producing flour or meal; 2 like meal; 3 starchy

farm /färm/ [F *ferme* < LL *firma* fixed payment] n 1 single portion of land under cultivation, with its buildings; 2 land where certain animals are raised, as *a fox farm* ‖ vt 3 to cultivate or till (land); 4 **farm out,** **a** to lease or let (a business, prospective revenue, or the like) in return for a fixed payment from the lessee; **b** to send (a baseball player) to a farm club ‖ vi 5 to follow the occupation of a farmer

farm' club' or **farm' team'** n minor league baseball team controlled by a major league team for the purpose of developing new players

farm'er n 1 one who farms, esp. one who cultivates or manages a portion of land; 2 one who undertakes the collection of taxes, customs, etc., paying a fixed sum and retaining the proceeds

farm'hand' n hired farm laborer

farm'house' (-hous·es /-ziz/) n main dwelling house on a farm

farm'ing n operation of a farm; agriculture

farm'stead' n farm, including buildings and land

farm'yard' n barnyard; also the area about or among various farm buildings other than the barn

far·o /fer'ō/ [< F *pharaon* Pharaoh] n card game in which the dealer bets against all the other players

far'-off' adj distant, remote

far'-out' adj slang 1 not conventional; 2 extreme; 3 esoteric

far·ra·go /fəräg'ō/ [L = mixed fodder] n (-goes) jumble; hodgepodge; medley

Far·ra·gut /far'əgət/, **David Glasgow** n (1801–70) U.S. admiral

far'-reach'ing adj 1 extending to a great distance in time or space; 2 causing significant or serious results

far·ri·er /far'ē·ər/ [< L *ferrum* iron] n blacksmith

far·row /far'ō/ [OE *fearth* little pig] n 1 litter of pigs ‖ vi 2 to give birth to pigs ‖ vt 3 to give birth to (pigs)

far·see·ing *adj* 1 able to see far; 2 prudent

far·sight·ed *adj* 1 able to see distant objects clearly; 2 able to look ahead and plan for the future || **far′sight′·ed·ly** *adv* || **far′sight′ed·ness** *n*

far·ther /fär′thər/ [ME *ferther* variant of *further*] *adj* 1 more distantly removed in space; more advanced; 2 additional, further || *adv* 3 to or at a more remote position in space; 4 moreover

far′ther·most′ *adj* most distant

far·thing /fär′thin/ [OE *fēorthing* < *fēortha* fourth] 1 former British coin equal to ¼ penny; 2 trifle; small amount

Far′ West′ *n* that part of the U.S.A. west of the Great Plains

fas·ces /fas′ēz/ [L = bundles] *npl* bundle of rods containing an ax, carried by the lictors before the high magistrates of ancient Rome as a symbol of authority

fas·ci·cle /fas′ikəl/ [L *fasciculus* dim. of *fascis* bundle] *n* 1 small bunch or bundle, cluster; 2 division of a printed work published in parts || **fas·cic·u·lar** /fəsik′yələr/ *adj*

fas·ci·nate /fas′ināt′/ [L *fascināre* (*-atus*) to enchant] *vt* 1 to bewitch with a mysterious and powerful charm; 2 to allure irresistibly; captivate || *vi* 3 to exercise a captivating or alluring power || **fas′ci·na′tion** *n*

fas·cism /fash′izəm, fash′-/ [It *fascismo* < L *fasces* the symbol of authority and order] *n* 1 political movement or system of government characterized by dictatorship, suppression of all dissent, complete regimentation, glorification of nation and race, and a belligerent foreign policy; 2 **Fascism** the fascist government established in Italy 1922–43 by Benito Mussolini || **fas′cist, Fas′cist** *adj & n* || **fa·scis′tic** /fə-/ *adj*

fash·ion /fash′ən/ [OF *façon* < L *factio* (*-onis*) way of making] *n* 1 shape or form of anything; 2 method of procedure, mode, manner, 3 prevalent style, particularly in dress; 4 general practice of good society; 5 people of polite society collectively; 6 **after** or **in a fashion** in a makeshift manner || *vt* 7 to mold or form || **fash′ion·er** *n* || SYN *n* custom, usage, style, vogue (see *mode*)

fash′ion·a·ble *adj* pert. or according to the prevailing mode or style || **fash′ion·a·bly** *adv*

fast[1] /fast′, fäst′/ [OE *fæst* secure] *adj* 1 securely fixed; 2 constant, faithful; 3 profound, as sleep; 4 unfading, as colors; 5 rapid, swift; 6 ahead of time, as a clock; 7 conducive to fast travel, as a *fast course*; 8 immoral, dissipated || *adv* 9 fixedly, firmly; 10 rapidly; 11 soundly, as *fast asleep* || SYN *adj* rapid, fleet,

hurried, swift, hasty, brisk, lasting, secure || ANT *adj* slow, movable, insecure

fast[2] [OE *fæstan* to keep a fast] *vi* 1 to take no food or abstain from certain foods || *n* 2 abstinence from all food or certain foods; 3 period of fasting

fast′ day′ *n* day set apart by civil or church authority for abstinence from food or certain kinds of food, as a devotional rite

fas·ten /fas′ən, fäs′-/ [< *fast*[1]] *vt* 1 to fix securely, as by tying, locking, or buttoning; 2 to keep fixed steadily, as the gaze; 3 to connect, attach || *vi* 4 to become fastened || **fas′ten·er** *n*

fas′ten·ing *n* something that fastens, as a bolt, lock, chain, or clasp

fast′-food′ *adj* specializing in the speedy preparation and service of hamburgers and the like

fas·tid·i·ous /fastid′ē·əs/ [L *fastidiosus*] *adj* difficult to please, finical, daintily particular || **fas·tid′i·ous·ly** *adv* || **fas·tid′i·ous·ness** *n*

fat /fat′/ [OE fǣtt] *adj* (**fat·ter; fat·test**) 1 possessing superfluous flesh; plump; 2 containing much oil or grease; 3 thick, broad; 4 lucrative; 5 prosperous, wealthy; 6 *slang* very little, as *fat chance* || *n* 7 semisolid, oily, yellow or white substance forming part of the tissue of animals; 8 *chem* compound ester formed by the union of organic acids and glycerine; 9 best of anything

fa·tal /fāt′əl/ [L *fatalis* according to fate] *adj* 1 fixed by fate; 2 foreboding; 3 causing death or destruction || **fa′tal·ly** *adv* || SYN destructive, prophetic, ominous (see *deadly*)

fa′tal·ism *n* 1 doctrine that all things are predetermined and happen regardless of one's efforts; 2 submission to events as unavoidable || **fa′tal·ist** *n* || **fa′tal·is′tic** *adj*

fa·tal·i·ty /fotal′itē/ *n* (**-ties**); 1 event resulting in death; 2 death

fat′ cat′ *n slang* 1 wealthy, influential person; 2 wealthy person who makes contributions to political campaigns

fate /fāt′/ [L *fatum* thing spoken < *fari* to speak] *n* 1 power or influence that predetermines events; destiny; 2 one's lot; unavoidable fortune; 3 final outcome; 4 the **Fates** *class. myth.* the three goddesses of destiny || **fat′ed** *adj* || SYN lot, doom, destiny, predestination, necessity, fortune, change (see *destiny*)

fate′ful *adj* 1 possessing fatal power; 2 momentous, significant; 3 prophetic || **fate′ful·ly** *adv* || **fate′ful·ness** *n*

fat′head′ *n slang* stupid person; fool, dolt

fa·ther /fäth′ər/ [OE *fæder*] *n* 1 male parent or ancestor; 2 one who stands in the general relation of a father; **3** originator or founder; **4** priest; **5** aged or reverend man or clergyman; **6** any religious writer of the early Christian church accepted as authentic; **7 Father** or **the Father God**, the first person of the Trinity ‖ *vt* **8** to beget or adopt; **9** to assume authorship of, or accept responsibility for ‖ **fa′ther·hood′** *n*

fa′ther-in-law′ *n* (**fathers-in-law**) father of one's husband or wife

fa′ther·land′ *n* land of one's birth or of one's ancestors

fa′ther·ly *adj* pert. to, like, or befitting a father ‖ **fa′ther·li·ness** *n*

Fa′ther's Day′ *n* third Sunday in June, devoted to honoring fathers and fatherhood

Fa′ther Time′ *n* representation of time as an old man with a beard and carrying a scythe

fath·om /fath′əm/ [OE *fæthm* length of the outstretched arms] *n* (**-oms** or **-om**) **1** *naut* measure of length equal to six feet ‖ *vt* **2** to measure the depth of; **3** to get to the bottom of, comprehend

fa·tigue /fətēg′/ [F *fatiguer* to tire < L *fatigare*] *n* **1** bodily or mental exhaustion; **2** *mech* weakness resulting from age, repeated vibration, or strain, as in metals; **3** *mil* nonmilitary labor done by soldiers; **4 fatigues** *pl* soldier's uniform worn on fatigue duty ‖ *vt* **5** to weary with bodily or mental effort; **6** *mech* to cause a condition of fatigue in ‖ SYN *n* lassitude, tiredness ‖ ANT *n* freshness, energy

fat′-sol′u·ble *adj* (vitamin) soluble in oils or fats or fat solvents

fat·ten /fat′ən/ *vt* **1** to make fat ‖ *vi* **2** to grow fat

fat′ty *adj* (**-ti·er; -ti·est**) **1** consisting largely of fat; **2** showing the characteristics of fat; greasy or oily

fat′ty ac′id *n* any of a series of acids, including the stearic and palmitic acids, occurring in natural fats

fat·u·ous /fach′ōō-əs/ [L *fatuus* foolish] *adj* vain and silly; complacently dull or inane ‖ **fat′u·ous·ly** *adv* ‖ **fa·tu·i·ty** /fət(y)ōō′itē/ *n* (**-ties**)

fau·cet /fôs′it/ [MF *fausset* vent peg] *n* device at the end of a pipe or container for drawing liquids; tap

fault /fôlt′/ [OF *faute* < L *fallere* to fail] *n* **1** failure to meet a task or duty; blame; **2** defect in character; **3** flaw in a structure, or in the appearance of a thing; **4** *geol* sliding displacement of rock structure along a fracture; **5** *tennis* service in which the ball fails to land in the proper court; **6 at fault** blameworthy; **7 find fault** to criticize ‖ *vt* **8** to blame ‖ *vi* **9** to err; **10** *geol* to fracture, said of rock structures ‖ SYN *n* error, weakness, flaw (see *failing*)

fault′find′ing *n* **1** criticism, esp. petty ‖ *adj* **2** captious, critical ‖ **fault′find′er** *n*

fault′less *adj* without defect ‖ **fault′-less·ly** *adv*

fault′y *adj* (**-i·er; -i·est**) **1** full of faults; **2** defective

faun /fôn′/ [L *Faunus* god of woodland] *n* *Rom myth.* one of the lesser deities of the woodland, represented as half man and half goat

fau·na /fôn′ə/ [L *Fauna* sister of Faunus] *n* (**-nas, -nae** /-nē/) **1** the animals characteristic of any particular region or period; **2** treatise on such a group of animals

Fau·nus /fôn′əs/ *n* *Rom myth.* god of the woodland, patron of animal life, hunting, and agriculture; identified with the Greek Pan

Faust /foust′/ *n* hero of various literary and other works of art, based on legends concerning Dr. Faustus, a German charlatan of the 16th century, who, wearying of his search for knowledge, sells his soul to the devil in return for worldly pleasures

faux pas /fō′ pä′/ [F = false step] *n* (**faux pas** /fō′ päz′/) blunder in manners

fa·vor /fāv′ər/ [L = favor, good will] *vt* **1** to regard with good will; **2** to show partiality to; **3** to resemble (a person) in appearance; **4** to help; support; **5** to oblige; **6** to treat with care (a sore or hurt part of the body) ‖ *n* **7** act of kindness; generous service; **8** approving regard; **9** partiality; **10** small gift received at social functions; **11 in favor of, a** in support of; **b** payable to ‖ SYN *n* graciousness, benevolence, kindness, bias

fa′vor·a·ble *adj* **1** propitious; **2** advantageous; **3** friendly ‖ **fa′vor·a·bly** *adv*

fa′vor·ite /-it/ *n* **1** one who or that which is preferred or particularly esteemed; **2** contestant considered to have the best chance of winning ‖ also *adj*

fa′vor·it·ism *n* partiality

Fawkes, Guy /fôks′/ *n* (1570–1606) English conspirator who attempted to blow up Parliament in 1605

fawn[1] /fôn′/ [MF *faon* < LL *feto* (-*onis*) fetus] *n* **1** deer less than one year old; **2** light yellowish brown

fawn[2] [OE *fagnian* to be glad] *vi* **1** to show pleasure or affection by crouching or cringing, as a dog; **2** to flatter someone meanly; cringe ‖ **fawn′er** *n* ‖ **fawn′ing·ly** *adv* ‖ SYN truckle, stoop, creep, cringe, grovel, curry favor

fay /fā′/ [MF *fee* < L *fata* fates] *n* elf, fairy

faze /fāz′/ [OE *fēsian* to drive away] *vt colloq* to disturb, disconcert

FBI Federal Bureau of Investigation

FCC Federal Communications Commission

FDA Food and Drug Administration

FDIC Federal Deposit Insurance Corporation

Fe [L *ferrum*] *chem* iron

fe·al·ty /fē'əltē/ [OE *feaulte* < L *fidelitas*] *n* (**-ties**) **1** loyalty, **2** *feudalism* pledge of fidelity of a tenant to his landlord or of a vassal to his superior

fear /fir/ [OE *fǣr* sudden danger] *n* **1** emotion characterized by dread or expectation of harm; **2** reverence for a supreme power ‖ *vt* **3** to regard with apprehension; dread; **4** to suspect or doubt; **5** to be afraid of; **6** to revere ‖ *vi* **7** to be afraid, be apprehensive ‖ SYN *n* (see *horror*) ‖ ANT *n* boldness, courage

fear'ful *adj* **1** affected with dread; feeling fear; **2** filled with awe and reverence; **3** causing fear; **4** *colloq* very big or intense ‖ **fear'ful·ly** *adv* ‖ **fear'fulness** *n* ‖ SYN shocking, terrible, frightful (see *afraid*)

fear'less *adj* without fear; bold; undaunted ‖ **fear'less·ly** *adv* ‖ **fear'less·ness** *n* ‖ SYN courageous, brave, daring, valorous, bold

fear'some *adj* **1** causing fear; **2** timorous; scared

fea·si·ble /fēz'ibəl/ [MF *faisible* < *faire* < L *facere* to do] *adj* capable of being done; practicable ‖ **fea'si·bly** *adv* ‖ **fea·si·bil'i·ty** /-bil'-/ *n* ‖ SYN practicable, possible, accomplishable

feast /fēst/ [OF *feste* < L *festa* festivals] *n* **1** elaborate repast, esp. one commemorating some event; banquet; **2** religious festival; **3** abundance of rich and palatable food ‖ *vt* **4** to entertain sumptuously; **5** to please or gratify, as *to feast one's eyes on a picture* ‖ *vi* **6** to have a feast; eat copiously ‖ SYN *n* banquet, entertainment, celebration, treat, repast

feat /fēt/ [MF *fait* deed] *n* difficult or striking act or deed displaying courage, strength, skill, or cunning ‖ SYN act, exploit, achievement

feath·er /feth'ər/ [OE *fether*] *n* **1** any of the light outgrowths from the skin that form the covering of a bird; **2** anything resembling such an outgrowth; **3** kind, species, as *birds of a feather*; **4** act of feathering an oar; **5** plumage; **6 a feather in one's cap** distinction, honor; **7 in fine** or **high feather** in good spirits ‖ *vt* **8** to supply with feathers; **9** to cover or line with feathers; **10** to turn (an oar) so that the blade is nearly horizontal while the oar is swung back into position for the next stroke; **11 feather one's nest** to take advantage of the situation to enrich oneself ‖ *vi* **12** to become covered with feathers; **13** to feather one's oar ‖ **feath'er·y** *adj*

feath·er·bed' *v* (**-bed'ded**; **-bed'ding**) *vi* to require an employer to hire more workmen than are needed ‖ **feath'er·bed'ding** *n*

feath'er·brain' *n* silly or weak-minded person ‖ **feath'er·brained'** *adj*

feath'er·edge' *n* **1** thin edge that bends or breaks easily, as of a board; **2** in a cutting tool, edge that is curled or turned over, or likely to be so ‖ **feath'er·edged'** *adj*

feath'er·weight' *n* **1** person of little importance; **2** least weight that can be put on a racehorse in a handicap; **3** boxer weighting 118 pounds and not more than 126 pounds

fea·ture /fēch'ər/ [MF *faiture* < L *factura* a making] *n* **1** striking or characteristic attribute; **2** trait that arouses interest; **3** any one part of the face; **4** prominent element or item, as of a game, show, or movie program; **5 features** *pl* face ‖ *vt* **6** to picture, delineate; **7** to give prominence to; **8** to be a feature of; **9** to conceive of ‖ SYN *n* trait, mark, attribute (see *characteristic*)

fea'tured *adj* principal, as *the featured actor*

Feb. February

fe·brile /fēb'rəl, feb'-/ [< L *febris* fever] *adj* characteristic of, or indicating, fever

Feb·ru·ar·y /feb'rōō·er'ē/ [L *Februarius* < *februa* purification] *n* second month of the year, having 28 days, or 29 days in leap years

fe·ces /fē'sēz/ [L *faeces* dregs] *npl* excrement ‖ **fe'cal** /-kəl/ *adj*

feck·less /fek'lis/ [< Sc *feck* abbr of *effect*] *adj* weak; without spirit; worthless

fe·cund /fēk'ənd, fek'-/ [L *fecundus*] *adj* fruitful; fertile ‖ **fe·cun·di·ty** /fikun'ditē/ *n*

fed /fed/ **1** *pt* & *pp* of **feed** ‖ *adj* **2 fed up** *colloq* bored

Fed. Federal

fed·er·al /fed'ərəl/ [F *fédéral* < L *foedus* (*-eris*) league] *adj* **1** pert. to, or of the nature of, a compact or union of sovereign states, which agree to delegate certain specific governmental powers to the central government; **2 Federal** designating or pert. to the government of the United States as distinguished from that of any state; **3** favoring the North during the Civil War ‖ *n* **4 Federal** partisan of the North during the Civil War

Fed'er·al De·pos'it In·sur'ance Cor·po·ra'tion *n* government agency which insures bank depositors against loss up to a certain amount

fed'er·al·ist *n* **1** advocate of the federal system of national organization; **2 Federalist** *U.S. hist* **a** before and immediately after the adoption of the Constitution, advocate of a strong centralized government; **b** supporter of the Union in the Civil War; **3 The Federalist** set of 85 articles published by Alexander Hamilton, James Madison, and John Jay in 1787 and 1788, explaining and advocating the adoption of the Constitution || **fed′·er·al·ism** n

fed′er·al·ize′ vt 1 to bring together in compact, as different states; 2 to bring under control of a federal government || vi 3 to unite under a federal government || **fed′er·al·i·za′·tion** n

Fed′er·al Re·serve′ Bank′ n one of 12 district banks set up under the Federal Reserve Board to regulate and aid the member banks in their respective districts

fed′er·ate′ [L *foederare (-atus)*] vt 1 to bring together into a union or federation || vi 2 to come into such a union || **fed′er·a′tion** n

fe·do·ra /fidôr′ə, -dōr′-/ [*Fedora*, play by V. Sardou (1831–1908)] n man's soft felt hat

fee /fē/ [OF *fé, fief*] n 1 charge for professional or other services rendered; 2 charge for admission or for membership; 3 legal charge for special privileges of a public nature; 4 tip or gratuity; 5 *feudalism* a land held from a superior on condition of rendering a specified kind of service in return; b tenure of such land; fief; 6 *law* inherited estate || SYN remuneration, charge, payment (see *salary*)

fee·ble /fēb′əl/ [OF *feble* < L *flebilis* lamentable] adj 1 weak, infirm; 2 deficient in power, vigor, or character || **fee′ble·ness** n || **fee′bly** adv || SYN slight, frail, decrepit, broken, debilitated

feed /fēd/ [OE *fēdan*] v (fed) vt 1 to give food or nourishment to; 2 to supply with what is needed, as a furnace with fuel; 3 to furnish for consumption, as fuel into a furnace; 4 to furnish with materials, as to *feed a machine;* 5 to gratify, satisfy || vi 6 to eat || n 7 food for animals; fodder; 8 a material furnished to a machine, to be operated upon or consumed; b motion that carries material to a machine; c mechanism causing this motion

feed′back′ n 1 return to the input of part of the output of a system or circuit; 2 input of an output signal into the microphone, causing noise

feed′ bag′ n bag containing grain, attached to the headstall of an animal in harness

feed′er n 1 one who or that which feeds; spec. person or device supplying material to a machine; 2 that which supplies the needs or increases the value of something else, as a *feeder bus line;* 3 *elec* wire connecting a central station or power house to secondary centers of distribution

feel /fēl/ [OE *fēlan*] v (felt) vt 1 to

perceive in any other way than by sight, hearing, taste, or smell, as *to feel hunger;* 2 to examine by touching; 3 to become aware of; be moved by; 4 to be conscious of (oneself) as being in a specific condition of mind or body; 5 to think; be convinced of; 6 **feel out** *colloq* to try cautiously to ascertain the opinions of || vi 7 to have perception by touch; 8 to be conscious of being, as *to feel hungry;* 9 to consider oneself to be, as *to feel insulted;* 10 to be stirred emotionally; 11 to seem (said of a given quality as perceived by touch), as *it feels soft;* 12 to grope; 13 **feel like** *colloq* to have a desire for; 14 **feel up to** *colloq* to be able to || n 15 sense of touch; 16 quality perceived by touch, as *the feel of silk;* 17 **get the feel of** to become adapted to

feel′er n 1 one who or that which feels; 2 organ of touch of an animal or insect; 3 remark designed to draw forth the view of others

feel′ing adj 1 possessing or showing great sensibility; 2 easily affected; sympathetic || n 3 any of the cutaneous senses, commonly called touch, by which contact, pressure, temperature, and pain are perceived; 4 act of perceiving or state of one who perceives by touch; 5 sensation received otherwise than through sight, hearing, taste, or smell; 6 emotion; 7 power to experience sympathy, tenderness, or the like; 8 belief or conviction; 9 animating spirit, as in a work of art, which calls forth an emotional response; 10 **feelings** pl sensitiveness or susceptibility || **feel′ing·ly** adv || SYN sense, sensation, sensitiveness, sensibility, susceptibility, emotion, sentiment, passion || DISCR *Feeling* is a general term for experience of the senses, and may include aspects of perception other than those derived from sight, hearing, smell, or taste. The means of awareness through bodily perceptions are called the *senses;* the power of these *senses,* regarded singly, as distinguished from the intellect or will, is called *sense. Sensation* is the physical *feeling* resulting from the operation of the *senses;* we have *sensations* of chill, creepiness, deafness, dizziness, and the like. *Sensibility,* popularly, is the quick and acute capacity for *feeling* of any kind; *sensibility* may make us aware of bodily heat or cold, or it may enable us to experience the higher mental or emotional agitations. *Sensitiveness* is a fine sort of *sensibility;* it is a very delicate responsiveness to any cause, however slight, as the *sensitiveness* of an artist to his subject, or of a thermômeter to changes of temperature. *Susceptibility* is a capacity for quick and strong response to emotional impressions; the *susceptible* youth easily falls in love. *Emotion* is strong, deep *feeling*. *Passion* is powerful *emotion*, the word most often connoting love or anger

fee′ sim′ple *n* (**fees simple**) inheritance in land without limitation as to heirs or restrictions as to sale

fee′ split′ting *n* the practice by a specialist of paying part of his fee to the referring doctor

feet /fēt′/ *pl of* **foot**

feign /fān′/ [OF *feindre* < L *fingere* to devise] *vt* 1 to simulate ‖ *vi* 2 to pretend, dissemble ‖ SYN sham, dissimulate, assume, affect (see *pretend*)

feint /fānt′/ [F *feinte* < OF *feindre* to feign] *n* 1 pretence of attack at one point while really attacking at another; 2 stratagem ‖ *vi* 3 to make a deceptive movement

feist·y /fīst′ē/ [< *dial. feist* small dog] *adj* (**-i·er; -i·est**) 1 full of nervous energy; 2 ill-tempered; touchy

feld·spar /feld′spär′/ [alter. of G *Feldspath*] *n* any of several minerals, chiefly silicates of aluminum, found in many rocks

fe·lic·i·tate /fílis′ítāt′/ *vt* to congratulate, wish happiness to ‖ SYN (see *congratulate*)

fe·lic′i·tous *adj* apt, appropriate, as words or expressions ‖ **fe·lic′i·tous·ly** *adv*

fe·lic′i·ty [L *felicitas* < *felix* happy] *n* (**-ties**) 1 happiness; 2 appropriateness, aptness; 3 pleasing power of expression; 4 that which makes happiness ‖ SYN bliss, enjoyment (see *happiness*)

fe·line /fē′līn/ [< *feles* cat] *adj* 1 of or pert. to a cat or the cat family; 2 stealthy; treacherous ‖ *n* 3 one of the cat family

fell¹ /fel′/ *pt of* **fall**

fell² [OE *fellan*] *vt* to cause to fall

fell³ [OF *fel* < L *fello* felon] *adj* cruel; destructive; barbarous

fel·lah /fel′ə/ [Ar] *n* (**-lahs, -la·hin** or **-la·heen** /fel′əhēn′/) Egyptian peasant

fel·loe /fel′ō/ [ME *felwe*] *n* rim or section of the rim of a wheel into which the outer ends of the spokes are fitted

fel·low /fel′ō/ [OE *fēolaga* partner] *n* 1 companion or associate; 2 one of the same kind or in the same position with others; 3 one of a pair; 4 *colloq* individual; 5 member of a society, esp. of a learned body; 6 graduate of a college or university who receives an honorary title or an annual sum for a stated period of study; 7 member of the governing body of a college or university; 8 *colloq* suitor, boyfriend ‖ *adj* 9 in companionship; associated

fel′low·ship′ *n* 1 association, esp. of a friendly character; comradeship; 2 common interest, as in fraternal orders; 3 organization of friends; 4 a endowment for the support of graduate students; b sum of money derived from such endowment paid to a graduate student; c position or title of honor without stipend conferred upon a graduate student ‖ SYN companionship, comradeship (see *acquaintance*)

fel′low trav′el·er *n* nonmember who supports the aims of a political party, esp. the Communist party

fel·on¹ /fel′ən/ [LL *fello* (-*lonis*)] *n* one who has committed a felony ‖ SYN criminal, convict, evildoer, malefactor

fel′on² [perh < L *fel* gall] *n* extremely painful abscess on a finger or toe, usu. near the nail

fel′o·ny *n* (**-nies**) major crime, more serious than a misdemeanor ‖ **fe·lo·ni·ous** /fílōn′ē·əs/ *adj*

felt¹ /felt′/ *pt & pp of* **feel**

felt² [OE] 1 fabric made of wool, or of wool, hair, and fur, forced together by pressure and/or heat; 2 any material resembling felt

fem. 1 feminine; 2 female

fe·male /fēm′āl/ [< L *femella* dim. of *femina* woman, influenced by *male*] *adj* 1 pert. to the sex that bears young or produces ova; 2 consisting of females; 3 *bot* having pistils without stamens, capable of being fertilized; 4 *mach* designating a part shaped to receive a corresponding male part ‖ 5 *n* female person, animal, or plant ‖ SYN *adj* feminine, womanly, womanlike, womanish ‖ DISCR To the sex of women we apply the word *female*; as opposed to *male*, it applies to animals and plants as well as to human beings. Though we still sometimes read of a *female* slave, *female* suffrage, or *female* education, *female* in nonbiological senses has been displaced by *feminine*. *Feminine* is applied to qualities distinguishing women, or things appropriate to them; we speak of *feminine* slightness or delicacy; *feminine* apparel; a truly *feminine* remark; *feminine* features. *Womanly* is applied to those qualities of womankind that are sweetly becoming or endearing; we speak of *womanly* sympathy or tact, but of *feminine* cattiness. *Womanish* is a contemptuous term, connoting, whether applied to men or women, the weaker and less likable qualities of the sex. Faults due to an excess of femininity are excused, often indulged, as *feminine* weakness at the sight of blood; such weakness in a man would be reproachfully termed *womanish*. *Womanlike* is used respectfully, like *womanly*, but it lacks the latter's warmth of tone, as *wom-*

anlike, she fainted when the danger was over

fem·i·nine /fem′inin/ [< L *femina* woman] *adj* 1 of or pert. to women; 2 delicate, tender, sensitive; 3 *gram* in some languages, designating the gender of words that denote females, and of other words classed with them || *n* 4 feminine gender; 5 feminine word || **fem′i·nin′i·ty** /-nin′-/ *n* || SYN womanly, womanlike (see *female)*

fem′i·nism *n* doctrine that women should be given every social freedom, advantage, and opportunity enjoyed by men || **fem′i·nist** *n*

femme fa·tale /fem′ fətal′/ [F = fatal woman] *n* (femmes fatales /fem′ fətalz′/) irresistibly seductive woman who leads men on, often to their doom

fe·mur /fēm′ər/ [L = thigh] *n* (femurs or fem·o·ra /fem′ərə/) thighbone

fen /fen′/ [OE *fenn*] *n* low flat marshland

fence /fens′/ [*abbr* of *defence*] *vt* 1 to enclose or surround with or as with a fence || *vi* 2 to practice the art of fencing; 3 to avoid making a direct reply; 4 *colloq* to deal in stolen goods || *n* 5 barrier consisting of posts, boards, wire, etc., as around a field; 6 *colloq* one who receives stolen goods; 7 **on the fence** uncommitted || **fenc′er** *n*

fenc′ing *n* art or sport of using a sword or foil

fend /fend′/ [*abbr* of *defend*] *vt* 1 to parry; 2 **fend off** to ward off || *vi* 3 **fend for oneself** to manage alone

fend′er *n* anything that fends or protects, as a guard in front of a fireplace, the mudguard of an automobile, or a bundle of rope or the like hung over a boat's side to lessen shock or prevent chafing

fen·nel /fen′əl/ [OE *finugl* < L *feniculum* < *fenum* hay] *n* fragrant plant *(Foeniculum vulgare)* of the carrot family, having yellow flowers

FEPC Fair Employment Practices Committee

-fer /-fər/ [L] *n comb form* bearer

fe·ral /fir′əl/ [< L *fera* wild beast] *adj* 1 wild, untamed; uncultivated; 2 *zool* reverted from the domestic to the savage state

fer-de-lance /fer′dəlans′, -läns′/ [F = iron head of lance] *n* large poisonous snake *(Trimeresurus atrox)* found in tropical America

Fer·di·nand II /furd′inand′/ *n* (1452–1516) king of Aragon 1479–1516; husband of Isabella and, as **Ferdinand V** (the Catholic) joint ruler of Castile 1474–1504

fer·ment /fur′ment/ [L *fermentum* leaven] *n* 1 substance that causes fermentation, as yeast, bacteria, etc.; 2 fermentation; 3 tumult; agitation || /fərment′/ *vt* 4 to produce fer-

mentation in; 5 to excite, stir up || *vi* 6 to undergo fermentation; 7 to be stirred up or excited

fer′men·ta′tion *n* 1 decomposition produced in an organic substance by the action of living organisms, such as certain fungi or bacteria; 2 agitation

fer·mi·um /fur′mē·əm/ [< Enrico *Fermi* (1901–54) It physicist] *n* transuranian element (Fm; at.no. 100)

fern /furn′/ [OE *fearn*] *n* any of a large order (Filicales) of flowerless plants, generally with broad and feathery fronds or leaves

fe·ro·cious /fərōsh′əs/ [< L *ferox (-ocis)* fierce] *adj* savage; cruel || **fe·ro′cious·ly** *adv* || **fe·ro′cious·ness** or **fe·roc′i·ty** /-ros′-/ *n* (-ties) || SYN brutal, fell, barbarous, fierce (see *inhuman)*

-fer·ous /-f(ə)rəs/ [< L *ferre* to bear] *adj comb form* producing; yielding; bearing, as *odoriferous*

fer·ret /fer′it/ [OF *furet* < *fur* robber] *n* 1 kind of weasel *(Mustela furo)* used to hunt rats and rabbits || *vt* 2 to hunt with ferrets; 3 **ferret out** to search perseveringly for

ferri- [< L *ferrum* iron] *comb form* iron, as *ferriferous*

fer·ric /fer′ik/ [< L *ferrum* iron] *adj* 1 pert. to, derived from, or containing iron; 2 *chem* designating a compound in which the valence of iron is higher than in ferrous compounds, as *ferric oxide*

fer′ric ox′ide *n* dark-red oxide of iron —Fe_2O_3— found in nature as hematite and rust, and used as a pigment and in polishing compounds

fer·rif·er·ous /fərif′ərəs/ *adj* containing or yielding iron

Fer′ris wheel′ [for′is/ [G. W. *Ferris* (d. 1896) Am engineer] *n* power-driven amusement device consisting of a vertical wheel revolving on a fixed axle and having in its rim pendent cars for passengers

ferro- /fer′ō/ *comb form* iron or steel, as *ferroconcrete*

fer′ro·con′crete *n* poured concrete containing steel bars, mesh, etc. to increase its strength

fer′ro·type′ *vt* 1 to make a glossy surface on (a photograph) by pressing the wet print on a metal sheet || *n* 2 tintype

fer·rous /fer′əs/ [< L *ferrum* iron] *adj* 1 pert. to, or derived from, iron; 2 *chem* designating a compound of iron in which iron is bivalent

fer·rule /fer′əl, -ōōl/ [MF *virole* < L *viriola* bracelet, altered by influence of L *ferrum* iron] *n* metal ring or cap placed at the end of a stick, tool handle, etc., to strengthen it

fer·ry /fer′ē/ [OE *ferian* to convey] *n* (-ries) 1 provision for carrying passengers or freight over comparatively narrow bodies of water by boats or rafts; 2 place where such a crossing is made; 3 ferryboat ‖ *v* (-ried) *vt* 4 to convey across a river or other body of water by boat or plane ‖ *vi* 5 to cross a body of water by boat

fer′ry‧boat′ *n* boat used for ferrying

fer‧tile /furt′əl/ [L *fertilis* < *ferre* to bear] *adj* 1 producing abundantly, fruitful; 2 inventive; 3 capable of developing because impregnated by the male element; 4 capable of reproducing; 5 promoting productiveness ‖ **fer‧til′i‧ty** /fərtil′itē/ *n* ‖ SYN prolific, plenteous, productive, rich, teeming

fer′ti‧lize′ *vt* 1 to render fruitful or productive; 2 to enrich with fertilizer; 3 to impregnate ‖ **fer′ti‧li‧za′tion** *n*

fer′ti‧liz′er *n* 1 any material used to fertilize the soil, as chemicals or manure; 2 *bot* carrier of the fertilizing agent, as a bee to a flower

fer‧ule /fer′il, -ōōl/ [L *ferula* fennel, rod] *n* flat stick, as a ruler, used in punishing children

fer‧vent /fur′vənt/ [L *fervens* (-*entis*) boiling] *adj* zealous; ardent; vehement ‖ **fer′vent‧ly** *adv* ‖ SYN impassioned, eager, impatient, fierce, intense

fer‧vid /fur′vid/ [L *fervidus* burning] *adj* burning; ardent; vehement ‖ **fer′vid‧ly** *adv* ‖ **fer′vid‧ness** *n* ‖ SYN impetuous, earnest, fiery, passionate, zealous

fer‧vor /fur′vər/ [L = heat] *n* intensity of feeling; zeal

-fest /-fest′/ [G *Fest* celebration] *n comb form* celebration or occasion marked by a particular activity, as *a songfest*

fes‧tal /fest′əl/ [< L *festum* feast] *adj* 1 pert. to a feast or holiday; 2 joyous, festive

fes‧ter /fes′tər/ [MF *festre* < L *fistula* ulcer] *vi* 1 to become inflamed and generate pus; ulcerate; 2 to grow virulent; rankle, as resentment; 3 to become corrupt or rotten ‖ *n* 4 pusforming children

fes‧ti‧val /fes′tivəl/ [see *festive*] *n* 1 celebration of some event or anniversary, either civil or religious; 2 entertainment of a specific sort, generally at regular intervals, as *the Handel festival*

fes′tive /-tiv/ [< L *festum* feast] *adj* 1 pert. to a feast or festival; 2 gay; joyous; convivial ‖ **fes′tive‧ly** *adv* ‖ SYN joyful, merry, festal, sportive, gay, mirthful

fes‧tiv′i‧ty *n* (-ties) 1 merrymaking; joyfulness; 2 celebration; festival

fes‧toon /festōōn′/ [F *feston* < It *festone*] *n* 1 decorative garland, as of leaves, draped between two points ‖ *vt* 2 to decorate with or form into a festoon

Fest‧schrift /fest′shrift′/ [G < *Fest* celebration + *Schrift* writing] *n*

(-schrift‧en /shrift′tən/ or -schrifts) volume of writings by many authors in honor of a colleague

fe‧tal /fēt′əl/ [< *fetus*] *adj* pert. to the fetus

fetch /fech′/ [OE *feccan*] *vt* 1 to go after and bring; get; 2 to be sold for; 3 to cause to come ‖ *vi* 4 to retrieve game; 5 *naut* to hold a course ‖ SYN accomplish, transport, convey (see *bring*)

fetch′ing *adj* pleasing, attractive

fete or **fête** /fāt′/ [F = feast] *n* 1 holiday; 2 religious festival; 3 festive celebration ‖ *vi* 4 to entertain or honor with festivities

fe‧ti‧cide /fēt′isid/ [*fetus* + -*cide*] *n* act of destroying a fetus

fet‧id /fet′id, fēt′-/ [< L *fetere* to stink] *adj* offensive in odor, stinking ‖ SYN noisome, rotten, disgusting, putrid, noxious

fe‧tish or **fe‧tich** /fet′ish, fēt′-/ [F *fétiche* < Port *feitiço* charm] *n* 1 any inanimate object that is worshiped or regarded with superstitious awe; 2 object having no intrinsic significance of sex, but arousing erotic feeling ‖ **fe′tish‧ism** ‖ **fe′tish‧ist** *n*

fet‧lock /fet′lok′/ [ME *fytlok*] *n* 1 on a horse, the tuft of hair just above the hoof at the back; 2 cushionlike projection that bears this tuft of hair; 3 also **fetlock joint** joint of the limb at this place

fet‧ter /fet′ər/ [OE *feter*] *n* 1 chain for binding the feet; 2 anything that restrains; hindrance ‖ *vt* 3 to place fetters on; 4 to hinder, restrain

fet‧tle /fet′əl/ [ME *fetlen* to shape] *n* condition or state, as in fine *fettle*

fe‧tus /fēt′əs/ [L = offspring] *n* 1 child in the uterus after the third month of gestation; 2 embryo in the uterus or egg after it is clearly defined

feud /fyōōd′/ [MF *fede* < OHG *fēhida* enmity] *n* 1 quarrel, generally hereditary or of long standing, between clans or families; 2 any prolonged quarrel ‖ *vi* 3 to conduct a feud ‖ **feud′ist** *n*

feu‧dal /fyōōd′əl/ [< ML *feudum* fief] *adj* of or pert. to feudalism

feu‧dal‧ism *n* 1 political and social system affecting almost every phase of life in Europe in the Middle Ages, referring spec. to the tenure of land and to the organization of military service and of the state, whereby the land was divided into fiefs, each held by a tenant or vassal as long as he rendered certain services to his superior lord, who might himself be a vassal either of a higher nobleman or of the king; 2 any political system similar to medieval feudalism ‖ **feu′dal‧is′tic** *adj*

feu′dal sys′tem *n* feudalism 1

feu′da‧to‧ry /-tôr′-, -tōr′-/ *n* (-ries) 1 feudal tenant or vassal ‖ *adj* 2 pert.

to the relation between a vassal and his lord

fe·ver /fēv′ər/ [OE *fēfer* < L *febris*] *n* 1 abnormal rise in body temperature; 2 any disease characterized by such high temperature; 3 extreme nervous excitement ‖ **fe′ver·ish** *adj*

fe′ver blis′ter or **sore′** *n* cold sore

few /fyoo′/ [OE *fēawe*] *adj* 1 small in number; not many ‖ *pron* 2 small number of persons or things; 3 **quite a few** *colloq* many

fey /fā′/ [OE *fǣge* fated] *adj* 1 *archaic* doomed or fated to death; 2 supernatural, elfin

fez /fez′/ [*Fez* city in Morocco] *n* (**fez·zes**) brimless felt hat, cone-shaped with a flat top, allowing the wearer to touch his forehead on the floor in prayer without removing it, worn chiefly by Mohammedan men

ff *mus* fortissimo

ff. 1 folios; 2 following; referring to more than one object

FHA Federal Housing Administration

fi·a·cre /fē·äk′ər/ [F] *n* small hackney coach

fi·an·cé /fē′änsā′/ [F] *n* man engaged to be married

fi·an·cée /-sā′/ [F] *n* girl or woman engaged to be married

fi·as·co /fē·as′kō/ [It] *n* (**-coes, -cos**) ignominious failure

fi·at /fī′ət, -at/ [L = let it be done] *n* 1 authoritative command; 2 arbitrary decree

fi′at mon′ey *n* paper currency made legal tender by law or fiat, but not having an intrinsic value equal to its nominal value

fib /fib′/ [perh *abbr* of dial. *fible-fable* nonsense] *n* 1 petty falsehood ‖ *v* (**fibbed; fib·bing**) *vi* 2 to tell fibs

fi·ber /fīb′ər/ [L *fibra*] *n* 1 one of the slender threadlike filaments forming certain organic tissues or textile fabrics; 2 tough substance that can be separated into threads and spun or woven; 3 fibrous structure; texture; 4 quality of character ‖ **fi′brous** *adj*

fi′ber·board′ *n* 1 material made of fibers compressed into sheets; 2 sheet of this material

fi′ber·glass′ *n* fabric made of finely spun glass used for sound absorption, insulation, and fireproofing

fi·broid /fī′broid/ [L *fibra* fiber + *-oid*] *adj* 1 fiberlike ‖ *n* 2 fibroma

fi·bro·ma /fībrōm′ə/ [LL] *n* (**-ma·ta** /-mətə/) tumor consisting chiefly of fibrous connective tissue

fi·bro·sis /-ōs′is/ *n pathol* development of excess fibrous tissue

fib·u·la /fib′yələ/ [L = brooch] *n* (**-lae** /-lē′/, **-las**) outer and smaller of the two bones of the lower leg ‖ **fib′u·lar** /-lər/ *adj*

-fic /-fik/ [L *-ficus*] *adj suf* making, as *honorific*

-fi·ca·tion /-fikāsh′ən/ *n suf* making, production, as *pacification*

fick·le /fik′əl/ [OE *ficol* deceitful] *adj* changeable, inconstant ‖ **fick′le·ness** *n* ‖ SYN freakish, changeable, crotchety, capricious, moody, whimsical, shifting, unsteady ‖ DISCR The *capricious* person yields to every impulse of a changing mind; he is inconstant in his emotions, fitful in his likes and dislikes, variable in his conduct. *Freakish* actions are so erratic and queer as to seem abnormal. *Whimsical* actions have their root in some kink or humor of the disposition rather than in instability or unsoundness; *whimsical* sayings are often of a droll turn; *whimsical* expressions or mannerisms often produce a chuckly sort of mirth; *whimsical* people are quaintly humorous in their desires or fancies ‖ ANT steady, constant, faithful, unchanging, resolute, firm

fic·tion /fik′shən/ [L *fictio* (*-onis*)] *n* 1 act of feigning or inventing; 2 that which is imagined or invented; 3 literature that narrates imaginary events and portrays imaginary characters, usu. in prose, as novels and romances ‖ **fic′tion·al** *adj* ‖ **fic′tion·al·ize′** *vt* ‖ **fic′tion·al·i·za′tion** *n* ‖ SYN fabrication, romance, myth, falsehood, fable

fic·ti·tious /fiktish′əs/ *adj* 1 of or pert. to fiction; 2 not genuine; false, pretended ‖ **fic·ti′tious·ly** *adv* ‖ SYN counterfeit, fabulous, assumed (see *artificial*)

fid /fid′/ [?] *n naut* 1 iron or wooden bar used to support a topmast; 2 tapering, pointed tool for spreading the strands of rope when splicing or for stretching grommets

fid·dle /fid′əl/ [OE *fithele* perh < LL *vidula*] *n* 1 *colloq* violin ‖ *vi* 2 *colloq* to play on a violin; 3 to trifle; tinker ‖ *vt* 4 *colloq* to play (a tune) on the violin ‖ **fid′dler** *n*

fid′dle-fad′dle /-fad′əl/ *colloq* *n* 1 nonsense [reduplication of *fiddle*]; trifling conversation ‖ *vi* 2 to talk nonsense; fuss about trifles ‖ *interj* 3 nonsense!

fid′dler crab′ *n* burrowing crab (genus *Uca*) of the Atlantic coast, having one claw much larger than the other

fid′dle·sticks′ *interj colloq* nonsense!

fid′dling *adj colloq* trifling; petty

fi·del·i·ty /fidel′itē, fi-/ [< L *fidelis* faithful] *n* (**-ties**) 1 faithfulness, loyalty; 2 exactness; 3 ability with which an electronic device accurately reproduces sound ‖ SYN allegiance, loyalty, devotion ‖ (see *constancy*)

fidg·et /fij′it/ [< obs. *fidge* to twitch] *vi* 1 to move about restlessly ‖ *vt* 2 to make uneasy ‖ *n* 3 one who fidgets; 4 **fidgets** *pl* nervous restlessness ‖ **fidg′et·y** *adj*

fi·du·ci·ar·y /fid(y)ōōsh′ē·er′ē, -shərē/ *n* (-**ies**) trustee, as *a fiduciary for a child's inheritance* ‖ also *adj*

fie /fī′/ [L *fi* phew!] *interj* for shame! (usu. a humorous pretense of horror)

fief /fēf′/ [OF < LL *feodum, feudum*] *n* feudalism 1 land held in return for service to a superior; feudal estate; 2 tenure of such an estate

field /fēld′/ [OE *feld*] *n* 1 piece of land cleared for cultivation, pasture, etc., generally enclosed; 2 plot of ground set aside for a special use, as *a baseball field*; 3 region yielding some natural product, as *an oil field*; 4 a site of a battle; **b** the battle itself; 5 sphere of action or scholarship; 6 wide expanse, as *a field of ice*; 7 area seen through a telescope or viewfinder, usu. *field of vision*; 8 open unenclosed country; 9 *phys* space over which some influence is extended, as *a magnetic field*; 10 stationary part of a motor or generator which produces a magnetic field around the armature; 11 *sports* **a** those who take part in a contest or sport, as in fox hunting; **b** in baseball, side that is not at bat; **c** in any contest among individuals, as horse racing, all the contestants except a specified one; 12 *heral* **a** surface of the escutcheon on which the device is drawn; **b** surface of a division of the shield ‖ *vt* 13 to give an answer to (a difficult question); 14 *baseball* to catch and return (a ball) from the field ‖ *vi* 15 *baseball* to catch and return balls batted to the field

field′ day′ *n* 1 military review; 2 day set for a series of outdoor athletic contests; 3 time of unusual success

field′er *n* baseball player other than the pitcher or catcher

field′er's choice′ *n baseball* option of a fielder catching a ground ball to retire a base runner instead of the batter at first base

field′ glass′ *nsg* or **field′ glass′es** *npl* small portable binocular telescope

field′ gun′ *n* cannon mounted on wheels

field′ hock′ey *n* hockey 2

field′ mag′net *n* magnet in a generator or motor which produces the magnetic field in which the armature rotates

field′ mar′shal *n* officer of the highest rank in many armies, equivalent to the U.S. five-star general of the army

field′ mouse′ *n* any of various wild mice that live in fields and meadows

field′ of′fi·cer *n* army officer of the grade of colonel, lieutenant colonel, or major

field′ of force′ *n* portion of space pervaded by some agent, as electricity, magnetism, or gravitation

field′ of hon′or *n* scene of a duel

field′piece′ *n* field gun

field′stone′ *n* undressed stone used for the exterior of buildings

field′ the′o·ry *n* detailed mathematical description of the physical properties of matter under the influence of a field, such as that of gravity

fiend /fēnd′/ [OE *fēond* enemy] *n* 1 evil spirit; demon; 2 wicked, cruel, and malicious person or foe; 3 one who is the victim of a harmful practice, as the excessive use of drugs; 4 one who is devoted to or very proficient in some activity, as *a poker fiend*

fiend′ish *adj* cruel, diabolical ‖ **fiend′-ish·ly** *adv* ‖ **fiend′ish·ness** *n*

fierce /firs′/ [OF *fiers* < L *ferus* savage] *adj* 1 furious; intense; violent; 2 eager, passionate, fervid ‖ **fierce′ly** *adv* ‖ **fierce′ness** *n*

fi·er·y /fī′ərē/ [see fire] *adj* (-**i·er**; -**i·est**) 1 of or pert. to fire; 2 glaring; burning; 3 passionate; easily aroused; 4 ardent; spirited ‖ **fi′er·i·ness** *n* ‖ SYN impetuous, fervid, torrid, hot, glowing, flaming

fi·es·ta /fē·es′tə/ [Sp] *n* 1 religious festival; holiday; saint's day; 2 any festive occasion

fife /fīf′/ [G *Pfeife* pipe] *n* shrill-toned transverse flute, used chiefly in military music ‖ **fif′er** *n*

fif·teen /fif′tēn′/ [OE *fiftēne*] *n* sum of five and ten (15; XV) ‖ also *adj* & *pron*

fif′teenth′ *n* 1 the one next in order after the fourteenth; 2 one of fifteen equal parts ‖ also *adj*

fifth /fifth′/ [OE *fifta*] *n* 1 the one next in order after the fourth; 2 one of five equal parts; 3 fifth part of a gallon; 4 *mus* **a** interval of three steps and a half step, as from C to G in the scale of C major; **b** fifth tone of a scale counting up from the tonic as first; the dominant ‖ also *adj*

fifth′ col′umn [allusion to secret Franco sympathizers in Madrid while four of his columns were advancing on the city during the Spanish Civil War 1939] *n* group of people who secretly sympathize with an invading enemy and stand ready to declare for and aid him when the opportunity presents itself ‖ **fifth′ col′umn-ist** *n*

fifth′ wheel′ *n* 1 spare wheel; 2 superfluous person

fif′ti·eth *n* 1 the one next in order after the forty-ninth; 2 one of fifty equal parts ‖ also *adj*

fif·ty /fif′tē/ [OE *fiftig*] *n* (-**ties**) 1 five times ten (50; L); 2 **the fifties** *pl* **a** the numbers from 50 to 59; **b** the years from 50 to 59 in a century or a lifetime ‖ also *adj* & *pron*

fif′ty-fif′ty *adj colloq* 1 shared equally; 2 so-so ‖ also *adv*

fig /fig′/ [OProv *figa* < L *ficus*] *n* 1 any of several trees bearing small pear-shaped, many-seeded fruit, esp. *Ficus carica*, native to SW Asia; 2 the fruit; 3 *colloq* trifle

fig. 337 **Filipino**

fig. 1 figurative(ly); **2** figure

fight /fīt'/ [OE *feohtan*] *v* (**fought**) *vi* **1** to contend in battle or with arms; engage in a physical contest; **2** to strive or contend for success against opposition or difficulty ‖ *vt* **3** to war or struggle against; **4** to strive for the mastery of; **5** to manage in battle; cause to struggle or contend; pit, as one cock against another ‖ *n* **6** combat, battle, conflict; **7** pugnacity, as *full of fight* ‖ **fight'er** *n* ‖ SYN *v* compete, contest, struggle, battle, dispute

fig' leaf' *n* **1** leaf of a fig tree; **2** device for concealing something indecent or thought to be indecent

fig·ment /fig'mənt/ [L *figmentum* fiction] *n* something imagined; invention of the mind

fig·ur·a·tive /fig'yərətiv/ *adj* **1** representing by a figure or emblem; **2** ornate, flowery; full of figures of speech; **3** symbolical, not literal ‖ **fig'ur·a·tive·ly** *adv*

fig·ure /fig'yər/ [L *figura* < *fingere* (*fig-*) to fashion] *n* **1** outline, shape, appearance; **2** prominent person; **3** impression or appearance made by a person's conduct or career; **4** image or representation of anything by means of painting, carving, modeling, drawing, or the like; **5** drawing made to illustrate a statement; **6** design or pattern in wall paper, fabrics, etc.; **7** symbol, esp. sign denoting a number; **8** movement in a dance; **9** price or value of a thing; **10** *mus* a smallest complete unit in musical form expressed in a few melody tones or chords and giving a distinctive idea; **b** type of melody or accompaniment sustained throughout a passage; **11** *geom* any combination of related lines, surfaces, or solids forming the subject of a discussion; **12** *rhet* figure of speech ‖ *vt* **13** to form in any determinate shape; **14** to represent, show by resemblance; **15** to adorn or cover with a pattern or design; **16** to imagine or form a mental image of; **17** to denote by, or indicate with, numerals or lines; compute; **18** to write or speak in metaphors; **19** **figure out, a** to understand; **b** to solve ‖ *vi* **20** to be prominent; take a part, as *to figure in politics;* **21** to calculate; **22** to contrive; **23** **figure on, a** to rely on; **b** to plan on ‖ **fig'ured** *adj* ‖ SYN *n* emblem, symbol, sign, metaphor, allegory

fig'ure·head' *n* **1** carved figure placed at the prow of a ship; **2** person with nominal but no real authority

fig'ure of speech' *n* expression using words in an unusual sense, as a simile or metaphor

fig·u·rine /-rēn'/ [It *figurina* dim. of *figura* figure] *n* small carved or molded figure

Fi·ji /fē'jē/ *n* island nation in S Pacific (620,000; 7,055 sq.m.; cap. Suva) ‖ **Fi'ji·an** *adj & n*

fil·a·ment /fil'əmənt/ [< L *filum* thread] *n* **1** fine thread or threadlike fiber; **2** metallic thread in a light bulb which is heated to incandescence by the electric current; **3** *electron.* such a filament in a vacuum tube which functions as a cathode and emits the electrons attracted by the plate

fil·bert /fil'bərt/ [< St. *Philibert*] *n* hazelnut

filch /filch'/ [ME *filchen*] *vt* to pilfer or steal, as trifling things ‖ **filch'er** *n*

file¹ /fī'(ə)l/ [L *filum* thread] *n* **1** any of various devices on or in which papers may be put for safekeeping or reference; **2** any collection of papers kept together and classified in an orderly way; **3** line of persons or things; **4** *chess* vertical row of squares ‖ *vt* **5** to place in a file; **6** to arrange in convenient order; **7** to transmit (news copy); **8** *law* **a** to deposit (a paper or document) with the proper officer; **b** to take as the first step in an action, as *to file a complaint* ‖ *vi* **9** to march in a file; **10** to register as a candidate

file² [OE *fēol*] *n* **1** hard steel tool with surface cut diagonally in sharp-edged ridges, used for smoothing or abrading; **2** anything used to polish or abrade ‖ *vt* **3** to smooth, clean, cut, or sharpen with a file

fi·let mi·gnon /filā' minyon'/ [F = 'dainty fillet] *n* (**filets mignons** /filā' minyonz'/) fillet cut from the thick end of a beef tenderloin

fil·i·al /fil'ē·əl, -yəl [< L *filius* son] *adj* **1** of or pert. to a son or daughter; **2** befitting a son or daughter in relation to a parent, as *filial devotion* ‖ **fil'ial·ly** *adv*

fil·i·a·tion /fil'ē·āsh'ən/ *n* **1** filial relationship; **2** determination of paternity; **3** relationship of a derivative to its source; **4** relationship of a language or culture to a prior state

fil·i·bus·ter /fil'ibus'tər/ [Sp *filibustero* < D *vrijbuiter* freebooter] *n* **1** military adventurer who engages in irregular warfare in a foreign country; **2** intentional obstruction of legislation by dilatory tactics, spec. by talking merely to consume time; **3** instance of such tactics ‖ *vi* **4** to act as a freebooter; **5** to delay legislation by a filibuster ‖ *vt* **6** to submit (legislation) to a filibuster ‖ **fil'i·bus'ter·er** *n*

fil·i·gree /fil'igrē'/ [< F *filigrane* < It *filigrana*] *n* **1** ornamental work in gold or silver wire, resembling lace; **2** something delicate or ornamental ‖ *vt* **3** to adorn with or form into filigree

fil'ings /fīl'iŋz/ *npl* fragments removed by a file

Fil·i·pi·no /fil'ipē'nō/ [Sp] *n* **1** native of the Philippine Islands ‖ *adj* **2** Philippine

fill /fil'/ [OE *fyllan*] *vt* **1** to make full; **2** to occupy completely; pervade; **3** to have or perform the duties of; **4** to supply with an incumbent, as an office; **5** to bring to a desired height or level, as a low place; **6** to feed; satisfy; **7** to execute or carry out, as a business order; **8** to stop up the crevices, pores, cavities, etc., of (wood, cloth, leather, teeth, etc.); **9** *pharm* to compound, as a prescription; **10 fill in, a** to supply with specific information; **b** to complete by adding something; **11 fill out** to supply specific information to (a document); **12 fill up** to fill to the top || *vi* **13** to become full; **14 fill in** to substitute; **15 fill out** to become larger || *n* **16** full supply, as much as produces satisfaction, as *to eat one's fill;* **17** that which is used to fill

fill'er *n* **1** one who or that which fills; **2** substance used for filling the pores in wood before painting; **3** tobacco used in the body of a cigar

fil·let /fil'it/ [F *filet* < L *filum* thread] *n* **1** narrow band of cloth or metal worn across the forehead to encircle or hold the hair; **2** thin, narrow strip or band; **3** *cookery* /filā'/ also **fi·let,** a boneless piece of meat or fish; **b** piece of meat boned, rolled, and tied for cooking || *vt* **4** to bind with a narrow band; **5** /filā'/ also **fi·let** to prepare (meat or fish) for cooking as a filet

fill'-in' *n* **1** substitute; **2** quick summary

fill'ing *n* that which is put in to fill a space, as in a pie or tooth

fil·lip /fil'ip/ [imit] *n* **1** a striking with the fingertip by releasing it forcefully from the ball of the thumb; **2** sharp stimulus || also *vt & vi*

Fill·more, Mil·lard /mil'ərd fil'môr, -mōr/ *n* (1800–74) 13th president of the U.S. 1850–53

fil·ly /fil'ē/ [ON *fylja* foal] *n* (**-lies**) **1** female foal; **2** *colloq* lively young girl

film /film'/ [OE *filmen* membrane] *n* **1** thin membrane or skin; **2** slight covering or layer; **3** haze or blur; **4** strip or sheet of cellulose acetate coated with a light-sensitive emulsion for receiving photographic impressions; **5** motion picture; **6** dimness of the eyes || *vt* **7** to cover with or as with a film; **8** to make a motion picture of || *vi* **9** to become covered or obscured with a film; **10** to be capable of reproduction (in a specified way) on a film, as *she films well*

film' clip' *n* strip of motion-picture film for insertion in a telecast

film'strip' *n* strip of film containing pictures, diagrams, printed matter, etc. for still projection

film'y *adj* (**-i·er; -i·est**) **1** like a film; gauzy; **2** covered by or as if by a film; hazy || **film'i·ness** *n*

fil·ter /filt'ər/ [OF *filtre* < LL *filtrum* < OLG *filt* felt] *n* **1** any porous material, as sand, cloth, or paper, through which a liquid is passed to remove solid particles or impurities; **2** device for clearing or purifying liquid or gaseous substances by filtering; **3** *elec* device for regulating or preventing the passage of current of certain frequencies or types while allowing other current to pass freely; **4** *photog* colored gelatine or glass mounted in front of a lens to control color balance or light intensity || *vt* **5** to act as a filter for; **6** to remove by means of a filter || *vi* **7** to move or pass through a filter || **fil'ter·a·ble** *adj*

fil'ter tip' *n* **1** mouthpiece of cigar or cigarette for filtering smoke; **2** cigar or cigarette with such a filter || **fil'ter-tipped'** *adj*

filth /filth'/ [OE *fylth*] *n* **1** foul matter; dirt; **2** anything that brings about physical or moral impurity; defilement

filth·y *adj* (**-i·er; -i·est**) **1** foul, dirty; **2** unclean morally or physically; **3** low; contemptible || **filth'i·ly** *adv* || **filth'i·ness** *n* || SYN muddy, soiled, stained; vile, obscene, squalid, nasty, impure || ANT clean, pure, uplifting, noble

fil'trate [see **filter**] *n* **1** liquid strained through a filter || *vt & vi* **2** to filter || **fil·tra'tion** *n*

fin¹ /fin'/ [OE *finn*] *n* **1** winglike extension from the body of a fish which helps to move, balance, or steer it; **2** one of the small vertical or horizontal plane surfaces or wings on an airplane used to stabilize it; **3** one of the projecting ridges on engine parts to aid in dissipating heat; **4** any finlike part, as on a ship || **finned'** *adj*

fin² [Yiddish *finif* five] *n slang* five-dollar bill

Fin. 1 Finland; **2** Finnish

fi·na·gle /fināg'əl/ [alter. of *fainaigue* to renege] *vt* **1** to wangle; **2** to swindle, trick || *vi* **3** to use devious and underhand methods || **fi·na'gler** *n*

fi·nal /fin'əl/ [< L *finis* end] *adj* **1** pert. to the end; finishing; last; **2** conclusive, decisive; **3** relating to an end or purpose || *n* **4** that which is final; **5** *sports* last and deciding heat or trial; **6** finals *pl* last examinations of a series || SYN *adj* ultimate, conclusive, definitive (see *last*)

fi·na·le /final'ē, -näl'ē/ [It = last] *n* **1** termination, end, or close, as of any series of events; **2** last act or scene of a performance; **3** *mus* last passage or movement in a composition

fi'nal·ist /fī'-/ *n* contestant in the last round of a contest

fi·nal·i·ty /final'itē/ *n* (**-ties**) **1** completeness; state of being fully settled;

2 decisive or conclusive action, utterance, or state

fi·nal·ize /fī′-/ vt to complete; put in final form

fi·nal·ly /fī′-/ adv **1** lastly; ultimately; **2** completely; unalterably; **3** at last

fi·nance /finans′, fī′-/ [MF *finer* to settle a debt] n **1** science of money, credit, and banking; **2** science of government budgets, revenues, and expenditures; **3** finances pl income, revenue, or money of a government, state, society, or individual || vt **4** to provide the capital or funds for || **fi·nan′cial** /-shəl/ adj || **fi·nan′cial·ly** adv

fin·an·cier /fin′ənsir′/ n **1** one trained in banking or money matters; **2** one who conducts private or public money affairs

fi·nanc′ing n **1** raising of funds; **2** funds thus raised

fin′back′ n whalebone whale (genus *Balaenoptera*), esp. a large species (*B. physalus*) common on the north Atlantic coast of the U.S.

finch /finch/ [OE *finc*] n any of many small songbirds (family Fringillidae) closely related to the sparrows, as the goldfinch, bullfinch, and canary

find /fīnd/ [OE *findan*] vt (found) vt **1** to discover by chance; **2** to obtain by searching; **3** to learn by experiment; **4** to regain, as something lost; **5** to arrive at, or reach, as a result; **6** *law* to decide upon, reach (a verdict); **7** find out, a to discover; learn; b to expose (a person) || vi **8** to reach a verdict || n **9** finding; discovery of something valuable

find′er n **1** one who or that which finds; **2** *photog* viewfinder

fin de siè·cle /faN′dəsyek′əl/ [F = end of the century] adj pert. to, or characteristic of, the end of the 19th century, esp. its artistic and literary sophistication and attitude of world-weariness

find′ing n **1** discovery; **2** decision of a judge, jury, or investigating body; **3** findings pl tools·and accessory materials used by certain artisans, as shoemakers and·dressmakers

fine¹ /fīn/ [OF *fin* settlement of dispute < L *finis* end] n **1** money paid as a penalty; **2** in fine, in conclusion; summing up || vt **3** to impose a fine on

fine² [OF *fin* exact < LL *finus* pure, refined < *finis* end] adj **1** pure; refined; **2** slender, thin; **3** keen, sharp; **4** light and delicate in fabric or material; **5** superior in character, excellent; **6** trained for maximum efficiency in an athletic contest; **7** handsome, beautiful; **8** pleasant, bright, **9** subtle, as *a fine distinction* || adv **10** very well; **11** finely || vt **12** to make finer || vi **13** to become finer || **fine′ly** adv || SYN adj sensitive,

smooth, thin, delicate, polished (see *exquisite*) || ANT adj coarse, unrefined, ugly

fi·ne³ /fē′nä/ [It] n *mus* the end of a repeated section

fine′ arts′ npl arts serving to please the aesthetic sense rather than for practical purposes, as painting, sculpture, and music

fine′ness n **1** condition or quality of being fine; **2** proportion of pure precious metal contained in an alloy, often expressed in parts per thousand

fin·er·y /fīn′ərē/ n (-ies) personal adornment, as elaborate or showy jewelry or clothing; display

fine′spun′ adj **1** drawn out or spun to extreme fineness; **2** impractical, too subtle, as *finespun theories*

fi·nesse /fines′/ [MF = fineness] n **1** artifice; strategy; **2** dexterity, artfulness; **3** *cards* the playing by a second or third player of the lower of two cards not in sequence, in the hope that the opponent on his right holds the card in between, so that the card played takes the trick or forces out an opposing card above his higher card || vt **4** to play (a card) in a finesse || vi **5** to make a finesse || SYN n ruse, trick, artifice, deceit (see *subterfuge*)

fin·ger /fiŋ′gər/ [OE] n **1** any one of the five terminal members of the hand, particularly one other than the thumb; **2** finger's breadth; **3** any mechanical device resembling a finger; **4** the part of a glove that accommodates one of the fingers || vt **5** to handle; **6** *slang* to inform on, identify || vi **7** to use the fingers in performing upon an instrument

fin′ger board′ n **1** strip of wood on which the strings are pressed in playing some stringed instruments; **2** keyboard

fin′ger bowl′ n small bowl for water in which to rinse the fingers after eating

fin′gered adj **1** having fingers; **2** *mus* so marked as to guide the fingers in playing

fin′ger·ing n **1** act of touching with the fingers; **2** manner of using the fingers on a musical instrument; **3** notation of the method of using the fingers in playing a musical composition

Fin′ger Lakes′ npl group of finger-shaped lakes in W New York

fin′ger·ling n young fish no longer than a man's finger

fin′ger man′ n *slang* person who designates someone to be the victim of a murder, robbery, or other act of violence

fin′ger post′ n post with directional signs usu. terminating in a pointed finger

fin′ger·print′ n **1** impression of the lines on the fingertips, used as a means of identification ‖ *vt* **2** to make a fingerprint of ‖ **fin′ger·print′ing** *n*

fin′ger·stall′ *n* cover to protect an injured finger

fin′ger·tip′ *n* **1** tip of a finger; **2** shield to protect end of a finger; **3 at one's fingertips, a** readily available; **b** immediately recallable; **4 to one's fingertips** through and through, altogether

fin′ger wave′ *n* wave in the hair formed with the fingers

fin·i·al /fin′ē·əl/ [< L *finis* end] *n* ornamental termination at the apex of a spire, pinnacle, or the like or at the top of a piece of furniture

fin·i·cal /fin′ikəl/ or **fin′ick·y** [< *fine²*] *adj* fastidious; too particular ‖ **fin′i·cal·ly** *adv* ‖ **fin′i·cal·ness** *n* ‖ SYN effeminate, foppish, fastidious

fi·nis /fin′is, fin′-/ [L = end] *n* end, conclusion

fin·ish /fin′ish/ [MF *finir* (-*niss*-) < L *finire*] *vt* **1** to complete; bring to an end; **2** to make perfect; **3** to put a finish on; **4** *colloq* to kill or render powerless; **5 finish off, a** to consume completely; **b** to kill; **6 finish up, a** to consume; **b** to end ‖ *vi* **7** to come to the end; stop ‖ *n* **8** last effort; **9** state of perfection or completion; **10** a surface coating, as on walls or furniture; **b** material used in such coating. ‖ **fin′ish·er** *n* ‖ **fin′ished** *adj* ‖ SYN *v* perfect, terminate, end, accomplish (see *close*)

fin′ish·ing school′ *n* school for teaching young ladies the social graces

fi·nite /fī′nīt/ *adj* **1** having a limit or limits, as opposed to *infinite*; restricted; **2** *gram* (verb form) showing changes for tense, number, and person ‖ *n* **3** that which is measurably limited

fink /fiŋk/ [?] *n slang* **1** informer; **2** contemptible person

Fin·land /fin′lənd/ *n* republic in N Europe (4,664,000; 130,119 sq.m.; cap. Helsinki) ‖ **Fin′land·er** *n*

Finn /fin/ [OE *Finnas* Finns] *n* **1** native or inhabitant of Finland; **2** member of a Finnish-speaking group of people

fin·nan had·die /fin′ən had′ē/ or **fin′nan had′dock** [Sc < town *Findon* + *haddock*] *n* smoke-cured haddock

Finn·ic /fin′ik/ *adj* of or pert. to the branch of the Uralic group of languages which includes Finnish, Estonian, and Lapp

Finn′ish *adj* **1** pert. to Finland, its inhabitants, or its language ‖ *n* **2** language of Finland

Fin·no-U·gric /fin′ō(y) oōg′rik/ *n* subfamily of the Uralic languages, including Finnish and Hungarian ‖ also *adj*

fiord /fyôrd′/ *n* var of **fjord**

fir /fur′/ [OE *fyrh*] *n* **1** any of various cone-bearing evergreen trees (genus *Abies*); **2** the timber of such a tree ‖ **fir′ry** *adj*

fire /fī′ər/ [OE *fyr*] *n* **1** visible heat or light developed by burning; flame; **2** wood, coal, etc. burning, as *a hot fire in the stove;* **3** destructive burning; conflagration; **4** quality of refracting light, as *the fire of a diamond;* **5** discharge, as of firearms or rockets; **6** spirit of enthusiasm; **7** fever; **8** trial by burning; **9** trial and affliction; **10 catch fire** to become ignited; **11 hang fire** to be delayed; **12 on fire,** a burning; **b** ardent; **13 under fire** under attack ‖ *vt* **14** to ignite; inflame; kindle; **15** to bake, as porcelain; **16** to discharge (a gun, a rocket); **17** to illuminate; **18** to animate; excite, as *to fire troops with enthusiasm;* **19** to stoke, as a locomotive; **20** *colloq* to throw; **21** *slang* to discharge from employment ‖ *vi* **22** to become ignited; **23** to start a fire, as in a boiler; **24** to be inflamed; **25** to discharge a firearm ‖ SYN *n* glow, warmth, brilliancy, ardor, blaze

fire′arm′ *n* hand weapon, as a revolver or rifle, which is discharged by an explosive

fire′ball′ *n* **1** large glowing meteor; **2** lightning that appears like a luminous ball; **3** central portion of a nuclear explosion

fire′ base′ *n* strongly armed position close to the enemy, seized in order to subject him to intense fire

fire′boat′ *n* boat equipped with apparatus for fighting fires along water fronts

fire′ bomb′ *n* bomb which sets fire to its target

fire′box′ *n* **1** in a stove, furnace, or boiler, the box holding the burning fuel; **2** box containing a device for transmitting fire alarms

fire′brand′ *n* **1** piece of burning wood; **2** agitator

fire′brick′ *n* brick made of material that withstands great heat, used to line furnaces

fire′ bug′ *n* person who intentionally sets fire to buildings or other property

fire′ clay′ *n* clay which resists intense heat, used for making crucibles, furnace linings, etc.

fire′ com′pa·ny *n* **1** group of men organized to extinguish fires; **2** organization issuing insurance against loss by fire

fire′crack′er *n* small paper cylinder filled with an explosive and having a fuse, used to make noise at celebrations

fire′damp′ *n* gas, principally methane, which forms in coal mines and which, mixed with air, explodes when ignited

fire′dog′ *n* andiron

fire′ drill′ *n* practice drill of the procedures to be followed in case of fire

fire′-eat′er *n* 1 performer who pretends to eat fire; 2 defiant, pugnacious person

fire′ en′gine *n* motor truck equipped to put out fires

fire′ es·cape′ *n* structure or stairway providing escape from a burning building

fire′ ex·tin′guish·er *n* portable extinguisher for small fires

fire′ fight′ *n mil* preliminary skirmish

fire′ fight′er *n* 1 fireman, member of a fire company; 2 one who fights forest fires ‖ **fire′ fight′ing** *n*

fire′fly′ *n* (**-flies**) any of the various small beetles (family Lampyridae) which emit phosphorescent light while flying at night

fire′ i′rons *npl* implements for tending a fire in a fireplace

fire′less cook′er *n* insulated container which cooks foods rapidly by sealing in heat

fire′lock′ *n* gunlock employing flame or sparks to ignite the charge, as a matchlock or flintlock

fire′man /-mən/ *n* (**-men** /-mən/) 1 stoker; 2 man whose work is fighting fires; 3 enlisted man who works with naval machinery

fire′ mark′ *n* metal plate, attached to a building, to indicate that the building is covered by fire insurance (used in London and E U.S. in the 18th century)

fire′place′ *n* open recess in a chimney in which a fire may be built; hearth

fire′plug′ *n* street hydrant from which water may be drawn for extinguishing fires

fire′ pow′er *n* capacity for delivering fire on a given target

fire′proof′ *adj* 1 unburnable ‖ *vt* 2 to make fireproof

fire′ sale′ *n* sale of goods damaged by fire

fire′ screen′ *n* wire screen placed in front of a fireplace for protection

fire′side′ *n* 1 space around a fireplace; 2 home

fire′ sta′tion *n* building housing fire engines and often firemen

fire′ tow′er *n* tower, usu. in forest areas, for watching for fires

fire′trap′ *n* highly combustible building, or one with inadequate fire escapes

fire′ wall′ *n* fireproof wall to prevent the spread of fire

fire′wa′ter *n colloq* liquor

fire′wood′ *n* wood for fuel

fire′works′ *npl* 1 combustible or explosive devices which produce brilliantly colored displays or loud noises; 2 violent outburst of temper

fir′ing line′ *n* 1 place where troops are stationed to fire on the enemy; 2

troops stationed at this place; 3 vanguard in any activity

fir′ing or′der *n* order in which ignition takes place in the cylinders of an internal-combustion engine

fir′ing pin′ *n* pin that strikes the cartridge primer in the chamber of a firearm when it is fired

fir′ing squad′ *n mil* detachment assigned to fire a volley, either as a salute or to carry out the death sentence

firm¹ /furm′/ [L *firmus*] *adj* 1 hard; solid; 2 rigid; immovable; 3 steady and vigorous, as a *firm step*; 4 enduring; steadfast; 5 resolute; positive ‖ *vt* 6 to compact; fix firmly ‖ **firm′ly** *adj* ‖ **firm′ness** *n* ‖ SYN *adj* solid, fixed, stable, steady, secure; resolute, rigid, determined, constant ‖ DISCR As here compared, that is *firm* which is settled, moved with difficulty, or not shaken easily from place, as a *firm* foundation; *firm* ground. That is *solid* which is hard and compact, substantial and unyielding, as a *solid* foundation is not only *firm* but strong; a *solid* wall. That which is *fixed* is *firm* because it is attached or fastened securely. That is *stable* which stands firmly in place. Figuratively, we speak of *firm* convictions, *solid* comfort, *fixed* habits, *stable* government

firm² [It *firma* signature < L *firmare* to confirm] *n* partnership or association of two or more persons, not a corporation, for doing business, each member being liable for all its debts

fir·ma·ment /furm′əmənt/ [see **firm**¹] *n* arch of the heavens

first /furst′/ [OE *fyrst*] *adj* 1 before all others in time, order, rank, or importance; 2 *auto* lowest (gear); 3 *mus* highest or chief (instrument or voice) ‖ *adv* 4 in advance of all others in order, place, rank, time, etc.; 5 sooner; rather; 6 for the first time ‖ *n* 7 beginning; 8 that placed before all others; 9 highest grade of an article of commerce; 10 winning place in a contest; 11 *auto* first gear ‖ SYN *adj* leading, foremost, chief, principal, primary

first′ aid′ *n* emergency treatment given to a suddenly ill or injured person before regular medical aid is available

first′-born′ *adj* 1 born first; eldest ‖ *n* 2 first-born child

first′ class′ *n* 1 first or highest class, grade, rank, or type of service or accommodations; 2 highest class of mail, including matter sealed against postal inspection and taking precedence in delivery ‖ **first′-class′** *adj* & *adv*

First′ day′ *n* among the Quakers, Sunday

first′ fruits′ *npl* 1 earliest gatherings

of the produce of the season; 2 earliest results or profits of any undertaking

first'hand' *adj & adv* obtained directly from the source

first' lieu·ten'ant *n* army or marine officer ranking between a captain and a second lieutenant

first'ly *adv* in the first place; first

first' mate' or **first' of'fi·cer** *n* officer in the merchant marine next in rank below the captain

first' name' *n* given name

first'-night'er *n* person who regularly attends the theater on opening nights

first' pa'pers *npl* papers filed by a resident alien as the first step to becoming naturalized

first' per'son *n gram* 1 person speaking; 2 form indicating such a person

first' quar'ter *n* time when, after new moon, half the moon's disk is lighted by the sun

first'-rate' *adj* of the highest excellence; preeminent

first'-run' *adj* of or pert. to the first showing of a motion picture in a particular area

first' ser'geant *n* a senior noncommissioned officer acting chiefly as administrative aid to the company commander

first'-string' *adj* being a regular (member or participant) and not a substitute

first' wa'ter *n* finest quality, esp. of precious stones

firth /furth/ /ON *fjörthr*/ *n* inlet of the sea at the mouth of a river

fis·cal /fis'kəl/ /< L *fiscus* treasury] *adj* 1 of or pert. to a the revenue, expenditures, and financial affairs of a government, or b financial affairs in general || *n* 2 revenue stamp || SYN *adj* financial (see *pecuniary*)

fish /fish/ /OE *fisc*/ *n* (**fish** or **fishes**) 1 vertebrate animal, usu. covered with scales and having gills for breathing the oxygen in water, reproducing by means of eggs usu. discharged into the water; 2 in general, any animal that lives wholly in water; 3 flesh of fish used as food; 4 *colloq* person; 5 **Fishes** sign (Pisces) of the zodiac || *vt* 6 to catch from in or under water; secure by angling; 7 to attempt to catch fish in, as *to fish the stream;* 8 to catch or get hold of, as if by fishing; 9 to seek for and bring to light; draw up || *vi* 10 a to catch fish; b to attempt or be able to catch fish; c to be employed in any way by which fish are taken; 11 to try to obtain through indirect methods

fish' and chips' *npl Brit* fried fish and French fried potatoes

fish'er *n* 1 one that fishes; 2 kind of weasel (*Martes pennanti*) found in North America

fish'er·man /-mən/ *n* (-men /-mən/) 1

one who catches fish as a sport or business; 2 vessel used in fishing

fish'er·y *n* (-ies) 1 business or act of catching fish; 2 place where, or season when, fish are taken regularly; 3 right to fish at a particular place or time

fish' hawk' *n* osprey

fish'hook' *n* barbed hook for catching fish

fish'ing ex·pe·di'tion *n* legal inquiry instituted in the hope of turning something up that may be used to partisan advantage

fish'joint' *n* joint of two railroad rails, held together end to end by a pair of iron plates

fish' meal' *n* dried ground fish, used as animal food or as fertilizer

fish'mon'ger /-muŋ'gər/ *n* one who deals in fish

fish'plate' *n* one of a pair of iron plates fitted at a joint to hold the rails in line

fish'pond' *n* small body of water stocked with edible fish

fish' sto'ry *n colloq* exaggerated lie; unbelievable story

fish'tail' *adj* 1 shaped like a fish's tail || *vi* 2 to swing an airplane or its tail from side to side for the retarding effect

fish'wife' *n* (-wives /-vz/) coarse, abusive woman

fish'y *adj* (-i·er; -i·est) 1 pert. to or like a fish; 2 *colloq* doubtful, questionable; 3 *colloq* vacant, expressionless

fis·sion /fish'ən/ /L *fissio* (-*onis*) a cleaving < *findere* (*fissus*) to cleave] *n* 1 act of splitting into parts; 2 *biol* cell division as a form of reproduction; 3 *phys* splitting of unstable radioactive atoms by bombarding them with neutrons with resultant release of great energy || **fis'sion·a·ble** *adj*

fis'sure /fish'ər/ /< L *findere* (*fissus*) to cleave] *n* narrow opening; crack

fist /fist/ /OE *fyst*/ *n* 1 hand closed or clenched; 2 *colloq* hand; 3 handwriting; 4 *typ* sign ☞ used for drawing attention

fist'ic *adj* pert. to boxing

fist'i-cuffs' *npl* encounter with the fists; boxing match

fis·tu·la /fis'chələ/ /L = pipe] *n* (-**las** or -**lae** /-lē'/) abnormal, ulcerous opening or passage, often leading into some internal organ

fit¹ /fit/ /OE *fitt* struggle] *n* 1 convulsion; 2 uncontrollable attack; 3 sudden impulse or manifestation of emotion; 4 **by fits and starts** in an irregular manner; 5 **throw a fit** *colloq* a to have a convulsion; b to become violently angry

fit² [ME] *adj* (**fit·ter;** **fit·test**) 1 adapted or qualified; 2 convenient; proper; 3 prepared; trained; 4 in good physical condition || *v* (**fit·ted;** **fit·ting**) *vt*

5 to make suitable; adapt; **6** to equip or supply, as with something of the right size; **7** to qualify; equip; prepare; **8** to be properly suited or adjusted to || *vi* **9** to be adapted to one, as *the suit fits;* **10** to be proper or suitable, be properly adjusted || *n* **11** adaptation of one thing to another; suitability || **fit′ly** *adv* || **fit′ness** *n* || SYN *adj* seemly, becoming, appropriate, adapted, pertinent; *v* suit, adapt, accommodate, adjust || DISCR To *fit* is to make or be of similar dimensions, so that one thing will combine or connect with another as it is supposed to do; we *fit* a garment to a person, a shelf to a particular space, a shade to a window. Figuratively, education *fits* us for life; their temperaments *fit* actors for certain parts. To *adapt* is a kind of fitting, requiring judgment, and a perception of the exact needs of the case. To *suit* is to make agreeable or conformable, as "*Suit* the action to the word." *Accommodate* involves conceding something voluntarily, often in an obliging spirit, as for the convenience or favor of another; we *accommodate* ourselves to the desires of our friends, or *accommodate* one another by lending money, extending credit, or the like. To *adjust* is to make fit or harmonious, usually by bringing a spirit of accommodation into the matter, as to *adjust* differences between friends. Mechanically, *adjust* means to secure such relative position of parts as to produce smooth motion or functioning, accuracy, or the like, as to *adjust* a carburetor || ANT *adj* unsuitable, improper, inappropriate

fit′ful *adj* **1** spasmodic; recurring irregularly; **2** restless || **fit′ful·ly** *adv* || **fit′ful·ness** *n* || SYN spasmodic, jerky, irregular, capricious, impulsive

fit′ter *n* **1** one who adapts, shapes, or adjusts; **2** one who tries on clothes; **3** one who adjusts or puts together pipes or machinery parts

fit′ting *adj* **1** suitable, appropriate || *n* **2** trying on of clothes for suitable fit; **3** anything used in adjusting or connecting, as part of a machine; **4** fittings *pl* equipment or necessary fixtures, as of a house or car || **fit′-ting·ly** *adv*

five /fiv′/ [OE fif] *n* **1** sum of four and one (5; V); **2** playing card or domino with five spots; **3** group of five units || *also adj & pron*

five′-and-ten′ *n* store selling a wide variety of inexpensive items, formerly costing five or ten cents

five′fold *adj* **1** having five times as much or as many || *adv* **2** five times as much or as many

Five′ Na′tions *spl* confederation of five Iroquoian tribes of NE United States

five′-spot′ *n* **1** playing card or die with five pips; **2** *slang* five-dollar bill

fix /fiks′/ [< L *figere* (*fixus*) to fasten] *vt* **1** to make fast or secure; fasten or attach; set or place permanently; **2** to settle definitely; **3** *colloq* to bribe or influence; **4** to direct or hold steadily, as *to fix one's attention;* **5** to prepare (a meal); **6** to assign (blame); **7** to convert (nitrogen) into stable compounds; **8** to adjust; repair; **9** *photog* to treat (a film or print) in a chemical bath in order to stabilize the image and prevent further development; **10** *colloq* to get even with; punish || *vi* **11** to become solid; **12** to settle down in a place; become stable || *n* **13** position, as of a ship or plane, obtained from bearings of two or more known points; **14** *colloq* awkward situation; dilemma; **15** *slang* injection of a narcotic || **fix′a·ble** *adj* || SYN *v* settle, decide, determine, establish, station, confirm, ratify, bind, fasten, attach, substantiate

fix·a′tion *n* **1** act of fixing; **2** state of being fixed; **3** *chem* process by which an element is combined in a stable compound so as to become available for commercial use; **4** *psychoanal* obsessive preoccupation with some idea or complex

fix′a·tive /-tiv/ *n* anything that serves to fix or make permanent, or prevents or retards fading or evaporation || *also adj*

fixed′ *adj* **1** firm; stable; permanent; **2** resolute; **3** unchanging; **4** *colloq* supplied, as with money || **fix′ed·ly** /-idlē/ *adv* SYN stable, rigid, permanent, unalterable (see *firm*[1])

fix′er *n* **1** one who or that which fixes; **2** one who induces officials to wink at illegal acts

fix′ings *npl colloq* things needed in any preparation; furnishings; trimmings

fix′ture /-chər/ *n* **1** that which is firmly fastened; **2** article of furniture attached to a house and considered as a part of it, as *a light fixture;* **3** one who seems permanent in his position

fizz /fiz′/ [imit] *n* **1** hissing noise; **2** effervescent or bubbling liquid, as soda water || *vi* **3** to make a hissing noise as if effervescing

fiz·zle /fiz′əl/ [imit] *vi* **1** to make a hissing noise; **2** *colloq* to fail miserably || *n* **3** sputtering; **4** state of restlessness; worry; **5** *colloq* complete and humiliating failure

fjord /fyôrd′/ [Norw] *n* narrow arm of the sea between high banks

Fla. Florida

flab·ber·gast /flab′ərgast′/ [?] *vt colloq* to confuse; bewilder; astonish

flab·by /flab′ē/ [obs *flappy* < *flap*] *adj* (**-bi·er**; **-bi·est**) 1 lacking firmness; flaccid; 2 feeble; lax; lacking force ‖ **flab′bi·ly** *adv* ‖ **flab′bi·ness** *n* ‖ SYN flaccid, limp, soft ‖ ANT strong, elastic, stiff

flac·cid /flak′sid/ [L *flaccidus*] *adj* lacking firmness; weak; flabby ‖ **flac·cid′i·ty** *n*

flac·on /flak′ən [F] *n* small stoppered bottle, as for perfume

flag¹ /flag′/ [15th-cent. Eng perh imit of flapping sound] *n* 1 piece of light cloth, bearing a design and chiefly used as a symbol or for signaling; 2 tail of a deer ‖ *v* (**flagged**; **flag·ging**) *vt* 3 to signal to, with a flag or light; 4 flag down to signal to stop

flag² [prob < OF *flac* < L *flaccus* flabby] *v* (**flagged**; **flag·ging**) *vi* 1 to hang loose; 2 to become languid; move or act slowly ‖ SYN droop, pine, languish, decline, fall, drag

flag³ [ME *flagge*] *n* any of various plants having long narrow leaves, esp. the iris and sweet flag

flag⁴ [ON *flaga*] *n* flagstone

Flag′ Day′ *n* June 14, the anniversary of the adoption in 1777 of the U.S. flag

flag·el·late /flaj′əlāt′/ [L *flagellare* (*-atus*)] *vt* to whip or scourge

flag·eo·let /flaj′əlet′, -lā/ [< OF *flajol* flute] *n* small flute resembling a recorder

flag′ging¹ [*flag⁴*] *n* pavement of flagstones

flag′ging² [< *flag²*] *adj* weary; losing force; failing ‖ SYN languid, drooping, languishing, pining, exhausted

flag′man /-mən/ *n* (**-men** /-mən/) one who uses flags or lights for signaling, as on a railroad

flag′ of con·ven′ience *n* flag of a nation under which foreign ship owners register to take advantage of lax regulations and operate at lower cost

flag′ of′fi·cer *n* naval officer above the rank of captain

flag′ of truce′ *n* white flag displayed to an enemy as an invitation to confer or a signal of surrender

flag·on /flag′ən/ [MF *flacon* bottle] *n* large vessel with a spout, handle, and sometimes a cover, used for liquors

flag′pole′ *n* pole on which a flag may be hoisted

fla·grant /flāg′rənt/ [L *flagrans* (*-antis*) blazing] *adj* openly wicked; outrageous; scandalous ‖ **fla′grant·ly** *adv* ‖ **fla′gran·cy** *n* ‖ SYN atrocious, monstrous, notorious (see *heinous*)

flag′ship′ *n* ship that leads a fleet and displays the flag of the commanding office

flag′staff′ *n* flagpole

flag′stone′ *n* large flat stone used for paving walks

flag′ stop′ *n* place where a public transport vehicle stops only on signal

flag′-wav′ing *n* ostentatious appeal to patriotism

flail /flāl′/ [OE *flegel*. < L *flagellum* whip] *n* 1 instrument consisting of a short wooden staff, from the end of which another piece hangs free, used for threshing grain by hand ‖ *vt* 2 to thresh with a flail; 3 to flog

flair /fler′/ [F = scent] *n* 1 fine critical sense; discernment; 2 aptitude

flak /flak′/ [G *Flugabwehrkanone* antiaircraft gun] *n* antiaircraft fire

flake /flāk′/ [ME] *n* 1 small thin flat fragment; chip ‖ *vi* 2 to break or separate into flakes; scale or peel off ‖ **flak′y** *adj* ‖ **flak′i·ness** *n*

flam·beau /flam′bō/ [F, *dim.* of *flambe* flame] *n* (**-beaus**, **-beaux** /-bōz/) 1 flaming torch used at night in processions; 2 large, often elaborate candlestick used in decorations

flam·boy·ant /flamboi′ənt/ [F = flaming] *adj* 1 having a wavy outline; 2 conspicuous, showy; 3 flowery (speech); 4 *arch.* having flamelike decorations, as French Gothic window design ‖ **flam·boy′ance** *n*

flame /flām′/ [OF *flambe* < L *flamma*] *n* 1 burning gas or vapor; blaze; state of visible combustion; 2 ardor of temper or passion; 3 *colloq* sweetheart ‖ *vi* 4 to burst into a blaze, rage, etc.; 5 to shine brightly ‖ *vt* 6 to burn; singe ‖ **flam′ing** *adj* ‖ SYN *n* glare, glow; zeal, fervor (see *light¹*)

fla·men·co /fləmeŋ′kō/ [Sp = Flemish] *n* 1 Andalusian gypsy dance style; 2 style of music accompanying it ‖ also *adj*

flame′-out′ *n* failure of an airplane jet engine

flame′throw′er *n* weapon that shoots forth a burning stream of incendiary fuel

fla·min·go /fləmiŋ′gō/ [Port] *n* (**-gos**, **-goes**) any of a family (Phoenicopteridae) of long-legged, long-necked, brightly colored tropical wading birds

flam·ma·ble /flam′əbəl/ [< *flame*] *adj* inflammable, easily set on fire

Flan·ders /flan′dərz/ *n* medieval country in W Europe along the North Sea, now divided between Belgium and France

flange /flanj/ [perh OF *flanche* flank] *n* 1 projecting rim on a wheel to keep it in place; 2 strengthening rib, as on a steel beam; 3 projecting collar to give a place for attachment, as on a pipe

flank /flaŋk/ [OF *flanc*] *n* 1 fleshy part of an animal's side between the ribs and the hip; 2 side of anything, esp. of an organized body of soldiers; 3 part of a fortification intended to defend another part ‖ *vt* 4 to border; 5 *mil* to pass around and threaten the side of

flan·nel /flan′əl/ [perh < Welsh *gwlan* wool] *n* 1 soft loosely woven cloth, usu. made of wool; **2 flannels** *pl* garment or garments made of this material

flan'nel·ette' [*dim.* of *flannel*] *n* soft cotton material resembling flannel

flap /flap'/ [ME *flappe*] *n* **1** anything broad and flat hanging loose, as the tail of a coat; **2** motion of anything hanging loose; **3** noise made by the motion of anything flapping; **4** slap || *v* (**flapped; flap·ping**) *vt* **5** to strike with or as with a flap; **6** to move (something) to and fro || *vi* **7** to move flatwise with a noisy beating motion; **8** to proceed by flapping

flap'jack' *n* pancake

flap'per [< *flap*] *n* **1** one who or that which flaps; **2** young woman of the 1920's who behaved with freedom from convention and moral restraints

flare /fler'/ [?] *n* **1** large, unsteady, dazzling light; **2** gaudiness, showiness; **3** a spreading outward or upward, as of the sides of a bell; **4** bright or blazing signal; **5** *photog* fogging of the image resulting from extraneous light reflected by the lens surfaces || *vi* **6** to burn with a broad unsteady light; **7** to become conspicuous; **8** to wave or flutter, as a flame in the wind; **9** to spread outward and upward; **10 flare up, a** to burst into flame; **b** to become violently angry || SYN blaze, glare, flame (see *light¹*)

flare' star' *n* star which suddenly and without apparent cause increases in brilliancy and after a few minutes returns to its normal state

flare'-up' *n* **1** sudden bursting into flame; **2** sudden outburst of anger or the like; **3** sudden intensification of something thought to be quiescent

flash /flash'/ [prob imit] *n* **1** sudden fleeting light; **2** sudden outburst, as of wit, merriment, or passion; **3** very short period; **4** gaudy display; **5** preliminary news report; **6** sudden flame and heat of an explosion; **7** brief intense artificial light by which photographs may be taken; **8 flash in the pan, a** intense effort that comes to naught; **b** person making such effort || *vt* **9** to cause to appear, gleam or act suddenly; **10** to send forth like a burst of light; communicate suddenly; **11** *colloq* to show, display || *vi* **12** to give forth a bright flame or light for an instant; **13** to burst into sudden but transient brilliancy; **14** to appear suddenly, or to pass at great speed || SYN *n* flame, spark, gleam, blaze (see *light¹*)

flash'back' *n* interruption of a narrative by the interjection of earlier events

flash' bulb' or **lamp'** *n* *photog* glass bulb containing wire which, when ignited, emits a brilliant light

flash' card' *n* card containing words, pictures, or numbers, held up by the teacher to elicit responses

flash'cube' *n* cube, attached to a camera, containing a flash bulb in each of its four vertical sides for taking flashes as it rotates

flash' flood' *n* sudden flood caused usu. by heavy rains or melting snow

flash' gun' *n* *photog* device that synchronizes the flash of a bulb with the opening of the shutter

flash'ing *n* sheets of metal or roofing paper used to make weatherproof joints, esp. where two surfaces meet at an angle

flash'light' *n* **1** flash **7**; **2** light that flashes; **3** small portable electric light operated by batteries

flash' point' *n* temperature at which the vapor given off by a volatile liquid ignites upon the application of a flame

flash'y *adj* (**-i·er; -i·est**) brilliant but empty; gaudy, showy || **flash'i·ly** *adv* || **flash'i·ness** *n*

flask /flask', fläsk'/ [LL *flasco* bottle] *n* **1** narrow-necked bottle used to hold liquids, powder, etc.; **2** metallic bottle with flat sides, shaped to fit in a pocket

flat¹ /flat'/ [ON *flatr*] *adj* (**flat·ter; flat·test**) **1** level, even, smooth; having a plane horizontal surface; **2** prostrate, laid low; **3** having breadth and smoothness but little thickness; **4** positive; unvarying; without discount, as a *flat rate*; **5** dull, monotonous; tasteless, insipid; **6** wanting in brilliancy or in the prominence of important features; **7** deflated (tire); **8** *mus* a lowered half a step in pitch; **b** below true pitch; **9** *colloq* broke || *adv* **10** in a level or prostrate position; **11** exactly, as *he did it in ten seconds flat*; **12** *mus* below true pitch || *n* **13** flat surface; **14** level plain; **15** shallow or shoal; **16** smooth wide part of a thing, as *the flat of a sword*; **17** *mus* **a** tone lowered half a step in pitch; **b** the symbol ♭ for this; **18** *theat* flat piece of scenery; **19** *colloq* flat tire || *v* (**flat·ted; flat·ting**) *vt* **20** to make flat; **21** *mus* to make lower in pitch by half a step || *vi* **22** to become flat; **23** to sing or play below the correct pitch || **flat'ly** *adv* || **flat'ness** *n* || SYN *adj* level; monotonous, characterless, dull; absolute || DISCR *Flat* country has no elevations, prominences, or curves; a *flat* roof has little inclination. *Level* country may be perfectly *flat;* on the contrary, it may be rugged or hilly, for *level* is a relative term, and may describe land that is *level* in contrast to that which is mountainous. *Flat,* applied to country, is often derogatory; *level* is neutral. Because flatness is akin to monotony, *flat* has acquired the meaning of colorless, unappealing, insipid, *dull*, as a *flat* lecture. *Flat*, meaning downright, or *absolute*, occurs in the expression a *flat* denial

flat² [OE *flet* floor] *n* apartment on one floor

flat'boat' *n* large boat with a flat bottom, used for freighting

flat'car' *n* railroad freight car having a flat bottom but no sides

flat'fish' *n* fish having a broad flat thin body, with both eyes on one side, as the flounder

flat'foot' *n* 1 (-feet) foot in which the arch of the instep is flattened so that the entire sole rests on the ground || *n* 2 (-foots) *slang* policeman

flat'foot'ed *adj* 1 having flat feet; 2 determined, unyielding; 3 off guard

flat'i'ron *n* iron for pressing, spec. the old-fashioned kind that had to be heated on a stove

flat-ten /flat'ən/ *vt* 1 to make flat; 2 to knock down || *vi* 3 to become flat; 4 **flatten out** to become straight or smooth; 5 to fly back into a horizontal position

flat-ter /flat'ər/ [perh OF *flater* to smooth] *vt* 1 to seek to please by insincere praise or attention; 2 to praise too highly; 3 to persuade with praise; encourage with false hopes; 4 to make more attractive than is so || *vi* 5 to use insincere praise || **flat'ter-er** *n* || **flat'ter-ing** *adj*

flat'ter-y *n* (-ies) 1 complimentary but insincere speech; false praise; blandishment; 2 act of one who flatters || SYN adulation, cajolery (see *compliment*)

flat'top' *n colloq* aircraft carrier

flat-u-lent /flach'ələnt/ [< L *flare* (*flatus*) to blow] *adj* 1 affected with or tending to produce gas in the stomach or intestines; 2 conceited || **flat'u-lence** *n*

fla-tus /flāt'əs/ [L = a blowing] *n* gas formed in the stomach or intestines

flat'ware' *n* plates, knives, or other more or less flat articles of china or metal

flat'wise' or **flat'ways'** *adv* with the flat side up or foremost

flat'work' *n* articles that in laundering can be ironed mechanically instead of by hand

flat'worm' *n* any of a phylum (Platyhelminthes) of unsegmented worms having a flattened body, many of which are parasitic, as liver flukes and tapeworms

flaunt /flônt'/ [prob ON] *vi* 1 to make a gaudy display, as in dress; be gaudy or ostentatious; 2 to behave in a forward manner || *vt* 3 to display with unnecessary show || **flaunt'-ing** *adj* || **flaunt'ing-ly** *adv* || SYN wave, brandish, display, parade, show off

flau-tist /flôt'ist, flout'-/ [< It *flauto* flute] *n* one who plays the flute

fla-vor /flāv'ər/ [MF *flaor*] *n* 1 that quality of a substance which affects the sense of taste; 2 *archaic* that quality which affects the sense of smell; 3 flavoring composition or substance; 4 pervasive characteristic || *vt* 5 to give a flavor or some distinguishing characteristic to || SYN *n* relish, savor, taste || DISCR *Taste*, the general term, denotes that quality of a substance which is perceived by the tongue, as a sweet *taste*; an acid *taste*. *Flavor* names a predominating quality of *taste*, often a delicate and pleasing quality; all cantaloupes *taste*, to a certain extent, alike; but certain varieties have a delicious *flavor* in addition to the ordinary cantaloupe *taste*. *Relish* is also a particular *taste*; plain food eaten by a hungry man has a wonderful *relish*; artificial aids to such enjoyment—condiments, spices, and odd, piquant, or distinctive *flavors*— are also *relishes*. *Relish* is added; *flavor* may be the property of the food itself. *Savor* appeals to both *taste* and *smell*, as the *savor* of a stew. Either a *flavor* or a *savor* may be disagreeable

fla'vor-ing *n* essence or extract for giving flavor

fla'vor-some *adj* full of flavor

flaw /flô'/ [ME < ON] *n* 1 blemish; defect; weak spot; 2 crack || *vt* 3 to make a defect in || *vi* 4 to develop a defect || **flaw'less** *adj* || SYN *n* crack, breach, imperfection (see *blemish*)

flax /flaks/ [OE *fleax*] *n* 1 slender blue-flowered plant (genus *Linum*) whose stem yields the fibers from which linen is made; 2 the fiber ready to be spun

flax'en *adj* 1 made of or resembling flax; 2 of a pale-yellow color

flax'seed' *n* seed of the flax, used in making linseed oil and in medicine

flay /flā/ [OE *flēan*] *vt* 1 to strip the skin from; 2 to torture; 3 to criticize harshly

flea /flē/ [OE *flēah*] *n* 1 any of an order (Siphonaptera) of small, wingless, bloodsucking jumping insects, parasitic on warm-blooded animals; 2 **flea in one's ear** irritating rebuke or warning

flea'bag' *n slang* run-down hotel

flea'bite' *n* 1 bite made by a flea; 2 *colloq* any slight discomfort or inconvenience

flea' mar'ket *n* street market where cheap and used articles are sold, usu. found in European cities

fleck /flek/ [< ON *flekkr*] *n* 1 spot; streak; splash || *vt* 2 to spot or splash; streak or stripe

fled /fled'/ *pt & pp* of **flee**

fledg'ling *n* /flej'liŋ/ 1 young bird just

learning to fly; 2 inexperienced person

flee /flē'/ [OE *flēon*] *v* (**fled**) *vt* 1 to run away from || *vi* 2 to hurry away, as from danger; 3 to vanish || SYN abscond, depart, run away, eschew, shun, avoid

fleece /flēs'/ [OE *flēos*] *n* 1 woolly coat of a sheep; 2 whole wool shorn from a sheep at one time; 3 anything resembling this coat of wool || *vt* 4 to shear or strip, as a sheep of its coat of wool; 5 to rob || **fleec'er** *n* || **fleec'y** *adj* (**-i-er; -i-est**)

fleet[1] /flēt'/ [OE *flēotan* to float] *adj* swift; rapid; nimble || **fleet'ness** *n* || SYN fast, speedy, quick, swift, nimble

fleet[2] [OE *flēot* ship] *n* 1 number of vessels in a group, under a single command; 2 the combined naval equipment of a nation; 3 any large group, as of ships, planes, or vehicles, under unified control

fleet' ad'mi-ral *n* highest rank in the U.S. navy

fleet'ing *adj* passing swiftly, transitory

Fleet' Street' [heart of the newspaper district of London, England] *n* the British press

Flem-ing /flem'iŋ/ [MD *Vlaming*] *n* Flemish-speaking Belgian

Flem'ing, Sir Alexander (1881-1955) *n* Scottish bacteriologist; codiscoverer of penicillin 1929; Nobel prize 1945

Flem'ing, Sir John Ambrose (1849-1945) *n* English electrical engineer, inventor of the diode 1904

Flem-ish /flem'ish/ [MD *Vlaemisch*] *adj* 1 pert. to the Flemings or to Flanders || *n* 2 language of the Flemings

flesh /flesh'/ [OE *flǣsc*] *n* 1 that part of an animal's body beneath the skin, composed of soft muscular tissue; 2 meat; 3 surface of the body; 4 bodily, as distinguished from spiritual, nature; 5 kindred, near relatives; 6 pulp of fruits or vegetables; 7 fatness; 8 **in the flesh** in person || *vt* 9 **flesh out** to elaborate, give substance to

flesh' and blood' *n* 1 close relatives; 2 human body

flesh'pots' *npl* 1 physical ease and comfort; 2 places offering luxurious entertainments

flesh'y *adj* (**-i-er; -i-est**) 1 plump, fat; 2 *bot* pulpy || **flesh'i-ness** *n* || SYN stout, fat, corpulent; pulpy, succulent

fleur-de-lis /flur'dəlis', floor'-/ [F = lily flower] *n* (**fleur-de-lis** or **fleurs-de-lis** /same as *sg/*) 1 iris; 2 stylized representation of it, as e.g., the emblem of the former royal family of France

flew /floo'/ *pt* of **fly**

flex /fleks'/ [< L *flectere* (*flexus*)] *vt* to bend or curve, as an arm

flex'i-ble *adj* 1 easily bent without breaking; pliant; 2 easily persuaded; 3 adaptable || **flex'i-bly** *adv* || **flex'i-bil'i-ty** /-bil'-/ *n* || SYN pliant, pliable, supple, elastic, ductile, limber, lithe, yielding, complaisant, tractable, servile || DISCR What can be bent, twisted, or warped without breaking is *flexible*, as a *flexible* willow rod; a *flexible* wrist. *Pliant* describes that which is so *flexible* that it can be bent in loops, like a strap, molded into forms, like clay, or laced back and forth in designs, like thread. *Pliable* contains with the idea of bending and folding, that of being workable, as soft wax or fondant. *Supple* means very *flexible* and *limber*; a *supple* motion is made by a rippling of the muscles, a bending without apparent effort; a *supple* branch can be bent double without breaking. Figuratively, *flexible* connotes adaptability or susceptibility, though a *flexible* disposition or will is not unduly impressionable. A character is *pliant* when it takes this or that shape at the will of another, *pliable* when it can be controlled or worked upon, often in an unfavorable way, by another || ANT inflexible, brittle, hard, unyielding

flex'or /-ər/ *n* muscle that bends or flexes a limb

flick /flik'/ [imit] *n* 1 light quick stroke, as with a whip; snap; flip || *vt* 2 to whip lightly || *vi* 3 to flutter; move with quick irregular vibrations

flick-er /flik'ər/ [OE *flicorian* to flutter] *vi* 1 to move with an unsteady and quick motion, as a flame in the wind; 2 to flutter, as with the wings || *n* 3 unsteady light or movement; flutter || **flick'er-ing** *adj & n*

fil-er or **fly'er** /flī'ər/ [< *fly*] *n* 1 aviator; 2 something that flies; 3 some part of a mechanism that moves rapidly; 4 step in a straight flight of stairs; 5 *colloq* speculative venture; 6 something that moves very rapidly, as an express train; 7 handbill

flight /flīt'/ [OE *flyht*] *n* 1 act, process, manner, or power of flying; 2 ascent of, or distance traveled by, anything that flies; 3 hasty departure; 4 birds flying together; 5 soaring forth, as *a flight of the imagination*; 6 any group of objects moving through the air together, as *a flight of arrows*; 7 connected series of steps; 8 scheduled trip on an airline

flight' con-trol' *n* system whereby the flight of an aircraft esp. on landing and takeoff is directed from the ground || **flight' con-trol'ler** *n*

flight' deck' *n* upper deck of aircraft carrier designed for takeoffs and landings

flight′ path′ *n* path of the center of gravity of a plane in flight

flight′y *adj* (-i·er; -i·est) 1 changeful, capricious; giddy; 2 unsteady, irresponsible ‖ **flight′i·ness** *n* ‖ SYN giddy, fanciful, half-witted, crazy, capricious

flim-flam /flim′flam′/ [prob ON] *colloq n* 1 trick; 2 act of cheating by deception ‖ *v* (-flammed; -flam·ming) *vt* 3 to trick or deceive

flim·sy /flim′zē/ [18th-cent. Eng] *n* 1 thin paper used for copies ‖ *adj* (-si·er; -si·est) 2 thin; weak; 3 ineffectual; lacking force ‖ **flim′si·ly** *adv* ‖ **flim′si·ness** *n* ‖ SYN *adj* feeble, frail, unsubstantial, superficial, vain, shallow ‖ ANT *adj* solid, substantial, strong

flinch /flinch′/ [MF *flenchir* to give way] *vi* 1 to shrink or draw back, as from pain; 2 to hesitate in undertaking a task ‖ *n* 3 act of flinching ‖ SYN *v* start, shrink, wince, startle ‖ DISCR To *start* is to move suddenly, usually in a forward leap or bound, as in fear or amazement; however, since it is natural to *start* back in surprise, away in horror, or aside to avoid something unexpected, we find *start* often used with *back*, *away*, and *aside*. To *startle* is to cause to *start* involuntarily, as by something sudden or unlooked for, as the noise *startled* him. To *startle* anyone is to cause his body to be momentarily convulsed from the effect of the unexpected or the frightening; to cause anyone to *shrink* is to make him recoil under the influence of fright or pain. To *flinch* is to show a loss of nerve, a wavering of courage, especially in the face of danger or at an unpleasant duty. A soldier may *flinch* before the enemy's attack, a parent from the proper discipline of his child. To *wince* is to draw back momentarily, and, usually, involuntarily, as under a stab of pain or the sting of a rebuke

fling /fliŋ/ [ON *flengja* to whip] *v* (flung) *vt* 1 to throw or hurl; 2 to throw to the ground; 3 to cast aside; throw off ‖ *vi* 4 to rush or move impatiently or angrily ‖ *n* 5 act of flinging; 6 period of unrestrained indulgence in pleasure; 7 kind of lively dance, as *the Highland fling*; 8 *colloq* attempt; trial, effort ‖ SYN *v* sling, toss, rush, hurl, dash (see *cast*)

flint /flint′/ [OE] *n* 1 hard crystalline or noncrystalline silica in various colors, found in chalk and limestone; 2 piece of this or other substance used for striking fire; 3 any extremely hard substance ‖ **flint′y** *adj* (-i·er; -i·est) ‖ **flint′i·ness** *n*

Flint *n* city in SE Michigan (197,000)

flint′ glass′ *n* heavy brilliant glass with a high index of refraction, used in lenses

flint′lock′ *n* 1 gunlock in which a spark from a stroke of flint on steel ignites the charge; 2 firearm having a lock of this type

flip /flip′/ [imit] *v* (flipped; flip·ping) *vt* 1 to flick with the fingers; strike with a short quick blow; 2 to cause to turn over in the air, as a coin; 3 to turn over rapidly ‖ *vi* 4 *colloq* to react strongly; 5 *colloq* to lose control of oneself ‖ *n* 6 act or instance of flipping; 7 somersault in the air; 8 mixed drink, spiced and served hot ‖ *adj* (flip·per; flip·pest) 9 flippant, impertinent

flip′-flop′ *n* 1 backward somersault; 2 flapping to and fro; 3 complete and sudden reversal in action or point of view ‖ *v* (-flopped; -flop·ping) *vi* 4 to execute a flip-flop

flip·pant /flip′ənt/ [prob < *flip*] *adj* 1 impertinent, disrespectful; 2 trifling, shallow; thoughtless ‖ **flip′pant·ly** *adv* ‖ **flip′pan·cy** *n*

flip′per [< *flip*] *n* 1 broad fin, arm, or paddle used in swimming, as that of a seal; 2 *slang* hand

flip′ side′ *n slang* the other and often less desirable side of a phonograph record

flirt /flurt′/ [imit] *vt* 1 to woo without serious intentions; 2 to trifle, play, as with an idea ‖ *n* 3 one who flirts ‖ **flirt′y** *adj* ‖ **flir·ta′tion** *n* ‖ **flir·ta′tious** *adj*

flit /flit′/ [ON *flytja* to remove] *v* (flit·ted; flit·ting) *vi* 1 to move suddenly about or away; 2 to fly swiftly; make short flights, dart

flitch /flich′/ [AS *flicce*] *n* strip or side of cured pork

flit′ter [G] *n* fine colored metallic fragments that glitter in the light, used for ornamentation

fliv·ver /fliv′ər/ [?] *n slang* small cheap automobile

float /flōt′/ [OE *flotian*] *vt* 1 to cause to be supported on the surface of a liquid or suspended in a volume of gas; 2 to cover with water; flood; 3 to level off, as a plaster surface; 4 to launch, start, or give currency to, as a rumor, a business, or a scheme; 5 to market (securities) ‖ *vi* 6 to be buoyed or held up on the surface of a liquid or within a volume of gas; 7 to glide without apparent effort; 8 to drift about aimlessly; hover ‖ *n* 9 anything that floats on the surface of a liquid, as a raft, a cork attached to a fishing line, a hollow ball that controls a valve in a flush tank, or the like; 10 plasterer's tool for spreading and smoothing; 11 low cart or platform on wheels, containing a group of objects or persons and exhibited in a procession or parade; 12 watertight structure attached to the underside of an airplane to enable it to float on the water; 13 milk shake containing a ball of unmelted ice cream; **14** *com* checks in transit, not yet collected; **15** in some water animals, sac or bladder filled with air or gas, to regulate the buoyancy of the body

floa·ta'tion *n* var of **flotation**

float'er *n* **1** one who or that which floats; **2** person with no fixed residence or employment; **3** one who votes illegally at several polling places

float'ing *adj* **1** free to move about; disconnected; **2** variable, not fixed or settled; **3** *com* **a** (capital) not permanently invested; **b** (debt) not funded

flock /flok'/ [OE *flocc* crowd] *n* **1** number of animals or birds of one kind keeping together; **2** large number; **3** church congregation in relation to its pastor ‖ *vi* **4** to congregate, come together in crowds ‖ SYN *n* company, congregation, family (see *herd*)

floe /flō'/ [perh Norw *flo*] *n* large mass of drifting ice from the polar ocean

flog /flog', flôg'/ [perh < L *flagellare*] *v* (**flogged; flog·ging**) *vt* to beat repeatedly with a whip or stick ‖ **flog'ging** *n* ‖ **flog'ger** *n*

flood /flud'/ [OE *flōd*] *n* **1** large mass of water overflowing the surface of a place or region; **2** rising or inflowing tide; **3** any great abundance resembling a deluge, as a *flood of letters*; **4** *theat* floodlight; **5** **the Flood** the great deluge of the days of Noah (Gen. 7, 8) ‖ *vt* **6** to overflow, inundate; **7** to fill completely or excessively ‖ *vi* **8** to rise in a flood, overflow

flood'gate' *n* **1** barrier or sluice in a waterway to regulate the flow of water; **2** any opening or opportunity for an outpouring

flood'light' *n* **1** artificial light casting a broad beam, as opposed to a *spotlight* ‖ *vt* **2** to illuminate with a floodlight

flood' plain' *n* level land adjacent to a river, subject to flooding

flood' tide' *n* rising tide

floor /flōr', flôr'/ [OE *flōr*] *n* **1** bottom surface of a room; **2** any similar surface on which one walks, as *the floor of a bridge*; **3** any bottom surface resembling a floor; **4** all the rooms on one level in a building; story; **5** the part of a legislative chamber assigned to the members; **6** right to address the assembly; **7** lower limit ‖ *vt* **8** to cover or provide with a floor; **9** to knock down; **10** to overwhelm, nonplus; **11** to press (the accelerator) to the floor

floor'ing *n* **1** materials for making floors; **2** floors collectively

floor' show' *n* entertainment presented in a night club

floor'walk'er *n* one who has general supervision over a department in a retail store

floo·zy /flōō'zē/ [?] *n* (**-zies**) tawdry woman of easy virtue

flop /flop'/ [var of *flap*] *v* (**flopped; flop·ping**) *vt* **1** to drop heavily; turn or let fall, as with a jerk or plump ‖ *vi* **2** to strike about; throw oneself about; **3** to change over quickly; **4** *slang* to fail miserably ‖ *n* **5** act or sound of flopping; **6** sudden change of allegiance; **7** *slang* failure ‖ **flop'py** *adj* (**-pi·er; -pi·est**)

flop'house' *n* (**-hous·es** /-zĭz/) cheap hotel for men with many beds in each room

flo·ra /flōr'ə, flôr'ə/ [< *Flora* Roman goddess of flowers] *n* (**-ras, -rae** /-rē/) **1** native plants of a particular region or period of the earth's history; **2** description of such plants

flo'ral [< L *flos* (*floris*) flower] *adj* pert. to, resembling, or consisting of flowers

Flor·ence /flor'əns, flôr'-/ *n* city in N central Italy on the Arno (440,000), leading city of Tuscany ‖ **Flor·en·tine'** /-tēn'/ *adj & n*

flori- *comb form* flower or flowers, as *floriculture*

flor·id /flōr'id, flor'-/ [L *floridus* blooming] *adj* **1** flushed; **2** brilliant with decorations; profusely embellished ‖ **flor'id·ly** *adv* ‖ **flor'id·ness** or **flo·rid'i·ty** /flə-/ *n*

Flor·i·da /flor'idə, flôr'-/ *n* state in SE U.S. between the Atlantic and the Gulf of Mexico (6,789,000; 58,560 sq.m.; cap. Tallahassee) ‖ **Flor·id·i·an** /flôrid'ē-ən/ *n*

flor·in /flôr'in, flor'-/ [It *fiorino* dim. of *fiore* flower; because coin was stamped with lily] *n* **1** originally, gold coin of Florence; **2** any of various European silver coins; **3** English silver coin worth two shillings

flo·rist /flōr'ist, flôr'-/ *n* one who sells flowers and plants

-flo·rous /-flōr'əs, -flôr'əs/ *adj comb form* flowered, as *uniflorous*

floss /flôs', flos'/ [perh OF *flosche* down] *n* **1** waste silk fibers; **2** soft, downy silken substance in the husks of certain plants; **3** untwisted soft silk used in embroidery

floss'y *adj* (**-i·er; -i·est**) **1** resembling floss; downy; silky; **2** *slang* flashy, loud, showy

flo·ta·tion /flōtā'shən/ *n* **1** act or state of floating; **2** *com* sale of securities of a new business; **3** *mining* method of ore separation whereby finely ground ore is separated in water containing fine bubbles and a reagent

flo·til·la /flōtil'ə/ [Sp, dim. of *flota* fleet] *n* **1** fleet of small vessels; **2** small fleet

flot·sam /flot'səm/ [AF *floteson* < OF *floter* to float] *n* goods lost in shipwreck and found floating

flounce[1] /flouns'/ [< earlier *frounce* <

OF *froncir* to wrinkle] *n* **1** narrow piece of cloth sewed to a petticoat or the skirt of a dress, with the lower border loose and spreading; deep ruffle || *vt* **2** to trim with a flounce or flounces

flounce² [perh Scand] *vi* **1** to move angrily and impatiently; **2** to move with exaggerated self-importance || *n* **3** act or instance of flouncing

floun·der¹ /floun′dər/ [perh < *founder*] *vi* **1** to struggle awkwardly; proceed with difficulty, as if hampered; **2** to make awkward efforts to get out of a difficult situation

floun·der² [OF *flondre* < Scand] *n* (-der or -ders) any of the flatfish family (Pleuronectidae) of fishes, including the halibut, characterized by great flatness of body

flour /flour′, flou′ər/ [early spelling of *flower*, in sense of finest part of wheat] *n* **1** fine meal of ground wheat or other grain; **2** any fine soft powder || *vt* **3** to sprinkle flour upon || **flour′y** *adj*

flour·ish /flur′ish/ [MF *florir* (-*riss*- < *florere* to bloom] *vi* **1** to prosper or thrive || *vt* **2** to brandish || *n* **3** figure formed by lines or strokes fancifully drawn; **4** decoration; **5** ostentatious or showy parade; **6** waving about, as of a sword; **7** *mus* fanfare || **SYN** *v* increase, grow, succeed; toss, flaunt, brandish

flour·ish·ing *adj* thriving; vigorous

flout /flout′/ [ME *flouten* to play the flute] *vt* **1** to treat contemptuously; jeer at || *vi* **2** to scoff; sneer || *n* **3** insult; contemptuous remark || **flout′-ing·ly** *adv* || **flout′er** *n*

flow /flō′/ [OE *flōwan*] *vi* **1** to run or spread, as *the river flows south;* **2** to glide; **3** to be uttered smoothly; **4** to rise, as the tide; **5** to melt; **6** to issue forth; **7** to hang freely; sway; **8** to abound, run over || *n* **9** act of flowing; **10** current or stream; **11** quantity of fluid that passes through a pipe, gate, or the like, under given conditions of pressure, cross section, etc.; **12** rise of the tide || **SYN** *v* gush, stream, pour, proceed, inundate, flood

flow·er /flou′ər/ [OF *flour* < L *flos* (*floris*)] *n* **1** that part of a seed-bearing plant that contains the reproductive organs; blossom; **2** plant cultivated for its blossoms; **3** choicest part of anything; **4** ornamental expression; **5** flowers *pl chem* fine powder produced esp. by sublimation; **6** in flower flowering, flourishing || *vi* **7** to blossom || **flow′ered** *adj*

flow·er·y *adj* **1** abounding in, or adorned with, flowers; **2** highly ornate or elaborate (language)

flown /flōn′/ *pp* of **fly**

flow′ sheet′ *n* diagram showing the successive stages of an industrial operation, a computer program, or the like

fl. oz. fluid ounce

flu /floo′/ [*abbr* of *influenza*] *n* influenza

flub /flub′/ [?] *v* (**flubbed; flub·bing**) *vt* & *vi* *colloq* **1** to bungle || *n* **2** blunder

fluc·tu·ate /fluk′chŏo·āt′/ [< L *fluctus* wave] *vi* **1** to roll to and fro, as a wave; **2** to rise and fall, as prices; **3** to be undecided || **fluc′tu·a′tion** *n* || **SYN** waver, oscillate, vacillate, vibrate, undulate, swerve, hesitate || **DISCR** *Oscillate* is used, literally, of the side-to-side swinging of a pendulum; figuratively, it is used of a swinging from one to the other between two fixed limits, as he *oscillated* between his desire to be generous and his wish for revenge. *Fluctuate* and *waver* suggest the to-and-fro or up-and-down movements of waves; a light in an unsteady hand *wavers;* the temperature of a malarial patient *fluctuates.* Figuratively, hesitating, indecisive characters *waver;* popularity *fluctuates;* prices *fluctuate.* *Vacillate,* now rarely used of physical things is applied to those whose purpose or attitude is frequently or easily changed

flue /floo′/ [?] *n* pipe or passage to convey away smoke, hot air, etc.

flu·ent /floo′ənt/ [L *fluens* (-*entis*) flowing] *adj* **1** possessing readiness and ease of speech; eloquent; **2** moving freely || **flu′ent·ly** *adv* || **flu′en·cy** *n*

fluff /fluf′/ [<*obs flue* down] *n* **1** light down or fur nap; **2** fluffy mass; **3** frivolous trifle; **4** *colloq* actor's slip of the tongue || *vt* **5** to shake or puff out, as feathers; **6** *colloq* to botch (one's lines in speaking) || *vi* **7** to become fluff or like fluff; **8** to bungle one's lines in speech || **fluff′y** *adj* (-i·er; -i·est)

flu·id /floo′id/ [L *fluidus* < *fluere* to flow] *adj* **1** able to flow, as a liquid or gas; **2** shifting, not stable || *n* **3** fluid substance || **flu·id′i·ty** *n* || **SYN** *n* liquid || **DISCR** Both *fluids* and *liquids* possess by nature the characteristic of flowing. *Fluids* include both *liquids* and gases; hence, all *liquids* are *fluids,* but not all *fluids* are *liquids.* Water, ordinarily, is both a *liquid* and a *fluid;* converted to steam, it is only a *fluid*

flu·id·ex′tract *n pharm* alcohol preparation containing one gram of dry drug per cubic centimeter

flu′id ounce′ *n* U.S. liquid measure equal to ⅟₁₆ pint

fluke¹ /flook′/ [OE *flōc*] *n* **1** flatfish; **2** parasitic flattened worm causing disease in sheep and other animals

fluke² [?] *n* **1** flattened end of an arm of an anchor; **2** one of the broad lobes on the tail of a whale; **3** head of a harpoon

fluke³ [?] *n* accidental stroke of luck || **fluk′y** *adj* (-i·er; -i·est)

flume /floom'/ [OF *flum* stream < L *flumen* river] 1 artificial channel for carrying water; 2 gap through which a torrent passes

flum·mox /flum'əks, -iks/ [?] *vt colloq* to bewilder

flung /fluŋ'/ *pt & pp* of **fling**

flunk /fluŋk'/ [?] *colloq n* 1 failure, as in a course or examination || *vi* 2 to fail in school; 3 to retire through fear; 4 **flunk out** to drop out of school because of failure || *vt* 5 to fail in; 6 to give a (student) the grade of failure

flun·ky /fluŋk'ē/ [Sc] *n* (-kies) also **flunkey** 1 *contemptuous* liveried servant; 2 toady; 3 performer of menial tasks

flu·o·resce /floo'ores', flōrës', flôres'/ [< L *fluere* to flow] *vt* 1 to give off (color) under the action of invisible radiation || *vn* 2 to become luminous when exposed to invisible radiation || **flu'o·res'cence** *n* || **flu'o·res'cent** *adj*

flu'o·res'cent lamp' *n* glass tube coated on the inside with a fluorescent material which becomes gaseous and emits light when an electric current passes through it

flu·or·ic /floo·ôr'ik/ [< *fluor*] *adj* pert. to or obtained from fluorine

fluor·i·date /floor'idat', flôr'-/ *vt* to treat with a fluoride

fluor·i·da'tion *n* treatment of a public water supply with fluorides in order to reduce tooth decay

flu·o·ride /floo'ərīd', floor'īd/ *n* salt of fluorine with a metal or a radical

fluor·i·nate /floor'ināt', flôr'-/ *vt* to treat or combine with fluorine

flu·o·rine /floo'ərēn', -rin, floor'ēn, -in/ *n* pale-yellow gaseous halogen element (F; at.no. 9; at.wt. 18.9984) of penetrating and disagreeable odor, capable of corroding glass and attacking with violence organic compounds

flu·o·rite /floo'ərīt', floor'īt/ *n* a common mineral, calcium fluoride —CaF₂— occurring in colored and sometimes transparent crystals, commonly in cubes; used as a flux and as the chief source of fluorine

flu·o·ro·car·bon /floo'ro·kar'bən/ *n* any of a number of inert compounds produced by replacing hydrogen by fluorine, used as aerosol propellants, refrigerants, lubricants, and fire extinguishers and in making resins and plastics

fluor·o·scope /floor'əskōp'/ *n* tube or box containing a screen covered with a fluorescent material upon which the shadows of objects exposed to X rays are focused || **fluor'o·scop'ic** /-skop'ik/ *adj* || **fluor·os'co·py** /-os'-kopē/ *n*

flu'or·spar' *n* fluorite

flur·ry /flur'ē/ [?] *v* (-ried) *vt* 1 to agitate, confuse, or bewilder || *n* (-ries) 2 sudden commotion; hurry; 3 sudden gust; squall; 4 light snowfall

flush¹ /flush'/ [imit perh *flash* + *blush*] *vt* 1 to redden; cause to blush; 2 to encourage, excite; thrill; 3 to wash or cleanse by means of a strong flow of water || *vi* 4 to blush; glow; 5 to become full of water || *n* 6 blush; glow; 7 sudden rush, as of water; 8 thrill, excitement; 9 even or unbroken surface || *adj* 10 full; 11 abundantly supplied, as with money; 12 vigorous; 13 even, level, forming a continuous surface || *adv* 14 evenly; straight; squarely

flush³ [ME *flusshen*] *vt* 1 to drive or startle from cover, as birds || *vi* 2 to rise or be startled from cover

flush³ [F *flux* run of cards] *n* 1 hand of cards all of one suit || *adj* 2 *poker* having cards of only one suit

flus·ter /flus'tər/ [perh ON *flaustr* hurry] *vt* 1 to confuse or agitate || *n* 2 agitation or confusion; excitement

flute /floot'/ [OF *fleüte*] *n* 1 tube-shaped orchestral instrument of the woodwind group, played by blowing across a hole near one end of the tube and opening and closing the finger holes and keys; 2 groove cut in the shaft of a column; 3 similar groove formed for decoration in wood, cloth, etc. || *vi* 4 to play on a flute; 5 to make a clear, flutelike noise || *vt* 6 to form flutes in || **flut'ed** *adj*

flut'ing *n* 1 channel or groove; 2 work decorated with grooves

flut'ist *n* flute player

flut·ter /flut'ər/ [OE *floterian*] *vi* 1 to move or flap the wings rapidly; 2 to move rapidly and irregularly; 3 to be in agitation or uncertainty || *vt* 4 to cause to flutter; 5 to throw into confusion || *n* 6 quick and irregular motion; vibration; 7 state of excitement or anxiety || **flut'ter·er** *n* || **flut'ter·ing·ly** *adv*

flu·vi·al /floo'vē-əl/ [< L *fluvius* river] *adj* pert. to, growing or living in, or caused by, rivers

flux /fluks'/ [L *fluxus* flowing] *n* 1 any flow or issue of matter; 2 flow of the tide; 3 continual change, as from indecision; 4 substance used to promote the fusion of metals or minerals, as in soldering or purifying; 5 *phys* rate of flow of fluids, particles, or energy || *vt* 6 to fuse; melt; make fluid; 7 to treat with a flux

fly /flī'/ [OE *fleogan*] *v* (flew; flown) *vi* 1 to move through or rise in the air with wings; 2 to pass swiftly; move rapidly; 3 to go quickly through the air as if propelled by some driving impulse; 4 to float in the air, as a flag; 5 to run away, flee; 6 to operate, or travel in, an aircraft; 7 **fly at** or **into** to assail violently; 8 **fly in the face of** to act in defiance of || *vt* 9 to avoid or shun; flee from; 10 to cause to float in the air; 11 to operate (an airplane); 12 to transport in an airplane; **13** to pass over in an aircraft, as *to fly the Atlantic* ‖ *v* (flied) *vt* **14** to raise (scenery or a curtain) above the stage ‖ *vi* **15** *baseball* to bat a fly ball; **16** fly out *baseball* to bat a fly ball that is caught ‖ *n* (flies) **17** two-winged insect of many kinds, including the common house fly; **18** hook dressed in imitation of an insect, used in fishing; **19** piece of cloth stretched over a tent, forming an extra roof; **20** flap which constitutes the door of a tent; **21** lap or flap on a garment to cover a row of buttons or a zipper; **22** horizontal dimension of a flag; opposite of *hoist;* **23** fly ball; **24** flight of a ball before it hits the ground; **25** flies *pl* space over a stage, with apparatus for handling scenery; **26** on the fly, **a** while in the air; **b** without stopping

fly′ ball′ *baseball n* batted ball that rises in the air

fly′by′ *n* (-bys) **1** low-altitude flight of one or more airplanes past a specified place; **2** passage of a spacecraft past a planet close enough to make useful observations

fly′-by-night′ *n* **1** shady businessman who intends to make a quick profit and leave; **2** venture that does not last ‖ also *adj*

fly′catch′er *n* any of the small birds that catch insects in midair, as the kingbird and the crested flycatcher

fly′er *n* var of flier

fly′-fish′ *vi* to fish with artificial flies for bait

fly′ing boat′ *n* seaplane the fuselage of which can float in the water

fly′ing but′tress *n arch.* arched brace against the wall of a building, resisting an outward thrust, as of the roof

fly′ing col′ors *npl* with flying colors victoriously; with honor

Fly′ing Dutch′man *n* **1** legendary Dutch sailor condemned for blasphemy to sail the seas until Judgment Day: the subject of a musical drama by Wagner; **2** his spectral ship, seen in bad weather, and regarded as an evil omen

fly′ing fish′ *n* fish of the family Exocoetidae whose winglike fins enable it to remain in the air for a short time

fly′ing fox′ *n* large fruit-eating bat (family Pteropodidae) of the Old World, with a foxlike face

fly′ing mare′ *n* wrestling maneuver in which a wrestler grasps the wrist of his opponent and throws him over his shoulder

fly′ing sau′cer *n* any of various allegedly extraterrestrial disk-shaped objects reported seen flying in the air

fly′ing squad′ *n* trained and highly mobile group of policemen, officials, etc., ready to be used in emergencies

fly′ing squir′rel *n* squirrel (genus *Glaucomys*) that makes very long, sailing leaps supported by folds of skin that stretch out between its fore and hind legs

fly′leaf′ *n* (-leaves) blank leaf at the beginning or end of a book

fly′pa′per *n* paper covered with an adhesive substance for catching flies, or soaked with a poison to kill flies

fly′speck′ *n* **1** spot made by the excrement of a fly; **2** any insignificant speck ‖ *vt.* **3** to soil with flyspecks

fly′trap′ *n* **1** device for catching flies; **2** plant that catches flies, as the pitcher plant

fly′way′ *n* migratory-bird route

fly′weight′ *n* boxer not exceeding 112 pounds in weight

fly′wheel′ *n* heavy wheel that renders more uniform the speed and motion of a machine, and esp. carries the crank over the dead centers

FM frequency modulation

Fm *chem* fermium

fm. **1** fathom; **2** from

fn footnote

f′ num′ber *n photog* number designating the ratio between the lens aperture and the focal length

F.O. **1** field officer; **2** Foreign Office

foal /fōl/ [OE *fola*] *n* **1** young of a horse, donkey, or camel ‖ *vt* **2** to bring forth (a foal) ‖ *vi* **3** to bring forth a foal

foam /fōm/ [OE *fām*] *n* **1** white substance formed on a liquid by violent shaking or fermentation; froth ‖ *vt* **2** to cause to froth ‖ *vi* **3** to gather froth; **4** to be enraged ‖ **foam′y** *adj* (-i-er; -i-est)

foam′ rub′ber *n* spongy synthetic rubber, used esp. in cushions and mattresses

fob¹ /fob/ [?] *n* **1** small pocket, esp. for a watch; **2** short watch chain or ribbon, often with some pendant attached

fob² [ME *fobben*] *v* (fobbed; fob-bing) *vt* fob off to get rid of, palm off

f.o.b. free on board, used with quotations of price with the name of a shipping point, to indicate that the price includes loading on railroad cars or trucks at that point, but no further transportation, as the price of an automobile *f.o.b. Detroit*

fo·cal /fōk′əl/ [see focus] *adj* pert. to or placed at a focus or central point

fo′cal length′ *n* distance from the lens or mirror to the focal plane

fo′cal plane′ *n* plane upon which the rays from the lens or mirror are brought to a focus

fo′cal ra′tio *n* f number

Foch /fôsh′/, **Ferdinand** *n* (1851–1929) French marshal, generalissimo of the Allied Armies in World War I

fo′c′s′le /fōk′səl/ *n naut* forecastle

fo·cus /fōk′əs/ [L = hearth] *n* (-cus-es,

-ci /-sī/) 1 point where rays, as of light, heat, sound, etc., meet, or from which they appear to diverge after being reflected or refracted; 2 focal length; 3 sharpness of the image at the focal plane, as *in focus, out of focus;* 4 starting point, as of infection or of an earthquake; 5 any central point ‖ *n* (**-ci**) 6 *math* a one of the points whose distances from any point on a plane curve depend upon some fixed law or laws; b one of the two points, as in the major axis of an ellipse, the sum of whose distances from any point on the curve is constant ‖ *v* (**-cused** or **-cussed; -cus·ing** or **-cus·sing**) *vt* 7 to bring to a focus or center; concentrate

fod·der /fod'ər/ [OE *fōdor*] *n* coarse food for horses, cattle, or sheep, esp. hay, cornstalks, and the like

foe /fō'/ [OE *fāh* hostile] *n* 1 personal enemy; ill-wisher; 2 enemy in war; 3 opposing or injurious factor ‖ SYN (see *enemy*)

foe·tus /fēt'əs/ *n* var of fetus

fog /fog', fôg'/ [< *foggy*] *n* 1 cloud of condensed water vapor near the surface of the earth; 2 any murkiness of the atmosphere or the substance causing it; 3 bewilderment; 4 *photog* haze obscuring a developed plate or film ‖ *v* (**fogged; fog·ging**) *vi* 5 to become clouded ‖ *vt* 6 to cover with mist; 7 to perplex; 8 to cloud (a photographic film)

fog' bank' *n* dense mass of fog on the surface of the sea

fog'bound' *adj* 1 enveloped by fog; 2 immobilized by surrounding fog

fog'gy [< *obs fog* long marsh grass] *adj* (**-gi·er; -gi·est**) 1 abounding in or filled with fog; 2 hazy, unclear; 3 bewildered ‖ **fog'gi·ly** *adv* ‖ **fog'gi·ness** *n*

Fog'gy Bot'tom *n* 1 former slum area of Washington, D.C., now the site of the State Department; 2 *colloq* the State Department

fog'horn' *n* horn for warning ships in a fog

fo·gy /fōg'ē/ [?] *n* (**-gies**) also **fo·gey** person of old-fashioned or overconservative habits and ideas (usu. preceded by *old*)

foi·ble /foib'əl/ [OF = weak] *n* minor failing or weakness of character; peculiarity ‖ SYN (see *failing*)

foil¹ /foi'l/ [OF < L *folium* leaf] *n* 1 paperlike sheet of metal used for wrapping, as *silver foil;* 2 thin leaf of metal placed under a gem to set it off; 3 person or thing that enhances by contrast

foil² [?] *n* long slender fencing weapon with a blunt point

foil³ [OF *fouler* to trample] *vt* to baffle or frustrate; defeat ‖ SYN circumvent, thwart, overthrow, balk, outwit, frustrate ‖ ANT assist, promote, encourage

foist /foist'/ [prob < D *dial. vuisten* to take in the hand] *vt* 1 to insert wrongfully or slyly; 2 to pass or palm off as genuine

fold¹ /fōld'/ [OE *fealdan*] *vt* 1 to double, bend over (part of something); 2 to enclose; wrap up; clasp; 3 to cross or intertwine (one's arms); 4 *cookery* to add (ingredients) gently, without stirring; 5 *colloq* to bring to an end ‖ *vi* 6 to become closed by folding; 7 *colloq* to close (said usu. of shows); 8 **fold up** *colloq* to go out of business ‖ *n* 9 part bent or doubled over another; 10 hollow or crease made by folding; 11 *geol* bend in rock strata

fold² [OE *fald*] *n* 1 pen for sheep; 2 flock of sheep; 3 members of a church or group sharing common beliefs ‖ *vt* 4 to shut up in a fold

-fold [OE *feald* multiplied] *suf* denoting multiplication; times, as *fourfold*

fold'er [< *fold¹*] *n* 1 one who or that which folds; 2 circular, map, or timetable that is conveniently folded; 3 folded cover or large envelope for letters and papers

fol·de·rol /fol'dərol'/ [nonsense refrain] *n* nonsense; trifle

fo·li·age /fōl'ē·ij/ *n* 1 growth of leaves; 2 leaves collectively; 3 artistic representation of leaves and flowers in decoration

fo·li·o /fōl'ē·ō'/ [< L *in folio* in a sheet] *n* 1 book of large size, with pages formed by folding a sheet of paper once; 2 page of manuscript or print; 3 two facing pages of a ledger, considered as one; 4 case for music, engravings, etc.; 5 *typ* page number ‖ *adj* 6 made up of sheets of paper folded once ‖ *vt* 7 to number or arrange consecutively the pages of (a book or manuscript)

folk /fōk'/ [OE *folc*] *n* 1 kindred tribe, race, or nation; 2 **folks** *pl colloq* a people in general; b one's relatives ‖ *adj* 3 of, pert. to, or originating among the common people, as *folk dancing*

folk' et'y·mol'o·gy *n* alteration of a word to fit popular though incorrect notions as to its etymology, as *cold slaw* for *cole slaw*

folk'lore' *n* 1 customs, traditions, and beliefs, esp. as handed down among the common people; 2 their study

folk'sy *adj* (**-si·er; -si·est**) sociable, casual, not standing on ceremony ‖ **folk'si·ness** *n*

folk' tale' *n* story or legend characteristic of the life and spirit of a people, usu. handed down by word of mouth

folk'ways' *npl* mode of living, thinking, and acting of a social group

fol·li·cle /fol'ikəl/ [L *folliculus* dim.

of *follis* bellows] *n* **1** *anat* very small sac or gland; **2** *bot* one-celled, dry-seed vessel that splits on the lower side

fol·low /fol'ō/ [OE *folgian*] *vt* **1** to go or come after; attend; pursue; **2** to succeed in order; be the consequence of; **3** to support the opinion or cause of; **4** to imitate or conform to; **5** to watch or attend to closely; **6** to practice, as *to follow a profession;* **7** to move along (a road); **8 follow suit, a** to play a card of the same suit as the card led; **b** to follow an example; **9 follow through** to pursue to completion; **10 follow up, a** to seek further details of; **b** to pursue to a conclusion ‖ *vi* **11** to go or come after another; **12** to result; **13 follow through** in golf, tennis, or other games, to allow the club or racket, after striking the ball, to swing on in the direction given the ball ‖ SYN pursue, chase, succeed, ensue; imitate, copy ‖ DISCR *Follow* is the general term. This verb has many idiomatic but familiar uses: to *follow* the hounds is to hunt; to *follow* an argument is to grasp it; to *follow* a path is to go along it; to *follow* a person, in the ordinary sense, is to keep in his wake. To *succeed,* said of persons, is to *follow* by taking the place of another, as the purchaser of a business *succeeds* the former proprietor. Events that *succeed* each other merely take place one after another, often regularly; an event that *ensues* has some orderly or logical connection with that which preceded; quarrels sometimes *ensue* from differences of opinion. *Follow* and *succeed* are used of both persons and things; *ensue* is used only of events or things. To *imitate* is to *follow* as in mannerisms, speech, or dress; we *imitate* those whom we admire or those with whom we are in contact. To *pursue* and *chase* are to follow with the intent to capture, kill, attack, or merely to overtake. Figuratively, we *pursue* aims for which we persistently work; we *chase* will-o'-the-wisps, unrealizable ideals, or the like

fol'low·er *n* **1** one who goes after another; **2** disciple, attendant, or dependent; **3** another of the same sect or party ‖ SYN partisan, adherent, attendant, retainer, satellite, disciple, imitator, pursuer, successor

fol'low·ing *adj* **1** succeeding; **2** *naut* (wind) blowing in the direction in which one is sailing ‖ *n* **3** group of followers, adherents, admirers, or patrons

fol'low-up' *n* **1** a repeating or supplementing of a previous action; **2** letter or circular sent to remind a person of the contents of a previous letter or circular, as for advertising purposes ‖ also *adj*

fol·ly /fol'ē/ [OF *folie* madness] *n* (**-lies**) **1** foolishness; **2** unbecoming conduct; **3** any foolish undertaking ‖ SYN foolishness, silliness, senselessness, levity, infatuation ‖ ANT wisdom, prudence, sense

fo·ment /fōment'/ [L *fomentum* poultice] *vt* **1** to foster, cultivate; **2** to incite, instigate ‖ **fo·ment'er** *n* ‖ **fo'men·ta'tion** *n*

fond /fond'/ [*pp* of *obs* fon to become tasteless] *adj* **1** affectionate, loving, ardently attached or devoted; **2** cherished; **3** partial; foolishly indulgent ‖ **fond'ly** *adv* ‖ **fond'ness** *n* ‖ SYN enamored, affectionate, ardent, passionate, doting ‖ ANT unfriendly, cold, undemonstrative

fon·dle /fon'dəl/ [*dim.* of *obs* fond to caress] *vt* to caress; touch or handle with tenderness

font¹ /font'/ [L *fons* (*fontis*) fountain] *n* **1** vessel to hold holy water, esp. that used in baptizing; **2** fountain; **3** oil vessel of a lamp

font² [F *fonte* founding of metal] *n* complete assortment of one size and style of type

food /fōod'/ [OE *fōda*] *n* **1** nutriment; nourishment; **2** that which is edible, as opposed to *drink;* **3** matter to discuss or dwell upon, as *food for thought* ‖ SYN diet ‖ DISCR *Food* is that which, taken into the body, builds up and nourishes, through chemical action, the normal structure of that body, or replaces its waste. *Diet* is *food* considered in its relation to laws of nutrition, or to the requirements of a given state of health, as a *diet* for a diabetic patient

food' chain' *n* chain of organisms in which each group consumes the next lower order in the series

food' cy'cle *n* group of food chains supplying all the food needed by a given ecological community

food' poi'son·ing *n* acute gastrointestinal upset caused by contaminated or poisonous foods

food'stuff' *n* anything of food value used as food or entering into the composition of food

fool /fōol/ [OF *fol* < L *follis* bellows] *n* **1** person lacking in reason or intelligence; **2** court jester; **3** one who acts in an unwise manner; **4** victim or butt; **5** enthusiast ‖ *vt* **6** to make a butt of; **7** to deceive; **8 fool away** to squander ‖ *vi* **9** to behave in a silly or frivolous manner; **10** to pretend; **11 fool around** to waste time, trifle; **12 fool with, a** to handle carelessly; **b** to meddle with

fool'er·y *n* (**-ies**) habitual folly; absurd conduct or action

fool'har'dy *adj* (**-di·er; -di·est**) having courage without judgment; rash ‖ **fool'har'di·ness** *n* ‖ SYN venturesome, adventurous, incautious, reckless, hasty ‖ ANT cautious, prudent, wary, careful

fool'ish *adj* **1** acting without judgment; **2** silly; ridiculous; absurd ‖ **fool'ish-ly** *adv* ‖ **fool'ish·ness** *n* ‖ SYN simple, witless, senseless, absurd, nonsensical

fool'proof' *adj* **1** designed to prevent thoughtless persons from harming themselves; **2** simple enough to be understood by anyone

fools'cap' *n* size of paper, about 14 x 17 inches, originally watermarked with a jester's cap and bells

fool's' er'rand *n* futile undertaking

fool's' gold' *n* iron pyrites; frequently mistaken for gold, which it resembles in color

foot /fŏŏt/ [OE fōt] *n* (feet) **1** that part of the leg on which a human being or an animal walks or stands; **2** lower part, base, foundation, or end of anything; **3** that part of a boot or stocking which receives the foot; **4** measure of length equal to twelve inches; **5** unmounted soldiers; **6** walking motion, step, swiftness; **7** part opposite the head of anything; **8** foots *pl* footlights; **9** *pros* a certain number of syllables making up a metrical unit in a verse; **10 on foot,** a afoot; b under way; **11 put one's foot down** take a firm stand; **12 put one's foot in it or in one's mouth** to commit a faux pas ‖ *vt* **13** to add a foot to, as a stocking; **14** to add figures in (a column) and place the total at the bottom; **15** *colloq* to pay, as to foot the bill; **16 foot it** to walk, run, or dance

foot'age /-ij/ *n* length in feet, as of lumber or motion-picture film

foot'-and-mouth' dis·ease' *n* acute infectious disease, characterized by an eruption of blisters in the mouth and on the hoofs; prevalent in wild animals, esp. ruminants and easily transmitted to cattle and pigs, and occasionally to man

foot'ball' *n* **1** any of various outdoor games in which two teams, usu. of eleven players each, try to carry or kick an inflated ball across the opponents' goal; esp. English rugby or a modified form of it played in America, and association football or soccer in which the use of hands and arms is generally prohibited; **2** ball used in any of these games

foot'board' *n* **1** board across the lower end of a bedstead; **2** board or platform on which to stand

foot' brake' *n* brake operated by the foot

foot'bridge' *n* bridge for pedestrians

foot'-can'dle *n* optics unit of illumination equal to one lumen per square foot: the illumination produced by a light of one international candle upon a surface one foot away

-foot'ed *comb form* having so many or such feet, as *four-footed, web-footed*

foot'fall' *n* **1** footstep; **2** sound of a footstep

foot'gear' *n* covering for the feet

foot'hill' *n* one of a range of low hills near the base of a mountain

foot'hold' *n* place where one may stand firmly; secure position; firm footing

foot'ing *n* **1** ground or support for the feet; **2** tread; act of moving on foot; **3** firm or assured position; **4** state or relative condition, as *a friendly footing;* **5** the part of a foundation in contact with the ground; **6** *com* a act of adding up a column of figures; b sum total of such a column

foot'less *adj* **1** without feet; **2** unsubstantial; **3** inept

foot'lights' *npl* **1** floor lights at the front of a theater stage; **2** the stage; the theater

foot'lock'er *n* small trunk at the foot of a soldier's bed

foot'-loose' *adj* free, unconfined

foot'man /-mən/ *n* (-men /-mən/) liveried servant who attends a carriage or automobile, waits on table, etc.

foot'note' *n* **1** explanatory or illustrative statement placed below the main text on a printed page ‖ *vt* **2** to add footnotes to

foot'pad' [*foot + obs pad* highwayman] *n* highwayman who robs on foot

foot'path' *n* narrow way for pedestrians

foot'-pound' *n* (**foot-pounds**) unit of energy or work equal to the work done by the force of one pound in moving its point of application one foot in the direction of the force

foot'-pound'al *n* unit of energy or work equal to the work performed by a force equal to one poundal producing a displacement of one foot in the direction in which it is applied

foot'-pound'-sec'ond *adj* (system of units) in which the foot is the unit of length, the pound the unit of mass, and the second the unit of time

foot'print' *n* mark made by a foot

foot'sie /-sē/ [dim. of *foot*] *n* play footsie with *colloq* **1** to be surreptitiously intimate with; **2** to curry favor with

foot' sol'dier *n* infantryman

foot'sore' *adj* having painful or tender feet, as from walking

foot'step' *n* **1** distance covered by a step; **2** action of the foot in stepping; **3** sound of a step; **4** footprint

foot'stone' *n* stone placed at the foot of a grave

foot'stool' *n* stool to rest the feet on

foot'-ton' *n* unit of energy equal to the work done in lifting one ton a distance of one foot

foot'wear' *n* foot covering, as shoes, slippers, and boots

foot'work' *n* 1 art or act of maneuvering the feet, as in certain sports; 2 skillful maneuvering

foot'worn' *adj* 1 wearied from walking; 2 worn down by being trod upon

foo-zle /foōz'əl/ [G *dial. fuseln* to work badly] *vt* 1 to bungle, do clumsily ‖ *vi* 2 to bungle, act clumsily ‖ *n* 3 clumsy, bungling action, esp. in golf

fop /fop'/ [ME *foppe*] *n* man who is devoted to fine dress; dandy ‖ **fop'-pish** *adj* ‖ SYN dude, beau, coxcomb, jackanapes, dandy

for /fôr', fər/ [OE] *prep* 1 in place of; 2 as being, as *I took him for someone else;* 3 in exchange against, as *two for ten cents;* 4 because of; 5 because of lack of, as *we are pressed for time;* 6 for the sake of; 7 in support of; 8 notwithstanding, in spite of; 9 to the number or amount of, as *a bill for five dollars;* 10 during, as *to stand for an hour;* 11 as regards, in consideration of; 12 introducing the subject of an infinitive, as *it is right for me to do this;* 13 in order to get, as *go for coffee;* 14 responsive to, as *an eye for beauty;* 15 intended to be used by; 16 intending to arrive at, as *leave for Boston;* 17 desirous of; 18 appropriate to; 19 after, as *he was named for his father* ‖ *conj* 20 because; since; seeing that; owing to the fact that

for-age /fôr'ij, for'-/ [OF *fourrage*] *n* 1 food for horses and cattle; 2 search for food or provisions for an army ‖ *vi* 3 to go in search of provisions ‖ *vt* 4 to supply with provisions; 5 to ravage, as a land in wartime ‖ **for'-ag-er**

for-a-min-i-fer /fôr'əmin'ifər/ [L *foramen* (-*minis*) hole + *ferre* to bear] *n* any of an order (Foraminifera) of rhizopods, small chiefly marine animals having pierced skeletons of limestone, remains of which form beds of rock, as the chalk cliffs of England

for-as-much as /fôr'əzmuch'əz/ *conj* because, since

for-ay /fôr'ā, for'-/ [ME *forray dial.* form of *forage*] *vt & vi* 1 to plunder, pillage ‖ *n* 2 raid; invasion for the sake of plunder

for-bade also **for-bad** /fôrbad', fər-/ *pt & pp* of **forbid**

for-bear¹ /fôr'bar'/ *n* var of **forebear**

for-bear² /fôrber'/ [*for* + *bear²*] *v* (-**bore;** -**borne**) *vt* 1 to abstain from ‖ *vi* 2 to restrain oneself; be patient

for-bear'ance *n* 1 patience, indulgence; 2 self-command ‖ SYN endurance, toleration, mercy (see *patience*)

for-bid /fôrbid', fər-/ [OE *forbēodan*] *v* (-**bade,** -**bad** /-bad'/, -**bid-den** /-bid'ən/, -**bid;** -**bid-ding**) *vt* 1 to prohibit; 2 to prevent, oppose

for-bid'ding *adj* repellent; disagreeable; repulsive

for-bore /fôrbôr'/ *pt* of **forbear²**

for-borne /fôrbôrn'/ *pp* of **forbear²**

force /fôrs', fôrs'/ [MF < L *fortis* strong] *n* 1 active power; vigor, strength, energy; violence; 2 power to produce conviction; persuasive power; 3 meaning, special significance, as of a word or expression; 4 troops; armament; 5 trained or organized body; 6 unlawful violence to property or person; 7 *phys* that which produces or tends to produce motion or a change in motion or shape in a body; 8 *baseball* force play; 9 **in force, a** with full strength; **b** in effect ‖ *vt* 10 to compel; overpower by strength; 11 to impel, push; 12 to produce by unnatural or excessive effort; strain; 13 to obtain (something) by force; 14 to break open; 15 *baseball* **a** to compel (a runner) to vacate a base in favor of a succeeding runner, as by hitting a grounder when first base is occupied; **b** to cause (a runner who has been forced) to be put out ‖ SYN *n* violence, dint, might (see *compulsion, energy*)

forced' *adj* 1 compulsory; 2 strained, as *a forced smile;* 3 driven by force or pressure, as *forced air;* 4 done under pressure or in an emergency, as *a forced march* ‖ **forc-ed-ly** /fôrs'-idlē, fôrs'-/ *adv*

force'-feed' *vt* to force food or ideas on

force'ful *adj* vigorous; strong; powerful ‖ **force'ful-ly** *adv* ‖ **force'ful-ness** *n*

force'meat' *n* [< obs *farce* spice + *meat*] *n* finely chopped meat, seasoned, commonly used for stuffing

force' play' *n* baseball play in which a runner is forced

for-ceps /fôr'səps/ [L = tongs] *nsg & npl* pincers or pliers for seizing and extracting

force' pump' *n* pump that operates under pressure

for'ci-ble /< *force*/ *adj* 1 having great mental or physical power; 2 attained or accomplished by force or compulsion ‖ **for'ci-ble-ness** *n* ‖ **for'ci-bly** *adv*

ford /fôrd', fôrd'/ [OE < *faran* to travel] *n* 1 shallow place in a stream that can be crossed by wading or in a vehicle ‖ *vt* 2 to wade through or pass over, as a stream, without swimming

Ford, Gerald R. /jer'əld/ *n* (1913–) 38th president of the U.S. 1974–77

Ford, Henry *n* (1863–1947) U.S. automobile manufacturer

for-done or **fore-done** /fôrdun'/ [< OE *fordōn* to destroy] *adj* utterly worn out, exhausted

fore¹ /fôr', fōr'/ [OE = forward, before] *n* 1 forward part ‖ *adj* 2 at or near the forward part ‖ *adv* 3 *naut* at or toward the bow

fore² [prob short for *before*] *interj golf* watch out! (cry of warning to persons ahead)

fore- [see fore¹] *comb form* **1** in front, as *forerunner;* **2** before or beforehand, as *foretell;* **3** front part of, as *forearm;* **4** near or at the front, as *foremost*

fore′-and-aft′ *adj naut* set lengthwise || **fore′ and aft′** *adv*

fore·arm′¹ [< *arm¹*] *n* arm from wrist to elbow

fore·arm′² [< *arm²*] *vt* to arm beforehand

fore′bear′ or **for·bear′** *n* ancestor

fore·bode /-bōd′/ [OE *fore* before + *bodian* to announce] *vi* **1** to presage evil; **2** to have a presentiment of evil; foresee || *vt* **3** to foretell (evil); **4** to have a presentiment of || **fore·bod′er** *n* || SYN betoken, portend, prophesy (see *foretell*)

fore·bod′ing *n* **1** feeling that evil is coming; **2** evil portent || SYN presentiment, misgiving || DISCR *Misgiving, foreboding,* and *presentiment* express degrees of expectation, *misgiving* and *foreboding* always, and *presentiment* almost always, of evil. *Misgiving* names a feeling of apprehension and dread about the future. *Foreboding* is more positive in its premonition of evil, and is tinged with the ominous. *Presentiment* is the least definite; one feeling a *presentiment* of evil is vaguely conscious of something unfortunate or unhappy in the air

fore′brain′ *n* **1** the front of the three divisions of the brain of the vertebrate embryo; **2** the part of the adult brain derived from it

fore′cast′ *n* **1** prediction || *v* (**-cast** or **-casted**) *vt* **2** to foresee; predict; **3** to foreshadow || *vi* **4** to make a forecast || **fore′cast′er** *n* || SYN *n* forethought, estimate, computation, premeditation, prophecy (see *foretell*)

fore·cas·tle /or *naut* fōk′səl/ *n* the part of the vessel forward of the foremast, where on merchant ships the seamen's quarters are located

fore·close /-klōz′/ [OF *forclore* (-*clos*)] *vt* **1** to cut off or debar (a person who has defaulted in payments due on a mortgage) from the right of redemption; **2** to enforce (a mortgage) || **fore·clo·sure** /-zhər/ *n*

fore·doom′ *vt* **1** to condemn beforehand; **2** to predestine to ruin

fore′ edge′ *n* outer edge of a book, opposite the backbone

fore′fa′ther *n* ancestor

fore·fend′ *vt* var of *forfend*

fore′fin′ger *n* finger next to the thumb; index finger

fore′foot′ *n* (-**feet**) one of the front feet of a quadruped or insect

fore′front′ *n* **1** place farthest forward; **2** foremost place

fore·gath′er *vi* var of *forgather*

fore·go′ *vt* var of *forgo*

fore·go′ing *adj* preceding; previous

fore·gone′ *adj* **1** previous; former; **2** predetermined; unavoidable

fore′gone′ con·clu′sion *n* **1** decision adopted in advance of due consideration; **2** inevitable result

fore′ground′ *n* that part of a landscape, picture, or scene near the observer

fore′hand′ *adj tennis* made, as a stroke, by holding the racket with the front of the hand toward the ball

fore′hand′ed *adj* **1** done in good season or beforehand; **2** done with a view toward the future || **fore′hand′-ed·ness** *n*

fore′head /also for′id, fôr′id/ *n* **1** that part of the face between the eyes and the scalp; **2** front part of anything

for·eign /for′in, fôr′-/ [OF *forain* < L *foris* outside] *adj* **1** belonging to or connected with another nation; alien; **2** belonging to other persons or things; **3** inappropriate || **for′-eign·ness** *n* || SYN outlandish, distant, extraneous, remote, alien

for′eign bill′ *n* bill of exchange payable in a foreign country

for′eign·er *n* citizen of a foreign country; alien

for′eign ex·change′ *n* **1** foreign currency or commercial paper payable in such currency; **2** process of settling accounts between persons or businesses of different nations

for′eign min′is·ter *n* cabinet minister in charge of relations with other countries

fore·judge′ *vt* to judge in advance; prejudge || **fore·judg′ment** *n*

fore·know′ *v* (-**knew**; -**known**) *vt* to know in advance || **fore·knowl′edge** *n*

fore′land′ /also -lənd/ *n* point of land projecting into the sea; headland

fore′leg′ *n* one of the front legs of an animal, esp. a mammal

fore′lock′¹ [< *lock¹*] *n* lock of hair growing on the forehead

fore′lock′² [< *lock²*] *n* **1** linchpin, key, or wedge to hold a wheel or nut in place || *vt* **2** to secure with such a device

fore′man /-mən/ *n* (-**men** /-mən/) **1** overseer; one having immediate charge of a group of workers; **2** chairman and spokesman of a jury || **fore′man·ship′** *n*

fore′mast′ /-mast′, -mäst′; *naut* -məst/ *n* mast nearest the bow of a vessel

fore′most′ [OE *formest* *superl.* of *forma* first] *adj* **1** chief; first in position, time, or rank || SYN chief, first, best, paramount, preeminent

fore′named′ *adj* aforementioned

fore′noon′ *n* time between sunrise and midday; morning

fo·ren·sic /fərən′sik/ [< L *forensis* of the forum] *adj* **1** pert. to or used in

courts of justice or public debate; 2 suitable for argument; **3** rhetorical || **4 forensics** nsg or npl art or study of formal argument or debating

fore'or·dain' vt to appoint beforehand; predestine; decree beforehand || **fore'or·di·na'tion** n

fore'part' n that part which is first or in front

fore'paw' n front paw

fore'quar'ter n forward end of half a carcass, as of beef

fore'run'ner n **1** messenger sent before; herald; **2** something that precedes a person or event; **3** premonitory sign || SYN harbinger, sign, omen, precursor, herald

fore'sail' /or naut -səl/ n **1** on a square-rigged ship or schooner, largest sail on the foremast; **2** on a sloop or yawl, sail carried on a forestay

fore·see' v (-saw; -seen) vt **1** to know beforehand; anticipate || vi **2** to show foresight || **fore·see'a·ble** adj

fore·shad'ow vt to suggest or indicate beforehand; presage || **fore·shad'ow·er** n

fore'sheet' n **1** one of the clew ropes attached to a foresail; **2 foresheets** pl front part of an open boat

fore'shore' n that part of a shore uncovered at low tide

fore·short'en vt **1** in drawing or painting, to shorten or make smaller, as objects, so that they will appear in proper perspective; **2** to reduce or abridge

fore'sight' n **1** power or act of seeing in advance; **2** heedful thought for the future; prudence || **fore'sight'ed** adj || SYN care, forethought, prevision (see wisdom)

fore'skin' n fold of skin covering the end of the penis; prepuce

for·est /for'ist, fôr'-/ [< LL (silva) forestis (woods) outside (the walls)] n **1** large extent of ground covered with trees; **2** the trees growing there; **3** uncultivated tract of land, more or less covered with trees and undergrowth; **4** thick cluster resembling a forest || vt **5** to cover with trees or woods || **for'est·a'tion** n

fore·stall' [< OE foresteall ambush] vt **1** to obstruct, hinder; prevent; **2** to anticipate; get ahead of || **fore·stall'er** n || SYN avert, anticipate, baffle, frustrate (see prevent)

fore'stay' n strong rope, usually of woven wire, reaching from the head of the foremast to the bow to support the foremast

for'est·er n **1** one skilled in knowledge of trees and timber; **2** officer who has charge of a forest; **3** any of several moths of the family Agaristidae; **4** Australian great gray kangaroo (Macropus canguru)

for'est·ry n science of caring for and cultivating trees, or of managing forests

fore·taste' vt **1** to anticipate; enjoy before possessing || **fore·taste'** n **2** brief anticipatory experience; anticipation; preconception

fore·tell' v (-told) vt **1** to predict or prophesy || vi **2** to utter a prophecy or prediction || SYN forecast, predict, presage, prophesy, forebode, portend || DISCR These words agree in the idea of telling beforehand what is to occur. Foretell is the general and familiar term, and requires only ordinary ability or intelligence. Predict is now used chiefly of events that can be calculated, as astronomical occurrences, and requires suitable mental training. Sometimes predict is used of those events which can be deduced from what has already happened, as to predict mutiny or war. Formerly predict connoted the possession of supernatural powers of foretelling, and this sense still lingers among those who tell fortunes, read palms, or the like. To prophesy is to foretell under the influence of inspiration; scripturally, to prophesy is to explain and interpret, as does one to whom God has revealed his truth. To forecast resembles predict, but it is more conjectural than inferential, though it is used almost entirely now of weather prognostications, and in this connection is, of course, calculative. To presage, forebode, and portend foretoken evil. To forebode is to apprehend evil in some obscure way; people "feel it in their bones." To portend is to foreshadow evil, especially in an ominous and threatening way, as these clashes portend civil war. To presage is often to draw a conclusion about the future from what the present is, as to presage the spread of a disease. Sometimes presage carries a note of warning, as the dead, still air presaged a storm. Forecast, foretell, prophesy, and predict are used only of persons; portend, only of things; forebode or presage, of either persons or things

fore'thought' n **1** planning beforehand; deliberate intention; **2** heed for the future; prudence || SYN premeditation, anticipation (see wisdom)

fore'top' /also -təp/ n naut platform at the head of a foremast

for·ev'er /also fər-/ adv **1** through eternity, everlastingly; **2** at all times || SYN endlessly, interminably, incessantly, unceasingly, always, everlastingly, eternally, perpetually

for·ev'er·more' adv for all eternity

fore·warn' vt to warn in advance || **fore·warn'ing** n

fore'wom'an /-woŏm'ən/ n (-women /-wim'ən/) female foreman

fore'word' n preface; introductory remark

for'feit /fôr'fit/ [OF forfait] n **1** fine

or penalty; **2** act of forfeiting; **3 forfeits** *nsg* game in which the losers perform ludicrous tasks ‖ *vt* **4** to lose, as a position, right, or advantage, by neglect ‖ *adj* **5** alienated or lost ‖ **for′feit·er** *n* ‖ **for′fei·ture** /-fichər/ *n*

for·fend /fôrfend′/ [< *for-* off + ME *fenden* to avert] *vt* **1** to defend, protect; **2** *archaic* to ward off, avert; prevent, as a disaster

for·gath′er [*for-* (intensive) + *gather*] *vi* **1** assemble; come together; **2** to associate

forge¹ /fôrj′/ [?] *vi* to advance slowly or with difficulty (often used with *ahead*)

forge² [OF *forgier* < L *fabricare* to contrive] *vt* **1** to shape or work (metal) while hot under a hammer or press; **2** to shape; form; invent; **3** to counterfeit with intent to defraud, as a signature on a check or the check itself ‖ *vi* **4** to be guilty of counterfeiting with intent to defraud ‖ *n* **5** open fire in which iron is treated by forced draft preparatory to shaping it; **6** smithy; **7** shop for heating and working iron ‖ **forg′er** *n* ‖ SYN *v* coin, falsify (see *counterfeit*)

for′ger·y *n* (-ies) **1** act of making a false or counterfeited document, as a check falsely signed or a fabricated historical or legal record; **2** article or writing counterfeited

for·get /fərget′/ [OE *forgietan*] *v* (-got; -got·ten or -got; -get·ting) *vt* **1** to fail to retain in one's memory or fail to recall; **2** to cease or omit to think of; **3** to omit to take; leave behind through oversight; **4** to pass over without notice; **5** to overlook willfully; disregard ‖ *vi* **6** to fail to remember

for·get′ful *adj* **1** apt not to remember; **2** negligent ‖ **for·get′ful·ly** *adv* ‖ **for·get′ful·ness** *n* ‖ SYN heedless, inattentive, careless (see *oblivious*)

for·get′-me-not′ *n* any of a genus (*Myosotis*) of small perennial herbs with pale-blue flowers and hairy leaves

forg′ing [< *forge²*] *n* any piece of metal which has been shaped while hot by hammering or pressing

for·give /fôrgiv′, fər-/ [OE *forgiefan*] *v* (-gave; -giv·en) *vt* **1** to pardon (an offense or an offender); **2** to remit (a debt or a debtor) ‖ *vi* **3** to display clemency or leniency ‖ **for·giv′a·ble** *adj* ‖ **for·giv′er** *n* ‖ SYN pardon, excuse, condone, remit, overlook, absolve ‖ DISCR To *forgive* is the act of one who has been offended or wronged; it not only lifts punishment or consequences from the offender, but restores him to an unresentful place in the affections of the offended one. Hence, *forgive* is the familiar term for the reestablishing of broken personal relationships. A *pardon* is

the act of a superior, and emphasizes the removal of the consequences of a fault or crime; it is a question of justice, and not of personal feelings: a governor or a judge may *pardon*, yet still harbor unforgiving feelings against the offender, if the wrong done touches him personally. A sinner restored to the grace of God through repentance is both *forgiven* and *pardoned*. To *condone* is to wink at an offense; one who *condones* sees the offense, but, expressly or tacitly, ignores it. To *excuse* is to release from blame in slight respects, as for a lack of ceremony, absence from school, or the like; *excuse* me, and, by courtesy, *pardon* me in the same sense, are used as conventional expressions of apology. To *remit* is to refrain from exacting a penalty or consequence; we may *remit* part of another's debt to us; a judge may *remit* part of a sentence

for·give′ness *n* **1** act of forgiving or state of being forgiven; **2** readiness to forgive ‖ SYN pardon, leniency, forbearance (see *mercy*)

for·giv′ing *adj* willing to forgive, showing forgiveness ‖ SYN charitable, clement, kind, merciful, lenient

for·go′ /fôr-/ [OE *forgān*] *v* (-went; -gone) *vt* to give up; deny oneself of; renounce; abstain from ‖ **for·go′er** *n* ‖ SYN quit, relinquish, resign, waive (see *abandon*)

fo·rint /fôr′int/ [Hung < It *fiorino* florin] *n* monetary unit of Hungary

for·judge′ *vt* var of **forejudge**

fork /fôrk′/ [OE *forca* < L *furca*] *n* **1** instrument with two or more prongs intended for picking up or holding a piece of food, a bunch of hay, or the like, or for digging into the soil; **2** anything resembling, or branching like, a fork; **3** angular opening or place of division caused by the meeting of two roads or rivers, of two branches of a tree, or the like; **4** any of the streams, roads, or the like, uniting or diverging at a fork ‖ *vt* **5** to make in the shape of a fork; **6** to raise, throw, or dig with a pronged tool; **7 fork over** *colloq* to hand over ‖ *vi* to branch off ‖ **forked′** *adj*

fork′ lift′ *n* machine for lifting heavy objects by means of forklike fingers

for·lorn /fôrlôrn′/ [*pp* of *obs forlese* to lose utterly < OE *forlēosan* to lose] *adj* **1** abandoned; deserted; destitute; **2** miserable; hopeless; wretched ‖ **for·lorn′ly** *adj* ‖ **for·lorn′ness** *n*

for·lorn′ hope′ [D *verloren hoop* lost troop] *n* **1** body of soldiers detached for a service of great danger; **2** hopeless enterprise; **3** vain hope

form /fôrm′/ [L *forma*] *n* **1** external appearance or shape of anything; **2** orderly arrangement; symmetry; **3**

pleasing appearance, beauty; **4** determinate shape or structure; **5** established practice or ritual; conventional behavior; **6** mold or pattern; **7** long backless bench; **8** class or grade in a preparatory school; **9** manner of doing something, style; **10** mannequin; **11** document with blank spaces to be filled in; **12** mold to contain freshly poured concrete; **13** *typ* types, plates, etc., locked in a frame ready for printing; **14** *gram* shape of a word in reference to spelling, inflection, or the like; **15** *sports* a physical condition as regards fitness to compete or perform; **b** conformity to any standard, as of grace or efficiency, in performing specific feats; **16** *philos* a essential nature; **b** idealized archetype; **c** that which determines the species or kind of something || *vt* **17** to give shape to, create; **18** to mold to a particular pattern; **19** to conceive or imagine; **20** to constitute; **21** to devise, adjust || *vi* **22** to take shape, become shaped || SYN *n* figure, shape, conformation, mold, fashion, semblance; rite, observance (see *ceremony*)

-form *adj comb form* **1** added to nouns, indicates "having the shape of," as *cruciform;* **2** added to adjectives, indicates "having the designated type of form," as *uniform, multiform*

for·mal *adj* **1** according to custom or established rules; precise; ceremonious; conventional; **2** having the outward shape without the inward reality || *n* **3** something formal, as a dance or gown || **for'mal·ly** *adv* || **for'mal·ize'** *vt* || SYN stiff, affected, punctilious (see *ceremonious*)

form·al·de·hyde /fôrmal'dəhīd'/ [*formic* + *alcohol* + *de* + *hyd*rogen] *n chem* pungent irritating gas —HCHO— used, often in solution, as an antiseptic, disinfectant, and preservative, and in industry

for'mal·ism *n* **1** exact observance of outward rites and customs, esp. in religious duties; **2** stiffness of manners or behavior || **for'mal·ist** *n*

for·mal·i·ty /-mal'-/ *n* (-ties) **1** ceremoniousness; strict adherence to external customs; state of being conventional; **2** ceremony; any conventionally required act || SYN· form, conventionality (see *ceremony*)

for·mat /fôr'mat/ [F < L *formatus* formed] *n* **1** whole style and size of a book, including the paper, type, and binding; **2** general organization and style, as of a television show

for·ma·tion *n* **1** act or process of forming; **2** that which is formed; **3** structure; **4** particular assemblage of troops; **5** *geol* group ·of strata or rocks of similar origin or composition

form'a·tive *adj* **1** giving shape to; tending to mold; **2** plastic or pliable || *n gram* **3** affix; **4** word made by adding an affix

form' class' *n* class of linguistic forms having one or more morphological or syntactical features in common and that can be substituted for each other in a construction

for·mer /fôr'mər/ [< ME *formest* foremost] *adj* **1** preceding in time or place; foregoing; prior; **2** first of two mentioned (correlative of *latter*); **3** erstwhile

for'mer·ly *adv* heretofore; in past time

form'fit'ting *adj* close-fitting

for·mic /fôr'mik/ [< L *formica* ant] *adj* derived from formic acid

For·mi·ca /fôrmīk'ə/ [trademark] *n* laminated heat-proof plastic, used for surfaces

for'mic ac'id *n* colorless fuming corrosive liquid —HCOOH— the irritant in the sting of insects, produced synthetically and used in industry and in medicine

for·mi·da·ble /fôrm'idəbəl/ [< L *formidare* to fear] *adj* **1** exciting dread; fearful; powerful; **2** hard to overcome or accomplish || SYN dangerous, terrible, threatening, tremendous, alarming, shocking || ANT powerless, helpless, weak

form'less *adj* without definite shape; lacking regularity of outline

For·mo·sa /fôrmōs'ə/ *n* former name of Taiwan

for·mu·la /fôrm'yələ/ [L *dim.* of *forma* shape] *n* (-las or -lae /-lē'/) **1** prescribed rule or model; **2** group of symbols expressing the composition or contents of a chemical compound; **3** orderly statement of faith or doctrine; **4** prescription, recipe; **5** infant's food consisting of a prescribed mixture of milk and other ingredients; **6** *math* a general equation; **b** rule or principle expressed in algebraic language or symbols

for'mu·late' *vt* **1** to put into the terms of, or reduce to, a formula; **2** to fix or state in definite terms; **3** to devise || **for'mu·la'tion** *n*

for·ni·cate /fôr'nikāt'/ [LL *fornicare* (-atus) < *fornix* brothel (arch, vault)] *vi* to commit fornication || **for'ni·ca'tor** *n*

for·ni·ca'tion *n* **1** sexual intercourse between unmarried persons; **2** *Bib* **a** unlawful sexual intercourse; **b** idolatry

for·sake /fôrsāk'/ [OE *forsacan*] *v* (-sook /-sŏŏk'/; -sak·en /-sāk'ən/) *vt* **1** to leave, desert, abandon; **2** to renounce, forswear || SYN desert, cast off, renounce (see *abandon*)

for·sooth /-sōōth'/ [OE *forsōth*] *adv* verily, in truth (usu. ironically), as *a gallant gentleman, forsooth!*

for·swear' [*for-* away + *swear*] *v* (-swore; -sworn) *vi* **1** to take an oath falsely || *vt* **2** to deny on oath; **3** to abjure, reject vehemently; **4** to perjure (oneself) || SYN abjure, reject, forgo, deny (see *perjure*)

for·syth·i·a /fôrsith'ē-ə, -sĭth'-/ [Wm. Forsyth (1737–1804) Brit botanist] *n* any of a genus (*Forsythia*) of ornamental shrubs, esp. any of several cultivated species bearing bright-yellow flowers in early spring before the leaves appear

fort /fôrt', fôrt'/ [< L *fortis* strong] *n* enclosed fortified place; fortress

fort. 1 fortification; **2** fortified

forte[1] /fôrt', fôrt'/ [< F *fort* strong] *n* one's strong point or special talent

for·te[2] /fôr'tā, fôrt'ē/ [It = strong] *adj & adv mus* loud

forth /fôrth', fōrth'/ [OE] *adv* **1** onward in time, position, order, or reckoning; forward **2** out, as from concealment or seclusion

Forth, Firth of *n* estuary of the Forth River in SE Scotland

forth'com'ing *adj* **1** ready or about to appear; **2** available when required || *n* a coming forth

forth'right' *adv* **1** straightforward; at once || *adj* **2** direct; decisive

forth'with' /-with', -with'/ *adv* at once, immediately; directly; now

for'ti·eth *n* **1** the one next in order after the thirty-ninth; **2** one of forty equal parts || also *adj*

for·ti·fi·ca'tion *n* **1** art or science of building or strengthening military defenses; **2** military work erected for defense; **3** strengthening || SYN fort, citadel, stronghold, defense

for·ti·fy /fôr'tifī'/ [F *fortifier* < L *fortificare*] *v* (**-fied**) *vt* **1** to strengthen by military works; **2** to make strong; **3** to encourage or confirm; **4** to add alcohol to (wine, etc.) || *vi* **5** to erect defenses || **for'ti·fi'er** *n*

for·tis /fôrt'is/ [L = strong] *adj phonet* **1** pronounced with relatively greater muscular tension: opposed to *lenis* || *n* (**-tes** /-tēz/) **2** consonant so pronounced

for·tis·si·mo /fôrtis'imō/ [It] *adj & adv mus* very loud

for'ti·tude' /-t(y)ood'/ [L *fortitudo* strength] *n* spiritual strength to endure suffering or adversity with courage || SYN endurance, resolution (see *bravery, patience*)

Fort' Knox' /noks'/ *n* military reservation in N Kentucky, repository of U.S. gold reserve

fort'night' /also Brit fôrt'nĭt/ [OE *fēorwertȳne niht* fourteen nights] *n* period of two weeks

fort'night'ly *adj* **1** occurring once a fortnight || *adv* **2** once a fortnight || *n* (**-lies**) **3** publication appearing every two weeks

for'tress /-tris/ [OF *forteresse* strength] *n* large place permanently fortified for defense; fort; castle

for·tu·i·tous /-t(y)oo'itəs/ [L *fortuitus*] *adj* **1** occurring by chance or accident; **2** lucky || **for·tu'i·tous·ly** *adv* || SYN contingent, incidental, accidental, casual, random, occasional || DISCR *Accidental, incidental, casual,* and *fortuitous* are terms descriptive of events or circumstances that happen without intention or premeditation. *Accidental* describes that which occurs without plan, as an *accidental* meeting; or as the result of carelessness or chance, as an *accidental* injury; an *accidental* bit of good fortune. *Incidental* describes a happening that occurs in connection with a greater or more important event. An *incidental* remark grows out of a discussion, and is relevant to it, but it is subordinate and unpremeditated, as are *incidental* expenses on a journey. *Fortuitous* describes events that occur wholly through chance; a *fortuitous* occurrence or coincidence is often a happy one. Columbus's discovery of America was *accidental* and *fortuitous,* and *incidental* to his main purpose as well. *Casual* describes that which occurs outside the regular course of events; a *casual* caller drops in unexpectedly. *Casual* carries relative unimportance as well as irregularity in its meaning; a *casual* remark is irrelevant and matters nothing; a *casual* warning falls on deaf ears. *Contingent* describes that which is unlooked for, and hence unprepared for; it is opposed to that which is definitely fixed. *Contingent* also describes a happening that is the result of unforeseen or unforeseeable conditions, and so gathers the meaning of *dependent,* as our success is *contingent* upon your cooperation. *Occasional,* like *casual,* describes that which is undesigned and comparatively infrequent; but the *occasional* happening grows out of some special juncture of events, while the *casual* event occurs without apparent cause || ANT planned, foreseen, premeditated

For·tu·na /fôrt(y)oo'nə/ *n Rom myth.* goddess of fortune or chance

for·tu·nate /fôr'chənit/ [< L *fortuna* chance] *adj* **1** happening by good fortune, opportune; **2** lucky, successful || **for'tu·nate·ly** *adv* || SYN (see *happy, lucky*) || ANT unlucky, calamitous

for'tune /-chən/ *n* **1** the good or ill that happens to mankind; chance, fate; **2** personified power regarded as determining good or ill luck; **3** estate, possessions, wealth; **4** forecast of one's future || SYN luck, fate, chance, destiny, property, possessions, riches || ANT misfortune, poverty, loss

for'tune cook'ie *n* folded wafer, often served in Chinese restaurants, containing a printed slip of paper, which tells a fortune or gives some other information

for′tune hunt′er *n* one who seeks wealth, esp. through marriage

for′tune-tell′er *n* one who claims ability to foretell events in the lives of others

Fort′ Wayne′ /‑wān′/ *n* city in NE Indiana (178,000)

Fort′ Worth′ *n* city in N Texas (393,-476)

for·ty /fôr′tē/ [OE *fēowertig*] *n* (-ties) 1 four times ten (40; XL); 2 **the forties** *pl* a the numbers from 40 to 49; b the years from 40 to 49 in a century or a lifetime ‖ also *adj & pron*

for′ty-nin′er *n* participant in the California gold rush of 1849

for′ty winks′ *nsg* short nap

fo·rum /fôr′əm/ [L = market place] *n* (-rums, -ra /-rə/) 1 one of the public places of meeting in Rome and other ancient cities where the law courts, public offices, etc. were situated; 2 place of public resort, or court of law; 3 a gathering for public discussion; 4 a medium for public discussion

for·ward /fôr′wərd/ [OE *foreweard*] *adv* 1 onward, in advance, toward the front ‖ *adj* 2 situated near the front; 3 early in season; advanced; precocious; 4 ready, prompt; 5 eager, earnest; 6 bold, impertinent; 7 radical, extreme; 8 of or pert. to the future ‖ *interj* 9 on! ‖ *n* 10 *sports* player in a forward position ‖ *vt* 11 to help or send onward; hasten; facilitate; 12 to transmit, transport to destination; 13 to prepare (a book) for the finisher ‖ **for′ward·er** *n* ‖ SYN *v* conduce, promote, further, facilitate, transmit

for′ward pass′ *n football* pass made toward the opponent's goal

for′wards *adv* forward

fos·sil /fos′əl/ [L *fossilis* dug up] *n* 1 animal, plant, or any trace of one, of prehistoric times, imbedded or preserved in a rock or in a cave; 2 person of fixed or antiquated ideas; 3 anything that holds out against change ‖ also *adj* ‖ **fos′sil·ize** *vt*

fos′sil fu′els *npl* oil, coal, and natural gas

fos·ter /fôs′tər, fos′-/ [OE *fōstor* nourishment] *vt* 1 to nourish, nurse, rear; 2 to support, cherish ‖ *adj* 3 giving, receiving, or sharing nurture or care, though not related by blood, as *foster mother*, *foster brother* ‖ SYN *v* tend, harbor, nurture; rear, support; promote, encourage ‖ ANT *v* discourage, neglect

fought /fôt/ *pt & pp* of **fight**

foul /foul′/ [OE *fūl* rotten] *adj* 1 morally or physically offensive, impure, filthy; 2 hateful, loathsome; 3 obscene or scurrilous (language); 4 unfair, contrary to rules; 5 not clean, clear, or fresh; impeded or choked with foreign matter; 6 a cloudy or stormy (weather); b contrary or adverse (wind); 7 obstructed or impeded by some entanglement or strained relationship, as *to fall foul of the law*; 8 *baseball* not fair; said of a batted ball which goes outside the angle made by the two base lines meeting at home plate ‖ *n* 9 *sports* act or play contrary to rules; 10 *baseball* foul ball ‖ *vt* 11 to make foul; 12 to come into collision with; 13 to entangle; 14 to disgrace; 15 **foul up** *colloq* to bungle ‖ *vi* 16 to become foul; 17 to become entangled; 18 *sports* a to collide; b to hit a foul ball ‖ **foul′ly** *adv* ‖ **foul′ness** *n* ‖ SYN *adj* unclean, scurrilous, obscene, soiled, smeared, odious ‖ ANT *adj* undefiled, pure, clean

fou·lard /fōōlärd′/ [F < Prov *foulat*] *n* 1 light washable satin-finished fabric of silk or silk and cotton; 2 wearing apparel made of this material

fouled′-up′ *adj colloq* badly disorganized

foul′mouthed′ /-mouᵺd′, -tht′/ *adj* using obscene or profane language

foul′ play′ *n* 1 treacherous dealing with another, esp. if involving murder; 2 *sports* unfair play, contrary to the rules

foul′ tip′ *n baseball* pitched ball that is deflected by the batter, giving the catcher an opportunity to catch it and retire the batter if it is the third strike

foul′-up′ *n colloq* breakdown of efficiency due to bungling

found¹ /found′/ 1 *pt & pp* of **find** ‖ *adj* 2 supplied with board and lodging, usu. in addition to money wages

found² [OF *fonder* < L *fundare*] *vt* 1 to lay the basis of, build; 2 to originate, establish, as a city, religion, or institution ‖ **found′ing** *n* ‖ SYN ground, fix, institute, rest, build, establish

found³ [MF *fondre* < L *fundere* to pour] *vt* to form, as a metal, by melting and pouring into a mold; to cast

foun·da′tion [see **found²**] *n* 1 basis or lowest part of a structure; groundwork; 2 principles or origin of anything; 3 a endowment or gift of money to support an institution; b institution so endowed; 4 substance or material on which other parts are overlaid ‖ SYN base, basis, groundwork, platform; fund

found′er¹ [see **found²**] *n* one who founds, establishes, or endows

foun′der² [MF *fondrer* < L *fundus* bottom] *vi* 1 to fill and sink; 2 to fall down, collapse; 3 to go lame ‖ *vt* 4 to cause to founder

found′er³ [see **found³**] *n* person who casts metal, glass, etc.

found′ling [*pp* of *find* + *-ling*] *n* child found after having been deserted by its unknown parents

found′ry [see **found**³] *n* (**-ries**) 1 place where metal casting is carried on; 2 act or process of casting metals

found′ry type′ *n* type cast for setting by hand

fount /fount′/ [MF *font* < L *fons* (*fontis*) spring] 1 spring of water; 2 original source, origin

foun′tain /-tən/ [OF *fontaine* < LL *fontana* < *fons* (*fontis*)] *n* 1 natural spring of water; 2 head or source of a river; 3 artificial jet or spout of water, or the structure surrounding it; 4 reservoir in a mechanism containing a liquid, as ink, which is drawn off as needed; 5 first cause or origin

foun′tain·head′ *n* 1 spring from which a stream flows; 2 first source

foun′tain pen′ *n* pen containing a reservoir of ink

four /fôr′, fōr′/ [OE fēower] *n* 1 sum of three and one (4; IV); 2 set of four persons or things; 3 playing card with four spots ‖ also *adj* & *pron*

four′bag′ger *n* baseball slang home run

four′ bits′ [< *four pieces (of eight)*] *nsg* slang fifty cents ‖ **four′-bit′** *adj*

four′-cy′cle *adj* (internal-combustion engine) having a cycle of four strokes: intake, compression, ignition (power), and exhaust

four′flush′er *n* 1 poker player who holds only four cards of the same suit but plays as if he had a flush; 2 *colloq* any person who cannot substantiate his claims; bluffer

four′fold′ *adj* 1 having four times as much or as many ‖ *adv* 2 four times as much or as many

four′-foot′ed *adj* having four feet

four′-hand′ed *adj* 1 cards for four players; 2 *mus* composed for four hands

Four′ Horse′men (of the A·poc′a·lypse) *npl* personification of the four plagues of mankind: war, famine, pestilence, and death (Rev. 6:2–8)

Four′ Hun′dred or **400** *n* social leaders of a city

four′-in-hand′ *n* 1 kind of necktie tied in a slipknot so that the ends hang down in front; 2 team of four horses under one driver or a coach drawn by it

four′-let′ter word *n* any of a number of monosyllabic words, usu. of four letters and of Old English provenience, referring to sex or the bodily functions and considered obscene

four′pence /-pəns/ *n* English silver coin worth four pennies

four′post′er *n* bed with four corner posts designed to support a canopy

four·ra·gère /fŏŏr′əzher′/ [F] *n* braided cord worn looped over the left shoulder of a military uniform, usu. awarded to an entire unit for bravery

four′score′ *adj* four times twenty; eighty

four′some /-səm/ *n* group containing four persons or things, or two couples or pairs

four′square′ *adj* 1 square-shaped; 2 upright and honest ‖ also *adv*

four′-strip′er /-strip′ər/ *n* navy officer whose insignia of rank is four stripes: captain

four′teen′ /-tēn′/ [OE fēowertēne] *n* sum of four and ten (14; XIV) ‖ also *adj* & *pron*

four′teenth′ *n* 1 the one next in order after the thirteenth; 2 one of fourteen equal parts ‖ also *adj*

fourth /fôrth′, fōrth′/ [OE fēortha] *n* 1 the one next in order after the third; 2 one of four equal parts; 3 *mus* a interval between the tonic and the fourth tone of a diatonic scale; b tone at the end of this interval; subdominant; c two tones, a fourth apart, sounded at once; d interval between any tone of a diatonic scale and the third tone above it ‖ also *adj*

fourth′ di·men′sion *n* dimension in addition to length, breadth, and depth, determined by a fourth rectangular coordinate; often thought of as time, as against the three spatial dimensions

fourth′ es·tate′ [by extension of the three estates of prerevolutionary France, that wielded political power: the clergy, the nobility, the commons] *n* journalism; the press

Fourth′ of Ju·ly′ *n* Independence Day

four′-wheel′er *n* four-wheeled vehicle

fowl /foul′/ [OE fugel bird] *n* (**fowls** or **fowl**) 1 bird; 2 hen or rooster; 3 any of several domesticated or wild gallinaceous birds, as ducks and turkeys; 4 meat of a fowl ‖ *vi* 5 to hunt wildfowl

fowl′ing piece′ *n* light gun for bird shooting and small game

fox /foks′/ [OE] *n* 1 any of several carnivorous animals of the dog family noted for cunning, esp. of the genus *Vulpes*; 2 fur of the fox; 3 sly, crafty person; 4 member of a tribe of Indians formerly living in Wisconsin ‖ *vt* 5 *colloq* to trick, deceive

fox′glove′ *n* any of a genus (*Digitalis*) of plants of the figwort family, having showy spikes of flowers, the leaves of one species (*D. purpurea*) being used in making digitalis

fox′hole′ *n* pit dug to provide cover from enemy fire

fox′hound′ *n* one of several breeds of dogs trained for fox hunting

fox′ ter′ri·er *n* small, intelligent dog, generally white with black patches, used as a pet and as a hunter of small game

fox′ trot′ *n* 1 dance in two-four or four-

four time, including walking steps, the two-step, etc.; **2** transitional pace of a horse between a walk and a trot ‖ **fox'-trot'** *v* (**-trot·ted; -trot·ting**) *vi* **3** to dance the fox trot

fox'y *adj* (**-i·er; -i·est**) **1** pert. to or like a fox; **2** cunning, crafty; **3** reddish-brown; **4** soured; **5** *slang* pretty, sexy ‖ **fox'i·ly** *adv* ‖ **fox'i·ness** *n*

foy·er /foi'ər/ [F = hearth, lobby] *n* lobby or entrance hall

F.P., f.p. foot-pound

fpm feet per minute

FPO 1 Fleet Post Office; **2** Field Post Office

fps 1 foot-pound-second; **2** frames per second

Fr *chem* francium

Fr. 1 father; **2** French; **3** Friar; **4** Friday

Fr., fr. French

fr. 1 fragment; **2** from; **3** franc

Fra /frä'/ [It, short for *frate*] *n* Brother, title used with the name of an Italian monk or brother, as *Fra Angelo*

fra·cas /frāk'əs/ [F < It *fracasso*] *n* uproar, noisy quarrel

frac·tion /frak'shən/ [LL *fractio* (*-onis*) a breaking] *n* **1** fragment; part; **2** *math* a part of a unity, as ¼; **b** a number of equal parts of unity, as ⅝ ‖ SYN division, portion, fragment (see *part*)

frac'tion·al *adj* **1** pert. to or constituting a fraction; **2** very small; **3** of or pert. to a process for separating out the components of a mixture through differences in their respective physical properties, as *fractional distillation* ‖ **frac'tion·al·ly** *adv*

frac'tious [< *fraction* in obsolete meaning of brawling] *adj* **1** unruly; rebellious; **2** peevish, irritable

frac'ture /-chər/ [L *fractura*] *n* **1** act of breaking; **2** break or rupture of a part of the body, esp. a bone; separation; **3** surface shown by breaking, esp. the texture, as of a mineral ‖ *vt* **4** to break or crack ‖ *vi* **5** to be fractured

frae /frā'/ [ON *frā*] *prep Scot* from

frag·ile /fraj'əl/ [L *fragilis* < *frangere* (*frag-*) to break] *adj* **1** delicate, easily broken; **2** flimsy, tenuous ‖ **fra·gil'i·ty** /frəjil'-/ *n* ‖ SYN frail, delicate, frangible (see *brittle*)

frag·ment /frag'mənt/ [L *fragmentum* < *frangere* to break] *n* **1** part broken away; **2** imperfect or unfinished part ‖ *vt & vi* **3** to break into fragments ‖ **frag'men·tar'y** /-ter'-/ *adj* ‖ **frag'men·ta'tion** *n* ‖ SYN portion, remnant, particle, piece (see *part*)

fra·grant /frā'grənt/ [L *fragrans* (*-antis*) < *fragrare* to smell sweet] *adj* having a pleasant odor; sweet-smelling ‖ **fra'grance** *n* ‖ SYN perfumed, aromatic, spicy, sweet-scented, odoriferous, redolent (see *odorous*)

frail /frāl'/ [OF *fraile* < L *fragilis*] *adj* **1** fragile, brittle; **2** weak, physically or morally ‖ **frail'ness** *n* ‖ SYN delicate, fragile, frangible (see *brittle*)

frail'ty *n* (**-ties**) **1** physical, mental, or moral weakness; **2** foible, failing

frame /frām'/ [< OE *framian* to be helpful] *vt* **1** to fit (one thing) into another; put together; **2** to devise, work up into proper form; **3** to adjust, adapt; **4** to surround or enclose with a frame, as a picture; **5** *colloq* to incriminate (an innocent person) with false evidence ‖ *n* **6** something constructed by framing; **7** that on which anything is held or stretched; **8** any contrivance for enclosing, admitting, or supporting something; **9** border for a picture or mirror; **10** shape, form, esp. a human form; **11** temper, state of mind; **12** each individual picture in a roll of movie film; **13** each complete scanning of the television field of vision; **14** *slang* frame-up ‖ **fram'er** *n* ‖ SYN *v* construct, forge, mold, fashion, fabricate

frame' house' *n* house constructed of wood

frame' of ref'er·ence *n* **1** arbitrary system, as of fixed lines, with reference to which the position or motion of an object can be determined; **2** set of accepted values by means of which an individual or group can evaluate its behavior

frame'-up' *n colloq* plot to incriminate a person falsely

frame'work' *n* **1** that which encloses or supports anything; **2** basis for a more complete structure

fram'ing *n* **1** act, style, or manner of putting something together; **2** that which frames; **3** framework

franc /fraŋk'/ [F perh < *Francorum* (rex) (king) of the Franks, inscription on early coin] *n* **1** coin and monetary unit of France; **2** any of the monetary units of various other countries, as Switzerland and Belgium

France /frans', fräns'/ *n* republic in W Europe (50,890,000; 211,208 sq.m.; cap. Paris)

fran·chise /fran'chīz/ [< OF *franc* free] *n* **1** right to vote; **2** particular privilege or right granted by a governmental body to an individual or group; **3** right granted by a company to represent it, sell its products, or use its name; **4** district over which such right extends ‖ *vt* **5** to grant a franchise to; **6** to enfranchise

Fran·cis·can /fransis'kən/ *adj* **1** pert. to the Order of Saint Francis, founded in 1209 by Saint Francis of Assisi ‖ *n* **2** member of this order, dedicated to poverty, celibacy, and obedience and engaged in missionary and charitable works

Fran′cis Fer′di·nand′ /fran′sis/ *n* (1863–1914) heir to the throne of Austria-Hungary, whose assassination at Sarajevo led directly to World War I

fran·ci·um /frans′ē·əm/ [< *France*] *n chem* radioactive metal of the alkali-metal group (**Fr;** at.no. 87)

Fran·co, Fran·cis·co /fraŋsis′kō fraŋk′ō/ *n* (1892–1975) Spanish general, leader of the victorious rebels in the Spanish Civil War 1936–39 and chief of state of Spain since 1939

Franco- [ML *Francus* Frenchman, Frank] *comb form* French, as *Franco-Prussian, Francophobe*

Fran·co·phile /fraŋk′əfīl/ *adj* having a strong love of France and things French ‖ also *n*

fran·gi·ble /fran′jibəl/ [< L *frangere* to break] *adj* breakable ‖ **fran′gi·bil′i·ty** /-bil′-/ *n*

frank¹ /fraŋk/ [LL *francus* free] *adj* 1 open or ingenuous; candid; 2 outspoken ‖ **frank′ly** *adv* ‖ **frank′ness** *n* ‖ **SYN** honest, plain, direct, straightforward (see *open*)

frank² [< *frank¹* in *obs* sense of free of charge] *n* 1 signature that exempts mail from postage; 2 mail privileged to go post-free; 3 privilege of franking mail ‖ *vt* 4 to send post-free through the use of one's signature; 5 to secure free passage of; 6 to exempt

frank³ *n slang* frankfurter

Frank [L *Francus* < OHG *franko* perh name of weapon] *n* 1 member of one of the Germanic tribes that set up the Frankish empire along the Rhine in the 3rd century and later spread into France, Germany, and Italy; 2 in the Levant, an inhabitant of western Europe

Frank·en·stein /fraŋk′ənstīn′/ *n* 1 in Mary Shelley's *Frankenstein*, a man who made a being that proved a torment to its maker; 2 one destroyed by his own creations; 3 the destroying being

Frank·fort /fraŋk′fərt/ *n* capital of Kentucky (19,000)

Frank·furt /fraŋk′fərt/ *n* city in W Germany (700,000)

frank·furt·er /< *Frankfurt*, Germany] *n* cooked and smoked sausage, wiener

frank·in·cense /fraŋk′insens′/ [< *frank¹* in *obs* sense of luxuriant + *incense*] *n* fragrant resin from several Old World trees of the balsam family, burned as incense

Frank′ish *adj* 1 of or pert. to the Franks ‖ *n* 2 language of the Franks

Frank·lin, Ben·ja·min /bən′jəmin fraŋk′lin/ *n* (1706–90) American statesman, diplomat, author, inventor, scientist; one of the founding fathers of the country

fran·tic /frant′ik/ [OF *frenetique* < Gk *phrenitikos* delirious] *adj* violently distracted; frenzied; wild ‖ **fran′ti·cal·ly** or **fran′tic·ly** *adv* ‖ **SYN** furious, raving, wild, insane, frenzied, phrenetic

frappe /frap′/ [< *frappé*] *n* thick milk-shake

frap·pé /frapā′/ [F, *pp* of *frapper* to strike, chill] *adj* 1 chilled, as beverages; 2 frozen or partly frozen, as fruit juice ‖ *n* 3 dessert consisting of sweetened fruit juice frozen to the consistency of mush

frat /frat′/ *n slang* college fraternity

fra·ter·nal /frətur′nəl/ [< L *frater* brother] *adj* 1 to, becoming, or like brothers; 2 of or pert. to a fraternity

fra·ter′nal twins/ *npl* twins from two ova, not necessarily resembling each other

fra·ter′ni·ty *n* (-ties) 1 brotherly relationship; 2 body of men banded together by common interests, as men of the same profession or class; 3 secret society, as of college men; 4 persons of the same character or class

frat·er·nize /frat′ərnīz′/ *vi* 1 to associate as brothers or members of the same fraternity; 2 to be on very friendly terms; 3 to meet on a plane of equality ‖ **frat′er·ni·za′tion** *n* ‖ **frat′er·niz′er** *n*

frat′ri·cide /-trisīd′/ [< L *frater* brother + *-cide*] *n* 1 killing of a brother or sister; 2 one who commits fratricide

Frau /frou′/ [G] *n* (**Frau′en** /-ən/) 1 married woman, wife; 2 Mrs.

fraud /frôd′/ [L *fraus* (*fraudis*)] *n* 1 deception or trickery intended to defraud; 2 one who or that which is not what is purported ‖ **SYN** deception, duplicity, imposition, sham, cheat

fraud·u·lent /frôj′ələnt/ *adj* 1 guilty of fraud; 2 characterized by or obtained by fraud ‖ **fraud′u·lent·ly** *adv* ‖ **fraud′u·lence** *n*

fraught /frôt′/ [*pp* of *obs* verb *fraught* to load with cargo] *adj* full of, accompanied by, as a *situation fraught with danger*

Fräu·lein /froi′līn/ [G] *n* (*pl* **Fräulein**) 1 unmarried woman; young lady; 2 Miss

Fraun′ho·fer lines′ /froun′hō′fər/ [Joseph von *Fraunhofer* (1787–1826) G optician] *npl* dark lines in the solar spectrum

fray¹ /frā′/ [< *affray*] *n* riot, brawl, quarrel

fray² [F *frayer* < L *fricare* to rub] *vt* 1 to chafe or wear away ‖ *vi* 2 to become frayed, as fabrics

fraz·zle /fraz′əl/ [< *fray²*] *vt* 1 to fray; 2 to exhaust the nerves of ‖ *vi* 3 to become frazzled ‖ *n* 4 state of being frazzled

freak /frēk′/ [?] *n* 1 capricious change of mind; whim; 2 any abnormal person, animal, plant, or occurrence

freak′ish *adj* 1 full of whims or pranks;

2 odd; abnormal || **freak′ish·ly** *adv* || SYN crotchety, whimsical, capricious (see *fickle*)

freck·le /frek′əl/ [< ON *frecknur*] *n* 1 brownish spot or fleck on the skin || *vt* 2 to mark (the skin) with freckles || *vi* 3 to become freckled || **freck′led** /-əld/ *adj*

Fred·er·ick the Great′ /fred′(ə)rik/ *n* (1712–86) king of Prussia 1740–86

Fred·er·ic·ton /fred′əriktən/ *n* capital of New Brunswick (20,000)

free /frē′/ [OE frēo] *adj* (fre′er; fre′est) 1 at liberty, not restrained or fettered; 2 not attached, as *the free end of a rope;* 3 independent; 4 uninfluenced, as *a free choice;* 5 (literary style or versification) not according to the conventional rules; 6 (translation) not following the original text literally; 7 a spirited, open (conduct); b unceremonious, familiar; c reckless, licentious; 8 lavish, generous, as *free with praise;* 9 abundant, as *a free flow of blood;* 10 voluntary, as *a free gift;* 11 permitted, as *you are free to go;* 12 accessible to all comers, as *a free port;* 13 open, clear of obstructions, as *free access;* 14 devoid, as *free of impurities;* 15 without charge; 16 having individual political or civil liberty; 17 designating a government not subject to some other government; 18 determined or acting through the exercise of one's individual volition, as *free will, a free agent;* 19 *chem* uncombined (element); 20 **free and clear** *law* without encumbrances; 21 **free and easy** informal, casual; 22 **free from** or **of** without || *v* (freed) *vt* 23 to set free; 24 to rid or exempt; clear || *adv* 25 without charge; 26 without restraint; 27 **make free with** to use freely || **free′ly** *adv* || **free′ness** *n* || SYN *adj* bounteous, frank, familiar, unconfined, unreserved, careless, unconcerned; *v* (see *liberate*)

free′board′ *n* that part of the side of a ship between the upper edge or gunwale and the water line

free′boot′er [D *vrijbuiter*] *n* pirate, buccaneer || **free′boot′** *vi*

freed′man /-mən/ *n* (-men /-mən/) *n* man freed from slavery

free′dom /-dəm/ [OE *frēodōm*] *n* 1 state of being free; 2 ease in performance; 3 particular privilege; 4 absence of conventionality; 5 undue familiarity; 6 power to act freely; 7 immunity; 8 unrestricted use; run || SYN unrestraint, franchise, exemption (see *liberty*)

free′ en′ter·prise′ *n* doctrine that business should be conducted by private individuals subject to free competition and the workings of supply and demand, with a minimum of government regulation

free′ fall′ *n* movement of a body subject only to gravity

free′-for-all′ *n* dispute, fight, or brawl joined in by all comers

free′ hand′ *n* freedom of action

free′-hand *adj* drawn by the hand without artificial aid

free′-hand′ed *adj* open-handed, generous

free′-heart′ed *adj* frank; generous; spontaneous

free′hold *n* 1 holding of land for life, or so that it is given to one's heirs; 2 land so held; also, land held without conditions || **free′hold′er** *n*

free′ lance′ *n* one who produces literary or artistic work without exclusive contractual commitments || **free′-lance′** *adj, adv, & vi*

free′-liv′ing *adj* unrestrained in the indulgence of appetite

free′ love′ *n* cohabitation without marriage or obligation

free′man /-mən/ *n* (-men /-mən/) 1 one who is free; 2 citizen

Free′ma′son *n* member of a secret society (*Free and Accepted Masons*) professing brotherly love, charity, and mutual aid

free′ma′son·ry *n* 1 natural sympathy; common interest; fraternity; 2 **Freemasonry** principles, institutions, rites, etc., of the Freemasons

free′ on board′ *adj* (manufactured product) loaded on railroad cars or trucks but with no further transportation, at a specified price || also *adv*

free′ port′ *n* 1 port open to all traders on the same terms; 2 port where merchandise may be stored free of duty, pending reexport or sale within the country

free′ rad′i·cal *n* atom or compound with at least one unpaired electron

Free′-Soil′ *adj* U.S. *hist* (political party) formed in Boston in 1848 to prevent the extension of slavery to the Territories || **Free′-Soil′er** *n*

free′-spo′ken *adj* frank; outspoken || **free′spo′ken-ness** *n*

free′stone′ *n* 1 a sandstone suitable for working or cutting without splitting; 2 peach in which the flesh, when ripe, does not stick to the stone

free′think′er *n* one who develops his opinions independently, esp. in regard to religious matters || **free′think′ing** *adj & n*

free′ thought′ *n* opinion that is independent of authority or established dogma, esp. in regard to religious matters

free′ trade′ *n* commerce with other countries free of tariffs, customs duties, or subsidies

free′ trad′er *n* believer in free trade

free′ verse′ *n* verse that does not follow a fixed meter

free′way′ *n* limited-access express highway

free′wheel′ing *n* 1 device that permits the drive shaft of a motor vehicle to become disengaged and rotate freely when its speed is greater than that of the engine shaft; **2** independent and irresponsible action or talk ‖ also *adj*

free′ will′ *n* **1** voluntary or unhampered choice or decision; **2** man's assumed power as a moral being to choose between good and evil ‖ **free′-will′** *adj*

freeze /frēz/ [OE *frēosan*] *v* (**froze**; **fro·zen**) *vt* **1** a to harden with cold; convert into ice; **b** to change from a liquid to a solid; **2** to kill by cold; **3** to transfix with fright; **4** to make rigid or inflexible; **5** to cause (assets, credit) to lose liquidity; **6** to fix (wages or prices) at the prevailing level; **7** to keep in an unchanging form; **8** to make adhere by or as by the action of cold; **9** to act toward in an icy or formal manner; **10** to anesthetize by freezing; **11** to photograph (an action) as a still ‖ *vi* **12** to be frozen; **13** to be very cold; **14** to adhere through cold; **15** to halt and remain motionless; **16** to become immobilized, as by fear or sudden emergency ‖ *n* **17** act or instance of freezing; **18** state of being frozen; **19** spell of weather below the freezing point; **20** legislative action to fix or control wages or prices

freeze′-dry′ *v* (**-dried**) *vt* to dry (blood plasma, foodstuffs, antibiotics) by freezing rapidly and then subliming the ice or other frozen solvent in a high vacuum at a low temperature ‖ **freeze′-dry′ing** *n*

freez′er *n* **1** compartment or room kept at −10°F or lower for a quick-freezing foods; **b** keeping foods frozen; **2** machine that freezes cream into ice cream or sherbet

freeze′-frame′ *n* frame of movie or tape that is held or repeated for a few seconds or longer

freez′ing point′ *n* temperature at which a liquid freezes or solidifies; of water, 32°F, 0°C

freight /frāt/ [MD *vrecht* < *vracht* cargo] *n* **1** goods with which a vessel, car, or other carrier is loaded; cargo; **2** method of transporting goods by common carriers; **3** sum charged for hauling goods; **4** *colloq* cost of anything ‖ *vt* **5** to load with goods for hauling; **6** to send (goods) by freight ‖ SYN *n* (see *cargo*)

freight′er *n* **1** one who receives and forwards freight; shipper; **2** vessel designed for carrying freight

French /french/ [AS *frencisc* Frankish] *adj* **1** pert. to France, its people, or its language ‖ *n* **2** language of France; **3 the French** *pl* the people of France

French′ Ca·na′di·an *n* French-speaking inhabitant of Quebec and adjoining

areas of Canada ‖ **French-Canadian** *adj*

French′ chalk′ *n* soft form of soapstone or steatite, used for ruling fabrics or removing grease spots

French′ cuff′ *n* doubled shirt cuff

French′ door′ *n* door or pair of doors with glass panes throughout its length

French′ dress′ing *n* salad dressing made with oil, vinegar, and seasoning

French′ fried′ po·ta′toes or **French′ fries′** *npl* deep-fried strips of potatoes

French′ Gui·an′a *n* former colony and present overseas department of France in NE coast of South America (30,000; 35,010 sq.m.; cap. Cayenne)

French′ horn′ *n* orchestral and band instrument of the brass group, consisting of a long coiled tube and a funnel-like mouthpiece

French′i·fy′ *v* (**-fied**) *vt* to make French in manners, characteristics, or customs ‖ **French′i·fi·ca′tion** *n*

French′ leave′ *n* hasty or secret departure

French′man /-mən/ *n* (**-men** /-mən/) native or inhabitant of France ‖ **French′wom′an** /-wŏŏm′ən/ *nfem* (**-wom′en** /-wim′ən/)

French′ pas′try *n* fancy filled pastry

French′ tel′e·phone *n* handset

French′ toast′ *n* slices of bread dipped in egg and milk, sautéed, and served usu. with cinnamon and syrup

French′ West′ In′dies *npl* French islands in the West Indies in the Caribbean, including the departments of Guadaloupe and Martinique

French′ win′dow *n* pair of casements extending to the floor and usu. opening like a French door

fre·net·ic /frənet′ik/ [see **frantic**] *adj* frenzied, frantic

fren·zy /fren′zē/ [OF *frenesie* < LL *phrenesis* madness] *n* (**-zies**) **1** violent agitation; temporary madness; fury ‖ *v* (**-zied**) *vt* **2** to throw into a frenzy ‖ **fren′zied** *adj* ‖ SYN *n* delirium, raving, wildness (see *insanity*)

Fre·on /frē′on/ [trademark] *n* any of a class of nonflammable hydrocarbons, containing fluorine, used as refrigerants

freq. frequent(ly)

fre·quen·cy /frēk′wənsē/ [see **frequent**] *n* (**-cies**) **1** rate of recurrence, as *the frequency of his heart attacks has greatly diminished;* **2** rate of recurrence with respect to the total number of occurrences; **3** also **fre′quence** rapid rate of recurrence, as *the frequency of crimes in that city;* **4** *phys* number of cycles per unit of time of a wave or other oscillation; **5** *statistics* a number of occurrences of a given type of event; **b** number of members of a population in a specified class

fre′quen·cy mod′u·la′tion *n* **1** *electron*

modulation of a carrier wave by varying its frequency; **2** *rad* broadcasting by means of such a carrier wave

fre·quent /frĕk'wənt/ [L *frequens* (-*entis*) crowded] *adj* **1** occurring or happening often; **2** habitual; persistent || /frĕkwĕnt', frĕk'wənt/ *vt* **3** to visit often, be often in || **fre'quent·ly** *adv* || **fre·quent'er** *n*

fre·quen'ta·tive *gram adj* **1** denoting persistent repetition of an action || *n* **2** frequentative verb

fres·co /frĕs'kō/ [It < OHG *frisc*] *n* (-**coes,** -**cos**) **1** method of wall painting in water colors on fresh plaster; **2** picture so painted || *vt* **3** to paint in fresco

fresh /frĕsh'/ [OE *fersc*] *adj* **1** new; recent; unfaded; **2** not yet used or sold; **3** not forgotten; **4** not wearied; **5** cool, refreshing; **6** not salt, as water; **7** inexperienced; **8** just arrived, as *fresh from the city*; **9** not preserved, as by canning, freezing, or storage; **10** not stale, decayed, or sour; **11** brisk (wind); **12** *slang* pert, forward || **fresh'ly** *adv* || **fresh'ness** *n* || SYN youthful, refreshing, cool, freshened, unused, strong, vigorous, sound, good (see *modern*) || ANT stale, old, withered, hackneyed, trite

fresh' breeze' *n* wind 19 to 24 miles per hour

fresh'en *vt* **1** to make like new; to revive || *vi* **2** to become strong, as a breeze; **3** to brighten; **4 freshen up** to make oneself fresh and spruce || **fresh'en·er** *n*

fresh'et /-ĭt/ [perh OF *freschet* fresh] *n* flood caused by melting snow or heavy rain

fresh' gale' *n* wind 39 to 46 miles per hour

fresh'man /-mən/ *n* (-**men** /-mən/) *n* **1** college or high-school student in his first year; **2** novice

fresh'-wa·ter *adj* **1** pert. to, living in, found in, or formed in fresh water; **2** accustomed to river navigation only; unskilled in seamanship; **3** provincial

fret' /frĕt'/ [OE *fretan* to eat] *v* (**fret·ted; fret·ting**) *vt* **1** to wear away by rubbing; **2** to vex, irritate || *vi* **3** to be worn away by friction or corrosion; **4** to be agitated or irritated; **5** to utter peevish complaints || *n* **6** irritation || SYN *v* harass, annoy, irritate, gall, chafe, vex

fret² [prob OF *frete* trelliswork] *n* **1** headdress of small bands or fillets crossing or meeting each other at right angles; **2** perforated or laced ornamental work || *v* (**fret·ted; fret·ting**) *vt* **3** to adorn with fretwork || **fret'ted** *adj*

fret³ [perh OF *frete* ferrule] *n* small ridge or bar on the finger board of certain stringed instruments

fret'ful [< *fret¹*] *adj* peevish, irritable || **fret'ful·ly** *adv* || **fret'ful·ness** *n* || SYN captious, testy, agitated, querulous, peevish (see *petulant*) || ANT serene, poised, patient, calm

fret'saw' *n* long, thin, narrow saw with fine teeth, used in cutting ornamental woodwork

fret'work' *n* carved, raised, or open ornamental work

Freud, Sig·mund /sig'mənd froid'/ *n* (1856–1939) Austrian neurologist, founder of psychoanalysis || **Freud'·i·an** *adj* & *n* || **Freud'i·an·ism** *n*

Frey·a /frā'ə/ [ON *Freyja*] *n Norse myth.* goddess of love and beauty

fri·a·ble /frī'əbel/ [< L *friare* to crumble] *adj* readily crumbled or reduced to powder

Fri. Friday

fri·ar /frī'ər/ [< OF *frere* < L *frater* brother] *n R C Ch* brother or member of certain religious orders, esp. of a mendicant order

fri'ar·y *n* (-**ies**) monastery of friars

fric·as·see /frik'əsē'/ [F] *n* **1** dish of chicken or other meat cut into small pieces, stewed or fried, and served with gravy or sauce || *vt* **2** to prepare as a fricassee

fric·a·tive /frik'ətiv/ [< L *fricare* to rub] *adj* **1** (consonant) produced by the forced passage of the breath through a narrow opening || *n* **2** fricative consonant, as *f, v, th,* or *z*

fric·tion /frik'shən/ [see *fricative*] *n* **1** act of rubbing; **2** irritation or disagreement caused by difference of opinion; **3** *mech* resistance to relative motion of two or more surfaces in contact with each other || **fric'tion·al** *adj*

fric'tion clutch' *n* clutch operated by friction between the parts

fric'tion tape' *n* black adhesive tape used esp. for insulating electric wires

Fri·day /frī'dē, -dā/ [OE *frīgedæg* Frigg's day] *n* sixth day of the week, following Thursday || **Fri'days** *adv*

fried /frīd'/ *adj slang* drunk

friend /frĕnd'/ [OE *frēond*] *n* **1** one devoted to another by affection, regard, or esteem; intimate acquaintance; **2** supporter or favorer of a cause; **3** ally; **4 Friend** member of the religious Society of Friends; Quaker || **friend'less** *adj* || SYN adherent, ally, comrade, companion

friend'ly *adj* (-**li·er; -li·est**) **1** pert. to a friend; **2** having the qualities of a friend; **3** ready to become acquainted; **4** not hostile; amicable, genial, affable; **5** favorable (breeze) || **friend'li·ness** *n* || SYN sociable, companionable, cordial, hearty, genial

friend'ship *n* **1** state of being friends; **2** mutual attachment; **3** good will

frieze¹ /frēz'/ [OF *frise* < L *Phrygium*

Phrygian] *n* any ornamental or sculptured band around a wall

frieze² [< MF *friser* to curl] *n* coarse woolen cloth with a shaggy nap on one side

frig·ate /frig′it/ [F *frégate* < It *fregata*] *n* **1** fast three-masted war vessel of the 18th and early 19th centuries; **2** U.S. warship intermediate between a cruiser and a destroyer

frig′ate bird′ *n* either of two large, rapacious, strong-winged, fish-eating sea birds (genus *Fregata*)

Frigg /frig′/ or **Frig′ga** *n* Norse myth. queen of the gods, wife of Odin

fright /frīt′/ [OE *fryhto*] *n* **1** sudden and extreme fear; alarm; **2** person whose dress or appearance is ridiculous || SYN dread, terror, dismay, panic (see *horror*)

fright′en *vt* **1** to terrify; alarm; terrorize; **2** frighten off or away to drive off by scaring

fright′ful /-fəl/ *adj* **1** terrifying; **2** shocking; **3** unpleasant; **4** extreme || **fright′ful·ly** *adv* || **fright′ful·ness** *n* || SYN fearful, dire, direful, terrific, terrifying, awful

frig·id /frij′id/ [L *frigidus*] *adj* **1** extremely cold; wintry; **2** cold in temperament; **3** stiff, formal, dull; **4** (woman) indifferent to or unresponsive during sexual intercourse || **frig′id·ly** *adv* || **frig′id·ness** or **fri·gid′i·ty** *n*

Frig′id Zone′ *n* either of the two areas about the earth's poles, extending to the edges of the temperate zones

fri·jol /frēhōl′/ [Sp] *n* (-jo·les /-hōl′ās/) seed of the kidney bean used extensively as food in Mexico and in SW United States

frill /fril′/ [perh < Flem *frull*] *n* **1** ruffle; **2** affectation of manner; ornamentation of dress; **3** superfluous detail intended to be ornamental || **frill′y** *adj* (-i·er; -i·est)

fringe /frinj′/ [MF *frenge* < L *fimbria* border] *n* **1** ornamental border of hanging threads or cords; **2** anything resembling a fringe; border; **3** optics light or dark band of light produced by interference or diffraction; **4** something that is secondary or marginal || *vt* **5** to border with or as with a fringe

fringe′ ben′e·fit *n* benefit received by an employee over and above his basic pay

frip·per·y /frip′ərē/ [OF *freperie* < *frepe* rag] *n* (-ies) **1** showy, gaudy finery; **2** ostentatious display

Fris·bee /friz′bē/ [trademark] *n* concave plastic disk used in a catching game

fri·sé /frizā′/ [F = curly] *n* carpeting or upholstery fabric with the pile in uncut loops

fri·seur /frēzur′/ [F] *n* hairdresser

Fri·sian /frizh′ən/ [< L *Frisius*] *n* **1** native or inhabitant of The Netherlands province of Friesland and of the Frisian Islands off the coast of The Netherlands and W Germany; **2** language of the Frisians || also *adj*

frisk /frisk′/ [OF *frisque* lively] *vi* **1** to gambol or dance in frolic || *vt* **2** to search (a person) for concealed articles, esp. weapons; **3** to rob in this manner || *n* **4** dance or frolic || **frisk′er** *n*

frisk′y *adj* (-i·er; -i·est) lively, sprightly, frolicsome || **frisk′i·ly** *adv* || **frisk′i·ness** *n*

frit·ter¹ /frit′ər/ [OF *friture* < L *frigere* (*frictus*) to fry] *n* small cake made of batter often with meat or fruit in it and deep-fried

frit′ter² [perh < OF *freture* < L *fractura* a breaking] *vt* **fritter away** to waste by degrees

fritz /frits′/ [?] *n* **on the fritz** *slang* out of order

friv·o·lous /friv′ələs/ [L *frivolus*] *adj* trifling, trivial; silly, not serious || **friv′o·lous·ly** *adv* || **fri·vol·i·ty** /frivôl′ itē/ *n* (-ties)

friz or **frizz** /friz′/ [F *friser*] *v* (**frizzed; friz·zing**) *vt* & *vi* **1** to form into small tight curls || *n* (**friz·zes**) **2** that which is frizzed, as hair || **friz′zy** *adj* (-zi·er; -zi·est)

friz′zle [< *fry²* + *sizzle*] *vt* **1** to fry until crisp || *vi* **2** to splutter in cooking

fro /frō′/ [ON *frā* from] *adv* **to and fro** back and forth

frock /frok′/ [OF *froc* perh < OHG *hroch* coat] *n* **1** monk's habit; **2** dress; **3** coarse overgarment; **4** frock coat || *vt* **5** to invest with the office of monk or priest

frock′ coat′ *n* close-fitting double-breasted coat for men, with wide skirts extending to the knees

frog¹ /frog′, frôg′/ [OE *frogga*] *n* **1** small tailless four-legged amphibian (order Anura) with smooth skin, webbed feet, and hind legs adapted for leaping; **2** mucus on the vocal chords, causing hoarseness

frog² [?] *n* plate used to guide the wheels of a railroad car where one track crosses another or at a switch

frog³ [perh < Port *froco* < L *floccus* flock of wool] *n* **1** spindle-shaped button that fits into a loop, used as a fastening for garments; **2** attachment at the belt for supporting a scabbard

frog′gy *adj* (-gi·er; -gi·est) **1** froglike; **2** full of frogs

frog′ kick′ *n* swimming kick in which the legs are bent at the knees, extended outward, and then brought together

frog′man′ /-man′, -mən/ *n* (-men /-men′, -mən/) swimmer equipped to stay under water for long periods, for salvage, reconnaisance, or demolition

frol·ic /frol'ik/ [D *vrolijk* < MD *vrō* glad] *n* 1 scene of merrymaking or gaiety; 2 sportive outburst; wild prank || *v* (-**icked; -ick·ing**) *vi* 3 to play pranks; gambol; make merry || **frol'ick·er** *n* || **frol'ic·some** *adj*

from /frum', frəm/ [OE < *fram* forth from] *prep* meaning primarily out, out of, forth, away; used with words indicating: 1 source or starting point in space or time, as *a letter from home, from two to ten* P.M.; 2 the first of two named limits, as *from eight to a dozen persons;* 3 starting point in measuring or stating distance, as *ten feet from the end;* 4 person that is deprived, or thing out of which something is taken, as *candy from a child, an apple from the barrel;* 5 reason or cause, as *weak from hunger;* 6 a thing distinguished or different, as *to tell real silk from imitation*

frond /frond'/ [L *frons (frondis)*] *n* leaf of a fern or certain palms

front /frunt'/ [L *frons (frontis)* forehead] *n* 1 the forehead or the entire face; 2 fore or foremost part of anything; 3 position directly before something; van; 4 expression of countenance; 5 shirt bosom; 6 land facing on the shore of a lake, bay, etc. 7 region where fighting is in progress during a war; 8 political party or movement uniting several groups; 9 person serving to give prestige to a group or society; 10 respectable or innocuous person or thing serving to mask illegal or shady persons or dealings; 11 external appearance of wealth or position; 12 *meteor.* advancing line of changing weather; 13 that part of a theater beyond the footlights when standing on the stage facing the audience; 14 **in front of** before; 15 **out front, a** outside the entrance; **b** in the van; **c** *theat* in the audience || *adj* 16 situated at the front; || *vt* 17 to stand or be situated opposite to; 18 to confront, meet; 19 to furnish with a front || *vi* 20 to have the front turned in a particular direction; 21 to serve as a front for nefarious persons or activities || *interj* 22 come forward! (serving to call a bellboy to attend a hotel guest)

front'age /-ij/ *n* 1 fore part of a building; 2 extent of a building or of land along a street or road; 3 space lying between a building and a roadway; 4 direction toward which a building faces

fron'tal *adj* 1 of or at the front; 2 pert. to the forehead; 3 pert. to the division between unlike air masses || **fron'tal·ly** *adv*

fron'tal bone' *n* one of a pair of membrane bones forming the forehead

fron'tal lobe' *n* anterior part of each cerebral hemisphere

front' bench' *n Brit* in the House of Commons, either of two seats near the Speaker, one to be occupied by a minister and the other by a leader of the opposition || **front' bench'er** *n*

front' foot' *n* foot measured along the front of a property

fron·tier /fruntir'/ [OF *frontiere* < LL *frontaria*] *n* 1 boundary of a country; 2 most remote settled part of a country, facing an unexplored region; 3 new or not fully explored realm of thought, research, etc.

fron·tiers·man /fruntirz'mən/ *n* (-**men** /-mən/) inhabitant of a newly settled region; pioneer

fron·tis·piece /frunt'ispēs'/ [< LL *frontispicium* countenance, influenced by Eng *piece*] 1 illustration facing the front page or title page of a book; 2 main face of a building; 3 ornamental pediment

front' mat'ter *n* everything preceding the main text in a book

front' of'fice *n* executive office of a company

front'-page' *adj* (news) of enough consequence to be put on the front page of a newspaper

frosh /frosh'/ [G *Frosch* frog; first-year student] *n* (*pl* **frosh**) freshman

frost /frôst', frost'/ [OE] *n* 1 formation of ice; 2 frozen water vapor; 3 temperature which causes freezing; 4 chilliness of manner || *vt* 5 to cover with, or as with, frost; 6 to damage by frost; 7 to ice (a cake) || *vi* 8 to freeze; 9 to become frosted

frost'bite' *n* 1 partially frozen condition of a part of the body || *v* (-**bit; -bit·ten**) *vt* 2 to injure with extreme cold

frost'ed *adj* 1 covered with frost; 2 injured by severe cold; 3 covered with icing; 4 having a dull or non-transparent finish, as glass || *n* 5 milk shake made with ice cream beaten in

frost'ing *n* 1 icing; 2 finish without luster for glass or metal

frost' line' *n* maximum depth to which soil freezes in winter

frost'y *adj* (-**i·er; -i·est**) 1 producing or accompanied by frost; 2 glistening with frost; 3 resembling frost, hoary; 4 cold or distant in manner || **frost'i·ly** *adv* || **frost'i·ness** *n*

froth /frôth', froth'/ [ON *frotha*] *n* 1 foam; 2 something superficial or shallow || *vt* 3 to cause to foam; 4 to give vent to, as foam; 5 to cover with foam || *vi* 6 to foam || **froth'y** *adj* (-**i·er; -i·est**)

fro·ward /frō'wərd/ [*fro* from + -*ward*] *adj* willful, disobedient, perverse || **fro'ward·ly** *adv* || **fro'ward·ness** *n* || SYN intractable, ungovernable, refractory, untoward

frown /froun'/ [OF *froignier*] *vi* 1 to

contract the brows; scowl; **2 frown on** or **upon** to disapprove ‖ *n* **3** scowl, stern look; **4** wrinkling of the brow expressive of displeasure

frowz·y or **frows·y** /frouz′ē/ [?] *adj* (**-i·er; -i·est**) **1** slovenly, untidy; **2** ill-smelling, musty; **3** unkempt

froze /frōz′/ *pt* of freeze

fro·zen /frōz′ən/ **1** *pp* of freeze ‖ *adj* **2** congealed by cold; **3** extremely cold; **4** injured or killed by frost; **5** not convertible temporarily into cash; **6** cold in manner; **7** fixed at the prevailing rates, as wages or prices

FRS Federal Reserve System

fruc·ti·fy /fruk′tifī′/ [OF *fructifier*] *v* (**-fied**) *vt* **1** to make productive; fertilize ‖ *vi* **2** to produce fruit ‖ **fruc′·ti·fi·ca′tion** *n*

fruc′tose /-tōs/ [< L *fructus* fruit] *n* a crystalline sugar —C₆H₁₂O₆— accompanying glucose in the juices of many fruits and in honey

fru·gal /frōōg′əl/ [L *frugalis*] **1** thrifty, economical; **2** used or supplied sparingly ‖ **fru′gal·ly** *adv* ‖ **fru′gal·ness** or **fru·gal′i·ty** /-gal′-/ *n* ‖ SYN prudent, sparing, saving, provident ‖ ANT lavish, spendthrift, wasteful, profuse

fruit /frōōt′/ [OF < L *fructus*] *n* **1** seed and all its enveloping parts; **2** edible part of a plant developed from a flower; **3** any vegetable product that is used for food, esp. that eaten raw as a dessert or cooked with sugar; **4** result or outcome ‖ *vi* **5** to bear fruit

fruit′ fly′ *n* any of various small two-winged insects of the family Trypetidae, whose larvae feed on fruit

fruit′ful /-fəl/ *adj* **1** yielding fruit; **2** productive, fertile ‖ **fruit′ful·ly** *adv* ‖ **fruit′ful·ness** *n*

fru·i·tion /frōō·ish′ən/ *n* **1** bearing of fruit; **2** realization, as of hopes or plans

fruit′less *adj* **1** bearing or having no fruit; **2** barren, unproductive; **3** vain, unprofitable ‖ **fruit′less·ly** *adv* ‖ SYN useless, idle, ineffectual, barren, sterile, vain

fruit′ sug′ar *n* fructose

fruit′y *adj* (**-i·er; -i·est**) **1** resembling fruit in flavor or odor; **2** rich in flavor, as wine; **3** cloyingly sweet

frump /frump/ [?] *n* dowdy, drab woman ‖ **frump′ish** or **frump′y** *adj*

frus·trate /frus′trāt/ [< L *frustrā* in vain] *vt* to defeat or disappoint, thwart or oppose, bring to nothing ‖ **frus′trat·ed** *adj* ‖ **frus·tra′tion** *n* ‖ SYN baffle, circumvent, thwart, defeat, balk

frus·tum /frus′təm/ [L = piece broken off] *n* (**-tums, -ta** /-tə/) **1** remainder of a cone or pyramid when the top is cut off by a plane parallel to the base; **2** the part of a solid included between two planes either parallel or inclined to each other

fry¹ /frī′/ [< ON *frīo* seed] *n* (*pl* **fry**) **1** young fish; **2** swarm of young fish or the like spawned or hatched in great numbers; **3** number of very small persons or objects

fry² [OF *frire* < L *frigere*] *v* (**fried**) *vt* **1** to cook with fat or oil in a pan or on a griddle ‖ *vi* **2** to be fried ‖ *n* (**fries**) **3** dish of something fried

fry′er *n* something intended for frying, as a young chicken

fry′ing pan′ *n* shallow pan with a long handle, used for frying

f.s. foot-second

f′ stop′ *n photog* lens aperture designated by an f number

ft. **1** foot, feet; **2** fort, fortification

FTC Federal Trade Commission

ft-lb foot-pound

ft-pdl foot-poundal

fuch·sia /fyōō′shə/ [L. *Fuchs* (1501–66) G botanist] *n* any of a genus (*Fuchsia*) of plants of the evening primrose family, with drooping, usu. red or pink flowers

fud·dle /fud′əl/ [?] *vt* **1** to intoxicate; **2** to confuse ‖ *n* **3** confused state

fud·dy-dud·dy /fud′ē-dud′ē/ [?] *n* (**-dies**) person who is stuffy, old-fashioned, conservative, and fussy ‖ also *adj*

fudge /fuj′/ [?] *n* **1** candy consisting of a stiff, sugary mixture flavored with chocolate, maple, or the like ‖ *interj* **2** nonsense! ‖ *vt* **3** to evade ‖ *vi* **4** to cheat; **5** to hedge

fu·el /fyōō′əl/ [OF *fouaille* < LL *focalia* brushwood] *n* **1** material for supplying a fire; **2** anything that serves to inflame or sustain passion or excitement ‖ *v* (**-eled** or **-elled; -el·ing** or **-el·ling**) *vt* **3** to furnish with fuel ‖ *vi* **4** to take in fuel

fu′el cell′ *n* device that produces a steady flow of electric current by the oxidation of hydrogen

fu·gal /fyōōg′əl/ [see *fugue*] *adj* pert. to or like a fugue

-fuge /-fyōōj′/ [< L *fuga* flight] *n suf* that drives away, as *vermifuge*

fu·gi·tive /fyōō′jitiv/ [< L *fugere* (-*itus*) to flee] *adj* **1** running away, as from pursuit; **2** fleeting ‖ *n* **3** one who flees from prosecution or prison ‖ SYN *adj* escaping, fleeing, evanescent, transitory

fugue /fyōōg/ [F < It *fuga* flight] *n mus* composition in which a definite number of parts or voices successively repeat the theme

füh·rer or **fueh·rer** /fyōōr′ər/ [G = leader] **1** der **Führer** title of Adolf Hitler; **2** any authoritarian leader

Fu·ji /fōō′jē/ or **Fu′ji·ya′ma** /-yäm′ə/ *n* extinct volcano on Honshu island, highest mountain in Japan (12,390 ft.)

-ful /-fəl/ [< *full*] *adj suf* **1** full of, abounding in, containing, characterized by, as *spiteful, graceful;* **2** having the qualities of, as *masterful;* **3** extremely, as *direful;* **4** able to, likely to, tending to, as *forgetful* ‖ /-fōŏl´/ *n suf* **5** amount that would fill, as *handful, cupful*

ful·crum /ful´krəm, fōōl´-/ [L = bedpost, prop] *n* (-**crums,** -**cra** /-krə/) **1** support on which a lever turns; **2** means by which influence is exerted

ful·fill or **ful·fil** /fōōlfil´/ [OE *fullfyllan*] *v* (-**filled;** -**fil·ling**) *vt* **1** to complete or accomplish; **2** to do; execute; perform or carry out (that which is promised, foretold, or expected); **3** to satisfy (requirements) ‖ **ful·fill´ment** *n* ‖ SYN effect, complete, realize, satisfy, gratify, execute, perform

ful·gent /ful´jənt/ [L *fulgens* (-*entis*)] *adj* shining, resplendent ‖ **ful´gent·ly** *adv*

full¹ /fōōl´/ [F *fouler*] *vt* **1** to scour and thicken, as cloth ‖ *vi* **2** to become thick by shrinking and pressing

full² [OE] *adj* **1** filled, having no empty space; **2** saturated, satiated; **3** copious; **4** rounded out, plump; **5** expressing much; **6** complete, entire; **7** having material arranged in folds, as *a full skirt;* **8** clear, distinct, sonorous ‖ *n* **9** highest state, extent, or measure; **10 in full,** a to the required amount; b without shortening; **11 to the full** thoroughly ‖ *adv* **12** completely; **13** to the utmost; **14** squarely ‖ **ful´ly** *adv* ‖ **full´ness** *n*

full´back´ *n* football player playing back of the scrimmage line between the two halfbacks and farther back

full´-blood´ed *adj* **1** full of vigor; hearty; **2** thoroughbred; of unmixed ancestry

full´-blown´ *adj* **1** in full bloom; **2** matured, completely developed

full´-bod´ied *adj* strong, rich in flavor, as wine

full´ dress´ *n* dress required for any specific formal or ceremonial occasion ‖ **full´-dress´** *adj*

full´er {< *full¹*} *n* one who fulls cloth

full´er's earth´ *n* soft clay-like mineral used in cleaning woolen goods and as a filter

full´-fash´ioned *adj* knitted or shaped to conform to body lines

full´-fledged´ *adj* **1** completely furnished with feathers; **2** entirely equipped; fully developed

full´ house´ *n* poker hand consisting of three of a kind and a pair

full´ moon´ *n* moon in the phase when its entire disk is illuminated

full´ mourn´ing *n* **1** somber garments worn as a show of bereavement; **2** long period in which they are worn

full´ nel´son *n* hold in which a wrestler passes his arms under the arms of his opponent from behind and locks his hands behind the opponent's neck

full´ sail´ *adv* ahead at full speed

full´-scale´ *adj* **1** same in size as the original; **2** using all facilities and resources; **3** of full size, as *a full-scale battle*

full´ stop´ *n* period, as at the end of a sentence

full´ swing´ *n* full capacity or activity

full´ tilt´ *adv* at full speed or capacity

full´ time´ *n* no less than the full amount of time considered normal in working at a particular pursuit or employment ‖ also *adv* ‖ **full´-time´** *adj*

ful·mi·nant /ful´minənt/ [L *fulminans* (-*antis*) lightening] *adj* occurring suddenly and with great severity

ful´mi·nate´ *vt* **1** to cause to explode; **2** to send out or utter, as a denunciation ‖ *vi* **3** to make a loud noise; explode; **4** to give out vehement denunciations ‖ *n* **5** explosive salt of fulminic acid, as *fulminate of mercury* ‖ **ful´mi·na´tion** *n*

ful·min´ic ac´id *n* unstable acid —HONC— forming salts which are extremely explosive

ful·some /fōōl´səm, ful´-/ *adj* **1** offensive from excess, esp. of acts or words; **2** gross, repulsive ‖ **ful´some·ly** *adv*

Ful·ton, Robert /fōōl´tən/ *n* (1765-1815) U.S. inventor, builder of the first practical steamboat

fu·mar·ic ac´id /fyōōmar´ik/ {< LL *fumaria* fumitory] *n* crystalline acid —HOOCCH=CHCOOH— occurring in many plants and used in making resins

fum·ble /fum´bəl/ [prob Scand] *vi* **1** to grope or search about awkwardly; **2** *sports* to fumble the ball ‖ *vt* **3** to do or handle awkwardly; **4** *sports* to drop (the ball) unintentionally ‖ *n* **5** act or instance of fumbling ‖ **fum´bler** *n*

fume /fyōōm´/ [L *fumus* smoke] *n* **1** vapor or gas, esp. if noxious or malodorous ‖ *vi* **2** to emit fumes; **3** to rage, rave angrily

fu·mi·gant /fyōōm´igənt/ *n* something used for fumigating

fu´mi·gate´ [L *fumigare*] *vt* to disinfect or purify by the action of smoke or vapor ‖ **fu´mi·ga´tion** *n* ‖ **fu´mi·ga´tor** *n*

fun /fun´/ [perh < *obs fon* to befool, < ?] *n* **1** pleasure, mirth, amusement, play; **2 for fun, in fun** jokingly; **3 like fun** *colloq* indeed not; **4 to make fun of** to make sport of, ridicule

func·tion /funk´shən/ {< L *fungi* (*functus*) to perform] *n* **1** act or performance of any duty, office, or business; **2** faculty, power; **3** role or office of any organ, animal, or vegetable; **4** public or official ceremony; **5** *math* quantity whose value depends upon the value of other quantities or whose changes in value depend upon the changes of others called its variables ‖ *vi* **6** to perform the duty or office for which a person or thing is intended; operate, work; **7 function as** to serve as, have the function of

func·tion·al *adj* **1** pert. to a function or its performance; **2** operational; **3** utilitarian, as *functional architecture*; **4** *pathol* not due to organic causes, as *a functional disease*

func·tion·ar·y *n* (**-ies**) one who holds an office or fills a responsible position; official

func′tion word′ *n* word expressing grammatical relationship rather than meaning

fund /fund′/. [L *fundus* bottom] *n* **1** permanent stock of something; **2** money set apart for carrying out some object; **3 funds** *pl* available financial resources ‖ *vt* **4** to place in or convert into a relatively permanent debt, bearing interest; **5** to provide money for

fun·da·ment /fun′dəmənt/ [L *fundamentum* foundation] *n* buttocks

fun′da·men′tal /-men′-/ *adj* **1** serving as a foundation or basis; **2** essential, primary ‖ *n* **3** primary or necessary principal; **4** *phys* lowest component of a complex wave; **5** *mus* note on which a chord is formed; root ‖ **fun′da·men′tal·ly** *adv*

fun′da·men′tal·ist *n* in modern Protestant churches, one who believes in the literal inspiration and inerrancy of the Bible ‖ **fun′da·men′tal·ism** *n*

fund′ed debt′ *n* debt running for a long period of time in the form of bonds

fu·ner·al /fyōon′ərəl/ [< L *funus* (*funeris*)] *n* **1** ceremony of burying a dead human body; **2** procession of mourners accompanying it ‖ *adj* **3** pert. to, or fit for, a funeral ‖ **fu′ner·ar′y** /-rer′-/ *adj*

fu′ner·al home′ or **par′lor** *n* place where the body of a deceased person reposes before the funeral and where it may be viewed by friends who come to pay their last respects

fu·ne·re·al /fyōonir′ē·əl/ *adj* **1** suitable for a burial; **2** mournful, gloomy

fun′fair *n* Brit amusement park

fun·gi /fun′jī/ *pl* of fungus

fungi- *comb form* fungus

fun·gi·cide /-jisīd/ [*fungi-* + *-cide*] *n* anything that destroys fungi ‖ **fun′gi·cid′al** *adj*

fun′gi·form′ *adj* mushroom-shaped

fun·go /fun′gō/ [?] *n* (**-goes**) ball hit by a batter who tossed it in the air himself

fun·gus /fun′gəs/ [L = mushroom] *n* (**fun·gus·es, fun·gi** /fun′jī/) **1** one of the plants, including bacteria, molds, mushrooms, toadstools, puffballs, smuts, and rusts, which lack chlorophyll and feed on organic matter; **2** *pathol* abnormal spongy growth ‖ **fun′gous** *adj*

fun′ house′ *n* building in an amusement park that has special devices for amusing and startling the patrons

fu·nic′u·lar rail′way /fyōonik′yələr/ [< L *funiculus* cord] *n* steep cable railway operating on two tracks on which one car is drawn up while the other is lowered

funk /funk/ [perh < early Flem *fonck*] *n* **1** panic, fright; **2** depressed mood

fun·nel /fun′əl/ [OProv *fonilh* < L *infundibulum*] *n* **1** wide-mouthed vessel shaped like a cone with a hole or spout at the little end for pouring liquids or powders into small openings; **2** funnel-shaped part; **3** smokestack of a steamship; **4** flue for ventilation ‖ *v* (**-neled** or **-nelled; -nel·ing** or **-nel·ling**) *vt* **5** to pour through a funnel; **6** to channel, concentrate ‖ *vi* **7** to pass through or as if through a funnel

fun·nies /fun′ēz/ *npl colloq* comic strips

fun′ny [< *fun*] *adj* (**-ni·er; -ni·est**) **1** comical, droll; **2** strange, odd ‖ **fun′ni·ly** *adv* ‖ **fun′ni·ness** *n* ‖ SYN laughable, comical, droll (see *ludicrous*)

fun′ny bone′ *n* **1** place on the elbow where a nerve near the surface tingles when struck; crazy bone; **2** *colloq* one's sense of humor

fun′ny busi′ness *n slang* somewhat mysterious behavior in which one suspects trickiness and deception

fur /fur′/ [< OF *forrer* to sheathe < Gmc] *n* **1** a thick soft hair covering certain animals; **b** skin of an animal with such covering; **2** any coating resembling fur; **3 furs** *pl* dressed skins of furbearing animals, used for clothing ‖ *v* (**furred; fur·ring**) *vt* **4** to cover, line, or trim with fur; **5** to cover with a coating, as the tongue; **6** to level, as flooring, by inserting furring ‖ **fur′ry** *adj* (**-ri·er; -ri·est**)

fur. furlong

fur·be·low /fur′bəlō/ [< F *falbala*] *n* **1** ruffle, flounce, or similar trimming on women's clothing; **2** showy ornamentation

fur·bish /fur′bish/ [OF *forbir* (*-biss-*) < OHG *forban* to polish] *vt* **1** to make bright by rubbing or polishing; **2** to renovate ‖ **fur′bish·er** *n*

fur·cate /fur′kāt/ [< L *furca* fork] *adj* **1** forked; branched ‖ *vi* **2** to form a fork, divide ‖ **fur·ca′tion** *n*

Fu·ries /fyōor′ēz/ *npl class. myth.* the three goddesses of vengeance: Alecto, Tisiphone, and Megaera

fu·ri·ous /fyōor′ē·əs/ [see **fury**] *adj* **1** very angry; **2** violent; **3** full of activity; **4** intense ‖ **fu′ri·ous·ly** *adv* ‖ SYN violent, vehement, fierce, boisterous, turbulent, mad ‖ ANT controlled, poised, serene, calm

furl /furl′/ [MF *ferler*] *vt* **1** to fold or roll up and fasten (a sail or flag) to something ‖ *vi* **2** to become furled

fur·long /fur′lôn, -lon/ [OE *furlang* <

furh furrow + *lang* long] *n* measure equal to an eighth of a mile or 220 yards

fur·lough /furʹlō/ [D *verlof*] *n* 1 leave of absence, esp. of a soldier || *vt* 2 to give a furlough to; 3 to lay off from work

fur·nace /furʹnis/ [OF *fornais* < L *fornax* (*-acis*)] *n* enclosed structure where fuel is burned to produce heat

fur·nish /furʹnish/ [OF *furnir* (*-niss-*)] *vt* 1 to fit out with what is needed; 2 to provide, give || **furʹnish·er** *n*

fur·nish·ings *npl* 1 necessary furniture and fittings of a house; 2 accessories of dress, wearing apparel

fur·ni·ture /furʹnichər/ [< F *fournir* to furnish] *n* 1 movable articles of a house used for general convenience, as beds, chairs, tables, etc.; 2 necessary equipment

fu·ror /fyo͞orʹôr/ [L = madness] *n* 1 rage; 2 great outburst of excitement or enthusiasm; stir; craze

fur·ri·er /furʹē̇-ər/ [see fur] *n* one who prepares or sells furs || **furʹri·er·y** *n* (*-ies*)

fur·ring also **furʹring strip** *n* strip of wood or metal used to level a wall for lathing or a floor for boarding

fur·row /furʹō/ [OE *furh*] *n* 1 trench made in the ground by a plow; 2 rut; 3 groove, wrinkle || *vt* 4 to plow, make furrows in || *vi* 5 to become wrinkled

fur·ther /furʹthər/ [OE *furthra*] *adj* 1 more distant in time or degree; 2 additional || [OE *furthor*] *adv* 3 to a greater distance in time or degree; 4 moreover, also || *vt* 5 to promote, help forward || SYN *v* advance, aid, assist, encourage, push

furʹther·ance *n* advancement; that which promotes or helps

furʹther·moreʹ *adv* besides, in addition

furʹther·mostʹ *adj* most distant; uttermost

furʹthest /*-thist*/ *adj* 1 most distant in time or degree || *adv* 2 at the most remote time; to the greatest degree

fur·tive /furʹtiv/ [L *furtivus* stolen < *furtum* theft] *adj* thieflike, stealthy || **furʹtive·ly** *adv* || **furʹtive·ness** *n* || SYN surreptitious, clandestine, stolen, stealthy, sly

fu·run·cle /fyo͞orʹuŋkəl/ [L *furunculus* petty thief] *n pathol* boil

fu·ry /fyo͞orʹē/ [L *furia*] *n* (*-ries*) 1 violent anger; rage, madness; 2 great violence; fierceness; 3 angry woman; stormy person; 4 Fury one of the Furies || SYN frenzy, violence, rage (see *anger*)

furze /furz/ [OE *fyrs*] *n* any of several spiny shrubs (genus *Ulex*) of the pea family, esp. an evergreen bushy species (*U. europaeus*) with yellow flowers

fuse[1] /fyo͞oz/ [L *fundere* (*fusus*) to pour] *vt* 1 to melt, esp. by heat; make

liquid; 2 to join or blend by melting or as if by melting || *vi* 3 to become melted, as by heat; 4 to blend, as if melted

fuse[2] [It *fuso* < L *fusus* spindle] *n* 1 small tube filled with a material easily set on fire or a cord saturated with such material, used for exploding gunpowder, etc.; 2 protective device in an electric circuit, usu. a conductor which melts and breaks the circuit when the current through it exceeds a safe strength; 3 fuze *1* || *vt* 4 to put a fuse in (an electric circuit); 5 to fuze

fu·see /fyo͞ozēʹ/ [F *fusée* < L *fusus* spindle] *n* 1 friction match that will burn in the wind; 2 signal consisting of a colored light that burns for a specified time, used on railroads; 3 fuse[2] *1*

fu·se·lage /fyo͞osʹəläzh', fyo͞ozʹ-/ [< F *fuselé* spindle-shaped] *n* main body of an airplane to which the wings and tail are attached

fuʹsel oil /fyo͞ozʹəl/ [G *fusel* bad liquor] *n* oily colorless poisonous liquid, a constituent of the residue after distillation of grain alcohol

fuse·tron /fyo͞ozʹtron/ *n* fuse that allows an overload for a short period when the current is first turned on

fuʹsi·form *adj* spindle-shaped; tapering toward each end

fu·sil·ier or **fu·si·leer** /fyo͞ozʹilir'/ [< F *fusil* musket] *n* 1 formerly, soldier armed with a flintlock; 2 member of any of several British regiments

fu·sil·lade /fyo͞osʹiläd', -läd', fyo͞ozʹ-/ [F < *fusiller* to shoot] *n* 1 discharge of a number of firearms in quick succession or at the same time; 2 general discharge or outburst

fu·sion /fyo͞ozhʹən/ [< *fuse*[1]] *n* 1 act or process of fusing; 2 union or result of things fused; 3 *politics* merging of different parties or factions; 4 *phys* transformation under the influence of intense heat of the nuclei of a light element into the nuclei of a heavier element with the sudden conversion of mass into great energy

fuʹsion·ist *n politics* advocate of fusion || **fuʹsion·ism** *n*

fuʹsion powʹer *n* controlled energy that may be obtained someday by harnessing the H-bomb

fuss /fus/ [perh imit] *n* 1 unnecessary or disturbing activity, esp. in small matters; 2 noisy dispute || *vi* 3 to worry; 4 to quarrel; 5 to be busy doing little or nothing || **fussʹer** *n*

fussʹy *adj* (*-i·er*; *-i·est*) 1 worrying or taking trouble about small matters; fidgety; 2 having much careful detail or requiring minute attention || **fussʹi·ly** *adv* || **fussʹi·ness** *n*

fus·tian /fusʹchən/ [OF *justaigne* < LL *fustaneus* < *fustis* cudgel] 1 kind of coarse twilled cotton cloth, as corduroy or velveteen; **2** high-sounding speech, bombast ‖ *adj* **3** made of fustian; **4** bombastic; **5** good-for-nothing

fus·ty /fus′tē/ [< OF *fust* wine cask] *adj* (**-ti·er; -ti·est**) **1** moldy; musty; **2** old-fashioned ‖ **fus·ti·ness** *n*

fut. future

fu·thark /fōō′thärk/ also **fu·thorc, fu·thork** /-thôrk/ [< the first six runes, *F, U, TH, A* or *O, R, C* or *K*] *n* runic alphabet

fu·tile /fyōōt′əl/ [L *futilis* leaky, futile] *adj* **1** ineffectual, useless; **2** unimportant, worthless ‖ **fu′tile·ly** *adv* ‖ **fu·til′i·ty** /-til′-/ *n* (**-ties**)

fu·ture /fyōōch′ər/ [L *futurus* about to be] *adj* **1** relating to time yet to come; about to take place ‖ *n* **2** time yet to come; **3** prospects; **4** *gram* tense denoting time yet to come; **5** **futures** *pl com* commodities sold or bought for future delivery

fu′ture·less *adj* without plan, prospect, or hope for the future

fu′ture per′fect *n gram* tense denoting past time from the point of view of a time in the future, as *he will have left when I arrive* ‖ also *adj*

fu·tur·ism *n* movement in art, literature, and music originating in Italy about 1906, aiming at self-expres-

sion unhampered by tradition or conventional form

fu′tur·ist *n* **1** advocate or follower of futurism; **2** one who believes that certain Biblical prophecies are yet to be fulfilled; **3** prophet who uses the new analytic techniques and the computer to make predictions

fu·tur·is′tic *adj* **1** pert. to the future; **2** pert. to futurism

fu·tu·ri·ty /-chōōr′-/ *n* (**-ties**) **1** time or state yet to come; **2** events of a time following the present; posterity

fu·tu′ri·ty race′ *n* horse race the entrants of which are selected well in advance, often at birth or before

fuze /fyōōz/ [var of *fuse*²] *n* **1** mechanical or electronic device for detonating artillery shells, mines, and missiles; **2** fuse² *1* ‖ *vt* **3** to provide with a fuze

fu·zee /fyōōzē′/ *n* var of **fusee**

fuzz /fuz′/ [?] *n* **1** fine, minute particles, as of down, wool, etc.; **2** *slang* police ‖ *vi* **3** to come off in fuzz ‖ *vt* **4** to make fuzzy; **5** to blur

fuzz′y *adj* (**-i·er; -i·est**) **1** like fuzz; **2** covered with fuzz; **3** blurred; **4** incoherent

fwd. forward

-fy /-fī′/ [< F *-fier* < L *facere* to do] *v suf* to make, cause, or form into, as *liquefy, satisfy*

G

G, g /jē′/ *n* (**G's** or **Gs; g's** or **gs**) seventh letter of the English alphabet

G 1 *mus* fifth tone in the scale of C major; **2** seventh in order or in a series; **3** something shaped like a G; **4** (**Gs** or **G's**) *slang* thousand dollars; **5** designation for a film recommended for general audiences

G, G. German

G. Gulf

g acceleration of gravity

g. **1** gauge; **2** gram(s)

Ga *chem* gallium

Ga. Georgia

gab /gab′/ [ME] *colloq n* **1** idle chatter ‖ *v* (**gabbed; gab·bing**) *vi* **2** to chatter idly

gab·ar·dine /gab′ərdēn′/ [MF *gauvardine* pilgrim's cloak] *n* firm durable cloth with a twilled weave

gab·ble /gab′əl/ [imit] *vt* **1** to say rapidly or senselessly ‖ *vi* **2** to jabber, cackle ‖ *n* **3** rapid meaningless talk; inarticulate sounds

gab·by /gab′ē/ [< *gab*] *adj* (**-bi·er; -bi·est**) *colloq* talkative

ga·ble /gāb′əl/ [ME < ON] *n* **1** triangular part of a wall between the slopes of a double-sloping roof; **2**

any triangular decorative construction ‖ **ga′bled** *adj*

ga′ble end′ *n* wall of a building with a gable at the top

ga′ble roof′ *n* ridged, double-sloping roof, each end of which encloses a vertical triangular portion of wall

Ga·bon /gabôn′/ *n* republic in W Central Africa, formerly a French colony (450,000; 103,000 sq.m.; *cap.* Libreville) ‖ **Gab·o·nese** /gab′ənēz′, -nēs′/ *adj & n* (**-nese**)

Ga·bri·el /gāb′rē·əl/ *n Bib* one of the archangels, sent as a herald of good tidings (Luke 1:26)

gad /gad′/ [ME *gadden*] *v* (**gad·ded; gad·ding**) *vi* to go about without purpose; ramble

Gad, gad /gad′/ [euphem for *God*] *interj* used as a mild oath

gad′a·bout′ *n* one who gads about aimlessly or in search of news and gossip

gad′fly′ [< ME *gad* goad] *n* (**-flies**) **1** any of various flies that bite cattle; **2** annoying person

gadg·et /gaj′it/ [< prob F *gâchette* catch of lock] *n* any small mechanical device

gad·o·lin·i·um /gad'əlin'ē·əm/ [J. *Gadolin* (1760–1852) Finnish chemist] *n* rare-earth metallic element (**Gd**; at. no. 64; at.wt. 157.25)

Gae·a /jē'ə/ *n Gk myth.* goddess of the earth

Gael /gāl'/ [Gael *Gaidheal*] *n* Celt of Ireland, Scotland, or the Isle of Man

Gael. Gaelic

Gael'ic *adj* 1 pert. to the Celtic peoples of Ireland, Scotland, and the Isle of Man ‖ *n* 2 their language

gaff /gaf'/ [F *gaffe* boat hook] *n* 1 large hook on the end of a pole for landing fish; 2 *naut* spar branching out from a mast, used as a support for a fore-and-aft sail; 3 **stand the gaff** *slang* to be able to take it ‖ *vt* 4 to land (fish) with a gaff

gaffe /gaf'/ [F] *n* faux pas

gaf·fer /gaf'ər/ [short for *godfather*] *n* old fellow

gag /gag'/ [ME *gaggen*] *n* 1 something placed in the mouth to hinder speech or to hold the mouth open; 2 any suppression of free speech; 3 *colloq* joke; 4 *colloq* clever or amusing remark or stunt introduced by an actor in his performance ‖ *v* (**gagged; gagging**) *vt* 5 to stop the mouth of; 6 to cause to retch; 7 to silence by force or law ‖ *vi* 8 to choke, as in an effort to vomit

gage¹ /gāj'/ [MF < Gmc] *n* 1 token, as a glove, thrown down as a challenge to combat; 2 challenge

gage² *n & vt* var of **gauge**

gag·gle /gag'əl/ [ME *gagelen*] *n* 1 flock of geese; 2 cackling sound; 3 band or flock of people; 4 number of things of any kind ‖ *vi* 5 to cackle like a goose

gag'man' /-man'/ *n* (-**men'** /-men'/) writer of comical material

gai·e·ty /gā'itē/ [F *gaieté*] *n* (-**ties**) 1 state or quality of being gay; merriment; 2 festivity; merrymaking ‖ SYN merriment, sportiveness, fun

gai·ly /gāl'ē/ *adv* in a gay manner

gain /gān/ [OF *gaaignier* to make profitable] *n* 1 advantage, profit; 2 increase; 3 acquisition; 4 ratio of output to input of an antenna or an electronic amplifier ‖ *vt* 5 to earn; 6 to win; 7 to obtain through an increase; 8 to get to ‖ *vi* 9 to make progress; 10 **gain on** to get nearer to ‖ **gain'er** *n* ‖ SYN *n* benefit, winnings, earnings, increase; *v* (see *get*) ‖ ANT *n* loss, privation, disadvantage, decrease

gain'ful *adj* yielding gain; profitable ‖ **gain'ful·ly** *adv*

gain'say' [*obs gain* against + *say*] *v* (-**said'** /-sed'/, -**sād'**/) *vt* 1 to contradict; 2 to deny; 3 to forbid

gait /gāt'/ [ME = way, gate] *n* manner of walking or running of people or animals, esp. horses

-gait'ed *adj comb form* having a particular gait, as *slow-gaited*

gai·ter /gāt'ər/ [F *guêtre*] *n* cloth or leather covering for the ankle, instep, and often the lower leg, worn over the shoe

gal /gal'/ [*dial.* for *girl*] *n colloq* girl

gal. gallon(s)

ga·la /gā'lə, gal'ə/ [F < It = finery] *n* 1 festival ‖ *adj* 2 festive

ga·lac·tic /gəlak'tik/ [< Gk *gala* (-*laktos*) milk] *adj* 1 pert. to milk; 2 pert. to the Milky Way, or to any galaxy

Gal·a·had /gal'əhad'/ *n Arthurian legend* the purest knight of the Round Table, who was successful in his quest for the Holy Grail

Ga·lá'pa·gos Is'lands /gəläp'əgōs'/ *npl* Pacific island group on the equator 600 miles W of and belonging to Ecuador (2,000; 2870 sq.m.)

gal·ax·y /gal'əksē/ [Gk *galaxias*] *n* (-**ies**) 1 independent system of stars held together by mutual gravitation; 2 brilliant assemblage; 3 **Galaxy** Milky Way

gale /gāl'/ [?] *n* 1 strong wind; 2 wind of 32–63 miles per hour; 3 outburst, as of laughter

Ga·len /gā'lən/ *n* 1 (ab. 130–200 A.D.) Greek physician and medical writer; 2 any physician

ga·le·na /gəlēn'ə/ [L = lead ore] *n* natural lead sulfide —PbS— the chief ore of lead

Ga·li·ci·a /gəlish'ē·ə, -lish'ə/ *n* 1 region now partly Polish and partly Russian; 2 Portuguese- and Spanish-speaking region and former province of NW Spain on the Atlantic Ocean ‖ **Ga·li'cian** *adj & n*

Gal·i·lee /gal'ilē/ *n* 1 ancient province of Palestine, now N Israel ‖ **Gal'i·le'an** *adj & n*

Gal'i·lee', Sea of *n* lake in N Israel

Gal·i·le·o /gal'ilē'ō/ *n* (Galileo Galilei) (1564–1642) Italian astronomer and physicist ‖ **Gal'i·le'an** *adj*

gall¹ /gôl/ [OE *gealla*] *n* 1 bile, esp. of the ox; 2 anything bitter or distasteful; 3 rancor; 4 insolence, impudence

gall² [ME *galle*] *n* 1 sore on the skin caused by chafing ‖ *vt* 2 to make sore by chafing; 3 to vex, irritate ‖ *vi* 4 to become chafed

gall³ [MF *galle* < L *galla* gallnut] *n* abnormal growth on plants, caused by insects, fungi, bacteria, or injury

gal·lant /gal'ənt/ [OF *galant* making merry] *adj* 1 showy, splendid; 2 brave, noble, chivalrous; 3 /also gəlant', -länt'/ showing elaborate courtesy to women ‖ /also gəlant', -länt'/ *n* 4 gallant man; 5 beau, suitor ‖ **gal'lant·ly** *adv* ‖ SYN *adj* bold, courageous, gay, intrepid, fine

gal'lant·ry *n* (-**ries**) 1 state of being gallant; 2 gallant conduct; 3 gallant act or speech ‖ SYN chivalrousness, fearlessness, valor (see *bravery*)

gall' blad'der *n* sac attached to the liver for storing excess bile

gal·le·on /gal'ē·ən/ [Sp *galeón*] *n* large broad-beamed vessel of the 15th and later centuries, used as a warship or merchantman, and esp. by the Spaniards as a treasure ship

gal·ler·y /gal'ərē/ [OF *galerie*] *n* (-ies) 1 covered walk, open on one or both sides; 2 long porch or veranda; 3 long narrow balcony along a building; 4 highest balcony in a theater; 5 building or room for the exhibition of art, etc.; 6 underground passageway, as in a mine

gal·ley /gal'ē/ [OF *galie* < LGk *galea*] *n* 1 seagoing vessel of former times, propelled mainly by oars; 2 ship's or plane's kitchen; 3 narrow tray for holding set type; 4 galley proof

gal'ley proof' *n* proof from a galley 3

gal'ley slave' *n* 1 slave or convict condemned to row a galley; 2 drudge

Gal·lic /gal'ik/ [< L *Gallus* Gaul] *adj* 1 pert. to Gaul or the Gauls; 2 pert. to France or the French

Gal'li·cism *n* French word or expression used in another language

Gal'li·cize' *vt* to Frenchify

gal·li·na·ceous /gal'ināsh'əs/ [< L *gallina* hen] *adj* like or belonging to an order (Galliformes) of birds including chickens, turkeys, grouse, and pheasants

gall·ing /gôl'iŋ/ [< gall²] *adj* chafing; vexing, exasperating

gal·li·um /gal'ē·əm/ [< L *gallus* cock; translation of *Lecoq* de Boisbaudran (d. 1912) F chemist] *n* rare metallic element (Ga; at.no. 31; at.wt. 69.72) notable for its low melting point (30°C)

gal·li·vant /gal'ivant'/ [perh < *gallant*] *vi* to gad about in pursuit of pleasure

gal·lon /gal'ən/ [ONF *galon*] *n* unit of liquid measure equal to four quarts; in the U.S. 231 cu.in. or 3.7853 liters

gal·lop /gal'əp/ [MF *galop*] *n* 1 rapid forward springing movement of a quadruped, esp. a horse; 2 act or instance of running or riding at this gait || *vi* 3 to run or ride at a gallop; 4 to go at top speed || *vt* 5 to cause to gallop

gal·lows /gal'ōz/ [OE *galga*] *n* (-lows or -lows·es) structure of two uprights and a crossbeam for hanging condemned criminals

gall'stone' *n* lump of solid matter formed in the gall bladder or biliary passages

ga·lore /gəlôr', -lōr'/ [Ir *go léor* to sufficiency] *adv* in abundance, as *pretty girls galore*

ga·losh /gəlosh'/ [F *galoche*] *n* high overshoe

gal·van·ic /galvan'ik/ [< Luigi *Galvani* (1737–98) It scientist] *adj* 1 producing or caused by an electric current; 2 stimulating, startling

gal·va·nism /gal'vəniz'əm/ *n* electricity produced by chemical action

gal'va·nize' *vt* 1 to subject to the action of an electric current; 2 to stimulate or excite; 3 to coat (iron or steel) with zinc by spraying, immersion, or electroplating

gal'va·nized' i'ron *n* iron coated with zinc to prevent rust

Gam·bi·a /gam'bē·ə/ *n* republic in W Africa, formerly a British colony (343,000; 4,361 sq.m.; cap. Banjul)

gam·bit /gam'bit/ [It *gambetto* act of tripping] *n* 1 chess opening in which a piece or pawn is intentionally sacrificed; 2 any maneuver from which one hopes to profit

gam·ble /gam'bəl/ [OE *gamenian*] *vi* 1 to play games of chance for stakes; 2 to risk something of value for possible profit || *vt* 3 to bet, wager; 4 **gamble away** to lose by betting || *n* 5 any undertaking involving high risk || **gam'bler** *n* || **gam'bling** *n* || SYN *n* risk, wager, hazard, venture, stake, game, waste

gam·bol /gam'bəl/ [< MF *gambade* leap] *n* dancing or skipping about; frolic || *v* (-boled or -bolled; -bol·ing or -bol·ling) *vi* to skip or dance about in play or frolic

gam·brel /gam'brəl/ [< OF *gambe* leg] *n* 1 hock joint of the hind leg of a horse; 2 bent stick used by butchers in suspending carcasses

gam'brel roof' *n* gable roof with two slopes on each side, the lower one being much steeper

game¹ /gām/ [OE *gamen*] *n* 1 amusement or pastime; 2 fun, sport; jest; 3 contest carried on by rules, with success dependent on strength, skill, or luck; 4 single match in such a contest; 5 number of points required to win; 6 scheme or strategy; 7 wild animals, birds, or fish pursued for sport or food; 8 any object of pursuit; 9 *colloq* profession or business; 10 **the game is up** victory is hopeless || *vi* 11 to gamble || *adj* 12 ready; spirited, plucky || **game'ly** *adv* || **game'ness** *n* || SYN *n* play, pastime, sport || DISCR *Play* is the general term for action or exercise for recreation, amusement, or diversion. *Games* and *sport* are forms of *play*; a *game* is a contest played according to rules and won by skill, strength, or luck. *Sport* names any of the outdoor pastimes, such as racing or hunting; athletic *sports* include jumping, running, football, and the like

game² [?] *adj colloq* lame (leg)

game'cock' *n* rooster bred and trained for fighting

game' fish' *n* edible fish sought after for the sport its capture provides

game' law' *n* law for the preservation of game, as by restricting the hunting season and/or the number or kind that can be taken

game′ plan′ *n* elaborate scheme for attaining a desired result

game′ster /-stər/ *n* habitual gambler

gam·ete /gam′ēt, gəmēt′/ [Gk = wife] *n* sexual cell that unites with another for reproduction or the formation of a new individual

game′ war′den *n* official who enforces game laws

gam·in /gam′in/ [F] *n* homeless street urchin

gam·ing /gām′iŋ/ *n* gambling

gam·ma /gam′ə/ *n* third letter of the Greek alphabet Γ, γ

gam′ma rays′ *npl* penetrating radiation of high frequency and short wave length emitted by radioactive substances

-g·a·mous /-gəməs/ [< Gk *gamos* wedding] *adj comb form* having a particular kind of marriage or so many mates, as *polygamous*

gam·ut /gam′ət/ [< ML *gamma ut*, last and first tones of the medieval musical scale] *n* 1 entire range or scale, as *the gamut of emotions*; 2 *mus* entire series of recognized notes

gam·y /gām′ē/ *adj* (-i-er; -i-est) 1 having the flavor of game; 2 slightly tainted; 3 smelly; 4 plucky

-g·a·my /-gəmē/ [see **-gamous**] *n comb form* marriage, as *polygamy*

gan·der /gan′dər/ [OE *gandra*] *n* 1 male goose; 2 *slang* look; glance

Gan·dhi, Mo·han·das K. /mō′həndäs′gän′dē, gan′-/ *n* (Mahatma Gandhi) (1869–1948) Indian spiritual leader, statesman, and patriot, who secured India's independence from Britain

gang /gaŋ/ [< OE *gangan* to go] *n* 1 group or band; 2 number of persons banded together, as for social or criminal purposes; 3 group of men working together; shift; squad ‖ *vi* 4 **gang up on** *colloq* to combine against

Gan·ges /gan′jēz/ *n* river in NE India, sacred to the Hindus

gan·gling /gaŋ′gliŋ/ [?] *adj* tall and awkward

gan·gli·on /gaŋ′glē-ən/ [Gk = tumor under the skin] *n* (-a /-ə/ or **-ons**) 1 collection of nerve-cell bodies and nerve fibers which transmits impulses; 2 globular swelling on a tendon sheath

gang′plank′ *n* movable plank or bridge for boarding or leaving a ship

gan·grene /gaŋ′grēn/ [Gk *gangraina* eating sore] *n* death of body tissue due to obstruction of the blood supply ‖ **gan′gre·nous** /-grinəs/ *adj*

gang′ster *n* member of a criminal gang

gang′way′ /n 1 passageway; 2 opening in a ship's rail or side; 3 gangplank ‖ *interj* 4 clear the way!

gan·net /gan′it/ [OE *ganot*] *n* any of

a small family (Sulidae) of large web-footed sea birds

gant·let /gônt′lit, gant′-/ *n* var of **gauntlet**[1,2]

gan·try /gan′rē/ [?] *n* (-tries) 1 bridge-like frame structure for supporting traveling cranes; 2 vertical structure for erecting large rockets; 3 bridge over railroad tracks carrying signals

Gan·y·mede /gan′imēd′/ *n* 1 *class. myth.* Trojan lad whom Zeus carried to Olympus to be his cupbearer; 2 *astron* one of the satellites of Jupiter

gaol /jāl′/ *n Brit* jail

gap /gap′/ [< ON *gapa* to open] *n* 1 opening; 2 disparity; 3 breach; 4 interval; hiatus; 5 pass in a mountain ridge ‖ *syn* hole, hollow, ravine, chasm, rift, notch

gape /gāp′, gap′/ [ON *gapa*] *vi* 1 to open the mouth wide, as from drowsiness, wonder, or hunger; 2 to stare with the mouth open; 3 to be wide open ‖ *n* 4 act of gaping; 5 wide opening

gap′-toothed′ *adj* having a gap between two teeth

gar /gär′/ [OE *gār* spear] *n* (gar or gars) also **gar′fish′** slender North American fresh-water fish (genus *Lepisosteus*) having a spearlike snout

G.A.R. Grand Army of the Republic, the organization of northern Civil War veterans

ga·rage /gəräzh′, -räj′/ [F] *n* 1 place for sheltering automobiles; 2 place for servicing and repairing automobiles ‖ *vt* 3 to place or keep in a garage

Gar′and ri′fle /gar′ənd/ [J. C. Garand (1888–) its inventor] *n* .30-caliber semiautomatic rifle, standard rifle of the U.S. Army in World War II

garb /gärb′/ [MF *garbe* grace < OIt *garbo*] *n* 1 dress, clothing; 2 style of dress, esp. of a distinctive kind ‖ *vt* 3 to clothe

gar·bage /gärb′ij/ [ME = entrails] *n* 1 kitchen refuse; 2 worthless, vile, or inferior matter of any kind

gar·ble /gärb′əl/ [OIt *garbellare* to sift < Ar *gharbala*] *vt* to distort or confuse, as a story, statement, or instructions, either innocently or intentionally

gar·den /gärd′ən/ [ONF *gardin*] *n* 1 plot of ground set apart for flowers or vegetables; 2 any rich or fruitful place; 3 cultivated grounds for public resort ‖ *vi* 4 to work in a garden ‖ **gar′den·er** *n* ‖ **gar′den·ing** *n*

gar·de·nia /gärdēn′yə/ [Alexander Garden (1730–91) Amer. botanist] *n* any of a large genus (*Gardenia*) of chiefly tropical plants cultivated for their fragrant waxlike white flowers

Gar·field, James A. /gär′fēld/ *n* (1831–81) 20th president of the U.S. 1881; assassinated

Gar·gan·tu·an /gärgan′chŏŏ·ən/ [< *Gargantua* voracious and amiable giant in satire of the same name by Rabelais] *adj* large beyond belief; enormous (esp. appetites or desires)

gar·gle /gärg′əl/ [MF *gargouiller*] *vt* 1 to rinse (the mouth or throat) with a liquid kept in motion by the slow expulsion of air from the lungs || *vi* 2 to use a gargle || *n* 3 liquid for gargling

gar·goyle /gär′goil/ [MF *gargouille* throat] *n* 1 grotesquely carved figure of an animal or human; 2 waterspout in the shape of a gargoyle

Gar·i·bal·di, Giu·sep·pe /jŏŏsep′ē gar′ibôl′dē/ *n* (1807–82) Italian patriot, unifier of modern Italy

gar·ish /gar′ish, ger′-/ [< ME *gauren* to stare] *adj* tastelessly gaudy; excessively ornate || SYN glaring, harsh, flashy, striking (see *showy*)

gar·land /gär′lənd/ [OF] *n* 1 wreath of flowers, leaves, or other material || *vt* 2 to decorate with garlands

gar·lic /gär′lik/ [OE *gārlēac* = spear leek] *n* 1 plant (*Allium sativum*) resembling a small onion, with pungent taste and odor; 2 its bulb, used in cooking || **gar′lick·y** *adj*

gar·ment /gär′mənt/ [OF *garniment* adornment] *n* article of clothing

gar·ner /gär′nər/ [OF *grenier* granary < L *granarium*] *vt* 1 to gather and store; 2 to acquire, gather

gar·net /gär′nit/ [MF *grenat*] *n* 1 any of a group of minerals consisting of silica with other constituents, occurring as a precious or semiprecious stone, generally red; 2 deep-red color

gar·nish /gär′nish/ [OF *garnir* (-*niss*-)] *vt* 1 to adorn, embellish; 2 to garnishee || *n* 3 ornament or decoration; 4 something laid about food as a decoration, as parsley || SYN *v* beautify, trim, deck, dress, embellish

gar′nish·ee′ *vt* 1 to attach (property or wages) in order to satisfy a debt || *n* 2 person served with a garnishment

gar′nish·ment *n* 1 act of garnishing; 2 act of garnisheeing

gar·ret /gar′it/ [OF *garite* watchtower] *n* attic

gar·ri·son /gar′isən/ [OF *garison* defense] *n* 1 troops stationed in a fortified place; 2 fortified place or military post || *vt* 3 to provide with a garrison

Gar′ri·son fin′ish [prob Snapper *Garrison* 19th-cent. jockey] *n* finish in a race in which the winner comes from behind at the last moment

gar·rote /gərōt′, gərot′/ [Sp] *n* 1 execution of Spanish origin by tightening an iron collar around the neck; 2 any device used for strangling || *vt* 3 to execute by the garrote; 4 to throttle

gar·ru·lous /gar′(y)ələs/ [< L *garrulus*] *adj* excessively talkative, esp.

about trivial things || **gar·ru·li·ty** /gərŏŏl′itē *n* || SYN loquacious, talkative, voluble, glib, fluent || DISCR These terms describe those who are able to express themselves freely and easily. *Talkative* people are fond of, and given to, talk; they are not necessarily boresome. *Loquacious* persons talk incessantly; they tire us. *Garrulous* people gabble constantly, usually on trivial topics, and repeat and relate reminiscences to such an extent that this word is applied frequently to the aged. *Voluble, fluent,* and *glib* describe those whose speech is ready and smooth. A *fluent* speaker uses easy, flowing language; a *voluble* talker fairly tumbles out the words. Speech so smooth that it persuades by its readiness rather than the soundness of its arguments is distrusted; hence both these words may be used in a derogatory sense; *voluble* is almost never used in a favorable sense. *Glib* describes one whose plausible, fluent words hide his insincerity and shallowness

gar·ter /gärt′ər/ [ONF *gartier*] *n* elastic band or strap by which a stocking is held up on the leg

gar′ter snake′ *n* any of a genus (*Thamnophis*) of small, harmless, usu. yellow-striped snakes common in North America

garth /gärth′/ [ON *gardhr* yard] *n* open space surrounded by a cloister

gas /gas′/ [coined from *chaos* by J. B. van Helmont, 17th-cent. Flemish chemist] *n* 1 completely elastic airlike fluid capable of indefinitely expanding; 2 any such fluid used as a fuel; 3 any such fluid used as an anesthetic; 4 poisonous gaseous mixture used in warfare or for executions; 5 *colloq* a gasoline; b automobile accelerator; 6 *slang* empty talk || *v* (**gassed; gas·sing**) *vt* 7 to cause to inhale poisonous gas || *vi* 8 *slang* to talk nonsense; 9 **gas up** to fill the gasoline tank of a vehicle || **gas′sy** *adj* (-**si·er; -si·est**)

gas′ chamber *n* room for the execution of condemned criminals by poison gas

Gas·co·ny /gas′kənē/ *n* former province in SW France || **Gas′con** *adj* & *n*

gas·e·ous /gas′ē·əs, gash′əs/ *adj* pert. to, like, or in the form of a gas

gas′guz′zler *n* car, usu. very big, that consumes a large amount of gasoline

gash /gash′/ [OF *garser*] *vt* 1 to cut deeply || *n* 2 deep cut

gas·ket /gask′it/ [?] *n* 1 thin piece or ring of rubber, metal, or fiber, placed between surfaces to make a joint airtight or watertight; 2 *naut* rope or flat plaited cord by which furled sails are tied fast to a spar

gas' main' *n* large underground pipe for conducting gas to individual buildings

gas' mask' *n* covering for the face to prevent the inhaling of gas

gas' me'ter *n* device for measuring the amount of gas used as fuel or for illumination

gas·o·hol /gas'əhôl', -hol'/ [*gasoline* + *alcohol*] *n* combustible liquid of nine parts of unleaded gasoline and one part of alcohol or anhydrous ethanol

gas·o·line /gas'əlēn', gas'əlēn'/ [*gas* + *-oline* < L *oleum* oil] *n* highly volatile and inflammable liquid distilled from petroleum, used chiefly as a fuel for internal-combustion engines

gasp /gasp/, gäsp'/ [ON *geispa* to yawn] *n* 1 quick painful effort to catch the breath || *vi* 2 to catch the breath with difficulty || *vt* 3 to utter in quick, painful breaths

gas' sta'tion *n* place that sells gasoline and oil for motor vehicles, and often other goods and services

gas·tric /gast'rik/ [see *gastro-*] *adj* affecting or pert. to the stomach

gas'tric juice' *n* digestive fluid secreted by the glands of the stomach

gas·tri·tis /gastrīt'is/ *n* inflammation of the stomach, esp. of its lining

gas·tro- [< Gk *gaster* (*-tros*) stomach] *comb form* stomach

gas·tron·o·my /-on'əmē/ [< *gastro-* + Gk *nomos* rule] *n* art of good eating || **gas'tro·nom'ic** (**-i·cal**) /-ənom'-/ *adj*

gas'tro·pod' /-əpod'/ *n* any of a class (Gastropoda) of mollusks, including the snails

gas'tro·scope' *n* instrument for viewing the interior of the stomach

gas'-tur'bine en'gine *n* internal-combustion engine in which the combustion which drives the turbine is attained by high compression

gas'works' *nsg* plant for the production of gas for distribution to homes and buildings

gat /gat'/ [< *Gatling gun*] *n* slang pistol

gate /gāt'/ [OE *geat*] *n* 1 opening to allow passage; 2 movable barrier giving access, as through a wall or fence, across railroad tracks, or onto a bridge or road; 3 gateway; 4 valve or door to control the flow of water; 5 total amount or number of paid admissions; 6 give the gate *slang* to get rid of

gate'-crash'er *n* person who enters a function without an invitation or without paying

gate'fold' *n* folded insert in a book or magazine

gate'-leg ta'ble *n* drop-leaf table which has legs that are swung out to support the leaves

gate' valve' *n* valve opened by a sliding plate

gate'way' *n* 1 that which gives access; 2 entrance closed by a gate

gath·er /gath'ər/ [OE *gaderian*] *vt* 1 to assemble or bring together; 2 to pick or harvest; 3 to amass, accumulate; 4 to summon or concentrate, as energies; 5 to infer or conclude; 6 to pucker or pleat || *vi* 7 to assemble; 8 to increase || *n* 9 fold or pleat

gath'er·ing *n* 1 act of assembling or bringing together 2 assemblage

Gat'ling gun' /gat'lip/ [R. J. *Gatling* (1818–1903) Am inventor] *n* early machine gun with a cluster of barrels discharged by a turning crank, first used in the Civil War

gauche /gōsh'/ [F = left, awkward] *adj* awkward; tactless || **gau'che·rie'** /-ərē'/ *n*

gau·cho /gou'chō/ [AmSp] *n* cowboy of Argentina, Uruguay, and S Brazil

gaud·y /gôd'ē/ [< ME *gaude* ornament] *adj* (**-i·er; -i·est**) showy, flashy || **gaud'i·ly** *adv* || **gaud'i·ness** *n* || SYN garish, flashy, spurious (see *showy*)

gauge /gāj/ [ONF] *n* 1 standard measure; 2 estimate or judgment; 3 any of various measuring or recording instruments or devices; 4 unit of measure of various dimensions, as the distance between railroad rails, the diameter of a shotgun barrel, the thickness of sheet metal, the diameter of screws or wire, or the fineness of knitted fabric || *vt* 5 to measure by any of various measuring standards or gauges; 6 to estimate

Gaul /gôl'/ *n* 1 ancient country of W Europe, essentially modern France and adjoining regions; 2 inhabitant of Gaul; 3 Frenchman

Gaul'ish *adj* 1 pert. to Gaul, its people, or its language || *n* 2 Celtic language of ancient Gaul

gaunt /gônt'/, gänt'/ [ME] *adj* 1 pinched and lean; 2 grim, desolate || **gaunt'ness** *n* || SYN emaciated, spare, lank, meager (see *lean*)

gaunt·let¹ /gônt'lit, gänt'-/ [MF *gantelet* dim. of *gant* glove] *n* 1 armored glove; 2 glove with a long cuff; 3 the cuff; 4 throw down the gauntlet to challenge to combat

gaunt·let² [< Sw *gatlopp*] *n* 1 two rows of men armed as with clubs with which to beat an offender made to run between them; 2 ordeal, crossfire

gauss /gous'/ [Karl F. *Gauss* (1777–1855) G scientist] *n* cgs unit of magnetic induction, equal to the intensity produced by a magnetic pole of unit strength at a distance of one centimeter

gauze /gôz'/ [F *gaze*] *n* 1 any thin, light, transparent fabric, as of cloth or wire; 2 surgical dressing of cotton gauze || **gauz'y** *adj* (**-i·er; -i·est**)

gave /gāv'/ *pt* of give

gav·el /gav'əl/ [?] *n* small mallet used by a judge or presiding officer to call for attention or order

ga·votte /gəvot'/ [F] *n* 1 French dance resembling a lively minuet; 2 piece of music for this dance in four-four tempo

gawk /gôk/ [?] *vi* 1 to stare stupidly || *n* 2 simpleton, booby

gawk'y *adj* (**-i·er; -i·est**) clumsy, ungainly || **gawk'i·ness** *n*

gay /gā/ [OF *gai*] *adj* 1 light-hearted; joyous; 2 showy, bright-colored; 3 dissipated, dissolute; 4 *colloq* homosexual || SYN lively, merry, sportive (see *cheerful, showy*)

gay·e·ty /gā'itē/ *n* var of **gaiety**

gay·ly /gāl'ē/ *adv* var of **gaily**

gaze /gāz/ [ME *gasen* < ON] *vi* 1 to look fixedly, stare || *n* 2 intent look || SYN *v* stare, gawk, glare, peer

ga·zelle /gəzel'/ [F < Ar *ghazāl*] *n* any of several small very swift antelopes of the genus *Gazella*

ga·zette /gəzet'/ [F < It *gazzetta*] *n* 1 newspaper; 2 *Brit* official government publication || *v* (**-zet·ted; -zet·ting**) *vt* 3 *Brit* to publish or announce in a gazette

gaz·et·teer /gaz'itir'/ *n* dictionary of geographical names

G.B. Great Britain

Gd *chem* gadolinium

Ge *chem* germanium

gear /gir/ [OE *gearwe*] *n* 1 **a** toothed wheel, disk, or part that meshes with another part with similar teeth, to transmit force or motion; **b** adjustment of such parts to each other, as in *or out of gear*; **c** specific adjustment of gears to change speed, power, or direction, as *high* or *reverse gear*; 2 unit of machinery with some specific purpose, as *steering gear*; 3 apparatus; implements; tools; 4 clothing and personal equipment; 5 **in** or **into high gear** at full speed || *vt* 6 to put cogs or teeth on; 7 to provide with or connect by gears; 8 to adapt to a particular purpose

gear'shift' *n* device for selecting or engaging gears in an automobile transmission

gear' wheel' *n* toothed wheel designed to mesh with another geared part; cogwheel

gee[1] /jē/ [?] *interj* 1 command to draft animals to turn to the right || *vi* 2 to turn to the right

gee[2] [< *Jesus*] *interj colloq* expression of amazement or enthusiasm

gee[3] [?] *vi colloq* to agree, harmonize

geese /gēs/ *pl* of **goose**

gee·zer /gēz'ər/ [prob < Sc *guiser* person in disguise] *n slang* eccentric man

Ge·hen·na /gihen'ə/ *n* 1 the valley of Hinnom near Jerusalem where the bodies of criminals were thrown; 2 hell; 3 place of torment

Gei'ger count'er /gīg'ər/ [Hans *Geiger* (1882–1947) G physicist] *n* instrument used to detect and measure radioactivity

gei·sha /gāsh'ə/ [Jap] *n* (**-shas** or **-sha**) Japanese girl trained to sing and dance and to be a companion for men

gel /jel/ [< *gelatin*] *n* 1 jellylike colloidal suspension or solution || *v* (**gelled; gel·ling**) *vi* 2 to form a gel

gel·a·tin also **gel·a·tine** /jel'ətən/ [F *gélatine* < It *gelatina*] *n* whitish, tasteless, and odorless translucent substance extracted from animal tissues and also from vegetables; soluble in water, it forms a jellylike mass when cooled, and is used in foods, confections, medicinal capsules, photographic films, etc. || **ge·lat·i·nous** /jəlat'ənəs/ *adj*

geld /geld/ [ON *gelda*] *v* (**geld·ed** or **gelt**) *vt* to castrate (an animal, esp. a horse)

geld'ing *n* castrated horse

gel·id /jel'id/ [L *gelidus*] *adj* very cold, frozen

gem /jem/ [OF *gemme* < L *gemma*] *n* 1 cut and polished precious stone; jewel; 2 any valuable or beautiful object

Gem·i·ni /jem'inī'/ [L = twins] *n* 1 a northern zodiacal constellation, the Twins; 2 third sign of the zodiac

-gen /-jən, also -jen/ [Gk *genes* born] *n comb form* producing, as *oxygen*

gen. 1 gender; 2 general; 3 genitive; 4 genus

Gen. 1 General; 2 Genesis

gen·darme /zhän'därm, jen'-/ [F] *n* 1 policeman in several European countries; 2 *slang* policeman

gen·der /jen'dər/ [MF *gendre* < L *genus* (*generis*) kind] *n* grammatical distinction applying in many Indo-European and other languages usu. to nouns, adjectives, and pronouns, determined by concord and often by distinctive endings || SYN SEX || DISCR *Sex* names the structural character, seen in both the animal and the plant world, of being either male or female. *Gender* is a grammatical classification by which nouns and pronouns are grouped in a rough correspondence with their *sex* if masculine or feminine, or lack of it if neuter

gene /jēn/ [Gk] *n* unit of heredity, attached to the chromosome, which transmits hereditary characters

ge·ne·al·o·gy /jēn'ē-al'əjē, jen'-, -äl'-/ [Gk *genea* race + -*logy*] *n* (**-gies**) 1 study of family descent; 2 record of such descent; list of ancestors; 3 descent from an ancestor; pedigree, lineage || **ge'ne·al'o·gist** *n* || **ge'ne·a·log'i·cal** /-əloj'ikəl/ *adj*

gen·er·a /jen'ərə/ *pl* of **genus**

gen·er·al /jen'(ə)rəl/ [L *generalis* < L *genus* (*generis*) class, race] *adj* 1 relating to a whole category or group; **2** pert. to the majority; **3** widespread; **4** not specific or particular; **5** usual, ordinary; **6** taken or viewed as a whole, as *the general situation;* **7** senior or highest, as *postmaster general* ‖ *n* **8** a second highest Army or Air Force officer, ranking above a lieutenant general; **b** any officer above the rank of colonel; **9 in general, a** usually; **b** as a whole; **c** without specific details ‖ SYN *adj* universal, customary, common, familiar, ordinary, normal, widespread, usual, prevalent ‖ DISCR *Common,* as here compared, means shared by many; hence, of ordinary occurrence, or happening frequently; we say a *common* fate; the *common* lot; a *common* experience. *General* emphasizes the idea of number rather than that of sharing; *general* includes the majority of cases, admitting some, perhaps many, exceptions, as a *general* rule; a *general* statement; hence, because so inclusive, it has come to mean widespread, as *general* opinion. *Universal* includes all cases or individuals concerned; it admits no exceptions

Gen'er·al As·sem'bly *n* **1** legislature of some states; **2** chief deliberative assembly of the United Nations, composed of delegations from all member nations

gen'er·al de·liv'er·y *n* mail held in a post office until called for

gen'er·al·is'si·mo' /-is'imō'/ [It *superl* of *generale* general] *n* supreme military commander

gen'er·al'i·ty /-al'itē/ *n* (-ties) **1** state of being general; **2** greatest part; majority; **3** nonspecific statement; **4** general principle

gen'er·al·ize' *vt* **1** to treat as general; **2** to derive (a general principle or inference) from particular instances; **3** to derive a general principle from (particular instances) ‖ *vi* **4** to formulate a general rule; **5** to draw general inferences ‖ **gen'er·al·i·za'tion** *n*

gen'er·al·ly *adv* **1** commonly; **2** extensively; **3** in a broad sense

gen'er·al of'fi·cer *n* officer above the grade of colonel

gen'er·al of the air' force' *n* highest rank in the U.S. Air Force

gen'er·al of the ar'my *n* highest rank in the U.S. Army

gen'er·al prac·ti'tion·er *n* physician who does not specialize

gen'er·al ses'sions *n* court of general jurisdiction in some states of the U.S.

gen'er·al·ship' *n* **1** office, rank, or military skill of a military commander; **2** skillful tactics in leadership

gen'er·al store' *n* store in a rural area that sells a large variety of goods

gen·er·ate /jen'ərāt'/ [L *generare* (*-atus*) to beget] *vt* **1** to bring into existence, as offspring; **2** to produce, as electricity; **3** to create, originate; spread around ‖ **gen'er·a'tive** /also jen'ərətiv/ *adj* ‖ SYN form, make, beget, create, originate, produce

gen·er·a'tion *n* **1** act or process of generating; **2** single succession in natural descent; **3** people of the same period; **4** average difference in age between parents and offspring, in man, about 30 years; **5** type of objects derived from a preceding type

gen·er·a'tion gap' *n* vast disparity between the outlook or aspirations of one age group of people and those of another

gen'er·a'tor *n* **1** one who or that which generates; **2** machine that converts mechanical energy into electrical energy; **3** apparatus that produces vapor or gas

ge·ner·ic /jəner'ik/ [< L *genus* (*generis*) class, race] *adj* **1** pert. to all members of a class or group; not specific; **2** *biol* pert. to a genus; **3** not trademarked ‖ **ge·ner'i·cal·ly** *adv*

gen·er·ous /jen'ərəs/ [OF < L *generosus* wellborn] *adj* **1** honorable; magnanimous; **2** unselfish, liberal; **3** ample, large; **4** bountiful ‖ **gen'er·os'i·ty** /-ros'itē/ *n* (-ties) ‖ SYN liberal, beneficent, bountiful, magnanimous, munificent, disinterested ‖ DISCR A *generous* giver is a free and warm-hearted giver, and his gift is large in proportion to his means. A *generous* person does not confine his noble-mindedness to the material world, but shows himself tolerant in spirit, lacking in prejudice, and free from meanness. A *liberal* giver is an open-handed one; a *liberal* gift is ample, though not extravagant; a *liberal* thinker, unshackled by conservatism, ranges freely; a *liberal* mind balks at narrowness or intolerance. A *munificent* gift is large, even vast, and is often made with a splendidly *generous* gesture. A *bountiful* gift is ample in amount and freely bestowed. *Beneficent* emphasizes the character of one who is actively kind; a *beneficent* deed really does good and comes from a warm heart. One who is *magnanimous* is great of mind and soul; he never allows himself to be petty or mean, and he generously overlooks weaknesses in others ‖ ANT base, avaricious, stingy

gen·e·sis /jen'əsis/ [Gk] *n* (-ses /-sēz'/) **1** origin, beginning; **2 Genesis** first book of the Old Testament, dealing with the Creation

ge·net·ic /jənet'ik/ [< *genesis*] *adj* **1** of or pert. to genetics; inherited; **2** of or pert. to genes

ge·net'ic en·gi·neer'ing *n* method of

directing genetic processes by the introduction of microbiological agents in the body in order to control its ultimate destiny

ge·net·ics *nsg* branch of biology that deals with heredity ‖ **ge·net′i·cist** *n*

Ge·ne·va /jənēv′ə/ *n* city in SW Switzerland (180,000) ‖ **Ge·ne′van** *adj & n*

Gen·ghis Khan /jeŋ′gis kän′/ *n* (1162–1227) Mongol conqueror of most of Asia and Russia

ge·ni·al /jēn′ē̄·əl, jēn′yəl/ [L *genialis* festive] *adj* 1 kindly and sympathetic; cordial; 2 agreeable, as climate ‖ **ge′ni·al·ly** *adv* ‖ **ge′ni·al′i·ty** /-al′-itē/ *n* ‖ SYN companionable, well-disposed, cordial, friendly

-gen·ic /jen′ik/ [see -**gen**] *adj comb form* producing or produced by, as *cryogenic*

ge·nie /jēn′ē̄/ [F < Ar *jinnī*] *n* jinn

gen·i·tal /jen′itəl/ [OF < L *genitalis*] *adj* 1 pert. to reproduction or the sexual organs ‖ *n* 2 **genitals** *pl* external sex organs

gen′i·ta′lia /-tāl′ē̄·ə, -yə/ *npl* genitals

gen·i·tive /jen′itiv/ [L *genetivus*] *n gram* 1 case expressing typically possession; 2 word in the genitive ‖ *also adj*

gen·ius /jēn′yəs/ [L = patron spirit] *n* 1 a remarkable natural fitness for some special pursuit; b extraordinary creative intellectual or artistic power; c person possessing such power; 2 distinctive spirit of quality, as of a nation or language ‖ SYN talent, turn, aptitude, intellect ‖ DISCR *Genius* is intellectual capacity of an extraordinary degree; it manifests itself as an instinctive power which is imaginative, creative, and spontaneous. *Talent* is exceptional mental ability in one field, capable of development through training

Gen·o·a /jen′ō̄·ə/ *n* seaport in NE Italy (780,000) ‖ **Gen′o·ese′** /-ēz′, -ēs′/ *adj & n* (-ese)

gen·o·cide /jen′əsīd′/ [Gk *genos* race + -*cide*] *n* 1 deliberate extermination of a race or nation; 2 person who practices genocide ‖ **gen′o·cid′al** *adj*

gen·re /zhän′rə/ [F = kind] *n* 1 kind, sort, or style, esp. in literature or art; 2 painting representing everyday life realistically ‖ *also adj*

gent /jent/ *n slang* gentleman

gen·teel /jentēl′/ [F *gentil*] *adj* 1 polite, well-bred; 2 affectedly so ‖ SYN refined, well-bred, cultivated (see *polite*)

gen·tian /jen′shən/ [L *gentiana* < *Gentius* king of Illyria] *n* 1 any of a genus (*Gentiana*) of herbs usu. bearing beautiful blue flowers; 2 root of the yellow gentian (*G. lutea*), the extract of which is used as a tonic

gen·tile or **Gen·tile** /jen′tīl/ [L *gentilis* of the same clan] *n* 1 one not a Jew; spec. a Christian; 2 (among Mormons) one not a Mormon; 3 pagan ‖ *also adj*

gen·til·i·ty /jentil′itē/ [see **gentle**] *n* (-ties) elegance of manner; good breeding

gen·tle /jent′əl/ [OF *gentil* of good birth < L *gentilis* of the same clan] *adj* 1 well-born; 2 courteous, refined; 3 kindly, amiable; 4 mild, not rough; 5 tractable, tame; 6 gradual (slope) ‖ SYN placid, soft, soothing, bland, docile, tame

gen′tle breeze′ *n* wind of 8–12 miles per hour

gen′tle·folk′ *npl* persons of good family and breeding

gen′tle·man /-mən/ *n* (-men /-mən/) 1 man of breeding and manners; 2 member of the British gentry 2; 3 respectable man of independent income who does not work for a living; 4 (polite term for) any man; 5 male servant; valet ‖ **gen′tle·man·ly** *adj* ‖ **gen′tle·wom′an** *nfem* (-wom′en)

gen′tle·men′s a·gree′ment *n* agreement based entirely on personal honor

gen′tle sex′ *n* women in general

gen·try /jent′rē/ [OF *genterise*] *n* 1 well-bred people in general; 2 *Brit* nonnobles with coats of arms and property, ranking next below the nobility; 3 people of a particular group

gen·u·flect /jen′yəflekt′/ [< L *genu* knee *flectere* to bend] *vi* to bend the knee in worship ‖ **gen′u·flec′tion** *n*

gen·u·ine /jen′yōō·in/ [L *genuinus* innate, real] *adj* 1 authentic, real; not counterfeit; 2 sincere ‖ **gen′u·ine·ly** *adv* ‖ **gen′u·ine·ness** *n* ‖ SYN true, pure, actual, authentic, unaffected, sincere

ge·nus /jēn′əs/ [L = race] *n* (**gen·e·ra** /jen′ərə/) *biol* subdivision of a family, itself divisible into species

ge·o- [< Gk *ge*] *comb form* earth

ge·o·cen·tric /jē′əsen′trik/ *adj* 1 pert. to or having the earth as a center; 2 pert. to the center of the earth ‖ **ge′o·cen′tri·cal·ly** *adv*

ge·od·e·sy /jē·od′isē/ [Gk *geodaisia* division of the earth] *n* science of measuring the size and shape of the earth, and of surveying areas so large that the earth's curvature must be considered ‖ **ge′o·des′ic** /-ədes′-, -ədēs′-/ *also* **ge′o·det′ic** /-ədet′-/ *adj*

ge·og·ra·phy /jē·og′rəfē/ [Gk *geographia*] *n* (-phies) 1 science dealing with the earth's surface features, climate, flora and fauna, populations, resources, industries, and political divisions; 2 topographical features of a region ‖ **ge·og′ra·pher** *n* ‖ **ge′o·graph′ic** (-i·cal) /-əgraf′-/ *adj*

ge·o·log·ic (-i·cal) /jē′əloj′ik(əl)/ *adj* of or pert. to geology

ge′o·log′ic time′ *n* long periods of

time, as epochs and eras, during which geologic changes take place

ge·ol·o·gy /jē·ol′ə jē/ [*geo-* + *-logy*] *n* (-gies) science which deals with the earth's crust, its successive physical changes, and the causes producing such changes ‖ **ge·ol′o·gist** *n*

ge·o·met·ric (-ri·cal) /jē′əmet′rik(əl)/ *adj* 1 pert. to or done by geometry; 2 characterized by lines, angles, circles, etc., as *geometric designs*

ge′o·met′ric pro·gres′sion *n math* sequence of terms in which the ratio between any two successive terms is the same, as 1, 2, 4, 8, 16

ge·om·e·try /jē·om′ itrē/ [Gk *geometria* measurement of the earth] *n* (-tries) branch of mathematics treating of the properties, measurements, and relations of lines, angles, surfaces, and solids ‖ **ge·om′e·tri′cian** /-trish/-ən/ *n*

ge′o·phys′ics /jē′ə-/ *nsg* physics relating to the earth in such matters as the tides, magnetism, temperature, meteorology, etc. ‖ **ge′o·phys′i·cal** *adj*

ge′o·pol′i·tics *nsg* 1 science of the relation between the domestic and foreign political life of a state and its physical environment; 2 national policy that is based on the interrelation of politics and geography ‖ **ge′o·po·lit′i·cal** *adj*

George III /jôrj′/ *n* (1738–1820) king of England (1760–1820), last sovereign of the American colonies

George′town′ *n* seaport and capital of Guyana (75,000)

Geor·gia /jôrj′ə/ *n* 1 state in SE United States (4,589,575; 58,876 sq. m.; cap. Atlanta); 2 constituent republic of the Soviet Union in Caucasia (4,000,000; 27,800 sq.m.; cap. Tiflis) ‖ **Geor′gian** *n*

ge·o·ther·mal /gē′əthurm′əl/ [*geo-* + *thermal*] *adj* 1 a pert. to the earth's internal heat; b (power) produced by such heat; 2 (energy) produced by the heat arising from the difference in temperature of two locations, one of which is under the surface of the earth

ge·ra·ni·um /jirān′ē·əm/ [L < Gk *geranion* crane's bill] *n* 1 common pink- or purple-flowered wild plant (genus *Geranium*) of E North America; 2 South African plant (*Pelargonium*), cultivated for its brilliantly colored or white flowers or for its fragrant foliage

ger·i·at·rics /jer′ē·at′riks/ [< Gk *geras* old age + *-iatrics*] *nsg* branch of medicine dealing with old age and the diseases of old age ‖ **ger′i·at′ric** *adj* ‖ **ger′i·a·tri′cian** /-ə·trish/ən/ *n*

germ /jurm′/ [F *germe* < L *germen* seed] *n* 1 rudimentary element of an organism; 2 sprout; seed; 3 microbe, bacterium, esp. disease-causing; 4 source, origin, as *the germ of an idea*

Ger·man /jur′mən/ [L *Germanus*] *adj* 1 of or pert. to Germany, its inhabitants, or their language ‖ *n* 2 native or inhabitant of Germany; 3 person of German descent; 4 language of the Germans

ger·mane /jərmān′/ [OF *germaine* < L *germanus* of the same parents] *adj* related, relevant

Ger′man Em′pire *n* empire which was established in 1871 by Bismarck under William I, king of Prussia, and which lasted until 1918

Ger·man·ic /jərman′ik/ *adj* 1 of or pert. to the Germans and allied peoples, as the Dutch, Scandinavians, and English; 2 German; 3 pert. to or designating the Germanic branch of languages ‖ *n* 4 a original language spoken by the Germanic people; b branch of the Indo-European family of languages descended from this

ger·ma·ni·um /jərman′ē·əm/ [< L *Germania* Germany] *n* rare gray-white metalloid element (Ge; at.no. 32; at. wt. 72.59), used chiefly as a semiconductor

Ger′man mea′sles *nsg* contagious virus disease resembling measles, usu. mild but damaging to the unborn child if contracted during pregnancy

Ger′man shep′herd *n* one of a breed of large shepherd dogs, intelligent and easily trained, used in police work and as Seeing Eye dogs

Ger′man sil′ver *n* any of several white alloys of nickel, copper, and zinc, used as a base for plated ware

Ger·ma·ny /-nē/ *n* region in N central Europe, divided since 1945 into East Germany and West Germany

ger·mi·cide /jurm′isīd′/ [< *germ* + *-cide*] *n* substance that kills germs ‖ **ger′mi·cid′al** *adj*

ger·mi·nate /jurm′ināt′/ [L *germinare* (-*atus*) to sprout] *vi* 1 to sprout or bud; 2 to begin to develop into a higher form ‖ *vt* 3 to cause to develop; produce ‖ **ger′mi·na′tion** *n* ‖ SYN propagate, develop, sprout, bud

germ′ war′fare′ *n* warfare in which bacteria, viruses, and other microorganisms are used to injure or destroy human beings, animals, or crops

ger·on·tol·o·gy /jer′əntol′əjē/ [< Gk *geron* (-*ontos*) old man] *n* science dealing with the aged and the processes of aging

ger·ry·man·der /jer′ē·man′dər, jer′-/ [Elbridge *Gerry* (1744–1814) gov. of Mass. + sala*mander*] *vt* 1 to create (an election district) in such a form as to give unfair advantage to one political party; 2 to manipulate unfairly ‖ *n* 3 act of gerrymandering; 4 gerrymandered district, often having a weird shape on a map

ger·und /jer′ənd/ [LL *gerundium*] *n* verbal noun; in English, the -*ing* form of verbs when used as a noun, as *writing letters is a chore*

Ge·sta·po /gəstäp′ō/ [G *geheime Staatspolizei*] *n* secret state police of Nazi Germany

ges·tate /jes′tāt/ [L *gestare (-atus)* to carry] *vt & vi* 1 to develop in the womb; 2 to develop slowly in the mind ‖ **ges·ta′tion** *n*

ges·tic·u·late /jestik′yəlāt′/ [L *gesticulari (-atus)*] *vi* to make gestures ‖ **ges·tic′u·la′tion** *n*

ges·ture /jes′chər/ [ML *gestura* posture, bearing] *n* 1 bodily movement expressing or emphasizing an idea or emotion; 2 act conveying intention ‖ *vi* 3 to make gestures ‖ *vt* 4 to express by gestures ‖ **SYN** *n* attitude, action, posture, gesticulation

get /get′/ [ON *geta*] *v* (**got**; **got** or **got·ten**; **get·ting**) *vt* 1 to come to have; obtain; receive; acquire; 2 to cause to be in some state or location, as *to get a machine started*, *to get the key in the keyhole*; 3 to prepare (a meal); 4 to persuade, as *to get her to go*; 5 to cause to be done, as *to get one's shoes shined*; 6 to catch or corner, as *you got me there*; 7 to capture; 8 *slang* to understand; 9 to find out; 10 to fetch; 11 to baffle; 12 to affect emotionally; 13 to hit, wound; 14 *colloq* to kill; 15 to be revenged on; 16 **get across** to make comprehensible; 17 **get it** *colloq* to be punished; 18 **get it over** to finish with something; 19 **get on** to put on; 20 **get off** to remove; 21 **have got to have** ‖ *vi* 22 to bring, take, or put oneself, as *to get into clothes*; 23 to succeed, contrive, as *she got to go after all*; 24 *colloq* to scram; 25 to become, as *I got hungry*; 26 to be, as *I got hit in the eye*; 27 to start, as *get going*; 28 to move from one place to another, as *get about, around, away, back, down, in, off, on, out, to, up*; 29 **get ahead** to be successful; 30 **get along, a** to leave; **b** to manage nicely; **c** to get on; 31 **get around** to circumvent; 32 **get at, a** to imply; **b** to determine; 33 **get away with** to do (something reprehensible) without being punished; 34 **get back at** to be revenged on; 35 **get by** to survive; 36 **get off** to escape punishment; 37 **get on, a** to proceed; **b** to be on good terms; **c** to make progress; 38 **get over** to recover from; 39 **get together, a** to congregate; **b** to agree; 40 **get up, a** to arise from bed; **b** to rise from a sitting or reclining position; 41 **get with** *slang* to keep abreast of ‖ *n* 42 offspring of an animal; 43 *tennis* very difficult return shot ‖ **SYN** *v* gain, acquire, attain, procure, win, achieve, secure ‖ **DISCR** To *get* is to come into the possession of in any way, as to *get* a fine salary, a promotion, a legacy, a disease, and an idea. To *gain* is to

get by labor, struggle, or effort that which is an advantage, a profit, or a goal, as to *gain* a livelihood, mastery over oneself. To *acquire*, like to *get*, means to come into full possession of in any manner; usually, however, *acquire* is used of those things *gained* slowly, as a collection of rarities, a language, a cultivated manner. One *earns* what he works for; we *earn* a living, or recognition in some field of endeavor. One *attains* who accomplishes the object of a lofty or worthy ambition; we *attain*, or *attain* to, greatness; some *attain* spiritual heights. To *procure* is to obtain, particularly through search, expenditure, or the services of others, as to *procure* advantageous seats, a copy of a book, a meal. To *win* is to *get* by struggle against hostile opposition, as in business, or in friendly competition, as in sport, love, or the like. To *achieve* is to *attain*, as by valor or industry, a great end, as to *achieve* glory, victory, success

get′a·way′ *n* 1 start, as of a race; 2 escape

Geth·sem·a·ne /gethsem′ənē/ *n* 1 garden near Jerusalem, the scene of Christ's agony and betrayal (Matt. 26:36); 2 any agonizing crisis

Get·tys·burg /get′izburg′/ *n* small town in S Pennsylvania, scene of crucial Civil War battle July 1–3, 1863

get′up′ *n colloq* 1 costume, dress; 2 format, style

gew·gaw /g(y)ōō′gô/ [?] *n* bauble, trinket

gey·ser /gīz′ər, gīs′-/ [Icel *geysir* gusher] *n* 1 hot spring which intermittently ejects jets of steam and water ‖ /gēz′-/ *n* 2 *Brit* hot-water heater

Gha·na /gän′ə/ *n* republic in W Africa (11,000,000; 92,000 sq.m.; cap. Accra) ‖ **Gha·na·ian** or **Gha·ni·an** /gänä′ən, gän′ē-ən/ *adj & n*

ghast·ly /gast′lē, gäst′-/ [OE *gāstlic* spiritual] *adj* (**-li·er**; **-li·est**) 1 deathlike; pale; 2 horrible; shocking ‖ *adv* 3 frightfully ‖ **ghast′li·ness** *n* ‖ **SYN** *adj* pallid, wan, cadaverous, hideous, gruesome

gher·kin /gurk′in/ [D *gurken* cucumbers] *n* 1 small prickly cucumber (*Cucumis anguria*) used for pickling; 2 immature common cucumber so used

ghet·to /get′ō/ [It] *n* (**-tos** or **-toes**) 1 quarter of a city in which formerly Jews were required to live; 2 slum inhabited chiefly by underprivileged minorities

ghost /gōst′/ [OE *gāst*] *n* 1 disembodied spirit of a dead person, supposed to haunt the living; 2 shadowy semblance; 3 ghost writer; 4 *telv* double image ‖ *vt & vi* 5 to ghostwrite ‖ **ghost′ly** *adj* (**-li·er**; **-li·est**) ‖

SYN *n* specter, phantom, phantasm, spirit, shade

ghost′ town′ *n* abandoned town

ghost′write′ *v* (-wrote′; -writ·ten) *vt* to write (books, articles, or speeches) for another whose name appears as the author || also *vi* || **ghost′ writ′er** *n*

ghoul /gōōl′/ [Ar *ghūl*] *n* 1 evil Oriental spirit that robs graves and feeds on the dead; 2 grave robber || **ghoul′ish** *adj*

GHQ, G.H.Q. General Headquarters

GI, G.I. [orig. galvanized *iron*, later taken to be government *issue*] *U.S. Army adj* 1 adhering to Army regulations and specifications; 2 of or pert. to enlisted men || *n* (GI's or GIs) 3 enlisted man

gi·ant /jī′ənt/ [OF *geant* < Gk *gigas* (-*antos*)] *n* 1 imaginary or legendary being of enormous size; 2 person or thing of great size, power, or importance || also *adj* || **gi′ant·ess** *nfem*

gi′ant·ism *n* condition causing growth to abnormal size of the entire body or of parts of the body

gi′ant pan′da *n* panda 2

gib·ber /jib′ər, gib′-/ [imit] *vi* to speak rapidly and incoherently; talk nonsense

gib′ber·ish *n* unintelligible chatter or writing

gib·bet /jib′it/ [OF *gibet*] *n* 1 gallows; 2 post with a projecting arm on which formerly the bodies of executed criminals were exhibited in chains || *vt* 3 to hang on a gallows; 4 to expose to public scorn

gib·bon /gib′ən/ [F] *n* any of a genus (*Hylobates*) of small, long-armed, arboreal anthropoid apes of SE Asia

gib·bous /gib′əs, jib′-/ [< L *gibbus* hump] *adj* 1 humpbacked; 2 (moon) convex at both edges, as it appears between half-moon (first quarter) and full moon and also between full moon and half-moon (last quarter)

gibe /jīb′/ [perh MF *giber* to treat roughly] *n* 1 taunt; sarcastic remark || *vt* & *vi* 2 to jeer, taunt || SYN *v* scoff, deride, flout, taunt, mock (see *jeer*)

gib·lets /jib′lits/ [< OF *gibelet* stew] *npl* edible internal organs of poultry, as the liver, gizzard, etc.

Gi·bral·tar /jibrôlt′ər/ *n* British crown colony on the Rock of Gibraltar (25,000; 1⅞ sq.m.)

Gi·bral·tar, Strait of *n* strait between Europe and Africa connecting the Atlantic with the Mediterranean

gid·dy /gid′ē/ [OE *gydig* insane] *adj* (-di·er; -di·est) 1 having or causing dizziness; 2 flighty, frivolous || **gid′di·ness** *n* || SYN unsteady, flighty, whirling, thoughtless, dizzy

Gide, An·dré /ăN′drā′zhēd′/ *n* (1869-1951) French writer; Nobel prize 1947

Gid·e·on /gid′ē·ən/ *n Bib* judge of Israel who delivered his people from the Midianites (Judges 6:11; 8:32)

Gid′e·on So·cí′e·ty *n* society of laymen of many denominations founded (1899) to place Bibles in hotel rooms

gift /gift′/ [OE] *n* 1 something given; present; 2 power or right of giving; 3 natural talent || SYN endowment, aptitude, talent, faculty, turn, bent; grant, alms, present, bribe, gratuity, boon, largess, donation || DISCR *Gift* and *endowment* name exceptional powers bestowed on us by nature. The two words are sometimes interchangeable; but *gift* is often used to name ability of a higher order than *endowment*, as the *gift* of eloquence; but beauty, charm, graciousness of manner are *endowments*, not *gifts*. *Talent*, in its specific sense, is a special mental *gift*, an *aptitude*, as for music or acting, capable of being developed by training, but falling short of genius. *Faculty* names a knack or *endowment*, as the *faculty* of managing men; the *faculty* of producing work. *Aptitude*, *turn*, and *bent* name inclinations or tendencies of the mind or character in certain directions. An *aptitude* may be natural or acquired; *turn* and *bent* more frequently name innate capacities, *bent* indicating a stronger and more positive inclination than *turn*. We speak of an *aptitude* for meeting people easily, a *turn* for mechanics, a *bent* for reading; a natural *bent* of the mind (see *boon*[1])

gift′ed *adj* 1 endowed with natural talent; 2 exceptionally intelligent

gift′ of gab′ *n colloq* ability and readiness to pour forth words

gift′-wrap′ *v* (-wrapped; -wrap·ping) *vt* to wrap with fancy paper and ribbon for presentation as a gift

gig /gig′/ *n* 1 one-horse, two-wheeled carriage; 2 light ship's boat

gi·gan·tic /jīgant′ik/ [< Gk *gigas* (-*antos*) giant] *adj* huge, colossal; of extraordinary size || SYN titanic, enormous, prodigious, vast, immense

gig·gle /gig′əl/ [imit] *n* 1 nervous silly laugh || *vi* 2 to laugh in a nervous tittering way || **gig′gler** *n*

gig·o·lo /jig′əlō/ [F] *n* man paid to be a woman's escort or lover

Gi′la mon′ster /hēl′ə/ [*Gila* River in Arizona] *n* large venomous black-and-orange lizard (*Heloderma suspectum*) of the SW United States and NW Mexico

gild /gild′/ [OE *gyldan*] *v* (gild·ed or gilt) *vt* 1 to coat with a layer of gold or something gold-colored; 2 to make attractive; adorn || **gild′ing** *n*

gill[1] /gil′/ [ME *gile*] *n* 1 breathing organ of most aquatic animals; 2 fleshy flap hanging below the beak of a fowl

gill[2] /jil′/ [MF *gille* wine measure] *n* one fourth of a pint

gil′ly·flow′er /jil′ē-/ [<ME *gilofre* <

OF *girofle*] *n* any of various cultivated garden plants, as the wall-
flower (*Cheiranthus cheiri*) or the
common stock (*Matthiola incana*)

gilt /gilt'/ 1 *pp & pt* of **gild** || *adj* 2
gilded; 3 gold-colored || *n* 4 gold
or gold-colored substance used to
gild a surface

gilt'-edged' *adj* of the highest quality,
as securities

gim·crack /jim'krak'/ [ME *gibecrake*]
n showy ornament; gewgaw || also
adj

gim·let /gim'lit/ [OF *guimbelet*] *n* small
boring tool with a pointed screw at
one end and a cross handle at the
other

gim'let-eyed' *adj* sharp-eyed

gim·mick /gim'ik/ [?] *n slang* 1 tricky
device; 2 something that attracts attention; 3 scheme kept hidden

gimp /gimp/ [?] *n* 1 limp; 2 cripple ||
gimp'y *adj*

gin[1] /jin'/ [*abbr* of *geneva* < D *gene-
ver* < L *juniperus* juniper] *n* alcoholic liquor distilled from grain and
usu. flavored with juniper berries

gin[2] [OF *engin* engine] *n* 1 cotton gin ||
v (**ginned; gin·ning**) *vt* 2 to clear (cotton) of seeds by a cotton gin

gin[3] [?] *n* gin rummy

gin·ger /jin'jər/ [OE *gingifer* < L *zingi-
ber*] *n* 1 any of a family (Zingiber-
aceae) of tropical plants esp. *Zingi-
ber officinale*, widely cultivated for
its pungent aromatic rootstock; 2
colloq vim; snap || *vt* **ginger up** to
liven

gin'ger ale' also *Brit* **gin'ger beer'** *n*
ginger-flavored carbonated soft drink

gin'ger·bread' *n* 1 molasses cake flavored with ginger; 2 gaudy and overelaborate ornamentation, esp. in
architecture

gin'ger·ly [?] *adj* 1 cautious, wary ||
adv 2 warily

ging·ham /giŋ'əm/ [F *guingan* < Malay *gingang* striped] *n* cotton dress
cloth dyed in the yarn before weaving

gin' mill' *n slang* bar, saloon

gin' rum'my *n cards* popular variety
of rummy

gi·raffe /jiraf', -räf'/ [F *girafe* < Ar
zurāfah] *n* very tall and very long-
necked ruminant (*Giraffa camelo-
pardalis*) of Africa

gird /gurd'/ [OE *gyrdan*] *v* (**girt** or
gird·ed) *vt* 1 to encircle or bind, as
with a belt; 2 to encircle; 3 to brace
(oneself) for action

gird'er *n* large beam, as of steel or
wood, used in structures for support, as of joists, floors, or masonry

gir·dle /gurd'əl/ [OR *gyrdel*] *n* 1 light
undergarment for supporting and
slimming the abdomen and hips; 2
belt, cord, or sash for the waist; 3
anything that surrounds like a belt
|| *vt* 4 to bind with, or as with, a
belt; 5 to enclose; encircle

girl /gurl'/ [ME *girle* young person]
n 1 female child; 2 young unmarried
woman; 3 female servant or employee; 4 sweetheart; 5 *colloq* wom-
an || **girl'ish** *adj* || **girl'hood'** *n*

girl' Fri'day [on model of *man Friday*]
n efficient and trustworthy female
worker, esp. in an office

girl' friend' *n* 1 female friend; 2 sweetheart

girl' scout' *n* member of the Girl
Scouts, an organization patterned
after the Boy Scouts, for general
outdoor training for girls

girt /gurt'/ 1 *pt & pp* of **gird** || *vt* 2
to gird 1

girth /gurth'/ [ON *gjörth* girdle] *n* 1
band by which the saddle is kept on
a horse; 2 circumference, as of a
waist or tree

gist /jist'/ [MF = it lies] *n* substance
of a matter; main point

give /giv'/ [OE *giefan*] *v* (**gave; giv·en**)
vt 1 to make a present of; donate;
bestow; 2 to hand over; deliver; 3
to offer or present, as a concert or
dinner; 4 to administer, as medicine;
5 to furnish or supply; 6 to grant; 7
to inflict, as punishment; 8 to allow,
as permission; 9 to pay; 10 to offer
as due, as *give him credit*; 11 to
yield, concede; 12 to utter, as a command; 13 to be the cause of, as *it
gives me a headache*; 14 to produce,
yield, as a result; 15 **give away, a**
to donate; **b** to present (the bride) to
the bridegroom; **c** to betray; 16 **give
it to** *colloq* to punish or reprimand;
17 **give off** to emit; 18 **give out, a**
to send out; **b** to announce; **c** to
distribute; 19 **give up, a** to renounce;
b to relinquish; **c** to devote (oneself)
|| *vi* 20 to present gifts; 21 to yield
to pressure; 22 **give in** to yield; 23
give out, a to become exhausted; **b**
to become used up; 24 **give up, a** to
despair; **b** to surrender || *n* 25 resil-
ience, elasticity || **giv'er** *n* || SYN *v*
grant, bestow, confer, present, offer,
supply, furnish, impart, cede, con-
vey || DISCR To *give* is a general term,
meaning primarily to make another
the receiver of something at our disposal or in our possession without
the idea of return or compensation,
as my father *gave* me a dollar. *Give*
is so widely used, however, that it
has in addition acquired the connotation of parting with something for
an equivalent, or of communicating
that which cannot be regarded as a
gift, as I'll *give* you five thousand
for the property; *give* a ransom; *give*
orders; *give* him a kick; *give* us the
facts. To *bestow* is to *give* what is
especially wanted or expressly needed, as to *bestow* gifts upon the
poor; to *bestow* is sometimes an act
of condescension or favor, as the
prince *bestowed* largess upon his
courtiers. To *grant* is to concede in-

dulgently, as to *grant* permission, a pardon, or an appeal; or to *give* formally or authoritatively, as the king *granted* tracts of land for settlement. To *confer* is to *give* respectfully, as a favor, title, or degree, that which is esteemed as an honor by the recipient. We say that a university *gives*, *grants*, or *confers* degrees; a judge may *give* or *grant*, but he never *confers*, a stay of sentence. To *offer* is to tender for refusal or acceptance; it may be a purely business proposition, as he *offered* to sell the property; it may be a gesture of humility, as he *offered* heartfelt apologies; or it may connote solemnity, as he *offered* sacrifice to the gods

give′-and-take′ *n* 1 act or practice of compromising; 2 good-natured exchange of ideas

give′a·way′ *n* 1 unintentional revelation; 2 something given free; 3 robbery, as of public funds or resources; 4 radio or television program in which prizes are given to contestants; 5 *colloq* game in which the goal is to lose points rather than win them

giv·en /giv′ən/ 1 *pp* of **give** ‖ *adj* 2 inclined, addicted, as *given to lying;* 3 stated, prearranged; 4 assumed, granted

giv′en name′ *n* name given to a person at birth or baptism, as contrasted with family name

giz·zard /giz′ərd/ [ONF *guisier* < L *gigeria* giblets] *n* second stomach of birds in which food is crushed by means of swallowed pebbles

Gk, Gk. Greek

gla·cé /glasā′/ [F = frozen] *adj* 1 iced (cake); 2 candied (fruit); 3 having a glossy surface ‖ *vt* 4 to make glacé

gla·cial /glāsh′əl/ [< L *glacies* ice] *adj* 1 pert. to, consisting of, or caused by ice or glaciers; 2 pert. to or produced by a glacial epoch; 3 frigid, icy

gla′cial ep′och or **pe′ri·od** *n* any period during which much of the Northern Hemisphere was covered by glaciers

gla·cier /glāsh′ər/ [F dial.] *n* mass of ice compacted from snow which flows slowly down valleys or over a large land area, either melting as it flows or reaching the sea and breaking off into icebergs

glad /glad′/ [OE *glæd*] *adj* (**glad·der; glad·dest**) 1 pleased; joyous; 2 cheerful, gay; 3 causing joy; 4 willing ‖ **glad′ly** *adv* ‖ **glad′ness** *n* ‖ SYN joyful, delighted, gratified (cf. *happy*) ‖ ANT sad, disheartened, unhappy

glad′den *vt* to make glad ‖ SYN cheer, comfort, exhilarate, gratify, please

glade /glād′/ [perh < *glad*] *n* open space in the woods

glad′ hand′ *n* cordial, and often hypocritical, welcome

glad·i·a·tor /glad′ē·ā′tər/ [L < *gladius*

sword] *n* 1 in ancient Rome, professional fighter or captive who fought to the death against men or animals in the public arena; 2 any valiant contestant ‖ **glad′i·a·to′ri·al** /-ətôr′-, -tōr′-/ *adj*

gla·di·o·lus /glad′ē·ōl′əs/ [L = small sword] *n* any of a genus (*Gladiolus*) of plants of the iris family having sword-shaped leaves and tall spikes of variously colored flowers

Glad′stone bag′ [William *Gladstone* (1809–98) Brit prime minister] *n* rectangular suitcase hinged to open flat

glam·our also **glam·or** /glam′ər/ [Sc < Eng *grammar* in early sense of occult science] *n* 1 fascinating allurement; enchantment; 2 romantic excitement ‖ **glam′or·ous** also **glam′our·ous** *adj* ‖ **glam′or·ize** also **glam′our·ize′** *vt*

glance /glans′, gläns′/ [< OF *glacier* to slip] *n* 1 quick look; 2 deflected movement or rebound ‖ *vi* 3 to take a quick look; 4 **glance off** to strike slantingly and fly off ‖ SYN *n* (see *glimpse*)

gland /gland′/ [OF *glande* < L *glans* (*glandis*) acorn] *n* group of cells or organ secreting a substance to be used by or eliminated from the body ‖ **glan′du·lar** /-jələr/ *adj*

glan·ders /glan′dərz/ [< OF *glandres* glandular swelling] *n* contagious and very destructive disease of horses, caused by the bacillus *Actinobacillus mallei* and marked by swelling of the glands of the lower jaw and a discharge of mucus from the nose

glare /gler′/ [ME *glaren*] *vi* 1 to shine with a dazzling light; 2 to stare fiercely ‖ *vt* 3 to express with a glare ‖ *n* 4 dazzling light; 5 overpowering luster; 6 fierce piercing look ‖ SYN *n* flame, flare, brilliance, blaze (see *light¹*)

glar′ing *adj* 1 sending forth or reflecting dazzling light; 2 conspicuous, flagrant; 3 fiercely staring

Glas·gow /glas′gō/ *n* largest city in Scotland, on the Clyde ‖ **Glas·we′gian** /-wēj′(ē)ən/ *adj* & *n*

glass /glas′, gläs′/ [OE *glæs*] *n* 1 hard brittle substance, usu. transparent, made by fusing mixtures of silicates with sodium and potassium carbonates, borates, etc.; 2 any substance of similar properties and composition; 3 article made of glass, as a mirror, windowpane, drinking utensil, or lens; 4 quantity contained in a drinking glass; 5 any of certain instruments made principally of glass, as telescopes, microscopes, and barometers; 6 **glasses** *pl* eyeglasses

glass′blow′er *n* one who or the machine which shapes molten glass by blowing it into the desired form ‖ **glass′blow′ing** *n*

glass·ine /glasēn′/ [*glass* + *-ine*] *n* nearly airtight transparent or semitransparent paper used for packaging

glass'ware' *n* articles of glass

glass'y *adj* (·i·er; ·i·est) 1 like glass in smoothness or transparency; 2 staring without expression || **glass'i·ly** *adv* || **glass'i·ness** *n*

glau·co·ma /glôkōm'ə/ [< Gk *glaukos* bluish gray] *n* disease of the eye marked by pressure within the eyeball, resulting in blindness

glaze /glāz'/ [ME *glasen*] *vt* 1 to furnish (a window) with glass; 2 to give a glassy finish to (pottery or the like); 3 to cover with a glossy coating; 4 to coat (food) with sugar or syrup || *vi* 5 to become glazed or glassy || *n* 6 glassy coating, as of pottery, certain fabrics, or food || **glaz'er** *n* || **glaz'ing** *n*

gla·zier /glāzh'ər/ *n* one whose trade is to set glass in windows

gleam /glēm'/ [OE *glæm*] *n* 1 flash or beam of light; 2 faint trace or manifestation, as *a gleam of hope* || *vi* 3 to emit a gleam; 4 to appear suddenly || SYN *n* beam, glow, glint, glimmer (see *light*[1])

gleam' in the eye' *n* faint trace of hope

glean /glēn'/ [OF *glener*] *vt* 1 to gather, as grain that the reapers have left; 2 to collect bit by bit, as facts || *vi* 3 to gather grain left by reapers; 4 to collect a little at a time || **glean'er** *n*

glean'ings *npl* that which is gleaned

glee /glē'/ [OE *glēo* entertainment] *n* 1 joy, exultation; 2 song for three or more voices || SYN cheeriness, cheerfulness, liveliness, merriment, joviality, mirth, hilarity || ANT sorrow, grief, dejection

glee' club' *n* group organized to sing choral music

glen /glen'/ [Gael *gleann*] *n* narrow secluded valley

glib /glib'/ [< *obs glibbery* slippery] *adj* (**glib·ber**; **glib·best**) plausibly fluent || **glib'ly** *adv* || **glib'ness** *n* || SYN facile, voluble, ready (see *garrulous*)

glide /glīd'/ [OE *glīdan*] *vi* 1 to flow or move smoothly and effortlessly; 2 (of aircraft) to move or descend gradually without power under the influence of air currents and gravity; 3 *mus* to slur two or more notes || *vt* 4 to cause to glide || *n* 5 act of gliding; 6 *phonet* nonsyllabic vowel sound heard as the second element of diphthongs, as the *i* sound heard in *buy, hay*, the *oo͞* sound heard in *now, no* || SYN *v* slip, slide, run, flow, shade, grade, slur

glid'er *n* 1 one who or that which glides; 2 motorless aircraft depending on air currents for flight

glim·mer /glim'ər/ [ME *glimeren*] *vi* 1 to shine or appear faintly and unsteadily || *n* 2 feeble unsteady light;

3 glimpse; faint perception || **glim'-mer·ing** *n* || SYN *n* glitter, glow, shimmer, sheen (see *light*[1])

glimpse /glimps'/ [ME *glimsen*] *n* 1 brief transient view or look; 2 inkling, faint idea || *vt* 3 to catch a momentary view of || *vi* 4 glimpse at to glance at || SYN *n* glance || DISCR A *glance* is a brief look at something; a *glimpse* is a momentary view of it.

glint /glint'/ [ME *glent* < Scand] *n* 1 gleam; 2 luster || *vi* 3 to gleam or flash out

glis·san·do /glisän'dō/ [It < F *glissant* sliding] *n* playing of a series of notes by sliding the fingers rapidly over the keys of a piano or the strings of a stringed instrument

glis·ten /glis'ən/ [OE *glisnian*] *vi* 1 to sparkle; shine, gleam || *n* 2 glitter, gleaming || **glis'ten·ing·ly** *adv*

glitch /glich'/ [?] *n* sudden departure from normal behavior of a device or a natural phenomenon

glit·ter /glit'ər/ [ON *glitra*] *vi* 1 to sparkle with reflected light; 2 to be showy or brilliant || *n* 3 sparkling light; 4 brilliant splendor; 5 small glittering colored specks used as ornaments || SYN *n* flash, sparkle, gleam, glimmer (see *light*[1])

gloam·ing /glōm'ing/ [OE *glōmung*] *n poet.* twilight; early evening

gloat /glōt'/ [prob < Scand] *vi* **gloat over** to look at or think about (something) with malevolent satisfaction

glob·al /glōb'əl/ *adj* world-wide

globe /glōb'/ [L *globus* ball] *n* 1 sphere, ball; 2 anything shaped somewhat like a sphere; 3 sphere on which is drawn a map of the earth or of the heavens; 4 **the globe** the earth

globe'-trot'ter *n* one who travels frequently all over the world

glob·u·lar /glōb'yələr/ *adj* 1 spherical; 2 composed of globules

glob·ule /glob'yo͞ol/ [L *globulus*] *n* small spherical body

glob·u·lin /glob'yəlin/ *n* any of a class of widely distributed proteins, similar to the albumins, found in animal and vegetable matter

glock·en·spiel /glok'ənspēl'/ [G] *n mus* instrument with tuned metal bars set in a frame and played with hammers

gloom /glo͞om'/ [ME *gloumen* to scowl] *n* 1 dimness, obscurity; 2 melancholy, depression || *vi* 3 to look sullen; frown; 4 to be melancholy; 5 to appear or become dim or somber

gloom'y *adj* (·i·er; ·i·est) 1 overspread with, or wrapped in, darkness; 2 depressing; causing gloom; 3 dismal; melancholy; dispirited; cheerless || **gloom'i·ly** *adv* || **gloom'i·ness** *n* || SYN dark, dusky, clouded; sullen, sulky, glum, surly, ill-tempered, ill-humored, morose, splenetic ‖ DISCR *Gloomy* describes one who is doleful, dejected, or dispirited. The *sullen* person is one who is kicking against the pricks of life in a resentful discontent; usually he is passive, but he makes no secret of his injured pride. The *sulky* person is displeased, poutily cross, obstinately unsociable. *Sullen* and *sulky* people are reserved and silent in their ill-humor. *Surly, morose,* and *splenetic* persons are harsh and bitter of speech, and uncivil in manner. The *surly* person will find cause for offense in your most casual remark. The *morose* are sour, crabbed, and apt to vent their spite upon others. The *splenetic* are sour and bitterly spiteful. *Glum* people are sometimes *sullen,* but may be only temporarily depressed

glo·ri·fy /glôr′ifī′, glōr′-/ [MF *glorifier* < L *glorificare*] *v* (-**fied**) *vt* 1 to make glorious; 2 to magnify and honor in worship; extol; 3 to make or make seem more splendid or excellent ‖ **glo′ri·fi·ca′tion** *n* ‖ SYN dignify, beatify, exalt, elevate, praise

glo·ri·ous /glôr′ē·əs, glōr′-/ *adj* 1 full of glory; 2 magnificent, splendid ‖ **glo′ri·ous·ly** *adv*

glo·ry /glôr′ē, glōr′-/ [OF *glorie* < L *gloria*] *n* (-**ries**) 1 distinction, fame, renown; 2 adoring praise; 3 splendor, magnificence; 4 heavenly bliss; 5 object of pride; 6 *art* halo ‖ *v* (-**ried**) *vi* 7 **glory in** to exult in, be proud of ‖ SYN *n* reputation, renown, honor (see *fame*)

gloss¹ /glôs′, glos′/ [< Scand] *n* 1 smooth glistening luster; 2 deceptive appearance ‖ *vt* 3 to put a gloss on; 4 **gloss over** to cover up or mitigate, as faults ‖ **gloss′y** *adj* (-**i·er; -i·est**)

gloss² [OF *glose* < Gk *glossa* tongue] *n* 1 explanation or comment, usu. in the margin or between the lines, concerning a difficult passage in a manuscript; 2 glossary; 3 willfully misleading explanation ‖ *vt* 4 to furnish with glosses; 5 to put in a gloss

glos′sa·ry /-ərē/ [L *glossarium*] *n* (-**ries**) list with explanations of obsolete, difficult, uncommon, or technical terms

glot·tal /glot′əl/ *adj* pert. to or articulated at the glottis

glot·tis /glot′is/ [Gk] *n* aperture between the vocal cords in the larynx

glove /gluv′/ [OE *glōf*] *n* 1 covering for the hand with a separate sheath for each finger; 2 boxing glove; 3 baseball player's mitt ‖ *vt* 4 to cover with or as with a glove

glow /glō′/ [OE *glōwan*] *vi* 1 to radiate heat and light; be incandescent; 2 to be red; show brilliant color; 3 to be warm or flushed; 4 to be animated by emotion ‖ *n* 5 intense or shining heat; incandescence; 6

brightness of color; 7 passion, ardor; 8 warmth of body ‖ SYN *n* ruddiness, fervidness, luminosity (see *light¹*)

glow·er /glou′ər/ [ME *glowren*] *vi* 1 to stare with sullen anger ‖ *n* 2 look of sullen anger

glow′worm′ *n* luminous wingless beetle or larva of the family Lampyridae, which gives forth a phosphorescent light

glu·cose /gloō′kōs/ [F < Gk *glykys* sweet] *n* 1 a sugar —C₆H₁₂O₆— found in honey and most sweet fruits; 2 syrup obtained by the hydrolysis of starch

glue /gloō′/ [OF *glu* < L *glus*] *n* 1 adhesive viscous liquid obtained from animal gelatin; 2 any adhesive liquid ‖ *v* (**glu·ing**) *vt* 3 to join or fasten, as with glue ‖ **glue′y** *adj* (**glu·i·er; glu·i·est**)

glue′pot′ *n* 1 double boiler for melting glue; 2 *Australian* stretch of back road full of mudholes

glum /glum′/ [ME *gloumen* to scowl] *adj* (**glum·mer; glum·mest**) gloomy; sullen; dejected ‖ **glum′ly** *adv* ‖ SYN dismal, silent, morose, dispirited (see *gloomy*)

glut /glut′/ [ME *gluten*] *v* (**glut·ted; glut·ting**) *vt* 1 to fill to repletion; 2 to oversupply, overstock ‖ *n* 3 superabundance; satiety; 4 excess of supply over demand ‖ SYN *v* stuff, overeat, surfeit, satiate (see *satisfy*)

glu·ten /gloōt′ən/ [L = glue] *n* protein, or the sticky albuminous part of wheat flour

glu·te·us /gloōt′ē·əs, gloōtē′-/ [< Gk *gloutos* rump] *n* (-**i** /-ī′/) any of three muscles forming the buttocks ‖ **glu′·te·al** *adj*

glu·ti·nous /gloōt′ənəs/ [see **gluten**] *adj* sticky; gluey

glut·ton /glut′ən/ [OF *glouton* < L *gluttire* to swallow] *n* one who eats to excess ‖ **glut′ton·ous** *adj* ‖ **glut′ton·y** *n*

glyc·er·in or **glyc·er·ine** /glis′ərin/ [< Gk *glykeros* sweet] *n* syrupy liquid —HOCH₂CHOHCH₂OH— obtained by the saponification of oils and fats; used in cosmetics and ointments, as a solvent, a food preservative, in inks and in antifreeze

glyc′er·ol′ /-rōl′, -rol′/ *n chem* glycerin

gly·co·gen /glīk′əjən/ [< Gk *glykys* sweet +-*gen*] *n* amorphous white substance —(C₆H₁₀O₅)n— formed in the liver from carbohydrates and converted into sugar as the body requires it

gm. gram(s)

G′-man′ /-man′/ [Government *man*] *n* (-**men** /-men′/) *n* FBI agent

Gmc, Gmc. Germanic

GMT, G.M.T. Greenwich Mean Time

gnarled /närld′/ [var of *obs* knurled < *knur* knot in wood] *adj* bent, twisted; weatherbeaten

gnash /nash'/ [ME *gnasten* < Scand] *vt* to grind (the teeth) in anger or pain

gnat /nat'/ [OE *gnæt*] *n* any of several small stinging or biting winged insects

gnaw /nô'/ [OE *gnagan*] *vt & vi* 1 to bite or eat away by degrees; 2 to corrode; consume; torment ‖ **gnaw'-ing** *adj & n*

gneiss /nīs'/ [G] *n* close-grained crystalline rock formed of parallel layers of feldspar, quartz, and mica

gnome /nōm'/ [F < NL *gnomus*] *n* one of the legendary dwarfs inhabiting the interior of the earth and guarding its treasures

gno-mon /nō'mon/ [Gk = indicator] *n* anything that points out the time of day by its shadow, as the arm of a sundial or a pillar

GNP gross national product

gnu /n(y)ōō'/ [Bushman *nqu*] *n* (**gnu** or **gnus**) any of a genus (*Connochaetes*) of South African antelopes with large oxlike head, long mane and tail, and curved horns; wildebeest

go /gō'/ [OE *gān*] *v* (**went; gone**) *vi* 1 to move forward or from one point to another; proceed; 2 to work or operate, as *the engine won't go;* 3 to depart; 4 to be abolished or relinquished, as *crime must go;* 5 to die; 6 to be transferred, as *the estate goes to the heirs;* 7 to pass into another condition, become, as *to go crazy;* 8 to continue in a specified state, as *to go hungry;* 9 to resort or repair, as *to go to court;* 10 to be guided or led, as *to go by his example;* 11 to be in harmony; be appropriate; 12 to extend, lead, as *the road goes to the city;* 13 to result, turn out; 14 to be sold, as *it went for ten dollars;* 15 to run, have a particular wording or tune, as *how does the first line go?;* 16 to elapse, as time; 17 to belong, as *the dishes go in the pantry;* 18 to bring oneself into a specified state, as *to go to sleep;* 19 to be contained without remainder; 20 to be known, as *he goes by the name of John;* 21 to be used up; 22 to proceed, progress; 23 to be allotted, as *my money goes for rent;* 24 to fail, as the senses or a dam; 25 **be going to** to be about to, intend to; 26 **go along** to concur; 27 **go around** to be enough for all; 28 **go back on** to fail to keep, as one's word; 29 **go for**, **a** to try for; **b** to assault; **c** to like, favor; 30 **go hard with** to be troublesome to; 31 **go in for** to indulge in; 32 **go in with** to go into partnership with; 33 **go off**, **a** to depart; **b** to explode, fire, or begin to function; 34 **go on**, **a** to continue; **b** to take place; 35 **go out**, **a** to be extinguished; **b** to cease to be in fashion; **c** to go on strike; **d** to be

active socially; 36 **go over**, **a** to scan, examine; **b** to repeat; **c** to be accepted; 37 **go through**, **a** to undergo; **b** to search; **c** to be accepted; 38 **go through with** to bring to completion; 39 **go under**, **a** to fail; **b** to sink; 40 **go up**, **a** to increase; **b** to be constructed; 41 **let go**, **a** to release one's hold; **b** to free, release; 42 **let oneself go** to free oneself from restraint; 43 **to go** *colloq* (food) to be taken out ‖ *vt* 44 *colloq* to pay, bid, wager, as *I'll go two dollars;* 45 **go bail for** to act as surety for; 46 **go one's way**, **a** to proceed in the same direction, as *going my way?;* **b** to continue in a certain mode of action, as *she goes her own way* ‖ *n* (**goes**) 47 energy, animation; 48 try; 49 **make a go** of make a success; 50 **no go** *colloq* futile; 51 **on the go** constantly active

goad /gōd'/ [OE *gād*] *n* 1 cattle prod; 2 compelling motive; spur ‖ *vt* 3 to urge on or drive, as with a goad ‖ SYN *v* stimulate, excite, instigate, arouse, pique

go-a-head' *n* signal to proceed

goal /gōl'/ [ME *gol* boundary] *n* 1 point or post aimed at in a race or contest; 2 place over, into, or across which a ball or puck must go in order to score; 3 score made in so doing; 4 any end aimed at

goal'ie /-ē/ *n* goalkeeper

goal'keep'er *n* player stationed at a goal to prevent the ball or puck from entering

goat /gōt'/ [OE *gāt*] *n* 1 any of several hollow-horned, cud-chewing mammals (genus *Capra*) related to the sheep; 2 *colloq* scapegoat; 3 lecherous man; 4 **get someone's goat** *colloq* to anger or annoy someone

goat-ee' *n* pointed beard on a man's chin

goat'herd' *n* one who tends goats

goat'skin' *n* 1 skin of a goat; 2 leather made from it

goat'suck'er *n* any of various medium-sized, long-winged, insect-eating birds, active at night, of the family Caprimulgidae, as the whippoorwill and nighthawk

gob¹ /gob'/ [MF *gobe* mouthful] *n* 1 clot or lump; 2 **gobs** *pl colloq* great amount

gob² [?] *n colloq* sailor in the U.S. Navy

gob-ble¹ /gob'əl/ [prob < *gob¹*] *vt* 1 to swallow hastily or greedily; 2 **gobble up** *colloq* to seize greedily

gob-ble² [imit] *vi* to make the cry of the turkey ‖ also *n*

gob'ble-de-gook' or **gob'ble-dy-gook'** /-dēgŏōk'/ [< *gobble²*] *n* incomprehensible bureaucratic jargon

gob'bler *n* male turkey

go'-be-tween' *n* intermediary

Go-bi /gōb'ē/ *n* large desert in E Asia, chiefly in Mongolia

gob·let /gob′lĭt/ [OF *gobelet*] *n* drinking glass with a stem

gob·lin /gob′lĭn/ [MF *gobelin*] *n* evil, mischievous, misshapen sprite

go′·by′ *n* intentional passing by or slight

god /gŏd/ [OE] **1** divine being, deity, esp. male; **2** idol; **3** person or thing deified; **4 God** the one Supreme and Absolute being, ultimate source of the universe

god′child′ *n* (**-chil·dren**) child for whom a person becomes sponsor at a baptism

god′daugh′ter *n* female godchild

god′dess *n* **1** female deity; **2** woman of superior beauty or charm

god′fa′ther *n* **1** man who acts as sponsor for a child at a baptism; **2** any sponsor ‖ *vt* **3** to act as godfather to

god′head′ *n* **1** state of being divine; **2 Godhead** Supreme Deity, or his essence, nature, or attributes

Go·di·va /gədīv′ə/ *n* English noblewoman of the 11th century who is said to have ridden naked through the streets of Coventry to win relief for the people from a tax levied by her husband

god′less *adj* **1** irreligious; **2** sinful

god′ly *adj* (**-li·er; -li·est**) devout, pious ‖ **god′li·ness** *n* ‖ SYN righteous, holy, religious, pious

god′moth′er *n* woman who acts as sponsor for a child at a baptism

god′par′ent *n* godfather or godmother

God′s′ a′cre *n* churchyard

god′send′ *n* unexpected but opportune assistance, esp. if badly needed

god′son′ *n* male godchild

God′speed′ [*God speed* you] *n* success: a wish for a prosperous journey

-go′er /-gō′ər/ [< *go*] *n comb form* one who attends frequently, as *a church-goer*

Goe·the, Jo·hann Wolf·gang von /yö′hän vôlf′gäŋ fən gœt′ə/ *n* (1749–1832) German poet, dramatist, and novelist ‖ **Goe′the·an** /-tē·ən/ *adj*

go′-get′ter *n colloq* aggressive and enterprising person

gog·gle /gog′əl/ [ME *gogelen* to squint] *vi* **1** to stare with bulging eyes; **2** (of the eyes) to stare wide open ‖ *n* **3 goggles** *pl* large spectacles, with shields around the rims, for protecting the eyes from dust, excessive light, wind, etc.

gog′gle-eyed′ *adj* having staring, prominent, or bulging eyes

Gogh, Vin·cent van /van gō′/ *n* (1853–90) Dutch painter

go′ing *n* **1** departure; **2** condition for locomotion, as of a road, as *it was tough going*; **3 goings on** *pl* a occurrences; **b** misbehavior ‖ *adj* **4** moving, operating ‖ *adv* **5** going on almost, as *going on ten*

go′ing-o′ver *n* (go·ings-o·ver) **1** examination; **2** reprimand; **3** beating

goi·ter /goit′ər/ [F *goitre*] *n* enlargement of the thyroid gland, causing a swelling in the front of the neck

gold /gōld/ [OE] *n* **1** precious yellow metal (**Au**; at.no. 79; at.wt. 196.967) remarkable for its density, malleability and ductility, and freedom from rust; found widely distributed in nature but always in small quantities; **2** coins made of gold; **3** wealth; **4** color of gold; **5** beautiful or precious quality ‖ also *adj*

gold′beat′er *n* one who makes gold leaf for gilding

gold′brick′ *n* **1** something worthless, as a brick painted to resemble gold, sold as something valuable; **2** *slang* one who shirks work ‖ *vt* **3** *slang* to cheat ‖ *vi* **4** *slang* to shirk work; to loaf

gold′ dig′ger *n colloq* woman who seeks to live with or marry a man for his wealth

gold′en *adj* **1** formed of, consisting of, like, or abounding in gold; **2** gold in color; **3** most valuable; excellent; **4** happy, prosperous; **5** fiftieth (anniversary)

gold′en age′ *n* period of greatest glory in the history, literature, etc., of a country, region, or city

gold′en ea′gle *n* large eagle of the Northern Hemisphere (*Aquila chrysaëtos*) with golden-brown feathers on the head and neck

Gold′en Fleece′ *n Gk myth.* fleece of gold guarded by a dragon and taken by Jason with the help of Medea

Gold′en Gate′ *n* strait connecting San Francisco Bay with the Pacific at San Francisco

Gold′en Horde′ *n* Tartar army that conquered Russia in the 13th century

Gold′en Horn′ *n* arm of the Bosporus that forms the harbor of Istanbul

gold′en mean′ *n* happy medium; moderation

gold′en·rod′ *n* **1** any of a genus (*Solidago*) of plants of the composite family with usu. small heads of yellow flowers; **2** any of several plants of allied genera

gold′en rule′ *n* principle of treating others as we wish them to treat us (Matt 7:12)

gold′en wed′ding *n* 50th anniversary of a wedding

gold′-filled′ *adj* having a layer of gold over a base metal

gold′finch′ *n* **1** European finch (*Carduelis carduelis*) having a patch of brilliant yellow on the wings; **2** any of several American finches (genus *Spinus*) having a lemon-yellow body

gold′fish′ *n* (**-fish** or **-fishes**) orange-colored fresh-water fish (*Carassius auratus*) of the carp family, usu. adaptable to aquariums and ponds

gold' foil' *n* gold beaten into sheets not as thin as gold leaf

gold' leaf' *n* gold beaten into very thin sheets

gold' mine' *n* **1** place where gold is or may be mined; **2** *colloq* source of great wealth or profit

gold' plate' *n* **1** gold tableware; **2** gold coating over base metal

gold'-plate' *vt* to plate (a base metal) with gold, as by electroplating

gold'smith' *n* one who makes and repairs articles of gold

gold' stand'ard *n* monetary system backed by and convertible into gold

golf /golf', gôlf'/ [ME] *n* outdoor game in which a small white ball must be driven into a succession of holes by long-handled clubs || also *vi* || **golf'er** *n*

Gol·go·tha /gol'gəthə/ *n Bib* Calvary, the hill outside Jerusalem where Jesus was crucified (Matt. 27:33)

Go·li·ath /gəli'əth/ *n Bib* Philistine giant killed by David with a stone from a sling (I Sam. 17:4)

gol·ly /gol'ē/ [*euphem* for *God*] *interj colloq* mild exclamation of puzzlement or surprise

Go·mor·rah /gəmôr'ə, -mor'-/ *n* **1** *Bib* ancient city in Palestine destroyed with Sodom for its wickedness (Gen. 19:24, 25); **2** any very wicked city

-gon /-gon', -gən/ [< Gk *gonia* corner] *n comb form* figure with a specified number of angles, as *pentagon*

go·nad /gō'nad, gon'-/ [< Gk *gonos* offspring] *n* sex gland; ovary or testis

gon·do·la /gon'dələ/ [It] *n* **1** long narrow flat-bottomed boat with high pointed ends, used on the canals of Venice; **2** open freight car with fixed sides; **3** passenger basket or car under a dirigible or balloon

gon'do·lier' /-lir'/ *n* boatman of a gondola

gone /gôn', gon'/ **1** *pp* of **go** || *adj* **2** departed; **3** ruined; **4** lost; **5** faint or weak; **6** dead; **7** used up; **8** past; **9 gone on** *slang* infatuated with

gon'er *n colloq* person or thing past saving

gon·fa·lon /gon'fələn/ [It *gonfalone*] *n* flag suspended from a crossbar, used by some of the Italian medieval states as their standard

gong /goŋ/ [imit] **1** disk or shallow bowl of metal producing a resonant tone when struck; **2** any bell similar in shape and sound

gon·or·rhe·a /gon'ərē'ə/ [< Gk *gonos* seed + *rhoia* flux] *n* infectious disease of the mucous membranes of the genital organs, communicated generally by sexual intercourse

goo /gōō'/ [?] *n colloq* any thick or sticky substance || **goo'ey** *adj* (goo-i·er; goo-i·est)

goo·ber /gōōb'ər/ [Afr] *n* peanut

good /gōōd'/ [OE *gōd*] *adj* (**bet·ter; best**) **1** adapted to the end in view, as *this powder is good for itching;* **2** competent; **3** of satisfactory quality, quantity, or degree; **4** pleasurable; **5** full, as *the job took a good hour;* **6** considerable, as *a good distance;* **7** reliable, honest; **8** genuine; **9** virtuous; having excellent moral qualities; **10** kind, merciful; **11** well-behaved; **12** favorable (weather); **13** beneficial, as *rest is good for you;* **14** in working order, as *a good engine, good eyesight;* **15** fitting; **16** valid; **17** attractive (looks, figure); **18** thorough (beating); **19** worthy, as *a good name, a good family;* **20** close (friend); **21** expertly done; **22 as good as** virtually; **23 make good, a** to repay or replace; **b** to fulfill; **c** to succeed; **24 no good** bad, worthless || *n* **25** merit, virtue; **26** benefit, profit; **27 for good** permanently; **28 to the good** ahead; **29 goods** *pl* **a** portable possessions; **b** textile fabric; **c** merchandise; **30 get the goods on** *slang* to discover something incriminating about || *interj* **31** expression of assent or pleasure || *adv* **32** *colloq* well; **33 good and** *colloq* very || SYN *adj* virtuous, righteous, upright, just, benevolent, decorous, honorable, ample, considerable, agreeable, pleasant, valid, profitable, wholesome || ANT *adj* bad, wicked, indecorous, unsound, insufficient

good'-by' or **good'-bye'** /-bī'/ [contr. of *God be with ye*] *interj* **1** farewell! || *n* **2** farewell

good'-fel'low·ship' *n* comradeship, geniality

good'-for-noth'ing *n* worthless person; rake || also *adj*

Good' Fri'day *n* Friday before Easter Sunday, observed by the Christian churches in commemoration of the Crucifixion

good'-heart'ed *adj* kind, generous

Good' Hope', Cape of *n* cape on the SW coast of the Republic of South Africa

good' hu'mor *n* cheery amiable mood || **good'-hu'mored** *adj* || **good'-hu'mored·ly** *adv*

good' looks' *npl* handsomeness, beauty || **good'-look'ing** *adj*

good'ly *adj* (-li·er; -li·est) **1** good-looking; **2** desirable, pleasant; **3** of considerable size

good' na'ture *n* amiability, kindness of disposition || **good'-na'tured** *adj* || **good'-na'tured·ly** *adv*

good'ness *n* **1** state or quality of being good || *interj* **2** expressing surprise or emphasis || SYN *n* uprightness, benevolence, chastity, purity, integrity, probity, rectitude, virtue, worth, kindness

good' Sa·mar'i·tan /səmar'itən/ [<

Bib parable (Luke 10:30–37)] *n* anyone who unselfishly helps others

good′-sized *adj* fairly large

good′ turn *n* favor, helpful act

good′ will′ *n* 1 benevolence; 2 hearty consent; 3 value of an established business over and above its material property, represented by its reputation, clientele, and other intangible assets

good′y *interj* 1 good! (usu. expressing childish delight) ‖ **goodies** *npl* 2 something pleasurable, esp. desserts or candy

goof /gōōf′/ [prob *obs goff* simpleton] *slang n* 1 stupid person; 2 careless blunder ‖ *vt* 3 to bungle, botch ‖ *vi* 4 to blunder; 5 **goof off** to evade work ‖ **goof′y** *adj* (**-i·er; -i·est**)

gook /gōōk′/ [?] *n* sludge; any gooey filth

goon /gōōn′/ [< dial. *gooney* simpleton, and cartoon character Alice the Goon] *n colloq* 1 roughneck; 2 hired thug

goose /gōōs′/ [OE *gōs*] *n* (**geese**) 1 any of numerous species of wild or domestic web-footed, flat-billed, large-bodied birds (subfamily *Anserinae*), with powerful wings, akin to the swans and ducks; 2 silly person; 3 **cook one's goose** *colloq* to ruin one's chances ‖ *n* (**goos·es**) 4 tailor's heavy smoothing iron with a curved handle; 5 *slang* poke between the buttocks ‖ *vt* 6 *slang* a to poke between the buttocks; b to feed spurts of gasoline to (a motor)

goose′ber′ry /also gōōz′-, -b(ə)rē/ *n* (**-ries**) 1 prickly shrub of the genus *Ribes*; 2 its edible acid fruit

goose′ egg′ *n colloq* score of zero

goose′ flesh′ or **pim′ples** or **skin′** *n* temporary roughness of the skin produced by cold or fear

goose′neck′ *n* rigid or flexible rod or pipe curved like the neck of a goose, used for various purposes

goose′ step′ *n* marching step in which the knees are not bent ‖ **goose′-step′** *v* (**-stepped; -step·ping**) *vi*

G.O.P. [Grand Old Party] *n* Republican party

go-pher /gōf′ər/ [perh F *gaufre* honeycomb] *n* 1 any of several ground squirrels (genus *Citellus*), burrowing rodents of the North American prairies; 2 any of several ratlike burrowing rodents (family *Geomyidae*) with large cheek pouches, of the southern U.S. and Central America

Gor′di·an knot′ /gôrd′ē·ən/ *n* knot tied by Gordius, king of Phrygia, so intricate that an oracle declared that he who loosed it should be master of Asia; cut through with a stroke of the sword by Alexander the Great

gore[1] /gôr′, gōr′/ [OE *gor* dirt] *n* blood, esp. thick or clotted ‖ **gor′y** *adj* (**-i·er; -i·est**)

gore[2] [OE *gāra* triangular piece of land] *n* 1 three-cornered piece of cloth sewn into a dress or sail; 2 one of the wedge-shaped panels making up a skirt or umbrella ‖ *vt* 3 to piece with gores

gore[3] [OE *gar* spear] *vt* to pierce with a horn or tusk

gorge /gôrj′/ [OF = throat] *n* 1 that which is swallowed; 2 overhearty meal; 3 obstruction which chokes up a channel; 4 narrow ravine with steep rocky sides ‖ *vt* 5 to stuff with food ‖ *vi* 6 to eat greedily ‖ SYN *v* glut, stuff, cram, overeat, satiate, surfeit

gor·geous /gôr′jəs/ [MF *gorgias* elegant] *adj* 1 splendid, showy; 2 delightful, enjoyable ‖ **gor′geous·ly** *adv*

Gor·gon /gôr′gon/ *n Gk myth.* one of three sisters, the most famous of whom was Medusa, whose appearance was so terrible that anyone who beheld them was turned to stone

go·ril·la /gəril′ə/ [Gk, prob < Afr] *n* 1 largest anthropoid ape (*Gorilla gorilla*) of W Africa; 2 *slang* thug, esp. one given to mayhem

gor·mand·ize /gôrm′əndiz′/ [F *gourmandise* gluttony] *vi* to eat like a glutton ‖ **gor′mand·iz′er** *n*

gorse /gôrs′/ [OE *gorst*] *n* furze

gosh /gosh′/ [euphem for God] *interj colloq* mild oath or exclamation

gos′hawk′ /gos′-/ [< *goosehawk*] *n* any of several fierce short-winged hawks with powerful bills, esp. *Accipiter gentilis*

Go·shen /gōsh′ən/ *n Bib* the part of Egypt allotted to the Hebrews (Gen. 45:10)

gos·ling /goz′liŋ/ [dim. < OE *gōs* goose] *n* young goose

gos·pel /gosp′əl/ [OE *gōdspel* good tidings] *n* 1 good news, esp. the announcement of the salvation of mankind by Jesus Christ; 2 teachings of Jesus and the apostles; 3 something received as absolutely true; 4 any doctrine earnestly advocated by its supporters; 5 **Gospel** any of the first four books of the New Testament ‖ also *adj*

gos·sa·mer /gos′əmər/ [ME *gossomer* goose summer] *n* 1 very fine cobweb; 2 filmy gauze; 3 any thin filmy material ‖ also *adj*

gos·sip /gos′ip/ [OE *godsibb* godparent] *n* 1 idle talk, esp. about other people's affairs; 2 one who habitually talks of other people and their affairs ‖ *vi* 3 to indulge in gossip ‖ **gos′sip·er** *n* ‖ **gos′sip·y** *adj* ‖ SYN *v* babble, chat, prate, tattle, repeat, tell

got /got′/ *pt & pp* of **get**

Goth /goth′/ [Gk *Gothoi* Goths < Gmc] *n* member of a Teutonic tribe that overran parts of the Roman Empire in the 3rd to 5th centuries A.D.

Goth′ic *adj* 1 pert. to the Goths or

their language; **2** *arch.* designating a style prevalent in W Europe from the 12th to the 16th centuries, with high pointed arches, steep roofs, windows large in proportion to the wall space, and lavish use of lacelike ornamental carving ‖ *n* **3** language of the Goths; **4** type face with strokes of uniform width

got·ten /got/ən/ *pp* of get

gouge /gouj/ [MF < LL *gubia*] *n* **1** chisel with a concave blade; **2** groove or cavity made by gouging; **3** fraud, extortion ‖ *vt* **4** to scoop out with or as with a gouge; **5** to cheat, overcharge, extort from ‖ **goug′er** *n*

gou·lash /gōō′läsh, -lash/ [Hung *gulyás* (hus) herdsman's (meat)] *n* highly seasoned stew of beef or veal, vegetables, and flour

gourd /gôrd′, gōōrd′/ [MF *gourde*] *n* **1** any of a family (Cucurbitaceae) of climbing plants bearing fleshy many-seeded fruit, as the melon and squash; **2** fruit of these plants, esp. a nonedible variety whose dried shell is used as a bottle

gourde /gōōrd′/ [F = heavy] *n* monetary unit of Haiti

gour·mand /gōōr′mənd/ [MF *gourmant*] *n* **1** gourmet; **2** glutton

gour·met /gōōr′mā/ [F] *n* connoisseur of fine food and drink

gout /gout′/ [MF *goute* drop < L *gutta*] *n* disease marked by an excess of uric acid in the blood and painful inflammation and swelling of the joints, esp. the big toe ‖ **gout′y** *adj*

gov., Gov. **1** government; **2** governor

gov·ern /guv′ərn/ [OF *governer* < L *gubernare* to steer] *vt* **1** to exercise authority over; **2** to guide, control; **3** *gram* to require the use of ‖ *vi* **4** to exercise authority ‖ SYN rule, command, sway, manage, control, direct, regulate, curb, restrain, influence ‖ DISCR To *command* is to exercise power or authority over one bound to obey. To *govern* is to secure obedience to such power or authority. To *control* is to have a dominating influence. A teacher who *commands* without exacting obedience neither *governs* nor *controls* her students. To *manage* a thing is to get into it and handle it to the last detail. To *direct* is to point out a course of action and order it followed. Those who *direct* issue the orders that define the policy of a company; those who *manage* the several departments carry out this policy in its details. To *manage* people or animals is to *control* them without arousing their antagonism. To *regulate* is to *control* by rule, to subject to restrictions, or to adapt to needs; we *regulate* traffic; public service commissions *regulate* rates for utility companies; villages *regulate* the speed of motor vehicles within their limits (cf. *conduct*)

gov′ern·ance *n* **1** exercise of authority; **2** system of governing

gov′ern·ess *n* woman who cares for or teaches children in their own home

gov′ern·ment *n* **1** established system of administering state affairs; **2** persons entrusted with the administration of the affairs of a state, as a prime minister and his cabinet; **3** act of governing; **4** guidance, control, or regulation, as of conduct or household affairs ‖ **gov′ern·men′tal** /-men′-/ *adj* ‖ SYN rule, state, control, restraint, direction, sway

gov′er·nor *n* **1** person appointed or elected to govern a province, state, colony, etc.; **2** person elected to be the chief executive of any of the States of the United States; **3** *Brit colloq* **a** father; **b** employer; **4** device for regulating the speed of an engine

govt., Govt. government

gown /goun′/ [OF *goune* < LL *gunna* fur garment] *n* **1** any loose, flowing outer garment; **2** woman's dress; **3** long robe, as worn officially by judges, clergymen, professors, and graduates ‖ *vt* **4** to attire in, or invest with, a gown

G.P. general practitioner

GP var of PG

gr. **1** grain(s); **2** gram(s); **3** gross

Gr. Greek

grab /grab′/ [perh MLG *grabben*] *v* (**grabbed; grab·bing**) *vt* **1** to seize suddenly; **2** to get possession of by dishonest methods ‖ *n* **3** sudden seizure; **4** acquisition by dishonest means; **b** thing grabbed

grab′ bag′ *n* **1** container from which one draws a gift without knowing what it is; **2** miscellaneous collection

grace /grās′/ [OF < L *gratia* favor] *n* **1** elegance or attractiveness of form, movement, manner, attitude, etc.; **2** favor, good will; **3** any pleasing natural endowment; **4** mercy; **5** prayer before or after a meal; **6** temporary relief from an obligation or the like, as *three days' grace;* **7** God's unmerited mercy toward mankind; **8** influence of God's spirit; **9** condition of one who enjoys God's special favor; **10** trait of special moral excellence; **11** Grace title of address applied to an archbishop, duke, or duchess; **12** Graces *pl class. myth.* goddesses of beauty, daughters of Zeus; **13 in someone's good graces** in someone's favor; **14 in someone's bad graces** in someone's disfavor; **15 with bad grace** grudgingly; **16 with good grace** willingly ‖ *vt* **17** to adorn; **18** to honor, favor

grace·ful *adj* displaying beauty in form, manner, movement, or expression ‖ **grace′ful·ly** *adv* ‖ **grace′ful·ness** *n* ‖

SYN comely, beautiful, felicitous, un-
constrained

grace′less *adj* **1** lacking grace; awkward, clumsy; **2** depraved; ill-mannered ‖ **grace′less·ly** *adv* ‖ **grace′·
less·ness** *n*

grace′ note′ *n mus* note immediately
preceding a harmony tone, added for
embellishment

gra·cious /grāsh′əs/ [L *gratiosus*] *adj*
1 showing or bestowing goodness,
kindness, or mercy; **2** affable, polite
‖ *interj* **3** expression of surprise ‖
gra′cious·ly *adv* ‖ **gra′cious·ness** *n* ‖
SYN *adj* favorable, kindly, benevo-
lent, courteous

grack·le /grak′əl/ [L *graculus* jackdaw]
n **1** any of various Old World birds
of the starling family (Sturnidae); **2**
any of several American blackbirds
with iridescent black plumage (genera *Quiscalus* and *Cassidix*]

grad. **1** graduate; **2** graduated

gra·da·tion /grədāsh′ən/ [< L *gradus*
step] *n* **1** act or process of arranging
in grades or steps; **2** any gradual
change by stages; **3** stage or degree
in such a series; **4** gradual blending
of one color into another

grade /grād/ [F < L *gradus* step] *n*
1 step or degree in a scale or pro-
gression; **2** group of persons or
things of the same quality or rank;
3 division by years of a school curriculum; **4** mark or rating of evaluation or classification; **5** measure or
degree of slope; **6** slope, as in a
road; **7 at grade** on the same level;
8 make the grade to succeed; **9 up to
grade** of sufficiently high quality ‖
vt **10** to level or slope (ground)
evenly; **11** to sort, as by size or quality; **12** to assign a grade or rating
to ‖ *vi* **13** to change gradually, blend

grade′ cross′ing *n* intersection of a railroad with a road or another rail-
road at the same level

grade′ school′ *n* elementary school

gra·di·ent /grād′ē·ənt/ [< L *gradi* to
step] *n* **1** incline of road or railway;
2 stretch, as of a highway, which is
not level; **3** *phys* a rate of change
from point to point of a physical
quantity, such as pressure, temperature, electrical potential; **b** curve
which represents this

grad·u·al /graj′ŏŏ·əl/ [ML *gradualis*]
adj proceeding or occurring by degrees; regular and slow ‖ **grad′u·al·
ly** *adv* ‖ SYN deliberate, moderate,
progressive, continuous ‖ ANT sudden, jerky, quick, immediate

grad′u·al·ism *n* policy of approaching
and reaching a goal by gradual stages

grad·u·ate /graj′ŏŏ·it/ [ML *graduare*
(-*atus*) to go step by step] *n* **1** one
who has received an academic degree or diploma; **2** container with
markings on the sides to indicate
capacity ‖ *adj* **3** of or pert. to stu-

dents or study beyond the bachelor's
degree ‖ /-āt′/ *vt* **4** to mark with
degrees, as a thermometer or container; **5** to arrange according to
degrees, as of quality, color, etc.; **6**
to confer a degree or diploma upon
‖ *vi* **7** to receive a degree or diploma

grad′u·ate school′ /-it/ *n* division of a
university granting degrees above
the bachelor's

grad′u·a′tion *n* **1** act of graduating or
state of being graduated; **2** ceremony of conferring degrees or diplomas

graf·fi·ti /grəfēt′ē/ [It] *npl* words,
often obscene, scrawled in public
places

graft /graft′, gräft/ [< MF *grafe* <
Gk *grapheion* stylus] *n* **1** bud or
shoot of a tree or plant inserted into
a slit in another where it continues to
grow; **2** piece of transplanted living
skin or other tissue; **3 a** use of one's
position to acquire dishonest gain; **b**
anything so gained; **4** act of grafting
‖ *vt* **5** to insert (a graft); **6** to obtain
by graft ‖ *vi* **7** to practice grafting

gra′ham crack′er /grā′əm/ ·[S. *Graham*
(1794–1851) Am nutritionist] *n* cracker made of whole-wheat flour

Grail /grāl/ [MF *graal* < ML *gradale*
platter] *n* **1** also **Ho′ly Grail′** in
medieval legend, cup used by Jesus
at the Last Supper, taken by Joseph
of Arimathea to England where it
disappeared, being revealed only to
those pure in spirit; **2** grail object
or goal of a long, arduous pursuit

grain /grān/ [OF < L *granum*] *n* **1**
any very small hard particle, as of
sand; **2** seed of a cereal plant, as
corn or wheat; **3** cereal plants; **4** any
small particle; **5** smallest unit of
weight, 1/437.5 of an ounce avoirdupois; **6** arrangement of particles
in a body; texture, as of marble; **7**
arrangement or direction of fibers
in a piece of wood; **8** granular surface or appearance; **9** disposition,
temper; **10 against the grain** in opposition to one's feelings or inclination; **11 with a grain of salt**
with reservations ‖ *vt* **12** to paint in
imitation of the grain of wood ‖
grain′y *adj* (-i·er; -i·est)

grain′ al′co·hol *n* alcohol *1*

grain′ el′e·va·tor *n* elevator *3*

gram or **gramme** /gram′/ [F *gramme* <
Gk *gramma* small weight] *n* metric
unit of mass or weight, equal to
15.432 troy grains and approximately
the weight of one cubic centimeter
of water at maximum density

-gram /-gram′/ [< Gk *gramma* letter]
comb form something written, as
telegram

gram·mar /gram′ər/ [OF *gramaire* <
Gk *grammatike*] *n* **1** phonology,
morphology, and syntax of a language which, taken conjointly, ac-

count for the distinctive features of that language; **2** the rules governing this; **3** study or account of these rules

gram·ma·ri·an /grəmer'ē-ən/ *n* **1** one who knows or teaches grammar; **2** one who sets himself up as the arbiter of correct grammatical usage

gram'mar school' *n* elementary or grade school

gram·mat·i·cal /grəmat'ikəl/ *adj* pert. to or in agreement with grammar or its rules || **gram·mat'i·cal·ly** *adv*

gram·pus /gramp'əs/ [ME *graundepose* < OF *grapois* fat fish] *n* small whale akin to the dolphins

gra·na·ry /gran'ərē/ [L *granarium*] *n* (-ries) **1** storehouse for grain; **2** region that produces an abundance of grain for export

grand /grand'/ [OF < L *grandis* full-grown] *adj* **1** large; imposing in size; **2** majestic, stately; **3** high in dignity, wealth, or power; **4** lofty or noble in character; **5** chief in importance; **6** including everything, as *grand total*; **7** very satisfactory; capital || *n* (*pl* **grand**) *colloq* thousand dollars || **grand'ly** *adv*

grand- /grand'-, gran'-/ *comb form* one generation removed, as *granduncle, grandnephew*

grand'aunt' *n* sister of one's grandparent

Grand' Banks' *npl* shoal and fishing grounds SE of Newfoundland

Grand' Can'yon *n* mile-deep gorge of the Colorado River in N Arizona, 200 miles long

grand'child' *n* (-chil·dren) child of one's son or daughter

grand'daugh'ter *n* daughter of one's son or daughter

grand' duke' *n* **1** sovereign ranking next below a king; **2** son or grandson of a czar || **grand' duch'ess** *nfem*

gran·dee /grandē'/ [Sp *grande*] *n* **1** Spanish nobleman of the highest rank; **2** any man of high rank

gran·deur /gran'jər, -jŏŏr/ *n* quality or state of being grand || SYN greatness, magnificence, splendor, sublimity || DISCR *Greatness*, figuratively applied, suggests importance, eminence, loftiness of character, or the like, as the *greatness* of a nation depends upon the integrity of its people; the *greatness* of Lincoln was not apparent to all of his own generation. *Grandeur* names a quality that impresses both eye and mind; it is imposing, stately, inspiring, as the *grandeur* of Mount Rainier; the *grandeur* of his sacrifice, his principles, his style of entertaining. *Magnificence* is full of beauty, color, sumptuousness, and is often *grandeur* on a warmer and more human plane, as the *magnificence* of his generosity, of his dress, of his retinue, of the scenery. *Splendor* is dazzling *mag-*

nificence. Sublimity is an exalted quality, awe-inspiring, noble, elevated, as the *sublimity* of certain passages in the Bible

grand'fa'ther *n* **1** father of either of one's parents; **2** male ancestor

grand'father's clock' *n* floor clock with a pendulum, enclosed in a very tall case

grand fi·na'le *n* colorful imposing finale to a theatrical performance or a sports event

gran·dil·o·quent /grandil'əkwənt/ [< L *grandiloquus* braggart] *adj* characterized by pompousness of style; bombastic || **gran·dil'o·quence** *n*

gran·di·ose /gran'dē·ōs'/ [F < It *grandioso*] *adj* **1** imposing, magnificent; **2** pompous, showy

grand' ju'ry *n* jury, usually of 12 to 23 persons, selected to weigh the state's case against an accused person, to return an indictment if the evidence seems persuasive, but to block prosecution if it is not

grand' lar'ce·ny *n* theft of property exceeding a specified limit

grand·ma /gran'mə, gram'ə/ *n colloq* grandmother

grand mal /gran'mal'/ [F = great sickness] *n* the severe form of an epileptic attack, characterized by convulsions and unconsciousness

grand'moth'er *n* **1** mother of either of one's parents; **2** female ancestor; **3** old woman

grand' op'er·a *n* serious drama in which the whole text is set to music

grand·pa /gran'pä, -pə, -gramp'ə/ *n colloq* grandfather

grand'par'ent *n* grandfather or grandmother

grand' pi·an'o *n* piano with a horizontal harp-shaped case

Grand' Rap'ids *n* city in SW Michigan (178,000)

grand' slam' *n* **1** *bridge* winning of all 13 tricks in a deal; **2** *baseball* home run with the bases loaded

grand'son' *n* son of one's son or daughter

grand'stand' *n* principle range of tiered seats at an outdoor arena

grand'stand play' *n* **1** *sports* spectacular play made to impress the public; **2** *colloq* anything done to make an impression and to win applause

grand' tour' *n* tour of continental Europe formerly taken by young British aristocrats as part of their education

grand'un'cle *n* brother of one's grandparent

grange /grānj'/ [MF < LL *granica*] *n* **1** farm; **2 Grange**, **a** association of farmers; **b** any of its local lodges

gran·ite /gran'it/ [It *granito* grained] *n* hard igneous rock composed of quartz, feldspar, and usu. mica

gran·ny or **gran·nie** *n* (-nies) *colloq* **1**

grandmother; **2** old woman; **3** fussy person

grant /grant′, gränt′/ [OF *greanter* to guarantee] *vt* **1** to give or confer; **2** to concede, admit as true; **3** to transfer the title of; **4** take for granted, **a** to consider or assume to be true; **b** to treat with indifference ‖ *n* **5** act of granting; **6** thing granted; **7** transfer of property ‖ **gran′tor** *n* ‖ **grantee′** *n* ‖ SYN *v* (see *give*); *n* (see *boon*[1])

Grant, U·lys·ses S. *n* (1822–85) U.S. commander in the Civil War; 18th president of the U.S. 1869–77

gran·u·lar /gran′yələr/ [see **granule**] *adj* composed of, or like, grains or granules

gran·u·late′ *vt* **1** to form into grains or granules, as sugar; **2** to roughen the surface of, as the eyelids ‖ *vi* **3** to become granular ‖ **gran′u·la′tion** *n*

gran·ule /gran′yōōl/ [LL *granulum*] *n* small grain or particle

grape /grāp′/ [OF = bunch of grapes] *n* **1** smooth green or purple berry, fruit of the grapevine, growing in clusters and used as a fruit and for making wine; **2** grapevine

grape′fruit′ *n* **1** large yellow citrus fruit with a juicy acid pulp; **2** its tree (*Citrus paradisi*)

grape′ hy′a·cinth *n* bulbous plant of the genus *Muscari* with blue spherical flowers that look like small grapes

grape′shot′ *n* small iron balls shot as a scattering charge from a cannon

grape′ sug′ar *n* dextrose

grape′vine′ *n* **1** any of a widely distributed genus (*Vitis*) of the vine family, which produces grapes; **2** secret means of conveying information

graph /graf′, gräf′/ [*graphic* formula] *n* **1** diagram or curve representing the successive values of a changing quantity; **2** written symbol of a sound; **3** diagram expressing a mathematical relation ‖ *vt* **4** to represent by a graph

-graph /-graf′, -gräf′/ [< Gk *graphein* to write] *n comb form* **1** something written, as *monograph*; **2** something that writes, as *telegraph*

graph·eme /graf′ēm/ *n* **1** letter or letters of an alphabet representing one sound, as *b* or *sh*; **2** all the letters or combinations of letters that represent a phoneme

graph·ic /graf′ik/ *adj* **1** pert. to or expressed in writing; **2** illustrating by graphs; **3** vividly described; **4** of or pert. to the graphic arts ‖ **graph′i·cal·ly** *adv* ‖ SYN forcible, lifelike, picturesque, striking, pictorial ‖ ANT dull, ordinary, flat, colorless, prosy

graph′ic arts′ *npl* drawing, painting, and other fine arts which represent objects on a flat surface

graph·ite /graf′īt/ *n* dark-gray natural form of carbon, used as lead in pencils and as a lubricant

graph′y *n* (-ies) **1** letter that functions as a diacritical mark; **2** variant spelling

-g·ra·phy /-g′rəfē/ *n comb form* **1** manner of writing or representing, as *stenography*; **2** science or study, as *geography*

grap·nel /grap′nəl/ [ME *grapenel*] *n* **1** small anchor with several flukes; **2** grappling iron

grap·ple /grap′əl/ [MF *grappelle* small hook] *vt* **1** to lay hold of, clinch ‖ *vi* **2** to struggle or contend in a close fight ‖ *n* **3** close hold, as in wrestling; **4** grappling iron

grap′pling hook′ or **i′ron** *n* device with hooks or claws for hooking onto objects

grasp /grasp′, gräsp′/ [ME *graspen*] *vt* **1** to seize or clasp, as by closing the hand on; **2** to seize, hold; **3** to understand, as an idea ‖ *vi* **4** grasp **at** to endeavor to seize; **5** to accept eagerly ‖ *n* **6** act of grasping; **7** hold, grip, possession; **8** comprehension ‖ SYN *v* clasp, clutch, grab, grip, embrace, hug, reach ‖ ANT *v* repel, lose, miss, let go, relinquish

grasp′ing *adj* avaricious, greedy

grass /gras′, gräs′/ [OE *græss*] *n* **1** green herbage, on which cattle feed; **2** plant of a large family (Gramineae) having hollow, jointed stalks, narrow leaves, and grainlike seeds; **3** pasture; **4** *slang* marijuana ‖ **grass′y** *adj* (-i·er; -i·est)

grass′hop′per *n* any of many species of leaping and flying insects (families Acrididae and Tettigoniidae), very destructive to vegetation, having narrow forewings and broad hind wings, folded when not in flight

grass′ roots′ *nsg & npl* the mass of common people making up the electorate of a community or nation ‖ **grass′-roots′** *adj*

grass′ wid′ow *n* woman divorced or separated from her husband

grate[1] /grāt′/ [OF *grater* to scratch < Gmc] *vt* **1** to grind into small particles by scraping against a rough body; **2** to rub together with a rasping sound ‖ *vi* **3** to make a rasping sound; **4** to be irritating

grate[2] [ML *grata*] *n* **1** framework of metal bars to hold burning fuel; **2** framework of metal bars for cooking over a fire; **3** partition made of bars, as in a window

grate′ful [< L *gratus* pleasing] *adj* **1** thankful, feeling gratitude; **2** refreshing, welcome ‖ **grate′ful·ly** *adv* ‖ **grate′ful·ness** *n*

grat′er *n* kitchen utensil with slits and openings, used for grating foods

grat·i·fy /grat′ifī′/ [L *gratificari*] *v* (-fied) *vt* to afford pleasure to; indulge; humor ‖ **grat′i·fi·ca′tion** *n* ‖

SYN indulge, humor, please, satisfy ‖ DISCR We *gratify* our desires, feelings, impulses, or curiosity for the pleasure we shall get out of it. We *indulge* our appetites or desires because we are too weak-willed to resist their influence. Any normal person likes occasionally to *gratify* a whim, or *indulge* in an extravagance. *Humor* is almost always used unfavorably; we *humor* invalids, fretful children, or, most unwisely, ourselves

grat·ing¹ /grāt'iŋ/ [< *grate¹*] *adj* harsh; irritating to the ear

grat·ing² [< *grate²*] *n* open framework of bars used to prevent passage

grat·is /grat'is, grāt'-/ [L] *adv & adj* without charge

grat·i·tude /grat'it(y)ood'/ [< L *gratus* thankful] *n* state of being thankful or grateful

gra·tu·i·tous /grət(y)oo'itəs/ [< L *gratuitus* spontaneous] *adj* 1 without cost; 2 without provocation; unwarranted

gra·tu'i·ty *n* (-ties) small gift of money for services rendered ‖ SYN present, donation, bounty, gift, tip (see *boon¹*)

grave¹ /grāv/ [OE *grafan* to dig] *v* (*pp* **graved** or **grav·en**) *vt* 1 to engrave, sculpture; 2 to impress indelibly on, as the mind ‖ *n* 3 excavation for the reception of a dead body; 4 place of burial; 5 death

grave² [MF < L *gravis* heavy] *adj* 1 important; serious; 2 solemn; sober; 3 critical, dangerous ‖ *n* 4 grave accent ‖ **grave'ly** *adv* ‖ SYN *adj* serious, solemn, earnest, sober, weighty, pressing, staid, momentous, melancholy, sad ‖ DISCR A *serious* person is thoughtful and reflective; a *serious* matter is important; a *serious* symptom calls for diagnosis. *Serious* is opposed to what is jocose or mirthful; *grave* is opposed to what is light, lively, or colorful. *Grave* people are slow-moving, not gay. Clergymen, judges, surgeons, are apt to be *grave*. Though chiefly used to characterize people, *grave* is also applied to weighty matters or affairs, gatherings of aged statesmen, momentous conferences, and the like. A *solemn* person is *grave*, and full of a sense of the importance of the moment, for solemnity is the product of an extraordinary occasion. A *solemn* warning is impressive; a *solemn* silence is mysterious; a *solemn* promise is sacred. *Earnest* is opposed to trifling; an *earnest* seeker is zealous, sincere, and intent. *Sober*, applied to people, describes those who are well-balanced, sane, and sedate, as opposed to those who perhaps are just as *serious* but more vivacious; applied to colors, *sober* means quiet, not

showy; *sober* garb is often mournful or drab (see *serious*) ‖ ANT *adj* lighthearted, giddy, insignificant, unimportant

grave' **ac'cent** *n* diacritical mark ` , used in Greek to show falling pitch, sometimes in English to show syllabic value, as in *belovèd*, and variously in other languages to show stress, vowel quality, or both

grav·el /grav'əl/ [OF *gravelle* dim. of *grave* pebbly shore] *n* 1 rounded fragments of rock coarser than sand, often mixed with sand ‖ *v* (**-eled** or **-elled**; **-el·ing** or **-el·ling**) *vt* 2 to cover with gravel

grav'el·ly *adj* 1 abounding in or containing much gravel; 2 harsh, grating (voice)

grav·en /grāv'ən/ 1 *pp* of **grave¹** ‖ *adj* 2 carved, sculptured; 3 deeply impressed

grav'en im'age *n* object of worship carved in wood or stone

grave'stone' *n* stone placed to mark a grave

grave'yard' *n* cemetery

grav·id /grav'id/ [L *gravidus* loaded] *adj* pregnant

grav·i·tate /grav'itāt'/ [see *gravity*] *vi* 1 to be attracted, as by gravitation; 2 to tend to a lower level

grav'i·ta'tion *n* 1 act of gravitating; 2 *phys* force of mutual attraction between all bodies in the universe, dependent on their respective masses, distance apart, and speed of motion relative to each other ‖ **grav'i·ta'tion·al** *adj*

grav'i·ty [L *gravitas* heaviness] *n* (-ties) 1 state of being grave; 2 gravitation, esp. the force which causes all terrestrial objects to be attracted downward toward the earth's center

gra·vure /grəvyoor'/ [< F *graver* to engrave + -*ure*] *n* 1 photomechanical reproduction of photographs by intaglio printing; 2 plate made for this purpose; 3 print made from such a plate

gra·vy /grā'vē/ [ME *gravey*] *n* (-vies) 1 juice that drips from meat in cooking, often thickened, as with flour, and used as a sauce; 2 *slang* something acquired with little or no effort

gra'vy train' *n slang* situation providing excessive and unearned profit or advantage

gray /grā/ [OE *grēg*] *n* 1 color resulting from mixing white and black; 2 something of this color, as an animal or clothing ‖ *adj* 3 of the color gray; 4 gray-haired; 5 dark, dismal; 6 old, mature; 7 vague; intermediate ‖ *vt* 8 to make gray ‖ *vi* 9 to become gray ‖ **gray'ness** *n*

gray'ish *adj* somewhat gray

gray'ling [< *gray*] *n* any of several species of a genus (*Thymallus*) of freshwater fishes allied to the trout

gray′ mat′ter *n* **1** grayish nerve tissue in the brain and spinal cord; **2** *colloq* brains, intelligence

graze¹ /grāz′/ [OE *grasian*] *vt* **1** to provide, as cattle, with growing herbage for food; **2** to feed on (grass, etc.) ‖ *vi* **3** to feed on growing herbage

graze² [?] *vt & vi* **1** to touch or rub lightly in passing ‖ *n* **2** a grazing

Gr. Br. or **Gr. Brit.** Great Britain

grease /grēs′/ [OF *graisse*] *n* **1** soft animal fat; **2** any thick oily matter; lubricant ‖ /grēs′, grēz′/ *vt* **3** to smear or lubricate with grease; **4** *colloq* to bribe

grease′ cup′ *n* small cup filled with grease, attached to and lubricating a bearing

grease′ gun′ *n* hand-held pump for forcing grease into bearings

grease′ mon′key *n* *slang* automobile mechanic

grease′ paint′ *n* theatrical make-up

greas′y /-sē, -zē/ *adj* (**-i·er; -i·est**) **1** resembling, containing, or covered with grease; **2** soiled with grease; **3** unctuous in manner; slippery

greas′y spoon′ *n* *slang* cheap unsanitary eating place

great /grāt′/ [OE] *adj* **1** large in size, number, quantity, extent, duration, etc.; vast; **2** extreme, as *great ignorance;* **3** weighty, important; **4** illustrious, prominent; **5** high-minded, noble; **6** sublime, magnificent, as *a great painting;* **7** being as designated in high degree, as *great friends;* **8** *colloq* first-rate, fine ‖ *adv* **9** very well ‖ *n* **10** great person ‖ **great′ly** *adv* ‖ **great′ness** *n* ‖ SYN *adj* big, huge, majestic, vast, grand, august, important, numerous, abundant, immense, eminent

great- *comb form* designating a relationship more remote by one generation, as *great-grandfather*

great′-aunt′ *n* sister of one's grandparent

Great′ Bear′ *n* constellation Ursa Major

Great′ Brit′ain *n* island NW of Europe comprising England, Scotland, and Wales (51,300,000; 89,047 sq.m.); the United Kingdom without Northern Ireland

great′ cir′cle *n* circle on a sphere whose plane passes through the center of the sphere, as the equator or any meridian on the earth

Great′ Dane′ *n* one of a breed of very large, powerful, short-haired dogs

Great′ Di·vide′ *n* chief watershed in North America, the Rocky Mountains

great′-grand′child′ *n* (**-chil·dren**) child of one's grandchild

great′-grand′par′ent *n* parent of one's grandparent

great′-heart′ed *adj* **1** magnanimous; generous; **2** brave

great′ horned′ owl′ *n* large North American owl (*Bubo virginianus*) with conspicuous hornlike ear tufts

Great′ Lakes′ *npl* chain of five large fresh-water lakes lying mainly between the central parts of the United States and Canada and emptying into the Atlantic through the St. Lawrence River

Great′ Plains′ *npl* semiarid plains east of the Rockies in North America

Great′ Salt′ Lake′ *n* large shallow salt lake in N Utah

great′-un′cle *n* brother of one's grandparent

grebe /grēb′/ [F] *n* any of several diving birds (family Podicipedidae) allied to the loon

Gre·cian /grēsh′ən/ [< L *Graecia* Greece] *adj & n* Greek

Gre·co- also **Grae·co-** /grēk′ō, grek′ō/ [< L *Graecus* Greek] *comb form* **1** Greece, Greeks; **2** Greek and, as *Greco-Roman*

Greece /grēs′/ *n* republic in SE Europe at the tip of the Balkan peninsula (8,614,000; 50,994 sq.m.; cap. Athens)

greed /grēd′/ [< *greedy*] *n* excessive desire for something; avidity ‖ SYN cupidity, avarice, covetousness ‖ DISCR *Greed, cupidity,* and *avarice* agree in expressing an insatiate longing for wealth. *Greed,* however, has a use extended beyond the passion for money; people entertain *greed* for food, drink, recognition, fame, and the like. *Cupidity* and *avarice* are confined to the desire for money and possessions: *cupidity* stresses the eagerness to get, *avarice* the tendency to hoard one's gains

greed′y [OE *grǣdig*] *adj* (**-i·er; -i·est**) **1** too eager for food and drink; gluttonous; **2** covetous, eagerly desirous ‖ **greed′i·ly** *adv* ‖ **greed′i·ness** *n* ‖ SYN rapacious, ravenous, insatiable (cf. *avaricious*)

Greek /grēk′/ [L *Graecus*] *n* **1** native or inhabitant of Greece; **2** language of the Greeks; **3** anything unintelligible ‖ also *adj*

Greek′ fire′ *n* substance that burns on or under water, used in naval warfare by the Byzantine Greeks

Greek′ Or′tho·dox Church′ *n* **1** Eastern Orthodox Church; **2** Church of Greece

green /grēn′/ [OE *grēne*] *n* **1** color of growing grass, composed of blue and yellow; **2** plot of grassy land, as *a village green, a putting green;* **3** **greens** *pl* **a** foliage cut for decoration; **b** leafy green vegetables ‖ *adj* **4** having the color green; **5** covered with grass or foliage, verdant; **6** fresh; flourishing; **7** unripe; **8** inexperienced; **9** naive; **10** wan or pale, as *green with envy;* **11** not seasoned, as *green wood* ‖ **green′ness** *n*

green′back′ *n* any U.S. legal-tender note printed in green on the back

green'er·y *n* (-ies) 1 green vegetation; 2 greenhouse

green'-eyed' *adj colloq* jealous

green'gro'cer *n* retailer of fresh fruits and vegetables || **green'gro'cer·y** *n* (-ies)

green'horn' *n* 1 inexperienced person; 2 *colloq* recent immigrant

green'house' *n* (-hous·es /-hou'ziz/) heated glass house for the cultivation of tender or out-of-season plants

green'house ef·fect' *n* rise in the temperature of the atmosphere resulting from the absorption of solar radiation by the earth and its conversion into infrared radiation, which is prevented from returning back to space by pollutants in the form of carbon dioxide, ozone, and water vapor

green'ish *adj* somewhat green

Green'land /-lənd/ *n* Danish island NE of North America (35,000; 840,000 sq.m.; *cap.* Godthaab), mostly ice-covered || **Green'land·er** *n* || **Green'land'ic** /-lan'dik/ *adj*

green' light' *n colloq* permission

green' pep'per *n* immature fruit of the garden pepper (*Capsicum frutescens*) used as a vegetable

green' rev·o·lu'tion *n* 1 planned arithmetical increase in agricultural production that could provide food for geometrically increasing human population; 2 huge increase in the growth of wheat and rice in the world brought about by the development since 1945 of new strains of these grains

green'sward' *n* turf well covered with grass

green' thumb' *n* gift of making plants grow

green' tur'tle *n* large sea turtle (*Chelonia mydas*) whose flesh is used for turtle soup

Green'wich /grin'ij, -ich, gren'-/ *n* London borough whose meridian is 0° longitude, from which all longitude is measured; formerly the site of the Royal Observatory (see *Herstmonceux*)

Green'wich (Civ'il or **Mean') Time'** *n* mean solar time of the meridian at Greenwich, England, used as the basis of standard time throughout most of the world

Green'wich Vil'lage /gren'ich/ *n* artistic and Bohemian quarter of New York City

green'wood' *n* wood or forest in its summer green

greet /grēt'/ [OE grētan] *vt* 1 to address salutations to; 2 to meet or receive; 3 to appear or be presented to

greet'ing *n* 1 salutation; welcome; 2 **greetings** *pl* expression of regard

gre·gar·i·ous /grigẽr'ē·əs/ [< L *grex* (*gregis*) flock] *adj* 1 (animals) living in herds; 2 fond of associating with others

Gre·go'ri·an cal'en·dar /grigôr'ē·ən, -gōr'-/ [< *Gregory*] *n* calendar now in use, correcting the Julian calendar by eliminating the centenary years as leap years, introduced by Pope Gregory XIII in 1582

Gre·go'ri·an chant' *n* plainsong of the Roman Catholic ritual

grem·lin /grem'lin/ [?] *n* mischievous goblin supposed to cause malfunctioning in machinery, esp. in aircraft

Gre·na·da /grənā'də/ *n* island nation in the West Indies (125,000; 133 sq. m.; *cap.* St. George's)

gre·nade /grinād'/ [F < Sp *granada* pomegranate] *n* 1 explosive shell detonated by a fuse and usu. thrown by hand; 2 glass missile which on breaking scatters tear gas or a fire extinguisher

gren·a·dier /gren'ədir'/ *n* 1 originally, soldier who threw grenades; 2 member of an elite infantry regiment in certain armies

gren·a·dine /gren'ədēn'/ [F < *grenade* pomegranate] *n* pomegranate syrup

Gresh'am's law' /gresh'əmz/ [Sir Thomas Gresham (1519–79) Eng financier] *n* tendency of bad money to drive out good money from circulation because of hoarding

grew /grōō'/ *pt* of **grow**

grey /grā'/ *n, adj, vt & vi* var of **gray**

grey'hound' [OE *grīghund*] *n* slenderbodied, long-legged, very swift dog

grid /grid'/ [< *gridiron*] *n* 1 grating or gridiron; 2 lead plate with perforations or other surface irregularities for supporting the active material in storage batteries; 3 system of high-tension power lines serving a large area; 4 electrode of a vacuum tube, consisting of a screen or coil of wire, which controls the flow of electrons from the filament to the plate or between other electrodes; 5 network of equally spaced rectangular lines, used as reference lines for locating points on charts, maps, etc.

grid·dle /grid'əl/ [OF *gredil* gridiron] *n* metal plate used for cooking pancakes, bacon, etc.

grid'dle·cake' *n* pancake

grid'i'ron [*griddle* + *iron*] *n* 1 grated iron utensil for broiling; 2 football field; 3 metal grid above a stage providing access to the rigging of scenery and curtains

grief /grēf'/ [OF *gref* heavy < L *gravis*] *n* 1 sorrow, mental distress, caused by affliction or loss; 2 cause of grief; 3 **come to grief** to fail; suffer disappointment || **SYN** sorrow, woe, affliction, tribulation, sadness, melancholy, trial, suffering || **DISCR** These words agree in expressing distress of mind or soul. *Sorrow* is occasioned by the ordinary disappointments, losses, regrets, or misfortunes which are the lot of people in general. *Grief* is deep *sorrow*, caused by an unusual loss, injury, or the like. *Grief* is more acute and more transitory than *sorrow*, and is apt to be marked by passionate demonstrations of feeling. *Affliction* is deep, keen, bitter suffering, occasioned by calamity or loss; *affliction* may name, also, the calamity or loss causing the distress. *Affliction* strikes more deeply into the soul than either *grief* or *sorrow*. *Tribulation* names a severe or grievous *affliction* extending through a long and trying period; it frequently refers to *suffering* regarded as discipline for the soul. *Woe* is like *grief* in that it is violent, and like *affliction* in that it is inconsolable. It is now used chiefly in poetry, though it has acquired also a facetious sense. *Sadness* is mental depression, either from a sorrowful event, or from a low condition of health or spirits; it may name a deep despondency, but it is often fleeting. *Melancholy* sometimes designates a not displeasing, pensive *sadness;* usually it is a habitual or constitutional tendency to despondency

grief'-strick'en *adj* overcome by grief

griev·ance /grēv'əns/ *n* 1 circumstance thought to be grounds for complaint; 2 complaint ‖ SYN injustice, injury, wrong

grieve /grēv'/ [OF *grever*] *vt* 1 to cause to feel grief ‖ *vi* 2 to feel grief

griev'ous *adj* 1 causing grief; 2 full of grief; 3 hard to be borne; 4 severe ‖ **griev'ous·ly** *adv* ‖ SYN mournful, sorrowful, distressing, severe

grif·fin /grif'in/ [MF *grifon*] *n* fabled animal with the body of a lion and the wings and head of an eagle

grill /gril'/ [F *gril*] *n* 1 gridiron; 2 grilled food; 3 room or restaurant specializing in grilled food ‖ *vt* 4 to cook on a grill; broil; 5 to subject to severe questioning

grille /gril'/ [F] *n* 1 grating or screen of metal bars placed before a window, or used as a gate or rail; 2 grating or screen for protecting and admitting air to an automobile engine or a radio

grim /grim'/ [OE] *adj* (**grim·mer; grim·mest**) 1 of a forbidding aspect; stern; 2 cruel; unyielding ‖ SYN ferocious, fierce, grisly, stern, relentless, terrible (see *sullen*) ‖ ANT benign, merciful, kind

gri·mace /grim'is, grimās'/ [F] *n* 1 facial expression indicating pain, disapproval, etc ‖ *vi* 2 to make a grimace

grime /grīm'/ [Flem *grijm*] *n* dirt embedded in a surface ‖ **grim'y** *adj* (**-i·er; -i·est**)

Grimm's' law' /grimz'/ [< Jacob Grimm (1785–1863) G philologist] *n* statement of a set of observed

consonant correspondences between Indo-European and Germanic, as exemplified by Greek *k, d, p, t,* which correspond respectively to English *h, t, f, th* (*kardia-heart; pater-father*)

grin /grin'/ [OE *grennian* to show the teeth] *v* (**grinned; grin·ning**) *vi* 1 to smile broadly, showing the teeth ‖ *vt* 2 to express by grinning ‖ *n* 3 act of grinning; broad smile

grind /grīnd'/ [OE *grindan*] *v* (**ground**) *vt* 1 to crush, pulverize; 2 to sharpen or smooth by abrasion; 3 to grate, as gears or the teeth; 4 to oppress, harass; 5 to turn the crank of ‖ *vi* 6 to grate or rub; 7 *colloq* to study hard ‖ *n* 8 act of grinding; 9 laborious and tedious work; 10 wearisome routine; 11 *colloq* laborious student ‖ **grind'er** *n*

grind'stone' *n* rotating stone wheel for sharpening blades

grin·go /griŋ'gō/ [Sp] *n* *disparaging* (in Spanish-speaking countries of the Western Hemisphere) foreigner, esp. a citizen of the U.S.

gri·ot /grē·ō', grē'ot/ [W Afr] *n* tribal poet, musician, or oral historian

grip /grip'/ [OE *gripe*] *n* 1 firm grasp; act of holding fast; 2 power of gripping; 3 small valise; 4 secret handclasp; 5 handle or hilt; 6 mental or physical mastery; 7 **come to grips with** to cope with; face ‖ *v* (**gripped** or **gript; grip·ping**) *vt* 8 to grasp or seize ‖ *vi* 9 to take fast hold

gripe /grīp'/ [OE *gripan* to seize] *vt* 1 to cause pain in the bowels of; 2 to vex, irritate ‖ *vi* 3 *colloq* to complain, grumble ‖ *n* 4 *colloq* complaint; 5 **gripes** *pl* spasmodic intestinal pain

grippe /grip'/ [F] *n* influenza

grip'ping *adj* holding one's interest; enthralling

gris·ly /griz'lē/ [OE *grislīc*] *adj* (**-li·er; -li·est**) hideous; horrible; gruesome ‖ SYN grim, hideous, gruesome, ghastly, horrible

grist /grist'/ [OE] *n* 1 grain for grinding; 2 ground grain; 3 **grist for** or **to one's mill** something appropriate or advantageous

gris·tle /gris'əl/ [OE] *n* cartilage ‖ **gris'tly** *adj* (**-tli·er; -tli·est**)

grit /grit'/ [OE *grēot*] *n* 1 fine abrasive particles, as sand; 2 coarsegrained sandstone; 3 pluck, spirit ‖ *v* (**grit·ted; grit·ting**) *vt* 4 to grate (the teeth) ‖ *vi* 5 to grate or grind ‖ **grit'ty** *adj* (**-ti·er; -ti·est**)

grits /grits'/ [OE *grytt*] *npl* coarsely ground hominy

griz·zle /griz'əl/ [MF *grisel* gray] *adj* 1 gray-haired; 2 gray

griz·zly /griz'lē/ *adj* (**-zli·er; -zli·est**) 1 grayish; streaked with gray ‖ *n* (**-zlies**) 2 grizzly bear

griz'zly bear' *n* large ferocious bear

(*Ursus horribilis*) of W North America

groan /grōn'/ [OE *grānian*] n 1 low deep sound uttered in pain or sorrow ‖ *vi* 2 to utter a groan; 3 to be weighed down; creak because of strain ‖ *vt* 4 to utter with groans

gro-cer /grōs'ər/ [OF *grossier* wholesale dealer] n one who sells groceries, as tea, flour, sugar, etc.

gro'cer-y n (-ies) 1 grocer's shop or business; 2 **groceries** pl food supplies sold by a grocer

grog /grog'/ [< *Old Grog*, nickname of Brit admiral Vernon (d. 1757)] n 1 alcoholic liquor mixed with water, esp. rum; 2 any alcoholic liquor

grog-gy /grog'ē/ adj (-gi-er; -gi-est) dazed, as from blows or fatigue

groin /groin'/ [ME *grynde*] n 1 lowest part of the abdominal wall near its junction with the thigh; 2 curved ridge made by the intersection of two arched ceilings or vaults

grom-met /grom'it/ [OF *gromette* curb] n 1 metal eyelet in cloth or leather; 2 insulating washer

groom /grōōm'/ [ME *grom*] n 1 man or boy who tends horses; 2 bridegroom ‖ *vt* 3 to tend (horses); 4 to make neat or tidy; 5 to prepare (someone), as for a higher position

grooms'man /-mən/ n (-men /-mən/) one who attends a bridegroom; best man

groove /grōōv'/ [MD *groeve*] n 1 channel or furrow, esp. as cut by a tool; 2 settled habit or routine ‖ *vt* 3 to put a groove in

groov'y adj (-i-er; -i-est) slang extremely attractive; highly pleasing

grope /grōp'/ [OE *grāpian* to grasp] vi 1 to feel one's way with the hands; 2 to feel blindly and uncertainly

gross /grōs'/ [OF *gros* large] adj 1 bulky, thick; 2 indelicate, coarse; 3 flagrant; 4 repulsively fat; 5 dull, witless; 6 without deductions; 7 broadly considered ‖ *n sg & npl* 8 twelve dozen ‖ *vt* 9 to earn, before deductions, a total income of ‖ **gross'ly** adv ‖ **gross'ness** n ‖ SYN glaring, sensual, vulgar, shameful, rough

gross' na'tion-al prod'uct n total value of all the goods and services produced in a country during one year

gro-tesque /grōtesk'/ [F < It *grottesca* cave (painting)] adj 1 fantastically formed; distorted; 2 bizarre; ridiculous ‖ n 3 whimsical ornamentation; grotesque object ‖ **gro-tesque'ly** adv ‖ **gro-tesque'ness** n ‖ SYN bizarre, comical, absurd (see *fanciful*)

grot-to /grot'ō/ [It < *grotta* < L *krypta* vault] n (-toes or -tos) 1 cave; 2 artificial cave or cavelike structure

grouch /grouch'/ [?] colloq n 1 fit of ill temper; sulkiness; 2 person with a grouch ‖ *vi* 3 to have a grouch ‖ **grouch'y** adj (-i-er; -i-est)

ground¹ /ground'/ *pt & pp* of **grind**

ground² [OE *grund*] n 1 earth or soil; 2 solid surface of the earth; 3 foundation, cause, or basis; 4 fundamental or preparatory part of an undertaking, as *to prepare the ground;* 5 neutral background, as in a design; 6 *elec* a that part of a circuit that is at zero potential with respect to the earth; b conducting body, such as the chassis of an automobile or a radio set, used as a general return of circuits and as an arbitrary zero potential; c connection of a conductor to a body at zero potential; 7 **grounds,** a tract of land, as about a building; b land for a special use, as *picnic grounds;* c dregs or sediment; d foundation or reason; 8 **break ground** to begin excavation for the construction of a building; 9 **gain ground,** a to advance; b to win acceptance; 10 **give ground** to retreat; 11 **hold** or **stand one's ground** to maintain one's position; 12 **lose ground,** a to fall back; b to lose acceptance; 13 **run into the ground** to overdo; 14 **shift one's ground** to change one's position, as in an argument ‖ *vt* 15 to set on the ground; 16 to fix firmly; establish; 17 to cause to run aground; 18 to teach the first principles to; 19 to cause (an airplane) to remain on the ground; 20 *elec* to connect with the ground ‖ *vi* 21 to alight, come to earth; 22 **ground out** *baseball* to be thrown out at first after hitting a grounder

ground' crew' n *mil* nonflying personnel who maintain aircraft, hangars, etc.

ground'er n *baseball* batted ball that bounds or rolls along the ground

ground' floor' n 1 floor of a building on the level of the ground; first floor; 2 *colloq* extremely advantageous position

ground' glass' n glass made translucent by having one of its surfaces ground or abraded

ground' hog' n woodchuck

ground'less adj without foundation or reason

ground'speed' n speed of an aircraft with reference to the ground beneath it

ground' swell' n heavy rolling of the sea caused usu. by a storm

ground' train'er n device for training a person on the ground, under simulated conditions of flight, in flying, gunnery, bombing, and other air activities

ground' wa'ter n water below the surface of the ground that has run off from the surface and that has risen from springs and wells

ground'work' n foundation; basis

ground' ze'ro n point on the surface

at which, or vertically above or below which, a nuclear bomb is detonated

group /grōōp'/ [F *groupe* < It *gruppo*] *n* 1 small crowd or assemblage; cluster; 2 collection of persons or things arranged or classified together; 3 *Air Force* operational unit higher than a squadron

group'er [< Port *garoupa*] *n* (-er or -ers) large sea bass of genera *Epinephelus*, *Mycteroperca*, and related genera of tropical and subtropical seas

group'ie [?] *n* female admirer and follower of male members of the beat generation

group' in·sur'ance *n* insurance available at low rates to a large group of persons

group' ther'a·py *n* psychotherapy in which a group of patients attempts to solve its problems by mutual discussion

grouse¹ /grous'/ [?] *n* (*pl* **grouse**) any of several dull-colored gallinaceous game birds of the family Tetraonidae

grouse² [?] *colloq vi* 1 to complain, grumble ‖ *n* 2 complaint

grout /grout'/ *n* 1 thin mortar or cement mixed with gravel; 2 fine plaster for ceilings ‖ *vt* 3 to surround or fill in with grout

grove /grōv'/ [OE *grāf*] *n* group of trees without undergrowth; small wood

grov·el /gruv'əl, grov-/ [< ME *grofling* with the face downward] *v* (-eled or -elled; -el·ing or -el·ling) *vi* 1 to lie or move abjectly with the face down; 2 to humble oneself meanly ‖ SYN crawl, creep, cringe, fawn, sneak, wallow

grow /grō'/ [OE *grōwan*] *v* (grew; grown) *vi* 1 to increase in size, strength, or maturity by natural development; 2 to arise or be produced naturally; 3 to flourish, thrive; become larger; 4 to become; change by degrees; 5 grow on to gain in favor with; 6 grow up to become fully mature ‖ *vt* 7 to cause or allow to grow ‖ grow'er *n* ‖ SYN develop, expand, wax, enlarge, augment

growl /groul'/ [prob imit] *n* 1 deep snarl or guttural noise such as is made by a dog ‖ *vi* 2 to utter a growl ‖ *vt* 3 to express with a growl

grown /grōn'/ 1 *pp* of **grow** ‖ *adj* 2 mature, fully developed

grown'up' *n* adult ‖ **grown'-up'** *adj*

growth /grōth'/ *n* 1 act or process of growing; 2 advancement; increase; 3 that which is grown; 4 formation of unhealthy tissue, as a tumor

growth' stock' *n* common stock of a company that has good prospects of steady growth in amount of business and profits

grub /grub'/ [ME *grubben* to dig] *v*

(**grubbed; grub·bing**) *vt* 1 to dig up, as earth; root out of the ground ‖ *vi* 2 to dig in the earth; 3 to drudge or toil ‖ *n* 4 larva of an insect; 5 plodder, drudge; 6 *colloq* food

grub·by /grub'ē/ *adj* (-bi·er; -bi·est) 1 dirty, untidy; 2 infested with grubs

grub'stake' *n* 1 money or supplies furnished to a prospector on condition of sharing in his discoveries ‖ *vt* 2 to furnish with a grubstake

grudge /gruj'/ [*obs grutch* < OF *groucier* to murmur] *n* 1 ill-will, resentment ‖ *vt* 2 to envy the good fortune of; 3 to grant reluctantly; begrudge ‖ **grudg'ing·ly** *adv* ‖ SYN *n* aversion, hatred, resentment (see *malice*)

gru·el /grōō'əl/ [OF] *n* thin porridge

gru'el·ing [< *obs gruel* punishment] *adj* exhausting, arduous

grue·some /grōō'səm/ [< *obs grue* to shudder] *adj* inspiring horror and loathing ‖ SYN ghastly, hideous, repulsive, dismal, frightful

gruff /gruf'/ [MF *grof* coarse] *adj* 1 rough, surly; 2 harsh, hoarse ‖ **gruff'ly** *adv* ‖ **gruff'ness** *n* ‖ SYN rugged, bluff, harsh, rude, disagreeable

grum·ble /grum'bəl/ [MF *grommeler*] *n* 1 growl; rumble; 2 complaint ‖ *vi* 3 to utter complainingly ‖ *vi* 4 to find fault; murmur discontentedly; 5 to growl ‖ **grum'bler** *n*

grump·y /grump'ē/ [< *obs grump* offense] *adj* (-i·er; -i·est) surly, peevish

grunt /grunt'/ [OE *grunettan*] *n* 1 deep guttural sound, as of a hog ‖ *vi* 2 to utter a grunt ‖ *vt* 3 to utter with a grunt

G'-string' [thickest string on a violin, tuned to the tone G] *n* small patch of cloth covering the genitalia of stripteasers

Gt. Br. or **Gt. Brit.** Great Britain

Guam /gwäm'/ *n* U.S. island in the Pacific E of the Philippines (68,000; 210 sq.m.; cap. Agaña) ‖ **Gua·ma·ni·an** /-män'ē·ən/ *adj & n*

gua·no /gwän'ō/ [Sp] *n* 1 solidified excrement of sea birds found at nesting places on Peruvian islands, valued as a fertilizer; 2 any similar fertilizer

gua·ra·ni /gwär'ənē'/ [name of Indian tribe] *n* monetary unit of Paraguay

guar·an·tee /gar'əntē'/ [see **guaranty**] *n* 1 guaranty; 2 pledge that something is or will perform as specified; 3 guarantor ‖ *vt* 4 to give a guarantee for; 5 to aver; undertake to bring about

guar·an·tor /gar'əntôr', -tər/ *n* one who guarantees or gives a guaranty

guar·an·ty /gar'əntē/ [AF *guarantie* < *guarant* warrant] *n* (-ties) 1 assumption of responsibility for the payment of another's debt or for the performance of some obligation by another; **2** that which is pledged as security ‖ *v* (**-tied**) *vt* **3** to warrant; insure; **4** to be responsible for (another's performance of an obligation)

guard /gärd′/ [OF *garder* to keep] *vt* **1** to watch over or protect; **2** to prevent from escaping ‖ *vi* **3 guard against** to take precautions against ‖ *n* **4** protection or defense; **5** any device for security, as *a mud guard;* **6** man or body of men that guards; **7** close watch; **8** *football* either of the two linemen stationed between a tackle and the center; **9 off (one's) guard** unwary; **10 on (one's) guard** wary, vigilant; **11 stand guard** to be on guard ‖ SYN *v* protect, ward, parry, watch, shield, cover, screen (see *defend*)

guard′ed *adj* **1** careful, cautious; **2** defended ‖ **guard′ed·ly** *adv*

guard′house′ (**-hous·es** /-ziz/) *n* **1** house occupied by guards; **2** *mil* jail for petty offenders

guard′i·an *n* **1** *law* one who has the care of the person or property of another; **2** one who or that which protects or guards ‖ **guard′i·an·ship′** *n*

guards′man /-mən/ *n* (**-men** /-mən/) **1** man employed as a guard; **2** member of the National Guard

Gua·te·ma·la /gwät′əmäl′ə/ *n* Spanish-speaking republic in Central America (4,717,000; 42,042 sq.mi.; cap. Guatemala City) ‖ **Gua′te·ma′lan** *adj & n*

gua·va /gwäv′ə/ [Sp *guayaba*] *n* **1** South American tree (*Psidium guajava*) bearing a pear-shaped fruit used for jelly; **2** its fruit

gu·ber·na·to·ri·al /g(y)ōōb′ərnətōr′ē·əl, -tōr′-/ [< L *gubernator* governor] *adj* pert. to a governor or to his office

Guern·sey /gurn′zē/ [one of the Channel Islands] *n* one of a breed of dairy cattle producing rich milk

guer·ril·la or **gue·ril·la** /gəril′ə/ [Sp, *dim.* of *guerra* war] *n* one of an irregular military force engaged in harassing an enemy in small bands ‖ also *adj*

guess /ges′/ [ME *gessen* < Scand] *vt* **1** to conjecture; judge at random; **2** to solve by conjecture; **3** to believe or think ‖ *vi* **4** to form an opinion without sound reason ‖ *n* **5** act of guessing; **6** conjecture

guess′work′ *n* **1** work performed by guessing; **2** action or opinion based on guessing

guest /gest′/ [OE *giest*] *n* **1** one who is entertained at the house or table of another; visitor; **2** one who is present by invitation; **3** lodger or boarder at a hotel, inn, etc.

guff /guf′/ [?] *n colloq* **1** insolent talk; **2** nonsense

guf·faw /gəfô′/ [?] *n* **1** loud burst of laughter ‖ *vi* **2** to utter guffaws

Gui·an·a /gē·an′ə, -än′ə/ *n* region on the N coast of South America on the Atlantic, including Guyana, Surinam, French Guiana, part of Venezuela, and part of Brazil (see *Guyana*)

guid·ance /gīd′əns/ *n* **1** act of guiding; direction, supervision; **2** counseling service, as for students

guide /gīd′/ [OF *guider*] *vt* **1** to lead or direct in a path or course; **2** to influence; govern by counsel ‖ *n* **3** one who or that which guides; **4** guidebook; **5** means of controlling a tool or other device ‖ SYN *v* rule, conduct, manage, pilot, train, control

guide′book′ *n* book of information for travelers

guid′ed mis′sile *n* aerial missile that is steered by radio signals or some sort of homing device

guide′line′ *n* **1** rope used to guide footsteps on rough terrain; **2** guide for courses of action laid down by higher authority

guide′post′ *n* post bearing a directional sign

guide′word′ *n* catchword on the top of a column, as in a dictionary

guild /gild′/ [ME *gilde*] *n* **1** association for mutual aid in a common trade or pursuit; **2** medieval association of merchants or skilled artisans

guil′der *n* monetary unit of The Netherlands, Surinam, and the Netherlands Antilles

guild′hall′ *n* **1** meeting place of a medieval guild; **2** town hall

guile /gil′/ [OF] *n* deceit, cunning, duplicity ‖ **guile′ful** *adj* ‖ SYN treachery, artfulness, trickery (see *deception*)

guile′less *adj* free of guile; artless, innocent ‖ SYN open, straightforward, honest, unsophisticated

guil·lo·tine /gil′ətēn′ / [J. I. *Guillotin* (1738–1814) F physician] *n* **1** apparatus for beheading a person by means of the fall of a heavy knife sliding in two upright guides ‖ /gil′ətēn′/ *vt* **2** to behead with the guillotine

guilt /gilt′/ [OE *gylt* offense] *n* state of one who has committed a crime or who is liable to a penalty; culpability ‖ **guilt′less** *adj*

guilt′y *adj* (**-i·er; -i·est**) **1** legally chargeable with a crime; wicked, criminal; **2** conscious of guilt; **3** *law* judged an offender against the law ‖ **guilt′i·ly** *adv* ‖ **guilt′i·ness** *n* ‖ SYN culpable, blameworthy, sinful, delinquent, criminal, wicked

guin·ea /gin′ē/ [< *Guinea*] *n* British unofficial monetary unit and former gold coin equal to 21 shillings

Guin·ea /gin′ē/ *n* republic in W

Africa (3,702,000; 94,926 sq.m.; cap. Conakry)

Guin'ea-Bis·sau' /bisou'/ *n* republic in W Africa (1,000,000; 13,948 sq. m.; cap. Bissau)

guin'ea fowl' *n* domesticated gallinaceous bird of the family Numididae, esp. *Numida meleagris,* having grayish-blue plumage with white spots

guin'ea hen' *n* 1 guinea fowl; 2 female guinea fowl

guin'ea pig' *n* 1 small tailless rodent of the genus *Cavia,* much used in scientific experiments; 2 subject of an experiment

Guin·e·vere /gwin'əvir'/ *n* Arthurian *legend* queen of King Arthur and mistress of Lancelot

guise /gīz/ [OF < OHG *wīsa* way] *n* 1 external appearance; garb; 2 semblance, false appearance

gui·tar /gitär'/ [Sp *guitarra* < Gk *kithara* zither] *n* six-stringed instrument plucked with the fingers or with a plectrum || **gui·tar'ist** *n*

gulch /gulch'/ [perh *obs* gulch to swallow] *n* deep narrow ravine

gul·den /gŏol'dən/ [D & G = golden] *n* 1 silver coin and monetary unit of The Netherlands; 2 any of various German and Austrian coins

gulf /gulf'/ [OF *golfe* < Gk *kolpos* bay of the sea] *n* 1 arm of the sea extending into the land, larger than a bay; 2 abyss; 3 wide separation

gulf' coast' *n* coast of the U.S. bordering on the Gulf of Mexico

Gulf' States' *npl* states of the U.S. bordering on the Gulf of Mexico

Gulf' Stream' *n* warm oceanic current flowing out of the Gulf of Mexico northeastward across the Atlantic and skirting the coast of Europe

gull¹ /gul'/ [perh < Welsh *gwylan*] *n* any of a large family (Laridae) of web-footed sea birds, white, gray, or marked with black

gull² [*obs gull* to gorge] *vt* 1 to cheat, impose upon, outwit || *n* 2 one easily deceived; dupe

gul·let /gul'it/ [OF *goulet*] *n* 1 esophagus; 2 throat

gul·li·ble /gul'ibəl/ [< *gull²*] *adj* easily deceived || **gul'li·bil'i·ty** /-bil'-/ *n*

gul·ly /gul'ē/ [prob< *gullet*] *n* (-lies) 1 channel worn by water; 2 ditch or gutter

gulp /gulp'/ [ME *gulpen*] *vt* 1 to swallow hastily in large drafts; 2 to suppress or choke back || *vi* 3 to catch the breath convulsively || *n* 4 act of gulping; 5 swallow, mouthful

gum¹ /gum'/ [OE *gōma* palate] *n* often **gums** *pl* firm fleshy tissue covering that part of the jawbones in which the teeth are embedded

gum² [OF *gomme* < Gk *kommi*] *n* 1 sticky substance that exudes from certain trees and shrubs and hardens on the surface; 2 tree or shrub that exudes and yields gum; 3 rubber; 4

any viscid substance that has become sticky and tough; 5 adhesive; 6 mucus on edge of eyelids; 7 chewing gum; 8 **gums** *pl* rubber overshoes || *v* (**gummed; gum·ming**) *vt* 9 to smear or fasten with gum; 10 **gum up** *slang* to ruin through incompetence || *vi* 11 to become stiff or sticky || **gum·my** *adj* (-mi·er; -mi·est)

gum' ar'a·bic *n* gum obtained from either of two species of acacia, used as an adhesive, in medicine, and in candy making

gum·bo /gum'bō/ [LaF] *n* 1 okra; 2 thick soup containing okra; 3 extremely sticky mud

gum'boil' *n* small abscess on the gums of the mouth

gum'drop' *n* candy made of vegetable gum or gelatin

gump·tion /gump'shən/ [Sc] *n* colloq 1 initiative, resourcefulness; 2 courage

gum'shoe' *n* 1 rubber overshoe; 2 sneaker; 3 *slang* detective || *vi* 4 to move stealthily, pry around

gun /gun'/ [ME *gunne*] *n* 1 weapon with a metal tube through which missiles are discharged by an explosive; 2 any device for discharging something under pressure; 3 **give the gun** to speed up, as a motor; 4 **jump the gun** to start or do something prematurely; 5 **stick to one's guns** to stand firm || *v* (**gunned; gun·ning**) *vi* 6 to shoot or hunt with a gun; 7 **gun for, a** to seek to kill; **b** to try to obtain || *vt* 8 to give gas to (an engine); 9 **gun down** to shoot

gun'boat' *n* small armed ship

gun'cot'ton *n* highly explosive substance made by treating cotton with nitric and sulfuric acids

gung ho /gun'hō'/ [Chin] *adj* overenthusiastic (group or person)

gun'man /-mən/ *n* (-men /-mən/) thug armed with a gun

gun' met'al *n* 1 variety of bronze, formerly used in making cannon; 2 dark-gray or blackish alloy, used for making all sorts of novelties; 3 color of this alloy || **gun'-met'al** *adj*

gun' moll' *n* *slang* gangster's girl

gun'ner *n* 1 artilleryman; 2 *nav* warrant officer who has charge of the ordnance and military supplies; 3 one who hunts game with a gun

gun'ner·y *n* 1 science of artillery; 2 the making and using of firearms

gun'play' *n* exchange of gunshots

gun'point' *n* at **gunpoint** under threat of being shot

gun'pow'der *n* explosive mixture of sulfur, charcoal, and saltpeter

gun'run'ner *n* smuggler of guns || **gun'-run'ning** *n*

gun'shot' *n* 1 range of a gun; 2 bullet fired from a gun; 3 firing of a gun

gun'smith' *n* one who makes or repairs firearms

gun·wale /gun'əl/ [*gun* + *wale* plank

on which guns were fixed on sailing ships] *n* upper edge of the side of a ship

gup·py /gup′ē/ [R. J. L. *Guppy*, donor of specimens to Brit Museum] *n* (**-pies**) small fresh-water fish (*Lebistes reticulatus*) remarkable for the brilliant coloration of the males

gur·gle /gurg′əl/ [?] *n* 1 broken bubbling sound, as of water flowing among pebbles ‖ *vi* 2 to make this sound

gu·ru /gŏŏr′ŏŏ/ [Hindi] *n* 1 Hindu religious teacher and spiritual guide; 2 *colloq* intellectual leader and counselor

gush /gush′/ [ME *guschen*] *vi* 1 to issue forth or flow suddenly and abundantly; 2 to display affection or enthusiasm in an exaggerated manner ‖ *vt* 3 to cause to gush ‖ *n* 4 sudden and violent flow of a liquid; 5 outburst, as of feelings ‖ SYN *v* flow, pour, issue, emit, send forth, eject

gush′er *n* 1 flowing oil well; 2 person who gushes

gush·y *adj* (**-i·er; -i·est**) excessively effusive ‖ SYN effusive, demonstrative, unrestrained

gus·set /gus′it/ [OF *gousset* < *gousse* nutshell] *n* small three-cornered piece inserted, as in a garment, to strengthen or enlarge a part

gust /gust′/ [ON *gustr*] *n* 1 sudden rush of wind; 2 sudden outburst or rush of fire, water, sound, etc.; 3 outburst of passion ‖ *vi* 4 to blow in gusts

gus·ta·to·ry /gust′ətôr′ē, -tōr′-/ [< L *gustus* taste] *adj* pert. to the sense of taste

gus·to /gust′ō/ [It] *n* zest; relish ‖ SYN appetite, taste, liking, fondness, enjoyment

gust′y *adj* (**-i·er; -i·est**) characterized by gusts

gut /gut′/ [OE *guttas* entrails] *v* (**gutted; gut·ting**) *vt* 1 to extract the entrails from; 2 to plunder; empty entirely; 3 to destroy the interior of, as by fire ‖ *n* 4 intestinal canal; 5 catgut; 6 **guts** *pl* a entrails; b *colloq* courage, spirit

gut′ course′ *n slang* extremely easy college course

Gu·ten·berg Bi′ble /gŏŏt′ənburg′/ [Johannes *Gutenberg* (1400?–68?) G printer and inventor of movable type] *n* Latin Bible printed at Mainz before 1456, thought to be the work of Gutenberg and the first book printed with movable type

gut·ta-per·cha /gut′əpur′chə/ [Malay *getah* gum + *percha* name of tree] *n* dried juice of any of certain trees (genera *Palaquium* and *Payena*) of the Malay Archipelago, extensively used in commerce, esp. for electrical insulation and in dentistry

gut·ter /gut′ər/ [OF *goutiere*] *n* 1 trough along the eaves of a building to carry off rain water; 2 channel at the side of a road to carry off surface water; 3 any shallow trough or trench; 4 white space formed by the inside margins of two facing pages of a book or other bound material; 5 place characterized by poverty, squalor, vice

gut′ter·snipe′ *n* one of the rabble

gut·tur·al /gut′ərəl/ [< L *guttur* throat] *adj* 1 pert. to or formed in the throat ‖ *n* 2 guttural sound

guy¹ /gī′/ [OF *guier* to guide] *n* 1 rope, wire, etc., to hold steady a pole or the like ‖ *vt* 2 to hold in place or keep steady with a guy

guy² [*Guy* Fawkes, Eng conspirator who sought to blow up Parliament in 1605] *colloq n* 1 fellow ‖ *vt* 2 to ridicule; 3 to tease

Guy·a·na /gī·an′ə, -än′ə/ *n* English-speaking nation in NE South America, formerly British Guinea (900,-000; 83,000 sq.m.; cap. Georgetown)

guz·zle /guz′əl/ [?] *vt & vi* to drink greedily and to excess ‖ **guz′zler** *n*

gym /jim′/ *n colloq* gymnasium

gym·na·si·um /jimnāz′ē·əm/ [L < Gk *gymnos* naked] *n* (**-ums** or **-a** /-ə/) 1 building or room equipped for athletic exercises; 2 in continental Europe, preparatory school with courses up to about the second year of an American college

gym·nas·tics /jimnas′tiks/ *npl* 1 athletic exercises; 2 *nsg* art of developing the physique by athletic exercises ‖ **gym·nas′tic** *adj*

gy·ne·col·o·gy /jīn′əkol′əjē, gīn′-, jin′-/ [< Gk *gyne* (*gynaikos*) woman] *n* branch of medical science which treats of diseases of women ‖ **gy′ne·col′o·gist** *n*

gyp /jip′/ [prob < *gypsy*] *v* (**gypped; gyp·ping**) *colloq vt & vi* 1 to swindle, cheat ‖ *n* 2 swindle; 3 swindler

gyp·sum /jip′səm/ [L < Gk *gypsos* chalk] *n* hydrous calcium sulfate —CaSO₄·2H₂O— used as a fertilizer and in making plaster of Paris

Gyp·sy /jip′sē/ [< *Egyptian* from supposed place of origin] *n* (**-sies**) 1 member of a swarthy wandering race of prob Hindu origin; 2 their language; 3 gypsy person who looks or lives like a Gypsy ‖ also *adj*

gyp′sy moth′ *n* moth (*Porthetria dispar*) whose larva feeds on foliage

gy·rate /jī′rāt, jīrāt′/ [L *gyrare* (*-atus*)] *vi* to revolve about a point or axis; rotate ‖ **gy·ra′tion** *n*

gy·ro /jī′rō/ *n* 1 gyrocompass; 2 gyroscope

gy·ro- [Gk *gyros* circle] *comb form* ring, circle, spiral

gy′ro·com′pass /jī′rō-/ *n* compass keeping its direction by using the principle of the gyroscope

gy′ro·scope′ /jīr′ə-/ *n* instrument consisting of a flywheel rotating about an axis arranged to move freely in one or more directions, used to sta-bilize vehicles and missiles moving through fluids ‖ **gy'ro·scop'ic** /-skop/-ik/ *adj*

H

H, h /āch'/ *n* (**H's** or **Hs; h's** or **hs**) eighth letter of the English alphabet

H 1 *chem* hydrogen; 2 eighth in order or in a series; 3 something shaped like an H; 4 *elec* henry

H., h. 1 height; 2 high; 3 *baseball* hit; 4 hour(s)

ha /hä/ [ME] *interj* exclamation expressing wonder, suspicion, mirth, joy, doubt, etc.

Ha *chem* hahnium

ha·be·as cor·pus /hāb'ē·əs kôrp'əs/ [L = (that) you have the body] *n law* writ or order to produce a prisoner at a stated time, to determine the justice of his detention

hab·er·dash·er /hab'ərdash'ər/ [< *obs haberdash* small wares] *n* one who deals in men's furnishings, as neckware, hats, etc. ‖ **hab'er·dash'er·y** *n* (-ies)

ha·bil·i·ments /həbil'əmənts/ [MF *habillement*] *npl* clothing, attire, accouterments esp. as worn by a particular profession or class

hab·it /hab'it/ [ME < L *habitus* condition, dress] *n* 1 distinctive dress, as in *riding habit, monk's habit;* 2 customary practice; 3 addiction; 4 usual physical or mental condition; 5 action so often repeated as to become a fixed characteristic or tendency ‖ SYN custom, routine, practice, fashion, use, wont ‖ DISCR *Custom* has its origin in the continued choice to keep on doing what has been done before. *Habit* is *custom* become so regular that it is automatic; so ingrained that it is spontaneous. *Custom* applies to groups of persons; *habit*, to the individual. It is an American *custom* to eat fruit for breakfast. We speak of the *habit* of smoking. *Routine* consists of the unvarying, mechanical performance of certain acts. *Practice*, like *custom*, stresses the actual repetition of an act rather than, like *habit*, the inclination to repeat it; but *practice* presents the act itself more vividly than *custom*, as the *practice* of early morning exercising

hab·it·a·ble [< L *habitare* to dwell] *adj* fit to live in

hab·it·ant *n* 1 inhabitant; 2 in Canada and Louisiana, farmer of French descent

hab·i·tat /hab'itat'/ [L = it dwells] *n* 1 natural abode of a plant or animal; 2 place where a person or thing is usually found

hab·i·ta'tion *n* 1 dwelling; 2 act of inhabiting

ha·bit·u·al /həbich'oo·əl/ *adj* 1 resulting from or acquired by habit; 2 customary, usual, regular; 3 given to a specified practice ‖ **ha·bit'u·al·ly** *adv*

ha·bit'u·ate' [L *habituare (-atus)*] *vt* to familiarize by use or repetition; accustom ‖ **ha·bit'u·a'tion** *n*

ha·bit·u·é /həbich'oo·a'/ [F] one who frequently visits a place

ha·ci·en·da /hä'sē·en'də/ [Sp] *n Sp Am* 1 landed estate, as a ranch or plantation; 2 house of the owner of such an estate

hack /hak'/ [OE *haccian*] *vt* 1 to cut or chop up roughly ‖ *vi* 2 to make rough cuts; 3 to give a short dry cough ‖ *n* 4 tool for hacking; 5 gash or notch; 6 dry, broken cough

hack² [< *hackney*] *n* 1 old worn-out horse; 2 carriage for hire; 3 writer or artist who turns out low-grade work in quantity for money; 4 *colloq* taxi ‖ *vi* 5 *colloq* to drive a taxi

hack·le /hak'əl/ [ME *hakell*] *n* 1 neck plumage of a domestic fowl; 2 long feather in the neck of a rooster, used for making artificial flies

hack·ney /hak'nē/ [ME *hakeney*] *n* 1 cab for hire; 2 horse for riding or driving; 3 drudge

hack'neyed *adj* trite, stale

hack'saw' *n* close-toothed saw with a narrow blade set in a frame, for cutting metal

had /had'/ *pt & pp of* have

had·dock /had'ək/ [ME *haddok*] *n* (-docks or -dock) North Atlantic food fish (*Melanogrammus aeglefinus*) of the cod family

Ha·des /hā'dēz/ *n* 1 *class. myth.* abode of the dead; 2 hell

hadn't /had'ənt/ had not

hadst /hadst'/ *archaic & poet.* 2nd *pers sg pres ind of* have

haemo- *comb form* var of **hemo-**

haf·ni·um /haf'nē·əm/ [< L *Hafnia* Copenhagen] *n chem* rare metallic element (**Hf**; at.no. 72; at.wt. 178.49) occurring in zirconium ores

haft /haft', häft'/ [OE *hæft*] *n* handle or hilt of a tool, knife, or sword

hag /hag'/ [ME *hagge*] *n* 1 ugly old woman; 2 witch

hag'fish' *n* (-fish·es or -fish) any of an order (Hyperotreta) of eellike, jaw-less fishes, which destroy fish by boring into their bodies

hag·gard /hag'ərd/ [MF *hagard* wild hawk] *adj* worn and wasted in appearance, gaunt ‖ SYN wasted, wan, wild-looking, gaunt, pale

hag·gis /hag'is/ [ME *hages*] *n* Scotch dish made of the internal organs of a sheep or calf, seasoned, mixed with oatmeal, and boiled in a sheep's stomach

hag·gle /hag'əl/ [ME *hagge* to chop] *vi* 1 to bargain by wrangling over trifles ‖ *n* 2 act of haggling

hag·i·og·ra·phy /hāj'ē·og'rəfē, hag'-/ [< Gk *hagios* saint + *-graphy*] *n* (-phies) 1 collection of biographies of saints; 2 writing of the lives of saints ‖ **hag'i·og'ra·pher** *n*

Hague, The /hāg'/ *n* one of the two capitals of The Netherlands; site of the Permanent Court of International Justice (592,841)

hah /hä'/ *interj* ha

hahn·i·um /hän'ē·əm/ [Otto *Hahn* (1879–1968) G physicist] *n* synthetic element (**Ha**; at. no. 105)

hail[1] /hāl'/ [OE *hago*] *n* 1 small pellets of ice precipitated from the sky; 2 shower of anything, as bullets ‖ *vt* 3 to pour down like hail ‖ *vi* 4 to pour down hail

hail[2] [ON *heill* healthy] *n* 1 salutation, greeting; 2 shout to attract attention ‖ *vt* 3 to greet, salute; 4 to call in order to stop, as a cab ‖ *vi* 5 to call out greetings; 6 **hail from** to be from ‖ *interj* 7 exclamation of greeting

hail'-fel'low well' met' *n* one who makes friends quickly with all whom he meets

hail'stone' *n* pellet of hail

hair /her'/ [OE *hēr*] *n* 1 one of the small filaments growing out of the skin of many animals; 2 mass of such hairs, as on the human head; 3 hairlike growth on a plant; 4 very small amount of space or time; 5 **get in someone's hair** *slang* to bother someone; 6 **let one's hair down** to relax, be informal; 7 **split hairs** to make overly fine distinctions

hair'breadth' or **hair's'breadth'** *n* minute distance

hair'cloth' *n* 1 fabric of camel's hair or horsehair used to cover furniture; 2 hair shirt worn for penance

hair'cut' *n* 1 act of cutting the hair; 2 style in which the hair is cut

hair'do' *n* manner of dressing the hair; coiffure

hair'dress'er *n* one who cuts or dresses hair

hair' dri'er *n* blower for drying hair

hair'line' *n* 1 very slender line; 2 lower edge of the hair on the forehead ‖ *adj* 3 thin, very narrow; 4 precise, exact

hair'piece' *n* toupee

hair'pin' *n* 1 two-pronged pin, as of

wire, for holding the hair or head-dress in place ‖ *adj* 2 U-shaped, as a curve in a road

hair'-rais'er *n* terrifying or thrilling story or experience

hair'-rais'ing *adj* terrifying; thrilling

hair' set' *n* act or result of fixing the hair by curling or waving with rollers when wet

hair' shirt' *n* garment of coarse hair-cloth worn next to the skin by penitents

hair' space' *n* thin metal strip used by printers to separate letters, words, lines, etc.

hair'split'ting *adj* making trivial or unnecessary distinctions ‖ also *n*

hair'spray' *n* spray from an aerosol to set the hair

hair'spring' *n* very delicate spring used to regulate the balance wheel of a timepiece

hair' trig'ger *n* trigger of a gun so adjusted that the slightest touch discharges the gun

hair'y *adj* (-i·er; -i·est) 1 of or like hair; 2 covered with hair ‖ **hair'i·ness** *n*

Hai·ti /hāt'ē/ *n* Creole- and French-speaking republic on the W third of the island of Hispaniola (4,581,000; 10,714 sq.mi.; cap. Port-au-Prince) ‖ **Hai'ti·an** /-tē·ən, -shən/ *adj & n*

hake /hāk'/ [ME] *n* (hakes or hake) any of several food marine fishes (genera *Urophycis* and *Merluccius*) related to the cod

hal·berd /hal'bərd/ [MF *hallebarde*] *n* former weapon consisting of a battle-ax attached near the point of a spear

hal'berd·ier' /-dir'/ *n* foot soldier armed with a halberd

hal·cy·on /hal'sē·ən/ [Gk (*h*)*alkyon* kingfisher, a fabled bird having the power of calming the seas] *adj* 1 peaceful, calm; 2 happy; prosperous

hale[1] /hāl'/ [OE *hāl* whole] *adj* healthy, robust

hale[2] [MF *haler* to haul] *vt* to bring as by dragging, as a person into court

half /haf', häf'/ [OE *healf*] *n* (halves /-vz/) 1 one of two equal parts; 2 half dollar; 3 **by half** by far; 4 **by halves, a** incompletely; **b** half-heartedly; 5 **go halves** to share or divide equally; 6 **in half** into halves ‖ *adj* 7 consisting of or forming a half; 8 partial; incomplete ‖ *adv* 9 to the extent of a half; 10 partially; 11 **not half** not at all

half'-and-half' *n* any of various mixtures of two substances combined in equal parts, as milk and cream or ale and porter

half'back' *n football* one of the two backs stationed on the side of the fullback

half'-baked' *adj* 1 immature; 2 not sufficiently thought through

half' bind'ing *n* binding in which only the back, and sometimes the corners of the book, are bound in leather

half'-breed' *n* one whose parents are of different races

half' broth'er *n* brother related through one common parent only

half'-caste' *n* **1** person of an East Indian parent on one side and a European on the other; **2** half-breed

half'-cocked' *adv* go off **half-cocked** to act rashly or without adequate preparation

half' dol'lar *n* coin of the U.S. and Canada worth 50 cents

half'-heart'ed *adj* lacking in interest or enthusiasm || **half'-heart'ed·ly** *adv*

half' hitch' *n* knot used for temporary fastening

half'life' *n* (**-lives**) time required for half the atoms of a radioactive substance to disintegrate

half'-mast' *n* position of a flag hung below the top of the staff as emblematic of mourning or as a distress signal

half'-moon' *n* **1** moon at the first or third quarter when half its disk is seen; **2** something shaped like a half-moon

half' mourn'ing *n*, **1** garb less somber than full mourning; **2** period in which it is worn

half' nel'son *n* hold in which a wrestler passes one arm under the corresponding arm of his opponent from behind and locks the hand on the back of the opponent's neck

half' note' *n mus* note half as long as a whole note

half·pen·ny /hăp'(ə)nē/ *n* (**half·pence** /hăp'əns/ or **-pen·nies**) British coin valued at half a penny

half' shell' *n* either half of a bivalve mollusk

half' sis'ter *n* sister related through one common parent only

half'-tim'bered *adj* having the framework of timber and the spaces between filled with masonry or plaster

half' ti'tle *n* **1** first printed page of a book which appears before the title page; **2** full page containing only the title of a subdivision

half'tone' *n* **1** photographic process of making plates for illustrations, by which the lights and shadows are reproduced by fine dots or lines; **2** picture so made; **3** intermediate tone in painting or engraving

half'-track' *n* military vehicle with rear wheels on caterpillar treads

half'-truth' *n* statement which is partly true but leaves something unsaid with the possible purpose of deceiving

half'way' *adj* **1** midway between two points; **2** partial || *adv* **3** at half the distance; midway; **4** partly; almost

half'-wit' *n* feeble-minded person || **half'-wit'ted** *adj*

hal·i·but /hal'əbət/ [ME *halybutte* holy flatfish (eaten on holy days)] *n* (**-but** or **-buts**) any of a subfamily of flounders, esp. the common halibut (*Hippoglossus hippoglossus*) of the North Atlantic, highly valued for food

hal·ide /hal'īd, hāl'-/ [*halogen* + *-ide*] *n chem* compound formed by a halogen with another element or a radical

Hal·i·fax /hal'əfaks'/ *n* capital of Nova Scotia (95,000)

hal·i·to·sis /hal'ətōs'is/ [< L *halitus* breath] *n* bad breath

hall /hôl/ [OE *heall*] *n* **1** corridor; **2** main living room of a castle; **3** large building or room for entertainments or the like; auditorium; **4** college or university building; **5** vestibule, lobby; **6** *Brit* manor house; **7** public building

hal·le·lu·jah /hal'ĭlōō'yə/ [Heb = praise ye Jehovah] *interj* **1** praise the Lord! || *n* **2** exclamation or song of praise to God

hall'mark' [< the stamp used by Goldsmiths' Hall in London attesting the quality of gold and silver articles] *n* **1** any mark or proof of genuineness; **2** any distinguishing feature

hal·lo /həlō'/ also **hal·loo** /-lōō'/ [?] *interj & n* **1** call to give greetings or attract attention || *vt* **2** to call or shout

hal·low /hal'ō/ [OE *hālgian*] *vt* **1** to consecrate; sanctify; **2** to honor as holy || SYN dedicate, consecrate, inscribe, address

Hal·low·een /hal'əwēn', häl'-/ [< *All Hallows Even*] *n* evening of October 31, the day before All Saints' Day

hal·lu·ci·na·tion /həlōōs'ənāsh'ən/ [< L *hallucinari* (*-atus*) to wander in mind] *n* **1** perception of sights, sounds, etc., not actually occurring; **2** false impression; delusion || **hal·lu'ci·na·to'ry** /-tôr'-, -tōr'-/ *adj* || SYN illusion, perception, impression (see *delusion*)

hal·lu·cin·o·gen /-nəjən, - nəjen'/ *n* substance, esp. one taken orally, that induces hallucinations

hall'way' *n* entrance hall or corridor in a building

ha·lo /hā'lō/ [Gk *halos* disk of sun or moon] (**-los**, or **-loes**) **1** luminous ring appearing to surround ice crystals or water droplets in the atmosphere; **2** bright ring represented in pictures as surrounding the heads of saints

hal·o·gen /hal'əjən/ [< Gk *hals* salt + *-gen*] *n* any of the elements chlorine, bromine, iodine, fluorine, and astatine, which form binary salts in direct combination with metals || **ha·log·e·nous** /həloj'ənəs/ *adj*

halt¹ /hôlt'/ [< G *halt*(machen) (to make) a stop] *n* 1 stop; 2 *vt & vi* to stop

halt² [OE *healt*] *adj* 1 lame || *vi* 2 to falter; to waver, to hesitate

hal·ter /hôlt'ər/ [OE *hælfter*] *n* 1 rope or strap for leading or holding an animal; 2 hangman's noose; 3 woman's garment for covering the breasts, secured by a loop around the neck

halve /hav'/, häv'/ [see **half**] *vt* 1 to divide into halves; 2 to lessen to half

halves /havz', hävz'/ *pl of* **half**

hal·yard /hal'yərd/ [ME *hallyer*] *n* tackle for hoisting or lowering a sail, yard, or flag

ham /ham'/ [OE *hamm* inner part of knee] *n* 1 back of the thigh; 2 a thigh of a hog; b meat from this; 3 *colloq* licensed amateur radio operator; 4 *colloq* actor who overacts || *v* (**hammed; ham·ming**) *vi* 5 *slang* to overact || *vt* 6 **ham it up** *slang* to overact

Ham /ham'/ *n Bib* second son of Noah (Gen. 10)

Ham·burg /ham'bərg/ *n* city in West Germany on the North Sea; largest seaport in continental Europe (1,900,000)

ham·burg·er [< *Hamburg*] *n* ground beef, served as steaks or in sandwiches

Ham·il·ton, Al·ex·an·der /ham'əltən/ *n* (1757–1804) American statesman, first Secretary of the Treasury 1789–97; killed in a duel by Aaron Burr

Ham·ite /ham'īt/ [< *Ham*] *n* 1 descendant of Ham; 2 member of the chief native race of N Africa, as an ancient Egyptian or a modern Berber || **Ham·it·ic** /-it'ik/ *adj & n*

ham·let /ham'lit/ [MF *hamelet*] *n* village of only a few houses

Ham·let /ham'lit/ *n* 1 tragedy by Shakespeare; 2 its hero

ham·mer /ham'ər/ [OE *hamor*] *n* 1 instrument with a handle and a metal head, used for driving nails, beating metals, etc.; 2 anything like this in shape or use, as the hammer in a gunlock, a padded mallet in a piano action, a gavel, etc.; 3 one of the bones in the middle ear || *vt* 4 to pound or drive with a hammer; 5 to assemble with or as with a hammer and nails; 6 **hammer home** to present (ideas) forcefully; 7 **hammer out,** a to arrive at by strong effort, as *to hammer out an agreement;* b to pound out, as a tune on a piano || *vi* 8 to strike heavy blows; 9 **hammer (away) at** to keep emphasizing

ham·mer and sick·le *n* emblem of Communism, which consists of crossed hammer and sickle and signifies the union of workers and peasants

ham·mer and tongs' *adv colloq* 1 making a great noise and racket; 2 with might and main; with all one's strength and power

ham·mer·head' *n* any of a family (Sphyrnidae) of sharks with hammershaped heads

ham·mock /ham'ək/ [Sp *hamaca*] *n* couch, usu. of network or canvas, suspended by ropes at the ends

ham·my *adj* (**-mi·er; -mi·est**) *colloq* 1 like a ham actor; 2 overacted

ham·per¹ /hamp'ər/ [ME *hampere*] *n* large wickerwork basket, usu. with a cover

ham·per² [ME *hampren*] *vt* to hinder, impede; interfere with

ham·ster /ham'stər/ [G] *n* burrowing ratlike rodent of the Old World, as *Cricetus cricetus,* having large cheek pouches

ham'string' *n* 1 one of the strong tendons at the back of the knee; 2 large tendon behind the hock in quadrupeds || *v* (**-strung**) *vt* 3 to disable by cutting the hamstring; 4 to thwart, cripple

hand /hand'/ [OE] *n* 1 lower part of the arm, connected at the wrist and adapted for grasping; 2 something resembling this in appearance or use; 3 pointer, as *the hands of a clock;* 4 measure of four inches; 5 skill, knack; 6 direction, side; 7 possession; control; 8 agency; 9 active participation, as *he had a hand in the work;* 10 aid, as *give me a hand;* 11 handwriting; 12 signature; 13 hired worker; 14 member of a ship's crew; 15 person considered as doing a specific thing, as *a good hand at figuring;* 16 *cards* a player; b cards held by each player on any deal; c round of play; 17 pledge, as of marriage; 18 source, as *at first hand;* 19 round of applause; 20 **at hand** within reach; 21 **force one's hand** to force a person to act; 22 **hand in hand,** a closely associated; b holding hands; 23 **hand over fist** *colloq* easily and in large amounts; 24 **hands down** easily; 25 **have one's hands full,** a to be overloaded, as with work; b to be unable to cope with a situation; 26 **off one's hands** out of one's care or responsibility; 27 **on hand** available; 28 **on the other hand** from the opposite point of view; 29 **out of hand,** a out of control; b at once; 30 **sit on one's hands,** a to fail to applaud; b to fail to take action; 31 **the upper hand** the advantage; 32 **with a heavy hand,** a severely; b clumsily || *vt* 33 to give or transmit with or as with the hand; 34 to lead or assist, as with the hand; 35 **hand down,** a to deliver (a judicial decision); b to transmit to posterity; 36 **hand it to** *colloq* to give credit to; 37 **hand out** to distribute

hand′bag′ *n* 1 woman's bag, as of leather, for carrying personal belongings, such as money and cosmetics; 2 valise

hand′ball′ *n* game in which a ball is struck with the hands and kept bounding against a wall

hand′bill′ *n* printed advertisement distributed by hand

hand′book′ *n* 1 small guidebook; 2 manual or concise outline of some subject

hand′car′ *n* small four-wheeled rail car propelled by a lever worked by hand

hand′cuff′ *n* 1 one of a pair of shackles connected with a chain for fastening the wrists together || *vt* 2 to put handcuffs on; 3 to restrain from free action

-hand′ed *adj comb form* 1 having a specified kind or number of hands, as *right-handed*; 2 requiring a specified number of people, as *three-handed pinochle*

Han·del, George Frederick /ˈhanˌdəl/ *n* (1685–1759) German-born English composer

hand′ful′ *n* 1 as much as a hand can hold; 2 a small number or quantity; 3 person or thing hard to control

hand·i·cap /ˈhandēˌkap/ [< *hand in cap* prob in reference to drawing of lots] *n* 1 hindrance; disadvantage; 2 specific disadvantage or advantage allotted a contestant to make the contest more even, as extra weight on a horse; 3 contest with a handicap || *v* (-capped; -cap·ping) *vt* 4 to give a handicap to; 5 to hinder; burden

hand′i·craft′ *n* 1 manual skill; 2 work requiring it; 3 articles made with the hands

hand′i·work′ *n* 1 work done by hand; 2 any work done by personal effort

hand·ker·chief /ˈhaŋkərchif, -chif′, -chēf′/ *n* 1 piece of cloth, usu. square, for wiping the nose or face; 2 neckerchief

han·dle /ˈhanˌdəl/ [OE] *n* 1 that part of a tool, vessel, etc., intended to be grasped by the hand; 2 *slang* name; 3 fly off the handle *colloq* to explode in anger || *vt* 4 to touch, hold, feel, examine, or move with the hand; 5 to manage, control; 6 to deal with; 7 to deal in || *vi* 8 to behave in a certain way when handled

han·dle·bar′ *n* or **han′dle·bars′** *npl* curved bar with handles on the ends for steering a bicycle or motorcycle

han′dler *n* person who assists in training a prize fighter

hand′maid′ *n* 1 female servant or attendant; 2 something subordinate

hand′-me-down′ *n* article of clothing handed down from a person who no longer wants it or has outgrown it

hand′ or′gan *n* portable barrel organ

hand′out′ *n* 1 anything given away free; 2 press release

hand′set′ *n* telephone unit consisting of a transmitter and receiver mounted on the ends of a handle

hand′shake′ *n* shaking of the right hands by two people, as in greeting, congratulations, or agreement

hand·some /ˈhansəm/ [ME *handsum* easily handled] *adj* 1 pleasing to look upon; well-formed; 2 generous, gracious; 3 ample

hand′spring′ *n* somersault in which one lands first on the hands and then on the feet

hand′-to-hand′ *adj* (combat) at close quarters

hand′-to-mouth′ *adj* barely making enough to keep alive

hand′writ′ing *n* 1 writing done by hand; 2 a style of such writing; b style of writing characteristic of an individual

hand′y *adj* (-i·er; -i·est) 1 skillful; 2 convenient, easily reached || **hand′i·ly** *adv*

hand′y·man′ /-ˌman′/ *n* (-men /-ˌmen′/) man hired for miscellaneous small jobs

Han·ford /ˈhanfərd/ *n* locality in SE Washington on the Columbia River, one of the sites where the atomic bomb was developed

hang /haŋ/ [OE *hōn* to hang *vt*; OE *hangian* to hang *vi*; & ON *hengjan* to cause to hang] *v* (hung) *vt* 1 to attach to something above; suspend; 2 to fasten so as to swing freely, as a door; 3 to attach or fasten to the wall, as wallpaper or pictures; 4 *slang* to strike (a blow); 5 to deadlock (a jury); 6 hang one on *slang* a to hit; b to become exceedingly drunk; 7 hang up, a to suspend, as from a hook or peg; b to delay || *vi* 8 to dangle, be suspended; 9 to depend or swing on supports; 10 to be dependent; 11 to be in a deadlock; 12 to jut out, as *to hang over the edge*; 13 to be in abeyance, as *let the matter hang*; 14 hang around *colloq* to loiter; 15 hang around with *colloq* to be constantly in the company of; 16 hang back to hesitate; 17 hang on, a to cling to; b to persevere; 18 hang out *slang* to loaf, spend much time; 19 hang over, a to hover threateningly; b to be postponed; 20 hang together, a to be loyal to each other; b to be logical; 21 hang up to end a telephone conversation by putting the receiver on the hook || *v* (hung or preferably hanged) *vt* 22 to suspend from the neck until dead, as with a rope || *vi* 23 to die by hanging || *n* 24 manner in which a thing hangs; 25 *colloq* manner of doing or using; knack; 26 general idea

han·gar /ˈhaŋər/ [F = shed] *n* shed for storing aircraft

hang′bird′ *n* 1 bird which builds a hanging nest, called hangnest; 2 Baltimore oriole

hang′dog′ *adj* 1 of degraded, ashamed, or sneaking appearance; 2 brow-beaten (appearance)

hang′er *n* 1 one who or that which hangs; 2 that by which something is hung; 3 shoulder-shaped frame, as of wood or wire, for hanging garments

hang′er-on′ *n* (**hang·ers-on**) unwelcome follower, parasite

hang′ing *n* 1 execution or death by hanging; 2 **hangings** *pl* draperies, curtains, etc., hung on the walls

hang′man /-mən/ *n* (**-men** /-mən/) man who hangs condemned criminals, public executioner

hang′nail′ [OE *angnǣgl* corn] *n* small piece of loose cuticle around a finger nail

hang′out′ *n colloq* place where a person spends a lot of time

hang′o′ver *n* sick aftereffects of drunkenness

hang′-up′ *n colloq* 1 fixation, inhibition; 2 psychological block

hank /haŋk/ [ME < Scand] *n* 1 skein of yarn or thread; 2 coil or loop

han·ker /haŋk′ər/ [prob Flem *hankeren*] *vi* to have an eager longing or craving ‖ **han′ker·ing** *n*

han·ky-pan·ky /haŋk′ē·paŋk′ē/ *n colloq* devious conduct; loose behavior

Han·ni·bal /han′ibəl/ *n* (247–138 B.C.) Carthaginian general who invaded Italy across the Alps

Ha·noi /hanoi′, hä-/ *n* capital of Vietnam (1,400,000)

han′som (cab′) /han′səm/ [J. A. *Hansom* (1803–82) Eng designer] *n* two-wheeled, one-horse cab with an outside driver's seat behind

hap·haz·ard /hap′haz′ərd/ [< *obs hap* chance + *hazard*] *adj* accidental; random ‖ **hap′haz′ard·ly** *adv* ‖ SYN *adj* promiscuous, random, accidental, casual

hap·less /hap′lis/ [< *hap* luck] *adj* luckless

hap′pen /hap′ən/ [ME *happenen*] *vi* 1 to chance; come or occur by chance; 2 to occur, take place; 3 to come or be by chance, as *he happened along as I sat there*; 4 to have a certain experience by chance, as *I happened to see your name in the paper*; 5 **happen on** to come upon by chance ‖ SYN *v* befall, chance, occur, betide, come about

hap′pen·ing *n* 1 event; occurrence; 2 gathering planned for the purpose of putting on a spontaneous act or show

hap·pi·ness /hap′ēnis/ *n* 1 quality or state of being happy; 2 good fortune; 3 natural elegance of address; felicity, as of language ‖ SYN joy, joyfulness, felicity, bliss, enjoyment, pleasure, satisfaction, gladness, delight, contentment ‖ DISCR *Pleasure*, the opposite of pain, is an agreeable emotion covering all degrees of the feeling. *Enjoyment* is the taking or experiencing of *pleasure*. *Happiness* is a state of glowing *pleasure*, of being radiantly contented with one's lot. *Joy* is vivid, profound, demonstrative, and, because of its intensity, often transient. *Gladness*, though as strong as *joy*, is more serene and is experienced over worthy causes; we speak of unholy *joy* over an enemy's downfall, not of unholy *gladness*. *Delight* is a high degree of *pleasure*, often bubbling and rapturous. *Felicity*, a word in rather elevated use, is intense *happiness*. *Bliss* is perfect *joy*. *Contentment* is a state of calm *pleasure* over what one has or is; *satisfaction* leaves nothing to be desired ‖ ANT unhappiness, wretchedness, misery, discontent, bitterness

hap·py /hap′ē/ [see **hapless**] *adj* (**-pi·er**, **-pi·est**) 1 enjoying pleasure or good; contented; 2 delighted, pleased; 3 favored by fortune, 4 giving or causing joy or gladness; 5 apt; felicitous ‖ **hap′pi·ly** *adv* ‖ SYN blissful, blithe, merry, gay, jolly, joyous, contented, cheerful, glad, sunny, fortunate, lucky, auspicious ‖ DISCR *Happy*, as compared with *lucky* and *auspicious*, means coming by good chance or fortune, as a *happy* outcome; a *happy* solution of difficulties; a *happy* accident. *Happy* emphasizes the favorable aspect of the chance; *lucky*, a familiar word, emphasizes the chance itself. A *lucky* man reaps benefits and success from what is apparently no labor of his own; a *lucky* circumstance brings fortune which might as easily have been turned away. *Fortunate* is a more dignified word than *lucky*; the *fortunate* man's status or good fortune is less striking, more in proportion to his labor, than that of the *lucky* man. *Auspicious* is not used of persons, but describes those casual and incidental circumstances that are of favorable omen for a journey, a new undertaking, etc., as an *auspicious* moment; an *auspicious* occasion ‖ ANT unhappy, unfortunate, sad

-hap′py *adj comb form* prone to use something to excess, as *trigger-happy*

hap′py-go-luck′y *adj* light-hearted, easy-going, trusting to luck

ha·ra·ki·ri /har′əkir′ē/ [Jap = cut the belly] *n* formerly in Japan, ritual suicide by disembowelment

ha·rangue /həraŋ′/ [MF *arenge* public address] *n* 1 noisy ranting speech; tirade ‖ *vi* 2 to deliver a harangue ‖ *vt* 3 to address in a harangue ‖ SYN *n* address, oration, declamation (see *speech*)

har·ass /har′əs, həras′/ [F *harasser* to tire out] *vt* to worry, tease, disturb, torment ‖ **har′ass·ment** *n* ‖ SYN besiege, fret, bother, pester, worry (see *annoy*)

har·bin·ger /här'binjər/ [MF *herber-gere*] *n* 1 messenger, forerunner; 2 any token of future events || *vt* 3 to announce; foretell; usher in

har·bor /här'bər/ [OE *hereboorg* army quarters] *n* 1 port or place of shelter for ships; 2 protected waterway equipped with docking facilities; 3 any place of refuge || *vt* 4 to shelter or protect; 5 to entertain, as thoughts or designs || SYN *n* shelter, security, haven, refuge, port

hard /härd'/ [OE *heard*] *adj* 1 compact and solid; firm and unyielding; 2 difficult to do or understand; 3 unsympathetic; unfeeling; 4 laborious, strenuous, fatiguing; 5 cruel, oppressive; 6 exacting; not easily complied with; 7 (water) containing mineral salts that retard lathering; 8 energetic; 9 powerful, as a blow; 10 (liquor) containing much alcohol; 11 unfriendly, as feelings; 12 (c and g) pronounced as in *come* and *go*; 13 **hard up** colloq urgently in need, esp. of money || *adv* 14 energetically; strenuously; 15 earnestly; diligently; 16 roughly; 17 to the utmost extent; 18 so as to become firm and solid; 19 with vexation, trouble, or sorrow; 20 **hard by** near; 21 **hard put to it** at a loss || **hard'ness** *n* || SYN *adj* difficult, arduous, harsh, laborious, severe, rigorous, exacting, trying, exhausting, obdurate, unfeeling, insensible, solid, firm, oppressive, unrelenting, callous || DISCR *Hard, difficult,* and *arduous* describe that which cannot be accomplished without labor or strain; *hard* describes a task that may require either physical or mental effort; *difficult* is used of tasks that require skill, cleverness, diplomacy, rather than physical exertion. Prisoners are condemned to *hard* rather than *difficult* labor; a problem that baffles the understanding may be termed either *hard* or *difficult. Arduous* describes that which is highly *difficult;* that is *arduous* which is high in aim, and attainable only through persevering toil of both body and mind, as an *arduous* enterprise. *Hard, obdurate, unfeeling,* and *insensible* designate an unyielding quality, as *hard* candy; a *hard* heart; an *obdurate* will or disposition; an *unfeeling* nature; *insensible* to pity || ANT *adj* soft, yielding, gentle, easy, sympathetic, lenient, submissive

hard'-and-fast' *adj* strict (rule)

hard'back' *n* hardcover || also *adj*

hard'-bit'ten *adj* tough, severe

hard'-boiled' *adj* 1 (egg) boiled until hard; 2 colloq tough, unfeeling

hard' ci'der *n* fermented apple juice

hard' coal' *n* anthracite

hard' core' *n* intransigent nucleus of a group or political party || **hard'-core'** *adj*

hard'cov'er *n* 1 book bound in a rigid cover || *adj* 2 (book) bound in a rigid cover; 3 pert. to hardcovers

hard'en *vt* 1 to make hard or harder || *vi* 2 to become hard or harder

hard'-fist'ed *adj* 1 miserly; 2 tough

hard'-hand'ed *adj* tyrannical

hard' hat' *n* light helmet of metal or plastic, worn as protection by construction workers and athletes

hard'-hat' colloq *n* 1 construction worker who wears a hard hat || *adj* 2 (work) requiring the wearing of a hard hat

hard'-head'ed *adj* 1 shrewd; 2 practical, unsentimental; 3 obstinate, stubborn

hard'-heart'ed *adj* 1 unfeeling; 2 cruel, merciless

har'di·hood' [< *hardy*] *n* 1 robustness; 2 daring, boldness; 3 effrontery, audacity

Har·ding, Warren Gamaliel /här'diŋ/ *n* (1865–1923) 29th president of the U.S. 1921–23

hard' la'bor *n* compulsory labor imposed upon prisoners

hard' lin'er *n* person who takes a tough and uncompromising position on the issues before him || **hard'-line'** *adj*

hard' lines' *npl* bad luck

hard' liq'uor *n* distilled liquor

hard'ly *adv* 1 scarcely; 2 barely; 3 improbably; 4 **hardly ever** almost never

hard'-nosed' *adj* tough, practical, unsentimental

hard'-of-hear'ing *adj* partly deaf

hard' pal'ate *n* the bony anterior part of the palate

hard'pan' *n* layer of hard earth underlying softer soil

hard'-pressed' *adj* heavily burdened with work or problems

hard' rub'ber *n* rubber vulcanized with a large amount of sulfur to become stiff and inelastic

hard' sauce' *n* butter mixed with powdered sugar and cream or brandy

hard'scrab'ble *adj* barren, miserable, unproductive in spite of great effort

hard' sell' *n* high-pressure salesmanship

hard'-shell clam' *n* edible clam (*Venus mercenaria*) with a hard rounded shell

hard'-shell crab' *n* edible crab that has not recently molted

hard'ship *n* privation, suffering, oppression || SYN exposure, suffering, misfortune, adversity

hard'tack' *n* hard, unsalted biscuit, formerly used aboard ship

hard'top' *n* automobile with no center posts between the windows

hard'wall' *n* gypsum plaster used on interior surfaces

hard'ware' *n* 1 articles of metal, as cutlery, utensils, tools, nails, etc.; 2 mechanical components of an activity; 3 weapons; 4 electronic equipment and machinery used in the performance of data processing

hard′wood′ *n* hard compact wood from broad-leaved trees

har·dy /härd′ē/ [OF *hardi* hardened, emboldened < Gmc] *adj* (**-di·er; -di·est**) 1 robust, capable of bearing hardship; 2 bold; resolute; 3 hot-headed; foolhardy; 4 (plant) able to survive the winter ‖ **har′di·ly** *adv* ‖ **har′di·ness** *n*

hare /her′/ [OE *hara*] *n* (**hare or hares**) any of several swift herbivorous rodents (genus *Lepus*) having a divided upper lip, long ears, a fluffy tail, and hind legs adapted for jumping, many American species being called rabbits

hare′brained′ *adj* giddy, rash

hare′lip′ *n* upper lip cleft in the middle, like a hare's

ha·rem /her′əm, har′-/ [Ar *harīm* forbidden place] *n* 1 that part of a Muslim house reserved for the females; 2 females of a harem

ha·ri·ka·ri /har′ēkar′ē/ *n* var of **harakiri**

hark /härk′/ [ME *herkien*] *vi* 1 *impv* listen!; 2 **hark back** to revert to a previous subject

hark·en /härk′ən/ *vi* var of **hearken**

har·le·quin /här′lək(w)in/ [MF < It *arlecchino*] *n* 1 buffoon; 2 comic performer in a comedy or pantomime who wears multicolored spangled garments

har·lot /här′lət/ [OF *herlot* rascal] *n* prostitute ‖ **har′lot·ry** *n*

harm /härm′/ [OE *hearm*] *n* 1 injury, damage; 2 moral evil ‖ *vt* 3 to do harm to ‖ **harm′ful** *adj* ‖ **harm′ful·ly** *adv* ‖ **harm′less** *adj* ‖ **harm′less·ly** *adv* ‖ **harm′less·ness** *n* ‖ SYN *n* mischief, hurt, loss, offense (see *injury*)

har·mon·ic /härmon′ik/ [see **harmony**] *adj* 1 marked by harmony; 2 pert. to harmony, as distinct from rhythm or melody; 3 having a rate of vibration which is an exact multiple of one regarded as fundamental ‖ *n* 4 *phys* wave having a frequency which is an exact multiple of a fundamental frequency; 5 *mus* overtone

har·mon′i·ca *n* hand instrument with metal reeds played by blowing and sucking air through them

har·mon′ics *nsg* science dealing with musical sounds

har·mo·ni·ous /härmōn′ē·əs/ *adj* 1 concordant; musical; 2 agreeing in action and feeling; 3 combined into a pleasing arrangement or whole ‖ **har·mo′ni·ous·ly** *adv* ‖ SYN congruous, peaceable, sweet, musical

har·mo·nize /här′məniz′/ *vt* 1 to make harmonious; 2 *mus* to add harmony to ‖ *vi* 3 to be or sing in harmony ‖ SYN accord, adjust, agree

har·mo·ny /här′mənē/ [Gk *harmonia* melody] *n* (**-nies**) 1 pleasing arrangement of parts to one another; 2 agreement in action, feeling, sentiment, or the like; 3 *mus* agreeable combination of simultaneous tones; 4 science treating of the composition of chords ‖ SYN agreement, accordance, unison, conformity, consonance, melody, concord, tunefulness

har·ness /här′nis/ [OF *harneis* armor] *n* 1 working equipment of a horse or other draft animal, used to attach it to a wagon, plow, or the like; 2 **in harness** at one's usual routine ‖ *vt* 3 to put a harness on; 4 to fasten with a harness; 5 to yoke, fasten together; 6 to utilize, make productive, as a waterfall

har′ness race′ *n* race of pacers or trotters hitched to sulkies

harp /härp′/ [OE *hearpe*] *n* 1 instrument played by plucking strings stretched across a triangular frame; 2 that part of a piano consisting of the strings and soundbox ‖ *vi* 3 **harp on** to dwell on persistently ‖ **harp′ist** *n*

har·poon /härpōōn′/ [D *harpoen*] *n* 1 barbed spear with a line attached to it for spearing whales ‖ *vt* 2 to strike or catch with a harpoon

harp·si·chord /härp′sikôrd′/ [*obs* F *harpechorde* < It *arpicordo*] *n* keyboard instrument similar to and the forerunner of the piano, in which the strings are plucked by quills or leather plectrums instead of being struck by hammers

Har·py /härp′ē/ *n* (**-pies**) 1 *class. myth.* any of three filthy winged monsters with the face of a woman and the body of a vulture; 2 **harpy** grasping rapacious person

har·que·bus /här′kwibəs/ [MF *harquebuse*] *n* ancient gun fired by a matchlock or wheel lock, forerunner of the musket

har·ri·dan /har′ədən/ [perh < F *haridelle* old jade] *n* shrewish old woman; hag

Har·ris·burg /har′isburg′/ *n* capital of Pennsylvania (80,000)

Har·ri·son, Benjamin /har′isən/ *n* (1833–1901) 23rd president of the U.S. 1889–93

Har·ri·son, William Henry *n* (1773–1841) 9th president of the U.S. 1841; grandfather of Benjamin Harrison

har·row /har′ō/ [ME *harwe*] *n* 1 farming instrument with sharp spikes or disks for breaking up clods or covering sown seed with earth ‖ *vt* 2 to drive a harrow over; 3 to torment, vex, distress

har′row·ing *adj* agonizing; vexing; tormenting

har·rumph /hərumf′/ [imit] *vt* 1 to say with a pompous throat-clearing sound; 2 to say disapprovingly ‖ also *vi*

har·ry /har′ē/ [OE *hergian*] *v* (**-ried**) *vt* 1 to plunder, lay waste; 2 to annoy, harass

harsh /härsh′/ [ME *harsk* < Scand]

adj **1** discordant; offensive to feelings or judgment; **2** rough to the hearing, taste, touch, or sight; **3** severe, stern, cruel ‖ **harsh′ly** *adv* ‖ **harsh′ness** *n* ‖ SYN rigorous, severe, gruff, relentless, austere

hart /härt/ [OE *heor(o)t*] *n* stag

Hart′ford /härt′fərd/ *n* capital of Connecticut (165,000)

har·um-scar·um /her′əmsker′əm/ [?] *adj* wild, reckless ‖ also *adv* & *n*

har′vest /här′vist/ [OE *hærfest* autumn] *vt* **1** to gather in or reap; **2** to receive as a reward ‖ *vi* **3** to gather in a crop ‖ *n* **4** season of harvesting; **5** season's crop; **6** result of effort

har′vest·er *n* reaping machine

har′vest moon′ *n* full moon at the time of the autumnal equinox

has /haz/ *3rd pers sg pres ind of* **have**

has′-been′ *n* person or thing whose popularity, usefulness, or effectiveness is past

hash /hash/ [F *hacher* to chop up] *vt* **1** to chop or mince, as meat; **2** to jumble, botch; **3 hash over** to review, go over ‖ *n* **4** dish of meat or vegetables chopped small; **5** jumble, muddle; **6 make a hash of** *colloq* to make a mess of; **7 settle one's hash** *colloq* to get the better of, subdue

hash′ house′ *n slang* cheap restaurant with unceremonious service

hash·ish /hash′ēsh, -ish/ [Ar = dry herb] *n* Oriental narcotic drug prepared from Indian hemp (*Cannabis indica*) and chewed or smoked for its intoxicating effect

hash′ mark′ *n mil* service stripe

has·n't /haz′ənt/ has not

hasp /hasp/, häsp/ [OE *hæpse* clasp] *n* clasp passing over a staple and secured with a pin or padlock

has·sle /has′əl/ [?] *n colloq* squabble ‖ also *vi*

has·sock /has′ək/ [OE *hassuc* coarse grass] *n* cushioned footstool

hast /hast/ *archaic & poet. 2nd pers sg pres ind of* **have**

haste /hāst/ [OF < Gmc] *n* **1** quickness of movement; speed; **2** unnecessary hurry; **3** urgency; **4 make haste** to hurry ‖ SYN nimbleness, dispatch, alacrity, hurry, expedition, bustle, flurry, rapidity, precipitancy

has·ten /hās′ən/ *vt* **1** to urge on; hurry; **2** to speed, accelerate ‖ *vi* **3** to move or act with speed; be quick ‖ SYN accelerate, quicken, expedite, speed

hast·y /hās′tē/ *adj* (**-i·er; -i·est**) **1** precipitate, rash; **2** hurried, quick; **3** cursory, superficial ‖ **hast′i·ly** *adv* ‖ **hast′i·ness** *n* ‖ SYN quick, speedy, swift, fleet, impetuous, eager, hurried, lively ‖ DISCR *Hasty* emphasizes the hurried quality of a motion or act, and has thus gathered the bad meaning of ill-considered. *Speedy* emphasizes rapidity, as a *speedy* gait.

Quick describes that which is prompt to respond, alert, lively in motion, sensitively intelligent; she was *quick* on her feet; *quick* at repartee

hat /hat/ [OE *hætt*] *n* **1** covering for the head, usu. with a crown and brim; **2 pass the hat** *colloq* to take up a collection; **3 talk through one's hat** *colloq* to utter nonsense; **4 under one's hat** confidential

hat′band′ *n* **1** ribbon around the crown of a hat just above the brim; **2** black hatband worn as a sign of mourning

hatch¹ /hach/ [OE *hæc* gate, rail] *n* **1** hatchway; **2** cover for a hatchway; **3** lower half of a divided door or gate

hatch² [ME *hacchen*] *vt* **1** to produce young from (eggs); **2** to produce (young) from eggs; **3** to plot or contrive ‖ *vi* **4** to yield young, as eggs; **5** to emerge from the egg

hatch³ [MF *hacher* to cut up] *n* **1** one of the system of fine crossed or parallel lines used in drawings or engraving, as for shading ‖ *vt* **2** to mark with hatches

hatch′er·y *n* (**-ies**) place where eggs, esp. of fish, are artificially incubated

hatch·et /hach′it/ [MF *hachette*] *n* **1** light short-handled axe used with one hand; **2 bury the hatchet** to make peace

hatch′ing *n drawing & engraving* shading with hatches

hatch′way′ *n* opening for a passage through the deck of a vessel, floor, roof, or the like

hate /hāt/ [OE *hatian*] *vt* **1** to abhor, abominate, detest; **2** to dislike ‖ *vi* **3** to feel hatred ‖ *n* **4** hatred; **5** object of hate or dislike ‖ **hat′er** *n*

hate′ful *adj* **1** exercising or exhibiting hatred; **2** deserving hatred; **3** distasteful ‖ **hate′ful·ly** *adv* ‖ **hate′ful·ness** *n* ‖ SYN odious, detestable, loathsome, abhorrent, offensive, obnoxious, repulsive ‖ DISCR That is *hateful* which awakens intense dislike or aversion; that is *odious* which not only excites aversion, but is disagreeable or repugnant besides, as *hateful* faults, vices, talebearing; *odious* remarks, legislation, behavior. That is *detestable* which awakens indignation or revulsion spiced with contempt, as *detestable* standards, cant, dissimulation. That is *loathsome* which is regarded with disgust, physical or moral, as a *loathsome* reptile, habit. *Abhorrent* describes that so repugnant as to cause a mental shrinking or recoil, as from fear, horror, or disgust. Unsightly or disgusting things are *offensive* to the senses; officious or ill-mannered people are *offensive* to others. *Obnoxious* adds to *offensive* the sense of extremely objectionable, and, as here

compared, is applied only to people
|| ANT pleasing, lovable

hate'mon'ger /-muŋ'gər/ n one who
arouses hate and prejudice in others

hath /hath'/ archaic & poet. 3d pers
sg pres ind of **have**

hat'pin' n long pin for fastening a
woman's hat to her hair

hat'rack' n frame or rack for holding
hats

ha-tred /hāt'rid/ n bitter aversion; ac-
tive hostility || SYN detestation, ani-
mosity, enmity (see antipathy)

hat-ter /hat'ər/ n maker or seller of
hats

haugh-ty /hôt'ē/ [< MF haut high] adj
(-ti·er; -ti·est) 1 proud; disdainful;
2 overbearing; contemptuous ||
haugh'ti·ly adv || **haugh'ti·ness** n ||
SYN supercilious, insolent, reserved
(see arrogant)

haul /hôl/ [var of hale²] vt 1 to pull,
drag; 2 to transport, as by truck or
train; 3 to bring, as before a judge;
4 **haul down** to lower, as a flag || vi
5 to change the course of a ship; 6
to tug, pull; 7 to transport goods;
8 **haul off** colloq to prepare to strike
by drawing the arm back || n 9 strong
pull; 10 catch; 11 distance over
which anything is hauled; 12 that
which is hauled || **haul'er** n

haunch /hônch'/, hänch'/ [OF hanche]
n 1 hip and buttock; 2 leg and loin
of an animal; hind quarter

haunt /hônt, hänt'/ [OF hanter] vt 1
to visit frequently or habitually; 2
to trouble by frequent appearances
or recurrences || n 3 place of fre-
quent or habitual refuge

haunt'ed adj 1 frequented by ghosts;
2 obsessed; distressed

haunt'ing adj sticking in the mind, not
easily forgotten

hau-teur /hōtūr'/ [F] n disdainful
pride, haughtiness

Ha-van-a /həvan'ə/ n 1 capital of
Cuba (1,000,000); 2 cigar made in
Cuba or of Cuban tobacco

have /hav'/ [OE habban] v (3rd pers
sg pres **has**; pt & pp **had**) vt 1 to
hold, possess; 2 to contain; include;
3 to get, take, as he had fish for dinner; 4 to affirm, declare, as rumor
has it that, etc.; 5 to engage in,
experience, as to have a good time; 6
to beget; 7 to hold as or where desired, as I have you where I want to;
8 to cause to be (done or the like),
as he had his shoes repaired; 9 to
engage in, as we had a fight; 10 to
permit, as he would not have it; 11 to
invite, as they had Jim for dinner;
12 **had better** ought to; 13 **had rather**
prefer; 14 **have got** to possess; 15
have got to to be obliged to; 16 **have
it coming** colloq to deserve something
unpleasant; 17 **have it in for** colloq
to bear a grudge against; 18 **have
it out** to settle a disagreement; 19

have on, a to wear; **b** to have
planned; 20 **have to** to be obliged
to; 21 **have to do with, a** to have
dealings with; **b** to be relevant to ||
v aux 22 used with the past parti-
ciple to form the perfect tenses || n
23 **haves** pl people possessing the
good things of life

have'lock' [Henry Havelock (1795–
1857) Eng general in India] n white
cloth cover for a military cap, with
a flap hanging down over the neck
as a protection against the sun and
the rain

ha-ven /hāv'ən/ [OE hæfen] n 1 harbor; 2 any place of shelter or refuge

have'-nots' npl people not possessing
the good things of life

have-n't /hav'ənt/ have not

hav-er-sack /hav'ərsak'/ [F havresac
< G Habersack oat bag] n canvas
bag for carrying rations and supplies, worn over the shoulder

hav-oc /hav'ək/ [OF havok] n 1 wide
and general devastation; 2 **cry havoc**
to warn of disaster

haw¹ /hô/ [imit] vi hem and haw to
hesitate in speaking; be evasive

haw² [?] vt & vi to turn toward the
left, said of draft animals || also
interj

Ha-wai-i /həwī'ē, -wä'yə/ n 1 state of
the U.S. consisting of the Hawaiian
Islands (769,913; 6,424 sq.m.; cap.
Honolulu); 2 largest of the Hawaiian
Islands || **Ha-wai'ian** adj & n

Ha-wai'ian Is'lands npl group of islands in the N Pacific 2000 miles SW
of California, making up the State
of Hawaii

hawk¹ /hôk'/ [OE hafoc] n 1 any of
several strong swift-flying birds of
prey (family Accipitridae) related to
the eagles; 2 any of several falcons
(family Falconidae); 3 colloq person
who takes a warlike stance

hawk² [< MLG haker retailer] vt to
peddle; cry out (wares) for sale in
the streets || **hawk'er** n

hawk³ [prob imit] vi 1 to force phlegm
from the throat by coughing; clear
the throat audibly || vt 2 to bring up
(phlegm) by hawking || n 3 noisy at-
tempt to clear the throat

hawk'-eyed' adj sharp-sighted

hawk'ish adj colloq favoring an unyielding position in international
matters; warlike

hawk'nosed' adj having a nose curved
like the beak of a hawk

hawks'bill tur'tle n sea turtle (Eret-
mochelys imbricata) from which tortoise shell is obtained

hawse'hole' n hole in the bow or stern
of a vessel through which a hawser
passes

haw-ser /hôz'ər/ [MF haucier to hoist]
n thick rope or cable used in towing
or mooring a vessel

haw-thorn /hô'thôrn'/ [OE haguthorn]

n any of a genus (*Crataegus*) of small thorny trees bearing fragrant flowers and small red berries

Haw·thorne, Na·than·iel /nəthan'yəl hô'thôrn'/ *n* (1804–64) U.S. novelist and short-story writer

hay /hā'/ [OE *hīeg*] *n* **1** grass, clover, etc., cut and dried for fodder; **2 hit the hay** *slang* to go to bed; **3 make hay while the sun shines** to take advantage of a situation while it lasts ‖ *vi* **4** to make hay

Hay·dn, Franz Jo·seph /fränts' yō'zəf hīd'ən/ *n* (1732–1809) Austrian composer

Hayes, Ruth·er·ford B. /ruth'ərfərd hāz'/ *n* (1822–93) 19th president of the U.S. 1877–81

hay' fe'ver *n* acute inflammation of the respiratory tract and eyes caused by an allergy to the pollen of certain plants

hay'loft' *n* loft in a barn or stable for the storage of hay

hay'mak'er *n colloq* wild punch delivered with great force

hay'ride' *n* pleasure outing in a wagon partly filled with hay

hay'seed' *n colloq* rustic, yokel

hay'stack' *n* stack or pile of hay in the open air

hay'wire' *adj colloq* **1** crazy; **2** out of order

haz·ard /haz'ərd/ [OF *hasard* game of dice] *n* **1** old game of chance from which craps is derived; **2** chance; **3** risk, danger; **4** *golf* bunker or other obstacle ‖ *vt* **5** to risk, chance, venture ‖ **haz'ard·ous** *adj* ‖ SYN *n* accident, casualty, peril (see *danger*)

haze[1] /hāz'/ [?] *n* **1** slight fog or mist; **2** vagueness of mind ‖ **ha'zy** *adj* (-zi·er; -zi·est)

haze[2] [MF *haser* to worry] *vt* to abuse and humiliate (freshmen and newcomers)

ha·zel /hāz'əl/ [OE *hæsel*] *n* **1** any shrub or tree of a genus (*Corylus*) of the birch family bearing a small rounded edible nut in a coarse husk; **2** hazelnut; **3** light reddish-brown color ‖ also *adj*

ha'zel·nut' *n* fruit of the hazel tree, filbert

H'-bomb' *n* hydrogen bomb

he /hē'/ [OE] *pron* (*3rd pers sg masc nom*) **1** previously designated male; **2** anyone, as *he who runs may read* ‖ *n* **3** man or male

He *chem* helium

HE, H.E. high explosive

he- *comb form* male, as *he-goat*

head /hed'/ [OE *hēafod*] *n* **1** the part of the body attached to the neck, comprising the face, brain, ears, nose, etc.; **2** top part of a plant, esp. when compact, as *a head of cabbage*; **3** intelligence, wits; **4** front or foremost part of anything; **5** leader or ruler; **6** position of authority or leadership; **7** upper end of anything;

8 separate topic or title; **9** origin or source, as of a river; **10** pressure, as of steam; **11** pressure as measured by the distance in feet between the surface of a liquid and any specified point; **12** froth on liquor; **13** promontory; **14** side of a coin showing a head; **15** striking part, as of a hammer; **16** membrane of a drum; **17** (*pl* head) unit of counting, as *ten head of cattle;* **18 come to a head** to reach a crisis; **19 give one his head** to allow one to do as he likes; **20 go to one's head, a** to intoxicate one; **b** to make one vain; **21 head over heels, a** headlong; **b** completely; **22 heads or tails** tossing of a coin to see if one can guess which side will come up; **23 keep one's head** to keep control of oneself; **24 lose one's head** to lose control of oneself; **25 not make head or tail of** to be unable to figure out; **26 out of one's head** crazy; **27 over one's head** beyond one's ability, understanding, or resources; **28 take it into one's head** to get a notion to; **29 turn one's head** to make one conceited ‖ *vt* **30** to lead, direct; **31** to take the first place in; **32** to direct the course of; **33** to supply with a head; **34** to deprive of a head; **35 head off** to intercept, get in front of ‖ *vi* **36** to move in a given direction ‖ *adj* **37** of or pert. to the head; **38** chief, principal; **39** located at the head or top; **40** coming from ahead

head'ache' *n* **1** pain in the head; **2** annoyance, cause for worry

head'band' *n* **1** band worn around the head; **2** band that connects two earphones

head'cheese' *n* chopped up portions of the head and feet of a pig or calf, seasoned and pressed into a loaf

head' cold' *n* common cold located in and near the nasal passages

head'dress' *n* **1** covering or ornament for the head; **2** manner of wearing the hair

-head'ed *adj comb form* having a head or heads of a specified kind or number, as *flat-headed, two-headed*

head'er *n* **1** plunge or fall headfirst

head'first' *adv* **1** with the head first; headlong; **2** in rash haste

head'gear' *n* anything worn upon the head

head'ing *n* **1** that which serves as a head or top; **2** title; stated topic at the head of a paragraph or section

head'land /-lənd/ *n* promontory, cape

head'light' *n* bright lamp at the head of a vehicle

head'line' *n* **1** heading in large type at the top of a newspaper column or at the beginning of an article ‖ *vt* **2** to supply with a headline; **3** to give top billing to

head'lin'er *show bus. n* performer

whose name appears in the largest letters; chief attraction

head/long [ME *headling*] *adv* 1 headfirst; 2 rashly || *adj* 3 rash; 4 plunging headfirst

head/ man/ *n slang* the one in charge

head/mas/ter *n* principal of a private boys' school

head/mis/tress *n* woman principal of a private school, esp. one for girls

head/ of gov/ern-ment *n* prime minister; president of the council of ministers

head/ of state/ *n* chief of state; titular head of a government

head/-on/ *adj & adv* with the front or head foremost

head/phones/ *npl* pair of telephone receivers held against the ears by a band across the head

head/quar/ters *nsg* or *npl* 1 office or residence of a commanding officer; 2 main office; center of operations

head/rest/ *n* support for the head, often adjustable, as on the back of a barber's or dentist's chair

head/set/ *n* headphones with or without a mouthpiece attached

head/ shrink/er *n slang* psychiatrist

head/stall/ *n* part of a bridle that fits over a horse's head

head/ start/ *n* advantage in a race or contest

head/stay/ *n* stay running from the head of the foremost mast to the end of the bowsprit

head/stock/ *n* 1 bearing for the revolving part of a machine; 2 part of a lathe that supports the chuck that turns the work

head/stone/ *n* stone marker at the head of a grave

head/strong/ *adj* stubborn, willful || SYN obstinate, stubborn, willful, wayward, perverse, intractable, determined || DISCR *Obstinate* describes one who holds to his own opinion or course in spite of reason, appeal, persuasion, or attack. *Obstinacy* lies in the will. A *stubborn* man, like the *obstinate* one, refuses to change, but *stubbornness* is more apt to be innate and hence habitual than *obstinacy*, and applies to an unyielding quality, inherent in facts as well as in persons. *Headstrong* describes a violently impetuous person. *Willful* people are more deliberate than the *headstrong*, and more *stubborn* than the *wayward*, who yield to caprice or whim. The *perverse* person is always different from what he should be, as in action, purpose, or desire

heads/-up/ *adj* alert, alive to opportunities as they present themselves

head/wait/er *n* man in charge of other waiters in a dining room or restaurant

head/wa/ters *npl* upper tributaries of a river

head/way/ *n* 1 forward motion; 2 progress; 3 time intervening between two trains, buses, etc., running in the same direction over the same route; 4 overhead clearance

head/wind/ *n* wind blowing opposite to the direction of a ship or plane

head/work/ *n* mental work; thinking

head/y *adj* (-i-er; -i-est) 1 precipitate, rash; 2 intoxicating || **head/i-ly** *adv* || **head/i-ness** *n*

heal /hēl/ [OE *hǣlan*] *vt* 1 to restore to health, cure; 2 to settle, as differences || *vi* 3 to become well or sound || **heal/er** *n*

health /helth/ [OE *hǣlth*] *n* 1 soundness of physical, mental, or moral condition; 2 freedom from disease; 3 toast to health and happiness

health/ food/ *n* food grown and processed for the preservation, improvement, and restoration of health, containing vitamins and other substances considered essential for normal bodily well-being

health/ful *adj* 1 promoting good health; 2 healthy || SYN hygienic, sanitary, wholesome (see *healthy*)

health/y *adj* (-i-er; -i-est) 1 possessing or pert. to good health; 2 healthful || SYN healthful, wholesome, vigorous, hale, hearty, salutary, sanitary, salubrious, nutritious, bracing || DISCR *Healthy* is most properly applied to that which has good health or is in a vigorous, thriving condition, as a *healthy* man or tree. *Healthy* also means conducive to health, and is applied to fresh air, exercise, climate, or other agents contributing to health, except food, to which *wholesome* is applied, as a *healthy* method of life; a *wholesome* diet. *Healthy* and *healthful* are to a degree interchangeable; but *healthful* is more commonly used of conditions that are health-giving, as air, climate, exercise. We do not say *healthy* food, but *healthful* food; we say a *healthy*, not a *healthful*, man. *Salubrious*, which carries a definite sense of improving the health, is applied chiefly to climate or air, rarely to food or exercise. *Salutary* measures produce good effects; *salutary* conditions are positively beneficial; unlike *salubrious*, *salutary* is now used chiefly in the moral sense

heap /hēp/ [OE = crowd] *n* 1 pile of things thrown together; 2 *colloq* large quantity || *vt* 3 to form into a heap, pile up; 4 to bestow generously; 5 to fill to overflowing

hear /hir/ [OE *hīeran*] *v* (**heard** /hurd/) *vt* 1 to perceive by ear; 2 to listen to; 3 to receive information of by hearing; 4 to obey; 5 *law* to conduct an examination of (a case) || *vi* 6 to have the sense of hearing; 7 **hear from** to get news of; 8 **not hear of** to refuse to allow || *interj* 9 *Brit* well said! || **hear/er** *n* || SYN *v* apprehend, learn, perceive, grant (see *listen*)

hear'ing *n* **1** act or process of perceiving sounds; **2** sense by which sound is perceived; **3** opportunity of being heard; **4** earshot; **5** formal examination conducted by an official, as a judge or commissioner

hear'ing aid' *n* small amplifier fitted to the ear to aid one's hearing

heark·en /härk'ən/ [OE *hercnian*] *vi* to listen, heed

hear'say' *n* unverified reports; rumor, gossip

hearse /hurs'/ [MF *herce* candle frame] *n* **1** vehicle for conveying dead bodies to church or to a cemetery; **2** frame over a coffin or tomb; **3** *R C Ch* triangular frame for holding candles at services on the last three days of Holy Week

heart /härt'/ [OE *heorte*] *n* **1** hollow muscular organ which maintains the circulation of the blood by rhythmic contractions and dilations; **2** seat of the affections, passions, and emotions; **3** tenderness, sympathy, affection; **4** courage, spirit, energy; **5** beloved; **6** one's personality as a vital or active force, as *with all my heart;* **7** vital part, center, core; **8** conventional design representing a heart; **9** playing card stamped with a heart; **10 hearts,** a *sg* or *pl* suit of cards so marked; **b** *sg* card game in which the object is to avoid taking heart tricks; **11 after one's own heart** that suits or pleases one perfectly; **12 at heart** basically; **13 by heart** memorized word for word; **14 have a change of heart** to change one's mind; **15 heart and soul** fervently; **16 set one's heart against** to be firmly opposed to; **17 set one's heart on** to desire strongly; **18 take to heart, a** to consider seriously; **b** to be deeply affected by; to sorrow over

heart'ache' *n* sorrow, grief; distress

heart' at·tack' *n* sudden malfunctioning of the heart

heart'beat' *n* complete cycle of contraction and dilation of the heart

heart'break' *n* overpowering grief ‖ **heart'break'ing** *adj*

heart'bro·ken *adj* overwhelmed by sorrow

heart'burn' *n* **1** burning sensation in the stomach and esophagus; **2** jealousy; envy

heart'en *vt* to encourage, cheer

heart' fail'ure *n* **1** failure of the heart to pump sufficient blood; **2** complete cessation of the heartbeat; death; **3** feeling of faintness

heart'felt' *adj* deeply felt; sincere

hearth /härth'/ [OE *heorth*] *n* **1** paved floor of a fireplace; **2** fireside; **3** home; **4** floor of a forge or furnace; **5** lowest part of a blast furnace

heart'land' *n* center area of a country which is the core of its economic, political, and military strength

heart'less *adj* unfeeling; harsh; cruel

heart' mur'mur *n* sound heard through a stethoscope revealing usu. a malfunction of the heart valves

heart'rend'ing *adj* causing extreme anguish or grief

heart'sick' *adj* distressed in mind; despondent

heart'strings' *npl* profoundest emotions or affections

heart'-to-heart' *adj* frank and intimate

heart'warm'ing *adj* moving; rewarding

heart'wood' *n* hard inner wood of a tree trunk

heart'y *adj* (**-i·er; -i·est**) **1** cordial; sincere; warm; **2** strong, vigorous; **3** abundant; nourishing; **4** keen in appetite ‖ *n* (**-ies**) **5** *naut* good fellow, pal ‖ **heart'i·ly** *adv* ‖ **heart'i·ness** *n* ‖ SYN sincere, cordial, earnest, ardent ‖ DISCR A *sincere* person is free from pretense; a *sincere* statement, feeling, or the like, is honest. *Hearty* adds to *sincere* a genial vigor of feeling, usually simple, even blunt in expression, appealing through its unvarnished genuineness, as a *hearty* welcome. *Cordial* adds to *sincere* a warmth of feeling, as *cordial* greetings

heat /hēt'/ [OE *hætu*] *n* **1** state of being hot; **2** degree to which a thing is heated; **3** sensation produced by a hot body; **4** highness of temperature; **5** hot weather; **6** artificial warming of interiors; **7** passion, ardor, vehemence; **8** maximum intensity, as *in the heat of passion;* **9** *phys* form of energy which raises temperature and which is transmitted by conduction, convection, and radiation; **10** *sports* **a** single course at a race or contest; **b** one of several preliminary elimination races; **11** period of sexual excitement in female animals; **12 the heat's on** *slang* laws and regulations are being enforced with especial zeal, making it difficult to get away with anything ‖ *vt* **13** to make hot; **14** to excite with passion or desire; make feverish; animate ‖ *vi* **15** to grow hot or warm; **16** to become feverish or excited

heat'ed·ly /-idlē/ *adv* with excited anger

heat'er *n* apparatus for heating water or rooms

heath /hēth'/ [OE *hæth*] *n* **1** *British Isles* tract of uncultivated land covered with heather or other coarse vegetation; **2** shrubby plant of a large family (Ericaceae), including the common heather

hea·then /hēth'ən/ [OE *hæthen* heath dweller, because people living remote from cities were the most resistant in adopting Christianity] *n*

(-then or -thens) **1** one who is not Christian, Jewish, or Mohammedan; pagan; **2** irreligious, uncultured person ‖ also *adj* ‖ **hea′then·ish** *adj*

heath·er /heth′ər/ [ME *hather*] *n* evergreen shrub (*Calluna vulgaris*) of the heath family, blooming profusely in late summer with white, pink, or carmine flowers

heat′ light′ning *n* distant lightning, without thunder, near the horizon

heat′ pros·tra′tion *n* physical collapse caused by prolonged exposure to high temperatures

heat′ pump′ *n* pump which, by compressing a refrigerant, transfers heat from or to a house or other building to or from the atmosphere, the earth, a body of water, etc. for the purpose of cooling or heating the house or building

heat′ shield′ *n* coating on the nose cone of a spacecraft, designed to absorb heat during reentry

heat′ wave′ *n* period of very hot weather

heave /hēv′/ [OE *hebban*] *v* (**heaved** or *naut* **hove**) *vt* **1** to lift up with effort; **2** to lift and throw; **3** to force from the breast, as a sigh; **4** to cause to rise or swell; **5** *naut* to draw or haul into a certain position, as an anchor ‖ *vi* **6** to be lifted up; **7** to swell; **8** to rise and fall alternately; **9** to strain; pant; **10** to vomit **11** *naut* to haul, pull, or push; **12** **heave into sight** *naut* to seemingly rise above the horizon and to come into view; **13** **heave to, a** *naut* to head into the wind and shorten sail and thus come to a stop; **b** to come to a stop ‖ *n* **14** act or effort of heaving; **15** rise, swell

heav·en /hev′ən/ [OE *heofon*] *n* **1** abode of God and of the blessed after death; **2** state or condition of bliss; **3** any place of supreme happiness or comfort; **4** **Heaven** the Deity; **5** **the heavens** *pl* the firmament or sky ‖ **heav′en·ward** *adj & adv* ‖ **heav′en·wards** *adv*

heav′en·ly *adj* **1** of or pert. to the abode of God; **2** beautiful, enchanting, like heaven; **3** of or pert. to the heavens, as *the heavenly bodies* ‖ **heav′en·li·ness** *n* ‖ SYN divine, sacred, blessed (see *celestial*)

heaves /hēvz′/ *nsg* asthmatic disease of horses

heav·y /hev′ē/ [OE *hefig*] *adj* (**-i·er**; **-i·est**) **1** of great weight; **2** of more than the usual weight; **3** large in size, quantity, extent, or effect, as *a heavy snowfall;* **4** on a large scale, as *a heavy buyer, heavy drinker;* **5** oppressive, burdensome; **6** grave, serious; **7** dejected, depressed; **8** powerful, deep, as a sound; **9** indigestible; **10** thick, coarse; **11** rough (going); **12** profound; **13** difficult to

do or cope with; **14** fraught, loaded; **15** dull, ponderous; **16** overcast (sky); **17** clumsy; **18** **heavy with child** in a state of advanced pregnancy ‖ *n* (**-ies**) **19** *theat* villain ‖ SYN ponderous, massive (see *onerous*)

heav′y·du′ty *adj* designed for heavy or excessive work, strain, or exposure

heav′y·hand′ed *adj* **1** clumsy; **2** oppressive

heav′y·heart′ed *adj* dejected, sorrowful

heav′y hy′dro·gen *n* deuterium

heav′y·set′ *adj* stocky, stout

heav′y wa′ter *n* water whose molecules contain heavy hydrogen

heav′y·weight′ *n* **1** very heavy person; **2** boxer or wrestler weighing over 175 pounds ‖ also *adj*

Heb., Hebr. Hebrew(s)

He·be /hē′bē/ *n Gk myth.* goddess of youth, daughter of Zeus and Hera, and cupbearer of the gods before Ganymede

He·bra·ic /hibrā′ik/ [Gk *Hebraikos*] *adj* pert. to the Hebrews or to their language

He·brew /hē′brōō/ [OF *Ebreu* < LGk *Hebraios*] *n* **1** member of one of the Semitic peoples inhabiting ancient Palestine; **2** language of the Hebrews; **3** **Hebrews** *sg* book of the New Testament ‖ also *adj*

Heb·ri·des /heb′ridēz′/ *npl* group of islands off the W coast of and belonging to Scotland

heck /hek′/ *interj euphem* hell!

heck·le /hek′əl/ [ME *hekelen*] *vt* to harass, annoy, badger (a public speaker) ‖ **heck′ler** *n*

hec·tare /hek′ter/ [F] *n* metric measure of 100 ares (10,000 sq. meters), or 2.471 acres

hec·tic /hek′tik/ [Gk *hektikos* habitual] *adj* characterized by feverish excitement or frenzied agitation

hec·to·graph /hek′təgraf, -gräf/ [< Gk *hekaton* hundred *-graph*] *n* apparatus for making copies from a gelatine surface

Hec′tor /hek′tər/ *n* **1** in Homer's *Iliad,* greatest Trojan hero, killed by Achilles ‖ *vt* **2** **hector** to bully, domineer; intimidate by threats

he′d /hēd′/ **1** he had; **2** he would

hedge /hej′/ [OE *hecg*] *n* **1** fence of bushes or shrubs; **2** any barrier or fence; **3** offsetting action to prevent total loss, as in a wager, argument, or investment ‖ *vt* **4** to enclose with a hedge; **5** to hinder, restrict, hem in; **6** to protect (one's stake or position) against total loss by making counterbalancing moves, as in wagering, arguing, or investing ‖ also *vi*

hedge′hog′ *n* **1** any of a genus (*Erinaceus*) of Old World mammals having spines on the back and sides; **2** porcupine; **3** *mil* one of a series of strongly fortified points

hedge′hop′ *v* (**-hopped; -hop·ping**) *vi* to fly close to the ground in an airplane

hedge′row′ *n* fence of small trees or shrubs

he·don·ism /hēd′əniz′əm/ [< Gk *hedone* pleasure] *n* 1 doctrine that pleasure and the gratification of desire constitute the chief good; 2 self-indulgence; living for pleasure || **he′don·ist** *n* || **he′do·nis′tic** *adj*

-he·dron /-hēd′rən/ [Gk *-edron* -sided] *n comb form* (**-drons** or **-dra** /-drə/) crystal or figure with a specified number of surfaces

heed /hēd′/ [OE *hēdan*] *vt & vi* 1 to notice carefully || *n* 2 careful attention; caution || **heed′ful** *adj* || **SYN** consideration, watchfulness (see *care*)

heed′less *adj* paying little or no heed or attention; careless || **SYN** inconsiderate, careless, unobserving, inattentive

hee·haw /hē′hô′/ [imit] *n* 1 bray; 2 coarse laughter || also *vi*

heel¹ /hēl′/ [OE *hieldan*] *vt* 1 to cause (a ship) to list || *vi* 2 to list

heel² [OE *hēla*] *n* 1 back part of the foot; 2 the part of a boot, shoe, or stocking at the heel; 3 anything shaped or positioned like a heel; 4 *colloq* contemptible person; 5 at one's heels close behind one; 6 down at the heel shabby; 7 take to one's heels to flee || *vt* 8 to furnish with a heel; 9 to strike (a golf ball) with the heel of the club; 10 to follow closely || *vi* 11 to follow at the heels, as a dog

heeled′ *adj* provided with funds

heft /heft′/ [< *heave*] *n* 1 heaviness, weight || *vt* 2 to try the weight of, as by lifting; 3 to lift

heft′y *adj* (**-i·er; -i·est**) 1 heavy; 2 strong, powerful

he·gem·o·ny /hijem′ənē, hej′imōn′ē, hēj′-/ [< Gk *hegemon* leader] *n* leadership, predominance, esp. of one state over another

He·gi·ra /hijir′ə, hej′ərə/ [Ar *hijrah* departure] *n* 1 flight of Mohammed from Mecca to Medina in 622, regarded as the beginning of the Muslim era; 2 **hegira** flight to a more hospitable place

Hei·del·berg /hīd′əlburg′/ *n* city in SW West Germany, seat of a famous university (130,000)

heif·er /hef′ər/ [OE *heahfore*] *n* young cow that has not yet calved

height /hīt′/ [OE *hiehtho*] *n* 1 extent from the base to the top; 2 altitude; 3 stature; 4 distance of an object above a fixed point; elevation; 5 eminence or hill; 6 highest point, summit; 7 highest degree; extreme; 8 **heights** *pl* hill, high place

height′en *vt* 1 to raise, make higher; 2 to intensify, enhance; increase || **SYN** intensify, inflate, augment, increase, aggravate

hei·nous /hān′əs/ [MF *haineus* < *haine* hatred] *adj* hateful, odious, atrocious || **SYN** odious, nefarious, villainous, flagrant, atrocious, outrageous, monstrous || **DISCR** *Heinous*, said of a crime or a criminal, connotes extreme wickedness; *heinous* sins or crimes are repulsively grievous. *Flagrant*, said of an offense or offender, means, literally, burning, and this meaning has been carried over into a figurative sense of glaring, or openly scandalous, as a *flagrant* breach of moral law. *Atrocious* means blackly, violently wicked or brutal. *Outrageous* carries the sense of exceeding the bounds of right, decency, or morality, as *outrageous* conduct; an *outrageous* affront

heir /er′/ [OF < L *heres*] *n* 1 one who inherits or is entitled to inherit the property or title of another; 2 anyone who receives a part of the property of a deceased person; 3 one who inherits qualities, reputation, or virtues from another

heir′ ap·par′ent *n* (**heirs apparent**) heir whose right of inheritance cannot be set aside

heir′ess *n* female heir, esp. one who has inherited or will inherit great wealth

heir′loom′ *n* any family possession handed down from generation to generation

heir′ pre·sump′tive *n* (**heirs presumptive**) one who will succeed as heir if his right is not voided by the birth of one nearer in succession

heist /hīst′/ [var of *hoist*] *slang vt* 1 to rob, esp. by burglary || *n* 2 robbery

held /held′/ *pt & pp* of **hold**

Hel·en (of Troy′) /hel′ən/ *n Gk myth.* beautiful daughter of Zeus and Leda, who was married to Menelaus, king of Sparta, and whose elopement with Paris caused the Trojan war

Hel·e·na /hel′ənə/ *n* capital of Montana (21,000)

hel·i·cal /hel′ikəl/ [see *helix*] *adj* pert. to or in the form of a helix

hel·i·cop·ter /hel′ikop′tər/ [< *helix* + Gk *pteron* wing] *n* aircraft propelled and sustained by horizontal propellers

he·li·o- [< Gk *helios*] *comb form* sun

he·li·o·cen·tric /hēl′ē·ōsent′rik/ [< *helio-* + Gk *kentron* center] *adj* pert. to or having the sun as a center || **he′li·o·cen′tri·cal·ly** *adv*

he·li·o·graph /hēl′ē·əgraf′, -gräf′/ [*helio-* + *-graph*] *n* apparatus for signaling by reflecting flashes of sunlight

he′li·o·trope′ /-ətrōp′/ [*helio-* + Gk *tropos* turn] *n* 1 any of a genus (*Helio-*

tropium) of plants of the borage family, esp. the sweet-scented cultivated species (*H. arborescens*) bearing purple flowers; 2 light-purple color

hel'i·port' /hel'i-/ [*helicopter* + *port*] *n* landing place for helicopters

he·li·um /hēl'ē·əm/ [< Gk *helios* sun] *n* very light, inert, colorless gaseous element (**He**; at.no. 2; at.wt. 4.0026) first discovered in the sun's atmosphere, occurring also in minerals and natural gas

he·lix /hē'liks/ [Gk = spiral] *n* (**-lix·es** or **hel·i·ces** /hel'isēz'/) anything in the shape of the thread of a screw or of a spiral

hell /hel'/ [OE *hel*] *n* 1 place of punishment for the wicked after death; 2 the evil spirits inhabiting hell; 3 any place or condition of extreme torment or misery; 4, **a hell of a** *slang* a very bad; b very great, extreme; c terribly, very; 5 **catch** or **get hell** *slang* to be severely reprimanded or punished; 6 **play hell with** *slang* to bring harm to; disrupt; 7 **raise hell** *slang* a to indulge in riotous action; b to object vehemently || *interj* 8 *slang* oath expressing irritation or anger

he'll /hēl'/ 1 he will; 2 he shall

hell'bent' *adj* recklessly determined to have one's way

hell'cat' *n* 1 shrewish and evil woman; 2 witch, sorceress

Hel·lene /hel'ēn/ [Gk *Hellen*] *n* Greek || **Hel·len·ic** /-len'ik/ *adj*

Hel·len·ism /hel'iniz'əm/ *n* 1 Greek culture and ideals; 2 admiration or imitation of the Greeks

Hel'len·is'tic *adj* of or pert. to the ancient Greeks, their language, culture, or architecture, after the time of Alexander the Great

Hel'len·ize' *vt* to make Greek in language and culture || also *vi*

hel·lion /hel'yən/ [< *hell*] *n colloq* troublemaker, rowdy

hell'ish *adj* 1 diabolical, infernal; 2 abominable, wretched

hel·lo /həlō', he-, hel'ō/ [var of *hallo*] *interj* 1 used to attract attention, answer the phone, or greet || *n* 2 this call or utterance

helm /helm'/ [OE *helma* rudder] *n* 1 wheel or tiller for steering a ship; 2 post of command or control

hel·met /hel'mit/ [MF] *n* protective head covering, usu. of metal, leather, or hard plastic || **hel'met·ed** *adj*

helms'man /-mən/ *n* (**-men** /-mən/) person who steers a ship

hel·ot /hel'ət, hēl'-/ [Gk *Heilotes* one of a slave caste of ancient Sparta] *n* slave, serf

help /help'/ [OE *helpan*] *vt* 1 to aid, assist; 2 to prevent, as *that is a misfortune that he cannot help*; 3 to keep from, refrain from, as *she could not help crying*; 4 to wait on, as customers; 5 to distribute food to at table; 6 to remedy; 7 **help oneself to** to take for oneself, usu. without asking; 8 **help out** to be of aid to; 9 **so help me** I'm telling the truth || *vi* 10 to be of aid or use || *n* 11 aid, assistance; 12 remedy; 13 one who or that which helps; 14 **the help** *pl* the servants; hired hands || **help'er** *n* || SYN *v* befriend, encourage, uphold, accommodate, cooperate, aid, assist, relieve, succor || DISCR *Help*, *aid*, and *assist* are to a degree interchangeable. *Help* is the strongest and most inclusive term, emphasizing the positiveness of the support rendered and the actual need for it. To *aid* is to further, often by cooperation, the work, struggles, or aim of another. To *assist* is to afford slight, casual, or subordinate service to another. We *help* the poor; we *aid* a reformed sinner to get a fresh start; we *assist* a feeble person to get off a bus. To *relieve* is to remove pain, or to free from anxiety; to *succor* is to render quick aid to one fallen into difficulty; we *relieve* suffering by medicine, the wants of the poor by contributions; we *succor* one found dying in the desert by giving him water || ANT *v* hinder, discourage, block, impede, balk, thwart

help'ful *adj* giving aid, useful

help'ing *n* portion of food served at a meal

help'ing hand' *n* assistance

help'less *adj* 1 unable to do for or help oneself; 2 lacking strength; incapacitated; 3 bewildered

help'mate' also **help'meet'** [< *meet²*] *n* 1 co-worker, helper; 2 spouse

Hel·sin·ki /hel'siŋkē/ *n* capital of Finland (519,326)

hel·ter-skel·ter /helt'ərskelt'ər/ [imit] *adj & adv* 1 in hurried confusion and disorder || *n* 2 disorder; confused and hasty action

Hel·ve·tia /helvēsh'ə/ *n poet.* Switzerland || **Hel·ve'tian** *adj & n*

hem¹ /hem'/ [OE] *n* 1 edge or margin of a cloth or garment turned back and sewed down to prevent fraying || *v* (**hemmed; hem·ming**) *vt* 2 to make a hem on; 3 to shut in, surround

hem² [imit] *interj* 1 utterance made to express hesitation or doubt, or to attract attention || *v* (**hemmed; hem·ming**) *vi* 3 to utter this sound; 4 **hem and haw** to hesitate in speaking; be evasive

he'-man' /-man'/ *n* (**-men'** /-men'/) strong virile man

hem·a·tite /hem'ətīt'/ [Gk *haimatites* bloodlike] *n* iron oxide —Fe_2O_3— a red to black mineral, the principal ore of iron

hemi- [Gk] *comb form* half

hem′i·sphere′ *n* **1** half of a globe or sphere; **2** any of the halves of the terrestrial globe, as the Eastern, Western, Northern, or Southern Hemisphere

hem′line′ *n* the lower edge of a skirt, coat, or dress

hem′lock′ [OE *hymlic*] *n* **1** tree of a genus (*Tsuga*) of large evergreens of the pine family; **2** poisonous herb (*Conium maculatum*), with finely divided leaves and white flowers; **3** poisonous drink made from this herb

hemo- [Gk *haima*] *comb form* blood

he·mo·glo·bin /hēm′əglōb′in, hem′-/ [*hemo-* + *globulin*] *n* coloring matter of the red blood corpuscles

he·mo·phil·i·a /hēm′efil′ē·ə, hem′-/ *n* hereditary abnormality of males in which the blood fails to clot, causing prolonged bleeding from any cut || **he′mo·phil′i·ac** /-ak′/ *n*

hem·or·rhage /hem′(ə)rij/ [Gk *haimorrhagia*] *n* **1** escape of blood from a blood vessel; profuse bleeding || *vi* **2** to bleed profusely

hem·or·rhoids /hem′(ə)roidz′/ [Gk *haimorrhoides* bleeding (veins)] *npl* painful swelling of the veins of the mucous membrane in the rectum

he·mo·stat /hēm′əstat′, hem′-/ [*hemo-* + *stat*] *n* clamp used by surgeons to stop bleeding

hemp /hemp/ [OE *henep*] *n* tall annual Asiatic herb (*Cannabis sativa*), or its tough fiber, used for making cordage and coarse fabrics

hem′stitch′ *n* ornamental stitching made by pulling out several parallel threads and drawing the cross threads together in small groups || also *vt*

hen /hen′/ [OE *henn*] *n* female of the domestic fowl, or of any gallinaceous bird

hence /hens′/ [ME *hennes*] *adv* **1** from this place, time, source, point of view, or the like; **2** for this reason

hence′forth′ *adv* from this time on

hench′man /-mən/ [ME] *n* (**-men** /-mən/) **1** supporter; trusted follower; **2** unscrupulous political supporter

hen·na /hen′ə/ [Ar *hinnā′*] *n* **1** Asiatic tree or shrub (*Lawsonia inermis*) with fragrant white flowers; **2** reddish-orange dye or cosmetic made from its leaves; **3** reddish orange || *vt* **4** to dye with henna

hen′peck′ *vt* to nag and find fault with (one's husband)

hen·ry /hen′rē/ [Joseph *Henry* (1797-1878) Am physicist] *n* (**-ries** or **-rys**) *elec* unit of inductance of a circuit in which an electromotive force of one volt is induced by a current varying at the rate of one ampere per second

Hen·ry, O. *n* pen name of William Sidney Porter (1862-1910) U.S. short-story writer

Hen·ry, Pat·rick *n* (1736-99) American patriot and statesman

Hen·ry VIII *n* (1491-1547) king of England 1509-47

hep /hep′/ *adj slang* hip²

he·pat·ic /hipat′ik/ [< Gk *hepar* (-*patos*) liver] *adj* of or pert. to the liver

hep·a·ti·tis /hep′ətīt′is/ *n* inflammation of the liver

hep′cat′ *n slang* jazz enthusiast or performer

Hep·ple·white /hep′əlw(h)īt′/ *n* piece of furniture made by or in the style of George Hepplewhite (d. 1786), English cabinetmaker, and influenced to some extent by Louis XVI || also *adj*

hep·ta- [Gk] *comb form* seven

hep·ta·gon /hep′təgon′, -gən/ [*hepta-* + -*gon*] *n* polygon having seven angles and seven sides || **hep·tag′o·nal** /-tag′ənəl/ *adj*

her /hur′, (h)ər/ [OE] *pron* **1** objective case of **she** || *adj* **2** possessive of **she**: of or belonging to her

He·ra /hir′ə/ *n Gk myth.* wife of Zeus, goddess of marriage and maternity, the Roman Juno

Her·a·cles /her′əklēz′/ *n* Greek form of Hercules

her·ald /her′əld/ [OF *heraut*] *n* **1** formerly, official or royal messenger; **2** one who announces important news; messenger; **3** forerunner, harbinger || *vt* **4** to introduce; proclaim publicly; usher in

he·ral·dic /heral′dik/ *adj* of or pert. to heralds or heraldry

her′ald·ry *n* (**-ries**) **1** office or duty of a herald; **2** science that treats of armorial bearings and coats of arms, and of determining pedigrees; **3** heraldic device; coat of arms; **4** heraldic pomp and ceremony

herb /(h)urb′/ [OF *erbe* < L *herba* grass] *n* **1** plant whose stem withers away annually after forming seed; **2** such a plant used for medicine, food, flavor, scent, or the like || **her·ba·ceous** /hərbāsh′əs/ *adj*

herb′age /-ij/ *n* herbs or green grasses collectively

herb′al *adj* **1** pert. to herbs || *n* **2** book on herbs and plants

her·bi·vore /hurb′ivôr′, -vōr′/ [< L *herba* grass + *vorare* to eat] *n* animal feeding on plants || **her·biv·o·rous** /hərbiv′ərəs/ *adj*

her·cu·le·an /hərkyōōl′ē·ən, hur′-kyəlē′ən/ [< *Hercules*] *adj* **1** of very great strength or power; **2** very difficult or dangerous (task); **3** Herculean of or pert. to Hercules

Her·cu·les /hurk′yəlēz′/ *n class. myth.* the most famous hero of classical antiquity, son of Jupiter, known for his great strength and for the 12

tasks or labors imposed on him by Juno

herd /hurd′/ [OE *heord*] *n* **1** group of cattle or other large animals feeding or traveling together; **2** rabble, mob; **3** the ignorant and uncultured ‖ *vi* **4** to flock together; **5** to crowd together; assemble ‖ *vt* **6** to form into a herd; **7** to drive or tend ‖ **herd′er** *n* ‖ SYN *n* flock, drove, pack, bevy, covey, shoal, school, gam, swarm ‖ DISCR A *herd* is a group of the larger animals, especially cattle, feeding or traveling together. A *pack* is a company of hounds, kept together, as for hunting, or of beasts, especially wolves, naturally keeping together, as in search of food. A *flock* is a number of birds or animals of a kind, feeding or flying together. *Bevy* is applied to a collection of birds, especially quail or larks, or of some small animals, as roes, and, properly also, to an animated band of women or children. *Covey*, also applicable to birds, is commonly confined to a brood of partridges. *Shoal* and *school* name large numbers of fish swimming in company. A *gam* is a *school* of whales. *Drove* names a *herd* or *flock*, driven or traveling together. *Swarm* is applied to a large number of small animals, especially insects in motion

-herd /hurd/ [OE *hirde*] *n comb form* herdsman, as *cowherd*

herds′man /-mən/ *n* (-men /-mən/) one who drives or tends a herd

here /hir′/ [OE *hēr*] *adv* **1** in or at this place; **2** to this place, in this direction; **3** at this point; now; **4** in the present life; **5** (used to draw attention to something, as) *here is the book, here comes John;* **6** **neither here nor there** irrelevant ‖ *n* **7** this place ‖ *interj* **8** used to command attention, to answer a roll call, etc.

here′a·bout′ also **here′a·bouts′** *adv* in this locality

here·af′ter *adv* **1** after this; from this time forth; **2** in the life to come ‖ *n* **3** time or state yet to come; future; **4** life after death

here·by′ also **here′by** *adv* by virtue of this; by means of this

he·red·i·tar·y /həred′iter′ē/ [< L *hereditare* to inherit] *adj* **1** passing, or capable of passing, legally from an ancestor to a descendant; **2** holding title or possession by inheritance; **3** transmitted naturally from parent to child

he·red·i·ty /həred′itē/ [MF *heredite* < L *hereditas* inheritance] *n* **1** transmission of genetic characteristics to descendants; **2** the transmitted characteristics

here·in′ *adv* in this; in this place

here′in·aft′er *adv* below; later in the same document or statement

here·of′ *adv* of this; about this

her·e·sy /her′əsē/ [OF *eresie* < Gk *hairesis* sect] *n* (-sies) opinion or doctrine in opposition to the orthodox and commonly held views and beliefs, esp. in religion

her·e·tic /her′ətik/ [MF *heretique* < Gk *hairetikos* able to choose] *n* **1** one who differs in doctrine from his church; **2** one who holds opinions contrary to customary views ‖ **he·ret·i·cal** /həret′ikəl/ *adj*

here′to·fore′ *adv* formerly; up to now

here′up·on′ *adv* **1** on this; **2** immediately following this

here·with′ *adv* with this, by means of this

her·it·age /her′itij/ *n* **1** estate that passes by descent; **2** inherited quality or lot

her·maph·ro·dite /hərmaf′rədīt′/ [Gk *Hermaphroditos* youth who became one with a nymph] *n* person, plant, or animal with both male and female sexual organs ‖ also *adj*

Her·mes /hur′mēz/ *n* Gk *myth.* messenger of the gods, and god of eloquence, science, and good luck, the Roman Mercury

her·met·ic (**-i·cal**) /hərmet′ik(əl)/ [ML *hermeticus* < *Hermes Trismegistus* Gk name of Egyptian god Thoth] *adj* perfectly airtight ‖ **her·met′i·cal·ly** *adv*

her·mit /hurm′it/ [OF *ermite* < Gk *eremites* desert dweller] *n* one who retires from society and lives alone; recluse

her′mit·age /-ij/ *n* abode of a hermit

her′mit crab′ *n* any of several crabs (families Paguridae and Parapaguridae) which occupy castoff shells

her·ni·a /hurn′ē-ə/ [L] *n* (-as or -ae /-ē/) protrusion of a loop, as of the intestine or a part of an internal organ, through an abnormal opening in the wall of its containing cavity

he·ro /hir′ō/ [Gk *heros*] *n* (-roes) **1** man of distinguished courage and nobility of character; **2** chief male character in a play, story, or poem; **3** chief personage in any great event

Her·od /her′əd/ *n* (the Great) (73?–4 B.C.) king of Judea 37–4 B.C.

He·rod·o·tus /hirod′ətəs/ *n* (484?–425? B.C.) Greek historian

he·ro·ic /hirō′ik/ *adj* **1** pert. to or like a hero; **2** brave, noble; **3** of or describing heroes or their deeds; **4** drastic, as *heroic measures;* **5** grand, high-flown, as language; **6** *art* larger than life-size ‖ *n* **7 heroics** *pl* extravagant or bombastic language

he·ro′ic verse′ *n* verse suited to exalted themes and used in epic poetry: in Greek and Latin, dactylic hexameter; in English and German, iambic pentameter; in French, Alexandrine

her·o·in /her′ō·in/ *n* white crystalline

addictive drug —C₁₇H₁₇(OC₂H₃O)₂
ON— derived from morphine; its
manufacture and importation is prohibited in the U.S.

her·o·ine /her′ō·in/ n female hero

her·o·ism /her′ō·iz′əm/ n 1 qualities or
attributes of a hero; 2 heroic actions
‖ SYN gallantry, prowess, courage
(see *bravery*)

her·on /her′ən/ [MF *hairon* < Gmc] n
any of a family (Ardeidae) of wading
birds with long neck and legs, frequenting marshy banks

her·pes /hur′pēz/ [Gk = shingles] n
acute inflammatory disease of the
skin, characterized by patches of
small clustered blisters

her·pe·tol·o·gy /hurp′itol′əjē/ [< Gk
herpeton reptile + *-logy*] n study of
reptiles ‖ **her′pe·tol′o·gist** n

Herr /her′/ [G] n (**Her′ren** /-ən/) 1
gentleman; 2 Mr., Sir

her·ring /her′iŋ/ [OE *hǣring*] n (*-ring*
or *-rings*) small edible fish (*Clupea
harengus*) found in great schools in
shallow North Atlantic waters

her′ring·bone′ n pattern composed of
rows of short parallel lines slanting
in opposite directions from a central
rib ‖ also *adj*

hers /hurz′/ [OE] *pron* that or those
belonging to her

her·self′ *pron* 1 reflexive form of **her**;
2 her normal self, as *she is herself
again*; 3 emphatic form of **she**, as
she did it herself

Herst·mon·ceux /hurst′mənsoo′/ also
Hurst- /hurst′-/ n village of SE Sus-
sex, England, site of the Royal Observatory and the British meteorological station

hertz /hurts′/ [< Heinrich R. *Hertz*, G
physicist (1857–1894)] n (**hertz** or
hertz·es) unit of frequency, equal to
one cycle per second

he's /hēz′/ 1 he is; 2 he has

hes·i·tate /hez′itāt′/ [L *haesitare*
(*-atus*)] vi 1 to waver, vacillate; 2 to
pause, delay; 3 to stutter, stammer;
4 to be reluctant ‖ **hes′i·tant** *adj* ‖
hes′i·tan·cy or **hes′i·ta′tion** n

Hes·sian /hesh′ən/ [< *Hesse* state in
Germany] n one of the mercenary
soldiers from Hesse employed by
Great Britain against the colonies in
the American Revolution ‖ also *adj*

het·er·o- [Gk *heteros*] *comb form*
other, different

het·er·o·dox /het′ərədoks′/ [< *hetero-*
+ Gk *doxa* opinion] *adj* unorthodox;
heretical

het·er·o·dyne /het′ərədīn′/ [*hetero-* +
Gk *dyna*(mis) force, power] vt *electron* to combine (an incoming series
of waves) with a local series of different frequency to produce a new
frequency equal to the difference between the two combining frequencies
‖ also *adj*

het·er·o·ge·ne·ous /het′ərəjēn′ē·əs/ [<

hetero- + Gk *genos* kind] *adj* 1 differing in kind, unlike; 2 composed
of parts of different kinds ‖ **het′er·o·
ge·ne′i·ty** /-jinē′itē/ n

het·er·o·sex′u·al n person whose sexual
desires and actions are directed toward the opposite sex ‖ also *adj*

hew /hyoo′/ [OE *hēawan*] v (*pp* **hewed**
or **hewn**) vt 1 to cut or shape, as
with an axe or other sharp-edged
tool; 2 to hack or chop; 3 to cut
down, as trees ‖ vi 4 to cut, chop;
5 **hew to** to conform to rigorously ‖
hew′er n

hex¹ /heks′/ [G *hexe* witch] n 1 evil
spell ‖ vt 2 to cast an evil spell on;
3 to bring bad luck to

hex² *adj colloq* hexagonal, as *hex nut*

hex·a- [Gk] *comb form* six

hex·a·gon /heks′əgon′, -gən/ [Gk *hex*
six + *-gon*] n polygon having six angles and six sides ‖ **hex·ag′o·nal**
/-ag′ənəl/ *adj*

hex·am′e·ter /-am′itər/ n line or verse
of six metrical feet

hex′a·pod′ /-əpod′/ *adj* 1 having six
feet ‖ n 2 true insect, member of
the class Insecta

hey /hā′/ [ME] *interj* used to express
surprise, joy, etc., or to attract attention

hey′day′ [prob < *high day*] n period of
greatest vigor, vitality, or prosperity

hey′ rube′ *interj carnival slang* come
help! (used to summon help in a
fight with the local townsmen)

Hf *chem* hafnium

Hg [L *hydrargyrum*] *chem* mercury

H′-hour′ n *mil* time set for an attack

hi /hī′/ [ME *hy*] *interj* hello!

H.I. Hawaiian Islands

hi·a·tus /hī·āt′əs/ [L = gap] n (*-tus·es*
or *-tus*) 1 space where something is
missing, as in a series; 2 break; gap;
3 juxtaposition of two vowels without an intervening consonant, as *he is*

Hi·a·wath·a /hī′əwŏ′thə, -wä′-/ n hero
of a poem by Longfellow, recounting
the life of a legendary leader among
the American Indians

hi·ber·nate /hīb′ərnāt′/ [L *hibernare*
(*-atus*)] vi 1 to winter; 2 to pass the
winter in a dormant or torpid state,
as the bears ‖ **hi′ber·na′tion** n

Hi·ber·ni·a /hīburn′ē·ə/ [L] n *poet.*
Ireland ‖ **Hi·ber′ni·an** *adj & n*

hi·bis·cus /hībisk′əs, hi-/ [Gk *hibiskos*]
n any of a genus (*Hibiscus*) of plants
of the mallow family, esp. those bearing large showy flowers of varied
colors

hic·cup also **hic·cough** /hik′əp/ [imit]
n 1 spasmodic inhalation of breath
accompanied by closure of the glottis, causing a sharp gasping sound; 2
hiccups *pl* this condition ‖ vi 3 to
give vent to hiccups

hick /hik′/ [nickname of *Richard*] n
unsophisticated person from the
country or a small town

hick·o·ry /hik′(ə)rē/ [< earlier *pohick-*

ery < Algonquian] *n* (-ries) 1 any of a genus (*Carya*) of nut trees of the walnut family; 2 its nut

hid /hid/ *pt & pp* of **hide²**

hid·den /hid'ən/ 1 *pp* of **hide²** || *adj* 2 concealed; not known || SYN invisible, latent, clandestine (see *obscure*)

hide¹ /hīd/ [OE *hyd*] *n* 1 raw or tanned skin of an animal; 2 **neither hide nor hair** not a trace (of someone or something missing)

hide² [OE *hydan*] *v* (**hid; hidden** or **hid**) *vt* 1 to conceal, put out of sight; 2 to keep secret; 3 to obstruct, as a view || *vi* 4 to conceal oneself, be concealed; 5 **hide out** to go into or be in hiding || SYN veil, cover (see *conceal*) || ANT disclose, divulge, uncover, reveal

hide'a·way' *n* refuge, retreat

hide·bound *adj* narrow-minded; extremely conservative

hid·e·ous /hid'ē·əs/ [OF *hidos* < *hisde* fear] *adj* 1 offensive to the sight, ear, or taste; 2 shocking, revolting || **hid'e·ous·ly** *adv* || **hid'e·ous·ness** *n* || SYN grim, ghastly, grisly, revolting, ugly, frightful

hide'out' *n* hiding place, esp. from the law

hid'ing¹ *n* colloq thrashing

hid'ing² *n* concealment

hie /hī/ [OE *hīgian* to strive] *v* (**hy·ing** or **hie·ing**) *vt & vi* to hasten

hi·er- or **hi·er·o-** [Gk *hieros*] *comb form* sacred, holy

hi·er·ar·chy /hī'ərär'kē/ *n* (-chies) 1 the body of clergy of a church, arranged according to rank; 2 government by such a body; 3 any system of persons or things arranged according to rank; 4 rank or order of holy beings, as angels || **hi'er·ar'chic** (**-chical**) *adj*

hi·er·o·glyph /hī'(ə)rəglif'/ [*hiero-* + Gk *glyphe* carving] *n* hieroglyphic

hi·er·o·glyph'ic *n* 1 pictorial symbol representing a word or sound, esp. one used in the writing system of ancient Egypt; 2 symbol with a hidden meaning; 3 written character hard to decipher || also *adj*

hi-fi /hī'fī'/ *n* 1 high fidelity; 2 sound-reproducing instrument with high fidelity || also *adj*

high /hī/ [OE *hēah*] *adj* 1 elevated in location; 2 extending far upward; 3 having (a specified) elevation or extent, as *a foot high*; 4 exalted; superior, as *high officials*; 5 chief, head; 6 advanced to completion, as *high tide*; 7 elated, lively, as *high spirits*; 8 grave, serious; 9 haughty; 10 expensive; 11 great in degree, force, number, or intensity, as *high speed*; 12 luxurious (living); 13 *colloq* drunk; 14 raised or shrill (pitch or voice); 15 at the highest ratio of wheel revolutions to engine revolutions, as *high gear*; 16 *phonet* (sound) produced with the tongue

in a raised position || *adv* 17 at or to a great altitude; 18 to a great degree; 19 at a great rate; 20 luxuriously; 21 **aim high** to have high aspirations; 22 **come high** to cost a great deal; 23 **flying high** elated; 24 **high and dry** stranded; 25 **high and low** everywhere || *n* 26 high gear; 27 high degree or level; 28 *meteor.* high-pressure system; 29 **on high** in heaven

high'ball' *n* 1 whiskey diluted with soda water or ginger ale and served in a high glass || *vi* 2 to move along at full speed (said of a railroad train)

high' blood' pres'sure *n* abnormally high arterial blood pressure

high'born' *adj* of noble birth or descent

high'boy' *n* high chest of drawers on legs

high'brow' *n* 1 person of refined tastes and intellect; 2 intellectual snob || also *adj*

high'chair' *n* chair for very young children, with high legs, arms, and a tray for food

High' Church' *adj* pert. to a party in the Anglican Church which advocates ritual and traditional dogma and lays much stress on church authority

high' com'e·dy *n* comedy dealing with the life of the upper social classes, characterized by witty, sophisticated dialogue

high' com·mand' *n* 1 supreme headquarters of a military force; 2 top authority in any organization

high·er ed·u·ca'tion *n* education above the high-school level

high'er-up' *n* colloq person in a position of authority

high' ex·plo'sive *n* powerful explosive in which the explosion is practically instantaneous

high'fa·lu'tin /-fəlōōt'ən/ [?] *adj* colloq pompous, pretentious

high' fi·del'i·ty *n* extremely faithful reproduction of sound over the whole range of audio frequencies || **high'-fi·del'i·ty** *adj*

high'-flown' *adj* 1 bombastic, inflated; 2 extravagant, pretentious

high' fre'quen·cy *n* radio frequency in the range between 3 and 30 megahertz || **high'-fre'quen·cy** *adj*

high' gear' *n* 1 gear that provides the highest ratio of wheel revolutions to engine revolutions; 2 state of extreme activity

High' Ger'man [because spoken in the high or mountainous regions] *n* 1 the German spoken natively in central and S Germany; 2 official and literary language of Germany, Austria, and Switzerland

high'-grade' *adj* of excellent quality

high'-hand'ed *adj* arbitrary; overbearing, oppressive || **high'-hand'ed·ly** *adv* || **high'-hand'ed·ness** *n*

high' hat' *n* man's tall silk black hat, worn esp. on formal occasions

high'-hat' *adj* 1 snobbish || *v* (-hat·ted; -hat·ting) *vt* 2 to snub, treat with disdain

high' horse' *n* haughty, contemptuous manner or attitude

high'jack' *vt* var of **hijack**

high' jinks' *npl slang* high-spirited pranks

high' jump' *n* field contest in which athletes jump for height over a horizontal bar

high'-keyed' *adj* 1 high-strung; excitable; 2 bright in color

high'land /-lənd/ *n* 1 elevated or mountainous land; 2 **the Highlands** mountainous district of N Scotland || **high'land·er** *n* || **High'land·er** *n*

high' life' *n* fashionable and expensive style of living

high'light *n* 1 lightest spot in a picture; 2 moment of special interest || *vt* 3 to direct attention to (a spot or object) by lighting effects; 4 to stress, emphasize

high'ly *adv* 1 to a high degree; 2 very favorably; 3 at a high price

High' Mass' *n R C Ch* celebration of the Eucharist, usu. at the high altar, accompanied by music

high'-mind·ed *adj* having high principles || **high'mind'ed·ness** *n*

high'ness *n* 1 state or quality of being high; 2 **Highness** title applied, with a possessive adjective, to members of a royal family

high' noon' *n* precise moment of noon

high'-pitched' *adj* 1 played or sung in a high pitch; 2 (roof) with a steep incline; 3 showing intense feeling; 4 lofty in thought

high'-pow'ered *adj* 1 having great drive and energy; 2 done with great drive and energy; 3 (optical device) with a high degree of magnification

high'-pres'sure *adj* 1 having, operated by, or suitable for a relatively high pressure; 2 aggressively persistent || *vt* 3 to use high-pressure tactics on, as in selling

high' priest' *n* 1 chief priest; 2 head priest of ancient Jewish priesthood; 3 leader in a movement

high'proof' *adj* high in alcoholic content

high'-rise' *adj* very tall (apartment or office building)

high'road' *n* 1 chief or much-traveled road; 2 easy method or course

high' school' *n* public school covering grades 9 (or 10) through 12 || **high'-school'** *adj*

high' seas' *npl* open waters of a sea or ocean, beyond the jurisdiction of any country

high' sign' *n colloq* stealthily given glance or signal of warning

high' so·ci'e·ty *n* fashionable, wealthy people; society 4

high'-sound'ing *adj* pompous; high-flown

high'-speed' *adj* 1 made to operate at high speed; 2 (film) suitable for photographing rapidly moving objects; 3 (steel) hard and tough enough to be used in tools that operate when made red-hot by the friction of high speeds

high'-spir'it·ed *adj* 1 mettlesome, animated; 2 courageous

high'-strung' *adj* tense, nervous, easily upset

high'-tail' *vi colloq* to leave rapidly; scamper away

high'-ten'sion *adj* carrying or having high voltage

high'-test' *adj* highly volatile (gasoline)

high' tide' *n* 1 highest level of the incoming tide; 2 culminating point

high' time' *n* 1 time just before it is too late; 2 *slang* celebration, spree, merrymaking

high'-toned' *adj* 1 high-principled; 2 pretentious, affectedly stylish

high' trea'son *n* treason against the state or sovereign

high' wa'ter *n* 1 water at its highest level, as in a flood; 2 high tide

high'way' *n* 1 main thoroughfare or route; 2 any public road or way on land or water

high'way·man /-mən/ *n* (-men /-mən/) robber who holds up travelers on a public road

hi'jack' [?] *vt* 1 to steal (goods in transit); 2 to commandeer (an airplane) in flight || **hi'jack'er** *n* || **hi'jack'ing** *n*

hike /hīk/ [?] *vi* 1 to tramp; take a long walk; march || *vt* 2 to pull up; 3 to raise (prices) || *n* 4 long walk or march; 5 rise, as in prices || **hik'er** *n*

hi·lar·i·ous /hiler'ē·əs, hī-/ [< L *hilaris* cheerful] *adj* 1 noisily gay and merry; 2 boisterously mirthful || **hi·lar'i·ous·ly** *adv* || **hi·lar'i·ty** /-lar'-/ *n* || SYN jolly, boisterous, romping (see *cheerful*)

hill /hil/ [OE *hyll*] *n* 1 natural elevation lower than a mountain; 2 small mound or heap of earth, as *an ant-hill;* 3 incline in a road; 4 **the Hill, a** the hill in Washington, D.C. on which the Capitol stands; **b** Congress; 5 **go over the hill** *slang* to desert || *vt* 6 to heap earth about, as plants, in a mound

hill'bil'ly [< *Billy*] *n* (-lies) uncouth person from the mountains or back-woods

hill·ock /hil'ək/ [ME *hilloc*] *n* small hill

hill'side' *n* side of a hill

hill'top' *n* top of a hill

hill'y *adj* (-i·er; -i·est) 1 abounding in hills; 2 steep, rugged || **hill'i·ness** *n*

hilt /hilt/ [OE] *n* 1 handle of a sword, dagger, or tool; 2 **up to the hilt** completely; fully

him /him/, im/ [OE] *pron* objective case of **he**

Him·a·la·yas /him'əlā'əz, himäl'yəz/

npl mountain range between India and Tibet, containing the highest mountains in the world ‖ **Him'e·la'·yan** *adj*

him·self' *pron* **1** reflexive form of **him**; **2** his normal self, as *he is not himself;* **3** emphatic form of **he,** as *he did it himself*

hind¹ /hīnd'/ [OE = deer] *n* female of the red deer, esp. in and after the third year

hind² [< OE *hinder* behind] *adj* (**hind·er; hind·most** or **hind·er·most**) situated in the rear, back

Hind. 1 Hindustan; 2 Hindustani

hind·er¹ /hīn'dər/ [*comp* of *hind²*] *adj* rear, posterior

hin·der² /hin'dər/ [OE *hindrian*] *vt* to obstruct, impede; thwart ‖ SYN clog, bar, block, check, embarrass, retard, impede (see *prevent*) ‖ ANT further, help, push, promote

Hin·di /hin'dē/ [Hindi *Hind* India] *n* principal language of northern India

hind'most' /hīnd'-/ *adj* farthest back

hind'quar'ter /hīnd'-/ *n* rear part of a halved carcass of beef, lamb, etc.

hin·drance /hin'drəns/ [< *hinder²*] *n* **1** act of hindering or state of being hindered; **2** thing or person that hinders ‖ SYN impediment, obstacle, obstruction, difficulty, encumbrance ‖ DISCR *Difficulty,* the general term, connotes that which is hard to do or overcome; a *difficulty* may be conquered usually by perseverance or effort, as the *difficulty* of scaling a cliff. A *hindrance* is that which pulls one back or puts a stop to progress. Rain or bashfulness may be a *hindrance.* That which bears down, burdens, hampers, is an *encumbrance;* heavy baggage is an *encumbrance.* An *impediment* is literally a stumblingblock; stones in the road are *impediments;* anything that slows us down or holds us back is an *impediment;* certain conditions are *impediments* to marriage; certain physical defects form *impediments* in one's speech. *Obstacles* and *obstructions* lie in our way; *obstacles* are *difficulties,* usually surmountable, of either a physical or a moral nature; an *obstacle* race is one in which physical barriers or *hindrances* must be passed; the path of success presents many *obstacles. Obstructions* are usually physical, and may be insurmountable. Torn-up roads form an *obstruction* to motorists

hind'sight' /hīnd'-/ *n* understanding of an event after it has happened

Hin·du /hin'dōō/ [Pers = Indian] *n* **1** native or inhabitant of India; **2** adherent of Hinduism ‖ also *adj*

Hin·du·ism *n* the Hindu social and religious system, the principal religious system of India

Hin'du·stan' /-stän', -stan'/ *n* Persian name of India

Hin·du·sta'ni /-nē/ *n* language of the Mohammedans in India, a dialect of Western Hindi, mixed with Arabic, Persian, and Turkish

hinge /hinj'/ [ME *heng*] *n* **1** joint on which a door or lid turns or swings; **2** natural joint, as of an oyster shell; **3** fundamental point on which anything depends ‖ *vt* **4** to hang by a hinge; **5** to furnish with a hinge ‖ *vi* **6** to turn or hang, as on a hinge; **7** **hinge on** or **upon** to depend for result on

hin·ny /hin'ē/ [L *hinnus*] *n* (**-nies**) offspring of a stallion and a female donkey

hint /hint'/ [OE *hentan* to seize upon] *n* **1** allusion, intimation, indirect suggestion ‖ *vt* **2** to give a hint of ‖ *vi* **3** **hint at** to intimate vaguely about ‖ SYN *v* indicate, mention, intimate, insinuate, imply, allude, point, advert, refer, signify, relate

hin·ter·land /hint'ərland'/ [G = hinder land] *n* **1** territory back of a river or seacoast region; **2** relatively inaccessible and primitive region

hip¹ /hip'/ [OE *hype*] *n* upper fleshy part of the thigh on each side of the pelvis

hip² [?] *adj slang* knowledgeable, informed; sophisticated

hipped' *adj colloq* greatly interested in or obsessed with

hip'pie *n* person who strives for unconventionality in behavior and dress and sometimes takes psychedelic drugs

hip·po /hip'ō/ *n colloq* hippopotamus

hip·po- [Gk *hippos*] *comb form* horse

Hip·poc·ra·tes /hipok'rətēz'/ *n* (460–377? B.C.) Greek physician, considered the Father of Medicine

Hip'po·crat'ic oath' /hip'əkrat'ik/ *n* solemn pledge usu. taken by those about to practice medicine, embodying a standard of medical ethics

hip·po·drome /hip'ədrōm'/ [*hippo-* + Gk *dromos* race course] *n* **1** ancient Greek or Roman course for chariot and horse races; **2** arena or building for circuses, games, or other spectacles

hip'po·pot'a·mus /-pot'əməs/ [*hippo-* + Gk *potamos* river] *n* (**-mus·es** or **-mi** /-mī'/) thick-skinned amphibious and herbivorous mammal (*Hippopotamus amphibius*) with short legs and a massive body, found in the rivers of Africa

hip'py *n* (**-pies**) var of **hippie**

hip'roof' *n* roof without gables, in which the sloping ends and sides meet in a sharp angle

hire /hī'(ə)r/ [OE *hyrian*] *vt* **1** to employ for wages; **2** to contract for the use of; **3** **hire out** to grant temporary use of for pay ‖ *vi* **4** **hire out** to take a job for pay ‖ *n* 5 act of hiring; 6 wages, pay; 7 for hire available for hiring ‖ SYN *n* (see *salary*); *v.* (see *employ*)

hire′ling /-liŋ/ *n* one who serves for wages; mercenary

hire′-pur′chase sys′tem *n Brit* installment plan

Hi·ro·shi·ma /hĭrōsh′ĭmə/ *n* seaport in Japan (500,000); destroyed August 6, 1945 by the first atomic bomb used in warfare

hir·sute /hur′sōōt, hers(y)ōōt′/ [L *hirsutus*] *adj* hairy; shaggy

his /hĭz′, ĭz/ [OE] *adj* 1 possessive of **he:** of or belonging to him ‖ /hĭz′/ *pron* 2 that or those belonging to him

His·pan·ic /hĭspan′ik/ [< L *Hispania* Spain] *adj* of or pert. to the Spanish language and culture, and to the Spanish-speaking peoples

His·pan·io·la /hĭsp′ənyōl′ə/ *n* island in the West Indies comprising Haiti and the Dominican Republic

hiss /hĭs′/ [OE *hyscan* to jeer at] *n* 1 prolonged sibilant noise, like the voiceless sound of *s* or of escaping steam; 2 such a sound made to express disapproval or derision ‖ *vi* 3 to utter a hiss ‖ *vt* 4 to express disapproval of by hissing

hist /hĭst′, st′/ *interj* hush!, listen!

hist. 1 historic(al); 2 history

his·ta·mine /hĭst′əmēn′/ [< Gk *histos* tissue + *amine*] *n* 1 amine compound —C₆H₉N₃— released in animal tissue by allergic reactions; 2 commercial form of this compound

his·to·gram /his′təgram′/ [< *histo*(ry) + *-gram*] *n statistics* diagram showing a frequency distribution with rectangles whose lengths represent the frequencies and whose widths represent the class intervals

his·tol′o·gy /-tol′əjē/ [< GK *histos* web, tissue + *-logy*] *n* 1 study of organic tissues; 2 microscopic structure of organic tissues

his·to·ri·an /hĭstôr′ē·ən, -stōr′-/ *n* writer of or expert in history

his·tor·ic /hĭstôr′ik, -stor′-/ *adj* 1 well-known in history; renowned, celebrated; 2 historical

his·tor′i·cal *adj* 1 of or pert. to history; 2 based upon or true to the facts of history ‖ **his·tor′i·cal·ly** *adv*

his·tor′i·cal pres′ent *n gram* present tense used for past narration

his·to·ry /hĭst′ərē/ [Gk *historia*] *n* (-ries) 1 complete story or narrative; 2 account of past events affecting one or more nations or peoples, arranged in due order; 3 branch of learning that studies past events; 4 past events in general ‖ SYN annals, story, record, account, recital, chronicle ‖ DISCR *A record* may be a brief note set down for remembrance or reference; it may be a piece of evidence or information preserved in writing, or in some other legible form, as in the traces of former geological periods found in rocks; or, a *record* may be a connected account of facts, preserved in a document, or on a monument or tablet. *Annals* and *chronicles* are kinds of *record; annals* narrate events year by year; *chronicles* set events down continuously over a certain period, long or short. *History* is a continuous, systematic *record* of public events. *Annals* and *chronicles* observe merely the order of time in presenting their material; *history* selects, emphasizes, and, usually, explains or interprets the events. *Annals* and *chronicles* set down that which happens, often regardless of subject, and always without perspective; *history* groups events, especially as they concern a certain nation, institution, or any center of interest, with regard to relative importance

his·tri·on·ic /his′trē·on′ik/ [< L *histrio*, (-onis)* actor] *adj* 1 pert. to acting or actors; 2 overacted; affected

his′tri·on′ics *npl* 1 acting, dramatics; 2 affected outburst

hit /hĭt′/ [ON *hitta*] *v* (**hit; hit·ting**) *vt* 1 to strike; give a blow to; 2 to touch (a mark); attain to; reach; 3 to coincide with, suit; 4 to meet with, find; 5 to impact against; 6 to propel by striking; 7 *baseball* to make (a base hit); 8 to affect severely; 9 *underworld slang* to murder; 10 **hit it off** *colloq* to get along ‖ *vi* 11 to clash or collide; 12 to strike out; deliver a blow; 13 to fire or explode, as a gasoline engine; 14 **hit on** or **upon** to discover, as by accident ‖ *n* 15 stroke or blow; 16 success, as *the song was a hit;* 17 *baseball* base hit; 18 *underworld slang* planned murder ‖ **hit′ter** *n*

hit′-and-run′ *adj* 1 fleeing after hitting, as a car involved in an auto accident; 2 *baseball* noting a play in which a base runner starts running as soon as the ball is pitched, hoping that the batter will hit the ball safely or bunt successfully

hitch /hich′/ [ME *hytchen*] *vt* 1 to fasten or tie; 2 to harness (a draft animal) to a vehicle; 3 to get (a ride) by hitchhiking; 4 **hitch up,** a to raise with short jerks; b to attach (a draft animal) to a vehicle; 5 **get hitched** *slang* to get married ‖ *vi* 6 **hitch on** to be attached to something ahead ‖ *n* 7 fastening, esp. temporary; 8 pulling or jerking upward; 9 obstacle, impediment; 10 inconsistency, as in a story; 11 *mil* period of enlistment; 12 kind of knot for temporary fastening

hitch′hike′ *vi* to travel by getting free rides from passing motorists ‖ **hitch′hik′er** *n*

hith·er /hith'ər/ [OE *hider*] *adv* **1** to this place ‖ *adj* **2** nearer

hith·er·to' *adv* up to this time

Hit·ler, A·dolf /ad'olf hit'lər, äd'-/ *n* (1889–1945) leader of the Nazis; chancellor and dictator of Germany 1933–45

hit' or miss' *adv* haphazardly

hit'-or-miss' *adj* haphazard; careless

Hit·tite /hit'īt/ [Heb *hittīm*] *n* **1** member of an ancient people dominant in Asia Minor 1900–1200 B.C.; **2** their language ‖ also *adj*

hive /hīv'/ [OE *hȳf*] *n* **1** beehive; **2** the bees living in a hive; **3** any place teeming with activity

hives /[?] *nsg* or *npl* skin eruption characterized by whitish elevations accompanied by intense itching

H.M. His (or Her) Majesty

H.M.S. 1 His (or Her) Majesty's Service; **2** His (or Her) Majesty's Ship

Ho *chem* holmium

hoard /hôrd', hōrd'/ [OE *hord*] *n* **1** store or treasure laid away in reserve ‖ *vi* & *vt* **2** to accumulate and store away

hoar'frost' /hôr'-, hōr'-/ [see hoary] *n* frozen dew

hoar'hound' *n* horehound

hoarse /hôrs', hōrs'/ [OE *hās*] *adj* **1** discordant, raucous; **2** having a husky or grating voice ‖ **hoarse'·ness** *n* ‖ **hoars'en** *vt* & *vi*

hoar·y /hôr'ē hōr'ē/ [OE *hār*] *adj* (·i·er; ·i·est) **1** white or gray with age; **2** ancient

hoax /hōks'/ [< *hocus*] *n* **1** humorous or mischievous deception ‖ *vt* **2** to deceive by a hoax ‖ SYN *v* deceive, take in, trick, bamboozle, cheat

hob /hob'/ [ME *Hob* < *Robin*] *n* play or raise hob with to disrupt, do mischief to

hob·ble /hob'əl/ [ME *hobelen*] *vi* **1** to limp; **2** to move haltingly ‖ *vt* **3** to make lame; **4** to tie the legs of (a horse) together to prevent movement; **5** to impede ‖ *n* **6** limping or awkward step; **7** rope or strap for hobbling horses

hob'ble skirt' *n* skirt made so tight below the knees as to prevent long steps

hob·by /hob'ē/ [ME *hoby* var of *Robin*] *n* (·bies) favorite pastime or leisure-time pursuit

hob'by·horse' *n* **1** stick with a horse's head on which children ride; **2** rocking horse

hob'gob'lin [< *hob* peg] *n* **1** impish elf; **2** bogy, bugbear

hob'nail' *n* nail with a large head for protecting the soles of heavy shoes ‖ **hob'nailed'** *adj*

hob·nob /hob'nob'/ [< *obs hab* or *nab* take or leave] *v* (·nobbed; ·nob·bing) *vi* hobnob with **1** to associate or talk on familiar terms with; **2** to chat or talk informally with

ho·bo /hō'bō/ [?] *n* (·bos or ·boes) **1** migratory worker; **2** tramp

Hob'son's choice' /hob'sənz/ [Thomas *Hobson* (1544–1631) Eng liveryman, who gave a customer only one choice, that of the horse nearest the door] *n* choice between what is offered and nothing

Ho Chi Minh /hō' chē' min'/ *n* **1** (1890?–1969) Vietnamese leader, president of Vietnam 1945–54 and of North Vietnam 1954–69; **2** (new name of) *Saigon*

hock¹ /hok'/ [OE *hōh* heel] *n* joint in the hind leg of some animals, corresponding to the ankle in man

hock² [D *hok* prison] *n* & *vt* colloq pawn¹

hock·ey /hok'ē/ [perh MF *hoquet* bent stick] *n* **1** game played on ice in which two teams try to drive the puck into their respective goals with curved sticks; **2** similar game played on a field with a ball

hock'shop' *n* colloq pawnshop

ho'cus /hōk'əs/ [< *hocus-pocus*] *v* (·cused or ·cussed; ·cus·ing or ·cus·sing) *vt* **1** to cheat or trick; **2** to drug (liquor)

ho·cus-po·cus /hōk'əs·pōk'əs/ [mock Latin, orig. a deliberate perversion of L *in hoc corpus* into this body] *n* **1** meaningless incantation used by conjurers and magicians; **2** sleight of hand; **3** trickery, deception

hod /hod'/ *n* **1** long-handled trough for carrying bricks or mortar; **2** coal scuttle

hod' car'ri·er *n* workman who carries mortar and bricks to the mason

hodge·podge /hoj'poj'/ [ME *hoche poche* thick stew] *n* confused mixture

Hodg'kin's dis·ease' /hoj'kinz/ [< Thomas *Hodgkin* (1798–1866) Eng physician] *n* progressive cancerous disease, characterized by inflammation and enlargement of the lymph nodes, spleen, liver, and kidneys

hoe /hō'/ [OF *houe* < Gmc] *n* **1** flat-bladed long-handled implement for loosening soil, weeding, etc. ‖ *vt* **2** to cut, till, or dig up with a hoe ‖ also *vi*

hoe'down' *n* dancing party with folk and square dances and hillbilly music

hog /hog', hôg'/ [OE *hogg*] *n* **1** full-grown domestic swine (family Suidae); **2** any of various animals resembling this, as the peccary, water hog, etc.; **3** colloq grasping, gluttonous, or filthy person; **4** go (the) whole hog colloq to go all the way ‖ *v* (hogged; hog·ging) *vt* **5** slang to take more than one's fair share of

hogs'head' *n* **1** liquid measure equal to 63 gallons; **2** large cask holding from 100 to 140 gallons

hog'tie' *v* (·ty·ing) *vt* **1** to tie together

all four extremities of; **2** *colloq* to hamper, immobilize

hog'wash' *n* **1** swill; **2** anything worthless; **3** nonsense

hog'wild' *adj colloq* overly enthusiastic

hoi pol·loi /hoi'pəloi'/ [Gk = the many] *npl* the crowd, the masses

hoist /hoist'/ [< ME *hissa* sailors' cry] *vt* **1** to lift or raise up with some lifting device || *n* **2** act of hoisting; **3** apparatus for hoisting; **4** vertical dimension of a flag; opposite of *fly*

hoi·ty-toi·ty /hoi'tētoi'tē/ [prob *obs hoit* to be riotously mirthful] *adj* **1** flighty; giddy; **2** haughty; condescending; **3** fussy; petulant

ho·kum /hōk'əm/ [prob < *hocus*] *n colloq* **1** nonsense; **2** stereotyped sentimentality in a play; **3** low comedy used by an actor or speaker to get laughs or attention

hold[1] /hōld'/ [< *hole*] *n* interior of a ship below decks, where the cargo is stored

hold[2] [OE *haldan*] *v* (**held**) *vt* **1** to grasp and keep in the hands or arms; clutch; **2** to retain, keep; **3** to possess, occupy, as an office; **4** to keep in a particular state or condition; **5** to detain; **6** to restrain, keep in check; **7** to judge, consider; **8** to believe or accept, as an opinion; **9** to have room for, contain; **10** to observe, celebrate, as a festival; **11** to call and conduct, as a meeting; **12** to uphold, support; **13** to decide legally; **14 hold back, a** to restrain; **b** to keep back; **15 hold down, a** to check; **b** to continue to hold, as a job; **16 hold off** to repel; **17 hold out** *slang* to withhold (something due); **18 hold over, a** to postpone; **b** to keep beyond the normal period; **19 hold up, a** to prop up; **b** to present, offer; **c** to delay; **d** to rob under threat of violence || *vi* **20** to keep a grasp on something; **21** to cling, adhere; **22** to remain firm and unbroken; **23** to be valid; **24** to remain in a specified state; **25 hold forth** to orate; **26 hold off** to defer action; **27 hold on, a** to keep going; **b** *colloq* to stop, as *hold on, there!*; **28 hold out, a** to last; **b** to refuse to surrender or quit; **c** *slang* to refuse to come to terms; **29 hold to** to endure in, continue in; **30 hold up** to endure, last; **31 hold with, a** to concur in; **b** to condone || *n* **32** act of holding; grasp, grip; **33** handle, support; **34** influence, domination; **35** *wrestling* grip on an opponent; **36 catch, get, lay,** or **take hold of** to seize, acquire || **hold'er** *n* || SYN *v* possess, comprehend, clasp, cherish, embrace, keep, restrain, contain, support, uphold, maintain

hold'ing *n* **1** farm or other real estate rented from another; **2 holdings** *pl* aggregate of owned property, esp. securities and real estate

hold'ing com'pa·ny *n* corporation which controls other corporations through the stocks and bonds it owns

hold'ing pat'tern *n* closed course in which an aircraft circles at a fixed altitude while waiting for landing instructions

hold'out' *n* person who delays signing a contract, seeking better terms

hold'o'ver *n* **1** person or thing remaining from a previous period; **2** play or movie held over beyond the original play date

hold'up' *n* **1** robbery under threat of violence; **2** delay

hole /hōl'/ [OE *hol*] *n* **1** opening through something; **2** cavity, depression; **3** tear, gap; **4** burrow of an animal; **5** dirty and dilapidated habitation; **6** a *golf* cup sunk in the green into which the ball must be played; **b** distance or section of a golf course from a tee to the next hole; **7 hole in the wall** very small quarters; **8 in a hole** *colloq* in trouble; **9 in the hole** *colloq* in debt || *vi* **10 hole up,** a hibernate; **b** *slang* to hide || SYN cavity, aperture, orifice, hollow, perforation, gap

hole' card' *n stud poker* card dealt face down

hol·i·day /hol'idā'/ [*holy* + *day*] *n* **1** religious festival; holy day; **2** any day set aside by law or custom as a day of rest from ordinary business and work; **3** period of recreation; vacation || *adj* **4** festive, gay

ho'li·er-than-thou' *adj* making a hypocritical show of virtue or piety

ho·li·ness /hō'lēnis/ [see **holy**] *n* **1** state or quality of being holy; **2 Holiness** title of the pope (used with *His* or *Your*) || SYN sanctity, piety, sacredness, righteousness, godliness || ANT impurity, impiety, unrighteousness

Hol·land /hol'ənd/ *n* The Netherlands || **Hol'land·er** *n*

hol·ler /hol'ər/ [var of *hollo*] *n* shout, yell || also *vt* & *vi*

hol·lo /hol'ō, həlō'/ *interj, n* & *vi* var of **hallo**

hol·low /hol'ō/ [OE *holh* hole] *adj* **1** having an empty space within; not solid; **2** concave, sunken; **3** insincere; **4** reverberating, muffled (sound) || *n* **5** cavity or pit; **6** basin, valley || *vt* **7** to make hollow || *vi* **8** to become hollow || SYN *adj* sunken, depressed, empty, worthless

hol·ly /hol'ē/ [OE *holegn*] *n* (**-lies**) **1** evergreen shrub or tree (genus *Ilex*) with glossy spiny leaves and red berries; **2** its leaves and berries, used for Christmas decorations

hol·ly·hock' [*holy* + OE *hoc* mallow] *n* tall perennial cultivated mallow (*Althaea rosea*) with large, decorative, varicolored flowers

Hol'ly·wood' *n* city in S California, center of the American motion-picture industry; now a part of Los Angeles

Holmes, Ol·i·ver Wen·dell /ol'ivər wen'dəl hōmz/ *n* **1** (1809–94) U.S. poet, novelist, and physician; **2** his son (1841–1935), U.S. jurist, associate justice of the Supreme Court 1902–32

Holmes, Sher·lock /shur'lok/ *n* famous fictional detective created by A. Conan Doyle (1859–1930), English writer

hol·mi·um /hōl'mē·əm/ [< *Holmia* Latinized form of *Stockholm*] *n* rare-earth element (**Ho**; at.no. 67; at.wt. 164.930)

hol·o- [Gk *holos*] *comb form* whole, entire

hol·o·caust /hol'əkôst', hōl'-/ [*holo-* + Gk *kauston* burnt] *n* complete or wholesale destruction, esp. by fire

hol'o·gram' *n* **1** three-dimensional pattern produced by holography; **2** photograph based on this pattern

hol'o·graph' *n* **1** document written entirely in the handwriting of the person whose signature it bears || *vt* **2** to reproduce by holography || **hol'·o·graph'ic** *adj*

ho·log·ra·phy /halog'rəfē/ *n* lensless system of producing three-dimensional photographs by using the single-frequency light waves of a laser

Hol·stein /hōl'stīn/ [name of G state] *n* one of a breed of large black-and-white dairy cattle

hol·ster /hōl'stər/ [D] *n* leather pistol case, worn on the person or attached to a saddle

ho·ly /hōl'ē/ [OE *hālig*] *adj* (**-li·er; -li·est**) **1** dedicated to the service of God, consecrated; **2** pure morally and spiritually; sinless; **3** worthy of reverence or worship || SYN devout, religious, blessed, hallowed, sacred || DISCR That is *holy* which by its own innate character is set up as spiritually or morally perfect. *Holy* is used in allusion to the special sacredness of whatever is associated with God, as *Holy* Ghost or *Holy* Spirit, *Holy* Family, *Holy* Land, *Holy* Bible. *Holy* is a stronger term than *sacred*, which describes that set apart by man for religious use, or that which is hallowed by association. *Sacred* songs, vessels, edifices, are those consecrated to the worship of God. That is *sacred*, too, which is to be kept free from profanation, violation, or harm. *Sacred* is opposed to secular and profane, as *sacred* history

Ho'ly Com·mun'ion *n* Communion 4
ho'ly day' *n* religious festival
Ho'ly Ghost' *n* third person of the Trinity
Ho'ly Land' *n* Palestine
ho'ly or'ders *npl* status of an ordained Christian minister or priest

Ho'ly Ro'man Em'pire *n* theoretical continuation of the Roman Empire or its W half, consisting mostly of Germany and N Italy, and dating from 962 to 1806

ho'ly rood' *n* **1** cross, crucifix; **2 Holy Rood** cross on which Jesus died

Ho'ly See' *n* see of Rome, the seat of the papacy; papal court

Ho'ly Spir'it *n* Holy Ghost

Ho'ly Thurs'day *n* **1** Ascension Day; **2** Maundy Thursday

ho'ly wa'ter *n* water blessed by a priest

Ho'ly Week' *n* week between Palm Sunday and Easter

Ho'ly Writ' *n* the Bible

hom·age /hom'ij/ [OF *ommage*] *n* **1** respect, reverence; **2** pay homage to give homage || SYN allegiance, loyalty, obeisance, respect

hom·bre /(h)om'brā/ [Sp] *n* man

hom·burg /hom'burg/ [*Homburg* Germany] *n* man's soft felt hat with a dented crown and a rolled brim

home /hōm/ [OE *hām*] *n* **1** one's abode or residence; **2** household and the life centered in it; **3** place of one's birth or youth; **4** one's country; **5** natural habitat; **6** benevolent or charitable institution; **7** *games* goal or destination; **8** home plate; **9** **at home, a** in one's residence; **b** disposed to receive visitors; **c** comfortable, at ease; **d** played on one's own field or grounds, said of a game || *adj* **10** pert. to one's abode or country; **11** carried on, or produced in, one's own house or country; **12** domestic; **13** *sports* played at home || *adv* **14** to or at home; **15** to the point aimed at; **16 bring something home to someone** to impress someone with something || *vi* **17** to go home; **18 home in on** to proceed to (the target), as a guided missile || **home'less** *adj* || **home'like'** *adj*

home' base' *n* **1** *baseball* home plate; **2** base of operations

home'bod'y *n* (**-ies**) person who likes to stay and work at home

home'-brew' *n* alcoholic beverage, esp. beer, made at home

home' e·co·nom'ics *nsg* study of managing a home and family in all its phases

home' fries' *npl* boiled potatoes sliced and fried

home'land' *n* land of one's birth or where one lives

home'ly *adj* (**-li·er; -li·est**) **1** simple, plain; **2** uncultured, crude; **3** plain-featured, unattractive || **home'li·ness** *n*

home'made' *adj* **1** made in, or for, the home; **2** of domestic, rather than foreign, manufacture; **3** plain; amateurish

home'mak'er *n* woman who manages a house; housewife; housekeeper

ho·me·o- [Gk *homoios*] *comb form* similar

home′ of′fice *n* 1 main office of a company; 2 **Home Office** department of the government in Great Britain that corresponds to the U.S. Department of the Interior

ho·me·op·a·thy /hōm′ē·op′əthē/ *n* system of medicine which seeks to cure disease by administering drugs which will produce effects on a healthy person similar to the symptoms of the disease treated ‖ **ho′me·o·path′ic** /-ə-path′ik/ *adj*

home′ plate′ *n* base at which the batter stands and which must be reached safely by a runner in order to score

hom′er *n* 1 home run ‖ *vi* 2 to hit a home run

Ho·mer /hōm′ər/ *n* Greek epic poet of the ninth century B.C., the reputed author of the *Iliad* and *Odyssey* ‖ **Ho·mer′ic** /-mer′ik/ *adj*

home′ rule′ *n* local self-government, as of a city, county, state, province, or dependency

home′ run′ *n baseball* run scored on a hit which enables the batter to make a circuit of the four bases, usu. because the ball has been hit out of the park

home′sick′ *adj* depressed because of absence from home or family ‖ **home′sick′ness** *n*

home′spun′ *adj* 1 (cloth) woven at home or made of yarn spun there; 2 rough; homely ‖ *n* 3 homespun cloth

home′stead′ *n* [OE *hāmstede*] 1 a home with the adjoining lands and buildings ‖ *vi* 2 to establish a home on a property

home′stretch′ *n* 1 that part of a race track from the last turn to the finish line; 2 final stage of a project or undertaking

home′town′ *n* town or city in which one lives or from which one comes ‖ also *adj*

home′ward /-wərd/ *adj* & *adv* toward home ‖ **home′wards** *adv*

home′work′ *n* 1 school work assigned for home study; 2 any work done at home

home′y *adj* (**hom·i·er**; **hom·i·est**) intimate; cozy; homelike ‖ **hom′i·ness** *n*

hom·i·cide /hom′isīd′/ *n* [L *homo* man + -*cide*] 1 killing of one human being by another; 2 person who kills another person ‖ **hom′i·cid′al** *adj*

hom·i·let·ics /hom′ilet′iks/ [see **homily**] *nsg* art of composing and delivering sermons ‖ **hom′i·let′ic** *adj*

hom·i·ly /hom′ilē/ [Gk *homilia* discourse] *n* (**-lies**) 1 religious discourse or sermon; 2 tedious moral dissertation

hom′ing de·vice′ *n* mechanism built into a missile that turns it toward a target emitting heat, radio waves, or other radiation

hom′ing pi′geon *n* pigeon trained and bred to fly home when released anywhere; used for racing and carrying messages

hom·i·ny /hom′inē/ [< Algonquian] *n* hulled and coarsely ground corn boiled for food

homo- [< Gk *homos*] *comb. form* same

ho·mo·ge·ne·ous /hōm′əjēn′ē·əs, hom′-/ [< *homo-* + Gk *genos* kind] *adj* 1 of the same kind; uniform; 2 composed of similar parts ‖ **ho′mo·ge·ne′i·ty** /-jənē′itē/ *n*

ho·mog·e·nize /həmoj′ənīz′/ *vt* 1 to make homogeneous; 2 to distribute the fat globules uniformly in (milk) by breaking them up

hom′o·graph′ /hom′ə-, hōm′ə-/ *n* one of two or more words identical in spelling but different in meaning and origin, as *lie* 'prevaricate' and *lie* 'recline' ‖ **hom′o·graph′ic** *adj*

hom·o·nym /hom′ənim, hōm′ə-/ [Gk *homonymon*] *n* 1 one of two or more words identical in sound but differing in meaning and spelling, as *pear, pair,* and *pare;* 2 homograph; 3 namesake ‖ **ho·mon·y·mous** /həmon′iməs/ *adj*

Ho·mo sa·pi·ens /hōm′ō sāp′ē·ənz/ [L = wise man] *n* genus and species to which modern man belongs; human being

ho′mo·sex′u·al /hōm′ə-/ *n* one who is sexually attracted to persons of the same sex ‖ also *adj* ‖ **ho′mo·sex′u·al′i·ty** /-al′-/ *n*

Hon. Honorable

Hon·du·ras /hond(y)ŏŏr′əs/ *n* Spanish-speaking republic in Central America (2,445,000; 43,277 sq.m.; cap. Tegucigalpa) ‖ **Hon·du′ran** *adj & n*

hone /hōn/ [OE *hān*] *n* 1 fine whetstone for sharpening razors ‖ *vt* 2 to sharpen on or as on a hone

hon·est /on′ist/ [L *honestus* honorable] *adj* 1 straightforward, trustworthy, upright; 2 genuine, unadulterated; 3 gained fairly; 4 honorable; truthful; 5 frank, open ‖ **hon′est·ly** *adv*

hon′es·ty *n* 1 freedom from deceit; 2 straightforwardness; fairness; 3 uprightness; 4 common garden plant (*Lunaria annua*) which has purple flowers and semitransparent pods ‖ SYN sincerity, fairness, honor, integrity, probity, uprightness, rectitude ‖ DISCR *Honesty* is that quality of man that shows him fair and truthful in speech, above cheating, stealing, misrepresentation, or any other fraudulent action. *Honor* adds to *honesty* a sturdy and splendid devotion to such standards of right, fidelity, courage, and conduct as society has crystallized throughout the centuries, as the *honesty* of the employees; the *honor* of a gentleman; his *honor* was at stake. *Uprightness* is that quality in man that carries him along a straight path of *honesty* and duty, as the *uprightness* of the judge was never questioned. *Integrity* emphasizes the wholeness of a man's moral nature; he is sound, incorruptible, and particularly strict about fulfilling the trusts reposed in him by others. *Probity* is virtue which has been put to the test and never found wanting; a man of *probity* is *honest* beyond mere care for the property of others; he regards their good name, their every advantage, with the same conscience as he would his own. *Probity, integrity, uprightness,* and *honor* are qualities of people; *honesty* may apply also to a thing, as an *honest* reply

hon·ey /hun′ē/ [OE *hunig*] n 1 sweet syrupy substance produced by bees from nectar and stored for food; 2 sweetness; 3 darling; 4 *colloq* something fine or excellent || v (-eyed or -ied) vt 5 to make sweet as with honey; 6 to address endearingly or flatteringly

hon′ey·bee′ n bee (*Apis mellifera*) which gathers nectar from flowers to make honey

hon′ey·comb′ n 1 wax structure of hexagonal cells made by bees for storing honey, pollen, eggs, and larvae; 2 anything similarly constructed || vt 3 to fill with holes like those of a honeycomb

hon′ey·dew′ (mel′on) n kind of muskmelon with smooth rind and sweet, greenish pulp

hon′ey·moon′ n 1 trip or vacation taken by a couple immediately after their wedding; 2 initial period of harmony in any relationship || vi 3 to go on a honeymoon || **hon′ey·moon′er** n

hon′ey·suck′le n any of a genus (*Lonicera*) of climbing shrubs, esp. *L. caprifolium,* a twining vine with sweet tubular flowers

Hong Kong /hoŋ′ koŋ′/ n British crown colony on the coast of S China near Canton (4,000,000; 391 sq.m.; cap. Victoria)

honk /hoŋk′, hôŋk′/ [imit] n 1 call of a goose; 2 any sound resembling this, as that of an automobile horn || vi 3 to make such a sound || vt 4 to sound (an automobile horn)

honk′y-tonk′ /-toŋk′, -tôŋk′/ [?] n cheap nightclub or dance hall

Hon·o·lu·lu /hon′əloō′loō/ n capital of Hawaii (324,871)

hon·or /on′ər/ [L] n 1 high esteem; 2 fame, reputation; 3 distinction; exalted rank; 4 integrity, honesty; 5 chastity; 6 mark of esteem, recognition of merit; 7 adornment; glory; credit; 8 *bridge* one of the five highest trump cards, or ace in no trumps; 9 *Honor* title of certain officials (with *Your* or *His*); 10 **honors** pl

distinguished standing in school or college; 11 **be on one's honor** to undertake to act honorably; 12 **do the honors** to serve as host || vt 13 to treat with respect or reverence; 14 to confer honor upon; 15 to accept as valid; 16 to accept and pay, as a check || SYN n (see *honesty, fame*); v reverence, esteem, admire || ANT v defame, despise, dishonor, revile

hon′or·a·ble [L *honorarius* pert. to honor] adj 1 worthy of esteem; illustrious; 2 in accord with honor; 3 distinguished in rank; characterized by marks of honor; 4 highminded; upright; noble || **hon′or·a·bly** adv || SYN creditable, illustrious, just, genuine, honest

hon′o·rar′i·um /-rer′ē-əm/ [L] n (-ums or -a /-ə/) 1 payment for services for which there is no set fee; 2 fee for professional services

hon′or·ar′y [L *honorarius* pert. to honor] adj 1 done or conferred as an honor; 2 possessing a title or position by courtesy, without giving service or receiving pay

Hon·shoo /hon′shoō/ n largest and most populous of the Japanese islands

hood¹ /hoŏd′/ [OE *hōd*] n 1 soft covering for the head and neck; 2 something resembling such a covering, as a folding cover for a carriage; 3 metal cover over an automobile engine; 4 fold hanging down the back of an academic gown, indicating by its color the wearer's degree or field of specialization || vt 5 to cover or furnish with or as with a hood || **hood′ed** adj

hood² [< *hoodlum*] n *slang* gangster, tough

-hood /-hoŏd, -hoŏd′/ [OE *-hād*] n suf. 1 state, quality, condition, or character of being, as *childhood;* 2 collective group or body, as *priesthood*

hood·lum /hoŏd′ləm/ [?] n rowdy, tough

hoo·doo /hoō′doō/ [Afr language] n 1 person or thing that brings bad luck || vt 2 to bring bad luck to

hood′wink′ /hoŏd′-/ vt to deceive, trick

hoo·ey /hoō′ē/ [?] n *colloq* nonsense, baloney

hoof /hoŏf′, hoōf′/ [OE *hōf*] n (**hoofs** or **hooves** /-vz/) 1 horny covering of the forepart of the feet of certain animals, as the horse and ox; 2 **on the hoof** live (livestock) || vi 3 *slang* to tap-dance || vt 4 **hoof it** *slang* to go on foot || **hoofed′** adj

hoof′er n *slang* tap-dancer

hook /hoŏk′/ [OE *hōc*] n 1 curved piece of metal, bone, or the like, with which to hold, pull, or catch something; 2 fishhook; 3 anything hook-shaped; 4 cape that turns inland at its extremity; 5 *sports* path of a ball that curves from a true path; 6 *boxing* curving blow; 7 **hooks**

pl slang hands; **8 by hook or (by) crook** by fair means or foul; **9 off the hook** *slang* released from difficulty or trouble; **10 on one's own hook** on one's own initiative || *vt* **11** to catch, fasten, or hang with or as with a hook; **12** to trick; ensnare; **13** to gore or attack with the horns; **14** *golf* to hit (the ball) so that it curves to the left; **15 get hooked** *slang* to become addicted; **16 hook up, a** to fasten with hooks; **b** to assemble and connect || *vi* **17** to bend like a hook; **18** to become fastened with a hook; **19** to be caught on or as on a hook

hook·ah /hŏŏk'ə/ [Ar *huqqah*] *n* pipe with a long tube for drawing tobacco smoke through water

hook' and eye' *n* fastener consisting of a hook which catches onto a loop

hook' and lad'der *n* fire engine, with a semitrailer, equipped with extension ladders and other devices

hooked' *adj* **1** curved like a hook; **2** furnished with hooks; **3** *slang* addicted, esp. to narcotics

hooked' rug' *n* rug made by drawing yarn or cloth through burlap or canvas

hook'er *n slang* streetwalker

hook'up' *n* **1** combination of related parts; **2 a** arrangement of parts and circuits, as in a radio; **b** diagram showing such an arrangement; **3** network of radio or television stations; **4** connection between several telephones for a conference; **5** *colloq* cooperative relationship between persons, nations, etc.

hook'worm' *n* **1** any of several roundworms of the family Ancylostomatidae, parasitic in the small intestine; **2** disease caused by hookworms

hook'y [< *hook it*] *n* **play hooky** to be absent from school without reason or permission

hoo·li·gan /hŏŏl'ĭgən/ [*Hooligan*, name of London rowdy] *n* hoodlum || **hoo'li·gan·ism** *n*

hoop /hŏŏp', hōōp'/ [OE *hōp*] *n* **1** circular band, as of wood or metal, to hold together the staves of a cask or tub, or used as a child's toy; **2** any circular band || *vt* **3** to bind or secure with a hoop; **4** to encircle; surround

hoop'skirt' *n* woman's skirt made to flare out by a framework of hoops underneath

hoo·ray /hŏŏrā'/ *interj* hurrah! || also *n & vi*

hoose·gow /hŏŏs'gou/ [Sp *juzgado* court] *n slang* jail

Hoo·sier /hŏŏzh'ər/ [?] *n* native or inhabitant of Indiana

hoot /hŏŏt'/ [ME *houten*] *vi* **1** to utter or imitate the cry of an owl; **2** to utter shouts of derision or contempt || *vt* **3** to jeer at, assail by hooting ||

n **4** cry of, or like that of, an owl; **5** shout of derision

hoot·en·an·ny /hŏŏt'ənan'ē/ [?] *n* (-nies) informal concert of folk music, singing, and dancing

Hoo·ver, Her·bert /hur'bərt hŏŏv'ər/ *n* (1874–1964) 31st president of the U.S. 1929–33

hoo·ver [H. Earl *Hoover* (1890–   ), U.S. manufacturer] *Brit n* **1** vacuum cleaner || *vt & vi* **2** to vacuum

hooves /hŏŏvz'/ *pl of* **hoof**

hop¹ /hop'/ [MD *hoppe*] *n* **1** perennial vine (*Humulus lupulus*) with conelike flowers; **2 hops** *pl* dried ripened cones of this plant, used to flavor malt liquors and in medicine || *v* (**hopped; hop·ping**) *vt* **3 hop up** *colloq* **a** to excite, make exuberant; **b** to make (an engine) more powerful

hop² [OE *hoppian*] *v* (**hopped; hop·ping**) *vt* **1** to leap over; **2** *colloq* to board (a vehicle) || *vi* **3** to leap on one foot; **4** to jump with both or all feet at once, as frogs; **5 hop down, over,** or **up** to make a short trip or flight || *n* **6** short brisk jump, esp. on one leg; **7** *colloq* dance; **8** *colloq* **a** airplane flight; **b** short trip; **9** bounce

hope /hōp'/ [OE *hopa*] *n* **1** expectation that what is desired will come to pass; **2** source of hope; **3** object of hope || *vt* **4** to expect with confidence; **5** to desire, believe || *vi* **6 hope for** to cherish a desire for, with anticipation || SYN *n* promise, reliance, trust, desire, expectation

hope' chest' *n* young woman's collection of clothing and other articles for her home in anticipation of marriage

hope'ful *adj* **1** full of hope; **2** inspiring hope || *n* **3** promising young person || **hope'ful·ly** *adv* || **hope'ful·ness** *n* || SYN *adj* assured, confident, optimistic (see *sanguine*) || ANT *adj* depressed, pessimistic, despairing

hope'less *adj* **1** without hope; **2** impossible to do or solve || **hope'less·ly** *adv* || **hope'less·ness** *n* || SYN despondent, desperate, forlorn, cheerless

hop'head' *n slang* drug addict

Ho·pi /hōp'ē/ [nat. *Hopitu* peaceful ones] *n* (-pis or -pi) member of a tribe of Pueblo Indians of N Arizona

hopped'-up' *adj slang* **1** overexuberant; **2** under the influence of a narcotic; **3** (engine) made more powerful

hop'per *n* **1** funnel-shaped container or bin for dry, loose material, loaded through the top and dispensed through the bottom; **2** open-top freight car with hoppers in the bottom for quickly unloading cargo; **3 a** tank of a flush toilet; **b** flush toilet

hop'scotch' *n* children's game involving tossing a stone into successive compartments of a design drawn on the sidewalk and bending over to pick it up while standing on one foot

Hor·ace /hôr′is, hor′-/ *n* (65–8 B.C.) Roman poet ‖ **Ho·ra·tian** /hərāsh′-ən/ *adj*

Ho·ra·tius /hərāsh′əs/ *n* Roman legend famous hero who guarded the bridge over the Tiber against the Etruscans

horde /hôrd′, hôrd′/ [Mongol *orda* camp] *n* multitude, gang, swarm

hore′hound′ /hôr′-, hōr′-/ [OE *hārhūne*] *n* 1 any of various plants of the mint family, esp. a species (*Marrubium vulgare*) used as a remedy for colds and coughs; 2 lozenge flavored with extract of horehound

ho·ri·zon /hərīz′ən/ [Gk = limiting] *n* 1 line where the sky and earth appear to meet; 2 limit or range of one's mental vision or interest; 3 *geol* rock deposit or formation definitely fixed as to time of origin

hor·i·zon·tal /hor′izont′əl, hôr′-/ *adj* 1 of, near, or pert. to the horizon; 2 parallel to the plane of the horizon; level; at right angles to the vertical; 3 reclining; 4 of the same or similar position or social status ‖ *n* 5 something horizontal

hor·mone /hôr′mōn/ [< Gk *hormaein* to set in motion, excite] *n* 1 chemical substance carried by the blood from one organ of the body to another, and capable of exciting the latter to increased functional activity; 2 synthetic substance which works like a natural hormone ‖ **hor·mo′nal** *adj*

horn /hôrn′/ [OE] *n* 1 bony, often pointed, projection growing on the head of various hoofed animals; 2 any similar projection, as the antler of a deer, tentacle of a snail, etc.; 3 bony substance of which animals' horns are made; 4 anything suggestive of a horn, as the pointed end of an anvil, the pommel of a saddle, the ends of a crescent moon, etc.; 5 *mus* a wind instrument; b French horn; 6 device sounded to give warning; 7 **blow one's own horn** to boast; 8 **lock horns** to fight each other ‖ *vi* 9 **horn in** *slang* to interrupt or intrude ‖ **horned′** *adj*

Horn, Cape *n* southernmost point of South America

horn′bill′ *n* any of several large Old World birds (family Bucerotidae) with large bills which in many species bear hornlike protuberances

hor·net /hôrn′it/ [OE *hyrnet*] *n* any of several large stinging wasps of the family Vespidae

horn′ of plen′ty *n* cornucopia

horn′pipe′ *n* lively dance, esp. popular with sailors, and music for it

horn′y *adj* (-i·er; -i·est) 1 made of horn; 2 having horns; 3 hard, like horn, calloused; 4 *slang* lustful

ho·rol·o·gy /hərol′əjē/ [< Gk *hora* time] *n* science of measuring time or of making timepieces ‖ **ho·rol′o·gist**

or **ho·rol′o·ger** *n* ‖ **hor·o·log·ic (-i·cal)** /hôr′əloj′ik(əl), hor′-/ *adj*

hor·o·scope /hôr′əskōp′, hor′-/ [Gk *horoskopos*] *n* 1 chart of the heavens showing the signs of the zodiac and the position of the planets; 2 prediction of the future based on such a chart

hor·ren·dous /horen′dəs, hôr-/ [< L *horrendus*] *adj* dreadful, horrible

hor·ri·ble /hor′ibəl, hôr′-/ [L *horribilis*] *adj* 1 terrible; causing horror; 2 severe; disagreeable ‖ **hor′ri·bly** *adv* ‖ **syn** awful, terrific, fearful, frightful, abominable

hor·rid /hor′id, hôr′-/ [L *horridus*] *adj* 1 horrible; 2 *colloq* disagreeable, unpleasant

hor·ri·fy /hor′ifī′, hôr′-/ [< L *horrificare*] *v* (-fied) *vt* to fill or strike with horror

hor·ror /hor′ər, hôr′-/ [L] *n* 1 excessive fear or abhorrence; extreme dread; 2 great aversion, antipathy, or disgust; 3 that which causes horror; 4 *colloq* something bad or in bad taste ‖ **syn** fright, fear, dread, terror, alarm, dismay, panic, apprehension, consternation, disquietude, affright ‖ **discr** *Fear* is the general term, and names a painful emotion springing from threatened danger or evil, accompanied by a desire to flee from it. *Fright* and *terror* are extreme *fear*; *fright* is sudden, shocking, but usually not lasting; *terror* is stark, violent, overwhelming. *Dread* is very great *fear*, aroused by an overpowering distrust of the future. *Apprehension*, akin to *dread*, is a more nervous and agitated, though really less serious, *fear*. *Disquietude* also is experienced over the future; it is a condition of worry, lack of peace, unrest. *Alarm* is an excited anticipation of danger. *Dismay* and *consternation* name violent states of *fear* in which the mind is confused, the heart discouraged, the future faced with helpless *terror*. *Panic* is excessive, frantic *fear*, often experienced by large numbers over a trifling cause or no cause at all. *Horror* is a terrified *fear* tinged by a shuddering abhorrence and repulsion

hors d'oeu·vre /ôr′ durv′/ [F = outside the work] *n* appetizer, as a canapé, served before dinner or at cocktail parties

horse /hôrs′/ [OE *hors*] *n* 1 large solid-hoofed quadruped (*Equus caballus*) with long mane and tail, used for riding or drawing burdens; 2 adult male of this animal; 3 cavalry; 4 framework or block for the support of anything; 5 *gymnastics* padded block on four legs used for vaulting, etc.; 6 *slang* heroin; 7 **beat** or **flog a dead horse** to continue to discuss a point that has been irrevocably settled; **8 from the horse's mouth** *slang* from an unimpeachable source; **9 hold one's horses** to check one's impatience; **10 horse of another color** something different; **11 play the horses** *colloq* to bet on horse races ‖ *vi* **12 horse around** *slang* to indulge in horseplay

horse'back' *n* **1 on horseback** astride a horse ‖ *adv* **2** on horseback

horse'car' *n* **1** streetcar drawn by a horse or horses; **2** car for transporting horses

horse' chest'nut *n* **1** tree (*Aesculus hippocastanum*) with large clusters of white or pink blossoms; **2** its nutlike seed

horse'flesh' *n* **1** horse meat; **2** riding and racing horses

horse'fly' *n* (**-flies**) any of several large flies (family Tabanidae) which suck blood from horses and cattle

horse'hair' *n* **1** hair of a horse, esp. from its mane or tail; **2** fabric woven of these hairs

horse'hide' *n* **1** hide of a horse; **2** leather made from it; **3** *slang* baseball

horse' lat'i·tudes *npl* latitudes about 30° N and S, marked by variable winds and clear weather

horse'laugh' *n* guffaw, esp. of derision ‖ also *vi*

horse'man *n* (**-men** /-mən/) **1** person on horseback; **2** one skilled in riding or caring for horses ‖ **horse'man·ship'** *n*

horse' op'er·a *n* hair-raising movie or radio play dealing with cowboy life in the Old West

horse'play' *n* rough boisterous fun

horse'play'er *n* one who bets on horse races

horse'pow'er *n* unit of power equal to 550 foot-pounds of work per second or 746 watts

horse'pow'er-hour' *n* unit of work, equal to the work done by one horsepower acting for one hour

horse'rad'ish *n* **1** large-leaved plant (*Armoracia rusticana*) of the mustard family; **2** its ground root, used as a relish

horse' sense' *n colloq* common sense

horse'shoe' *n* **1** U-shaped metal shoe to protect the hoof of a horse; **2** something U-shaped; **3 horseshoes** *nsg* game in which the players toss horseshoes at a stake

horse' trade' *n colloq* shrewd give-and-take and bargaining ‖ **horse'-trade'** *vi*

horse'whip' *n* **1** long whip for controlling a horse ‖ *v* (**-whipped**; **-whip·ping**) *vt* **2** to beat with a horsewhip

horse'wom'an *n* (**-wom'en**) **1** woman on horseback; **2** woman skilled in riding horses

hors'y *adj* (**-i·er**; **-i·est**) **1** pert. to or characteristic of horses; **2** (people)

devoted to horses, riding, breeding, racing, or fox hunting

hor·ta·to·ry /hôrt'ətôr'ē, -tōr'-/ [< L *hortari* to exhort] *adj* exhorting; urging some course of action

hor'ti·cul'ture /hôrt'ē-/ [< L *hortus* garden] *n* art or science of cultivating gardens or orchards ‖ **hor'ti·cul'tur·ist** *n* ‖ **hor'ti·cul'tur·al** *adj*

Ho·rus /hôr'əs, hōr'-/ *n* Egyptian solar deity, usually represented as a falcon or as a man with a falcon's head

ho·san·na /hōzan'ə/ [Gk < Heb *hoshi 'ahnna* save, we pray] *n* **1** shout of praise and glory to God ‖ *interj* **2** praise be to God!

hose /hōz/ [OE *hosa*] *n* (*pl* **hose**) **1** stocking, sock; **2** formerly, hip-length tights worn by men ‖ *n* (**hos·es**) **3** flexible tube for conveying liquids ‖ *vt* **4** to water with a hose; **5 hose down** to wash off or drench with a hose

ho·sier·y /hōzh'ərē/ *n* stockings in general

hos·pice /hos'pis/ [F < L *hospitium*] *n* shelter for travelers or pilgrims

hos·pi·ta·ble /hosp'itəbəl/ [< LL *hospitare* to entertain] *adj* **1** kind or attentive to guests or strangers; **2** receptive ‖ **hos'pi·ta·bly** *adv*

hos·pi·tal /hosp'itəl/ [LL *hospitale* place for guests] *n* institution for the treatment of the sick or wounded

hos'pi·tal'i·ty /-tal'-/ *n* (**-ties**) *n* act or practice of being hospitable

hos'pi·tal·ize' *vt* to place in a hospital ‖ **hos'pi·tal·i·za'tion** *n*

host¹ /hōst'/ [OF < L *hostis* enemy] *n* great number; throng

host² [MF *oste* < L *hospes* (-*itis*)] *n* **1** one who entertains guests; **2** innkeeper; **3** organism that gives nourishment to a parasite ‖ *vt* **4** to act as host to

Host /hōst'/ [LL *hostia* sacrifice] *n* consecrated bread or wafer used at Communion

hos·tage /host'ij/ [OF < L *obses* (-*idis*)] *n* person who remains in the hands of another as a pledge for the fulfillment of certain conditions

hos·tel /host'əl/ [OF < LL *hospitale*] *n* inn or hotel

hos'tel·ry [MF *ostelerie*] *n* (**-ries**) inn or hotel

host·ess /hōst'is/ *n* **1** female host; **2** woman employed in a restaurant to greet and seat patrons; **3** woman who looks after the comfort of travelers, as on an airplane

hos·tile /host'əl/ [L *hostilis*] *adj* **1** belonging to or characteristic of an enemy; **2** unfriendly, antagonistic

hos·til'i·ty /-til'-/ *n* (**-ties**) **1** state or condition of being hostile; **2** opposition; antagonism; **3 hostilities** *pl* warfare ‖ SYN bitterness, vindictiveness, animosity (see *enmity*)

hos·tler /(h)os'lər/ [OF *hostelier* innkeeper] *n* **1** one who takes care of horses at an inn or stable; **2** one who takes care of railroad locomotives after a run

hot /hot'/ [OE *hāt*] *adj* (**hot·ter; hot·test**) **1** having a high temperature; **2** producing the sensation of heat; **3** fiery; passionate; **4** violent; furious; **5** eager, enthusiastic; **6** lustful, sensual; **7** pungent, acrid; **8** fresh, strong, as *a hot scent;* **9** near to the object sought; **10** *slang* (person or thing) sought by the police; **11** electrically charged; **12** radioactive; **13** *slang* lucky, as *hot dice;* **14** much in demand, popular; **15** fresh, just out, as *hot news;* **16** **make it hot for** *colloq* to make things unpleasant for || *adv* **17** in a hot manner; while hot || **hot'ly** *adv*

hot' *air' slang* empty talk or writing

hot'bed' *n* **1** bed of earth covered with glass and heated usu. by manure to force the growth of plants; **2** any place or condition that promotes growth or activity, esp. of something bad

hot' cake' *n* **1** pancake; **2** **sell like hot cakes** to be sold effortlessly and in large quantities

hot' cross' bun' *n* bun marked with a cross, eaten during Lent

hot' dog' *n colloq* frankfurter, esp. one served in a split roll

ho·tel /hōtel'/ [F < OF *hostel* inn] *n* establishment providing lodging to travelers, and often eating and banquet facilities to the general public

hot'foot' *vi* **1** to go in haste || *n* (**-foots**) **2** surreptitious insertion of a lighted match between the sole and upper of someone's shoe

hot'head' *n* impetuous or fiery-tempered person || **hot'head'ed** *adj*

hot'house' *n* (**-hous·es** /-hou'ziz/) greenhouse

hot' line' *n* **1** telephone line that is always open and ready for immediate talk between two heads of government in case of extreme tension and the threat of atomic war; **2** similar line used for various kinds of emergency communications

hot' plate' *n* portable appliance for cooking, usu. heated by an electric coil

hot' po·ta'to *n colloq* difficult situation, having unpleasant repercussions

hot' rod' *n slang* old car with a souped-up engine || **hot' rod'der** *n*

hot' seat' *n slang* **1** electric chair; **2** embarrassing or ticklish situation

hot'shot' *n slang* highly efficient, aggressive, and successful person

hot' spot' *n* **1** *colloq* nightclub; **2** place of threatening conflict

hot' stuff' *n slang* **1** something extraordinary; **2** person who is extraordinary or thinks himself to be extraordinary

Hot·ten·tot /hot'əntot'/ [D] *n* **1** one of a South African race of men related to the Bushmen; **2** their language || also *adj*

hound /hound'/ [OE *hund* dog] *n* **1** any of various breeds of dog, typically droop-eared and deep-voiced, that hunt by scent or sight; **2** any dog || *vt* **3** to pursue unpityingly; **4** to nag, drive

hound's' tooth' *n* fabric pattern of broken checks || **hound's'-tooth'** *adj*

hour /ou'(ə)r/ [AF *oure* < Gk *hora*] *n* **1** 24th part of a day; 60 minutes; **2** time of day as marked by a clock; **3** particular or appointed time, as *the hour of adjournment;* **4** **hours** *pl* fixed or stated times for daily work, etc., as *office hours;* **5** **after hours** after the regular hours, as of work or business

hour'glass' *n* device for measuring time by the trickling of sand from an upper to a lower glass chamber through a narrow neck

hou·ri /hŏŏr'ē, hou'rē/ [F < Pers *hūrī*] *n* one of the beautiful maidens provided to Muslim men in paradise

hour'ly *adv* **1** every hour; **2** often || *adj* **3** occurring or done every hour; **4** frequent

house /hous'/ [OE *hūs*] *n* (**hous·es** /hou'ziz/) **1** building for residence; place of abode; **2** household; **3** building for some particular purpose, as *a house of worship;* **4** building in which a legislative or deliberative assembly meets; **5** business firm or place of business; **6** theater or its audience; **7** **House, a** family, esp. a reigning family, as *the House of Hanover;* **b** legislative assembly, as *the House of Representatives;* **8** **bring down the house** *colloq* to evoke thunderous applause; **9** **keep house** to manage a household; **10** **on the house** without charge || *adj* **11** of or pert. to a house; **12** suited for a house || /houz'/ *vt* **13** to provide lodging for; **14** to shelter; **15** to store

house' ar·rest' *n* confinement of an arrested person to his house

house'boat' *n* barge fitted up as a floating residence

house'break'er *n* one who breaks into and enters another's dwelling with intent to commit a felony || **house'-break'ing** *n*

house'bro'ken *adj* (pet) trained to excrete out of doors or in a place set aside

house'coat' *n* woman's long, one-piece garment for informal wear at home

house' cur'rent *n* the electricity supplied, as by a public utility, for domestic use, usually in the form of alternating current at sixty cycles

house' de·tec'tive *n* detective employed by a hotel to prevent lawbreaking by employees or patrons

house'fly' n (-files) common domestic fly (*Musca domestica*) breeding chiefly in manure and garbage

house'hold' n a house and all the people living in it || also *adj*

house'hold'er n 1 head of a household; 2 one who occupies a house as his own dwelling

house'hold word' n common, everyday word or phrase

house'keep'er n 1 woman who manages a household; 2 woman who takes care of a house || **house'keep'-ing** n

house'lights' npl lights that illuminate an auditorium before and after the performance

house'moth'er n woman in charge of a residence for young people, esp. young women, as female students or members of a sorority

house' of cards' n insubstantial plan or idea subject to imminent collapse

House' of Com'mons n lower house of the British or Canadian parliament

house' of ill' re-pute' n brothel

House' of Lords' n upper nonelective house of the British parliament

House' of Rep·re·sent'a·tives n lower house of the U.S. Congress, and of many states and some countries

house' par'ty n entertainment of guests in one's home overnight or for several nights

house'top' n 1 roof of a house; 2 **from the housetops** publicly; to all the world

house' trail'er n automotive vehicle in the form of a trailer, equipped with living quarters

house'wares' npl kitchen utensils, glassware, and other household equipment

house'warm'ing n party celebrating occupancy of a new house

house'wife' n (-wives /-vz/) 1 woman who manages the domestic affairs of her own household || /huz'if/ n (-wives /-ifs/) 2 small sewing pouch || **house'wife'ly** adj

house'work' n work connected with running a household

hous·ing /houz'iŋ/ n 1 lodging or shelter; 2 act of giving lodging or shelter; 3 casing or recess designed to receive or support a mechanism

Hous·ton /hyōōs'tən/ n 1 Sam (1793–1863) U.S. soldier and statesman, president of the Republic of Texas 1836–38; 2 city in SE Texas (1,232,-802)

hove /hōv'/ pt & pp of **heave**

hov·el /huv'əl, hov'-/ [ME] n 1 wretched and miserable little dwelling; 2 open shed for cattle

hov·er /huv'ər, hov'-/ [ME *hoveren*] vi 1 to flutter over or about; 2 to linger about uncertainly; 3 to waver

hov'er·craft' n motorized vehicle that travels on a cushion of air a few feet above the surface of land or water

how /hou'/ [OE *hū*] adv 1 in what manner; 2 to what degree or extent; 3 for what reason; 4 in what condition; 5 by what name; 6 with what meaning; 7 at what price; 8 used as an intensifier, as *how sad!*; 9 **how come?** *colloq* why?

how·be'it adv 1 *archaic* nevertheless || conj 2 obs although

how·dah /hou'də/ [< Hindi < Ar] n canopied seat on the back of an elephant or camel

how-do-you-do /hou'də-yədōō'/ also **how-de-do** /hou'dĕdōō'/ n fine or **pretty how-do-you-do** *ironic* very unpleasant situation or state of affairs

how·ev'er conj 1 in whatever manner; 2 to whatever degree or extent || adv 3 notwithstanding; yet; still

how·itz·er /hou'itsər/ [G *Haubitze* < Czech *houfnice* catapult] n short cannon throwing shells at a high angle

howl /houl'/ [ME *houlen*] vi 1 to utter a loud wailing cry like a wolf; 2 to utter a similar cry of pain or distress; 3 to make a sound like howling, as the wind || vt 4 to utter with howls; 5 **howl down** to suppress by howling || n 6 cry of a dog or wolf; 7 cry of distress or anguish; 8 loud laugh or shout of derision

howl'er n 1 one who or that which howls; 2 embarrassing or humorous blunder

howl'ing adj 1 uttering howls; 2 *colloq* tremendous (success)

how·so·ev'er adv 1 in whatsoever manner; 2 to whatever extent

hoy·den /hoid'ən/ [prob < MD *heiden* heathen] n rude boisterous girl; tomboy || **hoy'den·ish** adj

Hoyle, Ed·mond /ed'mənd hoil'/ n 1 (1672–1769) English authority on card games; 2 **according to Hoyle** according to the rules

hp, h.p., HP, H.P. horsepower

HQ, h.q., H.Q. headquarters

hr. hour

H.R.H. His (or Her) Royal Highness

ht. height

Hts. Heights

hub /hub'/ [prob < *hob* peg] n 1 central part of a wheel into which the axle fits and around which it revolves; 2 any central part; 3 center of activity and interest

hub·bub /hub'ub/ [< Celt] n 1 loud confusion of voices; 2 uproar, tumult || SYN (see *noise*)

hub'cap' n detachable metal cap that fits over the hub of an automobile wheel

hu·bris /h(y)ōō'bris/ [Gk = insolence] n overbearing pride

huck'le·ber'ry /huk'əl-/ [dial. var of *whortleberry*] n (-ries) 1 any of a genus (*Gaylussacia*) of low-growing shrubs bearing a berrylike fruit; **2** its berry

huck·ster /huk'stər/ [< obs huck haggle] *n* **1** peddler of small articles or of fruits and vegetables; **2** *colloq* person who works in advertising ‖ *vt* **3** to peddle

hud·dle /hud'əl/ [?] *vt & vi* **1** to crowd or draw together ‖ *n* **2** crowd or heap; **3** private conference; **4** *football* conference in a circle by the offensive team, usu. before each play

Hud·son /hud'sən/ [Henry *Hudson* (1576?–1611) Eng explorer] *n* river in E New York, flowing south into New York Bay

Hud'son Bay' *n* arm of the N Atlantic extending into E Canada

Hud'son seal' *n* muskrat fur dyed to resemble seal

hue[1] /hyōō'/ [OE *hiw*] *n* **1** color; **2** shade or tint ‖ SYN tint, shade, dye (see *color*)

hue[2] [MF *hu*] *n* **hue and cry** general outcry of alarm or pursuit

-hued /-hōōd'/ *adj comb form* -colored, as *red-hued*

huff /huf'/ [imit] *vi* **1** to puff, breathe heavily; **2** to become angry or offended ‖ *n* **3 in a huff** in a fit of ill humor or petulance ‖ **huff'y** *adj* (-i·er; -i·est)

hug /hug'/ [?] *v* (**hugged; hug·ging**) *vt* **1** to embrace closely; **2** to hold fast to, cling to; **3** to keep close to, as *to hug the shore* ‖ *n* **4** close embrace

huge /(h)yōōj'/ [OF *ahuge*] *adj* great, vast, of great bulk ‖ **huge'ly** *adv* ‖ **huge'ness** *n* ‖ SYN bulky, vast, colossal, immense (see *enormous*)

Hu·go, Vic·tor /hyōōg'ō/ *n* (1802–85) French poet, novelist, and dramatist

Hu·gue·not /hyōōg'ənot'/ [F] *n* French Protestant of the 16th and 17th centuries

huh /hu/ *interj* expressing surprise, disbelief, contempt, etc.

hu·la /hōōl'ə/ or **hu'la-hu'la** [Hawaiian] *n* native Hawaiian dance characterized by hip-swinging and intricate movement of the arms

hu'la skirt' *n* grass skirt worn by hula dancers

hulk /hulk'/ [OE *hulc*] *n* **1** body of an old or dismantled ship; **2** any unwieldy object, ship, or person; **3** wrecked or burned out shell, as of a building or vehicle

hulk'ing *adj* bulky; unwieldy, clumsy

hull /hul'/ [OE *hulu* husk] *n* **1** outer covering, as of various fruits, vegetables, and grains; husk; **2** hollow main body of a vessel, flying boat, or dirigible ‖ *vt* **3** to remove the hulls from (peas, etc.)

hul·la·ba·loo /hul'əbəlōō'/ [perh < *hullo* + Sc *baloo* lullaby] *n* uproar, tumult

hum /hum'/ [ME *hummen*] *v*

(**hummed; hum·ming**) *vi* **1** to make a continuous droning sound; **2** to sing with the lips closed; **3** to be continuously active and busy ‖ *vt* **4** to sing by humming ‖ *n* **5** sound of humming

hu·man /(h)yōōm'ən/ [L *humanus*] *adj* **1** of or pert. to man; **2** characteristic of or having the nature of mankind ‖ *n* **3** human being ‖ **hu'man·ness** *n* ‖ SYN *adj* (see *humane*)

hu·mane /(h)yōōmān'/ *adj* **1** kind; sympathetic; compassionate; **2** pert. to humanistic studies ‖ **hu·mane'ly** *adv* ‖ **hu·mane'ness** *n* ‖ SYN human ‖ DISCR That is human which characterizes man as such; that is *humane* which is actively benevolent. All persons are *human;* kindly persons are *humane*

hu'man·ism *n* **1** system of thought or action devoted to human interests and ideals; **2** also **Humanism** study of the cultures of classical Greece and Rome, instituted during the Renaissance by scholars who emphasized secular and individualistic thought ‖ **hu'man·ist** also **Hu'man·ist** *n* ‖ **hu'man·is'tic** *adj*

hu·man·i·tar·i·an /(h)yōōman'iter'ē·ən/ *n* **1** philanthropist; person devoted to improving the human condition; **2** one who bases religion on love for mankind rather than on faith in a supernatural revelation; **3** one who emphasizes the human nature of Jesus ‖ also *adj* ‖ **hu·man'i·tar'i·an·ism** *n*

hu·man·i·ty [L *humanitas*] *n* (-ties) **1** mankind as a whole; **2** state or quality of being human; **3** quality of being humane; **4 the humanities** *pl* a classical studies; **b** study of literature, art, and philosophy, as opposed to the sciences ‖ SYN kindness, sympathy (see *benevolence*)

hu'man·ize' *vt* **1** to make human or humane ‖ *vi* **2** to become human or humane

hu'man·kind' *n* mankind collectively

hu'man·ly *adv* **1** from a human viewpoint; **2** in a human manner; **3** within human power or knowledge

hum·ble /humb'əl/ [OF < L *humilis* lowly] *adj* **1** having a low estimate of oneself; modest; **2** lowly in condition; unassuming ‖ *vt* **3** to abase, humiliate; **4** to make humble ‖ **hum'ble·ness** *n* ‖ **hum'bly** *adv* ‖ SYN *adj* unassuming, subservient, self-depreciatory, modest, poor, plain, lowly, unpretentious, obscure, meek (see *lowly*) ‖ ANT *adj* haughty, proud, assertive

hum'ble pie' [earlier (an) *umble pie* < (a) *numble pie* < obs *numbles* entrails] *n* **eat humble pie** to make apologies, humiliate oneself

hum'bug' [?] *n* **1** fraud, sham; **2** impostor ‖ *v* (**-bugged; -bug-ging**) *vt* 3 to deceive, swindle

hum-ding-er /hum′diŋ′ər/ *n slang* someone or something very good of its kind

hum′drum′ [rhyming compound of *hum*] *adj* 1 dull, monotonous ‖ *n* 2 monotony

hu-mer-us /hyōōm′ərəs/ [L = shoulder] *n* (**-i** /-ī′/) bone of the upper arm, from the shoulder to the elbow ‖ **hu′mer-al** *adj*

hu-mid /(h)yōōm′id/ [L *humidus*] *adj* 1 damp, moist; 2 containing a relatively large amount of water vapor

hu-mid′i-fy *v* (**-fied**) *vt* to increase the moisture in; make humid

hu-mid′i-ty *n* 1 amount of water vapor in the air; 2 dampness

hu′mi-dor′ /-idôr′/ *n* container for cigars with provision for keeping them moist

hu-mil·l-ate /(h)yōōmil′ē-āt′/ [< L *humilis* low] *vt* to mortify, put to shame ‖ SYN humble, abase, mortify, disgrace, degrade

hu-mil′i-a′tion *n* 1 act of humiliating; 2 state of being humiliated ‖ SYN embarrassment, chagrin, disappointment, abasement, mortification

hu-mil′i-ty *n* (**-ties**) 1 state or quality of being humble; 2 humble act

hum′ming-bird′ /hum′iŋ-/ *n* any of many tiny, brilliantly colored birds (family Trochilidae), with long slender bills, whose rapidly moving wings enable them to hover while drinking nectar from flowers

hum-mock /hum′ək/ [?] *n* small hill or rounded mound

hu-mon-gous /(h)yōōmoŋ′gəs/ [prob < *huge* + *monstrous* + *great* + *tremendous*] *adj slang* huge, enormous

hu-mor /(h)yōōm′ər/ [L = fluid] *n* 1 state of mind, mood; 2 caprice; 3 capacity for perceiving or expressing what is amusing or funny; 4 any amusing element in a situation; 5 any of the four bodily fluids formerly believed to determine one's health and disposition ‖ *vt* 6 to yield to the mood of; indulge ‖ SYN *n* mood, disposition, wit ‖ DISCR *Wit* is a flashing perception that darts swiftly and unexpectedly among ideas, situations, or expressions, finding amusing incongruities, contrasts, or comical aspects which were not foreseen. *Wit* is keen, laughter-provoking, sometimes cutting in its deadly faculty for hitting upon a hidden truth. *Humor* is neither darting nor occasional, for it is more a turn of one's nature, a specific tendency of the disposition. *Wit* is intellectual; *humor* is sympathetic. Hence, *humor* is kindly, its mirth is of a generously human sort

hu′mor-ist *n* writer or teller of humorous stories

hu′mor-ous *adj* amusing, droll, funny ‖ **hu′mor-ous-ly** *adv* ‖ **hu′mor-ous-ness** *n* ‖ SYN amusing, facetious, funny, jocose, whimsical, witty, sportive ‖ ANT mournful, serious, sad, sober

hump /hump′/ [?] *n* 1 rounded protuberance, esp. that on the back of a camel or that formed by a crooked spine in man; 2 hummock; 3 **over the hump** past the worst part ‖ *vt* 4 to hunch (the back)

hump′back′ *n* 1 crooked back; 2 hunchback ‖ **hump′backed′** *adj*

humph /humf′/ *interj* 1 conventionalized representation of a snortlike sound expressing disgust or disbelief ‖ *n* 2 this exclamation ‖ *vi* 3 to utter a humph

hu-mus /(h)yōōm′əs/ [L = ground] *n* dark substance in soil formed by the decay of organic matter

Hun /hun′/ [LL *Hunnus*] *n* 1 one of a warlike people of Asia who overran and devastated Europe in the fifth century; 2 marauding, destructive person; vandal; 3 German soldier at the time of the wars with Germany

hunch /hunch′/ [?] *vt* 1 to bend or round (the back) ‖ *vi* 2 to lunge or bend forward ‖ *n* 3 hump; 4 *colloq* instinctive feeling or premonition

hunch′back′ *n* 1 person with a crooked back; 2 hunched back ‖ **hunch′-backed′** *adj*

hun-dred /hun′drid/ [OE] *n* ten times ten (100; C) ‖ also *adj*

hun′dred-fold′ *adj* 1 having 100 times as much or as many ‖ *adv* 2 a hundred times as much or as many

hun′dredth *n* 1 the one next in order after the ninety-ninth; 2 one of one hundred equal parts; 3 position of the second digit to the right of the decimal point ‖ also *adj*

hun′dred-weight′ *n* 20th part of a ton, equal to 100 pounds in the U.S. and 112 pounds in Britain

hung /huŋ′/ *pt* & *pp* of **hang**

Hung. 1 Hungarian; 2 Hungary

Hun-ga-ry /huŋ′gərē/ *n* republic in central Europe (10,231,000; 35,919 sq.mi.; cap. Budapest) ‖ **Hun-gar-i-an** /huŋger′ē-ən/ *adj* & *n*

hun-ger /huŋ′gər/ [OE *hungor*] *n* 1 appetite or desire for food; 2 discomfort caused by not eating; 3 any strong desire ‖ *vi* 4 to feel hunger; 5 to have a longing for something

hun′ger strike′ *n* continued refusal to eat, practiced as a protest or for publicity

hung′ ju′ry *n colloq* jury that cannot come to an agreement

hun-gry /huŋ′grē/ *adj* (**-gri-er; -gri-est**) 1 having a keen appetite; 2 feeling uneasiness for want of food; 3 eagerly desirous ‖ **hun′gri-ly** *adv*

hunk /huŋk/ [Flem *hunke*] *n colloq* large piece or chunk

hunk·y·do·ry /huŋk'ēdôr'ē, -dōr'-/ [?] *adj slang* fine; leaving nothing to be desired

hunt /hunt'/ [OE *huntian*] *vt* 1 to strive to catch or kill (game or wild animals); 2 to go through in search of something; 3 to use in the chase, as hounds; 4 to persecute, hound, follow closely; 5 to search after || *vi* 6 to follow the chase; 7 **hunt for** or **after** to seek || *n* 8 hunting of game or wild animals; 9 association of huntsmen; 10 search; 11 pursuit || SYN *v* seek, track, pursue, search, scour, follow

hunt'er *n* 1 one who hunts; 2 horse or hound trained for hunting

hunt'ing *n* 1 pursuit of game as a sport; 2 diligent pursuit of any object; 3 constant wavering of motion or speed about a given value as if in search of equilibrium

hunt'ress *n* woman that hunts

hunts'man /-mən/ *n* (-men /-mən/) 1 hunter; 2 one who has charge of the hounds in a hunt

hur·dle /hurd'əl/ [OE *hyrdel*] *n* 1 barrier to be leaped over in steeplechasing and racing; 2 obstacle || *vt* 3 to leap over; 4 to overcome || *vi* 5 to jump over an obstacle or hurdle

hur·dy·gur·dy /hurd'ēgurd'ē/ [prob imit] *n* (-dies) any musical instrument played by turning a crank

hurl /hurl'/ [ME *hurlen*] *vt* 1 to throw with violence; 2 to cast down; 3 to utter with vehemence; 4 to throw, fling || *n* 5 violent throw; fling; pitch || **hurl'er** *n* || SYN throw, drive, impel (see *cast*)

hurl·ing *n* Irish game resembling field hockey

hurl·y·burl·y /hur'lēbur'lē/ [?] *n* (-ies) tumult, uproar, hubbub

Hu·ron, Lake /hyŏŏr'ən, -on/ *n* one of the Great Lakes, between Michigan and Ontario

hur·rah /hərä', -rô'/ [G *hurra* interj] 1 expressing joy, triumph, encouragement, applause, etc. || *n* 2 exclamation of hurrah || *vi* 3 to shout hurrah

hur·ri·cane /hur'ĭkān'/ [Sp *huracán* < Carib] *n* violent cyclonic storm of the North Atlantic originating in the tropics

hur·ry /hur'ē/ [ME *horyen*] *v* (-ried) *vt* 1 to urge on; impel to greater speed; 2 to expedite || *vi* 3 to act or move with haste || *n* 4 haste; 5 urgency; precipitation || **hur'ried·ly** *adv* || SYN *v* dispatch, rush, expedite, quicken

hurt /hurt'/ [OF *hurter* to bruise] *v* (**hurt**) *vt* 1 to inflict pain on; wound; 2 to harm, impair; 3 to grieve, offend || *vi* 4 to be painful; 5 to suffer physical or mental pain || *n* 6 wound, injury; 7 damage, loss || SYN *n* wound, pain, bruise, loss, detriment,

damage, slight, stain, wrong (see *injury*)

hur·tle /hurt'əl/ [ME *hurtlen*] *vt* 1 to fling or impel violently || *vi* 2 to rush violently and with a rushing noise

hus·band /huz'bənd/ [OE *húsbonda* master of the house] *n* 1 married man in relation to his wife || *vt* 2 to manage with economy, conserve

hus'band·man /-mən/ *n* (-men /-mən/) farmer

hus'band·ry *n* 1 farming; 2 economical management; frugality

hush /hush/ [ME *hussht* quiet] *interj* 1 be still!, silence! || *vt* 2 to make silent; 3 to soothe, comfort; 4 **hush up** to suppress, conceal || *vi* 5 to be or become silent || *n* 6 silence; stillness

hush'-hush' *adj colloq* secret; confidential

hush' mon'ey *n* bribe to ensure silence or secrecy

husk /husk'/ [ME *huske*] *n* 1 dry outer covering of certain fruits or seeds, esp. of an ear of corn; 2 any rough and worthless outer covering || *vt* 3 to remove the husk from

husk'y[1] *adj* (-i·er; -i·est) 1 rough or hoarse (voice); 2 strong, burly || **husk'i·ly** *adv* || **husk'i·ness** *n*

hus'ky[2] [prob < *Eskimo*] *n* (-kies) Eskimo dog

hus·sar /hŏŏzär'/ [Hung *huszár* < OSerbian *husar* < It *corsaro* corsair'] *n* light-armed cavalryman of European armies, usu. wearing a colorful uniform

hus·sy /huz'ē, hus'ē/ [OE *húswíf* housewife] *n* (-sies) 1 bold or loose woman; 2 mischievous or misbehaving girl

hus·tings /hust'iŋz/ [OE < ODa *hústhing* house assembly] *nsg & npl* 1 electioneering platform; 2 proceedings of an election; 3 on the hustings campaigning for election

hus·tle /hus'əl/ [D *husselen* to shake] *vt* 1 to cause to move hurriedly and roughly; 2 to pressure (someone) into buying or doing something; 3 to get (money) by aggressive means or by begging || *vi* 4 to go or act rapidly; 5 *slang* to solicit clients (said of a prostitute) || *n* 6 energetic activity and speed in one's work

hus'tler *n* 1 one who hustles; 2 *colloq* person with energy and drive; 3 *slang* petty swindler; 4 *slang* prostitute

hut /hut'/ [F *hutte* < MHG *hütte*] *n* small house or cabin of simple construction

hutch /huch'/ [ME *hucche*] *n* 1 bin for storing grain, etc.; 2 coop or pen for animals; 3 hut, hovel

huz·za or **huz·zah** /həzä'/ [< earlier *hussa* sailor's cry] *interj* 1 hurrah! || *n* 2 hurrah || *vi* 3 to hurrah

hwan /(h)wän′/ *n* monetary unit of Korea (North and South)

hy·a·cinth /hī′əsinth′/ [Gk *hyakinthos*] *n* any of a genus (*Hyacinthus*) of plants of the lily family with sweet-scented bell-shaped flowers

hy·brid /hī′brid/ [L *hybrida* offspring of tame sow and wild boar] *n* 1 offspring of animals or plants of different species; 2 anything formed of heterogeneous elements || also *adj* || **hy′brid·ize′** *vt & vi* || **hy′brid·ism** *n*

hy·dr- or **hy·dro-** [Gk *hydor*] *comb form* 1 water; 2 hydrogen

hy′dra-head′ed /hī′drə-/ [Gk *Hydra* mythological sea serpent with 9 heads, each of which was replaced by 2 if cut off] *adj* 1 having many facets, branches, or divisions; 2 presenting numerous problems or difficulties

hy·dran·ge·a /hīdrān′jē·ə, -drān′-/ [*hydr-* + Gk *angeia* vessels] *n* any of a genus (*Hydrangea*) of shrubs or small trees with large showy clusters of flowers of many delicate colors

hy′drant /hī′drənt [< *hydr-* + *-ant*] *n* 1 standpipe with a valve and spout, usu. at the curb, for drawing water from a main for fire engines; 2 water faucet

hy·drate /hī′drāt/ [< *hydr-*] *n chem* 1 compound containing water || *vt & vi* 2 to combine with water || **hy·dra′tion** *n*

hy·drau·lic /hīdrôl′ik, -drol′-/ [Gk *hydraulikos* pert. to a water organ] *adj* 1 operated by the movement or pressure of a liquid; 2 of or pert. to hydraulics || *n* 3 **hy·drau′lics** *sg* science that deals with the action of water or other liquids in motion

hy·drau′lic brake′ *n* brake which is operated by a compressed fluid

hy·dric /hī′drik/ *adj* 1 pert. to or combined with hydrogen; 2 pert. to or requiring much moisture

hy·dride /hī′drīd, -drid/ *n* binary compound of hydrogen with an element or radical

hy·dro- *comb form* var of **hydr-**

hy′dro·car′bon /hī′drə-/ *n* one of a large and important group of compounds containing only hydrogen and carbon

hy′dro·chlo′ric ac′id /-klôr′ik, -klōr′-ik/ [< *hydro-* + *chlorine*] *n* colorless suffocating gas —HCl— soluble in water, much used in industry

hy′dro·dy·nam′ics *nsg* dynamics that deals with the action of fluids in motion || **hy′dro·dy·nam′ic** *adj*

hy′dro·e·lec′tric *adj* pert. to electric energy generated by water power

hy′dro·foil′ *n* 1 streamlined surface whose purpose is to support a body moving through the water; 2 wing-like attachment with such a surface, designed to raise the hull of a vessel in motion; 3 vessel with hydrofoils

hy′dro·gen /hī′drəjən/ *n* colorless, odorless, inflammable gaseous element (**H**; at.no. 1; at.wt. 1.00797), the lightest substance known; a constituent of all acids, of water, and of most organic compounds || **hy·drog·e·nous** /hīdroj′ənəs/ *adj*

hy′dro·gen bomb′ *n* extremely powerful bomb that derives its energy from the thermonuclear fusion of hydrogen isotopes

hy′dro·gen per·ox′ide *n* viscid, colorless, unstable liquid —H₂O₂— used in dilute solution as an antiseptic and as a bleach

hy′dro·gen sul′fide *n* colorless inflammable poisonous gas —H₂S— having the odor of rotten eggs

hy·drol·y·sis /hīdrol′isis/ *n chem* reaction produced by the decomposition of a compound, its elements taking up those of water

hy·drom·e·ter /hīdrom′itər/ *n* instrument for determining the specific gravity of liquids

hy′dro·pho′bi·a *n* 1 rabies; 2 abnormal dread of water

hy′dro·plane′ *n* 1 small high-powered motorboat with a stepped-up bottom designed to skim over the water at high speed; 2 airplane designed to land on and take off from water

hy′dro·pon′ics /-pon′iks/ [< *hydro-* + Gk *ponos* toil] *nsg* cultivation of plants in liquid solutions without soil

hy′dro·sphere′ *n* the water on the surface of the globe and in the atmosphere surrounding it

hy′dro·stat′ic *adj* pert. to the pressure and equilibrium of fluids

hy′dro·ther′a·py *n* treatment of disease by the use of water

hy·drous /hī′drəs/ *adj* containing water, esp. in chemical combination

hy·drox·ide /hīdrok′sīd, -sid/ *n* compound containing the hydroxyl radical

hy·drox′yl /-sil/ [*hydrogen* + *oxygen* + *ethyl*] *n* compound radical OH, existing in bases, acids, and many organic compounds, such as alcohols

hy·e·na /hī·ēn′ə/ [Gk *hyaina*] *n* any of a family (Hyaenidae) of carnivorous mammals native to Africa and Asia

hy·giene /hī′jēn/ [Gk *hygieine* (techne) (art) of health] *n* science which treats of the preservation of health and the prevention of disease

hy·gi·en·ic /hī′jē·en′ik, -jēn′ik/ *adj* 1 pert. to hygiene; 2 sanitary

hy·grom·e·ter /hīgrom′itər/ [< Gk *hygros* wet] *n* instrument for measuring atmospheric moisture

hy·men /hīm′ən/ [Gk] *n* thin membrane partly closing the external orifice of the vagina in virgins

hy′me·ne′al /-nē′əl/ [< *Hymen* Gk god of marriage] *adj* of or pert. to marriage

hymn /him'/ [Gk *hymnos*] *n* song in praise or honor, as of God or country

hym·nal /him'nəl/ also **hymn' book'** *n* book of hymns

hyp- *pref* var of **hypo-**

hy·per- [Gk = over] *pref* 1 over, beyond; 2 excessive

hy·per·bo·la /hīpur'bələ/ [NL < Gk *hyperbole* excess] *n* curve formed by the intersection of a plane with a right circular cone when the plane makes a greater angle with the base than does the line generating the cone

hy·per·bo·le /-lē/ [see **hyperbola**] *n* obvious exaggeration not meant to be taken literally

hy·per·bol·ic /hīp'ərbol'ik/ *adj* 1 of or pert. to a hyperbola; 2 having or using hyperboles

hy'per·sen'si·tive *adj* 1 excessively sensitive; 2 allergic

hy'per·son'ic *adj* of or pert. to speed that is equal to or exceeding five times the speed of sound in a given medium

hy'per·ten'sion *n* 1 excessive tension; 2 high blood pressure

hy'per·thy'roid·ism *n* overactivity of the thyroid gland, causing increased metabolism

hy·per·tro·phy /hīpur'trəfē/ [*hyper-* + Gk *trophe* food] *n* abnormal enlargement of an organ or body part ‖ also *v* (-phied) *vi*

hy·phen /hīf'ən/ [Gk = together] *n* the mark -, used to join the parts of compound words or to separate syllables, as at the end of a line

hy'phen·ate' *vt* to join or write with a hyphen

hyp·no- [< Gk *hypnos*] *comb form* 1 sleep; 2 hypnosis

hyp·no·sis /hipnōs'is/ *n* (-ses /-sēz/) 1 state resembling sleep, often artificially induced, in which the mind readily responds to external suggestion; 2 hypnotism

hyp·not'ic /-not'ik/ *adj* 1 pert. to or producing hypnosis; 2 inducing sleep; 3 susceptible to hypnotism ‖ *n* 4 person who can be hypnotized; 5 person in a state of hypnosis; 6 anything that produces sleep, as a drug ‖ **hyp·not'i·cal·ly** *adv*

hyp'no·tism /-nə-/ *n* science or practice of hypnotizing ‖ **hyp'no·tist** *n*

hyp'no·tize' *vt* 1 to put into a state of hypnosis; 2 to dazzle, fascinate, as by personal charm

hy·po¹ /hī'pō/ [< *hyposulfite*] *n* sodium thiosulfate, used in photography as a fixing agent

hy·po² *n colloq* 1 hypodermic syringe or injection; 2 stimulus

hy·po- /hī'pə, hi'pə/ [Gk = under] *pref* 1 under, below; 2 less than normal; 3 *chem* a indicating that the element to whose name in full or shortened form it is attached has a lower valence in an acid than in the corresponding acid in which the suffix *-ous* alone is used; b indicating that the word is the name of a salt and that the element to whose name in full or shortened form it is attached has a lower valence than in the corresponding salt with the suffix *-ite* alone

hy'po·chlo'rite /hīp'ə-/ *n* salt or ester of hypochlorous acid

hy'po·chlo'rous ac'id *n* acid —HClO— found only in solution, which with its salts is a powerful oxidizing and bleaching agent

hy'po·chon'dri·a /-kon'drē·ə/ [Gk = soft parts of the body under the cartilage of the ribs] *n* abnormal anxiety respecting one's state of health

hy'po·chon'dri·ac' /-ak'/ *n* one who is affected with hypochondria

hy·poc·ri·sy /hipok'rəsē/ [OF *ypocrisie* < Gk *hypokrisis* play acting] *n* (-sies) pretense of being what one is not, esp. assumption of an appearance of virtue which one does not possess ‖ SYN affectation, cant, sham, dissimulation

hyp·o·crite /hip'əkrit/ [OF *ypocrite* < Gk *hypokrites* actor] *n* one who pretends to be better morally than he really is ‖ **hyp'o·crit'i·cal** ‖ SYN dissembler, impostor, cheat, liar, pretender

hy·po·der·mic /hīp'ədurm'ik/ [*hypo-* + Gk *derma* skin] *adj* 1 pert. to the tissues under the skin, as *a hypodermic injection* ‖ *n* 2 hypodermic injection; 3 hypodermic syringe

hy'po·der'mic sy·ringe' *n* small glass syringe fitted with a hollow needle and operated by a piston for making hypodermic injections of medicines or withdrawing blood or other body fluids

hy'po·gly·ce'mi·a /-glīsēm'ē·ə/ [< *hypo-* + Gk *glykys* sweet] *n* abnormally low level of glucose in the blood ‖ **hy'po·gly·ce'mic** *adj*

hy·pot·e·nuse /hīpot'ən(y)ōōs'/ also **hy·poth'e·nuse** /-poth'-/ [< Gk *hypoteinein* to subtend] *n* that side of a right-angled triangle opposite the right angle

hy·poth·e·cate /hīpoth'ikāt', hi-/ [< Gk *hypotheke* mortgage] *vt* to pledge (property) as security for a debt; mortgage

hy·poth·e·sis /hīpoth'isis, hi-/ [Gk = foundation] *n* (-ses /-sēz/) 1 proposition or theory assumed as a basis for reasoning, argument, or investigation, or to explain certain phenomena; 2 supposition, conjecture ‖ **hy·poth'e·size'** *vt & vi*

hy·po·thet·i·cal /hīp'əthet'ikəl/ *adj* based on hypothesis; conjectural ‖ **hy'po·thet'i·cal·ly** *adv*

hy'po·thy'roid·ism *n* deficient activity of the thyroid gland, resulting in goiter and sluggishness

hys·sop /his′əp/ [Gk *hyssopos*] *n* fragrant medicinal herb of the mint family bearing blue flowers

hys·ter·ec·to·my /hist′ərek′təmē/ [Gk *hystera* womb + *-ectomy*] *n* (*-mies*) *surg* removal of the uterus

hys·te·ri·a /histir′ē-ə/ [< Gk *hystera* womb] *n* 1 nervous affection characterized by excessive emotional excitement with lack of control, as in fits of laughter and weeping; 2 any outbreak of wild excitement

hys·ter·ic /hister′ik/ *n* 1 person subject to hysteria; 2 **hysterics** *sg* fit of hysteria

hys·ter′i·cal *adj* 1 pert. to or affected by hysteria; 2 violently emotional; uncontrolled; 3 extremely funny || **hys·ter′i·cal·ly** *adv*

Hz hertz

I

I, i /ī/ *n* (**I's** or **Is**; **i's** or **is**) ninth letter of the English alphabet

I¹ /ī/ [OE *ic*] *pron* (*1st pers sg nom*) pronoun by which a speaker or writer designates himself

I² 1 *chem* iodine; 2 ninth in order or in a series; 3 something shaped like an I; 4 Roman numeral 1

I. 1 island(s); 2 isle(s)

-ia¹ [Gk & L *fem* ending] *n suf* 1 disease, as *anemia;* 2 genus, as *Forsythia*

-ia² [Gk & L *neut pl* ending] *pl suf* used to form the plural of certain words from Greek and Latin, as *amphibia*

Ia. Iowa

-ial [L *-ialis*] *adj suf* var of **-al¹**

i·am·bic /ī·am′bik/ [< Gk *iambos*] *n pros* foot of two syllables, consisting either of a short syllable followed by a long syllable or an unstressed syllable followed by a stressed syllable || also *adj*

-ian *suf* var of **-an**

-i·a·sis /-ī′əsis/ [Gk] *n suf* (*-ses* /-sēz′/) disease

-i·at·ric /ē·at′rik/ [< Gk *iatros* physician] *adj comb form* pert. to treatment or healing

-i·at′rics *n comb form* medical treatment

-i·a·try /ī′ətrē/ *n comb form* treatment, healing

ib. ibidem

I·be·ri·a /ībir′ē-ə/ *n* peninsula in SW Europe comprising Spain and Portugal || **I·be′ri·an** *adj & n*

i·bex /ī′beks/ [L] *n* (*-bex·es* or **ib·i·ces**/ib′isēz′/) any of several species of wild goats of the Old World, with large backward-curving horns

ibid. /ib′id/ ibidem

i·bi·dem /ībid′əm, ib′idəm/ [L] *adv* in the same place, as in a book, chapter, or passage

-i·bil·i·ty /əbil′itē/ *n suf* var of **-ability**

i·bis /ī′bis/ [Gk < Egypt.] *n* (*-bis·es* or **-bis**) any of several large storklike wading birds (family Threskiornithidae) related to the herons

-i·ble /-ībəl/ *adj suf* var of **-able**

Ib·sen, Hen·rik /hen′rik ib′sən/ *n* (1828–1906) Norwegian dramatist

-ic /-ik/ [Gk *-ikos*] *adj suf* 1 made up of, as *trochaic;* 2 like, as *angelic;* 3 of, pert. to, or belonging to, as *Celtic;* 4 resembling, as *classic;* 5 *chem* indicating that the element to whose name in full or shortened form it is attached has a higher valence in an acid than in the corresponding acid in which the suffix *-ous* is used; it corresponds to the suffix *-ate* of the name of a salt or ester || *n suf* 6 used a in nouns derived from the substantive use of adjectives in *-ic*, as *public;* b in nouns adopted in English from certain Greek adjectives, as *logic*

-i·cal /-ikəl/ [LL *-icalis* < *-ic* + *-al¹*] *adj suf* forming a variation of many adjectives in *-ic*, as *classical;* often differing in meaning from the form in *-ic*, as *historic* and *historical*, *comic* and *comical*

Ic·a·rus /ik′ərəs/ *n class. myth.* the young son of Daedalus, who, when escaping from Crete with his father, flew so high that the sun melted the wax with which his wings were attached and he fell into the sea and was drowned

ICBM, I.C.B.M. intercontinental ballistic missile

I.C.C., ICC Interstate Commerce Commission

ice /īs/ [OE *īs*] *n* 1 frozen water, a brittle, transparent solid; 2 any substance resembling this, as *menthol ice;* 3 frozen confection made of fruit juice, water, and sugar; 4 icing; 5 *slang* diamonds; 6 **break the ice, a** to make a start; **b** to overcome reserve; 7 **cut no ice** *colloq* to have no influence; 8 **on thin ice** in a risky position || *vt* 9 to freeze; 10 to cool by ice; 11 to cover with icing

Ice. 1 Iceland; 2 Icelandic

-ice /-is/ [L *-itia*] *n suf* quality or state of, as *justice, avarice*

ice′ age′ *n* glacial epoch

ice′ bag′ *n* rubber bag for holding ice,

applied to a part of the body which it is desired to cool

ice'berg' /-burg'/ [D *ijsberg* ice mountain] *n* huge mass of ice detached from a glacier and floating in the sea

ice'box' *n* refrigerator, spec. one using ice

ice'break'er *n* vessel designed for opening a channel through ice

ice'cap' *n* covering of ice over an area, as at the poles

ice' cream' *n* flavored cream or custard, sweetened and frozen

ice'-cream cone *n* cone-shaped wafer containing a scoop of ice cream

iced' *adj* 1 covered with ice; 2 cooled with ice; 3 covered with icing

ice' field' or **floe'** *n* large sheet of floating ice

ice' hock'ey *n* hockey *1*

Ice'land /-lənd/ *n* republic situated on an island in the North Atlantic, E of Greenland (193,215; 39,800 sq.m.; cap. Reykjavik) ‖ **Ice'land·er** *n*

Ice·lan'dic /-land'ik/ *adj* 1 of or pert. to Iceland or its people ‖ *n* 2 language of Iceland

ice' pick' *n* small sharp spike with a handle for chipping ice

ice' sheet' *n* thick sheet of ice covering a large land mass

ice' skate' *n* skate equipped with a metal blade for skating on ice ‖ **ice'-skate'** *vi*

ice' wa'ter *n* water chilled with ice

i·chor /ī'kôr/ [Gk] *n class. myth.* fluid which was supposed to flow in the veins of the gods instead of blood

ich·thy·o- [< Gk *ichthys*] *comb form* fish

ich·thy·ol·o·gy /ik'thē·ol'əjē/ *n* that branch of zoology that deals with fishes ‖ **ich'thy·ol'o·gist** *n*

i·ci·cle /īs'ikəl/ [OE *isgicel*] *n* tapering piece of ice formed when dripping water freezes

ic·ing /īs'iŋ/ *n* coating put on cake, made of sugar, egg white, etc.; frosting

i·con /ī'kon/ [Gk *eikon*] *n* 1 image, likeness; 2 *Orthodox Ch* sacred image or picture

i·con'o·clast' /-əklast'/ [*icon* + Gk *klastes* breaker] *n* 1 one hostile to the practice of worshiping icons; 2 one who attacks cherished beliefs and institutions ‖ **i·con'o·clasm** *n* ‖ **i·con'o·clas'tic** *adj*

I·con'o·scope' [trademark] *n* electronic scanning tube used in television cameras

-ics /-iks/ [see **-ic**] *n suf* science or art, as *physics*

i·cy /īs'ē/ *adj* (-ci·er; -ci·est) 1 pert. to, resembling, or covered with ice; 2 frigid in manner ‖ **i'ci·ly** *adv* ‖ **i'ci·ness** *n*

id /id'/ [L = it] *n psychoanal* the part

of the psyche which is the source of instinctive energy

I'd /īd'/ 1 I would; 2 I should; 3 I had

ID, I.D. 1 identification; 2 identity

-id¹ /-id/ [L *-idus*] *adj suf* forming descriptive words from Latin roots, as *fluid, morbid*

-id² [< Gk *-idai*] *adj suf* belonging to a specified biological family or class, as *arachnid*

-id³ [< Gk *-is* (*-idos*)] *n suf* used in the names of epic poems, as *Aeneid*

id. idem

Id. or **Ida.** Idaho

-i·dae /-idē'/ [Gk *-idai*] *npl suf zool* names of families, as *Hyaenidae*

I·da·ho /īd'əhō'/ *n* state in NW U.S. (713,000; 83,557 sq.m.; cap. Boise) ‖ **I'da·ho'an** *n*

-ide /-īd/ [*oxide*] *n suf chem* 1 indicating that the nonmetallic or more electronegative element to whose shortened name it is attached forms a binary compound with a metallic or more electropositive element or radical; 2 indicating some kind of relationship of a compound to an element, radical, or other element

i·de·a /īdē'ə/ [LL < Gk = appearance] *n* 1 mental picture or image; 2 purpose, intention; 3 belief, opinion

i·de·al /īdē'(ə)l/ [LL *idealis*] *adj* 1 expressing or embodying the perfect example or type; 2 very good, excellent; 3 existing in imagination only ‖ *n* 4 conception of something in its most perfect form; 5 standard of perfection; 6 person or thing embodying such a standard

i·de·al·ism /īdē'əliz'əm/ *n* 1 practice of idealizing; 2 pursuit of a mentally conceived standard of perfection; seeking after beauty or excellence ‖ **i·de'al·ist** *n* ‖ **i·de·al·is'tic** *adj*

i·de·al·ize' *vt* 1 to look upon as beautiful or perfect regardless of fact; 2 to see (a situation or condition) as it should be, not as it is; 3 to treat imaginatively, without regard to the limitations of real life, as in art or literature ‖ **i·de·al·i·za'tion** *n*

i·de'al·ly *adv* 1 perfectly; in an ideal manner; 2 in idea or thought; 3 in theory

i·dem /ī'dem or id'em/ [L] *pron & adj* 1 the same ‖ *adv* 2 in the same as above or before

i·den·ti·cal /īdent'ikəl/ [< ML *identicus*] *adj* 1 the very same; 2 exactly alike ‖ SYN uniform, interchangeable, selfsame (see *alike*)

i·den'ti·cal twins' *npl* twins from one ovum, generally resembling each other and of the same sex

i·den'ti·fi·ca'tion *n* 1 act of identifying or state of being identified; 2 something that identifies one

i·den'ti·fy' [LL *identificare*] *v* (-fied) *vt* 1 to establish the identity of; 2 to make, consider, or treat as the

same; **3** to join or associate closely
|| *vi* **4** to feel as one with another or
others

i·den'ti·ty [LL *identitas*] *n* (-ties) **1**
state of absolute resemblance; sameness; **2** distinctive individuality; condition of being a specific person or
thing; **3** condition of being what was
declared or asserted; **4** oneness; **5**
Australian & New Zealand person;
native, inhabitant

id'e·o·gram' /ĭd'ē-ə-, ĭd'-/ also **id'e·o·graph'** [< *idea* + *-gram* or *-graph*] *n*
1 symbol representing an object, action, or concept directly rather than
representing sounds; **2** any symbol
standing for a word or idea, as **2**, **&**,
or **$**

id·e·ol·o·gy /ĭd'ē-ŏl'ə-jē, ĭd'-/ *n* (-gies)
set of ideas, prejudices, beliefs, and
doctrines of an individual, group,
class, or movement || **id'e·o·log'i·cal**
/-əlŏj'-/ *adj* || **id'e·ol'o·gist** *n*

ides /īdz'/ [L *idus*] *npl* in the ancient
Roman calendar, the 15th of March,
May, July, and October, and the 13th
of the other months

id·i·o·cy /ĭd'ē-əsē/ [see **idiot**] *n* (-cies)
1 condition of being an idiot; **2**
utter foolishness; **3** extremely foolish act || SYN imbecility, stupidity,
senselessness, foolishness || ANT intelligence, sense, wisdom, brilliance

id·i·om /ĭd'ē-əm/ [Gk *idioma* peculiarity] *n* **1** language or style of speaking peculiar to an individual, group,
or people; **2** expression or phrase
the meaning of which is different
from the literal meanings of its components, as *shoot the breeze* || SYN
dialect, tongue, peculiarity (see *language*)

id'i·o·mat'ic /-mat'ik/ *adj* **1** peculiar
to or characteristic of a given language or style of speaking; **2** of the
nature of an idiom || **id'i·o·mat'i·cal·ly** *adv*

id'i·o·syn'cra·sy /-sĭŋk'rəsē/ [Gk *idiosynkrasia*] *n* (-sies) personal peculiarity of temperament, mannerism, or
habit || **id'i·o·syn·crat'ic** /-krat'-/ *adj*

id·i·ot /ĭd'ē-ət/ [Gk *idiotes* private person, layman] *n* **1** person in the lowest class of feeblemindedness; **2** very
foolish person; blockhead || **id'i·ot'ic**
/-ŏt'ik/ *adj*

id'i·ot card' *n* large card, kept out of
range of the television camera, with
words or phrases to prompt a speaker or performer

i·dle /īd'əl/ [OE *idel*] *adj* **1** useless,
futile; **2** vain, groundless; **3** unoccupied, inactive; **4** lazy, indolent; **5**
not used or employed || *vi* **6** to be
idle; **7** to act or move indolently;
8 *mach* to run slowly without transmitting power, as an automobile engine when the gear is in neutral || *vt* **9** to cause (a motor) to idle; **10**
idle away to pass (time) in idleness

|| **i'dle·ness** *n* || **i'dler** *n* || **i'dly** *adv*
|| SYN *adj* inactive, slothful, torpid,
sluggish, trifling, lazy, indolent, unoccupied, vain, futile, frivolous ||
DISCR An *idle* person may be inactive
in the general sense of doing nothing, or he may be frittering away
time in useless or ineffective action.
An *idle* tramp simply loafs; an *idle*
clerk may be intensely occupied with
something apart from his work. *Idle*
may or may not carry the tone of
reproach, but *lazy* is always disparaging. A *lazy* person is one who has an
aversion to work, though sometimes
physical laziness is accompanied by
a surprising mental alertness. The
indolent man is reluctant to think or
even to move. *Slothful* describes one
who has an intensified indolence. ||
ANT *adj* active, diligent

i·dol /īd'əl/ [Gk *eidolon*] *n* **1** image of
a divinity used as an object or medium of worship; **2** person or thing
loved or adored excessively

i·dol·a·try /īdŏl'ətrē/ [Gk *eidolatreia*]
n (-tries) **1** worship of idols; **2** excessive adoration or reverence of
any person or thing || **i·dol'a·ter** *n*
|| **i·dol'a·trous** *adj*

i'dol·ize' *vt* **1** to make an idol of ||
vi **2** to practice idolatry

i·dyll or **i·dyl** /īd'əl/ [Gk *eidyllion*] *n*
1 description in verse or prose of
a picturesque rural scene, rustic
episode, etc.; **2** such an episode

i·dyl·lic /īdĭl'ik/ *adj* **1** pert. to, or of
the nature of, an idyll; **2** pleasingly
simple

-ie /-ē/ [var of *-y*[1]] *dim. suf* implying
affection, as *lassie, dearie*

IE, I.E. Indo-European

i.e. [L *id est*] that is

-ier /-ir'/ [var of *-eer*] *n suf* person
concerned with or in charge of, as
financier, brigadier

if /ĭf'/ [OE *gif*] *conj* **1** on the condition that, as *if he did it, he's guilty;*
2 although, as *if the exam was hard,
it was fair;* **3** whether, as *ask if he
knows* || *n* **4** supposition or condition

if'fy *adj colloq* doubtful, questionable

-i·fy /-ĭfī'/ *v suf* var of *-fy*

ig·loo /ig'lōō/ [Eskimo = house] *n*
Eskimo dome-shaped hut made of
blocks of packed snow

ig·ne·ous /ig'nē-əs/ [< L *ignis* fire] *adj*
1 pert. to fire; **2** *geol* formed under
intense heat, as by volcanic action

ig·nite /ignīt'/ [L *ignire* (-*itus*)] *vt* **1**
to set on fire || *vi* **2** to take fire

ig·ni·tion /ignĭsh'ən/ *n* **1** act of igniting or state of being ignited; **2**
means of igniting; **3** device or process for exploding the charge in an
internal-combustion engine

ig·no·ble /ignōb'əl/ [L *ignobilis*] *adj*
1 not noble; inferior; **2** mean, base
|| **ig·no'bly** *adv*

ig'no·min'i·ous /-ē-əs/ *adj* **1** full of,

carrying, or incurring ignominy; shameful; **2** deserving disgrace; **3** humiliating ‖ ig'no·min'i·ous·ly adv ‖ SYN infamous, degrading, disgraceful, humiliating

ig·no·min·y /ig'nəmin'ē/ [L ignominia] n (-ies) **1** dishonor, public disgrace; **2** shameful or disgraceful conduct

ig·no·ra·mus /ig'nərām'əs, -ram-/ [L = we do not know] n ignorant person

ig·no·rant /ig'nərənt/ adj **1** lacking knowledge; uninstructed; **2** unaware, uninformed; **3** displaying or marked by lack of knowledge ‖ ig'no·rance n ‖ SYN illiterate, unlettered, uneducated, uninformed, untutored, unlearned ‖ DISCR One is ignorant who lacks knowledge. If he lacks that common knowledge which anyone might be reasonably expected to possess, he is ignorant in the general sense; if he is merely uninformed of a certain thing, he is ignorant in the particular sense. Ignorant is, therefore, far from an absolute term, for the best-informed man in the world is necessarily ignorant of many things, and the savage, deemed ignorant by the civilized man, is nevertheless wise in the ways of his environment. Illiterate means without letters, hence without the knowledge available through books and reading. Illiterate, especially in the census reports, or in regard to immigrants, means, specifically, unable to read or write. Unlettered is milder than illiterate. An uneducated person is one who has not had the advantage of systematic instruction or mind training. Though an uneducated person may be brilliant as far as the quality of his mind is concerned, he often lacks the ordered knowledge which is the basis of dependable judgments

ig·nore /ignôr', -nōr'/ [L ignorare not to know] vt to disregard; fail to recognize or notice

i·gua·na /igwän'ə/ [Sp < Arawak] n any of several large tropical American lizards of the genus Iguana

IHS [first 3 letters of Gk word for Jesus] **1** Jesus ‖ [L Iesus Hominum Salvator] **2** Jesus Savior of Men

il- /il-/ pref var of **in-**¹ or **in-**²

-il or **-ile** [L -ilis] adj suf of, like, or pert. to, as civil, juvenile

i·le·um /il'ē·əm/ [< L ilia entrails] n (-a/-ə/) lowest section of the small intestine, between the jejunum and the cecum

Il·i·ad /il'ē·əd/ [Gk Ilias (-ados) < Ilion Troy] n Greek epic poem describing the siege of Troy, ascribed to Homer

-il·i·ty /-il'itē/ [F -ilité < L -ilitas] suf forming nouns from adjectives end-

ing in -il(e), -able, -ible, as civility, agility, ability

Il·i·um /il'ē·əm/ n Latin name of ancient Troy

ilk /ilk'/ [OE ilca same] n family, kind, class

ill /il'/ [ON illr] adj (**worse; worst**) **1** sick, unwell; **2** evil, bad; **3** faulty, unsatisfactory; **4** unfavorable; **5** cross, unpleasant, as ill feeling; **6** ill at ease nervously uncomfortable ‖ n **7** evil; **8** harm; **9** misfortune; **10** sickness ‖ adv **11** badly; **12** imperfectly; **13** scarcely ‖ SYN adj sick, indisposed, unwell; harsh, unkind ‖ DISCR Ill and sick in general English usage have been interchangeable, but there is now a tendency in Great Britain to use sick of one suffering from nausea, while ill is employed in the wider sense to designate any disordered state of the body. In the United States, the words are still used with little distinction

I'll /il'/ I will or I shall

Ill. Illinois

ill'-ad·vised' adj imprudent

ill'-at-ease' adj attributive nervously uncomfortable

ill'-be'ing n state of being in poor health or circumstances

ill'-bred' adj **1** lacking good breeding; **2** rude, impolite

il·le·gal /ilēg'əl/ adj contrary to law ‖ il·le'gal·ly adv ‖ il'le·gal'i·ty /-gal'-/ n

il·leg'i·ble adj not legible; hard or impossible to read ‖ il·leg'i·bly adv ‖ il·leg'i·bil'i·ty /-bil'-/ n

il'le·git'i·mate adj **1** unlawful; **2** born out of wedlock; **3** contrary to good usage; not genuine ‖ il'le·git'i·ma·cy n

ill' fame' n bad name or reputation

ill'-fat'ed adj **1** destined to an unlucky end; **2** unlucky

ill'-fa'vored adj **1** not comely; ugly; **2** offensive

ill'-got'ten adj acquired by evil or dishonest means

il·lib'er·al adj not broad-minded; bigoted

il·lic·it /ilis'it/ [L illicitus] adj unlawful; not authorized

il·lim'it·a·ble adj without limit, immeasurable

Il·li·nois /il'inoi(z)'/ n state in N central U.S. (11,113,976; 56,400 sq.m.; cap. Springfield) ‖ Il'li·nois'an /-noi'(z)ən/ n

il·lit'er·ate adj **1** unable to read or write; **2** showing lack of learning or culture ‖ n **3** illiterate person ‖ il·lit'er·a·cy n ‖ SYN adj unlettered, uninstructed (see ignorant)

ill' na'ture n unpleasant disposition ‖ ill'-na'tured adj

ill'ness n sickness ‖ SYN ailment, indisposition, complaint (see disease)

il·log'i·cal *adj* not logical; contrary to sound reasoning

ill'-starred' *adj* ill-fated

ill'-tem'pered *adj* irascible, peevish

ill'-timed' *adj* inopportune; inappropriate

ill'-treat' *vt* to maltreat; misuse || **ill'-treat'ment** *n*

il·lu·mi·nant /ilŏŏm'inənt/ *n* substance which illuminates

il·lu·mi·nate /ilŏŏm'ināt'/ [L *illuminare* (-*atus*)] *vt* 1 to light up; 2 to enlighten; 3 to make clear, throw light on; 4 to adorn, as the initial letter of a manuscript, with designs in bright colors, silver, or gold

il·lu·mi·na·tion *n* 1 act of illuminating; 2 amount of light shed or supplied by a source of light || SYN enlightenment, embellishment (see *light*[1])

illus. or **illust.** 1 illustrated; 2 illustration

ill'-us'age *n* bad treatment, abuse

ill'-use' /-yōōz'/ *vt* 1 to abuse || /-yōōs'/ *n* 2 ill-usage

il·lu·sion /ilŏŏzh'ən/ [L *illusio* (-*onis*) irony] *n* 1 false or mistaken perception, as *an optical illusion*; 2 something that deceives by creating a false impression; 3 state of being deceived; 4 *psychol* perception in which sensory experiences are misinterpreted || **il·lu'so·ry** /-sərē, -zərē/ *adj* || SYN fallacy, unreality, hallucination (see *delusion*)

il·lus·trate /il'əstrāt, iləs'trāt/ [L *illustrare* (-*atus*) to light up] *vt* 1 to make clear by examples; 2 to furnish with pictures, as a book or magazine || **il'lus·trat'ed** *adj* || **il'lus·tra'tor** *n*

il'lus·tra'tion *n* 1 act or instance of illustrating; 2 that which illustrates, as a picture or example; 3 elucidation || SYN picture, cut, print, drawing, example

il·lus·tra·tive /iləs'trətiv, il'əstrāt'iv/ *adj* serving to illustrate

il·lus·tri·ous /iləs'trē·əs/ [< L *illustris* bright] *adj* distinguished, renowned, celebrated || SYN noted, glorious, noble (see *distinguished*)

ill' will' *n* hostility, enmity

I'm /īm'/ I am

im- /im-/ *pref* var of **in-**[1] or **in-**[2]

im·age /im'ij/ [OF < L *imago* (-*ginis*)] *n* 1 representation of the external form of a person or thing, as a picture or statue; 2 counterpart, exact resemblance; 3 figure of speech; 4 mental picture; 5 optical counterpart of an object formed by rays of light reflected from a mirror or refracted through a lens || *vt* 6 to form a likeness of, portray; 7 to mirror, reflect; 8 to imagine

im'age·ry /-ijrē/ *n* (-ries) 1 mental images considered collectively; 2 fanciful imagination; ability to make mental pictures; 3 figurative decoration in writing or speaking

im·ag'i·na·ble /imaj'inəbəl/ *adj* capable of being imagined

im·ag'i·nar'y *adj* existing only in the imagination; unreal || SYN ideal, fancied, fanciful, chimerical, illusory

im·ag'i·na'tion *n* 1 ability to create ideas or images independent of the external world; 2 creative faculty; 3 any product of the creative faculty; 4 fancy, notion; 5 ability to perceive a mental image created by another || SYN fancy, fantasy || DISCR The two words *fancy* and *imagination* name two aspects of that great power of the mind which creates, associates, combines, or alters mental images. Of the two, *fancy* is the lesser power; it may operate independently of the external world, but more often plays upon the objects or experiences of common life, to fill an idle moment or create a pleasing daydream. *Imagination* is more independent of the external world, and in a far deeper sense than *fancy* is truly creative. It presents images characterized by grandeur of conception, exaltation of mood, and that piercing vision which detects truth. The scientist, the poet, the wise parent, the great teacher, alike exercise it

im·ag'i·na·tive /-nətiv, -nāt'iv/ *adj* 1 proceeding from, exhibiting, or endowed with, imagination; 2 inventive; fanciful

im·ag'ine /-in/ [L *imaginari*] *vt* 1 to form a mental picture or an idea of; conceive; 2 to conjecture || *vi* 3 to form a mental picture; 4 to suppose, surmise || SYN deem, surmise, guess, conjecture, think, believe, picture, conceive, opine || ANT know, prove

im·bal'ance *n* lack of balance

im·be·cile /im'bəsəl, -sil/ [L *imbecillus* weak] *n* 1 feeble-minded person, just above the level of an idiot; 2 stupid person || **im'be·cil'ic** /-sil'-/ *adj* || **im'be·cil'i·ty** /-sil'-/ *n* (-ties)

im·bed /imbed'/ *vt* var of **embed**

im·bibe /imbīb'/ [L *imbibere* to drink in] *vt* 1 to drink; 2 to drink in, absorb || *vi* 3 to drink || **im·bib'er** *n*

im·bro·glio /imbrōl'yō/ [It] *n* 1 intricate and perplexing state of affairs; 2 bitter misunderstanding or disagreement

im·bue /imbyōō'/ [L *imbuere*] *vt* 1 to saturate; tinge deeply; 2 to permeate, as the mind with ideas

IMF International Monetary Fund

im·i·tate /im'itāt'/ [L *imitari* (-*atus*)] *vt* 1 to follow, or try to follow, the example of; 2 to mimic; 3 to reproduce or duplicate; 4 to simulate || **im'i·ta'tive** *adj* || **im'i·ta'tor** *n* || **im'i·ta·ble** *adj* || SYN mimic, mock, ape, impersonate, counterfeit, resemble, duplicate, simulate || DISCR To *imitate* is to pattern after another, either consciously or unconsciously. The things which imitation seeks to follow may or may not be praiseworthy, but its object is merely to make those things its own. To *mimic*, *mock*, and *ape* are all modes of *imitating;* they differ from it in their object, for the object of *mimicking* is to afford entertainment for others at the expense of the victim, the object of *mocking* is to affront or deride, and the object of *aping* is to improve oneself. One author may *imitate* the style of another in order to better his own, or because he lacks originality; admirers of great men strive to *imitate* them. People *mimic* the imperfect speech of a foreigner to excite laughter. A vulgar, ignorant person may *ape* his superiors. We *mock* a speech, showing up its hypocrisy, or bringing contempt upon it, sometimes unfairly and always insultingly (see *follow*)

im·i·ta'tion *n* 1 act of imitating; 2 result of imitating; copy; 3 counterfeit ‖ *adj* 4 made to resemble something superior or genuine ‖ SYN *n* impersonation, copy, likeness (see *duplicate*)

im·mac·u·late /imak'yəlĭt/ [L *immaculatus* spotless] *adj* 1 without blemish; 2 spotlessly clean; 3 errorless ‖ SYN unblemished, spotless, unsullied, stainless, pure

Im·mac'u·late Con·cep'tion *n* R C Ch dogma that the Virgin Mary, though naturally begotten, was, through divine favor, preserved from all stain of original sin

im·ma·nent /im'ənənt/ [L *immanens* (-*entis*) remaining in] *adj* indwelling; inherent ‖ **im'ma·nence** *n*

im'ma·te'ri·al *adj* 1 spiritual, incorporeal; 2 of no consequence ‖ SYN inconsequential, trifling, insignificant

im'ma·ture' *adj* not mature, ripe, grown, or developed ‖ **im'ma·tu'ri·ty** *n*

im·meas'ur·a·ble *adj* not capable of being measured; illimitable, vast ‖ **im·meas'ur·a·bly** *adv*

im·me·di·ate /imēd'ē·ĭt/ [ML *immediatus*] *adj* 1 next; succeeding; 2 close, not remote; 3 direct; acting without intervening agency; 4 not separated in time; instant; 5 pert. to the present; 6 not separated in space; adjoining

im·me'di·ate·ly *adv* 1 without delay; at once; 2 without intermediary ‖ SYN directly, instantly, instantaneously, presently, straightway, forthwith, promptly, soon, now ‖ DISCR *Immediately* expresses the idea that no time elapses between two events or actions; it means at once. *Directly* also, in its primary signification, means at once, but it has acquired now the secondary meaning of presently, in no long time, by and by; colloquially speaking, *directly* means pretty soon. *Immediately*, though far

less than *directly*, is also gathering a looser application, and sometimes now indicates soon instead of at once, as the time of the action. *Instantly* and *instantaneously* signify at this very moment, *now*, with no lapse of time, however brief. These words have kept the precision of their meaning. A slight difference in application is observable, indicating, in the case of *instantaneously*, that a small but imperceptible period of time has elapsed, as in the examples: he died *instantly;* the medicines affected the sick man *instantaneously*

im'me·mo'ri·al *adj* extending beyond the reach of memory or records

im·mense /imens'/ [L *immensus*] *adj* boundless, vast, very large ‖ **im·mense'ly** *adv* ‖ **im·men'si·ty** *n* (-ties) ‖ SYN huge, colossal, gigantic (see *enormous*)

im·merse /imurs'/ [L *immergere* (-*mersus*)] *vt* 1 to plunge or dip into a liquid; 2 to absorb or involve deeply; 3 to baptize by submerging in water ‖ **im·mer'sion** /-zhən, -shən/ *n*

im·mi·grate /im'igrāt'/ [L *immigrare* (-*atus*) to move in] *vi* to come into a country as a permanent resident ‖ **im'mi·gra'tion** *n* ‖ **im'mi·grant** /-grənt/ *adj & n*

im·mi·nence /im'inəns/ *n* 1 state or condition of being about to happen; 2 impending danger or evil

im'mi·nent [L *imminens* (-*entis*) overhanging] *adj* likely to occur at any moment ‖ SYN impending, threatening ‖ DISCR *Imminent* refers to an evil, danger, or disaster which is perilous and close at hand. *Impending* describes an evil as hanging over one; the time of its coming is more uncertain, but its arrival none the less sure than that described by *imminent*. *Threatening* describes that which has a menacing aspect, an ominous or evil-portending semblance; an evil *threatening* to happen may befall in the near future, in the distant future, or, sometimes, not at all

im·mo'bile *adj* 1 motionless; 2 not movable ‖ **im'mo·bil'i·ty** /-bil'-/ *n* ‖ **im·mo'bi·lize'** *vt*

im·mod'er·ate *adj* extreme, excessive; intemperate ‖ **im·mod'er·ate·ly** *adv* ‖ SYN inordinate, intemperate, excessive, unreasonable, extreme ‖ ANT restrained, reasonable, just

im·mod'est *adj* 1 not modest; indecent; 2 brazen, impudent ‖ **im·mod'es·ty** *n* ‖ SYN shameless, lewd, obscene, unchaste, indecent, sensual, impudent ‖ ANT modest, chaste, decent, pure

im·mo·late /im'əlāt'/ [L *immolare* (-*atus*) to sprinkle with grain] *vt* to make a sacrifice of ‖ **im'mo·la'tion** *n*

im·mor'al *adj* 1 not moral; 2 contrary to right conduct as conceived by any community or group || **im·mor'al·ly** *adv* || SYN bad, corrupt, depraved, loose, profligate, licentious, sinful, vicious, unprincipled, unrighteous || ANT moral, good, sinless, pure, virtuous, chaste

im'mo·ral'i·ty *n* (**-ties**) **1** state or quality of being immoral; **2** sexual misconduct; lewdness; **3** immoral act

im·mor'tal *adj* **1** not mortal; undying; **2** imperishable, everlasting || *n* **3** immortal person || **im'mor·tal'i·ty** *n* || SYN *adj* deathless, everlasting (see *eternal*)

im·mor'tal·ize' *vt* **1** to render immortal; **2** to confer everlasting fame upon

im·mov'a·ble *adj* **1** motionless; **2** not capable of being moved

im·mune /imyōon'/ [L *immunis* exempt] *adj* **1** exempt; **2** not liable to disease, as by inoculation || **im'mu·nize'** /-myə-/ *vt*

im·mu'ni·ty *n* (**-ties**) **1** exemption from natural, ordinary liabilities or misfortunes; **2** special privilege; **3** condition of not being susceptible to a given disease || SYN privilege, exemption, prerogative, advantage

im·mu·nol'o·gy /im'yənol'əjē/ *n* branch of medicine that deals with immunity from disease and the creation and preservation of immunity || **im'mu·nol'o·gist** *n* || **im·mu'no·log'i·cal** /-nəloj'ikəl/ *adj*

im·mure /imyōor'/ [ML *immurare* < L *murus* wall] *vt* to confine within or as within walls; seclude

im·mu·ta·ble /imyōot'əbəl/ [L *immutabilis*] *adj* unchangeable || **im·mu'ta·bly** *adv* || **im·mu'ta·bil'i·ty** /-bil'-/ *n*

imp /imp'/ [OE *impa* scion, graft] *n* **1** young devil; **2** mischievous child

im·pact' /impakt'/ [L *impingere* (*-pactus*) to press on] *vt* **1** to pack firmly; wedge closely || **im'pakt/** *n* **2** striking together of two objects; collision; **3** force of a collision; **4** forceful influence

im·pact'ed *adj* (tooth) so deeply embedded in the jawbone that it will not come through the gum

im·pac'tion *n* **1** act or state of being impacted; **2** condition of an impacted tooth

im·pair /imper'/ [MF *empeirer* to make worse] *vt* to lessen in excellence, value, or strength; damage || **im·pair'ment** *n* || SYN injure, diminish, mar, spoil, harm, blemish

im·pal·a /impal'ə, -päl'ə/ *n* African antelope (*Aepyceros melampus*), noted for its ability to leap

im·pale /impāl'/ [ML *impalare*] *vt* **1** to transfix with anything sharp; **2** to torture or put to death by thrusting through and fixing with a sharp stake

im·pal'pa·ble *adj* **1** not perceivable by touch; **2** (powder) too fine to be felt;

3 incapable of being readily understood || **im·pal'pa·bil'i·ty** /-bil'-/ *n*

im·pan'el *v* (**-eled** or **-elled; -el·ing** or **-el·ling**) *vt* **1** to enter on a list for jury duty; **2** to choose (a jury) from such a list

im·par'i·ty *n* lack of parity

im·part' [L *impartire* to share] *vt* **1** to bestow a share of; give; **2** to tell, make known; **3** to transmit, communicate || SYN reveal, disclose, divulge, yield, confer

im·par'tial *adj* fair, unbiased || **im·par'tial·ly** *adv*

im·par'ti·al'i·ty *n* quality or state of being impartial || SYN equity, disinterestedness, fairness (see *justice*)

im·pass'a·ble *adj* not to be passed or gone through; not admitting transit or travel

im·passe /im'pas, impas'/ [F] *n* position from which there is no way out; inescapable predicament

im·pas'si·ble [< L *pati* (*passus*) to suffer] *adj* **1** not subject to pain or harm; **2** impassive

im·pas'sioned *adj* ardent; showing deep feeling || SYN glowing, burning, fiery, intense, vehement

im·pas'sive *adj* **1** devoid of emotion; apathetic; **2** calm, serene || **im·pas'sive·ly** *adv* || SYN apathetic, insensible, invulnerable (see *stoical*)

im·pa'tient *adj* **1** not patient; **2** restless; eager; **3** impatient of intolerant of || **im·pa'tience** *n* || SYN peevish, fretful, hasty, choleric, testy, irritable

im·peach' [OF *empechier*] *vt* **1** to call in question; discredit; **2** to accuse (a public official) of misconduct in office || **im·peach'ment** *n* || SYN accuse, charge, arraign, censure, discredit

im·pec'ca·ble /impek'əbəl/ [LL *impeccabilis*] *adj* blameless, faultless

im·pe·cu·ni·ous /im'pikyōon'ē·əs/ [< *im-* + L *pecunia* money] *adj* without money, penniless

im·ped·ance /impēd'əns/ *n* resistance of a circuit to the flow of an alternating current

im·pede /impēd'/ [L *impedire* to entangle the feet] *vt* to obstruct, hinder

im·ped·i·ment /imped'imənt/ *n* **1** hindrance, obstruction; **2** organic obstruction to distinct speech || SYN obstacle, encumbrance, bar (see *hindrance*)

im·pel /impel'/ [L *impellere*] *v* (**-pelled; -pel·ling**) *vt* **1** to drive forward; urge on; **2** to propel, push on || SYN actuate, instigate, induce, move, excite, incite, embolden || ANT retard, deter, discourage

im·pend /impend'/ [L *impendere* to hang over] *vi* to be about to happen, be imminent || **im·pend'ing** *adj*

im·pen'e·tra·ble *adj* **1** unable to be penetrated; **2** not capable of being comprehended; **3** not susceptible to influences or ideas ‖ **im·pen'e·tra·bil'i·ty** /-bil'-/ n

im·pen'i·tent adj not penitent, unrepentant ‖ **im·pen'i·tence** n

im·per·a·tive /imper'ətiv/ [L imperativus] adj **1** authoritative; peremptory; **2** not to be shirked; urgent; **3** gram (verbal mood) expressing command ‖ n **4** command; **5 a** imperative mood; **b** imperative verb; **6** need, necessity ‖ SYN peremptory, commanding, authoritative, arbitrary, dictatorial, imperious, obligatory, urgent ‖ ANT adj gentle, submissive, docile, avoidable

im'per·cep'ti·ble adj **1** not perceptible; **2** very gradual ‖ **im'per·cep'ti·bly** adv

im·per'fect adj **1** incomplete; **2** defective, faulty; **3** gram (tense) that indicates past action going on but not completed ‖ n **4** imperfect tense ‖ **im·per'fect·ly** adv

im'per·fec'tion n **1** quality of being imperfect; **2** defect, blemish ‖ SYN weakness, fault, vice, flaw, deficiency, blemish

im·pe·ri·al /impir'ē·əl/ [L imperialis] adj **1** pert. to an empire, emperor, or empress; **2** of or pert. to a sovereign state as governing dependencies; **3** commanding, supreme; **4** domineering, imperious; **5** superior in size or quality; **6** designating the system of weights and measures of the United Kingdom ‖ n **7** tuft of hair beneath the lower lip ‖ SYN adj kingly, queenly, majestic, royal, sovereign

im·pe'ri·al·ism n policy of the extension of national power by the subjugation of foreign territories ‖ **im·pe'ri·al·ist** n ‖ **im·pe'ri·al·is'tic** adj

im·per'il v (-iled or -illed; -il·ing or -il·ling) vt to endanger, put in peril

im·pe·ri·ous /impir'ē·əs/ [L imperiosus] adj **1** dictatorial, overbearing; **2** overmastering, urgent ‖ **im·pe'ri·ous·ly** adv ‖ SYN arrogant, domineering, lordly, overbearing, arbitrary, dictatorial, imperative, compelling, despotic

im·per'ish·a·ble adj permanently enduring; immortal

im·per'ma·nent adj not permanent

im·per'me·a·ble adj not permitting passage, as of a fluid through a substance

im·per'son·al adj **1** not referring to any person; **2** having no distinct personality; **3** gram (verb) in the third person singular with meaningless it as the subject, as it snowed ‖ n **4** impersonal verb ‖ **im·per'son·al·ly** adv

im·per'son·ate' vt **1** to pretend to be (someone); **2** to assume the character of ‖ **im·per'son·a'tion** n ‖ **im·per'son·a'tor** n

im·per'ti·nent adj **1** not pertinent; **2** rude, presumptuous ‖ **im·per'ti·nence**

n ‖ SYN impudent, presumptuous, disrespectful, saucy

im'per·turb'a·ble adj not capable of being perturbed; calm

im·per·vi·ous /impur'vē·əs/ [< L im-·pervius] adj **1** impenetrable; **2** impervious to not affected or influenced by

im·pe·ti·go /imp'itī'gō/ [L] n skin disease characterized by pustules which become crusted

im·pet·u·ous /impech'ōō·əs/ [L impetuosus] adj **1** rushing with force and violence; **2** rash, impulsive ‖ **im·pet'u·ous·ly** adv ‖ **im·pet'u·os'i·ty** /-os'itē/ n ‖ SYN excitable, violent, furious, headlong, vehement, impulsive, rash, ardent ‖ ANT calm, deliberate, steady

im·pe·tus /imp'itəs/ [L = attack] n **1** momentum; **2** impulse; moving force; stimulus

im·pi·e·ty n (-ties) **1** lack of reverence for God; **2** impious act; **3** disrespect

im·pinge /impinj'/ [ML impingere to drive at] vi **1** to strike or dash; collide; **2** to encroach, infringe ‖ **im·pinge'ment** n

im·pi·ous /imp'ē·əs/ adj lacking reverence for God; irreligious ‖ SYN irreverent, ungodly, wicked, profane, blasphemous ‖ ANT devout, holy, reverent, godly

imp·ish /imp'ish/ adj like an imp; mischievous

im·plac·a·ble /implak'əbəl, -plāk'-/ adj not to be pacified or appeased; relentless ‖ **im·plac·a·bil'i·ty** /-bil'-/ n ‖ SYN unrelenting, inexorable, merciless, unappeasable, pitiless ‖ ANT forgiving, placable, mild, gentle

im·plant' vt to set in deeply; inculcate, instill

im·plau'si·ble adj not plausible

im·ple·ment /imp'ləmənt/ [LL implementum accomplishment] n **1** instrument, tool, or utensil ‖ /-ment'/ vt **2** to perform; fulfill, as a pledge; execute, as a policy; **3** to put into effect or to accomplish ‖ **im'ple·men·ta'tion** n

im·pli·cate /imp'likāt'/ [L implicare (-atus)] vt to involve, as a person in a crime

im'pli·ca'tion n **1** act of implying or state of being implied; **2** act of implicating or state of being implicated; **3** inference

im·plic·it /implis'it/ [L implicitus] adj **1** to be understood, though not directly expressed; implied; **2** essentially contained in; virtual; **3** unreserved, unquestioning ‖ **im·plic'it·ly** adv ‖ SYN tacit, implied, virtual, blind, absolute

im·plied /implīd'/ adj tacitly understood

im·plore /implôr', -plōr'/ [L implorare] vt to entreat earnestly; supplicate ‖

SYN supplicate, beseech, entreat, plead (see *pray*)

im·plo·sion /implōzh'ən/ [*im-* + explosion] *n* 1 collapse or bursting inward; 2 blockage of the breath in pronouncing a stop consonant

im·ply /implī'/ [MF *emplier* < L *implicare* to involve] *v* (-plied) *vt* 1 to involve as a consequence; 2 to hint, intimate || SYN include, impart, denote, mean, intimate, signify || ANT express, set forth, make explicit

im·po·lite /adj not polite; uncivil, rude || **im·po·lite'ly** *adv* || **im·po·lite'ness** *n*

im·pol'i·tic *adj* injudicious, inexpedient

im·pon'der·a·ble *adj* 1 that cannot be weighed or determined || *n* 2 something imponderable

im·port /impôrt', -pôrt'/ [L *importare*] *vt* 1 to bring from abroad, as merchandise; 2 to signify || /im'pôrt, -pôrt/ *n* 3 imported article; 4 meaning; 5 importance, consequence || **im·port'er** *n* || **im·por'ta·tion** *n*

im·por·tant /impôrt'ənt/ *adj* 1 of great consequence or significance; momentous; 2 of high position or authority || **im·por'tance** *n* || SYN grave, weighty, momentous, significant, valuable, influential, prominent, consequential, pompous (see *serious*) || ANT insignificant, unimportant, trifling

im·por·tu·nate /impôrch'ənit/ *adj* persistent in demand

im·por·tune /impôrt(y)ōōn', impôrch'ən/ [L *importunus* troublesome] *vt & vi* to urge persistently || **im·por'tu·ni·ty** *n* (-ties) || SYN beg, beseech, crave, entreat, implore, solicit

im·pose /impōz'/ [MF *imposer*] *vt* 1 to lay or inflict, as a burden, tax, or penalty; 2 to obtrude or thrust, as one's company on others || *vi* 3 **impose on** or **upon, a** to take advantage of; **b** to cheat

im·pos'ing *adj* strikingly impressive || SYN striking, majestic, noble, dignified || ANT featureless, unimpressive, commonplace, forceless

im·po·si·tion /im'pəzish'ən/ *n* [LL *impositio* (-onis)] *n* 1 act of imposing; 2 that which is imposed; 3 instance of taking unfair advantage

im·pos'si·ble *adj* 1 not possible; 2 not capable of occurring or being; 3 hopeless; not feasible; 4 unsuitable; objectionable || **im·pos'si·bil'i·ty** /-bil'-/ *n* (-ties)

im·post /im'pōst/ [LL *impostus*] *n* tax or duty

im·pos·tor /impos'tər/ [LL] *n* one who deceives others by an assumed character or false pretenses

im·pos·ture /impos'chər/ [LL *impostura*] *n* deception practiced by an impostor; fraud

im·po·tent /im'pətənt/ *adj* 1 lacking in physical, mental, or moral power;

2 (male) lacking sexual power || **im'po·tence** *n*

im·pound' *n* 1 to shut up in a pen or pound; 2 to confine within limits, as water; 3 *law* to seize and hold

im·pov·er·ish /impov'ərish/ [MF *empoverir* (-riss-)] *vt* 1 to make poor; 2 to use up the strength, richness, or fertility of || **im·pov'er·ish·ment** *n*

im·prac'ti·ca·ble *adj* 1 not to be effected by the means at hand; 2 impassable, as roads

im·prac'ti·cal *adj* not practical

im·pre·cate /imp'rikāt'/ [L *imprecari* (-atus)] *vt* to invoke (an evil or a curse)

im'pre·ca'tion *n* act of imprecating; curse || SYN curse, execration, anathema (see *malediction*)

im'pre·cise' *adj* not precise || **im'preci'sion** *n*

im·preg·na·ble /impreg'nəbəl/ *adj* not to be captured or overcome || **im·preg'na·bly** *adv* || **im·preg'na·bil'i·ty** /-bil'-/ *n*

im·preg·nate /impreg'nāt/ [LL *impraegnare* (-atus)] *vt* 1 to make pregnant; 2 to fertilize; 3 to saturate; 4 to imbue, as with feelings or ideas || **im'preg·na'tion** *n*

im·pre·sa·ri·o /imp'risär'ē·ō, -ser'-/ [It] *n* organizer, manager, or conductor of an opera or concert company

im·press'¹ [L *imprimere* (-pressus)] *vt* 1 to mark as with a die or stamp; 2 to stamp, imprint; 3 to affect or influence strongly || **im'press** *n* 4 act of impressing; 5 stamp, imprint; 6 distinguishing mark; characteristic

im·press'² [< *press²*] *vt* 1 to compel to enter the public service, as sailors; 2 to seize for public service || **im·press'ment** *n*

im·pres·sion /impresh'ən/ *n* 1 act of impressing or state of being impressed; 2 mark made by a stamp or mold; 3 effect produced on the mind by sensation, emotion, or intellect; 4 vague notion; 5 *publishing* whole number of copies printed at one time

im·pres'sion·a·ble *adj* easily impressed or influenced || SYN susceptible, moldable, sensitive

im·pres'sion·ism *n* 1 theory of painting in which the underlying aim is to record the vividness of the artist's first impression without elaborate detail; 2 broad treatment of a subject without much explanatory detail || **im·pres'sion·ist** *adj & n* || **im·pres'sion·is'tic** *adj*

im·pres'sive *adj* capable of making a strong impression on the mind; inspiring awe or admiration || **im·pres'sive·ly** *adv* || SYN stirring, exciting, moving, imposing

im·pri·ma·tur /imp'rimāt'ər/ [L = let it be printed] *n* 1 license to print a book, pamphlet, or the like; **2** sanction, approval

im·print /im'print/ *vt* **1** to mark or stamp; **2** to impress deeply ‖ **im'print** *n* **3** impression, impress, or mark left by something; **4** publisher's or printer's name, usu. with time and place of issue, on the title page or at the end of a book

im·pris'on *vt* to confine in or as in a prison ‖ **im·pris'on·ment** *n*

im·prob'a·ble *adj* not probable; unlikely ‖ **im·prob'a·bly** *adv* ‖ **im·prob'a·bil'i·ty** /-bil'-/ *n* (-ties)

im·promp·tu /impromp'tŌŌ/ [F < L *in promptu* in readiness] *adv* **1** without preparation; offhand ‖ *adj* **2** said, made, or done on the spur of the moment ‖ *n* **3** extemporaneous speech or performance

im·prop'er *adj* **1** unsuitable, inappropriate; **2** incorrect; **3** not according to good manners; unseemly; **4** contrary to law or morals ‖ **im·prop'er·ly** *adv*

im·pro·pri·e·ty /im'prəprī'itē/ *n* (-ties) **1** quality of being improper; **2** instance of that which is not in accordance with usage, custom, decency, or correctness

im·prove /improŌv'/ [AF *emprower* to turn into profit] *vt* **1** to make better or more profitable or desirable; **2** to use to advantage ‖ *vi* **3** to grow better; **4** **improve on** to make improvements in

im·prove'ment *n* **1** act of improving or state of being improved; **2** that by which a thing is improved or its value increased

im·prov'i·dent *adj* lacking foresight; not providing for the future ‖ **im·prov'i·dence** *n* ‖ SYN prodigal, wasteful, shiftless, thriftless, reckless

im·pro·vise /imp'rəvīz'/ [< It *improviso* improvised] *vt & vi* **1** *mus* to compose, perform, or sing on the spur of the moment and without preparation; **2** to make, provide, or do with whatever is at hand ‖ **im·prov'i·sa'tion** /improv'i-, im'prəvi-/ *n*

im·pru'dent *adj* not prudent; indiscreet ‖ **im·pru'dence** *n* ‖ SYN improvident, incautious, heedless, foolhardy, rash, inconsiderate, injudicious, indiscreet

im·pu·dent /imp'yədent/ [L *impudens* (-entis) shameless] *adj* insolent; disrespectful; brazen ‖ **im'pu·dent·ly** *adv* ‖ **im'pu·dence** *n*

im·pugn /impyŌŌn'/ [MF *impugner* < L *impugnare* to attack] *vt* to question, attack as false

im·pulse /imp'puls/ [L *impulsus*] *n* **1** force communicated suddenly, causing motion; impetus; **2** result of an impelling force; **3** incitement to action; **4** sudden determination to act; **5** *mech* effect of a force in changing the motion of a body, measured by the product of the force and the time during which it acts ‖ SYN incentive, incitement, motive, instigation, influence ‖ DISCR An *incentive* spurs or goads one to action; our desires, ambitions, or goals furnish *incentives*. A rich man may lack the *incentive* to earn money, but love of a certain profession may furnish a driving *incentive* to work. *Incentive* and *motive* are sometimes interchangeable, but *motive* implies the reason and will behind an action, rather than the stimulation that excited it. *Motive* determines what we shall do; *incentive* drives us to performance. Fear of punishment is often a child's *motive* for deceiving; detectives seek for the *motive* which may clear up an unexplained murder. An *impulse* is always mental; it is a sudden rush of feeling that incites to action without reflection; those who speak first and think afterward act on *impulse*; warm-hearted people yield to the *impulse* to be generous

im·pul'sive *adj* **1** swayed by impulse; **2** *mech* acting for a short time ‖ **im·pul'sive·ly** *adv* ‖ SYN impetuous, headlong, passionate, spontaneous

im·pu·ni·ty /impyŌŌn'itē/ [< L *impunis* without punishment] *n* freedom from punishment, injury, or loss

im·pure' *adj* **1** not pure or clean; **2** adulterated; **3** unclean, unhallowed

im·pu'ri·ty *n* (-ties) **1** condition of being impure; **2** that which makes impure

im·pute /impyŌŌt'/ [L *imputare*] *vt* to attribute or ascribe (esp. something discreditable) ‖ **im·put'a·ble** *adj* ‖ **im'pu·ta'tion** *n*

in /in'/, in/ [OE] *prep* **1** within the bounds of, as *in the woods;* **2** being surrounded by, as circumstances, activities, or interests, as *in business, in trouble;* **3** wearing; **4** in regard to; **5** done by, as *in ink;* **6** within a state, condition, occupation, situation, or time period, as *in pain, in winter, in two minutes;* **7** after, as *return in two days;* **8** at the time of, as *in the beginning;* **9** in the person or case of, as *you have a friend in me;* **10** within the capacity of, as *it isn't in him to do it;* **11** made of, as *a figure in porcelain;* **12** expressed in (a language); **13** as a means of, as *in explanation;* **14** from among, as *nine times in ten;* **15 in that** because, since ‖ *adv* **16** to or on the inside, as *he went in;* **17** in possession, power, or occupancy; **18** in style, as *vests are in this season;* **19** **be in for** to be obliged to undergo (something disagreeable); **20 be in for it** *slang* to be due to suffer the unpleasant consequences of one's actions; **21 in with** having influence with || *adj* **22** inner, internal; **23** incoming; **24** in power or office; **25** accepted; fashionable; **26** *slang* the richer by, as *he was in five dollars* || *n* **27** influence, as *he has an in at City Hall;* **28** the **ins** *pl* the political party in power; **29 ins and outs** details of any complicated matter or procedure

in-¹ /in-/ [L] *pref* in; into; toward; within; on

in-² [L] *pref* not; without; non-; un-

in-³ [OE] *pref* into; within; toward; on

-in /-in/ [L *-inus*] *suf chem* used in names of certain neutral compounds, as *albumin, fibrin*

in. inch(es)

In *chem* indium

in·a·bil·i·ty *n* lack of power or capacity || SYN incapacity, impotence (see *disability*) || ANT strength, ability, power

in ab·sen·tia /in'absen'shə/ [L] *adv* in absence

in·ac·ces·si·ble *adj* not accessible; unapproachable || **in·ac·ces·si·bil·i·ty** /-bil'-/ *n*

in·ac·cu·rate *adj* not accurate || **in·ac·cu·ra·cy** *n* (-cies)

in·ac·tion *n* **1** lack of action; **2** idleness

in·ac·ti·vate *vt* to render inactive

in·ac·tive *adj* **1** not active; inert; **2** sluggish; idle; **3** *mil* not in active service || **in·ac·tiv'i·ty** *n* || SYN inert, phlegmatic, lazy, idle, passive, supine, lifeless, indolent || DISCR *Inactive* people are not active; they may be lazy, and disinclined to act; they may be ill, and not able to exercise; they may be slow as opposed to lively or quick; they may be idle for the moment because there is nothing to do. *Inert* implies a disinclination to act, even to move, commonly inherent; *inert* natures, minds, bodies, are hard to prod or stimulate into motion or activity. *Inert* is applied figuratively to bodies in a state of torpor, as the senseless man lay *inert* upon the floor; a hibernating animal lies *inert* the winter long. Both *inactive* and *inert* are applied to things; we speak of an *inactive* volcano; matter is *inert. Phlegmatic* describes those who are born heavy, dull, and stolid of mind and temperament; they are unexcitable rather than lazy or lifeless

in·ad·e·quate *adj* not adequate or sufficient || **in·ad'e·qua·cy** *n* (-cies) || SYN incapable, deficient, insufficient, unsuitable

in·ad·mis·si·ble *adj* not to be allowed or admitted

in·ad·vert·ence /in'ədvurt'əns/ [ML *inadvertentia*] *n* **1** inattention; **2** oversight

in·ad·vert'ent *adj* **1** inattentive; careless; **2** unintentional || **in'ad·vert'-**

ent·ly *adv* || SYN unconsidered, heedless, thoughtless, inattentive, (see *negligent*) || ANT thoughtful, considerate, careful

in·ad·vis'a·ble *adj* not advisable

in·al·ien·a·ble *adj* incapable of being transferred to another || **in·al'ien·a·bly** *adv*

in·am·o·ra·ta /inam'ərät'ə/ [It] *n* **1** woman with whom one is in love; **2** mistress

in·ane /inān'/ [L *inanis*] *adj* empty; senseless, silly || **in·an'i·ty** /-nan'-/ *n* (-ties)

in·an'i·mate *adj* **1** lifeless; **2** dull, spiritless || SYN lifeless, dull, inert, soulless, spiritless (see *dead*)

in·ap'pli·ca·ble *adj* not applicable

in·ap·pre'ci·a·ble *adj* insignificant; of no consequence

in·ap·pro'pri·ate *adj* not suitable or proper

in·ap'ti·tude *n* lack of aptitude

in·ar·tic'u·late *adj* **1** not uttered in the form of intelligible speech; **2** unable to speak distinctly; **3** unspoken, dumb; **4** *zool* not composed of segments united by joints

in·ar·tis'tic *adj* **1** not artistic; **2** not graceful or skillful

in'as·much' as *conj* in view of the fact that; since

in·at·ten'tion *n* **1** lack of attention; **2** act of neglectful discourtesy

in·at·ten'tive *adj* not attentive; negligent || **in'at·ten'tive·ly** *adv* || SYN absent-minded, thoughtless (see *negligent*)

in·au'di·ble *adj* incapable of being heard

in·au·gu·ral /inôg'(y)ərəl/ *n* **1** inauguration; **2** inauguration speech || also *adj*

in·au'gu·rate' [L *inaugurare (-atus)*] *vt* **1** to induct into office with appropriate ceremonies; **2** to make a formal beginning of; **3** to initiate the public use of by some ceremony || **in·au'gu·ra'tion** *n* || SYN institute, initiate, begin, commence, induct

in'aus·pi'cious *adj* unfavorable; of bad omen

in'board' *adj & adv* inside or toward the center of a hull or aircraft

in'born' *adj* innate || SYN inbred, natural, ingrained (see *inherent*)

in'bred' *adj* **1** innate; native; **2** resulting from inbreeding || SYN (see *inherent*)

in·breed /in'brēd', inbrēd'/ *v* (**-bred**) *vt* to breed (closely related animals)

inc. **1** inclosure; **2** inclusive; **3** incorporated

In·ca /ink'ə/ [Sp < Quechua = royal prince] *n* **1** member of an Indian people whose empire, centered in Peru, was overthrown by the Spaniards in the 16th century; **2** member of the royal family of the Inca empire

in·cal·cu·la·ble *adj* very great or numerous; beyond reckoning

in·can·des·cent /ˌin·kəndesʹənt/ [L *incandescens (-entis)*] *adj* 1 glowing or white with heat; 2 brilliant, resplendent ‖ **in·can·desʹcence** *n*

inʹcan·desʹcent lamp *n* lamp in which light is produced by a filament rendered luminous by its resistance to an electric current

in·can·ta·tion /ˌin·kantashʹən/ [< L *incantare* to enchant] *n* 1 use of magical words for enchantment or exorcism; 2 formula so used; 3 magic, sorcery

in·ca·pa·ble *adj* not capable; incompetent; unfit ‖ SYN insufficient, unqualified, incompetent, inadequate (see *unable*) ‖ ANT able, sufficient, qualified

inʹca·pacʹi·tate *vt* 1 to render powerless or unfit; disable; 2 *law* to disqualify

inʹca·pacʹi·ty *n* (-ties) 1 lack of power; disability; 2 *law* disqualification ‖ SYN inability, disability, incompetency, incapability, disqualification ‖ ANT capacity, ability, qualification

in·car·cer·ate /ˌinkärʹsərāt/ [in-¹ + L *carcer* prison] *vt* to imprison, confine ‖ **in·carʹcer·aʹtion** *n*

in·car·nate /ˌinkärʹnit, -nāt/ [LL *incarnare (-atus)* to clothe with flesh] *adj* 1 embodied in human form; personified ‖ /-nāt/ *vt* 2 to embody in flesh; 3 to express in concrete form; actualize; 4 to be the type or embodiment of ‖ **inʹcar·naʹtion** *n*

in·cau·tious *adj* heedless; unwary ‖ SYN indiscreet, imprudent, thoughtless, foolhardy, rash ‖ ANT cautious, prudent, discreet, circumspect

in·cen·di·ar·y /ˌinsenʹdē·er'ē/ [< L *incendium* conflagration] *n* (-ies) 1 one who maliciously sets fire to property; 2 one who stirs up strife by inflaming people's passions; 3 bomb which sets fire to its target ‖ also *adj*

in·cense¹ /ˌinsensʹ/ [< L *incendere (-census)* to set on fire] *vt* to inflame with rage, make extremely angry ‖ SYN vex, exasperate, inflame, madden (see *irritate*)

in·cense² /ˌinʹsens/ [L *incensum* thing burned] *n* 1 substance, as aromatic gum, which gives off perfume when burned; 2 smoke or odor of this when burned, as in religious ceremonies; 3 any pleasant odor ‖ *vt* 4 to perfume, as with incense ‖ *vi* 5 to burn incense

in·cen·tive /ˌinsentʹiv/ [L *incentivus* setting the tune] *n* 1 that which arouses to action ‖ *adj* 2 stimulating, motivating; 3 stimulated by the prospect of a reward ‖ SYN *n* motive, stimulus, spur (see *impulse*)

in·cep·tion /ˌinsepʹshən/ [< L *incipere (-ceptus)* to begin] *n* beginning, origin

in·ces·sant /ˌinsesʹənt/ [< in-² + L *cessare* to cease]. *adj* unceasing; continual ‖ **in·cesʹsant·ly** *adv* ‖ SYN uninterrupted, unceasing (see *continual*)

in·cest /ˌinʹsest/ [L *incestus* impure] *n* sexual relations between persons too closely related to be legally married ‖ **in·cesʹtu·ous** /-cho͞o·əs/ *adj*

inch /ˌinchʹ/ [OE *ynce* < L *uncia*] *n* 1 measure of length equal to 1/12 foot or 2.54 centimeters; 2 small distance or degree ‖ *vt & vi* 3 to move by inches or by small degrees

in·cho·ate /ˌinkōʹit/ [L *inchoare (-atus)* to begin] *adj* 1 incipient; just begun; 2 incomplete; 3 amorphous; unorganized

in·ci·dence /ˌinʹsidəns/ [< L *incidere* to befall] *n* 1 range or degree of occurrence; 2 act or fact of falling upon or affecting something; 3 *geom* position of two figures in relation to each other when they partly coincide

inʹci·dent *adj* 1 falling or acting upon something from without, as light rays; 2 apt to occur; 3 naturally pertaining ‖ *n* 4 event or occurrence; 5 episode ‖ SYN *n* circumstance, occurrence (see *event*)

in·ci·den·tal /ˌinsidenʹtʹl/ *adj* 1 happening as a subordinate feature of something more important; casual; 2 relatively unimportant; 3 occurring as a necessary but minor result of something larger ‖ *n* 4 something incidental; 5 **incidentals** *pl* a miscellaneous items; b minor expenses ‖ SYN *adj* casual, accidental, chance (see *fortuitous*)

inʹci·denʹtal·ly *adv* 1 in an incidental manner; 2 by the way

in·cin·er·ate /ˌinsinʹərāt/ [ML *incinerare (-atus)*] *vt* to burn to ashes; consume by fire ‖ **in·cinʹer·aʹtion** *n*

in·cinʹer·aʹtor *n* furnace for incinerating

in·cip·i·ent /ˌinsipʹē·ənt/ [L *incipiens (-entis)*] *adj* beginning to be or to appear ‖ **in·cipʹi·ence** *n*

in·cise /ˌinsīzʹ/ [L *incidere (incisus)*] *vt* 1 to cut in or into; 2 to engrave; carve

in·ci·sion /ˌinsizhʹən/ *n* 1 act of incising; 2 cut made with a sharp instrument, as in surgery

in·ci·sive /-sīsʹiv/ *adj* 1 keen, acute; 2 sharply expressive; sarcastic ‖ **in·ciʹsive·ly** *adv* ‖ **in·ciʹsive·ness** *n*

in·ci·sor /-zər/ *n* one of the four front teeth in each jaw used for cutting

in·cite /ˌinsītʹ/ [L *incitare*] *vt* to move to action; stir up, rouse ‖ **in·citʹer** *n* ‖ SYN instigate, move, abet, animate, quicken, stir

in·citeʹment *n* 1 act of inciting; 2 state of being incited ‖ SYN spur, stimulation, incentive (see *impulse*)

in·ci·vil·i·ty /-sivilʹ-/ *n* (-ties) 1 lack of courtesy; 2 discourteous act ‖ SYN indignity, rudeness, unmannerliness

in·clem·ent /ˌinklemʹənt/ *adj* 1 harsh,

unmerciful; **2** bad, stormy (weather) ‖ **in·clem'en·cy** *n*

in·cli·na·tion /ˌinˈklĭnāshˈən/ *n* **1** inclined position or surface; **2** deviation from a given direction or position, usu. the vertical or horizontal; **3** act of bending; **4** disposition, bent; **5** preference, liking; **6** *geom* angle lying between two lines, planes, etc. ‖ SYN bias, affection, bent, propensity, proclivity, tendency, proneness, turn (see *disposition, desire*) ‖ ANT aversion, dislike, repulsion, disinclination

in·cline /inˈklīn/ [L *inclinare*] *vt* **1** to turn or lean from a given direction or position; **2** to bow; **3** to have a mental bent or tendency; **4** to have preference ‖ *vt* **5** to cause to lean; **6** to bow; **7** to direct, give a tendency to; dispose ‖ /ˈalso inˈklīn/ *n* **8** slope, grade ‖ **in·clined'** *adj*

in·close /inˈklōz/ *vt* var of **enclose**

in·clo·sure /inˈklōzhˈər/ *n* var of **enclosure**

in·clude /inˈklo͞od/ [L *includere* to shut in] *vt* **1** to enclose; **2** to contain as part of the whole; **3** to place in a class or category ‖ **in·clu'sion** *n* ‖ SYN contain, enclose, comprise (see *comprehend*)

in·clu·sive /-sĭv/ *adj* **1** comprehensive, all-embracing; **2** including the limits or extremes mentioned, as *from Monday to Saturday inclusive* ‖ **in·clu'sive·ly** *adv* ‖ **in·clu'sive·ness** *n* ‖ SYN comprehensive, comprising, surrounding

in·cog·ni·to /inˈkŏgˈnĭtō/ [It = unknown] *adj* & *adv* **1** under an assumed name; disguised ‖ *n* **2** state of being incognito; **3** person who is incognito

in·co·her·ent *adj* **1** without logical connection; disjointed, rambling; **2** not cohering; **3** without cohesion ‖ **in'·co·her'ence** *n*

in·come /ˈinˈkum/ *n* **1** amount, expressed in money, derived from one's labor, business, property, or capital; **2** annual receipts of a person or business ‖ SYN proceeds, profit, revenue, emolument, interest

in'come tax' *n* tax levied upon yearly receipts or profits

in'com'ing *adj* **1** coming in; **2** succeeding, as an official

in·com·mode /inˈkəmōd'/ [L *incommodare*] *vt* to inconvenience; disturb ‖ SYN annoy, trouble, molest, inconvenience, vex

in·com·mu·ni·ca·do /inˈkəmyo͞onˈi-käd'o/ [Sp *incomunicado*] *adj* held in solitary confinement without access to others ‖ *also adv*

in'com·mu'ni·ca·tive *adj* not communicative; taciturn, reticent

in·com'pa·ra·ble *adj* **1** not comparable; **2** unequaled, matchless ‖ **in·com'pa·ra·bly** *adv*

in'com·pat'i·ble *adj* **1** not compatible; **2** incapable of existing together in harmony ‖ **in'com·pat'i·bil'i·ty** /-bil'/-/ *n* ‖ SYN incongruous, conflicting (see *inconsistent*)

in·com'pe·tent *adj* **1** of inadequate ability or fitness; **2** *law* not legally qualified ‖ *n* **3** incompetent person ‖ **in·com'pe·tence** *n* ‖ SYN *adj* incapable, disqualified, unable, insufficient ‖ ANT *adj* sufficient, capable, qualified

in'com·plete' *adj* not complete; lacking a part or parts ‖ **in'com·plete'ly** *adv*

in'com·pre·hen'si·ble *adj* not understandable ‖ **in·com'pre·hen'si·bil'i·ty** /-bil'/-/ *n* ‖ SYN mysterious, baffling, inconceivable, unintelligible, unfathomable, recondite, inscrutable

in'com·press'i·ble *adj* not compressible

in'con·ceiv'a·ble *adj* not conceivable; unimaginable

in'con·clu'sive *adj* not conclusive; leading to no definite result

in·con'gru·ous *adj* inharmonious; unsuitable; inappropriate ‖ **in'con·gru'i·ty** *n* (-ties) ‖ SYN discordant, ill-matched (see *inconsistent*)

in'con·se·quen'tial *adj* **1** unimportant, of no consequence; **2** lacking sequence; irrelevant

in'con·sid'er·a·ble *adj* **1** not deserving consideration; unimportant; **2** of small value or quantity

in'con·sid'er·ate *adj* not considerate; thoughtless ‖ SYN negligent, heedless, improvident, incautious, rash ‖ ANT considerate, thoughtful, careful

in'con·sist'ent *adj* **1** not consistent; **2** self-contradictory, incompatible ‖ **in'con·sist'en·cy** *n* (-cies) ‖ SYN incongruous, incompatible, illogical, contradictory, conflicting, inharmonious, irreconcilable, unsuitable ‖ DISCR *Inconsistent, incongruous,* and *incompatible* agree in expressing discordance and disagreement. The idea under *inconsistent* is: unfit to be placed together; that under *incompatible* is: incapable of being suffered together; that under *incongruous* is: unsuitable, absolutely ill-matched. *Inconsistent* is applied to our actions or conduct when either is at variance with our principles. *Inconsistent* statements are contradictory. An *inconsistent* mode of life is not in keeping with one's income, standards, and the like. Colors that clash disagreeably are *incongruous.* Things, facts, natures, sentiments, that are *incompatible* cannot exist together. One cannot be at once serene and agitated—the states are *incompatible.* A man who adopts a certain course of action must discard all amusements or diversions that are *incompatible* with it ‖ ANT accordant, harmonious, agreeing, consistent, consonant

in'con·sol'a·ble *adj* not consolable

in·con·spic′u·ous *adj* not conspicuous, attracting little notice

in·con′stant *adj* changeable, variable; fickle || **in·con′stan·cy** *n* || SYN wavering, fluctuating, variable, disloyal, changeable, mutable, faithless || ANT constant, faithful

in′con·test′a·ble *adj* not admitting of question or dispute || **in′con·test′a·bly** *adv* || SYN certain, undeniable, incontrovertible, indubitable, unquestionable, indisputable || ANT doubtful, dubious, questionable, hypothetical, unverified

in·con′ti·nent *adj* 1 unrestrained; lacking control, esp. of the sexual passions; 2 unable to restrain a natural discharge || **in·con′ti·nence** *n*

in·con·tro·vert′i·ble *adj* not admitting of debate; indisputable || SYN incontestable, undeniable, indisputable, certain, positive, indubitable, irrefragable

in′con·ven′ience *n* 1 state of being inconvenient; 2 discomfort, lack of ease; 3 something inconvenient || *vt* to cause inconvenience to, put to trouble

in′con·ven′ient *adj* disadvantageous; awkward; inopportune || SYN unsuitable, inexpedient, inopportune, embarrassing, untimely || ANT convenient, suitable, fitting

in·cor·po·rate /ĭnkôr′ərāt/ [L *incorporare* (-*atus*) to embody] *vt* 1 to form into a corporation; 2 to charter legally, as a town or organization; 3 to embody; put in as a part; include || *vi* 4 to form a corporation || **in·cor′po·ra′tion** *n* || **in·cor′po·ra′tor** *n*

in′cor·rect′ *adj* not correct

in·cor·ri·gi·ble /ĭnkôr′ĭjĭbəl, -kŏr′-/ [LL *incorrigibilis*] *adj* 1 bad beyond correction or reform || *n* 2 incorrigible person

in′cor·rupt′i·ble *adj* 1 incapable of physical decay; 2 not liable to moral corruption or bribery

in·crease /ĭnkrēs′/ [MF *encreistre* < L *increscere*] *vi* 1 to become greater; multiply; grow || *vt* 2 to augment, enlarge; 3 to make more numerous || /ĭn′krēs/ *n* 4 act or fact of increasing; 5 amount or result of increasing || **in·creas′ing·ly** *adv* || SYN *n* extension, expansion, enlargement, accession, addition, growth, development; *v* extend, enlarge, dilate, expand, magnify, grow, multiply || DISCR These verbs agree in the idea of making bigger. *Increase*, the general term, is applied to quantity, number, and to size, especially as made greater by natural processes; we *increase* the quantity of a child's food as he grows older; as the child grows, he *increases* in height and weight; he is supposed to *increase* in wisdom. To *enlarge* is to make the dimensions of width, length, or height greater, and hence to *increase* the capacity, range, or bulk of a thing; we *enlarge* the docking facilities of a port; we *enlarge* a house, a business, a magazine, a room; we do not *increase* a room or a house. To *extend* is to make greater by stretching out to greater length, or into a greater space. We may *increase* our power by *extending* its influence || ANT *n* loss, diminution; *v* decrease, diminish, lessen

in·cred′i·ble *adj* not to be believed || **in·cred′i·bly** *adv*

in′cre·du′li·ty *n* refusal or inability to believe; disbelief || SYN unbelief, doubt, skepticism (see *disbelief*)

in·cred·u·lous *adj* unbelieving, skeptical || **in·cred′u·lous·ly** *adv*

in·cre·ment /ĭn′krəmənt, ĭŋ′-/ [L *incrementum*] *n* 1 increase, augmentation; 2 that which is added

in·crim·i·nate /ĭnkrĭm′ĭnāt/ [LL *incriminare* (-*atus*)] *vt* to accuse of, or implicate or involve in, a crime || **in·crim′i·na′tion** *n*

in·crust /ĭnkrŭst′/ *vt* 1 to cover with or as with a crust || *vi* 2 to form a crust || **in′crus·ta′tion** *n*

in·cu·bate /ĭn′kyəbāt, ĭŋ′-/ [L *incubare* (-*atus*)] *vt* 1 to sit upon and hatch (eggs); 2 to keep under conditions favorable for development, as bacteria or embryos || *vi* 3 to sit on eggs || **in′cu·ba′tion** *n*

in′cu·ba′tor *n* 1 apparatus for hatching eggs; 2 apparatus for rearing prematurely born babies; 3 apparatus for maintaining cultures, as of bacteria, at the proper temperature

in·cu·bus /ĭn′kyəbəs, ĭŋ′-/ [LL = nightmare] *n* (-*bus·es* or -**bi** /-bī′/) 1 demon believed to lie heavily on persons in their sleep; 2 nightmare; 3 any depressing weight or burden

in·cul·cate /ĭnkŭl′kāt, ĭn′kŭlkāt′/ [L *inculcare* (-*atus*) to tread on] *vt* 1 to impress upon the mind by persistent admonitions; 2 inculcate (someone) with, to instill, as ideas, in the mind of || **in′cul·ca′tion** *n*

in·cul·pate /ĭnkŭl′pāt, ĭn′kəlpāt′/ [L *inculpare* (-*atus*)] *vt* to censure; to blame, incriminate

in·cum·ben·cy /ĭnkŭm′bənsē/ *n* (-*cies*) 1 act or state of being incumbent; 2 term of an incumbent; 3 duty or obligation

in·cum·bent /ĭnkŭm′bənt/ [L *incumbens* (-*entis*) lying on] *adj* 1 holding office, as the *incumbent administration*; 2 **incumbent on** or upon obligatory on the part of || *n* 3 holder of an office

in·cu·nab·u·la /ĭn′kyŏŏnab′yələ/ [L = swaddling clothes] *npl* early books, esp. books printed before 1500

in·cur /ĭnkur′/ [L *incurrere* to run

into] *v* (**-curred; -cur-ring**) *vt* 1 to bring (something unpleasant or onerous) upon oneself; 2 to contract, as a debt

in-cur-a-ble /inkyŏŏr'əbəl/ *adj* 1 not curable || *n* 2 person afflicted with an incurable disease

in-cu'ri-ous *adj* not curious

in-cur-sion /ınkur'zhən/ [see **incur**] *n* inroad; raid; invasion

Ind. 1 independent; 2 index; 3 indicative

Ind. 1 India; 2 Indian; 3 Indiana

in-debt-ed /ındet'id/ *adj* 1 in debt; 2 under obligation; owing gratitude

in-debt'ed-ness *n* 1 state of being indebted; 2 amount owed

in-de'cent *adj* 1 not decent; unseemly; 2 vulgar, offensive, lewd || **in-de'cen-cy** *n* (**-cies**)

in'de-ci'pher-a-ble *adj* not decipherable

in'de-ci'sion *n* inability to decide || SYN vacillation, fluctuation (see *irresolution*)

in'de-ci'sive *adj* 1 not decisive; inconclusive; 2 irresolute; vacillating

in'de-clin'a-ble *adj gram* not declined

in-deed' *adv* 1 in fact, in truth || *interj* 2 denoting surprise, incredulity, irony, etc.

in-de-fat-i-ga-ble /ın'difat'igəbəl/ [L *indefatigabilis*] *adj* untiring || SYN assiduous, unremitting, unflagging, untiring

in'de-fen'si-ble *adj* 1 incapable of being defended; 2 incapable of being justified

in'de-fin'a-ble *adj* incapable of being described exactly or explained

in-def'i-nite *adj* 1 not precise, vague; 2 having no fixed limit || **in-def'i-nite-ly** *adv* || SYN indeterminate, undetermined, general, vague, unlimited, unmeasured, inexact, loose, lax

in-def'i-nite ar'ti-cle *n* article (in English, *a* or *an*) which does not make definite the noun it modifies

in-def'i-nite pro'noun *n* pronoun, like English *any, somebody*, which replaces in a vague and general way the persons or things to which it refers

in-del-i-ble /ındel'ibəl/ [< L *indelebilis* indestructible] *adj* 1 not to be blotted out, effaced, or forgotten; 2 that makes indelible marks || **in-del'i-bly** *adv*

in-del'i-cate *adj* lacking in refinement or modesty; coarse, indecent || **in-del'i-ca-cy** *n* (**-cies**)

in-dem-ni-fi-ca'tion *n* 1 act of indemnifying; 2 state of being indemnified; 3 reimbursement for loss, damage, or injury || SYN restitution, compensation, amends (see *redress*)

in-dem-ni-fy /indem'nifi'/ [< L *indemnis* free from loss] *v* (**-fied**) *vt* 1 to protect or insure against loss or damage; 2 to compensate for loss

in-dem'ni-ty *n* (**-ties**) 1 security against loss or damage; 2 payment for loss

or damage || SYN protection, compensation, remuneration

in-dent /ındent'/ [ML *indentare* to notch] *vt* 1 to make a notch or notches in; 2 to set in from the margin, as the first line of a paragraph || *vi* 3 to begin a line of print or writing with a blank space || **in'den-ta'tion** *n*

in-den-ture /ındench'ər/ *n* 1 written agreement, formerly in duplicate with correspondingly notched edges; 2 such an agreement binding an apprentice to service; 3 contract; formal certificate || *vt* 4 to bind by indenture

in'de-pend'ence *n* state of being independent; freedom from control or rule by others || SYN freedom, exemption, immunity (see *liberty*)

In'de-pend'ence Day' *n* July 4, U.S. holiday commemorating the adoption of the Declaration of Independence in 1776

in'de-pend'ent *adj* 1 not relying on, supported by, or governed by another; 2 having enough to live on; 3 self-reliant; 4 unattached to any political party; 5 not influenced by others || *n* 6 independent person || **in'de-pend'ent-ly** *adv*

in'de-scrib'a-ble *adj* that cannot be described

in'de-struct'i-ble *adj* not capable of being destroyed

in'de-ter'mi-na-ble *adj* not to be known or defined exactly

in'de-ter'mi-nate /-mınit/ *adj* 1 not settled; 2 indefinite, vague; 3 *math* having an indefinite number of values or solutions

in-dex /in'deks/ [L = that which indicates] *n* (**-dex-es** or **-di-ces** /-disēz'/) 1 forefinger; 2 pointer; 3 alphabetical table of the contents of a book; 4 that which serves to point out or indicate; 5 figure expressing a ratio or some property, as *index of intelligence*; 6 *typ* mark used to call attention; 7 **Index** *R C Ch* list of books not to be read without special permission || *vt* 8 to provide with an index; 9 to place in an index

in'dex fin'ger *n* forefinger

In-di-a /in'dē-ə/ *n* republic in S Asia, member of the British Commonwealth of Nations (630,000,000; 1,269,420 sq.m.; cap. New Delhi)

In'di-a ink' *n* permanent black ink made of lampblack

In'di-an *n* 1 member of any of the aboriginal races of the New World; 2 *colloq* any of the Indian languages of the New World; 3 native or citizen of India || also *adj*

In-di-an-a /in'dē-an'ə/ *n* state in central U.S. (5,193,669; 36,291 sq.m.; cap. Indianapolis) || **In'di-an'i-an** *n*

In-di-an-ap-o-lis /in'dē-ənap'əlis/ *n* capital of Indiana (744,624)

In'di-an club' *n* bottle-shaped club,

swung by the hands in gymnastic exercises

In'di•an file' *n* 1 single file || *adv* 2 in single file

In'di•an giv'er *n colloq* person who asks for and takes back a gift that he has given

In'di•an O'cean *n* ocean S of Asia between Africa and Australia

In'di•an sum'mer *n* period of mild weather occurring in the late fall or early winter

In'di•an wres'tling *n* contest in which two opponents sit facing each other with their right elbows on the table and grasping each other's right hand with the forearms straight up, the winner being the one who can force the other's hand down onto the table

In•dic /in'dik/ *adj* pert. to India or to the Indo-European languages spoken there

indic. indicative

in•di•cate /in'dikāt'/ [L *indicare* (*-atus*)] *vt* 1 to point out; 2 to be a sign of; show; make known; 3 to express briefly; hint; 4 *med* to show the need for || **in'di•ca'tion** *n* || SYN betoken, signify, denote, reveal, disclose, hint, suggest, intimate, manifest, exhibit, display, show

in•dic•a•tive /indik'ətiv/ *adj* 1 pointing out; suggestive; 2 *gram* (mood) of a verb used to assert or state a fact or ask a direct question || *n* 3 indicative mood; 4 verb in the indicative

in'di•ca'tor *n* one who or that which indicates, as a gauge or dial

in•di•ces /in'disēz'/ *pl* of **index**

in•dict /in'dīt/ [AF *enditer* influenced by Latin *dictare*] *vt* 1 to accuse of wrongdoing; 2 *law* (of a grand jury) to charge with a crime || **in•dict'a•ble** *adj* || **in•dict'ment** *n*

In•dies /in'dēz/ [*pl* of *obs Indy* India] *nsg* the Indies SE Asia in general, including India, Indochina, and the East Indies

in•dif•fer•ence *n* 1 state of being unconcerned; absence of feeling for or against; 2 unimportance; insignificance; 3 mediocrity || SYN apathy, listlessness, insensibility, unconcern, heedlessness, neglect, aloofness, coldness || DISCR *Apathy* is absence of feeling; primarily, *apathy* names a natural and permanent state, in which one is passionless and unexcitable, unfeeling, sluggish, phlegmatic; secondarily, *apathy* names a condition which resembles this state, induced or produced by some paralyzing shock or numbing influence, as the *apathy* of hopelessness. *Indifference* is the absence of interest or attention; it is often a transitory lack of feeling. *Insensibility* is a lack of mental feeling or emotion; if induced, it is temporary, as the condition following nervous shock; if it is nat-

ural, it is permanent. *Unconcern* is complacent disregard for the future. It may be the fruit of *apathy*, *insensibility*, or *indifference*

in•dif'fer•ent *adj* 1 unconcerned; 2 having no marked preference; 3 unimportant; 4 mediocre; 5 nonessential; 6 impartial || **in•dif'fer•ent•ly** *adv* || SYN careless, heedless, apathetic (see *stoical*)

in•dig•e•nous /indij'inəs/ [< LL *indigenus*] *adj* 1 born or produced in a particular country; native; 2 innate || SYN inborn, inherent, innate (see *native*)

in•di•gent /in'dijənt/ [L *indigens* (*-entis*)] *adj* destitute, needy || **in'di•gence** *n*

in•di•gest'i•ble *adj* not digestible

in•di•ges'tion *n* difficulty in digesting food

in•dig•nant /indig'nənt/ [< L *indignari* to be indignant] *adj* feeling anger or scorn at injustice, ingratitude, etc. || **in•dig'nant•ly** *adv*

in•dig•na'tion *n* anger at what is unworthy, dishonorable, or base || SYN wrath, resentment, fury, rage (see *anger*)

in•dig•ni•ty [L *indignitas* unworthiness] *n* (*-ties*) act intended to lower the dignity of another; insult || SYN affront, rudeness, discourtesy, outrage, offense || ANT honor, compliment, politeness

in•di•go /in'digō/ [Sp < Gk *indikon* Indian] *n* (*-gos* or *-goes*) 1 dark-blue dye obtained from various herbaceous shrubs or made synthetically; 2 deep-blue violet || *also adj*

in'di•rect' *adj* 1 not straight; 2 roundabout; 3 not straightforward; 4 secondary; not having direct bearing || **in'di•rect'ly** *adv* || **in'di•rec'tion** *n*

in'di•rect dis'course *n* quotation of what a speaker says, not in his exact words, but with words changed to suit the syntax required in a subordinate clause after a verb of saying or asking, as *where I was going* in *he asked me where I was going*

in'di•rect ob'ject *n gram* word or words representing the recipient to or for which a verbal action is performed, as *car* in *he gave the car a greasing*

in'dis•creet' *adj* not discreet; imprudent

in'dis•cre'tion *n* lack of discretion or an instance of it

in'dis•crim'i•nate /-nit/ *adj* 1 not discriminating; not choosing carefully; 2 confused; promiscuous || **in'dis•crim'i•nate•ly** *adv* || SYN confused, mingled, promiscuous, heterogeneous

in'dis•pen'sa•ble *adj* absolutely necessary or requisite || SYN essential, required, requisite (see *necessary*)

in'dis•posed' *adj* 1 slightly ill; 2 disinclined || **in'dis•po•si'tion** *n*

in'dis•put'a•ble /*also* indis'pyə-/ *adj* too evident to admit of debate

in•dis•sol•u•ble /in'disol'yəbəl/ *adj* 1

not capable of being dissolved; indestructible; **2** forever binding

in·dis·tinct/ /ˈɪn·dɪˈstɪŋkt/ *adj* **1** not easily distinguishable by the senses or the mind; **2** faint; indefinite

in'dis·tin'guish·a·ble *adj* **1** not distinguishable; **2** imperceptible

in·dite /ɪnˈdaɪt/ [OF *enditer* to make known] *vt* to compose, write

in·di·um /ˈɪn·dē·əm/ [< Gk *indikon* indigo] *n chem* rare, silver-white fusible metallic element (**In;** at.no. 49; at.wt. 114.82)

in·di·vid·u·al /ˌɪn·dɪˈvɪjˈōō·əl/ [< L *individuus* indivisible] *adj* **1** existing as a single and distinct thing or personality; **2** pert. to or characteristic of a single person or thing; **3** of a peculiar or striking character ‖ *n* **4** single or separate person, animal, or thing, as distinguished from a class or group; **5** person ‖ **in'di·vid'u·al·ly** *adv*

in'di·vid'u·al·ism *n* **1** egoism; the pursuit of personal ends; **2** social theory that favors the rights of the individual over those of the state; **3** individuality; **4** personal peculiarity ‖ **in'di·vid'u·al·ist** *n* ‖ **in'di·vid'u·al·is'tic** *adj*

in'di·vid'u·al'i·ty /-alˈ-/ *n* (-ties) **1** fact or condition of being individual; **2** individual existence; **3** sum of the distinctive characteristics that distinguish one person or thing from another; **4** individual thing or person

in'di·vis'i·ble *adj* not divisible

In·do- /ˈɪnˈdō-/ [Gk] *comb form* India

In'do·chi'na *n* peninsula in SE Asia stretching from India and China on the north to the southern tip of Malaya ‖ **In'do·Chi·nese'** *adj & n* (-nese)

in·doc·tri·nate /ɪnˈdɒkˈtrɪnāt/ [< *in-*¹ + *doctrine*] *vt* **1** to instruct in learning, principles, or doctrines; **2** to inculcate ‖ **in·doc'tri·na'tion** *n*

In'do·Eu'ro·pe'an *n* **1** family of languages of India, central and western Asia, and Europe, including the Armenian, Indo-Iranian, Hellenic, Celtic, Italic, Germanic, and Balto-Slavic branches; **2** prehistoric parent language of this family; **3** member of any of the peoples speaking an Indo-European language ‖ also *adj*

In'do·I·ra'ni·an *n* subfamily of Indo-European family of languages, including the Iranian branches and the Indo-European languages of the Indian subcontinent ‖ also *adj*

in·do·lent /ˈɪn·dələnt/ [LL *indolens* (-*entis*) insensitive to pain] *adj* **1** fond of idleness; laziness; **2** *pathol* causing little pain ‖ **in'do·lence** *n* ‖ SYN lazy, slothful, sluggish, inert (see *idle*)

in·dom·i·ta·ble /ɪnˈdɒmˈɪtəbəl/ [< L *indomitus* untamed] *adj* untamable; irrepressible; unconquerable

In'do·ne'sia /-nēzhˈə, -nēshˈə/ *n* republic in the Malay Archipelago, comprising Sumatra, Java, the Celebes, part of Borneo and New Guinea, and many smaller islands (100,795,000; 735,272 sq.m.; cap. Djakarta) ‖ **In'do·ne'sian** *adj & n*

in'door' [< *within door*] *adj* living, belonging, or done within doors

in·doors' *adv* inside or into the house

in·dorse /ɪnˈdôrs/ *vt* var of **endorse**

in·du·bi·ta·ble /ɪnˈd(y)ōōbˈɪtəbəl/ [L *indubitabilis*] *adj* too evident to be doubted; unquestionable ‖ **in·du'bi·ta·bly** *adv* ‖ SYN incontestable, indisputable, certain, evident

in·duce /ɪnˈd(y)ōōs/ [L *inducere* to lead in] *vt* **1** to influence (to do something); **2** to bring on, effect, cause; **3** *phys* to produce without contact, as a magnetic or electric effect; **4** to arrive at (a conclusion) by reasoning from particular cases to general principles ‖ SYN incite, persuade, influence, impel, urge, move

in·duce'ment *n* **1** act of inducing; **2** incentive

in·duct /ɪnˈdʌkt/ [L *inductus* led in] *vt* **1** to install in office; **2** to receive (a draftee) formally into the armed forces

in·duc'tance *n* **1** property of a circuit by virtue of which an electromotive force is produced in it by the variation of an electric current either in the circuit itself or in an adjacent circuit or by the fluctuation of an adjacent magnetic field; **2** device having this property

in·duc·tee' *n* person inducted into the armed forces

in·duc'tion *n* **1** installation of a person into office; **2 a** production of an electric charge, an electric current, or a magnetic field by a neighboring electric charge, electric current, or magnetic field without contact between the objects in which they are present; **b** electric charge, electric current, or magnetic field so produced; **3 a** process of reasoning from a part to a whole or of reaching a general conclusion from particular cases; **b** result so reached ‖ **in·duc'tive** *adj* ‖ SYN (see *deduction, conclusion*)

in·duc'tion coil' *n* transformer with soft-iron core around which are wound two concentric coils in the inner one of which, made of heavy wire, a low-voltage rapidly interrupted direct current is passed to produce in the outer one, made of fine wire, a high-voltage alternating current

in·duc'tion mo'tor *n* alternating-current motor in which the rotor is activated by the current induced in it by a rotating magnetic field in the stationary field magnets

in·duc·tor /induk′tər/ [see **induce**] n
1 one who inducts into office; 2 elec
device designed to introduce inductance into a circuit

in·dulge /indulj′/ [L indulgere to be
courteous to] vt 1 to give way to,
humor; 2 to yield to, give free rein to
‖ vi 3 to gratify one's tastes or desires ‖ SYN humor, pamper, spoil,
satisfy (see **gratify**)

in·dul′gence n 1 act or instance of indulging; 2 tolerance; 3 R C Ch
remission of temporal punishment
still due for sin after full repentance
and sacramental absolution

in·dul′gent adj characterized by indulgence to others; permissive

in·dus·tri·al /indus′trē·əl/ [see **industry**] adj 1 pert. to, of the nature of,
engaged in, or resulting from industry ‖ n 2 **industrials** pl stocks or
bonds of industrial enterprises

in·dus′tri·al·ist n owner or manager of
an industrial enterprise

in·dus′tri·al·ize′ vt to convert (an area)
into an economy based on industry ‖
in·dus′tri·al·i·za′tion n

in·dus·tri·al rev·o·lu′tion n social and
economic changes brought about by
the shift from handwork to large-
scale machine production that began
in England around the middle of the
18th century

in·dus′tri·al un′ion n labor union comprising all the workers in a particular industry

in·dus′tri·ous adj characterized by dili-
gence or application; hard-working,
‖ SYN assiduous, diligent, sedulous
(see **active, busy**) ‖ ANT indolent,
slothful, lazy

in·dus·try /in′dəstrē/ [L industria] n
(-tries) 1 steady application to a
task, business, or labor; 2 any form
of economic activity; 3 productive
enterprises generally; 4 productive
occupations as distinguished from finance and commerce; 5 particular
branch of work or trade

-ine [L -inus or -ina] adj suf 1 of the
nature of, pert. to, as asinine, marine; 2 like, as adamantine; 3 zool
belonging to the genus, as canine,
feline ‖ n suf 4 nouns from Latin, as
doctrine, medicine; 5 chem a forming names of alkaloids and basic
substances, as cocaine, aniline; b
names of the halogens, as chlorine

in·e·bri·ate /inēb′rē·āt′/ [L inebriare
(-atus) < ebrius drunk] vt 1 to intoxicate ‖ /-it/ n 2 drunkard ‖ **in·e′·
bri·a′tion** n

in·ed′i·ble adj not fit to be eaten

in·ef·fa·ble /inef′əbəl/ [L ineffabilis]
adj 1 unspeakable; inexpressible; 2
too sacred for utterance

in′ef·fec′tive adj 1 not producing or
incapable of producing the desired
result; 2 lacking in artistic effect ‖
SYN vain, useless, fruitless, inefficient,

inefficacious, futile ‖ ANT efficient,
fruitful, productive, operative

in′ef·fec′tu·al adj not producing the
desired result; unavailing; inefficient

in′ef·fi·ca·cy n inability to produce desired results ‖ **in′ef·fi·ca′cious** adj

in′ef·fi′cient adj not efficient ‖ **in′ef·fi′-
cien·cy** n ‖ SYN ineffective, incompetent, powerless, futile, unavailing,
fruitless, ineffectual, vain

in·el′e·gant adj lacking in beauty, refinement, elegance, or good taste

in·el′i·gi·ble adj 1 not eligible; 2 legally
unfitted for choice or election

in·ept /inept′/ [L ineptus] adj 1 not fit
or suitable; 2 absurd; 3 clumsy; 4
inefficient

in′e·qual′i·ty n (-ties) 1 lack of equality; 2 disparity; 3 unevenness, as in
a surface; 4 lack of due proportion;
uneven distribution; insufficiency; 5
math expression of the relation between unequal quantities ‖ SYN diversity, disproportion (see **disparity**)

in·eq′ui·ty n (-ties) lack of fairness or
justice ‖ **in·eq′ui·ta·ble** adj

in·er·rant /iner′ənt, -ur′-/ adj infal-
lible; free from error ‖ **in·er′ran·cy** n

in·ert /inurt′/ [L iners (-ertis)] unskill-
ful] adj 1 having no power of mo-
tion, action, or resistance; 2 sluggish; 3 having no active chemical or
medicinal properties ‖ SYN passive,
apathetic, dead, dull (see **inactive**)

in·er·tia /inursh′ə/ [L = lack of skill,
inactivity] n 1 tendency not to move
or act; 2 phys that property by virtue
of which a body remains at rest or
continues to move in a straight line,
unless acted upon by some external
force

in·er′tial guid′ance n automatic navigational system using gyroscopic devices, etc. for high-speed aircraft,
missiles, and spacecraft, which after
launching, adjusts the vehicle to a
predetermined flight path

in·es·cap′a·ble adj that cannot be
avoided or ignored

in′es·sen′tial adj 1 not essential ‖ n 2
inessential thing

in·es′ti·ma·ble adj 1 not to be computed; 2 beyond measure or price

in·ev·i·ta·ble /inev′itəbəl/ [L inevitabi-
lis] adj unavoidable ‖ **in·ev′i·ta·bly**
adv ‖ **in·ev′i·ta·bil′i·ty** /-bil′-/ n ‖
SYN unpreventable, unevadable (see
necessary)

in′ex·act′ adj not precise, correct, accurate, or punctual

in′ex·cus′a·ble adj not admitting of excuse; unpardonable ‖ **in′ex·cus′a·bly**
adv

in′ex·haust′i·ble adj 1 not to be used
up; unfailing; 2 tireless

in·ex·o·ra·ble /ineks′ərəbəl/ [L inex-
orabilis] adj unyielding; unrelenting
‖ **in·ex′o·ra·bly** adv ‖ SYN inflexible,
relentless, resolute, implacable

in·ex·pe′di·ent *adj* unsuitable to conditions; inadvisable

in′ex·pen′sive *adj* cheap, costing little

in′ex·pe′ri·ence *n* lack of experience and the knowledge gained from it ‖ **in′ex·pe′ri·enced** *adj*

in·ex·pert /in′ikspurt′, inek′spərt/ *adj* not expert, unskilled

in·ex·pi·a·ble /ineks′pē-əbəl/ *adj* not capable of being expiated or atoned for

in·ex′pli·ca·ble *adj* not capable of being explained

in′ex·press′i·ble *adj* incapable of being uttered or described

in ex·ten·so /in′iksten′sō/ [L] *adv* at full length; in full

in′ex·tin′guish·a·ble *adj* unquenchable

in ex·tre·mis /in′ikstrēm′is/ [L = at the very ends] *adv* at the point of death

in·ex′tri·ca·ble *adj* 1 involved beyond extrication; 2 incapable of being untied or disentangled; 3 unsolvable ‖ **in·ex′tri·ca·bly** *adv*

inf. 1 infantry; 2 infinitive

in·fal′li·ble *adj* 1 incapable of erring; 2 unfailing; 3 certain ‖ **in·fal′li·bil′i·ty** /-bil′-/ *n*

in·fa·mous /in′fəməs/ *adj* 1 having notoriously evil or vile repute; 2 scandalous ‖ **syn** shameful, disgraceful, detestable, ignominious, abominable, outrageous, wicked, villainous, atrocious

in·fa·my /in′fəmē/ [L *infamia* ill fame] *n* (-mies) 1 public disgrace; 2 baseness, vileness; 3 infamous act ‖ **syn** disgrace, ignominy, dishonor, reproach, baseness, opprobrium ‖ **ant** honor, dignity, respect

in·fan·cy /in′fənsē/ *n* (-cies) 1 state or period of being an infant; 2 first stage of anything; 3 period extending up to legal age

in·fant /in′fənt/ [L *infans* (-antis) not speaking] *n* 1 baby, very young child; 2 beginner; novice; 3 *law* person who has not yet attained legal age; minor

in·fan·ti·cide /infant′isid′/ [LL *infanticidium*] *n* 1 murder of an infant, esp. one just born; 2 person who murders an infant

in′fan·tile /-tīl′, -til/ *adj* 1 pert. to infants or infancy; 2 babyish

in′fan·tile′ pa·ral′y·sis *n* poliomyelitis

in·fan·try /in′fəntrē/ [F *infanterie* < It *infanteria*] *n* (-tries) branch of the army consisting of soldiers who fight on foot ‖ **in′fan·try·man** /-mən/ *n* (-men /-mən/)

in·fat·u·ate /infach′ōō-āt′/ [L *infatuare* (-atus) to make a fool of] *vt* to inspire with an extravagantly foolish passion ‖ **in·fat′u·at′ed** *adj* ‖ **in·fat′u·a′tion** *n*

in·fect /infekt′/ [L *inficere* (-fectus) to taint] *vt* 1 to contaminate; taint; 2 to communicate a disease, mood, or the like to

in·fec′tion *n* 1 act or process of infecting; 2 state of being infected; 3 infectious disease ‖ **syn** communication, epidemic (see *contagion*)

in·fec′tious or **in·fec′tive** *adj* 1 capable of communicating a disease by spreading germs; 2 readily communicated or spread

in·fe·lic′i·tous *adj* 1 unfortunate, unhappy; 2 inappropriate

in·fe·lic′i·ty *n* (-ties) 1 unhappiness; 2 inappropriate act or expression

in·fer /infur′/ [L *inferre* to bring in] *v* (-ferred; -fer·ring) *vt* 1 to derive by reasoning; conclude; 2 to guess; suppose ‖ *vi* 3 to draw conclusions ‖ **syn** deduce, derive, gather, conclude, imply ‖ **discr** *Infer* is often confused with *imply*. To *infer* is, chiefly, to derive, or come to, a conclusion; one who *implies* suggests, or affords tangible grounds for, a conclusion. What a speaker *implies*, his hearers may *infer*

in·fer·ence /in′fərəns/ *n* 1 process or act of inferring; 2 that which is inferred ‖ **in′fer·en′tial** /-rensh′-/ *adj* ‖ **syn** (see *conclusion*)

in·fe·ri·or /infir′ē-ər/ [L, *comp* of *inferus* low] *adj* 1 lower in place; nearer the bottom; 2 lower in rank, dignity, or office; 3 of lower quality, intelligence, ability, etc.; 4 less in quantity or number; 5 abject, servile ‖ *n* 6 inferior person or thing ‖ **in·fe′ri·or′i·ty** /-or′-, -ôr′-/ *n* ‖ **syn** *adj* subordinate, subservient; mediocre, second-rate

in·fer·nal /infurn′əl/ [< L *infernus* situated below] *adj* 1 of or pert. to hell; 2 hellish; fiendish; 3 outrageous ‖ **syn** diabolical, devilish, satanic, demoniac, hellish

in·fer·no /infurn′ō/ [It] *n* 1 hell; 2 place resembling hell; 3 *Inferno* first part of Dante's *Divine Comedy*, describing hell

in·fer′tile *adj* not fertile, barren

in·fest /infest′/ [L *infestare* to assail] *vt* to overrun; beset or annoy constantly ‖ **in′fes·ta′tion** *n*

in·fi·del /in′fidel/ [L *infidelis* faithless] *n* 1 one who rejects religion; 2 professed unbeliever in whatever religion is locally regarded as true, as a non-Christian or a non-Muslim ‖ **syn** unbeliever, disbeliever (see *skeptic*)

in′fi·del′i·ty /-del′-/ *n* (-ties) 1 breach of trust; disloyalty; 2 adultery

in′field′ *n* *baseball* 1 space within the base lines; 2 infielders collectively

in′field′er *n* *baseball* player stationed in the infield

in·fil·trate /in′filtrāt′, infil′trāt/ *vt* 1 to filter through, or cause to filter; 2 to pass through or into, as by filtering ‖ *vi* 3 to filter or pass through ‖ **in′fil·tra′tion** *n*

in·fi·nite /in′finit/ [L *infinitus* unbounded] *adj* 1 immeasurably great;

2 unlimited; immeasurable ‖ *n* **3** that which is infinite ‖ SYN *adj* limitless, illimitable, interminable, boundless, countless, fathomless, endless, vast, eternal

in·fin·i·tes·i·mal /in'finites'iməl/ [*infinite* + cent*esimal*] *adj* **1** immeasurably small; very minute; **2** of or pert. to very minute quantities; **3** *math* having a value less than any assignable value

in·fin·i·tive /infin'itiv/ [LL *infinitivus* indefinite] *n* verb form in many languages without limitation of person or number, often used as a noun. In English, the simple verb root, used after modal auxiliaries or the particle *to*, as go in *I must go* or *I wish to go* ‖ also *adj*

in·fin·i·tude /infin'it(y)ōod'/ *n* **1** infinity; **2** infinite number or extent

in·fin'i·ty *n* (-ties) **1** state or quality of being infinite; **2** that which is infinite; **3** infinite extent of time, space, or quantity; **4** indefinitely great quantity

in·firm' [L *infirmus*] *adj* **1** feeble, weak; **2** insecure; frail

in·fir·ma·ry /infurm'ərē/ *n* (-ries) place for the treatment of the sick and injured, esp. the quarters for the sick in a school, factory, etc.

in·fir'mi·ty *n* (-ties) **1** state of being infirm; **2** weakness; illness; frailty ‖ SYN foible, defect, disease, feebleness (see *debility*)

in'fix *n* **1** *gram* affix inserted in the body of a word, as *n* in the present tense of Latin *vincere* (root *vic-*) ‖ **in·fix'** *vt* **2** to fasten by piercing; to implant; **3** *gram* to insert as an infix

in·flame' [MF *enflammer* < L *inflammare*] *vt* **1** to fire with passion; **2** to excite; provoke; **3** to cause inflammation in ‖ *vi* **4** to become inflamed ‖ SYN anger, exasperate, enrage, arouse, kindle, fire

in·flam'ma·ble /-flam'əbəl/ *adj* **1** easily set on fire; **2** easily aroused to passion ‖ *n* **3** something inflammable

in·flam·ma·tion /in'fləmāsh'ən/ *n* **1** act of inflaming or condition of being inflamed; **2** unnatural condition of any part of the body due to irritation and shown by pain, redness, heat, and swelling

in·flam'ma·to·ry /-flam'ətôr'-, -tōr'-/ *adj* **1** tending to inflame the passions; **2** *pathol* pert. to, tending to produce, or showing inflammation

in·flate' /inflāt'/ [L *inflare* (-*atus*)] *vt* **1** to swell out, distend, as a balloon; **2** to puff up, make proud; **3** to expand or raise unduly, as prices ‖ *vi* **4** to become inflated

in·fla'tion *n* **1** act of inflating or state of being inflated; **2** sharp rise in prices accompanying an increase in the amount of money in circulation ‖ **in·fla'tion·ar·y** *adj*

in·flect /inflekt'/ [L *inflectere* to bend] *vt* **1** to vary the pitch or tone of (the voice); **2** *gram* to vary the form of (a word) by inflection ‖ *vi* **3** to undergo inflection

in·flec'tion *n* **1** variations undergone by words to mark case, number, gender, etc.; **2** change in pitch or tone of voice ‖ **in·flec'tion·al** *adj*

in·flex'i·ble [L *inflectere* (-*flexus*) to bend] *adj* **1** not flexible, rigid; **2** unalterable ‖ **in·flex'i·bil'i·ty** /-bil'-/ *n* ‖ SYN unbending, obstinate, obdurate, unappeasable, implacable, immovable, inexorable, resolute, rigorous

in·flict /inflict'/ [L *infligere* (-*flictus*) to strike on] *vt* **1** to cause by or as if by striking, as pain or a wound; **2** to cause to be suffered or borne; **3** to impose, as a punishment or something unpleasant ‖ **in·flic'tion** *n*

in'flow' *n* **1** act of flowing in; **2** that which flows in

in·flu·ence /in'flōō-əns/ [ML *influentia* astral emanation] *n* **1** power tending to produce effects by indirect or invisible means; **2** power arising from wealth or station, as *political influence;* **3** one who or that which has influence ‖ *vt* **4** to exert influence on; affect ‖ SYN *v* bias, sway, prejudice, alter, impel, affect, modify; *n* control, weight, authority, ascendancy

in'flu·ence ped'dling *n* the trading of one's contacts with corrupt politicians for personal gain

in'flu·en'tial /-ensh'əl/ *adj* having or exerting influence

in·flu·en·za /in'flōō-en'zə/ [It < ML *influentia* astral emanation] *n* acute contagious virus disease, frequently epidemic, characterized by inflammations of the air passages, severe muscular pains and headache, digestive and nervous disturbances, and prostration

in'flux' [LL *influxus* astral influence] *n* **1** inflow; **2** point at which a stream flows into another or into the sea

in·form' [L *informare* to give shape to] *vt* **1** to give (a person) knowledge, as of an event ‖ *vi* **2** to give incriminating information; **3** to enlighten ‖ SYN advise, notify, mention, tell, communicate, apprise, enlighten, vitalize, inspirit, animate

in·for'mal *adj* **1** not according to custom or rule; irregular; **2** without formality; unceremonious; **3** relaxed; casual ‖ **in'for·mal'i·ty** /-mal'-/ *n* (-ties)

in·form'ant /-ənt/ *n* **1** person from whom one gets information; **2** native speaker whose speech is used as a source of information by students of language

in·for·ma·tion /in'fərmāsh'ən/ *n* **1** knowledge given or acquired; **2** timely knowledge, esp. of facts; news; **3** *law* a lawsuit or accusation brought on behalf of the government; **b** declaration made before a magistrate requesting him to issue a summons or warrant || **in·for'ma·tion·al** *adj* SYN tidings (see *knowledge, intelligence*)

in·for·ma'tion re·triev'al *n* systematic recovery of information from any place where it has been stored, notably, a memory bank

in·form'a·tive *adj* giving knowledge; instructive

in·form'er *n* one who gives incriminating information

in·fra /in'fr∂/ [L] *adv* below, usu. in a text

in·fra- *pref* beneath, below, inferior to

in·frac'tion [< L *infractus* broken into] *n* breach, violation, as of a law or treaty

in'fra dig' *adj* beneath the dignity of a person

in'fra·red' *n* that part of the spectrum which lies beyond the visible range at the red end || also *adj*

in'fra·son'ic *adj* of, pert. to, or using vibrations with frequencies below the frequency of audible sound

in·fre'quent *adj* **1** seldom occurring; **2** occurring or placed only at long intervals || **in·fre'quent·ly** *adv* || **in·fre'quen·cy** *n*

in·fringe' [L *infringere* to break, weaken] *vt* **1** to break or violate, as a law || *vi* **2** **infringe on** to encroach or trespass on || **in·fringe'ment** *n* || SYN invade, transgress, violate, trespass, break

in·fu·ri·ate /infyŏŏr'ē·āt'/ [ML *infuriare* (*-atus*)] *vt* to enrage, madden

in·fuse' /infyŏŏz'/ [L *infundere* (*-fusus*) to pour in] *vt* **1** to introduce, as by pouring; **2** to fill; animate; **3** to impart or teach gradually; **4** to steep, as tea, in a liquid, in order to extract the soluble ingredients || **in·fu'sion** *n*

-ing¹ /-iŋ/ [OE *-ing, -ung*] *n suf* showing verbal action or its result, as *building*

-ing² [ME < OE *-ende*] *suf* forming the present participle of verbs, often used adjectively, as *singing canary*

in·gen·ious /injēn'y∂s/ [< L *ingenium* cleverness] *adj* **1** having inventive skill; clever; **2** skillfully contrived or made || **in·ge·nu·i·ty** /in'jən(y)ŏŏ'-itē/ *n* (*-ties*)

in·gé·nue /an'zhənŏŏ'/ [F = ingenuous] *n* **1** role of an inexperienced young girl in a play; **2** actress who portrays it

in·gen·u·ous /injen'yŏŏ∂s/ [< L *ingenuus* natural, free-born] *adj* **1** innocent, artless; **2** frank, open || **in·gen'u·ous·ly** *adv* || **in·gen'u·ous·ness** *n* || SYN unreserved, sincere; honorable (see *open*)

in·gest /injest'/ [L *ingestere* (*-gestus*) to pour in] *vt* to put or receive (food) into the stomach || **in·ges'tion** /-chən/ *n*

in·glo'ri·ous *adj* shameful, disgraceful

in·got /iŋ'gət/ [prob < MF *lingot*] *n* mass of metal cast into a mold, generally for storing and later recasting into some form for practical use

in·grained /ingrānd', in'grānd'/ [< *in* + *grain*] *adj* deep-seated; inherent; inveterate || SYN deep-seated, rooted (see *inherent*)

in·grate /in'grāt/ [L *ingratus*] *n* ungrateful person

in·gra·ti·ate /ingrāsh'ē·āt'/ [< L *gratia* grace] *vt* to bring (oneself) into the favor of another || **in·gra'ti·at'ing·ly** *adv*

in·grat'i·tude' *n* ungratefulness

in·gre·di·ent /ingrēd'ē·∂nt/ [< L *ingredi* to enter upon] *n* constituent part of a mixture or compound

in·gress /in'gres/ [L *ingressus* a going into] *n* **1** entrance, access; **2** liberty of access

in'grown' *adj* **1** growing within; **2** grown into adjacent flesh

in·hab'it [MF *enhabiter* < L *inhabitare*] *vt* to dwell in

in·hab'it·ant /-∂nt/ *n* person or animal that inhabits a place; resident

in·hal·ant /inhāl'∂nt/ *adj* **1** used for inhaling || *n* **2** medicine to be inhaled

in·hale' /inhāl'/ [*in-*¹ + L *halare* to breathe] *vt & vi* to breathe in || **in'ha·la'tion** /-∂-/ *n*

in·hal'er *n* apparatus for inhaling medicated vapors

in·har·mo'ni·ous *adj* not harmonious

in·here' /inhir'/ [L *inhaerere*] *vi* to be inherent

in·her'ent *adj* existing inseparably in something; essential; inborn || **in·her'ent·ly** *adv* || SYN innate, inbred, inborn, inseparable, ingrained, intrinsic, essential || DISCR That is *inherent* which exists in a person or thing as an inseparable or abiding quality; we speak of *inherent* characteristics; *inherent* properties. *Intrinsic* refers to the essential nature of a person or thing. *Inherent* and *intrinsic* are often used interchangeably, and both are opposed to the idea of accidental, merely apparent, adventitious, or transitory; but *inherent* emphasizes the permanent and connected, *intrinsic* the natural and constitutional aspect; we speak of an *inherent*, not an *intrinsic* love of luxury; we say *intrinsic* worth or virtue. That is *essential* without which a thing would not be what it is. *Inborn*, *inbred*, and *innate* are used only in connection with beings. *Innate* and *inborn* are almost exactly synonymous; but *innate* has the more extensive connotation; we say that properties are *innate* or *inborn*, in-

nate emphasizing their natural and *inherent* quality, *inborn* the mere fact that they are implanted in us from birth. *Inbred* emphasizes either the inherited or the cultivated aspect of a characteristic; a property or quality that is inherited and nurtured, as a talent, is both *inborn* and *inbred;* a habit, deeply rooted from birth, is *inbred;* characteristics secured in offspring from the cross-breeding of animals are *inbred. Ingrained* describes that which has seeped into the very being and has stamped itself as indelibly as a fast dye. We speak of *innate* ideas, *innate* shortcomings, *inborn* independence, *inborn* snobbishness, *inbred* considerateness, *inbred* feelings, *ingrained* selfishness

in·her·it /ĭnher′ĭt/ [MF *enheriter* to make heir < LL *inhereditare*] *vt* 1 to receive (property or rank) as an heir; 2 to receive (genetic characteristics) by heredity ‖ *vi* 3 to inherit property ‖ **in·her′i·tor** *n*

in·her·it·ance *n* 1 act of inheriting; 2 that which is or may be inherited

in·hib·it /ĭnhĭb′ĭt/ [L *inhibere* (*-hibitus*)] *vt* 1 to restrain; hold in check; 2 to forbid ‖ SYN prohibit, forbid, hinder, debar, preclude ‖ DISCR To *forbid* is the familiar term, and is both direct and personal; a mother *forbids* her child to cross the street. To *prohibit* is the formal, judicial term; it connotes more indirect, wide, and official action; the municipal government *prohibits* citizens from crossing the streets except at street intersections. A father *forbids* his boy to smoke; a garage owner *prohibits* smoking on his premises. The personal command in *forbid* has only personal force behind it; the prohibitions of a city or corporation are enforceable by law. To *inhibit*, in ordinary use, means to hold back or restrain; psychologists use the word to suggest repression, as *inhibited* feelings or instincts ‖ ANT further, permit, sanction, advance, promote

in·hi·bi′tion *n* 1 act of inhibiting or state of being inhibited; 2 *psychol* prevention of the exercise of one impulse by the exercise of another

in·hib′i·tor *n* substance added to another to inhibit chemical change

in·hos′pi·ta·ble *adj* 1 not hospitable; 2 barren, cheerless

in·hu′man *adj* 1 unfeeling; cruel, brutal; 2 lacking human qualities ‖ SYN ferocious, cruel, fierce, savage, merciless, ruthless, relentless, barbarous, bloodthirsty ‖ DISCR *Cruel* describes that indifference to the suffering of others, or pleasure therein, which characterizes many people in their natural state, as is evidenced by the desire of children to torment animals or each other. As people grow

civilized, or as children are molded by their environment, the disposition to be *cruel* is replaced by that kindness, gentleness, and tenderness to life which is known as humanity. Those who, civilized and mature, still lack the humanity to be expected of a decent human being, are *inhuman. Savage* implies the cruelty of the untamed, the natural bloodthirstiness and delight in prey of the uncivilized. *Ferocious* adds to *savage* the fire of anger, a beastlike violence; *ferocious* is indicative of a natural disposition to be murderously rapacious. *Fierce* describes a hotly combative nature, flaring, vehement, raging; fierceness differs from ferocity in being more the matter of a moment, hot but passing, and in being, often, latent or dormant. The quietest of women will instantly wax *fierce* in defense of her children. *Fierce* is now often used of feelings that are ardent, impetuous, almost angrily passionate, as *fierce* love or hate. *Brutal* describes an animal-like cruelty, formerly always malicious, now merely coarse, unfeeling, sensual. *Barbarous* is sometimes used to express the opposite of civilized, as *barbarous* tribes; it is also used to describe the coarse and *cruel* side of uncivilized life, as *barbarous* customs. *Ferocious, fierce,* and *savage* are used to describe the natural tempers of animals; *inhuman, brutal,* and *barbarous* describe people that act like animals

in·hu·mane′ *adj* lacking in kindness; cruel, brutal

in·hu·man′i·ty *n* (*-ties*) 1 quality of being unfeeling or unkind; 2 cruelty; 3 inhumane act

in·im·i·cal /ĭnĭm′ĭkəl/ [< L *inimicus*] *adj* 1 hostile, unfriendly; 2 opposed; antagonistic

in·im·i·ta·ble /ĭnĭm′ĭtəbəl/ [< *in-³* + *imitate*] *adj* beyond imitation; matchless

in·iq·ui·ty /ĭnĭk′wĭtē/ [L *iniquitas* unfairness] *n* (*-ties*) 1 wickedness; gross injustice; 2 wicked act; sin ‖ **in·iq′ui·tous** *adj* ‖ SYN crime, injustice, sin, abomination

in·i·tial /ĭnĭsh′əl/ [< L *initium* beginning] *adj* 1 of, pert. to, or placed at the beginning; first ‖ *n* 2 initial letter ‖ *v* (*-tialed* or *-tialled; -tial·ing* or *-tial·ling*) *vt* 3 to mark or sign with one's initials ‖ **in·i′tial·ly** *adv*

in·i′tial·ism *n* letterword

in·i·ti·ate /ĭnĭsh′ē·āt′/ [L *initiare* (*-atus*)] *vt* 1 to instruct in the first principles of anything; 2 to set on foot; begin; introduce; 3 to introduce into a club, secret society, or the like, by special ceremonies ‖ *-it/ n* 4 one who has been initiated ‖ **in·i′ti·a′tor** *n* ‖ **in·i′ti·a′tion** *n*

in·i·ti·a·tive /ĭnĭsh′(ē)ətĭv/ *n* 1 introductory or first step; **2** readiness to initiate action; enterprise; **3** procedure whereby a certain number of voters may force a referendum on proposed legislation

in·ject /injekt'/ [L *injicere* (-*jectus*) to throw into] *vt* **1** to force (a liquid) into a boiler under pressure or (fuel) into a combustion chamber; **2** to introduce (a liquid) into the body with a syringe; **3** to introduce (something different); **4** to interject, as a remark ‖ **in·jec'tion** *n*

in'jec·tor *n* device for injecting a liquid, as water into a boiler or fuel into a combustion chamber

in·ju·di·cious *adj* unwise; imprudent

in·junc'tion [< L *injungere* (-*junctus*) to enjoin] *n* **1** command, order; **2** *law* court order requiring or prohibiting a certain action

in·jure /in'jər/ *vt* to hurt, harm; damage physically or morally ‖ **in'jur·er** *n* ‖ **in·ju'ri·ous** /-jŏŏr'-/ *adj* ‖ SYN wrong, mar, sully, spoil, maltreat, violate

in·ju·ry [L *injuria*] *n* (-**ries**) **1** any hurt or harm, physical or moral; **2** any damage to or violation of one's rights or property ‖ SYN damage, detriment, loss, hurt, harm, mischief, impairment, injustice, wrong, evil, outrage, prejudice ‖ DISCR *Injury*, the general term, is applied to whatever affects one disadvantageously. We speak of an *injury* to the spine, to one's credit, to tires by a gravel road, to property adjoining garages or noisy factories. *Damage, harm, hurt,* and *mischief* are forms of *injury. Damage* connotes loss and diminished value; it is often partial, sometimes reparable, sometimes not; we insure against *damage* by fire. There is a note of blame in *damage,* suggesting carelessness or other fault in some agent. *Harm,* a word popularly used for *injury,* is practically interchangeable with it. *Harm* connotes loss or impairment, and though it may result from other causes, is frequently done by a living agent, with or without intention; false rumors often do *harm* to a candidate running for office; children unintentionally do *harm* to furniture. A broken arm, however, would be referred to as an *injury,* not a *harm;* undesirable neighbors would constitute an *injury,* not a *harm,* to the monetary value of property, but would be a *harm,* rather than an *injury,* to the morals of the children in the vicinity. *Mischief,* like *harm,* is often done by living agents, with or without intention. Children's sportive *mischief* vexes; the gossip's *mischief* produces evil; discontent is a great *mischief*-maker. *Hurt,* properly applied to such *injury* as affects sound-

ness of tissue, as a bruise, is also used of figurative and moral objects, as she carried that *hurt* in her heart for years

in·jus'tice *n* **1** quality of being unjust; **2** unjust act ‖ SYN grievance, unfairness, iniquity, injury, inequity ‖ ANT fairness, impartiality, justice, equity

ink /ink'/ [OF *enque* < Gk *enkauston* purple ink] *n* **1** colored fluid or viscous paste used for writing and printing ‖ *vt* **2** to spread, color, stain, or mark with ink

ink'ling [< *obs inkle* to whisper, hint] *n* **1** hint, suspicion; **2** partial knowledge

ink'well' *n* container for ink

ink'y *adj* (-**i·er; -i·est**) **1** very dark or black; **2** stained with ink; **3** resembling ink

in·laid /inlād', in'lād'/ **1** *pp* of *inlay* ‖ *adj* **2** set into a surface; **3** ornamented with inlaid materials

in·land /in'lənd/ *adj* **1** pert. to or situated in the interior of a country ‖ *adv* **2** in or toward the interior ‖ *n* **3** the interior of a country

in'-law' *n* relative by marriage

in·lay /inlā', in'lā'/ *v* (-**laid**) *vt* **1** to ornament (a surface) by setting in pieces of ivory, wood, etc. ‖ /in'lā'/ *n* **2** materials for inlaying; **3** inlaid work; **4** *dentistry* inlaid filling

in·let /in'let/ *n* narrow passage of water extending into the land

in'mate *n* one who is confined in a prison or institution

in me·mo·ri·am /in' məmôr'ē·əm -môr'-/ [L] *prep* in memory of

in'most' *adj* innermost; furthest within

inn /in'/ [OE = dwelling] *n* **1** small hotel; **2** tavern

in·nate /in'āt, ināt'/ [L *innatus*] *adj* inborn; native; natural ‖ **in·nate'ly** *adv* ‖ SYN original, natural, intrinsic (see *inherent*)

in·ner /in'ər/ [OE *innera*] *adj* **1** interior; farther within; **2** pert. to the mind or soul; **3** not easily perceived; **4** more intimate or secret

in'ner·most' *adj* farthest inward from outside

in'ner tube' *n* doughnut-shaped rubber tube kept inflated inside the carcass of a tire to carry the weight of the vehicle

in·ning /in'in/ [< *obs in* to lodge, include] *n* **1** *baseball* one of the nine divisions of the game in which each side has a turn at bat; **2** opportunity, turn

inn'keep'er *n* operator of an inn

in·no·cent /in'əsənt/ [L *innocens* (-*entis*) harmless] *adj* **1** sinless; **2** free from guilt or wrongdoing; **3** pure in heart; **4** foolishly ignorant; **5** without evil intent; **6** devoid, as *innocent of malice*; **7** harmless ‖ *n* **8** innocent person; **9** simpleton ‖ **in'-**

no·cence *n* || SYN *adj* guiltless, sinless, guileless, inoffensive, innocuous, virtuous, artless, ignorant || ANT *adj* guilty, sinful, wicked, unrighteous, impure

in·noc·u·ous /inok′yo͞o-əs/ [< L *innocuus*] *adj* harmless

in·no·vate /in′əvāt′/ [L *innovare* (-*atus*)] *vi* 1 to make changes in something established; introduce new things || *vt* 2 to introduce as new || **in′no·va′tive** *adj* || **in′no·va′tor** *n*

in′no·va′tion *n* 1 act of innovating; 2 new development or feature; change in method or procedure

Inns′ of Court′ *npl* 1 the four legal societies in London (Gray's Inn, Lincoln's Inn, the Inner Temple, and the Middle Temple) which have the exclusive right to call candidates to the English bar; 2 the buildings owned and used by these societies

in·nu·en·do /in′yo͞o-en′dō/ [L = by nodding at] *n* (-**does** or -**dos**) indirect reference, usu. derogatory

in·nu′mer·a·ble *adj* 1 incapable of being counted; 2 very numerous

in·oc·u·late /inok′yəlāt′/ [L *inoculare* (-*atus*) to implant] *vt* 1 to infect, as with disease or harmful ideas; 2 to inject with a disease in order to produce immunity || **in·oc′u·la′tion** *n*

in·of·fen′sive *adj* 1 not offending; 2 harmless; 3 not annoying

in·op′er·a·tive *adj* 1 not in operation; 2 not working; 3 ineffective

in·op′por·tune′ *adj* unsuitable; inappropriate; unseasonable || SYN inconvenient, ill-timed, inappropriate

in·or′di·nate *adj* excessive; immoderate; unrestrained || SYN excessive, immoderate, intemperate, disordered

in′or·gan′ic *adj* 1 without the organization or structure peculiar to living beings; pert. to lifeless matter; 2 *chem* pert. to substances not containing carbon as an essential element

in′put′ *n* 1 power or energy put into a machine or circuit; 2 data fed into a computer

in·quest /in′kwest/ [ML *inquesta*] *n* official inquiry with the aid of a jury into a special matter, as the cause of sudden death

in·quire /inkwī′(ə)r/ [OF *enquerre*] *vt* 1 to seek for or after by questions || *vi* 2 to seek information by questioning; 3 **inquire into** to investigate; 4 **inquire after** to ask about || **in·quir′er** *n* || SYN ask, interrogate, challenge (see *question*)

in·quir′ing *adj* 1 seeking information; 2 inquisitive || **in·quir′ing·ly** *adv*

in·quir·y /inkwir′ē, in′kwərē/ *n* (-**ies**) 1 act of inquiring; 2 investigation; 3 question || SYN examination, inquisition, query, interrogation

in·qui·si·tion /in′kwizish′ən/ [L *inquisitio* (-*onis*)] *n* 1 inquiry, examination, esp. one conducted harshly

without regard for justice or the rights of witnesses; 2 **Inquisition** *R C Ch* formerly, court for the discovery and punishment of heretics || **in·quis·i·to′ri·al** /-tôr′ē-əl, -tōr′ē-əl/ *adj*

in·quis·i·tive /inkwiz′itiv/ *adj* 1 prying; unduly curious; 2 active in the pursuit of knowledge || **in·quis′i·tive·ness** *n* || SYN prying, peeping, curious, meddlesome, searching

in re /in rē′/ [L] *prep* in the matter of

I.N.R.I. [L *Iesus Nazarenus Rex Iudaeorum*] Jesus of Nazareth, King of the Jews

in′road′ *n* 1 harmful encroachment; 2 hostile raid

in′rush′ *n* influx; rushing in

in·sane′ [L *insanus*] *adj* 1 mentally deranged, crazy; 2 utterly senseless; 3 intended for the insane || **in·sane′ly** *adv*

in·san′i·tar′y *adj* not sanitary

in·san′i·ty *n* (-**ties**) 1 condition of being insane; 2 extravagant folly || SYN dementia, derangement, alienation, feeble-mindedness, amentia, lunacy, delirium, frenzy, mania, hallucination, madness, fanaticism, fury, aberration || DISCR *Insanity* includes both deterioration of the mental functions (*dementia*), and disorder of these functions (*derangement* or *alienation*). Legal *insanity* in many States also includes *feeble-mindedness* (*amentia*). *Insanity*, as a scientific term, is falling into disuse and, like *lunacy*, is tending to become obsolete, retaining significance mainly in the legal sense. Underlying the common meaning and the legal use of the term *insanity* are concepts of social incompetence, maladjustment, and social nonconformity, involving ideas of mental incompetence, irrational or irresponsible conduct, and the like. The psychiatrist in a hospital for the insane treats many patients who are not legally insane. *Delirium*, which is present in certain mental disorders and may accompany a high fever, denotes a condition of being "out of one's mind"; it is a temporary or intermittent condition characterized by lack of orientation, incoherent ideas and speech, and other symptoms of *derangement*. *Delirium tremens*, an especially violent form, often following the excessive and prolonged use of intoxicants, is marked by delusions, hallucinations, and motor disturbance. *Frenzy* is excessive emotional agitation without self-control, and may, or may not, be pathological, as a *frenzy* of grief. *Mania* is mental disorder characterized by violent reactions, mental *derangement*, lack of self-control, etc., or it may name an obsession, as a suicidal *mania.* In their secondary senses, *mania* names an uncontrollable desire or craze for something, as a *mania* for bridge; *delirium,* a state of enthusiastic, rapturous, or wild excitement, as a *delirium* of joy; *lunacy* names a silly, foolish wantonness of conduct, and *frenzy,* wild or frantic excitement, as such folly is sheer *lunacy;* he acted in a *frenzy* of fear

in·sa·ti·a·ble /insā′shəbəl, -shē-əbəl/ *adj* incapable of being satisfied ‖ **in·sa′tia·bly** *adv*

in·scribe /inskrīb′/ [L *inscribere*] *vt* 1 to write or engrave; 2 to write or engrave upon; 3 to address (a written greeting, poem, or the like) to a person; 4 to enroll; 5 *geom* to draw, as a circle or polygon, within a figure in such a way that certain points of the figure drawn lie in the boundary of the original figure

in·scrip·tion /inskrip′shən/ *n* 1 act of inscribing; 2 something inscribed

in·scru·ta·ble /inskrōōt′əbəl/ [LL *inscrutabilis*] *adj* not to be understood; mysterious, enigmatic ‖ **in·scru′ta·bly** *adv* ‖ **in·scru·ta·bil′i·ty** /-bil′-/ *n*

in·sect /in′sekt/ [L *insectum* notched] *n* 1 any of a class of arthropods with segmented bodies, six legs, and usu. two pairs of wings; 2 any small arthropod, as a spider; 3 cur, contemptible person

in·sec′ti·cide /-isīd′/ *n* substance for killing insects

in·sec·tiv·o·rous /-tiv′ərəs/ [< *insect* + L *vorare* to eat] *adj* feeding on insects

in·se·cure′ *adj* 1 not firm; 2 unsafe; 3 not protected from danger; 4 beset with feelings of anxiety ‖ **in·se·cu′ri·ty** *n*

in·sem·i·nate /insem′ināt′/ [L *inseminare* (-atus)] *vt* to implant; insert; impregnate

in·sen·sate /insen′sāt, -sit/ [LL *insensatus*] *adj* 1 unfeeling; 2 stupid, foolish; 3 without sensation; 4 inanimate

in·sen′si·ble *adj* 1 incapable of feeling; 2 imperceptible; 3 apathetic, indifferent; 4 unconscious ‖ **in·sen′si·bly** *adv* ‖ **in·sen·si·bil′i·ty** /-bil′-/ *n* ‖ SYN numb, unfeeling, impassive, dull (see *hard*)

in·sen′si·tive *adj* not sensitive

in·sep′a·ra·ble *adj* incapable of being divided or parted

in·sert /insurt′/ [L *inserere* (-sertus)] *vt* 1 to put or fit in; cause to be included ‖ /in′sərt/ *n* 2 that which is inserted ‖ **in·ser′tion** *n*

in′set′ *n* something set in or inserted, as a small picture or map within the border of a larger one

in·shore /in′shôr′, -shōr′/ *adj* 1 being near, or moving in the direction of, the shore ‖ *adv* 2 toward the shore

in′side′ *adj* 1 interior; 2 known only to insiders ‖ /insīd′, in′sīd′/ *adv* 3 within; 4 indoors; 5 **inside of** within the space of; 6 **inside out,** a thoroughly; b with the inner side on the outside ‖ /insīd′/ *n* 7 that which is within; inner part; 8 inner side; 9 **insides** *pl* interior of the body, esp. the stomach and entrails ‖ /insīd′, in′sīd′/ *prep* 10 on the inner side of; within

in′side job′ *n colloq* crime committed with the collusion of or by a person employed by the victim

in·sid′er *n* one who is so situated as to be able to get reliable or special information not available to the general public

in′side track′ *n colloq* advantageous position

in·sid·i·ous /insid′ē-əs/ [L *insidiosus*] *adj* 1 treacherous; 2 sly, operating secretly ‖ **in·sid′i·ous·ly** *adv*

in·sight′ *n* 1 penetration; intuition; mental vision; 2 instance of this ‖ SYN discernment (see *discrimination, sagacity*)

in·sig·ni·a /insig′nē-ə/ [L, *pl* of *insigne* badge] *nsg & npl* distinguishing mark, as a badge of rank, office, or an organization

in·sig·nif′i·cant *adj* 1 without importance, force, influence, or meaning; 2 trifling; small ‖ **in·sig·nif′i·cance** *n* ‖ SYN immaterial, meaningless, irrelevant, trivial, contemptible, small, petty, paltry, unimportant

in·sin·cere′ *adj* not sincere ‖ **in·sin·cere′ly** *adv* ‖ **in·sin·cer′i·ty** /-ser′-/ *n* ‖ SYN artful, pharisaical, disingenuous, untrustworthy

in·sin·u·ate /insin′yōō-āt′/ [L *insinuare* (-atus)] *vt* 1 to push, work, or introduce by artful means, as into the confidence or affections; 2 to suggest or hint indirectly ‖ **in·sin′u·a′tion** *n*

in·sip·id /insip′id/ [L *insipidus*] *adj* 1 flat, without flavor; 2 uninteresting ‖ **in′si·pid′i·ty** /-sipid′-/ *n* ‖ SYN dull, flat, vapid, mawkish, pointless, prosaic, unsavory ‖ ANT bright, sparkling, lively, piquant

in·sist /insist′/ [L *insistere* to set foot on] *vi* 1 to be persistent; 2 **insist on** or **upon** to take a persistent stand on ‖ *vt* 3 to persist in demanding or asserting ‖ SYN persevere, persist, urge, demand, require ‖ DISCR We *insist* with force, argument, right, or authority, chiefly in a good sense; we *insist* that justice be done; that sanitary laws be enforced. The force behind *insist* is going outward; we are impelling others to do what they should do, or what we think they should do. To *persist* is to continue with firmness, even with obstinacy, in doing what we want to do. There is judgment back of *insisting;* there is mulishness and willfulness back of *persisting.* We *persist* in an ill-advised course, an unjust opinion, especially against protest or remonstrance. For such continuance in duty, or otherwise in the good sense, *persevere* is used. Reflection, determination in its courageous aspect, and virtue lie back of *persevere; we persevere* in unpleasant tasks, in a course of studies, in habits of daily exercise. To *urge* is to drive one to do a thing, but the force behind it is that of entreaty, or exhortation, or pressing advocacy; we *urge* people to act, or we *urge* the adoption of an action or a plan

in·sist'ent *adj* urgent; compelling attention ‖ **in·sist'ent·ly** *adv* ‖ **in·sist'·ence** *n*

in'so·far' as *conj* to the extent that

in'sole' *n* inner sole of a shoe

in·so·lent /in'sələnt/ [L *insolens* (-*entis*) unusual] *adj* 1 contemptuously offensive; 2 insulting ‖ **in'so·lent·ly** *adv* ‖ **in'so·lence** *n* ‖ SYN saucy, impudent, abusive, contemptuous (see *arrogant*) ‖ ANT respectful, mannerly, mild

in·sol'u·ble *adj* 1 not soluble; 2 unsolvable

in·sol'vent *adj* 1 unable to pay debts, bankrupt ‖ *n* 2 insolvent person ‖ **in·sol'ven·cy** *n* (-cies)

in·som·ni·a /insom'nē·ə/ [L < *insomnis* sleepless] *n* inability to sleep ‖ **in·som'ni·ac'** /-ak'/ *n*

in'so·much' as *conj* inasmuch as

in'so·much' that *conj* to such an extent that; so that

in·sou·ci·ant /insōōs'ē·ənt/ [F] *adj* unconcerned; carefree ‖ **in·sou'ci·ance** *n*

in·spect /inspekt'/ [L *inspicere* (-*spectus*)] *vt* 1 to examine closely and critically; 2 to review officially, as troops ‖ **in·spec'tion** *n*

in·spec'tor *n* 1 one who inspects; 2 (in some police forces) high-ranking officer, ranking above a captain

in·spi·ra·tion /in'spirāsh'ən/ *n* 1 inhalation; 2 act of inspiring or state of being inspired; 3 person or thing that inspires; 4 inspiring influence or impulse; 5 something inspired ‖ **in'·spi·ra'tion·al** *adj*

in·spire /inspī'(ə)r/ [L *inspirare* to breathe upon] *vt* 1 to animate or fill with ideas; 2 to control or guide by divine influence; 3 to kindle or arouse, as an idea, emotion, or impulse ‖ *vi* 4 to inhale; 5 to give inspiration ‖ SYN animate, cheer, stimulate, instill, impart, encourage, enliven ‖ ANT dispirit, depress, discourage

in·spir'it *vt* to give life or vitality to

inst. instant (of the present month)

Inst. Institution

in'sta·bil'i·ty /-bil'-/ *n* (-ties) 1 lack of stability; 2 inconstancy; vacillation ‖ SYN changeableness, mutability,

unsteadiness, unsubstantiality ‖ ANT constancy, steadiness, firmness

in·stall also **in·stal** /instôl'/ [ML *installare*] *vt* 1 to establish with ceremony in an office or position; 2 to put into position and connect for use ‖ **in'stal·la'tion** /-stə-/ *n*

in·stall·ment also **in·stal·ment** /instôl'mənt/ [< *obs estall* payment] *n* 1 portion of a sum of money or debt that is to be paid in parts at stated times; 2 one of a number of parts of anything, produced one part at a time, as *the first installment of a serial story*

in·stall'ment plan' *n* system of paying for purchases by installments over a period of time

in·stance /in'stəns/ [L *instantia* presence, urgency] *n* 1 something offered as an illustration or example; 2 at **the instance of** at the urging of; 3 **for instance** for example

in·stant /in'stənt/ [L *instans* (-*antis*) present, pressing] *adj* 1 urgent; 2 immediate; 3 imminent; 4 of the present month, as *the tenth instant* ‖ *n* 5 particular moment; 6 very small space of time

in·stan·ta·ne·ous /in'stəntăn'ē·əs/ *adj* 1 acting or occurring in an instant; 2 at a given moment ‖ **in'stan·ta'ne·ous·ly** *adv*

in'stant book' *n* paperback book produced in about a week's time by writers, editors, designers, and printers working twenty-four hours a day until copies have been delivered across the country, to tell the story of some news event of great interest for the moment

in'stant·ly *adv* at once ‖ SYN forthwith, directly (see *immediately*)

in'stant re'play *n sports* immediate playback of a short strip of video tape

in·stead /insted'/ *adv* 1 in place of someone or something; 2 **instead of** in place of

in'step' *n* upper side of the foot between the toes and the ankle

in·sti·gate /in'stigāt'/ [L *instigare* (-*atus*)] *vt* to provoke or urge on; incite ‖ **in'sti·ga'tion** *n* ‖ **in'sti·ga'·tor** *n* ‖ SYN impel, abet, goad, spur, tempt, stimulate

in·still also **in·stil** /instil'/ [L *instillare*] *v* (-stilled; -still·ing also -stil·ing) *vt* to introduce, as a principle, feeling, etc., gradually; impart slowly ‖ SYN infuse, implant, inculcate, inspire, engraft

in·stinct /in'stiŋkt/ [L *instinctus* impulse] *n* 1 natural involuntary urging to any action; 2 natural aptitude or skill ‖ **in·stinc'tive** *adj* ‖ **in·stinc'·tive·ly** *adv*

in·sti·tute /in'stit(y)ōōt'/ [L *instituere* (-*tutus*) to set up] *vt* 1 to establish, set up; 2 to start, initiate; 3 to put into operation || *n* 4 scientific, artistic, professional, or literary organization or place of education

in·sti·tu'tion *n* 1 act of instituting; 2 established rule, custom, principle, or the like, regulating social or civic conduct and organization; 3 organized body or society for promoting a particular object, esp. of a charitable or educational nature; 4 business concern, as a bank; 5 familiar thing, person, or practice || in·sti·tu'tion·al *adj*

in·struct /instrukt'/ [L *instruere* (-*structus*)] *vt* 1 to teach; educate; 2 to furnish with orders or directions; 3 to inform, apprise || in·struc'tive *adj* || SYN inform, direct, teach (see *advise*)

in·struc'tion *n* 1 act of instructing; 2 knowledge imparted; 3 **instructions** *pl* orders or directions || in·struc'tion·al *adj* || SYN direction, requirement (see *education, order*)

in·struc'tor *n* 1 teacher; 2 college teacher ranking below an assistant professor || in·struc'tor·ship' *n*

in·stru·ment /in'strəmənt/ [L *instrumentum* equipment] *n* 1 that by which anything is accomplished; agent, means; 2 mechanical device, tool; 3 contrivance for producing musical sounds; 4 legal document; 5 gauge or measuring device || SYN device, agent, medium, channel, apparatus

in·stru·men·tal /-ment'əl/ *adj* 1 serving as a means; 2 pert. to, performed on, or composed for musical instruments || in'stru·men·tal·ly *adv*

in'stru·men·tal'i·ty /-tal'-/ *n* (-ties) means, agency

in·sub·or'di·nate *adj* not following orders; not submitting to authority; disobedient || in·sub·or'di·na'tion *n* || SYN contumacious, unruly, rebellious

in'sub·stan'tial *adj* 1 not substantial; frail; 2 unreal

in·suf'fer·a·ble *adj* not to be borne; intolerable || in·suf'fer·a·bly *adv*

in·suf·fi'cient *adj* deficient in quality, amount, power, etc.; inadequate || SYN scanty, deficient, incapable, incompetent

in·su·lar /in's(y)ələr/ [< L *insula* island] *adj* 1 pert. to, situated or living on, or resembling an island; 2 isolated; 3 illiberal, narrow-minded || in'su·lar'i·ty /lar'itē/ *n*

in·su·late' *vt* 1 to isolate; segregate; 2 to separate (conducting bodies) with a nonconducting material in order to prevent leakage of electricity, heat, or sound; 3 to cover, as a pipe or wire, with nonconducting material

in'su·la'tion *n* 1 act of insulating, or state of being insulated; 2 material used for insulating

in'su·la'tor *n* 1 material of low conductivity; 2 device, as of glass or porcelain, for supporting charged wires

in·su·lin /in's(y)əlin/ [L *insula* island +-*in*] *n* preparation from the pancreas of oxen, sheep, and the like, used to retard the formation of sugar in the blood of diabetics

in·sult /insult'/ [L *insultare* to jump upon] *vt* 1 to treat with gross contempt or abuse; affront || /in'sult/ *n* 2 affront or indignity; 3 gross abuse in word or action || in·sult'ing *adj* || SYN *n* affront, abuse, indignity, contumely, outrage

in·su·per·a·ble /insōop'ərəbəl/ *adj* not to be overcome

in'sup·port'a·ble *adj* 1 not supportable; 2 not capable of being endured; insufferable

in·sur·ance /inshōor'əns/ *n* 1 system of protection against the risk of individual loss by distributing the burden of losses over a large number of individuals; 2 contract whereby one party agrees to indemnify the other party for loss, as by fire, accident, theft, death, etc., by the payment of a stated sum of money; 3 amount by which anything is insured

in·sur'ance pol'i·cy *n* contract of insurance

in·sure /inshōor'/ [var of *ensure*] *vt* 1 to guarantee against loss or harm; 2 to issue a contract of insurance to; 3 to ensure || in·sur'a·ble *adj*

in·sured' *n* one covered by an insurance policy

in·sur'er *n* company in the insurance business

in·sur·gent /insurj'ənt/ [L *insurgens* (-*entis*) rising up against] *n* person who rises up against lawful authority; rebel || also *adj* || in·sur'gence *n* || SYN *adj* mutinous, rebellious, insubordinate

in'sur·mount'a·ble *adj* incapable of being passed over or conquered; insuperable

in·sur·rec·tion /in'sərek'shən/ [< L *insurrectus* risen up against] *n* open rebellion; revolt || in'sur·rec'tion·ist *n* || SYN uprising, revolt, mutiny (see *revolution*)

in'swept' *adj* tapering toward the front

int. 1 interest; 2 interior; 3 internal; 4 international; 5 intransitive

in·tact /intakt'/ [L *intactus* untouchable] *adj* entire; unbroken, uninjured; untouched || SYN whole, unimpaired, perfect, entire, complete

in·ta·glio /intal'yō, -tāl'-/ [It] *n* 1 incised design or figure in any hard material; 2 gem or stone having a design cut into the surface

in'take' *n* 1 a taking in; 2 thing taken in; 3 amount taken in; 4 place where a fluid enters a pipe, channel, etc.

in·tan'gi·ble *adj* 1 incapable of being

touched; **2** vague, indefinite; **3** (business asset) not measurable by ordinary means, as good will ‖ **n 4** something intangible

in·te·ger /int′əjər/ [L = untouched] *n* **1** entity; **2** *math* whole number, not a fraction

in·te·gral /int′əgrəl/ *adj* **1** whole, complete; **2** necessary to the completeness of a whole; **3** pert. to an integer ‖ *n* **4** whole made up of parts ‖ **in′te·gral·ly** *adv*

in·te·grate /int′əgrāt′/ [L *integrare* (-*atus*) to make whole] *vt* **1** to bring together the parts of; **2** to give the sum total of; **3 a** to give (minority groups) the full rights of all citizens by removing segregation; **b** to cause (a place of public accommodation) to serve all citizens regardless of race ‖ *vi* **4** to become integrated ‖ **in′te·gra′tion** *n*

in·teg·ri·ty /integ′ritē/ [L *integritas* wholeness] *n* **1** uprightness, virtue, honesty; **2** soundness, uninjured state; **3** completeness ‖ SYN (see *justice, honesty*)

in·teg·u·ment /integ′yəmənt/ [L *integumentum* covering] *n* external covering, as the skin or a shell

in·tel·lect /int′əlekt′/ [L *intellectus* understood] *n* **1** powers of the mind or understanding that know and reason, distinguished from feeling and will; **2** power to reason; intelligence; **3** person of great intelligence ‖ SYN mind, intelligence, understanding, sense, reason, reasoning, genius, brains ‖ DISCR *Mind,* the general term for mental functioning, includes consciousness, thought, perception, cognition, feeling, volition, the subconscious, etc. Hence, we are aware of the world about us, we meditate, reason, and think things out, with the *mind.* We determine with the *mind,* as I have made up my *mind* to do it; we decide and resolve, as I know my own *mind* and shall stick to it; we feel disposed or inclined with our *minds,* as I have half a *mind* to do it; we have disordered *minds,* or have peace of *mind;* and we conceive of the *mind* as the self, soul, or spirit in contrast with the body, or physical self. *Intellect* is commonly limited to that power of the *mind* that knows or reasons, as opposed to the power of feeling and will; *mind* may be used in this limited sense, and then becomes synonymous with *intellect. Intelligence* commonly names the power to exercise the mental functions, the capacity to know, to apprehend. *Understanding* and *comprehension* emphasize *reason* and the functioning of *intelligence. Intellect* tends to become limited to the higher aspects of *intelligence,* abstract reasoning, purposeful thought, etc. One

who has this type of mind is an intellectual person. *Intellect* is found in man, but not in the lower animals, even those that have a fair degree of *intelligence*

in·tel·lec·tu·al /-chŏō-əl/ *adj* **1** pert. to, done by, or appealing to the intellect; **2** possessing or showing intelligence ‖ *n* **3** person of superior intellect; **4** person with intellectual pursuits ‖ **in′tel·lec′tu·al·ly** *adv* ‖ SYN *adj* intelligent, mental ‖ DISCR *Mental,* which is opposed to corporeal and bodily, is applied to those things that are of the mind, done by the mind, and distinguished by the mind, as *mental* enjoyments; *mental* discipline; *mental* endowments; *mental* arithmetic; a *mental* reservation. *Intellectual,* which, unlike *mental,* can also be applied to persons, applies to that which belongs to, appeals to, or demands the exercise of, the intellect, as opposed to the emotions, or the purely physical. *Intellectual* not only describes conversations which deal with thought-challenging or abstract subjects, but also the persons whose minds are so developed or gifted as to be able to handle such subjects. Such enlightened persons, taken collectively, are referred to as "the intellectuals." *Intelligent* describes, in the first place, those endowed with mind or intellect. It is also applied to animals, though bees and ants, in spite of their remarkably complex reaction patterns and the apparent purposefulness of their behavior, are not in the technical sense *intelligent.* It is applied further to those human beings who show the power to comprehend, as opposed to the idiotic or abnormal. Chiefly, however, *intelligent* describes those who comprehend quickly, show sagacity, a degree of shrewdness, and an all-round ability to understand. When we think of an *intellectual* man we think of a scholar; when we think of an *intelligent* man we picture a bright, active, quick mind working effectively

in·tel·li·gence /intel′igəns/ *n* **1** ability to learn, reason, or understand; **2** ability to direct one's thinking effectively; **3** intelligent being; **4** information; news; **5 a** secret information, as that secured by a government about another country; **b** government agency charged with gathering such information ‖ SYN information, news, tidings, advice ‖ DISCR *News* is the general term, connoting knowledge or report of recent events; timeliness and freshness characterize *news. Information* is specific knowledge; if it is recent and timely it is also *news;* but it may be a fact sought for a practical purpose, for direction, or the like. Hence, we have bureaus of *information*. *Tidings*, now chiefly a literary word, is a piece of *news*, as to bring glad *tidings*. *Intelligence* is *news* or *information* of a more formal coloring, with emphasis on the enlightening aspect of the facts so made known (see *intellect*)

in·tel'li·gence quo'tient *n* IQ

in·tel'li·gent [< L *intelligere* to understand] *adj* possessing or showing intelligence or comprehension ‖ **in·tel'li·gent·ly** *adv* ‖ SYN bright, quickwitted, sagacious, sensible, shrewd (see *intellectual*) ‖ ANT dull, stupid, ignorant

in·tel'li·gent'si·a /-gent'sē-ə, -jent'-/ [Russ] *npl* intellectuals collectively

in·tel'li·gi·ble *adj* understandable; clear ‖ in·tel'li·gi·bil'i·ty /-bil'-/ *n*

in·tem'per·ate *adj* 1 characterized by lack of moderation or self-restraint; 2 inclement; severe; 3 addicted to alcoholic liquors ‖ in·tem'per·ate·ly *adv* ‖ in·tem'per·ance *n* ‖ SYN immoderate, excessive, inordinate, unrestrained, drunken ‖ ANT temperate, controlled, moderate, mild

in·tend /intend'/ [MF *entendre* to understand < L *intendere* to direct] *vt* 1 to purpose; plan; 2 to design (a thing) for some purpose; 3 to mean; signify

in·tend'ed *adj* 1 done on purpose; 2 *colloq* prospective ‖ *n* 3 *colloq* person to whom one is engaged to be married

in·tense /intens'/ [L *intensus* stretched out] *adj* 1 extreme in degree; excessive; 2 intent; ardent, eager ‖ in·tense'ly *adv* ‖ SYN earnest, intent, fervid, rapt, glowing, ardent

in·ten'si·fy' *v* (-fied) *vt* to make more intense; strengthen ‖ in·ten'si·fi'er *n* ‖ in·ten'si·fi·ca'tion *n* ‖ SYN aggravate, enhance, increase, heighten

in·ten'si·ty *n* (-ties) 1 state or quality of being intense; 2 strength, force, or energy; 3 degree or amount of some condition, quality, or physical attribute, as of light or sound

in·ten'sive *adj* 1 increasing or causing to increase in intensity; 2 of or pert. to intensity; 3 thorough; 4 *gram* giving emphasis ‖ *n* 5 *gram* intensive word or element ‖ in·ten'sive·ly

in·tent /intent'/ [L *intentus*] *adj* 1 firmly fixed or directed, as a look; 2 having one's attention closely fixed on something ‖ *n* 3 purpose, aim; 4 meaning, import; 5 to all **intents and purposes** virtually; practically speaking ‖ in·tent'ly *adv* ‖ SYN *n* drift, aim, purport, view (see *design*)

in·ten'tion *n* 1 purpose, aim; 2 **intentions** *pl colloq* purpose with regard to, matrimony ‖ SYN aim, object, import, significance (see *design*)

in·ten'tion·al *adj* done on purpose ‖ in·ten'tion·al·ly *adv*

in·ter /intur'/ [MF *enterrer* < in-¹ + L *terra* earth] *v* (-terred; -ter·ring) *vt* to bury

in·ter- /int'ər-, int'ər-, intur'-, inter'-/ [L = between, among] *pref* 1 among, between; 2 together; mutually

in'ter·act' *vi* to act on each other ‖ in'ter·ac'tion *n*

in'ter·breed' *v* (-bred) *vt & vi* to propagate by crossing different varieties, kinds, or stocks

in·ter·ca·late /intur'kəlāt'/ [L *intercalare* (-*atus*)] *vt* 1 to insert (a day) in the calendar; 2 to interpolate ‖ in·ter·ca·la'tion *n*

in'ter·cede' *vi* 1 to mediate; 2 to plead in behalf of another ‖ in'ter·ces'sion *n* ‖ in'ter·ces'sor *n*

in·ter·cept' /-sept'/ [L *intercipere* (-*ceptus*)] *vt* 1 to seize or stop on the way; 2 to receive what was meant for another, as a message or forward pass; 3 to obstruct; interfere with the course of; come in the way of; 4 *math* to include between two points or lines ‖ in·ter·cept' *n* 5 a interception; b part intercepted ‖ in'ter·cep'tion *n*

in'ter·cep'tor or **in'ter·cept'er** *n* 1 person or thing that intercepts; 2 fastclimbing fighter plane used to intercept enemy aircraft

in'ter·change' *vt* 1 to give and receive reciprocally; exchange; 2 to exchange the position of, by putting one thing in the place of another; 3 to alternate ‖ in'ter·change' *n* 4 reciprocal exchange; 5 alternation; 6 road junction allowing access to or exit from a superhighway ‖ in'ter·change'a·ble *adj*

in'ter·col·le'giate *adj* between or among two or more colleges

in'ter·com' /-kom'/ *n colloq* two-way telephone system for local use

in'ter·com·mu'ni·cate' *vi* to communicate with one another ‖ in'ter·com·mu'ni·ca'tion *n*

in'ter·con·ti·nen'tal bal·lis'tic mis'sile *n* supersonic missile with a range great enough to reach another continent

in'ter·cos'tal /-kost'əl/ [*inter-* + L *costa* rib] *adj* between the ribs

in'ter·course [ML *intercursus* communication] *n* 1 communication or dealings between individuals, groups, or nations; 2 sexual connection, copulation ‖ SYN commerce, communication, reciprocation

in'ter·de·pend'ence *n* state of being mutually dependent ‖ in'ter·de·pend'ent *adj*

in'ter·dict' /-dikt'/ [OF *entredit* forbidden < L *interdictus*] *vt* 1 to restrain or forbid ‖ in'ter·dict' *n* 2 formal prohibition ‖ in'ter·dic'tion *n*

in·ter·est /int'(ə)rist/ [L = it matters] *n* 1 benefit; advantage; 2 attentive or sympathetic concern or regard; 3 consideration for personal or selfish profit; **4** personal influence over the action of others; **5** share in a business or other project; **6** *fin* a sum paid for the use of money; **b** rate percent per unit of time of such charge; **7 interests** *pl* persons concerned in some field of business or industry, taken collectively, as the *oil interests*; **8** in the interest(s) of in behalf of || *vt* **9** to engage the attention of; **10** to concern or involve; **11** to induce to participate

in·ter·est·ed *adj* **1** influenced by personal considerations or advantage; **2** feeling interest; concerned; **3** having a share, participating

in·ter·est·ing *adj* **1** engaging the attention or curiosity; **2** exciting the feelings or emotions

in·ter·fere /-fir'/ [MF (*s'*)*entreferir* to strike one another] *vi* **1** to come or be in opposition; **2** to meddle; **3** to hamper or hinder free action or movement; **4** *phys* to cause interference; **5** *rad* to prevent clear reception; **6** *sports* to intervene illegally

in·ter·fer·ence *n* **1** act or instance of interfering; **2** *phys* effect produced when two or more vibrations or trains of waves are superposed so as to strengthen or to neutralize one another; **3** *rad* intermixing of signals resulting in unintelligibility; **4 a** *sports* illegal hampering of an opposing player; **b** *football* blocking of opposing tacklers

in·ter·fer·on /-on/ *n* protein arising and acting in the midst of virus-infected cells to prevent the spread of the virus

in·ter·ga·lac·tic *adj* existing between galaxies

in·ter·im /int'ərim, -rim'/ [L = meanwhile] *n* **1** intervening time or period || *adj* **2** temporary

in·te·ri·or /intir'ē·ər/ [L, *comp* of *inter* between] *adj* **1** inner; internal; **2** inland || *n* **3** interior part; inside; **4** inside of a room or building; **5** internal or domestic affairs of a country

in·te'ri·or dec'o·ra'tor *n* person who designs and executes the interior finishing and embellishment of rooms and whole houses, including furnishings

interj. interjection

in·ter·ject /-jekt'/ [L *interjicere* (*-jectus*)] *vt* to insert; throw in; interpose

in·ter·jec'tion *n* **1** act or instance of interjecting; **2** something interjected; **3** *gram* word interjected without grammatical connection, to express sudden emotion

in·ter·lace /-lās'/ *vt* **1** to weave or lace together; **2** to mingle; intersperse

in·ter·lard /-lard'/ *vt* to vary by mingling with something different; diversify

in·ter·leaf *n* (-leaves /-vz/) blank leaf inserted between two leaves of a book

in·ter·leave /-lēv'/ *vt* **1** to provide (a book) with interleaves; **2** to insert interleaves between (the pages of a book)

in·ter·line'¹ [< *line*¹] *vt* to write in or insert between the lines of (something written or printed) || **in·ter·lin'e·ar** /-lin'ē·ər/ *adj*

in·ter·line'² [< *line*²] *vt* to fit (a garment) with an extra lining beneath the ordinary one || **in·ter·lin'ing** *n*

in·ter·lock' *vt* to fasten together by linking or engaging with one another || *also vi*

in·ter·loc'u·tor /-lok'yətər/ [< L *interloqui* (*-locutus*) to speak between] *n* **1** one who takes part in a conversation; **2** interrogator; **3** middle man in a minstrel troupe who acts as announcer and straight man for the end men

in·ter·loc'u·to·ry /-tôr'ē, -tōr'ē/ *adj law* **1** not final; **2** made or done during the process of an action

in·ter·lop'er /-lōp'ər/ [*inter-* + *lope*] *n* one who intrudes or thrusts himself into the affairs of others

in·ter·lude /-lood'/ [ML *interludium*] *n* **1** short, usu. farcical entertainment formerly given between acts of a play; **2** short musical passage played between the stanzas of a song or hymn, between the acts of an opera, etc.; **3** any interval of time between events

in·ter·lu'nar *adj* pert. to the period between the old moon and the new when the moon is invisible

in·ter·mar·riage *n* **1** marriage of individuals belonging to different classes, races, or religions; **2** marriage between persons closely related || **in·ter·mar·ry** *v* (-ried) *vi*

in·ter·me·di·ar·y /-mēd'ē·er'ē/ [see **intermediate**] *adj* **1** intermediate; **2** mediating || *n* (-ies) **3** agent; go-between

in·ter·me·di·ate /-mēd'ē·it/ [< L *inter-medius*] *adj* **1** in the middle; coming between || *n* **2** something intermediate; **3** intermediary

in·ter·med'i·ate fre'quen·cy *n* in superhetrodyne reception, frequency resulting from the combination of the received carrier frequency and the locally generated oscillator frequency || **in·ter·med'i·ate-fre'quen·cy** *adj*

in·ter·me'di·ate range' bal·lis'tic mis'·sile *n* supersonic missile which has a range of 800 to 1500 nautical miles

in·ter·ment /inturm'ənt/ [see **inter**] *n* burial

in·ter·mez'zo /-med'zō/ [It] *n* (-zos or -zi· /-zē/) **1** short piece of music or ballet performed between the acts of a play; **2** *mus* **a** interlude; **b** short composition

in·ter·mi·na·ble *adj* endless; without termination || SYN infinite, limitless, boundless (see *eternal*)

in·ter·min·gle *vt & vi* to mix or mingle together

in·ter·mis·sion [< L *intermissus* interrupted] *n* 1 short or temporary break; interruption; 2 interval of time between two parts, as acts of a play

in·ter·mit·tent /-mit'ənt/ [< L *intermittere* to interrupt] *adj* 1 stopping and starting; 2 periodic; 3 recurrent ‖ **in·ter·mit'tent·ly** *adv*

in·ter·mix *vt & vi* to intermingle, blend

in·tern /in'turn/ [F *interne* < L *internus* internal] *n* 1 recent graduate of a medical school serving an apprenticeship in a hospital ‖ *vt* 2 to serve as an intern ‖ /inturn'/ *vt* 3 to confine within fixed limits, as citizens of an enemy country or ships in a neutral port in war time

in·ter·nal /inturn'əl/ [L *internus*] *adj* 1 belonging to or situated on the inside; interior; 2 not foreign; domestic; 3 inherent; intrinsic; 4 subjective, pert. to the mind or soul; 5 (medicine) to be taken orally ‖ **in·ter'nal·ly** *adv*

in·ter·nal-com·bus'tion en'gine *n* engine in which power is generated within a cylinder or cylinders by the explosion of a mixture of air and fuel

in·ter'nal med'i·cine *n* branch of medicine dealing with nonsurgical treatment of diseases

in·ter'nal rev'e·nue *n* government revenue from domestic sources

in·ter·na·tion·al *adj* 1 pert. to or involving two or more nations ‖ *n* 2 International labor union with locals in more than one country ‖ **in·ter·na·tion·al·ly** *adv* ‖ **in·ter·na·tion·al·ize'** *vt*

in·ter·na·tion·al date' line' *n* imaginary line running roughly north and south through the Pacific Ocean, about 180° of longitude from Greenwich, and separating adjacent territories in which at any given time the calendar dates differ by one day

in·ter·na'tion·al law' *n* law of nations

In·ter·na·tion·al Mon'e·tar·y Fund' *n* agency of the United Nations, established at Bretton Woods in 1944 for the purpose of stabilizing the world's currencies and providing a pool for member nations to draw on

in·ter·na'tion·al Morse' code' *n* continental code

in·terne /in'turn/ *n* var of intern

in·ter·ne'cine /-nēs'in/ [< *inter-* + L *necare* to kill] *adj* 1 mutually destructive; 2 of or pert. to conflict within a group or nation; 3 characterized by great bloodshed

in·ter·nee /in'turnē'/ *n* person interned in war time

in·tern'ist *n* physician specializing in internal medicine

in·tern·ment /inturn'ment/ *n* act of interning or state of being interned in war time

in·tern·ship /in'turnship'/ *n* 1 service as an intern in a hospital; 2 service in a similar role in business

in·ter·plan'e·tar'y *adj* between planets

in·ter·play' *n* mutual action, play, or influence

In·ter·pol' /-pōl'/ [*International Police*] *n* international agency for exchanging police information among member nations

in·ter·po·late /inturp'əlāt'/ [L *interpolare* to polish] *vt* 1 to insert (new or unauthorized matter) into a book or writing; 2 to insert between other things or parts, as in a series in mathematics ‖ **in·ter·po·la'tion** *n*

in·ter·pose' [MF *interposer*] *vt* 1 to place between; 2 to put forth in order to interfere or mediate; 3 to introduce (a remark or opinion) into a conversation ‖ *vi* 4 to be between; 5 to mediate; 6 to interrupt by making a remark ‖ **in·ter·po·si'tion** *n* ‖ SYN intercede, arbitrate, intermeddle, intervene

in·ter·pret /inturp'rit/ [L *interpretari* to explain] *vt* 1 to explain the meaning of; 2 to translate orally; 3 to bring out the meaning of, by means of musical rendering, stage portrayal, or the like; 4 to regard from one's own viewpoint; construe ‖ *vi* 5 to act as an interpreter ‖ **in·ter'pret·er** *n* ‖ **in·ter'pre·ta'tion** *n* ‖ SYN explain, solve, unfold, elucidate, decipher, construe ‖ DISCR To *interpret* is to give the meaning of the language of one country or period in the language of another; or to explain in familiar terms that which is obscurely worded; or to bring out the meaning either by artistic presentation or sympathetic understanding, as to *interpret* a dream will make it intelligible; to *interpret* a character on the stage is to render it so that it lives to the audience; to *interpret* the testimony of a foreign-speaking witness is to give it in our native tongue. To *construe*, as here compared, is to *interpret* in the light of certain circumstances which reveal motives, give sense to, or otherwise explain a particular situation, as his silence was *construed* as consent. To *explain* is to clear up that which is not understood, is misunderstood, or is obscure; to *explain* is to make known meanings, account for conduct, make motives intelligible, solve difficulties, as to *explain* how to operate a radio set; to *explain* why we voted for so-and-so. To *elucidate* is to *explain*, especially by throwing light on, as by apt illustration, revealing comparison or the like

in·ter·ra'cial *adj* of, for, or involving different races

in·ter·reg'num /-reg'nəm/ [*inter-* + L *regnum* reign] *n* (-nums or -na

/-nə/) 1 interval between two consecutive reigns or governments; 2 any break in continuity

in'ter·re·lat'ed adj having a mutual connection or being relationship ‖ in'ter·re·la'tion n

in·ter·ro·gate /inter'əgāt/ [L interrogare (-atus)] vt 1 to question; examine by asking questions ‖ vi 2 to ask questions ‖ in·ter'ro·ga'tor n ‖ in·ter'ro·ga'tion n ‖ SYN ask, inquire, search, examine (see question)

in·ter'ro·ga'tion mark' or point' n question mark

in'ter·rog'a·tive /-rog'ətiv/ adj 1 indicating or containing a question ‖ n 2 gram interrogative word or element

in'ter·rog'a·to'ry /-tôr'-, -tōr'-/ adj 1 interrogative ‖ n (-ries) 2 question; 3 law question or questions formally put in writing

in'ter·rupt' /-rupt'/ [L interrumpere (-ruptus) to break apart] vt 1 to stop or hinder by breaking in upon; 2 to obstruct; 3 to cause to stop; end suddenly ‖ vi 4 to break into a conversation; 5 to interfere with an action

in'ter·rupt'er n 1 person or thing that interrupts; 2 device for intermittently and automatically opening and closing an electric circuit in a doorbell, induction coil, etc.

in'ter·rup'tion n 1 act of interrupting; 2 state of being interrupted; 3 obstacle; 4 sudden ceasing ‖ SYN discontinuance, break, hindrance, intervention

in'ter·scho·las'tic adj between schools

in'ter·sect' /-sekt'/ [inter- + L secare (sectus) to cut] vt 1 to divide or cut by passing through ‖ vi 2 to cross each other

in'ter·sec'tion n 1 act of intersecting, 2 place of intersecting; 3 place where two or more streets or roads meet or cross

in'ter·sperse' /-spurs'/ [L interspersus scattered among] vt 1 to vary by alternation or contrast; 2 to scatter about

in'ter·state' adj between states

in'ter·stel'lar adj between or among the stars

in·ter·stice /intur'stis [LL interstitium] n narrow space; crevice ‖ in'ter·sti'tial /-stish'əl/ adj

in'ter·twine' vt & vi to twine together

in'ter·ur'ban adj 1 between cities or towns ‖ n 2 interurban train or bus

in'ter·val /-vəl/ [L intervallum space between ramparts] n 1 time between events; 2 space between objects; 3 mus difference in pitch between two tones; 4 at intervals, a now and then; b here and there

in'ter·vene' /-vēn'/ [L intervenire] vi 1 to come between, intercede; 2 to occur between two things; 3 to interfere in the affairs of another; 4 law to become a party to a legal pro-

ceeding between two other parties ‖ in'ter·ven'tion /-ven'shən/ n

in'ter·view' n 1 personal conference or meeting; 2 a act of conversing with or being questioned by a reporter or writer; b published account of such a conversation ‖ vt 3 to have an interview with

in'ter·vo·cal'ic adj between vowels

in'ter·weave' v (-wove; -wo·ven) vt 1 to weave together; 2 to intermingle

in·tes·tate /intes'tāt, -tit/ [L intestatus] adj 1 not having made a will; 2 not disposed of by will ‖ n 3 one who dies intestate ‖ in·tes'ta·cy /-təsē/ n

in·tes·tine /intes'tin/ [L intestinus internal] n 1 any specific part of the intestines; 2 intestines pl lower part of the alimentary canal, from the stomach to the anus; bowels ‖ in·tes'·ti·nal adj

in·ti·mate[1] /int'imit/ [< L intimus innermost] adj 1 pert. to the inward nature of anything; 2 close in friendship; 3 familiar; confidential; 4 resulting from close study, as an intimate knowledge of art; 5 having had sexual relations; 6 private, innermost ‖ n 7 close friend ‖ in'ti·mate·ly adv ‖ in'ti·ma·cy /-məsē/ n (-cies)

in'ti·mate'[2] /-māt'/ [LL intimare (-atus)] vt to make known indirectly; hint ‖ in'ti·ma'tion n ‖ SYN hint, suggest, insinuate, allude, imply

in·tim'i·date /intim'idāt'/ [LL intimidare (-atus)] vt 1 to make afraid, esp. by threats; 2 to overawe ‖ in·tim'i·da'tor n ‖ in·tim'i·da'tion n

in·to /intō̄o, -to͝o, -tə/ [OE] prep 1 to the inside of; 2 in the direction of; 3 against, in contact with, as he bumped into the wall; 4 to the condition or state of, as to go into shock

in·tol'er·a·ble adj unbearable; not to be endured

in·tol'er·ant adj 1 not allowing difference of opinion or belief to others; 2 intolerant of unable to bear or endure ‖ in·tol'er·ant·ly adv ‖ in·tol'er·ance n

in·to·na·tion /int'ənāsh'ən/ n 1 pattern of pitch changes in speech; 2 manner of intoning

in·tone' [ML intonare] vt 1 to recite in a singing tone; 2 to utter in a monotone; chant ‖ vi 3 to chant; recite in singing tones or in a monotone

in·tox'i·cant /intoks'ikənt/ n that which intoxicates

in·tox'i·cate' /-kāt'/ [ML intoxicare (-atus)] vt 1 to smear with poison] vt 1 to make drunk; 2 to excite or stimulate exceedingly; 3 pathol to poison ‖ in·tox'i·ca'tion n

in·tra- /int'rə-/ [L=inside] pref within; inside

in·trac'ta·ble adj ungovernable; unruly; unmanageable ‖ in·trac'ta·bil'i·ty

/-bil'-/ *n* ‖ SYN disobedient, perverse, unruly

in·tra·mu·ral /-myōō'rəl/ *adj* within the limits of a building, city, organization, or university, as *intramural sports*

in·tran·si·gent /intrans'ijənt/ [Sp *intransigente*] *adj* 1 uncompromising, unyielding ‖ *n* 2 intransigent person ‖ in·tran'si·gence *n*

in·tran·si·tive *adj* (verb) not having a direct object to complete its meaning

in'tra·state' *adj* within a state

in'tra·ve'nous /-vēn'əs/ *adj* within or into a vein ‖ in'tra·ve'nous·ly *adv*

in·trench' *vt & vi* var of entrench

in·trep·id /intrep'id/ [L *intrepidus*] *adj* bold, fearless, daring ‖ in'tre·pid'·i·ty /-trəpid'-/ *n* ‖ SYN gallant, dauntless, courageous

in·tri·cate /int'rikit/ [L *intricatus* entangled] *adj* involved; perplexing; complicated ‖ in'tri·ca·cy /-kəsē/ *n* (-cies) ‖ SYN difficult, complex, involved, obscure

in·trigue /intrēg'/ [F *intriguer* < L *intricare* to entangle] *vi* 1 to carry on a secret plot; 2 to engage in secret love affairs ‖ *vt* 3 to interest keenly; 4 to puzzle ‖ *also* in'trēg/ *n* 5 secret plotting or scheming; 6 conspiracy; 7 secret love affair ‖ in·tri'guer *n*

in·trin·sic /intrins'ik/ [ML *intrinsecus* on the inside] *adj* pert. to the very nature of a thing; inherent ‖ in·trin'si·cal·ly *adv* ‖ SYN essential, innate, inbred (see *inherent*)

in·tro- /in'trə-/ [L] *pref* within, inward

in'tro·duce' /-d(y)ōōs'/ [L *introducere* to lead inside] *vt* 1 to conduct or bring in; 2 to bring into use or notice, as a style or fad; 3 to make known, as one person to another; cause to become acquainted; 4 to put into something; insert; 5 to give a first lesson in something to (a person), as *they introduced him to jogging;* 6 to present in a formal manner, as a resolution; 7 to open, begin

in'tro·duc'tion /-duk'shən/ *n* 1 act of introducing or state of being introduced; 2 something introduced; 3 preliminary section, as of a book or musical composition; 4 elementary treatise

in'tro·duc'to·ry /-duk'tərē/ *adj* serving to introduce; preliminary

in·tro·it /in'trō·it/ [L *introitus* entrance] *n* in liturgical churches, chant or that part of the service sung before the celebration of the Eucharist

in·tro·spec·tion /in'trəspek'shən/ [< L *introspectus* looked within] *n* act or process of examining one's own thoughts or feelings ‖ in'tro·spec'tive *adj*

in'tro·vert' /-vurt'/ [*intro-* + *invert'*] *vt* 1 to turn inward; 2 to direct the mind inward ‖ in'tro·vert' *n* 3 person who habitually directs his attention to his own feelings and thoughts, and who does not mix easily with others ‖ in'tro·ver'sion /-zhən or -shən/ *n*

in·trude /intrōōd'/ [L *intrudere* to push in] *vt* 1 to thrust or force without invitation or welcome ‖ *vi* 2 to come in without invitation or welcome ‖ in·trud'er *n* ‖ in·tru'sion /-zhən/ *n*

in·tru'sive *adj* 1 inclined to enter without right or welcome; forward; 2 forced or thrust in, as a foreign substance or element ‖ in·tru'sive·ly *adv* ‖ in·tru'sive·ness *n* ‖ SYN meddlesome, meddling, obtrusive, interfering, inquisitive, troublesome (see *officious*)

in·tu·i·tion /-t(y)ōō·ish'ən/ [< L *intuitus* contemplated] *n* 1 knowledge based on insight and spiritual perception rather than reasoning; 2 that which is known in this way

in·tu'i·tive /-t(y)ōō'itiv/ *adj* 1 perceiving or perceived by intuition; 2 possessing or acting by intuition ‖ in·tu'i·tive·ly *adv*

in·un·date /in'əndāt', inun'dāt/ [L *inundare* (-*atus*)] *vt* to fill to overflowing; flood ‖ in'un·da'tion *n*

in·ure /inyŏŏr'/ [AF *en ure* in use] *vt* 1 to accustom, habituate, as to pain or hardship ‖ *vi* 2 to take or have effect; 3 to redound; contribute

in·vade /invād'/ [L *invadere*] *vt* 1 to enter forcibly with a hostile army; 2 to encroach on; violate; 3 to attack; affect seriously ‖ *also vi* ‖ in·vad'er *n*

in·val·id¹ /inval'id/ [ML *invalidus*] *adj* not valid; without legal force

in·va·lid² /in'vəlid/ [L *invalidus* unsound] *n* 1 one who is weak or infirm in health ‖ *vt* 2 to dismiss from service as an invalid; 3 to make an invalid of

in·val'i·date' *vt* to make invalid or void ‖ in·val'i·da'tion *n*

in'va·lid'i·ty /-lid'-/ *n* lack of legal force

in·val'u·a·ble *adj* valuable beyond estimation; priceless

in·var'i·a·ble *adj* constant; unchanging ‖ in·var'i·a·bly *adv* ‖ SYN permanent, continual, uniform, constant

in·va·sion /invāzh'ən/ [see **invade**] *n* act or instance of invading

in·vec'tive /-vek'tiv/ [LL *invectivus* abusive] *n* 1 violent denunciation; 2 vituperation

in·veigh /invā'/ [L *invehi* to attack] *vi* inveigh against to rail at, speak violently against ‖ in·veigh'er *n*

in·vei·gle /invēg'əl, -vāg'-/ [AF *enveogler* to blind] *vt* to lure; cajole ‖ SYN decoy, allure, entice, wheedle, seduce

in·vent /invent'/ [L *invenire* (-*ventus*)] *vt* 1 to create; produce for the first time; originate; 2 to contrive; fabricate ‖ in·ven'tor *n* ‖ SYN originate, devise, fabricate (see *discover*)

in·ven'tion *n* 1 act or process of inventing; 2 something invented; 3 power of inventing; creative imagination

in·ven'tive *adj* 1 able to invent; 2 characterized by creative imagination || **in·ven'tive·ness** *n*

in·ven·to·ry /in'vəntôr'ē, -tōr'-/ [ML *inventorium*] *n* (-ries) 1 detailed, itemized list, as of property or a merchant's stock of goods; 2 things listed || *v* (-ried) *vt* 3 to make an inventory of; place in an inventory

in·verse /invûrs', in'vûrs/ [L *inversus*] *adj* 1 reversed in tendency, direction, or effect; inverted || *n* 2 direct opposite; contrary || **in·verse'ly** *adv*

in·ver'sion /-zhən, -shən/ *n* 1 act of inverting or state of being inverted; 2 something inverted; 3 *gram* change in the usual order of words in a sentence; 4 *meteor.* atmospheric condition occurring when a layer of cool air remains stationary over a layer of heavily polluted hot air and prevents the warmer air from rising

in·vert /invûrt'/ [L *invertere*] *vt* 1 to turn upside down, inside out, or in an opposite direction; 2 to reverse the meaning, order, or condition of || /in'vûrt/ *n* 3 homosexual

in·ver'te·brate *n* 1 animal without a backbone or spinal column || *adj* 2 having no backbone

in·vest /invest'/ [L *investire* to clothe in] *vt* 1 to bestow power or authority on; 2 *mil* to completely surround; besiege; 3 to apply (money) for profit or income; 4 to devote (time, effort, etc.) to achieve an end || *vi* 5 to invest money || **in·ves'tor** *n*

in·ves·ti·gate /invest'igāt'/ [L *investigare* (-atus) to track] *vt* 1 to inquire carefully concerning; examine systematically || *vt* 2 to pursue an inquiry || **in·ves'ti·ga·tive** *adj* || **in·ves'ti·ga'tor** *n* || **in·ves'ti·ga'tion** *n*

in·ves·ti·ture /-tichər/ [ML *investitura*] *n* act or right of giving possession or installing in office

in·vest'ment *n* 1 act of investing or state of being invested; 2 investing of money; 3 money invested; 4 that in which money is invested

in·vet·er·ate /invet'ərit/ [L *inveteratus* aged] *adj* 1 deep-rooted; 2 habitual

in·vid·i·ous /invid'ē-əs/ [< L *invidia* envy] *adj* 1 likely to cause ill will or envy; 2 unfairly discriminating

in·vig·or·ate /invig'ərāt'/ [< in⁻¹ + L *vigor* strength] *vt* to give vitality to; fill with energy || syn refresh, stimulate, energize, exhilarate

in·vin·ci·ble /invins'ibəl/ [< in⁻¹ + L *vincere* to conquer] *adj* unconquerable || **in·vin'ci·bil'i·ty** /-bil'-/ *n*

in·vi'o·la·ble *adj* 1 not to be profaned or injured; 2 to be kept unbroken, as a promise || **in·vi'o·la·bil'i·ty** /-bil'-/ *n*

in·vi'o·late /-lit, -lāt'/ *adj* 1 uninjured; unbroken; 2 not defiled; pure; 3 inviolable

in·vis'i·ble *adj* not visible || **in·vis'i·bil'i·ty** /-bil'-/ *n*

in·vi·ta·tion /in'vitāsh'ən/ *n* 1 act of inviting; 2 note or message used for inviting

in·vite /invīt'/ [L *invitare*] *vt* 1 to request courteously to go to some place or to do something; 2 to tempt; attract; 3 to give occasion for; 4 to make a formal request for || **in·vit'er** *n* || syn bid, summon, press, urge, allure (see *call*)

in·vit'ing *adj* tempting; attractive

in·vo·ca·tion /in'vəkāsh'ən/ *n* act of invoking

in·voice /in'vois/ [MF *envois* messages] *n* 1 itemized bill for goods sold or services rendered || *vt* 2 to present an invoice to; 3 to put on an invoice

in·voke /invōk'/ [L *invocare*] *vt* 1 to address in prayer or supplication; 2 to conjure; 3 to call on to be put into effect, as *to invoke the fifth amendment*

in·vol'un·tar'y *adj* 1 not under the control of the will; 2 not done by choice; 3 unintentional || **in·vol'un·tar'i·ly** *adv*

in·vo·lute /in'vəlōōt'/ [L *involutus* rolled up] *adj* 1 complicated; involved; 2 *bot* having edges rolled inward; 3 *zool* coiled spirally

in·vo·lu·tion *n* 1 act of folding or coiling in or round; 2 something which is intricate or complicated; 3 *biol* retrograde change, the reverse of evolution; degeneration; 4 *math* the process of raising a quantity to a given power

in·volve /involv'/ [L *involvere* to roll up] *vt* 1 to complicate; 2 to entangle; implicate; 3 to include as a consequence; entail; 4 to engage completely || **in·volve'ment** *n* || syn implicate, imply, complicate, include, entwine, wind, coil, envelop, surround

in·vul'ner·a·ble *adj* 1 incapable of being wounded or harmed; 2 immune to attack || **in·vul'ner·a·bil'i·ty** /-bil'-/ *n*

in·ward /in'wərd/ [OE *inweard*] *adj* 1 situated within; internal; 2 directed toward the inside; 3 spiritual || *adv* also **in'wards** 4 toward the center or interior; 5 into or toward the mind

in'ward·ly *adv* 1 internally; 2 in the mind or feelings; 3 secretly

i·o·dide /ī'ədīd', -did/ *n* salt of iodine with a metal or a radical

i·o·dine /ī'ədīn', -din, -dēn'/ [< Gk *iodes* violetlike] *n* 1 grayish-black, solid halogen element (I; at.no. 53; at.wt. 126.904), which, when heated, turns into a violet vapor; used in medicine and photography; 2 tincture of iodine, used as an antiseptic

i'o·dize' *vt* to combine or impregnate with iodine or an iodide

i·o·do·form /ī·ŏd'əfôrm', ī·od'-/ [*Io-dine* + *chloroform*] *n* yellow crystal-line powder —CHI₃— with a pene-trating odor, used as an antiseptic

i·on /ī'ən, -on/ [Gk = going] *n* atom or group of atoms electrically charged by having gained one or more electrons through attraction from the cathode to the anode (anion) or lost one or more elec-trons through attraction from the anode to the cathode (cation)

I·on·ic /ī·on'ik/ [< Gk *Ionia* W coast of Asia Minor and adjacent islands] *adj* pert. to or designating one of the orders of Greek architecture charac-terized by scroll-like decorations on the capitals of pillars

i·o·ni·um /ī·ōn'ē·əm/ [< *ion*] *n* radio-active isotope of thorium (Io; at.no. 90; at.wt. 230)

i·on·ize /ī'əniz/ *vt* **1** to dissociate into ions; **2** to produce ions in ‖ *vi* **3** to change into ions ‖ **i'on·i·za'tion** *n*

i·on'o·sphere /ī·on'ə-/ *n* that part of the earth's atmosphere above the stratosphere, consisting of ionized particles, 50 to 250 miles above the earth's surface

i·o·ta /ī·ōt'ə/ *n* **1** ninth letter of the Greek alphabet I, ι; **2** small or in-significant part; jot

IOU also **I.O.U.** /ī'ō'yōō'/ [= I owe you] *n* signed but informal acknowl-edgment of a debt

-ious [L *-iosus*] *adj suf* characterized by, having, as *religious*

I·o·wa /ī'əwə/ *n* state in central U.S. (2,825,000; 56,147 sq.m.; cap. Des Moines) ‖ **I'o·wan** *n*

ip·e·cac /ip'ikak'/ [< Port *ipeca-cuanha* < Tupi] *n* drug made from the dried root of a South American plant (*Cephaelis ipecacuanha*), used as an emetic and purgative

Iph·i·ge·ni·a /if'ijinī'ə/ *n* Gk *myth.* a daughter of Agamemnon, offered as a sacrifice to Artemis in order to se-cure favorable winds for the expedi-tion against Troy, but rescued by the goddess

ips inches per second

ip·so fac·to /ip'sō fak'tō/ [L] by the act or fact itself

IQ also **I.Q.** /ī'kyōō'/ [*intelligence quotient*] *n* index of intelligence, equal to mental age divided by chronological age, expressed in mul-tiples of 100

Ir¹ Irish

Ir² *chem* iridium

ir- /ir-/ *pref* var of **in-**¹ or **in-**²

I·ran /iran', i-/ *n* country in SW Asia (25,781,090; 636,300 sq.m.; cap. Teheran); formerly Persia ‖ **I·ra'ni·an** /-rän'ē·ən/ *adj & n*

I·raq /irak'/ *n* Arabic-speaking re-public in SW Asia (8,261,527; 167,887 sq.m.; cap. Baghdad) ‖ **I·ra'qi** /-ē/ *adj & n*

i·ras·ci·ble /īras'ibəl, iras'-/ [< L

irasci to get angry] *adj* easily ex-cited to anger; irritable ‖ **i·ras'ci·bil'i·ty** /-bil'-/ *n* ‖ SYN irritable, touchy, petulant, snappish, cross

i·rate /irāt', ī'rāt/ [L *iratus*] *adj* angry; enraged; incensed ‖ **i·rate'ly** *adv*

IRBM, I.R.B.M. intermediate range ballistic missile

ire /ī'(ə)r/ [OF < L *ira*] *n* anger, wrath ‖ SYN rage, passion, wrath (see *anger*)

Ire. Ireland

Ire·land /ī'(ə)rlənd/ *n* **1** English- and Gaelic-speaking island W of Britain, comprising Northern Ireland and the Republic of Ireland; **2** republic oc-cupying most of the island of Ire-land (2,884,000; 27,135 sq.m.; cap. Dublin)

ir·i·des·cent /ir'ides'ənt/ [see **iris**] *adj* having changing, shimmering, rain-bowlike colors ‖ **ir'i·des'cence** *n*

i·rid·i·um /irid'ē·əm, -irid'-/ [see **iris**] *n* hard silver-white metallic element (Ir; at.no. 77; at.wt. 192.2) of the platinum group, used to harden plati-num alloys

i·ris /ī'ris/ [Gk *Iris* the rainbow god-dess] *n* (**i·ris·es** or **ir·i·des** /ir'idēz', ī'r-/) **1** circular colored membrane surrounding the pupil of the eye; **2** any of a genus (*Iris*) of plants with sword-shaped leaves and showy flowers; **3** rainbow

I·rish /ī'rish/ [OE *Iras* the Irish] *adj* **1** pert. to Ireland, its people, or its language ‖ *n* **2** language of the Irish; **3** the Irish *pl* the people of Ireland

I'rish·man /-mən/ *n* (**-men** /-mən/) *n* man of Irish birth or race ‖ **I'rish·wom'an** *nfem* (**-wom'en**)

I'rish Sea' *n* arm of the Atlantic be-tween Ireland and Britain

irk /urk'/ [ME *irken* to weary < Scand] *vt* to worry, vex ‖ **irk'some** *adj*

i·ron /ī'ərn/ [OE *iren*] *n* **1** silver-white metallic element (Fe; at.no. 26; at.wt. 55.847), the most common metal; **2** utensil or weapon made of iron; **3** metal implement with a smooth flat bottom used, when heated, to press cloth; **4** anything especially hard, rigid, or strong; **5** any of several golf clubs with a metal head; **6 irons** *pl* fetters or shackles; **7 irons in the fire** matters in which one is interested; **8 strike while the iron is hot** to act before the opportunity passes ‖ *vt* **9** to press with a hot iron; **10 iron out** *colloq* to clear up or remove, as difficulties

I'ron Age' *n* period in the development of man, following the Bronze Age, when iron weapons and implements were made

i'ron-clad' *n* **1** warship of the 19th century cased with iron plates ‖ *adj* **2** unbreakable, not to be evaded, as a contract

I′ron Cur′tain *n* barrier to understanding and communication, imposed by censorship and travel restrictions, such as has existed between the communist bloc of E Europe and the countries to the west

i‑ron‑ic (‑i‑cal) /īron′ik(əl)/ [see *irony*] *adj* 1 pert. to, containing, or characterized by irony; 2 using irony ‖ **i‑ron′i‑cal‑ly** *adv*

I′ron lung′ *n* chamber encasing the chest, used to force air in and out of the lungs of patients whose chest muscles are paralyzed

I′ron‑mon′ger /‑muŋ′gər/ *n* chiefly *Brit* dealer in iron goods and hardware

I′ron py′rites /pī′rīts, pərīt′ēz/ *n* iron disulfide —FeS₂— a yellow mineral with a metallic luster, often mistaken for gold

I′ron‑ware′ *n* articles made of iron; hardware

I′ron‑work′ *n* objects made of iron, as gratings, rails, etc.

I′ron‑works′ *nsg* establishment where iron and steel products are made

i‑ro‑ny /īr′ənē/ [Gk *eironeia* pretended ignorance] *n* (‑nies) 1 covert sarcasm; ridicule in the guise of compliment or praise; 2 mode of speech meaning the opposite of what is said; 3 outcome of a situation which is the reverse of what would normally be expected ‖ SYN sarcasm, satire, banter (see *ridicule*)

Ir‑o‑quois /ir′əkwoi(z)′/ [F < Algonquian] *n* (*pl* ‑quois) member of one of the Indian tribes making up the Five Nations, formerly inhabiting central New York ‖ **Ir′o‑quoi′an** *adj & n*

ir‑ra′di‑ate′ /irād′‑/ [L *irradiare* (‑*atus*)] *vt* 1 to shed light upon; 2 to enlighten; 3 to radiate; 4 to expose to radiation ‖ **ir‑ra′di‑a′tion** *n*

ir‑ra′tion‑al *adj* 1 lacking or not exercising reasoning powers; 2 contrary to reason; absurd; 3 *math* not capable of being expressed as a ratio of two integers ‖ **ir‑ra′tion‑al′‑i‑ty** /‑nal′‑/ *n* (‑ties)

ir‑rec′on‑cil′a‑ble *adj* 1 not in agreement; incompatible; 2 uncompromising; implacable ‖ *n* 3 irreconcilable person

ir′re‑cov′er‑a‑ble *adj* not recoverable; irretrievable ‖ **ir′re‑cov′er‑a‑bly** *adv*

ir′re‑deem′a‑ble *adj* 1 incapable of being redeemed; 2 (paper money) not exchangeable for coins; 3 irreparable; not to be reformed ‖ **ir′re‑deem′a‑bly** *adv*

ir‑re‑den′tist /ir′ident′ist/ [< It *irredenta* unredeemed] *n* person advocating the return of a region from foreign jurisdiction to his own country by reason of ethnic ties ‖ **ir′re‑den′tism** *n*

ir‑re‑duc′i‑ble *adj* 1 incapable of being brought into a different condition or form; 2 incapable of being diminished or subdued; 3 *math* (fraction) not capable of simplification

ir‑ref‑u‑ta‑ble /iref′yətəbəl, ir′ifōoyt′‑əbəl/ *adj* not refutable; indisputable ‖ **ir′ref‑u′ta‑bly** *adv*

ir‑reg′u‑lar *adj* 1 not straight or unsymmetrical; not uniform in shape, proportion, duration, order, etc.; 2 not conforming to rule or established method; 3 *gram* deviating from the norm in inflection or usage ‖ **ir‑reg′u‑lar‑ly** *adv* ‖ **ir‑reg′u‑lar′i‑ty** /‑lar′‑/ *n* (‑ties)

ir‑rel′e‑vant *adj* not relevant, not bearing upon the case ‖ **ir‑rel′e‑vance** *n* also **ir‑rel′e‑van‑cy** *n* (‑cies)

ir‑re‑li′gious *adj* 1 lacking religion; 2 indifferent or hostile to religion

ir‑re‑me′di‑a‑ble *adj* not capable of being remedied or corrected

ir‑rep′a‑ra‑ble *adj* not capable of being repaired, restored, or made good ‖ **ir‑rep′a‑ra‑bly** *adv*

ir‑re‑place′a‑ble *adj* that cannot be replaced

ir‑re‑press′i‑ble /ir′ipres′ibəl/ *adj* incapable of being repressed or controlled ‖ **ir′re‑press′i‑bly** *adv*

ir‑re‑proach′a‑ble *adj* blameless; faultless

ir‑re‑sist′i‑ble *adj* incapable of being withstood; overpowering ‖ **ir′re‑sist′i‑bly** *adv*

ir‑res′o‑lute *adj* undecided; wavering

ir‑res′o‑lu′tion *n* lack of determination; hesitation ‖ SYN indecision, vacillation ‖ DISCR *Indecision* wavers because it does not know what to do. This state of mind, usually temporary, arises from the inability to judge between courses or actions presenting themselves as possible. *Indecision* therefore does not necessarily indicate weakness; *irresolution* and *vacillation* do. *Irresolution* cannot summon the courage to act or decide one way or the other; *vacillation* decides bravely enough, but directly changes to the opposite decision or action, and as quickly back again

ir′re‑spec′tive *adj* irrespective of regardless of

ir′re‑spon′si‑ble *adj* 1 lacking a sense of responsibility; 2 not accountable to anyone; 3 not capable of responsibility

ir′re‑triev′a‑ble *adj* not recoverable; irreparable

ir‑rev′er‑ent *adj* exhibiting lack of reverence or respect ‖ **ir‑rev′er‑ence** *n*

ir′re‑vers′i‑ble *adj* incapable of being reversed or changed ‖ **ir′re‑vers′i‑bly** *adv*

ir‑rev′o‑ca‑ble *adj* incapable of being revoked, repealed, or undone ‖ **ir‑rev′o‑ca‑bly** *adv*

ir‑ri‑gate /ir′igāt′/ [L *irrigare* (‑*atus*)] *vt* 1 to supply (land) with water by artificial means; 2 *med* to wash out (a wound or cavity) with a flow of liquid ‖ ir'ri·ga'tion *n*

ir·ri·ta·ble /ir'ĭtəbel/ *adj* easily irritated or provoked ‖ ir'ri·ta·bil'i·ty /-bil'-/ *n* ‖ SYN peevish, impatient, irascible, fretful, petulant

ir·ri·tant /ir'ĭtənt/ *adj* 1 causing irritation ‖ *n* 2 anything that irritates

ir'ri·tate' [L *irritare* (*-atus*) to provoke to anger] *vt* 1 to provoke or make angry; 2 to cause inflammation, redness, or pain in ‖ ir'ri·ta'tion *n* ‖ SYN vex, annoy, excite, incense, exasperate, provoke, offend, tease ‖ DISCR To *irritate* is to excite to anger, impatience, nervousness, or fretfulness, usually by something that grates on the sensibilities. We are *irritated* by being constantly crossed or nagged, or by having to listen to harsh or unnecessary noise. To *exasperate* is to *irritate* so thoroughly and intensely that hot, often bitter, anger results. We stand irritation as long as we can, and the "last straw" so *exasperates* us that we fly into a temper. To *annoy* is to disturb to the point of irritation; to *vex* is to *irritate* to the point of offense. We are *vexed* by the intentional slight of a friend, by the continued tardiness at appointments which so inconveniences us. To *provoke* is to arouse annoyance or vexation; we are *provoked* at ourselves when we act heedlessly and find ourselves in trouble; a constant stream of questions will *provoke* the most patient. *Provoke* is sometimes used in the sense of *tease*, as he pretended to have forgotten, just to *provoke* me. To *incense* is to incite one to maddened anger ‖ ANT pacify, tranquilize, placate, appease, soothe, calm

ir·rup·tion /irup'shən/ [< L *irruptus* broken into] *n* 1 a bursting or rushing in; 2 sudden invasion ‖ ir·rup'tive *adj*

IRS Internal Revenue Service

Ir·ving, Wash·ing·ton /ur'viņ/ *n* (1783–1859) U.S. novelist and historian

is /iz/ [OE] *3rd pers sg pres ind* of be

Is. 1 island; 2 isle

I·saac /iz'ək/ *n Bib* Hebrew patriarch, son of Abraham and Sarah, and father of Jacob and Esau (Gen. 21:3; 35:29)

Is·a·bel·la I /iz'əbel'ə/ *n* (1451–1504) queen of Castile 1474–1504, conqueror of Granada, and patron of Columbus

Is·a·iah /izā'ə/ *n Bib* 1 great Hebrew prophet of the 8th century B.C.; 2 book of the Old Testament

Is·car·i·ot /iskar'ē·ət/ *n Bib* surname of Judas, the apostle who betrayed Jesus (Matt. 10:4)

-ise /-īz'/ var of -ize

-ish /-ish/ [OE *isc*] *adj suf* 1 pert. to,

as *Scottish;* 2 like, as *girlish;* 3 somewhat, as *blackish;* 4 *colloq* about, as *fortyish*

Ish·ma·el /ish'mē·əl/ *n* 1 *Bib* exiled son of Abraham and Hagar (Gen. 16:11–16); 2 outcast

Ish·tar /ish'tär/ *n* Babylonian and Assyrian goddess of love and fertility

i'sin·glass' /ī'ziŋ-, iz'ən-/ [MD *huisenblas* sturgeon's bladder] *n* 1 gelatin prepared from the air bladders of certain fishes; 2 mica

I·sis /ī'sis/ *n* Egyptian goddess of fertility, the sister and wife of Osiris

Is·lam /is'ləm, iz'-, isläm'/ [Ar = submission] *n* 1 the religion of the Muslims, founded by Muhammad in the beginning of the 7th century; it embodies many Biblical teachings, but claims Muhammad was the greatest prophet of God; it denies the divinity of Jesus and makes the Koran the supreme written authority; 2 the whole body of Muslims and the countries in which they predominate ‖ Is·lam·ic /islam'ik, -läm'-/ *adj*

Is·lam·a·bad /isläm'əbäd/, iz-/ *n* capital of Pakistan (51,000)

is·land /ī'lənd/ [OE *igland* (*s* in spelling < *isle*)] *n* 1 tract of land surrounded by water that is smaller than a continent; 2 anything detached or isolated like an island

is'land·er *n* one born or living on an island

isle /īl/ [OF < L *insula*] *n* island, esp. a small one

is·let /ī'lit/ *n* very small island

ism /iz'əm/ [< -ism] *n* distinctive system, theory, or doctrine

-ism /-iz'əm/ [Gk *-ismos*] *n suf* 1 action of, as *baptism;* 2 state, condition, or quality of, as *heroism;* 3 system, doctrine, policy, etc., as *liberalism;* 4 characteristic or peculiarity, as *Britishism;* 5 morbid condition caused by excessive use of, as *alcoholism*

isn't /iz'ənt/ is not

i·so- [Gk *isos*] *comb form* equal; alike

i·so·bar /ī's'əbär'/ [*iso-+* Gk *baros* weight] *n* line on a map connecting places having the same barometric pressure

i·so·late /ī's'əlāt', is'-/ [It *isolato* < L *insula* island] *vt* 1 to place alone or in a detached position; separate from others; 2 *chem* to obtain in a pure or uncombined state ‖ i'so·la'tion *n*

i·so·la'tion booth' *n* small soundproof booth in a television studio or bulletproof booth in a court room

i'so·la'tion·ist *n* one who favors avoidance of political entanglements with other nations ‖ i'so·la'tion·ism *n*

i'so·mer /ī's'əmər/ [*iso-+* Gk *meros* part] *n chem* substance containing the same elements combined in the same proportions as another, but differing in arrangement and properties || **i'so·mer'ic** /-mer'-/ adj

i'so·met'ric adj 1 having equality of measure; 2 pert. to isometrics

i'so·met'ric pro·jec'tion n method of mechanical drawing showing measurements in three dimensions without regard to perspective

i'so·met'rics nsg exercises in which one muscle is employed against another or against an immovable object

i·sos·ce·les /īsos'ələz'/ [iso- + Gk skelos leg] adj (triangle) having two equal sides

i·so·therm /īs'əthurm'/ [iso- + Gk therme heat] n line on a map connecting places having the same temperature

i'so·tope' /-tōp'/ [iso- + Gk topos place] n one of two or more varieties of an element, almost identical as to chemical properties, but differing in atomic weight

Is·ra·el /iz'rē·əl/ n 1 republic in SW Asia on the Mediterranean (3,500,-000, 8,000 sq.m.; cap. Jerusalem); 2 Bib the Hebrew patriarch Jacob (Gen. 32); 3 the Jewish people; 4 northern kingdom of the ancient Hebrews

Is·rae·li /izrāl'ē/ n native or inhabitant of modern Israel || also adj

Is·ra·el·ite /iz'rē·əlīt'/ n 1 descendant of Jacob, esp., Hebrew of the ancient kingdom of Israel; 2 Jew, Hebrew

Is·sei /ē'sā'/ [Jap = first generation] nsg & npl Japanese born in Japan but resident in the U.S.

is·sue /ish'ŏŏ/ [MF < L exitus gone out] n 1 act of putting forth; 2 means of egress; outlet; 3 that which is published; 4 particular number of a periodical; 5 entire number or amount sent out at one time, as a government issue of banknotes; 6 something produced; 7 distribution, as of equipment or rations; 8 offspring; 9 final result, outcome; 10 discharge, as of blood or pus; 11 point of contention; 12 point at which a matter becomes ripe for decision; 13 at issue under dispute; 14 take issue with to disagree with || vt 15 to send out; emit; discharge; 16 to publish; put in circulation; 17 to distribute, as equipment or rations || vi 18 to come or pass forth; flow out; 19 to arise, as from a source; flow; 20 to be descended; 21 to accrue, as proceeds or revenue; 22 to result || is'su·ance n || SYN n outcome, event, consequence (see result)

-ist /-ĭst/ [Gk -istes] n suf 1 one who does or makes a practice of doing a given thing, as plagiarist; 2 one who pursues or is skilled in a given art or science, as geneticist; 3 adherent of a system, religion, or creed, as Buddhist; 4 one who holds to certain principles, as altruist

Is·tan·bul /is'tanbŏŏl', -bŏŏl', -tän-/ n Turkish port on both sides of the Bosporus (1,750,642)

isth·mus /is'məs/ [Gk isthmos] n (-mus·es or -mi /-mī/) neck of land connecting two larger bodies of land

-is·tic /-ist'ik/ [Gk -istikos] adj suf 1 pert. to or like, as characteristic; 2 corresponding to nouns ending in -ist, as altruistic

-is·ti·cal /-ist'ikəl/ [-istic + -al¹] adj suf 1 var of -istic in a few words, as patristical; 2 corresponding to nouns ending in -ic, as statistical

-is'tics [-ist + ics] n suf science or art, as ballistics

it /it/, it'/ [OE hit] pron used 1 to refer to a thing or animal previously mentioned; 2 as a substitute for any noun or noun clause mentioned or understood; 3 as the subject of an impersonal verb, as it is raining; 4 as apparent subject of a verb whose real subject follows, as it is time to go; 5 for an indefinite subject or object, as it was he who called, let's walk it; 6 to indicate a person of importance, as he thought he was it || n 7 in children's games, the one whom the other contestants oppose; 8 be with it slang to know what's going on; 9 get with it slang to do what is expected of one; 10 have it slang a to have the ability to do something well; b to have physical attraction

It. or **Ital.** 1 Italy; 2 Italian; 3 Italic **ital.** italic(s)

I·tal·ian /ital'yən/ [L Italianus] n 1 native or inhabitant of Italy; 2 language of Italy || also adj

i·tal·ic /ital'ik, īt-/ [Gk italikos Italian] adj 1 (style of printing type) that slopes to the right, as shown in this example: italics; 2 Italic pert. to Italy, esp. ancient Italy, or to the subfamily of Indo-European languages which includes Latin || n 3 italics nsg & npl italic type

i·tal'i·cize' vt 1 to print in italics; 2 to underline (letters or words) with a single line || vi to use italics

It·a·ly /it'əlē/ n republic in S Europe (52,334,000; 116,304 sq.m.; cap. Rome)

itch /ich'/ [OE giccan] vi 1 to feel a particular uneasiness in the skin, causing a desire to scratch; 2 to cause itching; 3 to have a constant and teasing desire; to long || vt 4 to cause to have an itch || n 5 sensation of itching; 6 constant and teasing desire for something; 7 the itch contagious skin disease characterized by intense itching || itch'y adj (-i·er, -i·est)

-ite /-ĭt, -īt'/ [Gk -ites] n suf 1 follower, descendant, or inhabitant of, as *Rooseveltite, Israelite;* **2** name of a commercial product, as *bakelite;* **3** fossil organism, as *tribolite;* **4** explosive, as *dynamite;* **5** *anat* part, segment, or joint; **6** *chem* indicating that the word is the name of a salt and that the element to whose name in full or shortened form it is attached has a lower valence than in the corresponding salt with the suffix *-ate;* it corresponds to the suffix *-ous* in the adjective part of the name of an acid

i·tem /ītˈəm/ [L = in like manner] *n* **1** separate article or particular; **2** newspaper paragraph; **3** *slang* sensational piece of news or gossip ‖ *adv* **4** also (used to introduce each article in an enumeration)

i′tem·ize′ *vt* to state or set down by items or individual parts

it·er·ate /itˈərāt′/ [L *iterare* (*-atus*)] *vt* to utter a second time; repeat ‖ **it′er·a′tion** *n*

i·tin·er·ant /ītinˈərənt/ [< L *itinerari* to travel] *adj* **1** traveling from place to place ‖ *n* **2** itinerant person

i·tin·er·ar′y *n* (*-ies*) **1** plan of a journey; **2** route; **3** record of a journey

-i·tis /-īˈtis/ [Gk] *n suf* inflammatory disease, as *tonsillitis*

its /its/, **its′** [*it* + his] *adj* **1** possessive of **it**: of or belonging to **it** ‖ *pron* **2** that or those belonging to **it**

it's /its/, **its′** /it is; **2** it has

it·self′ *pron* **1** reflexive form of **it**; **2** emphatic form of **it**; **3** its normal self, as *the canary is not itself today*

-i·ty /-itē/ [OF *-ite* < L *-itas*] *n suf* state or condition, as *hostility*

-ive /-iv/ [L *-ivus*] *adj* & *n suf* relating to; of the nature of, as *active, native*

I′ve /īv′/ I have

i·vied /īvˈēd/ [see **ivy**] *adj* covered or overgrown with ivy

i·vo·ry /īvˈ(ə)rē/ [OF *tvoire* < L *eboreus* of ivory] *n* (*-ries*) **1** hard white substance which forms the tusks of elephants and walruses; **2** creamy white color; **3** substance resembling ivory; **4** **ivories** *pl slang* **a** dice; **b** piano keys

I′vo·ry Coast′ *n* republic in W Africa (4,000,000; 124,504 sq.m.; cap. Abidjan)

i′vo·ry tow′er *n* **1** place withdrawn from everyday affairs; **2** aloofness from or refusal to deal with practical matters

i·vy /īvˈē/ [OE *ifig*] *n* (*-vies*) **1** any of several clinging evergreen or deciduous vines with ornamental leaves, as English ivy (*Hedera helix*) and Boston ivy (*Parthenocissus tricuspidata*); **2** any of various similar plants

I′vy League′ *n* group of colleges in NE U.S., characterized by high scholastic ratings and social prestige ‖ also *adj*

-ize /-īz′/ [OF *-iser* < Gk *-izein*] *v suf* **1** to subject or treat to the action denoted by the root, as *criticize;* **2** to make or make like, as *fossilize;* **3** to treat after the manner or method of, as *economize;* **4** to treat or combine with, as *oxidize*

J

J, j /jā′/ *n* (**J′s** or **Js**; **j′s** or **js**) **1** tenth letter of the English alphabet; **2** joule

J 1 tenth in order or in a series; **2** something shaped like a J

J. **1** Judge; **2** Justice; **3** Journal

jab /jab′/ [ME *jobben*] *v* (**jabbed; jab·bing**) *vt* **1** to poke; thrust something sharp into; **2** to punch with a short, sharp blow ‖ *vi* **3** to make a jabbing blow ‖ *n* **4** quick blow or thrust

jab·ber /jabˈər/ [prob imit] *vt* **1** to utter unintelligibly ‖ *vi* **2** to talk rapidly and indistinctly ‖ *n* **3** incoherent or unintelligible talk ‖ **jab′ber·er** *n*

ja·bot /zhabō′, ja-/ [F] *n* ruffle or frill, usu. of lace, worn down the front of a woman's blouse

jac·a·ran·da /jakˈəranˈdə/ [Port < Tupi-Guarani] *n* **1** Brazilian timber tree; **2** heavy dark wood of this tree; **3** tropical American tree with pale-purple flowers

jack /jak′/ [ME *Jacke* nickname of John] *n* **1** also **Jack** man or boy; **2** portable mechanism for lifting great weights; **3** male of several animals, esp. the ass; **4** playing card having the figure of a page boy; **5** small flag flown at the bow of a vessel to show nationality; **6** *elec* receptacle that accepts a plug; **7** *slang* money; **8** **a** six-pointed metal object used in the game of jacks; **b** **jacks** *sg* children's game in which jacks are tossed in the air and caught while a ball is being bounced ‖ *vt* **9** often **jack up,** **a** to lift with or as with a jack; **b** *colloq* to raise (costs, wages, or prices); **c** *colloq* to take to task

jack·al /jakˈəl, -ôl/ [Turk *çakal* < Pers *shagāl*] *n* **1** any of several doglike animals of the Old World (esp. *Canis aureus*) that hunt in packs at night; **2** one who does mean work for others

jack′ass′ *n* **1** male donkey; **2** blockhead

jack′boot′ *n* large boot reaching above the knee

jack′daw′ /-dô′/ [*jack* + ME *dawe*

jack·daw /jak′dô/ n European bird (*Corvus monedula*) of the crow family

jack·et /jak′it/ [MF *jaquet*] n 1 short tailless coat; 2 anything put on like a coat, as *a life jacket*; 3 covering for protection, insulation, etc., as for a book, record, engine, or machinery; 4 skin of a potato ‖ vt 5 to cover with a jacket

jack′-in-the-box′ n toy consisting of a grotesque figure which springs from within a box when the lid is released

jack′-in-the-pul′pit n American plant (*Arisaema triphyllum*) with inconspicuous flowers borne on a fleshy axis covered by a leaflike hood

jack′knife′ n (-knives /-vz/) 1 large pocketknife; 2 dive in which the diver bends his body during the dive and straightens out again before hitting the water ‖ vi 3 to form a sharp angle with each other, as two railroad cars jumping the track or a cab and trailer after a skid

jack′-of-all′-trades′ n (jacks-) one who is skillful at many kinds of work

jack′-o′-lan′tern /jak′ə-/ n lantern made from or in imitation of a hollowed pumpkin with holes cut out to resemble a face

jack′pot′ n 1 cumulative stakes in a game, contest, slot machine, etc.; 2 **hit the jackpot** slang to achieve immense success

jack′rab′bit n any of several species of large North American hares with long ears and long powerful hind legs

Jack·son /jak′sən/ n capital of Mississippi (150,000)

Jack·son, An·drew n (1767–1845) 7th president of the U.S. 1829–37

Jack·son, Thom·as J. n (Stonewall Jackson) (1824–63) Confederate general

Jack′son·ville′ /-vil′/ n city in NE Florida (528,865)

jack′-tar′ n sailor

Ja·cob /jāk′əb/ n Bib younger son of Isaac and ancestor, through his twelve sons, of the twelve tribes of Israel (Gen. 25:24–34)

Ja′cob′s lad′der n 1 Bib ladder reaching to heaven, seen by Jacob in a dream (Gen. 28:12); 2 naut rope ladder with wooden rungs

Ja′cob′s-lad′der n garden plant (*Polemonium caeruleum*) with leaves that resemble a ladder

jade¹ /jād′/ [?] n 1 inferior or worn-out horse; 2 vicious or disreputable woman ‖ vt 3 to tire by long-continued labor ‖ vi 4 to become weary; flag ‖ SYN v weary, fag, exhaust, fatigue, wear out

jade² [F < Sp (piedra de) *tjada* (stone of) the flank (because supposed to cure colic)] n 1 hard semiprecious stone, usu. green, used for gems and ornaments; 2 green color, ranging from bluish to yellowish ‖ also adj

jad·ed /jād′id/ [see jade¹] adj 1 tired-out by long-continued labor; 2 satiated from over-indulgence; 3 dissipated

jag /jag′/ [?] n colloq spree, binge

jag·ged /jag′id/ [?] adj irregularly notched or torn on the edges ‖ jag′-ged·ly adv ‖ SYN rough, pointed, broken, uneven, cleft, notched

jag·uar /jag′wär/ [Port < Tupi] n fierce forest cat (*Felis onca*) resembling the leopard, ranging from Texas to Patagonia

jai a·lai /hī′əlī′/ [Basque = merry game] n game of Spain and tropical America resembling handball and played with a basketlike racket attached to the wrist

jail /jāl′/ [OF *jaiole* cage] n 1 prison ‖ vt 2 to imprison

jail′bait′ n slang girl under the age of consent

jail′bird′ n inmate of a jail

jail′break′ n large-scale escape from a prison

jail′er or **jail′or** n person in charge of a jail

Jain /jīn′/ [Hindi = saint] n adherent of a reformed version of Hinduism founded in the 6th century B.C., characterized by the reverence paid to holy men of past times ‖ **Jain′ism** n

jake /jāk′/ [?] adj slang O.K.

ja·lop·y /jəlop′ē/ [?] n (-ies) old dilapidated automobile

jal·ou·sie /jal′əsē/ [F = slatted shutter] n window or door made of wooden, metal, or glass slats arranged as in a Venetian blind

jam¹ /jam′/ [prob imit] v (jammed; jam·ming) vt 1 to squeeze or wedge in so as to make movement impossible; 2 to press in tightly; 3 to crowd; 4 to crush; 5 to render (radio signals) unintelligible by sending out others on the same or nearly the same frequency ‖ vi 6 to become stuck or blocked; 7 to become unworkable because a part will not move as it should ‖ n 8 act of jamming or state of being jammed; 9 mass, as of vehicles, rendered immovable by jamming; 10 colloq trouble, embarrassing situation

jam² [?] n thick sweet fruit preserve

Ja·mai·ca /jəmāk′ə/ n island nation in the West Indies, member of the British Commonwealth of Nations (1,610,000; 4,415 sq.m.; cap. Kingston) ‖ **Ja·mai′can** adj & n

jamb /jam′/ [MF *jambe* leg] n one of the upright sides of a doorway, window, or other opening

jam·bo·ree /jam′bərē′/ [?] n 1 national or international gathering, as of Boy Scouts; 2 colloq uproarious spree

James /jāmz′/ n Bib 1 one of the twelve apostles, the son of Zebedee; 2 the James described as the Lord's brother (Gal. 1:19); 3 book of the New Testament

James I *n* (1566–1625) king of England and Ireland 1603–25; as James VI, king of Scotland 1567–1625; patron of the King James Version of the Bible

James II *n* (1633–1701) king of England, Ireland, and Scotland 1685–88

James'town' *n* village in E Virginia, first permanent English settlement in America 1607

jam'-packed' *adj* filled to overflowing

jam' ses'sion *n* impromptu jazz performance

Jan. January

jane /jān'/ *n slang* girl or woman

jan-gle /jaŋ'gəl/ [OF *jangler*] *vt* 1 to make a harsh discordant sound; 2 to wrangle ‖ *vi* 3 to cause to jangle ‖ *n* 4 jangling sound; 5 wrangle

Jan-is-sar-y /jan'iser'ē/ [Turk *yeniçeri* recruit] *n* (-ies) member of an elite corps in the army of the Ottoman Empire

jan-i-tor /jan'ĭtər/ [L = doorman] *n* caretaker of a building or apartment ‖ **jan'i-tress** *nfem*

Jan-u-ar-y /jan'yŏŏ-er'ē [L *Januarius* of Janus] *n* first month of the year, having 31 days

Ja-nus /jān'əs/ *n* Roman two-faced god of doorways, beginnings, and endings

Ja'nus-faced' *adj* 1 facing two ways; 2 having two contrasting aspects; 3 deceitful; hypocritical

ja-pan /jəpan'/ [< *Japan*] *n* 1 hard glossy black varnish ‖ *v* (-panned; -pan·ning) *vt* 2 to coat with japan or similar varnish

Ja-pan *n* island empire off the E coast of Asia (100,020,000; 142,727 sq.m.; cap. Tokyo) ‖ **Jap-a-nese** /jap'ənēz', -nēs'/ *adj & n* (-nese)

Jap'a-nese' bee'tle *n* small, bronzegreen, very destructive beetle (*Popillia japonica*)

jape /jāp'/ [ME *japen*] *vt* 1 to mock or trick ‖ *vi* 2 to jest or jeer ‖ *n* 3 jest or jibe

Ja-pheth /jāf'ĭth/ *n Bib* youngest son of Noah (Gen. 5:32)

jar¹ /jär'/ [prob imit] *v* (jarred; jar·ring) *vi* 1 to give out a harsh sound; 2 to shake; vibrate; 3 to clash; disagree; 4 to have a harshly irritating effect ‖ *vt* 5 to make discordant; 6 to cause to shake; 7 to jolt ‖ *n* 8 harsh sound; discord; 9 sudden shake or quivering; 10 conflict of opinion; 11 jolt, shock ‖ syn *v* tremble, jolt, quiver, disturb

jar² [MF *jarre* < Ar *jarrah* earthenware jar] *n* 1 broad-mouthed vessel of earthenware or glass; 2 contents or capacity of a jar

jar-di-niere /järd'ənir'/ [F] *n* ornamental stand or holder for flowers or plants

jar-gon /järg'ən/ [MF] *n* 1 unintelligible utterance; 2 pidgin; 3 special-

ized language of a group, profession, or trade ‖ syn gabble, argot, slang (see *language*)

Jas. James

jas-mine /jaz'mĭn/ [Pers *yāsmīn*] *n* 1 any of a genus (*Jasminum*) of shrubs of the olive family, bearing fragrant flowers; 2 any of various other shrubs

Ja-son /jās'ən/ *n Gk myth.* leader of the Argonauts, who retrieved the Golden Fleece with the help of the enchantress Medea

jas-per /jasp'ər/ [MF *jaspre*] *n* opaque variety of quartz, usu. red, brown, or yellow

ja-to /jāt'ō/ [jet-assisted takeoff] *n* takeoff assisted by a jet or a rocket

jaun-dice /jôn'dĭs, jän'-/ [OF *jaunice* < *jaune* yellow] *n* 1 abnormal condition characterized by yellowness of the eyes, skin, and urine, caused by bile in the blood ‖ *vt* 2 to affect with envy or prejudice

jaun'diced *adj* 1 affected or yellowed by or as if by jaundice; 2 exhibiting or embittered by envy, prejudice, malice

jaunt /jônt', jänt'/ [?] *n* 1 short excursion or pleasure trip ‖ *vi* 2 to take a short trip ‖ syn *n* excursion, journey, tour, trip, stroll

jaun-ty /jônt'ē, jänt'ē/ [F *gentil* genteel] *adj* (-ti-er; -ti-est) 1 sprightly; airy; 2 stylish ‖ **jaun'ti-ly** *adv*

Ja-va /jäv'ə/ *n* 1 main island of Indonesia ‖ *also* jav'ə/ *n* 2 *slang* coffee ‖ **Jav-a-nese** /jav'ənēz', -nēs'/ *adj & n* (-nese)

jave-lin /jav'(ə)lĭn/ [MF *javeline*] *n* light spear to be thrown by hand

jaw /jô'/ [OF *joue* cheek] *n* 1 one of the two bony structures which frame the mouth and in which the teeth are set; 2 the part of the face covering the jaws; 3 anything resembling a jaw in form or power of gripping, as *the jaws of a vise* ‖ *vt* 4 *slang* to talk ‖ *vt* 5 *slang* to scold

jaw'bone' *n* 1 bone of either jaw; 2 *slang* credit, trust

jaw'bon'ing *n* effort to control inflation by the exertion of presidential or other executive pressure against wage and price increases

jaw'break'er *n* 1 hard candy ball; 2 *colloq* word difficult to pronounce

jay /jā'/ [MF *jai*] *n* 1 any of several noisy, restless birds (subfamily Garrulinae); 2 bluejay

Jay, John *n* (1745–1829) first Chief Justice of the Supreme Court 1789–95

jay'walk' *vi* to cross a street anywhere except at a regular crossing ‖ **jay'walk'er** *n*

jazz /jazz'/ [?] *n* 1 music originating in New Orleans around 1900, characterized by syncopation and novel and acrobatic musical effects; 2 *slang* liveliness; 3 *slang* insincere talk ‖ *vt* 4 to play (music) in the manner of jazz; **5 jazz up** *slang* to enliven; speed up

jazz·y /jazˈy/ *adj* (**-i·er; -i·est**) **1** pert. to, or like, jazz; **2** *slang* lively, active; **3** *slang* sporty

jeal·ous /jelˈəs/ [OF *gelos*] *adj* **1** resentfully envious; **2** suspecting unfaithfulness; **3** vigilant, anxiously watchful ‖ **jealˈous·ly** *adv*

jeal·ous·y /jelˈəs·y/ (**-ies**) **1** envy; **2** resentment toward a rival; **3** insistence on exclusive affection; **4** watchful care ‖ SYN envy ‖ DISCR *Jealousy* is a passionate desire to keep what one has, intensified by the fear of losing it. In its noble sense, *jealousy* names a watchfulness and care that amounts to zeal, as the rights of a minor child should be preserved with *jealousy*. In its bad sense, *jealousy* is the green-eyed monster of fiction; it has the apprehensive or suspicious quality of fear, and is akin to anger, especially in its tendency to retaliation or revenge. *Envy* is a base passion, fed by the grudging hatred with which it covetously contemplates the advantages or possessions of others. *Envy* may be less intensely personal than *jealousy*, since one may feel *envy* of a friend without wishing him harm. *Jealousy* can be appeased, though often temporarily, by arguments, proofs, or the like, by the long-suffering object; *envy* is always sick over what others have and it lacks. *Envy* is found only between individuals; *jealousy* is also applicable to bodies of individuals, as democracies show a proper *jealousy* of their liberties

jeans /jēnz/ [ME *gene* Genoa] *npl* trousers or overalls made of a strong twilled cotton fabric

jeep /jēp/ [?] *n* small motor vehicle with four-wheel drive

jeer /jir/ [?] *vt* **1** to make loud fun of; ridicule ‖ *vi* **2** to scoff derisively ‖ *n* **3** coarse ridicule ‖ SYN *v* scoff, sneer, gibe, taunt, mock ‖ DISCR To *scoff* is to direct mockery or insolent derision, especially at serious and sacred things, particularly at religion, as exemplified in Goldsmith's famous line, "and fools who came to *scoff* remained to pray." To *sneer* is to show contempt as by curling the lip, smiling derisively, or by other facial expression; one may *sneer* also by uttering derisive remarks, usually ironical, often covert. *Sneers* may be cast at a person, thing, or cause. *Gibes* and *jeers*, which are always uttered, are directed only toward persons; a *gibe* is ill-natured, often disguised under fair speech, and usually reproachful. A *jeer* is insulting, satirical, and unsoftened, as he could stand the *jeers* of the crowd better than the privately bitter *gibes* of his wife. To *scoff* is irreverent; to *sneer*, *gibe*, and *jeer* are at best unfitting, at worst vulgar

Jef·fer·son, Thom·as /jefˈərsən/ *n* (1743–1826) 3rd president of the U.S. 1801–09 ‖ **Jefˈfer·soˈni·an** /-sōnˈē-ən/ *adj* & *n*

Jefˈfer·son Cit·y *n* capital of Missouri (29,000)

Je·ho·vah /jihōˈvə/ [erroneous rendering of Heb *YHVH*] *n* God ‖ SYN God, Lord, Almighty, Deity, Creator

je·june /jijo͞onˈ/ [L *jejunus* empty] *adj* uninteresting, dry, insipid

je·ju·num [< L *jejunum* neut of *jejunus* empty, because supposed to be empty after death] *n* (**-na**) middle section of the small intestine, between the duodenum and the ileum

jell /jel/ *vi* **1** to become like jelly; **2** to crystallize, become definite, as a plan

jel·ly /jelˈē/ [OF *gelee* frozen] *n* (**-lies**) **1** cooked, semisolid juice of meat, fruit, etc., containing gelatin or a similar coagulant; **2** any jellylike substance ‖ *v* (**-lied**) *vt* **3** to become jelly or like jelly ‖ *vt* **4** to make into jelly ‖ **jelˈlied** *adj*

jel·ly·bean' *n* brightly colored sugar-coated candy shaped like a bean

jel·ly·fish' *n* **1** any of several marine invertebrates (phylum Coelenterata) of dislike shape, varying size, and jellylike consistency; **2** *colloq* weak-willed person

jen·net /jenˈit/ [MF *genet* < Catalan = kind of horse] *n* **1** small Spanish horse; **2** female donkey

jen·ny /jenˈē/ [< *Janet*] *n* (**-nies**) **1** machine for spinning; **2** female donkey

jeop·ard·y /jepˈərdē/ [OF *jeuparti* divided game] *n* risk, peril, hazard ‖ **jeopˈard·ize'** *vt* ‖ SYN harm, risk, insecurity, peril (see *danger*)

jer·bo·a /jərbōˈə/ [Ar *yarbū'*] *n* any of a family (Dipodidae) of mouselike jumping rodents of the Old World with short forelegs and a long tail

jer·e·mi·ad /jerˈəmīˈad/ [< the prophecies of *Jeremiah*] *n* lamentation, tale of woe

Jer·e·mi·ah /jerˈəmīˈə/ *n* Bib **1** great Hebrew prophet of the sixth century B.C.; **2** book of the Old Testament

jerk¹ /jurk/ [?] *vt* **1** to give a quick pull, twist, or push to ‖ *vi* **2** to move convulsively ‖ *n* **3** sudden quick pull, twist, push, or throw; **4** convulsive movement; **5** *slang* fatuous, inconsequential person

jerk² [Sp *charqui* jerked beef] *vt* **1** to cut (meat, esp. beef) into strips and dry in the sun ‖ *n* **2** jerked meat

jer·kin /jurkˈin/ [?] *n* close-fitting jacket, often of leather and sleeveless, worn in the 16th and 17th centuries

jerk·wa·ter *adj* out-of-the-way, insignificant, as a town or a train

jerk′y *adj* (-i-er; -i-est) 1 moving in jerks; spasmodic; 2 characteristic of a jerk¹ 5

jer·o·bo·am /jer′əbō′əm/ [< *Jeroboam*, king of N Palestine (ab. 912 B.C.)] *n* wine bottle with a capacity of about ⅘ of a gallon

Je·rome, Saint /jərōm′/ *n* (ab. 340–420 A.D.) Church father, writer, and translator; compiler of the Vulgate

jer′ry-built′ /jer′ē-/ [< *slang Jerry* chamber pot] *adj* haphazardly put together; flimsily built

Jer·sey /jur′zē/ *n* 1 largest of the Channel Islands; 2 one of a breed of dairy cattle producing milk with a high butterfat content; 3 jersey close-fitting sweater or shirt

Jer′sey Cit′y *n* city in NE New Jersey (275,000)

Je·ru·sa·lem /jīrōō′sələm/ *n* capital of Israel (250,000); ancient holy city, site of the Hebrew Temple and of Christ's Passion

jes·sa·mine /jes′əmin/ *n* var of jasmine

jest /jest′/ [OF *geste* exploit] *n* 1 joke, pleasantry; 2 banter; ridicule; 3 butt of a joke ‖ *vi* 4 to joke; act, or speak banteringly

jest′er *n* 1 one who makes jokes; 2 professional fool at a medieval court

Jes·u·it /jezh′ōō-it, jez′yōō-it/ [< *Jesus*] *n* member of the Society of Jesus, a Roman Catholic order of priests founded in 1534 by Ignatius Loyola ‖ **Jes′u·it′ic** (-i-cal) /-it′-/ *adj*

Je·sus /jēz′əs/ [L < Gk *Iesous* < Heb *Yeshūa′*] also **Je′sus Christ′** *n* founder of the Christian religion

jet¹ /jet′/ [MF *jeter* to throw] *v* (**jet·ted**; **jet·ting**) *vt* 1 to spurt out ‖ *vi* 2 to shoot or spout out; 3 to travel by jet plane ‖ *n* 4 stream of fluid issuing under pressure from an opening; 5 that which issues in such a stream; 6 spout or nozzle for the emission of a fluid, as gas; 7 jet plane ‖ *adj* 8 of or pert. to a jet, jet propulsion, etc.

jet² [OF *jaiet*] *n* 1 hard black mineral akin to coal, used in making ornaments and buttons; 2 deep glossy black

jet′ en′gine *n* reaction engine that takes in air from outside as an oxidizer

jet′ lag′ *n* rapid change in time experienced by a person flying east or west in a jet

jet′ plane′ *n* plane operated by jet propulsion

jet′port′ *n* airport with runways designed for jet planes

jet′ pro·pul′sion *n* method of propelling a body based on its reaction to the high-speed ejection of a gas or fluid in the opposite direction

jet·sam /jet′səm/ [< *jettison*] *n* goods thrown overboard to ease a ship in peril

jet′ set′ *n* wealthy people who spend their time jetting between fashionable international resorts

jet′ stream′ *n* 1 high-altitude, fast-moving current of air that travels in undulating paths from west to east; 2 exhaust from a jet engine or rocket motor

jet·ti·son /jet′isən/ [OF *getaison* a throwing] *vt* 1 to throw (goods) overboard in order to lighten a ship or aircraft, or to improve stability; 2 to discard ‖ *n* 3 act of jettisoning

jet·ty /jet′ē/ [OF *jetee* projection] *n* (-ties) structure extending into the water, used as a pier or as a wall to protect a harbor or to direct currents

Jew /jōō/ [OF *gyu* < Gk *Ioudaios* < Heb *Yehūdī* Judean] *n* 1 adherent of Judaism; 2 Hebrew; 3 member of the ancient tribe of Judah; 4 subject of the ancient kingdom of Judea

jew·el /jōō′əl/ [OF *joel*] *n* 1 gem, precious stone; 2 ornament set with gems; 3 gem or similar hard substance used as a bearing in a timepiece; 4 person or thing especially excellent or precious ‖ *v* (-eled or -elled; -el·ing or -el·ling) *vt* 5 to furnish with jewels

jew′el·er or **jew′el·ler** *n* one who makes or deals in jewels

jew′el·ry *n* gems and articles of precious metals collectively

Jew′ish *adj* 1 pert. to or like the Jews ‖ *n* 2 *colloq* Yiddish

Jew′ry *n* the Jewish people collectively

jew′s′-harp′ [< D *jeugd-tromp* youth's trumpet] *n* small lyre-shaped musical instrument with a thin metal tongue placed between the teeth and struck by the finger

Jez·e·bel /jez′əbel, -bəl/ *n* 1 *Bib* evil wife of Ahab, king of Israel (2 Kings 9:30); 2 wicked, shameless woman

jg, j.g. junior grade

jib /jib′/ *n* 1 three-cornered sail extending beyond the bow of a vessel; 2 projecting arm of a crane or derrick; 3 **cut of one's jib** *colloq* one's appearance or way of acting

jib′ boom′ *n* spar which serves to prolong the bowsprit and to which a jib is fastened

jibe¹ /jīb′/ [?] *vi colloq* to harmonize, agree

jibe² *n, vt, & vi* var of gibe

jif·fy /jif′ē/ [?] *n* (-fies) *colloq* very short time

jig /jig′/ [? MF *giguer* to dance] *n* 1 rapid irregular dance or the music for it, often in triple time; 2 guiding tool; template; 3 **the jig is up** *slang* the situation is beyond remedy ‖ *v* (**jigged**; **jig·ging**) *vi* 4 to dance a jig ‖ *vt* 5 to sing or play in jig time

jig′ger *n* 1 measure of 1½ fluid ounce, used esp. in mixing alcoholic beverages; 2 *colloq* contrivance, gadget

jig·gle /jig′əl/ [< *jig*] *vt & vi* **1** to move jerkily back and forth || *n* **2** jiggling movement

jig′ saw′ *n* **1** saw with a narrow blade held in a frame, used to cut along curved or irregular lines || **jig′saw′** *vt* **2** to cut with a jig saw

jig′saw puz′zle *n* puzzle the object of which is to put together irregularly cut pieces to form a picture

ji·had /jihäd′/ [Ar] *n* **1** holy war against the enemies of the Muslim faith; **2** bitter war for religion or principle

jilt /jilt′/ [< Sc *jillet* flirtatious woman] *vt* to reject (a lover or one's betrothed)

Jim′ Crow′ /jim′/ [title of 19th-cent. minstrel song] *n* enforced segregation practiced against black people || **Jim′-Crow′** or **jim′-crow′** *adj*

Jim′-dan′dy *adj colloq* excellent

jim·my /jim′ē/ [< *James*] *n* (-mies) **1** short crowbar used by burglars || *v* (-mied) *vt* **2** to force open with or as with a jimmy

jim′son weed′ /jim′sən/ [< *Jamestown*, Virginia] *n* coarse, poisonous plant (*Datura stramonium*) having trumpet-shaped flowers and prickly fruit

jin·gle /jiŋ′gəl/ [imit] *vi* **1** to give a tinkling metallic sound || *vt* **2** to cause to jingle || *n* **3** jingling sound; **4** catchy succession of sounds or rhymes, as in verse

jin·go /jiŋ′gō/ [< phrase *by jingo* in 19th-cent. Brit patriotic song] *n* (-goes) one who favors an aggressive foreign policy, or who boasts of his country's warlike achievements || **jin′go·ism** *n* || **jin′go·is′tic** *adj*

jinks /jiŋks′/ [prob imit] *n high jinks pl slang* high-spirited pranks

jinn /jin′/ [Ar, *pl* of *jinnī* demon] *n Islamic myth.* supernatural being able to assume animal and human form, and to be subject to magic control

Jin·nah, Mohammed′ Ali /jin′ə/ *n* (1876–1948) Moslem leader; first governor general of Pakistan 1947–48

jin·rik·i·sha /jinrik′shô/ [Jap] *n* small two-wheeled carriage drawn by one man, used in the Far East

jinx /jiŋks′/ [prob < Gk *iynx* wryneck (bird used in divination)] *n* **1** person or thing supposed to bring bad luck || *vt* **2** *colloq* to bring bad luck to

jit·ney /jit′nē/ [?] *n* **1** *slang* five-cent coin; **2** conveyance, as an automobile or small bus, carrying passengers over a regular route for a small fare, originally five cents

jit·ter /jit′ər/ [imit] *vi* **1** to be extremely nervous || *n* **2** *the jitters pl* extreme nervousness || **jit′ter·y** *adj*

jit′ter·bug′ *n* **1** strenuously acrobatic dance; **2** one who dances the jitterbug || *v* (-bugged; -bug·ging) *vi* **3** to dance the jitterbug

jiu·jit·su /joōjit′soō/ *n* var of *jujitsu*

jive /jīv′/ [?] *n* **1** swing music; **2** *slang* jargon of jazz and of the world of entertainment || *vi* **3** to play, or dance to, jive music

Jno. John

Joan of Arc /jōn′əv ärk′/ *n* (1412–31) French national heroine, burned at the stake by the English

job /job′/ [?] *n* **1** piece of work, esp. of an odd or occasional kind or one undertaken for a fixed price; **2** specific task or responsibility; **3** specific employment; **4** thing or material worked on; **5** work, employment; **6** **on the job** *slang* doing one's work alertly || *v* (jobbed; job·bing) *vt* **7** to buy up (goods) for resale in smaller quantities; **8** to swindle; **9** **job out** to subcontract

Job /jōb′/ *n* **1** hero of a book of the Old Testament who patiently suffered much affliction; **2** book containing his story

job′ ac′tion *n* disruption of work by employees in order to enforce compliance with demands

job·ber /job′ər/ *n* **1** wholesaler who sells to dealers; **2** pieceworker

job′ber·y *n* dishonest conduct of public officials

job′-hop′ping *n colloq* constant moving from job to job in search of more satisfactory working conditions and better pay

job′less *adj* out of work; unemployed

job′ lot′ *n* **1** large assorted quantity of goods put up for sale in one lot; **2** miscellaneous lot of goods

job′ print′ing *n* miscellaneous printing of such material as letterheads, circulars, etc. || **job′ print′er** *n*

jock·ey /jok′ē/ [< Sc *Jock* Jack] *n* **1** one hired to ride a horse in a race || *vt* **2** to cheat or deceive; **3** to maneuver for advantage; manipulate cleverly

jock′strap′ *n* elastic athletic supporter for the genitals

jo·cose /jōkōs′/ [< L *iocus* jest] *adj* sportive, humorous, jesting || **jo·cos′i·ty** /-kos′-/ *n* || SYN facetious, droll, playful, waggish, funny, jocular || ANT doleful, sad, mournful, surly, dispirited, sober

joc·u·lar /jok′yələr/ [< L *ioculus* little joke] *adj* making jokes, jesting || **joc′u·lar′i·ty** /-lar′-/ *n* || SYN jocose, merry, blithe, sportive, good-humored

joc·und /jok′ənd, jōk′-/ [LL *iocundus*] *adj* jovial, sportive, gay || **jo·cun′di·ty** /-kun′-/ *n*

jodh·purs /jod′pərz/ [*Jodhpur*, India] *npl* riding breeches made to fit close from the knee to the ankle

Jod′rell Bank′ /jod′rəl/ *n* large, fully steerable radio telescope, located in NE Cheshire, England

jog¹ /jog′/ [prob < ME *shoggen* **to**

shake] *v* (**jogged; jog·ging**) *vt* 1 to push or shake lightly; 2 to nudge; 3 to stir up, as *to jog the memory* ‖ *vi* 4 to trot at a steady pace; 5 to walk at a fast, steady pace for exercise; 6 to move with a jolting motion; 7 to jog along to move forward at a slow, monotonous pace ‖ *n* 8 slight push or shake; 9 slow, steady trot ‖ **jog′ger** *n* ‖ **jog′ging** *n*

jog² [< *jag* notch] *n* 1 notch; 2 irregularity of line or surface

jog′ cart′ *n* narrow sulky with long shafts, used for training

jog·gle /jog′əl/ [< *jog¹*] *vt & vi* 1 to shake or move slightly ‖ *n* 2 shake or jolt

jog′ trot′ *n* slow regular gait

Jo·han·nes·burg /jōhän′is·burg′/ *n* largest city of South Africa (1,100,000)

John /jon′/ [Gk *Ioannes* < Heb *Yōhänän*] *n* 1 one of the twelve Apostles, reputed author of the fourth Gospel, three Epistles, and the Book of Revelation; 2 fourth book of the New Testament; 3 any of the three Epistles of the New Testament ascribed to John; 4 **john** *slang* a prostitute's customer; b toilet

John′ Bull′ *n* 1 typical Englishman; 2 the English collectively

John′ Doe′ *n* fictitious name for an unknown person, esp. in legal proceedings

john′ny·cake′ [?] *n* cake made of corn meal and milk or water

John′ny·come·late′ly *n* (**-lies**) newcomer to any endeavor

John·son, An·drew /jon′sən/ *n* (1808–75) 17th president of the U.S. 1865–69

John·son, Lyn·don B. /lin′dən/ *n* (1908–73) 36th president of the U.S. 1963–69

John·son, Sam·u·el *n* (1709–84) English writer and lexicographer

John′ the Bap′tist *n* Bib forerunner and baptizer of Jesus (Matt. 3)

join /join′/ [OF *joindre*] *vt* 1 to unite; connect; put or bring together; 2 to unite in marriage; 3 to unite with; 4 to become a member of; 5 to meet or accompany; 6 to engage in with others, as *to join battle*; 7 to be adjacent to, adjoin ‖ *vi* 8 to be in contact; be adjacent; 9 to become associated or united; 10 **join up** to enlist ‖ SYN unite, consolidate, couple, associate (see *combine*) ‖ ANT separate, detach, dissolve

join′er *n* 1 carpenter who finishes the inside woodwork for houses; 2 one who joins many clubs and organizations

joint /joint′/ [OF = joined] *n* 1 place where two things or parts are joined or united; 2 union of bones into a movable or immovable articulation; 3 large piece of meat cut for roasting; 4 *slang* disreputable night club, res-

taurant, or the like; 5 **out of joint, a** dislocated; b inappropriate ‖ *vt* 6 to form with joints; articulate; 7 to cut (meat) apart at the joint ‖ *adj* 8 united; combined; 9 used, held, or shared by two or more ‖ **joint′ly** *adv*

joist /joist′/ [OF *giste*] *n* horizontal timber to which the boards of a floor or the laths of a ceiling are attached

joke /jōk′/ [L *jocus*] *n* 1 something said or done to provoke mirth; 2 laughingstock; 3 something not to be taken seriously ‖ *vi* 4 to speak or act in a manner calculated to provoke mirth, or not to be taken seriously

jok′er *n* 1 one who jokes; 2 extra playing card, bearing the figure of a jester, used in certain games; 3 disguised nullifying clause, as in a legislative measure or legal contract; 4 any concealed obstruction or difficulty

jol·ly /jol′ē/ [OF *joli*] *adj* (**-li·er; -li·est**) 1 full of good spirits; merry, gay ‖ *v* (**-lied**) *vt* 2 to flatter; treat pleasantly in the hope of obtaining a favor; 3 to make good-humored fun of ‖ *adv* 4 Brit colloq very; uncommonly ‖ **jol′li·ty** *n* (**-ties**) ‖ SYN *adj* gay, festive, merry, jovial (see *joyful*)

jolt /jōlt′/ [prob blend of *obs joll* to bump and *obs jot* to jolt] *vt* 1 to shake by sudden jerks and jars; 2 to stun, as by a blow, electric current, or surprise; 3 to activate abruptly ‖ *vi* 4 to have a jerky or bumpy motion ‖ *n* 5 jolting bump, movement, or shock

Jo·nah /jōn′ə/ *n* 1 Bib minor prophet, swallowed by a large fish and later cast out unharmed; 2 jinx

Jones, John Paul /jōnz′/ *n* (1747–92) Scotch-born American naval hero of the Revolutionary War

jon·quil /jon′kwil, jon′-/ *n* plant (*Narcissus jonquilla*) of the amaryllis family, with fragrant yellow or white flowers

Jon·son, Ben /jon′sən/ *n* (1573–1637) English neoclassic dramatist, lyric poet, and actor ‖ **Jon·so′ni·an** /-sōn′ē·ən/ *adj*

Jor·dan /jôrd′ən/ *n* 1 river in SW Asia flowing between Israel and Jordan into the Dead Sea; 2 kingdom in SW Asia, E of Israel (2,101,000; 37,738 sq.m.; cap. Amman) ‖ **Jor·da′ni·an** /-dā′nē·ən/ *adj & n*

Jor′dan al′mond [ME *jardin* garden + *almond*] *n* 1 hard-shelled almond from Málaga, Spain; 2 almond covered with a hard sugar coating

Jo·seph /jōz′əf/ *n* Bib 1 son of Jacob, sold into slavery by his brothers (Gen. 37:28); 2 husband of Mary, the mother of Jesus (Matt. 1:18-25)

josh /josh′/ [?] *vt & vi* colloq to banter; ridicule good-naturedly

Josh·u·a /josh′ōō·ə/ *n* Bib successor to

Moses as the leader of the Israelites (Deut. 31:14-23; 34-9)

joss /jos'/ [pidgin Eng < Port *deus* god] *n* Chinese household divinity or idol

jos·tle /jos'əl/ [earlier *justle* < OF *juster* to joust] *vt & vi* 1 to push or shove roughly; elbow || *n* 2 jostling

jot /jot'/ [< Gk *iota* the letter *i*] *n* 1 very little bit || *v* (jot·ted; jot·ting) *vt* 2 **jot down** to make a brief note of

jot'ting *n* brief note or memorandum

joule /jōōl', joul'/ [J. P. Joule (1818-89) Brit physicist] *n* mks unit of work equal to 10^7 ergs

jounce /jouns'/ [ME *jouncen*] *vt & vi* 1 to jolt, bounce || *n* 2 jolt

jour·nal /jurn'əl/ [< L *diurnalis* < *dies* day] *n* 1 daily record; diary; 2 record of transactions kept by a legislative body or organization; 3 newspaper or magazine; 4 periodical of a learned society; 5 *bookkeeping* book in which each transaction is entered; 6 *mach* that portion of an axle or shaft that turns in a bearing

jour'nal·ese' *n* style of writing used by some journalists, esp. columnists, characterized by neologisms, coined words, and unusual syntax

jour'nal·ism *n* occupation of publishing, or writing for, newspapers or periodicals || **jour'nal·ist** *n* || **jour'nal·is'tic** *adj*

jour·ney /jurn'ē/ [OF *journee* day] *n* 1 trip, esp. one of rather long duration || *vi* 2 to take a trip || SYN *n* tour, trip, excursion, jaunt

jour'ney·man /-mən/ [< *journey* in obs sense of a day's work] *n* (-men /-mən/) worker who has served his apprenticeship or learned a trade

joust /just', joust'/ [OF *jouste*] *n* 1 combat between mounted knights with weapons such as lances, swords, or battle-axes || *vi* 2 to engage in a joust

Jove /jōv'/ [< L *Jove-* oblique stem of Jupiter] *n* the god Jupiter

jo·vi·al /jōv'ē·əl/ [L *jovialis* of the planet Jupiter (supposed to have a benign influence on men)] *adj* full of hearty good humor; convivial || **jo'vi·al'i·ty** /-al'-/ *n* || SYN festive, gay, mirthful, good-natured (see *joyful*)

Jo·vi·an /jōv'ē·ən/ *adj* pert. to the god Jupiter

jowl¹ /joul'/ [OE *ceafl* jaw] *n* 1 lower jaw; 2 cheek

jowl² [OE *ceole* throat] *n* 1 fold of flesh hanging from the jaw; 2 cheek of a hog

joy /joi'/ [OF *joie* < L *gaudium*] *n* 1 emotion of gladness; happiness; gaiety; 2 that which inspires joy || SYN (see *happiness*) || ANT grief, gloom

Joyce, James /jois'/ *n* (1882-1941) Irish novelist || **Joyc'e·an** /-ē·ən/ *adj & n*

joy'ful *adj* 1 full of joy; 2 showing joy;

3 causing joy || **joy'ful·ly** *adv* || **joy'-ful·ness** *n* || SYN festive, glad, happy, gay, joyous, jolly, jovial || DISCR *Joyful* describes that which produces or inspires keenly pleasurable emotions; it connotes, usually, expression or demonstration, as bells rang in the *joyful* tidings; he was wildly *joyful* over his success. *Joyous* describes rather an innate, bubbling quality, as the *joyous* smile of the proud mother; *joyous* laughter. *Jolly* and *jovial* often suggest good-natured mirth; a *jovial* company is festive; a *jolly* company is merry, often hilarious

joy'less *adj* without gladness; gloomy; despairing || **joy'less·ly** *adv*

joy'ous *adj* 1 full of joy; 2 showing joy; 3 causing joy || **joy'ous·ly** *adv* || **joy'-ous·ness** *n* || SYN (see *joyful*) || ANT doleful, sad, gloomy

joy' ride' *n colloq* 1 pleasure ride in an automobile; 2 short ride at reckless speed || **joy'-ride'** *v* (-rode; -rid·den) *vi*

J.P. Justice of the Peace

Jr., jr. junior

ju·bi·lant /jōōb'ilənt/ [< L *jubilum* shout] *adj* rejoicing; triumphant; exultant || **ju'bi·lant·ly** *adv*

ju·bi·la·tion /jōōb'ilāsh'ən/ *n* 1 act of rejoicing; 2 great joy; exultation; 3 joyful celebration

ju·bi·lee /jōōb'ilē', jōōb'ilē'/ [MF *jubilie* < LL *jubilaeus*] *n* 1 fiftieth anniversary of an event; its commemoration, or celebration; 2 celebration of certain other anniversaries, as the 25th, 60th, or 75th; 3 any occasion of rejoicing; 4 jubilation; 5 *R C Ch* year of special plenary indulgence granted by the Pope

Ju·dah /jōōd'ə/ *n Bib* 1 a son of Jacob and Leah; 2 one of the 12 tribes of Israel; 3 Hebrew kingdom in S Palestine (1 Kings 12:16-20)

Ju·da·ic /jōōdā'ik/ [< Gk *Ioudaios* Jew] *adj* pert. to the Jews or Judaism

Ju·da·ism /jōōd'ē·iz'əm/ *n* religion, culture, and ethos of the Jews || **Ju'da·ize'** *vt & vi* || **Ju'da·iz'er** *n*

Ju·das /jōōd'əs/ *n* 1 *Bib* a Judas Iscariot, the disciple who betrayed Jesus (Matt. 26:14, 48); b a man spoken of as a brother of Jesus (Matt. 13:55); c disciple identified by the phrase "not Iscariot" (John 14:22); 2 betrayer of a friend; traitor

Ju·de·a /jōōdē'ə/ *n* southern region of ancient Palestine, forming an independent kingdom of the tribes of Judah and Benjamin || **Ju·de'an** *adj & n*

judge /juj'/ [OF *juge* < L *judex*] *n* 1 presiding official in a court of law, having authority to hear and decide cases; 2 person appointed to determine the winner in a contest; 3 one who possesses critical judgment, as of art or wine; **4** one of the chief rulers of the Israelites from the death of Joshua to the kingship of Saul; **5 Judges** *sg* Old Testament book giving the history of the judges || *vt* **6** to hear and pass legal judgment on; **7** to estimate; form an opinion about || *vi* **8** to form an opinion; **9** to pass judgment || **judge′ship** *n*

judge′ ad′vo·cate *n mil* officer who acts as legal adviser to a commander and who administers military justice

judg′ment *n* **1** act or instance of judging; **2** judicial decision; **3** judicial order directing payment, as of a debt; **4** ability to make a decision or form an opinion; discernment, acumen; **5 Judgment** the Last Judgment || **syn** discernment, discretion (see *discrimination*)

Judg′ment Day′ *n* day of the Last Judgment

ju·di·cial /jŏŏdish′əl/ [< L *judicium* judgment] *adj* **1** pert. to a judge or to the administration of justice; **2** proceeding from, or inflicted by, a court of justice; **3** impartial; **4** functioning as a judge; involving judgment || **ju·di′cial·ly** *adv*

ju·di·ci·ar·y /jŏŏdish′ē-er′ē, -dish′ərē/ *n* (-ies) **1** judicial branch of a government; **2** judges collectively

ju·di′cious /-dish′əs/ *adj* prudent; exhibiting sound judgment || **ju·di′cious·ly** *adv* || **syn** wise, politic, discreet, sensible, well-advised

ju·do /jŏŏ′dō/ [Jap] *n* modified form of jujitsu, stressing the sport rather than the disabling of opponents

jug /jug/ [?] *n* **1** narrow-necked vessel for liquids, usu. with a handle; **2** *slang* jail || *v* (**jugged**; **jug·ging**) *vt* **3** to put into or cook in a jug; **4** *slang* to jail

jug·ger·naut /jug′ərnôt′/ [Hindi *Jagannāth* lord of the world (title of the god Vishnu)] *n* **1** any overpowering and inexorable force that crushes everything in its path; **2** anything demanding blind devotion and self-sacrifice

jug·gle /jug′əl/ [OF *jogler* to be a jester] *vt* **1** to keep (several objects) in the air by throwing and catching; **2** to almost fumble; **3** to falsify, as accounts, in order to embezzle || *vi* **4** to juggle objects; **5** to practice deceit or artifice || **jug′gler** *n* || **jug′glery** *n* (-ies)

Ju·go·slav /yŏŏg′ōsläv′, -slav′/ *adj* & *n* var of **Yugoslav**

Ju′go·sla′vi·a *n* var of **Yugoslavia**

jug·u·lar /jug′yələr, jŏŏg′-/ [< L *jugulum* throat] *adj* **1** pert. to the neck or throat; **2** designating or pert. to the jugular vein || *n* **3** jugular vein

jug′u·lar vein′ *n* one of the veins on the side of the throat which carry the blood from the head to the heart

juice /jŏŏs′/ [OF *jus* < L] *n* **1** fluid contained in or obtained from plant or animal tissues; **2** natural fluids of the body; **3** essence of anything; **4** *slang* electric current || *vt* **5** *colloq* to extract the juice from || **juic′er** *n*

juic′y *adj* (-i·er; -i·est) **1** full of juice; **2** spicy, scandalous

ju·jit·su /jŏŏjit′sŏŏ/ [Jap] *n* Japanese method of hand-to-hand combat without weapons, which uses the strength and weight of the opponent to defeat him

juke′box′ /jŏŏk′-/ [Gullah *juke* bawd] *n* coin-operated phonograph

Jul. July

ju·lep /jŏŏl′ip/ [MF < Ar *julāb*] *n* **1** drink composed of brandy or whisky sweetened and flavored; **2** mixture of sugar and water in which medicine is given

Jul′ian cal′en·dar /jŏŏl′yən/ [L *Julianus* pert. to Julius] *n* calendar established by Julius Caesar in 46 B.C. to give a civil year of 365 days with an extra day every four years, now superseded by the Gregorian calendar

ju·li·enne /jŏŏl′ē-en′/ [F] *adj* **1** designating vegetables, as potatoes, cut into thin strips || *n* **2** clear soup containing julienne vegetables

Ju·ly /jŏŏlī′, jə-/ [< L *Julius* Caesar] *n* seventh month of the year, having 31 days

jum·ble /jum′bəl/ *n* **1** confused mass, mixture, or collection || *vt* & *vi* **2** to mix in a confused mass

jum·bo /jum′bō/ [*Jumbo*, name of elephant in Barnum's show, reputed to be the largest in captivity] *n* **1** huge person or thing || *adj* **2** very large

jump /jump′/ [prob < Scand] *n* **1** spring or bound; **2** sudden rise, as in prices; **3** space covered by a jump; **4** involuntary start or jerk; **5** *checkers* act of capturing a piece by jumping over it; **6** get or have the jump on to get or have an advantage over, as by starting sooner than expected || *vt* **7** to leap over; **8** to cause to leap; **9** to leave (the tracks); **10** to take possession of (a mining claim) fraudulently; **11** to leave, flee from; **12** to increase sharply, as prices; **13** *checkers* to capture (a piece) by jumping over it; **14** *colloq* to attack from ambush; **15** to skip, omit; **16** to leap aboard in haste; **17 jump bail** to forfeit bail by not appearing when summoned; **18 jump ship** to desert from a ship; **19 jump the gun** to start before one should, as in a race || *vi* **20** to spring forward or upward; **21** to give a sudden or involuntary start; **22** to rise, as prices; **23** *colloq* to obey instantly; **24** to leap downward; **25 jump at** to take eagerly; **26 jump off** to start a major activity, as a military attack; **27 jump on** *colloq* to reprimand severely; **28 jump on the**

bandwagon to join a winning candidate or group

jump′er n 1 horse trained for jumping; 2 sleeveless dress with straps, worn over a blouse; 3 loose outer jacket worn by workmen; 4 piece of wire used to close a break or to short part of a circuit

jump′ seat′ n folding auxiliary seat in an automobile

jump′ spark′ n spark across an air gap or other dielectric, spec. between the points of a spark plug

jump′ suit′ n one-piece uniform worn by paratroopers

jump′y adj (-i·er; -i·est) nervous and apprehensive

Jun. 1 June; 2 Junior

jun·co /juŋ′kō/ [Sp] n (-cos or -coes) slate-gray finch of North America, esp. *Junco hyemalis*

junc·tion /juŋk′shən/ [< L *junctus* joined] n 1 act of joining or state of being joined; union; 2 point or place of union; 3 intersection of roads or railway lines

junc·ture /juŋk′chər/ n 1 junction; 2 point or line at which two bodies are joined; 3 concurrence of events producing a particular or critical occasion; 4 *gram* phonetic modification of sounds marking the boundaries between words

June /jōōn′/ [L *Junius* name of a Roman clan] n sixth month of the year, having 30 days

Ju·neau /jōō′nō/ n capital of Alaska (7,000)

June′ bug′ n in N U.S., reddish-brown beetle of the genus *Phyllophaga* that emerges from the ground at night in May and June

jun·gle /juŋ′gəl/ [Hindi *jangal*] n 1 any tract overrun with dense undergrowth and tangled vegetation, esp. in the tropics; 2 any tangled mass of objects; 3 any place of fierce dog-eat-dog competition or great physical danger

jun·ior /jōōn′yər/ [L = younger] adj 1 younger of two people in a family bearing the same name; 2 of lower standing or seniority; 3 for younger members; 4 later in date or occurrence || n 5 younger person; 6 one lower in rank or seniority; 7 student in the next to the last year of a high school or college

jun′ior col′lege n school offering the first two years of college instruction

jun′ior high′ school′ n school intermediate between elementary and high school, consisting of the 7th and 8th or the 7th to 9th grades

jun′ior var′si·ty n team composed of players not good enough to play on the varsity

ju·ni·per /jōō′nipər/ [L *juniperus*] n any of a genus (*Juniperus*) of ever-

green trees or shrubs, the berries of which are used in flavoring gin and in medicine

ju·ni·per ber′ry n 1 fruit of a juniper; 2 prostrate evergreen shrub (*Gaylussacia brachycera*) of SE U.S.

junk¹ /juŋk′/ [ME *jonke*] n 1 any old material no longer serviceable and discarded as worthless; 2 anything regarded as worthless; 3 *colloq* heroin || vt *colloq* to get rid of as worthless

junk² [Port *junco* < Javanese *jong*] n Chinese flat-bottomed vessel with a square bow and high stern

Jun·ker /yōōŋk′ər/ [G] n member of the landowning class of Prussia

jun·ket /juŋk′it/ [AF *jonquette* rush basket] n 1 dessert made of sweetened curdled milk and cream; 2 excursion; picnic; 3 trip at public expense, ostensibly on official government business || vi 4 to go on a junket

junk′ie n *colloq* drug addict, esp. one using heroin

junk′ mail′ n *colloq* unsolicited advertising sent through the mails

junk′man′ /-man′/ n (-men′ /-men′/) dealer in resalable junk

junk′yard′ n place where junk is deposited

Ju·no /jōō′nō/ n 1 *Rom myth.* wife of Jupiter, goddess of marriage and childbirth; 2 large asteroid

jun·ta /hŏōnt′ə, junt′ə/ [Sp = council] n small group, often of military officers, that rules a country after a coup d'état and before a legitimate government is formed

jun·to /jun′tō/ [Sp = conference] n group or faction that gathers for some common purpose, esp. political

Ju·pi·ter /jōō′pitər/ n 1 *Rom myth.* chief god of the heavens and of the weather; 2 largest planet in the solar system

Ju·ras·sic /jōōras′ik/ [< *Jura* Mountains] *geol* adj 1 designating or pert. to a period of the Mesozoic era, characterized by the existence of dinosaurs and the appearance of flying reptiles and birds || n 2 the Jurassic period

ju·rid·i·cal /jōōrid′ikəl/ [< L *juridicus*] adj pert. to law or the administration of justice

ju·ris·dic·tion /jōōr′isdik′shən/ [L *jurisdictio* (-onis)] n 1 right to exercise legal authority; 2 authority, control; 3 extent or range of authority; 4 territory over which authority is exercised || SYN dominion, power, authority, right, control

ju·ris·dic′tion·al adj 1 pert. to or involving jurisdiction; 2 pert. to the claim or the right of a union to exclusive labor jurisdiction in a factory, an industry, or a trade

ju·ris·pru′dence [L *jurisprudentia*] *n* **1** philosophy or science of law; **2** system of laws of a country

ju·rist /jŏŏr′ist/ [F *juriste* < L *jus* (*juris*) law] *n* **1** one skilled in the science of law; **2** judge; **3** lawyer

ju·ror /jŏŏr′ər/ [AF *jurour* < L *jurare* to swear] *n* member of a jury

ju′ry[1] [OF *juree* oath < L *jurare* to swear] *n* (**-ries**) **1** body of persons selected and sworn to inquire into or decide on the evidence in a case of law before them; **2** committee of experts selected to award prizes

ju′ry[2] [?] *adj naut* temporary, makeshift

just /just′/ [L *justus*] *adj* **1** right; fair; equitable; **2** in accordance with the facts; true; correct; **3** deserved ‖ *adv* **4** exactly, as *just right*; **5** a moment ago, as *he has just gone*; **6** only, barely, as *just a little*; **7** perfectly, quite, as *just beautiful*; **8** just now a moment ago; **9** just the same nevertheless ‖ **just′ly** *adv* ‖ SYN *adj* honest, honorable, fair, true, righteous

jus·tice /just′is/ [OF < L *justitia*] *n* **1** quality of being just; rectitude; integrity; **2** fairness, impartiality; **3** deserved reward or punishment; **4** administration of the law courts; **5** rightfulness; legality; **6** judge, magistrate; **7** bring to justice to cause to stand trial; **8** do justice to, a to treat fairly; b to appreciate ‖ SYN equity, right, honesty, integrity, justness, impartiality ‖ DISCR *Justice* and *equity* are here compared apart from their legal distinctions. *Justice* gives a man his strict due, deciding the case on its own merits, excluding the thought of others, and rendering decision on the basis of fairness, propriety, conformity to standards, adherence to fact, living worthily up to one's abilities, showing appreciation, or the like, as the *justice* of his punishment; the *justice* of her conduct; the *justice* of the criticism, or his resentment; the *justice* of his statement; to do oneself *justice*; do another *justice*. *Equity* does not exclude the thought of others, but rather entertains it, having for its purpose a fair apportionment, an even-handed distribution, of what there is. *Justice* is strict; *equity* has the elasticity of a spiritual quality, yielding where conditions demand or permit, and some-

times appearing to break the letter, while conserving the spirit, of a law. *Justness* can mean either *justice* or *equity*, but it usually connotes conformity to accuracy, truth, reasonableness, or the like. Just resentment is well grounded; just punishment is deserved; just divisions are fair. *Impartiality* is unbiased, unprejudiced, impersonal fairness ‖ ANT injustice, unfairness, dishonesty, partiality, untruth, wrong

jus′tice of the peace′ *n* public officer with varying duties, such as administering oaths, judging minor cases, and performing marriages

jus′ti·fy /just′ifī′/ [OF *justifier* < L *justus* just *facere* do] *v* (**-fied**) *vt* **1** to show or prove to be right; vindicate; warrant; **2** to free from blame; exonerate; **3** *typ* to make (lines of type) have even margins on both sides ‖ **jus′ti·fi′a·ble** *adj* ‖ **jus′ti·fi·ca′tion** *n* ‖ SYN vindicate, clear, exonerate, excuse, warrant, defend, absolve, acquit ‖ ANT condemn, blame, censure, convict

jut /jut′/ [var of *jet*[1]] *v* (**jut·ted; jut·ting**) *vi* jut out to stick out, project

jute /jōōt′/ [Bengali *jhuto*] *n* fiber of either of two East Indian plants (genus *Corchorus*), used for ropes, burlap, bagging, mats, etc.

Jute /jōōt′/ [ML *Jutae* Jutes] *n* member of a Germanic tribe living in Jutland who, with the Angles and Saxons, invaded Britain in the 5th century

Jut·land /jut′lənd/ *n* peninsula of continental Denmark

Ju·ve·nal /jōō′vənəl/ *n* (60–140 A.D.) Roman satirical poet

ju·ve·nile /jōō′vənəl, -nīl′/ [L *juvenilis*] *adj* **1** youthful; immature; **2** pert. to, characteristic of, or suitable to, young persons ‖ *n* **3** young person; **4** *theat* a youthful male role; b the actor who plays it

ju′ve·nile de·lin′quent *n* person who commits criminal acts but is too young to be tried in a regular court

ju′ve·nil′i·a /-nil′ē-ə, -nil′yə/ [L] *npl* **1** artistic or literary works produced in youth; **2** artistic or literary works suited or produced for the young

jux·ta·pose /juks′təpōz′/ [< *juxtaposition* < L *juxta* nearby + *position*] *vt* to place side by side; put close together ‖ **jux′ta·po·si′tion** *n*

K

K, k /kā′/ *n* (**K's** or **Ks; k's** or **ks**) eleventh letter of the English alphabet

K[1] **1** eleventh in order or in a series; **2**

something shaped like a K; **3** Kelvin; **4** *baseball* strike-out(s); **5** *chess* king

K[2] [NL *kalium*] *chem* potassium

k. **1** karat; **2** kilogram(s)

Ka·bul /käb′ŏŏl/ n capital of Afghanistan (440,000)

Kaf·ir or **Kaf·fir** /kaf′ər/ [Ar = infidel] n member of a native race of South Africa

kai·ser /kīz′ər/ [G < L caesar emperor] n title applied to the former emperors of Germany, Austria, and the Holy Roman Empire

kale /kāl/ [northern dial. form of cole cabbage] n 1 kind of cabbage with curled leaves (Brassica oleracea acephala); 2 colloq money

ka·lei′do·scope′ /kəlīd′ə-/ [< Gk kalos beautiful + eidos form + -scope] n 1 tube containing small bits of colored glass which, by an arrangement of mirrors, appear in a variety of symmetrical shapes when rotated; 2 anything that is continually changing || **ka·lei′do·scop′ic** /-skop′ik/ adj

Ka·li /kä′lē/ n Hindu goddess personifying creation and destruction

kal·so·mine /kal′səmīn′, -min/ n & vt calcimine

ka·mi·ka·ze /käm′əkäz′ē/ [Jap = divine wind] n Japanese pilot of World War II whose duty it was to crash his explosive-laden plane into enemy targets, esp. ships

Ka·nak·a /kənak′ə, kan′əkə/ [Hawaiian = man] n native Hawaiian

kan·ga·roo /kaŋ′gərŏŏ′/ [nat. name] n any of a family (Macropodidae) of herbivorous marsupials of Australia, having short forelegs, long powerful hind legs used for leaping, and a long strong tail

kan′ga·roo′ court′ n illegal mock court run by criminals inside a prison to enforce self-imposed regulations

Kans. Kansas

Kan·sas /kan′zəs/ n state in central U.S. (2,249,000; 82,158 sq.m.; cap. Topeka) || **Kan′san** n

Kan′sas Cit′y n 1 city in W Missouri (507,087); 2 city in NE Kansas, opposite Kansas City, Missouri (125,-000)

Kant, Im·man·u·el /iman′yŏŏ-əl kant′/ n (1724–1804) German philosopher || **Kant′i·an** adj & n || **Kant′i·an·ism** n

ka·o·lin /kā′əlin/ [F < Chin Kaoling mountain in China] n white clay from which porcelain is made

ka·pok /kā′pok/ [Malay kãpoq] n silky fibers within the seed pods of a tropical tree (Ceiba pentandra), used as a stuffing for mattresses and life jackets, for insulation, etc.

kap·pa /kap′ə/ n tenth letter of the Greek alphabet K, κ

ka·put /kəpŏŏt′/ [G] adj slang ruined; done for

Ka·ra·chi /kəräch̄ē/ n seaport in S West Pakistan (1,900,000); former capital

kar·a·kul /kar′əkəl/ n caracul

kar·at /kar′ət/ [var of carat] n twenty-fourth part: used to express the fineness of gold, 24 karat gold being 100 per cent pure

ka·ra·te /kərät′ē/ [Jap] n Japanese method of defending oneself by striking sensitive parts of an attacker's body with the feet, knees, elbows, and esp. the open hands

kar·ma /kär′mə/ [Skt = action] n 1 person's actions in one stage of his existence thought of as affecting his lot in the next; 2 destiny as determined by previous acts

Kash·mir /kash′mir, kashmir′/ n state in SW Asia, N of India, whose sovereignty is disputed between India and Pakistan (5,000,000; 82,500 sq.m.; cap. Srinagar) || **Kash·mir′i** /-ē/ also **Kash·mir′i·an** adj & n

Kat·man·du /kät′mändŏŏ′/ n capital of Nepal (125,000)

ka·ty·did /kāt′ēdĭd/ [imit] n large green grasshopper, the male of which makes a characteristic shrill sound

kay·ak /kī′ak/ [Eskimo] n Eskimo canoe made of sealskin stretched over a frame and kept watertight by a decklike covering laced about the paddler

kay·o /kā′ō′/ [< KO knock out] slang n 1 knockout || vt 2 to knock out

ka·zoo /kəzŏŏ′/ [?] n musical toy consisting of a metal tube with an opening on the side covered with wax paper, which makes a humming sound when one blows into the tube

kc kilocycle(s)

Keats, John /kēts′/ n (1795–1821) English poet

keel /kēl′/ [ON kjolr ship] n 1 chief and lowest timber or steel plate of a vessel extending from stem to stern along the bottom and supporting the whole frame; 2 ship; 3 longitudinal ridge on a leaf or bone; 4 on an even keel in a state of balance || vt 5 keel over, a to fall suddenly; b to faint, collapse

keel′haul′ vt 1 to drag (a person) from one side of a ship to the other, beneath the bottom; 2 to rebuke abusively

keen¹ /kēn′/ [OE cēne] adj 1 sharp-edged; 2 piercing, cutting, as a keen wind, keen sarcasm; 3 acute, intelligent; 4 eager, ardent, as a keen sportsman; 5 perceptive, as keen eyesight || keen′ly adv || keen′ness n || SYN cutting, penetrating, stinging, acute, shrewd

keen² [Ir caoine lamentation] n 1 wailing lament for the dead || vt 2 to utter a wailing lament

keep /kēp′/ [OE cēpan to observe] v (kept) vt 1 to tend, guard; 2 to preserve; 3 to support; maintain; 4 to manage, maintain in proper order, as to keep house; 5 to retain, hold; 6 to observe, fulfill; 7 to hold, detain; 8 to have on hand or in stock; 9 to maintain or cause to continue in a specified condition, as to keep the *light on;* **10** to make entries in, as *to keep records;* **11 keep back,** a to restrain, hold back; b to withhold, as information; **12 keep to oneself** to keep (something) secret; **13 keep up,** a to continue doing something, as *to keep up the payments;* b to keep in good condition ‖ *vi* **14** to remain or continue in a state or condition; **15** to continue fresh or unspoiled; **16** to continue, go on; **17 keep from** to refrain from; **18 keep on** to continue; **19 keep to,** a adhere to; b to remain in, as *he kept to his room;* **20 keep to oneself** to avoid contact with others; **21 keep up** to refrain from falling behind ‖ *n* **22** board and room; **23** stronghold or dungeon of a castle; **24 for keeps** *colloq* a for the winner to retain what he wins; b permanently ‖ SYN *v* save, support, hold (see *defend, celebrate*)

keep'er *n* **1** one who keeps; **2** person who has custody, as of prisoners, animals in a zoo, etc.; **3** one who guards or tends, as a doorway or entrance; **4** one who operates a retail business, as *a shopkeeper;* **5** iron bar across the poles of a permanent magnet

keep'ing *n* **in keeping with** in conformity with

keep'sake' *n* token held in memory of the giver; memento

keg /keg'/ [ON *kaggi*] *n* **1** small barrel holding five to ten gallons; **2** unit of weight for nails, equal to 100 pounds

Kel·ler, Hel·en /kel'ər/ *n* (1880–1968) U.S. lecturer, author, and teacher of the blind, herself deaf and blind from infancy

kel'ly green' /kel'ē/ [< name *Kelly*] *n* variable yellow green

kelp /kelp'/ [ME *culp*] *n* **1** any of several large brown seaweeds (family Laminariaceae); **2** their ashes

Kelt /kelt'/ *n* Celt ‖ **Kelt'ic** *adj & n*

Kel·vin /kel'vin/ [Lord *Kelvin* (1824–1907) Brit physicist] *adj* designating the degrees of the Kelvin scale

Kel'vin scale' *n* absolute scale of temperature, with zero at —273.16° Celsius

ken /ken'/ [OE *cennan*] *v* **(kenned; ken·ning)** *vt & vi* **1** *Scot* to know; understand ‖ *n* **2** knowledge; comprehension

Ken·ne·dy, John F. /ken'ədē/ *n* (1917–63) 35th president of the U.S. 1961–63; assassinated

ken·nel /ken'əl/ [ME *kenel* < LL *canile* < L *canis* dog] *n* **1** doghouse; **2** also **kennels** *pl* place where dogs are bred, reared, trained, or boarded

Ken'nel·ly-Heav'i·side' lay'er /ken'əlē hev'ēsīd'/ [A. W. *Kennelly* (1861–1939) Am electrical engineer and O. *Heaviside* (1850–1925) Brit physicist] *n* highly ionized radio-reflective layer of the upper atmosphere

Ken·tuck·y /kəntuk'ē/ *n* state in E central U.S. (3,219,000; 40,598 sq.mi.; cap. Frankfort) ‖ **Ken·tuck'i·an** *n*

Ken·ya /kēn'yə, ken'-/ *n* republic in E Africa, member of the British Commonwealth of Nations (9,948,-000; 224,960 sq.mi.; cap. Nairobi) ‖ **Ken'yan** *adj & n*

kep·i /kāp'ē, kep'ē/ [F < SwissG *käppi* little cap] *n* French military cap with a flat circular top and a visor

kept /kept'/ *pt & pp* of keep

ker·a·tin /ker'ətin/ [< Gk *keras* (*-atos*) horn] *n* albuminous substance found in hair, feathers, nails, hoofs, and horns

kerb /kurb'/ *n* Brit curb

ker·chief /kurch'if/ [OF *cuevrechief* cover the head] *n* **1** cloth worn on the head or about the neck; **2** handkerchief

ker·nel /kurn'əl/ [OE *cyrnel* dim. of *corn* grain] *n* **1** grain or seed; **2** the softer, sometimes edible portion of a nut, fruit stone, or the like; **3** nucleus of anything; core

ker·o·sene /ker'əsēn, ker'əsēn'/ [< Gk *keros* wax] *n* light colorless oil distilled from petroleum, coal, etc., and used as a fuel, as a solvent, and in lamps

ketch /kech'/ [ME *cache*] *n* small fore-and-aft-rigged sailing vessel

ketch·up /kech'əp/ [Malay *kechap* fish sauce] *n* any of various sauces for meat, esp. one prepared from tomatoes, onions, and spices

ke·tone /kē'tōn/ [G *Keton*] *n* any of a class of organic compounds, usu. volatile liquids or crystalline solids, allied to the aldehydes

ket·tle /ket'əl/ [OB *cetel* < L *catillus* small bowl] *n* metal vessel for boiling liquids, cooking foods, etc.

ket'tle·drum' *n* drum consisting of a large bowl of copper or brass with parchment stretched over the opening

key[1] /kē'/ [OB *cæg*] *n* **1** metal instrument for operating a lock by moving its bolt; **2** similar device for engaging a part, as in winding a clock or tightening skate clamps; **3** device which, when slipped into place, wedges, supports, or locks together different parts; **4** person or thing in a controlling position; **5** that by means of which a difficulty is removed or something unintelligible is explained; **6** explanation of marks, symbols, and abbreviations, as in a map or dictionary; **7** one of a set of levers by means of which certain instruments, as pianos and typewriters, are made to operate with the fingers; **8** style or tone of thought or expression; **9** device operated by the fingers for opening and closing an electric circuit; **10** *mach* straight piece of metal inserted into a keyway to prevent a wheel from turning on a shaft; 11 *mus* arrangement or series of musical tones bearing a fixed relation to the keynote || *vt* 12 to provide with a key or keys; 13 *mus* to regulate the key of; 14 to regulate; adjust; harmonize; 15 key up to stimulate; imbue with nervous energy || *adj* 16 strategically important; essential

key² [Sp *cayo*] *n* low, small reef or island

Key, Francis Scott *n* (1780–1843) *n* U.S. lawyer, author of *The Star Spangled Banner*

key′board′ *n* 1 row or set of keys, as on a piano, accordion, typewriter, or typesetting machine || *vt* 2 to set (copy) by operating a keyboard || also *vi*

key′hole′ *n* small opening in a door, lock, or the face of a clock for inserting a key

Keynes·l·an·ism /kān′zē-əniz′əm/ [John Maynard *Keynes* (1883–1946)] *n* advocacy of a policy of government intervention to maintain economic equilibrium

key′note′ *n* 1 *mus* basic note or tone of a scale; 2 central idea or ruling principle

key′note ad·dress′ or **speech′** *n* speech at a political convention that presents the basic principles of the party

key′ punch′ *n* keyboard machine that codes information on cards by punching holes in prescribed patterns || **key′punch′ vt** || **key′punch′er** *n*

key′ sig·na·ture *n mus* group of sharps or flats placed after the clef to indicate the key

key′stone′ *n* 1 central wedge-shaped stone of an arch, regarded as holding the arch together; 2 unifying principle

key′way′ *n* groove or slot in a shaft or hub for receiving the key that locks it in place with another part

Key′ West′ *n* 1 key or island off SW Florida; 2 southernmost city of continental U.S., a seaport on this island (34,000)

kg, kg. kilogram(s)

khak·i /kă′kē, kak′ē/ [Urdu = dusty] *n* 1 dull yellowish brown; 2 twilled cloth of this color; 3 uniform made of khaki

khan /kän′, kan′/ [Turk = prince] *n* 1 title applied to Genghis Khan and his successors as rulers over various Asiatic tribes and regions; 2 title applied to the rulers of certain semi-independent Asiatic states, and to various officers of lower rank; 3 in Afghanistan, India, and Iran, title of respect

Khar·toum /kärtōōm′/ *n* capital of Sudan (584,000)

khe·dive /kədēv′/ [< Turk *hidīv* < Pers *khidīw*] *n* viceroy of the sultan of Turkey in Egypt from 1867 to 1914

Khrush·chev, Ni·ki·ta /nikē′tə krōōsh′-chef, -chôf, krōōsh′-/ *n* (1894–1971) Russian political leader; premier of the U.S.S.R. 1958–64

kHz kilohertz

kib·butz /kĭbōōts′/ [ModHeb] *n* (-but-zim /-bōōtsēm′/) *n* collective farming community in Israel

kib·itz /kĭb′its/ [Yiddish < G *kiebitzen*] *vi* to give unsolicited advice, as a spectator, esp. at a card game || **kib′bitz·er** *n*

ki·bosh /kī′bosh, kĭbosh′/ [?] *n* put the kibosh on *colloq* to bring to a halt; squelch

kick /kĭk′/ [ME *kike*] *vt* 1 to strike with the foot; 2 to propel by kicking; 3 *football* to score (a goal) by kicking; 4 kick off *slang* to initiate; 5 kick out *colloq* to oust; 6 kick the habit *slang* to stop being addicted to a habit; 7 kick up *slang* to cause (a disturbance); 8 kick someone up·stairs *colloq* to promote someone to a nominally higher but relatively unimportant post in order to get rid of him || *vi* 9 to strike out with the foot; 10 to recoil; 11 *colloq* to protest vigorously; complain; 12 kick in *slang* to pay one's share; 13 kick off *slang* to start a football game or other undertaking; 14 kick over *colloq* to turn over (said of an internal combustion engine) || *n* 15 act of kicking; 16 recoil; 17 *colloq* objection or protest; 18 *colloq* intoxicating quality in an alcoholic drink; 19 *slang* pleasurable thrill; 20 *slang* temporary interest; 21 *slang* pocket

kick′back′ *n colloq* 1 disapproving response; 2 improper return of part of the money received as payment; 3 payment of a percentage of salary to an employer or supervisor; 4 money so paid or returned

kick′off′ *n* 1 *football* place kick used to start play; 2 *colloq* beginning of some enterprise

kid /kĭd′/ [prob ON *kith*] *n* 1 young goat; 2 leather made from the skin of a kid or goat; 3 *colloq* child; youth || *v* (**kid·ded; kid·ding**) *vt* 4 to humbug; 5 to banter with || *vi* 6 to jest; tease || **kid′der** *n*

kid′die also **kid′dy** *n* (-dies) *colloq* young child

kid′ gloves′ *npl* treat or handle with kid gloves to handle gingerly or with great tact

kid·nap /kid′nap/ [*kid* + *obs* nap to seize] *v* (-naped or -napped; -nap·ing or -nap·ping) *vt* to carry off (a person) by force, esp. in order to hold for ransom || **kid′nap·er** or **kid′nap·per** *n*

kid·ney /kid′nē/ [ME] *n* 1 either of two glandular organs which secrete urine; 2 meat of the kidney of an animal; 3 temperament, disposition; 4 sort or kind

kid′ney bean′ *n* 1 cultivated plant (*Pha-*

seolus vulgaris) which bears kidney-shaped seeds; **2** the seed

kid′ney stone′ *n* hard deposit that sometimes develops in the kidneys

Ki·ev /kē′ef/ *n* capital of the Ukraine in SW Russia (1,350,000)

kill /kil/ [ME *killen*] *vt* **1** to cause the death of; **2** to deaden; weaken; neutralize; **3** to use up (time); **4** to stop publication of (a news story); **5** to defeat (a legislative bill); veto; **6** to cut off or disconnect (a motor, an electric circuit); **7** *colloq* to drink all of (a bottle of liquor); **8 kill off** to kill all of || *vi* **9** to destroy life; **10** to be killed; **11 dressed to kill** dressed very stylishly || *n* **12** act of killing, esp. of game; **13** animal or animals killed || **kill′er** *n* || SYN *v* assassinate, execute, murder, slaughter, slay, massacre, dispatch || DISCR *To kill*, the general word, means to deprive of life, whether by accident, by law, by wrongdoing, or in self-defense; it refers equally to human beings, animals, or plants, and is as colorless as to method as it is to motive. To *execute* is to *kill*, according to law, one legally sentenced to death. *Assassinate*, *murder*, and *slaughter* are used in connection with the wrongful killing of human beings; to *assassinate* is to *kill* by treacherous, violent assault, whether secretly or openly; to *murder* is to *kill* with premeditated malice; to *slaughter* is to *kill* brutally, ruthlessly, and on a large scale. *Slaughter* as used in connection with the sweeping destruction of troops in battle does not connote brutality. *Slaughter* as applied to animals means to butcher them for food

kill′er whale′ *n* ferocious predatory dolphin (*Grampus orca*)

kill′ing *n* **1** *colloq* great unexpected profit || *adj* **2** exhausting; **3** *colloq* extremely funny

kill′-joy′ *n* person or thing that dampens or destroys the joy of others

kiln /kil/, kiln/ [OB *cylene* < L *culina* kitchen] *n* furnace or oven for burning, drying, or hardening, as bricks

kil·o /kil′ō/ *n* **1** kilogram; **2** kilometer

kil·o- /kil′ə-/ [F < Gk *chilioi*] *comb form* in metric system one thousand

kil′o·cy·cle *n* **1** one thousand cycles; **2** unit of radio frequency equal to one thousand cycles per second

kil′o·gram′ *n* basic metric unit of mass or weight equal to 1,000 grams or 2.2046 pounds

kil′o·gram′-me′ter *n* mks unit of work or energy, equal to the work done by the force of one kilogram in moving its point of application one meter in the direction of the force

kil′o·hertz′ *n* (-hertz, -hertz·es) unit of radio frequency equal to one thousand cycles per second

kil′o·li′ter *n* metric measure of capacity equal to 1,000 liters

kil·o·me·ter /kil′əmēt′ər, kilom′itər/ *n* unit of length or distance equal to 1,000 meters or 0.62137 mile || **kil′·o·met′ric** /-met′-/ *adj*

kil′o·ton′ *n* **1** one thousand tons; **2** explosive force equal to 1,000 tons of TNT

kil′o·watt′ *n* unit of electrical power equal to 1,000 watts

kil′o·watt′-hour′ *n* unit of electrical work or energy, equal to the work done by one kilowatt of power acting for one hour

kilt /kilt/ [ME *kylte*] *n* short, pleated skirt, as that worn by men in the Scottish Highlands

kil·ter /kilt′ər/ [?] *n* out of kilter not in good condition or order

ki·mo·no /kimōn′ə/ [Jap] *n* **1** loose, wide-sleeved robe with a wide sash; **2** woman's loose dressing gown

kin /kin/ [OB *cynn*] *n* **1** family; relatives; **2** relationship; **3** relative; related person or thing || *adj* **4** of the same ancestry or kind || **kin′ship** *n* || SYN *n* kinfolk, kinsmen, kindred, family, consanguinity, blood, connection, affinity, descent

-kin /-kin/ [ME < MD] *dim. suf*, as lambkin, mannikin

kind /kīnd/ [OB *gecynde* natural] *n* **1** class or natural group of people, animals, or objects; **2** variety, sort; **3** nature, character; **4 in kind** in the same way or with things of the same sort; **5 of a kind** of the same sort || *adj* **6** sympathetic; benevolent; **7** gracious; considerate; **8** mild, tractable || *adv* **9 kind of** somewhat || SYN *n* sort, description, nature, character; *adj* compassionate, friendly, gentle, tender, humane, charitable, good || DISCR *Kind* and *sort* are used interchangeably, but *sort* is often used when a tone of disparagement or slight is to be conveyed, as that *sort* of people should be kept out || ANT *adj* brutal, unmerciful

kin·der·gar·ten /kin′dərgärt′ən, -gärd′ən/ [G = children's garden] *n* school for four- to six-year-old children in which teaching is done mostly with games and handicraft and which serves as an introduction to the first grade

kind′-heart′ed *adj* full of kindness

kin·dle /kin′dəl/ [ON *kynda*] *vt* **1** to set fire to; ignite; **2** to stir up, animate || *vi* **3** to catch fire; **4** to become excited or inflamed

kin·dling /kind′liŋ/ *n* light combustible material for starting a fire

kind·ly /kīnd′lē/ *adj* (-li·er; -li·est) **1** gracious; sympathetic; benevolent; **2** agreeable; benign || *adv* **3** in a gracious manner; **4** readily; **5** favorably || **kind′li·ness** *n* || SYN *adj* gentle, pleasant, propitious, well-disposed || ANT *adj* ill-disposed, uncharitable, unforgiving

kind′ness *n* **1** state or quality of being

kind; 2 kind act ‖ SYN gentleness, benignity, clemency, tenderness, mildness ‖ ANT brutality, mercilessness, severity

kin·dred /kín'drid/ [ME] *n* **1** relationship by birth or marriage; kinship; **2** kin, kinfolk ‖ *adj* **3** related by blood or marriage; **4** of like nature or character

kine /kín'/ [< OE *cȳ*] *npl poet.* cows

ki·net·ic /kĭnet'ĭk/ [Gk *kinetikos*] *adj* pert. to, causing, or caused by, motion

ki·net·ic en'er·gy *n* energy possessed by a moving body because of its motion, as in a waterfall

ki·net'ics *nsg* branch of mechanics dealing with the changes of motion as produced by unbalanced forces

kin'folk' *npl* relations, relatives

king /kĭng'/ [OE *cyning*] *n* **1** male sovereign; **2** preeminent person or thing; **3** playing card representing a king; **4** *checkers* piece which reaches the opponent's last row and may then move in any direction; **5** *chess* principal piece; **6 Kings** *sg* one of the books of the Old Testament recording the reigns of the Jewish kings following David ‖ **king'ship** *n* ‖ **king'ly** *adj*

King, Mar·tin Lu·ther, Jr. *n* (1929–68) black American civil and human rights leader; Nobel peace prize 1964

king' crab' *n* large edible crab (*Paralithodes camtschatica*) of the N Pacific

king'dom *n* **1** country of which the head of state is a king or queen; **2** one of the main divisions of natural objects, as *the animal kingdom;* **3** any sphere of influence or activity

king'dom come' *n* the hereafter

king'fish'er *n* any of a family (Alcedinidae) of long-billed, fish-eating birds

King' James' Ver'sion *n* English translation of the Bible published in 1611 under authorization of James I

king'let *n* small crested bird of the genus *Regulus*

king'pin' *n* **1** vertical bolt pivoting the forward axle to the body of a vehicle; **2** pin at the apex in bowling and tenpins; **3** *colloq* essential person or thing

king'-size' also **king'-sized'** *adj* extra large

king'wood' *n* **1** Brazilian tree (*Dalbergia cearensis*); **2** hard, purplish-brown wood of this tree, used in cabinetwork

kink /kĭngk'/ [D = twist] *n* **1** twist, bend, or curl in a rope, wire, thread, or hair; **2** soreness in a muscle, esp. in the neck or back; **3** crotchet; odd whim or notion ‖ *vi* **4** to form a kink ‖ *vt* **5** to cause to kink ‖ **kink'y** *adj* (-i·er; -i·est)

Kin·sha·sa /kĭnshäs'ə/ *n* capital of Zaire (1,250,000)

kin'ship *n* relationship; affinity

kins·man /kĭnz'mən/ *n* (-men /-mən/) male relative ‖ **kins'wom'an** *nfem* (-wom'en)

ki·osk /kē-ŏsk', kĭ'ŏsk/ [F *kiosque* < Pers *kūshk* pavilion] *n* small, roofed, open newsstand or bandstand

Kip·ling, Rud·yard /rud'yərd kĭp'lĭng/ *n* (1865–1936) English author; Nobel prize 1907

kip·per /kĭp'ər/ [OE *cypera* spawning salmon] *vt* **1** to cure (herring or salmon) by salting and drying or smoking ‖ *n* **2** kippered herring or salmon

kirk /kurk'/ [ME < Scand] *n* Scot & N Eng church

kis·met /kĭz'mĭt, kĭs'-/ [Ar *qismat*] *n* fate; destiny

kiss /kĭs'/ [OE *cyssan*] *vt* **1** to touch with the lips in token of love, affection, or reverence; **2** to touch lightly ‖ *vi* **3** to kiss another on the lips; **4** to kiss each other ‖ *n* **5** act of kissing; **6** slight touch

kiss'er *n slang* face

kiss' of death' *n* token of approval which in reality greatly harms its recipient

kit /kĭt'/ [ME *kyt*] *n* **1** set or outfit, as of supplies, tools, or equipment, for a specific purpose; **2** container for these; **3** set of parts to be assembled to make a device such as a radio, toy, etc.; **4** the **whole kit and caboodle** *colloq* the whole lot

kitch'en /kĭch'ən/ [OE *cycene* < L *coquina*] *n* room or place where cooking is done

kitch'en·ette' /-net'/ *n* small, compact kitchen, usu. part of a larger room

kitch'en po·lice' *n mil* **1** duty of helping in the kitchen; **2** soldiers assigned to this duty

kite /kīt'/ [OE *cȳta* kite (bird)] *n* **1** any of several small birds related to the hawks (family Accipitridae); **2** light frame covered with paper or cloth for flying in the air at the end of a cord or string ‖ *vi* **3** to go or soar rapidly, like a kite ‖ *vt* **4** to draw (a check) with the intention of depositing funds to cover it before it is cashed

kith /kĭth'/ [OE *cȳth*] *n* **kith and kin** friends and relatives

kit·ten /kĭt'ən/ [ME *kitoun*] *n* young cat

kit'ten·ish *adj* **1** playful like a kitten; **2** coy, flirtatious

kit'ty[1] *n* (-ties) **1** kitten; **2** *pet name* cat

kit'ty[2] [< *kit*] *n* (-ties) **1** pool to which each player in a card game contributes for some special purpose; **2** fund or collection, to be used for a reserve or for some special purpose; **3** in some card games, cards left over after the deal, to be used by the winner of the bid

ki·wi /kē'wē/ [Maori] *n* any of a genus (*Apteryx*) of nocturnal flightless birds of New Zealand

KKK, K.K.K. Ku Klux Klan

klep·to·ma·ni·a /klep'tэmān'g̱·э, -mān'-yэ/ [< Gk *kleptes* thief + *mania*] *n* irresistible impulse to steal || **klep'to·ma'ni·ac'** /-ak'/ *n*

klieg' light' /klēg'/ [< *Kliegl* firm name] *n* electric arc light that gives very bright illumination, used in motion-picture photography

Klon·dike /klon'dīk'/ *n* region in the Yukon Territory of NW Canada, site of gold rush in 1897–98

km, km. kilometer(s)

knack /nak'/ [MB *kna(c)k*] *n* talent or aptitude

knap'sack' /nap'-/ [< LG *knapp* bite of food] *n* leather or cloth bag to hold supplies, carried on the back

knave /nāv'/ [OE *cnafa* boy] *n* 1 unprincipled rascal; 2 *cards* jack 4 || **knav'ish** *adj*

knav'er·y *n* (-ies) unprincipled rascality

knead /nēd'/ [OE *cnedan*] *vt* 1 to work into a smooth mass, as dough or clay, by squeezing and pressing; 2 to massage as by kneading

knee /nē'/ [OE *cnēow*] *n* 1 joint between the human leg and thigh; 2 corresponding part in an animal or insect; 3 the part of a garment covering the knee; 4 anything resembling a bent knee; 5 **bring someone to his knees** to force someone into submission || *vt* 6 to hit with the knee

knee' ac'tion *n* independent suspension of each front wheel of a vehicle

knee' breech'es /brich'ĭz/ *npl* trousers reaching to or just below the knee

knee'cap' *n* 1 movable bone on the front of the knee joint, patella; 2 protective covering for the knee

knee'-deep' *adj* 1 sunk to the knees in water, mud, snow, etc.; 2 deeply occupied or involved

knee'-high' *adj* rising up to the knees

knee'hole' *n* space for the knees and legs under a desk

knee' jerk' *n* involuntary extension of the leg caused by a tap on the tendon below the kneecap

kneel /nēl'/ [OE *cnēowlian*] *v* (knelt or kneeled) *vi* to bend down or rest on the knee or knees

knell /nel'/ [OE *cnyllan* to toll] *n* 1 sound of a bell rung slowly, as for a funeral; 2 any sound announcing the death of someone or the end of something || *vt* 3 to announce by a knell || *vi* 4 to toll dolefully

knelt /nelt'/ *pt* & *pp* of **kneel**

Knes·set /knes'et/ [< Heb = assembly] *n* parliament of Israel

knew /n(y)ōō'/ *pt* of **know**

knick·ers /nik'эrz/ also **knick'er·bock'-ers** /-bok'эrz/ [< D. *Knickerbocker* fictitious author of Washington Irving's *History of New York*] *npl* short loose breeches gathered below the knee

knick·knack /nik'nak'/ [< *obs knack* trinket] *n* ornamental trifle, trinket

knife /nīf'/ [OB *cnīf*] *n* (knives /-vz/) 1 cutting instrument consisting of a sharp-edged blade set in a handle; 2 blade forming part of an implement or machine || *vt* 3 to stab with a knife; 4 *colloq* to undermine by treachery

knife' switch' *n elec* switch consisting of a hinged blade which makes contact in a spring clip

knight /nīt'/ [OB *cniht* manservant] *n* 1 in medieval Europe, one admitted by solemn ceremonies to honorable rank and pledged to chivalrous conduct; 2 in Great Britain, one who is given a nonhereditary rank, entitling him to have *Sir* prefixed to his given name, in recognition of merit or patriotic service; 3 member of certain orders and societies; 4 *chess* piece bearing the figure of a horse's head || *vt* 5 to make (a man) a knight || **knight'hood** *n* || **knight'ly** *adj*

knight'-er'rant *n* (knights-errant) medieval knight who wandered about in search of adventure and to show his military prowess || **knight'-er'rant·ry** *n* (-ries)

Knight' Tem'plar /tem'plэr/ *n* (Knights Templars) member of a military order, founded about 1118 to protect pilgrims on the way to Jerusalem during the Crusades; suppressed in 1312

knit /nit'/ [OB *cnyttan*] *v* (knit·ted or knit; knit·ting) *vt* 1 to make (a fabric or garment) by looping or weaving thread or yarn; 2 to unite closely; tie or draw together; 3 to draw into wrinkles, as *to knit the brows* || *vi* 4 to knit a fabric of thread or yarn; 5 to become closely joined or united

knit'ting *n* knitted work

knives /nīvz'/ *pl* of **knife**

knob /nob'/ [MB *knobbe*] *n* 1 round swelling, lump, or mass; 2 rounded handle of a door, drawer, or the like; 3 rounded hill

knock /nok'/ [OB *cnocian*] *vt* 1 to strike or beat; give a blow to; 2 to bump, as one's head; 3 to make by striking, as a hole; 4 *colloq* to criticize; 5 **knock down, a** to indicate the sale of (an article) at an auction by a blow of the hammer: **b** to take apart (an assembled article); **c** *colloq* to reduce (prices); 6 **knock off** *slang* **a** to cease (work); **b** to complete, turn out; **c** to kill; **d** to hold up or burglarize; 7 **knock out, a** to render unconscious by a blow; **b** to put out of commission; 8 **knock together** to construct or assemble hastily; 9 **knock up, a** to injure, mar; **b** *slang* to make pregnant || *vi* 10 to strike a blow; 11 to rap on a door; 12 to bump or strike against something; 13 to make a pounding noise, as an auto engine; 14 **knock about or around** *slang* to wander idly or aimlessly; 15 **knock off** to stop working

‖ *n* 16 rap or blow; 17 act or sound of knocking; 18 *colloq* bit of adverse criticism

knock'down' 1 act or instance of being felled by a blow; 2 *colloq* price reduction; 3 *slang* introduction ‖ *adj* 4 capable of being readily disassembled

knock'er *n* 1 loose handle attached to a door, used for knocking; 2 *colloq* carping critic

knock'-kneed' *adj* having the legs bend inward at the knees

knock'out' *n* 1 act or instance of knocking out; 2 *colloq* stunningly attractive person or thing; 3 small piece of flat surface of metal or plastic prepared to be easily forced out where a hole is needed

knock'out drops' *npl slang* drug put in a drink to make the drinker unconscious

knoll /nōl'/ [OE *cnoll*] *n* rounded hillock

knot /not'/ [OE *cnotta*] *n* 1 interweaving or tying of the parts of one or more threads, cords, etc., so that they will not come apart; 2 anything resembling a knot or lump, as *a knot of muscles*; 3 entanglement; difficulty; 4 a hard knob or lump where a branch joins a tree trunk; b cross section of such a lump in lumber; 5 group or cluster of people or things; 6 tie, bond; 7 *naut* unit of velocity equal to one nautical mile per hour ‖ *v* (knot·ted; knot·ting) *vt* 8 to tie in a knot; form knots in; 9 to fasten with a knot ‖ *vi* 10 to become entangled; 11 to form knots ‖ SYN *n* tie, bend, hitch, splice ‖ DISCR *Tie* and *knot* are general terms, applied to any fastening or knoblike interlacing formed with a flexible cord. More specifically, a *knot* is a simple knob or lump formed by interweaving the strands of a single cord, as to prevent raveling; a *bend* is a *tie* by which one cord is fastened to another or to an object; a *hitch* is a *tie* forming a temporary fastening, easily undone. A *splice* is a joint between two cords, made by interweaving their strands

knot'hole' *n* hole in lumber caused by the falling out of a knot

knot'ty *adj* (-ti·er; -ti·est) 1 having many knots; 2 difficult, perplexing, as a problem

know /nō'/ [OE *cnāwan*] *v* (knew; known) *vt* 1 to perceive as true; understand clearly; 2 to have knowledge of; 3 to be acquainted or intimate with; 4 to be able to distinguish, as right from wrong; 5 know how to to have the ability, knowledge, and experience to; 6 know the ropes *colloq* to have knowledge and experience of a particular occupation or business ‖ *vi* 7 to be in-

formed; have certain knowledge about something ‖ *n* 8 in the know *colloq* having knowledge about a particular situation

know'-how' *n* ability to do a particular thing with skill and knowledge gained from study and experience

know'ing *adj* 1 having knowledge; 2 shrewd, cunning; 3 implying knowledge of certain events

know'ing·ly *adv* intentionally; with full knowledge of the circumstances or the consequences

knowl·edge /nol'ij/ *n* 1 clear perception of a truth or fact; 2 act or state of knowing; 3 that which is known; learning; 4 the sum of information or enlightenment of mankind, a group, or an individual; 5 practical understanding gained from experience; 6 awareness ‖ SYN acquaintance, comprehension, erudition, experience, learning, lore, information, enlightenment, intuition, conviction, wisdom, science, scholarship ‖ DISCR Broadly, *knowledge* is the sum of what is known, as every branch of *knowledge*. In a limited sense, *knowledge* is the body of facts, acquired or intuitive, known to a mind; referring to a single subject, such *knowledge* is an understanding of that subject, as a *knowledge* of botany. *Information* is *knowledge* of fact, usually not systematized, but gathered in a haphazard or casual way, as from instruction, reading, observation, or hearsay. *Experience* is the yield of life as it has been lived; it is the *knowledge* taught by all that one has enjoyed or suffered, viewed especially as a source of better judgment and increased skill for the future, as he learned by bitter *experience*; the lessons of *experience*. *Wisdom*, though consisting of *knowledge* plus *experience*, is a quality which transcends both: it unites with the facts of *knowledge* and the fruit of *experience* a genius for judgment; *wisdom* is both ideal and practical. *Science*, broadly, is systematized and formulated *knowledge* regarded as the result of the search for truth. In a more limited sense, *science* is the body of ordered *knowledge* available with reference to any particular subject, especially some aspect of the physical world, as the *science* of physics (see *learning*)

knowl'edge·a·ble *adj* possessing knowledge; perceptive; well-informed

known /nōn'/ *pp* of **know**

Knox·ville /noks'vil/ *n* city in E Tennessee (115,000)

knuck·le /nuk'əl/ [ME *knokel* prob *dim.* of MLG *knoke* bone] *n* 1 any of the joints of the fingers; 2 knee or the hock joint of an animal, used for food; 3 cylindrical projection of

a hinge, with a pin as axis; **4 knuckles**
nsg or *npl* brass knuckles ‖ *vi* **5**
knuckle down to apply oneself earnestly; **6 knuckle under** to yield or
submit

knurled /nurld′/ [< earlier *knur* hard
knob] *adj* having ridges on the edge,
as a thumbscrew, to provide a firm
grip for holding or turning

KO, K.O., k.o. /kā′ō′/ *v* (**KO′d;** **KO′-**
ing) *vt* **1** to knock out ‖ *n* **2** (**KO′s**)
knockout

ko·a·la /kō-äl′ə/ [native name] *n* arboreal marsupial of Australia (*Phas-*
colarctos cinereus), resembling a
teddy bear

Kö′chel list′ing /kœkh′əl/ *n* catalogue
of the authentic works (626 items)
of Wolfgang Amadeus Mozart, published in 1862 by Ludwig von Köchel
(1800–1877) and revised in 1937 by
Alfred Einstein

kohl /kōl′/ [Ar] *n* finely powdered
antimony sulfide, used in the East to
darken the eyelids

kohl·ra·bi /kōlrä′bē, kōl′rä′-/ [G < It
cavolrapa] *n* variety of cabbage
(*Brassica oleracea gongylodes*) with
an enlarged turniplike stem

koi·ne /koinā′/ [Gk = common] *n* the
Greek language of the Hellenistic
period, which spread throughout the
Near East and is the language of the
New Testament

kook /kōōk′/ [? < *cuckoo*] *n* slang
peculiar person; oddball ‖ **kook′y**
adj (**-i·er, -i·est**)

ko·peck /kō′pek/ [Russ *kopeika*] *n*
Russian coin equal to ⅟₁₀₀ rubble

Ko·ran /kôrän′, -ran′/ [Ar *qur'an* reci-
tation] *n* sacred book of Islam, regarded as containing the revelations
of God to Muhammad

Ko·re·a /kôrē′ə, kō-/ *n* country in E
Asia, divided in 1948 into North
Korea and South Korea ‖ **Ko·re′an**
adj & n

ko·ru·na /kôr′ənə/ [< L *corona* crown]
n monetary unit of Czechoslovakia

Kos·ci·us·ko, Thad·de·us /thad′ē-əs
kos′ē-us̄ kō/ *n* (1746–1817) Polish
patriot, general in the American
Revolutionary Army

ko·sher /kōsh′ər/ [Yiddish < Heb
kāshēr right] *adj* **1** (food) prepared
according to Jewish law; **2** slang **a**
authentic; **b** legitimate; legal

Kos·suth, Louis /kos′ōōth/ *n* (1802–
94) Hungarian statesman and patriot

kow·tow /kou′tou′/ [Chin *k'o-t'o* to
bump the head (on the floor)] *vi* to
display obsequious deference

K.P. kitchen police

Kr *chem* krypton

K′ ra′tion [A. Keys (1904–) American physiologist] *n U.S. Army* emergency field ration

Krem·lin /krem′lin/ [< Russ *kreml'*
fortress] *n* **1** inner citadel of Mos-

cow, seat of the chief government
offices of the Soviet Union; **2** government of the Soviet Union

Krem′lin·ol′o·gy *n* study of the policies
and activities of the Kremlin, esp. in
matters involving international relations ‖ **Krem′lin·ol′o·gist** *n*

Krish·na /krish′nə/ *n* an incarnation
of Vishnu, the second god of the
Hindu trinity

Kriss Krin·gle /kris′ krin′gəl/ [< G
Christkindel little Christ child] *n*
Santa Claus

kro·na /krōn′ə/ [< L *corona* crown] *n*
(-**nor** /-nər/) monetary unit of Sweden

kró·na /krōn′ə/ [< L *corona* crown] *n*
(-**nur** /-nər/) monetary unit of Iceland

kro·ne /krōn′ə/ [< L *corona* crown] *n*
(-**ner** /-nər/) monetary unit of Denmark and Norway

kryp·ton /krip′tən/ [Gk = hidden] *n*
rare gaseous element (Kr; at.no. 36;
at.wt. 83.80) present in very small
quantities in the atmosphere

Kua·la Lum·pur /kwä′lə lŏŏmpŏŏr′/ *n*
capital of Malaysia (325,000)

Ku·blai Khan /kōōb′lī kän′/ *n* (1216–
94) grandson of Genghis Khan and
founder of the Mongol dynasty of
China

ku·dos /k(y)ōō′dŏs, -dos/ [Gk] *n* glory;
fame; approval

Ku Klux Klan /k(y)ōō′ kluks′ klan′/ *n*
southern secret society after the
Civil War, whose aim was to regain
white political ascendancy in the
South; revived after World War I in
many parts of the U.S., advocating
the supremacy of the white, native-
born, Anglo-Saxon Protestants

küm·mel /kim′əl/ [G = caraway seed]
n cordial made usu. from rectified
alcohol and flavored with caraway
seed, anise, etc.

kum·quat /kum′kwot/ [Cantonese *kam*
kwat golden orange] *n* **1** small citrus
fruit the size and shape of a large
olive, used chiefly in preserves; **2** tree
(genus *Fortunella*) bearing this fruit

Kurd /kôōrd′, kurd′/ *n* member of the
people of Kurdistan, a region of
Turkey, Iran, Iraq, Syria, and the
Soviet Union

Kurd′ish *adj* **1** pert. to the Kurds or
their language ‖ **2** language of the
Kurds

Ku·wait /kōōwāt′, -wīt′/ *n* country,
former sheikdom in NE Arabia
(491,000; 6,200 sq.m.; cap. Kuwait
(100,000) ‖ **Ku·wai′ti** *adj & n*

kw. kilowatt

kwh., kW.H., K.W.H. kilowatt hour

Ky. Kentucky

Kyo·to /kē-ō′tō/ *n* city in central
Japan, former capital (1,400,000)

Kyr·i·e e·le·i·son /kir′ē-ā′elä′ē·son′/
[Gk = Lord have mercy] *n* **1** the first

words of a brief petition used at various places in the service in the Eastern Orthodox and Roman Catho-lic churches, and in the Anglican church, esp. as a response; 2 musical setting of these words

L

L, l /el′/ *n* (**L's** or **Ls**; **l's** or **ls**) twelfth letter of the English alphabet

L 1 twelfth in order or in a series; 2 Roman numeral 50; 3 something shaped like an L; 4 [*L libra*] pound; 5 (**L's** or **Ls**) *colloq* elevated railroad; 6 ell²

L, L. Latin

l. (*pl* **ll.**) line

L., l. 1 lake; 2 latitude; 3 left; 4 length; 5 liter; 6 lumen

la /lä′/ [It] *n mus* sixth tone in the diatonic scale

La *chem* lanthanum

La. Louisiana

L.A. /el′ā′/ *n colloq* Los Angeles

lab /lab′/ *n* laboratory

la·bel /lāb′əl/ [MF = ribbon] *n* 1 slip of paper or other material to be attached to an object, bearing an inscription indicating size, contents, price, ownership, or other pertinent facts; 2 classifying phrase or catchword ‖ *v* (-**beled** or -**belled**; -**bel·ing** or -**bel·ling**) *vt* 3 to mark with a label; 4 to classify; apply a label to

la·bi·al /lāb′ē-əl/ [< L *labium* lip] *adj* 1 of or pert. to the lips; 2 *phonet* formed or articulated by the lips ‖ *n phonet* labial sound

la·bi·al·ize′ *vt* to make (a sound) labial

la·bi·ate /lāb′ē-āt′, -it/ *adj* having parts like lips; lipped

la·bi·o- /lāb′ēō-/ *comb form* lip and, as *labiodental*

la·bor /lāb′ər/ [L = work] *n* 1 work, toil; physical or mental exertion; 2 the class of wage-earning workers; 3 the effort and pangs of childbirth ‖ *vi* 4 to toil or work; 5 to strive; take pains; 6 to operate or proceed with difficulty; move slowly; 7 to be in childbirth; 8 *naut* to pitch or roll heavily in a seaway; 9 labor **under** to act as if influenced by (a delusion, misunderstanding, etc.) ‖ *vt* 10 to overelaborate, as *to labor a point* ‖ SYN *n* work, toil, drudgery ‖ DISCR *Work*, the general term, names any output of energy or close application of effort to some purpose. Hence, its range is wide: *work* may be hard, easy, light, heavy, serious, pleasant, or burdensome. *Labor* is hard *work;* it may be mental, but is more apt to be physical exertion of a severe, tiring sort. *Toil* is even harder *work* than *labor;* it is painful as well as monotonous, exhausting rather than

merely wearing. *Work* may leave us agreeably or badly tired; *labor* leaves us painfully tired, heavy in body and mind from fatigue; *toil* leaves us frankly worn out. *Drudgery* is slavish, displeasing, often menial, *work; work,* light in itself, may be *drudgery* to one who hates routine ‖ ANT *n* idleness, sloth

lab·o·ra·to·ry /lab′(ə)rətôr′ē, -tōr′-, or *Brit* ləbôr′ətrē/ [< L *laborare* (-*atus*) to work] *n* (-**ries**) 1 building or room equipped for scientific work or for research; 2 any situation amenable to observation and experimentation

La′bor Day′ *n* first Monday in September, set apart in most states and in Canada as a legal holiday to honor labor

la′bored *adj* 1 done with difficulty; 2 forced, not natural

la′bor·er *n* one who labors, esp. one who does unskilled physical work for wages ‖ SYN workingman (see *artisan*)

la·bo·ri·ous /ləbôr′ē-əs, -bōr′-/ *adj* 1 requiring much exertion and toil; 2 painstaking; difficult

la′bor pains′ *npl* intense pains preceding childbirth, caused by the contraction of the uterus

la′bor un′ion *n* association of workers organized for mutual protection and benefit, and for collective bargaining with the employers

La·bour·ite /lāb′ərīt′/ *n* member of the British Labour Party, devoted to the interests of labor

Lab·ra·dor /lab′rədôr′/ *n* 1 large peninsula in E Canada; 2 the portion of the province of Newfoundland in the eastern end of this peninsula

la·bur·num /ləburn′əm/ [L] *n* any of a genus (*Laburnum*) of ornamental trees or shrubs, bearing hanging clusters of pea-shaped yellow flowers

lab·y·rinth /lab′ərinth/ [Gk *labyrinthos*] *n* 1 structure with many intricate and confusing passages; maze; 2 complicated or confusing situation; 3 **Labyrinth** *Gk myth.* bewildering maze constructed in Crete by Daedalus for King Minos to house the Minotaur ‖ **lab′y·rin′thine** /-rin′thin/ *adj*

lac /lak′/ [Hindi *lākh*] *n* dark-red resinous substance deposited by a scale insect (*Carteria lacca*) on trees in India, used in sealing wax, varnish, and shellac

lace /lās/ [OF *laz* < L *laqueus* noose] *n* **1** cord or string passed through holes to bind or fasten; **2** netlike ornamental fabric made from fine thread ‖ *vt* **3** to fasten with or as with a lace; **4** to pull together or compress by means of a lace; **5** to weave or twine together; **6** to provide with laces; **7** to lash, whip; **8** to streak; **9** to add a dash of liquor to ‖ *vi* **10** **lace into** to attack verbally or physically

lac·er·ate /las′ərāt′/ [L *lacerare* (-*atus*)] *vt* to tear or mangle ‖ **lac′-er·a′tion** *n*

lace′wing′ *n* any of various insects (family Chrysopidae) with delicately veined, lacelike wings, and brilliant eyes

Lach·e·sis /lak′isis/ *n class. myth.* that one of the three Fates who measures the thread of life

lach·ry·mose /lak′rimōs′ [< L *lacrima* tear] *adj* **1** tearful; **2** causing tears; mournful

lac′ing *n* **1** lace or cord; **2** thrashing

lack /lak′/ [ME *lak* fault] *vt* **1** to be without; not have; **2** to fall short by ‖ *vi* **3** to be wanting; be missing; **4** **be lacking in** to be deficient in ‖ *n* **5** want; deficiency; **6** that which is lacking

lack·a·dai·si·cal /lak′ədāz′ikəl/ [< *archaic interj alack-a-day!*] *adj* languishing; listless; lethargical ‖ **lack′-a·dai′si·cal·ly** *adv*

lack·ey /lak′ē/ [< MF *laquais*] *n* **1** male servant; **2** toady; servile follower

lack′ing *adj* **1** deficient ‖ *prep* **2** without

lack′lus′ter *adj* lacking luster; dull

la·con·ic /ləkon′ik/ [< Gk *Lakon* Spartan] *adj* saying much in a few words; concise ‖ **la·con′i·cal·ly** *adv* ‖ SYN succinct, brief, concise, pithy, terse (see *short*)

lac·quer /lak′ər/ [< Port *laca* lac] *n* **1** transparent varnish made by dissolving a resin or a cellulose ester in a volatile solvent; **2** any of various varnishes made with resin, esp. one made from the sap of certain Japanese trees; **3** woodwork coated with such a varnish and often inlaid ‖ *vt* **4** to coat with lacquer

la·crosse /ləcrôs′, -kros′/ [CanF = the crook] *n* game originated by North American Indians, in which two teams try to send a ball into each other's goal, using sticks with webbed pockets

lac·tate /lak′tāt/ [< L *lac* milk] *n* **1** salt or ester of lactic acid ‖ *vi* **2** to secrete milk ‖ **lac·ta′tion** *n*

lac·tic /lak′tik/ *adj* pert. to or derived from milk

lac′tic ac′id *n* colorless syrupy liquid —CH₃CHOHCOOH— occurring in sour milk and in the fermentation of vegetable juices

lac·tose /lak′tōs/ *n* white crystalline powder of sweetish taste —C₁₂H₂₂O₁₁— obtained from whey and used in pharmacy and in infant foods; also called **milk sugar**

la·cu·na /ləkyōōn′ə/ [L = ditch] *n* (-nas or -nae /-nē/) blank or gap

lac·y /lās′ē/ *adj* (-i·er; -i·est) lacelike

lad /lad′/ [ME *ladde* follower] *n* **1** boy, youth; **2** *colloq* chap

lad·der /lad′ər/ [OE *hlǣder*] *n* **1** device for climbing, consisting of two sidepieces connected by rungs; **2** any means of rising or climbing

lad′die *n Scot* boy, lad

lad·en /lād′ən/ *adj* loaded; burdened

la′dies′ man′ *n* man who seeks the company of women and strives to please them

la′dies′ room′ *n* public lavatory for women

La·di·no /lədēn′ō/ [Sp < L *Latinus* Latin] *n* dialect of Spanish spoken by the descendants of the Jews exiled from Spain and written in Hebrew characters

la·dle /lād′əl/ [OE *hlædel*] *n* **1** longhandled spoon or dipper for transferring liquids ‖ *vt* **2** to pour out with or as with a ladle

la·dy /lād′ē/ [OE *hlǣfdīge*] *n* (-dies) **1** woman of good family and position, or of refinement and breeding, corresponding to *gentleman*; **2** any woman; **3 Lady** *Brit* a title of the wife of any nobleman below the rank of duke; **b** courtesy title of the wife of a baronet or knight

la′dy·bug′ also **la′dy·bird′** *n* any of various small, brightly colored beetles of the family Coccinellidae

la′dy·fin′ger *n* small finger-shaped sponge cake

la′dy·in·wait′ing *n* (ladies-in-waiting) lady who attends a queen or princess

la′dy·kill′er *n* man who is peculiarly fascinating to women

la′dy·like′ *adj* befitting a lady

la′dy of the eve′ning *n* prostitute

la′dy·ship′ *n* **1** rank or dignity of a lady; **2** *Brit* title applied to ladies (preceded by *her* or *your*)

La·fa·yette, Mar·quis de /märkē′dəlaf′ē·et′/ *n* (1757–1834) French soldier, statesman, and patriot; general in the American Revolutionary Army

lag /lag′/ [prob < Scand] *v* (lagged; lag·ging) *vi* **1** to fall behind; fail to keep up ‖ *n* **2** a falling behind; **3** amount of this; **4** time lapse

lag′ bolt′ *n* bolt or screw with a square head

la′ger (beer′) /läg′ər/ [G *Lagerbier*] *n* beer aged from six weeks to six months after brewing

lag·gard /lag′ərd/ [< *lag*] *n* one who or that which lags behind

la·gniappe also **la·gnappe** /lanyap′/

[LaF] n southern U.S. small gratuity or present given by a tradesman to a customer

la·goon /ləgōōn′/ [It laguna] n 1 shallow water separated from the sea by sand dunes or coral reefs; 2 shallow channel, usu. an inlet of the sea

lag′ screw′ n wood screw with a square or hexagonal head to be driven by a wrench

La·gos /lä′gōs, lā′-/ n capital of Nigeria (675,000)

la·ic /lā′ik/ [Gk laikos of the people] adj 1 lay, secular || n 2 layman

laid /lād/ pt & pp of lay⁸

lain /lān/ pp of lie²

lair /ler′/ [OE leger bed] n 1 den of a wild beast; 2 hideout, as of criminals

laird /lerd/ [Sc form of lord] n Scot master of a landed estate

lais·sez faire /les′āfer′/ [F = let act] n noninterference, esp. by the government in economic affairs || **lais′-sez-faire′** adj

la·i·ty /lā′itē/ [< lay⁸] n laymen collectively

lake /lāk/ [OF lac < L lacus] n large body of water surrounded by land

Lake′ Coun′try or **Dis′trict** n region in NW England noted for its many beautiful lakes

Lake′ Po′ets npl Wordsworth, Coleridge, and Southey, who lived in the Lake Country

lake′ trout′ n large North American food fish (Salvelinus namaycush)

Lal′ly col′umn /läl′ē/ [trademark] n tubular steel column filled with concrete

lam /lam/ [< Scand] slang v (lammed; lam·ming) vt 1 to beat, thrash || vt 2 lam out of to leave in great haste, flee from || n 3 on the lam fleeing and in hiding from the police; 4 take it on the lam to leave in great haste; flee

la·ma /läm′ə/ [Tibetan] n priest or monk of Lamaism

La′ma·ism n the Buddhism of Tibet and Mongolia

lamb /lam/ [OE] n 1 young sheep; 2 flesh of young sheep used as food; 3 one who is gentle or innocent; 4 the Lamb Christ || vt 5 to give birth to a lamb

lam·baste /lambāst′/ [lam + baste beat] vt 1 to beat severely; 2 to excoriate

lamb·da /lam′də/ n eleventh letter of the Greek alphabet Δ, λ

lam·bent /lam′bənt/ [L lambens (-entis) licking] adj 1 playing lightly over the surface, as flame; 2 softly radiant; 3 gently brilliant, as wit || **lam′ben·cy** n

lam·bert /lam′bərt/ [J. H. Lambert (1728–77) G scientist] n cgs unit of brightness, being the brightness of a diffusing surface which emits one lumen per square centimeter

lamb′kin n little lamb

lame /lām′/ [OE lama] adj 1 crippled, esp. in a leg or foot, so that movement is difficult; 2 insufficient, ineffectual, as a lame excuse || vt 3 to cripple or disable

la·mé /lamā′/ [F] n fabric of metal threads mixed with silk, wool, or the like

lame′ duck′ n 1 officeholder who is serving out his time after failing of reelection; 2 weakling; ineffective person || **lame′-duck′** adj

la·ment /ləment′/ [L lamentari] vt 1 to mourn for; feel or express sorrow for || vt 2 to feel or express grief or sorrow; mourn || n 3 expression of grief or sorrow || **lam·en·ta·ble** /lam′əntəbəl/ adj || **lam′en·ta′tion** n || SYN v bewail, mourn, sorrow, grieve, beweep, bemoan, deplore || ANT v exult, triumph, rejoice

la·ment′ed adj mourned for

lam·i·nate /lam′ināt′/ [< L lamina thin plate] vt 1 to roll or press into a thin sheet; 2 to separate into thin layers by splitting; 3 to construct by joining several layers together || vt 4 to separate into thin layers || **lam′i·nat′ed** adj

lamp /lamp′/ [OF lampe < Gk] n 1 vessel in which an inflammable liquid is burned for light by means of a wick; 2 any device for furnishing light; 3 any of various devices for furnishing heat or therapeutic radiation || vt 4 slang to gaze at

lamp′black′ n fine soot of pure carbon formed by the imperfect combustion of oil, gas, etc., used as a pigment

lam·poon /lampōōn′/ [F lampon drinking song] n 1 sharp, often bitter satirical writing directed against persons or institutions || vt 2 to ridicule in a lampoon || **lam·poon′er** n

lam·prey /lamp′rē/ [OF lampreie] n any of various eellike fishes (order Hyperoartia) with a circular sucking mouth and rasplike teeth, very destructive to other fishes

lance /lans′, läns/ [OF < L lancea] n 1 thrusting weapon consisting of a long wooden shaft with a sharp spearhead; 2 lancer; 3 lancet || vt 4 to open with or as with a lancet

lance′ cor′po·ral n mil enlisted man ranking below a corporal

Lan·ce·lot /lan′səlot′, län′-/ n lover of Guinevere, bravest of King Arthur's knights

lanc′er n cavalry soldier armed with a lance

lan·cet /lan′sit, län′-/ n surgeon's small knife, with a sharp point and two edges

land /land/ [OE] n 1 the part of the earth's surface not covered by water; 2 country; region; 3 people; nation; 4 ground; soil; 5 real estate; 6 rural areas, as distinguished from the city || *vt* 7 to bring to, or set on, shore or the ground; 8 to bring to a place or condition, as *his actions landed him in jail;* 9 to get, secure, as a fish or a job || *vi* 10 to come or go ashore; 11 to come to land or a port; 12 to arrive at a place, as *to land in the hospital;* 13 to alight, come to earth

land′ breeze′ *n* evening breeze moving from land to sea

land′ed *adj* 1 owning land; 2 consisting of land

land′er *n* small spaceship, manned or unmanned, designed to land on the moon or a planet and sometimes return to a larger spaceship

land′fall′ *n* 1 first land sighted after a voyage; 2 act of sighting it; 3 landing by ship or plane; 4 landslide

land′-grant′ *adj* (college or university) receiving support from the U.S. government under certain laws

land′hold′er *n* holder, occupier, or owner of land

land′ing *n* 1 act of one who or that which lands; 2 place where goods or persons are landed from a ship; 3 platform at the end of a flight of steps

land′ing gear′ *n* wheels of an aircraft, which are lowered to permit it to land

land′la′dy *n* (**-dies**) 1 woman who leases land, buildings, or apartments to tenants; 2 woman who operates a rooming house or inn

land′locked′ *adj* 1 nearly or wholly enclosed by land; 2 (country or place) without access to the sea

land′lord′ *n* 1 one who leases land, buildings, or apartments to others; 2 master of an inn, rooming house, or the like

land′lub′ber *n* 1 one who has had little or no experience at sea; 2 one who is awkward on shipboard

land′mark′ *n* 1 something that marks a land boundary; 2 any conspicuous land feature, used as a guide by travelers and navigators; 3 any prominent feature or occurrence

land′mass′ *n* great extent of land in all directions

land′ mine′ *n* explosive charge placed under the surface of the ground and detonated by pressure

land′-of′fice busi′ness *n colloq* very profitable business

land′scape′ /-skāp′/ [MD *lantscap*] *n* 1 section of land seen as one view; 2 picture representing natural scenery || *vt* 3 to improve the appearance of (a plot of ground), as by planting lawns, trees, and shrubs

land′slide′ *n* 1 sliding of a mass of soil or rocks down a slope; 2 the mass itself; 3 overwhelming electoral victory

land′ward /-wərd/ *adj* & *adv* toward the land || **land′wards** *adv*

lane /lān′/ [OE] *n* 1 narrow way, road, or byway; 2 designated route followed by ships and airplanes; 3 marked-off path on a highway wide enough for one vehicle

lang·syne /laŋ′sīn′, -zīn′/ [Sc = long since] *adv* 1 long ago || *n* 2 the days of long ago

lan·guage /laŋ′gwij/ [AF] *n* 1 arbitrary system of vocal symbols by means of which human beings interact and communicate; 2 particular speech of a people or nation; 3 any conventionalized system of communication, as *the language of signs,* the *language of flowers;* 4 particular manner of expression; style; 5 particular speech of a group or profession || SYN speech, dialect, idiom, tongue, expression, diction, vernacular, patois, lingo, jargon, argot, slang || DISCR *Language* is, in its general sense, a means of conveying ideas. Among human beings ideas are conveyed by words, by expressive gestures, eyes, signs, or symbols. A nation which uses the same store of words in the same way possesses a *language;* we study the dead *languages* of ancient, vanished countries. We speak of the *language* of the eyes, of flowers. *Speech* is the power to utter articulate sound; also, the sound articulated or the thing said; in this latter sense *speech* and *language* are used interchangeably, as his *speech* was that of an educated man. The method of communication ascribed to animals, however, is their *language,* not their *speech.* A *tongue* is the *language* of a nation. *Idiom* is a distinguishing character peculiar to a *language,* perceived in the turn of its words and phrases, or in the nature of its construction. The way in which we use "shall" and "will" is idiomatic; such usages, the very bone of our English, are hardest for foreigners to grasp. *Vernacular* is the *language* belonging to one by birth; it is the mother tongue, conceived of particularly as unenriched by foreign additions and unweighted by the scholarly or heavy. A *dialect* is a *language* within a language, grown up or surviving in a district or in a certain class, with *idiom,* pronunciation, and vocabulary distinguishable from that of the main *language,* and admitted to it, though not recognized except as a subordinate part of, the main *language. Slang* consists of a body of words or phrases, or words in special senses, in a current, often rapidly passing, use. *Slang* may be coarse; it may be the characteristic cant of a club, a race track, or a group of students; or it may be merely colloquial, familiar *speech.* In the last-mentioned case, if it possesses aptness or force, it may become a part of standard English. *Lingo, jargon,* and *argot* are the special *languages* used by certain classes. *Jargon* is confused gibberish; it names a mode of *speech* full of unfamiliar terms, as that of baseball enthusiasts, students, or the like. *Argot* is particularly the secret *jargon* of thieves and tramps. A backwoodsman might style the *speech* of a scholar *lingo*; a foreign *language,* not understood, is sometimes contemptuously referred to as *lingo,* as is the vocabulary of an unfamiliar subject, as pugilists', scientists' *lingo. Jargon* also names *language* fallen into a barbarous state

lan·guid /laŋ'gwid/ [L *languidus*] *adj* 1 drooping; weak; 2 slow, spiritless; 3 feeble, without force ‖ SYN faint, flagging, listless, sluggish, inert, dull, wearied ‖ ANT active, eager, vigorous, energetic, fresh

lan·guish /laŋ'gwish/ [MF *languir* (-*guiss-*)] *vi* 1 to lose strength or animation; 2 to become slack or feeble; 3 to droop or pine away; 4 to assume a look of melancholy

lan·guor /laŋ'gər/ [L] *n* 1 weariness; lassitude, listlessness; 2 dreamy indolence ‖ **lan'guor·ous** *adj*

lank /laŋk/ [OE *hlanc*] *adj* 1 lean, thin; 2 (hair) without curl or wave ‖ **lank'ness** *n* ‖ SYN gaunt, thin, spare, meager, bony (see *lean²*)

lank'y *adj* (-i·er; -i·est) 1 gaunt; 2 lean and ungraceful ‖ **lank'i·ness** *n*

lan·o·lin /lan'əlin/ [< L *lana* wool + *oleum* oil] *n* fatty substance obtained from sheep's wool, used in ointments

Lan·sing /lan'siŋ/ *n* capital of Michigan (110,000)

lan·tern /lant'ərn/ [L *lanterna*] *n* 1 lamp, portable or fixed to a wall or post, consisting of a transparent or translucent case and an illuminating flame or a battery-powered electric light; 2 room at the top of a lighthouse containing the lamp; 3 partially open, towerlike structure on the roof of a building to give light and air to the interior

lan'tern-jawed' *adj* having a long thin face with hollow cheeks

lan'tern slide' *n* slide for a slide projector or magic lantern

lan·tha·num /lan'thənəm/ [< Gk *lanthanein* to lurk] *n* rare-earth metallic element (La; at.no. 57; at.wt. 138.91)

lan·yard /lan'yərd/ [MF *laniere* leather band] *n* 1 short cord for suspending something, as a whistle from the neck; 2 strong line with a hook attached, used in firing certain cannon

La·o·co·on /lā·ok'ō·on'/ [Gk] *n class. myth.* priest of Apollo who warned the Trojans against the wooden horse and with his two sons was

strangled by two serpents which Athena summoned from the sea

La·os /lä'ōs/ *n* people's republic in SE Asia (3,600,000; 91,400 sq.m.; cap. Vientiane) ‖ **La·o·tian** /lā·ōsh'ən/ *adj & n*

lap¹ /lap/ [OE *læppa*] *n* 1 front part of the body from the waist to the knees when seated; 2 the part of the clothing covering this; 3 place for supporting, sheltering, or rearing; 4 a that part of an object that overlaps another; b overlap; c measure or degree of overlap; 5 one complete circuit of a race course; 6 revolving disk used for cutting and polishing, as gems ‖ *v* (lapped; lap·ping) *vt* 7 to fold over; wrap; 8 to enfold, as *lapped in luxury*; 9 to overlap; 10 to get ahead of by a lap in a race; 11 to cut or polish with a lap ‖ *vi* 12 to be folded; 13 to overlap

lap² [OE *lapian*] *v* (lapped; lap·ping) *vt* 1 to take up (liquid) with the tongue, as an animal; 2 to wash or splash gently against, as waves; 3 lap up, a *colloq* to receive with enthusiasm; b to drink by lapping ‖ *n* 4 act of lapping

La Paz /ləpäz'/ *n* seat of government of Bolivia (360,000)

la·pel /ləpel'/ [*dim.* of *lap¹*] *n* fold at either side of a coat front, forming a continuation of the collar

lap·i·dar·y /lap'ider'ē/ [< L *lapis* (-*idis*) stone] *n* (-ies) 1 one who cuts, polishes, engraves, or sets jewels ‖ *adj* 2 pert. to the work of a lapidary; 3 pert. to or suitable for inscriptions on monuments

lap·is laz·u·li /lap'is laz'yəli'/ [L = stone of azure] *n* 1 opaque semiprecious stone of deep-blue color; 2 its color

Lap·land /lap'land'/ *n* region of the N Scandinavian peninsula and the adjoining part of Russia

Lap'land'er *n* native or inhabitant of Lapland

Lapp /lap/ *n* 1 Laplander; 2 language of the Lapps

Lap'pish *n* language of the Lapps

lapse /laps/ [L *lapsus* error] *vi* 1 to become void; terminate; 2 to fall or depart, as from virtue; 3 to elapse; 4 to fall into disuse; 5 lapse into to fall or subside into (a state or condition) ‖ *n* 6 interval of time; 7 slip, as of memory, tongue, or pen; 8 slight deviation from what is usual or right; 9 a passing into disuse; 10 termination of a claim or right through negligence or failure to exercise it ‖ SYN *n* default, error, mistake, deviation, decline

lar·ce·ny /lärs'ənē/ [MF *larcin* theft] *n* (-ies) unlawful taking away of another's property ‖ **lar'ce·nous** *adj*

larch /lärch/ [G *Lärche* < L *larix*] *n* any of a genus (*Larix*) of cone-bearing trees yielding a tough wood

lard /lärd/ [MF < L *lardum*] *n* 1 semisolid fat or grease prepared from melted hog's fat ‖ *vt* 2 to smear with lard; grease; 3 to enrich by the insertion of strips of pork or bacon before roasting; 4 to garnish or embellish

lar·der *n* place where food supplies are kept; pantry

lar·es and pe·na·tes /ler′ēz ənd pə-nāt′ēz/ [L] *npl* 1 household gods of the ancient Romans; 2 one's cherished household possessions

large /lärj/ [OF < L *largus* abundant] *adj* 1 great in size, scale, scope, or extent ‖ *n* 2 **at large,** a in full; in detail; b free, unconfined; c representing a whole state, county, or city rather than a specified district ‖ *adv* 3 **by and large** in general; in all respects ‖ **large′ness** *n* ‖ SYN big, broad, abundant, bulky, colossal, enormous, huge, massive, spacious, great, ample, immense

large′ in·tes′tine *n* shorter section of the intestines, comprising the cecum, colon, and rectum, which eliminates the waste matter of digestion

large′ly *adv* 1 mainly; 2 much

lar·gess /lärjes′, lär′jis/ [OF *largesse*] *n* 1 generous giving; 2 generous gift ‖ SYN present, gratuity, gift, bestowal, dole (see *boon*)

lar·go /lär′gō/ [It = slow] *mus adj & adv* 1 slow and stately ‖ *n* 2 largo movement

lar·i·at /lar′ē·ət/ [Sp *la reata* the lariat] *n* 1 rope for tethering horses; 2 lasso

lark¹ /lärk/ [OE *lāwerce*] *n* 1 any of various Old World songbirds (family Alaudidae), as the skylark; 2 any of various birds resembling larks

lark² [?] *n* 1 frolic; hilarious time ‖ *vi* 2 to frolic; have a hilarious time

lark′spur′ *n* any of a genus (*Delphinium*) of plants with showy spurred pink or blue flowers

lar·rup /lar′əp/ [prob < D *larp*] *vt colloq* to beat, thrash

lar·va /lär′və/ [L = ghost, mask] *n* (-vae /-vē/) 1 immature, often wormlike form of insects that undergo metamorphosis; 2 early form of any animal that is structurally unlike the adult, as a tadpole ‖ **lar′val** *adj*

lar·yn·gi·tis /lar′injīt′is/ [< *larynx*] *n* inflammation of the larynx

la·ryn′go·scope′ /ləriŋ′gə-/ *n* instrument for visually examining the larynx

lar·ynx /lar′iŋks/ [Gk] *n* (-ynx·es or la·ryn′ges /lərin′jēz/) upper part of the windpipe, a boxlike formation of cartilage and muscles in the throat containing the vocal cords

las·civ·i·ous /ləsiv′ē·əs/ [< L *lascivus* wanton] *adj* 1 lustful, lewd; 2 expressing or arousing lustful desires ‖ **las·civ′i·ous·ly** *adv* ‖ **las·civ′i·ous-**

ness *n* ‖ SYN unchaste, impure, lewd, licentious, sensual, salacious ‖ ANT chaste, pure, continent, restrained

la·ser /lāz′ər/ [light amplification by stimulated emission of radiation] *n* device that concentrates electromagnetic radiation into a narrow beam and amplifies it as visible light

lash¹ /lash/ [ME *lasshe*] *vt* 1 to beat or drive as with a whip; 2 to rebuke, berate ‖ *vt* 3 to strike out at someone or something, as with a whip or weapon; 4 **lash out at** to attack vigorously with weapons or words ‖ *n* 5 flexible part of a whip; 6 stroke of a whip; 7 goad; 8 eyelash

lash² [ME *laschen* to lace] *vt* to fasten or bind with a cord or rope

lass /las/ [ME *lasse*] *n* 1 girl or young woman; 2 sweetheart

las′sie *n* young girl

las·si·tude /las′it(y)o͞od′/ [L *lassitudo*] *n* weariness; lack of energy ‖ SYN languor, debility, exhaustion, droopiness, indifference ‖ ANT vigor, energy, vitality, freshness, briskness

las·so /las′ō/ [Sp *lazo*] *n* (-sos or -oes) 1 rope with a running noose for roping horses and cattle ‖ *vt* 2 to catch with a lasso

last¹ /last/, läst/ [OE *lǣste*] *n* wooden or metal model of the foot for making or repairing shoes

last² [OE *lætest, superl* of *læt* late] *adj* 1 being at the end, after all others; final; 2 only remaining; 3 next before the present, most recent; 4 least likely, as *he is the last man I would pick* ‖ *adv* 5 after all the others; 6 on the most recent occasion; 7 in conclusion; finally ‖ *n* 8 **at last** finally; 9 **breathe one's last** to die; 10 **the last of,** a the end of, as *the last of June;* b the remainder of, as *that's the last of the money;* c the final appearance of, as *we've seen the last of him* ‖ SYN *adj* final, latest, ultimate, conclusive ‖ DISCR That is *last* which comes after all others or comes at the end, as the *last* company in the parade; the *last* bus; trust a woman to have the *last* word. *Last* is also used to designate that which is nearest now or the present, as *last* week; it designates, too, the most recent, as his *last* story; her *last* baby. *Latest* differs from *last* as earliest differs from first; *latest* is applied only to the order of time; the *latest* news is up to the *latest* minute; the *latest* bus may also be the *last* bus; but "his *latest* book" may bear a different sense from "his *last* book." *Ultimate* designates that beyond which nothing more exists or is possible; *ultimate* may refer to the remote future, knowledge yet unplumbed, and the like, as the *ultimate* object, result, destiny; or it may refer to the remote past, or all that which has preceded regarded as a factor, as the *ultimate* cause; *ultimate* source; or it may describe the *last* that can be obtained, delved into, or traced out, as *ultimate* analysis. That is *final* which comes at the end, is terminating, is followed or can be followed by nothing else; the *final* performance of a play is the *last* performance; the *final* session of Congress; the *final* cause is, specifically, the end or purpose for which anything is done. That is *conclusive* which is convincing or decisive; a *conclusive* argument ends the discussion; a *conclusive* reply decides a matter one way or the other

last² [OE *læstan* to fulfil] *vi* 1 to continue in time or in existence; 2 to be sufficient; hold out; 3 to endure; wear well

last'ing *adj* durable; enduring; permanent ‖ SYN durable, stable (see *permanent*)

Last' Judg'ment *n* final judgment of all mankind, living and dead, at the end of the world

last'ly *adv* finally; in conclusion

last' name' *n* name that one has in common with other members of his family

last' quar'ter *n* time when, after full moon, half the moon's disk is lighted by the sun

last' sleep' *n* death

last' straw' [< the straw that broke the camel's back] *n* final crushing blow or insupportable irritation

Last' Sup'per *n* supper eaten by Jesus and his disciples on the night before the Crucifixion

last' word' *n* 1 final remark, as in an argument; 2 *colloq* latest style

lat. latitude

Lat. Latin

latch /lach'/ [OE *læccan* to grasp] *n* 1 fastening device for a door or gate, consisting of a bar that fits into a catch or groove ‖ *vt* 2 to fasten or close with a latch ‖ *vi* 3 to close by means of a latch; 4 **latch onto** *colloq* to get, obtain

late /lāt'/ [OE *læt*] *adj* 1 coming, occurring, or acting after the usual time; tardy; delayed; 2 occurring toward the end or close, as *a late hour*; 3 recent; 4 immediately preceding, as *the late mayor*; 5 deceased; 6 lasting far into the night, as *late parties*; 7 protracted, as *a late meeting*; 8 occurring at an advanced stage, as *late Victorian, late in life*; 9 of late lately ‖ *adv* 10 after the expected time; 11 recently, but no longer; 12 until after the usual time ‖ **late'ness** *n* ‖ SYN *adj* tardy, slow, delayed (see *modern*)

late' bloom'er *n* person, esp. a young person, whose abilities and interests are slow in developing

la·teen' sail' /lăten'/ [< L *latina*] *n* three-cornered sail attached to a long sloping yard

Late' Lat'in *n* the Latin of from the third to the seventh centuries, esp. as used by the early church fathers

late'ly *adv* recently

la·tent /lāt'ənt/ [L *latens* (-*entis*) hidden] *adj* 1 present but not apparent; not developed or active; 2 dormant (disease) ‖ **la'ten·cy** *n* ‖ SYN dormant, quiescent, hidden, potential, invisible, inactive ‖ ANT manifest, operative, developed

la'tent heat' *n* heat absorbed during a change of state from solid to liquid to gas, and radiated during the reverse process

lat·er·al /lat'ərəl/ [< L *latus* (*lateris*) side] *adj* 1 pert. to, proceeding from, or situated at or toward, the side ‖ *n* 2 *phonet* sound articulated with the breath passing on both sides of the tongue, as *l*; 3 *football* pass thrown parallel to the goal line

Lat·er·an /lat'ərən/ [L *Lateranus* Roman family name] *n* church of Saint John Lateran in Rome, the church of the Pope as bishop of Rome

la·tex /lā'teks/ [L = liquid] *n* milky juice secreted by certain plants, as the rubber tree

lath /lath', lăth'/ [OE *læt*] *n* (**laths** /-*thz*, -ths/) *n* 1 one of the thin, narrow strips of wood nailed to the framework of a house to support plaster; 2 coarse-meshed woven wire used similarly; 3 laths collectively ‖ *vt* 4 to cover with laths

lathe /lāth'/ [ME *lath* stand, support] *n* machine in which articles of wood or metal are shaped by turning against a cutting tool

lath·er /lath'ər/ [OE *lēathor* soap] *n* 1 foam made from soap and water; 2 profuse, foamy sweat ‖ *vi* 3 to form lather ‖ *vt* 4 to apply lather to ‖ **lath'er·y** *adj*

Lat·in /lat'ən/ [L *Latinus*] *n* 1 language of the ancient Romans; 2 native or inhabitant of ancient Latium, the province including Rome; 3 member of one of the peoples speaking a language derived from Latin, as the Spaniards, Argentines, and Rumanians ‖ also *adj*

Lat'in A·mer'i·ca *n* the part of the New World south of the U.S. in which Romance languages are spoken ‖ **Lat'in A·mer'i·can** *adj* & *n*

Lat'in Church' *n* Roman Catholic Church

Lat'in Quar'ter *n* section of Paris on the left bank of the Seine, frequented by students and artists

lat·i·tude /lat'ĭt(y)ōōd'/ [L *latitudo* breadth] *n* 1 angular distance of any point on the earth's surface north or south of the equator; 2 range; extent; **3** degree of freedom or independence of rules ‖ **lat′i-tu′di-nal** adj

la-trine /lətrēn′/ [F < L *latrina* place for washing] n toilet, esp. one consisting of a trench, as in a camp

-la-try /-lətrē/ [Gk *latreia*] n comb form worship, as *idolatry*

lat-ter /lat′ər/ [OE *lætra* comp of *læt* late] adj **1** more recent; later; **2** belonging to the end of a period of time; **3** second of two mentioned (correlative of *former*)

Lat′ter Day′ Saint′ n Mormon

lat′ter-ly adv **1** lately; **2** in a later period

lat-tice /lat′is/ [MF *lattis*] n **1** openwork made by crossed or interlaced strips of metal or wood; **2** door, window, or gate, having or made of a lattice

Lat-vi-a /lat′vē-ə/ n formerly independent country in NE Europe on the Baltic, now a constituent republic of the Soviet Union (2,100,000; 24,400 sq.m.; cap. Riga) ‖ **Lat′vi-an** adj & n

laud /lôd′/ [< L *laus* (*laudis*) praise] vt to praise highly; extol ‖ **laud′a-ble** adj

lau-da-num /lôd′(ə)nəm/ [< L *ladanum* gum resin] n tincture of opium

laud′a-to′ry /-tôr′-, -tōr′-/ adj expressing praise

laugh /laf′, läf′/ [OE *hlehhan*] vi **1** to express emotions such as mirth, ridicule, derision, or the like, by convulsive sounds accompanied by contortions of the face; **2 laugh at,** to be amused by; **b** to ridicule ‖ vt **3** to express or utter with laughter; **4** to move or affect by laughter, as *they laughed her out of her bad mood;* **5 laugh off** to dismiss as unfounded, ridiculous, or insignificant ‖ n **6** act or sound of laughing; **7** cause of laughter

laugh′a-ble adj mirth-provoking; causing hilarity; funny ‖ SYN droll, comical, amusing, witty, facetious, absurd, humorous; queer, odd (see *ludicrous*)

laugh′ing adj no **laughing matter** something too serious to be laughed off

laugh′ing gas′ n nitrous oxide, used as an anesthetic, esp. in dentistry

laugh′ing-stock′ n object of ridicule; butt of jokes

laugh′ter n action or sound of laughing

launch¹ /lônch′, länch′/ [AF *lancher* < L *lanceare* to throw a lance] vt **1** to hurl or discharge (a missile or rocket); **2** to cause (a newly constructed vessel) to glide into the water; **3** to set in the water, as a boat or launch; **4** to send forth; start; set in motion or operation ‖ vi **5 launch into** to plunge into; start with vigor

launch² [Sp *lancha* < Malay *lanchār*

speedy] n **1** large, open boat; **2** largest of the boats carried by a warship

launch′ing pad′ n platform from which a rocket or guided missile is launched

laun-der /lôn′dər, län′-/ [< MF *lavandier* washerwoman] vt **1** to wash or wash and iron (clothes) ‖ vi **2** to undergo laundering ‖ **laun′der-er** n ‖ **laun′dress** n*fem*

Laun′dro-mat′ /-drəmat′/ [trademark] n coin-operated self-service laundry

laun′dry n (-dries) **1** place where clothes are laundered; **2** articles of clothing laundered or to be laundered

laun′dry-man′ /-man′/ n (-men′ /-men′/) man who picks up and delivers laundry

lau-re-ate /lôr′ē-it/ [L *laureatus* crowned with laurel] adj **1** crowned with laurel as a mark of victory or distinction; **2** having great distinction; **3** having received special recognition (often placed after the noun), as *poet laureate* ‖ n **4** one who has been honored for achievement; **5** poet laureate ‖ **lau′re-ate-ship′** n

lau-rel /lôr′əl, lor′-/ [< OF *lorier* < L *laurus*] n **1** evergreen shrub (*Laurus nobilis*) of southern Europe; **2** any tree of the genus *Laurus*, or any of various similar trees; **3** wreath of laurel foliage, used for decoration or as an emblem of victory; **4 laurels** pl honor won

Lau-ren-ti-an /lôrensh′(ē)ən/ [< L *Laurentius* Lawrence] adj of or pert. to the St. Lawrence River

la-va /läv′ə, lav′ə/ [It] n **1** melted rock issuing from a volcano; **2** such substance solidified by cooling

lav-a-liere or **lav-a-llier** /lav′əlir′, läv′-/ [F *lavallière* loose flowing necktie] n ornamental pendant hanging from a chain worn around the neck

lav-a-to-ry /lav′ətôr′ē, -tōr′-/ [LL *lavatorium*] n (-ries) **1** washroom; **2** washbasin; **3** toilet

lave /läv′/ [L *lavare* to wash] vt & vi archaic to wash; bathe

lav-en-der /lav′əndər/ [AF *lavendre*] n **1** fragrant European plant (*Lavandula vera*) of the mint family; **2** its dried flowers and leaves, used in sachets; **3** pale purple

lav-ish /lav′ish/ [MF *lavasse* downpour] adj **1** giving or producing profusely; prodigal; **2** abundant; excessive ‖ vt **3** to bestow liberally ‖ **lav′ish-ly** adv ‖ SYN adj wasteful, profuse, bountiful, free-handed

law /lô′/ [OE *lagu* < Scand] n **1** binding rule of action established by authority; **2** enactment by a legislative body; **3** body of rules and regulations recognized as binding; **4** state of society produced by the existence and enforcement of such a body of rules; **5** rule of action or conduct established by custom, as *the laws of courtesy;* **6** authoritative injunction; **7** litigation; **8** jurisprudence; **9** legal profession; **10** legal knowledge, as *his law is sound;* **11** statement of the invariable occurrence of certain natural phenomena in the same way under specified conditions; established principle; **12** rules of procedure; recognized usage; **13** *Bib* moral and ceremonial code ascribed to Moses; **14 lay down the law** to give orders in no uncertain terms ‖ **SYN** edict, decree, code, commandment, enactment, mandate, order, ordinance, statute, regulation

law′ and or′der *n* state of obedience to the laws and resultant domestic tranquility

law′ful *adj* **1** permitted by law; **2** legal; legitimate ‖ **SYN** legal, legitimate, authorized,-allowable

law′less *adj* **1** contrary to law; **2** disorderly; unruly

law′mak′er *n* legislator

lawn¹ /lôn′/ [prob < *Laon* France] *n* fine, thin linen or cotton fabric

lawn² [MF *lande* heath < Celt] *n* plot of closely mowed grass

lawn′ mow′er *n* machine for mowing grass

lawn′ ten′nis *n* tennis played on a grass court

law′ of av′er·ag·es *n* **1** statistical principle of the proportional frequency between random drawings of an event and all the occurrences of the event; **2** idea that in the long run things will break even and, therefore, a hoped-for outcome will emerge

law′ of grav·i·ta′tion *n* statement that the attraction between any two particles in the universe is directly proportional to the products of their masses and inversely proportional to the distance between them

Law′ of Mo′ses *n* ancient law of the Hebrews, contained in the Pentateuch and attributed to Moses

law′ of na′tions *n* body of rules recognized by civilized nations as binding in their relations with each other

law′ of the jun′gle *n* behavior of wild animals and of human beings not restrained by any of the established laws of civilization

law·ren·ci·um /lôren′sē·əm/ [*Lawrence* Radiation Laboratory in Berkeley, Calif.] *n* synthetic radioactive metallic element (Lw; at.no. 103)

laws′ of mo′tion *npl* three laws in dynamics, formulated by Sir Isaac Newton—**a** first law: a body continues in a state of rest or of motion with constant velocity in a straight line unless acted upon by some external force; **b** second law: change in momentum is proportional to the

force causing the change and to the time during which it acts, and takes place in the same direction as the force; **c** third law: to every action there is an equal and opposite reaction

law′suit′ *n* action in a court for the settlement of a claim or the enforcement of a right

law′yer /-yər/ *n* one licensed to represent clients in court and to advise on legal matters

lax /laks/ [L *laxus* loose] *adj* **1** not firm or stiff; flabby; slack; **2** not strict; inexact; careless ‖ **lax′ness** *n* ‖ **SYN** yielding, relaxed, dissolute, loose, slack (see *negligent*) ‖ **ANT** severe, strict, energetic, heedful

lax·a·tive /laks′ətiv/ [< L *laxare* (-*atus*) to relax] *n* something that relieves constipation ‖ also *adj*

lax′i·ty *n* state or quality of being lax

lay¹ /lā/ [OF *lai*] *n* short poem meant to be sung

lay² [MF *lai* < Gk *laikos* of the people] *adj* of or pert. to laymen

lay³ [OE *lecgan*] *v* (**laid**) *vt* **1** to place, put, or deposit; cause to lie; **2** to place in orderly fashion, as bricks; **3** to construct or place in position, as foundations or floors; **4** to bring or beat down, as *a blow laid him low;* **5** to cause to subside, as dust; **6** to apply or place, as *to lay hands on someone;* **7** to cause to be in a given position or condition, as *to lay waste a country;* **8** to locate, as a scene; **9** to set (a table); **10** to impose, as a tax or penalty; **11** to ascribe or impute, as blame; **12** to present for consideration, as a claim or facts; **13** to devise, as a plan or plot; **14** to bet (someone); **15** to place on or over a surface, as a carpet; **16** to produce and deposit, as an egg; **17** *slang* to have sexual intercourse with; **18 lay aside, away,** or **by** to save or set aside for future use; **19 lay off, a** to dismiss (an employee) because of lack of work; **b** to measure; mark off; **20 lay open, a** to cut open; **b** to expose (oneself), as to criticism; **21 lay out, a** to spread out, arrange for use; **b** to plan or prepare; design; **c** *colloq* to spend; **d** to prepare (a corpse) for burial; **e** *slang* to knock (someone) unconscious; **f** to make a layout of; **22 lay up, a** to store for future use; **b** to cause to be confined in bed ‖ *vi* **23** to lay eggs; **24** *naut* to take up a specified position, as *to lay aft;* **25 lay into** *slang* to attack physically or verbally; **26 lay off** *slang* **a** to cease; **b** to stop annoying; **27 lay over** to make a temporary stop on a trip ‖ *v* (**layed**) *vt* **28** to bet, put up as a wager, as *I layed five dollars on that race* ‖ *n* **29** manner or position in which something lies, as *the lay of* *the land;* **30** *slang* a female partner in sexual intercourse; **b** act or instance of sexual intercourse

lay⁴ *pt* of **lie⁵**

lay'-by' *n Brit* siding on a highway to permit vehicles to stop without obstructing traffic

lay'er *n* **1** person or thing that lays; **2** one thickness, stratum, row, coating, or the like

lay'er cake' *n* cake made in layers, with a sweet filling between each layer

lay-ette' /-et'/ [F] *n* complete outfit of bedding, clothes, etc., for a newborn child

lay'man /-mən/ [< *lay⁵*] *n* (-men /-mən/) **1** one who is not a clergyman; **2** one who is not a member of a given profession or has no special knowledge of a given science or art

lay'off' *n* **1** act of laying off employees; **2** period of being without work

lay'out' *n* **1** act, process, or manner of laying something out; **2** arrangement or plan; **3** preliminary sketch of a newspaper page, advertisement, etc.

lay'o'ver *n* stopover

laz-a-ret-to /laz'əret'ō/ [It < Santa Maria di *Nazareth* hospital near Venice, influenced by *Lazaro* Lazarus] *n* **1** hospital for the care of persons with loathsome or contagious diseases, such as leprosy; **2** building or ship used as a quarantine station; **3** *naut* small space below deck, usually aft, where provisions and spare parts are kept

Laz-a-rus /laz'ərəs/ *n Bib* **1** brother of Mary and Martha, restored to life by Jesus (John 11); **2** beggar with loathsome sores in the parable of the rich man and the beggar (Luke 16:20–31)

laze /lāz'/ [< *lazy*] *vt* & *vi* to idle

la-zy /lāz'ē/ [?] *adj* (-zi-er; -zi-est) **1** indisposed to work or effort; indolent; **2** slow, sluggish || **la'zi-ly** *adv* || **la'zi-ness** *n* || SYN (see *idle*)

la'zy Su'san /sooz'ən/ *n* large revolving tray for holding several foods or condiments

lb. [< L *libra*] **1** pound; **2** also **lbs.** pounds

l.c. 1 *typ* lower case; **2** [L *loco citato*] in the place cited

lea /lē'/ [OE *lēah*] *n* grassy field, meadow

leach /lēch'/ [OE *leccan* to water] *vt* **1** to cause (a liquid) to drip or wash through something; **2** to extract by percolation || *vi* **3** to be extracted by percolation || *n* **4** substance through which water is percolated; **5** soluble substance obtained by leaching

lead¹ /led'/ [OE *lēad*] *n* **1** heavy, soft, malleable, bluish-white metallic element (Pb; at.no. 82; at.wt. 207.19), used for water pipes, roofing, bat-

teries, solder, radiation shielding, and in many alloys and compounds; **2** weight attached to a rope, as for measuring depths at sea; **3** stick of graphite used in pencils; **4** thin strip of metal used for separating lines of type; **5** bullets || *vt* **6** to cover, weight, line, treat, or join with lead

lead² /lēd'/ [OE *lædan*] *v* (led) *vt* **1** to guide or conduct; show the way to; **2** to guide the actions of, direct by influence; **3** to have control or direction of; command; **4** to go or be ahead of; be first among; **5** to induce, influence (to do something); **6** to spend, live, as a life of luxury; **7** *cards* to begin a game or trick by playing (a specific card or suit); **8** lead on to lure with falsehoods; mislead || *vi* **9** to act as guide, director, manager, or the like; conduct; **10** to have or take first place; **11** to be in the van; **12** to have the principal part, as in a play; **13** *boxing* to throw out a hand toward the opponent, as *he led with his left;* **14** to be capable of being led, as a horse; **15** *cards* to make the first play; **16** lead off to begin; **17** lead to, a to go to (a place), as a road; **b** to result in; **18** lead up to, a to prepare the way for; **b** to approach (a subject) gingerly and evasively || *n* **19** guidance, leadership, as *follow my lead;* **20** first place or position; **21** distance ahead; **22** clue; **23** leash; **24** short introductory summary in a newspaper story; **25** *cards* a right to play first; **b** play thus made; **26** a principal actor in a play; **b** his part; **27** wire connecting an instrument to an electric circuit

lead'en /led'-/ *adj* **1** of the color of lead; **2** heavy; **3** oppressive; **4** made of lead; **5** gloomy

lead'er /lēd'-/ *n* **1** one who or that which leads; **2** pipe to carry off water from a roof; **3** article of merchandise advertised and sold at a price to attract trade || **lead'er·ship'** *n* || SYN chief, commander, guide, head, conductor

lead'-in' /lēd'-/ *n* wire connecting a transmitting or receiving set to the antenna || also *adj*

lead'ing /lēd'-/ *adj* **1** that leads; **2** foremost, principal || SYN capital, first, chief, main, principal

lead'ing ques'tion *n* question worded to elicit a desired response

lead' pen'cil /led'/ *n* implement for drawing or writing made of a core of graphite incased in wood, metal, or paper

lead' poi'son·ing /led'/ *n* poisoning caused by the absorption of lead into the body, often occurring in children from eating lead paint

lead' time' /lēd'/ *n* time between the planning and completion of a project

leaf /lēf'/ [OE] *n* (leaves /-vz/) 1 one of the flat, thin, plant structures, usu. green, growing on a stem; 2 petal; 3 any of various thin flat objects, as a sheet of metal beaten very thin, a single sheet of a book with a page on each side, a removable section of a table top, one half of a folding door, or the like; 4 in leaf in foliage; 5 turn over a new leaf to make a fresh start ‖ *vi* 6 to put forth foliage; 7 leaf through to turn the pages of without reading carefully ‖ **leaf'y** *adj* (-i-er; -i-est)

leaf'let *n* 1 small sheet of printed matter; 2 small or young leaf; 3 *bot* one of the divisions of a compound leaf

leaf' spring' *n* long narrow spring composed of several layers of thin metal bound together

league[1] /lēg'/ [MF *ligue* < OIt *liga*] *n* 1 agreement between two or more persons, nations, or parties for their mutual good; 2 association of the parties to such an agreement; 3 group of athletic teams organized to play each other in regular schedules; 4 in league associated for a common purpose, not always good ‖ *vi* 5 to unite in a league ‖ **syn** *n* alliance, confederation, association, combination, confederacy, union, coalition; covenant, compact

league[2] [LL *leuga* < Celt] *n* former measure of distance, equal to about three miles

League' of Na'tions *n* international association established in January 1920 by the Treaty of Versailles to promote peace and dissolved in April 1946

Le·ah /lē'ə/ *n* Bib first wife of Jacob (Gen. 29:16)

leak /lēk'/ [ME *leken* < Scand] *n* 1 hole or crack which allows the unwanted entrance or escape of a fluid, light, etc.; 2 any means of unwanted entrance or escape; 3 act of leaking ‖ *vi* 4 to flow or pass through, or as through, a hole or crack; 5 to become known through unauthorized channels ‖ *vt* 6 to allow to leak ‖ **leak'y** *adj* (-i-er; -i-est)

leak'age /-ij/ *n* 1 act of leaking; leak; 2 that which leaks in or out; 3 amount leaked

lean[1] /lēn'/ [OE *hleonian*] *vi* 1 to incline or slant from the vertical; 2 to bend and rest against something for support; 3 to rely or depend; 4 to have a tendency or inclination ‖ *vt* 5 to cause to lean; 6 to incline or bend ‖ *n* 7 act of leaning

lean[2] [OE *hlǣne*] *adj* 1 (meat) lacking in fat; 2 thin, spare (person or animal); 3 scant; lacking in richness; meager ‖ *n* 4 meat without fat ‖ **syn** *adj* thin, meager, spare, gaunt, lank ‖ **discr** *Thin* people are noticeably without fat; *thin* usually describes a

skinny appearance, or the worn emaciation that follows illness or malnutrition; but we do hear the expression "naturally *thin*," describing those who are well but slim or slender. *Lean* is used of those who are "naturally *thin*," or who develop a muscular instead of a fat body; *lean* people usually look healthy. *Lean* is sometimes used in the less pleasing sense of *thin*. *Meager* applied to people suggests a starveling, blue-skinned look; a *gaunt* frame is bony, angular, full of unlovely hollows; a *gaunt* face is hollow and haggard. *Lank* people look long, whether they are tall or short, because of their characteristic shrunken thinness; the word is usually applied to tall, angular people, often with the suggestion of loose-jointedness, and, sometimes, of flabbiness ‖ **ant** *adj* stout, fat, full, corpulent

lean'ing *n* tendency, inclination

lean'-to' *n* building, shed, or the like, with a sloping roof, built against another structure

leap /lēp'/ [OE *hlēapan*] *v* (leaped or leapt) *vi* 1 to jump; spring; bound ‖ *vt* 2 to jump over; 3 to cause to jump ‖ *n* 4 jump, spring; 5 space cleared in leaping; 6 by leaps and bounds with great rapidity

leap'frog' *n* game in which one person bends over and another vaults over him

leapt /lept', lēpt'/ *pt* & *pp* of leap

leap' year' *n* year having 366 days, in which February has 29 instead of 28 days, occurring every fourth year, with the exception of the century years not divisible by 400

learn /lurn'/ [OE *leornian*] *v* (learned or learnt) *vt* 1 to acquire knowledge of or skill in; 2 to ascertain; be informed about; 3 to memorize ‖ *vt* 4 to gain knowledge or skill; 5 learn of to be informed of; hear about

learn·ed /lurn'id/ *adj* 1 having much learning; scholarly; 2 pert. to scholars and scholarly pursuits, as *learned journals* ‖ **syn** trained, scholarly, erudite, deeply read, scholastic, well-informed ‖ **ant** unscholarly, untrained

learn'ing *n* knowledge or skill gained by study or instruction; scholarship; erudition ‖ **syn** erudition, scholarship, lore ‖ **discr** *Learning* is knowledge obtained by study, commonly in the field of the languages, literature, history, or science. The amount of knowledge sufficient to be called *learning* is great, but *learning* shares the disadvantages of mere knowledge; it does not necessarily connote the power of efficient action or superior judgment. *Learning* has, in fact, been so often divorced from these more practical qualities as to gain for the learned a reputation for being remote and visionary. *Erudition* is profound *learning* in the abstruse studies beyond the interest or comprehension of ordinary people; it is more frequently applied to *learning* in literature and languages than in science. *Scholarship* is *learning* of an accurate, sometimes academic, always schooled and disciplined sort, commonly in the field of the liberal arts. Like *learning*, *scholarship* has been so much the possession of students that it is often unfavorably opposed to the practical ability of the average man. *Lore*, formerly another word for *erudition*, now is applied to a body of facts or traditions in connection with a certain subject, as bird *lore* (cf. *knowledge*)

learnt /lurnt'/ *pt & pp* of **learn**

lease /lēs'/ [OF *les*] *n* 1 written contract renting property to another, for a definite consideration and for a specified term || *vt* 2 to give possession of by a lease; 3 to get possession of by a lease

lease'hold' *n* 1 tenure of land by a lease; 2 land so held || **lease'hold'er** *n*

leash /lēsh'/ [OF *laisse*] *n* 1 thong or cord by which a dog is held; 2 curb; restraint || *vt* 3 to secure with or as with a leash; 4 to curb, restrain

least /lēst'/ [OE *læst superl* of *lǣs* less] *adj* 1 smallest in degree, size, value, importance, amount, etc. || *adv* 2 in the smallest degree || *n* 3 something that is least; 4 **at the least**, a no less than; b at any rate; 5 **not in the least** not at all

least' com'mon mul'ti·ple *n* smallest number that is exactly divisible by two or more numbers

leath·er /leth'ər/ [OE *lether*] *n* skin of an animal, tanned and prepared for use

Leath'er·ette' /-et'/ [trademark] *n* imitation leather

leath'ern *adj* made of or resembling leather

leath'er·neck' *n* slang U.S. marine

leath'er·y *adj* resembling leather in texture and toughness

leave¹ /lēv'/ [OE *læfan*] *v* (left) *vt* 1 to allow to remain, as *leave the book*; 2 to allow to remain or continue in the same place or condition, as *the appeal left him cold, leave the door open*; 3 to depart from; 4 to deliver, as *to leave a package*; 5 cease from; desist from; 6 to bequeath; 7 to refer for decision, as *I leave it to you*; 8 to have remaining after death; 9 **leave off** to stop; **leave out** to omit || *vi* 10 to depart; 11 **leave for** to set out for || SYN quit, forsake, desert, relinquish, surrender, forego (see *abandon, let³*)

leave² [OE *lēaf*] *n* 1 permission; 2 a permission to be absent; b time allowed for this; 3 **take leave of** to say good-by to; 4 **take one's leave** to depart || SYN liberty, license, allowance, permission

leav·en /lev'ən/ [MF *levain*] *vt* 1 to produce fermentation in by adding a fermenting agent; 2 to touch or tinge with something that modifies || *n* 3 substance that produces fermentation, esp. in dough, as yeast or fermenting dough; 4 any influence that causes change

leav'en·ing *n* leaven

leave' of ab'sence *n* leave² 2

leaves /lēvz'/ *pl* of **leaf**

leave'-tak'ing *n* farewell; parting

leav'ings *npl* remnant; remains

Leb·a·non /leb'ənən/ *n* Arabic-speaking republic in SW Asia on the Mediterranean (2,700,000; 4,000 sq.m.; cap. Beirut) || **Leb·a·nese** /leb'ənēz', -nēs'/ *adj & n* (-**nese**)

lech·er /lech'ər/ [OF *lecheor* glutton] *n* lewd or excessively sensual man || **lech'er·ous** *adj*

lech'er·y *n* excessive indulgence in sex acts

lec·tern /lek'tərn/ [OF *lettrun*] *n* stand with a slanted top to hold a book, used in churches and by lecturers

lec·ture /lek'chər/ [L *lectura* reading] *n* 1 instructive talk given before an audience or class; 2 lengthy reproof || *vi* 3 to deliver a lecture or lectures || *vt* 4 to deliver a lecture to

lec'tur·er *n* 1 one who lectures; 2 faculty position of varying levels and independent of academic rank

led /led'/ *pt & pp* of **lead**

ledge /lej'/ [OE *lecg*] *n* ridge, shelf, or bar projecting from a vertical surface, as from a building, cliff, or wall

ledg·er /lej'ər/ [ME *legger*] *n* bookkeeping book in which are recorded the final summaries of debits and credits

lee /lē'/ [OE *hlēo* shelter] *n* 1 shelter, esp. from inclement weather; 2 side or part sheltered from the wind; 3 *naut* direction toward which the wind blows; side away from the wind || also *adj*

leech /lēch'/ [OE *lǣce*] *n* 1 any of various bloodsucking flat worms of the class Hirudinea, formerly used for bleeding patients; 2 one who gets all he can out of another

leek /lēk'/ [OE *lēac*] *n* plant (*Allium porrum*) of the lily family resembling an onion, used for food or flavoring

leer /lir'/ [perh < OE *hlēor* cheek] *vi* 1 to look with a sidelong glance, slyly or lasciviously || *n* 2 sly or lascivious look

leer'y *adj* (-**i·er; -i·est**) wary; suspicious

lees /lēz'/ [< MF *lie* < LL *lia*] *npl* sediment, dregs, as of wine

lee·ward /lē'wərd or *naut* lōō'ərd/ *adj & adv* **1** at or toward the lee || *n* **2** direction toward which the wind blows; lee side

Lee'ward Is'lands /lē'wərd/ *npl* group of islands SE of Puerto Rico

lee'way' *n* **1** amount or angle of drift toward to leeward of a ship or aircraft, caused by cross winds; **2** room for freedom of action; **3** extra margin, as of time, space, material, etc.

left¹ /left'/ *pt & pp* of **leave¹**

left² [OE = weak] *adj* **1** of or pert. to the side of a person or thing that is turned toward the north when facing the sunrise; **2** (river bank) on the left of an observer facing downstream; **3** of or pert. to the political Left || *n* **4** left side; **5** *colloq* lefthand turn, as *make a left at the light;* **6** the Left the political party or movement more liberal, socialistic, or radical than the opposition || *adv* **7** toward the left

Left' Bank' *n* section of Paris on the south bank of the Seine, frequented by writers and artists

left' field' *n* baseball left side of the outfield

left'-hand' *adj* **1** situated on or to the left; **2** of, for, or with the left hand

left'-hand'ed *adj* **1** using the left hand in preference to the right; **2** done with or adapted to the left hand; **3** insincere or equivocal (compliment) || *adv* **4** toward or with the left hand; **5** in a left-handed manner || **left-hand'ed·ness** *n*

left'ist *n* member, advocate, or partisan of the Left || also *adj*

left'o'ver *n* **1** something remaining; **2** remnant of a meal to be eaten at another time

left' wing' *n* party, group, or portion of a party or group that leans to or is part of the Left || **left'wing'** or **left'-wing'** *adj* || **left'-wing'er** *n*

left'y *colloq n* (-ies) **1** left-handed person || *adj & adv* **2** left-handed

leg /leg'/ [ON *leggr*] *n* **1** one of the limbs by which men or animals walk; **2** lower limb in man, between the knee and the ankle; **3** anything resembling a leg in form or use; **4** the part of a garment covering the leg; **5** distinct portion of a trip; **6** one of the sides of a triangle other than the base; **7** not have a leg to stand on to be without any valid argument or excuse; **8** on one's or its last legs ready to give in or collapse; **9** pull someone's leg to fool or tease someone; **10** shake a leg *slang* to hurry up

leg·a·cy /leg'əsē/ [MF *legacie* legateship] *n* (-cies) **1** money or property willed to someone; **2** anything handed down from an ancestor or predecessor

le·gal /lēg'əl/ [< L *lex (legis)* law] *adj* **1** pert. to law or lawyers; **2** per-mitted or authorized by law || **le'gal·ly** *adv*

le'gal age' *n* period of life when one becomes qualified to assume full legal rights and responsibilities

le·gal·i·ty /ligal'itē/ *n* (-ties) **1** state of being in conformity with the law; lawfulness; **2** legal obligation or requirement

le'gal·ize' *vt* to make legal || **le'gal·i·za'tion** *n*

le'gal ten'der *n* lawful currency, which by law must be accepted in payment of all debts

leg·ate /leg'it/ [< L *legare (-atus)* to commission] *n* **1** envoy or delegate; **2** *R C Ch* special representative of the Pope

leg'a·tee' /-tē'/ [< L *legatus* bequeathed] *n* person to whom a legacy is bequeathed

le·ga·tion /ligāsh'ən/ *n* **1** diplomatic envoy of the rank of minister and his staff; **2** official residence of a diplomatic minister

le·ga·to /ligät'ō/ [It = tied together] *adj mus* smooth and flowing, without breaks between notes || also *adv*

leg·end /lej'ənd/ [ML *legenda* things to be read] *n* **1** story or body of stories handed down from the past, not documented but popularly believed to be true; **2** inscription, as on a coin or coat of arms, or under an illustration; **3** explanatory key, as on a map or chart

leg'end·ar'y /-der'-/ *adj* **1** of or pert. to legends; **2** based on or described in a legend or legends

leg·er·de·main /lej'ərdəmān'/ [MF = light of hand] *n* **1** sleight of hand; **2** deception; trickery

-leg·ged /-leg'id, -legd'/ *adj comb form* having so many or such legs, as *four-legged*

leg'gings *npl* outer coverings for the legs, as a protection from cold or wet

leg'gy *adj* (-gi·er; -gi·est) **1** having long legs; **2** having long, slender, eye-filling legs

leg'horn' [Leghorn, Italy] *n* **1** one of a breed of small chickens valued as prolific layers of white eggs; **2** hat made of Italian wheat straw

leg·i·ble /lej'ibəl/ [< L *legere* to read] *adj* capable of being read or deciphered || **leg'i·bly** *adv* || **leg'i·bil'i·ty** /-bil'-/ *n*

le·gion /lēj'ən/ [L *legio (-onis)*] *n* **1** basic army unit of ancient Rome, of from 3,000 to 6,000 men; **2** military force; army; **3** vast number; multitude || **le'gion·ar'y** /-ner'-/ *adj & n* (-ies)

le'gion·naire' /-ner'/ [F] *n* member of a legion

Le'gion of Hon'or *n* French honorary order founded by Napoleon as a reward for distinguished service

leg·is·late /lej'islāt'/ [< *legislator*] *vi*

l to enact laws ‖ *vt* **2** to bring about or regulate by law ‖ **leg'is·la'tion** *n* ‖ **leg'is·la'tive** *adj*

leg'is·la'tor [< L *lex* (*legis*) law + *lator* bringer] *n* member of a lawmaking body

leg'is·la'ture /-chər/ *n* lawmaking body

le·git /lejit'/ *adj* **1** *slang* legitimate ‖ *n* **2** *slang* legitimate theater

le·git·i·mate /lijit'imit/ [< L *legitimus* lawful] *adj* **1** lawful; in accord with the law; **2** born in wedlock; **3** genuine; not false; **4** reasonable; logical; **5** pert. to stage plays, as distinguished from vaudeville, motion pictures, television, etc. ‖ **le·git'i·ma·tize'** *vt* ‖ **le·git'i·ma·cy** *n*

leg'man' /-man', -mən/ *n* (**-men** /-men', -mən/) **1** subordinate who runs errands and performs other chores; **2** reporter who goes about in search of news

leg·ume /leg'yōom, ligyōom'/ [F < L *legumen*] *n* **1** any plant of the pea family, containing seeds in a pod; **2** the pod or seeds, used as food ‖ **le·gu'mi·nous** *adj*

leg'work' *n* work requiring much walking and moving from place to place, as of a newspaper reporter

le·i /lā', lā'ē/ [Hawaiian] *n* wreathe or garland for the neck or head

Leib·niz, Gott·fried Wil·helm von /gōt'frēt vil'helm fən līb'nits/ *n* (1646–1716) German philosopher and mathematician

Leip·zig /līp'tsik/ *n* city in East Germany (650,000)

lei·sure /lēzh'ər, lezh'-/ [OF *leisir*] *n* **1** free time to be spent as one sees fit, not given to work or duty; **2** at one's leisure at one's convenience ‖ *adj* **3** free, spare (time); **4** (class) not having to work

lei'sure·ly *adj* **1** deliberate, without haste ‖ *adv* **2** in a leisurely manner

leit·mo·tif /līt'mōtēf'/ [G = leading theme] *n mus* recurring phrase or theme, as in opera, that characterizes some person or idea

lem·ming /lem'iŋ/ [Norw] *n* any of several species of small mouselike rodents (genera *Lemmus* and *Dicrostonyx*) found in the arctic regions

lem·on /lem'ən/ [MF *limon* < Pers *līmūn*] *n* **1** citrus fruit (*Citrus limon*) with pale-yellow skin and acid juice; **2** its tree; **3** pale-yellow color; **4** *slang* person or thing extremely disappointing in performance ‖ **lem'on·y** *adj*

lem'on·ade' /-ād'/ *n* beverage of sweetened water and lemon juice

lem·pi·ra /lempir'ə/ [name of Indian chief] *n* monetary unit of Honduras

le·mur /lēm'ər/ [< L *lemures* ghosts] *n* any of several small arboreal mammals (genus *Lemur*) related to the monkeys, having a foxlike face, large eyes, and woolly fur, found mainly in Madagascar

lend /lend/ [OE *lǣnan*] *v* (lent) *vt* **1** to grant to another for temporary use, without compensation, or for a small fee, as a book, or at interest, as money; **2** to afford, provide, as *to lend aid, flowers lend beauty to the room;* **3** to devote or adapt (oneself or itself) ‖ *vi* **4** to make a loan ‖ **lend'er** *n*

length /leŋth/ [OE *lengthu*] *n* **1** measure of an object from end to end; **2** extent in space, time, or degree; **3** single piece of a certain length; **4** at length, a in full; b at last

length'en *vt* **1** to make long or longer ‖ *vi* **2** to become longer

length'wise' also **length'ways'** *adv & adj* in the direction of the length

length'y *adj* (-i·er; -i·est) long; long and tiresome

le·ni·ent /lēn'ē·ənt, lēn'yənt/ [L *leniens* (-entis*) soothing] *adj* not severe; indulgent; merciful ‖ **le'ni·en·cy** *n*

Len·in, Ni·ko·lai /nik'əlī' len'in/ *n* (1870–1924) leader of the Russian Revolution and premier of the Soviet Union 1918–24

Len'in·grad' /-grad'/ *n* seaport in NW Russia on the Baltic (3,750,000); formerly St. Petersburg (1703–1914) and Petrograd (1914–24)

le·nis /lē'nis, lā'-/ [L = soft] *adj phonet* **1** pronounced with relatively less muscular tension; opposed to *fortis* ‖ *n* (-nes /-nēz/) **2** consonant so pronounced

lens /lenz/ [L = lentil] *n* **1** piece of transparent substance, usu. glass, with one or two curved surfaces, having the property of converging or diverging beams of light and forming images of objects, used for magnification, correcting eye defects, etc.; **2** combination of such pieces, used in cameras and optical instruments; **3** convex body in the eye that focuses light rays on the retina

lens'man /-mən/ *n* (-men /-mən/) *colloq* photographer

lent /lent/ *pt & pp* of lend

Lent [OE *lengten* spring] *n* the forty weekdays preceding Easter Sunday, beginning with Ash Wednesday, observed by many Christian churches as a season of penitence and self-denial ‖ **Lent'en** *adj*

-lent /-lənt/ [L *-lentus*] *adj suf* full of, as *fraudulent*

len·til /lent'əl/ [OF *lentille* < L *lenticula*] *n* **1** plant (*Lens culinaris*) of the pea family, with small edible seeds; **2** the seed

len'to /lent'ō/ [It] *adv & adj mus* slow

Le·o /lē'ō/ [L = lion] *n* **1** a northern zodiacal constellation, the lion; **2** fifth sign of the zodiac

Le·o·nar·do da Vin·ci /lē'ənär'dō də vinch'ē/ *n* (1452–1519) Italian painter, sculptor, architect, philosopher, scientist, and inventor

le·o·nine /lē'ənīn'/ [< L *leo* (*leonis*) lion] *adj* pert. to or like a lion

leop·ard /lep'ərd/ [Gk *leopardos*] *n* 1 large ferocious cat-like mammal (*Felis pardus*) of Africa and S Asia, having a yellow skin dappled with black spots; 2 some similar animal, such as the jaguar, cheetah, or ounce

le·o·tard /lē'ətärd'/ [J. *Léotard* 19th-century F gymnast] *n* skin-tight garment used by dancers and acrobats

lep·er /lep'ər/ [OF *lepre* leprosy < Gk *lepra*] *n* person having leprosy

lep·re·chaun /lep'rəkon', -kôn'/ [Ir *leipreachan*] *n* Irish folklore sprite or fairy, usu. in the form of a little old man

lep·ro·sy /lep'rəsē/ *n* chronic infectious disease, marked by nodules, ulcers, white, scaly scabs, loss of fingers and toes, and loss of feeling in the nerves || **lep/rous** *adj*

les·bi·an /lez'bē·ən/ [< *Lesbos* Gk island in the Aegean] *n* female homosexual || **les/bi·an·ism**

lese/ maj/es·ty /lēz'/ [F *lèse majesté* = injured greatness] *n* crime against a sovereign or head of state, esp. against his dignity

le·sion /lēzh'ən/ [L *laesio* (-*onis*) attack] *n* hurt, wound, or local degeneration of an organ, causing a change in its function or structure

less /les'/ [*comp* of *little*, < OE *lǣssa*] *adj* 1 not so large in quantity, amount, or bulk; not so much; 2 fewer; 3 not so great in importance || *adv* 4 to a smaller extent, amount, or degree || *n* 5 a smaller amount || *prep* 6 minus

-less /-lis/ [OE *lēas* free from] *adj suf* 1 without, as *homeless*; 2 unable to be acted on, as *resistless*; 3 not acting in the manner indicated, as *ceaseless*

les·see /lesē'/ [AF] *n* person to whom a lease is granted

less/en *vt* 1 to make less; reduce || *vi* 2 to become less || SYN reduce, diminish, lower, abate (see *decrease*) || ANT aggravate, increase, expand, wax, swell, distend

less/er [< *less*] *adj* smaller; less

les·son /les'ən/ [OF *leçon* < L *lectio* (-*onis*) a reading] *n* 1 material assigned to a pupil for study; 2 that which is learned or taught by experience, observation, or the like; 3 rebuke, severe lecture; 4 portion of Scripture read as a part of divine worship

les·sor /les'ôr/ *n* one who grants a lease

lest /lest/ [< OE (thȳ) *lǣs* whereby less] *conj* for fear that

let¹ /let/ [OE *lettan* to hinder] *n* 1 *tennis* service in which the ball is served, although

it drops in the proper section of the court, is invalid because it touched the net in passing over it; 2 **without let or hindrance** without interfering or hindering

let² [OE *lǣtan*] *v* (let; let·ting) *vt* 1 to permit, allow; 2 to rent or hire; 3 to give out, assign, as a contract; 4 to cause (blood) to flow; 5 **let alone**, **a** to leave undisturbed or in solitude; **b** not to mention; much less; 6 **let be** to leave undisturbed or in solitude; 7 **let down**, **a** to disappoint; **b** to betray; 8 **let somebody in** on to share (a secret or inside information) with somebody; 9 **let off**, **a** to give forth, as steam; **b** to be lenient with; **c** to excuse from work; 10 **let out**, **a** to divulge; **b** to release; **c** to enlarge, as a garment; 11 **let someone have it** *colloq* **a** to hurt or injure someone by striking, shooting, insulting; **b** to scold someone severely || *vi* 12 to be leased or rented; 13 **let down** to slacken; 14 **let on**, **a** to pretend; **b** to admit, indicate one's awareness; **c** to make one's presence known; 15 **let out** to be over; be dismissed; 16 **let up**, **a** to cease; **b** to slacken, relax || *v aux* 17 a (to express a command): *let him enter;* **b** (to express a warning): *let him try to come in!;* **c** (to express in the first person plural a suggestion of sharing an action): *let us take a walk* || SYN allow, permit, suffer, endure, grant, give leave to, leave || DISCR *Let,* to permit or allow, is used without *to:* we *let* him go; we *let* the children decide. *Leave,* meaning to allow, especially with the idea of offering no interference, is used with *to:* we *leave* our guests to follow their own inclinations; we *leave* our students to decide upon their own courses. The use of *leave,* without *to,* in this sense for *let,* as in *leave* me have it, should be avoided

-let /-lit/ [MF -*elet*] *n suf* forming: 1 diminutives, as *streamlet;* 2 names of pieces of clothing or bodily ornaments, as *bracelet*

let/down/ *n* 1 slackening; 2 disappointment; 3 humiliation

le·thal /lēth'əl/ [< L *lethum* death] *adj* 1 fatal; 2 pert. to or causing death

leth·ar·gy /leth'ərjē/ [< Gk *lethargos* forgetful] *n* (-gies) 1 abnormal drowsiness; 2 listlessness; 3 state of apathy or indifference || **le·thar·gic** /li-thär'jik/ *adj*

let's /lets/ let us

Lett /let/ [G *Lette*] *n* Latvian

let·ter /let'ər/ [OF *lettre* < L *littera*] *n* 1 alphabetic symbol representing a speech sound; 2 written or printed communication; 3 exact word-for-word meaning; 4 emblem, usu. the initial letter of a school, awarded for outstanding performance in some sport; 5 **to the letter** (order executed) completely and precisely; **6 letters** *pl* a literature; **b** learning ‖ *vt* **7** to print or mark with letters; inscribe

let′ter-head′ *n* **1** printed form at the top of a sheet of paper, usu. containing the business name and address of the sender; **2** sheet so printed

let′ter-ing *n* letters, or an inscription, marked on an object

let′ter of cred′it *n* letter addressed by a bank to one or more of its correspondents, authorizing the honoring of drafts or bills of exchange drawn upon it

let′ter-per′fect *adj* **1** knowing something perfectly; **2** correct in every detail

let′ter-press′ *n typ* **1** printing done from raised type; **2** reading matter as distinguished from pictures, maps, etc.

let′ter-word′ *n* word in the form of an abbreviation which is pronounced by sounding the names of its letters in succession and which functions as a part of speech, as in *he MC′d the program; he has his Ph.D.*

Let-tish /let′ish/ [see Lett] *adj* **1** Latvian ‖ *n* **2** Latvian language

let-tuce /let′is/ [OF *laitues*] *n* **1** garden plant (*Lactuca sativa*) with crisp leaves used esp. in salads; **2** *slang* money

let′up′ *n colloq* **1** pause; stop; **2** slackening; relief

leu /lōō/ [Rumanian = lion] *n* (*lei* /lā′/) monetary unit of Rumania

leu-c- or **leu-co-, leu-k-** or **leu-ko-** [Gk *leukos*] *comb form* white

leu-ke-mi-a /lōōkēm′ē-ə/ [*leuk-* + *-emia*] *n* disease, usu. fatal, in which there is an uncontrolled multiplication of white blood cells

leu-ko-cyte /lōōk′əsīt′/ [*leuko-* + Gk *kytos* vessel] *n* white blood corpuscle, useful in destroying harmful bacteria

leu′kor-rhe′a /-rē′ə/ [*leuko-* + *-rrhea*] *n* white discharge from the female genital organ

lev /lef′/ [Bulgarian = lion] *n* (**lev-a** /lev′ə/) monetary unit of Bulgaria

Le-vant /livant′/ [MF] *n* region of the Near East comprising the countries around the E end of the Mediterranean, esp. Syria, Lebanon, Israel, and Jordan ‖ **Le-van-tine** /livan′tin, lev′əntīn′, lev′əntēn′/ *adj* & *n*

lev-ee¹ /lev′ē, levē′/ [F *levé, lever* rising] *n* **1** party, usu. in someone's honor; **2** reception held by the President of the U.S.; **3** in Great Britain, court assembly held in the afternoon for men

lev-ee² /lev′ē/ [F] *n* embankment, manmade or natural, to prevent a river from overflowing its banks

lev-el /lev′əl/ [MF *livel* < L *libella*] *adj* **1** smooth and flat; **2** having or lying in a horizontal surface or plane; horizontal; **3** having the same altitude, rank, importance, or condition; **4** judicious, well-balanced ‖ *n* **5** horizontal area, as of a field; **6** condition of being horizontal; **7** horizontal plane used as the basis from which to measure altitude, as *5,000 feet above sea level;* **8** rank; position relative to a given standard, as *a low level of conduct;* **9** instrument used to find a horizontal line or position, or to adjust something to the horizontal; **10** floor, story, as *track three is on the upper level;* **11** open stretch of water, as in a river or between two locks in a canal; **12** on the level *slang* honest and sincere ‖ *v* (*-eled* or *-elled; -el-ing* or *-el-ling*) *vt* **13** to make level; **14** to aim, as a gun; **15** to raze ‖ *vi* **16** *slang* to tell the truth, as *he didn't level with me;* **17** level off *aeron* to fly horizontally near the ground ‖ **lev′el-er** *n* ‖ syn *adj* horizontal, even, flush, plain, plane (see *flat¹*)

lev′el cross′ing *n Brit* grade crossing

lev′el-head′ed *adj* even-tempered and sensible

lev′el-ing rod′ *n* light pole, marked with graduations, used with a surveyor's level to measure differences in elevation

le-ver /lēv′ər, lev′-/ [OF *levier* lifter] *n* **1** bar used to pry or move a heavy object; **2** *mach* any rigid bar turning about a fixed point and having counteracting forces applied at two other points

le′ver ac′tion *n* rifle action in which the fired cartridge is ejected and a new one loaded into the firing chamber by means of a hand-operated lever in front of the trigger

le′ver-age /-ij/ *n* **1** action or application of a lever; **2** mechanical power gained by a lever; **3** power to act in a given situation; **4** *stock market* buying power generated by the purchase of securities on credit, as by buying on margin, selling short, or buying warrants

le-vi-a-than /ləvī′əthən/ [LL < Heb] *n* **1** Biblical sea monster; **2** anything huge of its kind

Le-vis /lē′vīz/ [trademark] *npl* closefitting denim pants reinforced with copper rivets

lev-i-ta-tion /lev′itāsh′ən/ [< L *levis* light] *n* *spiritualism* process or illusion of moving heavy objects, or of suspending them in the air, without natural agency

Le-vit-i-cus /livit′ikəs/ *n* third book of the Old Testament, containing the ceremonial laws administered by the priests

lev-i-ty /lev′itē/ [< L *levis* light] *n* (*-ties*) **1** lightness of conduct, frivolity; **2** inconstancy ‖ syn thoughtlessness, flightiness (see *lightness²*)

lev-y /lev′ē/ [MF *levee* raised] *n* (*-ies*)

1 act of raising by compulsion, as money or men; 2 amount or number raised || *v* (-led) *vt* 3 to impose (a tax); 4 to raise (troops); 5 to wage (war)

lewd /lood/ [OE *lǣwede* lay, unlearned] *adj* inciting to lust; obscene || **lewd′ness** *n* || SYN licentious, immodest, indecent, lascivious

Lew·is gun′ /loo′is/ [Col. I. N. *Lewis* (1858–1931) U.S. soldier and inventor] *n* light air-cooled machine gun with a circular magazine

lew′is·ite′ [W. L. *Lewis* (1878–1943) U.S. chemist] *n* blistering poison gas used in chemical warfare

lex·i·cal /leks′ikəl/ [< Gk *lexis* word] *adj* 1 pert. to the words of a language as distinguished from its grammar; 2 pert. to a dictionary or lexicon

lex·i·cog·ra·phy /lek′sikog′rəfē/ [Gk *lexikos* of words + -*graphy*] *n* the compiling of dictionaries || **lex′i·cog′·ra·pher** *n* || **lex′i·co·graph′ic** (-i-cal) -kōgraf′-, -kōgraf′-/ *adj*

lex′i·col′o·gy /-kol′-/ *n* study of word meanings and of idiomatic combinations of words || **lex′i·col′o·gist** *n*

lex′i·con /-kən, -kon′/ [Gk] *n* 1 dictionary, esp. of Greek, Hebrew, or Latin; 2 specialized vocabulary; 3 *ling* inventory of the morphemes of a language

LG, L.G. Low German

LGk, L.Gk. Late Greek

Lha·sa /läs′ə, las′ə/ *n* capital of Tibet (35,000); 12,000 ft. above sea level

Li *chem* lithium

L.I. Long Island

li·a·bil·i·ty /lī′əbil′itē/ *n* (-ties) 1 state of being liable; 2 something disadvantageous; 3 liabilities *pl* debts

li·a·ble /lī′əbel/ [< AF *lier* to bind < L *ligare*] *adj* 1 legally responsible; answerable; 2 liable to, a subject or exposed to (something undesirable); b likely to || SYN accountable, answerable (see *responsible*, *apt*)

li·ai·son /lē-āz′ən, -ā′zon, lē′əzon′/ [F] *n* 1 communication and close contact as between groups or units of an organization, military force, etc.; 2 illicit love affair; 3 *phonet* linking of the final sound of a word with the initial sound of the next

li·ar /lī′ər/ [OE *lēogere*] *n* one who tells lies || SYN hypocrite, dissembler, deceiver, prevaricator

li·ba·tion /lībāsh′ən/ [< L *libare* (-atus)* to pour] *n* 1 act of pouring out wine or other liquid in honor of a god; 2 liquid so poured; 3 *colloq* alcoholic drink

li·bel /lī′bəl/ [MF < L *libellus* little book] *n* 1 anything written or printed tending to defame or bring into ill repute; 2 crime of publishing a libel; 3 defamation; calumniation || *v* (-beled or -belled; -bel·ing or -bel·ling) *vt* 4 to publish a libel against; 5 to defame, slander || **li′bel·er** or

li′bel·ler *n* || **li′bel·ous** or **li′bel·lous** *adj*

lib·er·al /lib′ərəl/ [< L *liber* free] *adj* 1 not narrowly restricted, as *a liberal education*; 2 generous, openhanded; 3 plentiful, abundant; 4 unprejudiced; broad-minded; 5 a favoring progress and reform, as in politics and religion; b favoring egalitarianism || *n* 6 advocate of liberal principles, esp. in politics; 7 Liberal member of a political party devoted to liberal principles || **lib′er·al·ly** *adv* || **lib′er·al·ism** *n* || **lib′er·al·ize′** *vt & vi* || SYN *adj* abundant, ample, munificent, bounteous, free-handed (see *generous*)

lib′er·al arts′ *npl* courses of college instruction comprising the humanities, arts, natural sciences, and social sciences

lib·er·al·i·ty /lib′əral′itē/ *n* (-ties) 1 generosity; 2 open-mindedness

lib·er·ate′ [L *liberare* (-*atus*)] *vt* 1 to set free; 2 to free from combination, as a gaseous element || **lib′er·a′tor** *n* || **lib′er·a′tion** *n* || SYN extricate, unfasten, discharge, deliver, release, emancipate, free || DISCR We *free* by setting at liberty that which is bound, by ridding of or clearing away that which entangles or burdens; we *free* slaves, *free* our consciences from a sense of guilt, *free* land of mortgages, *free* ourselves from pain. To *liberate* is to set free from bondage, as a slave, or from confinement, as a prisoner; in these senses it is a more formal word than *free*. To *release* is to deliver from bondage, or set free from anything that restrains, fastens, or confines; we *release* acquitted prisoners, a friend from a promise, a debtor from his obligation. To *emancipate* is to *free* from legal, social, political, moral, or intellectual repression or restraint. We *emancipate* slaves by *freeing* them, unenfranchised citizens by giving them the suffrage, our minds by giving them range of thought. We *extricate* a person from a predicament or difficulty by literally disentangling the threads of his perplexities. To *discharge*, as here compared, is to *release* legally, as a prisoner, to dismiss from service, as an employee, or to clear, as a debt, by paying || ANT confine, restrain, hold

Li·be·ri·a /lībir′ē·ə/ *n* English-speaking republic in W Africa, founded in 1822 by freed American slaves (1,500,000; 43,000 sq.m.; cap. Monrovia) || **Li·be′ri·an** *adj & n*

lib′er·tar′i·an /-ter′ē·ən/ *n* 1 advocate of freedom for all; liberal; 2 one who believes in free will || also *adj*

lib·er·tine /lib′ərtēn′, -tin/ [L *libertinus* freedman] *n* 1 licentious person; rake || *adj* 2 loose in morals, dissolute || **lib′er·tin·ism** *n*

lib·er·ty /lib'ərtē/ [MF *liberte* < L *li-bertas*] *n* (**-ties**) 1 freedom from control or subjection; 2 freedom from restraint; 3 possession and use of the privilege of self-government; 4 instance of unwarranted familiarity; impertinence; 5 shore leave granted to a sailor; 6 **at liberty, a** out of work; **b** unconfined; **c** permitted (to do something) ‖ SYN freedom, independence, emancipation, license, exemption, franchise, immunity ‖ DISCR *Liberty* and *freedom* are used interchangeably; but *freedom* connotes an absence, want of, or the nonexistence of, compulsion or restraint; *liberty* connotes being freed from some sort of restraint or control, as captivity, despotism, or bondage. *Freedom* is wider of signification, and can be applied in the field of figurative oppression; we desire *freedom* from care, *freedom* from responsibility. "*Liberty* of conscience" is a phrase that suggests that once consciences were dictated to; "*liberty* of the press" has the echo of a one-time suppression; "personal *liberty*" suggests personal slavery. *Independence* is the name of that state of *freedom* in which nations are not dependent on, or subject to, the domination of others. *Emancipation* names the state of one set free from social, moral, intellectual, or political repression or restraint. *Emancipation* secures *liberty* of person for the slaves. *License*, in its better sense, is a permit issued by the government or other competent authority to carry on some certain business, or to marry, preach, or the like. In its unfavorable sense, *license* names an abuse of *freedom*. *Freedom* and *liberty* are also used in an unfavorable sense, meaning undue familiarity, a setting aside of rules or conventions, as to take *liberties* with; take the *liberty* of doing; to take *freedoms* with

li·bid·i·nous /libid'inəs/ [< *libido*] *adj* lewd, lustful

li·bi·do /libēd'ō, -bīd'ō/ [L = desire, lust] *n psychoanal* 1 sexual drive; 2 desire, urge, or personal interest directed toward a goal

Li·bra /līb'rə, lib'rə/ [L = scales] *n* 1 a southern zodiacal constellation; 2 seventh sign of the zodiac

li·brar·i·an /lībrer'ē·ən/ *n* one who has charge of a library

li·brar·y /lī'brerē, -brer'-/ [L *librarius* of book] *n* (**-ies**) 1 collection of books for reading or reference; 2 room or building containing such a collection; 3 place where books are rented or lent to patrons

li·bret·to /libret'ō/ [It, *dim.* of *libro* book] *n* (**-tos** or **-ti** /-tē/) text of an opera or other long dramatic musical composition ‖ **li·bret'tist** *n*

Lib·y·a /lib'ē·ə/ *n* Arabic-speaking republic in N Africa, W of Egypt (1,900,000; 679,375 sq.m.; caps. Tripoli and Benghazi) ‖ **Lib'y·an** *adj & n*

lice /līs'/ *pl* of **louse**

li·cense or **li·cence** /līs'əns/ [MF *li-cence* < L *licentia*] *n* 1 formal permission from government to do something; 2 document granting such permission; 3 legal permit; 4 right granted to another to use a patent; 5 excessive or unrestrained liberty; abuse of freedom; 6 intentional variation from a set form or rule, as *poetic license* ‖ *vt* 7 to grant legal permission or license to ‖ SYN *n* permission, authority, permit, privilege, excess, abuse (**see** *liberty*)

li·cen·see' or **li·cen·cee'** *n* one to whom a license is granted

li·cen·ti·ate /līsen'shē·it, -āt'/ *n* 1 one given authority by license to practice a profession; 2 in some foreign countries, academic degree roughly equivalent to a master's

li·cen·tious /līsen'shəs/ *adj* unrestrained by law or morality; lewd, libertine ‖ SYN unchaste, lustful, sensual, profligate, lewd

li·chen /līk'ən/ [Gk *leichen*] *n* any of a group (Lichenes) of plant formations composed of certain fungi growing in symbiosis with certain algae, found on trees, stones, etc.

lic·it /lis'it/ [L *licitus*] *adj* lawful; permitted

lick /lik'/ [OE *liccian*] *vt* 1 to pass the tongue over; 2 to play lightly over (said of flames); 3 *colloq* **a** to whip, thrash; **b** to defeat ‖ *n* 4 act of licking with the tongue; 5 small quantity; 6 salt lick; 7 *colloq* **a** quick stroke or blow; **b** brief burst of activity; 8 **lick and a promise** *colloq* barest attempt at doing something

lic·o·rice /lik'əris, lik'ərish, lik'rish/ [AF *lycorys* < Gk *glykyrrhiza* sweetroot (a plant)] *n* 1 leguminous plant (*Glycyrrhiza glabra*); 2 **a** its dried root or extract, used in medicine and candy; **b** candy flavored with it

lic·tor /lik'tər/ [L] *n ancient Rome* one of a body of officials who attended the chief magistrates, carrying the fasces before them

lid /lid/ [OE *hlid*] *n* 1 movable cover closing an opening, as of a box or trunk; 2 eyelid; 3 *slang* hat; 4 *colloq* curb, restraint

lie¹ /lī'/ [OE *lyge*] *n* 1 falsehood; 2 anything intended to mislead; 3 **give the lie to, a** to accuse of falsehood; **b** to belie ‖ *v* (**ly·ing**) *vi* 4 to utter a lie; 5 to make false representations ‖ *vt* 6 to accomplish, take, put, etc., by lying, as *he lied his way out of trouble* ‖ SYN *n* untruth, falsity, fabrication, quibble, prevarication, equivocation, mendacity, falsehood ‖ DISCR An *untruth* is something stated which is contrary to fact. A *falsehood* is the utterance of something known to be untrue; if it is the cloaking sort of refuge indulged in by frightened children, it is less culpable than an *untruth* told with intent to deceive. A *lie* is a deliberate, intentional *falsehood*. A *quibble* is an evasion of the truth, effected often by the shifting operation known as "side-stepping," or by making capital of ambiguity. An *equivocation* is a deliberate concealing of the truth behind words capable of a double interpretation. A *fabrication* is an invention; it is sometimes a plain *lie*; it is sometimes a fanciful embroidery of fact indulged in by the imaginative, and creative of more amusement than harm, as its nature is perfectly evident; sometimes it is a story told for its fictional or dramatic value. In this last-named sense, it is not of course comparable with the other words, as it is not meant to deceive. *Mendacity* is habitual, shameless lying; it bespeaks a falseness in the very nature of the person practicing it ‖ ANT *n* truth, fact, verity, reality

lie² [OE *licgan*] *v* (lay; lain; ly·ing) *vi* 1 to assume or be in a reclining position; 2 to be at rest, usu. horizontally (said of objects); 3 to be in a state of disuse, concealment, inactivity, or the like; 4 to exist or be situated; 5 to occupy a grave; 6 **lie down** to assume a reclining position; 7 **take lying down** *colloq* to submit without resisting ‖ *n* 8 way, position, or direction in which a thing lies

Liech·ten·stein /lĭk′tənstīn/ *n* tiny German-speaking principality between Austria and Switzerland (21,000; 61 sq.m.; cap. Vaduz)

lie′ de·tec′tor *n* polygraph 3

lief /lēf′/ [OE *lēof* pleasant, dear] *adv* willingly; gladly

liege /lēj′/ [OF *lige*] *adj* 1 owing allegiance to a feudal lord; 2 loyal ‖ *n* 3 feudal lord; 4 vassal

lien /lē′(ə)n/ [MF < L *ligamen* binding] *n* legal claim on a property until a debt is discharged

lieu /lōō′/ [MF = place < L *locus*] *n* **in lieu of** in place of

Lieut. Lieutenant

lieu·ten·ant /lōōten′ənt, Brit leften′-/ [MF = place holder] *n* 1 one who acts for a superior; 2 army officer ranking next below a captain; 3 navy officer ranking next below a lieutenant commander ‖ lieu·ten′an·cy *n* (-cies)

lieu·ten′ant colo′nel *n* army officer ranking next below a colonel

lieu·ten′ant com·man′der *n* navy officer ranking next below a commander

lieu·ten′ant gen′er·al *n* army officer ranking next below a general

lieu·ten′ant gov′er·nor *n* one next in rank below a governor, who suc-

ceeds to the office in case of the latter's death

lieu·ten′ant jun′ior grade′ *n* navy officer ranking next below a lieutenant

life /līf′/ [OB līf] *n* (lives /-vz/) 1 condition which marks the difference between an animal or plant and an inorganic body or dead organism; 2 state of being alive; 3 living person, as *three lives were lost in the storm;* 4 living things collectively, as *plant life;* 5 period during which one is alive; 6 manner of living, as *a life of pleasure;* 7 a biography; 8 animation; vivacity; 9 moving spirit, as *he was the life of the party;* 10 period of effectiveness or existence, as *the life of a car, of an insurance policy, etc.;* 11 particular type of existence, as *an active life;* 12 resilience, as of rubber; 13 life sentence; 14 **big as life** actually present; 15 **for the life of** one despite one's greatest efforts; 16 **not on your life!** *colloq* positively not! ‖ *adj* 17 of or pert. to life; animate; 18 provided for or lasting a lifetime; 19 for the protection of life; 20 working from nature

life′ belt′ *n* belt-like life preserver

life′blood′ *n* 1 the blood necessary to life; 2 any source of vital strength and energy

life′boat′ *n* boat specially constructed for rescue at sea or for escape from a shipwrecked vessel

life′ buoy′ *n* life preserver

life′ cy′cle *n* complete cycle of changes of an organism from one primary form to that of the next generation

life′guard′ *n* expert swimmer at a bathing beach, detailed to save people from drowning

life′ his′to·ry *n* 1 social history of an individual; 2 life cycle

life′ in·sur′ance *n* insurance providing for the payment of a stipulated sum to the beneficiary upon the death of the insured

life′ jack′et *n* buoyant jacket for supporting shipwrecked persons in the water

life′less *adj* 1 dead; 2 inanimate; 3 insensible; in a faint; 4 dull, listless ‖ SYN inanimate, torpid, inert, heavy (see *dead*)

life′like′ *adj* like the real thing; realistic

life′line′ *n* 1 rope thrown to a vessel in distress; 2 rope for raising and lowering a diver; 3 vital route for the transportation of supplies; 4 line in the palm of the hand which in palmistry is said to shed light on a person's future

life′long′ *adj* enduring or remaining throughout life

life′ of Ri′ley /rī′lē/ *n* slang life of ease and plenty

life′ pre·serv′er *n* jacket or belt of buoyant material for keeping a person afloat

lif·er /līf'ər/ *n slang* person serving a life sentence

life' sci'enc·es *npl* sciences concerned with the study of the phenomena of life, as botany, biology, biophysics, biochemistry, microbiology, and zoology

life' sen'tence *n* sentence condemning a convicted person to spend the rest of his life in prison

life'-size' *adj* of natural or original size

life'-style' *n* manner of living characteristic of a person throughout his life

life'time' *n* duration of one's life ‖ also *adj*

life'work' *n* undertaking to which one devotes his whole life

LI·FO /līf'ō/ [last-in, first-out] *adj* (method of inventory valuation) by which the cost of goods sold is based on the most recent prices of raw materials

lift /lift'/ [ON *lypta*] *vt* 1 to raise to a higher point; place in a higher position; 2 to exalt; raise to a higher degree or condition; 3 to remove or rescind; 4 to pay off (a mortgage); 5 to raise (one's voice); 6 to perform a face lifting on (a face); 7 *colloq* to steal ‖ *vi* 8 to exert strength in raising something; pull upward; 9 to rise and disperse, as fog ‖ *n* 10 act of lifting; 11 height to which something is lifted; 12 high position or carriage; 13 lifting force; 14 rise in spirits; 15 ride given to someone going in the same direction; 16 aid, assistance; 17 *Brit* elevator; 18 one thickness of leather in the heel of a shoe

lift'-off' *n* takeoff of a helicopter, rocket, or spacecraft

lift' truck' *n* small truck which mechanically lifts its load

lig·a·ment /lig'əmənt/ [L *ligamentum*] *n* band of fibrous tissue which connects the ends of bones or holds an organ in place

lig·a·ture /lig'əchŏŏr', -chər/ [< L *ligare* to bind] *n* 1 act of tying or binding; 2 thing that unites or binds, as a narrow bandage; 3 *mus* slur; 4 *typ* a two or more letters united to form a single character, as *æ*, *fi*; b stroke placed over two letters to indicate a ligature; 5 *surg* thread or wire used to tie blood vessels

light¹ /līt'/ [OB *lēoht*] *n* 1 condition of illumination necessary for vision; 2 luminous radiant energy which acts upon the eye to cause sight; 3 source of light; 4 sensation excited in the eye from which sight results; 5 brightness, illumination; 6 enlightenment; 7 window; 8 daylight; 9 appearance, aspect; 10 state of being in public view; 11 means of producing a flame to ignite something; 12 eminent or model person; 13 bright part of a painting or picture; 14 traffic light; 15 lighthouse; 16 **bring to light** to reveal; 17 **come to light** to be revealed; 18 **in the light of** considering; 19 **see the light**, a to be made public; b to understand; 20 **shed light on** to clear up ‖ *adj* 21 bright; illuminated; 22 pale in color; blond ‖ *v* (**lighted** or **lit**) *vt* 23 to set on fire, ignite; 24 to cause to shine; 25 to illuminate; 26 to brighten ‖ *vi* 27 to take fire; 28 **light up**, a to ignite a cigarette, etc.; b to become bright; c to brighten with joy ‖ SYN *n* blaze, flare, flame, flash, glare, gleam, glimmer, glitter, glow, sparkle, illumination ‖ DISCR *Blaze* and *flame* suggest light accompanied by heat; a *flame* is often sudden and intermittent; while a *blaze* is steadier both in heat and light, and is usually larger than a *flame*; thus, a candle *flame*, but the *blaze* of the sun. *Flare* suggests a sudden, unsteady, blinding light, as that of a torch; *flash*, a sudden light of short duration; *glare*, a steady, blinding, unpleasant light; *gleam*, a momentary, small light shining through darkness; *glimmer*, a faint wavering light; *glitter*, a hard, brilliant light; *glow*, a warm, soft, subdued, often rosy light; and *sparkle*, light in small, quick, sudden flashes. *Illumination* means either the general condition of light or brightness, or, specifically, the decoration of a house, a street, etc., with lights ‖ ANT *adj* dark, dim, gloomy

light² [OB *lēoht*, *līht*] *adj* 1 of little weight or specific gravity; not heavy; 2 less than usual in amount, weight, intensity, force, etc.; 3 delicate in structure or appearance; 4 easy to understand, perform, or endure, as *light reading, light tasks, light taxes*; 5 of little consequence; 6 (food) easy to digest; 7 (wine) containing little alcohol; 8 not heavy in movement or touch; nimble; graceful; 9 not heavily equipped, as *light infantry*; 10 carefree; gay; 11 frivolous; fickle; 12 morally loose; 13 unstable; flighty; 14 *cards* owing the pot money; 15 **make light of** to treat as unimportant ‖ *adv* 16 lightly ‖ **light'ly** *adv*

light³ [OB *līhtan* to make light] *v* (**lighted** or **lit**) *vi* 1 to come down, alight, as from a horse; 2 to settle from flight, as a bird; 3 **light on** or **upon** to come by chance on

light' breeze' *n* wind of 4–7 miles per hour

light'en¹ [< *light¹*] *vt* 1 to give light to; 2 to make bright or brighter ‖ *vi* 3 to gleam or flash with light; 4 to gleam with flashes of lightning; 5 to become lighter; brighten

light'en² [< *light²*] *vt* 1 to reduce in weight; 2 to alleviate, as cares or burdens; 3 to gladden or brighten ‖ *vi* 4 to become less heavy, burdensome, or severe

light′er¹ [< **light¹**] *n* **1** one who or that which lights; **2** device for lighting cigarets, etc.

light′er² [ME < MD] *n* large barge used to load vessels offshore, or to carry freight about a harbor

light′face′ *n typ* type with thin, light lines ‖ also *adj* ‖ **light′-faced′** *adj*

light′-fin′gered *adj* skillful at stealing and picking pockets

light′-foot′ed *adj* nimble of foot; fast-stepping

light′-head′ed *adj* **1** dizzy, giddy; **2** thoughtless; flighty

light′-heart′ed *adj* carefree, gay ‖ **light′-heart′ed·ness** *n*

light′ heav′y·weight′ *n* boxer or wrestler weighing between 160 and 175 pounds

light′house′ *n* (-hous·es /-ziz/) tower with a brilliant light at the top to guide ships at night

light′ing *n* **1** act or manner of illuminating; **2** arrangement of lights to achieve artistic effects, as in photography, the stage, and motion pictures

light′ me′ter *n photog* exposure meter

light′-mind′ed *adj* without seriousness; frivolous

light′ness¹ [< **light¹**] *n* **1** state of being illuminated; **2** loss of coloring; paleness

light′ness² [< **light²**] *n* **1** state of being light in weight; **2** lack of seriousness; frivolity; fickleness, delicacy; grace ‖ SYN gaiety, giddiness, flippancy, levity, flightiness, unsteadiness, inconstancy, volatility, buoyancy ‖ DISCR *Gaiety* is a proper lightness of heart apparent in speech and action. *Giddiness, flippancy, levity,* and *flightiness* are alike in being forms of *gaiety* carried to an extreme; but they differ in that *giddiness* usually means merely unsuitably wild or frivolous conduct; *flippancy* refers especially to speech that jests or trifles with a serious subject or upon a serious occasion; *levity* refers to inappropriately gay or trifling speech or conduct; as, in regard to so grave a decision his *levity* was ill-timed; and *flightiness* implies an unbalanced mental condition. *Unsteadiness, inconstancy,* and *volatility* are alike in suggesting lack of firmness; but *unsteadiness* suggests readiness to be moved from a purpose; *inconstancy* adds to this the idea of failure in loyalty; and *volatility* implies a fickle readiness to fly from one idea or plan to another. *Buoyancy,* taken literally, means lightness sufficient to enable a body to float on a liquid; but it suggests a lightness of spirit which can keep its possessor from sinking under trouble

light·ning /līt′niŋ/ [contr. of *lightening* < **lighten¹**] *n* **1** sudden discharge of electricity between clouds or between clouds and the ground ‖ *adj* **2** fast or sudden like lightning ‖ *v* (**light-ninged; light·ning**) *vi* **3** to discharge a flash or flashes of lightning

light′ning ar·rest′er *n* device for protecting electrical instruments from lightning by carrying the discharge to the ground

light′ning bug′ *n* firefly

light′ning rod′ *n* metal rod fastened high above a building to protect it from lightning by grounding discharges

light′ship′ *n* vessel carrying a warning light and moored at a specific spot, to warn or guide shipping

light′-struck′ *adj photog* (film) fogged by unintentional exposure to light

light′weight′ *n* **1** boxer weighing between 126 and 135 pounds; **2** *colloq* person of little importance or influence ‖ *adj* **3** below average in weight; **4** light in texture; **5** of little account

light′-year′ *n* distance traversed by light in one year, about 5,878,000,000,000 miles

lig·ne·ous /lig′nē-əs/ [< L *lignum* wood] *adj* composed of, or like, wood

lig·nin /lig′nin/ *n* substance that forms the main part of wood in woody stems

lig′nite /-nīt/ *n* soft brownish coal with a woody texture

lik·a·ble or **like·a·ble** /līk′əbəl/ *adj* pleasing, easily liked

like¹ /līk/ [OE *gelīc*] *adj* **1** similar; equal, as *in like manner* ‖ *prep* **2** in the manner of; **3** similar to, resembling; **4** characteristic of; **5** in the mood for, as *I feel like reading*; **6** showing evidence of, as *it looks like rain* ‖ *adv* **7** *slang* as if one is, as *he drove like crazy* ‖ *conj* **8** *colloq* **a** as; **b** as if ‖ *n* **9** that which is equal or similar; counterpart, as *where will you find his like?*; **10** the like something similar, as *they make nails, screws, and the like*; **11** the like of the equal of

like² [OE *līcian* to please] *vt* **1** to have a taste for; enjoy; find agreeable; **2** to find congenial; be attracted to; **3** to wish, want ‖ *vi* **4** to choose, as *do as you like* ‖ *n* **5** likes *pl* things one fancies

-like *adj suf* similar to, resembling, as *boylike, fishlike*

like′li·hood′ *n* probability

like′ly [ON *līkligr*] *adj* (-li·er; -li·est) **1** credible, plausible; **2** suitable, as *a likely place*; **3** favorable, promising; **4** likely to reasonably expected to, as *likely to happen* ‖ *adv* **5** probably ‖ SYN *adj* probable, credible, plausible ‖ DISCR A *likely* event is one that might in the circumstances happen; a *likely* rumor is such as might prove true; a *likely* prophecy is one that is apt to be justified by events. *Probable* is not so emphatic as *likely*; it connotes less assurance, more of doubt, although carrying the idea that the odds are in favor of the thing specified; a *probable* event may be expected to happen; a *probable* rumor is apt to prove true; a *probable* story has more evidence for it than against it (see *apt*)

lik·en /līk′ən/ [< *like*[1]] *vt* to compare

like′ness *n* 1 state or quality of being like; 2 portrait; copy; 3 guise; external appearance ‖ SYN resemblance, similarity, identity, agreement, parallel, portrait, effigy ‖ DISCR *Likeness, resemblance,* and *similarity* are often used one for another. *Likeness,* however, connotes an essential and specific sameness in the qualities or properties under discussion. *Resemblance* may suggest merely a fleeting or superficial correspondence. *Similarity* expresses a degree of *likeness,* but it is also casual, contingent, external in its nature. There is at times a startling *likeness* between father and son; a mirror reflects our *likeness.* A stranger's faint *resemblance* to some one we know bothers us until we can recall the one we are reminded of; a *resemblance* in form or shape is noticeable among natural objects, especially as seen in different lights or from different angles. *Similarity* is observable between characters, circumstances, reactions, styles of speech, modes of making decisions, ages, or the like

like′wise′ *adv* 1 in a similar manner; 2 also

lik′ing *n* 1 preference, inclination; 2 fondness; affection

li·lac /līl′ək/ [Sp < Ar *lilak* < Pers *nilak* bluish] *n* 1 any of a genus (*Syringa*) of shrubs of the olive family, with large clusters of fragrant white or purple flowers; 2 pinkish purple

Li·li·a·ceous /lil′ē·āsh′əs/ [< L *lilium* lily] *adj* 1 pert. to or resembling lilies; 2 *bot* pert. to or belonging to the lily family

Lil·li·pu·tian /lil′ēpyōōsh′ən/ [< *Lilliput,* fictitious country inhabited by tiny people in Swift's *Gulliver's Travels*] *n* 1 very small person; 2 person who is petty and narrow ‖ also *adj*

lilt /lilt/ [ME *lulte*] *n* 1 rhythmic movement or cadence, as in a tune; 2 lilting tune ‖ *vt* & *vi* 3 to sing or play in a rhythmic or gay manner

lil·y /lil′ē/ [OB *lilie* < Gk *leirion*] *n* (-ies) 1 any of a genus (*Lilium*) of plants having a bulblike root and conical, showy flowers; 2 any of various related plants resembling the lily; 3 fleur-de-lis

lil′y-liv′ered *adj* cowardly

lil′y of the val′ley *n* (lilies of the valley) low-growing perennial herb (*Convallaria majalis*) bearing racemes of fragrant white bell-shaped flowers

lil′y pad′ *n* wide, floating leaf of a water lily

lil′y-white′ *adj* 1 white as a lily; 2 pure, uncorrupted; 3 designating persons or groups opposed to the inclusion of Negroes in organizations or places of public accommodation

Li·ma /lēm′ə/ *n* capital of Peru (2,650,000)

li′ma bean′ /līm′ə/ [< *Lima*] *n* bean (*Phaseolus limensis*) or its flat seed, prized for food

limb[1] /lim/ [OE *lim*] *n* 1 arm, leg, or wing; 2 main branch of a tree; 3 **out on a limb** *colloq* in a vulnerable position

limb[2] [L *limbus* edge] *n astron* edge of the disk of the sun, moon, or a planet

lim·ber /lim′bər/ [?] *adj* 1 flexible; pliable; 2 supple, lithe ‖ *vt* 3 **limber up** to make limber ‖ *vi* 4 **limber up** to make oneself limber ‖ SYN *adj* pliable, supple, lithe, pliant (see *flexible*) ‖ ANT *adj* stiff, rigid, brittle, firm, unbending

lim·bo /lim′bō/ [< L *in limbo* on the edge (of hell)] *n* 1 abode of the souls of unbaptized infants and of the righteous who died before the coming of Christ; 2 place of oblivion or confinement

Lim′burg·er (cheese′) /lim′burg′ər/ [< *Limburg* province of The Netherlands] *n* soft cheese with a strong odor

lime[1] /līm′/ [OE *līm*] *n* 1 calcium oxide —CaO— a white earthlike substance obtained by the action of heat on limestone, marble, sea shells, etc., used in making cement, mortar, etc., and to neutralize acid soil ‖ *vt* 2 to treat (soil) with lime

lime[2] [F < Ar *līm*] *n* 1 small spiny tree (*Citrus aurantifolia*) with evergreen leaves and white flowers; 2 greenish-yellow, lemonlike acid fruit of this tree

lime′kiln′ *n* furnace for burning limestone or shells to obtain lime

lime′light′ [means of stage illumination produced by playing a hot flame on lime, used before the invention of the electric arc lamp] *n* notoriety; prominent position before the public

lim·er·ick /lim′ərik/ [< *Limerick,* county in Ireland] *n* humorous verse of five anapestic lines, often obscene, in which the first and second lines rhyme with the fifth, and the third line with the fourth

lime′stone′ *n* stone consisting essentially of calcium carbonate, used for building and as a source of lime

lim·ey /līm′ē/ [< *lime-juicer* British sailor, formerly required to drink lime juice to prevent scurvy] *n slang* Englishman

lim·it /lĭm′ĭt/ [MF *limite* < L *limes* (-*itis*)] *n* **1** boundary; **2** line or point beyond which extent is not possible (used of space, time, quantity, etc.); **3** utmost extent; **4 limits** *pl* space or region enclosed by boundaries || *vt* **5** to set a limit to; restrict

lim·i·ta·tion *n* **1** act of limiting or state of being limited; **2** that which limits; restriction; **3** inability; incapacity

lim·it·ed *adj* **1** restricted; circumscribed; **2** (train or bus) making a limited number of stops; **3** *Brit* (company) owned by stockholders whose liability is limited to the percentage of stock owned by each; **4** (monarchy) whose powers are restricted by a constitution and a legislature

lim·it·ed-ac·cess high·way *n* superhighway with access limited to specific interchanges and entrance and exit ramps

lim·it·less *adj* having no limit; unconfined; immeasurable || SYN infinite, boundless, illimitable, unrestricted

limn /lĭm′/ [< OF *luminer* to illuminate] *vt* **1** to paint or draw; **2** to portray, depict

lim·ou·sine /lĭm′əzēn′/ [F] *n* **1** large luxurious automobile with a separate compartment for the chauffeur; **2** small bus for transporting passengers to and from an airport

limp¹ /lĭmp′/ [< OE *lemphealt* limping] *vi* **1** to walk with or as with a lame leg; **2** to proceed haltingly or in a faltering manner || *n* **3** lameness in walking

limp² [?] *adj* **1** lacking stiffness or firmness; **2** weak in character; lacking vigor || SYN loose, elastic, drooping, limber, soft, flabby, flaccid || ANT stiff, substantial, firm, rigid, unbending

lim·pet /lĭm′pĭt/ [< AS *lempedu* < LL *lampreda*] *n* marine mollusk with a cone-shaped shell, found sticking tightly to rocks and piles and often used for food

lim·pid /lĭm′pĭd/ [L *limpidus*] *adj* transparent; sparklingly clear || **lim·pid·i·ty** *n* || SYN lucid, pellucid, crystalline (see *transparent*)

lin·age /lĭn′ĭj/ [< *line¹*] *n* number of agate lines contained in a newspaper or magazine article or advertisement

linch·pin /lĭnch′-/ [< OE *lynis*] *n* pin through the end of an axle to keep the wheel in place

Lin·coln /lĭnk′ən/ *n* capital of Nebraska (129,000)

Lin·coln, A·bra·ham *n* (1809–65) 16th president of the U.S. 1861–65; assassinated by John Wilkes Booth

Lind·bergh, Charles A. /lĭn(d)′burg/ *n* (1902–74) U.S. aviator; made first solo, nonstop flight across the Atlantic Ocean 1927

lin·den /lĭnd′ən/ [OE] *n* any of a genus (*Tilia*) of large trees with heart-shaped leaves and small clusters of cream-colored flowers, prized as shade trees

line¹ /lĭn′/ [OE < L *linea* string] *n* **1** slender string, rope, wire, cord, or the like; **2** mark drawn by a pen, pencil, or the like; **3** any mark resembling this, as a wrinkle in the skin; **4** wire or pipe for conducting electricity or fluids; **5** telephone connection; **6** a transportation or transit system; **b** particular route or track; **7** agate line; **8** row of persons or things; **9** queue; **10** *slang* glib conversation used to influence people to their detriment; **11** row of printed or written words; **12** verse; **13** short note or letter; **14** course of thought or conduct; **15** business or profession; **16** lineage; **17** *math* figure which has extent in one direction without breadth or thickness; **18** *mil* **a** forward position facing the enemy; **b** series of connected fortifications; **19** fighting forces of an army; **20** *nav* officers in charge of the fighting forces of a warship; **21** branch of business; **22** stock of goods; **23** the line the equator; **24** lines, **a** words of a part in a play; **b** contour, outline; **25** bring into line to make conform; **26** draw the line to impose a restriction, as *he drew the line at drinking*; **27** get into line to conform; **28** hold the line to stand firm, not give way; **29** in line, a straight; **b** in conformity; **30** in (the) line of duty while executing one's work or duty; **31** out of line *slang* not conforming to what is right or proper; **32** toe the line to do what is expected; follow orders || *vt* **33** to draw lines on; **34** to show by lines; outline; **35** to form a line along; **36** *baseball* to bat (the ball) swiftly and close to the ground; **37** line up, a to bring into a line or row; **b** to secure, get hold of || *vt* **38** line up to form into a line

line² [OE *līn* flax] *vt* **1** to cover on the inside, as a garment; **2** to serve as the inside covering of; **3** to put something inside, fill, as *line one's pockets*

line·age /lĭn′ĭj/ [AF *linage* < L *linea* line] *n* **1** descent from an ancestor; **2** family, pedigree

lin·e·al /lĭn′ē-əl/ [LL *linealis*] *adj* **1** linear; **2** pert. to direct descent from an ancestor; **3** hereditary

lin·e·a·ments /lĭn′ē-əmĕnts/ [L *lineamenta*] *npl* distinctive features, esp. of the face

lin·e·ar /lĭn′ē-ər/ [< L *linea* line] *adj* **1** pert. to or consisting of a line or lines; **2** pert. to length; **3** having length only; **4** resembling a line

lin·e·ar meas·ure *n* **1** system of measuring length; **2** any unit of measurement in linear measure, as the inch or foot

line′ drive′ *n baseball* batted ball that travels at great speed and near the ground

line′man /-mən/ *n* (-men /-mən/) **1** man who installs and repairs electrical, telephone, and telegraph wires; **2** *football* player in the line

lin·en /lĭn′ən/ [OE = made of flax] *n* **1** thread or fabric made of flax; **2** often **linens** *pl* **a** articles made of linen, as sheets, table cloths, etc.; **b** similar articles made of cotton

lin·er /līn′ər/ *n* **1** ship or plane on a regular schedule; **2** *baseball* line drive

line′up′ *n* **1** arrangement of persons or things in a line; **2** police procedure whereby suspects are lined up for identification; **3** *sports* list of starting players with their positions

-ling /-lĭŋ/ [OE] *n suf* **1** one connected or related, as *hireling*; **2** forming diminutives, as *duckling*

lin·ger /lĭŋ′gər/ [OE *lengan* to lengthen] *vi* **1** to remain or stay longer than usual; **2** to delay; dally; **3** to remain alive, though waning, dying, or the like

lin·ge·rie /län′zhərā′, lan′zhərē′/ *n* women's underwear

lin·go /lĭŋ′gō/ [< *lingua franca*] *n* (-goes) language, esp. one strange or foreign || SYN jargon, cant, dialect (see *language*)

lin·gua fran·ca /lĭŋ′gwə frăŋk′ə/ [It = Frankish tongue] *n* **1** jargon formerly common in the E Mediterranean region as a trade language, based mostly on Italian, with elements of other languages spoken in the area; **2** any language used as a medium of communication by speakers of other languages

lin·gual /lĭŋ′gwəl/ [< L *lingua* tongue] *adj* **1** pert. to or articulated with the tongue || *n* **2** lingual sound

lin′guist /-gwist/ *n* **1** polyglot; **2** person skilled in linguistics

lin·guis·tic /lĭŋ·gwĭs′tĭk/ *adj* **1** of or pert. to language; **2** of or pert. to linguistics || *n* **3 linguistics** *sg* science of language

lin·i·ment /lĭn′imənt/ [L *linimentum*] *n* liquid rubbed on the skin to soothe or stimulate it

lin·ing /līn′ĭŋ/ *n* that with which something is lined

link /lĭŋk′/ [ME *linke*] *n* **1** single loop or division of a chain; **2** single part of a connected series; **3** connection, tie; **4** one section of a chain of sausages || *vt* **5** to join by, or as by, a link || *vi* **6 link (up)** with to join with, be united to

link′age /-ĭj/ *n* **1** act of linking or state of being linked; **2** *mach* assembly of rods linked together to transmit motion

links′ [OE *hlincas* ridges of land] *npl* golf course

Link′ train′er [Edwin A. Link (1904–) Am inventor] *n* swiveling device for training airplane pilots on the ground, which simulates actual flying conditions

Lin·nae·an or **Lin·ne·an** /linē′ən/ [Carolus *Linnaeus* (1707–78) Sw botanist] *adj* of or pert. to Linnaeus (Linné) or the taxonomic classification and binomial nomenclature he devised

lin·net /lĭn′ĭt/ [OF *linette* < *lin* flax] *n* **1** small Old World finch (*Carduelis cannabina*); **2** finch of W U.S. and N Mexico (*Carpodacus mexicanus*)

li·no·le·um /lĭnō′lē·əm/ [< L *linum* flax + *oleum* oil] *n* floor covering made of ground cork and linseed oil with a backing of burlap or canvas

Lin·o·type /lĭn′ətīp/ [trademark < *line of type*] *n* keyboard-operated type-setting machine which casts each line of type in one piece || **lin′o·typ′ist** *n*

lin′seed′ /-sēd′/ [OE *līn* flax] *n* flaxseed

lin′seed oil′ *n* pale-yellow oil pressed from linseed, used in making paint, linoleum, printer's inks, etc.

lint /lĭnt′/ [ME] *n* **1** soft down obtained by scraping linen, used for dressing wounds; **2** raveling and bits of thread from textiles

lin·tel /lĭnt′əl/ [MF = threshold] *n* horizontal crosspiece over the top of a door or window

li·on /lī′ən/ [OF < Gk *leon*] *n* **1** large powerful cat (*Felis leo*) found in Africa and S Asia; **2** man of great courage; **3** much sought-after celebrity || **li′on·ess** *nfem*

li′on·heart′ed *adj* bold, courageous

li′on·ize′ *vt* to make much of, treat as a celebrity

lip /lĭp′/ [OE *lippa*] *n* **1** one of the two fleshy borders of the mouth; **2** flaring edge of a container; **3** rim or edge; **4** liplike part; **5** *slang* insolent talk; **6 button one's lip** *slang* to keep silent about something; **7 keep a stiff upper lip** to face distress or misfortune bravely

lip·id /lĭp′ĭd, līp′-/ also **lip·ide** /lĭp′ĭd, lĭp′īd/ [< F *lipide* < Gk *lipos* fat + *-id*] *n* any of a class of fats or fatlike substances, insoluble in water but soluble in organic solvents, that constitute the principal structural components of living cells

lip′ read′ing *n* comprehension of what a speaker is saying, as by a deaf person, by watching the movement of the lips || **lip′-read′** *v* (-read /-red/) *vt & vi*

lip′ serv′ice *n* insincere profession of loyalty or friendship

lip′stick′ *n* crayonlike stick of rouge for reddening the lips

liq·ue·fac·tion /lĭk′wĭfak′shən/ [see

liquefy] *n* act of liquefying or state of being liquefied

liq·ue·fy /lik′wifī′/ [L *liquefacere*] *v* (**-fied**) *vt & vi* to change into a liquid

li·queur /likur′/ [F] *n* strong, sweet, and variously flavored alcoholic liquor; cordial

liq·uid /lik′wid/ [L *liquidus*] *adj* 1 freely flowing; fluid; not solid or gaseous; 2 clear and smooth in sound; 3 colorless; transparent; 4 readily converted into cash ‖ *n* 5 liquid substance; 6 liquid consonant (*l* or *r*) ‖ **li·quid′i·ty** /likwid′-/ *n* ‖ SYN (see *fluid*)

liq′uid air′ *n* air liquefied by compression and cooling; used as a refrigerant

liq′ui·date′ *vt* 1 to settle or pay off, as debts; 2 to break up, as a partnership; 3 to eliminate permanently; kill; 4 to settle and wind up the affairs of (a company, estate, or the like); 5 to convert into cash ‖ *vi* 6 to liquidate debts ‖ **liq′ui·da′tor** *n* ‖ **liq′ui·da′tion** *n*

liq′uid meas′ure *n* system of units of capacity used for liquid commodities, as milk or gasoline

liq′uid ox′y·gen *n* oxygen liquefied by compression and cooling; used as an oxidizer of a liquid-fuel rocket

liq·uor /lik′ər/ [L = fluidity] *n* 1 alcoholic beverage, esp. one distilled, as whisky or brandy; 2 liquid in which meat or other food has boiled; 3 *pharm* solution of a nonvolatile substance

li·ra /lir′ə/ [It < L *libra* pound] *n* (**li·re** /lir′ā/) 1 monetary unit of Italy; 2 monetary unit of Turkey

Lis·bon /liz′bən/ *n* capital of Portugal (850,000)

lisle /līl′/ [*Lisle*, former spelling of Lille, France] *n* fine hard-twisted cotton thread or fabric

lisp /lisp/ [OE *āwlyspian* to lisp] *n* 1 speech defect characterized by the pronunciation of /s/ like /th/, and of /z/ like /th/ ‖ *vt & vi* 2 to pronounce with a lisp ‖ **lisp′ing·ly** *adv*

lis·some also **lis·som** /lis′əm/ [< *lithesome*] *adj* limber; supple; lithe

list¹ /list′/ [OE = border] *n* 1 series of names, words, or items arranged in a sequence; catalogue; roll; 2 list price ‖ *vt* 3 to set down in a list; 4 to register (a stock) in an exchange ‖ *vi* 5 to be offered for sale at a specified price, as *what does the camera list for?*

list² [?] *vi* 1 to tilt over to one side ‖ *vt* 2 to cause (a ship) to list ‖ *n* 3 tilting to one side

list³ [OE *hylstan*] *archaic vt* 1 to listen to ‖ *vi* 2 to listen

lis·ten /lis′ən/ [OE *hlysnan*] *vi* 1 to give close attention so as to hear; hearken; 2 to heed, obey; 3 **listen in**, **a** to eavesdrop on a telephone conversation; **b** to listen to a broadcast program ‖ **lis′ten·er** *n* ‖ SYN hear; attend, hark, heed ‖ DISCR To *hear* is to perceive by the ear, as a sound, cry, etc. To *listen* is to make the effort to *hear*, to try consciously to *hear*. We may *hear* without *listening* and we may *listen* without *hearing*

list′less [ME *lystles*] *adj* languid; spiritless; lacking energy ‖ **list′less·ly** *adv* ‖ SYN languid, dull, flagging, unconcerned, unheeding

list′ price′ *n* established retail price

lists′ [ME *listes*] *npl* 1 enclosure where tournaments were held; 2 any place of combat or competition; 3 **enter the lists** to engage in conflict or controversy

Liszt, Franz /fränts′ list′/ *n* (1811–86) Hungarian composer and pianist

lit /lit′/ *pt & pp* of **light¹** and **light³**

lit. 1 liter(s); 2 literal(ly); 3 literature

lit·a·ny /lit′ənē/ [Gk *litaneia*] *n* (**-nies**) 1 prayer consisting of a series of petitions with responses by the congregation; 2 any solemn supplication; 3 droning and monotonous account

li′tchi /lēch′ē/ [Chin *li chih*] *n* 1 Chinese tree (*Litchi chinensis*); 2 also **litchi nut** edible dried fruit of this tree

li·ter /lēt′ər/ [F *litre* < Gk *litra* pound] *n* metric unit of capacity, equal to 1000 cubic centimeters; equivalent to 1.0567 liquid quarts

lit·er·a·cy /lit′ərəsē/ [see **literate**] *n* ability to read and write

lit·er·al /lit′ərəl/ [< L *littera* letter] *adj* 1 according to the natural or primary meaning of a word, not figurative; 2 consisting of or pert. to letters; 3 exactly following the words of the original, as *a literal translation*; 4 not exaggerated, as *the literal truth*; 5 matter-of-fact, prosaic ‖ **lit′er·al·ly** *adv* ‖ **lit′er·al·ism** *n*

lit′er·ar·y *adj* 1 pert. to literature or to men of letters; 2 having a knowledge of, or engaged in, literature

lit′er·ate /-it/ [L *litteratus* learned] *adj* 1 knowing how to read and write; 2 educated; well-read; 3 pert. to, or having knowledge of, letters or literature ‖ *n* 4 literate person

lit·e·ra·ti /lit′ərät′ī, -rät′ē/ [L] *npl* men of letters; intellectuals

lit·er·a·ture /lit′(ə)rəchər, -chŏŏr′/ [L *litteratura* grammar] *n* 1 all the writings of a people, country, or period, esp. those prized for beauty or force of style; 2 the body of writings on a given subject; 3 any printed matter, as advertising circulars, etc.

lith- or **litho-** [Gk *lithos*] *comb form* stone

-lith /-lith′/ *comb form* stone

lithe /līth′/ [OE = soft] *adj* limber; gracefully nimble; supple

lithe′some *adj* lithe, lissome

lith·i·a /lith′ē·ə/ *n* white crystalline oxide of lithium (Li₂O)

lith′i·um [< Gk *lithos* stone] *n* silver-white metallic element (Li; at.no. 3; at.wt. 6.939), the lightest known metal

lith′o·graph′ /lith′ə-/ *n* 1 impression of a picture or of printed matter reproduced from a specially treated surface of stone or other material ‖ *vt* 2 to reproduce by lithograph ‖ **lith′o·graph′ic** *adj* ‖ **li·thog·ra·phy** /lithŏg′rəfē/ *n* ‖ **li·thog′ra·pher** *n*

lith′o·sphere′ *n* crust of the earth

Lith·u·a·ni·a /lith′ōō·ān′ē·ə/ *n* formerly independent country on the E shore of the Baltic, now a constituent republic of the Soviet Union (2,800,000; 31,623 sq.m.; cap. Vilna ‖ **Lith′u·a/ ni·an** *adj & n*

lit·i·gant /lit′igənt/ *n* party to a lawsuit

lit′i·gate′ [L *litigare* (*-atus*) < *lis* (*litis*) lawsuit] *vi* 1 to bring to court for settlement ‖ *vt* 2 to engage in a lawsuit ‖ **lit′i·ga′tion** *n*

li·ti·gious /litij′əs/ [MF *litigieux* < L *litigiosus*] *adj* 1 given to engaging in lawsuits; 2 subject to litigation; 3 quarrelsome, contentious

lit·mus /lit′məs/ [< Scand] *n* violet-blue coloring matter obtained from lichens, which is turned red by an acid and is restored to blue by an alkali

lit′mus pa′per *n* paper saturated with litmus, used to test solutions

li·to·tes /lit′ətēz′, lit′-, lītō′tēz/ [Gk = plainness] *n* understatement by denial of the opposite, as *a man of no mean ability*

Litt. D. [L *Litterarum Doctor*] Doctor of Letters

lit·ter /lit′ər/ [OF *litiere* bed, litter] *n* 1 curtained couch with projecting shafts for carrying; 2 stretcher for a sick or wounded person; 3 straw, hay, or the like, used as bedding for animals; 4 objects or rubbish scattered about untidily; 5 young of animals produced at one time ‖ *vt* 6 to scatter carelessly; 7 to render untidy by scattering rubbish about ‖ *vi* 8 to scatter around; 9 to bring forth young, said of animals

lit′ter·bug′ *n colloq* person who scatters waste paper and rubbish about at random

lit·tle /lit′əl/ [OE *lȳtel*] *adj* (less or *lesser* or **lit·tler**; *least* or **lit·tlest**) 1 small in size, quantity, dignity, importance, or power; 2 brief in time; 3 young; 4 mean; petty; 5 a little an appreciable amount of ‖ *adv* (*less*; *least*) 6 in a small degree; not much; 7 (used before a verb) not at all, as *he little knew that was going on;* 8 a little slightly, somewhat; 9 little by little gradually ‖ *n* 10 small amount, quantity, or degree; 11 a little, a a small amount; b a small distance; c a brief

time; 12 make little of to belittle ‖ SYN *adj* small, diminutive, tiny, minute ‖ DISCR *Little* is the opposite of great or big, and usually is applied to that which is of natural size, condition, or amount, as a *little* book of poems; the *little* finger. *Little* also connotes, in certain connections, tenderness, indulgence, condescension or the like, as *little* woman; you generous *little* simpleton; your *little* favor was appreciated. *Small* is opposed rather to large, and describes that which is either definitely or comparatively lacking, or deficient in size or strength as set by a standard; a *small* number is less than we expected; so is a *small* contribution; we say a dress is too *small*, not too *little*. Unlike *little*, *small* does not carry a favorable emotional connotation; a bereaved parent speaks of a *little* grave, not a *small* grave; an annoyed old gentleman refers to *small* boys' mischief, not to that of dear *little* boys. Both *small* and *little* connote the unimportant, the paltry, or contemptible; we speak of *small* significance; *little* minds; *small* change; *little* trials are harder to bear than big ones. *Tiny* is a child's word for very *small;* it is conversationally used also for *minute*, which means exceedingly small, and, as applied to details or particulars, precise, exact, accurate. *Diminutive* means relatively *small;* a *diminutive* person is *smaller* than he ought to be

Lit′tle Bear′ *n* constellation Ursa Minor

Lit′tle Rock′ *n* capital of Arkansas (110,000)

lit′tle slam′ *n bridge* winning of all tricks but one

lit·to·ral /lit′ərəl/ [< L *litus* (*litoris*) shore] *adj* 1 pert. to, near, or situated on a shore ‖ *n* 2 coastal region

lit·ur·gy /lit′ərjē/ [Gk *leitourgia* public worship] *n* (*-gies*) set form of service or ritual for public worship ‖ **li·tur·gi·cal** /litur′jikəl/ *adj*

liv·a·ble also **live·a·ble** /liv′əbəl/ *adj* 1 capable of being lived through; endurable; 2 fit or agreeable to live in or with

live[1] /liv′/ [OE *libban*] *vt* 1 to be alive, have life; 2 to pass life in a particular manner, as *to live happily;* 3 to reside; 4 to win a livelihood; 5 to survive or endure, as *they lived through hard times;* 6 to enjoy life to the full; 7 live high to live luxuriously; 8 live in to reside at one's place of employment, as a servant; 9 live up to to come up to the expectation of (an ideal, standard, or the like) ‖ *vt* 10 to experience or pass, as *to live a happy life;* 11 to practice or express constantly, as *to live one's religion;* 12 live down to cause to be forgotten, as *to live down disgrace;* 13 **live it up** *colloq* to live extravagantly

live² /līv′/ [< *alive*] *adj* 1 alive, living; 2 pert. to living things; 3 effective; operative; 4 unexploded, as a shell; 5 electrically charged; 6 still burning, as a coal; 7 *sports* (ball) in play; 8 bright, striking (color); 9 energetic; full of enthusiasm; 10 of present interest, as *a live topic;* 11 (radio or television program) broadcast when heard or seen, not taped or prerecorded; 12 **live one** *slang* ready spender

-lived /-līvd′/ *comb form* having a specified kind of life, as *long-lived*

live·li·hood /līv′-/ [ME *livilod*] *n* means of existence, support; employment || SYN living, maintenance, subsistence, support

live′long /liv′-/ [OE *lēof lang* dear long] *adj* lasting long (of time); tedious; whole, entire

live·ly /līv′-/ [OE *līflīc* vital] *adj* (-li·er; -li·est) 1 active; vigorous; 2 brisk; full of spirit; 3 vivid; keen; 4 cheering, exhilarating, as *a lively tune;* 5 resilient, as a ball || *adv* 6 briskly || **live′li·ness** *n* || SYN *adj* merry, sportive, sprightly, vivacious, spirited, gay, alive || ANT *adj* slow, languid, sluggish, dull

liv·en /līv′ən/ *vt* 1 to make lively || *vi* 2 **liven up** to become lively

live′ oak′ /līv′/ *n* evergreen oak (*Quercus virginiana*) of the southern U.S.

liv·er /liv′ər/ [OE *lifer*] *n* organ of the body, the chief functions of which are to secrete bile and to form glycogen from the digested food material

liv·er·ied /liv′ərēd/ [< *livery*] *adj* clothed in livery

Liv·er·pool *n* seaport in NW England (750,000) || **Liv′er·pud′li·an** /-pud′-lē·ən/ *adj & n*

liv·er·wurst /-wurst′, -wŏŏrst′/ [< G *wurst* sausage] *n* sausage containing mostly ground liver

liv·er·y /liv′ərē/ [OF *livree* clothing allowance] *n* (-ies) 1 distinctive costume worn by servants or by any special group of persons; 2 maintenance of horses for hire

liv·er·y·man /-mən/ *n* (-men /-mən/) keeper or employee of a livery stable

liv·er·y sta′ble *n* stable where horses and vehicles are cared for or let out for hire

lives /līvz′/ *pl* of life

live′ steam′ /līv′-/ *n* steam under full pressure

live′stock′ *n* domestic animals raised for use or profit

live′ wire′ *n* 1 wire carrying an electric current; 2 *slang* extremely energetic person

liv·id /liv′id/ [L *lividus*] *adj* 1 black-and-blue; discolored, as by a bruise; 2 ashy-pale

liv·ing /liv′-/ *adj* 1 alive; 2 in actual

use, as *a living language;* 3 vigorous, active, as *a living hope;* 4 of or pert. to existing persons or things, as *within living memory;* 5 true to life; 6 pert. to life, as *living conditions;* 7 (wage) sufficient for life; 8 designed for living in, as *living accommodations* || *n* 9 livelihood; 10 mode of life; 11 state of existence; 12 **the living** *pl* those who are alive

liv′ing death′ *n* unbearable state of existence

liv′ing room′ *n* room in a residence for lounging, visiting, and social activity

liv′ing wage′ *n* wage sufficient to make life fairly tolerable

liz·ard /liz′ərd/ [MF *lesard*] *n* reptile (suborder Lacertilia) having a scaly body, a long tail, and typically, four well-developed legs

'll /-l, -əl/ 1 will, as *he'll come;* 2 *colloq* till, as *wait'll I see him*

LL, L.L. 1 Late Latin; 2 Low Latin

lla·ma /läm′ə/ [Sp < Quechua] *n* South American ruminant (genus *Lama*) with a woolly coat, used as a beast of burden

lla·no /län′ō/ [Sp] *n* broad grassy plain of Spanish America

LL.B. [L *Legum Baccalaureus*] Bachelor of Laws

LL.D. [L *Legum Doctor*] Doctor of Laws

lo /lō′/ [OE *lā*] *interj* poet. behold!, look!

load /lōd′/ [OE *lād*] *n* 1 burden; 2 amount carried at one time; 3 customary unit or measure of weight of certain substances; 4 that which is held up or borne, as *the load on an arch;* 5 mental burden; 6 charge of ammunition; 7 work that has to be done by a machine, person, or group; 8 **have a load on** *slang* to be drunk; 9 **get a load of** *slang* to look at; 10 **loads** *colloq* plenty, lots, as *loads of fun* || *vt* 11 to put a load on or in; 12 to put (freight, cargo, etc.) on or in a vehicle or carrier; 13 to burden, weigh down; 14 to give to in great abundance; 15 to put a charge in (a firearm); 16 to put (film) in a camera || *vi* 17 to put on or take on a load; 18 to load a firearm || *adv* 19 **loads** *colloq* a lot || **load′er** *n* || SYN *n* pack, weight, burden (see *encumbrance*)

load′ed *adj* 1 fraudulently weighted (dice); 2 *slang* very rich; 3 *slang* drunk

load′stone′ *n* var of lodestone

loaf¹ /lōf′/ [OE *hlāf*] *n* (**loaves** /-vz/) 1 shaped mass of bread or cake; 2 shaped mass of food, as of meat or sugar

loaf² [< *loafer*] *vt* 1 to waste time; lounge about doing nothing || *vt* 2 **loaf away** to pass (time) in idleness

loaf·er [prob < D *landlooper* vagabond] *n* 1 one who loafs; 2 casual moccasinlike shoe

loam /lōm′/ [OE *lām*] *n* rich fertile soil composed of sand, clay, and decayed organic matter ‖ **loam′y** *adj* (-i-er; -i-est)

loan /lōn′/ [ON *lān*] *n* 1 something lent, esp. money at interest; 2 act of lending ‖ *vt & vi* 3 to lend

loan′ shark′ *n colloq* one who lends money at exorbitant interest and ensures collection by threats of violence

loan′ trans-la′tion *n* 1 creation of a compound from native elements translated from the corresponding elements of a compound in a foreign language; 2 the compound thus created, as *loan translation* from German *Lehnübersetzung*

loan′ word′ *n* word adopted into a language from another language, as *hotel* from French

loath /lōth′, lōth′/ [OE *lāth* hostile] *adj* unwilling, reluctant ‖ SYN reluctant, averse, indisposed, disinclined, unwilling, opposed

loathe /lōth′/ [OE *lāthian*] *vt* to detest, abhor

loath′ing /-th-/ *n* aversion, intense disgust

loath′some /-th-/ *adj* disgusting, revolting ‖ SYN abominable, offensive, abhorrent, detestable, revolting (see *hateful*)

loaves /lōvz′/ *pl* of **loaf**

lob /lob′/ [*obs lob* something hanging] *v* (lobbed; lob-bing) *tennis vt* 1 to hit (the ball) in a high arc ‖ *vi* 2 to lob the ball ‖ *n* 3 lobbed ball

Lo-ba-chev′ski-an ge-om′e-try /lō′-bəchef′skē-ən/ [N. I. *Lobachevski* (1793–1856) Russ mathematician] *n* non-Euclidean geometry of a space in which parallel lines steadily diverge from each other

lo-bar /lōb′ər, lō′bär/ [see **lobe**] *adj* of or pert. to a lobe

lo′bar pneu-mo′ni-a *n* acute pneumonia, involving a lobe or lobes of the lungs, caused by the pneumococcus

lob-by /lob′ē/ [ML *lobia* gallery] *n* (-bies) 1 entrance hall, as to a theater, apartment, or public building; 2 group of persons who try to influence the votes of members of a lawmaking body ‖ *v* (-bied) *vi* 3 to try to influence the votes of legislators ‖ *vt* 4 to try to get (a bill) passed by lobbying ‖ **lob′by-ist** *n*

lobe /lōb′/ [Gk *lobos*] *n* 1 any rounded projection or part, as the soft hanging part of the ear; 2 subdivision of an organ marked off by a fissure or connective tissue

lob-ster /lob′stər/ [OE *loppestre*] *n* (-ster or -sters) 1 any of various edible crustaceans, esp. any of a genus (*Homarus*) having five pairs of legs, the first developed into powerful claws; 2 spiny lobster

lob′ster pot′ *n* trap for catching lobsters

lo-cal /lōk′əl/ [< L *locus* place] *adj* 1 pert. to place; 2 relating to, or characteristic of, a particular place; 3 pert. to or for a particular part of the body, as *a local anesthetic;* 4 making all stops ‖ *n* 5 local train or bus; 6 local branch, as of a labor union

lo′cal col′or *n* distinctive characteristics of a place or period that set it apart from others

lo-cale /lōkal′/ [F *local*] *n* 1 place with reference to some characteristic condition; 2 scene, as of a play or story

lo-cal-i-ty /lōkal′itē/ *n* (-ties) 1 general region or position; vicinity; 2 definite place ‖ SYN neighborhood, district, vicinage, place, position

lo′cal-ize′ *vt* to limit or trace to a particular place

lo′cal op′tion *n* right of choice granted to a political subdivision, esp. as to permission to sell alcoholic beverages

lo-cate /lō′kāt, lōkāt′/ [L *locare* (-*atus*) to place] *vt* 1 to place in a particular spot; establish; 2 to mark out and determine the position of; 3 to discover the location of ‖ *vi* 4 to settle

lo-ca′tion *n* 1 act of locating or state of being located; 2 position or place; 3 area or tract with definite limits; 4 **on location** motion pictures away from the studio, in an actual locale

loc-a-tive /lok′ətiv/ [< *locate*] *gram adj* 1 designating a case in some languages which indicates place where ‖ *n* 2 locative case; 3 word in the locative

lo-ca-tor /lō′kātər/ *n* 1 person who fixes boundaries; 2 filing card that shows the location of records, personnel, etc.; 3 device for locating airborne aircraft

lo′ca-tor map′ *n* small map that is inserted with a geographical entry in a dictionary or encyclopedia to supplement and illustrate the definition

loc. cit. [L *loco citato*] in the place cited

loch /lok′, lokh′/ [Gael] *n Scot* 1 lake; 2 bay or arm of the sea

lo-ci /lō′sī/ *pl* of **locus**

lock¹ /lok′/ [OE *locc*] *n* 1 tuft or curl of hair; 2 **locks** *pl* head of hair

lock² [OE *loc*] *n* 1 device for securing something closed, as a lid, door, drawer, safe, or the like, so that it cannot be opened without a key or combination; 2 any device that fastens; 3 enclosure between two gates in a canal for raising and lowering boats from one water level to another; 4 mechanism for firing a gun; 5 any of several holds in wrestling ‖ *vt* 6 to fasten or secure with a lock; 7 to make fast by interlocking, as *locked in an embrace;* 8 to make rigid by the linking of parts, as gears; 9 to jam, make immovable; 10 **lock horns** to dispute, clash head-on; 11 **lock in** to confine as with a lock; 12 **lock out, a** to keep out as by a lock;

b to subject to a lockout; **13 lock up,** a to secure by locking; b to incarcerate ‖ *vi* **14** to become locked; **15** to become interlocked; **16 lock up** to lock all the doors of a place

lock'er *n* drawer, cupboard, compartment, or chest secured by a lock

lock'et /-ǐt/ [MF *locquet* small lock] *n* small case, usu. worn on a necklace, holding a portrait or keepsake

lock'jaw' *n* form of tetanus in which the jaws lock together

lock' nut' *n* **1** nut specially made so that it will not work loose when holding a bolt; **2** second nut used to keep the first nut tight

lock'out' *n* refusal by an employer to allow employees to continue to work for him unless they accept his terms as to wages and working conditions

lock'smith' *n* maker or mender of locks

lock' step' *n* march in very close file, in which the leg of each marcher stays closely behind the leg of the marcher in front of him

lock'up' *n* jail

lo·co /lō̄'kō/ [Sp] *adj slang* crazy

lo'co·mo'tion /lō̄k'ə-/ [< *locus* + *motion*] *n* act or power of motion

lo'co·mo'tive *adj* **1** pert. to locomotion ‖ *n* **2** self-propelled vehicle for pulling railway trains

lo'co·weed' /lō̄k'ō-/ *n* any of various plants (genera *Astragalus* and *Oxytropis*) that cause erratic behavior and paralysis in animals

lo·cus /lō̄k'əs/ [L = place] *n* (-ci /-sī/) **1** place, locality; **2** *geom* the collection of all points, lines, or surfaces which satisfy a given condition; **3** *genetics* linear position of a gene on a chromosome

lo·cust /lō̄k'əst/ [L *locusta*] *n* **1** any of a family (Acrididae) of grasshoppers destructive to vegetation, which migrate in great swarms; **2** cicada; **3** any of several large deciduous trees (genus *Robinia*), esp. the common locust (*R. pseudoacacia*) having rough bark, yellow-white flowers, and weak thorns

lo·cu·tion /lōkyō̄osh'ən/ [< L *loqui* (*locutus*) to speak] *n* **1** particular style of speech; **2** peculiar phrase; idiom

lode /lōd/ [OE *lād* course] *n* deposit of metallic ore found in a vein in rocks

lode'star' *n* **1** guiding star; **2** North Star

lode'stone' *n* **1** magnetite that possesses magnetic polarity; **2** piece of this used as a magnet; **3** person or thing that attracts

lodge /loj/ [OF *loge*] *n* **1** small house; cottage; hut; **2** house for seasonal or special use, as *a hunting lodge;* **3** porter's or gamekeeper's cottage on a large estate; **4** hut of an American Indian; **5** local chapter or meeting place of a fraternal organization; **6** resort hotel ‖ *vt* **7** to furnish with dwelling space; **8** to deposit, as for safekeeping; **9** to settle or put in some spot; **10** to place formally before the proper authorities, as a complaint; **11** to confer or vest, as power ‖ *vi* **12** to live for a time; **13** to live in a rented room or rooms; **14** to be deposited or come to rest

lodg'er *n* one who lives in a rented room in another's home

lodg'ing *n* **1** sleeping accommodation; **2** temporary residence; **3 lodgings** *pl* room or rooms rented as living quarters

lodg'ment *n* **1** act of lodging or state of being lodged; **2** place of lodging; **3** occupation of a military position

lo·ess /lō̄'es, les', lus'/ [G] *n* loamy yellowish-brown earth found in river valleys in the Northern Hemisphere

loft /lôft/ [OE < Scand] *n* **1** room directly beneath a roof; **2** gallery raised above the main floor, as an organ loft or a hayloft; **3** upper floor in a warehouse or factory; **4** *golf* a slope on the face of a club to cause the ball to rise; b stroke made with such a club ‖ *vt* **5** *golf* to hit (a ball) high in the air ‖ *vi* **6** to loft the ball

loft'y *adj* (-i·er; -i·est) **1** very high; **2** exalted in dignity or rank; **3** proud; haughty; **4** stately, sublime ‖ SYN haughty, insolent, superior, dignified, exalted, tall, high, soaring ‖ ANT meek, lowly, low, abject

log¹ /log', lôg/ [ME *logge*] *n* **1** unhewn piece of felled timber; **2** device for measuring the speed of a ship through the water; **3** book in which the record of a ship's or aircraft's daily progress and other items of interest are entered; **4** record of progress and accomplishment kept in various other industries ‖ *v* (**logged; log·ging**) *vt* **5** to fell and trim (trees); **6** to fell the timber of (a tract of woodland); **7** to enter in a log; make a record of; **8** to go at (a certain speed), as a ship or plane; **9** to cover (a certain distance) ‖ *vi* **10** to cut down and get out trees ‖ **log'ger** *n*

log² *n* logarithm

log- or **logo-** [Gk *logos*] *comb form* word, speech

lo'gan·ber'ry /lō̄g'ən-/ [J. H. *Logan* (1841–1928) Am horticulturist] *n* (-ries) **1** plant obtained by crossing the red raspberry with the California blackberry; **2** its fruit

log·a·rithm /log'ərĭth'əm, lôg'-, -rĭth'əm/ [*log-* + Gk *arithmos* number] *n* exponent of the power to which a base number must be raised to give a required number, as *the logarithm of 100 to the base 10 is 2* ‖ **log'a·rith'·mic** *adj*

log'book' *n* log¹ **3**

loge /lōzh/ [F] *n* **1** separate section in

front of the lowest balcony in a theater; 2 theater box

log′ger-head′ /lŏg′-, lôg′-/ [< dial. *logger* block of wood] *n* at loggerheads, quarreling

log-gia /lŏj′(ē)ə, lôj′-/ [It] *n* (-gias or -ge /-jä/) covered gallery or arcade having at least one side open to the air

log-ic /lŏj′ĭk/ [Gk *logike* of reason] *n* 1 science of correct reasoning; 2 correct reasoning or inference; 3 particular way of reasoning; 4 system of classification of thought in any branch of knowledge

log′i-cal *adj* 1 pert. to logic; 2 according to the rules of logic; 3 reasonable; to be expected; 4 skilled in using the principles of logic || **log′i-cal-ly** *adv*

lo-gi-cian /lōjĭsh′ən/ *n* one skilled in logic

lo-gis-tics /lōjĭs′tĭks/ [F *logistique* < *loger* to lodge] *nsg* branch of military operations dealing with the moving, quartering, and provisioning of troops || **lo-gis′tic** (-ti-cal) *adj*

log′jam′ /lŏg′-, lôg′-/ *n* 1 mass of floating logs jammed immovably together; 2 any blockage or deadlock

log′o-gram′ also **log′o-graph′** /lŏg′-, lôg′-/ *n* conventional symbol representing a word, as & for *and* or $ for *dollar* || **log′o-graph′ic** *adj*

log′roll′ing *n* 1 sport of rotating a log in the water with the feet while maintaining one's balance; 2 mutual exchanging of favors, as by legislators

-logue or **-log** /-lŏg′, -lôg′/ [Gk *-logos*] *comb form* specified kind of speech or writing, as *dialogue*

log′wood′ *n* 1 West Indian and Central American tree (*Haematoxylon campechianum*); 2 heartwood of this tree; 3 dark-red coloring principle of this heartwood, much used in dyeing

lo-gy /lōg′ē/ *adj* (-gi-er; -gi-est) sluggish, lethargic

-l·o·gy /-ləjē/ [Gk *-logia*] *comb form* 1 science, doctrine, theory, as *zoology*; 2 kind of speaking or writing, as *phraseology*

loin /loin′/ [MF *loigne* < VL *lumbea*] *n* 1 cut of meat from the front of the hindquarters, as of beef, pork, etc.; 2 **loins** *pl* a lower part of the body on either side of the spine between the lowest rib and the hip bone; but *literary* hips and lower abdominal region, regarded as the seat of strength and of procreation; 3 **gird up one's loins** to get ready for strenuous action

loin′cloth′ *n* cloth worn over the lower part of the loins, the sole article of clothing of many primitive tribes

loi-ter /loit′ər/ [perh < MD *loteren*] *vi* 1 to spend time idly; delay; saunter || *vt* 2 loiter away to pass (time) idly || **loi′ter-er** *n*

loll /lŏl′/ [ME *lollen*] *vi* 1 to lounge about at ease; 2 to hang out loosely, as a dog's tongue || *vt* 3 to permit to hang loosely or droop

lol-li-pop or **lol-ly-pop** /lŏl′ēpop′/ [?] *n* piece of hard candy on a stick

Lom-bard /lŏm′bərd, lum′-, -bärd′/ [OIt *Lombardo* < LL *Langobardus*] *n* 1 native or inhabitant of Lombardy, a region of N Italy; 2 one of a Germanic tribe that settled in N Italy in the 6th century

Lom-bard-y /lŏm′bərdē, lum′-/ *n* region and former province in N Italy (cap. Milan)

Lom′bard-y pop′lar *n* poplar (*Populus nigra italica*) remarkable for its slender form and upcurved branches, popular as a shade tree in narrow streets

lon. longitude

Lon-don /lun′dən/ *n* 1 capital of the United Kingdom and of the British Commonwealth, comprising the administrative county of London, composed of the cities of London and Westminster and 27 boroughs (3,250,-000); 2 **City of London** small area in the heart of London, one square mile in extent, nucleus of the larger city, bailiwick of the Lord Mayor, and financial center of Britain; 3 **Greater London** the metropolitan area of which London is the nucleus (7,913,600; 693 sq.m.) || **Lon′don-er** *n*

Lon′don broil′ *n* plank steak broiled and cut into thin slices

lone /lōn′/ [< *alone*] *adj* 1 solitary; unaccompanied; 2 apart, isolated; 3 sole

lone-ly *adj* (-li-er; -li-est) 1 solitary; without a companion; 2 desolate; remote; 3 isolated; 4 lonesome || **lone′li-ness** *n* || SYN solitary, alone, lone, lonesome, desolate, deserted || DISCR To be *alone* is to be all by oneself. *Solitary* describes the condition of being *alone*, as *solitary* confinement; a *solitary* stroll. *Solitary* applied to places means secluded, unfrequented, as *solitary* haunts. He who is *lonely* is *solitary* and *alone* and regrets it. A *lonely* place is remote, hard to reach, or not frequented by human beings. *Lone* is a poetical word for *lonely*, though we still speak ordinarily of a *lone* hand in cards. He is *lonesome* who feels *lonely*; that is *lonesome* which makes us feel *lonely*, as the *lonesome* cry of the whippoorwill. A place is *lonesome* that is secluded. *Desolate* describes the state of one forlorn because he is left alone

lon′er *n colloq* lone wolf

lone′some *adj* 1 depressed because alone; 2 remote; isolated || **lone′some·ly** *adv* || **lone′some·ness** *n* || SYN forlorn, alone, deserted, desolate (see *lonely*)

lone' wolf' *n colloq* one who lives and acts alone

long[1] /lôŋ′, loŋ′/ [OE *lang, long*] *adj* (**long-er** /lôŋ′gər, loŋ′gər/; **long-est** /lôŋ′gist, loŋ′gist/) 1 having great extent or duration; 2 tedious; tiresome; 3 in length, as *a yard long;* 4 continued to a great extent, as *a long list;* 5 far-reaching; 6 designating measure, quantity, weight, etc., in excess of the standard, as *a long half hour;* 7 *fin* owning stocks or commodities; 8 high (odds); 9 *phonet* a (any of the English vowels) sounded like its name; b (vowels and consonants) prolonged in pronunciation; 10 long on well supplied with ‖ *adv* 11 to a great length or period; 12 at a distant time, as *long before;* 13 for a length of time, as *to stay long;* 14 throughout the duration of, as *all his life long;* 15 as long as, a while; b inasmuch as; c provided that ‖ *n* 16 garment made for tall people; 17 *fin* person who owns stocks or commodities in expectation of a rise; 18 **before long** soon; 19 **for long** for a long time

long[2] [OE *langian*] *vi* 1 long for to desire (something) eagerly; 2 long to to desire eagerly to (do something) ‖ SYN hanker, crave, yearn, want, desire

long. longitude

Long' Beach' *n* city in SW California (358,633)

long' dis'tance *n* 1 telephone service between distant points; 2 operator or exchange that makes connections for distant calls ‖ **long'-dis'tance** *adj & adv*

long' di·vi'sion *n* arithmetical division, with divisors of two or more digits, in which each step is written down in a conventional pattern

long'-drawn' also **long'-drawn'-out'** *adj* prolonged

lon·gev·i·ty /lonjev′itē/ [< L *longus* long + *aevum* age] *n* 1 great length of life; 2 seniority; tenure ‖ **lon·ge'vous** /-jē′-/ *adj*

long' face' *n* glum expression ‖ ‖ **long'-faced'** *adj*

Long'fel'low, Henry Wadsworth *n* (1807–82) U.S. poet

long'hair' *n colloq* person devoted to intellectual pursuits and to classical art and music

long'hand' *n* ordinary handwriting

long'-head'ed *adj* farseeing; shrewd

long'horn' *n* one of a breed of long-horned cattle of the southwestern U.S.

long'ing *n* earnest desire; strong craving ‖ SYN appetite, yearning, inclination (see *desire*)

Long' Is'land *n* island in SE New York, separated from Connecticut by Long Island Sound

lon·gi·tude /lon′jit(y)ood′/ [L *longi-*

tudo] *n* angular distance east or west on the earth's surface measured from the meridian of Greenwich, England

lon·gi·tu·di·nal *adj* 1 pert. to longitude; 2 pert. to length; 3 extending lengthwise

long'-lived' /-līvd′, -livd′/ *adj* 1 lasting a long time; 2 living to a great age

long'-play'ing rec'ord *n* disk record playing at 33⅓ revolutions per minute

long'-range' *adj* 1 designed to fire at a great range; 2 taking the future into account

long'shore'man /-mən/ [< *along shore*] *n* (**-men** /-mən/) one who works on the docks loading and unloading boats

long' shot' *n* 1 anything given little chance of success; 2 **not by a long shot** by no means

long' stand'ing *n* great length of existence ‖ **long'-stand'ing** *adj*

long'-suf'fer·ing *adj* patient under injury or offense ‖ also *n*

long' suit' *n* 1 *cards* suit in which the most cards are held; 2 that in which one excels

long'-term' *adj* covering or extending to a long period of time

long' ton' *n* 2,240 pounds

long'-wind'ed *adj* 1 speaking or writing at great length; 2 tedious, long-drawn-out ‖ **long'-wind'ed·ness** *n*

look /look′/ [OE *lōcian*] *vi* 1 to direct the eyes in order to see; 2 to gaze with a certain manner or feeling, as *to look sadly at someone;* 3 to face or front; 4 to appear or seem; 5 **look after** to take care of; 6 **look at** to observe; 7 **look down on** to regard with contempt; 8 **look for**, a to seek; b to expect; 9 **look forward to** to anticipate with pleasure; 10 **look in** to visit briefly; 11 **look in on** to drop in on; 12 **look into** to investigate; 13 **look on** to watch as a spectator; 14 **look out** to be watchful; 15 **look out for**, a to be on the watch for; b to be concerned about; 16 **look sharp**, a to be alert; b to be stylish; 17 **look to**, a to give attention to; b to put one's hopes or expectations in; 18 **look up** *colloq* to improve; 19 **look up to** to admire ‖ *vt* 20 to show by one's expression, as *he looked his contempt;* 21 to turn the eyes on, as *he looked her up and down;* 22 to have an appearance appropriate to, as *he looks every inch a king;* 23 **look over** to examine; 24 **look up** to seek out, as a number in the phone book or a friend for a visit ‖ *n* 25 act or instance of looking; 26 appearance, aspect; 27 expression of face; 28 **looks** *pl* general appearance ‖ also **look here** *interj* 29 come now!, stop that nonsense! ‖ SYN *v* behold, see, appear, discern, perceive, gaze, regard, inspect, scan, view, stare (see *seem*)

look′er *n slang* good-looking woman

look′er-on′ *n* (**lookers-on**) spectator; bystander ‖ SYN spectator, beholder, inspector, eyewitness

look′ing glass′ *n* mirror

look′out′ *n* 1 act of keeping watch; 2 place or keeping watch; 3 person stationed to keep watch; 4 *colloq* concern or interest

loom¹ /lōŏm′/ [OE *gelōma* tool] *n* frame or machine for weaving cloth

loom² [?] *vi* 1 to come into view indistinctly and appear huge; 2 to suddenly come into sight; to seem imminent

loon/lōŏn′/ [Scand] *n* any of several northern diving birds of the genus *Gavia*

loon·y or **loon·ey** /lōŏn′ē/ [< *lunatic*] *adj* (**-i·er; -i·est**) *slang* lunatic ‖ *n* (**-ies**) *slang* lunatic

loop /lōŏp′/ [ME *loupe*] *n* 1 a doubling or folding upon itself, as of a cord, ribbon, etc., forming a ring or eye; 2 anything resembling or shaped like a loop; 3 *aeron* maneuver in which a plane describes a vertical loop; 4 **the Loop** the downtown section of Chicago, within the loop formed by the elevated railroad ‖ *vt* 5 to form into, furnish with, or secure with loops ‖ *vi* 6 to make a loop

looped′ *adj slang* drunk

loop′hole′ *n* 1 narrow opening for observation or shooting through; 2 means of escape or evasion

loop′-the-loop′ *n aeron* loop 3

loose /lōŏs′/ [ON *lauss*] *adj* 1 not firmly fastened; 2 unbound; 3 not tightly fitted; 4 lacking in accuracy; not exact; 5 not close or compact in substance or texture; 6 lax in morals; 7 not packaged; 8 not rigid or taut; 9 free, unconfined; 10 **turn loose** to free from confinement or restraint ‖ *adv* 11 loosely; 12 **break loose** to escape from confinement ‖ *vt* 13 to set free; 14 to unbind, undo; 15 to relax; render less strict; 16 to loosen; 17 to release, as an arrow ‖ *n* 18 **on the loose, a** free, unconfined; **b** *colloq* dissolute ‖ **loose′ly** *adv* ‖ **loose′ness** *n* ‖ SYN *adj* slack, free, indefinite, lewd, dissolute ‖ ANT *adj* tight, confined, clear, definite, good, pure

loose′ ends′ *npl* 1 unsettled details; 2 **at loose ends** in an unsettled state or position

loose′-leaf′ *adj* having removable leaves held by clasps or rings, as a notebook

loos′en *vt* 1 to make loose or looser; 2 to unfasten, undo ‖ *vi* 3 to become loose or looser; 4 **loosen up** *colloq* to relax, become less tense

loot /lōŏt′/ [Hindi *lūṭ*] *vt* & *vi* 1 to plunder ‖ *n* 2 stolen or plundered articles; 3 *colloq* valuables; 4 *slang* money ‖ SYN *n* plunder, booty, spoil, pillage, gain, rapine

lop /lop′/ [ME *loppen*] *v* (**lopped; lop·ping**) *vt* to cut off or trim

lope /lōp′/ [ON *hlaupa* to leap] *n* 1 easy, swinging gait, as of a horse ‖ *vi* 2 to run with a lope

lop′-eared′ [< *obs lop* to hang] *adj* having drooping ears

lop′sid′ed [see lop-eared] *adj* 1 leaning to one side; 2 unsymmetrical; 3 disproportionate

lo·qua·cious /lōkwāsh′əs/ [< L *loquax* (-*acis*)] *adj* talkative, garrulous ‖ **lo·quac′i·ty** /-kwas′-/ *n* ‖ SYN voluble, fluent, glib, chatty (see *garrulous*)

lo·ran /lôr′ən, lōr′-/ [*long-range navigation*] *n* navigation system for determining position by means of radio signals from two known points

lord /lôrd′/ [OE *hlāford* loaf keeper] *n* 1 one supreme in authority; master; sovereign, ruler; 2 master of a feudal estate; 3 leader in a business or profession, as *a press lord;* 4 British nobleman; 5 **Lord, a** God; **b** Jesus Christ; **c** title given to British noblemen and bishops; **d** courtesy title given to the sons of high-ranking British lords ‖ *vt* 6 **lord it over** to behave imperiously towards

lord′ly *adj* (**-li·er; -li·est**) 1 suited to or like one of high rank; noble; 2 imperious, haughty ‖ *adv* 3 in a lordly manner ‖ SYN *adj* imperious, domineering, haughty, arrogant, dictatorial, despotic, arbitrary, tyrannical, insolent

lor·do·sis /lôrdōs′is/ [< Gk *lordos* bent] *n* abnormal forward curvature of the spine

lord′ship *n* 1 rank or dignity of a lord; 2 *Brit* title applied to lords, bishops, and judges (preceded by *his* or *your*)

Lord′s′ Prayer′ *n* prayer beginning with the words *Our Father* (Matt. 6:9–13)

lore /lôr′, lōr′/ [OE *lār*] *n* 1 traditional knowledge; 2 learning; erudition ‖ SYN knowledge, scholarship (see *learning*)

lor·gnette /lôrnyet′/ [F < *lorgner* to peep] *n* pair of eyeglasses or opera glasses mounted on a handle

lor·ry /lôr′ē, lor′-/ [?] *n* (**-ries**) 1 *Brit* truck, large motor truck; 2 long four-wheeled wagon without sides; 3 mine car running on rails

Los An·ge·les /lôsan′jəlis, -lēz′, los-, -aŋ′gə-/ *n* city in SW California, the metropolis of the West Coast (2,816,061)

lose /lōŏz′/ [OE *losian* to be lost] *v* (**lost**) *vt* 1 to cease to have, or to be deprived of, as by death, separation, accident, negligence, etc.; 2 to fail to keep, as health, temper, interest, or the like; 3 to mislay or miss; 4 to wander from, as to *lose the trail;* 5 to leave far behind; 6 to be obliged to give up the possession of, as to *lose money in business;* 7 to waste, let go by, as *to lose an opportunity;* 8 to fail to keep in sight or to follow mentally; 9 to fail to win; 10 to fail to catch, see, or hear; 11 to cause the loss of; 12 be lost to be ruined or destroyed; 13 lose oneself to be submerged; disappear ‖ *vi* 14 to experience loss; 15 to fail of success; 16 lose out *colloq* to fail to obtain something ‖ los′er *n* ‖ SYN forfeit, squander, ruin, mislay, overlook

los′ing *adj* 1 involving loss; 2 involved in loss ‖ *n* 3 losings *pl* losses, esp. in gambling

loss /lôs′, los′/ [OE *los* destruction] *n* 1 state or fact of being lost or destroyed; 2 that which is lost, or its value; 3 losses, a number of men killed, captured, or wounded in battle; b amount lost, as in business or gambling; 4 at a loss perplexed ‖ SYN damage, failure, forfeiture, deprivation, defeat

loss′ lead′er *n* article sold at a loss in order to attract trade to a retail store

lost /lôst′, los′t/ *pt & pp* of lose

lot /lot′/ [OE *hlot*] *n* 1 object, as a straw or a slip of paper, used in deciding a question by chance; 2 method of so deciding, as *to choose by lot;* 3 choice arrived at; 4 fortune, fate; 5 parcel of land; 6 motion picture studio; 7 a number of things or persons collectively; 8 kind, sort, as *a sorry lot;* 9 a lot (of) also lots (of) a great quantity (of); a great deal (of); 10 draw or cast lots to decide by lot ‖ SYN doom, fate, portion (see *destiny*)

Lot /lot′/ *n Bib* Abraham's nephew, whose wife was turned into a pillar of salt (Gen. 19:26)

Lo·thar·i·o /lōthěr′ē·ō′/ [character in Nicholas Rowe's *The Fair Penitent* 1703] *n* gay seducer of women

lo·tion /lōsh′ən/ [L *lotio* (*-onis*) a wash] *n* liquid preparation for application to the skin, as for cleaning and soothing, or for medication

lot·ter·y /lot′ərē/ [MF *loterie* < MD] *n* (*-ies*) gambling game in which prizes are distributed by lot, usu. among the holders of numbered tickets

lo·tus /lōt′əs/ [Gk *lotos*] *n* 1 water lily of the genus *Nymphaea;* 2 any of a genus (*Lotus*) of plants bearing purple, yellow, or white flowers; 3 *Gk myth.* legendary plant, the fruit of which caused a state of forgetfulness and euphoria

loud /loud′/ [OE *hlūd*] *adj* 1 strongly audible; 2 insistent; emphatic; 3 vulgarly showy in dress or manner; 4 vivid or strong (colors) ‖ *adv* 5 loudly ‖ loud′ly *adv* ‖ loud′ness *n* ‖ SYN clamorous, thunderous, raucous, shrieking, clangorous, boister-

ous ‖ ANT soft, subdued, low

loud′mouth′ or loud′-mouth′ *n* (*-mouths* /-*thz*, -*ths*/) person who talks too loud or too much ‖ loud′mouthed′ /-*thd*, -*tht*/ *adj*

loud′speak′er *n* electronic device for amplifying the sound of speech or music

Lou·is XIV /lōō′ĭs, lōō′ē/ *n* (1638–1715) king of France 1643–1715

Lou·is XVI *n* (1754–93) king of France 1774–92; guillotined during the French Revolution

Lou·i·si·an·a /lōō-ēz′ē·an′ə, lōō′(ē)-/ *n* state in the S United States (3,643,-000; 48,506 sq.m.; cap. Baton Rouge) ‖ Lou·i′si·an′i·an *n*

Lou·is·ville /lōō′ēvĭl′/ *n* city in N Kentucky on the Ohio (361,472), seat of the Kentucky Derby

lounge /lounj/ [?] *vi* 1 to pass time indolently: loaf; 2 to loll, recline at ease ‖ *vt* 3 lounge away to pass (time) idly ‖ *n* 4 couch or sofa; 5 waiting room in a hotel, club, or the like ‖ loung′er *n*

lounge′ liz′ard *n slang* 1 hanger-on; parasite; 2 parasitic ladies' man

loupe /lōōp′/ [F] *n* small jeweler's magnifying glass, often made like a cup to fit the eye socket

louse /lous′/ [OE *lūs*] *n* (lice) 1 any of several small wingless sucking insects (order Anoplura) parasitic on man and animals; 2 any of various other insects, crustaceans, and arachnids living on plants and animals ‖ *n* (lous·es) 3 *slang* mean contemptible person ‖ *vt* 4 louse up *slang* to botch

lous·y /louz′ē/ *adj* (*-i·er; -i·est*) 1 infested with lice; 2 *colloq* a badly done; b contemptible; 3 lousy with *slang* a overrun with; b well-supplied with

lout /lout′/ [?] *n* clumsy, ill-mannered person ‖ lout′ish *adj*

lou·ver /lōō′vər/ [MF *lovier*] *n* 1 series of slats or fins arranged horizontally over an opening, and angled so as to admit air but not rain or the sun; 2 any individual slat of such an opening; 3 any arrangement of slits or openings to admit air, as in an automobile hood

Lou·vre /lōō′rə, lōō′(ə)r/ *n* former palace in Paris, now a museum

love /luv′/ [OE *lufu*] *n* 1 strong feeling of affection; fond and tender attachment; 2 passionate devotion to one of the opposite sex; 3 love affair; 4 strong liking, as *love of learning;* 5 state of feeling kindly and benevolent toward others; 6 object of affection; sweetheart; 7 *tennis* zero score; 8 in love feeling love; 9 make love, a to embrace and kiss; b to indulge in sexual intercourse ‖ *vt* 10 to have love for; 11 to make love to ‖ *vi* 12 to be in love ‖ lov′a·ble or love′a·ble *adj* || SYN *n* fondness, tenderness, friendship, liking, affection (see *attachment*)

love' af·fair' *n* 1 romantic attachment; 2 amour, liaison

love'bird' *n* 1 any of various small parrots, esp. of the genus *Agapornis*, that show marked affection for their mates; 2 *colloq* pair of deeply enamored lovers

love' feast' *n* 1 among the early Christians, meal eaten together as a symbol of brotherly love; 2 similar meal in imitation of this; 3 any banquet or meeting marked by exceptional good feeling

love'lorn' /-lôrn'/ [< OE *loren* lost] *adj* forsaken by or longing for one's love

love'ly *adj* (-li·er, -li·est) 1 having physical or mental traits that arouse affection or admiration; 2 beautiful; 3 *colloq* delightful || *n* (-lies) 4 *colloq* beautiful young woman || **love'li·ness** *n* || SYN *adj* comely, fair, exquisite, attractive, enchanting, captivating (cf. *beautiful*)

lov·er /luv'ər/ *n* 1 one who loves, esp. a man in love with a woman; 2 paramour; 3 one deeply attached to anything, as *a lover of art*; 4 lovers *pl* couple in love with each other

love' seat' *n* small sofa for two

love'sick' *adj* languishing with love || **love'sick'ness** *n*

lov'ing *adj* feeling or expressing great affection or love || **lov'ing·ly** *adv*

lov'ing cup' *n* large drinking cup or bowl with handles, often awarded as a prize

lov'ing-kind'ness *n* affectionate sympathy; tenderness; mercy

low¹ /lō/ [ON *lāgr*] *adj* 1 not high; having little elevation; 2 below the normal elevation or level, as *low tide*; 3 deep in pitch; 4 (heavenly body) near the horizon; 5 relatively small in amount, intensity, value, etc., as *low heat*; 6 of humble rank or position; 7 lacking bodily or mental vigor; 8 unfavorable, as *a low opinion*; 9 unrefined; vulgar; 10 not highly developed; 11 décolleté (dress); 12 *phonet* (vowel) articulated with the tongue low in the mouth; 13 at the lowest ratio of wheel revolutions to engine revolutions, as *low gear* || *adv* 14 in or to a low level, position, degree, point, amount, etc.; 15 lay low, a to overpower, knock down; b *slang* to lie low; 16 lie low to be or go into hiding || *n* 17 low level, position, degree, point, amount, etc.; 18 low gear; 19 *meteor.* low-pressure system; 20 point of greatest decline, as *prices hit a new low* || SYN *adj* deep, soft, inferior, abject, commonplace, vulgar, unrefined || ANT *adj* lofty, superior, noble, high

low² [OE *hlōwan*] *vi* 1 to moo like cattle || *n* 2 act or sound of lowing

low'born' *adj* of humble parentage

low'boy' *n* low chest of drawers on legs

low'brow' *n* *colloq* nonintellectual || also *adj*

Low' Church' *adj* pert. to a party in the Anglican Church which advocates a simple ritual and lays little stress on church authority

low' com'e·dy *n* comedy characterized by farce, burlesque, and horseplay

Low' Coun'tries *npl* collective name for the region of The Netherlands, Belgium, and Luxembourg

low'down' *n* the lowdown *colloq* the true facts of a situation

low'-down' *adj* *colloq* mean, contemptible

Low·ell, James Russell /lō'əl/ *n* (1819–91) U.S. poet, essayist, and diplomat

low·er¹ /lō'ər/ *vt* 1 to let or bring down; let fall; 2 to reduce in price or value; 3 to weaken; reduce in strength or intensity; 4 to degrade, humble; 5 *mus* to change to a less high pitch or volume || *vi* 6 to become less high; go down; decrease

low·er² /lou'ər/ [ME *louren*] *vi* 1 to scowl, frown; 2 to appear threatening, as *the sky* || *n* 3 scowling look

Low'er Cal·i·for'nia /lō'-/ *n* peninsula in NW Mexico, south of California

low'er case' /lō'-/ *n typ* letters which are not capitals; small letters || **low'er-case'** *adj*

low'er mid'dle class' /lō'-/ *n* social class below the middle class and above the working class

low'est com'mon de·nom'i·na·tor *n* least common multiple of two or more denominators

low' fre'quen·cy *n* radio frequency in the range between 30 and 300 kilohertz || **low'-fre'quen·cy** *adj*

low' gear' *n* 1 gear that gives the lowest ratio of wheel revolutions to engine revolutions; 2 state of little activity

Low' Ger'man [because spoken in the lowland regions] *n* the West Germanic languages and dialects spoken in The Netherlands, Belgium, and N Germany

low'-grade' *adj* of low quality

low'-key' also **low'-keyed'** *adj* 1 of low intensity; 2 understated

low'land /-lənd/ *n* 1 low, flat country, below the level of the surrounding country; 2 the Lowlands *pl* the lowland region of Scotland || **low'land·er** *n* || **Low'land·er** *n*

Low' Lat'in *n* later form of Classical Latin, esp. the Latin used during the Middle Ages

low'ly *adj* (-li·er, -li·est) 1 low in rank or size; humble; modest || *adv* 2 modestly, humbly; 3 softly; in a low voice || SYN *adj* humble, modest, unpretending || DISCR *Humble* and *lowly* are interchangeable in the sense of poor, that is, in the condition or of the sort of those who have no money, or very little. To be born in a *humble* or *lowly* cottage, of *humble* or *lowly* parents, has been the lot of many a great man; Jesus himself had a *humble* woman for his mother, and chose the *lowly* station of carpenter. But *lowly*, not at all derogatory in sense, is often applied to conditions rather than to people; and *humble* often connotes a false meekness or unworthy abjectness

Low' Mass' *n* R C Ch Mass said without music by one priest, with less ceremony than a High Mass

low'-mind'ed *adj* having a coarse vulgar mind || **low'-mind'ed•ness** *n*

low'-necked' *adj* (dress) cut low about the neck

low'-pitched' *adj* 1 low in tonal range; 2 (roof) with little slope

low' pro'file *n* inconspicuous posture or stance

low'-spir'it•ed *adj* depressed, downhearted

low' tide' *n* 1 lowest level of the outgoing tide; 2 lowest point; decline

lox¹ /loks/ [Yiddish < G *lachs* salmon] *n* kind of smoked salmon

lox² [liquid oxygen] *n* 1 liquid oxygen || *vt* 2 to load (a missile or rocket) with liquid oxygen

loy•al /loi'əl/ [MF < L *legalis* legal] *adj* 1 faithful to one's country, employer, friends, or cause; 2 of, pert. to, or displaying loyalty || **loy'al•ly** *adv*

loy'al•ist *n* 1 one loyal to the legal government in time of revolt; 2 one who was loyal to the British during the American Revolution; 3 Loyalist one who remained loyal to the Republic during the Spanish Civil War (1936-39)

loy'al•ty *n* (-ties) state, quality, or instance of being loyal || SYN allegiance, fidelity, faithfulness, trust, constancy

loz•enge /loz'inj/ [MF *losenge*] *n* 1 diamond-shaped figure; 2 confection or cough drop originally of this shape

LP [trademark < Long Playing] *n* (LPs or LP's) long-playing record

LSD [lysergic acid diethylamide] *n* crystalline solid —C₁₆H₁₆N₂CON(C₂H₅)₂— which produces hallucinations and psychotic states similar to those of schizophrenia

Lt. Lieutenant

Ltd., ltd. limited 3

Lu *chem* lutetium

Lu•an•da /lōō•an'də/ *n* capital of Angola (225,000)

Luang Pra•bang /lwäŋ' präbäŋ'/ *n* royal capital of Laos (30,000)

lu•au /lōō'ou/ [Hawaiian] *n* feast of Hawaiian food

lub•ber /lub'ər/ [ME *lobre*] *n* 1 big clumsy oaf; 2 landlubber

lu•bri•cant /lōō'brikənt/ [< L *lubricus* slippery] *n* substance that reduces friction, as oil or grease

lu'bri•cate' [L *lubricare* (*-atus*)] *vt* 1 to reduce friction in, make slippery; 2 to apply a lubricant to || **lu'bri•ca'tion** *n* || **lu'bri•ca'tor** *n*

lu•bri•cious /lōōbrish'əs/ or **lu•bri•cous** /lōō'brikəs/ [< L *lubricus* slippery] *adj* 1 oily, slippery; 2 shifty, elusive; 3 lewd, lecherous

lu•cid /lōō'sid/ [L *lucidus*] *adj* 1 clear, transparent; 2 readily understood; 3 sane, rational; 4 shining || **lu•cid'i•ty** /-sid'-/ *n* || SYN perspicuous, sound, sane, pellucid, clear, limpid, translucent, luminous (see *transparent*)

lu•ci•fer /lōō'sifər/ [L = morning star] *n* 1 match lit by striking the head; 2 Lucifer rebellious archangel who was cast out of heaven; Satan (Isa. 14:12)

Lu•cite /lōō'sīt/ [trademark] *n* transparent plastic material used as a substitute for glass

luck /luk/ [MD *luc*] *n* 1 chance; accident; fortune; 2 good fortune; 3 in luck lucky; 4 out of luck unlucky || **luck'less** *adj*

luck'y *adj* (-i•er; -i•est) having, resulting in, or bringing good luck || **luck'i•ly** *adv* || SYN fortunate, successful, prosperous, favored, auspicious, well-omened || DISCR *Lucky* and *fortunate* are applied to those things that happen through favorable or advantageous chance, without the effort of the person whose fortunes or affairs are thus furthered; he who is benefited by such occurrences is also termed *fortunate* or *lucky*. *Fortunate* is used especially of an extremely opportune happening which falls in admirably with one's plans and purposes. *Lucky* describes that which strikes like a bolt from the blue, without apparent cause, unexpectedly, unaccountably, at exactly the right time. *Fortunate* is used soberly, gravely, rather of serious affairs; *lucky* is a more ordinary, everyday word. We say that we had a *lucky* turn, made a *lucky* guess; we made very *fortunate* connections in this distant city. *Successful* describes one who has obtained what he started out to get, or a life or career marked by such attainments or achievements. *Prosperous* is used of a flourishing, thriving condition, attended by continued success, or of a person who is enjoying such a condition. A *successful* person has striven; a *prosperous* person may have striven, or may have been *fortunate*

lu•cra•tive /lōō'krətiv/ [MF *lucratif*] *adj* profitable, remunerative

lu·cre /lōōk′ər/ [L *lucrum*] *n* money or profits

lu·cu·brate /lōōk′yəbrāt′/ [L *lucubrare* (*-atus*)] to work by lamplight] *vi* to study or write with severe exertion, esp. at night

lu·cu·bra′tion *n* 1 close and earnest study; 2 writing produced by long toilsome study

lu·di·crous /lōōd′ikrəs/ [L *ludicrum* stage play] *adj* 1 comical; 2 ridiculous; 3 provoking derisive laughter ‖ SYN funny, laughable, ridiculous, comical, comic, droll ‖ DISCR That is *laughable* which excites laughter or merriment, as a humorous anecdote. *Ludicrous* describes that which excites scornful laughter, or deserves derisive laughter, usually because of some incongruity, exaggeration, or the like. All manifestations of human vanity and pretentiousness are *ludicrous*, though the word is applied also to situations and predicaments in which fate has played the trick, rather than the people concerned. Crabbe quotes Pope in this connection: " Let an ambassador speak the best sense in the world, and deport himself in the most graceful manner before a prince, yet if the tail of his shirt happen . . . to hang out behind, more people will laugh at that than attend to the other.' This is the *ludicrous*." *Ridiculous* is applied to that which deserves contemptuous, scornful laughter; we make fun of the *ridiculous*, which we usually find in the unreasonableness, the absurdities, the disadvantages, of another. Ridicule is usually biting and sarcastic. That is *funny* which makes us laugh in spontaneous enjoyment, as a *funny* story; the *funny* attempts of a baby to imitate grown people. *Funny* has also acquired the meaning of odd, difficult to understand, as a *funny* way to end a story; a *funny* place to put it. That is *comical* which provokes a feeling of mirth in us, as the lifted eyebrow gave him a *comical* expression. That is *comic* which makes us laugh or is supposed to make us laugh; *comic* strips in the daily papers, a *comic* song, and the like, are purposely *funny* and facetious. That is *droll* which makes us smile in amused surprise over some odd quirk or hidden incongruity, brought out, usually, in a rather dry or slyly joking fashion

luff /luf′/ [ME] *naut vi* 1 to steer or sail nearer or into the wind ‖ *n* 2 act of luffing; 3 forward edge of a fore-and-aft sail

lug /lug′/ [< Scand] *n* (**lugged; lugging**) *vt* 1 to pull, drag, or carry with effort ‖ *n* 2 projecting part for supporting or grasping; 3 *slang* big clumsy fellow

lug·gage /lug′ij/ [< *lug*] *n* suitcases, valises, trunks; baggage

lug′ nut′ *n* one of the large nuts used to attach automobile wheels

lu·gu·bri·ous /lōōg(y)ōōb′rĕ·əs/ [< L *lugubris*] *adj* excessively mournful; dismal, doleful

Luke /lōōk′/ *n Bib* 1 early Christian disciple, reputed author of the third Gospel and of the Acts; 2 third book of the New Testament

luke′warm′ /lōōk′-/ [< *obs luke* tepid] *adj* 1 moderately warm; tepid; 2 unenthusiastic

lull /lul′/ [ME *lullen*] *vt* 1 to soothe to sleep; 2 to quiet ‖ *vi* 3 to become quiet gradually ‖ *n* 4 state of being lulled; 5 calm lasting for a short time ‖ SYN *v* still, calm, hush, compose, tranquilize, quiet

lull·a·by /lul′əbī′/ [ME] *n* (**-bies**) song used to lull a young child to sleep; cradlesong

lum·ba·go /lumbā′gō/ [< L *lumbus* loin] *n* pain in the muscles of the lumbar region of the back

lum·bar /lum′bər, -bär/ *adj* pert. to the region of the loins

lum·ber¹ /lum′bər/ [?] *n* timber sawed into planks and boards, ready for market

lum·ber² [ME *lomeren*] *vi* to move clumsily and heavily ‖ **lum′ber·ing** *adj*

lum′ber·jack′ *n* man who works at cutting and preparing timber

lum′ber·man /-mən/ *n* (**-men** /-mən/) dealer in lumber

lum′ber·yard′ *n* place for storing and selling lumber

lu·men /lōōm′ən/ [L = light] *n* unit of luminosity equal to the light emitted per unit of solid angle by a uniform point source of one international candle

lu·mi·nar·y /lōōm′iner′ĕ/ [ML *luminaria* lamp] *n* (**-ies**) 1 body giving forth light, esp. a heavenly body; 2 eminent person; leader in some field

lu·mi·nes′cence /-nes′əns/ [< L *lumen* light] *n* emission of light by a body, not caused by incandescence ‖ **lu′mi·nes′cent** *adj*

lu′mi·nous *adj* 1 giving forth light; 2 shining; 3 brightly lit; 4 clear; easily understood; 5 enlightening ‖ **lu′mi·nos′i·ty** /-nos′-/ *n* ‖ SYN radiant, glowing, clear, lucid (see *bright*)

lump /lump′/ [ME *lompe*] *n* 1 small shapeless mass; 2 swelling; protuberance; 3 collection of things; 4 *colloq* slow-moving, dull-witted person ‖ *vi* 5 to unite in one mass; 6 to treat collectively; 7 **lump it** *colloq* to put up with something one does not like ‖ *adj* 8 in the form of a lump; 9 total, complete (sum)

lump′y *adj* (**-i·er; -i·est**) 1 full of lumps; 2 like a lump; 3 choppy (sea)

lu·na·cy /lōōn′əsĕ/ [< *lunatic*] *n* (**-cies**)

insanity ‖ SYN madness, craziness, frenzy (see *insanity*)

lu·nar /lōōn′ər/ [< L *luna* moon] *adj* 1 pert. to or resembling the moon; 2 measured by the moon's revolutions

lu·nar mod·ule *n* small self-contained, rocket-powered spaceship, attached to and integral with a larger ship, that can be detached for landing on the moon and returning to the larger ship while the latter is in lunar orbit

lu′nar month′ *n* interval from one new moon to the next, about 29½ days

lu′nar year′ *n* year of twelve lunar months, or about 355 days, used in some calendars

lu·na·tic /lōōn′ətik/ [< L *luna* moon, thought to cause madness] *adj* 1 insane; 2 extremely foolish ‖ *n* 3 insane person

lu′na·tic fringe′ *n* persons who make up the fanatically extreme or radical minority of some political, social, or religious groups

lunch /lunch′/ [< *luncheon*] *n* 1 light meal, esp. one around noon ‖ *vi* 2 to eat lunch

lunch′eon /-chən/ [perh < *dial. noncheon* snack] *n* formal lunch held in connection with a meeting, as of a club or convention

lunch′eon·ette′ /-net′/ *n* restaurant specializing in light meals and lunches

lung /lung′/ [OE *lungen*] *n* one of the two organs of breathing in air-breathing vertebrates

lunge /lunj′/ [< F *allonger* to lengthen] *n* 1 sudden thrust, as with a sword; 2 sudden leap or plunge forward ‖ *vi* 3 to make a lunge

lu·pine /lōō′pin/ [< L *lupus* wolf] *adj* 1 of or like a wolf; 2 savage; ravenous ‖ /lōō′pin/ *n* 3 garden or fodder plant of the genus *Lupinus*, with blue, pink, or white flowers

lurch¹ /lurch′/ [?] *n* 1 sudden pitch or swing to one side; 2 staggering motion ‖ *vi* 3 to roll or pitch suddenly; 4 to move with lurches

lurch² [MF *lourche* an old game] *n* leave in the lurch to leave in a difficult situation; desert (someone)

lure /lōōr/ [MF *loire* bait] *n* 1 anything that entices or allures; 2 artificial bait; decoy ‖ *vt* 3 to entice, allure ‖ SYN *v* allure, decoy, tempt, seduce, coax, mislead

lu·rid /lōōr′id/ [L *luridus* pale-yellow] *adj* 1 gruesome, ghastly; 2 resembling flames seen through smoke; 3 shocking; vivid; sensational

lurk /lurk′/ [ME *lurken*] *vi* 1 to lie in wait; lie concealed; 2 to move furtively

lus·cious /lush′əs/ [ME *lucius* perh < *delicious*] *adj* 1 sweet, delicious; 2 delightful, extremely pleasing to the senses; 3 voluptuous

lush¹ /lush′/ [ME *lusch* soft] *adj* 1 succulent; 2 rich in luxuriant vegetation; 3 luxurious

lush² [?] *n slang* drunkard

lust /lust′/ [OE = pleasure] *n* 1 strong desire to possess and enjoy; 2 sexual desire; lecherousness ‖ *vi* 3 to have overpowering sexual desire; 4 **lust for** or **after** to have a strong craving for

lus·ter /lust′ər/ [MF *lustre*] *n* 1 gloss, sheen; 2 brightness, splendor; 3 brilliance, renown

lust′ful *adj* full of sinful and impure desires ‖ SYN licentious, lascivious, lewd, sensual, unchaste

lus′trous *adj* 1 having luster or sheen; 2 brilliant, radiant ‖ SYN radiant, sheeny, glossy, shining (see *bright*)

lust′y *adj* (-i·er) -i·est) robust; vigorous; healthy

lute /lōōt/ [MF *lut* < Ar *al′ud* the wood] *n mus* stringed instrument with a mandolin-shaped body and a neck bent to form a sharp angle ‖ *lut′ist n*

lu·te·ti·um /lōōtēsh′ē·əm/ [< *Lutetia* L name of Paris] *n* rare-earth metallic element (Lu; at.no. 71; at.wt. 174.97)

Lu·ther·an /lōōth′ərən/ [< Martin *Luther* (1483–1546) leader of the Reformation in Germany] *adj* 1 pert. to Martin Luther or to the Protestant church he founded ‖ *n* 2 member of the Lutheran Church ‖ **Lu′ther·an·ism** *n*

Lux. Luxembourg

Lux·em·bourg /luks′əmburg′/ *n* small German- and French-speaking grand duchy SE of Belgium (335,000; 999 sq.m.; cap. Luxembourg)

lux·u·ri·ant /lugzhŏŏr′ē·ənt, luksh-/ [< L *luxuriare* to luxuriate] *adj* 1 fertile; fruitful; 2 producing abundantly; 3 profuse; florid ‖ **lux·u′ri·ance** *n* ‖ SYN exuberant, teeming, rank, fertile, luxurious ‖ DISCR *Luxuriant* growth is profuse; *luxuriant* display tends toward the superfluous. *Luxuriant* often carries with the idea of abundance that of loveliness, perfection, pleasing excellence; *exuberant* carries the idea of excess. *Exuberant* growth is often rank; *exuberant* joy is overflowing; *exuberant* spirits are bounding, effusive; *exuberant* style is lavish, given to copiousness and superabundance. *Luxurious* as a synonym for *luxuriant* is now rare; *luxurious* has come to mean voluptuous, steeped in luxury. We speak of a *luxuriant* head of hair; the *luxuriant* imagery of a poem

lux·u·ri·ate /-āt/ *vi* 1 to grow abundantly; 2 to live extravagantly; 3 to revel unrestrainedly or without stint

lux·u·ry /luk′shərē, lugzh′-/ [L *luxuria*] *n* (-ries) 1 extravagant indulgence in pleasure or ease; 2 anything conducive to a life of luxury, esp. if not a necessity ‖ **lux·u·ri·ous** /-ŏor'ē-əs/ adj

Lw chem lawrencium

-ly /-lē/ [OE -līc like] adj suf 1 like or characteristic of, as manly; 2 every, as weekly ‖ adv suf 3 in a specified manner or degree, as greatly

ly·cée /lēsā'/ [F < lyceum] n French high school, attended by students preparing for the university

ly·ce·um /lisē'əm, lis'ē-/ [L < Gk lykeion Lyceum] n 1 academy; 2 institution providing lectures and concerts; 3 lycée; 4 **Lyceum** grove near Athens where Aristotle and other philosophers taught

lye /lī/ [OE lēag] n alkaline solution obtained by leaching, used in washing, making soap, cleaning drains, etc.

ly·ing /lī'iŋ/ prp of lie[1] and lie[2]

ly'ing-in' n period or state of confinement at the time of childbirth

lymph /limf/ [L lympha water] n transparent yellowish fluid found in the body tissues resembling blood plasma

lymph- or **lympho-o-** comb form lymph

lym·phat'ic /-fat'ik/ adj 1 pert. to or carrying lymph; 2 sluggish; phlegmatic

lym·phat'ic gland' n any of the gland-like masses which secrete lymphocytes

lym'pho·cyte' /-əsīt'/ [lympho- + Gk kytos vessel] n small cell derived from a lymphatic gland, which becomes a white corpuscle when it passes into the blood

lym'phoid adj 1 of or like lymph; 2 pert. to the tissues of the lymph glands

lynch /linch/ [prob < an 18th-cent. Judge Lynch of Virginia] vt to kill or execute (a suspect) by mob action

without due process of law ‖ **lynch'·ing** n

lynx /liŋks/ [Gk] n any of a genus (Lynx) of large, fierce wildcats with a short tail and tufted ears

lynx'-eyed' adj sharp-sighted

ly'on·naise' po·tə'toes /lī'ənāz'/ [F = of Lyons] npl slices of boiled potatoes fried with onions

Ly·ra /lī'rə/ [see lyre] n small northern constellation, the Lyre

lyre /līr/ [Gk lyra] n mus hand-held harplike instrument used by the ancients to accompany singing or recitation

lyre'bird' n Australian bird of the genus Menura, the tail of the male resembling a lyre when spread

lyr·ic /lir'ik/ [< lyre] n 1 lyric poem; 2 lyrics pl words of a song ‖ also **lyr'i·cal** adj 3 a songlike (poetry); b (poetry) expressive of emotion and sentiment; 4 (poet) of lyric verse; 5 a (voice) of light volume and modest range; b having such a voice ‖ **lyr'i·cal·ly** adv

lyr·i·cism /lir'isiz'əm/ n 1 lyric quality or style; 2 intense expression of lyrical feeling

lyr'i·cist n 1 person who writes the words of songs; 2 lyric poet

Ly·sen·ko·ism /lisen'kō·iz'əm/ [T. D. Lysenko (1898–) Russ biologist] n genetic doctrine that acquired characters are inherited

-ly·sis /-lisis/ [Gk lysis loosening] n comb form (-ses /-sēz'/) dissolution, breaking down, as electrolysis

-lyte /-līt/ [Gk lytos soluble] n comb form substance that can undergo decomposition, as electrolyte

-lyze /-līz'/ [< -lysis] vt comb form to subject to dissolution, decomposition, or breakdown, as electrolyze

M

M, m /em'/ n (M's or Ms; m's or ms) 13th letter of the English alphabet

M 1 13th in order or in a series; 2 Roman numeral 1000; 3 something shaped like an M; 4 designation for a film recommended for mature audiences; 5 typ em

M. 1 Monday; 2 (pl **MM.**) Monsieur; 3 mountain

M., m. 1 meridian; 2 minute(s); 3 married; 4 meter(s); 5 mile(s); 6 masculine; 7 male; 8 month

m. mech mass

M'·1' n (M-1's) Garand rifle

ma /mä'/ [< mama] n colloq mamma, mother

M.A. [L Magister Artium] Master of Arts

ma'am /mam', mäm', məm/ [< madam] n colloq madam (used in direct address)

Mac- /mak-, mək-/ [Gael = son] pref in Scotch or Irish names, son

ma·ca·bre /məkäb'(rə), -ər/ [MF danse macabre dance of death] adj 1 pert. to or symbolizing death; 2 grim; gruesome

mac·ad·am /məkad'əm/ [J.L. McAdam (1756–1836) Sc engineer] n roadway of crushed stone, compacted with tar or asphalt ‖ **mac·ad'am·ize'** vt

mac·a·ro·ni /mak'ərōn'ē/ [It maccaroni] n 1 food composed of wheat paste formed and dried in long thin tubes; 2 (-nis or -nies) 18th-century English dandy

mac·a·ron·ic /-ron′-/ *adj* 1 (writing) characterized by a mixture of non-Latin words with Latin endings and genuine Latin words; 2 composed of a mixture of languages

mac·a·roon /mak′ərōōn′/ [MF *macaron*] *n* cooky made of egg whites, sugar, and almonds or coconut

ma·caw /məkô′/ [Port *macao*] *n* any of numerous large tropical American parrots (chiefly genus *Ara*) noted for gaudy plumage

Mac·beth /məkbeth′, mak-/ *n* 1 king of Scotland who died in 1057; 2 tragedy of Shakespeare; 3 its hero

Mac·ca·bees /mak′əbēz′/ *npl* 1 family of Jewish patriots who led a successful revolt (175–164 B.C.) against Syria; 2 books of the Old Testament Apocrypha relating this struggle

mace¹ /mās′/ [OF] *n* 1 heavy war club with a spiked head; 2 staff carried by or before an official as a symbol of authority ∥ *vt* 3 to coerce into making a contribution, esp. to a political fund

mace² [MF *macis*] *n* spice ground from the outer shell of the nutmeg

Mace /mās′/ [trademark] *n* 1 temporarily disabling liquid sprayed in the face to cause tears, dizziness, and sometimes nausea ∥ *vt* 2 to attack with Mace

Mac·e·do·ni·a /mas′idōn′ē-ə, -yə/ *n* region adjoining the N shore of the Aegean Sea, in ancient times a region that became dominant in Greece in the reign of Alexander the Great; now divided between Greece, Yugoslavia, and Bulgaria ∥ **Mac′e·do′ni·an** *adj & n*

mac·er·ate /mas′ərāt′/ [L *macerare* (-*atus*) to soften] *vt* 1 to soften or separate the parts of by soaking or digestion; 2 to cause to grow thin ∥ *vi* 3 to grow thin ∥ **mac′er·a′tion** *n*

mach. 1 machine; 2 machinery

ma·chet·e /məshet′ē, -chet′ē/ [Sp] *n* large heavy knife used in Latin America for cutting sugar cane, for clearing underbrush, and as a weapon

Mach·i·a·vel·li·an /mak′ē-əvel′ē-ən/ [< Niccolò *Machiavelli* (1469–1527) Florentine statesman and writer] *adj* 1 pert. to Machiavelli or to his doctrine that any means, however treacherous and despotic, are justifiable when employed to maintain a strong central government; 2 crafty, double-dealing ∥ also *n*

mach·i·nate /mak′ināt′/ [L *machinari* (-*atus*) to contrive] *vt* to plan, contrive, usu. with evil intent ∥ **mach′i·na′tion** *n*

ma·chine /məshēn′/ [L *machina*] *n* 1 any contrivance designed to utilize available energy, or to convert energy from one form to another; 2 mechanical apparatus consisting of various moving parts working to-gether to perform a specific operation; 3 vehicle operated by a machine or motor; 4 one who acts mechanically or at the bidding of another; 5 combination of persons acting together for a common purpose, as *the machine of government*; 6 political organization which controls the policies and activities of a party; 7 device that transmits, or modifies the application of, force or motion ∥ *vt* 8 to form or finish with a machine

ma·chine′ gun′ *n* small automatic gun capable of firing a rapid and continuous stream of bullets ∥ **ma·chine′-gun** *vt* ∥ **ma·chine′ gun′ner** *n*

ma·chine′ lan′guage *n* system of signs, symbols, and numbers used in the operation of a computer

ma·chin′er·y *n* (-ies) 1 machines collectively or their parts; 2 any means or combination by which something is kept in action, as *the machinery of government*

ma·chine′ screw′ *n* screw with thread designed to fit into a threaded hole

ma·chine′ shop′ *n* shop where parts and objects are made or shaped by machine tools

ma·chine′ tool′ *n* power-driven tool, as a lathe, for cutting and shaping metals

ma·chin′ist *n* 1 one who makes or repairs machines; 2 one who operates machinery or machine tools

ma·chis·mo /mächēz′mō/ [< MexSp < Sp *macho* male] *n* strong sense of pride at being a male

Mach′ num′ber /mäk′, mak′/ [Ernst *Mach* (1838–1916) Austrian physicist] *n* number indicating the ratio of speed of a body to the speed of sound at a given altitude

mack·er·el /mak′(ə)rəl/ [OF *makerel*] *n* (-el or -els) 1 oily food fish (*Scomber scombrus*) found in schools in the North Atlantic; 2 any of various similar fishes

mack′er·el sky′ *n* sky covered with fleecy clouds that look like the bars of a mackerel's back

mack·i·naw also **Mack′i·naw′ coat′** /mak′inô′/ [*Mackinac* Island in N Lake Huron] *n* short, heavy, usu. plaid, coat made of wool

mack·in·tosh /mak′intosh′/ [Charles *Macintosh* (1766–1843) Sc designer] *n* raincoat made of rubberized cloth

macro- [Gk] *comb form* 1 long; 2 large

mac·ro·cosm /mak′rəkoz′əm/ [*macro-* + *cosmos*] *n* the universe; the world at large, exterior to man ∥ **mac′ro·cos′mic** *adj*

ma·cron /mäk′ron, mak′-, -rən/ [Gk = long] *n* mark placed over a vowel, as in ē and ō, to indicate that it is long

mad /mad′/ [< OE *gemǣd* maddened] *adj* (mad·der; mad·dest) 1 insane; 2

angry; **3** infatuated; **4** furious or frenzied, as with rage or terror; **5** rabid; **6** imprudent, foolish; **7** like mad *slang* with great speed or energy ‖ **mad′ly** *adv* ‖ **mad′ness** *n* ‖ SYN crazy, delirious, rabid, violent, frantic, rash, infatuated ‖ ANT sane, rational, reasonable

Mad·a·gas·car /mad′əgas′kər/ *n* large island in the Indian Ocean off the SE coast of Africa, main island of the Malagasy Republic

mad·am /mad′əm/ [OF *madame* my lady] *n* **1** courteous term of address for a lady; **2** housewife; **3** woman in charge of a brothel

mad·ame /mad′əm, mədam′, ma-/ [F] *n* (**mes·dames** /mādam′, -däm′/) title used in addressing or referring to a married woman who is not American or British

mad′cap′ *n* rash impulsive person ‖ also *adj*

mad·den /mad′ən/ *vt* **1** to make insane or furious ‖ *vi* **2** to become insane or furious ‖ **mad′den·ing** *adj*

mad·der /mad′ər/ [OB *mæddre*] *n* **1** any of a genus (*Rubia*) of herbs, esp. *R. tinctorum*, from the root of which a red dye is extracted; **2** the dye

made /mād/ **1** *pt & pp* of make ‖ *adj* **2** artificially produced; **3** assured of success

Ma·dei·ra /mədir′ə, məder′ə/ *n* **1** group of islands in the North Atlantic W of Morocco belonging to Portugal; **2** rich dessert wine of Madeira, or one like it made elsewhere

mad·e·moi·selle /mad′(ə)m(w)əzel′/ [F] *n* (**-selles** or **mes·de·moi·selles** /mād′(ə)m(w)əzel′/) title used in addressing or referring to an unmarried woman who is not American or British

made′-to-meas′ure *adj* made to one's individual measurements

made′-to-or′der *adj* made to one's individual specifications

made′-up′ *adj* **1** concocted; **2** put together; **3** wearing make-up

mad′house′ *n* (**-hous·es** /-ziz/) *n* **1** insane asylum; **2** wild, noisy, disorganized place

Mad·i·son /mad′isən/ *n* capital of Wisconsin (130,000)

Mad·i·son, James *n* (1751–1836) 4th president of the U.S. 1809–17

Mad′i·son Av′e·nue [street in New York City] *n* center of the advertising industry in the U.S.

mad′man′ /-man′, -mən/ *n* (**-men** /-men′, -mən/) lunatic ‖ **mad′·wom′an** *nfem* (**-wom′en**)

mad′ mon′ey *n slang* **1** small sum of money carried by a woman on a date to supply her with carfare in case she quarrels with her companion and must get home alone; **2** pin money

Ma·don·na /mədon′ə/ [It = my lady] *n* **1** the Virgin Mary; **2** picture or statue of the Virgin

Ma·don′na lil′y *n* lily (*Lilium candidum*) having white, trumpet-shaped flowers

mad·ras /mad′rəs, mədras′, -dräs′/ [*Madras*] *n* **1** fine cotton fabric, often of fancy design; **2** curtain material with raised figures, often in color

Ma·dras /mədras′, -dräs′/ *n* seaport in S India on the Bay of Bengal (1,800,000)

Ma·drid /mədrid′/ *n* capital of Spain (2,600,000)

mad·ri·gal /mad′rigəl/ [It *madrigale*] *n* **1** short love poem; **2** unaccompanied part song for four to eight voices, popular in the 15th and 16th centuries

Mae·ce·nas /mīsēn′əs, mī-/ [Gaius *Maecenas* (70–8 B.C.) patron of Vergil and Horace] *n* supporter or patron, esp. of the arts

mael·strom /māl′strəm/ [early D = grinding stream] *n* **1** large and violent whirlpool; **2** any tumultuous and agitated state or condition

maes·tro /mī′strō/ [It] *n* master in any art, esp. a great composer, conductor, or teacher of music

Ma·fi·a /mäf′ē·ə/ [Sicilian] *n* international crime organization, reputed to control racketeering, gambling, and prostitution, and trafficking in narcotics, in many parts of the world

mag. **1** magazine; **2** magnetism

mag·a·zine /mag′əzēn, mag′əzēn′/ [F *magasin* < Ar *makhāzin* storehouses] *n* **1** periodical publication containing various articles, stories, poems, etc., often illustrated, and frequently specializing in one subject, as news, detective stories, hobbies, etc.; **2** warehouse; **3** place for storing military supplies; **4** cartridge chamber of a gun; **5** room in a fort or warship in which ammunition is stored; **6** reservoir or supply chamber in any of various machines and implements

Ma·gel·lan, Fer·di·nand /məjel′ən/ *n* (ab. 1480–1521) Portuguese navigator, leader of the first expedition to circumnavigate the globe

ma·gen·ta /məjent′ə/ [battle of *Magenta*, Italy, 1859, year of discovery] *n* **1** purplish-red dye and pigment derived from coal tar; **2** purplish red ‖ also *adj*

mag·got /mag′ət/ [< ME *mathek* < Scand] *n* **1** wormlike larva of certain insects, as the fly; **2** whim ‖ **mag′got·y** *adj*

Ma·ghrib /mu′grib/ [Ar = West] *n* the ancient Arab littoral of NW Africa, including present-day Morocco, Algeria, and Tunisia

Ma·gi /mā′ji/ [L < Gk *magos* magician] *npl* (*sg* **-gus** /-gəs/) Bib the three wise men who came from the East to see the child Jesus (Matt. 2:1–12)

mag·ic /maj′ik/ [Gk *magike*] *n* 1 art of working by supernatural power; sorcery, witchcraft; 2 sleight of hand; 3 any mysterious power, as *the magic of beauty* ‖ also *adj* ‖ **mag′i·cal** *adj* ‖ **mag′i·cal·ly** *adv* ‖ SYN *n* enchantment, necromancy, sorcery, witchery, witchcraft, charm, incantation

ma·gi·cian /məjish′ən/ [MF *magicien*] *n* one skilled in magic or sleight of hand

mag′ic lan′tern *n* slide projector

mag·is·te·ri·al /maj′istir′ē-əl/ [< L *magister* master, teacher] *adj* 1 pert. to a magistrate or to his office; 2 authoritative; 3 domineering ‖ SYN august, pompous, dignified, stately, commanding

mag′is·tra·cy /-trəsē/ *n* (-cies) 1 office, function, or jurisdiction of a magistrate; 2 body of magistrates

mag′is·trate /-trāt′, trit/ *n* 1 civil officer who has executive authority; 2 minor judicial officer, as a police judge or justice of the peace

mag·ma /mag′mə/ [Gk = kneaded mass] *n* (-mas or -ma·ta /-mətə/) molten matter deep inside the earth, from which igneous rock is formed

Mag·na Char·ta or **Car·ta** /mag′nə kärt′ə/ [L = Great Charter] *n* 1 charter of English civil liberty, forced from King John by the English barons in 1215; 2 any constitution safeguarding personal rights

mag·na cum lau·de /mag′nə kum lôd′ē/ [L = with great praise] *adj & adv* with great academic distinction

mag·nan·i·mous /magnan′iməs/ [< L *magnanimus* great-souled] *adj* 1 high-minded; noble; 2 generous; free from petty vindictiveness ‖ **mag′na·nim′i·ty** /-nənim′-/ *n* (-ties) ‖ SYN unselfish, altruistic, benevolent (see *generous*)

mag·nate /mag′nāt, -nit/ [LL *magnas* (-*atis*)] *n* person of high rank, influence, or importance

mag·ne·sia /magnēzh′ə, -shə/ [Gk = of *Magnesia*, town in Asia Minor] *n* magnesium oxide —MgO— a white tasteless powder, used as an antacid and as a laxative

mag·ne·si·um /zē-əm, -shē-əm, -zhəm/ [< *magnesia*] *n* extremely light, silver-white metallic element (Mg; at.no. 12; at.wt. 24.312) that burns with an intense white light; used in lightweight alloys and in flash bulbs and flares

mag·net /mag′nit/ [Gk *magnes* (-*etos*) of Magnesia] *n* 1 lodestone; 2 body, as a piece of iron or steel, that has the property of attracting iron and steel; 3 electromagnet; 4 person or thing that attracts

mag·net′ic /-net′ik/ *adj* 1 having the properties of, or capable of being given the properties of, a magnet; 2 pert. to the earth's magnetism; 3 pert. to, actuated by, causing, or caused by, magnetism; 4 having power to attract people ‖ **mag·net′i·cal·ly** *adv*

mag·net′ic field′ *n* region near a magnet or electric current where magnetic force is exerted

mag·net′ic flux′ *n* total inductive effect exerted through a given area by a magnetic field

mag·net′ic nee′dle *n* magnetized steel bar mounted so as to turn freely in the direction of the magnetic poles of the earth

mag·net′ic pole′ *n* 1 point in each polar region where a magnetic needle mounted on a horizontal axis stands vertical; 2 either of the two poles of a magnet, where the lines of force are most intense

mag·net′ic tape′ *n* tape, usu. plastic, coated on one or both sides with a substance containing iron oxide to make it sensitive to an electromagnet, used in tape recorders

mag′net·ism *n* 1 the property of attraction possessed by magnets; 2 the force to which this attraction is due; 3 science that treats of magnetic phenomena; 4 personal attraction

mag′net·ite′ *n* mineral form of black iron oxide —Fe₃O₄— one of the most important iron ores

mag′net·ize′ *vt* 1 to give magnetic properties to; 2 to attract; charm ‖ **mag′net·i·za′tion** *n*

mag·ne·to /magnēt′ō/ [*magneto*electric generator] *n* small generator in which the magnetic field is produced by one or more permanent magnets

mag·ne·to- /-magnēt′ō-/ *comb form* 1 magnetic; 2 magnetism

mag·ne·tom·e·ter /mag′nitom′itər/ *n* device for measuring the intensity of a magnetic field and also for detecting the presence of objects of iron and steel on persons or in their baggage

mag·ne′to·mo′tive force′ *n* force that produces magnetic flux

mag·ne·tron /mag′nitron′/ [*magnet* + *electron*] *n* two-element vacuum tube in which the flow of electrons is controlled by an external electromagnetic field, used to generate high-power microwaves

mag·nif·i·cence /magnif′isəns/ [L *magnificentia*] *n* 1 grandeur of appearance; splendor; 2 impressiveness; great beauty ‖ **mag·nif′i·cent** *adj* ‖ **mag·nif′i·cent·ly** *adv* ‖ SYN sumptuousness, beauty, majesty (see *grandeur*)

mag·nif′i·co /-kō/ [It] *n* (-coes) person of rank or distinction

mag·ni·fy /mag′nifī/ [L *magnificare*] *v* (-fied) *vt* 1 to increase the apparent size of, as with a lens; **2** to enlarge; **3** to exaggerate ‖ *vi* **4** to increase the apparent size of an object ‖ **mag′ni•fi′er** *n* ‖ **mag′ni•fi•ca′tion** *n*

mag•ni•fy′ing glass′ *n* lens which enlarges the apparent dimensions of objects viewed through it

mag•nil•o•quent /magnil′əkwənt/ [< L *magniloquentia* high-flown speech] *adj* pompous in style or speech; boastful ‖ **mag•nil′o•quence** *n*

mag′ni•tude [L *magnitudo*] *n* **1** greatness of size, extent, or importance; **2** size or extent; **3** *astron* degree of brightness of a star as viewed from the earth, varying by a ratio of 2.512, the brightest being of the first magnitude ‖ **SYN** bulk, mass, extent, bigness, largeness, hugeness, vastness, size, greatness, immensity, dimension

mag•no•li•a /magnōl′ē•ə, -nōl′yə/ [< Pierre *Magnol* (1638–1715) F botanist] *n* **1** any of a genus (*Magnolia*) of trees having large fragrant pink or white blossoms and aromatic bark; **2** its blossom

mag•num /mag′nəm/ [L = great] *n* large wine bottle holding ⅖ of a gallon

mag′num o′pus [L = great work] *n* chief work, as of an author

mag′pie′ [*Mag* Margaret + *pie*] *n* **1** any of several noisy birds (genus *Pica*) with black and white plumage; **2** chatterbox

Mag•yar /mag′yär, mô′dyôr/ [Hung] *n* **1** member of the chief ethnic people of Hungary, who speak a Finno-Ugric language; **2** Finno-Ugric language of Hungary ‖ also *adj*

ma•ha•ra•ja(h) /mä′hərä′jə/ [Hindi = great king] *n* ruling prince of an Indian state, equivalent to a king ‖ **ma′ha•ra′nee**, -ni /-nē/ *nfem*

ma•hat•ma /məhät′mə/ [Skt = greatsouled] *n* in Hinduism, man revered for wisdom and saintliness

mah-jongg /mä′jôŋ′, -joŋ′, -zhôŋ′, -zhoŋ′/ *n* game of Chinese origin, played with small tiles resembling dominoes

mahl′stick′ /mäl′-, môl′-/ [< D *maalstok* < *malen* to paint + *stok* stick] *n* stick used as a rest for the hand in painting

ma•hog•a•ny /məhog′ənē/ [?] *n* (**-nies**) **1** tree (*Swietenia mahogani*) of tropical America, valued for its hard wood; **2** any of various other trees producing a similar wood; **3** wood of any of these trees; **4** dark-reddish brown

ma•hout /məhout′/ [Hindi *mahāut*] *n* elephant driver or keeper

maid /mād′/ [< *maiden*] *n* **1** young unmarried woman; girl; **2** female servant

maid′en [OE *mægden*] *n* **1** unmarried

girl or woman; **2** virgin; **3** something untried or unused; **4** horse that has never won a race ‖ *adj* **5** earliest or first, as *a maiden voyage* ‖ **maid′en•ly** *adj & adv*

maid′en•hair′ *n* any of a genus (*Adiantum*) of delicate ferns found in damp woods

maid′en•head′ *n* **1** virginity; **2** hymen

maid′en•hood′ *n* state or time of being a maiden or virgin

maid′en name′ *n* woman's surname before marriage

maid′ of hon′or *n* **1** unmarried woman who acts as a bride's chief attendant; **2** unmarried noble lady who attends a queen

maid′serv′ant *n* woman servant

mail¹ /māl′/ [OF *maille* < L *macula* mesh] *n* flexible body armor of steel rings, net, or scales ‖ **mailed′** *adj*

mail² [OF *male* bag] *n* **1** letters, packages, etc., delivered by the post office; **2** also **mails** *pl* system for collecting and delivering the mail ‖ *vt* **3** to deposit in a mailbox; send through the mails ‖ **mail′a•ble** *adj*

mail′box′ *n* **1** public box for the deposit of mail for the post office; **2** box into which the mailman puts mail for the recipient

mailed′ fist′ *n* **1** naked power; **2** superior force used as a threat

mail′man′ /-man′/ *n* (**-men′** /-men′/) employee of the post office who picks up and delivers the mails

mail′-or•der house′ *n* firm that takes orders and delivers goods through the mail

maim /mām′/ [ME *mayme*] *vt* to cripple; mutilate

main /mān′/ [OE *mægen* strength] *n* **1** principal conduit or pipe, as *a water main*; **2** *poet.* ocean; **3** *archaic* mainland; **4** in **the main** for the most part; **5** with **might and main** with all one's strength ‖ *adj* **6** chief, principal; **7** by **main force** or **strength** by sheer strength ‖ **main′ly** *adv* ‖ **SYN** *adj* first, principal, leading (see *chief*)

main′ chance′ *n* choice that will be to one's greatest advantage

main′ clause′ *n gram* clause that is a complete sentence by itself

Maine /mān′/ *n* state in the NE U.S. in New England (993,000; 33,465 sq.m.; *cap.* Augusta) ‖ **Main′er** *n*

main′land /-lənd, -land′/ *n* principal land mass, as of a continent, distinguished from adjacent islands ‖ also *adj*

Main′ Line′ *n* fashionable residential area extending for about 20 miles west of Philadelphia ‖ **Main′ Lin′er** *n*

main′mast /-mast′, -mäst′, *naut* -məst/ *n* principal mast of a vessel

main′sail /-sāl′, *naut* -səl/ *n* principal sail on the mainmast of a vessel

main′spring *n* **1** principal spring in a

mechanism, as a watch; **2** chief motivation or driving force

main′stay′ *n* **1** any of the lines that secure the mainmast forward; **2** chief support

main′stem′ *n colloq* main street

main′stream′ *n* prevailing course or trend of events

main′ street′ *n* principal street of a city or town

main·tain /măntān′/ [OF *maintenir*] *vt* **1** to support, sustain; keep up; **2** to support or bear the expense of; **3** to defend by argument; **4** to keep in due condition; keep in repair; **5** to retain possession of; hold to ‖ SYN conserve, support, allege, uphold (see *assert*)

main·te·nance /mānt′ənəns/ *n* **1** act of maintaining or state of being maintained; **2** means of sustenance; upkeep, support; **3** *law* unlawful meddling in a civil suit

maî·tre d′ /māt′ər dē′/ *n* (**maî·tre d′s**) *colloq* maître d′hôtel

maî·tre d′hô·tel /māt′ər dōtel′/ [F = master of the hotel] *n* (**maîtres d′hôtel**) **1** headwaiter; **2** butler, steward; **3** hotel manager; **4** sauce of melted butter, minced parsley, and lemon juice

maize /māz/ [Sp *maíz* < WInd *mahís*] *n* **1** *Brit* corn; **2** pale yellow

Maj. Major

ma·jes·tic /məjes′tik/ *adj* noble; grand; imposing, stately ‖ **ma·jes′ti·cal·ly** *adv* ‖ SYN royal, regal, sublime, splendid, stately, elevated, lofty, magnificent

maj·es·ty /maj′istē/ [MF *majeste*] *n* (**-ties**) **1** sovereignty; grandeur; nobility; sublimity; **2** Majesty title applied to a reigning sovereign (preceded by *his, her,* or *your*)

ma·jol·i·ca /məjol′ikə/ [< It < *Majorca,* where first made] *n* **1** Italian decorative earthenware with an opaque glaze; **2** earthenware made in imitation of this

ma·jor /māj′ər/ [L = greater] *adj* **1** greater or great in number, extent, dignity, or quality; **2** of legal age; **3** *mus* a (scale) having the half steps between the third and fourth between the seventh and eighth tones; **b** (interval) between the tonic and the second, third, sixth, and seventh tones of a major scale; **c** characterized by the use of major scales, intervals, and tones ‖ *n* **4** subject or field in which a college student specializes; **5** one of legal age; **6** army officer next in rank above a captain; **7** **the majors** *pl sports* the major leagues ‖ *vi* **8** major in to specialize in (a subject or field of college study)

ma·jor-do·mo /-dōm′ō/ [Sp *mayordomo*] *n* **1** chief steward in charge of a great household; **2** butler

ma′jor gen′er·al *n* army officer ranking next below a lieutenant general

ma·jor·i·ty /məjôr′itē, -jôr′-/ [ML *majoritas*] *n* (**-ties**) **1** the greater of two numbers, more than half; **2** amount by which the greater number, constituting more than half, exceeds the remainder; **3** legal age; **4** *mil* rank or office of a major ‖ SYN plurality ‖ DISCR *Majority,* though having considerable common ground with *plurality,* must not be used for it indiscriminately. A *majority* must be a portion greater than one half of the total number (of votes cast, or the entire electorate). In computing votes, it is usually reckoned according to the excess of votes which the candidate or measure receiving it has over the combined number of votes cast for all other candidates or alternative measures. A *plurality* is the margin which one candidate (or, less frequently, measure) has over another; unless otherwise specified, the term is always used with respect to the leader and the nearest rival. *Majority* may be qualified for parliamentary purposes, as a two-thirds *majority*

ma′jor league′ *n* one of the main leagues of professional teams, as of baseball ‖ **ma′jor-lea′guer** *n*

ma′jor scale′ *n mus* scale having a series of whole steps except for half steps between the third and fourth and the seventh and eighth degrees

make /māk/ [OE *macian*] *v* (**made**) *vt* **1** to create; fashion; compose; frame; produce; bring about; **2** to prepare for use, as *to make a bed;* **3** to acquire, as *friends* or a *fortune;* **4** to earn (money); **5** to compute to be, as *I make the amount fifty dollars;* **6** to amount to, as *three feet make a yard;* **7** to cause the success of, as *this venture will make him;* **8** to score (points) in a game; **9** to reach, as *to make port;* **10** to have the qualities to become, as *he'll make a good husband;* **11** to cause to be or become, as *to make her happy;* **12** to cause or compel, as *to make a child obey;* **13** to constitute, as *one swallow does not make a summer;* **14** to understand, take to be; **15** to perform, execute, as *to make a gesture* or *a speech;* **16** *colloq* to get a position on (a team); **17** to cause or bring about, as war or trouble; **18** to go at a certain speed, as *we made 60 on the road today;* **19** to arrive in time for, as a show or train; **20** *slang* to seduce; **21** **make believe** to pretend; **22** **make a play for** *slang* to try to get; **23** **make book** *slang* to take bets; **24** **make good on,** a to fulfill, as a promise; b to make restitution for; **25** **make it** *colloq* a to succeed; b to stay alive; c to reach a specific goal; **26** **make out,** a to fill out (a blank); **b** to decipher; **c** to impute that one is, as *they made him out a thief;* **27 make over, a** to remodel; **b** to transfer (property); **28 make up, a** to put together; constitute; **b** to invent; **c** to arrange; **d** to repeat (a course one has failed in or an exam one has missed) ‖ *vi* **29** to put something into a specified condition, as *to make ready, make sure;* **30** to act in a specific manner, as *to make merry;* **31 make away with, a** to steal; **b** to get rid of; **c** to kill; **32 make** (**so**) **bold** to dare, have the temerity; **33 make do** to do as best one can with what is available; **34 make for, a** to go toward; **b** to attack; **c** to promote or cause, as misunderstanding; **35 make like** *slang* to imitate; **36 make off** to flee, depart in haste; **37 make off with** to steal; **38 make out, a** *colloq* to manage; **b** *slang* to neck, pet; **39 make up, a** to become reconciled; **b** to dress in costume and put on make-up for a part in a play; **c** to apply make-up; **40 make up for** to compensate for; **41 make up to** *colloq* to fawn on ‖ *n* **42** act or process of making; **43** brand; **44** shape, style; construction, build; **45** amount of output; **46** *elec* closing of a circuit; **47 on the make** *slang* a seeking to advance one's fortunes or stature by any means; **b** seeking sexual relations

make' and brake' *n* **1** mechanical device which opens and closes an electric circuit; **2** electrical device which automatically opens and closes a circuit as long as a supply of current is present ‖ **make'-and-brake'** *adj*

make'-be-lieve' *n* pretense, sham ‖ also *adj*

mak'er *n* **1** one who makes; **2** signer of a promissory note; **3** Maker the Creator, God

make'shift' *n* temporary substitute or improvisation for want of something better ‖ also *adj*

make'-up *n* **1** way in which something is put together; composition; **2** character or nature; **3** costume and paint put on by an actor for a part; **4** facial cosmetics; **5** general appearance of a printed page, as of a book or newspaper, with reference to the type used, illustrations, etc.

make'-work' *n* work of a kind that keeps a person busy but does not accomplish anything of value

mak'ing *n* **1 in the making** being made; **2 makings** *pl* **a** that from which something is made; **b** potential

mal- /mal-/ [F] *comb form* badly; wrong; ill

mal'ad-just'ed *adj* badly adjusted to one's environment ‖ **mal'ad-just'ment** *n*

mal'ad-min'is-ter *vt* to administer badly ‖ **mal'ad-min'is-tra'tion** *n*

mal'a-droit' *adj* lacking skill; clumsy

mal-a-dy /mal'ədē/ [OF *maladie*] *n* (-dies) disease or illness, esp. a deep-seated or lingering disorder ‖ SYN infirmity, complaint (see *disease*)

Mal-a-ga /mal'əgə/ [*Málaga,* Spain] *n* **1** a sweet white wine; **2** a white grape

Mal-a-gas-y /mal'əgas'ē/ *n* (-y or -ies) **1** native of Malagasy; **2** language of Malagasy ‖ also *adj*

Mal'a-gas'y (**Re-pub'lic**) *n* republic consisting of Madagascar and minor islands in the Indian Ocean (8,050,000; 226,444 sq.m.; cap. Tananarive)

ma-laise /malāz'/ [F] *n* vague feeling of uneasiness and discomfort

mal-a-prop-ism /mal'əpropiz'em) [< Mrs. *Malaprop* in Sheridan's *The Rivals* (1775)] *n* ridiculous misuse of words

mal-ap-ro-pos /mal'əprəpō'/ *adj* **1** inappropriate ‖ *adv* **2** inappropriately

ma-lar-i-a /məler'ē-ə/ [It = bad air] *n* febrile disease, caused by a protozoan parasite deposited in the blood by the bite of a mosquito of the genus *Anopheles* ‖ **ma-lar'i-al** *adj*

ma-lar-key /məlärk'ē/ [?] *n* colloq baloney, bunkum

Ma-la-wi /mälä'wē/ *n* republic in SE Africa, member of the British Commonwealth of Nations (4,042,412; 45,483 sq.m.; cap. Zomba)

Ma-lay /māl'ā, məlā'/ *n* **1** one of the race dominant in the Malay Peninsula and the adjacent islands; **2** language of the Malays ‖ also *adj* ‖ **Ma-lay-an** /məlā'ən/ *adj & n*

Ma-lay-a /məlā'ə/ *n* the southern and greater part of the Malay Peninsula, comprising the mainland part of the Federation of Malaysia

Ma'lay Ar'chi-pel'a-go *n* group of islands in the Indian Ocean and the Pacific Ocean

Ma'lay Pen-in'su-la *n* peninsula in SE Asia, including Malaya and the S part of Thailand

Ma-lay-sia /məlāzh'ə, melāsh'ə/ *n* independent federation in SE Asia, comprising Malaya, Sarawak, and Sabah; member of the British Commonwealth of Nations (11,000,000; 128,430 sq.m.; cap. Kuala Lumpur) ‖ **Ma-lay'sian** *adj & n*

Mal-colm X /mal'kəm eks'/ *n* (né Malcolm Little) (1925–65) black American leader, advocating black pride and self-reliance; assassinated

mal'con-tent' *n* person who is discontented and dissatisfied, esp. with the prevailing order ‖ also *adj*

mal de mer /mal'dəmer'/ [F] *n* seasickness

Mal'dive Is'lands /mal'dīv/ *n* independent sultanate consisting of a group of small islands SW of the S tip of India (110,883; 115 sq.m.; cap. Malé)

male /māl'/ [MF < L *masculus*] *adj* **1** pert. to the sex that begets young by fertilizing the female; **2** consisting of males; **3** *bot* having organs, as stamens, capable of fertilizing; **4** *mach* designating a part shaped to fit a corresponding female part ‖ *n* **5** male person, animal, or plant

mal·e·dic·tion /mal´ĭ-/ *n* **1** curse; imprecation; **2** slander ‖ SYN anathema, oath, blasphemy, imprecation, curse, execration, profanity ‖ DISCR A *malediction* is a calling down or declaration of evil against someone; it is a general word for strong denunciation, as in his rage he cast *maledictions* on friends and foes alike. *Malediction* is the opposite of *benediction*. A *curse*, as spoken by man, is a solemn prayer to God to punish with vengeance, destruction, or other evil; or, conceived as pronounced by God, a decree of such evil. An *imprecation* is also a prayer that calamity or evil may fall on one; it is uttered only by man, and is vindictive. An *execration* is an evil-wishing expression colored by horror and detestation; it is bitter and full of hatred. *Curses* and *imprecations* are sometimes merely coarse or profane expressions

mal·e·fac·tor /mal´ĭ-/ *n* **1** evildoer; **2** criminal ‖ **mal´e·fac´tress** *nfem* ‖ **mal´e·fac´tion** *n* ‖ SYN criminal, culprit, felon, convict

ma·lef·i·cent /məlef´ĭsənt/ /< L *maleficus* wicked] *adj* causing or doing evil ‖ **ma·lef´i·cence** *n*

ma·lev·o·lent /məlev´ələnt/ [L *malevolens* (*-entis*)] *adj* malicious; spiteful; wishing evil to others ‖ **ma·lev´o·lence** *n*

mal·fea·sance /malfēz´əns/ [*mal-* + *obs feasance* doing] *n* performance by a public official of an illegal or wrongful act

mal·for·ma·tion *n* faulty or abnormal structure of any body or part of the body ‖ **mal·formed´** *adj*

mal·func·tion *n* failure to function properly ‖ also *vi*

Ma·li /mäl´ē/ *n* republic in W Africa (5,000,000; 464,000 sq.m.; cap. Bamako)

mal·ice /mal´ĭs/ [OF < L *malitia* evil] *n* **1** ill will; spiteful desire to inflict harm; **2** *law* intent to do evil ‖ SYN rancor, grudge, spite, resentment, hostility, ill will, revenge, animosity, pique ‖ DISCR *Malice* loves to injure because of its very nature, needing no special provocation. *Spite* is a mean desire to thwart or hurt others in petty ways; one may be spiteful by nature, or· be goaded to *spite* by some external irritation. *Grudge* and *resentment* are born of anger over personal injury; a *grudge* is ill will nursed in a bitter heart, and ready to act on opportunity, as I have long held a *grudge* against him. *Resentment* is a sullen anger continued by

brooding over its cause. *Rancor* is a deep-seated bitterness made of spite and *malice*, as an unholy *rancor* soured their hearts ‖ ANT benignity, kindness, good will

mal·ice a·fore·thought *n law* deliberate intent to commit a crime, as murder

ma·li·cious /məlish´əs/ *adj* bearing, showing, characterized by, or caused by malice ‖ SYN spiteful, resentful, rancorous, malevolent, malign, malignant, virulent, evil-minded, ill-disposed ‖ ANT benevolent, humane, kind, merciful, well-disposed, loving

ma·lign /məlīn´/ [MF *maligne* < L *malignus*] *adj* **1** malevolent, malicious; **2** baleful, evil ‖ *vt* **3** to speak evil of, slander ‖ SYN v revile, vilify, abuse, asperse (see *calumniate*) ‖ ANT *v* compliment, praise, laud, eulogize

ma·lig·nant /məlig´nənt/ *adj* **1** having or showing strong and active enmity; **2** intending or bringing about evil; **3** (disease or condition) so severe as to endanger life; tending to get worse ‖ **ma·lig´nan·cy** *n* (-cies)

ma·lig·ni·ty *n* (-ties) **1** state or condition of being malign; **2** malignant act or event

ma·lin·ger /məlĭŋ´gər/ [F *malingre* sickly] *vi* to pretend or protract illness to escape work or duty ‖ **ma·lin´ger·er** *n*

mall /môl/ [var of *maul*] *n* **1** shaded public walk or promenade; **2** street lined with shops and not open to vehicles; **3** strip of land dividing the lanes of a highway

mal·lard /mal´ərd/ [OF *malart*] *n* (-lards or -lard) the common wild duck

mal·le·a·ble /mal´ē-əbəl/ [< L *malleare* to hammer] *adj* **1** capable of being extended or shaped by hammering or rolling; **2** tractable, easily influenced ‖ **mal·le·a·bil´i·ty** /-bil´-/ *n*

mal·let /mal´ĭt/ [MF *maillet*] *n* **1** short-handled hammer with usu. a wooden head, used esp. for driving tools; **2** long-handled implement for driving the balls in croquet or polo

mal·le·us /mal´ē-əs/ [L = *hammer*] *n* (-i /-ī´/) outermost of the three small bones in the middle ear

mal·low /mal´ō/ [OE *mealwe* < L *malva*] *n* **1** any of a large family (Malvaceae) of herbs, shrubs, and trees, including the marsh mallow; **2** any of a genus (*Malva*) of plants of this family

mal·nu·tri·tion *n* undernourishment from lack of food, an ill-balanced diet, or poor digestion

mal·oc·clu·sion *n dentistry* failure of the teeth of the upper jaw to meet correctly the corresponding teeth of the lower jaw

mal·o·dor·ous *adj* having a disagreeable smell

mal·prac·tice *n* wrong or neglectful

treatment of a client by a professional person, esp. a surgeon or physician

malt /môlt′/ [OE *mealt*] *n* 1 barley or other grain partially germinated and dried for brewing; 2 beer or ale; 3 *colloq* malted milk

Mal·ta /môlt′ə/ *n* self-governing British island in the Mediterranean S of Sicily (335,000; 92 sq.m.; cap. Valletta) ‖ **Mal·tese**′ /-tēz′, -tēs′/ *adj & n* (-tese)

malt′ed *n colloq* malted milk

malt′ed milk′ *n* 1 soluble powder made of malt and powdered milk; 2 beverage made of this powder dissolved in milk, often with flavoring and/or ice cream

Mal·thu·si·an /malthōōz′ē-ən/ [< Thomas R. *Malthus* (1766–1834) Eng economist] *adj* of or pert. to the theories of Malthus, stating that population tends to increase faster than the means of subsistence and that poverty is inevitable unless the growth of population is checked ‖ also *n*

mal·treat′ *vt* to treat roughly, abuse ‖ **mal·treat′ment** *n*

mam·bo /mäm′bō/ [AmSp] *n* fast ballroom dance of West Indian origin, similar to the rumba ‖ also *vi*

mam·ma[1] also **ma·ma** /mäm′ə, məmä′/ [instinctive] *n* mother

mam·ma[2] /mam′ə/ [L = breast] *n* (-mae /-mē/) organ that secretes milk, found in all female mammals; breast, udder

mam·mal /mam′əl/ *n* member of the highest class of vertebrate animals, the Mammalia, which nourish their young with milk from the mammae ‖ **mam·ma′li·an** /-māl′ē-ən/ *adj*

mam·ma·ry /mam′ərē/ *adj* of or pert. to the mammae or breasts

mam·mon /mam′ən/ [Aram *māmōnā* riches] *n* 1 wealth; worldly riches; 2 **Mammon** cupidity personified

mam·moth /mam′əth/ [Russ *mamot*] *n* 1 huge hairy-skinned elephant of the extinct genus *Mammuthus* with long tusks curving upward ‖ *adj* 2 gigantic, immense

man /man′/ [OE] *n* (men /men′/) 1 human being; 2 the human race; 3 adult male person; 4 male employee or subordinate; 5 male servant; valet; 6 one possessed of manly qualities; 7 husband; 8 one of the pieces in chess, checkers, or similar games; 9 players in a game; 10 **as one man** all in unison; 11 **to a man** none being excepted ‖ *vt* (**manned**) **man·ning** *vt* 12 to furnish with men; 13 to occupy a post or posts in, on, or at; 14 to brace; strengthen

Man, Isle of *n* semiautonomous island in the Irish Sea, part of the United Kingdom (50,000; 227 sq.m.; cap. Douglas)

-man /-mən, -man′/ *comb form* 1 member of a specified nation; 2 one doing a specified kind of work

Man. Manitoba

man′ a·bout town′ *n* man who has the entrée in the most fashionable places

man·a·cle /man′əkəl/ [MF *manicle*] *n* 1 shackle for the hand; handcuff ‖ *vt* 2 to handcuff; 3 to restrain

man·age /man′ij/ [It *maneggiare* to handle (horses)] *vt* 1 to administer; direct; 2 to handle; control; 3 to contrive or bring about ‖ *vi* 4 to conduct or direct affairs; 5 to make use of available resources, get along ‖ **man′age·a·ble** *adj* ‖ SYN direct, regulate, govern, superintend, engineer, control, supervise (see *conduct, govern*)

man′age·ment *n* 1 act or manner of managing; administration; control; 2 skillful managing; 3 persons in charge of and managing a business or institution; 4 managers as a class, as distinguished from *labor* ‖ SYN superintendence, direction, economy, conduct, guidance, control, care, charge, regulation

man′ag·er *n* one who manages, esp. a person who directs an enterprise or business ‖ **man′a·ge′ri·al** /-jir′ē-əl/ *adj*

Ma·na·gua /mənäg′wə/ *n* capital of Nicaragua (240,000)

ma·ña·na /mənyän′ə/ [Sp] *n* 1 tomorrow ‖ *adv* 2 tomorrow; soon; in the future

man·a·tee /man′ətē′, man′ətē′/ [Sp *manatí* < Carib] *n* any of several aquatic herbivorous mammals (genus *Trichechus*) with two flippers and a broad rounded tail

Man·ches·ter /man′chistər, -ches-/ *n* city in NW England (675,000)

Man·chu /manchōō′/ *n* 1 member of the native Mongolian race of Manchuria that conquered China in 1644; 2 language of the Manchus ‖ also *adj*

Man·chu·ri·a /-chōōr′ē-ə/ *n* large region in NE China, original home of the Manchus ‖ **Man·chu′ri·an** *adj & n*

man·da·mus /mandām′əs/ [L = we command] *n* writ issued by a superior court directing the person, corporation, or inferior court addressed, to perform some act

man·da·rin /man′dərin/ [Port *mandarim* < Malay] *n* 1 high-ranking public official of the former Chinese Empire; 2 small orange (*Citrus reticulata*) with a loose rind and sweet pulp; 3 **Mandarin** chief Chinese dialect, the official language of China

man·date /man′dāt, -dit/ [L *mandare* (-*atus*) to command] *n* 1 order, command; 2 official charge or injunction; 3 will of a constituency expressed to its elected representative; 4 a commission to a nation, granted by the former League of Nations to administer territory taken from the Central Powers after World War I; **b** mandated territory || /-dāt/ *vt* **5** to assign (territory) to a nation under a mandate || SYN *n* law, decree, edict, ordinance, statute

man·da·to·ry /-tôr'-, -tōr'-/ *adj* **1** containing or pert. to a mandate; **2** obligatory

man'-day' *n* work done in one day by one man

man·di·ble /man'dĭbəl/ [LL *mandibula* jaw] *n* **1** bone of the lower jaw; **2** in arthropods, the first pair of mouth parts, variously modified for biting, crushing, chewing, sucking, or piercing; **3** either part of a bird's beak

man·do·lin /man'dəlĭn/ [It *mandolino*] *n mus* instrument of the lute variety, with a pear-shaped sound box, a fretted neck, and metal strings in pairs, played with a plectrum

man·drake /man'drāk/ [ME *mandrage* < Gk *mandragoras*] *n* narcotic plant (*Mandragora officinarum*) with a large forked root and a white or purple flower

man·drel /man'drəl/ [< F *mandrin*] *n* **1** shaft inserted into a piece to hold it while it is being machined, as in a lathe; **2** shaft on which a circular saw or grindstone is mounted

man·drill /man'dril/ [*man* + *drill* baboon] *n* large and ferocious W African baboon (*Papio sphinx*) with large canine teeth

mane /mān/ [OE *manu*] *n* the long hair on the upper side or about the neck of certain animals, as the horse and lion || **maned'** *adj*

man'-eat'er *n* animal that eats human flesh || **man'-eat'ing** *adj*

ma·nège /manezh'/ [F < *maneggio*] *n* **1** school for horsemanship; **2** art of training, riding, or driving horses; **3** the paces of a trained horse

ma·neu·ver /mənōō'vər/ [F *manœuvre* < L *manu operari* to work by hand] *n* **1** controlled movement, as of troops or war vessels; **2** artful proceeding or course of action; stratagem; **3** maneuvers *pl mil* tactical field exercises involving large bodies of troops, simulating war || *vi* **4** to perform maneuvers; **5** to scheme, make crafty moves || *vt* **6** to move or change the position of; **7** to handle skillfully; manipulate; **8** to make, move, or place by skillful maneuvers || SYN *n* artifice, stratagem (see *subterfuge*)

man' Fri'day [< devoted servant in *Robinson Crusoe*] *n* faithful and efficient helper

man'ful *adj* courageous; resolute; bravely determined || **man'ful·ly** *adv* || SYN noble, brave, manly, manlike,

mannish || DISCR *Manly* connotes the possession of such qualities as befit a man, as courage, stamina, boldness, hardiness. *Manlike* describes the appearance and the qualities, good or bad, that distinguish a man; it usually stresses his finer qualities, however, as *manlike* determination. *Manful* emphasizes the fighting qualities, the bravery and resolution characteristic of men, as a *manful* spirit. *Mannish* describes those who ape the fashions or manners of men, as a *mannish* girl

man·ga·nese /man'gənēs, -nēz'/ [F < *magnesia*] *n* hard, brittle, grayish-white metallic element (**Mn**; at.no. 25; at.wt. 54.938) used in steel manufacture, in alloys, as a deoxidizing agent, etc.

mange /mānj'/ [MF *manjue* itch] *n* any of various diseases affecting the skin of animals and sometimes man, resulting in loss of hair and scaly eruptions

man·ger /mān'jər/ [MF *maingeure*] *n* box or trough from which horses and cattle eat

man·gle¹ /man'gəl/ [D *mangel*] *n* **1** machine for pressing cloth, esp. damp linen, between rollers || *vt* **2** to press in a mangle

man·gle² [AF *mangler*] *vt* **1** to cut to pieces; mutilate by cutting and hacking; **2** to make a botch of || **man'gler** *n*

man·go /man'gō/ [Port *manga* < Tamil *mankay*] *n* (-**goes** or -**gos**) **1** slightly acid fruit of a tropical tree (*Mangifera indica*), eaten ripe or pickled; **2** the tree

man·grove /man'grōv, maŋ'-/ [?] *n* any of a genus (*Rhizophora*) of low tropical shore trees that send down roots which ultimately cause the tree to spread over large areas

man·gy /mān'jē/ [< *mange*] *adj* (-**gi·er**, -**gi·est**) **1** having, caused by, or similar to mange; **2** shabby, squalid; **3** mean, low

man'han'dle *vt* to handle roughly

Man·hat·tan /manhat'ən/ *n* **1** island at the mouth of the Hudson River in SE New York, coextensive with the Borough of Manhattan, part of and the nucleus of New York City (1,750,000); **2** cocktail of whiskey and sweet vermouth

Man·hat'tan Proj'ect *n* secret government program that was set up during the Second World War to develop the atomic bomb

man'hole' *n* opening, usu. having a cover, to admit a man, as into a tank or sewer

man'hood' *n* **1** state of being a man; **2** manly qualities; **3** men collectively

man'-hour' *n* work done by one man in one hour

ma·ni·a /mān′ē·ə, -yə/ [Gk = madness] *n* 1 excessive desire or enthusiasm; craze; 2 mental disorder characterized by emotional exaltation, high excitability, and a tendency to violent reactions accompanied by impulses to a special type of behavior, as *a suicidal mania* || SYN frenzy, madness, lunacy (see *insanity*)

-ma·ni·a /-mān′ē·ə/ *comb form* mania

ma·ni·ac /mān′ē·ak′/ *n* violently insane person || **ma·ni·a·cal** /mənī′əkəl/ *adj*

man·ic /man′ik, mān′-/ *adj* exhibiting or affected by mania

man′ic-de·pres′sive *n* person who alternates between periods of elation and depression || also *adj*

man·i·cure /man′ikyŏŏr′/ [F] *n* 1 care of the hands and fingernails; 2 person who cares for the hands and fingernails of others || also *vt* & *vi* || **man′i·cur′ist** *n*

man·i·fest /man′ifest′/ [L *manifestus*] *n* 1 list of the cargo transported by land, sea, or air; 2 passenger list of an airplane || *adj* 3 obvious, clear, apparent to the senses || *vt* 4 to make manifest || **man′i·fest′ly** *adv* || SYN *adj* visible, overt, unmistakable, evident; *v* demonstrate, prove, reveal, display

man′i·fes·ta′tion *n* 1 act of manifesting or state of being manifested; 2 that which is manifested; 3 public demonstration || SYN exhibition, indication, display, disclosure

man′i·fes′to /-tō/ [It] *n* (-**toes**) proclamation of intentions or objectives by a government, group, or prominent person

man·i·fold /man′ifōld′/ [OE *manigfeald*] *adj* 1 various in kind or quality; numerous; 2 comprehensive; 3 many-sided; 4 (business form) having several copies with interleaved carbons || *vt* 5 to make copies of, as with carbon paper || *n* 6 copy made by manifolding; 7 tissuelike paper for making carbon copies; 8 *mach* chamber with several outlets or inlets || *adv* 9 many times; greatly || SYN *adj* sundry, divers, various, multifarious

man·i·kin /man′ikin/ [D *mannekin* puppet] *n* 1 dwarf; little man; 2 model of the human body for teaching medical students; 3 mannequin

Ma·nil·a /mənil′ə/ *n* 1 largest city and capital of the Philippines (1,400,000); 2 Manila hemp; 3 Manila paper

Ma·nil′a hemp′ *n* strong fiber obtained from the leaves of a Philippine plant, *Musa textilis*, used for making rope, paper, and fabrics

Ma·nil′a pa′per *n* strong brown paper made from Manila hemp and also from other material

Ma·nil′a rope′ *n* strong rope made from Manila hemp

man′ in the street′ *n* average citizen

ma·nip·u·late /mənip′yəlāt′/ [< F *manipulation* manipulation] *vt* 1 to operate, work, or manage skillfully; 2 to influence artfully; control the actions of by skillful management; 3 to falsify, as books and records || **ma·nip′u·la′tor** *n* || **ma·nip′u·la′tion** *n*

Man·i·to·ba /man′itōb′ə/ *n* province in central Canada (963,066; 251,000 sq.m.; cap. Winnipeg) || **Man′i·to′ban** *n*

man′kind′ *n* 1 the human race; human beings collectively || **man′kind′** *n* 2 men, not women

man′ly *adj* (-**li·er**; -**li·est**) 1 having the qualities befitting a man; courageous; virile; 2 pert. to or suitable for a man || **man′li·ness** *n* || SYN intrepid, determined, frank (see *manful*)

Mann, Thom·as /män′/ *n* (1875–1955) outstanding German novelist and essayist; Nobel prize 1929

man·na /man′ə/ [Gk < Heb *mān*] *n* 1 *Bib* the food miraculously supplied to the Israelites in the wilderness (Ex. 16:15); 2 any necessities apparently supplied by a miracle

Mann′ Act′ /man′/ [James R. *Mann* (1856–1922) U.S. Congressman] *n* federal law passed in 1910 making it illegal to transport a woman across a state line for immoral purposes

man·ne·quin /man′ikin/ [F < D *mannekin*] *n* 1 model of the human body used to display clothes in shop windows; 2 person who models clothes

man·ner /man′ər/ [AF *manere*] *n* 1 method; way of acting or happening; 2 bearing, mien; 3 sort, kind, species; 4 aspect, style, as in literature or art; 5 **manners** *pl* a social behavior, as *good* or *bad manners*; b polite behavior; c prevailing customs, as of a people, class, or period; 6 by no manner of means certainly not; 7 in a manner of speaking in a way, as it were || SYN behavior, demeanor, address, mode, system

man′nered *adj* affected

-man′nered *comb form* having manners as specified, as *ill-mannered*

man′ner·ism *n* peculiarity of style, action, or bearing, esp. if affected or carried to excess || SYN affectation, air || DISCR A *mannerism* is an excessive adherence to some distinctive trait or singularity, particularly some trick or oddity of style in literature or art. An *affectation* is a trick of behavior or style consciously assumed. *Affectations* are hence usually artificial, unnatural, and without sincerity; a *mannerism*, though peculiar, may be a perfectly natural trait of its possessor. An *affectation* so consistently assumed that it is displayed unconsciously becomes a

mannerism, and a *mannerism* put on for display is an *affectation*

man·ner·ly *adj* 1 polite, courteous || *adv* 2 politely; respectfully

man·nish *adj* masculine; characteristic of a man, as *a mannish voice* || SYN (see *manful*) || ANT effeminate, womanish

ma·noeu·vre /məno͞ov′ər/ *n, vi, & vt* var of **maneuver**

man′ of all′ work′ *n* domestic who does all kinds of work around the house

man′ of parts′ *n* man who stands out in many divergent areas

man′ of the cloth′ *n* clergyman

man′ of the world′ *n* sophisticated, experienced, broad-minded man

man′-of-war′ *n* (**men-of-war** /men′-/) 1 warship; 2 Portuguese man-of-war

man′ on horse′back [nickname of Georges Boulanger (1837–91) F general] *n* military leader who threatens to become or becomes a dictator

man·or /man′ər/ [OF *manoir* < L *manere* to stay] *n* 1 in England, landed estate; 2 in Middle Ages, feudal estate; 3 mansion on an estate or plantation

man′ pow′er *n* the power supplied by the work of human beings

man′pow′er *n* the number of men available or required, as for the armed forces, industry, or a specific task

man·sard (roof′) /man′särd/ [François Mansart (1598–1666) F architect] *n* roof with a double slope, the lower being steeper than the upper

manse /mans/ [ML *mansus* house] *n* parsonage

man′serv′ant *n* (**men-serv·ants** /men′-/) male servant

man·sion /mansh′ən/ [L *mansio* (-onis)] *n* stately residence

man′-sized′ *adj colloq* of a goodly size, as befitting a man

man′slaugh′ter *n law* unlawful killing of a human being without malice aforethought

man·tel /mant′əl/ [see **mantle**] *n* 1 the facing around and above a fireplace; 2 mantelpiece

man′tel·piece′ *n* projecting shelf above a mantel

man·til·la /mantil′ə/ [Sp] *n* lace head scarf worn by women, esp. in Spanish-speaking countries

man·tis /mant′is/ [Gk = prophet] *n* (-tis·es or -tes /-tēz/) any of various insects (order Mantidae) which prey on other insects and are noted for folding the front legs as if praying

man·tis·sa /mantis′ə/ [L = addition] *n* decimal part of a logarithm

man·tle /mant′əl/ [OE *mæntel* < L *mantellum*] *n* 1 loose sleeveless cloak; 2 anything that covers or envelopes; 3 mesh hood that fits over a flame and gives light by glowing; 4 outer fold of skin covering the body of mollusks; 5 the part of the earth between the crust and the core || *vt* 6 to cover with or as with a cloak; disguise; conceal || *vi* 7 to be overspread, as with a covering; 8 to blush, flush

man·u·al /man′yoo̅-əl/ [< L *manus* hand] *adj* 1 pert. to or done by the hands || *n* 2 handbook; small book of directions; 3 *mil* prescribed drill in the use of a weapon; 4 keyboard of an organ

man·u·al train′ing *n* training in manual arts and crafts, esp. in woodworking

man·u·fac·ture /man′yəfak′chər/ [< LL *manufactus* handmade] *n* 1 the making, usu. on a large scale, of articles by hand or by machinery; 2 making of anything; 3 manufactured product || *vt* 4 to make by hand, machinery, or other processes; 5 to work, as raw materials, into useful forms; 6 to invent or fabricate with intent to deceive || **man′u·fac′tur·er** *n*

man·u·mit /man′yəmit′/ [L *manumittere*] *v* (-**mit·ted;** -**mit·ting**) *vt* to give freedom to (a slave) || **man′u·mis′·sion** /-mish′ən/ *n*

ma·nure /mən(y)oo̅r′/ [MF *manouvrer* to do work by hand] *n* 1 animal excrement used as a fertilizer || *vt* 2 to put manure on (land)

man·u·script /man′yəskript′/ [ML *manuscriptum* something written by hand] *adj* 1 written by hand or typewritten || *n* 2 book or paper written by hand; 3 handwritten or typewritten author's work, ready to be submitted for printing or editorial consideration; 4 writing, as opposed to printing

Manx /manks/ [earlier *Manisk* < Scand] *adj* 1 pert. to the Isle of Man || *n* 2 the Manx language; 3 the Manx *pl* the Manx people

manx′ cat′ *n* tailless domestic cat

Manx′man /-mən/ *n* (-men /-mən/) native or inhabitant of the Isle of Man

man·y /men′ē/ [OE *manig*] *adj* (**more; most**) 1 numerous; 2 **many a** a lot of, as *he spent many a gay hour there* || *n* 3 a great number; multitude || *pron* 4 many persons or things

man′y-sid′ed *adj* 1 having many sides; 2 having many aspects; 3 versatile

Mao·ism /mou′izəm/ [Mao Tse-tung (1893–1976) Chin communist] *n* personal political, economic, social, and military theories of Mao Tse-tung concerning world-wide revolution, guerrilla warfare, etc. || **Mao′ist** *adj & n*

Ma·o·ri /mou′rē/ *n* 1 member of the native population of New Zealand; 2 language of the Maoris || *also adj*

map /map/ [ML *mappa* mundi map of the world < L *mappa* napkin] *n* 1 representation of the physical or political features of the earth or some portion of it; **2** chart of the heavens; **3** *slang* face; **4** **off the map** out of existence ‖ *v* (**mapped; map-ping**) *vt* **5** to make a map of; **6** **map out** to plan ‖ SYN (see *chart*)

ma-ple /māp′əl/ [OE *mapul*trēow maple tree] *n* any of a large genus (*Acer*) of trees, valued for their shade, their wood, and in some species, their sap

ma′ple syr′up *n* syrup made from maple sap

ma-quette /maket′/ [F < It *macchietta* sketch] *n* small-size model of a building, monument, or a piece of sculpture

ma-quis /mäkē′/ [F < Corsican] *n* (*pl* -**quis** /kē′/) fighter in the French resistance in World War II

mar /mär/ [OE *merran* to hinder] *v* (**marred; mar-ring**) *vt* **1** to disfigure; **2** to impair ‖ SYN injure, blemish, impair, deface, hurt, scratch

Mar. March

mar-a-bou /mar′əbōō′/ [F < Ar *murabit* hermit] *n* **1** any of several large Old World storks (genus *Leptoptilus*), of which the soft under-wing feathers are used for dress trimmings; **2** marabou feather

ma-rac-a /məräk′ə/ [Port < Tupi] *n* gourd filled with seeds or pebbles, used as a rhythm instrument

mar-a-schi-no /mar′əskēn′ō/ [It] *n* cordial made from cherries

mar′a-schi′no cher′ry *n* cherry cooked in a syrup flavored with maraschino

mar-a-thon /mar′əthon′, -thən/ [*Marathon* plain in central Greece from which Pheidippides ran over 26 miles to Athens to report the Greek victory over the Persians 490 B.C.] *n* **1** foot race of 26 miles, 385 yards; **2** any contest requiring prolonged endurance

ma-raud /mərôd′/ [F = rogue] *vt & vi* to raid and plunder ‖ **ma-raud′er** *n*

mar-ble /märb′əl/ [OF *marbre* < Gk *marmaros*] *n* **1** hard crystalline limestone found in various colors and capable of taking a fine polish; **2** something resembling marble in hardness, smoothness, or coldness; **3** sculptured piece of marble; **4** small clay, glass, stone, or metal ball used in games; **5** **marbles,** a *sg* game played with marbles; **b** *pl slang* mental faculties ‖ *vt* **6** to give a veined or mottled appearance to in imitation of marble

mar-cel /märsel′/ [*Marcel* Grateau (1852–1936) F hairdresser] *v* (-**celled;** -**cel-ling**) *vt* **1** to form (the hair) into regular even waves ‖ *n* **2** marcelled hair-do

march¹ /märch′/ [OF *marche*] *n* **1** frontier; borderland ‖ *vi* **2** to border

march² [F *marchier* to trample] *n* **1** regular measured step or walk, as of

a body of soldiers; **2** a movement, as of troops, from one place to another; **b** distance covered; **3** steady advance; **4** *mus* composition to accompany marching; **5** **on the march** moving ahead; **6** **steal a march on** to get the advantage over, esp. secretly ‖ *vt* **7** to cause to march ‖ *vi* **8** to move with regular steps, as in a military formation ‖ **march′er** *n*

March /märch/ [AF *marche* < L *Martius*] *n* third month of the year, having 31 days

mar-chion-ess /märsh′ənis/ [ML *marchionissa*] *n* **1** wife or widow of a marquis; **2** lady of the rank of a marquis

march′-past′ *n* parade past a reviewing stand

Mar-co-ni, Gu-gliel-mo /gōōlyel′mō märkōn′ē/ *n* (1874–1937) Italian inventor, developer of wireless telegraphy; Nobel prize in physics 1909

Mar-di gras /märd′ēgrä′/ [F = fat Tuesday] *n* day before Lent, celebrated in New Orleans, Paris, and other cities with gay carnivals; Shrove Tuesday

mare¹ /mer′/ [OE *mere* horse] *n* female of the horse and other equine animals

ma-re² /mer′ē, mär′ē/ [L = sea] *n* (-**ri-a** /-rē-ə/) one of the dark plains of the moon, thought to be seas before the advent of high-powered telescopes

mare′s′-nest′ /merz′-/ *n* **1** spectacular hoax; **2** place or situation of extreme confusion or disorder

mare′s′-tail′ *n* **1** long, narrow tufted cirrus cloud, the first indication of an approaching warm front; **2** aquatic plant (*Hippuris vulgaris*) with dense whorls of tapering leaves

mar-ga-rine /märj′(ə)rin/ [F < Gk *margaron* pearl] *n* butter substitute made usu. from vegetable oils

mar-gin /märj′in/ [L *margo* (-*ginis*)] *n* **1** border, edge; **2** limit; **3** amount in reserve, as of money, time, or space; **4** blank border of a page; **5** difference between the cost and the selling price of an article; **6** *stock market* percentage of the cost of a stock bought on credit that must be paid in cash ‖ **mar′gin-al** *adj* ‖ SYN reservation, provision, verge (see *border*)

Ma-rie An-toi-nette /mərē′ an′twənet′/ *n* (1755–93) queen of France 1774–93, wife of Louis XVI; guillotined during the French Revolution

mar-i-gold /mar′igōld′/ [the Virgin *Mary* + *gold*] *n* any of several plants (genera *Tagetes* and *Calendula*) with strongly scented leaves and showy yellow or orange flowers

ma-ri-hua-na or **ma-ri-jua-na** /mar′iwän′ə/ [MexSp *mariguana, marihuana*] *n* **1** hemp plant (*Cannabis* *sativa*); **2** its dried leaves, smoked in cigarets as a narcotic

ma·rim·ba /mərim′bə/ [W African] *n* *mus* instrument resembling the xylophone, with resonators under the bars to reinforce the sound

ma·ri·na /mərēn′ə/ [Sp = marine *adj*] *n* boat basin for small craft

mar·i·nade /mar′ināď/ [F < Sp *marinada*] *n* **1** spiced wine or vinegar in which meat or fish is steeped; **2** meat or fish steeped in it ‖ /mar′-ināď/ *vt* **3** to marinate

ma·ri·na·ra /mär′inär′ə/ [It] *n* sauce made of tomatoes, spice, and garlic

mar·i·nate /mar′ināt′/ [prob It *marinato* marinated] *vt* to steep (meat or fish) in a marinade

ma·rine /mərēn′/ [MF *marin* < L *marinus*] *adj* **1** pert. to, living in, or formed by, the sea; **2** pert. to shipping or navigation; nautical, maritime ‖ *n* **3** soldier serving on shipboard and on land; **4** member of the U.S. Marine Corps; **5** in some countries, department of naval affairs; **6** collective shipping of a country, as *the merchant marine* ‖ SYN *adj* nautical, naval (see *maritime*)

Ma·rine′ Corps′ *n* branch of the U.S. Navy, the members of which are trained as soldiers and used for amphibious operations and as ready combat troops

mar·i·ner /mar′inər/ *n* sailor; seaman

Mar·i·ol·a·try /mer′ē·ol′ətrē/ [*Mary* + *-latry*] *n* excessive veneration of the Virgin Mary, esp. if carried to the point of idolatry

mar·i·o·nette /mar′ē·ənet′/ [F] *n* puppet with jointed limbs manipulated by strings from above

mar·i·tal /mar′itəl/ [< L *maritus*] *adj* of or pert. to marriage

mar·i·time /mar′itim′/ [L *maritimus*] *adj* **1** living or situated near the sea; **2** connected with the sea in respect to navigation or trade ‖ SYN marine, nautical, naval ‖ DISCR *Marine* describes that found in, belonging to, or produced by, the sea, as *marine* animals or plants. It is sometimes used in connection with naval affairs, as *marine* stores; but it usually has to do with commerce at sea, as *marine* insurance, or with things for use at sea, as a *marine* compass. *Maritime* is applied to places bordering on or near the sea, as *maritime* states; or things connected with the sea, as *maritime* law. Occasionally *marine* and *maritime* overlap; we say *marine* or *maritime* insurance, but more often *marine*; we say *marine* or *maritime* law, but more frequently *maritime*. *Naval* refers sometimes to ships as used in commerce, but usually to a navy. *Nautical* refers to sailors or the art of navigation, as a *nautical* chart or

almanac. The *naval* force of a nation is the complement of the military

mar·jo·ram /märj′ərəm/ [ML *majorana*] *n* any of several plants of the mint family (genera *Origanum* and *Majorana*), used in cooking

mark¹ /märk/ [OE *mearc*] *n* **1** target; **2** visible imprint, as a line, stain, scratch, written word, or the like; **3** brand; label; stamp; **4** indication; trait; distinguishing feature; **5** character made by one who cannot write his name; **6** written or printed symbol, as *an exclamation mark*; **7** figure or letter indicating a student's grade; **8** high position; distinction, as *men of mark*; **9** set standard; **10** line, object, or the like, serving to indicate position; **11 beside the mark** irrelevant; **12 easy mark** gull, dupe; **13 make one's mark** to achieve success; **14 wide of the mark** very inaccurate or wrong ‖ *vt* **15** to put or make a mark on; **16** to characterize; identify or indicate, as by a mark; **17** to single out or select, as by a mark; destine; **18** to notice, observe; **19** to heed; **20** to rank or grade, as examination papers; **21** to record, as a score; **22** to supply with a tag or sign indicating price; **23 mark down** to reduce in price; **24 mark off** to set apart, as by a boundary; **25 mark out** to trace or outline, as by marks; **26 mark up, a** to raise the price of; **b** to put marks on

mark² [OE *marc*] *n* monetary unit of Germany

Mark /märk/ *n Bib* **1** one of the twelve Apostles, reputed author of the second Gospel; **2** second book of the New Testament

Mark′ An′to·ny /ant′ənē/ *n* (83–30 B.C.) Roman general, friend of Caesar and lover of Cleopatra

mark′down′ *n* **1** amount deducted from the original price of a product to arrive at the selling price; **2** decrease in price

marked′ *adj* **1** noticeable; conspicuous; **2** having a mark or marks ‖ **mark′-ed·ly** /-idlē/ *adv*

mark′er *n* **1** something that marks or indicates; **2** counter used in card playing; **3** *slang* IOU for a gambling debt

mar·ket /märk′it/ [ONF < L *mercatus*] *n* **1** meeting of people for selling or buying; **2** public or private place for the sale or purchase of merchandise; **3** shop for the sale of food; **4** trade in a particular commodity; **5** group to which or region where something can be sold, as *the teenage market, the European market*; **6** demand as shown by rate or price; **7 at the market** at the prevailing price; **8 in the market for** looking to buy; **9 on the market** up for sale ‖ *vt* **10** to buy or sell goods ‖ *vt* **11** to offer for sale or to sell || **mar′ket·a·ble** *adj* || **mar′ket·a·bil′i·ty** /-bil′-/ *n*

mar′ket·ing *n* 1 act of buying or selling; 2 things bought at a market; 3 all the activities involved in the advertising, display, selling, shipping, storing, etc. of a product

mar′ket·place′ *n* 1 building or open area where goods are offered for sale; 2 world of business and commerce

mar′ket price′ *n* prevailing price of anything

mar′ket val′ue *n* actual value of anything if placed on the market

mark′ing *n* often **mark′ings** *pl* pattern of marks, as on fur or feathers

mark·ka /märk′kä/ [Finnish < Sw *mark*] *n* monetary unit of Finland

marks·man /märks′mən/ *n* (-men /-mən/) one who shoots well

mark′up′ *n* 1 amount added to the cost of a product to arrive at the selling price; 2 increase in price

marl /märl′/ [OF *marle* < LL *margila*] *n* 1 crumbly deposit of clay or sand containing much lime, used as a fertilizer || *vt* 2 to fertilize with marl || **marl′y** *adj*

mar·lin /mär′lin/ [< *marline*spike] *n* large marine game fish (genus *Makaira*) having a long spearlike upper jaw

mar′line·spike′ also **mar′lin·spike′** /mär′lin-/ [ME *marlyne* loosely twisted cord] *n naut* pointed iron tool used for separating the strands of a rope and in splicing

mar·ma·lade /mär′məlād′, mär′məläd′/ [Port *marmelada* quince jam] *n* thick preserve made from the pulp and often the rind of fruit

Mar·ma·ra /mär′mərə/ also **Mar·mo·ra** /mär′mərə, -mōr′-/, Sea of *n* sea between the Bosporus and the Dardanelles

mar·mo·set /mär′məzet′/ [OF = grotesque image] *n* any of various small tropical American monkeys of several genera, having soft fur and long, hairy, nonprehensile tails

mar·mot /mär′mət/ [F *marmotte*] *n* any of a genus (*Marmota*) of hibernating, burrowing rodents, as the woodchuck

Mar·o·nite /mar′ənīt′/ [< St. *Maron* 4th-cent. monk] *n* member of a Uniat sect of Lebanon and Syria

ma·roon¹ /mərōōn′/ [< Sp *cimarrón* wild] *vt* 1 to leave alone and abandoned, as on a desolate shore or island; 2 to leave without resources or a way out

ma·roon² [F *marron* < It *marrone* chestnut] *n* dark brownish red

mar′plot′ *n* one who spoils some plan by meddling interference

mar·quee /märkē′/ [assumed *sg* of *marquise*, thought to be *pl*] *n* rooflike structure projecting over the sidewalk at an entrance to a public building, as a hotel or theater

mar·quess /mär′kwis/ *n Brit* var of **marquis**

mar·que·try /mär′kitrē/ [MF] *n* (-tries) woodwork, as furniture or floors, inlaid with various colored woods, ivory, metal, mother-of-pearl, etc.

mar·quis /mär′kwis, märkē′/ [MF] *n* (-quis·es or -quis /-kēz′/) nobleman ranking next below a duke

mar·quise /märkēz′/ [F] *n* 1 marchioness (applied to non-British ladies); 2 gem cut, or ring having gems set, in a double-pointed oval; 3 marquee

mar·qui·sette /mär′k(w)izet′/ [F] *n* sheer fabric with an open square mesh, used for curtains

mar·riage /mar′ij/ [OF *mariage*] *n* 1 state of being married; wedlock; 2 any close union; 3 *pinochle* meld of a king and queen of the same suit || **mar′riage·a·ble** *adj* || SYN matrimony, wedlock, wedding, espousal, nuptials || DISCR *Matrimony* names the state of those united in the relationship of husband and wife. *Marriage* is used chiefly of the act or ceremony of joining two persons. *Wedlock* denotes the married state. *Wedding* may name the marriage ceremony only, or the *marriage* and the festivities that accompany it. *Nuptials* is a more formal and less familiar word for *wedding*

mar·row /mar′ō/ [OE *mearg*] *n* 1 fatty tissue that fills the cavities of the bones; 2 innermost or essential part

mar·ry /mar′ē/ [OF *marier* < L *maritare*] *v* (-ried) *vt* 1 to unite in marriage; 2 to take as husband or wife; 3 to bring together in close union; 4 **marry off** to give in marriage || *vi* 5 to get married

Mars /märz′/ *n* 1 *Rom myth.* god of war; 2 planet whose orbit lies next outside the earth's, notable for its reddish color

Mar·seil·laise /mär′sä·ez′/ [pert. to Marseilles, because first sung on the road from Marseilles to Paris 1792] *n* French national anthem

Mar·seilles /märsālz′, märsā′/ *n* seaport in SE France on the Mediterranean (893,771)

marsh /märsh′/ [OE *mersc*] *n* swampy tract of land || **marsh′y** *adj* (-i·er; -i·est)

mar·shal /märsh′əl/ [OF *mareschal* < Gmc] *n* 1 official in charge of ceremonies and parades; 2 in many armies, officer of the highest rank, equivalent to the U.S. general of the army; 3 officer of a U.S. judicial district, with duties similar to those of a sheriff; 4 policeman or sheriff || *v* (-shaled or -shalled; -shal·ing or

-shal·ling *vt* **5** to arrange or dispose in order, as troops, facts, etc.; **6** to lead; manage

Mar·shall, George Cat·lett /jôrj′ kat′- lĭt märsh′əl/ *n* (1880–1959) U.S. general and diplomat; Secretary of State 1947–49; Nobel peace prize 1953; proponent of the Marshall Plan to aid the European nations in economic recovery after World War II

Mar·shall, John *n* (1755–1835) U.S. Chief Justice 1801–35

marsh′ gas′ *n* methane given off by decaying vegetable matter

marsh′ mal′low *n* perennial wild herb (*Althaea officinalis*), which has pink flowers and grows in marshy places

marsh′mal′low *n* soft spongy candy originally made from the root of a mallow growing in swampy areas, now made from gelatin, sugar, syrup, and flavoring and dusted with powdered sugar

marsh′ mar′i·gold *n* marsh plant (*Caltha palustris*) of the crowfoot family

mar·su·pi·al /märsōōp′ē-əl/ [< L *marsupium* pouch] *n* any mammal of a low order (Marsupialia) that carries its young in an abdominal pouch || also *adj*

mart /märt′/ [MD *markt* < L *mercatus*] *n* market; marketplace

mar·ten /märt′ən/ [MF *martrine* marten fur] *n* **1** any of several small carnivorous arboreal mammals (genus *Martes*) like, but larger than, a weasel; **2** its fur

mar·tial /märsh′əl/ [L *martialis* of Mars] *adj* **1** of or pert. to war and military affairs; **2** warlike

mar′tial law′ *n* law imposed by the military in time of emergency, when civil authority breaks down

Mar·tian /märsh′ən/ [< L *Martius*] *adj* **1** of or pert. to the planet Mars || *n* **2** supposed inhabitant of Mars

mar·tin /märt′ən/ [St. *Martin*] *n* any of various swallows

mar·ti·net /märt′inet′/ [Jean *Martinet* 17th-cent. F general] *n* strict disciplinarian

mar·tin·gale /märt′ingāl′/ [< F (chausses à la) *martingualle* trousers in the manner of a native of *Martigue*, Prov village] *n* **1** strap in a horse's harness, passing from the girth forward between the forelegs and up to the bit or reins, to hold the head down; **2** any system of trying to recover betting losses by progressively increasing the stakes; **3** *naut* a rope or small chain for staying the jib boom to the dolphin striker; **b** the dolphin striker

mar·ti·ni /märtēn′ē/ [?] *n* cocktail made usu. with gin and dry vermouth, often served with an olive

mar·tyr /märt′ər/ [OE < Gk = witness] *n* **1** one who accepts death in preference to renunciation of a faith, cause, or principle; **2** one who suffers keenly for a cause or principle; **3** constant sufferer, as from disease || *vt* **4** to put to death as a martyr; **5** to make a martyr of; **6** to persecute; torture || **mar′tyr·dom** *n*

mar·vel /mär′vəl/ [OF *merveille* < L *mirabilia* wonderful things] *n* **1** object of surprise or astonishment; prodigy || *v* (-veled or -velled; -vel·ing or -vel·ling) *vi* **2** to feel astonishment; wonder

mar·vel·ous also **mar′vel·lous** *adj* **1** causing wonder or astonishment; **2** extraordinary; incredible; **3** great; wonderful || **mar′vel·ous·ly** *adv*

Marx·ism /märks′izəm/ [Karl *Marx* (1818–83) G socialist] *n* theory of the inevitable class struggle that will lead to the overthrow of capitalism and the advent of socialism and the classless society || **Marx′i·an** *adj* || **Marx′ist** *adj & n*

Mar·y /mer′ē/ *n* mother of Jesus, the Virgin Mary

Mar′y·land /-lənd/ *n* state in the E U.S. at the head of the Chesapeake Bay (3,922,000; 10,577 sq.m.; cap. Annapolis) || **Mar′y·land′er** *n*

Mar′y Mag′da·lene /mag′dələn′/ *n Bib* the repentant woman forgiven by Jesus (Luke 7:37–50)

Mar′y Stu′art /st(y)ōō′ərt/ *n* (1542–87) queen of Scotland 1542–67; beheaded by Elizabeth I of England

mar·zi·pan /mär′zipan′/ [G < It *marzapane*] *n* confection made of almond paste

-mas /-məs/ [< *mass*] *comb form* used for certain Christian holidays, as *Christmas*

mas., masc. masculine

mas·car·a /maskar′ə/ [Sp *máscara* mask] *n* **1** preparation for darkening the eyelashes and eyebrows || *vt* **2** to apply mascara to

mas·cot /mas′kot, -kət/ [F *mascotte* < Port *mascota* charm] *n* **1** person, animal, or object supposed to bring good luck; **2** a emblem of a group; **b** person considered as a symbol, as of a ball team; **3** small boy who works for a baseball team

mas·cu·line /mask′yəlin/ [L *masculinus* < *masculus* manly] *adj* **1** of or pert. to men; **2** manly, virile; **3** *gram* in some languages, designating the gender of words that denote males, and of other words classed with them || *n* **4** masculine gender; **5** masculine word || **mas′cu·lin′i·ty** /-lin′-/ *n*

ma·ser /māz′ər/ [microwave amplification by stimulated emission of radiation] *n* device that generates and amplifies electromagnetic waves

mash /mash′/ [OE *māsc* mixture] *n* **1** mixture of ground grain and water, used in brewing and distilling; **2** warm mixture of bran and water fed to horses and cattle; **3** any soft pulpy mass || *vt* **4** to crush; **5** to beat or squeeze into a soft pulpy state

mash′er *n slang* man who makes advances to women he does not know

mash·ie /mash′ē/ [?] *n* iron-headed golf club with a deeply slanted face

mask /mask′, mäsk′/ [MF *masque*] *n* **1** full or partial cover for the face in order to disguise or protect it; **2** cast or model of the face done in plaster or wax, as after death; **3** anything that conceals; pretense; **4** masque || *vt* **5** to cover with a mask; **6** to conceal; disguise

masked′ ball′ *n* ball at which masks are worn

mask′ing tape′ *n* adhesive tape used to protect a surface that is not to be painted where it meets an adjacent surface, as when painting a dado

mas·och·ism /mas′əkiz′əm, maz′-/ [< L. von Sacher-*Masoch* (1835–95) Austrian writer] *n* **1** abnormal sexual gratification derived from physical abuse at the hands of others; **2** any pleasure derived from being abused or humiliated || **mas′och·ist** *n* || **mas′-och·is′tic** *adj*

ma·son /mās′ən/ [OF *maçon*] *n* **1** construction worker in brick or stone; **2** Mason Freemason

Ma′son-Dix′on line′ /diks′ən/ [Charles *Mason* Eng astronomer and Jeremiah *Dixon* Eng surveyor] *n* boundary between Pennsylvania and Maryland surveyed in 1763–67, forming with the Ohio River the boundary between the free and slave states before the Civil War, and popularly considered to be the boundary between the North and the South

Ma·son·ic /məson′ik/ *adj* of or pert. to the Freemasons

Ma·son·ite /mās′ənīt′/ [trademark] *n* material of wood fiber in hard sheets, used for partitions, as insulation, etc.

Ma′son jar′ [John L. *Mason* 19th-cent. Am inventor] *n* glass jar with an airtight cap, used in home canning

ma′son·ry *n* (-ries) **1** occupation of a mason; **2** stonework or brickwork; **3** Masonry Freemasonry

masque /mask′, mäsk′/ [var of *mask*] *n* **1** masquerade; **2** form of dramatic spectacle with music and dancing, usu. on a mythological or allegorical theme, popular in the 16th and 17th centuries

mas·quer·ade /mask′ərād′/ [Sp *mascarada*] *n* **1** ball where masks and disguising costumes are worn; **2** acting or living under false pretenses; **3** disguise || *vi* **4** to take part in a masquerade; **5** to take the part of another; assume under false pretenses || **mas′quer·ad′er** *n*

mass /mas′/ [F *masse* < Gk *maza* barley cake] *n* **1** quantity or lump of matter of indefinite shape; **2** large

quantity or number; **3** bulk; size; **4** main part; **5** *phys* quantity of matter in a body that is a measure of its inertia; **6** the masses *pl* the common people || *vt* **7** to gather or assemble into a mass || *vi* **8** to form or come together in a mass || SYN *n* amount, bulk, total, agglomeration, body

Mass /mas′/ [OE *mæsse* < L *missa* discharged] *n R C Ch* celebration of the Eucharist

Mass. Massachusetts

Mas·sa·chu·setts /mas′əchōōs′its/ *n* state in NE U.S., in New England (5,689,000; 8266 sq.m.; cap. Boston) || **Mas′sa·chu′setts·an** *n*

mas·sa·cre /mas′əkər/ [MF] *n* **1** merciless, indiscriminate slaughter of many people || *vt* **2** to slaughter indiscriminately and in great numbers || **mas′sa·crer** /-krər/ *n* || SYN *n* butchery, murder (see *carnage*)

mas·sage /məsäzh′, -säj′/ [F] *n* **1** a rubbing or kneading of a part of the body to increase circulation and relax the muscles || *vt* **2** to give a massage to

mas·seur /məsur′/ *n* man whose occupation is massaging || **mas·seuse′** /-sōōs′, -sōōz′/ *n*fem

mas·sive /mas′iv/ [MF *massif*] *adj* **1** weighty; bulky; **2** consisting of or forming a large mass; **3** imposing, impressive; **4** large in amount or extent || **mas′sive·ly** *adv* || SYN bulky, ponderous, solid, substantial, large, unwieldy || ANT flimsy, unsubstantial, light, frail

mass′ me′di·a *npl* communications media that reach the mass of the people, as newspapers, magazines, and television

mass′ meet′ing *n* general assembly of people open to all, as for public discussion

mass′ noun′ *n gram* noun that denotes typically a homogeneous substance or material, as *wine* or *leather*, or an abstract concept, as *humility*, and cannot be used in English in the plural or with the indefinite article, except when used in a particularized sense

mass′ pro·duc′tion *n* production of goods in great quantity, esp. by machinery and the use of assembly lines || **mass′-pro·duce′** *vt*

mast /mast′, mäst′/ [OE *mæst*] **1** tall vertical spar on a ship that supports the sails, yards, rigging, booms, etc.; **2** any upright pole, as the main post of a derrick; **3** before the mast as a common sailor

mas·tec·to·my /mastek′təmē/ [< Gk *mastos* breast + -*ectomy*] *n* (-mies) surgical removal of a breast

mas·ter /mast′ər, mäst′-/ [OE *magister* and OF *maistre* < L *magister*] *n* **1** person who rules or commands others; **2** employer of servants; **3**

owner of a slave or animal; **4** one who has control of something; **5** male head of a household, college, school, or the like; **6** worker to whom an apprentice is bound; **7** one able to train others in skilled work; **8** skilled workman; expert; craftsman; **9** winner in a contest; victor; **10** great artist; **11** commander of a merchant vessel; **12** court officer appointed to assist the judge; **13 Master**, a holder of a master's degree; **b** title used before the names of boys; **c** official title, as *Master of the Hounds* ‖ *vt* **14** to overcome, conquer; **15** to rule, direct; **16** to learn thoroughly, excel in ‖ *adj* **17** principal; **18** controlling; **19** characteristic of the authority, power, and skill of a master

mas′ter-at-arms′ *n* (**masters-at-arms**) *nav* petty officer responsible for discipline aboard ship

mas′ter-ful *adj* **1** domineering; **2** indicating mastery; expert, skillful ‖ SYN domineering, imperious, lordly, dictatorial

mas′ter key′ *n* key that will open several different locks, as for all the doors of a hotel

mas′ter-ly *adj* **1** characteristic of a master; skillful ‖ *adv* **2** in a masterly manner

mas′ter-mind′ *vt* **1** to plan and direct (the activities of a group) ‖ *n* **2** originator and executor of a particular plan or project

Mas′ter of Arts′ *n* **1** master's degree in the humanities or the social sciences; **2** holder of this degree

mas′ter of cer′e-mo-nies *n* director of entertainment at a show, party, banquet, or the like

Mas′ter of Sci′ence *n* **1** master's degree in mathematics or the natural sciences; **2** holder of this degree

mas′ter-piece′ *n* **1** anything made with surpassing excellence, as a work of art or a piece of writing; **2** one's best work

mas′ter's de-gree′ *n* university degree ranking above the bachelor's and below the doctorate

mas′ter ser′geant *n* second-highest non-commissioned officer in the Army, Air Force, and Marine Corps

mas′ter-y *n* (**-ies**) **1** dominion; control; **2** victory; **3** expert skill; intellectual command ‖ SYN ascendancy, supremacy, victory, rule, sway

mast′head′ *n* **1** *naut* topmost point of a mast to which the flag is raised; **2** name of a newspaper or periodical, printed at the top of the front page; **3** statement printed in a newspaper or periodical, giving the publisher, address of publication, and directing staff

mas-ti-cate /mast′ikāt′/ [LL *masticare* (-*atus*)] *vt* **1** to chew; **2** to reduce to a paste or pulp by grinding ‖ **mas′ti-ca′tion** *n*

mas-tiff /mast′if, mäst′-/ [ME *mastif*] *n* one of a breed of large short-haired dogs with drooping ears

mas-to-don /mast′ədon′/ [< Gk *mastos* breast + *odous* (*odontos*) tooth] *n* any of several species of large extinct elephants (chiefly genus *Mammut*)

mas-toid /mas′toid/ [Gk *mastos* breast + -*oid*] *n* projection of the temporal bone of the skull behind the ear

mas-toid-i-tis /mas′toidī′tis/ *n* inflammation of the mastoid

mas-tur-bate /mast′ərbāt′/ [L *masturbari*] *vi* **1** to achieve orgasm by manipulating one's own genitals ‖ *vt* **2** to cause (another) to achieve orgasm by manipulation of the genitals ‖ **mas′tur-ba′tor** *n* ‖ **mas′tur-ba′tion** *n*

mat¹ /mat′/ [OE *meatte* < LL *matta*] *n* **1** flat piece of coarse woven fabric, as of straw or rushes, or of other material, as rubber, used as a protective covering, for wiping the shoes, etc.; **2** anything thickly overgrown or entangled ‖ *v* (**mat-ted; mat-ting**) *vt* **3** to cover with or as with a mat; **4** to form into a mat ‖ *vi* **5** to become entangled

mat² [F] *adj* **1** dull, lusterless in finish or surface ‖ *n* **2** dull finish or surface; **3** border around a picture ‖ *v* (**mat-ted; mat-ting**) *vt* **4** to produce a dull surface on

mat³ [< *matrix*] *n typ* papier-mâché impression of a cut or of type, from which a stereotype plate is cast

mat-a-dor /mat′ədôr′/ [Sp = killer] *n* bullfighter, spec. the one who kills the bull

match¹ /mach′/ [OE *gemæcca* companion] *n* **1** anything that agrees with or is exactly like another thing; **2** equal; one able to cope with another; **3** game or contest; **4** marriage; **5** one considered as to suitability for marriage ‖ *vt* **6** to unite in marriage; **7** to compete with successfully; **8** to equal; **9** to suit; correspond to; be compatible with; **10** to get a counterpart or the equal of; **11** to place in opposition; **12** to provide with an opponent; **13** a to flip or toss (coins) in order to decide a bet or something of the sort; **b** to do this with (someone) ‖ *vi* **14** to be equal; **15** to correspond with the counterpart

match² [OF *mesche* wick] *n* **1** slender piece of wood or paper tipped with a material that is easily ignited by friction or by rubbing on a specially treated surface; **2** wick, fuse

match′less *adj* having no equal

match′mak′er *n* **1** one who arranges marriages for others; **2** one who arranges sports contests, esp. between boxers or wrestlers ‖ **match′mak′ing** *adj* & *n*

mate[1] /māt′/ *n* **1** checkmate *I* ‖ *vt* **2** to checkmate *3*

mate[2] [ME < MLG] *n* **1** companion or associate; fellow worker; comrade, (often in compounds, as *classmate*); **2** one of a pair; **3** spouse; **4** one of a pair of mated animals; **5** ship's officer ranking below the captain; **6** *nav* petty officer ‖ *vt* **7** to match; **8** to marry; **9** to pair (animals) for breeding ‖ *vt* **10** (of animals) to copulate; **11** to match; **12** to marry

ma·té or **ma·te**[3] /mä′tā, ma′-/ [Sp *mate*] *n* aromatic tealike beverage made from the dried leaves of a South American plant (*Ilex paraguayensis*)

ma·te·ri·al /mətir′ē-əl/ [< L *materia* matter] *adj* **1** consisting of, or pert. to substance; physical, not spiritual; **2** pert. to bodily wants; **3** important; **4** pertinent ‖ *n* **5** substance of which anything is made; **6** crude matter or elements for further elaboration, as *raw material, material for an article*; **7** cloth, fabric ‖ SYN *adj* bodily, physical, temporal; momentous, significant ‖ ANT *adj* spiritual, unsubstantial

ma·te·ri·al·ism *n* **1** doctrine that all the phenomena of the universe, including thought, are explainable only in terms of matter; **2** tendency to emphasize material things and to ignore spiritual values ‖ **ma·te′ri·al·ist** *n* ‖ **ma·te′ri·al·is′tic** *adj*

ma·te′ri·al·ize′ *vt* **1** to give material form to ‖ *vt* **2** to become a fáct; to actually appear; **3** to assume bodily or material form

ma·te′ri·al·ly *adv* **1** physically; **2** considerably, to a great degree

ma·té·ri·el or **ma·te·ri·el** /mətir′ē·el′/ [F] *n* supplies and equipment, esp. for military use; distinguished from *personnel*

ma·ter·nal /məturn′əl/ [< L *mater* mother] *adj* **1** of, pert. to, characteristic of, or derived from a mother; **2** related through a mother ‖ **ma·ter′nal·ly** *adv*

ma·ter·ni·ty /məturn′itē/ [ML *maternitas*] *n* **1** motherhood; **2** motherliness; **3** hospital or department of a hospital devoted to the care of women before and after childbirth and to the newborn children ‖ *adj* **4** of or pert. to pregnant women or women who have just given birth

math /math′/ *n* colloq mathematics

math·e·mat·i·cal /math′əmat′ikəl/ *adj* **1** of, pert. to, or concerned with mathematics; **2** exact; precise ‖ **math′e·mat′i·cal·ly** *adv*

math′e·mat′ics [< Gk *mathemata*] *nsg* science that treats of quantities, magnitudes, and forms, and their relationships, by the use of numbers and symbols ‖ **math′e·ma·ti′cian** /-mətish′ən/ *n*

mat·in /mat′ən/ [OF = morning] *n* **1** *poet.* morning song; **2 matins,** a service of morning prayer; **b** *R C Ch* one of the daily offices, properly recited at midnight

mat·i·née or **mat·i·nee** /mat′ənā′/ [F = morning] *n* afternoon performance, as of a play or motion picture

matri- [L] *comb form* mother

ma·tri·arch /māt′rē·ärk′/ *n* **1** woman who rules a family or tribe; **2** woman who rules with authority in place of a man; **3** very old and dignified woman ‖ **ma′tri·ar′chal** or **ma′tri·ar′chic** *adj*

ma′tri·ar′chy *n* (-chies) social organization in which the mother is the head of the family and in which descent is reckoned through the mother

ma·tri·ces /māt′rīsēz′, mat′-/ *pl* of **matrix**

mat·ri·cide /mat′rīsīd′, māt′-/ *n* **1** murder of a woman by her son or daughter; **2** one who kills his mother ‖ **mat′ri·cid′al** *adj*

ma·tric·u·late /mətrik′yəlāt′/ [< LL *matricula* register] *vt* **1** to enroll, as a student in a college ‖ *vi* **2** to be matriculated ‖ /-lit/ *n* **3** one who has been matriculated ‖ **ma·tric′u·la′tion** *n*

mat·ri·mo·ny /mat′rimō′nē/ [L *matrimonium*] *n* (-nies) rite or state of marriage ‖ **mat′ri·mo′ni·al** *adj* ‖ SYN (see **marriage**)

ma·trix /māt′riks, mat′-/ [L = womb] *n* (-trix·es or -tri·ces -trisēz′/) **1** something holding within it another object to which it gives shape or form; **2** die or mold, as for the face of type; **3** rock in which a fossil, mineral, or gem is embedded

ma·tron /māt′rən/ [L *matrona*] *n* **1** married woman; **2** mature woman, esp. one of social position; **3** woman who superintends the housekeeping in a hospital or other institution; **4** female guard or attendant in a woman's prison ‖ **ma′tron·ly** *adj*

ma′tron of hon′or *n* married woman who acts as a bride's chief attendant

mat·ro·nym·ic /mat′rənim′ik/ [< *matri-* + *-onym*] *n* name derived from that of the mother

MATS Military Air Transport Service

Matt. *Bib* Matthew

mat′ted *adj* tangled; in a thick mass

mat·ter /mat′ər/ [OF *matere* < L *materia* timber, stuff] *n* **1** that which occupies space and of which any material body is composed; substance; **2** indefinite amount, as *a matter of a few cents*; **3** subject for discussion or action; **4** affair; business; **5** cause of difficulty; **6** mail; **7** pus; **8** *phys* substance of the physical universe that is characterized by inertia, extension, etc.; **9** *typ* material set up in type or that has been printed from type; **10** as a matter of

fact in fact, actually; **11 for that matter** as far as that is concerned; **12 no matter** it's not important ‖ *vi* **13** to be of importance

mat′ter-of-fact′ *adj* sticking close to facts; literal; practical; not imaginative

Mat·thew /math′yōō/ *n Bib* **1** one of the twelve Apostles; **2** first book of the New Testament

mat′ting *n* **1** coarse fabric of straw, rushes, or the like, used for floor covering; **2** material for making mats

mat·tock /mat′ək/ [OE *mattuc*] *n* tool for digging the soil similar to a pick-axe, but having one end flat like an adz

mat·tress /mat′ris/ [OF *materas* < L *materasso* < Ar] *n* **1** sack of heavy cloth filled with hair, felt, foam rubber, coiled springs, or the like, used as a pad for a bed; **2** mat made of interwoven trees, poles, or shrubs, used to protect embankments and jetties from erosion

mat·u·rate /mach′ərāt′, mat′yə-/ [L *maturare* (-*atus*) to ripen] *vi* **1** to ripen; **2** to form pus ‖ **mat′u·ra′tion** *n*

ma·ture /məchŏŏr′, -t(y)ŏŏr′/ [L *maturus* ripe] *adj* **1** ripe; full-grown; **2** fully developed; **3** *fin* due, payable ‖ *vi* **4** to become mature ‖ *vt* **5** to make mature ‖ **ma·ture′ly** *adv* ‖ **ma·tu′ri·ty** *n* ‖ SYN grown, developed, ripe, perfect, prime (see *mellow*) ‖ ANT *adj* immature, green

ma·tu·ti·nal /mət(y)ōōt′inəl/ [< L *matutinus*] *adj* **1** pert. to the morning; **2** occurring early in the day

mat·zo /mät′sə, -sō/ [Yiddish < Heb *massāh*] *n* (-**zos** or -**zoth** /-sōt′, -sōth′, -sōs′/) thin cracker of unleavened bread eaten by Jews during Passover

maud·lin /môd′lin/ [ME *Maudelen* (Mary) Magdalene, portrayed as a weeping penitent] *adj* **1** mawkishly sentimental; **2** mawkishly drunk

maul /môl′/ [OF *mail*] *n* **1** heavy hammer for driving stakes ‖ *vt* **2** to handle roughly or abusively; **3** to injure, bruise ‖ **maul′er** *n* ‖ **maul′ing** *n*

maul·stick /môl′stik′/ *n* mahlstick

Mau Mau /mou′mou′/ [Kikuyu] *n* member of a terrorist society in Kenya, established in the 1950's for the purpose of gaining independence

Mau·na Lo·a /moun′ə lō′ə, môn′-/ *n* active volcano in Hawaii (13,680 ft.)

maun·der /môn′dər/ [?] *vi* to talk, act, or walk foolishly and aimlessly ‖ **maun′der·er** *n*

Maun′dy Thurs′day /môn′dē/ [< OF *mande* command] *n* Holy Thursday, the day before Good Friday, commemorating the new command given at the time of the washing of the feet of the disciples by Christ (John 13:5,14,34)

Mau·ri·ta·ni·a /môr′itān′ē·ə/ *n* republic in W Africa, SW of Algeria (1,200,-000; 418,140 sq.m.; cap. Nouakchott)

Mau·ri·ti·us /môrish′ē·əs/ *n* country on islands E of Madagascar (920,-000; 788 sq.m.; cap. Port Louis)

mau·so·le·um /môs′əlē′əm/ [L < Gk *Mausoleion* the magnificent tomb of Mausolus (d. ab. 350 B.C.) king of Caria] *n* (-**ums** or -**a** /-ə/) grand and imposing tomb

mauve /mōv′/ [F < L *malva* mallow] *n* delicate reddish-purple color

mav·er·ick /mav′(ə)rik/ [Samuel *Maverick* (1803–70) Texas rancher, whose unbranded cattle ran at large] *n* **1** unbranded animal running at large, esp. a motherless calf; **2** dissenter, esp. in politics

maw¹ /mô′/ [OE *maga* stomach] *n* **1** craw or crop of a bird; **2** throat, gullet, or jaws of an animal; **3** gaping opening or cavity

maw² [var of *ma*] *n dial.* mother

mawk·ish /môk′ish/ [< *obs mawk* maggot < Scand] *adj* **1** causing disgust; insipid; **2** foolishly sentimental ‖ **mawk′ish·ly** *adv* ‖ **mawk′ish·ness** *n*

max·il·la /maksil′ə/ [L] *n* (-**lae** /-lē/) **1** one of the jawbones, esp. the upper; **2** one of the paired mouth parts below or behind the mandibles of arthropods ‖ **max′il·lar′y** /-ler′-/ *adj*

max·im /maks′im/ [L *maxima* (propositio) greatest (proposition)] *n* established principle or truth, as of manners or morals, expressed in concise form; adage ‖ SYN proverb, aphorism, precept, saw (see *truism*)

max·i·ma /maks′imə/ *pl* of **maximum**

max′i·mal *adj* largest; highest; pert. to a maximum

max′i·mize′ *vt* to increase to the maximum size, amount, or degree

max′i·mum /-məm/ [L = greatest] *n* (-**mums** or -**ma** /-mə/) **1** greatest number, quantity, or degree possible; greatest value or quantity attained or attainable by a variable quantity ‖ *adj* **2** greatest in quantity or highest in degree; **3** highest permitted by law or other authority

may /mā′/ [< OE *mæg*, *pres ind* of *magan* to be able] *v* (**might**) *modal aux* **1** am, are, or is; **a** allowed to; **b** likely but not certain to; **c** able to; **2** expressing the earnest desire or wish of the speaker, as *may you enjoy good health* ‖ SYN can ‖ DISCR *Can* expresses the ability to do; *may* expresses permission, as man *can* walk or think; you *may* go. The use of *can* to ask permission is incorrect, as in: *Can* I go? To grant the permission by saying, You *can* go, has colloquial standing, but is better avoided

May /mā′/ [F *mai* < L *Maius*] *n* fifth month of the year, having 31 days

Ma·ya /mä′yə/ *n* **1** member of an Indian people of Yucatán, who had reached a relatively high state of civilization before the coming of Columbus; 2 their language ‖ **Ma·yan** *adj*

may·be /māb'ē/ [< *may it be*] *adv* perhaps; possibly

May' Day' *n* 1 May 1, traditionally a festival in honor of spring; 2 in many countries, a day honoring labor or socialism ‖ **May'-day'** *adj*

May'day' [F *m'aidez* help me] *n* international distress signal of ships and planes

May'flow'er *n* 1 any of several plants flowering in May or early spring; 2 vessel that brought the Pilgrims from England to the New World in 1620

may·hem /mā'hem, mā'əm/ [AF *mahaym*] *n law* crime of willfully crippling or mutilating someone

may·n't /mā'ənt, mānt'/ may not

may·on·naise /mā'ənāz, mā'ənāz'/ [F] *n* salad dressing made of the raw yolks of eggs, olive oil, vinegar, and seasoning

may·or /mā'ər, mer'/ [OF *matre* < L *maior* greater] *n* chief executive of a municipality ‖ **may'or·al** *adj*

may'or·al·ty /-əltē/ *n* (-ties) office or tenure of a mayor

May'pole' *n* pole decorated with flowers and streamers, around which May-day celebrations are held

May' queen' *n* young girl, chosen for her beauty, who presides over May-day festivities and is crowned with flowers

mayst /māst'/ *archaic 2nd pers sg pres ind* of **may**

maze /māz'/ [< *amaze*] *n* 1 intricate and confusing network of passages; labyrinth; 2 state of bewilderment and confusion

ma·zur·ka /məzurk'ə, -zoork'ə/ [Pol = woman of Mazury province] *n* 1 lively Polish dance in moderate triple measure; 2 music for it

M.B.A. Master of Business Administration

MC Marine Corps

M.C. Master of Ceremonies

MC /em'sē'/ *n* 1 emcee ‖ *v* (**MC'd**; **MC'ing**) *vt & vi* 2 to emcee

McCar·thy·ism /məkärth'ē-iz'əm/ [Joseph R. *McCarthy* (1909–57) U.S. senator] *n* 1 public accusation of wrongdoing on flimsy or nonexistent evidence, esp. of treasonous conduct; 2 any grossly unfair investigative procedure

Mc·Kin·ley, Mount /məkin'lē/ *n* mountain in Alaska (20,300 ft.); highest in North America

Mc·Kin·ley, Wil·liam *n* (1843–1901) 25th president of the U.S. 1897–1901; assassinated

Md *chem* mendelevium

Md. Maryland

MD, M.D. Middle Dutch

M.D. [L *Medicinae Doctor*] Doctor of Medicine

M'·day' *n* mobilization day

me /mē', mē/ [OE] *pron* objective case of **I**

ME, M.E. Middle English

mead /mēd'/ [OE *medu*] *n* alcoholic liquor made of fermented honey

mead·ow /med'ō/ [OE *mǣdwe*] *n* 1 field used for pasture or for growing hay; 2 low land near a body of water, often swampy and covered with coarse grass

mead'ow·lark' *n* any of several American songbirds (genus *Sturnella*) having a yellow breast marked with black

mea·ger or **mea·gre** /mēg'ər/ [OF *maigre*] *adj* 1 lacking fertility, richness, or strength; poor, scanty; 2 emaciated; lean ‖ SYN gaunt, poor, barren (see *lean²*)

meal¹ /mēl'/ [OE *melu*] *n* 1 the edible part of grain coarsely ground; 2 unsifted flour made from corn or wheat

meal² [OE *mēl* fixed time] *n* 1 occasion of taking food; 2 food so taken

meal' tick'et *n* 1 ticket issued by some restaurants entitling the purchaser to meals until the value of the ticket is used up; 2 *slang* one who provides sustenance for others, as *she married only because she wanted a meal ticket*

meal'time' *n* hour fixed for serving or eating a meal

meal'y *adj* (-i·er; -i·est) 1 covered with coarse meal; floury; 2 like meal; powdery; friable; 3 pale; sallow; 4 mealy-mouthed

meal'y-mouthed' /-mouthd', -tht/ *adj* afraid or unwilling to use plain language

mean¹ /mēn'/ [OE *mǣnan*] *v* (**meant**) *vt* 1 to intend; 2 to signify, denote; 3 to intend to express, as *what do you mean by that?*; 4 to designate, as *she means me* ‖ *vi* 5 **mean well** to have good intentions

mean² [OE *gemǣne* common] *adj* 1 lacking in distinction; humble; plebeian; 2 lacking in dignity; ignoble; 3 low in grade or quality; 4 stingy, niggardly; 5 shabby, sordid; 6 contemptible, base; 7 disagreeable; disobliging; 8 *slang* with great skill, as *he plays a mean piano* ‖ **mean'ly** *adv* ‖ **mean'ness** *n* ‖ SYN niggardly, abject, vile, base, ignoble, degraded, contemptible, sordid, pitiful ‖ ANT generous, noble

mean³ [MF *meien* < L *medianus*] *adj* 1 in an intermediate position; between two extremes; 2 medium, average, as to quality, degree, or bulk ‖ *n* 3 condition, quality, course of action, or the like, which is near the middle point between two extremes; 4 *math* a quantity intermediate between the extremes of a set of quantities; b one of the two middle terms in a proposition; c average; d square root of the product of two quantities; 5 *logic* middle term of a syllogism; 6 **means**, a *sg* instrumentality, agency; b *pl* resources; wealth; 7 by all means, a without fail; b certainly; 8 by means of through the agency of; 9 by no means not at all || SYN *adj* average || DISCR As here compared, *mean* describes a condition intermediate between two opposite extremes, as in size or quality, as of *mean* height or ability. *Average* expresses a usual, prevalent standard, or the common or ordinary type or kind

me·an·der /mē·an'dər/ [Gk *Maiandros* winding river in Asia Minor] *vi* 1 to follow a winding course; 2 to ramble aimlessly || *n* 3 winding course

mean·ing /mēn'ĭŋ/ *adj* 1 expressive; full of significance; 2 intending, as *well-meaning* || *n* 3 purpose, object; 4 significance || SYN *n* purport, import, sense, acceptation, significance (see *signification*)

mean'ing·ful *adj* having meaning or import || SYN weighty, consequential, significant, important

mean'ing·less *adj* lacking in meaning; senseless

mean' so'lar time' *n* time measured by the mean sun and, therefore, having equal divisions

mean' sun' *n* imaginary sun thought of as moving uniformly around the celestial equator and taking the same time as the true sun does in the ecliptic

meant /ment'/ *pt & pp* of mean

mean'time' also mean'while' *adv* 1 during an interval; between times || *n* 2 intervening time

mea·sles /mēz'əlz/ [ME *maseles*] *nsg* contagious disease, esp. of children, marked by fever, catarrhal symptoms, and a rash of small red spots

mea·sly /mēz'lĭ/ *adj* (·sli·er; ·sli·est) *colloq* slight, contemptible

meas·ure /mezh'ər/ [MF *mesure* < L *mensura*] *n* 1 quantity, dimensions, or capacity of a thing; 2 standard for determining this; 3 unit of measurement; 4 any standard of comparison, judgment, or estimation; 5 instrument used for measuring; 6 act of measuring; 7 definite quantity measured; 8 system of measurements; 9 amount or degree, as *a measure of praise*; 10 stated amount; allotment; 11 legislative enactment, law; 12 *mus* a series of tones in regular rhythm from one primary accent to the next; b the notes between two bars; c tempo; 13 *pros* single metrical unit; 14 *typ* width of a column or page; 15 measures *pl* course of action, steps; 16 beyond measure immeasurably; 17 for good measure in

addition; 18 in a measure to some extent || *vt* 19 to compute as to quantity or extent by a fixed standard; 20 to estimate by comparison; appraise; 21 to serve as a measure for; 22 measure off or out to allot; set apart; mark off || *vi* 23 to take measurements; 24 to be of a specific measure; 25 measure up to be sufficiently capable; 26 measure up to to be as good as || meas'ur·a·ble *adj*

meas'ured *adj* 1 uniform, regular, rhythmical; 2 carefully considered; calculated

meas'ure·less *adj* unlimited; vast

meas'ure·ment *n* 1 act of measuring; 2 size or quantity determined by measuring; 3 system of measuring

meat /mēt/ [OE *mete* food] *n* 1 animal flesh used as food; 2 edible part, as of a fruit or nut; 3 gist; substance || meat'y *adj* (·i·er; ·i·est)

meat'ball' *n* 1 chopped meat cooked in the form of a ball; 2 *slang* clumsy lout

Mec·ca /mek'ə/ *n* 1 city in W Saudi Arabia, one of the two capitals (160,000); birthplace of Mohammed and holy city of Islam; 2 also mecca place that many people visit or hope to visit || Mec'can *adj & n*

mech. 1 mechanical; 2 mechanics

me·chan·ic /məkan'ik/ [< Gk *mechane* machine] *n* one skilled in the use of tools and in the operation and repair of machinery || SYN workman (see *artisan*)

me·chan'i·cal *adj* 1 pert. to or operated by machinery; 2 pert. to the use of tools and machinery; 3 pert. to the science of mechanics; 4 automatic; routine; 5 done without thought, machinelike; spiritless || me·chan'i·cal·ly *adv*

me·chan'i·cal ad·van'tage *n* ratio between the force exerted by a machine and the force that actuates it

me·chan'i·cal draw'ing *n* drawing, as of a plan or design of machinery, made with compasses, rules, etc.

me·chan·ics /məkan'iks/ *nsg* 1 a science that treats of forces and their effects in producing and changing motion; b application of this science to machines; 2 *npl* routine procedures, as *the mechanics of the presidency*

mech·a·nism /mek'əniz'əm/ *n* 1 structure and arrangement of the parts of a machine; 2 system of interdependent parts working in or as in a machine; 3 agency or process by which something is accomplished; 4 routine procedure

mech'a·nize' *vt* 1 to equip, as an industry, with machines to replace manual labor; 2 to equip (an army) with tanks and motor vehicles || mech'a·ni·za'tion *n*

med·al /med'əl/ [MF *medaille* < It *medaglia*] *n* small flat piece of metal, often disk-shaped, marked with a design or words commemorating some event, act, or occasion, and sometimes given as a reward for valor or merit

med·al·ist or **med·al·list** *n* recipient of a medal

me·dal·lion /mədalʹyən/ [F *médaillon*] *n* **1** large medal; **2** tablet or panel bearing a figure or design drawn, sculptured, or engraved

Med·al of Hon·or *n* highest U.S. military decoration, awarded in the name of Congress for conspicuous gallantry in combat above and beyond the call of duty

med·dle /medʹəl/ [MF *medler*] *vi* to interfere impertinently in another's affairs ‖ **med·dler** *n*

med·dle·some *adj* interfering; inclined to meddle ‖ SYN officious, interfering, obtrusive, impertinent

me·di·a /mēdʹē·ə/ *pl* of **medium**

me·di·ae·val /mēdʹē·ēvʹəl, mid'-, med'-/ *adj* var of **medieval**

me·di·al /mēdʹē·əl/ [<L *medius* middle] *adj* **1** middle; **2** average; ordinary ‖ **me·di·al·ly** *adv*

me·di·an /-ən/ [L *medianus*] *adj* **1** intermediate; middle ‖ *n* **2** middle number in a series; **3** straight line drawn from the vertex of a triangle to the center of the opposite side; **4** center strip, as of lawn, dividing opposing traffic lanes in a dual highway

me·di·an strip/ *n median* 4

me·di·ate /-it/ [L *mediare* (-*atus*) to intervene] *adj* **1** connected through or involving an intermediate agency ‖ /-āt'/ *vi* **2** to act to effect a settlement of a dispute; **3** to be in an intermediate position ‖ *vt* **4** to bring about, as peace, by acting as an intermediary ‖ **me·di·a·tion** *n* ‖ **me·di·a·tor** *n*

med·ic /medʹik/ [L *medicus* physician] *n colloq* **1** doctor or member of the medical corps; **2** medical student

med·i·cal /medʹikəl/ *adj* pert. to the practice or study of medicine ‖ **med·i·cal·ly** *adv*

me·dic·a·ment /mədikʹəmənt, medʹi-/ *n* medicine, remedy

Med·i·care or **med·i·care** /medʹiker/ *n* government-sponsored medical and health insurance, esp. for the aged

med·i·cate/ [L *medicare* (-*atus*)] *vt* **1** to treat with medicine; **2** to put medicine into (a liquid or other substance)

me·dic·i·nal /mədisʹinəl/ *adj* pert. to or having the properties of medicine; curative

med·i·cine /medʹisin/ [L *medicina*] *n* **1** art or science of treating disease, illness, and abnormal physical and mental conditions, esp. by nonsurgical means; **2** any substance used for the prevention, treatment, and cure of disease; **3** medical profession; **4**

good medicine *slang* person or thing regarded as an influence for good; **5 take one's medicine** *slang* **a** to undergo punishment for wrongdoing; **.b** to bear the consequences of an unwise decision

med·i·cine ball/ *n* large, heavy ball thrown back and forth for exercise

med·i·cine man/ *n* among American Indians and other primitive tribes, priest of the local religion thought to possess supernatural powers

med/i·co/ /-kō'/ *n colloq* **1** medical doctor; **2** medical student

me·di·e·val /mēdʹē·ēvʹəl, mid'-, med'-/ [< L *medius* middle + *aevum* age] *adj* pert. to or characteristic of the Middle Ages

me·di·e·val·ism *n* **1** spirit, customs, or practices of the Middle Ages; **2** interest in or imitation of medieval customs and institutions; **3** medieval custom or practice ‖ **me·di·e·val·ist** *n*

me·di·o·cre /mēdʹē·ōkʹər/ [MF <L *mediocris*] *adj* of medium quality; commonplace; of only moderate worth

me·di·oc·ri·ty /-okʹritē/ *n* (-ties) **1** state or quality of being mediocre; **2** person of only average ability

med·i·tate /medʹitāt'/ [L *meditari* (-*atus*)] *vt* **1** to intend, plan ‖ *vi* **2** to ponder, contemplate ‖ **med·i·ta·tion** *n* ‖ **med·i·ta·tive** *adj* ‖ SYN ponder, reflect, contemplate (see *muse*)

Med·i·ter·ra·ne·an (Sea/) /medʹitərān'-ē·ən/ *n* large sea between Europe and Africa, connected with the Atlantic Ocean at the Strait of Gibraltar

me·di·um /mēdʹē·əm/ [L = middle] *n* (-ums or -a /-ə/) **1** that which lies between extremes; mean; **2** middle or intervening state; **3** intervening substance, as air, through which some physical action takes place; **4** environment; **5** agency, means; **6** nutritive substance for the cultivation of microorganisms ‖ *n* (-ums) **7** person supposed to be able to communicate with the dead ‖ *n* (-a) **8** channel or means of mass communication, as the press, television ‖ *adj* **9** occupying a middle position; moderate ‖ SYN mean, instrument, means, channel, agency

med·ley /medʹlē/ [MF *medlee*] *n* **1** mass of heterogeneous elements; **2** *mus* parts of different selections combined into one piece ‖ SYN variety, diversity, jumble, miscellany

me·dul·la /midulʹə/ [L = marrow] *n* (-las, -lae /-lē/) **1** marrow or marrowlike substance; **2** medulla oblongata

me·dul·la ob·long·a·ta /ob'lôŋgätʹə/ *n* lowest part of the brain, a continuation of the spinal cord

Me·du·sa /məd(y)o͞osʹə/ *n* **1** Gk myth.

one of the three Gorgons, slain by Perseus; **2 medusa** (**-sas** or **-sae** /-sē/) a jellyfish

meek /mēk/ [ME *meke* < Scand] *adj* **1** gentle; patient; **2** submissive; spiritless || **meek'ly** *adv* || **meek'ness** *n* || SYN unassuming, submissive, mild, long-suffering, spiritless

meer·schaum /mir'shŏm, -shəm, -shoum/ [G = seafoam] *n* **1** white claylike mineral used for ornamental carvings; **2** tobacco pipe having a meerschaum bowl

meet¹ /mēt/ [OE *mētan*] *v* (**met**) *vt* **1** to come up to or approach from a different direction; **2** to come face to face with; **3** to join at an appointed place, as *meet me for lunch*; **4** to be present at the arrival of, as *to meet a train*; **5** to come into contact with; **6** to intersect; **7** to oppose in a contest; **8** to be introduced to; **9** to experience; encounter; **10** to be perceived by; **11** to satisfy or pay, as one's obligations; **12** to conform to, as a requirement; **13** to refute; **14** meet halfway to compromise with || *vi* **15** to come together; assemble; **16** to come in contact with another; **17** to unite; **18** to contend; **19** to become acquainted; **20 meet with, a** to encounter; **b** to experience, receive || *n* **21** assemblage for an athletic contest

meet² [OE *gemǣte*] *adj* suitable, fitting

meet'ing *n* **1** act of coming together; **2** assembly for a specific purpose; **3** junction or union

meg·a- /meg'ə-, meg'ə-/ [Gk] *comb form* **1** large; **2** a million of

meg'a·cy'cle *n* **1** one million cycles; **2** unit of radio frequency equal to one million cycles per second

meg'a·hertz' *n* (**-hertz** or **-hertz·es**) meg-acycle **2**

meg'a·lith /-lĭth/ *n* huge stone or boulder used in making prehistoric monuments || **meg'a·lith'ic** *adj*

meg'a·lo·ma'ni·a /meg'əlō-/ [< Gk *megalos* great + *-mania*] *n* obsession or mental illness characterized by delusions of grandeur || **meg'a·lo·ma'ni·ac'** /-ak'/ *n*

meg'a·lop'o·lis /-lop'əlĭs/ [Gk = great city] *n* large urban area consisting of several adjoining cities and their suburbs

meg'a·phone' *n* conical trumpetlike instrument for directing and magnifying the voice of a speaker

meg'a·ton' /-tun'/ *n* **1** one million tons; **2** explosive force of one million tons of TNT

meg·ohm /meg'ōm'/ *n* unit of electrical resistance equal to one million ohms

mei·ot·ic /mī·ot'ik/ [Gk *meiotikos* lessening] *adj* depreciatory, disparaging

mel·an·cho·li·a /mel'ənkōl'ē·ə/ [Gk = black bile] *n* mental disorder marked by depression of spirits and brooding || **mel'an·chol'ic** /-kol'ik/ *adj*

mel'an·chol'y /-kol'ē/ [< *melancholia*] *n* (**-ies**) **1** dejection; depression of spirits; **2** pensive sadness || *adj* **3** causing melancholy; **4** showing melancholy || SYN *adj* dispirited, sad; *n* (see *grief, dejection*)

Mel·a·ne·sia /mel'ənēzh'ə, -nēsh'ə/ *n* chain of islands in the South Pacific about 1,000 miles east of Australia || **Mel'a·ne'sian** *adj* & *n*

mé·lange /mälänzh'/ [F] *n* mixture; jumble

mel·a·no·ma /mel'ənōm'ə/ [Gk *melas* (*-anos*) black + *-oma*] *n* dark-pigmented tumor, esp. of the skin

Mel'ba toast' /mel'bə/ [Nellie *Melba* (1861–1931) Australian soprano] *n* thin slices of dry toast

Mel·bourne /mel'bərn/ *n* seaport in SE Australia (1,950,000)

meld /meld'/ [G = *melden* to announce] *vt* **1** to combine, to merge; **2** *pinochle* to declare and display (certain card combinations) for a score || *vi* **3** to combine, to merge; **4** *pinochle* to meld a combination of cards || *n* **5** act of melding; **6** melded cards

me·lee /mā'lā, mālā'/ [F] *n* **1** confused general hand-to-hand fight; **2** general confusion

mel·io·rate /mēl'yərāt'/ [L *meliorare* (*-atus*)] *vt* & *vi* to ameliorate

mel·lif·lu·ous /məlif'lōo·əs/ [< L *mel* honey + *fluere* to flow] *adj* smooth and sweet (words, voices, or sounds); honeyed || **mel·lif'lu·ous·ly** *adv*

mel·low /mel'ō/ [ME *melwe*] *adj* **1** soft and full-flavored from ripeness; **2** well-matured, as wine; **3** full, pure; not harsh, as color, sound, etc.; **4** softened by age or maturity; **5** *colloq* genial; somewhat tipsy || *vt* **6** to make mellow || *vi* **7** to become mellow || **mel'low·ness** *n* || SYN *adj* mature, ripe, soft, softened, delicate || DISCR Literally, that is *mature* which is fully developed; that is *ripe* which is ready to be harvested, gathered, or used; that is *mellow* which is soft, juicy, and sweet in its ripeness. Figuratively, plans completely thought out may be termed *mature;* the product of a *mature* mind is *mature* judgment. *Ripe* carries the idea of full readiness into its figurative sense; *ripe* for mischief; *ripe* scholarship; *ripe* beauty is that of a grown woman, usually in her prime, as contrasted with that of a girl. *Mellow* character is the product of experience; *mellow* judgment is wise, temperate, and understanding; *mellow* wine is old; *mellow* light is soft and soothing || ANT *adj* immature, green, hard, unripe, bitter

me·lo·de·on /məlōd'ē·ən/ [G] *n* small reed organ

me·lod·ic /məlŏd′ĭk/ [see melody] adj
1 pert. to melody; 2 melodious

me·lo·di·ous /məlŏd′ḗ·əs/ adj 1 containing or producing melody; 2 musical; tuneful ‖ SYN tuneful, harmonious, dulcet, sweet, pleasing, musical
‖ ANT discordant, jarring, dissonant

mel·o·dra·ma /mel′ə-/ [F mélodrame]
n 1 highly sensational or romantic
play with a happy conclusion; 2
behavior which makes a violent appeal to the emotions ‖ **mel′o·dra·
mat′ic** adj

mel·o·dy /mel′ədḗ/ [Gk meloidía
choral singing] n (-dies) 1 agreeable
succession of single tones in musical
compositions; 2 air or principal part
in harmonized music; 3 song or tune
‖ SYN harmony ‖ DISCR Melody is an
arrangement of single notes in succession, serving to express a musical
idea; melody also names the principal part or air thus musically formed.
Harmony names a combination of
notes of different pitch produced simultaneously to form chords

mel·on /mel′ən/ [LL melo (-onis) <
Gk melopepon apple-shaped gourd]
n 1 muskmelon; 2 watermelon; 3
cut a melon to distribute an extra
dividend to the stockholders of a
corporation

Mel·pom·e·ne /melpom′ĭnḗ/ n Gk
myth. Muse of tragedy

melt /melt/ [OE meltan, mieltan] vt
1 to change (a solid) to a liquid, as by
heat; fuse; 2 to dissolve; 3 to soften,
as the heart or feelings ‖ vi 4 to be
melted; 5 to dissolve; 6 to be weakened or softened; 7 melt away to
dwindle away; disappear ‖ n 8
amount melted at one time

melt′down′ n phys melting of rods containing pellets of uranium fuel, or of
such pellets themselves; a catastrophic nuclear accident in which
the reactor core could sink deep into
the ground with massive release of
radiation into the atmosphere

melt′ing point′ n temperature at which
a solid melts and a liquid of the
same substance freezes

melt′ing pot′ n 1 crucible; 2 country
or locality in which people of diverse
backgrounds are fused into one culture

mem·ber /mem′bər/ [L membrum
limb] n 1 one of the individuals composing an organization, group, or
community; 2 individual unit or constituent part of any whole; 3 limb or
organ of the body

mem′ber·ship′ n 1 state of being a
member; 2 members of an organization collectively; 3 total number of
members

mem·brane /mem′brān/ [L membrana
parchment] n any thin pliable sheet
of animal or vegetable tissue ‖
mem′bra·nous /-brənəs/ adj

me·men·to /məment′ō/ [L, impv of
meminisse to remember] n (-tos or
-toes) 1 reminder of something past;
souvenir; 2 reminder of something
to come; warning

mem·oir /mem′wär/ [F mémoire note]
n 1 official memorandum; 2 memoirs
pl a a history written from personal
experience; b autobiography

mem·o·ra·bil·i·a /mem′ərəbil′ē·ə/ [L]
npl things worthy of remembrance
or record

mem·o·ra·ble /mem′ərəbəl/ [< L
memorare to bring to mind] adj
worthy of remembrance; notable ‖
mem′o·ra·bly adv ‖ SYN signal,
marked, noteworthy, outstanding

mem·o·ran·dum /mem′əran′dəm/ [L
= thing to be remembered] n (-dums
or -da /-də/) 1 note to assist one to
remember; reminder; 2 informal
written message sent between people or departments of the same company or organization; 3 diplomacy
informal statement or summary regarding some subject of discussion
between two governments; 4 com
statement of terms of sale with the
privilege of return; 5 law informal
document stating the terms of a
contract or transaction

me·mo·ri·al /məmôr′ḗ·əl, -mōr′-/ [L
memorialis pert. to memory] adj 1 in
remembrance; commemorative ‖ n
2 thing intended to keep in mind a
certain person or event; 3 written
statement of facts addressed to a
government or public body usu. as
the basis of a request

Me·mo′ri·al Day′ n May 30, a legal
holiday in most states, observing the
memory of those who died in the
wars of the U.S., now generally
changed to the last Monday in May

me·mo′ri·al·ize′ vt 1 to address a petition or remonstrance to, with a statement of supporting facts; 2 to commemorate

mem·o·rize /mem′əriz′/ vt to commit
to memory

mem·o·ry /mem′ərḗ/ [L memoria] n
(-ries) 1 mental function which
makes it possible to retain and recall
past experiences; 2 remembrance;
recollection; 3 period of time covered by remembrance; 4 state of
being remembered; 5 commemoration ‖ SYN remembrance, recollection, retrospect, reminiscence ‖
DISCR Memory is the faculty of retaining or reproducing past images,
impressions, or thoughts. Remembrance is the act of recalling past
images or impressions, the state of
their being recalled, or the act of
keeping them before the mind. Both
memory and remembrance can be
involuntary, as from association, as
his face brings childhood scenes to
remembrance; or they can function

deliberately, as the events of that day came at the call of *memory*. *Recollection* is remembering by act of will, or the conscious dwelling on the recalled occurrence. *Reminiscence* is the recollection or, especially, the narrative, of one's *memories*. *Memory*, *remembrance*, and *recollection* are all used to name the period within which *memory* operates ‖ ANT forgetfulness, oblivion

mem′o·ry bank′ *n* device, as in a computer, in which data are recorded and stored for later retrieval

Mem·phis /mem′fis/ *n* 1 city in SW Tennessee on the Mississippi (623,-530); 2 ancient capital of Egypt, on the Nile, now in ruins

men /men/′ *pl* of **man**

men·ace /men′is/ [MF < L *minax* (-*acis*) threatening] *n* 1 impending danger or evil; threat ‖ *vt* 2 to threaten; imperil ‖ *vi* 3 to threaten; impend ‖ SYN *v* (see *threaten*)

mé·nage /mānäzh′/ [F] *n* 1 household; 2 household management

me·nag·er·ie /mənaj′ərē/ [F = housekeeping] *n* place where wild or strange animals are kept for exhibition

mend /mend/′ [< *amend*] *vt* 1 to repair, make whole; to patch; 2 to rectify; reform ‖ *vi* 3 to improve; 4 to recover one's health ‖ *n* 5 act of mending; 6 mended place; 7 **on the mend** improving, esp. in health

men·da·cious /mendash′əs/ [< L *mendax* (-*acis*)] *adj* 1 untrue; 2 lying ‖ **men·dac′i·ty** /-das′-/ *n* (-**ties**)

men·de·le·vi·um /men′dəlēv′ē-əm/ [Dmitri Ivanovich *Mendeleev* (1834-1907) Russian chemist] *n* synthetic radioactive element (Md; at.no. 101)

Men′del's laws′ /men′dəlz/ [Gregor *Mendel* (1822-84) Austrian botanist] *npl* basic principles of heredity discovered by Mendel, modified by subsequent discoveries ‖ **Men·de′li·an** /-dēl′ē-ən/ *adj*

Men·dels·sohn, Fe·lix /fā′liks men′-dəlsən/ *n* (1809-47) German composer

men·di·cant /men′dikənt/ [< L *mendicus* beggar] *adj* 1 practicing begging ‖ *n* 2 beggar; 3 mendicant friar ‖ **men′di·can·cy** *n*

Men·e·la·us /men′əlā′əs/ *n* Gk myth. king of Sparta, brother of Agamemnon, and husband of Helen

men·ha·den /menhād′ən/ [< Algonquian] *n* (*pl* -**den**) nonedible fish (genus *Brevoortia*) of the herring family, caught in large numbers off the Atlantic coast, used for fertilizer and oil

me·ni·al /mēn′ē-əl, -yəl/ [< OF *mesnie* household] *adj* 1 pert. to or suitable for servants; 2 servile, degrading ‖ *n* 3 domestic servant; 4 servile person

me·nin·ges /minin′jēz/ [*pl* of Gk *meninx* membrane] *npl* the three membranes that envelop the brain and spinal cord ‖ **me·nin′ge·al** *adj*

men·in·gi·tis /men′injīt′is/ *n* inflammation of the meninges

me·nis·cus /minisk′əs/ [Gk *meniskos* crescent] *n* (-**nis·ci** /-nis′ī/ or -**nis·cus·es**) 1 crescent-shaped body; 2 lens one surface of which is concave and the other convex; 3 surface of a column of liquid that is made either concave or convex by surface tension

Men·non·ite /men′ənīt′/ [< *Menno* Simons (1492-1559) G reformer] *n* member of an evangelical Protestant sect that rejects infant baptism and is noted for plainness of life and dress and refusal to take oaths, resist violence, or hold political office

men·o·pause /men′əpôz′/ [F < Gk *men* month + *pausis* cessation] *n* final cessation of menstruation

men·ses /men′sēz/ [L, *pl* of *mensis* month] *nsg* or *npl* periodic flow of blood and other matter from the uterus, occurring normally every four weeks

men's′ room′ *n* public lavatory for men

men·stru·al /men′strōō-əl/ [L *menstrualis* monthly] *adj* pert. to the menses

men′stru·ate′ [L *menstruare* (-*atus*)] *vi* to discharge the menses ‖ **men′stru·a′tion** *n*

men·su·ra·tion /men′shərāsh′ən/ [< L *mensura* measure] *n* 1 act or process of measuring; 2 division of geometry dealing with the measurement of lengths, areas, and volumes

mens′wear′ also **men's′ wear′** *n* clothing for men; men's furnishings

-ment /-mənt/ [OF < L *-mentum*] *suf* 1 act or fact of doing something, as *enforcement*; 2 condition or state resulting from an act, as *excitement*; 3 means or instrument, as *adornment*; 4 result or outcome, as *attachment*

men·tal /ment′əl/ [< L *mens* (*mentis*) mind] *adj* 1 pert. to the mind; 2 characterized by or pert. to illness of the mind ‖ **men′tal·ly** *adv* ‖ SYN (see *intellectual*)

men·tal′i·ty /-tal′-/ *n* (-**ties**) intellectual ability; mental capacity; mind

men′tal re·tar·da′tion *n* subnormal intelligence characterized by general inadequacy

men·thol /men′thol, -thôl/ [< L *mentha* mint + *oleum* oil] *n* solid, white, volatile, crystalline alcohol —$CH_3C_6H_9(C_3H_7)OH$— obtained from oil of peppermint; used in medicines and toilet preparations

men·tion /men′shən/ [L *mentio* (-*onis*)] *n* 1 brief reference; 2 formal recognition for meritorious service or achievement ‖ *vt* 3 to speak briefly of; 4 to refer to by name; **5** to cite formally for meritorious service or achievement || **men'tion·a·ble** *adj* || SYN *v* tell, communicate, impart, name

men·tor /ment'ər/ [*Mentor*] loyal adviser of Odysseus] *n* wise and faithful adviser

men·u /men'yŏō, mān'-/ [F] *n* **1** list of the dishes served at a meal; **2** the food served

me·ow /mē·ou', myou'/ [imit] *n* **1** sound made by a cat || *vi* **2** to make the sound of a cat

Meph·i·stoph·e·les /mef'istof'ilēz'/ [G] *n* medieval legend one of the seven chief devils, to whom Faust sold his soul

me·phi·tis /məfīt'is/ [L] *n* **1** foul and poisonous emanation from the earth, as from a mine; **2** any noxious odor || **me·phit'ic** /-fit'ik/ *adj*

mer·can·tile /murk'əntēl', -til', -til/ [F < It] *adj* **1** of or pert. to merchants and trade; **2** pert. to mercantilism

mer·can·til'ism *n* doctrine and practice by a nation of maintaining the greatest possible surplus of exports over imports, thus gaining economic and political power over other nations

mer·cap·tan /mərkap'tan/ [L *mercurium captans* capturing mercury] *n chem* one of a class of compounds analogous to alcohol, but containing sulfur instead of oxygen, and characterized by an offensive garlicky odor

Mer·ca·tor pro·jec·tion /mərkāt'ər/ [Gerhardus *Mercator* (1512–94) Flem geographer] *n* map projection in which meridians and parallels are drawn as straight lines at right angles to each other and in which the scale varies increasingly away from the equator, causing great distortion in area and distances; this projection is useful to navigators because rhumb lines are always straight

mer·ce·nar·y /murs'əner'ē/ [L *mercenarius*] *adj* **1** acting only for reward or money; **2** hired (soldiers) || *n* (-ies) **3** soldier hired by a foreign country

mer·cer /murs'ər/ [AF < L *merx* (*mercis*) merchandise] *n Brit* dealer in textiles

mer'cer·ize' [J. *Mercer* (1791–1866) Eng calico printer] *vt* to treat (cotton fabrics) with caustic alkali to strengthen them and give them a silky sheen

mer·chan·dise /murch'əndīz'/ [OF *marchandise*] *n* **1** goods, wares, or articles bought and sold in trade || *vi* **2** to buy and sell merchandise || *vt* **3** to buy and sell; trade in; **4** to promote the sale of || **mer'chan·dis'·ing** *n*

mer·chant /murch'ənt/ [OF *marcheant*] *n* **1** retailer; shopkeeper; **2** dealer, trader || *adj* **3** mercantile; **4** pert. to the merchant marine

mer'chant·man /-mən/ *n* (-men /-mən/) *n* trading vessel

mer'chant ma·rine' *n* that part of a nation's shipping engaged in trade

mer·ci·ful /murs'ifəl/ [see **mercy**] *adj* full of, or exercising, mercy || **mer'ci·ful·ly** *adv* || SYN lenient, tender, compassionate, gracious, benignant, mild, charitable || ANT merciless, cruel, inexorable, hard-hearted, unyielding

mer'ci·less *adj* having or showing no mercy; pitiless || **mer'ci·less·ly** *adv* || SYN hard-hearted, pitiless, relentless, remorseless, unrelenting, implacable || ANT merciful, kind, humane

mer·cu·ri·al /mərkyŏŏr'ē·əl/ [see **mercury**] *adj* **1** volatile; lively; **2** fickle, changeable; **3** pert. to mercury; **4** Mercurial pert. to Mercury

mer·cu'ric *adj* pert. to or containing mercury, esp. with a valence of two

Mer·cu'ro·chrome' *n* [trademark] *n* solution of a mercuric compound —C₂₀H₈Br₂HgNa₂O₆— used as an antiseptic

mer·cu·ry /murk'yərē/ [L *Mercurius*] *n* **1** heavy silvery metallic element (Hg; at.no. 80; at.wt. 200.59), liquid at ordinary temperatures, extensively used in industry, in thermometers and scientific instruments, and in medicinal drugs; **2** Mercury, a *Rom myth.* son of Jupiter and messenger of the gods, god of commerce and eloquence and patron of thieves and travelers; **b** innermost and smallest planet of the solar system

mer'cu·ry-va'por lamp' *n* lamp producing a bright light by means of an electric arc in mercury vapor, much used for street lighting

mer·cy /murs'ē/ [OF *merci* < L *merces* reward] *n* (-cies) **1** willingness to forgive or treat an offender leniently; clemency; forbearance; **2** disposition to be merciful; **3** act of kindness; **4** at the mercy of in the power of || SYN benevolence, clemency, forgiveness, pardon, lenity, leniency, forbearance, pity, gentleness || DISCR *Mercy* is compassion and gentle treatment shown to an offender who expects no kindness and is wholly in one's power; *mercy* is also compassion toward those who, through no fault of their own, are in trouble, and in one's power. *Clemency* is a tendency to mildness toward offenders, usually shown by superiors; *clemency* may be exercised through kindness, or it may be dictated by self-interest, worldly wisdom, or the like. Judges, royalty, political bosses, show *clemency*. *Pardon* remits the penalty, usually for a serious offense; *pardon* has a specific legal usage, naming that official release which frees an offender from the legal consequences of his act. *Forgiveness* connotes a change of heart in the offended person, whereby he wipes out displeasure and resentment toward the offender. *Lenity* and *leniency* designate a sympathetic mildness of temper; teachers, parents, show *leniency*; a mistress shows *lenity* toward servants ‖ ANT cruelty, severity

mer′cy kill′ing *n* euthanasia

mere /mir′/ [L *merus* unmixed] *adj* nothing but; no more than; this only

mere′ly *adv* only; simply

mer·e·tri·cious /mer′ĭtrish′əs/ [< L *meretrix* harlot] *adj* attracting by false show; tawdry; deceitfully alluring

mer·gan·ser /mərgans′ər/ [< L *mergus* diver + *anser* goose] *n* any of several fish-eating ducks (subfamily Merginae) having a long hooked bill bearing toothlike serrations

merge /murj′/ [L *mergere* to dip] *vt* 1 to cause to combine; unite; swallow up ‖ *vi* 2 to be absorbed; lose individuality or identity; 3 to unite into one ‖ SYN unite, blend, coalesce, join, amalgamate (see *mix*)

merg′er *n* 1 act or instance of merging; 2 combination of two or more enterprises, organizations, or corporations into a single entity

me·rid·i·an /mərid′ē·ən/ [MF *meridien* < L *meridies* midday] *n* 1 great circle of the celestial sphere, passing through its poles and the zenith of any given point on earth; 2 highest point reached by a heavenly body in the sky; 3 acme; zenith of success; 4 a great circle of the earth, passing through the poles; b half of a great circle, passing through a given place; longitude ‖ also *adj*

me·ringue /mərang′/ [F] *n* icing or garnish made of beaten white of egg and sugar

me·ri·no /mərēn′ō/ [Sp < L *majorinus* of a larger kind] *n* 1 one of a Spanish breed of sheep with a fine silky wool; 2 wool or cloth from a merino

mer·it /mer′it/ [OF *merite* < L *meritum*] *n* 1 worth; excellence; that which deserves commendation; 2 **merits** *pl* essential right or wrong, to be used as a basis of judgment ‖ *vt* 3 to deserve

mer′i·toc′ra·cy /-tok′rə·sē/ *n* (-cies) system of education in which talent is nurtured and rewarded ‖ **mer′it·o·crat′ic** /-əkrat′ik/ *adj*

mer′i·to′ri·ous /-tôr′ē·əs, -tōr′-/ *adj* worthy of praise or reward

Mer·lin /mur′lin/ *n* Arthurian legend famous magician and seer at King Arthur's court

mer′maid /mur′-/ [< OE *mere* sea] *n* legendary sea creature with the head, arms, and trunk of a woman and the tail of a fish

Mer·o·vin·gi·an /mer′əvin′jē·ən/ [< LL *Merovingi* descendants of Merovaeus] *adj* 1 pert. to or designating the first Frankish dynasty in France, founded by Clovis in 481 and lasting until 752 ‖ *n* 2 member of this dynasty

mer·ri·ment /mer′imənt/ *n* mirth, fun, gaiety

mer·ry /mer′ē/ [OE *myrige* pleasant] *adj* (-ri·er; -ri·est) 1 mirthful; gay; joyous; 2 festive; jolly; 3 **make merry** to be gay, have a good time ‖ **mer′ri·ly** *adv* ‖ **mer′ri·ness** *n* ‖ SYN mirthful, cheerful, blithe, sportive, jocular, hilarious, gay, vivacious ‖ ANT sad, dispirited, cheerless

mer′ry-go-round′ *n* 1 revolving circular platform fitted with wooden animals and seats, on which persons ride for amusement; 2 rapid whirl or round of activity

mer′ry-mak′er *n* participant in gay festivities ‖ **mer′ry·mak′ing** *n*

me·sa /mās′ə/ [Sp = table] *n* land formation common in the Southwest, having a flat top and steep sides

mes·ca·line /mes′kəlēn, -lin/ [< AmSp *mescal* < Nahuatl *mexcalli maguey*] *n* white crystalline powder —C₁₁H₁₇NO₃— that produces hallucinations

mes·dames /mādäm′, -dam′/ *pl* of **madame**

mes·de·moi·selles /mād′(ə)m(w)əzel′/ *pl* of **mademoiselle**

mesh /mesh′/ [prob < OE *mæscre*] *n* 1 one of the openings between the threads of a net; 2 any openwork fabric; 3 network; 4 engagement of gear teeth; 5 **meshes** *pl* a interlaced threads that form a mesh; b clutches, trap ‖ *vt* 6 to entangle in, or as in, a net; 7 to make into a net or network; 8 to engage (gears); 9 to coordinate; interlock ‖ *vi* 10 to become entangled; 11 to be engaged, as gears; 12 to match; interlock

mes·mer·ize /mez′mərīz, mes′-/ [< F.A. *Mesmer* (1734–1815) Austrian physician] *vt* 1 to hypnotize; 2 to charm, fascinate ‖ **mes′mer·ism** *n*

meso- [Gk *mesos*] *comb form* middle

me·son /mē′zon, -son, mez′on, mes′-/ [*meso-* + electron] *n phys* elementary particle intermediate between an electron and a proton

Mes·o·po·ta·mi·a /mes′əpətäm′ē·ə/ *n* ancient country in W Asia between the Tigris and the Euphrates rivers, coinciding roughly with modern Iraq ‖ **Mes′o·po·ta′mi·an** *adj & n*

Mes·o·zo·ic /mes′əzō′ik, mez′-, mēs′-, mēz′-/ [*meso-* + Gk *zoe* life] *n geol* era between the Paleozoic and the Cenozoic, characterized by the dinosaurs ‖ also *adj*

mes·quite /meskēt′, mes′kēt/ [Sp *mez-*

quite < Nahuatl] *n* small tree or shrub (*Prosopis glandulosa*) of SW North America having fragrant flowers, feathery leaves, and sugary pods used as fodder

mess /mes'/ [OF *mes* dish] *n* **1** a group of persons taking their meals together; **b** place where they eat; **c** the meal itself; **2** disagreeable concoction; **3** state of dirt or confusion; **4** muddle; botch; **5** enough for a dish or a meal; **6** untidy jumble; **7** serious trouble; **8** *colloq* **a** untidy person; **b** confused or disordered person || *vt* **9** often **mess up, a** to befoul, soil; **b** to muddle, botch || *vi* **10** to eat in a mess; **11 mess around** *colloq* to putter; **12 mess around with** *slang* to associate with (someone) for immoral or dishonest purposes; **13 mess in** or **with** to meddle in

mes·sage /mes'ij/ [OF] *n* **1** communication delivered by any means; **2** formal communication of a chief executive to a legislative body; **3** inspired utterance, as of a prophet; **4** point, moral, or teaching

mes·sen·ger /mes'ənjər/ [OF *messagier*] *n* **1** bearer of a message; **2** one who runs errands; **3** harbinger, forerunner

Mes·si·ah /məsī'ə/ [Heb *māshīah* anointed one] *n* **1** the awaited savior of the Jews; **2** Jesus Christ; **3** messiah any expected deliverer

mes·sieurs /mes'ərz/ *pl* of **monsieur**

mess' jack'et *n* man's short tailless jacket

mess' kit' *n* compact set of utensils and a metal dish, used by soldiers in the field, campers, etc.

Messrs. /mes'ərz/ *pl* of **Mr.**

mess·y *adj* (**-i·er; -i·est**) **1** dirty; untidy; **2** causing a mess; **3** embarrassing || **mess'i·ly** *adv* || **mess'i·ness** *n*

mes·ti·zo /mestēz'ō/ [Sp] *n* person of mixed blood, esp. one of Spanish and Indian blood

met /met'/ *pt* & *pp* of **meet**

meta- or **met-** [Gk = among, with, after] *comb form* **1** after, behind, beyond, as *metaphysics;* **2** change, as *metamorphosis*

me·tab·o·lism /mətab'əliz'əm/ [< Gk *metabole* change] *n* process by which a living cell transforms food materials into protoplasm and by which food material and protoplasm are broken down by oxidation into waste matter || **me·tab'o·lize'** *vt* || **met·a·bol·ic** /met'əbol'ik/ *adj*

met·al /met'əl/ [OF < Gk *metallon* mine] *n* **1** any of a class of elements, crystalline when solid, and usu. hard, opaque, ductile, conductive, and characterized by a peculiar luster; **2** mixture made wholly or partly from such elements, as an alloy; **3** spirit; temper; mettle; **4** *chem* any element that can replace the hydrogen of an acid || **me·tal·lic** /mətal'ik/ *adj*

met'a·lan'guage /met'ə-/ *n* kind of language used to describe, analyze, or define a language

met'al·loid' *n* **1** nonmetal; **2** nonmetal that can form an alloy with a metal, as carbon with iron to form steel; **3** member of a group of elements that share the properties of metals and nonmetals, as arsenic, bismuth, boron, or silicon || also *adj*

met·al·lur·gy /met'əlur'jē/ *n* **1** science of separating metals from their ores; **2** treating and working metals to develop particular shapes or qualities; **3** making alloys || **met'al·lur'gic** (**-gi·cal**) *adj* || **met'al·lur'gist** *n*

met·a·mor·phism /met'əmôrf'izəm/ *n* **1** metamorphosis; **2** *geol* process by which minerals and rocks are changed from their original constitution || **met'a·mor'phic** also **met'a·mor'phous** *adj*

met'a·mor'phose /-fōz, fōs/ *vt* **1** to change the form or nature of; **2** to cause to undergo metamorphosis or metamorphism || *vi* **3** to undergo metamorphosis or metamorphism

met'a·mor·pho·sis /-əsis/ [Gk] *n* (**-ses** /-sēz'/) **1** complete change of form, shape, or structure; **2** person or thing so changed; **3** *zool* change or succession of changes in the form and habits of many lower animals before they reach maturity, as caterpillar to pupa to butterfly, or tadpole to frog

met'a·phase' *n* stage of mitosis in which the chromosomes lie along the equator of the spindle

met·a·phor /met'əfôr', -fər/ [< Gk *metapherein* to transfer] *n* figure of speech in which a name, action, or descriptive term characteristic of one object is applied to another to suggest a likeness between them, as *he was a lion in battle* || **met'a·phor'i·cal** /-fôr'-, -for'-/ *adj*

met'a·phys'ics [< Gk ta *meta* ta *physika* the works (of Aristotle) placed after the physical sciences] *nsg* **1** branch of philosophy dealing with the nature, character, and causes of being and knowing, the existence of God, etc.; **2** abstract speculative philosophy in general || **met'a·phys'i·cal** *adj* || **met'a·phy·si'cian** *n*

me·tas·ta·sis /mətas'təsis/ [Gk = change] *n* (**-ses** /-sēz'/) transfer of disease or malignancy from one part of the body to another through the blood stream || **me·tas'ta·size'** *vi* || **met·a·stat·ic** /met'əstat'ik/ *adj*

met'a·tar'sal *n* bone in the metatarsus || also *adj*

met'a·tar'sus /-tär'səs/ [*meta-* + Gk *tarsos* flat surface] *n* that part of the lower or hinder limb between the ankle and toes, consisting in man of five long bones in the foot

me·tath·e·sis /mətath'isis/ [Gk = transposition] *n* (**-ses** /-sēz'/) transposition of letters or sounds in a word, as *bird* for older *brid* || **me·tath'e·size'** *vt & vi*

mete /mēt'/ [OE *metan* to measure] *vt* **mete out** to allot, apportion

me·tem·psy·cho·sis /mətem(p)'sĭkōs'ĭs, met'əmsī-/ [Gk] *n* (-ses /-sēz/) 1 passage of the soul from one body to another; 2 rebirth of the soul at death in another body, either human or animal

me·te·or /mēt'ē·ər/ [Gk *meteoros* raised] *n* mass of matter from outer space which enters the earth's atmosphere at very high speed and becomes incandescent; a falling or shooting star

me·te·or·ic /-ôr'ik, -or'ĭk/ *adj* 1 of or pert. to meteors; 2 swift; dazzling; momentarily brilliant

me·te·or·ite' *n* mass of stone or metal from outer space that has survived passage through the atmosphere; fallen meteor

me·te·or·oid' *n* meteor in outer space before it enters the atmosphere

me·te·or·ol·o·gy /-ol'-/ *n* science of atmospheric phenomena and weather forecasting || **me'te·or·ol'o·gist** *n* || **me'te·or·o·log'i·cal** /-əloj'-/ *adj*

me·ter¹ /mēt'ər/ [OE < Gk *metron* measure] *n* 1 *pros* a rhythm; measured arrangement in verse of groups of syllables having a time unit and a regular beat; b specific arrangement of metrical groups; 2 that part of a musical composition or structure which depends on time values

me·ter² [< *mete*] *n* 1 instrument for measuring and recording, as the rate of flow or consumption of liquids, gases, or electric current || *vt* 2 to measure with a meter

me·ter³ [F *mètre* < Gk *metron* measure] *n* standard unit of length in the metric system, equal to 39.37 inches, originally intended to be one ten-millionth of the distance on a meridian from equator to pole but now defined as 1,650,763.73 wavelengths of the orange-red light of krypton 86

-me·ter /-mĭtər, also -mēt'ər/ [< Gk *metron* measure] *comb form* measuring instrument, as *thermometer*

me·ter-kil'o·gram'-sec'ond *adj* (system of units) in which the meter is the unit of length, the kilogram the unit of mass, and the second the unit of time

me·ter maid' *n* policewoman who writes tickets for parking violations

meth·a·done /meth'ədōn'/ [< *meth-* + *a(mino)* + *d(iphenyl)* + *-one*] *n* narcotic drug —$C_{21}H_{27}NO$— used, in the form of its hydrochloride, for relieving pain and treating heroin addiction

meth·ane /meth'ān/ [< *meth(yl)* + *-ane²*] *n* colorless, odorless, highly inflammable gas —CH_4— found in

natural gas, and the main constituent of firedamp and marsh gas

me·thinks /mĭthĭngks'/ *v* (**me·thought**) *v impers archaic* it seems to me

meth·od /meth'əd/ [Gk *methodos*] *n* 1 use of a defined or regular plan; 2 established form of systematic procedure, as *a method of teaching*; 3 orderly arrangement, classification, or the like; 4 habitual orderliness; 5 **the Method** method of acting developed by the Russian director Stanislavski, in which the actor identifies with the character he portrays || SYN way, system, manner, plan, design

me·thod·i·cal /məthod'ĭkəl/ *adj* systematic; orderly; painstaking || **me·thod'i·cal·ly** *adv*

Meth'od·ist *n* member of an evangelical denomination, an offshoot of the Anglican Church, founded by John Wesley || **Meth'od·ism** *n*

me·thought /mĭthôt'/ *pt* of **methinks**

Me·thu·se·lah /məthōōz'(ə)lə/ *n Bib* patriarch who is recorded to have lived 969 years (Gen. 5:27)

meth·yl /meth'əl/ [< Gk *methy* wine + *hyle* wood] *n* hydrocarbon radical —CH_3— present in wood alcohol and other compounds

meth'yl al'co·hol *n* volatile, inflammable, poisonous liquid —CH_3OH— obtained synthetically and by the distillation of wood; used as a solvent, as an antifreeze, and as a fuel

meth'yl·at'ed spir'its *npl* ethyl alcohol denatured by mixing with methyl alcohol to prevent its use as a beverage

me·tic·u·lous /mətik'yələs/ [< L *meticulosus* fearful] *adj* extremely careful about even unimportant details

mé·tier /mātyā'/ [F] *n* 1 profession, trade; 2 forte

me·ton·y·my /mĭton'ĭmē/ [Gk *metonymia* change of name] *n* figure of speech in which not the literal word but one associated with it is used, as *the sword* for war (cf. *synecdoche*)

met·ric /met'rĭk/ *adj* 1 of or pert. to the meter or the metric system; 2 metrical

met'ri·cal *adj* 1 pert. to or composed in meter or verse; 2 metric

met'ri·ca'tion *n* adoption or introduction of the metric system

met'rics *nsg* art or science of meter and metrical composition

met'ric sys'tem *n* decimal system of weights and measures, having the meter (39.37 inches) as the basic unit of length, the are (a square of ten meters on each side or 119.6 square yards) as the unit of surface, the liter (a cube nearly one tenth of a meter on each edge, or 1.0567 quarts) as the unit of capacity, and the gram (approximately equivalent to the weight of a cubic centimeter of water, or 15.432 grains) as the unit of weight

met'ric ton' *n* metric unit of weight of

1000 kilograms, equal to 2204.62 pounds

met·ro /met′rō/ [F *métro* < *Chemin de fer métropolitain* Metropolitan Railway] *n* subway in European cities and Montreal, Canada

met·ro·nome /met′rənōm′/ [Gk *metron* measure + *nomos* law] *n* instrument for clicking off exact intervals of time, for marking rhythm in music

me·trop·o·lis /mətrop′əlis/ [Gk = mother city] *n* 1 principal or largest city of a country, state, or region; 2 parent city or state of a colony, esp. in ancient Greece

met·ro·pol·i·tan /met′rəpol′itən/ *adj* 1 pert. to a metropolis || *n* 2 resident of a metropolis; 3 chief bishop in an ecclesiastical province

-me·try /-mitrē/ [Gk *metria*] *comb form* measurement, as *trigonometry*

met·tle /met′əl/ [var of *metal*] *n* 1 temperament; disposition; 2 ardor, spirits || **met′tle·some** *adj*

mew /myōō′/ [imit] *n* 1 cry of a cat *vi* 2 to utter this sound

mewl /myōōl′/ [imit] *vi* to whimper like a young child

mews /myōōz′/ [*Mews* at Charing Cross, London] *nsg* or *npl* stables built around a court, now converted into apartments or originally built as apartments

Mex. 1 Mexico; 2 Mexican

Mex·i·co /meks′ikō/ *n* Spanish-speaking republic bordering on the SW United States (50,671,000; 761,604 sq.m.; cap. Mexico City) || **Mex′i·can** *adj* & *n*

Mex′i·co Cit′y *n* capital of Mexico (3,287,334)

Mex′i·co, Gulf of *n* arm of the Atlantic between the U.S., Mexico, and Cuba

mez·za·nine /mez′ənēn′, mez′ənēn′/ [F < It *mezzanino*] *n* 1 low floor between two main floors, esp. the floor between the first and second, often a gallery; 2 lowest balcony, or the front part of it, in a theater

mez·zo /met′sō, mez′ō/ [It = middle] *adj mus* moderate; half

mez′zo·so·pran′o /-(-os or -i /-ē/)/ *n* voice, or person having a voice, between soprano and contralto

MF, M.F. Middle French

mfg. manufacturing

mfr. 1 manufacture; 2 manufacturer

mg, mg. milligram(s)

Mg *chem* magnesium

MGk, MGr. Medieval Greek

mgr. 1 manager; 2 monsignor

MHG, M.H.G. Middle High German

mi /mē/ [It] *n mus* third tone in the diatonic scale

mi. 1 mile(s); 2 mill(s)

Mi·am·i /mī·am′ē, -am′ə/ *n* city in SE Florida on the Atlantic (334,859); famous winter resort

mi·as·ma /mī·az′mə/ [Gk = pollution] *n* (-mas or -ma·ta /-mətə/) 1 noxious vapor from rotting organic matter; 2 any evil emanation or atmosphere || **mi·as′mal** or **mi·as′mic** *adj*

mi·ca /mīk′ə/ [L = crumb] *n* any of a large group of minerals, complex silicates of aluminum, resistant to heat and electricity, and readily separated into thin transparent sheets

mice /mīs′/ *pl* of **mouse**

Mich. Michigan

Mi·chael /mīk′əl/ *n Bib* one of the archangels, leader in the war against Satan (Rev. 12:7–9)

Mi·chel·an·ge·lo /mīk′əlan′jəlō′/ *n* (1475–1564) Italian painter, sculptor, and architect

Mich·i·gan /mish′igən/ *n* state in the N central U.S. (8,875,000; 57,980 sq.m.; cap. Lansing) || **Mich′i·gan′der** /-gan′dər/ *n*

Mich·i·gan, Lake *n* one of the Great Lakes, between Wisconsin and Michigan

Mick·ey Finn /mik′ē fin′/ [?] *n* drink containing a drug which acts quickly to produce illness or unconsciousness

mi·cra /mīk′rə/ *pl* of **micron**

mi·cro- [Gk *mikros* small] *comb form* 1 small, as *microbe*; 2 enlarging what is small, as *microphone*; 3 one millionth part, as *microampere*

mi·crobe /mī′krōb/ [*micro-* + Gk *bios* life] *n* microorganism, esp. a bacterium instrumental in producing disease

mi′cro·bi·ol′o·gy /mīk′rō-/ *n* the biology of microorganisms

mi·cro·cosm /mīk′rəkoz′əm/ [*micro-* + *cosmos*] *n* 1 a world in miniature; 2 man regarded as combining in himself the elements of the universe || **mi′cro·cos′mic** *adj*

mi′cro·far′ad *n* unit of capacitance, equal to one millionth of a *farad*

mi′cro·fiche′ /-fēsh′/ [F *fiche* filing card] *n* sheet of microfilm suitable for filing

mi′cro·film′ *n* 1 film bearing greatly reduced photographs, as of books, newspapers, or documents, and which must be enlarged by projection for viewing || *vt* 2 to make a microfilm of

mi′cro·groove′ *n* 1 very narrow needle groove, as on a long-playing record; 2 record with such a groove

mi·crom·e·ter /mīkrom′itər/ *n* instrument for measuring minute distances and angles

mi·cron /mī′kron/ [Gk = small] *n* (-crons or -cra /-krə/) one millionth of a meter

Mi·cro·ne·sia /mīk′rənēzh′ə, -nēsh′ə/ *n* group of small islands in the Pacific E of the Philippines || **Mi′cro·ne′sian** *adj* & *n*

mi′cro·or′gan·ism /-rō-/ *n* microscopic organism, as a bacterium, fungus, virus, or protozoan

mi′cro·phone′ /-rə-/ *n* device in which sound waves produce corresponding variations in an electric current, used in telephonic and radio transmission

mi′cro·phys′ics *nsg* branch of physics dealing with the ultimate particles of matter

mi′cro·scope′ *n* optical instrument for magnifying objects too small to be seen or seen in detail by the naked eye

mi′cro·scop′ic /-skop′ik/ *adj* 1 pert. to, seen by, or involving a microscope; 2 very minute; 3 so small as to be invisible to the naked eye ‖ **mi′cro·scop′i·cal·ly** *adv*

mi·cros·co·py /mīkros′kəpē, mīk′res·kōp′ē/ *n* use of the microscope

mi′cro·switch′ /-krə-/ *n* small, highly sensitive switch used in automatic-control devices

mi′cro·wave′ *n* very short electromagnetic wave, esp. one shorter than 100 cm. in wavelength

mic·tu·rate /mik′chərāt′/ [< L *micturire* to have to make water] *vi* to urinate ‖ **mic′tu·ri′tion** /-rish′ən/ *n*

mid¹ /mid′/ [OE *midd* middle] *adj* being in or at the middle of

mid² or **′mid** *prep* amid

mid- *comb form* the middle of, as *midafternoon*

mid′air′ *n* point in the air high above the ground

Mi·das /mīd′əs/ *n Gk myth.* Phrygian king to whom the power was granted to change everything he touched into gold

mid′brain′ *n* that part of the brain developed from the middle brain of the embryo

mid′day′ *n* noon ‖ also *adj*

mid·dle /mid′əl/ [OE *middel*] *adj* 1 equally distant from the extremes; mean; medial; 2 intermediate; intervening; 3 **Middle** intermediate (stage of a language), between Old and Modern ‖ *n* 4 point or part equidistant from the two extremes; 5 that which is intermediate; 6 middle part of the body

mid′dle age′ *n* period of life between youth and old age ‖ **mid′dle-aged′** /-ājd′/ *adj*

Mid′dle Ag′es *npl* period between ancient and modern times, from the fall of the Roman empire in the west to the Renaissance, about 500 to 1500

Mid′dle At·lan′tic States′ *npl* New York, New Jersey, and Pennsylvania

mid′dle class′ *n* social class intermediate between the highest and the lowest ‖ **mid′dle-class′** *adj*

mid′dle ear′ *n* middle portion of the ear, a cavity separated from the outer ear by the eardrum

Mid′dle East′ *n* region extending from Turkey to Iraq and Iran, and S to the Red Sea and the Gulf of Aden

Mid′dle Eng′lish *n* the English language approximately from 1150 to 1500

mid′dle·man′ /-man′/ *n* (**-men** /-men′/) 1 one acting as intermediary between producer and consumer; 2 intermediary

mid′dle-of-the-road′ *adj* moderate in one's views ‖ **mid′dle-of-the-road′er** *n*

mid′dle·weight′ *n* 1 one who is of average weight; 2 boxer weighing from 147 to 160 pounds

Mid′dle West′ *n* N central region of the U.S., extending roughly from the W border of Pennsylvania to the Rocky Mountains, and from Canada and the Great Lakes to the Ohio and the N border of Arkansas and Oklahoma ‖ **Mid′dle West′ern** *adj* ‖ **Mid′dle West′ern·er** *n*

mid·dling /mid′liŋ/ [see **middle**] *adj* 1 of moderate rank, size, or quality ‖ *adv* 2 moderately

mid·dy /mid′ē/ [< *midshipman*] *n* (**-dies**) 1 *colloq* midshipman; 2 middy blouse

mid′dy blouse′ *n* loose blouse with a sailor collar

midge /mij′/ [OE *mycg*] *n* 1 any very small fly or gnat; 2 midget

midg′et /-it/ *n* very small person or thing

Mi·di /mēdē′/ [F = midday] *n* south, esp. the south of France

mid′land /-lənd/ *n* 1 interior or central part of a country; 2 **Midlands** *pl* central counties of England

mid′night′ *n* 1 middle of the night; twelve o'clock at night; 2 intense darkness or gloom ‖ also *adj*

mid′riff /-rif/ [OE *midhrif*] *n* 1 diaphragm; 2 middle part of the body between the chest and the waist

mid′sec′tion *n* 1 middle part; 2 *colloq* midriff

mid′ship′man /-mən/ *n* (**-men** /-mən/) student officer at the naval or coast-guard academy, ranking next below a warrant officer

midst /midst′/ [< *amidst*] *n* 1 middle; central place ‖ *prep* 2 amidst

mid′stream′ *n* middle of a stream

mid′sum′mer *n* middle of the summer ‖ also *adj*

mid′term′ *n* 1 middle of a term, as of school or office; 2 **midterms** *pl colloq* midterm exams ‖ also *adj*

mid′-Vic·to′ri·an *adj* 1 pert. to the middle period (ab. 1850–80) of the reign of Queen Victoria; 2 characteristic of the old-fashioned customs and rigid social standards of this period ‖ *n* 3 person who lived or flourished during this period; 4 person with the tastes, standards, or ideas of this period

mid′way′ *adj & adv* 1 in the middle; halfway ‖ **mid′way′** *n* 2 amusement section of an exposition or fair

mid′week′ *n* middle of the week ‖ also *adj*

mid'week'ly *adj* & *adv* occurring in the middle of the week

Mid'west' *n* Middle West || **Mid'west'ern** *adj* || **Mid'west'ern·er** *n*

mid'wife' [OE *mid* with + *wif* woman] *n* (-**wives** /-vz/) woman who assists women in childbirth

mid'win'ter *n* middle of the winter || also *adj*

mid'year' *n* 1 middle of a calendar or academic year; 2 examination at the middle of an academic year; 3 **mid·years** *pl* midyear exams || also *adj*

mien /mēn/ [prob < *demean*, influenced by F *mine* look] *n* appearance; demeanor

miff /mif/ [?] *vt colloq* to offend, displease

might¹ /mīt/ [< *meahte*, *pt* of *magan* to be able] *v* (*pt* of **may**) *modal aux* used to express: 1 possibility, as *I might go if it doesn't rain*; 2 permission, as *might I come in?*

might² [OE *miht*] *n* 1 force, power, strength; 2 superior strength; 3 **with might and main** with all one's strength

might'y *adj* (-**i·er**; **-i·est**) 1 powerful, strong; 2 of extraordinary size, consequence, amount, etc. || *adv* 3 *colloq* very

mi·gnon·ette /min'yənet'/ [F, *dim.* of *mignon* delicate] *n* any of a genus (*Reseda*) of plants, esp. a fragrant cultivated species (*R. odorata*) with greenish-white flowers

mi·graine /mī'grān/ *n* headache, usu. affecting one side of the head only and accompanied by nausea

mi·grant /mī'grənt/ *n* 1 roving; migrating || *n* 2 person or animal that migrates; 3 worker who migrates in search of work

mi·grate /mī'grāt/ [L *migrare* (-*atus*) to wander] *vi* 1 to move from one country or locality to another; 2 to move periodically from one climate or feeding ground to another || **mi'gra·to'ry** /-grətôr'-, -grətōr'-/ *adj*

mi·gra'tion *n* 1 act of migrating; 2 group of migrating individuals || **mi·gra'tion·al** *adj*

mi·ka·do /mikäd'ō/ [Jap] *n* emperor of Japan

mike /mīk/ *n colloq* microphone

mil /mil/ [L *mille* thousand] *n* unit of length equal to .001 of an inch

mil. 1 military; 2 militia

mi·la·dy /mīlād'ē/ [*my lady*] *n* (-**dies**) 1 English noblewoman (used in Europe as a term of address); 2 fashionable lady

Mi·lan /mīlan'/ *n* city in N Italy (1,672,800); commercial center of Italy || **Mil·an·ese** /mil'ənēz', -nēs'/ *adj* & *n* (-**ese**)

milch' cow' /milch'/ [OE -*milce*] *n* cow kept for milking

mild /mī'(ə)ld/ [OE *milde*] *adj* 1 gentle in temper and disposition; 2 moder-

ate in quality, degree, or taste; not harsh, severe, or bitter || **mild'ly** *adv* || **mild'ness** *n* || SYN tender, merciful, soft, lenient, meek, serene

mil·dew /mil'd(y)ōō'/ [OE *mildēaw* honeydew] *n* 1 any of various fungi found on plants or decaying substances; 2 any of numerous diseases of plants produced by such parasites; 3 spot or discoloration caused by various fungi on cloth, leather, paper, etc., usu. when exposed to dampness || *vt* 4 to affect with mildew || *vi* 5 to become mildewed

mile /mīl/ [OE *mīl* < L *milia* passuum thousand paces] *n* 1 unit of linear measure containing 5,280 feet; 2 nautical mile

mile'age /-ij/ *n* 1 allowance for traveling expenses at a specified rate per mile; 2 aggregate distance in miles; 3 *colloq* advantage, use; service

mile'stone' *n* 1 stone marker indicating the distance in miles from one point to another; 2 event marking a significant advance

mi·lieu /mīlyōō', mēl-/ [F] *n* environment; setting

mil·i·tant /mil'itənt/ [< L *militare* to serve as a soldier] *adj* 1 aggressive; combative; 2 warring || *n* 3 militant person || **mil'i·tan·cy** *n*

mil'i·ta·rism *n* 1 disposition to maintain national power by means of strong military forces; 2 warlike policy; 3 exaltation of military ideals || **mil'i·ta·rist** *n* || **mil'i·ta·ris'tic** *adj*

mil'i·tar'y /-ter'ē/ [L *militaris* < *miles* soldier] *adj* 1 pert. to soldiers, arms, or warfare; 2 martial; 3 soldierly; 4 performed by soldiers || *n* 5 **the military** *pl* soldiers collectively; **the armed forces** || **mil'i·tar'i·ly** *adv*

mil'i·tar'y po·lice' *npl* soldiers who act as police within the army

mil'i·tate' [see **militant**] *vi* **militate against** to operate against

mi·li·tia /mīlish'ə/ [L = soldiery] *n* body of citizens enrolled and trained for military purposes but not called except in time of emergency || **mi·li'tia·man** /-mən/ *n* (-**men** /-mən/)

milk /milk/ [OE *milc*] *n* 1 white fluid produced by the mammary glands of female mammals for the nourishment of their young; 2 this fluid from cows, used by man as a food; 3 any fluid resembling milk, as the milk of a coconut || *vt* 4 to draw milk from, as *to milk a cow*; 5 to exploit, plunder || **milk'er** *n*

milk'maid' *n* woman who works in a dairy or milks cows

milk'man' /-man'/ *n* (-**men** /-men'/) one who sells or delivers milk

milk' of mag·ne'sia *n* milky suspension of magnesium hydroxide —$Mg(OH)_2$— in water, used as a laxative and antacid

milk' shake' *n* beverage made of milk

whipped with flavoring and some-times ice cream

milk′sop′ n weak, effeminate man

milk′ sug′ar n lactose

milk′ tooth′ n one of the temporary set of teeth in the young of mammals

milk′weed′ n any of a large family (Asclepiadaceae) of plants with entire leaves and milklike sap

milk′y adj (-i-er; -i-est) 1 containing, or like, milk; 2 giving milk; 3 white like milk

Milk′y Way′ n broad, luminous band encircling the heavens, consisting of countless stars not separately visible to the naked eye; part of the galaxy containing the solar system

mill¹ /mĭl′/ [< L millesimum thousandth] n the tenth of a cent, used as a money of account

mill² [OE mylen < LL molina] n 1 building equipped with machinery to grind grain; 2 any machine for grind-ing solid substances; 3 manufactur-ing plant; 4 **through the mill** colloq through severe trial and discipline ‖ vt 5 to subject to any operation like that performed by a mill; 6 to make a raised border around the edges of (a coin); 7 to put radial grooves on the edges of (a coin) ‖ vi 8 **mill around** or **about** to move around aim-lessly and in great confusion

mil·len·ni·um /mĭlen′ē-əm/ [< L mille thousand + biennium two-year pe-riod] n (-ums or -a /-ə/) 1 period of a thousand years; 2 period of joy and prosperity; 3 **the millenium** the thou-sand years when Christ will reign on earth (Rev. 20:1–5) ‖ **mil·len′ni·al** adj

mill′er n 1 one who owns or operates a grain mill; 2 moth whose wings ap-pear as if covered with flour

mil·les·i·mal /mĭles′imǝl/ [L millesi-mus] adj & n thousandth

mil·let /mĭl′it/ [MF milet] n 1 cereal grass (Panicum miliaceum) native to India, bearing minute seeds used for human food and for fodder; 2 any of various grasses resembling millet

mil·li- [L] comb form 1 thousandth part of; 2 rarely, thousand, as milli-pede

mil′li·am′pere n unit of measure of electrical current, equal to one thou-sandth of an ampere

mil·liard /mĭl′yərd, -yärd/ [F] n Brit billion, one thousand millions

mil·li·bar /mĭl′ibär′/ n cgs unit of pres-sure equal to one thousandth of a bar or 1000 dynes per square centi-meter

mil′li·cur′ie n unit of radioactivity (one thousandth of a curie)

mil′li·gram′ n thousandth part of a gram, equal to 0.0154 grain

mil′li·me′ter n lineal measure equal to the thousandth part of a meter or .03937 of an inch

mil′line′ [million + line] n unit of measurement used in determining ad-vertising cost, equivalent to one agate line in one million copies

mil·li·ner /mĭl′inər/ [var of obs Mila-ner native of Milan] n designer, maker, and/or seller of women's hats

mil′li·ner′y /-ner′ē, -nərē/ n (-ies) 1 articles such as women's hats sold by milliners; 2 business or shop of a milliner

mill′ing n raised edge of a coin, or the radial grooves cut in it

mill′ing ma·chine′ n machine tool with revolving cutters, for cutting gear teeth and producing formed sur-faces on metal pieces

mil·lion /mĭl′yən/ [MF < OIt millione] n 1 ten hundred thousand (1,000,-000); 2 indefinitely large number; 3 **the million** the mass of common peo-ple ‖ also adj ‖ **mil′lionth** adj & n

mil′lion·aire′ /-ner′/ n 1 one whose total wealth comes to at least one million dollars, pounds, or other cur-rency; 2 very rich person

mil·li·pede /mĭl′ipēd′/ [< L mille thou-sand + pes (pedis) foot] n any ar-thropod of the class Diplopoda, hav-ing a body composed of up to 100 or more segments, each with two pairs of legs

mill′pond′ n lake or pond where water is stored to provide power for a mill

mill′race′ n channel through which water is conducted to a mill wheel

mill′stone′ n 1 one of two flat circular stones used for grinding grain; 2 any oppressive burden

mill′stream′ n the stream in a millrace

mill′work′ n woodwork fabricated in a planing mill

mill′wright′ n one who builds mills or installs their machinery

mi·lord /mĭlôrd′/ [< my lord] n Eng-lish nobleman (used in Europe as a term of address)

milque′toast′ /mĭlk′-/ [cartoon char-acter] n meek person who is easily intimidated

milt /mĭlt′/ [OE milte spleen] n 1 male reproductive glands of a fish when filled with seminal fluid; 2 the fluid itself

Mil·ton, John /mĭlt′ən/ n (1608–74) English poet

Mil·wau·kee /mĭlwôk′ē/ n city in SE Wisconsin (741,000)

mime /mīm/ [Gk mimos imitator] n 1 pantomime; 2 mimic; 3 clown ‖ vi 4 to act or play a part, usu. without words ‖ vt 5 to mimic ‖ **mim′er** n

mim′e·o·graph′ /mĭm′ē·ə-/ [former trademark] n 1 apparatus for making copies of anything drawn, written, or typewritten by means of a stencil and an ink roller ‖ vt 2 to make copies of, on a mimeograph

mi·met·ic /mĭmet′ĭk/ [< Gk mimetes

imitator] *adj* pert. to, characterized by, or showing mimicry

mim·ic /mim'ik/ [Gk *mimikos*] *adj* 1 mimetic; 2 mock, simulating the real ‖ *n* 3 imitator; one skilled in mimicry ‖ *v* (**-icked; -ick·ing**) *vt* 4 to ridicule by copying (a person's manners, characteristics, etc.); 5 to copy closely; 6 to simulate ‖ **mim'ick·er** *n* ‖ SYN *v* mock, ape, copy (see *imitate*)

mim'ic·ry *n* (**-ries**) practice, art, or act of mimicking

mi·mo·sa /mimōs'ə, -mōz'ə/ [< Gk *mimos* imitator] *n* any of a genus (*Mimosa*) of herbs, shrubs, and trees growing in warm regions, having small flowers in cylindrical spikes

min. 1 minimum; 2 minute(s)

min·a·ret /min'əret', min'əret'/ [Ar *manārat* lighthouse] *n* tall slender tower attached to a Muslim mosque, containing balconies from which the muezzin calls the faithful to prayer

min·a·to·ry /min'ətôr'ē, -tōr'-/ [< L *minari* to threaten] *adj* threatening; menacing

mince /mins/ [MF *mincier* < LL *minutia* small piece] *vt* 1 to cut or chop into minute pieces; 2 to utter with unnatural and assumed elegance; 3 **not mince words** or **matters** to be blunt ‖ *vi* 4 to behave, act, or speak with affected elegance

mince'meat' *n* 1 finely chopped mixture of raisins, apples, spices, etc., and sometimes meat, used as a filling for pie; 2 anything chopped very fine; 3 **make mincemeat of** *colloq* to chop up, destroy completely

mince' pie' *n* pie with a filling of mincemeat

minc'ing *adj* affectedly dainty (speech, action, or walk)

mind /mīnd/ [< OE *gemynd* memory] *n* 1 remembrance; recollection; 2 seat of consciousness, contemplation, thought, opinion, and feeling; 3 understanding or intellect; 4 sanity; 5 intention; purpose; 6 inclination; choice; 7 person, esp. with regard to his mental attributes; 8 *psychol* entirety of mental experience; aggregate of processes connected with the functioning of the brain and nervous system; 9 spiritual being, opposite of *matter*; 10 **bear** or **keep in mind** to remember; 11 **be in one's right mind** to be sane; 12 **cross one's mind** to occur to one; 13 **have in mind** to intend; 14 **make up one's mind** to decide; 15 **put in mind** to remind ‖ *vt* 16 to pay attention to; 17 to regard with attention; note; 18 to object to, dislike, feel annoyance at; 19 to obey; 20 to watch, tend; 21 *dial.* to remember ‖ *vi* 22 to be obedient; 23 to care, object; 24 to be careful; 25 **never mind** it is nothing; don't bother ‖ SYN *n* understanding, brain (see *intellect*)

-mind'ed *adj* disposed or inclined

-mind'ed *adj comb form* having a specific kind of mind, as in **strongminded**

mind'ful *adj* mindful of heedful of

mind'less *adj* 1 senseless; 2 **mindless of** heedless of-

mind' read'ing *n* ability to read another's thoughts without normal communication ‖ **mind' read'er** *n*

mind's' eye' *n* imagination

mine¹ /mīn/ [MF] *n* 1 excavation from which minerals, precious stones, etc., are dug out; 2 deposit of ore or coal; 3 inexhaustible supply; 4 tunnel run under an enemy's trench or fortification in which a charge of high explosive is fired; 5 device containing a high explosive, on or near the surface of the water, intended to blow up enemy shipping; 6 land mine ‖ *vt* 7 to extract (ore, coal, etc.) from the ground; 8 to dig into, as for ore or coal; 9 to place military mines in or under ‖ *vi* 10 to dig a mine; 11 to extract ore, coal, etc., from the earth; 12 to place military mines ‖ **min'er** *n*

mine² [OE *mīn*] *pron* 1 that or those belonging to me ‖ *adj* 2 (used archaically before a vowel sound or after the noun it modifies) my

mine' de·tec'tor *n* electromagnetic device for locating land mines

mine'field' *n* land or water area sown with explosive mines

mine'lay'er *n* *nav* ship equipped for laying mines in the water

min·er·al /min'(ə)rəl/ [< ML *minera* mine] *n* 1 any substance not animal or vegetable in origin; anything inorganic; 2 any of a large group of natural inorganic substances having a homogeneous structure, a specific chemical composition, uniform physical characteristics, and usu. a definite form of crystal; 3 any substance exhibiting similar properties as the result of inorganic processes, as coal; 4 ore ‖ *adj* 5 pert. to, of the nature of, or containing a mineral or minerals; 6 inorganic

min·er·al·ize *vt* 1 to transform (a metal) into an ore; 2 to impregnate with minerals

min·er·al·o·gy /-rol'əjē, -ral'-/ *n* science of minerals ‖ **min'er·al·o·gist** *n*

min·er·al oil' *n* colorless oil distilled from petroleum, used as a lubricant and as a laxative

min·er·al wa'ter *n* water containing dissolved mineral salts or gases, used for medicinal purposes

min·er·al wool' *n* insulating material made from molten slag or rock

Mi·ner·va /minurv'ə/ *n* *class. myth.* goddess of wisdom and handicrafts or invention

min·e·stro·ne /min'istrōn'ē/ [It] *n* rich, thick soup containing meat and vegetables

mine′ sweep′er *n nav* ship equipped for destroying or removing mines from the water

Ming /miŋ′/ *n* Chinese dynasty (1368–1644) noted for the development of the arts, esp. in porcelain and painting

min·gle /miŋ′gəl/ [OE *mengan* to mix] *vt* **1** to combine by mixing; blend; **2** to prepare by mixing; concoct ‖ *vi* **3** to associate; come together; participate; **4** to become mixed or united ‖ SYN unite, intermingle, join, merge (see *mix*)

min·i·a·ture /min′(ē)əchər/ [It *miniatura*] *n* **1** very small painting, esp. a portrait on ivory; **2** something greatly reduced in size; **3 in miniature** on a greatly reduced scale ‖ *adj* **4** done on a very small scale; minute

min′i·a·tur·ize′ *vt* to produce in microscopic form, as electronic circuits and equipment ‖ **min′i·a·tur·i·za′tion** *n*

Min·ié ball′ /min′ē/ [C. E. *Minié* (1814–79) F inventor] *n* muzzle-loading bullet with a hollow base which expands when fired, the standard rifle bullet of the Civil War

min·im /min′im/ [L *minimus* smallest] *n* **1** smallest liquid measure, one sixtieth of a fluid dram, about one drop; **2** tiny quantity of anything ‖ *adj* **3** smallest

min·i·ma /min′imə/ *pl* of **minimum**

min′i·mize′ *vt* **1** to reduce to, or estimate at, a minimum; **2** to belittle

min′i·mum /-məm/ [L] *n̄* (**-mums** or **-ma** /-mə/) **1** least quantity; **2** lowest point reached or recorded; **3** least quantity admissible ‖ *adj* **4** lowest; least possible or allowable ‖ **min′i·mal** *adj*

min·ing /mīn′iŋ/ *n* **1** act, process, or business of extracting ore, coal, etc. from the ground; **2** the placing of military mines

min·ion /min′yən/ [MF *mignon* darling] *n* **1** obsequious favorite, attendant, or dependent; **2** subordinate; minor official

min′i·skirt′ /min′ē-/ *n* extremely short skirt, ending a couple of inches above the knee

min·is·ter /min′istər/ [L = servant] *n* **1** in some countries, official entrusted by the head of a government with the direction of a government department; **2** diplomatic agent, of lower rank than an ambassador; **3** clergyman or pastor ‖ *vi* **4** to serve as pastor of a church; **5 minister to** to serve, attend to ‖ *vt* **6** to administer ‖ **min′is·te′ri·al** /-tir′ē-əl/ *adj*

min′is·ter with·out′ port·fo′li·o *n* government minister not assigned to a specific department

min′is·trant *adj* **1** ministering ‖ *n* **2** one who ministers

min′is·tra′tion *n* **1** act of serving as a

pastor; **2** act of helping, aiding, attending, or the like; service; aid

min′is·try *n* (**-tries**) **1** ministration; service; **2** service, office, or tenure of a minister; **3** clergy; **4** a government department in some countries; **b** building which houses it

min·i·um /min′ē-əm/ [L = cinnabar] *n* red lead

mink /miŋk/ [ME] *n* **1** semiaquatic weasellike mammal (*Mustela vison*); **2** its valuable fur; **3** woman's mink coat

Minn. Minnesota

Min·ne·ap·o·lis /min′ē-ap′əlis/ *n* city in SE Minnesota (434,400)

min·ne·sing·er /min′isiŋ′ər/ [G] *n* medieval German troubadour

Min·ne·so·ta /min′isōt′ə/ *n* state in the N central U.S. (3,805,000; 84,068 sq. m.; cap. St. Paul) ‖ **Min′ne·so′tan** *n*

min·now /min′ō/ [OE *myne*] *n* **1** any of several fresh-water fishes of the carp family; **2** any similar small fish

Mi·no·an /minō′ən/ *adj* of or pert. to the pre-Greek civilization of Crete, ab. 3000 to 1100 B.C. ‖ also *n*

mi·nor /mīn′ər/ [L = less] *adj* **1** less in quantity, number, importance, or extent; **2** of little consequence or importance; **3** under legal age; **4** *mus* lower by a half tone than the corresponding major ‖ *n* **5** one under legal age; **6** subject complementary to a student's major; **7 the minors** *pl sports* the minor leagues ‖ *vi* **8 minor in** to take a (minor subject) in college

mi·nor·i·ty /minor′itē, -nôr′-, mī-/ [ML *minoritas*] *n* (**-ties**) **1** smaller part or number; **2** group differing from the majority of a population, as in race or religion; **3** state or period of being under legal age

mi′nor league′ *n* professional sports league of less than the top rank ‖ **mi′nor lea′guer** *n*

mi′nor scale′ *n mus* scale having half steps between the second and third, fifth and sixth, and seventh and eighth degrees

Min·o·taur /min′ətôr′/ *n Gk myth.* monster with a bull's head and a man's body, kept in the Cretan Labyrinth, which periodically devoured seven youths and seven maidens sent as tribute from Athens, until slain by Theseus

min·ster /min′stər/ [OE *mynster*] *n Brit* **1** church monastery; **2** cathedral

min·strel /min′strəl/ [OF *menestrel*] *n* **1** medieval traveling poet and musician; **2** poet or musician; **3** one of a troupe of singers and comedians made up as black people

min′strel·sy *n* (**-sies**) **1** art or practice of minstrels; **2** collection of minstrels' ballads or lyrics

mint¹ /mint′/ [OE *minte* < Gk *minthe*] *n* **1** any of a large family (Labiatae) of aromatic-leaved herbs, esp. any of a genus (*Mentha*) extensively used in condiments and as the source of flavoring extracts; 2 mint-flavored confection

mint² [OE *mynet* coin < L *moneta*] n 1 place where money is coined or printed under government authority; 2 vast amount, as of money || vt 3 to coin or stamp (money); 4 to invent, make

mint′age /-ij-/ n 1 act of minting money; 2 coinage; 3 cost of minting; 4 imprint upon a coin

mint′ con·di′tion n **in mint condition** new and unused, as if just made in a mint

mint′ ju′lep n julep made with bourbon and garnished with mint

min·u·end /min′yōō·end′/ [L *minuendus* to be diminished] n number from which another number is to be subtracted

min·u·et /min′yōō·et′/ [F *menuet*] n 1 slow and stately dance in triple measure in vogue from the 17th to the 19th century; 2 music for it

mi·nus /mīn′əs/ [L = less] prep 1 less, decreased by; 2 without || adj 3 negative || n 4 minus sign; 5 minus quantity; 6 deficiency

mi′nus sign′ n symbol —, indicating subtraction or a negative quantity

min·ute¹ /min′it/ [ML *minuta* small] n 1 sixtieth part of an hour; 2 sixtieth part of a degree of arc; 3 short time, moment; 4 **minutes** pl proceedings of a meeting as officially recorded; 5 **up to the minute** up-to-date

mi·nute² /min′yōōt′, mī-/ [L *minutus* small] adj 1 very small; 2 of trifling importance; 3 exact, precise || **mi·nute′ly** adv

min′ute·man′ /-man′/ n (-**men** /-men′/) in the American Revolution, citizen ready to take up arms against the British at a minute's notice

mi·nu·ti·ae /min(y)ōōsh′ē·ē′/ [< L *minutia* smallness] npl small or trivial details

minx /minks′/ [?] n bold or saucy girl

Mi·o·cene /mī′əsēn′/ [< Gk *meion* less + *kainos* recent] n geol epoch of the Tertiary period of ten to 25 million years ago, characterized by the presence of grazing mammals

mir·a·cle /mir′əkəl/ [OE *miracul* < L *miraculum*] n 1 act or happening in the physical world that departs from the laws of nature; supernatural occurrence; 2 marvel, wonder || **mi·rac·u·lous** /mirak′yələs/ adj

mir′a·cle play′ n medieval dramatic representation of events related in the Bible

mi·rage /miräzh′/ [F] n 1 optical illusion caused by heat inversion in the atmosphere, whereby objects beyond the horizon appear close by, often distorted or inverted; 2 something illusory

mire /mī′(ə)r/ [ON *myrr*] n 1 deep mud; wet earth; slush; dirt || vt 2 to soil; 3 to cause to be stuck in mud || vi 4 to stick; sink into mud || **mir′y** adj (-i·er; -i·est)

mir·ror /mir′ər/ [OF *mirour* < LL *mirare* to look at] n 1 reflecting surface of silvered glass; 2 any smooth surface that reflects images; 3 anything that represents a true likeness; 4 model, pattern || vt 5 to reflect, as in a mirror

mirth /murth′/ [OE *myrigth*] n hilarity; gaiety, merriment || **mirth′ful** adj || SYN hilarity, glee, joyousness, jollity, gladness

MIRV /murv′/ [multiple independently targeted reentry vehicle] n missile with separate warheads designed to strike separate enemy targets on re-entering the atmosphere

mis- /mis-, mis′-/ [OE] pref bad(ly); wrong(ly); mistaken(ly)

mis′ad·ven′ture n 1 mishap; piece of bad luck; 2 misfortune

mis′al·li′ance [modeled on F *mésalliance*] n improper or undesirable alliance, esp. in marriage

mis·an·thrope /mis′ənthrōp′/ [< Gk *misein* to hate + *anthropos* man] n one who hates mankind || **mis′an·throp′ic** (-i·cal) /-throp′-/ adj || **mis·an′thro·py** /-an′thrəpē/ n

mis′ap·ply′ v (-plied) vt to apply badly or wrongly || **mis′ap·pli·ca′tion** n

mis′ap·pre·hend′ vt to misunderstand || **mis′ap·pre·hen′sion** n

mis′ap·pro′pri·ate′ vt to apply to a wrong or dishonest use or purpose, as money || **mis′ap·pro′pri·a′tion** n

mis′be·got′ten adj wrongfully begotten; illegitimate

mis′be·have′ vi 1 to behave badly or wrongly || vt 2 to conduct (oneself) badly or wrongfully || **mis′be·hav′ior** n

mis′be·lief′ n wrong or false opinion or conviction

misc. 1 miscellaneous; 2 miscellany

mis·cal′cu·late′ vt & vi to calculate incorrectly; misjudge || **mis·cal′cu·la′tion** n

mis·call′ vt to call by a wrong name

mis·car′riage n 1 failure to reach a just or desired result; 2 abortion; premature expulsion of a nonviable fetus

mis·car′ry v (-ried) vi 1 to go wrong; go astray; 2 to have a miscarriage of a fetus

mis·cast′ v (-cast) vt 1 to cast (an actor) in an unsuitable part; 2 to cast (a play) with unsuitable actors

mis·ce·ge·na·tion /mis′ijənāsh′ən/ [< L *miscere* to mix + *genus* race] n marriage or sexual relations between persons presumed to be of different races

mis·cel·la·ne·a /mis′əlān′ē·ə/ [L = mixed things] npl assortment, collection, as of writings

mis·cel·la·ne·ous adj 1 consisting of

several kinds; **2** many-sided; consisting of various qualities

mis'cel·la'ny *n* (**-nies**) miscellaneous collection of things, as of literary writings

mis·chance' *n* misfortune; mishap ‖ SYN accident, calamity, misadventure, hardship

mis·chief /mis'chif/ [OF *meschief* calamity] *n* **1** harm; injury, damage; **2** source of vexation or annoyance; **3** tendency to vex or annoy; **4** vexatious or annoying action ‖ SYN detriment, damage, prank (see *injury*)

mis'chief-mak'er *n* **1** troublemaker; **2** one who stirs up discord

mis'chie·vous *adj* **1** causing mischief; **2** full of pranks; causing annoyance to others

mis·ci·ble /mis'ibəl/ [< L *miscere* to mix] *adj* capable of being readily mixed ‖ **mis'ci·bil'i·ty** /-bil'-/ *n*

mis'con·ceive' *vt* & *vi* to misunderstand

mis'con·cep'tion *n* erroneous conception; mistaken idea ‖ SYN delusion, misapprehension, mistake

mis·con'duct *n* **1** improper or wrong behavior ‖ **mis'con·duct'** *vt* **2** to manage badly; **3** to conduct (oneself) improperly ‖ SYN *n* misdemeanor, misdeed, misbehavior, impropriety, deliquency, mismanagement

mis'con·strue' *vt* to misinterpret ‖ **mis'con·struc'tion** *n*

mis·cre·ant /mis'krē·ənt/ [OF *mescreant* unbelieving] *n* **1** villain; evildoer ‖ *adj* **2** villainous ‖ SYN *n* evildoer, rascal, caitiff, ruffian, scoundrel

mis·cue' *n* **1** *sports* error; **2** *theat* wrong cue ‖ *v* (**-cu·ing**) *vi* **3** to make a miscue

mis·deal' *v* (**-dealt** /-delt'/) *cards vt* & *vi* **1** to deal wrongly ‖ *n* **2** wrong deal

mis·deed' *n* wrong or wicked deed ‖ SYN misconduct, offense, misdemeanor, trespass

mis'de·mean'or *n* **1** ill conduct; **2** *law* indictable offense of less seriousness than a felony ‖ SYN misconduct, offense, misbehavior, misdeed, transgression, fault, trespass

mis'di·rect' *vt* **1** to direct wrongly or badly; **2** to address wrongly, as a letter ‖ **mis'di·rec'tion** *n*

mi·ser /mīz'ər/ [L = wretched] *n* one who accumulates money for its own sake; stingy, covetous person

mis·er·a·ble /miz'(ə)rəbəl/ *adj* **1** wretched; unhappy; pitiable; **2** causing misery; **3** worthless, mean ‖ **mis'er·a·bly** *adv* ‖ SYN distressed, afflicted, lamentable, worthless, paltry, forlorn, wretched, abject ‖ ANT happy, worthy

mi·ser·ly /mī'-/ *adj* characteristic of a miser; grasping ‖ SYN close, penurious, mean, stingy

mis·er·y /miz'ərē/ *n* (**-ies**) **1** extreme pain, distress, or misfortune; wretchedness; **2** cause of distress ‖ SYN wretchedness, despondency, suffering, anguish, privation, destitution ‖ ANT happiness, health, comfort

mis·fea·sance /misfēz'əns/ [MF *mesfaisance*] *n* *law* **1** doing of a lawful act in an illegal manner; **2** wrongful exercise of lawful authority

mis·fire' *vi* **1** to fail to explode or be discharged, as a gun or shell, or the fuel in a cylinder; **2** to fail to do what is expected or hoped for ‖ *n* **3** instance of misfiring

mis·fit' *n* **1** clothing which is too large or too small; **2** person not suited to his environment or position

mis·for'tune *n* **1** adversity, trouble; **2** calamity, mishap ‖ SYN hardship, calamity, mishap (see *trouble*)

mis·giv'ing *n* feeling of doubt or anxiety; apprehension ‖ SYN presentiment, doubt, anxiety, premonition, presage (see *foreboding*)

mis·gov'ern *vt* to govern badly ‖ **mis·gov'ern·ment** *n*

mis·guid'ed *adj* misled

mis·hap /mis'hap/ [*mis-* + ME *hap* to happen] *n* unlucky accident ‖ SYN mischance, misfortune, calamity (see *trouble*)

mish·mash /mish'mash'/ [reduplication of *mash*] *n* confused mixture, hodgepodge

mis'in·form' *vt* to give false information to ‖ **mis'in·for·ma'tion** *n*

mis'in·ter'pret *vt* to interpret wrongly ‖ **mis'in·ter'pre·ta'tion** *n*

mis·judge' *vt* & *vi* to judge wrongly

mis·lay' *v* (**-laid**) *vt* to put in a wrong or forgotten place

mis·lead' *v* (**-led**) *vt* **1** to deceive; delude; misguide; **2** to lead in the wrong direction; **3** to lead into wrongdoing ‖ **mis·lead'ing** *adj*

mis·man'age *vt* & *vi* to manage badly ‖ **mis·man'age·ment** *n*

mis·match' *vt* **1** to match badly ‖ *n* **2** bad match

mis·name' *vt* to call by a wrong name

mis·no·mer /misnōm'ər/ [MF *mesnomer* to misname] *n* name applied in error

miso- [Gk] *comb form* hatred of

mi·sog·a·my /misog'əmē/ [< *miso-* + Gk *gamos* marriage] *n* hatred of marriage ‖ **mi·sog'a·mist** *n*

mi·sog·y·ny /misoj'inē/ [< *miso-* + Gk *gyne* woman] *n* hatred of women ‖ **mi·sog'y·nous** *adj* ‖ **mi·sog'y·nist** *n*

mis·place' *vt* **1** to put in a wrong or forgotten place; **2** to place wrongly or unwisely ‖ **mis·place'ment** *n*

mis·print' *vt* **1** to print incorrectly ‖ **mis'print'** *n* **2** typographical error

mis·pri·sion /misprizh'ən/ [OF *mesprision* mistake] *n* *law* **1** wrongful act by a public official; **2** concealment of a crime, or failure to prevent its commission, esp. the crime of treason

mis'pro·nounce' *vt* & *vi* to pronounce

incorrectly ‖ **mis′pro·nun′ci·a′tion** n

mis·quote′ vt & vi to quote incorrectly ‖ **mis′quo·ta′tion** n

mis·read′ v (**-read** /-red′/) vt to misinterpret; read incorrectly ‖ **mis-read′ing** n

mis′rep·re·sent′ vt to represent falsely; give a wrong impression of ‖ **mis′-rep·re·sen·ta′tion** n ‖ SYN equivocate, lie, deceive (see *prevaricate*)

mis·rule′ vt 1 to misgovern ‖ n 2 misgovernment

miss[1] /mis′/ [OE *missan*] vi 1 to fail to hit, find, attain, catch, or the like; 2 to feel the need of; feel the loss or absence of; 3 to omit or pass by; fail to observe, keep, etc.; 4 to avoid or escape, as *he just missed getting hit* ‖ vi 5 to fail to make a hit; fly wide of the mark; 6 to fail ‖ n 7 failure to hit, reach, see, or obtain ‖ SYN v overlook, lose, omit, escape, fail, skip ‖ ANT v notice, keep, succeed, get, obtain, achieve

miss[2] [< *mistress*] n 1 young girl or unmarried woman; 2 **Miss** title used before the name of, or in addressing, a young girl or unmarried woman

Miss. Mississippi

mis·sal /mis′əl/ [< LL *missa* mass] n R C Ch 1 book containing the order of service for the Mass; 2 any book of devotions

mis·shap·en /mis·shāp′ən/ [*mis-* + *shape*] adj deformed; distorted

mis·sile /mis′əl/ [L *missilis* something thrown] n 1 projectile, weapon, or other object suitable for hurling or shooting; 2 guided missile

mis′sile gap′ n disparity between the nuclear striking power of one nation and that of another

mis′sile·ry also **mis′sil·ry** n science dealing with the building and use of guided missiles and rockets

miss′ing adj lost; lacking; absent

miss′ing link′ n 1 hypothetical creature assumed to have existed between the anthropoid ape and man; 2 gap in a series or sequence

miss′ing per′son n person who cannot be found or accounted for after an accident or military engagement

mis·sion /mish′ən/ [L *missio* (*-onis*) a sending] n 1 act of sending or state of being sent, with certain powers, to do some special service; 2 assigned task; 3 diplomatic delegation; 4 calling, esp. to preach and spread religion; 5 series of special religious services; 6 organization for doing religious and charitable work; 7 body of people sent to perform a special work; 8 a body of missionaries; b their organization and residence

mis′sion·ar′y n (**-ies**) 1 person who is sent to spread the knowledge of a religion and convert people to it, esp. in foreign lands; 2 person who propagandizes ‖ also adj

Mis·sis·sip·pi /mis′isip′ē/ n state in the

S U.S. on the Gulf of Mexico (2,217,000; 47,716 sq.m.; cap. Jackson) ‖ **Mis′sis·sip′pi·an** n

Mis′sis·sip′pi Riv′er n river flowing from N Minnesota to the Gulf of Mexico in Louisiana, principal river of the U.S.

mis·sive /mis′iv/ [MF *lettre missive* sent letter] n letter or written message

Mis·sour·i /mizŏŏr′ē, -zŏŏr′ə/ n state in the central U.S. (4,677,000; 69,674 sq.m.; cap. Jefferson City) ‖ **Missour′i·an** n

Mis·sour′i Riv′er n one of the major rivers of the U.S., flowing from Montana into the Mississippi at St. Louis

mis·spell′ v (**-spelled** or **-spelt** /-spelt′/) vt & vi to spell incorrectly ‖ **mis-spell′ing** n

mis·spent′ adj squandered; wasted

mis·state′ vt to state falsely or incorrectly ‖ **mis·state′ment** n

mis·step′ n 1 wrong step; 2 error in conduct

mist /mist′/ [OE] n 1 visible watery vapor in the atmosphere at or near the earth's surface; 2 fog; 3 anything that dims or obscures ‖ vi 4 to rain in fine drops; 5 to become misty ‖ vt 6 to make misty

mis·take′ [ON *mistaka*] v (**-took; -tak-en**) vt 1 to misunderstand; 2 to identify wrongly in place of another person or thing ‖ vi 3 to err ‖ n 4 error; 5 fault; misunderstanding ‖ **mis·tak′a·ble** adj ‖ SYN n oversight, misapprehension (see *blunder*)

mis·tak′en adj 1 incorrect, wrong; 2 wrong in judgment; 3 misunderstood; misinterpreted ‖ **mis·tak′en·ly** adv

mis·ter /mist′ər/ [< *master*] n 1 colloq sir; 2 **Mister**, a title prefixed to a man's name or office, usu. written *Mr.*; b title used in addressing warrant officers and cadets in the armed forces, and naval officers below the rank of commander

mis·tle·toe /mis′əltō′/ [OE *mistiltān* mistletoe twig] n 1 semiparasitic European evergreen plant (*Viscum album*) that bears waxy white berries; 2 similar plant (*Phoradendron flavescens*) found in the U.S.

mis·took′ pt of **mistake**

mis·tral /mist′rəl, misträl′/ [Prov = master wind] n dry, violent wind coming from the north in the Mediterranean departments of France

mis·treat′ vt to treat badly, abuse ‖ **mis·treat′ment** n

mis·tress /mis′tris/ [MF *maistresse*] n 1 female head of a family, school, or the like; 2 female owner, as of an animal; 3 female employer of servants; 4 woman or nation having the mastery or control of anything; 5 female paramour; 6 **Mistress** title formerly used before a woman's name, now superseded by *Mrs.*, *Miss*, or *Ms.*

mis·tri/al *n* court trial which is void because of an error in procedure or inability of the jury to agree

mis·trust/ *n* 1 lack of trust or confidence ‖ *vt & vi* 2 to doubt; suspect; distrust ‖ **mis·trust/ful** *adj* ‖ SYN *n* doubt, suspicion, misgiving, question

mist·y /mist/ē/ [< *mist*] *adj* (**-i·er; -i·est**) 1 characterized by, or hidden by, mist; 2 dim, obscure ‖ **mist/i·ness** *n*

mis/un·der·stand/ *v* (**-stood**) *vt* to take in a wrong sense, misinterpret

mis/un·der·stand/ing *n* 1 disagreement, quarrel; 2 mistake as to meaning

mis·use/ /-yōōs/ *n* 1 wrong or improper use ‖ /-yōōz/ *vt* 2 to use wrongly; 3 to abuse ‖ **mis·us/age** /-yōōs/ij, -yōōz/ij/ *n*

mite[1] /mīt/ [OE] *n* any of a large variety of arachnids (order Acarina) infesting plants, animals, stored foods, etc.

mite[2] [MD] *n* 1 very small amount of money; 2 very small person, thing, or amount; 3 **a mite** somewhat

mi·ter /mīt/ər/ [Gk *mitra* fillet, turban] *n* 1 tall clefted hat worn by bishops and abbots; 2 dignity or office of a bishop; 3 covering over a chimney to keep out the rain; 4 *carp* beveled surface in contact with a similar surface on another piece, the contact forming a right-angled joint between the two pieces ‖ *vt* 5 to raise to the rank of bishop; to bestow a miter upon; 6 to join, as moldings, on a beveled surface or line at a corner

mi/ter box/ *n* device for guiding a handsaw in making cuts at various angles

mi/ter joint/ *n* right-angled joint between two pieces

mi/ter square/ *n* instrument with two arms or blades for marking pieces for a miter joint

mit·i·gate /mit/igāt/ [L *mitigare* (**-atus**)] *vt* 1 to lessen in force, intensity, severity, or painfulness ‖ *vi* 2 to abate; moderate ‖ **mit/i·ga/tor** *n* ‖ **mit/i·ga/tion** *n* ‖ SYN assuage, alleviate, relieve, abate, allay ‖ DISCR These words have in common the idea of giving relief. We *alleviate* suffering, distress, want, by doing as much as possible to remove the cause. We *assuage* by comforting, as grief; by quieting, as passion; by calming or appeasing, as appetite. We *allay* suffering, passion, excitement, by soothing and quieting. To *mitigate* is to make pain, grief, punishment, or the like, milder

mi·to·sis /mītōs/is, mi-/ [< Gk *mitos* thread] *n* series of changes that take place in the nucleus and protoplasm of a cell in the usual process of division

mi/tral value/ /mīt/rəl/ [< *miter*] *n* valve that controls the flow of blood between the left auricle and left ventricle of the heart

mitt /mit/ [< *mitten*] *n* 1 baseball glove with a thick pad over the palm; 2 mitten; 3 *slang* hand

mit·ten /mit/ən/ [MF *mitaine*] *n* 1 glove covering the four fingers together and the thumb separately; 2 *slang* boxing glove

mix /miks/ [< F *mixte* mixed] *vt* 1 to blend into one mass; 2 to join, associate; 3 to make by mixing; 4 **mix up** to confuse; 5 **mix up in** to involve in; 6 **mix it up** *slang* to engage in a fight, esp. with the fists ‖ *vi* 7 to become mixed; 8 to mingle ‖ *n* 9 act of mixing; 10 mixture; 11 *colloq* muddle ‖ SYN *v* compound, amalgamate, fuse, incorporate, mingle, blend, merge, coalesce, unite ‖ DISCR To *unite* is to bring together or make one, as to *unite* broken fragments with cement or a torn page with glue, to *unite* common interests in a common company, to *unite* by a bridge cities separated by a river. To *mix* is to *unite*, as two or more substances, so that the one substance is thoroughly permeated with the other in a promiscuous body, as to *mix* the dry ingredients of a cake. The States in this Union are *united;* the population is a *mixed* group from all other nations. To *mingle* is to join, as one substance or color with another, so that the two elements joined are distinguishable, as a complexion of *mingled* white and pink; people received the news with *mingled* joy and pain. To *blend* is to *mix* elements or parts into a whole in which they are inseparable and indistinguishable, as to *blend* coffees, colors; to *blend* type characteristics by intermarriage. To *merge* is to lose utterly, or to cause an utter loss of, identity in the whole; several companies *merge*, or are *merged* to form one. *Coalesce* stresses the act or process of forming one, as the opposing parties *coalesced* to gain strength ‖ ANT *v* separate, divide, part, scatter

mixed/ *adj* 1 blended; 2 composed of unlike parts or elements; 3 (stock market) moving in both directions; irregular; 4 made up of or designed for persons of both sexes; 5 *gram* inflected by change in both root and suffix; 6 **mixed up** muddled, confused

mixed/ mar/riage *n* marriage between persons of different religions or races

mixed/ met/a·phor/ *n* expression consisting of two or more figures of speech incongruous with each other

mixed/ num/ber *n* number consisting of a whole number and a fraction

mix/er *n* 1 one who or that which mixes; 2 kitchen appliance for blending foods; 3 mixing faucet; 4 one who readily adapts himself in any company

mix′ing fau′cet *n* faucet that mixes hot and cold water in any desired proportion

mix′ture /-chər/ *n* 1 act of mixing or state of being mixed; 2 that which is mixed; 3 *chem* aggregate of different substances which are not chemically united into one compound

mix′-up′ *n* tangle; confused muddle

miz·zen /miz′ən/ *n* 1 mizzenmast; 2 fore-and-aft sail on a mizzenmast

miz′zen-mast′ /-mast′, -mäst′, *naut* -məst/ *n* the aftermost mast of a vessel having three or more masts

mks meter-kilogram-second

ML, M.L. Medieval Latin

MLG, M.L.G. Middle Low German

Mlle. (Mlles.) Mademoiselle

mm. millimeter(s)

Mme. (Mmes.) Madame

Mn *chem* manganese

mne·mon·ic /nimon′ik/ [< Gk *mneme* memory] *adj* 1 aiding or improving the memory; 2 pert. to the memory ‖ *n* 3 **mnemonics** *sg* art or science of improving the memory

Mne·mos·y·ne /nĕmos′ənē, -moz′-/ *n* Gk *myth.* goddess of memory, mother of the Muses

Mo *chem* molybdenum

Mo. 1 Missouri; 2 Monday

mo. (mos.) month

M.O. 1 money order; 2 method of operation

mo·a /mō′ə/ [< Maori] *n* any of several extinct species (family Dinornithidae) of flightless birds of New Zealand, resembling the ostrich

moan /mōn/ [ME *mone*] *n* 1 long low sound expressing sorrow or pain; 2 any similar sound, as the sighing of the wind ‖ *vi* 3 to utter moans ‖ *vt* 4 to utter in a moaning voice; 5 to bewail

moat /mōt/ [OF *mote* mound] *n* defensive ditch around a castle or fortress, usu. containing water

mob /mob/ [< L *mobile vulgus* excitable crowd] *n* 1 riotous crowd bent on lawless violence; 2 any group of people crowded together; 3 the masses; 4 criminal gang ‖ *v* **(mobbed; mob·bing)** *vt* 5 to attack in a disorderly mob; 6 to crowd about riotously ‖ SYN *n* crowd, multitude, rabble (see *throng*)

mo·bile /mōb′əl, mō′bēl/ [L *mobilis* movable] *adj* 1 movable; easily moved; 2 easily changing in expression ‖ *n* 3 piece of sculpture suspended in midair with parts balanced so as to move independently ‖ **mo·bil′i·ty** /-bil′-/ *n*

Mo·bile /mō′bēl/ *n* seaport in Alabama (205,000)

mo′bile home′ *n* trailer designed and used as a permanent dwelling

mo′bi·lize′ /mō′biliz′/ *vt* 1 to call (troops) into service; 2 to put (industry, transport, etc.) on a war footing; 3 to marshal (forces, energy, wealth, etc.) for action ‖ *vi* 4 to be mobilized ‖ **mo′bi·li·za′tion** *n*

mob′ rule′ *n* seizure and control of government by a mob

mob·ster /mob′stər/ *n* member of a criminal gang

moc·ca·sin /mok′əsin/ [< Algonquian] *n* 1 heelless shoe of soft leather, without laces; 2 cottonmouth, water moccasin

mo·cha /mok′ə/ [*Mocha* Arabia] *n* 1 superior kind of coffee originally from Arabia; 2 flavor made from coffee, usu. with chocolate added

mock /mok/ [MF *mocquer*] *vt* 1 to ridicule; 2 to deride by mimicking; 3 to disappoint; 4 to mimic; counterfeit; 5 to defy ‖ *vi* 6 to jeer, scoff ‖ *adj* 7 imitation ‖ **mock′er** *n* ‖ SYN *v* ridicule, ape, mimic (see *taunt, imitate*)

mock′er·y *n* (**-ies**) 1 act of mocking; 2 derision; ridicule; 3 impertinent mimicry; 4 sham, travesty ‖ SYN derision, mimicry (see *ridicule*)

mock′ing·bird′ *n* grayish songbird (*Mimus polyglottos*) of the S U.S., noted for its ability to imitate the songs of other birds

mock′up′ *n* full-size scale model of a new machine or weapon, usu. made for testing

mod /mod/ [< *modern*] *n* 1 ultrastylish and sophisticated young person aping Edwardian manners and dress ‖ *adj* 2 ultrastylish and sophisticated; unconventional

mod·al /mōd′əl/ [see **mode**] *adj* 1 pert. to mode, manner, or form; 2 *gram* pert. to or expressing mood

mod′al aux·il′ia·ry *n* any of a small set of English auxiliary verbs, as *can, shall, must,* that have only finite forms and are used with infinitives (without the preposition *to*) to express mood and tense

mo·dal′i·ty /-dal′-/ *n* (**-ties**) 1 characteristic or fact of consisting of manner or form only; 2 *logic* quality of a proposition as expressing a sequence which is possible, contingent, impossible, or necessary

mode /mōd/ [L *modus* manner] *n* 1 method; manner; form; 2 custom; 3 fashion; 4 *gram* mood¹; 5 *mus* scale ‖ SYN fashion, style, vogue, way, method ‖ DISCR *Fashion* is the prevailing custom according to the current conventional usage of polite society, especially in dress, as short sleeves are in *fashion;* bright colors are the *fashion. Mode* names the general *fashion,* especially of a particular time, as her sleeves were in the *mode* of yesterday. *Style* is *fashion* so distinctively followed that there is a superiority and lack of commonplaceness in the result, as her clothes had a touch of Parisian *style. Vogue* is the latest, generally current *style;* it is usually expressive of the temporary gusts of *fashion*

mod·el /mod'əl/ [MF *modelle* < OIt *modello*] *n* 1 pattern or example of something to be made, copied, or imitated; 2 small-sized representation of something to be made; 3 style, type, or design; 4 one who poses for a painter or sculptor; 5 person who displays clothes or demonstrates products by wearing or using them for potential customers ‖ *v* (-eled or -elled; -el·ing or -el·ling) *vt* 6 to form after a pattern; 7 to make a model of; 8 to fashion; 9 to wear (clothes) for display ‖ *vi* 10 to make models; 11 to serve as a model ‖ *adj* 12 serving as a model; 13 worthy of being imitated ‖ **mod'el·er** *n*

Mod'el T' *n* 1 car manufactured by the Ford Motor Company in the period 1908–28; 2 *colloq* flivver ‖ *adj* 3 primitive, rudimentary; 4 outmoded

mod·er·ate /mod'ərit/ (-*atus*) to regulate] *adj* 1 kept or staying within reasonable bounds, not extreme or excessive; 2 limited; medium ‖ *n* 3 person of moderate views in politics or religion ‖ /-āt'/ *vt* 4 to make moderate; 5 to preside over (a public forum) ‖ *vi* 6 to become moderate ‖ **mod'er·ate·ly** *adv* ‖ **mod'er·a'tion** *n* ‖ SYN *adj* temperate, abstemious, sober, gentle, reasonable ‖ ANT *adj* intemperate, unrestrained

mod·e·ra·to /mod'ərät'ō/ [It] *adj mus* medium or moderate in tempo ‖ also *n*

mod·er·a'tor *n* 1 one who presides over a public forum, panel discussion, or quiz show; 2 presiding official of the Presbyterian Church; 3 substance, such as graphite, used for slowing down neutrons in a reactor

mod·ern /mod'ərn/ [LL *modernus*] *adj* 1 pert. to the present time; recent; 2 up-to-date, not antiquated; 3 pert. to contemporary styles of art, music, and literature ‖ *n* 4 person of present or recent times; 5 person of modern views and tastes ‖ SYN *adj* recent, new, novel, late, fresh ‖ DISCR That is *new* which has not existed before or long, as a *new* periodical; a *new* recipe. *New* also describes that which is for the first time made, perceived, brought into use, discovered, or experienced, as a *new* discovery, fashion, sensation; or that which is unfamiliar, or appearing for the first time in season, as a *new* face; *new* peas. That is *fresh* which has just been made or received, as *fresh* butter, a *fresh* copy, or is young, vigorous, tonic, or active, as *fresh* faces; *fresh* air; *fresh* energy. *Recent* is applied to things that have happened in the near past, or are in

a comparatively *new* state, as a *recent* discovery. *Late* is like *recent* in applying to that just past, as of *late* years; but it is especially used in the sense of former but not present or current, as the *late* president; and also in the sense of lately deceased, as her *late* husband. *Modern* describes the present period in contrast with times quite remote. A *modern* invention is a thing of today; a book on *modern* warfare would go back to the beginning of what is now prevalent. A *novel* idea is strange, not before conceived; a *novel* experiment has been hitherto unknown

Mod'ern Eng'lish *n* the English language from about 1500 to the present

mod·ern·ism *n* 1 thing of recent date, esp. a usage, method, or characteristic of present times; 2 **Modernism**, a R C Ch theological method based on modern scholarship, which attempts to reconcile the church dogmas with modern science and philosophy, and with modern Biblical criticism; condemned by Pope Pius X in 1907; **b** liberal theological movement of the 20th century in Protestantism ‖ **mod'ern·ist** *n* ‖ **mod'ern·is'tic** *adj*

mo·der·ni·ty /modurn'itē/ *n* (-ties) 1 something modern; 2 quality of being modern

mod'ern·ize *vt* 1 to make modern ‖ *vi* 2 to become modern

mod·est /mod'ist/ [L *modestus* moderate] *adj* 1 having a humble estimate of oneself, not vain; 2 unpretentious; 3 decent and decorous in dress and behavior; 4 moderate ‖ **mod'est·ly** *adv* ‖ **mod'es·ty** *n*

mod·i·cum /mod'ikəm/ [L = moderate] *n* small amount

mod·i·fy /mod'ifī'/ [MF *modifier* < L *modificare*] *v* (-fied) *vt* 1 to change slightly in form; vary; 2 to limit, reduce; 3 *gram* **a** to qualify or limit the meaning of, as a noun by an adjective; **b** to change (a vowel) by umlaut ‖ **mod'i·fi'er** *n* ‖ **mod'i·fi·ca'tion** *n* ‖ SYN alter, temper, soften, change (see *qualify*)

mod·ish /mōd'ish/ *adj* fashionable, stylish

mo·diste /mōdēst'/ [F] *n* fashionable dressmaker, dealer in women's apparel

mod·u·lar /moj'ələr/ [see **module**] *adj* 1 pert. to a module; 2 designating a construction characterized by easily interchanged parts or units

mod·u·late /moj'ələāt'/ [L *modulari* (-*atus*) to measure] *vt* 1 to vary the sound of, as the voice; 2 to tone down; regulate; 3 *electron.* to impress upon (a carrier wave) the low-frequency pattern of sound waves or other signals by varying the amplitude, frequency, or phase of the carrier wave; **4** *mus* to cause to pass to a new related key **||** *vi* **5** *mus* to pass from one key to a related key **|| mod′u·la′tor** *n* **|| mod′u·la′tion** *n*

mod·ule /moj′ōōl/ [L *modulus* measure] *n* **1** standard unit of measurement; **2** *arch.* variable unit of length for expressing the proportions of the parts of a building; **3** any self-contained interchangeable part or unit, as of a computer, electronic device, etc.; **4** working model

mo·dus ο·pe·ran·di /mōd′əs op′əran′-dī/ [L] *n* method of operating

mo′dus vi·ven′di /viven′dī/ [L] *n* **1** manner of living; **2** practical method of getting along; **3** temporary arrangement pending a settlement

Mo·ga·di·shu /mōg′ədēsh′ōō/ *n* capital of Somalia (170,000)

Mo·gul /mō′gul, mōg′əl/ [Pers *Mugul* Mongol] *n* **1** one of the Mongol conquerors of India in the 16th century; **2 mogul** magnate

mo′hair /mō′-/ [It *moccaiaro* < Ar *mukhayyar* choice] *n* **1** hair of the Angora goat; **2** material woven from it

Mo·ham·med /mōham′id/ *n* Muhammad

Mo·ham′med·an *adj* **1** pert. to Muhammad or to Islam **||** *n* **2** Muslim **|| Mo·ham′med·an·ism** *n*

Mo′hawk /mō′-/ [< Algonquian] *n* one of a tribe of American Indians, formerly resident in the Mohawk Valley of central New York, the leading tribe of the Iroquois Confederacy

moire /mwär′, môr′, mōr′/ [F < Eng *mohair*] *n* watered silk or mohair fabric

moist /moist′/ [MF *moiste*] *adj* slightly wet, damp **|| moist′ness** *n* **|| mois·ten** /mois′ən/ *vt* & *vi*

mois·ture /mois′chər/ [MF *moistour*] *n* **1** slight dampness; **2** water or other liquid in small quantity

mo′lar (tooth′) /mōl′ər/ [< L *mola* millstone] *n* tooth with a flat surface for grinding

mo·las·ses /məlas′iz/ [Port *melaço*] *n* the dark sticky syrup left after refining cane sugar

mold¹ /mōld′/ [OE *molde* dust] *n* fine soft soil, rich in decayed matter

mold² [< OF *modle* < L *modulus* measure] *n* **1** hollow form in which anything molten or plastic is cast or shaped; **2** shape in which a thing is cast; **3** something formed in a mold; **4** pattern or model; **5** kind, character; **6** form or shape **||** *vt* **7** to make in or on a mold; **8** to form or shape **||** SYN *v* frame, shape, model, ornament, knead

mold³ [ME *mowlde*] *n* **1** any of many fungi which produce a furry coat on dead organic matter; **2** this furry coat **||** *vt* **3** to cover with mold **||** *vi* **4** to become covered with mold

mold′er [< *mold¹*] *vt* & *vi* to turn to dust, decay

mold′ing [< *mold²*] *n* **1** narrow decorative surface on a cornice, door jamb, or the like; **2** strip of material used for such ornamentation

mold′y *adj* (**-i·er**; **-i·est**) **1** covered with mold; **2** musty, stale **|| mold′i·ness** *n*

mole¹ /mōl/ [OE *māl*] *n* **1** dark-colored raised spot or growth on the skin; **2** nevus

mole² [ME *molle*] *n* any of several small, insectivorous, underground mammals, esp. of the family Talpidae, with soft fur, rudimentary eyes, and broad feet with which they dig long underground burrows

mole³ [MF < L *moles* mass] *n* **1** massive breakwater, esp. of stone, as at the mouth of a harbor; **2** inner harbor

mo·lec·u·lar /mōlek′yələr, mə-/ *adj* pert. to, caused by, or consisting of molecules

mo·lec′u·lar bi·ol′o·gy *n* branch of biology which deals with the molecular structure and development of biological systems

mol·e·cule /mol′əkyōōl′/ [LL *molecula* dim. of L *moles* mass] *n* smallest particle of a substance, whether an element or compound, which can exist independently and still retain its physical and chemical identity

mole′hill′ *n* little ridge made by the burrowing of a mole

mole′skin′ *n* **1** fur of the mole; **2** strong twilled cotton fabric

mo·lest /məlest′/ [L *molestare*] *vt* **1** to interfere with, annoy; disturb maliciously; **2** to make indecent advances to **|| mo′les·ta′tion** /mōl′-, mol′-/ *n* **||** SYN incommode, plague, vex, trouble, pester, disturb

Mo·lière /mōlyer′/ *n* (Jean-Baptiste Poquelin) (1622–73) French writer of comedies

moll /mol′/ [< name *Moll*] *n slang* gangster's girl friend

mol·li·fy /mol′ifī′/ [MF *mollifier* < L *mollificare* to soften] *v* (**-fied**) *vt* **1** to soothe; appease; **2** to mitigate, lessen

mol·lusk or **mol·lusc** /mol′əsk/ [L *molluscus* soft] *n* invertebrate of the phylum Mollusca, typically having a soft body covered with a hard shell, as snails and oysters

Mol·ly /mol′ē/ [trademark] *n* (**-lies**) expansion bolt designed to be fastened into holes drilled in masonry

mol′ly·cod′dle [*Molly* (< *Mary*) + *coddle*] *n* **1** man or boy used to being coddled; milksop **||** *vt* **2** to pamper, coddle

Mo·loch /mō′lok, mol′ək/ *n Bib* fire god of the ancient Phoenicians and Ammonites, to whom human sacrifices were offered

Mo′lo·tov cock′tail /mol′ətôf′, -tof′, môl′-/ [V.M. Molotov (1890–   )

Russ statesman] *n* home-made incendiary bomb consisting of a gasoline-filled bottle that is thrown at the target

molt /mōlt'/ [< ME *mouten* < L *mutare* to change] *vi* 1 to shed feathers, skin, horns, or the like, for replacement by a new growth ‖ *vt* 2 to shed (feathers or the like) ‖ *n* 3 act or instance of molting; 4 that which is molted

mol·ten /mōlt'ən/ [*archaic pp* of *melt*] *adj* 1 fused by heat, melted; 2 cast of melted metal

mo·lyb·de·num /məlib'dinəm/ [< Gk *molybdaina* galena] *n* hard, silvery, metallic element (**Mo;** at.no. 42; at.wt. 95.94), used as an alloy in the manufacture of steel for cutting tools

mom /mom'/ *n colloq* mother

mo·ment /mōm'ənt/ [L *momentum* movement] *n* 1 portion of time; instant; 2 importance, as *news of great moment;* 3 *mech* a tendency, as of a force or velocity, to cause motion around a central point; **b** product of a quantity and its perpendicular distance from an axis; 4 *statistics* mean value of a power of a random variable; 5 **at the moment** right now ‖ SYN importance, weight, consequence, significance

mo'men·tar'i·ly /-ter'-/ *adv* 1 for a moment; 2 from moment to moment

mo'men·tar'y /-ter'-/ *adj* 1 lasting only for a moment; 2 apt to occur at any moment ‖ SYN transitory, passing, transient, fugitive

mo'ment of truth' *n* 1 moment in a bullfight when the matador kills the bull; 2 decisive moment on which everything depends

mo·men·tous /mōment'əs/ *adj* very important, of great consequence

mo·men·tum /mōment'əm/ *n* (**-ta** /-tə/ or **-tums**) [L] 1 *mech* quantity of motion in a moving body, as measured by the product of its mass and its velocity; 2 impetus due to motion

mom·ma /mom'ə/ *n* mama

Mo·mus /mōm'əs/ *n class. myth.* god of ridicule and censure

mon- or **mono-** [Gk] *comb form* one; alone; single

Mon. 1 Monday; 2 Monsignor

Mon·a·co /mon'əkō'/ *n* tiny principality on the Mediterranean, bordering SE France (23,000; ½ sq.m.; cap. Monaco); famous for its gambling casino ‖ **Mon·e·gasque** /mon'əgask'/ *adj & n*

mon·arch /mon'ərk/ [Gk *monarches* sole ruler] *n* 1 hereditary ruler, as a king, queen, or emperor; 2 sole ruler; 3 large migratory butterfly (*Danaus plexippus*) with black-and-white markings ‖ **mo·nar·chal** /mənärk'əl/ or **mo·nar'chic** (**-chi·cal**) *adj*

mon'ar·chism *n* the principles or advocacy of monarchy ‖ **mon'ar·chist** *n* ‖ **mon·ar·chis'tic** *adj*

mon'ar·chy *n* (**-chies**) 1 government by a monarch; 2 nation the head of which is a monarch

mon·as·ter·y /mon'əster'ē/ [LGk *monasterion*] *n* (**-ies**) home to which persons, esp. monks, retire to live in seclusion under religious vows ‖ SYN cloister, abbey, convent, hermitage

mo·nas·tic /mənast'ik/ [Gk *monastikos*] *adj* 1 pert. to monasteries or to monks; 2 withdrawn, secluded ‖ **mo·nas'ti·cal·ly** *adv* ‖ **mo·nas'ti·cism** *n*

mon·au·ral /monōr'əl, mōn-/ *adj* 1 of or pert. to sound reproduction from one signal only; 2 pert. to perception of sound by one ear only

Mon·day /mun'dē, -dā/ [OE *mōnan dæg* moon's day] *n* second day of the week, following Sunday ‖ **Mon'days** *adv*

Mon'day morn'ing quar'ter·back [from fact that American football games were played on weekends] *n colloq* one who by hindsight criticizes the doings of others and offers solutions to their problems

mon·e·tar·y /mon'iter'ē, mun'-/ [< L *moneta* money] *adj* 1 of or pert. to currency or coinage; 2 pecuniary ‖ SYN financial, fiscal (see *pecuniary*)

mon·ey /mun'ē/ [MF *moneie* < L *moneta*] *n* (**-eys** or **-ies**) 1 coins and paper currency issued by a government and used as a medium of exchange; 2 any negotiable instrument readily convertible into cash; 3 wealth; 4 **in the money** *slang* **a** affluent; **b** first, second, or third in a horse race

mon'ey·bags' *nsg slang* very rich person

mon'eyed *adj* wealthy

mon'ey·man' /-man'/ *n* (**-men** /-men'/) man whose business is dealing in money; financier

mon'ey of ac·count' *n* monetary denomination not actually issued, but used in reckoning, as the mill

mon'ey or'der *n* order for the payment of a stated sum, sold at one post office or bank and payable at another

-mon·ger /-mung'gər/ [OE *mangere* *comb form* 1 chiefly *Brit* dealer, trader, as *fishmonger;* 2 contemptible busybody, as *scandalmonger*

Mon·gol /mong'gəl/ *n* 1 member of the native race of Mongolia; 2 any Mongolian language ‖ also *adj*

Mon·go·li·a /mongōl'ē·ə/ *n* region in E central Asia, comprising the Chinese-controlled Inner Mongolia and the Mongolian People's Republic ‖ **Mon·go'li·an** *adj & n*

Mon·go'li·an id'i·ot *n* one afflicted with Mongolism

Mon·go'li·an Peo'ple's Re·pub'lic *n*

republic in E central Asia (1,300,000; 604,000 sq.m.; cap. Ulan Bator)

Mon′gol·ism *n* abnormal condition of a person born with a flattened skull, slanting eyes, and mental deficiency

Mon′gol·oid′ *adj* of or pert. to one of the principal divisions of mankind, characterized by a yellowish skin, slanting eyes, prominent cheekbones, and straight black hair, including most of the peoples of central and E Asia and the aborigines of the New World || also *n*

mon·goose /moŋ′gōōs/ [Marathi *mangūs*] *n* (-goos·es) any of several species (genus *Herpestes*) of small ferretlike mammals, esp. *H. edwardsii* of India, noted for its ability to kill rats and venomous snakes

mon·grel /muŋ′grəl, moŋ′-/ [< OE *mang*- mixture] *n* 1 animal or plant of mixed breed, esp. a dog; 2 *disparaging* person or thing of mixed origin || **mon′grel·ize′** *vt*

mon·ies /mun′ēz/ *pl* of **money**

mon·i·ker /mon′ikər/ [?] *n slang* name or nickname

mon·ism /mon′izəm, mōn′-/ [< Gk *monos* one] *n* 1 any theory that seeks to trace phenomena of many different kinds to a single source or principle; 2 theory that all phenomena in the universe arise from a single underlying principle || **mon′ist** *n*

mon·i·tor /mon′itər/ [L = counselor] *n* 1 one who warns or advises; 2 pupil selected to help instruct or keep order among other pupils; 3 *rad & telv* receiver used for monitoring a transmission; 4 any of several large lizards (family Varanidae) of tropical regions of the Old World; 5 former armored vessel with very low freeboard and revolving turrets || *vt* 6 to oversee; keep a check on; 7 to observe and record; 8 *rad & telv* to listen to or watch (a transmission) in order to check technical quality or for censorship

monk /muŋk′/ [OE *munuc* < Gk *monachos* solitary] *n* one of a body of men bound by vows to a religious life and usu. to celibacy, obedience, and poverty || **monk′hood** *n* || **monk′ish** *adj*

mon·key /muŋk′ē/ [prob LG] *n* 1 any mammal of the order Primates, excluding man and, usu. the anthropoid apes and the lemurs; 2 mischievous person, esp. a child; 3 **have a monkey on one′s back** *slang* to be addicted to heroin; 4 **make a monkey (out) of** to make a fool of || *vi* 5 **monkey with** to play, trifle, or meddle with

mon′key busi′ness *n slang* 1 improper or illegal conduct; 2 misbehavior

mon′key·shine′ *n slang* mischievous or frolicsome prank

mon′key suit′ *n slang* 1 man′s dress suit; 2 uniform

mon′key wrench′ *n* 1 wrench with a sliding jaw adjusted by turning a screw; 2 *colloq* something that complicates or obstructs an action or operation

monk′s′ cloth′ *n* heavy cotton fabric with a basket weave, used chiefly for curtains

monks′hood *n* any of a genus (*Aconitum*) of plants having a hood-shaped upper sepal

mono- *see* **mon-**

mon′o·ba′sic /mon′ə-/ *adj* (acid) containing one replaceable hydrogen atom

mon′o·chro·mat′ic *adj* 1 having a single color; 2 *optics* consisting of light of a single wavelength or of a very limited range of wavelengths

mon′o·chrome′ *n* picture in one color or in different shades of one color

mon·o·cle /mon′əkəl/ [< **mon-** + L *oculus* eye] *n* eyeglass for one eye

mon′o·cot′y·le′don *n* seed plant having a single cotyledon in the embryo

mo·noc·u·lar /mənok′yələr/ [*see* **monocle**] *adj* 1 pert. to, or fitted for the use of, one eye; 2 one-eyed

mo·nog·a·my /mənog′əmē/ *n* 1 marriage with only one person at a time; 2 *zool* pairing with a single mate through life || **mo·nog′a·mous** *adj*

mon·o·gram /mon′əgram′/ *n* character or design formed by the interweaving of two or more letters, as the initials of a name

mon′o·graph′ *n* treatise on one particular subject or some branch of it

mon′o·ki′ni /-kēn′ē/ *n* woman′s bikinilike topless bathing suit

mon′o·lin′gual *adj* 1 spoken or written in only one language; 2 speaking only one language || *n* 3 person fluent in only one language

mon′o·lith *n* 1 single large block of stone; 2 pillar, statue, etc., formed from a single stone; 3 something huge and intractable || **mon′o·lith′ic** *adj*

mon·o·log or **mon·o·logue** /mon′əlog′, -lôg′/ *n* 1 dramatic scene in which only one person speaks; 2 long speech by one person; 3 literary work in the form of a soliloquy || **mon′o·log′ic** (-i·cal) /-loj′-/ *adj* || **mo·nol·o·gist** /mənol′əjist, mon′əlog′ist, -lôg′-/ *n*

mon′o·ma′ni·a *n* 1 mania in regard to a single subject; 2 extravagant pursuit of one idea || **mon′o·ma′ni·ac′** /-ak′/ *n*

mo·no·mi·al /mōnōm′yē·əl, mə-/ [*mono*- + *binomial*] *n* 1 *alg* expression consisting of a single term; 2 *biol* name consisting of a single word || also *adj*

mon′o·nu′cle·o′sis /-n(y)ōōk′lē·ōs′is/ [*mono*- + *nuclear* + *-osis*] *n* condition of having an abnormally large number of leukocytes with a single nucleus in the blood

mon'o·phon'ic /-fon'-/ *adj* 1 monaural 1; 2 *mus* having a single melodic line and no accompaniment

mon'oph·thong' /-əfthôṇ', -əfthoṇ'/ [*mono-* + Gk *phthongos* sound] *n* simple vowel sound, not combined in the same syllable with a semivocalic sound ‖ **mon'oph·thon'gal** /-gəl/ *adj* ‖ **mon'oph·thong·ize** /-gīz/ *vt & vi*

Mo·noph·y·site /mənof'isīt'/ [< *mono-* + Gk *physis* nature] *n* adherent of the doctrine that Christ had but a single nature in which the human and divine elements were combined

mon'o·plane' *n* airplane with a single wing on each side

mo·nop·o·ly /mənop'əlē/ [Gk *monopolion*] *n* (**-lies**) 1 exclusive control of, or right to control, some commodity or service; 2 company that possesses such control; 3 subject of a monopoly; 4 sole possession of anything ‖ **mo·nop'o·list** *n* ‖ **mo·nop'o·lis'tic** *adj* ‖ **mo·nop'o·lize'** *vt*

mon'o·rail' *n* 1 single rail on which railway cars are run or from which they are suspended; 2 railroad using this system

mon'o·so'di·um glu'ta·mate' /glōot'-əmāt'/ [< *gluten*] *n* white crystalline powder —HOOC(CH₂)₂CH-(NH₂)COONa— used in cooking to intensify flavor

mon'o·syl'la·ble *n* word of one syllable ‖ **mon'o·syl·lab'ic** *adj*

mon'o·the'ism *n* doctrine of or belief in the existence of but one God ‖ **mon'o·the'ist** *n* ‖ **mon'o·the·is'tic** *adj*

mon'o·tone' *n* 1 speech or utterance on a single note or key; 2 single note used continuously for speech, recitation, intoning, or the like; 3 lack of variety in style, as of a written composition

mo·not·o·ny /mənot'ənē/ *n* 1 dull sameness of tone; similarity in cadence; 2 lack of variety; tedious uniformity ‖ **mo·not'o·nous** *adj*

mon'o·treme' /-trēm'/ [*mono-* + Gk *trema* opening] *n* any member of the lowest order (Monotremata) of mammals, the females laying large shelled eggs hatched outside the body, as the platypus

Mon'o·type' *n* [trademark] keyboard-operated typesetting machine which through the intermediary of punched paper tape casts and sets each individual type ‖ **mon'o·typ'er** *n*

mon·o·va·lent /mon'əvā'lənt/ [< *mono-* + L *valens* (*-entis*) worth] *adj* 1 *chem* a having a valence of one; b having one valence; 2 *bacteriol* effective against only one pathological organism ‖ **mon'o·va'lence** *n*

mon·ox'ide /mon-, mən-/ *n* oxide containing one atom of oxygen in each molecule

Mon·roe, James /mənrō'/ *n* (1758–

1831) 5th president of the U.S. 1817–25

Mon·roe' Doc'trine *n* policy announced by President Monroe in 1823 to the effect that the United States would view as an unfriendly act any attempt of a European nation to intervene in American affairs or to increase its holdings in the New World

Mon·ro·vi·a /mənrōv'ē-ə/ *n* capital of Liberia (81,000)

mon·sieur /məsyœ'/ [F = my lord] *n* (**mes·sieurs** /mes'ərs, F māsyœ'/) French title of courtesy equivalent to *Sir* or *Mr.*

Mon·si·gnor or **mon·si·gnor** /monsēn'-yər/ [It = my lord] *n* 1 title conferred on certain Roman Catholic prelates; 2 the person bearing this title

mon·soon /monsōōn'/ [*obs* D *monssoen* < Port *monção* < Ar *mawsim* season] *n* 1 wind, esp. in the Indian Ocean and S Asia, blowing from the southwest in summer and from the northeast in winter; 2 rainy season that accompanies the summer monsoon

mon·ster /mon'stər/ [MF *monstre* < L *monstrum* portent] *n* 1 any animal, plant, or thing of abnormal form or structure; 2 animal or plant remarkably deformed or hideous; 3 person remarkable for extreme wickedness, cruelty, or ugliness; 4 animal or thing of huge size; 5 fabulous creature of form or features not found in nature ‖ *adj* of unusual size, enormous

mon·strance /mon'strəns/ [< *monstrare* to show] *n R C Ch* vessel in which the consecrated Host is shown at the altar and in processions

mon·stros·i·ty /monstros'itē/ [see **monstrous**] *n* (**-ties**) 1 state or quality of being monstrous; 2 anything monstrous

mon'strous [< L *monstrosus*] *adj* 1 abnormal; 2 enormous, huge; 3 horrible, hideous; 4 revolting; shocking ‖ **SYN** immense, hateful, shocking, hideous (see *heinous*) ‖ **ANT** small, ordinary, attractive

mons ve·ne·ris /monz' ven'əris/ [L = mount of Venus] *n* (**mon·tes veneris** /mon'tēz/) rounded prominence of fatty tissue just above the cleft of the vagina in the human female

Mont. Montana

mon·tage /montäzh'/ [F = mounting] *n* bits of many pictures arranged or superimposed to produce a particular effect

Mon·tan·a /montan'ə/ *n* state in the NW U.S. (694,000); 147,138 sq.m.; cap. Helena ‖ **Mon·tan'an** *n*

mon·te /mont'ē/ [Sp = mountain] *n* gambling game resembling faro, played with a deck of 40 cards

Mon·te Car·lo /mont'ē kär'lō/ *n* town

in Monaco (10,000); famous gambling resort

Mon·te·vi·de·o /mont'əvidā'ō/ n capital of Uruguay (1,158,632)

Mon·te·zu·ma /mont'izōom'ə/ n (1470–1520) last Aztec emperor of Mexico 1502–20

Mont·gom·er·y /montgum'(ə)rē/ n capital of Alabama (135,000)

month /munth'/ [OE *mōnath*] n 1 one of the twelve parts into which the calendar year is divided; 2 solar month; 3 lunar month; 4 period of about four weeks or 30 days

month'ly adj 1 continued for a month; 2 performed, happening, or published once a month ‖ adv 3 once each month ‖ n (-lies) 4 periodical published each month; 5 the month·lies colloq the menstrual period

Mont·mar·tre /mônmär'trə/ n hilly district in Paris frequented by artists and famous for night life

Mont·par·nasse /mônparnäs'/ n district on the Left Bank of the Seine in Paris, frequented by artists and writers

Mont·pel·ier /montpēl'yər/ n capital of Vermont (9,000)

Mont·re·al /mont'rē·ôl'/ n city in S Quebec on the St. Lawrence, largest city in Canada (135,000)

mon·u·ment /mon'yəmənt/ [L *monumentum*] n 1 anything that keeps alive the memory of a person or event, as a pillar, statue, or the like; 2 striking and lasting example or instance; 3 any work of lasting significance; 4 stone or other object set to mark a boundary ‖ SYN memorial, record, cenotaph

mon·u·men·tal /-ment'əl/ adj 1 serving, or fitted, to keep alive the memory of a person or event; 2 resembling a monument; 3 huge; massive; 4 exceptionally great

moo /mōō'/ [imit] vi 1 to make the sound of a cow ‖ n 2 lowing of a cow

mooch /mōōch'/ [OF *muchier* to skulk] vt & vi slang to cadge, sponge ‖ mooch'er n

mood¹ /mōōd'/ [< *mode*] n gram set of verb forms or periphrastic devices used to express the speaker's attitude in terms of certainty, uncertainty, wish, doubt, command, etc.

mood² [OE *mōd* feeling] n state or temper of the feelings or emotions; humor

mood'y adj (-i·er; -i·est) 1 sullen; ill-humored; 2 given to quick changes in mood; temperamental

moon /mōōn'/ [OE *mōna*] n 1 natural satellite of the earth, revolving around it once a month at a distance of about 240,000 miles; 2 any planetary satellite; 3 month; 4 anything resembling the moon in shape ‖ vi 5 to wander about in an absent-minded and listless manner

moon'beam' n ray of moonlight

moon'-faced' adj having a full round face like a full moon

moon'light' n 1 light from the moon ‖ vi 2 colloq to work at another job after one's regular full-time work, esp. at night ‖ moon'light'er n ‖ moon'light'ing n

moon'lit' adj lighted by the moon

moon'quake' n disturbance on the surface of the moon similar to an earthquake

moon'shine' n 1 moonlight; 2 empty talk; 3 colloq whiskey or other alcoholic beverage smuggled or made illegally ‖ moon'shin'er n

moon'shot' n the launching of a missile to the moon

moon'stone' n any of several translucent varieties of feldspar with an opalescent sheen, used as gems

moon'struck' adj crazed through the supposed influence of the moon

moor¹ /mōōr'/ [OE *mōr*] n Brit broad tract of wasteland covered with heather or bushes

moor² [ME *more*] vt 1 to secure; 2 to secure in a particular place by a cable or anchor, as a ship ‖ vi 3 to be secured in this way; 4 to moor a ship

Moor [MF *More* < Gk *Mauros*] n 1 Arabic-speaking Muslim of Morocco; 2 one of the Saracens who invaded Spain in the Middle Ages ‖ Moor'ish adj

moose /mōōs'/ [< *Algonquian*] n (pl moose) North American herbivorous mammal (*Alces americanus*), the largest member of the deer family, with large flattened antlers

moot /mōōt'/ [OE *mōt* meeting] vt 1 to propose for discussion ‖ adj 2 debatable; 3 academic; 4 theoretical

moot' court' n mock court held by students for practice in legal procedure

mop /mop'/ [ML *mappula* cloth] n 1 implement for washing floors, decks, etc., consisting of a bundle of cloth or yarn on a long handle; 2 any similar loose, tangled bunch, as a mop of hair ‖ v (mopped; mop·ping) vt 3 to clean or dry with a mop; 4 mop up, a mil to clear of remaining hostile soldiers after the main enemy forces have retreated or been captured; b slang to finish up

mope /mōp'/ [?] vi 1 to be dull and listless ‖ n 2 the mopes pl colloq the blues, low spirits ‖ mop'ey or mop'y (-i·er; -i·est) adj ‖ mop'er n

mo·ped /mō'ped/ [*motor* + *pedal*] n strongly built bicycle with a light motor

mop·pet /mop'it/ [dim. of obs mop pet child] n baby; young child

mop'-up' n act of mopping up

mo·raine /mərān'/ [F] n ridge or heap of rocks and gravel deposited by a glacier

mor·al /môr′əl, mor′-/ [L *moralis*] *adj* 1 pert. to man's conception of what is right and just; 2 ethical, discriminating between right and wrong; 3 chaste, virtuous; 4 capable of being influenced by a sense of right; 5 verified by reason, logic, or probability, as a *moral certainty;* 6 teaching a pious lesson; 7 sympathetic but not active, as *moral support* || *n* 8 lesson taught by a fable, story, or event; 9 **morals** *pl* a behavior, conduct, or habits with respect to what is right or wrong; b theory of right conduct; ethics || *adj* 10 **morals** pert. to or dealing with sexual immorality, as *a morals charge*

mo·rale /məral′/ [F] *n* mental state as regards zeal, determination, and confidence

mor′al·ist *n* 1 one who professes or teaches morality; 2 one who wants to guard over the morals of others, as by imposing censorship || **mor′al·is′tic** *adj*

mo·ral·i·ty /məral′itē/ *n* **(-ties)** 1 the teaching of the rules of right behavior; 2 moral conduct; virtue; 3 system of morals

mor′al·ize′ *vi* to talk about right and wrong || **mor′al·iz′er** *n*

mor′al·ly *adv* 1 in a moral manner; 2 regarding morals; 3 virtually

mo·rass /məras′/ [D *moeras*] *n* bog, swamp

mor·a·to·ri·um /môr′ətôr′ē·əm, mor′-, -tōr′-/ [L = causing delay] *n* **(-ums** or **-a** /-ə/) 1 legal authorization to delay payment of money due; 2 period of such delay; 3 temporary cessation of some activity

Mo·ra·vi·a /mōrāv′ē·ə, mə-/ *n* province of the former kingdom of Bohemia, now part of Czechoslovakia

Mo·ra′vi·an *adj* 1 of or pert. to Moravia || *n* 2 native or inhabitant of Moravia; 3 Czech dialect of Moravia; 4 member of a Protestant denomination originating in Moravia, which bases its theology strictly on the Scriptures

mo·ray /môr′ā, mərā′/ [Port *moréia*] *n* any of a large family (Muraenidae) of pugnacious marine eels with knifelike teeth, found in all warm seas

mor·bid /môr′bid/ [L *morbidus* diseased] *adj* 1 pert. to or caused by disease; 2 sick, unhealthy; 3 mentally gloomy or unwholesome || **mor′bid·ly** *adv* || **mor·bid′i·ty** *n* || SYN diseased, sick, unwholesome, unsound, abnormal

mor·dant /môrd′ənt/ [MF = biting] *n* 1 corrosive substance used in etching; 2 substance used to fix colors in dyeing || *adj* 3 sarcastic, biting

more /môr′, mōr′/ [OE *māra*] *adj* 1 greater in number, quantity, amount, measure, or degree; 2 additional; longer || *adv* 3 to a greater degree; 4 again; in addition; 5 **more or less,** a somewhat; b approximately || *n* 6 greater quantity or number; 7 something further or additional; 8 *pl* a greater number of persons or things

more·o′ver *adv* besides, further

mo·res /môr′ēz/ [L, *pl* of *mos* custom] *npl* folkways; unwritten laws of conduct having the sanction of usage

mor·ga·nat·ic /môr′gənat′ik/ [ML *matrimonium ad morganaticam* marriage with a morning gift] *adj* pert. to or designating the marriage of a man of royal or other high rank with a woman of lower degree, in which the wife and children do not share the husband's rank or property

morgue /môrg′/ [F] *n* 1 place where the bodies of unidentified persons are kept temporarily; 2 reference department of a newspaper

mor·i·bund /môr′ibund′/ [L *moribundus*] *adj* at the point of death; dying

Mo·ris·co /məris′kō/ [Sp] *n* **(-cos** or **-coes)** 1 Moor; 2 Moor living in Spain || *adj* Moorish

Mor·mon /môr′mən/ [*Mormon,* character in the *Book of Mormon* sacred book of the sect] *n* member of the Church of Jesus Christ of Latter-day Saints, founded in 1830 by Joseph Smith (1805–44) || **Mor′mon·ism** *n*

morn /môrn′/ *n poet.* morning

morn′ing [OE *morgen,* modeled on *evening*] *n* 1 early part of the day; 2 the part of the day from dawn to noon or from midnight to noon; 3 any early part, as *the morning of life* || also *adj*

morn′ing-glo′ry *n* **(-ries)** 1 any of a genus (*Ipomaea*) of twining plants with heart-shaped leaves and funnel-shaped blue, pink, lavender, or white flowers; 2 any of various related plants

morn′ings *adv* during the morning regularly

morn′ing sick′ness *n* feeling of nausea occurring in the morning, often a symptom of pregnancy

morn′ing star′ *n* any of the brighter planets seen in the eastern sky just before sunrise

Mo·ro /môr′ō, mōr′-/ [Sp = Moor] *n* native Mohammedan of the S Philippines

Mo·roc·co /mərok′ō/ *n* 1 Arabic-speaking kingdom in NW Africa (15,400,000; 171,897 sq.m.; cap. Rabat); 2 **morocco** fine grained leather made from goatskin tanned with sumac; 3 any imitation of this || **Mo·roc′can** *adj & n*

mo·ron /môr′ən, mō′ron/ [< Gk *moros* foolish] *n* 1 person below normal in mentality but ranking above an imbecile; 2 *colloq* stupid person || **mo·ron·ic** /məron′ik/ *adj*

mo·rose /mərōs′/ [L *morosus* peevish] *adj* sullen, gloomy; unsociable || SYN sulky, splenetic, crabbed (see *gloomy, sullen*)

mor·ph- or **mor·pho-** [Gk] *comb form* form

-morph /-môrf'/ [< Gk *morphe* form] *comb form* having a specified form

mor·pheme /môr'fēm/ [F] *n* smallest meaningful unit in a language, as *cat* and *s* in *cats* || **mor·phem'ic** *adj*

Mor·phe·us /môr'fē·əs, -fyōōs/ *n class. myth.* god of dreams and of sleep

mor·phine /môr'fēn/ [< *Morpheus*] *n* crystalline alkaloid —C₁₇H₁₉NO₃· H₂O— extracted from opium and used in medicine to produce sleep and insensibility to pain

mor·phol·o·gy /môrfol'əjē/ *n* 1 branch of biology dealing with the form and structure of plants and animals; 2 branch of grammar dealing with the changes words undergo to show inflection and derivation || **mor'pho·log'i·cal** /-fəloj'-/ *adj*

Mor'ris chair' /môr'is, mor'-/ [William *Morris* (1834–96) Eng poet and craftsman] *n* large armchair with heavy cushions and an adjustable back

mor'ris dance' [< *morys* var of *Moorish*] *n* English pastoral dance in four-four measure in which the participants are costumed, carry tambourines, and wear ankle bells

mor·row /mor'ō, môr'ō/ [ME *morwe*] *n* 1 the next day after any given day; 2 tomorrow; 3 *archaic* morning

Morse' code' /môrs'/ [Samuel F. B. *Morse* (1791–1872) U.S. inventor of the telegraph] *n* system of dots, dashes, and spaces, or of visual or aural representations of them, used in telegraphy and in visual signaling to represent the letters of the alphabet, numerals, etc.

mor·sel /môrs'əl/ [OF] *n* 1 bite, mouthful; 2 small portion of anything

mor·tal /môrt'əl/ [L *mortalis* < *mors* (*mortis*) death] *adj* 1 subject to death; 2 fatal; 3 to the death, as *mortal combat, mortal enemies*; 4 pert. to human beings; 5 dire, as *mortal peril*; 6 of this world; 7 extreme;·8 pert. to death || *n* 9 human being || **mor'tal·ly** *adv* || SYN *adj* implacable, fatal; human (see *deadly*)

mor·tal'i·ty /-tal'-/ *n* (-ties) 1 condition of being subject to death; 2 death; destruction; 3 death rate

mor'tal'i·ty ta'ble *n* table giving statistical information regarding the number of persons of a given age that may be expected to die during a given period

mor·tar¹ /môrt'ər/ [OE *mortere* < L *mortarium*] *n* 1 bowllike vessel in which substances are pounded or crushed to a powder with a pestle; 2 short cannon for firing shells at a high angle

mor·tar² [OF *mortier* < L *mortarium*] *n* 1 building cement made of lime, sand, and water || *vt* 2 to cement with mortar

mor'tar·board' *n* 1 square board for holding mortar; 2 academic cap with a square flat top and a tassel worn on ceremonial occasions

mort·gage /môrg'ij/ [OF = dead pledge] *n* 1 pledge of property to a creditor as security for the payment of a debt; 2 document which details the terms of this pledge || *vt* 3 to place (property) under a mortgage; 4 to pledge; stake

mort·ga·gee /môrg'əjē'/ *n* person who holds a mortgage on someone's property

mort·ga·gor also **mort·gag·er** /môrg'əjər/ *n* person who mortgages his property

mor·ti·cian /môrtish'ən/ [*mort*uary + *physician*] *n* undertaker

mor·ti·fy /môrt'ifī'/ [MF *mortifier* < L *mortificare* to put to death] *v* (-fied) *vt* 1 to humiliate, embarrass; 2 to subdue by self-denial, as the passions; 3 to cause gangrene in || *vi* 4 to become gangrenous || **mor'ti·fi·ca'tion** *n* || SYN humiliate, chagrin, confuse, vex, disconcert

mor·tise /môrt'is/ [MF *mortaise*] *n* 1 hole or hollowed-out space, as in a piece of wood, to receive a tenon of the same size and shape || *vt* 2 to fasten with a mortise and tenon

mor'tise lock' *n* lock fitted in a mortise

mor·tu·ar·y /môrch'ōō·er'ē/ [ML *mortuarium*] *adj* 1 pert. to the dead or the burial of the dead || *n* (-ies) 2 funeral home

mo·sa·ic /mōzā'ik/ [ML *mosaicus* < Gk *mouseios* of the Muses] *n* 1 design or picture made by inlaying very small pieces of glass, stone, etc., of various colors; 2 piece of work decorated in this manner; 3 anything that is pieced together

Mo·sa·ic /mōzā'ik/ [< *Moses*] *adj* pert. to Moses or to the laws and writings ascribed to him

Mos·cow /mos'kō, -kou/ *n* capital of the Soviet Union (6,395,000)

Mo·selle /mōzel'/ [river in Germany] *n* mild white wine made in the valley of the Moselle in W Germany

Mo·ses /mōz'iz, -is/ *n Bib* the great prophet and lawgiver who led the Israelites out of Egypt

mo·sey /mōz'ē/ [?] *vi colloq* to stroll leisurely, amble

Mos·lem /moz'ləm, mos'-/ *n* & *adj* Muslim

mosque /mosk'/ [It *moschea* < Ar *masjid*] *n* Muslim place of worship

mos·qui·to /məskēt'ō/ [Sp, *dim.* of *mosca* fly] *n* (-toes) any of a family (Culicidae) of two-winged insects, the female of which sucks the blood of man and animals, and certain species of which transmit malaria and yellow fever

moss /môs′, mos′/ [OE *mos*] *n* **1** any of a phylum (Bryophyta) of small-leaved plants forming mats on rocks, tree trunks, and moist ground; **2** any of numerous lichens similar to moss ‖ **moss′y** *adj* (**-i·er**; **-i·est**)

moss′back′ *n* **1** old turtle; **2** person who resists new ideas

most /mōst′/ [OE *mǣst*] *adj* **1** greatest in number, quantity, amount, size, or degree; **2** in the majority of cases ‖ *n* **3** the majority, as *he is wiser than most*; **4** most of the greatest number or part of; **5 at (the) most** at the maximum; **6 make the most of** to use to full advantage; **7 the most,** **a** the greatest quantity, amount, or degree; **b** *slang* the ultimate, the best, as *as a singer, she's the most* ‖ *adv* **8** in the greatest or highest degree

-most /-mōst′/ [OE *-mest superl suf*] *adj* & *adv suf* most or most towards, as *uppermost*

most′-fa′vored-na′tion clause′ *n* clause in a treaty by which a nation grants another nation the same favorable terms it grants to any other nation

most′ly *adv* **1** for the most part; **2** chiefly

mot /mō′/ [F = word] *n* witty remark

mote /mōt′/ [OE *mot*] *n* small particle; speck

mo·tel /mōtel′/ [*motor* + *hotel*] *n* roadside hotel providing rooms with adjacent parking spaces for motorists

mo·tet /mōtet′/ [MF] *n* unaccompanied vocal composition in elaborate counterpoint and with Biblical text

moth /môth′, moth′/ [OE *moththe*] *n* (**moths** /-*thz*, -ths/) **1** any of numerous insects (order Lepidoptera) closely resembling the butterflies but chiefly nocturnal and having antennae without knobs; **2** clothes moth

moth′ball′ *n* **1** small ball usu. of naphthalene used to repel moths from wool or fur; **2 in mothballs** in storage

moth′eat′en *adj* **1** damaged by the larvae of clothes moths; **2** worn; full of holes; **3** out of style

moth·er /muth′ər/ [OE *mōdor*] *n* **1** female parent; **2** origin, source; **3** elderly woman (used as a term of affectionate address) ‖ *vt* **4** to act as a mother to

Moth′er Goose′ *n* legendary author of a collection of old nursery rhymes first published in English in 1760

moth′er·hood′ *n* **1** state of being a mother; **2** feelings or spirit of a mother; **3** mothers collectively

Moth′er Hub′bard /hub′ərd/ [character in a nursery rhyme] *n* loose beltless garment for women

moth′er-in-law′ *n* (**mothers-in-law**) mother of one's husband or wife

moth′er·land′ *n* land of one's birth or of one's ancestors

moth′er·ly *adj* pert. to, like, or befitting a mother ‖ **moth′er·li·ness** *n*

moth′er-of-pearl′ *n* hard iridescent lining of the shell of various mollusks ‖ also *adj*

Moth′er's Day′ *n* second Sunday in May, devoted to honoring mothers and motherhood

moth′er su·pe′ri·or *n* (**mothers superior** or **mother superiors**) head of a female religious house

moth′er tongue′ *n* **1** one's native language; **2** language from which another language is derived

moth′er wit′ *n* natural intelligence; innate humor

mo·tif /mōtēf′/ [F = motive] *n* central theme or subject, as in a work of art or literature, or in a musical composition

mo·tile /mōt′il/ [< L *motus* moved] *adj* capable of spontaneous motion ‖ **mo·til′i·ty** /-til′-/ *n*

mo′tion /mōsh′ən/ [L *motio* (-*onis*)] *n* **1** act, process, or state of moving or changing position; **2** action, as opposed to rest; **3** gesture; **4** manner of moving; **5** formal proposal made in a deliberative meeting; **6** *law* application to a court for an order or ruling; **7** movement of voice parts in harmony; **8 in motion** moving ‖ *vi* **9** to make a meaningful gesture ‖ *vt* **10** to guide or invite by a gesture ‖ **mo′tion·less** *adj* ‖ SYN *n* action, change, movement, move, transition; transit; gesticulation; proposal

mo′tion pic′ture *n* series of persons or things in action, photographed in rapid succession, so that when projected on a screen at the same speed the illusion of natural movement is created ‖ **mo′tion-pic′ture** *adj*

mo·ti·vate /mōt′ivāt′/ *vt* to provide with a motive or incentive

mo·tive /mōt′iv/ [ML *motivum*] *n* **1** that which urges to action; incentive; **2** motif ‖ *adj* **3** causing or pert. to motion ‖ SYN *n* (see *cause, impulse*)

-mo′tive *comb form* moving, motion

mo′tive pow′er *n* **1** power used to impart motion to machinery; **2** all the locomotives of a railroad; **3** driving force

mot·ley /mot′lē/ [ME] **1** consisting of different colors; **2** composed of heterogeneous elements ‖ *n* **3** garment of various colors formerly worn by jesters

mo·tor /mōt′ər/ [L = one who moves] *n* **1** internal-combustion engine; **2** machine that converts electrical energy into mechanical energy; **3** automobile ‖ *adj* **4** imparting or causing motion; **5** involving or pert. to muscular movement ‖ *vi* **6** to travel by automobile

mo′tor·boat′ *n* boat propelled by a motor

mo′tor·cade′ *n* procession of automobiles

mo′tor·car′ *n* automobile

mo′tor·coach′ *n* bus

mo′tor·court′ *n* motel

mo′tor·cy′cle *n* **1** two-wheeled vehicle similar to a bicycle but heavier and driven by a motor ‖ *vi* **2** to ride in a motorcycle ‖ **mo′tor·cy′clist** *n*

mo′tor·ist *n* one who drives or rides in an automobile

mo′tor·ize′ *vt* **1** to equip with motor-driven vehicles; **2** to furnish with a motor or motors ‖ **mo′tor·i·za′tion** *n*

mo′tor·man /-mən/ *n* (**-men** /-mən/) one who operates a streetcar or rapid-transit train

mo′tor sail′er *n* boat using both sail and motor power

mo′tor scoot′er *n* scooter propelled by a small motor and provided with a seat

mo′tor ship′ *n* ship driven by internal-combustion engines, usu. diesel engines, rather than steam

mo′tor·way′ *n Brit* superhighway

mot·tle /mot′əl/ [< *motley*] *vt* to mark with spots or splotches of various colors ‖ **mot′tled** *adj*

mot·to /mot′ō/ [It] *n* (**-toes** or **-tos**) **1** maxim adopted as a guiding principle; **2** legend inscribed on something as appropriate to its character ‖ SYN saw, saying, adage, precept (see *truism*)

mould /mōld/ *n, vt, & vi* var of **mold**

moult /mōlt/ *vi, vt, & n* var of **molt**

mound /mound/ [?] *n* **1** elevation of earth, stone, sand, or rubble; **2** heap; **3** small hill; **4** *baseball* slight elevation on which the pitcher stands

mount¹ /mount/ [OE *munt* < L *mons* (*montis*)] *n* **1** *poet.* mountain; **2 Mount** designation preceding the name of some mountains

mount² [OF *monter* to climb] *vt* **1** to ascend, climb; **2** to climb up on; **3** to place in or on a suitable setting or backing; **4** to set on an elevation; **5** to furnish with a horse or horses; **6** to arrange for exhibition, as a stuffed or preserved animal or skeleton; **7** to set up for use, as a gun or lens ‖ *vi* **8** to ascend, rise; **9** to get on top of something; **10** also **mount up** to rise in amount ‖ *n* **11** act of mounting; **12** riding horse; **13** structure, setting, or backing on which something is mounted ‖ SYN v rise, ascend, climb, scale, soar, elevate, raise

moun·tain /mount′ən/ [OF *montaigne*] *n* **1** natural elevation rising to a considerable height above the surrounding country; **2** great mass or amount ‖ **moun′tain·ous** *adj*

moun′tain chain′ *n* series of connected mountains

moun′tain·eer′ *n* **1** dweller in the mountains; **2** mountain climber

moun′tain goat′ *n* white goatlike ruminant (*Oreamnos americanus*) of the Rocky Mountains

moun′tain li′on *n* cougar

moun′tain sick′ness *n* condition characterized by difficult breathing and nausea, caused by the thin air of high altitudes

moun·te·bank /mount′əbaŋk′/ [It *montimbanco* one who mounts a bench] *n* charlatan or quack, esp. one who sells quack remedies in public places

mount′ed *adj* seated or serving on horseback

Moun′tie *n colloq* member of the Royal Canadian Mounted Police

mount′ing *n* setting or mount for something

Mount′ Ver′non /vur′nən/ *n* home and tomb of George Washington, in Virginia on the Potomac, south of Washington

mourn /môrn′, mōrn′/ [OE *murnan*] *vi* **1** to grieve for the dead; **2** to feel or express sorrow ‖ *vt* **3** to grieve or sorrow for; lament; **4** to utter in a lamenting manner ‖ SYN bemoan, bewail, sorrow, grieve, lament, deplore ‖ ANT triumph, exult, rejoice, delight, joy

mourn′er *n* **1** person who attends a funeral to mourn the death of a friend or relative; **2** person who repents and shows publicly a desire for salvation

mourn′er′s bench′ *n* front seat in a church reserved for those expressing a desire for salvation

mourn′ful *adj* **1** expressing sorrow; **2** doleful; overcome with grief; **3** causing sorrow; arousing grief ‖ **mourn′-ful·ly** *adv* ‖ SYN sad, sorrowful, grievous, lugubrious, dolorous ‖ ANT happy, light-hearted, gay, joyous, glad

mourn′ing *n* **1** state of expressing grief; **2** expression of grief for one who has died, as by black drapes on buildings, flags at half-mast, or wearing black garments; **3** black clothes or a black sleeve band expressing grief

mourn′ing dove′ *n* North American wild dove, *Zenaidura macrura*, so called from its plaintive note

mouse /mous′/ [OE *mūs*] *n* (**mice**) **1** any of several small rodents (family Muridae), esp. those of the genus *Mus* that infest houses; **2** *slang* black eye ‖ /mouz′/ *vi* **3** to hunt for mice

mous·er /mouz′ər/ *n* animal that catches mice, esp. a cat

mousse /mōōs′/ [F] *n* dessert made of whipped cream, whites of eggs, sugar, etc., flavored and chilled

mous·tache /məstash′, mus′tash/ n
mustache

mous·y /mouz′ē, mous′ē/ adj (-i·er;
-i·est) 1 resembling a mouse; 2 overrun with mice; 3 quiet as a mouse; 4
drab

mouth /mouth′/ [OE mūth] n (mouths
/-thz/) 1 opening through which animals and men take food; space between the lips and the throat; 2 this
opening as the channel of speech; 3
entrance or exit; 4 opening through
which something is emptied or filled;
5 down in the mouth colloq de-
pressed; 6 give mouth to to utter ||
/mouth′/ vt 7 to utter pompously; 8
to mumble; 9 to seize in or with the
mouth

mouth′ful n 1 as much as can be
or usually is put in the mouth at one
time; 2 small quantity; 3 to say a
mouthful slang to say something of
special significance

mouth′ or′gan n harmonica

mouth′piece′ n 1 part or piece, as of a
wind instrument or pipe, that is
placed in the mouth; 2 spokesman;
3 slang lawyer

mouth′wash′ n solution for gargling, as
for a sore throat or to sweeten the
breath

mouth′-wa·ter·ing adj appetizing enough
to cause salivation

mou′ton /mōō′ton/ [F = sheep] n
sheepskin dyed to resemble beaver
or seal

mov·a·ble also move·a·ble /mōōv′əbəl/
adj 1 capable of being moved in
space or time || n 2 something mov-
able; 3 movables law movable articles of personal property

move /mōōv′/ [MF movoir] vt 1 to
cause to change place or position; 2
to set in motion; 3 to cause to act;
impel; 4 to stir the feelings of;
arouse the emotions or sympathies
of; 5 to offer for formal action, as
in a court or deliberative assembly;
6 to cause (the bowels) to operate; 7
com to cause (goods) to be bought
or sold || vi 8 to change place or
position; 9 to advance; 10 to change
one's residence; 11 to take action;
begin to act; 12 to engage in activities; 13 to make an application; 14
com to be sold || n 15 act of moving;
16 act in the execution of a plan; 17
chess, checkers right or turn to move
a piece; 18 change of residence; 19
get a move on colloq a to start; b to
hurry; 20 on the move colloq a ac-
tive; b moving from place to place ||
SYN v induce, persuade, impel, propel, actuate, instigate, stimulate, incite, goad, influence, stir, convey

move′ment n 1 act or result of moving;
2 manner of moving; 3 joint effort
of people or groups toward some
end; 4 definite or organized trend, as
in literature or thought; 5 evacuation of the bowels; 6 specific arrangement of moving parts, as in a
watch; 7 mus a rhythm; tempo; b
one of the parts or complete units of
a major musical composition; 8 activity, life; 9 price change

mov′er n one whose business or work
is moving household effects of people who change their residence

mov′ie n colloq 1 motion picture; 2 the
movies npl a motion pictures; b
motion-picture theater; c motion-
picture industry

mov′ing adj 1 having influence; causing
action; 2 stirring the feelings or af-
fections; pathetic || SYN impressive,
imposing, stirring, exciting, touching, affecting

mov′ing van′ n large covered truck for
moving furniture and other movable
possessions

mow¹ /mō/ [OE māwan] v (pp mowed
or mown /mōn′/) vt 1 to cut down,
as grass or grain; 2 to cut grass or
grain from; 3 mow down to kill in
great numbers || vi 4 to cut grass or
grain || mow′er n

mow² /mou/ [OE mūga] n 1 heap of
hay or grain stored in a barn; 2
compartment in a barn for hay or
grain

mox·i·bus·tion /moks′ēbus′chən/ [Eng
moxa flammable herb + L uro
(ustus) to burn] n art of treating
disease with herbs, roots, bark,
leaves, and animal extracts, practiced esp. in China

mox·ie /moks′ē/ [name of soft drink]
n slang 1 pep, vigor; 2 courage

Mo·zam·bique /mōz′əmbēk′/ n republic in SE Africa (9,300,000; 799,380
sq.m.; cap. Can Phumo)

Moz·ar·ab /mōzar′əb/ [Sp mozárabe
< Ar musta′rib would-be Arab] n
Christian in Moorish Spain during
the occupation || Moz·ar′a·bic adj

Mo·zart, Wolf·gang A·ma·de·us
/wōōlf′gaŋ am′ədā′əs mō′tsärt/ n
(1756–91) Austrian composer

MP, M.P. Military Police

mph, m.p.h miles per hour

Mr. /mist′ər/ n (pl Messrs. /mes′ərz/)
Mister, title used before a man's
name or position

Mrs. /mis′iz/ n (pl Mmes. /mādäm′,
-dam′/) title used before the name
of a married woman

Ms. /miz′, miz/ n title sometimes used
before the name of a married or unmarried woman

MS motor ship

MS., ms. (pl MSS., mss.) manuscript

M.S., M.Sc. Master of Science

Msgr. Monsignor

M.Sgt., M/Sgt. Master Sergeant

MST Mountain Standard Time

Mt. 1 Mount; 2 Mountain

mu /m(y)ōō′/ n twelfth letter of the
Greek alphabet M μ

much /much/ [OE *micel*] *adj* (**more; most**) **1** great in quantity, measure, amount, or degree || *adv* **2** to a great degree or extent; **3** about, approximately || *n* **4** great quantity; **5** something considerable or unusual; **6 make much of** to treat as of great importance

mu·ci·lage /myōōˈsˈilij/ [LL *mucilago* moldy juice] *n* **1** gummy substance found in certain plants; **2** adhesive fluid made of a gum or like substance mixed with water || **mu'ci·lag'i·nous** /-laj'-/ *adj*

muck /muk/ [ME *muk* dung < Scand] *n* **1** moist manure; **2** mixture of rich black earth and decayed matter, often used as fertilizer; **3** dirt, filth

muck'rake' *vi* to search out and expose corruption, dishonesty, or wrongdoing on the part of public men || **muck'rak'er** *n*

mu·cous /myōōˈkəs/ [< *mucus*] *adj* pert. to, resembling, or secreting mucus

mu'cous mem'brane *n* moist lining of those cavities and canals of the body that communicate with the exterior

mu·cus /myōōˈkəs/ [L = snot] *n* viscid secretion of the mucous membranes

mud /mud/ [ME *mode*] *n* soft wet earth; mire

mud'der *n* race horse that runs well on a muddy track

mud·dle /mudˈəl/ [< *mud*] *vt* **1** to confuse or stupefy, as with liquor; **2** to bungle; mix up; **3** to stir, as a cocktail || *vi* **4 muddle through** to come to a successful end despite lack of planning or directed effort || *n* **5** mixup, mess

mud'dle·head'ed *adj* confused; stupid

mud'dler *n* **1** one who muddles; **2** stick for stirring drinks

mud'dy *adj* (**-di·er; -di·est**) **1** full of or covered with mud; **2** clouded; **3** confused; vague || *v* (**-died**) *vt* **4** to make muddy; **5** to make turbid; **6** to make confused

mud'guard' *n* guard or shield over a wheel, as of an automobile, to check dirt flying from below

mud'sling'ing *n* spreading of malicious gossip about one's opponent or competitor || **mud'sling'er** *n*

mu·ez·zin /m(y)ōōˈezˈin/ [Ar *mu'adhdhin*] *n* Muslim public crier who calls the faithful to prayer from a minaret

muff /muf/ [D *mof* < MF *moufle* mitten] *n* **1** warm, soft, cylindrical cover into the ends of which the hands are thrust for protection from the cold; **2** *sports* failure to hold on to a ball; **3** bungle || *vt colloq* **4** to bungle; **5** to fail to catch (a ball)

muf·fin /mufˈin/ [?] *n* small round sometimes sweetened quick bread served usu. with butter and often eaten hot

muf·fle /mufˈəl/ [ME *muflen*] *vt* **1** to wrap up closely and warmly; **2** to cover up so as to deaden the sound of; **3** to deaden (sound)

muf'fler *n* **1** heavy scarf for the neck; **2** any of various devices for muffling sound, as the sound of the exhaust gases of an internal-combustion engine

muf·ti /mufˈtē/ [Ar] *n* **1** Muslim interpreter of the law; **2** civilian dress, esp. when worn by one who usually wears a uniform

mug /mug/ [?] *n* **1** cup of earthenware or metal, usu. with a handle; **2** quantity it contains; **3** *slang* **a** face; **b** grimace; **c** ruffian || *v* (**mugged; mug·ging**) *vt* **4** to attack and beat (a person) for the purpose of robbing; **5** *slang* to photograph the face or profile of, as for police files || *vi* **6** to grimace

mug'ger *n* one who assaults people for the purpose of robbing them || **mug'ging** *n*

mug'gy [< *dial.* *mug* drizzle] *adj* (**-gi·er; -gi·est**) humid and oppressive (weather) || **mug'gi·ness** *n*

Mu·ham·mad /mōōhamˈəd/ *n* (570–632) Arab founder of Islam

Mu·ham'mad·an *adj* & *n* Muslim

mu·lat·to /m(y)ōōlatˈō, mə-/ [Sp *mulato*] *n* (**-toes**) person with a light-brown skin pigmentation of mixed African and Caucasian ancestry

mul·ber·ry /mulˈberˈē, -bərē/ [OE *mōrberie* < L *morum*] *n* (**-ries**) **1** any of a genus (*Morus*) of trees bearing a sweet berry and broad leaves; **2** fruit of this tree

mulch /mulch/ [ME *molsh* soft] *n* **1** layer of dried leaves, straw, etc., used to protect the roots of plants || *vt* **2** to cover with mulch

mulct /mulkt/ [L *mulcta*] *n* **1** fine, penalty || *vt* **2** to fine; **3** to obtain by fraud; **4** to cheat, defraud

mule[1] /myōōl/ [OF < L *mula*] *n* **1** offspring of a male donkey and a mare; **2** *colloq* obstinate person

mule[2] [MF < L *mulleus* red shoe] *n* slipper that leaves the heel bare

mule' skin'ner *n colloq* muleteer

mu·le·teer' /-lətir'/ [MF *muletier*] *n* mule driver

mul'ish *adj* obstinate, stubborn

mull[1] /mul/ [?] *vt* to warm, spice, and sweeten, as ale or wine

mull[2] [?] *vi* **mull over** to ponder, study

mul·lah /mulˈə, mōōlˈə/ [Pers *mulla* < Ar] *n* complimentary title given to scholars and religious teachers in Islamic countries

mul·lein /mulˈən/ [< AF *moleine* < *mol* soft] *n* coarse plant (*Verbascum thapsus*) with large woolly leaves and yellow flowers in tall spikes

mul·let /mulˈit/ [MF *mulet*] *n* (**-let** or **-lets**) **1** any of a family (Mugilidae) of food fishes of Europe and America; **2** any of various other freshwater fishes, generally suckers

mul'li·ga·n (stew') /mul'igən/ [< name *Mulligan*] *n slang* stew made from scraps of meat and vegetables

mul·li·ga·taw·ny /mul'igətŏn'ē/ [Tamil *milakutanni* pepper water] *n* East Indian soup made of meat and curry

mul·lion /mul'yən/ [MF *moinel*] *n* **1** upright bar or slender column, esp. one of stone, forming a division between the lights of a window; **2** upright piece between panels, as in a door

mul·ti- /mult'i-, mult'i-/ [L < *multus* much, many] *comb form* many; more than two; more than one

mul'ti·cel'lu·lar *adj* having or composed of many cells

mul'ti·far'i·ous /-fer'ē-əs/ [LL *multifarius* manifold] *adj* having much variety; diverse

mul'ti·fold *adj* numerous; manifold

mul'ti·form' *adj* having many different shapes or forms

mul'ti·lat'er·al *adj* **1** many-sided; **2** involving more than two nations

mul'ti·lin'gual *adj* **1** speaking more than two languages; **2** spoken or written in more than two languages

mul'ti·mil'lion·aire' *n* one who possesses at least several million dollars, pounds, pesos, etc.

mul'ti·na'tion·al *adj* **1** pert. to or involving more than two nations || *n* **2** corporation that has divisions in more than two nations

mul·tip'a·rous /-tip'ərəs/ [< *multi-* + L *parere* to produce] *adj* giving birth to more than one offspring at a time

mul'ti·par'tite /-pär'tīt/ [< *multi-* + L *pars* (*partis*) part] *adj* **1** having many parts or divisions; **2** participated in by more than two nations

mul·ti·ple /mult'ipəl/ [F < LL *multiplus*] *n* **1** number which contains another an exact number of times || *adj* **2** having or involving elements or parts

mul'ti·ple-choice' *adj* (examination) listing several answers for each question from which the correct one must be chosen

mul'ti·ple scle·ro'sis *n* neurological disease characterized by weakness and lack of muscular coordination, caused by sclerosis of parts of the spinal cord

mul'ti·plex' /-pleks'/ [< L *multi-* + *plex* fold] *adj* **1** manifold; **2** equipped to transmit two or more sets of signals in one or both directions simultaneously over the same wire or radio band; **3** pert. to an aerial stereoscopic method whereby with three cameras maps are prepared that give a three-dimensional effect || *n* **4** multiplex electronic sys-

tem; **5** multiplex topographic instrument || *vt* & *vi* **6** to transmit by multiplex

mul'ti·pli·cand' /-plikand'/ [L *multiplicandum* to be multiplied] *n* number to be multiplied by another

mul'ti·pli·ca'tion [< *multi-* + L *plicare* to fold] *n* **1** act or process of multiplying or state of being multiplied; **2** *math* operation by which any given number or quantity is increased a given number of times

mul'ti·pli·ca'tion sign' *n* symbol × or ·, indicating multiplication

mul'ti·plic'i·ty /-plis'itē/ [LL *multiplicitas*] *n* (*-ties*) **1** condition or quality of being manifold or various; **2** a great number

mul'ti·pli'er /-plī'ər/ *n* **1** one who or that which multiplies; **2** number by which another is multiplied

mul'ti·ply' /-plī'/ [OF *multiplier* < L *multiplicare*] *v* (*-plied*) *vt* **1** to increase the number or quantity of; **2** *math* to find the product of by multiplication || *vi* **3** to increase in number or extent; **4** to perform multiplication

mul'ti·stage' *adj* **1** (rocket) having more than one stage; **2** *electron* (amplifier) of more than one stage

mul'ti·tude' /-t(y)ōod'/ [L *multitudo*] *n* **1** numerousness; **2** great number; **3** crowd || **mul'ti·tu'di·nous** *adj* || SYN crowd, mob, populace, rabble

mul·ti·va·lent /mult'ivāl'ənt, multiv'ələnt/ [*multi-* + L *valens* (*-entis*)] *adj* *chem* having a valence of three or higher || **mul'ti·va'lence** *n*

mum¹ /mum'/ [ME *momme*] *adj* **1** silent; **2** keep mum to say nothing; **3** mum's the word! say nothing!

mum² *colloq* chrysanthemum

mum³ *n* Brit **1** mother; **2** madame

mum·ble /mum'bəl/ [ME *momele*] *vt* **1** to utter indistinctly || *vi* **2** to speak indistinctly; mutter in a low tone || *n* **3** mumbled utterance

mum'ble·ty·peg' /-tĕpeg'/ [< *mumble the peg*] *n* children's game in which the blade of a pocket knife must stick in the ground after being tossed in the air in various prescribed ways

mum·bo jum·bo /mum'bō jum'bō/ [WAfr] *n* **1** meaningless incantation or ritual; **2** purposely confusing language

mum'mer *n* one who wears a disguise or fancy costume, as at a New Year's revel; **2** actor or pantomimist

mum'mer·y *n* (*-ies*) **1** mummers' performance; **2** ceremonies or performance regarded as ridiculous or insincere

mum'mi·fy' *v* (*-fied*) *vt* **1** to make into a mummy || *vi* **2** to shrivel; dry up || **mum'mi·fi·ca'tion** *n*

mum·my /mum'ē/ [ML *mummia* < Ar *mūmiyah*] *n* (*-mies*) **1** body of a human being or animal embalmed

as in the ancient Egyptian manner;
2 any well-preserved corpse; 3 dried-
up, shrunken human being

mumps /mumps'/ [< *dial. mump* to
grin] *nsg* contagious disease marked
by swelling of the salivary glands,
esp. the parotid

munch /munch'/ [ME *monchen*] *vt &
vi* to chew with a crunching noise ||
munch'er *n*

mun·dane /mundān'/, mun'dān/ [LL
mundanus < L *mundus* world] *adj* 1
worldly; 2 common, ordinary || SYN
secular, temporal, worldly, terrestrial, earthly

Mu·nich /myōō'nik/ *n* city in W Germany, capital of Bavaria (1,200,000)

mu·nic·i·pal /myōōnis'ipəl/ [< L *mu-
niceps* (*-cipis*) citizen] *adj* of or pert.
to a city or town or to its government

mu·nic'i·pal'i·ty /-pal'itē/ *n* (*-ties*)
town, city, or other similar entity
having a separate corporate existence

mu·nif·i·cent /myōōnif'isənt/ [< L *mu-
nificentia* generosity] *adj* very gen-
erous in giving; bountiful; lavish ||
mu·nif'i·cence *n* || SYN large, vast,
princely, lavish (see *generous*)

mu·ni·tion /myōōnish'ən/ [L *munitio*
(*-onis*) fortress] *vt* 1 to supply with
munitions || *n* 2 **munitions** *pl* weap-
ons and ammunition used in warfare

mu·ral /myōōr'əl/ [< L *murus* wall]
adj 1 pert. to or resembling a wall;
2 on or against a wall || *n* 3 paint-
ing on the surface of a wall

mur·der /mur'dər/ [OE *morthor*] *n* 1
law unlawful killing of a human
being, usu. with malice aforethought;
2 *slang* something dangerous, diffi-
cult, or extremely unpleasant || *vt* 3
to kill (a human being) with deliberate malice; 4 to destroy; 5 to ruin;
spoil || **mur'der·er** *n* || **mur'der·ess**
nfem || SYN *v* slay, assassinate,
slaughter (see *kill*)

mur'der·ous *adj* 1 pert. to, guilty of, or
causing murder; 2 brutal; 3 very
trying

mu'ri·at'ic ac'id /myōōr'ē·at'ik/ [< L
muria brine] *n* hydrochloric acid

murk /murk'/ [ME *mirke*] *n* darkness

murk'y *adj* (*-i·er*; *-i·est*) 1 dark; obscure; gloomy; 2 hazy, misty; 3 con-
fused; not clear || **murk'i·ly** *adv* ||
murk'i·ness *n*

mur·mur /mur'mər/ [L *murmurare*] *n*
1 low indistinct sound, as of a running stream or of low voices; 2
complaint in a low muttering tone; 3
med abnormal sound of the heart
heard through a stethoscope || *vi* 4
to make a murmur; 5 to mutter in
discontent || *vt* 6 to utter in a mur-
mur || **mur'mur·er** *n* || SYN *v* growl,
mutter, whine (see *complain*)

Mur'phy bed' /murf'ē/ [W. L. *Murphy*
Am inventor] *n* bed that folds into
a cabinet or closet when not in use

mus·cat /musk'ət, mus'kat/ [MF =
musk-flavored] *n* 1 any of several
musk-flavored grapes; 2 vine yielding these grapes; 3 wine made from
them

mus·ca·tel /musk'ətel'/ [*dim.* of *muscat*] *n* sweet wine made from the
muscat grape

mus·cle /mus'əl/ [L *musculus* little
mouse] *n* 1 organ of fibrous tissue
capable of contracting and producing movements of the body; 2 mus-
cular strength; 3 coercive force || *vt*
4 **muscle one's way into** to force
one's way into || *vi* 5 **muscle in** to
force one's way in

mus'cle·bound' *adj* having enlarged
and inelastic muscles from too much
exercise

mus'cle·man' /-man'/ *n* (*-men* /-men'/)
thug hired by a gangster to carry out
acts of violence

Mus·co·vy /musk'əvē/ *n archaic &
poet.* 1 Moscow; 2 Russia || **Mus'-
co·vite'** /-vīt'/ *adj & n*

mus·cu·lar /musk'yələr/ [see **muscle**]
adj 1 of or pert. to muscles; 2
strong; vigorous

mus'cu·lar dys'tro·phy /dis'trəfē/ [*dys-
+ -trophy*] *n* disease of unknown
origin that causes progressive wasting of the muscles

mus'cu·la·ture /-ləchər/ *n* muscular
system of the body

muse /myōōz'/ [MF *muser*] *vi* to medi-
tate in silence || SYN consider, reflect,
ponder, meditate, dream, deliberate,
brood, contemplate || DISCR We *con-
template* by regarding thoughtfully,
by studying; we *contemplate* our finished work to appraise it; we *contemplate* the future, while hazy plans
outline themselves. We *consider* by
viewing mentally; we *consider* a
change of occupation with caution
and prudence; we can forget our disadvantages by *considering* our advantages; we *consider* ways and
means, and the practical aspects of
a situation. To *reflect* is to *consider*
what is past or what is to happen to
us in the light of its moral value or
spiritual meaning; we may with
profit *reflect* upon the brevity of life,
the improvement of our inner selves,
the mistakes we have made. We
deliberate by thinking carefully,
slowly, weighing the pros and cons
of the argument or question in question. We *ponder* by examining seriously, often anxiously, what has
taken place, or some future course,
as he *pondered* the motives Foster
might have had for betraying him,
we *pondered* our next move. *Muse*
suggests freely wandering thoughts;
we *muse* on the past, what is now
going on, or what may happen tomorrow, drowned in imaginative, not
too serious, reflection

Muse /myōz′/ [Gk *Mousa*] *n* 1 *class. myth.* any of the nine goddesses who presided over the arts and sciences; 2 muse guiding genius of a poet

mu·sette′ bag′ /myōōzet′/ [< MF *muse* bagpipe] *n* small bag with a shoulder strap carried by army officers for their personal belongings

mu·se·um /myōōzē′əm/ [L < Gk *mouseion* seat of the Muses] *n* building or place for exhibiting artistic, scientific, or historical objects

mush[1] /mush′/ [prob var of *mash*] *n* 1 porridge of boiled corn meal; 2 any thick mixture like mush; 3 anything lacking in firmness; 4 mawkishness

mush[2] [prob CanF *moucher* to hurry] *vi* to travel over snow with a dog sled

mush′room′ [MF *mousseron*] *n* 1 any of various forms of fleshy fungi of rapid growth, having a thick stem and usu. an umbrella-shaped top, esp. one of the edible species of the family Agaricaceae; 2 anything resembling a mushroom in shape and esp. in rapid growth || *vi* 3 to grow rapidly like a mushroom

mush′room cloud′ *n* large cloud shaped like a mushroom, resulting from a nuclear explosion in the air

mush′y *adj* (-i·er; -i·est) 1 soft; yielding like porridge; 2 *colloq* mawkish; effusively sentimental

mu·sic /myōōz′ik/ [Gk *mousike* (techne) (art) of the Muses] *n* 1 art of making harmonious combinations of tones; 2 harmony or melody; 3 musical composition; 4 such a composition written or printed; 5 such compositions collectively; 6 any harmonious sounds; 7 **face the music** to accept the consequences of one's actions

mu·si·cal *adj* 1 pert. to music; 2 producing music; 3 melodious; harmonious; 4 having an appreciation of or a talent for music; 5 set to music || **mu′si·cal·ly** *adv* || **SYN** tuneful, melodious, harmonious, dulcet, sweet || **ANT** discordant, inharmonious, unmusical

mu′si·cal com′e·dy *n* light amusing play, interspersed with songs, duets, choruses, and dancing

mu·si·cale /myōōz′ikal′/ *n* private entertainment of vocal and instrumental music

mu′sic box′ *n* 1 box containing a musical instrument that plays automatically; 2 jukebox

mu′sic hall′ *n* 1 concert hall; 2 *Brit* vaudeville theater

mu·si·cian /myōōzish′ən/ *n* one skilled in music, esp. a performer, composer, or conductor || **mu·si′cian·ship′** *n*

mu′si·col′o·gy /-kol′əjē/ *n* study of the history, theory, and science of music || **mu′si·col′o·gist** *n*

musk /musk′/ [L *muscus* < Pers *mushk*] *n* 1 strong-scented substance of persistent fragrance obtained from the male musk deer; 2 odor of this substance or something resembling it || **musk′y** *adj* (-i·er; -i·est)

musk′ deer′ *n* small hornless deer (*Moschus moschiferus*) of central Asia, the male of which secretes musk

mus·keg /mus′keg/ [< Algonquian] *n* Canadian & N U.S. sphagnum swamp

mus·kel·lunge /musk′əlunj′/ [< Ojibwa] *n* (-lunge or -lunges) large edible pike (*Esox masquinongy*) of central North America, prized as a game fish

mus·ket /musk′it/ [MF *mousquet* < It *moschetto* sparrow hawk] *n* 1 heavy large-caliber shoulder gun, predecessor of the modern rifle; 2 any shoulder gun used by infantry soldiers

mus′ket·eer′ *n* soldier armed with a musket

mus′ket·ry *n* 1 fire of small arms; 2 art of firing such arms; 3 muskets collectively

musk′mel′on *n* edible fruit of any of several varieties of a trailing vine (*Cucumis melo*), as the canteloupe

musk′ ox′ *n* heavyset American arctic ox (*Ovibos moschatus*)

musk′rat′ *n* (-rat or -rats) cat-sized aquatic rodent (*Ondatra zibethica*) of North America, with a glossy dark brown fur and a musky odor

Mus·lim /muz′lim, mōōz′-, mōōs′-/ [Ar = one who submits] *n* adherent of Islam || also *adj*

mus·lin /muz′lin/ [F *mousseline* < It *mussolina* of Mosul, Mesopotamia] *n* 1 any of various fine cotton fabrics; 2 any of various heavier fabrics, used for sheets, etc.

muss /mus′/ [prob blend of *mess* and *fuss*] *colloq n* 1 disorder, mess || *vt* 2 to disorder; rumple || **muss′y** *adj* (-i·er; -i·est)

mus·sel /mus′əl/ [OE *muscle* < LL *muscula*] *n* 1 any of several bivalve mollusks; 2 edible mollusk of the family Mytilidae

Mus·so·li·ni, Be·ni·to /benē′tō mōōs′-selē′nē, mōōs′-/ *n* (Il Duce) (1883–1945) Fascist leader; premier of Italy 1922–1943

Mus·sul·man /mus′əlmən/ [Pers *Mus-ulmān* Muslims] *n* (-men /-mən/ or -mans /-mənz/) Muslim

must[1] /must′/ [L *mustum*] *n* grape juice pressed for making wine but not yet fermented

must[2] [< OE *mōste pt* of *mōt* may] *modal aux* 1 am, are, or is: **a** obliged or compelled to; **b** likely to, as *he*

must have gone, it must be raining;
c certain to, as *we all must die* || *adj*
2 vitally necessary, as *this is must
legislation* || *n* **3**, **a must** something
that must be done || SYN *v* (see
ought¹)

mus·tache /mus′tash, məstash′/ [MF
moustache < It *mostaccio* < MGk
moustaki] *n* the hair worn on a man's
upper lip

mus·ta·chio /məstash′ō, -stash′ē·ō′,
-stäsh′ō, -stäsh′ē·ō′/ [Sp *mostacho*
< It *mostaccio*] *n* mustache, esp. if
extending beyond the lip

mus·tang /mus′taŋ/ [Sp *mestengo*] *n*
1 small hardy half-wild horse of the
prairies of America, descended from
Spanish stock; **2** *navy slang* officer
commissioned from the ranks

mus·tard /mus′tərd/ [OF *moustarde*] *n*
1 any of a genus (*Brassica*) of plants
whose pungent seeds in powder or
paste form are used as a condiment
and in plasters; **2** condiment prepared from the ground or powdered
seed of a mustard plant

mus′tard gas′ *n* oily liquid —(ClCH₂·
CH₂)₂S— having a mustardlike odor,
and causing severe blistering, blindness, and death, used in chemical
warfare in World War I

mus′tard plas′ter *n* poultice made of a
paste of mustard, flour, and water
spread on a piece of cloth or paper

mus·ter /mus′tər/ [OF *mostre*] *vt* **1** to
assemble and array, as troops for
review or roll call; **2** to collect and
show, as *to muster one's courage;*
3 muster in to enlist, as troops; **4
muster out** to discharge from mili-
tary service || *vi* **5** to be assembled ||
n **6** assembly or gathering, esp. of
troops; **7** roll of troops thus assembled; **8** assemblage or collection; **9
pass muster** to be approved or accepted

must·n't /mus′ənt/ must not

mus·ty /mus′tē/ [?] *adj* (-ti·er; -ti·est)
1 having a stale or moldy flavor or
odor; **2** antiquated, obsolete || **mus′·
ti·ness** *n*

mu·ta·ble /myōōt′əbəl/ [< L *mutare*
(-*atus*) to change] *adj* **1** capable of
or susceptible to change; **2** fickle, in-
constant || **mu′ta·bil′i·ty** /-bil′-/ *n* ||
SYN changeable, variable, inconstant,
undependable, wavering, unsteady,
unstable

mu·tant /myōōt′ənt/ *adj* **1** undergoing
mutation || *n* **2** new type or organism
resulting from mutation

mu′tate *vt & vi* to change

mu·ta′tion *n* **1** alteration, change; variation; **2** *biol* a sudden variation in
an inheritable characteristic in a
plant or animal, caused by a change
in a gene or chromosome; **b** mutant

mu·ta·tis mu·tan·dis /myōōtät′is myōō-
tan′dis/ [L] *adv* the necessary
changes having been made

mute /myōōt′/ [MF *muet* < *mutus*] *adj*
1 speechless; silent; **2** lacking the
power of speech; dumb; **3** silent (let-
ter) || *n* **4** one who cannot speak or
who remains silent; **5** *phonet* stop;
6 *mus* device for deadening tone ||
vt **7** to muffle or deaden the sound
of || **mute′ly** *adv*

mu·ti·late /myōōt′ilāt′/ [L *mutilare*
(-*atus*)] *vt* **1** to cut off a limb or necessary part of; maim; **2** to render
incomplete or imperfect || **mu′ti·la′·
tion** *n* || **mu′ti·la′tor** *n* || SYN cripple,
disfigure, destroy, maim, expunge,
delete

mu·ti·nous *adj* disposed to or guilty of
rebellion against authority; insubor-
dinate || **mu′ti·nous·ly** *adv* || SYN in-
surgent, insubordinate, seditious, tur-
bulent, riotous || ANT obedient, trac-
table, submissive

mu·ti·ny /myōōt′inē/ [MF *mutin* re-
bellious] *n* (-nies) **1** rebellion against
authority, esp. of soldiers or sailors
against their officers || *v* (-nied) *vi* **2**
to commit mutiny || **mu′ti·neer′** *n* ||
SYN *n* insurrection, riot, revolt (see
revolution)

mutt /mut′/ [*muttonhead*] *n* *slang* mongrel dog

mut·ter /mut′ər/ [ME *moteren*] *vi* **1**
to utter words in a low voice with
the lips almost closed; murmur; **2** to
make a low rumbling sound || *vt* **3**
to utter low and indistinctly || *n* **4**
act of muttering; **5** something mut-
tered || **mut′ter·er** *n*

mut·ton /mut′ən/ [OF *moton* sheep]
n flesh of sheep used as food

mut′ton·chops′ *npl* side whiskers that
are narrow at the top and broad and
turned toward the corners of the
mouth at the bottom

mut′ton·head′ *n* *colloq* stupid person;
oaf, dolt

mu·tu·al /myōōch′ōō·əl/ [< L *mutuus*
borrowed] *adj* **1** done or felt by each
toward the other; interchanged; given
and received; **2** possessed or shared
by, or affecting, two or more per-
sons; **3** joint, common || **mu′tu·al·ly**
adv || **mu′tu·al′i·ty** /-al′-/ *n* || SYN
common, reciprocal, joint, correlative
|| DISCR That is *common* which be-
longs to, issues from, or is done by
or shared alike with, more than one;
as *common* consent; *common* knowledge; *common* property. That is
mutual which is felt by each toward
the other, as *mutual* love, hatred;
or which is done by each toward the
other, as *mutual* aid, advantage; or
which is experienced in common, as
mutual misery. Mutual, in the sense
of *common* to two or more persons,
as in the expression *our mutual
friend*, is not sanctioned by the best
usage, though the word is used in
this sense by writers of excellent
standing. *Mutual* and *reciprocal* are

sometimes used interchangeably, as *reciprocal* help; *mutual* aid; *mutual* or *reciprocal* love. *Reciprocal* is more often used in connection with an act or thought performed in return for something previously done by another, as *reciprocal* recriminations; *reciprocal* responsibilities

mu·tu·al fund' *n* investment company that issues and sells shares without limit and stands ready to repurchase them on demand

mu·tu·al in·duc'tion *n* production of a flow of current in a conductor by a varying flow of current in an adjacent conductor

muu-muu /mōō'mōō'/ [Hawaiian] *n* loose dress, often with colorful patterns

mu·zhik /mōōzhik', mōō'zhik/ [Russ] *n* Russian peasant

muz·zle /muz'əl/ [MF *musel* snout] *vt* 1 to secure or enclose the mouth or snout of (an animal) to prevent eating or biting; 2 to prevent from talking; silence ‖ *n* 3 the projecting mouth, lips, and nose of an animal; snout; 4 cover or guard to put over an animal's muzzle; 5 mouth of the barrel of a firearm

muz'zle-load'er *n* gun that is loaded through the muzzle

my /mī'/ [OE *mīn*] *adj* possessive of I: of or belonging to me

my·col·o·gy /mīkol'əjē/ [< Gk *mykes* fungus + -*logy*] *n* branch of botany dealing with fungi ‖ **my·col'o·gist** *n* ‖ **my'co·log'i·cal** /-əloj'-/ *adj*

my·e·lin /mī'əlin/ [< Gk *myelos* marrow] *n* fatty substance encasing the central portion of certain nerve fibers

my'e·li'tis /-līt'is/ *n* inflammation of the spinal cord or of the bone marrow

my·na, my·nah /mīn'ə/ [Hindi *mainā*] *n* any of several Asian birds of the starling family (Sturnidae), several species of which have the ability to mimic human speech

my·o·pi·a /mī-ōp'ē-ə/ [Gk] *n* 1 nearsightedness; 2 lack of foresight ‖ **my·op'ic** /-op'-/ *adj*

myr·i·ad /mir'ē-əd/ [Gk *myrias* (-*ados*) 10,000] *n* 1 very large number; 2 very large number of persons or things ‖ *adj* 3 innumerable

myr·mi·don /murm'idən, -don'/ [name of ancient Gk tribe] *n* one who is unquestioning and unscrupulous in executing the orders of a superior

myrrh /mur'/ [OE *myrre* < Gk *myr·rha*] *n* aromatic resinous substance exuded by various species of plants (genus *Commiphora*) of Arabia and E Africa, used in perfumery and incense

myr·tle /murt'əl/ [ML *myrtillus*] *n* 1 any of a genus (*Myrtus*) of evergreen shrubs, esp. a species (*M. communis*)

with white or rosy flowers and glossy leaves of S Europe; 2 any of several unrelated American plants

my·self /mīself'/ *pron* 1 reflexive form of me; 2 emphatic form of me, as *I myself did it*; 3 my normal self, as *I am not myself today*

mys·te·ri·ous /mistir'ē-əs/ *adj* 1 containing, involving, or characterized by mystery; 2 obscure; unexplained ‖ **mys·te'ri·ous·ly** *adv* ‖ **mys·te'ri·ous·ness** *n* ‖ SYN dark, secret, mystic, unfathomable, baffling

mys·ter·y /mist'ərē/ [Gk *mysterion*] *n* (-ies) 1 something secret, hidden, or unexplained; 2 obscurity, secrecy; 3 that which is beyond human understanding; 4 mystery play; 5 sacrament; 6 story or play about a mystery; 7 **mysteries** *pl* among the ancients, sacred rites to which only certain persons were admitted after the imposition of vows of secrecy

mys'ter·y play' *n* medieval play based on a Biblical story

mys·tic /mist'ik/ [Gk *mystikos* secret] *adj* 1 beyond human understanding; 2 involving some secret meaning; allegorical; 3 mysterious; 4 of or pert. to mystics or mysticism ‖ *n* 5 person who strives to attain knowledge of mysteries beyond the understanding of ordinary mortals, as by meditation or a state of spiritual ecstasy ‖ SYN *adj* mysterious, hidden, recondite

mys'ti·cal *adj* 1 mystic; 2 spiritually symbolic

mys'ti·cism *n* 1 quality or character of being mystic; 2 belief in direct spiritual union with God through meditation and surrender to His will; 3 belief in the attainment of ultimate truth through intuition

mys'ti·fy' [F *mystifier*] *v* (-fied) *vt* 1 to involve in mystery; 2 to bewilder, puzzle ‖ **mys'ti·fi·ca'tion** *n* ‖ SYN confuse, baffle, puzzle (see *perplex*) ‖ ANT clear up, explain, elucidate, unravel, disentangle

mys·tique /mistēk'/ [F] *n* mystical beliefs and attitudes suffusing a person, group, idea, or object, causing an aura of mystical power to surround him or it

myth /mith'/ [Gk *mythos* word] *n* 1 traditional, legendary story, often founded on some event in the early history of a people and embodying some religious belief of that people; 2 false belief held by a people to justify social institutions such as slavery; 3 imaginary person, thing, or event ‖ **myth'i·cal** *adj*

my·thol·o·gy /-thol'-/ *n* (-gies) 1 a body of the myths of a people or person; 2 science or study of myths ‖ **my·thol'o·gist** *n* ‖ **myth'o·log'i·cal** /-loj'-/ *adj*

N

N, n /en'/ *n* (**N's** or **Ns**, **n's** or **ns**) 14th letter of the English alphabet

N 1 North(ern); 2 New; 3 *chem* nitrogen; 4 something shaped like an N; 5 14th in order or in a series; 6 *chess* knight; 7 *typ* en

n indefinite number, esp. a constant integer denoting degree, power, number of a term in a series, or the like

N. 1 Navy; 2 Norse; 3 November

n. 1 [L *natus*] born; 2 neuter; 3 nominative; 4 noun

N., n. 1 new; 2 noon; 3 north(ern); 4 *chem* normal (solution)

Na [L *natrium*] *chem* sodium

N.A. North America

NAACP or **N.A.A.C.P.** *n* National Association for the Advancement of Colored People

nab /nab'/ [?] *v* (**nabbed; nab·bing**) *vt colloq* 1 to seize unexpectedly; 2 to arrest

na·bob /nā'bob/ [Hindi *nawwāb* governor] *n* rich and/or prominent man

na·celle /nəsel'/ [F = small boat] *n aeron* basket, cabin, or other enclosure for carrying passengers or crew or housing motors on aircraft

na·cre /nāk'ər/ [F] *n* mother-of-pearl ‖ **na·cre·ous** /nā'krē-əs/ *adj*

na·dir /nād'ər/ [Ar = opposite] *n* 1 *astron* point opposite the zenith; 2 lowest point

nag¹ /nag'/ [ME *nagge* small horse] *n colloq* decrepit horse

nag² [prob Scand] *n* 1 one who scolds constantly ‖ *v* (**nagged; nag·ging**) *vt* 2 to find fault with continually; 3 to urge ‖ *vi* 4 to scold or urge constantly ‖ **nag'ger** *n* ‖ **nag·ging** *adj*

Na·ga·sa·ki /näg'əsäk'ē/ *n* seaport city, Kyushu island, Japan (350,000) destroyed August 9, 1945 by the second atomic bomb used in warfare

nai·ad /nā'əd, nī'ad/ [Gk *naias* (-*ados*)] *n* (**nai·ads** or **nai·a·des** /-dēz'/) 1 *class. myth.* water nymph; 2 aquatic larva of certain insects, as the dragonfly

nail /nāl/ [OE *nægel*] 1 horny substance at the ends of the fingers and toes; 2 slender pointed piece of metal, driven with a hammer to hold pieces together; 3 **hit the nail on the head** to sum up exactly ‖ *vt* 4 to fasten with nails; 5 *colloq* a to catch, trap; b to detect, expose; 6 to hit with a blow or weapon; 7 **nail down** to settle definitively

nail' pol'ish *n* lacquer or enamel for giving a sheen to the fingernails

Nai·ro·bi /nīrōb'ē/ *n* capital of Kenya (270,000)

na·ive, na·ïve /nä·ēv'/ [F] *adj* 1 artless, simple, unaffected; 2 credulous ‖ **na·ive'ly, na·ïve'ly** *adv* ‖ **na·ive·té, na·ïve·té** /nä·ēvtä'/ *n*

na·ked /nāk'id/ [OE *nacod*] *adj* 1 unclothed, nude; 2 bare, uncovered; 3 without concealment, obvious; 4 plain, unadorned, as *the naked truth*; 5 unaided, as *the naked eye* ‖ **na'ked·ness** *n* ‖ SYN nude, denuded, uncovered, exposed, barren, simple ‖ ANT covered, clothed, draped, robed

NAM or **N.A.M.** *n* National Association of Manufacturers

nam·by–pam·by /nam'bē-pam'bē/ [nickname of Eng writer of sentimental verse, *Ambrose Philips* (1675–1749)] *adj* 1 weakly sentimental (person or writing); 2 affectedly nice ‖ *n* (**-bies**) 3 namby-pamby person

name /nām'/ [OE *nama*] *n* 1 term or title by which a person or thing is called or known; 2 character, reputation, fame; 3 something having merely nominal existence, as, *truth had become a name*; 4 disparaging epithet; 5 famous person; 6 **in name** only having the appearance, not the reality; 7 **in the name of,** a by authority of; b in appeal to ‖ *adj* 8 having an established reputation, as *a name band* ‖ *vt* 9 to give a name to, call; 10 to specify, appoint for a special purpose, as, *name the day;* 11 to mention, call by name; 12 to identify; 13 to appoint, nominate ‖ SYN *n* appellation, epithet, designation, title, denomination, reputation ‖ DISCR *Name*, in its general sense, includes all these other terms; in its limited sense, it is that particular word by which an individual, place, animal, or thing, is spoken of or to; one's Christian or given *name* is his first, or personal, *name*; his last *name*, or surname, is his family *name*. An *appellation* is a particular *name*, given because of, or growing out of, peculiar circumstances; Lincoln won the *appellation* of "The Rail-splitter"; Aristides, a Greek philosopher, bore the *appellation* of "The Just." A *title* is a distinctive, personal *name*, bestowed or inherited as a mark of honor or rank, or falling to one assuming a certain office, as Lord, Lady, King, Judge, etc. An *epithet* as an adjective, or a word or phrase used as an adjective, is attached to a person or thing as significant of a certain characteristic. Homer refers to Dawn as the "*rosy-fingered* goddess of the morning"; Corbett, the prizefighter, won the *epithet* of "Gentleman Jim." An *epithet* frequently, but by no means always, emphasizes a bad characteristic. A *designation* is a *name* that distinguishes or marks out in a more general way than an *appellation*; classes, grades, or groups bear *designations* significant of their standing. *Denomination* names a particular class or kind, especially in a collective sense, as coins of several *denominations*

name′ day′ *n* day sacred to the saint whose name one bears, observed like a birthday in Continental Europe

name′-drop′per *n* person who implies in conversation and writing that widely known persons are his close associates or friends

name′·less *adj* 1 without a name; 2 unknown; without the author's name; 3 unmentionable; 4 without legal right to a name, illegitimate; 5 inexpressible, as a *nameless fear*

name′·ly *adv* to wit, that is to say

name′ of the game′ *n* the essential thing; what is bound to happen

name′sake *n* 1 one having the same name as another; 2 one called after another

Na·mib·i·a /nämib′ē-ə/ *n* African country, formerly South West Africa (1,500,000; 318,261 sq.m.; cap. Windhoek)

nan·keen, nan·kin /nankēn′/ [*Nanking,* China] *n* buff-colored cotton cloth

nan·ny /nan′ē/ [*Nanny,* nickname for Anne] *n* (**-nies**) 1 *Brit* nursemaid; 2 nanny goat

nan′ny goat′ *n* female goat

nap¹ /nap′/ [OE *hnæppian*] *v* (**napped; nap·ping**) *vi* 1 to take a short slumber, to doze; 2 to be off one's guard || *n* 3 short slumber, doze

nap² [ME *noppe*] *n* 1 short, projecting hairs or fibers forming the surface of some materials and lying smoothly in one direction; 2 *bot* downy covering of some plants

na·palm /nā′päm/ [*naphthalene* + *palmitate*] *n* jellied gasoline used in incendiary bombs, flamethrowers, etc.

nape /nāp/ [ME] *n* back of the neck

naph·tha /naf′thə/ [Gk] *n* volatile inflammable liquid hydrocarbon solvent used chiefly in dry cleaning

naph·tha·lene /naf′thəlēn′/ *n* crystalline coal-tar derivative —C₁₀H₈— used as a moth repellant and in dyes

naph·thol /naf′thōl/ [*naphtha* + L *oleum* oil] *n chem* any of a group of naphthalene derivatives used in making dyes and antiseptics

Na·pier′i·an log′a·rithm /nəpir′ē-ən/ [John Napier (1550–1617) Scot inventor of logarithms] *n* natural logarithm

nap·kin /nap′kin/ [ME *nappekin*] *n* small cloth or paper square, esp. one used at table

nap′kin ring′ *n* band of wood, metal, etc., for holding a folded table napkin

Na·ples /nāp′əlz/ *n* seaport in SW Italy (1,200,000)

Na·po·le·on I /nəpōl′ē-ən/ or **Napoleon Bo·na·parte** /bōn′əpärt′/ *n* (1769–1821) emperor of France 1804–15 || **na·po·le·on′ic** /-on′ik/ *adj*

na·po·le·on *n* 1 oblong custard-filled pastry; 2 former French gold coin

Na·po·le·on III *n* Louis Napoleon Bonaparte (1808–73), nephew of Napoleon I, emperor of France 1852–70

nap·py /nap′ē/ [< *napkin* + -y] *n* (**-pies**) *Brit* diaper

nar·cism /när′sizəm/ *n* narcissism || **nar·cis′tic** *adj*

nar·cis·sism /när′sisiz′əm/ *n* 1 abnormal love of one's own body; 2 self-love || **nar′cis·sist** *adj & n* || **nar′cis·sis′tic** *adj*

nar·cis·sus /närsis′əs/ [L < Gk] *n* (**-sus** or **-sus·es** or **-si** /-sī/) 1 bulbous plant of the genus *Narcissus,* such as the daffodil and the jonquil; 2 **Narcissus** *Gk myth.* youth doomed to pine away for love of his own reflection until finally changed into the narcissus

narco- [Gk *narke* numbness, stupor] *comb form* stupor, narcosis

nar·co′sis /-kōs′is/ [Gk] *n* (**-ses** /-sēz/) stupor produced by drugs || **nar′cose** /-kōs/ *adj*

nar·cot′ic /-kot′ik/ [Gk *narkotikos* numbing] *adj* 1 producing stupor or sleep || *n* 2 drug that dulls the senses esp. to pain and induces sleep or, in excessive doses, causes stupor or coma; 3 anything that soothes and induces a dreamy state; 4 person who makes habitual use of narcotics

nar·es /ner′ēz/ [L] *npl anat* nostrils

Nar′ra·gan′sett Bay′ /nar′əgan′sit/ *n* inlet of Atlantic Ocean, Rhode Island

nar·rate /narāt′, nar′āt/ [L *narrare* (-*atus*)] *vt* to tell, recite, relate || **nar′ra·tor** *n* || SYN detail, recite, recount, relate, report, tell

nar·ra′tion *n* 1 act of narrating; 2 narrative, tale

nar·ra·tive /nar′ətiv/ *n* 1 act of storytelling; 2 recital of a story or event; 3 story || also *adj* || SYN account, narration, relation, story, tale

nar·row /nar′ō/ [OE *nearu*] *adj* 1 not wide; 2 limited in size, amount, or scope; 3 illiberal, prejudiced; 4 with little margin, as a *narrow escape*; 5 exact, searching, as *narrow scrutiny* || *vt* 6 to decrease the width of; 7 to restrict || *vi* 8 to contract, become less broad || **nar′row·ly** *adv* || **nar′row·ness** *n*

nar′row-mind′ed *adj* illiberal, bigoted || **nar′row-mind′ed·ly** *adv* || **nar′row-mind′ed·ness** *n*

nar′rows *nsg & npl* narrow water passage; strait

nar·y /ner′ē/ [*ne′er a*] *adj dial.* not any

NAS·A /nas′ə/ *n* National Aeronautics and Space Administration

na·sal /nāz′əl/ [< L *nasus* nose] *adj* 1 pert. to the nose; 2 pronounced through the nose ‖ *n* **3** nasal sound, **4** *anat* either of two bones in the nose ‖ **na·sal·i·ty** /nāzal′itē/ *n* ‖ **na′sal·ize**′ *vt & vi*

nas·cent /nas′ənt, nās′-/ [L *nascens* (*-entis*) being born] *adj* **1** beginning to exist or grow; **2** *chem* just released from combination ‖ **nas·cence** /-əns/ *n*

Nash·ville /nash′vil/ *n* capital of Tennessee (447,877)

nasi-, naso- [L *nasus* nose] *comb form* nose, nasal

nas·tur·tium /nəstur′shəm, nas-/ [L] *n* any of a genus (*Tropaeolum*) of plants of the mustard family with pungent stem and seeds and with showy red and yellow flowers

nas·ty /nast′ē/ [ME] *adj* (**-ti·er; -ti·est**) **1** filthy; **2** disgusting; **3** obscene; **4** troublesome, harmful, as *a nasty cut;* **5** ill-natured; **6** unpleasant, as *a nasty day* ‖ **nas′ti·ly** *adv* ‖ **nas′ti·ness** *n*

na·tal /nāt′əl/ [L *natalis*] *adj* **1** pert. to one's birth; **2** native ‖ SYN (see *native*)

Na·tal /nətal′, -täl′/ *n* **1** province of the Republic of South Africa (2,950,-000; 35,284 sq.m.; cap. Pietermaritzburg); **2** city and seaport in NE Brazil (160,000)

na·tion /nāsh′ən/ [MF < L *natio* (*-onis*) race] *n* **1** independent country; **2** cultural group with a common history, language, and traditions ‖ SYN people, tribe ‖ DISCR *People* is often employed as the plural of *person;* but in a different usage it is a singular, referring to the aggregate of individuals making up a given community and regarded as a group or unit, whether they compose a *nation* or not. *Nation* emphasizes the organization of a *people* into a unified political body. When we speak of the American *people* we speak of a group gathered from all parts of the globe to form the American *nation. Tribe* emphasizes the idea of common descent, and is used chiefly of primitive or undeveloped *peoples*

na·tion·al /nash′(ə)nəl/ *adj* **1** of or pert. to a nation; **2** nationwide; not local ‖ *n* **3** citizen or subject of a nation ‖ **na′tion·al·ly** *adv*

Na′tion·al Guard′ *n* state militia equipped by the U.S. government and subject to call to federal service

na′tion·al·ism *n* **1** devotion to the interests or glory of one's own country; **2** advocacy of national independence ‖ **na′tion·al·ist** *adj & n* ‖ **na′tion·al·is′tic** *adj*

Na′tion·al·ist Chi′na *n* the noncommunist part of China on Taiwan (13,383,357; 13,885 sq.m.; cap. Taipei)

na·tion·al·i·ty /-nal′-/ *n* (**-ties**) **1** membership in a nation; **2** the character or traits of the people of a country as a whole; **3** people united by customs, institutions, etc.; **4** national descent

na′tion·al·ize′ *vt* **1** to make national; **2** to place under the ownership or control of the national government ‖ **na′tion·al·i·za′tion** *n*

na′tion·hood′ /nāsh′-/ *n* state of being a nation

Na′tion of Is′lam *n* U.S.-based organization that emphasizes black self-reliance, now open to all races and renamed World Community of Al-Islam in the West

na′tion·wide′ *adj* extending throughout the whole nation

na·tive /nāt′iv/ [MF *natif* < L *nativus*] *adj* **1** belonging to a person by reason of his birth, as *one's native land;* **2** belonging to a place by birth, production, or growth, as *native plants;* **3** innate; **4** natural, unaffected; **5** occurring in nature, not artificial, as *native copper* ‖ *n* **6** one that is born, or that which is grown, in a particular place; **7** aborigine; **8** *colloq* local resident ‖ SYN *adj* natal, natural, original, innate, indigenous ‖ DISCR *Natural* describes that existing in, or produced by, one's nature, not artificial, affected, assumed, or acquired; some possess *natural* grace; others are *naturally* awkward. *Native* also stresses the idea of that which is born in us, as opposed to that which is acquired or cultivated. *Native* differs from *natural* in being applied always to that which is desirable; we speak of *natural,* not *native,* clumsiness. *Native* also describes that which belongs to us by birth, as our *native* land. *Natal* is used exclusively of that connected with the circumstances of birth, as the *natal* hour. *Indigenous* is used particularly of that which belongs naturally to a climate, soil, country, as fruits *indigenous* to America. Figuratively, *indigenous* approaches the sense of inborn, inherent, as traits *indigenous* to humanity

Na′tive A·mer′i·can *n & adj* American Indian

na′tive-born′ *adj* born in a particular place

na′tiv·ism *n* **1** policy of favoring native citizens over immigrants; **2** revival or perpetuation of indigenous cultures

na′tiv·ist *n* **1** one who advocates the policy of favoring native citizens over immigrants; **2** one who considers heredity as the overwhelming influence in the development of an individual or a group rather than environment ‖ also *adj*

na·tiv·i·ty /nətiv′itē/ [MF *nativité*] *n* (**-ties**) **1** birth; **2 the Nativity, a** the birth of Christ; **b** Christmas

NA·TO /nāt′ō/ *n* North Atlantic Treaty Organization

nat·ty /natʹē/ [?] *adj* (**-ti·er; -ti·est**) smart and trim in dress ‖ **natʹti·ly** *adv* ‖ **natʹti·ness** *n*

nat·u·ral /nachʹ(ə)rəl/ [MF < L *naturalis*] *adj* **1** inborn (trait); **2** normal, not unusual; **3** life-like; **4** produced by nature, not artificial; **5** illegitimate (offspring); **6** pert. to nature **7** unaffected in manner; **8** *mus* neither sharp nor flat ‖ *n* **9** *colloq* person or thing sure to succeed; **10** *mus* a sign that cancels preceding sharp or flat; **b** natural note; **11** seven or eleven on the first throw of the dice in craps ‖ **natʹu·ral·ness** *n* ‖ SYN *adj* normal, regular, ordinary, usual, typical, common, original ‖ DISCR That is *natural* which exists in or by nature, as the *natural* color of one's hair. That is *normal* which conforms to a standard or norm, as a *normal* pulse; *normal* mental processes (see *native*) ‖ ANT *adj* abnormal, monstrous, unusual, unnatural

nat·u·ral gas *n* gas composed largely of methane and other hydrocarbons obtained from natural earth fissures or from wells, and used chiefly as a fuel

nat·u·ral his·to·ry *n* study of plant and animal life, esp. in popularized form

nat·u·ral·ism *n* **1** action based on natural instincts; **2** doctrine that scientific laws account for everything in the universe; **3** realism in art and literature without idealization ‖ **natʹu·ral·is·tic** *adj*

natʹu·ral·ist *n* **1** student of plants and animals, esp. field biologist; **2** advocate of naturalism

natʹu·ral·ize *vt* **1** to confer citizenship upon (an alien); **2** to adopt (a foreign word or custom); **3** to acclimatize (plants or animals) ‖ **natʹu·ral·i·za·tion** *n*

natʹu·ral law *n* body of law deemed to be derived from nature and binding upon human society in the absence of and sometimes in spite of positive law

natʹu·ral log·a·rithm *n* logarithm to the base *e* (2.718 +)

nat·u·ral·ly /nachʹ(ə)rəlē, -ərlē/ *adv* **1** by nature, innately; **2** not artificially or with artificial aid; **3** without affectation; **4** as might be expected; of course

natʹu·ral num·ber *n* *math* any positive whole number

natʹu·ral re·sourc·es *npl* coal, oil, forests, water power, etc., which constitute the natural wealth of a region

natʹu·ral sci·ence *n* organized knowledge concerning the physical universe, as physics, chemistry, and biology

natʹu·ral se·lec·tion *n* natural process by which only those forms of plant and animal life survive which are able to adapt to their environment

na·ture /nāchʹər/ [MF < L *natura*] *n* **1** the force that creates the phenom-

ena of the material world; **2** universe; **3** inherent and essential quality; **4** kind, sort; **5** primitive state of man; **6** physical constitution of an organism; **7** inherent character or disposition; **8** natural scenery; **9** **by nature** inherently

naught /nôt/ [OE *nāwiht*] *n* **1** nothing; **2** zero; the arithmetical symbol *0*

naugh·ty /nôtʹē/ [< *naught* worthless] *adj* (**-ti·er; -ti·est**) **1** mischievous; disobedient; **2** improper, risqué, off-color ‖ **naughʹti·ly** *adv* ‖ **naughʹti·ness** *n* ‖ SYN perverse, mischievous, wayward (see *bad*)

nau·se·a /nôzʹē·ə, nôsʹ-, nôshʹ(ē)ə/ [L] *n* **1** sickness at the stomach with a desire to vomit; **2** disgust, loathing

nau·se·ate /-āt'/ *vt* to affect with nausea; ‖ *vi* to feel nausea ‖ **nauʹse·at·ing** *adj*

nau·seous /nôshʹəs, nôzʹē·əs/ *adj* **1** feeling sick in the stomach; **2** causing nausea; **3** disgusting, repulsive ‖ SYN disgusting, distasteful, offensive, repugnant

nautch /nôch/ [Hindi *nāch* dance] *n* entertainment in India in which trained girl dancers perform

nau·ti·cal /nôtʹikəl/ [< Gk *nautikos*] *adj* pert. to ships and/or sailors ‖ SYN marine, naval, oceanic (see *maritime*)

nau·ti·cal mile *n* any of various units of distance used in navigation: **1** British unit = 6080 ft.; **2** former U.S. unit = 6080.2 ft.; **3** international unit = 6076.116 ft. or 1852 meters, used by U.S. since 1959

nau·ti·lus /nôtʹləs/ [Gk *nautilos* sailor] *n* **1** any of a genus (*Nautilus*) of mollusks of the S Pacific and Indian oceans with a flattened spiral shell; **2** small marine mollusk (*Argonauta argo*) resembling and related to the octopus

Nav·a·ho or **Nav·a·jo** /nävʹəhō, navʹ-/ [Apache Ind = broad field] *n* (**-ho, -jo, -hos,** or **-jos**) **1** member of an Indian tribe inhabiting northern New Mexico and Arizona; **2** their language ‖ also *adj*

na·val /nāvʹəl/ [L *navalis*] *adj* pert. to a navy ‖ SYN marine, nautical, oceanic (see *maritime*)

naʹval stores *npl* products obtained from pine trees, as pitch, turpentine, or rosin

nave /nāv/ [L *navis* ship] *n* main part of a church between the side aisles

na·vel /nāvʹəl/ [OE *nafela*] *n* pit in the middle of the abdomen where the umbilical cord was attached to the fetus

naʹvel or·ange *n* seedless orange having a navel-like depression in the rind at the apex

nav·i·gate /navʹigāt'/ [L *navigare* (-*atus*)] *vt* **1** to travel on or through by ship or plane; **2** to direct the course of (a ship or plane) ‖ *vi* **3** to sail; 4 *colloq* to get about || **nav′i‧ga‧ble** /-gəbəl/ *adj* || **nav′i‧ga′tion** *n* || **nav′i‧ga′tor** *n*

na‧vy /nāv′ē/ [MF *navie*] *n* (-**vies**) 1 the warships of a nation; 2 often **Navy** entire naval establishment of a nation, including personnel; 3 navy blue

na′vy bean′ *n* small, white variety of the kidney bean, dried and then soaked for cooking

na′vy blue′ *n* dark blue || **na′vy-blue′** *adj*

Na′vy Cross′ *n* U.S. decoration for extraordinary heroism in action against an armed enemy

na′vy yard′ *n* shipyard for naval construction and repairs

nay /nā′/ [ON *nei*] *n* 1 negative vote or voter || *adv* 2 no; 3 not only this, but also, as *he was happy, nay, ecstatic*

Naz‧a‧rene /naz′ərēn′/ [Gk *Nazarenos*] *n* 1 native of Nazareth, Palestine; 2 Christian; 3 **the Nazarene** Jesus Christ

Na‧zi /nät′sē, nat′sē/ [G *Nationalsozialist*] *n* member of, believer in, or supporter of, the German fascist political party, which ruled Germany 1933–45 under Adolf Hitler || **Na′zi‧fi‧ca′tion** *n* || **Na′zi‧fy′** *vt* || **Na′zi‧ism** or **Na′zism** *n*

Nb *chem* niobium

N.B. New Brunswick

N.B., n.b. [L *nota bene* note well] observe carefully

N′-bomb′ *n* neutron bomb

N.C. North Carolina

N.C.O. *n* noncommissioned officer

Nd *chem* neodymium

n.d. no date

N.Dak. North Dakota

NE northeast(ern)

Ne *chem* neon

N.E. 1 New England; 2 northeast(ern)

Ne‧an‧der‧thal /nē‧an′dərthôl′, -tôl/ [name of valley in W Germany] *adj* 1 pert. to an extinct species of Stone Age man; 2 crude in manner and actions

Ne‧a‧pol‧i‧tan /nē′əpol′itən/ [L *neapolitanus* < Gk] *adj* 1 of Naples, Italy || *n* 2 native or inhabitant of Naples

neap′ tide′ /nēp′/ [OE *nēp*flod] *n* either of the two lowest high tides of the month, occurring at the quarters of the moon

near /nir′/ [OE] *adj* 1 close in time, space, or degree; 2 a closely related; b intimately associated; 3 by a close margin; barely avoided; 4 left-hand (wheel or horse); 5 direct, short, as *the nearest road*; 6 closely resembling a prototype || *adv* 7 not far in time or space; 8 almost || *prep* 9 close to || *vt* & *vi* 10 to approach || **near′ness** *n* || syn *adj* adjacent, contiguous, narrow, nigh; stingy

near′-by′ or **near′by′** *adj* 1 close; not remote || *adv* 2 in the vicinity

Near′ East′ *n* the countries around the E Mediterranean, including SW Asia and sometimes the Balkans

near′ly *adv* 1 almost, all but; 2 closely, as *nearly related*

near′ miss′ *n* something that narrowly misses the target

near′sight′ed *adj* seeing clearly close objects only || **near′sight′ed‧ly** *adv* || **near′sight′ed‧ness** *n*

neat /nēt′/ [MF *net* < L *nitidus*] *adj* 1 clean and orderly; 2 tastefully simple; 3 skillful, clever; 4 precise; 5 net (profit); 6 undiluted (drink); 7 *slang* admirable || syn cleanly, dapper, orderly, prim, shapely, spruce, tidy || ant careless, dirty, disorderly, untidy

neath, ′neath /nēth/ *prep poet.* beneath

neat′s′-foot′ oil′ /nēts′-/ [AS *nēat* cattle] *n* leather dressing made from cattle bones

neb /neb′/ [OE *nebb* face] *n* 1 beak, bill; 2 snout; 3 nib, tip

Neb. or **Nebr.** Nebraska

Ne‧bras‧ka /nəbrask′ə/ *n* state in central U.S. (1,483,791; 77,227 sq.m.; cap. Lincoln) || **Ne‧bras′kan** *n*

Neb‧u‧chad‧nez‧zar /neb′(y)əkədnez′ər/ or **Neb‧u‧chad‧rez‧zar** /-kədrez′ər/ *n* *Bib* king of Babylon 604–561 B.C., who destroyed Jerusalem and enslaved the Jews (2 Kings 24, 25)

neb‧u‧la /neb′yələ/ [L = mist] *n* (-**las** or -**lae** /-lē′/) *astron* any of numerous luminous formations in the heavens resembling haze or clouds and consisting either of vast clouds of gas and/or dust or of clusters of stars too distant to be separately distinguishable || **neb′u‧lar** /-lər/ *adj*

neb′u‧lar hy‧poth′e‧sis *n* *astron* theory that the solar system evolved from a gaseous nebula

neb′u‧lous /-ləs/ *adj* 1 hazy, indistinct; 2 nebular; 3 clouded || syn confused, indefinite, mixed, shadowy, vague

nec‧es‧sar‧i‧ly /nes′əser′ilē/ *adv* 1 of necessity; 2 unavoidably

nec‧es‧sar‧y /nes′əser′ē/ [L *necessarius*] *adj* 1 existing from the nature of the case, as *a necessary conclusion*; 2 essential, indispensable; 3 unavoidable, inevitable, as *the necessary result*; 4 obligatory, imperative || *n* 5 usu. **necessaries** *pl* indispensable items, as *the necessaries of life* || syn *adj* essential, indispensable, needful, requisite, inevitable, expedient, required, needed, compulsory, unavoidable, intrinsic || DISCR *Necessary* may describe that which must exist in the course of nature, or must be true according to logic, or must be present if a desired end is to be accomplished, or must be so because of our point of view, as it is *neces-*

sary to live in order to die; a *neces-sary* consequence; a *necessary* element; polite usage makes many little courtesies *necessary*. *Essential* does not involve the idea of point of view or of circumstances; *essential* means absolutely *necessary;* a thing is not complete or whole if deprived of any *essential* part. A motor is *essential* if an automobile is to go by its own power; shock absorbers are *necessary* from the point of view of comfort. *Indispensable* is applied to that which may be not be done without; money is *indispensable;* clothing is *indispensable. Requisite* is less absolute than either *necessary* or *indispensable;* it applies to that which is *required,* but requirements vary with the minds dealing with them, so that *requisite* gains a relative tone. What is *requisite* for the comfort of a fine lady would seem unnecessary to a man who needed food. *Needful* reflects the idea of actual want, though it differs from *necessary* in a degree; if new clothes are merely *needful,* we may perhaps get along for a time by patching and care; if new clothes are *necessary,* there is no alternative to getting them. That is *inevitable* which is *necessary* because one cannot get away from it; what goes up must come down—an *inevitable* result; what is born must die—an *inevitable* end. That is *expedient* which is *necessary* because of aptness, suitability, or advantage.

ne·ces·si·tate /nəses'itāt'/ *vt* 1 to imply as a condition or result; to make unavoidable; 2 to compel (a course of action)

ne·ces'si·tous /-təs/ *adj* 1 needy, destitute; 2 urgent; 3 necessary, unavoidable

ne·ces'si·ty [MF *necessité* < L *necessi-tas*] *n* (**-ties**) 1 state of being necessary; 2 something necessary; 3 poverty; 4 compulsion; 5 **of necessity** necessarily ‖ SYN exigency, urgency, emergency, occasion, extremity, fate, want (see *need*)

neck /nek'/ [OE *hnecca*] *n* 1 that part of the body connecting the head with the trunk; 2 the long slender extended part of an object, as of a bottle or of land; 3 strait, channel; 4 the part of a garment through which the neck protrudes; 5 **by a neck** with a very narrow margin of victory ‖ *vi* 6 *slang* to kiss and caress

neck' and neck' *adj & adv* very close in a contest, as a race

neck'band' *n* 1 band worn around the neck; 2 part of garment that encircles the neck

neck'er·chief /-ərchif/ [*neck* + *ker-chief*] *n* square of cloth worn around the neck

neck'lace /-lis/ *n* ornamental chain of gold, jewels, beads, etc., worn around the neck

neck'line' *n* neck opening of a garment

neck'piece' *n* garment, as a scarf, worn around the neck

neck'tie' *n* narrow cloth worn around the neck and tied in front

necr-, necro- [Gk *nekros* dead] *comb form* pert. to the dead or death

ne·crol·o·gy /nəkrol'əjē/ [*necro-* + *-logy*] *n* (**-gies**) 1 obituary; 2 list of the dead ‖ **nec·ro·log·ic** (-i·cal) /nek'-rəloj'ik(əl)/ *adj* ‖ **ne·crol'o·gist** /-jist/ *n*

nec·ro·man·cy /nek'rəman'sē/ [MF *nigromancie* black art + LL *necro-mantia* divination through the dead] *n* 1 divination by communication with the dead; 2 sorcery ‖ **nec'ro·man'cer** *n* ‖ **nec'ro·man'tic** *adj* ‖ SYN conjuration, magic, sorcery, witchcraft

ne·crop·o·lis /nəkrop'əlis/ [Gk = city of the dead] *n* (**-lises** or **-les** /-lēz'/) cemetery, esp. a large one built in ancient times

ne·cro·sis /nəkrōs'is/ [Gk = making dead] *n* (**-ses** /-sēz/) localized death of body tissue ‖ **ne·crot·ic** /-krot'ik/ *adj*

nec·tar /nek'tər/ [Gk] *n* 1 *Gk myth.* drink of the gods; 2 any delicious drink; 3 sweet plant secretion from which bees make honey

nec·tar·ine /nek'tərēn'/ *n* smooth-skinned peach

nee, née /nā'/ [F = born] *adj* (married woman) whose maiden name was

need /nēd'/ [OE *nied*] *n* 1 lack, want; 2 straitened circumstances; 3 necessity; 4 **if need be** if necessary ‖ *vt* 5 to stand in want of, require ‖ *vi* 6 to be necessary, as *it needs to be done* ‖ *modal aux* 7 to be obliged to, as *he need not come* ‖ SYN *n* necessity, want, essential, compulsion, urgency ‖ DISCR *Need* is a state of circumstances requiring something, or the something required. *Necessity,* as compared with *need,* is more urgent, has, in fact, the element of *compulsion* in it. We may be in *need* of diversion, but if we cannot afford it, we go without it; the *necessities* of life are things without which life cannot be maintained. *Need* implies that you can get what is required; *necessity* implies that you must get it; *want* simply implies that you do not have it. One in *want* of money has no money; one in *need* of money may be longing for luxuries. A house in *need* of paint does not look its best; a house in *want* of paint has depreciated in worth. An *essential* is an element without which a thing cannot be complete or whole; an *essential* is therefore in the highest degree a *necessity* to the thing of which it is a part (see *poverty*)

need′ful *adj* necessary, required ‖ SYN requisite, needed, required (see *necessary*)

nee·dle /nēd′əl/ [OE *nǣdl*] *n* 1 small, slender, sharp-pointed steel sewing instrument with an eye for thread; 2 slender rod of steel, bone, or plastic for knitting or crocheting; 3 short slender piece that moves in the groove of a phonograph record and transmits vibrations; 4 thin, hollow, pointed metal tube at the end of a hypodermic syringe; 5 pointer on an instrument dial, gauge, or compass; 6 pine leaf; 7 anything resembling a needle, as a sliver of rock or an obelisk ‖ *vt* 8 a to goad by repeated gibes; b to tease; 9 to strengthen (a beverage) by adding alcohol

nee′dle point′ *n* 1 lace made with a needle on a paper pattern; 2 embroidery of woolen threads on canvas ‖ **nee′dle-point′** *adj*

need′less *adj* unnecessary ‖ **need′less·ly** *adv* ‖ **need′less·ness** *n*

nee′dle valve′ *n* valve containing a needle-shaped rod controlling the flow of a liquid

nee′dle·work′ *n* 1 hand sewing; embroidery done by hand; 2 the occupation of sewing ‖ **nee′dle·work′er** *n*

needn′t /nēd′ənt/ need not

needs /nēdz′/ [OE *nēdes*] *adv* necessarily

need′y *adj* (-i·er; -i·est) very poor ‖ **need′i·ness** *n*

ne′er /ner′/ *adv poet.* never

ne′er′-do-well′ *n* one who does nothing worth while ‖ *adj* shiftless, irresponsible

ne·far·i·ous /nifer′ē·əs/ [L *nefarius*] *adj* very wicked ‖ **ne·far′i·ous·ly** *adv* ‖ **ne·far′i·ous·ness** *n* ‖ SYN criminal, iniquitous, heinous, detestable

ne·gate /nigāt′/ [L *negare* (-*gatus*)] *vt* 1 to deny; 2 to nullify

ne·ga′tion *n* 1 act of denying; contradiction; the opposite of affirmation; 2 lack of positive qualities; 3 negative statement or doctrine

neg·a·tive /neg′ətiv/ *adj* 1 (response) that denies or refuses, saying no; 2 a lacking positive qualities, as a *negative personality*; b offering nothing constructive; 3 opposite in nature to something considered positive, as a *negative force*; 4 *math* a (number) less than zero; b (number) to be subtracted; 5 *chem* (element or radical) that gains electrons; 6 *elec* a having a preponderance of electrons, as a *negative particle*; b (point in a circuit) that has a lower potential; c pert. to the south pole of a magnet; 7 (test or reaction) showing the absence of a suspected condition or organism; 8 *photog* with light and shadows reversed ‖ *n* 9 negative expression; 10 a negative vote or reply;

b refusal; 11 side that attacks the proposition in a debate; 12 *elec* battery plate that has the lower potential; 13 *gram* word or affix expressing negation; 14 *math* a quantity less than zero; b number to be subtracted; 15 *photog* a negative image; b film or plate containing a negative image ‖ *vt* 16 to deny the truth of, contradict; 17 to refuse assent to; veto; 18 to disprove; 19 to counteract ‖ **neg′a·tive·ly** *adv*

neg′a·tiv·ism *n* tendency to speak or act in a way exactly opposite to that desired

ne·glect /niglekt′/ [L *negligere* (-*lectus*)] *vt* 1 to fail to do; 2 to disregard; 3 to leave uncared for ‖ *n* 4 failure to do what should be done; 5 state of being neglected; 6 disregard, indifference ‖ **ne·glect′ful** *adj* ‖ **ne·glect′ful·ly** *adv* ‖ **ne·glect′ful·ness** *n* ‖ SYN carelessness, inattention, neglectfulness, negligence, oversight, heedlessness, thoughtlessness, inadvertence, remissness ‖ DISCR *Neglect* and *negligence* are often used interchangeably to name the act of slighting, or omitting, a duty, attention, or other thing that should have been heeded or performed, as a single instance of *neglect* cost him his life; the gateman's criminal *negligence*. Certain differences, however, appear in their usage; we speak of the *neglect*, not *negligence*, of duty, studies, business, or health. *Neglect* of one's clothes means not taking care of them; *negligence* in attire means a careless disregard of how it is arranged and worn. *Negligence* is ordinarily used to name habitual *neglect*

neg·li·gee /neg′lizhā′/ [F *négligé*] *n* 1 woman's loose-fitting dressing gown; 2 carelessly informal dress

neg·li·gence /neg′lijəns/ *n* 1 habit of not doing that which should be done; 2 carelessness, thoughtlessness; 3 *law* failure to exercise ordinary and reasonable care under the circumstances, as a result of which injury is caused to another person

neg′li·gent [L *negligens* (-*entis*)] *adj* 1 inclined to leave undone what should be done; 2 careless, inattentive ‖ **neg′li·gent·ly** *adv* ‖ SYN remiss, lax, inattentive, regardless, inadvertent, neglectful, thoughtless ‖ DISCR The *negligent* person is careless; he fails, through laziness, lack of will power, or for no reason at all, to do what he should do. One who is *remiss* lacks the energy to remember what he should do, or the force to do it if he does remember. He is *inadvertent* who lets things slip by him unintentionally while he is thinking of something else; if such preoccupation becomes constant, the individual is termed *inattentive*. *Regardless* describes one heedless of consequences, *negligent* of others in inconsiderate ways, as *regardless* of safety; *regardless* of other people's feelings, he spoke his mind. *Lax*, literally the opposite of tense and rigid, is figuratively the opposite of severe, strict, and stringent; in its figurative sense it means loose and *negligent*, and is applied chiefly to a lack of fiber in morals, discipline, standards, or the like

neg·li·gi·ble /-jĭbəl/ *adj* so small or unimportant that one may disregard it; of little account ‖ **neg′li·gi·bly** *adv*

ne·go·ti·ate /nĭgōsh′ē·āt′/ [L *negotiari* (*-atus*)] *vt* 1 to sell or transfer to another, as commercial paper or securities; convert into cash; 2 **a** to put through (any deal or agreement); **b** to conclude by treaty or agreement, as *negotiate a peace;* 3 to succeed in crossing, passing, or getting through ‖ *vi* 4 to deal or bargain with others in order to come to terms ‖ **ne·go′ti·a·ble** /-sh(ē)əbəl/ *adj* ‖ **ne·go′ti·a′·tion** *n* ‖ **ne·go′ti·a′tor** *n*

Ne·gri·to /nĭgrēt′ō/ [Sp *dim.* of *negro* black] *n* (*-tos* or *-toes*) member of any of the dwarf Negroid races of Oceania and SE Asia

Ne·gro /nē′grō/ [Sp and Port = black] *n* (*-groes*) often *offensive* 1 member of any of the black races, esp. those of Africa; 2 person with some black ancestors ‖ also *adj*

Ne·groid /nē′groid/ [*Negro* + *-oid*] *adj* resembling the black races in appearance and characteristics

Neh·ru, Ja·wa·har·lal /jəwä′hərläl′ ner′ōō, nä′rōō/ *n* (1889–1964) prime minister of India 1950–64

neigh /nā′/ [OE *hnǣgan*] *vi* 1 to make a long loud cry (said of a horse) ‖ *n* 2 cry of a horse

neigh·bor /nāb′ər/ [OE *neāhgebūr*] *n* 1 one who lives close to another; 2 *colloq* friend, fellow being (familiar mode of address) ‖ *vt* 3 to adjoin; 4 to live or be near to ‖ *vi* 5 to live as a neighbor; 6 to be on friendly terms

neigh′bor·hood′ *n* 1 region near-by, vicinity; 2 district of a city having its own characteristics, as *a run-down neighborhood;* 3 **in the neighborhood of, a** near; **b** about; more or less ‖ SYN community, district, environs, locality, vicinity

neigh·bor·ing /nāb′(ə)rĭŋ/ *adj* near, adjoining

neigh′bor·ly *adj* 1 characteristic of neighbors; 2 friendly, helpful ‖ *adv* 3 in friendly fashion

nei·ther /nēth′ər, nīth′-/ [OE *nāhwæther* not whether] *pron* 1 not the one nor the other ‖ *adj* 2 not either ‖ *conj* 3 not either; 4 and not, also not

Nejd /nejd′/ *n* region in central and E Saudi Arabia

nel·son /nel′sən/ [?] *n* wrestling hold

in which leverage is applied to the opponent's arm, neck, and head

Nel·son, Viscount Horatio *n* (1758–1805) British admiral, victor of Trafalgar

nem·e·sis /nem′əsis/ [Gk] *n* (*-ses* /-sēz′/) 1 retribution, just punishment; 2 one who inflicts just punishment; 3 hard-to-beat rival; 4 **Nemesis** *Gk myth.* goddess of retributive justice

neo- [Gk *neos* new] *comb form* 1 new, recent; 2 new and different

Ne·o·cene /nē′əsēn′/ [*neo-* + Gk *kainos* new] *n* latter portion of the Tertiary period ‖ also *adj*

ne′o·clas′sic (**-si·cal**) /nē′ō-/ *adj* pert. to a revival of classic Greek and Roman style, esp. in literature and the arts ‖ **ne′o·clas′si·cism** *n* ‖ **ne′o·clas′si·cist** *n*

ne′o·dym′i·um /-dĭm′ē·əm/ [*neo-* + *didymium*] *n* rare-earth element (**Nd**; at.no. 60; at.wt. 144.24), used to give a violet color to glass and porcelain

ne′o·im·pres′sion·ism *n* late 19th-cent. theory of certain French painters who sought to develop impressionistic methods through the rigid application of scientific principles

Ne′o-Lat′in *n* 1 New Latin; 2 the Romance languages, individually or collectively

Ne′o·lith′ic /-lĭth′ĭk/ [*neo-* + *-lith*] *adj* of or pert. to the late Stone Age, characterized by polished stone implements, the initial stages of agriculture, and the domestication of animals

ne·ol·o·gism /nē·ol′əjĭz′əm/ *n* 1 new word or meaning; 2 its use

ne·o·my·cin /nē′ōmīs′in/ *n* antibiotic (*Streptomyces fradiae*) produced by a soil actinomycete

ne·on /nē′on/ [< Gk *neos* new] *n* colorless, odorless, inert gaseous element (**Ne**; at.no. 10; at.wt. 20.183) present in the earth's atmosphere and used chiefly in display signs

ne′o·na′tal *adj* of or pert. to newborn children

ne′o·phyte′ /-fīt′/ [Gk *neophytos* newly planted] *n* 1 beginner, novice; 2 recent convert

Ne′o·pla′to·nism *n* system of philosophy, founded by Plotinus and prevalent from the 3rd to the 5th century, combining the idealistic philosophy of the Greeks with Oriental mysticism, influenced by the Jewish, Gnostic, and Christian philosophies ‖ **Ne′o·pla·ton′ic** *adj* ‖ **Ne′o·pla′to·nist** *n*

ne′o·prene′ /-prēn′/ [*neo-* + *chloroprene*] *n* a synthetic rubber with superior resistance to oil, sunlight, and heat

Ne′o-Scho·las′ti·cism *n* present-day Catholic movement seeking to modernize the teachings of medieval scholasticism

Ne·pal /nəpôl′, -päl′, -pal′/ *n* monarchy in the Himalayas (10,294,484; 54,363 sq.m.; cap. Katmandu) || **Nep·a·lese** /nep'əlēz', -lēs/ adj & n (-lese)

ne·pen·the /nĭpen'thē/ [Gk *nepenthes* griefless] n **1** potion used by the ancient Greeks to drive away pain and sorrow; **2** anything inducing forgetfulness of sorrow

neph·ew /nef'yōō/ [OF *neveu*] n son of a brother or sister, or of a brother-in-law or sister-in-law

nephr- or **nephro-** comb form kidney

ne·phrit·ic /nəfrit'ik/ adj **1** pert. to the kidneys; **2** pert. to or affected with nephritis

ne·phri·tis /nəfrīt'is/ [Gk] n inflammation or disease of the kidneys

ne plus ul·tra /nē'plus'ul'trə/ [L = no farther] n **1** highest or uttermost point attainable; **2** height of achievement; acme, perfection

nep·o·tism /nep'ətiz'əm/ [It *nepotismo* < L] n favoritism to relatives, as by giving jobs

Nep·tune /nep't(y)ōōn/ n **1** Rom myth. god of the sea, identified with the Greek Poseidon; **2** astron eighth planet in order from the sun, invisible to naked eye || **Nep·tu'ni·an** adj

nep·tu·ni·um /nept(y)ōōn'ē·əm/ [NL < *Neptune*] n radioactive element (Np; at.no. 93; at.wt. 237), not occurring free in nature but produced artificially by the neutron bombardment of U-238 in the process of making plutonium

nerd /nurd'/ [?] n slang gauche, tacky, or uncool person; creep; drip

Ne·re·id /nir'ē·id/ [Gk *Nereis* (-eidos) daughter of Nereus] n Gk myth. any of the fifty daughters of Nereus who attended Poseidon as sea nymphs

Ne·ro /nir'ō, nē'rō/ n (37–68) Roman emperor 54–68

nerve /nurv'/ [L *nervus*] n **1** anat one of the white cords, made up of bundles of nerve fibers, which transmit nervous impulses between all parts of the body and the brain and spinal cord; **2** bodily vigor, energy; **3** mental strength or control; coolness; **4** sinew, tendon, as *strain every nerve*; **5** one of the vascular ribs or veins forming the framework of a leaf; **6** one of the ribs or veins in an insect's wing; **7** colloq impudent boldness; **8** sore or sensitive point; **9** sensitive pulp of a tooth; **10** nerves pl hysterical attack of excitement or timidity || vt **11** to fill with vigor or courage || SYN v encourage, energize, invigorate, stimulate

nerve' cell' n cell of which the nervous tissue is formed

nerve' cen'ter n **1** group of nerve cells having a common function; **2** center of leadership or control

nerve' fi'ber n one of the slender filaments of which the nerves are formed

nerve' im'pulse n progressive alteration in the protoplasm of a nerve fiber that, when stimulated, transmits sensations or instructions

nerve'less adj **1** biol without nerves; **2** lacking force or courage, spineless; **3** poised; without nervousness

nerve'-rack'ing or **nerve'-wrack'ing** /-rak'iŋ/ adj extremely trying to one's patience

nerv·ous /nurv'əs/ adj **1** a pert. to or made of nerves; **b** pert. to the nervous system; **2** having weak nerves, easily excited, timid; **3** forceful, energetic; **4** a restless, uneasy; **b** excitable, jumpy || **nerv'ous·ly** adv || **nerv'ous·ness** n || SYN irritable, excitable, forceful, tense, spirited

nerv'ous break'down n nervous exhaustion or prostration, marked by abnormal fatigue

nerv'ous sys'tem n the system in an organism that includes all the nerve cells and nervous tissue and, in the vertebrates, the brain, spinal cord, and nerves

nerv'y adj (-i·er; -i·est) **1** bold, courageous; **2** presumptuous, brazen || **nerv'i·ness** n

-ness /-nis/ n suffix [OE -nes] quality, state, condition, or degree, as *sickness, goodness*

nest /nest'/ [OE] n **1** bed or dwelling made or chosen by a bird for its eggs and young; **2** home or hatching place of insects and reptiles; **3** cozy retreat; **4** resort or its denizens, as *a nest of thieves*; **5** hotbed; **6** number of similar boxes, bowls, etc., each one fitting inside the larger one || vi **7** to build or live in a nest; **8** to hunt birds' nests || vt **9** to place in, or as in, a nest; **10** to build a nest for; **11** to pack (e.g., tables) one inside the other

nest' egg' n **1** real or artificial egg placed in a nest to induce a hen to continue laying eggs; **2** money laid aside as a reserve fund

nes·tle /nes'əl/ [OE *nestian*] vi **1** to make and use a nest; **2** to lie closely and cozily, snuggle; **3** to lie half hidden || vt **4** to cuddle; **5** to place as in a nest, shelter

nest·ling /nest'liŋ/ n young bird still living in natal nest

Nes·tor /nest'ər, -ôr/ n **1** class. myth. ancient Greek king who fought at Troy, famed for his wisdom; **2** wise old man

net¹ /net'/ [OE] n **1** fabric made of twine, knotted into meshes, used for catching fish, birds, etc.; **2** fine openwork fabric, as silk, used for bridal veils, laces, etc.; **3** any of various other meshed fabrics, used for covering, protecting, or confining, as *a net for the hair;* **4** canvas for catching persons jumping into a building; **5** mental or moral entanglement; snare; **6** scheme to entrap ‖ *v* (**net·ted; net·ting**) *vt* **7** to make into a net or network; **8** to catch in a net; **9** to entrap by clever stratagem; snare; **10** to cover or protect with, or as with, a net ‖ **net′like′** *adj*

net² [MF = clean < L *nitidus*] *adj* **1** free from all charges and deductions; **2** remaining after deducting all expenses, as *net profit;* **3 a** (weight) remaining after deducting waste, refuse, etc.; **b** (weight) remaining after deducting the weight of the container; **4** final, as *the net result* ‖ *n* **5** net amount ‖ *v* (**net·ted; net·ting**) *vt* **6** to earn as clear profit; **7** to produce as profit; yield

Neth. Netherlands

neth·er /neth′ər/ [OE *nithera*] *adj* **1** situated below, beneath; lower; **2** pert. to the regions below the earth's surface; infernal

Neth·er·lands, The /neth′ərləndz/ *nsg* or *npl* kingdom of NW Europe (13,200,000; 12,978 sq.m.; cap. Amsterdam; seat of government The Hague); also called Holland

Neth′er·lands An·til′les *npl* autonomous island territory of The Netherlands in the Caribbean Sea NE of Venezuela (223,000; 370 sq.m.; cap. Willemstad)

neth′er·most′ *adj* lowest

neth′er·world′ *n* world of the dead; Hades

net·ting /net′iŋ/ *n* **1** act or method of making or using nets; **2** fabric made of twine knotted into meshes, as *fish netting;* **3** any of various other types of netlike fabric or openwork, as *fine dress netting;* **4** netlike fabric of wire, as for fences; **5** any system of crossed lines; network

net·tle /net′əl/ [OE *netel*] *n* **1** any of various plants having prickles or stinging hairs; **2 a** any of a genus (*Urtica*) of coarse herbs with stinging, prickly leaves and small green flowers; **b** any of a family (Urticaceae) of plants typified by this genus ‖ *vt* **3** to sting, as with nettles; **4** to provoke, irritate

net′tle rash′ *n* a burning, itching eruption on the skin, appearing in patches and resembling the effects of a nettle sting

net′work′ *n* **1** meshwork; an openwork fabric made by interlacing threads of any material; **2** any system of crossed or interlaced lines; **3** process of making any sort of meshwork; **4** *elec* combination of resistance, inductance, and capacity, made to obtain certain electrical characteristics; **5** *rad & telv* chain of transmitting stations

neur- or **neuro-** [Gk *neuron* sinew] *comb form* nerve

neu·ral /n(y)ŏŏr′əl/ *adj* pert. to the nerves or nervous system

neu·ral′gia /-ral′jə/ *n* acute and intermittent pain, usu. of the face or head, along the course of and over a nerve ‖ **neu·ral′gic** *adj*

neu′ras·the′ni·a /-əsthēn′ē·ə/ [*neur-* + Gk *asthenia* sickness] *n* nerve exhaustion or nervous prostration; nervous disorder marked by abnormal fatigue ‖ **neu′ras·then′ic** /-then′ik/ *adj & n*

neu·ri′tis /-rīt′is/ *n* inflammation of a nerve or nerves, accompanied by pain and impaired reflexes ‖ **neu·rit·ic** /-rit′ik/ *adj & n*

neu·rol′o·gy /-rol′əjē/ *n* branch of medical science dealing with the nervous system and its diseases ‖ **neu′ro·log′i·cal** /-rələjikəl/ *adj* ‖ **neu·rol′o·gist** *n*

neu′ron /-ron/ [Gk = sinew] *n* nerve cell with all its extensions, regarded as the fundamental structural unit of the nervous system

neu′ro·sci′ence /n(y)ŏŏr′ō-/ *n* science that deals with the anatomy and physiology of the brain, with its functions and the relations between its parts, and with consciousness, learning, memory, and behavior ‖ **neu′ro·sci·en·tif′ic** *adj* ‖ **neu′ro·sci′en·tist** *n*

neu·ro′sis /-rōs′is/ *n* (**-ses** /-sēz/) functional disturbance accompanied by disorder of the nervous system, not traceable to any physical cause

neu·rot′ic /-rot′ik/ *adj* **1** of or pert. to neurosis; **2** affected with neurosis; emotionally unstable ‖ *n* **4** neurotic person ‖ **neu·rot′i·cal·ly** *adv*

neu·ter /n(y)ŏŏt′ər/ [MF *neutre* < L *neuter*] *adj* **1** gram pert. to the gender which is neither masculine nor feminine; **2** *entom* without fully developed reproductive organs in adult life; **3** castrated; sterile; **4** *bot* sexless, having neither pistils nor stamens; **5** taking no sides; neutral ‖ *n* **6** grammatical form of the neuter gender; **7** insect or plant that does not develop sex organs; **8** castrated or spayed animal

neu·tral /n(y)ŏŏ′trəl/ [MF] *adj* **1** taking neither side in a dispute; **2** of or pert. to a neutral country; **3** having no inclination or interest in a difference of opinion; indifferent; **4** neither good nor bad; so-so; **5 a** of no decided color or characteristic, as *a neutral gray;* **b** colorless, achromatic; **6** sexless, sterile; **7** without stamens or pistils; **8** *chem* neither acid nor basic; **9** *elec* uncharged; neither positive nor negative ‖ *n* **10** neutral person or nation; **11** *mach* position of disengagement of gears ‖ **neu′tral·ly** *adv*

neu′tral·ism *n* **1** neutrality; **2** advocacy

or policy of neutrality, esp. in foreign affairs || **neu′tral·ist** *n* || **neu′-tral·ist′ic** *adj*

neu·tral′i·ty /-tral′itē/ *n* 1 state of being neutral; 2 inviolability of national territory to attack by belligerents

neu′tral·ize′ *vt* 1 to make of no effect, counteract; 2 to declare (a country) by treaty to be neutral, making its territory inviolable to belligerents; 3 to make chemically neutral; 4 *elec* to make inert by equalizing the positive and negative quantities; 5 to make neutral by blending with the complementary color || **neu′tral·i·za′-tion** *n* || **neu′tral·iz′er** *n*

neu′tral spir′its *npl* ethyl alcohol of 190 or higher proof used esp. for blending whiskies

neu·tri·no /n(y)ōōtrē′nō/ [It] *n* elementary particle with zero mass at rest and no electric charge

neu′tron /-tron/ [prob < *neutral*] *n phys* minute particle of matter of approximately the mass of a proton but without either positive or negative charge and present in all atomic nuclei except those of hydrogen

neu′tron bomb′ *n* nuclear bomb that would release death-dealing neutrons but cause limited contamination in the atmosphere

neu′tron star′ *n* hypothetical celestial body that is formed when a giant star exhausts its nuclear fuel and collapses inward on itself, crushing much of its matter into a ball of neutrons

Nev. Nevada

Ne·vad·a /nəvad′ə, -väd′-/ *n* state in W U.S. (488,738; 110,540 sq.m.; cap. Carson City) || **Ne·vad′an** *n*

nev·er /nev′ər/ [OE nǣfre] *adv* 1 not at any time; 2 in no degree, not at all

nev′er·more′ *adv* never again

nev′er·the·less′ *adv* in spite of that; yet; however; still

ne·vus /nēv′əs/ [L *naevus* mole] *n* (-vi /-vī/) pigmented mark on the skin, usu. congenital; birthmark

new /n(y)ōō′/ [OE nīwe] *adj* 1 lately made, invented, or discovered; 2 modern, novel; 3 unfamiliar, strange; 4 changed, different; 5 unused; 6 refreshed, renewed; 7 beginning afresh, recurring, as *a new day;* 8 New modern (language), as *New Latin* || *adv* 9 recently; 10 anew, afresh || SYN *adj* fresh, novel (see *modern*)

New′ Am′ster·dam′ *n* Dutch colonial name for New York

New·ark /n(y)ōō′ərk/ *n* 1 city in NE New Jersey (382,417); 2 city in N Delaware (11,000)

New′ Bed′ford /bed′fərd/ *n* seaport in SE Massachusetts (109,000)

new′born′ *adj* 1 just born; 2 reborn

New′ Bruns′wick /brunz′wik/ *n* prov-ince in E Canada (616,788; 28,354 sq.m.; cap. Fredericton)

new′com′er *n* recent arrival

New′ Deal′ *n* economic and governmental policies of President Franklin D. Roosevelt in the 1930's, aiming at economic recovery and social security || **New′ Deal′er** *n*

New′ Del′hi /del′ē/ *n* capital of India (314,377)

new′el (post′) /n(y)ōō′əl/ [MF *nouel* kernel] *n* 1 central pillar supporting the steps of a winding stairway; 2 post supporting the handrail at the foot or head of a stairway

New′ Eng′land *n* NE portion of U.S., comprising Maine, New Hampshire, Vermont, Massachusetts, Rhode Island, and Connecticut || **New′ Eng′land·er** *n*

new′fan′gled /-fang′gəld/ [*new* + OE *-fangen* caught] *adj* 1 new, novel; 2 inclined to novelty

New·found·land /n(y)ōō′fəndlənd/ *n* 1 large island in E Canada (450,000; 42,734 sq.m.); 2 province of Canada, consisting of the island of Newfoundland and Labrador (458,000; 154,734 sq.m.; cap. St. John's); 3 large shaggy intelligent breed of dog

New′ Guin′ea *n* large island in the East Indies, north of Australia (2,100,000; 306,600 sq.m.)

New′ Hamp′shire /ham(p)′shər/ *n* state in NE U.S. (737,681; 9,304 sq.m.; cap. Concord) || **New′ Hamp′shir·ite′** *n*

New′ He′brew *n* present-day language of Israel

New′ Jer′sey *n* state in E U.S. (7,168,000; 7,836 sq.m.; cap. Trenton) || **New′ Jer′sey·ite′** or **New′ Jer′sey·an** *n*

New′ Lat′in *n* Latin used in modern times, esp. for scientific terminology

New′ Left′ *n U.S.* leftist trend, esp. among the young, from dissent towards libertarian, egalitarian, and pacific goals, and their attainment by political action, and sometimes by anarchistic activities

new·ly /n(y)ōō′lē/ *adv* 1 recently, lately; 2 in a new way

new′ly·wed′ *n* person recently married

new′ math·e·mat′ics *nsg* noncompartmentalized method of teaching mathematics from arithmetic through calculus, launched around 1950

New′ Mex′i·co *n* state in SW U.S. (1,016,000; 121,666 sq.m.; cap. Santa Fe) || **New′ Mex′i·can** *n*

new′ moon′ *n* the moon when it is between the earth and the sun so that its dark side is toward the earth, showing only a thin crescent a few days later shortly after sunset

New′ Or′le·ans /ôr′lē·ənz, ôrlēnz′/ *n* seaport city in SE Louisiana on the Mississippi river (960,000)

news /n(y)ōōz/ *nsg* 1 recent tidings; 2 report of recent events; 3 newsworthy event ‖ also *adj* ‖ SYN tidings (see *intelligence*)

news′ a′gen·cy *n* **1** organization that gathers news for news media; **2** business which sells newspapers and magazines at retail

news′beat′ *n* piece of news obtained by a newspaper ahead of other newspapers and news media

news′boy′ *n* boy or man who sells or delivers newspapers

news′break′ *n* newsworthy event

news′cast′ *n* news broadcast on radio or television ‖ **news′cast′er** *n*

news′let′ter *n* printed circular containing news sent to a special group

news′mag′a·zine′ *n* periodical, usu. weekly, recapitulating and commenting on current events

news′mong·er /-muŋ′gər/ *n* a gossip

news′pa′per *n* **1** paper published periodically, usu. daily or weekly, containing news, editorials, advertisements, and other features; **2** newsprint

news′print′ *n* thin, unsized paper used chiefly for newspapers

news′reel′ *n* short motion picture of current news events

news′ re·lease′ *n* statement prepared in advance and distributed to the news media by or in behalf of public figures, companies, government agencies, etc.

news′ serv′ice *n* news-gathering agency

news′stand′ *n* booth where newspapers and magazines are sold

New′ Style′ *adj* (date) according to the Gregorian calendar

news′wor′thy *adj* interesting enough to be reported in a newspaper or to be broadcast

news′y *adj* (-i·er; -i·est) *colloq* **1** full of news; **2** full of gossip

newt /n(y) о̄оt′/ [ME *an ewte* a newt] *n* any of several small salamanders found in damp places

New′ Tes′ta·ment *n* **1** the second of the two great divisions of the Bible, which contains the Gospels and the writing based on them; **2** covenant of God to mankind embodied in the coming of Christ and in his life, teachings, and sacrifice

New·ton /n(y)о̄оt′ən/, **Sir Isaac** *n* (1642–1727) English mathematician and philosopher, who formulated the law of universal gravitation ‖ **New·to′ni·an** /-to̅n′ē·ən/ *adj & n*

New′ World′ *n* Western Hemisphere ‖ also *adj*

New′ Year′s′ or **New′ Year′s′ Day′** *n* first day of January, usually celebrated as a legal holiday

New′ Year′s′ Eve′ *n* night of December 31

New′ York′ /yôrk′/ *n* **1** state in NE U.S. (18,190,740; 49,576 sq.m.; cap. Albany); **2** commercial metropolis of the U.S. at the mouth of the Hudson, divided into the boroughs of the Bronx, Brooklyn, Manhattan, Queens, and Staten Island (8,200,000) ‖ **New′ York′er** *adj & n*

New′ Zea′land /zēl′ənd/ *n* member of British Commonwealth made up of two large and several small islands in S Pacific (2,800,000; 103,736 sq. m.; cap. Wellington) ‖ **New′ Zea′land·er** *n*

next /nekst′/ [OE *niehst*] *adj* **1** immediately preceding or following; **2** soonest come to, as *the next man you see;* **3** *next to,* **a** besides, adjacent to; **b** very nearly; **4** *to get next to* slang to ingratiate oneself with ‖ *adv* **5** immediately succeeding; **6** on the first occasion hereafter ‖ *prep* **7** beside, adjacent to

next′-door′ *adv* at, in, or to the next house or building or, within a building, the next room ‖ **next′-door′** *adj*

next′ of kin′ *nsg & npl* person or persons nearest in relationship

nex·us /nek′səs/ [L = bound] *n* (-uses or -us) **1** link, tie; **2** linked series or group

Nez Per·cé /nez′ purs′/ [F = pierced nose] *n* **1** member of American Indian tribe of Idaho, Oregon, and Washington; **2** their language ‖ also *adj*

N.F., N.Fld. Newfoundland

N.G. 1 National Guard; **2** New Guinea

N.G., n.g. /en′jē′/ *adj slang* no good

N.H. New Hampshire

Ni *chem* nickel

ni·a·cin /nī′əsin/ [*nicotinic acid* +-*in*] *n* nicotinic acid

Ni·ag·a·ra /nī·ag′(ə)rə/ *n* **1** river between Ontario and New York State running from Lake Erie to Lake Ontario; **2** *fig* flood, torrent

Ni·ag′a·ra Falls′ *n* **1** celebrated falls on Niagara River; **2** city in W New York State on the Niagara River (102,000); **3** city on the Canadian side of falls (22,000)

nib /nib′/ [prob OE *nebb*] *n* **1** point of anything, esp. of a pen; **2** bird's beak

nib·ble /nib′əl/ [?] *vt* **1** to bite a little at a time; **2** to continue to bite gently and quickly ‖ *vi* **3** to bite little bits ‖ *n* **4** act of nibbling

Ni·be·lung /nē′bəlo̅о̅ŋ′/ [G] *n Teut myth.* **1** one of a race of dwarfs whose hoard and ring were taken by Siegfried; **2** one of the race of Burgundians who stole the hoard from Siegfried's widow

nib·lick /nib′lik/ [?] *n* iron-headed golf club with slanted face for short lofts

Nic·a·ra·gua /nik′ərä′gwə/ *n* Spanish-speaking republic of Central America (1,783,000; 50,200 sq.m.; cap. Managua) ‖ **Nic′a·ra′guan** *adj & n*

nice /nīs′/ [OF = foolish < L *nescius* ignorant] *adj* **1** precise, accurate; **2** fine, subtle; **3** fastidious; **4** refined; of good taste; **5** delicately sensitive; **6** socially agreeable, pleasant; **7**

pleasing to the senses ‖ **nice′ly** *adv* ‖ **nice′ness** *n* ‖ SYN accurate, fastidious, discriminating, finical

Ni′cene Creed′ /nī′sēn, nīsēn′/ [< *Nicaea*, anc city in NW Asia Minor] *n* 1 creed of Christian belief promulgated by first council at Nicaea, 325 A.D.; 2 slightly changed version, used since the Middle Ages by the Roman and Anglican churches and accepted by evangelical Protestant denominations

ni·ce·ty /nī′sətē/ [MF *nicete* foolishness] *n* (-ties) 1 very small distinction or detail; 2 quality of delicacy or subtlety; 3 careful discrimination and precision; 4 fastidiousness; 5 **to a nicety** with the greatest precision ‖ SYN delicacy, exactness, fineness, minuteness

niche /nich′/ [F] *n* 1 recess in a wall, as for a statue; 2 position or condition especially adapted to a person occupying it

Nich·o·las, Saint /nik′ələs/ *n* fourth-century bishop of Myra, Asia Minor; patron saint of Russia and of children, often identified with Santa Claus

Nich·o·las II *n* (1868–1918) last czar of Russia 1894–1917; executed by the Bolsheviks

nick /nik′/ [ME *nyke*] 1 slight cut or notch; 2 critical point (of time) ‖ *vt* 3 to cut notches in; 4 to hit upon exactly; 5 *colloq* to overcharge, cheat

nick·el /nik′əl/ [< G Kupfer*nickel* copper demon] *n* 1 hard, white, malleable and ductile metallic element (Ni; at.no. 28; at.wt. 58.71) notable for resistance to corrosion and much used in alloys and in plating; 2 U.S. or Canadian five-cent coin, made of copper and nickel ‖ *v* (-eled or -elled; -el·ing or -el·ling) *vt* 3 to plate with nickel

nick′el-cad′mi·um cell′ *n elec* cell in which the positive pole is nickel, the negative pole cadmium, the electrolyte 40 per cent potassium hydroxide by weight, and the voltage approximately 1.2

nick·el·o′de·on /-lŏd′ē·ən/ [*nickel* + *odéon* concert hall] *n* coin-operated player piano or phonograph

nick′el sil′ver *n* hard white alloy of copper, nickel, and zinc

nick′nack′ *n* var of **knickknack**

nick′name′ [ME a*n ekename* an additional name] *n* 1 familiar form of a given name; 2 substitute, often descriptive, name given in derision, sport, or familiarity ‖ *vt* 3 to give a nickname to

Nic·o·de·mus /nik′ədē′məs/ *n* Pharisee and ruler of the Jews, who consulted Jesus at night and was told that he must be born again to be saved (John 3:1–8)

Nic·o·si·a /nik′əsē′ə/ *n* capital of Cyprus (103,000)

nic·o·tine /nik′ətēn′/ [< J. *Nicot,* who introduced tobacco into France 1560] *n* poisonous oily alkaloid —$C_{10}H_{14}$-N₂— present in tobacco

nic′o·tin′ic ac′id /nik′ətin′ik/ *n* acid —$C_6H_5NO_2$— that is part of the vitamin-B complex and used in the prevention of pellagra

niece /nēs′/ [OF] *n* daughter of one's brother or sister, or of one's brother-in-law or sister-in-law

Nie·tzsche /nēch′ə, nēch′ē/, **Friedrich Wilhelm** *n* (1844–1900) German philosopher, expounder of the doctrines of the superman and the will to power ‖ **Nie′tzsche·an** /-chē·ən/ *adj & n* ‖ **Nie′tzsche·an·ism** or **Nie′tzsche·ism** *n*

nif·ty /nif′tē/ [?] *adj* (-ti·er; -ti·est) *slang* fine, attractive, stylish

Ni·ger /nī′jər/ *n* 1 river in W Africa, flowing 2600 m. to Gulf of Guinea; 2 republic in W Africa (3,546,000; 489,200 sq.m.; cap. Niamey)

Ni·ge·ri·a /nījir′ē·ə/ *n* republic in W Africa, member of British Commonwealth (61,450,000; 356,669 sq.m.; cap. Lagos) ‖ **Ni·ge′ri·an** *adj & n*

nig·gard /nig′ərd/ [ME < Scand] *n* stingy, covetous person; miser ‖ *adj* ‖ **nig′gard·li·ness** *n* ‖ **nig′gard·ly** *adj*

nigh /nī′/ [OE nēah] *adj, adv, & prep* near

night /nīt′/ [OE *niht*] *n* 1 the period of darkness between sunset and sunrise; 2 any period of darkness or gloom

night′ blind′ness *n* abnormally diminished vision in dim light

night′-bloom·ing ce′re·us /sir′ē·əs/ [L *cera* wax] *n* any of several cacti with flowers which open about midnight (*Hylocereus undatus, Selenicereus pteranthus, S. grandiflorus,* and *Nyctocereus serpentinus)*

night′cap′ *n* 1 cap worn in bed; 2 drink, usu. alcoholic, taken at bedtime; 3 *baseball* final game of a doubleheader

night′clothes′ *npl* bed garments

night′ club′ *n* place of evening diversion furnishing usu. food, liquor, entertainment, and dancing

night′dress′ *n* 1 nightclothes; 2 nightgown

night′fall′ *n* end of the day

night′ glass′es *npl* field glasses of low power for seeing objects in the dark

night′gown′ *n* long loose gown worn in bed

night′hawk′ *n* 1 any of a genus (*Chordeiles*) of American birds related to the whippoorwill, feeding on the wing on night-flying insects; 2 *colloq* night owl

night·in·gale /nīt′iṇgāl′, nīt′ən-/ [OE *nihtegale*] *n* any of several small Old World thrushes (genus *Luscinia*) noted for the melodious nocturnal song of the male

Night′in·gale′, Florence n (1820–1910) Eng nurse, pioneer in modern nursing

night′ latch′ n door lock with a spring bolt opened by a key from the outside and by a knob from the inside

night′ let′ter n telegram sent at night at reduced rates, to be delivered the following morning

night′ly adj 1 pert. to the night; 2 occurring every night ‖ adv 3 at night; 4 every night

night′mare′ [night + OE mare evil spirit] n 1 terrifying dream accompanied by oppression in the chest and a feeling of helplessness; 2 any situation causing terror and anxiety ‖ **night′mar′ish** adj

night′ owl′ n colloq person who stays up late at night

night′shade′ n any of· a genus (Solanum) of plants including the potato plant and the eggplant; esp. any of several poisonous and medicinal species

night′shirt′ n long-tailed shirt worn in bed

night′stick′ n policeman's club

night′time′ n night 1

night′walk′er n person abroad at night for an evil purpose

night′watch′ n 1 nocturnal period of guard duty; 2 period of night watching; 3 guard keeping watch by night

ni·hil·ism /nī′həliz′əm/ [L nihil nothing] n 1 doctrine that nothing can be known, because nothing exists; 2 rejection of traditional beliefs in religion and morals; 3 political or social doctrine that totally rejects society and all authority, and holds that in the interest of progress all present social institutions should be destroyed; 4 violent revolution, anarchism; 5 Nihilism program of a 19th-cent. Russian political party seeking to destroy existing institutions through terrorism and assassination ‖ **ni′hil·ist** adj & n ‖ **ni′hil·is′·tic** adj

ni·hil ob·stat /nē′hil ob′stat/ [L = nothing stands in the way] n R C Ch official certification by a diocesan censor that a book contains nothing contrary to faith and morals

Ni·ke /nī′kē/ [Gk goddess of victory] n radio-directed antiaircraft missile

nil /nil/ [L, contr. of nihil nothing] n nothing

Nile /nīl/ n river in E Africa, flowing 3,485 m. north from Lake Victoria through Egypt to the Mediterranean Sea

nim·ble /nim′bəl/ [OE numol holding much] adj 1 swift; lively in movement; 2 alert; quick-witted ‖ **nim′·ble·ness** n ‖ **nim′bly** adv ‖ SYN agile, dextrous, deft, spry, brisk

nim·bo·stra·tus /nim′bōstrāt′əs, -strat′-/ [< L nimbus + stratus] n (-ti /-tī/) low-altitude, dark-gray rain cloud

nim·bus /nim′bəs/ [L = rain cloud] n (-bus·es, -bi /-bī/) 1 heavy gray rain cloud; 2 halo or cloud of light surrounding the heads of saints and divinities in pictures and statues

Nim·rod /nim′rod/ n 1 Bib greatgrandson of Noah, a mighty hunter (Gen. 10:8,9); 2 hunter

nin·com·poop /nin′kəmpo͞op′/ [?] n silly, stupid person; fool

nine /nīn/ [OE nigon] n 1 sum of eight and one (9; IX); 2 group formed of nine units, as, a baseball team; 3 playing card with nine spots ‖ also adj & pron

nine′fold′ adj 1 having nine times as much or as many ‖ adv 2 nine times as much or as many

nine′pins′ nsg bowling game played with nine pins

nine′teen′ /-tēn′/ [OE ningontene] n sum of nine and ten (19; XIX) ‖ also adj & pron

nine′teenth′ n 1 the one next in order after the eighteenth; 2 one of nineteen equal parts ‖ also adj

nine′ti·eth n 1 the one next in order after the eighty-ninth; 2 one of ninety equal parts ‖ also adj

nine′ty [OE nigontig] n (-ties) 1 nine times ten (90; XC); 2 the nineties pl a the numbers from 90 to 99; b the years from 90 to 99 in a century or a lifetime ‖ also adj & pron

Nin·e·veh /nin′əvə/ n ancient capital of Assyria on the Tigris ‖ **Nin·e·vite** /nin′əvīt′/ adj & n

nin·ny /nin′ē/ [perh an innocent] n (-nies) fool, simpleton

ninth /nīnth/ n 1 the one next in order after the eighth; 2 one of nine equal parts; 3 Mus a interval embracing an octave and a second; b chord containing a ninth ‖ also adj

ni·o·bi·um /nī·ō′bē·əm/ [< Niobe, character in Gk myth.] n gray metallic element (Nb; at.no. 41; at.wt. 92.9) found with tantalum and used as an alloy

nip¹ /nip/ [ME nippen] v (nipped; nip·ping) vt 1 to pinch; 2 to cut off the end of; 3 to blight, destroy, as frost does; 4 nip in the bud to stop (something) before it can get started ‖ n 5 pinch, bite; 6 sharp cold; 7 sharp comment; 8 little bit

nip² [prob < nipperkin wine measure] n 1 sip of liquor ‖ v (nipped; nip·ping) vi 2 to take a nip

nip′ and tuck′ adj & adv extremely close (contest)

nip·per /nip′ər/ n 1 horse's incisor; 2 claw of a crustacean; 3 young boy; 4 nippers pl tool for nipping, as pincers

nip·ple /nip′əl/ [prob dim. of nib] n 1 protuberance on a breast containing the orifices of the milk ducts; 2 rubber teat used as the mouthpiece of nursing bottles; 3 a device regulating the discharge of a liquid; b small orifice through which grease is injected; **4** short piece of pipe threaded, usu. externally, on both ends

Nip·pon /nipon'/ *n* native name of Japan ‖ **Nip·pon·ese** /nip'ənēz', -nēs'/ *adj & n* (-ese)

nip·py /nip'ē/ [< nip¹] *adj* (-pi·er; -pi·est) biting, sharp

nir·va·na, Nir·va·na /nirvän'ə nər-/ [Skt = extinction] *n* **1** *Buddhism* highest religious state, when all desire for existence is extinguished and the soul becomes one with the Creator; **2** freedom from pain and worry

Ni·sei /nē'sā'/ [Jap = 2d generation] *n* person of Japanese parents born outside Japan, esp. in the U.S.

ni·si /nī'sī/ [L = unless] *adj law* taking effect at a specified time unless modified or avoided, as by subsequent proceedings, as *a decree nisi*

Nis'sen hut' /nis'ən/ [Peter N. *Nissen* Brit military engineer] *n* prefabricated corrugated iron shelter shaped like a barrel

nit /nit'/ [OE *hnitu*] *n* **1** egg of a louse or flea; **2** the young insect; **3** insignificant speck

ni·ter /nī'tər/ [MF < Gk *nitron*] *n* **1** potassium nitrate; **2** sodium nitrate; saltpeter

nit'-pick'ing *n colloq* petty faultfinding

nitr- [< *niter*] *comb form* **1** nitrogen; **2** nitrate; **3** indicating the univalent group NO₂

ni·trate /nī'trāt/ [*nitr-* + *-ate*] **1** salt or ester of nitric acid, esp. sodium or potassium nitrate, used as a fertilizer ‖ *vt* **2** a to subject to the action of nitric acid; **b** to convert into a salt by combination with nitric acid ‖ **ni·tra'tion** *n*

ni·tric /-trik/ *adj* pert. to or containing nitrogen, esp. in compounds with more oxygen than the corresponding nitrous compounds

ni'tric ac'id *n* corrosive acid —HNO₃— used as an oxidizing agent, in making explosives, fertilizers, and dyes, and in etching

ni'tric ox'ide *n* colorless poisonous gas —NO— obtained by oxidizing ammonia in the making of nitric acid

ni'tride /-trīd/ *n* binary compound in which nitrogen is the more electronegative element

ni'tri·fy' [F *nitrifier*] *v* (-fied) *vt* **1** to combine or saturate with nitrogen; **2** to impregnate with nitrates, as soils, for plant growth ‖ **ni'tri·fi·ca'tion** *n*

ni'trite /-trīt/ *n* salt of nitrous acid, containing less oxygen than a nitrate

ni·tro /nī'trō/ *adj* **1** containing the univalent group NO₂ ‖ *n* **2** any of various nitrated products, esp. nitroglycerine

nitro- var of **nitr-**

ni'tro·bac·te'ri·a *npl* bacteria which cause nitrification in the soil

ni'tro·cel'lu·lose' *n* compound of nitrogen and cellulose used in making explosives, collodion, and lacquer

ni'tro·gen /-trəjən/ *n* colorless, odorless, tasteless gaseous element (N; at.no. 7; at.wt. 14.0067), constituting 78 percent of the atmosphere by volume and occurring in all living tissue and as a constituent of soils ‖ **ni·trog·e·nous** /-troj'inəs/ *adj*

ni'tro·gen cy'cle *n* the natural processes by which nitrogen passes from the soil to the air and back again

ni'tro·gen fix·a'tion *n* **1** process of combining atmospheric nitrogen with any of various stable compounds, used esp. for making fertilizers and explosives; **2** process whereby bacteria and other soil microorganisms convert atmospheric nitrogen into nitrates, which become available to growing plants

ni'trog·en·ize' /-troj'inīz'/ *vt* to combine, impregnate, or saturate with nitrogen or compounds containing nitrogen

ni'tro·glyc'er·in or **-ine** *n* heavy, oily, poisonous liquid —C₃H₅(ONO₂)₃— used in explosives and as a heart stimulant

ni'trous /-trəs/ *adj* **1** resembling, obtained from, or containing niter; **2** designating nitrogen compounds containing less oxygen than nitric compounds

ni'trous ox'ide *n* colorless gas —N₂O— used as an anesthetic, esp. in dentistry; also called *laughing gas*

nit·wit /nit'wit'/ [prob < *nit* + *wit*] *n* simpleton

nix /niks'/ [G *nichts* nothing] *slang n* **1** nothing ‖ *adv* **2** no ‖ *vt* **3** to veto

Nix·on, Rich·ard Mil·hous /mil'hous nik'sən/ *n* (1913–) 37th president of the U.S. 1969–74 ‖ **Nix·o'ni·an** /-sōn'ē-ən/ *adj & n*

N.J. New Jersey

NL New Latin

NLRB National Labor Relations Board

N.M. or **N. Mex.** New Mexico

N.N.E. north-northeast

N.N.W. north-northwest

no /nō'/ [OE nā] *adv* **1** expressing refusal or denial, as *no, I don't*; **2** not any, not at all, as *he is no better*; **3** not, as, *whether or no* ‖ *adj* **4** not any, as *I have no money* ‖ *n* (noes, nos) **5** reply of refusal or denial; **6** a negative vote; **b** person voting in the negative ‖ *interj* **7** expressing doubt or incredulity

No or **no** /nō'/ [Jap] *n* classic Japanese dance-drama

No., no. number

No·ah /nō'ə/ *n* Hebrew patriarch, builder of the ark in which he, his family, and many animals survived the great deluge (Gen. 6–9)

nob /nob'/ [< *knob*?] *n* **1** *cribbage* jack of trumps when in hand or crib;

2 *slang* head; **3** *Brit colloq* person of means and note

nob·by /nob′ē/ *adj* (**-bi·er; -bi·est**) *colloq* stylish, smart

no·bel·i·um /nōbel′ē-əm/ [*Nobel* institute] *n* radioactive element (**No; at.no. 102**) produced artificially

No·bel′ prize′ /nōbel′/ [Alfred B. *Nobel* (1833–96) Sw manufacturer and philanthropist, inventor of dynamite] *n* one of six prizes awarded annually in the fields of physics, chemistry, literature, medicine or physiology, economics, and in the promotion of peace

no·bil·i·ty /nōbil′itē/ [L *nobilitas* via MF] *n* **1** state or quality of being great, excellent, or worthy; **2 a** high birth or rank as denoted by a title; **b** the body of persons of rank above the common people; peerage ‖ SYN aristocracy, peerage, rank, grandeur, loftiness

no·ble /nō′bəl/ [OE < L *nobilis*] *adj* **1** high in excellence or worth; illustrious; **2** high in rank; of ancient lineage; aristocratic; **3** stately, imposing, as *noble architecture;* **4** *chem* pure, inert, not readily combined with oxygen, as *the noble metals or gases* ‖ *n* **5** person bearing a title of nobility ‖ **no′ble·ness** *n* ‖ **no′bly** *adv* ‖ SYN *adj* lofty, elevated, magnificent, aristocratic, honorable, renowned, famous, magnanimous, generous ‖ ANT *adj* narrow, small, insignificant, obscure

no′ble·man /-mən/ *n* (**-men** /-mən/) person of noble rank; peer ‖ **no′ble·wom′an** *nfem* (**-wom′en**)

no·blesse o·blige /nōbles′ ōblēzh′/ [F = nobleness obliges] rank entails responsibility; honorable or generous conduct is expected from those of high rank or high-minded principles

no·bod·y /nō′bod′ē, -bədē/ *pron* **1** no one ‖ *n* (**-ies**) **2** person of no importance, influence, or rank

nock /nok′/ [ME *nocke*] *n* **1** notch at the end of an arrow to receive the bowstring; **2** groove for the bowstring at either end of the bow ‖ *vt* **3** to set (the arrow) on the bowstring

noct- or **nocti-** or **nocto-** [L *nox* (*noctis*)] *comb form* night

noc·tur·nal /nokturn′əl/ [L *nocturnus*] *adj* **1** pert. to or happening at night; **2** active at night, as *nocturnal animals*

noc·turne /nok′turn/ [F = nocturnal] *n* **1** painting of a night scene; **2** quiet, dreamy musical composition, usu. for the piano

nod /nod′/ [ME *nodden*] *v* (**nod·ded; nod·ding**) *vt* **1** to incline or bend forward with a quick movement, as *to nod the head* in token of assent, salutation, invitation, etc., or from drowsiness; **2** to signify by a quick inclination of the head, as *to nod*

assent ‖ *vi* **3** to incline or bend forward the top with a quick motion; **4** to bend the head in token of assent, salutation, etc.; **5** to bend the head drowsily; **6** to make an error because of momentary abstraction ‖ *n* **7** act of nodding

node /nōd′/ [L *nodus* knot] *n* **1** knot, knob, swelling; **2** dilemma or complicated situation, as in a story; **3** either of the two points where the orbit of one celestial body intersects a specific plane; **4** point at which a curve cuts or crosses itself; **5** point on the stem of a plant from which a leaf springs; **6** swelling or protuberance, as on a bone or tendon; tumor; **7** *phys* stationary point, line, or plane in a vibrating body ‖ **nod′al** *adj*

nod·ule /noj′ool/ [L *nodulus*] *n* **1** little knot or irregular, rounded lump; **2** small node or tumor; **3** small joint on a stem ‖ **nod′u·lar** *adj* ‖ **nod′u·lose′** /-lōs′/ *adj*

no·el /nō-el′/ [F *noël* Christmas] **1** Christmas carol; **2** Noel Christmas season

no′-fault in·sur′ance *n* automobile insurance that covers injuries and losses directly regardless of the cause of an accident

nog /nog′/ [?] *n* **1** a strong English ale; **2** eggnog

nog·gin /nog′in/ [< *nog* ?] *n* **1** small cup or mug; **2** liquid measure equal to one gill; **3** *colloq* head

no′-hit′ *adj* (baseball game) in which one pitcher does not allow the opposing team a hit

no′how′ *adv* in no way

noise /noiz′/ [OF = quarrel < L *nausea*] *n* **1** sound, esp. when confused or disagreeable; **2** clamor, outcry; **3** *acoustics* sound resulting from discordant vibrations; **4** *electronic communication* unwanted signal ‖ *vt* **5** to spread by rumor ‖ *vi* **6** to make a noise; **7** to talk loudly or noisily ‖ SYN *n* sound, clamor, hubbub, racket, uproar, tumult, outcry, din ‖ DISCR *Sound,* the general term, names what is or may be heard. *Noise* is harsh, grating *sound. Sound* may name sweet music; *noise* is discordant. To indicate a break in silence, however, any little *sound* may also be referred to as a *noise,* as he started at a *sound;* he started at a *noise. Clamor, hubbub, racket, uproar,* and *tumult* are all species of *noise,* usually made by a confusion of *sounds,* but including, too, the natural commotion other than *noise* that exists when numbers of agitated people are together. *Clamor* emphasizes bawling, yelling, or shouting. Voices calling in opposition, loud expressions as of protest or amusement, all coming at once, produce an *uproar.* The noisy uprising of a mob, or the confused cries of a milling multitude, create a *tumult. Hubbub* and *racket* name a *din* that is distracting and disturbing; *hubbub* is a more riotous, *racket* a more clattering, *noise*

noise·less *adj* making no noise ‖ **noise′·less·ly** *adv* ‖ **noise′less·ness** *n*

noi·some /noi′səm/ [< OF *anoi* annoyance] *adj* **1** noxious, injurious to health; **2** foul-smelling, offensive ‖ SYN unwholesome, deleterious, noxious, fetid, pestilential ‖ ANT healthful, salubrious, beneficial

nois·y /noiz′ē/ *adj* (**-i·er; -i·est**) **1** full of noise; **2** making noise ‖ **nois′i·ly** *adv* ‖ **nois′i·ness** *n*

nol·le pros·e·qui /nol′ēpros′əkwī′/ [L = not to be willing to pursue] *n* plaintiff's or prosecutor's formal notice that he will drop a suit either wholly or in part

no·lo con·ten·de·re /nō′lōkənten′dərē/ [L = I do not wish to contest] *n* plea by the defendant refusing to defend himself but not admitting his guilt

nol·pros /nol′pros′/ [*nolle prosequi*] *v* (**-prossed; -pros·sing**) *vt* to drop (a suit) by entering a nolle prosequi

no·mad /nō′mad/ [Gk *nomas* (*-ados*) roaming] *n* **1** one of any unsettled tribes who wander about in search of pasture, game, etc. **2** person who roams about without a fixed abode ‖ **no·mad′ic** *adj* ‖ **no′mad·ism** *n*

no′ man′s′-land′ *n* **1** land to which no one has valid or superior rights of ownership; **2** the contested area between two armies at war; **3** indefinite, ill-defined area

nom de guerre /nom′dəger′/ [F = war name] *n* (**noms de guerre**) pseudonym

nom de plume /nom′dəplōōm′/ [F = pen name] *n* (**noms de plume**) **1** pen name; **2** pseudonym

no·men·cla·ture /nōm′ənklāch′ər/ [L *nomenclatura* name calling] *n* **1** collection of words and terms or system of names for things used in any art or science; **2** any specified system of naming

nom·i·nal /nom′inəl/ [ML *nominalis*] *adj* **1 a** in name only, not actual; **b** small, negligible; **2** pert. to or being a noun in form or use; noun-like; **3 a** of or pert. to a name or names; **b** bearing or mentioning a personal name ‖ *n* **4** *ling* noun or word or phrase used as a noun ‖ **nom′i·nal·ly** *adv*

nom′i·nal·ize′ *vt* to convert into a noun

nom·i·nate /nom′ināt/ [L *nominare* (*-atus*)] *vt* **1** to appoint to an office or position; **2** to name as a candidate for an office or honor ‖ **nom′i·na′tion** *n* ‖ **nom′i·na′tor** *n*

nom·i·na·tive /-nətiv/ [L *nominativus*] *adj* **1** pert. to the case of the subject

of a verb; **2** chosen by nomination; **3** bearing a person's name ‖ *n* **4** a nominative case; **b** word in this case

nom′i·nee′ /-nē′/ *n* person who has been nominated

-n·o·my /-nəmē/ [Gk *-nomia*] *n comb form* system of laws governing a specific field of knowledge, as *astronomy*

non- /usu. non′-/ [MF < L] *pref* **1** with adjectives: not, as *nonpaying, noncompetitive, non-English;* **2** with nouns: **a** not (a), as *nondrinker, nonelectrolyte, nonmembers;* **b** lack of, failure of, as *noncompliance, nonenforcement, noncompletion*

non·age /non′ij, nōn′-/ [MF] *n* **1** minority; period when one is legally under age; **2 a** period of youth; **b** immaturity

non·a·ge·nar·i·an /non′əjəner′ē·ən/ [< L *nonageni* · ninety each] *n* person 90 years old or between 90 and 100 years old ‖ also *adj*

non·a·gon /non′əgon′, -gən/ [L *nonus* nine + *-gon*] *n* polygon having nine angles and nine sides ‖ **non·ag′o·nal** /-ag′ənəl/ *adj*

non′a·ligned′ *adj* (nation) not aligned with the U.S.A., the Soviet Union, or Communist China ‖ **non′a·lign′ment** *n*

nonce /nons′/ [ME *nanes*] *n* present occasion or time; time being, as *for the nonce*

nonce′ word′ *n* word coined and used only once for a particular occasion

non·cha·lant /non′shəlänt′, non′shələnt/ [F] *adj* without interest or enthusiasm, indifferent ‖ **non′cha·lance′** *n*

non′com′ /-kom′/ *n colloq* noncommissioned officer

non·com′bat·ant /-kom′bətənt/ *n* **1** member of the armed forces whose duties do not include fighting, as a chaplain; **2** civilian ‖ also *adj*

non′com·mis′sioned of′fi·cer *n* enlisted man in the armed forces with a rank above that of the two lowest grades

non′com·mit′tal /-kəmit′əl/ *adj* **1** not revealing one's opinion or purpose; **2** unwilling to commit oneself ‖ **non′·com·mit′tal·ly** *adv*

non com·pos men·tis /non′comp′əs ment′is/ [L = not master of one's mind] *adj law* not of sound mind

non′con·duc′tor *n* substance conducting little or no electricity, heat, or sound

non′con·form′i·ty *n* **1** failure or refusal to make one's conduct or opinions conform to those prevailing generally; **2** lack of correspondence or agreement; **3 Nonconformity** doctrine of Protestant dissent against the Church of England ‖ **non′con·form′ist** *adj & n* ‖ **Non′con·form′ist** *adj & n*

non′co·op′er·a′tion *n* refusal to cooperate, esp. with a government, through civil disobedience

non'de·nom'i·na'tion·al *adj* not sponsored or controlled by a religious denomination

non'de·script' /-diskript'/ [*non-* + L *descriptus* described] *adj* difficult to describe; of no special kind or class ‖ also *n*

none /nun'/ [OE nān] *pron* 1 not any; no part, as *I want none*; 2 nobody; no one, as *none came* ‖ *adv* 3 in no way, as *none the worse*

non·en'ti·ty *n* (-ties) 1 nonexistence; 2 something not existing, or existing only in the imagination; 3 insignificant person

none'such' *n* person or object that has no rival or equal; paragon

none'the·less' *adv* nevertheless

non'-Eu·clid'e·an ge·om'e·try *n* geometry of spaces differing from the space we feel we are familiar with

non·fea'sance /-fēz'əns/ [*non* + OF *faisance* doing] *n law* neglect or omission of some duty which one is legally bound to perform

non·fic'tion *n* narrative prose literature other than fiction, as biography, history, the essay ‖ **non·fic'tion·al** *adj*

non'in·ter·ven'tion *n* policy of not intervening, esp. in the affairs of another nation

non·mem'ber *n* person who is not a member

non·met'al *n* element that combines with hydrogen, cannot replace the hydrogen of an acid, and lacks most other metallic properties, as phosphorus, carbon, oxygen, bromine, nitrogen ‖ **non'me·tal'lic** *adj*

non·pa·reil' /-pərel'/ [MF] *adj* 1 without equal ‖ *n* 2 person or thing of unequaled excellence; 3 a sugar pellet of various colors; b small chocolate disk covered on one side with white sugar pellets; 4 *typ* a 6-point type; b 6-point space between lines

non·par'ti·san *adj* 1 unbiased; objective; 2 not following a person, cause, or party

non·plus' [L = no more] *n* (-plus·es or -plus·ses) 1 state of extreme perplexity ‖ *v* (-plused or -plussed; -plus·ing or -plus·sing) *vt* 2 to put into a state of utter perplexity; to confound

non·prof'it *adj* not conceived or organized for making a profit

non'pro·lif'er·a'tion trea'ty *n* agreement among the nations of the world to not spread knowledge of the nuclear bomb—among nations who do not possess it, including an agreement among those who do not possess it to not develop it

non'-pros' /-pros'/ [L *non prosequitur*] *v* (-prossed; -pros·sing) *vt* to enter a non prosequitur against

non' pro·se'qui·tur /prəsek'witər/ [L =

he does not pursue] *n* judgment entered against the plaintiff in a suit in which he fails to appear

non're·sis'tance *n* policy of not resisting violence or unjust authority by force ‖ **non're·sis'tant** *adj* & *n*

non're·stric'tive clause' *n* parenthetical descriptive clause not essential to the meaning of a sentence, as that man, *whose name I do not know*, came in late

non·rig'id air'ship *n* lighter-than-air craft having a flexible gas container maintaining its shape by the pressure of the contained gas

non'sched'uled air'line *n* airline that is not required to operate on a regular schedule, but operates as the traffic warrants

non·sec·tar'i·an *adj* not confined to any one sect or religion

non·sense /-sens, -səns/ *n* 1 words or ideas having no sense; absurdity; 2 things of little worth, trifles ‖ *interj* 3 absurd! ‖ **non·sen'si·cal** *adj* ‖ **non·sen'si·cal·ly** *adv* ‖ SYN *n* silliness, absurdity, folly, rubbish, tomfoolery

non se'qui·tur /sek'witər/ [L = it does not follow] *n* inference or conclusion that does not follow from the facts stated

non·sked' /-sked'/ [*nonscheduled*] *n* nonscheduled airline

non'skid' *adj* (tire) constructed to resist skidding

non·stand'ard *adj* 1 not standard; 2 not conforming to the speech and writing of educated native speakers of a language

non'stop' *adj* & *adv* without stopping en route

non'suit' [AF *nounsute*] *n* withdrawal of a suit during trial, voluntarily or by judgment of the court, on discovery of error or defect in the case ‖ also *vt*

non'sup·port' *n* failure to provide maintenance for a legal dependent

non·un'ion *adj* 1 not belonging to a labor union; 2 not in favor of unions ‖ *n* 3 *surg* failure of a bone to unite

non·vi'o·lence *n* policy or practice of seeking one's ends without resort to violence ‖ **non·vi'o·lent** *adj*

noo·dle¹ /nōōd'əl/ [G *Nudel*] *n* narrow ribbon of dried dough, boiled and served with a sauce or in soups

noo·dle² [*noddle* head + *noodle¹*] *n colloq* 1 simpleton; 2 head, pate

nook /nŏŏk'/ [ME *nok*] 1 interior corner; 2 small secluded retreat

noon /nōōn'/ [OE *nōn* < L *nona* ninth hour] *n* 1 midday; twelve o'clock in the daytime; 2 time of greatest brilliance or power

noon'day' *n* midday

no' one' *pron* nobody

noon'tide' *n* noon

noon'time' *n* midday

noose /nōōs'/ [L *nodus* knot via Prov?]

n 1 loop with a slipknot that tightens as it is drawn ‖ *vt* 2 to secure by a noose; 3 to make a slipknot in

nope /nōp/ *adv colloq* no

nor /nôr´, nər/ [ME, contr. of *nother* neither] *conj* 1 and not—a negative connective used: **a** as a correlative of a preceding negative, as *I eat neither pie nor cake;* **b** following, but not as a correlative of, a preceding negative, as *I said I would not fall, nor did I;* 2 *dial.* than

Nor·dic /nôr´dik/ [F *nordique*] *adj* 1 of or pert. to the Germanic peoples of northern Europe and esp. of Scandinavia; 2 of or pert. to the tall, blond, long-headed, blue-eyed subtype of the Caucasian race ‖ *n* 3 member of this race

Nor·folk /nôr´fək/ *n* seaport city and naval base in SE Virginia (307,951)

Nor·folk jack´et *n* man's loose-fitting belted jacket with side pockets

norm /nôrm´/ [L *normal* carpenter's square] *n* 1 accepted standard, authoritative model; 2 **a** average; **b** a designated standard of average performance; 3 *statistics* quantitative standard determined by the average, median, or other measure of the central tendency among the varying individuals of a type or species

nor·mal [L *normalis*] *adj* 1 conforming to a norm; regular; natural; 2 serving as a standard; 3 **a** average in intelligence and emotional adjustment; **b** sane; 4 *geom* perpendicular; 5 *med* free from disease, malformation, or malfunction; 6 *chem* **a** not associated; **b** having a straight-chain structure ‖ *n* 7 that which is normal or regular; 8 that which is regarded as the norm; standard; 9 *geom* perpendicular line or plane, esp. to a tangent at the point of tangency; 10 *phys* average or mean value of observed quantities ‖ **nor·mal´i·ty** -mal´-/ *n* ‖ SYN *adj* regular, typical, usual (see *natural*)

nor·mal·cy /-sē/ *n* normality, esp. of political and economic conditions

nor·mal·ize /ˈ *vt* 1 to make normal; 2 to heat (a steel alloy) to a temperature above the transformation range and then allow it to cool ‖ *vi* 3 to return to normal ‖ **nor´mal·i·za´tion** *n*

nor·mal·ly *adv* 1 in a normal manner; 2 **a** under normal circumstances; **b** as a rule

nor´mal school´ [< F *école normale* model school] *n* formerly, a two-year school training public-school teachers, now replaced by four-year liberal-arts colleges

nor´mal so·lu´tion *n* a solution having a concentration of one gram equivalent of solute per liter

Nor·man /nôr´mən/ [OF *Normant*] *n* 1 native or inhabitant of Normandy; 2 one of the Scandinavian invaders

of Normandy in the 10th century who adopted the French language and who conquered England in 1066; 3 dialect of French spoken and written by the Normans in the Middle Ages; 4 dialect of French spoken in Normandy in modern times ‖ also *adj*

Nor´man ar´chi·tec·ture *n* Romanesque style first appearing in Normandy in the 10th century and introduced into England by the Normans

Nor´man Con´quest *n* conquest of England by the Normans under William the Conqueror in 1066

Nor´man·dy /-dē/ *n* region and former province of N France along the English Channel, named for the Normans who conquered it; a medieval duchy whose duke, William the Conqueror, became also king of England in 1066

Nor´man French´ *n* 1 medieval Norman (person and dialect); 2 modern dialect of Normandy ‖ **Nor´man-French´** *adj*

nor´ma·tive /-ətiv/ [F *normatif*] *adj* 1 of or pert. to a norm; 2 prescribing norms, as *normative grammar*

Norse /nôrs´/ [prob D *noordsch*] *adj* 1 of or pert. to ancient Scandinavia and its language; 2 Norwegian ‖ *n* 3 **a** language of Norway; **b** any of the western Scandinavian dialects and languages; 4 *npl* **a** Norwegians; **b** Scandinavians generally, esp. of ancient times

Norse´man /-mən/ *n* (-men /-mən/) ancient Scandinavian

north /nôrth´/ [OE] *n* 1 one of the four cardinal points of the compass, the direction away from the equator along any meridian in the Northern Hemisphere and towards the equator in the Southern; 2 often **North** region or territory lying in this direction; 3 **the North** the region of the U.S., north of the Ohio river and the Mason-Dixon line, which was the heart of the resistance against Secession during the Civil War ‖ *adj* 4 situated in, directed toward, or facing the north; 5 (wind) blowing from the north ‖ *adv* 6 in or toward the north

North´ A·mer´i·ca *n* northernmost continent in the Western Hemisphere, extending north from Central America (265,000,000; ab. 8,450,000 sq.m.) ‖ **North´ A·mer´i·can** *adj & n*

North´ At·lan´tic Trea´ty Or·gan·i·za´-tion *n* defensive organization of noncommunist countries of Europe and America (1949)

north´bound´ *adj* headed north

North´ Cape´ *n* point of land at the northern tip of Norway, the northernmost point of Europe

North´ Car·o·li·na /kar´əlīn´ə/ *n* state in SE U.S. (5,082,000; 52,712 sq.m.;

cap. Raleigh) || **North′ Car′o·lin′i·an** /-lin′ē-ən/ n

North′ Da·ko′ta n state in N central U.S. (617,761; 70,665 sq.m.; cap. Bismarck) || **North′ Da·ko′tan** n

north′east′ /also naut nôr′ēst′/ n **1** compass point halfway between north and east; **2** region lying in this direction; **3 the Northeast** the northeastern part of the U.S., esp. New England || adj **4** situated in, directed toward, or facing the northeast; **5** (wind) blowing from the northeast || adv **6** toward the northeast || **north′-east′er·ly** adj & adv || **north′east′ern** adj || **north′east′ward** /-wərd/ adj & adv || **north′east′wards** /-wərdz/ adv

north′east′er /naut nôr′-/ n storm or gale from the northeast

North′east′ern·er n native or inhabitant of the Northeast

north·er /nôr′thər/ n strong, cold north wind, esp. in the Gulf Coast region

north′er·ly /-th-/ adj & adv **1** in the direction of or moving toward the north; **2** (wind) from the north || n (-lies) **3** north wind

north′ern /-th-/ adj **1** situated in, directed toward, or facing the north; **2** (wind) blowing from the north; **3 North′ern** of or pert. to the North || **north′ern·er** n || **North′ern·er** n

North′ern Hem′i·sphere′ n that part of the earth north of the equator

North′ern Ire′land n division of the United Kingdom in the NE of Ireland (1,425,000; 5238 sq.m.; cap. Belfast)

north′ern lights′ npl aurora borealis

north′ern·most′ adj farthest north

North′ern Spy′ n American variety of apple with red stripes that ripens in late autumn

North′ Frig′id Zone′ n that part of the earth between the Arctic Circle and the North Pole

North′ Is′land n the northernmost and smaller of the two principal islands of New Zealand

North′ Ko·re′a n country in NE Asia formed in 1948 by the division of Korea at 38° N (12,700,000; 46,540 sq.m.; cap. Pyongyang) || **North′ Ko·re′an** adj & n

north′land /-lənd/ n northern part of a country

north′ pole′ n **1** the pole of a magnet that points toward the north magnetic pole; **2 North Pole,** a northern end of the earth's axis; **b** point of the celestial sphere near the North Star directly above the earth's North Pole

North′ Sea′ n arm of the Atlantic between Great Britain on the west and northern Europe on the east

North′ Star′ n Polaris, the polestar, toward which the North Pole points

North′ Tem′per·ate Zone′ n the part of the earth between the tropic of Cancer and the Arctic Circle

north′ward /-wərd/ adj & adv toward the north || **north′ward·ly** adj & adv || **north′wards** adv

north′west′ /naut nôr′-/ n **1** compass point halfway between north and west; **2** region lying in this direction; **3 the Northwest** the northwestern region of the U.S. between the Rocky Mountains and the Pacific || adj **4** situated in, directed toward, or facing the northwest; **5** (wind) blowing from the northwest || adv **6** toward the northwest || **north′west′er·ly** adj & adv || **north′west′ern** adj || **north′west′ward** /-wərd/ adj & adv || **north′west′wards** /-wərdz/ adv

north′west′er /also naut nôr′-/ n storm or gale from the northwest

North′west′ern·er n native or inhabitant of the Northwest

North′west Pas′sage n water route along the Arctic coast of Canada and Alaska, from the Atlantic to the Pacific; first navigated 1903–06

North′west Ter′ri·to·ries npl territory in NW Canada (23,000; 1,304,903 sq.m.; cap. Yellowknife)

Norw. 1 Norway; **2** Norwegian

Nor·way /nôr′wā/ n kingdom in W part of the Scandinavian Peninsula (3,784,000; 125,181 sq.m.; cap. Oslo) || **Nor·we′gian** /-wēj′ən/ adj & n

nos- var of **noso-**

nose /nōz/ [OE nosu] n **1** the prominent portion of the face above the mouth in which the nostrils and the olfactory nerves are situated; **2** corresponding part in animals; snout, muzzle; **3** sense of smell; **4** any projecting part, as a ship's prow, the front end of a bullet, or the working end of a tool; **5 by a nose** slang by the narrowest of margins; **6 follow one's nose** to guide oneself by instinct; **7 lead by the nose** to reduce to a state of abject subjection; **8 look down one's nose at** to look disdainfully upon; **9 on the nose** slang precisely; **10 pay through the nose** to pay an excessive price; **11 turn up one's nose at** to scorn || vt **12** to scent; discover by the sense of smell; **13 a** to pry into curiously; **b** to find out by prying; **14** to rub with the nose; nuzzle; **15** to push or move with or as with the nose; **16 nose out** to defeat by a nose || vi **17** to smell or scent; sniff; **18** to pry inquisitively; **19** to push forward slowly, as the ship nosed into the harbor

nose′ bag′ n feed bag

nose′bleed′ n bleeding from the nose

nose′ cone′ n cone-shaped forward end of a rocket or guided missile, designed to withstand the heat of reentry into an atmosphere

nose′ dive′ n **1** maneuver in which an airplane dives at great speed; **2** fig

sudden drop or decline ‖ **nose′-dive′**
vi

nose′gay′ *n* small bunch of flowers

no′-show′ *n colloq* passenger who fails
to notify the company that he is not
going to occupy the seat he has reserved

noso- [Gk *nosos*] *comb form* disease

nos·tal·gi·a /nostal′j(ē)ə/ [Gr *nostos*
return home + *-algia*] *n* 1 homesick-
ness; 2 yearning for the return of
past happier times or circumstances
‖ **nos·tal′gic** *adj* ‖ **nos·tal′gi·cal·ly** *adv*

nos·tril /nos′trəl/ [OE *nosthyrl*] *n* one
of the two external openings of the
nose

nos·trum /nos′trəm/ [L = ours] *n* 1
quack medicine; 2 a medicine recommended as a cure-all; b pet remedy
for political or social ills, panacea

nos′y /nōz′ē/ *adj* (**-i·er; -i·est**) *colloq*
prying into someone else's affairs ‖
nos′i·ly *adv* ‖ **nos′i·ness** *n*

not /not′/ [ME < *nought*] *adv* used to
negate that which it modifies, as *I
do not; not here*

no·ta be·ne /nōt′ə ben′ē/ [L] note well;
pay particular attention

no·ta·ble /nōt′əbəl/ [ME < L *nota-
bilis*] *adj* 1 noteworthy, remarkable;
2 distinguished, eminent ‖ *n* 3 prominent or important person ‖ **no′ta-
bil′i·ty** /-bil′-/ *n* ‖ **no′ta·bly** *adv* ‖
SYN *adj* distinguished, signal, striking, rare, evident, remarkable ‖ ANT
adj obscure, usual, ordinary

no·ta·rize /nōt′əriz′/ *vt* to acknowledge
or attest (a document) officially as a
notary ‖ **no′ta·ri·za′tion** *n*

no·ta·ry /nōt′ərē/ [L *notarius* secre-
tary] *n* (**-ries**) or **no′ta·ry pub′lic**
(**notaries public** or **notary publics**)
official authorized by law to attest or
acknowledge deeds and contracts, administer oaths, take affidavits and
depositions, and protest bills of exchange ‖ **no·tar′i·al** /-ter′-/ *adj*

no·ta·tion /nōtāsh′ən/ [L *notatio*
(*-onis*)] *n* 1 a system of signs or symbols used in place of ordinary writing
for brevity or clearness, esp. in the
arts and sciences; b act, method, or
practice of using such a system; 2
written note or jotting ‖ **no·ta′tion·al**
adj

notch /noch′/ [ME *an otch* a notch
< OF *oche*] *n* 1 V-shaped cut or in-
dentation, often made to keep score;
2 short, narrow pass or defile; 3
colloq score or grade ‖ *vt* 4 to make
a notch in; 5 to record by making
notches; 6 *colloq* to score (a victory)

note /nōt′/ [L *nota* mark] *n* 1 brief
memorandum to assist the memory;
2 explanatory comment or reference
set apart from the text; 3 short, informal letter; 4 formal official or diplomatic communication; 5 significant
mark or feature; characteristic quality, as a *note of languor in her voice;*
6 reputation, fame; 7 heed, attention;

8 bird's musical cry or call; 9 **notes**
pl series of memoranda, giving an
outline of facts, topics, impressions,
etc., as of a lecture; 10 *mus* a written sign or character representing the
pitch and relative length of a tone; b
musical tone; 11 legal paper acknowledging a debt and promising
payment; 12 piece of paper money;
bank note; 13 **compare notes** to exchange views and impressions; 14
make note of to mark down for study
or future reference ‖ *vt* 15 to make
a memorandum of; 16 to make mention of; 17 to observe, notice; 18 to
pay careful attention to; 19 to set
down in musical notation ‖ SYN *n* remark, comment, observation, annota-
tion, explanation

note′book′ *n* book for notes and memoranda

not′ed *adj* well-known, celebrated ‖
SYN (see *notorious, distinguished*)

note′wor′thy *adj* worthy of notice or
attention; remarkable ‖ **note′wor′-
thi·ness** *n*

noth·ing /nuth′iŋ/ [OE *nāthing*] *n* 1 no
thing, nought; 2 nothingness; 3 thing
or person of no significance or importance; 4 **make nothing of,** a to
treat lightly; b not to understand
(something); 5 **nothing doing** *colloq*
a certainly not; b no activity ‖ *adv*
by no means

noth′ing·ness *n* 1 state of nonexistence;
2 worthlessness, unimportance; 3 unconsciousness or death; 4 thing of no
importance

no·tice /nōt′is/ [MF < L *notitia* ac-
quaintance] *n* 1 knowledge, information; 2 a notification, warning; b
state of being notified or warned, as
*he was put on notice that he would
be discharged if he was late;* 3 notification of the termination or non-
renewal of employment or of a contract or agreement, as *he was given
two weeks' notice;* 4 observation or
attention, as *he took notice of her
new hat;* 5 a posted sign or placard
giving information, warning, or directions; b announcement in a newspaper; 6 press criticism or review of
a book or theatrical presentation ‖
vt 7 to observe, take notice of; 8 to
comment on, mention; 9 to pay polite
attention to ‖ SYN *n* notification, intelligence, news, advice, observation,
respect; *v* heed, observe, remark,
perceive, note ‖ DISCR We may *notice*
things casually; we *remark* with an
awakened mind some particular aspect or characteristic of the thing
noticed or seen. We *notice* some
morning that our neighbor has left
at an earlier hour than usual; later
we *remark* that he is no longer habitually
leaving at this earlier hour. We *observe* by judging or drawing inferences from what we have watched.
What we *notice* or *remark* may be

thrust upon our attention; what we *observe* we watch of our own accord. To *perceive* is to lay hold of a thing by the mind or senses. We *perceive* differences, resemblances, bases for comparison, changes in temperature, and the like

no·tice·a·ble *adj* 1 capable of being noticed; 2 conspicuous, significant || **no′tice·a·bly** *adv*

no′ti·fy′ /nōt′ifī′/ [MF *notifier* < L *notificare*] *v* (**-fied**) *vt* 1 to inform or give notice to; 2 to give formal notice to || **no′ti·fi·ca′tion** *n* || SYN acquaint, advise, declare, inform, warn

no′tion /nōsh′ən/ [L *notio -onis*] *n* 1 general concept or idea; 2 theory or belief; 3 inclination, whim; 4 knick-knack; 5 notions *pl* small household articles, as buttons, thread, and pins || SYN conception, apprehension, opinion, caprice

no′tion·al *adj* 1 pert. to or conveying an idea, fancy; 2 speculative; 3 imaginary; 4 given to whims; 5 *gram* having full meaning, not relational || **no′tion·al′i·ty** /-nal′-/ *n* || **no′tion·al·ly** *adv* || SYN fanciful, whimsical, capricious, changeable, fickle || ANT steady, constant, predictable, practical

no·to·chord /nōt′əkôrd/ [Gk *noton* back + *chord*] 1 in the lower chordates, an elastic rodlike structure lying below the nerve chord and functioning like a backbone; 2 similar structure in the early embryonic stages of vertebrates, later replaced by the backbone

no·to·ri·e·ty /nōt′ərī′itē/ *n* (**-ties**) 1 state of being publicly known, esp. in an undesirable sense; 2 one who is widely known, esp. for some sensational or scandalous reason

no·to·ri·ous /nōtôr′ē·əs, -tōr′-/ [L *notorius* evident] *adj* widely known, usu. in a bad sense, as a *notorious criminal* || **no·to′ri·ous·ly** *adv* || SYN noted || DISCR *Noted*, meaning well or generally known, is used in either a good or an unfavorable sense. We may refer to a *noted* clergyman or a *noted* gambler. *Notorious* is used always in the unfavorable sense; a *notorious* liar is widely known as such, and generally acknowledged to deserve the name

not′with·stand′ing *prep* 1 in spite of || *conj* 2 although || *adv* 3 nevertheless, however

nou·gat /nōōg′ət/ [F] *n* confection of pasty consistency containing almonds or other nuts and sometimes fruit

nought /nôt′/ *n* var. of **naught**

noun /noun′/ [AF *noun* name < L *nomen*] *n* member of a class of words, excluding the pronouns, which in English are generally inflected for the possessive case and for number, and function as subjects or objects of verbs and as objects of prepositions;

in traditional grammar, nouns are thought of as naming persons, places, and things

nour·ish /nur′ish/ [OF *norir* (-*risse*)] *vt* 1 to feed (a living organism or an emotion); 2 to foster, promote the growth of || **nour′ish·ment** *n* || SYN nurture, feed, cherish, sustain, foster, promote

nour′ish·ing *adj* nutritious

nou·veau riche /nōō′vō′rēsh′/ [F = new rich] *n* (**nouveaux riches** /same as *sg*/) newly rich and usu. vulgar person

Nov. November

no·va /nōv′ə/ [L = new] *n* (**-vas** or **-vae** /-vē/) star which suddenly flashes to thousands of times its former brightness and then gradually fades again

No·va Sco·tia /nōv′ə skōsh′ə/ *n* peninsula and maritime province in SE Canada (760,000; 21,425 sq.m.; cap. Halifax) || **No′va Sco′tian** *n*

nov·el¹ /nov′əl/ [OF = new] *adj* 1 new, unprecedented; 2 new, unusual || SYN (see *modern*) || ANT ancient, old, outworn

nov·el² [It *novella* tale] *n* fictional prose narrative of considerable length, involving a continuous plot and ostensibly presenting a picture of real life || **nov·el·ist** *n* || **nov·el·is′tic** *adj* || **nov·el·i·za′tion** *n* || **nov′el·ize** *vt*

nov·el·ette /nov′əlet′/ *n* short novel

no·vel·la /nōvel′ə/ *n* 1 novelette || *n* (*pl* **-vel·le** /-vel′ā/) *n* 2 short story of great compactness and with a sharply pointed plot

nov′el·ty /nov′əltē/ *n* (**-ties**) 1 quality or state of being novel; 2 something new or unusual; 3 novelties *pl* new superficially attractive and chiefly decorative articles of trade, usu. of small value

No·vem·ber /nōvem′bər/ [L = ninth month (of Roman calendar)] *n* eleventh month of the year, having 30 days

no·ve·na /nōvēn′ə/ [ML < L = nine each] *n* R C Ch devotion of nine consecutive days

nov·ice /nov′is/ [MF] *n* 1 beginner, tyro; 2 newly admitted member of a religious order who has not yet taken vows

no·vi·ti·ate /nōvish′ē·it, -āt′/ [MF *noviciat*] *n* 1 state or period of being a novice; 2 quarters set aside for religious novices

No·vo·caine /nōv′əkān′/ *n* [trademark] procaine hydrochloride

now /nou′/ [OE nū] *adv* 1 at the present time; 2 quite recently, as *he left just now*; 3 under the circumstances, as *now what will you do?* 4 sometimes, as *now one, now the other*; 5 at this moment, as *he was now ready to go*; 6 used as a mark of transition without temporal force, as *now what do you mean?* 7 used to introduce a command ȯr entreaty, as *now don't* *do that;* **8 now and then** occasionally; **9 now that** seeing that, since ‖ *conj* **10** since, as *I need not stay, now you're here* ‖ *n* the present, as *up to now*

now'·a·days' [ME *nou adayes*] *adv* at the present time

no'way' or **no'ways'** *adv* not at all

no'where' *adv* no place ‖ also *n*

no'wheres' *adv dial.* nowhere

no'wise' *adv* in no way

nox·ious /nok′shəs/ [L *noxius*] *adj* physically or morally harmful or injurious ‖ SYN hurtful, noisome, corrupting, pestiferous

noz·zle /noz′əl/ [*dim.* of *nose*] *n* **1** projecting mouthpiece or spout through which a liquid may be discharged, as on a hose or teapot; **2** in a jet engine or rocket, duct through which the velocity of a liquid or gas is increased; **3** *slang* nose

Np *chem* neptunium

N.S. Nova Scotia

NT, NT., or **N.T.** New Testament

-n't /-ənt/ *comb form* not

nth /enth′/ *adj* **1** *math* representing an indefinitely large or small ordinal number; **2** extreme, utmost, as *to the nth degree*

nu /n(y)o͞o′/ Gk < Sem] *n* thirteenth letter of the Greek alphabet N, *ν*

nu·ance /n(y)o͞o′äns, n(y)o͞o·äns′/ [F = shade of color] *n* delicate shading, as of tone, color, meaning, feeling, or expression

nub /nub′/ [MLG *knubbe* knob] *n* **1** knob, lump; **2** gist

nub·bin /nub′in/ [*dim.* of *nub*] *n* **1** imperfect ear of corn; **2** something small or stunted

Nu·bi·a /n(y)o͞o′bē·ə/ *n* region in S Egypt and N Sudan inhabited by mixed Negroid tribes, which formed a powerful empire in the Middle Ages ‖ **Nu′bi·an** *adj* & *n*

nu·bile /n(y)o͞o′bəl, -bīl/ [L *nubilis*] *adj* marriageable (girl or woman) ‖ **nu·bil′i·ty** *n*

nucle- [< *nucleus*] *comb form* **1** nucleus; **2** nucleic acid

nu·cle·ar /n(y)o͞o′klē·ər/ *adj* **1** of, pert. to, or constituting a nucleus; **2** pert. to, making use of, or involving the atomic nucleus, atomic energy, or atomic weapons, as *nuclear reactor, nuclear submarine, nuclear war*

nu′cle·ar fis′sion *n* fission 3

nu′cle·ar fu′sion *n* fusion 4

nu′cle·ar phys′ics *nsg* branch of physics dealing with the structure and behavior of atomic nuclei

nu′cle·ar pro·pul′sion *n* method of propulsion of a body based on the release of power by controlled rearrangement of atomic nuclei

nu·cle′ic ac′id /-klē′ik/ *n* any of two groups of complicated acids containing nitrogen, sugar, and phosphoric acid, one obtained from the

thymus gland and the other first prepared from yeast

nu′cle·in /-in/ *n* any of a class of phosphorus-bearing protein substances found in cell nuclei

nucleo- var of **nucle-**

nu′cle·on′ /-on′/ *n* proton or neutron esp. in the nucleus of an atom ‖ **nu′cle·on′ic** *adj*

nu′cle·on′ics *nsg* branch of physics that deals with atomic nuclei

nu′cle·us /-əs/ [L = kernel] *n* (-i /-ī′/) **1 a** core or central part about which matter is collected, or to which accretion is made; **b** any body or thing that serves as the center of growth or development; **2** central, rounded, or oval mass of protoplasm in a cell, regarded as essential to metabolism, growth, reproduction, and heredity; **3** group of nerve-cell bodies in the brain or spinal chord, from which arise nerve fibers that are distributed to one limited part of the body, as the motor nerves of the eye; **4** small bright central point in a comet's head; **5** positively charged central portion of an atom consisting of nucleons and having nearly all the mass of the atom, around which the electrons revolve

nude /n(y)o͞od′/ [L *nudus*] *adj* **1 a** bare, naked, unclothed; **b** without the usual covering; **2** *law* (contract) without consideration and therefore void ‖ *n* **3** state of being nude, as *in the nude;* **4** nude person; **5** *art* representation of a nude figure ‖ **nu′di·ty** *n*

nudge /nuj′/ [? OE *cnucian* to knock] *vt* **1** to touch or push gently ‖ *n* **2** gentle touch

nud′ism *n* practice of going and living in the nude ‖ **nud′ist** *adj* & *n*

nug·get /nug′it/ [? *obs* nug lump] *n* lump of native gold or other precious metal

nui·sance /n(y)o͞o′səns/ [AF < OF *nuisir* to harm] *n* **1** annoying, disagreeable, or vexatious person or thing; **2** something obnoxious or injurious to a community or an individual for which legal remedy may be sought

nui′sance tax′ *n* consumer tax paid in small amounts

null /nul′/ [L *nullus* none] *adj* **1** of no legal force; invalid; **2** trivial; of no value; **3** having no existence; equal to nothing; **4** indicating zero reading on a scale; **5** being or pert. to zero; **6** *math* (set) having no members ‖ *n* **7** zero

null′ and void′ *adj* null *l*

nulli- [L *nullus*] *comb form* none, null

nul′li·fy′ [LL *nullificare*] *v* (-fied) *vt* **1** to deprive of legal force, annul; **2** to destroy, make ineffective ‖ **nul′li·fi·ca′tion** *n* ‖ SYN invalidate, quash, repeal, annul (see *cancel*)

nul′li·ty [ML *nullitas*] *n* (-ties) **1** quality or state of being null; **2** something null; **3** something having no legal standing

numb /num'/ [OE *numen* taken] *adj* **1** weakened in or deprived of the power of sensation or motion ‖ *vt* **2** to make numb ‖ **numb'ly** *adv* ‖ **numb'-ness** *n*

num·ber /num'bər/ [OF *nombre* < L *numerus*] *n* **1** total count of a collection or aggregate of units; **2** symbol representing this total; numeral representing the point where the count of an aggregate ends; **3** quantity or amount considered as an aggregate of units, as *a large number of people came;* **4** numeral; **5** any of a series of numerals affixed in regular order to a series of things, as *a house number;* **6** single issue of a periodical; **7** class, lot, caste, as *we count her among our number;* **8 a** one of a group of musical compositions; **b** part of a theatrical program made up of similar parts; **c** distinct act or performance within a show; **9** article of merchandise, esp. wearing apparel; **10** *gram* category of certain word classes (principally nouns in English) which indicates whether one or more than one are referred to; **11 numbers** *pl* a considerable amount; **b** *obs* arithmetic; **12 the numbers** numbers game; **13 by the numbers, a** in unison to a special cadence; **b** in a systematic or routine manner; **14 have one's number** *slang* to have knowledge of someone's real character or motives; **15 without number** very numerous ‖ *vt* **16** to ascertain the number of; **17** to assign a number to; **18** to amount to, comprise; **19** to include, as *I number him among my friends;* **20** to fix or limit the number of ‖ *vi* **21** to count; **22** to total ‖ SYN *v* count, reckon, designate (see *calculate*)

num'ber·less *adj* **1** having no number; **2** countless, very many

num'ber one' *n* **1** *colloq* oneself; one's welfare ‖ *adj* **2** *colloq* the first or most important

Num'bers *nsg* fourth book of the Old Testament

num'bers game', **pool'**, or **rack'et** *n* an illegal lottery in which small bets are placed on a sequence of three or more numbers appearing daily in financial reports, game scores, etc.

numb'skull' *n* var of **numskull**

nu'mer·a·ble /n(y)o͞om'ərəbəl/ *adj* capable of being counted or numbered

nu'mer·al [LL *numeralis* pert. to numbers] *n* **1** word expressing a number; **2** conventional symbol or symbols used to express a number ‖ also *adj*

nu·mer·ate /n(y)o͞om'ərāt'/ [L *numerare* (-*atus*)] *vt* **1** to enumerate; **2** to read (a numerical expression) in words ‖ **nu'mer·a'tion** *n*

nu'mer·a'tor *n* **1** one who numerates; **2** *math* the part of a fraction above

the line that shows how many parts of the denominator are taken, as *the numerator of ¾ is 3*

nu·mer·i·cal /-mer'-/ *adj* **1** pert. to or indicating number; **2** designated by numbers; **3** expressed by numbers instead of letters ‖ **nu·mer'i·cal·ly** *adv*

nu'mer·ol'o·gy /-mərol'əjē/ *n* study of the occult meaning of numbers, esp. of the date of one's birth or those derived from the letters of one's name

nu'mer·ous [L *numerosus*] *adj* **1** consisting of a great number of units; **2** a great many

Nu·mid·i·a /n(y)o͞omid'ē·ə/ *n* ancient country in N Africa ‖ **Nu·mid'i·an** *adj & n*

nu·mis·mat·ic /n(y)o͞om'izmat'ik, -is-/ [< Gk *nomisma* (-*atos*) coin] *adj* **1** pert. to or consisting of coins or medals; **2** pert. to numismatics ‖ **nu'mis·mat'ics** *nsg* **3** study or collecting of coins or medals ‖ **nu'mis'ma·tist** /-mətist/ *n*

num'skull' /num'-/ *n colloq* dunce, blockhead

nun /nun'/ [OE *nunne* < L *nonna*] *n* female member of a religious order under vows of poverty, chastity, and obedience, usu. living in a convent

nun·ci·o /nun'shē·ō'/ [It] *n* permanent papal ambassador to a foreign government

nun'ner·y *n* (-ies) convent of nuns

nup·tial /nup'shəl/ [L *nuptialis*] *adj* **1** of or pert. to marriage or the marriage ceremony ‖ *n* **2 nuptials** *pl* marriage ceremony ‖ SYN *n* ceremony, wedding (see *marriage*)

Nurn·berg /nurn'burg'/ *n* city in Bavaria, W Germany (470,000), scene of the war-crimes trials of Nazi leaders 1945–46

nurse /nurs'/ [OF *nurice*] *n* **1** one who takes care of the sick or infirm; **2** one who cares for young children; **3** wet nurse; **4** one who or that which protects or fosters; **5** worker that attends the young of social insects ‖ *vt* **6** to care for or wait upon in sickness; **7** to suckle (an infant); **8** to rear, bring up; **9** to promote growth or vigor in; **10** to encourage, cherish, foster, as a grudge; **11** to take care of, treat, as *to nurse a cold;* **12** to clasp, fondle ‖ *vi* **13** to suckle a child; **14** to take the breast; **15** to care for the sick or infirm

nurse'maid *n* girl or woman employed to care for children

nurs'er·y *n* (-ies) **1** room or apartment for young children; **2** place where young plants are raised for transplanting or sale; **3** any place, practice, or condition which fosters, develops, or educates

nurs'er·y school' *n* prekindergarten school

nurse's aide' *n* helper in a hospital

who assists the nurses by performing routine menial tasks not requiring professional skills or knowledge

nurs'ing bot'tle n bottle with a rubber nipple for feeding infants

nurs'ing home' n institution for taking care of the aged, infirm, or chronically ill

nurs'ling n 1 infant, child; 2 anything that is tenderly fostered

nur·ture /nur'chər/ [MF *nourriture*] n 1 food, nourishment; 2 education, training, upbringing || vt 3 to rear, educate; 4 to nourish, foster || SYN v cherish, foster, promote, develop, train

nut /nut'/ [OE *hnutu*] n 1 the dry fruit of certain trees, consisting of a kernel or seed enclosed in a hard shell; 2 the kernel itself; 3 one-seeded fruit of certain trees and shrubs, having a woody, bony, or leathery covering, as the acorn; 4 perforated block, usu. of metal, having an internal screw thread, as for securing or adjusting a bolt; 5 a problem; b person or thing hard to deal with; 6 *slang* a enthusiast; b queer or foolish person; c insane person; 7 *slang* head; 8 *show bus.* net expenses of a production or show; 9 *mus* in stringed instruments, ridge supporting the strings at the upper end of the finger board || v (nut·ted; nut·ting) vi 10 to seek nuts || nut'like' adj

nu·ta·tion /n(y)ōōtāsh'ən/ [L *nutatio* (-*onis*)] n 1 act of nodding the head; 2 a oscillation of the axis of a rotating body; b oscillation of the earth's pole of rotation; 3 movement of plant parts due to unequal rates of growth

nut'brown' adj chestnut-colored

nut'crack'er n 1 instrument for cracking nuts; 2 European bird (*Nucifraga caryocatactes*) of the crow family, feeding principally on nuts

nut'hatch' n any of several small related birds (family Sittidae) that creep on tree trunks and feed on nuts and insects

nut'meat' n edible kernel of a nut

nut·meg /nut'meg/ [*nut* + OF *mugue* musk] n 1 the hard aromatic kernel of the fruit of an East Indian tree (*Myristica fragrans*) used as a spice; 2 tree that bears this fruit

nu·tri·a /n(y)ōō'trē·ə/ [Sp = otter] n 1 coypu; 2 its fur

nu·tri·ent /n(y)ōō'trē·ənt/ [L *nutriens* (-*entis*)] adj 1 containing or conveying nutrition; 2 nutritious || n 3 nutritious substance

nu'tri·ment /-trimənt/ [L *nutrimentum*] 1 that which affords nourishment; food; 2 anything which promotes growth || **nu'tri·men'tal** /-men'-/ adj

nu·tri'tion /-trish'ən/ [LL *nutritio* (-*onis*)] n 1 act or process of nourishing or being nourished; 2 process by which an animal or plant uses food to repair wasted tissues and promote growth and development || **nu·tri'·tion·al** adj

nu·tri'tion·ist n specialist in nutrition

nu·tri'tious adj providing nourishment

nu'tri·tive /-tiv/ adj 1 of or pert. to nutrition; 2 nutritious, nourishing

nuts' *slang* adj 1 crazy; 2 enthusiastic || *interj* 3 used to express strong disapproval or rejection

nut'shell' n 1 shell of a nut; 2 **in a nutshell** expressed concisely

nut'ty adj (-ti·er; -ti·est) 1 abounding in or flavored with nuts; 2 nutlike; 3 *slang* crazy, foolish || **nut'ti·ness** n

nux vom·i·ca /nuks' vom'ikə/ [NL = vomiting nut] n 1 poisonous seed of an East Indian tree (*Strychnos nux-vomica*) yielding strychnine and brucine; 2 the tree

nuz·zle /nuz'əl/ [ME *noselen*] vt 1 to burrow, rub, or snuff with the nose; 2 to root up with the nose, as a hog || vi 3 to press or rub the nose into or against something; 4 to go with the nose toward the ground; 5 to nestle, lie snug

NW, N.W. northwest(ern)

N.W.T. Northwest Territories

N.Y. New York

N.Y.C. New York City

ny·lon /nī'lon/ [coined word] n 1 very tough, elastic synthetic material used for yarn, bristles, etc.; 2 **nylons** stockings of this material

nymph /nimf'/ [Gk *nymphe*] n 1 *class. myth.* any of numerous lesser divinities, represented as beautiful maidens living in the mountains, forests, meadows, and waters; 2 beautiful young woman; 3 immature stage of insects that undergoes incomplete metamorphosis

nym'pho·ma'ni·a /-fəmān'ē·ə/ n uncontrolled sexual desire in women || **nym'pho·ma'ni·ac'** /-ak'/ adj & n

N.Z. New Zealand

O

O, o /ō'/ n (O's or Os; o's, oes, or os) 15th letter of the English alphabet

O¹ 1 15th in order or in a series; 2 something shaped like an O; 3 *chem* oxygen; 4 the Arabic cipher, zero; 5 blood type

O² /ō'/ [ME] *interj* **1** *archaic & poet.* used before a noun in direct address, as *O God on high!* **2** oh!

O, 'O. Old

O. **1** Ohio; **2** Ocean

o' /ō', ə/ *prep* abbreviation of *of*, as *two o'clock*

O' /ō'/ [Ir *ō*] *pref* descendant (in Irish names), as *O'Neill*

oaf /ōf'/ [*obs auf* < ON *älfr* elf] *n* clumsy, stupid person ‖ **oaf'ish** *adj*

O·a·hu /ō-ä'hoo, wä'-/ *n* most important of the Hawaiian Islands, on which Honolulu is located

oak /ōk'/ [OE *āc*] *n* **1** any of a large genus (*Quercus*) of valuable timber-yielding trees; **2** the hard wood of these trees ‖ **oak'en** *adj*

Oak'land /-lənd/ *n* seaport in Northern California on San Francisco Bay (361,561)

oak' leaf' clus'ter *n* U.S. military decoration consisting mainly of four bronze oak leaves, placed on the ribbon of another decoration to signify a second award of the same medal

Oak' Ridge' *n* city in E Tennessee, one of the sites where the atomic bomb was developed (27,000)

oa·kum /ōk'əm/ [OE *ācumbe* prunings] *n* loose hemp fiber obtained by untwisting old ropes, used for caulking boats

oar /ôr', ōr'/ [OE *ār*] *n* **1** long pole with a flattened blade at one end for rowing or steering a boat; **2** oarsman; **3 rest on one's oars,** **a** to raise the oars out of the water by bearing down on the handles; **b** to stop striving for further success after achieving a reputation in one's business or profession

oar'lock' *n* swiveled device for holding an oar on the gunwale

oars'man /-mən/ *n* (**-men** /-mən/) one who rows

OAS Organization of American States

o·a·sis /ō-ās'is/ [Gk prob < Egypt.] *n* (**-ses** /-sēz/) fertile verdant place in a desert

oat /ōt'/ [OE *āte*] *n* **1** cereal plant (*Avena sativa*) cultivated in cool climates for its seed; **2 oats** *pl* the seed, used for food; **3 feel one's oats** *colloq* **a** to feel lively; **b** to become cognizant of one's latent powers

oath /ōth'/ [OE *āth*] *n* (**-ths** /-thz, -ths/) **1** solemn declaration that one speaks the truth or that one will keep a promise, God or some object or person held sacred being appealed to as a witness; **2** form of words in which such a declaration is made; **3** the name of God or of anything sacred spoken irreverently or blasphemously; **4** curse; swearword

oat'meal' *n* **1** meal made of oats; **2** porridge made of it

ob·bli·ga·to /ob'ligät'ō/ [It] *mus adj* **1** required, indispensable; (accompaniment) that cannot be omitted ‖ *n* **2** obbligato part

ob·du·rate /ob'd(y)ŏŏrit/ [L *obduratus* hardened] *adj* **1** hard-hearted, unyielding; **2** impenitently wicked; **3** unbending, obstinate ‖ **ob'du·ra·cy** /-rəsē/ *n* ‖ SYN callous, inflexible, hard-hearted, unyielding (see *hard*) ‖ ANT yielding, compliant, submissive, obedient, humble

O.B.E. Order of the British Empire

o·be·di·ent /ōbēd'ē·ənt/ [L *oboediens* (*-entis*)] *adj* **1** obeying or willing to obey; **2** submissive to authority ‖ **o·be'di·ence** *n* ‖ SYN yielding, submissive, docile, compliant, tractable, dutiful ‖ ANT disobedient, insubordinate

o·bei·sance /ōbās'əns, ōbēs'-/ [< MF *obeir* to obey] *n* **1** bow or a bend of the knee as an expression of obedience or submission; **2** deference; homage

ob·e·lisk /ob'əlisk/ [Gk *obeliskos* small spit] *n* tall four-sided stone pillar with a pyramidal top

O·ber·on /ōb'əron/ *n* medieval folklore king of the fairies

o·bese /ōbēs'/ [L *obesus* having eaten] *adj* grossly overweight ‖ **o·bes'i·ty** *n* ‖ SYN corpulent, stout, portly, adipose

o·bey /ōbā'/ [OF *obeir* < L *oboedire* to listen to] *vt* **1** to conform to the rule or authority of; **2** to comply with the orders of; **3** to carry out, as orders ‖ *vi* **4** to be obedient ‖ SYN serve, keep, follow, observe, submit, yield, defer

ob·fus·cate /obfus'kāt, ob'fəskāt'/ [L *obfuscare* (*-atus*) to darken] *vt* to bewilder; perplex; confuse ‖ **ob'fus·ca'tion** *n*

o·bi /ōb'ē/ [Jap] *n* wide sash with a bow behind, worn over a kimono

o·bit /ōb'it, ob'-/ [L *obitus* death] *n* obituary

ob·i·ter dic·tum /ob'itər dik'təm/ [L] *n* (**obiter dic·ta** /-tə/) passing remark or opinion

o·bit·u·ar·y /ōbich'ŏŏ·er'ē/ [< L *obitus* death] *adj* **1** pert. to or recording a death or deaths ‖ *n* (**-ies**) **2** printed notice of a death, often accompanied by a brief biographical sketch

obj. **1** object; **2** objection; **3** objective

ob·ject /ob'jekt, -jikt/ [< L *objicere* (*-jectus*) to hurl] *n* **1** anything that can be seen or touched; **2** anything perceived or thought of; **3** person or thing affected by an action, or arousing feeling; **4** motive, end, aim; **5** *gram* nominal that receives the action of a verb or is governed by a preposition ‖ /əbjekt'/ *vt* **6** to urge in opposition ‖ *vi* **7** to offer opposition; **8** to feel or express disapproval || **ob·jec′tor** *n* || SYN *n* intention, purpose, design, motive, end goal, aim (see *design*)

ob·jec·tion /əbjek′shən/ *n* 1 act of objecting; 2 feeling or expression of feeling of opposition or disapproval; 3 reason for objecting || SYN exception, difficulty, impediment, scruple

ob·jec′tion·a·ble *adj* 1 liable or open to objection; 2 offensive; 3 insulting; 4 unpleasant, as an odor

ob·jec′tive *adj* 1 existing outside of the mind; having independent existence; real; 2 dealing with outward facts rather than with thoughts or feelings; 3 unbiased; 4 *gram* designating the case of the object || *n* 5 end or goal toward which any action is directed; 6 *gram* case of the object; 7 lens or group of lenses that form the image in an optical instrument or camera || **ob·jec′tive·ly** *adv* || **ob′jec·tiv′i·ty** /ob′jektiv′itẽ/ *n*

ob′ject les′son *n* anything which exemplifies a principle in a concrete manner

ob·jet d′art /obzhä′ där′/ [F] *n* (**objets d′art** /same as *sg*/) object of artistic merit

ob·jur·gate /ob′jərgāt′, objur′gāt/ [L *objurgare* (-*atus*)] *vt* to rebuke, upbraid || **ob′jur·ga′tion** *n* || **ob·jur′ga·to′ry** -jurg′ətôr′ẽ, -tōr′-/ *adj*

ob·late /ob′lāt, oblāt′/ [L *oblatus* offered] *adj* 1 (sphere) flattened at the poles || *n* 2 R C Ch lay member of a monastery or of a religious society

ob·la′tion *n* 1 act of making an offering to God or to the gods; 2 offering of the bread and wine of the Eucharist

ob·li·gate /ob′ligat′/ [L *obligare* (-*atus*)] *vt* to bind, as by contract, promise, or a sense of duty

ob′li·ga′tion *n* 1 act of obligating or state of being obligated; 2 binding power of a vow, promise, or a sense of duty; 3 any duty imposed by law, social relations, or good will; 4 responsibility; 5 *law* contract; 6 *com* bond; 7 indebtedness; 8 debt of gratitude

ob·li·ga·to·ry /ob′ligatôr′ẽ, əblig′-, -tōr′-/ *adj* 1 morally or legally binding; 2 compulsory

o·blige /əblīj′/ [OF *obligier* < L *obligare* to bind] *vt* 1 to compel morally, legally, or physically; 2 to bind by some favor or kindness; 3 to render a favor to; gratify; accommodate

o·blig′ing *adj* willing to do favors; accommodating || **o·blig′ing·ly** *adv*

ob·lique /əblēk′, əblīk′/ [L *obliquus* bent] *adj* 1 neither horizontal nor vertical; slanting; 2 not straightforward; evasive, indirect; 3 *gram* (case) neither nominative nor vocative || **ob·lique′ly** *adv* || **ob·liq′ui·ty** -lik′-witẽ/ *n* (-ties)

ob·lique′ an′gle *n* acute or obtuse angle

ob·lit·er·ate /əblit′ərāt′/ [L *obliterare* (-*atus*) to erase] *vt* 1 to erase or blot out; 2 to destroy, efface completely || **ob·lit′er·a′tion** *n* || SYN expunge, wipe out, destroy, efface (see *erase*)

ob·liv·i·on /əbliv′ẽ·ən/ [< L *oblivisci* to forget] *n* state of utter forgetfulness or of being forgotten

ob·liv′i·ous *adj* 1 forgetful; 2 **oblivious of** or **to** unaware of || SYN forgetful, abstracted, absorbed, absent-minded || DISCR A poor memory makes one *forgetful; oblivious* describes rather the state of one lost in deep forgetfulness. One who is *forgetful* cannot recall what he wishes, is guilty of inadvertent omissions, neglectfulness, or the like. One is *oblivious* through preoccupation, weakness, age, sleep, or some similar cause, as *oblivious* of the passage of time. That usage of *oblivious* which makes it mean merely "not conscious" is not sanctioned; we say he seemed unconscious of my resentment, not *oblivious* to it.

ob·long /ob′lôŋ, ˝ -loŋ/ [L *oblongus* rather long] *n* a more or less rectangular figure that is longer than it is broad || also *adj*

ob·lo·quy /ob′ləkwẽ/ [L *obloquium* contradiction] *n* (-quies) 1 widespread reproach or censure; 2 disgrace resulting from public censure || SYN ignominy, shame, scandal, disgrace, dishonor, infamy || ANT honor, eulogy, credit, renown, glory

ob·nox·ious /əbnok′shəs/ [L *obnoxiosus* submissive] *adj* hateful; offensive || SYN odious, objectionable, detestable (see *hateful*)

o·boe /ō′bō/ [It < F *hautbois*] *n* woodwind instrument with a plaintive penetrating tone produced by a double reed mouthpiece || **o′bo·ist** *n*

obs., Obs. 1 obsolete; 2 observatory

ob·scene /əbsēn′/ [L *obscenus*] *adj* 1 indecent, lewd; 2 disgusting, repulsive || **ob·scene′ly** *adv* || SYN foul, filthy, unclean, vile, scurrilous, dirty

ob·scen′i·ty /-sen′-/ *n* (-ties) 1 quality of being obscene; 2 something obscene; 3 obscene word

ob·scu·rant·ism /əbskyōōr′əntiz′əm/ [< L *obscurans* (-*antis*) one who darkens] *n* 1 opposition to the spread of learning; 2 deliberate obscurity of style in speech or writing || **ob·scu′rant·ist** *n*

ob·scure /əbskyōōr′/ [OF *obscur* < L *obscurus* dark] *adj* 1 not clear or distinct; 2 shadowy, dim; 3 not easily understood; incomprehensible; 4 humble, lowly; 5 not well known || *vt* 6 to make obscure || **ob·scure′ly** *adv* || **ob·scu′ri·ty** *n* (-ties) || SYN *adj* ambiguous, indistinct, vague, hidden, unintelligible, difficult, abstruse, profound || DISCR *Obscure*, as here compared, describes that which is not clearly expressed, and hence is doubtful, unintelligible, or illegible, as *obscure* meanings or passages in a text; *obscure* inscriptions on monuments. *Vague* ideas are ill-defined, hazy, clouded; *vague* ambitions are indefinite; *vague* explanations carry no clear meaning to be grasped by the mind. *Ambiguous* phrases or passages have two possible senses. (see *equivocal*.) That is *difficult* which is hard for the mind to get at, and hence is perplexing or puzzling, as a problem or course of action. The *hidden*, *profound*, and *abtruse* are hard to understand. *Hidden* meanings are often revealed by the second reading of a good book. *Abstruse* thoughts are far away from the ordinary paths of the average man's thinking. *Profound* reflections or subjects require deep study and thought for their comprehension

ob·se·quies /ob'sikwēz/ [LL *obsequiae*] *npl* funeral rites or ceremonies

ob·se·qui·ous /əbsēk'wē·əs/ [L *obsequium* compliance] *adj* meanly submissive; servile, fawning

ob·serv·a·ble /əbzurv'əbel/ *adj* 1 capable of being observed, discerned, measured; 2 deserving observance; 3 remarkable; noteworthy

ob·serv·ance /əbzurv'əns/ [see **observe**] *n* 1 act of keeping or of paying attention to, as laws or customs; 2 rite, ceremony, or sacrament; 3 custom to be followed or heeded ‖ SYN observation; rite, form (see *ceremony*)

ob·serv'ant *adj* 1 quick to notice, attentive; 2 obedient to rules or customs; 3 alert; watchful ‖ SYN watchful, heedful, regardful, noting, attentive

ob·ser·va·tion /ob'zərvāsh'ən/ *n* 1 act, power, or habit of observing; careful notice; 2 that which is observed; 3 remark, comment; 4 scientific examination and recording of facts

ob'ser·va'tion·al *adj* based on observation rather than experiment

ob·serv·a·to·ry /əbzurv'ətôr'ē, -tōr'-/ *n* (-ries) 1 building equipped for astronomical or meteorological observations; 2 tower or other high place giving an extensive view

ob·serve /əbzurv'/ [MF *observer* < L *observare*] *vt* 1 to see and note; 2 to watch closely, look at attentively; 3 to comply with, adhere to; 4 to keep appropriately; celebrate; 5 to remark, comment; 6 to examine closely for a scientific purpose ‖ *vi* 7 to take notice; 8 to comment; 9 to act as an observer ‖ **ob·serv'er** *n* ‖ SYN perceive, scrutinize (see *celebrate*, *notice*)

ob·sess /əbses'/, ob-/ [L *obsessus* besieged] *vt* to preoccupy, haunt, or trouble the mind of

ob·ses'sion *n* 1 state of being obsessed; 2 that which obsesses

ob·sid·i·an /əbsid'ē·ən/ [<L *Obsius* reputed discoverer] *n* a dark, glassy, volcanic rock

ob·so·les·cent /ob'sələs'ənt/ [< *obsolescere* to fall into disuse] *adj* becoming obsolete ‖ **ob'so·les'cence** *n*

ob·so·lete /ob'səlēt'/ [L *obsoletus*] *adj* 1 gone out of use; no longer practiced or accepted; 2 outmoded; discarded ‖ SYN old-fashioned, outworn, discarded, ancient, antiquated ‖ ANT new, fresh, modern, recent

ob·sta·cle /ob'stəkəl/ [OF < *obstaculum*] *n* that which blocks the way; obstruction ‖ SYN barrier, difficulty, obstruction (see *hindrance*)

ob·ste·tri·cian /ob'stitrish'ən/ *n* physician specializing in obstetrics

ob·stet·rics /obstet'riks/ [< L *obstetrix* (-icis) midwife] *n* branch of medicine dealing with the treatment and care of women in pregnancy and childbirth ‖ **ob·stet'ric (-ri·cal)** *adj*

ob·sti·nate /ob'stinit/ [L *obstinare* (-atus) to persist in] *adj* 1 headstrong; stubborn; adhering to one's opinion or purpose; 2 not yielding to treatment, as a disease ‖ **ob'sti·na·cy** /-nəsē/ *n* ‖ SYN self-willed, perverse, inflexible (see *headstrong*)

ob·strep·er·ous /əbstrep'ərəs/ [< L *obstrepere* to make a noise] *adj* 1 clamorous, noisy; 2 unruly; turbulent

ob·struct /əbstrukt'/ [L *obstruere* (-structus) to build against] *vt* 1 to block up, close, or fill with obstacles, so as to prevent passage; 2 to impede or prevent from progress; 3 to be in the way of, cut off from sight ‖ **ob·struc'tor, ob·struct'er** *n* ‖ **ob·struc'tive** *adj* SYN bar, check, oppose, retard, impede, hinder (see *prevent*) ‖ ANT help, promote, further, facilitate

ob·struc'tion *n* 1 anything that stops, closes, or bars the way; 2 that which prevents or hinders progress ‖ SYN bar, obstacle, impediment (see *hindrance*)

ob·struc'tion·ist *n* one who deliberately hinders progress, as by parliamentary maneuvering in a legislative body ‖ **ob·struc'tion·ism** *n*

ob·tain /əbtān'/ [MF *obtenir* < L *obtinere*] *vt* 1 to get possession of; gain by effort ‖ *vi* 2 to be established in use; prevail ‖ **ob·tain'a·ble** *adj* ‖ **ob·tain'ment** *n* ‖ SYN achieve, secure, procure, earn, gain

ob·trude /əbtrōōd'/ [L *obtrudere*] *vt* 1 to thrust forth; push out; 2 to offer with unreasonable persistence and without invitation ‖ *vi* 3 to force oneself upon others; intrude ‖ **ob·tru'sion** /-zhən/ *n*

ob·tru'sive *adj* inclined to push oneself into undue prominence; intrusive ‖ **ob·tru'sive·ly** *adv* ‖ **ob·tru'-sive·ness** *n* ‖ SYN bold, pushing, impertinent (see *officious*)

ob·tuse /obt(y)ōōs'/ [L *obtusus* blunt] *adj* **1** blunt, not pointed or sharp; **2** (angle) greater than 90 degrees; **3** dull, slow of perception; **4** indistinct, as sound ‖ SYN rounded, stupid, insensible, thick (see *blunt*)

ob·verse /obvurs', ob'vurs/ [L *obversus* turned toward] *adj* **1** facing the observer; **2** forming a counterpart ‖ /ob'vurs/ *n* **3** side of a coin or medal having the principal design on it; **4** counterpart

ob·vi·ate /ob'vē·āt'/ [L *obviare* (*-atus*) to withstand] *vt* to dispose of, as difficulties; render unnecessary

ob·vi·ous /ob'vē·əs/ [L < *obvius* at hand] *adj* evident; plain ‖ SYN open, apparent, unmistakable, clear, evident, patent, manifest, unconcealed, overt, indubitable ‖ DISCR That is *obvious* which lies so open to the eye or mind that it cannot be escaped, as the reason, conclusion, connection is *obvious*. That is *manifest* which is strikingly, indubitably evident, as a *manifest* difference; a *manifest* absurdity, miracle, lie. That is *patent* which is apparent to all, as his modesty was *patent*

oc·a·ri·na /ok'ərēn'ə/ [It < *oca* goose] *n* small wind instrument shaped like a sweet potato, with a mouthpiece and finger holes

oc·ca·sion /əkazh'ən/ [OF < L *occasio* (*-onis*)] *n* **1** favorable chance or opportunity; **2** particular or important event or celebration; **3** special occurrence; **4** cause; **5** justification; reason; **6 on occasion** at times ‖ *vt* **7** to cause ‖ SYN *n* opportunity ‖ DISCR An *occasion* is an event or such a juncture of events as seems to require action, as I had *occasion* to reprove him. *Occasion* is also a fitting time, as a suitable *occasion* never offered. An *opportunity* is a chance to act, an opening with favorable or advantageous coloring, which perhaps never will happen again; it invites action, as the boy eagerly embraced the *opportunity* to go to college. *Occasion* and *opportunity* agree in naming a suitable time; *occasion* has a faint urge of need; *opportunity* invites by the chance of success (see *cause*)

oc·ca·sion·al *adj* **1** incidental or casual; **2** happening now and then; **3** intended for or serving particular occasions ‖ **oc·ca'sion·al·ly** *adv*

Oc·ci·dent /ok'sidənt/ [MF < L (sol) *occidens* (*-entis*) the setting (sun)] *n* **the Occident** Europe and the Western Hemisphere ‖ **Oc'ci·den'tal** /-den'-/ *adj & n*

oc·ci·put /ok'siput', -pət/ [L] *n* (-puts or **oc·cip·i·ta** /oksip'itə/) back part of the skull ‖ **oc·cip'i·tal** *adj*

oc·clude /əklōōd'/ [L *occludere* (*-clusus*) to shut up] *vt* **1** to shut up or out; **2** to close or stop up, as an opening or passage ‖ *vi* **3** *dentistry* to close with the opposing cusps fitting together

oc·clu·sion /-zhən/ *n* **1** act or state of occluding; **2** *phonet* complete closure at some point of the vocal tract in the pronunciation of stops

oc·clu·sive *adj* **1** characterized by or having occlusion ‖ *n* **2** *phonet* stop

oc·cult /əkult', ok'ult/ [L *occultus* covered over] *adj* **1** secret, mysterious; **2** supernatural; **3** of or pert. to magic, astrology, and other arcane sciences ‖ *n* **4 the occult** occult practices ‖ *vt* **5** *astron* to hide (a body) by passing between it and the earth ‖ *vi* **6** to become concealed

oc·cul·ta·tion *n* **1** concealment; disappearance; **2** the obscuring of a star or planet by the passage of the moon or another planet between it and the observer

oc·cult·ism *n* **1** belief in the supernatural or magical; **2** practices based on such belief ‖ **oc·cult'ist** *n*

oc·cu·pan·cy /ok'yəpənsē/ [see **occupy**] *n* (-cies) **1** act of occupying; **2** possession or tenancy of a property; **3** term of occupying

oc'cu·pant *n* one who occupies a property or office

oc'cu·pa·tion *n* **1** act of occupying or state of being occupied; **2** one's regular business or calling ‖ **oc'cu·pa'tion·al** *adj* ‖ SYN occupancy, tenure, vocation (see *business*)

oc'cu·pa·tion·al ther'a·py *n* therapy consisting of light work for mental diversion or for the exercise of affected parts

oc·cu·py /ok'yəpī'/ [MF *occuper* < L *occupare*] *v* (-pied) *vt* **1** to take possession of; **2** to dwell in; **3** to fill or cover the time or space of; **4** to employ (oneself, one's mind, etc.); **5** to hold (an office or position) ‖ **oc'cu·pi'er** *n*

oc·cur /əkur'/ [L *occurrere* to run against] *v* (-curred; -cur·ring) *vi* **1** to happen or take place; **2** to be found; exist; **3** to happen to come into one's mind

oc·cur·rence *n* **1** act or fact of occurring; **2** happening; event; **3** appearance or presence of some phenomenon at a particular time or place, as *the occurrence of this word on the first page* ‖ SYN circumstance, incident, accident (see *event*)

OCD Office of Civilian Defense

o·cean /ōsh'ən/ [Gk *okeanos* stream encircling the earth] *n* **1** the vast body of salt water covering more than three fifths of the globe; **2** any of its five chief divisions; **3** immense expanse or amount ‖ **o·ce·an·ic** /ōsh'ē·an'ik/ *adj*

o'cean lin'er *n* large passenger ship

crossing the ocean on a regular schedule

o·cean·og·ra·phy /-og'rəfē/ n physical geography dealing with the ocean ǁ **o′cean·og′ra·pher** n

o·ce·lot /os'əlot', ōs'-/ [F < Nahuatl *ocelotl* jaguar] n leopardlike spotted cat (*Felis pardalis*) found in the Americas from Texas south

o·cher /ōk′ər/ [OF *ocre* < Gk *ochra*] n any of several earthy varieties of iron ore used as pigments, ranging in color from yellow to red

o′clock′ /ə-/ [of (*the*) *clock*] adv **1** according to or by the clock, as *four o′clock*; **2** at an angle or position indicated by an imaginary hour hand on an imaginary horizontal or vertical clock face, as *an airplane approaching at eleven o′clock*

OCS Officer Candidate School

Oct. October

oct-, oc·ta-, or oc·to- [< Gk *okto*] *comb form* eight

oc·ta·gon /ok'təgon', -gən/ [*octa-* + *-gon*] n polygon having eight angles and eight sides ǁ **oc·tag′o·nal** /-tag′-ənəl/ adj

oc′tane num′ber or **rat′ing** /ok'tān/ [*oct-* + *-ane*] n number designating the antiknock quality of gasoline

oc·tave /ok'tiv, -tāv/ [L *octavus* eighth] n mus **1** interval of twelve half steps; **2** tone at this interval; eighth tone of a diatonic scale; **3** series of tones or keys of an instrument, comprised in such a scale

oc·ta·vo /octā'vō, -tä'-/ [< L in *octavo* in an eighth] n **1** book size, about 6 by 9 inches, made by printing on large sheets folded to form eight leaves or sixteen pages; **2** octavo book ǁ adj **3** in octavo

oc·tet /oktet'/ [*oct-* + *duet*] n **1** any group of eight persons or things; **2** mus a composition for eight instruments or voices; **b** the eight performers rendering such a composition

Oc·to·ber /oktōb′ər/ [= eighth month (of Roman calendar)] n tenth month of the year, having 31 days

oc·to·ge·nar·i·an /ok'təjəner′ē·ən/ [< L *octogeni* eighty each] n person 80 years old or between 80 and 90 years old ǁ also adj

oc·to·pus /ok'təpəs/ [Gk *oktopous* eight-footed] n (**-puses** or **-pi** /-pī′/) any of a genus (*Octopus*) of sea animals having a saclike body with eight arms provided with suckers

oc·to·roon /ok'tərōōn′/ [*octo-* + *quadroon*] n person who by descent is seven-eighths white and one-eighth black

oc·u·lar /ok'yələr/ [< L *oculus* eye] adj **1** pert. to the eye or to eyesight; **2** visual ǁ n **3** eyepiece

oc′u·list n **1** physician specializing in the treatment of the eyes; **2** optometrist

odd /od′/ [ME *odde*] adj **1** not matched

or paired with another; **2** (number) not even, not exactly divisible by two; **3** left over after equal division; extra; **4** not appropriated or occupied, as *a few odd moments*; **5** unusual; **6** peculiar; eccentric; **7** occasional, miscellaneous, as *odd jobs*; **8** (round number) and a few more, as *fifty odd* ǁ **odd′ly** adv ǁ SYN unmatched, uneven, strange, grotesque, fantastic, uncommon, droll (see *eccentric*) ǁ ANT common, usual, ordinary, normal, matched

odd′ball′ n slang nonconforming, eccentric person ǁ also adj

odd′i·ty n (**-ties**) **1** peculiar or eccentric person, thing, or quality; **2** peculiarity; eccentricity

odd′ lot′ n **1** stock market quantity of stock traded less than the standard quantity (100 shares for active issues); **2** any quantity less than the standard unit of trading

odds′ npl **1** advantage in favor of one as compared with another; **2** probability; **3** ratio of probability; **4** this ratio applied in betting to equalize the chances of all the bettors; **5** sports handicap; **6** at odds in dispute or at variance

odds′ and ends′ npl bits, remnants

odds′-on′ adj **1** more likely to win or succeed than not; **2** fairly safe (bet, chance, risk)

ode /ōd′/ [MF < Gk *ōide* song] n lyric poem expressing lofty sentiment in an elevated style

-ode /-ōd′/ [< Gk *hodos*] *comb form* road, way

O·des·sa /ōdes′ə/ n seaport on the Black Sea in the S Ukraine in SW Russia (750,000)

o·de·um /ōdē′əm/ [Gk *ōideion*] n (**-ums** or **-a** /-ə/) **1** roofed theater for musical performances in ancient Greece and Rome; **2** any structure devoted to musical or dramatic representations

O·din /ōd′in/ n Norse myth. chief of the gods and god of war, culture, art, and the dead

o·di·ous /ōd′ē·əs/ [< *odium*] adj **1** hateful, detestable; **2** repulsive; offensive ǁ SYN invidious, detestable, disagreeable (see *hateful*)

o′di·um /-əm/ [L = hatred] n **1** hatred; **2** discredit or blame; reproach ǁ SYN disgrace, ignominy, opprobrium, detestation

o·dom·e·ter /ōdom′itər/ [Gk *hodos* way + *-meter*] n instrument for measuring the distance traveled by a vehicle

o·dont- or **o·don·to-** [< Gk *odous* (*odontos*)] *comb form* tooth

o·dor /ōd′ər/ [L] n **1** smell, scent, aroma; **2** in good odor in good repute; **3** in bad odor in bad repute

o·dor·if·er·ous /-rif′ərəs/ [< L *odorifer*] adj giving off an odor ǁ SYN fragrant, sweet-scented, perfumed (see *odorous*)

o′dor·ous *adj* odoriferous ‖ SYN odoriferous, redolent, fragrant, aromatic, perfumed ‖ DISCR These words describe that which diffuses a scent. *Odorous* and *odoriferous* ordinarily refer to a sweet smell, though they may describe that which is disagreeable. *Redolent* applies to that which gives forth a strong smell, as a room *redolent* of tobacco smoke; *redolent* is now chiefly used in its figurative sense, as *redolent* with memories. *Fragrant* describes that which is sweet-smelling and sense-delighting in an exquisite way, as *fragrant* odors drifted from the wisteria vine; *fragrant* flowers. *Aromatic* odors are spicy, pungent, and agreeable, as those of a pine forest, coffee, cinnamon. That is *perfumed* which smells sweet. *Perfumed* can be applied in an unfavorable sense as *fragrant* cannot; *fragrance* appeals to a refined taste, but *perfume* may be too strong to be pleasing

O·dys·seus /ōdis′yo͞os, -ē·əs/ *n Gk myth.* king of Ithaca, the wisest and shrewdest of the Greeks who fought against Troy; hero of the *Odyssey*

Od·ys·sey /od′isē/ *n* 1 epic poem attributed to Homer, describing the ten years' wanderings of Odysseus to Ithaca after the siege of Troy; 2 often **odyssey** any long adventurous journey

oe- [L, transliteration of Gk *oi-*] variant spelling of *e-* in some words of Latin and Greek origin

OE, O.E. Old English

O.E.D., OED Oxford English Dictionary

Oed·i·pus /ed′ipəs, ēd′-/ *n Gk myth.* king of Thebes who unwittingly killed his father and married his mother

Oed′i·pus com′plex *n* fixation of a child's sex phantasies upon the parent of the opposite sex, accompanied by feelings of antagonism toward the other parent, which often persists into adult life

o′er /ôr/ *prep & adv poet.* over

of /uv′, əv/ [OE] *prep* 1 from (denoting removal, origin, etc.), as *south of Mexico, men of the West;* 2 separated from, as *bereft of his mother;* 3 as a result of, as *he died of his wounds;* 4 concerning; 5 in respect to, as *quick of speech;* 6 belonging or related to, or connected with, as *the house of my father, the streets of Paris;* 7 by, as *the plays of Shakespeare;* 8 containing, having, or consisting of, as *a glass of milk;* 9 made from, as *a crown of gold;* 10 possessing, as *a man of means;* 11 specified, as *a weight of five pounds;* 12 among, as *one of you is a traitor;* 13 indicating apposition or identity, as *the city of London, that brute of a con-*

vict; 14 indicating the object of a gerund preceded by an article, as *the blowing of whistles;* 15 a indicating time, as *of late;* b before, as *ten minutes of four;* 16 on, as *he came of a Friday;* 17 on the part of, as *that's good of you*

OF, O.F. Old French

off /ôf′, of′/ [var spelling of *of*] *adj* 1 farther (horse or wheel); 2 not up to standard; 3 disconnected, not in operation; 4 on the way; starting, as *off to Florida;* 5 a completing or having completed one's tour of work or duty, as *I'm off at five;* b away from work, as *I'm off on weekends;* 6 remote (chance); 7 in specified circumstances or condition, as *he was worse off than before;* 8 (hours) free from work; 9 wrong, as *you're way off;* 10 not completely sane; 11 of less than full activity or business, as *the off season;* 12 no longer in effect, as *the deal is off* ‖ *adv* 13 away; so as not to be on, against, near, etc., as *take off your hat, he stood far off;* 14 from the list price, as *five percent off;* 15 in the future, as *my graduation is a year off;* 16 out of operation, discontinued, as *turn off the light;* 17 away from work or duty; 18 completely, as *to cut something off;* 19 into unconsciousness, as *he dozed off;* 20 be or take off to depart; 21 **off and on** or **on and off** intermittently ‖ *prep* 22 not on or attached to; away from; 23 below the usual standard of, as *off one's game;* 24 away from, distant from, as *a mile off the highway;* 25 away from (one's job or duty); 26 to seaward of, as *off Sandy Hook;* 27 colloq abstaining from, as *off liquor* ‖ *interj* 28 begone!, away!

of·fal /ôf′əl, of′-/ [*off* + *fall*] *n* 1 waste meat of a butchered animal; 2 refuse or garbage

off′beat′ *adj* unconventional, nonconformist, unexpected

Off′ Broad′way *n* experimental and low-cost drama produced outside the Broadway theater district in New York City ‖ **Off′-Broad′way** *adj*

off′ chance′ *n* remote possibility

off′-col′or *adj* 1 not of a natural or satisfactory color; 2 risqué; in bad taste

Of·fen·bach, Jacques /zhäk′ ôf′ənbäk′, of′-/ *n* (1819–80) French composer of operettas, born in Germany

of·fend /əfend′/ [MF *offendre* < L *offendere* (-*fensus*) to strike] *vi* 1 to displease or make angry; vex or annoy; 2 to insult, affront ‖ *vi* 3 to transgress, sin; 4 to give offense ‖ **of·fend′er** *n* ‖ SYN irritate, affront, pique, nettle, provoke, insult

of·fense or **of·fence** /əfens′, of′ens/ *n* 1 sin, wrong, crime, or misdemeanor; 2 cause of wrongdoing or sin; 3 act of offending; 4 any cause of anger or displeasure; insult, injury; 5 state of feeling offended; **6** attack or assault; **7** attacking side; **8 take offense** to become offended ‖ SYN trespass, transgression, misdeed, delinquency, misdemeanor, affront, indignity, insult, outrage

of·fen·sive *adj* **1** causing displeasure; annoying; **2** disagreeable; disgusting; **3** insulting; **4** used in or pert. to attack ‖ *n* **5** attitude or position of attack; **6** attack or attacking movement; **7 take the offensive** to attack ‖ SYN *adj* insolent, obnoxious, displeasing, offending, aggressive, attacking (see *hateful*)

of·fer /ôf′ər, of′-/ [OE *offrian* & OF *offrir*, both < L *offerre*] *vt* **1** to present for acceptance or refusal; proffer; **2** to propose, as a plan or suggestion; **3** to propose (to do something); **4** to present for display or sale; **5** to present in worship or sacrifice, as *to offer a prayer*; **6** to bid as a price; **7** to attempt to make or give, as *to offer assistance* ‖ *vi* **8** to occur, present itself ‖ *n* **9** act or instance of offering; **10** proposal or bid; **11** that which is offered ‖ SYN *v* extend, present, proffer, tender (see *give*)

of·fer·ing *n* **1** something offered, as a gift, contribution, or worship; **2** something presented for inspection, exhibition, or sale

of·fer·to·ry /-tôr′ē, -tōr′-/ *n* (**-ries**) **1** offering of the unconsecrated bread and wine in the Eucharist; **2** **a** that part of a church service at which the collection is taken; **b** the accompanying music

off·hand′ *adv* **1** without preparation, extempore; **2** brusquely; cavalierly ‖ *adj* **3** done offhand; **4** brusque; casual

of·fice /ôf′is, of′-/ [OF < L *officium* duty] *n* **1** position of trust or authority, as *the office of president*; **2** function; **3** place for the transaction of business or the practice of a profession; **4** persons collectively who work in an office; **5** form ordained for a religious ceremony or right; **6 the office** *slang* signal or sign, as *give me the office when the cop turns the corner*; **7 offices** *pl* something done in behalf of another

of·fice boy′ *n* young man employed to run errands and do menial tasks in an office

of·fice-hold·er *n* one holding a government office

of·fi·cer [MF *officier*] *n* **1** one who holds a commission in the armed forces; **2** policeman; **3** mate on a civilian vessel; **4** one of the persons elected to administer the affairs of an organized body, as a club or corporation ‖ *vt* **5** to furnish with officers; **6** to direct, command

of·fi·cial /əfish′əl/ *n* **1** one who holds an office or performs public duties ‖ *adj* **2** pert. to an office or public duty;

3 authoritative; authorized ‖ **of·fi′·cial·ly** *adv* ‖ **of·fi′·cial·dom** *n*

of·fi·ci·ate /əfish′ē·āt′/ *vi* **1** to perform the duties of an office; **2** to preside; **3** to perform the office of a priest or minister at a divine service

of·fi·cious /əfish′əs/ *adj* too bold in offering unwanted services or advice ‖ **of·fi′·cious·ly** *adv* ‖ **of·fi′·cious·ness** *n* ‖ SYN meddlesome, intrusive, obtrusive, impertinent ‖ DISCR *Officious, intrusive,* and *obtrusive* agree in the idea of forcing oneself unwanted upon others. The *officious* person is given to offering his services where they are frankly not wanted; sometimes in his zeal he even does or undertakes to do that which is none of his business. The *officious* person frequently has good intentions; the *intrusive* person is not so bent on helping others as on doing what he wishes or thinks desirable to do. He forces himself into the presence or conversation of others, offers advice, or invites himself where he is unwelcome. The *obtrusive* person presses his opinions, his advice, his personality so persistently upon others as to cause annoyance. Any of these words may apply either to a person or to his conduct

off·ing *n* **in the offing, 1** in the somewhat remote future; **2** far but not out of sight

off′·ish *adj colloq* aloof, distant in manner

off′·lim′its *adj* (area) forbidden to be entered, as by soldiers or students

off′-peak′ *adj* occurring or in service when demand is less than maximum

off′print′ *n* reprint of an article appearing in a book or periodical ‖ also *vt*

off′-sea′son *adj* **1** out of season ‖ *n* **2** season of slowest activity, as in business or a resort

off′set′ *n* **1** that which develops from or is set off from something; **2** compensating equivalent; **3** *mach* sharp curve or jog, as in a pipe or rod, to avoid an obstacle; **4** printing process by which an inked impression is made on a rubber roller and then transferred to paper ‖ **off′set′, off′set′** *v* (**-set; -set·ting**) *vt* **5** to balance; compensate for; **6** *typ* to print by offset

off′set print′ing *n* offset 4

off′shoot′ *n* that which branches off a family, race, stem, discussion, etc.

off′shore′ *adj* **1** (wind or breeze) moving away from the shore and toward the sea; **2** situated or taking place away from the shore but not on the high seas ‖ *adv* **3** away from the shore

off′side′ *adj* & *adv sports* beyond a prescribed line that a player must not pass

off′spring′ *n* (**-spring** or **-springs**) **1**

child or children; issue; descend-
ant(s); **2** product or result

off′·stage′ *adv* **1** off or away from the
stage; in the wings ‖ *adj* **2** out of
view of the audience; in the wings or
backstage

off′-the-cuff′ *adj* impromptu

off′-the-rec′ord *adj* not to be divulged
or published ‖ also *adv*

off′-white′ *n* color consisting of white
mixed with a small amount of some
light color ‖ also *adj*

off′ year′ *n* **1** poor year in yield of any
kind; **2** year that does not have a
major election ‖ **off′-year′** *adj*

oft /ôft/, oft′/ [OE] *adv poet.* often

of·ten /ôf′(t)ən, of′/(t)ən/ [ME *oftin*]
adv **1** many times; **2** in many cases

of′ten·times′ *adv* often

O′ gauge′ *n* model railroad gauge of
1¼ inches

o·gee /ōjē′, ō′jē/ [< MF *ogive* rib or
arch] *n* molding with an S-shaped
profile

og·ham /og′əm, ôg′-, ōg′-/ [Ir] *n* alphabet used in Old Irish inscriptions on
tombstones, consisting of lines for
the consonants and notches for the
vowels

o·give /ō′jīv, ōjīv′/ *n* **1** diagonal rib
crossing in a Gothic vault; **2** pointed
arch; **3** a shape of a projectile between its point and its bearing surface; **b** shape of the nose cone of a
guided missile or rocket

o·gle /ōg′əl/ [prob < LG *oegeln*] *vt* **1**
to look at flirtatiously and impertinently ‖ *vi* **2** to give ogling looks ‖ *n*
3 ogling look

o·gre /ōg′ər/ [F] *n* **1** imaginary man-
eating monster of folklore and fairy
tales; **2** cruel or hideous person ‖
o′gress *nfem*

oh /ō′/ [< O²] *interj & n* (**oh's** or **ohs**)
exclamation of wonder, sorrow,
shame, pain, or anxiety

OHG, O.H.G. Old High German

O·hi·o /ōhī′ō/ *n* state in the Midwest
(10,652,000; 41,222 sq.m.; cap. Columbus) ‖ **O·hi′o·an** *n*

O·hi′o Riv′er *n* river in E central U.S.
flowing SW from Pittsburgh, Pa. to
the Mississippi in S Illinois

ohm /ōm′/ [G.S. *Ohm* (1787–1854) G
physicist] *n* the practical mks unit of
electric resistance, being the resistance of a circuit in which a difference of potential of one volt moves
a current of one ampere ‖ **ohm′ic**
adj

ohm′me′ter /-mēt′ər/ *n* instrument for
measuring electrical resistance in
ohms

O.H.M.S. On His (or Her) Majesty's
Service

-oid /-oid′/ [< Gk *eidos* form] *adj &
n suf* denoting (something) like; in
the form of or resembling, as *anthropoid*

oil /oi′(ə)l/ [OF *oile* < L *oleum*] *n* **1**

any of a class of greasy, combustible,
generally liquid substances of complex structure, soluble in alcohol or
ether but not in water, used for lubricating, heating, illuminating, anointing, etc.; **2** any substance of similar consistency; **3** petroleum; **4** oil
color; **5** oil painting; **6** *slang* unctuous
flattery; **7 pour oil on troubled waters**
to calm down a potentially troublesome situation; **8 strike oil, a** to discover oil; **b** to have a great success ‖
vt **9** to lubricate or supply with oil;
10 to bribe ‖ **oil′er** *n*

oil′cloth′ *n* (**-cloths** /-ths, -thz/) cloth
made waterproof by treating with oil
or oil paint, used for covering shelves
and for table covers

oil′ col′or *n* paint made by grinding
pigment in oil

oil′cup′ *n* small cup for holding and
supplying lubricant to a bearing

oil′ paint′ing *n* **1** picture painted with
oil colors; **2** art of painting with oil
colors

oil′skin′ *n* **1** cloth treated with oil to
render it waterproof; **2 oilskins** clothing made of such cloth

oil′ well′ *n* hole bored through rock
to an underground supply of crude
oil

oil′y *adj* (**-i·er; -i·est**) **1** containing or
like oil; **2** covered with oil; **3** smooth
in speech or manner; fawning ‖ **oil′-
i·ness** *n*

oint·ment /oint′mənt/ [OF *oignement*
< L *unguentum*] *n* unctuous prep-
aration, often medicated, applied to
the skin for soothing and healing

O.K., OK, or **okay** /ō′kā′/ [prob <
O.K. Club, Democratic club of New
York in 1840, for *Old* Kinderhook,
birthplace of Martin Van Buren]
colloq adj **1** all right; correct; approved ‖ *v* (**O.K.'d; O.K.'ing**) *vt* **2** to
mark as O.K.,; approve ‖ *n* (**O.K.'s**)
3 approval

o·ka·pi /ōkäp′ē/ [native name] *n* (**-pis**
or **-pi**) small mammal (*Okapia john-
stoni*) akin to the giraffe, found in
central Africa

oke /ōk′/ *adj colloq* O.K.

o·key-doke /ō′kē′ēdōk′/ also **o′key-do′-
key** *adj colloq* O.K.

O·kie /ō′kē/ [*Oklahoma*] *n* migrant
worker from Oklahoma

Okla. Oklahoma

O·kla·ho·ma /ōk′ləhōm′ə/ *n* state in
the S central U.S. (2,559,000; 69,919
sq.m.; cap. Oklahoma City) ‖ **O′kla-
ho′man** *n*

O′kla·ho′ma Cit′y *n* capital of Oklahoma (366,481)

o·kra /ōk′rə/ [WAfr] *n* **1** West Indian
plant (*Hibiscus esculentus*) cultivated
for its mucilaginous pods, used as
a vegetable, in soups, etc.; **2** soup or
stew made of it; gumbo

-ol¹ /-ol′, -ōl′/ [alcohol] *suf* denoting
an alcohol or a phenol, as *methanol*

-ol² [L *oleum*] *suf* denoting an oil or an oil derivative, as *benzol*

old /ōld/ [OE (e)ald] *adj* (**old·er** or **eld·er; old·est** or **eld·est**) 1 having existed or lived many years; 2 having an appearance of age; 3 pert. to aged people; 4 having reached a certain age, as *three years old*; 5 decayed by time; 6 ancient; out of date; 7 worn out; long used; not new; 8 of long standing; 9 former; 10 experienced, as *an old hand*; 11 designating which one of two or more things of the same kind existed before the other, as *the old country*; 12 implying familiarity or intimacy, as *old fellow;* 13 *colloq* great, as *a high old time* ‖ *n* 14 former times, as *days of old*; 15 **the old**, a that which is old; b *pl* old people collectively ‖ SYN *adj* ancient, antique, antiquated, old-fashioned, obsolete, archaic, venerable ‖ ANT *adj* young, new

old′ boy′ *n* 1 oldster, full of pep; 2 alumnus of a British public school

Old′ Church′ Sla·von′ic *n* the oldest form of Slavic, used in Bible translations and other ecclesiastical documents of the late 9th century

old′en *adj archaic & poet.* old, ancient

Old′ Eng′lish *n* 1 the English language approximately from 450 to 1150; 2 style of black-faced type

old′ fash′ioned *n* cocktail made with whiskey, bitters, sugar, fruit, and water

old′-fash′ioned *adj* 1 having or adhering to ideas or customs that are out of date; 2 out of style ‖ SYN quaint, obsolete ‖ ANT modern, new

old′ fo′gy *n* also **old′ fo′gey** person of old-fashioned or overconservative habits and ideas

Old′ French′ *n* the French language from the fourth to the thirteenth century

Old′ Glo′ry *n* flag of the United States

old′ goat′ *n slang* 1 mean old fellow; 2 lecherous old fellow

Old′ Guard′ *n* 1 imperial guard of Napoleon; 2 conservative element of a political party, group, or movement

old′ hand′ *n* one who knows a lot about something, esp. from long experience

Old′ Har′ry *n* Satan

old′ hat′ *adj colloq* old-fashioned; behind the times

old′ish *adj* somewhat old

Old′ Lat′in *n* Latin before the first century B.C.

old′ maid′ *n* 1 old or confirmed spinster; 2 prudish, fussy person; 3 card game ‖ **old′-maid′ish** *adj*

old′ man′ *n colloq* 1 father; 2 husband

old′ mas′ter *n* 1 great painter of before the 19th century; 2 painting by an old master

old′ moon′ *n* the moon when it is between the earth and the sun so that

its dark side is toward the earth showing only a thin crescent which is waning

Old′ Norse′ *n* language of Scandinavia before the 13th century

old′ rose′ *n* grayish rose color ‖ **old′-rose′** *adj*

old′ school′ *n* adherents of the old scheme of things ‖ **old′-school′** *adj*

old′ school′ tie′ *n* 1 tie of a special striped pattern worn by graduates of the various British public schools; 2 a snobbishness; b great conservatism

old′ster *n colloq* old or elderly person

Old′-Style′ *adj* (date) according to the Julian calendar

Old′ Tes′ta·ment *n* 1 the first of the two great divisions of the Bible, which contains the Law, the Prophets, and the Hagiographa; 2 covenant between God and Israel on Mount Sinai

old′-time′ *adj* 1 pert. to former times; 2 long-established

old′tim′er *n* 1 old person; 2 person of great seniority; 3 old-fashioned person

old′ wives′′ tale′ *n* traditional belief that has no basis in fact

Old′ World′ *n* Eastern Hemisphere ‖ also *adj*

old′-world′ *adj* 1 pert. to the ancient world; 2 old-fashioned; antique; 3 Old World

o·lé /ōlā′/ [Sp] *interj* used to express approval or to encourage or incite, as a bullfighter ‖ also *n*

o·le·ag·i·nous /ōl′ē·aj′ines/ [< L *oleaginus* < *olea* olive] *adj* 1 oily; 2 oily in manner; unctuous

o·le·an·der /ōl′ē·an′dər/ [ML] *n* subtropical evergreen shrub (*Nerium oleander*) with handsome, fragrant, red or white flowers

o·le′ic ac′id /ōlē′ik/ [< L *oleum* oil] *n* acid —CH₃(CH₂)₇CH = CH(CH₂)₇COOH— found in most fats as a colorless, oily liquid with a pungent taste, used in making soap

o·le·o /ōl′ē·ō′/ *n* oleomargarine

o′le·o·mar′ga·rine /-märj′(ə)rin/ [F] *n* butter substitute extracted from animal or vegetable fats

o′le·o·res′in *n* 1 natural mixture of resins and volatile essential oils; 2 liquid extract made up of an essential oil holding resin in solution

ol·fac·to·ry /olfak′tərē/ [< L *olfactor* one who smells] *adj* pert. to or used in smelling

ol·i·garch /ol′igärk′/ [Gk *oligos* few + *-arch*] *n* one of the rulers in an oligarchy

ol′i·gar′chy *n* (**-chies**) 1 government in which the supreme power is in the hands of a few; 2 state so governed; 3 the few who rule ‖ **ol′i·gar′chic** (**-chi·cal**) *adj*

ol·ive /ol′iv/ [OF < L *oliva*] *n* 1 any of a genus (*Olea*) of trees and shrubs, esp. an evergreen Old World tree

(*O. europaea*) cultivated for its fruit; 2 its small oval fruit, valued for its oil and as a relish; 3 dull yellowish green ‖ also *adj*

ol′ive branch′ *n* 1 branch of the olive tree, regarded as the emblem of peace; 2 token of peace or reconciliation

ol′ive drab′ *n* 1 deep olive color; 2 cloth or uniform of this color ‖ **ol′ive-drab′** *adj*

ol′ive oil′ *n* oil pressed from ripe olives, used medicinally and in foods

ol′i·vine′ /-vēn′/ [< G *Olive* olive + *-ine*] *n* 1 silicate of magnesium and iron —(MgFe)₂SiO₄—, a mineral constituent of igneous rocks; 2 transparent green variety, used as a gem

O·lym·pi·a /ōlimp′ē-ə/ *n* 1 plain in NW Peloponnesus, where the Olympic Games of ancient Greece were held; 2 capital of Washington (19,000)

O·lym·pi·ad, o·lym·pi·ad /ōlimp′ē-ad′/ [Gk *olympias* (*-ados*)] *n* 1 period of four years between celebrations of the ancient Olympic Games; 2 celebration of the modern Olympic Games

O·lym′pi·an [< *Olympus*] *adj* 1 pert. to Olympus; 2 pert. to, like, or suitable to the gods on Olympus; 3 majestic; godlike ‖ *n* 4 any of the twelve great gods who dwelt on Olympus; 5 contender in the modern Olympic Games

O·lym′pic *adj* 1 pert. to the Olympic Games; 2 Olympian ‖ *n* 3 the **Olym′pics** *pl* the Olympic Games

O·lym′pic Games *npl* 1 athletic games of ancient Greece, celebrated every four years in honor of Zeus; 2 modern revival of these games, open to participants from every nation and held every four years

O·lym·pus /ōlimp′əs/ *n* mountain in N Greece, reputed home of the ancient Greek gods

-o·ma /-ōm′ə/ [Gk] *n suf* (**-o·mas** or **-o·ma·ta** /-ōm′ətə/) tumor, as *carcinoma*

O·ma·ha /ōm′əhô′, -hä′/ *n* city in E Nebraska (347,328)

om·buds·man /om′bədzmən/ [Sw = commissioner] *n* (**-men** /-mən/) 1 public official appointed to investigate complaints by private citizens against bureaucrats; 2 one who investigates complaints, as of students, and brings about adjustments

o·me·ga /ōmēg′ə, -māg′ə, -meg′ə/ [Gk = big *o*] *n* 1 twenty-fourth and last letter of the Greek alphabet Ω ω; 2 the last; the end

om·e·let also **om·e·lette** /om′(ə)lit/ [F *omelette*] *n* eggs beaten and cooked in a pan, often with other ingredients added, as cheese or tomatoes

o·men /ōm′ən/ [L] *n* 1 prophetic sign of some future event; portent ‖ *vt* 2 to portend

om·i·cron /om′ikrən, -kron′/ [Gk = small *o*] *n* fifteenth letter of the Greek alphabet O o

om·i·nous /om′/nəs/ [< *omen*] *adj* portending evil; foreboding

o·mis·sion /ōmish′ən/ *n* 1 act of omitting or state of being omitted; 2 something omitted

o·mit /ōmit′/ [L *omittere* (*-missus*)] *v* (**o·mit·ted; o·mit·ting**) *vt* 1 to leave out; 2 to neglect; fail to do

om·ni- [< L *omnis*] *comb form* all

om·ni·bus /om′nibəs, -bus′/ [L = for all] *n* 1 bus 1 ‖ *adj* 2 covering many items, as *an omnibus bill*

om·nip·o·tent /omnip′ətənt/ [L *omnipotens* (*-entis*)] *adj* all-powerful ‖ **om·nip′o·tence** *n*

om·ni·pres′ent /om′ni-/ *adj* present everywhere at the same time

om·nis·cient /omnish′ənt/ [*omni-* + L *sciens* (*-entis*) knowing] *adj* knowing all things ‖ **om·nis′cience** *n*

om·niv·o·rous /omniv′ərəs/ [*omni-* + L *vorare* to eat] *adj* 1 eating both animal and vegetable food; 2 eating anything; 3 taking in everything, as *an omnivorous reader*

on /ôn′, on′/ [OE *an*, *on*] *prep* 1 upon; supported by; in contact with; 2 covering, as *a hat on his head*; 3 located at, as *the shop on Main Street*; 4 in the act or state of, as *on a journey, on fire*; 5 forming part of, as *on the team*; 6 as a result of, as *a loss on the deal*; 7 by the agency of, as *to live on fruit*; 8 with respect to, as *have pity on her*; 9 in the direction of, as *the door opens on the lawn*; 10 about, as *a talk on peace*; 11 at the time of, as *on June first*; 12 denoting cause or basis, as *on purpose; on my honor*; 13 denoting the instrument of an action, as *to play on the harp*; 14 upon the event of, as *on his arrival*; 15 *colloq* at the expense of, as *have one on me* ‖ *adv* 16 forward, as *go on*; 17 in or into a position to cover, support, etc., as *put on your coat*; 18 in or into action or use, as *turn on the gas*; 19 in progress, as *the fight is on*; 20 toward something, as *the crowd looked on*; 21 continuously, as *he talked on*; 22 **on and off** intermittently; 23 **on and on** interminably ‖ *adj* 24 in operation; 25 taking place; 26 performing, as *you're on in ten minutes*; 27 planned, as *do you have anything on for tonight?*; 28 **on to** *colloq* informed about, aware of, as *the police were on to him*

ON, O.N. Old Norse

o·nan·ism /ōn′əniz′əm/ [< *Onan* (Gen.38:9)] *n* 1 withdrawal before ejaculation in sexual intercourse; 2 male masturbation

once /wuns′/ [OE *ānes*] *adv* 1 formerly; 2 one time only; 3 at any time, ever; 4 by one step or degree, as *a* *cousin once removed;* **5 once and for all** decisively; conclusively; **6 once upon a time** once long ago ‖ *n* **7** one time; **8 at once, a** simultaneously; **b** immediately; **9 all at once** suddenly ‖ *conj* **10** if ever; whenever

once'-o'ver *n colloq* quick appraisal

on'com'ing *adj* approaching

one /wun'/ [OE *ān*] *adj* **1** being a single unit, being, or object; individual; **2 a** certain, as *one John Jones;* **3** single; united, as *they answered with one voice;* **4** the same; **5** on an unspecified occasion in the past, as *one day last month;* **6** on an unspecified occasion in the future, as *she'll come one day* ‖ *n* **7** number expressing unity (1; I); **8** single person or thing; **9 at one** in agreement; attuned; **10 one and all** everyone ‖ *pron* **11** any person, anyone, as *one must live;* **12** used to nominalize an adjective, as *I want a ripe one; I threw the bad ones out*

-one /-ōn/ [Gk = *fem n suf*] *n suf chem* used in the name of certain hydrocarbons and ketones

one'-a-cat' *n* one old cat

one' an·oth'er *pron* each one the other

one'-armed ban'dit *n* slot machine for gambling, operated by a long handle at the side

one'-base hit' *n* baseball hit which allows the batter to reach first base safely

one'-horse town' *n colloq* small and backward community

one'ness *n* **1** unity; singleness; **2** agreement; concord

one old cat /wun'əkat'/ *n* simplified form of baseball played when there are not enough players to form two teams

on·er·ous /on'ərəs, ōn'-/ [< L *onus* (*-eris*) burden] *adj* burdensome; oppressive ‖ SYN difficult, heavy, toilsome, wearisome, arduous, oppressive, burdensome, weighty ‖ DISCR Literally, that is *heavy* which is hard to lift; figuratively, *heavy* has in common with the other words here compared the idea of being hard to bear, hard to stand, grievous, as a *heavy* fate, trial; a *heavy* load on my heart. *Burdensome* describes that which weights one down with an actual load, as a light package carried a long way may become *burdensome;* figuratively, *burdensome* means wearying and oppressive to the heart and mind as well as to the body, as *burdensome* obligations, duties. *Arduous* is applied to that which is hard to achieve save through persistent, laborious exertion; the smooth style of a writer is usually the result of *arduous* toil. *Onerous* is used chiefly in the figurative sense of *burdensome*, though it adds to

burdensome the idea of annoyance, trouble, and tediousness, as the *onerous* work of classifying notes

one·self' also **one's self'** *pron* **1** a person's self (often used reflexively or emphatically); **2 be oneself, a** to be one's normal self; **b** to be sincere and unaffected; **3 by oneself, a** alone; **b** unaided

one'-sid'ed *adj* **1** having or appearing on only one side; **2** very unequal, as a contest; **3** partial; unfair

one'-step' *n* round dance of quick movement to two-four time

one'time' *adj* of a previous time, former

one'-to-one' *adj* corresponding part by part

one'-track' *adj* **1** having a single track; **2** *colloq* obsessed with, or incapable of dealing with, more than one thing or idea

one'-way' *adj* **1** moving or permitting movement in one direction only; **2** for travel only in one direction

on·ion /un'yən/ [OF *oignon* < L *unio* (*-onis*)] *n* **1** any of several plants (genus *Allium*) of the lily family, esp. *A. cepa,* having a strong-smelling edible bulb used as a vegetable; **2** its bulb; **3 know one's onions** *slang* to know one's subject or business thoroughly

on'ion·skin' *n* a thin translucent paper

on'look'er *n* spectator

on·ly /ōn'lē/ [OE *ānlīc*] *adj* **1** alone; sole; **2** one and no more; **3** unique; superior ‖ *adv* **4** exclusively; **5** merely; **6** singly; **7** just, as *only yesterday;* **8** as a result, as *you will only be sorry;* **9 only too** extremely ‖ *conj* **10** except that

on·o·mat·o·poe·ia /on'əmat'əpē'ə/ [< Gk *onoma* (*-atos*) name + *poiein* to make] *n* **1** formation of words in imitation of natural sounds, as *hiss, bang;* **2** word so formed ‖ **on'o·mat'o·poe'ic** *adj*

on'rush' *n* forward rush or flow

on'set' *n* **1** start; **2** attack

on'slaught' /-slôt'/ [D *aanslag*] *n* furious attack

on'stage' *adv* **1** on or to the stage ‖ *adj* **2** pert. to or used on a stage in view of the audience

Ont. Ontario

On·tar·i·o /onter'ē·ō'/ *n* province in E central Canada bordering on the Great Lakes (7,000,000; 412,582 sq.m.; cap. Toronto) ‖ **On·tar'i·an** *adj & n*

On·tar'i·o, Lake *n* one of the Great Lakes, lying between New York and Ontario

on·to /ôn'tōō, on'-/ *prep* **1** to a position on; **2** *colloq* aware of

on·tog·e·ny /ontoj'ənē/ [< Gk *on* (*ontos*) being + *-genes* producing] *n* *biol* history or development of an individual organism o·nus /ōn′əs/ [L = burden] *n* burden; responsibility

on′ward /-wərd/ *adj* 1 advancing ‖ also on′wards *adv* 2 toward a point ahead; forward

-o·nym /-ənim/ [Gk -*onymos*] *comb form* name, word

on·yx /on′iks, ōn′-/ [Gk] *n* 1 variety of chalcedony in layers of various colors; 2 jet black

oo·dles /ōōd′əlz/ [?] *npl colloq* a large amount

oo·long /ōō′lông, -loŋ/ [Chin *wulung*] *n* fragrant brown or amber tea, mainly from Taiwan

oomph /ōōmf′/ [prob imit of expression of admiration] *n slang* 1 sex appeal; 2 vitality, vigor

ooze[1] /ōōz′/ [OE *wāse* puddle] *n* 1 soft slimy mud; 2 bog or marsh; 3 soft deposit on the ocean floor of the calcareous remains of marine animals

ooze[2] [OE *wās* juice] *vi* 1 to flow gently; exude; 2 to escape or come out gradually ‖ *vt* 3 to exude slowly ‖ *n* 4 act of oozing; 5 that which oozes

o·pac·i·ty /ōpas′itē/ [see opaque] *n* (-ties) 1 quality or state of being opaque; 2 something opaque

o·pal /ōp′əl/ [L *opalus*] *n* 1 form of silica, opaque or transparent, with a wide range of color; 2 the translucent variety, notable for an iridescent play of colors, prized as a gem

o′pal·esce /ōp′ələs′/ *vi* to give out a display of variegated colors, as an opal ‖ o′pal·es′cence *n* ‖ o′pal·es′cent *adj*

o·paque /ōpāk′/ [L *opacus* shaded] *adj* 1 not transparent or translucent; not allowing light to pass through; 2 not transmitting heat, sound, radiation, etc.; 3 (color) having no luster or brightness; 4 unintelligible; 5 obtuse, dull-witted

op′ art′ /op′/ *n* style of abstract art using geometric figures to create optical effects and illusions

op. cit. /op′ sit′/ [L *opere citato*] in the work cited

OPEC Organization of Petroleum Exporting Countries

o·pen /ōp′ən [OE = raised up] *adj* 1 not shut; not closed, sealed, barred, locked, covered, or obstructed; 2 exposed to the outside, as *an open porch;* 3 in operation, as *the store is open till five; school is open now; the bridge is open to traffic;* 4 clear of trees, as *open country;* 5 unfilled, unoccupied, as *the job is open; there is an open place at the poker table;* 6 undecided, unsettled; 7 not surrounded or enclosed, as *the open sea;* 8 not restricted as to participants, as *an open meeting;* 9 unfolded, as *an open newspaper;* 10 not hidden, as *an open scandal; open lawlessness;* 11 (mind) not made up; 12 generous; 13 frank, sincere, as *an open manner;* 14 *phonet* a (vowel) articulated with the mouth relatively open; b (syllable) not ending in a consonant; 15 open to willing to listen to, as a suggestion ‖ *vt* 16 to cause to become open, unbarred, unlocked, unfolded, uncovered, unsealed, or unobstructed; 17 to begin; 18 to reveal, expose; 19 to pierce or make a hole in; 20 to make accessible or available, as *to open a region to settlement* ‖ *vi* 21 to become open; 22 to commence; 23 to lead, as *the door opens into the hall;* 24 to expand, develop; 25 to become more clearly visible; 26 *cards* to make the first play or bet ‖ *n* 27 the open the outdoors; 28 in the open in public view ‖ o′pen·ly *adv* ‖ SYN *adj* frank, candid, ingenuous, plain, artless, free, sincere, aboveboard, truthful ‖ DISCR An *open* countenance is a true index of what is going on behind it; an *open* statement keeps nothing back. A *frank* statement, while it lacks the nakedness of an *open* one, is yet blunt and true. *Candid* shares the disagreeable connotation of *frank,* though the motive behind *candor* is that of impartiality and fairness, rather than savage truthtelling. An *ingenuous* remark is naïve; the speaker is so innocent that his lack of experience or tact is indulgently forgiven or smiled at. *Plain* is allied to *open,* in that you cannot escape its meaning; *plain* speaking is unvarnished and discouragingly truthful; a *plain* direction is clear. *Artless,* like *ingenuous,* is undesigning and guileless in its disclosures

o′pen-air′ *adj* taking place out of doors; outdoor

o′pen-and-shut′ *adj* obvious, not requiring further investigation

o′pen cit′y *n* city declared to be of no military value in time of war, neither to be defended nor bombarded

o′pen door′ *n* free and easy access to all, as for trade or immigration ‖ o′pen-door′ *adj*

o′pen-end′ *adj* 1 subject to further change or negotiation, as an agreement; 2 (investment company) that operates as a mutual fund

o′pen·er *n* 1 one who or that which opens; 2 opening event; 3 openers *pl poker* pair, as jacks or better, giving the holder the right to make the first bet; 4 for openers *slang* to start with

o′pen-faced′ *adj* 1 having a sincere countenance; 2 (watch) having a dial covered only by a crystal; 3 (sandwich or pie) with filling uncovered by bread or dough

o′pen-hand′ed *adj* generous, liberal

o·pen-heart' *adj* (surgery) performed with the heart open while its functions are taken over by an external mechanical device

o·pen-heart'ed *adj* 1 frank; 2 generous

o·pen-hearth' *adj* designating a process for making steel that removes the impurities from a bath of molten iron lying on the open hearth of the furnace

o·pen house' *n* 1 house where all visitors are welcome; 2 time during which a school or institution is open to visitors

o·pen·ing *n* 1 act or instance of opening; 2 aperture, hole; 3 beginning, commencement; 4 unfilled job; 5 first performance of a show; 6 opportunity or chance

o·pen let'ter *n* letter addressed to an individual which is made public

o·pen-mind'ed *adj* 1 having no preconceptions; 2 receptive to new ideas

o·pen reel' *n* set of two reels of magnetic tape that are not enclosed in a cartridge or cassette and that are placed manually on the spindles

o·pen sea'son *n* period when game may be hunted without restrictions

o·pen se'cret *n* supposed secret that everybody knows

o·pen ses'a·me [phrase used by Ali Baba to gain entrance to the robbers' cave] *n* unfailing means of entrance or access

o·pen shop' *n* shop or factory that employs both union and nonunion labor

o·pen·work' *n* carving, metal work, embroidery, etc., so made that it shows open spaces in its pattern

op·er·a[1] /op'(ə)rə/ [It < L = work] *n* 1 drama in which all parts are sung to orchestral accompaniment, usu. containing arias, duos, choruses, and recitatives; 2 theater in which it is performed

o·pe·ra[2] /ōp'ərə, op'-/ *pl* of **opus**

op·er·a·ble /op'ərəbəl/ [< *operate*] *adj* amenable to treatment by surgical operation

o·pé·ra bouffe /op'ərə bōōf'/ [F] *n* comic opera, esp. of a farcical nature

op·er·a glass'es *npl* small binoculars of low power for viewing shows, sports events, etc.

op·er·a hat' *n* man's collapsible top hat

op·er·ate /op'ərāt'/ [L *operari* (*-atus*) to work] *vi* 1 to work, act, or function; 2 to work a machine or apparatus; 3 to produce a certain effect, exert an influence; 4 to produce a desired result; 5 to perform military, commercial, or other operations; 6 to treat the body surgically || *vt* 7 to cause (a machine, device, vehicle, etc.) to operate; 8 to man-

age, direct, or conduct, as *to operate a business*

op·er·at'ic /-rat'ik/ *adj* pert. to, suitable for, or like opera

op·er·a'tion *n* 1 act or way of operating; 2 surgical treatment of the body to remedy disease, repair injury, or correct deformity; 3 power to act; 4 process, course, or procedure in producing any specific thing or result, as in industry, mathematics, or warfare; 5 **in** or **into operation** in or into an operative state

op·er·a'tion·al *adj* 1 in working condition; 2 able to function effectively

op·er·a'tions re·search' *n* mathematical and scientific analysis of the purpose, performance, and efficiency of a proposed or actual military or commercial operation

op·er·a·tive /op'(ə)rətiv, op'ərāt'iv/ *adj* 1 in operation; 2 in effect; 3 pert. to or engaged in work; 4 pert. to surgical operations || *n* 5 skilled worker; 6 private detective; 7 secret agent

op·er·a'tor *n* 1 one who operates a machine or device; 2 person who operates a telephone switchboard; 3 person or company that operates a business or industrial enterprise; 4 *math* symbol indicating a mathematical process to be performed; 5 *slang* person adept at gaining advantage, enriching himself, or evading responsibilities by slick and often dubious methods

op·er·et'ta /-ret'ə/ [It, *dim.* of opera] *n* short opera, usu. of a light and humorous character

oph·thal·mic /ofthal'mik/ [< Gk *ophthalmos* eye] *adj* pert. to the eye

oph'thal·mol·o·gy /-mol'əjē/ *n* branch of medical science which treats of the functions and diseases of the eye || **oph'thal·mol'o·gist** *n*

-o·pi·a /ōp'ē·ə/ [Gk] *n comb form* condition of sight, as myopia

o·pi·ate /ōp'ē·it, -āt'/ [see **opium**] *n* 1 medicine containing opium for relieving pain or inducing sleep; 2 anything that induces inaction or dulls the feelings || *also adj*

o·pine /ōpīn'/ [L *opinari*] *vt* 1 to express as an opinion || *vi* 2 to conjecture, guess

o·pin·ion /əpin'yən/ *n* 1 belief or judgment; 2 estimation or appraisal; 3 statement of the law bearing on a case, made by a judge || SYN view, estimate, idea, notion, conviction, sentiment, impression, judgment, belief, conclusion

o·pin'ion·at'ed *adj* firm or obstinate in one's ideas or beliefs || SYN conceited, egotistical, dogmatic, obstinate, stubborn, arrogant, dictatorial, imperious, domineering || DISCR The *opinionated* man thinks so highly of his own judgments that he not only clings to them tenaciously, but spreads them for all to hear. He is arrogant and dictatorial, and hence not popular. The *egotistical* man has one beloved subject—himself. The *conceited* man has such an opinion of his abilities and qualities that he is inordinately vain. The *dogmatic* man thinks that there is but one way to do a thing—his || ANT modest, humble, meek, retiring

o·pi·um /ōp′ē-əm/ [L < Gk *opion* poppy juice] *n* powerful narcotic and addictive drug obtained from the juices of a poppy (*Papaver somniferum*)

o·pos·sum /əpos′əm/ [< Algonquian] *n* any of a family (Didelphidae) of small American marsupials, esp. *Didelphis virginiana*, of nocturnal and arboreal habits, which pretends to be dead if threatened

op·po·nent /əpōn′ənt/ [< L *opponere* to oppose] *n* one who opposes; adversary

op·por·tune /op′ərt(y)ōōn′/ [L *opportunus*] *adj* 1 fit, suitable; 2 timely; convenient || SYN convenient, timely, favorable, advantageous

op′por·tun′ist *n* one who takes advantage of circumstances regardless of principle || **op′por·tun′ism** *n*

op′por·tu′ni·ty *n* (-ties) 1 convenient time or occasion; 2 chance; 3 favorable opening, as in business || SYN (see *occasion*)

op·pose /əpōz′/ [OF *opposer* < L *opponere* + OF *poser* to pose] *vt* 1 to place opposite, as in contrast; 2 to act against; contend with; 3 to resist; 4 to set up as an obstacle || **op·pos′a·ble** *adj* || SYN withstand, thwart, defy, obstruct, gainsay (see *prevent*) || ANT agree, yield, further, promote

op·po·site /op′əzit, -sit/ [MF < L *oppositus*] *adj* 1 situated in front of or over against; 2 contrary, opposed; 3 proceeding the other way; 4 very different || *n* 5 one who or that which is opposite || *prep* 6 across from; *theat* in a complementary role to || SYN *adj* contrary, contradictory || DISCR *Opposite* and *contrary* are sometimes interchangeable, being applied to things diametrically different from each other, as to go in *opposite*, or *contrary*, directions; a result *opposite*, or *contrary*, to what was expected. *Opposite*, however, is likely to be used of position in space, *contrary* of opposition in nature, meaning, or opinion, as *opposite* sides of the street, *contrary* hopes or views. *Contradictory* describes things in direct opposition, and mutually exclusive, as *contradictory* statements or terms

op′po·site num′ber *n* either one of two persons who occupy corresponding positions in two organizations

op′po·si′tion /-zish′ən/ *n* 1 act of opposing or state of being opposed; 2 antagonism; resistance; 3 *astron* situation of two heavenly bodies when the angular distance between their longitudes is 180°; 4 **the opposition,** a the person, group, or organization opposing or in competition with the efforts of one's own group or organization; b the political party out of power || SYN resistance || DISCR *Opposition* and *resistance* agree in the idea of setting one thing up against another. Applied to persons, *opposition* may name an unvoiced disapproval of a course of action: it may take the form of plain balking; it may be a mere declaration of opinion; or it may be actively hostile. *Resistance* is called forth by opposing plans, and may be either passive or active; we offer *resistance* to an enemy's advance || ANT assistance, promotion, encouragement

op·press /əpres′/ [MF *oppresser* < L *oppressus* crushed] *vt* 1 to burden; crush by hardship or severity; 2 to weigh heavily upon physically or mentally || **op·pres′sor** *n*

op·pres′sion /-shən/ *n* 1 act of oppressing or state of being oppressed; 2 cruel and unjust treatment by those in authority; 3 distress of the mind or body

op·pres′sive *adj* 1 burdensome; unjust; despotic; 2 overpowering, causing physical or mental distress

op′pro·bri·ous /əprōb′rē-əs/ *adj* 1 abusive; 2 disgraceful || SYN insulting, abusive, offensive, vulgar, gross

op·pro′bri·um /-əm/ [L] *n* 1 disgrace; scorn; reproach; 2 cause of such disgrace

opt /opt′/ [F *opter*] *vi* to make a choice

op·ta·tive /op′tətiv/ [< L *optare* (-*atus*) to choose] *adj* 1 designating a mood of the verb, as in Greek, which expresses a wish || *n* 2 optative mood, or a verb form in it

op·tic /op′tik/ [Gk *optikos*] *adj* 1 pert. to the eye or to vision; 2 optical || *n* 3 **optics** *sg* branch of physics that deals with vision and the properties of light

op′ti·cal *adj* 1 pert. to optics; 2 pert. to vision; 3 visual; 4 intended to correct vision

op′ti·cal read′er *n* device for the photoelectric conversion of printed characters into electrical impulses that are recorded on magnetic tape

op·ti·cian /optish′ən/ *n* one who makes or sells eyeglasses, lenses, and/or optical instruments

op′tic nerve′ *n* nerve running from the eye to the optic centers of the brain

op·ti·mism /op′timiz′əm/ [< L *optimus* best] *n* 1 belief that everything is ordered for the best, and that eventually good will triumph over evil; **2** inclination to look on the best side of life or to expect success || **op′ti·mist** *n* || **op′ti·mis′tic** *adj* || **op′ti·mis′ti·cal·ly** *adv*

op·ti·mum /op′timəm/ [L] *n* (**-mums** or **-ma** /-mə/) best or most favorable degree, number, condition, or the like

op·tion /op′shən/ [< L *optare* to choose] *n* **1** right or power of choosing; **2** act of choosing; choice; **3** privilege to buy or sell property within a stated period and upon terms and conditions agreed to in advance || SYN preference, selection, alternative, right, privilege (see *choice*)

op′tion·al *adj* left to one's choice

op·tom·e·try /optom′itrē/ [Gk *optos* visible + *-metry*] *n* practice or profession of testing the eyes in order to prescribe corrective glasses if needed || **op·tom′e·trist** *n*

op·u·lent /op′yələnt/ [L *opulens* (*-entis*)] *adj* **1** wealthy; **2** abundant, plentiful || **op′u·lence** *n*

o·pus /ōp′əs/ [L = work] *n* (**o·pus·es** or **o·pe·ra** /ōp′ərə, op′-/) musical composition, usu. numbered

or /ôr′, ər/ [< *obs conj other* < OE *ôththe*] *conj* **1** suggesting an alternative, as *this or that;* **2** also, in other words, as *a triangle or three-sided figure*

-or /-ər, sometimes -ôr/ [OF *-eur, -eor* & L *-or*] *n suf* person or thing that, as *sailor, actor*

or·a·cle /ôr′əkəl, or′-/ [L *oraculum*] *n* **1** in ancient Greece, **a** reply, often ambiguous, of a god to some inquiry, delivered through a priest or priestess; **b** agency transmitting such replies; **c** place where they were given; **2** anyone speaking with wisdom, inspiration, or authority; **3** advice or opinion of such a person

o·rac·u·lar /ōrak′yələr, ōr-/ *adj* **1** of the nature of or pert. to an oracle; **2** authoritative, wise; **3** having the power to utter wise sayings or prophecies; **4** enigmatic; ambiguous

o·ral /ôr′əl, ōr′-/ [< L *os* (*oris*) mouth] *adj* **1** uttered by the mouth; spoken; **2** pert. to the mouth; **3** *phonet* pronounced without nasal resonance || *n* **4** oral examination for a higher degree in a university

or·ange /or′inj, ôr′-/ [OF < Ar *nâranj*] *n* **1** evergreen tree (*Citrus aurantium* and *C. sinensis*) with fragrant white flowers and juicy reddish-yellow fruit; **2** the sweet or subacid fruit; **3** reddish-yellow color || *adj* **4** orange-colored

or′ange·ade′ /-ād′/ *n* cooling drink made from orange juice and water

Or′ange·man /-mən/ [William of *Orange* (1650–1702) Protestant king of England 1689–1702, who defeated the Catholic James II in 1690] *n* (**-men** /-mən/) **1** member of an Irish secret society founded in 1795 to uphold Protestantism in Ireland; **2** Northern Irish Protestant

o·rang·u·tan /ôraŋ′ōōtan′, ôr-/ [Malay = man of the forest] *n* large reddish-brown arboreal ape (*Pongo pygmaeus*) of Borneo and Sumatra, with very long arms

o·rate /ôrāt′, ōr-/ [< *oration*] *vi* to declaim pompously

o·ra·tion /ôrāsh′ən, ōr-/ [< L *orare* to speak] *n* formal speech, esp. one delivered at a public ceremony || SYN address (see *speech*)

or·a·tor /ôr′ətər, or′-/ [L] *n* **1** one who makes an oration; **2** speaker of great eloquence

or·a·tor·i·cal /ôr′ətôr′ikəl, or′-, -tor′-/ *adj* pert. or suitable to an orator or oratory

or·a·to·ri·o /ôr′ətôr′ē·ō′, or′-, -tōr′-/ [It = small chapel] *n mus* elaborate composition, usu. on a sacred theme, operatic in form but sung without action, scenery, or costumes

or′a·to·ry *n* [L *oratorius* oratorical] *n* (**-ries**) **1** art of public speaking; **2** eloquence in speaking; **3** small chapel, esp. one for private devotion; **4 Oratory** society of priests without vows organized for the purpose of holding popular services with simple preaching

orb /ôrb′/ [L *orbis*] *n* **1** globe, sphere; **2** heavenly body; **3** eye or eyeball; **4** the globe as a symbol of sovereignty

or·bit /ôrb′it/ [L *orbita* wheel track] *n* **1** path, usu. elliptical, described by any body in space subject to the gravity of another body; **2** course of one's life or activities; **3** eye socket || *vi* **4** to travel in an orbit || *vt* **5** to travel around (a body) in an orbital path; **6** to put (an artificial satellite) in an orbital path || **or′bit·al** *adj*

or·chard /ôrch′ərd/ [OE *ortgeard*] *n* ground planted with fruit trees

or·ches·tra /ôrk′istrə/ [Gk = space for the chorus to dance] *n* **1** company of musicians playing a full range of instruments, as strings, brass, woodwinds, drums, etc.; **2** main floor of a theater || **or·ches·tral** /ôrkes′trəl/ *adj*

or′ches·tra pit′ *n* space near the stage in the front part of a theater where the orchestra sits

or′ches·trate′ *vt* to compose or arrange (music) for an orchestra || **or′ches·tra′tion** *n*

or·chid /ôrk′id/ [< Gk *orchis* testicle] *n* **1** any of a large family (Orchidaceae) of plants of tropical and temperate regions, bearing showy flowers; **2** bluish to reddish purple || **or′chi·da′ceous** /-dāsh′əs/ *adj*

or·dain /ôrdān′/ [OF *ordener* < L *ordinare* to order] *vt* **1** to appoint to the Christian ministry; confer holy orders upon; **2** to decree, give orders for; **3** to appoint authoritatively; establish; **4** to destine, as by fate or Providence

or-deal /ôr′dēl, ôrdēl′/ [OE *ordāl*] *n* **1** severe trial or test; trying circumstance; **2** ancient method of trial by fire, water, combat, etc., to determine the guilt or innocence of the accused

or-der /ôrd′ər/ [OF *ordre* < L *ordo* row] *n* **1** regular arrangement, as in a row or series; sequence; **2** social rank; **3** fraternal, monastic, or military society or brotherhood; **4** honorary society in which membership is conferred for meritorious service, as *the Order of the Garter;* **5** badge of distinction worn by members of such groups; **6** regular or settled method of action; system; **7** established custom; **8** regular or harmonious arrangement; **9** satisfactory condition; **10** authoritative command; **11** public tranquility or observance of law; **12** direction to purchase or supply something; **13** the goods purchased or supplied; **14** written direction to pay money or give over property; **15** *arch.* any arrangement of columns with an entablature, esp. one of the classical arrangements; **16** any of the degrees of priesthood; **17** *bot & zool* group next larger than a family and smaller than a class; **18** **orders** *pl* rite or sacrament of ordination; **19** **a tall order** a difficult task; **20** **in order, a** in satisfactory condition; **b** fitting; **21** **in order that** so that; **22** **in order to** for the purpose of; **23** **on order** (goods) ordered; **24** **on the order of** similar to; **25** **out of order, a** not operating; **b** inappropriate; **c** not acting within the rules of parliamentary procedure ‖ *vt* **26** to give an order to; **27** to regulate or manage; direct; **28** to command; **29** to give directions for the purchase of; **30** to arrange systematically ‖ *vi* **31** to give an order ‖ SYN *n* instruction, command, direction, requirement, rule, regulation, mandate, precept, injunction ‖ DISCR *Order, instruction, command, direction,* and *requirement* agree in expressing authoritative demands. *Requirements* for college entrance are set forth by the colleges; *instructions* as to how to fulfill these *requirements* will be given by teachers or office employees. Superiors commonly give *instructions* as to what shall be done; but army officers, naval officers, men in charge of construction gangs, employers, give the less elastic *order. Orders* are imperative, often arbitrary. *Directions* are explicit, more of a guiding and managing nature, and usually given in connection with business administration or superintendence. A college professor leaves *instructions*

for his laboratory assistants; a ship captain issues *orders;* the mistress of a house leaves *directions* for the servants, for young children. *Command* is reserved for the bidding of those in supreme authority. It contains the force of an *order* and the pressing moral quality that attaches to superiority

or′der-ly *adj* **1** neat, tidy; **2** methodical, systematic; **3** peaceable, law-abiding ‖ *adv* **4** properly; **5** methodically, systematically ‖ *n* (-lies) **6** male hospital attendant; **7** soldier who acts as a servant or messenger ‖ **or′der-li-ness** *n*

Or′der of the Gar′ter *n* highest order of British knighthood, instituted about 1348

or-di-nal /ôrd′inəl/ [< L *ordo* (-*dinis*) row] *adj* **1** pert. to ordinal numbers; **2** *bot & zool* pert. to an order ‖ *n* **3** ordinal number

or′di-nal num′ber *n* number expressing degree or order in a series, as *first, second,* etc.

or-di-nance /ôrd′inəns/ [OF *ordenance*] *n* **1** decree or command, as of God; **2** law or statute

or-di-nar-i-ly /ôrd′iner′ilē/ *adv* **1** usually; **2** in an ordinary way

or′di-nar′y *adj* [L *ordinarius* according to rule] *adj* **1** usual, customary; **2** commonplace; undistinguished ‖ *n* (-ies) **3** *R C Ch* established order for saying the part of the Mass that precedes the canon; **4** **out of the ordinary** unusual ‖ SYN *adj* regular, common, normal, average, mediocre

or′di-nate /-dinit/ [L (linea) *ordinate* (applicata) (line applied) in order] *n math* vertical coordinate of a point measured parallel to the y-axis

or-di-na′tion [LL *ordinatio* (-*onis*)] *n* act, fact, or ceremony of ordaining or being ordained

ord-nance /ôrd′nəns/ [< *ordinance*] *n* **1** artillery; **2** weapons, ammunition, and supplies; **3** department having charge of them

or-dure /ôr′jər, -dyŏŏr/ [OF] *n* excrement, dung

ore /ôr′, ōr′/ [OE *ār* brass] *n* metal-bearing mineral or rock

Ore., Oreg. Oregon

o-reg-a-no /əreg′ənō′/ [Sp] *n* plant (genus *Origanum*) of the mint family related to marjoram and used as a spice

Or-e-gon /ôr′əgən, -gon′, or′-/ *n* state in the NW U.S. on the Pacific (2,091,000; 96,981 sq.m.; cap. Salem) ‖ **Or-e-go-ni-an** /ôr′əgō′nē-ən/ *n*

or-gan /ôr′gən/ [Gk *organon* tool] *n* **1** part of an animal or plant fitted to perform a specific function; **2** means of making known the opinions or acts of a person or party, as a newspaper; **3** means by which an action is performed; **4** musical instrument having pipes sounded by compressed air and played by means of one or more keyboards; **5** any of various similar instruments without pipes

or·gan·dy or **or·gan·die** /ôr′gəndē/ [F *organdi*] *n* very fine transparent muslin dress goods

or′gan grind′er *n* street musician who plays a hand organ

or·gan·ic /ôrgan′ik/ *adj* **1** pert. to a body organ; **2** having an organized structure; **3** pert. to a living organism; **4** containing carbon as an essential ingredient; **5** constitutional; inherent ‖ **or·gan′i·cal·ly** *adv*

or·gan′ic chem′is·try *n* the chemistry of carbon compounds

or·gan′ic food′ *n* food grown and processed without the use of pesticides, preservatives, and other artificial agents

or·gan·ism /-gən-/ *n* **1** any form of plant and animal life; **2** any organized body or system resembling a living being

or′gan·ist *n* person who plays the organ

or·gan·i·za′tion *n* **1** act or process of organizing or state of being organized; **2** that which is organized; **3** body of persons united for a specific purpose ‖ **or·gan·i·za′tion·al** *adj*

Or·gan·i·za′tion of A·mer′i·can States′ *n* organization founded in 1948 comprising the U.S. and most of the nations to the south for the purpose of economic and military cooperation

or·gan·ize′ *vt* **1** to give organic structure to; **2** to systematize; **3** to set up, establish, make viable; **4** to get (workers) to join a union; **5** to get the workers of (a shop, factory, or industry) to form a union ‖ *vi* **6** to become organized ‖ **or′gan·iz′er** *n*

or·gasm /ôr′gazəm/ [Gk *orgasmos* excitement] *n* climax of the sexual act

or·gy /ôr′jē/ [MF *orgie* < Gk *orgia* secret rites] *n* (**-gies**) **1** wild licentious revelry; **2** any unbridled passionate outburst, as *an orgy of murders;* **3** orgies *pl* in ancient Greece, secret rites in honor of a god, characterized by wild dancing, singing, and revelry

o·ri·el /ôr′ē·əl, ôr′-/ [< OF *oriol* gallery < ML *oriolum*] *n* projecting window structure supported by corbels or brackets

o·ri·ent /ôr′ē·ent, ôr′-/ [MF < L *oriens* (*-entis*) east] *vt* **1** to adjust, as to a new environment; **2** to direct or position toward an object or with reference to the points of the compass; **3** **orient oneself** to get one's bearings ‖ /ôr′ē·ent, ôr′-/ *n* **4** east; **5** **the Orient,** **a** the Far East; **b** the countries to the E and SE of the Mediterranean

o·ri·en·tal *adj* **1** eastern; **2** **Oriental** of or pert. to the Orient ‖ *n* **3** **Oriental** native of the Orient

o·ri·en·ta′tion *n* **1** act of orienting or state of being oriented; **2** instruction

designed to make one adjusted to new surroundings or employment

or·i·fice /ôr′ifis, or′-/ [LL *orificium*] *n* small opening; vent

orig. 1 origin; **2** origin(al)

o·ri·ga·mi /ôr′igäm′ē/ [Jap] *n* **1** Japanese process of folding paper into decorative figures; **2** figure made by this process

or·i·gin /ôr′ijin, or′-/ [L *origo* (*-inis*) source] *n* **1** beginning of anything; source; birth; **2** parentage; **3** cause; **4** derivation ‖ SYN commencement, inception, occasion, root

o·rig·i·nal /ərij′inəl/ *adj* **1** of or pert. to the beginning or origin of something; **2** first in existence or order; **3** not copied; **4** able to create that which is new; **5** novel, new ‖ *n* **6** that from which anything is copied or translated; **7** original work; **8** person of original thought or action ‖ **o·rig′i·nal·ly** *adv* ‖ **o·rig′i·nal′i·ty** /-nal′-/ *n*

o·rig′i·nal sin′ *n* innate depravity, considered as man's heritage from Adam

o·rig′i·nate /*vt* **1** to bring into existence; invent; create ‖ *vi* **2** to begin to exist, start; **3** to start (at a given place), said of public transport ‖ **o·rig′i·na′·tor** *n*

O·ri·no·co /ôr′ənō′kō, ōr′-/ *n* river in Venezuela flowing into the Atlantic

o·ri·ole /ôr′ē·ōl′, ōr′-/ [OF *oriol* < L *aureolus* golden] *n* **1** any of a family (Oriolidae) of brightly colored birds of the Old World; **2** any of various American birds (family Icteridae), mostly yellow or orange and black

O·ri·on /ôrī′ən, ōr·-/ *n* **1** *Gk myth.* a mighty hunter beloved of Artemis, who accidentally killed him and placed him in the sky among the constellations; **2** constellation on the celestial equator, noted for its three bright stars in a line forming Orion's belt

or·i·son /ôr′tzən, or′-/ [OF < LL *oratio* (*-onis*)] *n* prayer

Or·lon /ôr′lon/ [trademark] *n* synthetic fiber resistant to wrinkling and weathering

or·mo·lu /ôr′məlōō′/ [F *or moulu* ground gold] *n* **1** imitation gold made of an alloy of copper and zinc; **2** brass finished to resemble gold; **3 a** gold powder formerly used in gilding; **b** metal gilded with this powder

or·na·ment /ôrn′əmənt/ [L *ornamentum*] *n* **1** anything that adorns or beautifies; **2** article or person that adds beauty, honor, or grace to the surroundings ‖ /-ment′/ *vt* **3** to furnish with ornaments; **4** to be an ornament to ‖ **or′na·men′tal** *adj* ‖ **or′na·men·ta′tion** *n*

or·nate /ôrnāt′/ [< L *ornare* (*-atus*) to adorn] *adj* excessively adorned or embellished

or·ner·y /ôrn′ərē/ [< *ordinary*] *adj colloq* mean-tempered; vile

or·ni·thol·o·gy /ôr′nithol′əjē/ [Gk *ornis*

(-*ithos*) bird + -*logy*] *n* branch of zoology dealing with birds ‖ **or'ni·thol'o·gist** *n* ‖ **or'ni·tho·log'i·cal** /-thǝloj'-/ *adj*

oro- [Gk *oros*] *comb form* mountain

o·ro·tund /ōr'ǝtund/, ōr'-/ [L *ore rotundo* with round mouth] *adj* **1** full, clear, rich (voice); **2** pompous, grandiloquent (speaking style)

or·phan /ôrf'ǝn/ [Gk *orphanos* bereaved] *n* **1** child who has lost a parent, or more commonly both parents, by death ‖ *vt* **2** to make an orphan of

or'phan·age /-ij/ *n* **1** institution for the care of orphans; **2** state of being without a parent

Or·pheus /ôr'fyoōs, -fē-ǝs/ *n Gk myth.* musician who played with such charm that he won the consent of Pluto for the return of his wife, Eurydice, from Hades, provided he did not look back at her until they returned to earth, but he did and thereby lost her

or'ris·root' /ôr'is-, or'is-/ [*orris* var of *iris* + *root*] *n* fragrant rootstock of the orris (*Iris florentina*), used in perfumery and cosmetics

or·th- or **or·tho-** [Gk *orthos*] *comb form* **1** straight; **2** correct

or'tho·chro·mat'ic /ôr'thǝ/ *adj* (photographic emulsion) sensitive to all colors except red

or'tho·don'tics /-dont'iks/ also **or'tho·don'tia** /-don'shǝ/ [*ortho-* + Gk *odous* (*odontos*) tooth] *nsg* branch of dentistry concerned with correcting or preventing irregular teeth ‖ **or'tho·don'tist** *n*

or·tho·dox /ôr'thǝdoks'/ [*ortho-* + Gk *doxa* opinion] *adj* **1** conventional; approved; **2** conforming to approved or traditional doctrine or practice; **3** Orthodox of or pert. to the Eastern Orthodox Church ‖ **or'tho·dox'y** *n*

Or'tho·dox' Church' *n* Eastern Orthodox Church

or·tho·e·py /ôr'thō·ep'ē, ôrthō'ǝpē/ [Gk *orthoepeia*] *n* art or study of correct pronunciation

or·thog·ra·phy /ôrthog'rǝfē/ [Gk *orthographia*] *n* (**-phies**) **1** correct spelling; **2** study of spelling; **3** any system of representing sounds by symbols ‖ **or·tho·graph·ic** /ôr'thǝgraf'ik/ *adj*

or·tho·pe·dics /ôr'thǝpēd'iks/ [< *ortho-* + Gk *pais* (*paidos*) child] *nsg* prevention or treatment of deformities, esp. in young children ‖ **or'tho·pe'dic** *adj* ‖ **or'tho·pe'dist** *n*

-o·ry /-ôr'ē, -ōr'ē, -ǝrē/ [L -*orius*] *n suf* **1** where, place for, as *dormitory, factory* ‖ *adj suf* **2** pert. to, tending to, characterized by, as *obligatory, illusory*

Os *chem* osmium

O·sa·ka /ōsäk'ǝ/ *n* city in S Japan (3,250,000)

Os·can /osk'ǝn/ *n* **1** one of an Italic people inhabiting ancient Italy S of Rome; **2** their language ‖ also *adj*

Os·car /osk'ǝr/ [< name] *n* one of a group of statuettes awarded annually by the Academy of Motion Picture Arts and Sciences for distinguished achievement in film-making and acting

os·cil·late /os'ilat'/ [L *oscillare* (-*atus*)] *vi* **1** to swing backward and forward, as the pendulum of a clock; vibrate; **2** to pass back and forth from one state to another; fluctuate ‖ *vt* **3** to cause to oscillate ‖ **os'cil·la'tion** *n* ‖ SYN vibrate, vacillate (see *shake, fluctuate*)

os'cil·la'tor *n* nonrotating device for producing audio-frequency or radio-frequency oscillations

os·cil'lo·gram' /ǝsil'ǝ-/ *n* recording made by an oscillograph

os·cil'lo·graph' *n* device for recording the wave forms of an electric quantity

os·cil'lo·scope' *n* device which shows visually the changes in a varying electric current, as on a cathode-ray tube or fluorescent screen

os·cu·late /osk'yǝlat'/ [L *osculari* (-*atus*)] *vt* & *vi* **1** to kiss; **2** *geom* to touch, as two curves, at three or more points ‖ **os'cu·la'tion** *n*

-ose¹ /-ōs', -ōs'/ [L -*osus*] *adj suf* like, full of, as *verbose*

-ose² [*glucose*] *n suf chem* carbohydrate or sugar, as *cellulose, maltose*

o·sier /ōzh'ǝr/ [ML *aussarium* willow bed] *n* **1** any of several willows, esp. *Salix viminalis* and *S. purpurea*, used for basketry and wickerwork; **2** twig from such a willow

O·si·ris /ōsīr'is/ *n* chief Egyptian god of the underworld, brother and husband of Isis and father of Horus

-o·sis /-ōs'is, -ǝsis/ [Gk] *n suf* condition, process, or state, as *cyanosis, metamorphosis*

-os·i·ty /-os'itē/ [L -*ositas*] *n suf* used to form nouns from adjectives in -*ose* and -*ous*, as *generosity*

Os·lo /oz'lō, os'-/ *n* capital of Norway (483,196)

os·mi·um /oz'mē·ǝm/ [< Gk *osme* smell] *n* hard, heavy, bluish-white metallic element (Os; at.no. 76; at.wt. 190.02) used chiefly in alloys and electric-light filaments

os·mo·sis /ozmōs'is, os-/ [< Gk *osmos* push] *n* diffusion, or tendency to diffuse, of fluids through a membrane so as to equalize the concentration on both sides

os·prey /osp'rē/ [MF *offraie*] *n* large hawk (*Pandion haliaetus*) that feeds on fish

os·se·ous /os'ē·ǝs/ [< L *os* bone] *adj* consisting of, like, or capable of forming bone; bony

os'si·fied' *adj* **1** hardened into bone; **2** *slang* drunk

os·si·fy /os'ifī/ [L *os* bone + -*fy*] *vt*
1 to change into bone or similar hard
substance ‖ *vi* 2 to become bone; 3
to become hardened and unyielding
in opinions or viewpoint ‖ **os'si·fi·
ca'tion** *n*

os·ten·si·ble /ostens'ibəl/ [< L *ostendere* (-*tensus*) to show] *adj* 1 professed; pretended; 2 apparent ‖ **os·
ten'si·bly** *adv* ‖ SYN seeming, apparent, evident (see *plausible*)

os·ten·ta·tion /ost'əntāsh'ən/ [< L *ostentare* (-*atus*) to show] *n* unnecessary show, vainglorious display ‖
SYN pomp, boast, flourish, pretentiousness, show

os·ten·ta'tious *adj* fond of show; pretentious; gaudy

os·te·o- [Gk *osteon*] *comb form* bone

os·te·op·a·thy /ost'ē·op'əthē/ *n* system
of therapy which is based on the
theory that structural derangement,
esp. of the spinal column, is the
chief cause of disease and which lays
stress on restoring health by manipulation ‖ **os'te·o·path'ic** /-əpath'ik/
adj ‖ **os'te·o·path'** *n*

ost'mark' /ôst'-, ost'-/ [G = east mark]
n monetary unit of East Germany

os·tra·cize /os'trəsīz'/ [< Gk *ostrakon*
tile used in voting] *vt* 1 in ancient
Greece, to banish by popular vote;
2 to bar from public or private favor,
as *he was ostracized by his friends*
‖ **os'tra·cism** *n*

os·trich /os'trich, ôs'-/ [OF *ostruce* <
LL *avis struthio*] *n* any of a genus
(*Struthio*) of two-toed, swiftly running, flightless birds of Africa, the
largest living birds

Os·tro·goth /os'trəgoth'/ [LL *Ostrogothus*] *n* member of the tribe of
East Goths who established a kingdom in Italy in the sixth century ‖
Os'tro·goth'ic *adj*

OT, OT., or **O.T.** Old Testament

O·thel·lo /ōthel'ō, əth-/ *n* in Shakespeare's *Othello*, a Moor in the service of Venice who killed his wife
Desdemona in a fit of jealousy

oth·er /uth'ər/ [OE *ōther*] *adj* 1 not the
same, different, as *other matters*; 2
additional, more, as *I have other
sisters*; 3 remaining, as *the other
men may leave*; 4 former, as *other
times*; 5 every other every second;
6 **the other day (night, week)** on a
day (night, week) recently passed ‖
adv 7 other than otherwise than ‖
pron 8 other person or thing; 9 different person or thing

oth'er·wise' [OE (*on*) *ōthre wīsan* (in)
another way] *adv* 1 differently; 2 in
another respect ‖ *adj* 3 different

oth'er world' *n* world after death;
world to come

oth'er·world'ly *adj* 1 not of this world;
2 abstracted; absent-minded; 3 concerned with the spirit or mind

o·ti·ose /ōsh'ē·ōs'/ [< L *otium* leisure]
adj 1 lazy, idle; at leisure; 2 having
no practical use

o·to- [< Gk *ous* (*otos*)] *comb form* ear

o·tol·o·gy /ōtol'əjē/ *n* science of the
ear and its diseases ‖ **o·tol'o·gist** *n*

Ot·ta·wa /ot'əwə/ *n* capital of Canada
(290,741)

ot·ter /ot'ər/ [OE *otor*] *n* (-ter or -ters)
any of several fish-eating mammals
(genus *Lutra*), related to the weasels,
valued for their brown fur

Ot·to·man /ot'əmən/ [F < Ar *'Othmän* founder of dynasty] *adj* 1 of or
pert. to the Ottoman Empire ‖ *n* 2
subject of the Ottoman Empire; 3
Turk; 4 **ottoman** low cushioned seat
or footstool

Ot'to·man Em'pire *n* Turkish empire
founded ab. 1300, which at its height
spread from the gates of Vienna to
Morocco, succeeded in 1919 by the
republic of Turkey

Oua·ga·dou·gou /wäg'ədōog'ŏŏ/ *n* capital of Upper Volta (60,000)

ouch /ouch'/ [?] *interj* exclamation signifying sudden pain

ought[1] /ôt'/ [OE *ahte pt* of *agan* to
owe] *modal aux* used to express:
obligation, fitness, necessity, duty, or
probability, as *I ought to go, this nail
ought to hold* ‖ SYN must, should
‖ DISCR Ought expresses the obligation of duty, moral necessity, or
rightness, as we *ought* to pay our
debts promptly; we *ought* to tell the
truth. *Should* also expresses the idea
of bounden duty or the constraint
of necessity, as you *should* love
your neighbor as yourself; but in
general it is both milder and weaker
than *ought*, and stresses advisability,
fitness, advantageousness, as you
should be more careful; you *should*
have more respect for your elders.
Ought also approaches the meaning
of advisability or strong probability;
we occasionally say, "the telegram
ought to reach him within three
hours," or "he *ought* to think before
he speaks." *Must* emphasizes compulsion, physical, moral, or logical,
as he *must* hang for first degree murder; he *must* take better care of himself; he *must* be mad to suggest such
a thing

ought[2] *n & adv* var of **aught**[1,2]

ought·n't /ôt'ənt/ ought not

oui /wē'/ [F] *adv* yes

Oui·ja (board') /wē'jə/ [F *out* + G *ja*
yes; trademark] *n* device consisting of
a flat board containing the alphabet
and other characters, and a movable
pointer, used, as at spiritualistic
séances, to spell out words in answer
to questions

ounce /ouns'/ [MF *unce* < L *uncia*] *n*
1 weight of 1/16 of a pound avoirdupois; 2 weight of 1/12 of a pound
troy; 3 fluid ounce; 4 small or insignificant quantity

our /ou'(ə)r, är'/ [OE *ūre*] *adj* possessive of **we;** of or belonging to us

ours /ou'(ə)rz, ärz'/ *pron* that or those belonging to us

our·self' *pron* myself (used by a person, as a sovereign or editor, who refers to himself as *we*)

our·selves' *pron* **1** reflexive form of **us; 2** our normal selves, as *we are not ourselves today;* **3** emphatic form of **us,** as *we did it ourselves*

-ous /-əs/ [OF < L *-osus*] *adj suf* **1** full of, of the nature of, like, as *poisonous, amorous;* **2** *chem* indicating that the element to whose name in full or shortened form it is attached has a lower valence in an acid than in the corresponding acid in which the suffix *-ic* is used; it corresponds to the suffix *-ite* of the name of a salt or ester

oust /oust'/ [OF *oster* to take away] *vt* to eject; turn out; dispossess || **SYN** dislodge, drive out, evict, eject, dismiss

oust'er *n* ejection; dispossession

out /out'/ [OE *ūt*] *adv* **1** outside; not within doors; **2** abroad; away; forth; as *to go out to Wyoming;* **3** *baseball* so as to count as an out, as *he struck out;* **4** to be done by others, as *she gives her wash out;* **5** so as to clear from obstruction or refuse, as *to sweep out a room;* **6** loudly, as *to speak out;* **7** to a conclusion or end, as *to burn out, fight it out;* **8** idle; on strike, as *the workers are out;* **9** disclosed, as *the secret is out;* **10** to depletion, as *drained out;* **11** into society, as *she comes out in the fall;* **12** extended, as *he stretched out his arms;* **13** into active existence, as *war broke out;* **14** from a stock, as *pick one out;* **15** completely, as *her form filled out;* **16** blotted, as *paint it out;* **17** all **out** *colloq* completely; **18 out** for trying to get, openly seeking; **19 out of,** a away from, as *out of town;* b from the inside of; c from a specified material, as *made out of wood;* d because of, as *out of the goodness of his heart* || *adj* **20** absent, away; **21** beyond regular limits; **22** in error; **23** out of pocket, losing, as *out ten dollars;* **24** unconscious; **25** *baseball* retired, as *out at first;* **26** no longer holding employment or office; **27** ended, as *before the year is out;* **28** extinguished; **29** not in fashion; **30 out of,** a beyond, as *out of reach;* b short of, as *out of sugar;* c on the outside of; d fooled by || *prep* **31** through (a window, a door); **32** along (a road) || *interj* **33** begone! || *n* **34** outer nook or corner; **35** excuse or justification; **36** *baseball* put-out; **37 outs** *pl* people out of political power; **38** on the **outs** not friendly || *vi* **39** to become public; **40** to utter, as *out with it!*

out- *pref* **1** more than, beyond, exceeding, as *outlast, outbid;* **2** outside, exterior, as *outhouse;* **3** out, away, as *outbound*

out'age *n* **1** temporary failure in the supply of electrical power; **2** shortage in a shipment of merchandise

out'-and-out' *adj* thorough-going, complete

out'back' *n Australian* back country, remote from the cities on the coast

out'bid' *v* (-**bid;** -**bid·den** or -**bid;** -**bid·ding**) *vt & vi* to exceed or go beyond in bidding

out'board' *adj* located on the outside surface or away from the center of a ship, boat, or aircraft

out'bound' *adj* outward bound

out'break' *n* sudden bursting forth, as of an epidemic or a revolt or riot

out'build'ing *n* structure apart from the main building, as a barn or shed

out'burst' *n* outbreak, as of sentiment or passion

out'cast' *n* one who is cast out or rejected, esp. socially

out'class' *vt* to surpass in class or quality

out'come' *n* result or consequence || **SYN** issue, upshot, consequence, effect

out'crop' *n geol* coming of a stratum to the surface of the ground

out'cry' *n* (-**cries**) clamor; uproar; loud protest || **SYN** noise, hubbub, uproar, clamor, tumult

out'dat'ed *adj* out-of-date

out'dis'tance *vt* to outstrip; excel in speed

out'do' *v* (-**did;** -**done**) *vt* to surpass, excel

out'door' *adj* in the open air

out'doors' *adv* **1** out of doors || *adj* **2** outdoor || *n* **the outdoors** *sg* the world outside of buildings

out'doors'man /-mən/ *n* (-**men** /-mən/) one who lives outdoors or likes outdoor life and activities

out'er *adj* **1** farther out; **2** external

Out'er Mon·go'li·a *n* Mongolian People's Republic

out'er·most' *adj* farthest out

out'er space' *n* space beyond the earth's atmosphere

out'face' *vt* to stare (one) out of countenance; defy

out'field' *n baseball* **1** space outside and beyond the base lines; **2** outfielders collectively

out'field'er *n baseball* player stationed in the outfield

out'fit' *n* **1** all the articles necessary for any undertaking; **2** complete costume; **3** *colloq* any group associated together || *v* (-**fit·ted;** -**fit·ting**) *vt* **4** to furnish with an outfit || **out'-fit'ter** *n*

out'flank' *vt* **1** to go around the flank of; **2** to bypass; outmaneuver

out'fox' *vt* to outsmart

out'go' *n* (-**goes**) **1** that which goes out; **2** expenditure, disbursement

out·go'ing *adj* 1 departing; 2 friendly; responsive

out'grow' *vt* 1 to excel in growing; 2 to grow away from, as a habit; 3 to become too big for, as clothes

out'growth' *n* anything that grows out of or proceeds from anything else; offshoot; result

out'guess' *vt* to anticipate correctly the intensions or the behavior of

out'house' *n* (**-hous·es** /-ziz/) privy

out'ing *n* short excursion or pleasure trip

out·land'ish *adj* 1 strange, unfamiliar; bizarre; 2 foreign-looking

out'last' *vt* 1 to last longer than; 2 to outlive

out'law' [OE *ūtlaga* < Scand] *n* 1 criminal sought by the police || *vt* 2 to declare to be an outlaw; 3 to make illegal

out'lay' *n* expenditure, disbursement

out'let /-let, -lit/ *n* 1 exit; vent; 2 receptacle for plugging a device into an electric circuit; 3 market for goods; 4 store selling a particular product; 5 means of self-expression; 6 local radio or television station of a network

out'line' *n* 1 line that shows the outer limits or shape of a figure; 2 sketch that shows the shape of a figure without light and shade; 3 first draft or sketch; 4 **outlines** *pl* main principles; chief features || *vt* 5 to draw or give an outline of

out'live' *vt* 1 to live longer than; survive; 2 to last longer than

out'look' *n* 1 view from a place; 2 future prospect; 3 mental viewpoint; 4 lookout; watchtower

out'ly'ing *adj* apart from the main body; remote; lying beyond the limits

out·ma·neu'ver *vt* to defeat by more clever maneuvering

out'mod'ed *adj* 1 out of style; 2 obsolete

out'most' *adj* outermost

out'num'ber *vt* to exceed in number

out' of bounds' *adv* beyond the established limits || **out'-of-bounds'** *adj*

out'-of-date' *adj* no longer current; outmoded

out' of doors' *adv* outside; in the open || **out'-of-door(s)'** *adj*

out'-of-pock'et *adj* paid out in cash, as expenses

out' of print' *adj* 1 no longer published; 2 (book) not now available; sold-out

out'-of-the-way' *adj* 1 remote; difficult to find or reach; 2 deviating from the usual form or manner; irregular; 3 questionable; improper

out·pa'tient *n* ambulatory patient receiving treatment in a hospital but not remaining there

out'post' *n* 1 soldier or body of troops stationed in advance of the main army; 2 position so occupied

out'pour'ing *n* outflow or effusion

out'put' *n* 1 quantity produced; yield; 2 quantity produced in a given time; 3 power delivered by a machine or an electric circuit

out'rage [OF] *n* 1 gross insult or injury; 2 immoral or unlawful violence || *vt* 3 to abuse violently; injure grievously; 4 to offend grossly; 5 to rape || SYN *n* abuse, violence, affront, insult, indignity

out·ra'geous /-rāj'əs/ *adj* 1 violent; atrocious; 2 without regard for decency, shocking; 3 uncalled-for, as *outrageous prices* || **out·ra'geous·ly** *adv* || SYN abominable, infamous, atrocious (see *heinous*)

out'rank' *vt* to exceed in rank

out'rid'er *n* mounted attendant who rides in advance of or beside a carriage

out'rig'ger *n* framework projecting at the side of a boat to keep it from capsizing

out'right' *adv* 1 altogether, completely; 2 instantly, at once; 3 straightforwardly || *adj* 4 downright; 5 total, complete

out'run' *v* (**-ran**; **-run**; **-run·ning**) *vt* 1 to run faster or farther than; 2 to escape from, as by running

out'set' *n* start, beginning

out'shine' *v* (**-shone**) *vt* 1 to be brighter than; 2 to surpass

out'side' *n* 1 outer side, part, or surface; 2 external appearance; 3 **at the outside** at the maximum; 4 **on the outside** in the world beyond the walls of a prison || *adj* 5 outer; 6 coming from without; 7 done outside of class; 8 remote, barely possible (chance); 9 *colloq* maximum (price; estimate) || /out'sīd', out'sīd'/ *adv* 10 on or to the outside; 11 outdoors; 12 externally; 13 **outside of**, a beyond the limits of; b *colloq* excepting || *prep* 14 on or toward the outside of; 15 beyond the limits of; 16 *colloq* outside of, excepting

out'sid'er *n* 1 one who does not belong to a given party, set, company, or family; 2 uninvited guest

out'size' *n* 1 uncommon size, esp. if larger than usual; 2 garment of such size || *adj* also **out'sized'** 3 being of an outsize

out'skirts' *npl* outlying sections of a city

out'smart' *vt* to outwit

out'spo'ken *adj* candid, frank; unreserved in speech

out'spread' *adj* spread out; stretched out

out'stand'ing *adj* 1 standing out, prominent, conspicuous; 2 unpaid

out'stretched' *adj* stretched out, extended

out'strip' *v* (**-stripped**; **-strip·ping**) *vt* 1 to outdo; 2 to go faster than

out'ward /-wərd/ [OE *ūtweard*] *adj* 1 external, outer; visible; 2 proceeding or directed out or away; 3 super-

ficial ‖ adv also **out′wards** 4 away
from an inner place; toward the
outside; 5 externally; apparently ‖
out′ward·ly adv

out′weigh′ vt 1 to weigh more than; 2
to surpass in value or importance

out′wit′ v (-wit·ted; -wit·ting) vt to
get the better of by superior cunning
or cleverness ‖ SYN overreach, foil,
baffle, circumvent, thwart

out′worn′ 1 worn out; 2 obsolete, out-
of-date

ou·zo /ōōz′ō/ [ModGk] n anise-fla-
vored Greek liqueur

o·va /ōv′ə/ pl of ovum

o·val /ōv′əl/ [< ovum] adj 1 elliptical; 2 egg-shaped ‖ n 3 anything
oval-shaped

O′val Of′fice n the President's private
office in the White House

o·va·ry /ōv′ərē/ [NL ovarium < ovum]
n (-ries) 1 organ in the female animal in which the ova are formed;
2 bot lower part of the pistil in which
the seeds form ‖ **o·var·i·an** /ōver′-
ē·ən/ adj

o·vate /ōv′āt/ [< ovum] adj 1 oval;
2 bot (leaf) having the base broader
than the apex

o·va·tion /ōvāsh′ən/ [L ovatio (-onis)]
n 1 tumultuous demonstration of
public esteem; 2 Rom hist lesser
triumph celebrating a minor victory

ov·en /uv′ən/ [OE ofen] n heated
chamber, as in a stove, for baking,
roasting, drying, heating, etc.

o·ver /ōv′ər/ [OE ofer] prep 1 above
in position, authority, dignity, excellence, or value; 2 across, to the
other side of; 3 covering, upon, as
a cape over the shoulders; 4 more
than; 5 during, throughout, as over
the weekend; 6 back and forth upon,
as to wander over the plains; 7 concerning, in regard to; 8 upon, affecting, as what came over him? 9 all
through, as let's go over this again;
10 across, as over the sea; 11 reaching higher than, as over his head;
12 in preference to; 13 by means of,
as over the radio; 14 **over and
above** in addition to ‖ adv 15 from
beginning to end, as talk the matter
over; 16 from one to another, as
hand it over; 17 from one side to
the other, as to go over to the enemy;
18 in excess, in addition; 19 so as
to bring the opposite side up, as turn
the card over; 20 so as to be no
longer upright, as to topple over; 21
once again; 22 across or above; 23
covering the whole surface, as
painted over; 24 to a place, as come
on over; 25 all over everywhere;
26 **over again** once more ‖ adj 27
upper; higher; superior; 28 excessive; 29 finished, done; 30 outer
(covering or garment); 31 extra,
surplus

o·ver- pref expressing: 1 excess, as
overconfident; 2 outer or upper position, as overcoat, overlord; 3
motion from one side to the other,
from edge to edge, across the brim,
etc., as overstep, overlap; 4 motion
passing beyond, as overflow, over-
shoot; 5 completeness, as overawe,
overjoyed

o′ver·act′ vt & vi to act with exaggeration

o′ver·age′¹ /-āj′/ adj over the required age

o′ver·age² /-ij/ n excess

o′ver·all′ adv & adj 1 from end to end;
2 including everything ‖ n 3 o′ver-
alls′ pl loose trousers, usu. with a
bib attached, worn over other clothes
to protect them

o′ver·awe′ vt to intimidate by inspiring
awe

o′ver·bal′ance vt 1 to upset the balance
of; 2 to outweigh

o′ver·bear′ing adj arrogantly domineering

o′ver·blown′ adj 1 excessive; 2 over-
inflated; 3 bombastic

o′ver·board′ adv 1 over the side of a
ship; 2 **go overboard** to go to extremes, as in opinion or interest

o′ver·cast′ adj 1 covered almost entirely with clouds ‖ n 2 condition of
heavy clouds in the sky

o′ver·charge′ vt 1 to charge too much;
2 to overload ‖ **o′ver·charge′** n 3
excessive charge or load

o′ver·coat′ n coat worn for warmth
over the regular clothing

o′ver·come′ v (-came; -come) vt 1 to
defeat; prevail over ‖ vi 2 to be
victorious

o′ver·com′pen·sate′ vi to conceal an
undesirable character trait by emphasizing an opposite one ‖ o′ver-
com′pen·sa′tion n

o′ver·do′ v (-did; -done) vt 1 to do or
carry to excess ‖ vi 2 to go beyond
one's strength

o′ver·done′ adj cooked too much

o′ver·dose′ n 1 dose in excess of the
prescribed amount ‖ o′ver·dose′ vt
2 to administer too large a dose to

o′ver·draft′ n 1 act of overdrawing an
account; 2 overdrawn check; 3
amount overdrawn

o′ver·draw′ v (-drew; -drawn) vt 1 to
make checks upon (an account) for
a greater amount than is on deposit;
2 to exaggerate

o′ver·dress′ vt to dress to excess

o′ver·drive′ n auto device that automatically reduces the ratio of the
crankshaft speed to the drive-shaft
speed

o′ver·due′ adj 1 past due; 2 too long
awaited

o′ver·flight′ n air flight high over an
area

o′ver·flow′ vi 1 to flow or run over;
2 to be abundant ‖ vt 3 to flood; 4
to flow over the banks or edges of

‖ **o'ver·flow'** *n* **5** an overflowing; **6** that which overflows; **7** superabundance; **8** people excluded by crowding, as *the overflow from the art gallery went to the museum;* **9** outlet for excess liquid

o'ver·fly' *v* (-flew; -flown) *vt* **1** to fly high over; **2** to fly farther than

o'ver·grown' *adj* **1** grown too large; **2** grown over, as with weeds ‖ **o'ver·growth'** *n*

o'ver·hand' *adj* **1** done with the hand raised above the shoulder ‖ *adv* **2** done in an overhand manner

o'ver·hang' *v* (-hung) *vt* **1** to hang over; **2** to project beyond and above; **3** to menace ‖ *vi* **4** to jut or project over something; hang over ‖ **o'ver·hang'** *n* **5** projection or jutting out; amount of overhang

o'ver·haul' *vt* **1** to make complete repairs on; recondition; **2** to overtake ‖ **o'ver·haul'** *n* **3** thorough repair or reconditioning

o'ver·head' *adv* **1** over one's head; above; up in the air ‖ **o'ver·head'** *adj* **2** situated or passing above or over the head ‖ *n* **3** fixed expenses of a business, not directly connected with the cost of the product, as rent, interest, heat, etc.

o'ver·hear' *v* (-heard) *vt* to hear (a person or thing) without the speaker's knowledge or intention

o'ver·heat' *vt* to heat to excess

o'ver·joyed' *adj* transported with joy

o'ver·kill' *n* **1** nuclear capacity to destroy more of an enemy than necessary for victory; **2** excess of zeal ‖ **o'ver·kill'** *vt* **3** to attack and destroy with more nuclear force than necessary ‖ also *vi*

o'ver·land' /-land', lənd/ *adj* & *adv* by, across, or over land

o'ver·lap' *v* (-lapped; -lap·ping) *vt* **1** to extend over the edge of; lap over; **2** to coincide with ‖ *vi* **3** to lap over ‖ **o'ver·lap'** **4** act or instance of overlapping; **5** amount of overlapping; **6** part that overlaps

o'ver·lay' *v* (-laid) *vt* **1** to lay or place over; **2** to cover, as with a layer ‖ **o'ver·lay'** *n* **3** something laid or applied over something else

o'ver·leaf' *adv* on the other side of the page

o'ver·load' *vt* to load to excess

o'ver·look' *vt* **1** to look down upon from above; **2** to fail to notice; **3** to excuse ‖ **o'ver·look'** *n* **4** high place that affords a view

o'ver·lord' *n* **1** one who is lord over other lords or people; **2** powerful, influential person

o'ver·ly *adv* excessively

o'ver·much' *adj, adv,* & *n* too much

o'ver·night' *adv* **1** for or during the night or the previous night; **2** almost instantly, as *she became famous overnight* ‖ **o'ver·night'** *adj* **3** done,

occurring for the duration of the night; **4** staying all night; **5** valid for one night; **6** occurring almost instantly

o'ver·pass' *n* bridge carrying a railroad or highway over another

o'ver·pay'ment *n* **1** payment of more than is due; **2** amount of overpayment

o'ver·play' *vt* **1** to overemphasize or exaggerate; **2 overplay one's hand** to outsmart oneself

o'ver·pow'er *vt* **1** to subdue by superior force; **2** to affect greatly ‖ **o'ver·pow'er·ing** *adj*

o'ver·pro·duc'tion *n* creation of supply in excess of needs and demand

o'ver·rate' *vt* to rate too highly

o'ver·reach' *vt* **1** to reach above or beyond; **2** to get the better of by trickery; cheat; **3 overreach oneself** to fail of success by attempting too much ‖ syn deceive, baffle, outwit, circumvent, gull, dupe

o'ver·ride' *v* (-rode; -rid·den) *vt* **1** to trample down; **2** to set aside or disregard; **3** to prevail over ‖ **o'ver·ride'** *n* **4** commission paid to a sales manager on the total sales in his district; **5** *mach* manual device for bypassing automatic operation

o'ver·rid'ing *adj* that takes precedence over everything else

o'ver·rule' *vt* to rule or decide against

o'ver·run' *v* (-ran; -run·ning) *vt* **1** to grow or spread over in great quantity or numbers; **2** to invade; infest; **3** to defeat decisively; **4** to run beyond; **5** to overflow

o'ver·seas' *adv* **1** across the sea; abroad ‖ *adj* **2** across the sea; **3** pert. to countries across the sea

o'ver·see' *v* (-saw; -seen) *vt* to direct, supervise ‖ **o'ver·se'er** /-sē'ər, -sir'/ *n*

o'ver·sexed' *adj* exhibiting excessive sexual desire or need

o'ver·shad'ow *vt* **1** to throw a shadow over; darken; **2** to tower over; render less conspicuous

o'ver·shoe' *n* outer shoe, as of rubber, worn over another shoe for protection against wet or cold

o'ver·shoot' *v* (-shot) *vt* **1** to send or shoot over or beyond; **2** to go beyond ‖ *vi* **3** to shoot beyond the mark; **4** to go too far

o'ver·shot' *adj* **1** having the upper jaw protruding over the lower; **2** (water wheel) operated by water flowing over the top

o'ver·sight' *n* **1** failure to see or notice; **2** error or omission due to inattention; **3** watchful care; management, direction ‖ syn superintendence, surveillance, charge, supervision, direction

o'ver·size' *adj* also **o'ver·sized'** **1** of excessive size; **2** too large ‖ *n* **3** size larger than usual

o'ver·sleep' v (-slept) vt to sleep beyond the proper time for waking

o'ver·spread' v (-spread) vt to spread or cover over

o'ver·state' vt to express too forcefully; exaggerate || o'ver·state'ment n

o'ver·step' v (-stepped; -step·ping) vt to go beyond

o'ver·strung' adj excessively nervous, jittery

o'ver·stuffed' adj (furniture) with the entire frame covered with stuffing and upholstery

o'ver·sub·scribe' vt to subscribe for in excess of what is available

o·vert /ōv'ərt, ōvurt'/ [OF = opened] adj open to view; publicly seen or known || o·vert'ly adv

o·ver·take' v (-took; -tak·en) vt 1 to catch up with; 2 to come suddenly upon

o'ver·tax' vt to make too great demands on

o'ver-the-coun'ter adj 1 (transaction) not effected on an organized securities exchange; 2 (stocks and bonds) traded independently of an organized securities exchange; 3 (drugs) legally obtainable without a prescription

o'ver·throw' v (-threw; -thrown) vt 1 to defeat; turn out of power || o'ver·throw' n 2 ruin, defeat; deposition from power

o'ver·time' n 1 time beyond the stipulated hours of work or of certain games; 2 pay for work done in overtime || also adv

o'ver·tone' n 1 mus accompanying tone that is higher in frequency than the fundamental; 2 often pl implied connotation

o'ver·trick' n bridge trick taken by the declarer in excess of his contract

o'ver·trump' vt to take with a higher trump than one already played || also vi

o'ver·ture' /-choor', -chər/ [OF = opening] n 1 opening offer or proposal; 2 mus a music played as an introduction to an opera; b independent orchestral composition of similar nature

o'ver·turn' vt 1 to conquer, overthrow; 2 to turn over, upset || vi 3 to turn over, capsize || o'ver·turn' n 4 act of overturning or state of being overturned

o'ver·ween'ing adj 1 conceited, arrogant; too self-confident; 2 excessive, immoderate, exaggerated || SYN conceited, presumptuous, prideful

o'ver·weight' n 1 excess weight beyond the legal or usual amount; 2 preponderance || adj 3 weighing too much

o'ver·whelm' /-w(h)elm'/ [ME overwhelmen] vt 1 to overpower; overcome completely; 2 to cover over completely || o'ver·whelm'ing adj

o'ver·work' vi 1 to work too hard || vt 2 to cause to work too hard; 3 to overdo || o'ver·work' n 4 excessive work

o'ver·wrought' adj 1 excessively excited, overstrained; 2 elaborated to excess

o·vi- also ov- [< ovum] comb form egg

Ov·id /ov'id/ n (43 B.C.–17 A.D.) Roman poet

o·vi·duct /ōv'idukt'/ n one of the two tubes through which the matured ova pass from the ovary to the uterus or the egg sac

o'vi·form' adj egg-shaped

o·vip·a·rous /ōvip'ərəs/ [< ovi- + L parere to beget] adj producing offspring from eggs which hatch outside the body

o·vi·pos·i·tor /ōv'ipoz'itər/ n organ for depositing eggs, found at the extremity of the abdomen of many female insects

o'void adj egg-shaped

o·vu·late /ōv'yəlāt'/ vi to produce eggs or to discharge them from the ovary

o·vule /ōv'yōōl/ [L ovulum little egg] n spore case of a seed plant in which the egg and surrounding structures develop which form the seed

o·vum /ōv'əm/ [L = egg] n (o·va /-və/) female reproductive cell

owe /ō'/ [OE āgan to possess] vt 1 to be obliged to pay; 2 to be obliged or indebted for; 3 to be in debt to || vi 4 to be in debt

ow'ing adj 1 due; 2 owing to on account of; ascribable to

owl /ou'(ə)l/ [OE ūle] n 1 any of numerous nocturnal birds of prey (order Strigiformes) with large heads and eyes and short hooked beaks; 2 person who keeps late hours || owl'ish adj

owl'et /-it/ n young or small owl

own /ōn'/ [OE āgen] adj & pron (preceded by a possessive) 1 belonging to oneself or itself; 2 peculiar or private, no one else's, as my own affair; 3 hold one's own to maintain one's position or condition; 4 on one's own colloq independently, by one's own efforts || vt 5 to possess; 6 to admit or acknowledge, as a fault || vi 7 own up to confess || own'er n || own'er·ship' n

ox /oks'/ [OE oxa] n (ox·en /oks'ən/) 1 any bovine animal (genus Bos), including cattle; 2 castrated bull || n (ox·es) 3 clumsy oaf

ox·al'ic ac'id /oksal'ik/ [F oxalique] n violently poisonous crystalline substance —HOOCCOOH·2H₂O— found in many plants and used principally for cleaning and bleaching

ox'blood n deep dull red

ox'bow' /-bō'/ n 1 U-shaped piece of wood in an ox yoke; 2 U-shaped or S-shaped bend in a river

Ox'bridge' n 1 Oxford or Cambridge University or both combined; 2 British intellectual life as exemplified at these universities ‖ also *adj*

ox·en /oks'ən/ *pl* of ox

ox·ford /oks'fərd/ [*Oxford*, England] *n* low shoe laced over the instep

Ox·ford *n* city in S England (110,000), seat of the famous university founded in the 12th century

Ox'ford gray' *n* dark gray

ox·i·da·tion /oks'idāsh'ən/ *n* act of oxidizing or state of being oxidized

ox·ide /oks'īd/ [F < *oxygène* + *acide*] *n* compound of oxygen with another element or a radical

ox'i·dize' /-id-/ *vt* **1** to cause to combine with oxygen; convert into an oxide; **2** to rust ‖ *vi* **3** to become oxidized

ox'i·diz'er *n* propellant component, such as air, liqnid oxygen, nitric acid, and fluorine, which supports combustion when combined with a fuel

Oxon. Oxonian

Ox·o·ni·an /oksōn'ē·ən/ [< L *Oxonia* Oxford] *adj* **1** of or pert. to Oxford or Oxford University ‖ *n* **2** student or graduate of Oxford University

ox'tail' *n* skinned tail of a steer, used in soups and stews

ox·y- /oks'i-/ [Gk *oxys*] *comb form* **1** sharp; pointed; **2** acid

ox'y·a·cet'y·lene' torch' *n* blowpipe burning a mixture of oxygen and acetylene, used for cutting steel

ox'y·gen /-jən/ *n* colorless, odorless, gaseous element (O; at.no. 8; at.wt. 15.9994), constituting one fifth of the volume of the atmosphere and widely found in nature in combination; it supports combustion and combines readily with most of the elements to form oxides, and is essential to all life

ox'y·gen·ate' also **ox'y·gen·ize'** *vt* to combine or impregnate with oxygen ‖ ox'y·gen·a'tion *n*

ox'y·gen mask' *n* mask with tube attached for inhaling oxygen

ox'y·gen tent' *n* enclosed canopy placed over a patient in bed to supply pure oxygen for the purpose of facilitating breathing

ox'y·mo'ron *n* (-ra /-rə/) *n* figure of speech combining incongruous or contradictory ideas, as *studied carelessness* or *make haste slowly*

ox'y·tone' *n* word stressed on the final syllable ‖ also *adj*

o'yer and ter'mi·ner /ō'yər, oi'ər, turm'inər/ [AF = to hear and settle] *n* in some states, any of various higher criminal courts

o·yez /ō'yes, -yez/ [AF] *interj* attention! (used in court to command attention)

oys·ter /oist'ər/ [MF *oistre* < Gk *ostreon*] *n* any of a family (Ostreidae) of edible sea mollusks having two unequal hinged shells

oys'ter bed' *n* place where oysters breed or are bred

oys'ter crack'er *n* small rounded cracker served with soups or oysters

oys'ter fork' *n* small three-pronged fork used for eating raw oysters, shrimp cocktails, etc.

oz. ounce(s)

O'zark Moun'tains /ō'zärk/ also **the O'zarks** *npl* group of low mountains in S Missouri and N Arkansas

o·zone /ō'zōn/ [F < Gk *ozein* to smell] *n* **1** form of oxygen, O₃, having marked oxidizing properties, produced by the discharge of electricity through air or oxygen, chiefly used in bleaching and in purifying water; **2** *colloq* pure fresh air

P

P, p /pē'/ *n* (P's or Ps; p's or ps) **1** 16th letter of the English alphabet; **2** mind one's p's and q's to be careful in what one does

p [It *piano*] *mus* softly

P 1 16th in order or in a series; **2** something shaped like a P; **3** *chem* phosphorus; **4** *chess* pawn

p. 1 page; **2** participle; **3** past; **4** per; **5** *baseball* pitcher

pa /pä', pô'/ *n colloq* papa, father

Pa *chem* protactinium

Pa. Pennsylvania

PA public-address system

PA, P.A. press agent

pab·u·lum /pab'yələm/ [L] *n* food, for nourishment or thought

pa·ca /päk'ə, pak'ə/ [Sp & Port <

Tupi] *n* large South American rodent (*Cuniculus paca*) resembling the guinea pig

pace /pās'/ [OF *pas* < L *passus* step] *n* **1** step; **2** space covered by a step in walking; **3** gait, manner of stepping; **4** gait of a horse in which the legs on the same side move simultaneously in the same direction; **5** rate of speed, activity, or progress; **6** put one through his paces to test one's skills or abilities; **7** set the pace to set the example for others to emulate ‖ *vt* **8** to measure by paces; **9** to walk back and forth over; **10** to set the pace for ‖ *vi* **11** to walk with regular steps; **12** to move at a pace (said of horses)

pace′mak′er *n* 1 one who sets the pace; 2 device implanted under the skin to stimulate and regulate the heart muscle

pac′er *n* horse trained to pace in harness racing

pach·y·derm /pak′idurm′/ [< Gk *pachys* thick + *derma* skin] *n* 1 any of various thick-skinned mammals such as the elephant and hippopotamus; 2 elephant; 3 thick-skinned person

pach′y·san′dra /-san′drə/ [< Gk *pachys* thick + *andros* stamens] *n* plant (*Pachysandra*) much used as a ground cover, as on lawns

pa·cif·ic /pəsif′ik/ [L *pacificus*] *adj* 1 peacemaking, conciliatory; 2 peaceful, tranquil || *n* 3 **the Pacific** the Pacific Ocean || SYN *adj* calm, gentle, still, tranquil, smooth, peaceable || ANT *adj* stormy, belligerent, quarrelsome, contentious

Pa·cif′ic O′cean *n* the largest ocean, stretching westward from the Americas to Asia and Australia

pac·i·fi·er /pas′ifī′ər/ *n* 1 one who or that which pacifies; 2 rubber nipple given to babies to suck in order to quiet them

pac·i·fist /pas′ifist/ *n* one who on principle opposes war as wrong || **pac′i·fism** *n*

pac′i·fy′ *v* (-fied) *vt* 1 to calm or appease; 2 to bring or restore to peace || **pac′i·fi·ca′tion** *n* || SYN soothe, compose, tranquilize, placate, propitiate, allay || ANT excite, disturb, irritate, agitate, provoke

pack /pak′/ [ME *packe* < LG] *n* 1 bundle tied up for carrying; 2 collection or quantity, as *a pack of lies*; 3 standard number of things in a package, as *a pack of matches*; 4 number of animals associated together for hunting; 5 group of people or things classed together, as *a pack of thieves*; 6 number of floating cakes of ice driven close together; 7 therapeutic measure in which the patient is wrapped in hot or cold wet cloths || *vt* 8 to stow away, arrange compactly, or press into a bundle; 9 to fill (a receptacle) entirely; 10 to package for marketing; 11 to cram or crowd; 12 to press into a compact mass; 13 to load, as with packs; 14 to fill tightly with waterproof or gasproof material, as the joints in a pipe; 15 to arrange to suit one's own ends, as *to pack a jury*; 16 to carry or wear, as *to pack a gun*; 17 **pack off** to send away, dismiss || *vi* 18 to press together into a compact mass; 19 to stow things for safety or carrying; 20 to put one's clothes and personal items into luggage; 21 to crowd together || SYN *n* set, band, gang, drove; burden, load (see *herd*)

pack′age /-ij/ *n* 1 something packed, wrapped, or boxed; parcel; 2 group of related things that come as a unit || *vt* 3 to put into a package or packages || SYN parcel, packet (see *bundle*)

pack′age deal′ *n* deal involving an entire group of related products or services

pack′age store′ *n* store selling liquor for consumption off the premises

pack′ an′i·mal *n* animal used for carrying loads

pack′er *n* one whose business or occupation is packing foods

pack′et /-it/ [MF *pacquet*] *n* 1 small bundle or package; 2 ship carrying passengers, mails, and merchandise on a regular route

pack′horse′ *n* horse used for carrying loads

pack′ing *n* 1 act of one that packs; 2 materials used to cushion packed goods; 3 material used to fill small spaces to prevent leaking, as between a piston rod and a stuffing box

pack′ rat′ *n* large North American rodent (*Neotoma cinerea*) noted for hoarding small articles in its nest

pack′sad′dle *n* saddle for carrying the load on a pack animal

pack′train′ *n* line of pack animals

pact /pakt′/ [L *pactum*] *n* compact or agreement

pad¹ /pad′/ [D = path] *n* 1 dull sound, as of footsteps || *v* (**pad·ded; pad·ding**) *vi* 2 to walk making a dull sound with the feet

pad² [?] *n* 1 soft cushionlike material used to fill a hollow space, lessen pressure or friction, protect from blows, etc.; 2 cushionlike part of anything, as the under part of the toes of some animals; 3 block of sheets of paper; 4 floating leaf of the water lily; 5 platform from which a rocket is launched; launching pad; 6 *slang* one's home || *v* (**pad·ded; pad·ding**) *vt* 7 to stuff or line with pad·ding; 8 to increase in size by adding unnecessary material, as *to pad a story*; 9 to add fraudulent items to (an expense account)

pad′ded cell′ *n* room in a mental hospital with walls padded to prevent inmates from harming themselves

pad′ding *n* 1 material used to pad something; 2 unnecessary matter added to speech or writing

pad·dle /pad′əl/ [ME *paddel*] *n* 1 short oar with a broad blade at one or both ends, used without a rowlock; 2 similar instrument used for stirring, mixing, or spanking || *vt* 3 to propel with a paddle, as a canoe; 4 to spank, as with a paddle || also *vi*

pad′dle wheel′ *n* large wheel for propelling a steamboat, having paddles arranged radially around its rim

pad·dock /pad′ək/ [OE *pearroc* enclosure] *n* 1 small field for pasture;

2 enclosure at a race track where horses are saddled and mounted; **3** *Australian* extensive pasture land, often fenced in

pad·dy /pad′ē/ [Malay *pādī*] *n* (**-dies**) **1** rice in the husk; **2** rice field

pad′dy wag′on [prob Eng slang *Paddy* policeman] *n slang* patrol wagon

pad′lock′ [ME *padlok*] *n* **1** portable lock with a jointed link to pass through a staple or ring ‖ *vt* **2** to fasten with a padlock; **3** to lock up; close

pa·dre /pä′drē/ [Sp, Port, & It] *n* **1** father; priest; **2** military chaplain

pae·an /pē′ən/ [L < Gk *paian* Apollo] *n* loud and joyous song of praise or triumph

paed-, paedo- var of ped-², pedo-

pa·el·la /pə·el′ə, -ā′yə/ [Sp < Cat] *n* Spanish dish of chicken and rice, with vegetables, seasoning, and often meat and shellfish

pa·gan /pāg′ən/ [L *paganus* peasant] *n* **1** heathen; **2** idolater or worshiper of many gods; **3** one who is not a Christian, Jew, or Muslim; **4** one who has no religious beliefs ‖ also *adj* ‖ **pa′·gan·ism** *n*

page¹ /pāj′/ [OF < It *paggio*] *n* **1** in the Middle Ages, boy training for knighthood by attending on a person of rank; **2** boy servant; **3** uniformed attendant acting as an usher, messenger, and errand boy; **4** one employed to carry messages and run errands for the members of a legislative body ‖ *vt* **5** to summon (a person) by calling out his name in a public place

page² [MF < L *pagina*] *n* **1** one side of a leaf, as of a book; **2** the entire leaf; **3** historical event or period ‖ *vi* **4** page through to leaf through ‖ *vt* **5** to mark or number in pages

pag·eant /paj′ənt, pāj′-/ [ME *pagent, pagen* < L *pagina* page] *n* **1** brilliant or stately display or procession, with a series of scenes acted in costume, often celebrating some historical event; **2** empty show; mere display ‖ SYN spectacle, sight, exhibition, show, parade

pag′eant·ry *n* (**-ries**) **1** splendid display; pomp; **2** unsubstantial show

page′boy′ *n* **1** page¹ **3**; **2** hair style in which the hair is rolled under at shoulder length

page′ proof′ *n* proof from type that has been arranged in a page or pages

pag·i·nate /paj′ināt′/ [< L *pagina* page] *vt* to number the pages of ‖ **pag′i·na′tion** *n*

pa·go·da /pəgōd′ə/ [Port *pagode* < Pers *but* idol + *kadah* dwelling] *n* Oriental temple built like a pyramidal tower with many stories

paid /pād′/ **1** *pt* & *pp* of **pay** ‖ *adj* **2** receiving pay, as *a paid assistant*

pail /pāl′/ [OE *pægel* wine vessel < ML *pagella*] *n* container, cylindrical or nearly so, with a hooped handle for carrying liquids; bucket

pail′ful′ *n* as much as a pail will hold

pain /pān′/ [OF *peine* < Gk *poine* penalty] *n* **1** distress or suffering of body or mind; **2** pains *pl* a diligent effort; **b** sufferings borne in childbirth; **3** on, upon, or under pain of subject to the penalty of ‖ *vt* **4** to cause physical pain to; hurt; **5** to cause mental suffering to; grieve ‖ *vi* **6** to cause pain ‖ **pain′less** *adj* ‖ SYN *n* suffering, agony, anguish, pang, ache, affliction ‖ ANT *n* comfort, relief, pleasure, ease

pain′ful *adj* **1** full of or causing pain; **2** distressing; difficult

pain′kill′er *n colloq* remedy that relieves pain; analgesic

pains′tak′ing *adj* taking much trouble; careful; laborious

paint /pānt′/ [OF *peint* painted] *n* **1** substance composed of pigment in a liquid vehicle, applied as a protective or decorative coating or in making pictures; **2** the dried pigment after the liquid evaporates; **3** cosmetics; **4** *western U.S.* pinto ‖ *vt* **5** to coat or cover with or as with paint; **6** to portray with paint; **7** to decorate with paint; **8** to depict, describe; **9** to apply medicated liquid to (a sore or wound) with a brush; **10** paint the town red *slang* to celebrate by going to night clubs and bars ‖ *vi* **11** to paint pictures; **12** to put on rouge

paint′er¹ *n* **1** one whose occupation is to cover with paint, as *a house painter*; **2** artist who paints pictures

paint′er² [MF *paynter* prob < MF *pentoir* rope for hanging clothes] *n* bow line by which a small boat is towed or made fast to a mooring

paint′ing *n* **1** painted picture; **2** work of one who paints; **3** pictures painted at a particular time or place

pair /per′/ [OF *paire* < L *paria*] *n* (**pair** or **pairs**) **1** two similar things used together or corresponding to each other, as *a pair of gloves*; **2** single thing composed of two joined parts, as *a pair of scissors*; **3** married couple; **4** two people or animals associated together; **5** two members on opposite sides in a legislative body who agree that neither will vote on a given motion ‖ *vt* **6** to arrange in pairs; **7** to match; **8** to mate ‖ *vi* **9** to form a pair or pairs; **10** pair off to come together in couples

pais·ley /pāz′lē/ [*Paisley*, Scotland] *n* **1** wool or silk material woven or printed with colorful and intricate designs; **2** scarf of this material

pa·ja·mas /pəjäm′əz, -jam′-/ [Hindi *pāejāma*] *npl* sleeping garment consisting of a jacket and loose trousers

Pa·ki·stan /pak′istan′/ *n* republic in S Asia, formerly West Pakistan

(53,990,173; 310,403 sq.m.; cap. Islamabad ‖ **Pa'ki·sta'ni** /-nē/ *adj & n*

pal /pal'/ [Gypsy = brother] *n* 1 intimate friend, chum ‖ *v* (**palled; palling**) *vi* 2 **pal around with** to associate with as a pal

pal·ace /pal'is/ [OF *palais* < L *palatium* house of Augustus on the Palatine hill] *n* 1 official residence of a sovereign, bishop, or other person of high rank; 2 magnificent house or building

pal·a·din /pal'ədin/ [F < It *paladino*] *n* 1 one of the twelve chief knights of Charlemagne; 2 notable champion or defender of a cause

pa·lae·o- var of **paleo-**

pal·an·quin /pal'ənkēn'/ [Port < Hindi *palang* bed] *n* in India and China, covered carriage for one passenger, carried on the shoulders of men by means of a pole

pal·at·a·ble /pal'ətəbəl/ [see **palate**] *adj* 1 pleasing to the taste, appetizing; 2 agreeable; acceptable ‖ SYN delicious, savory, pleasing, agreeable

pal·a·tal /pal'ətəl/ *adj* 1 of or pert. to the palate; 2 *phon* articulated with the blade of the tongue against the hard palate ‖ *n* 3 palatal consonant ‖ **pal'a·tal·ize'** *vt*

pal·ate /pal'it/ [L *palatum*] *n* 1 roof of the mouth; 2 sense of taste

pa·la·tial /pəlāsh'əl/ [< L *palatium* palace] *adj* 1 pert. to, suitable to, or resembling a palace; 2 stately, magnificent

pa·lat·i·nate /pəlat'ən·āt'/ [< *palatine*] *n* territory ruled by a palatine

pal·a·tine /pal'ətīn/, -tin/ [L *palatinus* imperial] *adj* 1 (noble) having royal privileges ‖ *n* 2 palatine noble; 3 **the Palatine** the one of the seven hills of Rome on which the imperial palace stood

pa·lav·er /pəlav'ər/ [Port *palavra* word] *n* 1 idle talk, chatter; 2 conference, parley ‖ *vi* 3 to talk idly; 4 to confer, parley

pale¹ /pāl'/ [MF < L *pallidus*] *adj* 1 lacking in color; whitish; 2 not bright; dim; 3 feeble ‖ *vt* 4 to make pale ‖ *vi* 5 to become pale ‖ SYN *adj* pallid, white, ashen, bloodless, haggard, ghastly ‖ ANT *adj* rosy, healthy, flushed, rubicund

pale² [MF *pal* stake < L *palus*] *n* 1 pointed stake used for fences; 2 district or territory within set bounds; restricted locality; 3 **beyond the pale** beyond the limit of what is acceptable

pale'face' *n* white person, in alleged parlance of North American Indians

pa·le·o- [Gk *palaios*] *comb form* old

Pa·le·o·cene /pāl'ē·əsēn', pal'-/ [*paleo-* + Gk *kainos* new] *n* epoch of the Tertiary period 60,000,000 years ago, characterized by the appearance of birds and mammals ‖ also *adj*

pa·le·og·ra·phy /pāl'ē·og'rəfē, pal'-/ *n* 1 ancient forms of writing; 2 study of ancient writings ‖ **pa'le·o·graph'ic** /-əgraf'-/ *adj*

pa'le·o·lith'ic /pāl'ē·ə-, pal'-/ *adj* pert. to the early Stone Age, marked by the development of bone and flint tools

pa'le·on·tol'o·gy /-əntol'-/ [*paleo-* + Gk *onta* beings + -*logy*] *n* science dealing with life in past geological periods as shown by fossils ‖ **pa'le·on·tol'o·gist** *n*

Pa·le·o·zo·ic /pāl'ē·əzō'ik, pal'-/ [*paleo-* + Gk *zoe* life] *n* era of from 200,-000,000 to 600,000,000 years ago, characterized by the appearance of fish, reptiles, and insects ‖ also *adj*

Pal·es·tine /pal'istīn'/ *n* region in SW Asia at the SE corner of the Mediterranean, ancient home of the Jews, the *Holy Land*; comprising parts of modern Israel, Jordan, and Egypt ‖ **Pal'es·tin'i·an** /-tin'ē·ən/ *adj & n*

pal·ette /pal'it/ [MF < It *paletta* small shovel] *n* thin oval or oblong board with a thumb hole, used by artists for mixing and holding colors

pal·frey /pôl'frē/ [OF *palefrei*] *n* saddle horse, esp. one for a woman

Pa·li /pāl'ē/ [Skt *pāli* bhāsa canonical language] *n* language of the Buddhist scriptures

pal·imp·sest /pal'impsest'/ [Gk *palimpsestos* scraped again] *n* parchment manuscript from which the writing has been erased and new writing put on

pal·in·drome /pal'indrōm'/ [Gk *palindromos* recurring] *n* word or sentence which reads the same backward as it does forward, as *Madam I'm Adam*

pal·ing /pāl'ing/ [< *pale²*] *n* 1 pale fence; 2 pales for a fence

pal·i·sade /pal'isād'/ [F *palissade*] *n* 1 fence or fortification formed of a line of pointed stakes set in the ground; 2 **palisades** *pl* line of sheer cliffs

pal'ish *adj* slightly or somewhat pale; not having much color

pall¹ /pôl'/ [OE *pæll* < L *pallium* cloak] *n* 1 covering for a coffin, hearse, or tomb; 2 any darkening covering, as of smoke or gloom; 3 coffin

pall² [< *appall*] *vi* 1 to become insipid or wearisome; 2 to become distasteful

pal·la·di·um /pəlād'ē·əm/ [< L *Pallas* (-*adis*) name of asteroid] *n* rare silver-white metallic element (**Pd**; at. no. 46; at.wt. 106.4), used as a catalyst and in alloys

Pal·las /pal'əs/ *n* 1 *Gk myth.* name often prefixed to that of the goddess Athena; 2 largest of the asteroids

pall'bear'er *n* one of the persons who carry or attend the coffin at a funeral

pal·let[1] /pal′ĭt/ [< *palette*] *n* 1 any of various mechanical tools or devices, as a wooden tool used in making pottery, a pawl that regulates the movement of a ratchet wheel, etc.; 2 platform or frame for storing and transporting goods

pal·let[2] [AF *paillette* < OF *paille* straw] *n* small rough bed, as of straw

pal·li·ate /pal′ē-āt′/ [L *palliare* (-*atus*) to cloak] *vt* 1 to lessen or abate the severity or painfulness of; 2 to excuse or cause to appear less wrong ‖ **pal′li·a′tion** *n* ‖ **pal·li·a·tive** /pal′ē-āt′ĭv, pal′ē-ŏtĭv/ *adj* & *n* ‖ SYN extenuate, cover, conceal, screen, excuse, soften, gloss, mitigate ‖ DISCR To *excuse* is to offer a plea which will partially free the offender from the blame attached to a fault or offense, as they *excused* his preoccupation by saying that business worried him. To *extenuate* and to *palliate* both attempt to lessen admitted fault or wrongfulness. To *extenuate* is to try to make the fault seem smaller than it is, or the blame less, by presenting circumstances or reasons for the doing of it, as to *extenuate* a guilty act by citing the bad youthful environment of the offender. To *palliate* is to try to hide, rather than to *soften*, the degree of blameworthiness. One *palliates* a crime by calling it by a softer name, or concealing part of it ‖ ANT aggravate, magnify

pal·lid /pal′ĭd/ [L *pallidus*] *adj* pale, wan ‖ SYN ghastly, pale, bloodless, ashen, white, wan

pal·lor /pal′ər/ [L] *n* lack of color, as in the face; paleness

palm[1] /päm′/ [L *palma*] *n* 1 inner surface of the hand between the wrist and the base of the fingers; 2 the part of a glove that covers the palm; 3 linear measure of from 3 to 4 inches or from 7 to 9 inches; 4 **cross** or **grease the palm of** to bribe ‖ *vt* 5 to conceal in the palm; 6 **palm off** to dispose of by fraud

palm[2] [OE < L *palma* palm tree] *n* 1 any of various species of tropical trees (family Palmaceae) characterized by large leaves radiating from the summit of a tall branchless trunk; 2 leaf of this tree, used as an emblem of victory; 3 victory

pal·mate /pal′māt, -mĭt/ *adj* 1 (leaf or antlers) shaped like a hand with the fingers spread; 2 web-footed; 3 *bot* having several leaflets diverging from the summit of one petiole

palm′er *n* pilgrim of the Middle Ages who carried a palm branch as a sign that he had been to the Holy Land

pal·met·to /palmet′ō/ [Sp *palmito*] *n* (-**tos** or -**toes**) any of several palm trees with fan-shaped leaves, of the West Indies and the S United States

palm′is·try *n* art of reading character and telling fortunes by the lines of the palm ‖ **palm′ist** *n*

Palm′ Sun′day *n* the Sunday before Easter, celebrated in commemoration of Christ's entry into Jerusalem, when palm branches were strewn before him

palm′y *adj* (-**i·er**; -**i·est**) flourishing, prosperous, as *palmy days*

pal·o·mi·no /pal′əmēn′ō/ [Sp] *n* breed of horse of a pale-yellow color and flaxen mane and tail

pa·loo·ka /pəlōōk′ə/ [?] *n slang* 1 clumsy stupid person; 2 clumsy incompetent boxer

pal·pa·ble /pal′pəbəl/ [< L *palpare* to touch] *adj* 1 capable of being touched or felt; 2 obvious; plain ‖ **pal′pa·bly** *adv* ‖ SYN manifest, obvious, apparent, evident, tangible

pal·pate /pal′pāt/ [see **palpable**] *vt* to investigate by touch, as in diagnosing certain diseases

pal·pi·tate /pal′pĭtāt′/ [L *palpitare* (-*atus*) to throb] *vi* to beat or throb rapidly, flutter, as the heart ‖ **pal′pi·ta′tion** *n*

pal·sy /pôl′zē/ [< MF *paralisie*] *n* (-**sies**) 1 paralysis; 2 muscular condition accompanied by tremors ‖ **pal′sied** *adj*

pal·try /pôlt′rē/ [LG *paltrig* ragged] *adj* (-**tri·er**; -**tri·est**) 1 small, trifling; 2 worthless; contemptible ‖ SYN base, petty, insignificant, trifling, despicable, trashy, worthless ‖ ANT noble, generous, admirable

pam·pas /pamp′əz/ [Sp < Quechua *bamba* plain] *npl* great treeless plains of Argentina

pam·per /pamp′ər/ [MD *pamperen*] *vt* to treat overindulgently, coddle

pam·phlet /pamf′lĭt/ [< ML *pamphletus dim.* of *Pamphilus* title of a 12th-cent. poem] *n* 1 small unbound book, usu. with a paper cover; 2 brief treatise or essay, generally on a controversial subject

pam′phlet·eer′ *n* 1 writer of controversial pamphlets ‖ *vi* 2 to write and issue such pamphlets

pan[1] /pan′/ [OE *panne*] *n* 1 broad shallow vessel of metal, used for cooking and other household purposes; 2 any vessel or receptacle of similar shape; 3 *slang* face; 4 depression in the lock of a muzzleloader in which the priming powder is placed ‖ *v* (**panned**; **pan·ning**) *vt* 5 to wash (gravel or sand) in a pan to cause the gold to settle out; 6 to cause (gold) to settle out by panning; 7 *colloq* to criticize severely ‖ *vi* 8 **pan out** *colloq* to turn out

pan[2] [*panorama*] *v* (**panned**; **pan·ning**) *vi* 1 to operate a motion picture camera while swinging it horizontally or vertically in order to get a panoramic view or to keep a person or thing in view ‖ *vt* **2** to cause (a camera) to pan

Pan /pan′/ *n* Gk *myth.* god of the woodlands and of flocks and herds, represented as having the legs, ears, and horns of a goat

pan- /pan-/ [Gk] *comb form* all

pan·a·ce·a /pan′əsē′ə/ [Gk *panakeia*] *n* **1** remedy for all ills and diseases; **2** solution to all problems

pa·nache /pənash′, -näsh′/ [F < It *pennacchio* plume] *n* **1** plume on a hat or helmet; **2** verve; flamboyant manner

Pan·a·ma /pan′əmä′, -mô′/ *n* Spanish-speaking republic at the S end of Central America, connecting it with South America (1,329,000; 29,209 sq.m.; cap. Panama City) ‖ **Pan′a·ma′ni·an** /-män′ē-ən/ *adj* & *n*

Pan·a·ma, Isth·mus of *n* isthmus in Panama separating the Atlantic and Pacific Oceans

Pan·a·ma Ca·nal′ *n* canal connecting the Atlantic and Pacific Oceans at the Isthmus of Panama in the Canal Zone; opened 1914

Pan·a·ma (Cit′y) *n* capital of Panama (300,000)

Pan′a·ma (hat′) *n* lightweight hat made of the plaited leaves of a palmlike tree (*Cardulovica palmata*) of Central and South America

Pan′-A·mer′i·can *adj* pert. to all the countries and peoples of the Americas ‖ **Pan′-A·mer′i·can·ism** *n*

pan′cake′ *n* **1** thin flat cake made of batter and fried in a pan or on a griddle; **2** *aeron* abrupt, nearly vertical landing ‖ *vi* **3** *aeron* to make a pancake landing

pan′cake make′·up *n* make-up in cake form applied with a sponge

pan′chro·mat′ic *adj* (film) sensitive to all colors

pan·cre·as /paŋk′rē-əs, pan′krē-/ [*pan-* + Gk *kreas* flesh] *n* large fleshy gland below and behind the stomach, which secretes a digestive fluid into the small intestine and produces the hormone insulin ‖ **pan′cre·at′ic** /-at′-/ *adj*

pan·da /pan′də/ [< Nepalese] *n* **1** Himalayan mammal (*Ailurus fulgens*) about the size of a cat and rusty red in color; **2** also **gi′ant pan′da** Himalayan carnivore (*Ailuropoda melanoleuca*) resembling a small bear, white with black legs, shoulders, ears, and eye patches

pan·dem·ic /pandem′ik/ [*pan-* + Gk *demos* people] *adj* **1** epidemic over a wide area; **2** general, universal ‖ *n* **3** pandemic disease

pan·de·mo·ni·um /pan′dimōn′ē-əm/ [*Pandaemonium*, palace in Hell in Milton's *Paradise Lost*, < *pan-* + Gk *daimon* devil] *n* wild uproar; tumultuous chaos

pan·der /pan′dər/ [< *Pandarus* Trojan who acted as go-between in the love affair of Troilus and Cressida] *n* **1** panderer ‖ *vi* **2** pander to to cater to (base instincts or desires)

pan′der·er *n* **1** pimp; go-between; **2** one who caters to and exploits the base instincts or desires of others

P. & L. profit and loss

Pan·do·ra′s box′ /pandôr′əz, -dōr′-/ [*Pandora*, according to Gk myth, the first woman, whose curiosity impelled her to open a forbidden box, allowing all the world's evils to escape to afflict mankind] *n* source of unforeseen and expanding troubles

pane /pān′/ [MF *pan* < L *pannus* cloth] *n* sheet of glass in the frame of a window

pan·e·gyr·ic /pan′ijir′ik/ [< Gk *panegyris* formal assembly] *n* **1** praise formally written or spoken in honor of some person or event; **2** any high praise ‖ **pan′e·gyr′i·cal** *adj* ‖ **pan′e·gyr′ist** *n*

pan·el /pan′əl/ [OF = small piece] *n* **1** rectangular piece of material, as of cloth or wood; **2** division or section, as of a wall, ceiling, or door; **3** strip of contrasting material put lengthwise in a skirt; **4** list of persons summoned to serve as jurors; **5** body of persons selected to perform some public service, as conducting a discussion, judging a contest, or acting as advisors; **6** board or mount containing dials, switches, or controls, as for an engine, electrical device, or switchboard ‖ *v* (-eled or -elled; -el·ing or -el·ling) *vt* **7** to furnish with panels

pan′el dis·cus′sion *n* public discussion conducted by a panel of invited guests

pan′el heat′ing *n* heating of interiors by means of heating pipes or electric conductors concealed behind panels

pan′el·ist *n* member of a panel **5**

pan′el truck′ *n* small delivery truck with an enclosed body

pan·e·tel·la /pan′itel′ə/ [Sp *panetela*] *n* long slender cigar

pang /paŋ′/ [?] *n* sudden sharp physical or mental pain

pan′han′dle *n* **1** strip of territory in certain states projecting between two other states ‖ *vi* **2** to accost and beg money from passers-by ‖ *vt* **3** to accost and beg from

pan·ic /pan′ik/ [Gk *panikos* of Pan] *n* **1** extreme, sudden, and unreasoning fright, spreading quickly through groups of persons or animals; **2** sudden general condition of distrust in financial quarters, marked by the precipitate attempt to withdraw funds from banks and to convert all holdings into cash; **3** *slang* someone or something considered hilarious ‖ *v* (-icked; -ick·ing) *vt* **4** to affect with panic; **5** *slang* to cause to laugh hilariously ‖ *vi* **6** to be overcome with panic || **pan'ick·y** *adj* || SYN fear, terror, alarm (see *horror*)

pan'ic bar' or **bolt'** *n* horizontal bar on the inside of an exit door of a public place that opens the door when depressed

pan'ic-strick'en *adj* filled with overwhelming fear

pan·nier /pan'yər, -ē-ər/ [MF *panier* < L *panarium* bread basket] *n* **1** large basket; **2** one of two baskets suspended across the back of an animal

pan·o·ply /pan'əplē/ [Gk *panoplia*] *n* (-plies) **1** complete suit of armor; **2** any splendid enveloping array

pan·o·ram·a /pan'əram'ə, -räm'ə/ [*pan-* + Gk *horama* view] *n* **1** wide view in all directions; **2** picture seen in several scenes unrolled before the spectator; **3** continuously changing scene of events || **pan'o·ram'ic** *adj*

pan·sy /pan'zē/ [MF *pensee* thought] *n* (-sies) **1** common garden plant (*Viola tricolor*) of the violet family, having blossoms of velvety texture; **2** *slang* male homosexual

pant /pant'/ [MF *pantaisier*] *vi* **1** to breathe rapidly; gasp; heave; **2 pant for** or **after** to desire ardently || *vt* **3** to utter with a gasp || *n* **4** short rapid breath; **5** throb || **pant'ing·ly** *adv*

pan·ta·loons /pant'əlōōnz'/ [It *pantalone* nickname for a Venetian < St. *Pantaleone* patron saint of Venice] *npl* **1** man's hip-length hose; **2** trousers

pan·tech·ni·con /pantek'nikon', -kən/ [orig. a London 19th-cent. bazaar < *pan-* + Gk *technikon* artistic] *n* *Brit* **1** warehouse, esp. for furniture; **2** moving van

pan·the·ism /pan'thē·iz'əm/ *n* doctrine that God exists not as a person, but as manifested in the material universe and in man and every natural object || **pan'the·ist** *n* || **pan'the·is'tic** *adj*

pan·the·on /pan'thē·on'/ [Gk *pantheion*] *n* **1** temple dedicated to all gods; **2** all the gods of a people collectively; **3** place where the famous dead of a nation are buried; **4** heroes and idols of a nation or group collectively; **5 Pantheon** circular temple built 120 A.D. at Rome, used as a church since 609

pan·ther /pan'thər/ [Gk] *n* **1** cougar; **2** leopard

pant·ies /pant'ēz/ [*dim.* of *pants*] *npl* women's and children's underpants

pan·to- var of pan-

pan'to·graph' /pant'ə-/ *n* **1** jointed framework on the roof of an electric vehicle making contact with an overhead electric wire; **2** instrument in the form of a parallelogram for the mechanical copying of drawings, maps, signatures, etc. on any predetermined scale

pan'to·mime' *n* **1** play in which there is no speaking; **2** *Brit* musical play at Christmas written around a popular fairy tale; **3** meaningful action without speech || *vt* & *vi* **4** to represent or act in pantomime || **pan'to·mim'ist** *n* || **pan'to·mim'ic** /-mim'-/ *adj*

pan·try /pant'rē/ [OF *paneterie* bread room] *n* (-tries) **1** room or closet for bread and other foods, silverware, etc.; **2** small room off the kitchen from which food is served

pants /pants'/ [< *pantaloons*] *npl* **1** trousers; **2** drawers, panties

pants' suit' *n* woman's suit consisting of slacks with a jacket to match

pant'y /pant'ē/ [*sg* of *panties*] *n* panties

pant'y hose' *n* one-piece combination of panties and hose

pant'y·waist' *n* **1** child's undergarment consisting of drawers buttoned to an undershirt; **2** *colloq* sissy, weakling

pan·zer /pan'zər/ [G] *n* armored vehicle or tank || also *adj*

pap /pap'/ [prob repetition of infant's hunger cry] *n* **1** soft food for infants; **2** idea devoid of substance

pa·pa /päp'ə, pəpä'/ [MF < L] *n* father

pa·pa·cy /pāp'əsē/ *n* (-cies) **1** office, dignity, or authority of the Pope; **2** popes collectively; **3** system of church government based on the authority of the Pope

pa·pal /pāp'əl/ [ML *papalis*] *adj* pert. to the Pope or the papacy

pa·pa·raz·zo /päp'ärä'tsō/ [It] *n* (-zi /-tsē/) society news photographer

pa·paw /pô'pô, pəpô'/ [< *papaya*] *n* sweet, many-seeded fruit of a tree (*Asimina triloba*) of the central and S United States

pa·pa·ya /pəpä'yə/ [Sp] *n* melonlike fruit of a tropical palmlike tree (*Carica papaya*)

pa·per /pāp'ər/ [MF *papier* < Gk *papyros* papyrus] *n* **1** material in the form of thin flexible sheets, made of finely divided fibers, as from rags or wood, used for writing, printing, wrapping, and various other purposes; **2** piece or sheet of this; **3** newspaper; **4** essay or article; **5** legal or commercial document; **6** banknotes or bills of exchange; **7** wallpaper; **8** stationery; **9** *slang* free tickets of admission; **10 papers** *pl* documents of identification; **11 on paper, a** in theory; **b** existing in plans only || *adj* **12** flimsy, frail; **13** not realized, existing only in writing, as *paper profits* || *vt* **14** to cover with wallpaper; **15** *slang* to fill (a theater) by issuing passes || **pa'per·y** *adj*

pa'per·back' *n* **1** book bound in flexible paper || *adj* **2** (book) bound in flexible paper; **3** pert. to paperbacks

pa'per·board' *n* thick, stiff cardboard

pa'per·boy' *n* newsboy

pa'per clip' *n* wire bent double into a flat clip for attaching papers together

pa'per·hang'er *n* **1** one whose work is applying wallpaper; **2** *slang* passer of bad checks ‖ **pa'per·hang'ing** *n*

pa'per knife' *n* instrument with a flat blade for opening envelopes

pa'per prof'its *npl* profits not realized because the holdings have not been sold

pa'per ti'ger *n* one who or that which appears huge and powerful but is in reality small and weak

pa'per·weight' *n* weighted object, usu. ornamental, placed on papers to keep them from scattering

pa'per work' *n* clerical work, as keeping records, filing reports, etc.

Pa·pia·men·to /päp'yəment'ō/ [?] *n* creolized language based on Spanish, spoken on the West Indian island of Curaçao

pa·pier-mâ·ché /pāp'ərməshā'/ [F = chewed paper] *n* paper pulp mixed with glue, casein, or the like, molded into various shapes ‖ *also adj*

pa·pil·la /pəpil'ə/ [L = nipple] *n* (-lae -lē̵̷) any small nipplelike projection such as is found on the tongue ‖ **pap·il·lar·y** /pap'fler'ē̵, pəpil'ərē̵/ *adj*

pa·pist /pāp'ist/ [< *papal*] *n disparaging* adherent of Roman Catholicism ‖ *also adj* ‖ **pa'pist·ry** *n*

pa·poose /papōōs'/ [< Algonquian] *n* North American Indian baby

pap·py /pap'ē̵/ [< *papa*] *n* (-pies) *dial.* papa, father

pap·ri·ka /pap'rikə, paprēk'ə, pə-/ [Hung] *n* pungent red condiment ground from dried sweet peppers

Pap' test' /pap'/ [George N. Papanicoleau (1883–1962) U.S. scientist, born in Greece] *n* use of a smear of bodily secretions, esp. from the cervix and vagina, for early detection of cancer

Pap'u·a New Guin'ea /päp'ōō-ə/ *n* country in the SW Pacific, on New Guinea and smaller islands (3,000,000; 178,704 sq.m.; cap. Port Moresby)

pap·ule /pap'yōōl/ [L *papula*] *n* pimple

pa·py·rus /pəpīr'əs [L < Gk *papyros*] *n* (-ri -rī/) **1** tall Egyptian sedge (*Cyperus papyrus*) from the fibers of which the ancients made paper; **2** paper made from the pith of this plant; **3** manuscript or writing on papyrus

par /pär/ [L = equal] *n* **1** face value of stocks and bonds; **2** equality, as *he is not on a par with the others;* **3** rate of exchange at which the money unit of one country may be exchanged for that of another using the same metal as a standard of value; **4** average state or condition, as *above par, below par;* **5** *golf* score set as a standard for a hole or course

par·a- [Gk = beside] *pref* **1** beyond;

b against; **2** *chem* designating a compound which is structurally closely related to another, as *paraldehyde;* **3** a protecting against, as *parachute;* **b** associated with parachutes, as *paratrooper*

par·a·ble /par'əbəl/ [Gk *parabole* comparison] *n* short allegorical story teaching a moral ‖ SYN comparison (see *allegory*)

pa·rab·o·la /pərab'ələ/ [L < Gk *parabole* setting aside] *n* curve formed by the intersection of a cone with a plane parallel to its side

par·a·bol·ic /par'əbol'ik/ *adj* **1** of or pert. to a parable; **2** pert. to or formed like a parabola

par·a·chute /par'əshōōt'/ [F < It *para* stop! + *chute*] *n* **1** folded pack attached to a body harness which opens into a large fabric umbrella when a ring is pulled, allowing a person who jumps from an aircraft to land safely ‖ *vi* **2** to descend by parachute ‖ *vt* **3** to drop (troops, equipment, etc.) by parachute ‖ **par'a·chut'ist** *n*

pa·rade /pərād'/ [MF < Sp *parada* stopping place] *n* **1** public procession, usu. with band music, honoring an anniversary, person, or event; **2** ostentatious display; **3** military display or review of troops ‖ *vt* **4** to make a display of; **5** to walk over or through **6** to form, as in military order, for display ‖ *vi* **7** to walk about to show oneself; **8** to take part in a parade; **9** to form in military order ‖ **pa·rad'er** *n* ‖ SYN *n* pomp, show, ostentation, display, pageantry

par'a·di·chlo'ro·ben'zene /par'ədīklōr'ō, -klōr'-/ [*para-* + *di-* + *chlorine* + *benzene*] *n* white, crystalline, flaky substance —$C_6H_4Cl_2$— prepared from benzene, used as a moth repellant

par'a·did'dle [imit] *n* snare-drum roll

par'a·digm /-dīm, -dīm/ [Gk *paradeigma* pattern] *n* **1** example or model; **2** *gram* set of inflected forms of a word arranged in a fixed order

par'a·dise /-dīs'/ [OE *paradis* < Gk *paradeisos* park] *n* **1** Garden of Eden; **2** abode of the souls of the righteous after death; heaven

par'a·dox' /-doks'/ [Gk *paradoxon*] *n* **1** something that seems unbelievable yet may be true; **2** self-contradictory statement; **3** any person or thing with a contradictory nature ‖ **par·a·dox'i·cal** *adj* ‖ **par'a·dox'i·cal·ly** *adv*

par·af·fin /par'əfin/ [G < L *parum* little + *affinis* related] *n* **1** odorless, colorless, waxy substance obtained from crude petroleum, used in making candles, as a waterproofing material for paper, wood, etc., to seal preserving jars, and the like; **2** *chem* any one of a group of hydrocarbons having the general formula C_nH_{2n+2}

par·a·gon' /-gon', -gən/ [MF < It *paragone* touchstone] *n* model or pattern of perfection

par·a·graph' [Gk *paragraphe* marked passage] *n* 1 distinct section of a writing, usu. beginning with an indented line; 2 brief item or article in a newspaper or magazine; 3 reference mark ¶ indicating a paragraph or the need of one ‖ *vt* 4 to arrange in paragraphs

Par·a·guay /par'əgwā', -gwī'/ *n* Spanish- and Guarani-speaking republic in central South America (2,500,000; 157,046 sq.m.; cap. Asunción) ‖ **Par·a·guay'an** *adj* & *n*

par·a·keet /par'əkēt'/ [MF *perroquet* parrot] *n* any of numerous small parrots with long tails, popular as pets

par·al·lax' /-əlaks'/ [Gk *parallaxis* change] *n* 1 apparent displacement of an object caused by change in the position of the observer; 2 *photog* difference between the view seen through a taking lens and that seen through a separate viewfinder

par·al·lel' /-əlel'/ [Gk *parallelos* side by side] *adj* 1 having the same course; 2 similar; corresponding; 3 extending in the same direction and equidistant at all points, never meeting, as lines and planes ‖ *n* 4 counterpart; 5 anything resembling or parallel to another; 6 parallel line or plane; 7 one of the imaginary lines on the globe parallel to the equator and indicating latitude; 8 *typ* mark ‖ used as a reference or as a divider; 9 **in parallel** *elec* connected with one set of poles or terminals in one line and the other set in another ‖ *v* (-leled or -lelled; -lel·ing or -lel·ling) *vt* 10 to state the likeness of; 11 to be parallel with; 12 to correspond to; 13 to match

par·al·lel bars' *npl* two raised horizontal bars, parallel to each other, designed for physical exercises

par·al·lel·o·gram' /-əgram'/ [Gk *parallelogrammon*] *n* four-sided plane figure whose opposite sides are equal and parallel

pa·ral·y·sis /pəral'isis/ [Gk] *n* (-ses /-sēz'/) 1 loss of the power of sensation or movement in one or more parts of the body; 2 stoppage or crippling of activities ‖ **par·a·lyt·ic** /par'əlit'ik/ *adj* & *n*

par·a·lyze /par'əliz'/ *vt* 1 to affect with paralysis; 2 to render useless or ineffective ‖ **par·a·ly·za'tion** *n*

par·a·me'ci·um /-mēs'ē·əm, -mēsh'-ē·əm/ [< Gk *paramekes* oval] *n* (-a /-ə/) any of a genus (*Paramecium*) of one-celled, oval-shaped, ciliated protozoans, common in stagnant pools

par·a·med'ic *n* 1 physician or surgeon who parachutes to where his services are needed; 2 medical technician

par·a·med'i·cal *adj* 1 designating or pert. to activities that supplement the work of regular medical personnel; 2 pert. to a paramedic or paramedics

pa·ram·e·ter /pəram'itər/ *n* 1 *math* quantity which may have various values, each fixed within the limits of a stated case or discussion; 2 standard or determining factor; 3 *colloq* limit

par·a·mil'i·tar'y *adj* designating or pert. to a military force operating outside the regular organized forces

par·a·mount' [< OF *par* by + *amont* above < L *ad montem* to the mountain] *adj* above all others; supreme, chief ‖ SYN dominant, superior, principal, foremost, preeminent, chief ‖ ANT minor, secondary

par·a·mour' /-moŏr'/ [OF *par amour* by love] *n* illicit lover

par·a·noi'a /-noi'ə/ [Gk] *n* mental disorder marked by systematized delusions, especially of grandeur or persecution ‖ **par·a·noid'** *adj* & *n* ‖ **par·a·noi'ac** /-ak/, *adj* & *n*

par·a·pet /par'əpit, -pet'/ [It *parapetto*] *n* 1 low wall at the edge of a roof, bridge, or the like; 2 a barrier raised along the top of a wall or rampart; **b** mound of earth, sandbags, etc., protecting troops in a trench

par·a·pher·na'li·a /-fə(r)nāl'ē·ə/ [ML < *para-* + Gk *pherne* dowry] *npl* 1 personal accessories; 2 equipment; apparatus

par·a·phrase' *n* 1 rewording of a text, giving the meaning in another form ‖ 2 *vt* & *vi* to reword ‖ **par·a·phras'·tic** /-frast'-/ *adj*

par·a·ple'gi·a /-plēj'ē·ə/ [Gk] *n* paralysis of the lower part of the body ‖ **par·a·ple'gic** /-plēj'-, -plej'-/ *adj* & *n*

par·a·psy·chol'o·gy *n* branch of psychology dealing with clairvoyance, extrasensory perception, and psychic phenomena

par·a·site' [Gk *parasitos* one who eats at another's table] *n* 1 one who lives at the expense of others; 2 animal or plant that lives on or in another animal or plant at the latter's expense or to its detriment ‖ **par·a·sit'ic** /-sit'-/ *adj*

par·a·si·tol'o·gy /-sīt-, -sit-/ *n* branch of biology dealing with parasites

par·a·sol /par'əsôl', -sol'/ [MF < It *parasole*] *n* small light umbrella used as a lady's sunshade

par·a·troop'er *n* member of a military unit whose function is to parachute into combat areas or behind the enemy's lines

par·a·ty'phoid *n* infectious disease similar to but milder than typhoid ‖ also *adj*

par'boil' [MF *parboillir* to cook well]

vt **1** to cook partially by boiling; **2** to subject to extreme heat

par·cel /pärs′əl/ [MF *parcelle* small piece] *n* **1** small bundle or package; **2** separate distinct part; share, as *a parcel of land*; **3** group of persons or things ‖ *v* (-celed or -celled; -cel·ing or -cel·ling) *vt* **4 parcel out** to divide or apportion ‖ SYN *n* package, packet (see *bundle*)

par′cel post′ *n* **1** branch of the postal service that delivers packages under a certain size; **2** packages handled by this branch

parch /pärch′/ [ME *parchen*] *vt* **1** to scorch, burn slightly; **2** to dry with heat; **3** to make hot or thirsty

Par·chee·si /pärchēz′ē/ [Hindi *pachisi*; trademark] *n* board game originating in India in which the moves are determined by the throw of dice

parch′ment [MF < L *pergamena* (charta) (paper) of Pergamum] *n* **1** skin of a sheep, goat, etc., prepared for writing; **2** writing or document on parchment

pard·ner /pärd′ner/ *n dial.* partner

par·don /pärd′ən/ [OF *pardoner*] *vt* **1** to release from penalty; **2** to forgive; **3** to overlook, excuse ‖ *n* **4** forgiveness; **5** release from punishment; **6** polite indulgence; **7** *law* a release from penalty for an offense; **b** document granting a pardon ‖ **par′don·a·ble** *adj* ‖ SYN *v* absolve, acquit (see *forgive*); *n* (see *mercy*)

pare /per′/ [MF *parer* to trim] *vt* **1** to cut off or remove the outer layer or skin of; peel; **2** to cut away little by little; reduce or lessen; **3** to remove by cutting off

par·e·gor·ic /par′əgôr′ik, -gor′-/ [Gk *paregorikos* soothing] *n* **1** anodyne; **2** camphorated tincture of opium, used to relieve diarrhea in children

par·ent /par′ənt, per′-/ [L *parens* (-*entis*)] *n* **1** father or mother; **2** progenitor; **3** source or cause ‖ **pa·ren′tal** /pərent′əl/ *adj*

par′ent·age /-ij/ *n* **1** birth or descent; origin; **2** state or position of a parent

par·en·ter·al /pərent′ərəl/ [*para-* + *enteral*] *adj* administered or to be administered otherwise than through the digestive tract ‖ **par·en·ter·al·ly** *adv*

pa·ren·the·sis /pəren′thisis/ [Gk] *n* (-ses /-sēz′/) *n* **1** explanatory word, phrase, or clause injected into a sentence without affecting its syntactical construction; **2** either or both of the marks ( ) used to set this off ‖ **par·en·thet′ic** (-i·cal) /par′ənthet′-/ *adj*

pa·re·sis /pərēs′is, par′i-/ [Gk = letting go] *n* **1** syphilitic brain disorder marked by progressive loss of mental and physical powers; **2** partial paralysis ‖ **pa·ret′ic** /-ret′-, -rēt′-/ *adj & n*

par·fait /pärfā′/ [F = perfect] *n* **1** frozen dessert of whipped cream, beaten eggs, syrup, etc.; **2** fruit sundae

pa·ri·ah /pərī′ə/ [Tamil *paraiyan* one of low caste] *n* despised outcast

pa·ri·e·tal /pərī′ətəl/ [F < L *paries* wall] *adj* **1** (bone) at the sides and top of the skull; **2** pert. to living within the walls or on the campus of a college

par·i·mu·tu·el /par′imyōōch′ōō-əl/ [F = mutual wager] *n* system of betting at race tracks in which the winners divide the total money bet on each race, less track expenses, in proportion to the amount of their wagers

par′ing /per′-/ *n* piece or part pared off

par′ing knife′ *n* small knife used for paring vegetables and fruit

Par·is¹ /par′is/ *n* capital of France (2,790,091) ‖ **Pa·ri·sian** /pərizh′ən, -rēzh′-/ *adj & n*

Par·is² *n Gk myth.* son of Priam, king of Troy, whose abduction of Helen precipitated the Trojan War

Par′is green′ *n* emerald-green pigment obtained from copper acetate and arsenic trioxide, used as a pigment and an insecticide

par·ish /par′ish/ [OF *paroche* < Gk *paroikia* neighborhood] *n* **1** ecclesiastical district under the charge of one clergyman; **2** congregation and the locality covered by its activities; **3** in England, civil district organized for self-government in local matters; **4** in Louisiana, county

pa·rish·ion·er /pərish′ənər/ *n* member of a parish

par·i·ty /par′itē/ [L *paritas*] *n* **1** like state or degree; equality; equal value; **2** *fin* equality in the value of the currency of two countries; **3** system of giving farmers the same purchasing power they had in a selected base period by government price supports for their products

park /pärk/ [OF *parc* enclosure] *n* **1** tract of land of varying extent, set apart and beautified as a public place for out-of-door recreation ‖ *vt* **2** to place and leave (a vehicle) temporarily; **3** *colloq* to deposit temporarily, as *he parked his hat in the hall* ‖ *vi* **4** to park a vehicle

par·ka /pärk′ə/ [< Aleut] *n* heavy cold-weather jacket with an attached hood

Par′ker House′ roll′ [*Parker House*, Boston hotel] *n* roll made by folding a flat piece of dough in half

park′ing me′ter *n* meter at a parking space, designed to time the duration of parking of an automobile, actuated by a coin inserted by the motorist

Par′kin·son's dis·ease′ /pärk′insənz/ [James *Parkinson* (1755–1824) Eng

surgeon] *n* nerve disease marked by tremors, muscular rigidity, and slowness of movement

Par'kin·son's law' [Cyril Northcote *Parkinson* (1909-   ) Eng historian] *n* observation that work expands as more time is made available for it

park'way' *n* wide thoroughfare having a divider and/or side strips planted with grass and trees

par·lance /pär'ləns/ [AF] *n* 1 way of speaking; 2 language, jargon

par·lay /pär'lā, -lē/ [< F *paroli* double of one's winnings] *n* 1 amount bet plus one's winnings || *vt* 2 to bet (an original wager and its winnings) on a subsequent race, contest, etc.; 3 to manage (one's resources, talents, etc.) with great profit or advantage

par·ley /pär'lē/ [MF *parlee*] *n* 1 conference or talk, especially with an enemy || *vi* 2 to hold a parley, confer || SYN *n* conference, discussion (see *conversation*)

par·lia·ment /pär'ləmənt/ [OF *parlement* speaking] *n* 1 meeting or assembly; 2 legislature; 3 **Parliament** the legislature of Great Britain, Canada, and many other countries and of the Canadian provinces

par'lia·men·tar'i·an /-ter'-/ *n* one who is versed in the rules of procedure of deliberative bodies

par'lia·men'ta·ry *adj* 1 according to the rules of procedure governing deliberative assemblies; 2 of, pert. to, or enacted by a parliament

par·lor /pär'lər/ [OF *parleor* < *parler* to speak] *n* 1 room for the reception and entertainment of guests; living room; 2 lounge in a hotel or club

par'lor car' *n* in U.S., railroad car fitted out in a more luxurious manner than an ordinary coach

par·lous /pär'ləs/ [var of *perilous*] *adj* 1 dangerous; risky || *adv* 2 exceedingly

Par'me·san (**cheese'**) /pär'mizan', -zän/, -zən/ [MF < It *parmigiano* of Parma] *n* hard dry Italian cheese, usu. grated

Par·nas·sus /pärnas'əs/ *n* 1 mountain in Greece sacred to Apollo and the Muses; 2 any center of poetic and artistic activity

pa·ro·chi·al /pərōk'ē̇-əl/ [< LL *parochia* parish] *adj* 1 pert. to a parish; 2 narrow, provincial || **pa·ro'chi·al·ism** *n*

pa·ro'chi·al school' *n* church-run elementary or high school

par·o·dy /par'ədē/ [Gk *parōidia* burlesque song] *n* (-**dies**) 1 humorous or farcical imitation, as of a literary or musical work or a person; 2 poor imitation || *v* (-**died**) *vt* 3 to make a parody of || **par'o·dist** *n* || SYN *n* mimicry, exaggeration, imitation, representation, burlesque, caricature,

travesty || DISCR *Imitation* is a serious attempt to reproduce an original. *Burlesque, travesty, parody*, and *caricature* pervert or exaggerate certain aspects of the original in order to deride or ridicule it. *Burlesque* and *travesy* may be written or acted; *parody* is written; *caricature* may be literary, but is usually pictorial. A *burlesque* obtains an extravagant or absurd effect, usually incongruous, by treating a serious subject with levity, or a trifling subject seriously. A *burlesque* may be written independently of any actual play, poem, etc., but even so it is imitative, presenting in an absurd way such a portrayal as the life of a countryman on his arrival in a big city. A *caricature* overemphasizes certain distinguishing marks or traits; *caricatures* of Theodore Roosevelt capitalized his smile and teeth; former President Wilson was made to look overbookish. A *parody* changes the subject matter of some work, usually well known, but retains the style, especially in its tricks or affectations. A *travesty* retains the subject matter, but so alters the style that the effect is ridiculous. *Mimicry* is such a copying of its original as to be comical through its very faithfulness. Both *travesty* and *mimicry* are sometimes the product of innocence rather than deliberate effort

pa·role /pərōl'/ [MF *parole* (d'honneur) word (of honor)] *n* 1 release of a prisoner from jail before his sentence has expired, conditioned on his good behavior; 2 promise given by a prisoner of war that in return for conditional freedom he will either refrain from bearing arms against his captors or will return to prison at a stated time; 3 on parole in the state of being paroled || *vt* 4 to put on parole

pa·rol·ee' *n* person on parole

pa·rot·id /pərot'id/ [Gk *parotis* (-*idos*) tumor near the ear] *n* salivary gland below and in front of each ear || also *adj*

-p·a·rous /-pərəs/ [L -*parus* < *parere* to bear] *adj comb form* giving birth to

par·ox·ysm /par'əksiz'əm/ [Gk *paroxysmos* irritation] *n* 1 sudden outburst; fit; 2 sudden or periodic recurrence of pain or other symptoms of a disease || **par'ox·ys'mal** *adj*

par·ox·y·tone' /par-/ *n* word stressed on the next to the last syllable || also *adj*

par·quet /pärkā'/ [F, *dim.* of *parc* park] *n* 1 flooring made of wooden inlay; 2 main floor of a theater between the orchestra rail and the parquet circle

par·quet' cir'cle *n* part of the main

floor of a theater that lies under the balcony

par·ra·keet /par'əkēt'/ *n* var of **parakeet**

par·ri·cide /par'isīd'/ [L *parricidum* kin murder] *n* **1** murder of a parent or other close relative, esp. one's father; **2** one who commits parricide ‖ **par'ri·cid'al** *adj*

par·rot /par'ət/ [var of *parakeet*] *n* **1** any of many tropical birds (order Psittaciformes) with hooked bill and brilliant feathers, able to make sounds resembling words; **2** person who repeats words without understanding their meaning ‖ *vt* **3** to repeat mechanically ‖ *vi* **4** to prattle

par·ry /par'ē/ [F *parez!* parry!] *v* (-ried) *vt* **1** to ward off, as a blow; **2** to evade, as a question ‖ *n* (-ries) **3** act or instance of parrying

parse /pärs/ [L *pars* (orationis) part (of speech)] *vt* to analyze (the words in a sentence) grammatically and syntactically

par·sec /pär'sek'/ [*parallax* + *second*] *n astron* unit of stellar distance, equal to the distance from the earth to a star with a heliocentric parallax of one second of arc, equivalent to about 3¼ light-years

Par·see or **Par·si** /pär'sē/ [Pers *Pārsī* Persian] *n* descendant of the old Persians who fled Persia in the 8th century to escape Muslim persecution, now living mostly in India and following the Zoroastrian religion

par·si·mo'ni·ous *adj* showing parsimony ‖ **par'si·mo'ni·ous·ly** *adv* ‖ SYN penurious, niggardly, grasping (see *avaricious*)

par·si·mo·ny /pärs'imōn'ē/ [L *parsimonia* frugality] *n* stinginess; extreme unnecessary economy ‖ SYN frugality, miserliness, niggardliness, avariciousness, penuriousness ‖ ANT prodigality, extravagance

pars·ley /pärs'lē/ [OF *peresil* < Gk *petroselinon* rock parsley] *n* garden plant (*Petroselinum crispum*) the leaves of which are used as a garnish and for flavoring

pars·nip /pärs'nip/ [ME *passenep* < L *pastinaca*] *n* plant (*Pastinaca sativa*) of the parsley family with white edible roots

par·son /pärs'ən/ [ML *persona* parish priest] *n* **1** clergyman of a parish; **2** minister or preacher

par'son·age /-ij/ *n* dwelling provided by a church for its clergyman

part /pärt/ [OE & MF < L *pars* (*partis*)] *n* **1** portion or section of a whole; **2** share in action, duty, or responsibility, as *to do one's part;* **3** essential element, as *a body part, auto parts;* **4** side or party, as *they took his part;* **5** concern or interest, as *I had no part in this;* **6** character or role played by an actor; **7** divi-

sion of the hair; **8** *mus* **a** one of the melodies in a harmony; **b** one of the voices or instruments which form a concerted piece; **c** written score for one of these; **9** parts *pl* a quarter, region, as *they live in these parts;* **b** ability or talent, as *a man of parts;* **10** for one's part as far as one is concerned; **11** for the most part mostly, in most cases; **12** in part partly; **13** on the part of, a in behalf of; **b** by; **14** take part to participate ‖ *vt* **15** to divide into parts; **16** to comb (the hair) so as to leave a part; **17** to disunite, force to go apart; **18** to separate ‖ *vi* **19** to be separated or divided; **20** to separate; withdraw; **21** part with to give up ‖ *adv* **22** partly, as *he is part Japanese* ‖ SYN *v* sever, remove, disjoin, divide, disunite, sunder; *n* division, portion, share, fraction, piece, fragment, particle ‖ DISCR *Part,* the general term, denotes some, but not all, of a thing or things, whether actually separated from the whole, or viewed as separate, as I divided the apple into four *parts;* the *parts* of the human body. A *portion* is a *part* of a whole, regarded especially as assigned to one person, as a stepchild's *portion* of the money. A *division* is a certain *part* of a whole, especially as seen by one who is classifying, distributing, or cutting it, as the natural *division* of the twenty-four hours into night and day; geographical *divisions; division* of the estate among the heirs; *division* of labor according to the strength of the performers; *division* of an apple into *parts.* A *fraction* is properly a *part* contained by the whole an integral number of times; loosely, it names any *part,* especially a little *part,* as a bit or scrap. A *share* is an equitable *portion,* separated from a common source for one individual as his rightful amount, or contributed by him to a common fund as his just proportion, borne by him as his just *division* of joint expenses, or the like; as, *share* and *share* alike. A *piece* is a *part* cut off from the rest, as a *piece* of cake; a *piece* of glass suggests a broken *fragment;* a *piece* of poetry names a detached but complete *part;* a *piece* of glassware suggests that which is complete in itself. A *particle* is a tiny *part,* or minute *portion;* it is often used figuratively to denote the smallest possible amount, as he has not a *particle* of humor ‖ ANT *v* join, unite, keep together

par·take' [*part* + *take*] *v* (-took; -taken) *vi* **1** to take part; **2** partake of, a to have a share of; **b** to share in the nature or character of

par·terre /pärter'/ [F = on the ground]

par·the·no·gen'e·sis /pärth'ənō-/ [Gk *parthenos* virgin + *genesis*] *n* reproduction from eggs that have not been fertilized, as in certain insects

Par·the·non /pärth'ənon', -nən/ *n* temple of Athena Parthenos on the Acropolis at Athens

par·tial /pär'shəl/ [LL *partialis*] *adj* 1 inclined to favor one side or party; biased; 2 incomplete, in part only; 3 pert. to or constituting a part; 4 **partial to** fond of, favoring ‖ **par'tial·ly** *adv*

par·ti·al·i·ty /pärsh(ē)al'itē/ *n* (-ties) 1 state or quality of being biased; favoritism; 2 strong liking

par·tic·i·pant /pärtis'ipənt/ *adj* 1 participating ‖ *n* 2 one who participates

par·tic'i·pate' [L *participare* (-*atus*)] *vt* to partake with others; take part; share ‖ **par·tic'i·pa'tion** *n* ‖ **SYN** share ‖ **DISCR** We *participate* with others in joys or sorrows, in debates, discussions, sympathy, or the like. We *share* one another's sorrows also, but we do not *share* debates; we *share* one another's experience, shelter, money. In these cases we could not use *participate*; but we could *share* or *participate* in a conversation

par·ti·ci·ple /pärt'isip'əl/ [MF < L *participium*] *n* word derived regularly from a verb which is used to form various compound tenses, as in *is writing*, *has written*, and also adjectives, as in *writing instrument*, *the written word* ‖ **par'ti·cip'i·al** *adj*

par·ti·cle /pärt'ikəl/ [L *particula*] *n* 1 very small piece or bit; 2 *gram* a short subordinate indeclinable part of speech, as a conjunction or preposition; **b** prefix or suffix ‖ **SYN** atom, mite, scrap, jot, shred, iota (see *part*)

par'ti·col'ored /pärt'ē-/ [MF *parti* variegated] *adj* having varied colors

par·tic·u·lar /pərtik'yələr/ [MF *particuler* < LL *particularis*] *adj* 1 distinct from others; individual; 2 unusual; 3 exact, precise; 4 exacting; fastidious ‖ *n* 5 individual case or instance; 6 **particulars** *pl* details; 7 **in particular** especially ‖ **par·tic'u·lar·ly** *adv* ‖ **par·tic'u·lar'i·ty** /-lar'-/ *n* ‖ **SYN** *adj* precise, exact, definite, accurate, appropriate, peculiar, singular, individual, finicky, critical

par·tic'u·lar·ize' *vt* 1 to give the details of; specify; 2 to make particular ‖ *vi* 3 to treat specifically

par·tic'u·lates *npl* minute particles, spec. dust and soot in the air

part'ing *n* 1 departure; leave-taking; 2 separation; division

par·ti·san /pärt'izən/ [MF < It *partigiano*] *n* 1 adherent or follower of a person, cause, or party; 2 member of a guerrilla group fighting, or engaged in acts of sabotage, against an enemy army of occupation ‖ also *adj*

par·ti·tion /pärtish'ən/ [< L *partitus* divided] *n* 1 act of dividing or state of being divided; 2 interior dividing wall; 3 section or division ‖ *vt* 4 to divide into parts; 5 to divide by partitions

par·ti·tive *adj* 1 serving to divide into parts; 2 *gram* denoting a part, as a *partitive genitive* ‖ *n* 3 *gram* partitive word or case

part'ly *adv* not wholly; to some extent

part'ner /-nər/ [AF *parcener* coheir] *n* 1 one who takes part in an activity with another; 2 one who is associated with another or others, as a joint owner in a business; associate; 3 *games* one who plays with another against opponents; 4 one who dances with another; 5 spouse ‖ **SYN** associate, colleague, coadjutor, accomplice, confederate, sharer, mate, companion (see *ally*)

part'ner·ship' *n* 1 state of being a partner; 2 joint interest or ownership; 3 association of partners in a business or profession

part' of speech' *n* any of the form classes into which words are traditionally divided, according to meaning, form, and function

par·took /pärtŏŏk'/ *pt* of partake

par·tridge /pär'trij/ [MF *pertris* < Gk *perdix*] *n* 1 any of various Old World gallinaceous game birds (chiefly genus *Perdix*) allied to the quails and pheasants; 2 any of a number of similar game birds of America, as the bobwhite, quail, and ruffled grouse

part' time' *n* less than the usual time for a given occupation ‖ **part'-time'** *adj & adv*

par·tu·ri·tion /pär't(y)ŏŏrish'ən, -chŏŏr-/ [< L *parturire* to give birth] *n* childbirth

par·ty /pärt'ē/ [OF *partie* part] *n* (-ties) 1 group of persons engaged in a particular activity, as *a hunting party*; 2 political organization of people with a common philosophy of government; 3 person or persons on one side of a dispute or court case; 4 participant; 5 social gathering; 6 *colloq* person ‖ *vi* 7 **go partying** *colloq* to attend parties

par'ty girl' *n* 1 attractive young woman hired to entertain men at parties; prostitute; 2 girl or woman who goes to parties all the time

par'ty lead'er *n* 1 head of a political party; 2 first secretary of the Communist Party

par'ty line' *n* 1 telephone line shared by several subscribers; 2 official policy of a totalitarian party, followed without question by its members; **3** line defining the boundary between properties belonging to different persons

par′ty lin′er *n* person who follows the party line of a totalitarian party

par′ty wall′ *n* common wall shared by contiguous buildings

par′ val′ue *n* face value *1*

par·ve·nu /pär′vən(y)o͞o′/ [F = newcomer] *n* one who has recently risen to unaccustomed wealth or social position

pas·chal /pask′əl/ [< Gk *pascha* Easter < Heb *Pesach* Passover] *adj* of or pert. to Easter or to the Passover

pas de deux /pä də du′/ [F] *n* (*pl* **pas de deux** /pä də du′/) ballet figure danced by two partners

pa·sha /pəshä′, pash′ə, päsh′ə/ [Turk] *n* formerly in Turkey, a civil or military official of high rank

pass /pas′, päs′/ [OF *passer* < LL *passare*] *vi* **1** to go; proceed; move along; **2** to go by; **3** to go from one state or condition to another; **4** to elapse or go by, as time; **5** to go unnoticed, as *his action passed without rebuke;* **6** to circulate; **7** to be barely adequate; **8** to be enacted; **9** to depart, go away; **10** to go through a test successfully; **11** *cards* **a** to relinquish the right or opportunity of playing or bidding; **b** to throw in one's hand; **12** to be conveyed or transferred; **13** **bring to pass** to cause to happen; **14** **come to pass** to happen; **15** **pass away, a** to end; **b** to die; **16** **pass for** to be taken as; **17** **pass on, a** to give an opinion on; **b** to die; **18** **pass out** *colloq* to lose consciousness; **19** **pass over** to disregard ‖ *vt* **20** to go by, through, beyond, etc.; **21** to allow to pass; **22** to undergo; **23** to get through successfully, as *to pass an exam;* **24** to cause or allow to go; **25** to cause to go; to hand, as *pass the butter;* **26** to cause to circulate, as bad money or rumors; **27** to spend (time); **28** to give as a judgment, as *to pass sentence;* **29** to utter, as a remark; **30** to enact (legislation); **31** to obtain legislative sanction from, as *the bill passed the house;* **32** to express (judgment); **33** to excrete; **34** to omit, as a dividend; **35** **pass off** to present fraudulently or under a false identity; **36** **pass on** to hand on, convey; **37** **pass over** to refrain from granting recognition to, as for promotion; **38** **pass up** *colloq* to reject ‖ *n* **39** act of passing; **40** narrow passage or defile across a mountain range; **41** permit allowing free admission or passage; **42** *mil* a permit to enter a restricted area or pass through military lines; **b** leave of specified short duration granted to a soldier; **43** *sports* transfer of a ball or puck to a teammate;

44 state of affairs, as *things have come to a dreadful pass;* **45** undergoing successfully of a test or examination; **46** movement of the hands, as in hypnotism or sleight of hand; **47** *fencing* thrust, lunge; **48** *colloq* invitation by word or gesture to sexual intimacy; **49** *cards* act of not bidding or raising another's bid; **50 a pretty pass** *colloq* an awkward or difficult state of affairs ‖ **pass′er** *n*

pass. **1** passive; **2** passenger; **3** passim

pass′a·ble *adj* **1** capable of being passed; **2** acceptable, adequate

pas·sage /pas′ij/ *n* **1** act of going from one place or condition to another; **2** permission to pass; **3** course or progress, as *the passage of time;* **4** journey, voyage; **5** legal enactment; **6** portion of a written work or musical composition; **7** way or means of passing; passageway; **8** conflict, encounter ‖ syn channel, path, hall, entry, corridor (see *way*)

pas′sage·way′ *n* hall, corridor, or alley

pass′book′ *n* bankbook

pas·sé /pasā′/ [F = past] *adj* past; out-of-date

passed′ ball′ in baseball pitched ball which the catcher should but does not catch, allowing a runner to advance

pas·sel /pas′əl/ [var of *parcel*] *n* large group or number

pas·sen·ger /pas′ənjər/ [MF *passager* passer-by] *n* one who is conveyed in an automobile or a public conveyance, as a train, ship, or plane

pas′sen·ger pi′geon *n* extinct pigeon (*Ectopistes migratorius*) once very numerous in North America, noted for migrating in great flocks

pass′er-by′ *n* (**passers-by**) one who passes by

pas·ser·ine /pas′ərin, -rīn′, -rēn′/ [< L *passer* sparrow] *n* bird belonging to the order Passeriformes, comprising more than half of all birds, marked by having the feet adapted for perching ‖ also *adj*

pas·sim /pas′im/ [L] *adv* here and there, throughout (in a text)

pass′ing *adj* **1** going by, beyond, or through; **2** fleeting, as *a passing fancy;* **3** casual, cursory; **4** (grade) sufficient to pass an exam ‖ *n* **5** act of one who or that which passes; **6** way or means of passing; **7** death; **8 in passing** incidentally

pass′ing bell′ *n* **1** bell that announces the death or funeral of a person; **2** harbinger of the passing away of something

pas·sion /pash′ən/ [OE < L *passio* (*-onis*) suffering] *n* **1** fit of violent anger; **2** intense emotional upheaval or excitement; **3** sexual excitement or desire; lust; **4** love, desire, as a *passion for music;* **5** object of love or desire; **6 Passion** Christ's suffering during the last days of his life ‖ SYN enthusiasm, affection, emotion, feeling, ardor

pas·sion·ate /-it/ *adj* 1 capable of intense feeling; 2 ardent; 3 sensual, lustful ‖ **pas′sion·ate·ly** *adv*

Pas′sion play′ *n* representation of the Passion of Christ

pas·sive /pas′iv/ [L *passivus* submissive] *adj* 1 submissive; 2 not acting but acted upon; 3 inactive, inert; quiescent; 4 *gram* designating the voice or form of the verb which represents the subject as the recipient of the action asserted by the verb ‖ *n* 5 passive voice ‖ **pas′sive·ly** *adv* ‖ **pas·siv′i·ty** *n*

pas′sive re·sist′ance *n* resistance, as to a law or government action or policy, by nonviolent means, such as boycotts and noncompliance

pass′key′ *n* 1 master key; 2 skeleton key; 3 private key

Pass′o·ver *n* Jewish feast commemorating the exodus of the Jews from Egypt (Ex. 12)

pass′port′ *n* [MF *passeport*] *n* 1 document given by a government to a citizen traveling abroad, authenticating identity and citizenship; 2 anything that opens the way to success or the accomplishment of a purpose

pass′word′ *n* secret word identifying authorized persons and permitting them to enter or pass

past /past′, päst′/ [var of *passed*] *adj* 1 having formerly been, gone by, as *the past generation;* 2 just gone by, as *the past hour;* 3 having formerly served, as *past president;* 4 *gram* designating a tense of the verb which expresses action, state, etc. in the past ‖ *n* 5 time gone by; 6 previous life or history; 7 *gram* past tense ‖ *adv* 8 by, beyond, as *walk past* ‖ *prep* 9 after in time; 10 beyond, as *past the bridge*

pas·ta /päst′ə/ [It] *n* thin unleavened dough produced in a variety of shapes, usu. boiled and served with a sauce

paste /päst′/ [MF < Gk = porridge] *n* 1 mixture, often made of flour and water, used for sticking things together; 2 dough in a moist sticky condition; 3 preparation, as of fish or nuts, reduced to a creamy consistency; 4 fruit-flavored jellylike confection; 5 a heavy glass used to make artificial gems; **b** gems so made; 6 *slang* blow on the face ‖ *vt* 7 to stick with paste; 8 to cover by or as by pasting; 9 *slang* to land a blow on

paste′board′ *n* thick stiff material made of layers of paper or wood pulp pasted together

paste′ gem′ *n* imitation gem made of glass

pas·tel /pastel′/ [F < It *pastello* dim. of *pasta* paste] *n* 1 soft subdued shade; 2 crayon made by mixing ground paints with gum water; 3 picture drawn with such crayon ‖ also *adj*

pas·tern /past′ərn/ [MF *pasturon*] *n* that part of a horse's foot between the fetlock and the footbone

pas·teur·ize /pas′chəriz/, past′ə-/ [< Louis *Pasteur* (1822–95) F chemist and biologist] *vt* to expose (milk, cheese, or fermented liquids) to a high temperature but below the boiling point for a given period of time, to kill bacteria and arrest fermentation ‖ **pas′teur·i·za′tion** *n*

pas·tiche /pastĕsh′, pä-/ [F < It] *n* 1 miscellany of artistic, literary, musical, or other borrowings; 2 literary or musical imitation; parody

pas′time′ /pas′-, päs′-/ [*pass* + *time*] *n* something which causes the time to pass agreeably; diversion ‖ SYN recreation, entertainment (see *amusement*)

past′ mas′ter *n* masterful or consummate practitioner of some art or profession ‖ **past′ mis′tress** *nfem*

pas·tor /past′ər/ [L = shepherd] *n* clergyman in charge of a church

pas′to·ral /-əl/ *adj* 1 pert. to shepherds; 2 pert. to rustic life; rural; 3 pert. to the duties of a clergyman ‖ *n* 4 poem, play, or story showing the life and customs of shepherds; 5 picture showing rural life or scenes

pas′tor·ate /-it/ *n* 1 office or tenure of a pastor; 2 body of pastors

past′ par′ti·ci·ple *n* participle with past meaning

past′ per′fect *n* tense formed with the past tense of *have* and a past participle, as *I had seen* ‖ also *adj*

pas·tra·mi /pəsträm′ē/ [Yiddish < Rumanian] *n* cut of smoked or pickled beef, highly seasoned

pas·try /päst′rē/ [see **paste**] *n* (-**tries**) desserts, as pies, tarts, etc., made with a rich crust of shortened paste

pas·tur·age /pas′chərij, päs′-/ *n* pasture

pas·ture /pas′chər, päs′-/ [MF < LL *pastura*] *n* 1 grass on which cattle feed; 2 ground covered with such grass ‖ *vt* 3 to put (livestock) to graze on a pasture

past·y /päst′ē/ *adj* (-**i·er**; -**i·est**) resembling paste in appearance or texture ‖ **past′i·ness** *n*

pat[1] /pat′/ [ME] *n* 1 light tap or blow with the hand; 2 small shaped lump, as of butter; 3 light sound or tap ‖ *v* (**pat·ted**; **pat·ting**) *vt* 4 to strike gently with a flat surface or with the hand or fingers; 5 to stroke gently; 6 **pat on the back** *colloq* to praise; compliment

pat[2] [?] *adj* 1 apt, fitting; 2 excessively glib; 3 thoroughly mastered, as *to have it pat* ‖ *adv* 4 perfectly; 5 **stand pat, a** *poker* to play the cards dealt without drawing; **b** to hold firmly to one's line of conduct

pat. patent(ed)

Pat·a·go·ni·a /pat'əgōn'ē-ə, -yə/ *n* large flat region in S South America extending from the Andes to the Atlantic, lying mostly in Argentina || **Pat'a·go'ni·an** *adj & n*

patch /pach'/ [ME *pacche*] *n* **1** piece of material put on to mend a tear, cover a hole, strengthen a worn place, or protect a wounded part, etc.; **2** small piece of anything, as of ground or clouds; **3** beauty spot *1* || *vt* **4** to put a patch on; **5** often **patch up, a** to mend or repair hastily; **b** to settle, as a quarrel || **patch'y** *adj* (**-i·er; -i·est**)

patch·ou·li /pəchŏŏl'ē, pach'ŏŏlē/ [F < Tamil *pacculi*] *n* strong perfume made from the fragrant oil of either of two East Indian plants, *Pogostemon heyneanus* and *P. cablin*

patch' pock'et *n* pocket made by sewing a piece of material on the outside of a garment

patch' test' *n* allergy test made by applying an allergy-impregnated patch to the skin

patch'work' *n* **1** fabric made of pieces of cloth of various shapes and colors sewed together; **2** any work thrown together haphazardly; jumble

pate /pāt'/ [ME] *n* top of the head

pâ·té de foie gras /pätā' də fwä' grä'/ [F] *n* paste made of the livers of fattened geese, used as a table delicacy

pa·tel·la /pətel'ə/ [L, dim. of *patena* pan] *n* (**-lae -lē/**) kneecap

pat·ent /pat'ənt/ [L *patens* (*-entis*) lying open] *n* **1** right or privilege granted by the government as the sole right to make, use, or sell an invention for a certain number of years; **2** document granting this right; **3** that which is patented || *vt* **4** to take out a patent on || *adj* **5** patented; **6** also /pāt'ənt/ **a** obvious; **b** lying open || **pat'ent·ly** /pāt'-/ *adv* || SYN *adj* manifest, clear, unobscured (see *obvious*)

pat·ent·ee' /pat'-/ *n* person to whom or company to which a patent has been granted

pat'ent leath'er /pat'-/ *n* leather with a hard, smooth, glossy surface

pat'ent med'i·cine /pat'-/ *n* **1** patented medicine; **2** medicine sold in drugstores without a prescription

pat'ent right' /pat'-/ *n* exclusive right conferred by a patent

pa·ter·nal /pəturn'əl/ [< L *pater* father] *adj* **1** of or pert. to a father; **2** received from a father; **3** related through the father || **pa·ter'nal·ly** *adv*

pa·ter'nal·ism *n* benevolent despotism,

whereby the state, corporation, or other authority seeks to maintain with the governed or employed a relationship like that between a father and his dependent children

pa·ter'ni·ty [L *paternitas* < *pater* father] *n* **1** fatherhood; **2** male parentage; **3** authorship, source

pa·ter·nos·ter /pät'ərnost'ər, pat'-/ [L = our father] *n* **1** the Lord's Prayer, esp. the Latin version; **2** any formula used as a prayer; **3** every eleventh bead in a rosary, indicating that the Lord's Prayer is to be said

Pat·er·son /pat'ərsən/ *n* city in NE New Jersey (145,000)

path /path', päth'/ [OE *pæth*] *n* (**paths** /-*thz*, -ths/) **1** road worn by the feet of men or animals; **2** walk or way; **3** course or route

path- [Gk *pathos* suffering] *comb form* disease

-path /-path'/ [< -*pathy*] *n comb form* **1** practitioner of a particular system of medicine, as *osteopath*; **2** one suffering from a specific ailment, as *psychopath*

pa·thet·ic /pəthet'ik/ [Gk *pathetikos* sensitive] *adj* **1** arousing sorrow and pity; **2** pert. to the feelings; **3** woefully inadequate || **pa·thet'i·cal·ly** *adv*

path'find'er *n* one who finds or makes a way through unexplored territory

-path·ic /-path'ik/ *adj suf* forming adjectives from nouns in **-pathy**

patho- var of **path-**

path·o·gen /path'əjən/ *n* disease-producing organism || **path'o·gen'ic** /-jen'-/ *adj*

path·o·log·i·cal /path'əloj'ikəl/ *adj* **1** of or pert. to pathology; **2** pert. to disease; **3** diseased; **4** inveterate (liar)

pa·thol·o·gy /pəthol'əjē/ *n* (**-gies**) **1** science that treats of diseases; **2** physical condition of an organ or body part, caused by disease || **pa·thol'o·gist** *n*

pa·thos /pā'thos/ [Gk = suffering] *n* **1** that quality in an experience, or in literature or music, that excites sympathy and pity; **2** pity

path'way' *n* path

-pa·thy /-pəthē/ [Gk *patheia* suffering] *n comb form* **1** disease, as *neuropathy*; **2** system of therapy, as *osteopathy*; **3** feeling or emotion, as *sympathy*

pa·tience /pāsh'əns/ *n* **1** the quality of suffering without complaint; **2** endurance and perseverance; **3** power to wait calmly; **4** *cards* solitaire || SYN perseverance, calmness, composure, fortitude, endurance, forbearance, resignation, submission || DISCR *Patience* bears the troubles of life without complaint in looks, manner, or speech. *Endurance* bears suffering and hardship with determined firmness. *Patience* is the outgrowth of mind and soul; *endurance* requires physical stamina as well. *Fortitude* combines high courage with the habit and power of *endurance;* we face periods of unrelieved pain or of adversity with *fortitude*. *Forbearance* consists in refraining from a justly provoked action; *forbearance* does not repay injury in kind, not from supineness or unawareness, but by exercise of the will. *Resignation* is an uncomplaining acceptance of sorrow or evil on a loftier plane than that of *patience* or *endurance; endurance* may endure in frank displeasure; *patience* may yield to harassment; *resignation* submits unfalteringly. *Submission* names the obedient spirit in which great trials or serious affairs are met || ANT impatience, peevishness, anger, intolerance

pa·tient /pāsh′ənt/ [MF *pacient* < L *patiens* (*-entis*) suffering] *adj* 1 suffering pain, hardship, affliction, insult, or the like, with meekness or calmness; 2 persevering; 3 waiting with calmness || *n* 4 one under the care of a doctor || **pa′tient·ly** *adv*

pat·i·na /pat′(ĭ)nə/ [It = coating] *n* 1 green coating of oxides and carbonates which forms on copper, brass, and bronze after exposure to the weather; 2 similar film formed by exposure on any metal or wooden surface

pa·ti·o /pat′ē·ō′/ [Sp] *n* 1 courtyard within a house or other building; 2 paved unroofed area adjoining a house

pat·ois /pat′wä/ [F] *n* (**-ois** /-wäz/) local dialect

pat. pend. patent pending

patri- [Gk & L *pater*] *comb form* father

pa·tri·arch /pāt′rē·ärk′/ [Gk *patriarches*] *n* 1 founder or head of a family or tribe; 2 one of the early ancestors of the Jews, as Abraham, Isaac, and Jacob; 3 aged and venerable man; 4 head of one of the autonomous branches of the Eastern Orthodox Church; 5 highest-ranking Roman Catholic bishop after the Pope; 6 head of any of certain independent churches of the East; 7 high dignitary of the Mormon Church || **pa′tri·ar′chal** *adj*

pa′tri·ar′chate /-ĭt/ *n* 1 office, jurisdiction, or residence of a patriarch; 2 patriarchy

pa′tri·ar′chy *n* (**-chies**) social organization in which the father is the head of the family

pa·tri·cian /pətrish′ən/ [< L *patricius*] *n* 1 member of the ancient Roman aristocracy; 2 aristocrat || also *adj*

pat·ri·cide /pat′risīd′/ *n* 1 murder of

one's father; 2 one who murders his father

Pat·rick /pat′rik/, **Saint** *n* (389?–461?) bishop and patron saint of Ireland

pat·ri·mo·ny /pat′rimōn′ē/ [L *patrimonium*] *n* (**-nies**) 1 property or estate inherited from one's father or ancestors; 2 heritage

pa·tri·ot /pāt′rē·ət, -ot′/ [MF *patriote* < Gk *patriotes* fellow countryman] *n* one who loves and supports his country and its interests || **pa′tri·ot·ism** *n* || **pa′tri·ot′ic** /-ot′-/ *adj*

pa·tris·tic /pətrist′ik/ also **pa·tris′ti·cal** *adj* of or pert. to the early fathers of the Christian church or to their writings

pa·trol /pətrōl′/ [F *patrouiller*, orig. to tramp in the mud] *v* (**-trolled; -trol·ling**) *vt* 1 to make regular rounds in (an area) for protection or surveillance || *vi* 2 to go on patrol || *n* 3 act of patrolling; 4 one or more persons, vehicles, ships, or planes assigned to patrol; 5 subdivision of a Boy Scout troop

pa·trol′man /-mən/ *n* (**-men** /-mən/) policeman assigned to patrol on foot

pa·trol′ wag′on *n* police van for transporting arrested persons to the police station

pa·tron /pāt′rən/ [L *patronus*] *n* 1 guardian or protector; 2 upholder or supporter, as of music or the arts; 3 customer or client; 4 one who supports a social or charitable event; 5 patron saint || **pa′tron·ess** *nfem*

pa·tron·age /pāt′rənij, pat′-/ *n* 1 support; guardianship; protection; 2 condescension; 3 offices and jobs given out by a politician in return for political loyalty and support

pa′tron·ize /pāt′-, pat′-/ *vt* 1 to support or sponsor; 2 to treat with condescension; 3 to trade with as a regular customer || SYN promote, support, countenance, aid, favor

pa′tron·iz′ing *adj* condescending

pa′tron saint′ *n* saint regarded as the guardian of an individual, church, or institution

pat·ro·nym·ic /pat′rənim′ik/ *n* 1 family name; 2 family name derived from the name of an ancestor by the addition of an affix indicating descent, as *Johnson*, *MacAndrew*

pa·troon /pətrōōn′/ [D < L *patronus* patron] *n* one who received a large tract of land with manorial rights under the old Dutch government of New York and New Jersey

pat·sy /pat′sē/ [?] *n* (**-sies**) *slang* 1 dupe; 2 scapegoat; 3 butt of a joke

pat·ter[1] /pat′ər/ [< *pater*noster] *vt* & *vi* 1 to speak glibly and rapidly || *n* 2 glib and rapid speech, as of an entertainer, salesman, or circus barker; 3 chatter, meaningless talk

pat·ter[2] [< *pat*[1]] *n* 1 quick succession of light tapping sounds || *vi* 2 to run with quick short steps; **3** to make a patter || *vt* **4** to cause to patter

pat·tern /pat'ərn/ [MF *patron* < ML *patronus*] *n* **1** model from which to copy; **2** anything cut out or formed into a shape to be copied; **3** decorative design; **4** style or type; **5** consistent or characteristic arrangement or design || *vt* **6** to make or fashion after a pattern; **7** to supply or ornament with a pattern

pat·ty /pat'ē/ [F *pâté* pastry] *n* (**-ties**) **1** small pie; **2** thin round piece of food, as of hamburger; **3** food fried or baked in a shell of dough

pat'ty-cake' *n* children's game consisting of mutual palm-slapping accompanied by a nursery rhyme

pau·ci·ty /pôs'itē/ [L *paucitas*] *n* **1** smallness of number; **2** scarcity

Paul /pôl/ *n Bib* apostle of Christ and missionary to the Gentiles (Acts 9: 3–32), whose epistles are contained in several books of the New Testament || **Paul'ine** /-īn/ *adj*

Paul' Bun'yan /bun'yən/ *n* legendary giant American lumberjack

paunch /pônch', pänch'/ [AF *paunche*] *n* belly, esp. if protruding || **paunch'y** *adj* (**-i·er; -i·est**)

pau·per /pôp'ər/ [L = poor] *n* very poor person, esp. if supported by public welfare

pau'per·ize' *vt* to make a pauper of || **pau'per·i·za'tion** *n*

pause /pôz'/ [L *pausa*] *n* **1** temporary stop or rest; **2** *mus* mark over or under a note or rest to show that it is to be prolonged; **3** give pause to to cause to hesitate || *vi* **4** to make a short stop; wait; hesitate || SYN *n* cessation, stay, delay, suspension, stop

pave /pāv'/ [MF *paver*] *vt* **1** to cover the surface of (a street or road) with bricks, asphalt, concrete, etc.; **2 pave the way** to prepare the way

pave'ment [OF < L *pavimentum*] *n* **1** paved surface of a street or road; **2** sidewalk

pa·vil·ion /pəvil'yən/ [OF *paveillon*] *n* **1** large tent, esp. one supported on posts; **2** temporary open building for shelter, entertainment, etc.; **3** one of a group of adjacent or attached buildings, as in a hospital

pav·ing /pāv'iŋ/ *n* **1** pavement; **2** material for a pavement

Pav·lov, I·van Pe·tro·vich /ivän' petrô'vich pav'lov/ *n* (1849–1936) Russian physiologist, pioneer in the study of conditioned reflexes

paw¹ /pô'/ [MF *poue* < Gmc] *n* **1** foot of a four-footed animal with claws; **2** *colloq* hand || *vt* **3** to touch or scrape with the forefeet; **4** *colloq* to handle clumsily or roughly or with too much familiarity || also *vi*

paw² *n dial.* pa

pawl /pôl'/ [?] *n* tonguelike piece hinged to engage the teeth of a

ratchet wheel so as to impart or prevent motion

pawn¹ /pôn'/ [OF *pan* pledge] *n* **1** something given as security for a loan; **2** state of being so pledged || *vt* **3** to give as security for a loan

pawn² [AF *poun*] *n* **1** *chess* piece of the lowest value; **2** one who is manipulated for the advantage of another

pawn'bro'ker *n* one whose business is to lend money on goods deposited with him as security

pawn'shop' *n* pawnbroker's shop

pawn' tick'et *n* receipt for goods left with a pawnbroker

paw'paw' *n* papaw

pay /pā'/ [OF *paier* < L *pacare* to appease] *v* (**paid**) *vt* **1** to satisfy the claims of; **2** to recompense for labor or work done; **3** to discharge, as a debt, by giving what is required; **4** to be profitable to, as *it pays you to study;* **5** to defray (expenses); **6** to yield, as interest or dividends; **7** to render (a compliment, attention, regards, etc.); **8** to make (a visit); **9 pay back** to retaliate upon; **10 pay down** to give (a partial payment) at the time of purchase; **11 pay off, a** to pay (a debt) in full; **b** to pay (a person) full wages due, as when discharging him; **12** *slang* to bribe; **13 pay out** to disburse || *vi* **13** to make recompense; discharge a debt; **14** to be profitable or worth while; **15 pay up** to make full payment || *v* (**payed** /pād'/) *vt* **16 pay out** to pass out (a rope) by slackening || *n* **17** payment; **18** wages or salary; **19** paid employment; **20** person from the standpoint of his ability or willingness to pay, as *he is good pay* || **pay'er** *n* || SYN *v* remunerate, compensate, repay, reimburse, requite, defray, indemnify; *n* (see **salary**)

pay'a·ble *adj* **1** to be paid; due; **2** that can be paid

pay'check' *n* **1** bank check given in payment of wages; **2** wages

pay' dirt' *n* **1** gravel containing gold that can be extracted at a profit; **2 hit pay dirt** *slang* to be successful in an endeavor

pay·ee' *n* one to whom money is or is to be paid

pay' en've·lope *n* **1** envelope in which wages are delivered; **2** wages

pay'load' *n* **1** revenue-producing cargo or paying passengers; **2** warhead of a guided missile, rocket, or aircraft

pay'mas'ter *n* person charged with paying wages

pay'ment *n* **1** act of paying; **2** that which is paid; **3** recompense or punishment

pay'off' *n* **1** payment of money due, as for a bet or debt; **2** reckoning or settlement; **3** reward, retribution; **4** climax or culmination

pay·o·la /pā-ōl'ə/ *n slang* bribe paid

for the promotion of a commercial product, esp. to a disk jockey to play certain records

pay'out' *n* disbursement; distribution of money

pay'roll' *n* 1 list of persons receiving pay, with the amount due each; 2 total amount of a payroll; 3 the cash for it

pay' sta'tion *n* coin-operated public telephone

Pb [L *plumbum*] *chem* lead

P.B.A. Patrolmen's Benevolent Association

p.c., pct. percent

Pd *chem* palladium

pd. paid

P.D.Q. [pretty damn quick] *adv slang* right away

pea /pē²/ [< *pease* < OE *pise* < LL *pisa*] *n* (peas or *archaic* pease) 1 pod-bearing vine (*Pisum sativum*); 2 edible seed of this vine; 3 any of various other plants or their seed similar to the pea; 4 something small and round like a pea

peace /pēs²/ [OF *pais* < L *pax*] *n* 1 freedom from or cessation of war; 2 friendly international relations; 3 any state of calm or tranquillity; 4 public order; 5 **hold one's peace** to keep silent; 6 **keep the peace** to maintain public order; 7 **make one's peace** to become reconciled || **peace'a·ble** *adj* || **peace'ful** *adj* || SYN quiet, rest, calm, concord, agreement

peace'mak'er *n* one who tries to restore peace between two unfriendly parties

peace' pipe' *n* calumet

peace'time' *n* period of peace

peach¹ /pēch²/ [MF *peche* < L *persicum* (malum) Persian (apple)] *n* 1 the fleshy juicy fruit of an orchard tree, *Prunus persica*; 2 the tree itself; 3 light pinkish yellow; 4 *colloq* someone or something approved of for excellence or beauty

peach² [earlier *appeach* < AF *apecher*] *vi slang* to inform against an accomplice

peach'y *adj* (-i·er; -i·est) *colloq* excellent; fine

pea'cock' [OE *pēa* peafowl < L *pavo*] *n* 1 male of the peafowl, noted for its long handsome erectile tail, marked with iridescent eyelike spots; 2 any peafowl; 3 vain strutting person

pea'fowl' *n* any of a genus (*Pavo*) of fowls with greenish-blue plumage

pea' green' *n* yellowish green || **pea'-green'** *adj*

pea'hen' *n* female peafowl

pea' jack'et [< D *pij* coarse woolen cloth] *n* short double-breasted coat of thick woolen cloth, as worn by sailors

peak /pēk²/ [perh < *pike*] *n* 1 pointed summit of a mountain; 2 mountain with a pointed summit; 3 pointed top or end of anything; 4 highest point; 5 visor of a cap; 6 period of maximum intensity, volume, load, or the like || *vi* 7 to reach a maximum

peak'ed /-id/ [?] *adj* wan, sickly

peal /pēl²/ [prob < *appeal*] *n* 1 long, loud sound, as of bells, thunder, or laughter || *vi* 2 to ring or resound

pea'nut' *n* 1 nutlike fruit of a vine (*Arachis hypogaea*) of the pea family, which ripens underground in shell-like pods; 2 the vine itself; 3 **work for peanuts** *slang* to receive very low pay

pea'nut but'ter *n* paste made from ground roasted peanuts, used chiefly as a spread

pea'nut gal'ler·y *n colloq* rearmost or topmost balcony of a theater

pear /per²/ [OE *peru* < L *pirum*] *n* 1 the fleshy edible fruit of an orchard tree, *Pyrus communis*, typically rounded at the base and narrow at the stem; 2 the tree itself

pearl /purl²/ [MF *perle* < LL *perla*] *n* 1 small rounded mass of lustrous, satiny substance, creamy or silvery white to black in color, formed within the shells of certain bivalves to cover irritating substances that get inside the shell; valued as a gem; 2 anything resembling this; 3 pale-grayish-white color; 4 mother-of-pearl; 5 something that is a fine example of its kind || *vt* 6 to adorn with pearls || *vi* 7 to fish for pearls || **pearl'y** *adj* (-i·er; -i·est)

Pearl' Har'bor *n* large U.S. naval base near Honolulu, scene of the Japanese surprise attack Dec. 7, 1941 that precipitated U.S. entry into World War II

peas·ant /pez²ənt/ [MF *paisant* < L *pagensis* of a province] *n* in many countries, uneducated farm laborer or petty farmer; low-class rustic

peas'ant·ry *n* the class of peasants; peasants collectively

pease /pēz²/ *n archaic pl* of **pea**

pea'shoot'er *n* toy consisting of a slender tube through which dried peas or the like are blown

pea' soup' *n* 1 soup of split peas; 2 *colloq* impenetrable yellowish fog

peat /pēt²/ [ML *peta*] *n* carbonaceous deposit occurring principally in marshy places, composed of partly decayed vegetable matter and forming a valuable fuel when dried

peat' moss' *n* moss, esp. of the genus *Sphagnum*, from which peat is formed

peb·ble /peb²əl/ [OE *papolstān* pebble stone] *n* 1 small rounded stone, worn smooth as by the action of water || *vt* 2 to grain (leather) so as to produce an uneven surface || **peb'bly** *adj*

pe·can /pikan², -kän², pē²kan/ [Cree *pakan*] *n* 1 sweet nut with a smooth oval shell, fruit of a hickory tree (*Carya illinoensis*) of the S U.S.; **2** the tree

pec·ca·dil·lo /pek'ədil'ō/ [Sp *pecadillo*] *n* (-**los** or -**loes**) petty or trifling sin or fault

pec·ca·ry /pek'ərē/ [< Carib] *n* (-**ries**) genus (*Tayassu*) of hoglike animals of nocturnal, gregarious, and pugnacious habits, of tropical and subtropical America

peck[1] /pek'/ [OF *pek*] *n* **1** dry measure of 8 quarts or one quarter of a bushel; **2** a great deal, as *a peck of trouble*

peck[2] [var of **pick**[2]] *vt* **1** to strike with the beak, as a bird; **2** to strike with a pointed instrument; **3** to make (a hole) by pecking; **4** to pick up (food) with the beak || *vi* **5** to make strokes with the beak or a sharp instrument; **6 peck at**, a to nibble at (food); **b** to nag || *n* **7** quick sharp stroke, as with the beak; **8** *colloq* quick light kiss

pec·tin /pek'tin/ [< Gk *pektos* congealed] *n* carbohydrate occurring in many fruits and vegetables, the cause of the formation of jelly in jams and preserves

pec·to·ral /pek'tərəl/ [< L *pectus* (-*oris*) breast] *adj* **1** pert. to, located at, or worn on the chest || *n* **2** something worn on the chest

pec·tose /-tōs/ [< *pectin*] *n* the pulpy part of fleshy, unripe fruits, convertible into pectin by heat or the process of ripening

pec·u·late /pek'yəlāt'/ [L *peculari* (-*atus*)] *vt* & *vi* to embezzle || **pec'u·la'tion** *n*

pe·cu·liar /pikyōōl'yər/ [L *peculiaris* of private property] *adj* **1** distinctive; individual; **2** strange; queer; **3 peculiar to** characteristic of || **pe·cu'liar·ly** *adv* SYN queer, singular, odd, unusual, rare, strange

pe·cu'li·ar'i·ty /-ē·ar'-/ *n* (-**ties**) **1** state or quality of being peculiar; **2** peculiar trait or characteristic; **3** eccentricity, oddness

pe·cu·ni·ar·y /pikyōōn'ē·er'ē/ [< L *pecunia* money] *adj* relating to or involving money || SYN monetary, fiscal, financial || DISCR *Pecuniary* affairs concern and involve money; a *pecuniary* reward consists of money. *Monetary* is applied to money itself, as the *monetary* standard of a coinage. *Financial* refers to the science of managing money, especially in large sums. *Fiscal* ordinarily applies to public revenue or accounts, or to the *financial* affairs of government when their official nature is stressed. *Fiscal* and *financial* are interchangeable in the expression, the *fiscal* year; but *fiscal* is more common in American, *financial* in English, usage.

ped[1] or **pedi-** [L *pes* (*pedis*)] *comb form* foot

ped[2] or **pedo-** [Gk *pais* (*paidos*)] *comb form* child, boy

-ped /-ped', -pəd/ also **-pede** /-pēd'/ [L *pes* (*pedis*)] *comb form* foot

ped·a·gogue also **ped·a·gog** /ped'əgog', -gôg'/ [Gk *paidagogos*] *n* **1** schoolmaster, teacher; **2** pedant || **ped'a·gog'ic** /-goj'ik, -gōj'-/ *adj*

ped·a·go·gy /-gō'jē, -goj'ē/ *n* **1** teaching; **2** science or art of teaching

ped·al /ped'əl/ [L *pedalis* of the feet] *n* **1** foot-operated lever or treadle || *v* (-**aled** or -**alled**; -**al·ing** or -**al·ling**) *vt* **2** to operate by treading on the pedals; **3** to drive by operating pedals || *vi* **4** to use pedals || /also pēd'əl/ *adj* **5** of or pert. to the feet

ped'al push'ers /ped'-/ *npl* slacks extending half way down the calf of the leg, worn by women or girls

ped·ant /ped'ənt/ [It *pedante* teacher] *n* **1** one who makes a needless display of learning; **2** one who insists on strict adherence to rules and picayune details || **pe·dan·tic** /pədant'ik/ *adj* || **pe·dan'ti·cal·ly** *adv*

ped'ant·ry *n* (-**ries**) **1** state or condition of being a pedant; **2** instance of this

ped·dle /ped'əl/ [< ME *pedlere* peddler] *vi* **1** to travel about selling small wares; **2** to do a small business || *vt* **3** to sell from door to door; hawk; **4** to deal out in small quantities, as candy, gossip, favors || **ped'dler** *n*

ped·er·as·ty /ped'əras'tē/ [Gk *paiderastia* love for boys] *n* anal intercourse, esp. with a boy || **ped'er·ast'** *n*

ped·es·tal /ped'istəl/ [MF *piedestal* < It *piedistallo* foot of a stall] *n* base, foot, or support, esp. for a column or statue

pe·des·tri·an /pədest'rē·ən/ [< L *pedester* on foot] *adj* **1** going on foot; walking; **2** dull, unimaginative; banal || *n* **3** one who goes on foot

pedi- var of **ped**[1]

pe·di·at·rics /pēd'ē·at'riks, ped'-/ *nsg* branch of medicine dealing with the care of children and the treatment of their diseases || **pe'di·at'ric** *adj* || **pe'di·a·tri'cian** /-ətrish'ən/ *n*

ped'i·cab' /ped'ē-/ *n* three-wheeled vehicle for two passengers pedaled by a driver in front

ped'i·cure' /ped'ē-/ *n* care and treatment of the feet

ped·i·gree /ped'igrē'/ [MF *pie de grue* crane's foot < shape of genealogical tree] *n* **1** record of ancestry; **2** lineage, descent

ped'i·greed' *adj* having a known pedigree

ped'i·ment [earlier *peremint* < *pyramid*] *n* **1** ornamented, usu. triangular low space or gable over the front of a building; **2** similar decoration over a door, window, or the like

ped·lar /ped'lər/ *n* var of **peddler**

pedo- var of **ped**[2]

pe·dom·e·ter /pidom'itər/ *n* instrument for recording the distance covered in walking

pe·dun·cle /pidunk'əl/ [< NL *pedunculus* little foot] *n* 1 primary flower stalk supporting either a solitary flower or a cluster of flowers; 2 *zool* stalklike process

peek /pēk'/ [MF *pike*] *vi* 1 to glance furtively, esp. through a crevice or crack || *n* 2 quick furtive look

peek'a·boo' [children's peeping game] *adj* 1 (woman's blouse or dress) made of transparent materials or cut away so as to reveal the body; 2 pert. to a method of retrieving documents through the light shining through matching holes in index cards

peel /pēl'/ [OE *pilian* < L *pilare* to remove hair from] *vt* 1 to strip off (skin, rind, bark, etc.); 2 to strip the skin, rind, bark, etc. from; 3 **keep one's eyes peeled** *colloq* to keep a close watch || *vi* 4 to come off, as skin, rind, or bark; 5 to lose an outer covering; 6 *colloq* to undress || *n* 7 skin or rind

peen /pēn'/ [prob < Scand] *n* spherical or wedge-shaped end of a hammer head, opposite the face

peep¹ /pēp'/ [ME *pepen*] *vi* 1 to chirp or cry, as a young bird || *n* 2 cry of a young bird; chirp, squeak

peep² [ME *pepe*] *vi* 1 to look through a crack or from a hiding place; 2 to look slyly or furtively; 3 to begin to appear, as the sun || *n* 4 quick, furtive look; 5 glimpse; 6 first appearance

peep'hole' *n* hole to peep through

peep'ing Tom' [tailor who peeped at Lady Godiva as she rode naked through the streets of Coventry] *n* person who gains sexual gratification from watching others from hiding

peep' show' *n* exhibition viewed through a small opening, sometimes fitted with a magnifying glass

peep' sight' *n* rear sight on a firearm consisting of a flat plate with a small hole through which the gunner peeps when aiming

pee·pul /pē'pəl/ *n* var of **pipal**

peer¹ /pir'/ [OF *per* < L *par* equal] *n* 1 equal, as in rank or ability; 2 nobleman || **peer'ess** *nfem* || **peer'age** /-ij/ *n*

peer² [?] *vi* 1 to look narrowly or closely, as if to see more clearly; 2 to peep out

peer'less *adj* without equal, matchless

peeve /pēv'/ [< *peevish*] *vt* 1 to irritate, vex || *n* 2 source of annoyance; vexation; 3 grievance; complaint

peev·ish [ME *pevish*] *adj* fretful, querulous || SYN irritable, querulous, petulant, pettish, captious, ill-humored, testy, fretful, cross || ANT good-humored, forbearing, gentle, patient, controlled

pee·wee /pē'wē'/ [< *wee*?] *n* person, animal, or thing much smaller than normal

peg /peg'/ [ME *pegge* < MD] *n* 1 pin or bolt, often of wood, used to hold things together, hang things on, make fast tent ropes, stop up holes, mark scores, etc.; 2 *mus* pin in the neck of a stringed instrument, which, when turned, tightens or loosens the string which is attached to it; 3 *colloq* step or degree; 4 *colloq* leg; 5 *baseball* throw at a base or home in an attempt to put out a runner; 6 **take down a peg** to humble || *v* (pegged); peg·ging) *vt* 7 to fasten, mark, or pierce with pegs; 8 *baseball* to throw (the ball) fast and low; 9 to fix (prices) || *vi* 10 **peg away** to work steadily and persistently

Peg·a·sus /peg'əsəs/ *n* 1 *class. myth.* winged horse, used by Bellerophon in overcoming the Chimera; 2 *astron* large northern constellation, its three brightest stars forming part of the square of Pegasus

peg' leg' *n* 1 wooden leg; 2 person with a wooden leg

peg'-top' *adj* (dress or trousers) wide at the hips and narrow at the ankles

P.E.I. Prince Edward Island

peign·oir /pānwär', pen-, pān'wär, pen'-/ [F] *n* woman's dressing gown

pe·jo·ra·tive /pijōr'ətiv, -jor'-, pej'-ərāt'iv, pēj'-/ [< L *pejorare* (*-atus*) to make worse] *adj* 1 disparaging (word or affix), depreciating in meaning || *n* 2 pejorative word or form || **pej'o·ra'tion** /pej'-, pēj'-/ *n*

Pe·kin /pēk'in'/ [*Peking*] *n* one of a large breed of flightless domestic ducks

Pe·king /pēk'iŋ/ *n* capital of the People's Republic of China (8,000,000)

Pe·king·ese or **Pe·kin·ese** /pēk'inēz', -nēs/ *n* (-ese) 1 small pugnosed, long-haired toy dog, originating in China; 2 native or inhabitant of Peking; 3 Chinese dialect of Peking || also *adj*

pe·koe /pēk'ō, pek'ō/ [Chin *pek ho* white down] *n* a choice black tea from India, Ceylon, and Java

pe·lag·ic /pəlaj'ik/ [< Gk *pelagos* sea] *adj* 1 of or pert. to the sea or ocean; 2 living or growing near the surface of the ocean, far from shore

pelf /pelf'/ [OF *pelfre* booty] *n* disparaging wealth, esp. if ill-gotten

pel·i·can /pel'ikən/ [OE *pellican* < Gk *pelekan*] *n* any of certain large web-footed water birds (genus *Pelecanus*) with a huge bill, the lower part of which has a large pouch for storing food

pel·la·gra /pəlag'rə, -lāg'-, läg'-/ [It] *n* disease caused by niacin deficiency, characterized by skin rashes and serious disturbance of the nervous system

pel·let /pel'it/ [MF *pelote*] *n* 1 any small, densely formed ball, as of clay or food; 2 small shot or bullet

pel·li·cle /pel'ikəl/ [L *pellicula*] *n* very thin skin or film

pell-mell also **pell-mell** /pel'mel'/ [MF *pelemele*] *adv* in a confused and disorderly manner; headlong || also *adj*

pel·lu·cid /pəloos'id/ [L *pellucidus*] *adj* 1 perfectly clear; transparent; 2 easily understood

pe·lo·ta /pəlō'tə/ [Sp] *n* 1 game of jai alai; 2 ball used in this game

pelt[1] /pelt'/ [ME] *n* undressed skin of a fur-bearing animal

pelt[2] [?] *vt* 1 to strike by throwing missiles at; 2 to hurl; 3 to beat repeatedly || *vi* 4 to strike repeated blows; 5 to beat down heavily, as rain or hail; 6 to hurry

pel·vis /pel'vis/ [L = basin] *n* (-**vis·es** or -**ves** /-vēz/) basin-shaped, bony hip girdle in the lower part of the trunk, supporting the spinal column and resting on the lower extremities || **pel'vic** *adj*

pem·mi·can /pem'ikən/ [Cree *pimikan*] *n* American Indian food made of meat, fat, and sometimes fruit, dried, pounded, and pressed into cakes

pen[1] /pen'/ [OE *penn*] *n* 1 enclosure, as for confining animals || *v* (**penned** or **pent; pen·ning**) *vt* 2 to confine in or as in a pen

pen[2] [MF *penne* < L *penna* feather] *n* 1 any of various writing instruments using ink || *v* (**penned; pen·ning**) *vt* 2 to write with or as with a pen

pen[3] *n slang* penitentiary

pen- (L *paene*) *pref* almost

pe·nal /pēn'əl/ [< L *poena* penalty] *adj* of, pert. to, or liable to punishment

pe·nal·ize *vt* 1 to inflict punishment on; 2 to make subject to punishment or penalty; 3 to put at a disadvantage

pen·al·ty /pen'əltē/ [LL *poenalitas*] *n* (-**ties**) 1 legal punishment; 2 fine or forfeit paid by a party to an agreement for failure to fulfill his part; 3 *sports* disadvantage incurred by a player or team for an infraction of the rules

pen·ance /pen'əns/ [AF *penaunce*] *n* 1 self-imposed suffering as an expression of sorrow for sin; 2 *R C Ch* sacrament in which, after repentance, confession, and performance of penalties imposed by the priest, absolution for sin is received

pence /pens'/ *npl Brit pl* of **penny**

pen·chant /pench'ənt/ [F] *n* strong leaning or inclination

pen·cil /pen'səl/ [MF *pincel* painter's brush] *n* 1 slender rod containing a core of graphite or crayon, used for writing and drawing; 2 anything shaped or used like a pencil, as for

applying make-up; 3 *optics* group of rays of light proceeding from or converging to a point || *v* (-**ciled** or -**cilled; -cil·ing** or -**cil·ling**) *vt* to write, sketch, or mark with or as with a pencil

pend /pend'/ [L *pendere* to hang] *vi* to await settlement

pen'dant [MF] *n* 1 anything hanging for ornamentation; 2 earring or locket

pen'den·cy *n* (-**cies**) state of being pending or undecided

pen'dent [see **pend**] *adj* 1 suspended; 2 jutting over; 3 undetermined; impending || *n* 4 pendant

pend'ing *adj* 1 not yet finished or decided; impending || *prep* 2 during; 3 until; awaiting

pen·du·lous /pen'jələs, -d(y)ələs/ [< L *pendulus*] *adj* hanging or swinging freely

pen·du·lum /-jələm, -d(y)ə-/ *n* 1 body suspended from a fixed point so that it swings freely, as in certain clocks; 2 alternation, as of public opinion

Pe·nel·o·pe /pənel'əpē/ *n Gk myth.* the faithful wife of Ulysses

pen·e·trate /pen'ətrāt'/ [L *penetrare* (*-atus*) to pierce] *vt* 1 to pierce; enter; make a way into; 2 to reach the interior of; 3 to understand; detect; 4 to pervade; 5 to affect deeply || *vi* 6 to pass or pierce into something; 7 to affect the emotions deeply || **pen'e·tra·ble** *adj*

pen'e·trat'ing *adj* 1 piercing; sharp; 2 discerning; knowing

pen'e·tra'tion *n* 1 act of penetrating; 2 permeation of one culture into another; 3 depth reached by a projectile in a target; 4 mental acuteness or keenness; insight; analytic power || SYN (see *discrimination, sagacity*)

pen·guin /pen'gwin, peŋ'-/ [?] *n* any of an order (Sphenisciformes) of large flightless sea birds of the Antarctic, with flipperlike wings

pen'hold'er *n* 1 holder for a penpoint; 2 rack for holding pens

pen·i·cil·lin /pen'isil'in/ [< L *penicillus* brush] *n* antibiotic produced by the mold *Penicillium notatum*, effective in the treatment of many bacterial infections, esp. those caused by various cocci, as pneumonia and gonorrhea

pen·in·su·la /pənin's(y)ələ/ [*pen-* + *insula* island] *n* piece of land extending from the mainland and almost surrounded by water || **pen·in'su·lar** *adj*

pe·nis /pēn'is/ [L = tail, penis] *n* (-**nis·es** or -**nes** /-nēz/) male organ of urination and sexual intercourse

pen·i·tent /pen'itənt/ [< L *paenitere* to repent] *adj* 1 sorry for sin; repentant || *n* 2 penitent person; 3 one who has confessed his sin and is doing penance || **pen'i·tent·ly** *adv* | **pen'i-**

ten'tial /-ten'shəl/ *adj* || **pen'i-tence** *n*

pen'i-ten'tia-ry /-shərē/ *n* (**-ries**) state or federal prison

pen'knife' /< orig. use for sharpening quill pens/ *n* (**-knives** /-vz/) small pocketknife

pen'man-ship' /'-mən-/ *n* 1 art of handwriting; 2 style of writing'

Penn, Wil-liam /pen'/ *n* (1644–1718) English Quaker, founder of Pennsylvania 1682

Penn., Penna. Pennsylvania

pen' name' *n* name used by a writer instead of his real name

pen-nant /pen'ənt/ [*pennon* + *pendant*] *n* 1 long narrow flag or streamer; 2 flag used as an emblem of victory, as in baseball

pen'ni-less *adj* without money

pen-non /pen'ən/ [MF *penon* < L *penna* feather] *n* 1 swallow-tailed or triangular flag, borne by a knight on his lance; 2 pennant; 3 any flag; 4 wing or pinion

Penn-syl-va-ni-a /pen'sĭlvān'ē̇-ə, -yə/ *n* state in the E U.S. (11,793,909; 45,333 sq.m.; cap. Harrisburg) || **Penn'syl-va'ni-an** *n*

Penn'syl-va'ni-a Av'e-nue *n* wide avenue in Washington that runs from the Capitol past the White House

Penn'syl-va'ni-a Dutch' *npl* 1 descendants of 17th- and 18th-century German settlers in E Pennsylvania; 2 *sg* their language || **Penn'syl-va'ni-a-Dutch'** *adj*

pen-ny /pen'ē/ [OE *pening*] *n* (**-nies** or *Brit* pence denoting amount in value) 1 cent; 2 coin of the United Kingdom, formerly ¹⁄₂₄₀ of the pound but since 1971, ¹⁄₁₀₀ of the pound; 3 any insignificant amount of money, as *not a penny*; 4 **bad penny** someone or something worthless; 5 **a pretty penny** a considerable sum

-pen'ny *adj suf* denoting size of nails

pen'ny ar-cade' *n* building or hall, as in an amusement park, having amusement devices operated for a penny or other small sum

pen'ny pinch'er *n* stingy miserly person || **pen'ny-pinch'ing** *adj*

pen'ny-roy'al /< OF *poliol* < L *puleium* pennyroyal + *roial* royal/ *n* 1 fragrant American herb (*Hedeoma pulegioides*) of the mint family, found in old pastures; 2 somewhat similar Eurasian plant (*Mentha pulegium*)

pen'ny-weight' *n* unit of weight equal to 24 grains or ¹⁄₂₀ of an ounce troy

pe-nol-o-gy /pēnol'əjē/ [< L *poena* penalty] *n* scientific study of punishment for crime, of prison management, etc.

pen' pal' *n* person who corresponds regularly with someone at a great distance whom he has never met and is not likely to meet

pen'point' *n* point of a pen, esp. a removable nib set in a penholder

pen-sion /pen'shən/ [L *pensio* (-*onis*) payment] *n* 1 fixed sum paid periodically to a retired or disabled person, or to the surviving dependents of one who died in service || *vt* 2 to grant a pension to; 3 **pension off** to cause someone to retire on a pension || **pen'sion-er** *n*

pen-sive /pens'iv/ [MF] *adj* reflective; musing || SYN meditative, reflective, dreamy, contemplative

pent /pent'/ 1 *pt & pp* of **pen**[1] || *adj* 2 shut up; closely confined

penta- or **pent-** [< Gk *pente*] *comb form* five

pen-ta-gon /pent'əgon'/ [*penta-* + *-gon*] *n* 1 polygon having five sides and five angles; 2 **the Pentagon** pentagonal building in Virginia near Washington, headquarters of the Department of Defense || **pen-tag'o-nal** /pentag'ənəl/ *adj*

pen'ta-gram' *n* five-pointed star made by extending the sides of a regular pentagon till they intersect

pen'ta-he'dron *n* (**-drons** or **-dra** /-drə/) solid having five plane faces || **pen'ta-he'dral** *adj*

pen-tam-e-ter /pentam'itər/ *n* verse of five feet

pen-tane /pen'tān/ *n* colorless, flammable, very volatile liquid hydrocarbon —$CH_2(CH_2)_3CH_3$— obtained by the distillation of petroleum, used as a solvent and as an anesthetic

pen'ta-prism' *n* prism with five faces that deflects all rays parallel to the major face exactly 90°, used in range-finders and in the viewfinders of single-lens reflex cameras

Pen'ta-teuch' /-t(y)ook'/ [*penta-* + Gk *teuchos* tool] *n* first five books of the Old Testament

pen-tath-lon /pentath'lən/ [*pent-* + Gk *athlon* contest] *n* athletic contest consisting of five events

pen-ta-va-lent /pent'əvāl'ənt, pentav'ə-/ *adj chem* having a valence of five || **pen'ta-va'lence** *n*

Pen-te-cost /pent'əkôst', -kost'/ [Gk *pentekoste* (hemera) fiftieth (day)] *n* Christian feast celebrated on the seventh Sunday after Easter, commemorating the descent of the Holy Ghost upon the apostles || **pen'te-cos'tal** *adj*

pent'house' /-hous-es /-ziz/] [< ME *pentis* < LL *appendicium* appendage] 1 separate dwelling on the roof of a building; 2 enclosure on a roof to conceal elevator machinery, etc.; 3 shed or slanting roof projecting from a main wall or building; 4 slanting roof over a doorway

pent'-up' *adj* curbed, restrained, held back

pe-nult /pē'nult/ or **pe-nul-ti-ma** /pinult'imə/ [*pen-* + L *ultima* last] *n* last syllable but one of a word

pe-nul'ti-mate /-mit/ *adj* 1 next to the last || *n* 2 penult

pe·num·bra /pǐnumˈbrə/ [*pen-* + L *umbra* shadow] *n* (**-bras** or **-brae** /-brē/) **1** partially lighted part of a shadow, as that of the earth on the moon during an eclipse; **2** vague, undetermined area or condition

pe·nu·ri·ous /pən(y)ŏŏrˈē-əs/ *adj* **1** miserly; **2** poor; **3** scanty

pen·u·ry /penˈyərē/ [L *penuria*] *n* **1** miserliness, stinginess; **2** want; destitution, extreme poverty ‖ SYN need, privation, destitution (see *poverty*)

pe·on /pēˈən, -on/ [Sp = laborer] *n* **1** in Spanish America, peasant; **2** farm laborer forced to work to pay off debts ‖ **pe·on·age** /-ij/ *n*

pe·o·ny /pēˈənē/ [MF *pioine* < Gk *paionia*] *n* (**-nies**) **1** any of a genus (*Paeonia*) of plants of the crowfoot family with large showy flowers; **2** flower of one of these plants

peo·ple /pēpˈəl/ [OF *pueple* < L *populus*] *npl* **1** inhabitants, population; **2** individuals of a collective group; **3** general public; **4** persons in relation to a leader or ruler; **5** persons, as *three people came*; **6** relatives or family; **7** human beings; **8** persons in an indefinite sense, as *people will talk* ‖ *nsg* (**peoples**) **9** body of persons united into a community, race, tribe, or nation, as *the peoples of Europe* ‖ *vt* **10** to populate ‖ SYN population, populace, race, tribe (see *nation*)

pep /pep/ [< *pepper*] *colloq n* **1** liveliness, energy, vim ‖ *v* (**pepped**) **pep·ping**) *vt* **2** pep up to enliven; invigorate ‖ **pep·py** *adj* (**-pi·er; -pi·est**)

pep·er·o·ni /pepˈərōnˈē/ [It] *n* highly seasoned sausage made of pork and beef

pep·lum /pepˈləm/ [L < Gk *peplos* shawl] *n* flounce or short, fitted overskirt attached about the waist of a woman's dress

pep·per /pepˈər/ [OE *piper* < L < Gk *peperi*] *n* **1** pungent spice obtained from plants of the genus *Piper*, esp. *P. nigrum*; **2** capsicum or red pepper; **3** garden plant (*Capsicum frutescens*) which bears large podlike fruit ‖ *vt* **4** to season with pepper; **5** to sprinkle thickly; **6** to pelt with small missiles

pep·per-and-salt *adj* (cloth, hair, etc.) of closely spotted black and white

pep·per-box *n* small container with a perforated top for sprinkling pepper on food

pep·per·corn *n* dried berry of the black pepper plant *Piper nigrum*

pep·per·grass *n* any pungent plant of the genus *Lepidium*, including garden cress (*L. sativum*)

pep·per·mint *n* **1** very pungent herb (*Mentha piperita*) of the mint family; **2** its oil; **3** peppermint-flavored candy

pep·per pot *n* **1** highly flavored stew of tripe and vegetables; **2** West In-

dian stew of meat or fish, vegetables, and a preparation of cassava sap

pep·per·y *adj* **1** pungent or sharp; **2** irritable, hot-tempered

pep·pill *n* pill containing a stimulant

pep·sin /pepˈsǐn/ [< Gk *pepsis* digestion] *n* **1** enzyme secreted in the stomach that helps digest proteins; **2** peptic preparation obtained from the stomachs of hogs, used in medicine and as a digestive

pep talk *n* talk or speech designed to arouse enthusiasm or prevent it from flagging

pep·tic /pepˈtik/ [Gk *peptikos*] *adj* **1** pert. to digestion; **2** pert. to pepsin

peptic ul·cer *n* ulcer of the stomach or of the duodenum, caused by the corrosive action of gastric juices

pep·tone /pepˈtōn/ [< Gk *pepton* cooked] *n* any of a class of substances formed by the action of dilute acids or of pepsin on albuminous matter in food

per /pər/ [L] *prep* **1** for or in each, as *five dollars per day*; **2** through, by means of

per- /pər-/ [L] *pref* **1** over all of, as *pervade*; **2** thoroughly, as *perturb*; **3** to distruction, as *perdition*; **4** *chem* **a** indicating that the element to whose name in full or shortened form it is attached has a higher valence in an acid than in the corresponding acid in which the suffix *-ic* alone is used; **b** indicating that the word is the name of a salt and that the element to whose name in full or shortened form it is attached has a higher valence than in the corresponding salt with the suffix *-ate* alone

Per·sia(n)

per·ad·ven·ture *adv* **1** *archaic* perhaps, it may be ‖ *n* **2** doubt, question

per·am·bu·late /-lāt/ *vt* **1** to walk through or over, esp. to inspect ‖ *vi* **2** to walk or stroll about ‖ **per·am·bu·la·tion** *n*

per·am·bu·la·tor *n* baby carriage

per an·num /anˈəm/ [L] *adv & adj* yearly

per·cale /pərkāl/ [F < Pers *pargālah* rag] *n* closely woven cotton cloth with a smooth finish

per cap·i·ta /kapˈitə/ [L = by heads] *adv & adj* by or for each person

per·ceive /pərsēv/ [OF *perceive*] *vt* **1** to become aware of through the senses; **2** to see and understand; grasp mentally ‖ SYN observe, apprehend, grasp (see *discern, notice*)

per·cent /*per-* + L *centum* hundred] *n* (*pl* **percent**) **1** one one-hundredth part; **2** percentage ‖ *adv* **3** of each hundred

per·cent·age /-ij/ *n* **1** rate or proportion per hundred; **2** portion or part; **3** number of hundredths of a total; **4** *colloq* advantage

per·cent·ile /-tīl, tǐl/ *n* any of the 100 numbers which divide a series of values arranged in order of frequency into 100 equal parts

per·cept /pur'sept/ [L *perceptum*] *n* 1 that which is perceived; 2 mental impression perceived by the senses || **per·cep·tu·al** /pərsep'choo·əl/ *adj*

per·cep·ti·ble /pər-/ *adj* capable of being perceived; discernible || **per·cep·ti·bly** *adv*

per·cep·tion *n* 1 act or faculty of perceiving; 2 mental apprehension; understanding; 3 mental impression; percept

per·cep·tive *adj* 1 of or pert. to perception; 2 capable of perceiving; 3 marked by intelligent understanding and insight

perch¹ /purch/ [MF *perche* < Gk *perke*] *n* (perch or perches) any of several small, edible, spiny-finned fresh-water fishes of the genus *Perca*

perch² [OF *perche* < L *pertica* pole] *n* 1 anything, as a rod or pole, on which birds sit or roost; 2 any high seat or resting place || *vi & vt* 3 to rest on or as on a perch

per·chance' [AF *par chance*] *adv literary* by chance; perhaps

Per·che·ron /purch'əron, pursh'-/ [F < *Perche* district in France] *n* one of a breed of large strong draft horses

per·cip·i·ent /pərsip'ē·ənt/ [< L *percipere* to perceive] *adj* 1 perceptive, discerning || *n* 2 one who perceives

per·co·late /purk'əlāt'/ [L *percolare* (-*atus*) to filter] *vi* 1 to filter through a porous substance; 2 to become brewed in a percolator || *vt* 3 to cause to pass through a porous substance; filter; 4 to brew (coffee) in a percolator || **per'co·la'tion** *n*

per'co·la'tor *n* coffee pot in which coffee is made by forcing boiling water up through a tube and allowing it to return to the bottom of the pot by filtering through a perforated basket containing ground coffee

per·cus·sion /pərkush'ən/ [< L *percussus* struck hard] *n* 1 striking of two bodies against each other; 2 *med* tapping of part of the body for diagnostic purposes; 3 *mus* production of a tone by a stroke or blow

per·cus'sion cap' *n* small metal cuplike cap containing an explosive, used before the advent of metallic cartridges to fire the powder charge in firearms by being struck by the hammer

per·cus'sion in'stru·ment *n mus* instrument which produces sound by being struck, as the drum or piano

per di'em /dī'əm/ [L] *adv & adj* 1 by the day, daily || *n* 2 allowance for daily expenses

per·di·tion /pərdish'ən/ [L *perditio* (-*onis*) destruction] *n* 1 total loss or destruction; 2 loss of one's soul or hopes of heaven; 3 hell

per·e·gri·na·tion /per'əgrināsh'ən/ [L *peregrinatio* (-*onis*) travel abroad] *n* 1 traveling about; 2 journey

per·emp·to·ry /pəremp'tərē, per'əmptôr'ē, -tōr'-/ [L *peremptorius* destructive] *adj* 1 imperative; not to be denied or questioned; 2 dictatorial, imperious; 3 *law* decisive; final || **per·emp'to·ri·ly** *adv* || **per·emp'to·ri·ness** *n*

per·en·ni·al /pəren'ē·əl/ [< L *perennis*] *adj* 1 lasting through the year; 2 enduring; unceasing; 3 *bot* surviving more than two years || *n* 4 perennial plant

per·fect /purf'ikt/ [L *perfectus*] *adj* 1 flawless; 2 complete; exact in every detail; 3 impossible of improvement; 4 utter, as *perfect* strangers; 5 *bot* (flower) having both stamens and pistils; 6 *gram* designating a verb form or tense expressing action or state completed with regard to some temporal point of reference || *n* 7 *gram* a perfect tense; b verb form in that tense || /pərfekt'/ *vt* 8 to complete or finish; 9 to bring to perfection; 10 to improve || **per'fect·ly** *adv* || **per·fect'i·ble** *adj* || SYN *adj* accurate, faultless, correct, complete, entire, whole, sinless, pure, stainless, ideal, unblemished || DISCR That is *unblemished* which is not marred, disfigured, or spoiled in any way affecting its beauty or soundness. That is *complete* which, according to the intention of the maker, the entirety of the thing in question, or the fulfillment of a given object, lacks nothing, as the new gas extension is *complete*; a *complete* radio set; a *complete* success. *Accurate* describes that which conforms to a standard or rule through the exercise of positive care to the end of insuring rightness and comprehensiveness; an *accurate* statement is truthful and *complete*. *Perfect* describes that which is *complete*, *unblemished*, without lack according to its kind, and distinguished by worth and excellence

per·fec'tion *n* 1 state or quality of being perfect; 2 act of perfecting; 3 highest degree of excellence; 4 perfect embodiment of some quality; 5 to perfection perfectly

per·fec'tion·ist *n* one who demands and strives for perfection || **per·fec'tion·ism** *n*

per·fec'tive *gram adj* 1 designating a verbal aspect, as in Russian, denoting completed action or state || *n* 2 perfective aspect or verb

per·fec·to /pərfek'tō/ [Sp = perfect] *n* cigar thick in the middle and tapering at both ends

per·fer'vid *adj* very fervid

per·fid·i·ous /pərfid'ē·əs/ *adj* faithless; guilty of perfidy || **per·fid·i·ous·ly** *adv* || SYN deceitful, traitorous, treacherous, false

per·fi·dy /purf'idē/ [L *perfidia*] *n* (-**dies**)

1 treachery; breach of faith; disloyalty; 2 act of treachery

per·fo·rate /purf'ərāt'/ [L *perforare* (-atus)] *vt* to pierce through; make a hole or holes through

per'fo·ra'tion *n* 1 act of perforating or state of being perforated; 2 hole bored or punched through something

per·force' *adv* of necessity; necessarily

per·form /pərfôrm'/ [MF *parfournir* to furnish] *vt* 1 to do or carry out; execute; 2 to discharge or fulfill, as a vow; 3 to portray, as a character in a play; 4 to render by the voice or a musical instrument || *vi* 5 to execute or complete an undertaking; 6 to act a part in a play; 7 to perform music; 8 to do what is expected of a person or machine || **per·form'er** *n* SYN execute, discharge, accomplish (see *effect*)

per·form'ance *n* 1 act of performing; 2 manner in which a mechanical device performs its function; 3 thing done; deed or feat; 4 public exhibition, as of a play or musical entertainment

per·form'ing arts' *npl* arts performed in· public, as drama, music, ballet, through such media as the stage, film, radio, and television

per·fume /pərfyōōm'/ [F *parfumer*] *vt* 1 to scent, make fragrant || /also pur'fyōōm/ *n* 2 pleasing odor, fragrance; 3 substance or extract producing a pleasing odor

per·fum'er·y *n* (-ies) 1 perfumes in general; 2 place where perfumes are made; 3 art of preparing perfumes

per·func·to·ry /pərfuŋk'tərē/ [L *perfunctorius* carelessly done] *adj* 1 done in a half-hearted or careless manner; 2 done merely to discharge a duty || **per·func'to·ri·ly** *adv*

per·go·la /purg'ələ/ [It] *n* latticework covering a walk or veranda and used as a trellis for climbing plants

per·haps /pərhaps'/ [*per-* + *obs hap* chance] *adv* possibly; maybe

peri- [Gk = around] *pref* 1 around, about; 2 near

per·i·car·di·um /per'ikärd'ē·əm/ [Gk *perikardios* surrounding the heart] *n* (-a /-ə/) membrane that encloses the heart || **per'i·car'di·al** also **per'i·car'di·ac'** /-ak'/ *adj*

per'i·carp' /-kärp'/ [*peri-* + Gk *karpos* fruit] *n* layers forming the wall of a fruit

Per·i·cles /per'iklēz'/ *n* (490–429 B.C.) Athenian statesman || **Per'i·cle'an** *adj*

per'i·gee' /-jē'/ [*peri-* + Gk *ge* earth] *n* point in the orbit of the moon or a satellite circling the earth which is closest to the earth

per'i·he'li·on /-hēl'ē·ən, -yən/ [*peri-* + Gk *helios* sun] *n* point in the orbit of a planet or comet which is closest to the sun

per·il /per'əl/ [OF < L *periculum*] *n*

1 exposure to injury; danger, risk || *v* (-iled or -illed; -il·ing or -il·ling) *vt* 2 to expose to danger; risk || **per'il·ous** *adj* || **per'il·ous·ly** *adv* SYN *n* hazard, jeopardy, risk (see *danger*)

pe·rim·e·ter /pərim'itər/ *n* 1 outer boundary of a plane figure; 2 length of this boundary

pe·ri·od /pir'ē·əd/ [Gk *periodos* period of time, circuit] *n* 1 definite portion of time with fixed limits; 2 any space of time; 3 indefinite part of a continued series of events, as *a critical period of history*; 4 concluding point of a cycle of events or of a specified length of time; 5 dot . used as a mark of punctuation, as at the end of a declarative sentence or after an abbreviation; 6 menses; 7 specific length of time into which a school day or certain games are divided; 8 basic unit of geological time, a subdivision of an era; 9 *phys* duration of one complete cycle of a wave; 10 time of revolution of a planet, satellite, or comet around its primary; 11 complete musical sentence eight measures long, ending with a cadence || *adj* 12 characteristic of a style current at a certain time in history, as *period furniture*

pe·ri·od·ic /-od'ik/ *adj* 1 intermittent; 2 occurring at regular intervals; 3 recurring at intervals; 4 *phys* recurring at equal intervals of time || **pe'ri·od'i·cal·ly** *adv* || **pe'ri·o·dic'i·ty** /-ədis'itē/ *n*

pe·ri·od'i·cal *adj* 1 periodic || *n* 2 magazine or journal published at regular intervals of more than a day

pe·ri·od'ic law' *n chem* statement of the observed relationship among the elements, to the effect that their properties are periodic functions of their atomic numbers

pe·ri·od'ic ta'ble *n* table in which the elements are arranged according to their atomic numbers, illustrating the periodic law

per·i·o·don·tics /per'ē·ədon'tiks/ [*peri-* + *odont-* + *-ics*] *nsg* branch of dentistry that deals with the tissue, gum, and bone structure that surrounds and supports the teeth || **per'i·o·don'tal** *adj*

per·i·pa·tet·ic /per'ipətet'ik/ [< Gk *peripatein* to walk] *adj* 1 itinerant; walking about; 2 **Peripatetic** pert. to the philosophy of Aristotle, who taught while walking in the Lyceum at Athens || also *n*

pe·riph·er·y /pərif'ərē/ [Gk *periphereia* circumference] *n* (-ies) 1 perimeter or boundary line of a plane figure; 2 outside surface of a solid; 3 environs, surrounding space || **pe·riph'er·al** *adj*

pe·riph·ra·sis /pərif'rəsis/ [Gk] *n* (-ses /-sēz'/) roundabout way of speaking; circumlocution; wordiness

|| SYN indirection, redundancy (see *circumlocution*)

per·i·phras·tic /per'ifras'tik/ *adj* 1 roundabout; expressed in too many words; 2 *gram* designating a construction of two or more words having the same function as a single word

per'i·scope' *n* instrument for viewing objects above the line of sight or around an obstruction, consisting of a tube with mirrors or prisms and lenses

per'i·scop'ic *adj* (lens) taking in an extended lateral range of view

per·ish /per'ish/ [OF *perir* (-*riss*-)] *vi* 1 to die an untimely or violent death; 2 to be destroyed or ruined

per'ish·a·ble *adj* 1 liable to decay, injury, or death; 2 easily spoiled || *n* 3 something perishable, as food

per'i·stal'sis /-stal'sis, -stôl'-/ [*peri-* + Gk *stalsis* contraction] *n physiol* wavelike muscular contraction occurring in some tubular structures, esp. the alimentary canal, serving to propel the contents onward || **per'i·stal'tic** *adj*

per'i·to·ne'um /-tənē'əm/ [Gk *peritonaion* that which is stretched around] *n* (-**ums** or -**a** /-ə/) serous membrane lining the abdominal cavity || **per'i·to·ne'al** *adj*

per'i·to·ni'tis /-nīt'is/- *n* inflammation of the peritoneum

per'i·wig' [MF *perruque*] *n* peruke

per'i·win'kle¹ /-wiŋk'əl/ [OE *pervince* < L *pervinca*] *n* any of a genus (*Vinca*) of creeping evergreen plants, esp. the common myrtle (*V. minor*) with shiny leaves and solitary blue or white flowers

per·i·win·kle² [OE *pinewincle*] *n* any of various snails, esp. a genus (*Littorina*) of marine forms, including an edible European species (*L. littorea*)

per·jure /pur'jər/ [L *perjurare*] *vt* **jure oneself** to commit perjury || **per'jured** *adj* || **per'jur·er** *n* || SYN forswear || DISCR To *forswear*, now seldom used, is to reject or deny upon oath, as to *forswear* wealth. To *perjure* oneself is to swear falsely under oath in a court of justice. Used reflexively, *forswear* is synonymous with *perjure*, as he *forswore* himself for her sake

per'ju·ry *n* (-ries) *law* willful utterance of a false statement under oath

perk¹ /purk'/ [ME *perken* to preen] *vi* 1 **perk up** to become jaunty or lively || *vt* 2 **perk up** to raise briskly, as the head

perk² *vt & vi colloq* to percolate

perk'y *adj* (-i·er; -i·est) jaunty; pert; lively || **perk'i·ly** *adv*

per·ma·frost' /purm'ə-/ [*permanent* + *frost*] *n* permanently frozen subsoil, as in arctic regions

per·ma·nent /purm'ənənt/ [L *permanens* (-*entis*)] *adj* 1 lasting; fixed; 2 intended to last indefinitely; 3 long-lasting || *n* 4 permanent wave || **per'ma·nen·cy** *n* (-cies) || **per'ma·nent·ly** *adv* || SYN stable, steadfast, changeless, perpetual, lasting, enduring, durable, fixed, invariable, unchangeable || DISCR That is *permanent* which is not temporary, not apt to change, is supposed to last, or does last, until the end, as an annuity provides one with a *permanent* income; *permanent* institutions; *permanent* arrangements. *Lasting* may describe the eternal quality connoted by *everlasting*, and apply to the spiritual, as the *lasting* blessedness of the peace of God; or it may be used, like *permanent*, in the sense of *unchanging*, and apply to the material, as a *lasting* texture, color, structure, foundation. *Durable* is used chiefly in the material sense, and connotes the wearing or lasting qualities of things, as *durable* dress goods. *Stable* refers to what is firmly fastened in place; a desk which does not shake when leaned upon is *stable*. *Enduring* suggests the quality of wearing well, as oak is an *enduring* wood; but it more frequently describes that quality which bears up under annoyance or suffering, as *enduring* patience; it also applies in the sense of everlasting to that which is to continue forever, as the *enduring* goodness of God

per'ma·nent mag'net *n* magnet that retains its magnetism after it has been removed from the magnetizing field

per'ma·nent wave' *n* wave in the hair, produced artificially to last a long time

per·me·a·ble /purm'ē·əbəl/ *adj* capable of allowing penetration by fluids; porous || **per'me·a·bil'i·ty** /-bil'-/ *n*

per'me·ate' /-āt'/ [L *permeare* (-*atus*)] *vt* 1 to pass through the pores and crevices of; 2 to spread through or mingle with || **per'me·a'tion** *n*

Per·mi·an /pur'mē·ən/ [< *Perm* former province in Russia] *n* last period of the Paleozoic era || also *adj*

per·mis·si·ble /pərmis'ibəl/ [see *permit*] *adj* allowable; tolerable || **per·mis'si·bly** *adv*

per·mis·sion /pərmish'ən/ *n* 1 act of permitting; 2 leave; consent || SYN license, sufferance, consent, authority, allowance || ANT refusal, opposition, denial, prohibition

per·mis'sive *adj* 1 giving permission; not forbidding; 2 tolerant; lenient

per·mit /pərmit'/ [L *permittere* (-*missus*) to let through] *v* (-**mit·ted**; -**mit·ting**) *vt* 1 to allow; consent to; tolerate; 2 to give leave to, authorize || *vi* 3 to give consent, allow ||

/purm′it/ *n* 4 official written warrant or license; 5 postal permit || SYN *v* suffer, empower, authorize (see *allow*)

per·mu·ta·tion /purm′yətāsh′ən/ [< L *permutare* to change throughout] *n* 1 alteration, change; 2 *math* a any of the ways in which a number of objects, letters, etc., may be arranged in a definite order in a series; b rearrangement to effect all possible variations in order of the elements of a series

per·ni·cious /pərnish′əs/ [< L *perniciosus* ruinous] *adj* 1 highly injurious or hurtful; 2 deadly || SYN deleterious, destructive, baneful, deadly, harmful, evil, ruinous || ANT beneficial, wholesome, good

per·ni′cious a·ne′mi·a *n* disease characterized by a marked decrease of the red blood cells, caused by the failure to absorb vitamin B₁₂

per·o·ra·tion /per′ərāsh′ən/ [< L *perorare* to sum up] *n* summing up or conclusion of a speech

per·ox·ide /pər-/ *n* 1 oxide which contains more oxygen than some other oxide of the same element; 2 hydrogen peroxide || *vt* 3 to bleach with peroxide, esp. the hair

per·pen·dic·u·lar /purp′əndik′yələr/ [L *perpendicularis*] *adj* 1 at right angles to a given line or surface; 2 upright, vertical || *n* 3 perpendicular line or plane

per·pe·trate /purp′ətrāt′/ [L *perpetrare* (*-atus*) to carry through] *vt* to do, perform, commit, as a crime, a hoax, a blunder, etc. || **per′pe·tra′tion** *n* || **per′pe·tra′tor** *n*

per·pet·u·al /pərpech′ŏŏ-əl/ [< L *perpetuus*] *adj* 1 never-ceasing, continuous; 2 everlasting || **per·pet′u·al·ly** *adv* || SYN incessant, interminable, enduring (see *eternal*)

per·pet′u·ate′ *vt* to make perpetual; keep from oblivion; preserve || **per·pet′u·a′tion** *n* || **per·pet′u·a′tor** *n*

per·pe·tu·i·ty /purp′ət(y)ŏŏ′itē/ *n* (-ties) 1 state of being perpetual; 2 eternity; 3 in perpetuity forever

per·plex /pərpleks′/ [L *perplexus* confused] *vt* to puzzle, bewilder; confuse || **per·plex′ing** *adj* || **per·plex′i·ty** *n* (-ties) || SYN confuse, confound, bewilder, puzzle, distract, involve, mystify || DISCR He is *puzzled* who is brought to a mental standstill by something complicated or baffling; we are *puzzled* over the demeanor of a friend who is effusively cordial one day and cool the next. He is *perplexed* who is not only *puzzled* but indecisive, doubtful, or in suspense as to what to do, think, or say. Difficulty or intricacy *puzzles;* contradictions, uncertainty *perplex.* To *confuse* one is to put his mental processes to rout; one *confused* cannot think straight. One *confounded*

is worse; he is overwhelmed utterly; he cannot, for the moment, even speak; his mind is paralyzed. Proof of the duplicity of a trusted friend might *confound* one. To *bewilder* is to plunge one into a dazed state in which the faculties are staggered, but not so utterly as in *confusion;* a child is *bewildered,* then frightened, on waking in a strange place at night. To *mystify* is to throw into confusion or bewilderment purposely, especially one prone to believe what most people would recognize as incredible; magicians *mystify* their youthful audiences. To *distract* is to *bewilder* by dividing the attention, as by making conflicting claims upon it || ANT explain, expound, elucidate

per·qui·site /purk′wizit/ [L *perquisitus* carefully sought] *n* 1 incidental profit or extra privilege over and above the regular salary or income; 2 customary gratuity

per se′ /sē′/ [L] *adv* by or in itself; inherently; as such

per·se·cute /purs′ikyŏŏt′/ [L *persequi* (*-secutus*) to pursue] *vt* 1 to pursue in order to injure or afflict; harass or ill-treat, as for religious opinions; 2 to annoy, vex || **per′se·cu′tor** *n* || **per′se·cu′tion** *n*

Per·seph·o·ne /pərsef′ənē/ *n* Gk myth. queen of the lower world, daughter of Demeter and Zeus, and wife of Hades

Per·seus /pur′sŏŏs, -sē-əs/ *n* Gk myth. Greek hero who slew Medusa and saved Andromeda from the sea monster

per·se·vere /pur′sivir′/ [MF *perseverer* < L *perseverare*] *vi* to persist; continue steadfastly in any enterprise || **per′se·ver′ance** *n* || SYN continue, endure (see *persist, insist*)

Per·shing, John J. /pursh′iŋ/ *n* (1860-1948) U.S. general of the armies, commander of the A.E.F. in World War I

Per·sia /purzh′ə, pur′shə/ *n* 1 ancient empire in W Asia; 2 former name of Iran || **Per′sian** *adj* & *n*

Per′sian Gulf′ *n* inlet of the Arabian Sea between Arabia and Iran

Per′sian lamb′ *n* fur of the caracul lamb

Per′sian mel′on *n* round muskmelon with a green rind and orange flesh

per·si·flage /purs′ifläzh′/ [F] *n* banter, raillery

per·sim·mon /pərsim′ən/ [< Algonquian] *n* astringent plumlike fruit of a tree of the genus *Diospyros* of North America and the Orient

per·sist /pərsist′, -zist′/ [L *persistere* to stand firm] *vi* 1 to continue steadily in any course commenced; persevere; 2 to continue fixed; endure || SYN persevere || DISCR To *persevere* is to continue steadfastly in a certain course in spite of discouragement, obstacles, or difficulties; *persevere* is used always in a good sense, or a worthy cause, and reflects honor on its subject. To *persist* is also to continue steadfastly, but it often has an unfavorable connotation; people *persist* in courses better abandoned, against advice, pleadings, and opposition. We *persevere* in doing our duty, *persevere* with a task once begun; we *persist* in neglecting our work, in being late, in refusing to do what we should (see *insist*) ‖ ANT desist, fail, cease

per·sist'ent *adj* 1 persisting; persevering; 2 enduring; 3 continuing; repeated ‖ **per·sist'ence** also **per·sist'-en·cy** *n*

per·snick·et·y /pərsnik'itē/ [?] *adj colloq* fussy, fastidious

per·son /purs'ən/ [OF *persone* < L *persona* mask; actor's part] *n* 1 human being; 2 individual; 3 one's actual self; personality; 4 body of a human being; bodily appearance; 5 *gram* any of the three categories used in many languages to distinguish between the speaker, the person spoken to, and the person or thing spoken of; applied in English to the personal pronouns, and appearing vestigially in verbs; 6 *theol* mode of being in the Trinity: the Father, the Son, and the Holy Ghost; 7 **in person** in one's bodily presence

per'son·a·ble *adj* attractive, handsome

per'son·age /-ij/ *n* 1 person of importance; 2 person; 3 part or character in a play

per'son·al *adj* 1 relating or peculiar to an individual and his private affairs; 2 pert. to the outward appearance or looks; 3 done in person; 4 referring offensively to someone's character, conduct, or appearance; 5 *gram* pert. to person ‖ *n* 6 private notice in a newspaper or magazine containing special information about or for some person

per'son·al ef·fects' *npl* one's own clothing and other possessions such as toilet articles and papers that one carries on a trip

per'son·al e·qua'tion *n* what has to be taken into account to balance the difference between an observer's bias and what is generally considered to be the true facts

per·son·al'i·ty /-al'-/ *n* (-ties) 1 sum of one's qualities of mind and character; 2 individuality; personal identity; 3 prominent person, celebrity; 4 **personalities** *pl* offensive remarks made about a person

per'son·al·ize *vt* 1 to make personal; 2 to personify, typify; 3 to mark or have marked with one's name or initials

per'son·al·ly *adv* 1 with regard to oneself; 2 as if directed at oneself; 3 as a person; 4 in person

per'son·al pro'noun *n* any of the pronouns indicating grammatical person

per'son·al prop'er·ty *n law* property consisting of movable articles

per·so·na non gra·ta /pərsōn'ə nongrät'ə/ [L] *n* (**personae non gratae** /-ē/) unacceptable or unwelcome person, as a diplomat who is expelled from the country to which he is accredited

per·son·i·fy /pərson'ifī/ *v* (-fied) *vt* 1 to treat or regard (a thing or an abstract idea) as a person; 2 to be a striking example of; typify ‖ **per·son'i·fi·ca'tion** *n*

per·son·nel /purs'ənel'/ [F] *n* (*pl* **per·sonnel**, used collectively) 1 body of persons employed in any business, service, or enterprise; 2 administrative division concerned with the selection, training, and placement of personnel

per'son-to-per'son *adj* (telephone call) charged for only if the person making it speaks with the specific person asked for ‖ also *adv*

per·spec·tive /pərspek'tiv/ [ML *perspectivus* optical] *n* 1 technique of representing objects on a flat surface to show depth and relative distance; 2 picture in perspective; 3 view including distance as well as foreground; 4 far-reaching mental view; 5 right proportion

per·spi·ca·cious /pur'spikāsh'əs/ [< L *perspicax* (-*acis*) sharp-sighted] *adj* keen of mind; discerning ‖ SYN astute, shrewd, acute, sagacious

per'spi·cac'i·ty /-kas'-/ *n* keenness of sight and brain; penetration; acumen ‖ SYN insight, acuteness (see *sagacity*)

per·spi·cu·i·ty /pur'spikyōō'itē/ [< L *perspicuitas* transparency] *n* 1 lucidity, as of thought or expression; 2 perspicacity ‖ SYN plainness, intelligibility, explicitness, lucidity

per·spic·u·ous /pərspik'yōō-əs/ *adj* 1 clear to the understanding; plainly expressed; 2 perspicacious

per·spi·ra·tion /pur'spirā'shən/ *n* 1 sweat; 2 act or process of sweating

per·spire /pərspī'ər/ [L *perspirare* to breathe through] *vt & vi* to sweat; to exude through the pores

per·suade /pərswād'/ [L *persuadere* (-*suasus*)] *vt* to prevail upon; induce; convince ‖ **per·suad'er** *n* ‖ SYN entice, influence, incline (see *convince*)

per·sua·sion /pərswāzh'ən/ *n* 1 act of persuading or state of being persuaded; 2 conviction, belief; 3 particular sect or religion; 4 persuasive ness

per·sua·sive /-siv/ *adj* having the power to persuade ‖ **per·sua'sive·ly** *adv*

pert /purt'/ [ME = *open* < L *apertus*] *adj* 1 saucy, bold; 2 lively, spry; 3 chic, smart

per·tain /pərtān′/ [MF *partenir*] *vi* 1 to belong, be appropriate; 2 to relate or refer ‖ SYN relate, appertain, concern, belong, refer

per·ti·na·cious /purt′ənāsh′əs/ [< L *pertinax* (*-acis*)] *adj* 1 holding stubbornly to any opinion or design; 2 extremely persistent ‖ **per′ti·na′·cious·ly** *adv* ‖ **per′ti·nac′i·ty** /-nas′-/ ‖ SYN inflexible, dogged, stubborn, persistent, pressing, importunate ‖ ANT yielding, pliable, tractable

per·ti·nent /purt′ənənt/ [L *pertinere* to pertain to] *adj* relating to the matter at hand; relevant ‖ **per′ti·nent·ly** *adv* ‖ **per′ti·nence** *n* ‖ SYN pat, timely, appertaining, related (see *relevant*)

per·turb /pərturb′/ [L *perturbare*] *vt* 1 to agitate; disturb greatly; 2 *astron* & *phys* to cause deviations in the orbit of (a celestial body or an electron) as the result of the attraction of a body or bodies other than the primary ‖ **per′tur·ba′tion** /purt′ərb-/ *n*

Pe·ru /pərŏŏ′/ *n* Spanish-speaking republic in W South America (13,285,-000; 496,224 sq.m.; cap. Lima) ‖ **Pe·ru′vi·an** *adj* & *n*

pe·ruke /pərŏŏk′/ [F *perruque* < It *perruca*] *n* wig, esp. as worn by men in the 17th and 18th centuries, and still worn by British lawyers and judges in court

pe·rus·al /pərŏŏz′əl/ *n* act of perusing

pe·ruse /pərŏŏz′/ [ME = use up < *per-* + *use*] *vt* 1 to read with care; 2 to read

per·vade /pərvād′/ [L *pervadere* (*-vasus*)] *vt* to pass or spread through every part of; permeate ‖ **per·va·sion** /pərvāzh′ən/ *n* ‖ **per·va′sive** /-siv/ *adj*

per·verse /pərvurs′/ [L *perversus* awry] *adj* 1 willfully wrong; wicked; 2 wayward; fractious; 3 obstinate ‖ **per·verse′ly** *adv* ‖ **per·ver′si·ty** *n* (*-ties*) ‖ SYN contrary, refractory, willful (see *headstrong*)

per·ver·sion /pərvurzh′ən/ *n* 1 act of perverting or state of being perverted; 2 abnormal sex habits or practices

per·vert /pərvurt′/ [L *pervertere* (*-versus*) to overturn] *vt* 1 to turn from the right course; lead astray; 2 to misconstrue, distort; 3 to misapply; 4 to debase ‖ /pur′vərt/ *n* 5 perverted person, esp. one who practices sexual perversion ‖ **per·vert′ed** *adj*

pe·se·ta /pəsāt′ə/ [Sp] *n* monetary unit of Spain

pes·ky /pes′kē/ [prob < *pest*] *adj* (*-ki·er; -ki·est*) *colloq* troublesome, annoying

pe·so /pās′ō/ [Sp = weight] *n* monetary unit of Argentina, Colombia, Cuba, the Dominican Republic,

Mexico, Paraguay, the Philippines, and Uruguay

pes·si·mism /pes′imiz′əm/ [< L *pessimus* worst] *n* 1 belief that the world is bad and that existence is an evil; 2 tendency to look on the dark side of life or to expect failure ‖ **pes′si·mist** *n* ‖ **pes′si·mis′tic** *adj* ‖ **pes′si·mis′ti·cal·ly** *adv*

pest /pest′/ [L *pestis* plague] 1 anything or anyone very destructive, annoying, or troublesome; 2 destructive insect; vermin; 3 nuisance; 4 pestilence

pes′ter [MF *empestrer* to hobble, entangle] *vt* to annoy, bother; irritate with little vexations

pest′hole′ *n* place subject to pestilence

pest′house′ *n* (*-hous·es* /-ziz/) house for people having infectious or contagious diseases

pest′i·cide′ *n* preparation that kills pests, as insects and rodents

pes·tif·er·ous /pestif′ərəs/ [L *pestiferus* plague-bearing] *adj* 1 carrying contagion; 2 *colloq* mischievous; annoying

pes·ti·lence /pest′iləns/ [MF < L *pestilentia*] *n* 1 fatal epidemic disease; 2 bubonic plague; 3 anything considered harmful ‖ **pes′ti·len′tial** /-len′shəl/ *adj*

pes′ti·lent *adj* 1 pestilential; 2 bad for health or morals; 3 making mischief; vexatious

pes·tle /pes′əl/ [MF *pestel* < L *pistillum*] *n* instrument used for crushing and grinding substances in a mortar

pet¹ /pet′/ [?] *n* 1 tame animal kept, treated kindly, and played with; 2 person treated with special affection; favorite; 3 anything particularly favored ‖ *v* (**pet·ted; pet·ting**) *vt* 4 to fondle or indulge; caress ‖ *vi* 5 *colloq* to fondle or caress one of the opposite sex

pet² [?] *n* fit of peevishness

pet·al /pet′əl/ [Gk *petalon* leaf] *n* one of the divisions or leaflike parts of a blossom

pe·tard /pĭtärd′/ [< MF *peter* to break wind] *n* 1 explosive device formerly used to blow in doors or make breaches in walls; 2 hoist with or by one's own petard caught in one's own trap

pet′ cock′ or **pet′cock′** *n* small faucet or valve for draining pipes, cylinders, etc.

pe·ter /pēt′ər/ [?] *vi* peter out to diminish gradually and then disappear

Pe·ter /pēt′ər/ *n* 1 one of the twelve apostles, also called *Simon Peter*; 2 either of two books of the New Testament, traditionally ascribed to Peter

Peter I *n* (Peter the Great) (1672–1725) czar of Russia 1682–1725

Pe′ter Pan′ *n* hero of James Barrie's

play of the same name, about a boy who never grew up

pet·i·ole /petˈē-ōl′/ [L *petiolus* little foot] *n* slender stem that bears the broad part of a leaf

pe·tite /pətēt′/ [F = small] *adj* (woman) having a small trim figure

pe·tite′ bour′geoi·sie′ *n* lower middle class

pet·it four /petˈē fôr′, fōr′/ [F = small oven] *n* (petits fours /fôrz′, fōrz′/) small teacake

pe·ti·tion /pətishˈən/ [L *petitio* (-onis) < *petere* to seek] *n* 1 formal request to someone in authority; 2 earnest request or prayer; 3 document containing a request signed by many persons ‖ *vt* 4 to present a petition to; 5 to solicit earnestly ‖ *vi* 6 to make a petition ‖ **pe·ti′tion·er** *n*

pe·tit mal /patē′ mal′/ [F = small illness] *n* mild form of epileptic seizure, characterized by short intervals of unconsciousness

Pe·trarch /pēˈträrk/ *n* (1304–74) Italian poet and scholar ‖ **Pe·trar′chan** /pĭ-/ *adj*

pet·rel /petˈrəl/ [ME *pitteral*] *n* any of various strong-winged sea birds of the family Procellariidae

petri- or **petro-** [Gk *petra* rock] *comb form* stone, rock

pet·ri·fy /petˈrĭfī/ [MF *petrifier*] *v* (-fied) *vt* 1 to change into stone or a stony substance; 2 to harden; 3 to paralyze, as with fear ‖ *vi* 4 to become petrified ‖ **pet′ri·fac′tion** *n*

Pe·trine /pēˈtrīn, -trin/ *adj* pert. to the apostle Peter

pet·ro·chem′i·cal /petˈrō-/ *n* chemical derived from petroleum or natural gas ‖ also *adj*

pet·ro·dol′lars *npl* surplus earned by the oil-exporting countries

pet·rol /petˈrəl/ [< *petroleum*] *n* Brit gasoline

pet·ro·la·tum /petˈrəlāt′əm/ also **pe·tro′le·um jel′ly** *n* jellylike substance derived from petroleum, used as a lubricant and in ointments

pe·tro·le·um /pətrōlˈē-əm/ [*petro-* + L *oleum* oil] *n* inflammable liquid mixture of highly complex hydrocarbons, of great economic importance, occurring naturally and obtained in various parts of the earth by drilling into the earth or rock, used as a fuel and by fractional distillation and other processes to yield benzine, gasoline, kerosene, lubricating oils, petrolatum, naphtha, paraffin, asphalt, etc.

pet′ti·coat′ /petˈē-/ [*petty coat*] *n* 1 underskirt; 2 *colloq* woman, girl, ‖ *adj* 3 feminine; 4 of or by women

pet′ti·fog′ger /-fog′-, -fôg′-/ [prob *petty* + *obs* *fogger* pettifogger] *n* 1 lawyer who handles small or mean cases, often using unscrupulous methods; 2 one who quarrels over trifling details ‖ **pet′ti·fog′ging** *adj*

pet′tish [< *pet²*] *adj* fretful, cross ‖ SYN peevish, petulant, ill-tempered

pet·ty /petˈē/ [MF *petit* little] *adj* (-ti·er; -ti·est) 1 trifling, unimportant; 2 of less or secondary importance, as *a petty offense;* 3 mean, small-minded ‖ **pet′ti·ness** *n* ‖ SYN trivial, insignificant, small, inconsiderable, mean, paltry ‖ ANT important, weighty, big, generous

pet′ty cash′ *n* small cash fund for paying minor bills

pet′ty ju′ry *n* jury that hears the cases of persons indicted by a grand jury

pet′ty lar′ce·ny *n* theft of property the value of which is below a certain amount

pet′ty of′fi·cer *n* enlisted man in the navy with a rank above that of seaman

pet·u·lant /pechˈələnt/ [< L *petulantia* impudence] *adj* snappish, cross, impatient, esp. over trifling vexations ‖ **pet′u·lance** *n* ‖ SYN querulous, fretful, peevish ‖ DISCR *Fretful* describes a state of irritation or vexation in which a chafing, worrying distress or whining impatience is displayed. *Querulous* is applicable to a state of irritation that manifests itself chiefly in faultfinding or impatient complaining. A feverish child, or a nervous invalid, will be *fretful;* the speech of a spoiled, discontented wife, or a chronic invalid who is "enjoying poor health" will be *querulous. Petulant* suggests a head-tossing kind of fretfulness, usually temporary and capricious. *Peevish* implies ill humor of waspish, snapping, irritable sort

pe·tu·nia /pət(y)ōōn′yə/ [< *obs* F *petun* tobacco < Tupi] *n* any of a genus (*Petunia*) of hairy tropical plants with showy funnel-shaped single or double flowers

pew /pyōō/ [MF *puie* balcony] *n* one of the fixed benches with backs, arranged in rows in a church

pe·wee /pē′wē/ [imit] *n* 1 wood pewee; 2 phoebe

pew·ter /pyōōt′ər/ [MF *peutre*] *n* 1 alloy of tin with varying quantities of lead or other metals; 2 pewter vessel; 3 pewter vessels collectively

pe·yo·te /pā-ō′tē/ [Sp < Nahuatl *peyotl*] *n* 1 cactus of Mexico and the SW U.S. (*Lophophora williamsii*) containing a narcotic drug; 2 the drug

Pfc. private first class

pfen·nig /fen′ĭg/ [G = penny] *n* German coin, 1/100 of a mark

Pg, Pg. Portuguese

PG designation of a film recommended for all ages, but with parental guidance suggested

PGA, P.G.A. Professional Golfers' Association

pH *chem* negative logarithm of hydrogen-ion concentration in gram atoms per liter, used to express acidity or alkalinity of solutions

-phage /-fāj'/ [Gk -*phagos*] *n comb form* one that eats

-ph·a·gous /-fəgəs/ [Gk -*phagos*] *adj comb form* eating

-ph·a·gy /-fəjē/ [Gk -*phagia*] *n comb form* eating

pha·lan·ges /fəlan'jēz/ [*pl* of *phalanx*] *npl* small bones of the fingers and toes

pha·lanx /fā'laŋks, fal'-/ [Gk] *n* 1 close battle formation of the ancient Greek heavy infantry, presenting to the enemy a row of interlocked shields and a hedge of spears; 2 compact mass of individuals; 3 group of people united for some purpose; 4 one of the phalanges

phal·lus /fal'əs/ [Gk *phallos*] *n* (**phal·lus·es** or **phal·li** /-lī/) 1 penis; 2 symbol of the penis as the organ of generation, used in some rituals as the emblem of the generative power in nature ‖ **phal'lic** *adj*

phan·tasm /fan'tazəm/ [Gk *phantasma* apparition] *n* 1 specter; ghost; 2 illusory mental image ‖ **phan·tas'mal** *adj*

phan·tas'ma·go'ri·a /-məgôr'ē·ə, -gôr'-/ [*phantasm* + prob Gk *agora* assembly] *n* 1 fantastic or spectacular effects or dissolving views produced by a magic lantern; 2 changing group of figures or images, seen as if in a dream ‖ **phan·tas'ma·go'ric** *adj*

phan·ta·sy /fant'əsē/ *n* (**-sies**) fantasy

phan·tom /fant'əm/ [MF *fantosme* < Gk *phantasma*] *n* 1 apparition; specter; 2 something having appearance without substance

phan'tom cir'cuit *n elec* additional circuit derived from existing circuits without the use of additional wires

Phar·aoh /fer'ō/ [Gk *pharaon* < Heb *Phar'oh*] *n* title of the rulers of ancient Egypt

Phar·i·see /far'īsē/ [Gk *Pharisaios* < Heb *pārūsh* separated] *n* 1 one of a religious sect among the Jews in the Maccabean and New Testament periods that laid especial stress on the exact interpretation and literal observance of the law; 2 **pharisee** self-righteous person; sanctimonious hypocrite ‖ **Phar'i·sa'ic** (-i-cal) /-sā'-/ *adj* ‖ **phar'i·sa'ic** (-i-cal) *adj*

phar·ma·ceu·tics /färm'əsōōt'iks/ [< Gk *pharmakeuein* to administer drugs] *nsg* science or profession of preparing and dispensing drugs ‖ **phar'ma·ceu'tic** (-ti-cal) *adj*

phar·ma·cist *n* one licensed to practice pharmacy; druggist

phar·ma·co- [Gk *pharmakon*] *comb form* drug

phar'ma·col'o·gy /-kol'əjē/ *n* science of the preparation, administration, and effects of drugs ‖ **phar'ma·col'o·gist** *n*

phar'ma·co·poe'ia /-kəpē'ə/ [*pharmaco-* + Gk *poiein* to make] *n* 1 official book describing drugs and medicines; 2 stock of drugs

phar'ma·cy /-sē/ [Gk *pharmakeia* druggists' work] *n* (**-cies**) 1 pharmaceutics; 2 drugstore

phar·yn·gi·tis /far'injīt'is/ *n* sore throat; inflammation of the pharynx

phar·ynx /far'iŋks/ [Gk] *n* (**-ynx·es** or **phar·yn·ges** /fərin'jēz/) cavity or passage connecting the mouth and nose with the larynx and esophagus ‖ **pha·ryn·ge·al** /fərin'j(ē)əl, far'injē'-əl/ *adj*

phase /fāz/ [Gk *phasis* appearance] *n* 1 any one of the changing aspects in which an object of varying conditions appears; 2 any one stage or period in the development of anything; 3 one side or view of a subject; 4 appearance presented by the moon or a planet at a particular time; 5 *phys* position or stage which a periodic phenomenon, such as a wave, has reached at a given time with reference to a starting point; 6 *chem* portion of a heterogeneous system which is homogeneous, as the ice in a mixture of ice and water; 7 **in phase** in a state of synchronous operation ‖ *vt* 8 to put in phase; 9 **phase in** to put into use gradually; 10 **phase out** to withdraw from use gradually

Ph.D. [L *Philosophiae Doctor*] Doctor of Philosophy

pheas·ant /fez'ənt/ [AF *fesaunt* < Gk *Phasianos* (ornis) (bird) of the Phasis River] *n* 1 any of numerous large gallinaceous Old World birds (family Phasianidae) with brilliant plumage; 2 any of various similar birds, as the ruffed grouse

phe'no·bar'bi·tal' /fēn'ō-, fēn'ə-/ [*phainos* shining + *barbital*] *n* white crystalline powder —C₁₂H₁₂N₂O₃— used as a sedative and hypnotic

phe·nol /fē'nōl, -nol/ [< Gk *phainos* shining + L *oleum* oil] *n* carbolic acid

phe·nom /finom'/ *n slang* person of extraordinary prowess in any sport

phe·nom·e·na /finom'ənə/ *pl* of **phenomenon**

phe·nom'e·nal *adj* 1 pert. to or of the nature of a phenomenon; 2 extraordinary, prodigious

phe·nom'e·non' /-non'/ [Gk *phainomenon* appearing] *n* 1 something strange or uncommon; 2 remarkable thing or person ‖ *n* 3 (-na /-nə/) any physically observable fact or event; 4 that which appears to be real to the senses whether it exists or not

phen·yl /fēn'il, fen'-/ [*obs phene* benzene + *-yl*] *n chem* univalent radical —C₆H₅— found in phenol, benzene, etc.

phew /fyōō′/ *interj* exclamation showing disgust, impatience, discomfort, etc.

phi /fī′/ *n* twenty-first letter of the Greek alphabet Φ, φ

phi·al /fī′əl/ *n* vial

Phi′ Be′ta Kap′pa *n* 1 national honor society consisting of persons who achieved high academic distinction while college undergraduates; 2 member of Phi Beta Kappa

phil- [Gk *philos* friendly, loving] *comb form* loving, having affinity for

Phil·a·del·phi·a /fil′ədelf′ē·ə/ *n* city in SE Pennsylvania (1,948,609)

Phil′a·del′phi·a law′yer *n colloq* shrewd lawyer, well-versed in the law

phi·lan·der /f'lan′dər/ [Gk *Philandros* fictional lover] *vi* to make love without serious intentions; flirt ‖ **phi·lan′der·er** *n*

phi·lan·thro·py /f'lan′thrəpē/ [Gk *philanthropia*] *n* (-pies) 1 love of mankind; desire to help men, esp. by acts of charity; 2 philanthropic act; 3 philanthropic agency ‖ **phi·lan′thro·pist** *n* ‖ **phil·an·throp·ic** /fil′ənthrop′ik/ *adj*

phi·lat·e·ly /f'lat′əlē/　[*phil-* + Gk *ateleia* exemption from payment] *n* collection and study of postage stamps ‖ **phi·lat′e·list** *n*

-phile /-fīl′/ also **-phil** /-fil′/ [see **phil-**] *n comb form* lover, friend, one having an affinity for

phil·har·mon·ic /fil′här-, fil′ər-/ *adj* 1 fond of or devoted to music (frequently used in the names of musical societies) ‖ *n* 2 symphony orchestra

-phil·i·a /-fil′ē·ə/ [Gk = friendship] *n comb form* abnormal liking for or tendency toward

phi·lip·pic /-fil'ip′ik/ [Gk *Philippikos* one of the orations of Demosthenes attacking Philip II of Macedon] *n* speech bitterly denouncing someone

Phil·ip·pines /fil′ipēnz/ also **Phil′ip·pine′ Is′lands** *npl* island republic in the W Pacific consisting of an archipelago NE of Borneo and SE of China (28,000,000; 114,830 sq.m.; cap. Manila) ‖ **Phil′ip·pine′** *adj*

Phil·is·tine or **phil·is·tine** /fil′istēn′, -stīn′, f'lis′tin, -tēn/ [*Philistine* inhabitant of ancient Philistia in SW Palestine, an early enemy of the Israelites] *n* person devoid of and indifferent or hostile to culture ‖ also *adj*

Phil′lips head′ /fil′ips/ [trademark] *n* screw head with two partial slots in the form of a cross to keep the special screwdriver from slipping out of the slots

philo- var of **phil-**

phil·o·den·dron /fil′ədən′drən/ [*philo-* + Gk *dendron* tree] *n* tropical American climbing plant (family Araceae), popular as a house plant

phi·lol·o·gy /f'lol′əjē/ [Gk *philologia* love of learning] *n* 1 study of written documents; 2 linguistics ‖ **phi·lol′o·gist** *n* ‖ **phil·o·log·i·cal** /fil′əloj′ikəl/ *adj*

phi·los·o·phize /f'los′əfīz′/ *vi* 1 to reason as a philosopher; 2 to speculate superficially

phi·los·o·phy [Gk *philosophia* love of wisdom] *n* (-phies) 1 study and knowledge of the principles that cause, control, or explain facts or events; 2 study of the basic principles of a particular field of knowledge; 3 practical wisdom that comes from knowledge of general laws and principles; 4 system of general beliefs or views; 5 serenity; composure ‖ **phi·los′o·pher** *n* ‖ **phil·o·soph·ic** /fil′əsof′ik(əl)/ *adj*

phil·ter /filt′ər/ [Gk *philtron*] *n* magical potion, esp. one that has the power to excite love

phle·bi·tis /fləbīt′is/　[< Gk *phleps* (*phlebos*) vein] *n* inflammation of a vein

phlegm /flem′/ [Gk *phlegma* (-*atos*) inflammation, flame] *n* 1 thick mucus discharged from the throat; 2 apathy; 3 coldness; calmness

phleg·mat·ic /flegmat′ik/ *adj* 1 sluggish, apathetic; 2 cool, not easily excited

phlo·em /flō′em/ [G < Gk *phloos* bark] *n* in higher plants, that portion of a vascular bundle having perforated or relatively thin-walled cells, and devoted to food carrying

phlox /floks′/ [Gk = flame] *n* any of a genus (*Phlox*) of annual and perennial herbs bearing showy clusters of flowers

Phnom Penh /nôm′ pen′, pənôm′ pen′/ *n* capital of Cambodia (403,500)

-phobe /-fōb′/ [Gk *phobos* fear] *n comb form* one fearing and hating

pho·bi·a /fōb′ē·ə/ [< -*phobia*] *n* abnormal fear or dread

-pho·bi·a [Gk] *n comb form* abnormal fear or dread of something or someone

phoe·be /fēb′ē/ [imit, influenced in spelling by *Phoebe* Gk goddess of the moon] *n* any of several American flycatchers (genus *Sayornis*), esp. *S. phoebe* of E North America, with a plaintive note

Phoe·ni·cia /finish′ə, -nēsh′ə/ *n* ancient country at the E end of the Mediterranean, in what is now Lebanon and Israel, which established a commercial empire about ten centuries B.C. ‖ **Phoe·ni′cian** *adj* & *n*

phoe·nix /fēn′iks/ [Gk *Phoinix*] *n* 1 mythical bird, said to live 500 years in the desert of Arabia and, after being consumed by fire, to rise again from its ashes; symbol of immortal life; 2 person or thing of great beauty or excellence

Phoe·nix *n* capital of Arizona (581,562)

phon- [< Gk *phone*] *comb form* sound, voice

phone¹ /fōn′/ [Gk *phone* sound] *n* discrete speech sound

phone² *colloq n* 1 telephone ‖ *vt & vi* 2 to telephone

-phone /-fōn′/ [Gk *-phonos*] *n comb form* 1 sound; 2 instrument producing sound

pho·neme /fō′nēm/ [Gk *phonema* sound] *n* one of the functional units of sound which contrast in the same environment with all others, enabling the speakers to distinguish one utterance from another. Each phoneme generally has several distinct varieties or phones, called *allophones*, whose occurrence is predictable and automatic, which never contrast in the same environment, and which consequently are not heard by native speakers, for whom only the phoneme has reality ‖ **pho·ne′mic** /fə-, fō-/ *adj*

pho·ne′mics *nsg* study of phonemes and the theory of phonemes

pho·net·ics /fənet′iks, fō-/ *nsg* science of the production, reception, analysis, classification, and transcription of speech sounds or phones ‖ **phonet′ic** *adj* ‖ **pho·net′i·cal·ly** *adv* ‖ **pho·ne·ti·cian** /fōn′ətish′ən/ *n*

phon·ic /fon′ik, fōn′ik/ *adj* pert. to speech sounds

phon′ics *nsg* method of teaching reading based on the sounds of the letters in a word rather than on the word as a unit

phono- var of **phon-**

pho′no·graph′ /fōn′ə-/ *n* instrument that reproduces sound from grooves in a record ‖ **pho′no·graph′ic** *adj*

pho·nol·o·gy /fənol′əjē, fō-/ *n* 1 sound system of a language; the phonemes and their phonetic description; 2 history of sound changes in a language ‖ **pho·nol′o·gist** *n* ‖ **pho′no·log′ic** (**-i·cal**) /fōn′-/ *adj*

pho·ny or **pho·ney** /fōn′ē/ [?] *adj* (**-ni·er; -ni·est**) 1 spurious, fake, counterfeit ‖ *n* (**-nies** or **-neys**) 2 fake

phoo·ey /foo′ē/ *interj colloq* exclamation indicating disgust or rejection

phos·gene /fos′jēn/ [Gk *phos* light + *-genes* born] *n* colorless poisonous gas —COCl₂— with the odor of musty hay, used in chemical warfare

phos·phate /fos′fāt/ [see **phosphorus**] *n* 1 salt or ester of phosphoric acid; 2 fertilizer containing phosphates; 3 carbonated drink containing a little phosphoric acid

phos·pho·res·cence /fosfəres′əns/ *n* 1 property of emitting light without incandescence, resulting from slow oxidation; 2 light thus emitted; 3 continued emission of light by some substances after the stimulus has been removed ‖ **phos′pho·resce′** *vi* ‖ **phos′pho·res′cent** *adj*

phos·phor·ic /fosfôr′ik, -for′-/ *adj* pert. to, like, obtained from, or containing phosphorus, esp. in its higher valence

phos·pho·rous /fos′fərəs, fosfôr′əs, -fōr′-/ *adj* pert. to, like, obtained from, or containing phosphorus, esp. in its lower valence

phos·pho·rus /fos′fərəs/ [L < Gk *phos* light + *-phoros* bringing] *n* waxy, poisonous, phosphorescent nonmetallic element (P; at.no. 15; at.wt. 30.974), occurring in rocks, soil, and animal tissue, igniting spontaneously when warm, and used in matches, fertilizers, and medicine

pho·to /fōt′ō/ *n colloq* photograph

pho·to- [< Gk *phos* (*photos*) light] *comb form* 1 light, 2 photography; photographic

pho′to·cell′ *n* photoelectric cell

pho′to·cop′i·er *n* machine that makes photocopies

pho′to·cop′y *n* (**-ies**) 1 photographic reproduction ‖ *v* (**-ied**) *vt* 2 to reproduce (printed, typed, written material, etc.) photographically

pho′to·e·lec′tric /fōt′ō-/ *adj* pert. to the electric or electronic action of light or other radiation, spec. in increasing electric conduction

pho′to·e·lec′tric cell′ *n* 1 electric cell which, when acted upon by light, allows an electric current to pass which increases with the intensity of the light; used to measure light intensity, operate mechanisms, reproduce sound from sound tracks, operate alarm systems, etc.; 2 phototube

pho′to·en·grav′ing *n* 1 process by which a photograph is reproduced in relief upon a metal plate for printing; 2 picture printed from such a plate ‖ **pho′to·en·grave′** *vt*

pho′to fin′ish *n* finish in a race so close that the winner can be determined only by examining a photograph of it

pho′to·fin′ish·er *n* one whose business is to develop films and make prints ‖ **pho′to·fin′ish·ing** *n*

pho′to·flood′ lamp′ *n* very bright lamp used in photography

pho·to·gen·ic /fōt′əjen′ik/ *adj* 1 photographing well; 2 *biol* phosphorescent; 3 *pathol* caused by light

pho′to·graph′ *n* 1 picture produced by photography ‖ *vt* 2 to make a photograph of ‖ *vi* 3 to make photographs; 4 to be photographed ‖ **pho·tog·ra·pher** /fətog′rəfər/ *n*

pho′to·graph′ic *adj* 1 pert. to photography; 2 reproducing life or nature in all its details ‖ **pho′to·graph′i·cal·ly** *adv*

pho·tog·ra·phy /fətog′rəfē/ *n* art or process of making pictures by the action of light on sensitized surfaces

pho′to·gra·vure′ *n* 1 any of several processes for printing pictures from an intaglio plate prepared photographically; 2 such a plate; 3 picture so printed

pho′to·jour′nal·ism *n* journalism in which the news is told chiefly by means of photographs

pho′to·me·chan′i·cal *adj* pert. to the mechanical printing of pictures from plates made photographically

pho·tom·e·try /fətom′itrē/ *n* measurement of the intensity of light ‖ **pho′-to·met′ric** *adj*

pho′to·off′set′ *n* method of printing in which the material to be printed is transferred to a plate photographically and then reproduced by offset

pho′to·play′ *n* screenplay

pho′to·sphere′ *n* the luminous visible surface of the sun

Pho′to·stat′ /-stat′/ [trademark] *n* 1 camera making facsimile copies of papers; 2 also **photostat** copy so made ‖ *v* **photostat** (**-stat·ed** or **-stat·ted**; **-stat·ing** or **-stat·ting**) *vt* 3 to make a photostat of ‖ **pho′to·stat′ic** *adj*

pho′to·syn′the·sis *n* synthesis of carbohydrates in plants from water and carbon dioxide by the action of sunlight and with the aid of chlorophyll as a catalyst

pho′to·tube′ *n* diode whose cathode when struck by light emits· electrons which are drawn to the anode

phras·al /frāz′əl/ *adj* constituting or in the form of a phrase

phras′al prep·o·si′tion *n* preposition made of two particles of which the first is usu. an adverb and the second a simple preposition, as *out of*

phras′al verb′ *n* spaced verb made of a simple verb (usu. of Anglo-Saxon origin) and a short adverb (usu. a preposition used as an adverb)

phrase /frāz′/ [Gk *phrasis* speech] *n* 1 brief pithy expression containing a single idea; 2 characteristic style or manner of speech; 3 group of related words not containing a subject and a predicate and acting as a grammatical unit; 4 *mus* portion of a period, generally four measures in length ‖ *vt* 5 to put into words; 6 *mus* a to bring out the phrases of; b to group (notes) into a phrase

phra·se·ol·o·gy /frāz′ē·ol′əjē/ *n* style, manner, or peculiarity of expression ‖ SYN language, style (see *diction*)

phre·net·ic /frinet′ik/ [Gk *phrenetikos*] *adj* 1 frantic; frenzied; 2 wildly excited; fanatic ‖ *n* 3 phrenetic person

phren·ic /fren′ik/ [< Gk *phren* mind, diaphragm] *adj* 1 pert. to the mind; 2 pert. to the diaphragm

phre·nol·o·gy /frinol′əjē/ [< Gk· *phren* mind] *n* system of character reading based on the form of the skull

Phryg·i·a /frij′ē·ə/ *n* region settled in NW Asia Minor in the 13th cent. B.C. ‖ **Phryg′i·an** *adj* & *n*

phyl- [Gk *phylon*] *comb form* race, tribe; phylum

phy·la /fil′ə/ *pl* of phylum

phy·lac·ter·y /filak′tərē/ [Gk *phylakterion* amulet] *n* (**-ies**) 1 charm or talisman; 2 small square box containing a strip of parchment on which texts from the law are inscribed, worn by Jewish men during prayer

phyl·i- or **phyl·lo-** [Gk *phyllon*] *comb form* leaf

-phyll also **-phyl** /-fil′/ [Gk *phyllon*] *n comb form* leaf

phylo- var of phyl-

phy·log·e·ny /filoj′ənē/ [< *phylo-* + *genesis*] *n* (**-nies**) 1 historical development of a race or tribe; 2 evolutionary development of a species of plant or animal

phy·lum /fil′əm/ [L < Gk *phylon* race] *n* (**-la** /-lə/) major subdivision of the animal kingdom, consisting of one or more classes

phys·ic /fiz′ik/ [Gk *physike* (episteme) (knowledge) of nature] *n* 1 cathartic ‖ *v* (**-icked**; **-ick·ing**) *vt* 2 to administer a cathartic to; 3 to act as a cathartic upon

phys′i·cal *adj* 1 relating to physics and physical science; 2 material as opposed to moral and spiritual; 3 pert. to the body ‖ *n* 4 physical examination ‖ **phys′i·cal·ly** *adv* ‖ SYN (see *corporal³*) ‖ ANT unreal, spiritual

phys′i·cal an′thro·pol′o·gy *n* branch of anthropology concerned with human body structure, its evolution, and its measurements

phys′i·cal ed′u·ca′tion *n* systematic instruction in exercises and sports given in a school

phys′i·cal ge·og′ra·phy *n* study of the natural features of the earth, as climate, soils, land forms, drainage, and the changes caused by erosion

phys′i·cal ther′a·py *n* therapy by physical means, as massage, baths, and exercise, rather than by drugs ‖ **phys′i·cal ther′a·pist** *n*

phy·si·cian /fizish′ən/ [OF *fisicien*] *n* doctor of medicine

phys·ics /fiz′iks/ [see **physic**] *nsg* science dealing with matter and energy, esp. such changes as do not involve chemical or physiological change ‖ **phys′i·cist** *n*

phys·i·o- [Gk] *comb form* 1 physics; 2 physical

phys·i·og·no·my /fiz′ē·og′nəmē/ [< Gk *physiognomoia* judging of persons by their features] *n* (**-mies**) 1 the face as expressive of character; 2 outward appearance; 3 art of judging character from outward appearance, esp. of the face

phys′i·og′ra·phy /-og′rəfē/ *n* 1 physical geography; 2 study of nature in general

phys′i·ol′o·gy /-ol′əjē/ *n* 1 science dealing with the functions or life processes of animals and plants; 2 functions of the human body ‖ **phys′i·ol′-**

o·gist *n* ‖ **phys'i·o·log'i·cal** /-əloj'-/ *adj*

phys'i·o·ther'a·py /fiz'ē-ō-/ *n* physical therapy ‖ **phys'i·o·ther'a·pist** *n*

phy·sique /fizēk'/ [F < Gk *physikos* natural] *n* formation of the body; constitution; appearance

phy·tog·ra·phy /fītog'rəfē/ [< Gk *phyton* plant + *-graphy*] *n* branch of botany dealing with the naming, description, and classification of plants

pi¹ /pī'/ *n* **1** sixteenth letter of the Greek alphabet Π π; **2 a** the symbol π designating the ratio of the circumference of a circle to its diameter; **b** the ratio itself, 3.1415926 +

pi² [?] *n* **1** jumbled printing type ‖ *vt* **2** to jumble (type)

P.I. Philippine Islands

pi·a·nis·si·mo /pē'ənis'imō/ [It] *adj* & *adv mus* very soft

pi·a·no¹ /pē·än'ō, pyän'ō/ [It] *adj* & *adv mus* soft

pi·an·o² /pē·an'ō, pyan'ō/ [< *pianoforte*] *n mus* large keyboard instrument in which the keys actuate hammers which strike metal strings ‖ **pi·an·ist** /pē·an'ist, pyan'-, pē'ən-/ *n*

pi·an'o·for'te /fôrt'ē, -fôr'tā/ [It = softloud] *n* piano²

pi·an'o wire' *n* very thin, strong steel wire

pi·as·ter /pē·ast'ər/ [F *piastre* < It *piastra* coin, metal plate] *n* **1** monetary unit of Vietnam; **2** coin of certain countries in the eastern end of the Mediterranean

pi·az·za /pē·az'ō/ [It < Gk *plateia*] *n* **1** in Italy, open square; **2** veranda

pi·ca /pīk'ə/ [ML = collection of church rules] *n* large size of type, 12 point, making about six lines to the inch, or ten characters to the linear inch in typewriters

pic·a·dor /pik'ədôr'/ [Sp] *n* horseman in a bullfight who incites the bull to rage and action by jabbing it with a lance

pic·a·resque /pik'əresk'/ [< Sp *pícaro* rogue] *adj* **1** pert. to rogues and rascals; **2** (fiction) having a rogue as hero

Pi·cas·so, Pa·blo /päb'lō pikäs'ō/ *n* (1881–1973) Spanish painter and sculptor

pic·a·yune /pik'ə·yŏŏn'/ also **pic'a·yun'ish** [F *picaillon* coin of small value] *adj* petty, trifling; of no account

Pic'ca·dil'ly Cir'cus /pik'ədil'ē/ *n* traffic circle and square in London, noted as an amusement and theater center

pic·ca·lil·li /pik'əlil'ē/ [?] *n* relish of finely chopped vegetables and hot spices

pic·co·lo /pik'əlō'/ [It = small] *n* small flute pitched an octave higher than the ordinary flute ‖ **pic'co·lo'ist** *n*

pick¹ /pik'/ [ME *pikk*] *n* **1** heavy tool for breaking earth and rock, con-

sisting of a pointed iron bar with a wooden handle set at right angles to it in the middle; **2** any of various sharp-pointed instruments, as *ice pick, toothpick;* **3** plectrum

pick² [ME *pikken* to prick] *vt* **1** to strike or break with a sharp instrument, or with the beak, as *to pick a hole;* **2** to open (a lock) without a key, as with a wire or picklock; **3** to pluck or gather; **4** to clean of something, pluck, as *to pick a chicken;* **5** to eat fastidiously or in small bits; **6** to choose or select; **7** to provoke, as a quarrel; **8** to rob, as *to pick a pocket;* **9** to pluck the strings of (a musical instrument); **10** to probe or scratch in order to clean, as *to pick one's teeth;* **11** pick off, a to remove by picking; **b** to shoot, hit; **12** pick out, **a** to select; **b** to make out, recognize; **13** pick up, **a** to lift from the ground or floor; **b** to come across, as by chance; **c** to take along in a vehicle; **d** *colloq* to accost and induce to accompany one; **e** *slang* to arrest; **f** to get casually ‖ *vi* **14** to pilfer; **15** to choose carefully; **16** to find fault; **17** pick at *colloq* **a** to find fault with; **b** to eat sparingly; **c** to handle; **18** pick on, a *colloq* to tease, harass; **b** to choose; **19** pick up, **a** to accelerate; **b** to improve ‖ *n* **20** stroke, as with a point; **21** act of choosing; **22** choice; **23** the best ‖ **pick'er** *n* ‖ SYN *v* choose, select, cull (see *elect*)

pick'a·back' [earlier a *pick pack*] *adv* & *adj* piggyback

pick'ax or **pick'axe'** *n* pick¹ *1*

picked' *adj* chosen, carefully selected

pick·er·el /pik'(ə)rəl/ [*dim.* of *pike²*] *n* (*-el* or *-els*) any of several freshwater food fishes (genus *Esox*) of the pike family

pick·et /pik'it/ [F *piquet*] *n* **1** upright pointed stake used for fences, tying a horse; etc.; **2** person, or one of a group of persons, stationed at a public place to demonstrate for or against a government action or policy, in favor of union demands, as for better pay or working conditions; **3** soldier or soldiers stationed forward to warn of an enemy advance ‖ *vt* **4** to enclose within a picket fence; **5** to tether a horse to a picket; **6 a** to place pickets at (a factory, store, or public building); **b** to stand or walk as a picket at; **7** *mil* **a** to guard with pickets; **b** to post for picketing ‖ *vi* **8** to serve as a picket

pick'et fence' *n* fence made of a row of pickets or stakes fastened together

pick'et line' *n* line of strikers or other demonstrators standing or walking up and down as pickets

pick'ings *npl* **1** scraps or remains; **2** advantage gained by dishonest means; spoils

pick·le /pik'əl/ [MF *pekel*] *n* 1 brine or vinegar used for preserving foods; 2 cucumber preserved in vinegar; 3 other vegetables, meat, fruit, etc., preserved in pickle; 4 *colloq* embarrassment or difficulty; 5 acid bath used to remove scale from metal ‖ *vt* 6 to preserve in brine or vinegar; 7 to immerse in an acid bath to remove scale, etc.

pick'lock' *n* 1 instrument for picking locks; 2 person who picks locks; thief

pick'-me-up' *n colloq* 1 refreshment; light lunch; cup of coffee; 2 drink of liquor taken as a restorative

pick'pock'et *n* one who steals from another's pockets

pick'up' *n* 1 act of picking up; 2 power or process of rapid acceleration; 3 pickup truck; 4 *colloq* stranger picked up casually, usu. with a view to sexual intimacy; 5 *colloq* improvement; 6 device which transforms the undulations of the grooves of a phonograph record by means of the vibrations of a needle into audiofrequency voltages to be converted into sound

pick'up truck' *n* small open delivery truck

pick'y *adj* (-i·er; -i·est) fussy; choosy

pic·nic /pik'nik/ [F *pique-nique*] *n* 1 outing by a group taking food along to eat in the open; 2 *colloq* pleasant experience ‖ *v* (-nicked; -nick·ing) *vi* 3 to go on or hold a picnic ‖ **pic'nick·er** *n*

pi·cot /pēk'ō/ [F] *n* one of the small projecting loops forming the edge of certain laces, ribbons, etc.

pic·ric ac'id /pik'rik/ [< Gk *pikros* bitter] *n* yellow, crystalline, bitter and poisonous acid —$C_6H_2(NO_2)_3OH$— chiefly used in explosives

Pict /pikt/ [< L *Picti* painted ones] *n* one of an ancient pre-Celtic people of N Britain, who merged with the Scots in the ninth century

pic·to·ri·al /piktōr'ē-əl, -tōr'-/ < L *pictorius*] *adj* 1 pert. to, of the nature of, shown by, or containing pictures; 2 vividly described ‖ *n* 3 periodical featuring pictures

pic·ture /pik'chər/ [L *pictura* painting] *n* 1 painting, drawing, or photograph of a person, object, or scene; 2 likeness or image; 3 mental image; 4 representation; embodiment; 5 scene or group suitable to be a subject for an artist; 6 motion picture ‖ *vt* 7 to represent in a picture; 8 to describe vividly; 9 to form a mental image of

pic'ture hat' *n* woman's hat with a very wide flexible brim

pic'tur·esque' /-esk'/ *adj* 1 giving a vivid impression; graphic; 2 charming, quaint

pic'ture win'dow *n* large window taking up almost the whole wall

pid·dle /pid'əl/ [?] *vi* 1 to dawdle,

waste time ‖ *vt* 2 also **piddle away** to fritter away

pid'dling *adj* trifling, insignificant

pidg·in /pij'in/ [corruption of Eng *business*] *n* auxiliary language developed chiefly for commercial purposes when two or more peoples come into contact, based usu. on one language with a modified phonology and simplified morphology and on vocabulary and syntactic elements from the other languages

pidg'in Eng'lish *n* pidgin based on English with Chinese elements, used as a commercial language in parts of the Orient

pie¹ /pī'/ [ME] *n* dish consisting of meat, fruit, or the like, baked between two layers of pastry or on one lower crust

pie² *n* & *vt* var of **pi³**

pie'bald' [< *obs* pie magpie] *adj* 1 mottled with different colors, esp. black and white ‖ *n* 2 piebald horse

piece /pēs/ [OF *pece* < Gaulish] *n* 1 part of anything, fragment, as *a piece of bread, a piece of land*; 2 quantity regarded as a unit in manufacture, as *a piece of goods*; 3 single example or unit, as *a piece of advice, a piece of baggage*; 4 single object of a group, as *each piece in the set*; 5 single distinct literary, musical, or artistic work; 6 amount of work done as a distinct job; 7 coin; 8 gun; 9 one of the counters or men used in playing chess, checkers, and similar games; 10 **go to pieces** to lose self-control; 11 **speak one's piece** *colloq* to express one's thoughts and opinions ‖ *vt* 12 to enlarge or mend by adding material; 13 also **piece together** to make by joining sections together ‖ SYN *n* fragment, portion, section (see *part*)

pièce de ré·sis·tance /pē-es' də rizis-täns'/ [F] *n* 1 main dish; 2 main event

piece' goods' *npl* fabrics sold at retail in lengths requested by the customer

piece'meal' [ME *pecemele*] *adv* 1 gradually, piece by piece ‖ *adj* 2 done piecemeal

piece' of eight' *n* former Spanish coin equal to eight reals, once current in Latin America and the gulf coast of the U.S. (see **bit²** 3)

piece'work' *n* work done and paid for by the piece ‖ **piece'work'er** *n*

pied /pīd'/ [see *piebald*] *adj* spotted, usu. in large areas; piebald

Pied·mont /pēd'mont/ *n* 1 plateau between the Appalachians and the coastal plain in the SE U.S.; 2 region in NW Italy bordering on the Alps

pier /pir'/ [LL *pera* dike] *n* 1 masonry support of adjacent spans of a bridge; 2 support, as of timbers or iron, in the structure of a building or bridge; 3 structure built out over the water for docking, or as an amusement area or promenade; 4 portion of wall between two openings

pierce /pirs'/ [OF *percer*] *vt* 1 to penetrate or perforate; 2 to bore through or into; 3 to penetrate with the mind or eye; 4 to sound shrilly through; 5 to affect deeply ‖ *vi* 6 to enter, penetrate

Pierce, Frank·lin *n* (1804–69) 14th president of the U.S. 1853–57

pierc'ing *adj* penetrating; sharp, keen ‖ **pierc'ing·ly** *adv*

pier' glass' *n* tall mirror occupying the space between two windows

Pierre /pir'/ *n* capital of South Dakota (10,000)

Pie·tà /pē'ätä'/ [It = pity] *n* representation of the Virgin Mary mourning the dead body of Christ on her lap

pi·e·tism /pī'itiz'əm/ *n* 1 the stressing of personal piety over formality in religion; 2 intense religious devotion; 3 exaggerated piety ‖ **pi'e·tist** *n* ‖ **pi'e·tis'tic (-ti·cal)** *adj*

pi·e·ty /pī'itē/ [MF *piete* < L *pietas*] *n* (-ties) 1 devotion to religion; 2 reverence for God; 3 honor and obedience to parents; 4 pious act ‖ SYN holiness, devoutness, sanctity, godliness, religion ‖ ANT ungodliness, irreligion, irreverence

pi·e·zo·e·lec·tric'i·ty /pī·ēz'ō-/ [< Gk *piezein* to press] *n* electricity produced in certain crystals by pressure ‖ **pi·e'zo·e·lec'tric** *adj*

pif·fle /pif'əl/ [?] *n colloq* 1 nonsense; 2 nonsensical talk

pig /pig'/ [ME *pigge*] *n* 1 swine; 2 *colloq* greedy or filthy person; 3 *slang* policeman; 4 oblong mass of metal which has been poured into a mold; 5 mold for such a mass

pi·geon /pij'ən/ [MF *pijon*] *n* 1 any of a family (Columbidae) of swift-flying birds of many species, having short heads and plump bodies; 2 *slang* one who is easily tricked

pi'geon·hole' *n* 1 small open compartment, as in a desk, for filing papers ‖ *vt* 2 to place in a pigeonhole; 3 to lay aside and forget; shelve; 4 to assign to a definite place

pi'geon-toed' *adj* having the toes or feet turned in

pig·gish /pig'ish/ *adj* piglike; greedy; dirty ‖ **pig'gish·ness** *n*

pig·gy /pig'ē/ *n* (-gies) young or small pig

pig'gy·back' [< *pickapack*] *adv* 1 on the back or shoulders ‖ *adj* 2 carried on the back or shoulders; 3 pert. to a method of carrying trucks on flatcars

pig'gy bank' *n* small receptacle with a slot for saving coins, often in the shape of a pig

pig'head'ed *adj* stupidly obstinate or stubborn

pig' i'ron *n* iron cast into pigs

Pig' Lat'in *n* disguised form of English used as a secret language by children, formed by moving initial consonants to the end of words and adding the sound /ā/

pig·ment /pig'mənt/ [L *pigmentum*] *n* 1 any substance used to impart color; 2 insoluble dry coloring matter mixed in a liquid vehicle to form paint or ink; 3 coloring matter in animals and plants ‖ *vt* 4 to color

pig'men·ta'tion *n biol* coloration, esp. of the skin

Pig·my /pig'mē/ *n* (-mies) var of Pygmy

pig'skin' *n* 1 leather made from the hide of a pig; 2 *colloq* football

pig'sty' *n* (-sties) pen for pigs

pig'tail' *n* 1 braid of hair hanging down the back of the head; 2 long twist of tobacco; 3 short strip of stranded copper wire

pike¹ /pīk'/ [OE *pīc* point] *n* weapon consisting of a long wooden shaft with a spearhead at one end, formerly used by infantrymen

pike² [< *pikefish* < *pike¹*] *n* (**pike** or **pikes**) any of a genus (*Esox*) of voracious fresh-water fishes having a long snout

pike³ [< *turnpike*] *n* 1 toll road; 2 highway

pik·er /pīk'ər/ [?] *n colloq* 1 one who does things in a small niggardly way; 2 cheapskate

pike'staff' (-**staves** /-stāvz'/) *n* shaft with a spike at the end, as that carried by mountaineers

pi·laf /pīläf'/ [Pers *pilāw*] *n* Levantine dish consisting of rice steamed in bouillon, often with meat or chicken

pi·las·ter /pilas'tər/ [MF *pilastrum*] *n* rectangular column with a base and capital, built partly in a wall

Pi·late, Pon·tius /pon'shəs pīl'ət/ *n* Roman governor of Judea under whom Christ was crucified (John 18: 29; 19:22)

pile¹ /pīl'(ə)l/ [MF < L *pila* pillar] *n* 1 mass or heap; 2 large building; 3 *phys* reactor; 4 pyre; 5 *colloq* great quantity; 6 *colloq* fortune ‖ *vt* 7 to load with a pile of something; 8 **pile up**, a to put in a pile; b to accumulate ‖ *vi* 9 to go in a confused mass into, out of, or off someplace; 10 **pile up** to accumulate into a pile

pile² [OE *pīl* shaft < L *pilum* javelin] *n* timber, metal, or concrete column driven into the ground to form a foundation or support, as for a building, wharf, or retaining wall

pile³ [L *pilus* hair] *n* 1 nap of cloth; 2 hair, esp. soft hair or fur; 3 fiber or filament, as of cotton, etc. ‖ **piled'** *adj*

pile' driv'er *n* machine for driving piles into the ground

piles' [< L *pila* ball] *npl* hemorrhoids

pile'up' *n* collision of several vehicles that have piled into each other

pil·fer /pilf′ər/ [MF *pelfre* booty] *vt* to steal (small amounts or trifling objects) ‖ also *vi* ‖ **pil′fer·er** *n* ‖ **pil′fer·age** /-ij/ *n*

pil·grim /pil′grim/ [OF *peligrin* < L *peregrinus* stranger] *n* 1 one who travels from a distance to visit a sacred place or shrine; 2 traveler; 3 **Pilgrim** one of the Puritan settlers of Plymouth Colony in 1620 ‖ **pil′grim·age** /-ij/ *n*

pill /pil′/ [< L *pilula* small ball] *n* 1 pellet containing medicine, to be swallowed whole; 2 something disagreeable that must be accepted; 3 *slang* boring person; 4 *sports slang* baseball or golf ball; 5 **the pill** women's oral contraceptive

pil·lage /pil′ij/ [MF] *vt & vi* 1 to plunder, loot, esp. in war ‖ *n* 2 act of pillaging; 3 plunder, booty ‖ **pil′lag·er** *n* ‖ SYN *v* plunder, despoil, steal, rob, strip, sack

pil·lar /pil′ər/ [OF *piler* < ML *pilare*] *n* 1 upright shaft to support a structure or to serve as a monument; 2 any upright mass similar to this; 3 support or mainstay; 4 **from pillar to post** aimlessly

pill′box′ *n* 1 small container for pills; 2 *mil* small low concrete structure armed with machine guns and small cannon, used for defense; 3 **small** round flat-topped woman's hat

pil·lion /pil′yən/ [Gael *pillean* **cush-ion**] *n* extra saddle or seat **behind** the main one on a horse or **motor-cycle,** to carry a passenger

pil·lo·ry /pil′ərē/ [OF *pilori*] *n* (-ries) 1 wooden frame on an upright post having holes for the head and hands, formerly used to subject offenders to public shame ‖ *v* (-ried) *vt* 2 to place in a pillory; 3 to expose to public disgrace or abuse

pil·low /pil′ō/ [OE *pylu* < L *pulvinus*] *n* 1 cloth bag filled with feathers or other soft material to support the head of a person lying down; 2 any rest for the head ‖ *vt & vi* 3 to rest on or as on a pillow

pil′low block′ *n* support for a shaft which drives machinery

pil′low-case′ or **pil′low-slip′** *n* removable cloth covering for a pillow

pi·lot /pil′ət/ [MF *pillote* < It *pilota*] *n* 1 one who steers a vessel; 2 one licensed to conduct a vessel in and out of a port or in difficult waters; 3 guide or leader; 4 mechanical regulating device; 5 cowcatcher; 6 pilot light; 7 one who operates an aircraft ‖ *adj* 8 serving as a guide; 9 serving as a preliminary experimental unit or model ‖ *vt* 10 to steer; 11 to guide through difficulties

pi′lot film′ *n* film exemplifying a series of television shows, shown to prospective sponsors

pi′lot·house′ *n* (-hous·es /-ziz/) enclosed structure from which a ship is steered

pi′lot lamp′ *n* small electric lamp which is used to show whether a given circuit is open or closed

pi′lot light′ *n* small flame kept burning on a gas stove from which the main burners are lighted

pi·men·to /piment′ō/ [< *pimiento*] *n* unripe fruit of the allspice tree, dried and used as a flavoring

pi·mien·to /pimyent′ō/ [Sp] *n* variety of sweet pepper used as a vegetable and as a relish

pimp /pimp′/ [?] *n* 1 man who solicits customers for prostitutes in return for a share of the proceeds ‖ *vi* 2 to act as a pimp

pim·per·nel /pimp′ərnel′, -nəl/ [OF < LL *pipinella*] *n* plant of the genus *Anagallis* with white, blue, or scarlet flowers, one species of which (*A. arvensis*) closes with the approach of bad weather

pim·ple /pimp′əl/ [?] *n* small swelling of the skin containing pus ‖ **pim′pled** *adj* ‖ **pim′ply** *adj* (-pli·er; -pli·est)

pin /pin′/ [OE *pinn*] *n* 1 short piece of wire with a sharp point at one end and a round head at the other, used for fastening; 2 ornament, badge, or jewel fitted with a pin and clasp; 3 bolt or peg; 4 *bowling* wooden peg to be knocked down by the ball; 5 **pins** *pl colloq* legs ‖ *v* (**pinned; pin·ning**) *vt* 6 to fasten with or as with a pin; 7 to hold fast in one position; 8 *colloq* to give one's fraternity pin to (a girl) as a sign of going steady; 9 **pin down, a** to hold fast; b to force (someone) to commit himself; 10 **pin something on someone** *slang* to fasten the blame for something on someone

pin·a·fore /pin′əfōr′, -fôr′/ [*pin* + *afore*] *n* sleeveless garment worn over a blouse or sweater

pin′ball ma·chine′ *n* device actuated usu. by a coin for playing a game, called pinball, in which balls are shot up a groove by a lever-actuated spring, then allowed to roll down an inclined plane, hitting pins and bumpers which electrically record the score of the players

pince-nez /pans′nā′, pins′-/ [F = pinch nose] *n* (**pince-nez** /-nāz′/) pair of eyeglasses kept on the nose by a spring

pin·cers /pins′ərz/ [ME *pynceours*] *nsg & npl* 1 instrument for gripping and holding, having two handles and two hinged jaws; 2 *zool* organ resembling pincers

pinch /pinch′/ [OF *pincier*] *vt* 1 to squeeze between two surfaces or edges, or between the thumb and a finger; 2 to press or squeeze painfully; 3 to oppress or distress; 4 to make thin or wan; 5 *slang* to arrest; 6 *slang* to steal; 7 **pinch pennies** to be extremely frugal || *vi* 8 to squeeze painfully; 9 **pinch and scrape** to economize unduly || *n* 10 squeeze or nip; 11 painful pressure; distress; 12 sudden need or emergency; 13 as much as can be held between the thumb and a finger; 14 *slang* arrest; 15 *slang* theft

pinch·bot′tle *n* bottle with concave sides for easy grasping

pin′chers *nsg & npl* pincers

pinch′ hit′ *n* hit made by person pinchhitting

pinch′-hit′ *v* (-hit; -hit·ting) *vi* 1 to substitute at bat for a teammate; 2 to substitute for another in an emergency || **pinch′ hit′ter** *n*

pin′cush′ion *n* small cushion in which pins are stuck for storage

Pin·dar /pin′dər/ *n* (522?–443?) Greek lyric poet

pine¹ /pīn′/ [OE *pīn* < L *pinus*] *n* 1 any of a genus (*Pinus*) of cone-bearing evergreen trees with needlelike leaves; 2 its wood

pine² [OE *pīnian*] *vi* 1 to long intensely; 2 **pine away** to fail in health and vigor from grief or longing || SYN languish, droop, wither, flag

pin′e·al bod′y /pin′ē·əl, pīn′-/ [< L *pinea* pine cone] *n* small body of unknown function situated in the brain of all vertebrates having a cranium

pine′ap′ple *n* 1 large cone-shaped fruit of a low-growing tropical plant (*Ananas comosus*) with spiny leaves; 2 the plant itself; 3 *slang* hand grenade

pine′ cone′ *n* fruit of the pine tree

pin′feath′er *n* feather just beginning to grow

ping /piŋ′/ [imit] *n* 1 sharp sound, as from a bullet || *vi* 2 to make a ping

Ping-Pong /piŋ′poŋ′/ [trademark] *n* table tennis

pin′head′ *n* 1 head of a pin; 2 anything small and trifling; 3 *slang* stupid person; fool

pin′hole′ *n* tiny hole made by or as if by a pin

pin·ion¹ /pin′yən/ [F *pignon*] *n* 1 small gear that meshes with a larger one; 2 toothed shaft that engages with a gear

pin·ion² [MF *pignon*] *n* 1 last group of bones of a bird's wing, corresponding to the human hand and wrist; 2 wing; 3 feather || *vt* 4 to bind the wings of, or to clip the pinions of (a bird); 5 to bind; 6 to confine or fetter

pink¹ /piŋk/ [?] *n* 1 pale red; 2 any of a genus (*Dianthus*) of plants, esp. any of several garden flowers of this genus, with sharp-pointed leaves and a sweet spicy fragrance; 3 leftwinger; 4 condition of supreme excellence; 5 **in the pink** in excellent condition || *adj* 6 pale-red; 7 leftist

pink² [ME *pinken*] *vt* 1 to stab; prick; 2 to pierce with small holes; 3 to scallop the edge of, as cloth

pink′eye′ *n* acute contagious conjunctivitis marked by redness of the eyeball and eyelids

pink′ie or **pink′y** [D *pinkje*] *n* (-ies) *colloq* little finger

pink′ish *adj* somewhat pink

pink′o *n* (-os or -oes) *disparaging* leftish person; left-winger

pink′ slip′ *n* notice of dismissal from one's employer

pin′ mon′ey *n* allowance of money for small expenditures, as from a husband to his wife

pin·nace /pin′is/ [< Sp *pinaza* (made of) pine] *n* 1 small, light schooner-rigged or oar-propelled sailing vessel; 2 ship's boat

pin·na·cle /pin′əkəl/ [MF *pinacle* < LL *pinnaculum* peak] *n* 1 small tower or spire above the rest of a building; 2 highest point; 3 peak, summit

pin·nate /pin′āt/ [< L *pinna* feather] *adj bot* arranged like a feather along two sides of an axis, as the veins in a leaf or the leaflet arrangement of a compound leaf

pin′ oak′ *n* oak (*Quercus palustris*) exhibiting pyramidal growth in the arrangement of its branches

pi·noch·le /pē′nukəl, -nok-/ [?] *n* 1 card game played with a 48-card deck having two sets of the face cards, aces, tens, and nines; 2 meld of the queen of spades and the jack of diamonds

pi·ñon /pin′yon, -yon/ [Sp] *n* 1 pine tree of W North America and Mexico bearing edible nutlike seeds; 2 the seed

pin′point′ *n* 1 point of a pin || *vt* 2 to locate precisely

pin′prick′ *n* tiny puncture made by or as by a pin

pins′ and nee′dles *npl* 1 tingling sensation in a limb that has been numb; 2 **on pins and needles** worried and anxious about something impending

pin′ set′ter *n* device that automatically replaces the pins in a bowling alley after they have been knocked down in play

pin′ stripe′ *n* 1 very thin strip in a fabric pattern; 2 garment with such a stripe

pint /pīnt′/ [ME *pinte*] *n* liquid and dry measure of capacity equal to half a quart

pin·tle /pin′təl/ [< OE *pintel* penis] *n* 1 pin or bolt on which a hinge turns; 2 pin or bolt by which a gun is attached to a towing vehicle; 3 *naut* pin upon which a rudder swings

pin·to /pínt′ō/ [AmSp] *adj* 1 mottled; piebald ‖ *n* 2 pinto horse

pint′-size(d)′ *adj colloq* smaller than standard

pin′up′ *n colloq* 1 large picture of a pretty young girl usu. nude or in scanty attire; 2 girl in such a picture ‖ also *adj*

pin′wheel′ *n* 1 toy consisting of paper or plastic vanes rotating on the end of a stick; 2 fireworks device that revolves rapidly on a pin when ignited

pin′worm′ *n* small threadlike roundworm infesting the rectum, esp. in children

pin·y /pín′ē/ *adj* (-i·er; -i·est) pert. to or abounding in pine trees

pi·o·neer /pī′ənir′/ [OF *peonier* foot soldier] *n* 1 one who goes before to prepare the way for others, as a settler in a new country or a researcher in a new field; 2 soldier engaged in road building and repairing ‖ *vi* 3 to be a pioneer ‖ *vt* 4 to open up, as a way or road; 5 to take the lead in

pi·on·i·um /pī·ōn′ē·əm/ *n* quasi-atom, composed of a pi meson and a mu meson bound together

pi·ous /pī′əs/ [L *pius* dutiful] *adj* 1 showing reverence for God; religious; 2 done under pretense of religion; 3 sacred; nonsecular ‖ SYN dutiful, godly, upright, virtuous, religious

pip¹ /pip′/ [< *pippin*] *n* 1 small seed, as of an apple or orange; 2 *slang* someone or something extraordinary

pip² [< *obs peep* spot] *n* 1 one of the spots on playing cards, dice, or dominoes; 2 one of the metal lozenges on the shoulder straps of British officers as insignia of rank; 3 spot of light on a radarscope produced by the echo from a distant object

pip³ [< L *pituita* phlegm] *n* 1 disease of poultry; 2 *slang* mild human illness; used humorously

pi·pal /pē′pəl/ [Hindi] *n* fig tree (*Ficus religiosa*) of India, considered sacred by Buddhists

pipe /pīp′/ [OE < L *pipa*] *n* 1 any long hollow tube for conveying liquids and gases; 2 tube of clay, wood, etc., with a bowl at one end for smoking tobacco; 3 as much as the bowl of a pipe will hold; 4 large cask of varying capacity; 5 wine measure equal to two hogsheads or 126 wine gallons; 6 note or call of a bird or insect; 7 tube or reed producing musical sounds, as a flute or clarinet; 8 tube of a pipe organ; 9 cylindrical vein of ore; 10 **pipes** *pl* bagpipes ‖ *vt* 11 to play (music) on a pipe or pipes; 12 to utter in a high key; 13 to furnish with pipes; 14 to convey through pipes; 15 to trim with piping; 16 *naut* to call by means of a whistle; 17 *slang* to look at ‖ *vi* 18

to play on a pipe; 19 to utter a shrill sound; 20 to whistle; 21 **pipe down** *slang* to become quiet

pipe′ clay′ *n* fine white clay used in making tobacco pipes and in various industrial processes

pipe′ dream′ *n colloq* fantastic notion; vain hope

pipe′ line′ *n* 1 pipe for conveying water, natural gas, oil, etc., esp. from a long distance and often underground; 2 direct channel of information

pipe′ or′gan *n* organ 4

pip′er *n* 1 one who plays a pipe or bagpipes; 2 **pay the piper,** a to pay the cost of something; b to face the consequences of one's actions

pi·pette /pīpet′, pī-/ [F] *n* small tube used for measuring and transferring liquids from one vessel to another

pipe′ wrench′ *n* wrench with toothed jaws, one of which can be screwed tight, for turning pipes

pip′ing *adj* 1 shrill (voice) ‖ *adv* 2 **piping hot** very hot (food) ‖ *n* 3 music of a pipe or the act of producing it; 4 network of pipes; 5 tubular strip of material along a seam or fold

pip·pin /pip′in/ [OF *pepin* seed] *n* 1 any of several varieties of apple; 2 *slang* someone or something extraordinary

pip′-squeak′ *n colloq* insignificant person

pi·quant /pēk′ənt/ [F = pricking] *adj* 1 agreeably sharp to the taste; 2 agreeably interesting or stimulating ‖ **pi′quant·ly** *adv* ‖ **pi′quan·cy** *n* ‖ SYN keen, spirited, lively, tart, pungent, spicy ‖ DISCR *Pungent* describes that which is sharp or biting (primarily to the sense of taste or smell); *piquant,* that which is agreeably *pungent* or, figuratively, that which is sharp and stimulating, as a *pungent* flavor, *pungent* satire, a *piquant* sauce, *piquant* wit or repartee. *Spicy* means full of spice, aromatic, highly flavored, *pungent*

pique /pēk′/ [MF] *n* 1 slight anger or resentment; wounded pride ‖ *vt* 2 to wound the pride of; displease; 3 to stir (curiosity, interest) ‖ SYN *n* resentment, vexation, irritation

pi·qué /pikā′/ [F] *n* heavy ribbed or figured cotton cloth

pi·ra·cy /pīr′əsē/ [Gk *peirateia*] *n* (-cies) 1 robbery, or the practice of robbing vessels, on the high seas; 2 unauthorized use of a copyrighted or patented work

pi·ra·nha /pirän′yə/ [Port < Tupi] *n* small voracious and extremely ferocious fish (genus *Serrasalmus*) of South America

pi·rate /pīr′ət/ [Gk *peirates*] *n* 1 one who practices piracy; 2 pirate ship; 3 predator, plunderer ‖ *vt* 4 to commit piracy upon; **5** to obtain by piracy ‖ **pi·rat'i·cal** /-rat'-/ *adj*

pir·ou·ette /pir'ōō·et'/ [F] *n* **1** whirl or turn made on the toes; **2** quick turn or whirl of a horse ‖ *vi* **3** to perform a pirouette

pis·ca·to·ri·al /pis'kətôr'ē·əl, -tōr'-/ or **pis'ca·to'ry** [< L *piscator* fisherman] *adj* **1** pert. to fishes or fishing; **2** living by fishing

Pis·ces /pī'sēz, pis'ēz/ [L = fishes] *n* **1** a southern zodiacal constellation, the Fishes; **2** twelfth sign of the zodiac; **3** *zool* class of vertebrates comprising the true fishes

pis·ta·chi·o /pistash'ē·ō', -stäsh'-/ [It *pistacchio*] *n* **1** nut of a tree (*Pistacia vera*) with an edible, greenish, almond-flavored kernel, used for flavoring; **2** the kernel; **3** the tree

pis·til /pist'il/ [L *pistillum* pestle] *n* central organ of a flower, bearing seed in its enlarged base or ovary

pis·tol /pist'əl/ [MF *pistole*] *n* small short gun for use with one hand

pis'tol grip' *n* handle or grip shaped like a pistol butt, as on some tools and weapons

pis'tol-whip' *v* (-whipped; -whip·ping) *vt* to beat with a pistol

pis·ton /pist'ən/ [F < It *pistone*] *n* **1** solid disk or cylinder fitting exactly inside a hollow cylinder, either moved by fluid pressure and imparting motion to a rod connected to it, or compressing or moving a fluid by the motion of the rod; **2** sliding valve in a wind instrument that changes the pitch

pis'ton ring' *n* metal ring around a piston to maintain a close fit and prevent the escape of fluid from the cylinder

pit¹ /pit/ [OE *pytt* < L *puteus* well] *n* **1** hole in the earth; **2** shaft of a mine; **3** pitfall; **4** enclosure in which animals are set to fight each other; **5** natural hollow in the body; **6** small hole left, as by smallpox; **7** indentation in a surface; **8** special section in a commodity exchange for trading in a particular commodity, as the *wheat pit;* **9** place where the orchestra sits in front of the stage; **10** place where racing cars are serviced during a race; **11** the pit hell ‖ *v* (pit·ted; pit·ting) *vt* **12** to mark with pits; **13** to match or set to fight against another ‖ *vi* **14** to become marked with pits

pit² [D = kernel] *n* **1** kernel of certain fruits, as the peach ‖ *v* (pit·ted; pit·ting) *vt* **2** to remove the pit from

pit·a·pat /pit'əpat'/ [imit] *adv* **1** with quick beating; flutteringly ‖ *n* **2** succession of light quick sounds or taps ‖ *v* (-pat·ted; -pat·ting) *vi* **3** to go pitapat

pitch¹ /pich'/ [OE *pic* < L *pix* (*picis*)] *n* **1** thick, tenacious black substance, left as a residue of coal tar after distillation, used for calking and paving; **2** any of various other bituminous substances and resins ‖ *vt* **3** to cover or smear with pitch

pitch² [ME *pichen*] *vt* **1** to set up, as a tent or camp; **2** to place or fix at a particular level; **3** to throw or fling; **4** *baseball* **a** to serve (the ball) to the batter; **b** to pitch the ball in (a game) ‖ *vi* **5** to fall headlong; **6** to rise alternately forward and aft, as a ship in a heavy sea; **7** *baseball* to act as pitcher; **8** to dip, slope; **9 pitch in** *colloq* **a** to contribute, as to a collection; **b** to set energetically to work; **c** to start to eat heartily; **10 pitch into** *colloq* to attack vigorously ‖ *n* **11** act or manner of pitching; **12** throw or toss; **13** pitching motion of a ship; **14** *slang* a sales talk; **15** angle, approach, point of view; **15** that which is pitched; **16** degree or rate; **17** tone of a voice; **18** distance between two successive threads of a screw; **19** distance between the centers of two successive gear teeth; **20** slope, as the *pitch of a roof;* **21** *mus* **a** elevation or depression of a tone, depending on the number of vibrations per second; **b** standard number of tonal vibrations accepted as a basis for tuning instruments

pitch'-black' *adj* black as pitch; very black

pitch'blende' /-blend'/ [*pitch¹* + G *Blende* zinc sulfide] *n* lustrous black mineral, an oxide of uranium; a source of radium and uranium

pitch'-dark' *adj* dark as pitch; very dark

pitched' bat'tle *n* full-scale battle or encounter

pitch'er¹ /-/ [< *pitch²*] *n* baseball player who pitches

pitch'er² [OF *pichier*] *n* vessel for liquids, usu. with a spout and handle

pitch'er plant' *n* any of a number of insectivorous plants whose leaves are formed in the shape of a pitcher

pitch'fork' *n* large fork with a long handle for tossing hay and straw

pitch'man /-mən/ *n* (-men /-mən/) **1** high-pressure salesman; **2** itinerant street vendor

pitch'out' *n* baseball ball purposely pitched too wide of the plate for the batter to hit

pitch' pipe' *n* mus small pipe producing one designated note, used in tuning instruments or for setting the pitch in unaccompanied singing

pit·e·ous /pit'ē·əs/ [< *pity*] *adj* exciting or deserving pity ‖ **pit'e·ous·ly** *adv*

pit'fall' *n* **1** concealed pit used as a trap; **2** any unsuspected source of danger

pith /pith'/ [OE *pitha*] *n* **1** soft spongy substance in the center of the stems of certain plants; **2** heart or essence

pit·head' *n* entrance to a mine

pith·y *adj* (-i·er; -i·est) *adj* 1 like or full of pith; 2 forcible; full of meaning; terse || **pith'i·ly** *adv* || **pith'i·ness** *n* || SYN pointed, concise, succinct, terse (see *short*)

pit·i·a·ble /pit'ē-əbəl/ [OF *piteable*] *adj* 1 deserving pity; 2 contemptible || **pit'i·a·bly** *adv* || SYN sorrowful, wretched, sad, miserable (see *pitiful*)

pit'i·ful /pit'ifəl/ *adj* 1 deserving or arousing pity; 2 contemptible; meager || SYN piteous, pitiable, abject, base, miserable, despicable, lamentable, pathetic, wretched, woeful, sorrowful || DISCR That is *piteous* which awakens pity because of its need, as a *piteous* cry. *Pitiful* in the sense "full of pity" is a synonym for compassionate, and is seldom used in modern English; it applies rather to that which calls for pity because it is helpless, sad, or pathetic, as *pitiful* poverty. *Pitiful* sometimes connotes contempt as well as pity; a *pitiful* story may be shabby and mean as well as mournful. *Pitiable* also applies to that which deserves pity, as a *pitiable* plight. *Pitiable* and *pitiful* are sometimes interchanged, as a *pitiful* or a *pitiable* condition || ANT admirable, noble, sublime

pit'i·less *adj* without pity; merciless || SYN implacable, cruel, unforgiving, relentless

pit·tance /pit'əns/ [OF *pitance*] *n* 1 small allowance; 2 meager amount of money

pit·ter-pat·ter /pit'ər-pat'ər/ [imit] *n* 1 succession of light quick sounds or taps || *vi* 2 to make this sound || *adv* 3 with a pitter-patter

Pitts·burgh /pits'burg/ *n* city in W Pennsylvania (520,117)

pi·tu·i·tar·y (gland') /pit(y)oŏ'iter'ē/ [< L *pituita* phlegm] *n* small rounded endocrine gland on the under side of the brain, secreting several hormones

pit·y /pit'ē/ [OF *pite* < L *pietas*] *n* (-ies) 1 feeling of sorrow for the distress of others; 2 reason for regret or grief || *v* (-ied) *vt* 3 to feel pity for; feel sorry for || SYN *n* compassion, tenderness (see *sympathy*)

piv·ot /piv'ət/ [F] *n* 1 pin or shaft on which something rotates; 2 person or thing on which something hinges or depends; 3 pivoting movement || *vt* 4 to place on or supply with a pivot || *vi* 5 to turn on or as on a pivot

piv'ot·al *adj* 1 like a pivot; 2 critically important

pix·ie or **pix·y** /piks'ē/ [?] *n* (-ies) sprite; fairy

pix·i·lat·ed /piks'ilāt'id/ [< *pixie*] *adj* 1 a bit unbalanced mentally; 2 whimsical; 3 *slang* drunk

piz·za /pēt'sə/ [It] *n* baked dish consisting of a flat crust topped with tomato sauce and cheese, often with additional ingredients

piz·zazz /pizaz'/ [?] *n slang* glamour, flamboyance

piz·ze·ri·a /pēt'sərē'ə/ *n* place making and serving pizzas

piz·zi·ca·to /pit'sikät'ō/ [It] *adj & adv* played by plucking the strings with the finger instead of drawing a bow across them

pk. 1 pack; 2 park; 3 peck

pkg. package

pl. 1 place; 2 plural

plac·a·ble /plak'əbəl, plāk'-/ [L *placabilis*] *adj* capable of being placated; willing to forgive

plac·ard /plak'ärd, -ərd/ *n* 1 notice posted in a public place; poster || *vt* 2 to place placards on or in; 3 to advertise by means of placards

pla·cate /plā'kāt, pla'-/ [L *placare* (-*atus*)] *vt* to pacify; appease

place /plās'/ [MF < Gk *plateia* broad street] *n* 1 open space or square in a city; 2 court or short street; 3 particular location; special spot or locality; 4 particular community or region; 5 residence; 6 building or location devoted to a special purpose; 7 location of a given body, as *out of place*; 8 room to stand or sit in, as *save me a place*; 9 rank, social position; 10 duty; responsibility; 11 position, job; 12 position in order, as *in first place*; 13 space, room; 14 second place in a horse race; 15 **give place to, a** to be replaced by; **b** to give precedence to; 16 **in place in** the proper place; 17 **in place of** in lieu of; 18 **put someone in his place** to humble someone; 19 **take place** to occur || *vt* 20 to put in a particular place, situation, or relation; 21 to indicate the place of; 22 to identify by recalling; 23 to finish in a specified standing in a competition; 24 to arrange for, as a loan or an order || *vi* 25 to finish second in a horse race || **place'ment** *n* || SYN *n* post, station, room, location, situation

pla·ce·bo /pləseb'ō/ [L = I shall please] *n* (-bos or -boes) substance, as a pill containing no medicine, given as a control in an experiment or to please or humor a patient who supposes it to be medicine

place' card' *n* card with the name of a guest, used to indicate his place at table

place' kick' *n football* play in which the ball is kicked after being placed or held on the ground || **place'-kick'** *vt & vi*

place' mat' *n* mat used for a table setting for one person

pla·cen·ta /pləsent'ə/ [L < Gk *plakoeis* (-*koentos*) flat cake] *n* organ developed in the pregnant uterus of most mammals, to nourish the fetus and eliminate its waste products, being expelled after birth

plac·er /plas'ər/ [Sp] n place where loose surface soil contains gold or other valuable minerals

plac·id /plas'id/ [L *placidus*] adj calm; peaceful ‖ **plac·id·ly** adv ‖ **pla·cid'·i·ty** /pləsid'-/ n ‖ SYN gentle, serene, tranquil, unruffled (see *calm*)

plack·et /plak'it/ [?] n slit at the top of a skirt or dress to make it easy to put on

pla·gi·a·rism /plāj'(ē)əriz'əm/ [< L *plagiarius* kidnaper] n 1 act of stealing and using as one's own the ideas or the expression of the ideas of another; 2 that which is thus stolen ‖ **pla·gi·a·rist** n ‖ **pla·gi·a·rize'** vt & vi

plague /plāg'/ [L *plaga* wound, blow] n 1 affliction or calamity; 2 nuisance; 3 deadly epidemic disease; 4 infectious epidemic disease caused by the bacterium *Pasteurella pestis* and transmitted by fleas carried by rats ‖ vt 5 to afflict with disease or evil; 6 to annoy greatly ‖ SYN v distress, trouble, harass, torment, disturb

plaid /plad/ [Gael *plaide* blanket] n 1 cloth woven with a crossbarred pattern; 2 crossbarred pattern

plain /plān/ [OF < L *planus* flat] adj 1 clear, evident; 2 sheer; utter; 3 easily understood; 4 unlearned; unpolished; 5 simple in manners; 6 frank, sincere; 7 not luxurious; 8 without ornament; 9 all of one color; 10 without beauty; homely; 11 not rich (food); 12 uncomplicated; 13 ordinary ‖ adv 14 clearly ‖ n 15 wide stretch of level land ‖ **plain'ly** adv ‖ **plain'ness** n ‖ SYN adj obvious, apparent, guileless, intelligible, explicit (see *open*) ‖ ANT adj obscure, indistinct, vague, ambiguous, equivocal

plain'clothes'man /-mən/ n (-men /-mən/) detective who wears civilian clothes while on duty

Plain' Peo'ple npl members of a sect stressing plain dress and simple living, as the Amish and Mennonites

Plains' In'di·ans npl American Indians belonging to any of several nomadic tribes that inhabited the Great Plains, hunting the buffalo

plains'man /-mən/ n (-men/-mən/) inhabitant of the plains

plain'song' also **plain'chant'** n early Christian church music sung without accompaniment, still used in the Anglican and Catholic services

plain'-spo'ken adj blunt, candid

plaint /plānt'/ [MF] n 1 complaint; 2 lament

plain·tiff /plān'tif/ [ME *plaintif*] n one who brings suit in court

plain·tive /plān'tiv/ [ME *plaintif* complainant] adj expressing sorrow; mournful, sad

plait /plāt'/ plat'/ [OF *pleit* < L *plicitus* folded] n 1 pleat; 2 braid ‖ vt 3 to pleat; 4 to braid; 5 to form by braiding

plan /plan'/ [F < L *planus* flat] n 1 scale drawing of a horizontal section of a building or machine; 2 diagram or map; 3 arrangement of parts according to a fixed design; 4 scheme or project; 5 method of procedure; 6 **plans** pl working drawings, as of a house ‖ v (planned; plan·ning) vt 7 to make a plan of; 8 to arrange beforehand ‖ vi 9 to make plans ‖ **plan'ner** n ‖ SYN n project, purpose, sketch (see *design, scheme*)

plane¹ /plān/ [MF < LL *plana*] n 1 carpenter's tool for smoothing wood ‖ vt 2 to smooth or make even with a plane

plane² [L *planus* flat] n 1 geom surface such that if any two points in it are joined by a straight line, the line will lie wholly in the surface; 2 any flat or even surface; 3 grade or level; 4 airplane; 5 one of the flat supporting surfaces of an airplane ‖ adj 6 flat; level; even; without irregularities of surface; 7 geom lying wholly in a plane

plane' ge·om'e·try n geometry that treats of points, lines, and surfaces in one plane

plan·et /plan'it/ [Gk *planetes* wanderer] n 1 any of the larger celestial bodies of the solar system revolving around the sun and shining by reflected light; 2 astrol any heavenly body regarded as influencing the affairs of men ‖ **plan'e·tar'y** /-ter'-/ adj

plan·e·tar·i·um /plan'iter'ē·əm/ [< LL *planetarius* of a planet] n (-ums or -a /-ə/) 1 instrument by which spots of light, representing heavenly bodies and moving appropriately, are projected upon the inner surface of a dome representing the sky; 2 the building housing it

plane' tree' [MF < Gk *platanos*] n any of a genus (*Platanus*) of large trees with broad leaves, including the sycamore

plan·gent /plan'jənt/ [< L *plangens* (-entis) beating the breast] adj 1 loud, reverberating; 2 having a plaintive sound

plank /plaŋk'/ [ONF *planke* < L *planca*] n 1 long flat piece of timber thicker than a board; 2 item in the platform of a political party ‖ vt 3 to cover with planks; 4 to broil on a board

plank'ton /-tən/ [G < Gk *planktos* wandering] n drifting microscopic organisms on the surface of the ocean

plant /plant'/ [OE *plante* < L *planta*] n 1 vegetable organism; 2 herb or small vegetable growth as distinguished from a tree or shrub; 3 tools, machinery, fixtures, and sometimes buildings of any trade or business, as *a manufacturing plant*; 4 total equipment necessary for the conduct of any institution; **5** complete equipment for a particular operation, as *a cooling plant;* **6** *slang* trick, snare, trap; **7** person placed in a seemingly innocent position for purposes of deception or robbery ‖ *vt* **8** to put in the ground for growth, as seed; **9** to stock with plants, as *to plant a garden;* **10** to fix firmly, place; **11** to found, establish, as a colony; **12** to post or station; **13** to conceal for the purpose of tricking or trapping someone

plan·tain[1] /plant′ən/ [Sp *plátano*] *n* tropical broad-leaved tree (*Musa paradisiaca*) of the banana family, yielding a fruit larger than and less sweet than the banana

plan·tain[2] [OF *plantein*] *n* any of a genus (*Plantago*) of stemless herbs, esp. a common weed (*P. major*) having a rosette of broad leaves and central stalks

plan·ta·tion /plantāsh′ən/ [L *plantatio* (*-onis*) planting] *n* large farm or estate where tropical and semitropical products are cultivated, as cotton, rubber, coffee, etc.

plant′er *n* **1** owner or cultivator of a plantation; **2** one who or that which plants; **3** decorative plant container

plant′ louse′ *n* small juice-sucking parasitic insect infesting plants

plaque /plak′/ [F] *n* **1** flat piece of metal or other material containing a picture, design, or legend, used as a wall ornament or to commemorate a person or an event; **2** brooch or similar ornament; **3** accumulation that stains the teeth, formed from bacteria and mucus in the saliva; **4** abnormal deposit on the wall of a blood vessel

-plasm /-plaz′əm/ [< *plasma*] *n comb form* something shaped or molded

plas·ma /plaz′mə/ [Gk = something molded] *n* **1** liquid part of the blood exclusive of the corpuscles; **2** protoplasm; **3** *phys* gas containing equal concentrations of positive ions and electrons

plas·ter /plas′tər, pläs′-/ [OE < Gk *emplastron*] *n* **1** pasty mixture of lime, sand, and water, which dries hard, used for coating walls and ceilings; **2** plaster of Paris; **3** medicinal preparation spread on cloth and applied to the body ‖ *vt* **4** to cover with plaster, as walls; **5** to treat with plaster of Paris; **6** to apply a plaster to; **7** to cover thickly, as with posters ‖ **plas′ter·er** *n*

plas′ter·board′ *n* board used in interior construction consisting of sheets of gypsum and felt covered with paper

plas′ter cast′ *n* **1** piece of sculpture cast in plaster of Paris; **2** dressing made of gauze and plaster of Paris to immobilize a broken bone

plas′tered *adj slang* drunk

plas′ter of Par′is *n* quick-setting mixture of gypsum and water, used as a plaster and in making casts

plas·tic /plas′tik/ [Gk *plastikos*] *adj* **1** capable of being molded; **2** produced by molding; **3** giving form to matter, as *plastic art;* **4** quick to receive impressions, as a *plastic mind;* **5** pert. to molding or modeling ‖ *n* **6** also **plastics** *sg* any of a group of synthetic or natural materials, shaped when soft and then hardened, used as substitutes for many other materials ‖ **plas·tic′i·ty** /-tis′-/ *n*

plas′tic sur′ger·y *n* surgery for the restoration of deformed or mutilated parts of the body

plat du jour /plä′ də zhŏōr′/ [F = dish of the day] *n* (**plats du jour** /plä′/) featured dish in a restaurant

plate /plāt′/ [OF] *n* **1** shallow dish for food; **2** contents of a dish; **3** food and service for one person; **4** thin flat piece of some rigid substance, as glass or metal; **5** sheet of metal used for armor; **6** piece of metal on which something is engraved or printed; **7** metal surface engraved with something drawn or written from which a print is to be made; **8** full-page illustration in a book; **9** metallic ware overlaid with gold or silver; **10** tableware of gold or silver; **11** denture fitting in the mouth and containing artificial teeth; **12** dish for collecting money in a church; **13** *baseball* home plate; **14** metallic grid filled with active material which constitutes individually or in groups a negative or positive element of a storage battery; **15** anode of a vacuum tube in the form of a sheet of metal which receives the electrons emitted by the filament; **16** *photog* sheet of glass coated with a sensitized emulsion ‖ *vt* **17** to coat (metal) with another metal, as gold or tin; **18** to cover with sheets of metal; **19** to make an electrotype or a stereotype of

pla·teau /platō′/ [F] *n* (**-teaus** or **-teaux** /-tōz′/) **1** broad elevated tract of flat land; **2** period of halted activity, as depicted by a flat line on a graph

plate′ glass′ *n* thick glass rolled in plates, ground flat, and polished on both sides

plat·en /plat′ən/ [MF *platine* flat object] *n* **1** flat plate or cylinder in a printing press that brings the paper against the type; **2** typewriter roller

plat·form /plat′fôrm/ [MF *platte form* flat form] *n* **1** raised horizontal structure or floor, as for a stage for speakers, or along a railroad track to permit access to cars; **2** principles and policies, as of a political party

plat·i·na /plat′ənə, plətēn′ə/ [Sp] n native alloy of platinum

plat·ing /plāt′iŋ/ n coating of metal or of thin metal sheets

plat·i·num /plat′ənəm/ [< platina] n rare, heavy, grayish-white metallic element (Pt; at.no. 78; at.wt. 195.09), ductile and malleable, fused with great difficulty, and unattacked by oxygen and most acids; used in chemical utensils, in jewelry, in dentistry, in electrical and electronic apparatus, etc.

plat′i·num blonde′ n 1 pale bluish-silver color; 2 girl or woman having hair of this color

plat·i·tude /plat′it(y)ōōd′/ [F = flatness] n trite or commonplace remark ‖ **plat′i·tu′di·nous** adj

Pla·to /plāt′ō/ n (427–347 B.C.) Greek philosopher ‖ **Pla′to·nism** /plāt′ən-/ n ‖ **Pla′ton·ist** n

Pla·ton·ic /pləton′ik/ adj 1 pert. to or characteristic of Plato or his philosophy; 2 also **platonic** spiritual (love), free from physical desire

pla·toon /plətōōn′/ [F peloton] n 1 mil component part of a company consisting of two or more squads; 2 football group of players who specialize in one aspect of the game and are put in as needed

Platt·deutsch /plät′doich′/ [G = lowland German] n the Low German spoken in N Germany

plat·ter /plat′ər/ [AF plater < OF plat plate] n 1 large flat dish for serving food; 2 slang phonograph record

plat·y·pus /plat′ipəs/ [Gk platypous broad-footed] n small egg-laying water mammal (Ornithorhynchus anatinus) of Australia, having a duck-like bill

plau·dits /plôd′its/ [< L plaudite (impv) applaud] npl 1 applause; 2 expression of approval

plau·si·ble /plôz′ibəl/ [L plausibilis deserving applause] adj 1 having the appearance of truth; 2 worthy of confidence ‖ **plau′si·bly** adv ‖ **plau′-si·bil′i·ty** n /-bil′-/ ‖ SYN specious, ostensible, apparent, colorable ‖ DISCR That is specious which appears fine and right on the surface, but is not so in reality. Plausible arguments or pretences are also fair-seeming; they sound reasonable or probable, but usually are a means of deceiving, though they may be innocently made. The ostensible is that which is pushed to the front, made apparent, or is professed, often with the intent to conceal the reality lurking behind, as an ostensible purpose ‖ ANT genuine, true, honest, actual, trustworthy

play /plā′/ [OB pleg(i)an] vi 1 to move lightly or capriciously; flicker; 2 to sport or frolic; engage in a pastime; 3 to take part in a game; 4 to gamble; 5 to perform on a musical instru-

ment; 6 to act on the stage; 7 to behave in a specific way, as to play fair; 8 to dally, trifle; 9 play at to do (something) without being serious about it; 10 play fast and loose to act irresponsibly; 11 play into the hands of to act in such a way as to give the advantage to (one's opponent); 12 play up to colloq to try to gain the favor of by flattery ‖ vt 13 to take part in (a game or sport); 14 to lay a wager on; 15 to compete with in a game; 16 to put into action in a game or contest, as a player, a ball, or a card; 17 to make believe that one is, as to play cops and robbers; 18 to perform, as to play a comedy, play a waltz on the piano; 19 to perform music on; 20 to act in the character of; 21 to work, set in action, as to play a trick, play a hose; 22 to maneuver, as to play a fish; 23 play back to reproduce (a phonograph record or tape recording, esp. one that has just been made); 24 play down to treat as unimportant; 25 play it by ear to improvise; 26 play up to magnify the importance of ‖ n 27 brisk motion; 28 elusive or irregular movement, as of light; 29 freedom or room to act or move, as in a mechanism; 30 exercise, esp. in a contest of strength or skill; 31 exercise of mental powers; 32 amusement; recreation; sport; 33 gambling; 34 any single action in a game; 35 one's turn to play; 36 fun, jest; 37 manner of acting, as fair play; 38 drama; dramatic performance; 39 bring into play to introduce and make use of ‖ SYN n pastime, diversion, recreation (see game)

play′act′ vi 1 to act in a play; 2 to behave in an affected manner

play′back′ n 1 device for reproducing a phonograph or tape recording; 2 the recording

play′bill′ n 1 poster or circular announcing a play; 2 program of a play, with the names of the actors

play′boy′ n wealthy man who spends his time in the pursuit of pleasure

played′ out′ adj 1 tired out; exhausted; 2 used up

play′er n 1 person who plays a game; 2 actor; 3 performer on a musical instrument; 4 device that operates a player piano; 5 device that reproduces music recorded on disks or tape; 6 gambler; 7 trifler

play′er pi·an′o n mechanical piano playing music from a perforated roll

play′ful adj 1 sportive, full of fun; 2 humorous ‖ **play′ful·ly** adv

play′go′er n one who habitually goes to the theater

play′ground′ n 1 ground used for games and recreation, esp. by children; 2 locality suitable for relaxation and vacationing

play′house′ *n* (-hous·es /-ziz/) 1 theater; 2 small house for children to play in; 3 toy house

play′ing card′ *n* one of the cards of a pack used for playing games

play′mate′ *n* companion in play

play′-off′ *n* game or series of games played to decide a tie

play′ on words′ *n* pun

play′pen′ *n* small pen for the safe play of an unattended child

play′thing′ *n* means of diversion; toy

play′wright′ *n* writer of plays

pla·za /plaz′ə, pläz′ə/ [Sp] *n* open square in a city

plea /plē′/ [< OF *plaid*] *n* 1 excuse; 2 entreaty; 3 *law* defendant's answer to the charges against him; 4 **cop a plea** *slang* to plead guilty to a lesser charge in order to escape punishment for a more serious one || SYN argument, pretext, justification, subterfuge

plea′-bar′gain *vi* to make a deal to avoid a trial on a serious charge by pleading guilty to lesser charges || **plea′-bar′gain·ing** *n*

plead /plēd′/ [Of *plaidier* to sue, plead] *v* (**plead·ed** or **plead** /pled′/ or **pled**) *vi* 1 to argue or reason in support of something; 2 to supplicate, beg earnestly; 3 to make a plea in court || *vt* 4 to offer as an excuse; 5 *law* a to argue (a case); b to answer ("guilty" or "not guilty") to a charge || **plead′er** *n* || SYN beg, beseech, advocate, allege (see *pray*)

pleas·ant /plez′ənt/ [MF *plaisant*] *adj* 1 pleasing; agreeable; delightful; 2 characterized by attractive ways; cheerful; amiable || SYN pleasing, comfortable, merry, amiable, kindly, accommodating, obliging || ANT disagreeable, displeasing, unkind, troublesome, rude, cross

pleas′ant·ry *n* (-ries) 1 merriment, gaiety; 2 jest, quip || SYN raillery, banter, playfulness, facetiousness

please /plēz′/ [MF *plaisir*] *vt* 1 to give enjoyment or satisfaction to; 2 to be the wish or pleasure of, as *it pleases him to stay*; 3 to be so kind as to (used in polite commands), as *please come in* || *vi* 4 to like, as *do as you please*; 5 to afford satisfaction or enjoyment || SYN satisfy, gratify, gladden, indulge, delight, charm, entertain, amuse || ANT offend, vex, dissatisfy, bore

pleas′ing *adj* giving satisfaction; agreeable

pleas·ur·a·ble /plezh′ərəbəl/ *adj* gratifying; delightful || **pleas′ur·a·bly** *adv*

pleas·ure /plezh′ər/ [MF *plaisir*] *n* 1 feeling of being pleased; 2 delight, joy; 3 choice; wish || SYN delectation, felicity, satisfaction, comfort; delight; gratification; gladness (see *happiness*)

pleat /plēt′/ [var of **plait**] *n* 1 fold of even width in cloth, pressed or stitched in place || *vt* 2 to form pleats in

plebe /plēb′/ [< *plebeian*] *n* member of the lowest or freshman class in the U.S. Military Academy and the U.S. Naval Academy

ple·be·ian /plibē′ən/ [< L *plebeius* < *plebs* commoner] *n* 1 member of the common people || *adj* 2 of or pert. to the common people; 3 coarse, vulgar

pleb·i·scite /pleb′isit, -sīt′/ [F < L *plebiscitum* decree of the plebeians] *n* direct vote of all qualified voters on a measure, as to determine a form of government

plec·trum /plek′trəm/ [L < Gk *plektron*] *n* (-trums or -tra /-trə/) piece of thin ivory, metal, or shell, used to pluck the strings of certain instruments

pled /pled′/ *pt* & *pp* of **plead**

pledge /plej′/ [MF *plege* hostage, security] *n* 1 anything given as a security or guarantee; 2 solemn promise to do or not do something; 3 token of good will; 4 person tentatively accepted for membership, as in a fraternity, pending formal approval; 5 **take the pledge** to vow to stop drinking alcoholic beverages || *vt* 6 to give as security; 7 to pawn; 8 to bind by a promise; 9 to promise solemnly; 10 to accept as a tentative member || **pledg′er** *n*

Ple·ia·des /plē′ədēz′, plī′-/ [< Gk *myth.* the seven daughters of Atlas, who turned into stars] *npl* cluster of small stars in the constellation Taurus

Pleis·to·cene /plīs′təsēn′/ [< Gk *pleistos* most + *kainos* new] *n* geol epoch of about one million years ago, characterized by the spread of glacial ice and the appearance of man || also *adj*

ple·na·ry /plē′nərē, plen′-/ [LL *plenarius*] *adj* 1 full; complete; unqualified; 2 (session) attended by all the members, as of an assembly

plen·i·po·ten·ti·ar·y /plen′əpoten′shēer′ē, -shərē/ [ML *plenipotentiarius*] *adj* 1 having full power; unlimited || *n* (-ies) 2 diplomatic agent having full power and authority to negotiate

plen·i·tude /plen′it(y)ōōd′/ [L *plenitudo*] *n* fullness; abundance

plen·te·ous /plent′ē·əs/ [see **plenty**] *adj* abundant, copious || SYN ample, exuberant, fertile, abundant, rich

plen·ti·ful /plent′ifəl/ *adj* 1 abundant; 2 fruitful || SYN ample, copious, unstinted, exuberant

plen·ty /plent′ē/ [OF *plente* < L *plenitas* fullness] *n* (-ties) 1 abundant supply; 2 sufficient quantity; 3 abundance; 4 plenty of an abundance of || *adj* 5 *colloq* plentiful || *adv* 6 *colloq* fully, sufficiently

ple·o·nasm /plē′ənaz′əm/ [Gk *pleonasmos*] *n* 1 use of more words than are necessary; redundancy; **2** redundant word or expression ‖ **ple'o·nas'·tic** *adj*

pleth·o·ra /pleth'ərə/ [LL < Gk *pleth-ore* fullness] *n* overabundance; excess

pleu·ra /ploŏr'ə/ [Gk = side of body, rib] *n* (-rae /-rē/) delicate membrane lining each half of the chest cavity and covering the lungs ‖ **pleu'ral** *adj*

pleu·ri·sy /-rĭsē/ [OF *pleurisie* < Gk *pleuritis*] *n* inflammation of the pleura, characterized by difficult breathing

plex'i·glass' /plek'sĭ-/ [*Plexiglas*; trademark] *n* lightweight transparent thermoplastic polymer, used as a glass substitute

plex·us /plek'səs/ [L = interweaving] *n* (-us·es or -us) **1** network of veins, nerves, etc.; **2** any intricate network

pli·a·ble /plī'əbəl/ [F] *adj* **1** easily bent; flexible; **2** easily influenced ‖ **pli'a·bil'i·ty** /-bĭl'-/ *n* ‖ SYN limber, supple, docile, compliant (see *flexible*)

pli·ant /plī'ənt/ [OF] *adj* **1** subject to easy bending; **2** yielding, compliant ‖ **pli'an·cy** *n* ‖ SYN supple, pliable, lithe, tractable (see *flexible*)

pli·ers /plī'ərz/ [< *ply*³] *nsg* or *npl* small pincers for bending wire or for holding small objects

plight¹ /plīt/ [ME var of *plait* influenced by ME *plite* < OE *pliht* danger] *n* unfavorable or dangerous situation

plight² [OE *pliht* danger] *vt* **1** to promise earnestly; pledge, as one's faith; **2** to engage to marry, betroth

plinth /plinth/ [Gk *plinthos*] *n* square slab at the base of a column or pedestal

Pli·o·cene /plī'əsēn/ [< Gk *pleion* more + *kainos* new] *n geol* epoch preceding the Pleistocene, characterized by the growth of mountains and the increased size and number of mammals ‖ also *adj*

Pli'o·film' /plī'ə-/ [trademark] *n* clear, pliable, waterproof film used esp. for protective packaging

P.L.O. Palestine Liberation Organization

plod /plod/ [imit] *v* (**plod·ded; plod·ding**) *vi* **1** to walk slowly and heavily; **2** to drudge or toil ‖ *vi* **3** to walk over heavily and slowly ‖ **plod'der** *n*

plonk /plonk/ [?] *n Australian* cheap wine or liquor

plop /plop/ [imit] *v* (**plopped; plop·ping**) *vi* **1** to make a sound like that of a flat object falling into a liquid; **2** to fall heavily ‖ *vt* **3** to drop heavily ‖ *adv* **4** with a plop ‖ *n* **5** plopping sound

plot /plot/ [OE] *n* **1** small well-marked piece of ground; **2** scheme or secret plan, esp. one with evil purpose; **3** plan or story line of a play, novel, etc. ‖ *v* (**plot·ted; plot·ting**) *vt* **4** to make a plan or map of; **5** to locate or show on a map or chart; **6 a** to mark (points), as on a graph; **b** to connect such points with lines; **7** to lay secret plans for, esp. something nefarious; **8** to construct the plot of (a novel or the like) ‖ *vi* **9** to scheme, conspire ‖ **plot'ter** *n* ‖ SYN *n* complication, entanglement, machination, intrigue; *v* conspire, plan, contrive, scheme

Plo·ti·nus /plōtīn'əs/ *n* (205?–270?) Egyptian-born Roman philosopher; founder of Neoplatonism

plov·er /pluv'ər, plō̆v'-/ [OF *plovier* rainbird] *n* **1** any of a family (Charadriidae) of snipelike shore birds; **2** any of several allied birds

plow also *Brit* **plough** /plou'/ [OE *plōh* plowland] *n* **1** farm implement for turning up the soil in preparation for planting; **2** any machine or tool that works in a similar way, by cutting, shoving, furrowing, etc., as a snowplow ‖ *vt* **3** to turn up (soil) with a plow; **4** to make (a furrow) with a plow; **5 plow back** to reinvest (profits) in a business; **6 plow up** to make furrows in ‖ *vi* **7** to till soil with a plow; **8 plow into, a** to crash into; **b** to begin to work vigorously on; **9 plow through** to go or move through

plow'boy' *n* **1** boy who guides or leads a team pulling a plow; **2** country lad, rustic

plow'share' *n* pointed steel blade of a plow

ploy /ploi'/ [?] *n* maneuver or stratagem intended to outwit an opponent

pluck /pluk/ [OE *pluccian*] *vt* **1** to pull off, out, or up; **2** to pull or tug at; **3** to strip completely of feathers; **4** to sound by pulling or twitching (the strings of a musical instrument); **5** *slang* to fleece, rob; **6 pluck up, a** to uproot; **b** to summon (one's courage) ‖ *vi* **7 pluck at** to pull, tug ‖ *n* **8** tug; **9** spirit, courage ‖ SYN *n* confidence, courage, gameness, spirit, intrepidity, resolution (see *bravery*)

pluck'y *adj* (-i·er; -i·est) brave, courageous

plug /plug/ [MD *plugge*] *n* **1** piece of wood, metal, or the like, used to fill or stop a hole; **2** cake of pressed tobacco; **3** hydrant; **4** *slang* broken-down horse; **5** device for connecting an electric cord to a source of electricity, or one telephone line to another; **6** spark plug; **7** *colloq* publicity for a product worked into a news story, radio or television show, etc. ‖ *v* (**plugged; plug·ging**) *vt* **8** to stop or make tight with a plug; **9** *colloq* to give publicity to; **10** *slang* to shoot; **11** *slang* to hit; **12 plug in** to connect (an electric device or telephone) to an outlet ‖ *vi* **13** also **plug along** to work doggedly ‖ **plug'ger** *n*

plug'board' *n* **1** switchboard in which the current is switched by means of plugs; **2** panel in a computer in which connections for programing are made with plugs

plug·ug·ly n (-lies) colloq roughneck, tough

plum /plum′/ [OE plūme < L prunum] n 1 smooth, oval, drupaceous fruit of a tree of the genus Prunus; 2 the tree itself; 3 raisin when used in baking; 4 something choice or desirable; 5 reddish purple

plum·age /plōōm′ij/ [see plume] n 1 feathers collectively; 2 bright costume

plumb /plum′/ [L plumbum lead] n 1 small heavy weight fastened to a cord and suspended to indicate a vertical line or the depth of water; 2 out of plumb not truly vertical || adj 3 perpendicular; 4 colloq out-and-out; absolute || adv 5 perpendicularly; 6 colloq completely || vt 7 to test with a plumb line; 8 to make vertical; 9 to get to the bottom of, understand, as a mystery

plumb·er /plum′ər/ [AF plummer < LL plumbarius < plumbum lead] n one who installs, repairs, and maintains water and drainage systems, and often gas and steam systems

plumb·ing /plum′iŋ/ n 1 occupation or trade of a plumber; 2 all the pipes and fixtures for conveying water and liquid wastes in a building

plumb′ line′ n line to which a plumb is attached

plume /plōōm/ [OE plūme < L pluma down] n 1 long and beautiful feather or tuft of feathers; 2 feather worn as an ornament; 3 feather or tuft of feathers or hair worn on a hat or helmet; 4 something like a feather in shape or lightness; 5 prize, mark of honor || vt 6 to preen (itself), as a bird; 7 to adorn with feathers or fine clothes; 8 plume oneself on or upon to feel proud of oneself because of

plum·met /plum′it/ [MF plommet < plomb lead] n 1 plumb; 2 heavy burden, as of sorrow || vi 3 to plunge vertically; 4 to drop sharply

plump[1] /plump′/ [ME plompe dull, coarse] adj 1 well-filled or rounded out || vi 2 plump out to become plump || vt 3 plump out or up to make plump

plump[2] [prob imit] vi 1 to fall or sink down heavily and abruptly; 2 plump for to come out in favor of || vt 3 to cause to fall heavily || adj 4 blunt, direct || adv 5 heavily; 6 straight down || n 7 a sudden heavy fall; b sound made by such a fall

plun·der /plun′dər/ [D plunderen] vt 1 to take from by force; 2 to despoil, rob || vi 3 to pillage, rob || n 4 booty, pillage; 5 act of plundering || plun′-der·er n || SYN v ravage, pillage, despoil, rifle; n robbery, spoil, rapine, loot, booty, pillage, spoliation

plunge /plunj′/ [MF plonger] vt 1 to

put suddenly into a liquid or into any substance that can be penetrated; 2 to put suddenly into an unexpected condition, as to plunge a country into war || vi 3 to fall or rush headlong into something; 4 to enter suddenly and quickly; 5 to descend abruptly, as a road; 6 colloq to bet heavily || n 7 act of plunging; 8 dive or leap; 9 headlong dash; 10 swim; 11 take the plunge to enter suddenly on a course of action

plung·er n 1 one who plunges; 2 colloq reckless gambler; 3 cylindrical piece used as a piston in a pump or hydraulic device; 4 rubber suction cup on a handle, used to clear clogged drains

plunk /pluŋk′/ [imit] vt 1 to pluck (a stringed instrument or its strings); 2 plunk down colloq to put down quickly or forcefully || vi 3 to twang; 4 plunk down colloq to drop heavily || n 5 act or sound of plunking || adv 6 colloq exactly; b with a plunk

plu·per·fect /plōō-/ [< L plus quam perfectum more than perfect] n & adj past perfect

plu·ral /plŏŏr′əl/ [L pluralis] adj 1 consisting of more than one; 2 gram designating more than one, or in some languages, more than two || n 3 gram a plural number; b form in the plural

plu·ral·ism n 1 condition of being plural; 2 philos the teaching that there is more than one ultimate principle || plu′ral·is′tic adj

plu·ral·i·ty /plŏŏral′itē/ n (-ties) 1 state or quality of being plural; 2 majority; 3 excess of votes cast for one candidate over those cast for any other || SYN (see majority)

plu′ral·ize′ vt to make plural

plus /plus′/ [L = more] adj 1 more (by a certain quantity); 2 positive, as a plus quantity; 3 pert. to positive electricity; 4 indicating addition || prep 5 increased by; with the addition of || n 6 plus quantity; 7 plus sign

plush /plush′/ [F p(e)luche] n 1 soft fabric with a pile longer than that of velvet || adj 2 luxurious

plus′ sign′ n sign +, indicating addition or a positive quantity

Plu·tarch /plŏŏt′ärk/ n (46?–120? A.D.) Greek biographer

Plu·to /plŏŏt′ō/ n 1 class. myth. god of the lower world; 2 outermost planet of the solar system

plu·toc·ra·cy /plŏŏtok′rəsē/ [Gk ploutokratia] n (-cies) 1 rule or government by the rich; 2 the wealthy class

plu·to·crat /plŏŏt′əkrat′/ n member of the plutocracy || plu′to·crat′ic adj

plu·to·ni·um /plŏŏtōn′ē·əm/ [< Pluto] n radioactive element (Pu; at.no. 94) not occurring free in nature but produced by two successive beta-ray transformations from an isotope of uranium

plu·vi·al /plōō′vē-əl/ [< L *pluvia* rain] *adj* pert. to rain; rainy

ply[1] /plī′/ [< *apply*] *v* (**plied**) *vt* 1 to work at steadily; 2 to use diligently; 3 to address insistently, as *to ply a person with questions;* 4 to urge, offer insistently, as *to ply one with food* || *vt* 5 to keep at work; 6 to run regularly between two places, as a steamer

ply[2] [MF *pli* fold] *n* (**plies**) web or layer, as in a carpet or tire

-ply /-plī′/ *comb form* ply[2], as *four-ply tires*

Plym′outh Rock′ /plim′əth/ *n* 1 rock at Plymouth, Mass., on which the Pilgrims are said to have landed in 1620; 2 American breed of domestic fowl

ply′wood′ *n* construction material made of two or more layers of wood glued together

Pm *chem* promethium

P.M., **p.m.** [L *post meridiem* after noon] period from 12 noon to 12 midnight

pneu·mat·ic /n(y)ōōmat′ik/ [< Gk *pneuma* (-*atos*) air, wind] *adj* 1 pert. to, consisting of, or containing air; 2 inflated with or operated by air; 3 pert. to pneumatics || *n* 4 **pneumatics** *sg* branch of physics dealing with the physical properties of air and other gases

pneu·mo·coc′cus /n(y)ōōmə-/ [< Gk *pneumon* lung + *coccus*] *n* (-**ci** /-sī/) bacterium (*Diplococcus pneumoniae*) causing lobar pneumonia

pneu·mo·ni·a /n(y)ōōmōn′ē-ə, -yə/ [Gk] *n* 1 inflammation of the lungs; 2 lobar pneumonia

Po *chem* polonium

P.O. 1 Post Office; 2 petty officer

poach[1] /pōch′/ [MF *poche* bag] *vt* to cook in a simmering liquid, as eggs

poach[2] [MF *pocher*] *vi* to trespass, esp. to obtain game unlawfully on another's property || **poach′er** *n*

pock /pok′/ [OE *poc*] *n* 1 slight skin pustule, as in smallpox; 2 scar left by such a pustule

pock·et /pok′it/ [ONF *pokete*] *n* 1 small pouch in a garment for carrying small articles; 2 any pocket-like receptacle, cavity, or opening; 3 ore-bearing cavity in a mine; 4 air hole *1;* 5 financial means; 6 **in one's pocket** under one's control; 7 **line one's pocket** to profit, often at the expense of others; 8 **out of pocket, a** having paid out money; **b** having suffered a financial reverse || *adj* 9 that can be carried in a pocket; 10 relatively small || *vt* 11 to put in a pocket; 12 to take possession of, esp. unlawfully; 13 to receive (an insult) without showing feeling; 14 to suppress, as pride

pock′et·book′ *n* small pouch or case, as of leather, for money, papers, etc., carried either in the pocket or by an attached handle

pock′et·knife′ *n* (-**knives** /-vz/) small knife with blades that fold into the handle, for carrying in the pocket

pock′et mon′ey *n* small sum for current expenses; spending money

pock′et ve′to *n* veto effectuated by the failure of a chief executive to sign a bill within ten days of adjournment of the legislative body

pock′mark′ *n* 1 scar or pit, as left by smallpox || *vt* 2 to mark with or as with pockmarks

po·co /pōk′ō/ [It = little] *adv mus* a little; somewhat

pod /pod′/ [?] *n* any seed vessel which dries and opens when ripe, as that of the bean or the pea

-pod /-pod′/ [Gk -*podos*] *comb form* -footed, as *cephalopod*

po·di·um /pōd′ē-əm/ [L < Gk *podion* little foot] *n* (-**ums** or -**a** /-ə/) raised platform for an orchestra conductor or a public speaker

Poe, Ed·gar Al·lan /pō′/ *n* (1809–49) U.S. poet and short-story writer

po·em /pō′əm/ [Gk *poiema*] *n* 1 composition in verse. marked by beauty of thought and language; 2 any imaginative piece of writing in beautiful language; 3 anything resembling a poem in beauty or imaginative suggestion

po·e·sy /pō′əzē/ [Gk *poiesis*] *n* (-**sies**) *archaic & poet.* poetry

po·et /pō′it/ [Gk *poietes* = maker] *n* 1 one who composes poems; 2 any writer gifted with imagination, creative power, and ability to express poetic ideas in beautiful language || **po′et·ess** *nfem* || SYN dreamer, bard, troubadour, minstrel, singer

po′et·as′ter /-as′tər/ [*poet* + L -*aster* expressing contempt] *n* writer of inferior verses

po·et·ic (-**i·cal**) /pō-et′ik(əl)/ *adj* 1 pert. to or characteristic of poets or poetry; 2 gifted with the faculties or feelings of a poet; 3 suitable as a subject for poetry; 4 expressed in poetry

po·et′ic jus′tice *n* reward or punishment that ideally fits the circumstances

po·et′ic li′cense *n* deviation from formal rules or conventions in writing, done for special effect

po·et·ics *nsg* 1 branch of literary study dealing with poetry and its technique and criticism; 2 treatise dealing with this subject

po′et lau′re·ate *n* 1 poet acclaimed as the most representative of a country, region, or class; 2 in Great Britain, official poet of the royal court

po′et·ry *n* 1 the composition of poems;

2 poems, verse; 3 poetic quality or feeling

po'go stick' /pō'gō/ n pole with a footrest near the bottom attached to a spring, enabling a person to leap like a kangaroo

po·grom /pəgrom', pŏg'rəm/ [Russ = devastation] n organized massacre, originally of Jews in Russia

po·i /pō'ē, poi'/ [Hawaiian] n fermented food of Hawaii made from the taro root

poign·ant /poin'(y)ənt/ [MF = piercing] adj 1 keenly appealing to the emotions; 2 distressing to the mind or feelings || **poign'an·cy** n

poin·ci·an·a /poin'sē·an'ə/ [M. de Poinci 17th-cent. F governor in the West Indies] n shrub of the genus Poinciana with showy scarlet or orange flowers

poin·set·ti·a /poinset'(ē)ə/ [J.R. Poinsett, Am minister to Mexico, who discovered the plant there] n any of a genus (Euphorbia) of Mexican and Central American plants with large red petallike leaves clustered around small flowers

point /point'/ [MF pointe] n 1 sharp end of a thing, as of a pin; 2 something which projects, as the tip of a cape; 3 essential question or idea; 4 speck or dot; 5 mark of punctuation; 6 decimal point; 7 particular spot or location; 8 exact place or time; 9 particular detail or item; 10 aim or purpose; 11 exact degree, as in temperature; 12 unit of scoring in certain games or sports; 13 degree or step; 14 distinguishing feature or characteristic; 15 craps number that must be thrown with the dice to win; 16 position of a hunting dog when indicating the presence of game; 17 contact in the distributor of an internal-combustion engine that makes and breaks the current to the spark plugs; 18 geom that which has position but not length, breadth, or thickness; 19 one of the 32 divisions of a compass, equal to one eighth of a right angle; 20 typ unit of measurement for type, equal to ab. ¹⁄₇₂ of an inch; 21 com unit of price quotation, usu. equal to one dollar; 22 at or on or upon the point of close to; 23 beside the point irrelevant; 24 in point that is pertinent; 25 make a point of to insist on; 26 to the point pertinent || vt 27 to put a point on; 28 to show the purpose of, as to point a moral; 29 to show the direction of; 30 to direct or aim; 31 to fill the joints of (masonry) with mortar and smooth with a trowel; 32 to show the presence of (game) by assuming a certain position, as a hunting dog; 33 point out to direct the attention to; 34 point up to give emphasis to || vi 35 to call attention by extending the finger; 36 to face; tend; be directed; 37 to point game; 38 naut to sail close to the wind

point'-blank' adj 1 straight to the mark; so close to the target that it is impossible to miss; 2 direct and abrupt || also adv

point'ed adj 1 sharp; 2 having a personal application, as a remark || **point'ed·ly** adv

point'er n 1 one who or that which points; 2 hand on a watch, meter, or instrument; 3 long tapering stick used to point out things, as on a blackboard; 4 breed of dog trained to point game; 5 timely hint or piece of advice; 6 the Pointers pl two stars of the Big Dipper which guide the eye to the North Star

poin·til·lism /pwant'iliz'əm/ [F pointillisme] n pictorial representation by means of small dots of pure color applied with the point of a brush

point' lace' n fine kind of lace made wholly with the needle

point'less adj 1 blunt, dull; 2 meaningless, without relevance; 3 without scoring a point in a game || SYN flat, irrelevant, inane, insipid, dull, blunt

point' of hon'or n something that affects one's honor or self-respect

point' of or'der n question raised as to the correctness of any parliamentary procedure

point' of view' n 1 standpoint; 2 opinion

poise /poiz'/ [MF pois weight] n 1 balance; 2 self-possession; 3 stability || vt 4 to balance; 5 to hold in a raised position || vi 6 to remain or hang balanced or suspended

poi·son /poiz'ən/ [OF puison < L potio (-onis) potion] n 1 substance which destroys life or health; 2 destructive influence || vt 3 to give poison to; 4 to injure or kill by poison; 5 to put poison in or on; 6 to corrupt || **poi'son·er** n || **poi'son·ous** adj § SYN n pestilence, pest, bane, venom, malignity

poi'son i'vy n any of several sumacs (genus Rhus) having white berries and glossy green leaves which on contact can cause severe irritation to the skin

poi'son-pen' let'ter n anonymous letter sent with malicious intent to damage another's reputation or happiness

poke¹ /pōk'/ [MD] n archaic & dial. 1 bag or sack; 2 pocket

poke² [MD poken] vt 1 to prod or push against, esp. with a pointed object; 2 to thrust in or out; 3 to make (a hole; one's way) by poking; 4 slang to strike, hit; 5 poke fun at to ridicule; 6 poke one's nose into to meddle in || vi 7 to thrust or push; 8 to move lazily, dawdle; 9 poke around to pry; to rummage; to putter || n 10 thrust or jab; 11 slang blow with the fist; **12 a** projecting rim on a woman's bonnet; **b** also **poke′ bon′net** the bonnet itself; **13** *slang* slow, lazy person; dawdler

pok·er[1] /pōk′ər/ *n* metal rod for poking and stirring fires

po′ker[2] [?] *n* any of several card games in which the players place bets on their hands, the various combinations of cards being given specific values

po′ker face′ [adopted by poker players so that their opponents cannot guess what cards they hold] *n* face not revealing any expression

pok·ey[1] /pōk′ē/ [?] *n slang* jail

pok·y or **pok·ey**[2] /pōk′ē/ [< *poke*[2]] *adj* (**-i·er; -i·est**) **1** dull, slow, tedious; **2** small, cramped; shabby

Pol. 1 Poland; **2** Polish

Po·land /pōl′ənd/ *n* republic in E central Europe (31,944,000; 120,665 sq.m.; cap. Warsaw)

po·lar /pōl′ər/ [see **pole**[1]] *adj* **1** pert. to or situated near either of the poles of the earth; **2** passing repeatedly over the earth's or another planet's north and south poles, as *an artificial polar satellite*; **3** of or pert. to the poles of a magnet, electric cell, etc.; **4** exactly opposite, as in action or character; **5** acting or serving as a guide

po′lar bear′ *n* large white bear (*Thalarctos maritimus*) of the arctic regions

Po·la·ris /pəlar′is/ [L = polar] *n* the polestar or North Star, in the constellation Ursa Minor, at which the North Pole points

po·lar·i·ty /pōlar′itē/ *n* **1** property possessed by electrified or magnetized bodies by which they exert directly opposite forces in opposite directions; **2** presence of two opposite or opposed tendencies

po·lar·i·za·tion /pō′lərizāsh′ən/ *n* **1** act of polarizing or state of being polarized; **2** a pulling apart of two groups of people into tensely opposing stances

po·lar·ize′ *vt* **1** to provide with two opposite poles; **2** to give polarity to; **3** to cause (electromagnetic waves, esp. light) to oscillate in a definite plane; **4** *elec* to deposit gas on (one or both electrodes of a battery), increasing the resistance of the circuit ‖ *vi* **5** to acquire polarity; **6** to become polarized

po·lar·iz′er *n* device, as a prism or crystal, which converts ordinary light into a beam of light consisting of vibrations in a single plane

Po′lar·oid′ [trademark] *n* material that polarizes light passing through it, used to reduce glare

pole[1] /pōl/ [Gk *polos* pivot, axis] *n* **1** either of the two ends of the axis of the earth or any sphere; **2** either of

two opposed forces or principles; **3** either of two regions of a magnet or electric battery, etc., in which opposite forces are manifested; **4** celestial pole

pole[2] [OE *pāl* < L *palus* stake] *n* **1** long staff or rod, as *a fishing pole*; **2** narrow cylindrical pillar, usu. of wood or metal, as *a telephone pole* ‖ *vt* **3** to push or propel with a pole

Pole /pōl/ [G] *n* native or inhabitant of Poland

pole′ax′ [ME *pollax* = head ax] *n* **1** battle-ax having a long handle and a head with a spike or hook on one side and a blade on the other; **2** ax used in slaughtering animals ‖ *vt* **3** to kill or strike down with or as with a poleax

pole′cat′ [ME *polcat*] *n* **1** European weasellike mammal (*Mustela putorius*) that throws out an offensive odor; **2** skunk

po·lem·ic /pəlem′ik, pō-/ [Gk *polemos* war] *n* **1** disputatious argument; **2** person who argues against another; **3** polemics *sg* art or practice of disputation ‖ also **po·lem′i·cal** *adj* **4** disputatious; involving dispute ‖ **po·lem′i·cal·ly** *adv*

pole′star′ *n* **1** Polaris, the North Star; **2** something that serves as a guiding principle

pole′ vault′ *n* field event consisting of a vault over a high bar with the aid of a pole ‖ **pole′-vault′** *vi*

po·lice /pəlēs′/ [MF < Gk *politeia* government] *n* **1** organized force of the government that enforces the laws, keeps order, and investigates crimes; **2** any body of men employed to guard property and maintain order; **3** *pl* members of a police force ‖ *vt* **4** to guard, keep order, or regulate, as with police; **5** *mil* to maintain cleanliness in (a camp, barracks, etc.)

po·lice′ dog′ *n* German shepherd

po·lice′man /-mən/ *n* (**-men** /-mən/) member of a police force ‖ **po·lice′·wom′an** *nfem* (**-wom′en**)

po·lice′ state′ *n* nation in which the government uses the police to suppress all dissent

po·lice′ sta′tion *n* headquarters of the police in a city or precinct, to which arrested persons are brought to be booked

pol·i·cy[1] /pol′isē/ [MF *policie*] *n* (**-cies**) **1** course of conduct; **2** line of action in relation to some special issue; **3** line of conduct adapted to given circumstances

pol′i·cy[2] [MF *police* < It *polizza*] *n* (**-cies**) **1** insurance contract; **2** numbers game

po·li·o /pōl′ē·ō′/ *n* poliomyelitis

po·li·o·my·e·li·tis /pōl′ē·ōmī′əlīt′is/ [< Gk *polios* gray + *myelos* marrow] *n* acute virus disease attacking the spinal cord esp. of young children, often resulting in paralysis and deformity

Po·lish /pōl′ish/ *adj* **1** of or pert. to Poland, its inhabitants, or their language ‖ *n* **2** language of the Poles

pol·ish /pol′ish/ [MF *polir* (*-liss-*)] *vt* **1** to make smooth or glossy by rubbing; **2** to make polite or refined; **3 polish off** *slang* **a** to dispose of quickly; **b** to get rid of ‖ *n* **4** substance used for polishing; **5** act of polishing or state of being polished; **6** gloss; **7** elegance, refinement ‖ **pol′ish·er** *n* ‖ SYN *v* shine, rub, burnish, furbish, perfect, refine

po·lite /pəlīt′/ [L *politus* polished] *adj* **1** courteous, showing good manners; **2** refined, cultivated ‖ **po·lite′ly** *adv* ‖ **po·lite′ness** *n* ‖ SYN civil, courtly, courteous, polished, urbane, cultured, genteel, affable, refined, complaisant ‖ DISCR To be *civil* requires one only to refrain from rudeness, to observe the least of those laws that govern social intercourse. *Polite* sometimes implies a merely mechanical observance of propriety, but often describes a person of good breeding and of sympathy, tact, and natural kindliness. *Courteous* suggests a particularly appealing politeness; *courteous* behavior is distinguished by dignity, grace, and charming deference. *Urbane* adds to *courteous* the idea of smoothness, blandness, and suavity. *Affable* adds to *courteous* the idea of approachableness, ease of address, sociability, or amiability. *Complaisant* describes one deferentially obliging to the wishes of others. *Polished* suggests the result of having been perfected, smoothed, or the finished manner of a person expert in any walk of life, as a *polished* gentlewoman, a *polished* villain. *Polished* as applied to verse, works of art, or the like, connotes the finish that exquisite care and workmanship have imparted. *Genteel* in serious use is often either ironical or vulgar; it is applied to those who are shabbily stylish, or who make crude attempts at elegance and refinement ‖ ANT boorish, rude, impolite

pol·i·tic /pol′itik/ [MF *politique* < Gk *politikos* civil] *adj* **1** prudent; shrewd; **2** expedient; **3** political, as in *body politic* ‖ *n* **pol′i·tics** *sg* or *pl* **4** science or art of government; **5** political affairs; **6** political methods; **7** party affiliation; **8** intrigue used to gain one's ends ‖ SYN *adj* sagacious, artful, wily, discreet, judicious, diplomatic ‖ ANT *adj* impolitic, unwary, indiscreet

po·lit·i·cal /pəlit′ikəl/ *adj* **1** of, pert. to, or concerned with politics; **2** pert. to or advocating a particular system of politics or government, as a *political party*, *political machine*; **3** of

or pert. to the civil government, as *a political subdivision*, *political office* ‖ **po·lit′i·cal·ly** *adv*

po·lit′i·cal sci′ence *n* science of government and politics

pol·i·ti·cian /pol′ətish′ən/ *n* **1** one engaged in party politics; **2** office holder more interested in advancing the fortunes of his party than in the general welfare; **3** one who seeks to advance himself by political intrigues

po·lit·i·cize /pəlit′isīz′/ *vt* **1** to make political; inject politics into ‖ *vi* **2** to become political; discuss politics

po·lit·i·co /pəlit′ikō′/ [Sp and It] *n* politician

po·lit·i·co- *comb form* political

pol·i·ty /pol′itē/ [Gk *politeia* government] *n* (*-ties*) **1** organization of the government of a state, church, etc.; **2** any community living under an organized system of government

Polk, James K. /pōk′/ *n* (1795–1849) 11th president of the U.S. 1845–49

pol·ka /pōlk′ə, pōk′ə/ [Czech < Pol = Polish woman] *n* lively dance of Bohemian origin, or the music for it ‖ *also vi*

pol′ka dot′ /pōk′ə/ *n* **1** one of a number of spots or dots on a plain background in a fabric; **2** pattern of such dots

poll /pōl/ [MLG *polle*] *n* **1** head, esp. the top or back part of it; **2** list of persons, esp. those entitled to vote at an election; **3** the voting at an election; **4** number of votes recorded; **5** record of the views of selected individuals of a group on a given topic; **6 polls** *pl* place where votes are cast ‖ *vt* **7** to clip or shear, as hair or wool; **8** to lop off, as the top of a tree; **9** to record the votes of; **10** to receive the votes of; **11** to cast in a ballot box; **12** to take a poll of the opinions of

pol·len /pol′ən/ [L = fine flour, dust] *n* yellow grains or spores, growing in the anthers of flowers, which fertilize the cells in the ovary

pol′len count′ *n* count of the number of pollen grains in a given volume of air in a given period of time, usu. 24 hours

pol·li·nate /pol′ənāt′/ [< *pollen*] *vt* to fertilize (a flower) by placing pollen on the stigma ‖ **pol′li·na′tion** *n*

pol·li·wog or **pol·ly·wog** /pol′ēwog/ [ME *polwygle*] *n* **1** tadpole; **2** *colloq* person who in crossing the equator in a boat for the first time is initiated by the shellbacks

poll′ster *n* person who takes public-opinion polls

poll′ tax′ *n* tax that formerly had to be paid in some states by voters before being permitted to vote

pol·lu·tant /pəlō̄ot′ənt/ [< *pollute*] *n* something that pollutes, esp. the air, water, and soil

pol·lute /pəlōōt'/ [L *polluere* (*-utus*)] *vt* to make unclean; defile

pol·lu'tion *n* 1 act of polluting or state of being polluted; 2 contamination of the air, water, and soil by the waste products of modern technology

Pol·ly·an·na /pol'ē·an'ə/ [heroine of *Pollyanna*, 1913 novel] *n* person of unquenchable optimism

po·lo /pōl'ō/ [Balti (Tibetan *dial.*) = ball] *n* game, somewhat resembling field hockey, played on horseback with long-handled mallets ‖ **po'lo·ist** *n*

Po·lo, Mar·co /märk'ō pōl'ō/ *n* (ab. 1254–1324) Venetian traveler who left an account of his journey to the Far East

po'lo coat' *n* double-breasted belted coat, usu. of camel's hair

po·lo·ni·um /pəlōn'ē·əm/ [ML *Polonia* Poland] *n* radioactive element (**Po;** at.no. 84)

po'lo shirt' *n* short-sleeved pull-over sport shirt

pol·ter·geist /pōlt'ərgīst'/ [G = noise ghost] *n* ghost or spirit supposed to cause unexplained noises and to move tables and other objects

pol·troon /poltrōōn'/ [MF < OIt *poltrone*] *n* craven coward ‖ **pol·troon'·er·y** *n*

poly- [Gk] *comb form* much, many

pol·y·an·dry /pol'ē·an'drē, pol'ē·an'drē/ [< *poly-* + Gk *aner* (*andros*) man] *n* practice of having more than one husband at the same time ‖ **pol'y·an'drous** *adj*

pol'y·clin'ic *n* hospital or clinic for the treatment of all diseases

pol·y·es·ter /pol'ē·es'tər, pol'ē·es'tər/ *n* a polymer used in the manufacture of synthetic resins, plastics, and fibers

pol'y·eth'yl·ene' /-eth'əlēn'/ *n* a polymer —(-CH₂CH₂-)ₙ— used chiefly in packaging and electrical insulation

po·lyg·a·my /pəlig'əmē/ *n* practice or state of having several spouses, esp. wives, at one time ‖ **po·lyg'a·mist** *n* ‖ **po·lyg'a·mous** *adj*

pol·y·gen·e·sis *n* descent of a race or species from more than one species ‖ **pol'y·ge·net'ic** /-jənet'ik/ *adj*

pol'y·glot' /-glot'/ [Gk *polyglottos* many-tongued] *adj* 1 containing or written in several languages; 2 knowing several languages ‖ *n* 3 book, often the Bible, with the same text in several languages; 4 one who speaks several languages

pol'y·gon' /-gon'/ [Gk *polygonon*] *n* closed plane figure having three or more sides and angles ‖ **po·lyg·o·nal** /pəlig'ənəl/ *adj*

pol'y·graph' *n* 1 machine which produces many copies of a drawing or writing; 2 writer of many books or of many types of books; 3 instrument which records bodily variations and reflexes and is used as a lie detector

pol'y·he'dron /-hēd'rən/ [Gk *polyedron*] *n* (-**drons** or -**dra** /-drə/) solid figure bounded by many plane faces ‖ **pol'y·he'dral** *adj*

Pol'y·hym'ni·a /-him'nē·ə/ *n* Gk myth. Muse of oratory and sacred poetry

pol·y·mer /pol'imər/ [Gk *polymeres* having many parts] *n chem* compound in which two or more small molecules have combined to form larger molecules that consist of repeating structural units

pol'y·mer'ic /-mer'ik/ *adj* pert. to, of the nature of, or constituting a polymer

pol·y·mer·ize /pol'imərīz', pəlim'ərīz'/ *vt* 1 to render polymeric ‖ *vi* 2 to become polymeric

Pol'y·ne'sia /-nēzh'ə, nēsh'ə/ *n* the islands of the Central and South Pacific E of Melanesia and Micronesia, extending from the Hawaiian Islands S to New Zealand ‖ **Pol'y·ne'sian** *adj & n*

pol'y·no'mi·al /-nōm'ē·əl/ [*poly-* + binomial] *adj* 1 having many names ‖ *n* 2 *alg* expression consisting of two or more terms; 3 *biol* name consisting of more than two terms

pol·yp /pol'ip/ [Gk *polypous* many-footed] *n* 1 simple invertebrate animal consisting of a sac with a mouth surrounded by tentacles at one end, and a means of attachment to a foreign body at the other; 2 *pathol* projecting growth from a mucous surface of the body

pol'y·phon'ic *adj* 1 consisting of a variety of sounds or voices; 2 designating a style of composition in which two or more melodies are harmoniously intertwined; 3 producing two or more tones at once, as the piano

pol'y·sty'rene /-stī'rēn/ [*poly-* + styrax a plant] *n* plastic foam —[-CH(C₆H₅)CH₂-]ₙ— used in insulation

pol'y·syl'la·ble *n* word of three or more syllables ‖ **pol'y·syl·lab'ic** /-lab'-/ *adj*

pol'y·tech'nic [F *polytechnique*] *adj* 1 pert. to, including, or giving instruction in industrial arts and technical subjects ‖ *n* 2 polytechnic school

pol'y·the'ism *n* doctrine or belief in more than one god or in many gods ‖ **pol'y·the'ist** *n* ‖ **pol'y·the·is'tic** *adj*

pol'y·un·sat'u·rat'ed *adj* denoting fats and oils whose molecules are unsaturated by hydrogen atoms

pol·y·va·lent /pol'ival'ənt, pəliv'ələnt/ *adj* having more than one valence

po·made /pəmād', -mäd', pō-/ [F *pommade* < It *pomata*] *n* 1 perfumed ointment for the hair ‖ *vt* 2 to apply pomade to

pome /pōm'/ [MF < L *pomum* apple] *n* fleshy many-celled fruit with a membranous core enclosing several seeds, as the apple and pear

pome·gran·ate /pom'(ə)gran'it, pum'-/ [MF *pomegrenate*] *n* 1 edible fruit with a thick rind and a very seedy, crimson, pleasantly acid pulp, borne by a tree (*Punica granatum*) widely grown in warm regions; 2 the tree itself

Pom·er·a·ni·an /pom'ərān'ē·ən, -yən/ [< *Pomerania* region of Poland and East Germany] *n* small dog with long silky hair, a bushy curled-up tail, and a pointed muzzle

pom·mel /pum'əl, pom'-/ [MF *pomel*] *n* 1 knob on a sword hilt; 2 rounded hump on the front of a saddle || *v* (-meled or -melled; -mel·ing or -mel·ling) *vt* 3 to beat severely

pom·my /pom'ē/ [?] *n Australian & New Zealand* Englishman, esp. one recently arrived

pomp /pomp'/ [Gk *pompe* procession] *n* showy display; grandeur; splendor || SYN display, ostentation, pageantry, ceremony

pom·pa·dour /pomp'ədôr', -dōr', -dŏŏr'/ [Marquise de *Pompadour* (1721–64) mistress of Louis XV of France] *n* style of hairdo in which the hair is brushed back straight from the forehead without a part, and often, in a woman's coiffure, over a roll

pom·pa·no /pomp'ənō'/ [Sp] *n* food fish (genus *Trachinotus*) of the Gulf Coast and the West Indies

pom-pom /pom'pom'/ [imit] *n* automatic antiaircraft gun

pom·pon /pom'pon/ [F] *n* 1 ornamental tuft or ball, as of ribbon, for women's wear; 2 tuft or plume, as on a cap; 3 kind of chrysanthemum or dahlia with buttonlike flowers

pom·pous *adj* affectedly stately; self-important || **pom'pous·ly** *adv* || **pom·pos'i·ty** /-pos'itē/ *n* || SYN ostentatious, showy, pretentious, haughty, boastful, conceited, vainglorious, consequential

Ponce de Le·ón /pons' də lē'ən/ *n* (ab. 1460–1521) Spanish explorer and discoverer of Florida 1513

pon·cho /pon'chō/ [Sp] *n* blanketlike cloak with a hole in the middle for the head

pond /pond'/ [OE] *n* small body of standing water

pon·der /pon'dər/ [MF *ponderer*] *vt* 1 to consider carefully; think about || *vi* 2 to reflect, think deeply || SYN examine, revolve, study, meditate (see *muse*)

pon'der·ous *adj* 1 heavy, unwieldy; 2 labored, dull

pone /pōn'/ [< Algonquian] *n* southern U.S. corn bread

pon·gee /ponjē'/ [< Chin] *n* soft, thin silk fabric in usu. its natural tan color

pon·iard /pon'yərd/ [F *poignard*] *n* dagger

pon·tiff /pont'if/ [F *pontife* < L *ponti-fex*] *n* 1 high priest; 2 bishop; 3 pope

pon·tif·i·cal /-tif'-/ *adj* 1 of or pert. to a pontiff; 2 pompous or dogmatic || *n* **pon·tif'i·cals** *pl* vestments and insignia of a pontiff

pon·tif·i·cate /pontif'ikit/ *n* 1 office or tenure of a pontiff || /-kāt'/ *vi* 2 to speak pompously or dogmatically

pon·toon /pontoŏn'/ [F *ponton*] *n* 1 low flat boat; 2 floating structure, as a boat or hollow cylinder, used as one of the supports of a floating bridge; 3 seaplane float

pon'toon bridge' *n* temporary bridge supported by pontoons

po·ny /pōn'ē/ [Sc *powney* < OF *poulenet* little foal] *n* (-nies) 1 horse of any of certain small breeds; 2 slang race horse; 3 slang literal translation of a passage in a foreign language, used dishonestly in school; 4 small liquor glass || *v* (-nied) *vt* 5 **pony up** to pay (money owed)

po'ny tail' *n* hairdo in which the hair is drawn back tightly, fastened at the back of the head, and allowed to hang down the back like a horse's tail

pooch /pōōch'/ [?] *n slang* dog

poo·dle /pōōd'əl/ [G *Pudel*] *n* one of a breed of intelligent black or white curly-haired dogs

pooh /pōō'/ *interj* exclamation of scorn or contempt

pooh'-pooh' *vt* to treat contemptuously; make light of

pool[1] /pōōl'/ [OE *pōl*] *n* 1 pond; 2 stretch of deep still water in a stream; 3 puddle; 4 swimming pool; 5 any small amount of still liquid, as *a pool of blood*

pool[2] [F *poule* stakes] *n* 1 game played by driving balls with a cue into the pockets of a pool table; 2 stakes in certain gambling games; 3 accumulated wagers of a group of persons betting as on a race; 4 combination of stockholders for joint speculation; 5 combination of competing industries to control markets, fix prices, etc.; 6 shared facility, as *a car pool* || *vt* 7 to put (money, resources) into a common fund; 8 to form a pool of

pool' hall' or **pool'room'** *n* place for playing pool or billiards

pool' ta'ble *n* billiard table with six pockets, for playing pool

poop[1] /pōōp'/ [MF *pouppe*] *n* superstructure at the stern of a vessel

poop[2] [?] *vt slang* to exhaust

poor /pōōr'/ [OF *povre* < L *pauper*] *adj* 1 having little or no means of support; needy; 2 lacking in good qualities; inferior; inadequate, faulty, unsatisfactory; 3 scanty, meager; 4 unfortunate, worthy of pity || *n* 5 **the poor** *pl* the needy people || SYN *adj* humble, meager, scanty, destitute, cheap

poor'house' *n* (-hous·es /-hou'ziz/) public institution for paupers

poor'ly adv 1 in a poor manner; in an imperfect way || adj 2 dial. in poor health, ill

pop¹ /pop'/ [imit] n 1 short sharp quick sound; 2 shot from a firearm; 3 effervescent nonintoxicating drink || v (popped; pop-ping) vi 4 to make the sound of a pop; 5 to move quickly; 6 to come suddenly into view; 7 to burst open with a pop; 8 to shoot with a gun; 9 pop up baseball to hit a pop fly; 10 pop off slang to express oneself loudly or indiscreetly; 11 pop out baseball to be put out by hitting a pop fly that is caught || vt 12 to thrust suddenly; 13 to cause to burst open with a pop; 14 to fire (a gun); 15 slang to hit; 16 pop the question to propose marriage || adv 17 suddenly; with a pop

pop² [< poppa] n colloq father

pop³ adj colloq popular

pop. 1 popular(ly); 2 population

pop' art' n style of art using commercial art forms, such as posters and comic strips

pop' con'cert n concert of popular and semiclassical music

pop'corn' n 1 any of several varieties of corn the kernels of which pop into a white puffy mass when heated; 2 the popped corn

pope /pōp'/ [OE pāpa < L] n 1 Russian priest; 2 Eastern Orthodox patriarch of Alexandria; 3 usu. Pope bishop of Rome and head of the Roman Catholic Church

Pope, Al·ex·an·der /pōp'/ n (1688–1744) English poet

pop'eyed' adj 1 having protruding eyes; 2 wide-eyed with amazement

pop' fly' n baseball short high fly that can be easily caught

pop'gun' n toy which shoots harmless pellets by air pressure with a loud pop

pop·in·jay /pop'injā'/ [MF papingai parrot] n fop who chatters like a parrot

pop·ish /pōp'ish/ adj disparaging pert. to the Roman Catholic Church

pop·lar /pop'lər/ [MF pouplier] n any of a genus (Populus) of trees with light soft wood and heart-shaped leaves

pop·lin /pop'lin/ [F popeline < It papalina papal, because made in the papal town of Avignon] n finely ribbed fabric made of various materials

pop'o'ver n light muffin with a hollow center

pop·pa /pop'ə/ [< papa] n colloq father

pop'pet (valve') /pop'it/ [< puppet] n lift valve operated by a stem that rises and falls

pop·py /pop'ē/ [OE popæg < L papaver] n (-pies) any of a genus (Papaver) of plants with showy flowers, one species (P. somniferum) yielding opium

pop'py·cock' [D pappekok soft dung] n colloq nonsense

pop'py seed' n seed of the poppy, used in baking

pop·u·lace /pop'yəlis/ [F < It popolaccio] n 1 common people; 2 population of a place || syn rabble, people, multitude (see throng)

pop·u·lar /pop'yələr/ [< L populus people] adj 1 pert. to or consisting of the common people; 2 regarded with approval, as she's very popular; 3 held in favor by large numbers of people; 4 pert. tō, suitable for, or intended for all the people; 5 (prices) within the means of ordinary people; 6 prevailing; common || **pop'u·lar·ly** adv

pop·u·lar·i·ty /-lar'-/ n state or quality of being pleasing to or esteemed by many

pop·u·lar·ize' vt to make popular; make intelligible and interesting to the layman

pop·u·late [ML populare (-atus)] vt 1 to furnish with inhabitants; 2 to inhabit

pop·u·la'tion n 1 act of populating; 2 total number of people in a place; 3 any group of inhabitants separately distinguished; 4 any aggregation of individuals subject to statistical study

pop'u·lous adj heavily populated

pop'-up' n pop fly

por·ce·lain /pōrs'(ə)lin, pōrs'-/ [F porcelaine < It porcellana] n 1 fine, white, translucent glazed earthenware; 2 ware made of porcelain

porch /pôrch', pōrch'/ [OF porche < L porticus] n 1 roofed approach to a doorway, usu. extending from the main wall; 2 veranda; 3 portico

por·cine /pôr'sin, -sín/ [L porcinus] adj of or pert. to swine

por·cu·pine /pôrk'yəpin'/ [MF porc espin spiny pig] n any of several rodents of the families Hystricidae and Erethizontidae, covered with sharp erectile quills

pore¹ /pôr', pōr'/ [Gk poros passage] n minute hole, as in a leaf or the skin, for perspiration, absorption, etc.

pore² [ME poren] vi pore over to ponder, study intently

por·gy /pôrg'ē/ [Sp or Port pargo] n (-gy or -gies) 1 small marine food fish (Pagrus pagrus) of the Mediterranean and N Atlantic; 2 any of several similar fishes

pork /pôrk', pōrk'/ [OF porc < L porcus hog] n flesh of swine used as food

pork' bar'rel n slang government bill or appropriation designed to provide states or localities with improvements, jobs, and patronage with the ulterior purpose of winning favor with constituents

pork′er *n* hog, esp. when fattened for food

pork′pie (**hat′**) *n* snap-brim hat with a round flat crown

por·nog·ra·phy /pôrฺtog′rəfē/ [< Gk *porne* harlot] *n* obscene writings or pictures || **por·nog′ra·pher** *n* || **por′-no·graph′ic** /-əgraf/ *adj*

po·rous /pôr′əs, pōr′əs/ [< *pore*[1]] *adj* having tiny holes through which a fluid may pass || **po·ros′i·ty** /-ros′-/ *n*

por·phy·ry /pôr′fərē/ [< Gk *porphyros* purple] *n* (**-ries**) hard stone having a dark igneous base with feldspar and quartz crystals embedded in it

por·poise /pôrp′əs/ [MF *porpeis* < L *porcus* hog + *piscis* fish] *n* (**-poise** or **-poises**) 1 any of several small gregarious cetaceans (genus *Phocaena*) from five to eight feet long; 2 dolphin

por·ridge /por′ij, pôr′-/ [var of *pottage*] *n* food made of oatmeal or other meal boiled in milk or water

Por′ro prism′ /pôr′ō/ [I. *Porro* (1801–75) It engineer] *n* prism used in reflex cameras and binoculars to erect the final image

port[1] /pôrt′, pōrt′/ [OE < L *portus*] *n* 1 harbor; 2 city with a harbor

port[2] [L *porta* gate] *n* 1 porthole; 2 *mach* small aperture or outlet, as for steam, exhaust gases, etc.; 3 small aperture through which a gun may be fired, as in armor plate; 4 left side of a ship or aircraft || *vt* & *vi* 5 to turn to the left

port[3] [F *porter* to carry] *vt mil* to carry diagonally, as a rifle, in front of the body, holding the upper end to the left

port[4] [< *Oporto* city in Portugal] *n* strong sweet wine, usu. ruby red in color

Port. 1 Portugal; 2 Portuguese

port′a·ble [< *port*[3]] *adj* 1 capable of being easily carried || *n* 2 something portable || **port′a·bil′i·ty** /-bil′-/ *n*

por·tage /-tij/ *n* 1 carrying of goods and boats overland from one waterway to another; 2 place where this is done || *vt* 3 to carry on a portage || *vi* 4 to make a portage

por·tal [ML *portale*] *n* gate, door, or entrance, esp. one that is imposing

Port-au-Prince /pôrt′ō prins′, pōrt′-/ *n* capital of Haiti (250,000)

port·cul·lis /pôrtkul′is, pōrt-/ [MF *porte coleice* sliding door] *n* strong grating hung over the gateway of a fortified place and lowered to prevent passage

por·tend /pôrtend′, pōr-/ [L *portendere*] *vt* to presage; forebode || SYN presage, prophesy, predict, augur (see *foretell*)

por·tent /pôr′tent, pōr′/ [L *portentum*] *n* omen or sign, esp. of something momentous or ominous || **por·ten′tous** *adj*

por·ter[1] /pôrt′ər, pōrt′-/ [AF < LL *portarius*] *n* doorkeeper or gatekeeper

por·ter[2] [MF *porteour* carrier] *n* 1 one who carries baggage, as at stations and hotels; 2 one who waits on passengers in sleeping and parlor cars; 3 one who works at cleaning, as in buildings or offices

por·ter[3] [< *porter's* ale] *n* a heavy dark ale

por′ter·house′ steak′ [*obs porterhouse* ale house] *n* choice cut of steak between the tenderloin and sirloin

port·fo·li·o /pôrtfōl′ē·ō′, pōrt-/ [It *portafoglio*] *n* 1 case for loose papers, drawings, etc., esp. government documents; 2 office of a government minister; 3 list of securities held by an investor

port′hole′ *n* 1 round opening or window on the side of a ship; 2 hole or slit, as in a wall, through which to shoot

por·ti·co /pôrt′ikō′, pōrt′-/ [It < L *porticus*] *n* (**-coes** or **-cos**) porchlike structure consisting of a roof borne by columns

por·tiere or **por·tière** /pôrt′ē·er′, pōrt′-, pōrtyer′, pōr-/ [F = carriage door] *n* curtain hung in a doorway

por·tion /pôr′shən, pōr′-/ [OF *porcion*] *n* 1 piece or part of anything; 2 share given or allotted; 3 part of an estate descending to an heir; 4 dowry; 5 serving (of food); 6 one's lot or fate || *vt* 7 to divide into portions; 8 **portion out** to distribute shares of || **por′tion·less** *adj* || SYN *n* share, allotment, parcel (see *part*)

Port′land /-lənd/ *n* 1 seaport in NW Oregon (382,619); 2 seaport in SW Maine (72,500)

port′ly [< *port*[3]] *adj* (**-li·er; -li·est**) 1 corpulent, stout; 2 stately, dignified || **port′li·ness** *n*

port·man·teau /pôrtman′tō, pôrt′mantō′, pōrt′-/ [F *portemanteau* cloak carrier] *n* (**-teaus** or **-teaux** /-tōz/) suitcase or small trunk that opens into two halves

Port′ Mores′by /môrz′bē, mōrz′-/ *n* capital of Papua (28,000)

port′ of call′ *n* stop on the route of a ship

port′ of en′try *n* seaport, or city or town at a land boundary, containing a customs house and through which people and goods may enter a country

Port′-of-Spain′ *n* city in Trinidad, capital of Trinidad and Tobago (93,954)

Por·to No·vo /pôrt′ō nōv′ō/ *n* capital of Benin (120,000)

Por′to Ri′co /rēk′ō/ *n* former name (before 1932) of Puerto Rico || **Por′to Ri′can** *adj* & *n*

por·trait /pôr′trāt, -trit, pōr′-/ [MF] *n* 1 picture of a person, esp. of the face, as a drawing, painting, or photograph; 2 vivid word picture || **por′trait·ist** *n*

por·trai·ture /-trĭchər/ *n* 1 art of portraying; 2 portrait

por·tray' /-trā'/ [MF *portraire*] *vt* 1 to make a portrait of; 2 to describe in words; 3 to represent by acting

por·tray'al *n* 1 act of portraying; 2 representation, portrait

Por·tu·gal /pôrch'əgəl, pōrch'-/ *n* republic in SW Europe, W of Spain (9,335,000; 35,510 sq.m.; cap. Lisbon) || **Por'tu·guese'** /-gēz', -gēs'/ *adj & n* (-guese)

Por·tu·guese' man'-of-war' *n* any of several large marine coelenterates (genus *Physalia*) having a bladder or float that supports them on the surface and from which numerous poisonous tentacles are suspended for the capture of prey

pose /pōz'/ [MF *poser* to place] *vt* 1 to lay down, as a proposition; put or set forth, as a question; 2 to place in a suitable attitude, as for a picture || *vi* 3 to assume and keep an attitude, as for a picture; 4 to put on a certain manner for effect; make a pretense || *n* 5 bodily attitude or position; 6 mental attitude; 7 affectation

Po·sei·don /pəsīd'ən, pō-/ *n* Gk myth. god of the sea, the Roman Neptune

pos·er [< *obs appose* to put to] *n* puzzling problem or question

po·seur /pōzur'/ /[F] *n* one who affects a pose of superiority or elegance

posh /posh'/ [?] *adj colloq* luxurious, sumptuous

pos·it /poz'ĭt/ [L *ponere* (*positus*) to place] *vt* 1 to place, set; 2 to declare or present as true; affirm

po·si·tion /pəzish'ən/ *n* 1 location, situation; 2 standing or rank; 3 office or employment; 4 posture; 5 proper or usual place or arrangement; 6 mental attitude toward any subject; 7 act of positing; 8 thing posited; 9 place occupied by troops || *vt* 10 to place in a particular or appropriate position || SYN *n* locality, place, rank, status, circumstance, stand

po·si'tion pa'per *n* document setting forth one's position as a basis for discussion or negotiation

pos·i·tive /poz'ĭtiv/ [L *positivus*] *adj* 1 clearly affirmed or expressed; 2 leaving no doubt; 3 having distinct characteristics; marked by the possession of qualities rather than the lack of them; 4 confident; sure; 5 cock-sure, aggressively certain; 6 *math* (number) greater than zero; 7 *chem* (element or radical) that loses electrons; 8 *gram* designating the simple form of an uncompared adjective or adverb; 9 *elec* a having a deficiency of electrons; b (point in a circuit) that has a higher potential; c pert. to the north pole of a magnet; 10 (test or reaction) showing the presence of a suspected condition or organism; 11 *photog* corresponding with the object photographed in respect to light and shadows; 12 *colloq* out-and-out, absolute || *n* 13 something positive; 14 *elec* battery plate that has the higher potential; 15 *math* a quantity more than zero; b number to be added; 16 *photog* positive image; 17 *gram* simple form of adjective or adverb || SYN *adj* sure, absolute, actual, incontestable

pos'i·tive·ly *adv* 1 in a positive way; 2 undoubtedly || /poz'ĭtiv'lē/ *interj* 3 absolutely yes!

pos'i·tiv·ism *n* system of philosophy founded by Auguste Comte (1798–1857), which teaches that scientific fact is the only sure source of truth, dismissing as immaterial the search for ultimate causes || **pos'i·tiv·ist** *n*

pos'i·tron /-tron'/ [*positive* + *electron*] *n* particle produced in atomic disintegration, having the charge and mass of an electron but with the charge positive instead of negative

poss. possessive

pos·se /pos'ē/ [ML = power] *n* body of men given legal authority to assist in carrying out the law, as for the apprehension of criminals

pos·sess /pazes'/ [MF *possessier*] *vt* 1 to be the owner of; own; 2 to have as a quality or faculty; 3 to occupy, seize; 4 to gain control of, said of evil spirits, passions, beliefs, etc. || **pos·ses'sor** *n*

pos·sessed' *adj* 1 frenzied; 2 controlled as by evil spirits; 3 seized, overpowered; 4 calm

pos·ses·sion /pazesh'ən/ *n* 1 act of possessing; 2 state of being possessed; 3 ownership; occupancy; 4 thing owned; 5 self-control; 6 foreign territory under the control of a nation; 7 **possessions** *pl* property, wealth

pos·ses'sive *adj* 1 designating ownership or right; 2 desiring possession excessively; 3 *gram* designating that form of nouns or pronouns showing possession || *n* 4 *gram* a possessive case; b form in the possessive

pos·si·ble /pos'ĭbəl/ [L *possibilis*] *adj* 1 capable of existing, being, happening, being done; etc.; 2 conceivable, not known to be untrue; 3 optional || **pos'si·bly** *adv* || **pos'si·bil'i·ty** /-bil'-/ *n* (-ties) || SYN practicable, feasible, potential, latent

pos·sum /pos'əm/ *n* 1 opossum; 2 **play possum** *colloq* a to play dead; b to pretend to be asleep; c to pretend ignorance

post[2] /pōst'/ [OE < L *postis*] *n* 1 upright piece of timber, metal, or the like, used to support, as a street lamp, display posters, etc.; 2 pole at a race track indicating the starting and finishing point of a race || *vt* 3 to fasten, as a placard, to a wall or the like; 4 to make known by means of placards; 5 to place (a person's name) on a notice; 6 to fasten notices on

post² [F *poste* < It *posta*] *n* **1** the mail; **2** *Brit* any of the appurtenances of the postal system, as a post office, mail carrier, or letter box ‖ *vi* **3** to rise and fall in the saddle when riding, esp. when trotting ‖ *vt* **4** a to send by mail; **b** to drop into a letter box; **5** *bookkeeping* **a** to transfer (an entry or item) from journal to ledger; **b** to enter (an item) in the proper place; **6** to inform fully ‖ *adv* **7** speedily

post³ [F *poste* < It *posto*] *n* **1** place where a person or thing is stationed; **2** position of trust, employment, or duty; **3** trading settlement; **4** branch of a veterans' organization; **5** military station ‖ *vt* **6** to station or place; **7** *mil* to appoint to a station, command, or office

post- /pōst-/ [L] *pref* behind; after

post′age /-ĳ/ *n* amount charged for sending letters, etc. by mail

post′age me′ter *n* machine that prints the postmark on mail, records the amount, and keeps a record until the total prepaid postage has been used up

post′age stamp′ *n* official stamp affixed to mail matter as a sign that the postage has been paid

post′al *adj* pert. to the post office or mail service

post′al card′ or **post′ card′** *n* **1** card for mailing with a stamp printed on it, sold at post offices; **2** commercially printed card to which a stamp must be affixed, usu. with a picture on one side

post′al per′mit *n* postal marking on mail that indicates instead of stamps that postage has been paid

post′al sav′ings bank′ *n* savings bank run by a government through local post offices

post′date′ *vt* **1** to mark (a document or check) with a date later than the time of writing, rendering it inoperative or uncashable until the marked date; **2** to assign to a later date; **3** to follow in time

post′ed *adj* informed

post′er *n* [< *post*¹] *n* **1** advertising placard or bill; **2** one who posts such bills

pos·te·ri·or /postir′ē·ər/ [L, *comp* of *posterus* following] *adj* **1** later; **2** hinder; rear ‖ *n* **3** buttocks

pos·ter·i·ty /poster′itē/ [L *posteritas*] *n* **1** future generations collectively; **2** one's descendants collectively

pos·tern /pōst′ərn/ [OF *posterne*] *n* **1** back door or gate; **2** private entrance

post′ ex·change′ *n* store on an army post selling goods at cost to army personnel

post′grad′u·ate *adj* **1** pert. to or engaged in studies after graduation from school or college ‖ *n* **2** one pursuing studies after graduation

post′haste′ *adv* quickly; with speed

post·hu·mous /pos′chəməs, -chŏŏm-/ [L *postumus* latest born] *adj* **1** born after the death of the father; **2** published after the death of the author; **3** happening or continuing after one's death

post′im·pres′sion·ism *n* theory and practice of various painters who, since the late 19th century, in revolt against the scientific aspects of impressionism and the formalism of academic painting, have striven for self-expression through mass and form ‖ **post′im·pres′sion·ist** *n* ‖ **post′im·pres′sion·is′tic** *adj*

post′lude′ /-lōōd/ [*post-* + *prelude*] *n mus* concluding phrase or movement

post′man /-mən/ *n* (-**men** /-mən/) letter carrier

post′mark′ *n* **1** official mark stamped on mail canceling the stamp and showing the date and place of sending or receiving ‖ *vt* **2** to place a postmark on

post′mas′ter *n* person in charge of a post office ‖ **post′mis′tress** *nfem*

post′mas′ter gen′er·al *n* (**postmasters general** or **postmaster generals**) national head of the postal system

post′me·rid′i·an /-mərid′ē·ən/ [L] *adj* **1** of or pert. to the afternoon; **2** occurring after noon

post′ me·rid′i·em /-ē·əm/ [L] *adj* P.M., in the period between noon and 12 midnight

post-mor′tem /-môrt′əm/ [L = after death] *adj* **1** occurring or done after death, or after an event ‖ *n* **2** postmortem examination

post′na·sal drip′ *n* trickling of mucus from behind the nose onto the pharynx, caused by a cold, allergy, etc.

post·na′tal *adj* happening after birth

post′ of′fice *n* **1** government department which handles the mails; **2** station of the postal system where mail is sorted for transmission or distribution, stamps are sold, and other postal services are rendered

post′-of′fice box′ *n* numbered compartment at a post office where mail is kept until called for by the renter, who holds the key

post′paid′ *adj* having the postage paid in advance

post·pone′ /-pōn′/ [L *postponere*] *vt* to put off till later ‖ **post·pone′ment** *n* ‖ SYN delay, put off, procrastinate (see *defer*)

post·pran·di·al /-pran′dē·əl/ [*post-* + L *prandium* lunch] *adj* following a meal, esp. dinner

post′script′ [L *postscriptum*] *n* **1** something added to a letter after it has been finished and signed; **2** anything added to a writing or speech

post′ time′ *n* time at which all the horses in a race must be at the starting post

pos·tu·lant /pos'chələnt/ [< L *postulare* (-*atus*) to demand] *n* 1 one who makes a request or petition; 2 candidate for admission into a religious order

pos'tu·late' *vt* 1 to assume without proof, as a basis for argument; 2 to take for granted; 3 to claim as one's right ‖ /-lĭt, -lāt'/ *n* 4 self-evident statement; 5 proposition accepted without proof; 6 prerequisite; 7 fundamental principle

pos·ture /pos'chər/ [F] *n* 1 carriage of the body; bearing; 2 pose; 3 mental attitude ‖ *vi* 4 to take a certain position; pose ‖ **pos'tur·er** *n*

post'war' *adj* pert. to a period after a war

po·sy /pōz'ē/ [< *poesy*] *n* (-**sies**) flower or bunch of flowers

pot /pot'/ [OE *pott*] *n* 1 metal or earthenware vessel for holding or cooking liquids or other substances; 2 vessel, usu. of earthenware, for holding growing plants; 3 chamber pot; 4 total money bet in a gambling game; 5 *slang* large sum of money; 6 *slang* marijuana; 7 *slang* potbelly; 8 go to pot to deteriorate ‖ *v* (**pot·ted**; **pot'ting**) *vt* 9 to preserve, plant, or place in a pot; 10 to shoot, as game

po·ta·ble /pōt'əbəl/ [L *potabilis*] *adj* drinkable

pot'ash' *n* 1 any of various potassium salts, esp. impure potassium carbonate, obtained from wood ashes; 2 potassium hydroxide

po·tas·si·um /pətas'ē·əm/ [< F *potasse* potash < D *potasch*] *n* silvery white, soft metallic element (**K**; at.no. 19; at.wt. 39.102) found widely diffused in soils and mineral deposits

po·tas'si·um car'bon·ate' *n* white granular powder —K_2CO_3— used chiefly in making soap, glass, etc.

po·tas'si·um cy'a·nide *n* white poisonous compound —KCN— used in electroplating and photography

po·tas'si·um hy·drox'ide *n* white, deliquescent solid —KOH— which generates heat when dissolved in water, used as a bleach and as a caustic

po·tas'si·um ni'trate *n* crystalline substance —KNO_3— produced by nitrification of the soil, used to make gunpowder, fertilizer, etc.

po·tas'si·um per·man'ga·nate' /pər·man'gənāt'/ *n* dark purple crystalline salt —$KMnO_4$— used as an oxidizer, disinfectant, and antiseptic

po·ta·to /pətāt'ō, -tāt'ə/ [Sp *patata*] *n* (-**toes**) edible tuber of a common plant, *Solanum tuberosum*

po·ta'to chip' *n* thin crisp slice of fried potato, salted and eaten cold

pot'bel'ly *n* (-**lies**) protuberant belly ‖ **pot'bel'lied** *adj*

pot'boil'er *n* *colloq* mediocre literary or artistic work turned out for money

pot' cheese' *n* cottage cheese

Po·tem'kin vil'lage /pō·tem'kin/ [< fake villages built along a road to deceive and impress Catherine II by Grigori A. *Potemkin* (1739–91) Russ statesman] *n* elaborate display that conceals something shabby or unpleasant; false front

po·tent /pōt'ənt/ [L *potens* (-*entis*) *adj* 1 powerful; mighty; 2 (man) capable of sexual intercourse ‖ **po'ten·cy** *n* (-**cies**)

po'ten·tate' *n* one who has great power; monarch

po·ten·tial /pətensh'əl/ *adj* 1 capable of being or becoming; 2 possible ‖ *n* 3 possibility; 4 latent ability or excellence; 5 *elec* degree of electrification of a point with respect to some other point in the same system ‖ **po·ten'ti·al'i·ty** /-shē·al'-/ *n* (-**ties**)

po·ten'tial en'er·gy *n* energy possessed by a body because of its position or configuration, as in a coiled spring

po·ten'ti·om'e·ter /-om'itər/ *n* 1 instrument for measuring voltage; 2 variable or adjustable resistor; 3 voltage divider

poth·er /poth'ər/ [?] *n* 1 confusion; turmoil ‖ *vt & vi* 2 to bother

pot'hold'er *n* small thick pad, as of woven cloth, for handling hot pots and pans

pot'hole' *n* 1 hole in a road or street, formed by cold weather or excessive use; 2 any cylindrical hole in the ground or in rock

pot'hook' *n* 1 hook for hanging a pot over an open fire; 2 hooked rod for lifting hot pots and stove lids; 3 S-shaped stroke in writing, as by one learning to write

po·tion /pōsh'ən/ [L *potio* (-*onis*)] *n* drink, esp. one that is medicinal, magical, or poisonous

pot' liq'uor *n* broth left in a pot after cooking meat and/or vegetables

pot'luck' *n* take potluck to eat whatever may chance to be on hand

Po·to·mac /pətōm'ək/ *n* river rising in West Virginia and flowing SE to the Chesapeake Bay between Maryland and Virginia, and on which the District of Columbia is situated

pot'pie' *n* 1 meat pie made in a deep dish; 2 meat stew with dumplings

pot·pour·ri /pō'poŏrē', pō'poŏrē'/ [F = rotten pot] *n* medley or mixture; miscellany

pot' roast' *n* meat, usu. beef, browned in a pot and boiled slowly in very little water

pot'sherd' /-shurd'/ [*pot* + *sherd*, var of *shard*] *n* piece of broken earthenware esp. one found at an archaeological excavation

pot'shot' *n* 1 casual, random, or aimless shot; 2 easy shot at close range

pot'tage /-ij/ [OF *potage* soup] *n* stew

or thick soup of meat and/or vegetables

pot′ted *adj* 1 placed in a pot; 2 planted in a pot; 3 *slang* drunk

pot′ter *n* maker of pottery

pot′ter's field′ [allusion to Matt. 27:7] *n* cemetery for unknown persons and paupers

pot′ter's wheel′ *n* rotating horizontal disk on which clay is shaped by a potter

pot′ter·y *n* (-ies) 1 ceramic ware; 2 place where such ware is made; 3 art or business of making pottery

pouch /pouch′/ [ONF *pouche*] *n* 1 small bag or sack, usu. of leather, for carrying change, tobacco, ammunition, etc.; 2 mailbag; 3 *anat & bot* baglike receptacle or cavity; 4 *zool* bag or sac of an animal, usually for carrying its young, as in the kangaroo

poul·tice /pōlt′is/ [L *pultes* thick pap] *n* soft moist mass, as of cloth, flaxseed, or the like, applied like a plaster to a sore or inflamed part of the body

poul·try /pōl′trē/ [MF *pouleterie* < *poule* fowl] *n* domestic fowls collectively, as chickens, turkeys, ducks, etc.

pounce /pouns/ [ME = talon] *vi* 1 to swoop down suddenly; 2 **pounce on** or **upon** to swoop down on and seize || *n* 3 sudden swoop and seizure

pound¹ /pound′/ [OE *pund* < L *pondus* weight] *n* 1 unit of weight equal to 16 ounces avoirdupois, used in everyday commerce; 2 unit of weight equal to 12 ounces troy, formerly used for weighing gold and silver, which are now weighed in troy ounces; 3 monetary unit of the United Kingdom; 4 monetary unit of various other countries, some former dominions or possessions of Great Britain, others in Africa and the Near East

pound² [ME] *n* place for confining and keeping stray animals, as *a dog pound*

pound³ [OE *pūnian*] *vt* 1 to strike forcibly and repeatedly; 2 to pulverize or crush by pounding; 3 to produce by pounding, as a tune on the piano || *vi* 4 to deal repeated blows; 5 to throb violently, as the heart; 6 to make the sound of heavy blows; 7 to go or move with heavy steps or with great force

pound·al /pound′əl/ *n phys* the footpound-second unit of force which, if applied for one second to a mass of one pound, will change its velocity by one foot per second

pound′ cake′ *n* rich cake made with large proportions of butter, flour, and sugar (originally one pound of each)

-pound′er *comb form* weighing (so many) pounds, as *the fish was a six-pounder*

pound′ ster′ling *n* pound¹ 3

pour /pôr′, pōr′/ [ME *pouren*] *vt* 1 to cause to flow in a stream; 2 to send forth freely; 3 **pour out** to utter in a steady stream || *vi* 4 to come or flow forth in a great stream, as *the people poured out of the building;* 5 to rain heavily

pousse-ca·fé /pōōs′kəfā′/ [F = coffee pusher] *n* 1 liqueur served after coffee; 2 small glass of liqueurs of different colors arranged in layers by means of their several specific gravities

pout /pout′/ [ME *pouten* to swell out] *vi* 1 to push out the lips in sullenness or displeasure; 2 to look sulky || *vt* 3 to push out (the lips) || *n* 4 fit of sullenness; 5 act of pouting || **pout′er** *n*

pout′er pi′geon *n* one of a breed of pigeons that puff out the crop

pov·er·ty /pov′ərtē/ [OF *poverte*] *n* 1 state of being poor; want, necessity; 2 any lack of richness in quality; need; scarcity || SYN destitution, need, penury, privation, mendicancy, indigence, pauperism, beggary, want || DISCR *Poverty*, a state the opposite of riches, is hence somewhat relative in the stringency it connotes; it can name the condition of being really poor, wanting the means to procure the necessaries of life—a bare, unlovely condition; or it can name an uncomfortable, but not a crying, lack. One whose income has been suddenly cut in two is plunged into comparative *poverty*, but he may have to go without cars and golf rather than food or clothing. *Destitution* is a want of the necessaries of life and a lack of the resources with which to buy them; it often connotes a sudden deprivation, as by fire, flood, or famine. *Destitution* may, therefore, be temporary, though extreme, *poverty*. *Penury* is abject *poverty*, and connotes a permanent state of utter want and wretchedness. *Need* may be a condition of continued *poverty*, though there is always a suggestion of urgency about *need;* or it may be the requirement of an occasion, easily satisfied, as batteries in *need* of recharging; a child in *need* of correction. *Indigence* is politely applied to the *poverty* of those fallen in station; but it can mean a lack of necessities as well as of luxuries. *Privation* is the state of needing badly that which is not procurable and is much to be desired; castaways after a shipwreck may suffer *privations*. *Mendicancy* is such *poverty* that those suffering from it habitually beg for relief || ANT wealth, abundance, riches, affluence, opulence, substance, property, treasure

pov′er·ty-strick′en *adj* very poor; destitute

POW, P.O.W. prisoner of war

pow·der /poud′ər/ [OF *poudre*] *n* **1** any dry substance in fine particles; dust; **2** specific preparation in powder form, as gunpowder or face powder; **3 take a powder** *slang* to leave precipitously || *vt* **4** to reduce to a powder; **5** to sprinkle with powder; **6** to apply powder to || *vi* **7** to be reduced to a powder; **8** to apply powder to the face or body || **pow′der·y** *adj*

pow′der blue′ *n* pale, grayish blue

pow′der·horn′ *n* container for gunpowder used for muzzle-loaders

pow′der puff′ *n* soft fluffy pad for applying powder to the face or body

pow′der room′ *n* **1** ladies′ room; **2** second washroom in a house, generally without a bathtub

pow·er /pou′ər/ [AF *poeir* < LL *potere* to be able] *n* **1** ability to do or act; **2** strength, vigor; **3** rule or authority; **4** ability to command or control; **5** nation having international influence because of military strength; **6** source of energy which imparts motion to machinery; **7** *math* a number of times a quantity is to be multiplied by itself as indicated by an exponent; **b** product thus obtained; **8** *phys* product of work and a unit of time, measured in watts, horsepower, etc.; **9** magnifying capacity of a lens, expressed as the number of times it multiplies the diameter of an object; **10** legal authority || *vt* **11** to supply with power; **12** to supply power to (a machine) || SYN strength, vigor, force, puissance, potency, might, efficiency, ability, capacity, efficacy, authority, competency, ascendancy (see *energy*) || ANT weakness, feebleness, helplessness, impotence, inability

pow′er am′pli·fi′er *n* amplifier that increases the power output of a circuit

pow′er brake′ *n* brake applied by compressed air or some other power source with little pressure on the pedal

pow′er dive′ *n* *aeron* steep dive with the engines delivering full or nearly full power || **pow′er-dive′** *vt* & *vi*

-pow′ered *adj* *comb form* having a specified source of power or fuel, as *gasoline-powered*

pow′er·ful *adj* having great power, strength, or influence || SYN effectual, influential, commanding, efficient, efficacious, potent, puissant, vigorous, sturdy, strong

pow′er·house′ *n* (**-hous·es** /-ziz/) **1** building where electric power is generated; **2** *sports* team noted for its aggressiveness; **3** *colloq* **a** person full of energy; **b** person or group wielding great influence

pow′er·less *adj* **1** weak; helpless; **2** ineffectual; unable || SYN ineffectual, impotent, feeble, weak, unable

pow′er of at·tor′ney *law* authority to act for another person

pow′er pack′ *n* unit consisting of transformer, rectifier, and filter for converting alternating current into direct current at the several high and low voltages needed by an electronic circuit

pow′er plant′ *n* **1** powerhouse *1*; **2** motor, machine, or machinery supplying the power for a particular operation or vehicle

pow′er pol′i·tics *nsg* or *npl* international diplomacy that depends on military strength for the realization of national aims

pow′er shov′el *n* machine for excavating and removing debris, operated by a source of power

pow′er struc′ture *n* the influential people of a community, state, or nation who, because of their great wealth and/or positions of authority, effectively control all political, economic, and social life

pow·wow /pou′wou′/ [< Algonquian] *n* **1** formerly, council or conference of or with Indians; **2** *colloq* any conference || *vi* **3** to hold a powwow

pox /poks/ [*pocks* pl of *pock*] *n* any of various diseases marked by skin eruptions

pp. 1 pages; **2** past participle; **3** pianissimo

p.p., P.P. 1 parcel post; **2** postpaid

P.P.S. [L *post postcriptum*] additional postscript

P.Q. Province of Quebec

PR public relations

Pr 1 *chem* praseodymium; **2** Provençal

pr. 1 pair; **2** present; **3** price; **4** pronoun

P.R. Puerto Rico

prac·ti·ca·ble /prak′tikəbəl/ [< ML *practicare* to practice] *adj* capable of being done or used; feasible || **prac′ti·ca·bil′i·ty** /-bil′-/ *n* || SYN feasible, usable, possible

prac·ti·cal /prak′tikəl/ [< Gk *praktikos* active] *adj* **1** pert. to or resulting from practice or use; **2** having useful ends in view; capable of useful action; **3** keeping possible results in mind, as *let's be practical*; **4** matter-of-fact; **5** in essence or effect, virtual || **prac′ti·cal′i·ty** /-kal′-/ *n*

prac′ti·cal joke′ *n* trick played on a person usu. to his disadvantage or embarrassment

prac′ti·cal·ly *adv* **1** in a practical manner; **2** from a practical viewpoint; **3** virtually; **4** almost; **5** more or less

prac′ti·cal nurse′ *n* nurse experienced in caring for the sick but who has not graduated from an accredited school of nursing

prac·tice /prak'tis/ [ML *practicare*] *vt* 1 to do frequently or as a rule; 2 to work at or pursue as a profession; 3 to perform often in order to learn; 4 to teach by frequent repetition; drill; 5 to observe the tenets of (a religion) ‖ *vi* 6 to do something habitually; 7 to follow a profession; 8 to do something often in order to learn ‖ *n* 9 custom; habit; 10 customary performance; 11 action or process of doing something; 12 exercise of any profession; 13 business or clientele of a professional man; 14 regular exercise as a means to learning; 15 skill gained by such exercise ‖ SYN custom, usage, manner, exercise (see *habit*)

prac'ticed *adj* skilled through much practice; experienced

prac·ti'tion·er *n* 1 one who practices something specific, esp. a profession; 2 Christian Scientist who practices healing

Prae·to'ri·an Guard' /prētôr'ē·ən/ [< L *praetor* magistrate] *n* bodyguard of the emperors of ancient Rome

prag·mat·ic /pragmat'ik/ [Gk *pragmatikos*] *adj* 1 practical; 2 active; busy; 3 meddlesome, officious; 4 *philos* dealing with, based on, or judging from the actual working of an idea in experience rather than theory ‖ **prag'ma·tism** /-mə-/ *n* ‖ **prag'ma·tist** *n*

Prague /präg/ *n* capital of Czechoslovakia (1,020,000)

prai·rie /prer'ē/ [F = meadow] *n* large treeless tract of level or slightly undulating grassland, esp. in the central U.S.

prai'rie dog' *n* small burrowing rodent (genus *Cynomys*) with a doglike bark, living in colonies on the prairies

prai'rie schoon'er *n* large covered wagon used by the pioneers who settled the West

praise /prāz/ [OF *preisier* to prize] *vt* 1 to bestow approval upon, extol; 2 to worship; glorify ‖ *n* 3 expression of approval; commendation; 4 glorification of God ‖ SYN *v* commend, applaud, eulogize, extol, flatter, laud; *n* commendation, approval, encouragement, worship, eulogy, panegyric, encomium ‖ ANT *v* blame, abuse, defame, upbraid, asperse, vilify, malign; *n* disapproval, reproach, censure, defamation, blame

praise'wor'thy *adj* deserving praise

pra·line /prä'lēn, prā'-, prälēn'/ [F < Field Marshal du Plessis-*Praslin* (1598–1675), whose cook invented the confection] *n* confection made of nuts cooked in syrup

pram /pram/ *n* Brit *colloq* perambulator

prance /prans', präns'/ [ME] *vi* 1 to rear and caper, as a horse; 2 to ride on a prancing horse; 3 to strut, caper ‖ *n* 4 prancing movement

prank /praŋk/ [?] *n* mischievous or playful trick ‖ **prank'ish** *adj* ‖ **prank'ster** *n*

pra·se·o·dym·i·um /prās'ē·ōdim'ē·əm, präz'-/ [< Gk *prasios* green + *didymos* twin] *n* rare-earth metallic element (Pr; at.no. 59; at.wt. 140.91)

prat /prat/ [?] *n slang* buttocks

prate /prāt/ [ME < MD *praeten*] *vt* to prattle, babble; talk idly and foolishly ‖ **prat'er** *n*

prat'fall' *n slang* fall on the buttocks

prat·tle /prat'əl/ [MLG *pratelen*] *vi* 1 to chatter, babble, talk foolishly ‖ *vt* 2 to utter by prattling ‖ *n* 3 act of prattling; 4 chatter, babble ‖ **prat'tler** *n*

prawn /prôn'/ [ME *prane*] *n* any of several shrimplike crustaceans extensively used for food (genera *Peneus, Palaemon, Pandalus*, etc.)

pray /prā'/ [OF *preier*] *vi* 1 to ask earnestly or with reverence; 2 to speak to God, in request, confession, or praise ‖ *vt* 3 to request; 4 to ask earnestly for; 5 to beseech, implore ‖ SYN entreat, implore, beg, beseech, plead ‖ DISCR These words agree in being different modes of asking. To *beg* is to ask earnestly or humbly, or out of such need as compassion must heed, as he *begged* for work; he *begged* for food. One who habitually asks for, and lives by, alms *begs* in a special sense. To *entreat* is to ask urgently, frequently by using what personal influence or other persuasive power one has, as he *entreated* me, in the name of our friendship, to spare him. To *beseech* is even more urgent than *entreat*; it is earnest, fervent, passionate entreaty. To *implore* is to ask supplicatingly, desperately, often in humiliation; distracted mothers *implore* pardons at the last moment for sons convicted of murder. To *plead*, as here compared, is to make an earnest appeal to a person for another, or for something much desired. Except in the conventional *"pray excuse me,"* a way in which *beg*, also, is used, *pray* is not often employed in modern usage, save in reference to communing with God. We may *pray* God to forgive us, *beg* him for mercy, *implore* his help

prayer /prer'/ [OF *preiere*] *n* 1 act of praying; 2 thanks and praise given to God and requests made of him; 3 formula or words used in praying; 4 that which is prayed for; 5 form of religious service for public worship ‖ **prayer'ful** *adj* ‖ SYN supplication, invocation, entreaty, importunity

pray'ing man'tis *n* mantis

pre- /L *prae-*/ *pref* before in place, time, or standing

preach /prēch/ [OF *prechier*] *vi* 1 to deliver a sermon; 2 to give advice, as on religious or moral subjects, esp. in a sanctimonious manner ‖ *vt* 3 to declare or teach by public discourse; 4 to advocate urgently; 5 to deliver (a sermon) ‖ **preach′ing** *n* ‖ **preach′ment** *n*

preach′er *n* 1 one who preaches; 2 clergyman

preach′y *adj* (-i-er; -i-est) *colloq* inclined to long tiresome discourses

pre-am-ble /prē′am′bəl/ [ML *praeambulum* that which goes before] *n* introduction or preface, esp. one to a law or constitution stating its intent or the reasons for it

pre-amp also **pre-amp** /prē′amp′/ *n colloq* preamplifier

pre-am′pli-fi′er /prē-/ *n* auxiliary device in the amplifier circuit of a radio or phonograph that increases the strength of a weak audiofrequency signal

pre′ar-range′ *vt* to arrange beforehand ‖ **pre′ar-range′ment** *n*

pre-car-i-ous /priker′ē-əs/ [< L *precarius* obtained through care] *adj* 1 depending upon circumstances; uncertain; 2 risky, dangerous ‖ SYN uncertain, risky, perilous, doubtful, dubious, insecure, hazardous, unsettled, unstable, unsteady ‖ DISCR *Uncertain* is opposed to the fixed, the determined, the definite, the assured, the sure-to-happen, as *uncertain* weather, fate, meaning; her coming is *uncertain*; they trusted to an *uncertain* wind; *uncertain* profits. *Precarious* describes that sort of uncertainty that depends on the will of others, or on events still hidden in the future, or on the hazards of the perilous. He who holds a position only while his political party is in power holds a *precarious* position ‖ ANT assured, certain

pre-cau′tion /pri-/ *n* 1 caution taken beforehand; 2 measures taken in advance to secure good results or to prevent danger or failure ‖ **pre-cau′tion-ar′y** /-ner′-/ *adj*

pre-cede /prisēd′/ [L *praecedere*] *vt* 1 to go before in time, place, rank, or importance ‖ *vi* 2 to have precedence

pre-ced′ence /prisēd′əns/ also **pre-ce-dence** /pres′idəns/ *n* act or right of preceding

prec-e-dent /pres′idənt/ *n* 1 something said or done that provides a pattern for similar cases; 2 rule for action established by previous action ‖ also **pre-ced-ent** /prisēd′ənt/ *adj* 3 preceding ‖ SYN *n* antecedent, case, instance, example, pattern

pre-ced′ing *adj* that precedes ‖ SYN previous, foregoing, prior, antecedent

pre-cept /prē′sept/ [L *paeceptum*] *n* 1 rule of action or moral conduct; maxim; 2 *law* writ, warrant ‖ SYN (see *truism*)

pre-cep-tor /prisep′tər/ *n* instructor or teacher

pre-ces-sion /prisesh′ən/ [< L *praecessus* preceded] *n* 1 act of preceding; 2 *mech* regular change in direction of the axis of a rotating body

pre-ces′sion of the e′qui-nox-es *n astron* slow retrograde or westward motion of the equinoctial points on the ecliptic, due to the slow and regular shifting of the direction of the earth's axis in space

pre-cinct /prē′sinkt/ [L *praecinctus* surrounded] *n* 1 place with fixed boundaries; 2 outward limit or boundary; 3 police district; 4 election district; 5 **precincts** *pl* surrounding regions

pre-ci-os-i-ty /presh′ē-os′itē/ *n* (-ties) fastidiousness or affectation, as in language or style

pre-cious /presh′əs/ [L *pretiosus* valuable] *adj* 1 of great price or value; costly; 2 dear; esteemed; 3 overnice; 4 thorough, extreme, as *a precious nuisance* ‖ *adv* 5 *colloq* very ‖ **pre′cious-ly** *adv* ‖ **pre′cious-ness** *n* ‖ SYN *adj* valuable, rare, expensive, costly, dear

pre′cious stone′ *n* mineral that, because of its rarity, beauty, luster, iridescence, etc., is used for jewelry

prec-i-pice /pres′ipis/ [MF < L *praecipitium*] *n* almost vertical cliff or its edge

pre-cip-i-tant /prisip′itənt/ *adj* 1 falling headlong; 2 moving with rash haste ‖ *n* 3 *chem* anything that causes precipitation

pre-cip′i-tate′ [L *praecipitare* (-atus) to throw down headfirst] *vt* 1 to hurl headlong; 2 to send with force; 3 to bring on hastily or prematurely; 4 to cause to condense from vapor and fall as rain or snow; 5 *chem* to cause to separate out, as a solid from a solution ‖ *vi* 6 *chem* to be precipitated; 7 to fall to the earth as precipitation ‖ /also -tit/ *n* 8 *chem* substance precipitated from a solution; 9 condensed moisture in the form of rain, snow, or hail ‖ *adj* 10 overhasty, rash; 11 hurried, sudden; 12 descending steeply

pre-cip′i-ta′tion *n* 1 act of precipitating or state of being precipitated; 2 rashness; rash haste; 3 **a** moisture precipitated from the atmosphere, as rain, snow, or hail; **b** amount precipitated

pre-cip′i-ta′tor *n* 1 person who precipitates or hastens; 2 electrostatic device for removing dust, smoke, pollen, etc. from the air of an interior by ionizing the particles and precipitating them on charged plates

pre·cip'i·tous *adj* 1 very steep; 2 precipitate; hasty; rash

pré·cis /prāsē', prā'sē/ [F] *n* (**-cis** /-sēz', -sēz/) summary, abstract

pre·cise /prisīs'/ [L *praecisus* cut off] *adj* 1 accurate; definite; 2 exact; no more, no less; 3 being that and no more; 4 keeping closely to rule; exact to excess ‖ **pre·cise'ly** *adv* ‖ **pre·ci'sion** /-sizh'ən/ *n* ‖ SYN explicit, definite, exact, particular (see *correct*)

pre·clude /priklōōd'/ [L *praecludere* to shut off] *vt* 1 to shut out, exclude; 2 to prevent; render ineffectual ‖ **pre·clu'sion** /-klōōzh'ən/ *n*

pre·co·cious /prikōsh'əs/ [< L *praecox* prematurely ripe] *adj* developed earlier than usual or prematurely, as a child or the mind of a child ‖ **pre·coc'i·ty** /-kos'-/ *n*

pre·con·ceive /prē'-/ *vt* to form an idea of beforehand ‖ **pre'con·cep'-tion** *n*

pre·cur·sor /prikurs'ər/ [L *praecursor* forerunner] *n* 1 predecessor; 2 harbinger ‖ **pre·cur'so·ry** *adj*

pre·date' /prē'-/ *vt* 1 to date ahead; 2 to precede in date

pred·a·tor /pred'ətər/ [L = plunderer] *n* 1 one who preys on others; 2 animal that lives by preying on other animals ‖ **pred'a·to'ry** /-tōr'-, -tôr'-/ *adj*

pred·e·ces·sor /pred'isesˌər, pred'-isesˌər/ [AF *predecessour* < LL *praedecessor*] *n* 1 one who precedes another in an office or position; 2 that which precedes another, as in a position or location; 3 ancestor, forefather

pre·des·ti·na·tion /pri-/ *n* 1 act of predestining or state of being predestined; 2 fate, destiny; 3 *theol* doctrine that from all eternity God has ordered whatever comes to pass, esp. with reference to the salvation or damnation of souls

pre·des·tine /-tin/ *vt* to decree or determine beforehand; foreordain

pre'de·ter'mine /prē'-/ *vt* 1 to determine or decide beforehand; 2 to predestine ‖ **pre'de·ter'mi·na'tion** *n*

pre·dic·a·ment /pridik'əmənt/ [L *praedicamentum* that which is proclaimed] *n* difficult or unfortunate plight ‖ SYN quandary, plight, dilemma

pred·i·cate /pred'ikāt'/ [L *praedicare* (-*atus*) to proclaim] *vt* 1 to affirm as belonging to, or characteristic of, something; 2 to assert, declare; 3 to signify, connote; 4 **predicate on** or **upon** to base on ‖ /-kit/ *n* 5 *gram* the part of the sentence which makes a statement about the subject, as the verb, including its modifiers and object; 6 *logic* that which is asserted or denied

pre·dict /pridikt'/ [L *praedicere* (-*dictus*)] *vt* to foretell, prophesy ‖ **pre·dic'tor** *n* ‖ SYN forecast, foreshow, presage, augur (see *foretell*)

pre·dic'tion *n* 1 the foretelling of a future event; 2 prophecy

pre·di·lec·tion /prē'dilek'shən, pred'-/ [< L *praedilectus* preferred] *n* preference; partiality ‖ SYN prepossession, partiality (see *prejudice*)

pre'dis·pose' /prē'-/ *vt* 1 to incline beforehand; 2 to make liable or susceptible ‖ **pre·dis'po·si'tion** *n*

pre·dom·i·nate' /pri-/ *vi* 1 to be superior in strength, power, or influence; 2 to prevail; preponderate ‖ **pre·dom'i·nant** *adj* ‖ **pre·dom'i·nance** *n*

pre·em'i·nent also **pre-em'i·nent** /prē-/ *adj* superior to all others; surpassing ‖ **pre·em'i·nence** also **pre-em'i·nence** *n*

pre·empt also **pre-empt** /prē-empt'/ [L *praeemere* (-*emptus*) to bring beforehand] *vt* 1 to seize or appropriate in advance of others; 2 to establish a right or claim to, as by occupying public land ‖ **pre·emp'tive** also **pre-emp'tive** *adj* ‖ **pre·emp'tion** also **pre-emp'tion** *n*

preen /prēn/ [ME *prenen*] *vt* 1 to clean and smooth (the feathers) with the beak; 2 to dress (oneself) up; adorn (oneself); 3 to pride (oneself) on something

pre'ex·ist' also **pre'-ex·ist'** *vi* 1 to exist beforehand; 2 to have a prior existence ‖ *vt* 3 to precede in existence ‖ **pre'ex·ist'ence** also **pre'-ex·ist'ence** *n* ‖ **pre'ex·ist'ent** also **pre'-ex·ist'ent** *adj*

pre·fab /prē'fab'/ *adj* 1 prefabricated ‖ *n* 2 something prefabricated

pre·fab'ri·cate' /prē'-/ *vt* to manufacture standardized parts of (a house or other bulky object) so that they may be shipped to the place of assembly and easily assembled

pref·ace /pref'is/ [MF < L *praefatio*] *n* 1 introduction to a book, speech, etc., preceding the body of the work; 2 anything introductory ‖ *vt* 3 to provide with a preface; 4 to be a preface to ‖ **pref'a·to'ry** /-tôr'-, -tōr'-/ *adj*

pre·fect /prē'fekt/ [L *praefectus*] *n* 1 in ancient Rome, any of various civil or military officials; 2 civil governor of a French department

pre'fec·ture /-chər/ *n* office, jurisdiction, or residence of a prefect

pre·fer /prifur'/ [L *praeferre*] *v* (**-ferred; -fer·ring**) *vt* 1 to regard or esteem more than other persons or things; 2 to choose instead of someone or something else; 3 to offer for consideration, as a charge in court ‖ SYN choose, elect, favor, select, promote, submit

pref·er·a·ble /pref'ərəbəl/ *adj* 1 more desirable; 2 worthy to be preferred ‖ **pref'er·a·bly** *adv*

pref·er·ence /pref'ərəns/ *n* 1 act of

preferring or state of being preferred; **2** that which is preferred ‖ **pref'er·en'tial** /-ensh'əl/ *adj* ‖ SYN alternative, election, pick (see *choice*)

pref'er·en'tial bal'lot *n* ballot on which the voter may indicate several choices for the same office in the order of preference

pre·fer'ment *n* **1** act of preferring or state of being preferred; **2** promotion, advancement

pre·ferred' stock' *n* stock which pays usu. a fixed rate of dividend and has prior claim over that of common stock to dividends and in the case of liquidation to assets

pre·fix /prē'fiks/ [L *praefixus* placed before] *n* **1** affix placed before the beginning of a word, as *dis* in *disbelief;* **2** something prefixed ‖ /also prēfiks'/ *vt* **3** to add a prefix to; **4** to add as a prefix

preg·na·ble /preg'nəbəl/ [MF *prenable* < *prendre* to take] *adj* susceptible of being taken or conquered ‖ **preg'na·bil'i·ty** /-bil'-/ *n*

preg·nant /preg'nənt/ [L *praegnans* (*-antis*)] *adj* **1** having offspring developing in the uterus; **2** filled, abounding; **3** inventive, fertile; **4** fruitful; **5** full of meaning, significant ‖ **preg'nan·cy** *n* (*-cies*)

pre·hen·sile /prihens'il/ [F < L *prehendere* (*-hensus*) to grasp] *adj* adapted for grasping, as the limbs, toes, and tail of certain animals

pre'his·tor'ic (*-i·cal*) /prē'-/ *adj* pert. to a period before recorded history

pre·judge' /prē-/ *vt* to judge beforehand or without sufficient consideration ‖ **pre·judg'ment** *n*

prej·u·dice /prej'ədis/ [OF < L *praejudicium* prejudgment] *n* **1** bias, favorable or unfavorable; **2** unreasoning objection to or hatred of persons or things; **3** injury or harm as a result of another's action or judgment; **4** **without prejudice** *law* without affecting a case or any rights involved ‖ *vt* **5** to cause to have prejudice; **6** to hurt, injure, or damage ‖ SYN *n* unfairness, preconception, bias, partiality, prepossession, predilection, presumption ‖ DISCR *Prejudice, predilection,* and *presumption* are words which express anticipation in thought. *Prejudice* usually names a bias against a person or thing; it clogs our understanding, and makes us unfair to those for whom it is entertained. Sufficient knowledge of that toward which it is directed would often remove *prejudice.* A *prepossession* is a prejudgment in favor of its object. It is based upon feeling rather than upon reason or understanding, and it is not so far-reaching as *prejudice;* a *prepossession* in favor of an unseen person would not do him so much

good as a *prejudice* against him would do harm. A *predilection* is a mental preference for a person or thing one is yet unacquainted with

prej'u·di'cial /-dish'əl/ *adj* injurious; damaging ‖ SYN detrimental, damaging, injurious derogatory

prel·ate /prel'it/ [ML *praelatus*] *n* high-ranking churchman

pre·lim /prilim'/ *n slang* preliminary

pre·lim·i·nar·y /prilim'iner'ē/ [< *pre-* + L *limen* threshold] *adj* **1** introductory; preparatory ‖ *n* (*-ies*) **2** preliminary act or step; **3** *sports* event taking place before the main event

prel·ude /prel'yōōd, prāl'-, prē'lōōd, prā'-/ [ML *praeludium* foreplay] *n* **1** preface, preliminary; **2a** a phrase, section, or short piece of music serving as introduction to the main portion of a composition; **b** short independent composition ‖ *vt* **3** to serve as or be a prelude to

pre·mar'i·tal /prē-/ *adj* pert. to the period before marriage

pre·ma·ture /prēm'ət(y)ōōr', -əchōōr', prēm'əchōōr'/ *adj* arriving, occurring, or done before the usual or proper time ‖ **pre'ma·ture'ly** *adv*

pre·med /prēmed'/ *n colloq* **1** premedical studies; **2** premedical student

pre·med'i·cal /prē-/ *adj* of or pert. to college study preparatory to and before entering medical school

pre·med'i·tate' /pri-/ *vt & vi* to consider carefully or plan beforehand ‖ **pre·med'i·ta'tion** *n*

pre·mier /prim(y)ir', prēm'ē·ər/ [F = first] *adj* **1** foremost, chief; **2** earliest ‖ *n* **3** prime minister ‖ **pre·mier'·ship** *n*

pre·miere /primir', -myer'/ [F = first] *n* **1** first public performance, as of a play; **2** leading lady ‖ *vi* **3** to have the first performance ‖ *vt* **4** to give the first performance of; **5** to appear for the first time in a leading role

prem·ise /prem'is/ [ML *praemissa* (*propositio*) (*proposition*) set in front] *n* **1** *logic* statement from which a conclusion is to be drawn; **2 premises** *pl* building with its grounds ‖ /also primīz'/ *vt* **3** to state in advance as an explanation; **4** to assume as a premise

pre·mi·um /prēm'ē·əm/ [L *praemium* reward] *n* **1** prize or award offered as an inducement to purchase or enter a contest; **2** payment for an insurance policy; **3** amount paid in excess of the nominal value, as for securities, interest, or currency; **4** high value; **5 at a premium** at a high price because of short supply

pre·mo·ni·tion /prē'mənish'ən, prem'-/ [L *praemonitio* (*-onis*)] *n* **1** forewarning; **2** presentiment ‖ **pre·mon·i·to·ry** /primon'ĭtôr'ē, -tōr'-/ *adj*

pre·na·tal /prē-/ *adj* occurring or existing before birth pre·oc·cu·py /prē-/ vt to absorb; completely engage the attention of || pre-oc'cu·pied' adj || pre·oc'cu·pa'tion n

pre'or·dain' /prē'-/ vt to foreordain

prep /prep'/ n colloq preparatory school

prep. 1 preposition; 2 preparation; 3 preparatory

prep·a·ra·tion /prep'ərāsh'ən/ [see pre-pare] n 1 act of preparing or state of being prepared; 2 any steps taken to prepare for something; 3 something prepared or manufactured, esp. something curative or medicinal

pre·par·a·to·ry /pripar'ətôr'ē, -tôr'-/ adj 1 serving to prepare; 2 introductory

pre·par'a·to·ry school n 1 private high school; 2 Brit private elementary school

pre·pare /priper'/ [L praeparare (-atus)] vt 1 to make ready, fit, or suitable; 2 to make; compound; give form to || vi 3 to make things or oneself ready || SYN adapt, adjust, arrange, qualify, provide

pre·par'ed·ness /-idnis, -perd'nis/ n state of being prepared, esp. for war

pre·pay' /prē-/ v (-paid) vt to pay, or pay the cost of, in advance || pre·pay'ment n

pre·pense /pripens'/ [< OF purpenser to meditate] adj (malice) thought out beforehand; intended

pre·pon·der·ate /pripon'dərāt'/ [L praeponderare (-atus) to outweigh] vi to have superiority in weight, influence, or the like; predominate || pre·pon'der·ant adj || pre·pon'der·ance n

prep·o·si·tion /prep'əzish'ən/ [L prae-positio setting before] n any of a class of words used before a noun or pronoun to form phrases modifying verbs or substantives, and expressing various relations || prep'o·si'tion·al adj

pre'pos·sess' /prē'-/ vt 1 to fill (the mind) beforehand; 2 to predispose to a favorable opinion or impression || pre'pos·ses'sion n

pre'pos·sess'ing adj impressing favorably; attractive

pre·pos·ter·ous /pripost'(ə)rəs/ [L praeposterus reversed] adj contrary to common sense; ridiculous; absurd

pre·puce /prē'pyōōs/ [L praeputium] n foreskin covering the end of the penis

pre're·cord'ed /prē'-/ adj (radio or television program) recorded in advance of the time of its broadcast

pre·req'ui·site /pri-/ adj 1 required beforehand || n 2 something prerequisite

pre·rog·a·tive /prirog'ətiv/ [L praerogativa previous choice, privilege] n exclusive right or privilege inherent in a certain office, position, person, group, or class

pres. present

Pres. President

pres·age /pres'ij/ [L praesagium] n 1 feeling that something is to happen; presentiment or foreboding; 2 omen or sign || pre·sage /prisāj'/ vt 3 to foretell; give warning of; 4 to have a foreboding of || SYN v prophesy, forebode, predict (see foretell)

pres·by·o·pi·a /prez'bē-ōp'ē-ə/ [< Gk presbys old man -opia] n defect of vision due to the inability of the eye to focus on near objects, usu. appearing with age

pres·by·ter /prez'bitər, pres'-/ [Gk presbyteros elder] n 1 priest; 2 elder of a Presbyterian church

pres'by·te'ri·an /-tir'ē-ən/ adj 1 pert. to or characterized by government of a church by elders; 2 Presbyterian pert. to or designating any of several branches of a Calvinistic Protestant denomination having a presbyterian form of government || n 3 Pres'by·te'ri·an member of the Presbyterian church

pres'by·ter'y /-ter'ē/ n (-ies) 1 a organized body in the Presbyterian church having judicial power and composed of the ministers and ruling elders of the churches in a given district; b district so represented; 2 R C Ch priest's residence

pre·sci·ence /prēsh'(ē)əns, presh'-/ [LL praescientia] n 1 foreknowledge; 2 foresight || pre'sci·ent adj

pre·scribe /priskrīb'/ [L praescribere (-scriptus) to hold by prescription] vt 1 to set down as a guide or rule of action; 2 to order the use of (a medicine or treatment) || vi 3 to lay down rules; 4 to give directions for the administration of a remedy

pre·script /prē'skript/ n order, precept

pre·scrip·tion /priskrip'shən/ n 1 written direction for the preparation and administration of a remedy; 2 the prescribed medicine; 3 act of prescribing; 4 that which is prescribed; 5 law a obtaining of a right to property by long-continued use; b right thus obtained || pre·scrip'tive adj

pres·ence /prez'əns/ [MF < L prae-sentia] n 1 state or fact of being present; 2 immediate vicinity, as in the presence of danger; 3 attendance, as your presence is required; 4 one's appearance or bearing; 5 spirit, ghost

pres'ence of mind' n quickness of thinking in time of stress

pres·ent[1] /prez'ənt/ [L praesens (-entis)] adj 1 being in attendance at a given place; 2 existing at this time; 3 gram designating a tense which mainly expresses time that now is, or action now going on; 4 being here under consideration, as the present paper || n 5 present time; 6 gram a present tense; b form in the present; 7 at present now; 8 for the present for now

pre·sent[2] /prizent'/ [OF presenter <

L *praesentare* to place before] *vt* **1** to bring before someone; **2** to introduce (a person); **3** to bring to view or notice; **4** to display; exhibit; **5** to offer as a gift; **6** to furnish (someone) with a gift; **7** to submit for consideration; **8** to proffer or deliver formally; **9** to convey, as greetings or compliments ‖ **pres·ent** /prez′ənt/ *n* **10** gift or donation ‖ SYN *n* gift, donation (see *boon*¹)

pre·sent′a·ble *adj* **1** that can be presented; **2** fit to be seen or to appear ‖ **pre·sent′a·bil·i·ty** /-bil′-/ *n*

pre·sent′ arms′ *n mil* salute with a rifle held vertically before the body

pres′en·ta′tion /prez′-, prēz′-/ *n* **1** act of presenting or state of being presented; **2** that which is presented

pres′ent-day′ *adj* current, of today

pre·sen′ti·ment /prizent′-/ [F] *n* **1** apprehension, as of evil; **2** foreboding ‖ SYN misgiving, apprehension (see *foreboding*)

pres′ent·ly *adv* **1** soon; **2** now

pre·sent′ment /prizent′-/ [< *present*²] *n* **1** presentation; **2** *law* report or statement of a grand jury concerning an offense of which it has personal knowledge, but for which no indictment has been presented

pres′ent par′ti·ci·ple *n* participle with present meaning

pres′ent per′fect *n* tense formed by the present tense of *have* with a past participle, as *I have seen* ‖ also *adj*

pre·serv·a·tive /prizurv′ətiv/ *adj* **1** tending to preserve ‖ *n* **2** anything that preserves, as a chemical added to food to keep it from spoiling

pre·serve /prizurv′/ [L *praeservare* to guard] *vt* **1** to keep from injury; save; **2** to keep (food) from spoiling, as by heat or by the use of sugar, salt, vinegar, etc.; **3** to maintain, as *to preserve peace;* **4** to protect (game) or reserve (land), as for hunting ‖ *vi* **5** to make preserves; **6** to preserve game ‖ *n* **7** place set apart for keeping game, fish, etc., for sport; **8 preserves** *pl* fruit preserved by cooking with sugar ‖ **pre·serv′er** *n* ‖ **pres′er·va′tion** /prez′ər-/ *n* ‖ SYN *v* keep, guard, shield (see *defend*)

pre·side /prizīd′/ [L *praesidere*] *vi* **1** to act as chairman of an assembly or meeting; **2** **preside over** to exercise direction of

pres·i·dent /prez′idənt/ *n* **1** chief executive officer of an organized body, as a corporation, club, society, or college; **2 President, a** chief executive of the United States and of certain other republics as those of the New World; **b** head of state of parliamentary republics, as Germany and Italy ‖ **pres′i·den′tial** /-shəl/ *adj* ‖ **pres′i·den·cy** *n* (-cies)

pres′i·dent of the coun′cil of min′is·ters *n* prime minister, as of France and Italy

press¹ /pres′/ [L *pressare*] *vt* **1** to act on with a steady force; **2** to bear heavily down on; **3** to squeeze or compress; **4** to hug or embrace; **5** to thrust by pushing against; **6 a** to squeeze (juice), as from grapes; **b** to squeeze juice from; **7** to urge; **8** to compel; **9** to force to hurry; **10** to make smooth by bearing down upon, as cloth with a hot iron ‖ *vi* **11** to exert pressure; **12** to bear heavily; **13** to crowd; **14** to be urgent or insistent; **15 press on** to push forward with determination ‖ *n* **16** any of various devices for pressing, crushing, or stamping; **17** printing machine; **18** newspapers and periodicals collectively; **19** news reporters collectively; **20** publicity, critical comment, as *the play had a good press;* **21** process or art of printing; **22** crowd, throng; **23** act of crowding forward; pressure; **24** hurry or urgency; **25** smooth crease on the front of trouser legs; **26 go to press** to begin being printed

press² [OF *prest* loan] *vt* **1** to force into service, esp. naval service ‖ *n* **2** compulsory recruitment

press′ a′gent *n* person hired to gain favorable publicity for a client

press′ con′fer·ence *n* interview between newsmen and some public figure

press′ gang′ *n* formerly, squad of men detailed to kidnap men, as from a tavern, for forced service in the navy

press′ing *adj* urgent

press′man /-mən/ *n* (-men /-mən/) one who operates a printing press

press′ re·lease′ *n* news release

pres·sure /presh′ər/ [L *pressura*] *n* **1** force exerted on a surface by something in contact with it; **2** exertion of mental or moral force; **3** oppression; distress; **4** urgency; **5** electromotive force; **6** *phys* force per unit area ‖ *vt* **7** to exert pressure on (a person, group, or government)

pres′sure cook′er *n* pot for cooking foods quickly by means of steam under pressure

pres′sure group′ *n* special interest group that seeks to pressure officials or legislators into doing what it wants

pres′sur·ize′ *vt* to maintain sea-level pressure in (the cabin of a plane that flies at high altitudes)

press′work′ *n* **1** management or operation of a printing press; **2** work done by or on a press, as distinguished from composition

pres·ti·dig·i·ta·tion /prest′idij′itāsh′ən/ [F] *n* sleight of hand ‖ **pres′ti·dig′i·ta′tor** *n*

pres·tige /prestēzh′, -tēj′/ [F] *n* authority or influence due to reputation or achievements ‖ **pres·tig′ious** /-tij′-(ē)əs, -tēj′-/ *adj*

pres·to /pres′tō/ [It] *adv & adj* quick, fast

pre·sume /prizo͞om'/ [L *praesumere*] *vt* 1 to take for granted, suppose; 2 to venture (to do something); 3 to seem to prove || *vi* 4 to behave with improper boldness; 5 **presume on** or **upon** to take advantage of, as *to presume on one's good nature* || **pre·sum'a·ble** *adj* || **pre·sum'a·bly** *adv*

pre·sump·tion /prizump'shən/ *n* 1 act of presuming; 2 assumption; 3 that which is presumed; 4 bold forwardness; 5 *law* inference that an act has been committed, or that a fact exists || SYN effrontery, arrogance, impudence, assurance; assumption, expectation (see *prejudice*)

pre·sump'tive *adj* affording reasonable ground for belief; probable

pre·sump'tu·ous /-cho͞o-əs/ *adj* forward, bold, impertinent || SYN self-assured, arrogant, rash, impertinent, bold

pre·sup·pose' /prē'-/ *vt* 1 to take for granted; assume in advance; 2 to require as a foregoing condition || **pre·sup·po·si'tion** *n*

pre·tend /pritend'/ [L *praetendere* to stretch forth] *vt* 1 to make a false show of; feign; 2 to profess falsely; 3 to make believe || *vi* 4 to make believe; 5 **pretend to** to lay claim to || **pre·tend'er** *n* || SYN affect, assume, feign, counterfeit, sham, simulate || DISCR *Pretend* and *feign* are both used of that which is opposed to the real or true. *Pretend* is used in an unfavorable sense; beggars sometimes *pretend* to be deaf and dumb; sinners *pretend* to repent. *Feign* is used in both the bad and the indifferent sense, as he *feigned* illness so that he could stay at home; he *feigned* a composure which he did not feel. People *feign* madness; like the simulation of those who *pretend* to be deaf and dumb, this sort of feigning is open and deliberate scheming. *Feign* is also used in connection with the invention of poets or dramatists, and asserts that to be true which all know to be false but accept for its literary or story value, as the stories of mythology are by common consent *feigned* to be true.

pre·tense /pritens', prē'tens/ *n* 1 deception; make-believe; 2 false show; sham; 3 false allegation; 4 unwarranted claim || SYN assumption, disguise, plea, simulation, hypocrisy, pretension, pretext || ANT fact, honesty, sincerity

pre·ten'sion *n* 1 claim made; 2 state of having some justifiable claim; 3 pretentiousness; 4 **pretensions** *pl* claim to excellence in something

pre·ten'tious *adj* 1 making claim to superiority; 2 ostentatious || **pre·ten'tious·ly** *adv* || **pre·ten'tious·ness** *n* || SYN ostentatious, vainglorious, parading (see *showy*)

pret·er·it or **pret·er·ite** /pret'ərit/ [L

praeteritus past] *gram adj* 1 past || *n* 2 past tense; 3 verb in the preterit

pre·ter·nat·u·ral /prēt'ər-/ [ML *praeternaturalis*] *adj* 1 extraordinary; 2 supernatural

pre·text /prē'tekst/ [L *praetextum*] *n* pretense or excuse

Pre·to·ri·a /pritôr'ē·ə, -tōr'-/ *n* capital of the province of Transvaal and administrative capital of the Republic of South Africa (303,689)

pret·ty /prit'ē, purt'ē/ [OE *prættig* cunning] *adj* (-ti·er; -ti·est) 1 pleasing to the eye because of grace and daintiness; 2 pleasing to the ear or mind; 3 *ironic* fine; 4 *colloq* considerable || *adv* 5 fairly; rather; quite; 6 **sitting pretty** *colloq* in a good position || *v* (-tied) *vt* **pretty up** to make pretty || **pret'ti·ly** *adv* || **pret'ti·ness** *n* || SYN fair, comely, good-looking (see *beautiful*)

pret·zel /pret'səl/ [G] *n* hard, dry, salted biscuit made in the form of a knot

pre·vail /privāl'/ [L *praevalere* to be more able] *vi* 1 to gain the advantage; obtain influence or superiority; 2 to be prevalent; 3 to predominate; 4 **prevail on** or **upon** to persuade

pre·vail'ing *adj* 1 having greater influence or strength; controlling; 2 prevalent

prev·a·lent /prev'ələnt/ *adj* common; current; widespread || **prev'a·lence** *n*

pre·var·i·cate /privar'ikāt/ [L *praevaricari* (-*atus*) to straddle] *vi* to stray from the truth; lie || **pre·var'i·ca'tor** *n* || **pre·var'i·ca'tion** *n* || SYN equivocate, misrepresent, evade, deceive || DISCR These words agree in expressing the idea of getting away from the truth; they differ, however, in method and intent. To *evade* is cleverly to avoid answering a question, telling something we prefer not to tell, or the like. To *evade*, therefore, may or may not be deceptive; if by *evading* we produce a false or wrong impression, it is; if we are merely noncommittal, or successful in changing the subject, it is not. To *equivocate* is deliberately to conceal the truth by resorting to ambiguity; one who has been *evaded* is likely to know that he has been tricked into dropping the subject. To *prevaricate* is to speak or act in such a way as to deceive; prevarication is usually accomplished by shuffling, shifting, or quibbling, or by using vague or indefinite statements. *Lie* is an outright word; *prevaricate* is a softer word than *lie*, and throws part of the blame upon the trustful receiver of vague phrases, but the effect of prevaricating is practically that of lying. To *misrepresent* may or may not be blameworthy, according to the motive of the agent; to *misrepresent* is to give a false impression or account of, as through intent to deceive, lack of knowledge, or the like, as being poor, he *misrepresented* the life of the rich

pre·vent /privent'/ [L *praevenire* (-*ventus*)] *vt* 1 to stop or keep from happening; 2 to hinder ‖ *vi* 3 to stand in the way ‖ **pre·vent'a·ble** or **pre·vent'i·ble** *adj* ‖ SYN hinder, obstruct, resist, oppose, avert, preclude, intercept, forestall, frustrate, stop, check ‖ DISCR To *hinder* is to keep one from his purpose. We are *hindered* usually only for a time; the thought of delay and postponement is dominant. If we are *hindered* by a shower from starting on time, we may start later; whereas if we are *prevented* from going, we do not go at all. To *obstruct*, *oppose*, and *resist* are modes of *hindering*; to *obstruct* is to place something in the way of accomplishment; it is often used of important actions that are blocked or checked. *Hinder* is used of any delay, however trifling. We are *hindered*, not *obstructed*, in our day's work by interruptions; the path of an army is *obstructed*, not *hindered*, by barricades or fallen logs, or by flooded roads. To oppose is to *hinder* by setting oneself against something, by summoning contending force against; we *oppose* lawbreakers in actuality when we fight them as individuals in the courts; we *oppose* the idea of lawbreaking in general by doing our own individual best to uphold the law. *Resist* is stronger than *oppose*, and suggests contending against that which is offering active force or energy against us. We *resist* efforts to infringe upon our liberty; hard woods *resist* wear better than soft

pre·ven'tion *n* 1 act of preventing; 2 preventive

pre·ven'tive *adj* 1 serving to prevent or hinder ‖ *n* 2 something that prevents, as a medicine that prevents disease

pre'view' /prē'-/ *vt* 1 to show or look at beforehand ‖ *n* 2 advance look; 3 also **pre·vue**, a advance showing of a movie or play before the regular run; b advance showing of scenes from a forthcoming motion picture for the purpose of advertising it

pre·vi·ous /prēv'ē̇-əs/ [< L *praevius*] *adj* 1 going before in time; prior; 2 *colloq* premature ‖ *adv* 3 **previous to** prior to ‖ **pre'vi·ous·ly** *adv*

pre'vi·ous ques'tion *n* motion that a vote be taken at once on the main issue, esp. as a means to end debate

pre'war' *adj* before the war

prex·y /prek'sē̇/ *n* (-ies) *slang* president of a college or university

prey /prā'/ [OF *preie*] *n* 1 animal hunted for food; 2 any victim of

violence, sharp practices, disease, etc.; 3 act of preying, as *a beast of prey* ‖ *vi* 4 **prey on** or **upon, a** to take as prey; b to victimize; c to raid for plunder; d to exert a baleful influence on, as the mind

Pri·am /prī'əm/ *n Gk myth.* last king of Troy, slain in the sack of the city

Pri·a·pus /prī·āp'əs/ *n* 1 *class. myth.* son of Dionysus and Aphrodite and god of procreation; 2 **priapus** phallus

price /prīs'/ [OF *pris* < L *pretium*] *n* 1 something of value, usu. money, given or asked in exchange for a thing; 2 reward for the capture or death of an outlaw; 3 cost in money or effort in order to achieve something; 4 odds 4; 5 **beyond price** priceless ‖ *vt* 6 to fix the price of; 7 to ask the price of

price'-earn'ings ra'tio *n* measure of the value of a common stock, determined by dividing the current market price of a share by the company's net earnings per share for the most recent twelve months

price'less *adj* 1 invaluable; having a worth too great to be measured; 2 *colloq* highly amusing

price' sup·port' *n* government subsidy paid to maintain the price of a commodity

prick /prik'/ [OE *prica* point] *n* 1 act of pricking or the state of being pricked; 2 puncture with a sharp instrument; 3 sharp pain, as one caused by a pointed instrument; 4 slender, pointed object capable of piercing, as a thorn ‖ *vt* 5 to pierce with something pointed; 6 to pain or sting, as with remorse; 7 to erect (the ears), as a dog; 8 **prick up one's ears** to become suddenly attentive

prick'ly [< OE *pricel* sharp point] *adj* (-li·er; -li·est) 1 full of thorns or sharp points; 2 stinging, smarting

prick'ly heat' *n* itching skin eruption caused by inflammation of the sweat glands

pride /prīd'/ [OE *prȳde*] *n* 1 undue self-esteem; conceit; 2 haughtiness; disdain; 3 sense of personal dignity; self-respect; 4 that of which one is proud; 5 best part of anything; 6 group of lions; 7 mettle in horses ‖ *vt* 8 **pride oneself on** to be proud of ‖ **pride'ful** *adj* ‖ SYN *n* vanity, conceit, complacency, vainglory ‖ DISCR *Pride* is a term which may include *conceit* and *vanity*, but it has also a meaning apart from these. *Pride* may be a feeling noble, dignified, and admirable; such *pride* is that which forbids us to show our hurt, however much we are humiliated; which bids us keep doggedly on, when we are about to fall, or otherwise works through our natural self-respect to compel us to be our best. Such *pride* is the envy of the weak, for it is the possession only of the strong. Unworthy *pride* is haughty, overbearing, arrogant, hate-producing. *Pride* in this bad sense is also connected with the idea of strength, for this characteristic makes people overweening, irritable, and apt to be violent in their claims for themselves. *Vanity* and *conceit* are cardinal weaknesses. *Vanity* is felt over trifling things; and the *vanity* felt over one's fashionable clothes is a much more empty and frivolous feeling than that connoted by the unfavorable sense of *pride*. *Vanity* must not only consider itself fine, but must have the open adulation of others; *vanity* wilts under disapproval, where sometimes *pride* would wax so much the fiercer. *Conceit* is sometimes based on actual achievement or possession, but oftener it is the fruit of excessive self-love, and is boastfully puffed up and lofty over what does not even exist. Frivolous people are *vain;* usually youth is *conceited*. *Vainglory* is *vanity* pompous, strutting, and boastful. *Complacency* is a calm and composed self-approval, often irritating to others || ANT *n* humility, self-distrust, self-depreciation, meekness, lowliness, humbleness, self-abasement

prie-dieu /prē'dyōō'/ [F = pray God] *n* small kneeling desk for prayer with a shelf above for a book

priest /prēst'/ [OE *prēost* < Gk *presbyteros* elder] *n* 1 one devoted to the service of God or a god, with authority to perform religious rites; 2 one ordained to the Christian ministry; 3 in liturgical churches, minister of the second rank, between bishop and deacon || **priest'ess** *nfem* || **priest'hood** *n* || **priest'ly** *adj*

priest'-rid'den *adj* dominated or tyrannized over by priests

prig /prig'/ [?] *n* person who self-righteously affects airs of superior virtue || **prig'gish** *adj*

prim /prim'/ [?] *adj* (**prim·mer; prim·mest**) precise; nice; formally neat || **prim'ly** *adv* || SYN tidy, neat, trim, stiff, formal, demure

pri·ma bal'le·ri·na /prēm'ə/ *n* chief ballerina in a ballet company

pri·ma·cy /prīm'əsē/ [ML *primatia*] *n* (**-cies**) 1 state of being first in rank or importance; 2 office or dignity of an ecclesiastical primate

pri·ma don·na /prēm'ə don'ə, prim'-/ [It = first lady] *n* 1 principal female singer in an opera; 2 temperamental person who has tantrums if he doesn't get his way

pri·ma fa·ci·e /prīm'ə fāsh'ē·ē', fāsh'ē, fāsh'ə/ [L = at first view] *adj* 1 at first sight; as far as at first appears; 2 obvious; self-evident || also *adv*

pri·mar·i·ly /prīmer'īlē, prī'mer-, prīm'-

ər-/ *adv* 1 in the first place; originally; 2 essentially; fundamentally

pri·ma·ry /prī'merē, prīm'ərē/ [L *primarius* of the first rank] *adj* 1 first in order of origin, time, or place; original; 2 fundamental, basic; 3 first in order of development; belonging to the first stage; 4 first in rank; principal; 5 *elec* designating the inducing current or the circuit designed for it; 6 pert. to the large flight feathers in a bird's wings || *n* (**-ries**) 7 that which is first in rank, place, or importance; 8 primary election; 9 celestial body around which a satellite revolves; 10 *elec* winding in a transformer or the like, carrying current that induces a current in a separate winding called the secondary || SYN *adj* original, fundamental, chief, first, prime, primeval, primordial, primitive, pristine

pri·ma·ry ac'cent *n* the main stress of a word

pri·ma·ry cell' *n elec* cell that converts chemical energy into electrical energy and cannot be recharged

pri·ma·ry e·lec'tion *n* preliminary party election for choosing convention delegates or nominees for office

pri·ma·ry school' *n* elementary school

pri·mate /prī'māt, prīm'it/ [LL *primas* (-*atis*) of the first rank] *n* 1 highest-ranking archbishop or bishop in a country or province; 2 member of the highest order of mammals (Primates), which includes man and the apes, monkeys, lemurs, and marmosets || **pri'mate·ship'** *n*

prime /prīm'/ [OE *prīm* < L *prima* (hora) first (hour)] *adj* 1 first in order of rank, time, or importance; 2 original; early; 3 excellent, first-rate; 4 being at the highest point of life; vigorous; 5 (meat) of the best quality; 6 having the highest credit rating; 7 (TV time) of the highest value || *n* 8 most vigorous and flourishing stage; 9 prime number; 10 first or best part of anything; 11 mark ' placed above and to the right of a figure or letter, to indicate a minute, inch, etc. or to make a distinction || *vt* 12 to prepare for a particular task or operation, as by pouring a liquid into a pump or putting powder behind the main charge in a firearm; 13 to cover with a preparatory coat of paint; 14 to supply with information, answers, etc.

prime' me·rid'i·an *n* meridian passing through Greenwich, England, from which longitude is reckoned east and west

prime' min'is·ter *n* chief minister of the cabinet in the government of countries the head of which is a monarch or a ceremonial president

prime' num'ber *n* number not divisible

without a remainder by any number except itself or *1*

prim·er[1] /prim'ər/ *n* 1 one who or that which primes; 2 explosive cap, esp. on the rear end of a cartridge, which fires it when struck by the hammer or pin actuated by the trigger

prim·er[2] /prim'ər/ [ML *primarium*] *n* elementary textbook, esp. one for teaching children to read

prime' rate' /prīm'/ *n* minimum rate of interest on short-term loans that commercial banks charge to their most credit-worthy borrowers

pri·me·val /prīmēv'əl/ [< L *primaevus* young] *adj* pert. to the earliest age or time, esp. of the world

prim'ing /prīm'-/ *n* 1 act of one who primes; 2 first or preparatory coat of paint; 3 powder or other substance used to ignite a charge

prim·i·tive /prim'itiv/ [MF < L *primitivus*] *adj* 1 pert. to the beginning; original; 2 savage; uncivilized; 3 simple or crude; old-fashioned; 4 original; primary; 5 *biol* rudimentary

pri·mo·gen·i·ture /prīm'əjen'ichər/ [< L *primogenitus* first-born] *n* 1 state of being first-born; 2 inheritance of the entire estate by the eldest son

pri·mor·di·al /prīmôrd'ē-əl/ [LL *primordialis*] *adj* 1 existing from the beginning; original; 2 *biol* earliest formed; primitive

primp /primp/ [perh < *prim*] *vt* 1 to dress with exaggerated care ‖ *vi* 2 to groom oneself with exaggerated care

prim'rose' [ML *prima rosa* first rose] *n* 1 any of a widely distributed genus (*Primula*) of plants bearing showy, variously colored flowers; 2 pale yellow

prim'rose path' *n* life devoted to heedless indulgence, usu. leading to disaster

prince /prins'/ [OF < L *princeps* principal person] *n* 1 ruler or sovereign; 2 ruler of a principality or small state; 3 son of a king or emperor; 4 one who is a very distinguished member of his class, as *a merchant prince;* 5 man of exceptionally fine character ‖ **prin'cess** /-sis, -ses/ *nfem* ‖ **prince'dom** *n*

Prince' Al'bert [*Albert* Edward (1841–1910) Prince of Wales (later Edward VII of Great Britain)] *n* double-breasted frock coat

prince' con'sort *n* husband of a reigning female sovereign

Prince' Ed'ward Is'land /ed'wərd/ *n* island and province in E Canada in the Gulf of St. Lawrence (109,000; 2184 sq.m.; cap. Charlottetown)

prince'ling *n* young or insignificant prince

prince'ly *adj* (-li·er; -li·est) 1 pert. to a prince; 2 noble, magnificent; lavish

Prince' of Dark'ness *n* Satan

Prince' of Peace' *n* Jesus Christ

Prince' of Wales' *n* title conferred on the eldest son of the British sovereign

prin·ci·pal /prins'ipəl/ [L *principalis*] *adj* 1 first or highest in rank, value, character, degree, or importance; chief ‖ *n* 2 principal person or thing; 3 chief or head; 4 actor in a leading part; 5 head of a public school; 6 sum of money drawing interest or earning dividends; 7 main part of an estate, as distinguished from income; 8 *law* **a** person authorizing another to act as his agent; **b** actual perpetrator of a crime; **c** party to a contract ‖ **prin'ci·pal·ly** *adv* ‖ SYN *adj* main, first, highest (see *chief*)

prin·ci·pal·i·ty /-pal'-/ *n* (-ties) 1 territory ruled by a prince or from which his title is derived; 2 position or authority of a prince

prin'ci·pal parts' *npl* set of inflected forms of a verb from which all others can be derived, as *sing, sang, sung*

prin·ci·ple /prins'ipəl/ [< MF *principe* < L *principium* beginning] *n* 1 source or cause from which a thing comes; 2 settled rule of action or conduct; 3 fundamental or general truth upon which others are founded; 4 uprightness, integrity, as *a man of principle;* 5 method of operation or procedure; 6 natural law by which something operates; 7 **principles** *pl* basic tenet; basis of conduct

prin'ci·pled *adj* having high principles; acting with integrity

print /print'/ [OF *preinte*] *n* 1 mark made by pressure; 2 stamp or die; 3 something stamped out, as a pat of butter; 4 printed letters; 5 printed matter; 6 anything produced by type or from an engraved plate; 7 *photog* picture reproduced from a negative; 8 printed or dyed design or pattern on cloth; 9 printed cloth; 10 garment made of printed cloth; 11 **in print,** in printed form; **b** (book) still available; 12 **out of print** (book) no longer available ‖ *vt* 13 to make an impression on; 14 to fix or stamp in or on something; 15 to stamp (cloth) with patterns, etc.; 16 to reproduce from type, engraved plates, etc., as books, pictures, and newspapers; 17 to cause (written material) to be published; 18 to write in letters like those of type; 19 to produce (a photograph) from a negative ‖ *vi* 20 to make impressions from type, plates, or the like; 21 to publish books, etc.; 22 to make letters resembling type

print'ed cir'cuit *n* electrical circuit in which the wires are replaced by conductive strips of metal deposited on a nonconductive sheet

print'ed mat'ter *n* matter that is printed from type on a press and is acceptable for special postal rates

print'er *n* 1 one whose occupation is printing; 2 mechanism of a computer that produces printed matter

print′er's dev′il *n* devil 5

print′ing *n* 1 setting of reading matter in type; 2 printed matter; 3 all the copies of a book, etc., printed at one time

print′ing press′ *n* machine for printing from type, plates, etc.

print′-out′ *n* printed output of a computer

pri·or /prī′ər/ [L = former, elder, superior] *adj* 1 preceding in time or order; previous || *adv* 2 **prior to** before || *n* 3 head of a priory; 4 in an abbey, officer next in rank to the abbot || **pri′or·ess** *nfem*

pri·or′i·ty /-or′-, -ôr′-/ *n* (-ties) 1 state of being prior; 2 precedence; 3 prior right

pri′or·y *n* (-ies) religious house governed by a prior or prioress

prism /priz′əm/ [Gk *prisma* (-*matos*) thing sawed] *n* 1 *geom* solid whose bases are similar, equal, and parallel polygons, and whose lateral faces are parallelograms; 2 *optics* transparent body at least two faces of which are plane surfaces inclined to each other; used to produce deviation or dispersion of light || **pris·mat·ic** /priz·mat′ik/ *adj*

pris·on /priz′ən/ [OF < L *prensio* (-*onis*) seizure] *n* 1 building for the confinement of arrested and convicted persons; 2 any place of confinement

pris·on·er /priz′(ə)nər/ *n* 1 one who is confined under restraint, esp. in prison; 2 prisoner of war

pris′on·er of war′ *n* member of the armed forces captured by the enemy in time of war

pris·sy /pris′ē/ [*prim* + *sissy*] *adj* (-si·er; -si·est) overly prim and prudish

pris·tine /pris′tēn, -tĭn, -tīn/ [L *pristinus* former, earlier] *adj* pert. to the earliest time or state; original

prith·ee /prith′ē/ [< I *pray thee*] *interj* *archaic* please

pri·va·cy /prīv′əsē/ *n* (-cies) 1 state of being private; 2 seclusion; 3 secrecy || SYN seclusion, solitude, retreat (see *retirement*)

pri·vate /prīv′it/ [L *privatus*] *adj* 1 personal; not public; 2 away from public view; secret; 3 not holding public office; 4 not open to the public; 5 belonging to individuals || *n* 6 lowest rank in the army or marines; 7 **privates** *pl* external genitals; 8 **in private** in seclusion; secretly || **pri′vate·ly** *adv*

pri·va·teer′ [*private* + *volunteer*] *n* 1 privately owned vessel licensed by a government to attack enemy shipping; 2 commander or one of the crew of such a vessel

pri′vate eye′ *n* slang private detective

pri·va′tion *n* 1 lack of the necessities of life; need; 2 act of depriving or state of being deprived || SYN want, lack, destitution, need (see *poverty*)

priv·et /priv′it/ [?] *n* any of several shrubs of the olive family, esp. *Ligustrum vulgare*, having dark green leaves and white flowers, much used for hedges

priv·i·lege /priv′ĭlij/ [L *privilegium* special law] *n* 1 special advantage, favor, or right granted to some to the exclusion of others; 2 any advantage or special favor || *vt* 3 to grant a privilege to; 4 to exempt (from something) || SYN *n* immunity, benefit, exemption, advantage

priv′i·leged *adj* 1 enjoying a privilege or privileges; 2 (information received from a client by a lawyer or from a penitent by a priest) not required to be divulged in court; 3 (utterance made on the floor of a legislative assembly) not liable to prosecution for libel or slander

priv·y /priv′ē/ [OF *prive* private] *adj* 1 **privy to** privately informed of || *n* (-ies) 2 small outside shed containing one or two holes or seats for defecating and urinating

priv′y coun′cil *n* body of advisers, as of a sovereign

prize¹ /prīz/ [MF *prise* reward] *n* 1 reward offered in a contest or lottery; 2 anything of value or worth striving for; 3 something captured from an enemy in war, as a ship at sea || *vt* 4 to value highly || *adj* 5 that has won a prize; 6 that could win a prize; 7 given as a prize; 8 egregious, glaring, as *a prize blunder*

prize² also **prise** /prīz′/ [MF *prise* grasp] *vt* to pry³

prize′ fight′ *n* professional boxing match || **prize′ fight′er** *n*

prize′ ring′ *n* boxing ring

pro¹ /prō′/ [L] *prep* 1 in favor of || *adv* 2 in favor of the side that affirms a question in debate || *n* 3 person or argument upholding a proposition or favoring the affirmative in a debate

pro² *adj* & *n* colloq professional

pro-¹ [L] *pref* 1 in front of, as *protection;* 2 to the front, as *proceed;* 3 favoring, as *pro-British;* 4 instead of, as *pronoun*

pro-² [Gk] *pref* before in time, place, rank, etc., as *prologue*

prob. 1 probable; 2 probably

prob·a·bil·i·ty /prob′əbil′itē/ *n* (-ties) 1 quality or state of being probable; 2 something likely; strong likelihood; 3 chances of an event's occurring in proportion to those against its occurring; 4 **in all probability** most likely, very probably

prob·a·ble /prob′əbəl/ [L *probabilis*] *adj* 1 likely to occur or to be true; 2 giving grounds for belief || **prob′a·bly** *adv* || SYN reasonable, apparent, presumable (see *likely*)

pro·bate /prō′bāt/ [L *probare* (-*atus*)

to prove, test] *vt* **1** to authenticate (a will) ‖ *n* **2** legal validation of a will

pro·ba'tion *n* **1** testing or trial; **2** period of such testing; **3** conditional release of an offender from jail; **4** trial period allowing students to make up educational deficiencies or improve their behavior ‖ **pro·ba'tion·ar'y** /-nər'-/ *adj*

pro·ba'tion·er *n* one on probation

probe /prōb/ [LL *proba* test] *n* **1** *surg* slender instrument for exploring a wound or cavity; **2** searching inquiry ‖ *vt* **3** to examine with a probe; **4** to investigate

pro·bi·ty /prōb'itē, prob'-/ [L *probitas*] *n* virtue; integrity; honesty ‖ SYN honor, uprightness, virtue, rectitude, integrity (see *honesty*) ‖ ANT sin, evil, dishonesty, dishonor

prob·lem /prob'ləm/ [Gk *problema*] *n* **1** difficult matter to be settled; **2** question set forth for solution or discussion

prob'lem·at'ic (-i·cal) /-at'-/ *adj* questionable; doubtful; contingent

pro·bos·cis /prōbos'is/ [Gk] *n* **1** elephant's trunk or the long flexible snout of certain other animals; **2** elongated mouth parts of certain insects; **3** *slang* nose

pro'caine hy'dro·chlo'ride /prō'kān, prōkān'/ [*pro-* + *cocaine*] *n* crystalline powder —C₁₃H₂₀O₂N₂·HCl— less toxic than cocaine, used as a local and spinal anesthetic

pro'ca·the'dral /prō'-/ *n* church used temporarily as a cathedral

pro·ce·dure /prəsēj'ər/ [see **proceed**] *n* **1** process, or manner of proceeding; **2** course of action or conduct ‖ SYN course, method, manner, process, proceeding

pro·ceed /prəsēd'/ [L *procedere (-cessus)*] *vi* **1** to go on or forward; continue; **2** to carry on or continue an action; **3** to carry on a legal action; **4 proceed from** to originate or emanate from

pro·ceed'ing *n* **1** action, course of action, or conduct; **2 proceedings** *pl* **a** course of action in a law case; **b** records of the transactions of a society, board of directors, or the like ‖ SYN performance, procedure, action, transaction

pro·ceeds /prō'sēdz/ *npl* money or profit derived from a transaction or sale

proc·ess /pros'es, prōs'-/ *n* **1** action which continues and progresses; **2** operation or succession of operations leading to some result; **3** passage or lapse of time; **4** *anat & biol* outgrowth or projecting part; **5** court order issued as a part of a legal action ‖ *vt* **6** to cause to undergo some operation; **7** to prepare by a particular process; **8** to go through and dispose of systematically, as correspondence, applications, etc.; **9** *law* to serve with a court order

pro·ces·sion /prəsesh'ən/ *n* **1** regular or orderly process; **2** line of persons or things moving in such a manner; **3** act of going on or forward

pro·ces'sion·al *adj* **1** pert. to processions ‖ *n* **2** hymn sung at the beginning of a church service while the clergy and choir are passing to their places; **3** solemn music composed to accompany a ceremonial procession

proc'ess serv'er *n* person who serves legal processes, as subpoenas

proc'ess shot' *n* *motion pictures* scene shot before a projected background to simulate a distant location

pro·claim /prəklām', prō-/ [L *proclamare* to cry out] *vt* to make known publicly; announce officially

proc'la·ma'tion /prok'lə-/ *n* **1** official public announcement; **2** that which is proclaimed

pro·clit·ic /prōklit'ik/ [NL *procliticus* < Gk *pro-* + *klinein* to lean] *n* word joined to a following word and pronounced without accent ‖ *also adj*

pro·cliv·i·ty /prōkliv'itē/ [L *proclivitas*] *n* natural inclination, tendency ‖ SYN inclination, disposition, propensity, proneness, bent ‖ ANT disinclination, dislike, aversion, repugnance

pro·con·sul /prō-/ *n* *Rom hist* **1** official who performed the duties of a consul outside of Rome, as in conducting a war or governing a province; **2** any administrator of a dependency

pro·cras·ti·nate /prōkrast'ināt'/ [L *procrastinare (-atus)* to put off till tomorrow] *vi* **1** to delay; postpone ‖ *vt* **2** to put off from day to day ‖ **pro·cras'ti·na'tion** *n* ‖ **pro·cras'ti·na'tor** *n* ‖ SYN (see *defer¹*)

pro·cre·ate' [L *procreare (-atus)*] *vt* to produce, engender, or beget ‖ **pro'cre·a'tion** *n* ‖ **pro'cre·a'tor** *n* ‖ **pro'cre·a'tive** *adj*

Pro·crus·te·an /prōkrust'ēən/ [< *Procrustes* mythical robber who stretched or cut off part of the legs of his victims to make them fit his bed exactly] *adj* forcing conformity by any means

proc·tol·o·gy /proktol'əjē/ [Gk *proktos* anus + *-logy*] *n* branch of medical science dealing with the rectum and the anus and their diseases ‖ **proc·tol'o·gist** *n*

proc·tor /prok'tər/ [contr. of *procurator*] *n* person who supervises students at examinations ‖ *also vt & vi*

proc·u·ra·tor /prok'yərāt'ər/ [L = manager] *n* *Rom hist* any of various provincial administrators

pro·cure /prəkyŏŏr'/ [L *procurare* to take care of] *vt* **1** to get or obtain; **2** to cause or bring about; **3** to get (females) for immoral purposes ‖ *vi* **4** to act as a procurer ‖ **pro·cur'a-**

ble *adj* || **pro·cure′ment** *n* || SYN attain, acquire, earn, win, gain (see *get*)

pro·cur′er *n* pimp || **pro·cur′ess** *nfem*

Pro·cy·on /prō′sē·on′/ [*pro-* before + Gk *kyōn* dog] *n* bright star in the constellation Canis Minor

prod /prod′/ [?] *v* (**prod·ded; prod·ding**) *vt* 1 to poke with or as with a pointed instrument; 2 to goad or urge || *n* 3 poke; 4 pointed implement for prodding

prod·i·gal /prod′igəl/ [< L *prodigus* wasteful] *adj* 1 recklessly extravagant; wasteful; 2 lavish, bountiful || *n* 3 spendthrift || **prod′i·gal′i·ty** /-gal′-/ *n* (**-ties**) || SYN *adj* extravagant, profuse, improvident, lavish

pro·di·gious /prədij′əs/ [< *prodigy*] *adj* 1 unusually great in size, extent, degree, or quantity; 2 marvelous, amazing || SYN extraordinary, excessive, huge, portentous, astonishing, wonderful, vast

prod·i·gy /prod′ijē/ [L *prodigium* portent] *n* (**-gies**) 1 wonder, marvel; 2 person, esp. a child, who is remarkably gifted || SYN miracle, portent, wonder

pro·duce /prəd(y)ōōs′/ [L *producere* (*-ductus*)] *vt* 1 to exhibit or bring to view, as *produce your passport;* 2 to bear; bring forth; yield; 3 to manufacture or make; 4 to make ready for exhibition, as a play or motion picture; 5 to extend or lengthen, as a line || *vi* 6 to yield products, offspring, profits, or the like || **prod·uce** /prod′(y)ōōs, prōd′-/ *n* 7 that which is produced, esp. farm or garden products || **pro·duc′er** *n*

prod·uct /prod′əkt/ *n* 1 that which is produced by nature, labor, thought, chemical change, etc.; 2 consequence or result; 3 result obtained by multiplying two or more quantities || SYN crop, harvest, yield, outcome, fruit, effect, result, consequence, proceeds, return, production, produce

pro·duc·tion /prəduk′shən/ *n* 1 act of producing; 2 that which is produced; 3 performance on the stage

pro·duc·tive *adj* 1 having the quality or power of producing; 2 fertile; 3 productive of bringing about || **pro·duc′tive·ly** *adv*

pro·duc·tiv·i·ty /prō′-/ *n* 1 ability to produce; 2 fertility of the land; 3 output of the means of industrial production; 4 output per man-hour

prof /prof′/ *n colloq* professor

Prof. Professor

pro·fane /prəfān′, prō-/ [L *profanus* outside the temple] *adj* 1 not sacred or holy; secular; 2 showing disrespect or irreverence toward God or sacred things; blasphemous || *vt* 3 to treat (something sacred) with irreverence, contempt, or abuse; 4 to put to an improper use; debase || **prof′a·na′-**

tion /prof′ə-/ *n* || SYN *adj* impious, irreligious, secular, temporal, worldly, wicked, unsanctified, unholy, irreverent, blasphemous || ANT *adj* consecrated, holy, sacred, pious, reverent, devout

pro·fan′i·ty /prəfan′-, prō-/ *n* (**-ties**) 1 contempt for holy things; irreverence; 2 blasphemy, swearing

pro·fess /prəfes′/ [L *profiteri* (*-fessus*) to confess] *vt* 1 to declare openly; avow; 2 to pretend; 3 to declare belief in; 4 to claim to be an authority in || *vi* 5 to make an avowal || **pro·fessed′** *adj* || **pro·fess′ed·ly** /-idlē/ *adv*

pro·fes·sion /-fesh′ən/ *n* 1 act of professing; avowal; 2 religious faith professed; 3 calling or vocation, esp. one that requires specialized learning and mental rather than manual labor; 4 all the persons engaged in any one calling || SYN acknowledgment, declaration (see *business*)

pro·fes′sion·al *adj* 1 pert. to a profession, esp. one of the learned professions; 2 following an occupation as a means of livelihood rather than as a pastime or sport; 3 participated in for gain, as *a professional football match* || *n* 4 one who makes his living by an occupation, as distinguished from an amateur; 5 person belonging to a learned profession || **pro·fes′sion·al·ism** *n*

pro·fes′sor /-fes′ər/ *n* 1 a teacher of the highest rank in a college or university; **b** title of such a teacher; 2 any teacher; 3 instructor in an art or sport || **pro·fes·so·ri·al** /prōf′əsôr′ē·əl, -sōr′-/ *adj* || **pro·fes′sor·ship′** *n*

prof·fer /prof′ər/ [AF *profrer*] *vt* 1 to offer for acceptance || *n* 2 offer

pro·fi·cient /prəfish′ənt/ [L *proficiens* (*-entis*)] *adj* thoroughly qualified or skilled in any work; expert || **pro·fi′cien·cy** *n* || SYN skillful, versed, expert, adept, trained, dexterous || ANT awkward, bungling, clumsy, untrained, inexpert

pro·file /prō′fīl/ [It *profilo*] *n* 1 outline or contour; 2 side view of a face; 3 concise and vivid biographical sketch || *vt* 4 to draw or write a profile of

prof·it /prof′it/ [MF < L *profectus*] *n* 1 monetary gain; 2 ratio of the amount by which income exceeds expense in a given time; 3 benefit or advantage; 4 **profits** *pl* that part of the return from invested capital that is left after all costs have been paid || *vt* 5 to benefit; be of profit to || *vi* 6 to make profits; to be of use; benefit

prof′it·a·ble *adj* 1 yielding gain or profit; paying; 2 useful; beneficial || **prof′it·a·bly** *adv* || SYN beneficial, advantageous, desirable, remunerative, lucrative || ANT harmful, undesirable, worthless

prof'it and loss' *n* account of net gain and loss over a given period of time or in a given transaction ‖ **prof'it-and-loss'** *adj*

prof'it-eer' *vi* 1 to make exorbitant profits by taking advantage of shortages and/or strained economic conditions to charge excessive prices ‖ *n* 2 one who profiteers

prof'it shar'ing *n* plan in which employees receive a share in the profits of a business

prof'it squeeze' *n* decrease in profit caused by the diminishing gap between the cost of production and the income from sales

prof'it tak'ing *n* selling while one's holdings show a gain

prof·li·gate /prof'ligit, -gāt'/ [L *profligatus*] *adj* 1 given up to vice; wicked; 2 recklessly extravagant ‖ *n* 3 profligate person ‖ **prof'li·ga·cy** *n* ‖ SYN *adj* dissolute, licentious, depraved, vicious

pro for'ma in'voice /prō fôr'mə/ *n* invoice filled out for the guidance of the customer, not as an actual bill

pro·found /prəfound'/ [AF < L *profundus*] *adj* 1 very deep; 2 intellectually deep; 3 intense (emotional state or feeling); 4 of deep significance ‖ **pro·found'ly** *adv* ‖ **pro·fun'di·ty** /-fun'-/ *n* (-ties) ‖ SYN intense, unqualified, abstruse (see *obscure*)

pro·fuse /prəfyŏŏs'/ [L *profusus*] *adj* 1 pouring forth freely; giving or given with great liberality; lavish; 2 abundant ‖ **pro·fuse'ly** *adv* ‖ **pro·fu'sion** /-fyŏŏzh'ən/ *n* ‖ SYN redundant, extravagant, plentiful, prodigal

pro·gen·i·tor /prōjen'itər/ [L] *n* ancestor, forefather

prog·e·ny /proj'ənē/ [MF *progenie*] *n* (-nies) offspring; children; descendants

prog·na·thous /prog'nəthəs, prognā'-/ [*pro-³* + Gk *gnathos* jaw] *adj* having the jaws projecting

prog·no·sis /prognōs'is/ [Gk] *n* (-ses /-sēz/) forecast or prediction, esp. as to the outcome of a disease

prog·nos·tic /prognost'ik/ *adj* 1 of or pert. to prognosis ‖ *n* 2 omen or sign; 3 prediction

prog·nos'ti·cate' *vt* 1 to foretell, predict ‖ *vi* 2 to make a forecast ‖ **prog·nos'ti·ca'tor** *n* ‖ **prog·nos'ti·ca'tion** *n*

pro·gram also **pro·gramme** /prō'gram, prō'gram/ [Gk *programma* writing] *n* 1 brief outline giving in order the features making up a public entertainment, ceremony, or the like; 2 features included in such an outline; 3 radio or television performance; 4 regular plan or schedule; 5 prospectus or syllabus; 6 sequence of instructions fed into a computer for the solution of a problem ‖ *v* (-gramed or -grammed) -gram·ing or -gram·ming) *vt* 7 to schedule on a

program; 8 to prepare a program for (a computer)

pro'gram·mer /-gram-/ *n* person who prepares programs for a computer

pro'gram mu'sic *n* instrumental music that suggests certain topics, such as scenes or narratives, and depends to a certain extent on them for its interest

prog·ress /prog'res, *Brit* prōg'res/ [L *progressus*] *n* 1 proceeding forward; advancement; improvement; 2 growth or development; 3 course taken by something; 4 forward movement; 5 **in progress** under way ‖ **pro·gress** /prəgres'/ *vi* 6 to move forward; advance; 7 to develop; improve ‖ SYN *n* increase, development, attainment

pro·gres·sion /prəgresh'ən/ *n* 1 movement forward; 2 succession, as of events; 3 *math* series of numbers each of which bears a fixed relation to the next preceding one

pro·gres'sive *adj* 1 moving forward, esp. by gradations or steps; 2 making or favoring advancement or improvements; 3 favoring progress, change, and reform in politics; 4 spreading, increasingly serious (disease); 5 *gram* designating a tense or aspect of the verb that indicates action going on at a given time ‖ *n* 6 one who is progressive, esp. in politics

pro·gres'sive tax' *n* tax in which the rate increases with the rise in taxable income

pro·hib·it /prōhib'it/ [L *prohibere* (-*hibitus*)] *vt* 1 to forbid by law; 2 to forbid an action of (a person); 3 to hinder, prevent

pro·hi·bi·tion /prō'əbish'ən/ *n* 1 act of prohibiting; 2 law that prohibits; 3 the forbidding by law of the manufacture and sale of alcoholic drinks; 4 period from 1920 to 1933, when such a law was in effect in the U.S.

pro'hi·bi'tion·ist *n* one who favors the prohibition of liquor ‖ **pro'hi·bi'tion·ism** *n*

pro·hib'i·tive *adj* 1 that prohibits; 2 (price) so high that no one can afford to buy

pro·ject /prəjekt'/ [L *projicere* (-*jectus*) to fling forth] *vt* 1 to throw, shoot, or cast forward; 2 to plan or contemplate; 3 *geom* to construct (a figure, line, or the like) on a given surface so that it corresponds point by point on the same or a different scale to a given figure; 4 *psychol* to perceive (an idea or image) as an external object perceptible to the senses; 5 to calculate (what something will be in the future), as *to project costs*; 6 to cause to protrude ‖ *vi* 7 to jut out; extend forward; 8 to present a likable image of oneself, esp. to an audience ‖ **proj·ect** /proj'ekt/ *n* 9 design, scheme, or plan; 10

undertaking ‖ SYN *n* design, plan, purpose, device (see *scheme*)

pro·jec·tile /prəjĕk'təl/ [L = projecting] *n* 1 body thrown or shot forward; 2 bullet, shell, rocket, or the like, fired by an explosive charge

pro·jec·tion *n* 1 act or state of projecting; 2 that which juts out; 3 representation on a plane surface of the curved surface of the earth; 4 *psychol* reference of perception to the object perceived or to some definite location; 5 reproduction on a screen of the image of a film by means of lenses and an intense light; 6 calculation of something in the future

pro·jec'tion booth' *n* room in the rear of a theater housing the motion picture projectors and spotlights

pro·jec'tion·ist *n* person who operates a motion-picture projector

pro·jec'tor *n* machine for projecting images onto a screen from a motion-picture film or slide

pro·le·tar·i·at /prōl'ətər'ē·ət/ [F < L *proletarius* citizen of the lowest class] *n* the unpropertied working class ‖ **pro'le·tar'i·an** *adj* & *n*

pro·lif·er·ate /prōlĭf'ərāt'/ [< ML *prolifer* bearing offspring] *vt* & *vi* 1 to grow by rapid production of new parts; 2 to spread wildly and rapidly ‖ **pro·lif'er·a'tion** *n*

pro·lif·ic /prōlĭf'ĭk/ [ML *prolificus*] *adj* producing abundantly, as young, fruit, ideas, or mental work

pro·lix /prōlĭks', prō'lĭks/ [L *prolixus* extended] *adj* 1 wordy, long-drawn-out (speech); 2 wordy, diffuse (speaker) ‖ **pro·lix'i·ty** *n*

pro·log or **pro·logue** /prō'lŏg, -lôg/ [Gk *prologos*] *n* 1 introduction or preface, as to a novel, poem, or discourse; 2 introductory speech or scene in a play; 3 any introductory event

pro·long /prəlông', -lŏng'/ [LL *prolongare*] *vt* to lengthen in time or space ‖ **pro'lon·ga'tion** /prō'-/ *n*

prom /prŏm/ [*promenade*] *n* school or college dance

prom·e·nade /prŏm'ənād', -näd'/ [F < LL *prominare* (*-atus*) to drive (beasts)] *n* 1 walk for pleasure or display; 2 public place for walking ‖ *vi* 3 to take a promenade ‖ *vt* 4 to take a promenade through; 5 to show off; parade

Pro·me·the·us /prəmēth'(y)ōōs, -ē·əs/ *n* Gk *myth.* a Titan who stole fire from heaven for men and who, as punishment, passed many years chained to Mt. Caucasus with an eagle tearing at his liver until freed by Hercules ‖ **Pro·me'the·an** /-ē·ən/ *adj*

pro·me·thi·um /prəmēth'ē·əm/ [< *Prometheus*] *n* rare-earth metallic element (**Pm**; at.no. 61)

prom·i·nence /prŏm'ĭnəns/ *n* 1 state of being prominent; 2 protuberance; 3 cloud of gas extending beyond the sun's disk, visible during solar eclipses

prom·i·nent [L *prominens* (*-entis*) jutting out] *adj* 1 standing or jutting out beyond a regular line or surface; 2 conspicuous, noticeable; 3 leading; widely known ‖ **prom'i·nent·ly** *adv* ‖ SYN important, eminent, noted (see *distinguished*)

pro·mis·cu·ous /prəmĭs'kyōō·əs/ [< L *promiscuus* mixed up] *adj* 1 confused; mixed up without order; 2 having sexual relations with many casual partners ‖ **prom·is·cu·i·ty** /prom'ĭskyōō'ĭtē, prōm'-/ *n* (*-ties*) ‖ SYN haphazard, confused, indiscriminate

prom·ise /prŏm'ĭs/ [ML *promissa*] *n* 1 engagement to do or not to do something; 2 ground for expectation of excellence or success in the future ‖ *vt* 3 to engage or pledge (to do or not to do); 4 to make a promise of; 5 to make a promise of something to; 6 to furnish reason to expect ‖ *vi* 7 to make a promise; 8 to betoken, augur

Prom'ised Land' *n* 1 Canaan, promised by God to Abraham and his descendants (Gen. 12:7); 2 **promised land** place of expected lasting happiness

prom·is·ing *adj* giving hope of turning out well or successfully ‖ SYN auspicious, hopeful, encouraging (see *propitious*)

prom'is·so'ry note' /-sôr'-, -sōr'-/ *n* written agreement to pay a specified sum of money at a fixed date or on demand, to a designated person or to the bearer

prom·on·to·ry /prŏm'əntôr'ē, -tōr'-/ [L *promunturium*] *n* (*-ries*) high point of land jutting into a body of water; headland

pro·mote /prəmōt'/ [L *promovere* (*-motus*) to move forward] *vt* 1 to help the development of; advance; further; 2 to raise to higher rank; 3 to advance (a pupil) to a higher class; 4 to foster the sale of (a product) through advertising and publicity; 5 *slang* to wangle ‖ **pro·mo'tion** *n* ‖ SYN aid, elevate, patronize, assist, foster, push, dignify, accelerate ‖ ANT discourage, hinder, deter

pro·mot'er *n* 1 one who organizes new businesses or projects or who raises money for them; 2 one who pushes schemes for enriching himself at others' expense

prompt /prŏmpt/ [L *promptus*] *adj* 1 quick to act as occasion demands; 2 immediate, done without delay ‖ *vt* 3 to move to action; 4 to suggest, inspire; 5 to recall or suggest words to (a speaker or actor) ‖ **prompt'ly** *adv* ‖ **prompt'ness** also **promp'ti·tude'** /-t(y)ōōd'/ *n* ‖ SYN *adj* instant, unhesitating, alert, ready, punctual

prompt′er *n* 1 one who rouses to action; 2 person employed to recall forgotten lines to the actors during a play or opera

prom·ul·gate /prom′əlgāt′, prəmul′gāt/ [L *promulgare (-atus)*] *vt* 1 to make known formally and officially; publish; 2 to disseminate (a teaching, creed, etc.) || **prom′ul·ga′tion** /prom′-, prōm′-/ *n* || SYN declare, proclaim, spread, publish

pron. 1 pronoun; 2 pronunciation

prone /prōn′/ [L *pronus* inclined forward] *adj* 1 lying face or front downward; 2 **prone** to inclined or tending to

prong /prôŋ′, proŋ′/ [ME *pronge*] *n* any pointed projecting part, as the tines of a fork or the tip of an antler || **pronged′** *adj*

prong′horn′ *n* swift ruminant (*Antilocapra americana*) resembling an antelope, found on the western plains of North America

pro·nom′i·nal /prō-/ [L *pronominalis*] *adj* 1 pert. to or like a pronoun || *n* 2 pronominal word

pro′noun′ *n* any of a small class of words that may replace nouns and noun phrases, as *he, his, him, it, this, who*

pro·nounce /prənouns′/ [MF *prononcier*] *vt* 1 to articulate (sounds, words, etc.); 2 to speak or utter solemnly or formally, as *to pronounce a benediction;* 3 to declare to be, as *he was pronounced a failure* || *vi* 4 to utter words; 5 to speak with confidence or authority || **pro·nounce′a·ble** *adj* || SYN affirm, declare, deliver, recite, utter

pro·nounced′ *adj* strongly defined; emphatic, decided

pro·nounce′ment *n* formal or authoritative statement

pron·to /pront′ō/ [Sp] *adv slang* quickly, at once

pro·nun·ci·a·men·to /prənun′sē·əment′ō, -shē·ə-/ [Sp *pronunciamiento*] *n* manifesto, declaration

pro·nun·ci·a·tion /prənun′sē·āsh′ən/ [L *pronuntiatio (-onis)* delivery (of a speech)] *n* 1 act of uttering speech sounds; 2 manner of uttering the sounds of a language; 3 phonemic or phonetic transcription

proof /prōōf′/ [OF *prueve* < LL *proba* test] *n* 1 means by which something is shown to be true; 2 state of having been tested and found worthy; 3 convincing argument or evidence; 4 test or trial; 5 standard of strength for distilled liquors; 6 process for testing the correctness of an arithmetical calculation; 7 *typ* trial impression taken from type for correction; 8 *photog* trial print || *adj* 9 being of a standard strength or purity; 10 **proof against** impervious to

-proof *comb form* impervious to or protected from, as *shockproof*

proof′ coin′ *n* one of a small number of coins of a new issue, struck from polished dies on a polished or mat blank

proof′read *v* (-read /-red′/) *vt* 1 to read (printer's proof) in order to indicate corrections || *vt* 2 to read printer's proof in order to indicate corrections || **proof′read′er** *n*

prop¹ /prop/ [ME *proppe*] *n* 1 support or stay || *v* (**propped; prop·ping**) *vt* 2 to support with or as with a prop; 3 to rest against a support

prop² [*property*] *n theat* property 4

prop³ *n aeron* propeller

prop·a·gan·da /prop′əgan′də/ [L (congregatio de) *propaganda* (fide) (congregation for) propagating (the faith)] *n* purported news or facts deliberately spread to propagate a particular ideology or to influence public opinion || **prop′a·gan′dist** *n* || **prop′a·gan′dize** *vt*

prop·a·gate /prop′əgāt′/ [L *propagare (-atus)*] *vt* 1 to cause to increase or multiply by successive production; 2 to circulate, disseminate; 3 to cause to extend or spread in space, as light || *vi* 4 to be produced by generation or other means; 5 to have offspring || **prop′a·ga′tion** *n*

pro·pane /prō′pān/ *n* colorless flammable gas —CH₃CH₂CH₃— found in natural gas and petroleum, used as a fuel

pro·pel /prəpel′/ [L *propellere*] *v* (**-pelled; -pel·ling**) *vt* to drive onward; urge forward; push

pro·pel′lant *n* 1 mixture of a fuel and an oxidizer, used to propel rockets; 2 any propelling agent

pro·pel′ler *n* 1 device with rotating blades for propelling an airplane or ship; 2 any similar device

pro·pen·si·ty /prəpens′itē/ [< L *propensus* inclined] *n* (-ties) natural inclination or tendency || SYN bent, bias, disposition, inclination

prop·er /prop′ər/ [OF *propre* < L *proprius* one's own] *adj* 1 suitable, fitting, appropriate; 2 belonging naturally to some person or thing; 3 according to accepted usage; correct; 4 conventional; respectable; 5 in the strict sense of the word, as *Paris proper* has a small area; 6 Brit thorough || **prop′er·ly** *adv* || SYN convenient, appropriate, seemly, congruous

prop′er frac′tion *n* fraction having the numerator less than the denominator

prop′er noun′ *n* noun referring to a unique person, place, or thing, usu. spelled with an initial capital, as *James, Trenton*

prop′er·tied /-tēd/ *adj* owning substantial property

prop′er·ty [MF *properte*] *n* (-ties) 1 the

things owned by a person; possessions; 2 real estate; 3 essential or characteristic attribute, as of an element; 4 *theat* article required in a play, as a piece of furniture, an ornament, or something used by an actor ‖ SYN peculiarity, characteristic; estate, land, wealth

proph·e·cy /prof'ise̱/ [OF *prophecie* < Gk *propheteia*] *n* (-**cies**) 1 prediction of future events; 2 that which is predicted; 3 any inspired utterance of truths divinely revealed

proph·e·sy /prof'isī'/ [MF *prophesier*] *v* (-**sied**) *vt* 1 to foretell or predict, esp. under divine influence ‖ *vi* 2 to make predictions; 3 to speak under divine inspiration ‖ SYN predict, prognosticate, foreshow (see *foretell*)

proph·et /prof'it/ [Gk *prophetes*] *n* 1 one who predicts the future; 2 one inspired by God to teach his will to men and announce future events; 3 *Bib* person chosen by God to lead the people of Israel; 4 **the Prophet** Muhammad; 5 **the Prophets** *sg* group of books of the Old Testament ‖ **proph'et·ess** *nfem*

pro·phet·ic /prəfet'ik/ *adj* 1 of or pert. to a prophet; 2 of or pert. to prophecy; 3 portentous ‖ **pro·phet'i·cal·ly** *adv*

pro·phy·lac·tic /prō'f'ilak'tik, prof'-/ [Gk *prophylaktikos* guarding] *adj* 1 preventing or guarding against, esp. disease ‖ *n* 2 prophylactic device or medicine, esp. against venereal disease

pro·pin·qui·ty /prōpiŋk'witē/ [L *propinquitas*] *n* nearness in time, space, or blood relationship ‖ SYN vicinity, neighborhood, proximity, nearness

pro·pi·ti·ate /prəpish'ē·āt'/ [L *propitiare* (-*atus*)] *vt* to conciliate or appease ‖ **pro·pi'ti·a'tion** *n* ‖ **pro·pi'ti·a·to'ry** /-tôr'-, -tōr'-/ *adj* ‖ SYN pacify, conciliate, mollify, appease

pro·pi·tious [< L *propitius*] *adj* 1 favorably inclined; 2 favorable ‖ SYN auspicious, promising, prosperous, lucky, friendly, kindly, timely ‖ DISCR That is *auspicious* which is of happy or favorable omen, as an *auspicious* day for a picnic. *Propitious* means favorable, or of favoring influence, as a *propitious* wind aided our journey

prop'jet' *n* 1 turboprop engine; 2 airplane driven by turboprop engine

pro·po·nent /prəpōn'ənt/ [< L *proponere* to propose] *n* 1 one who makes a proposal; 2 advocate; adherent

pro·por·tion /prəpôrsh'ən, -pōrsh'-/ [L *proportio* (-onis) symmetry] *n* 1 comparative relation in size, amount, or degree; ratio; 2 proper relation of all the parts; 3 proportionate share; 4 symmetry; harmony; 5 *math* statement of equality between ratios; 6 **proportions** *pl* dimensions ‖ *vt* 7 to put into proper proportion ‖ **pro·por'tion·al** *adj*

pro·por'tion·al rep're·sen·ta'tion *n* system of voting whereby each party gets legislative representation in proportion to the total votes cast for it

pro·por'tion·ate /-it/ *adj* in correct proportion; proportioned

pro·pos·al /prəpōz'əl/ *n* 1 act of offering something for acceptance; 2 that which is offered; 3 offer of marriage

pro·pose /prəpōz'/ [MF *proposer*] *vt* 1 to offer for consideration or acceptance; 2 to suggest; 3 to intend, purpose; 4 to present (a person) for acceptance, as into membership of a club ‖ *vi* 5 to make an offer of marriage; 6 to form a plan ‖ **pro·pos'er** *n*

prop·o·si·tion /prop'əzish'ən/ [L *propositio* (-onis)] *n* 1 that which is offered for consideration; 2 offer of terms; proposal; 3 plan proposed; 4 presentation of a topic to be discussed in a debate; 5 *logic* statement whose truth or falsity is to be demonstrated; 6 *math* statement of a theorem or problem for solution; 7 *colloq* proposal of illicit sexual relations ‖ *vt* 8 to propose a deal or plan to; 9 *colloq* to propose sexual relations to ‖ SYN *n* plan, intention, measure, topic, proposal

pro·pound' /prə-/ [var of ME *propone*] *vt* to present for consideration

pro·pri·e·tar·y /prəprī'iter'ē/ [ML *proprietarius* owner] *adj* 1 pert. to a proprietor; 2 held under patent or copyright by a private owner, as *a proprietary medicine*

pro·pri'e·tor /-tər/ *n* owner ‖ **pro·pri'e·tor·ship'** *n* ‖ **pro·pri'e·tress** *nfem*

pro·pri'e·ty [L *proprietas*] *n* (-**ties**) 1 state of being proper; 2 conforming to established rule or custom; correctness; 3 **the proprieties** the customs and standards of polite society ‖ SYN appropriateness, decorum, fitness, becomingness

pro·pul·sion /prəpulsh'ən/ [< L *propulsus* propelled] *n* 1 act of propelling or state of being propelled; 2 means of propelling ‖ **pro·pul'sive** *adj*

pro ra·ta /prō rāt'ə, rät'-/ [ML] *adv* proportionately; according to a certain rate ‖ **pro-ra'ta** *adj*

pro·rate /prō'rāt', prōrāt'/ [< *pro rata*] *vt & vi* to divide or assess proportionately ‖ **pro·rat'a·ble** *adj*

pro·rogue /prōrōg'/ [MF *proroger* < L *prorogare*] *vt* 1 to adjourn; 2 to discontinue for an indefinite time, as a session of the British parliament ‖ SYN terminate, suspend (see *adjourn*)

pro·sa·ic /prōzā′ik/ [LL *prosaicus*] *adj* 1 pert. to or resembling prose; 2 commonplace, dull || SYN unimaginative, matter-of-fact, uninteresting

pro·sce·ni·um /prōsēn′ē·əm/ [L < Gk *proskenion*] *n* (-ums or -a /-ə/) *theat* arch separating the stage from the auditorium

pro·sciut·to /prōshoōt′ō/ [It] *n* spiced ham, usu. smoked, served in very thin slices

pro·scribe /prōskrīb′/ [L *proscribere* (-*scriptus*)] *vt* 1 to declare to be outlawed; 2 to forbid; prohibit; 3 to outlaw; banish || **pro·scrip′tion** /-skrip′shən/ *n* || **pro·scrip′tive** *adj*

prose /prōz′/ [L *prosa* (oratio) straightforward (discourse)] *n* 1 ordinary spoken or written language, not verse; 2 tiresome and commonplace talk

pros·e·cute /pros′ikyoōt′/ [L *prosequi* (-*secutus*) to pursue] *vt* 1 to pursue in order to accomplish, as *to prosecute a war*; 2 *law* a to bring suit against in court; b to seek to secure or enforce by court action; c to seek to obtain a conviction against || *vi* 3 to carry on a lawsuit; 4 to conduct a criminal case against a defendant

pros·e·cu′tion *n* 1 act of prosecuting; 2 **the prosecution** the prosecutor and his aids in a criminal case

pros′e·cu′tor *n* 1 district attorney; 2 one who carries on a lawsuit against another

pros·e·lyte /pros′əlīt′/ [Gk *proselytos*] *n* 1 convert to a religion or opinion || *vt & vi* 2 also **pros′e·lyt·ize′** /-li-/ to convert

pros·o·dy /pros′ədē/ [Gk *proso(i)dia* song sung with accompaniment; tone] *n* 1 patterns of stress and intonation in speech; 2 study of meters and versification; 3 system of metrical structure; style of versification

pros′pect /pros′pekt/ [L *prospectus* view] *n* 1 view, scene; 2 anticipation, expectation; 3 potential customer or client; 4 **prospects** *pl* a probability of success or profit; b future outlook || *vt* 5 to explore (a region) for valuable minerals || also *vi* || **prospec·tor** /prospektər/ /prəspek′tər/ *n*

pro·spec·tive /prəspek′tiv/ *adj* 1 likely; expected; 2 future

pro·spec′tus [L = prospect] *n* report outlining or advertising something, as a new issue of stock, a new literary work, etc.

pros·per /pros′pər/ [< L *prosperus* fortunate] *vi* to thrive, flourish

pros′per·ous *adj* 1 prospering; 2 wealthy, well-to-do || **pros·per′i·ty** /-per′-/ *n* || SYN fortunate, successful, auspicious (see *lucky*)

pros′tate (gland′) /pros′tāt/ [Gk *prostates* one who stands before] *n* in males, gland lying around the neck of the bladder and its duct

pros·the·sis /pros′thisis/ [Gk = addition] *n* (-ses /-sēz′/) 1 addition of a letter or syllable to a word, esp. by prefixing; 2 a replacement of an absent part of the body by an artificial one; b the artificial part || **pros·thet′ic** /-thet′-/ *adj*

pros·ti·tute /pros′tit(y)oōt′/ [L *prostituere* (-*tutus*)] to offer for sale] *vt* 1 to put to base use for gain; 2 to offer (oneself) as a prostitute || *n* 3 person who enters into sexual relations for pay || **pros′ti·tu′tion** *n*

pros·trate /pros′trāt/ [L *prostratus* prostrate] *vt* 1 to lay flat, throw down from a standing position; 2 to destroy, ruin; 3 to exhaust; 4 **prostrate oneself** to lie face down on the ground in submission || *adj* 5 lying at full length; 6 lying face down in submission; 7 exhausted; 8 overthrown; helpless

pros·tra′tion *n* 1 act of prostrating or state of being prostrated; 2 great physical or mental depression or exhaustion

pros·y /prōz′ē/ [< *prose*] *adj* (-i·er, -i·est) prosaic

prot- var of proto-

pro·tac·tin·i·um /prō′taktin′ē·əm/ [*prot-* + *actinium*] *n* radioactive metallic element (Pa; at.no.91)

pro·tag·o·nist /prōtag′ənist/ [Gk *protagonistes*] *n* 1 central figure of a literary work; 2 chief supporter or leader of a cause or movement

prot·a·sis /prot′əsis/ [Gk = proposition] *n* (-ses /-sēz′/) clause containing the condition in a conditional sentence

pro·te·an /prōt′ē·ən/ [< *Proteus*, Gk sea god who could change his form at will] *adj* readily taking on different shapes or forms

pro·tect /prətekt′/ [L *protegere* (-*tectus*) to cover in front] *vt* 1 to keep in safety; guard; 2 to shield (home products) from foreign competition by high tariffs || **pro·tec′tor** *n* || **pro·tec′tive** *adj* || **pro·tec′tion** *n* || SYN guard, shield, shelter (see *defend*)

pro·tec′tive tar·iff′ *n* tariff designed to protect home products by raising the price of imports

pro·tec′tor·ate /-it/ *n* 1 control exercised by a strong nation over a weak one; 2 state so controlled

pro·té·gé /prōt′əzhā′, prōt′əzhā′/ [F = protected] *n* one who is under the protection, patronage, or care of another || **pro′té·gée′** *nfem*

pro·te·in /prōt′ē·in, prō′tēn/ [G < Gk *proteios* primary] *n* any of a class of complex organic compounds that contain amino acids as part of their basic structure and are found in all living organisms and required by all life processes

pro tem /prō tem′/ *adv & adj* pro tempore

pro tem·po·re /prō temp′ərē/ [L] *adv* 1 for the time being ‖ *adj* 2 temporary

Prot·er·o·zo·ic /prot′ərəzō′ik, prōt′-/ [< Gk *proteros* former + *zoe* life] *n* era preceding the Paleozoic, having the oldest known animal fossil forms ‖ also *adj*

pro·test /prətest′/ [F *protester* < L *protestari* to declare publicly] *vi* 1 to object strongly; remonstrate ‖ *vt* 2 to make a solemn declaration of; assert; 3 to declare formally to be dishonored by nonpayment or non-acceptance, as a note or bill of exchange; 4 to object strongly to; remonstrate against ‖ /prō′test/ *n* 5 statement or declaration of objection, disapproval, or dissent; 6 notarized declaration that a note, check, or the like has been presented and payment or acceptance refused ‖ **pro·test′er** *n* ‖ **prot·es·ta·tion** /prot′istā′shən/ *n* ‖ SYN *v* assert, affirm, declare, object, disagree

Prot·es·tant /prot′istənt/ *n* member of one of the branches of the Christian church which separated from the Roman Catholic Church during the Reformation in the 16th century ‖ also *adj* ‖ **Prot′es·tant·ism** *n*

Prot·es·tant E·pis′co·pal Church′ *n* independent American church in communion with, and having the same doctrine and forms of worship as the Anglican Church

pro·thon·o·tar·y /prōthon′əter′ē, prōth′-ənōt′ərē/ [Gk *protonotarios*] *n* (-ies) 1 in some states, chief court clerk; 2 R C Ch one of twelve officials who record important pontifical proceedings; 3 *Orthodox Ch* chief secretary of the patriarch of Constantinople

pro·to- [Gk *protos*] *comb form* 1 first, foremost; 2 earliest; 3 *chem* a first of a series of compounds; b containing the smallest amount of an element

pro·to·col /prōt′əkôl, -kol′, -kōl′/ [LGk *protokollon* first leaf glued to a papyrus roll and containing the contents] *n* 1 first draft on which a permanent document, as a treaty, is based; 2 formal code of etiquette for affairs of state

pro·to·lan′guage /prōt′ə-/ *n* hypothetical reconstructed language postulated as the parent form from which a language or group of languages is descended

pro·ton /prō′ton/ [Gk = first] *n* a fundamental constituent of all atomic nuclei, carrying a unit positive charge equal to that of the electron

pro·to·plasm /prōt′əplaz′əm/ *n* complex semifluid substance, the living matter of all plant and animal cells and tissues ‖ **pro′to·plas′mic** *adj*

pro′to·type′ *n* 1 original or pattern; 2 exemplar ‖ **pro′to·typ′i·cal** *adj*

pro·to·zo′an /-zō′ən/ [*proto-* + Gk *zoe* life] *n* microscopic one-celled animal of the phylum Protozoa, which includes the most primitive forms of animal life ‖ also *adj*

pro·to·zo·ol′o·gy *n* branch of zoology dealing with protozoa

pro′to·zo′on /-on, -ən/ *n* (-a /-ə/) *n* protozoan

pro·tract /prōtrakt′/ [L *protrahere* (-*tractus*) to draw forth] *vt* 1 to draw out, prolong; 2 *anat* to protrude, extend; 3 *math* to draw and map with a scale and a protractor ‖ **pro·trac′tion** *n*

pro·trac′tor *n* 1 instrument for plotting and measuring angles on paper; 2 muscle that extends a limb

pro·trude /prōtrōod′/ [L *protrudere* (-*trusus*)] *vt* 1 to thrust forward ‖ *vi* 2 to project ‖ **pro·tru′sion** /-zhən/ *n* ‖ **pro·tru′sive** /-siv/ *adj*

pro·tu·ber·ance /prōt(y)ōob′ərəns/ [< L *protuberans* (-*antis*) protruding] *n* something that protrudes; knob; swelling ‖ **pro·tu′ber·ant** *adj*

proud /proud′/ [OE *prūd* arrogant] *adj* 1 overbearing, haughty; 2 having worthy self-respect, as *too proud to beg;* 3 having a feeling of glad satisfaction, as *proud of a friend's success;* 4 of great dignity, as *a proud name;* 5 spirited, mettlesome, as *the the knight's proud steed;* 6 majestic, stately, as *proud cities* ‖ **proud′ly** *adv* ‖ SYN insolent, disdainful, lordly, arrogant, stately

proud′ flesh′ *n* excessive granulation on an inflamed area in a sore or a healing wound

prove /prōov′/ [OF *prover* < L *probare* to test] *v* (**proved**; **proved** or **prov·en** /prōov′ən/) *vt* 1 to test or try by experiment; 2 to establish the truth of by argument or evidence; 3 to demonstrate the accuracy of (a calculation) ‖ *vi* 4 to turn out to be; 5 prove to be to turn out to be ‖ **prov′a·ble** *adj* ‖ SYN justify, substantiate, manifest, confirm, fix

Pro·ven·çal /prov′ənsäl′, prōv′-/ [< *Provence* district and former province in SE France] *n* 1 local vernacular of S France, a distinct Romance language; 2 speaker of Provençal ‖ also *adj*

prov·en·der /prov′əndər/ [OF *provendre*] *n* 1 dry feed for livestock; 2 food, provisions

pro·ve·ni·ence /prōven′ē·əns, -yəns/ [< L *proveniens* coming forth] *n* source; origin

prov·erb /prov′ərb/ [MF < L *proverbium*] *n* 1 short familiar saying expressing some well-known truth; 2 **Proverbs** *sg* poetical book of the Old Testament ‖ **pro·ver·bi·al** /prəvurb′-**

ē·əl/ *adj* ‖ SYN axiom, precept, maxim, aphorism (see *truism*)

pro·vide /prəvīd'/ [L *providere* to foresee] *vt* 1 to furnish or supply; 2 to stipulate beforehand ‖ *vi* 3 **provide for,** a to support financially; b to take measures to ensure the success of; c to take measures against; 4 **provide against** to take measures against ‖ **pro·vid'er** *n*

pro·vid'ed *conj* on condition that

prov·i·dence /prov'idəns/ [L *providentia* foresight] *n* 1 prudent management; prudence; 2 the care of God for mankind; 3 manifestation of God's care; 4 **Providence** God thought of as watching over mankind

Prov·i·dence *n* capital of Rhode Island (210,000)

prov'i·dent *adj* 1 providing for the future; 2 thrifty ‖ SYN prudent, watchful, thrifty (see *economical*)

prov'i·den'tial /-densh'əl/ *adj* 1 effected by or showing divine providence; 2 fortunate

pro·vid'ing *conj* provided

prov·ince /prov'ins/ [L *provincia*] *n* 1 large administrative division of certain countries, as of Canada, Argentina, and Spain; 2 sphere of action or authority; 3 department of knowledge or activity; 4 district administered by an archbishop; 5 **the provinces** *pl* the parts of a country beyond the capital and the largest cities

pro·vin·cial /prəvinsh'əl/ *adj* 1 of or pert. to a province; 2 rural; unsophisticated; 3 narrow, illiberal ‖ *n* 4 inhabitant of a province; 5 member of a religious order presiding over his order within an ecclesiastical province

pro·vin'cial·ism *n* 1 word, expression, mannerism, or way of thinking peculiar to an outlying district; 2 devotion to the ideas and customs of one special region; 3 narrowness of view; prejudice

prov'ing ground' *n* place for testing something, as a weapon, vehicle, idea, etc.

pro·vi·sion /prəvizh'ən/ [L *provisio* (-*onis*) foreseeing] *n* 1 act of providing something, as food; 2 something provided; 3 care taken beforehand; forethought; 4 clause in a statute or legal instrument stipulating a particular thing; 5 **provisions** *pl* supplies of food

pro·vi'sion·al *adj* temporary; conditional; tentative ‖ **pro·vi'sion·al·ly** *adv*

pro·vi·so /prəvīz'ō/ [L = it being provided] *n* (-sos or -soes) conditional clause or stipulation, as in a legal instrument or statute

prov·o·ca·tion /prov'əkāsh'ən/ [see *provoke*] *n* 1 act of provoking; 2 that which provokes; incitement; instigation

pro·voc·a·tive /prəvok'ətiv/ *adj* tending to provoke; inciting to action, anger, etc. ‖ **pro·voc'a·tive·ly** *adv*

pro·voke /prəvōk'/ [L *provocare*] *vt* 1 to excite or stir up, as emotions or actions; 2 to stir to action; 3 to enrage; offend; irritate ‖ SYN rouse, evoke, vex, exasperate (see *irritate*)

pro·vok'ing *adj* irritating, annoying

prov·ost /prov'əst, prō'vōst/ [OE *profost* < L *propositus* prefect] *n* 1 high executive officer in a university, usu. ranking next to the president; 2 chief ecclesiastical dignitary in a cathedral or collegiate church

pro'vost mar'shal /prōv'ō/ *n* 1 officer in charge of military police; 2 officer in the Navy in charge of prisoners pending and during court-martial

prow /prou/ [MF *proue*] *n* bow of a ship

prow·ess /prou'is/ [OF *proece*] *n* 1 daring bravery; 2 superior ability ‖ SYN gallantry, courage, valor (see *bravery*)

prowl /proul/ [ME *prollen* to search] *vi* 1 to wander stealthily, as for prey or plunder ‖ *vt* 2 to roam over or through, as in search of prey ‖ *n* 3 act of prowling; 4 **on the prowl** in the act of prowling ‖ **prowl'er** *n*

prowl' car' *n* police car that roams the streets to keep order and catch malefactors

prox·im·i·ty /proksim'itē/ [< L *proximus* nearest]. *n* nearness in place, time, or other relation ‖ SYN propinquity, vicinity, neighborhood, nearness

prox·im'i·ty fuze' *n* fuze that detonates a charge in the vicinity of the target rather than on contact

prox·y /prok'sē/ [contr. of *procuracy* a procuring] *n* (-ies) 1 position or powers of one authorized to act for another; 2 person so authorized; 3 document granting such power

prude /prood'/ [F] *n* person excessively modest or proper in dress, conduct, and speech ‖ **prud'ish** *adj* ‖ **prud'er·y** *n*

pru·dent /prood'ənt/ [L *prudens* (-*entis*)] *adj* 1 wise in practical things; 2 careful, cautious; 3 careful for the future ‖ **pru'dent·ly** *adv* ‖ **pru'dence** *n* ‖ SYN practical, frugal, farseeing, forehanded (see *careful*) ‖ ANT careless, indiscreet, unmindful, heedless

prune[1] /proon'/ [MF *proognier*] *vt* 1 to trim off unwanted twigs and branches from; 2 to cut and clear away (anything considered superfluous)

prune[2] [MF < L *prunum* plum] *n* dried plum

pru·ri·ent /proor'ē·ənt/ [L *pruriens* (-*entis*) itching] *adj* lewd in thought or desire; lustful; lascivious ‖ **pru'-ri·ence** *n*

pru·ri·tus /prŏŏrīt′əs/ [L] *n* itching

Prus·sia /prush′ə/ *n* former powerful kingdom in N central Europe, archetype of the ruthless militaristic state; nucleus of the German Empire of 1871–1918 and chief state of the Weimar republic; dissolved in 1947 || **Prus′sian** *adj & n*

pry[1] /prī′/ [ME *prien*] *v* (**pried**) *vi* to look inquisitively, esp. into something that is not one's business

pry[2] [< *prize*[2]] *v* (**pried**) *vt* 1 to raise, open, or detach with a lever; 2 to separate, get away, or ferret out, as *he pried the secret from her* || *n* (**pries**) 3 bar used as a lever; 4 leverage

P.S. Public School

P.S., p.s. postscript

psalm /säm′/ [OE < Gk *psalmos* song with the harp] *n* 1 sacred song or hymn, esp. one contained in the Book of Psalms; 2 **Psalms** *sg* book of the Old Testament containing psalms and prayers || **psalm′ist** *n*

psal·mo·dy /säm′ədē, sal′mə-/ [Gk *psalmo(i)dia* singing to the harp] *n* (**-dies**) 1 writing or singing of psalms; 2 psalms collectively

Psal·ter /sôlt′ər/ [Gk *psalterion* stringed instrument] *n* the Book of Psalms, esp. when arranged for use in church services

pseu·do /sōōd′ō/ [< *pseudo-*] *adj* false, spurious

pseu·do- [< Gk *pseudes* false] *comb form* false, spurious

pseu′do·nym /sōōd′ə-/ *n* 1 fictitious name; 2 pen name || **pseu·don′y·mous** /-don′iməs/ *adj*

pshaw /shô′/ *interj* expression of contempt, impatience, etc.

psi /sī′/ *n* twenty-third letter of the Greek alphabet Ψ, ψ

psi, p.s.i. pounds per square inch

psit·ta·co·sis /sit′əkōs′is/ [< Gk *psittakos* parrot] *n* severe infectious disease transmitted to man by parrots

pso·ri·a·sis /sərī′əsis/ [< Gk *psora* itch] *n* chronic skin disease characterized by scaly red patches

psych. 1 psychological; 2 psychology

psych- [< *psyche*] *comb form* 1 mind, mental processes; 2 psychological; 3 mental

Psy·che /sīk′ē/ [Gk = soul] *n* 1 *Gk myth.* beautiful maiden symbolic of the soul, beloved of Eros, god of love; 2 **psyche,** a soul; b mind

psych·e·del·ic /sīk′idel′ik/ [*psych-* + Gk *delos* manifest; coined by Humphry Osmond in 1956] *adj* 1 noting a mental state of euphoria and heightened perception bordering on hallucination; 2 (drug) producing this effect

psy·chi·a·try /sīkī′ətrē, sī-/ *n* branch of medicine dealing with the treatment of mental disorders || **psy·chi′a·trist** *n* || **psy·chi·at·ric** /sīk′ē·at′rik/ *adj*

psy·chic /sīk′ik/ *adj* 1 pert. to the soul or mind; 2 pert. to occult nonphysical phenomena; 3 pert. to mental phenomena unexplainable by physical means; 4 (person) sensitive to supernatural forces || *n* 5 psychic person

psy·cho /sīk′ō/ *slang adj* 1 psychopathic || *n* 2 psychopath

psy·cho- var of **psych-**

psy′cho·a·nal′y·sis *n* (**-ses** /-sēz′/) method of treating psychoneuroses by analyzing unconscious mental processes and bringing them out to the consciousness of the patient || **psy′cho·an′a·lyst** *n* || **psy′cho·an′a·lyze′** *vt*

psy′cho·log′i·cal mo′ment /sī′kələj′ikəl/ *n* critical time to take action for maximum effect

psy′cho·log′i·cal war′fare *n* organized effort to create confusion among the enemy or opposition by means of threats and propaganda

psy·chol·o·gy /sīkol′əjē/ *n* (**-gies**) 1 science of the mind and of human nature; 2 science of human and animal behavior; 3 mental characteristics of an individual or group; 4 a system of psychology; 5 use **psychology on** *colloq* to take subtle advantage of the known weaknesses or predilections of || **psy·chol′o·gist** *n*

psy′cho·neu·ro′sis /sīk′ō-/ *n* (**-ses** /-sēz′/) emotional disorder characterized by anxiety, obsession, and psychosomatic complaints

psy·cho·path /sī′kəpath′/ *n* 1 mentally ill person; 2 psychopathic personality

psy′cho·path′ic per′son·al′i·ty *n* person characterized by antisocial behavior and extreme selfishness, and by inability to establish a meaningful relationship with other people

psy′cho·pa·thol′o·gy /-pəthol′-/ *n* science dealing with mental diseases and abnormalities

psy′cho·sci′enc·es *npl* sciences dealing with the mind and mental behavior, with mental diseases and disorders, and with the treatment and cure of mental diseases and disorders, as psychology, psychoanalysis, and psychiatry

psy·cho·sis /sīkōs′is/ [Gk = giving of life] *n* (**-ses** /-sēz′/) any severe mental disorder || **psy·chot′ic** /-kot′-/ *adj & n*

psy′cho·so·mat′ic *adj* pert. to symptoms of physical illness due to the mental and emotional state of the patient rather than physical causes

psy′cho·ther′a·py *n* treatment of mental disorders by psychological and psychoanalytical methods || **psy′cho·ther′a·pist** *n*

Pt *chem* platinum

pt, p.t. past tense

pt. 1 part; 2 pint(s); 3 point; 4 preterit

P.T. Pacific Time

P.T.A. Parent-Teacher Association

ptar·mi·gan /tär'migən/ [Gael *tarmachan*] *n* a grouse (genus *Lagopus*) of northern regions, having feathered feet

P'T' boat' *n* torpedo boat

pter·o·dac·tyl /ter'ədak'til/ [< Gk *pteron* wing + *daktylos* finger] *n* extinct flying reptile having featherless wing membranes between the body, arm, and elongated fifth finger

Ptol·e·my /tol'əmē/ *n* (ab. 100–170 A.D.) Hellenistic astronomer, geographer, and mathematician, formulator of the theory of the geocentric solar system ‖ **Ptol'e·ma'ic** /-mā'ik/ *adj*

pto·maine /tō'mān, tōmān'/ [It *ptomaina* < Gk *ptoma* dead body] *n* any of a class of alkaloid substances found in decaying organic matter, often highly poisonous

Pu *chem* plutonium

pub /pub'/ *n Brit colloq* public house

pub. 1 public; 2 publication; 3 publisher

pu·ber·ty /pyōōb'ərtē/ [L *pubertas* age of maturity] *n* earliest age at which a person can beget or bear children

pu·bes·cent /pyōōbes'ənt/ [< L *pubescere* to attain puberty] *adj* 1 arrived at puberty; 2 *bot & zool* covered with soft downy hairs ‖ **pu·bes'cence** *n*

pu·bic /pyōōb'ik/ [< L *pubes* groin, pubic hair] *adj* pert. to or situated at the lower part of the abdomen adjacent to the genitals

pub·lic /pub'lik/ [L *publicus*] *adj* 1 of, pert. to, affecting, belonging to, done for, open to, or in the name of all the people; 2 open, generally known, as *a public scandal*; 3 maintained at public expense ‖ *n* 4 the **public,** a the people as a whole, all the people; b that portion of the public with a specified common interest, as *the stock-buying public*; 5 **go public** to make a publicly-owned corporation of a private one by selling stock to the public; 6 **in public** openly, publicly ‖ **pub'lic·ly** *adv*

pub'lic-ad·dress' sys'tem *n* communications system with a microphone and loudspeakers making speech, music, etc. audible to many people distant from the source, as in a large auditorium or arena, or in the halls of a hospital to summon a doctor

pub'li·can /-ən/ [L *publicanus*] *n* 1 in ancient Rome, tax collector; 2 *Brit colloq* keeper of a public house

pub'li·ca'tion /< L *publicare* to make public] *n* 1 act of publishing or state of being published; 2 public announcement; 3 that which is published, esp. a magazine or journal

pub'lic con·ven'ience *n* rest room available to the public, sometimes for a charge

pub'lic con·vey'ance *n* scheduled

means of transportation available to the public at fixed rates

pub'lic de·fend'er *n* lawyer appointed to represent indigent defendants in criminal cases at public expense

pub'lic do·main' *n* 1 condition of an author's or composer's work not protected by copyright or on which the copyright has expired; 2 land owned by the state or the national government

pub'lic house' *n Brit* tavern or inn

pub'li·cist *n* 1 press agent; 2 writer on public or political affairs; 3 expert in international law

pub·lic'i·ty /-lis'-/ *n* 1 public notice; state of being widely known; 2 process or business of procuring public notice; 3 news stories, pictures, etc., issued to secure public notice

pub'li·cize *vt* to give publicity to

pub'lic re·la'tions *npl* 1 public opinion regarding a specific person, company, government, or other entity; 2 *sg* art or business of promoting good will

pub'lic school' *n* 1 tax-supported elementary or high school open to and compulsory for all children; 2 *Brit* private boarding secondary school for boys ‖ **pub'lic-school'** *adj*

pub'lic serv'ant *n* government official; anyone whose salary comes from taxes

pub'lic-spir'it·ed *adj* having zeal for the public welfare

pub'lic u·til'i·ty *n* business that supplies an essential commodity to the public, as water, electricity, telephones, or transportation, and is regulated by the government, esp. as to rates

pub'lish /pub'lish/ [MF *puplier*] *vt* 1 to make known; announce or proclaim; 2 to have printed and offer for sale or distribution to the public ‖ *vi* 3 to publish or cause to be published books, periodicals, or articles ‖ **pub'lish·er** *n*

puck /puk'/ [< *poke*²] *n* hard rubber disk used in hockey

puck'er [prob < *poke*¹] *vt* 1 to gather into small folds; wrinkle ‖ *vi* 2 to wrinkle; 3 **pucker up** *slang* to protrude the lips for kissing

puck'ish [OE *pūca* sprite] *adj* impish; mischievous

pud·ding /pōōd'iŋ/ [ME *poding*] kind of sausage] *n* soft dessert made of flour, milk, eggs, and various other ingredients

pud·dle /pud'əl/ [OE *pudd* ditch] *n* 1 small pool, esp. of dirty water left after a rain ‖ *vt* 2 to make muddy; 3 to subject (iron) to puddling ‖ **pud'dler** *n*

pud'dling *n* conversion of molten pig iron into wrought iron by oxidation of silicon and carbon through the action of the flame or by the addition of scale and scrap iron, and the ultimate elimination of carbon and other impurities

pu·den·dum /pyōōden'dəm/ [L = thing to be ashamed of] *n* (**-da** /-də/) 1 vulva; 2 **pudenda** *pl* external genitals

pudg·y /puj'ē/ [?] *adj* (**-i·er**; **-i·est**) short and fat; dumpy

pueb·lo /pweb'lō/ [Sp = town] *n* 1 in SW U.S., Indian communal dwelling of adobe, often several stories high; 2 **Pueblo** member of one of the tribes of Indians living in pueblos

pu·er·ile /pyōō'ərǐl/ [< L *puer* boy] *adj* 1 pert. to childhood; 2 foolish; childish || **pu'er·il'i·ty** /-ǐl'-/ *n* (**-ties**)

pu·er'per·al fe'ver /pyōō·urp'ərəl/ [< L *puer* child + *parus* bearing] *n* infection occurring during or immediately after childbirth

Puer·to Ri·co /pwert'ō rēk'ō/ *n* Spanish-speaking island in the West Indies E of the Dominican Republic, a commonwealth associated with the U.S. (3,000,000; 3435 sq.m.; cap. San Juan) || **Puer'to Ri'can** *adj & n*

puff /puf'/ [OE *pyffan*] *n* 1 short quick blast, as of wind or breath; 2 short emission, as of smoke or vapor; 3 draw, as on a pipe or cigar; 4 powder puff; 5 swelling; 6 pastry shaped like a ball filled with cream; 7 exaggerated praise || *vt* 8 to send out air, smoke, breath, etc., in short puffs; 9 to breathe quick and hard; 10 to take puffs, as at a cigar; 11 to move with puffs, as a locomotive; 12 **puff up, a** to swell up; **b** to swell with importance || *vt* 13 to blow, drive, etc., with whiffs or puffs, 14 to smoke, as a cigar; 15 to praise exaggeratedly; 16 **puff up** to swell, distend, as with air || **puff'y** *adj* (**-i·er**; **-i·est**)

puff'ball' *n* any of various ball-shaped fungi which emit a cloud of spores when broken

puf·fin /puf'in/ [ME *puffyn*] *n* any of various northern sea birds (genera *Fratercula* and *Lunda*) with duck-shaped bodies and large bills

puff' paste' *n* dough used in making light flaky pastries

pug[1] /pug'/ [?] *n* one of a breed of small dogs with a short broad nose, wrinkled face, and tightly curled tail

pug[2] *n slang* pugilist

pu·gil·ism /pyōō'jǐliz'əm/ [< L *pugil* boxer] *n* art or practice of boxing || **pu'gil·ist** *n* || **pu'gil·is'tic** *adj*

pug·na·cious /pugnāsh'əs/ [< L *pugnax* (-*acis*)] *adj* inclined to fight; quarrelsome, bellicose || **pug·nac'i·ty** /-nas'-/ *n* || SYN belligerent, disputatious, contentious, fighting

pug' nose' *n* nose turned up and broadened at the tip || **pug'-nosed'** *adj*

pu·is·sant /pyōō'isənt, pyōō·is'ənt, pwis'ənt/ [< ME < MF < VL *po-*

tiens (-*entis*) < L *posse* to be able] *adj* powerful; mighty; strong || **pu'·is·sance** *n*

puke /pyōōk'/ [?] *vt & vi slang* to vomit

Pu·las·ki, Cas·i·mir /kaz'imir' pōōlas'-kē/ *n* (1748-79) Polish patriot and general in the American Revolutionary army

pul·chri·tude /pulk'rǐt(y)ōōd'/ [L *pulchritudo*] *n* beauty || **pul'chri·tu'di·nous** *adj*

Pu·litz·er Prize' /pōōl'itsər, pyōōl'-/ [Joseph *Pulitzer* (1847-1911) Hungarian-born Am journalist] *n* one of several annual prizes in journalism, literature, music, etc.

pull /pōōl'/ [OE *pullian* to pluck] *vt* 1 to draw toward a particular direction; 2 to draw or tug at; 3 to drag, haul; 4 to draw out, as a tooth or knife; 5 to remove; 6 to attract (votes); 7 to rend or tear; 8 to pluck; 9 to restrain (a race horse); 10 to soften the effect of (punches); 11 to strain (a muscle); 12 to hit (a ball) so as to cause it to curve from a straight path; 13 *typ* to make (a proof) by taking an impression of type; 14 **pull off** *slang* to accomplish (something spectacular); 15 **pull oneself together, a** to recover from adversity; **b** to regain one's composure; 16 **pull someone's leg** to tease a person || *vi* 17 to draw forcibly; tug; 18 to inhale, as through a pipe or cigar; 19 to move (away, ahead, back, etc.); 20 **pull back, a** to withdraw; **b** to fall back, retreat; 21 **pull for** *colloq* to support; encourage; 22 **pull in** to arrive at a station, as a bus or train; 23 **pull out** to depart; 24 **pull over** to drive a vehicle to the curb or roadside and stop; 25 **pull through** to survive, as from an illness; 26 **pull up** to halt || *n* 27 act of pulling; 28 pulling power; 29 sustained effort; 30 *slang* influence by which one attains favors, advantage, etc.; 31 handle of a doorbell, drawer, etc.

pull'back' *n* 1 act of pulling back; 2 restraint; curtailment; 3 orderly withdrawal of troops; 4 device that holds or pulls something back

pul·let /pōōl'it/ [MF *poulet*] *n* young hen

pul·ley /pōōl'ē/ [MF *polie*] *n* 1 wheel with a broad flat rim, used with a belt to transmit power; 2 wheel with a grooved rim turning in a frame, used with a rope or chain for raising or moving heavy weights

Pull·man (car') /pōōl'mən/ [George M. *Pullman* (1831-97) U.S. inventor] *n* railroad parlor car or sleeping car

pull'o'ver *n* sweater or shirt that must be pulled over the head

pul·mo·nar·y /pul'mənər·ē, pōōl'-/ [< L *pulmo* (-*onis*) lung] *adj* pert. to or affecting the lungs

Pul'mo'tor /pul'-, pōōl'-/ [trademark] *n* device for artificial respiration by forcing oxygen into the lungs

pulp /pulp'/ [L *pulpa*] *n* **1** soft fleshy part of an animal or vegetable body, as of fruit; **2** any soft formless mass; **3** soft mass of ground linen, cotton, or wood, from which paper is made; **4** inner sensitive substance of a tooth; **5** magazine or book printed on cheap paper, containing lurid stories of small literary value ‖ *vt* **6** to make into pulp; **7** to remove the pulp from ‖ *vi* **8** to become pulpy ‖ **pulp'y** *adj* (-i·er; -i·est)

pul·pit /pōōlp'it, pulp'-/ [L *pulpitum* platform] *n* **1** raised stand in a church from which the clergyman delivers the sermon or conducts the service; **2** the clergy collectively

pul·que /pōōl'ke̯/ [MexSp] *n* fermented drink made from the sap of certain Mexican plants

pul·sar /pul'sär/ [*pulsate* + stell*ar*] *n* galactic source of radio energy of short duration

pul·sate /pul'sāt/ [L *pulsare* (-*atus*) to beat] *vi* **1** to expand and contract rhythmically; throb; **2** to vibrate ‖ **pul·sa'tion** *n*

pulse /puls'/ [L *pulsus* beat] *n* **1** regular throbbing in an artery, which may be felt with the finger; **2** regular stroke or beat ‖ *vi* **3** to pulsate

pul·ver·ize /pul'vəriz'/ [< L *pulvis* (-*eris*) dust] *vt* **1** to reduce to powder or dust by crushing, grinding, etc.; **2** *slang* to defeat utterly ‖ *vi* **3** to be reduced to powder or dust ‖ **pul'ver·i·za'tion** *n*

pu·ma /pyōōm'ə/ [Sp < Quechua] *n* cougar

pum·ice /pum'is/ [MF *pomis*] *n* porous volcanic rock, used as an abrasive and polish

pum·mel /pum'əl/ [var of *pommel*] *v* (-meled or -melled; -mel·ing or -mel·ling) *vt* to beat, pound

pump¹ /pump'/ [ME *pumpe*] *n* **1** device for raising, circulating, moving, compressing, or exhausting fluids, by means of a piston or rotating vanes ‖ *vt* **2** to raise or move with a pump; **3** to remove water or other fluids from; **4** to inflate (a tire); **5** to operate by moving a lever similar to a pump handle; **6** to draw out by artful questions; **7** to question persistently ‖ **pump'er** *n*

pump² [?] *n* low shoe without lacing

pump'-ac'tion *adj* (rifle or shotgun) having an action that ejects the fired cartridge and loads a new one into the firing chamber by means of a lever that slides back and forth under the barrel

pum'per·nick'el [G dial. = a devil breaking wind] *n* dark bread made of coarse rye flour

pump' gun' *n* pump-action rifle or shotgun

pump·kin /pump'kin, puŋk'in/ [*dim.* of ME *pumpion*] *n* **1** plant (*Cucurbita pepo*) of the gourd family, with large, round, orange-yellow, edible fruit; **2** the fruit

pump' prim'ing *n* spending of government funds in commercial enterprises in an effort to stave off or recover from an economic recession

pump' room' *n* room or hall at a spa where mineral water flows

pump'-stor'age plant' *n* electric power plant in which water is pumped up above a river or reservoir when demand is low and released to generate power when demand is greatest

pun /pun'/ [?] *n* **1** humorous play on the different meanings of a word or on the similar meaning and/or sound of different words ‖ *vt* (**punned; pun·ning**) *vi* **2** to make puns ‖ *vt* **3** to ply or annoy with puns

punch¹ /punch'/ [ME *punchen*] *n* **1** blow or thrust, as with the fist; **2** *colloq* force, energy ‖ *vt* **3** to strike with the fists; **4** *W U.S. colloq* to drive (cattle); **5** to depress (a key, as on a typewriter or adding machine, or a button, as on a computer)

punch² [< *obs puncheon*] *n* **1** tool for making dents or holes; **2** machine tool for stamping and forming sheet-metal articles ‖ *vt* **3** to perforate, stamp, or form with a punch

punch³ [Hindi *pānch* five < original number of ingredients] *n* drink made with fruit juices, sugar, spices, etc., often with wine or spirits added

Punch [< *Punchinello* character in It puppet show] *n* **1** hunchbacked puppet with a hooked nose, hero in a farcical puppet show; **2 pleased as Punch** highly delighted

punch'board' *n* gambling game consisting of a small board filled with perforated disks containing concealed lucky numbers which are punched out by the players

punch' bowl' *n* large bowl from which a beverage is served with a ladle

punch' card' *n* card in which holes have been punched in order to record and reproduce all kinds of data

punch'-drunk' *adj* **1** suffering concussion from repeated blows on the head; **2** *colloq* dazed, bewildered

punched' tape' *n* paper tape with holes punched in it to store and retrieve information

punch'ing bag' *n* inflated or stuffed ball suspended so that it may be struck with the fists for exercise

punch' line' *n* phrase or sentence which sums up a statement or a humorous story with telling effect

punch'y *adj* (-i·er; -i·est) punch-drunk

punc·til·i·o /puŋktil'ē·ō'/ [It *puntiglio*]

n precise point in conduct or ceremony; meticulous exactness

punc·til·i·ous *adj* strict or precise in conduct; very formal || **punc·til′i·ous·ly** *adv* || SYN scrupulous, correct, particular, ceremonious

punc·tu·al /puŋk′chōō-əl/ [< L *punctum* point] *adj* precisely on time; prompt || **punc′tu·al′i·ty** /-al′-/ *n*

punc′tu·ate [ML *punctuare* (-*atus*) to define] *vt* 1 to mark with punctuation marks; 2 to emphasize; 3 to interrupt || **punc′tu·a′tion** *n*

punc′tu·a′tion mark′ *n* any of a group of conventional marks, as the period, comma, question mark, etc., used to clarify meaning by transferring to writing certain phenomena of speech not shown by the alphabet, as juncture, pauses, pitch, and stress

punc·ture /puŋk′chər/ [LL *punctura*] *vt* 1 to pierce or perforate; 2 to make (a hole) by perforating || *vi* 3 to become punctured || *n* 4 act of puncturing; 5 hole made by puncturing

pun·dit /pun′dit/ [Hindi *pandit* scholar] *n* 1 Brahman learned in Sanskrit and Hinduism; 2 any man of great learning; 3 solemn commentator

pun·gent /pun′jənt/ [< L *pungere* to prick] *adj* 1 stinging or biting to the taste or smell; 2 sarcastic, caustic; 3 mentally stimulating || **pun′gen·cy** *n* || SYN acrid, sharp, stimulating, bitter (see *piquant*)

Pu·nic /pyōō′ik/ [L *Punicus* Phoenician] *adj* 1 of or pert. to the ancient Carthaginians; 2 treacherous; deceitful

Pu′nic Wars′ *npl* wars waged by Rome against Carthage (264–241; 218–201; 149–146 B.C.) as a result of which Carthage was defeated and annexed

pun·ish /pun′ish/ [MF *punir* (-*niss*-)] *vt* 1 to cause to pay the penalty of a crime or fault, as by fine, imprisonment, pain, or death; 2 to impose a penalty for (an offense) || **pun′ish·a·ble** *adj* || **pun′ish·ment** *n* || SYN discipline, chastise, castigate (see *chasten*)

pu·ni·tive /pyōō′nitiv/ *adj* pert. to, involving, or inflicting punishment

punk¹ /puŋk′/ [?] *n* 1 partly decayed wood; tinder; 2 prepared substance in stick form that smolders when lit; used to light fuses

punk² [?] *slang n* 1 inexperienced youngster; 2 petty criminal; 3 worthless person, good-for-nothing || *adj* 4 of very poor quality; 5 low, weak

pun′ster *n* one given to punning

punt /punt′/ [OE < L *ponto* pontoon] *n* 1 flat-bottomed boat with square ends propelled with a pole; 2 *football* kick in which the ball is dropped and kicked before it reaches the ground || *vt* 3 to propel (a boat) with a pole; 4 to kick (a dropped

football) before it touches the ground || *vi* 5 to punt a boat; 6 to punt a football || **punt′er** *n*

pu·ny /pyōō′ē/ [AF *puisne* (child) born after] *adj* (-**ni·er**; -**ni·est**) small in strength, size, or importance; weak, feeble

pup /pup′/ [< *puppy*] *n* 1 young dog, puppy; 2 young of several other animals, as the seal

pu·pa /pyōō′pə/ [L = girl, doll] *n* (-**pae** /-pē/ or -**pas**) quiescent stage in the metamorphosis of many insects, spent usu. within a chrysalis or cocoon, during which the larva changes into an adult || **pu′pal** *adj*

pu·pil¹ /pyōō′pəl/ [MF *pupille* < L *pupillus* orphan, ward] *n* young person in the care of a teacher || SYN student, learner, youth (see *scholar*)

pu·pil² [L *pupilla*] *n* expanding and contracting opening in the iris of the eye, through which rays of light pass to the retina

pup·pet /pup′it/ [MF *poupette*] *n* 1 small doll representing a human being or animal, moved by wires, rods, or the hands, usu. appearing with others on a small stage; 2 one who is under the influence and control of another; 3 doll

pup′pet·eer′ *n* one who manipulates puppets or marionettes, esp. for entertainment

pup′pet gov′ern·ment *n* government which on the surface seems to be autonomous but which is actually controlled by another power

pup·py /pup′ē/ [MF *poupee* doll] *n* (-**pies**) young dog

pup′py love′ *n* adolescent infatuation

pup′ tent′ *n* small portable tent for two people

pur·blind′ /pur′-/ [ME *pur blind* pure blind] *adj* 1 almost blind; 2 mentally shortsighted; obtuse

pur·chase /purch′əs/ [AF *purchaser* to seek, procure] *vt* 1 to buy; 2 to acquire by effort || *n* 3 act of purchasing; 4 thing purchased; 5 firm grasp or footing; 6 effective hold or leverage in raising or moving heavy bodies || **pur′chas·er** *n* || **pur′chas·a·ble** *adj*

pur·dah /purd′ə/ [Hindi *pardah* curtain] *n* 1 curtain or screen used in India to hide women from public view; 2 custom of thus secluding women

pure /pyōōr′/ [OF *pur* < L *purus*] *adj* 1 free from foreign or adulterating matter; 2 utter; sheer; 3 chaste; innocent; 4 clean, unsullied; 5 guiltless; 6 genuine; 7 abstract, theoretical, as *pure science*; 8 simple, chaste (language, style); 9 monophthongal (vowel) || **pure′ly** *adv* || **pure′ness** *n* || SYN undefiled, chaste, guileless, stainless, absolute, mere, genuine || ANT polluted, adulterated, impure

pure′bred′ *n* animal whose ancestors

derive for many generations from a recognized breed ‖ also *adj*

pu·rée /pyŏŏrā′, pyŏŏr′ā/ [F] *n* 1 cooked food strained through a sieve; 2 soup of puréed ingredients ‖ *vt* 3 to make a purée of

pur·ga·tive /purg′ətiv/ [LL *purgativus*] *adj* 1 purging or cleansing ‖ *n* 2 purging medicine; cathartic

pur·ga·to·ry /purg′ətôr′ē̆, -tōr′-/ [ML *purgatorium*] *n* (-ries) 1 R C Ch state or place in which souls are purified after death from venial sins by suffering; 2 any place of torment or misery

purge /purj′/ [OF *purger*] *vt* 1 to cleanse or free of impurities or of anything undesirable; 2 to rid (a nation, party, organization, etc.) of persons regarded as disloyal; 3 to clear of guilt; 4 to wipe from one's record, as an accusation or offense; 5 to empty (the bowels) by the action of a cathartic ‖ *n* 6 act or process of purging; 7 purgative

pu·ri·fy /pyŏŏr′-/ *v* (-fied) *vt* 1 to make pure; free from that which contaminates, adulterates, or debases; 2 to free from guilt; 3 to make ceremonially clean ‖ **pu′ri·fi·ca′tion** *n*

Pu·rim /pŏŏr′im/ [Heb = lots] *n* Jewish feast celebrated about March 1 to commemorate the deliverance of the Jews in Persia from destruction (Esther 8:3–14)

pur·ist /pyŏŏr′ist/ *n* one who observes and insists on the strictest purity in language, style, etc. ‖ **pu·ris′tic** *adj* ‖ **pur′ism** *n*

pu·ri·tan /pyŏŏr′itən/ [< *purity*] *n* 1 one who is excessively strict in religion and morals; 2 Puritan one of a sect rising in the 16th and 17th centuries within the Church of England who sought reforms in doctrine and worship and strictness in morals ‖ **pu′ri·tan/i·cal** /-tan′-/ *adj*

pu′ri·ty [OF *purte* < L *puritas*] *n* state or quality of being pure

purl /purl′/ [*obs* pirl to twist] *n* 1 embroidered or puckered border; 2 reversed stitch in knitting, used to produce a ribbed effect ‖ *vt* 3 to ornament with an embroidered border; 4 to reverse (stitches) in knitting ‖ *vi* 5 to reverse stitches in knitting

pur·lieus /pur′l(y)ōōz/ [< AF *purale* a going through (influenced by F *lieu* place)] *npl* adjacent districts; environs

pur·loin /pərloin′/ [OF *purloignier*] *vt* & *vi* to steal

pur·ple /purp′əl/ [OE < L *purpura*] *n* 1 color resulting from the blending of blue and red; 2 deep crimson; 3 robe of this color, formerly worn by royalty; 4 royal power and dignity; 5 rank or office of a cardinal; 6 **born to the purple** of high or royal birth ‖ *adj* 7 of the color purple; 8 regal;

9 excessively ornate (prose) ‖ *vt* 10 to color purple ‖ *vi* 11 to become purple

Pur′ple Heart′ *n* medal awarded to members of the U.S. Armed Forces for wounds received in action

pur′plish *adj* somewhat purple

pur·port /pur′pôrt, -pōrt/ [AF *purporter* to convey] *n* 1 apparent purpose, intention; import ‖ /also purpôrt′, -pōrt′/ *vt* 2 to profess, claim; 3 to signify; imply

pur·pose /purp′əs/ [OF *purposer* to propose] *vt* 1 to intend; 2 to resolve ‖ *n* 3 design, intention; 4 end or aim desired; 5 resoluteness; 6 **on purpose** intentionally ‖ **pur′pose·ful** *adj* ‖ SYN *n* plan, intent, object, aim (see *design*)

pur′pose·ly *adv* intentionally; deliberately

purr /pur′/ [imit] *n* 1 low murmuring of a cat when pleased ‖ *vi* 2 to utter a purr

purse /purs′/ [OE *purs* < ML *bursa*] *n* 1 small bag or pouch for money; 2 woman's handbag; 3 sum of money offered as a prize or present; 4 treasury; wealth ‖ *vt* 5 to pucker or wrinkle

purs′er *n* ship's officer in charge of accounts

purse′ strings′ *npl* control of the disposition of money, as in a household

pur·su·ance /pərsōō′əns/ *n* carrying out, as of a plan or order

pur·su′ant *adj* & *adv* **pursuant to** in accordance with

pur·sue /pərsōō′/ [AF *pursuer*] *vt* 1 to chase with the aim of overtaking; 2 to stick to, attend, as *ill luck pursued him*; 3 to seek; 4 to follow, continue, as *studies or a course of action*; 5 to continue to annoy or trouble ‖ **pur·su′er** *n* ‖ SYN seek, chase, hunt (see *follow*)

pur·suit /pərsōōt′/ *n* 1 act of pursuing; 2 quest; 3 occupation ‖ SYN employment, profession (see *business*)

pu·ru·lent /pyŏŏr′(y)ələnt/ [L *purulentus*] *adj* pert. to, consisting of, containing, like, or discharging pus ‖ **pu′ru·lence** *n*

pur·vey /pərvā′/ [AF *purveier*] *vt* to provide, as food, provisions, information, gossip, etc. ‖ **pur·vey′ance** *n* ‖ **pur·vey′or** *n*

pur·view /pur′-/ *n* 1 extent or scope of anything; 2 range of vision, experience, or the like

pus /pus′/ [L] *n* yellowish viscid substance occurring in abscesses and inflamed sores

push /pŏŏsh′/ [MF *pousser*] *vt* 1 to press against with force for the purpose of moving; 2 to make by pushing, as one's way; 3 to urge; 4 to press by persistent effort; 5 to press hard on (a person) in order to make him do something ‖ *vi* 6 to exert steady effort; shove; **7 push ahead** to advance steadily; **8 push off** *colloq* to depart; **9 push on** to continue forward ‖ *n* **10** thrust, shove; **11** vigorous effort or attack; **12** *colloq* enterprise; energy ‖ SYN *v* shove, thrust, force, drive, prosecute, extend

push′ but′ton *n* small knob which, when pushed, closes and/or opens an electric circuit directly or through a relay

push′-but′ton *adj* **1** operated by a push button or as by a push button; **2** using automatic or remote-control means for performing a mission against an enemy

push′ cart′ *n* cart pushed by hand as by a vendor or by a customer in a self-service store

push′er *n slang* narcotics peddler

Push·kin, Alexander /pŏosh′kin/ *n* (1799–1837) Russian poet and dramatist

push′o′ver *n slang* **1** something easily done; **2** person or group easily persuaded or defeated

push′-pull′ *n* circuitry in which two vacuum tubes are connected in such a way that their grid voltages complement each other in the combined amplified plate voltage ‖ also *adj*

push′up′ *n* exercise in which a person raises his body from a prone position by bending his arms while keeping his hands on the floor and his back straight

push′y *adj* (**-i·er; -i·est**) *colloq* obnoxiously forward and presuming ‖ **push′i·ness** *n*

pu·sil·lan·i·mous /pyŏo′sǝlan′imǝs/ [< LL *pusillanimis* petty-spirited] *adj* cowardly ‖ **pu′sil·la·nim′i·ty** /-lǝnim′-/ *n* ‖ SYN weak, timid, cowardly, mean-spirited (see *recreant*) ‖ ANT brave, faithful, spirited, courageous

puss¹ /pŏos′/ [?] *n* cat

puss² [Ir *pus*] *n slang* face

pus·sy¹ /pus′ē/ *n* (**-si·er; -si·est**) containing or like pus

puss′y² /pŏos′ē/ *n* (**-ies**) cat; kitten

puss′y·foot′ *vi* **1** to move in a cautious or stealthy manner; **2** to avoid committing oneself on an issue

puss′y wil′low *n* American dwarf willow (*Salix discolor*) bearing furry gray spikes

pus·tule /pus′chǝl/ [L *pustula* pimple] *n* small circumscribed elevation of the skin containing pus ‖ **pus′tu·lar** *adj* ‖ **pus′tu·late′** *vt & vi*

put /pŏot/ [ME *putten*] *v* (**put; put·ting**) *vt* **1** to throw or hurl, as *to put the shot;* **2** to cause to be in any situation or position; place, lay; **3** to set (to doing something), as *to put him to work;* **4** to cause to be in a state or condition, as *to put him to shame;* **5** to state, propose, as *to put a question;* **6** to apply, set, as *to put one's mind to a task;* **7** to

assign, ascribe; **8** to express, as *to put a thought into words;* **9** **put across** *colloq* **a** to make (an idea) understood; **b** to ensure the success of (a project); **10** **put aside** to store for the future; **11** **put away, a** to return (something) to its usual place; **b** to give up, renounce; **c** to commit, as to an institution; **12** **put by** to save, as money; **13** **put down, a** to write down; **b** to suppress; **c** *slang* to humble, humiliate; **14** **put forward** to propose; **15** **put in, a** to spend (time); **b** to contribute, as *to put in a good word for him;* **16** **put off, a** to postpone; **b** to rebuff; **17** **put on, a** to assume, as airs; **b** to produce (a show); **c** to clothe or cover oneself with; **d** to apply (a brake); **e** *slang* to tease, pull the leg of; **18** **put out, a** to vex; **b** to inconvenience; **c** to disconcert; **d** to send forth, as buds or shoots; **e** to lend, as money at interest; **f** to extinguish; **g** to publish; **h** *baseball* to retire (a runner); **i** to produce; **19** **put over, a** to accomplish, bring about; **b** to postpone; **20** **put something over on** to deceive; **21** **put through, a** to carry out successfully; **b** to subject to; **22** **put up, a** to offer for sale; **b** to can or preserve; **c** to offer or advance (funds); **d** to lodge; **e** to nominate; **f** to set (the hair); **23** **put up to** to incite (a person) to ‖ *vi* **24** to go or move, as *to put for school;* **25** *naut* to arrive, as *the ship put into port;* **26** **put about** *naut* to reverse one's course; **27** **put down** *aeron* to land; **28** **put forth** to sprout; **29** **put in** to enter a harbor; **30** **put in for** to apply for; **31** **put on** to make a pretense; **32** **put out** to go out to sea; **33** **put up** to lodge; **34** **put upon** to impose upon; **35** **put up with** to endure, tolerate ‖ *n* **36** agreement to deliver a specified amount of stock at a fixed price and date ‖ *adj* **37** **stay put** *colloq* to not move, to not go away

put′-and-take′ *n* any of various gambling games using some device, as the spin of a top, to determine how much each player puts in or takes out of the pot.

pu·ta·tive /pyŏo′tǝtiv/ [L *putativus*] *adj* supposed; reputed

put′-down′ *n* act that humiliates someone or puts him in his place

put′-on′ *adj* **1** feigned ‖ *n* **2** act of teasing or pulling someone's leg, as *his pretending to be rich was a big put-on*

put′-out′ *n baseball* play causing a batter or runner to be put out

pu·tre·fy /pyŏo′trifī′/ [MF *putrefier*] *v* (**-fied**) *vt* **1** to cause to rot ‖ *vi* **2** to rot ‖ **pu′tre·fac′tion** *n*

pu·tres·cent /pyŏotres′ǝnt/ *adj* rotting; becoming rotten ‖ **pu·tres′cence** *n*

pu·trid /pyōōt′rid/ [L *putridus*] *adj* 1 rotten, decaying; 2 stinking ‖ **pu·trid′i·ty** *n*

putt /put′/ [var of *put*] *n golf* 1 stroke on the putting green to play a ball into the hole ‖ *vt* 2 to strike (a ball) with such a stroke ‖ *vi* 3 to make a putt

put·tee /put′ē/ [Hindi *patti* bandage] *n* 1 cloth gaiter wrapped spirally from ankle to knee; 2 leather legging

putt·er[1] /put′ər/ *n* 1 short club used for putting; 2 one who putts

put·ter[2] [< *dial. pote* to push] *vi* to work or move idly or ineffectually

putt′ing green′ *n golf* plot of smooth turf around a hole

put·ty /put′ē/ [F *potée* potful] *n* (-ties) 1 plastic mixture of powdered chalk and linseed oil used to fill cracks, hold panes in window sashes, etc. ‖ *v* (-tied) *vt* 2 to fill or secure with putty

put′up′ /pŏŏt′-/ *adj* planned beforehand

put′-up·on′ *adj* ill-treated; taken advantage of

puz·zle /puz′əl/ [?] *n* 1 something that perplexes or causes bewilderment; 2 toy made to tax one's skill in arranging its parts; 3 problem; riddle ‖ *vt* 4 to perplex; baffle; mystify; 5 **puzzle out** to solve by clever thinking ‖ SYN *v* confuse, bewilder, mystify (see *perplex*)

puz′zle·ment *n* 1 perplexity; 2 something puzzling

puz′zler *n* puzzling problem

Pvt. Private

PW prisoner of war

PX (PXs) post exchange

Pyg·ma·li·on /pigmāl′ē·ən, -yən/ *n class. myth.* sculptor who fell in love with his masterpiece, a statue of a beautiful maiden, to which, in answer to his prayer, Aphrodite gave life

pyg·my /pig′mē/ [Gk *pygmaios*] *n* (-mies) 1 dwarf; 2 anything small of its kind; 3 **Pygmy** one of the dwarf races of Africa or SE Asia ‖ also *adj*

py·ja·mas /pəjăm′əz/ *npl Brit* pajamas

py·lon /pī′lon/ [Gk = gateway] *n* 1 gateway in Egyptian temples in the form of one or two truncated pyramids; 2 post or tower for guiding aviators; 3 steel tower supporting electrical or telephone cables

py·lo·rus /pīlōr′əs -lōr′-, pī-/ [Gk *pyloros* gatekeeper] *n* (-ri /-rī/) opening of the stomach into the small intestine

Pyong·yang /pyuŋ′yăŋ′/ *n* capital of North Korea (650,000)

py·or·rhe·a /pī′ərē′ə/ [< Gk *pyon* pus + -*rrhea*] *n* discharge of pus; *spec.* inflammatory infection of the gums accompanied by loosening of the teeth

pyr·a·mid /pir′əmid/ [Gk *pyramis* (-*idos*)] *n* 1 *geom* solid body with triangular sides meeting in a point; 2 any structure of similar shape; 3 one of the huge pyramidal structures in Egypt having a square base, built by the ancient Egyptians as royal tombs; 4 any group of persons or things arranged in a pyramid ‖ *vi* 5 to take the form of a pyramid ‖ *vt* 6 to arrange in the form of a pyramid; 7 to pile up (costs, stock, speculations, etc.) one on top of the other ‖ **py·ram·i·dal** /piram′idəl/ *adj*

pyre /pī′ər/ [Gk *pyra*] *n* pile of wood or other combustible material, usu. for burning a dead body

Pyr·e·nees /pir′ənēz′/ *npl* mountain range separating France from Spain ‖ **Pyr′e·ne′an** *adj*

py·re·thrin /pīrēth′rin/ [< *pyrethrum* a chrysanthemum from which it is extracted] *n* either of two viscous liquids —$C_{21}H_{28}O_3$— and —$C_{22}H_{28}O_5$— used as insecticides

Py·rex /pī′reks/ [trademark] *n* variety of glassware used in cooking, possessing great strength and resistance to heat, chemicals, and electricity

py·rite /pī′rīt/ [Gk *pyrites* of fire] *n* iron pyrites

py·ro- /pīr′ə-/ [Gk *pyr* fire] *comb form* fire; heat

py·ro·ma·ni·a *n* compulsion to set fire to something ‖ **py·ro·ma′ni·ac′** /-ak′/ *n*

py·ro·tech′nics /-tek′niks/ *nsg* or *npl* 1 art of making fireworks; 2 fireworks display; 3 brilliant display, as of wit ‖ **py′ro·tech′nic** *adj*

Pyr′rhic vic′to·ry /pir′ik/ [< *Pyrrhus* (ab. 318–272 B.C.) king of Epirus whose defeat of the Romans at Asculum so weakened his army that it was subsequently easily destroyed] *n* victory won at too great a cost

Py·thag·o·re′an the′o·rem /pithag′ərē′ən/ [< *Pythagoras* (ab. 582–500 B.C.) Gk philosopher and mathematician] *n geom* theorem that the square of the hypotenuse of a right triangle is equal to the sum of the squares of the other two sides

Pyth·i·as /pith′ē·əs/ *n* see **Damon and Pythias**

py·thon /pī′thon, -thən/ [Gk = mythical serpent slain by Apollo] *n* 1 one of several Old World nonvenomous constrictors of the family Boidae; 2 sooth-saying or familiar spirit; 3 person possessed by such a spirit

py′tho·ness *n* 1 woman possessed of the power of foretelling events; 2 one of the priestesses of Apollo's temple at Delphi

pyx /piks′/ [Gk = box] *n* 1 R C Ch box or container in which the consecrated wafer is kept; 2 box in which coins are placed to be tested at the mint

Q

Q, q /kyōō′/ *n* (**Q's** or **Qs; q's** or **qs**) 17th letter of the English alphabet

Q 1 17th in order or in a series; **2** something shaped like a Q; **3** *chess* queen; **4** medieval Roman numeral 500 (now D)

q. 1 quart; **2** question

Q. 1 Quebec; **2** Queen

Q.E.D. [L *quod erat demonstrandum*] which was to be shown or proved

QM, Q.M. Quartermaster

qt. 1 quantity; **2** quart

q.t. [*quiet*] *n slang* **on the q.t.** quietly, without letting it be known

qua /kwā′, kwä′/ *prep* as; in the manner or capacity of

quack[1] /kwak′/ [imit] **1** cry of a duck, or a harsh sound like it ‖ *vi* **2** to utter a quack

quack[2] [< earlier *quacksalver* < D] *n* **1** fraudulent pretender to medical skill; **2** charlatan ‖ **quack′er·y** *n* (**-ies**)

quad[1] /kwod′/ *n colloq* quadrangle 1

quad[2] *n colloq* quadruplet

quad·ran·gle /kwo′draŋ′gəl/ [LL *quadrangulum* four-cornered] *n* **1** foursided area surrounded by buildings, as on a college campus; **2** in U.S. Geological Survey maps, rectangular division of land charted on one sheet; **3** plane figure having four sides and four angles ‖ **quad·ran′gu·lar** *adj*

quad·rant /kwo′drənt/ [L *quadrans* (-*antis*) fourth part] *n* **1** quarter of a circle or arc of 90 degrees; **2** area bounded by such an arc and the radii at its extremities; **3** instrument with a 90-degree graduated arc for measuring altitudes, used in astronomy and navigation

quad·ra·phon·ic /kwod′rəfon′ik/ *adj* designating a system of sound reproduction in which signals are picked up by four microphones and reproduced by four speakers, the microphones and the speakers being located so as to provide a binaural effect in depth as well as breadth

quad′rate /-drāt, -drit/ [L *quadratus* squared] *adj* **1** square; rectangular ‖ /-drāt/ *vi* **2** to agree, correspond ‖ *vt* **3** to cause to agree or correspond

quad·rat·ic /kwodrat′ik/ *adj* **1** square; **2** *alg* involving the second but no higher power of an unknown quantity ‖ *n* **3** quadratic equation

quad·rat′ic e·qua′tion *n alg* equation in which the highest power of the unknown quantity is a square

quad·ren′ni·al /-dren′ē·əl/ [< L *quadriennis*] *adj* **1** occurring once in four years; **2** comprising four years ‖ *n* **3** fourth anniversary

quad·ri- or **quad·r-** [L] *comb form* four

quad′ri·lat′er·al /kwo′dri-/ *adj* **1** having four sides ‖ *n* **2** plane figure bounded by four straight lines

qua·drille /k(w)ədril′/ [F < Sp *cuadrilla* troop, gang] *n* **1** square dance for four couples; **2** the music for it

quad·ril·lion /kwodril′yən/ [*quadr-* + *million*] *n* **1** in U.S. and France, number represented by one followed by 15 zeros; **2** in Great Britain and Germany, number represented by one followed by 24 zeros

quad·riv′i·um /-driv′ē-əm/ [L = place where four roads meet] *n* (**-a** /-ə/) *medieval education* the advanced course in the liberal arts, consisting of arithmetic, geometry, astronomy, and music

quad·roon /-drōōn′/ [< Sp *cuarterón*] *n* person one-fourth black

quad·ru·ped /kwo′drōōped/ [L *quadrupes* (-*pedis*)] *n* fourfooted animal

quad·ru·ple /kwo′drōōpəl, kwodrōōp′-əl/ [L *quadruplus*] *adj* **1** fourfold; **2** four times as great ‖ *n* **3** quantity four times as great as another ‖ *vt* **4** to make four times as great ‖ *vi* **5** to become four times as great

quad·ru·plet /kwo′drōōplit, kwodrōōp′-lit/ *n* **1** combination of four of a kind; **2** one of four children born in the same birth

quad·ru·pli·cate /kwodrōōp′likāt′/ *vt* **1** to quadruple ‖ /also -kit/ *adj* **2** fourfold ‖ *n* **3** one of four like things; **4 in quadruplicate** in four identical copies

quaff /kwäf′, kwaf′, kwôf′/ [?] *vt* & *vi* **1** to drink heartily and copiously; **2** *n* hearty drink

quag·mire /kwag′mī(ə)r, kwog′-/ [? + *mire*] *n* **1** soft miry ground, bog; **2** perplexing predicament

qua′hog /kwô′-, kō′-, kwəhôg′, -hog′/ [<AmInd] *n* hard-shell clam

quai /kā′/ [see **quay**] *n* one of the streets running along the quays in Paris

Quai d'Or·say /kādôrsā′/ *n* **1** quai on the south bank of the Seine in Paris where the department of foreign affairs is located; **2** French foreign office or its policies

quail[1] /kwāl′/ [OF *quaille*] *n* any of various small gallinaceous game birds, as of the Old World genus *Coturnix* or the New World genus *Colinus*, including the bobwhite

quail[2] [ME] *vi* to shrink from pain or danger; lose heart; cower

quaint /kwānt′/ [OF *cointe* clever] *adj* **1** pleasingly odd or unusual; **2** attractive because of an old-fashioned daintiness or prettiness ‖ **quaint′ly** *adv* ‖ **quaint′ness** *n*

quake /kwāk′/ [OE *cwacian*] *vi* **1** to

tremble or shake, as from cold or emotion; **2** to shake from internal shock or convulsion ‖ *n* **3** earthquake

Quak·er /kwāk′ər/ *n* member of the Society of Friends ‖ **Quak′er·ess** *nfem* ‖ **Quak′er·ism** *n*

Quak′er meet′ing *n* **1** gathering of Quakers for worship in which there is little speaking; **2** *colloq* meeting in which there is little conversation

qual·i·fi·ca·tion /kwol′ifikāsh′ən/ [see **qualify**] *n* **1** act of qualifying or state of being qualified; **2** training, ability, or aptitude for a particular job or function; fitness; **3** restriction; modification

qual′i·fied′ *adj* **1** competent, fit; **2** limited or restricted

qual′i·fy′ [ML *qualificare* to endue with a quality] *v* (**-fied**) *vt* **1** to make fit or competent; **2** to moderate or soften; **3** to limit; modify ‖ *vi* **4** to be or become fit or competent for something; **5** to be empowered legally; **6** to demonstrate enough ability in a trial contest to be admitted to the final ‖ **qual′i·fi′er** *n* ‖ SYN prepare, change, abate, diminish, temper, modify, mitigate, soften ‖ DISCR To *change* is to make, or become, different, as to *change* color; *change* one's mind; to *change* to a new course of action; to *change* one's tactics. To *modify* is to make partial, usually minor, changes in; we *modify* an estimate discovered to be higher or lower than it should be. To *qualify* is to subject to reserves or limitations, usually with a softening or mitigating effect; we *qualify* the severity of a reproof by accompanying it with some sign of gentleness. *Modify* is used, also, in the latter sense of *mitigate, soften*

qual′i·ta′tive *adj* pert. to quality, rather than quantity

qual·i·ty /kwol′itē/ [OF *qualite* < L *qualitas*] *n* (**-ties**) **1** that which distinguishes one person or thing from others; attribute; characteristic; **2** essential nature; kind; **3** degree of excellence; **4** excellence, superiority; **5** character of a tone, based on its overtones, which distinguishes it from other tones of the same pitch and intensity ‖ SYN attribute, property, trait, characteristic ‖ DISCR *Quality* names an essential, inherent part of the nature of a thing or being, as the *qualities* of a judge; the *qualities* of physical matter. If a *quality* is changed, the whole is changed in that one respect, as isolation from his kind altered the *quality* of his thinking. An *attribute* is a *quality* assigned by us to a being or object. If our thinking has been right, and the *quality* so ascribed is in fact inherent, the *attribute* is truly an essential *quality;* if our judgment is at fault, the *attribute* is not truly a *quality* (see *characteristic*)

qualm /kwäm′/ [?] *n* **1** sudden doubt or misgiving; **2** compunction; twinge of conscience; **3** feeling of sickness, esp. in the stomach

quan·da·ry /kwon′dərē/ [?] *n* (**-ries**) state of hesitation or doubt; dilemma

quan·ta /kwont′ə/ *pl* of **quantum**

quan·ti·ta·tive /kwont′itāt′iv/ *adj* pert. to quantity

quan·ti·ty /kwont′itē/ [OF *quantite* < L *quantitas*] *n* (**-ties**) **1** that property of a thing which permits its measurement with reference to a fixed standard, as of volume, weight, length, or the like; **2** size, magnitude; **3** amount; measure; **4** any unspecified amount; **5** large amount; **6** *math* **a** anything that can be increased, divided, or measured; **b** symbol representing this; **7** *phonet* length or duration of a sound

quan·tum /kwont′əm/ [L = how much] *n* (**-ta** /-tə/) *phys* smallest quantity of radiant energy, varying according to the frequency of the radiator

quan′tum the′o·ry *n* theory originated in 1900 by the German physicist Max Planck, stating that emission and absorption of radiant energy are not continuous but take place in small finite amounts or quanta

quar·an·tine /kwor′əntēn′, kwôr′-/ [It < *quaranta* forty] *n* **1** period of detention and isolation imposed on ships or persons suspected of having a contagious disease upon arrival at a port or frontier; **2** any isolation imposed to prevent contagion from spreading; **3** place of such isolation ‖ *vt* **4** to place under quarantine

quar·rel /kwor′əl, kwôr′-/ [OF *querele* < L *querela* complaint] *n* **1** angry dispute; **2** disagreement or falling out ‖ *v* (**-reled** or **-relled;** **-rel·ing** or **-rel·ling**) *vi* **3** to dispute angrily; **4** to disagree; fall out; **5** **quarrel with** a to dispute with; fight with; **b** to find fault with ‖ **quar′rel·some** *adj* ‖ SYN *n* dispute, controversy, feud, wrangle, fuss, altercation, contention ‖ DISCR *Dispute*, in its good sense, is a calling in question of something claimed or asserted by another; hence, it may name a difference of opinion as to the validity of a will, or it may be a friendly debate. In its bad sense, *dispute*, commonly oral, is a hot wrangle, usually undignified and sharp, as a *dispute* over precedence. The idea underlying *controversy* is that of opposition to the opinion of another; a *controversy* may be a neutral discussion on an abstract subject, as a *controversy* over the superiority of democratic government to paternalistic government; in its ordinary sense, a *controversy*, usually in words and often in writing, is bitter and angry in its ill feeling. The idea underlying *contention* is that of maintaining a stand against another; hence, *contention* is personal, and ill feeling is unavoidable; it is commonly in words, though sometimes in acts, and is bitterly conflicting, as they spend their days in *contention* and strife. *Altercation* names a hot *dispute* or a stormy, wordy *contention*. *Quarrel* names an angry *dispute*, in word or act, usually accompanied by a rupture of friendly relations, though *quarrel* applies also to trifling differences, like those arising among children. *Quarrel* may also name the cause of complaint or ground for differences, as I have no *quarrel* with you.

quar·ry[1] /kwor′ē, kwôr′ē/ [ML *quareia*] *n* (**-ries**) 1 open excavation from which stone is obtained by cutting and blasting ‖ *v* (**-ried**) *vt* 2 to take (stone) from a quarry

quar·ry[2] [OF *cuiree*] *n* (**-ries**) any object of pursuit, esp. game pursued by a hunter

quart /kwôrt′/ [OF *quarte* fourth] *n* 1 liquid measure of capacity equal to one fourth of a gallon; 2 dry measure equal to one eighth of a peck; 3 container of one quart capacity

quar·ter /kwôrt′ər/ [OF < L *quartarius*] *n* 1 one of the four equal parts into which a thing is or may be divided; 2 one fourth of a year; 3 a one fourth of a dollar; b coin of this value; 4 one of the four cardinal points of the compass; 5 *sports* any one of the four periods that make up a game; 6 a period of fifteen minutes or a fourth of an hour; b moment at the beginning or end of such a period; 7 district of a city; 8 one of the four legs of an animal with the parts near it, as *a quarter of beef*; 9 *astron* a fourth part of the moon's monthly revolution; b phase when before or after full moon half the moon's disk is lighted by the sun; 10 *heral* one of the four parts into which a shield is divided; 11 mercy; 12 usu. **quarters** *pl* lodgings, esp. military; 13 part of a community, class, or group, as *word from the highest quarter* ‖ *vt* 14 to divide into four equal parts; 15 to dismember (a condemned criminal); 16 to furnish with lodging; 17 *heral* to place or bear (a coat of arms) in quarters on a shield ‖ *adj* 18 consisting of, or equal to, a fourth part

quar′ter·back′ *n* 1 *football* back, usu. behind the center, who calls the plays ‖ *vt* 2 to act as a quarterback of ‖ *vi* 3 to play quarterback

quar′ter·deck′ *n* the part of the upper deck of a ship between the stern and the mainmast

quar′ter·ly *adj* 1 occurring once every three months ‖ *adv* 2 once every three months ‖ *n* (**-lies**) 3 periodical issued every three months

quar′ter·mas′ter *n* 1 *mil* officer in charge of providing lodging, clothing, and supplies; 2 *nav* petty officer who assists the navigator and has charge of signals, steering, etc.

quar′ter note′ *n mus* note equal to one fourth of a whole note

quar′ter round′ *n* molding the cross section of which is a quarter circle

quar′ter sec′tion *n surveying* square tract of land containing 160 acres or one fourth of a square mile

quar·tet also **quar·tette** /kwôrtet′/ [It *quartetto*] *n* 1 any group of four persons or things; 2 *mus* a composition for four instruments or voices; b the four performers rendering such a composition

quar·to /kwôrt′ō/ [< L (in) *quarto* (in) the fourth (of a sheet)] *n* 1 page size (ab. 9 by 12 inches) obtained by folding a sheet twice so as to form four leaves or eight pages; 2 book of this size

quartz /kwôrts′/ [G *Quarz*] *n* silicon dioxide —SiO_2— one of the commonest minerals, occurring in crystals or masses, found in sand and in many rocks

quartz′ glass′ *n* silica glass, which is highly transparent to ultraviolet radiation

quartz′ lamp′ *n* ultraviolet lamp contained in a vitreous silica bulb to reduce absorption

qua·sar /kwā′sär, -sər, -zər/ [*quasi* stell*ar*] *n* one of a group of very distant celestial objects of unknown composition that are powerful sources of radio energy

quash /kwosh′/ [OF *quasser* < L *quassare* to shake and L *cassare* to annul] *vt* 1 to subdue or crush, as a rebellion; 2 *law* to annul or set aside, as an indictment ‖ SYN nullify, annul, invalidate

qua·si /kwā′sī, -zī, kwä′sē/ [L = as if; almost] *adj* seeming, apparent

qua·si- *comb form* almost; seemingly, apparently

quat·rain /kwo′trān/ [F] *n* stanza or poem of four lines

qua·ver /kwāv′ər/ [ME] *vi* 1 to shake or tremble; 2 to have a tremulous sound ‖ *vt* 3 to utter or sing with a tremulous voice ‖ *n* 4 shaking or trembling, as of the voice; 5 trill in singing or playing

quay /kē′/ [OF *kay*] *n* permanent wharf, usu. of masonry

quea·sy /kwēz′ē/ [ME *coisy*] *adj* (**-si·er; -si·est**) 1 nauseated; sick at the stomach; 2 causing nausea; 3 fastidious; squeamish; 4 delicate, ticklish ‖ **quea′si·ly** *adv* ‖ **quea′si·ness** *n*

Que·bec /kwibek′/ *n* 1 French- and

English-speaking province in E Canada (5,780,845; 594,860 sq.m.; cap. Quebec; 2 capital of Quebec (175,-000)

Quech·ua /kech'wə/ *n* 1 Indian language of the Andean regions from Ecuador to Bolivia; 2 speaker of Quechua ‖ **Quech'uan** *adj & n*

queen /kwēn'/ [OE *cwēn*] *n* 1 wife of a king; 2 female sovereign; 3 woman who is a leader in or who is pre-eminent in her sphere, as *a movie queen*; 4 fully developed female of bees, ants, or termites; 5 playing card bearing a picture of a queen; 6 *chess* most powerful piece, able to move in a straight or diagonal direction across unoccupied squares; 7 *slang* male homosexual ‖ *vi* 8 to behave as a queen; act in an imperious manner ‖ *vt* 9 **queen it** to dominate ‖ **queen'ly** *adj* (**-li·er; -li·est**)

queen' bee' *n* 1 fertile female bee; 2 *slang* domineering woman

queen' ol'ive *n* large delicately flavored olive, esp. the variety grown in Spain

Queens' *n* one of the constituent boroughs of New York City

queer /kwir'/ [G *quer* crosswise] *adj* 1 differing from the normal; peculiar, strange; 2 giddy, faint; 3 mentally deranged; 4 suspicious; open to question; 5 *slang* counterfeit; 6 *slang* homosexual ‖ *vt* 7 to spoil, ruin; jeopardize ‖ *n* 8 counterfeit money; 9 *slang* homosexual ‖ SYN *adj* droll, odd, funny, strange, unique, peculiar

quell /kwel'/ [OE *cwellan* to kill] *vt* 1 to suppress or subdue; crush; 2 to quiet or allay ‖ SYN overpower, suppress, crush, reduce

quench /kwench'/ [ME *quenchen*] *vt* 1 to put out or extinguish; 2 to slake or satisfy, as thirst

quer·u·lous /kwer'(y)ələs/ [< L *querulus*] *adj* 1 complaining; 2 peevish, fretful ‖ SYN (see *petulant*)

que·ry /kwir'ē/ [L *quaere* (*impv*) ask] *n* (**-ries**) 1 question, inquiry; 2 doubt ‖ *v* (**-ried**) *vt* 3 to inquire into, ask about

quest /kwest'/ [MF *queste* < L *quaesita*] *n* 1 seeking, search; 2 expedition for a particular object ‖ *vi* 3 to search or seek

ques·tion /kwes'chən/ [AF *questiun*] *n* 1 act of asking; inquiry; 2 that which is asked; interrogation; 3 subject under discussion; 4 problem; difficulty; 5 dispute; 6 **beyond question** beyond dispute; 7 **out of the question** impossible; unthinkable ‖ *vt* 8 to interrogate, ask questions of; 9 to consider doubtful; 10 to challenge; take exception to ‖ *vi* 11 to ask questions ‖ **ques'tion·er** *n* ‖ SYN *n* (see *doubt*); *v* ask, dispute, inquire, interrogate, examine, challenge ‖ DISCR To *ask*, the general term, is to call for an answer, to request,

seek a favor, or desire help, as I *asked* the reason; I *asked* cooperation from my partners. *Inquire, question,* and *interrogate* seek to obtain information. *Inquire* is a more formal, though no better, word than *ask,* as the committee *inquired* into the cause of the disaster. To *examine* is to test by questions aimed to bring out all the facts, as to *examine* a witness. To *interrogate* and to *question* are to try to get information by close examination; a justice *interrogates* or *questions* those officially brought before his court. *Question,* in the sense of receiving with doubt or objection, comes close to the sense of *challenge,* as to *question* the truth of a statement; to *challenge* the honesty of a candidate

ques'tion·a·ble *adj* 1 open to question; 2 doubtful as to character, morality, propriety, etc.

ques'tion mark' *n* 1 punctuation mark ? indicating a question; 2 person or thing that is an unknown quantity

ques·tion·naire /-ner'/ [F] *n* series of questions submitted to a number of people for the purpose of eliciting information

quet·zal /ketsäl'/ [AmSp < Nahuatl] *n* 1 handsome bird (*Pharomachrus mocinno*) of Central America, with a crest and long hanging tail; 2 monetary unit of Guatemala

queue /kyōō'/ [F = tail] *n* 1 braid of hair hanging down the back; 2 line of persons waiting their turn ‖ *vi* 3 **queue up** to get in line

Que'zon Cit'y /kā'zon/ *n* capital of the Philippines since 1948 (482,400)

quib·ble /kwib'əl/ [?] *n* 1 evasion of the point in question by advancing trifling arguments; 2 petty objection or criticism ‖ *vi* 3 to avoid the truth by a quibble ‖ **quib'bler** *n*

quick /kwik'/ [OE *cwicu* living] *adj* 1 rapid, swift; 2 prompt; 3 of short duration; 4 alert; prompt to understand; 5 prompt to perceive, as *a quick ear;* 6 hasty; impatient ‖ *adv* 7 quickly ‖ *n* 8 flesh under the nails; 9 seat of the feelings, as *hurt to the quick;* 10 **the quick and the dead** the living and the dead ‖ **quick'ly** *adv* ‖ **quick'ness** *n* ‖ SYN *adj* prompt, agile, lively, fleet, brisk, expeditious (see *hasty*) ‖ ANT *adj* (see *slow*)

quick' bread' *n* bread, biscuits, etc., made with a quick-acting leavening agent

quick'en *vt* 1 to bring life to; 2 to revive; give new life to; 3 to hasten ‖ *vi* 4 to give indications of life, as a fetus in the womb; 5 to act or move more quickly; 6 to become more sensitive, as the emotions or perceptions ‖ SYN animate, revivify, hurry, hasten, accelerate, urge, incite ‖ ANT retard, discourage, drag

quick'-freeze' *v* (**-froze**; **-fro·zen**) *vt* to freeze (food) very rapidly, avoiding formation of large ice crystals which cause cell rupture, and allowing it to be stored for very long periods at temperatures well below freezing

quick'ie *n slang* anything made or done quickly

quick'lime' *n* lime¹

quick'sand' *n* soft, loose, wet bed of sand that quickly engulfs any heavy object that comes upon it

quick'sil'ver *n* mercury

quick'-wit'ted *adj* alert, nimble-witted

quid¹ /kwid'/ [OE *cwidu* cud] *n* piece of something to be chewed, esp. of tobacco

quid² [?] *n* (*pl* **quid**) *Brit colloq* the sum of one British pound

quid pro quo /kwid' prō kwō'/ [L = something for something] *n* something given or done in return for something else

qui·es·cent /kwī·es'ənt/ [L *quiescens* (*-entis*) becoming quiet] *adj* resting; inactive; calm; still

qui·et /kwī'it/ [L *quietus*] *adj* 1 free from agitation or disturbance; 2 free from noise; silent; 3 tranquil; 4 at rest, motionless; 5 inactive; 6 subdued; 7 not ostentatious ‖ *vt* 8 to make quiet ‖ *vi* 9 to become quiet ‖ *n* 10 freedom from motion, noise, or disturbance; 11 peace, tranquillity ‖ **qui'et·ly** *adv* ‖ SYN *n* tranquillity, serenity, peace, calmness, repose, quietude ‖ ANT *n* noise, uproar, disturbance

qui'e·tude' /-t(y)ōōd'/ *n* state of being quiet; repose, tranquillity

qui·e·tus /kwī·ē'ēt'əs/ [ML *quietus* (est) (he is) quit] *n* 1 anything that puts an end to action, esp. death; 2 period of inactivity and quiet

quill /kwil'/ [ME *quil*] *n* 1 large feather of a bird's wing or tail; 2 hollow shaft of a feather; 3 pen made from a feather; 4 spine of a hedgehog or porcupine

quilt /kwilt'/ [OF *cuilte*] *n* 1 bed covering made by stitching a layer of soft cotton or wool between two layers of fabric; 2 any quilted material ‖ *vt* 3 to fasten together (two layers of fabric) with stitches, often in an ornamental pattern, with a soft material between ‖ *vi* 4 to make a quilt ‖ **quilt'ed** *adj*

quilt'ing *n* 1 material for making quilts; 2 quilted material

quince /kwins'/ [MF *cooin* < Gk *kydonion*] *n* 1 hard, acid, yellowish fruit, much used for preserves, of a small bushy tree (*Cydonia oblonga*); 2 the tree

qui·nine /kwī'nīn/ [Sp *quina* < Quechua *kina* bark] *n* 1 bitter alkaloid —$C_{20}H_{24}N_2O_2$— obtained from the bark of the cinchona tree, used as a tonic and in the treatment of ma-

laria; 2 salt of this alkaloid, esp. the sulfate

qui'nine wa'ter *n* carbonated beverage flavored with quinine, lemon, and lime

quin·quen·ni·um /kwinkwen'ē·əm/ [L] *n* (**-ums** or **-a** /-ə/) period of five years ‖ **quin·quen'ni·al** *adj*

quin·sy /kwin'zē/ [ML *quinancia*] *n* suppurative inflammation of the tonsils and throat

quint /kwint/ *n colloq* quintuplet

quin·tes·sence /kwintes'əns/ [ML *quinta essentia* the fifth essence (alluding to the supposed fifth element of the ancient and medieval philosophers)] *n* 1 pure and concentrated essence of anything; 2 most perfect embodiment of some quality or thing ‖ **quin'tes·sen'tial** /-isensh'əl/ *adj*

quin·tet also **quin·tette** /kwintet'/ [F *quintette* < It *quintetto*] *n* 1 any group of five persons or things; 2 *mus* a composition for five instruments or voices; b the five performers rendering such a composition

quin'tile /-til, -til/ *n statistics* 1 any of the four numbers which divide a distribution of values arranged in order of magnitude into five equal parts; 2 one of the five equal parts of a distribution of values

quin·tu·ple /kwint'(y)ōōpəl, kwint(y)ōōp'əl, -tup'-/ [F < L *quint*us fifth + quadr*uple*] *adj* 1 fivefold; 2 five times as great ‖ *n* 3 quantity five times as great as another ‖ *vt* 4 to make five times as great ‖ *vi* 5 to become five times as great

quin·tu·plet /kwint'(y)ōōplit, kwint(y)ōōp'lit, -tup'-/ *n* 1 combination of five of a kind; 2 one of five children born in the same birth

quin·tu·pli·cate /kwint(y)ōōp'likāt'/ *vt* 1 to quintuple ‖ /*also* -kit/ *adj* 2 fivefold ‖ *n* 3 one of five like things; 4 **in quintuplicate** in five identical copies

quip /kwip/ [< *obs quippy* perh < L *quippe* forsooth] *n* 1 witty or sarcastic remark ‖ *v* (**quipped**; **quipping**) *vi* 2 to utter quips ‖ *vt* 3 to say quippingly ‖ **quip'ster** *n*

quire /kwī'ər/ [MF *quaer* < LL *quaternum* set of four sheets] 1 *n* set of 24 or 25 uniform sheets of paper; 2 set of folded printed sheets numbered in sequence

Quir·i·nal /kwir'ənəl/ *n* 1 one of the seven hills of Rome, site of the Quirinal Palace; 2 also **Quirinal Palace** residence of the President of Italy

quirk /kwurk'/ [?] *n* 1 peculiarity of manner; 2 twist or turn, as of fate ‖ **quirk'y** *adj* (**-i·er; -i·est**)

quirt /kwurt'/ [Sp *cuarta*] *n* riding whip with a short handle and a lash of braided rawhide

quis·ling /kwiz'liŋ/ [Vidkun *Quisling*

(1887–1945) head of the collaborationist Norwegian government during the Nazi occupation] *n* one who traitorously assists an enemy power to invade his country

quit /kwit′/ [OF *quitter*] *v* (**quit** or **quit·ted; quit·ting**) *vt* 1 to resign; relinquish; 2 to depart from; 3 to cease; discontinue ‖ *vi* 4 to stop; 5 to quit one's job; 6 to stop doing what one is supposed to carry to completion ‖ *adj* 7 free; clear ‖ SYN *v* surrender, relinquish, cease, leave

quit′claim′ *law n* 1 relinquishing of a claim or a right to property ‖ *vt* 2 to give up claim to, as an estate

quite /kwit′/ [ME] *adv* 1 completely, wholly; 2 tô a considerable extent; very

Qui·to /kēt′ō/ *n* capital of Ecuador (375,000)

quits /kwits′/ [< *quit*] *adj* 1 even (with someone), as after retaliation or repayment; 2 **call it quits,** a to stop or discontinue what one is doing; b to give up or abandon an effort

quit′tance [OF] *n* 1 discharge or release from a debt or obligation; 2 recompense; repayment

quit′ter *n* one who shrinks or gives up before a task is finished

quiv·er[1] /kwiv′ər/ [OF *quivre*] *n* portable case or sheath for arrows

quiv′er[2] [ME] *n* 1 act of trembling; tremor ‖ *vi* 2 to tremble or shake; vibrate ‖ SYN *v* (see *shake*)

qui vive /kē vēv′/ [F = whoever it may be] *n* 1 sentry's challenge; 2 **on the qui vive** on the alert

quix·ot·ic /kwiksot′ik/ [< Don *Quixote*] *adj* chivalrous or romantic to an absurd or extravagant degree

quiz /kwiz′/ [?] *n* (**quiz·zes**) 1 questioning; 2 informal examination of students ‖ *v* (**quizzed; quiz·zing**) *vt* 3 to examine or test (students); 4 to question

quiz′ pro·gram or **show′** *n* television or radio program in which contestants compete by answering questions

quiz′zi·cal *adj* 1 puzzled, as a look or expression; 2 humorously serious; odd ‖ **quiz′zi·cal·ly** *adv*

quoit /kwoit′, kwät′/ [ME *coyte*] *n* 1 flat iron ring used in the game of quoits; 2 **quoits** *sg* game in which players pitch these rings at a short peg

quon·dam /kwon′dam/ [L] *adj* former, erstwhile

Quon′set hut′ /kwons′it/ [trademark] *n* building consisting of a prefabricated semicylindrical metal shed with end walls

quo·rum /kwôr′əm, kwōr′-/ [L = of whom] *n* proportion of members of an organization or group that must be present if a meeting is to transact business legally

quo·ta /kwōt′ə/ [< L *quota* (pars)] how great (a part)] *n* proportional share alloted or required

quo·ta·tion /kwōtāsh′ən/ [see **quote**] *n* 1 act of quoting; 2 that which is quoted; 3 a statement of the current price of a security or commodity; b price stated

quota′tion mark′ *n* mark of punctuation used to set off a quotation, usu. " at the beginning and " at the end

quote /kwōt′/ [ML *quotare* to divide into chapters or parts] *vt* 1 to repeat (a passage from a book, speech, or the like); 2 to repeat the words of; 3 to enclose in quotation marks; 4 to give the current market price of ‖ *vi* 5 to repeat the words of another ‖ *n* 6 quotation mark; 7 quotation ‖ **quot′a·ble** *adj*

quoth /kwōth′/ [< OE *cwethan* to speak] *vt archaic* said (followed by a subject of the first or third person)

quo·tid·i·an /kwōtid′ē·ən/ [L *quotidianus*] *adj* 1 daily; 2 (fever) recurring daily ‖ *n* 3 something recurring daily, as a fever

quo·tient /kwōsh′ənt/ [< L *quotiens* how often] *n math* result of division; number of times a given number is contained in another

q.v. [L *quod vide*] which see

R

R, r /är′/ *n* (**R's** or **Rs; r's** or **rs**) 18th letter of the English alphabet

R 1 18th in order or in a series; 2 something shaped like an R; 3 *chess* rook; 4 designation for a film to which persons under 16 are not admitted without an accompanying adult; 5 **the three R's** reading, 'riting (writing), and 'rithmetic (arithmetic), the primary essentials of education

R. [L *rex*] 1 king; 2 [L *regina*] queen

R., r. 1 rabbi; 2 radius; 3 railroad; 4 railway; 5 right; 6 river; 7 road

Ra 1 *chem* radium ‖ /rä′/ *n* 2 sun god of ancient Egypt

R. A. Royal Academy

Ra·bat /räbät′/ *n* seaport and capital of Morocco (355,000)

rab·bet /rab′it/ [OF *rabat*] *n* 1 groove or slot made in the edge or face of one piece of wood to receive the edge of another piece; 2 joint thus made ‖

vt 3 to cut a rabbet in; 4 to join by a rabbet

rab·bi /ra′bī/ [Heb = my master] *n* chief religious official of a Jewish synagogue and spiritual leader of the congregation ‖ **rab·bin·i·cal** /rəbin′-ikəl/ *adj*

rab·bit /rab′it/ [ME *rabet*] *n* 1 burrowing rodent (*Lepus cuniculus*) resembling the hare; 2 any of various hares; 3 fur of the rabbit

rab′bit ears′ *npl* indoor television antenna consisting of two swiveling telescoping rods

rab′bit punch′ *n* short sharp punch to the nape of the neck

rab·ble /rab′əl/ [ME *rabel*] *n* 1 mob; 2 **the rabble** the lowest rank of society ‖ SYN crowd, populace (see *throng*)

rab·ble-rous′er *n* person who rouses the passions of the mob

Rab·e·lais, Fran·çois /fräns′wä rab′-əlā′/ *n* (1490–1553) French satirist, whose work is characterized by coarse humor ‖ **Rab′e·lai′si·an** /-läz′ē·ən, -läzh′ən/ *adj*

rab·id /rab′id/ [L *rabidus*] *adj* 1 furious, raging; 2 fanatical, over-zealous; 3 pert. to or affected with rabies

ra·bies /rāb′ēz, -ē·ēz′/ [L = madness] *n* acute infectious and often fatal disease of dogs, cats, and other animals, transmitted to man by the bite of an infected animal

rac·coon /rakōōn′/ [< Algonquian] *n* (-coons or -coon) small nocturnal North American omnivore (*Procyon lotor*) having grayish-brown fur, black markings on the head, and a bushy tail

race¹ /rās′/ [ON *rās*] *n* 1 swift current of water or the channel for such a current; 2 watercourse made for industrial purposes; 3 competitive contest of speed; 4 any competition or contest; 5 channel or slot along which some part of a machine moves; 6 **the races** the program of horse or dog races run at a track ‖ *vi* 7 to run swiftly; 8 to compete in a race; 9 to run too fast, as a machine because of lightened load; 10 to engage in the business of racing horses or dogs ‖ *vt* 11 to cause to move swiftly; 12 to contend with in a race; 13 to cause to run in a race

race² [F < It *razza*] *n* 1 class of persons having common interests, characteristics, etc., as *the race of poets;* 2 division of mankind, made up of tribes and nations descended from a common stock; 3 branch of such a division; 4 mankind

race′ horse′ *n* horse bred for racing

ra·ceme /rāsēm′, rə-/ [ML *racemus* bunch of berries or grapes] *n* flower cluster in which blooms grow singlestemmed at almost regular distances on a stalk

race′ ri′ot *n* riot arising from racial antagonism

race′ track′ *n* course laid out for horse or auto races

race′way′ *n* 1 water channel; 2 tube for protecting electric wires; 3 race track for harness races

Ra·chel /rāch′əl/ *n Bib* wife of Jacob and mother of Joseph and Benjamin (Gen. 30:25; 35:16–19)

ra·chit·ic /rəkit′ik/ [< Gk *rachitis* inflammation of the spine] *adj* pert. to or suffering from rickets

ra·cial /rāsh′əl/ *adj* pert. to a race or family of men ‖ **ra′cial·ly** *adv*

rac′ing form′ *n* published sheet giving information on horse races, betting odds, performance of horses and jockeys, etc.

rac′ism *n* 1 belief in the inherent superiority and inferiority of races; 2 policy or practice of persecution or deprivation of rights based on race

rack¹ /rak′/ [MD *rec* rail] *n* 1 framework on or in which articles are hung or arranged; 2 wrenching or straining, as by storms; 3 *mach* bar having teeth on one side that engage the teeth of a gear; 4 *pool* triangular frame for arranging the balls before play; 5 medieval instrument for torturing the body by stretching the limbs; 6 physical or mental anguish; 7 **on the rack, a** under pressure; **b** in torment ‖ *vt* 8 to torture, torment; 9 to subject to physical or mental anguish; 10 **rack one's brains** to strain in mental effort ‖ SYN *v* torment, wrench, rend (see *break*)

rack² [var of *wrack*] *n* **rack and ruin** destruction; decay

rack³ [ME < OProv *arracer* to drain off] *vt* to draw off (liquor) from the dregs at the bottom

rack·et¹ /rak′it/ [?] *n* 1 clattering uproar; noise, din; 2 scene of excitement or gaiety; 3 *colloq* organized illegal activity ‖ SYN hubbub, uproar, commotion (see *noise*)

rack·et² also **rac·quet** /rak′it/ [MF *raquette*] *n* 1 network bat used in tennis and similar games; 2 **rac·quets** *sg* game for two or four persons played in a four-walled court

rack′et·eer′ *n* person engaged in an organized illegal activity

rac·on·teur /rak′ontur′/ [F] *n* one who tells interesting stories and anecdotes

rac·y /rās′ē/ [< *race²*] *adj* (-i·er; -i·est) 1 rich, fragrant, as wine; 2 lively, spirited, as *a racy style;* 3 risqué; ribald

rad /rad′/ [< *radiation*] *n* unit of radiation absorbed by the whole body (rather than by a single organ)

ra·dar /rā′där/ [*radio directing and ranging*] *n* device for detecting objects, not directly visible, by measuring the time it takes for a radio beam to be reflected back from the object

ra′dar·scope′ *n* viewing screen of a radar apparatus, on which the reflected radio beams appear as blips

ra·di·al /rād′ē·əl/ [< L *radius* spoke] *adj* 1 spreading out from a center, as rays of light or radii; 2 pert. to radii; 3 *anat* pert. to the radius ‖ **ra′di·al·ly** *adv*

ra′di·al tire′ *n* pneumatic tire with cords at right angles to the center of the tread

ra·di·an /rād′ē·ən/ *n* angle at the center of a circle subtending an arc of the circle equal in length to the radius, the angle being equal to 57°17′44.8″

ra·di·ant /rād′ē·ənt/ [*see* **radiate**] *adj* 1 emitting rays of light; shining; 2 beaming, joyful; 3 emitted by radiation, as *radiant heat* ‖ **ra′di·ance** *n* ‖ SYN beaming, shining, brilliant (*see* **bright**)

ra′di·ant en′er·gy *n* energy transmitted in the form of electromagnetic waves

ra′di·ate′ [L *radiare (-atus)*] *vt* 1 to emit in rays; 2 to give forth, as happiness or love ‖ *vi* 3 to spread out like radii from the center; 4 to emit rays, as of heat or light; 5 to beam or glow, as with love

ra·di·a′tion *n* 1 act of radiating; 2 that which is radiated; 3 *phys* a propagation of energy in the form of waves or particles; b energy so propagated

ra′di·a′tion sick′ness *n* illness caused by overexposure to X rays or radioactive materials

ra′di·a′tor *n* 1 body that radiates; 2 device for radiating heat from steam or hot water into a room; 3 device for cooling, as engines, by transferring heat from circulating water to the outer air

rad′i·cal /rad′ikəl/ [< L *radix (-icis)* root] *n* 1 word root; 2 one who wants to make fundamental changes, as in government or society, by going to the root of things; 3 extremist; 4 *chem* specific arrangement of atoms which acts in combination as a single atom; 5 *math* a quantity considered as the root of another quantity; b radical sign ‖ *adj* 6 pert. to the root or origin; 7 fundamental; 8 thoroughgoing, extreme; 9 extreme in politics ‖ **rad′i·cal·ly** *adv* ‖ **rad′i·cal·ism** *n*

rad′i·cal·ize′ *vt* 1 to make radical, esp. in politics; 2 *colloq* to stir up, incite ‖ **rad′i·cal·i·za′tion** *n*

rad′i·cal sign′ *n* the symbol √⁻ indicating that the following quantity is to have its root extracted

ra·di·i /rād′ē·ī′/ *pl* of **radius**

ra·di·o /rād′ē·ō′/ [*radio*telegraphy] *n* 1 wireless telegraphy or telephony; 2 apparatus for receiving radio broadcasts; 3 radio broadcasting as a business or as an entertainment medium ‖ *adj* 4 pert. to, employed in, or sent by radio; 5 of or pert. to radiant energy ‖ *vi* 6 to transmit something by radio ‖ *vt* 7 to send by radio; 8 to communicate with by radio

ra·di·o- /rād′ē·ō-/ [< L *radius* ray] *comb form* 1 radio; 2 radioactive; 3 radiant-energy; 4 radial; 5 radium

ra′di·o·ac′tive *adj* having the property of spontaneously emitting radiation from the disintegration of atomic nuclei ‖ **ra′di·o·ac·tiv′i·ty** *n*

ra′di·o·ac′tive de·cay′ *n* spontaneous disintegration or transformation of a radioactive nucleus

ra′di·o as·tron′o·my *n* branch of astronomy that bases its observations on the entire spectrum of electromagnetic radiation instead of visible light alone

ra′di·o·bea′con *n* radio station that continually emits signals to tell ships and airplanes of their location

ra′di·o·car′bon *n* 1 radioactive isotope of carbon; 2 carbon 14

ra′di·o·e·col′o·gy *n* study of the ecological interactions between plant and animal life and radioactive substances

ra′di·o fre′quen·cy *n* frequency of electromagnetic waves, used in the transmission of signals, between approximately 15,000 cycles per second and the frequencies of infrared ‖ **ra′di·o-fre′quen·cy** *adj*

ra′di·o·gram′ *n* message sent by radio

ra′di·o·i′so·tope′ *n* artificially produced radioactive isotope

ra′di·ol′o·gy /-ol′əjē/ *n* science dealing with X rays, X-ray photographs, and their interpretation ‖ **ra′di·ol′o·gist** *n*

ra′di·o·tel′e·gram′ *n* message sent by radiotelegraphy

ra′di·o·tel′e·graph′ *n* telegraph for transmitting messages or signals by radio waves ‖ **ra′di·o·te·leg′ra·phy** *n*

ra′di·o·tel′e·phone′ *n* telephone for transmitting speech by radio waves ‖ **ra′di·o·te·leph′o·ny** *n*

ra′di·o tel′e·scope *n* concave reflector that detects radio waves of extraterrestrial origin

ra′di·o·ther′a·py *n* use of X rays or radioactive substances for the treatment of disease

ra′di·o wave′ *n* electromagnetic wave of radio frequency

rad·ish /rad′ish/ [OE *rēdic* < L *radix (-icis)* root] *n* garden plant (*Raphanus sativus*) with a pungent root, eaten raw

ra·di·um /rād′ē·əm/ [< L *radius* ray] *n* highly radioactive metallic element (Ra; at.no. 88; at.wt. 226) that spontaneously disintegrates into radon and alpha rays

ra·di·us /rād′ē·əs/ [L = staff, spoke] *n* (-i /-ī/ or -us·es) 1 straight line from the center of a circle or sphere to the circumference or surface; 2 length of this line; 3 circular area defined by a radius, as *within a radius of two miles;* **4** limit of travel without re-fueling, as of a boat or plane; **5** *anat* shorter bone of the forearm on the thumb side

ra·di·us vec´tor *n* **1** line drawn from a central point or origin to a variable point on a curve; **2** *astron* **a** straight line joining two bodies traveling in relative orbits; **b** its length

ra·dome /rā´dōm/ *n* domelike housing for a radar antenna

ra·don /rā´don/ [< *radium*] *n* gase-ous, highly radioactive element (Rn; at.no. 86; at.wt. 222) formed by the disintegration of radium

RAF, R.A.F. Royal Air Force

raf·fi·a /raf´ē-ə/ [< Malagasy] *n* **1** palm of Madagascar (genus *Raphia*) with long plumelike leaves; **2** its fiber, used in weaving baskets, hats, etc.

raff·ish /raf´ish/ [< *riffraff*] *adj* **1** taw-dry; flashy; **2** disreputable

raf·fle /raf´əl/ [MF *rafle* a game of chance] *n* **1** kind of lottery in which the participants buy chances on a prize || *vt* **2** also **raffle off** to dispose of by a raffle

raft[1] /raft´, räft´/ [ON *raptr* rafter] *n* **1** floating framework or platform of buoyant materials, as logs, planks, inflated rubber, etc. || *vt* **2** to trans-port on a raft

raft[2] [ME *raff* heap] *n colloq* **a raft of** a lot of

raft·er /raf´tər, räf´-/ [OE *ræfter*] *n* sloping beam that helps to support the roof of a house

rag[1] /rag´/ [ON *rögg* tuft] *n* **1** worn or torn piece of cloth of no value; **2** cloth for washing or dusting; **3** *con-temptuous* newspaper or magazine; **4** **rags** *pl* tattered or worn-out gar-ments; **5** **chew the rag** *slang* to chat, gossip idly

rag[2] [?] *v* (**ragged; rag·ging**) *vt colloq* **1** to scold; **2** to tease severely

rag´a·muf´fin /rag´ə-/ [ME *Ragamof-fyn* demon in medieval poem *Piers Plowman*] *n* **1** ragged, disreputable fellow; **2** child in ragged clothes

rage /rāj´/ [OF < LL *rabia*] *n* **1** un-controlled anger; **2** extreme violence; fury; **3** enthusiasm, great eagerness; **4** anything excessively popular; fad || *vi* **5** to be furiously incensed; storm; **6** to act or speak violently; **7** to have furious force or effect, as a battle or a fever || SYN *n* fury, wrath, violence (see *anger*)

rag·ged /rag´id/ *adj* **1** torn; tattered; **2** clothed in tattered garments; **3** rough, jagged; **4** shaggy || **rag´ged·y** *adj*

rag·lan /rag´lən/ [Lord *Raglan* (1788–1855) Brit general] *n* loose overcoat with no shoulder seams, the sleeves extending to the collar

ra·gout /ragoo´/ [F] *n* highly seasoned stew of meat and vegetables

rag´tag´ *n* rabble; riffraff

rag´time´ *n mus* **1** rhythm having strong syncopation in the melody with the accompaniment in two-four time; **2** music in ragtime

rag´weed´ [< the appearance of the leaves] *n* any of several coarse, com-mon herbs (genus *Ambrosia*), the pollen of which is the chief cause of hay fever

rah /rä´/ *interj* hurrah

raid /rād´/ [OE *rād* road] *n* **1** sudden attack; foray, as by aircraft or a band of soldiers on enemy territory, or by the police on a building in search of criminals or evidence of crime; **2** any concerted effort to effect some purpose at someone's expense || *vt* **3** to make a raid on || *vi* **4** to take part in a raid

rail[1] /rāl´/ [MF *reille* bar < L *regula* straight piece of wood] *n* **1** bar of wood or metal placed in a horizontal position as a support, guard, or fence; **2** one of the two metal bars forming a track for the wheels of a railroad vehicle; **3** **rails** *pl* formerly, stocks or bonds of railroad compa-nies; **4 by rail** by railroad || *vt* **5 rail in** or **off** to enclose with rails

rail[2] [MF *raale*] *n* any of several spe-cies of widely distributed birds (fam-ily Rallidae) having a rather heavy body, long legs, weak wings, and a harsh cry

rail[3] [MF *railler* to deride] *vi* **rail at** or **against** to complain about bitterly; denounce vehemently

rail´car´ *n* self-propelled railroad pas-senger car, which sometimes carries also baggage, mail, and other goods

rail´head´ *n* farthest point to which the rails of a railroad extend

rail´ing *n* **1** fence of horizontal rails; **2** banisters

rail´ler·y *n* (-**ies**) good-humored banter

rail´road´ *n* **1** one or more tracks each formed by two parallel rails, along which cars are propelled for trans-porting passengers, freight, and mails; **2** such a road with all its roll-ing stock, stations, repair yards, etc.; **3** organization and persons operating a railroad || *vt* **4** to rush, as a bill, through a legislature; **5** *colloq* to convict (someone) hastily and un-justly

rail´road flat´ *n* apartment with no hall and in which the rooms are all in a row like the cars of a passenger train

rail´road´ing *n* construction and opera-tion of railroads || **rail´road´er** *n*

rail´way´ *n* **1** railroad; **2** railroad for light traffic, as *a street railway;* **3** any track with a runway for wheels

rai·ment /rām´ənt/ [< *obs arrayment*] *n* clothing; wearing apparel

rain /rān´/ [OE *regn*] *n* **1** water falling in drops condensed from moisture in the air; **2** the fall of such drops; **3** fall or shower of anything, as a *rain of bullets* ‖ *vi* **4** to fall in drops of water from the clouds; **5** to send down rain, as the sky or the clouds; **6** to fall like rain, as tears ‖ *vt* **7** to send down like rain; **8** to bestow freely, shower, as favors; **9** to deal, as blows or insults; **10 be rained out** to be postponed on account of rain; **11 rain cats and dogs** *colloq* to rain heavily

rain'bow' /-bō′/ *n* **1** arc revealing the colors of the spectrum, formed in the sky opposite the sun by the reflection and refraction of the sun's rays from drops of falling rain, spray, or mist; **2** any brilliant array of colors

rain'bow trout' *n* multicolored food fish (*Salmo gairdnerii*) of W North America

rain' check' *n* **1** ticket for future admission to an outdoor event postponed by rain; **2** postponement of an invitation to another time

rain'coat' *n* waterproof overcoat

rain'fall' *n* **1** shower of rain; **2** amount of rain that falls in a definite period on any given area, expressed in inches

rain'mak'ing *n colloq* cloud seeding

rain'out' *n* outdoor event canceled or postponed because of rain

rain'y *adj* (-i·er; -i·est) having or bringing copious rain ‖ **rain'i·ness** *n*

rain'y day' *n* future time of possible need

raise /rāz′/ [ON *reisa*] *vt* **1** to elevate, lift; **2** to set upright; **3** to restore to life; **4** to rouse (game) from cover; **5** to construct, erect; **6** to cause, set in motion, as *to raise a storm*; **7** to grow, breed; **8** to procure, collect, muster, as money, armies, etc.; **9** to give rise to, set going, as strife, rumors, expressions of feeling, etc.; **10** to rouse or stir up; incite; **11** to bring up for consideration, as a question, objection, etc.; **12** to advance in rank; **13** to increase in degree, amount, intensity, etc., as prices, the voice, the spirits, etc.; **14** to cause (dough) to rise; **15** to increase fraudulently the amount of (a check); **16** to make radio contact with; **17** to put an end to (a blockade or siege); **18** *poker* to bet higher than (another player); **19** to utter, as a cry; **20** *naut* to cause (land) to appear by approaching it; **21** to rear, bring up ‖ *n* **22** act of raising; **23** increase in pay ‖ SYN *v* erect, exalt, heighten, increase, enhance, promote, originate ‖ ANT *v* lower, depress, humble

rai·sin /rāz′in/ [OF < L *racemus* bunch of grapes] *n* special variety of grape, dried in the sun or artificially

rai·son d'être /rāzôn′ de′tr∂/ [F] *n* (*raisons d'être*) reason for being

ra·jah or **ra·ja** /räj′∂/ [Hindi *rājā* king] *n* prince or ruler in India and the East Indies

rake¹ /rāk′/ [OE *raca*] *n* **1** agricultural implement with teeth at one end for gathering hay, leaves, etc., or for smoothing the soil; **2** any implement similar in make and use ‖ *vt* **3** to gather or smooth with a rake; **4** to use a rake on; **5** to search through carefully; **6** to fire along the length of; **7 rake in** to gather in large amounts; **8 rake up** to make known (something discreditable) ‖ *vi* **9** to use a rake; **10** to make a close search

rake² [< earlier *rakehell*] *n* dissolute, licentious man; roué

rake³ [?] *n* **1** inclination from the perpendicular or the horizontal ‖ *vi* **2** (of a ship's mast or funnel) to incline sternward from the perpendicular ‖ *vt* **3** to cause to incline from the perpendicular

rake'-off' *n* share received illicitly; **2** share of gross income; **3** rebate

rak'ish¹ [prob < *rake³*] *adj* **1** smart and fast-looking (ship); **2** smart, dashing, jaunty ‖ **rak'ish·ly** *adv*

rak·ish² [< *rake²*] *adj* debauched; dissolute

Ra·leigh /rôl′ē, räl′ē/ *n* capital of North Carolina (95,000)

Ra·leigh, Sir Wal·ter *n* (ab. 1552–1618) English explorer and author

ral·ly /ral′ē/ [F *rallier*] *v* (-lied) *vt* **1** to reassemble and restore to order, as troops in flight; **2** to call together for any purpose; **3** to revive, restore, as one's spirits ‖ *vi* **4** to return to order, as troops; **5** to come together for united action; **6** to recover strength; **7** to score runs after being behind; **8** to rise sharply, as the price of stocks ‖ *n* (-lies) **9** act or fact of rallying; **10** mass meeting of partisans, as of a political party or sports team; **11** also **rallye** sports car race

ram /ram′/ [OE] *n* **1** male sheep; **2** battering ram; **3** a vessel with a steel beak for ramming enemy ships; **b** the beak itself; **4 Ram** the constellation Aries ‖ *v* (**rammed; ram·ming**) *vt* **5** to strike or butt against with great force; **6** to press or force by heavy blows; **7** to press or cram (a person or thing) into something; **8** to cram or stuff ‖ *vi* **9 ram into** to collide violently with

Ram·a·dan /ram′∂dän/ [< Ar *ramada* to be hot] *n* the ninth month of the Muslim year, observed by fasting daily from dawn to sunset; **2** the fasting

ram·ble /ram′b∂l/ [perh < ME *romen* to roam] *n* **1** aimless, leisurely stroll ‖ *vi* **2** to wander or rove aimlessly about; **3** to talk or write aimlessly and at length; **4** to grow or spread aimlessly

ram'bler *n* **1** one who or that which rambles; **2** any of several varieties of climbing roses

ram·bunc·tious /rambuŋk'shəs/ [?] *adj* boisterous; unruly

ram·e·kin or **ram·e·quin** /ram'ikin/ [F *ramequin* pastry made with cheese] *n* 1 small dish in which food is baked and served; 2 baked food made chiefly of cheese, eggs, and bread crumbs

ram·i·fy /ram'ifī'/ [MF *ramifier*] *v* (-**fied**) *vt & vi* to divide or spread into parts or branches ‖ **ram'i·fi·ca'tion** *n*

ram'jet' (**en'gine**) *n* jet engine having the fuel injected into a stream of air compressed by the speed of the aircraft

ramp /ramp'/ [OF *ramper* to climb] *n* 1 slope joining two levels; 2 entrance to or exit from a limited-access highway; 3 movable staircase for entering or leaving an airplane

ram·page /ram'pāj/ *n* 1 state of excitement or rage; 2 violent behavior ‖ /rampāj'/ *vi* 3 to dash about violently; 4 to storm; rage

ramp'ant [OF] *adj* 1 growing or spreading unchecked; unbridled; 2 violent, raging; 3 *heral* reared on the hind legs with one foreleg raised above the other, as *a lion rampant*

ram·part /ram'pärt, ramp'ərt/ *n* 1 embankment surmounted by a parapet, surrounding a fortified place; 2 any protection from danger; defense

ram'rod' *n* rod for ramming down the charge of a muzzleloader

ram'shack'le [*dial. ransackle* to ransack] *adj* loose, shaky, rickety

ran /ran'/ *pt of* **run**

ranch /ranch'/ [Sp *rancho*] *n* 1 farm for the raising of cattle, sheep, or horses in large numbers ‖ *vi* 2 to conduct or work on a ranch ‖ **ranch'er** *n*

ran·cid /ran'sid/ [L *rancidus* stinking] *adj* having a rank, tainted smell or taste of spoiled fat ‖ **ran·cid'i·ty** /-sid'-/ *n*

ran·cor /raŋk'ər/ [MF *rancour* < L *rancor* rancidity] *n* inveterate malice, vindictive enmity ‖ **ran'cor·ous** *adj* ‖ SYN malignity, ill will, grudge, hatred (see *malice*)

R & D research and development

rand /rand'/ [D = border] *n* monetary unit of South Africa

ran·dom /ran'dəm/ [OF *randon* violence, rapidity] *adj* 1 done without aim or purpose; aimless, haphazard ‖ *n* 2 **at random** aimlessly, haphazardly ‖ SYN *adj* haphazard, casual, fortuitous

ran'dom var'i·a·ble *n statistics* quantity which may take any of the values of a specified set with a specified relative frequency or probability

rang /raŋ'/ *pt of* **ring²**

range /rānj'/ [MF *ranger* to set in a row] *vt* 1 to set or arrange in a row or regular order; 2 to place (oneself) within a given group; 3 to classify; 4 to wander over or along; 5 to sail along ‖ *vi* 6 to wander, roam; 7 to go over or through a place; 8 to go or extend in a line; 9 to vary within certain limits; 10 to be found or occur over a certain area, as plants or animals ‖ *n* 11 line or row; series; 12 chain of mountains; 13 scope, extent; 14 great tract of land over which cattle graze; 15 region in which an animal or plant lives; 16 class or order; 17 limits within which a thing may vary in degree or amount; 18 distance to which a missile can be sent; 19 distance of the target from a weapon; 20 place for shooting at a target; 21 cooking stove; 22 distance to which a vehicle can go without refueling

range' find'er *n* instrument for determining the distance of an object from the observer

rang·er /rān'jər/ *n* 1 one of an armed band of men patrolling a region; 2 forest warden; 3 **Ranger** U.S. soldier in World War II trained for commando duty

Ran·goon /raŋgōōn'/ *n* capital of Burma (1,850,000)

rang·y /rān'jē/ *adj* (-**i·er; i·est**) long-limbed and slender

ra·ni or **ra·nee** /rä'nē/ [Hindi *rānī*]) *n* 1 wife of a rajah; 2 Hindu female ruler or princess

rank¹ /raŋk'/ [OF *ranc* row < Gmc] *n* 1 row or line of objects or persons; 2 orderly formation; 3 high station or position; 4 grade of social or official position; 5 relative standing; 6 line of soldiers drawn up side by side; 7 *chess* horizontal row of squares; 8 **the ranks** *pl* a the army as a whole; b the body of enlisted men; 9 **pull rank on** *slang* to use one's higher rank to gain an advantage over (another person) ‖ *vt* 10 to arrange in ranks; 11 to assign to a certain class, order, or division; 12 to outrank (esp. others of the same grade by reason of seniority) ‖ *vi* 13 to hold a certain rank; 14 to hold the highest rank ‖ SYN *n* dignity, nobility, condition, degree, character, class, description, order, distinction, eminence

rank² [OE *ranc* bold] *adj* 1 very plentiful and coarse in growth; 2 offensively strong in taste or smell; 3 offensive, loathsome; 4 utter; extreme ‖ SYN exuberant, luxuriant, gross, indecent, rancid

rank' and file' *n* 1 the common people in a nation; 2 the general membership of an organization

rank'ing *adj* that outranks all others

ran·kle /raŋk'əl/ [MF *rancler* < LL *dracunculus* a sore] *vi* 1 to continue to fester in the mind; 2 to cause mental pain or irritation ‖ *vt* **3** to cause bitter resentment in

ran·sack /ran'sak/ [ON *rannsaka* to search a house] *vt* **1** search thoroughly through; **2** to pillage

ran·som /rans'əm/ [OF *rançon* < L *redemptio* (*-onis*) redemption] *n* **1** redemption of a captive or seized property by payment of a consideration; **2** the sum paid or demanded ‖ *vt* **3** to free from prison, slavery, or punishment by a payment; **4** to redeem; set free

rant /rant/ [MF *ranten* to rave] *vi* to rave in extravagant or violent language; declaim vehemently ‖ **rant'·ing** *n*

rap[1] /rap/ [name of an 18th-cent. Irish counterfeit halfpenny] *n* the least bit

rap[2] [ME *rappen*] *v* (**rapped; rap·ping**) *vi* **1** to knock or tap quickly and sharply ‖ *vt* **2** to strike sharply; **3** to make a rapping sound with (the hand, part of the hand, or something held in the hand) against or on something, *as the policeman rapped his knuckles on the door;* **4** *colloq* to criticize; **5** **rap out** to utter sharply ‖ *n* **6** quick blow or tap; **7** **beat the rap** *slang* to be cleared of a criminal charge; **8** **bum rap** *slang* frame-up; **9** **take the rap** *slang* to take the blame for something

ra·pa·cious /rəpāsh'əs/ [< L *rapax* (*-acis*)] *adj* **1** plundering; **2** greedy, grasping; **3** predatory (animal) ‖ **ra·pac'i·ty** /-pas'-/ *n* ‖ **SYN** avaricious, extortionate, grasping, voracious, ravenous, greedy ‖ **ANT** generous, moderate, bountiful

rape[1] /rāp/ [L *rapere* to seize] *vt* **1** to force (a woman) to have sexual intercourse; **2** to seize and carry off by force ‖ *n* **3** act of raping a woman; **4** abduction

rape[2] [L *rapum* turnips] *n* plant (*Brassica napus*) of the mustard family, used as forage, from the seeds of which an oil is obtained

Raph·a·el /raf'ē·əl, räf'-/ *n* (1483–1520) Italian painter

rap·id /rap'id/ [L *rapidus*] *adj* **1** very quick or swift; **2** moving or acting with speed; **3** progressing or accomplished quickly ‖ *n* **4** usu. **rapids** *pl* place in a river where the water descends rapidly ‖ **rap'id·ly** *adv* ‖ **ra·pid'i·ty** /rəpid'-/ *n* ‖ **SYN** *adj* fast, swift, speedy, fleet, flying, prompt

rap'id trans'it *n* off-street public transportation in large cities by means of subways and/or elevated railways

ra·pi·er /rāp'ē·ər/ [MF (espee) *rapiere* = rasping sword] *n* light, slender, sharp-pointed sword used chiefly for thrusting

rap·ine /rap'in/ [L *rapina*] *n* violent seizure of another's property; plunder ‖ **SYN** plunder, spoliation, pillage, robbery

rap·pel /rapel'/ [F = recall] *n* **1** descent over a cliff by means of a double rope passed under one thigh and over the opposite shoulder ‖ *v* (**-pelled; -pel·ling**) *vi* **2** to descend by means of a rappel

rap·port /rapôr', -pōr'/ [F] *n* sympathetic relationship; harmony

rap·proche·ment /ra'prôsh'mäN'/ [F] *n* the establishing or reestablishing of cordial relations

ras·cal·lion /raskal'yən/ [earlier *rascallion* < *rascal*] *n* rascal, scamp, rogue

rapt /rapt/ [L *raptus* seized] *adj* **1** carried away with emotion; enraptured; **2** engrossed, absorbed

rap·ture /rap'chər/ *n* **1** ecstatic joy; **2** expression of this ‖ **rap'tur·ous** *adj* ‖ **SYN** ecstasy, transport, delight, joy, bliss ‖ **DISCR** These words agree in expressing a state of exalted or ardent feeling. *Ecstasy* is joy so profound, and often so sudden, that it paralyzes with sheer delight; one experiencing *ecstasy* is as one entranced. *Rapture* is as profound, but is less transient; it has its roots in quieter causes, is exultant while it is serene, is impassioned, even though lasting. *Ecstasy* silences; *rapture* forces expression; *ecstasy* paralyzes; *rapture* stimulates to action. *Ecstasy* visits anyone of an ardent or fervent nature, granting the exciting cause; only those capable of grasping deep significances experience *rapture*. *Transport* carries one out of himself in vehement emotion; but, unlike *ecstasy* and *rapture*, the feeling governing a *transport* may be either rage or sorrow. *Transports* are sudden seizures, and urge men sometimes to unconsidered actions, good or bad

rare[1] /rer'/ [L *rarus* thin, loose] *adj* **1** thin, not dense; **2** scarce, uncommon; **3** excellent, choice ‖ **rar'i·ty** *n* (**-ties**) ‖ **SYN** extraordinary, incomparable (see *exquisite*)

rare[2] [OE *hrer* underdone (eggs)] *adj* (meat) cooked slightly, partially raw

rare'bit *n* Welsh rabbit

rare'-earth' met'als *npl* group of closely related metallic elements (atomic numbers 57 to 71) with generally similar properties, used chiefly in making high-quality lenses

rar·e·fy /rer'ifi'/ [MF *rarefier*] *v* (**-fied**) *vt* **1** to make rare or less dense; **2** to refine, purify ‖ *vi* **3** to become thin or less dense ‖ **rar'e·fac'tion** *n*

rare'ly *adv* **1** seldom, infrequently; **2** uncommonly, exceptionally

rar·ing /rer'in/ [< *rear*[2]] *adj colloq* intensely eager

ras·cal /rask'əl/ [OF *rascaille* rabble] *n* **1** mean fellow; scoundrel; **2** mischievous person or animal ‖ **ras'cal·ly** *adj* ‖ **ras·cal'i·ty** /-kal'-/ *n* (**-ties**)

rash[1] /rash'/ [OF *rache* scurf] *n* **1**

eruption of spots on the skin; **2** great number of instances of the same thing

rash² [ME] *adj* recklessly hasty in thought or act ‖ **rash′ly** *adv* ‖ **rash′-ness** *n* ‖ SYN foolhardy, heedless, careless, impetuous, venturous, incautious, inconsiderate, mad

rash′er [perh < *obs rash* to slice] *n* **1** thin slice of bacon for frying; **2** single serving of bacon slices

rasp /rasp′, räsp/ [OF *rasper* to scrape, grate] *vt* **1** to rub or scrape with or as with a rough instrument; **2** to irritate or grate on; **3** to utter with a grating noise ‖ *vi* **4** to scrape or grate roughly; **5** to make a grating noise ‖ *n* **6** coarse file having a toothed surface; **7** any similar tool; **8** harsh grating noise ‖ **rasp′y** *adj* (-i•er; -i•est)

rasp•ber•ry /raz′ber′ē, -berē, räz′-/ *n* (-ries) **1** any of various rosaceous shrubs (genus *Rubus*) bearing juicy, finely flavored, cup-shaped fruit; **2** the red, black, or yellow fruit of these plants; **3** *colloq* **a** jeers, heckling; **b** rude sound made with the tongue and lips expressing derision

ras•tle /ras′əl/ *vt & vi* dial. to wrestle

rat /rat′/ [OE *ræt*] *n* **1** any of several rodents (family Muridae) related to but larger than the mouse; **2** *slang* a contemptible person; **b** informer; **3** small pad over which the hair is rolled; **4 smell a rat** *colloq* to suspect something ‖ *v* (**rat•ted; rat•ting**) *vi* **5** to catch or hunt rats; **6** *slang* to turn informer; **7 rat on** *slang* to inform on

rat•a•ble or **rate•a•ble** /rāt′əbəl/ [see **rate**] *adj* **1** capable of being rated; **2** proportional; **3** *Brit* liable to taxation

rat′bag′ *n Australian* disagreeable eccentric

ratch•et /rach′it/ [F *rochet* kind of lance head] *n* **1** toothed bar or wheel with which a pawl engages; **2** such a bar or wheel together with the pawl

ratch′et wheel′ *n* toothed wheel which is prevented from turning backwards by a pawl

rate¹ /rāt′/ [ML *rata* share] *n* **1** amount or number of one thing measured by units of another; **2** fixed relation of amount, number, or degree between two things; **3** fixed charge per unit of quantity; **4** price, cost; **5** relative quality or condition; rank, class; **6** degree of speed of working or acting; **7 rates** *pl Brit* local property tax; **8 at any rate** in any event ‖ *vt* **9** to estimate or appraise; **10** to give a rating to; **11** to consider, regard; **12** *colloq* to deserve ‖ *vi* **13** to be placed in a certain class or rank; **14** to have value

rate² [< ME *raten*] *vt & vi* to scold sharply ‖ SYN reprove, rail at, upbraid, chide (see *scold*)

rate′ of ex•change′ *n* ratio of the value of one currency to that of another

rate′pay′er *n Brit* one who pays rates or local taxes

rat′fink′ *n slang* thoroughly contemptible person

rath•er /rath′ər, räth′-/ [OE *hrather*] *adv* **1** more willingly; **2** on the contrary; **3** more properly, more accurately; **4** to a certain extent; **5** with more propriety; with better reason ‖ /rathur′/ *interj* **6** *Brit colloq* decidedly!

rat•i•fy /rat′ifī′/ [MF *ratifier*] *v* (-fied) *vt* to approve formally (the action of another or others, as a treaty or amendment) ‖ **rat′i•fi•ca′tion** *n* ‖ SYN approve, sanction, validate, accept, endorse, corroborate, confirm (see *substantiate*)

rat•ing /rāt′in/ [see **rate**] *n* **1** classification according to grade, quality, etc.; **2** credit standing; **3** designated limit of capacity or load, as of a motor; **4** *Brit* enlisted man in the navy

ra•tio /rāsh′ō, -ē•ō′/ [L = reckoning] *n* **1** relation of number, degree, or quantity; proportion; **2** *math* quotient of one quantity divided by another of like kind

ra•ti•o•ci•na•tion /rash′ē•os′ināsh′ən/ [< L *ratiocinari* (-*atus*) to calculate] *n* process of reasoning or logical thinking ‖ **ra′ti•oc′i•nate′** *vi*

ra•tion /rash′ən, rāsh′-/ [F < L *ratio* (-*onis*) reckoning] *n* **1** definite quantity of food for a soldier's meal; **2** any fixed or stated share; **3 rations** *pl* provisions ‖ *vt* **4** to furnish with rations; **5** to limit the supplies of (a scare item), as in war time; **6** to impose rationing on

ra•tion•al /rash′ənəl/ [L *rationalis*] *adj* **1** pert. to reason; **2** having the power to reason; **3** able to exercise reason; **4** agreeable to reason; sensible ‖ **ra′tion•al′i•ty** /-al′-/ *n* ‖ SYN reasonable, sensible, sound ‖ DISCR *Rational* describes one endowed with reason, one who has the faculty of reason, as man is a *rational* animal. Rarely, *reasonable* is also used in this abstract sense; but as a rule *reasonable* describes one who uses the faculty of reason, or such things as are thought out according to reason. Hence, we speak of a man of *sound* judgment, who will listen intelligently to both sides of a question, as a *reasonable* man. A compromise fair to both parties is *reasonable*.

ra•tion•ale /rash′ənal′/ [L = rational] *n* **1** exposition of basic principles; **2** statement of the reasons for something

ra′tion•al•ism *n* **1** habit or principle of thinking for oneself instead of conforming to accepted authority; **2** *theol* doctrine that places reason above revelation as the guide in matters of belief; **3** *philos* theory that ultimate truth must be discovered by reason rather than by experience ‖ **ra′tion·al·ist** *n* ‖ **ra′tion·al·is′tic** *adj*

ra′tion·al·ize′ *vt* **1** to explain according to reason; **2** to make conformable to reason; **3** to assign a plausible explanation to (one's actions or attitudes, of which the real motive may be suppressed or unconscious); **4** *math* to remove radical signs from ‖ *vi* **5** to rely on reason for guidance; **6** to rationalize one's thoughts or actions ‖ **ra′tion·al·i·za′tion** *n*

ra′tion·al num′ber *n math* number that can be expressed as an integer or the quotient of two integers

rat·line /rat′lin/ [ME *ratling*] *n* one of the short horizontal ropes in the shrouds of a ship that serve as a ladder

rat′ race′ *n colloq* the competitive and unremitting grind of everyday existence or of some regular assignment or task

rats′ *interj slang* exclamation of disgust or disappointment

rats′bane′ *n* **1** rat poison; **2** spec., white arsenic

rat′-tail file′ *n* long, narrow, round file, for enlarging holes

rat·tan /ratan′/ [Malay *rōtan*] *n* **1** any of several climbing palms (genus *Calamus*); **2** stem of such a palm, used for wickerwork, chair bottoms, etc.

rat·tle /rat′əl/ [ME *rateln*] *vi* **1** to produce short sharp noises in quick succession; **2** to move with a clatter; **3 rattle on** to talk rapidly and monotonously ‖ *vt* **4** to cause to rattle; **5** to confuse or disconcert; **6 rattle off** to utter rapidly ‖ *n* **7** series of short, sharp, clattering sounds in quick succession; **8** rattling sound in the throat; **9** child's toy for making a rattling sound; **10** horny plates at the end of a rattlesnake's tail

rat′tle·brain′ *n* giddy empty-headed person ‖ **rat′tle·brained′** *adj*

rat′tler *n* rattlesnake

rat′tle·snake′ *n* any of several poisonous American snakes (family Crotalidae) with a series of horny ringlike plates at the end of the tail which rattle when shaken

rat′tle·trap′ *n* old, rickety, rattling vehicle

rat′ty *adj* (**-ti·er, -ti·est**) shabby

rau·cous /rôk′əs/ [< L *raucus* hoarse] *adj* hoarse, harsh-sounding

raun·chy /rônch′ē/ [?] *adj* (**-chi·er, -chi·est**) *slang* **1** careless, unkempt; **2** obscene; **3** lecherous

rav·age /rav′ij/ [F] *n* **1** often **ravages** *pl* destruction; ruin; havoc ‖ *vt* **2** to lay waste, pillage; ruin ‖ *vi* **3** to work havoc ‖ SYN *v* overrun, desolate, devastate, destroy, despoil, violate, desecrate, sack, pillage, plunder

rave /rāv′/ [ME *raven*] *vt* **1** to utter

in frenzy ‖ *vi* **2** to talk wildly, as in delirium; **3** to speak enthusiastically ‖ *n* **4** extravagantly favorable review or criticism

rav·el /rav′əl/ [prob MD *ravelen*] *v* (**-eled** or **-elled**; **-el·ing** or **-el·ling**) *vt* **1** to draw out the threads of (a woven fabric); **2** to unravel; make plain or clear ‖ *vi* **3** to become unwoven; fray; **4** to become tangled ‖ *n* **5** snarl, tangle

ra·ven /rāv′ən/ [OE *hræfn*] *n* **1** large bird of the crow family, of a glossy, black color ‖ *adj* **2** lustrous and black

rav·en·ous /rav′ənəs/ [OF *ravineus*] *adj* **1** furiously hungry; **2** voracious

ra·vine /rəvēn′/ [MF = torrent] *n* narrow valley with steep sides

rav′ing /rāv′-/ *n* **1** irrational talk; delirium ‖ *adj* **2** delirious; talking wildly; **3** extraordinary (beauty)

ra·vi·o·li /rav′ē·ōl′ē/ [It] *nsg & npl* small squares of pasta stuffed with meat or cheese

rav·ish /rav′ish/ [MF *ravir* (-*viss*-) to seize] *vt* **1** to seize and remove by force; **2** to rape; **3** to transport with delight or rapture ‖ **rav′ish·er** *n* ‖ **rav′ish·ment** *n* ‖ SYN entrance, enrapture, delight, enchant

rav′ish·ing *adj* entrancing

raw /rô′/ [OE *hrēaw*] *adj* **1** uncooked; **2** with the skin rubbed off; **3** natural; unprocessed; not manufactured, as *raw silk*; **4** crude, inexperienced, as *raw troops*; **5** cold and damp; **6** harshly unfair; **7** undiluted (whiskey); **8** crude, unrefined, as humor ‖ *n* **9** in the raw, **a** in the natural state; **b** *slang* naked ‖ SYN *adj* unfinished, unpolished, boorish, undisciplined, green, inexperienced, untempered, unprepared

raw′boned′ *adj* gaunt; lean

raw′ deal′ *n slang* case of unfair treatment

raw′hide′ *n* **1** untanned skin, as of cattle; **2** whip made of it

raw′ ma·te·ri·al *n* material before it is processed into a finished product

ray¹ /rā′/ [OF *rai* < L *radius*] *n* **1** narrow beam of light; **2** one of a number of lines spreading from a common center; **3** small amount, as *a ray of hope*; **4** *phys* beam of energy propagated through space in the form of waves or particles; **5** *bot* outer flowers of certain composite plants; **6** one of the supporting spines of a fish's fin; **7** one of the radiating arms of a starfish

ray² [L *raia*] *n* any of various fishes (suborder Batoidei) having a broad flat body and a thin tail

ray·on /rā′on/ [F] *n* lustrous elastic cellulose spun into thread from which various fabrics closely resembling silk are made

raze /rāz′/ [MF *raser* < L *rasus*

scraped] *vt* to level to the ground; obliterate ‖ SYN (see *destroy*)

ra·zor /rāz′ər/ [OF *rasor*] *n* sharp-edged instrument used for shaving hair from the skin

ra′zor·back′ *n* long-legged hog with a ridged back, common in the South

razz /raz′/ [< *raspberry*] *vt* slang to tease, heckle, or ridicule

raz·zle·daz·zle /raz′əl daz′əl/ *n* colloq 1 showy activity; 2 confusion; commotion

Rb *chem* rubidium

R.B.I., RBI *baseball* run(s) batted in

R.C., RC 1 Red Cross; 2 Roman Catholic

Rd. Road

Re *chem* rhenium

re¹ /rā′/ [It] *n mus* second tone of the diatonic scale

re² /rē′/ [L] *prep* in the matter of, with reference to

're are, as *we're, they're*

re- [L] *pref* 1 against; 2 back, backward; 3 again

reach /rēch′/ [OE *rǣcan*] *vt* 1 to stretch out, as the hand; 2 to touch or grasp, as with the extended hand; 3 to arrive at, attain; 4 to extend as far as, penetrate to; 5 to influence, affect; 6 to hit with an object thrown, wielded, or fired; 7 to get in touch with; 8 to amount to ‖ *vi* 9 to extend the hand, foot, or the like, so as to touch or seize something; 10 to endeavor to obtain something; 11 to extend in time, space, amount, or the like ‖ *n* 12 act or instance of reaching; 13 extent or range of reaching; 14 unbroken stretch, as of water

re·act /rē·akt′/ *vi* 1 to act in return; act reciprocally; 2 to respond to an influence or stimulus; 3 to act in a reverse direction; 4 *chem* to exert mutual chemical action; 5 *phys* to resist the action of a body by an opposing force

re·ac′tance *n* opposition of a circuit to the flow of an alternating current because of inductance and capacity

re·ac′tion *n* 1 opposing or return action or influence; 2 political movement in the direction of extreme conservatism or rightism; 3 action in response to a stimulus; 4 chemical change

re·ac′tion·ar·y /-ner′-/ *n* (-ies) one who favors or is a partisan of political reaction ‖ also *adj*

re·ac′tion en′gine *n* engine that derives thrust by expelling a stream of gases of combustion to the rear; it works in accordance with Newton's third law of motion

re·ac′tion time′ *n* time elapsed between stimulus and response

re·ac′ti·vate *vt* to render active again; make operational again ‖ **re·ac′ti·va′tion** *n*

re·ac′tor *n* apparatus in which a con-

trolled chain reaction of atomic fission may be maintained for the production of fissionable material, radioactive isotopes, or power

read¹ /rēd′/ [OE *rǣdan* to interpret, read] *v* (**read** /red′/) *vt* 1 to interpret and understand (written or printed words, notes of music, etc.); 2 to peruse and understand (other significant signs, marks, etc.), as *to read a barometer, read the sky;* 3 to hear and understand the broadcast signal or message of; 4 to interpret, as a person's thoughts; 5 to foretell; 6 to read aloud (something written or printed); 7 to attribute (an additional meaning) into what is being read; 8 to study (law); 9 to register, as a gauge; 10 to impress upon, as *he read them a lesson;* 11 **read out of** to expel from (an organization or political party) ‖ *vi* 12 to read written or printed matter; 13 to utter aloud what is written; 14 to have a specified wording; 15 to give a public reading; 16 to be subject to interpretation, as *how does the law read?;* 17 **read about** or **of** to learn of by reading; 18 **read for** to try out for (a part in a play); 19 **read up on** to make a study of

read² /red′/ 1 *pt & pp* of **read** ‖ *adj* 2 informed by reading, as *widely read*

read′a·ble /rēd′-/ *adj* 1 easy and interesting to read; 2 legible ‖ **read′-a·bil′i·ty** /-bil′-/ *n*

read′er *n* 1 one who reads; 2 one who evaluates manuscripts offered for publication; 3 professor's assistant who reads themes for him; 4 schoolbook for instruction and practice in reading

read′i·ly /red′-/ *adv* 1 promptly, easily; 2 willingly

read′ing /rēd′-/ *n* 1 perusal of written or printed matter; 2 utterance aloud of written words; 3 academic study, scholarship; 4 public recitation; 5 version or form of a particular passage in a book, as *various readings of a passage in different editions;* 6 written or printed matter to be perused; 7 manner of interpreting something written, as *an actor's reading of his lines;* 8 that which is indicated by a graduated instrument

read·y /red′ē/ [ME *redy*] *adj* (-i·er; -i·est) 1 in condition to act or to be used immediately; 2 willing, as *ready to obey;* 3 liable, likely, as *the tree was ready to fall;* 4 quick in action or perception, prompt, as *a ready wit;* 5 immediately available, as *ready cash;* 6 with repairs or adjustments completed, as *the car is ready;* 7 disposed, as *ready to laugh;* 8 **make ready** to prepare ‖ *v* (-ied) *vt* 9 to make ready ‖ **read′i·ness** *n* ‖ SYN *adj* apt, facile, opportune, ingenious, ripe

read′y-made′ *adj* 1 not made to individual order or measure; made in standard forms; **2** prepared beforehand; **3** conventional; lacking in originality

read′y-to-wear′ *adj* **1** made in advance and ready for immediate wear; **2** dealing in ready-to-wears ‖ *n* **3** ready-made piece of clothing

re·a′gent *n chem* substance which, because of its reaction with other substances, is used in analysis and synthesis

re·al /rē′əl, rēl′/ [LL *realis* of the thing itself] *adj* **1** actually existing; true; **2** genuine, authentic ‖ *adv* **3** *colloq* very ‖ *n* **4** for real *slang* a actually; **b** really in existence ‖ SYN *adj* actual, certain, sure, authentic, veritable, true

re′al es·tate′ *n* property in land and buildings ‖ **re′al-es·tate′** *adj*

re·al·ism /rē′əliz′əm/ *n* **1** tendency to concern oneself with actuality or fact; **2** *philos* **a** doctrine that objects that can be perceived have a real existence independent of perception; **b** doctrine that class terms or concepts have a real existence apart from the objects included under them; **3** *art & literature* practice of presenting people and things as they are in real life without idealization ‖ **re′al·ist** *n* ‖ **re′al·is′tic** *adj* ‖ SYN (see *reality*)

re·al·i·ty /rē·al′itē/ *n* (**-ties**) **1** state or quality of being real; **2** that which exists or is actual; fact; truth; **3** in reality actually; in fact ‖ SYN truth, actuality, verity, verity, truthfulness, realism ‖ DISCR *Reality* is the property of being real, of really existing; *reality* is what is, despite appearances. It is opposed to the imaginary, the make-believe, the fictitious, the merely apparent, the artificial, the ostensible. It is a rest to tired minds to escape from *reality* into the world of make-believe. Some diamonds, apparently genuine, are in *reality* paste. *Actuality* is *reality* regarded as fact; *actuality* is opposed to what may be, what has been, or what might have been, or what somebody thought, said, or supposed to be the case. *Truth* is that quality of a person which compels him to make his acts and statements conform to fact, without insincerity or equivocation. *Truth* inheres also in things, and is evidenced in their *reality*, *actuality*, or mechanical accuracy or exactness. We speak of the *truth* of a statement. *Veracity* is the quality of a person who is disposed to, and habitually does, speak the *truth*; a veracious man might tell something untrue, but it would not be meant as falsehood. *Truth* is sometimes used in this sense of *veracity*; we speak of a person of *veracity* or of *truth*, indicating a

basic trend of his character. *Truthfulness* may apply to the quality that makes a man veracious, but it oftenest refers to the innate *truth* of a statement, or the sincerity underlying a belief or stand. *Verity*, like *truth*, is an exact conformance to fact; it is a habit of thought, manifested in speech. *Reality*, *realism*, and *verity* are often used of representations in art or literature of life or things. Something reproduced with *reality* is so strikingly real that the observer feels the reaction of *actuality*; "startling *reality*" is a well-worn phrase. *Verity* is such truthful representation as convinces, is sincere, impresses with its *reality*. *Realism*, opposed to *idealism*, presents every detail in a practical way, sparing nothing, revealing everything

re·al·ize /rē′əliz′/ *vt* **1** to bring into actual existence; accomplish; **2** to bring clearly before the mind; feel fully and keenly; **3** to convert into money; **4** to obtain as a profit ‖ *vi* **5** to sell property for ready money ‖ **re′al·i·za′tion** *n* ‖ SYN comprehend, appreciate, conceive, get, obtain

re·al·ly /rē′(ə)lē/ *adv* **1** actually; **2** genuinely; **3** indeed

realm /relm′/ [OF *reialme*] *n* **1** kingdom; **2** domain or sphere

re′al prop′er·ty *n* property consisting of land, buildings, and all appurtenances, as crops, timber, etc.

re·al·tor /rē′əltər, -tôr′/ *n* dealer in real estate associated with the National Association of Real Estate Boards

re′al·ty *n* real estate

re′al wag′es *npl* wages estimated in purchasing power rather than money

ream[1] /rēm′/ [MF *reime* < Sp *rezma* < Ar] *n* **1** twenty quires or 500 sheets of paper; **2** usu. **reams** *pl* a large quantity

ream[2] [OE *rēman* to open up] *vt* to enlarge (a hole) with a reamer

ream′er *n* any of various tools with sharp edges for enlarging or tapering holes

reap /rēp′/ [OE *repan*] *vt* **1** to cut down (grain), as with a sickle; **2** to gather in (a crop); **3** to receive as a reward or in return for effort ‖ also *vi*

reap′er *n* **1** one who reaps; **2** reaping machine

re′ap·por′tion·ment /rē′-/ *n* realignment of legislative districts, usu. done to allow for population shifts

rear[1] /rir′/ [< *arrear*] *n* **1** back part; **2** place or position behind; **3** buttocks; **4** bring up the rear to be at the end ‖ *adj* **5** pert. to or situated at the rear

rear[2] [OE *rēran* to raise] *vt* **1** to raise or lift up; elevate; **2** to construct, erect; **3** to bring up and educate (children) ‖ *vi* **4** to rise up on the hind legs, as a horse; **5** to rise up in anger; **6** to rise, tower ‖ SYN construct, establish, breed, foster, instruct

rear′ ad′mi·ral *n* naval officer ranking next below a vice admiral

rear′ end′ *n* **1** hindmost end; **2** *colloq* buttocks

re·arm′ /rē-/ *vt* **1** to arm again; **2** to provide with better and more modern weapons ‖ **re·ar′ma·ment** *n*

rear′most′ *adj* farthest back; last

rear′ward /-wərd/ *adj* **1** located at or directed toward the rear ‖ *adv* **2** also **rear′wards** at or toward the rear

rea·son /rēz′ən/ [OF *raisun* < L *ratio* (*-onis*)] *n* **1** power or faculty of understanding and inferring; **2** sanity; common sense; **3** cause or motive for an act or opinion; **4** explanation for a belief, remark, act, or the like; **5 by reason of** because of; **6 in** or **within reason** reasonable; **7 stand to reason** to be logical ‖ *vi* **8** to think logically; **9** to draw conclusions; **10** to argue or discuss ‖ *vt* **11 reason out** to come to a conclusion about by logical thinking

rea·son·a·ble *adj* **1** endowed with reason; **2** moderate, not excessive; **3** sensible, logical ‖ **rea′son·a·bly** *adv* ‖ SYN equitable, sound, moderate (see *rational*)

rea·son·ing *n* **1** act of one who reasons; **2** line of argument; presentation of reasons ‖ SYN argument, ratiocination, thought, thinking

re·as·sure′ *vt* **1** to restore confidence in; **2** to assure again ‖ **re′as·sur′ance** *n*

re·bate /rĭbāt′/ [OF *rabattre* to put down] *vt* **1** to make a reduction from; **2** to allow a discount to ‖ /rē′bāt/ *n* **3** discount; partial refund

re·bec /rē′bek/ [OF *rebebe* < Ar *rabāb*] *n* medieval stringed instrument having a pear-shaped body and one to three strings, played with a bow

Re·bek·ah also **Re·bec·ca** /rĭbek′ə/ *n Bib* wife of Isaac and mother of Esau and Jacob (Gen. 25:20–26)

re·bel /rĭbel′/ [OF *rebelle*] *v* (**-belled; -bel·ling**) *vi* **1** to resist or take up arms against the government; **2** to revolt against any authority; **3** to feel aversion or repugnance ‖ **reb·el** /reb′əl/ *n* **4** one who resists the authority of his government or takes up arms against it; **5** one who resists any authority

re·bel·lion /rĭbel′yən/ *n* **1** act of rebelling; **2** resistance to or defiance of any authority; revolt ‖ SYN insurrection, mutiny, resistance (see *revolution*)

re·bel′lious *adj* **1** opposing or resisting authority of any kind; **2** pert. to rebels or rebellion; **3** unmanageable, as *rebellious hair* ‖ SYN mutinous,

seditous, intractable, ungovernable, contumacious ‖ ANT yielding, tractable, manageable

re·birth /rĭburth′, rē′burth′/ *n* **1** second birth; **2** revival; renewed existence

re·bound /rĭbound′/ [MF *rebondir*] *vi* **1** to spring or fly back from impact ‖ /rē′bound′/ *n* **2** act of rebounding; recoil; **3** *basketball* ball that bounces off the backboard; **4 on the rebound** as a reaction to a crisis such as an unhappy love affair

re·broad′cast′ /rē/-/ *v* (**-cast** or **-cast·ed**) *vt* **1** to broadcast (a program) again; **2** to broadcast (a program picked up from another station) ‖ *n* **3** broadcast that is repeated; **4** broadcast that is picked up from another station

re·buff /rĭbuf′, rē′buf/ [MF *rebuffer* < It *ribuffare*] *n* **1** blunt refusal or rejection; snub; **2** sudden check; defeat ‖ /rĭbuf′/ *vt* **3** to repel curtly; refuse bluntly; **4** to check suddenly

re·built′ /rē-/ *adj* disassembled and repaired with new parts added, as an appliance or motor

re·buke /rĭbyōōk′/ [AF *rebuker* to defeat] *n* **1** sharp reproof; reprimand ‖ *vt* **2** to reprove sharply ‖ SYN *v* admonish, reprimand, reprehend, check

re·bus /rēb′əs/ [L = by things] *n* puzzle in which words or syllables are represented by pictures or symbols, the names of which, when sounded in sequence, afford the solution

re·but /rĭbut′/ [OF *rebouter*] *n* (**-but·ted; -but·ting**) *vt* **1** to refute by argument, evidence, or proof ‖ *vi* **2** to offer a rebuttal

re·but′tal *n* **1** act of rebutting; **2** *law* presentation of evidence which contradicts testimony already given by the opposing side in a trial

re·cal·ci·trant /rĭkal′sĭtrənt/ [< L *recalcitrare* to oppose strongly] *adj* refusing to comply; refractory; stubborn ‖ **re·cal′ci·trance** *n*

re·call /rĭkôl′/ *vt* **1** to order or summon back; **2** to remember, recollect; **3** to take back, revoke ‖ /rē′kôl/, rĭkôl′/ *n* **4** act of recalling; **5** removal of, or the right to remove, an elected official from office by petition and vote of the electors

re·cant /rĭkant′/ [L *recantare*] *vt* to retract formally (an opinion or belief); renounce ‖ also *vi* ‖ **re′can·ta′tion** /rē′-/ *n*

re·cap¹ /rē′kap′, rē′kap′/ *v* (**-capped; -cap·ping**) *vt* **1** to cement a new tread on (a tire) ‖ /rē′kap′/ *n* **2** recapped tire ‖ **re·cap′pa·ble** *adj*

re·cap′² *v* (**-capped; -cap·ping**) *vt* **1** to recapitulate ‖ *n* **2** recapitulation

re·ca·pit′u·late′ /rē′-/ *vt & vi* to sum up; restate briefly ‖ **re′ca·pit′u·la′tion** *n*

recd., rec′d. received

re·cede /rĭsēd′/ [L *recedere*] *vi* **1** to

fall back; retreat; retire; **2** to slope backward

re·ceipt /risēt'/ [AF *receite*] *n* **1** act of receiving or fact of being received; **2** recipe; **3** written acknowledgment of anything obtained from another; **4 receipts** *pl* cash received from the sale of goods or services ‖ *vt* **5** to acknowledge in writing the payment of (a bill)

re·ceiv·a·ble /risēv'əbəl/ *adj* **1** capable of being received; **2** awaiting payment, as *accounts receivable*

re·ceive /risēv'/ [ONF *receivre* < L *recipere*] *vt* **1** to take (something offered or delivered); **2** to get knowledge of, as *to receive reports*; **3** to admit to one's company, entertain; **4** to hold, contain; **5** to admit as credible, accept, as *they received the faith;* **6** to sustain, be subjected to, as a shock or blow; **7** to experience; **8** to admit into membership; **9** to admit into a place ‖ *vi* **10** to receive something; **11** to take the sacrament; **12** to receive guests; **13** to pick up broadcast signals

Re·ceived' Stand'ard Eng'lish *n* the English spoken in British public schools and at Oxford and Cambridge universities and accepted as the standard English of educated Englishmen

re·ceiv'er *n* **1** one who or that which receives; **2** receptacle; **3** one who knowingly receives stolen goods; **4** device for converting electrical signals into sound and/or sight, as a radio, television set, or telephone earpiece; **5** *law* person appointed by a court to administer property in bankruptcy or that is subject to litigation

re·ceiv'er·ship' *n law* **1** state of being bankrupt; **2** position or function of a receiver

re·ceiv'ing line' *n* a number of persons standing in line at a formal reception to welcome the guests as they file by and sometimes to present them to a guest of honor

re·cent /rē'sənt/ [L *recens* (*-entis*)] *adj* **1** not long past; **2** of origin or occurrence near the present; new, modern; **3 Recent** *geol* designating the era extending from the close of the Pleistocene to the present ‖ **re'cent·ly** *adv* ‖ **re'cen·cy** *n* ‖ SYN new, late (see *modern*)

re·cep·ta·cle /risep'təkəl/ [L *receptaculum*] *n* **1** container; **2** box with an electrical fitting for receiving a plug connected to a lamp, appliance, or other electric device; **3** that part of the stalk to which the floral organs are attached

re·cep·tion /risep'shən/ [L *receptio* (*-onis*)] *n* **1** act of receiving or state of being received; **2** formal entertainment of a large number of guests;

3 formal or official greeting of a person; **4** quality of reproduction of radio or television signals

re·cep'tion·ist *n* office employee who answers the telephone and receives callers

re·cep'tive *adj* **1** having the quality of taking in or receiving; **2** quick to take in ideas or impressions ‖ **re'cep·tiv'i·ty** /rē'-/ *n*

re·cess /rises', rē'ses/ [L *recessus* receded] *n* **1** hollowed-out space, as in a wall; **2** temporary stopping of work or school; short intermission; **3 recesses** *pl* inner or secluded area ‖ *vi* **4** to take a recess

re·ces·sion /risesh'ən/ *n* **1** act of receding; withdrawal; **2** procession of withdrawal, as at the end of a church service; **3** decline sufficiently deep, prolonged, and widespread to cause a significant decrease in aggregate economic activity

re·ces'sion·al *adj* **1** pert. to a withdrawing procession ‖ *n* **2** hymn sung or played during a recession, as at the close of a church service

re·ces'sive *adj* **1** receding; **2** *genetics* pert. to characteristics which do not appear in the immediate offspring, but which may be transmitted

re·cid·i·vist /risid'ivist/ [< L *recidivus* relapsing] *n* chronic repeater of criminal or antisocial offenses ‖ **re·cid'i·vism** *n*

rec·i·pe /res'ipē'/ [*impv* of L *recipere* = receive] *n* **1** set of directions for preparing a dish or drink; **2** any method or formula for attaining something, as *recipe for success*

re·cip·i·ent /risip'ē·ənt/ [L *recipiens* (*-entis*) receiving] *n* **1** one who or that which receives ‖ *adj* **2** receiving

re·cip·ro·cal /risip'rəkəl/ [< L *reciprocus*] *adj* **1** done, given, or offered by each to the other; mutual; **2** offered in return for something done or given; **3** able to be exchanged for one another; **4** *gram* (pronoun) showing mutual action or relation ‖ *n* **5** that which is given or done by each to the other; **6** *math* quotient of unity divided by any quantity, as *the reciprocal of 3 is ⅓* ‖ **re·cip'ro·cal·ly** *adv* ‖ SYN *adj* interchangeable, complementary, correlative (see *mutual*)

re·cip'ro·cate' [L *reciprocare* (*-atus*) to move back and forth] *vt* **1** to give to and receive from one another, as *they reciprocate favors;* **2** to return in kind, as *he reciprocates her affection;* **3** to cause to move alternately back and forth ‖ *vi* **4** to interchange something; make an exchange; **5** to pay back an act or feeling; **6** to move alternately back and forth ‖ **re·cip'ro·ca'tion** *n*

re·cip'ro·cat'ing en'gine *n* engine in which the pistons move back and forth in a straight line in the cylinders

rec·i·proc·i·ty /res′ipros′itē/ [see reciprocal] n 1 reciprocal state or relationship; 2 mutual exchange; 3 relationship between two nations in which each grants the other special advantages in trade

re·cit·al /risit′ol/ [see recite] n 1 act of reciting; 2 account of events; narration; 3 performance of music or dancing, usu. by a single artist or by the students of a teacher

rec·i·ta·tion /res′itāsh′ən/ n 1 act of reciting; 2 public rendering of prose or poetry committed to memory; 3 response by students to a teacher's questions on a prepared lesson; 4 classroom instruction

rec·i·ta·tive /res′itətēv′/ [It recitativo] n 1 words of a song spoken to music with rhythm but without pitch; vocal rendition intermediate between speech and singing; 2 passage rendered in this style ‖ also adj

re·cite /risīt′/ [L recitare (-atus) to read aloud] vt 1 to repeat aloud from memory, as a lesson in the classroom; 2 to tell in detail; relate; ‖ vi 3 to recite something ‖ SYN narrate, relate, recount, rehearse, repeat

reck·less /rek′lis/ [OE reccelēas] adj heedless of consequences; rash ‖ SYN foolhardy, careless, daring, regardless, remiss

reck·on /rek′ən/ [ME rekenen] vt 1 to count or compute; 2 to consider as being; 3 to think, suppose ‖ vi 4 **reckon on** to depend or rely on; 5 **reckon with, a** to take into consideration; **b** to deal with

reck′on·ing n 1 computation, count; 2 settling of accounts; 3 an accounting

re·claim′ /ri-/ vt 1 to reform; bring back from vice; 2 to bring to use or under cultivation, as swamp or wild land; 3 to recover (useful substances) from waste products ‖ rec′la·ma′tion /rek′lə-/ n ‖ SYN redeem, restore, reform, tame, civilize

re·cline /riklīn′/ [L reclinare] vt 1 to cause to lean or lie back ‖ vi 2 to lie down

re·clin′er n reclining chair with adjustable back and footrest

rec·luse /rek′lōōs, riklōōs′/ [OF reclus] n one who lives alone; hermit

rec·og·ni·tion /rek′əgnish′ən/ [< L recognitus recognized] n 1 act of recognizing or state of being recognized; 2 formal acknowledgment or commendation

re·cog·ni·zance /rikog′nizəns, -kon′-/ n law 1 agreement entered into before a magistrate or court to do some particular act; 2 sum of money to be forfeited if the obligation is not fulfilled

rec·og·nize /rek′əgnīz′/ [recognition + -ize] vt 1 to take formal notice of;

acknowledge; 2 to concede as true, admit; 3 to know the identity of; recall as having been previously known; 4 to admit acquaintance with; salute; 5 in a deliberative assembly, to give the floor to ‖ **rec′og·niz′a·ble** adj

re·coil /rikoil′/ [OF reculer] vi 1 to draw back, as in dismay or fear; 2 to spring back, kick, as a gun when fired; 3 to retreat, fall back ‖ /also rē′koil′/ n 4 act of recoiling

rec·ol·lect /rek′əlekt′/ vt & vi to remember

rec·ol·lec′tion n 1 act of recollecting; 2 thing recollected ‖ SYN remembrance, reminiscence (see memory)

rec·om·mend /rek′əmend′/ vt 1 to speak in favor of, commend, as for a job; 2 to advise; suggest; urge; 3 to make attractive ‖ **rec′om·men·da′tion** n

re·com·mit′ /rē′-/ v (-mit·ted; -mit·ting) vt 1 to commit again; 2 to refer again, as to a committee

rec·om·pense /rek′əmpens′/ [MF recompenser] vt 1 to remunerate; reward; 2 to give compensation for ‖ n 3 remuneration; reward; 4 compensation ‖ SYN remuneration, requital (see salary)

rec·on·cile /rek′ənsīl′/ [L reconciliare to reestablish] vt 1 to restore harmony or friendship between; 2 to adjust; settle, as differences; 3 to make compatible or consistent; 4 **reconcile one** to to bring one to accept (something unpleasant or unwanted), as to reconcile a person to his losses ‖ **rec′on·cil′a·ble** adj ‖ **rec′on·cil′i·a′tion** /-sil′ē·ā′shən/ n

rec·on·dite /rek′əndīt/ [L reconditus] adj 1 too difficult for the ordinary mind to understand;′ profound or abstruse; 2 obscure ‖ SYN abstruse, hidden, secret, mysterious, occult

re·con·di′tion /rē′-/ vt to restore to good condition, as by cleaning, repairing, replacing worn parts, etc.

re·con·nais·sance /rikon′isəns/ [F] n 1 act of reconnoitering; 2 survey of a region, esp. for military information

rec·on·noi·ter /rek′ənoit′ər, rēk′-/ [MF reconoistre to recognize] vt to survey and inspect (a region, an enemy position) for scientific or military purposes ‖ also vi

re·con′quest /rē′-/ n conquest of something formerly held and later lost

re·con·sid′er /rē′-/ vt to consider again, esp. with a view to changing a decision ‖ **re′con·sid′er·a′tion** n

re·con·struct′ vt 1 to construct again; rebuild; 2 to recreate from available evidence

re′con·struc′tion n 1 act of reconstructing; 2 **Reconstruction** process of restoring to the Union, after the Civil War, the states that had seceded (1865–77)

re·con·vert vt to change back to a former status, function, belief, etc ‖ **re·con·ver·sion** n

re·cord /rĭkôrd'/ [L recordari to remember] vt 1 to write or set down an account of (events); 2 to register, as on a graph or gauge; 3 to register (sound) permanently, as by grooves on a disk or magnetically on tape, for the purpose of reproduction at will; 4 to make a recording of ‖ **rec·ord** /rĕk'ərd/ n 5 act of recording or state of being recorded; 6 permanent account of events; 7 official list of achievements good or bad, as a scholastic record, police record; 8 remembrance, souvenir; 9 criminal record; 10 official report of public acts; 11 cylinder or disk for reproducing sounds in phonographs; 12 law official copy of all documents and proceedings in a case; 13 best attained performance; 14 records pl public documents; 15 **on record, a** publicly known; **b** officially attested; 16 **off the record** confidential or unofficial ‖ adj 17 surpassing all previous events of the same nature ‖ SYN n register, chronicle, entry (see history)

rec·ord chang·er n mechanism of a record player that automatically drops or puts in place and plays one record at a time of a stack of records

re·cord·er n 1 one who records; 2 official who keeps public records; 3 device for recording or registering; 4 end-blown flute with a mellow tone

re·cord·ing n 1 phonograph record; 2 that which is recorded on it

rec·ord play·er n mechanical or electrical machine for playing phonograph records; phonograph

re·count /ri-/ [MF reconter] vt 1 to tell in detail; narrate; 2 to enumerate

re·count /rē-/ vt 1 to count again ‖ /rē'kount'/ n 2 second count, as of votes

re·coup /rĭkōōp'/ [MF recouper to cut again] vt 1 to make good, regain, as a loss; 2 to indemnify ‖ **re·coup·ment** n

re·course /rē'kôrs, rĭkôrs'/ [OF recours] n 1 resort or appeal to something for aid or protection; 2 person or thing appealed to; 3 liability of the endorser of a negotiable instrument

re·cov·er /ri-/ [MF recovrer] vt 1 to get back or regain; 2 to make up for; make good the loss or damage of; 3 to regain (one's strength, balance, composure, etc.); 4 to salvage (by-products, auxiliary materials, and leavings); 5 law to obtain by judgment in a court, as damages ‖ vi 6 to regain health or strength, or any former state; 7 to regain one's balance or composure ‖ **re·cov·er·a·ble** adj ‖ **re·cov·er·y** n (-ies) ‖ SYN re-

take, repossess, retrieve, recuperate, reanimate, recruit ‖ ANT lapse, fail, sink, die

rec·re·ant /rĕk'rē-ənt/ [OF] adj 1 cowardly ‖ n 2 coward ‖ SYN adj cowardly, craven, dastardly, pusillanimous, traitorous ‖ DISCR These words agree in describing an ignoble lack of courage, either moral or physical. One who is cowardly is soft of fiber in the face of danger, shrinks unduly from pain. Craven and pusillanimous describe base cowardliness, craven connoting an abject, crushed condition of the spirit, pusillanimous a mean, feeble, contemptible absence of pluck, grit, or endurance. Dastardly describes one not only cowardly but skulking, one who commits a crime or is guilty of a malicious act safe from detection or observation. Recreant is another word for craven, and, like craven, connotes avowed defeat and surrender; it is also used in the sense of faithless, apostate. Recreant, dastardly, and craven are harsh, condemning adjectives ‖ ANT adj courageous, spirited, noble, faithful

rec·re·a·tion /rĕk'rē-āsh'ən/ [MF < L recreatio (-onis) restoration to health] n 1 refreshment of mind or body after toil or weariness; 2 any occupation that diverts ‖ SYN pastime, diversion, play (see amusement)

re·crim·i·nate /rikrim'ināt'/ [< re- + L criminari (-atus) to accuse] vi to answer one accusation with another ‖ **re·crim'i·na'tion** n

re·cru·des·cence /rē'krōōdes'əns/ [< L recrudescere to become raw again] n breaking out afresh; renewal of activity ‖ **re·cru·des'cent** adj

re·cruit /rikrōōt'/ [F] n 1 man newly enlisted in the armed forces; 2 new member of any group ‖ vt 3 to enlist (people) into the armed forces; 4 to enlist (new members, workers, etc.) ‖ vi 5 to recruit soldiers, members, etc.; 6 to recover health and strength ‖ **re·cruit'er** n ‖ **re·cruit'ment** n ‖ SYN v enlist, reenforce, replenish, supply, renew, reinvigorate ‖ ANT v disperse, scatter, lose, reduce

rect- or **recti-** [L rectus] comb form 1 right; 2 straight

rec·tal /rĕk'təl/ [< rectum] adj of or pert. to the rectum

rec·tan·gle /rĕk'taŋ'gəl/ n four-sided plane figure having four right angles ‖ **rec·tan'gu·lar** adj

rec·ti·fi·er /rĕk'tifi'ər/ n device for changing alternating current into direct current

rec·ti·fy [MF rectifier] v (-fied) vt 1 to correct; set right; 2 to purify by distillation; 3 to change (alternating current) to direct ‖ **rec'ti·fi·ca'tion** /-fi-/ n ‖ SYN correct, reform, amend, improve, mend, repair ‖ DISCR Cor-

rect and *rectify* are often used interchangeably in the sense of setting right, amending, or making good. We *correct* or *rectify* errors. When a distinction between these words is observed, it lies in the fact that *correct* connotes the idea of making right according to a standard, as of accuracy, convention, or the like, and in this respect is more definite than *rectify*, which carries the idea of making a wrong thing right, as a mistake, or of setting right, as a false judgment. We *correct* a wrong statement; we *rectify* the wrong opinion which produced it. We *correct*, not *rectify*, printer's proof. To *reform* is to make a more sweeping change than that underlying either *correct* or *rectify*, though in order to *reform*, that which is wrong must be *corrected* or *rectified*. A city government in which bad practices have been *corrected* or a country in which conditions of riot and general disregard of law and order have been *rectified* is *reformed*

rec·ti·lin·e·ar /rīkum′bənt/ *adj* 1 moving in a straight line; 2 bounded by straight lines; 3 characterized by straight lines

rec·ti·tude /rek′tit(y) oŏd′/ [MF < LL *rectitudo*] *n* 1 honesty; moral uprightness; 2 correctness || SYN justice, integrity, virtue, righteousness, goodness || ANT dishonesty, iniquity, partiality

rec·tor /rek′tər/ [L = ruler] *n* 1 clergyman in charge of an Episcopal parish; 2 head of certain universities and colleges

rec·to·ry *n* (**-ries**) clergyman's residence

rec·tum /rek′təm/ [L *rectum* (intestinum) straight (intestine)] *n* (**-tums** or **-ta** /-tə/) lower end of the large intestine

re·cum·bent /rīkum′bənt/ [L *recumbens* (-*entis*)] *adj* leaning; lying, reclining || **re·cum′ben·cy** *n*

re·cu·per·ate /rīk(y)ōōp′ərāt′/ [L *recuperare* (-*atus*) to recover] *vt* 1 to restore to former strength; 2 to regain (health, wealth, position, etc.) || *vi* 3 to regain health; recover from illness, pecuniary loss, etc. || **re·cu′per·a′tion** *n* || **re·cu′per·a′tive** /-āt′iv, -ətiv/ *adj*

re·cur /rīkur′/ [L *recurrere* to run back] *v* (**-curred; -cur·ring**) *vi* 1 to occur again or at intervals; 2 to go or come back, as in memory or in speech || **re·cur′rent** *adj* || **re·cur′·rence** *n*

re·cy·cle /rē-/ *vt* 1 to run through a cycle again; 2 to convert (trash) into usable products || *vi* 3 to stop a countdown and go back to an earlier point in the count

red /red/ [OE *rēad*] *adj* (**red·der; red·dest**) 1 of the color red || *n* 2 the color of blood; 3 red pigment or coloring; 4 something red; 5 Red

revolutionary socialist, esp. a communist; 6 **in the red** operating at a loss; 7 **see red** *colloq* to become enraged || **red′ness** *n*

re·dact /rīdakt′/ [L *redigere* (-*dactus*)] *vt* 1 to frame, draw up; 2 to edit || **re·dac′tor** *n* || **re·dac′tion** *n*

red′bait′ing *n* act or practice of denouncing people as radicals or communists || **red′bait′er** *n*

red′-blood′ed *adj* brave; virile

red′breast′ *n* 1 American or European robin; 2 fresh-water sunfish (*Lepomis auritus*) of E and SE U.S.

red′cap′ *n* porter in a railroad station

red′ car′pet [< the strip of red carpeting laid out for dignitaries to walk on when entering a building on ceremonial occasions] *n* ceremonious deference shown to visitors, esp. those of high rank

red′ cent′ *n colloq* something of trivial value, as *not worth a red cent*

red′coat′ *n* British soldier, esp. during the American Revolution

Red′ Cross′ *n* international society for helping the sick and wounded in war, and for administering aid and relief in times of natural calamities, its emblem being a red cross on a white background

red′den *vt* 1 to make red || *vi* 2 to become red; 3 to blush, flush

red′dish *adj* somewhat red

re·deem /rīdēm′/ [MF *redimer* < L *redimere*] *vt* 1 to buy back; 2 to pay off, as a promissory note; 3 to recover (something pledged or mortgaged) by payment; 4 to free from captivity by paying ransom; 5 to turn in (coupons) for premiums; 6 to free from sin and its consequences; 7 to make good, fulfill, as a promise; 8 to make up for, atone for, as a fault || **re·deem′a·ble** *adj* || SYN convert, rescue, restore, regain, deliver, liberate, recover, ransom, compensate, offset, reclaim

re·deem′er *n* 1 one who redeems; 2 **the Redeemer** Jesus Christ

re·demp·tion /rīdemp′shən/ *n* act of redeeming or state of being redeemed || **re·demp′tive** *adj*

re·de·ploy /rē′diploi′/ *vt* & *vi* to move from one theater of war to another || **re′de·ploy′ment** *n*

red′ gi′ant *n* reddish star having a large volume and low surface temperature

red′-hand′ed *adj* & *adv* in the act or in possession of incriminating evidence

red′head′ *n* person with red hair || **red′-head′ed** *adj*

red′ her′ring [< practice of drawing a smoked herring across a track to throw hounds off the scent] *n* false clue deliberately planted to mislead or divert attention

red′-hot′ *adj* 1 heated to redness; 2 greatly excited; 3 furious; 4 very new

re′di·rect′ /rē′-/ *adj* 1 *law* designating the examination of a witness after cross-examination by the opposing attorney ‖ *vt* 2 to direct anew

re·dis′count /rē-/ *n* 1 advancement of money or credit on negotiable paper that has already been discounted ‖ *vt* 2 to discount again

re·dis′trict /rē-/ *vt* to divide anew into districts ‖ **re·dis′trict·ing** *n*

red′ lead′ /led′/ *n* lead oxide —Pb_3O_4— a scarlet-colored powder used in making glass and storage batteries and as a pigment

red′-let′ter day′ [< practice of marking Sundays and holidays in red on calendars] *n* memorable or lucky day

red′-light′ dis′trict *n* section of a city occupied by houses of prostitution, formerly designated by red lights

red′ man′ *n* American Indian

red′neck′ *n southern U.S.* uncouth, uneducated tenant farmer or laborer

red·o·lent /red′ələnt/ [L *redolens* (-*entis*) giving off an odor] *adj* 1 giving off a pleasing odor; 2 **redolent of,** a smelling of; b suggestive of ‖ **red′o·lence** *n* ‖ SYN scented, fragrant, strong-smelling (*see odorous*)

re·dou′ble /rē-/ *vt* 1 to double; 2 to go back over; 3 *bridge* to double the opponent's double ‖ *vi* 4 to be doubled; 5 to reecho

re·doubt′ /ri-/ [F *redoute*] *n* 1 small enclosed fortification erected to defend a pass, hilltop, or the like; 2 central work inside a fortification

re·doubt′a·ble [MF *redoutable*] *adj* 1 formidable; 2 commanding respect ‖ SYN dreadful, terrible, tremendous, fearful

re·dound /ridound′/ [MF *redonder* < L *redundare* to overflow] *vi* to flow back as a consequence; contribute, as *his acts redounded to his glory*

red′ pep′per *n* 1 any of a genus (*Capsicum*) of plants of the nightshade family, including sweet pepper and cayenne; 2 condiment made from the seeds and pods of cayenne

re·dress′ /ri-/ *vt* 1 to correct or do away with, as abuses; 2 to make right, repair, as a wrong or injury; 3 to make amends to ‖ /usu. rē′dres/ *n* 4 compensation for or reparation of a wrong; 5 act of redressing a wrong ‖ SYN *n* repayment, amends, reparation, requital, indemnification, restitution, reward, satisfaction ‖ DISCR Literally, *repayment* is the return of an exact amount in kind, as of money borrowed. Figuratively, *repayment* may name any sort of return. *Indemnification* names a security or protection against harm or loss, such as is bought in accident- or fire-insurance policies; it also names the money paid in compensation for such loss or harm. Compensation for loss or harm may be *restitution, reparation, redress,* or *requital. Restitution* emphasizes the fact that something owed has been paid to the proper person, or that something unjustly taken away has been restored to the proper owner. *Reparation* emphasizes the repairing of something damaged; one country makes *reparation* to another by apologizing for an indignity, reimbursing for actual damage, or otherwise satisfying the claim. *Redress* is *reparation* for wrongs or grievances; it has in addition the connotation of making up for, as we expected no *redress* from so bitter an enemy. *Requital* may mean the return of good for good, but it oftener carries the sense of retaliation or vengeance. *Amends* is a more informal word for *reparation* or *restitution. Reward,* like *requital,* can mean a recompense for good or evil; unlike *requital,* a *reward* may be under or over that which is merited. *Satisfaction* is more general than any of these words; it may mean the *repayment* of a debt, the *amends* offered for an injustice, the fulfillment of an obligation, or that which is accepted or offered as atonement

Red′ Sea′ *n* narrow arm of the Indian Ocean between Africa and the Arabian Peninsula and connected to the Mediterranean by the Suez Canal

red′ shift′ *n* 1 increase in the wavelength of light coming from rapidly receding celestial bodies in accordance with the Doppler effect; 2 increase in the wavelength of a radiation caused by an opposing gravitational field

red′skin′ *n* American Indian

red′ snap′per *n* large food fish (*Lutjanus blackfordi*) of the Gulf of Mexico

red′ tape′ [< tape used to tie official papers] *n* excessive formality and rigid adherence to regulations in the conduct of business, esp. government business ‖ **red′-tape′** *adj*

re·duce /rid(y)ōōs′/ [L *reducere* to lead back] *vt* 1 to make less in value, quantity, size, or the like; lessen; lower; 2 to bring to a lower position; degrade; 3 to subdue, conquer; 4 to lower in price; 5 to bring into a different physical state, as *to reduce sugar to syrup;* 6 to dilute; 7 *math* to change (numbers or quantities) from one form to another; 8 *chem* a to deoxidize; b to change from a higher to a lower degree of oxidation; 9 *surg* to restore (a displaced part) to its rightful position; 10 **be reduced to** to be driven to (doing something) ‖ *vi* 11 to become reduced; 12 to lose weight by dieting ‖ **re·duc′i·ble** *adj* ‖ **re·duc′tion** /-duk′-/

n || SYN diminish, lessen, minimize, curtail, conquer, subject, abase, weaken, allay, alleviate

re·duc'ing a'gent *n* *chem* substance that removes oxygen in some degree from a compound and is oxidized itself

re·duc·ti·o ad ab·sur·dum /rĭduk'shē-ō' ad absŭr'dəm/ [L = reduction to absurdity] *n* refutation of a proposition by showing the absurdity of its implications

re·dun·dan·cy /rĭdun'dənsē/ [see **redound**] *n* (**-cies**) 1 state of being redundant; 2 unnecessary repetition; verbiage; 3 instance of such repetition; 4 portion of a signal that is repeated for use in case of failure || SYN excess, superfluity (see *circumlocution*)

re·dun·dant *adj* 1 exceeding what is needed; 2 superfluous (words), unnecessary to the sense

red'wood' *n* 1 any of various trees having a reddish wood or yielding a red dye; 2 very large California tree (*Sequoia sempervirens*) having reddish wood

re·ech·o /rē-ek'ō/ *vt* 1 to echo or repeat the sound of again || *vi* 2 to resound, reverberate || *n* (**-oes**) 3 repeated echo; second echo

reed /rēd/ [OE *hrēod*] *n* 1 the jointed hollow stem of any of certain coarse grasses that grow in wet places, esp. of the genera *Phragmites* and *Arundo*; 2 musical pipe made from such stems; 3 *mus* a elastic tongue of reed, wood, or metal, that vibrates at the opening of a pipe, as in an organ, or is fastened to the mouthpiece, as in the clarinet; b any reed instrument, as an oboe || **reed'y** *adj* (**-i·er; -i·est**)

reef¹ /rēf/ [ME *riff*] *n* 1 that part of a sail that can be drawn in and secured to lessen the area exposed to the wind || *vt* 2 to shorten (a sail) by tying off reefs

reef² [D *rif*] *n* sandbar or shelf of rock lying level with or just below the surface of the water

reef'er *n* 1 short jacket or coat, usu. double-breasted; 2 *slang* marijuana cigarette

reek /rēk/ [OE *rēc* smoke] *n* 1 disagreeable odor || *vi* 2 to smell strongly and offensively; 3 to send out vapor, steam, or fumes

reel¹ /rēl/ [OE *hrēol*] *n* 1 any of various devices consisting of a revolving frame for winding yarn, rope, fishlines, motion picture film, tape, garden hose, etc.; 2 bobbin; 3 amount of motion picture film held by one reel, usu. 1,000 feet || *vt* 4 to wind on a reel; 5 **reel in** to pull in by winding a line on a reel, as fish; 6 **reel off** to tell or write rapidly and easily

reel² [ME *relen*] *vi* 1 to stagger or sway, as from blows or intoxication; 2 to turn round and round; 3 to feel the sensation of whirling; 4 to give way, waver || *n* 5 act of reeling; 6 lively country or folk dance or the music for it

re·en'try /rē-/ *n* (**-tries**) 1 act of entering again; 2 return to earth's atmosphere of a rocket or artificial satellite

reeve /rēv/ [?] (**reeved** or **rove**) *vt naut* to pass (a rope) through a hole or ring

re·fec·to·ry /rĭfek'tərē/ [ML *refectorium*] *n* (**-ries**) dining hall in a college or religious house

re·fer /rĭfur'/ [L *referre* to bring back] *v* (**-ferred; -fer·ring**) *vt* 1 to submit to another for information or decision; 2 to direct for information, help, or the like || *vi* 3 to direct attention; allude; 4 to appeal; apply; 5 to indicate relation; 6 to direct one person to another for information or recommendation || **re·fer'ral** *n* || SYN attribute, ascribe, advert, point, allude, submit

ref·er·ee /ref'ərē'/ *n* 1 one to whom a matter is referred for decision and settlement; 2 judge or umpire in certain sports; 3 *law* person to whom a question in a case is sent by a court to be investigated and decided or reported back to the court || *vt* 4 to act as a referee in || *vi* 5 to act as a referee

ref·er·ence /ref'ərəns/ *n* 1 act of referring; 2 direction of attention to something; 3 passing allusion; 4 a direction in a book or writing to some other book or passage; b book or passage to which attention is directed; 5 person to whom inquiries may be directed regarding another person; 6 written statement of the ability of a person given by another; 7 relation, regard, as *with reference to this* || *adj* 8 suitable for use in securing special information, as *a reference book*

ref·er·en·dum /ref'ərən'dəm/ [L = to be referred] *n* (**-dums** or **-da** /-də/) 1 right of the people to vote directly on proposed legislation; 2 such a vote

ref·er·ent /ref'ərənt/ *n* that which is referred to by a term or symbol

re·fill' /rē'-/ *n* supply of the same substance to replace what has been used up, as *a refill for a ball-point pen*

re·fine /rĭfīn'/ *vt* 1 to free from impurities; 2 to free from coarseness or rudeness; educate, make cultured || *vi* 3 to become fine or pure; improve in quality || **re·fined'** *adj* || **re·fine'ment** *n*

re·fin·er·y *n* (**-ies**) building and equipment for refining a crude material, as ore, oil, or sugar

re·fin'ish /rē-/ *vt* to give a new finish to, as wood or furniture

re·fit' *v* (-fit·ted; -fit·ting) *vt* 1 to repair, make ready for use again; 2 to equip with supplies again || *vi* 3 to be refitted

re·flect /riflekt'/ [L *reflectere* to bend back] *vt* 1 to throw back, as heat, light, or sound; 2 to give back an image of; to mirror; 3 to bring back as a result, as *his acts reflect honor upon him* || *vi* 4 to be reflected; 5 to mediate, ponder; 6 **reflect on** to cast reproach, shame, blame, etc. on || SYN reproduce, show, contemplate (see *muse*)

re·flec'tance *n* percentage of radiation falling on a surface that is reflected from it

re·flect'ing tel'e·scope' *n* telescope which functions by means of the reflection of light rays by a concave mirror

re·flec'tion *n* 1 act of reflecting or state of being reflected; 2 anything reflected; image; 3 attentive consideration, thought; 4 criticism, reproach || SYN deliberation, musing, thinking (see *criticism*)

re·flec'tor *n* 1 anything that reflects light, sound, heat, etc.; 2 reflecting telescope

re·flex /rē'fleks/ [L *reflexus* bent back] *n* 1 reflection, as of light, sound, or color; 2 reflected image; 3 that which reproduces certain essential qualities of something; 4 reflex action || *adj* 5 reflected, as light or color; 6 pert. to, or caused by, reflex action

re'flex ac'tion *n* involuntary action of certain muscles, organs, etc., occurring when the excitation of a sensory nerve is transmitted to a nerve center, and thence reflected along an efferent nerve to the muscle or organ

re'flex cam'er·a *n* camera in which the image to be photographed is reflected by a mirror to a ground-glass viewer

re·flex·ive /riflek'siv/ *adj* 1 (verb) having an identical subject and object, as *he loves himself*; 2 (pronoun) used as the object of a reflexive verb || *n* 3 reflexive verb; 4 reflexive pronoun

re·for'est /rē-/ *vt* to replant (deforested land) with trees || also *vi* **re·for'est·a'tion** *n*

re·form' /ri-/ [MF *reformer*] *vt* 1 to change into another and better form; 2 to make better by the removal of faults or abuses; 3 to put an end to, as abuses; 4 to induce (a person) to abandon an evil course of conduct || *vi* 5 to give up evil ways || *n* 6 change for the better; removal of evil and abuse; 7 an instance of this; 8 change from an evil to an upright character || SYN *v* better, reclaim, improve (see *rectify*)

ref·or·ma·tion /ref'ərmāsh'ən/ *n* 1 act of reforming or state of being reformed; 2 **the Reformation** the religious movement begun by Martin Luther in the 16th century, having for its aim the reform of the Roman Catholic Church and resulting in the formation of the Protestant Churches

re·for'ma·to·ry /-tōr'-, -tôr'-/ *n* (-ries) also **re·form' school'** penal institution for reforming youthful offenders and minors

Re·formed' Church' *n* any of several Protestant churches which separated from the Lutherans and adopted the religious doctrines of Calvin, Zwingli, and others in the 16th century

re·formed' spell'ing *n* revised English spelling in which each letter represents with approximate precision only one sound and in which all silent letters are eliminated

re·form'er *n* one who seeks to reform morals, as in behavior and politics

re·fract /rifrakt'/ [L *refringere* (-*fractus*) to break up] *vt* to subject to refraction || **re·frac'tive** *adj*

re·fract'ing tel'e·scope' *n* telescope which functions by means of the refraction of light rays through a lens

re·frac'tion *n* 1 the bending of rays, as of light, in passing obliquely from one medium to another of different density; 2 *astron* apparent increase in elevation of a heavenly body, greatest at the horizon, caused by the refraction of light by the atmosphere

re·frac'tor *n* refracting telescope

re·frac'to·ry *adj* 1 disobedient; unmanageable; 2 resisting heat; hard to work or fuse, as ore or metals; 3 not yielding to treatment || *n* (-ries) 4 heat-resistant substance used in the construction of furnaces, ovens, etc.

re·frain[1] /rifrān'/ [OF] *n* 1 phrase or verse repeated at intervals, esp. at the end of each stanza of a poem or song; 2 musical setting for these words; 3 melody

re·frain[2] [OF *refrener* to bridle] *vi* 1 to forbear; hold back; 2 **refrain from** to abstain from || SYN abstain, withhold, forbear, restrain, cease || ANT continue, persist, persevere, keep on

re·fran·gi·ble /rifran'jəbəl/ [see **re·fract**] *adj* capable of being refracted

re·fresh' /ri-/ *vt* 1 to make fresh again, as by wetting or cooling; 2 to revive after fatigue or exhaustion; 3 to quicken (the memory) || SYN invigorate, enliven, strengthen, cheer

re·fresh'ing *adj* 1 reviving or making fresh again; 2 stimulating; 3 cool and pleasant, as a drink || **re·fresh'·ing·ly** *adv*

re·fresh'ment *n* 1 act of refreshing or state of being refreshed; 2 that which refreshes, as food or drink; 3 **refreshments** *pl* food and drink served at a reception, dance, or the like

re·frig·er·ant /rifrij'ərənt/ n any substance used to refrigerate, as ice or a volatile liquid that cools by evaporation

re·frig·er·ate [L refrigerare (-atus) to chill] vt to make or keep cold, as in a refrigerator || **re·frig·er·a'tion** n

re·frig·er·a'tor n chest or room where food and other perishables are chilled and kept cold

re·fu'el /rē-/ v (-eled or -elled; -el·ing or -el·ling) vt 1 to provide with a new supply of fuel || vi 2 to take on a new supply of fuel

ref·uge /ref'yōōj/ [MF < L refugium] n 1 place of safety from trouble or danger; 2 one who or that which protects and defends || SYN cover, shelter, protection, retreat, sanctuary

ref'u·gee [F refugié] n one who flees for protection to a foreign land, esp. from war or from political or religious persecution

re·ful·gent /riful'jənt/ [L refulgens (-entis)] adj shedding a brilliant light || **re·ful'gence** n || SYN flashing, brilliant, bright, radiant, shining

re·fund'¹ /ri-/ [L refundere to pour back] vt 1 to return (a payment) || /rē'-/ n 2 repayment

re·fund'² /rē-/ [re- + fund] vt to discharge, as a loan, through credit secured by a new loan

re·fur'bish /rē-/ vt to renovate

re·fus·al /rifyōōz'əl/ n 1 act or instance of refusing; 2 right or opportunity to accept or reject before others

re·fuse¹ /rifyōōz'/ [OF refuser] vt 1 to decline to accept; 2 to decline to grant; deny; 3 to decline (to do something); 4 mil to bend back (a flank) so that it faces to the side || vi 5 to decline action or acceptance || SYN reject, deny, renounce, repel, decline || ANT accept, assent, admit, take, claim, acknowledge

ref·use² /ref'yōōs/ [OF refus rejection] n waste material; trash, rubbish || SYN dregs, sediment, scum, leavings, scraps, waste

re·fute /rifyōōt'/ [L refutare] vt to prove to be false or wrong || **re·fut'-a·ble** adj || **ref'u·ta'tion** /ref'yōō-/ n || SYN deny, confound (see confute)

reg. 1 register(ed); 2 regular; 3 regiment

re·gain' vt 1 to get possession of again; 2 to get back to

re·gal /rēg'əl/ [L regalis royal] adj 1 of, like, or befitting a king; 2 splendid, stately

re·gale /rigāl'/ [OF = feast] vt to entertain in a lavish manner; feast; delight || **re·gale'ment** n

re·ga·li·a /rigāl'ē-ə, -yə/ [L = royal things] npl 1 royal rights or privileges; 2 emblems of royalty; 3 personal decorations or insignia indicating an order or office; 4 finery; fine clothes

re·gard /rigärd'/ [MF regarder to look at] vt 1 to observe, look at; 2 to consider; 3 to heed, respect; 4 to esteem, care for; 5 to relate to, concern; 6 to take into account; 7 **as regards** concerning || n 8 look or gaze; 9 consideration, care; 10 affection, respect; 11 particular point, as **in this regard**; 12 **regards** pl good wishes; 13 **in** or **with regard to** relating to; 14 **without regard to** ignoring, not considering || SYN n esteem, affection, respect, deference, favor, attention, heed, observance, notice || DISCR Esteem is high opinion, based on a mental valuation of the person who is its object, and tinged with interest, cordiality, or approval. It is therefore a warmer term than respect, which is deference yielded without any seasoning of personal favor; we entertain esteem for a clergyman whom we warmly admire as well as respect; we yield respect sometimes to the office of a clergyman whose personal qualities do not appeal to us at all. Regard is esteem deepened by affection; it is often mutual, whereas esteem and respect can be entertained by one person for another who is quite unaware of it

re·gard'ful adj 1 heedful; attentive; 2 respectful

re·gard'ing prep concerning, about

re·gard'less adj 1 heedless; careless || adv 2 anyway; in spite of adverse conditions; 3 **regardless of** without paying attention to; in spite of || SYN adj inattentive, indifferent (see negligent)

re·gat·ta /rigat'ə/ [It] n 1 boat race; 2 series of boat races

re·gen·cy /rēj'ənsē/ [see regent] n (-cies) 1 office, jurisdiction, government, or tenure of a regent; 2 **Regency** period in Britain (1811–20) during which the Prince of Wales (later George IV) was regent || adj 3 **Regency** pert. to a style of architecture and furniture developed during the British Regency

re·gen'er·ate' /ri-/ vt 1 to produce anew; fill with new life or power; 2 to make better, reform; 3 to renew spiritually; 4 biol to regrow (a lost limb or part) || /-it/ adj 5 made over; 6 reformed; 7 born again spiritually || **re·gen'er·a·tive** adj || **re·gen'er·a'tion** n

re·gent /rēj'ənt/ [L regens (-entis) ruling] n 1 one who governs during the youth, absence, or unfitness of the rightful ruler; 2 member of the governing board of certain state universities or school systems

reg·i·cide /rej'isīd'/ [< L rex (regis) king + -cide] n 1 murder of a king; 2 murderer of a king

re·gime also **ré·gime** /rāzhēm', rə-/ [F] n 1 mode or system of government or direction; **2** period of rule or direction

reg·i·men /rej'imen', -mən/ [L] **1** government, rule; **2** *med* regular system of diet, exercise, and general habits, prescribed for some special purpose; **3** *gram* government

reg·i·ment /rej'imənt/ [LL *regimentum* government] *n* **1** army unit, generally consisting of two or more battalions ‖ -ment'/ *vt* **2** to form into orderly, disciplined, or standardized classes; **3** to subject to strict discipline ‖ **reg'i·men·ta'tion** *n*

reg'i·men'tal *adj* **1** of or pert. to a regiment ‖ **regimentals** *npl* **2** regimental uniform

Re·gi·na /rijīn'ə/ *n* capital of Saskatchewan (126,000)

re·gion /rēj'ən/ [AF *regiun* < L *regio* (-*onis*)] *n* **1** indefinitely large section of the earth, as *a tropical region;* **2** distinct district of a state, country, or city; **3** sphere or realm; **4** division or part of the body; **5** one of the portions into which the sea or air is thought of as divided, as according to its flora and fauna ‖ **re'gion·al** *adj*

re'gion·al·ism *n* **1** theory or practice of dividing a nation into regions on a specific basis, as politics; **2** devotion to the welfare of one's own region; **3** trait, custom, word, or accent peculiar to a region; **4** practice or style in literature or art emphasizing regional characteristics

reg·is·ter /rej'istər/ [< LL *regesta* things recorded] *n* **1** official written record; roll or list, as of births; **2** any of various devices for recording data; **3** cash register; **4** device for regulating the entrance of heated air to a room; **5** *mus* compass or range of a voice or instrument; **6** in (or out of) register in (or out of) exact alignment, as in printing or color photography ‖ *vt* **7** to enter formally in a register; **8** to enroll, as a student or voter; **9** to indicate on a scale; **10** to show (emotion) by facial expression; **11** to ensure safe delivery of (a letter or package) by having it recorded at the post office ‖ *vi* **12** to have one's name registered on an official list; **13** to be in register; **14** to make an impression ‖ SYN *n* list, category, history, annals, archives

reg'is·tered nurse' *n* nurse graduated from an accredited school and licensed by the state

reg'is·trar' /-trär'/ [ML *registrarius*] *n* official who keeps records, esp. of academic grades in a college

reg'is·tra'tion *n* **1** act or instance of registering; **2** enrollment; **3** entry in a register; **4** certificate attesting to one's having registered ownership of something, as a car

reg'is·try *n* (-tries) **1** act of registering; **2 a** official list or register; **b** place

where it is kept; **3** nationality of a merchant ship

re·gress /rē'gres/ [L *regressus* returned] *n* **1** return; going back; **2** right of returning ‖ /rigres'/ *vi* **3** to go back, return; **4** to revert to a less advanced state ‖ **re·gres'sive** *adj* ‖ **re·gres'sion** *n*

re·gret /rigret'/ [MF *regreter*] *v* (-gret·ted; -gret·ting) *vt* **1** to remember with remorse or distress; **2** to feel sorry about, as the loss or lack of something ‖ *n* **3** sorrow or concern for the loss or lack of something; **4** distress over some past event; **5** vexation; disappointment; **6** regrets *pl* polite expression of refusal of an invitation ‖ **re·gret'ful** *adj* ‖ **re·gret'ta·ble** *adj* ‖ SYN *n* compunction, grief, misgiving (see *sorrow*)

reg·u·lar /reg'yələr/ [MF < L *regularis*] *adj* **1** according to a rule, order, or custom; **2** usual; **3** symmetrical; even; **4** recurring at fixed times; **5** habitual, constant; **6** orderly, methodical; **7** duly qualified for an occupation; **8** following the usual pattern; **9** (polygon) having all sides and angles equal; **10** belonging to a religious order and bound by its rules; **11** designating the permanent standing army or its troops; **12** *colloq* a thorough, complete, as *a regular bookworm;* **b** full-scale ‖ *n* **13** regular soldier; **14** habitual client; **15** average-sized garment; **16** anyone or anything that is regular ‖ **reg'u·lar·ly** *adv* ‖ **reg'u·lar·ize'** *vt* ‖ **reg'u·lar'i·ty** /-lar'-/ *n* ‖ SYN *adj* symmetrical, normal, typical, usual, habitual ‖ ANT *adj* crooked, uneven, unnatural, devious, abnormal, fitful, irregular, varying

reg'u·late' [LL *regulare* (-*atus*) to make regular] *vt* **1** to control or direct by rule, method, or principle; **2** to cause to conform to regulations; **3** to adjust to a desirable or standard condition; **4** to adjust so as to achieve accuracy ‖ **reg'u·la'tor** *n* ‖ **reg'u·la'to·ry** /-letôr'-, -lətōr'-/ *adj* ‖ SYN adjust, dispose, manage, govern, systematize

reg'u·la'tion *n* **1** act of regulating or state of being regulated; **2** prescribed rule, direction, or law ‖ *adj* **3** conforming to regulations; **4** customary, usual

Reg·u·lus /reg'yələs/ [L = little king] *n* star of the first magnitude in the constellation Leo

re·gur·gi·tate /rigur'jitāt'/ [ML *regurgitare* (-*atus*)] *vt* to pour or throw back, as liquids, gases, or partly digested food from the stomach ‖ also *vi* ‖ **re·gur'gi·ta'tion** *n*

re·ha·bil·i·tate /rē'həbil'itāt'/ [< L *habilis* fit, suitable] *vt* **1** to restore to a former state, rank, or privilege; **2** to reestablish the good reputation of;

3 to restore to sound operation ‖ re'ha·bil'i·ta'tion n

re·hash' /rē-/ vt 1 to work (old material) into a new form ‖ /rē'hash'/ n 2 act of rehashing; 3 that which is rehashed

re·hearse /rĭhurs'/ [MF *rehercier* to repeat] vt 1 to practice in private as a preparation for a public performance; 2 to cause (an actor or musician) to rehearse; 3 to recount in detail ‖ vi 4 to rehearse a part, play, etc. ‖ re·hears'al n ‖ SYN relate, describe, recount, detail, practice, repeat

Reich /rīk'/ [G = realm] n the German state or nation

reign /rān'/ [OF *regne* < L *regnum* rule] n 1 royal power; sovereignty; 2 time during which a ruler occupies the throne; 3 control, sway, as *the reign of law* ‖ vi 4 to head a monarchy as king or queen; 5 to hold sway, prevail ‖ SYN v prevail, predominate, control, govern, rule, command ‖ ANT v obey, submit, comply

re·im·burse /rē'imburs'/ [re- + L *imbursare* to pay] vt 1 to refund, pay back, as expenses or loss; 2 to make repayment to for expenses or loss ‖ re'im·burse'ment n ‖ SYN recompense, compensate, repay, refund

rein /rān'/ [OF *resne* < L *retinere* to hold back] n 1 leather strap fastened to each end of the bit of a horse as a means of controlling it; 2 reins pl any means of restraint or control, as *the reins of government;* 3 give (free) rein to to free from restraint; indulge freely ‖ vt 4 to restrain, guide, or control, as with reins ‖ SYN v repress, check, govern, restrain, control

re'in·car'nate /rē'-/ vt 1 to give another body to ‖ /-nĭt/ adj 2 given another body

re'in·car·na'tion n rebirth of the soul in a new body

rein'deer' /rān'-/ [ON *hreindȳri*] n (pl reindeer) any of various species of deer (genus *Rangifer*) of northern regions, both male and female having antlers

re·in·force /rē'infôrs', -fōrs'/ [re- + var of *enforce*] vt 1 to strengthen by adding material, props, or pieces; 2 to strengthen (a military force) by adding troops or matériel; 3 to strengthen; augment

re'in·forced con'crete n ferroconcrete

re'in·force'ment n 1 act of reinforcing or state of being reinforced; 2 anything that reinforces; 3 reinforcements pl additional troops or matériel

re·in·state /rē'instāt'/ vt to restore to a former state, station, or authority ‖ re'in·state'ment n

re·it'er·ate' /rē-/ vt to do or say repeatedly ‖ re·it'er·a'tion n ‖ re·it'er·a'tive /-āt'ĭv, -ətĭv/ adj

re·ject /rĭjekt'/ [L *rejicere* (-*jectus*) to throw back] vt 1 to discard; 2 to refuse to take; decline; 3 to refuse to grant, believe, or agree to; 4 to refuse to receive (a person), rebuff ‖ /rē'jekt/ n 5 person or thing rejected ‖ re·jec'tion n ‖ SYN v repel, deny, decline, renounce, eliminate ‖ ANT v acknowledge, accept, take, defend, maintain

re·joice /rĭjois'/ [OF *rejouir* (-*jouiss*-)] vi 1 to feel joy; delight ‖ vt 2 to gladden ‖ re·joic'ing n

re·join'¹ /rē-/ vt & vi to join again

re·join'² /rĭ-/ [AF *rejoyner*] vt 1 to say in answer to a reply; 2 to retort ‖ vi 3 to make answer to a reply; 4 to retort, reply

re·join·der /rĭjoin'dər/ n 1 answer, esp. to a reply; 2 quick, sharp, cutting reply; 3 law defendant's answer to plaintiff's reply ‖ SYN reply, retort, repartee, response, answer

re·ju·ve·nate /rĭjōōv'ənāt'/ [< re- + L *juvenis* young] vt to make young again; restore to youthful vigor ‖ re·ju've·na'tion n ‖ re·ju've·na'tor n

re·lapse /rĭlaps'/ [L *relapsus* slid back] vi 1 to fall back into a former state; 2 to backslide, as into vice; 3 to become ill again after partial recovery ‖ n 4 act of relapsing; 5 return of a disease after partial recovery

re·late /rĭlāt'/ [L *relatus* carried back] vt 1 to tell, recite, narrate; 2 to connect; establish a relation between ‖ vi 3 to interact with others in a sympathetic relationship; 4 relate to to have connection or association with ‖ SYN recount, report, rehearse, narrate, describe, detail ‖ ANT deny, suppress, withhold

re·lat'ed adj connected, as by association, kinship, or marriage

re·la'tion n 1 act of narrating; 2 narrative; 3 state of being mutually or reciprocally connected; 4 kind of connection, correspondence, or feeling existing between two or more persons or things; 5 kinship; 6 relative, kinsman; 7 math ratio, proportion; 8 relations pl a dealings, affairs, as *foreign relations;* b sexual intercourse; 9 in or with relation to regarding ‖ SYN analogy, connection, kinship; narration, report

re·la'tion·ship' n 1 kinship; 2 connection or involvement

rel·a·tive /rel'ətĭv/ [LL *relativus*] adj 1 comparative, not absolute, as *relative value;* 2 having meaning only in connection with something else; 3 relative to relating or pertinent to ‖ n 4 person related to another by blood or marriage

rel'a·tive clause' n clause that modifies an antecedent

rel'a·tive hu·mid'i·ty n ratio of the

amount of water vapor present in the air to the greatest amount possible at the same temperature

rel'a·tive pro'noun *n* pronoun that refers to an antecedent, as *who, which,* etc.

rel·a·tiv'i·ty *n* 1 state of being relative; 2 interdependence on one another; 3 *phys* theory elaborated by Albert Einstein that all position, motion, etc., can be defined only by means of some selected frame of reference, that all statements of physical laws take exactly the same form in all systems of reference in whatever way such systems may be moving relatively to one another, and that space and time are relative

re·lax /rĭlaks'/ [L *relaxare* to loosen] *vt* 1 to slacken, loosen; 2 to render less strict, mitigate; 3 to lessen the tenseness of; 4 to relieve from strain or tension ‖ *vi* 5 to become relaxed ‖ **re·lax'ing** *adj* ‖ SYN ease, relieve, open, abate, unbend ‖ ANT bind, tighten, strain, intensify

re'lax·a'tion /rē'-/ *n* 1 act of relaxing or state of being relaxed; 2 restful recreation or diversion

re'lax·a'tion of ten'sion *n* lessening of international strained relations between nations; détente

re·lay /rē'lā/ [MF *relais*] *n* 1 supply of fresh men, horses, or dogs held ready to replace others; 2 *elec* device by which the opening or closing of one circuit opens or closes another; 3 automatic control for actuating switches, valves, etc.; 4 relay race ‖ /also rĭlā'/ *vt* 5 to send by relay or as by relays

re'lay race' *n* race in which a series of contestants succeed one another, each covering a part of the course

re·lease /rĭlēs'/ [OF *relessier* < L *relaxare* to loosen] *vt* 1 to free from confinement, obligation, penalty, pain, or trouble; 2 to free from anything that holds back; 3 to let go of; 4 to permit the showing or sale of, as *to release a film;* 5 *law* to surrender, as a claim ‖ *n* 6 act of releasing; 7 a releasing for publication, performance, or sale; 8 news release; 9 *law* surrender, as of a claim ‖ SYN *v* acquit, discharge, exculpate (see *liberate*)

rel·e·gate /rel'igāt'/ [L *relegare* (*-atus*) to send away] *vt* 1 to send or consign to a less desirable place or position; 2 to refer (a matter or task) to a person for decision or performance ‖ **rel'e·ga'tion** *n* ‖ SYN commit, banish, consign, transfer, refer

re·lent /rĭlent'/ [ME *relenten*] *vi* 1 to become less cruel, become more compassionate; 2 to become less severe, slacken ‖ SYN mollify, soften, yield, relax

re·lent'less *adj* unmoved by pity; indifferent to the pain of others; unyieldingly harsh ‖ **re·lent'less·ly** *adv* ‖ SYN austere, grim, harsh, implacable, unpitying

rel·e·vant /rel'əvənt/ [ML *relevans* (*-antis*) lifting up] *adj* relating to the case in hand; pertinent ‖ **rel'e·vance** or **rel'e·van·cy** *n* ‖ SYN pertinent, adapted, congruous, apt, apropos, fitting, suitable ‖ DISCR *Relevant* and *pertinent* agree in expressing fitness, logical relationship, and propriety between the matter or subject in hand and that which is said concerning it, as *relevant* testimony; *pertinent* suggestions. *Pertinent* has also gathered the meaning of fitted or adapted to a proposed end or aim, and thus comes into comparison with *apropos,* meaning to the purpose, appropriate, opportune, as *pertinent* remarks; a remark *apropos* and happy ‖ ANT inappropriate, unsuitable, irrelevant, incongruous

re·li·a·ble /rĭlī'əbəl/ [see *rely*] *adj* dependable; that can be relied on ‖ **re·li'a·bly** *adv* ‖ **re·li'a·bil'i·ty** /-bil'-/ *n* ‖ SYN trustworthy, dependable, responsible ‖ ANT untrustworthy, heedless, irresponsible, unreliable

re·li'ance *n* 1 trust; confidence; 2 dependence; 3 someone or something relied on ‖ SYN confidence, dependence (see *trust*)

re·li'ant *adj* 1 trusting; having confidence; 2 dependent

rel·ic /rel'ik/ [OF *relique* < L *reliquiae* remains] *n* 1 survival from the past, as *a relic of the stone age;* 2 anything held in religious reverence, as the remains of a martyr or saint; 3 object cherished for its age or historical associations

rel·ict /rel'ikt/ [ML *relicta*] *n* 1 archaic widow; 2 plant or animal of an otherwise extinct genus living on in an environment that has undergone great change

re·lief /rĭlēf'/ [OF] *n* 1 alleviation of or release from pain, discomfort, distress, monotony, etc.; 2 instrument or means by which relief is given; 3 money or food given to those in need; 4 release from a post or duty by discharge or substitution; 5 person so substituted; 6 raising of a siege; 7 vividness or sharpness of outline due to contrast; 8 projection of a design from a plane surface, as in sculpture; 9 work so produced; 10 effect of elevation or projection obtained by shading, colors, etc., as on a map; 11 **on relief** receiving financial assistance from the government because of need ‖ SYN mitigation, help, assistance, remedy, rescue

re·lieve /rĭlēv'/ [MF *relever*] *vt* 1 to remove or alleviate (pain, discomfort, distress, monotony, etc.); 2 to free from burden, distress, pain, or the like; **3** to raise the siege of; **4** to release from a post by replacing or providing a replacement; **5** to right (a wrong) by judicial or legislative interposition; **6** to set off or enhance by contrast; **7** to break the monotony of; vary; **8** to reduce, as pressure or load; **9** *baseball* to replace (a pitcher) || SYN aid, assuage, ease, remove, allay (see *help*)

re·li·gion /rĭlíj'ən/ [L *religio (-onis)* piety] *n* **1** any system of belief and worship based on revelation and faith; **2** outward acts or practices of life by which men indicate their recognition of faith in God or gods; **3** conformity to the teachings of religion || SYN devotion, faith, belief, piety, worship

re·li·gious *adj* **1** feeling and living in accordance with religion; devout, pious; **2** of, pert. to, or concerned with religion; **3** pert. to a monastic order; **4** conscientious, scrupulously faithful || *n* **5** person who is bound by monastic vows; monk; nun; **6** **religious** *pl* such persons collectively || **re·li'gious·ly** *adv* || SYN *adj* godly, holy, pious, god-fearing, devout

re·lin·quish /rĭlíŋk'wĭsh/ [MF *relinquir (-quiss-)*] *vt* **1** to retire from; abandon; **2** to give up, surrender; **3** to let go || **re·lin'quish·ment** *n* || SYN surrender, resign, forego, quit (see *abandon*)

rel·i·qua·ry /rel'ĭkwer'ē/ [MF *reliquaire*] *n* (-ies) casket or receptacle in which relics are kept

rel·ish /rel'ĭsh/ [OF *reles* aftertaste] *n* **1** fondness; liking; zest; **2** flavor, esp. when pleasing or distinctive; **3** condiment taken with food to render it more enjoyable, as chopped sweet pickle || *vt* **4** to take pleasure in || SYN *n* fondness, taste, gusto, zest, flavor, enjoyment

re·lo·cate /rē-/ *vt* & *vi* to settle in a new place

re·luc·tance /rĭluk'təns/ *n* **1** unwillingness, disinclination; **2** *elec* resistance that a magnetic circuit offers to magnetic flux

re·luc·tant [L *reluctans (-antis)* struggling against] *adj* unwilling, disinclined || SYN averse, unwilling, indisposed, loath, opposed, backward || ANT eager, disposed, willing, inclined

re·ly /rĭlī'/ [MF *relier* to bind] *v* (-lied) *vi* rely on to trust; depend on || SYN confide, repose, lean, depend, trust

rem /rem'/ [roentgen equivalent, man] *n* the quantity of radiation that will have the same biological effect on man as the exposure to one roentgen of ordinary X ray

re·main /rĭmān'/ [OF *remaindre*] *vi* **1** to stay behind or in the same place;

2 to endure; persist; **3** to continue in the same state or condition; **4** to be left after a part has been used up, taken away, lost, or destroyed; **5** to be left to be done || **remains** *npl* **6 a** that which remains; **b** dead body || SYN *v* abide, continue, last, endure, halt, stand, stop, tarry || ANT *v* leave, flee, depart, perish

re·main·der *n* **1** portion or number left; **2** *math* **a** the part, less than the divisor, left over after division; **b** the quantity left after subtraction; **3** copy of a book left in a publisher's stock after its sale has ceased || *vt* **4** to dispose of (unsold books) || SYN *n* leavings, surplus, remnant, residue, balance || DISCR *Remainder*, *remnant*, and *residue* agree in naming that which is left when the other part, often the greater part, has been taken away. *Remainder* is general in its application; we speak of the *remainder* obtained by the process of subtraction; the *remainder* of our life. *Remnant* usually names a fragment, as a *remnant* of cloth left at the end of a bolt; figuratively, *remnant* may name a scattered few, or a small surviving group of people, the rest of whom have suffered dispersion, calamity, or extinction. *Residue* technically is a residuum, or residual product left from some process; ordinarily it is that which remains after a separation, removal, settlement, or the like. The *residue* of an estate is that which is left when all debts and previous requirements are settled. *Balance* in the sense of the rest or the *remainder* is incorrectly used. The difference between one's credits and debits is a *balance* struck; the unpaid part of a debt, a *balance* due; but this is a different idea from that carried by *remainder*, *residue*, and *remnant*. It is correct to call a deficiency in an account the *balance* due; it is incorrect to say that you are going to refrain from work for the *balance* of the day

re·make /rē'-/ *n* motion picture that is a refilming of one previously made

re·mand /rĭmand'/ [OF *remander*] *vt* **1** to call, order, or send back; **2** *law* to recommit to custody after a preliminary examination

re·mark /rĭmärk'/ [MF *remarquer* to note] *vt* **1** to note, observe; **2** to say briefly and casually || *vi* **3** **remark on** to make a comment on || *n* **4** brief comment or statement; **5** note, notice || SYN *v* perceive, observe, express (see *notice*)

re·mark·a·ble *adj* noteworthy, extraordinary || **re·mark'a·bly** *adv* || SYN observable, notable, eminent, extraordinary || ANT common, usual, ordinary

Rem·brandt /rem'brant/ *n* (1606–69) Dutch painter

re·me·di·al /rĭmēd′ē·əl/ *adj* 1 affording a remedy; 2 corrective

rem·e·dy /rem′ədē/ [AF *remedie* < L *remedium*] *n* (**-dies**) 1 any medicine, application, or treatment which cures or relieves sickness or a bodily disorder; 2 that which removes or corrects an evil; 3 legal redress ‖ *v* (**-died**) *vt* 4 to cure or heal; 5 to repair, make right ‖ **re·me′di·a·ble** /rĭmēd′ē-/ *vt* ‖ SYN *n* restorative, corrective, medicine, redress

re·mem·ber /rĭmem′bər/ [OF *remembrer* < LL *rememorari*] *vt* 1 to recall to mind; think of again; 2 to keep in mind; not forget; 3 to carry greetings from, as *remember me to your father;* 4 to tip, give a present to ‖ *vi* 5 to possess or use the faculty of memory

re·mem′brance *n* 1 act or power of remembering; 2 state of being remembered; 3 length of time within which one has memories; 4 anything that recalls or keeps in mind a particular memory; memento; 5 **remembrances** *pl* greetings ‖ SYN souvenir, reminder, reminiscence (see *memory*)

re·mind /rĭmīnd′/ [*re-* + *mind*] *vt* 1 to cause (someone) to remember; 2 to put (someone) in mind (of someone or something), as *he reminds me of my uncle* ‖ **re·mind′er** *n*

rem·i·nisce /rem′ĭnis′/ [< *reminiscent*] *vi* to engage in recollection of the past

rem′i·nis′cence *n* 1 act or faculty of recalling past experiences; 2 that which is recalled; 3 that which is remembered and told; recollection; 4 something that reminds or suggests some other thing ‖ SYN retrospection, recollection (see *memory*)

rem′i·nis′cent [L *reminiscens* (*-entis*) remembering] *adj* 1 pert. to or of the nature of reminiscence; 2 given to reminiscence; 3 **reminiscent of** suggestive of

re·miss /rĭmis′/ [L *remissus* sent back] *adj* careless; neglectful; slack ‖ **re·miss′ness** *n* ‖ SYN slack, slothful, behindhand (see *negligent*)

re·mis′sion *n* 1 act of remitting; 2 forgiveness, pardon; 3 abatement or subsidence of the virulence of a disease

re·mit /rĭmit′/ [L *remittere* to send back] *v* (**-mit·ted; -mit·ting**) *vt* 1 to forgive, pardon, as a sin or offense; 2 to refrain from inflicting (a punishment) or exacting (a fine); 3 to slacken, relax, as watchfulness; 4 to restore or replace, as to a former status; 5 to postpone, defer; 6 to send (money) in payment; 7 to send back (a case) to a lower court; 8 to return (a fine) ‖ *vi* 9 to moderate, abate, as a fever; 10 to send money in payment

re·mit′tance *n* 1 sending of money; 2 the money sent

re·mit′tance man′ *n* man sent out from England, esp. to Australia and Canada, and provided with remittances to make sure he does not return home

re·mit′tent *adj* abating temporarily or at intervals, as a fever

rem·nant /rem′nənt/ [OF *remenant* remaining] *n* 1 that which is left; 2 little bit, fragment; 3 short piece of fabric, as at the end of a bolt of cloth; 4 vestige ‖ SYN residue, scrap, portion (see *remainder*)

re·mod′el /rē-/ *v* (**-eled** or **-elled; -el·ing** or **-el·ling**) *vt* to reconstruct, make over

re·mon·strate /rĭmon′strāt/ [ML *remonstrare* (*-atus*) to show, exhibit] *vi* to put forth strong reasons in complaint; object; protest ‖ **re·mon′strance** *n* ‖ SYN protest, complain (see *expostulate*)

re·morse /rĭmôrs′/ [MF *remors* < L *remorsus* bitten again] *n* mental pain or anguish caused by the sense of guilt ‖ **re·morse′ful** *adj* ‖ **re·morse′less** *adj* ‖ SYN anguish, grief, repentance (see *sorrow*)

re·mote /rĭmōt′/ [L *remotus* moved back] *adj* 1 distant in space or time; 2 distant in relationship or connection; 3 out-of-the-way; 4 slight, faint ‖ **re·mote′ly** *adv* ‖ **re·mote′ness** *n* ‖ SYN distant, alien, foreign, unrelated, secluded, retired, abstracted ‖ ANT immediate, near, relevant

re·mote′ con·trol′ *n* electrical or radio operation of a device at a distance ‖ **re·mote′-con·trol′** *adj*

re·mount′ /rē-/ *vt* & *vi* 1 to mount again ‖ /rē′mount′/ *n* 2 fresh horse

re·mov′al *n* 1 act of removing; 2 change of residence or business; 3 dismissal, as from office; 4 *Brit* transportation of furniture from one residence or business to another or from or to a warehouse

re·move /rĭmōōv′/ [OF *remouvoir*] *vt* 1 to move (something) from a place; 2 to take off or away; 3 to put out of an office or position; 4 to eliminate, put an end to ‖ *vi* 5 to move, change residence ‖ *n* 6 act of removing; 7 step or interval ‖ **re·mov′a·ble** *adj*

re·moved′ *adj* separated by degrees in relationship, as *a first cousin once removed is the child of a first cousin*

re·mu·ner·ate /rĭmyōōn′ərāt′/ [L *remunerari* (*-atus*) to reward] *vt* to pay; recompense; compensate ‖ **re·mu′ner·a′tion** *n* ‖ **re·mu′ner·a′tive** /also *-ətiv*/ *adj* ‖ SYN requite, reward, recompense, reimburse, satisfy

Re·mus /rēm′əs/ *n Rom myth.* one of the legendary founders of Rome, slain by his twin brother Romulus for leaping scornfully over the walls of the newly built city

ren·ais·sance /ren′ĭsäns′/ [F] *n* 1 birth; renewal; 2 **Renaissance,** a period of the great revival of classical learning and art in Europe from the 14th to the 16th centuries, marking the transition from the medieval to the modern world; **b** style of art and architecture of that period ‖ also *adj*

re·nal /rēn′əl/ [< L *renes* kidneys] *adj* of or pert. to the kidneys

re·nas·cent /rinas′ənt, -nās′-/ [L *renascens* (*-entis*)] *adj* being born again; reviving

rend /rend′/ [OE *rendan*] *v* (**rent**) *vt* **1** to tear apart with force or violence; **2** to split apart, divide; **3** to distress (the heart) ‖ *vi* **4** to become rent ‖ SYN rupture, lacerate, cleave, rip, slit (see *break*)

ren·der /ren′dər/ [MF *rendre* to give back] *vt* **1** to give in return, pay back; **2** to pay as due, as *to render tribute or obedience;* **3** to present for consideration, deliver; **4** to state, utter as final, as a decision; **5** to cause to be or to become; make; **6** to furnish, give, as *to render aid;* **7** to translate; **8** to express, perform, depict, interpret, as in music or painting; **9** to purify or separate by melting, as lard

ren·dez·vous /rän′dəvōō′/ [MF = betake yourselves] *n* (**-vous** /-vōōz′/) **1** appointed place of meeting; **2** appointment for a meeting at a fixed time and place; **3** prearranged meeting of space vehicles in outer space ‖ *v* (**-vouses** /-vōōz′/; **-voused** /-vōōd′/; **-vous·ing** /-vōō′iŋ/) *vt* & *vi* to assemble at a specified time and place

ren·di·tion /rendish′ən/ [MF < LL *redditio* (*-onis*)] *n* **1** act of rendering; **2** translation; **3** style of performing or interpreting

ren·e·gade /ren′igād′/ [Sp *renegado*] *n* **1** apostate; **2** turncoat; deserter

re·nege /rinig′/ [ML *renegare*] *vt* cards **1** to play a card not of the suit led; **2** to fail to keep one's word ‖ *n* **3** cards act of reneging

re·new /vt **1** to make new again; revive; **2** to begin again, resume; **3** to grant or obtain an extension of; **4** to replace, replenish ‖ **re·new′a·ble** *adj* ‖ **re·new′al** *n*

ren·net /ren′it/ [ME] *n* **1** inner membrane of the stomach of calves and certain other young animals; **2** preparation made from this, used to curdle milk, as in making cheese; **3** rennin

ren·nin /-in/ [< *rennet*] *n* enzyme forming the active principle of rennet

Re·noir, Pierre Au·guste /pyer′ ōgust′ ren′wär/ *n* (1841–1919) French painter

re·nounce /rinouns′/ [MF *renoncer*] *vt* **1** to disown; **2** to give up formally, as a claim; **3** to give up, abandon ‖ **re·nounce′ment** *n* ‖ SYN repudiate, surrender, disclaim (see *abandon*)

ren·o·vate /ren′əvāt′/ [L *renovare* (*-atus*)] *vt* to make as if new; restore; repair ‖ **ren′o·va′tion** *n* ‖ **ren′o·va′-**

tor *n* ‖ SYN purify, revive, renew, regenerate, refresh

re·nown /rinoun′/ [AF *renoun*] *n* fame; widespread and exalted reputation ‖ SYN glory, honor, distinction (see *fame*)

re·nowned′ *adj* having a wide and honorable reputation; famed ‖ SYN glorious, celebrated, distinguished, honored

rent[1] /rent′/ **1** *pt* & *pp* of rend ‖ *n* **2** tear, hole, or slit; **3** split or division of opinion or belief ‖ SYN breach, division, schism, fissure, rupture

rent[2] [OF *rente*] *n* **1** fixed amount payable at a stated time by a tenant to a landlord for the use of property ‖ *vt* **2** to give the use of (property) in return for rent; **3** to get or hold the use of (property) in return for rent ‖ *vi* **4** to be leased or let ‖ **rent′er** *n*

rent′al *n* **1** amount paid or received as rent; **2** property offered for rent

re·nun·ci·a·tion /rinun′sē-āsh′ən, -shē-āsh′ən/ [L *renunciatio* (*-onis*) proclamation] *n* act or instance of renouncing ‖ SYN abandonment, rejection, recantation, repudiation ‖ ANT acknowledgment, proclamation, vindication

re·or·der *n* **1** repeated order of a product or a service ‖ *vt* **2** to give a reorder for; **3** to change the order or sequence of

re·or·gan·ize′ /rē′-/ *vt* **1** to organize again; **2** to change to a more satisfactory form or system ‖ **re′or·gan·i·za′tion** *n*

rep[1] /rep′/ [F *reps*] *n* fabric having a surface of fine horizontal cords

rep[2] *n* slang reputation

Rep. 1 Republican; **2** Representative

re·pair[1] /riper′/ [OF *repairier* < L *re·patriare* to go back to one's native land] *vi* to go, betake oneself, as *to repair to one's home*

re·pair[2] [MF *reparer*] *vt* **1** to put into good condition again after decay or damage; mend; **2** to remedy, set right; **3** to heal, mend; **4** to make amends for ‖ *n* **5** also **repairs** *pl* act of repairing; **6** in **repair** in good condition resulting from being repaired ‖ **re·pair′a·ble** *adj* ‖ SYN *v* restore, amend, mend, renew, recruit ‖ ANT *v* harm, impair, injure, destroy, damage

rep·a·ra·ble /rep′ərəbəl/ [L *reparabilis*] *adj* capable of being repaired or remedied

rep·a·ra·tion /rep′ərāsh′ən/ *n* **1** act of making amends; **2 reparations** *pl* compensation payable by a defeated country to the victors for losses incurred during a war ‖ SYN restitution, indemnity, amends (see *redress*)

rep·ar·tee /rep′ərtē′/ [F *repartie*] *n* **1** clever, quick-witted retort; **2** clever, witty conversation; **3** skill in making clever retorts ‖ SYN answer, response, rejoinder, retort, reply

re·past /rĭpast′, -päst′/ [OF < LL *repastus* fed] *n* meal

re·pa·tri·ate /rĭpāt′rē̇·āt′/ [LL *repatriare* (-*atus*) to restore to native land] *vt* **1** to bring or send back to the country of which one is a citizen, as a refugee or war prisoner || /-it/ *n* **2** one who has been repatriated || **re·pa′tri·a′tion** *n*

re·pay′ /rĭ-/ *v* (-**paid**) *vt* **1** to pay back; **2** to make return to, as *to repay a creditor*; **3** to make return for, as *to repay a kindness* || *vi* **4** to make payment or return || **re·pay′a·ble** *adj* || **re·pay′ment** *n* || SYN reward, recompense, requite, compensate

re·peal /rĭpēl′/ [AF *repeler*] *vt* **1** to cancel, annul, or revoke, as a law || *n* **2** act of repealing; abrogation || SYN *v* revoke, rescind, reverse, nullify, abolish (see *cancel*) || ANT *v* continue, renew, sustain

re·peat /rĭpēt′/ [MF *repeter*] *vt* **1** to say again; **2** to make, do, or cause to happen again; **3** to tell (something heard) to someone else; **4** to say after another || *vi* **5** to say or do something again || *n* **6** act of repeating; repetition; **7** anything said or done over again; **8** *mus* a sign : directing a part within two such signs to be played twice; **b** passage thus marked; **9** *radio, telv* transcribed program that is repeated || **re·peat′er** *n*

re·peat′ed *adj* done, made, or said again and again || **re·peat′ed·ly** *adv*

re·peat′ing ri′fle *n* rifle from which several shots can be fired without reloading

re·pel /rĭpel′/ [L *repellere*] *v* (-**pelled; -pel·ling**) *vt* **1** to drive back; check the advance of; **2** to resist; **3** to oppose, reject; **4** to cause aversion in; **5** *phys* to drive away || *vi* **6** to act with force against force; **7** to cause aversion || **re·pel′lent** *adj* & *n* || SYN repulse, resist, oppose, reject, decline || ANT accept, take, favor, encourage, grant, embrace, allure

re·pent /rĭpent′/ [OF *repentir*] *vi* **1** to feel regret or sorrow for something done or left undone; be penitent; **2** to do penance || *vt* **3** to feel regret or sorrow for

re·pent′ance *n* regret or sorrow felt for some wrongdoing, along with determination to reform || **re·pent′ant** *adj* || SYN compunction, regret, remorse, penitence, sorrow, contrition || ANT stubbornness, hardness, impenitence

re′per·cus′sion /rē′-/ [L *repercussio* (-*onis*) a striking back] *n* **1** recoil; rebound; **2** state of being forced or thrown back; **3** reverberation, as of sound; **4** widespread effect of an event or action, often unforeseen and indirect

rep·er·toire /rep′ərtwär′/ [F] *n* list of plays, operas, songs, etc., that a performer or company has ready to render

rep·er·to·ry /rep′ərtôr′ē̇, -tōr′-/ [L *repertorium* inventory] *n* (-**ries**) **1** collection or stock of anything; **2** repertoire; **3** theatrical company that has a repertoire of several plays, operas, or the like, which it presents in regular sequence

rep·e·ti·tion /rep′ĭtish′ən/ [L *repetitio* (-*onis*)] *n* **1** act of repeating; **2** that which is repeated || **re·pet·i·tive** /rĭpet′itiv/ *adj*

rep′e·ti′tious *adj* characterized by tedious repetition

re·pine /rĭpīn′/ [*re-* + *pine*²] *vi* to fret oneself; complain; feel discontent

re·place′ /rĭ-/ *vt* **1** to put back in place; **2** to take or fill the place of; substitute for; **3** to restore; return || **re·place′a·ble** *adj* || **re·place′ment** *n*

re·play /rēplā′/ *vt* to play (a game, a video tape, etc.) again || /rē′play′/ *n*

re·plen·ish /rĭplen′ish/ [MF *replenir* (-*niss-*)] *vt* **1** to refill; make complete again; **2** to supply again || **re·plen′ish·ment** *n*

re·plete /rĭplēt′/ [L *repletus* filled up] *adj* **1** completely filled; abounding; **2** gorged || **re·ple′tion** *n* || SYN full, abounding, surfeited, gorged, sated, satisfied

re·plev·in /rĭplev′in/ [AF < OF *replevir* to give security] *n law* **1** action for the recovery of goods wrongfully seized or held; **2** writ or order making such return || *vt* **3** to recover (goods) by replevin

rep·li·ca /rep′lika/ [It] *n* exact copy; reproduction || SYN duplicate, facsimile, copy, model, reproduction

rep′li·cate /-kit/ [< *replicare* (-*atus*) to fold back] *adj* **1** laid or folded back over itself || /-kāt′/ *vt* **2** to fold over; **3** to make a replica of; to reproduce; **4** to reply

re·ply /rĭplī′/ [MF *replier* to fold back, reply] *v* (-**plied**) *vi* **1** to answer, respond || *vt* **2** to say in answer || *n* (-**plies**) **3** answer, response || SYN *n* rejoinder, repartee, retort, answer, response

re·port /rĭpôrt′, -pōrt′/ [MF *reporter* < L *reportare* to carry back] *vt* **1** to give or prepare a formal account of; **2** to bring back, as an answer; **3** to relate, as the results of an investigation; **4** to write an account of for publication; **5** to state as an ascertained fact, as *to report the presence of sharks*; **6** to present a formal statement of; **7** to make a charge against, to a superior; **8** to announce the conclusions reached concerning (a pending bill) in a legislature || *vi* **9** to make, prepare, or present a report; **10** to present oneself at a given place || *n* **11** official or authorized presentation of facts, as *a government report*; **12** statement; **13** account, esp. for publication; **14**

something widely talked of; rumor; 15 loud explosive noise ‖ SYN *v* narrate, record, announce, relate, recount

re·port¹ card´ *n* written report of a student's grades and behavior, sent periodically to his parents

re·port´ed·ly /-idlē/ *adv* according to rumor

re·port´er *n* 1 one who reports; 2 one who prepares official reports; 3 one who gathers and reports news, as for a newspaper ‖ **rep·or·to·ri·al** /repˊərtôrˊē·əl, -tōrˊ-/ *adj*

re·pose¹ /ripōzˊ/ [L *reponere* (-*positus*) to replace] *vt* to place (trust, faith, confidence, etc.) in someone or something

re·pose² [MF *reposer* < LL *repausare* to pause, rest] *vi* 1 to lie at rest; be calm or peaceful; 2 to lie dead; 3 to lie or rest on a support ‖ *n* 4 state of being at rest; sleep; 5 calmness; composure; peace of mind ‖ SYN *n* rest, sleep, calmness, ease, peace, relaxation ‖ DISCR *Rest* is a ceasing from exertion, a stopping of that which has wearied or worn one; we may crave *rest* from social activities as well as from painful drudgery. *Rest*, too, may be obtained by change, either for mind or muscles; one may feel the refreshing *rest* that comes when the mind is relieved from worry; one using his eyes on close work may afford them *rest* by glancing now and then at distant objects. Perfect *rest*, like perfect *repose*, is *sleep*; but *repose* is a far deeper, more complete relaxation than *rest*. *Repose* connotes not only a ceasing from toil, but a flooding of the being with tranquillity and peace, refreshing and harmonious in effect. *Repose* is a composure that springs from an understanding view of life ‖ ANT *n* agitation, unrest

re·pos·i·to·ry /ripozˊitôrˊē, -tōrˊ-/ [L *repositorium*] *n* (-ries) 1 place for the storing and safe-keeping of goods; 2 person in whom one confides

re·pos·sess´ /rēˊ-/ *vt* to recover possession of, esp. for nonpayment of money due ‖ **re·pos·ses´sion** *n*

rep·re·hend /repˊrihendˊ/ [L *reprehendere* to check, blame] *vt* 1 to blame; 2 to rebuke, censure ‖ **rep´re·hen´sion** *n* ‖ SYN blame, reprimand, rebuke, reproach, censure ‖ ANT approve, exculpate, praise, commend

rep´re·hen´si·ble *adj* deserving rebuke or censure

rep·re·sent /repˊrizentˊ/ [L *repraesentare*] *vt* 1 to place vividly before the mind; 2 to portray, depict; 3 to make a statement about, esp. with the idea of influencing public opinion; 4 to describe or portray in words; 5 to act or speak for, act in behalf of; 6 to act as the elected

representative of (a district or constituency); 7 to take or act the part of; impersonate; 8 to stand for; symbolize; 9 to stand as a type or specimen of; 10 to correspond to; 11 **represent as** to describe as

rep´re·sen·ta´tion *n* 1 act or fact of representing; 2 state or fact of being represented; 3 number or body of representatives; 4 picture or image; 5 often **representations** *pl* statement of reasons for protesting something ‖ SYN image, emblem, picture, delineation, portraiture

rep´re·sent´a·tive *adj* 1 representing; 2 based or founded on representation of constituencies by delegates; 3 typical of a group or class ‖ *n* 4 typical example or specimen; 5 one who represents another or others; agent; 6 member of a legislative body representing a definite constituency; 7 **Representative** member of the lower house of Congress or of certain state legislatures

re·press /ripresˊ/ [L *reprimere* (-*pressus*)] *vt* 1 to keep under control; check; 2 to subdue, quell; 3 *psychoanal* to suppress (painful thoughts or memories) from the conscious mind ‖ **re·pres´sion** *n* ‖ **re·pres´sive** *adj* ‖ SYN restrain, check, curb, rein, stay, suppress ‖ ANT agitate, enliven, arouse, stimulate, express

re·prieve /riprēvˊ/ [< earlier *reprived* prob < F *repris* taken back] *vt* 1 to suspend temporarily the execution of (a condemned criminal); 2 to free temporarily from pain, danger, or the like ‖ *n* 3 temporary delay in carrying out a sentence; 4 warrant granting such delay; 5 any temporary relief

rep·ri·mand /repˊrimandˊ, -mändˊ/ [F *réprimande*] *n* 1 severe or official rebuke ‖ *vt* 2 to rebuke severely or officially ‖ SYN reproof, reproach, censure; *v* (*scold*)

re·print´ /rēˊ-/ *vt* 1 to print again ‖ **re´print´** *n* 2 new impression of a printed work; facsimile copy; 3 offprint

re·pris·al /riprīzˊəl/ [OF *reprisaille*] *n* retaliation for injuries received, esp. in war, as for enemy attacks on the home front, acts of sabotage against an occupying army, etc. ‖ SYN requital, retaliation, compensation, indemnity

re·pro /rēˊprō/ *n* proof on glossy paper to be photographed for making a plate

re·proach /riprōchˊ/ [OF *reprochier*] *vt* 1 to upbraid; rebuke, blame; 2 to bring shame or dishonor upon ‖ *n* 3 censure; 4 disgrace or dishonor incurred; 5 cause of blame or dishonor ‖ **re·proach´ful** *adj*

rep·ro·bate /repˊrəbātˊ/ [L *reprobatus* disapproved] *adj* 1 given up to sin, depraved ‖ *n* 2 depraved person ‖

SYN *adj* abandoned, condemned, profligate, depraved

rep'ro·ba'tion *n* 1 disapproval; condemnation; 2 rejection

re'pro·duce' /rē'-/ *vt* 1 to produce again; 2 to produce a copy or duplicate of; 3 to produce (offspring) ‖ *vi* 4 to produce offspring

re'pro·duc'tion *n* 1 act or process of reproducing, or state of being reproduced; 2 copy or duplicate; 3 generation of their own kind by plants and animals ‖ **re'pro·duc'tive** *adj*

re·proof' /ri-/ *n* act of reproving; censure, rebuke ‖ SYN admonition, reprimand, chiding, criticism

re·prove /riprōōv'/ [OF *reprover* < L *reprobare*] *vt* 1 to chide, rebuke; 2 to express disapproval of (something said or done) ‖ **re·prov'ing·ly** *adv* ‖ **re·prov'al** *n* SYN reprehend, rebuke (see *scold, blame*)

rep·tile /rep'til, -tīl/ [< L *reptilis* crawling] *n* 1 animal of a class (Reptilia) of cold-blooded vertebrates, as the snake, lizard, turtle, and alligator; 2 mean, groveling person ‖ **rep·til'i·an** *adj & n*

Repub. 1 Republic; 2 Republican

re·pub·lic /ripub'lik/ [< L *res publica* public matter, the state] *n* 1 state in which the supreme power is held by the citizens qualified to vote, through their elected representatives and executive officers; 2 any nation of which the head of government is a president rather than a hereditary monarch

re·pub'li·can *adj* 1 of, pert. to, characteristic of, or favoring a republic; 2 Republican pert. or belonging to the Republican party ‖ *n* 3 partisan of a republican form of government; 4 Republican member of the Republican party ‖ **re·pub'li·can·ism** *n*

Re·pub'li·can par'ty *n* one of the two major political parties of the U.S., founded in 1854

Re·pub'lic of Ire'land *n* Ireland 2

re·pu·di·ate /ripyōōd'ē·āt'/ [L *repudiare* (-*atus*) to reject] *vt* 1 to refuse to recognize; cast off; disown; 2 to refuse to acknowledge or to pay (a debt or obligation) ‖ **re·pu'di·a'tion** *n* ‖ **re·pu'di·a'tor** *n* ‖ SYN disclaim, disavow, renounce, discard, recant, retract, resign ‖ DISCR One *disavows* a statement which he did not make, a principle which he does not hold, an act which he did not commit. One *disclaims* a connection of which he is ashamed, a character falsely attributed to him, the authorship of a book which he did not write. To *renounce*, *repudiate*, and *resign* are more forceful terms, connoting a positive, sometimes a public, casting aside or giving up of that before held or approved. One *renounces*

formally that which he no longer believes, as a doctrine, or that to which he has some right, as a claim, or that which should in consistency by him be foregoing, as celibates *renounce* marriage. One *repudiates* with a gesture of rejection; among the ancients, a wife unwanted or faithless was *repudiated*. A tincture of the repulsion thus attached to the word still clings to it, whether one *repudiates* a dogma, the authority back of it, a prodigal son, a gift, or an obligation. To *resign* is formally to give up a position to which one has been elected or for which one has been selected. To *recant* and *retract* refer to *disclaiming* that which has been said or maintained; to *recant* is to withdraw, usually publicly, a formerly sponsored belief, opinion, or declaration. To *retract* is to take back openly what was said of another, as an untrue statement or false charge. To *discard* is to throw away what is considered valueless, as old clothes; figuratively, one *discards* outgrown desires, false friends, unworthy ambitions ‖ ANT acknowledge, own, admit, keep

re·pug·nant /ripug'nant/ [< L *repugnare* to resist] *adj* 1 highly distasteful or disagreeable; repulsive; 2 incompatible, contradictory; 3 antagonistic, unfriendly ‖ **re·pug'nance** *n*

re·pulse /ripuls'/ [L *repellere* (-*pulsus*)] *vt* 1 to drive back, repel; 2 to reject; rebuff ‖ *n* 3 act of repelling or state of being repelled; 4 rejection; rebuff

re·pul'sion *n* 1 act of repelling or state of being repelled; 2 aversion, repugnance; 3 *phys* force that tends to separate two bodies of like electrical charge or magnetic polarity

re·pul'sive *adj* 1 loathsome, offensive; 2 repelling ‖ SYN repellent, offensive ‖ ANT alluring, attractive

rep·u·ta·ble /rep'yətəbəl/ *adj* having a good reputation; respectable; creditable ‖ **rep'u·ta·bly** *adv* ‖ **rep'u·ta·bil'i·ty** /-bil'-/ *n* ‖ SYN estimable, honorable, creditable, respectable

rep·u·ta·tion /rep'yətāsh'ən/ *n* 1 repute in which one is generally held; 2 good name or standing ‖ SYN credit, distinction, respectability (see *fame*)

re·pute /ripyōōt'/ [MF *reputer* < L *reputare*] *n* 1 estimation in which a person is held; 2 good name or character ‖ *vt* 3 to be reputed to be to be considered to be

re·put'ed *adj* 1 having the reputation of being; 2 supposed to be but probably nonexistent, as *his reputed fortune* ‖ **re·put'ed·ly** *adv*

re·quest /rikwest'/ [OF *requeste*] *n* 1 act or instance of asking for something; 2 thing asked for; 3 condition of being asked for; demand; 4 by

request in response to requests ‖ *vt* 5 to ask for, esp. with politeness; 6 to ask (a person) to do something

req·ui·em /ˈrek′wē-əm, ˈrēk′-/ [L = rest] *n* 1 Mass for the repose of the soul of the dead; 2 music for such a Mass; 3 any musical service or hymn for the dead

req·ui·es·cat /ˌrek′wē-es′kat/ [L *requiescat* (in pace) may he (or she) rest (in peace)] *n* prayer for the repose of the soul of the dead

re·quire /riˈkwīr′(ə)r/ [L *requirere*] *vt* 1 to need; 2 to demand, as by authority; insist upon; compel; 3 to call for, as *that suit requires a matching tie*

re·quire′ment *n* 1 something needed; 2 something required or demanded; 3 condition that must be met to satisfy a rule, standard, or the like ‖ SYN demand, need, requisite (see *order*)

req·ui·site /ˈrek′wizit/ [L *requisitus* demanded] *adj* 1 required; necessary; indispensable ‖ *n* 2 something requisite ‖ SYN *adj* required, essential, needed (see *necessary*)

req·ui·si′tion /-zish′ən/ *n* 1 act of requiring; 2 authoritative, formal demand or summons; 3 written order, as for supplies ‖ *vt* 4 to demand or take, as by right or authority

re·quit′al /-kwit′-/ [see **requite**] *n* 1 act of repaying or making return for good or evil; 2 just return for good or evil; 3 repayment for a loss ‖ SYN compensation, return, retribution (see *redress*)

re·quite /riˈkwīt′/ [re- + *obs* quite to pay] *vt* 1 to repay or return good or evil to (a person); 2 to repay or return good or evil for; reward or avenge; 3 to make a fit return for; compensate ‖ SYN retaliate, reciprocate, revenge, remunerate, recompense, satisfy, repay, compensate, reward

re′run′ /ˈrē′-/ *n* reshowing of a film or video tape ‖ **re·run′** *v* (**-ran; -run; -run·ning**) *vt* to reshow (a film or video tape)

re·scind /riˈsind′/ [L *rescindere* to tear off] *vt* to abrogate; annul; cancel ‖ **re·scis′sion** /-sizh′ən/ *n*

res·cue /ˈres′kyoo/ [OF *rescourre*] *vt* 1 to set free from danger, imprisonment, or evil ‖ *n* 2 act of rescuing ‖ **res′cu·er** *n* ‖ SYN *v* retake, recover, recapture, reclaim, release

re·search /riˈsurch/, ˈrē′surch/ [OF *recercher*] *n* 1 systematic inquiry or investigation in a particular subject or science ‖ *vt* 2 to investigate or study exhaustively ‖ *vi* 3 to make researches ‖ **re·search′er** *n*

re·sec′tion /ri-/ [L *resectio* (*-onis*) a cutting off] *n* surg operation of cutting out a part, as of a bone

re·sem·blance /rizem′bləns/ *n* quality or state of resembling; likeness;

similarity ‖ SYN semblance, similarity, similitude (see *likeness*)

re·sem·ble /rizem′bəl/ [OF *resembler* < L *simulare* to imitate] *vt* to be like or similar to

re·sent /rizent′/ [F *ressentir* to feel] *vt* to feel, express, or show anger because of; be indignant at ‖ **re·sent′-ful** *adj*

re·sent′ment *n* strong feeling of anger or displeasure because of a real or fancied wrong, insult, etc. ‖ SYN offense, rancor, bitterness, anger, pique, grudge, spite, animosity, ill will, envy (see *malice*)

res·er·va·tion /ˌrez′ərvāsh′ən/ *n* 1 act of reserving; holding back or hiding; 2 anything held back; 3 keeping back for oneself, as of a right or interest; 4 express or tacit limitation or qualification, as *a mental reservation*; 5 tract of public land kept for some public use; 6 granting or securing of hotel accommodations, a seat on a plane, train, etc.

re·serve /rizurv′/ [MF *reserver*] *vt* 1 to set aside or withhold for future use or disposal; 2 to retain control of by stipulation; 3 to set apart for a particular use; 4 to secure the use of for a specific occasion, as a seat in a theater, train, or plane, or hotel accommodations ‖ *n* 5 act of reserving; restriction; qualification; 6 that which is reserved; extra stock; 7 tract of land set apart for a special purpose; 8 restraint in speech and manner, aloofness; reticence; 9 *fin* a funds kept on hand by a bank; b cash set aside for expected or unexpected expenses; 10 body of troops kept out of action and ready to aid as needed; 11 also **reserves** *pl* troops not on active duty but subject to call; 12 **in reserve** put aside to be used when needed; 13 **without reserve** without restraint ‖ SYN *n* qualification, limitation, pride, reticence, coldness, backwardness, coyness ‖ ANT *n* frankness, indiscretion, pertness, loquacity, presumption

re·served′ *adj* 1 secured for a specific occasion; 2 reticent; undemonstrative ‖ SYN distant, taciturn, uncommunicative

re·serv′ist *n* member of the reserve military force

res·er·voir /ˈrez′ərvwär′, -vôr′/ [F < LL *reservatorium* storehouse] *n* 1 place where water is collected and stored for use; 2 reserve quantity; store

re′set′ /ˈrē′-/ *n* device for resetting or restarting a motor or mechanism that has been automatically turned off by an overload

re·show′ /ˈrē′-/ *vt* to show (a motion picture or video tape) again

re·side /riˈzīd′/ [L *residere*] *vi* 1 to dwell, live; 2 to be inherent; rest or be vested

res·i·dence /ˈrez′idəns/ *n* 1 act or fact

of residing; **2** place where one resides; **3** period during which one lives in a place || **res'i·den'tial** /-denshǝl/ *adj* || SYN habitation, house, dwelling, domicile, mansion

res'i·den·cy *n* (**-cies**) **1** official residence of certain diplomatic agents; **2** position or tenure of a medical resident

res'i·dent *adj* **1** residing; **2** residing where one works; **3** nonmigratory (bird) || *n* **4** one who resides in a place; **5** diplomatic agent living at a foreign court; **6** physician who lives at or works on the staff of a hospital as part of his training

re·sid·u·al /rizij'ŏŏ-ǝl/ *adj* **1** pert. to, consisting of, or like a residue or remainder; **2** remaining, left over || *n* **3** remainder; **4** residuals *pl* continued payment to a performer for the repeated showing of a television film in which he appears

res·i·due /rez'id(y)ŏŏ'/ [MF *residu* < L *residuum*] *n* that which remains after a part has been removed; remainder || SYN rest, remnant, leavings (see *remainder*)

re·sign /rizīn'/ [L *resignare* to cancel] *vt* **1** to give up (a position or office); **2** to relinquish (a claim or right); **3** to submit or reconcile (oneself) || *vi* **4** to give up a position or office || SYN renounce, abdicate (see *abandon, repudiate*)

res·ig·na·tion /rez'ignāsh'ǝn/ *n* **1** act of resigning; **2** document conveying this act; **3** uncomplaining submission || SYN submissiveness, endurance (see *patience*)

re·signed' *adj* submissive; patiently uncomplaining

re·sil·i·ent /rizil'ē-ǝnt, -yǝnt/ [< L *resilire* to leap back] *adj* **1** springing back to a former position or shape; elastic; **2** having or showing power of recovery || **re·sil'i·ence** or **re·sil'i·en·cy** *n*

res·in /rez'in/ [MF *resine* < L *resina*] *n* **1** any of a class of uncrystallizable vegetable substances obtained as exudations from certain plants or produced synthetically, used in making varnishes and plastics; **2** rosin || **res'in·ous** *adj*

res'in·ate' *vt* to impregnate or treat with resin

re·sist /rizist'/ [L *resistere* to stand back] *vt* **1** to oppose, withstand; strive against || *vi* **2** to offer opposition, refuse to obey or agree || **re·sist'er** *n* || **re·sist'i·ble** *adj* || SYN withstand, thwart, oppose (see *prevent*)

re·sist'ance *n* **1** act or capacity of resisting; **2** *elec* **a** opposition offered by a conductor to the passage of an electric current, measured in ohms; **b** conductor that offers such opposition; **3** force that acts to prevent or retard motion, as the resistance of

the air to bodies passing through it; **4 Resistance** underground organization in an occupied country that resists the occupying forces by sabotage and guerrilla warfare || **re·sist'ant** *adj* || SYN antagonism, hindrance (see *opposition*) || ANT surrender, acquiescence, passivity, quiescence

re·sis'tor *n* device providing resistance for an electric circuit

res·o·lute /rez'ǝlŏŏt'/ [L *resolutus* resolved] *adj* determined; firm in purpose || **res'o·lute'ly** *adv* || **res'o·lute'ness** *n* || SYN firm, brave, obstinate, inflexible, steadfast, persevering, unshaken || ANT indecisive, flexible

res'o·lu'tion *n* **1** act of separating into constituent parts; **2** resoluteness; fixed determination; **3** that which is decided upon; resolve; **4** formal proposal or expression of opinion by a legislative assembly or public meeting; **5** solution, solving; **6** *optics* process or capability of distinguishing between two closely adjacent images or sources of light || SYN decision, steadfastness (see *determination*)

re·solve /rizolv'/ [L *resolvere* to loosen] *vt* **1** to separate into constituent parts; **2** to change or convert (oneself or itself); **3** to cause to decide (to do something); **4** to reduce to simpler form; **5** to clear up, solve; **6** to make a firm decision (to do something); **7** to decide or adopt by formal vote; **8** to dispel, as fear or doubts; **9** *optics* to render distinguishable the elements of (an image) || *vi* **10** to separate into constituent parts; **11** to come to a determination; decide firmly || *n* **12** steadfast purpose; **13** resolution, determination || SYN *n* conclusion, resolution (see *determination*)

re·solved' *adj* firm in purpose; determined; resolute

res·o·nance /rez'ǝnǝns/ [MF < L *resonantia*] *n* **1** prolongation of sound by reflection; **2** full vibrating quality of sound; **3** *phys* **a** energetic vibrations of a body produced by application of a periodic force of nearly the same frequency as that of the free vibration of the affected body; **b** reinforcement of a sound by a body tuned to the same pitch || **res'o·nant** *adj*

re·sort /rizôrt'/ [OF *resortir* to go out again] *vi* **1 resort to, a** to go habitually, often, or in great numbers to; **b** to have recourse to || *n* **2** place much visited for rest and recreation; **3** recourse; **4** person or thing resorted to

re·sound /rizound'/ [MF *resoner* < L *resonare*] *vi* **1** to sound loudly; **2** to reecho, reverberate; **3** to be famous || *vt* **4** to cause to sound loudly; **5** to cause to echo; **6** to proclaim loudly

re·source /risôrs′, rē′sôrs/ [F *res-source*] *n* 1 that on which one depends for help or support; 2 ability to cope with an emergency; 3 **resources** *pl* skill in devising expedients; practical ingenuity; 4 money, means; assets; 5 natural wealth of a country ‖ SYN means, contrivance, resort, ingenuity, skill, expedient, device, shift, wit; *pl* funds, money, wealth

re·source·ful *adj* capable of dealing skillfully with unusual problems ‖ **re·source′ful·ness** *n*

re·spect /rispekt′/ [L *respicere* (*-spectus*) to look back at] *vt* 1 to show consideration for; 2 to avoid intruding upon; 3 to hold in honor and esteem; 4 to have relation to; concern ‖ *n* 5 honor and esteem; 6 consideration; deference; 7 special point or particular; 8 reference; regard, as *with respect to this*; 9 **respects** *pl* expression of good will or regard ‖ SYN *v* (see *esteem*); *n* bias, partiality, consideration, notice (see *deference, regard*) ‖ ANT *n* disregard, disrespect, contempt, dislike, scorn

re·spect′a·ble *adj* 1 worthy of regard or esteem; 2 of good name or repute; 3 fairly numerous; 4 of moderate excellence or size ‖ **re·spect′a·bly** *adv* ‖ **re·spect′a·bil′i·ty** /-bil′-/ *n*

re·spect′ful *adj* showing or marked by proper regard, esteem, or courtesy; deferential ‖ **re·spect′ful·ly** *adv*

re·spect′ing *prep* about, concerning

re·spec′tive *adj* relating to each of several persons or things

re·spec′tive·ly *adv* with respect to each in the order named

res·pi·ra·tion /resp′irāsh′ən/ [see **re·spire**] *n* act or process of breathing ‖ **res·pi·ra·to·ry** /resp′irətôr′ē̇, -tôr′-, rispīr′-/ *adj*

res′pi·ra·tor *n* 1 device, as of gauze, placed over the nose or mouth to prevent the inhalation of noxious substances; 2 apparatus for producing artificial respiration

re·spire /rispī′ər/ [L *respirare*] *vt & vi* to breathe

res·pite /resp′it/ [OF *respit* < L *respectus*] *n* interval of relief, as from trouble, pain, or the like ‖ SYN pause, stop, cessation, intermission, delay, letup

re·splend·ent /risplen′dənt/ [< L *resplendere* to shine brightly] *adj* shining brilliantly; dazzling; splendid ‖ **re·splend′ence** *n* ‖ SYN gorgeous, refulgent, radiant, vivid, lustrous

re·spond /rispond′/ [L *respondere*] *vi* 1 to reply; 2 to react (to a stimulus); 3 to act in return or in answer ‖ *vt* 4 to reply; say in answer

re·spond′ent *adj* 1 responsive; answering ‖ *n* 2 one who replies; 3 *law* one who answers to a suit; defendant

re·sponse /rispons′/ [L *responsum*] *n*

1 answer, reply; 2 *eccl* verse, sentence, etc., said or sung by the congregation or choir in reply to the clergyman; 3 reaction to a stimulus ‖ SYN answer, retort, repartee, replication, rejoinder

re·spon′si·bil′i·ty /-bil′-/ *n* (-ties) 1 state of being responsible; 2 that for which one is responsible; 3 duty, obligation

re·spon′si·ble *adj* 1 involving trust, duty, or obligation; 2 answerable, accountable; 3 trustworthy, dependable; 4 capable of distinguishing between right and wrong; 5 able to discharge an obligation ‖ **re·spon′si·bly** *adv* ‖ SYN answerable, accountable, dependable, liable ‖ DISCR We are *responsible for* something *to* someone; the United States post office is *responsible to* the public *for* the safe and prompt delivery of mail. *Liable* in the sense of *responsible* is followed by *for*. He who indorses a note is *liable*, on the defection of the dráwer, *for* the sum named in the note ‖ ANT untrustworthy, heedless

re·spon′sive *adj* 1 making responses; 2 reacting readily, as to influences, stimuli, or appeals

rest¹ /rest′/ [OE] *n* 1 freedom from disturbance of mind or spirit; tranquillity; 2 sleep; 3 death; 4 cessation of motion or effort; repose; 5 stopping place; lodging; 6 support; base; 7 *mus* **a** interval of silence; **b** sign indicating this; 8 **at rest, a** resting; **b** tranquil; **c** motionless; **d** dead; 9 **lay to rest** to bury ‖ *vi* 10 to cease motion, labor, or exertion; 11 to remain without change or further notice; 12 to take repose; sleep; 13 to be quiet or still; be at peace; 14 to lie; lean; be spread out; be supported; 15 *law* to terminate voluntarily the introduction of evidence; 16 **rest on** or **upon, a** to be based on; **b** to rely on; **c** to be the responsibility of ‖ *vt* 17 to give rest to; 18 to stop, halt; 19 to place on a support; lay; lean; 20 to base or ground; 21 to terminate the introduction of evidence on ‖ SYN *n* intermission, quiet, peace (see *repose*)

rest² [F *rester* to remain < L *restare*] *vi* 1 to continue to be, stay, as *rest assured* ‖ *n* 2 **the rest, a** that which is left, the remainder; **b** *pl* the others

res·tau·rant /rest′ərənt, -ränt′/ [F] *n* place where meals are served to customers

res·tau·ra·teur /rest′ərətur′/ [F] *n* proprietor or operator of a restaurant

rest′ cure′ *n* system of treatment, esp. of nervous disorders, involving complete rest

rest′ful *adj* 1 full of, or giving, rest; 2 being in repose; quiet ‖ **rest′ful·ly** *adv*

res·ti·tu·tion /rest′it(y)o͞osh′ən/ [L *res-*

titutio (-onis)] n 1 restoration to the rightful owner of that which has been taken away; 2 indemnification for loss, injury, or damage; 3 restoration to a former place or condition || SYN compensation, indemnification (see redress)

res·tive /rest′iv/ [OF restif] adj 1 unwilling to go forward; balky, stubborn; 2 unruly; 3 restless; uneasy

rest′less adj 1 finding no rest; 2 uneasy, restive; 3 always active or in motion; 4 affording no rest || SYN discontented, roving, unsettled, wandering, agitated, unquiet || ANT contented, steady, calm, quiet, restful, composed

res·to·ra·tion /rest′ərāsh′ən/ [see restore] n 1 act of restoring or state of being restored; 2 the Restoration the return of Charles II to the throne of England in 1660, and the period following to 1685

re·stor·a·tive /ristôr′ətiv, -stōr′-/ adj 1 having power to restore || n 2 something that restores

re·store /ristôr′, -stōr′/ [OF restorer < L restaurare] vt 1 to give back to the owner (something previously lost or taken); 2 to reinstate in a former office, dignity, or the like; 3 to bring back to health or a normal condition; 4 to reestablish, as order; 5 to repair and alter, as a building, painting, or the like, so as to bring it to its original condition; 6 to reproduce (something ancient) in its original condition || SYN reinstate, recover, refund, reclaim, repair

re·strain /ristrān′/ [MF restraindre] vt 1 to hold back from action; 2 to keep under control; repress; 3 to limit, restrict; 4 to deprive of liberty || SYN constrain, suppress, restrict, hold, confine, circumscribe || ANT excite, impel, free

re·straint /ristrānt′/ n 1 act of restraining or state of being restrained; 2 confinement, loss of liberty; 3 means of restraining; 4 reserve, constraint || SYN repression, restriction (see compulsion)

re·strict /ristrikt′/ [L restringere (-strictus) to hold back] vt to keep within bounds; confine; limit || re·strict′ed adj || re·stric′tion n

re·stric·tive adj tending to restrict or limit

re·stric·tive clause′ n gram clause that is essential to the meaning of a sentence, as I do not know the name of the man who came in late

rest′ room′ n room in a public place having toilets, washbowls, etc.

re·sult /rizult′/ [L resultare to rebound] vi 1 to follow as a consequence or effect; 2 result in to terminate or conclude in as a consequence || n 3 the consequence of some action; outcome; 4 math that which is obtained by calculation || SYN n termination, issue, event, product, conse-

quence, upshot, outcome || DISCR These words agree in expressing that which follows a cause or a given set of circumstances. Result stresses the effect of an action or an effort as a whole. We speak of the result of an experiment, of a mathematical calculation, of an educational campaign. Consequence emphasizes the logical or natural order of that which follows; consequences are often unforeseeable and unforeseen, are direct or indirect, and are restricted to the moral field. We speak of the consequences of leading an evil life, or of disregarding the rules of health. An act may have many consequences, but only one result. Issue names the final outcome of a set of circumstances or happenings. We speak of the issue of an argument, a battle, a conference. Event shares the finality of issue, but emphasizes the idea of fact; event is what actually does happen as the upshot of foregoing circumstances

re·sult′ant adj 1 following as a result or consequence || n 2 that which results

re·sume /rizoom′/ [L resumere to take again] vt 1 to take up again after interruption; begin again; 2 to take or occupy again; 3 to go back to using || vi 4 to start again || re·sump′tion /-zump′-/ n

ré·su·mé /rez′oomā′, rez′oomā′/ [F] n 1 summary; 2 brief written account of one's qualifications and experience, as in a job application

re·sur·gent /risurj′ənt/ [< L resurgere to rise again] adj rising or tending to rise again || re·sur′gence n

res·ur·rect /rez′ərekt′/ [< resurrection] vt 1 to raise from the dead; 2 to bring back to notice or use

res·ur·rec·tion [ME < LL resurrectio (-ionis) < L resurgere to rise again] n 1 a rising again from the dead; 2 state of those risen from the dead; 3 restoration, revival; 4 the Resurrection the rising of Christ from the dead

re·sus·ci·tate /risus′itāt′/ [L resuscitare (-atus) to raise again] vt to revive from unconsciousness or apparent death || re·sus′ci·ta′tion n

ret /ret/ [MD reten to soak] v (ret·ted; ret·ting) vt to soak, as flax, hemp, or wood, so as to remove the natural juices or to loosen the fibers

re·tail /rē′tāl/ [OF = piece cut off] n 1 sale of goods directly to the consumer, usu. in small quantities || adj 2 pert. to retail || adv 3 at a retail price; in small quantities || vt & vi 4 to sell in small quantities || /ritāl′/ vt 5 to tell and retell, as gossip || re′tail·er n

re·tain /ritān′/ [OF retenir] vt 1 to persist in holding or keeping in use, possession, practice, control, etc.; 2 to engage beforehand by a fee, as a lawyer; **3** to keep in mind

re·tain·er *n* **1** one in the service of a person of high rank or position; **2** retaining fee, as to a lawyer

re·tain·ing wall' *n* wall to prevent a bank of earth from sliding

re·take' /rē-/ *n* **1** scene or sequence in a movie that has been filmed again ‖ **re·take'** *vt* **2** to take again; take back; **3** to photograph again; film again

re·tal·i·ate /rĭtal'ē·āt'/ [L *retaliare* (-*atus*)] *vi* to give like for like, esp. evil for evil ‖ **re·tal'i·a'tion** *n* ‖ **re·tal'i·a·to'ry** /-ətôr'ē, -tōr'-/ *adj*

re·tard /rĭtärd'/ [L *retardare*] *vt* **1** to slow up; **2** to hinder, delay ‖ *vi* **3** to be delayed ‖ *n* **4** delay ‖ **re'tar·da'tion** /rē'-/ *n* ‖ **SYN** *v* hinder, delay, defer, obstruct, impede

re·tard'ate /-āt/ *n* person who is mentally retarded

re·tard'ed *adj* (person) of slowed mental or emotional development

retch /rech/ /[OE *hrᴂcan* to spit up] *vi* to try to vomit; strain, as in vomiting

re·ten·tion /rĭtensh'ən/ [L *retentio* (-*onis*)] *n* **1** act of retaining or state of being retained; **2** capacity for retaining; **3** act or power of remembering; memory ‖ **re·ten'tive** *adj*

ret·i·cent /ret'isənt/ [< L *reticere* to be silent] *adj* disposed to be silent; reserved, taciturn ‖ **ret'i·cence** *n* ‖ **SYN** silent, reserved, uncommunicative, taciturn

ret·i·cle /ret'ikəl/ [L *reticulum* little net] *n* network of fine lines placed in the eyepiece of a telescope or transit

ret·i·na /ret'inə/ [ML < L *rete* net] *n* (-nas or -nae /-nē'/) innermost coat of the back of the eyeball that receives through the lens the image which is transmitted to the brain by the optic nerve ‖ **ret'i·nal** *adj*

ret·i·nue /ret'in(y)ळ'/ [MF] *n* body of retainers

re·tire /rĭtī'ər/ [MF *retirer* to withdraw] *vi* **1** to go to a place of privacy; **2** to withdraw, retreat; **3** to withdraw from business, office, or active life; **4** to go to bed ‖ *vt* **5** to withdraw; **6** to withdraw from circulation or from the market, as stocks or currency; **7** to remove from active service; **8** *baseball* to put out

re·tire'ment *n* **1** act of retiring; **2** state of being retired, spec. from one's former occupation; **3** privacy; seclusion; **4** place removed from public notice ‖ **SYN** seclusion, solitude, privacy, isolation, retreat ‖ **DISCR** These words agree in expressing a withdrawing into private life, *seclusion*, or security. One in *retirement*, as a widow in mourning, does not mingle freely with her former associates, though she may see her intimates. Businessmen beyond the age of active work go into a *retirement* that is merely the quiet opposite of public life. *Seclusion* is a cloistered *retirement*, very strict, though broken perhaps by association with relatives or servants. *Solitude* connotes the presence of no one else; *privacy* is the opposite of publicity. People beset by crowds long for *privacy*; reflective, independent minds crave *solitude*. *Retreat* names a drawing back into *retirement*, *privacy*, or *solitude*. *Retreat* and *retirement* may also name a place of refuge

re·tir'ing *adj* shy, reserved

re·tool' /rē-/ *vt* to replace the stamping machinery of a factory in order to produce a new model

re·tort¹ /rĭtôrt'/ [L *retorquere* (-*tortus*) to bend back] *n* **1** quick or pointed reply ‖ *vt* **2** to say as a retort; **3** to fling back (an accusation, epithet, etc.) ‖ *vi* **4** to make a retort ‖ **SYN** *n* response, reply, rejoinder, repartee

re·tort² /rĭtôrt', rē'tôrt'/ [L *retorta* bent back] *n* **1** vessel in which substances are subjected to a high temperature for purposes of distillation or decomposition; **2** spherical glass vessel with a long neck bent downward, used for this purpose

re·touch /rē-/ *vt* to touch up or improve, as a photograph or painting

re·trace /rĭ-/ *vt* **1** to trace backward; **2** to follow again from the beginning

re·tract /rĭtrakt'/ [L *retrahere* (-*tractus*) to draw back] *vt* **1** to draw back or in; **2** to recall or withdraw; take back ‖ *vi* **3** to withdraw or take back something said or written; **4** to withdraw or recede ‖ **re·tract'a·ble** *adj* ‖ **re·trac'tion** *n* ‖ **SYN** recall, disavow, recant (see *repudiate*)

re·trac'tile /-tĭl/ *adj* capable of being withdrawn, drawn back, or drawn in

re·trac'tor *n* **1** one who or that which retracts; **2** muscle that retracts an organ or part; **3** *surg* instrument for holding back the edges of a wound

re·tread /rētred'/ *vt* **1** to put a new tread on (a tire) ‖ /rē'tred'/ *n* **2** retreaded tire

re·treat /rĭtrēt'/ [OF *retraite*] *n* **1** act of withdrawing or retiring; **2** retirement or seclusion; **3** asylum or shelter; **4** forced withdrawal of troops; **5** *mil* a flag-lowering ceremony at sunset; **b** bugle call for this ceremony; **6** *eccl* retirement for prayer and meditation; **7** beat a retreat to retreat hurriedly ‖ *vi* **8** to withdraw, draw back ‖ **SYN** *n* refuge, shelter, solitude (see *retirement*)

re·trench' /rĭ-/ [F *retrencher*] *vi* to cut down expenses ‖ **re·trench'ment** *n* ‖ **SYN** curtail, abridge, decrease, diminish, reduce, economize ‖ **ANT** expand, lavish, waste, increase

ret·ri·bu·tion /ret'rĭby͞oōsh'ən/ [L retributio (-onis)] n reward or punishment for good or bad actions, esp. loss or suffering inflicted as a just punishment ‖ **re·trib·u·tive** /rĭtrĭb'yətĭv/ adj

re·trieve /rĭtrēv'/ [OF retrover to find again] vt 1 to recover, regain; 2 to revive, restore; 3 to repair the harm done by; make amends for; 4 to recover (data) stored in the memory of a computer; 5 hunting to fetch (killed or wounded game) ‖ vi 6 hunting to retrieve game ‖ **re·triev'a·ble** adj ‖ **re·triev'al** n

re·triev'er n 1 one who or that which retrieves; 2 dog trained to retrieve game

ret·ro- [L] pref back, backward

ret'ro·ac'tive /ret'rō-/ adj operative or effective with reference to past occurrences or a past date

ret'ro·fir'ing n ignition of the retrorockets of a space vehicle

ret'ro·grade' /ret'rə-/ adj 1 directed or moving backward, reversed; retreating; 2 going from a better to a worse condition; 3 astron (planet) moving westward relative to the fixed stars ‖ vi 4 to go backward; 5 to decline ‖ **ret'ro·gra·da'tion** /-grə-/ n

ret·ro·gress /ret'rəgres', ret'rəgres'/ [< L retrogressus gone back] vi to go backward into an earlier or worse stage ‖ **ret'ro·gres'sion** n

ret'ro·rock'et /ret'rō-/ n small rocket whose function it is to decelerate a larger rocket by producing thrust in the direction opposite to the motion of the larger rocket

ret·ro·spect /ret'rəspekt'/ [L retrospectus looked back at] n **in retrospect** in looking back on the past ‖ SYN remembrance, reminiscence (see memory)

ret'ro·spec'tion n 1 act of meditating upon things past; 2 a recalling to memory ‖ **ret'ro·spec'tive** adj

ret·rous·sé /ret'r͞oōsā'/ [F] adj turned up (nose)

re·turn /rĭturn'/ [MF retorner] vi 1 to come or go back; 2 to reply ‖ vt 3 to send, bring, or put back; restore; 4 to repay, do in reciprocation; 5 to render (a verdict); 6 to elect or reelect to a seat in a legislative body; 7 to produce or yield, as a profit; 8 to report officially; 9 to send (an answer) in reply; 10 games to strike or play (the ball) back ‖ n 11 act or fact of returning; 12 that which is returned; 13 recurrence; 14 yield, profit; 15 formal report or statement of result; 16 response; 17 **in return** in exchange or reciprocity ‖ adj 18 repeated; 19 of, pert. to, or for a return; 20 (game) played to provide a loser with a chance to win from a previous opponent; 21 (mail)

that is sent immediately on receipt of a letter; 22 (ticket) a that is good for a return journey; b that is good for a round trip; 23 (trip) to a place and back again ‖ **re·turn'a·ble** adj

re·u·ni·fy' /rē-/ v (-fied) vt to restore the unity of (a country, political party, etc.) ‖ **re'u·ni·fi·ca'tion** n

re·un'ion /rē-/ n 1 act of reuniting or state of being reunited; 2 festive gathering of friends, classmates, associates, or relatives

re'u·nite' /rē'-/ vt & vi to unite again

rev /rev/ [revolution] v (revved; revving) vt 1 to speed up the revolutions of (an engine) ‖ vi 2 to be revved

Rev. Reverend

re·vamp' /rē-/ vt to reconstruct, revise, renovate

re·veal /rĭvēl'/ [MF reveler] vt 1 to disclose; divulge; unveil; 2 to display, exhibit ‖ SYN publish, announce, disclose, divulge

rev·eil·le /rev'ələ/ [F réveillez (impv) awaken] n early morning drumbeat or bugle call that rouses military personnel for the day's duty

rev·el /rev'əl/ [MF reveler] v (-eled or -elled; -el·ing or -el·ling) vi 1 to take part in boisterous merrymaking; 2 **revel in** to take great delight in ‖ n 3 riotous festivity, revelry ‖ **rev'el·er** or **rev'el·ler** n

rev·e·la·tion /rev'əlāsh'ən/ [< L revelatus revealed] n 1 act of revealing, disclosure; 2 that which is revealed; 3 theol manifestation by God of His will and truths to man; 4 **Revelation** last book of the New Testament

rev'el·ry n (-ries) uproarious merrymaking

re·venge /rĭvenj'/ [MF revenger < re + L vindicare to lay claim to] vt 1 to inflict pain or punishment for; avenge; 2 to avenge the wrongs done to ‖ n 3 act of avenging; 4 that which is done in vengeance; 5 vindictiveness ‖ SYN v requite, retaliate, vindicate (see avenge)

re·venge'ful adj full of revenge; avenging ‖ SYN malicious, vengeful, vindictive, resentful ‖ ANT forgiving, humane, merciful, kindly, well-disposed

rev·e·nue /rev'ən(y)͞oō/ [MF] n income, esp. that of a government collected from taxes, duties, and excises

rev'e·nue cut'ter n small armed government vessel used chiefly to prevent smuggling

rev'e·nu'er n revenue agent charged with preventing illegal distillation of liquor

rev'e·nue stamp' n stamp used on a commodity to show that a government tax has been paid on it

re·ver·ber·ate /rĭvurb'ərāt'/ [L reverberare (-atus) to strike back] vi 1 to resound, reecho; 2 to rebound or be reflected ‖ *vt* **3** to cause (a sound) to reecho; **4** to reflect, as heat or light ‖ re·ver'ber·a'tion *n* ‖ re·ver'·ber·a·to'ry /-ətôr'ē, -tōr'-/ *adj*

re·vere /rivir'/ [L *revereri*] *vt* to regard with respectful and affectionate awe; venerate

Re·vere, Paul /rivir'/ *n* (1735–1818) American patriot, who rode through the Massachusetts countryside to warn the Americans of the approach of British troops on April 18, 1775

rev·er·ence /rev'(ə)rəns/ *n* **1** deep respect together with awe and affection; veneration; **2** act or sign of respect; **3** state of being revered; **4** Reverence title given to the clergy (with *his* or *your*) ‖ *vt* **5** to revere ‖ SYN veneration, honor, homage, respect, deference (see *awe*)

rev·er·end /rev'(ə)rənd/ *adj* **1** worthy of reverence; **2** pert. to the clergy; **3** the Reverend used to modify the name of a clergyman, as *the Reverend John Miller* or *the Reverend Dr. John Miller* ‖ *n* **4** *colloq* clergyman

rev'er·ent *adj* showing or expressing reverence ‖ rev'er·ent·ly *adv*

rev·er·en'tial /-ensh'əl/ *adj* proceeding from, expressing, or inspiring reverence

rev·er·ie or rev·er·y /rev'ərē/ [F < *rêver* to dream] *n* (-ies) **1** deep musing; state of being lost in thought; **2** daydream ‖ SYN daydream, reflection, musing (see *dream*)

re·ver·sal /rivurs'əl/ *n* act or instance of reversing, or state of being reversed

re·ver'sal film' *n* film in which the negative is processed into a positive transparency

re·verse /rivurs'/ [MF *revers* < L *reversus*] *adj* **1** turned backward; opposite; **2** causing an opposite motion; **3** backward, reversed; **4** *typ* (printed matter) with the black and white reversed ‖ *n* **5** the contrary or opposite; **6** back or less important side of a coin or medal; **7** change for the worse, misfortune; **8** check, defeat; **9** *mach* a backward motion; **b** reverse gear ‖ *vt* **10** to turn back, inside out, or upside down; **11** to cause to move in an opposite direction; **12** to change to an opposite condition; **13** to exchange, transpose; **14** to annul or revoke, as a judicial decision ‖ *vi* **15** to move in an opposite direction; **16** to put into reverse gear ‖ re·vers'i·ble *adj*

re·verse' gear' *n* gear which changes the motion of an automobile or other vehicle to the backward direction

re·ver'sion /-zhən/ *n* **1** act or instance of reverting; **2** reversal

re·vert /rivurt'/ [L *revertere* to turn back] *vi* **1** to go back; recur; **2** *law* to return to the grantor or his heirs, as property; **3** to return to a former practice or belief; **4** *biol* to return to an earlier type

re·vet·ment /rivet'mənt/ [< F *revêtir* to line] *n* **1** covering of stone, cement, or other material, to hold in place a sloping embankment; **2** veneer of stone or other hard substance over less durable or less ornamental material

re·view' /ri-/ [MF *revue*] *n* **1** going over anything again for study or examination; **2** general consideration of the past; **3** criticism, esp. of a new publication or work of art; **4** magazine or paper specializing in such criticisms or in timely essays; **5** formal inspection of a military force; **6** *theat* revue; **7** reexamination of a judicial decision by a higher court ‖ *vt* **8** to study, consider, or examine again; **9** to look back on; **10** to write a critical review of; **11** to inspect formally; **12** to survey, go over; **13** to reexamine (a decision of a lower court) ‖ re·view'er *n*

re·vile /rivīl'/ [MF *reviler*] *vt* **1** to heap abuse on ‖ *vi* **2** to use abusive language ‖ re·vile'ment *n* ‖ re·vil'er *n* ‖ SYN abuse, malign, asperse, slander, vilify, vituperate, calumniate ‖ ANT extol, honor, magnify, praise

re·vise /rivīz'/ [L *revisere* to revisit] *n* **1** act of revising; **2** revised form; **3** proof containing corrections made in a former proof ‖ *vt* **4** to change and correct; improve ‖ re·vi'sion /-vizh'ən/ *n*

re·vi'sion·ism *n* **1** movement designed to modify Marxism in theory or practice; **2** advocacy of any kind of revision ‖ re·vi'sion·ist *adj* & *n*

re·viv·al /rivīv'əl/ [see *revive*] *n* **1** act of reviving or state of being revived, **2** restoration to life, vigor, or activity; **3** restoration of public attention, interest, or use; **4** renewal of interest in religion; religious awakening; **5** meeting or series of meetings to arouse interest in religion; **6** new production, as of an old play

re·viv'al·ism *n* spirit or methods that characterize religious revivals ‖ re·viv'al·ist *n*

re·vive /rivīv'/ [L *revivere* to live again] *vi* **1** to come back to life, consciousness, vigor, or activity ‖ *vt* **2** to restore to life or animation; give new force or activity to; **3** to produce again, as an old play

re·viv·i·fy /rivīv'ifī'/ [F *révivifier*] *v* (-fied) *vt* **1** to renew life or interest in; **2** to restore life to

re·voke /rivōk'/ [L *revocare* to call again] *vt* **1** to take back, cancel, repeal ‖ *vi* **2** *cards* to fail to follow suit when one should ‖ *n* **3** *cards* act or instance of revoking ‖ rev'o·ca·ble /rev'əkəbəl/ also re·vok'a·ble /rivōk'-/ *adj* || **rev·o·ca·tion** /rev'əkāsh'-ən/ *n* || SYN *v* recall, abrogate, renounce, annul, rescind, abolish (see *cancel*) || ANT *v* proclaim, uphold

re·volt /rivōlt'/ [MF *revolter*] *n* 1 uprising against authority, rebellion || *vi* 2 to rise, rebel; 3 **revolt at** to feel disgust at; 4 **revolt from** to turn away from in abhorrence or disgust || *vt* 5 to fill with disgust or loathing || SYN *n* mutiny, insurrection, sedition, rebellion (see *revolution*)

re·volt'ing *adj* 1 disgusting, loathsome; 2 rebelling; seditious

rev·o·lu·tion /rev'əlōōsh'ən/ [LL *revolutio* (-onis)] *n* 1 course or motion of a heavenly body around another; 2 succession of changes or events happening in a cycle; 3 overthrow of one form of government and the setting up of another; 4 any decided and sudden change; 5 **the Revolution** the Revolutionary War || **rev·o·lu·tion·ar·y** /-ner'-/ *adj* & *n* (-ies) || **rev'o·lu'tion·ist** *n* || SYN sedition, mutiny, anarchy, insurrection, revolt, rebellion, riot, confusion || DISCR The idea underlying *revolution*, in a political sense, is a fundamental change of government brought about by those governed. A *revolution* may be accomplished, therefore, by bloody violence or without a struggle. *Rebellion* connotes actual fighting; it is organized, armed resistance to established government. A *revolution* peaceably accomplished through common consent has nothing in common with *rebellion*; but a *revolution* brought about by battle is a *rebellion* while it is in the fighting state, a *revolution* when the ends are attained. The point of view may determine whether *revolution* or *rebellion* shall be used; the Revolution of 1776 would seem to the British to be a *rebellion*. *Revolt* is an uprising against constituted authority, which, in intention at least, lacks the scope of *rebellion*. An *insurrection*, as the word is applied to uprisings of tyrannically governed or enslaved peoples, is, like a *revolt*, a *rebellion* in its early or initial stage. *Mutiny* is *revolt* against constituted authority, commonly on the part of soldiers or sailors against officers. A *riot* is an outbreak of lawlessness or disorder on the part of a crowd, though the intention of the crowd is not necessarily unlawful. *Sedition* is the stirring up, plotting, or inciting of such rebellious agitation as tends to treason

Rev'o·lu'tion·ar·y War' *n* the revolt of the American Colonies against Great Britain (1775–83)

rev'o·lu'tion·ize' *vt* 1 to cause a political revolution in; 2 to alter completely and radically

re·volve /rivolv'/ [L *revolvere* to roll backward] *vt* 1 to cause to rotate; 2 to cause to move in a circular course, as in an orbit; 3 to turn over in the mind || *vi* 4 to move in an orbit; 5 to rotate; 6 to move in cycles; recur || SYN turn, roll (see *rotate*)

re·volv'er *n* pistol having chambers in a rotating cylinder for holding several cartridges that may be fired in succession

re·volv'ing door' *n* door consisting of four leaves set at right angles to each other and revolving about a central pivot, designed to keep drafts from entering a building

re·volv'ing fund' *n* fund from which new loans are made from moneys provided by repayments of previous loans

re·vue /rivyōō'/ [F = review] *n* 1 musical show in which current foibles are parodied; 2 any show with music, dances, and skits

re·vul·sion /rivulsh'ən/ [< L *revulsus* torn away] *n* 1 violent change, esp. of feeling; 2 strong reaction of repugnance and distaste

re·ward /riwôrd'/ [ONF *rewarder* to look at] *n* 1 something given in appreciation of praiseworthy conduct; 2 money offered for services or for the return of something lost || *vt* 3 to give a reward to, recompense; 4 to give a reward for || SYN *n* pay, requital, prize, return (see *redress*)

re·ward'ing *adj* 1 useful, valuable; 2 gracious, pleasing

re·write' /rē-/ *v* (-wrote; -writ·ten) *vt* 1 to write in a new form; revise; 2 to write up (a news account) in suitable form for publication || **re'write'** *n* 3 the story thus written up

Rey·kja·vik /rāk'yəvēk'/ *n* capital of Iceland (80,000)

r.f. radio frequency

Rf *chem* rutherfordium

R.F.D., RFD Rural Free Delivery

Rh *chem* rhodium

rhap·so·dy /rap'sədē/ [Gk *rhapso(i)-dia* recital of epic poetry] *n* (-dies) 1 part of an epic poem suitable for a single recitation; 2 disconnected, extravagant piece of literature marked by exaggerated feeling; 3 any rapturous utterance; 4 highly emotional instrumental composition suggestive of improvisation || **rhap'so·dize'** *vt* || **rhap·sod'ic** (-i·cal) /-sod'-/ *adj*

rhe·a /rē'ə/ [*Rhea*, Gk goddess] *n* any of a genus (*Rhea*) of flightless three-toed birds of South America, resembling but smaller than the ostrich

Rhen·ish /ren'ish/ [< L *Rhenus* the Rhine] *adj* of or pert. to the river Rhine or the country about it

rhe·ni·um /rēn'ē·əm/ [< L *Rhenus* the Rhine] *n* rare metallic element (Re; at.no. 75; at.wt. 186.2) having a very high melting point

rhe·o·stat /rē'əstat'/ [< Gk *rheos* stream + *-stat*] *n* variable resistance for controlling the current in a circuit

rhe·sus (**mon'key**) /rēs'əs/ [*Rhesus* Thracian ally of Troy] *n* small monkey (*Macaca mulatta*) of India, used in medical experiments

rhet·o·ric /ret'ərik/ [< Gk *rhetorike* (techne) (art) of speaking] *n* 1 art of using language effectively; 2 exaggerated language; bombast || **rhe·tor·i·cal** /ritôr'ikəl, -tōr'-/ *adj* || **rhet'o·ri'cian** /-rish'ən/ *n*

rhe·tor'i·cal ques'tion *n* question asked only for rhetorical effect and not to elicit a response

rheum /rōm/ [Gk *rheuma* flow] *n* watery discharge from a mucous surface, as of the eye or nose || **rheum'y** *adj* (**-i·er; -i·est**)

rheu·mat'ic /-mat'-/ *adj* 1 of or pert. to rheumatism; 2 affected with rheumatism || *n* 3 person with rheumatism

rheu·mat'ic fe'ver *n* serious disease, usu. of children, with fever, swelling of the joints, and inflammation of the heart valves

rheu'ma·tism /-mətiz'əm/ *n* 1 any painful condition of the joints and muscles; 2 rheumatic fever || **rheu'ma·toid'** *adj*

Rh' fac'tor /är'' āch'/ [*rhesus* monkey] *n* agglutinating substance, the absence of which in some blood (Rh-negative) makes the blood incompatible with the much more common blood (Rh-positive)

Rhine /rīn'/ *n* river flowing from Switzerland through W Germany and The Netherlands into the North Sea

Rhine'land /-land', -lənd/ *n* that part of West Germany lying along the Rhine || **Rhine'land·er** *n*

rhine'stone' *n* paste gem, usu. imitating a diamond

Rhine' wine' *n* any of numerous white dry wines produced in the Rhine valley, or one resembling them

rhi·ni·tis /rīnīt'is/ [< Gk *rhis* (*rhinos*) nose + *-itis*] *n* inflammation of the mucous membrane of the nasal passages

rhi·no /rīn'ō/ *n* rhinoceros

rhi·no- [Gk *rhis* (*rhinos*) nose] *comb form* nose

rhi·noc·er·os /rīnos'ərəs/ [Gk *rhinokeros* = nose horn] *n* any of a family (Rhinocerotidae) of massive, thick-skinned, three-toed herbivorous mammals of tropical Asia and Africa, having on the snout one or two hornlike projections

rhi·zo- [< Gk *rhiza*] *comb form* root

rhi·zome /rī'zōm/ [Gk *rhizoma* root] *n* elongated underground stem which produces roots below and leaves above

rhi·zo·pod /rīz'əpod'/ *n* any of a class (Rhizopoda) of protozoans with temporary footlike extensions of the body for locomotion and feeding

rho /rō/ *n* seventeenth letter of the Greek alphabet P, ρ

Rhode' Is'land /rōd'/ *n* one of the New England states, smallest in area in the U.S. (949,723; 1214 sq.m.; cap. Providence) || **Rhode' Is'land·er** *n*

Rho·de·sia /rōdēzh'ə/ *n* see Zimbabwe-Rhodesia

Rhodes' schol'ar·ships' /rōdz'/ [Cecil *Rhodes* (1853–1902) Eng administrator and businessman in South Africa] *npl* scholarships to Oxford University established by the will of Cecil Rhodes and awarded to students in the U.S. and the British Commonwealth

rho·di·um /rōd'ē·əm/ [< Gk *rhodon* rose] *n* rare, white, lustrous metallic element (**Rh**; at.no. 45; at.wt. 102.905) used to electroplate precision instruments

rho·do·den·dron /rōd'əden'drən/ [Gk = rose tree] *n* any of various shrubs (genus *Rhododendron*) with large, handsome clusters of white, pink, or variously colored flowers

rhom·boid /rom'boid/ [< *rhombus* + *-oid*] *n* parallelogram with oblique angles and only two of the opposite sides equal

rhom·bus /rom'bəs/ [L < Gk *rhombos*] *n* (**-bus·es** or **-bi** /-bī/) equilateral parallelogram with oblique angles

Rhone /rōn'/ *n* river flowing from Switzerland through the Lake of Geneva and SE France into the Mediterranean

rhu·barb /rōō'bärb/ [OF *reubarbe*] *n* 1 any of a genus (*Rheum*) of plants with long, fleshy acid leafstalks, used in cookery; 2 extract from the roots of some species, used as a cathartic and tonic; 3 *slang* noisy squabble

rhumb' line /rum(b)'/ [Sp *rumbo*] *n* curved line on the surface of the earth that cuts all meridians at the same angle; it is represented by a Mercator chart by a straight line, and is always longer than a great circle

rhyme /rīm'/ [OF *rime*] *n* 1 agreement in final sounds of two or more words, esp. at the ends of related lines of verse; 2 word agreeing in final sound with another; 3 verse or line in which the final sound of the last word corresponds with that of another verse; 4 verse in which the last words of some of the lines correspond in sound || *vi* 5 to accord in sound; 6 to end in the same sound; 7 to make verses || *vt* 8 to make to correspond in sound; 9 to express in verse

rhyme'ster *n* writer of inferior verses

rhythm /rith′əm/ [Gk *rhythmos* measured motion] *n* **1** regular recurrence, as in poetry or music, of stress, accent, or quantity; **2** movement marked by some regular measured recurrence of beat or sound, as of a dance, machine, or pulse; **3** regularity and harmony of movement, as in the dance; **4** harmonious balance of treatment, as in art; **5** balancing or grouping of tone lengths within a measure ‖ **rhyth′mic (-mi·cal)** *adj*

rhythm′ meth′od *n* method of birth control by abstaining from sexual intercourse during the period of the woman's ovulation

R.I. Rhode Island

ri·al /rī′əl/ [Pers < Ar < Sp *real*] *n* monetary unit of Iran

Ri·al·to /rē·al′tō/ [It = business district of Venice] *n* **the Rialto** the theater distrct of a city, esp. of New York

rib /rib′/ [OE] **1** one of the set of long curved bones attached laterally to the spine and encircling the cavity of the chest; **2** anything like a rib in shape or function, as a ridge in fabrics, a rod in an umbrella frame, or an archlike member supporting a vault; **3** *colloq* act of ribbing ‖ *v* **(ribbed; rib·bing)** *vt* **4** to enclose, strengthen, or mark with or as with ribs; **5** *colloq* to badger, tease ‖ **ribbed′** *adj*

rib·ald /rib′əld/ [OF *ribault*] *adj* indecent; coarse, vulger ‖ **rib′ald·ry** *n*

rib·bon /rib′ən/ [OF *riban*] *n* **1** fine fabric woven in a narrow strip with two selvages, used for adornment; **2** *mil* strip of the ribbon of a medal or decoration worn in lieu of the medal, as on a service uniform; **3** long narrow strip of cloth impregnated with ink, for inking the type on a typewriter or office machine; **4** **ribbons** *pl* shreds

ri·bo·fla·vin /rī′bōflāv′in/ [< *ribose* a kind of sugar + *flavin* a ketone < L *flavus* yellow] *n* yellow pigment —$C_{17}H_{20}N_4O_6$— a component of the vitamin B complex, found esp. in whey, eggs, and green leaves

rice /rīs′/ [OF *ris* < It *riso*] *n* **1** cereal grain produced in warm climates and extensively used for food; **2** the grass (*Oryza sativa*) bearing this grain ‖ *vt* **3** to reduce to the size of rice

rich /rich′/ [OE *rīce* or OF *riche*] *adj* **1** having many possessions or resources; wealthy; **2** expensive, valuable; **3** great in amount, abundant, as *rich crops*; **4** fertile, productive; **5** abounding in pleasing, desirable, or valuable qualities, as perfumes or food; **6** deep, vivid (colors); **7** mellow and full in sound; **8** *colloq* a very amusing; **b** ridiculous; **9** **rich in** or

with abounding in, abundantly supplied with ‖ *n* **10** **the rich** *pl* wealthy people collectively ‖ **rich′ly** *adv*

Rich·ard I /rich′ərd/ *n* (Richard the Lion-Hearted) (1157–99) crusader and king of England 1189–99

Rich·e·lieu, Cardinal /rish′(ə)lōō′/ *n* (1585–1642) French statesman and cardinal

rich′es [OF *richesse*] *npl* many possessions, wealth

Rich′mond /rich′mənd/ *n* capital of Virginia (255,000); capital of the Confederacy 1861–65

Rich′ter scale′ /rik′tər/ [Charles F. *Richter* (1900–) U.S. seismologist] *n* logarithmic scale of the energy dissipated in seismic disturbances, ranging from 1.5 (smallest earthquake that can be felt) to 8.5 (extremely severe and devastating earthquake)

rick /rik′/ [OE *hrēac*] *n* **1** stack, as of hay or grain ‖ *vt* **2** to stack in a rick

rick·ets /rik′its/ [?] *n* disease of children caused by improper utilization of calcium salts and/or by vitamin D deficiency, marked by softness and curving of the bones

rick′et·y *adj* **1** affected with rickets; feeble; shaky; falling apart

rick·ey /rik′ē/ [< a Col. *Rickey*] *n* cold drink made with lime juice, carbonated water, and liquor, esp. gin

ric·o·chet /rik′əshā′/ [F] *n* **1** rebound or deflection of an object, as a stone or bullet, hitting a glancing blow on a flat surface ‖ *v* **(-cheted /-shād′/; -chet·ing /-shā′iŋ/)** *vi* **2** to move in this manner

ri·cot·ta /rikot′ə/ [It] *n* a soft Italian cottage cheese

rid /rid′/ [ON *rythja* to clear (land)] *v* **(rid or rid·ded; rid·ding)** *vt* **1** to free; clear; deliver; **2** **get rid of** to dispose of, become free from

rid·dance /rid′əns/ *n* **1** act of ridding or state of being rid; **2** **good riddance** relief at getting rid of something

rid·den /rid′ən/ *pp* of **ride**

rid·dle[1] /rid′əl/ [OE *rēdelse* counsel] *n* **1** question or statement requiring ingenuity to answer or fathom; **2** puzzling or perplexing question, person, or thing; enigma ‖ *vt* **3** to propound riddles ‖ SYN *n* conundrum, paradox, enigma, puzzle

rid·dle[2] [OE *hriddel* sieve] *vt* **1** to pierce with holes in many places; **2** to sift through a riddle; **3** to disprove, refute successfully; **4** to permeate, overrun, corrupt, as *an army riddled with treason* ‖ *n* **5** coarse sieve

ride /rīd′/ [OE *rīdan*] *v* **(rode; rid·den)** *vi* **1** to be carried on the back of a horse or other animal; **2** to sit on and manage a horse; **3** to be borne along in or on a vehicle or any conveyance; **4** to float or move on the water; **5** to rest or turn on something; **6** to serve for riding in a specified way, *this car rides well;* **7** let **ride** to allow to continue without interference; **8** ride up to rise out of place, as a necktie over a collar ‖ *vt* **9** to sit upon and manage, as a horse; **10** to be carried on, through, or over; **11** to traverse or cover, as a specified distance; **12** to do or perform, as a race; **13** to harass by teasing or criticism; **14** to domineer, as *he was ridden by fear;* **15** ride down to overtake (someone or something pursued); **16** ride herd on to control strictly; **17** ride out to endure successfully ‖ *n* **18** journey on horseback or on any kind of conveyance; **19** vehicle or device at an amusement park for the entertainment of the public, as a roller coaster; **20** take someone for a ride *slang* **a** to abduct and murder; **b** to trick, swindle

rid′er *n* **1** one who rides; **2** usu. unrelated section or clause added to a legislative bill

ridge /rij′/ [OE *hrycg* spine, ridge] *n* **1** range of hills or mountains; **2** extended projection where two slopes meet; **3** any raised or projecting strip or line, as on the earth, in cloth, or in the roof of the mouth ‖ *vt* **4** to mark or provide with ridges ‖ *vi* **5** to form ridges

ridge′pole′ *n* horizontal timber at the peak of a roof, to which the upper ends of the rafters are secured

rid·i·cule /rid′ikyōōl′/ [L *ridiculus* laughable] *n* **1** speech or action intended to cause a person or thing to be laughed at contemptuously ‖ *vt* **2** to make fun of, treat with derision ‖ SYN *v* (see *taunt*); *n* sarcasm, satire, derision, irony, mockery, raillery ‖ DISCR *Ridicule*, the holding up as a laughingstock, may be playful, merely inconsiderate, or hostile. Hence *ridicule* may or may not be mean and malicious, and the merriment which it arouses may be jestingly or deliberately contemptuous of its object. *Derision* is the hostile sort of *ridicule*. *Mockery*, as here compared, is *derision* mingled with the considered design to insult and contemn. Mobs howl with *derision* when their victim suffers. *Irony* is the expression of one's meaning in language which conveys a different, usually the opposite, signification; it is *ridicule* subtly and covertly conveyed. *Irony* may be bitingly severe; it may be mildly humorous. *Sarcasm* is sharp; it is intended to hurt. Usually *sarcasm* wounds through taunts and reproaches disguised rather than open, or through *irony* of the cutting sort. *Satire* is commonly formal composition in which follies or vices are held up to *ridicule* with the idea of preventing their recurrence

ri·dic·u·lous /ridik′yələs/ *adj* deserving or exciting ridicule ‖ SYN comical, funny, droll, grotesque (see *ludicrous*)

rid·ing /rīd′iŋ/ [ME *triding* < Scand] *n* **1** one of the three administrative divisions into which the county of York in N England is divided; **2** any similar division

riel /rēl′/ [?] *n* monetary unit of Cambodia

Rie·mann′i·an ge·om′e·try /rēmän′-ē̄-ən/ [G. F. B. *Riemann* G mathematician (1826–1866)] *n* non-Euclidean geometry of a space in which parallel lines intersect at some point

Ries′ling /rēs′liŋ, rēz′-/ [G] *n* **1** variety of grape grown in Europe and California, from which a fragrant white dry wine is made; **2** the wine

rife /rīf′/ [OE] *adj* **1** prevalent; **2** rife with abounding in

rif·fle /rif′əl/ [var of *ripple*] *n* **1** ripple on the surface of water; **2** act or instance of riffling cards ‖ *vt* **3** to look at hastily by shuffling, as a stack of papers; **4** to shuffle (cards) by the half of a deck in each hand and causing them to fall alternately together

riff·raff /rif′raf′/ [OF *rif et raf* things of small value] *n* rabble; the scum of society

ri·fle[1] /rif′əl/ [OF *rifler* to plunder] *vt* to ransack and rob; plunder, strip bare

ri·fle[2] [< LG *rifeln* to groove] *n* firearm with the barrel spirally grooved inside to give the projectile a spin for greater distance and accuracy

ri′fle·man /-mən/ *n* (-men /-mən/) man armed with a rifle

ri′fling *n* set of spiral grooves on the inner surface of the barrel of a gun

rift /rift′/ [ME < Scand] *n* **1** split, cleft; **2** opening; **3** break in friendly relations

rig /rig′/ [ME *riggen* < Scand] *v* (rigged; rig·ging) *vt* **1** to furnish (a ship) with the equipment necessary for service; **2** to fit out, equip; **3** to manipulate dishonestly; **4** rig out to furnish with equipment or clothing; **5** rig up to set up for operation ‖ *n* **6** arrangement of the sails, masts, etc., of a ship; **7** vehicle drawn by a horse or horses; **8** *colloq* odd style of dress; **9** outfit, gear; **10** oil-well drilling equipment

Ri·ga /rēg′ə/ *n* capital of Latvia (675,000)

Ri·gel /rīj′əl, rīg′-/ [Ar *rijl* foot, because in the foot of Orion] *n* brilliant bluish-white star in the constellation Orion

rig′ging *n* **1** ropes, cables, etc., by which the masts of a ship are supported and the sails set; **2** ropes used to support and fly the curtains and drops on a theater stage; **3** gear, tackle

rig′ging loft′ *n* space over a theater stage for flying curtains and drops

right /rīt′/ [OE *riht*] *adj* **1** straight; **2** *geom* having the axis perpendicular to the base; **3** in accordance with truth, justice, or propriety; **4** correct; **5** sound (mind); **6** fit, suitable; **7** of or pert. to the side of a person or thing that is turned toward the south when facing the sunrise; **8** (river bank) on the right of a person facing downstream; **9** in good condition; well; **10** exposed to the eye in use, as *the right side of a carpet;* **11** most convenient; satisfactory; **12** of or pert. to the political Right || *adv* **13** in a straight line; directly; **14** justly; righteously; **15** suitably; **16** correctly; **17** precisely, exactly; **18** to, toward, or on the right hand; **19** completely; **20** promptly; **21** favorably; **22 right away** or **off** immediately || *n* **23** that which is correct, just, or legal; **24** that to which one has a moral or legal claim; **25** interest or ownership; **26** *fin* privilege of buying a specified amount of a security; **27** right-hand side; **28** right turn; **29** right hand; **30** the **Right** the political party or movement more conservative and reactionary than the opposition; **31 by rights** in all fairness; **32 to rights** into proper order || *vt* **33** to restore to proper condition; **34** to correct; **35** to set upright; **36** to do justice to || *vi* **37** to resume an upright position || **right′ness** *n* || SYN *n* justice, advantage, immunity, license, privilege; *adj* lawful, true, fair, good, honest, virtuous

right′ a·bout′ face′ *n* **1** *mil* command to turn about to the right and face in the opposite direction; **2** complete reversal of opinion or action

right′ an′gle *n* angle of 90 degrees || **right′-an′gled** *adj*

Right′ Bank′ *n* section of Paris on the north bank of the Seine

right·eous /rīch′əs/ [OE *rihtwīs*] *adj* **1** blameless; virtuous; upright; **2** justifiable; **3** just, worthy || **right′eousness** *n* || SYN good, godly, moral, upright, virtuous, just

right′ face′ *n* *mil* command to turn 90 degrees to the right

right′ field′ *n* *baseball* right side of the outfield

right′ful *adj* **1** having a lawful claim; legitimate; **2** just; fair || **right′ful·ly** *adv*

right′-hand′ *adj* **1** on or to the right; **2** pert. to the right hand; **3** chiefly relied on, as *a right-hand man*

right′-hand′ed *adj* **1** done or used with the right hand; **2** able to use the right hand more easily than the left; **3** turning clockwise || *adv* **4** toward or with the right hand; **5** in a right-handed manner

right′ist *n* member, advocate, or partisan of the Right || *also adj*

right′ly *adv* **1** uprightly; **2** properly; suitably; **3** correctly

right′-of-way′ *n* **1** right of a vehicle or plane to proceed ahead of another; **2** right of passage; **3** strip of land on which railroad tracks are laid

right′-to-work′ law′ *n* state law in the U.S. which gives workers freedom to work without the obligation of union membership

right′ wing′ *n* the most conservative segment of a legislature, group, organization, or party || **right′-wing′** *adj* || **right′-wing′er** *n*

right′y *colloq n* (**-ies**) **1** right-handed person || *adj & adv* **2** right-handed

rig·id /rij′id/ [L *rigidus*] *adj* **1** unyielding; stiff, inflexible; **2** strict; severe || **ri·gid′i·ty** /rijid′-/ *n* || SYN firm, hard, stern, harsh (see *austere*)

rig·ma·role /rig′mərōl′/ [< *ragman roll*] *n* **1** foolish talk; nonsense; **2** needlessly elaborate procedure

rig′or /rig′ər/ [L = stiffness] *n* **1** strictness; harshness; **2** severity; **3** hardship || SYN inclemency, asperity, harshness, exactness, austerity || ANT softness, gentleness, tenderness

ri·gor mor·tis /rig′ər môrt′is, rig′ôr/ [L = stiffness of death] *n* stiffening of the body after death

rig′or·ous *adj* **1** marked by sternness or severity, as discipline; **2** exact, strict; **3** harsh; bitter, as climate || SYN stiff, unyielding, relentless (see *austere*)

Rig-Ve·da /rig′vād′ə, -vēd′-/ [Skt] *n* collection of ancient Hindu hymns; first and most important of the sacred books of the Hindus

rile /rīl/ [var of *roil*] *vt colloq* to vex; irritate

Ri·ley, James Whit·comb /jāmz′ (h)wit′-kəm rīl′ē/ *n* (1849–1916) U.S. poet

rill /ril/ [LG *rille*] *n* **1** small stream or rivulet; **2** one of the long narrow depressions on the surface of the moon

rim /rim′/ [OE *rima*] *n* **1** border, edge, or margin, esp when round or raised; **2** outer hoop of a wheel || *v* (**rimmed; rim·ming**) *vt* **3** to furnish with a rim; **4** to serve as a rim around; **5** to roll around the rim of without going in || SYN *n* edge, margin, bank, verge (see *border*)

rime¹ /rīm′/ [OE *hrīm*] *n* **1** hoarfrost, white frost || *vt* **2** to coat with rime

rime² *n, vi, & vt* var of **rhyme**

rim′fire′ /rim′-/ *adj* **1** (cartridge) having the primer in the rim at its base; **2** (rifle) that uses such cartridges

rind /rīnd′/ [OE] *n* firm outer skin or coat, as of fruit

ring¹ /riŋ'/ [OE *hring*] *n* **1** ornamental circular band, usu. of a precious metal and often adorned with gems, worn on the finger; **2** any small circular band; **3** any circular line or mark; **4** anything with a circular shape; **5** any circular arrangement, as of smoke, bushes, persons, etc.; **6** arena or enclosed space for contests or displays, as at a circus or bullfight; **7** square canvas-covered platform bordered by ropes, for boxing and wrestling contests; **8** combination of persons usu. for illegal or unethical purpose; **9 the ring** prize fighting; **10 run rings around** to be far superior to; **11 toss one's hat in the ring** to enter a political contest ‖ *vt* **12** to encircle; hem in; **13** to strip the bark off (a tree) in the form of a ring; **14** to encircle (the peg) with a ring, quoit, or horseshoe

ring² [OE *hringan*] *v* (**rang; rung**) *vi* **1** to give out a resonant sound, as a bell; **2** to cause a bell to sound, as a summons; **3** to sound loudly and clearly; **4** to have the sensation of a buzzing sound, as the ears; **5** to resound, echo, as a place; **6 ring off** to terminate a telephone conversation; **7 ring out** to resound; **8 ring true** (or **false**) to appear to be genuine (or spurious) ‖ *vt* **9** to cause (a bell) to ring; **10** to sound by striking; **11** to announce or proclaim by ringing; **12 ring down the curtain on** to bring to an end; **13 ring up, a** to call by telephone; **b** to register on a cash register; **14 ring up the curtain on** to initiate, inaugurate ‖ *n* **15** act or instance of ringing; **16** sound of ringing; **17** telephone call; **18** any echoing or repeated sound; **19** set or peal of bells; **20** characteristic sound or quality of utterance, as *a ring of sincerity*

ring·er¹ /riŋ'ər/ [< *ring¹*] *n* quoit or horseshoe that rings the peg

ring·er² [< *ring²*] *n slang* **1** race horse or player fraudulently substituted for another; **2** person or thing closely resembling another; **3 be a dead ringer for** to look exactly like

ring' fin'ger *n* finger on which the engagement ring or wedding band is worn, traditionally the third finger on the left hand

ring'lead'er *n* one who leads others, esp. in illegal activities or in opposition to authority

ring'let /-lit/ *n* curl of hair

ring'mas'ter *n* master of ceremonies at a circus performance

ring' road' *n Brit* highway that runs around an urban area

ring'side' *n* **1** area immediately adjacent to the ring at a prize fight; **2** place that provides a close view ‖ also *adj*

ring'worm' *n* contagious skin disease marked by scaly circular patches, caused by a parasitic fungus

rink /riŋk'/ [MF *renc* row, rank] *n* **1** smooth expanse of ice for ice skating; **2** smooth floor for roller skating; **3** building housing a rink

rinse /rins'/ [MF *rincer*] *vt* **1** to wash lightly, esp. to wash with clean water to remove soap; **2 rinse off** or away to remove, as soap or dirt, with clear water ‖ *n* **3** act or instance of rinsing

Ri·o de Ja·nei·ro /rē'ō dē'zhəner'ō/ *n* seaport in SE Brazil, former capital (3,500,000)

Ri·o Grande /rē'ō grand'/ *n* river rising in Colorado, flowing through New Mexico, and forming the boundary between Texas and Mexico to the Gulf of Mexico

ri·ot /rī'ət/ [OF *riote* brawl] *n* **1** violent public disorder engaged in by a number of persons; **2** boisterous festivity; revelry; **3** unrestrained behavior, display, or growth; **4** *law* disturbance of the public peace by a number of persons who are unlawfully assembled; **5** *colloq* someone or something extremely funny; **6 run riot** to act or grow without restraint ‖ *vi* **7** to take part in a riot; **8** to act without restraint ‖ **ri'ot·er** *n* SYN disorder, uproar, tumult (see *revolution*)

Ri'ot Act' *n* **1** in Great Britain, act providing that if twelve or more persons unlawfully or riotously assemble and refuse to disperse within an hour after the reading of a specified portion of the act by a competent authority, they shall be considered as felons; **2 read the riot act** to state with authority a line of conduct that must be followed

ri·ot·ous *adj* **1** engaging in a riot; seditious; noisy; **2** indulging in revelry; wanton ‖ **ri'o·tous·ly** *adv* ‖ SYN noisy, uproarious, clamorous ‖ ANT quiet, orderly, peaceful

rip /rip'/ [ME prob < Flem *rippen*] *v* (**ripped; rip·ping**) *vt* **1** to tear apart violently; **2** to open up the seam of; **3** to tear out or remove by cutting; **4** to saw (wood) with the grain; **5 rip up** or **open** to tear or cut up or open; **6 rip out, a** to tear or cut out; **b** to utter violently ‖ *vi* **7** to become ripped; **8** *colloq* to rush along violently; **9 rip into** *colloq* to assail violently ‖ *n* **10** rent or tear

R.I.P. [L *requiesca(n)t in pace*] may he (or she or they) rest in peace

ri·par·i·an /rīper'ē·ən, rī-/ [L *riparius* < *ripa* bank] *adj* of, on, or pert. to the banks of a river or other body of water

rip' cord' *n* **1** cord which, when pulled, opens a parachute; **2** cord pulled to release gas from a balloon or dirigible to cause descent

ripe /rīp'/ [OE] *adj* **1** grown to maturity; ready for harvest; **2** ruddy and plump, as *ripe lips;* **3** brought to the most fit state for use; mellow; **4** advanced to a high degree of development; matured; **5** advanced (age); **6** ready to act, as *ripe for mischief;* **7** ready for action, as plans; **8** sufficiently advanced, as time ‖ SYN consummate, complete, perfected, seasoned (see *mellow*) ‖ ANT green, immature, sour

rip·en /rīp′ən/ *vt* **1** to make ripe; mature ‖ *vi* **2** to become ripe; mature

rip′-off *n colloq* **1** theft; **2** questionable appropriation, as of fashions and styles

ri·poste /rĭpōst′/ [F < It *risposta* response] *n* **1** *fencing* return thrust given after parrying a lunge; **2** quick, clever reply ‖ *vi* **3** to make a riposte

rip′ping *adj Brit slang* splendid

rip·ple /rĭp′əl/ [?] *n* **1** any slight curling wave, as on the surface of water or in hair ‖ *vt* **2** to make ripples in ‖ *vi* **3** to become ruffled or slightly waved on the surface; **4** to sound like water running over a rough surface

rip′-roar′ing *adj colloq* lively, boisterous; riotously exciting

rip′saw′ *n* coarse-toothed saw for cutting wood with the grain

rip′snort′er *n colloq* someone or something very strong, intense, or remarkable

rip′tide′ *n* **1** running tide that breaks against an opposing tide and results in violent agitation of the water; **2** *fig* violent encounter of conflicting forces

rise /rīz′/ [OE *rīsan*] *v* (**rose; ris·en** /rĭz′ən/) *vi* **1** to go from a lower position to a higher; ascend; **2** to extend upward; **3** to get up from bed in the morning; **4** to be constructed; **5** to originate, spring; **6** to go higher, as the level of water; **7** to slope upward; **8** to get up from kneeling, sitting, or lying down; stand up; **9** to ascend above the horizon; **10** to come into view or existence; **11** to swell, as dough; **12** to increase in value, force, intensity, or the like; **13** to thrive, prosper; **14** to be promoted in rank; **15** to revolt; **16** to come back to life ‖ *n* **17** act or instance of rising; **18** the distance anything ascends; **19** small hill; **20** appearance above the horizon; **21** source, origin; **22** increase in value, force, amount, or the like; **23** advance in power, distinction, or rank; **24** revolt; **25 get a rise out of** *colloq* to provoke an angry reaction from; **26 give rise to** to cause, bring about ‖ SYN *v* arise, ascend, spring, flow

ris′er *n* upright part of a step

ris·i·bil·i·ty /rĭz′ibil′ĭtē/ *n* (**-ties**) **1** inclination to laughter; **2 risibilities** *pl* sensitiveness to the ridiculous

ris′i·ble [LL *risibilis*] *adj* **1** having the faculty or power of laughing; **2** laughable, ridiculous; **3** pert. to, or used in, laughing ‖ SYN ridiculous, ludicrous, laughable ‖ ANT grave, serious

ris·ing /rīz′ĭŋ/ *n* **1** act of one who or that which rises; **2** projection, eminence; **3** revolt

risk /rĭsk′/ [F *risque* < It *risco*] *n* **1** possibility of loss or injury; danger; **2** *insurance* probability or amount of loss; **3 run the risk of** to hazard, take the chance of ‖ *vt* **4** to expose to danger; **5** to take a chance on, venture upon ‖ **risk′y** *adj* (**-i·er; -i·est**) ‖ SYN *n* jeopardy, hazard, exposure (see *danger*)

ris·qué /rĭskā′/ [F = risked] *adj* suggestive of impropriety or indecency, as a song or joke

rite /rīt′/ [L *ritus*] *n* prescribed form of religious or other solemn ceremony ‖ SYN observance, sacrament (see *ceremony*)

rit·u·al /rich′ōō·əl/ [L *ritualis*] *n* **1** set form for the performance of a religious or other rite; **2** book of such forms; **3** body of ceremonies used in a church or order ‖ **rit′u·al·ly** *adv*

rit′u·al·ism *n* adherence to or insistence on ritual ‖ **rit′u·al·ist** *n* ‖ **rit′u·al·is′tic** *adj*

ritz·y /rĭt′zē/ [César *Ritz* Swiss founder of elegant hotels + -*y*] *adj* (**-i·er; -i·est**) *slang* swanky; plush; sumptuous

ri·val /rīv′əl/ [L *rivalis* one who has the same mistress] *n* **1** one who strives to equal or surpass another; competitor; **2** one who or that which equals or excels another ‖ *v* (**-valed** or **-valled; -val·ing** or **-val·ling**) *vt* **3** to try to equal or surpass; **4** to be or become the equal of ‖ SYN *n* competitor, antagonist (see *enemy*)

ri′val·ry *n* (**-ries**) act of trying to equal or excel ‖ SYN contention, opposition, contest, competition, antagonism, jealousy (see *emulation*)

riv·en /rĭv′ən/ [ME < Scand] *adj* rent, split apart

riv·er /rĭv′ər/ [OE *rivere* < LL *riparia* shore, river] *n* **1** large natural stream of water flowing in a definite channel into another river, a lake, or the sea; **2** any stream similar to a river, as of lava; **3** copious flow of something

riv′er ba′sin *n* area drained by a river and its tributaries

riv·et /rĭv′ĭt/ [< MF *river* to fasten] *n* **1** metal bolt with a head on one end, used to hold together two or more pieces by passing it through holes and hammering the plain end ‖ *v* (**-et·ed** or **-et·ted; -et·ing** or **-et·ting**) *vt* **2** to fasten with a rivet or rivets; **3** to clinch or fix firmly; **4** to fix (the eyes, mind, etc.) attentively ‖ **riv′et·er** *n*

Riv·i·er·a /riv'ē·er'ə/ *n* coastal resort area on the Mediterranean, extending on both sides of the French-Italian border from Toulon to La Spezia

riv·u·let /riv'yəlit/ [It *rivoletto*] *n* small brook

Ri·yadh /rē·yäd'/ *n* city in central Saudi Arabia, one of the two capitals (275,000)

ri·yal /rēyäl'/ [Ar < Sp *real*] *n* monetary unit of Saudi Arabia

rm. room

Rn *chem* radon

R.N. 1 registered nurse; 2 Royal Navy

RNA [ribonucleic acid] *n* a nucleic acid found chiefly in the cytoplasm of cells

roach /rōch'/ *n* cockroach

road /rōd'/ [OE *rād*] *n* 1 public highway, usu. paved, for traveling by vehicles; 2 any way or course; 3 railroad; 4 **roads** *pl* roadstead; 5 **hit the road** *slang* to start traveling; 6 **on the road, a** traveling; **b** on tour, as a theatrical company ‖ SYN highway, thoroughfare, passage, path (see *way*)

road'a·bil'i·ty /-bil'-/ *n* ability of an automobile to ride smoothly over all kinds of roads

road'bed' *n* foundation laid to receive the ties and rails of a railroad or the surfacing of a highway

road'block *n* 1 obstruction set up across a road to halt traffic; 2 anything that obstructs progress

road' com'pa·ny *n* theatrical company on tour

road' hog' *n* driver who impedes traffic by driving on parts of two lanes

road'house' *n* (-hous·es /-ziz-/) tavern or nightclub located on a highway in a suburban or rural area

road'run'ner *n* large terrestrial bird of the cuckoo family (*Geococcyx californianus*), found in the SW U.S. and noted for its running speed

road' show' *n* show given by a road company

road'side' *n* area adjoining a road ‖ also *adj*

road'stead' *n* partly sheltered anchorage for ships near the shore

road·ster /rōd'stər/ *n* open automobile with a seat for two and a rumble seat in the rear

road'way' *n* road, esp. the part used by vehicles

road'work' *n* exercise consisting of running in the open, indulged in chiefly by boxers in training

roam /rōm'/ [ME *romen*] *vi* 1 to wander about without any definite goal ‖ *vt* 2 to wander over ‖ SYN range, prowl, stroll, rove, saunter, loiter

roan /rōn'/ [MF < OSp *roano*] *adj* 1 (horse) having a coat whose main color of bay, sorrel, or chestnut is sprinkled with gray or white ‖ *n* 2 roan color; 3 roan horse

roar /rôr', rōr'/ [OE *rārian*] *vi* 1 to give forth a loud, deep, rumbling sound, as thunder, the wind, or traffic; 2 to shout or bellow, as in pain or wrath; 3 to laugh loudly ‖ *vt* 4 to utter by roaring ‖ *n* 5 deep full cry, as of a lion; 6 loud cry, as of distress or rage; 7 any loud rumbling sound; 8 loud laugher ‖ SYN *v* clamor, bawl, boom, howl, resound, shout

roast /rōst'/ [OF *rostir*] *vt* 1 to cook (meat) by exposure to fire; 2 to bake or cook in an oven; 3 to heat to excess; 4 to dry by the action of heat; parch, as *to roast peanuts*; 5 *colloq* to criticize or ridicule unsparingly ‖ *vi* 6 to be roasted; 7 to roast meat or other food ‖ *n* 8 act of roasting; 9 piece of meat that is roasted or intended for roasting; 10 *colloq* unsparing criticism or ridicule

rob /rob'/ [OF *robber*] *v* (**robbed; rob·bing**) *vt* 1 to deprive of something by force or intimidation; 2 to steal from; 3 to pillage, as a house; 4 to deprive unjustly; defraud ‖ *vi* 5 to commit theft ‖ **rob'ber** *n* ‖ **rob'ber·y** *n* (-ies)

robe /rōb'/ [OF] *n* 1 long loose outer garment, often indicating rank or office; 2 any long loose garment, as for dressing or lounging; 3 covering, as for the lap, made of cloth or fur ‖ *vi* 4 to put on a robe ‖ *vt* 5 to dress, esp. in a robe

Robes·pierre /rōbz'pir, -pē·er'/ *n* (1758–94) French lawyer, a leader of the French Revolution

rob·in /rob'in/ [OF, dim. of *Robert*] *n* 1 small European bird (*Erithacus rubecula*) having a red breast; 2 large American thrush (*Turdus migratorius*) with a dull red breast

Rob'in Hood' *n* legendary English outlaw of the 12th century, who robbed the rich and gave to the poor

Rob·in·son Cru·soe /rob'insən krōō'sō/ *n* title hero of the novel (1719) by Daniel Defoe, who was shipwrecked and lived for years on a small deserted island

ro·bot /rōb'ot, rob'-/ [coined by Karel Čapek in his play R.U.R. (1920) < Slavic root for 'work'] *n* 1 machine built in the form of a man that does work on command; 2 person who works like a machine, mechanically and on orders; 3 any device that operates automatically, performing humanlike functions

ro'bot bomb' *n* bomb delivered by a rocket-propelled, pilotless plane

Rob' Roy' /roi'/ *n* cocktail made with Scotch, sweet vermouth, and bitters

ro·bust /rōbust'/ [L *robustus* oaken, strong] *adj* 1 hardy, strong, vigorous; 2 rich, full-bodied, as flavor

Ro·cham·beau, Jean Bap·tiste /zhän' batēst' rō'shambō'/ *n* (1725–1807) French general, commander of the

French forces aiding the Americans in the Revolutionary War

Roch·es·ter /roch′estər, -istər/ *n* city in W New York (320,000)

rock[1] /rok′/ [ME *rokke*] *n* 1 large mass of stone; 2 cliff; crag; 3 firm support; defense; 4 *geol* a any mineral matter; b bed or mass of one mineral; 5 stone; 6 *slang* diamond or gem; 7 **on the rocks** *colloq* a (beverage) served with ice cubes; b ruined; bankrupt

rock[2] [OE *roccian*] *vt* 1 to move to and fro or from side to side; 2 to shake or sway violently; 3 to stun, affect deeply ‖ *vi* 4 to move to and fro or from side to side; 5 to be deeply moved, as with emotion; 6 to rock-'n'-roll ‖ SYN swing, sway, oscillate, lull (see *shake*)

rock′ and rye′ *n* drink made with rye whiskey, rock candy, and fruit

rock′ bot′tom *n* the lowest level ‖ **rock′-bot′tom** *adj*

rock′-bound′ *adj* full of or hemmed in by rocks

rock′ can′dy *n* boiled sugar crystallized in large chunks

rock′ crys′tal *n* transparent quartz, esp. when colorless

rock′er *n* 1 one of the curved pieces on which a cradle or rocking chair rocks; 2 rocking chair; 3 any of several devices that operate by rocking back and forth; 4 **off one's rocker** *slang* crazy

rock·et /rok′it/ [F *roquet* < It *rocchetta*] *n* 1 device propelled by the liberation of gases resulting from the ignition of combustible material, used in fireworks, signaling, hurling explosives, and launching space capsules ‖ *vi* 2 to shoot upward; move like a rocket

rock′et en′gine *n* reaction engine that carries its own oxidizer with it

rock′et·ry *n* science of rocket design and flight ‖ **rock′et·eer′** *n*

Rock·ies /rok′ēz/ *npl* the Rockies the Rocky Mountains

rock′ing chair′ *n* chair mounted on rockers or springs, which permit the occupant to rock back and forth

rock′ing horse′ *n* toy horse mounted on rockers

rock′-'n'-roll′ *n* 1 jazz characterized by a heavy beat and much repetition; 2 dance to this music ‖ *vi* 3 to dance to or play rock-'n'-roll

rock′-ribbed′ *adj* 1 having ridges of rock; 2 firm, unyielding

rock′ salt′ *n* common salt occurring in solid masses

rock′ wool′ *n* woollike material made from molten rock, used for insulation

rock′y[1] [< *rock*[1]] *adj* (-i·er; -i·est) 1 full of, like, or consisting of rock; 2 inflexible; unfeeling

rock′y[2] [< *rock*[2]] *adj* (-i·er; -i·est) 1 shaky, unsteady; 2 uncertain

Rock′y Moun′tains *npl* principal mountain chain of North America, extending from Alaska to New Mexico

ro·co·co /rəkōk′ō/ [F < *rocaille* pebblework] *n* 1 overelaborate style of decoration representing shells, leaves, scrolls, etc., massed together, popular in the 17th and 18th centuries; 2 anything ornate or florid in art or literature ‖ also *adj*

rod /rod′/ [OE *rodd*] *n* 1 straight slender wand or stick of wood or other material; 2 fishing pole; 3 switch or whip; 4 correction or discipline; 5 scepter; 6 measure of length equal to 5½ yards; 7 slender bar for holding curtains, towels, etc.; 8 *slang* pistol; 9 rodlike cell in the retina

rode /rōd′/ *pt* of **ride**

ro·dent /rōd′ənt/ [L *rodens* (-*entis*) gnawing] *n* mammal of the order Rodentia, characterized by teeth adapted for gnawing, as squirrels, rabbits, and mice

ro·de·o /rōd′ē·ō′, rōdā′ō/ [Sp = a going round] *n* public contest in cowboy skills, as cattle roping and broncho busting

Ro·din, Au·guste /ōgust′ rōdan′/ *n* (1840–1917) French sculptor

rod′man /-mən/ *n* (-men /-mən/) man who carries and holds the leveling rod in surveying

rod·o·mon·tade /rod′əmontād′, rōd′-, -täd/ [MF < It *Rodomonte*, the boastful Saracen leader in Ariosto's *Orlando Furioso*] *n* vainglorious boasting; bluster, bragging

roe[1] /rō′/ [ME *rowe*] *n* fish eggs, esp. when massed in the ovarian membrane

roe′buck′ *n* male of the roe deer

roe′ deer′ [OE *rāhdēor*] *n* small agile Old World deer (*Capreolus capreolus*)

roent·gen /rent′gən/ [W.K. Roentgen (1845–1923) G physicist and Nobel prize winner, discoverer of X rays] *n* unit of X radiation and gamma radiation in the air

roent′gen rays′ or **Roent′gen rays′** *npl* X rays

rog·er /roj′ər/ [communications code word for R] *interj* 1 message received and understood; 2 *colloq* O.K.

rogue /rōg′/ [?] *n* 1 dishonest person; scoundrel; 2 mischievous, playful person; 3 vicious animal living separately from the herd ‖ **ro′guish** *adj* ‖ **ro′guer·y** /-gərē/ *n* (-ies)

rogues′ gal′ler·y *n* collection of photographs of criminals filed for police reference

roil /roil′/ [?] *vt* 1 to make muddy by stirring; 2 to vex, disturb

roist·er /roist′ər/ [OF *rustre* ruffian] *vi* to swagger; act in a noisy or blustering way ‖ **roist′er·er** *n*

Ro·land /rōl′ənd/ *n* Charlemagne's nephew, hero of the Old French epic *Chanson de Roland* and other legends, slain in 778 while fighting against the Saracens

role also **rôle** /rōl'/ [F = roll (of paper)] *n* 1 part or character taken by an actor in a play; 2 function assumed by anyone

roll /rōl'/ [OF *roller* < LL *rotulare*] *vt* 1 to move by turning over and over; 2 to move along on casters or wheels; 3 to cause to turn over and over; 4 to wrap upon itself or some other object; make into the form of a ball or cylinder; 5 to move with an up-and-down or side-to-side motion; 6 to utter or express with a deep vibrating sound; 7 to spread flat with a roller; 8 to beat (a drum) in a quick manner; 9 to pronounce with a trill; 10 to throw (dice); 11 to rob (a drunk) by going through his pockets; 12 **roll back, a** to reduce (prices) to a former level; **b** to drive back (an advancing enemy); 13 **roll out, a** to spread out flat; **b** to bring out by rolling; 14 **roll up, a** to form into a coil or cylinder; **b** to accumulate ‖ *vi* 15 to move by turning over and over; 16 to move on wheels; 17 to turn from side to side; 18 to rock; 19 to wallow, as *to roll in wealth*; 20 to sweep along, go smoothly; 21 to give forth a deep rumbling sound, as thunder or drums; 22 to take, through winding, the form of a ball or cylinder; 23 to undulate, as land; 24 to flatten or spread out under a roller; 25 to revolve or make a complete circuit; 26 to reel ‖ *n* 27 act of rolling or state of being rolled; 28 that which rolls; roller; 29 reeling gait; 30 rolling motion; 31 anything rolled up in a coil or cylinder; 32 list or register; 33 kind of raised biscuit or bread, often doubled over; 34 continued deep sound, as of a drum or thunder; 35 **a** *slang* bundle of paper money; **b** bankroll; 36 throw of the dice

roll'back' *n* 1 act, instance, or result of rolling back prices, costs, services, wages, an enemy, etc.; 2 return to a less menacing stance, esp. in the matter of nuclear armaments

roll' call' *n* act or instance of calling out a list of names of those belonging to an organization, as soldiers or pupils

roll'er *n* 1 cylinder used for grinding, smoothing, flattening, inking, reducing friction, etc.; 2 small wheel or caster on which something moves; 3 cylinder on which something is rolled; 4 hollow cylindrical piece, as of plastic, for rolling the hair into waves; 5 long heavy wave

roll'er bear'ing *n* bearing which uses rollers to lessen the friction

roll'er coast'er *n* amusement railway

in which small cars run along sharply inclined tracks

roll'er der'by *n* race between two teams of roller skaters on a short circular track

roll'er skate' *n* skate equipped with four small wheels ‖ **roll'er-skate'** *vi* ‖ **roll'er skat'er** *n*

rol·lick·ing /rol'ikiŋ/ [?] *adj* boisterously jolly

roll'ing mill' /rōl'-/ *n* 1 mill in which hot metal is forced through rollers for shaping into rails, plates, etc.; 2 set of rollers for shaping metal

roll'ing pin' *n* smooth cylinder of wood or other material, for rolling out dough

roll'ing stock' *n* the cars and locomotives of a railroad

roll'top desk' *n* desk with a flexible cover that slides back and up under the top

ro·ly-po·ly /rōl'ēpōl'ē/ [rhyming formation on *roll*] *adj* short and fat; pudgy

Rom. 1 Roman; 2 Romans

Ro·ma·ic /rōmā'ik/ [Gk *Rhomaikos* Roman] *n* 1 the vernacular of modern Greece ‖ *adj* 2 pert. to modern Greece or its language

ro·maine' let'tuce /rōmān'/ [F = Roman] *n* variety of lettuce (*Lactuca sativa longifolia*) with long easily detached leaves

Ro·man /rōm'ən/ [L *Romanus*] *n* 1 native or citizen of Rome; 2 **Romans** *sg* book of the New Testament; 3 **roman** the ordinary type used in printing, distinguished from *italics* ‖ *adj* 4 pert. to the city of Rome; 5 pert. to the ancient kingdom, republic, or empire of Rome; 6 pert. to the Roman Catholic Church; 7 **roman** pert. to or written in Roman numerals

ro·man à clef /rōmäⁿ'äklā'/ [F = novel with a key] *n* (**romans à clef** /rōmäⁿ'äklā'/) novel whose purported fictional events and characters are based on real events and persons

Ro'man can'dle *n* tube which shoots out a series of balls of fire when ignited, used in fireworks

Ro'man Cath'o·lic *n* member of the church of which the Pope in Rome is the head ‖ also *adj* ‖ **Ro'man Ca·thol'i·cism** *n*

ro·mance /rōmans'/ [OF *romanz* < LL *romanice* in the vernacular] *n* 1 medieval prose or poetical tale of love, adventure, and chivalry, originally written in a Romance dialect; 2 form of idealistic prose fiction stressing adventure and extravagant incident rather than reality or character analysis; 3 disposition or tendency to delight in fancifulness, adventure, sentiment, or idealized love; 4 falsehood; 5 love affair; 6 *mus* short simple melody of a sentimental character; **7 Romance** the Romance languages ‖ *vt* **8** to invent fanciful or extravagant stories; **9** to indulge in visions or dreamy imaginings ‖ *vt* **10** *colloq* to make love to; woo ‖ **11 Ro′mance** *adj* (language) descended from Latin ‖ **ro·manc′er** *n*

Ro′mance lan′guag·es *npl* the languages descended from Latin, as French, Italian, Spanish, Portuguese, and Rumanian

Ro′man Em′pire *n* the empire established by the ancient Romans (27 B.C.–476 A.D.), ruled from Rome and later Constantinople, extending at its height from Britain to Arabia

Ro·man·esque /rōm′ənesk′/ [< *Roman*] *n* style of architecture and ornamentation developed during the period from the 8th to the 12th century and characterized by the round arch and a solid substantial appearance ‖ also *adj*

Ro·ma′ni·a *n* see **Rumania**

Ro·man·ic /rōman′ik/ *adj* **1** Roman; **2** Romance (language)

Ro′man·ize *vt* **1** to make Roman; **2** to make Roman Catholic

Ro′man nose′ *n* nose with a high bridge

Ro′man nu′mer·als *npl* numerals used before the adoption of the Arabic notation and still used for certain purposes, based on the following letters or combinations of them: I = 1; V = 5; X = 10; L = 50; C = 100; D = 500; and M = 1000

Ro·ma′no (*cheese′*) /rōmän′ō/ [It = Roman] *n* sharp, hard Italian cheese made from sheep's milk

Ro·ma·nov /rōm′ənôf′/ *n* last imperial dynasty of Russia (1613 to 1917)

Ro·mansh /rōmänsh′, -mänsh′/ [< LL *romanice* in Romance] *n* Romance language spoken in SE Switzerland, one of the four official languages of the country ‖ also *adj*

ro·man·tic /rōmant′ik/ [F *romantique*] *adj* **1** pert. to, like, or characterized by romance; **2** fanciful; **3** visionary; impractical; **4** inclined to sentimentalize love; **5** ardent; passionate; **6** following fancy and free interpretation rather than set forms; **7 Romantic** (literature) emphasizing picturesqueness and beauty of subject, imagination and emotion, and love of nature and the common man, rather than regularity of form ‖ *n* romantic person ‖ **ro·man′ti·cal·ly** *adv* ‖ SYN *adj* fictitious, improbable, wild, chimerical, dreamy, poetic ‖ ANT *adj* exact, precise, literal

ro·man′ti·cism *n* **1** quality or characteristic of being romantic; **2 Romanticism** the 19th century Romantic movement in literature

Rom·a·ny /rom′ənē, rōm′-/ [Gypsy *Romain* Gypsy woman] *n* (**-nies**) **1** Gypsy; **2** Gypsies collectively; **3** language of the Gypsies ‖ also *adj*

Rome /rōm′/ *n* capital of Italy (2,200,000); capital of the ancient Roman Empire and site of the Holy See

Ro·me·o /rōm′ē·ō′/ *n* Juliet's lover in Shakespeare's *Romeo and Juliet*

romp /romp′/ [var of obs *ramp* bold woman] *vi* **1** to play in a boisterous manner; **2** *sports* to win effortlessly ‖ *n* **3** boisterous play; **4** effortless pace

romp′ers *npl* child's garment consisting of a waist with short loose pants attached

Rom·u·lus /rom′yələs/ *n* Rom. myth. founder and first king of Rome, abandoned as a baby and suckled by a she-wolf with his twin brother Remus, whom he later slew

rood /rŏŏd′/ [OE *rōd*] *n* **1** crucifix; **2** land measure equal to one fourth of an acre or 40 square rods

rood′ screen′ *n* ornamental screen, usu. surmounted by a rood, which separates the choir or chancel from the nave of a church

roof /rŏŏf′, rŏŏf′/ [OE *hrōf*] *n* **1** top covering of a building; **2** any similar covering or upper part, as of a car or of the mouth; **3** house; **4 raise the roof** *slang* **a** to complain vehemently; **b** to make a lot of noise ‖ *vt* **5** to cover with or as with a roof

roof′ gar′den *n* garden on the flat top of a building, esp. when combined with a public restaurant or theater

roof′ing *n* material for roofs

rook¹ /rŏŏk′/ [OE *hrōc*] *n* **1** gregarious European crow (*Corvus frugilegus*) ‖ *vt* **2** *colloq* to cheat, swindle

rook² [OF *roc* < Pers *rukh*] *n* chess piece resembling a castle that can be moved any unobstructed distance vertically or horizontally across the board

rook′er·y *n* (**-ies**) **1** breeding place or colony of rooks or crows; **2** any place where gregarious birds or animals congregate in large numbers to breed; **3** crowded tenement

rook′ie /-ē̱/ [< *recruit*] *n* **1** raw recruit; **2** beginner; neophyte

room /rŏŏm′, rŏŏm′/ [OE *rūm*] *n* **1** space occupied or that can be occupied; **2** enclosure separated by partitions from the rest of the structure in which it is located; **3** persons in a room, as *the whole room applauded;* **4 rooms** *pl* living quarters ‖ *vi* **5** to lodge

room′er *n* one who rents a room to live in

room·ette′ /-et′/ *n* small private compartment in a sleeping car, containing a folding bed and toilet facilities

room′ful *n* **1** what a room will hold; **2** the people that fill or almost fill a room

room'ing house' n house with furnished rooms for renting

room'mate' n person who shares a room or apartment with one

room' serv'ice n the serving of food, ice, drinks, etc., to guests in hotel rooms

room'y adj (-i·er; -i·est) having plenty of room; spacious ‖ **room'i·ness** n

Roo·se·velt, Frank·lin D. /rōz'ə·velt', -vəlt/ n (1882–1945) 32nd president of the U.S. 1933–45; elected to four terms, the only president to serve more than two terms

Roo·se·velt, The·o·dore /thē'ə·dôr'/ n (1858–1919) 26th president of the U.S. 1901–09; Nobel peace prize 1906

roost /rōōst/ [OE hrōst] n 1 place, as a pole or perch, where a bird rests at night; 2 any resting place ‖ vi 3 to rest, as for the night

roost'er n male of the domestic fowl

root[1] /rōōt/, rŏŏt/ [OE rōt < Scand] n 1 underground part of a plant, serving to fix it in the earth, absorb moisture, and store nourishment; 2 the part of an organ that is most deeply imbedded, as of a finger nail or tooth; 3 source or origin; 4 essential part; 5 math a value which, if substituted for the unknown quantity in an equation, satisfies the equation; b quantity which when multiplied by itself a specified number of times, produces a given quantity; 6 mus first or lowest member of a common chord or triad; 7 gram a basic part of a word to which affixes are added; b reconstructed form from which forms in related languages are derived; 8 roots pl place where a person has grown up and where his family, friends, and interests lie; 9 take root, a to begin to grow by sending out roots; b to become established ‖ vi 10 to take root ‖ vt 11 to fix in a place as by roots; 12 to implant deeply; 13 root out, a to tear or dig up by the roots; b to eradicate

root[2] [OE wrōtan] vi 1 to turn up the earth with the snout; 2 to rummage ‖ vt 3 root up, a to dig up with the snout; b to unearth

root[3] [?] vi 1 to give encouragement by cheering; 2 root for, a to encourage by cheering; b to be a partisan of ‖ **root'er** n

root' beer' n carbonated beverage made with the extract of roots or bark

root'let /-lit/ n 1 little root; 2 secondary root thrown out by a climbing plant

root'stock' n 1 root with its buds; 2 rhizome

rope /rōp/ [OE rāp] n 1 thick stout cord made of several strands of hemp or other fiber, wire, etc., twisted together; 2 collection of things strung together, as a rope of pearls; 3 death by hanging; 4 know the ropes to know the details of a business, operation, or procedure; 5 on the ropes, a (prize fighter) helpless and leaning against the ropes; b slang facing defeat or failure ‖ vt 6 to bind or tie with a rope; 7 to lasso; 8 rope in slang to entice by deception; 9 rope off to set aside or enclose as by ropes

Roque'fort (cheese') /rōk'fərt/ [town in France] n strong cheese veined with blue mold, made from sheep's milk

Ror'schach test' /rôr'shäk, rôr'-/ [Hermann Rorschach (1884–1922) Swiss psychiatrist] n test to reveal a person's personality by noting his reaction to a series of ink blots

ro·sa·ceous /rōzāsh'əs/ [L rosaceus] adj 1 roselike; 2 belonging to the rose family (Rosaceae); 3 having a five-petaled corolla

ro·sa·ry /rōz'ər̄ē/ [ML rosarium < L = rose garden] n (-ries) R C Ch 1 string of beads for counting a series of prayers to be said in a certain order; 2 the series of prayers thus counted

rose[1] /rōz/ [OE < L rosa] n 1 any of a genus (Rosa) of shrubs, esp. of the thorny varieties, erect or climbing, bearing showy fragrant flowers; 2 the flower; 3 light crimson or crimson pink

rose[2] pt of **rise**

ro·sé /rōzā'/ [F = pink] n a pink, dry table wine

ro·se·ate /rōz'ē·it/ [< L roseus] adj rosy

rose'-col'ored adj 1 rosy; red or pink like a rose; 2 optimistic; 3 providing a cheerful outlook on life

rose' fe'ver n hay fever caused by the inhalation of rose pollen

rose·mar·y /rōz'mer'ē/ [L ros marinus marine dew] n (-ies) fragrant evergreen shrub (Rosmarinus officinalis) of the mint family with aromatic leaves, used as a seasoning and in perfumes

ro·se·o·la /rōzē'ələ/ [LL, dim. of roseus rose-colored] n 1 any pinkish eruption of the skin; 2 measles

Ro·set'ta stone' /rōzet'ə/ [town in Egypt] n stone tablet discovered in 1799, bearing an inscription in Egyptian hieroglyphics and in Greek, which provided the key for the decipherment of the ancient Egyptian writings

ro·sette /-zet'/ [F = little rose] n 1 ornament, as a knot or bunch of ribbon, in the shape of a rose; 2 arch. circular ornament, as leaves arranged in a circle around a bud; 3 any arrangement, formation, or part resembling a rose

rose' wa'ter n toilet water having the odor of roses

rose'-wa'ter *adj* **1** having the odor of rose water; **2** affectedly nice

rose' win'dow *n* circular stained-glass window with divisions in elaborate tracery radiating from or arranged around its center

rose'wood' *n* **1** hard, dark-red wood, often rose-scented, yielded by various tropical trees and used for fine furniture; **2** tree from which such wood is obtained

Rosh Ha·sha·na /rōsh' həshän'ə, rôsh', -shôn'-/ [Heb = head of the year] *n* the Jewish New Year, the first of the month Tishri

ros·in /roz'in/ [var of *resin*] *n* **1** hard, brittle amber substance that remains after distilling crude turpentine, used in varnishes and printing inks, and for rubbing on the bows of stringed instruments; **2** resin

ros·ter /rost'ər/ [D *rooster* list] *n* **1** list or roll, as of personnel or equipment; **2** schedule or program of procedure

ros·trum /ros'trəm/ [L = beak of bird, ship's prow (in plural, speaker's platform because it was decorated with ramming beaks from captured warships)] *n* (-**trums** or -**tra** /-trə/) platform or stage for public speaking

ros·y /rōz'ē/ *adj* (-**i·er**, -**i·est**) **1** red or pink like a rose; **2** roselike; **3** favorable, promising; **4** optimistic

rot /rot/ [OE *rotian*] *v* (**rot·ted**; **rot·ting**) *vt & vi* **1** to decay, decompose ‖ *n* **2** process of rotting or state of being rotten; **3** rotting matter; **4** moral decay; **5** any of various plant and animal diseases characterized by decay; **6** *colloq* nonsense

ro·ta·ry /rōt'ərē/ [LL *rotarius* < L *rota* wheel] *adj* **1** turning around on an axis, as a wheel; **2** having rotating parts ‖ *n* (-**ries**) **3** traffic circle

ro·tate /rō'tāt, rōtāt'/ [L *rotare* (-*atus*)] *vt* **1** to cause to turn on an axis; **2** to cause to alternate or change about ‖ *vi* **3** to turn around on or as on an axis; **4** to alternate, or succeed by turn in a series ‖ **ro·ta'tion** *n* ‖ SYN *v* revolve, turn, roll, recur ‖ DISCR *Rotate* is used of motion about an axis within the turning body; *revolve* is occasionally so used, but more specifically of motion about an axis outside the body. The earth *rotates* on its axis daily and *revolves* about the sun annually

R.O.T.C. Reserve Officers' Training Corps

rote /rōt/ [ME] *n* **1** fixed routine; **2** by **rote** by sheer memory, without attention to meaning or understanding

rot'gut' *n* *slang* cheap, vile liquor

ro·ti·fer /rōt'ifər/ [< L *rota* wheel + -*fer*] *n* any of a class (Rotifera) of microscopic water animals having a wheellike appendage at the front end

ro·tis·ser·ie /rōtis'ərē/ [F] *n* small broiler with a rotating spit

ro·to·gra·vure' /rō'tə-/ [< L *rota* wheel + *gravure*] *n* **1** photomechanical process for printing illustrations from plates etched on copper cylinders; **2** illustration so printed; **3** section of a newspaper printed by this process

ro·tor /rōt'ər/ [abbr of *rotator*] *n* rotating part of a motor, generator, turbine, etc.

rot·ten /rot'ən/ [ME *roten* < Scand] *adj* **1** putrid, decayed; **2** foul-smelling; **3** corrupt; **4** despicable; **5** *colloq* very bad; disgusting; **6** *slang* weak, miserable ‖ SYN putrified, decomposed, fetid, tainted, offensive, treacherous ‖ ANT healthful, pure, sweet, sound

rot'ter *n* *Brit slang* mean, contemptible person

Rot·ter·dam /rot'ərdam'/ *n* seaport in the SW part of The Netherlands (750,000)

ro·tund /rōtund'/ [L *rotundus* round] *adj* **1** round, rounded; **2** plump; **3** full-toned ‖ **ro·tun'di·ty** *n* (-**ties**)

ro·tun'da /-ə/ [It *rotonda*] *n* **1** circular building, esp. one with a dome; **2** large circular room

rou·é /rōō-ā'/ [F = broken on the wheel] *n* libertine, dissipated man, rake

rouge /rōōzh'/ [F < L *rubeus* red] *n* **1** red cosmetic for coloring the cheeks and lips; **2** powdered ferric oxide for polishing glass or metal ‖ *vt* **3** to apply rouge to

rough /ruf'/ [OE *rūh*] *adj* **1** having an uneven surface; not smooth; **2** shaggy; **3** characterized by turbulence, as *a rough flight*; **4** unpleasant, as *a rough time*; **5** not finished or perfected, as *a rough sketch*; **6** not polished; crude; **7** not refined; rude; **8** harsh to the ear; jarring; **9** uncivil; harsh; **10** violent; characterized by violent action; **11** stormy; **12** approximate, as *a rough guess* ‖ *n* **13** *golf* long grass between and bordering the fairways; **14** **in the rough** in a crude or unfinished condition ‖ *adv* **15** roughly ‖ *vt* **16** to make rough; **17** to subject to physical violence; **18** **rough** **it** to do without comforts and conveniences; **19** **rough out** to make a rough sketch of; **20** **rough up** to subject to physical violence ‖ **rough'ly** *adv* ‖ SYN *adj* jagged, rugged, rude, rustic, uneven, uncivil, harsh (see *abrupt*)

rough'age /-ij/ *n* the part of a diet that affords bulk rather than nourishment

rough' breath'ing *n* *Gk gram* the symbol ' placed over an initial vowel or rho to indicate aspiration

rough'en *vt* **1** to make rough ‖ *vi* **2** to become rough

rough'hewn' *adj* roughly shaped; crudely formed; coarse

rough'house' *n* **1** horseplay; rough disorderly playing ‖ /-hous', -houz'/ *v* (-housed /-houst', -houzd'/; -hous·ing /-hous'iŋ, -houz'iŋ/) *vt* 2 to subject to horseplay ‖ *vi* 3 to engage in horseplay

rough'neck' *n colloq* rowdy, tough

Rough' Rid'ers *npl* volunteer cavalry regiment that fought in the Spanish-American War in 1898 under Theodore Roosevelt

rough'shod' *adv* **ride roughshod over** to crush all resistance from; treat harshly

rough' stuff' *n slang* violence; physical assault

rou·lade /roolad'/ [F] *n* 1 dish made with slices of meat rolled with bacon and steamed; 2 rapid succession of notes sung to one syllable

rou·lette' /-let'/ [F *dim.* of *rouelle* wheel] *n* game of chance played with a rotating bowl-like disk marked off in sections that are numbered and colored red and black

Rou·ma·ni·a /roomān'ē·ə, -nyə/ *n* Rumania ‖ **Rou·ma'ni·an** *adj & n*

round /round'/ [OF *rond* < L *rotundus*] *adj* 1 shaped like a circle, sphere, or cylinder; 2 having a curved contour or surface; 3 whole, complete, as *a round dozen;* 4 large, considerable, as *a round sum;* 5 full in sound; 6 **in round numbers** expressed in whole numbers or in tens, hundreds, thousands, etc. ‖ *n* 7 round shape or object; 8 customary course or route; 9 series of events or acts, as *a round of parties;* 10 circular dance; 11 action in which a number of persons take part at one time, as *a round of cheers;* 12 *cards* complete play in which each player has his turn dealing; 13 *golf* playing of the complete course; 14 three-minute period of a boxing match; 15 portion distributed or served at one time, as *a round of drinks;* 16 cut of beef between the rump and the leg; 17 single shot from a firearm; 18 simultaneous discharge from a number of guns; 19 single charge of ammunition; 20 song sung by several voices starting one after the other at regular intervals; 21 **in the round**, a (theater) with the stage completely surrounded by the audience; b (sculpture) carved on all sides, not attached; 22 **make the rounds** to go routinely from one place to another, as *they make the rounds of the night spots* ‖ *vt* 23 to make round; 24 to fill out, make plump; 25 to pass around, as *to round a corner;* 26 to surround, encircle; 27 to pronounce (a vowel) with the lips rounded; 28 **round off**, a to complete or finish; b to express as a round number; 29 **round out** to complete or finish; 30 **round up** to assemble, gather ‖ *vi* 31 to become round; 32 **round out** to

fill out, become plump ‖ *adv* 33 around; 34 through a recurring period, as *all year round* ‖ *prep* 35 around ‖ **round'ness** *n* ‖ SYN *adj* curved, curvilinear, circular, spherical, globose, globular, orbed, rotund, plump

round'a·bout' *adj* 1 indirect; circuitous ‖ *n* 2 short jacket for men or boys; 3 *Brit* merry-go-round; 4 *Brit* traffic circle

roun·de·lay /roun'dəlā'/ [MF *rondelet* something round] *n* song in which a line or phrase is continually repeated

round'er *n colloq* habitual drunkard; wastrel, drifter

Round'head' *n* in 17th-century England, a Puritan or supporter of Parliament, who wore his hair cropped short

round'house' *n* (-hous·es /-ziz/) 1 circular building for storing and repairing locomotives, each stall of which is entered from the center by means of a turntable; 2 *slang* wild punch in which the fist describes a horizontal arc

round' lot' *n* standard quantity of stocks traded (100 shares for active issues)

round'ly *adv* 1 in a round manner; 2 completely; 3 vigorously; 4 severely

round' rob'in *n* 1 petition or the like bearing signatures written in a circle so as not to show who signed first; 2 letter circulated from person to person in a group or organization; 3 tournament in which each contestant plays all other contestants

round'-shoul'dered *adj* having stooping shoulders

Round' Ta'ble *n* Arthurian legend table at which King Arthur and his knights sat, made circular so that none might claim precedence

round-ta'ble *adj* pert. to a discussion or conference in which the participants have equal opportunity to air their views

round' trip' *n* trip to a given place and back again ‖ **round'-trip'** *adj*

round'up' *n* 1 gathering together and driving in of herds of cattle; 2 any gathering together

round'worm' *n* any of a class (Nematoda) of worms resembling the earthworms, some species being parasitic in man and other mammals

rouse /rouz'/ [ME] *vt* 1 to waken from sleep; 2 to stir to thought or action ‖ *vi* 3 to become roused ‖ *n* 4 a rousing

rous'ing *adj* stirring, exciting

Rous·seau, Jean Jacques /zhän' zhäk' rooso'/ *n* (1712–78) French philosopher and writer

roust /roust'/ [var of *rouse*] *vt* 1 to rout out of bed; 2 *slang* (of police) to stop and search (a suspect)

roust'a·bout' *n* 1 unskilled worker, as

on a pier or ship; **2** circus laborer; **3** transient laborer in an oil field

rout[1] /rout/ [OF *route* broken] *n* **1** overwhelming defeat and flight || *vt* **2** to defeat overwhelmingly; **3** to put to flight || SYN *v* overpower, conquer, repulse (see *vanquish*)

rout[2] [var of *root*[2]] *vt* **1** to root as with the snout; **2 rout out, a** to scoop out, dig out; **b** to bring to view, turn up; **c** to drag or force out

route /root, rout/ [OF < L (via) *rupta* broken (road)] **1** road or way; **2** customary or regular course, as of a ship, plane, or salesman || *vt* **3** to send or forward by a certain route; **4** to fix the route of

rou·tine /root̄ēn/ [F] *n* **1** customary or regular procedure; **2** unvarying and boring actions gone through regularly and mechanically; **3** performer's act, as *a song and dance routine* || *adj* **4** of or relating to customary procedure; **5** dull, unimaginative || **rou·tine/ly** *adv* || SYN *n* habitude, practice, system, round (see *habit*)

rove[1] /rōv/ [ME *roven*] *vi* **1** to wander aimlessly || *vt* **2** to ramble over or through

rove[2] /rōv/ *pt* & *pp* of **reeve**

rov·er *n* **1** wanderer; nomad; **2** motor vehicle designed for travel on the moon; **3** *Brit* person holding a ticket at a concert for standing room only

row[1] /rō/ [OE *rāw*] *n* **1** series of persons or things in a line; **2** line of seats in a theater

row[2] [OE *rōwan*] *vi* **1** to employ oars in propelling a boat || *vt* **2** to propel by means of oars; **3** to carry in a rowboat || *n* **4** act or instance of rowing; **5** ride in a rowboat || **row/er** *n*

row[3] /rou/ [?] *n* **1** noisy disturbance or quarrel; **2** clamor || *vi* **3** to take part in a noisy quarrel

row/boat/ /rō-/ *n* boat propelled by oars

row·dy /roud̄ē/ [?] *n* (**-dies**) **1** rough disorderly fellow || *adj* (**-di·er; -di·est**) **2** rough and disorderly || **row/dy·ism** *n*

row·el /rou/əl/ [MF *rouelle* small wheel] *n* small spiked wheel at the end of a spur

row/ house/ /rō/ *n* one of a row of adjoining and usu. similar houses, each having its side walls in common with its neighbors

roy·al /roi/əl/ [MF < L *regalis*] *adj* **1** of or pert. to a king or queen; **2** related to by blood or descended from a king or queen; **3** kingly; regal; **4** often **Royal** pert. to, established by, under the patronage of, or in the service of a king, queen, or monarch || **roy/al·ly** *adv* || SYN imperial, majestic, sovereign, supreme || ANT base, inferior, paltry, servile

roy/al flush/ *n poker* the five highest cards of a suit held in one hand

Roy/al High/ness *n* **1** title bestowed on members of a royal family; **2** *Brit* title bestowed on the children and grandchildren of a reigning monarch

roy/al·ist *n* supporter or adherent of the monarchical form of government, or of a specific king || **roy/al·ism** *n*

roy/al jel/ly *n* larval food secreted by honeybees and fed to those larvae which will develop into queens

roy/al·ty *n* (**-ties**) **1** royal state or status; **2** royal persons collectively; **3** member of a royal family; **4** kingliness; **5** share of the product or profit, as from a mine, paid to the owner; **6** percentage paid to an inventor or author for the use of a patent or copyright

rpm, r.p.m. revolutions per minute

R.R. railroad

-r·rhe·a, -r·rhoe·a /-rē/ə/ [Gk *rhoia*] *comb form* flow, discharge

R.S.V.P. [F *répondez s'il vous plaît*] please reply

Ru *chem* ruthenium

rub /rub/ [ME *rubben*] *v* (**rubbed; rub·bing**) *vt* **1** to cause (a surface) to undergo friction and pressure; **2** to apply with friction and pressure, as wax on a floor; **3** to cause to move over something with pressure, as *to rub one's hand over one's face*; **4 rub down, a** to massage; **b** to polish; smooth; **5 rub it in** *colloq* to keep repeating or emphasizing something unpleasant; **6 rub out, a** to erase; **b** *slang* to murder; **7 rub the wrong way** to irritate or annoy || *vi* **8** to rub something; **9** to become worn or sore with friction; **10 rub off** to disappear with rubbing || *n* **11** act or instance of rubbing; **12** obstacle; annoyance

rub/ber[1] [from its use in erasing] *n* **1** one who rubs; **2** elastic, tenacious substance prepared from the solidified sap or latex of various tropical trees (as of the genera *Hevea* and *Ficus*) or made synthetically, used for waterproofing, insulating, and in the manufacture of numerous products; **3** low overshoe of rubber; **4** rubber band; **5** eraser of rubber || **rub/ber·y** *adj*

rub·ber[2] [?] *n cards* **1** series of games played till one side wins; **2** deciding game

rub/ber band/ *n* narrow elastic band of rubber for holding things together

rub/ber check/ *n colloq* worthless check

rub/ber·ize/ *vt* to impregnate with rubber

rub/ber·neck/ *colloq vi* **1** to indulge in sightseeing; crane the neck in order to see more || *n* **2** tourist

rub/ber plant/ *n* popular house plant (*Ficus elastica*) with long shiny leaves

rub/ber stamp/ *n* **1** device with a rubber surface that is inked for stamping; **2** *colloq* one who approves automatically anything brought before him || **rub/ber-stamp/** *vt*

rub·bish /rub′ish/ [ME *robys*] *n* 1 anything thrown out as worthless; trash; 2 nonsense

rub·ble /rub′əl/ *n* 1 rough broken stones or bricks; 2 broken bits and pieces, as of demolished buildings

rub′down′ *n* massage

rube /rōōb′/ [< *Reuben*] *n slang* hick

ru·bel·la /rōōbel′ə/ [L = reddish] *n* German measles

Ru·bens, Pe·ter Paul /rōōb′ənz/ *n* (1577–1640) Flemish painter

Ru·bi·con /rōōb′ikon′/ *n* 1 river in N Italy, ancient boundary between Cisalpine Gaul and Italy, the crossing of which committed Caesar to civil war; 2 **cross the Rubicon** to perform any act that commits one irrevocably

ru·bi·cund /rōōb′ikund′/ [L *rubicundus*] *adj* ruddy, reddish

ru·bid·i·um /rōōbid′ē·əm/ [< L *rubidus* red] *n chem* rare, soft silverwhite metallic element (**Rb**; at.no. 37; at.wt. 85.47), used in vacuum tubes and photoelectric cells

ru·ble /rōōb′əl/ [Russ *rubl′*] *n* monetary unit of Russia

ru·bric /rōōb′rik/ [L *rubrica* red ocher] *n* 1 title or heading in a printed work appearing in red to give it prominence; 2 heading of a section or chapter; 3 any rule of conduct

ru·by /rōōb′ē/ [MF *rubi* < L *rubeus* red] *n* (**-bies**)1 highly valued precious stone, a red variety of corundum; 2 deep red ‖ also *adj*

ruck′sack′ /ruk′-/ [G] *n* knapsack carried slung over the shoulder or back

ruck·us /ruk′əs/ [?] *n colloq* noisy fracas

rud·der /rud′ər/ [OE *rōther*] *n* vertical piece at the rear of a vessel or aircraft, used for steering

rud·dy /rud′ē/ [OE *rudig*] *adj* (**-di·er; -di·est**) 1 red or reddish; 2 having a healthy red color; 3 *Brit slang* damned ‖ **rud′di·ness** *n* ‖ SYN fresh, glowing, rosy, reddish, bronzed

rude /rōōd′/ [L *rudis*] *adj* 1 barbarous; uncultivated; 2 impolite; insolent; 3 rugged (health); 4 crude, roughly done; 5 harsh, violent ‖ **rude′ly** *adv* ‖ **rude′ness** *n* ‖ SYN impudent, discourteous, impolite, uncouth, barbarous, rough, gruff, rustic, violent, fierce, rugged, sturdy, vigorous ‖ ANT polite, civil, polished, gentle

rude′ a·wak′en·ing *n* sudden and shocking awareness of something very unpleasant

ru·di·ment /rōōd′imənt/ [L *rudimentum* beginning] *n* 1 usu. **rudiments** *pl* **a** anything in its first undeveloped state; beginning; **b** first or introductory principles of an art or science ‖ **ru′di·men′ta·ry** /-ment′ərē/ *adj*

rue¹ /rōō′/ [MF < L *ruta*] *n* any of a genus (*Ruta*) of Old World plants, esp. a yellow-flowered species (*R.*

graveolens) with strong odor and bitter taste, formerly used medicinally

rue² [OE *hrēowan*] *vt* 1 to lament or be sorry for; 2 to look upon with regret; wish undone ‖ *vi* 3 to feel regret

rue′ful *adj* 1 causing or inspiring sorrow or pity; 2 feeling or expressing sorrow or pity; 3 glum, morose ‖ **rue′ful·ly** *adv* ‖ SYN sorrowful, regretful, pitiable, lamentable, mournful, deplorable ‖ ANT joyful, pleased

ruff¹ /ruf′/ [prob < *ruffle*] *n* 1 large fluted starched collar worn in the 16th and 17th centuries; 2 anything like such a collar, as a prominent growth of feathers or hair around the neck of an animal ‖ **ruffed**′ *adj*

ruff² [MF *roffle*] *cards n* 1 act or instance of trumping ‖ *vt* 2 to trump ‖ *vi* 3 to play a trump

ruffed′ grouse′ *n* North American game bird (*Bonasa umbellus*) with tufts of feathers on the sides of its neck

ruf·fi·an /ruf′ē·ən, -yən/ [MF *rufian* rake] *n* brutal lawless fellow

ruf·fle /ruf′əl/ [ME *ruffelen*] *vt* 1 to draw into folds or gathers; 2 to erect (the feathers); 3 to make ripples in; 4 to disarrange, disorder; 5 to annoy, vex ‖ *vi* 6 to be or become ruffled ‖ *n* 7 plaited or gathered strip of material; 8 vexation, irritation; 9 ripple, undulation

rug /rug′/ [< Scand] *n* 1 heavy floor covering usu. over only part of the floor; 2 *Brit* lap robe or coverlet

Rug·by /rug′bē/ [school in *Rugby*, England] *n* kind of football, the predecessor of American football

rug·ged /rug′id/ [ME < Scand] *adj* 1 having a rough uneven surface; 2 steep and rocky; 3 uncouth, unpolished; 4 furrowed, irregular (features); 5 harsh; stern; austere; 6 stormy; 7 strong, tough ‖ SYN uneven, craggy, wooded; crabbed (see *abrupt*)

ru·in /rōō′in/ [MF < L *ruina*] *n* 1 destruction; downfall; 2 that which causes destruction or decay; 3 state of decay or desolation; 4 loss of wealth, health, position, etc.; 5 something or someone ruined; 6 **ruins** *pl* remains of a destroyed or decayed building or city ‖ *vt* 7 to bring to ruin ‖ *vi* 8 to come to ruin ‖ **ru′in·a′tion** *n* ‖ SYN *n* perdition, desolation, wreck, downfall, collapse, subversion, seduction; *v* deface, raze, demolish (see *destroy*) ‖ ANT *n* prosperity, recovery, success

ru·in·ous *adj* 1 showing decay or downfall; dilapidated; 2 causing destruction; hurtful ‖ SYN pernicious, baneful, disastrous, destructive

rule /rōōl′/ [OF *riule* < L *regula*] *n* 1 standard, principle, regulation, guide, or formula for procedure or conduct; **2** established method; accepted usage; **3** government; dominion; reign; **4** ruler 2; **5** regulations governing a religious order; **6 as a rule** generally ‖ *vt* **7** to govern or control; **8** to settle, decree; **9** to mark with lines with the aid of a straightedge; **10 rule out** to exclude from consideration ‖ *vi* **11** to exercise authority; **12** *law* to decide a point ‖ SYN *n* maxim, formula, guide, order, direction, regulation, standard, government, reign

rule' of law' *n* strict adherence to law as the guiding principle of government

rule' of thumb' *n* practical or approximate method of procedure based on experience rather than book learning

rul'er *n* **1** one who rules; sovereign; **2** thin strip, as of wood or metal, with a straight edge marked off in inches or centimeters, for measuring or for drawing straight lines

rul'ing *adj* **1** governing; **2** controlling ‖ *n* **3** decision by authority or by a court

rul'y Eng'lish *n* English designed for the computer in which one word has only one meaning and one meaning can be expressed by only one word

rum¹ /rum'/ [prob < *obs* rumbullion] *n* **1** alcoholic liquor distilled from molasses or the juice of sugar cane; **2** any intoxicating drink

rum² [perh < Gypsy *rom* male Gypsy] *adj Brit slang* queer; peculiar; strange

rum³ *n* rummy¹

Rum. Rumania(n)

Ru·ma·ni·a /rōōmān'ē·ə, -yə/ *n* republic in the Balkans in SE Europe (20,300,000; 91,634 sq.m.; cap. Bucharest) ‖ **Ru·ma'ni·an** *adj & n*

rum·ba /rum'bə/ [Sp] *n* ballroom dance of Cuban origin ‖ also *vi*

rum·ble /rum'bəl/ [ME *romblen*] *vi* **1** to make a low, heavy, continued sound; **2** to move with such a sound ‖ *vt* **2** to cause to make or move with a rumbling sound ‖ *n* **4** low, heavy, rolling sound; **5** seat for servants or place for baggage at the back of a carriage; **6** *slang* street fight between teenage gangs

ru·mi·nant /rōōm'inənt/ *n* **1** any of a suborder (Ruminantia) of hoofed mammals that chew the cud, as cattle, deer, and camels ‖ *adj* **2** ruminating

ru'mi·nate' [L *ruminari* (-*atus*) to chew again] *vi* **1** to chew the cud; **2** to meditate; muse ‖ *vt* **3** to chew again; **4** to ponder over, meditate on ‖ **ru'mi·na'tive** *adj* ‖ **ru'mi·na'tion** *n*

rum·mage /rum'ij/ [MF *arrumage* stowage] *vt* **1** to search thoroughly through by turning over the contents ‖ *vi* **2** to make a thorough search ‖ *n* **3** rummaging search; **4** miscellaneous odds and ends ‖ **rum'·mag·er** *n*

rum'mage sale' *n* sale of miscellaneous articles, as for charity

rum·my¹ /rum'ē/ [?] *n* any of various card games the object of which is to match sets and sequences of cards

rum·my² [< *rum¹*] *n* (**-mies**) *slang* drunkard; alcoholic

ru·mor /rōōm'ər/ [L] *n* **1** hearsay; gossip; **2** unverified current story ‖ *vt* **3** **be rumored** to be circulated as a rumor ‖ **ru'mor·mon'ger** /-muŋ'gər/ *n*

rump /rump'/ [ME *rumpe* < Scand] *n* **1** hind part of an animal; **2** buttocks

rum·ple /rum'pəl/ [< LG *rumpen*] *vt* **1** to wrinkle, crumple ‖ *vi* **2** to become creased or wrinkled ‖ *n* **3** wrinkle or irregular crease

rum·pus /rum'pəs/ [?] *n* commotion, uproar

rum'pus room' *n* room used for games and parties

run'run'ner *n* **1** person who brings liquor illegally ashore or across a border; **2** ship engaged in such traffic ‖ **rum'run'ning** *n*

run /run'/ [OE *rinnan*] *v* (**ran; run; run·ning**) *vi* **1** to move or go at a pace swifter than a walk; **2** to hurry, rush; **3** to flee, depart suddenly; **4** to travel, proceed, as *the train runs on the track;* **5** to make regular trips, ply; **6** to flow; **7** to melt and flow, as butter; **8** to function; operate, as an engine; **9** to extend in a certain direction, as *the railroad runs north;* **10** to continue in time, keep going, as *the play ran a year;* **11** to pass into a different state or condition, as *to run into luck;* **12** to ravel, as a thread in a stocking; **13** to be a candidate for office; **14** to follow a line of descent, as *laziness runs in his family;* **15** to climb or creep, as a vine; **16** to have a certain quality; average, as *the potatoes run large;* **17** *law* to continue in force; **18** to have recourse, as *to run to the law;* **19** to make a quick short trip; **20** to spread, as a color in a fabric; **21** to flow as a discharge, as tears or pus; **22** to be expressed in a certain manner, as *the passage runs as follows;* **23** to total, as a bill; **24** to appear in the press, as a story; **25 run across** to meet by accident; **26 run afoul of** to incur the wrath or penalty of; **27 run after** to pursue; **28 run around with** *colloq* to consort with; **29 run away** to flee, escape; **30 run away with, a** to elope with; **b** *colloq* to win easily, as prizes or honors; **31 run down to** stop operating; **32 run for it** to flee; **33 run into, a** to meet up with; **b** to collide with; **34 run off** to depart quickly; **35 run on** to go on without stopping; **36 run out** to terminate, be used up; **37 run out of** to use up, be left without; **38 run out on** *colloq* to abandon; **39 run over, a** to knock down and pass over; **b** to exceed; **c** to repeat ‖ *vt* **40** to operate, drive, or cause to work; **41** to move (finger, hand, eye, etc.) along or over something: **42** to perform or accomplish by running, as *run a race, run errands;* **43** to cover (a specified distance), as *to run fifty yards;* **44** to enter in a race; **45** to cause to ply; **46** to transport in a vehicle; **47** to print, as a story; **48** to conduct, as tests; **49** to sponsor (a candidate); **50** to cause to flow, as water from a tap; **51** to cause to unravel, as a stocking; **52** to thrust or drive, as a nail; **53** to extend, as an electric wire; **54** to cost approximately; **55** to chase after, hunt; **56** to pour forth, as *the earth ran blood;* **57** to go through (something dangerous) as *to run a blockade, run the rapids;* **58** to expose oneself to, as *run a risk;* **59** to smuggle; **60** to discharge, as pus; **61** to sew in a continuous row, as a seam; **62** to mark out, as a line or boundary; **63** to manage; direct; **64 run down, a** to fell by striking with a vehicle; **b** to pursue and capture; **c** to search out; **d** *colloq* to disparage; **65 run in, a** to break in, as a new car, new machinery; **b** *typ* to add without indenting; **c** *slang* to arrest and detain; **66 run off, a** to drive away; **b** to print or duplicate; **67 run on** *typ* to add (something) at the end of a text or article; **68 run out** to expel; **69 run through, a** to pierce with a sword; **b** to consume rapidly; **c** to rehearse rapidly; **70 run up, a** to incur (debts); **b** to cause to increase ‖ *n* **71** act, instance, or period of running; **72** trip; **73** act of flowing or that which flows, as *a run of maple sap;* **74** continued course or succession, as *a run of ill luck;* **75** sudden pressing demand, as *a run on a bank;* **76** average kind, as *the ordinary run of people;* **77** place passed over frequently by animals; **78** enclosed space to confine and feed animals; **79** brook; **80** period of operation, or the work turned out in that period; **81** *baseball* point scored by crossing home plate; **82** series of points made in succession in certain sports and games; **83** *mus* quick succession of rapid notes; **84** free use or enjoyment, as *to have the run of the place;* **85** continued series of performances, as *the play had a long run;* **86** sequence of cards of the same suit; **87** slope, as for skiing; **88** upstream movement of fish in the spawning season; **89** line, as in a stocking, where a series of stitches have come undone; **90 run for one's money,** a good sport; **b** keen competition; **91 in the long run** in the end; **92 on the run** *colloq* a while running; **b** pursued by the police

run'·a·round' *n colloq* series of evasions, esp. in answer to a request

run'a·way' *n* **1** fugitive; **2** horse or vehicle out of control ‖ *adj* **3** escaping from control; **4** brought about by running away or eloping; **5** won easily

run'down' *n* **1** quick summary of all pertinent facts; **2** *baseball* play in which a runner is caught off base between two of the opposing team who proceed to run him down

run'-down' *adj* **1** in poor physical condition; **2** dilapidated; **3** unwound; **4** discharged (battery)

rune /rōōn/ [OE *rūn* secret] *n* **1** character in one of the alphabets of the ancient Germanic tribes; **2** something written in runes; **3** magical saying used in casting a spell ‖ **ru'nic** *adj*

rung¹ /ruŋ/ *pp* of **ring**

rung² [OE *hrung*] *n* crosspiece of a ladder or chair

run'-in' *n* **1** *colloq* quarrel; **2** *typ* matter added to a text without indenting or starting a new paragraph

run'ner *n* **1** one who runs; **2** messenger; **3** one of the pieces on which a sleigh, skate, or sled slides; **4** *bot* a slender trailing branch that takes root at the end or at its joints; **b** plant that spreads in this way; **5** something on which something else moves; **6** rocker; **7** long narrow piece of carpeting; **8** strip of embroidery, lace, linen, or other cloth to place across a table, bureau, etc.; **9** run **89;** **10** smuggler

run'ner-up' *n* **(runners-up)** person or team finishing second

run'ning *adj* **1** linear (measurement); **2** sustained, as *a running commentary;* **3** performed while running; **4** discharging pus ‖ *adv* **5** in succession ‖ *n* **6 in the running** having a chance to win in a contest; **7 out of the running,** a not among the winners; **b** not competing; **c** having no chance to win

run'ning mate' *n* candidate for a lesser office running with one for the principal office

run'ny *adj* **(-ni·er; -ni·est) 1** that is inclined to run, as *a runny paint;* **2** (nose or eyes) that discharge mucus

Run·ny·mede /run'imēd/ *n* meadow on the Thames, W of London, where King John is said to have signed the Magna Charta in 1215

run'off' *n* **1** that which drains off, as melting snow in the spring; **2** deciding contest to determine the winner among the top two contestants

run'-of-the-mill' *adj* mediocre; ordinary; commonplace

run'-of-the-mine' *adj* **1** crude, unsorted (coal or ore); **2** mediocre; ordinary; run-of-the-mill

run'-on' *n* **1** *pros* line that continues a preceding line without a syntactical break; **2** *typ* matter that is added to run on ‖ *also adj*

runt /runt′/ [?] *n* person, animal, or plant that is small or stunted for its kind ‖ **runt′y** *adj* (-i·er; -i·est)

run′way *n* 1 way or path over which something runs; 2 smooth strip on an airfield on which planes land and take off; 3 ramp projecting out into the audience from a stage, as in a burlesque theater

ru·pee /rōōpē′, rōō′pē/ [Hindi *rūpiyā*] *n* monetary unit of India, Pakistan, Ceylon, Mauritius, Trucial Oman, and Oman

ru·pi·ah /rōōpē′ə/ [see rupee] *n* monetary unit of Indonesia

rup·ture /rup′chər/ [L *ruptura*] *n* 1 act of breaking or bursting, or state of being broken or burst; 2 breach of friendly relations; 3 hernia ‖ *vt* 4 to break or burst; 5 to bring about a breach of; 6 to cause a hernia in ‖ *vi* 7 to undergo a breach or break

ru·ral /rōōr′əl/ [MF < L *ruralis*] *adj* 1 pert. to, like, or living in, the country; 2 pert. to agriculture ‖ **SYN** pastoral, arcadian, bucolic, rustic, countrified

Rus. Russia(n)

ruse /rōōz′/ [MF] *n* trick, stratagem ‖ **SYN** artifice, feint, trick, stratagem (see *subterfuge*)

rush¹ /rush′/ [OE *risc*] *n* any plant of the family Junaceae, having long stems and growing on wet ground, used in making chair bottoms, baskets, and the like

rush² [AF *russher*] *vi* 1 to move or act with great speed; press forward with violent haste; 2 to appear or go rapidly ‖ *vt* 3 to cause to move or act with great speed; hurry; 4 to convey hurriedly; 5 to attack and occupy; 6 *football* to advance (the ball) by carrying it; 7 *colloq* to pay marked attention to, as a girl or a desirable candidate for a fraternity ‖ *n* 8 act of rushing; 9 impetuous or violent forward movement; 10 sudden migration, as to a newly discovered gold field; 11 busy activity, as *the Christmas rush*; 12 state of being hurried, as *in a rush*; 13 attention paid to a girl or fraternity candidate; 14 great demand, as *a rush on bonds*; 15 *football* play in which the ball is carried forward ‖ *adj* 16 requiring haste; 17 done in haste

rush′ hour′ *n* peak traffic hour, as in the morning when people are going to work and in the evening when they are returning home ‖ **rush′-hour′** *adj*

Russ. Russia(n)

Rus·sell, Bert·rand /burt′rənd rus′əl/ *n* (Lord Russell) (1872–1970) British philosopher, mathematician, and social reformer; Nobel prize in literature 1950

rus·set /rus′it/ [OF *rousset*] *n* 1 reddish brown; 2 variety of winter apple having a rough, greenish-brown skin ‖ *adj* 3 reddish-brown; 4 made of coarse, reddish-brown cloth; homespun

Rus·sia /rush′ə/ *n* country in E Europe, largest constituent republic of the Soviet Union (140,000,000; 6,645,000 sq.m.; cap. Moscow) ‖ **Rus′sian** *adj* & *n*

Rus′sian dress′ing *n* mayonnaise with chili sauce, pimientos, etc.

Rus′sian rou·lette′ *n* game with a revolver having only one bullet, in which each player in turn spins the cylinder, places the muzzle against his head, and pulls the trigger

rust /rust′/ [OE] *n* 1 red oxide of iron formed on iron and steel by exposure to air and moisture; 2 any formation appearing on other metals through corrosion; 3 any of a group of fungi growing parasitically on green plants and resembling a coating of rust; 4 reddish brown ‖ *vi* 5 to become rusty ‖ *vt* 6 to affect with rust

rus·tic /rust′ik/ [L *rusticus*] *adj* 1 rural; 2 artless, unsophisticated; 3 of rude make, unpolished ‖ *n* 4 unsophisticated countryman ‖ **rus·tic′i·ty** /-tis′-/ *n* ‖ **SYN** *adj* rough, coarse, boorish, countrified ‖ **ANT** *adj* polished, refined, urbane, cultured, polite

rus′ti·cate′ *vi* 1 to reside in or go to the country ‖ *vt* 2 to send to the country; 3 to make rustic ‖ **rus′ti·ca′tion** *n*

rus·tle /rus′əl/ [ME] *vi* 1 to make a soft crackling sound as that made by rubbing silk or leaves together; 2 *colloq* to move energetically ‖ *vt* 3 to cause to rustle; 4 *colloq* **a** to get or obtain by energetic action; **b** to steal (cattle); 5 **rustle up** *colloq* to procure ‖ *n* 6 sound of rustling

rus′tler *n* 1 one who rustles or hustles; 2 *colloq* cattle thief

rust′y *adj* (-i·er; -i·est) 1 covered with rust; 2 impaired by inactivity or neglect; 3 out of practice; 4 rust-colored

rut¹ /rut′/ [?] *n* 1 track worn in the ground by wheels; 2 fixed habit, dull routine ‖ *v* (rut·ted; rut·ting) *vt* 3 to make ruts in ‖ **rut′ted** *adj*

rut² [MF] *n* 1 periodic sexual exitement of various mammals, as cattle, deer, etc. ‖ *v* (rut·ted; rut·ting) *vi* 2 to be in a state of rut ‖ **rut′tish** *adj*

ru·ta·ba·ga /rōōt′əbāg′ə/ [Sw *dial. rotabagge*] *n* kind of turnip of a yellowish color (*Brassica napobrassica*)

Ruth /rōōth′/ *n Bib* 1 wife of Boaz, who left her own people out of devotion to her mother-in-law Naomi; 2 book of the Old Testament

ru·the·ni·um /rōōthēn′ē·əm/ [< *Ruthenia* region in the U.S.S.R.] *n* rare, silvery-white, brittle metallic element (**Ru**; at.no. 44; at.wt. 101.07), very infusible and resembling platinum in its resistance to acids

ruth·er·ford·i·um /ruth′ərfôrd′ē·əm/

[Ernest *Rutherford* (1871–1937) Eng physicist] *n* (tentative name of a) synthetic element (**Rf**; at. no. 104)

ruth·less /rŏŏth'-/ [< ME *ruthe* pity] *adj* cruel, pitiless, merciless

Rwan·da /rŏŏ·än'də/ *n* republic in central Africa between Tanganyika and the Congo (3,500,000; 10,150 sq.m.; cap. Kigali)

Rwy. Railway

Rx *n* [< L *recipe* take] prescription

Ry. Railway

rye /rī'/ [OE *ryge*] *n* 1 hardy cereal plant (*Secale cereale*) or its seed, used in making bread, in distilling whiskey, and as fodder; 2 rye bread; 3 rye whiskey

rye' bread' *n* bread made from rye flour

rye' whis'key *n* whiskey distilled from mash containing at least 51 per cent rye

S

S, s /es'/ *n* (S's or Ss; s's or ss) 19th letter of the English alphabet

S 1 *chem* sulfur; 2 19th in order or in a series; 3 something shaped like an S

s. 1 second(s); 2 shilling(s); 3 singular

S. 1 Saturday; 2 Sea; 3 September; 4 Socialist; 5 Sunday

S., s. 1 Saint; 2 school; 3 south; 4 southern

-s¹ /-z, -s, or -iz/ [OE *-as*] regular plural ending of nouns, as *bags*, *books*, *races*

-s² /-z, -s, or -iz/ [OE *-es, -eth*] ending of the 3rd person singular present indicative of verbs, as *prays*, *cuts*, *splices*

's¹ /-z, -s, or -iz/ [OE *-es*] possessive morpheme attached to most singular and plural nouns, as *men's*, *Jack's*, *judge's*

's² /-z, -s/ 1 contraction of *is*, as *he's coming*; 2 contraction of *has*, as *he's seen it*; 3 contraction of *us*, as *let's stay*

S.A. 1 South Africa; 2 South America

Sab·bath /sab'əth/ [Gk *sabbaton* < Heb *shābath* to rest] *n* 1 Saturday, the seventh day of the week, observed by the Jews and some Christian sects as a day of rest and worship; 2 the Christian Sunday, or first day of the week

Sab·bat·i·cal /səbat'ikəl/ *adj* 1 pert. to or like the Sabbath; 2 **sabbatical** bringing a period of rest || *n* 3 sabbatical year

sab·bat'i·cal year' *n* year's leave with pay granted for study, travel, and research, esp. to professors and usu. every seventh year

sa·ber /sāb'ər/ [F *sabre*] *n* heavy cavalry sword having a slightly curved blade

sa'ber rat'tling *n* threatening display of military power by a nation in order to intimidate other nations

sa·ble /sāb'əl/ [OF] *n* 1 weasellike carnivorous mammal, either *Mustela zibellina* in the Old World or *Mustela americana* in the New, valued for its dark brown fur; 2 its fur; 3 *heral* black; 4 **sables** *pl* mourning

clothes || *adj* 5 dark; black; mourning

sab·o·tage /sab'ətäzh'/ [F < *sabot* wooden shoe < practice of throwing wooden shoes in factory machinery to cause breakdowns during early labor disputes] *n* 1 deliberate destruction of or interference with production or with the machinery of plants or public facilities, as railroads, communications, and water supplies, as by workmen during labor disputes or enemy agents in time of war; 2 undermining of any venture || *vt* 3 to cause sabotage in

sab·o·teur /sab'ətur'/ [F] *n* one who engages in sabotage

sa·bra /säb'rə/ [ModHeb *sābrāh*] *n* native-born Israeli

SAC Strategic Air Command

sac /sak'/ [L *saccus* sack] *n* baglike part of a plant or animal, sometimes containing fluid

sac·cha·rin /sak'ərin/ [< Gk *sakcharon* sugar] *n* white crystalline powder —C₆H₄COSO₂NH— produced synthetically, 500 times sweeter than sugar, and used as a sugar substitute

sac·cha·rine /-rin, -rīn'/ *adj* 1 of, pert. to, or producing sugar; 2 cloyingly sweet, as a voice or manner

sac·er·do·tal /sas'ərdōt'əl/ [< L *sacerdos* (*-otis*) priest] *adj* priestly

sa·chem /sāch'əm/ [AmInd] *n* chief in some American Indian tribes

sa·chet /sashā'/ [F = small bag] *n* small bag or cushion filled with perfumed powder

sack¹ /sak'/ [OE *sacc* < L *saccus*] *n* 1 bag, esp. a large one of coarse cloth for holding grain, potatoes, etc.; 2 *baseball slang* base; 3 **hit the sack** *slang* to go to bed; 4 **get the sack** *slang* to be dismissed from a job; 5 **the sack** *slang* a bed; b dismissal from a job || *vt* 6 to put into sacks; 7 *slang* to dismiss from a job

sack² [MF < It *sacco* sack for holding loot] *n* 1 plundering of a captured place || *vt* 2 to plunder or pillage (a place captured in battle) || **sack'er** *n* || SYN *v* ravage, plunder, pillage, loot

sack³ [< F *sec* dry] *n* any of several dry

light wines formerly imported from Spain and the Canary Islands

sack'cloth' *n* 1 coarse cloth for making sacks; 2 coarse cloth formerly worn as a token of mourning or repentance

sack' coat' *n* man's jacket with a loose back that hangs straight

sack' dress' *n* loose dress that hangs straight from the shoulder to the seam

sac·ra·ment /sak'rəmənt/ [L *sacramentum* oath, consecration] *n* 1 *eccl* visible sign of spiritual grace, spec. a holy rite regarded as in itself a means of grace, including baptism and the Eucharist in Protestant churches, and also confirmation, penance, holy orders, matrimony, and extreme unction in the Catholic and Orthodox churches; 2 the consecrated elements of the Eucharist; 3 something regarded as sacred; 4 **the Sacrament** the Eucharist or Lord's Supper || **sac'ra·men'tal** /-ment'əl/ *adj*

Sac·ra·men·to /sak'rəment'ō/ *n* capital of California (200,000)

sa·cred /sāk'rid/ [*pp* of *obs sacre* < L *sacrare* to consecrate] *adj* 1 set apart or dedicated to holy or religious uses; consecrated; 2 pert. to religion; not secular; 3 not to be profaned; inviolable || SYN hallowed, consecrated, inviolable (see *holy*)

sa'cred cow' *n* someone or something held in such popular esteem as to be exempt from close examination or criticism

sac·ri·fice /sak'rifīs/ [OF < L *sacrificium*] *n* 1 act of presenting to God or to a deity some offering, as a slaughtered animal or incense, in worship or expiation; 2 that which is so consecrated and offered; 3 giving up something cherished or precious for the sake of someone or something having a higher claim to one's loyalty; 4 thing thus given up; 5 *baseball* sacrifice hit; 6 *com* steep price reduction || *vt* 7 to offer as a sacrifice; 8 to sell or dispose of at a loss || *vi* 9 to offer up a sacrifice; 10 *baseball* to make a sacrifice hit || **sac'ri·fi'cial** /-fish'əl/ *adj*

sac'ri·fice fly' *n baseball* fly that enables a runner on third to score after it is caught

sac'ri·fice hit' *n baseball* short hit or bunt on which the batter is put out but which permits a runner to advance

sac·ri·lege /sak'rilij/ [OF < L *sacrilegium*] *n* desecration or profanation of anything held sacred || **sac'ri·le'gious** /-lij'əs, -lēj'-/ *adj*

sac·ris·tan /sak'ristən/ [LL *sacristanus*] *n* one who has the care of church vessels, vestments, etc.

sac·ris·ty /sak'ristē/ [ML *sacristia*] *n* (-ties) apartment in a church where the sacred vessels, vestments, robes, etc., are kept

sac·ro·il·i·ac /sak'rō·il'ē·ak'/ [< *sacrum* + L *ilia* intestines] *n* joint where the sacrum and pelvic bone meet

sac·ro·sanct /sak'rōsaŋkt'/ [L *sacrosanctus*] *adj* most sacred; inviolable

sa·crum /sāk'rəm, sak'-/ [L (os) *sacrum* sacred (bone) from use in sacrifice] *n* (-cra/-krə/) composite triangular bony structure forming the back of the pelvis, made of five vertebrae joined together || **sa'cral** *adj*

sad /sad/ [OE *sæd*] *adj* (**sad·der; sad·dest**) 1 full of grief; downcast; mournful; sorrowful; 2 causing sorrow or mournfulness; distressing; 3 *colloq* bad; sorry || **sad'ly** *adv* || **sad'ness** *n* || SYN unhappy, downcast, melancholy, mournful, unfortunate || ANT gay, merry, cheerful, glad, jocose

sad'den *vt* 1 to make sad || *vi* 2 to become sad

sad·dle /sad'əl/ [OE *sadol*] *n* 1 padded leather seat on an animal, bicycle, etc.; 2 cut of meat consisting of the two loins; 3 **in the saddle** in command or in authority || *vt* 4 to put a saddle on; 5 to burden or encumber

sad'dle·bag' *n* one of a pair of bags attached to a saddle

sad'dle·bow' /-bō'/ *n* arched front part of a saddle

sad'dle horse' *n* horse specially trained to carry a rider

sad'dle shoe' *n* flat-heeled shoe with a band of contrasting-colored leather across the instep

sad'dle soap' *n* mild soap made with added neat's-foot oil, used for cleaning and preserving leather

Sad·du·cee /saj'əsē'/ [Gk *Saddoukaios* < Heb] *n* one of an ancient aristocratic Jewish sect obeying only the Mosaic law; opposed to the Pharisees in politics and in certain religious opinions || **Sad'du·ce'an** *adj*

sad·ism /sad'izəm, sād'-/ [< Marquis de *Sade* (1740–1814) F writer of stories featuring perverted sexual practices] *n* 1 sexual gratification from inflicting pain on others; 2 any enjoyment gained from mistreating others || **sad'ist** *n* || **sa·dis'tic** *adj*

sad' sack' *n colloq* well-meaning but pathetically inept person

S.A.E. Society of Automotive Engineers

sa·fa·ri /səfär'ē/ [Swahili < Ar = pert. to a journey] *n* expedition or journey, esp. for hunting big game

safe /sāf/ [OF *sauf* < L *salvus* uninjured] *adj* 1 free from danger, injury, or harm; 2 out of danger; unharmed; 3 in secure custody, as *safe in jail*; 4 involving no risk, as *a safe dose*; 5 reliable, trustworthy; 6 cautious, prudent; 7 *baseball* reaching base without being put or forced out || n 8 iron or steel chest for keeping money or valuables || **safe′ly** adv || **safe′ness** n

safe′-con′duct n 1 guarantee of safe passage, esp. in war time; 2 document authorizing this; 3 act of conducting safely

safe′-crack′er n burglar who specializes in breaking safes open

safe′-de-pos′it box′ n box in a bank vault that may be rented by individuals to hold their valuables

safe′guard′ n 1 something that guards or protects; 2 defense, precaution || vt 3 to protect, guard

safe′keep′ing n 1 keeping or guarding in safety; 2 protection, care

safe′ty n (-ties) 1 state of being safe; 2 device for preventing damage to machinery or injury to workers; 3 device which, when set, prevents the accidental firing of a gun; 4 football play in which the player with the ball is tackled and downs the ball in his own end zone; 5 baseball base hit

safe′ty glass′ n shatterproof glass

safe′ty lamp′ n miner's lamp in which the flame is prevented from igniting inflammable gases by being enclosed in wire gauze

safe′ty match′ n match that will not ignite unless struck on a prepared surface

safe′ty pin′ n pin bent back on itself with the point locked inside a sheath

safe′ty ra′zor n razor with a replaceable blade held inside a guard with only the edge exposed

safe′ty valve′ n 1 valve, as on a boiler, which automatically releases steam if the pressure exceeds a predetermined level; 2 means of relief from worry or strong feeling

saf′flow′er /saf′-/ [D saffloer] n Asiatic plant (Carthamus tinctorius) resembling the thistle and bearing yellowish-red flowers

saf′flow·er oil′ n oil extracted from safflower seeds, used in cookery, in salads, and as a paint vehicle

saf·fron /saf′rən/ [MF safran < Ar za′farān] n 1 a crocus (Crocus sativus) bearing purple flowers; 2 one of the dried orange-colored stigmas of this plant, which yield a deep-yellow dye and are used in medicine and in cookery; 3 deep-yellow or orange color

S. Afr. South Africa(n)

sag /sag/ [ME saggen] v (sagged; sag-ging) vi 1 to sink or droop in the middle from pressure or weight; 2 to lean to one side, as a door; 3 to yield, weaken; 4 to drop in price || n 5 act, fact, or instance of sagging; 6 amount of sagging

sa-ga /säg′ə/ [Icel] n 1 medieval Icelandic narrative relating heroic legends and historical traditions, often

centering around one family; 2 any long narrative of heroic deeds

sa-ga-cious /səgāsh′əs/ [< L sagax (-acis)] adj wise, shrewd; discerning || SYN (see wise, politic)

sa-gac′i-ty /-gas′-/ n keen practical judgment; shrewd mental penetration || SYN penetration, judiciousness, keenness, acumen, perspicacity, insight, acuteness, astuteness, shrewdness || DISCR These words name varying degrees of the power of mental perception. Penetration is extraordinary discernment, which enters at lightning speed into the essence of a matter, uncovering that which was concealed, observing pretexts in their true colors, unshrouding artifice. Acuteness and acumen name a still higher degree of intellectual capacity; acuteness characterizes a more general capability than penetration; acumen adds comprehensiveness and judicious discrimination to acuteness. A man of penetration sees through problems or difficulties with a glance; acuteness will enable him in addition to observe the subtleties of the situation; acumen will enable him to perceive its every angle, and to select those aspects which are most important. Perspicacity, like penetration, names that power of the mind which gets at the substance of things. Sagacity unites penetrative keenness with judicious foresight, to the end that the one possessing sagacity seems sometimes uncannily prescient. Sagacity exercises itself usually in the ordinary affairs of everyday life; it is a sensible sort of judgment, below the level of wisdom, but above that of shrewdness. Shrewdness is a sharply discriminating aptitude for practical affairs—so sharp, indeed, that it leans toward the crafty; the word connotes that kind of cleverness that can pick and keep a bargain. If we are beaten by sagacity, we are inclined to admire the technique of our defeat; if we are beaten by shrewdness, we resent the method. Astuteness is like perspicacity in that it is sharp, like sagacity in that it is foreseeing and farseeing; it uses its qualities often to the end of artfulness or craftiness, and sometimes bears the unfavorable connotation of shrewdness. Insight is discernment plus that intuition which plumbs character at a glance

sage¹ /sāj/ [F] adj 1 wise, judicious || n 2 profoundly wise man || **sage′ly** adv || SYN adj wise, prudent, profound, learned, serious

sage² [MF sauge < L salvia] n 1 any of several plants (genus Salvia) of the mint family, esp. S. officinalis, the spicy leaves of which are used in cookery; 2 sagebrush

sage'brush' *n* any of various low shrubs (genus *Artemisia*) of the composite family, grayish-green in color, found on the W plains of the U.S.

Sag·it·ta·ri·us /saj'iter'ē·əs/ [L = archer] *n* 1 a southern zodiacal constellation, the Archer; 2 ninth sign of the zodiac

Sa·har·a /səher'ə/ *n* desert in N Africa; largest desert in the world

sa·hib /sä'ib/ [Urdu < Ar *çāhib* friend] *n* sir, master; title formerly applied to Europeans in colonial India

said /sed/ 1 *pt & pp* of **say** ‖ *adj* 2 aforesaid

Sai·gon /sīgon'/ *n* city in Vietnam, renamed *Ho Chi Minh* (3,806,000)

sail /sāl'/ [OE *segl*] *n* 1 sheet of canvas or other fabric which is extended on masts and spars to catch enough wind to drive a vessel forward; 2 sails collectively; 3 anything suggestive of a sail; 4 voyage or trip in a vessel, esp. a sailing ship; 5 **set sail** to begin a sea voyage; 6 **under sail** sailing ‖ *vi* 7 to travel on a ship; 8 to move over the water, as a ship; 9 to begin a voyage by water; 10 to glide along like a boat; float smoothly along; 11 to sail a boat; 12 **sail into**, a to begin vigorously; b to attack with fury; c to assault verbally ‖ *vt* 13 to pass over (a body of water) in a ship; 14 to navigate (a vessel)

sail'boat' *n* boat propelled by sails

sail'fish' *n* any of a genus (*Istiophorus*) of large fishes with a swordlike upper jaw and a large saillike dorsal fin

sail'or /-ər/ *n* 1 one whose occupation is sailing; 2 seaman below the rank of officer; 3 straw hat with a flat brim and low flat crown

sail'plane' *n* light glider

saint /sānt'/ [OF < L *sanctus* sacred] *n* 1 person of exceptional holiness, recognized by most Christian churches as having attained a special position in heaven; 2 person of exceptional patience and charity; 3 person of holy life; 4 *R C Ch* exceptionally godly person who, after death, has been canonized and is officially recognized as being capable of interceding with God for sinners ‖ **saint'hood** *n* ‖ **saint'ly** *adj* (-li·er; -li·est) ‖ **saint'li·ness** *n*

Saint' An'drew's Cross' *n* X-shaped cross

Saint' Ber·nard' /bərnärd'/ [< hospice of St. Bernard in the Swiss Alps] *n* one of a large breed of dogs, formerly bred for the purpose of rescuing snow-bound travelers

saint'ed *adj* 1 canonized; 2 saintly; 3 blessed in heaven; dead

Saint' Pat'rick's Day' /pat'riks/ *n* March 17, observed by the Irish in honor of the patron saint of Ireland

Saint' Val'en·tine's Day' *n* February 14, observed in honor of an early Christian martyr by exchanging valentines

saith /seth'/ *archaic 3rd pers sg pres ind* of say

sake¹ /sāk'/ [OE *sacu* affair] *n* **for the sake of** 1 for the interest or benefit of; 2 for the purpose of

sa·ke² or **sa·ki** /säk'ē/ [Jap] *n* Japanese fermented liquor made from rice

sal /sal'/ [L] *n pharm* salt

sa·laam /səläm'/ [Ar = peace] *n* 1 Oriental greeting; 2 obeisance with a low bow and the right palm on the forehead ‖ *vi* 3 to make a salaam ‖ *vt* 4 to greet with a salaam

sal·a·ble or **sale·a·ble** /säl'əbəl/ *adj* 1 capable of being sold; 2 easily sold; marketable

sa·la·cious /səlāsh'əs/ [< L *salax* (-*acis*)] *adj* 1 lustful, lecherous; 2 lewd, obscene

sal·ad /sal'əd/ [MF *salade* < VL *salata* salted] *n* cold dish of raw foods, as vegetables or fruits, with or without cooked foods, served with a dressing as a side or main dish

sal'ad days' *npl* days of one's youth and innocence

sal'ad dress'ing *n* sauce for salads, usu. based on oil and vinegar or mayonnaise

Sal·a·din /sal'ədin/ *n* (1137–93) a leader of the Saracens against the Crusaders, and sultan of Egypt 1175–93

sal·a·man·der /sal'əman'dər/ [Gk *salamandra*] *n* 1 any of tailed, lizardlike amphibians (order Urodeles) with moist scaleless skin; 2 mythical reptile able to live in fire; 3 small portable stove

sa·la·mi /səläm'ē/ [It] *n* spiced sausage, often flavored with garlic

Sal·a·mis /sal'əmis/ *n* island SE of Greece, near which the Greeks defeated the Persians in a naval battle 480 B.C.

sal·a·ry /sal'ərē/ [AF *salarie* < L *salarium* soldier's salt money] *n* (-ries) regular periodic payment for services rendered ‖ **sal'a·ried** *adj* ‖ SYN wage, hire, pay, compensation, remuneration, stipend, recompense, fee ‖ DISCR *Salary* names the fixed periodical payment made to those who do professional or mental work; *wage* is applied to payment made for manual or mechanical work. A *wage* is also fixed and periodical, but is considered less permanent and stable, and is paid usually at shorter intervals, than *salary*. *Pay* is used frequently in the sense of *wages*, sometimes in the sense of *salary; pay* suggests definitely the actual money given for goods bought, services rendered, or debts discharged. *Wage* and *pay* are supposed to wipe out debt or obligation. *Compensation* is a general term which means that which is given in return; it may mean plain *pay;* or it may name amends, restoration for loss, indemnification for injury, etc. Hence, it may include *remuneration* and *recompense* as well as *pay, hire,* and *salary.* The basic idea of *remuneration* is reward; it is, however, often loftily used for *salary* or other pecuniary return, such as royalties. *Remuneration* falls short of the general sense of *recompense; recompense* lacks the commercial or pecuniary tone, and enters rather the field of satisfaction, requital, atonement, or retribution given. The *compensation* given by the government to the widows of soldiers who died in action can be termed a *remuneration;* there can be no fitting *recompense* for a life lost. *Fee* names the *remuneration* which a professional man, such as a lawyer, asks for his services; it is also applied to the money a public officer, as a notary, gets for performing his function; sometimes it is a gratuity, as the *fee* given to a clergyman at a marriage. *Stipend* formerly applied to the regular *salary* of a clergyman; it now applies to the fixed payment for a university scholarship or fellowship

sale /sāl′/ [OE *sala*] *n* 1 act of selling; 2 chance to sell; market; 3 disposal of goods at a low price; 4 transfer of property in exchange for money

sales′ *adj* of or pert. to selling, as *sales promotion*

sales- *comb form* concerned with selling, as *salesman, salesroom*

sales′man·ship′ *n* skill in or the technique of selling

sales′ re·sist′ance *n* resistance to sales talk

sales′ talk′ *n* 1 argument aimed at a prospective buyer to induce him to buy something offered; 2 any argument intended to persuade someone

sales′ tax′ *n* tax on the retail price of goods, and often services, paid by the purchaser

Sal′ic law′ /sal′ik/ [< LL *Salii* tribe of Franks] *n* law excluding women from succession to the throne

sal′i·cyl′ic ac′id /sal′isil′ik/ [< F *salicine* < L *salix* (*-icis*) willow] *n* white crystalline powder —C₆H₄(OH)(COOH)— used in aspirin and as a food preservative, and in the treatment of rheumatism

sa·li·ent /sāl′ē·ənt, -yənt/ [L *saliens* (*-entis*) leaping] *adj* 1 conspicuous, outstanding; 2 projecting outward || *n* 3 salient angle or part || **sa′li·ence** *n*

sa·line /sā′līn, -lēn/ [< L *sal* salt] *adj* consisting of, resembling, or con-

taining salt; salty || **sa·lin′i·ty** /səlin′-/ *n*

Salis·bur·y /sôlz′ber′ē, -bərē/ *n* 1 city in county of Wiltshire, in S England, north of which Stonehenge is located (35,000); 2 capital of Zimbabwe-Rhodesia (625,000)

Salis′bur·y steak′ [J. H. *Salisbury,* 19th-cent. Eng dietician] *n* hamburger patty of ground beef, broiled or fried and often served with a sauce

sa·li·va /səlīv′ə/ [L] *n* watery fluid secreted by glands in and behind the mouth and discharged into the mouth to aid in tasting, chewing, and swallowing, and in the digestion of starchy foods || **sal.i.var.y** /sal′-iver′ē/ *adj*

sal·i·vate /sal′ivāt′/ [L *salivare* ⟨*-atus*⟩] *vi* to secrete saliva || **sal′i·va′tion** *n*

Salk′ vac·cine′ /sô(l)k′/ [Jonas *Salk* (1914–) U.S. bacteriologist] *n* oral vaccine producing immunity against poliomyelitis, prepared from three types of viruses

sal·low /sal′ō/ [OE *salo*] *adj* pale, sickly yellow (complexion)

sal·ly /sal′ē/ [MF *saillie*] *n* (-lies) 1 sortie of troops from a fortified place against a besieging enemy; 2 any rushing forth; 3 sudden outburst of wit or fancy || *v* (-lied) *vi* 4 to rush out suddenly, as besieged troops; 5 to set out, as on a journey; 6 to set out energetically

sal·ma·gun·di /sal′məgun′dē/ [F *salmigondis*] *n* 1 dish of chopped meats and other ingredients, spiced and seasoned; 2 miscellaneous collection, medley

salm·on /sam′ən/ [OF *saumon* < L *salmo* (*-onis*)] *n* 1 silver-scaled sea or fresh-water fish (*Salmo salar*) with pink flesh, which ascends rivers from the North Atlantic to spawn; 2 any of several related fishes of the genus *Oncorhynchus* of the North Pacific; 3 yellowish pink

sal·mo·nel·la /sal′mənel′ə/ [Daniel E. *Salmon* (1850–1914) U.S. veterinarian] *n* any of several rod-shaped bacteria (genus *Salmonella*) that cause food poisoning in man and other warm-blooded animals

salm′on trout′ *n* 1 European sea trout (*Salmo trutta*); 2 any of various large salmonlike fishes of North America

Sa·lo·me /səlōm′ē/ *n* Bib the daughter of Herodias, who received from Herod, as a reward for her dancing, the head of John the Baptist (Matt. 14:8)

sa·lon /səlon′/ [F < It *salone* large hall] *n* 1 large room for the reception of guests; 2 periodic gathering of persons of note in artistic, literary, and political circles

sa·loon /səlōōn′/ [earlier var of *salon*]

n **1** bar, tavern; **2** public room for special uses, as on a ship

salt /sôlt'/ [OE *sealt*] *n* **1** sodium chloride —NaCl— a white crystalline substance found in sea water, subterranean beds, etc., and used for seasoning foods, preserving meats, and in industry; **2** anything which gives flavor or pungency; **3** piquant wit; **4** *chem* compound formed by the replacement of the hydrogen of an acid by a metal or a radical acting like a metal; **5** *colloq* sailor; **6 salts** *pl* saline cathartic; **7 with a grain of salt** with reserve or allowance, as for exaggeration; **8 worth one's salt** worth what one is paid || *vt* **9** to season, preserve, or cure with salt; **10** to add extraneous rich ore deceptively to (a mine); **11 salt away** *colloq* to put away for future use, as money

salt'cel'lar [*salt* + OF *saliere* saltcellar] *n* salt shaker

Salt' Lake' Cit'y *n* capital of Utah (190,000)

salt' lick' *n* place to which animals come to lick a natural salt deposit

salt' marsh' *n* marsh bathed by tidal sea water

salt' of the earth' *n* uncommonly good and noble person or group

salt'pe'ter [ME *sal petre* < L *sal petrae* rock salt] *n* **1** naturally occurring potassium nitrate —KNO₃—; **2** sodium nitrate

salt' pork' *n* pork cured with salt

salt' shak'er *n* container for salt with a perforated top

salt' wa'ter *n* very salty water, esp. sea water || **salt'-wa'ter** *adj*

salt'y *adj* (**-i-er; -i-est**) **1** pert. to, tasting of, or containing salt; **2** of the sea or sailing; **3** piquant, witty, racy

sa·lu·bri·ous /səlōōb'rē-əs/ [< L *salubris*] *adj* healthful || **sa·lu'bri·ty** *n* || SYN favorable, wholesome (see *healthy*)

sal·u·tar·y /sal'yətər'ē/ [L *salutaris*] *adj* **1** healthful; **2** beneficial || SYN salubrious, beneficial, wholesome (see *healthy*)

sal·u·ta·tion /sal'yətāsh'ən/ [see **salute**] *n* **1** greeting; **2** a gesture of greeting; **b** written or uttered word of greeting; **3** prefatory greeting in a letter, as *Dear Sir*

sa·lu·ta·to·ri·an /səlōōt'ətôr'ē-ən, -tōr'-/ *n* student who delivers the opening oration at a commencement, usu. ranking second in the class

sa·lute /səlōōt'/ [L *salutare* to greet] *n* **1** greeting; **2** act, word, or gesture of respect or good will; **3** *mil* a prescribed gesture or position of body or arms as a sign of respect, esp. the raising of the hand to the head; **b** discharge of cannon, dipping of a flag, or the like, as a sign of greeting or respect || *vt* **4** to greet with a gesture or expression of respect or

good will; **5** to give a military salute to || *vi* **6** *mil* to execute a salute

Sal·va·dor /sal'vədôr'/ *n* see **El Salvador** || **Sal'va·dor'an** *adj* & *n*

sal·vage /sal'vij/ [MF = saving] *n* **1** act of saving property from damage or destruction, as a ship or its cargo from the dangers of the sea; **2** payment to those who help save property under such circumstances; **3** property so saved; **4** price received for goods recovered from a fire || *vt* **5** to save from shipwreck, fire, or other danger

sal·va·tion /salvāsh'ən/ [L *salvatio* (*-onis*)] *n* **1** act of saving or state of being saved from loss or calamity; **2** that which saves; **3** *theol* saving of the soul from sin and death; redemption

Sal·va'tion Ar'my *n* religious body organized on military lines for the purpose of evangelism and the relief of poverty

salve /sav', säv'/ [OE *sealf*] *n* **1** ointment; **2** anything that soothes or pacifies || *vt* **3** to apply a salve to; **4** to soothe, palliate

sal·ver /sal'vər/ [Sp *salva* tasting of food for poison] *n* tray for food or beverages

sal·vo /sal'vō/ [It *salva* < L *salve* hail] *n* (**-vos** or **-voes**) **1** simultaneous discharge of a number of guns, esp. in salute; **2** any welcoming round, as of applause or cheers

SAM surface-to-air missile

S.Am. South America

sa·mar·i·um /səmer'ē-əm/ [< Col. *Samarski* 19th-cent. Russ inspector of mines] *n* rare-earth metallic element (Sm; at.no. 62; at.wt. 150.35)

sam·ba /säm'bə, sam'-/ [Port < Afr] *n* Brazilian ballroom dance or the music for it || also *vi*

same /sām'/ [ON *samr*] *adj* **1** identical; **2** alike in kind, quality, or degree; equal; **3** unchanged; **4** just mentioned || *pron* **5** identical person or thing; **6** person or thing previously mentioned || *adv* **7** in the identical manner; **8 all the same** or **just the same** nevertheless; in spite of everything || **same'ness** *n* || SYN *adj* equivalent, selfsame, alike, interchangeable, corresponding, identical, similar

S.Amer. South America

Sa·mo·a /səmō'ə/ *n* group of islands in the S Pacific, divided between American Samoa and Western Samoa || **Sa·mo'an** *adj* & *n*

sam·o·var /sam'əvär'/ [Russ] *n* metal urn with a spigot for heating water for tea

Sam·o·yed /sam'ə·yed'/ *n* **1** Uralic language spoken in NW Siberia and on NE coast of the Soviet Union in Europe; **2** medium-sized Russian dog used for herding reindeer and pulling sleds

sam·pan /sam′pan/ [Chin *san pan* three boards] *n* small boat of the Orient, usu. propelled by a single scull over the stern

sam·ple /samp′əl, sämp′-/ [MF *es-sample*] *n* 1 part of anything, or one of a number, taken to show the quality of the whole; specimen ‖ *vt* 2 to test, take a sample of

sam′pler *n* 1 piece of ornamental needlework made as an exhibition of skill; 2 collection of samples

Sam·son /sam′sən/ *n Bib* one of the judges of Israel, noted for his great strength (Judges 13–16)

Sam·u·el /sam′yōō-əl/ *n Bib* 1 Hebrew prophet, the last of the judges; 2 either of two books of the Old Testament, which give his history

sam·u·rai /sam′ŏŏrī′/ [Jap] *n* (-rai) member of the military class in feudal Japan

San An·to·ni·o /san′ antōn′ē-ō′/ *n* city in S Texas, site of the Alamo (654,-153)

san·a·to·ri·um /san′ətôr′ē-əm, -tōr′-/ [L = curative] *n* (-ums or -a /-ə/) 1 hospital for certain chronic diseases, as tuberculosis and nervous disorders; 2 sanitarium

San·cho Pan·za /san′chō pan′zə/ *n* the ignorant but shrewd and amusing squire of Don Quixote

sanc·ti·fy /saŋk′tifī/ [LL *sanctificare*] *v* (-fied) *vt* 1 to purify, make free from sin; 2 to set apart as holy; consecrate; 3 to make productive of spiritual blessing; 4 to lend sanctity to; justify ‖ **sanc′ti-fied′** *adj* ‖ **sanc′-ti-fi·ca′tion** *n*

sanc·ti·mo·ny /saŋk′timōn′ē/ [L *sanctimonia* holiness] *n* pretended devoutness, hypocritical show of piety ‖ **sanc′ti-mo′ni-ous** *adj*

sanc′tion /saŋk′shən/ [L *sanctio* (-onis)] *n* 1 authorization; 2 ratification; 3 *law* provision of a law for securing obedience by penalty or reward; 4 **sanctions** *pl* punitive measures by one or more nations against a nation that defies international law ‖ *vt* 5 to authorize; 6 to confirm; approve ‖ SYN *v* confirm, justify, authorize, ratify, approve, allow ‖ ANT *v* disapprove, disavow, deny, forbid

sanc′ti·ty /< L *sanctus* holy] *n* (-ties) 1 holiness; 2 sacredness; 3 sacred object

sanc·tu·ar·y /saŋk′chōō-er′ē/ [L *sanctuarium*] *n* (-ies) 1 consecrated or holy place; 2 the part of a church nearest the altar; 3 place of shelter, protection, or refuge; 4 immunity granted by such a place ‖ SYN refuge, asylum, immunity, shelter

sanc·tum /saŋk′təm/ [L = sacred] *n* (-tums or -ta /-tə/) 1 sacred place; 2 inviolably private room or study

sand /sand′/ [OE] *n* 1 mineral substance composed of small grains of rock, usu. quartz, found chiefly on beaches and in deserts; 2 **sands** *pl* a stretch of sand; b moments; time ‖ *vt* 3 to sprinkle with sand, as an icy street; 4 to fill up with sand; 5 to smooth or polish with sand or sandpaper

san·dal /san′dəl/ [F *sandale* < Gk *sandalion*] *n* 1 shoe consisting of a sole fastened to the foot by straps or thongs; 2 loose slipper or low shoe

san′dal·wood′ [< Gk *sandalon*] *n* 1 any of several tropical trees, esp. of the genus *Santalum;* 2 the close-grained fragrant wood of these trees

sand′bag *n* 1 bag filled with sand, used for ballast, in fortifications, etc. ‖ *vt* 2 to strike or stun with a sandbag; 3 *colloq* to coerce

sand′bar′ *n* bar of sand formed in a river or sea

sand′blast′ *n* sand driven by a blast of air or steam, used to clean, cut, polish, or engrave hard substances ‖ also *vt*

sand′box′ *n* 1 container for sand; 2 box of sand for children to play in

sand′er *n* machine for sanding or sandpapering

sand′fly′ *n* (-flies) any of several bloodsucking flying insects that infest beaches

sand′hog′ *n* man who works in digging tunnels under compression and, esp. under water

San Di·e·go /san′dē-āg′ō/ *n* seaport in S California; naval base (696,769)

sand′lot′ *adj* (sport, esp. baseball) played by boys on vacant city lots

sand′man′ /-man′/ *n* (-men /-men′/) nursery character supposed to make children sleepy by sprinkling sand in their eyes

sand′pa′per *n* 1 strong paper coated with a layer of sand or other abrasive, used for smoothing and polishing ‖ *vt* 2 to smooth or polish by rubbing with sandpaper

sand′pip′er *n* any of various small shore birds (family Scolopacidae) with long legs and bills

sand′ shark′ *n* any of several small sharks of the family Carchariidae, found in shallow waters of the Atlantic coast

sand′stone′ *n* rock composed chiefly of quartz sand hardened into a solid mass by a natural cement, as silica, iron oxide, or calcium carbonate

sand′storm′ *n* strong wind that raises and drives along great clouds of sand

sand′ trap′ *n golf* hazard consisting of a shallow sandy pit, usu. near a green

sand′wich /sand′wich, san′-/ [Earl of Sandwich (1718–92)] *n* 1 two or three slices of bread with a layer of meat, cheese, jelly, etc., between them; 2 anything resembling a sandwich ‖ *vt*

3 to insert or place between two other things

sand·wich board' *n* two connected sign-boards that hang in front of and be-hind a person and carry advertising

sand·wich man' *n* man carrying a sand-wich board

sand·y *adj* (-i·er; -i·est) **1** of, containing, or like sand; **2** of a yellowish-red color

sane /sān'/ [L *sanus* healthy] *adj* **1** mentally sound, rational; **2** showing sound judgment

San·for·ized /san'fərīzd'/ [trademark] *adj* noting a process of preshrinking of fabrics

San Fran·cis·co /san' fransis'kō/ *n* sea-port in central California (715,674) || **San' Fran·cis'can** *n*

sang /saŋ'/ *pt* of sing

sang-froid /sän frwä'/ [F = cold blood] *n* calm indifference; coolness, com-posure

san·gui·nar·y /saŋ'gwiner'ē/ [L *sangui-narius*] *adj* **1** accompanied by great bloodshed, as a battle; **2** bloodthirsty, cruel || SYN bloody, inhuman, savage || ANT kind, humane

san·guine /saŋ'gwin/ [L *sanguineus* bloody] *adj* **1** ruddy, as *a sanguine complexion*; **2** confident; optimistic, cheerful || SYN optimistic, buoyant, warm, ardent, hopeful, confident, cheerful || DISCR A *cheerful* person is contented of heart, unruffled of temper, equable in disposition; hence he is usually *hopeful* and generally *optimistic. Sanguine* connotes habit-ual hopefulness; *sanguine*, in an older meaning, carried the idea of full-bloodedness, abundant and active cir-culation, and ruddiness of complex-ion. Such a state of health was con-sidered as productive of optimism, since those who possessed it were usually *cheerful* and inclined to look on the bright side of things. An *ar-dent* temper is glowingly enthusiastic

san·i·tar·i·um /san'iter'ē·əm/ [< L *sanitas* health] *n* (-ums or -a -/-ə/) **1** health resort; **2** sanatorium *l*

san·i·tar·y /san'iter'ē/ *adj* **1** pert. to health; **2** hygienic; clean and germ-free

san'i·tar·y nap'kin *n* small pad worn to absorb the menstrual flow

san'i·ta'tion /san'ita'shən/ *n* practical application of sanitary measures for the preservation of health, applied esp. to sewage disposal

san'i·tize' *vt* to make sanitary

san·i·ty /san'itē/ [L *sanitas* health] *n* **1** state of being sane; **2** soundness of judgment

San Jo·se /san' hōzā'/ *n* city in W Cali-fornia (445,779)

San Jo·sé /sän' hōsā'/ *n* capital of Costa Rica (177,969)

San Juan /san' hwän'/ *n* capital of Puerto Rico (440,000)

sank /saŋk'/ *pt* of sink

San Ma·ri·no /san' mərēn'ō/ *n* small independent Italian-speaking repub-lic entirely inside E Italy (17,464; 23 sq.m.; cap. San Marino)

San Mar·tín, Jo·sé de /hōsā' dā sän-märtēn'/ *n* (1778–1850) Argentine general and statesman, a leader in the South American revolt against Spain

sans /sanz'/ [OF] *prep archaic & lit-erary* without

Sans., Sansk. Sanskrit

San·skrit /san'skrit/ [Skt *samskrta* perfected] *n* ancient sacred language of India, oldest known Indo-Euro-pean language || *also adj*

sans' ser'if *n* typeface that does not have serifs

San·ta Claus /sant'ə klôz'/ *also* San·ta [D *Sint Klaas* Saint Nicholas] *n* the jolly, chubby, white-bearded old man who brings gifts to children on Christmas Eve

San·ta Fe /sant'ə fā'/ *n* capital of New Mexico (40,000)

San·ti·a·go /sant'ē·äg'ō/ *n* capital of Chile (2,248,378)

San·to Do·min·go /sant'ō dōmiŋ'gō/ *n* capital of the Dominican Republic (560,636)

São Pau·lo /souɴ pou'lŏŏ/ *n* city in S Brazil; large industrial center (3,-350,000)

sap[1] /sap'/ [OE *sæp*] *n* **1** the circulat-ing fluid of a plant; **2** *slang* dupe, fool

sap[2] [OIt *zappa* hoe] *v* (**sapped; sap-ping**) *vt* **1** to undermine; **2** destroy in-sidiously; weaken

sa·pi·ent /sāp'ē·ənt/ [L *sapiens* (*-entis*) *adj* wise, sagacious || **sa'pi·ence** *n*

sap'ling *n* young tree

sa·pon·i·fy /səpon'ifī'/ [< L *sapo* (*-onis*) soap + *-ify*] *v* (**-fied**) *vt* **1** to convert (a fat) into soap || **2** *vi* to become soap || **sa·pon'i·fi·ca'tion** *n*

sap'per /< *sap[2]*] *n* Brit mil engineer

sap·phire /saf'īər/ [Gk *sappheiros*] *n* **1** hard transparent precious stone of deep-blue color; **2** the deep-blue color of this gem

sap·py *adj* (**-pi·er; -pi·est**) *slang* foolish; silly || **sap'pi·ness** *n*

sap·ro·phyte /sap'rəfīt'/ [< Gk *sapros* rotten + *phyton* plant] *n* any organ-ism that feeds on dead organic mat-ter, as some bacteria and fungi || **sap'ro·phyt'ic** /-fit'ik/ *adj*

sap'suck'er *n* either of two American woodpeckers (genus *Sphyrapicus*) which drill holes in trees to drink the sap

sar·a·band /sar'əband'/ [Sp *zara-banda*] *n* slow and stately Spanish dance or the music for it

Sar·a·cen /sar'əsən/ [LGk *Sarakenos*] *n* Muslim or Arab, esp. one of those who fought the Crusaders during the Middle Ages

Sar·ah /ser'ə/ *n Bib* wife of Abraham

and mother of Isaac (Gen. 17:15, 19)

Sa·ran /sə́ran/ [trademark] *n* thermoplastic material used as a fiber and for transparent packaging

sar·casm /sär′kazəm/ [Gk *sarkasmos*] *n* **1** cutting irony or scornful derision; **2** bitter cutting remark or taunt || SYN (see *ridicule*)

sar·cas·tic /särkast′ik/ *adj* **1** pert. to or characterized by sarcasm; **2** using or given to the use of sarcasm || **sar·cas′ti·cal·ly** *adv*

sar·co·ma /särkōm′ə/ [Gk = tumor] *n* (-mas or -ma·ta /-mətə/) malignant tumor originating in connective tissue

sar·coph·a·gus /särkof′əgəs/ [Gk *sarkophagos* flesh-eating, because limestone was thought to consume the flesh of corpses] *n* (-gi /-jī′/ or -gus·es) stone coffin, usu. elaborately carved, made for the remains of a distinguished personage

sar·dine /särdēn′/ [L *sardina*] *n* **1** small European fish (*Sardina pilchardus*) of the herring family, edible when preserved in oil; **2** one of several related fishes

Sar·din·i·a /särdin′ē·ə/ *n* large Italian island in the Mediterranean W of Italy || **Sar·din′i·an** *adj & n*

sar·don·ic /särdon′ik/ [< Gk *sardonios* Sardinian] *adj* derisive; sneering; disdainful || **sar·don′i·cal·ly** *adv*

sa·ri /sär′ē/ [Hindi] *n* Hindu woman's garment consisting of a long cloth wrapped around the body

sa·rong /sərôŋ′, -roŋ′/ [Malay] *n* garment worn by men and women in the Malay Archipelago and some South Sea Islands, resembling a loose skirt

sar·sa·pa·ril·la /särs′(ə)peril′ə, sas′pə-/ [Sp *zarzaparilla*] *n* **1** any of various climbing or trailing tropical American plants (genus *Smilax*); **2** the dried roots, used medicinally; **3** soft drink flavored with an extract from the dried roots

sar·to·ri·al /särtôr′ē·əl, -tōr′-/ [< L *sartor* tailor] *adj* **1** pert. to a tailor or his work; **2** pert. to men's clothing

Sar·tre, Jean Paul /zhän′ pôl′ särt′(rə)/ *n* (1905–) French novelist and essayist

sash¹ /sash′/ [Ar *shāsh* muslin] *n* band, ribbon, or scarf worn around the waist or over the shoulder

sash² [< *chassis*] *n* window frame or part of a door made to hold panes of glass

sa·shay /sashā′/ [F *chassé* dance step] *vi* **1** to move boldly and with self-assurance; **2** to take a gliding step in dancing

Sask. Saskatchewan

Sas·katch·e·wan /saskach′əwon′/ *n* province in W Canada (956,000; 251,700 sq.m.; cap. Regina)

sass /sas′/ [< *sassy*] colloq *n* **1** impudent back talk || *vt* **2** to answer impudently

sas·sa·fras /sas′əfras′/ [Sp *sasafrás*] *n* **1** small American tree (*Sassafras albidum*) of the laurel family; **2** the aromatic bark of its roots, used medicinally and for flavoring

sas·sy /sas′ē/ [*dial.* var of *saucy*] *adj* (-si·er; -si·est) saucy; impudent

sat /sat′/ *pt & pp* of **sit**

Sat. **1** Saturday; **2** Saturn

Sa·tan /sāt′ən/ [Heb = adversary] *n* the Devil

sa·tan·ic /sətan′ik/ *adj* **1** pert. to or like Satan; **2** devilish; infernal; malevolent

satch·el /sach′əl/ [OF *sachel*] *n* small bag, as for carrying personal belongings

sate /sāt′/ [?] *vt* **1** to fully satisfy (an appetite or desire); **2** to glut, surfeit || SYN glut, surfeit, cloy, satiate (see *satisfy*)

sa·teen /satēn′/ [< *satin*] *n* woolen or cotton fabric made to simulate satin

sat·el·lite /sat′əlīt′/ [L *satelles* (-litis*) attendant] *n* **1** body in orbit around a larger one, as a moon around a planet; **2** man-made object launched to orbit the earth, another planet, or the sun; **3** earth-orbiting satellite designed to relay radio and television signals; **4** someone or something attendant upon or under the influence of someone or something more powerful, as a follower of an important man or a country controlled by a larger one || also *adj*

sa·ti·ate /sāsh′ē·āt′/ [L *satiare* (-atus*) to satisfy] *vt* **1** to satisfy fully; **2** to surfeit; gratify beyond wish or appetite || **sa·ti·a′tion** *n* || **sa′ti·a·ble** *adj* || SYN sate, glut, surfeit, cloy, weary (see *satisfy*)

sa·ti·e·ty /səti′ətē/ [L *satietas*] *n* state of being satiated

sat·in /sat′ən/ [MF] *n* closely woven silk, nylon, or rayon fabric having a glossy face || **sat′in·y** *adj*

sat·ire /sa′tīər/ [L *satira*] *n* **1** literary composition in which vice and folly are held up to ridicule; **2** sarcasm or ridicule used to expose vice and folly || **sa·tir·ic** (-i·cal) /sətir′ik(əl)/ *adj* || **sat·i·rist** /sat′ərist/ *n* || **sat·i·rize** /sat′ərīz′/ *vt* || SYN irony, mockery, sarcasm (see *ridicule*)

sat·is·fac·tion /sat′isfak′shən/ [see *satisfy*] *n* **1** act of satisfying or state of being satisfied; **2** that which satisfies; **3** opportunity to avenge a wrong or insult, as by a duel; **4** payment or discharge, as of an obligation || SYN gratification, indemnification, reparation, enjoyment, comfort, complacency (see *happiness*, *redress*)

sat·is·fac·to·ry /-tərē/ *adj* **1** giving satisfaction; satisfying; **2** sufficient to meet demands, desires, or requirements || **sat·is·fac′to·ri·ly** *adv*

sat·is·fy /OF *satisfier* < L *satisfacere* to do enough/ vt 1 to make content; give enough to; fulfill the wishes of; gratify; 2 to free from doubt, convince; 3 to pay in full, discharge, as a debt; 4 to expiate, make atonement for; 5 to meet the conditions or requirements of ‖ vi 6 to give satisfaction ‖ SYN sate, satiate, cloy, surfeit, suffice, glut ‖ DISCR That *satisfies* which fills a demand, pleases a taste, fulfills a desire, or provides contentment. It is not too much, but there is no feeling that it is inadequate or scanty. That *suffices* which is merely enough, barely adequate. To *satiate* is to fill a demand to the full, or gratify desire completely; to *sate* is even more emphatic; one whose greed for power is *satiated*, or whose appetite for vengeance or amusement is *sated*, is wearied of what he previously longed for. To *cloy* is to sicken with sameness, particularly with overabundance, sweetness, or luxury; to *surfeit* is to get too much, or cause to take too much, particularly of food. Both *cloy* and *surfeit* connote revulsion. To *glut* is to fill disgustingly full; *glut* expresses the extreme of satisfaction, or repletion; it sickens the offender. An ordinary meal *satisfies* a normal person; much less than an ordinary meal would *suffice* one lost in the mountains. Children released from restrictions will *cloy* themselves with sweets; naturally greedy persons will *glut* themselves with food. One sensible and sensitive will never *surfeit* himself with anything ‖ ANT check, stint, deny, restrain, starve

sa·trap /sā′trap, sa′-/ [Gk *satrapes* < OPers] n 1 governor of a province in ancient Persia; 2 any despotic subordinate ruler ‖ sa′trap·y n (-ies)

sat·u·rate /sach′ərāt′/ [L *saturare* (-*atus*)] vt 1 to cause to be thoroughly impregnated, imbued, or soaked to the limit of capacity for absorbing; 2 to cover completely, as a target with bombs or an area with police ‖ sat′u·ra′tion n

Sat·ur·day /sat′ərdē, -dā′/ [OE *Saternesdæg* Saturn's day] n seventh and last day of the week, following Friday ‖ Sat′ur·days adv

Sat·urn /sat′ərn/ n 1 Roman god of seedtime and harvest; 2 second largest planet of the solar system, characterized by flat concentric rings that surround it and are visible when viewed through a telescope

Sat·ur·na·li·a /sat′ərnāl′ē·ə, -yə/ [< *Saturn*] nsg & npl 1 in ancient Rome, annual feast of Saturn, characterized by unrestrained revelry; 2 **saturnalia** sg any occasion of riotous and dissolute merrymaking ‖ Sat′ur·na′li·an adj

sat′ur·nine′ /-nīn′/ [< supposed influence of the planet Saturn] adj gloomy; grave; phlegmatic

sat·yr /sat′ər, sāt′-/ [Gk *satyros*] n 1 class. myth. lecherous woodland deity, half man half goat; 2 lecher ‖ sa·tyr·ic /-i·cal/ /sətir′ik(ə)l/ adj

sat′y·ri′a·sis /-rī′əsis/ n uncontrollable sexual desire in men

sauce /sôs′/ [MF < LL *salsa*] n 1 liquid dressing or seasoning for food; 2 anything that adds zest or piquancy; 3 stewed fruit, as *apple sauce*; 4 slang liquor

sauce′pan′ n small pot with a long handle for stewing or boiling

sau′cer [OF *saussier*] n small shallow dish to hold a cup

sau′cy adj (-ci·er; -ci·est) 1 pert, bold; 2 insolent, impudent; 3 gay, sprightly ‖ sau′ci·ly adv ‖ sau′ci·ness n ‖ SYN impertinent, pert, insolent, forward, uncivil

Sa·u·di A·ra·bi·a /sä-ōōd′ē, soud′ē, sôd′ē/ n Arabic-speaking kingdom comprising most of Arabia (6,870,-000; ab. 830,000 sq.m.; cap. Riyadh) ‖Sa·u′di A·ra′bi·an adj & n

sau·er·bra·ten /sou′ərbrät′ən/ [G] n pot roast marinated in vinegar, sugar, and seasoning

sau′er·kraut′ /-krout′/ [G = sour cabbage] n chopped cabbage fermented in a brine made of its own juice with salt

Saul /sôl′/ n Bib 1 the first king of Israel (1 Sam. 10); 2 original name of the apostle Paul before his conversion (Acts 9:11; 13:9)

sau·na /sôn′ə/ [Finn] n 1 Finnish dry-heat bath for which steam is produced by throwing water on red-hot stones; 2 bathhouse for such a bath

saun·ter /sônt′ər, sänt′-/ [ME *santren* to muse] vi 1 to stroll idly; walk in a leisurely fashion ‖ n 2 leisurely stroll; 3 leisurely gait

sau·ri·an /sôr′ē·ən/ [< Gk *sauros* lizard] n zool reptile of the suborder Sauria, comprising the lizards ‖ also adj

sau·sage /sôs′ij/ [OF *saussiche*] n minced meat, as beef or usu. pork or a combination of meats, highly seasoned and usu. stuffed into a section of gut or other casing

sau·té /sōtā′, sō-/ [F] adj browned in a pan containing a little grease ‖ also v (-téed) vt

sau·terne /sōturn′, sō-/ [*Sauternes*, France] n semisweet white wine of the district of Bordeaux

sav·age /sav′ij/ [MF '*sauvage*] adj 1 untamed, ferocious; 2 uncivilized, primitive; 3 cruel, inhuman; 4 crude, unpolished; 5 ill-tempered, enraged ‖ n 6 uncivilized, primitive person; 7 fierce, brutal person; 8 rude person ‖ sav′age·ly adv ‖ sav′age·ness n ‖ SYN adj barbarous, fierce, enraged, sanguinary (see *inhuman*) ‖ ANT adj civilized, gentle

sav'age·ry *n* (-ries) savage state, condition, conduct, or act

sa·van·na /sə·van'ə/ [Sp *sabana*] *n* grassy plain with few trees, generally bordering a jungle area

sa·vant /səvänt', sav'ənt/ [F] *n* man of profound learning

sa·vate /səvät'/ [F] *n* kind of boxing in which kicks to the body are used as well as blows with the hands

save¹ /sāv'/ [OF *sauver* < L *salvus* safe] *vt* 1 to deliver from danger, injury, loss, or destruction; rescue; 2 to spare, as trouble; 3 to prevent the waste of, as time; 4 to refrain from spending, lay aside, as money; 5 to keep from wearing out, as *moderate speed saves tires*; 6 *theol* to free from the power and results of sin || *vi* 7 to refrain from spending or wasting; 8 to lay something aside for future use || **sav'er** *n*

save² [OF *sauf*] *prep* except, but

sav'ing *adj* 1 redeeming, as *a saving grace* || *n* 2 economy or reduction in expenditure; 3 **savings** *pl* money laid away || *prep* 4 except; 5 with all due respect for || SYN *adj* delivering, qualifying (see *economical*)

sav'ings ac·count' *n* bank account which draws interest

sav'ings bank' *n* bank that pays interest on savings accounts

sav·ior /sāv'yər/ [OF *saveour*] *n* 1 one who saves or delivers; 2 **the Savior** or **the Saviour** Jesus Christ

sa·voir-faire /sav'wär fer'/ [F = knowing how to do] *n* knowledge of what to do in any situation

sa·vor /sāv'ər/ [OF *savour*] *n* 1 flavor; taste; relish; 2 essential or particular quality or characteristic || *vt* 3 to taste or smell with delight; appreciate; 4 to season; relish; flavor || *vi* 5 **savor of** to smack of

sa'vor·y¹ *adj* pleasing to taste or smell; palatable

sa·vor·y² [ME *saverey*] *n* (-ies) fragrant herb (genus *Satureia*) of the mint family, used in cooking

sav·vy /sav'ē/ [Sp *¿sabe?* do you know?] *slang n* 1 shrewdness, intelligence || *v* (-vied) *vt* & *vi* 2 to understand

saw¹ /sô'/ [OE *saga*] *n* 1 cutting tool with a thin blade and a toothed edge || *v* (*pp* **sawed** or **sawn**) *vt* 2 to cut or shape with a saw || *vi* 3 to be cut with a saw; 4 to cut with or as with a saw

saw² [OE *sagu*] *n* proverb, adage || SYN maxim, saying, adage (see *truism*)

saw³ *pt* of **see**

saw'bones' *nsg slang* surgeon, doctor

saw'buck' *n* 1 sawhorse; 2 *slang* ten-dollar bill

saw'dust' *n* dust or fine particles of wood produced in sawing

saw'horse' *n* rack or trestle on which wood is placed for sawing

saw'mill' *n* mill where logs are sawed into lumber

sawn /sôn'/ *pp* of **saw**

saw'-toothed' *adj* serrate; having teeth like those of a saw

saw'yer /-yər/ *n* one whose occupation is sawing

sax /saks'/ *n colloq* saxophone

Sax·on /saks'ən/ [L *Saxo* (-*onis*)] *n* 1 member of a Teutonic tribe that participated in the conquest of what is now England in the 5th and 6th centuries; 2 their language; 3 Anglo-Saxon; 4 inhabitant of modern Saxony || also *adj*

Sax'o·ny *n* 1 former kingdom, later a state of Germany, now a region in S East Germany; 2 indeterminate region in N Germany inhabited by the ancient Saxons

sax'o·phone' /saks'ə-/ [A. J. **Sax** (1814–94) Belgian inventor] *n* keyed wind instrument consisting of a metal tube with a reed mouthpiece

say /sā'/ [OE *secgan*] *v* (**said**; *3rd pers sg pres ind* **says** /sez'/) *vt* 1 to speak, utter; 2 to express in words; tell; 3 to state as an opinion; assert; 4 to estimate; assume; 5 to recite; 6 **go without saying** to be self-evident beyond the need to explain; 7 **that is to say** in other words || *vi* 8 to express an opinion; declare, assert || *n* 9 something said, or what one has to say; 10 one's turn or right to express an opinion; 11 **have the say** to have the authority

say'ing *n* that which is said, esp. an adage or maxim || SYN saw, byword, maxim (see *truism*)

say'-so' *n* **on the say-so of** by the authority of

Sb [L *stibium*] *chem* antimony

Sc [L *scandium*] *chem* scandium

S.C. South Carolina

scab /skab'/ [ON *skabb*] *n* 1 crust formed over a wound or sore; 2 worker who takes the place of a striker || *v* (**scabbed**; **scab·bing**) *vi* to act as a scab || **scab'by** *adj* (-bi·er; -bi·est)

scab·bard /skab'ərd/ [AF *escaubers*] *n* sheath for a sword or bayonet

sca·bies /skāb'ēz, -ē·ēz'/ [L = the itch] *n* contagious skin disease of man and animals caused by parasitic mites

scab·rous /skab'rəs/ [< L *scaber* rough] *adj* 1 difficult; 2 rough (surface); 3 obscene

scads /skadz/ [?] *npl slang* a large amount

scaf·fold /skaf'əld, -ōld/ [OF *escadafault*] *n* 1 temporary structure to allow workmen to reach high places, as in the construction, painting, cleaning, and repairing of buildings; 2 raised platform for executing criminals

scaf'fold·ing *n* 1 scaffold or series of

scaffolds; **2** material for erecting scaffolds

scal·a·wag /skal'əwag'/ [?] *n* **1** scamp; **2** native white Southerner who was a Republican during Reconstruction

scald /skôld'/ [ONF *escalder* < LL *excaldare* to wash in hot water] *vt* **1** to burn or injure with hot liquid or steam; **2** to expose to heat over steam or hot liquid; **3** to bring near to boiling, as milk; **4** to blanch (fruits or vegetables) || *n* **5** burn or injury from hot liquid or steam

scale¹ /skāl'/ [ME < Scand] *n* **1** one of the pans of a balance; **2** often **scales** *pl* balance or any instrument or machine for weighing; **3** **tip the scales at** to weigh; **4** **turn the scales** to pass from defeat to victory || *vt* **5** to weigh

scale² [MF *escale*] *n* **1** one of the thin horny plates forming the outer covering of many fishes, lizards, and snakes; **2** any thin plate resembling such a covering; **3** one of the thick leaves protecting the bud of a plant in winter; **4** film of oxide which forms on metals when heated; **5** incrustation on the inside of a boiler || *vt* **6** to strip the scales from || *vi* **7** to drop scales; **8** to form scales; **9** to become encrusted with scale || **scal'y** *adj* (-i·er; -i·est)

scale³ [L *scala* ladder] *n* **1** graduated measure, esp. a series of marks laid down at definite distances along a line; **2** basis for a system of numbering, as *the decimal scale*; **3** any progressive series or graded system, as *the social scale*; **4** relative dimensions between a representation and what it represents, as on a map; **5** table or series of graduated rates, as *a wage scale*; **6** *mus* series of tones in consecutive order, generally within the interval of an octave || *vt* **7** to climb up or over; **8** **scale down** to reduce in accordance with a settled ratio

scale' in·sect *n* any of many plant-sucking insects (family Coccidae), the females of which are often attached to the plant and covered with a waxy scale

sca·lene /skālēn'/ [< Gk *skalēnos* uneven] *adj* **1** (triangle) that has three unequal sides and angles; **2** (cone) that has the axis oblique to the base

scal·lion /skal'yən/ [OF *escalogne* < L (caepa) *Ascalonia* (onion of) Ascalon] *n* **1** onion with an almost bulbless root; **2** shallot; **3** leek

scal·lop /skol'əp, skal'-/ [OF *escalope* shell] *n* **1** any of numerous bivalve mollusks with hinged, fluted shells; **2** large muscle in certain of these mollusks, valued as food; **3** shell of any of these mollusks; **4** shallow dish in which oysters, fish, etc., are cooked; **5** one of a series of curves forming an ornamental edge, as on lace || *vt* **6** to cut scallops in (an edge); **7** to cook or serve in scallop shells; **8** to mix with milk and crumbs and bake until brown

scalp /skalp'/ [ME < Scand] *n* **1** the skin on top of the head from which the hair grows; **2** portion of the skin with the attached hair, taken by some North American Indians in token of victory || *vt* **3** to cut or tear the scalp from; **4** to buy and resell (admission tickets) at a higher than the official price || **scalp'er** *n*

scal·pel /skalp'əl/ [L *scalpellum*] *n* surgeon's small straight knife

scamp /skamp'/ [prob OF *escamper* to decamp] *n* **1** rascal, rogue || *vt* **2** to perform carelessly

scam'per *vi* **1** to run or go quickly; **2** to frolic about

scan /skan'/ [LL *scandere* to scan verse] *v* (**scanned**; **scan·ning**) *vt* **1** to examine carefully; **2** to give a quick glance at; **3** to examine (verse) for metrical form and divide into metrical feet; **4** to pass a beam of light or a stream of electrons over (a surface, view, portion of space, soundtrack, etc.) for conversion into an electrical current, for transmission, and finally for reproduction of the original image or sound || *vi* **5** to scan verse; **6** to conform to a metrical pattern || also *n*

Scan., Scand. Scandinavia(n)

scan·dal /skan'dəl/ [Gk *skandalon* snare] *n* **1** reproach caused by shameful actions; public disgrace; **2** cause of reproach; discreditable conduct; **3** slander; malicious gossip || SYN aspersion, calumny, detraction (see *slander*)

scan'dal·ize' *vt* to offend or shock by scandalous conduct

scan'dal·mon·ger /-muŋ'gər/ *n* one who spreads scandal

scan'dal·ous *adj* **1** (speech or writing) containing defamatory information; **2** causing or bringing scandal || **scan'dal·ous·ly** *adv* || SYN shameful, disgraceful, infamous, shocking

scan'dal sheet' *n* newspaper or magazine that plays up scandal

Scan·di·na·vi·a /skan'dināv'ē·ə/ *n* Norway, Sweden, Denmark, and Iceland, with the adjacent islands || **Scan'di·na'vi·an** *adj & n*

scan·di·um /skan'dē·əm/ [< L *Scandia* Scandinavia] *n* rare metallic element (Sc; at.no. 21; at.wt. 44.956) of the rare-earth group

scan·sion /skansh'ən/ [L *scansio* (-*onis*)] *n* metrical analysis of verse

scant /skant'/ [ON *skamt* short] *adj* **1** meager, inadequate; **2** scarcely enough || *vt* **3** to cut down, stint

scant'ies *npl* very short panties

scant·ling /skant'liŋ/ [< OF *eschantillon* gauge, scale] *n* **1** stud, upright; **2** studs, uprights; **3** size of a building stone or lumber; **4** width and thickness of frames, planking, or other elements of a boat's hull; **5** small amount; modicum

scant·y /-i·er; -i·est/ *adj* **1** barely sufficient; **2** meager, sparing ‖ **scant′·ly** *adv* ‖ **scant′i·ness** *n* ‖ SYN pinched, insufficient, bare, sparse, deficient ‖ ANT plenty, sufficient, ample, abundant, generous

scape′goat′ /skāp′-/ [*escape* + *goat* < goat let loose in the wilderness by the ancient Jews on Yom Kippur after symbolically taking the blame for the people's sins (Lev. 16:8–22)] *n* one made to bear the blame for others

scape′grace′ [*escape* + *grace*] *n* unprincipled person; rogue

scap·u·la /skap′yələ/ [L = shoulder] *n* (-lae /-lē′/ or -las) shoulder blade

scap′u·lar /-lər/ *adj* **1** pert. to the scapula ‖ *n* **2** loose sleeveless garment worn by monks; **3** two small pieces of cloth fastened by strings passing over the shoulders, worn next to the body front and back, from motives of devotion

scar /skär/ [Gk *eschara* scar of a burn] *n* **1** mark left after a wound, burn, or sore has healed; **2** any mark or blemish ‖ *v* (**scarred; scarring**) *vt* **3** to mark with a scar ‖ *vi* **4** to form a scar

scar·ab /skar′əb/ [L *scarabaeus*] *n* **1** beetle (genus *Scarabaeus*), esp. *S. sacer*, held sacred by the ancient Egyptians; **2** gem or seal in the form of a scarab beetle, worn as a charm by the ancient Egyptians

scarce /skers′/ [ONF *escars*] *adj* **1** rare, seldom seen; **2** not plentiful; not equal to the need

scarce′ly *adv* not quite; hardly; barely

scar·ci·ty /skers′itē/ *n* (-ties) state or condition of being scarce ‖ SYN lack, scantiness, insufficiency, penury, dearth

scare /sker/ [ON *skirra*] *vt* **1** to frighten, terrify; **2** **scare away** or **off** to drive off by frightening; **3** **scare up** *colloq* to look for and get ‖ *vi* **4** to take fright ‖ *n* **5** sudden fright or alarm

scare′crow′ *n* **1** crude representation of a man set up to frighten birds away from crops; **2** person grotesquely or wretchedly dressed

scared·y-cat /skerd′ēkat′/ *n colloq* person who is easily scared

scare′head′ *n colloq* headline in very large type

scarf /skärf′/ [ONF *escarpe* sash, sling] *n* (**scarfs** or **scarves** /-vz/) **1** long broad piece of cloth worn for ornament or warmth around the neck, head, or shoulders; **2** long covering for a bureau or table

scar·la·ti·na /skär′lətēn′ə/ [It *scarlattina*] *n* scarlet fever, esp. a mild form of it

scar·let /skär′lit/ [ML *scarlettum* < Pers *saqalāt* scarlet cloth] *n* **1** bright-red color of orange tinge; **2** cloth of such color ‖ also *adj*

scar′let fe′ver *n* contagious febrile disease accompanied by a severe sore throat and a scarlet rash

scar′let tan′a·ger /tan′əjər/ [< Tupi *tangara*] *n* American passerine bird (*Piranga olivacea*) the male of which is scarlet with black wings and tail during the mating season

scarp /skärp′/ [It *scarpa*] *n* sharp, steep slope

scar′ tis′sue *n* connective tissue forming a scar that has become fibrous

scar·y /sker′ē/ *adj* (-i·er; -i·est) *colloq* **1** easily frightened; **2** causing fright

scat /skat′/ [a hiss + *cat*] *v* (**scat·ted; scat·ting**) *vi* **1** to go off hurriedly ‖ *interj* **2** get out of here!

scath·ing /skāth′iŋ/ [< ON *skathi* harm] *adj* scorching; bitterly severe, as *scathing remarks* ‖ **scath′ing·ly** *adv*

sca·tol·o·gy /skətol′əjē/ [Gk *skor* (*skatos*) dung + -*logy*] *n* preoccupation with obscenity or excrement ‖ **scat·o·log·i·cal** /skat′ələj′ikəl/ *adj*

scat·ter /skat′ər/ [ME *scateren* < Scand] *vt* **1** to strew about aimlessly; **2** to drive in several directions; disperse ‖ *vi* **3** to disperse ‖ *n* **4** act of scattering; **5** that which is scattered

scat′ter·brain′ *n* one incapable of serious concentrated thought ‖ **scat′ter-brained′** *adj*

scat′ter rug′ *n* small rug, as for under a table or chair

scav·enge /skav′inj/ [< *scavenger*] *vt* **1** to remove filth and garbage from, as streets; **2** to collect (usable materials), as from a junk pile ‖ *vi* **3** to act as a scavenger

scav′en·ger [AF *scawager* inspector] *n* **1** animal that feeds on carrion; **2** one who scavenges; **3** person or company employed in garbage removal

sce·nar·i·o /siner′ē·ō′, -när′-/ [It] *n* manuscript of a motion picture play, giving the incidents, scenes, characters, and dialogue ‖ **sce·nar′ist** *n*

scene /sēn/ [L *scena* stage < Gk *skene* tent] *n* **1** setting of a play or story; **2** place or circumstances in which any event takes place; **3** stage scenery; **4** division of an act in a play; **5** episode or situation in real life; **6** landscape; view, scenery; **7** **make a scene** to have an embarrassing outbreak of emotion or bad manners; **8** **make the scene** *slang* to go to some public place

scen·er·y /sēn′ərē/ *n* (-ies) **1** general appearance of a locality; general character of a landscape; **2** painted screens, hangings, etc., used as backgrounds on a stage

sce·nic /sēn′ik, also sen′-/ *adj* **1** having beautiful natural scenery; **2** of or pert. to stage scenery

scent /sent'/ [MF *sentir* to smell] *vt* 1 to smell, discern by the sense of smell; 2 to get an intimation of; 3 to perfume ‖ *n* 4 odor, fragrance; 5 sense of smell; 6 odor by which a person or animal can be traced; 7 clue by which any pursuit or investigation can be aided

scep·ter /sep'tər/ [Gk *skeptron*] *n* ruler's staff, emblematic of sovereignty

scep·tic /skep'tik/ *n* var of **skeptic**

sched·ule /skej'ool, Brit shej'-/ [LL *schedula* small sheet of paper] *n* 1 timetable; 2 written or printed list or inventory; 3 plan listing the steps necessary for the completion of a project and the time allotted for each step; 4 listing of events to occur in a specific time and order ‖ *vt* 5 to place or include in a schedule; 6 to plan to occur or be done at a certain time or date

sche·mat·ic /skēmat'ik/ *adj* 1 of the nature of or pert. to a plan, outline, or diagram ‖ *n* 2 diagram or plan

scheme /skēm'/ [Gk *schema* form] *n* 1 systematic arrangement or plan; 2 underhand plot or device; 3 sketch; diagram; map ‖ *vt* 4 to devise, contrive ‖ *vi* 5 to form plans; plot ‖ **schem'er** *n* ‖ SYN *n* plan, project, design ‖ DISCR *Design* includes not only the end to be accomplished, but a method of doing it with the means at hand. A *plan* is a detailed method by which a design is worked out. Both these words may name something indefinitely proposed to the mind as an aim, but *scheme* and *project* are the words usually employed to connote the airy or the visionary. *Scheme*, the more indefinite of the two, is also narrower in scope; often it names an artful, underhand *plan*, as for getting even for an injury. A *project* may be tentative or visionary, or may be a concrete proposal, as the *project* to build cotton mills near the cotton fields (cf. *design*)

scher·zo /sker'tsō/ [It = jest] *n* (-zos or -zi /-tsē/) *mus* sprightly movement following a slow one, as the third movement in a sonata or symphony

Schick' test' /shik'/ [Béla *Schick* (1877–1967) U.S. pediatrician, born in Hungary] *n* method for determining a person's susceptibility to diphtheria by the injection of a dilute diphtheria toxin under the skin

schiff·li /shif'lē/ [Swiss G = little ship] *n* 1 machine for embroidering textiles and making lace patterns; 2 lace and embroidery produced by such a machine

schil·ling /shil'iŋ/ [G] *n* monetary unit of Austria

schism /siz'əm/ [Gk *schisma* rent, tear] *n* 1 split or division into opposing parties, esp. within a church over doctrinal differences; 2 state of being so divided

schis·mat·ic /sizmat'ik/ *adj* 1 pert. to, characteristic of, or guilty of schism ‖ *n* 2 promoter of schism or adherent of a schismatic body

schist /shist'/ [Gk *schistos* splitting] *n* crystalline metamorphic rock in which the component minerals are arranged in parallel layers

schiz·o /skits'ō, skiz'ō/ *n slang* schizoid

schiz'oid *adj* 1 pert. to schizophrenia ‖ *n* 2 schizophrenic person

schiz·o·phre·ni·a /skitz'əfrēn'ē-ə, skiz'-/ [< Gk *schizein* to split + *phren* heart, mind] *n* psychosis characterized by withdrawal, delusions, and personality deterioration ‖ **schiz'o·phren'ic** /-fren'-/ *adj*

schle·miel /shləmēl'/ [Yiddish < Heb] *n slang* hapless person who makes a mess of everything he puts his hand to

schmaltz /shmälts/ [Yiddish = rendered fat] *n colloq* anything cloyingly sentimental ‖ **schmaltz'y** *adj* (-i-er; -i-est)

schnapps /shnäps'/ [G] *n* hard liquor

schnau·zer /shnouz'ər/ *n* one of a German breed of dogs having a wiry coat

schnei·der /shnīd'ər/ [G = tailor]· *gin rummy vt* 1 to keep (an opponent) from scoring any point in a game ‖ *n* 2 act of schneidering

schnit·zel /shnits'əl/ [G = a shaving] *n* veal cutlet

schol·ar /skol'ər/ [OE *scolere* < LL *scholaris*] *n* 1 very learned person, esp. in a particular field; 2 student, pupil ‖ **schol'ar·ly** *adj & adv* ‖ SYN pupil, student ‖ DISCR *Scholar* is nowadays applied chiefly to those who have perfected themselves in some branch of learning; the term implies profundity of knowledge as opposed to a casual acquaintance with a subject. The word is used frequently of those versed in the liberal arts, particularly in the languages. *Scholar* is still occasionally used in America to name one going to school, as in the nursery rhyme about the "ten-o'clock *scholar*"; but this use is old-fashioned even here. However, we speak of one apt at learning as a good *scholar*, or of one rather dull as a poor *scholar*. *Pupil* has supplanted *scholar* as the name for the schoolboy or schoolgirl, and is also used for one under the instruction of a tutor. *Pupil* connotes dependence on, and subordination to, the teacher. *Student* names one who studies independently of the close supervision or authority of a teacher; hence it, rather than *pupil*, is used of learners in the higher educational institutions. *Student* does not connote erudition as does *scholar*

schol·ar·ship' *n* **1** quality of work done by a student; **2** academic attainments of a scholar; **3** erudition; **4** financial or other aid granted to a student || SYN erudition, knowledge (see *learning*)

scho·las·tic /skəlas′tik/ [Gk *scholastikos* studious, learned] *adj* **1** of or pert. to schools and education; **2** of or pert. to secondary schools; **3** pert. to the medieval schoolmen || *n* **4** schoolman

scho·las′ti·cism *n* **1** system of philosophy and theology of the medieval schoolmen; **2** dogmatic adherence to traditional doctrines and methods

school[1] /skool′/ [OE *scōl* < Gk *scholē* leisure, study] *n* **1** place or institution of learning; **2** body of the students of a school; **3** regular session during which instruction is given; **4** division of a university giving instruction in a particular field; **5** any channel through which knowledge or training is gained; **6** followers, imitators, or disciples of any teacher or leader || *vt* **7** to train or instruct

school[2] [D = troop] *n* great number of fish feeding or swimming together || SYN company, shoal (see *herd*)

school′ board′ *n* elected or appointed committee that runs a local school system

school′ing *n* instruction in school; education

school·man /-mən/ *n* (**-men** /-mən/) **1** one of the medieval philosophers, usu. teachers in the universities, who treated religious and philosophical questions strictly according to the authority of the church fathers and Aristotle; **2** professional educator

school′marm′ /-märm′/ [< *ma′am*] *n colloq* woman schoolteacher

school′mas′ter *n* man who teaches in or heads a school || **school′mis′tress** *n fem*

school′ ship′ *n* training ship for future naval or merchant marine officers

school′teach′er *n* teacher in a school below the college level

school′ year′ *n* period in which school is open and regular classes are held

schoon·er /skoon′ər/ [?] *n* **1** sailing vessel with two or more masts rigged fore and aft; **2** *colloq* tall beer glass

schoon′er-rigged′ *adj* rigged as a schooner

schot·tische /shot′ish/ [G = Scottish] *n* round dance similar to the polka, or the music for it

Schu·bert, Franz /fränts′ shoob′ərt/ *n* (1797–1828) Austrian composer

Schu·mann, Robert /shoo′män/ *n* (1810–56) German composer

schuss /shoos′/ [G = shot] *n* **1** *skiing* straight downhill run on a steep course || *vi* **2** to execute a schuss

schwa /shwä′/ [G < Heb *shewā*] *n* **1** mid-central vowel sound characteristic of many unstressed syllables in English as the two *a*'s in *aroma;* **2** its symbol ə

Schweit·zer, Al·bert /shwīt′sər/ *n* (1875–1965) Alsatian musician and writer; doctor and missionary in Africa; Nobel peace prize 1952

sci·at·i·ca /sī·at′ikə/ [< LL *sciaticus* pert. to the back of the hip] *n* **1** neuralgia of the sciatic nerve in the hip or thigh; **2** any painful condition in the region of the hip

sci·ence /sī′əns/ [MF < L *scientia* knowledge] *n* **1** knowledge, as of general truths or particular facts, obtained and shown to be correct by accurate observation; **2** knowledge coordinated, arranged, and systematized with reference to general truths or laws; **3** skill or proficiency; **4** particular branch of knowledge || SYN skill, efficiency (see *knowledge*)

sci′ence fic′tion *n* imaginative fiction based on highly speculative and fantastic predictions of developments in science, often dealing with space travel

sci·en·tif·ic /-tif′ik/ [LL *scientificus*] *adj* **1** pert. to, or used in, science; **2** in accord with the rules or methods of science; systematic; exact || **sci′en·tif′i·cal·ly** *adv*

sci·en·tist *n* expert or specialist in science

scil·i·cet /sil′iset′/ [< L *scire licet* it is permitted to know] *adv* namely; to wit

scim·i·tar /sim′itər/ [It *scimitarra*] *n* Oriental sword with a curved blade

scin·til·la /sintil′ə/ [L = spark] *n* **1** shining spark; **2** particle, slightest trace

scin·til·late /sint′ilāt′/ *vi* **1** to give off sparks; **2** to twinkle; **3** to flash, sparkle || **scin′til·la′tion** *n*

scin·til·la′tion count′er *n* device for detecting and counting scintillations produced by radioactivity

sci·on /sī′ən/ [OF *cion* shoot, twig] *n* **1** sprout or shoot, esp. one cut for grafting; **2** descendant

scis·sor /siz′ər/ *vt* to cut with scissors

scis′sors [MF *cisoires*] *npl* cutting instrument having two blades pivoted together that slide over each other as they close

scis′sors kick′ *n* kick in swimming in which the legs move somewhat like the blades of a pair of scissors

scle·ra /sklir′ə/ [Gk *sklera* hard] *n* fibrous membrane that covers all the eyeball except the area covered by the cornea

scle·ro·sis /sklirōs′is/ [Gk = hardening] *n* (**-ses** /-sēz/) hardening of a tissue or body part || **scle·rot′ic** /-rot′ik/ *adj*

scoff /skof′, skôf′/ [ME *scof* < Scand] *n* **1** expression of scorn; **2** object of scorn or derision || *vi* **3**

to mock or jeer; **4 scoff at** to mock or jeer at ‖ **scoff′er** *n* ‖ SYN *v* taunt, mock, deride (see *jeer*)

scoff′law′ *n* *slang* person who flouts the law

scold /skōld′/ [ME *scald* abusive person < Scand] *vi* **1** to chide sharply or rudely; **2** to speak abusively ‖ *vt* **3** to rebuke, reprimand severely ‖ *n* **4** one who habitually finds fault, esp. a rude quarrelsome woman ‖ **scold′er** *n* ‖ SYN *v* reprove, rate, berate, chide, reprimand, rebuke, upbraid ‖ DISCR To *reprove* is to blame for some fault or irregularity; it is sometimes tenderly or mildly reproachful, as the mother *reproved* her child; but it may be stern and forceful, as the judge *reproved* the attorney from the bench. *Rebuke* connotes more sharpness and severity than *reprove*; we *rebuke* for more serious cause, and we place the stress on the idea of blame rather than on dissatisfaction or disapproval. To be *rebuked* cuts us; to be *reproved* makes us reproach ourselves. *Reprimand* is stronger than *rebuke*. A manager *reprimands*, not *reproves* or *rebukes*, a subordinate who has blundered; an officer is *reprimanded* by his superior. *Chide*, though not used officially or authoritatively as is *reprimand*, is nevertheless a stronger word; there is sometimes faultfinding implied in it, and the sense of blame it conveys is deep. When we *chide* those we love, there is present a note of admonition. *Scold* is the most severe of all these words. It connotes noisy faultfinding, railing, and violence of tone. *Rate* and *berate* add to *scold* the heat of anger and, too often, unreasonableness. To *upbraid* is to blame severely for that which justly deserves blame, as something disgraceful or wicked; it is often reproachful, as her father *upbraided* her for her disobedience

sconce /skons′/ [MF *esconse* hiding place, screened lantern] *n* wall bracket for candles or other lights, often backed with a mirror

scone /skōn′/ [MF *schoonbrot* fine bread] *n* thick batter cake of barley, oatmeal, or wheat

scoop /skōōp′/ [MF *schope*] *n* **1** small utensil with a handle resembling a deep-sided shovel or a hollow hemisphere, for taking up flour, ice cream, etc.; **2** amount dipped up in one scoop; **3** bucket of a dredge or steam shovel; **4** act of scooping; **5** news item printed or broadcast before any rival ‖ *vt* **6** to be first with a news item ahead of (rivals); **7 scoop out** to dig or hollow out; **8 scoop up** to take or gather up as with a scoop

scoot /skōōt′/ [< Scand] *vi* to dart, scurry; dash off

scoot′er *n* **1** child's toy vehicle hung low on two wheels and propelled by pushing one foot against the ground; **2** motor scooter

scope /skōp′/ [It *scopo* aim, purpose < Gk *skopos*] *n* **1** extent or range of view, intent, or action; **2** opportunity for action or achievement ‖ SYN compass, sweep, range, reach, extent, field, capacity

-scope /-skōp′/ [Gk -*skopion*] *n comb form* instrument for observing, as *telescope*

-sco·py /-skəpē/ [Gk *skopia* viewing] *n comb form* observation, as *microscopy*

sco·pol·a·mine /skəpol′əmēn′, -mĭn/ [G. A. *Scopoli* (1723–88) It naturalist + *amine*] *n* vegetable alkaloid —$C_{17}H_{21}NO_4$— used to produce dilation of the pupils of the eyes and to produce twilight sleep

scor·bu·tic /skôrbyōōt′ĭk/ [< ML *scorbutus* scurvy] *adj* of, pert. to, or affected with scurvy

scorch /skôrch′/ [< Scand] *vt* **1** to burn slightly so as to cause a change in color, taste, or texture; **2** to shrivel or parch with heat; **3** to attack with caustic criticism; **4** to destroy by fire ‖ *vi* **5** to be scorched ‖ *n* **6** superficial burn ‖ SYN parch, dry, wither, shrivel, singe (see *burn*)

scorched′-earth′ pol′i·cy *n* military policy of laying waste, as by fire, of a countryside belonging to the enemy

scorch′er *n* **1** *colloq* extremely hot day; **2** something caustic, as severe criticism

scorch′ing *adv* **scorching hot** excessively hot; burning

score /skōr′, skôr′/ [OE *scoru*] *n* **1** notch, line, or groove, esp. one made for keeping tally; **2** tally so kept; **3** account; debt; **4** grudge; **5** motive, reason; **6** number of points, runs, etc., made in a game or contest; **7** *mus* copy of a composition showing all the parts for all the instruments and/or voices; **8** grade in an examination; **9** set of twenty; **10 scores** *pl* a large number ‖ *vt* **11** to mark with lines, scratches, or notches; **12** to keep record or account of, as by notches; **13** to make (points, runs, etc.) in a game or contest; **14** to record the score of; **15** to make a score of; **16** to evaluate in a test or examination; **17** to upbraid; **18** *mus* to adapt for an instrument; transcribe; orchestrate ‖ *vi* **19** to keep score; **20** to make a point or points in a game; **21** to achieve a success ‖ **scor′er** *n*

score′board′ *n* large board in a sports arena showing the current score

score′card′ *n* card for keeping score, and, esp. in a baseball game, indicating the names and positions of the players

scorn /skôrn′/ [OF *escarn*] *n* **1** contempt, disdain; **2** object of contempt or derision ‖ *vt* **3** to hold in contempt or disdain; **4** to reject with contempt ‖ **scorn′ful** *adj* ‖ **SYN** *v* abhor, detest, contemn, mock, deride ‖ **ANT** *v* admire, honor, respect

Scor·pi·o /skôrp′ē-ō′/ [L < Gk *skorpios* scorpion] *n* **1** a southern zodiacal constellation; **2** eighth sign of the zodiac

scor′pi·on /-ən/ *n* any of an order (*Scorpionida*) of arachnids of warm regions, having the two front legs equipped with pincers and the slender, jointed tail ending in a poisonous sting

Scot /skot′/ [LL *Scottus*] *n* native or inhabitant of Scotland

Scot. **1** Scotch; **2** Scotland; **3** Scottish

scotch /skoch′/ [ME *scocchen* to gash] *vt* **1** to wound, disable; **2** to put an end to, as rumors

Scotch /skoch′/ [< *Scottish*] *adj* **1** Scottish ‖ *n* **2** dialect of English spoken in Scotland; **3** Scotch whisky; **4** the Scotch *pl* the people of Scotland

Scotch′-I′rish *adj* of or pert. to the Protestant descendants of Scotch immigrants to northern Ireland ‖ the Scotch-I′rish *npl*

Scotch′man /-mən/ *n* (-men /-mən/) Scot ‖ **Scotch′wom′an** *nfem*

Scotch′ tape [trademark] *n* thin transparent adhesive tape

Scotch′ ter′ri·er *n* one of a breed of small terriers with wiry hair and short legs

Scotch′ ver′dict *n* **1** verdict of not proven instead of not guilty, sometimes allowed in Scotch criminal law; **2** *colloq* inconclusive decision or outcome

Scotch′ whis′ky *n* whiskey distilled in Scotland from barley and having a distinctive smoky flavor

scot′-free′ [< ME *scot* = tax < Scand] *adj* without due payment, penalty, or harm

Sco·tia /skōsh′ə/ [L] *n poet.* Scotland

Scot′land /-lənd/ *n* country in the N part of Great Britain, a constituent of the United Kingdom (5,250,000; 29,795 sq.m.; cap. Edinburgh)

Scot′land Yard′ [street in Westminster, London, site of former headquarters] *n* **1** London police headquarters; **2** detective branch of the London police

Scots /skots′/ [< *Scottis* N variant of *Scottish*] *adj* **1** Scotch or Scottish ‖ *n* **2** Scottish 2

Scots′man /-mən/ *n* (-men /-mən/) Scot ‖ **Scots′wom′an** *nfem*

Scot′tish [ME < LL *Scottus*] *adj* **1** of or pert. to Scotland, its people, or its language ‖ *n* **2** dialect of English spoken in Scotland; **3** the Scottish *pl* the people of Scotland

scoun·drel /skoun′drəl/ [?] *n* man without honor or virtue ‖ **scoun′drel·ly** *adj*

scour¹ /skou′(ə)r/ [ME *scouren*] *vt* **1** to clean or polish by hard rubbing, as with some abrasive material; **2** to clean grease or dirt from; **3** to wash or clear out by flooding or flushing, as a channel or pipe ‖ *vi* **4** to scrub anything thoroughly; **5** to become clean and bright through rubbing

scour² [OF *escourre*] *vt* **1** to pass over swiftly; **2** to go through thoroughly, as on a search

scourge /skurj′/ [AF *escorge*] *n* **1** whip; **2** affliction or calamity ‖ *vt* **3** to whip or flog; **4** to torment; harass

scout¹ /skout′/ [OF *escoute* listener] *n* **1** person sent out to obtain information; **2** soldier, vessel, or plane sent out to reconnoiter; **3** *sports* person who seeks to recruit new talent for a team; **4** Boy Scout or Girl Scout ‖ *vi* **5** to act as a scout ‖ *vt* **6** to reconnoiter; **7** **scout out** *colloq* to seek

scout² [ON *skūta* taunt] *vt* to reject with scorn, scoff at

scout′mas′ter *n* adult leader of a troop of Boy Scouts

scow /skou′/ [D *schouw*] *n* large flat-bottomed boat with square ends

scowl /skou′(ə)l/ [ME *scoulen* < Scand] *vi* **1** to wrinkle the brow in displeasure; look sullen or angry ‖ *vt* **2** to express with a scowl ‖ *n* **3** scowling look or aspect

scrab·ble /skrab′əl/ [D *schrabbelen* to scratch] *vi* **1** to scramble; scrape, scratch, or paw with the hands, as if to find or collect something ‖ *vt* **2** to gather hurriedly, scrape together; **3** to scribble ‖ *n* **4** scramble; hasty gathering up or together; **5** hasty careless writing; **6** eager, rude struggle for the possession of something

scrag·gly /skrag′lē/ [var of *craggy*] *adj* (-gli·er; -gli·est) **1** unkempt, shaggy; **2** rough, jagged

scram /skram′/ [< *scramble*] *v* (**scrammed; scram·ming**) *vi colloq* to be off, go away at once

scram·ble /skram′bəl/ [prob var of *scrabble*] *vi* **1** to clamber, wriggle, or move along on the hands and feet; **2** to struggle unceremoniously for the purpose of getting something; **3** *mil* (of planes) to take off quickly to intercept enemy aircraft ‖ *vt* **4** to toss together at random; **5** to prepare (eggs) by stirring the whites and yolks together; **6** to render (a radio or telephone message) incomprehensible except with a special receiving device that changes the frequencies; **7** **scramble up** or **together** to collect or gather up hurriedly and unsystematically ‖ *n* **8** unceremonious struggle after gain or position; **9** laborious progress over rough ground; **10** *mil* quick take-off of planes to intercept enemy aircraft

scram'bler *n* device that scrambles radio and telephone messages

scrap¹ /skrap'/ [ME *scrappe* < Scand] *n* **1** small piece; fragment; **2** discarded material; **3 scraps** *pl* bits of leftover food || *v* (**scrapped; scrapping**) *vt* **4** to break up, make into scrap; **5** to discard || *adj* **6** in the form of fragments or pieces; **7** (paper) not wanted, to be discarded

scrap² [?] *n* **1** fight, quarrel || *v* (**scrapped; scrap·ping**) *vi* **2** to fight, quarrel || **scrap'per** *n*

scrap'book' *n* blank book in which to paste clippings or pictures

scrape /skrāp'/ [ON *skrapa*] *vt* **1** to rub over a surface gratingly; **2** to rub smooth or clean as with an abrasive tool; **3** to clean or remove with an abrasive tool; **4 scrape up** or **together** to gather or accumulate in small amounts or with difficulty || *vi* **5** to rub something gratingly; **6** to save money by being extremely economical; **7 scrape through** to barely get by || *n* **8** act, noise, or effect of scraping; **9** scraped place; **10** difficulty, predicament || **scrap'er** *n*

scrap' i'ron *n* iron scraps for remelting

scrap·ple /skrap'əl/ [< *scrap¹*] *n* corn meal boiled with pork, seasoned, and served in fried slices

scrap'py *adj* (**-pi·er; -pi·est**) combative

scratch /skrach'/ [ME *cracchen*] *vt* **1** to mark or tear the surface of with something rough or pointed; **2** to tear or dig with the nails or claws; **3** to cancel, erase, or strike out, as by drawing a line through; **4** to relieve itching; **5** to rub on a rough surface || *vi* **6** to use the nails or claws in rubbing, tearing, or digging; **7** to rub the head or body to relieve itching; **8** to cause irritation or pain by rubbing, as *the collar scratches;* **9** to make a scraping noise || *n* **10** mark, tear, or wound made by scratching; **11** act or sound of scratching; **12** canceled entry in a horse race; **13 from scratch, a** from the beginning; **b** from nothing; **14 up to scratch** up to satisfactory standards || *adj* **15** *colloq* hastily gathered together, as *a scratch team* || **scratch'y** *adj* (**-i·er; -i·est**)

scratch' hit' *n* baseball poorly hit ball barely allowing the batter to reach first safely

scratch' pad' *n* pad of scratch paper

scratch' pa'per *n* paper for jotting down notes

scratch' sheet' *n* racing publication giving the day's entries, jockeys, scratches, and odds

scratch' test' *n* test for allergic susceptibility, made by rubbing allergens into small scratches or breaks in the skin

scrawl /skrôl'/ [ME *scraule*] *vt* **1** to write or draw irregularly or hastily; scribble || *n* **2** careless, illegible writing

scraw·ny /skrôn'ē/ [?] *adj* (**-ni·er; -ni·est**) lean, skinny || **scraw'ni·ness** *n*

scream /skrēm'/ [ME *scremen*] *vi* **1** to utter a sharp shrill cry, as of fear or pain; **2** to cry out in a shrill piercing voice; **3** to laugh uncontrollably || *vt* **4** to utter with or as with a scream || *n* **5** sharp shrill cry; **6** *colloq* something or someone hilarious

screech /skrēch'/ [ME *scrichen*] *vi* **1** to utter or make a shrill high-pitched sound || *vt* **2** to utter with a screech || *n* **3** shrill high-pitched cry or sound || **screech'y** *adj* (**-i·er; -i·est**)

screech' owl' *n* any owl that utters a screeching cry, esp. a small American owl of the genus *Otus*

screed /skrēd'/ [ME *screde* < Scand] *n* long tiresome speech or writing

screen /skrēn'/ [AF *screne*] *n* **1** covered framework, partition, or curtain, for shelter, protection, or privacy; **2** something that protects or conceals; **3** frame covered with a mesh to keep out insects; **4** sieve for separating the finer and coarser parts, as of coal or sand; **5** white or silvery surface on which motion pictures or slides are projected; **6** medium of motion pictures || *vt* **7** to shelter, protect, or conceal, as behind a screen; **8** to sift through a screen; **9** to project (a motion picture) on a screen; **10** to provide with screens *3;* **11** to select or test, as for suitability or loyalty, by investigation or interviews || SYN *v* cover, shelter, conceal, shield, protect, hide

screen'play' *n* **1** motion picture scenario; **2** motion picture

screen' test' *n* test on film to determine a person's suitability for a part in a motion picture

screw /skrōō'/ [ME] *n* **1** metal fastener threaded in an advancing spiral and usu. having a slotted head; **2** anything with a spiral form; **3** screw propeller; **4** *slang* prison guard; **5 have a screw loose** *slang* to be slightly crazy; **6 put the screws on** or **to** to coerce || *vt* **7** to tighten or fasten with or as with a screw; **8** to attach with a screw; **9** to make tight (something with a spiral thread) by turning; **10** to twist, turn, move spirally; **11** *slang* to cheat, swindle; **12 screw up, a** to intensify (one's courage); **b** to contort (one's face); **c** *slang* to bungle badly || *vi* **13** to turn like a screw; **14** to fasten or go on with a screwing motion

screw'ball' *n* **1** baseball pitched ball that curves toward the same side from which it was thrown; **2** *slang* eccentric or erratic person || also *adj*

screw′ cap′ n cap made to screw on the threaded neck of a bottle or the opening of a gasoline tank

screw′driv′er n 1 tool for turning screws; 2 drink made with vodka and orange juice

screw′ eye′ n wood screw with a ring as a head

screw′ jack′ n jack operated by a screw-threaded shaft

screw′ pro·pel′ler n propeller for a ship or plane having a number of spirally pitched blades around a hub

screw′y adj (-i·er; -i·est) slang 1 crazy, irrational; 2 queer, odd

scrib·ble /skrĭb′əl/ [ML scribillare] vt 1 to write in a careless or hurried manner; 2 to cover with illegible or meaningless writing ‖ vi 3 to write carelessly or meaninglessly ‖ n 4 scribbled writing ‖ **scrib′bler** n

scribe¹ /skrīb′/ [L scriba clerk] n 1 writer; clerk; secretary; 2 one whose work was copying manuscripts; 3 Bib ancient teacher of the Jewish law; Jewish theologian and lawyer ‖ **scrib′al** adj

scribe² [perh < inscribe] vt to mark or score (wood, metal, etc.) with a tool with a hard, sharp point

scrim /skrĭm′/ [?] n theat drop of thin gauzelike material that appears opaque when lit from the front but is transparent when lit from behind

scrim·mage /skrĭm′ĭj/ [var of skirmish] n 1 general fight; confused struggle; 2 football any play begun by snapping the ball back from a position on the ground; 3 sports practice play or session

scrimp /skrĭmp′/ [< Scand] vt 1 to allow too little of; make too small; 2 to be niggardly to; stint ‖ vi 3 to be sparing, frugal, or niggardly

scrip /skrĭp′/ [< script] n 1 certificate for a fractional share of stock; 2 certificate entitling the bearer to goods or cash; 3 paper currency formerly issued in denominations of less than one dollar

script /skrĭpt′/ [L scriptum thing written] n 1 ordinary handwriting; 2 any system of writing; 3 copy of the text of a play or show; 4 type in imitation of handwriting

scrip·ture /skrĭp′chər/ [L scriptura writing] n 1 any sacred writing; 2 the Scriptures pl the Bible ‖ **scrip′-tur·al** adj

script′writ′er n author of scripts for movie plays or television shows

scrod /skrŏd′/ [?] n young codfish cut apart for cooking

scrof·u·la /skrŏf′yələ/ [LL = swelling of the glands] n disease marked by tuberculous enlargement of the lymphatic glands, usu. of the neck ‖ **scrof′u·lous** adj

scroll /skrōl′/ [ME scrowle] n 1 roll of paper or parchment, esp. with writing on it; 2 ornamental spiral design resembling a parchment roll

scro·tum /skrōt′əm/ [L] n (-ta /-tə/ or -tums) pouch of skin containing the testicles

scrounge /skrounj′/ [?] vt 1 to cadge; bum; 2 to borrow or take without serious intention of returning or paying ‖ vi 3 **scrounge around** to search about in a haphazard fashion ‖ **scroung′er** n

scrub¹ /skrŭb′/ [MD schrobben] v (scrubbed; scrub·bing) vt 1 to wash by rubbing, as on a washboard; 2 to rub hard with a wet cloth or brush, as a floor; 3 to cleanse (a gas) of impurities; 4 colloq to cancel ‖ vi 5 to scrub something ‖ n 6 act or process of scrubbing

scrub² [N Eng var of shrub] n 1 stunted trees or shrubs; 2 area covered with such trees or shrubs; 3 anything inferior in size, quality, or breed; 4 sports player not good enough for or not playing on the regular team ‖ adj 5 small, undersized ‖ **scrub′by** adj (-bi·er; -bi·est)

scrub′wom′an n (-wom′en) cleaning woman, esp. one who scrubs floors and does other similar work

scruff /skrŭf′/ [var of scuff] n nape of the neck

scrump·tious /skrŭmp′shəs/ [? < sumptious] adj colloq splendid, first-rate

scru·ple /skrōō′pəl/ [L scrupulus small pebble] n 1 very small quantity; 2 apothecaries′ weight of one third of a dram or twenty grains; 3 doubt or hesitation arising from difficulty in deciding what is right or wrong ‖ vi 4 to have scruples ‖ vt 5 to have scruples about

scru·pu·lous /skrōō′pyələs/ adj 1 having or showing scruples; 2 punctilious; minutely attentive to details; exact ‖ **scru′pu·lous·ly** adv ‖ SYN punctilious, cautious, exact, qualmish, squeamish

scru·ti·nize /skrōōt′ĭnīz′/ vt to inspect closely, subject to minute inspection

scru′ti·ny [< L scrutari to search] n (-nies) 1 close inspection or examination; 2 searching look ‖ SYN inquiry, investigation, examination, inspection

scu·ba /skōō′bə/ [self-contained underwater breathing apparatus] n portable diver′s apparatus with compressed-air tanks that strap to the back for breathing under water

scud /skŭd′/ [Norw skudda to push] v (scud·ded; scud·ding) vi 1 to run, fly, or move swiftly; 2 naut to run before a gale with little or no sail spread ‖ n 3 act of scudding; 4 clouds or spray driven by the wind

scuff /skŭf′/ [prob Sw skuffa to shove] vi 1 to become rough on the surface; 2 to shuffle, drag the feet ‖ vt 3 to wear a rough place on the surface of; scratch or spoil the surface or finish of; 4 to move with a dragging motion; shuffle, as the feet ‖ *n* 5 act of scuffing; 6 rough or worn spot

scuf·fle /skuf′əl/ [< *scuff*] *vi* 1 to fight or struggle confusedly; 2 to shuffle; scuff the feet ‖ *n* 3 confused or disorderly fight

scull /skul′/ [ME *sculle*] *n* 1 one of a pair of oars used by one person; 2 oar used at the stern of a boat with a twisting motion to propel it; 3 light racing boat propelled by one to four oarsmen using sculls ‖ *vt* 4 to propel with a scull or sculls ‖ *vi* 5 to scull a boat ‖ **scull′er** *n*

scul·ler·y /skul′ərē/ [MF *escuelerie*] *n* (**-ies**) room where cooking utensils are cleaned and kept

scul·lion /skul′yən/ [MF *escouvillon* swab] *n* 1 servant who cleans cooking utensils and does other menial service in the kitchen; 2 low, disreputable wretch

sculp·tor /skulp′tər/ [L] *n* one who sculptures ‖ **sculp′tress** *nfem*

sculp·ture /-chər/ [L *sculptura*] *n* 1 art of fashioning figures or other objects in the round or in relief by chiseling stone, casting metal, carving wood, modeling clay, etc.; 2 any work of sculpture; 3 such works collectively ‖ *vt* 4 to make (a work of sculpture), as by carving, modeling, or casting; 5 to represent or portray in sculpture; 6 *phys geog* to change in form by erosion ‖ **sculp′tur·esque** *adj*

scum /skum′/ [MD *schume*] *n* 1 layer of impurities on the surface of a liquid; 2 refuse; 3 rabble, riffraff ‖ *v* (**scummed**; **scum·ming**) *vt* 4 to remove the scum from ‖ *vi* 5 to become covered with scum

scum′my *adj* (**-mi·er**; **-mi·est**) 1 covered with scum; 2 *colloq* vile, contemptible

scup·per /skup′ər/ [ME *skopper*] *n* hole, tube, or gutter at the side of a ship to carry off water from the deck

scurf /skurf′/ [OE] *n* 1 small white scales of dead skin, as dandruff; 2 anything like flakes or scales sticking to a surface

scur·ri·lous /skur′iləs/ [< L *scurrilis* adj grossly or obscenely vulgar or abusive ‖ **scur·ril′i·ty** /skəril′-/ *n* (**-ies**) ‖ SYN foul, vulgar, opprobrious, coarse, abusive

scur·ry /skur′ē/ [< *hurry-scurry*] *v* (**-ried**) *vi* 1 to hasten or move rapidly along ‖ *n* (**-ries**) 2 hurried movement, scampering

scur·vy /skur′vē/ [< *scurf*] *n* 1 disease caused by lack of vitamin C, marked by weakness, thinness, and bleeding gums ‖ *adj* (**-vi·er**; **-vi·est**) 2 mean, contemptible ‖ **scur′vi·ly** *adv*

scutch·eon /skuch′ən/ *n* escutcheon

scut·tle¹ /skut′əl/ [? < *scud*] *vi* 1 to hasten or hurry away; scurry ‖ *n* 2 hasty flight; scampering

scut·tle² [OF *escoutille* hatchway < Sp *escotilla*] *n* 1 small opening with a lid, as on the roof of a house, or on the deck, side, or bottom of a ship ‖ *vt* 2 to sink (a vessel) by opening seacocks or cutting holes in the bottom or sides; 3 to destroy, ruin

scut·tle³ [OE *scutel* platter] *n* deep bucket for holding coal

scut′tle·butt′ *n* 1 drinking fountain or water cask aboard ship; 2 *colloq* rumor, gossip

Scyl·la /sil′ə/ *n* 1 *class. myth.* she-monster, dangerous to navigation, living on a promontory on the S coast of Italy; 2 **between Scylla and Charybdis** between two evils, one of which must be accepted

scythe /sīth/ [OE *sithe*] *n* cutting instrument with a long curved blade attached to a long bent handle, used for mowing grass, grain, hay, etc.

S.D., S.Dak. South Dakota

SDR special drawing rights

Se *chem* selenium

SE, S.E. southeast(ern)

sea /sē′/ [OE *sǣ*] *n* 1 large body of salt water, smaller than an ocean, and more or less enclosed by land; 2 large inland body of water; 3 the great expanse of salt water that covers most of the earth's surface; 4 large wave; 5 condition of the sea's surface; 6 very large extent, as *a sea of troubles*; 7 life of a sailor; 8 **at sea**, **a** on a sea voyage; **b** bewildered, uncertain; 9 **put (out) to sea** to embark on a voyage ‖ *adj* 10 of or pert. to the sea

sea′ a·nem′o·ne *n* any of numerous polyps, often beautifully colored, the outspread tentacles of which resemble petals

sea′ bass′ /bas′/ *n* any of various saltwater fishes (family Serranidae) of the Atlantic, many species of which are valuable for food

Sea·bee′ [*Construction Battalion*] *n* member of a naval construction battalion established to build military installations in combat zones

sea′board′ *n* seacoast

sea′ change′ *n* 1 marked change, usu. for the better; 2 change that the sea has brought about

sea′coast′ *n* land bordering on the sea

sea′ cow′ *n* any of several large herbivorous aquatic mammals, as the manatee and dugong

sea′ dog′ *n* old sailor

sea·far′er /-fer′ər/ *n* 1 traveler on the sea; 2 sailor

sea′far′ing *adj* 1 traveling by sea; 2 following the life of a sailor

sea′ food′ *n* shellfish or salt-water fish used for food

sea′go′ing *adj* 1 seafaring; 2 suitable or fitted for use in the open sea

sea′ green′ *n* rich bluish green ‖ **sea′-green′** *adj*

sea′ gull′ *n* gull

sea horse′ *n* 1 any of various small fishes (genus *Hippocampus*) with head and fore part of the body resembling the head and neck of a horse, that swim with the body in an upright position; 2 hippopotamus; 3 *class. myth.* creature with a horse's head and fish's tail, ridden by Neptune and other sea gods

seal¹ /sēl′/ [OE *sēolh*] *n* (seal or seals) 1 any of various marine carnivorous mammals (suborder Pinnipedia), some species yielding a valuable fur; 2 the fur; 3 leather made from sealskin; 4 dark grayish brown ‖ *vi* 5 to hunt seals

seal² [OF *seel*] *n* 1 stamp or die engraved with some device, motto, or image for impressing paper, wax, etc., as a mark of authenticity on a letter or document; 2 impression so made; 3 anything that approves or confirms; 4 anything that seals, closes firmly, or secures, as a gasket to prevent the escape of gases; 5 wax, lead, or the like, placed on an envelope, box lid, or door, to show that it has not been opened; 6 anything that keeps a thing secret, as *a seal of silence*; 7 any of several devices to prevent the entrance of gas or air into a pipe; 8 special decorative stamp, as *Christmas seals* ‖ *vt* 9 to affix a seal to; 10 to ratify or confirm; 11 to close with a device that reveals tampering if broken; 12 to shut tightly as with a seal, as a letter with a glued envelope flap or a valve housing with a gasket; 13 to determine irrevocably, as someone's fate

seal′ant *n* 1 sealing agent, such as sealing wax; 2 paint and other liquids used to form a watertight coating

sea′ legs′ *npl* ability to adapt oneself to the pitching and rolling motion of a ship

sea′ lev′el *n* level of the surface of the sea at mean tide

seal′ing wax′ *n* resinous substance that softens when heated, used for sealing letters, documents, etc.

sea′ li′on *n* any of several large seals of the Pacific with external ear openings, esp. *Zalophus californianus*

seal′skin′ *n* 1 skin of a seal; 2 fur of the fur seal, prepared for use; 3 garment made from this fur

seam /sēm′/ [OE *sēam*] *n* 1 line formed by sewing two pieces of material together; 2 edges left, usu. on the inside, after making a seam; 3 any line formed by two edges that join; 4 scar; wrinkle; 5 layer of mineral or rock ‖ *vt* 6 to join or sew together, forming a seam; 7 to mark with a seam or line ‖ *vi* 8 to crack open ‖ **seam′less** *adj*

sea′man /-mən/ *n* (**-men** /-mən/) *n* 1 sailor; 2 *nav* sailor below the rank of petty officer

sea′man·ship′ *n* skill in the management of a vessel

sea′ mile′ *n* nautical mile

sea′ mon′ster *n* any hideous or terrifying marine creature, esp. a mythical one

seam·stress /sēm′stris/ [OE *sēamestre*] *n* woman who sews for a living

seam′y *adj* (**-i·er; -i·est**) 1 showing or having seams; 2 a less attractive; b sordid, wretched

sé·ance /sā′äns/ [F = session] *n* meeting at which a spiritualist attempts to communicate with the dead

sea′ ot′ter *n* marine otter (*Enhydra lutris*) of the N Pacific having a valuable fur coat

sea′plane′ *n* airplane adapted to land on and take off from the water

sea′port′ *n* city or town with a harbor or port for ocean-going vessels

sea′ pow′er *n* 1 nation having naval power; 2 naval power of a nation

sear¹ /sir′/ [OE *sēarian*] *vt* 1 to dry up, wither; 2 to scorch; 3 to burn or char the surface of; 4 to render callous or unfeeling ‖ *adj* 5 sere; dry, withered

sear² [MF *serre* grasp] *n* small catch in the lock of a gun to hold the hammer at half or full cock

search /surch′/ [OF *cercher*] *vt* 1 to go over and examine carefully; 2 to examine (a person) in order to find something concealed; 3 to examine, test; probe; 4 **search me** *slang* I haven't the slightest idea ‖ *vi* 5 to seek; make search; 6 to investigate; 7 **to search for** to try to find ‖ *n* 8 act or fact of searching; 9 careful investigation; examination ‖ **search′-er** *n* ‖ SYN *v* hunt, examine, explore, scrutinize, seek

search′ing *adj* penetrating, sharp ‖ **search′ing·ly** *adv*

search′light′ *n* large light with a reflector that throws a powerful beam in any direction

search′ war′rant *n* court order giving the police authority to search private premises

sea′ rob′in *n* any of several small marine fishes (genus *Prionotus*) of a reddish color and distinguished by having three rays below the pectoral fins on each side

sea′scape′ [*sea* + landscape] *n* picture showing a scene at sea

sea′ ser′pent *n* enormous snakelike sea monster said to live in the ocean

sea′ shell′ *n* shell of any marine mollusk

sea′shore′ *n* land bordering the sea

sea′sick′ *adj* suffering from nausea and

dizziness caused by the pitching and rolling of a ship at sea ‖ **sea′sick′ness** *n*

sea′side′ *n* seashore, seacoast ‖ also *adj*

sea′ snake′ *n* any of numerous venomous fish-eating snakes (family Hydrophidae) found in warm seas

sea-son /sēz′ən/ [OF *se(i)son*] *n* 1 one of the four periods into which the year is divided by the annual changes in the sun's declination: spring, summer, autumn, and winter; 2 definite or particular period of the year, as *the rainy season, the holiday season;* 3 appropriate or fitting time; 4 any period of time; 5 **in season** available, as certain fruits; 6 **out of season** not in season ‖ *vt* 7 to add seasoning to; 8 to add zest to; 9 to fit for use by time or habit; inure; acclimate; 10 to bring to the best state for using, as *to season timber* ‖ *vi* 11 to become seasoned

sea′son-a-ble *adj* 1 timely, opportune; 2 in keeping with the season of the year

sea′son-al *adj* of, pert. to, or dependent on the season

sea′son-ing *n* salt, pepper, herbs, spices, or the like added to food to heighten its flavor

sea′son tick′et *n* ticket valid for a specified number of events or times, usu. sold at a reduced rate

seat /sēt/ [ON *sǣti*] *n* 1 something on which to sit, as a chair; 2 that part of a chair, stool, etc., on which one sits; 3 buttocks; 4 the part of a garment covering the buttocks; 5 location, site; 6 membership, as in a legislative body or stock exchange; 7 sitting accommodation for one person, as *a seat for a play;* 8 manner of sitting, as on a horse; 9 *mach* part or surface supporting another part or surface, as in a valve ‖ *vt* 10 to place in a seat or seats; 11 to have seats for (a specified number of people); 12 to install in office; 13 *mach* to adjust or place on a seat ‖ *vi* 14 *mach* to fit well on its seat, as a valve

seat′ belt′ *n* belt attached to the seat of an airplane or automobile and secured around the waist of the passenger as a safety measure

seat′ing *n* 1 arrangement of seats in an auditorium or stadium; 2 assignment of seats, as at a table ‖ also *adj*

SEATO /sē′tō/ *n* Southeast Asia Treaty Organization

sea′ trout′ *n* any of several species of marine trout prized for their tender flesh

Se-at-tle /sē-at′əl/ *n* seaport in W Washington (530,831)

sea′ wall′ *n* wall or embankment for checking the encroachment of the sea or for use as a breakwater

sea′ward /-wərd/ *adj* & *adv* toward the sea

sea′way′ *n* 1 channel or waterway connecting an inland port with the ocean; 2 forward motion of a ship through the waves; 3 **in a seaway** in a rough sea

sea′weed′ *n* 1 any plant growing in the sea; 2 marine alga

sea′wor′thy *adj* (ship or boat) fit or safe for a sea voyage ‖ **sea′wor′thi-ness** *n*

se-ba′ceous glands′ /sibāsh′əs/ [< L *sebaceus* < *sebum* tallow] *npl* glands in the skin that secrete oily matter to lubricate the hair and skin

seb-or-rhe-a /seb′ərē′ə/ [L *sebum* + *-rrhea*] *n* disease characterized by an excessive discharge from the sebaceous glands, resulting in scales on the skin and other skin abnormalities

sec¹ /sek/ [F = dry] *adj* dry (wine, esp. champagne)

sec² secant

sec. 1 second; 2 secretary

SEC, S.E.C. Securities and Exchange Commission

se-cant /sē′kant, sēk′ənt/ [L *secans* (-*antis*) cutting] *n* 1 straight line intersecting a curve at two or more points; 2 *trig* ratio of the hypotenuse of a right triangle to the side adjacent to a given angle

se-cede /sisēd′/ [L *secedere*] *vi* to withdraw formally from membership in a body, group, federation, or organization

se-ces-sion /sisesh′ən/ *n* 1 act or instance of seceding; 2 **Secession** withdrawal from the Union of the eleven southern states in 1860–61, which precipitated the Civil War ‖ **se-ces′sion-ist** *n*

se-clude /siklōōd′/ [L *secludere*] *vt* to withdraw from others; keep apart ‖ **se-clud′ed** *adj*

se-clu′sion /-zhən/ *n* 1 withdrawal from the society of others; 2 secluded spot ‖ SYN privacy, retreat, solitude (see *retirement*)

sec-ond¹ /sek′ənd/ [OF < L *secundus*] *adj* 1 immediately following the first; 2 next to the first in place, time, value, excellence, rank, or importance; 3 another, as *a second chance*; 4 *mus* rendering a part that is lower in pitch than another voice or instrument; 5 *auto* next to lowest (gear) ‖ *n* 6 one that is second; 7 backer or assistant; 8 aide or attendant, as to a boxer or duelist during a match or duel; 9 article of merchandise not of first quality; 10 formal approval of a motion in an assembly; 11 **seconds** *pl* second helping of food ‖ *vt* 12 to support; assist; 13 to give formal approval to (a motion) so that it can be discussed and voted on ‖ *adv* 14 in second place ‖ **sec′ond·er** *n* ‖ **sec′ond·ly** *adv*

sec′ond[2] [ML *secunda* (minuta) second (minute), that is, the one resulting from the second sexagesimal division of the hour or the degree] *n* **1** one sixtieth of a minute of time; **2** one sixtieth of a minute of angular measure "; **3** moment

sec′ond·ar′y /-der′ē̩/ *adj* **1** second in order, rank, or importance; **2** subordinate, minor; **3** derivative, not primary; **4** *elec* pert. to or designating an induced current or its circuit ‖ *n* (-ies) **5** that which is inferior in rank, place, or importance; **6** *elec* winding in a transformer or the like, carrying current that is induced by a current in a separate winding called the primary ‖ **sec′ond·ar′i·ly** *adv*

sec′ond·ar·y ac′cent *n* the stress of a word that is weaker than the primary accent but stronger than no accent at all

sec′ond·ar·y boy′cott *n* boycott of union workers against their employer not because of a dispute with him but because of a dispute with another company having the same union

sec′ond·ar·y cell′ *n* *elec* cell in which electrical energy can be stored by passing a current through it from an outside source

sec′ond·ar·y school′ *n* high school or prep school

sec′ond child′hood *n* senility

sec′ond class′ *n* **1** accommodations, as on a ship, intermediate in cost and luxury between first and third class; **2** class of mail including newspapers and periodicals

sec′ond-class′ *adj* **1** pert. to second class; **2** inferior, second-rate

sec′ond cous′in *n* child of a first cousin

sec′ond fid′dle *n* play second fiddle to be in a subordinate role or position

sec′ond-guess′ *vt* **1** to use hindsight in criticizing (a person or thing); **2 a** to predict (an event); **b** to outguess (a person)

sec′ond-hand′ *adj* **1** received from someone else; not original; **2** not new; used before; **3** dealing in secondhand goods ‖ also *adv*

sec′ond lieu·ten′ant *n* lowest-ranking commissioned officer in the Army, Marines, or Air Force

sec′ond mate′ *n* officer of a merchant ship ranking third after the captain

sec′ond na′ture *n* ingrained habit

sec′ond pa′pers *npl* final documents certifying the naturalization of an alien

sec′ond per′son *n* *gram* **1** person spoken to; **2** form indicating such a person

sec′ond-rate′ *adj* not of first quality; mediocre; inferior ‖ **sec′ond-rat′er** *n*

sec′ond sheet′ *n* sheet of paper of inferior quality for making carbon copies

sec′ond sight′ *n* clairvoyance

sec′ond-sto′ry man′ *n colloq* burglar who enters a house through an upstairs window

sec′ond thoughts′ *npl* reservations about a previous decision

sec′ond wind′ /wind// *n* restoration of normal breathing after hard physical effort

se·cre·cy /sēk′rise̩/ *n* (-cies) **1** state or quality of being secret; **2** ability to keep secrets; **3** secretive habits

se·cret /sēk′rit/ [L *secretus* hidden] *adj* **1** concealed; not revealed; **2** secluded; retired; **3** mysterious, occult; **4** working in secrecy, as *a secret agent, secret police* ‖ *n* **5** something kept secret; **6** mystery; **7** key or formula for solving some mystery or puzzle; **8 in secret** secretly ‖ **se′cret·ly** *adv* ‖ SYN *adj* private, hidden, furtive (see *clandestine*)

sec·re·tar·i·at /sek′riter′ē̩·it/ [F] *n* office, duties, and staff of a secretary charged with administrative duties, esp. of an international organization

sec·re·tar·y /sek′riter′ē̩/ *n* (-ies) [ML *secretarius*] *n* **1** person employed to take care of correspondence, typing, records, filing, etc., in an office; **2** official of an organization or corporation charged with correspondence, keeping the records, taking down minutes of meetings, etc.; **3** writing desk; **4 Secretary** member of the president's cabinet in charge of a department of the government ‖ **sec′re·tar′i·al** *adj* ‖ **sec′re·tar′y·ship′** *n*

se·crete[1] /sikrēt′/ *vt* to hide or conceal ‖ SYN mask, cloak, shroud, hide (see *conceal*)

se·crete[2] [L *secernere* (*secretus*) to discern] *vt* to separate or elaborate from blood or sap and make into a new substance ‖ **se·cre′tion** *n*

se·cre·tive /sēk′ritiv, sikrēt′-/ *adj* reticent, inclined to secrecy

Se′cret Serv′ice *n* U.S. government agency charged with apprehending counterfeiters and guarding the life of the President

sect /sekt′/ [L *secta* faction] *n* **1** a number of persons adhering to a specific doctrine or set of beliefs; **2** religious denomination, esp. a faction of dissenters from an established church ‖ SYN faction, denomination, communion, body, party

sec·tar·i·an /-ter′ē̩·ən/ *adj* **1** of, pert. to, or adhering to a sect; **2** narrow-minded ‖ *n* **3** member of a sect ‖ **sec·tar′i·an·ism** *n*

sec·tion /sek′shən/ [L *sectio* (-*onis*)] *n* **1** act of cutting; separation by cutting; **2** part cut off; **3** distinct or separate part or subdivision of anything; **4** drawing or representation of an object as if cut in two by an intersecting plane; **5** *U.S. W of Ohio* subdivision of land one mile square, 1/36 of a township; **6** *mil* subdivision of a platoon; **7** *railroads* a portion of railway track assigned to one maintenance crew; **b** sleeping car compartment including an upper and lower berth; **c** train running on the same schedule as another; **8** *surg* a the making of an incision; **b** the incision || *vt* **9** to divide or cut into sections

sec·tion·al *adj* **1** of or pert. to a section of a country; **2** made up of several sections

sec·tion·al·ism *n* exaggerated devotion to sectional interests

sec·tor /sek'tər/ [L = cutter] *n* **1** part of a circle bounded by two radii and the included arc; **2** distinct area of a combat zone; **3** part or division, as of a city

sec·u·lar /sek'yələr/ [LL *saecularis* worldly < L *saeculum* age] *adj* **1** pert. to worldly affairs or to things not religious; **2** (clergy) not bound by monastic vows; **3** not concerned with religion or churches || SYN mundane, earthly, terrestrial, temporal

sec·u·lar·ize *vt* **1** to make secular; **2** to transfer (property) from religious to civil control || **sec·u·lar·ism** *n* || **sec·u·lar·i·za·tion** *n*

se·cure /sikyŏŏr'/ [L *securus* carefree] *adj* **1** free from fear or danger; safe; **2** free from care or worry; **3** free from doubt; assured; **4** firm, steady; **5** in safe keeping; in custody || *vt* **6** to make safe; protect; **7** to make certain, assure, guarantee; **8** to close; make fast; **9** to obtain; **10** a to assure payment of, as by a bond or mortgage; **b** to assure payment to, as by a bond or mortgage; **11** to seize and confine || **se·cure'ly** *adv* || SYN *v* get, attain, obtain, catch; *adj* sure, assured, preserved, certain || ANT *adj* unsafe, undefended

se·cu·ri·ty *n* (-ties) **1** state or quality of being secure; **2** protection, defense; **3** measures taken to prevent burglary, theft, sabotage, etc.; **4** one who becomes surety for the debt or default of another; **5** bond or share of stock; **6** collateral

se·cu·ri·ty an·a·lyst *n* person who studies and sometimes predicts the value of stocks and bonds on the basis of the earnings and the quality of the management of the companies

Se·cu·ri·ty Coun·cil *n* committee of the United Nations responsible for the maintenance of international peace, composed of five permanent members and ten elected members

secy., sec'y. secretary

se·dan /sidan'/ [?] *n* closed automobile with two or four doors and two full-width seats

se·dan' chair' *n* enclosed chair for one person borne on two poles by two men

se·date /sidāt'/ [< L *sedare* (-*atus*) to make calm] *adj* **1** calm, composed; unruffled || *vt* **2** to place under sedation || SYN *adj* decorous, demure, staid, settled, serene

se·da'tion *n* quieting of excitement or hysteria, esp. by the administration of drugs

sed·a·tive /sed'ətiv/ *adj* **1** tending to calm or soothe; **2** allaying excitement or pain || *n* **3** sedative agent

sed·en·tar·y /sed'ənter'ē/ [L *sedentarius*] *adj* **1** accustomed to inactivity; **2** marked by or requiring much sitting; **3** (animals) remaining in one place or attached, as barnacles

sedge /sej/ [OE *secg*] *n* any of a large family (Cyperaceae) of grasslike herbs growing in damp places

sed·i·ment /sed'imənt/ [L *sedimentum*] *n* **1** solid matter that settles at the bottom of a liquid; **2** *geol* matter deposited by water, ice, or air

sed·i·men·ta·ry /-ment'ərē/ *adj* **1** pert. to or composed of sediment; **2** *geol* formed by the deposit of sediment, as rocks

sed·i·men·ta·tion *n* precipitation or accumulation of sediment

se·di·tion /sidish'ən/ [L *seditio* (-*onis*)] *n* action, as speech or writing, but short of overt acts, inciting rebellion against the government || SYN disorder, agitation, commotion (see *revolution*)

se·di'tious *adj* **1** of or pert. to sedition; **2** guilty of sedition || SYN rebellious, factious, turbulent, mutinous

se·duce /sid(y)ŏŏs'/ [L *seducere* to lead aside] *vt* **1** to lead from the path of right, duty, or virtue, by flattery or promises; **2** to persuade to have illicit sexual relations || **se·duc'er** *n* || **se·duc'tion** /-duk'shən/ *n* || **se·duc'tive** *adj*

sed·u·lous /sej'ələs/ [L *sedulus* careful] *adj* steadily industrious and persevering; persistent || SYN assiduous, diligent, persevering (see *busy*)

see¹ /sē/ [OE *sēon*] *v* (**saw; seen**) *vt* **1** to perceive by the eye; behold; view; **2** to discern mentally; comprehend; **3** to escort or accompany; **4** to find out, ascertain; **5** to have knowledge of; experience; **6** to make sure, as *see that you do it*; **7** to visit, meet with; **8** to receive, as *Mr. Smith will see you now*; **9** to imagine, as *he couldn't see her married to Paul*; **10** to have dates with; **11** *poker* to match (a bet or a bettor); **12** to prefer (someone or something) in a specified condition, as *I'll see him dead first*; **13** see off to accompany (someone) to the train, plane, etc.;

14 see through to stay with (a task) to completion ‖ *vi* **15** to have the power of sight; **16** to comprehend; perceive mentally; **17** to find out by inquiry; **18** to consider, reflect; **19 see about, a** to investigate; **b** to take care of; **20 see after** to take care of; **21 see through** to see the true nature of; **22 see to** to take care of

see² [OF *sie* < L *sedes* seat] *n* **1** official seat, office, or jurisdiction of a bishop; **2** diocese

seed /sēd/ [OE *sǣd*] *n* **1** fertilized and mature ovule of a flowering plant containing the embryo from which a new plant can grow; **2** any small seedlike fruit; **3** any generative part of a plant, including the true seeds, seedlike fruits, bulbs, tubers, etc.; **4** first principle or source, germ, as *seeds of discord*; **5** offspring, descendants; **6** semen; **7 go to seed, a** to shed seeds; **b** to deteriorate ‖ *vi* **8** to sow seeds; **9** to produce or shed seeds ‖ *vt* **10** to sow with seed; **11** to remove the seeds from; **12** *sports* **a** to arrange (the drawing for places of contestants in a tournament) so that the superior contestants will not meet in the early rounds; **b** to distribute (players or teams) in this manner ‖ **seed'less** *adj* ‖ **seed'er** *n*

seed' leaf' *n* cotyledon

seed'ling *n* **1** plant grown from a seed; **2** young plant, esp. a small or young tree

seed' pearl' *n* pearl weighing less than ¼ grain

seed'y *adj* (**-i-er; -i-est**) **1** full of seed; **2** shabby, threadbare; **3** spiritless, out of sorts

see'ing *conj* **1** inasmuch as; considering, since ‖ *n* **2** *astron* ability to see celestial bodies clearly because of low air turbulence, as *there is good seeing tonight*

See'ing Eye' dog' *n* dog trained by the Seeing Eye corporation of Morristown, N.J. to guide blind persons

seek /sēk/ [OE *sēcan*] *v* (**sought**) *vt* **1** to go in search of; look for; **2** to resort to, go to; **3** to attempt, as *he sought to do good*; **4 seek out** to look for; single out ‖ *vi* **5 seek after** to seek ardently

seem /sēm/ [ME *semen* < Scand] *vi* **1** to appear to be; look; **2** to appear to exist, as *there seems no need to hurry*; **3** to appear to one's own mind, as *I seemed to float through the air* ‖ SYN appear, look ‖ DISCR To *appear* is to be in view, or present to the senses. *Appear* is used of the existing, of the positive. The sun *appears* above the horizon in the early morning. *Look* is used of that toward which the eyes are directed; she *looks* pale; it *looks* now as if it would rain. What *seems* does so to the mind, and has been the subject of at least brief reflection, from which a conclusion has been drawn. The stars *appear* in the sky on clear nights; they *seem* nearer than they are; they *seem* to twinkle. *Seem* is often used not of the actual, but of the apparent, the probable, or the dubious. What *appears* to be a short distance to a vigorous man may *seem* long to the weary or discouraged. All these words are in ordinary use interchangeable, particularly so in their figurative employment; a thing may *look*, *appear*, or *seem* strange

seem'ing *adj* ostensible; apparent ‖ **seem'ing·ly** *adv*

seem'ly *adj* (**-li·er; -li·est**) fit or becoming; appropriate ‖ SYN decorous, suitable, decent (see *becoming*)

seen /sēn/ *pp* of **see**

seep /sēp/ [OE *sīpian*] *vi* to leak slowly; ooze; trickle ‖ **seep'age** /-ij/ *n*

se·er /sē'ər/ *n* **1** one who sees ‖ /sir'/ *n* **2** one who foretells future events; prophet; crystal gazer; **3** one who has keen moral and spiritual insight; sage ‖ **seer'ess** *n* fem

seer'suck·er /sir'-/ [Pers *shīr o shakkar* milk and sugar] *n* thin linen or cotton fabric usu. having alternating stripes and a crinkled surface

see'saw' [prob < *saw¹*] *n* **1** game in which children sitting on opposite ends of a balanced plank move alternately up and down; **2** the apparatus for this game; **3** any up-and-down or back-and-forth motion ‖ *vi* **4** to move like a seesaw

seethe /sēth/ [OE *sēothan* to boil] *vi* **1** to boil; **2** to bubble or froth as from boiling; **3** to be violently agitated

see'-through' *adj* (garment) of transparent material, as mesh or net

seg·ment /seg'mənt/ [L *segmentum*] *n* **1** any of the parts into which an object naturally separates or is divided; **2** *geom* part cut off from a figure by a line or plane ‖ /segment'/ *vt & vi* **3** to divide into segments ‖ **seg·men·ta'tion** *n* ‖ **seg·men'tal** *adj*

seg·re·gate /seg'rigāt/ [L *segregare* (-*atus*) to separate from the flock] *vt* **1** to separate from others; set apart; **2** to compel (a racial or religious minority) to live apart from the dominant group, usu. under oppressive conditions ‖ *vi* **3** to be or become segregated ‖ **seg're·ga'tion** *n*

se·gue /sāg'wā, seg'-/ [*impv* of It *seguire* < L *sequi* to follow] *mus vi* **1** to proceed without pause ‖ *n* **2** act of segueing

sei·gneur·y /sēn'yərē/ [F] *n* (**-ies**) Canadian land held by a grant from the king of France, until 1854

seign·ior /sēn'yər/ [ME] *n* feudal lord

seign·ior·age /sēn'yərij/ [ME] *n* profit arising from the difference between the monetary and the metal value of coins

seine /sān/ [OE *segne* < Gk *sagene* fishing net] *n* 1 large encircling fishing net having floats at the top and weights at the bottom ‖ *vt & vi* 2 to fish with a seine

Seine /sān/ *n* river in N France flowing through Paris to the English Channel

seis·mic /sīz'mik/ [< Gk *seismos* earthquake] *adj* pert. to, produced by, or characteristic of an earthquake

seis·mo·graph /sīz'mə-/ *n* instrument that records the time, duration, direction, and intensity of earthquakes

seis·mol·o·gy /-mol'əjē/ *n* scientific study of earthquakes and their causes and results ‖ **seis·mol·o·gist** *n*

seize /sēz/ [OF *saisir*] *vt* 1 to take possession of by force; 2 to take by legal authority, confiscate; 3 to capture; arrest; 4 to grasp, snatch; 5 to avail oneself of, as *to seize an opportunity* ‖ *vi* 6 **seize on** to grasp forcibly and suddenly ‖ SYN catch, snatch, take, capture, arrest, clutch, grasp, comprehend ‖ ANT lose, drop, release, relinquish

sei·zure /sēzh'ər/ *n* 1 act or instance of seizing; 2 sudden attack; fit, spell

sel·dom /sel'dəm/ [OE *seldum, seldan*] *adv* rarely, not often

se·lect /silekt'/ [L *seligere* (-*lectus*)] *vt* 1 to pick out, choose ‖ *adj* 2 chosen for special excellence or fitness; 3 of great excellence; choice; 4 exclusive, discriminating ‖ SYN v choose, cull, take (see *elect*)

se·lect·ee /n one chosen by draft for military service

se·lec·tion *n* 1 act of selecting or state of being selected; 2 thing or things selected; 3 group of things, as at a store, from which a choice may be made

se·lec·tive *adj* of, pert. to, resulting from, or characterized by selection

se·lec·tive serv·ice *n* compulsory military service

se·lect·man /-mən/ *n* (-men /-mən/) one of a board of officials chosen annually in most New England towns to transact public business

se·lec·tor *n* 1 person or mechanism that makes selections; 2 electrical device which automatically selects the terminal when has been signaled to select

se·le·ni·um /silēn'ē·əm/ [< Gk *selene* moon] *n* nonmetallic element (Se; at.no. 34; at.wt. 78.96) chemically resembling sulfur, used in photometers because of its variable electrical resistance when exposed to light

self /self/ [OE] *n* (selves) 1 a person's own distinct individuality; one's own person or character; 2 personal welfare; selfishness ‖ *pron* (selves) 3 myself, himself, oneself, etc.

self- *comb form* by, in, on, of, to, or with oneself or itself, as *self-destruction*

-self *comb form* (-selves) added to personal pronouns to give emphatic or reflexive force, as *she did it herself, he injured himself*

self'-a·buse' *n* 1 abuse of oneself; 2 masturbation

self'-ad·dressed' *adj* addressed to oneself

self'-as·sur'ance *n* self-confidence ‖ **self·as·sured'** *adj*

self'-cen'tered *adj* concerned only with oneself; selfish

self'-com·mand' *n* self-control

self'-con·ceit' *n* exaggerated vanity ‖ **self'-con·ceit'ed** *adj*

self'-con'fi·dence *n* confidence in oneself, in one's abilities, judgment, etc. ‖ **self'-con'fi·dent** *adj*

self'-con'scious *adj* 1 acutely conscious of oneself as an object of interest; 2 ill-at-ease ‖ **self'-con'scious·ly** *adv* ‖ **self'-con'scious·ness** *n*

self'-con·tained' *adj* 1 self-controlled; 2 reserved; uncommunicative; 3 *mach* complete in itself

self'-con·trol' *n* control of one's feelings and emotions ‖ **self'-con·trolled'** *adv*

self'-de·fense' *n* 1 act of defending oneself; 2 *law* plea that injury or death to another was unavoidably caused in defense of one's own life

self'-de·ni'al *n* 1 sacrifice of one's own desires; unselfishness; 2 instance of doing without something one needs or likes

self'-de·struct' *vi* to disintegrate at a preset time or in an emergency

self'-de·ter'mi·na'tion *n* determination by the people of a country or region of their own form of government

self'-de·vo'tion *n* selfless devotion to the interests of others

self'-ef·face'ment *n* keeping oneself out of the limelight ‖ **self'-ef·fac'ing** *adj*

self'-em·ployed' *adj* working for oneself; being one's own employer

self'-es·teem' *n* 1 self-respect; 2 self-conceit ‖ SYN self-respect, self-approbation (see *egotism*)

self'-ev'i·dent *adj* evident without need of proof; obvious

self'-ex·plan'a·to'ry *adj* obvious, needing no explanation

self'-i·den'ti·fi·ca'tion *n* identification of oneself with someone or something else

self'-im·por'tant *adj* having an exaggerated opinion of one's own importance ‖ **self'-im·por'tance** *n*

self'-in·duc'tance *n* inductance *l*

self'-in·duc'tion *n* *elec* production of a flow of current in a conductor by a varying flow of current in the same conductor

self'-in'ter·est *n* 1 personal interest or advantage; 2 undue regard for one's own interest; selfishness ‖ **self'-in'ter-est-ed** *adj*

self'ish *adj* actuated by or absorbed in one's own interests, regardless of others ‖ **self'ish-ly** *adv* ‖ **self'ish-ness** *n*

self'less *adj* having no thought for oneself; unselfish

self'-load'ing *adj* (firearm) loading bullets into the firing chamber automatically

self'-made' *adj* 1 made by oneself; 2 having attained wealth or position unaided

self'-pos-sessed' *adj* having or showing composure and calmness ‖ **self'-pos-ses'sion** *n*

self'-pres'er-va'tion *n* desire possessed normally by all animals to preserve themselves from harm or destruction

self'-re-li'ance *n* reliance on or confidence in one's own ability, efforts, or judgment ‖ **self'-re-li'ant** *adj*

self'-re-spect' *n* proper regard for one's own character and dignity ‖ **self'-re-spect'ing** *adj*

self'-re-straint' *n* self-control; restraint imposed by oneself

self'-right'eous *adj* upright in one's own estimation; smugly righteous ‖ **self'-right'eous-ness** *n*

self'-sac'ri-fice' *n* sacrifice of one's own self or one's interests or welfare for the sake of duty or other high motive ‖ **self'-sac'ri-fic'ing** *adj*

self'same' *adj* exactly the same; identical

self'-sat'is-fied' *adj* feeling or showing satisfaction with oneself ‖ **self'-sat'is-fac'tion** *n*

self'-seek'ing *n* 1 selfish ‖ *n* 2 selfishness

self'-serv'ice *n* 1 waiting on oneself, as at a cafeteria or supermarket ‖ *adj* 2 (store, restaurant, etc.) operated by self-service

self'-serv'ing *adj* furthering one's own interests in disregard of others

self'-start'er *n* small electric motor for starting an internal-combustion engine

self'-styled' *adj* called as specified by oneself, as *a self-styled doctor*

self'-suf-fi'cient *adj* 1 able to supply all needs without assistance; 2 having confidence in one's own abilities ‖ **self'-suf-fi'cien-cy** *n*

self'-willed' *adj* obstinate, stubborn

sell /sel'/ [OE *sellan*] *v* (**sold**) *vt* 1 to give in return for a consideration, esp. money; 2 to offer for sale, deal in; 3 to cause to be accepted, as an idea; 4 to persuade to buy; 5 to betray for money or other reward; 6 to win (someone) over; 7 **sell off** to sell cheaply in order to be rid of; 8 **sell out, a** to dispose of completely by selling; **b** *colloq* to betray ‖ *vi* 9 to make a sale; 10 to be on sale; 11 to engage in selling; 12 **sell out** to

turn traitor ‖ *n* 13 *stock market* order to sell ‖ **sell'er** *n* ‖ SYN *v* barter, bargain, betray (see *trade*)

sell'out' *n* 1 show or athletic contest for which all seats have been sold; 2 act or instance of treason

Selt-zer /selt'sər/ [G *Selterser* from Selters, village in Germany] *n* 1 effervescent alkaline mineral water with medicinal properties; 2 also **seltzer** artificially carbonated water of similar composition

sel-vage /sel'vij/ [*self* + *edge*] *n* edge of cloth woven to prevent raveling and different in material or finish from the surface of the cloth

selves /selvz'/ *pl* of **self**

se-man'tics /simant'iks/ [Gk *semantikos* significant] *nsg* study of word meanings and their historical development ‖ **se-man'tic** *adj* ‖ **se-man'ti-cist** /-sist/ *n*

sem-a-phore /sem'əfôr', -fōr'/ [< Gk *sema* sign + *phoros* bearer] *n* 1 apparatus for signaling railroad trains by showing a bar or row of lights in a vertical, diagonal, or horizontal position; 2 system of communication in which letters, numbers, etc., are represented by various positions of small flags held in the extended hands ‖ **sem'a-phor'ic** *adj*

sem-blance /sem'bləns/ [MF] *n* 1 image, representation; 2 resemblance; 3 outward appearance, pretense; 4 slight amount; modicum

se-men /sēm'ən/ [L = seed] *n* fluid produced in the male reproductive organs, which contains spermatozoa

se-mes-ter /simes'tər/ [G < L (*cursus*) *semestris* (period) of six months] *n* one of the two terms of the academic year

sem-i- /sem'ē-, -ī-, -i-, sem'-/ [L = half] *pref* 1 half; 2 partly; 3 twice in a specified period

sem'i-an'nu-al /-mē-, -mī-/ *adj* occurring twice a year; half-yearly ‖ **sem'i-an'nu-al-ly** *adv*

sem'i-cir'cle /-mi-/ *n* half of a circle ‖ **sem'i-cir'cu-lar** *adj*

sem'i-co'lon /-mi-/ *n* punctuation mark ; indicating a separation in the parts of a sentence greater than that marked by a comma

sem'i-con-duc'tor /-mē-, -mī-/ *n* solid, such as germanium and silicon, whose electric conductivity is weak but greater than that of insulators ‖ **sem'i-con-duc'ting** *adj*

sem'i-de-tached' /-mē-, -mī-/ *adj* designating either of two houses sharing a party wall but detached from other buildings

sem'i-fi'nal /-mē-, -mī-/ *n* 1 *sports* elimination round preceding the final one in a tournament; 2 *boxing* match preceding the main event ‖ also *adj* ‖ **sem'i-fi'nal-ist** *n*

sem'i-month'ly /-mē-, -mī-/ *adj* 1 occurring or done twice a month ‖ *n*

(-lies) 2 semimonthly publication ‖ *adv* 3 twice a month

sem·i·nal /sem′inəl/ [< L *semen* (-*inis*) seed] *adj* 1 pert. to, containing, or consisting of semen; 2 *bot* pert. to seed; 3 original (work or idea) that influences later works or ideas

sem·i·nar /sem′inär′/ [G < L *seminarium* seed plot] *n* 1 group of students pursuing an advanced course of study, esp. original research; 2 course of study for such a group; 3 any group study

sem·i·nar·i·an /sem′inerˌē·ən/ *n* student in a theological seminary

sem′i·nar′y [L *seminarium* seed plot] *n* (-ies) 1 school for the training of clergymen; 2 school for young women of the secondary level or higher

Sem·i·nole /sem′inōl′/ [Creek *simanole* runaway] *n* one of a tribe of American Indians living in Florida and Oklahoma

sem′i·pre′cious /mē-, -mi-/ *adj* (gems, as the garnet and onyx) inferior in value to precious stones

sem′i·pro′ /-mē-, -mi-/ *n colloq* semiprofessional

sem′i·pro·fes′sion·al *n* person who engages part-time in a sport for pay

Sem·ite /sem′it/ [Gk *Sem* < Heb *Shem* a son of Noah] *n* 1 one of the peoples originating in SW Asia, including the ancient Phoenicians and the modern Arabs and Jews; 2 Jew

Se·mit·ic /simit′ik/ *adj* 1 pert. to the Semites or their languages ‖ *n* 2 language family which includes Arabic, Aramaic, and Hebrew

sem′i·vow′el /-mē-/ *n* consonant sound that is spelled with a letter that in some words represents a vowel sound, as /w/ in *wet* and *one* and /y/ in *year, onion,* and *unite*

sem′i·week′ly /-mē-, -mi-/ *adj* 1 occurring or done twice a week ‖ *n* (-lies) 2 semiweekly publication ‖ *adv* 3 twice a week

sem·per fi·de·lis /semp′ər fidel′is/ [L] always faithful (motto of the U.S. Marines)

sen /sen/ [Jap] *n* (*pl* **sen**) Japanese money of account, 1/100 of a yen

sen., Sen. 1 senate; 2 senator; 3 senior

sen·ate /sen′it/ [L *senatus* council of elders] *n* 1 legislative assembly; 2 **Senate** upper house of the legislature of the U.S., many other countries, and most states

sen·a·tor /sen′ətər/ [L] *n* member of a senate ‖ **sen′a·to′ri·al** /-tôr′ē·əl, -tōr′-/ *adj*

send /send/ [OE *sendan*] *v* (**sent** d) *vt* 1 to drive; impel; direct; 2 to cause to go; dispatch, as *send a messenger;* 3 to cause to be conveyed or transmitted; 4 *slang* to thrill; 5 **send forth** to produce or yield; 6 **send in** to cause to be delivered; 7 **send off** to

dismiss; 8 **send out, a** to issue, emit; **b** to dispatch; 9 **send packing** to dismiss in disgrace; 10 **send up** please to send to prison ‖ *vi* 11 to transmit messages; 12 **send for, a** to summon; **b** to order ‖ **send′er** *n* ‖ SYN forward, project, discharge, emit, dispatch, transmit, throw, hurl ‖ ANT keep, hold, bring

send′-off′ *n* 1 start given to someone or something; 2 demonstration of good will to one going away

Sen·e·gal /sen′igôl′/ *n* republic in W Africa (3,900,000; 76,084 sq.m.; cap. Dakar) ‖ **Sen′e·ga·lese′** /-lēz′, -lēs′/ *adj & n* (-lese)

se·nes·cent /sənes′ənt/ [L *senescens* (-*entis*)] *adj* growing old, aging

se·nile /sē′nil/ [L *senilis* old] *adj* of, pert. to, resulting from, or characteristic of old age, esp. pert. to the mental and physical deterioration accompanying it ‖ **se·nil′i·ty** /sinil′-/ *n*

sen·ior /sēn′yər/ [L = older] *adj* 1 superior in age, rank, dignity, or office; 2 of prior appointment or election; 3 older of two people in a family bearing the same name ‖ *n* 4 person superior to others in years, dignity, rank, office, or seniority; 5 student in the final year of a high school or college

sen′ior cit′i·zen *n* elderly person; one who is retired or old enough to be retired

sen′ior high′ school′ *n* public school, consisting of the 10th to 12th grades

sen·ior·i·ty /senyor′itē, -yôr′-/ *n* 1 state of being senior; 2 precedence by reason of length of service

sen·na /sen′ə/ [L < Ar *sanā*] *n* 1 any of certain plants (genus *Cassia*) of the pea family; 2 purgative drug made from the leaves of certain species

sen·sa·tion /sensāsh′ən/ [ML *sensatio* (-*onis*) < L *sensus* sense] *n* 1 any feeling, process, or condition of mind or body resulting from stimulation of the sense organs; 2 vague feeling without reference to external stimuli; 3 emotion, as *a sensation of triumph;* 4 condition of general excitement, enthusiasm, or interest; 5 cause of such condition, as *her hat was a sensation* ‖ SYN perception ‖ DISCR *Sensation,* according to the psychologist, is the elementary process in *perception,* which is the faculty of combining sensations so as to form a mental picture of an object, but a percept or mental image when studied analytically is found to be complex even when apparently simple, so that a pure sensation is almost never alone in consciousness. *Sensations* may be aroused by the immediate stimulation of a sense organ, or by the functioning of a brain center. So simple a process as the seeing that one line is longer than another is *perception*, involving visual and kinesthetic sensations and previous experience of spatial relations. The simplest conscious impressions of objects of sense are percepts rather than *sensations* (see *feeling*)

sen·sa′tion·al *adj* 1 tending to stimulate great interest or excitement; startling; lurid; 2 extremely good, phenomenal ‖ **sen·sa′tion·al·ly** *adv*

sen·sa′tion·al·ism *n* a catering to the sensational in speech, writing, or actions

sense /sens′/ [L *sensus* perception, feeling] *n* 1 faculty of receiving impressions through outside stimuli, as heat, cold, etc.; 2 perception or consciousness as a result of outside stimuli; 3 any of the faculties through which sensation is aroused, as sight, smell, hearing, taste, or touch; 4 sensation, feeling, as *a sense of pleasure*; 5 faculty of perceiving relations of a particular kind, as *a moral sense*; 6 intuitive perception, as *a sense of humor*; 7 normal understanding, rationality; 8 sound mind; good judgment; 9 meaning; 10 consensus; 11 that which is sensible; 12 **senses** *pl* sanity; 13 **in a sense** to an extent; 14 **make sense, a** to be reasonable; **b** to be intelligible ‖ *vt* 15 to perceive by the senses; 16 to become aware of ‖ *syn* (see *signification, feeling*)

sense′less *adj* 1 unconscious; 2 foolish, stupid; 3 meaningless; 4 unreasonable ‖ *syn* dull, stupid, absurd, meaningless, foolish

sen·si·bil·i·ty /sens′ibil′itē/ *n* (**-ties**) 1 capacity for sensation or feeling; 2 mental discernment; 3 capacity for intellectual, moral, or aesthetic feelings; 4 **sensibilities** *pl* **a** feelings; **b** touchiness ‖ *syn* susceptibility, sensitiveness (see *feeling*)

sen′si·ble [L *sensibilis*] *adj* 1 capable of being perceived by the senses; 2 appreciable in quantity or magnitude to the senses; 3 cognizant; 4 conscious; 5 having or showing good sense or good judgment ‖ **sen′si·bly** *adv*

sen·si·tive /sens′itiv/ [MF *sensitif* < ML *sensitivus*] *adj* 1 sensory; 2 acutely susceptible to external stimuli; 3 adjusted so as to respond quickly to slight changes, as a measuring instrument; 4 readily responsive to the action of certain agents, as a photographic film; 5 having keen sensibilities; 6 touchy, easily offended; 7 involving great secrecy or delicate negotiations ‖ **sen′si·tiv′i·ty** *n*

sen′si·tize′ *vt* to make sensitive or responsive

sen·sor /sen′sər/ *n* device that detects

various forms of energy, which it transmits for interpretation or measurement or for operating some kind of control

sen·so·ry /sens′ərē/ *adj* of or pert. to sensation or the senses

sen·su·al /sen′shōō·əl/ [LL *sensualis*] *adj* 1 sensory; 2 pert. to or preoccupied with the gratification of the senses or appetites; voluptuous, licentious, carnal ‖ **sen′su·al′i·ty** /-al′-/ *n* ‖ *syn* licentious, carnal, fleshly, brutish, gross

sen′su·al·ism *n* 1 sensuality; licentiousness; 2 *ethics* belief that in the satisfaction of the senses lies the greatest good; 3 *aesthetics* emphasis on the sensual aspects of beauty; 4 *philos* doctrine that all ideas have their origin in sensation or sense perceptions ‖ **sen′su·al·ist** *n*

sen′su·ous *adj* 1 of, pert. to, derived from, or appealing to the senses; 2 readily susceptible to sense impressions

sent /sent′/ *pt & pp* of **send**

sen′tence /sent′əns/ [OF < L *sententia* opinion] *n* 1 *law* **a** decision of a court; **b** penalty inflicted; 2 *gram* series of words, bounded by pauses and typical intonation patterns, expressing a complete thought ‖ *vt* 3 to pronounce sentence upon ‖ **sen′tenc·er** *n*

sen·ten·tious /sentensh′əs/ *adj* 1 full of or given to the use of pithy sayings or maxims; 2 self-righteous

sen·tient /sensh′ənt/ [L *sentiens* (*-entis*) feeling] *adj* 1 having the faculty of sense perception; 2 experiencing sensation or feeling ‖ **sen′tience** *n*

sen·ti·ment /sent′imənt/ [OF < ML *sentimentum*] *n* 1 opinion or state of mind based on feeling; 2 refinement of feeling; 3 tendency to form emotional judgments; 4 exhibition or manifestation of a refined or delicate feeling; 5 thought expressed in words but distinct from them; 6 thought; judgment; attitude ‖ *syn* sentimentality ‖ *discr* *Sentiment*, ordinarily used in a good sense, is compounded of both thought and feeling. It manifests itself as a mental view, tendency, or bias, warmed, colored, prompted by, or based on, emotion. Such a view or tendency is noble or lofty in thought, artistic, delicate, sometimes tender, in feeling. Taken as a whole such views or tendencies influence the will and govern action, as the *sentiment* of patriotism; the *sentiment* of honor; a person's *sentiments* with regard to a given proposal. The susceptibility to such mental feelings is also called *sentiment*, as a man of *sentiment*. Less often *sentiment* is used in an unfavorable sense, that denoting mawkishness, weepy, emotional weakness or the display of it, or the tendency to be swayed by emotion rather than thought; it is in this unfavorable sense that *sentiment* and *sentimentality* are synonyms. *Sentimentality* sometimes adds to mawkishness the idea of affected feeling, of artificial, almost vulgar, susceptibility to feeling, as "he had a tonic quality of mind that always attacked *sentimentality*"; "she was attracted by the *sentimentality* of stories which described long, unhappy attachments"

sen·ti·men·tal /-ment'əl/ *adj* 1 having, expressing, or given to sentiment; 2 appealing to, or based on, sentiment; 3 affectedly emotional; mawkish

sen·ti·men·tal·i·ty /-tal'-/ *n* (-ties) 1 state or quality of being sentimental; 2 affectation of fine or tender feeling; 3 weak or affected emotionalism; 4 instance of being sentimental ‖ SYN emotionalism, mawkishness (see *sentiment*)

sen·ti·nel /sent'inəl/ [MF *sentinelle* < It *sentinella*] *n* guard, sentry

sen·try /sent'rē/ [< *centrinel* var of *sentinel*] *n* (-tries) soldier or guard stationed to guard against unauthorized entry, surprise attack, etc.

sen'try box' *n* small cabinlike structure for sheltering a sentry

Seoul /sōl'/ *n* capital of South Korea (3,800,000)

sep. separate

se·pal /sēp'əl/ [L *separ* separate + *petal*] *n* one of the divisions or parts of a calyx

sep·a·ra·ble /sep'(ə)rəbəl/ *adj* capable of being separated

sep·a·rate /sep'ərāt'/ [L *separare* (-*atus*)] *vt* 1 to keep or set apart; divide; 2 to set apart by coming in between; 3 to sort, divide, as grain; 4 to remove from association, as *to separate someone from the army* ‖ *vi* 5 to part; withdraw from one another; 6 to become detached; 7 to become disconnected; 8 to part company and go in different directions ‖ /sep'ərit/ *adj* 9 divided from the rest; disconnected; 10 distinct; unconnected; 11 not shared, as *separate checks, separate rooms* ‖ **sep'·a·rate·ly** *adv* ‖ SYN *v* sever, remove, detach, split, estrange, withdraw ‖ ANT *v* unite, connect, join, mix

sep·a·ra'tion *n* 1 act of separating or state of being separated; 2 place of separation; gap, opening; 3 *law* divorce from bed and board without the dissolution of marriage, by common consent or by judicial decree

sep·a·ra·tist /-rətist/ *n* advocate of separation, esp. from a nation or church

sep'a·ra'tor *n* 1 one who or that which separates; 2 device for separating, as cream from milk

Se·phar·dim /sifär'dim/ [Heb] *npl* the Jews of Spain and Portugal and their descendants, many of whom speak a dialect of Spanish ‖ **Se·phar'dic** *adj*

se·pi·a /sēp'ē·ə/ [Gk = cuttlefish] *n* 1 dark-brown pigment obtained from the secretion of the cuttlefish; 2 dark brown ‖ *adj* 3 dark-brown

se·poy /sē'poi/ [Urdu *sipahi*] *n* formerly, native soldier of the British Army in India

sep·sis /sep'sis/ [Gk = decay] *n* poisoning caused by the presence of bacteria in the blood

Sept. September

Sep·tem·ber /septem'bər/ [L = seventh month (of Roman calendar)] *n* ninth month of the year, having 30 days

sep·tet /septet'/ [L *septem* seven + *duet*] *n* 1 any group of seven persons or things; 2 *mus* a composition for seven instruments or voices; b the seven performers rendering such a composition

sep·tic /sep'tik/ [Gk *septikos* putrefactive] *adj* 1 infective, as by bacteria; 2 infected by bacteria

sep·ti·ce·mi·a /sep'tisēm'ē·ə/ [*septic* + -*emia*] *n* invasion of the blood stream by pathogenic bacteria

sep'tic tank' *n* large sewage tank in which waste matter is decomposed by bacteria

sep·tu·a·ge·nar·i·an /sep'chōō·əjener'-ē·ən/ [< L *septuageni* seventy each] *n* person 70 years old or between 70 and 80 years old ‖ also *adj*

Sep·tu·a·gint /sep'tu(y)ōō·əjint, sep'chōō·/ [L *septuaginta* seventy < tradition that translation was made by 70 scholars each working independently] *n* earliest Greek version of the Old Testament

sep·tum /sep'təm/ [L = enclosure] *n* (-ta /-tə/) wall or partition in a plant or animal structure

sep·ul·cher /sep'əlkər/ [OF *sepulcre* < L *sepulcrum*] *n* grave or tomb; burial vault

se·pul·chral /səpulk'rəl/ *adj* 1 of or pert. to a sepulcher or to a burial; 2 gloomy or funereal; 3 deep or hollow in tone

seq. [L *sequentes, sequentia*] that which follows

se·quel /sēk'wəl/ [L *sequela* what follows] *n* 1 that which follows; continuation; 2 literary work complete in itself but that continues the narrative of a preceding work

se·quence /sēk'wəns/ [LL *sequentia*] *n* 1 following or succession; 2 number or series of things following one another; 3 *cards* set of three or more cards of the same suit following one another in value; 4 single episode of a motion picture film shown without interruptions or breaks ‖ **se·quen'tial** /sikwensh'əl/ *adj*

se·ques·ter /sikwest′ər/ [L = trustee, agent] *vt* 1 to cause to withdraw into obscurity; seclude; 2 *law* to seize, as the property and income of a debtor, until some claim is satisfied; 3 to confiscate; appropriate ‖ **se′ques·tra′tion** /sē′-/ *n*

se·quin /sēk′win/ [It *zecchino* former gold coin of Venice] *n* small coin-like spangle used in dress trimmings

se·quoi·a /sikwoi′ə/ [*Sequoya* (ab. 1770–1843) Cherokee scholar] *n* either of two tall evergreen trees (genera *Sequoia* and *Sequoiadendron*) of California

se·ra·glio /siral′yō, -räl′-/ [It *serraglio* enclosure] *n* 1 a palace of the former sultans of Turkey; 2 harem

se·ra·pe /sərăp′ē/ [MexSp *sarape*] *n* small bright-colored blanket used as a wrap, esp. in Mexico and Guatemala

ser·aph /ser′əf/ [< Heb *serāphīm*] (-**aphs** or -**a·phim** /-əfim/) 1 one of the celestial beings surrounding God's throne (Isa. 6); 2 highest order of angels ‖ **se·raph′ic** (-**i·cal**) /siraf′ik(əl)/ *adj*

Serb /surb′/ [Serbian *Srb*] *adj* & *n* Serbian

Ser·bi·a /surb′ē·ə/ *n* former kingdom in the Balkans, now a constituent republic of Yugoslavia ‖ **Ser′bi·an** *adj* & *n*

Ser·bo·Cro·a′tian /surb′ō-/ *n* principal language of Yugoslavia, written in the Latin alphabet in Croatia and in the Cyrillic in Serbia ‖ also *adj*

sere /sir′/ [var of *sear*[1]] *adj* dry, withered

ser·e·nade /ser′ənād′/ [F < It *serenata* evening song] *n* 1 musical composition sung or played by a lover under the window of his lady; 2 piece of music fitted to such an occasion ‖ *vt* & *vi* 3 to entertain by singing or playing beneath a window ‖ **ser′e·nad′er** *n*

ser·e·na·ta /ser′ənät′ə/ [It] *n* 1 composition resembling a symphony but of simpler construction; 2 cantata or poem set to music; 3 serenade

ser·en·dip·i·ty /ser′ondip′itē/ [coined by Horace Walpole, Eng author < *Serendip* former name of Ceylon] *n* gift of finding without seeking ‖ **ser′en·dip′i·tist** *n* ‖ **ser′en·dip′i·tous** *adj*

se·rene /sərēn′/ [L *serenus*] *adj* 1 clear, fair; 2 placid, unruffled ‖ **se·rene′ly** *adv* ‖ **se·ren′i·ty** /-ren′-/ *n* ‖ **SYN** reposeful, quiet, unperturbed, tranquil (see *calm*) ‖ **ANT** disturbed, ruffled, agitated

Se·rene′ High′ness *n* title applied to certain European princes of less than royal rank

serf /surf′/ [MF < L *servus* slave] *n* 1 in medieval Europe, and in Russia until 1861, peasant attached to the land and transferred with it; 2 slave

‖ **serf′dom** *n* ‖ **SYN** thrall, vassal, bondman, drudge (see *slave*)

serge /surj′/ [F < L *serica* silken] *n* twilled woolen fabric used for clothing

ser·geant /sär′jənt/ [OF *sergent* servant] *n* 1 police officer ranking next below a lieutenant; 2 noncommissioned officer ranking next above a corporal in the Army or the Marines, and in the Air Force next above an airman first class ‖ **ser′gean·cy** *n* (-**cies**)

ser′geant at arms′ *n* officer in a deliberative body whose duty is to preserve order

ser′geant ma′jor *n* highest-ranking noncommissioned officer in the U.S. Army and the U.S. Marine Corps

se·ri·al /sir′ē·əl/ [< *series*] *adj* 1 of, pert. to, or arranged in a series; 2 published, broadcast, or screened in installments at regular intervals ‖ *n* 3 serial story, play, or motion picture; 4 consecutively numbered periodical

se′ri·al num′ber *n* identification number, as of an automobile or a soldier, issued seriatim

se·ri·a·tim /sir′ē·ăt′im, ser′-/ *adv* in regular order, one after the other

se·ries /sir′ēz/ [L] *n* (pl -**ries**) 1 number of related things or events succeeding one another in order; 2 connected succession or sequence; set; 3 **in series** *elec* connected end to end to form a single continuous conductor

se′ries-wound′ /-wound′/ *adj* (electric generator or motor) in which the armature winding and the field winding are connected in series

ser·if /ser′if/ [?] *n typ* fine cross stroke at the top or bottom of a letter, or across the end of a stroke, as in the letter F

se·ri·ous /sir′ē·əs/ [LL *seriosus* < L *serius*] *adj* 1 grave in character or conduct; 2 thoughtful; 3 sincere; in earnest; 4 important, weighty; 5 alarming; causing anxiety ‖ **se′ri·ous·ly** *adv* ‖ **SYN** earnest, grave, sedate, solemn, sober, important, momentous ‖ **DISCR** *Serious* people are not given to trifling or frivolity, but are *sedate*, thoughtful, and responsible. *Serious* affairs have consequence, are important, or demand consideration, as a *serious* step; a *serious* accident; a *serious* subject. People who carry heavy responsibilities are *grave* in manner; *serious* symptoms, dangerous faults, threatening ill fortune, are *grave* matters. *Grave* and *sober* alike describe somber colors and *sedate* mien; they are both opposed to the gay. *Sober* people are not vehement, not excited, not vivacious; they are sane, well-balanced, temperate. *Earnest* is opposed to *trifling*.

Important is applied to affairs or times of significance, moment, and weight, which require attention and consideration. A *solemn* person is *grave* in manner; he is full of the *important* occasion that has given rise to solemnity. A *solemn* warning is impressive; a *solemn* promise is sacred; a *solemn* silence is mysterious, sometimes depressing (see *grave* ²) ‖ ANT trifling, frivolous, flippant, gay, hilarious

ser·mon /surm′ən/ [L *sermo* (-*onis*) speech] *n* 1 formal talk on a moral or religious subject, often based on Scripture and delivered from the pulpit by a clergyman; 2 any serious address; admonition; 3 tedious speech ‖ **ser′mon·ize** *vt* & *vi* ‖ SYN discourse, lecture, exhortation (see *speech*)

Ser′mon on the Mount′ *n* discourse of Jesus containing the Beatitudes and considered the best complete statement of Christian ethics and principles (Matt. 5-7; Luke 6:20-49)

se·rol·o·gy /sirol′əjē/ [see **serum**] *n* study of serums and their use in the treatment of disease

se·rous /sir′əs/ *adj* 1 pert. to, producing, or containing serum; 2 thin and watery

ser′pent /surp′ənt/ [L *serpens* (-*entis*) creeping] *n* 1 snake; 2 sly, treacherous person

ser′pen·tine′ /-tēn′, -tīn′/ *adj* 1 pert. to or like a snake; 2 winding, sinuous; 3 crafty, cunning

ser·rate /ser′it, -āt/ [< L *serrare* (-*atus*) to saw] *adj* notched along the edge like a saw, as some leaves ‖ **ser·ra′tion** *n*

ser·ried /ser′ēd/ [< MF *serrer* to place close together] *adj* close together, as serried ranks of soldiers

se·rum /sir′əm/ [L = whey] *n* (-**rums** or -ra /-rə/) 1 yellowish clear watery fluid of blood remaining after coagulation; 2 such fluid taken from the blood of an animal which has been made immune to a given disease by inoculation, used as an antitoxin

serv·ant /surv′ənt/ [OF = serving] *n* one who works for another, esp. one who performs domestic duties

serve /surv′/ [OF *servir*] *vt* 1 to work for, be in the service of; 2 to give service to; aid; 3 to give homage to; 4 to put on the table and distribute, as food; 5 to wait upon at table; 6 to wait on, as in a shop; 7 to meet the needs of; answer the purpose of; 8 to render active service to; 9 to promote, contribute to; 10 to treat, act toward; 11 to undergo, spend (a term in office, imprisonment, etc.); 12 to operate (artillery); 13 *law* a to deliver (a writ or summons); b to deliver a writ or summons to; 14 *tennis* to put (the ball) into play; 15

serve one right to give one his just deserts ‖ *vi* 16 to work as a servant; 17 to wait on table; 18 to serve meals; 19 to discharge the duties of an office or employment; 20 to be sufficient; 21 to answer the purpose; 22 to suit, be favorable; 23 *tennis* to put the ball in play ‖ *n* 24 *tennis* act or turn of serving the ball ‖ SYN *v* promote, aid, assist, help, minister, obey

serv·ice /surv′is/ [OF < L *servitium*] *n* 1 state or position of a domestic servant; 2 rendering of any labor, office, or duty to another; 3 set of dishes or table utensils; 4 public exercises of worship; 5 liturgical form prescribed for public worship or for some special ceremonial, as the *marriage service*; 6 official duty or work of public servants; 7 operation of an organized system for supplying public needs, as *bus service, telephone service, repair service*; 8 legal delivery of a writ or process; 9 *tennis* act or manner of serving; 10 public employment, as *government service*; 11 department of the government, as *the postal service*; 12 *mil* a armed forces; b particular branch of the armed forces; 13 act of breeding animals; 14 often **services** *pl* a work done for another; b duty required or performed in any office; c employment, aid, or kindness rendered to another; 15 **at the service of** at the disposal of; 16 **be of service** to be helpful ‖ *vt* 17 to restore to good condition; 18 to perform routine maintenance tasks on, as an automobile; 19 to supply services to; 20 to copulate with (a female animal) ‖ *adj* 21 serviceable; useful; 22 for servants; 23 providing repair and maintenance; 24 of or pert. to the armed forces

serv·ice·a·ble *adj* 1 useful; 2 having good wearing qualities

serv·ice·man′ /-man′/ *n* (-**men** /-men′/) 1 member of the armed forces; 2 repairman

serv′ice sta′tion *n* gas station

serv′ice stripe′ *n* stripe worn on the sleeve of the uniform of enlisted men indicating each period of enlistment and reenlistment

ser·vile /sur′vəl, -vīl/ [L] *adj* 1 of, pert. to, or befitting a slave; 2 slavishly humble; cringing; fawning; 3 submissive; abject ‖ **ser·vil′i·ty** /sərvil′-/ *n*

serv′ing *n* portion of food or drink served at one time; helping

ser·vi·tor /sur′vitər/ [L] *n* servant; attendant

ser′vi·tude′ /-t(y)ōōd′/ [L *servitudo*] *n* 1 bondage, slavery; 2 compulsory service or labor enforced as punishment

ser·vo /sur′vō/ or **ser′vo·mech·an·ism**

[< L *servus* slave] *n* device for applying considerable power by the exertion of much smaller power and for maintaining the steady performance of a mechanism by means of sensors

ses·a·me /ses′əmē/ [Gk] *n* 1 tropical herb (*Sesamum indicum*) bearing edible seeds from which an oil is expressed that is used in cookery, medicines, and cosmetics; 2 the seeds

ses′qui·cen·ten′ni·al /ses′kwi-/ [< L *sesqui* one and a half times] *n* 150th anniversary or its celebration

ses·sion /sesh′ən/ [L *sessio* (*-onis*)] *n* 1 meeting of a court, legislature, organization, etc. to transact business; 2 single uninterrupted meeting of such a body; 3 continuous series of such meetings; 4 period of study or lessons; 5 any period of time given to group activity

set /set/ [OE *settan*] *v* (set; set·ting) *vt* 1 to put in a particular place, position, or condition; 2 to cause to be in a certain condition, as *to set a house on fire;* 3 to make ready, as *to set a trap;* 4 to render rigid or firm, as jelly; 5 to make fast, as a color; 6 to regulate, as a timepiece; 7 to reduce (a bone) from a state of fracture or dislocation; 8 to assign or fix, as a price, a time, a limit, or a quota; 9 to start, employ, as *to set a man to work;* 10 to furnish (an example); 11 to mount (a gem); 12 to fix with settled purpose, as *to set one's heart on something;* 13 to direct, start aright; 14 *naut* a to spread (sails); b to fix (a course); 15 *mus* to fit (music) to words or (words) to music; 16 *typ* a to arrange (type) in the proper order; b to put into type; 17 to place the plates and silverware on (a table); 18 to arrange (the hair) in a particular style; 19 *theat* to prepare (the stage) for a particular scene; 20 *bridge* to defeat by a specified number of tricks; 21 **set back**, a to hinder; b *colloq* to cost; 22 **set down**, a to put in writing; b to humiliate; 23 **set forth** to state, describe; 24 **set off**, a to explode; b to contrast; 25 **set on** to cause to attack, as *they set the dogs on him;* 26 **set up**, a to raise; b to erect; c to bring about; d to establish || *vi* 27 to sink below the horizon; 28 to harden, become firm or permanent; 29 to have a certain direction; tend; 30 to fit, as clothes; 31 to sit on eggs, as a hen; 32 **set down** to land in an airplane; 33 **set in** to begin, come to pass, as *a reaction set in;* 34 **set off** to leave on a journey; 35 **set out**, a to leave on a journey; b to begin a course of action; 36 **set upon** to attack || *adj* 37 fixed or established; 38 deliberate, formal, as a *set speech;* 39 determined; obstinate;

40 fixed; rigid; 41 ready || *n* 42 act of setting or state of being set; 43 number of persons associated or drawn together by common interests, as *the younger set;* 44 number of things intended to be used together or that complement each other, as *a set of drill bits;* 45 carriage, build; 46 fit, as of clothes; 47 any series of related things, as *a set of books;* 48 bent or inclination; 49 radio or television receiver; 50 *tennis* group of six or more games won by a margin of two or more games; 51 scenery or construction made to represent a scene in a play; 52 *math* group of elements classed together || SYN *v* adapt, establish, fix, settle, station, put, appoint, start, prepare, adjust, arrange || ANT *v* disturb, overthrow, disorder, disarrange

set′back′ *n* reverse, check; defeat

set′screw′ *n* machine screw, usu. without a head, used to prevent the part against which it presses from slipping

set·tee /setē′/ [perh var of *settle²*] *n* seat with a back for two or more persons

set′ter *n* 1 one who or that which sets; 2 one of a kind of long-haired hunting dogs which stand rigidly and point on scenting game

set′ting *n* 1 act of one who or that which sets; 2 that in which something is set, as a gem; 3 scene of a story or play; 4 scene in which anything takes place; environment

set·tle¹ /set′əl/ [OE *setlan*] *vt* 1 to establish in life or in a home or business; 2 to free from doubt or uncertainty; 3 to quiet, compose, as the nerves; 4 to set or fix; put in order; 5 to clarify (a liquid) by depositing dregs; 6 to colonize; 7 to cause to sink and make compact; 8 to decide, as a dispute; 9 to appoint or set, as a date; 10 to dispose of, set in order, as an estate; 11 to adjust the balance of; liquidate; 12 *law* to bestow legally; 13 to pay, as a bill || *vi* 14 to become fixed in one spot, as a pain; 15 to come to rest; alight; 16 to establish a residence; 17 to grow calm or clear; 18 to sink gradually to the bottom; 19 to adjust differences or accounts; come to an agreement; 20 to become firm, compact, or solid; 21 to sink, as a building's foundation; 22 to resolve or determine, as *to settle on a course of conduct;* 23 **settle down**, a to enter on an even life or routine; b to become tranquil; 24 **settle up** to pay, liquidate a debt || SYN regulate, conclude, fix, locate, decide, quiet (see *substantiate*) || ANT disorder, agitate, confuse, disturb

set·tle² [OE *setl*] *n* long high-backed bench with arms

set'tle·ment *n* 1 act or state of settling or state of being settled; 2 colonization; 3 colony, esp. in its early stages; 4 adjustment of an account, dispute, etc.; 5 sparsely settled village; 6 welfare and community center for underprivileged persons

set'tler *n* one who settles, esp. in a new colony or region

set'-to' *n colloq* altercation

set'up' *n* 1 arrangement, organization; 2 task or contest deliberately made easy; 3 opponent easy to defeat; 4 everything needed for a mixed drink except the liquor

sev·en /sev'ən/ [OE *seofon*] *n* 1 sum of six and one (7; VII); 2 set of seven persons or things; 3 playing card with seven spots ‖ also *adj & pron*

sev'en dead'ly sins' *npl* the seven sins of pride, covetousness, lust, anger, gluttony, envy, and sloth

sev'en·fold' *adj* 1 having seven times as much or as many ‖ *adv* 2 seven times as much or as many

sev'en seas' *npl* all the navigable waters of the world

sev·en·teen' /-tēn'/ [OE *seofontēne*] *n* sum of seven and ten (17; XVII) ‖ also *adj & pron*

sev'en·teenth' *n* 1 the one next in order after the sixteenth; 2 one of seventeen equal parts ‖ also *adj*

sev'en·teen'-year' lo'cust *n* a cicada (*Magicicada septendecim*) of the E U.S. that emerges in great numbers after spending 17 years in the nymph stage

sev'enth *n* 1 the one next in order after the sixth; 2 one of seven equal parts; 3 *mus* interval between any degree of a scale and the one preceding its octave above ‖ also *adj*

sev'en·ti·eth *n* 1 the one next in order after the sixty-ninth; 2 one of seventy equal parts ‖ also *adj*

sev·en·ty [OE *seofontig*] *n* (-ties) 1 seven times ten (70; LXX); 2 the **seventies** *pl* the numbers from 70 to 79; b the years from 70 to 79 in a century or a lifetime ‖ also *adj & pron*

sev'er /sev'ər/ [MF *severer* to separate] *vt* 1 to cut off; 2 to divide into parts; 3 to break off, disjoin ‖ *vi* 4 to become severed ‖ SYN part, separate, detach, disjoin, break, rend

sev·er·al /sev'(ə)rəl/ [AF < ML *separalis*] *adj* 1 individual, respective; 2 a few; more than two but not many; 3 different, diverse ‖ *npl* 4 several persons or things ‖ **sev'er·al·ly** *adv*

sev'er·ance pay' *n* lump sum other than salary paid to an employee dismissed through no fault of his own, usu. based on his years of service

se·vere /sivir'/ [L *severus*] *adj* 1 strict, harsh; 2 extremely plain, as style; 3 grave; stern; 4 extreme, violent, as a pain or the weather; 5 hard to bear

or undergo; trying; 6 critical, dangerous, as an illness ‖ **se·ver'i·ty** /-ver'-/ *n* (-ties) ‖ SYN strict, stern, unrelenting, harsh, sharp, plain (see *austere*) ‖ ANT lax, mild, merciful, easy, gentle

sew /sō/ [OE *siwian*] *v* (*pp* **sewed** or **sewn**) *vt* 1 to join or fasten together with stitches; 2 to make or mend by sewing; 3 **sew up, a** to close or mend by sewing; **b** *colloq* to get exclusive control of ‖ *vi* 4 to work with needle and thread

sew·age /sōo'ij/ [< *sewer*] *n* waste matter carried off by a sewer

sew·er¹ /sōo'ər/ [OF *seuwiere* sluice] *n* pipe or channel, usu. underground, for carrying off water and waste matter

sew·er² /sō'ər/ *n* one who or that which sews or stitches

sew·er·age /sōo'ərij/ *n* 1 drainage by sewers; 2 system of sewers; 3 sewage

sew·ing /sō'ij/ *n* 1 act of one who sews; 2 things to be sewn

sewn /sōn/ *pp* of **sew**

sex /seks/ [L *sexus*] *n* 1 the sum of the anatomical and physiological characteristics that make an animal or plant male or female; 2 one of the two divisions into which people are grouped as being male or female; 3 attraction of one sex for the other

sex- [L = six] *comb form* six

sex' act' *n* sexual intercourse

sex·a·ge·nar·i·an /sek'səjəner'ē·ən/ [< L *sexageni* sixty each] *n* person who is 60 years old or between 60 and 70 years old ‖ also *adj*

sex' ap·peal' *n* quality of attracting the opposite sex

sex'ism *n* prejudice against women ‖ **sex'ist** *adj & n*

sex' pot' *n slang* one who is the embodiment of sexiness

sex·tant /seks'tənt/ [L *sextans* (-*antis*) sixth part] *n* instrument for measuring altitudes and angular distances between heavenly bodies, used in navigation

sex·tet also **sex·tette** /sekstet'/ [It *sestetto*] *n* 1 any group of six persons or things; 2 *mus* a composition for six instruments or voices; **b** six performers rendering such a composition

sex·ton /seks'tən/ [< MF *secrestein*] *n* minor church official who takes care of church property and who formerly dug graves

sex·u·al /sek'shōo·əl/ [LL *sexualis*] *adj* 1 of or pert. to sex; 2 involving the two sexes; 3 (reproduction) characterized by the union of gametes ‖ **sex'u·al'i·ty** /-al'-/ *n*

sex'u·al in'ter·course' *n* genital contact, esp. between humans

sex'y *adj* (-i·er; -i·est) *colloq* 1 exuding sexual attraction; 2 risqué ‖ **sex'i·ness** *n*

Sey·chelles /sāshel′,-shelz′/ *n* republic in the Indian Ocean (65,000; 171 sq. m.; cap. Victoria)

Sgt. Sergeant

shab·by /shab′ē/ [< OE *sceabb* scab] *adj* (**-bi·er**; **-bi·est**) 1 worn or threadbare; 2 seedy, unkempt; 3 dilapidated; decayed; 4 mean, petty, unworthy ‖ **shab′bi·ly** *adv* ‖ **shab′bi·ness** *n*

shack /shak′/ [?] *n* 1 crude cabin, shanty ‖ *vi* 2 **shack up** *slang* a to cohabit; b to have illicit sexual relations

shack·le /shak′əl/ [OE *sceacul*] *n* 1 one of a pair of rings or a similar device for confining the wrists or ankles; 2 anything that confines, restrains, or impedes; 3 any of various fastenings, as the bow of a padlock or a link for coupling cars ‖ *vt* 4 to restrain or confine with shackles; 5 to restrain or impede the free action of; 6 to join or fasten with a shackle

shad /shad′/ [OE *sceadd*] *n* (**shad** or **shads**) any of several fishes (genus *Alosa*) of the herring family, esp. an American species (*A. sapidissima*)

shade /shād′/ [OE *sceadu*] *n* 1 darkness caused by cutting off the rays of light; 2 area from which direct rays of light are excluded by an intervening object; 3 something which cuts off or softens direct light, as *a window shade, a lamp shade;* 4 degree of darkness of a color; 5 slight degree of difference; 6 little bit; 7 comparative obscurity; 8 ghost ‖ *vt* 9 to screen from light; 10 to darken, dim; 11 to represent shadows and shade in (a picture) ‖ *vi* 12 to blend or change by slight degrees ‖ SYN *n* darkness, gloom, screen (see *color*)

shad′ing *n* 1 slight variation; 2 representation of light and shade in a picture

shad·ow /shad′ō/ [OE *sceaduwe*, form of *sceadu* shade] *n* 1 dark image cast by a body intercepting light; 2 partial darkness or shade; 3 inseparable companion; 4 darker portion of a picture; 5 weakened or diminished counterpart; 6 faint suggestion, trace; 7 ghost; 8 dim foreshadowing or premonition; 9 gloom; 10 one keeping a close watch on another by following constantly; 11 **shadows** *pl* darkness ‖ *vt* 12 to cast a shadow on; 13 to keep under close surveillance by following constantly; 14 **shadow forth** to represent faintly and prophetically ‖ **shad′ow·y** *adj*

shad′ow·box′ *vi* to go through the motions of boxing without an opponent ‖ **shad′ow·box′ing** *n*

shad′ow cab′i·net *n* in some countries, notably Britain, the members of the opposition in Parliament who would become members of the cabinet on the return of their party to power

shad′ow·land′ *n* region of obscurity and uncertainty

shad·y /shād′ē/ *adj* (**-i·er**; **-i·est**) 1 full of or causing shade; 2 *colloq* questionable; of doubtful honesty; 3 **on the shady side of** *colloq* older than (a specified age)

shaft /shaft′, shäft′/ [OE *sceaft*] *n* 1 long straight stem or handle, as on an arrow, spear, or hammer; 2 something that moves toward its mark like an arrow, as *a shaft of ridicule, a shaft of light;* 3 one of the poles between which a horse is harnessed to a vehicle; 4 body of a column between the base and the capital; 5 vertical or slanted entrance to a mine; 6 any narrow well-like space, as *an elevator shaft;* 7 *mach* round straight bar for transmitting motion, as *a drive shaft, a propeller shaft;* 8 **give the shaft to** *slang* to betray, sell out

shag·gy /shag′ē/ [< OE *sceacga* hair of the head] *adj* (**-gi·er**; **-gi·est**) 1 having rough or bushy hair; 2 rough, tangled, as hair; 3 unkempt; 4 having a rough nap

shah /shä′/ [Pers = king] *n* title of the former rulers of Iran

shake /shāk′/ [OE *sceacan*] *v* (**shook**; **shak·en** /shāk′ən/) *vt* 1 to cause to tremble; move with a quick short motion; 2 to loosen, dislodge; 3 to cause to waver, sway, or totter; 4 to agitate, disturb; 5 to brandish; 6 to mix by agitating; 7 to mix (dice) by rolling in the hand; 8 to get rid of (a person); 9 to elude (a pursuer); 10 **shake down,** a to knock down by shaking; b to give a test run to; c *slang* to extort money from; 11 **shake off** to outdistance (a pursuer); 12 **shake up,** a to mix by shaking; b to jar, treat roughly; c to shock, upset; d to reorganize ‖ *vi* 13 to move; tremble, sway; 14 to shake something; 15 to shake hands ‖ *n* 16 act or instance of shaking; 17 tremor; 18 milk shake; 19 *colloq* deal or treatment, as *a fair shake;* 20 **the shakes** *pl* fit of trembling; 21 **no great shakes** *colloq* mediocre; unimportant; 22 **two shakes (of a lamb's tail)** instant, moment ‖ SYN *v* agitate, rock, swing, oscillate, sway, vibrate, tremble, shiver, quiver, shudder, jar, rattle ‖ DISCR To *shake* is to move violently up and down, back and forth, or from side to side, with rapid, short motions; that which is *shaken* may be a large body, as the earth *shaken* by a quake, or it may be a rug *shaken* by the hands, or a leaf *shaken* by a breeze. To *agitate* is to *shake* in an irregular manner. *Shake* and *agitate* are often used interchangeably, though we say that the ocean is *agitated,* not *shaken,* by the tempest, and that the kernels of corn in a popper are *shaken* rather than *agitated*. Figuratively, *agitate* is used of less profound disturbance than *shake*; our feelings are *agitated* by the news of a great public disaster; we are *shaken* by a personal affliction. To *rock* is to move to and fro on a base, as to *rock* a cradle; or from a deep foundation that acts as a pivot, as the house *rocked*. *Rocking* is a slower, less jerky movement than *shaking*. Figuratively, to *rock* indicates a deep-seated upheaval of all that was firm and substantial, as his world *rocked* about him. To *swing* is to move to and fro from a support above, as does a pendulum, or from a fixed point or points at the sides, as a door on its hinges. To *oscillate* is to *swing* like a pendulum, moving to and fro between two points. To *sway* is to *oscillate* irregularly, or to *swing* back and forth unsteadily, as branches in the wind. *Vibrate*, like *oscillate*, indicates the regular motion to and fro of the pendulum; *vibrate* is also used to express the rapid motion produced when a taut string is plucked, when a bell is struck, when a heavy footstep *shakes* the floor. Flames of fire dancing with a rapid, vibrating motion are said to *quiver*, as are leaves that move in the breeze, voices that tremble with emotion. *Shiver* is used of a trembling, vibrating, momentary motion such as runs over the body from cold, down the spine from horror, or from thrilling anticipation. To *shudder* is to experience a kind of shivering; to *shudder* connotes loathing or repugnance

shake'down' *n* 1 extortion ‖ *adj* 2 (cruise or flight) intended to test new equipment and train new and unaccustomed crews

shak'er *n* 1 one who or that which shakes; 2 container with a perforated top for sprinkling sugar, salt, flour on food; 3 device or container for shaking or mixing various beverages; 4 **Shaker** one of a religious celibate sect living in community settlements, so called from the motions of a dance in their ritual

Shake·speare, William /shāk′spir/ *n* (1564–1616) English dramatist and poet ‖ **Shake·spear′e·an** /-ē̯-ən/ *adj & n*

shake'-up' *n* thorough and far-reaching reorganization

shak·o /shak′ō, shāk′ō/ [Hung *csákó*] *n* tall stiff military hat, having a visor and a plume

shak·y /shāk′ē/ *adj* (-i·er; -i·est) 1 trembling; 2 infirm, tottering; 3 wavering, undecided; 4 of questionable credit or solvency

shale /shāl′/ [OE *scealu* shell] *n* stone of clayey origin, easily split into thin layers

shall /shal′, shəl/ [OE *sceal*] *v* (**should**) *modal aux* used to express: 1 simple futurity in formal usage, as *I shall arrive at two o'clock;* 2 permission, promise, determination, command, threat, etc., as *shall I come early?, thou shalt not kill*

shal·lot /shəlot′/ [OF *eschalote*] *n* kind of small onionlike vegetable (*Allium ascalonicum*) allied to garlic but of milder flavor

shal·low /shal′ō/ [ME *schalowe*] *adj* 1 not deep; 2 superficial, having no mental depth ‖ *n* 3 often **shallows** *sg* or *pl* shallow body of water

shalt /shalt′/ *archaic 2nd pers sg* of **shall**

sham /sham′/ [perh *dial.* var of *shame*] *n* 1 fraud, imitation; 2 ornamental, trimmed covering, as for a pillow or bolster ‖ *adj* 3 feigned, counterfeit ‖ *v* (**shammed; shamming**) *vi* 4 to make false pretenses; feign ‖ *vt* 5 to make a pretense of; dissemble ‖ SYN *v* pretend, delude, cheat, trick, feign

sha·man /shäm′ən, sham′-/ [< Turkic] *n* medicine man or priest of one of the primitive religions of N Asia ‖ **sha′man·ism** *n*

sham·ble /sham′bəl/ [< OE *sceamel* stool] *vi* 1 to walk awkwardly, shuffle ‖ *n* 2 shambling gait

sham'bles [< *obs* **shamble** butcher's bench] *nsg* 1 slaughterhouse; 2 place of carnage or destruction; 3 scene of great disorder

shame /shām′/ [OE *sc(e)amu*] *n* 1 painful feeling of humiliation caused by the consciousness of guilt, immodesty, or dishonor; 2 sensitiveness to such feelings; 3 dishonor; disgrace; 4 something sad or unfortunate; 5 **for shame!** you should be ashamed of yourself!; 6 **put to shame**, a to cause to be ashamed; b to outdo ‖ *vt* 7 to cause to feel shame; 8 to disgrace; 9 to drive or force by a sense of shame ‖ **shame′ful** *adj* ‖ **shame′less** *adj* ‖ SYN ignominy, mortification, humiliation, reproach, disgrace (see *chagrin*)

sham·poo /shampo͞o′/ [< Hindi *chāmpnā* to press] *vt* 1 to wash (the hair and scalp); 2 to clean (a rug, upholstery, etc.) ‖ *n* 3 act of shampooing; 4 preparation used for shampooing

sham·rock /sham′rok/ [Ir *seamróg*] *n* any of several three-leaved plants, one species (*Trifolium dubium*) of which is the national emblem of Ireland

sha·mus /shäm′əs/ [Ir *Séamas* James] *n slang* detective

shang·hai /shaŋ′hī, shaŋhī′/ [< *Shanghai*] *vt* to kidnap for enforced service as a sailor

Shang·hai /shaŋhī′/ *n* seaport in China (11,000,000)

shank /shaŋk'/ [OE *scanca*] *n* 1 the leg from the knee to the ankle; 2 the entire leg; 3 cut of meat from the top part of the leg of an animal; 4 the portion of a tool or implement between the cutting or acting part and the part by which it is held; 5 a the early part of a period of time; b the latter part of a period of time; 6 the narrow part of the sole of a shoe

shank's' mare' *n* 1 the legs as a means of locomotion; 2 **ride shank's mare** to go on foot

shan't /shant', shänt/ shall not

shan·ty /shant'ē/ [CanF *chantier* shed] *n* (**-ties**) shack crudely put together with cast-off materials

shan'ty·town' *n* town or part of a town made up of shanties

shape /shāp'/ [OE *scieppan* to form, create] *n* 1 form or figure of a person or thing; outline, contour; 2 that which has form or figure; 3 person or object indistinctly seen; 4 apparition; 5 mold or pattern; 6 concrete or definite embodiment or form; 7 condition; 8 physique or body, esp. of a woman; 9 **take shape** to assume a definite form ‖ *vt* 10 to make into a certain form; mold, fashion; 11 to adapt, adjust; 12 to aim or direct (one's course) ‖ *vi* 13 to take form, develop; 14 **shape up** *colloq* a to assume a satisfactory form; b to line up for assignment to the day's work, as longshoremen ‖ **shape'less** *adj*

SHAPE /shāp'/ *n* Supreme Headquarters Allied Powers, Europe

shape'ly *adj* (**-li·er, -li·est**) of pleasing shape, as a woman's figure

shap·ka /shäp'kə/ [Russ] *n* round brimless fur hat

shard /shärd'/ [OE *sceard*] *n* piece or fragment, esp. of earthenware

share /sher'/ [OE *scearu* cutting, division] *n* 1 portion or part allotted to, belonging to, or owed by an individual; 2 one of the equal fractions into which a company's capital stock is divided ‖ *vt* 3 to divide and distribute; apportion; 4 to possess in common; partake of or experience with others ‖ *vi* 5 to participate ‖ SYN *n* (see *part*); *v* (see *participate*)

share'crop'per *n* tenant farmer who pays part of his crop as rent ‖ **share'crop'** *v* (**-cropped'; -crop'ping**) *vt & vi*

share'hold'er *n* stockholder

shark¹ /shärk'/ [?] *n* any of various sharp-toothed voracious marine fishes of elongated form and tough skin

shark² [G *dial. Schork* scoundrel] *n* 1 swindler, usurer; 2 *colloq* one unusually able in some field

shark'skin' *n* smooth lightweight fabric of worsted or rayon

sharp /shärp'/ [OE *scearp*] *adj* 1 having a fine edge or point for cutting

or piercing; 2 well-defined, distinct; 3 abrupt, as a turn, rise, or drop; 4 quick, keen, as *a sharp eye*; 5 shrewd, keen-witted; 6 close in dealing; unscrupulous; 7 severe, intense, as pain; 8 violent, fierce, as *a sharp struggle*; 9 piercing, penetrating; 10 pungent; 11 sarcastic, caustic; 12 *slang* flashily stylish; 13 *mus* a raised half a step in pitch; b above true pitch ‖ *adv* 14 sharply; 15 punctually; 16 *mus* above true pitch ‖ *n* 17 sharper; 18 *mus* a tone raised half a step in pitch; b the symbol ♯ for this ‖ *vt* 19 *mus* to make higher in pitch by half a step ‖ *vi* 20 to sing or play above the correct pitch ‖ **sharp'ly** *adv* ‖ **sharp'ness** *n* ‖ SYN *adj* keen-edged, acrimonious, stinging, penetrating, shrill, violent, severe, clever, astute, angular

sharp'en *vt* 1 to make sharp or sharper ‖ *vi* 2 to become sharp or sharper

sharp'er *n* cheat, swindler

sharp'ie *n* 1 sharper; 2 shrewd, alert person; 3 *slang* sharp dresser

sharp'shoot'er *n* 1 one expert in marksmanship; 2 *slang* sharper

shat·ter /shat'ər/ [ME *schateren*] *vt* 1 to break into pieces; 2 to destroy the health or power of; 3 to defeat; ruin ‖ *vi* 4 to fly into pieces

shat'ter·proof' *adj* (glass) sandwiched with plastic so as to resist shattering

shave /shāv'/ [OE *scafan*] *v* (*pp* **shaved** or **shav·en**) *vt* 1 to remove (hair) from with a razor; 2 to cut in very thin slices or shavings; 3 to graze; 4 to cut or trim, as prices; 5 to scrape the surface of ‖ *vi* 6 to use the razor to remove hair ‖ *n* 7 act or operation of shaving

shav'er *n* 1 one who or that which shaves; 2 *colloq* boy, lad

shave'tail' *n* *slang* second lieutenant

shav'ing *n* thin slice pared off, as of wood

Shaw, George Ber·nard /burn'ərd shō'/ *n* (1856–1950) Irish dramatist and novelist; Nobel prize 1925 ‖ **Sha·vi·an** /shäv'ē·ən/ *adj & n*

shawl /shôl'/ [Pers *shāl*] *n* square or oblong piece of cloth used chiefly by women as a wrap for the shoulders

she /shē'/ [OE *sēo fem* of *dem pron se*] *pron* (3rd pers sg fem nom) 1 previously designated feminine; 2 anything considered feminine, as *she's a good ship* ‖ *n* 3 woman or female

she- /shē'-/ *comb form* female, as *she-goat*

sheaf /shēf'/ [OE *scēaf*] *n* (**sheaves** /-vz/) 1 bound bundle of cut grain; 2 any bundle, as of papers or arrows

shear /shir'/ [OE *sceran*] *v* (*pp* **sheared** or **shorn**) *vt* 1 to cut as with shears; 2 to remove by cutting, as hair or wool; 3 to cut or clip something from, as *to shear sheep;* 4 to strip or deprive of something ‖ *vi* 5 to use scissors, shears, or the like; 6 **shear off** to break off by sliding against another part; 7 **shear through** to cut through, as *the boat sheared through the water* ‖ *n* 8 act or process of shearing; 9 machine for cutting or clipping metal; 10 **shears** *pl* large scissors; 11 any of various large cutting instruments working by the crossing of opposed blades

sheath /shēth/ [OE *scēath*] *n* (-**ths** /-thz or -ths/) 1 case for the blade of a sword or knife; 2 any similar close-fitting case or covering

sheathe /shēth/ *vt* 1 to put into a sheath; 2 to encase or cover with sheathing

sheath'ing /shēth'-/ *n* covering layer applied to protect less durable material, as metal on a roof, hull, or cable

sheave[1] /shiv, shēv/ [ME *sheeve*] *n* pulley or wheel with a grooved rim for holding a chain, cable, or belt in place

sheave[2] /shēv/ [< *sheaf*] *vt* to gather and bind into sheaves

She·ba, Queen of /shēb'ə/ *n* queen who visited Solomon in order to test his wisdom (I Kings 10:1–13)

she·bang /shibaŋ/ [?] *n* the whole shebang *colloq* the entire outfit, structure, or contrivance

shed[1] /shed/ [OE *scēadan*] *v* (**shed; shed·ding**) *vt* 1 to pour out; 2 to cause to flow; 3 to throw off; resist penetration by, as *this fabric sheds water;* 4 to throw off (a natural growth, as hair, feathers, leaves, skin, etc.); 5 to pour forth, spread about, as *to shed light;* 6 **shed blood,** a to cause blood to flow; b to slaughter, kill ‖ *vi* 7 to shed hair, leaves, etc.

shed[2] [var of *shade*] *n* 1 small building, often with the front or sides open, for shelter or storage; 2 small rude cabin

she'd /shēd/ 1 she had; 2 she would

sheen /shēn/ [OE *scīene* beautiful] *n* brightness, luster

sheep /shēp/ [OE *scēap*] *n* (*pl* **sheep**) 1 any of various cud-chewing mammals (genus *Ovis*) related to the goats, esp. a domesticated species (*O. aries*) valued for its wool and flesh; 2 meek timid person

sheep' dog' *n* dog trained to herd sheep

sheep'ish *adj* abashed; awkwardly bashful

sheep's' eyes' *npl* **make sheep's eyes** to cast amorous glances

sheep'skin' *n* 1 skin of a sheep; 2 leather or parchment made from it; 3 *colloq* diploma

sheer[1] /shir/ [OE *scēr* clear] *adj* 1

absolute, utter, as *sheer folly;* 2 very thin or transparent (fabric); 3 steep, vertical ‖ *adv* 4 perpendicularly; straight; 5 quite, completely ‖ **sheer'ness** *n*

sheer[2] [?] *vi* 1 to turn from the proper course, swerve ‖ *vt* 2 to cause to sheer ‖ *n* 3 deviation from a course; 4 upward curve of the deck, gunwale, and lines of a ship toward the bow and stern

sheet[1] /shēt/ [OE *scēte*] *n* 1 broad thin piece of any substance, as paper, metal, cloth, etc.; 2 large piece of cotton or linen used as bedding; 3 single piece of paper; 4 newspaper; 5 broad expanse or surface, as of water or fire; 6 sail

sheet[2] [OE *scēatline*] *n* rope or chain attached to a sail to extend it or haul it in

sheet' light'ning *n* lightning appearing as a momentary and widely diffused glow, usu. the reflection of a flash from a distant thunderstorm

sheet' met'al *n* metal in thin sheets

sheet' mu'sic *n* music printed on unbound sheets of paper

sheik or **sheikh** /shēk/ [Ar *shaikh* old man] *n* 1 head of an Arab family, tribe, or village; 2 *slang* accomplished and masterful lover; ladies' man ‖ **sheik'dom** or **sheikh'dom** *n*

shek·el /shek'əl/ [Heb *sheqel*] *n* 1 ancient Hebrew gold or silver coin; 2 **shekels** *pl slang* money

shelf /shelf/ [OE *scylfe*] *n* (**shelves** /-vz/) 1 flat ledge set horizontally against a wall or in a frame to hold things; 2 something resembling a shelf, as a sand bank, reef, or projecting ledge; 3 **on the shelf** inactive, out of use

shell /shel/ [OE *sciell*] *n* 1 hard outside covering encasing a fruit, seed, nut, egg, animal, or part of an animal; 2 anything like a shell in being concave, hollow, empty, or in affording protection; 3 tortoise shell; 4 light, long, narrow racing boat; 5 cartridge; 6 explosive projectile for a cannon ‖ *vt* 7 to remove the shell of; 8 to fire shells at, bombard; 9 **shell out** *slang* to pay

she'll /shēl/ 1 she will; 2 she shall

shel·lac /shəlak'/ [*shell* + *lac*] *n* 1 refined lac in thin sheets for making varnish; 2 solution of shellac, esp. in alcohol, used as a varnish ‖ *v* (-**lacked; -lack·ing**) *vt* 3 to coat or treat with shellac; 4 *slang* a to trounce; b to thrash

shel·lack'ing *n slang* 1 decisive defeat; 2 thrashing, beating

shell'back' *n* 1 veteran sailor; 2 person who has crossed the equator in a boat

shelled' *adj* 1 with the shells removed; 2 having a shell

Shel·ley, Per·cy Bysshe /pur'sē bish' shel'ē/ *n* (1792–1822) English poet

shell'fish n (-fish or -fishes) invertebrate water animal having a shell

shell' game' n 1 swindling game in which spectators bet on the location of a pea concealed under one of three inverted shells; 2 any swindle

shell' shock' n mental disorder brought on by prolonged exposure to battle

shel·ter /shelt'ər/ [?] n 1 place of protection, as from danger or exposure to inclement weather; 2 state of being protected or shielded; protection; 3 one's home || vt 4 to protect, give shelter to || SYN n refuge, retreat, sanctuary, security, defense

shelve /shelv'/ vt 1 to place on a shelf; 2 to dismiss from service; 3 to postpone indefinitely

shelves /shelvz'/ pl of shelf

shelv'ing n 1 shelves collectively; 2 material for shelves

Shem /shem'/ n Bib Noah's eldest son; reputed ancestor of the Semites

she·nan·i·gans /shənan'igənz/ [?] npl colloq prankishness, mischief

shep·herd /shep'ərd/ [sheep + -herd] n 1 one who tends sheep; 2 pastor, clergyman || vt 3 to tend, guard, or lead, as a shepherd || **shep'herd·ess** nfem

Sher·a·ton /sher'ətən/ [Thomas Sheraton (1751–1806) Eng designer] adj designating a style of English furniture of the 18th century characterized by straight lines and light and simple construction

sher·bet /shurb'it/ [Pers sharbat beverage] n flavored water ice with milk or egg white added

sher·iff /sher'if/ [OE scīrgerēfa] n chief law-enforcement officer of a county

Sher·pa /shur'pə/ n (-pas or -pa) Tibetan in N Nepal, who sometimes serves as a porter in mountain-climbing expeditions

sher·ry /sher'ē/ [older sheris < Xeres (modern Jerez) town in Spain] n (-ries) amber wine of varying sweetness produced in Spain and elsewhere

she's /shēz'/ 1 she is; 2 she has

Shet'land po'ny /shet'lənd/ [Shetland Islands N of Scotland] n one of a breed of hardy shaggy ponies with long manes and tails

Shi·ah /shē'ə/ [Ar < sect] n (pl Shiah) 1 member of that one of the two chief divisions of Islam which considered Ali, the son-in-law of Muhammad, as the rightful successor of the Prophet; 2 branch of Islam formed by the Shiah

shib·bo·leth /shib'əlith, -leth'/ [Heb] n 1 Bib Hebrew word used by the Gileadites to distinguish the fleeing Ephraimites, who could not pronounce the sound sh (Judges 12:4–6); 2 password; test or watchword of a party or faction

shield /shēld'/ [OE scield] n 1 piece of armor of various sizes, shapes, and materials, usu. carried on the left arm to protect the body; 2 any person or thing that protects; 3 escutcheon; 4 police official's badge; 5 any protective covering || vt 6 to protect with or as with a shield; 7 to screen, conceal

shift /shift'/ [OE sciftan to divide] vt 1 to transfer from one person, place, or position to another; 2 to exchange one specimen of for another; substitute; 3 to change the ratio of (gears) || vi 4 to change position; veer; 5 to shift gears; 6 **shift for oneself** to get along on one's own || n 7 change, substitution, or alteration of one thing, kind, or position for another; 8 scheduled period of work; 9 workers working during this period; 10 transfer; 11 straight, loose-fitting dress; 12 gearshift

shift' key' n typewriter key that shifts the characters of the top half of the typeface to the printing position

shift'less adj lazy; irresponsible; improvident || **shift'less·ly** adv || SYN improvident, thriftless, lazy

shift'y adj (-i·er; -i·est) 1 tricky; evasive; 2 resourceful

shill /shil'/ [?] slang n 1 person who poses as a patron, to lure others to participate, as at an auction or in gambling || vi 2 to act as a shill

shil·le·lagh also **shil·la·lah** /shəlāl'ē, -ə/ [Shillelagh, town in Ireland] n stout cudgel or club

shil·ling /shil'iŋ/ [OE scilling] n 1 former monetary unit of the United Kingdom and of various countries; 2 monetary unit of several former British colonies, as Kenya and Uganda

shil·ly-shal·ly /shil'ēshal'ē/ [< obs shill I?, shall I?] v (-lied) vi to be irresolute; vacillate

shim /shim'/ [?] n 1 thin piece of metal, wood, etc., used to raise a part, as for leveling or to compensate for wear || vt 2 to insert a shim into or under

shim·mer /shim'ər/ [OE scrimrian] vi 1 to shine tremulously with a faint light; glimmer; 2 to quiver, as heat waves || n 3 faint wavering light; gleam; flicker

shim·my /shim'ē/ [< chemise] n (-mies) 1 vibration; wobble; 2 dance performed with a shaking motion || v (-mied) vi 3 to wobble, vibrate; 4 to dance the shimmy

shin /shin'/ [OE scinu] n 1 front part of the leg between the ankle and knee || v (shinned; shin·ning) vt & vi 2 to climb by gripping with the hands and legs and pulling oneself up

shin'bone' n tibia

shin·dig /shin'dig/ [?] n colloq dance; party; festivity

shin·dy /shin′dē/ [< *shindig*] *n colloq*
(-dies) 1 brawl, uproar; 2 shindig

shine /shīn′/ [OE *scīnan*] *v* (shone or
shined) *vi* 1 to give out or reflect rays
of light; beam; glow; 2 to be noted ||
v (shined) *vt* 3 to cause to shine; 4 to
direct the light of; 5 to polish, put
a gloss on || *vi* 6 **shine up to** *colloq*
to be attentive to (a person) for
ulterior motives || *n* 7 radiance; 8
polish; 9 sunshine; 10 shoeshine; 11
take a shine to *colloq* to take a liking to

shin′er *n slang* black eye

shin·gle /shin′gəl/ [var of *shindle*
< L *scindula*] *n* 1 one of the thin
oblong pieces of wood, slate, etc.
used in overlapping rows for roofing
and siding; 2 haircut in which the
hair at the back of the head lies in
overlapping rows; 3 *colloq* small
signboard, as of a doctor or lawyer
|| *vt* 4 to cover with shingles; 5 to
cut the hair in a shingle

shin′gles [OF *cengle* < L *cingulum*
girdle] *nsg* or *npl* acute virus disease
of the skin, characterized by groups
of small blisters following the line of
a cutaneous nerve

shin′ing *adj* 1 giving or reflecting light;
2 bright, resplendent; 3 illustrious,
distinguished || SYN radiant, lumi-
nous, gleaming, lustrous, brilliant,
refulgent, conspicuous (see *bright*)

Shin·to /shin′tō/ [Jap < Chin *shin
tao* way of the gods] *n* native religion of the Japanese, emphasizing
worship of ancestors and dead
heroes || **Shin′to·ism** *n* || **Shin′to·ist** *n*

shin·y /shin′ē/ *adj* (-i·er, -i·est) 1 polished, glossy; 2 bright; 3 worn
smooth and glossy

ship /ship′/ [OE *scip*] *n* 1 any vessel
of considerable size navigating deep
water; 2 sailing vessel with a bowsprit and three or more square-
rigged masts; 3 aircraft || *v* (shipped;
ship·ping) *vt* 4 to place or receive on
board a vessel; 5 to send or transport by any means of transportation,
as by ship, plane, rail, or truck; 6
to put in the proper place or position
on a boat, as oars; 7 to hire for
service on a ship; 8 **ship off** *colloq*
to send away; 9 **ship out** to send (a
person) to a far-off place || *vi* 10 to
engage to serve on a ship; 11 to go
aboard; 12 **ship out** to leave for
other parts

-ship /-ship′/ [OE -*scipe*] *n suf* 1
state or quality of being, as *friendship*; 2 office, dignity, or profession,
as *clerkship*; 3 art or skill, as *horsemanship*

ship′board′ *n* 1 on shipboard aboard a
ship || *adj* 2 occurring or existing on
a ship

ship′fit′ter *n* one who fits together the
plates and girders of a ship for welding or riveting

ship′mas′ter *n* captain of a ship other
than a war vessel

ship′mate′ *n* one who serves with another on a ship

ship′ment *n* 1 act or instance of shipping goods; 2 the goods shipped

ship′ of state′ *n poet. & literary* nation

ship′per *n* one who ships goods

ship′ping *n* 1 act or business of shipping goods; 2 ships collectively;
tonnage

ship′shape′ *adj* 1 neatly arranged, in
good order || *adv* 2 in a shipshape
manner

ship′side′ *adj* 1 located at the side of
a ship || *adv* 2 at the side of a ship
|| *n* 3 area alongside a ship that is
used for loading and unloading
passengers and freight

ship′worm′ *n* any of several wormlike
mollusks that bore into ship timbers,
wharf piles, etc.

ship′wreck′ *n* 1 destruction or loss of
a ship at sea; 2 remains of a
wrecked ship; 3 utter ruin || *vt* 4 to
cause to suffer shipwreck; 5 to ruin,
destroy

ship′wright′ *n* one who builds or repairs ships

ship′yard′ *n* place where ships are built
or repaired

shire /shīr′/ [OE *scīr* administration,
district] *n* county in Great Britain

shirk /shurk′/ [var of *shark²*] *vt* to
evade (work, duty, or obligation) ||
also *vi* || **shirk′er** *n*

shirr /shur′/ [?] *n* 1 puckering produced in a fabric by means of paral-
lel gathers || *vt* 2 to draw up (cloth)
by gathering on parallel-running
stitches; 3 to cook (eggs) in a but-
tered dish or casserole

shirt /shurt′/ [OE *scyrte* tunic] *n* 1
man's blouse of lightweight material,
usu. having a collar and often worn
with a necktie under a jacket; 2
keep one's shirt on *slang* to remain
calm; 3 **lose one's shirt** *slang* to
undergo a heavy financial loss

shirt′waist′ *n* woman's sleeved, tailored
blouse

shish ke·bab /shish′kəbäb′/ [Turk] *n*
small pieces of meat broiled on a
skewer with tomatoes, onions, peppers, or other vegetables

shiv /shiv′/ [?] *n slang* knife

shiv·a·ree /shiv′ərē′/ [F *charivari*] *n*
mock serenade to newlyweds with
kettles, pans, horns, etc.

shiv·er /shiv′ər/ [ME *chiveren*] *vi* 1
to tremble, as from cold or fright ||
n 2 act or condition of shivering; 3
the shivers *pl* fit of shivering || **shiv′-
er·y** *adj*

shoal¹ /shōl′/ [OE *scolu* troop, host]
n 1 large company; 2 school of fish
|| SYN crowd, company, multitude
(see *herd*)

shoal² [OE *sceald*] *adj* 1 shallow || *n*
2 shallow place in a body of water;

3 sand bank or bar which shows only at low tide

shoat /shōt'/ [ME *shote*] *n* young pig

shock¹ /shok'/ [MF *choc*] *n* 1 sudden violent blow or impact; 2 unexpected and violent jarring or disturbance of the feelings, mind, etc.; 3 cause of such disturbance; 4 effect produced by the passage of an electric current through the body; 5 state of prostration following severe injury, loss of blood, or disease || *vt* 6 to strike with surprise, horror, disgust, etc.; 7 to give an electric shock to || *vi* 8 to be subjected to a shock || **shock'er** *n*

shock³ [ME] *n* 1 stack of sheaves of grain set upright together in a field; 2 bushy tangled mass, as of hair

shock' ab·sorb'er *n* device for damping rebounding motion, as of the springs in an automobile

shock'-head'ed *adj* having a thick mass of hair

shock'ing *adj* highly offensive; disgusting

shock' ther'a·py *n* treatment of certain mental disorders by inducing shock with drugs or electricity

shock' troops' *npl* troops specially trained to lead and deliver assaults

shock' wave' *n* wave front of abrupt change of pressure caused by an intense explosion or by an object moving faster than the speed of sound

shod /shod'/ *pt* & *pp* of **shoe**

shod·dy /shod'ē/ [?] *n* (**-dies**) 1 inferior material made from rags and waste cloth; 2 anything of a quality inferior to that which is affirmed || *adj* (**-di·er; -di·est**) 3 inferior in grade; 4 mean; contemptible

shoe /shōō'/ [OE *scōh*] *n* 1 covering for the human foot, usu. made of leather and reaching about to the ankle; 2 horseshoe; 3 something resembling a shoe in form, use, or position; 4 the part of a brake that presses against the wheel or drum; 5 outer covering of a pneumatic tire; 6 piece that slides against the third rail to supply current to an electric train; 7 **fill someone's shoes** to take someone's place; 8 **in someone's shoes** in another's place || *v* (**shod** or **shoed**) *vt* 9 to furnish with a shoe or shoes

shoe'horn' *n* curved smooth piece of metal or other material slipped into the back of a shoe to aid in putting it on

shoe'lace' *n* string or cord for lacing and fastening a shoe

shoe'mak'er *n* one who makes or mends shoes

shoe'shine' *n* act or instance of polishing shoes

shoe'string' *n* 1 shoelace; 2 **on a shoestring** on very little money

shoe'tree' *n* form for stretching a shoe or for preserving its shape

sho·gun /shō'gun/ [Jap] *n* one of the former hereditary military governors of Japan, who usurped the powers of the emperor until 1868, when the emperor's power was restored

shone /shōn'/ *pt* & *pp* of **shine**

shoo /shōō'/ [imit] *interj* 1 get out of here! || *vt* 2 to drive or frighten away, as by crying "shoo"

shoo'-in' *n* *colloq* someone or something regarded as certain to win a contest or election

shook /shŏōk'/ 1 *pt* of **shake** || *adj* 2 also **shook' up'** *slang* emotionally upset

shoot /shōōt'/ [OE *scēotan*] *v* (**shot**) *vt* 1 to discharge (a missile) from a weapon; 2 to discharge (a weapon); 3 to strike, kill, or wound with a missile discharged from a weapon; 4 to move, as a bolt, into a fastening; 5 to put forth; fling; propel; 6 to cause to protrude; stick out; 7 to pass or rush rapidly over, as *shoot the rapids;* 8 to variegate by the intermixture of different colors; 9 to photograph or film; 10 to direct or move quickly; 11 *sports* a to throw or propel (a ball, puck, etc.); b to score (a goal or point); 12 to pull (shirt cuffs) below the sleeve of a jacket; 13 to take the altitude of (a heavenly body); 14 **shoot down** to bring down by shooting; 15 **shoot up** *colloq* to spray bullets recklessly at || *vi* 16 to rush or flash along swiftly; 17 to dart with a stabbing sensation, as pains; 18 to project; protrude; 19 to discharge missiles from a weapon; 20 to indulge in hunting or target shooting; 21 to photograph; 22 **shoot for** *colloq* to strive for; 23 **shoot up** to grow suddenly and rapidly || *n* 24 new growth or sprout; 25 shooting match; 26 chute; 27 launching of rocket or missile || **shoot'er** *n*

shoot'ing *n* act or instance of shooting someone

shoot'ing gal'ler·y *n* place where one may shoot at targets for a fee

shoot'ing star' *n* meteor visible in the night sky

shoot'ing stick' *n* stick that resembles a cane, with a spike at one end and a folding seat at the other, for use at races and other outdoor events

shoot'-out' *n* shooting affray between two gangs or between a gang and the police, usu. continued until one side gives up

shop /shop'/ [OE *sceoppa* booth] *n* 1 retail store; 2 workshop of a mechanic or artisan; 3 factory; 4 **set up shop** to go into business; 5 **talk shop** to talk about one's work after working hours || *v* (**shopped; shop·ping**) *vi* 6 to visit shops to look over or to purchase goods || *vt* 7 *colloq* to shop in

shop'keep'er *n* owner or operator of a retail shop

shop'lift'ing *n* theft of goods on display in a retail shop ‖ **shop'lift'er** *n*

shop'per *n* 1 one who shops; 2 person hired to shop in competitors' stores to compare goods and prices

shop'ping cen'ter *n* large plaza with retail shops and parking facilities for people who shop by auto

shop' stew'ard *n* union member chosen to represent the workers in a factory or department

shop'talk' *n* act of talking about one's work after working hours

shop'worn' *adj* soiled, faded, or worn from having been handled or exposed in a store

sho·ran /shō'ran, shō'-/ [*short range navigation*] *n* navigation aid by which a ship or aircraft determines its position by the relative time taken by two signals to go to and come back from two known ground stations

shore¹ /shôr', shōr'/ [OE *scora*] *n* 1 land bordering on a large body of water or large river; 2 land as opposed to sea, as *stationed on shore* ‖ *adj* 3 of, pert. to, or located on land along the water ‖ SYN (see *border*)

shore² [ME] *n* 1 prop or support set obliquely against or beneath a ship, wall, etc. ‖ *vt* 2 **shore up** to support by shores

shore' din'ner *n* dinner consisting mostly of seafood

shore' leave' *n* 1 permission to go ashore for a short time; 2 the time spent ashore

shore' pa·trol' *n* detachment acting as military police for sailors and marines on shore leave

shor'ing *n* 1 act of shoring up; 2 shores collectively

shorn /shôrn', shōrn'/ *pp* of **shear**

short /shôrt'/ [OE *scort*] *adj* 1 of brief duration; 2 not long; limited in length; 3 small of stature, not tall; 4 scant, deficient; 5 insufficiently supplied; 6 failing to come up to a standard measure, requirement, etc.; 7 (memory) of limited retentive power; 8 curt, abrupt; 9 crisp, flaky, as pastry; 10 *fin* a not possessing at the time of sale the property or securities one has contracted to deliver; b designating or pert. to the sale of stock which the seller does not possess but which he hopes to buy at a lower price; 11 **short for** being a shorter form for; 12 **short of**, a inferior to; b in want of; c excluding ‖ *n* 13 something that is short; 14 short subject; 15 garment size shorter than average; 16 short circuit; 17 *baseball* position played by the shortstop; 18 *fin* short seller; 19 **shorts** *pl* a loose trousers reaching to the knee or higher; b men's short drawers; 20 **for short** as an abbreviation; 21 **in short**, a briefly; b in summary ‖ *adv* 22 abruptly; suddenly; 23 not quite reaching an intended goal or target; 24 **so as to be short**; 25 **cut short** to end before time; 26 **fall short**, a to fail to reach a standard; b to be insufficient; 27 **run short of** to begin to be deficient in; 28 **sell short** to sell stock one does not possess in the hope of buying it for less ‖ *vt & vi* 29 often **short out** to short-circuit ‖ **short'ness** *n* ‖ SYN *adj* concise, laconic, pithy, compact, condensed, terse, succinct, little, insufficient, inadequate, brief, curt ‖ DISCR We may say a *brief* or a *short* interval, a *brief* or a *short* speech, but we say a *short* man, a *short* trip. *Short* can also mean abrupt, especially snappishly, or reticently so, as he was so *short* with me that I asked no more questions. *Brief* and *short* in their synonymous sense commonly refer to duration, less often to manner, though sometimes *brief* connotes reduction or abridgment, and *short* suggests incompleteness. The other words refer to manner or style, to the person given to such style, or the speech or writing marked by it. Conciseness is decisive brevity; a *concise* speech is cut down to the pith of the matter; *concise* writing contains no unnecessary words, and has a brisk and bracing quality. *Laconic* adds to *concise* the tendency to use language so compressed that it is axiomatic. "Many words darken speech," a maxim taken from an old copy book, probably originated in a mind that loved *laconic* expression. A *pithy* saying is one that so presents the kernel of a matter as to give it force and effectiveness by its very compression. To be *brief* one needs only to compass one's subject quickly; to be *concise*, one has only to be sparing and precise with his words; to be *laconic*, one must be a niggard with words; but to be *pithy* requires wit and intelligence. *Terse* adds to *pithy* smoothness and finish, a polished lack of superfluity. *Succinct* combines the precision of *concise* and the elegance of *terse*. *Curt* may connote the clean brevity of *concise*, or it may mean *short* in the sense of discourteously abrupt

short'age /-ij/ *n* 1 deficiency; 2 deficit

short'bread' *n* rich butter cake or cooky

short'cake' *n* sweet cake or biscuit split into layers and served with fruit between the layers, often covered with whipped cream

short'-change' *vt* 1 to give less than the correct change to; 2 *colloq* to cheat

short' cir'cuit *n* accidental contact between wires of an electric system, resulting in lowered resistance and excessive flow of current ‖ **short'-cir'cuit** *vt & vi*

short'com'ing *n* failing; fault; defect

short′ cov′er·ing *n* purchase of stock made to close out a short sale

short′cut′ *n* shorter or quicker way

short′en *vt* 1 to make short or shorter || *vi* 2 to become short or shorter || **short′en·er** *n*

short′en·ing /-niŋ/ *n* butter, lard, etc., used to make baked goods crisp and flaky

short′fall′ *n* amount by which there is a shortage; deficit

short′hand′ *n* one of various systems of rapid writing in which characters, symbols, and abbreviations are used for letters, words, and phrases

short′-hand′ed *adj* short of workers

short′horn′ *n* one of a large, heavy breed of short-horned beef cattle, originally from Durham in N England

short′ in′ter·est *n fin* total amount by which all traders are short in a given stock or commodity or in the whole market on a given day

short′-lived′ /-līvd′, -livd′/ *adj* living or lasting a short time

short′ly *adv* 1 soon; 2 abruptly; curtly; 3 briefly

short′ or′der *n* food quickly prepared on order, as at a diner || **short′-or′der ed** *adj*

short′ po·si′tion *n fin* position of a trader who is short in a stock or commodity that he has sold

short′-range′ *adj* of limited extent or duration

short′ sale′ *n* sale for future delivery of property or securities not owned by the seller || **short′ sell′er** *n*

short′ shrift′ /-shrift′/ [OE *scrift* penance] *n* very little consideration or attention

short′-sight′ed *adj* 1 nearsighted; 2 marked by lack of foresight

short′stop′ *n* baseball infielder stationed between second and third base

short′ sto′ry *n* prose fiction characterized by relative brevity and unity of plot || **short′-sto′ry** *adj*

short′ sub′ject *n* short film, as a cartoon or travelogue, used to supplement a motion-picture program

short′-tem′pered *adj* easily angered; irascible

short′-term′ *adj* applying to, or maturing in, a short period of time

short′ ti′tle *n* abbreviated bibliographical entry consisting of author's name, book's title curtailed if possible, date and place of publication, and publisher's or printer's name

short′wave′ *n* electromagnetic wave of 60 meters or less || also *adj*

short′-wind′ed /-wind′id/ *adj* easily put out of breath by exercise

shot¹ /shot/ 1 *pt & pp* of **shoot** || *adj* 2 variegated or streaked with color; 3 *colloq* worn out, ruined

shot² [OE *scot*] *n* 1 act of shooting; 2 discharge, as of a firearm; 3 projectile or missile; 4 such missiles collectively; 5 small pellet of lead, or a number of such pellets combined in one charge and used in a shotgun; 6 reach or range; 7 *sports* stroke or throw; 8 marksman; 9 spherical weight to be put or thrown in competition for distance; 10 try, attempt; 11 hypodermic injection; 12 small drink, usu. an ounce, of liquor; 13 pointed remark; 14 guess; 15 photograph; 16 single film sequence; 17 **like a shot** instantly; 18 **shot in the arm** *slang* stimulus; renewed vigor; 19 **shot in the dark** wild guess

shot′ glass′ *n* small glass for holding a shot of whiskey

shot′gun′ *n* 1 smoothbore gun for firing shot of various sizes, used for shooting birds and small quadrupeds || *adj slang* 2 coercive; 3 haphazard, hit-or-miss; 4 broad; inclusive

shot′gun rid′er *n* armed guard on a stagecoach

shot′gun wed′ding *n slang* wedding forced on the groom by the pregnant bride's relatives

shot′ put′ *n* 1 athletic contest in which a heavy ball is thrown for distance; 2 single throw of the shot || **shot′-put′ter** *n*

shot′ tow′er *n* tower from the top of which molten lead is dropped into a tank of water at the bottom, forming round shot

should /shood′/ [OE *sc(e)olde*] *v* (*pt* of **shall**) *modal aux* used to express: 1 condition, supposition, hesitation, etc., as *if it should rain, do not go; I should hardly say so;* 2 moral obligation or duty, as *you should try harder* || SYN (see **ought**)

shoul·der /shōl′dər/ [OE *sculdor*] *n* 1 either of the two projecting parts of the human body formed by the bones and muscles between the neck and the place where the arm joins the trunk; 2 corresponding part in animals; 3 cut of meat comprising the upper portion of the foreleg; 4 shoulderlike projection; 5 the part of a garment that covers the shoulder; 6 border along the edge of a road; 7 **shoulders** *pl* a the two shoulders and the part of the back between them; b *colloq* strength to bear heavy burdens or to sustain responsibility or blame; 8 **cry on someone's shoulder** to tell someone one's troubles || *vt* 9 to take upon the shoulder; 10 to assume the responsibility of; 11 to push with or as with the shoulder

shoul′der blade′ *n* one of the two flat triangular bones of the back of the shoulder, to which the bone of the upper arm is jointed

shoul′der patch′ *n* cloth patch worn on a uniform sleeve near the shoulder, identifying the wearer's unit

should·n't /shoŏd'ənt/ should not

shouldst /shoŏdst'/ *archaic 2nd pers sg of* should

shout /shout'/ [ME *shoute*] *vi* 1 to utter a loud and sudden cry ‖ *vt* 2 to utter or express in a loud voice ‖ *n* 3 loud, sudden outcry ‖ **shout'er** *n*

shove /shuv'/ [OE *scūfan*] *vt* 1 to push along carelessly or roughly; 2 to crowd or jostle; 3 to push or thrust ‖ *vi* 4 to push; 5 **shove off,** a to push a boat away from the shore; b *slang* to leave ‖ *n* 6 act or instance of shoving

shov·el /shuv'əl/ [OE *scofl*] *n* 1 implement consisting of a broad blade with turned-up sides and a long handle, for lifting and throwing loose material ‖ *v* (**-eled** *or* **-elled; -el·ing** *or* **-el·ling**) *vt* 2 to take up and throw with or as with a shovel; 3 to clear or dig with a shovel ‖ *vi* 4 to use a shovel

show /shō'/ [OE *scēawian* to scrutinize] *v* (*pp* **shown** *or* **showed**) *vt* 1 to present to view; exhibit; display; 2 to make clear, explain; teach; 3 to prove, demonstrate; 4 to direct; conduct, usher; 5 to reveal, make evident; 6 to indicate, point out; 7 **show off** to make an ostentatious display of; 8 **show up,** a to expose, as faults; b to outdo ‖ *vi* 9 to put in an appearance; 10 to be visible or noticeable; 11 to finish third in a horse race; 12 **show off** to make a vain display of one's good points; 13 **show up,** a to appear, be seen; b *colloq* to put in an appearance ‖ *n* 14 act or instance of showing; 15 exhibition; demonstration; display; 16 spectacle; 17 ostentatious display; 18 appearance, semblance; 19 sign or indication; 20 public performance or exhibition of any kind; 21 movie theater; 22 *colloq* chance; 23 third finish in a horse race; 24 **run the (whole) show** to be in complete charge of an enterprise; 25 **steal the show** to draw more attention than the main attraction; 26 **stop the show** to win such enthusiastic applause that the show is interrupted ‖ SYN *v* display, exhibit, disclose, reveal, prove

show' bill' *n* poster which advertises a show or play

show' boat' *n* large boat in which theatrical performances are given

show' busi'ness *n* the entertainment industry, comprising acting, producing, managing, etc.

show'case' *n* 1 glass case or cabinet for displaying objects, as goods for sale; 2 representative model; 3 any place of display

show'down' *n* 1 *cards* laying down of one's hand with the cards exposed; 2 any final confrontation

show·er /shou'ər/ [OE *scūr*] *n* 1 brief fall of rain, sleet, or hail; 2 fall of any objects in considerable number; 3 number of gifts given together, as for a prospective bride; 4 abundant supply of anything; 5 shower bath ‖ *vt* 6 to water abundantly, as with a shower; 7 to pour out; 8 to bestow liberally; 9 to give (oneself) a shower bath ‖ *vi* 10 to fall in a shower; 11 to take a shower bath ‖ **show'er·y** *adj*

show'er bath' *n* 1 device for spraying water over the body from above; 2 bath taken with this device

show' girl' *n* young woman in lavish costume appearing in a musical show

show'ing *n* 1 display; exhibition; 2 presentation of a fact, condition, or the like; 3 performance, record

show'man /-mən/ *n* (**-men** /-mən/) 1 one whose business is the presentation and production of shows; 2 one skilled in presenting things in a striking or dramatic manner ‖ **show'man·ship'** *n*

shown /shōn/ *pp of* **show**

show'-off' *n* one who shows off

show'piece' *n* 1 something put on display; 2 object that is exhibited because of its unusual characteristics

show'place' *n* building, garden, or other place, generally open to the public, that is famed for its beauty, taste, and distinction

show'room' *n* room where goods to be sold are displayed

show'y *adj* (**-i·er; -i·est**) 1 of imposing appearance; 2 gaudy, ostentatious ‖ SYN gaudy, gay, flashy, garish, tawdry, pretentious ‖ DISCR Brilliantly colored flowers in a garden, the bright red of the flying cardinal, are *showy* in a favorable sense. That which attracts the eye or attention by a gay or apparently fine exterior, but which is really cheap, worthless, or artificial, is *showy* in an unfavorable sense, as *showy* jewels; *showy* manners which do not disguise the boor. *Gaudy*, like *showy*, connotes brilliance of color, but it suggests inappropriateness and lack of taste rather than worthlessness. *Gaudy* clothes might be expensive, but they would be badly chosen and of striking colors. *Gaudy* can mean conspicuous in a bad sense, as *gaudy* raiment; it is also unfavorably suggestive of the overdone, overdecorated, as a *gaudy* literary style. *Gay* lacks the unfavorable connotation of *gaudy; gay* colors, though bright, are pleasing; *gay* clothes are well chosen as to color and appropriateness. *Flashy* adds to *showy* and *gaudy* the note of vulgarity; that which is *flashy* is cheap, shallow, and common. *Garish* describes the obtrusively bright; that which is *garish* attracts the eye by gaudiness, or dazzles it by glare and harshness. That is *tawdry* which is cheap, showily worthless, overornamented, flimsy, or frail in nature, as *tawdry* furnishings. A *pretentious* style, a *pretentious* display, claim a merit they do not possess, or a significance not actual; a *pretentious* braggart is unable to sustain his boastings; a *pretentious* style of living is often adopted by the newly rich

shrank /shraŋk´/ *pt of* **shrink**

shrap·nel /shrap´nəl/ [H. *Shrapnel* (1761–1842) Brit general] *n* 1 bullets or pieces of iron in a shell, timed to explode and scatter over a desired point; 2 shell containing shrapnel

shred /shred´/ [OE *scrēade*] *n* 1 narrow strip torn or cut off; 2 bit, fragment ‖ *v* (**shred** *or* **shred·ded; shred·ding**) *vt* 3 to tear or cut into shreds ‖ **shred´der** *n*

shrew /shrōō´/ [OE *scrēawa*] *n* 1 any of several small mouselike animals (family Soricidae) feeding chiefly on insects and worms; 2 nagging brawling woman ‖ **shrew´ish** *adj*

shrewd /shrōōd´/ [ME *schrewed* accursed] *adj* 1 sharp-witted or clever in practical affairs; 2 indicative of cleverness, as *a shrewd glance* ‖ **shrewd´ly** *adv* ‖ **shrewd´ness** *n* ‖ SYN astute, subtle, knowing, sagacious, discerning, discriminating, penetrating (cf. *sagacity*)

shriek /shrēk´/ [ME *shrichen*] *vi* 1 to utter a sharp shrill cry ‖ *vt* 2 to utter with a shriek ‖ *n* 3 piercing scream; shrill and inarticulate outcry

shrike /shrīk´/ [OE *scrīc*] *n* any of a group of ferocious birds of the family Laniidae, having a strong hooked beak, which feed on insects, mice, and smaller birds

shrill /shril´/ [ME *shrille*] *adj* 1 sharp, piercing, and high-pitched in tone ‖ *vt & vi* 2 to cry shrilly ‖ **shril´ly** *adv*

shrimp /shrimp´/ [< OE *scrimman* to be bent] *n* (**shrimp** *or* **shrimps**) 1 any of various small mostly marine crustaceans (esp. genus *Crangon*) related to the lobsters; 2 *colloq* small or insignificant person ‖ *vi* 3 to catch shrimp ‖ **shrimp´er** *n*

shrine /shrīn´/ [OE *scrīn* < L *scrinium* coffer] *n* 1 reliquary; 2 saint's tomb; 3 any place or object hallowed by some association

shrink /shriŋk´/ [OE *scrincan*] *v* (**shrank** *or* **shrunk; shrunk** *or* **shrunk·en**) *vi* 1 to contract; become smaller or shorter; 2 to draw back, flinch ‖ *vt* 3 to cause to shrink ‖ SYN shrivel, wither, blight, fade ‖ ANT bloom

shrink·age /-ij/ *n* 1 act or amount of shrinking; 2 decrease in value

shrive /shrīv´/ [OE *scrīfan*] *v* (**shrived** *or* **shrove; shriv·en** /shriv´ən/ *or* shrived) *vt archaic* to hear the confession of and give absolution to

shriv·el /shriv´əl/ [?] *v* (**-eled** *or* **-elled; -el·ing** *or* **-el·ling**) *vt & vi* 1 to wrinkle, contract; 2 to wither

shroud /shroud´/ [OE *scrūd* dress, garment] *n* 1 cloth in which a corpse is wrapped for burial; 2 anything that envelops and conceals; 3 one of a set of ropes stretched from the side of ship to a masthead ‖ *vt* 4 to dress in a shroud; 5 to conceal, veil, obscure

shrove /shrōv´/ *pt of* **shrive**

Shrove´ Tues´day *n* Tuesday before Ash Wednesday, the last day before Lent

shrub /shrub´/ [OE *scrybb* brushwood] *n* woody perennial plant smaller than a tree, usu. divided into several primary stems at or near the ground

shrub´ber·y *n* (**-ies**) 1 shrubs collectively; 2 a planting of shrubs

shrug /shrug´/ [ME *schruggen*] *v* (**shrugged; shrug·ging**) *vt* 1 to contract or draw up (the shoulders) to express doubt, indifference, etc. ‖ *vi* 2 to raise and contract the shoulders ‖ *n* 3 raising and contraction of the shoulders

shrunk /shruŋk´/ *pt & pp of* **shrink**

shrunk´en *pp of* **shrink**

shuck /shuk´/ [?] *n* 1 husk, shell, or pod ‖ *vt* 2 to remove the shucks from

shucks´ *interj* exclamation of disgust or disappointment

shud·der /shud´ər/ [ME *shoderen*] *vt* 1 to tremble or shake with fear, repugnance, or horror ‖ *n* 2 act of shuddering ‖ SYN *v* (see *shake*)

shuf·fle /shuf´əl/ [prob < LG *schuffeln*] *vt* 1 to drag (the feet) along the ground in walking or dancing; 2 to mix (cards); 3 to move or mix up (objects) ‖ *vi* 4 to walk clumsily without lifting the feet; 5 to mix the cards in a deck; 6 **shuffle off** to move away or depart by or as if by shuffling ‖ *n* 7 act or instance of shuffling; 8 shuffling gait

shuf´fle·board´ *n* 1 game in which disks are shoved by hand toward certain marks along the surface of a long rimmed board standing on legs; 2 similar game in which disks are shoved by long cues onto numbered squares on a floor or deck

shun /shun´/ [OE *scunian* to avoid, fear] *v* (**shunned; shun·ning**) *vt* to avoid, keep clear of ‖ SYN *avoid*, evade ‖ DISCR We sometimes *avoid* trouble simply by not happening to get into it; we also *avoid* people whom we do not like, or embarrassing situations, by some contrivance or excuse. In this latter sense *avoid* is particularly like *shun*; we *shun* things by taking care not to get in contact with them; we can either *avoid* or *shun* trouble. *Shun*, not *avoid*, is used of the turning away or keeping away from a person or a thing out of loathing or repugnance; we *shun* those who have contagious diseases. *Evade* adds to *avoid* the idea of clever, noncommittal escape; *evading* is done with skill rather than artifice. One who *evades* the law is often within it; we *evade* answering unwelcome questions by an apparently satisfying, but actually baffling, reply

shunt /shunt'/ [ME *shunten*] *vt* 1 to turn to one side; 2 to switch, as a car or train; 3 to evade, put aside; 4 *elec* to supply an additional path for (a current) ‖ *n* 5 act of shunting; 6 *elec* conductor joining two points of a circuit over which part of the current may be diverted; 7 railroad switch

shunt'-wound' /-wound'/ *adj* (electric generator or motor) in which the armature winding and the field winding are connected in parallel

shush /shush'/ [imit] *interj* 1 hush! ‖ *vt* 2 to say "shush" to; cause to be quiet

shut /shut'/ [OE *scyttan*] *v* (shut; shut-ting) *vt* 1 to close so as to prevent entrance or exit; 2 to close, as by pushing or pulling a cover, door, window, etc., into place; 3 to bar, exclude; 4 to fold or bring together the parts of, as an umbrella or book; 5 to confine; 6 **shut down** to close, cause to stop operating; 7 **shut in** to enclose; 8 **shut off, a** to turn off; **b** to isolate; 9 **shut out, a** to exclude; **b** *sports* to keep (the other side) from scoring; 10 **shut up, a** to confine; **b** to close up; **c** *colloq* to silence ‖ *vi* 11 to close; 12 **shut down** to close, cease operations; 13 **shut up** *colloq* to become silent ‖ *adj* 14 closed; made fast

shut'down' *n* act or instance of stopping work for a time, as in a factory

shut'-eye' *n slang* sleep

shut'in' *n* invalid confined to a house, hospital, or the like

shut'off' *n* device for shutting off something

shut'out' *n sports* game in which the losing side fails to score

shut'ter *n* 1 movable cover for a window; 2 any of various devices for covering an aperture; 3 *photog* device for opening and closing an aperture in a camera for a predetermined time in order to expose a film or plate ‖ *vt* 4 to close or supply with shutters

shut·tle /shut'əl/ [OE *scyttel* bar, bolt] *n* 1 instrument used in weaving to carry the thread of the woof back and forth through the warp; 2 sliding holder which carries the lower thread in a sewing machine; 3 public conveyance that makes frequent trips between comparatively close points

‖ *vt & vi* 4 to move back and forth

shut'tle·cock' *n* rounded piece of cork stuck with feathers and driven with a battledore in badminton

shy¹ /shī'/ [OE *scēoh*] *adj* (**shi·er** or **shy·er**; **shi·est** or **shy·est**) 1 easily scared; timid; 2 bashful, reserved; 3 suspicious, wary; 4 short, lacking ‖ *v* (**shied**) *vi* 5 to start aside from fear, as a horse; 6 to hesitate, turn away ‖ **shy'ly** *adv* ‖ **shy'ness** *n* ‖ SYN *adj* timorous, reserved (see *diffident*)

shy² [?] *v* (**shied**) *vt* to throw with a jerk; fling, as a stone

Shy·lock /shī'lok/ [relentless money-lender in Shakespeare's *Merchant of Venice*] *n* usurer

shy·ster /shī'stər/ [?] *n colloq* one who carries on business by sharp practices, esp. and unethical lawyer

si /sē'/ [It] *n mus* seventh tone of the diatonic scale

Si *chem* silicon

Si·am /sī·am'/ *n* former name of Thailand ‖ **Si'a·mese'** /-əmēz', -əmēs'/ *adj & n* (**-mese**)

Si'a·mese cat' *n* one of a breed of short-haired cats with a grayish fur and the face, paws, and tail of a darker shade

Si'a·mese twins' [< *twins* born in *Siam* in 1811] *npl* twins born joined together

Si·be·ri·a /sībir'ē·ə/ *n* the part of the Soviet Union in N Asia ‖ **Si·be'ri·an** *adj & n*

sib·i·lant /sib'ilənt/ [L *sibilans* (-*antis*) whistling, hissing] *adj* 1 hissing; 2 *phonet* making, representing, or sounded with a hissing sound, as the sounds *s*, *z*, *sh*, and *zh* ‖ *n* 3 sibilant consonant

sib·ling /sib'liŋ/ [< OE *sib* relative] *n* brother or sister ‖ *also adj*

sib·yl /sib'əl/ [Gk *Sibylla*] *n* 1 *class. myth.* any of certain women, priestesses of shrines, who were inspired to foretell future events; 2 sorceress; witch

sic¹ /sik'/ [L] *adv* so, thus (often inserted in a quoted passage to indicate that it is quoted verbatim)

sic² or **sick** /sik'/ [var of *seek*] *v* (**sicked**; **sick·ing**) *vt* 1 to incite (a dog) to attack; 2 **sic 'im!** attack him! (said to a dog)

Sic·i·ly /sis'ilē/ *n* largest island in the Mediterranean, off the toe of and belonging to Italy ‖ **Si·cil·ian** /sisil'yən, -ē·ən/ *adj & n*

sick /sik'/ [OE *sēoc*] *adj* 1 ill; affected with disease; 2 nauseous, inclined to vomit; 3 disgusted; surfeited, as *sick of waiting;* 4 deeply affected, as with sorrow, longing, or weariness; 5 neurotic or psychotic; 6 used by or set apart for the sick; 7 *colloq* mortified, chagrined ‖ *n* 8 **the sick** *pl* sick people collectively ‖ SYN *adj* diseased, unhealthy, unwell, frail, ill (see *ill*) || ANT *adj* healthy, sound, well

sick′ bay′ *n* hospital area aboard a ship

sick′bed′ *n* bed of a sick person

sick′en *vi* 1 to become sick || *vt* 2 to make sick

sick′en·ing *adj* 1 nauseating; 2 repulsive, disgusting

sick·le /sik′əl/ [OE *sicol*] *n* instrument for cutting grain and grass, having a semicircular blade fitted into a short handle

sick′ leave′ *n* leave with pay granted because of illness

sick′ly *adj* (-li·er; -li·est) 1 ailing, in poor health; 2 characteristic of or suggesting sickness; 3 weak, faint, pale; 4 mawkish; sickening

sick′ness *n* 1 illness; 2 malady, disease; 3 nausea || SYN ailment, illness, qualmishness (see *disease*)

sick′room′ *n* room occupied by a sick person

side /sīd′/ [OE] *n* 1 any of the bounding lines of a surface; 2 any of the lateral surfaces of an object; 3 either surface of a flat object, as of a door or paper; 4 the part lying either to the right or left of the observer; 5 either longitudinal half of a person or animal, especially of the trunk; 6 longitudinal section of a carcass as prepared for the butcher; 7 position to the right or left of, or nearer or farther than, a dividing line, as *this side of the road*; 8 one of the parties in a contest or conflict; 9 position held by a faction; 10 line of descent with reference to parentage; 11 aspect; 12 slope of a hill or mountain; 13 **on the side** *colloq* **a** in addition; **b** as a side dish; 14 **side by side** next to each other, together; 15 **take sides** to join one ′side in a dispute || *adj* 16 situated at, coming from, or directed to the side; 17 minor, incidental || *vi* 18 **side against** to oppose (one of the parties to a dispute); 19 **side with** to join (one of the parties to a dispute)

side′ arm′ *n* weapon carried at the side or in the belt, as a pistol or sword

side′board′ *n* piece of dining-room furniture for holding articles used on the table

side′burns′ [alter. of *burnsides* < A. E. *Burnside* Civil War general] *npl* the strips of hair growing on the cheeks in front of the ears below the hairline

side′car′ *n* 1 small car attached to the side of a motorcycle for one passenger; 2 cocktail made of brandy, orange liqueur, and lemon juice

side′ ef·fect′ *n* unlooked-for harmful effect of a drug or medicine in addition to its intended effect

side′kick′ *n colloq* buddy; confederate

side′light′ *n* 1 one of the two lights, red on the port side, green on the starboard, of a vessel under way at night; 2 light falling from the side; 3 incidental information or revelation

side′line′ *n* 1 auxiliary line of goods; 2 business or occupation carried on in addition to one's regular occupation; 3 **sidelines** *pl* lines marking the side boundaries of an athletic field; 4 in Canada, secondary road at right angles to main road; 5 **on the sidelines** not participating || *vi* 6 *colloq* to put temporarily out of action, as by an injury

side′long′ *adj* lateral; indirect; sideways || also *adv*

side′man′ /-man′, -mən/ *n* (-**men** /-men′, -mən/) instrumentalist in a jazz band or orchestra, esp. in support of a soloist

si·de·re·al /sīdir′ē̇·əl/ [< *sidus* (-*eris*) star] *adj* 1 pert. to the stars; 2 measured by the apparent motion of the stars, as time

side′sad′dle *n* 1 saddle enabling a woman wearing a skirt to sit with both feet on the same side of the horse || *adv* 2 seated on a sidesaddle

side′ show′ *n* 1 minor show given in connection with the principal one, as at a circus; 2 any subordinate event

side′slip′ *v* (-slipped; -slip·ping) *vi* 1 to slip sideways || *vt* 2 to cause to sideslip || *n* 3 act or instance of sideslipping

side′split′ting *adj* uproariously funny

side′-step′ *v* (-stepped; -step·ping) *vt* & *vi* to dodge by or as if by stepping aside

side′swipe′ *vt* 1 to strike with a glancing blow along the side in passing || *n* 2 such a blow

side′track′ *vt* 1 to transfer (a car or train) from the main track to a siding; 2 to lead away from the main subject; 3 to postpone consideration of || *n* 4 short track connected with the main track; siding

side′walk′ *n* walk, usu. paved, along the side of a street, for pedestrians

side′walk su·per·in·tend′ent *n* bystander who is an interested spectator at the site of the erection or demolition of a building or other construction and sometimes comments on the work to other bystanders

side′wall′ *n* the part of a tire between the wheel rim and the tread

side′ways′ also **side′wise′** *adv* 1 from or toward one side; 2 with one side foremost; 3 scornfully, askance || also *adj*

side′-wheel′er *n* steamboat propelled by paddle wheels on each side

side′wind′er /-wīnd′-/ *n* 1 rattlesnake (*Crotalus cerastes*) of the SW U.S. and Mexico that moves sideways

sid·ing /sīd′iŋ/ *n* 1 short railroad track connected with the main track; 2 weatherproof boarding or shingles that form the outer covering of a frame house

si·dle /sīd′əl/ [< OE *sidling* sidelong] *vi* to move sideways or unobtrusively

siege /sēj′/ [OF = seat] *n* 1 surrounding of a fortified place by an army to compel its surrender; 2 prolonged or persistent attempt to gain something; 3 long period of distress or annoyance; 4 **lay siege to** to besiege

si·en·na /sē-en′ə/ [It (terra di) *Siena* (earth of) Siena] *n* 1 a clay used as a pigment; 2 color of this pigment: brownish orange when raw and reddish brown when burned

si·er·ra /sē-er′ə/ [Sp < L *serra* saw] *n* mountain range rising in long jagged peaks suggestive of the teeth of a saw

Si·er·ra Le·o·ne /sē-er′ə lē̱-ōn′/ *n* republic in W Africa, member of the British Commonwealth of Nations (2,600,000; 27,699 sq.m.; cap. Freetown)

si·es·ta /sē-est′ə/ [Sp < L *sexta* (hora) sixth (hour)] *n* midday or afternoon nap, common in hot countries

sieve /siv′/ [OE *sife*] *n* utensil with a meshed or perforated bottom for separating the finer from the coarser parts of a substance

sift /sift′/ [OE *siftan*] *vt* 1 to separate, as the fine parts from the coarser, with a sieve; 2 to pass through or as through a sieve; 3 to examine critically; 4 to separate as with a sieve; 5 to scatter or sprinkle with or as with a sieve ‖ *vi* 6 to pass through or as through a sieve ‖ **sift′er** *n*

sigh /sī′/ [OE *sīcan*] *vi* 1 to breathe deeply and audibly, as from fatigue, sorrow, relief, etc.; 2 to make a sound like sighing; 3 **sigh for** to yearn for, pine for ‖ *vt* 4 to express by sighs ‖ *n* 5 act or sound of sighing

sight /sīt′/ [OE *gesiht*] *n* 1 power or faculty of seeing; vision; 2 act of seeing or being seen; 3 view, glimpse; 4 something worth seeing; spectacle; 5 range of vision; 6 any of several devices for guiding the eye or aim, as on a gun or optical instrument; 7 observation taken with an instrument to ascertain position or direction; 8 something that attracts attention by its odd or distressing appearance; 9 a **sight** for sore eyes *colloq* someone or something that one is glad to see; 10 **at sight**, **a** as soon as seen; **b** *com* on presentation; 11 **know by sight** to recognize by appearance, not by name; 12 **not by a long sight** *colloq* not nearly; **b** definitely not; 13 **on sight** as soon as seen; 14 **out of sight**, **a** too far to be seen; **b** away from one's presence; **c** *colloq* extremely expensive; 15 **sight unseen** without first seeing ‖ *vt* 16 to see, find by looking; 17 to take a sight of; 18 to aim by means of a sight; 19 to adjust the sights of ‖ *vi* 20 to aim or observe by a sight; 21 to gaze in a certain direction

sight′ draft′ *n* draft payable on presentation

sight′ gag′ *n* bit of visual comedy

sight′less *adj* blind

sight′ly *adj* (**-li·er**; **-li·est**) pleasing to the eye, attractive

sight′-read′ *v* (**-read** /-red′/) *vt & vi* to read or perform without preparation

sight′see′ing *n* act of visiting objects and places of interest ‖ **sight′se′er** *n*

sig·ma /sig′mə/ *n* eighteenth letter of the Greek alphabet Σ, σ and ς

sign /sīn′/ [OF *signe* < L *signum*] *n* 1 symbol or emblem; 2 any written word, character, or the like used to express a familiar meaning; 3 character used in mathematical or musical notation; 4 mark, token; 5 omen, portent; 6 gesture or motion used to express some thought, command, or wish; 7 lettered board or plate, publicly displayed, giving warning or directions, or advertising a business or profession; 8 trace or indication; 9 one of the twelve equal divisions of the zodiac ‖ *vt* 10 to affix one's signature to; 11 to write (one's name); 12 to hire by getting the signature of; 13 **sign away** to dispose of by signing a document; 14 **sign on** to hire; 15 **sign over** to turn (property) over ‖ *vi* 16 to write one's signature, as on a check or document; 17 **sign off** to cease broadcasting for the day; 18 **sign on**, **a** to obligate oneself to work for a particular employer; **b** to begin broadcasting for the day; 19 **sign up**, **a** to join an organization; **b** to enlist in the armed forces ‖ **sign′er** *n* ‖ SYN *n* (see **emblem**)

sig·nal /sig′nəl/ [L *signalis* of a sign] *n* 1 sign, light, act, or the like for conveying information, warning, or commands; 2 initial cause; that which incites action; 3 token or sign; 4 *rad & telv* sound or picture transmitted or received ‖ *adj* 5 memorable, outstanding ‖ *v* (**-naled** or **-nalled**; **-nal·ing** or **-nal·ling**) *vt* 6 to make a signal to; 7 to communicate by a signal ‖ *vi* 8 to communicate by signals ‖ **sig′nal·er** or **sig′nal·ler** *n*

sig′nal·ize′ *vt* 1 to make conspicuous or prominent; 2 to point out, indicate

sig·na·to·ry /sig′nətôr′ē, -tōr′-/ [< L *signare* (-*atus*) to mark] *n* (-ries) signer of a document, esp. a nation signing a treaty

sig′na·ture /-chər/ *n* 1 person's signed name or mark, as on a letter or document; 2 *mus* signs at the beginning of a staff showing the key and time; 3 *typ* one of the large printed sheets which, when folded, contains a set of pages of a book in proper order

sig·net /sig′nit/ [ML *signetum*] *n* 1 small seal, as on a finger ring; 2 impression made by a signet

sig·nif·i·cance /signif′ikəns/ [see *signify*] *n* 1 state or quality of being expressive; 2 what is meant to be expressed; meaning; often hidden or underlying meaning, as *the full significance of his remark escaped me*; 3 quality of being noteworthy; consequence, as *how he feels is of no significance* ‖ SYN expressiveness, importance (see *signification*)

sig·nif′i·cant *adj* 1 having a meaning; 2 meaningful; 3 noteworthy, consequential

sig′ni·fi·ca′tion *n* 1 that which is expressed or suggested; implication; 2 meaning of a sign, symbol, character, etc. ‖ SYN sense, meaning, import, purport, significance ‖ DISCR *Meaning* is that which one intends to express, or what one has in mind, as when I spoke, this was my *meaning*. *Meaning* is general in its connotation, however, and can be used for each of the other words. *Sense* is the special *meaning* or way in which a word is to be understood, as in a literal *sense; in* an exact *sense. Sense* can also be used to mean intelligibility, or to indicate the presence or absence of *meaning,* as what *sense* is there in the passage?; this verse has no *sense. Signification* is the exact *meaning* or *sense* of a word, phrase, or any part thereof, usually without implied or covert *meanings; significance* is used for the whole thought conveyed by the word or phrase, especially as indicative of moment or weight, and including all the subtleties of *meaning* that radiate from it. *Import* is like *significance* in including all implications, and also in referring to the *meaning* of the word or phrase as a whole. We speak of the *signification* of a prefix, the *significance* of the introductory paragraph, the real *import* of what seems a casual remark. *Purport* names the general drift or tenor, as the *purport* of the argument or document

sig·ni·fy′ [OF *signifier* < L *significare*] *v* (-fied) *vt* 1 to make known by words, signs, or acts; 2 to denote, mean ‖ *vi* 3 to be of consequence, to matter

sign′post′ *n* 1 post to which a sign is affixed; 2 indication; clue

Sikh /sēk′/ [Hindi = disciple] *n* one of a warlike religious sect in India, a reformed offshoot of Hinduism that rejects the caste system and priestly supremacy

si·lage /sil′ij/ [< *silo*] *n* fodder preserved in a silo

si·lence /sil′əns/ [OF < L *silentium*] *n* 1 state of being silent; muteness; 2 taciturnity; 3 absence of sound; stillness; 4 absence or omission of mention ‖ *vt* 5 to cause or force to be silent; 6 to quiet, put to rest; 7 to put (enemy guns) out of commission ‖ *interj* 8 be silent!

si′lenc·er *n* 1 one who or that which silences; 2 device for deadening the sound of a gun

si·lent /sil′ənt/ *adj* 1 saying nothing, mute; 2 taciturn; 3 not making any noise, quiet; 4 unspoken; unexpressed; 5 omitting mention; happening without notice; 6 (letter) not sounded ‖ si′lent·ly *adv*

si′lent part′ner *n* partner having no active role in a business

sil·hou·ette /sil′ōō·et′/ [E. de *Silhouette* (1709–67) F minister of finance] *n* 1 solid black outline drawing, esp. a profile; 2 dark shape outlined against a light background ‖ *vt* 3 to cause to appear in or as in a silhouette

sil·i·ca /sil′ikə/ [< L *silex* (-*licis*) flint] *n* hard white or colorless mineral substance, silicon dioxide —SiO_2— occurring as quartz, agate, flint, etc., used in making glass, abrasives, and ceramics

sil′i·ca gel′ *n* gelatinous form of silica that is highly adsorbent, used as a drying agent

sil·i·cate /sil′ikit, -kāt′/ *n* salt or ester of silicic acid, used extensively in making glass

si·lic′ic ac′id /silis′ik/ *n* weak gelatinous acid formed by combination of silica and water

sil·i·con /sil′ikən, -kon′/ *n* nonmetallic element (Si; at.no. 14; at.wt. 28.086) found abundantly in nature in combination with oxygen as a constituent of rocks, sand, etc.

sil′i·cone′ /-kōn′/ *n* any of several polymers containing silicon and oxygen atoms, used as lubricants, adhesives, in insulation, etc.

sil′i·co′sis /-kōs′is/ *n* disease of the lungs caused by inhaling silica dust, as by quarry workers

silk /silk′/ [OE *sioloe* < Gk *serikon*] *n* 1 fine, soft, lustrous fabric made from threads spun by silkworms to form their cocoons; 2 thread or fiber produced by these worms; 3 any similar thread, as that spun by spiders; 4 anything like silk in texture, such as the hairlike tuft on an ear of corn; 5 **silks** *pl* blouse and cap of a jockey, bearing the colors of the horse's owner; **6 hit the silk** *slang* to parachute || *adj* **7** pert. to or made of silk || **silk′en** *adj* || **silk′y** *adj* (**-i·er; -i·est**)

silk′ hat′ *n* man's tall cylindrical hat covered with black silk plush, worn with formal dress

silk′screen′ *n* **1** process for making prints and posters in which colors are forced through a mesh screen onto the paper || *vt* **2** to print by silkscreen

silk′-stock′ing *n* **1** aristocratic or wealthy person; **2** person who dresses richly and elegantly || also *adj*

silk′worm′ *n* larva of certain moths that are cultivated for the silk they spin into cocoons, esp. that of a Chinese moth (*Bombyx mori*)

sill /sil/ [OE *syl*] *n* **1** horizontal piece forming the foundation of a structure; **2** horizontal piece forming the bottom of a doorway or window

sil·ly /sil′ē/ [OE *sēlig* blessed] *adj* (**-li·er; -li·est**) **1** lacking good sense; foolish; witless; **2** unwise; absurd; **3** *colloq* dazed || **sil′li·ness** *n* || SYN *adj* childish, fatuous, ridiculous, senseless

si·lo /sī′lō/ [Sp] *n* **1** pit or cylindrical tower for storing fodder; **2** underground structure of steel and concrete for housing ballistic missiles

silt /silt/ [ME *cylte*] *n* **1** mud or fine earth suspended in or deposited by running water || *vt* **2** to choke or fill up with silt || *vi* **3** to become choked or filled with silt

sil·ver /sil′vər/ [OE *siolfor*] *n* **1** soft, lustrous, white, malleable, and ductile metallic element (Ag; at.no. 47; at.wt. 107.870), used for coins, tableware, jewelry, ornaments, etc., its compounds being used in medicine and photography; **2** anything made of this metal, as silverware or money; **3** anything like silver; **4** luster or color of silver || *vt* **5** to cover or coat with silver or a silverlike substance; **6** to give the color of silver to || *vi* **7** to turn silvery white

sil′ver·fish′ *n* wingless silver-colored insect (*Lepisma saccharina*) that feeds on the starch in wallpaper and books

sil′ver foil′ *n* foil made of silver or a silvery metal

sil′ver fox′ *n* red fox in the period when its fur is black with silvery tips on the hairs

sil′ver i′o·dide *n* yellow precipitate —AgI— that turns dark on exposure to light and is used in photography, medicine, and rainmaking

sil′ver lin′ing *n* pleasant side of an unfortunate or sad situation

sil′ver ni′trate *n* white crystalline poisonous powder —AgNO₃— used in photographic emulsions and as an antiseptic

sil′ver plate′ *n* **1** silver tableware; **2** silver coating over base metal

sil′ver-plate′ *vt* to plate (a base metal) with silver, as by electroplating

sil′ver screen′ *n* motion pictures

sil′ver·smith′ *n* one who makes and repairs articles of silver

sil′ver spoon′ *n* **born with a silver spoon in one's mouth** born into wealth

Sil′ver Star′ *n* medal awarded to U.S. soldiers for bravery, ranking below the Distinguished Service Cross

sil′ver-tongued′ *adj* eloquent; persuasive (speaker)

sil′ver·ware′ *n* articles, esp. tableware, made of silver, silver-plated metal, or other metals

sil′ver wed′ding *n* 25th anniversary of a wedding

sil′ver·y *adj* **1** covered with or containing silver; **2** resembling silver; **3** like the sound of a silver bell, soft and clear in tone

sim·i·an /sim′ē·ən/ [< L *simia* ape] *adj* **1** pert. to or like an ape or monkey || *n* **2** ape or monkey

sim·i·lar /sim′ilər/ [< L *similis*] *adj* **1** having resemblance; analogous; **2** *geom* having the same shape but differing in size || **sim′i·lar′i·ty** /-lar′-/ (**-ties**) || SYN (see *alike*)

sim·i·le /sim′ilē/ [L] *n* figure of speech expressing likeness between unlike objects, differing from a metaphor in form by the use of *like* or *as*, as *she is like a flower*

si·mil·i·tude /simil′it(y)ood′/ [L *similitudo*] *n* **1** similarity, likeness; **2** guise, outward show

sim·mer /sim′ər/ [ME *simper*] *vt* **1** to cook in a liquid at or just below the boiling point || *vi* **2** to cook at or just below the boiling point; **3** to make a gentle murmuring sound; **4** to be in a state of suppressed emotion; **5 simmer down** *slang* to become calm || *n* **6** act or state of simmering

Si·mon Le·gree /sīm′ən ligrē′/ [brutal slaveowner in Harriet Beecher Stowe's *Uncle Tom's Cabin*] *n* any harsh taskmaster

si′mon-pure′ /sīm′ən/ [*Simon Pure* character in 18th-cent. play] *adj* real, genuine

si·mo·ny /sīm′ənē, sim′-/ [LL *simonia* < *Simon* Magus, sorcerer who sought to buy the power of the Holy Ghost (Acts 8:9-24)] *n* act or sin of buying or selling church offices or positions of honor

sim·pa·ti·co /simpat′ikō′/ [It] *adj* congenial, having the knack of being liked by others

sim·per /simp′ər/ [prob < Scand] *vi* **1** to smile in a silly or self-conscious manner || *vt* **2** to express with a simper || *n* **3** silly, affected smile

sim·ple /simp′əl/ [OF < L *simplus*] *adj* **1** single, not compound or complex; **2** mere, unqualified; **3** unassuming; **4** common, ordinary; **5** plain, unadorned; **6** sincere, straightforward; **7** unpretentious; **8** humble; of low rank; **9** unlearned; unsophisticated; **10** foolish, lacking sense; **11** unimportant; insignificant ‖ **sim·plic′i·ty** /-plĭs′-/ *n* (-ties) ‖ SYN innocent, guileless, unsophisticated, straightforward, uninvolved, intelligible

sim′ple frac′tion *n* fraction whose terms are whole numbers

sim′ple frac′ture *n* fracture in which the broken bone does not project through the skin

sim′ple in′ter·est *n* interest paid only on the principal

sim′ple-mind′ed *adj* **1** feebleminded; **2** lacking good sense; **3** artless; unsophisticated

sim′ple sen′tence *n* sentence that does not have a coordinate or subordinate clause

sim′ple·ton /-tən/ *n* foolish person

sim′pli·fy′ [F *simplifier*] *v* (-fied) *vt* to make easier; reduce from the complex to the simple ‖ **sim′pli·fi·ca′·tion** *n*

sim·plis·tic /sĭmplĭs′tĭk/ *adj* naively oversimplified ‖ **sim·plis′ti·cal·ly** *adv*

sim′ply /-plē/ *adv* **1** in a simple manner; **2** only, merely; **3** quite, absolutely

sim·u·la·crum /sĭm′yəlāk′rəm/ [L = likeness] *n* (-cra /-krə/) **1** image or representation; **2** superficial or unreal likeness

sim·u·late /sĭm′yəlāt′/ [L *simulare* (-*atus*)] *vt* **1** to feign or counterfeit; **2** to act like; imitate ‖ **sim′u·la′tion** *n*

si′mul·cast′ /sīm′əl-/ [*simultaneous* + broad*cast*] *v* (-cast) *vt* **1** to broadcast (a program) simultaneously on radio and television or on FM and AM radio ‖ *n* **2** simulcast program

si·mul·ta·ne·ous /sīm′əltăn′ē·əs, sĭm′-/ [ML *simultaneus*] *adj* happening, done, or existing at the same time

sin /sĭn/ [OE *synn*] *n* **1** willful breaking of divine law or violation of the principles of morality; **2** any serious fault or offense ‖ *v* (**sinned; sinning**) *vi* **3** to commit a sin

Si·nai, Mount /sī′nī/ *n* Bib mountain on which Moses received the Ten Commandments (Ex.19)

since /sĭns′/ [< *obs sithence* < OE *siththan* after that] *adv* **1** from then until now, as *he left on Monday and has not been seen since;* **2** at some time between then and now, subsequently, as *he has since been promoted;* **3** before this, ago, as *not long since* ‖ *prep* **4** continuously from, as *since this morning;* **5** between then and now, as *twice since noon* ‖ *conj* **6** from and after a time when, as *I haven't seen him since that happened;* **7** seeing that, because

sin·cere /sĭnsĭr′/ [L *sincerus* clean, pure] *adj* **1** true, genuine; **2** without hypocrisy or deceit ‖ **sin·cere′ly** *adv* ‖ SYN true, real, unassumed, genuine (see *hearty*)

sin·cer′i·ty /-ser′-/ *n* state or quality of being sincere ‖ SYN honesty, unaffectedness, frankness, straightforwardness (see *candor*)

sine /sīn′/ [L *sinus* curve] *n trig* ratio which, when a perpendicular is dropped from any point on one side of an angle to the other side, the length of the perpendicular bears to the distance from the vertex to the point from which the perpendicular is dropped

si·ne·cure /sīn′ĭkyŏŏr′, sĭn′-/ [L *sine cura* without care] *n* any office or position having a salary or fees but entailing little work or responsibility

sine′ curve′ /sīn′/ *n math* serpentine plane curve of the equation $y = \sin x$

si·ne di·e /sīn′ē dī′ē/ [L = without day] *adv* without setting a day or time for reassembling, as a legislative assembly or convention

si·ne qua non /sīn′ē kwā′ non′/ [L = without which not] *n* indispensable condition; absolute necessity

sin·ew /sĭn′yŏŏ/ [OE *sinu*] *n* **1** tendon; **2** strength; energy; **3** anything supplying strength; mainstay

sin′ew·y *adj* **1** pert. to or like a sinew; **2** vigorous, tough

sin′ful *adj* wicked; full of sin ‖ **sin′ful·ly** *adv* ‖ **sin′ful·ness** *n* ‖ SYN guilty, immoral, iniquitous, unholy (cf. *bad*)

sing /sĭŋ/ [OE *singan*] *v* (**sang; sung**) *vi* **1** to make musical sounds with the voice; **2** to produce melodious sounds, as birds or certain insects; **3** to make a humming, buzzing, or whistling noise, as bullets; **4** to celebrate some event in verse or song; **5** to ring with a buzzing sound, as the ears; **6** *slang* to squeal, inform; **7 sing out** *colloq* to call out loudly ‖ *vt* **8** to utter with musical inflections of the voice; **9** to celebrate in song or verse; **10** to bring into a certain condition by singing, as *to sing a child to sleep;* **11** to speak warmly of, as *he sang their praises* ‖ *n* **12** gathering together of persons for the purpose of singing ‖ **sing′er** *n* ‖ SYN *v* carol, warble, hum, chant, intone

Sin·ga·pore /sĭŋ′(g)əpôr′, -pōr′/ *n* republic occupying an island just S of the Malay Peninsula, member of the British Commonwealth (2,000,000; 222 sq.m.; cap. Singapore)

singe /sĭnj′/ [OE *sengan*] *v* (**singe·ing**) *vt* **1** to burn slightly or on the surface; scorch; **2** to burn the tips of (the hair); **3** to burn the feathers off the carcass of (a fowl) ‖ *n* **4** act of singeing; **5** superficial burn ‖ SYN *v* scorch, scar, char (see *burn*)

Sin·gha·lese /siŋ'gəlēz', -lēs'/ [< Skt *Sinhala* Ceylon] *n* (-lese) 1 one of the native people of Ceylon; 2 their language ‖ also *adj*

sin·gle /siŋ'gəl/ [MF *sengle* < L *singulus*] *adj* 1 consisting of only one; 2 alone; 3 unmarried; 4 having only one on each side, as a contest or combat; 5 unique, as *the single instance;* 6 of or for one person, unit, or thing; 7 having only one part or component; 8 sincere, undivided ‖ *vt* 9 *baseball* to advance (a base runner) by hitting a single; 10 **single out** to pick out from all the others ‖ *vi* 11 *baseball* to hit a single ‖ *n* 12 single person or thing; 13 *baseball* one-base hit; 14 *colloq* one-dollar bill; 15 **singles** *sg* match, as in tennis, between two players ‖ **sin'gly** *adv*

sin·gle-ac'tion *adj* (revolver) that must be cocked by hand before each shot

sin·gle-breast'ed *adj* (coat) having a single row of buttons down the center of the front

sin'gle file' *n* line of persons or things one behind the other

sin·gle-hand'ed *adj* 1 having, using, or requiring only one hand; 2 done without aid or assistance ‖ *adv* 3 without help ‖ **sin'gle-hand'ed·ly** *adv*

sin·gle-lens' re'flex (cam'er·a) *n* reflex camera that has only one lens, in which the viewing mirror swings out of the way when the shutter is actuated to allow the image to fall on the film

sin·gle-mind'ed *adj* 1 having but one purpose; 2 steadfast ‖ **sin'gle-mind'ed·ly** *adv* ‖ **sin'gle-mind'ed·ness** *n*

sin'gle·ness *n* 1 state of being single; 2 state of being unmarried; 3 exclusive attention, as *singleness of purpose*

sin'gle-space' *vt & vi* to typewrite leaving no blank line between lines

sin'gle tax' *n* tax, usu. on land, constituting the sole source of public revenue

sin'gle·ton /-tən/ *n* 1 the only card of a suit held in one hand; 2 something occurring singly

sin'gly *adv* 1 individually; one by one; 2 without others; alone

sing'song' *n* 1 singing or poetry marked by an unvaried monotonous rhythm; 2 monotonous drawling tone

sin·gu·lar /siŋ'gyələr/ [L *singularis*] *adj* 1 unique; 2 peculiar, strange; 3 remarkable, exceptional; 4 *gram* denoting one person or thing ‖ *n* 5 *gram* a singular number; b form in the singular ‖ **sin'gu·lar·ly** *adv*

sin·gu·lar'i·ty /-lar'-/ *n* (-ties) 1 state or quality of being singular; 2 peculiarity

sin·is·ter /sin'istər/ [L = left, inauspicious] *adj* 1 ill-omened, boding evil; 2 corrupt, evil; 3 unfortunate; 4 *archaic & heral* on the left side

sink /siŋk/ [OE *sincan*] *v* (**sank** or **sunk; sunk**) *vi* 1 to become wholly or partly submerged, as in water or quicksand; 2 to descend lower and lower; 3 to incline downward; 4 to descend from sight, as the sun; 5 to decline or degenerate gradually; 6 to appear depressed or hollow; 7 to enter or penetrate deeply; 8 to make a lasting impression, as *to sink into the mind;* 9 to subside or settle gradually; 10 to fall or lapse gently, as into sleep or thought; 11 to decrease or diminish in intensity, value, or the like; 12 to become lower in tone or pitch, as a voice; 13 to approach death ‖ *vt* 14 o cause to sink; 15 to dig or excavate, as a well; 16 to place in an excavation thus made, as a pipe; 17 to lower in value or amount; 18 to degrade, debase; 19 to conceal, prevent revelation of; 20 to invest unprofitably; 21 to lower the level of, as a road; 22 *sports* to cause (the ball) to go in the basket, cup, or pocket ‖ *n* 23 basin, as in a kitchen, usu. with a water supply and drain; 24 place of vice and corruption; 25 depression in the land, esp. one from which water escapes by evaporation or percolation

sink'er *n* 1 weight attached to a fishing line; 2 *slang* doughnut; 3 *baseball* pitched ball that sinks as it reaches the plate

sink'hole' *n* 1 low land in which drainage collects; 2 hole formed in rock by water

sink'ing fund' *n* money set aside to pay off bonds or other obligations

sin'less *adj* free from sin

sin·ner /sin'ər/ *n* one who sins; wrongdoer

Si·no- [LGk *Sinai* the Chinese] *comb form* Chinese

Si·nol·o·gy /sīnol'əjē, si-/ *n* study of the history, language, and culture of the Chinese ‖ **Si·nol'o·gist** *n*

Si'no-Ti·bet'an /sīn'ō-/ *n* family of languages that includes Chinese, Tibetan, Burmese, Thai, etc. ‖ also *adj*

sin·ter /sint'ər/ [G = cinder] *vt* to cause (metal parts) to adhere into one mass by heating without melting

sin·u·ous /sin'yōō-əs/ [L *sinuosus*] *adj* 1 curving in and out, winding; 2 twisting, devious ‖ **sin'u·os'i·ty** /-os'-/ *n* (-ties)

si·nus /sīn'əs/ [L = curve, bent surface] *n* natural cavity, pocket, or hollow in a bone or other body tissue, esp. one of the air cavities in the skull communicating with the nose

si'nus·i'tis /-īt'is/ *n* inflammation of the sinuses in the head

-sion /-shən, -zhən/ [L -*sio* (-*onis*)] *suf* indicating 1 act of, as *expulsion;* 2 state of being, as *fusion;* 3 result or product of an act, as *pension*

Sioux /sōō′/ [F < Ojibwa] *n* (*pl* **Sioux**) member of any of several American Indian tribes, esp. the Dakota tribe ‖ also *adj* ‖ **Siou′an** *adj & n*

sip /sip′/ [ME *sippe*] *v* (**sipped; sip-ping**) *vt & vi* 1 to drink a little at a time ‖ 2 act or instance of sipping; 3 small quantity sipped

si·phon /sīf′ən/ [Gk = tube] *n* 1 tube shaped like an inverted U having one leg longer than the other, used for drawing off liquids from one container into another at a lower level by atmospheric pressure; 2 siphon bottle ‖ *vt* 3 to draw off or transfer with a siphon

si′phon bot′tle *n* bottle for carbonated water fitted with a bent tube extend-ing to the bottom with a stopcock at the top, upon opening which the water is forced out by the pressure of the contained gas

sir /sur′/ [var of *sire*] *n* 1 term of re-spect in addressing a man without speaking his name; 2 **Sir** formal salutation to a man in a letter, as *Dear Sir* ‖ **Sir** /sər/ *n* 3 title used with the first name of a knight or baronet

sire /sī′ər/ [OF < L *senior* elder] *n* 1 title used in addressing a sovereign; 2 *archaic* father or forefather; 3 male progenitor of beasts ‖ *vt* 4 to beget

si·ren /sī′rən/ [L < Gk *seiren*] *n* 1 *class. myth.* any of several sea nymphs, half woman and half bird, said to lure sailors to destruction by their beauty and sweet singing; 2 alluring and seductive woman; 3 de-vice for producing a loud wailing sound, used as a foghorn, whistle, or warning horn, as on a fire engine or ambulance

Sir·i·us /sir′ē·əs/ [L < Gk *seirios* scorching] *n* the Dog Star, the brightest star in the sky, in the constellation Canis Major

sir·loin /sur′loin/ [< OF *sur* over + *longe* loin] *n* choice cut of beef, taken from the upper part of the loin in front of the rump

si·roc·co /sirok′ō/ [It < Ar *sharq* east] *n* 1 hot dust-laden wind blow-ing north from the African deserts; 2 moist, warm southeast wind that sweeps over Italy; 3 any strong hot wind

sir·up /sir′əp/ *n* syrup

sis /sis′/ *n colloq* sister

si·sal (**hemp′**) /sis′əl, sis′-/ [*Sisal* port of Yucatán] *n* fiber obtained from a tropical plant (*Agave sisalana*) used in making rope

sis·sy /sis′ē/ [< *sis*] *n* (-**sies**) 1 effemi-nate boy or man; 2 excessively timid person ‖ **sis′si·fied** *adj*

sis·ter /sist′ər/ [OE *sweoster*] *n* 1 female in relation to another off-spring of the same parents; 2 female fellow member; 3 nun; 4 *Brit* head nurse ‖ *adj* 5 regarded as femi-nine and having close relationship or resemblance to another, as *sister ships*

sis′ter·hood *n* 1 quality or state of being a sister; 2 group of women united by a common interest, as in a religious community

sis′ter·in-law′ *n* (**sisters-in-law**) 1 hus-band's or wife's sister; 2 a brother's wife; 3 wife of the brother of one's husband or wife

sis′ter·ly *adj* 1 like or pert. to a sister; 2 affectionate, kind ‖ **sis′ter·li·ness**

Sis·y·phus /sis′ifəs/ *n Gk myth.* king of Corinth who was condemned to keep rolling to the top of a hill a huge stone which always rolled down again

sit /sit′/ [OE *sittan*] *v* (**sat**; **sit·ting**) *vi* 1 to rest with the weight of the body on the buttocks; 2 to take a seat; 3 to perch; 4 to rest inactive or pas-sive; 5 to be situated; 6 to fit, suit, as *the dress sits well;* 7 to press or weigh, as sorrow; 8 to occupy a seat or place officially, as a judge or leg-islator; 9 to convene or hold a ses-sion, as a court; 10 to cover eggs to be hatched, as a fowl; 11 to pose, as for a portrait; 12 to baby-sit; 13 to be acceptable, as *this doesn't sit well;* 14 **sit down** to take a seat; 15 **sit in** to take part in something; 16 **sit in on** to participate in (a discussion, an event, etc.); 17 **sit on, a** to inquire into; **b** *colloq* to suppress; **c** *colloq* to rebuke; 18 **sit tight** to bide one's time; 19 **sitting pretty** in an advan-tageous position; 20 **sit up, a** to rise to a sitting position, as one lying in bed; **b** to sit erect; **c** to stay up be-yond one's usual bedtime ‖ *vt* 21 to have or keep a seat on (a horse); 22 to seat (oneself); 23 **sit out** to fail to take part in, as *he sat out the war in Washington*

si·tar /sitär′/ [Hindi] *n* lute of India with a long broad neck

sit′-down strike′ *n* strike in which the workers refuse to leave their place of employment

site /sīt′/ [L *situs*] *n* 1 position or loca-tion ‖ *vt* 2 to place into position, as artillery

sit′-in′ *n* organized demonstration, as against segregation, in which the participants install themselves in a place and refuse to leave

sit′ter *n* baby-sitter

sit′ting *n* 1 position or act of one who sits; 2 session or meeting; 3 time during which one sits, as for a por-trait

sit′ting duck′ *n slang* one who is an easy target

sit′ting room′ *n* small living room, as one adjoining a bedroom in a hotel suite

sit·u·ate /sich′ŏŏ-āt′/ [LL *situare* (-*atus*)] *vt* to locate ‖ **sit′u·at′ed** *adj*

sit′u·a′tion *n* **1** position, locality; **2** condition, state; **3** employment; job; **4** state of affairs

sitz′ bath′ /sits′/ [< G *Sitzbad* sit bath] *n* **1** tub in which one may bathe while seated; **2** bath taken in such a tub

Si·va /sēv′ə, shēv′ə/ [Skt = auspicious one] *n* Hindu god of destruction and reproduction, forming with Brahma and Vishnu the supreme trinity

six /siks′/ [OE] *n* **1** sum of five and one (6; VI); **2** set of six persons or things; **3** playing card with six spots ‖ *also adj & pron*

six′fold′ *adj* **1** having six times as much or as many ‖ *adv* **2** six times as much or as many

six′pence /-pəns/ *nsg* **1** British coin worth six pennies ‖ *nsg* or *npl* **2** *Brit* sum of six pennies

six′-shoot′er *n* revolver holding six bullets

six′teen′ /-tēn′/ [OE *sixtēne*] *n* sum of six and ten (16; XVI) ‖ *also adj & pron*

six′teenth′ *n* **1** the one next in order after the fifteenth; **2** one of sixteen equal parts ‖ *also adj*

six′teenth′ note′ *n mus* note with one sixteenth the duration of a whole note

sixth /siksth′/ *n* **1** the one next in order after the fifth; **2** one of six equal parts; **3** *mus* sixth tone of a diatonic scale ‖ *also adj*

sixth′ sense′ *n* intuitive perception

six′ti·eth *n* **1** the one next in order after the fifty-ninth; **2** one of sixty equal parts ‖ *also adj*

six′ty [OE *sixtig*] (-ties) *n* **1** six times ten (60; LX); **2** the sixties *pl* **a** the numbers from 60 to 69; **b** the years from 60 to 69 in a century or a lifetime ‖ *also adj & pron*

siz·a·ble or **size·a·ble** /sīz′əbəl/ *adj* of considerable size; fairly large

size¹ /sīz′/ [ME *sise*] *n* **1** any of various thin glutinous preparations made from glue or starch for filling pores and glazing the surface of walls, paper, or cloth ‖ *vt* **2** to prepare, stiffen, or cover with size

size² [OF *sise*] *n* **1** dimensions, magnitude, or bulk; **2** one of a series of standard graduated measures for various articles, as *a size seven hat*; **3** *that's about the size of it colloq* that is the actual fact of the matter ‖ *vt* **4** to arrange according to size; **5** to make or shape to size; **6 size up** *colloq* to form an estimate of ‖ *vi* **7 size up** *colloq* to come up to requirements

-sized *comb form* having a specified size, as *large-sized*

siz′ing *n* **1** size¹; **2** act of applying size¹

siz·zle /siz′əl/ [imit] *vi* **1** to make a hissing sound, as in frying; **2** *colloq* to be intensely hot ‖ *n* **3** sizzling sound

S.J. Society of Jesus

skate¹ /skāt′/ [ON *skata*] *n* any of various broad flat-bodied fishes (esp. genus *Raja*) with narrow tails and cartilaginous skeletons

skate² [D *schaats*] *n* **1** shoe, or frame fitting under a shoe, equipped with a metal blade for gliding over ice or with small wheels for rolling over floors or paved surfaces ‖ *vi* **2** to glide or roll on skates; **3 skate on thin ice** to be in a precarious or delicate position ‖ **skat′er** *n*

skate³ *n* [?] fellow; guy; chap

skate′board′ *n* child's toy consisting of an oblong board mounted on skate wheels on which the rider balances himself while moving

ske·dad·dle /skidad′əl/ [?] *vi colloq* to run off in haste, decamp

skeet′ /skēt′/ *n* form of trapshooting in which the shooter shoots at targets thrown at various angles, elevations, and speeds

skein /skān′/ [MF *escaigne*] *n* quantity of thread or yarn coiled together or wound on a spindle

skel·e·ton /skel′ətən/ [Gk = mummy] *n* **1** bony framework of man and animals; **2** supporting framework of anything; **3** outline, as of a play; **4** emaciated animal or person; **5 skeleton in the closet** scandalous secret out of one's past ‖ *adj* **6** reduced to a minimum, as *a skeleton crew* ‖ **skel′-e·tal** /-təl/ *adj*

skel′e·ton key′ *n* key with the bit filed down so that it can be used as a master key

skep·tic /skep′tik/ [Gk *skeptikos* thoughtful] *n* **1** person characterized by a doubting attitude; **2** one who questions the truth or validity of generally accepted conclusions and beliefs in science, natural phenomena, and religion; **3 Skeptic** adherent of one of the ancient Greek philosophical schools that doubted the possibility of real knowledge of anything ‖ **skep′ti·cal** *adj* SYN doubter, infidel, agnostic, atheist, freethinker ‖ DISCR A *doubter* is one who is inclined to disbelieve; especially, in a religious sense, a *doubter* is one so overwhelmed by uncertainty that he withholds assent. A *skeptic* is one who doubts so emphatically that he denies the truth of Christianity, of divine revelation, or of all religious doctrines. An *infidel*, literally one without faith, is, in general, an unbeliever. The *skeptic* denies; the *infidel* rejects and refuses. Historically, any non-Christian, particularly during the Crusades, any Mohammedan, was an *infidel*. Now the term, which carries opprobrium, is applied according to point of view; for instance, from a Mohammedan or Jewish point of view, a Christian is an *infidel*. An *agnostic* is one who maintains that nothing is, or can actually be, known about anything not materially real and present. The *agnostic* neither doubts nor denies; he merely says, "I do not know." An *atheist* is one who denies the existence of a God. A *freethinker* may be a radical or he may be one throwing off justly resented religious authority. He who calls himself a *freethinker* is apt to be merely rejecting what he has a right to reject; but the same name, if applied to him by the body with which he disagrees, connotes, from their viewpoint, radicalism and rebellion

skep'ti·cism *n* 1 incredulous, doubting, or critical state of mind; 2 doubt or denial with regard to a religion, esp. Christianity; 3 **Skepticism** doctrines and beliefs of the Skeptics

sketch /skech'/ [D *schets* < It *schizzo*] *n* 1 simple, quickly made drawing, often merely an outline; 2 outline, rough draft; 3 short simple piece of literature or music; 4 brief, slight dramatic performance ‖ *vt* 5 to make a sketch of ‖ *vi* 6 to make a sketch

sketch'y *adj* (-i·er; -i·est) brief; incomplete; superficial

skew /skyōō'/ [ONF *escuer* to avoid] *adj* 1 oblique, slanting ‖ *n* 2 oblique movement; distortion ‖ *vi* 3 to move in sidelong fashion; swerve; 4 to glance obliquely ‖ *vt* 5 to shape obliquely; 6 to give an oblique direction to

skew·er /skyōō'ər/ [?] *n* 1 long pin for keeping meat in shape for roasting or for fastening it to a spit ‖ *vt* 2 to fasten with or as with a skewer

ski /skē'/ [Norw] *n* (**skis** or **ski**) 1 one of a pair of long slender runners attached to each foot for gliding over snow ‖ *vi* 2 to travel on skis ‖ *vt* 3 to travel on skis over ‖ **ski'er** *n*

skid /skid'/ [prob < Scand] *n* 1 wedge or drag used on a wheel to check its motion; 2 one of a pair of logs, planks, or the like, used to form a track along which heavy objects may be rolled or pushed; 3 runner on the landing gear of some airplanes; 4 act or instance of skidding; 5 **hit the skids** to lose one's wealth and position; 6 **on the skids** on the way to social and economic ruin ‖ *v* (**skidded; skid·ding**) *vi* 7 to slip sideways; 8 to slide without turning, as a wheel on a slippery road; 9 *aeron* to slide sideways and outward when turning

skid' row' /-rō'/ *n* run-down section of a city, frequented by vagrants and alcoholics

skiff /skif'/ [MF *esquif* < OHG *skif* ship] *n* small, light boat for sailing and rowing

ski·jor·ing /skējôr'iŋ, -jôr'-/ *n* sport in which the skier is drawn by a horse or motor vehicle

ski' jump' *n* steep snow-covered drop on the side of a hill that levels off to a horizontal ramp so that skiers may speed down and jump off into space before landing on the slower slope of the hill

ski' lift' *n* chair suspended from a cable for carrying skiers to the top of a slope or ski jump

skill /skil'/ [ON *skil* discernment] *n* 1 proficiency derived from aptitude and practice; 2 craft or art requiring dexterity and training; 3 expertness; competence ‖ **skilled'** *adj* ‖ SYN expertness, aptitude, dexterity (see *ability*)

skil·let /skil'it/ [ME *skelet*] *n* 1 frying pan; 2 cooking vessel with a handle and sometimes legs

skill'ful or **skil'ful** *adj* 1 having skill; 2 showing or requiring skill ‖ **skill'ful·ly** *adv* ‖ SYN able, handy, proficient, able, deft (see *clever*) ‖ ANT awkward, clumsy, maladroit, inexpert

skim /skim'/ [var of *scum*] *v* (**skimmed; skim·ming**) *vt* 1 to remove floating substances from the top of (a liquid); 2 to remove from the top of a liquid; 3 to glide lightly over the surface of; 4 to read or glance at hurriedly or superficially; 5 to cause to skip, as a stone on water ‖ *vi* 6 to pass lightly over or near a surface; 7 to read rapidly and superficially ‖ *n* 8 act or process of skimming; 9 any substance skimmed off

ski' mask' *n* storm hood worn by skiers

skim'mer *n* 1 perforated ladle for skimming; 2 long-winged marine bird of the genus *Rynchops* that flies close to the water with the lower mandible immersed for skimming up fish as food; 3 stiff straw hat with a flat crown and straight brim

skim' milk' *n* milk from which the cream has been skimmed

skimp /skimp'/ [?] *vt & vi* to scrimp

skimp'y *adj* (-i·er; -i·est) 1 scanty; 2 stingy

skin /skin'/ [ON *skinn*] *n* 1 outer covering of the body of man and animal; 2 pelt; 3 rind, peel; 4 anything like a skin, as the covering of an aircraft; 5 vessel made of an animal's hide to hold liquids; 6 **get under the skin** of *slang* to irritate ‖ *v* (**skinned; skin·ning**) *vt* 7 to remove the skin of; 8 to scrape the skin from (a part of the body); 9 *slang* to defraud, fleece; 10 **skin alive** *colloq* **a** to reprimand severely; **b** to defeat decisively

skin'-deep' *adj* 1 not profound, superficial || *adv* 2 superficially

skin' div'ing *n* sport in which a swimmer submerges under water for spearfishing or exploring, using a mask, foot fins, and a snorkel or air cylinder || **skin'-dive'** *vi* || **skin'-div'er** *n*

skin' flick' *n* motion picture featuring nudity and sex

skin'flint' *n* miser

skin' game' *n* swindling scheme or trick

skin'ny [< *skin*] *adj* (-ni·er; -ni·est) very thin, emaciated || **skin'ni·ness** *n*

skip /skip/ [< Scand] *v* (skipped; skip·ping) *vi* 1 to leap or bound lightly; pass along rapidly; 2 to pass from one thing to another, omitting what intervenes; 3 to move by alternately hopping and stepping; 4 *colloq* to leave hurriedly without notice; 5 to bounce along a surface || *vt* 6 to jump lightly over; 7 to pass over or omit; 8 to cause to bound or jump over a surface; 9 *colloq* to flee hurriedly and secretly from || *n* 10 omission; 11 act of skipping; 12 light leap or bounce; 13 gait of alternating hops and steps

skip' bomb'ing *n* bombing by low-flying planes in which the bombs hit the surface repeatedly before finally hitting the target

ski'plane' /skē'-/ *n* airplane equipped with skis for landing on and taking off from snow

skip·per /skip'ər/ [MD *schipper*] *n* 1 captain of a ship; 2 captain or leader, as of a team || *vi* 3 to act as a skipper

skip' trac'er *n* locator of persons who skip town to avoid paying their debts

skirl /skurl'/ [ME *scrille* < Scand] *vi* 1 to play the bagpipe || *n* 2 sound of a bagpipe

skir·mish /skur'mish/ [OF *eskermir* (-*miss*-)] *n* 1 fight between small detachments of opposing armies; 2 any slight encounter || *vi* 3 to take part in a skirmish || **skir'mish·er** *n* || SYN *n* attack, contest, engagement (see *battle*)

skirt /skurt'/ [ON *skyrta* shirt] *n* 1 the part of a garment that extends below the waist; 2 garment for women and girls covering the body below the waist; 3 skirtlike edge or border; 4 *slang* female || *vt* 5 to border; pass along the edge of; 6 to turn away from, avoid, as a controversial issue

ski' run' *n* sloping course used for skiing

skit /skit'/ [?] *n* short humorous theatrical sketch or act

ski' tow' *n* moving rope for towing skiers up a hill

skit'tish *adj* 1 restless; nervous; 2 coy, timid, shy; 3 capricious; fickle; 4 fearful; wary; 5 (horse) easily frightened

skiv·vy /skiv'ē/ [?] *n* (-vies) T-shirt

skoal /skōl'/ [< Scand] *interj* your health! (used as a toast)

Skt, Skt., Skr., Skrt. Sanskrit

sku·a /skyoo'ə/ [Faeroese *skūgvur*] *n* large fierce gull-like bird (*Catharacta skua*) of Arctic and Antarctic regions

skul·dug·ger·y /skuldug'ərē/ [?] *n* dishonest and dishonorable proceedings

skulk /skulk'/ [< Scand] *vi* 1 to lurk about or keep hidden; 2 to move in a stealthy manner

skull /skul'/ [< Scand] *n* skeleton or bony framework of the head

skull'cap' *n* soft close-fitting brimless cap

skunk /skuŋk'/ [< Algonquian] *n* 1 small American mammal (*Mephitis mephitis*), black with a white stripe down the back, able to eject at will a very offensive odor; 2 *colloq* contemptible person || *vt* 3 *slang* to beat (an opponent in a game) very badly

skunk' cab'bage *n* swamp plant (*Symplocarpus foetidus*) with broad leaves, which emits a skunklike odor

sky /skī'/ [< Scand] *n* (skies) 1 the heavens or upper atmosphere; 2 often **skies** *pl* climate or weather; 3 heaven; 4 **out of a clear sky** unexpectedly, abruptly

sky' blue' *n* color of the clear sky || **sky'-blue'** *adj*

sky'div'ing *n* sport of parachute jumping with delayed opening of the parachute || **sky'dive'** *vi* (-dived or -dove; -dived) || **sky'div'er** *n*

sky'-high' *adj* & *adv* very high

sky'jack' *vt* to hijack (an airplane) || **sky'jack'er** *n* || **sky'jack'ing** *n*

sky'lark' *n* 1 small Old World lark (*Alauda arvensis*) that sings continuously in flight || *vi* 2 *colloq* to frolic boisterously

sky'light' *n* 1 window in a roof or ceiling; 2 diffuse light of the sky, distinguished from direct sunlight

sky'line' *n* 1 outline of the buildings of a city seen against the sky; 2 horizon

sky' mar'shal *n* armed guard who travels incognito on an airplane to guard against skyjacking

sky' pi'lot *n slang* chaplain; clergyman

sky'rock'et *n* 1 kind of fireworks, a rocket that mounts high into the air and explodes || *vi* 2 to rise spectacularly || *vt* 3 to cause to rise, esp. in fame and fortune

sky'scrap'er *n* very high building

sky'ward /-wərd/ *adj* & *adv* toward the sky || **sky'wards** *adv*

sky'writ'ing *n* 1 process whereby an aviator releases a trail of smoke that forms letters in the sky; 2 the letters so formed || **sky'writ'er** *n*

slab /slab'/ [ME *slabbe*] *n* relatively broad thick piece or slice of anything, as of marble or stone

slack /slak′/ [OE *sleac*] *adj* 1 slow; sluggish; inactive; 2 loose, not tight or taut; 3 careless, negligent || *n* 4 that part of a stretched wire, rope, etc., that is not taut; 5 period of inactivity; 6 slack condition or part || *vt* 7 also **slack off** to slacken || *vi* 8 also **slack up** to slacken || *adv* 9 in a slack manner || SYN *adj* lax, loose, sluggish, remiss, negligent

slack′en *vi* 1 to become slack || *vt* 2 to make slack; 3 to retard, slow down || SYN abate, languish, fail, relax, loosen

slack′er *n* one who shirks work or duty, esp. military service

slack′-jawed′ *adj* having the mouth open

slacks′ *npl* trousers for informal wear

slack′ suit′ *n* 1 man's suit consisting of slacks with shirt or loose jacket to match; 2 woman's suit consisting of slacks with a jacket to match

slag /slag′/ [MLG *slagge*] *n* 1 fused refuse that separates out from a metal during smelting; 2 fused lava

slain /slān′/ *pp* of **slay**

slake /slāk′/ [OE *slacian*] *vt* 1 to quench or appease; 2 to mix (lime) with water, forming slaked lime

slaked′ lime′ *n* white crystalline powder —Ca(OH)₂— made by adding water to lime, used in mortar and cement

sla·lom /släl′əm/ [Norw] *n* skiing race down a steep zigzag course around and between artificial obstacles

slam /slam′/ [< Scand] *v* (**slammed; slam·ming**) *vt* 1 to shut violently and noisily; 2 to throw down and strike with force and noise; 3 *colloq* to criticize with severity || *vi* 4 to bang noisily in closing || *n* 5 violent and noisy closing or impact; 6 *bridge* winning of all the tricks or all the tricks but one

slan·der /slan′dər/ [OF *esclandre*] *n* 1 utterance of false and defamatory statements about another; 2 false and defamatory statements || *vt* 3 to defame by slander || **slan′der·er** *n* || **slan′der·ous** *adj* || SYN *n* aspersion, scandal || DISCR *Slander* consists of lies or false reports circulated maliciously, usually behind the back of the person concerned, with the purpose of injuring his character or reputation. *Aspersion* is accomplished by insinuating, by casting reflections, by making damaging implications, by discrediting, especially in a slighting or belittling way. To admit that a piece of work is very good, but imply at the same time that any normal person could do it as well with little effort is to cast an *aspersion*. *Scandal* consists of gossip, perhaps true, perhaps false, repeated either from malice or thoughtlessness, and spread abroad

slang /slaŋ′/ [?] *n* 1 popular words, phrases, or usage not acceptable in formal language, often ephemeral, but sometimes becoming colloquial or standard; 2 argot, jargon || **slang′y** *adj* (**-i·er; -i·est**) || SYN jargon, cant (see *language*)

slant /slant′, slänt′/ [< Scand] *vt* 1 to slope || *vt* 2 to give a sloping direction to; 3 to twist or distort (a story) in order to give a particular interpretation to it || *n* 4 slanting line, surface, or direction; 5 point of view || **slant′ing** *adj*

slant′ line′ *n* virgule

slap /slap′/ [LG *slapp(e)*] 1 blow with something flat, as with the open hand; 2 sharp rebuke || *v* (**slapped; slap·ping**) *vt* 3 to strike, as with the open hand; 4 to throw down with violence; 5 *colloq* to place quickly and carelessly, as *he slapped paint on the wall* || *adv* suddenly; abruptly

slap′dash′ *adj* 1 hasty and careless || *adv* 2 in a hasty and careless manner

slap′hap′py *adj* (**-pi·er; -pi·est**) *colloq* dazed, befuddled; punch-drunk

slap′stick′ *n* 1 combination of two flat sticks, used by comedians in low comedy skits, that make a loud noise when striking other performers; 2 broad comedy characterized by horseplay and physical contact

slash /slash′/ [ME *slaschen*] *vt* 1 to cut by striking violently and at random, as with a knife; 2 to cut slits in; 3 to reduce, curtail; 4 to lash || *vi* 5 to strike violently and at random; 6 to make a sweeping stroke || *n* 7 long cut or stroke; 8 slit; gash; 9 slit in a garment revealing another material beneath; 10 reduction; 11 virgule

slash′ing *adj* 1 cutting violently or at random; 2 severe, merciless; 3 dashing, reckless

slat /slat′/ [MF *esclat*] *n* 1 thin narrow strip, as of wood or metal || *v* (**slat·ted; slat·ting**) *vt* 2 to provide with slats

slate /slāt′/ [MF *esclate*] *n* 1 fine-grained rock that splits into thin smooth plates; 2 thin plate of this rock or a similar material, used as roofing or a writing tablet; 3 dark bluish-gray color; 4 list of proposed candidates; 5 **clean slate** good record || *vt* 6 to designate or plan

slat·tern /slat′ərn/ [?] *n* untidy, slovenly woman || **slat′tern·ly** *adj* & *adv*

slaugh·ter /slôt′ər/ [ON *slātr* butchered meat] *n* 1 great and violent destruction of life; massacre; 2 butchering of animals for food || *vt* 3 to kill with violence; massacre; 4 to butcher (animals) for the market; 5 *colloq* to trounce, defeat || SYN *n* butchery, bloodshed, massacre (see *carnage*)

slaugh′ter·house′ *n* (**-hous·es** /-ziz/)

place where animals are butchered for the market

Slav /släv′, slav′/ [LGk *Sklabos*] *n* 1 member of the race occupying central and Eastern Europe, as the Czechs, Slovaks, Poles, Russians, Serbs, Croats, and Bulgarians ‖ *adj* 2 Slavic

slave /släv′/ [LGk *Sklabos* Slav (because so many Slavs were made captives)] *n* 1 human being owned by another; 2 drudge; 3 one under the power of a habit or vice ‖ *vi* 4 to work like a slave; drudge ‖ SYN *n* serf, vassal, thrall, subject ‖ DISCR A *serf* is one who is attached to the soil or estate on which he lives; he is transferred, if the land is sold, to the new owner, like the land itself. A *slave* is the actual legal property of another person, and is absolutely subject to his owner. *Vassal*, historically the word for one who held land under legal tenure, and *thrall*, now in historical or literary use, are both synonyms for *slave*. All these words are used in picturesque figurative senses; any humble dependent is a *vassal;* one mentally enslaved to the will of another is a *thrall;* one speaks of the *slaves* of power or desire

slave′ brace′let *n* bracelet or chain worn around the ankle

slave′ driv′er *n* overbearing taskmaster

slav·er¹ /slav′ər/ [< Scand] *vi* 1 to let saliva run from the mouth ‖ *vt* 2 to cover or dribble with saliva ‖ *n* 3 saliva running from the mouth

slav·er² /slā′vər/ *n* vessel or person engaged in the slave trade

slav′er·y *n* 1 condition of being a slave; 2 practice or institution of keeping slaves; 3 drudgery ‖ SYN bondage, vassalage, captivity, enthrallment

slav·ey /slā′vē/ *n* Brit maid of all work

Slav·ic /släv′ik, slav′-/ *adj* 1 of or pert. to the Slavs or their language ‖ *n* 2 group of languages spoken by the Slavs

slav·ish /slā′vish/ *adj* 1 submissive; servile; 2 base, ignoble; 3 lacking originality; blindly imitative

Sla·vo·ni·a /sləvō′nē·ə/ *n* region in N Yugoslavia, the former military frontier of Austria-Hungary against the Turks ‖ **Sla·vo′ni·an** *adj & n*

Sla·von·ic /sləvon′ik/ *adj* 1 Slavic; 2 Slavonian

slay /slā′/ [OE *slēan*] *v* (slew; slain) *vt* to kill by violence ‖ **slay′er** *n*

slea·zy /slēz′ē/ [?] *adj* (-zi·er; -zi·est) 1 thin, flimsy, as cloth; 2 poorly made; 3 cheap, contemptible

sled /sled′/ [MLG *sledde*] *n* 1 small vehicle on runners, for coasting or being drawn over snow; 2 sledge ‖ *v* (sled·ded; sled·ding) *vt* 3 to carry on a sled ‖ *vi* 4 to ride or be carried on a sled

sledge¹ /slej′/ [var of *sled*] *n* vehicle on runners for carrying loads over snow

sledge′² (ham′mer) [OE *slecg*] *n* large, heavy hammer requiring the use of both hands

sleek /slēk′/ [var of *slick*] *adj* 1 smooth, glossy; 2 well-groomed; 3 suave ‖ *vt* 4 to make sleek

sleep /slēp′/ [OE *slēp*] *n* 1 temporary, normal suspension of consciousness occurring periodically; 2 death ‖ *v* (slept) *vi* 3 to take rest in sleep; 4 to be quiescent or inactive; 5 to be dead; 6 to be numb as the result of pressure; 7 sleep in to sleep at one's place of employment; 8 sleep out to sleep away from home ‖ *vt* 9 to repose in (sleep), as *he slept a sound sleep;* 10 to have sleeping accommodations for; 11 sleep away or out to pass in sleep; 12 sleep off to rid oneself of through sleep

sleep′er *n* 1 one who sleeps; 2 horizontal beam serving as a support for some superstructure; 3 sleeping car; 4 colloq unexpected success

sleep′ing bag′ *n* large padded and zippered bag for sleeping in the open

sleep′ing car′ *n* railroad car equipped with berths and sleeping compartments

sleep′ing pill′ *n* sedative in the form of a pill for inducing sleep

sleep′ing sick′ness *n* 1 usu. fatal disease prevalent in parts of Africa, characterized by pronounced mental lethargy and caused by a parasite transmitted by a species of tsetse fly; 2 virus disease of the brain causing apathy and sleepiness

sleep′less *adj* 1 not sleeping; 2 spent without sleep; 3 always active ‖ **sleep′less·ness** *n*

sleep′walk′ing *n* act or state of walking in one's sleep ‖ **sleep′walk′er** *n*

sleep′y *adj* (-i·er; -i·est) 1 inclined to sleep; drowsy, 2 quiet, idle; 3 causing drowsiness ‖ **sleep′i·ness** *n*

sleep′y·head′ *n* sleepy person

sleet /slēt′/ [ME *slete*] *n* 1 frozen raindrops; 2 thin coating of ice on the ground ‖ *vi* 3 to shower sleet ‖ **sleet′y** *adj* (-i·er; -i·est)

sleeve /slēv′/ [OE *slēfe*] *n* 1 the part of a garment that covers the arm; 2 *mach* sleevelike part; 3 laugh up or in one's sleeve to be inwardly amused; 4 up one's sleeve kept hidden but close at hand ‖ **sleeve′less** *adj*

sleigh /slā′/ [D *slee*] *n* vehicle equipped with runners for traveling over snow, usu. horse-drawn

sleight′ of hand′ /slīt′/ [ME *slegth* dexterity, artifice] *n* 1 dexterity in the use of the hands, as in juggling or doing card tricks; 2 feat or trick performed by such dexterity

slen·der /slen′dər/ [ME *s(c)lendre*] *adj* 1 narrow in proportion to length or height; **2** thin, slim; **3** feeble, slight; **4** small, meager

slen'der·ize' vt **1** to make slender || vi **2** to become slender

slept /slept/ pt & pp of **sleep**

sleuth /slooth/ [< sleuthhound < ME slooth trail, track] colloq n **1** detective || vi **2** to track or trail

slew¹ /sloo/ pt of **slay**

slew² [Ir sluagh] n multitude, great number

slice /slis/ [OF esclicier to splinter] n **1** thin broad piece cut from something; **2** share or portion; **3** sports a path of a ball that curves toward the side from which it is hit; **b** ball that goes in a slice || vt **4** to cut into slices; **5** to cut (a piece or pieces) from something; **6** sports to hit (the ball) so that it goes in a slice || vi **7** sports to slice the ball; **b** to be sliced, as a ball || **slic'er** n

slick /slik/ [OE slician to make smooth] adj **1** adroit, dexterous; **2** smooth, sleek; **3** slippery; **4** sly, wily, suave; **5** slang first-class || vt **6** to make sleek or smooth; **7 slick up** colloq to make neat or trim || adv **8** smoothly; deftly || n **9** smooth area, as a film of oil on water; **10** colloq smart magazine printed on fine, glossy paper

slick'er n **1** oilskin raincoat; **2** shifty, sophisticated person, as a city slicker

slick'pa'per adj (magazine) printed on glossy paper, aimed at affluent and sophisticated readers

slide /slid/ [OE slīdan] v (**slid** /slid/; **slid** or **slid·den** /slid'ən/) vi **1** to move along a surface without leaving it; **2** to glide; **3** to slip, skid; **4** to pass imperceptibly or gradually; **5** to move or proceed quietly or easily, as he slid into a seat; **6 let slide** to allow (something) to take its course; neglect || vt **7** to push along, cause to slide; **8** to put quietly and unobtrusively, as he slid his hand into his pocket || n **9** act of sliding; **10** smooth inclined surface for sliding; **11** small glass plate for holding objects to be examined with a microscope; **12** piece of transparent glass or film having an image on it for projection; **13** sliding part; **14** fall of a mass of rock or snow down a mountain

slide'-ac'tion adj pump-action

slide' fas'ten·er n zipper

slide' pro·jec'tor n lantern that projects images from slides on a screen

slide' rule' n rule graduated in two or more scales used for making mathematical calculations

slide' valve' n valve that slides back and forth in the cylinder of a steam engine, alternately opening the intake and exhaust ports and thus imparting reciprocating motion to the piston

slid'ing scale' n schedule of income or

costs that vary with other income or costs, as wages with the cost of living

slight /slit/ [ME] adj **1** slender, not husky; **2** small in amount, degree, or quantity; **3** unimportant, trivial || n **4** action displaying intentional neglect or discourtesy || vt **5** to treat with indifference or contempt; snub; **6** to neglect or do carelessly || **slight'·ing** adj || SYN v contemn, disregard, neglect, scorn, disdain

slight'ly adv **1** slenderly; **2** to a small degree

slim /slim/ [MD = crafty] adj (**slim·mer; slim·mest**) **1** slender; **2** scant, meager || v (**slimmed; slim·ming**) vt **3** to make slim || vi **4** to become slim

slime /slim/ [OE slīm] n **1** thin mud; **2** any moist, oozy substance, esp. that which is dirty and offensive; **3** sticky substance secreted by certain animals and plants || **slim'y** adj (-i·er; -i·est)

sling¹ /sling/ n **1** implement whirled by hand for hurling missiles, as stones; **2** act of slinging; **3** any of various devices for hoisting heavy articles; **4** strap for suspending a gun, pack, etc., from the shoulder; **5** supporting bandage, as for a wounded arm || v (**slung**) vt **6** hurl, cast, fling; **7** to hang by or as by a sling

sling² [?] n iced drink made of brandy, gin, or other spirits, and water, sweetened and flavored

sling'shot' n Y-shaped stick with an elastic band between the prongs for hurling stones, etc.

slink /slingk/ [OE slincan to creep] v (**slunk**) vi **1** to move furtively, sneak along; **2** colloq to walk sinuously in a slow, provocative manner, as a woman || **slink'y** adj (-i·er; -i·est)

slip¹ /slip/ [MD slippen] v (**slipped; slip·ping**) vi **1** to glide or slide easily; move with little or no friction; **2** to lose one's footing, as on a slippery surface; **3** to go or come stealthily or unobserved, as to slip into the room; **4** to move or slide out of place; **5** to escape or pass; **6** to deteriorate in quality or standing, as his work is slipping; **7** to blunder, err; **8 let slip** to say unintentionally; **9 slip out, a** to leave surreptitiously; **b** to be revealed unintentionally; **10 slip up** to blunder || vt **11** to put on or off with ease, as a ring or garment; **12** to cause to move with a sliding action, as a bolt; **13** to cause to slide off, as the dog slipped his leash; **14** to convey or withdraw quickly or steadily; **15** to escape or pass from (the memory, attention, etc.); **16** to dislocate, as a disk in the vertebrae; **17 slip one's mind** to be forgotten; **18 slip something over on** colloq to trick || n **19** act or instance of slipping; **20** blunder; oversight; **21** space between wharves for vessels; **22** woman's undergarment; **23** pillowcase; **24** *geol* fault or displacement of one section of strata; **25** *give someone the slip* to elude someone, escape from someone

slip² [ME *slippe*] *n* **1** piece or strip, as of paper; **2** cutting from a plant for grafting or planting; **3** *a slip of a* a slender young (person)

slip′ cov′er *n* removable cloth cover made to fit over a piece of furniture

slip′knot′ *n* knot tied so that it slips along the rope or cord around which it is formed

slip′page /-ij/ *n* act or amount of slipping

slip′per *n* low comfortable shoe easily slipped on or off

slip′per·y /-(ə)rē/ *adj* (**-i·er; -i·est**) **1** liable to cause slipping or sliding; **2** affording no firm hold; not easily caught or held; **3** shifty, untrustworthy

slip′per·y elm′ *n* **1** American elm (*Ulmus fulva*) having a sticky inner bark; **2** the bark, used as a soothing application

slip′shod′ *adj* slovenly, careless; unsystematic

slip′stream′ *n* current of air driven aft by an airplane propeller

slip′-up′ *colloq* blunder; oversight

slit /slit′/ [ME *slitten*] *v* (**slit; slit·ting**) *vt* **1** to cut lengthwise or into long strips; **2** to cut a lengthwise opening in; split || *n* **3** straight narrow cut or opening

slith·er /slith′ər/ [OE *slidrian*] *vi* **1** to slide, slip, or glide with an irregular motion || *n* **2** slithering motion

slit′ trench′ *n mil* narrow trench

sliv·er /sliv′ər/ [OE *slīfan* to split] *n* **1** sharp, thin, pointed piece broken off, as of wood; splinter || *vt & vi* **2** to split into slivers

sliv·o·vitz /sliv′əvits/ [Serbo-Croatian *slīvovica*] *n* plum brandy

slob /slob′/ [Ir *slab*] *n slang* sloppy, slovenly boor

slob·ber /slob′ər/ [ME *sloberen*] *vi* **1** to let saliva dribble from the mouth; **2** to act with mawkish sentimentality || *vt* **3** to wet by slobbering || *n* **4** saliva dribbling from the mouth

sloe /slō′/ [OE *slā*] *n* **1** small, bitter plum of the blackthorn tree (*Prunus spinosa*); **2** the tree

sloe′-eyed′ *adj* having dark and/or slanted eyes

sloe′ gin′ *n* cordial flavored with sloe

slog /slog′/ [?] *v* (**slogged; slog·ging**) *vi* to plod heavily, as in thick mud || *vt* to hit hard

slo·gan /slōg′ən/ [Gael *sluaghgairm* battle cry, as of a Highland clan] *n* rallying cry; catchword; motto

sloop /slōōp′/ [D *sloep*] *n* one-masted vessel with fore-and-aft rig

slop /slop′/ [ME *sloppe*] *n* **1** liquid carelessly spilled; **2** *slang* unappetizing food; **3** swill; **4** liquid mud; **5** *slops pl* a dirty water or liquid refuse; **b** distillery mash after removal of the alcohol || *v* (**slopped; slop·ping**) *vt* **6** to spill; **7** to spill liquid on; **8** to feed swill to (swine) || *vi* **9** to spill liquid; **10** *slop over* to spill over

slope /slōp′/ [< ME *aslope* slanting] *n* **1** inclined line; slant; **2** inclined surface; **3** inclined ground || *vi* **4** to incline from the horizontal or the perpendicular || *vt* **5** to give a sloping direction to

slop′py *adj* (**-pi·er; -pi·est**) **1** wet and splashy; muddy; **2** messy, dirty; **3** slovenly, careless || **slop′pi·ly** *adv* || **slop′pi·ness** *n*

slosh /slosh′/ [prob *slop* + *slush*] *vi* **1** to splash, flounder, as to slosh through a puddle; **2** to splash about inside a container, as a liquid in a partly filled bottle || *vt* **3** to throw or splash (a liquid) about; **4** to agitate in a liquid, as a mop in water

slot /slot′/ [MF *esclot* hollow between the breasts] *n* **1** narrow slit, groove, or opening; **2** position in a series or sequence || *v* (**slot·ted; slot·ting**) *vt* **3** to cut a slot in

sloth /slôth′, slōth′/ [ME *slouthe* slowness] *n* **1** any of various slow-moving mammals (order Edentata) of tropical America, which cling upside down to branches; **2** laziness, indolence

sloth′ful *adj* lazy, indolent; slow || SYN inert, unoccupied, vacant, trifling, futile (see *idle*)

slot′ ma·chine′ *n* machine actuated by the insertion of a coin, for vending small articles or for gambling

slouch /slouch′/ [?] *n* **1** stooping of the head or shoulders; ungainly carriage; **2** ungainly slovenly person; **3** no *slouch* able person in some specified activity || *vi* **4** to have an awkward drooping posture; **5** to move with an ungainly posture || **slouch′y** *adj* (**-i·er; -i·est**)

slouch′ hat′ *n* soft hat with a wide flexible brim

slough¹ /slou′/ [OE *slōh*] *n* **1** place full of deep mud; bog; **2** situation from which it is difficult to get out || /slōō′/ *n* **3** marshy pond or inlet

slough² /sluf′/ [ME *slouth*] *n* **1** cast-off skin of a snake; **2** mass of dead tissue cast off from living tissue; **3** *cards* discard || *vi* **4** to come off or be shed, as the slough of a snake; **5** *cards* to discard || *vt* **6** also *slough off* to discard; throw off; get rid of

Slo·vak /slō′vak, -väk/ [Czechoslovak *Slovák* a Slav] *n* **1** native or inhabitant of Slovakia; **2** language of the Slovaks || also *adj*

Slo·va′ki·a /-kē·ə/ *n* region in E Czechoslovakia || **Slo·va′ki·an** *adj & n*

Slo·vene /slō′vēn, slōvēn′/ [< OSlav

Slovene] *n* **1** native or inhabitant of Slovenia; **2** language of the Slovenes || also *adj*

Slo·ve'ni·a /-nē-ə, -nyə/ *n* constituent republic of Yugoslavia, in the NW part || **Slo·ve'ni·an** *adj & n*

slov·en·ly /sluv'ənlē/, [< MFlem *sloovin* slattern] *adj* **1** untidy, not clean, not neat; **2** careless, slipshod || *adv* **3** in a slipshod or untidy manner || **slov'en·li·ness** *n*

slow /slō/ [OE *slāw* sluggish] *adj* **1** not rapid in motion; **2** not prompt; tardy; **3** requiring a long time; **4** not rash or hasty; **5** dull, tedious; **6** not busy; **7** behind time, as a clock; **8** tending to hinder rapid movement, as *a slow track*; **9** mentally dull; **10** behind the times || *adv* **11** slowly || *vt* **12** often **slow down** or **slow up** to retard, reduce the speed of || *vi* **13** often **slow down** or **slow up** to become slow or slower || **slow'ly** *adv* || **slow'ness** *n* || SYN *adj* sluggish, tardy, tedious, dilatory, inactive, deliberate, moderate, dull, backward || DISCR *Slow* trains take a longer time than fast trains to go the same distance; *slow* wits comprehend with difficulty what a lively mind grasps instantly; a watch that is *slow* is behind the correct time; *slow* growth takes place gradually. *Sluggish* means *slow* to move or rouse, as *sluggish* circulation; inert or inclined to be inactive, as a *sluggish* person; almost without movement or current, as *sluggish* air; a *sluggish* stream. *Tardy* means *slow* in getting where we ought, promised, or hoped, to be; *tardy* pupils are late for school. *Tardy* means also *slow* in coming, arriving, or putting in an appearance, as *tardy* amends; *tardy* recognition. *Tedious* describes that which is irksomely or boresomely *slow* || ANT *adj* fast, punctual, quick, alert, nimble-witted

slow'burn' *n slang* anger that develops slowly

slow'down' *n* intentional slowing down of work by workers attempting to enforce demands on their employers

slow' mo'tion *n* action in a motion picture sequence deliberately slowed down to an unnaturally slow pace || **slow'-mo'tion** *adj*

slow'poke' *n colloq* one habitually slow in action or movement

slow'up' *n* slowing up of progress or activity

sludge /sluj/ [ME *sluche*] *n* **1** mire; sticky mud; **2** any deposit of mudlike sediment, as that formed on the inside of a boiler or that deposited in a crankcase by the mixture of water and oil || **sludg'y** *adj* (**-i·er; -i·est**)

slug /slug/ [ME *slugge* slothful] *n* **1** any of various snails without external shells; **2** small unshaped piece of metal; **3** metal disk used as a coin;

4 lead bullet; **5** *typ* a piece of metal thicker than type, used for spacing; **b** line of type in one piece; **6** *slang* shot of liquor || *v* (**slugged; slug·ging**) *vt* **7** *colloq* to hit hard, esp. with the fist; **8** to hit (a baseball) far enough for at least a two-base hit || *vi* **9** to hit hard || **slug'ger** *n*

slug'gard /-ərd/ *n* lazy person

slug'gish *adj* **1** dull, inactive; **2** lazy, indolent; **3** slow, torpid || SYN heavy, torpid, inactive, languid, idle (see *slow*)

sluice /sloos/ [OF *escluse* floodgate] *n* **1** artificial channel for water, having a gate to regulate the flow; **2** also **sluice' gate'** the gate in a sluice; **3** a stream of water issuing through a floodgate; **b** the water held back by such a gate; **4** inclined trough for washing gold ore, carrying logs, etc. || *vt* **5** to wash with water from or as from a sluice; **6** to draw off by a sluice, as water; **7** to transport by a sluice, as logs || *vi* **8** to flow or run out, as through a sluice

slum /slum/ [?] *n* **1** squalid run-down quarter of a city; **2** the **slums** *pl* slums collectively || *v* (**slummed; slum·ming**) *vi* **3** go **slumming** to visit slums out of curiosity or for vicarious thrills || **slum'my** *adj* (**-mi·er; -mi·est**)

slum·ber /slum'bər/ [< OE *slūma* slumber] *vi* **1** to sleep; **2** to be inactive || *n* **3** sleep; **4** period of inactivity

slum'lord' *n* owner of slum property which he refuses to take care of and for which he charges excessive rents

slump /slump/ [< Scand] *vi* **1** to sink down heavily; **2** to fall or decline suddenly, as prices; **3** to assume a drooping posture || *n* **4** act or instance of slumping; **5** pronounced economic decline

slung /slung/ *pt & pp* of **sling**

slunk /slungk/ *pt & pp* of **slink**

slur /slur/ [MD *sleuren* to drag in mud] *v* (**slurred; slur·ring**) *vt* **1** to speak slightingly of, disparage; **2** to pronounce indistinctly; **3** *mus* **a** to sing or execute without breaks between two or more tones; **b** to mark with a slur || *vi* **4** **slur over** to pass over quickly without proper consideration || *n* **5** slurred speech; **6** aspersion; **7** *mus* a mark ⌢ or ⌣ connecting notes that are to be sung or played without a break; **b** slurred tones

slurp /slurp/ [D *slurpen*] *n* **1** loud sucking noise made while eating or drinking || *vt & vi* **2** to eat or drink with a slurp

slush /slush/ [perh Norw *slusk*] *n* **1** partly melted snow; **2** silly sentimental talk or writing || **slush'y** *adj* (**-i·er; -i·est**)

slut /slut/ [ME *slutte*] *n* **1** dirty untidy

woman; **2** promiscuous woman ||
slut′ish *adj*

sly /slī′/ [ON *slǣgr* clever] *adj* (**sly·er**
or **sli·er; sly·est** or **sli·est**) **1** crafty;
wily; **2** deceitful; **3** roguish || *n* **4 on
the sly** secretly; without being ob-
served || **sly′ly** or **sli′ly** *adv* || **sly′ness**
n || **SYN** surreptitious, artful, roguish
(see *wily*)

Sm *chem* samarium

smack¹ /smak′/ [OE *smæc*] *n* **1** slight
taste or flavor; **2** smattering; tinge ||
vi **3 smack of** to have a taste or suggestion of

smack² [MD *smakken* to strike] *n* **1**
sharp noise, as one made with the
lips in kissing or tasting; **2** loud
hearty kiss; **3** resounding blow || *vt*
4 to kiss with a loud noise; **5** to make
a loud noise with (the mouth or lips);
6 to strike with a sharp blow || *vi* **7**
to make a noise with the lips in kiss-
ing or tasting || *adv* **8** with sudden
violence; **9** straight, directly

smack³ [D *smak*] *n* fishing vessel having a well for keeping the fish alive

small /smôl′/ [OE *smæl*] *adj* **1** comparatively little in size, value, quantity, degree, etc.; not large; **2** unimportant or insignificant; **3** petty,
mean-spirited; **4** lower-case (letter);
5 feel small to feel ashamed || *adv* **6**
in a small way || *n* **7** the small part
of a thing || **small′ness** *n* || **small′ish**
adj || **SYN** *adj* insignificant, diminu-
tive, fine, miniature, puny, tiny (see
little)

small′ arms′ *npl* firearms that are fired
while held in one or both hands

small′ cap′ or **cap′i·tal** *n* letter having
the form of a capital letter but the
size of a smaller letter

small′ change′ *n* **1** loose coins; **2** insignificant thing or person

small′ fry′ *npl* **1** little or young fish; **2**
children; **3** unimportant persons

small′ hours′ *npl* the early morning
hours after midnight

small′ in·tes′tine *n* longer section of
the intestines, comprising the duodenum, jejunum, and ileum, which di-
gests the food coming from the
stomach

small′ po·ta′toes *nsg colloq* insignificant
person or thing

small′pox′ *n* acute contagious virus
disease marked by an eruption of
pustules, often leaving permanent
scars

small′-scale′ *adj* **1** having all dimensions greatly reduced, as a map or
model; **2** of small extent or scope

small′ screen′ *n* television

small′ talk′ *n* light unimportant conversation; idle gossip

small′-time′ *adj* of little importance or
influence

smart /smärt′/ [OE *smeart*] *vi* **1** to feel
or be the source of a stinging sensa-
tion; **2** to cause a stinging sensation

or pain; **3** to have one's feelings
wounded || *tr* **4** to cause to smart ||
n **5** sharp stinging pain; **6** keen grief
|| *adj* **7** causing a stinging sharp sen-
sation; **8** severe, sharp, as a pain or
blow; **9** brisk, fresh, as a breeze; **10**
bright, capable, shrewd; **11** witty,
clever; **12** flip, pert, saucy; **13** stylish,
spruce; **14** fashionable, elegant ||
smart′ly *adv* || **smart′ness** *n*

smart′ al′eck /al′ik/ [< *Alexander*] *n*
wise guy || **smart′-al′eck·y** *adj*

smart′en *vt* **smarten up, 1** to make
stylish or spruce; **2** to make more
knowledgeable; **3** to make brisker,
as a pace || also *vi*

smart′ mon′ey *n* money wagered or
invested by knowledgeable people
who know what they are doing

smart′ set′ *n* the most fashionable and
elegant segment of society

smash /smash′/ [perh *smack* + *mash*]
vt **1** to break to pieces by violence;
shatter; **2** *tennis* to strike (the ball)
very hard with an overhand stroke;
3 to defeat; break up; destroy; **4** to
hit or strike with great force || *vi* **5**
to break to pieces, as from a violent
blow or collision; **6** to collide violently with something; **7** to go into
bankruptcy suddenly || *n* **8** act or
instance of smashing; **9** heavy blow;
10 collision; **11** utter destruction; **12**
colloq great success; **13** drink composed of liquor, crushed ice, and
sugar, variously flavored, esp. with
mint; **14** bankruptcy; **15** *sports* hard-
hit ball || *adj* **16** *colloq* successful;
sensational

smashed′ *adj slang* drunk

smash′ing *adj colloq* terrific, sensational

smash′up′ *n* **1** violent collision; **2** total
ruin

smat·ter·ing /smat′əriŋ/ [< Scand] *n*
slight, superficial knowledge

smear /smir′/ [OE *smerian*] *vt* **1** to
spread or daub with something
greasy, sticky, or wet; **2** to spread
or daub a greasy, sticky, or wet substance on; **3** to defame; sully; **4**
slang to defeat overwhelmingly; **5**
to bribe; **6** to make dirty with grease
or the like || *n* **7** blot or stain;
smudge; **8** substance placed on a
slide for examination with a microscope; **9** defamation

smear′case′ [G *Schmierkäse*] *n* cottage
cheese

smell /smel′/ [ME *smellen*] *v* (**smelled**
or **smelt**) *vt* **1** to perceive the odor
of through the nose; **2** to discern or
detect as if by a scent, as *to smell
trouble;* **3 smell up** to pervade with
an offensive odor || *vi* **4** to use the
sense of smell; **5** to give off an odor,
as *this smells good, this smells like
a rose;* **6** to have an offensive odor,
as *skunks smell;* **7** *colloq* to be badly
done, as *her singing smells;* **8 smell**

about to pry into; 9. **smell of, a** to smell like; b to smack of || *n*.10 sense of smell; 11 act or instance of smelling; 12 odor, scent; 13 suggestion, trace; 14 aura, as *the smell of success* || SYN *n* fragrance, scent, perfume, aroma, odor

smell'ing salts' *n* carbonate of ammonia prepared aromatically, used to relieve faintness, headache, etc.

smell'y *adj* (-i-er; -i-est) having an offensive odor

smelt[1] /smelt/ [OE] *n* (**smelt** or **smelts**) any of certain small silvery food fishes (family Osmeridae), found in northern waters

smelt[2] *pt & pp* of **smell**

smelt[3] [prob < MD *smelten*] *vt* 1 to fuse or melt (ore) to extract the metal; 2 to obtain (metal) by this process

smelt'er *n* 1 one who or that which smelts; 2 place where ores are smelted

smi·lax /smīl'aks/ [Gk] *n* 1 delicate trailing green plant (*Asparagus medeoloïdes*) much used for decoration; 2 any of several prickly vines or herbs of a genus (*Smilax*) of the same family

smile /smīl'/ [ME *smilen*] *vi* 1 to turn up the corners of the mouth to indicate pleasure, amusement, affection, contempt, disdain, or the like; 2 to present a gay or cheerful aspect; 3 **smile at, a** to direct a smile towards; b to be amused by; 4 **smile on** or **upon** to regard with favor || *vt* 5 to express with a smile; 6 to affect by smiling || *n* 7 act or instance of smiling; 8 smiling expression; 9 favorable regard; 10 pleasing aspect || **smil'ing** *adj* || **smil'ing·ly** *adv*

smirch /smurch'/ [ME *smorchen*] *vt* 1 to soil, stain; 2 to bring disgrace upon || *n* 3 smear or stain; 4 blot on the reputation

smirk /smurk'/ [OE *smearcian*] *vi* 1 to smile in an offensively satisfied way || *n* 2 smirking smile

smite /smīt'/ [OE *smītan*] *v* (**smote**; **smit·ten**) *vt* 1 to strike hard; 2 to destroy; afflict; put to death; 3 to affect with the abruptness of a blow; 4 to cast down; punish; trouble; 5 **be smitten** to be affected by a strong emotion, as love or fear

smith /smith'/ [OE] *n* 1 one who works or shapes metal; 2 blacksmith

smith·er·eens /smith'ərēnz'/ [?] *npl colloq* tiny fragments

smith'y /-thē, thē/ [OE *smiththe*] *n* (-ies) 1 blacksmith; 2 his workshop

smit·ten /smit'ən/ 1 *pp* of **smite** || *adj* 2 afflicted; 3 enamored

smock /smok'/ [OE *smoc*] *n* 1 long loose outer garment to protect the clothing || *vt* 2 to dress in a smock

smog /smog', smôg'/ [*smoke* + *fog*] *n* fog heavily contaminated with industrial smoke and chemical fumes || **smog'gy** *adj* (-gi·er; -gi·est)

smoke /smōk'/ [OE *smoca*] *n* 1 visible finely divided matter or vapor formed during combustion; 2 any visible fumes or vapor; 3 act of smoking tobacco; 4 cigar or cigarette || *vt* 5 to expose to smoke in order to blacken or cure; 6 to inhale or puff out the smoke of (a pipe, cigar, etc.); 7 **smoke out, a** to force out by or as by smoke; b to expose, unmask || *vi* 8 to emit or give out smoke; 9 to smoke a cigar, etc.

smoke' bomb' *n* bomb that emits smoke when detonated

smoke'house' *n* (-hous·es /-ziz/) place where meats, fish, etc. are cured by smoking

smoke'less *adj* 1 being free of smoke; 2 producing or emitting little or no smoke, as certain powders

smok'er *n* 1 one who smokes; 2 smoking car; 3 informal social gathering of men

smoke' screen' *n* 1 dense smoke cloud formed to conceal the movements of ships, troops, etc.; 2 something intended to conceal the truth

smoke'stack' *n* pipe for discharging smoke into the air, as from a factory or locomotive

smok'ing car' *n* railroad car in which passengers may smoke

smok'ing jack'et *n* man's indoor lounging jacket

smok'y *adj* (-i·er; -i·est) 1 emitting smoke, esp. excessively; 2 soiled or stained by smoke; 3 pert. to or filled with smoke; 4 hazy; 5 like smoke in color or appearance

smol·der or **smoul·der** /smōl'dər/ [ME *smolderen*] *vi* 1 to burn or smoke without flame; 2 to exist in a stifled or suppressed condition || *n* 3 slow, suppressed combustion or its resultant smoke

smooch /smōōch'/ [?] *slang vi* 1 to kiss and pet || *n* 2 kiss || **smooch'er** *n*

smooth /smōōth'/ [OE *smōth*] *adj* 1 not rough to the touch or the sight; even and uniform in surface and texture; 2 free from lumps; 3 unruffled; calm; 4 free from sharpness, bland to the taste; 5 flattering, as *smooth words;* 6 easy and polished (diction); 7 steady in motion; free from jolts; 8 easy-running; 9 without hair, beardless; 10 free from difficulties or interruptions || *adv* 11 smoothly || *vt* 12 to make smooth; 13 **smooth away** to remove, as difficulties or hindrances; 14 **smooth out** to make smooth; 15 **smooth over** to extenuate; make light of || **smooth'ly** *adv*

smooth'bore' *n* gun with an unrifled bore

smooth' breath'ing *n Gk gram* the symbol ' placed over an initial vowel to indicate lack of aspiration

smooth/ie *n colloq* very suave fellow, esp. in dealing with women

smor·gas·bord /smôr′gəsbôrd′/ [Sw *smörgasbord* = sandwich table] *n* buffet of hors d'oeuvres, salads, meats, etc.

smote /smōt′/ *pt* of **smite**

smoth·er /smuth′ər/ [ME *smorther*] *vt* 1 to suffocate; 2 to stifle; 3 to suppress or conceal; 4 *cookery* a to cover, as with onions; b to cook in a covered dish ‖ *vi* 5 to be suffocated; 6 to be stifled

smudge /smuj′/ [ME *smogen* to smear] *n* 1 dirty or blurred mark; 2 suffocating smoke; 3 smoky fire used in keeping off insects or in preventing frost ‖ *vt* 4 to smear or stain; 5 to fill with smoke from a smudge ‖ *vi* 6 to become smudged ‖ **smudg′y** *adj* (-i·er; -i·est)

smudge′ pot′ *n* container for burning a smoky fuel to produce smudge to guard against frost

smug /smug′/ [perh LG *smuk* neat] *adj* (**smug·ger**; **smug·gest**) self-satisfied, self-righteously complacent ‖ **smug′ly** *adv* ‖ **smug′ness** *n*

smug·gle /smug′əl/ [LG *smugeln*] *vt* 1 to bring or send (goods) to or from a country secretly and illegally; 2 to carry or introduce secretly ‖ *vi* 3 to smuggle goods ‖ **smug′gler** *n*

smut /smut′/ [OE *smitte*] *n* 1 particle of soot; 2 black stain or smudge; 3 any of various fungi that attack corn, wheat, etc., producing black spores; 4 indecent language or talk ‖ **smut′·ty** *adj* (-ti·er; -ti·est)

Sn [L *stannum*] *chem* tin

snack /snak′/ [MD *snacken* to snap] *n* light quickly eaten meal

snack′ bar′ *n* lunchroom for light meals

snaf·fle /snaf′əl/ [?] *n* bit, usu. jointed in the middle, for a bridle

sna·fu /snaf′ōō, snafōō′/ [situation normal all fouled up] *n* 1 chaotic, badly disorganized situation ‖ *vt* 2 to foul up badly

snag /snag′/ [< Scand] *n* 1 stump of a branch projecting from the trunk; 2 some part of a tree sticking up from the bottom of a river or lake and dangerous to boats; 3 any dangerous projection; 4 hole in a stocking or garment made by snagging; 5 any unsuspected obstacle or difficulty ‖ *v* (**snagged**; **snag·ging**) *vt* 6 to catch, damage, or destroy on a snag ‖ *vi* 7 to be caught or entangled on something

snail /snāl′/ [OE *snægl*] *n* 1 any of numerous land or water mollusks, having a spiral shell from which the head and a large foot are protruded when the animal is in motion; 2 slow-moving person

snake /snāk′/ [OE *snaca*] *n* 1 any of various limbless reptiles having long slim bodies, a few species of which are venomous; 2 treacherous person; 3 *plumbing* flexible metal band or wire that can be fed into curved pipes to dislodge obstructions; 4 length of flexible wire fed through an electric conduit to pull wires through ‖ *vi* 5 to wind, move, or twist like a snake

snake′ dance′ *n* procession in single file in which each participant holds on to the person in front and moves in a snakelike course ‖ **snake′-dance′** *vi*

snake′ eyes′ *n craps* cast in which the two dice show one spot each

snake′ in the grass′ *n* treacherous friend

snap /snap′/ [D *snappen*] *v* (**snapped**; **snap·ping**) *vi* 1 to break suddenly; 2 to make a sharp sudden sound; crackle; 3 to flash or sparkle, as the eyes; 4 to close, move, catch, or strike with a sharp sound; 5 to jump or act with alacrity; 6 **snap at**, a to snatch at suddenly, esp. with the teeth; b to seize or accept eagerly; c to speak sharply and crossly to; 7 **snap into it** *colloq* to act with vigor; 8 **snap out of it** *colloq* a to regain one's good spirits, b to recover from depression or a period of low or poor productivity ‖ *vt* 9 to seize suddenly, as with the teeth; 10 to break off suddenly or short; 11 to cause to make a sudden sharp sound, as *snap the fingers*; 12 to close with a sudden sharp sound; 13 to throw with a jerk, to flip, as a ball; 14 to take a snapshot of; 15 **snap up** to seize or accept eagerly; 16 **snap one's fingers** at to flout; 17 **snap someone's head off** to speak very harshly to, esp. in reprimand ‖ *n* 18 act or instance of snapping; 19 short sharp sound or report; 20 fastener or catch that closes with a click; 21 thin crisp cooky; 22 *colloq* energy or vim; 23 brief intense period, as of cold weather; 24 *colloq* anything easily performed or acquired; 25 snapshot; 26 **not give** or **care a snap** to be utterly indifferent ‖ *adj* 27 easy; 28 offhand, with little thought, as *snap judgment*

snap′ brim′ *n* hat brim that can be turned down or up

snap′drag·on *n* any of several plants (genus *Antirrhinum*), some cultivated for their showy racemes of flowers of various colors

snap′ fas·ten·er *n* device in two parts for fastening two pieces, as of a garment, one part having a projection that snaps into a hole in the other part

snap′per *n* 1 any of various large edible marine fishes of the family Lutjanidae; 2 snapping turtle

snap′ping tur′tle *n* one of several large

fresh-water turtles of the New World (family Chelydridae) having powerful jaws

snap'pish *adj* short-tempered, irritable || SYN testy, fretful, petulant, impatient, touchy

snap'py *adj* (-pi·er; -pi·est) 1 snappish; 2 *colloq* a full of energy, brisk; b stylish; 3 **make it snappy** *slang* to hurry

snap'shot' *n* 1 instantaneous informal photograph; 2 *hunting* quick shot made without taking careful aim

snare¹ /sner'/ [OE *sneara* < Scand] *n* 1 noose for catching an animal or bird; 2 anything that entraps || *vt* 3 to catch or entangle with or as with a snare; 4 to entice; involve by trickery

snare² [MLG = string] *n* one of the strings of gut or wire stretched across the lower head of a snare drum

snare' drum' *n* small drum with snares stretched across one head to produce a rolling or rattling sound

snarl¹ /snärl'/ [< *obs snar* < LG] *vi* 1 to growl viciously, as a dog; 2 to speak in a snarling manner || *vt* 3 to utter in a snarling manner || *n* 4 act of snarling; 5 snarling tone or utterance

snarl² [ME < Scand] *vt & vi* 1 to tangle || *n* 2 tangle

snatch /snach'/ [ME *snacchen*] *vt* 1 to seize suddenly, rudely, or eagerly; grab; 2 *slang* to kidnap || *vi* 3 **snatch at** to grab at, attempt to grab || *n* 4 act or instance of snatching; 5 hasty grab; 6 small fragment; 7 brief spell of action; 8 *slang* a kidnaping

sneak /snēk'/ [OE *snīcan* to creep] *vi* 1 to move or act in a furtive or stealthy manner || *vt* 2 to put, pass, take, remove, etc., in a furtive or stealthy manner || *n* 3 act of sneaking; 4 sneaky contemptible person; 5 **sneaks** *pl colloq* sneakers || **sneak'y** *adj* (-i·er; -i·est)

sneak'er *n* canvas shoe with a soft, usu. rubber, sole

sneak'ing *adj* 1 sneaky; 2 secret, unavowed

sneak' pre'view *n* unannounced showing of a film, usu. to get the audience's reaction

sneer /snir'/ [ME *sneren*] *vi* 1 to show contempt by an expression of the face, as by curling the lips; 2 to speak or write contemptuously || *vt* 3 to utter in a sneering manner || *n* 4 act of sneering; 5 contempt or scorn shown in speech or manner; 6 contemptuous insinuation || SYN *v* gibe, scoff, ridicule (see *jeer*)

sneeze /snēz'/ [ME *snesen*] *vi* 1 to expel the breath suddenly by an involuntary spasm through the nose and mouth; 2 **sneeze at** *colloq* to

scorn || *n* 3 act or instance of sneezing

snick·er /snik'ər/ [imit] *n* 1 half-suppressed laugh || *vi* 2 to laugh in a sly or suppressed manner

snide /snīd'/ [?] *adj* maliciously derogatory

sniff /snif'/ [ME] *vi* 1 to draw in the breath audibly through the nose; 2 **sniff at** to show disdain for || *vt* 3 to smell or inhale by sniffing; 4 to perceive by or as by smelling || *n* 5 act of sniffing; 6 odor, scent

snif·fle /snif'əl/ [< *sniff*] *vi* 1 to sniff repeatedly, as to clear mucus from the nose || *n* 2 act or sound of sniffling; 3 **the sniffles** *pl* head cold causing sniffling

snif'ter *n* 1 large goblet for holding a small quantity of brandy, shaped to intensify the aroma; 2 *slang* small drink of liquor

snig·ger /snig'ər/ *vi* 1 to snicker || *n* 2 snicker

snip /snip'/ [D *snippen*] *v* (snipped; snip·ping) *vt* 1 to cut or cut off with a short quick stroke or series of strokes || *n* 2 act of snipping; 3 small cut; 4 small piece; bit; 5 *colloq* small, young, or insignificant person; 6 **snips** *pl* metal shears

snipe /snip'/ [ME < Scand] *n* 1 any of several long-billed game birds (genera *Gallinago* and *Limnocryptes*) found in marshy places; 2 small sign pasted on a theatrical poster, giving such information as "held over," "starts Sunday," etc. || *vi* 3 to hunt snipes; 4 to shoot at people from a hidden or distant position; 5 to attack or criticize a person or his work, esp. anonymously || **snip'er** *n*

snip·pet /snip'it/ [< *snip*] *n* 1 small piece snipped off; 2 fragment; 3 *colloq* insignificant person

snip'py *adj* (-pi·er; -pi·est) *colloq* curt; disdainful; tart

snit /snit'/ [?] *n* state of agitation

snitch /snich'/ [?] *colloq* *vi* 1 **snitch on** to inform on, squeal on || *vt* 2 to steal || *n* 3 informer || **snitch'er** *n*

sniv·el /sniv'əl/ [< OE *snofl* mucus] *v* (-eled or -elled; -el·ing or -el·ling) *vi* 1 to run at the nose; 2 to cry or fret in an affected or hypocritical manner; 3 to sniffle || *n* 4 act of sniveling || **sniv'el·er** or **sniv'el·ler** *n*

snob /snob'/ [dial. = cobbler's apprentice < ?] *n* 1 one who is servile to persons of wealth and position and condescending to those he considers inferior; 2 one who fancies himself an expert in some field and is disdainful of those who are uninformed || **snob'ber·y** *n* || **snob'bish** *adj* || **snob'bish·ly** *adv* || **snob'bish·ness** *n*

snood /snōōd'/ [OE *snōd*] *n* netlike bag worn at the back of the head to hold the hair

snook /snōōk', snŏŏk'/ [?] *n* 1 gesture

of derision and defiance; **2 cock a snook** at to thumb one's nose at

snook·er /snook′ər/ *n* kind of pool played with fifteen red balls and six other balls, having various point values

snoop /snoop′/ [D *snoepen* to sneak food] *colloq vi* **1** to sneak about seeking information on other people's affairs; pry ‖ *n* **2** one who snoops ‖ **snoop′y** *adj* (-i·er; -i·est)

snoot /snoot′/ [var of *snout*] *n* **1** *slang* nose ‖ *vt* **2** *colloq* to condescend to

snoot′ful′ *n colloq* enough liquor imbibed to make one drunk

snoot′y *adj* (-i·er; -i·est) *colloq* snobbish

snooze /snooz′/ [?] *colloq vi* **1** to nap, doze ‖ *n* **2** nap

snore /snor′, snôr′/ [ME *snoren*] *vi* **1** to breathe with a coarse rasping sound during sleep ‖ *n* **2** act or sound of snoring ‖ **snor′er** *n*

snor·kel /snôrk′əl/ [G *Schnorkel*] *n* **1** device connected by hoses to a submerged submarine, that floats on the surface and has valves that allow air to be taken in and exhausted but that does not permit water to enter; **2** breathing tube which permits swimming face down or beneath the surface

snort /snôrt′/ [ME *snorten*] *vi* **1** to expel air forcefully through the nose; **2** to express feeling in this way, as *to snort with anger* ‖ *vt* **3** to utter with a snort ‖ *n* **4** sound of snorting; **5** *slang* shot of liquor ‖ **snort′er** *n*

snot /snot′/ [< OE *gesnot*] *n* **1** *vulgar* nasal mucus; **2** *slang* supercilious person ‖ **snot′ty** *adj* (-ti·er; -ti·est)

snout /snout′/ [ME *snoute*] *n* **1** the long protruding nose and jaws of an animal; **2** *slang* nose

snow /snō′/ [OE *snāw*] *n* **1** frozen water vapor in the form of white feathery flakes or crystals; **2** *poet.* whiteness; white blossoms; **3** *slang* cocaine or heroin; **4** spots on a television screen from a weak signal ‖ *vi* **5** to fall as snow ‖ *vt* **6** *slang* to persuade by salesmanship; **7 snow in** or **under** to obstruct, cover, or shut in with or as if with masses of snow

snow′ball′ *n* **1** ball made of packed snow; **2** shrub with round white flowers of the genus *Viburnum*, esp. *V. opulus* ‖ *vi* **3** to increase rapidly at an accelerating rate ‖ *vt* **4** to throw snowballs at; **5** to cause to snowball

snow′bank′ *n* mass of heaped snow

snow′bell′ *n* small tree with clusters of white flowers (*Styrax grandifolia*)

snow′ber′ry *n* (-ries) **1** shrub with clusters of white berries (*Symphoricarpus albus*); **2** West Indian shrub (*Chiococca alba*)

snow′bound′ *adj* shut in or confined by snow

snow′-capped′ *adj* topped with snow, as mountains

snow′drift′ *n* mass of snow heaped up by the wind

snow′drop′ *n* bulbous plant (*Galanthus nivalis*) with nodding bell-like white flowers

snow′fall′ *n* **1** fall of snow; **2** amount of snow falling in a given time or in a given area

snow′flake′ *n* white feathery crystal of snow

snow′ goose′ *n* white North American goose (*Chen hyperborea*)

snow′ job′ *n slang* deception practiced to convince someone of the merits of something

snow′ line′ *n* the line above which a mountain is covered with snow the year round

snow′man′ /-man′/ *n* (-men′ /-men′/) figure of a man molded in snow

snow′mo·bile′ /-məbēl′/ [*snow* + *automobile*] *n* vehicle designed to travel over or through snow

snow′plow′ *n* machine or engine used to clear roads, tracks, etc., of heavy snow

snow′shoe′ *n* network of rawhide stretched on a racket-shaped frame for walking over deep snow

snow′suit′ *n* child's outer garment for cold weather, fitting snugly at the wrists and ankles

snow′ tire′ *n* automobile tire with a deep tread and sometimes metal studs, to improve traction on snow and ice

snow′y *adj* (-i·er; -i·est) **1** covered with, full of, or characterized by snow; **2** white like snow; **3** pure, unsullied

snow′y owl′ *n* diurnal white owl of the arctic regions (*Nyctea scandiaca*)

snub /snub′/ [ME] *v* (**snubbed; snubbing**) *vt* **1** to treat with scorn; ignore; slight intentionally; **2** to check suddenly, usu. by means of a rope ‖ *n* **3** intentional slight; **4** check

snub′ nose′ *n* short nose turned up at the tip ‖ **snub′-nosed′** *adj*

snuck /snuk′/ *dial. pt & pp of* **sneak**

snuff¹ /snuf′/ [MD *snuffen* to blow the nose] *vt* **1** to draw in through the nose; **2** to smell, sniff ‖ *vi* **3** to sniff; **4** to take snuff ‖ *n* **5** act of snuffing; **6** powdered tobacco to be inhaled through the nose; **7 up to snuff** *colloq* up to the usual standard

snuff² [ME *snuffen*] *n* **1** burned part of a candlewick ‖ *vt* **2** to cut the snuff from; **3 snuff out, a** to extinguish; **b** to suppress, destroy

snuff′box′ *n* small, often ornamental holder for snuff

snuff′er¹ *n* person who uses snuff

snuff′er² *n* usu. **snuffers** *pl* **1** instrument for trimming a charred wick; **2** metal cone with a handle for extinguishing a candle

snuf·fle /snuf′əl/ [< *snuff¹*] *vi* **1** to

sniffle ‖ *vt* **2** to utter through the nose ‖ *n* **3** act of snuffling

snug /snug'/ [< Scand] *adj* (**snug·ger; snug·gest**) **1** sheltered, safe; cozy and comfortable; **2** compact and convenient; trim; **3** fitting closely; **4** private, hidden

snug'gies *npl* women's and children's long knitted underpants

snug·gle /snug'ǝl/ *vi & vt* to cuddle or nestle close for warmth and comfort

so[1] /sō'/ [OE *swā*] *adv* **1** to the extent indicated, as *he is not so tall;* **2** to such a degree (that); **3** just as indicated, as *hold the ball so;* **4** likewise, as *so have I;* **5** therefore, as *the door was open, so he went in;* **6** more or less, as *back in an hour or so;* **7** then, as *so you are back;* **8** too (used in emphatic contradiction), as *I can so;* **9** very, as *she is so beautiful;* **10** very much, as *I love you so;* **11** **and so forth** or **and so on,** a continuing in this way; **b** etcetera; **12 so as** to in order to; **13 so that, a** in order that; **b** with the result that ‖ *conj* **14** in order that; **15** with the result that ‖ *interj* **16** exclamation of surprise, shocked discovery, etc.

so[2] /sō'/ *n mus* sol[1]

soak /sōk'/ [OE *sōcian*] *vt* **1** to cause to absorb moisture; **2** to steep in a fluid; **3** to wet through and through; **4** *slang* to strike, punch; **5** *slang* to overcharge; **6 soak up** to absorb ‖ *vi* **7** to be steeped in a fluid; **8** to become thoroughly wet; **9** to enter by pores or small openings, as a liquid; **10 soak in** to penetrate into the mind or consciousness ‖ *n* **11** act of soaking or state of being soaked; **12** *slang* drunkard

so'-and-so' *n* **1** someone or something not known or named; **2** euphemism for an offensive name

soap /sōp'/ [OE *sāpe*] *n* **1** substance for washing and cleansing, made by combining a fatty acid with an alkali such as potash or soda; **2 no soap** *slang* nothing doing ‖ *vt* **3** to cover, rub, or wash with soap ‖ **soap'y** *adj* (**-i·er; -i·est**)

soap'box' *n* **1** box on which a speaker stands to harangue a street crowd; **2** any public forum for expressing one's ideas ‖ also *adj*

soap' op'er·a [< fact that such serials were often sponsored by soap manufacturers] *n radio & telv* serialized drama of domestic trials and tribulations

soap'stone' *n* massive rock form of talc with a greasy feel, used for ornamental carvings, table tops, etc.

soar /sôr', sōr'/ [MF *essorer*] *vi* **1** to fly upward in the air; **2** to glide along high in the air; **3** to rise high, as mountains; **4** to rise above what is usual, as prices or hopes

sob /sob'/ [ME *sobben*] *v* (**sobbed; sob·bing**) *vi* **1** to weep while catching the breath convulsively; **2** to make a sound like sobbing ‖ *vt* **3** to utter with sobs ‖ *n* **4** act or sound of sobbing

so·ber /sōb'ǝr/ [OF *sobre*] *adj* **1** temperate by habit; **2** not drunk; **3** steady, sedate; **4** solemn, grave; **5** subdued, as colors ‖ *vt* **6** also **sober up** to make sober; **7** also **sober down** to steady, calm, make serious ‖ *vi* **8 sober down** to become steady, calm, or serious; **9 sober up** to recover from drunkenness ‖ **so'ber·ness** or **so·bri·e·ty** /sǝbrī'ǝtē, sō-/ *n* ‖ SYN *adj* thoughtful, sedate (see *serious, grave*)

so'ber·sid'ed *adj* grave, serious-minded, solemn-looking

so·bri·quet /sō'brikā', -ket', sō'brikā', -ket'/ [F] *n* nickname

sob' sis'ter *n* journalist who writes sentimental human-interest stories

sob' sto'ry *n* **1** story of personal hardship; **2** excuse intended to arouse sympathy

so'-called' *adj* so named or termed, often incorrectly

soc·cer /sok'ǝr/ [association + -*er*] *n* kind of football in which the ball is driven by the feet, legs, body, or head, the use of hands or arms being prohibited except for the goalkeepers

so·cia·ble /sōsh'ǝbǝl/ [L *sociabilis*] *adj* **1** fond of the society of others; companionable; **2** friendly; characterized by friendly companionship ‖ **so'cia·bil'i·ty** /-bil'-/ *n*

so·cial /sōsh'ǝl/ [< L *socius* companion] *adj* **1** fitted or accustomed to live in organized communities with mutual cooperation; **2** pert. to the relationship and problems of human beings living in a community; **3** inclined or disposed to friendly intercourse, sociable; **4** pert. to fashionable society; **5** (insects) living in organized communities; **6** pert. to social work ‖ *n* **7** informal party ‖ **so'cial·ly** *adv*

so'cial an·thro·pol'o·gy *n* var of **cultural anthropology**

so'cial climb'er *n* person who is ambitious to be accepted in fashionable society

so'cial·ism *n* **1** doctrine that there should be public ownership and operation of the means of production and distribution; **2** application of this doctrine; **3** political movement advocating it ‖ **so'cial·ist** *adj & n* ‖ **so'cial·is'tic** *adj*

so'cial·ite' *n* member of fashionable society

so'cial·ize' *vt* **1** to make social; **2** to make socialistic; put under government control or ownership ‖ *vi* **3** to mingle sociably

so'cial·ized' med'i·cine *n* system of providing complete medical care to all citizens at government expense or through deductions from salaries

so'cial reg'is·ter *n* directory of prominent society people

so'cial sci'ence *n* 1 sociology; 2 field of study not a natural science or one of the humanities, as history or economics

So'cial Se·cu'ri·ty *n* old-age pension and disability plan maintained by the U.S. government through compulsory payments by employers and deductions from employees' salaries and through payments by the self-employed

so'cial stud'ies *npl* courses in elementary and secondary schools comprising history, geography, civics, etc.

so'cial work' *n* work for the promotion of the welfare of the community, esp. of the poor, children, etc. ‖ **so'cial work'er** *n*

so·ci·e·tal /səsīʹitəl/ *adj* pert. to large social groups

so·ci·e·ty /səsīʹitē/ [MF *societe* < L *societas*] *n* (-ties) 1 people in general, considered as living in relationship with one another; 2 group of people bound together by a common interest or relationship; 3 company, companionship; 4 the wealthy, fashionable social class and their life; 5 organized body of persons united by a common interest and purpose, as *a debating society* ‖ also *adj*

So·ci'e·ty of Friends' *n* Christian sect, founded in England in 1650, that is opposed to war, oathtaking, and ritual in church services (see *Quaker*)

So·ci'e·ty of Je'sus *n* organization of the Jesuits, founded by Ignatius Loyola in 1534

so·ci·ol·o·gy /sōsʹē·olʹəjē, sōshʹ-/ [< L *socius* companion + -*logy*] *n* science that deals with human society, its development, forms, and functions ‖ **so'ci·ol'o·gist** *n* ‖ **so'ci·o·log'i·cal** /-əloj'-/ *adj*

sock[1] /sok'/ [OE *socc* < L *soccus* low-heeled shoe] *n* short stocking usu. not reaching the knee

sock[2] [?] *slang vt* 1 to hit hard; 2 **sock away** to save ‖ *n* 3 hard blow; 4 *theat* great success

sock·et /sok'it/ [ME *soket* < AF] *n* hollow into which something is fitted or secured, as *an eye socket, a lamp socket*

Soc·ra·tes /sok'rətēz'/ *n* (469?-399 B.C.) Athenian philosopher

So·crat·ic /səkrat'ik/ *adj* 1 pert. to Socrates; 2 pert. to his method of teaching by questions

sod /sod'/ [MD *sode*] *n* 1 grassy top layer of the soil; turf ‖ *v* (**sod·ded; sod·ding**) *vt* 2 to cover with sod

so·da /sōd'ə/ [It] *n* 1 sodium carbonate; 2 sodium bicarbonate; 3 sodium hydroxide; 4 soda water; 5 drink made from soda water and syrup, often with ice cream added

so'da ash' *n* crude sodium carbonate

so'da crack'er *n* thin crisp cracker, leavened with baking soda

so'da foun'tain *n* counter equipped to serve soda and ice cream

so'da jerk' *n colloq* one who works at a soda fountain

so·dal·i·ty /sōdal'itē/ [L *sodalitas*] *n* (-ties) 1 association or society; 2 lay association organized for religious and charitable purposes

so'da pop' *n* flavored carbonated water

so'da wa'ter *n* carbonated water, taken plain, flavored with syrup, or added to whiskey

sod·den /sod'ən/ [*archaic pp of seethe*] *adj* 1 soaked through; 2 soggy from improper cooking; 3 stupid or dull, as from drunkenness; 4 listless, inert

so·di·um /sōd'ē·əm/ [< *soda*] *n* alkaline metallic element (Na; at.no. 11; at.wt. 22.9898), always occurring in combination

so'di·um bi·car'bon·ate' *n* white crystalline powder —NaHCO₃— used in baking powder, in manufacturing, and as an antacid

so'di·um car'bon·ate' *n* grayish-white powder —Na₂CO₃— used in washing and in the manufacture of glass, soap, paper, etc.

so'di·um chlo'ride *n* salt 1

so'di·um hy·drox'ide *n* white water-soluble solid —NaOH— which generates heat when dissolved in water, used in manufacturing and as a caustic

so'di·um ni'trate *n* crystalline substance —NaNO₃— used in fertilizers and explosives

so'di·um thi·o·sul'fate *n* white translucent powder —Na₂S₂O₃·5H₂O— used as a bleach and in photography as a fixing agent

so'di·um-va'por lamp' *n* street lamp which lights when an electric current flows through sodium vapor in its interior

Sod·om /sod'əm/ *n Bib* city which was destroyed with Gomorrah because of its wickedness (Gen. 19:24,25)

sod·om·y /sod'əmē/ [< *Sodom*] *n* unnatural sexual intercourse between human males or between a human being and an animal ‖ **sod'om·ite'** *n*

-so·ev'er *comb form* added to *who, what, where, when, how*, etc., to make them more general or indefinite, as *whatsoever*

so·fa /sōf'ə/ [Ar *suffah*] *n* upholstered couch with back and arms

sof·fit /sof'it/ [It *soffitto*] *n* undersurface of a part of a building, as of a cornice, arch, or marquee

So·fi·a /sōf'ē·ə, sōfē'ə/ *n* capital of Bulgaria (894,487)

soft /sôft', soft'/ [OE *sōfte*] *adj* 1 lacking in hardness; 2 easily cut or shaped; **3** smooth and yielding to the touch; **4** not glaring; subdued (light or color); **5** not harsh or loud, as voices or music; **6** gentle; **7** lenient; **8** tender, sympathetic, as *a soft heart*; **9** not sharp or abrupt, as *soft outlines*; **10** delicate, weak; not robust; **11** occurring without destructive impact, as *a soft landing*; **12** (water) lathering easily with soap; **13** (*c* and *g*) pronounced as in *cell* and *gem*; **14** *colloq* easy (job); **15** soft in the head mentally weak; **16** be soft on *colloq* to have a crush on ‖ *adv* **17** gently; quietly ‖ soft′ly *adv* ‖ soft′ness *n* ‖ SYN *adj* mild, gentle, bland, malleable, ductile, delicate, conciliatory, courteous, placid, susceptible, tender, weak ‖ ANT *adj* hard, harsh, stiff, crude

soft′ball′ *n* **1** kind of baseball played on a smaller diamond by ten players on each side with a larger and softer ball; **2** the ball

soft′-boiled′ *adj* (egg) not boiled long enough to solidify the yolk

soft′ coal′ *n* bituminous coal

soft′ drink′ *n* nonalcoholic beverage

sof•ten /sôf′ən, sof′ən/ *vt* **1** to make soft ‖ *vi* **2** to become soft ‖ SYN allay, mitigate, enervate, palliate, chasten

soft′-head′ed *adj* weak-minded; stupid

soft′-heart′ed *adj* compassionate; generous-minded

soft′ land′ing *n* landing of a spacecraft, as on the moon, at a speed that avoids destructive impact ‖ soft′-land′ *vt* & *vi*

soft′ pal′ate *n* the soft back part of the palate

soft′-ped′al [< piano *pedal*] *v* (-aled or -alled; -al•ing or -al•ling) *vt* to play down, make less prominent or emphatic

soft′ sell′ *n* subtle salesmanship that avoids high pressure

soft′-shell clam′ *n* edible clam (*Mya arenaria*) with a thin, whitish shell

soft′-shell crab′ *n* edible crab that has recently molted and still has a soft shell, esp. the blue crab (*Callinectes sapidus*)

soft′-shoe′ *adj* (dancing) performed in soft-soled shoes without taps

soft′ shoul′der *n* unpaved and soft side of a road

soft′ soap′ *colloq n* flattery; persuasion ‖ soft′-soap′ *vt*

soft′-spo′ken *adj* speaking in a mild gentle tone

soft′ spot′ *n* weakness for something, special fondness

soft′ touch′ *n slang* **1** person easily duped; **2** person or team easily defeated; **3** person easily persuaded to give or lend money

soft′ware′ *n* written or printed material used in data-processing programing

soft′wood′ *n* wood easy to cut, from coniferous trees

soft′y *n* (-ies) *colloq* sentimental or compassionate person

sog•gy /sog′ē/ [< Eng *dial.* sog to become soaked] *adj* (-gi•er; -gi•est) wet and soft ‖ sog′gi•ness *n*

soil¹ /soil/ [AF < L *solium* seat] *n* **1** loose top layer of the earth's surface; **2** ground, earth; **3** land, country

soil² [OF *soillier*] *vt* **1** to make dirty, stain; **2** to mar or sully ‖ *vi* **3** to become stained or dirty ‖ *n* **4** dirt or stain; **5** compost; manure ‖ SYN *v* pollute, besmear, daub, defile, stain

soi•ree or **soi•rée** /swärā′/ *n* evening party or reception

so•journ /sō′jurn/ [OF *sojorn*] *n* **1** temporary stay ‖ /also sōjurn′/ *vi* **2** to dwell for a time, stay

sol¹ /sôl/ [It] *n mus* fifth tone of the diatonic scale

sol² /sol′, sōl′/ [hydro*sol*] *n* colloidal suspension of a solid in a liquid

sol³ /sōl′, sol′/ [Sp = sun] *n* monetary unit of Peru

sol•ace /sol′is/ [OF *solas*] *n* **1** comfort in sorrow or disappointment; lessening of grief; **2** that which gives solace ‖ *vt* **3** to give solace to

so•lar /sōl′ər/ [L *solaris < sol* sun] *adj* pert. to, measured by, proceeding from, or produced by the sun

so′lar bat′ter•y *n* group of photoelectric cells for converting solar energy into electricity

so•lar•i•um /sōler′ē•əm, sə-/ [L = balcony or terrace] *n* (-ums or -a /-ə/) porch or room enclosed with glass and exposed to the sun

so′lar month′ *n* one twelfth of a solar year, about 30½ days

so′lar plex′us *n* network of nerves lying back of the stomach

so′lar prom′i•nenc•es *npl* eruptions of luminous gas rising far above the surface of the sun

so′lar sys′tem *n* the sun together with all the planets and other bodies subject to its gravity

so′lar year′ *n* year extending between one vernal equinox and the next

sold /sōld/ *pt & pp* of **sell**

sol•der /sod′ər/ [OF *soldure*] *n* **1** easily fusible alloy, used, when melted, to join metal surfaces or to mend breaks in metals ‖ *vt & vi* **2** to join with or as with solder

sol′der•ing i′ron *n* tool for melting and applying solder

sol•dier /sōl′jər/ [OF *soldeier* < L *solidus* pay] *n* **1** one who serves in an army; **2** enlisted man; **3** private; **4** person of military skill; **5** worker in any cause; **6** ant or termite with powerful jaws, specialized to defend the colony; **7** *colloq* loafer; malingerer ‖ *vi* **8** to serve as a soldier; **9** *colloq* to loaf on the job

sol'dier of for'tune n 1 adventurer; 2 mercenary

sold' out' adj 1 completely sold; 2 having none left to sell

sole[1] /sōl/ [ML < L *solea* sandal, flatfish] n 1 any of a family (Soleidae) of flatfishes, esp. *Solea solea*, esteemed as food; 2 any of various flounders

sole[2] [OE < L *solea*] n 1 underside of the foot; 2 corresponding part of a shoe, stocking, etc. ‖ vt 3 to furnish with a sole

sole[3] [L *solus*] adj being or acting alone; only; single ‖ **sole'ly** /sōl'lē/ adv

sol·e·cism /sol'isiz'əm/ [Gk *soloikismos* < *Soloi* town noted for its corrupt Greek] n mistake in grammar; incorrect usage ‖ **sol'e·cist** n

sol·emn /sol'əm/ [MF *solemne* < L *sollemnis*] adj 1 attended with formal or sacred rites or ceremonies; 2 impressive; awe-inspiring; 3 earnest; grave ‖ **so·lem·ni·ty** /səlem'nitē/ n (-ties) ‖ **sol'emn·ly** adv ‖ SYN (see *serious, grave*)

sol'em·nize /-niz'/ vt 1 to perform or celebrate with ceremonies and rites; 2 to render serious or grave ‖ SYN honor, observe, dignify (see *celebrate*)

so·le·noid /sōl'inoid'/ [< Gk *solen* channel + -*oid*] n coil of wire wound in the form of a helix of one or more layers, used to produce a magnetic field

sol-fa /sōl'fä'/ [*sol* + *fa*] mus n 1 the syllables *do, re, mi, fa, sol, la,* and *ti* used in singing the scale; 2 use of these in singing ‖ vt & vi 3 to sing using these syllables

sol·feg·gio /sōlfej'ō, -fej'ē-ō'/ [It] n (-gios or -gi /-jē/) mus vocal exercise sung to the sol-fa syllables

so·lic·it /solis'it/ [MF *soliciter*] vt 1 to ask with earnestness; entreat; 2 to endeavor to obtain, as trade; 3 to accost and importune for immoral purposes ‖ also vi ‖ **so·lic'i·ta'tion** n ‖ SYN ask, importune, invite, beg, implore, crave

so·lic'i·tor n 1 one who solicits business, contributions, etc.; 2 law officer of a city; 3 Brit lawyer who practices in the lower courts, gives legal advice, and assists barristers

so·lic'i·tor gen'er·al n (solicitors general) law officer of the federal government or of a state, ranking next to the attorney general

so·lic'i·tous adj 1 eager; 2 anxious; 3 careful; 4 concerned; apprehensive ‖ **so·lic'i·tous·ly** adv

so·lic'i·tude /-t(y)ood'/ n state of being solicitous ‖ SYN uneasiness, anxiety, concern (see *care*)

sol·id /sol'id/ [L *solidus*] adj 1 not liquid or gaseous; 2 cubic; having three dimensions; 3 not hollow; 4 hard, compact; 5 weighty; sound, genuine; 6 sound morally or financially; 7 unbroken, as a *solid wall*; 8 dense, thick; 9 of the same material throughout, as *solid gold*; 10 strongly built, substantial; 11 not hyphenated or separated by a space, as the two elements of a compound word; 12 undivided; unanimous; 13 uninterrupted, continuous, as a *solid hour, a solid row*; 14 uniform (shade or color); 15 slang excellent; 16 in solid colloq looked upon favorably, as *he's in solid with the boss* ‖ n 17 solid body; 18 body having three dimensions ‖ **sol'id·ly** adv ‖ SYN adj massive, firm, compact, rigid, stable, unbroken, sound, strong, substantial (see *firm*)

sol'i·dar'i·ty /-där'-/ n condition of being united in opinion and effort

sol'id ge·om'e·try n geometry that treats of points, lines, and surfaces in three dimensions

so·lid·i·fy /səlid'ifī'/ v (-fied) vt 1 to make solid; 2 to unite, consolidate ‖ vi 3 to become solidified ‖ **so·lid'i·fi·ca'tion** n

so·lid'i·ty n (-ties) 1 state or quality of being solid; 2 firmness; 3 soundness

sol'id-state' adj 1 (physics) which deals with the electronic properties of solids and esp. crystals; 2 (device) made of semiconducting materials, which controls the flow of electric current without the use of heated elements or vacuums

so·lil·o·quy /səlil'əkwē/ [LL *soliloquium*] n (-quies) 1 talking to oneself; 2 utterance not addressed to any one ‖ **so·lil'o·quize'** vi

sol·i·taire /sol'iter'/ [F] n 1 any of various card games played by one person; 2 gem, esp. a diamond, mounted alone; 3 piece of jewelry mounted with a single gem

sol·i·tar·y /sol'iterē'/ [L *solitarius*] adj 1 alone; without companions; 2 sole, only; 3 far removed; unfrequented ‖ n (-ies) 4 hermit; 5 colloq solitary confinement ‖ SYN adj only, sole, individual, lonesome, deserted, alone, retired, remote, desolate, unfrequented (see *lonely*) ‖ ANT adj numerous, frequented, social

sol'i·tar'y con·fine'ment n confinement of a prisoner alone by himself

sol·i·tude /sol'it(y)ood'/ [MF < L *solitudo*] n 1 state of being by oneself; seclusion; 2 remote, lonely place ‖ SYN isolation, retreat, seclusion (see *retirement*)

sol·mi·za·tion /sol'mizāsh'ən/ [< *sol*[1] + *mi*] n method or practice of using the sol-fa syllables to represent the tones of the scale

so·lo /sō'lō/ [It < L *solus* alone] n (-los or -li /-lē/) 1 mus leading part performed by one person, with or without accompaniment; 2 any performance or act by one person alone || *vi* 3 to perform or act alone || also *adj & adv* || **so′lo·ist** *n*

Sol·o·mon /sol′əmən/ *n* 1 *Bib* son of David, king of Israel in the tenth century B.C., and builder of the first temple; 2 any very wise person

Sol′o·mon Is′lands *n* island nation in W Pacific (215,000; 11,015 sq.m.; cap. Honiara)

So·lon /sōl′ən/ *n* 1 Athenian lawgiver of the sixth century B.C.; 2 often **solon** wise lawmaker; legislator

so′ long′ *colloq* *n* 1 good-by || *interj* 2 good-by!

sol·stice /sol′stis/ [OF < L *solstitium*] *n* either of the two times per year when the sun is farthest from the equator: June 21, the longest day of the year in the Northern Hemisphere and Dec. 22, the shortest day

sol·u·ble /sol′yəbəl/ [LL *solubilis*] *adj* 1 capable of being dissolved; 2 capable of being solved || **sol′u·bil′i·ty** /-bil′-/ *n*

sol·ute /sol′yōōt, sōl′ōōt/ [L *solutus* loosened] *n* the substance dissolved in a solution

so·lu·tion /səlōōsh′ən/ *n* 1 act of solving a problem; 2 state of being solved; 3 explanation, answer; 4 a act of mixing one or more substances in another to form a homogeneous mixture; b such a mixture

solve /solv′/ [L *solvere* to loosen] *vt* 1 to explain, clear up; 2 to find the answer to || **solv′a·ble** *adj* || **solv′a·bil′i·ty** /-bil′-/ *n*

sol·vent /solv′ənt/ [L *solvens* (-*entis*) loosening] *adj* 1 having the power of causing solution; 2 able to pay all debts || *n* 3 any liquid in or by which a substance can be dissolved || **sol′ven·cy** *n*

So·ma·li·a /sōmäl′ē·ə/ *n* republic in E Africa (3,500,000; 246,201 sq.m.; cap. Mogadishu)

so·mat·ic /sōmat′ik/ [< Gk *soma* (-*matos*) body] *adj* 1 pert. to the body; physical; 2 *anat* of or pert. to the body

so·ma·tol·o·gy /sō′mətol′əjē/ *n* branch of anthropology concerned with human anatomy and physiology

som·ber /som′bər/ [F *sombre*] *adj* 1 dull, dark; 2 sad, gloomy; 3 grave, serious

som·bre·ro /sombrer′ō/ [Sp = hat] *n* broad-brimmed and often high-crowned hat, worn esp. in Latin America and the SW U.S.

some /sum′, səm/ [OE *sum*] *adj* 1 certain but unspecified, as *some people came;* 2 of a certain unspecified number, amount, or degree, as *I have some money;* 3 certain, as *some days I stay in bed;* 4 about, as *some ten came;* 5 *colloq* remarkable, as *she has some voice* || *pron* 6 a partial number or quantity, as *some came*

-some¹ /-səm/ [OE *-sum*] *adj suf* 1 pert. to, producing, as *quarrelsome;* 2 to a considerable degree, as *lithesome;* 3 likely to, as *tiresome*

-some² /-sōm′/ [Gk *soma*] *comb form* body, as *chromosome*

some·bod′y /-bod′ē, -bud′ē, -bədē/ *pron* 1 some person || *n* (-**ies**) 2 person of importance

some·day′ *adv* at some time in the future

some·how′ *adv* in one way or another not specified or known

some·one′ *pron* some person, somebody

some·place′ *adv* somewhere

som·er·sault /sum′ərsôlt′/ [OF *sombresault*] *n* 1 acrobatic feat in which the body makes a complete revolution, rolling end over end; 2 complete reversal, as of thought || *vi* 3 to perform a somersault

some·thing *pron* 1 thing not definitely known or specified; 2 unknown amount or degree, as *to give something* || *n* 3 **be something** to be a person or thing of importance || *adv* 4 somewhat; 5 *colloq* quite

some·time′ *adv* 1 at some indefinite or unspecified time || *adj* 2 former

some·times′ *adv* now and then, occasionally

some·what′ *adv* a little, to some extent

some·where′ *adv* 1 in, to, or at an unknown or unspecified place; 2 approximately, as *he has somewhere around a million dollars*

som·me·lier /sum′əlyā′/ [F] *n* wine steward in a restaurant

som·nam·bu·late /somnam′byəlāt′/ [< L *somnus* sleep + *ambulare* (-*atus*) to walk] *vi* to walk in one's sleep

som·nam′bu·lism *n* sleepwalking || **som·nam′bu·list** *n*

som·no·lent /som′nələnt/ [L *somnolentus*] *adj* 1 sleepy; 2 inducing sleepiness || **som′no·lence** *n*

son /sun′/ [OE *sunu*] *n* 1 male child in relation to his parents; 2 male descendant; 3 male person regarded as the product of a particular background, as *a son of Ireland, a son of Harvard;* 4 **the Son** the second person of the Trinity, Jesus Christ

so·nar /sō′när/ [*so*und *na*vigation *r*anging] *n* apparatus for detecting and locating underwater objects by the sound waves they reflect or produce

so·na·ta /sənät′ə/ [It] *n mus* composition in three or four related but contrasting movements for one or two instruments

song /sôŋ′, soŋ′/ [OE] *n* 1 composition to be rendered by the voice; 2 tuneful musical sounds made by certain birds and insects; 3 act or art of singing; 4 that which is sung; 5 poetry suited to musical expression, as the lyric or ballad; **6 for a song** at a very low price

song'bird' n 1 bird that sings; 2 female singer

Song' of Sol'o·mon n poetical book of the Old Testament

song'ster [OE *sangestre* songstress] n 1 one who sings; 2 songbird; 3 writer of songs and poems || **song'-stress** *nfem*

son·ic /son'ik/ [< L *sonus* sound] *adj* 1 pert. to sound; 2 pert. to the speed of sound in air

son'ic boom' n loud noise like a thunderclap caused by the shock wave generated by an object traveling through the atmosphere at supersonic speed

son'-in-law' n (**sons-in-law**) husband of one's daughter

son·net /son'it/ [It *sonetto*] n poem of fourteen lines, arranged according to any of several rhyme schemes, generally on a single theme

so·no·rant /sənôr'ənt, -nōr'-/ [< L *sonorus* sounding] n *phonet* consonant, as *l* or *m*, produced without stoppage of the breath stream or without friction noise

so·no'rous *adj* 1 deep and resonant, as a sound; 2 giving a full sound; resonant; 3 impressive, imposing (speech or language) || **so·nor'i·ty** n

soon /sōon/ [OE *sōna*] *adv* 1 in a short time; shortly; 2 in the near or immediate future; 3 quickly; promptly; 4 willingly; readily, as *just as soon as not*; 5 **sooner or later** eventually

soot /sŏot', sŏot'/ [OE *sōt*] n black powder, a form of carbon, deposited in chimneys, pipes, etc., resulting from imperfect combustion || **soot'y** *adj* (**-i·er; -i·est**)

sooth /sōoth/ [OE *sōth*] n *archaic* truth

soothe /sōoth'/ [OE *sōthian* to assert the truth] *vt* 1 to make quiet or calm; comfort or console; 2 to make less severe, relieve, as pain || **sooth'-ing·ly** *adv* || SYN quiet, assuage, mitigate, pacify, tranquilize

sooth'say'er n one who claims to foretell the future || **sooth'say'ing** n

sop /sop'/ [OE *sopp*] n 1 anything soaked, dipped, or softened in a liquid, as bread in milk; 2 something given to pacify or bribe || *v* (**sopped; sop·ping**) *vt* 3 to dip or soak in a liquid; 4 **sop up** to absorb (a liquid)

S.O.P. Standard Operating Procedure

soph /sof'/ n *colloq* sophomore

soph·ism /sof'izəm/ [Gk *sophisma*] n 1 plausible but unsound argument intended to deceive; 2 any subtly fallacious argument

soph'ist n 1 person who engages in sophism; 2 **Sophist** one of a group of teachers in ancient Greece, famous for their sophisms

so·phis·ti·cate /səfist'ikāt'/ [ML *sophisticare* (*-atus*) to contrive cleverly] *vt* 1 to mislead; pervert; 2 to make sophisticated || *also -kit/* n 3 sophisticated person || **so·phis'ti·ca'tion** n

so·phis'ti·cat'ed *adj* 1 worldly-wise; not naive; 2 intricate (machinery, process, etc.)

soph'ist·ry n (**-ries**) 1 sophism; 2 plausible but unsound reasoning || SYN fallacy, casuistry, evasion, chicanery

Soph·o·cles /sof'əklēz'/ n (495?–406) Greek dramatist || **Soph'o·cle'an** *adj*

soph·o·more /sof'(ə)môr', -mōr'/ [< Gk *sophos* wise + *moros* foolish] n student in the second year of high school or college

soph'o·mor'ic *adj* immature, half-baked; conceited

-so·phy /-səfē/ [Gk *sophia* wisdom] *comb form* science or knowledge, as *theosophy*

so·po·rif·ic /sŏp'ərif'ik, sop'-/ [< L *sopor* sleep + -*fic*] *adj* 1 causing or tending to induce sleep || n 2 anything that causes sleep, as a drug or medicine

sop'ping /sop'ing/ *adv* **sopping wet** drenched, soaked

so·pran·o /səpran'ō/ -prän'ō/ [It = highest] n 1 highest singing voice; 2 singer with such a voice; 3 part for a soprano || *also adj*

sor·cer·y /sôrs'ərē/ [ML *sorceria*] n (**-ies**) witchcraft, necromancy, black magic || **sor'cer·er** n || **sor'cer·ess** *nfem*

sor·did /sôr'did/ [L *sordidus* dirty] *adj* 1 mean, vile, base; 2 wretched, squalid || SYN mean, gross, contemptible, ignoble, despicable

sore /sôr', sōr'/ [OE *sār*] *adj* 1 tender or painful to the touch; inflamed; 2 grieved, afflicted; 3 causing sorrow; distressing; 4 angry, resentful, annoyed || n 5 sore spot on the body; 6 bruise or break on the skin; 7 cause of annoyance or distress || **sore'ness** n

sore'head' n *colloq* 1 disgruntled or dissatisfied person; 2 poor loser

sore'ly *adv* 1 grievously; 2 urgently

sor·ghum /sôr'gəm/ [< It *sorgo*] n 1 canelike grass (*Sorghum vulgare*) yielding a sweet juice from which syrup is made; 2 the syrup

so·ror·i·ty /sərôr'itē, -ror'-/ [< L *soror* sister] n (**-ties**) women's or girls' club, esp. in a school or college

sor·rel[1] /sôr'əl, sor'-/ [OF *surele*] n 1 any of several species of herbs (genus *Rumex*) having acid leaves used in salads; 2 any of several acid-juiced herbs (genus *Oxalis*); 3 any of various other herbs

sor·rel[2] [OF *sorel*] n 1 reddish brown; 2 horse of this color || *also adj*

sor·row /sor'ō, sôr'ō/ [OE *sorg*] n 1 distress and pain caused by loss, regret, disappointment, etc.; 2 anything that causes grief or affliction ‖ *vi* **3** to grieve, feel sorrow ‖ SYN *v* grieve, mourn; *n* compunction, regret, remorse, grief, sadness, lamentation, repentance, affliction, trial, tribulation ‖ DISCR *Sorrow* is a deep and lasting *sadness* or mental pain felt for misfortune, sin, the loss of some one dear to us, or other serious source of distress. *Regret* can be as deep and moving a feeling as *sorrow*, *as regret* over the loss of a friend. But commonly *regret* names a feeling of annoyance, disappointment, vexation; we feel *regret* over forgetting an appointment, over a social blunder, or any painful situation. *Sorrow* for sin is deeper than *regret* over sin. *Compunction* is slight *regret*, felt over a committed or a contemplated act; *compunction* is colored by scruple, by a tiny pricking of conscience, as the instant I had spoken so harshly, I felt *compunction* in my heart. *Remorse* is bitter *sorrow* and *repentance* over wrongdoing; guilt weighs heavily on the remorseful, often with the sense of helplessness, of irreparableness. No matter how sorry a murderer may be, he cannot restore life to his victim; hence, in addition to *sorrow*, in spite of *repentance*, he will be eaten by *remorse* (see **grief**) ‖ ANT *n* glee, mirth, happiness, rejoicing, hilarity

sor'row·ful *adj* **1** feeling sorrow; **2** expressing sorrow; **3** causing sorrow ‖ **sor'row·ful·ly** *adv* ‖ SYN disconsolate, lamentable, grievous, dismal, mournful, sad, rueful, dreary, doleful ‖ ANT joyous, merry, gleeful, happy, pleasant, gay, hilarious

sor·ry /sor′ē, sôr′ē/ [OE *sārig*] *adj* (**-ri·er; -ri·est**) **1** feeling sorrow, pity, or regret; **2** wretched, miserable

sort /sôrt′/ [MF] *n* **1** kind, class, species; **2** manner, way; **3** nature, quality; **4** of **sorts** of poor or mediocre quality; **5** out of **sorts**, **a** in a bad temper; **b** not feeling well; **6** sort of *colloq* rather, somewhat ‖ *vt* **7** to arrange according to classes; classify; **8** sort out to pick out or separate from others ‖ SYN *n* group, class, order, species (see **kind**)

sor·tie /sôrt′ē/ [F < *sortir* to go out] *n* **1** sudden attack of troops from a defensive or besieged position; **2** single tactical mission of a combat plane

SOS /es′ō′es′/ [< the letters of the international Morse code represented by the signal] *n* **1** international signal of distress . . . — — — . . . used esp. by ships at sea; **2** any call for help

so'-so' *adj* **1** neither very good nor very bad; indifferent ‖ *adv* **2** passably

sos·te·nu·to /sos′tənōōt′ō/ [It] *adj mus* sustained, prolonged

sot /sot′/ [ME] *n* confirmed drunkard

sot·to vo·ce /sot′ō vōch′ē/ [It = beneath the voice] *adv* in an undertone, so as not to be overheard

sou /sōō′/ [F] *n* former French coin of very little value

sou·brette /sōōbret′/ [F < Prov *soubret* conceited] *n* coquettish lady's maid in a play or opera

souf·flé /sōōflā′, sōō′flā′ [F = puffed up] *cookery n* **1** baked dish made light and fluffy by adding beaten egg whites ‖ *adj* **2** also **souf·fléed'** light and fluffy ‖ *vt* **3** to make light and fluffy like a soufflé

sough /suf′, sou′/ [< OE *swōgan* to sound] *n* **1** murmur or rustling, as of wind ‖ *vi* **2** to murmur or rustle, as the wind

sought /sôt′/ *pt* & *pp* of **seek**

soul /sōl′/ [OE *sāwol*] *n* **1** the spiritual, immaterial, and immortal part in man, as distinguished from the body; **2** that part of a man's nature where feelings, ideals, and morals center; **3** expression of fine feelings or ideals; high-mindedness; **4** necessary or central part of anything; **5** person who leads and inspires; **6** person, as *not a soul was there*; **7** disembodied spirit; **8** personification, model, as *he is the soul of honor*

soul'ful *adj* full of or expressing deep feeling

soul'less *adj* **1** lacking a soul; **2** lacking nobility of nature

sound¹ /sound′/ [OE *gesund*] *adj* **1** free from injury, damage, defect, decay, or disease; healthy; firm; strong; **2** profound; uninterrupted (sleep); **3** founded on truth or right; free from error; **4** legal, valid, as *a sound title*; **5** in good financial condition; solvent; **6** thorough, hearty, as *a sound thrashing*

sound² [AF *soun*] *n* **1** the sensation perceived through the ear; **2** vibrations in an elastic medium, as the air; **3** any distinctive or characteristic noise, as *a sound of exultation*; **4** distance to which a sound is audible, as *within sound of the bell*; **5** meaningless noise; **6** *phonet* any of the series of articulate utterances of which speech is made up; **7** mental impression, as *I don't like the sound of this* ‖ *vt* **8** to cause to make a sound; **9** to emit, as *to sound a high note*; **10** to order or announce by sound, as an alarm; **11** to examine or test by causing to give forth sound, as *to sound the walls*; **12** to pronounce, articulate ‖ *vi* **13** to make a sound; **14** to give a certain impression, as *this sounds bad*; **15** **sound off** *slang* **a** to air one's ideas loudly; to complain loudly; **c** to boast ‖ SYN *n* (see **noise**)

sound³ [MF *sonder*] *vt* **1** to measure the depth of (water), as by lowering a weight on the end of a line; **2** *med* to examine with a sound; **3**

often **sound out** to seek to ascertain the views of, often indirectly ‖ *vt* 4 to take soundings; 5 to dive deeply, as a whale ‖ *n* 6 *surg* long, slender instrument for exploring body cavities

sound⁴ [OE *sund*] *n* 1 stretch of water connecting two large bodies of water or lying between the mainland and an island; 2 inlet of the sea

sound′ bar·ri·er *n* aerodynamic drag as the speed of sound is approached by an aircraft

sound′ booth′ *n* 1 soundproof booth in which the acuity and range of a person's hearing is tested; 2 soundproof enclosure in which a person is isolated from outside sounds

sound′ ef·fects′ *npl* sounds and noises produced by artificial means on the stage or behind the scenes to give the impression of the real thing

sound′ing *n* act or instance of measuring the depth of water or of using a probe

sound′ing board′ *n* 1 resonant plate forming part of a musical instrument; 2 board used to reflect sound, as on a stage; 3 person or group used to test the effectiveness of or reaction to something

sound′proof′ *adj* 1 impervious to sound ‖ *vt* 2 to make soundproof

sound′ track′ *n* narrow strip containing the recorded sound on the edge of a motion picture film

sound′ track′ *n* truck with a loudspeaker for broadcasting music, speeches, etc., for advertising or electioneering

sound′ wave′ *n* longitudinal pressure wave in a material medium

soup /sōōp′/ [F *soupe*] *n* 1 liquid food made by boiling or simmering meat, vegetables, etc.; 2 *slang* nitroglycerine ‖ *vt* 3 **soup up** *slang* to increase the power and speed of (an engine or motor)

soup·çon /sōōpsôn′/ [F] *n* 1 suspicion; intimation; 2 minute amount

sour /sou′(ə)r/ [OE *sūr*] *adj* 1 having a tart or acid taste, as vinegar; 2 acid, esp. as a result of fermentation; 3 unpleasant, disagreeable; 4 irritable, ill-tempered; 5 acid (soil) ‖ *vt* 6 to cause to become sour; 7 to make cross or disagreeable; 8 to embitter ‖ *vt* 9 to become sour ‖ **sour′ness** *n* ‖ SYN *adj* acid, crabbed, morose (see *bitter*) ‖ ANT *adj* sweet, pleasant, agreeable, good-natured

sour′ball′ *n* 1 small round piece of hard candy, usu. with a tart fruit flavor; 2 grouch; unpleasant person

source /sôrs′, sōrs′/ [OF *sorse*] *n* 1 point of origin of a stream or river, as a spring; 2 that from which anything rises or originates; 3 person or writing cited as authority

source′ lan′guage *n* 1 language of the

learner of a foreign language; 2 language from which a translation is made (opposite of *target language*)

sour′dough′ *n* 1 leaven, esp. fermented dough; 2 prospector in Alaska or Canada

sour′ grapes′ [< fable by Aesop] *npl* pretended scorn for something unattainable

sour·puss /sour′pŏos′/ *n* *colloq* extremely grouchy person

souse /sous′/ [MF *souce* pickled] *n* 1 act of steeping in brine or pickle, or of plunging into water or other liquid; 2 anything preserved in pickle, as pig's feet; 3 *slang* drunkard ‖ *vt* 4 to steep in brine; 5 to plunge into water; soak thoroughly; 6 to dash, as water; 7 *slang* to intoxicate

soused′ *adj* *slang* drunk

sou·tane /sōotän′/ [F < It *sottana*] *n* cassock

south /south′/ [OE *sūth*] *n* 1 one of the four cardinal points of the compass, the direction away from the equator along any meridian in the Southern Hemisphere and towards the equator in the Northern; 2 often **South** region or territory lying in this direction; 3 **the South** the region of the U.S. south of Pennsylvania and the Ohio River, most of which seceded in 1861 to form the Confederacy ‖ *adj* 4 situated in, directed toward, or facing the south; 5 (wind) blowing from the south ‖ *adv* 6 in or toward the south

South′ Af′ri·ca, Re·pub′lic of *n* (Azania) Afrikaans- and English-speaking republic in S Africa (18,733,000; 471,879 sq.m.; caps. Pretoria and Capetown) ‖ **South′ Af′ri·can** *adj* & *n*

South′ A·mer′i·ca *n* southernmost continent in the Western Hemisphere, extending south from Panama (165,-000,000; ab. 7,000,000 sq.m.) ‖ **South′ A·mer′i·can** *adj* & *n*

south′bound′ *adj* headed south

South′ Car·o·li′na /kar′əlīn′ə/ *n* state in the SE U.S. (2,590,516; 31,055 sq.m.; cap. Columbia) ‖ **South′ Car′o·lin′i·an** /-lin′ē·ən/ *n*

South′ Da·ko′ta *n* state in the N central U.S. (662,000; 77,047 sq.m.; cap. Pierre) ‖ **South′ Da·ko′tan** *n*

south′east′ *n* 1 compass point halfway between south and east; 2 region in this direction; 3 **the Southeast** the southeastern region of the U.S. ‖ *adj* 4 situated in, directed toward, or facing the southeast; 5 (wind) blowing from the southeast ‖ *adv* 6 toward the southeast ‖ **south′east′·er·ly** *adj* & *adv* ‖ **south′east′ern** *adj* ‖ **south′east′ward** /-wərd/ *adj* & *adv* ‖ **south′east′wards** /-wərdz/ *adv*

south′east′er *n* storm or gale from the southeast

South′east′ern·er *n* native or inhabitant of the Southeast

south′er·ly /*suth*′-/ *adj & adv* 1 toward the south; 2 (wind) from the south ‖ *n* (-lies) 3 south wind

south·ern /*suth*′ərn/ *adj* 1 situated in, directed toward, or facing the south; 2 (wind) blowing from the south; 3 South′ern of or pert. to the South ‖ **south′ern·er** *n* ‖ **South′ern·er** *n*

South′ern Hem′i·sphere′ *n* that part of the earth south of the equator

south′ern lights′ *npl* aurora australis

south′ern·most *adj* farthest south

South′ern Rho·de′sia *n* Rhodesia

South·ey, Robert /*suth*′ē, *south*′ē/ *n* (1774–1843) English poet; poet laureate 1813–43

South′ Frig′id Zone′ *n* that part of the earth between the Antarctic Circle and the South Pole

South′ Is′land *n* the larger of the two principal islands of New Zealand

South′ Ko·re′a *n* country in SE Asia formed in 1948 by the division of Korea at 38° N (30,010,000; 38,000 sq.m.; cap. Seoul) ‖ **South′ Ko·re′an** *adj & n*

south·land /-lənd/ *n* southern part of a country

south′paw′ *n* colloq left-handed person, esp. in sports

south′ pole′ *n* 1 the pole of a magnet that points toward the south magnetic pole; 2 **South Pole**, a southern end of the earth′s axis; b point on the celestial sphere directly above the earth′s South Pole

South′ Sea′ Is′lands *npl* the islands of the South Pacific

South′ Tem′per·ate Zone′ *n* the part of the earth between the tropic of Capricorn and the Antarctic Circle

south·ward /-wərd/ *adj & adv* toward the south ‖ **south′ward·ly** *adj & adv* ‖ **south′wards** *adv*

south′west′ /also *naut* sou′-/ *n* 1 compass point halfway between south and west; 2 region lying in this direction; 3 the Southwest the southwestern region of the U.S. ‖ *adj* 4 situated in, directed toward, or facing the southwest; 5 (wind) blowing from the southwest ‖ *adv* 6 toward the southwest ‖ **south′west′er·ly** *adj & adv* ‖ **south′west′ern** *adj* ‖ **south′west′ward** /-wərd/ *adj & adv* ‖ **south′west′wards** /-wərdz/ *adv*

South′west′ern·er *n* native or inhabitant of the Southwest

sou·ve·nir /soov′ənir′, soov′ənir′/ [F = to remember] *n* memento; keepsake; remembrance

sov·er·eign /sov′(ə)rin/ [OF *soverain*] *adj* 1 supreme, chief; 2 royal; 3 supreme in power or rank; 4 independent (state) ‖ *n* 5 monarch; supreme ruler; 6 British gold coin formerly equal to one pound, but now worth much more ‖ **SYN** *adj* royal, imperial, majestic, supreme

sov′er·eign·ty *n* (-ties) 1 state, quality, or status of being sovereign; 2 independent power or dominion

so·vi·et /sōv′ē-it, -et′/ [Russ *sovet* council] *n* 1 any of various governing councils in Russia, starting at the local level and culminating in the Supreme Soviet ‖ *adj* 2 of or pert. to a soviet; 3 **Soviet** of or pert. to the Soviet Union

So′vi·et·ol′o·gist *n* person who is well-informed regarding the Soviet government, its activities and its ideology

So′vi·et Un′ion *n* federal union of 15 republics in E Europe and N Asia, of which the largest by far is Russia (235,543,000; 8,649,550 sq.m.; cap. Moscow)

sow[1] /sou/ [OE *sū*] *n* 1 adult female swine; 2 adult female of some other animals, as the bear

sow[2] /sō/ [OE *sāwan*] *v* (*pp* **sown** /sōn/ or **sowed**) *vt* 1 to strew (seed) upon the earth; 2 to strew seed over; 3 to disseminate, as ideas ‖ *vi* 4 to sow seed ‖ **sow′er** *n*

soy /soi/ [Jap *shōyu* < Chin] *n* 1 soybean; 2 soy sauce

soy′bean′ *n* 1 small leguminous plant (*Glycine soja*); 2 its seed, used as food, and yielding an oil also used as food and in making paints, varnishes, plastics, etc.

soy′ sauce′ *n* sauce made from fermented soybeans, much used in Oriental cookery

Sp. 1 Spain; 2 Spaniard; 3 Spanish

spa /spä/ [< *Spa* Belgian resort] *n* 1 mineral spring; 2 town having such springs

space /spās/ [OF *espace* < L *spatium*] *n* 1 the limitless three-dimensional expanse in which all material things exist; 2 room; distance or area between things; 3 extent or area; 4 unoccupied place; 5 length of time; 6 *mus* one of the open places between the lines of a staff; 7 the limitless region beyond the earth′s atmosphere containing the rest of the universe ‖ *vt* 8 to arrange with open spaces; separate by means of spaces ‖ **spac′er** *n*

space′ bar′ *n* horizontal bar on a typewriter that advances the carriage when depressed

space′ charge′ *n* electric charge in a vacuum or near vacuum distributed three-dimensionally rather than over a surface

space′craft′ *n* (*pl* **-craft**) vehicle that can travel in outer space

space′far′ing *adj* (capable of) traveling in outer space, as *the two spacefaring nations*

space'man /-mən/ *n* (**-men** /-mən/) astronaut

space' probe' *n* **1** exploration of outer space or of celestial bodies other than the earth; **2** spacecraft designed to carry out such exploration

space'ship' *n* vehicle designed to travel to other planets in outer space

space' sta'tion *n* manned satellite used for observation of the earth, other planets, and the sun and for the assembling and launching of other satellites

space'suit' *n* sealed and pressurized suit with a helmet enabling the wearer to exist in outer space or in a very thin atmosphere outside a pressurized cabin or spaceship

space'-time' con·tin'u·um *n* continuum containing one temporal and three spatial coordinates, by which any object or event can be located

space' walk' *n* activity of an astronaut outside a spacecraft in orbit

spa·cial /spāsh'əl/ *adj* var of **spatial**

spa·cious /spāsh'əs/ *adj* **1** capacious, roomy; **2** vast, broad ‖ SYN large, capacious, vast, ample, expansive

spade¹ /spād'/ [OE *spadu*] *n* **1** flat-bladed digging tool with a long handle; **2 call a spade a spade** to call a thing by its right name; speak bluntly ‖ *vt* **3** to dig or work with a spade

spade² [It *spada*] *n* **1** black figure shaped like an inverted heart with a stem at the cleft, marking one of the four suits of playing cards; **2** playing card stamped with this mark; **3 spades** *sg* or *pl* suit of cards so marked; **4 in spades** *slang* in full measure, in the extreme

spade'work' *n* difficult and necessary preliminary work

spa·ghet·ti /spəget'ē/ [It] *n* long dried strings of paste, cooked by boiling and usu. served with a sauce

Spain /spān/ *n* kingdom in SW Europe (32,275,434; 194,885 sq.m.; cap. Madrid)

spake /spāk/ *archaic pt* of **speak**

span¹ /span'/ [OE] *n* **1** distance between the tips of the thumb and little finger when fully extended; **2** this distance as a unit of length, equal to nine inches; **3** short space of time; **4** any extent having two definite bounds; **5** horizontal distance between the two supports of an arch, or between any two consecutive supports of a bridge ‖ *v* (**spanned**) **span·ning**) *vt* **6** to measure by the length of the extended thumb and fingers; **7** to extend span or across; **8** to arch over; bridge over

span² [D *spannen* to unite] *n* pair of horses or other animals harnessed together

span·gle /spaŋ'gəl/ [ME *spangel*] *n* **1** small thin piece of glittering metallic substance, used esp. on garments ‖ *vt* **2** to decorate with spangles; **3** to sprinkle or strew with small shiny objects

Span·iard /span'yərd/ [OF *Espaignart*] *n* native or inhabitant of Spain

span·iel /span'yəl/ [OF *espaignol* Spanish (dog)] *n* any of several breeds of small dogs with hanging ears and long silky hair

Span·ish /span'ish/ [< *Spain*] *adj* **1** pert. to Spain, its language, or its people ‖ *n* **2** language of Spain and Spanish America; **3 the Spanish** *pl* the people of Spain

Span·ish A·mer'i·ca *n* the Spanish-speaking countries of the New World ‖ **Span·ish-A·mer'i·can** *adj* & *n*

Span'ish fly' *n* **1** bright green beetle (*Cantharis vesicatoria*) of S Europe; **2** powdered preparation made from this beetle and used to raise blisters and as a diuretic and aphrodisiac

Span'ish in'flu·en'za *n* pandemic influenza

Span'ish mack'er·el *n* any of several mackerels, esp. a small-scaled food fish (*Scomberomorus maculatus*) found off the Atlantic coast

Span'ish Main' *n* **1** originally, mainland of northern South America bordering on the Caribbean; **2** Caribbean Sea

Span'ish moss' *n* nonparasitic plant (*Tillandsia usneoides*) of the southern U.S., growing on the branches of trees and hanging in long festoons

Span'ish om'e·let *n* omelet made with tomatoes, onions, and green peppers

Span'ish on'ion *n* large mild onion, often eaten raw

spank /spaŋk/ [imit] *vt* **1** to punish by striking, esp. the buttocks with the open hand ‖ *n* **2** slap or blow given in spanking

spank'er [?] *n naut* fore-and-aft sail attached to the aftermast of a vessel with three or more masts

spank'ing [?] *adj* **1** moving quickly and briskly; **2** *colloq* unusually fine or big ‖ *adv* **3** *colloq* very, as *spanking new*

span·ner /span'ər/ [< *span¹*] *n Brit* wrench

span'-new' *adj* brand-new

spar¹ /spär'/ [OE *spæren* gypsum] *n* any of certain crystalline minerals of definite cleavage and shiny luster

spar² [ME *sparre*] *n* stout round pole; mast, yard, or boom

spar³ [ME] *v* (**sparred**) **spar·ring**) *vi* **1** to box with much feinting and parrying, without striking decisive blows; **2** to engage in a contest of words

spare /sper'/ [OE *sparian*] *vt* **1** to refrain from using severely or with full power, as *don't spare the horses*; **2** to withhold or refrain from, omit, as *spare no expense*; **3** to give or lend without inconvenience, as *can you spare a dime?*; **4** to refuse to injure or punish; treat leniently, be merciful to; **5** to spare left over, that can be spared, as *not a moment to spare* ‖ *adj* **6** lean; **7** scanty; **8** frugal; **9** additional, held in reserve; **10** extra, as *spare cash* ‖ *n* **11** spare thing or part; **12** *bowling* knocking down of all the pins in two tries ‖ SYN *adj* gaunt, lean, meager, lank, bony, thin

spare'rib' [MLG *ribbespēr* rib cut] *n* cut of pork consisting of the ribs with the meat closely trimmed

spar'ing *adj* **1** frugal, economical; **2** limited ‖ **spar'ing·ly** *adv* ‖ SYN frugal, stingy, scant, slight (see *economical*)

spark¹ /spärk/ [OE *spearca*] *n* **1** tiny burning particle thrown off by fire or two hard bodies striking together; **2** any bright small flash of light; **3** small particle or trace; **4** electric discharge across a gap, as in a spark plug; **5** *sparks sg slang* ship's radio operator ‖ *vi* **6** to emit sparks ‖ *vt* **7** *colloq* to stimulate or animate

spark² [?] *vt & vi colloq* to woo

spark' coil' *n* induction coil used to produce the spark in a spark plug

spark' gap' *n* space between two electrodes across which sparks are made to pass, as in a spark plug

spar·kle /spärk'əl/ [< *spark¹*] *vi* **1** to give off sparks; **2** to glisten, flash, twinkle; **3** to be lively; flash with wit; **4** to bubble up, effervesce ‖ *n* **5** flashing; scintillation; **6** bubbling, effervescence ‖ SYN *n* flash, glitter, scintillation (see *light¹*)

spar'kler *n* **1** kind of fireworks that gives off sparks; **2** *colloq* diamond

spar'kling *adj* **1** glittering, flashing; **2** bubbling, effervescing, as wine; **3** brilliant, vivacious

spark' plug' *n* **1** device screwed into the end of each cylinder of an internal-combustion engine, containing two electrodes between which an electric spark jumps that ignites the fuel; **2** *colloq* person who inspires and animates an organization

spar'ring part'ner *n* boxer hired to spar with and help train another boxer

spar·row /spar'ō/ [OE *spearwa*] *n* any of numerous species of small, prolific, and pugnacious gray and brown or black and brown birds of the finch family, found in most parts of the world

spar'row·hawk' *n* any of several small hawks or falcons that prey on small birds, esp. *Accipiter nisus* of the Old World and a small falcon (*Falco sparverius*) of America

sparse /spärs/ [L *sparsus* scattered] *adj* **1** thinly scattered or distributed; **2** scanty, meager

Spar·tan /spärt'ən/ [< *Sparta*, city in Greece noted in ancient times for the toughness and discipline of its inhabitants] *n* person unflinching in courage and endurance ‖ also *adj*

spasm /spaz'əm/ [Gk *spasmos*] *n* **1** sudden involuntary contraction of the muscles; **2** any sudden brief movement, activity, or emotion

spas·mod·ic /spazmod'ik/ *adj* **1** sudden but short-lived; done or acting in fits and starts; **2** pert. to or characterized by spasms ‖ **spas·mod'i·cal·ly** *adv* ‖ SYN fitful, variable, jerky, violent, convulsive, intermittent, unstable, impulsive, transitory

spas·tic /spas'tik/ [Gk *spastikos*] *adj* **1** of or characterized by muscular spasms ‖ *n* **2** person suffering from spasms, esp. those caused by cerebral palsy

spat¹ /spat/ [?] *n* **1** petty quarrel ‖ *v* (**spat·ted**; **spat·ting**) *vi* **2** to engage in a spat

spat² [< *spatterdash* legging] *n* ankle-high legging

spat³ *pt & pp* of **spit**

spate /spāt/ [?] *n* **1** sudden heavy outpouring; **2** large amount; **3** *Brit* **a** heavy downpour; **b** inundation

spa·tial /spāsh'əl/ [< L *spatium* space] *adj* pert. to, taking up, or having existence in space

spat·ter /spat'ər/ [perh < D *spatten* to burst, spout] *vt* **1** to splash a liquid or a wet substance on; **2** to scatter in drops or by splashing ‖ *vi* **3** to scatter or splash in drops ‖ *n* **4** act or sound of spattering; **5** spot or splash made by something splattered

spat'ter·dash' *n* legging reaching up to the knee, worn as protection from mud

spat·u·la /spach'ələ/ [L = broad blade] *n* instrument with a broad flat blade, used for mixing food and drugs, removing foods from cooking utensils, spreading plaster, etc.

spav·in /spav'in/ [OF *espa(r)vain*] *n* disease of horses, marked by a bony deposit in the hock joint and causing lameness ‖ **spav'ined** *adj*

spawn /spôn/ [prob < AF *espaundre* to pour out] *vi* **1** to lay eggs in the water, as fish ‖ *vt* **2** to produce (spawn); **3** to bring forth; give rise to ‖ *n* **4** the eggs of fish, oysters, and other water animals; **5** *contemptuous* numerous offspring

spay /spā/ [AF *espeier* to cut with a sword] *vt* to remove the ovaries of (an animal)

S.P.C.A. Society for the Prevention of Cruelty to Animals

S.P.C.C. Society for the Prevention of Cruelty to Children

speak /spēk/ [OE *sp(r)ecan*] *v* (**spoke** or *archaic* **spake**; **spo·ken**) *vi* **1** to utter words; talk; **2** to make a speech; **3** to convey ideas; signify; **4** **speak for**, **a** to speak in behalf of; **b** to stake a claim to; **5** **speak of** to mention, talk about; **6 speak out** to speak without reserve; **7 speak up** to speak so that one can be heard; **8 speak well for** to testify to the good qualities of; **9 to speak of** worth mentioning, as *he has no money to speak of* || *vt* **10** to utter; **11** to express in words; **12** to converse in (a language)

speak'-eas'y *n* (-ies) place that illegally sells alcoholic drinks

speak'er *n* **1** one who is speaking; **2** one who makes a speech; **3** loudspeaker; **4 Speaker** presiding officer of the lower house of many legislatures, as of the House of Representatives

speak'ing *adj* **1** having the power of speech; **2** vivid, lifelike, as *a speaking likeness*; **3 on speaking terms** casually acquainted; **4 not on speaking terms** estranged because of a quarrel or dislike

spear /spir'/ [OE *spere*] *n* **1** weapon to be thrown or thrust, having a sharp pointed head at the end of a long shaft; **2** slender blade, as of grass || *vt* **3** to pierce or catch with or as with a spear

spear'fish' *vi* to catch fish with a spear

spear'head' *n* **1** pointed head of a spear; **2** person at the forefront, as of an attack or activity || *vt* **3** to act as a spearhead for

spear'mint' *n* pungent spicy herb (*Mentha spicata*), used in flavoring

spe·cial /spesh'əl/ [L *specialis* individual, particular] *adj* **1** distinguishing; **2** designed or formed for a particular purpose; **3** specific; **4** different from others, uncommon; **5** distinctive, exceptional || *n* **6** special person or thing; **7** item on sale at a reduced price; **8** special edition of a newspaper; **9** train run for a special purpose || **spe'cial·ly** *adv*

spe'cial de·liv'er·y *n* delivery of mail by special messenger for an additional fee

spe'cial draw'ing rights' *npl* reserve assets issued as a supplement or substitute for gold through the International Monetary Fund for adjusting the balance of payments among nations

spe'cial ef·fect' *n* imitation of a natural phenomenon, such as lightning, thunder, an earthquake, introduced in a motion-picture, television, or radio scene or episode

spe'cial·ist *n* **1** one who specializes in a particular study, work, or branch of science or medicine; **2** *U.S. Army* private who gets the pay of a noncommissioned officer because of special qualifications

spe'cial·ize' *vi* to concentrate on and be expert in a particular line of study, work, or branch of science or medicine || **spe'cial·i·za'tion** *n*

spe'cial·ty *n* (-ties) **1** study, work, or branch of science or medicine in which one specializes; **2** article dealt in exclusively or receiving particular attention; **3** special quality or feature

spe·cie /spēsh'ē, spēs'ē/ [L (in) *specie* (in) kind] *n* coin; gold or silver money as opposed to paper money

spe·cies /spēsh'ēz, spēs'-/ [L = appearance, kind] *nsg & npl* **1** kind, sort; **2** *biol* major subdivision of a genus, made up of individuals having common inherited characteristics and able to breed only with other members of the same subdivision

spe·cif·ic /spisif'ik/ [ML *specificus*] *adj* **1** of or pert. to a species; **2** specified; definite or particular; **3** of a particular kind; **4** (remedy) curing or arresting a definite disease or condition || *n* **5** something specific; **6** specific remedy

spec·i·fi·ca·tion /spes'ifikāsh'ən/ *n* **1** act of specifying; **2** definite and full statement of particulars; **3 specifications** *pl* **a** detailed statement of requirements for carrying out a construction contract; **b** statement of the dimensions, characteristics, etc., of an appliance or apparatus

spe·cif'ic grav'i·ty *n* relative weight of a given volume of matter as compared with the weight of an equal volume of a standard substance, as water for liquids and solids and air or hydrogen for gases

spec·i·fy /spes'ifī'/ [OF *specifier* < ML *specificare*] *v* (-fied) *vt* **1** to mention or name particularly; state in detail; **2** to state as a condition

spec·i·men /spes'imən/ [L = characteristic mark] *n* **1** sample; **2** part or individual that typifies the whole or all; **3** *colloq* person who typifies some ridiculous or humorous quality || SYN example, instance, sample, pattern, model, illustration || DISCR An *example* is illustrative; a *specimen* is representative; an *instance* is demonstrative. *Example* is general; it can be used for either *specimen* or *instance*. An *example* of a man's workmanship illustrates the type of work he ordinarily does; the Scriptures afford many *examples* of conduct; history furnishes *examples* which should instruct the present. A *specimen* is an *example* that represents a class or whole, as a *specimen* of copper ore; a splendid *specimen* of manhood, generosity, the fighting spirit. We speak of an *example* or *specimen* of workmanship, skill, or type; but of a *specimen* of ore, an *example* of conduct, a *specimen* of the oriole, an *example* of a man's duplicity. An *instance* is an *example* that serves to confirm or prove a certain point. It applies only to actions or proof, and not, as does *ex-*

ample, to the moral or intellectual field as well. We may cite Lincoln as an *example* to be followed; we may prove his good qualities by giving *instances* of his loyalty, his truthfulness, or his charity

spe·cious /spēsh'əs/ [L *speciosus* good-looking, plausible] *adj* appearing good or right at first sight, but not really so ‖ SYN ostensible, apparent (see *plausible*)

speck /spek'/ [OE *specca*] *n* 1 small spot or mark; 2 little bit or particle ‖ *vt* 3 to spot with specks

speck·le /spek'əl/ [ME] *n* 1 small speck or spot of a different color or substance than the thing it is on ‖ *vt* 2 to mark with speckles

speck'led trout' *n* brook trout

specs /speks'/ *npl colloq* 1 spectacles; 2 specifications

spec' sheet' /spek'/ *n colloq* sheet containing the specifications of an appliance or apparatus

spec·ta·cle /spek'təkəl/ [L *spectaculum* show] *n* 1 something striking or impressive displayed to public view; 2 grand exhibition or public show; 3 deplorable public display; 4 **spectacles** *pl* eyeglasses ‖ SYN pageant, exhibition, display, parade, show

spec'ta·cled *adj* 1 wearing spectacles; 2 (animal) marked in such a way as to suggest spectacles

spec·tac'u·lar /-tak'yələr/ *adj* 1 dramatically impressive; thrilling ‖ *n* 2 spectacular display; 3 elaborate television show

spec·ta·tor /spek'tātər, spektāt'ər/ [L] *n* 1 one who looks on, esp. at a public exhibition; 2 observer, witness

spec·ter /spek'tər/ [L *spectrum* image] *n* 1 ghost, apparition; 2 menacing threat ‖ SYN phantom, spirit, shade, ghost, apparition

spec·tral /spek'trəl/ [see **specter**] *adj* 1 pert. to or like a specter; 2 pert. to, produced by, or like a spectrum

spec·tro- /spek'trə-/ *comb form* spectrum

spec'tro·gram' *n* representation of a spectrum

spec'tro·scope' *n* optical instrument for producing and observing spectra of light or other radiation ‖ **spec'tro·scop'ic** /-skop'-/

spec'trum /-trəm/ [L = image] *n* (**-tra** /-trə/ or **-trums**) 1 image in which the constituents of a beam of light or other radiant energy are separated into bands of different waves according to their wavelengths; 2 continuous range of activities, characteristics, values, or objects that are associated in some way

spec·u·late /spek'yəlāt/ [L *speculari* (-*atus*) to spy out, examine] *vi* 1 to meditate, ponder, reflect; 2 to en-

gage in risky business ventures in the hope of making big profits ‖ **spec'u·la'tor** *n* ‖ **spec'u·la'tion** *n* ‖ **spec'u·la'tive** /-lāt'iv, -lətiv/ *adj* ‖ SYN invest, gamble ‖ DISCR To *speculate* is to lay out money in such a way as to assume an economic risk that would exist normally, whereas to *gamble* is to attempt to gain from buying and selling accompanied by wholly unnecessary risks. On the other hand, to *invest* is to lay out money for profit or income without any risk except of a business failure. Money placed in a savings bank or in bonds is an investment. The buying of stocks, except perhaps preferred, is sometimes considered speculation; selling short, a gamble

sped /sped'/ *pt & pp* of **speed**

speech /spēch'/ [OE *sp(r)æc*] *n* 1 the power to speak; 2 act of speaking; 3 manner of speaking; 4 that which is spoken; conversation; 5 language or dialect; 6 formal discourse, oration; 7 field of study devoted to the theory and practice of speaking ‖ SYN address, harangue, oration, discourse, disquisition, sermon ‖ DISCR These words agree in expressing the idea of utterance. *Speech* is the general term for the public utterance of thoughts or sentiments. One may make a formal or an informal *speech;* an *address* is generally set and formal, and carries a grave and dignified connotation. The Gettysburg *Address* exemplifies this usage; we speak of an after-dinner *speech.* An *oration* is formal, elaborate, and not infrequently solemn, since it is delivered, often, on the occasion of some ceremony. The style of an *oration* is polished; an *oration* is always carefully prepared. The *orations* of Cicero have been admired for centuries in their written form. A *harangue* is a noisy, passionate, unrestrained appeal, often polemical and disputatious as well as overardent, as the *speech* proved to be a *harangue* on government ownership. *Discourse* names a set *speech;* a *discourse* is usually full and adequate, and on a definite subject; sometimes it is a treatise intended to give instruction. A *disquisition* is a particularly elaborate *discourse;* it is long, detailed, systematic; often it becomes the statement of an inquiry or investigation. A *sermon* is a *discourse* usually delivered by a clergyman. Any *discourse* or informal talk which is morally uplifting can properly be called a *sermon* (see *language*)

speech' clin'ic *n* clinic where speech disorders are treated

speech'less *adj* 1 struck dumb; 2 silent; 3 incapable of speech ‖ **speech'-**

less·ly *adv* ‖ SYN dumb, silent, mute, inarticulate, still

speed /spēd/ [OE *spēd* success] *n* 1 act or state of moving rapidly; swiftness; 2 rate of motion or progress; velocity; 3 *photog* a sensitivity of an emulsion to light; b duration of the opening of a shutter; c lens aperture; 4 *auto* gear ratio; 5 *slang* amphetamine pills ‖ *v* (**sped** or **speed·ed**) *vi* 6 to move rapidly; 7 to exceed the speed limit; 8 **speed up** to go at a faster pace ‖ *vt* 9 to cause to speed; 10 to expedite; 11 **speed up** to cause to go or run faster ‖ SYN *n* celerity, haste, rapidity, expedition

speed·er *n* driver who exceeds the speed limit

speed·ing *adj* 1 moving with speed ‖ *n* 2 driving at an illegally high speed

speed' lim'it *n* maximum speed permitted by law on certain roads, in certain areas, and under certain weather conditions

speed·om·e·ter /-dom′itər/ *n* device for indicating speed, as the miles per hour that an automobile is traveling and often the distance traveled

speed'ster *n colloq* 1 one who speeds; 2 automobile designed for speed, esp. a sports car

speed' trap' *n* section of road with hidden police ready to spring out at unwary motorists and catch them speeding

speed'up' *n* 1 act or instance of speeding up; 2 increase in production without increase in pay

speed'way' *n* track or course for fast driving or racing

speed'y *adj* (**-i·er; -i·est**) 1 swift; rapid; 2 prompt, without delay ‖ **speed'i·ly** *adv* ‖ **speed'i·ness** *n* ‖ SYN swift, fast, rapid, quick (see *hasty*)

spe·le·ol·o·gy /spēl′ē·ol′əjē/ [< Gk *spelaion* cave] *n* study and exploration of caves ‖ **spe'le·ol'o·gist** *n*

spell[1] /spel/ [OE = recital] *n* 1 incantation; charm; 2 fascination

spell[2] [OF *espeller*] *v* (**spelled** or **spelt**) *vt* 1 to name or write in order the letters of (a word); 2 to form (a word), as *d o g* spells dog; 3 to indicate or mean, as *war spells hardship*; 4 **spell out**, a to read with difficulty; b to explain explicitly step by step ‖ *vi* 5 to spell words; 6 to spell correctly

spell[3] [OE *spelian*] *n* 1 period of work, duty, or activity; 2 any continuous period of time; 3 attack or fit, as *a spell of dizziness* ‖ *v* (**spelled**) *vt* 4 to take the place of (another) for a time

spell'bind' [< *spellbound*] *v* (**-bound**) *vt* to hold as by a spell, fascinate, esp. by oratory ‖ **spell'bind'er** *n*

spell'bound' *adj* fascinated, enchanted

spell'ing *n* 1 the act of spelling; 2 the way words are spelled; orthography

spell'ing bee' *n* spelling contest between individuals or teams

spelt /spelt/ *pt & pp* of **spell**[2]

spe·lunk /spiluŋk′/ [L *spelunca* cave] *vi* to explore caves as a hobby ‖ **spe·lunk'er** *n*

spend /spend/ [OE *aspendan* < L *expendere*] *v* (**spent**) *vt* 1 to pay out, as money; expend in purchases; 2 to squander; use wastefully; 3 to exhaust, use up; 4 to use, consume; 5 to pass (time) ‖ *vi* 6 to spend money, energy, etc. ‖ **spend'er** *n*

spend'thrift' *n* one who is wasteful and extravagant ‖ also *adj*

spent /spent/ 1 *pt & pp* of **spend** ‖ *adj* 2 exhausted; worn out; without energy or force

sperm /spurm′/ [Gk *sperma* seed] *n* 1 semen; 2 spermatozoon

sper·ma·cet·i /spurm′əset′ē, -sēt′ē/ [ML = sperm of the whale] *n* white waxy substance obtained from the oil in a sperm whale's head, used in making ointments and candles

sper·ma·to·zo·on /spurm′ətəzō′ən/ [< Gk *sperma* (-*atos*) sperm + *zoon* living being] *n* (-**zo·a** /-zō′ə/) male germ cell found in semen, which fertilizes the *ovum*

sperm' whale' *n* large whale (*Physeter catodon*) valued for its spermaceti and oil

spew /spyōō′/ [OE *spīwan*] *vt & vi* 1 to throw up from the stomach; vomit; 2 to cast forth, eject ‖ *n* 3 that which is spewed

sphag·num /sfag′nəm/ [< Gk *sphagnos* moss] *n* any of a genus (*Sphagnum*) of mosses found on the surface of bogs

sphere /sfir′/ [Gk *sphaira*] *n* 1 solid round body the surface of which is everywhere equidistant from the center; 2 any similarly shaped body; 3 celestial body; 4 field, extent, or range of control, influence, or the like; 5 surroundings; 6 *astron* celestial sphere ‖ **spher'i·cal** /sfer′-/ *adj*

sphe·roid /sfir′oid/ *n* 1 body that is nearly a sphere in shape; 2 *geom* figure generated by the revolution of an ellipse about one of its axes ‖ also *adj* ‖ **sphe·roi'dal** *adj*

sphinc·ter /sfiŋk′tər/ [Gk] *n* ringlike voluntary or involuntary muscle that surrounds an opening of the body, expanding to open it and contracting to close it

sphinx /sfiŋks′/ [Gk] *n* (**sphinx·es** or **sphin·ges** /sfin′jēz/) 1 reticent and inscrutable person; 2 **Sphinx**, a *Gk myth.* monster at Thebes, Greece, with the head and breast of a woman and the body of a winged lion, who slew passers-by unable to solve the riddle she propounded; b colossal statue near Cairo built by the ancient Egyptians, having the face of a man and the body of a recumbent lion

spice /spīs'/. [OF *espice* < LL *species* spices] *n* 1 any of various aromatic vegetable substances used for seasoning, as cinnamon, nutmeg, and pepper; 2 relish; zest; piquancy ‖ *vt* 3 to season with spices; 4 to give zest to

spick'-and-span' /spik'-/ [< *obs* spick spike + *span*-new brand new] *adj* 1 clean and neat; 2 fresh and new

spic·y /spīs'ē/ *adj* (-i·er; -i·est) 1 flavored with, containing, or having the qualities of spice; 2 fragrant; aromatic; 3 pungent; piquant; 4 racy, risqué ‖ SYN stimulating, lively, pungent (see *piquant*)

spi·der /spīd'ər/ [OE *spīthra*] *n* 1 any of various arachnids (order Araneae), most of which spin webs to catch prey; 2 anything suggestive of a spider in form; 3 *mach* any of various parts having radiating members, esp. if the ends are not connected

spi'der·y *adj* resembling a spider or its web

spiel /spēl/ [G = play] *n* sales talk; pitch ‖ **spiel'er** *n*

spiff·y /spif'ē/ [?] *adj* (-i·er; -i·est) *slang* fine; spruce

spig·ot /spig'ət/ [ME] *n* 1 faucet; 2 plug to stop up the vent in a cask

spike[1] /spīk'/ [ME] *n* 1 fastener resembling a large nail; 2 any sharp point or projection, as on a weapon or on the sole of a shoe to prevent slipping ‖ *vt* 3 to fasten with spikes; 4 to pierce with or impale on a spike; 5 to injure with the spikes of a shoe, as a baseball player; 6 to thwart or frustrate, as a scheme or rumor; 7 to disable (a muzzle-loading cannon) by driving a spike into the touchhole; 8 *colloq* to add liquor to (a drink)

spike[2] [L *spica*] *n* 1 ear of grain; 2 arrangement of flowers on a stalk in which the flowers are attached directly, without stems, along the end of the stalk

spill /spil'/ [OE *spillan* to destroy] *v* (**spilled** or **spilt**) *vt* 1 to cause or permit to run over or fall out of a container, esp. accidentally; 2 to scatter, as papers; 3 to shed (blood); 4 *colloq* to throw, as a rider from his horse; 5 *slang* to disclose or tell ‖ *vi* 6 to be spilled ‖ *n* 7 act of spilling or state of being spilled; 8 throw or tumble, as from a horse or vehicle

spill'way' *n* channel for conveying excess water, as from a reservoir

spilt /spilt'/ *pt & pp* of **spill**

spin /spin'/ [OE *spinnan*] *v* (**spun**; **spin·ning**) *vt* 1 to draw out and twist (various fibers) into thread or yarn; 2 to make (yarn) by drawing out and twisting fibers; 3 to form, as a web or cocoon, by drawing out threads of fluid from a gland, said of spiders, silkworms, etc.; 4 to cause to whirl rapidly, as a top; 5 to relate at length, as a tale or story; 6 **spin off**

com to transfer (some of the activities of a company) to a new and subsidiary company; 7 **spin out** to draw out, protract ‖ *vi* 8 to spin thread or yarn; 9 to form a web or cocoon; 10 to whirl, twirl; 11 to move quickly and easily ‖ *n* 12 act of spinning; 13 spinning motion; 14 sudden downward movement, as of prices; 15 short pleasure drive; 16 tailspin

spin·ach /spin'ich/ [MF *espinache* < Sp < Ar] *n* 1 common garden herb (*Spinacia oleracea*), the leaves of which are boiled and eaten as a vegetable; 2 the leaves

spi·nal /spīn'əl/ [< *spine*] *adj* 1 of or pert. to the spine, the spinal column, or any thornlike structure ‖ *n* 2 spinal anesthetic

spi'nal col'umn *n* the series of jointed vertebrae forming the axis of the skeleton and containing the spinal cord

spi'nal cord' *n* large cord of nervous tissue running lengthwise through the spinal column

spi'nal tap' *n* withdrawal of fluid from the spine for analysis or for injection of an anesthetic

spin·dle /spin'dəl/ [OE *spinel*] *n* 1 long thin rod used for twisting and holding the spun thread in spinning; 2 slender rod or pin on which a part turns or which revolves; axle or shaft; 3 anything very slender or thin; 4 thin pointed rod set point up on a base for attaching papers, cards, etc.; 5 *biol* fine threads bundled like a spindle during mitosis ‖ *vt* 6 to impale (a paper, card, etc.) on a spindle 4 ‖ *vi* 7 to grow into a slender stalk or stem

spin·dly /spind'lē/ *adj* (-dli·er; -dli·est) long and thin

spin'dry' *v* (**-dried**) *vt* to dry by whirling rapidly, as in a washing machine

spine /spīn'/ [L *spina*] *n* 1 stiff pointed growth on a plant or animal, as a thorn or quill; 2 spinal column; 3 stamina, backbone; 4 back of a book cover

spine'less *adj* 1 having no spine or backbone; 2 without courage or the will to resist; 3 without spines

spin·et /spin'it/ [F *espinette* < G. *Spinetti* It inventor] *n* 1 early form of piano resembling a small harpsichord; 2 small upright piano

spin·na·ker /spin'ikər/ [?] *n* large triangular sail, used chiefly by racing vessels running before the wind

spin'ner *n* 1 one who or that which spins; 2 any of various attachments to a fishhook that twirl to attract fish

spin'ner·et' /-et'/ [dim. of *spinner*] *n* silk-spinning organ of silkworms and spiders

spin'ning wheel' *n* domestic machine used for spinning cotton, wool, etc., in which a spindle is turned by a large wheel operated by hand or foot

spin'-off' n 1 com transfer of some of the activities of a company to a subsidiary company for which the original stockholders receive stock of the subsidiary without having to pay income tax; 2 something derived or extracted from a larger entity to continue to have an independent existence

Spi·no·za, Ba·ruch /bərōōk' spinōz'ə/ n (1632–77) Dutch philosopher

spin·ster /spins'tər/ [ME spinnestere female spinner] n woman who remains unmarried beyond the usual age of marriage

spin·y /spīn'ē/ adj (-i·er; -i·est) 1 spinelike; 2 full of thorns or spines; 3 full of difficulty or perplexity

spin'y lob'ster n edible crustacean of the family Palinuridae, resembling the lobster but having a spiny shell and without the large pincers

spi·ral /spīr'əl/ [< Gk speira coil] n 1 geom a plane curve traced by a point moving around a fixed point from which it continually recedes, as in a watch spring; b similar curve traced by a point moving around an axis, and continually receding from a plane cutting the axis, as in the thread of a screw; 2 anything shaped like or resembling a spiral; 3 continuous increase or decrease in prices and costs || adj 4 pert. to or shaped like a spiral || v (-raled or -ralled; -ral·ing or -ral·ling) vi 5 to take a spiral form; 6 to move in a spiral course || vt 7 to cause to spiral

spire /spīr'ər/ [OE spīr stalk] n 1 slender leaf or blade; 2 body that tapers to a point, esp. the tapering top of a tower or steeple; 3 steeple; 4 highest point, pinnacle || vi 5 to shoot up in, or as in, a spire

spir·it /spir'it/ [L spiritus breath] n 1 life; the principle of life regarded as a mysterious entity separable from the body; 2 soul; 3 supernatural being, as a ghost or fairy; 4 person with reference to qualities of mind or temper, as a noble spirit; 5 temper, mood, disposition; 6 enthusiasm for an object, as school spirit; 7 intent, as the spirit of the law; 8 pervading character, as the spirit of the age; 9 pharm alcoholic solution of a volatile substance; 10 **Spirit** Holy Spirit; 11 **spirits** pl a mood or feeling, as high spirits; b distilled alcoholic liquor || vt 12 to carry suddenly and secretly, as he was spirited away by the police

spir'it·ed adj lively, full of vigor || SYN bold, ardent, fiery, vivacious, mettlesome || ANT lifeless, dull, unanimated, dead, heavy

spir'it gum' n glue used by actors to fasten a false beard or mustache to the skin

spir'it lev'el n instrument for determining the true horizontal by centering a bubble in a glass tube filled with alcohol or ether

spir·it·u·al /spir'ichŏŏ·əl/ [ML spiritualis] adj 1 not material; incorporeal; 2 of or pert. to the spirit or soul, not physical; 3 holy, divine; 4 pert. to sacred or religious things; ecclesiastical || n 5 religious song || **spir'it·u·al·ly** adv || **spir'it·u·al'i·ty** /-al'-/ n || **spir'it·u·al·ize'** vt

spir'it·u·al·ism n 1 belief that disembodied spirits communicate with the living, esp. through a medium; 2 doctrine that nothing exists except soul and spirit || **spir'it·u·al·ist** n || **spir'it·u·al·is'tic** adj

spir'it·u·ous adj containing or of the nature of alcohol or distilled alcoholic liquors

spi·ro·chete /spīr'əkēt'/ [< Gk speira coil + chaite hair] n any of several spiral-shaped bacteria, some of which are pathogenic to man

spit¹ /spit'/ [OE spitu] n 1 long pointed rod which is used to hold meat for roasting before an open fire; 2 small point of land, or long narrow shoal, extending out into the sea || v (spit·ted; spit·ting) vt 3 to push a spit through; impale

spit² [OE spittan] v (spit or spat; spit·ting) vt 1 to eject from the mouth; 2 to eject or emit like saliva; 3 to utter in an angry snarl || vi 4 to eject saliva from the mouth; 5 to make a hissing noise like a cat; 6 to rain or snow lightly || n 7 saliva; 8 act of spitting; 9 spit and image exact likeness

spit'ball' n 1 paper chewed into a pellet; 2 baseball ball moistened on one side with saliva by the pitcher to make it curve; now illegal

spit' curl' n tight curl of hair, usu. pressed against the cheeks or the forehead

spite /spīt'/ [abbr of despite] n 1 ill will with the desire to injure; malice; 2 in spite of in defiance of, notwithstanding || vt 3 to treat with spite; try to injure or thwart; 4 to annoy; disappoint || **spite'ful** adj || SYN n bitterness, pique, rancor, malevolence, grudge, enmity (see malice)

spit'fire' n quick-tempered person, esp. a woman

spit'ting im'age n colloq exact likeness

spit·tle /spit'əl/ [OE spætl] n saliva, spit

spit·toon /spitŏŏn'/ [spit² + -oon as in balloon] n bowl-shaped receptacle for spit, ashes, cigar butts, etc.

spitz /spits'/ [G = pointed] n any of several dogs with long silky hair, erect pointed ears, and a bushy tail

splake /splāk'/ [speckled trout + lake trout] n (splake or splakes) Canadian game fish hybrid between brook trout and lake trout

splash /splash'/ [OE plæsc] vt 1 to

spatter with a liquid, mud, etc.; 2 to spatter (a liquid, mud, etc.) on; 3 to cause to appear spattered; 4 to make (one's way) by splashing through something || *vi* 5 to dash or spatter a liquid about; 6 to fall or fly in scattered drops; 7 **splash down** (of a returning space vehicle) to land with a splash in the water || *n* 8 act or sound of splashing; 9 something splashed; 10 spot caused by splashing; 11 irregular spot of color; blotch; 12 **make a splash** *colloq* to make a big show, attract attention || **splash′y** *adj* (**-i·er; -i·est**)

splash′down′ *n* landing of a spacecraft in the water

splat·ter /splat′ər/ [*splash* + *spatter*] *vt* & *vi* to splash, spatter

splay /splā′/ [*abbr* of *display*] *vt* 1 to dislocate; 2 to slope or slant || *vi* 3 to slope or slant; 4 to spread out || *n* 5 surface at an oblique angle to another

splay′foot′ *n* (**-feet**) *n* broad flat foot that turns outward || **splay′foot′ed** *adj*

spleen /splēn′/ *n* 1 ductless glandular organ situated at the left of the stomach, serving to form lymphocytes and to store blood; 2 ill temper, spite; 3 **vent one's spleen** to give vent to one's anger or spite

splen·did /splen′did/ [L *splendidus* brilliant] *adj* 1 magnificent, gorgeous; 2 grand, glorious; 3 fine, excellent || **splen′did·ly** *adv* || SYN majestic, imposing, inspiring, glorious

splen·dor /splen′dər/ [L] *n* 1 brilliance, magnificence; 2 grandeur, glory || **splen′dor·ous** or **splen′drous** *adj* || SYN gorgeousness, magnificence, luster, showiness, parade, sumptuousness, display (see *grandeur*)

sple·net·ic /splinet′ik/ [LL *spleneticus*] *adj* 1 pert. to the spleen; 2 fretful, peevish || SYN morose, spiteful, churlish, sour, crabbed, testy, gruff (see *sullen, gloomy*)

splice /splīs′/ [MD *splissen*] *vt* 1 to unite (the ends of two ropes) by interweaving the ends of the strands; 2 to unite (pieces of wood, film, etc.) by overlapping and fastening the ends together; 3 *slang* to unite in marriage || *n* 4 act or place of splicing

spline /splīn′/ [?] *n* one of the parallel ridges on a shaft fitting into grooves in the hub of a gear, to transmit torque

splint /splint′/ [MD *splinte* metal plate or pin] *n* 1 thin strip of wood for basketwork, chair seats, etc.; 2 thin strip, as of wood, for holding in place an injured part, as a fractured bone

splin·ter /splint′ər/ [MD] *n* 1 sliver broken or split off; 2 faction separated from the main group || *vi* 3 to break off or be broken in splinters

|| *vt* 4 to break into splinters; 5 to split (a group) into small factions

splin′ter group′ *n* dissident element of an organization that separates from the main body

split /split′/ [MD *splitten*] *v* (**split; split·ting**) *vt* 1 to divide or cut lengthwise, as wood with the grain; 2 to rend or tear apart; 3 to divide or break up into parts; 4 to divide, share; 5 to separate, disunite; 6 to divide (each existing share of stock of a company) into two or more new shares, the total value of the new shares having the same value as the old shares before the division || *vi* 7 to break apart; 8 to divide or break lengthwise; 9 to divide or share; 10 often also **split up** to part or separate || *n* 11 act of splitting; 12 rupture; separation; 13 small bottle of wine; 14 performance in which the legs are separated while the body descends to the floor until the legs extend at right angles to the body; 15 *bowling* arrangement of pins after the first bowl in which there is such a gap between them as to make a spare extremely improbable || SYN *v* separate, tear, divide, cut (see *break*)

split′ de·ci′sion *n boxing* nonunanimous decision

split′ in·fin′i·tive *n* infinitive construction in which some qualifier, usu. an adverb, is intercalated between *to* and the verb

split′-lev′el *adj* 1 (house) in which some rooms are about half a story above or below adjacent rooms || *n* 2 such a house

split′ per·son·al′i·ty *n psychol* double consciousness in which an individual lives alternately two separate lives

split′ screen′ *n* motion picture or television screen showing two or more scenes projected simultaneously side by side

split′ sec′ond *n* small fraction of a second

split′ tick′et *n* ballot cast for candidates of more than one party

split′ting *adj* intensely painful, as a headache

split′-up′ *n* splitting or separation; dissociation

splotch /sploch′/ [?] *n* 1 large irregular spot or stain || *vt* 2 to mark with splotches || **splotch′y** *adj* (**-i·er; -i·est**)

splurge /splurj′/ [?] *n* 1 showy display || *vi* 2 to spend money on a luxury or costly pleasure

splut·ter /splut′ər/ [*splash* + *sputter*] *vt* 1 to utter in a quick and incoherent manner || *vi* 2 to speak hastily and confusedly; 3 to make a hissing or sputtering noise || *n* 4 a spluttering noise or talk || **splut′ter·er** *n*

spoil /spoil′/ [MF *espoillier*] *v* (**spoiled** or **spoilt**) *vt* 1 to damage; impair the good qualities of; 2 to overindulge, with harmful effects on character, as *to spoil a child* || *vi* 3 to become bad, tainted, or rotten, as food; 4 be **spoiling for a fight** *colloq* to be eager to fight || *n* 5 usu. **spoils** *pl* a pillage, plunder; **b** public offices and the gain derived from them, appropriated by the successful party in an election || **spoil′er** *n* || **spoil′age** /-ij/ *n* || SYN *v* plunder, injure, impair, destroy, corrupt

spoil′sport′ *n* person whose actions spoil the pleasure of others

spoils′ sys′tem *n* distribution of public offices among the members of the victorious party

spoilt /spoilt′/ *pt & pp* of **spoil**

spoke¹ /spōk′/ *pt* of **speak**

spoke² [OE *spāca*] *n* 1 one of the bars of a wheel connecting the hub with the rim; 2 rung of a ladder

spo·ken /spōk′ən/ 1 *pp* of **speak** || *adj* 2 uttered in speech, oral

-spo′ken *comb form* having a specified kind of voice, as *soft-spoken*

spokes′man /-mən/ *n* (-men /-mən/) one who speaks for another or others

spo·li·ate /spō′lē-āt′/ [L *spoliare* (-*atus*) to spoil] *vt & vi* to rob, plunder || **spo′li·a′tion** *n*

spon·dee /spon′dē/ [<Gk *spondeios*] *n pros* foot of two long syllables or of two stressed syllables || **spon·da′ic** /-dā′ik/ *adj*

sponge /spunj′/ [OE < Gk *spongia*] *n* 1 porous highly elastic mass of horny fibers forming the skeleton of certain invertebrate marine animals (phylum Porifera), which when wet becomes soft and highly absorbent; used in washing and bathing; 2 any porous absorbent substance resembling a sponge; 3 **throw in the sponge** *slang* to give up, admit defeat || *vi* 4 to suck in like a sponge; 5 to gather sponges; 6 **sponge off** or on *colloq* to live at the expense of || *vt* 7 to clean, wipe, or dampen as with a sponge; 8 to obtain by imposing on someone; 9 **sponge off** to wipe off as with a sponge; 10 **sponge up** to soak up as with a sponge || **spon′gy** *adj* (-gi·er; -gi·est)

sponge′ bath′ *n* bath taken by using a wet sponge or cloth without immersing oneself in water

sponge′ cake′ *n* light cake with a spongy texture

spong′er *n* 1 boat engaged in sponging; 2 *colloq* one who lives off others

sponge′ rub′ber *n* foam rubber

spon·sor /spons′ər/ [L] *n* 1 one who is responsible for, endorses, or vouches for a person or thing; 2 godfather or godmother; 3 person or company that buys time on a radio or television show to advertise something || *vt* 4 to be a sponsor of || **spon′sor·ship** *n*

spon·ta·ne·i·ty /spont′ənē′itē/ *n* (-ties) 1 quality or state of being spon-

taneous; 2 **spontaneities** *pl* spontaneous movements or actions

spon·ta·ne·ous /spontän′ē-əs/ [< L *sponte* of one's own accord] *adj* 1 done or acting from natural impulse or desire; 2 produced naturally by internal causes; self-generated; 3 growing naturally, without cultivation || **spon·ta′ne·ous·ly** *adv*

spon·ta′ne·ous com·bus′tion *n* combustion occurring in a body by internal chemical change without the application of external heat

spoof /spoof′/ [name of game invented by A. Roberts (1852–1933) Eng comedian] *vt* 1 to deceive by a hoax; 2 to kid good-humoredly || *vi* 3 to scoff lightly || *n* 4 good-humored satire; 5 hoax

spook /spook′/ [D] *colloq n* 1 ghost || *vt* 2 to haunt; 3 to scare || **spook′y** *adj* (-i·er; -i·est)

spool /spool′/ [MD *spoele*] *n* 1 rimmed cylinder with a hole through the center on which thread, wire, or the like is wound; 2 any similar device || *vt* 3 to wind on a spool

spoon /spoon′/ [OE *spōn* chip] *n* 1 utensil with a small shallow bowl at the end of a handle, used for eating, stirring, serving, etc.; 2 anything resembling a spoon; 3 *golf* wooden club having the face so pitched as to loft the ball || *vt* 4 to take up or out with or as with a spoon || *vi* 5 *colloq* to show love and affection as by kissing and hugging

spoon′er·ism [< W.A. *Spooner* (1844–1930) Eng clergyman] *n* inadvertent interchange of sounds, usu. initial, in two or more words, as in *dickens and chucks*

spoon′-feed′ *v* (-fed) *vt* 1 to feed (someone) with a spoon; 2 to pamper, to coddle; 3 to give (a person) no chance to think or act for himself || **spoon′-fed′** *adj*

spoon′y *adj* (-i·er; -i·est) *colloq* foolishly demonstrative in lovemaking

spoor /spoor′/ [D] *n* track or trail, esp. of a wild animal

spo·rad·ic /spôrad′ik, spōr-/ [Gk *sporadikos* scattered] *adj* 1 occurring here and there in a scattered manner; occasional; 2 single, isolated || **spo·rad′i·cal·ly** *adv* || SYN isolated, rare, occasional, uncommon, separate

spo·ran·gi·um /spôran′jē-əm, spōr-/ [< Gk *spora* seed + *angeion* vessel] *n* (-a /-ə/) sac in which spores in flowerless plants are produced

spore /spôr′, spōr′/ [Gk *spora* seed, sowing] *n* 1 asexual reproductive cell capable of growing into a new plant, as in fungi and many flowerless plants; 2 germ or seed || *vi* 3 to bear or produce spores

spor·ran /spor′ən/ [Gael *sporan*] *n*

large purse, usu. of fur, worn in front of a Scotch Highlander's kilt

sport /spôrt, spōrt/ [contr. of *disport*] *n* **1** pastime, diversion; **2** object of derision; **3** toy or plaything, as *to be a sport of fate*; **4** outdoor play or recreation, as hunting, shooting, etc.; **5** athletic game or activity requiring skill and done in competition; **6** *biol* animal or plant, or part of either, which exhibits a sudden and spontaneous variation from the usual or normal type; **7** *colloq* one interested in sports, esp. a gambler; **8** *colloq* sportsmanlike person; **9 make sport of** to mock, ridicule; **10 in sport** in jest || *adj* **11** of or pert. to sports; **12** for outdoor or casual wear, as *sport clothes, sport shirt* || *vi* **13** to play; frolic; **14** to jest; trifle; **15** to engage in outdoor sports || *vt* **16** *colloq* to show off or wear ostentatiously || SYN *n* pastime, play, frolic, mirth, recreation, diversion (see *game*[1])

sport'ing *adj* **1** of or pert. to sports; **2** sportsmanlike; **3** of or pert. to sports or games involving gambling

sport'ing chance' *n* risk that a good loser is willing to take

sport'ing house' *n colloq* brothel

spor'tive *adj* **1** frolicsome; playful; **2** relating to sports; **3** done in sport || SYN merry, gleeful, playful, mirthful, frolicsome

sports' *adj* sport **11** & **12**

sports' car' *n* small high-powered automobile with two seats

sports'cast' *n* broadcast devoted to a sports event or to giving news of sports || **sports'cast'er**

sports'man /-mən/ *n* (**-men** /-mən/) **1** one who engages in field sports, as hunting, racing, fishing, etc.; **2** one who is fair and honorable in sports and is a good loser and gracious winner || **sports'wom'an** *nfem* || **sports'man-like'** *adj* || **sports'man-ship'** *n*

sports'wear' *n* casual and informal clothing, often worn for such sports as tennis and golf

sports'writ'er *n* newspaperman who writes about sporting events

sport'y *adj* (**-i-er; -i-est**) *colloq* **1** trim and smart; **2** showy, flashy; **3** gay, dissipated

spot /spot/ [ME *spotte* < MD] *n* **1** blot; stain; **2** blemish; flaw; **3** definite locality, place; **4** small portion of a surface different from the rest, as in color, texture, etc.; **5** *cards* one of the conventional designs identifying the suit; **6** pip on a die or domino; **7** *colloq* spotlight; **8** *colloq* a small quantity; **b** drink, as of liquor; **9 hit the spot** to be satisfying; **10 in a spot** *slang* in an uncomfortable predicament; **11 on the spot** *slang* in a position of great difficulty || *v* (**spot·ted; spot·ting**) **12** to mark with spots; **13** to stain; **14** to

mar; **15** to place on a particular spot, as an observer, a billiard ball, etc.; **16** *colloq* to locate or identify; **17** *sports slang* to allow as a handicap || *vi* **18** to become spotted; **19** to make a spot or stain || **spot'ted** *adj*

spot' an·nounce'ment *n* brief television or radio announcement or commercial inserted or spotted by a local station in a network program

spot' cash' *n* ready cash on hand

spot' check' *n* check or investigation made at random and restricted to a few samples or instances || **spot'-check'** *vt* & *vi*

spot'less *adj* **1** without a stain or flaw; **2** blameless, irreproachable; **3** immaculately clean || SYN pure, immaculate, unblemished, unsullied

spot'light' *n* **1** brilliant concentrated light that can be aimed in any direction to illuminate a small area, as at a theatrical performance or mounted on an automobile or ship; **2** publicity; prominence || *vt* **3** to light with a spotlight; **4** to direct attention to

spot' news' *n* late news, reported as it occurs

spot'ter *n* **1** one who watches for enemy planes; **2** one who secretly checks on the honesty and behavior of employees; **3** *mil* forward observer who reports on the accuracy of artillery fire or who spots targets

spot'ty *adj* (**-ti·er, -ti·est**) **1** full of or occurring in spots; **2** uneven in performance or quality || **spot'ti·ness** *n*

spot'-weld' *vt* **1** to weld (two pieces of metal) together in a small spot by applying a high current at low voltage || *n* **2** place so welded

spouse /spouz/, spous'/ [OF *spus* < L *sponsus* betrothed] *n* either one of a married couple

spout /spout'/ [ME *spouten*] *vt* **1** to throw out forcibly in a jet or stream; **2** *colloq* to utter pompously || *vi* **3** to come forth with violence in a jet or stream; **4** *colloq* to speak in a pompous manner || *n* **5** projecting tube, trough, nozzle, or the like through which a liquid is poured; **6** stream or jet of liquid

sprain /sprān/ [?] *vt* **1** to injure (the muscles or ligaments around a joint) by straining, wrenching, or twisting || *n* **2** injury caused by spraining

sprang /sprang/ *pt* of **spring**

sprat /sprat/ [OE *sprott*] *n* small herringlike European fish (*Clupea sprattus*)

sprawl /sprôl'/ [OE *spreawlian*] *vi* **1** to lie or sit with the body and limbs awkwardly stretched out; **2** to spread in an irregular straggling manner, as a plant, buildings, or handwriting || *vt* **3** to cause to sprawl || *n* **4** sprawling position; **5** irregular straggling array

spray[1] /sprā′/ [ME] *n* **1** small branch of a tree or plant bearing leaves or flowers; **2** slender graceful sprig of flowers or foliage

spray[2] [MD *spraeien*] *n* **1** water or other liquid driven in small particles by wind, dashing of waves, etc.; **2** jet of liquid particles emitted by an atomizer or spray gun, as paint, perfume, insecticide, etc.; **3** spray gun or atomizer || *vt* **4** to apply a spray to; **5** to scatter in fine drops || *vi* **6** to discharge a spray; **7** to break up into a spray || **spray′er** *n*

spray′ gun′ *n* device for spraying liquids by means of air pressure from a pump

spread /spred′/ *v* (**spread** /spred′/) *vt* **1** to cause to cover a surface, as *to spread butter on bread;* **2** to cover with a thin layer, as *to spread bread with butter;* **3** to divulge, circulate; **4** to unfold, open, stretch out, as leaves, wings, a map on a table, etc.; **5** to diffuse, emit; **6** to disseminate, as a disease; **7** to display, exhibit, as *to spread out goods;* **8** to set (a table); **9** to push apart (rails, the arms, etc.); **10** to distribute about, as hay; **11** to flatten, as the end of a rivet; **12** **spread oneself thin** to dissipate one's effectiveness by trying to do too many things simultaneously || *vi* **13** to extend over a large area; expand; **14** to be dispersed, scattered, or distributed; **15** to become circulated or widely known; **16** to be propagated; **17** to diffuse; **18** to be forced apart; **19** to lie displayed, as a scene; **20** to admit of being spread, as *cold butter doesn't spread easily* || *n* **21** act or extent of spreading; **22** extent, expanse; **23** covering for a bed, table, etc.; **24** *colloq* table set with abundant food; feast; **25** any substance used to spread on bread; **26** *stock market* difference between the bid and asked price of a security or commodity || **spread′er** *n* || SYN *v* disperse, disseminate, publish, circulate

spread′-ea′gle *vt* **1** to stretch (something) out in the form of an eagle with its wings spread || *vi* **2** to assume this position

spree /sprē′/ [?] *n* **1** merry frolic; **2** drinking bout; **3** period or bout of overindulgence or great activity

sprig /sprig′/ [ME *sprigge*] *n* **1** small twig or shoot of a tree or plant; spray; **2** youth; scion

spright·ly /sprīt′lē/ [< *spright* var of *sprite*] *adj* (-**·l·er;** -**·l·est**) brisk, animated, gay || also *adv* || SYN vivacious, spirited, lively (see *cheerful*)

spring /spring′/ [OE *springan*] *v* (**sprang** or **sprung; sprung**) *vi* **1** to leap, bound; dart; **2** to arise or appear suddenly; **3** to escape from or

as from restraint; recoil, rebound; **4** to become warped or bent; **5** to issue, proceed; **6** **spring up** to rise, come into being || *vt* **7** to cause to spring; **8** to reveal or produce unexpectedly, as a joke or surprise; **9** to cause to snap closed, as a trap; **10** to cause to warp or crack; **11** to cause by springing, as *to spring a leak;* **12** *slang* to obtain the release of, as from jail; **13** to leap over || *n* **14** leap, bound; **15** elastic contrivance that returns to its original shape after being bent or compressed; **16** elasticity; resilience; **17** recoil; **18** origin, source; **19** natural supply of water rising to the surface of the earth; **20** season when plants begin to grow; in the Northern Hemisphere from March 21 to June 22; **21** first and freshest period || *adj* **22** of or pert. to spring or springtime

spring′board′ *n* **1** flexible springy board used to give impetus to acrobats in leaping or to swimmers in diving; **2** point of departure to a better state or condition

spring′ chick′en *n* **1** young chicken that yields tender meat; **2** **no spring chicken** *colloq* not young any more

spring′ fe′ver *n* listless feeling experienced with the coming of spring

spring′-load′ed *adj* (machine part, trunk lid, etc.) held to a certain position by a spring

spring′ tide′ *n* highest high tide of the month, occurring at the time of the full and the new moon

spring′time′ also **spring′tide′** *n* **1** spring season; **2** earliest season; youth

spring′y *adj* (-**·i·er;** -**·i·est**) elastic, resilient || **spring′i·ness** *n*

sprin·kle /spring′kəl/ [D *sprenkelen*] *vt* **1** to scatter in small drops or particles; **2** to cover with small drops or particles || *vi* **3** to rain lightly; **4** to scatter something so that it falls in small particles || *n* **5** act or instance of sprinkling; **6** that which is sprinkled; **7** light rain; **8** small quantity

sprin′kler *n* **1** device for sprinkling; **2** one of a system of valves connected to water pipes in or near the ceiling that open to sprinkle water if the temperature rises to a predetermined point

sprin′kling *n* **1** small quantity, as of drops or particles, sprinkled about; **2** small number found here and there; **3** small amount, as of knowledge

sprint /sprint′/ [< Scand] *n* **1** short run at full speed || *vi* **2** to run at full speed || *vt* **3** to run (a specified distance) at full speed || **sprint′er** *n*

sprite /sprīt′/ [OF *esprit* spirit] *n* elf, goblin, fairy

sprock·et /sprok′it/ [?] *n* **1** any of the

teeth, as on the outer rim of a wheel, that engage with the links of a drive chain; 2 also **sprock′et wheel′** wheel having such teeth

sprout /sprout′/ [OE *sprūtan*] *vi* 1 to begin to grow or develop; 2 to put forth shoots ‖ *vt* 3 to cause to sprout; 4 to remove the sprouts from ‖ *n* 5 new shoot; bud; 6 **sprouts** *pl* Brussels sprouts

spruce /sproos′/ [ME < OF *Pruce* Prussia] *n* 1 any of a genus (*Picea*) of evergreen trees of the pine family, bearing pendulous cones and needle-shaped leaves; 2 any of various related trees, as the hemlock ‖ *adj* 3 smart, trim, neat ‖ *vt* 4 **spruce up** to make spruce ‖ *vi* 5 **spruce up** to become spruce

sprung /sprung′/ *pt & pp* of **spring**

spry /sprī′/ [?] *adj* (spri·er or spry·er; spri·est or spry·est) nimble, active, agile

spud /spud′/ [ME *spuddle* dagger] *n* 1 *colloq* potato; 2 sharp, narrow spade, esp. for digging up large-rooted weeds

spume /spyoom′/ [L *spuma*] *n* froth, foam; scum

spu·mo·ne or **spu·mo·ni** /spəmōn′ē/ [It] *n* smooth-textured Italian ice cream in layers of different colors, usu. containing chopped fruits and/or nuts

spun /spun′/ *pt & pp* of **spin**

spunk /spunk′/ [prob Gael *spong* tinder] *n colloq* mettle; spirit; pluck ‖ **spunk′y** *adj* (-i·er; -i·est)

spur /spur′/ [OE *spura*] *n* 1 rowel, or blunt or sharp projection, worn on the heel of a horseman to urge the horse on; 2 anything that urges to action; stimulus; 3 any spurlike projection; 4 projecting ridge extending laterally from a mountain range; 5 sharp spine, as on the legs of a rooster; 6 sharp metallic point fastened to the spur of a gamecock's leg; 7 short railroad track branching from the main track; 8 **on the spur of the moment** abruptly on an impulse; 9 **win one's spurs** to prove one's worth ‖ *v* (spurred; spur·ring) *vt* 10 to prick with a spur; 11 to incite, goad ‖ *vi* 12 to urge a horse on with spurs; 13 to hasten or press onward ‖ **spurred** *adj* ‖ SYN *v* excite, stimulate, urge, goad, incite

spurge /spurj′/ [MF *espurge*] *n* any of a large genus (*Euphorbia*) of flowering plants, mostly shrubby, many of which secrete a bitter milky juice

spu·ri·ous /spyoor′ē-əs/ [< L *spurius*] *adj* 1 not genuine; not as claimed; counterfeit; 2 illegitimate ‖ SYN bogus, fraudulent, sham (see *artificial*)

spurn /spurn′/ [OE *spurnan*] *vt* 1 to reject with scorn; 2 to treat with disdain or contempt

spurt /spurt′/ [OE *spryttan* to sprout] *vi* 1 to gush forth suddenly in a stream or jet; 2 to exhibit a burst of speed or energy ‖ *vt* 3 to throw out, as a liquid, in a stream or jet ‖ *n* 4 sudden forcible outpouring of liquid

sput·nik /spoot′nik, sput′-/ [Russ = fellow traveler] *n* any of the satellites launched into earth orbit by Russia, esp. the first 1957

sput·ter /sput′ər/ [perh < D *sputteren*] *vi* 1 to emit particles explosively, as sparks, hot fat, etc.; 2 to spit scattered drops of saliva, as in rapid or excited speech; 3 to utter words rapidly and incoherently ‖ *vt* 4 to emit or utter sputteringly ‖ *n* 5 act or sound of sputtering ‖ **sput′ter·er** *n*

spu·tum /spyoot′əm/ [L] *n* (-ta /-ta /-tə/) 1 saliva, spittle; 2 any expectorated matter

spy /spī′/ [OF *espier*] *n* (spies) 1 one who keeps secret watch on the doings of others; 2 one employed by a government to ferret out secret information in another country, esp. on military affairs ‖ *v* (spied) *vt* 3 to gain sight of, espy; 4 to discover by looking carefully; detect; 5 **spy out** to examine or explore secretly ‖ *vi* 6 to act as a spy; 7 **spy on** or **upon** to observe closely and secretly

spy′glass′ *n* small telescope

sq., Sq. square

squab /skwob′/ [< Scand] *n* nestling pigeon

squab·ble /skwob′əl/ [< Scand] *vi* 1 to wrangle, dispute noisily ‖ *n* 2 wrangle, dispute

squad /skwod′/ [F *esquadre* < It *squadra* square] *n* 1 any small group of persons engaged in a common effort; 2 smallest organized army unit, generally ten men or less headed by a corporal

squad′ car′ *n* police car connected by shortwave with headquarters

squad·ron /skwod′rən/ [It *squadrone* band of men] *n* 1 subdivision of a cavalry regiment; 2 subdivision of a fleet; 3 basic tactical unit of the Air Force

squal·id /skwol′id/ [L *squalidus*] *adj* 1 extremely dirty through neglect; 2 wretched, foul

squall¹ /skwôl′/ [perh < *squall²*] *n* 1 sudden and violent gust of wind, often accompanied by rain, sleet, or snow; 2 sudden trouble or danger ‖ *vi* 3 to blow as a squall ‖ **squall′y** *adj* (-i·er; -i·est)

squall² /skwôl′/ [< Scand] *vi* 1 to scream or cry out violently ‖ *vt* 2 to utter with squalls ‖ *n* 3 act or sound of squalling

squal·or /skwol′ər/ [L] *n* 1 wretched and filthy condition; 2 foulness, dirt

squan·der /skwon′dər/ [?] *vt* to spend prodigally; lavish; waste

square /skwer'/ [OF *esquarre*] n 1 equilateral rectangle; 2 anything of, or resembling, this form; 3 city block; 4 open area, as formed by two or more intersecting streets, often used as a small park; 5 any of various instruments used for measuring or laying out right angles; 6 math product obtained by multiplying a number or quantity by itself; 7 slang conventional, conservative, unsophisticated person; 8 **on the square** colloq just; honest; 9 **out of square** not at right angles || vt 10 to form into a square; 11 to form into a right angle, cause to make a right angle with something else; 12 to push (the shoulders) back; 13 to balance, pay off, as *to square accounts;* 14 to even the score of; 15 to cause to conform to a given standard; adjust to a given measure; 16 math to multiply (a number or quantity) by itself; b to determine or express the area of in square measure; 17 to make straight or even; 18 slang a to influence; bribe; b to adjust (a matter), as by influence or bribery; 19 **square off** to cut or reduce to a square or rectangular form || vi 20 **square off** to assume a boxing attitude, as for a fist fight; 21 **square up** to settle a bill; 22 **square with** to accord or agree with || adj 23 having four equal sides and four right angles; 24 approximating a square in form; 25 forming a right angle; rectangular; 26 perpendicular; 27 thickset (build); 28 upright, honest; just; 29 straightforward; direct; 30 stated in terms of square measure; 31 colloq full or satisfying (meal); 32 slang conventional, conservative || adv 33 squarely

square' dance' n dance consisting of a series of set figures or steps for an even number of couples

square' deal' n colloq fair and just treatment

square' knot' n common knot, used for tying the ends of two ropes together

square'ly adv 1 in a square manner; 2 directly; 3 fairly

square'-rigged' adj (ship) having square sails stretched along yards suspended horizontally at the middle || **square'-rig'ger** n

square' root' n quantity of which a given quantity is the square

square' sail' n four-sided sail set on a yard suspended horizontally across the mast

square' shoot'er n colloq straight shooter

squash¹ /skwosh'/ [< AmInd askuta-*squash*] n 1 edible fruit of any of various plants (genus *Cucurbita*); 2 plant bearing such fruit

squash² [MF *esquasser*] vt 1 to crush or squeeze into a flat mass or pulp;

2 to quash, suppress; 3 colloq to silence (a person) by a crushing argument or retort || vi 4 to be crushed into a mass or pulp; 5 to make a splashing sound || n 6 act or sound of squashing; 7 crushed object or mass; 8 game played in a walled court with a racket and ball || **squash'y** adj (-i·er; -i·est)

squat /skwot'/ [OF *esquatir* to flatten] v (squat·ted or squat; squat·ting) vi 1 to crouch or sit on the hams or heels; 2 to crouch, cower, as a rabbit; 3 to settle on public land under government lease; 4 to settle on land without right or permission || vt 5 to cause to squat || adj 6 short and thickset || n 7 squatting position

squat'ter n 1 one who settles on land without right or permission; 2 one who settles on land under government regulation with a view to gaining title to it

squat'ter's right' n right to acquire legal title to land which one has openly and continuously occupied for a certain number of years

squaw /skwô'/ [< AmInd] n 1 North American Indian woman or wife; 2 any girl or woman

squawk /skwôk'/ [?] n 1 loud harsh cry; 2 loud complaint || vi 3 to utter a squawk; 4 to complain loudly || **squawk'er** n

squeak /skwēk'/ [ME *squeken*] n 1 sharp, shrill, high-pitched sound; 2 **narrow** or **close squeak** colloq narrow escape || vi 3 to utter or emit a squeak; 4 **squeak by** or **through** to succeed or attain a goal by the narrowest of margins || vt 5 to utter with a squeak || **squeak'y** adj (-i·er; -i·est)

squeal /skwēl'/ [ME *squelen*] vi 1 to utter a shrill, prolonged cry; 2 slang to turn informer || vt 3 to utter with a squeal || n 4 shrill, prolonged cry || **squeal'er** n

squeam·ish /skwēm'ish/ [ME *squem-ish*] adj 1 easily nauseated; 2 excessively prudish; 3 fastidious, particular || **squeam'ish·ness** n || SYN fastidious, scrupulous, finical, queasy, sickish

squee·gee /skwē'jē/ [perh related to *squeeze*] n 1 tool with a cross piece edged with rubber for removing water from a flat surface; 2 similar device with a rubber roller for pressing the water from photographic prints || vt 3 to press or scrape with a squeegee

squeeze /skwēz'/ [< OE *cwȳsan*] vt 1 to press, compress; 2 to extract by pressure, as juice; 3 to force into place by pressure; 4 to oppress, burden; 5 to hug, embrace; 6 baseball to cause (a runner on third base) to score by executing a squeeze play || vi 7 to press, push, as *to squeeze* *through a crowd*; **8** to exert pressure ‖ *n* **9** pressure; crush, jam; **10** act of squeezing; **11** hug, embrace; **12** *colloq* threat, intimidation, coercion

squeeze′ bot′tle *n* soft plastic container the contents of which can be squeezed out

squeeze′ play′ *n* **1** *baseball* hit-and-run play executed or attempted with the runner on third base; **2** in bridge, a play that forces an opponent to discard a card that might have taken a trick; **3** pressure brought to bear in order to force an issue

squeez′er *n* utensil for squeezing juice from fruit or vegetables

squelch /skwelch′/ [prob imit] *vt* **1** to crush, suppress, or silence completely, as by a crushing retort ‖ *n* **2** act of squelching; **3** crushing retort

squib /skwib′/ [?] *n* **1** firecracker that burns with a hissing noise, ending with a slight explosion or none at all; **2** witty or sarcastic lampoon; **3** short news item, used as a column filler

squid /skwid′/ [?] *n* any of various marine cephalopod mollusks, of the genera *Loligo, Ommastrephes*, and others, having a cigar-shaped body and ten arms, varying in length from four inches to 80 feet

squint /skwint′/ [D *schuinte* slant] *n* **1** act of squinting; **2** sidelong stealthy glance; **3** condition characterized by crossed eyes; **4** *colloq* look, glance ‖ *vi* **5** to see or look obliquely; **6** to look with eyes half closed; **7** to be cross-eyed ‖ *vt* **8** to cause to look obliquely; **9** to half close (the eyes)

squint′-eyed′ *adj* **1** cross-eyed; **2** with squinting eyes; **3** prejudiced; malignant

squire /skwī′ər/ [*abbr* of *esquire*] *n* **1** formerly, a young man of noble birth attendant upon a knight; **2** English landowner, esp. the chief landed proprietor of a district; **3** justice of the peace or local judge; **4** lady′s escort ‖ *vt* **5** to attend or serve as a squire; **6** to escort (a lady)

squirm /skwurm′/ [?] *vi* **1** to wriggle, writhe; **2** to show embarrassment or chagrin

squir·rel /skwur′əl/ [AF *escuirel*] *n* **1** any of various small bushy-tailed arboreal rodents (family Sciuridae) feeding on grains or nuts; **2** its fur ‖ *vt* **3** squirrel away to hoard

squir′rel·ly *adj* *slang* peculiar, eccentric

squirt /skwurt′/ [ME *squirten*] *vi* **1** to shoot out in a jet; spurt; **2** to eject liquid in a jet ‖ *vt* **3** to cause to squirt; **4** to wet by squirting ‖ *n* **5** act of squirting; **6** small stream or jet squirted forth; **7** *colloq* small, insignificant but conceited person

Sr *chem* strontium

Sr. senior

Sri Lan·ka /srēlän′kə/ *n* (Ceylon) island republic off the southern coast of India (11,491,000; 25,332 sq.mi.; cap. Colombo); member of the British Commonwealth

S.R.O. standing room only

SS, S.S. steamship

SS. Saints

SSR, S.S.R. Soviet Socialist Republic

St. **1** Saint; **2** Street; **3** Strait

stab /stab′/ [ME] *v* (**stabbed; stabbing**) *vt* **1** to pierce or wound with or as with a pointed weapon; **2** to thrust or plunge (a pointed weapon); **3** to wound, as a person′s feelings or conscience ‖ *vi* **4** to pierce something with or as with a pointed weapon ‖ *n* **5** thrust with a sharp-pointed weapon; **6** wound so made; **7** *colloq* attempt; **8** sharp pain; **9** stab in the back *colloq* treacherous act

sta·bil·i·ty /stəbil′itē/ [L *stabilitas*] *n* **1** state or quality of being stable; **2** firmness; **3** permanence; **4** firmness of character; steadiness

sta·bi·lize /stāb′əliz/ *vt* **1** to make stable or firm ‖ **sta′bi·li·za′tion** *n*

sta′bi·liz′er *n* **1** any of various devices for maintaining the equilibrium of an airplane; **2** gyroscopically controlled fin used to keep ships from rolling in a heavy sea; **3** constituent added to an explosive to reduce its liability to spontaneous decomposition; **4** any of various substances added to goods, chemicals, paint, etc., to prevent deterioration

sta·ble¹ /stāb′əl/ [OF *estable* < L *stabilis*] *adj* **1** firmly established; **2** having permanence; not easily moved or changed; **3** firm in purpose; steadfast; **4** *chem* **a** (element) not readily reacting; **b** (compound) not easily decomposed; **5** *mech* (body) tending to return to its original position ‖ **sta′bly** *adv* ‖ SYN inflexible, steady, steadfast (see *firm*)

sta·ble² [OF *estable* < L *stabulum*] *n* **1** building in which horses, cows, etc., are housed; **2** the race horses belonging to a particular owner ‖ *vt* **3** to put or keep in a stable ‖ *vi* **4** to be lodged in a stable

stac·ca·to /stəkät′ō/ [It = separated] *adj* **1** abrupt, discontinuous; **2** *mus* sharp, crisp (notes), not legato ‖ *n* (**-tos** or **-ti** /-tē/) **3** *mus* staccato performance; **4** something abrupt and discontinuous ‖ *adv* **5** in a staccato manner

stack /stak′/ [ON *stakkr* haystack] *n* **1** orderly pile or heap, as of hay, books, etc.; **2** smokestack; **3** rack with shelves for books; **4** *colloq* large amount or number; **5** blow one′s stack *slang* to lose one′s temper ‖ *vt* **6** to arrange in a stack; **7** to keep (airplanes) flying in a circle above an airport at various altitudes waiting their turn to land; **8** *colloq* to load unfairly with biased people, as an investigating committee or jury; **9 stack the deck** or **cards,** a to secretly arrange the cards so as to cheat; b to rig things unfairly || vi **10 stack up** slang a to be plausible, square with the facts; b to compare

stacked' adj **to be stacked** slang to have a voluptuous figure

sta·di·um /stād'ē·əm/ [L < Gk stadion] n (-ums or -a /-ə/) 1 ancient Greek linear measure equal to about 600 feet; 2 outdoor sports arena usu. oval or horseshoe-shaped, with tiers of seats for the spectators

staff /staf', stäf'/ [OE stæf] n 1 body of assistants to a manager or executive; 2 specific group of workers; 3 mil body of officers assisting a commander in his executive and administrative duties || n (**staffs** or **staves** /stāvz'/) 4 stick carried for support in walking or climbing, as a weapon, or as an emblem of authority; 5 shaft or pole serving as a support, as for a flag; 6 mus set of five lines and four spaces on which the notes are written || vt 7 to provide with a staff of workers or assistants || adj 8 full-time auxiliary or organizational (work or personnel)

staff' of life' n bread

staff' ser'geant n noncommissioned officer in the Army, Marines, or Air Force, ranking above a sergeant

stag /stag'/ [ME stagge] n 1 adult male deer; 2 colloq man who does not escort a lady at a social function || adj 3 for men only, as a stag dinner || adv 4 **go stag** to attend a social function as a stag

stage /stāj'/ [OF estage] n 1 raised platform, as in a theater, for a play or spectacle, for public speakers or performers, etc.; 2 place or field of action; 3 place of rest on a journey; station; 4 distance between any two stations; 5 point or period of development, as the first stage of a disease, an insect's larval stage; 6 stagecoach; 7 section of an outer-space rocket containing engines and propellant, which usu. separates from other similar sections when its fuel is exhausted; 8 electron part of an amplifier, of which the principal element is a tube or transistor, which provides a step in the radio-frequency, intermediate-frequency, or audio-frequency amplification of a signal; 9 **the stage** the theater, the theatrical profession || vt 10 to represent as on a stage; 11 to plan and carry out

stage'coach' n horse-drawn conveyance traveling on a regular route with passengers, mail, and freight

stage'craft' n art or skill in the writing and staging of plays

staged' adj contrived

stage' fright' n extreme nervousness

felt by an inexperienced speaker or performer before an audience

stage'hand' n person employed to set up and change scenery, lighting, etc., on a stage

stage'-man'age vt to arrange or stage (some event) to produce a particular effect

stage' pres'ence n self-assured bearing of an actor or speaker before an audience

stage'-struck' adj 1 being an eager fan of all things theatrical; 2 intensely desirous of a theatrical career

stage' whis'per n loud whisper uttered by an actor, meant to be heard by the audience but supposedly not heard by the other actors on the stage

stag·fla·tion /stagflāsh'ən/ [stagnation + inflation] n steady rise in the cost of living accompanied by a decline in business and employment

stag·ger /stag'ər/ [ON stakra to push continuously] vi 1 to totter, reel; 2 to waver, hesitate || vt 3 to cause to totter or reel; 4 to shock, astonish; 5 to cause to doubt or waver; 6 to set in zigzag order on either side of a central line; 7 to spread (times of arrival or departure, lunch periods, etc.) so as to prevent crowding || n 8 reeling or tottering motion; 9 staggered arrangement; 10 **staggers** sg disease of horses and cattle marked by staggering and falling

stag'ing n 1 scaffolding; 2 act or art of putting plays on stage; 3 concentration of troops or supplies for transport

stag·nant /stag'nənt/ [L stagnans (-antis)] adj 1 not flowing; 2 stale or foul from long standing, as water; 3 inactive; dull, sluggish

stag·nate /stag'nāt/ [L stagnare (-atus)] vi to be or become stagnant || **stag·na'tion** n

stag·y /stāj'ē/ adj (-i·er; -i·est) 1 theatrical in manner; 2 appearing staged; not natural

staid /stād'/ [archaic pt & pp of stay] adj sober, sedate || **staid'ly** adv || SYN grave, decorous, settled, composed, sedate

stain /stān'/ [ME steinen] vt 1 to blot or spot; 2 to corrupt, tarnish; 3 to color or dye with something that penetrates, or that combines with, the substance colored || vi 4 to take or make a stain || n 5 discoloration, spot, or blot; 6 cause for reproach; taint; 7 dye

stained' glass' n window glass pigmented by the fusion into it of certain metallic oxides || **stained'-glass'** adj

stain'less steel' n steel made highly resistant to rust or chemical action by alloying it with chromium

stair /ster'/ [OE stæger] n 1 any one

of a set of steps connecting different levels; **2 stairs** usu. *pl* flight of steps

stair'case' *n* flight of steps with handrail, banisters, etc.

stair'way' *n* **1** flight of steps; **2** staircase

stair'well' *n* vertical shaft inside a building containing a stairway

stake /stāk/ [OE *staca*] *n* **1** pointed post or stick driven in the ground as a marker, support, etc.; **2** post to which a condemned person was tied for burning; **3** one of a number of vertical posts at the edge of the platform of a vehicle to retain loads; **4** investment or share in something; **5** often **stakes** *pl* **a** that which is wagered on a game or contest; **b** prize offered in a contest; **6 at stake** involved; in danger of being lost; **7 pull up stakes** *colloq* to move one's domicile or business || *vt* **8** to wager, bet; **9** *colloq* to furnish with capital or supplies; **10 stake out, a** to mark the boundaries of; **b** to claim or reserve for oneself; **c** *colloq* to place (a suspect or hideout) under surveillance; **d** *colloq* to station (police) to maintain constant watch

stake'out' *n colloq* surveillance of a place by the police watching for a suspect or in anticipation of a crime

sta·lac·tite /stəlak'tīt/ [< Gk *stalaktos* dripping] *n* iciclelike formation of carbonate of lime hanging from the roof of a cave, caused by dripping water containing the mineral

sta·lag·mite /stəlag'mīt/ [< Gk *stalagma* drop] *n* cone of carbonate of lime on the floor of a cave, formed usu. under a stalactite and often uniting with it

stale /stāl/ [ME] *adj* **1** not fresh; flat, tasteless; dry and hard; **2** worn out by use or familiarity; trite; **3** having vigor or ability impaired from prolonged activity or from surfeit || *vt* **4** to make stale || *vi* **5** to become stale

stale'mate' *n* **1** *chess* situation in which the only moves possible will place one's king in check, resulting in a draw; **2** any deadlock || *vt* **3** to subject to a stalemate

Sta·lin, Jo·seph V. /stäl'in, -ēn/ *n* (1879–1953) Russian leader in the Revolution and premier of the U.S.S.R. 1941–53

stalk¹ /stôk/ [ME *stalke* < OE *stæla*] *n* **1** stem of a plant; **2** any stem or part resembling this

stalk² [OE *bestealcian*] *vt* **1** to approach (game or a quarry) stealthily || *vi* **2** to stalk game or a quarry; **3** to walk in a stiff and haughty manner || *n* **4** act of stalking; **5** stiff and haughty stride

stalk'ing-horse' *n* **1** horse or figure of a horse behind which a hunter conceals himself; **2** pretense; blind; **3** candidate put forward to conceal the candidacy of a more important candidate or to divide and defeat the opposition

stall /stôl/ [OE *steall*] *n* **1** stable; **2** enclosed space in a stable for one animal; **3** any marked-off space, as for cars; **4** booth where goods are sold; **5** *Brit* orchestra seat in a theater; **6** *colloq* evasion; **7** unintentional stopping of an engine or vehicle || *vt* **8** to place or keep in a stall; **9** to cause to stick fast, as in mud; **10** to cause (an engine or vehicle) to stop unintentionally; **11** also **stall off** to put off, delay, as by evasion or pretexts || *vi* **12** to stick fast, as in mud; **13** to be stalled, as an engine or vehicle

stal·lion /stal'yən/ [OF *estalon*] *n* adult male horse

stal·wart /stôl'wərt/ [OE *stælwirthe* serviceable] *adj* **1** sturdy, strong; **2** brave, daring; **3** firm, steadfast || *n* **4** firm, loyal partisan

sta·men /stām'ən/ [L = warp in an upright loom] *n* pollen-bearing part of a flower, consisting of the filament and the anther

stam·i·na /stam'inə/ [L = threads] *n* strength or staying power; power of endurance

stam·mer /stam'ər/ [OE *stamerian*] *vt* **1** to speak with spasmodic breaks and repetitions || *vt* **2** to utter with a stammer || *n* **3** stammering speech; **4** stammered utterance

stamp /stamp/ [ME *stampen* to stamp the foot] *vt* **1** to mark, as a coin, with a figure or design by means of a die; **2** to put a postage or other official stamp on; **3** to label, brand, characterize; **4** to imprint, impress; **5** to shape or cut out as with a die or stamp; **6** to set (the foot) down loudly and heavily; **7** to beat with the bottom of the foot; **8** to crush or grind as with a pestle; **9** to grind into powder, as ore; **10 stamp out** to destroy or end, as if by stamping with the foot || *vi* **11** to strike or beat the foot forcibly downward || *n* **12** act or instance of stamping; **13** impression, pattern, device, or special mark imprinted upon a surface; **14** engraved block or die for making such impressions or imprints; **15** machine for crushing ore; **16** postage stamp; **17** official mark indicating validity, payment of a fee, etc.; **18** trading stamp; **19** sanction, authority; **20** characteristic quality or nature; **21** sort, kind, brand

stam·pede /stampēd'/ [Sp *estampida*] *n* **1** sudden panicky headlong flight of a herd of animals; **2** any disorganized flight or rush || *vt* **3** to cause to stampede; **4** to rush or overrun || *vi* **5** to start off in a panic; **6** to act together from a sudden impulse

stamp'ing ground' *n colloq* favorite haunt

stance /stans'/ [F < It *stanza* position] *n* 1 posture, position of the body; 2 intellectual or emotional attitude; 3 *golf* position of a player's feet

stanch[1] /stônch', stanch', stänch'/ [OF *estanchier*] *vt* 1 to stop the flow of, as blood; 2 to stop a flowing from, as a wound || *vi* 3 to stop flowing

stanch[2] *adj* var of **staunch**[2]

stan·chion /stansh'ən/ [OF *estanchon*] *n* upright supporting post or bar

stand /stand'/ [OE *standan*] *v* (**stood**) *vi* 1 to be stationary on the feet in an erect position; 2 to be upright; 3 to cease to move, stop; 4 to be at rest or lie stagnant, as water; 5 to be placed in a specified condition, attitude, or position, as *he stands acquitted, he stands at the head of his class;* 6 to be located; 7 *Brit* to be a candidate; 8 to remain in force; 9 to remain in existence, endure, last; 10 to step or move, as *stand aside;* 11 to be of a certain height when erect; 12 to maintain a certain attitude, as toward an issue; 13 *naut* to hold a course at sea, as *to stand to the harbor;* 14 **stand by,** a to support, adhere to; b to stand aside and wait; 15 **stand for,** a to represent; b to advocate; c *colloq* to tolerate; 16 **stand in with** *colloq* to have influence with; 17 **stand off** to keep at a distance; 18 **stand on,** a to rest on; b to demand; 19 **stand out,** a to project; b to be prominent; 20 **stand up,** a to assume an erect position; b to prove valid; c to be durable; 21 **stand up for,** a to support, defend; b to be a best man for at a wedding; 22 **stand up to** to hold one's ground against || *vt* 23 to be upright; put in place; 24 to put up with, endure; 25 to undergo; bear; 26 *colloq* to pay for; 27 **stand off** to repel; 28 **stand up** *slang* to fail to keep an appointment with || *n* 29 stop or halt; 30 stop for the purpose of offering resistance; 31 position on an issue; 32 witness stand; 33 position, station; 34 outdoor platform for speakers, a band, dignitaries reviewing a parade, etc.; 35 any habitual booth or station for business, as *a cab stand;* 36 small table or rack for holding various articles; 37 standing growth, as of grain or trees; 38 *theat* town where a company halts for a performance; 39 **stands** *pl* tiered platform with seats for spectators; 40 **make a stand** to stop and fight

stand·ard /stan'dərd/ [OF] *n* 1 figure, flag, etc., used as an emblem of a military unit, sovereign, or high official; 2 established or authorized measure of weight, length, quality, etc.; 3 authorized proportion of weight of fine metal and of alloy in coins; 4 any type, example, or model generally accepted as correct; 5 upright support || *adj* 6 serving as an accepted model for comparison, basis for measurement, etc.; 7 of recognized excellence; 8 common, customary; 9 fulfilling the requirements of law or custom || SYN *n* type, model, test, gauge, ideal (see *criterion*)

stand'ard-bear'er *n* 1 one who carries the standard of a military unit; 2 leader of a movement or political party

stand'ard-bred' *n* one of a breed of trotting and pacing horses used for harness racing || **stand'ard-bred'** *adj*

stand'ard·ize *vt* to make standard || **stand'ard·i·za'tion** *n*

stand'ard of liv'ing *n* level of everyday life relating to food, clothing, shelter, and recreation enjoyed by an individual, class, or region

stand'ard time' *n* official civil time of any of the 24 time zones into which the earth is divided

stand'-by' *n* (**-bys**) 1 one who or that which can be depended upon; 2 person or thing standing by ready to substitute; 3 passenger standing by in the hope of filling a reservation canceled at the last minute, as for a seat on a plane || also *adj*

stand·ee' *n colloq* one who stands because no seats are available

stand'-in' *n* 1 one who substitutes for a motion-picture actor during tedious nonacting chores such as setting up lights and cameras; 2 any substitute; 3 influence, drag

stand'ing *n* 1 continuance, duration, as *a habit of long standing;* 2 reputation; rank; status || *adj* 3 in an upright position; 4 stagnant, not flowing, as water; 5 lasting, continuing, as *a standing rule;* 6 performed from an upright position, as *a standing jump*

stand'ing ar'my *n* permanent army of a nation

stand'ing room' *n* room for standing where no seats are available

stand'-off' *n* 1 tie or draw; 2 that which counterbalances and results in inaction, sometimes strained

stand'-off'ish *adj* reserved, aloof

stand'out' *n* someone or something outstanding

stand'pipe' *n* high pipe or reservoir into which water is pumped to secure pressure in a water system

stand'point' *n* point of view

stand'still' *n* ceasing of action; halt or stop

stand'-up' *adj* 1 standing upright; 2 done or taken while standing; 3 characterized by boldness regardless of consequences, as *a stand-up fight*

stand'-up' co·me'di·an *n* comedian who delivers a comic monologue while standing alone on the stage

stank /staŋk/ *pt* of **stink**

stan·nic /stan'ik/ [< L *stannum* tin] *adj* of or pert. to tin, esp. with a valence of four

stan·za /stan'zə/ [It = room] *n* division of a poem, consisting of a group of lines, usu. of a fixed length, meter, and/or rhyme scheme

staph·y·lo·coc·cus /staf'ĭlokok'əs/ [< Gk *staphyle* bunch of grapes + *coccus*] *n* (-**coc·ci** /-kok'sī/) any of several bacteria of the genus *Staphylococcus*, some of which are pathogenic for man

sta·ple[1] /stāp'əl/ [MD *stapel* market] *n* 1 chief commodity produced in a district; 2 principal or basic item; 3 raw material; 4 commodity in steady demand; 5 basic food item; 6 fiber of cotton, flax, or wool || *adj* 7 chief; basic; regularly produced

sta·ple[2] [OE *stapol* pillar] *n* 1 small U-shaped piece of metal driven into wood to hold or fasten something; 2 wire similarly bent to fasten papers together by being driven through with a special device and having the ends clinched on the other side || *vt* 3 to fasten with a staple or staples || **sta'pler** *n*

star /stär/ [OE *steorra*] *n* 1 any celestial body visible in the night sky other than the moon; 2 one of the distant self-luminous bodies that remain practically always in the same position relative to one another, distinguished from the planets; 3 any self-luminous celestial body, including the sun; 4 conventional representation of a star, having five or six points radiating from the center; 5 such a figure used as a badge, decoration, medal, ornament, award, etc.; 6 brilliant or prominent person, esp. in the theatrical profession; 7 *astrol* celestial body, esp. a planet, regarded as influencing a person's life; 8 destiny; 9 **thank one's (lucky) stars** to acknowledge one's good luck || *v* (**starred**; **star·ring**) *vt* 10 to ornament with stars; 11 to mark with an asterisk; 12 to feature as a star of a play or movie || *vi* 13 to shine like a star, be illustrious; 14 to appear as a star in a play or movie || *adj* 15 of or pert. to a star; 16 distinguished; preeminent

star'board' /also -bərd/ [OE *stēorbord*] *n* 1 right side of a vessel or airplane when one faces forward || *adj* 2 pert. to or lying on the starboard || *vt* 3 to turn (the helm) to the right || also *adv*

starch /stärch'/ [OE *stearc* stiff] *n* 1 white tasteless solid carbohydrate —(C₆H₁₀O₅)n— an important constituent of plants; 2 commercial preparation of this used to stiffen fabrics in manufacturing and laundering; 3 stiffness of manner; 4 *colloq* courage or backbone || *vt* 5 to stiffen with or as with starch || **starched'** *adj* || **starch'y** *adj* (-**i·er**; -**i·est**)

Star' Cham'ber *n* 1 former English court dealing chiefly with offenses against the Crown, notorious for its severity and arbitrary methods; 2 any arbitrary and unfair tribunal or investigating committee

Star' Cit'y *n* site of the Soviet missile test center, north of Moscow

star'-crossed' *adj* ill-fated

star' cut' *n* gem having a hexagonal top surface surrounded by six facets with the form of equilateral triangles

star'dom *n* status of a star 6

star' drill' *n* chisellike masonry drill having a pointed, faceted head

stare /ster'/ [OE *starian*] *vi* 1 to look with wide open eyes; gaze steadily; 2 to be conspicuous or prominent || *vt* 3 to influence by staring || *n* 4 fixed, intent look || SYN *v* look, gaze (see *gape*)

star'fish' *n* (-**fish** or -**fishes**) any of a large class (Asteroidea) of marine animals having a star-shaped body with five or more rays

star'gaze' *vi* 1 to gaze at the stars; 2 to daydream || **star'gaz'er** *n*

stark /stärk/ [OE *stearc* strong, stiff] *adj* 1 stiff, rigid, as in death; 2 utter, downright; 3 harsh, grim || *adv* 4 completely, as **stark mad**

stark'-nak'ed [< OE *steort* tail] *adj* completely naked

star'let /-lit/ *n* budding young actress

star·ling /stär'liŋ/ [OE *stærlinc*] *n* one of a widespread family of birds, of which one European species (*Sturnus vulgaris*) with black, partly irridescent plumage has been introduced into North America

star'ry *adj* (-**ri·er**; -**ri·est**) 1 of or pert. to the stars; 2 set with or decked with stars; 3 lighted by stars; 4 shining like stars

Stars' and Stripes' *npl* flag of the U.S.

Star'-Span'gled Ban'ner *n* 1 flag of the U.S.; 2 official anthem of the U.S.

start /stärt/ [ME *sterten*] *vi* 1 to spring suddenly; leap, bound; 2 to make a sudden involuntary movement; 3 to set out, begin; 4 to commence an action or activity; 5 **start in** to begin; 6 **start out** to begin a journey || *vt* 7 to set into motion or action; 8 to rouse suddenly, as game; 9 to bring into being or operation; 10 to cause to begin running, as a horse in a race; 11 to begin, enter on, as a new action or program; 12 to enable to begin (a journey, career, etc.); 13 to loosen or cause to give way; 14 to set flowing, as wine; 15 **start up** to set in motion || *n* 16 sudden leap or bound; **17** involuntary twitch or jerk; **18** beginning or first motion, as of a race, journey, or course of action; **19** point of beginning; **20** lead or advantage, as in a race or competition; **21** opportunity to begin a career ‖ SYN *v* spring, move, jerk, twitch (see *flinch*)

start′er *n* **1** one who signals to the operator of an elevator, bus, etc. the time to move; **2** one who gives the signal to start a race; **3** person or animal that starts in a race; **4** self-starter

star·tle /stärt′əl/ [OE *steartlian* to stumble] *vt* **1** to cause to start suddenly from fright or alarm ‖ *vt* **2** to be startled ‖ *n* **3** shock, as of surprise or alarm ‖ **star′tling** *adj* SYN *v* frighten, alarm, excite, start (see *flinch*)

starve /stärv′/ [OE *steorfan* to die] *vi* **1** to suffer or die from extreme hunger; **2** *colloq* to be famished; **3 starve for** to feel a great need for ‖ *vt* **4** to cause to starve; **5** to force by hunger, as *to starve a city into surrender* ‖ **star·va′tion** *n*

starve·ling *n* **1** one who suffers from lack of food or is poorly nourished; **2** thin weak animal or plant ‖ *adj* **3** hungry; weak

stash /stash′/ [?] *vt* also **stash away** *colloq* to put away for future use

-stat /-stat′/ [Gk *-states*] *comb form* that checks the status of, as *rheostat*

state /stāt′/ [OF *estat*] *n* **1** condition in which a person or thing is; situation; **2** condition with respect to structure and form, as *solid state*; **3** political or social standing; rank; style of living; **4** ceremonious style or formal dignity; pomp; **5** body of people united under one government; nation; **6** the civil powers of a state, as contrasted with the church; **7** any of several semiautonomous territories forming part of a federal union, as the states of the American Union; **8** activities of a national government, as *affairs of state*; **9 State** *colloq* Department of State; **10 the States** *pl* the United States (generally used abroad); **11 lie in state** to be exhibited publicly before interment ‖ *adj* **12** pert. to a national government, as *state papers*; **13** used on formal or ceremonious occasions; **14 State** pert. to one of the United States ‖ *vt* **15** to declare definitely; **16** to set forth formally ‖ SYN *v* tell, declare, affirm, allege, narrate, express

state′craft′ *n* art of government

stat′ed *adj* **1** fixed, regular; **2** declared, set forth

state′hood′ *n* status or condition of a state in the U.S.

state′house′ *n* (**-hous·es** /-ziz/) capitol of a state in the U.S.

state′less *adj* having no nationality

state′ly *adj* (**-li·er**; **-li·est**) **1** imposing, majestic; **2** dignified ‖ **state′li·ness** *n* ‖ SYN grand, majestic, impressive, lofty, dignified

state′ment *n* **1** something stated; **2** formal communication or declaration; **3** *com* abstract of an account, esp. one showing money due

state′room′ *n* private sleeping room on a passenger vessel or sleeping car

state′s′ ev′i·dence *n* testimony presented by the prosecution in a criminal case, esp. that given by a participant in the crime who testifies against his accomplices

state′side′ *adj* & *adv* in or toward the U.S.

states′man /-mən/ *n* (**-men** /-mən/) one skilled in public affairs and the art of government ‖ **states′man·ship′** *n*

state′ troop′er *n* member of the police force under state jurisdiction in any of the states of the United States

stat·ic /stat′ik/ [Gk *statikos*] *adj* **1** pert. to bodies at rest, or forces in equilibrium; **2** motionless, unchanging; **3** pert. to static electricity; **4** acting without motion, as *static pressure* ‖ *n* **5** a static or atmospheric electricity; **b** interference with broadcast signals caused by such electricity

stat′ic e·lec·tric′i·ty *n* electricity contained in or produced by stationary charges

stat′ics *nsg* branch of science that deals with bodies at rest or forces in equilibrium

sta·tion /stāsh′ən/ [L *statio* (*-onis*) a standing] *n* **1** place where a person or thing usu. remains or is assigned; **2** rank, standing; **3** place devoted to a particular kind of work or service, as *a gasoline station, police station*; **4 a** regular stopping place on a railroad, bus line, etc.; **b** building associated with it; **5** place from which radio and television programs are broadcast ‖ *vt* **6** to set or place; assign to a station

sta′tion·ar′y *adj* **1** not moving; fixed; **2** unchanging in state or condition

sta′tion break′ *n* interruption in a radio or television program for identifying the station or making an announcement

sta′tion·er [ML *stationarius* one who has a permanent shop] *n* one who deals in stationery

sta′tion·er′y /-er′ē/ *n* **1** paper, ink, and other writing materials; **2** writing paper

sta′tion i·den′ti·fi·ca′tion *n* name that is announced periodically to identify a broadcasting station

sta′tions of the cross′ *n* series of 14 representations of the stages of Christ's passion, placed around the walls of a church or on the road to a church or shrine

sta'tion-to-sta'tion *adj* (long-distance telephone call) chargeable if the person making it speaks to anyone at the number called ‖ also *adv*

sta'tion wag'on *n* passenger car with rear seats that fold out of the way or can be removed, and having a tailgate

sta·tis·tic /stətist'ik/ [NL *statisticus* < L *status* standing] *n* 1 numerical datum; 2 statistics, a *pl* numerical facts systematically collected and classified, regarding a large group of persons or things; b *sg* science that deals with the collecting, classifying, and interpretation of such data ‖ **sta·tis'ti·cal** *adj* ‖ **sta·tis'ti·cal·ly** *adv* ‖ **stat·is·ti·cian** /stat'istish'ən/ *n*

sta·tor /stāt'ər/ [NL] *n* fixed or stationary part of a motor, generator, turbine, etc.

stat·u·ar·y /stach'ōō·er'ē/ [L *statuarius*] *n* statues collectively

stat·ue /stach'ōō/ [L *statua*] *n* sculptured, molded, or cast figure of a person or animal, or of an abstract form

stat'u·esque' /-esk'/ *adj* having the beauty or formal dignity of a statue

stat'u·ette' /-et'/ *n* small statue

stat·ure /stach'ər/ [L *statura*] *n* 1 height of a person or animal; 2 level of achievement attained

sta·tus /stāt'əs, stat'-/ [L] *n* 1 state or condition of affairs; 2 rank; social position; 3 legal standing; 4 high prestige in relation to others

sta'tus quo' /-kwō'/ [L = condition in which] *n* existing condition or state

sta'tus seek'er *n* person who seeks to attain a high or higher standing in the group in which he works or lives ‖ **sta'tus seek'ing** *n*

sta'tus sym'bol *n* something a person possesses or claims to possess by which he attains or hopes to attain a higher social or economic status

stat·ute /stach'ōōt/ [L *statutus* established] *n* 1 law passed by a lawmaking body; 2 any rule established by some authority

stat'ute mile' *n* ordinary mile, containing 5,280 feet

stat'ute of lim'i·ta'tions *n* statute limiting the period within which legal action may be taken

stat'u·to'ry /-tôr'-, -tōr'-/ *adj* 1 authorized, enacted, or imposed by statute; 2 (offense) made punishable by statute

stat'u·to'ry rape' *n* sexual intercourse with a girl under the age of consent

staunch¹ /stônch'/ *vt & vi* var of **stanch¹**

staunch² /stônch'/, stänch'/ *adj* 1 sound, firm; 2 constant, loyal, steadfast

stave /stāv'/ [ME] *n* 1 pole, staff; 2 one of the curving strips of wood forming the sides of a barrel; 3 verse or stanza ‖ *v* (staved or stove) *vt* 4 **stave in** to break or crush inward; 5 **stave off** to hold or ward off

staves /stāvz'/ *pl* of **staff**

stay¹ /stā'/ [OF *estayer* to prop] *vt* 1 to hold up, prop ‖ *n* 2 flat strip of metal, plastic, etc., used to stiffen corsets, collars, etc.; 3 **stays** *pl* corset

stay² [OE *stæg*] *naut n* 1 strong rope or wire used to steady or support a mast, spar, or funnel ‖ *vt* 2 to hold or support with stays

stay³ [AF *estaier* < OF *ester* < L *stare*] *v* (stayed or *archaic* staid) *vi* 1 to remain; 2 to dwell, abide; 3 to continue being, as *he stayed honest;* 4 to stop, halt; 5 to linger ‖ *vt* 6 to check, hold back; 7 to put off, postpone; 8 to suppress, as anger; 9 to appease, as hunger; 10 to endure ‖ *n* 11 stop, halt; 12 sojourn; 13 suspension of judicial proceedings

stay'ing pow'er *n* ability to last and hold out

Ste. [F *Sainte*] Saint (referring to a woman)

stead /sted'/ [OE *stede* place] *n* 1 **in one's stead** in one's place; 2 **stand in good stead** to be of use or advantage (to)

stead'fast' *adj* 1 fixed; steady; 2 unwavering, constant ‖ SYN resolute, unswerving, staunch, unwavering

stead·y /sted'ē/ *adj* (-i·er; -i·est) 1 firm in position; well balanced; 2 resolute, unwavering; 3 regular, uniform; 4 firm, unfaltering; 5 sober, reliable; 6 calm, unexcited; 7 continuous, unchanging; 8 *naut* (ship) keeping its direction unchanged; keeping nearly upright; 9 **go steady** to date one person exclusively ‖ *n* (-ies) 10 *colloq* one with whom one goes steady ‖ *v* (-ied) *vt* 11 to make or keep steady ‖ *vi* 12 to become steady ‖ **stead'i·ly** *adv* ‖ **stead'i·ness** *n*

steak /stāk'/ [ME *steike* < Scand] *n* slice of beef or other meat cooked or to be cooked by broiling or frying

steal /stēl'/ [OE *stelan*] *v* (stole; sto·len) *vt* 1 to take by theft; take without leave or right; 2 to take by craft or surprise, as *to steal a kiss, a glance, someone's heart;* 3 to move, convey, or put stealthily; 4 *baseball* to suddenly run to and reach (a base) safely, without the help of a batted ball or error; 5 **steal the show** to win the most applause because of a spectacular performance ‖ *vi* 6 to commit theft; 7 to move or act stealthily or secretly ‖ *n* 8 *colloq* theft; 9 *colloq* terrific bargain ‖ SYN *v* abstract, filch, pilfer, rob, swindle, purloin

stealth /stelth'/ [ME *stelthe*] *n* secret, furtive way of acting or proceeding ‖ **stealth'y** *adj* (-i·er; -i·est) ‖ **stealth'·i·ly** *adv*

steam /stēm'/ [OE *stēam*] *n* 1 the vapor into which water is converted by boiling; 2 visible mist of condensed water vapor; 3 any vapor or exhalation; 4 *colloq* force; energy; 5 **blow off steam** *slang* to give vent to one's emotions ‖ *vi* 6 to give off steam; 7 to move under the power of steam; 8 *colloq* to be very angry; 9 also **steam up** to become covered with condensed steam ‖ *vt* 10 to expose to or treat with steam ‖ **steam'y** *adj* (-i·er; -i·est)

steam'boat' *n* steamship, esp. a small one plying rivers and lakes

steam' en'gine *n* engine operated by steam

steam'er *n* 1 something operated by steam; 2 steamship; 3 apparatus in which articles are steamed

steam' fit'ter *n* one who installs and repairs boilers and steam pipes

steam' heat' *n* heat obtained by the circulation of steam, as in radiators

steam'roll'er *n* 1 heavy roller driven by steam, used to smooth the surface of roads; 2 any overpowering force, used to crush opposition ‖ *vt* 3 to move, crush, or override, as opposition

steam' room' *n* heated steam-filled room to induce sweating

steam'ship' *n* large steam-propelled ship

steam' shov'el *n* large steam-powered machine for digging and excavating

steam' ta'ble *n* table with a compartment for steam or hot water above which containers of food are placed to be kept warm, used in restaurants and cafeterias

ste·ar'ic ac'id /stē-ar'ik, stir'ik/ [< Gk *stear* fat] *n* solid white fatty acid —CH₃(CH₂)₁₆COOH— present in most animal and vegetable fats and oils; used in making soaps, candles, medicines, and suppositories

steed /stēd'/ [OE *stēda* stallion] *n poet.* spirited riding horse

steel /stēl'/ [OE *stȳle*] *n* 1 alloy of iron and carbon, capable of being hardened, toughened, and otherwise altered by the addition of various elements, as nickel, manganese, and chromium; 2 instrument or weapon made of steel; 3 **steels** *pl* stocks or bonds of steel-producing companies ‖ *vt* 4 to make hard, strong, or unfeeling ‖ **steel'y** *adj* (-i·er; -i·est)

steel' wool' *n* fine shavings of steel, used to clean or smooth surfaces

steel·yard /stēl'yärd', -yərd, stil'yərd/ *n* weighing apparatus consisting of a movable weight on a graduated arm, which balances a shorter arm from which the article to be weighed is suspended

steep¹ /stēp'/ [OE *stēap* lofty] *adj* 1 having a sharp pitch or slope; precipitous; 2 *colloq* exorbitant ‖ SYN precipitous, high, sheer (see *abrupt*)

steep² [ME *stepen* < Scand] *vt* 1 to soak in a liquid in order to clean, soften, or extract some element; 2 to imbue or saturate ‖ *vi* 3 to be soaked in a liquid

steep'en *vt* 1 to make steeper ‖ *vi* 2 to become steeper

stee·ple /stēp'əl/ [OE *stēpel* tower] *n* tapering tower, esp. one standing above the roof of a building and usu. topped by a spire

stee'ple·chase' *n* 1 horse race over a turf course provided with obstacles, as ditches, hedges, etc. ‖ *vi* 2 to ride or run in a steeplechase

stee'ple·jack' *n* man who works on high structures, as smokestacks, steeples, etc.

steer¹ /stir'/ [OE *stēor*] *n* 1 castrated male bovine from two to four years old; 2 ox of any age

steer² [OE *stēoran*] *vt* 1 to direct the course of by means of a tiller, wheel, etc.; 2 to control the direction or course of; 3 to follow (a course); 4 to guide (a person) ‖ *vi* 5 to direct something in its course; 6 to go in a given direction; 7 to be susceptible of being guided or steered, as *this automobile steers easily;* 8 **steer clear of** to avoid ‖ *n* 9 *colloq* piece of advice; tip, hint, as *a bum steer*

steer'age /-ij/ *n* the part of a ship for the passengers who pay the lowest rates

steer'ing com·mit'tee *n* committee that prepares the agenda of a meeting or session

steer'ing gear' *n* steering mechanism of a vehicle

steer'ing wheel' *n* wheel with which the driver controls the steering, as on an automobile or ship

steers'man /-mən/ *n* (-men /-mən/) helmsman

stein /stīn'/ [G = stone] *n* mug, usu. earthenware, esp. for beer

ste·le /stēl'ē, stēl'/ [Gk] *n* upright slab or pillar bearing an inscription, used as a gravestone, marker, etc.

stel·lar /stel'ər/ [< L *stella* star] *adj* 1 of or like a star; 2 pert. to a preeminent performer

stem¹ /stem'/ [OE *stemn*] *n* 1 main stalk of a plant; 2 stalk that bears a leaf, flower, or fruit; 3 slender part or projection, as of a pipe or wineglass; 4 main line of descent of a family; 5 forward part of a vessel; 6 *mus* vertical line joined to the head of a note; 7 the part of a word to which inflectional endings are attached ‖ *v* (**stemmed; stem·ming**) *vt* 8 to remove the stems from; 9 to make headway against ‖ *vi* **10 stem from** to derive from

stem[3] [ON *stemma*] *v* (**stemmed; stemming**) *vt* **1** to stop, check; **2** to dam up, as a stream

stem′ware′ *n* glassware, as for desserts and wines, having a bowl mounted on a stem

stench /stench′/ [OE *stenc* smell] *n* foul odor, stink

sten·cil /stens′əl/ [OF *estenceler* to sparkle] *n* **1** thin sheet, as of metal or cardboard, with letters or a design cut out, so that when held against a surface and ink or paint is applied, the letters or design are reproduced on the surface beneath; **2** letters or design so made ‖ *v* (**-ciled** or **-cilled; -cil·ing** or **-cil·ling**) *vt* **3** to mark or paint with a stencil

ste·nog·ra·phy /stənog′rəfē/ [< Gk *stenos* narrow + -*graphy*] *n* art or practice of writing in shorthand ‖ **ste·nog′ra·pher** *n* ‖ **sten·o·graph·ic** /sten′əgraf′ik/ *adj*

sten·o·type /sten′ətīp′/ *n* machine resembling a typewriter for writing in special shorthand symbols

sten·to·ri·an /stentôr′ē·ən, -tōr′-/ [< *Stentor* Gk herald in the *Iliad* with a loud voice] *adj* very loud, booming, as the voice

step /step′/ [OE *steppan*] *v* (**stepped; step·ping**) *vi* **1** to move the foot or the feet alternately, as in walking; **2** to walk, esp. a short distance; **3** to execute dance steps; **4** to move briskly; **5 step down** to give up one's position; **6 step in** to intervene; **7 step into**, **a** to place the foot into; **b** to come by (something) easily; **8 step on it**, **a** *colloq* to step on the accelerator to increase the speed; **b** *slang* to hurry up; **9 step out** to go to places of entertainment; **10 step up** to come closer ‖ *vt* **11** to set or place, as the foot; **12 step down**, **a** to decrease the rate of; **b** to decrease the voltage of (a current) by means of a transformer; **13 step off** to measure by steps; **14 step up**, **a** to increase the rate of; **b** to increase the voltage of (a current) by means of a transformer ‖ *n* **15** movement made in raising or setting down the foot; **16** distance covered by a step; **17** rank, level, degree; **18** short distance; **19** footprint; **20** sound or manner of walking; **21** support for the foot in ascending or descending, as a tread in a stairway; **22** one of a series of actions or measures; **23** one of a sequence of movements in a dance; **24 in step**, **a** in rhythm; **b** in conformity; **25 keep step** to keep pace; **26 out of step**, **a** out of rhythm; **b** not in conformity; **27 step by step** gradually; in sequence; **28 take steps** to take measures; **29 watch one's step** *colloq* to be careful

step- /step′-/ [OE *stēop-* orphaned] *comb form* designating relationship not by blood, but by the remarriage of a parent

step′broth′er *n* son by a previous marriage of one's stepfather or stepmother

step′child′ *n* (**-chil·dren**) child by a previous marriage of one's spouse

step′daugh′ter *n* daughter by a previous marriage of one's spouse

step′-down′ trans·form′er *n* transformer that reduces voltage

step′fa′ther *n* husband of one's mother by a marriage subsequent to her marriage with one's own father

step′lad′der *n* ladder having flat steps instead of rungs, esp. one with four legs hinged at the top so that it will stand up by itself

step′moth′er *n* wife of one's father by a marriage subsequent to his marriage with one's own mother

step′par′ent *n* stepfather or stepmother

steppe /step′/ [Russ *step′*] *n* vast treeless plain, esp. of Russia or Siberia

step′per *n* **1** horse that lifts its front feet high; **2** switch that makes a sequence of contacts by remote control; **3** *colloq* dancer

step′ping·stone′ *n* **1** stone for stepping on, as in crossing a stream; **2** any means of advance

step′sis′ter *n* daughter by a previous marriage of one's stepfather or stepmother

step′son′ *n* son by a previous marriage of one's spouse

step′-up′ trans·form′er *n* transformer that increases voltage

-ster /-stər/ [OE -*estre*] *n suf* denoting **1** occupation, as *teamster*; **2** one that makes, as *trickster*; **3** participant, as *gangster*; **4** one that is, as *youngster*

ster·e·o /ster′ē·ō′, stir′-/ *n* **1** stereoscopic photography or photograph; **2** stereophonic sound reproduction or a set that reproduces such sound ‖ also *adj*

ster·e·o- [Gk *stereos* solid] *comb form* **1** solid; **2** three-dimensional

ster·e·o·phon·ic /ster′ē·əfon′ik, stir′-/ *adj* designating a system of sound reproduction in which signals which have been picked up by two or more microphones are reproduced by two or more speakers located so as to give a binaural effect

ster·e·o·scope′ *n* optical instrument with two lenses, through which photographs taken in pairs from slightly different angles appear as one picture in three dimensions ‖ **ster′e·o·scop′ic** /-skop′-/ *adj*

ster·e·o·type′ *n* **1** printing plate cast in a papier-mâché mold made from the original type; **2** fixed or conventional conception or type ‖ *vt* **3** to make a stereotype of; **4** to give a set form to ‖ **ster′e·o·typed′** adj

ster·ile /ster′il/ [L *sterilis* barren] adj **1** not fertile, unfruitful; **2** without power to reproduce offspring; **3** free from living microorganisms; **4** barren mentally or spiritually ‖ **ste·ril′i·ty** /stəril′-/ n

ster′i·lize′ vt **1** to make unproductive or barren; **2** to destroy bacteria in, as by heat ‖ **ster′i·liz′er** n ‖ **ster′i·li·za′tion** n

ster·ling /stur′liŋ/ [ME = a silver coin] n **1** standard of weight and purity of British gold and silver coins; **2** sterling silver ‖ adj **3** of or pert. to British money; **4** genuine, excellent

ster′ling sil′ver n silver having a fineness of .925; **2** articles made of this, as tableware and jewelry

stern¹ /sturn′/ [OE *styrne*] adj **1** severe, harsh; **2** forbidding, grim ‖ **stern′ly** adj ‖ SYN grim, unyielding, strict, repelling (see *austere*) ‖ ANT submissive, gentle, yielding, compassionate

stern² [ME *sterne* < Scand] n **1** rear part of a vessel; **2** rear of anything

ster·num /sturn′əm/ [LL < Gk *sternon* breast] n (**-na** /-nə/ or **-nums**) generally flat bony or cartilaginous plate to which the ends of most of the ribs are attached; present in most vertebrates above the fishes ‖ **ster′nal** adj

stern′wheel′er n steamboat with a paddle wheel at the stern

stet /stet′/ [3d pers sg pres subj of L *stare* to stand] v (**stet·ted; stet·ting**) vt **1** to mark (a manuscript or proof) with the word *stet* ‖ vi impv **2** (used as a printer's direction in proofreading to cancel a correction or deletion) let it stand

steth′o·scope′ /steth′ə-/ [< Gk *stethos* chest + -*scope*] n med instrument for listening to chest sounds, as of the heart or lungs

ste·ve·dore /stēv′ədôr′, -dōr′/ [Sp *estibador*] n one who loads and unloads ship cargoes

stew /st(y)ōō′/ [MF *estuve* hot bath] vt **1** to boil slowly, simmer ‖ vi **2** to be stewed; **3** colloq to worry; **4** slang to simmer with suppressed anger ‖ n **5** dish prepared by stewing, esp. of meat and vegetables; **6** colloq nervous anxiety; stew

stew·ard /st(y)ōō′ərd/ [OE *stigweard*] n **1** one who manages the property and financial affairs of another; **2** person employed at a hotel or club or on a ship to superintend the buying and distribution of food; **3** one who waits on passengers ‖ **stew′ard·ess** n*fem* ‖ **stew′ard·ship′** n

stewed adj slang drunk

St.′ He·le·na /həlēn′ə/ n British island in the S Atlantic W of southern Africa, place of Napoleon's exile 1815–21 (5,000; 47 sq.m.)

stib·nite /stib′nīt/ n lead-gray, crystalline mineral —Sb_2S_3— the most important ore of antimony

stick¹ /stik′/ [OE *sticca*] n **1** relatively long and slender piece of wood; **2** small branch or shoot broken or cut off from a tree or shrub; **3** something long and slender, like a rod or wand, a piece of chewing gum, a piece of dynamite, a cane, a baton, a club, a lever, etc.; **4** colloq stiff or dull person; **5** compulsion, coercion; **6 the sticks** pl colloq the country; rural regions

stick² [OE *stician*] v (**stuck**) vt **1** to pierce with something pointed; **2** to impale; **3** to cause to enter or pierce; **4** to put in a specified position; **5** to put, push, or thrust, as *to stick one's head out the window*; **6** to cause to adhere; **7** to detain so as to be unable to proceed, as *we got stuck in traffic*; **8** to puzzle, pose; **9 stick it out** colloq to endure something disagreeable to the end; **10 stick someone with** colloq to impose (something onerous or disagreeable) on someone; **11 stick up** slang to rob at gunpoint ‖ vi **12** to have its point stuck; **13** to persist, persevere; **14** to protrude or extend; **15** to adhere closely; **16** to be checked, hindered, or jammed; **17** to have misgivings, hesitate, as *he'll stick at nothing*; **18** to remain firm and faithful; **19 stick around** slang to linger; **20 stick by** or **to** to remain faithful to; **21 stick out, a** to protrude; to project; **b** to persist, hold out; **c** colloq to be noticeable or outstanding; **22 stick up for** to uphold, come to the defense of

stick′ball′ n children's street game resembling baseball, played usu. with a rubber ball and a broomstick

stick′er n **1** gummed label; **2** colloq puzzling situation or problem

stick·ler /stik′lər/ [< obs *stickle* to insist, haggle] n **1** one who stubbornly insists, esp. on things of little importance; **2** puzzling or difficult problem

stick′up′ n slang holdup, robbery

stick′y adj (**-i·er; -i·est**) **1** adhesive, gluey; **2** hot, muggy; **3** difficult, awkward (situation or problem)

stick′y-fin′gered adj given to thievery

stiff /stif′/ [OE *stif*] adj **1** rigid, hard to bend; **2** not moving or working freely or smoothly; **3** taut, drawn tight; **4** not fluid, thick; **5** awkward, constrained (manner); **6** strong, powerful (breeze, drink, or blow); **7** difficult, hard to accomplish; **8** high, excessive (price); **9** sore, not supple, as muscles or joints; **10** harsh, as a penalty ‖ n **11** slang dead body; **12** slang formal unresponsive person; **13** slang fellow, as *lucky stiff*; **14** slang contestant that has no chance

|| SYN *adj* stark, unbending, formal, awkward

stiff'en *vt* 1 to make stiff || *vi* 2 to become stiff || **stiff'en·er** *n*

stiff'-necked' *adj* haughty, obstinate

sti·fle /stīf'əl/ [< *Scand*] *vt* 1 to suffocate, smother; 2 to check, suppress || *vi* 3 to be stifled

stig·ma /stig'mə/ [Gk = prick, mark] *n* (**-mas** or **-ma·ta** /-mətə/) 1 mark of disgrace or infamy; 2 *bot* the part of the pistil on which the pollen falls; 3 spot on the skin that bleeds periodically; 4 **stigmata** *pl* marks corresponding to the wounds on the crucified body of Christ, said to appear supernaturally on the bodies of certain saints and ecclesiastics || **stig·mat'ic** /-mat'-/ *adj*

stig'ma·tize' *vt* 1 to mark with disgrace; brand with infamy; 2 to produce stigmata on the body of || **stig'ma·ti·za'tion** *n*

stile /stīl/ [OE *stigel*] *n* set of steps leading over a fence or wall

sti·let·to /stilet'ō/ [It] *n* (**-tos** or **-toes**) small sharp dagger having a slender blade

still¹ /stil/ [OE *stille*] *adj* 1 motionless, at rest; 2 peaceful, calm; 3 without sound; silent, hushed; 4 not sparkling, as wine || *adv* 5 till then or till now, as previously; 6 for all that, nevertheless; 7 even; yet, as *louder still*; 8 without movement; quietly || *conj* 9 yet, nevertheless || *vt* 10 to make still || *n* 11 *poet.* quiet, stillness; 12 photograph of a scene from a motion picture || **still'ness** *n* || SYN *v* lull, allay, subdue, appease, restrain, tranquilize || ANT *v* arouse, agitate, disturb, incite

still² [< *distill*] *n* apparatus for distilling liquids, esp. to obtain alcoholic liquors

still' a·larm' *n* fire alarm given by telephone or any means other than by pulling the lever of a fire-alarm box

still'born' *adj* dead at birth

still' life' *n* (**lifes**) picture of inanimate objects, as flowers or fruit

Still'son wrench' /stil'sən/ [trademark] *n* wrench with a pivoted toothed jaw for turning pipes, that tightens its grip when pressure is applied to the handle

stilt /stilt/ [ME *stilte*] *n* 1 one of two poles with a foot rest attached to the side to elevate the foot in walking; 2 post for supporting a structure above the ground and above water

stilt'ed *adj* pompous, stiffly formal

stim·u·lant /stim'yələnt/ [see **stimulate**] *adj* 1 stimulating || *n* 2 something that stimulates, as coffee, tea, or certain drugs

stim'u·late' [L *stimulare* (-*atus*) to goad on] *vt* 1 to rouse to activity, animate; encourage; 2 *med* to produce greater activity in, affect as by an intoxicant || *vi* 3 to act as a stimulant || **stim'-**

u·la'tor *n* || **stim'u·la'tion** *n* || SYN stir, goad, inspirit, awaken, provoke, excite

stim'u·lus /-ləs/ [L = goad] *n* (**-li** /-lī'/) 1 something that rouses the mind or senses; 2 *physiol* anything that excites an organ or tissue to a specific activity

sting /stiŋ/ [OE *stingan* to pierce] *v* (**stung**) *vt* 1 to prick or wound with a stinging organ; 2 to cause a sharp smarting pain to; 3 to spur or incite to action || *vi* 4 to inflict a sharp smarting wound; 5 to be sharply painful, give pain || *n* 6 the sharp often poisonous organ of defense or offense of certain animals; 7 one of the sharp piercing hairs of certain plants; 8 act or instance of stinging; 9 pain or wound caused by stinging; 10 keen, smarting mental or physical pain; 11 that which goads to action, as *the sting of conscience* || **sting'ing·ly** *adv*

sting'er *n* 1 stinging organ, as of a bee; 2 cocktail made of brandy and crème de menthe

stin·gy /stin'jē/ [< *sting*] *adj* (**-gi·er; -gi·est**) 1 miserly, extremely ungenerous; 2 scanty, meager || **stin'gi·ly** *adv* || **stin'gi·ness** *n* || SYN close, niggardly, penurious (see *avaricious*)

stink /stiŋk/ [OE *stincan*] *v* (**stank** or **stunk; stunk**) *vi* 1 to throw off a strong offensive smell; 2 *slang* to be very bad, as *that show stinks*; 3 **stink of,** a to expel an offensive odor of; b *slang* to have an excessive amount of (money); || *vt* 4 **stink up** to cause to stink; 5 **stink out** to drive out with an offensive odor || *n* 6 offensive odor; 7 *slang* fuss, scandal

stink' bomb' *n* device that emits a foul odor when released or broken

stink'er *n* *slang* despicable person

stink'ing *slang adj* 1 very drunk; 2 very rich || *adv* 3 offensively, as *stinking drunk*

stink'weed' *n* any of various plants with an offensive scent

stint /stint/ [OE *styntan* to dull] *vt* 1 to restrict, limit || *vi* 2 to be frugal; economize, pinch || *n* 3 limit or bound; 4 something allotted or assigned as a quantity or task

sti·pend /stī'pend/ [L *stipendium* soldier's pay] *n* 1 fixed pay for services; 2 periodic fixed payment, as for a university fellowship || SYN compensation, allowance, wage (see *salary*)

stip·ple /stip'əl/ [D *stippelen*] *vt* 1 to draw, engrave, or print by means of light touches or dots || *n* 2 art or method of stippling; 3 effect produced by stippling

stip'pling *n* 1 method of painting or engraving by dots or light touches; 2 something stippled

stip·u·late /stip'yəlāt'/ [L *stipulari* (-*atus*)] *vi* 1 to make an agreement, to insist ‖ *vt* **2** to arrange or settle definitely; **3** to specify, as part of an agreement

stip′u·la′tion *n* **1** act of stipulation; **2** something stipulated; something agreed to ‖ SYN arrangement, covenant, condition, agreement (see *contract*)

stir¹ /stur′/ [OE *styrian*] *v* (**stirred**; **stir·ring**) *vt* **1** to move an implement or the hand continuously in a circular motion so as to mix (a liquid or other substance) thoroughly; **2** to change the position of; move; **3** to put into motion; agitate; **4** to bestir (oneself); **5** to incite, rouse; **6 stir up, a** to cause to rise, as dust; **b** to give rise to, as trouble ‖ *vi* **7** to move, change position; **8** to be in motion, be active; **9** to be current; **10** to be incited or roused ‖ *n* **11** act or result of stirring; **12** bustle, activity; **13** agitation or excitement ‖ SYN *v* incite, stimulate, arouse, animate, actuate, encourage, upset, provoke ‖ ANT *v* calm, assuage, soothe, still, quiet

stir² [?] *n* slang prison

stir′ring *adj* **1** busy, bustling; **2** exciting, rousing; thrilling

stir·rup /stir′əp, stur′-/ [OE *stigrāp*] *n* loop-shaped support for a rider's foot, usu. of metal and hung from the saddle by a strap

stitch /stich′/ [OE *stice* pricking] *n* **1** *sewing* a single pass of a threaded needle in and out of a fabric; **b** the section of thread left in the fabric; **2** *knitting & crocheting* a single complete movement of the needle or hook; **b** link or loop of thread or yarn so formed; **3** particular arrangement of threads in needlework; **4** bit or piece of clothing; **5** sudden sharp pain, as in the side; **6** least amount or portion ‖ *vt* **7** to unite by stitches; sew ‖ *vi* **8** to sew

St.′ John′s′ *n* capital of Newfoundland (64,000)

St.′ Law′rence, Gulf of /lor′əns, lôr′-/ *n* arm of the Atlantic between Newfoundland and SE Canada

St.′ Law′rence Riv′er *n* river starting at Lake Ontario and flowing between Ontario and New York and NE through SE Canada to the Gulf of St. Lawrence

St.′ Law′rence Sea′way *n* seaway permitting seagoing vessels to go up the St. Lawrence and into all the Great Lakes

St.′ Lou′is /lo͞o′is/ *n* city in E Missouri on the Mississippi (750,000)

stoat /stōt′/ [ME *stote*] *n* ermine (*Mustela erminea*) in its summer coat of reddish brown

stock /stok′/ [OE *stocc* trunk, log] *n* **1** trunk or principal stem of a tree or plant; **2 a** trunk or plant in which a graft is placed; **b** plant from which cuttings are taken; **3** race, family, or relationship; **4** founder of a family; **5** livestock; **6 a** capital of a company or corporation in the form of shares; **b** any share or shares of such capital; **7** accumulation or supply of goods; **8** wide close-fitting band or collar worn about the neck; **9** any raw material for manufacture; **10** *cookery* water in which meat, fish, etc., has been boiled, used as a foundation for soups; **11** *theat* stock company; **12** handle of a whip, fishing rod, etc.; **13** piece, usu. of wood, to which the barrel and lock of a gun are attached; **14** *typ* specific quality or weight of paper; **15** commonly cultivated herb of the genus *Mathiola*, esp. *M. incana*, bearing terminal racemes of showy, single or double flowers of various colors; **16** *mach* wrench for holding dies for cutting threads; **17 stocks** *pl* a frame with holes for the legs and sometimes the wrists, formerly used to confine petty offenders and expose them to public ridicule; **b** frame on which a ship lies while being built; **18 in stock** on hand for immediate sale; **19 out of stock** not on hand; **20 take stock** to inventory goods on hand; **21 take stock of** to appraise; **22 take** or **put stock in** to attach credence to, have faith in ‖ *vt* **23** to furnish with a stock or supply; **24** to furnish with livestock; **25** to store for future use ‖ *vi* **26 stock up** to lay in a supply ‖ *adj* **27** kept on hand; **28** trite, commonplace; **29** pert. to breeding livestock; **30** pert. to the stock or shares of a company

stock·ade /stokād′/ [Sp *estacada*] *n* **1** line of posts or timbers set up as a barrier for defense or as an enclosure; **2** prison for military offenders ‖ *vt* **3** to defend or surround with a stockade

stock′breed′er *n* one who raises livestock

stock′bro′ker *n* broker who buys and sells securities for customers

stock′car′ *n* latticed boxcar for carrying livestock

stock′ car′ *n* standard model automobile adapted for racing

stock′ com′pa·ny *n* **1** company whose capital is divided into shares of stock; **2** *theat* group of actors more or less permanently associated under one management and playing a repertoire

stock′ ex·change′ *n* **1** association of stock brokers; **2** place where securities are bought and sold

stock′hold′er *n* one who owns shares of stock

stock′hold·er of rec′ord *n* stockholder who is registered on the books of the company as such at the close of a certain business day

Stock·holm /stok'hō(l)m/ *n* capital of Sweden (1,247,254)

stock·ing /stok'iŋ/ [*dim.* of *obs* stock hose] *n* close-fitting woven or knitted covering for the foot and leg

stock' in **trade'** *n* 1 goods that are kept for sale; 2 any kind of resources of a person or group of persons

stock' mar'ket *n* 1 stock exchange; 2 market for securities in general; 3 prices offered for stocks and bonds

stock'pile' *n* 1 reserve supply of goods, esp. if subject to shortages || *vt & vi* 2 to accumulate for a stockpile

stock'-still' *adj* motionless

stock'tak'ing *n* examination and reappraisal

stock'y *adj* (**-i·er; -i·est**) short and stoutly built; thickset

stock'yard' *n* large enclosure for cattle, hogs, and sheep awaiting slaughter

stodg·y /stoj'ē/ [< *obs* stodge heavy food] *adj* (**-i·er; -i·est**) dull, tedious; lacking in vivacity

sto·gy /stōg'ē/ [< *Conestoga* town in Pennsylvania] *n* (**-gies**) long, coarse, slender cigar

sto·ic /stō'ik/ [< Gk *stoikos* < *stoa* porch] *n* 1 stoical person; 2 **Stoic** adherent of the Greek philosopher Zeno, who taught that man should be governed by reason, subdue all passions, and be indifferent to pleasure or pain || *also adj* || **sto'i·cism** *n* || **Sto'i·cism** *n*

sto·i·cal *adj* impassive; indifferent to pain, grief, or joy || **sto'i·cal·ly** *adv* || SYN stolid, indifferent, impassive || DISCR The *indifferent* man lacks interest; he shows no inclination for or against; he is neutral, apathetic, unconcerned. The *impassive* man lacks feeling; he is not subject to emotion. One might shrink from being tried by an *indifferent* jury; one could be sure that an *impassive* jury would at least be calmly reasonable. A *stolid* man is wooden; he may be *impassive*, or he may be concealing sorrow or elation. The *stoical* man intentionally exercises control, fortitude, indifference to either pleasure or pain, and hence his appearance is as masklike as that of the *stolid* man. The apathy of an *indifferent* or an *impassive* man is unwilled. The seeming apathy of a *stolid* person is also inborn. The stoniness of a *stoical* person is acquired

stoke /stōk/ [D *stoken* to feed a fire] *vt* to tend (a fire or furnace); supply with fuel

stok'er *n* 1 one employed to tend and feed a furnace or boiler; 2 device for automatically feeding coal to a furnace

stole¹ /stōl/ *pt* of steal

stole² [Gk = garment] *n* 1 long wide scarf, often of fur, worn about the neck and shoulders; 2 long narrow scarf, fringed at the edges and worn over the shoulders by clergymen

sto·len /stōl'ən/ *pp* of steal

stol·id /stol'id/ [L *stolidus* dull] *adj* not easily aroused; impassive || **sto·lid'i·ty** /stəlid'-/ *n* || SYN unexcitable, heavy, wooden, dull (see *stoical*)

sto·ma /stōm'ə/ [Gk = mouth] *n* (**sto·ma·ta** /stōm'ətə, stom'-/) 1 *bot* minute hole or pore, as in the outer covering of leaves or stems; 2 *zool* mouth or mouthlike opening

stom·ach /stum'ək/ [Gk *stomachos*] *n* 1 saclike organ of digestion at the end of the esophagus; 2 appetite; 3 inclination; 4 abdomen, belly || *vt* 5 to eat without repugnance; 6 to put up with, tolerate

stom'ach·er *n* ornamented or jeweled garment worn over the stomach and chest in the 15th and 16th centuries by men and women and later as an underbodice by women

stomp /stomp'/ [var of *stamp*] *colloq* *vt* 1 to stamp on with the feet || *vi* 2 to tread heavily

stone /stōn'/ [OE *stān*] *n* 1 bit or piece of rock; 2 the hard nonmetallic mineral matter of which rock is composed; 3 piece of rock cut and shaped for a special use, as for building or grinding; 4 gem; 5 something resembling a stone in hardness or shape, as the pit of a peach; 6 abnormal stony formation, as in the kidney or bladder; 7 (*pl* stone) Brit unit of weight equal to 14 pounds avoirdupois; 8 **leave no stone unturned** to do everything possible || *vt* 9 to pelt with stones; 10 to remove the stone from, as fruit

stone- *comb form* completely, as *stone-deaf*

Stone' Age' *n* period in the development of man, preceding the Bronze Age and the Iron Age, when stone weapons and implements were made

stone'-broke' *adj colloq* completely out of money

stoned' *adj slang* drunk

Stone·henge /stōn'henj/ *n* prehistoric ruin on the plain north of Salisbury, England, consisting mainly of a large circle of huge megalithic stones

stone' mar'ten *n* marten (*Mustela foina*) of the Old World, with a white mark on the breast and throat

stone's' throw' *n* short distance

stone'wall' *vt* 1 to block, obstruct || *vi* 2 to block, obstruct all interference

ston'y *adj* (**-i·er; -i·est**) 1 full of or containing stones; 2 pert. to or like stone; 3 hard, unyielding; merciless || **ston'i·ly** *adv*

stood /stŏŏd'/ *pt & pp* of stand

stooge /stŏŏj'/ [?] *n colloq* 1 foil for a comedian or the butt of his jokes; 2 underling, puppet, yes man || *vi* 3 to act as a stooge

stool /stŏŏl'/ [OE *stōl*] *n* 1 single seat

without a back; **2** bench or rest for the feet or knees; **3** matter discharged from the bowels ‖ *vi* **4** to act as a stool pigeon

stool' pi'geon also **stool'ie** [< *stool* in obsolete sense of decoy bird] *n slang* criminal who informs on other criminals

stoop[1] /stōōp/ [OE *stūpian*] *vi* **1** to bend the body down and usu. forward; **2** to carry the head and shoulders habitually bowed forward; **3** to condescend or deign; **4** to submit ‖ *vt* **5** to bend down ‖ *n* **6** act or instance of stooping; **7** stooping position

stoop[2] [D *stoep*] *n* small platform or porch with a short flight of stairs at the entrance to a house

stop /stop/ [< OE *forstoppian* < L *stuppa* < Gk *styppē* oakum] *v* (**stopped**; **stop·ping**) *vt* **1** to close by filling, stuffing, covering, etc.; **2** to obstruct; make impassable; **3** to cause to cease motion or activity; **4** to cause to cease; **5** to suspend, discontinue; **6** to prevent; **7** *sports* to defeat; **8** to desist from; **9 stop down** *photog* to close down (the aperture of a camera); **10 stop up** to plug ‖ *vi* **11** to cease; discontinue; desist; halt; **12** to halt for a short time; **13** to lodge; **14 stop by** to make a brief visit in passing; **15 stop in** to drop in for a visit; **16 stop off** to stop briefly in passing; **17 stop over** to stay over ‖ *n* **18** act of stopping; **19** obstruction; **20** pause or delay; **21** halt; stay; **22** place where public conveyances stop for passengers; **23** punctuation mark, esp. a period; **24** device to regulate or check motion or to keep a movable part in place; **25** finger hole on a wind instrument closed to change the pitch; **26 a** set of organ pipes producing tones of the same quality; **b** lever that actuates organ stops; **27** *phonet* consonant sound formed by complete closure of the vocal tract; **28** order to stop payment on a check; **29** *photog* f number ‖ **SYN** *v* cease, check, arrest, obstruct, end, suspend

stop'cock' *n* faucet or valve that regulates the flow of a liquid or gas

stop'gap' *n* makeshift, temporary substitute

stop'light' *n* **1** taillight that lights up when the driver depresses the brake pedal; **2** traffic light

stop' num'ber *n photog* f number

stop' or'der *n* order to a broker to sell a stock if the price descends to a predesignated level

stop'o'ver *n* **1** temporary stop in the course of a journey; **2** stopover privilege with the right to continue later, on a railroad, airplane, or bus ticket

stop'page /-ij/ *n* **1** act or instance of stopping or state of being stopped; **2** obstruction, block

stop' pay'ment *n* order to a bank not to cash a specified check

stop'per *n* **1** one who or that which stops; **2** plug, as a cork, for closing a bottle, cask, etc. ‖ *vt* **3** to close with a stopper

stop' street' *n* street, marked with a stop sign, at which all traffic must stop and yield the right of way before proceeding

stop'watch' *n* watch with a hand that can be instantly started and stopped, for use in timing races, etc.

stor·age /stôr'ij, stôr'-/ [see **store**] *n* **1** act of storing or state of being stored; **2** space for storing; **3** price charged for storing

stor'age bat'ter·y *n* **1** voltaic battery consisting of storage cells; **2** storage cell

stor'age cell' *n* voltaic cell which is recharged by passing through it an electric current in the reverse direction

store /stôr', stōr'/ [OF *estor*] *n* **1** great quantity or number; **2** supply, esp. one kept in reserve or ready for use; **3** retail shop; **4 stores** *pl* supplies of necessities; **5 in store, a** in waiting; **b** in readiness; **6 set or lay store by** to value or esteem ‖ *vt* **7** to furnish or stock; **8** to accumulate or collect; **9** to put away for safekeeping, as in a warehouse

store'house' *n* (**-hous·es** /-ziz/) **1** building where goods are stored; **2** person or thing that is an abundant source of knowledge, wisdom, etc.

store'keep'er *n* shopkeeper

store'room' *n* room for storage

sto·rey /stôr'ē, stōr'-/ *n Brit* story[1]

sto·ried /stôr'ēd, stōr'-/ [see **story**[2]] *adj* celebrated in story or history

stork /stôrk/ [OE *storc*] *n* any of a family (Ciconiidae) of wading birds with long legs and neck and a long bill

storm /stôrm/ [OE] *n* **1** strong wind accompanied by thunder, lightning, rain, snow, or the like; **2** wind with force 11 or 64–72 miles per hour on Beaufort scale; **3** anything like a storm, as *a storm of applause*; **4** outburst of passion or excitement; **5** violent commotion; **6** *mil* violent assault on a fortified place ‖ *vt* **7** *mil* to attack by frontal assault; **8** to subject as if to a storm, as *the crowd stormed the doors* ‖ *vi* **9** to blow, hail, rain, or snow violently; **10** to rage; **11** to rush violently

storm' cel'lar *n* underground structure or cellar providing refuge during a severe storm, cyclone, etc.

storm' cen'ter *n* person or place that is a center of troubles, tumult, or agitation

storm' door' *n* extra door outside the regular door to protect against cold and drafts

storm' hood' *n* knitted hood covering

the head and neck with openings for the eyes

storm′ sew′er *n* sewer for carrying off excess rainfall from streets or roads

storm′ sig′nal *n* signal, as a flag, displayed in coastal areas to warn of a storm

storm′ win′dow *n* extra window outside the regular one to protect against cold and drafts

storm′y *adj* (**-i·er**; **-i·est**) 1 characterized by or subject to storms; 2 turbulent, violent, raging

storm′y pet′rel *n* 1 any of several small sea birds of the family Hydrobatidae; 2 any person who causes strife and controversy

sto·ry¹ /stôr′ē, stōr′-/ [ME *storie*] *n* (**-ries**) space or set of rooms between two floors of a building

sto·ry² [Gk *historia*] *n* (**-ries**) 1 history; 2 narration of real or imagined events; 3 short tale or romance; 4 anecdote; 5 plot of a narrative; 6 facts about someone or something; 7 report; rumor; 8 *colloq* falsehood; 9 article in a newspaper ‖ SYN account, legend, incident, narrative, recital, tale, novel, fable (see *anecdote*)

sto′ry line′ *n* plot of a play, novel, or the like

sto′ry·tell′er *n* 1 one who tells stories; 2 *colloq* liar ‖ **sto′ry·tell′ing** *n*

stoup /stoop′/ [ME *stowp*] *n* basin for holy water at the entrance of a church

stout /stout′/ [OF *estout* brave, proud] *adj* 1 bold, brave, resolute; 2 sturdy, firm, powerful; 3 large and bulky; 4 stocky, thickset ‖ *n* 5 very strong ale or porter ‖ **stout′ly** *adv*

stout′-heart′ed *adj* brave, courageous, undaunted

stove¹ /stōv′/ [OE *stofa* bathroom] *n* apparatus, using fuel or electricity, that furnishes heat for cooking or for warmth and comfort

stove² *pt* & *pp* of **stave**

stove′pipe′ *n* 1 pipe for carrying off the smoke and gases from a stove; 2 also **stove′pipe′ hat′** *colloq* tall silk hat

stow /stō′/ [OE = place] *vt* 1 to put away in the proper place, esp. without loss of space; 2 to fill by packing closely; 3 *slang* to stop; 4 **stow away** to put away, as for storage ‖ *vi* 5 **stow away** to hide, as aboard a ship, in order to avoid paying for passage

stow′age /-ij/ *n* 1 act of stowing or state of being stowed; 2 space or place for stowing; 3 that which is stowed; 4 charge for stowing

stow′a·way′ *n* one who hides on a vessel or airplane to avoid paying the fare or to evade pursuit

St.′ Paul′ *n* capital of Minnesota (309,-980)

St.′ Pierre′ and Miq′ue·lon′ /pyer′ ən

mik′əlon′/ *n* small group of islands belonging to France off the S coast of Newfoundland

stra·bis·mus /strəbiz′məs/ [Gk *strabismos*] *n pathol* condition of being cross-eyed

strad·dle /strad′əl/ [< OE *strād* strode] *vi* 1 to stand, sit, or walk with the legs wide apart; 2 *colloq* to appear to favor both sides of a question ‖ *vt* 3 to stand or sit across, bestride; 4 to spread (the legs) wide; 5 *colloq* to appear to favor both sides of (a question) ‖ *n* 6 act of straddling; 7 space between the legs when wide apart; 8 *stock exchange* arrangement by which one buys the option of either calling for or delivering stock at a stated price; 9 *colloq* noncommittal position on a question

Strad·i·var·i·us /strad′iver′ē·əs/ [L form of *Stradivari*] *n* any of the violins made by Antonio Stradivari (1644–1737) of Cremona, Italie

strafe /strāf′, sträf′/ [G *strafen* to punish] *vt* 1 to punish or harass by heavy fire or bombardment; 2 to subject (ground troops) to machine-gun and cannon fire from low-flying aircraft

strag·gle /strag′əl/ [ME *straglen*] *vi* 1 to wander out of the direct course; stray away from others; 2 to roam idly; wander; 3 to spread about in scattered fashion ‖ **strag′gler** *n* ‖ **strag′gly** *adj* (**-gli·er**; **-gli·est**)

straight /strāt′/ [< OE *streccan* to stretch] *adj* 1 not crooked or curved; 2 perfectly vertical or horizontal; 3 honorable, upright; 4 orderly; properly placed or arranged; 5 *colloq* direct from the source, reliable; 6 plain; unmodified; 7 undiluted (liquor); 8 correct, right, as *straight thinking;* 9 unbroken (succession); 10 *slang* normal, not homosexual ‖ *adv* 11 in a straight manner or direction; 12 each, as *ten cents straight;* 13 at once, forthwith; 14 **set someone straight** to inform one of the true facts of a situation; 15 **straight ahead** in a straight forward direction; 16 **straight off** or **away** immediately, without delay; 17 **to go straight** to mend one's ways ‖ *n* 18 *poker* sequence of five cards

straight′ and nar′row (path′) *n* way of virtue

straight′a·way′ *adj* 1 without curves or turns ‖ *n* 2 straightaway race track or part of a track ‖ *adv* 3 at once

straight′edge′ *n* strip of wood or metal having a perfectly straight edge with which to test or draw straight lines

straight′en *vt* also **straighten out** 1 to make straight; 2 to clear up, disentangle; 3 to impart the facts or truth to ‖ *vi* also **straighten out** 4 to become straight; 5 to become decent, reliable, etc. ‖ **straight′en·er** *n*

straight′ face′ *n* serious facial expression that conceals a desire to laugh at something ludicrous ‖ **straight'-faced'** *adj*

straight' flush' *n poker* sequence of five cards of the same suit

straight'for'ward *adj* 1 leading directly onward; 2 honest, open, frank ‖ *adv* 3 in a straightforward manner ‖ SYN *adj* honest, frank, open, candid, direct

straight' from the shoul'der *adv* directly, without evasion ‖ **straight'-from-the-shoul'der** *adj*

straight' jack'et *n* var of strait jacket

straight' man' *n show bus.* foil for a comedian

straight' ra'zor *n* razor with a large blade that folds into the handle

straight' shoot'er *n* upright honorable person

straight'way' *adv* at once

straight' whis'key *n* unblended whiskey 80 to 110 proof

strain¹ /strān/ [OE *strēon* product, progeny] *n* 1 stock, race, line of descent; 2 hereditary tendency or trait; 3 trace, streak; 4 variety, as of a species

strain² [OF *estreindre*] *vt* 1 to stretch to the utmost; 2 to stretch beyond proper limits; 3 to weaken or injure by excessive use or overexertion; sprain; 4 to overload, make excessive demands on, as *to strain one's luck;* 5 to embrace; 6 to filter; 7 to remove by filtering; 8 to deform, as by stress ‖ *vi* 9 to make a violent effort, strive; 10 to be filtered; 11 to become injured by overuse or overexertion ‖ *n* 12 act of straining or state of being strained; 13 great exertion; 14 injury due to overexertion; sprain; 15 excessive demands, as on resources, emotions, physical strength, etc.; 16 musical passage; 17 flight or burst of the imagination, as a song, tune, or poem; 18 alteration in the shape of a body due to stress

strained' *adj* 1 forced; not relaxed or natural; 2 weakened, impaired (friendship)

strain'er *n* filter or sieve for straining liquids

strait /strāt/ [OF *estreit*] *n* often **straits** *pl* 1 narrow stretch of water connecting two larger bodies of water; 2 perplexity, difficulty

strait'en *vt* to put into difficulties; embarrass, distress

strait' jack'et *n* 1 strong tight coat made so as to prevent the use of the arms, used to restrain the violently insane; 2 anything that restrains freedom of action

strait'-laced' *adj* strict in manners or morals; puritanical, prudish

strake /strāk/ [ME < *stretch* or *streak*] *n naut* continuous line of planks or plates extending from stem

to stern along the bottom or sides of a vessel

strand¹ /strand/ [OE] *n* 1 shore ‖ *vt* 2 to drive ashore, run aground, as a ship; 3 to leave in a state of embarrassment or difficulty ‖ *vi* 4 to run aground

strand² [?] *n* 1 one of a number of flexible strings, as of wire or fiber, twisted together into a cable or rope; 2 similar string, as of pearls, beads, or hair; 3 thread or threadlike part

strange /strānj/ [OF *estrange*] *adj* 1 of or belonging to others; not one's own; 2 belonging to some other place; 3 not known or seen before; 4 odd, unusual, out of the ordinary; 5 reserved, shy, as *to feel strange in company;* 6 unversed, unacquainted, as *she is strange to that kind of work* ‖ *adv* 7 in a strange manner ‖ SYN *adj* uncommon, extraordinary, unnatural, irregular, marvelous, queer, fantastic (see *eccentric*)

stran'ger *n* 1 person whom one does not know; 2 one who is unfamiliar with something; 3 newcomer

stran-gle /straŋ'gəl/ [OF *estrangler* < L *strangulare*] *vt* 1 to choke; kill by squeezing the throat; 2 to suppress or stifle ‖ *vi* 3 to be choked or suffocated ‖ **stran'gler** *n* ‖ **stran-gu-la-tion** /straŋ'gyəlāsh'ən/ *n*

strap /strap/ [OE *stropp* thong] *n* 1 narrow band, as of leather, used to fasten objects or hold them in place; 2 any narrow strip or band, as one of metal to hold parts of a frame together, a watchband, a band of cloth on the shoulder of a jacket, or the leaf of a hinge; 3 razor strop ‖ *v* (strapped; strap'ping) *vt* 4 to fasten with a strap; 5 to beat with a strap; 6 to strop

strap'hang'er *n colloq* standee in a bus or subway who steadies himself by holding onto an overhead strap or bar

strapped' *adj colloq* lacking, hard up, as *strapped for cash*

strap'ping *adj* strong, robust; large

stra-ta /strāt'ə, strat'ə/ *pl* of **stratum**

strat-a-gem /strat'əjəm/ [Gk *strategema* piece of generalship] *n* trick or ruse, esp. for deceiving the enemy in war ‖ SYN artifice, maneuver, ruse (see *subterfuge*)

stra-te-gic /strətēj'ik/ *adj* 1 pert. to or serving the ends of strategy; 2 skillfully adapted to the end in view; 3 essential to the conduct of war, as *strategic materials* ‖ **stra-te'gi-cal-ly** *adv*

strat-e-gy /strat'ijē/ [Gk *strategia* generalship] *n* (-gies) 1 art or science of planning and directing large-scale military operations; 2 skill in using stratagems; 3 plan for securing a desired end ‖ **strat'e-gist** *n*

strat·i·fy /ˈstratəˌfī/ [< *stratum* + *-fy*] *v* (-fied) *vt* 1 to form or arrange in strata or layers || *vi* 2 to form layers || **strat'i·fi·ca'tion** *n*

strato- [L *stratus* spread out] *comb form* 1 stratus; 2 stratosphere

strat'o·cu'mu·lus /ˌstratˈō-, stratˈō-/ *n* (-li /-lī'/) low cloud formation characterized by dark masses in waves or layers

strat'o·sphere' /ˈstratə-/ *n* the part of the earth's atmosphere between the troposphere and the ionosphere, from about seven to about fifteen miles above the surface, where there are no clouds, no strong currents, and no changes of temperature with altitude || **strat'o·spher'ic** /-sferˈik/ *adj*

stra·tum /ˈstratəm, stratˈ-/ [L = something spread] *n* (-ta /-tə/ or -ums) 1 layer of material of any kind; 2 geol layer or bed, as of rock or sand; 3 level or gradation, as of society

stra·tus /ˈstratˈəs, stratˈ-/ [L = spread out] *n* (-ti /-tī/) continuous horizontal layer of cloud, generally of uniform thickness and low altitude

Strauss, Jo·hann /ˈyōhän' strousˈ/ *n* (1825–99) Austrian composer of operettas and waltzes

Strauss, Richard *n* (1864–1949) German composer of operas, tone poems, songs, etc.

straw /strô/ [OE *strēaw*] *n* 1 stalk of grain; 2 mass of such stalks when cut and threshed; 3 fibers of such stalks used in making hats, baskets, etc.; 4 small tube for sucking beverages || *adj* 5 made of straw; 6 of the color of straw; 7 worthless, paltry

straw'ber·ry /-berˈē, -bərē/ *n* (-ries) 1 red, acid fruit of any of several low-growing plants (genus *Fragaria*); 2 plant that bears this fruit

straw'ber·ry mark' *n* reddish, slightly raised birthmark

straw' boss' *n colloq* head of a work crew

straw' man' *n* 1 figure of a man filled with straw, sometimes used as a scarecrow; 2 inconsequential or non-existent person used by another as a front or cover

straw' vote' *n* unofficial vote to ascertain the trend of opinion on an issue or a candidate

stray /strā/ [MF *estraier*] *vi* 1 to wander from the direct or proper path or course; 2 to roam, wander; 3 to wander from the path of right or duty || *n* 4 one who or that which strays; 5 domestic animal lost and wandering about || *adj* 6 lost, wandering about; 7 incidental, casual

streak /strēk/ [OE *strica* stroke, mark] *n* 1 line of color; stroke or stripe; 2 flash (of lightning); 3 vein, tendency, as *a streak of sadism*; 4 layer; 5 *colloq* run, as of luck; 6 like a

streak *colloq* very swiftly || *vt* 7 to mark with streaks || *vi* 8 to become streaked; 9 to move swiftly; 10 to flash; 11 to race naked in public || **streak'y** *adj* (-i·er; -i·est)

stream /strēm/ [OE *strēam*] *n* 1 current of water or other fluid; 2 brook or river; 3 continuous flow, as of light, cars, etc.; 4 continued course or drift || *vi* 5 to flow or move as in a stream; 6 to emit a stream, as *eyes streaming with tears*; 7 to stretch out with a waving motion, as a flag || *vt* 8 to throw off or pour out in a stream

stream'er *n* 1 anything that floats or streams out, as a long narrow flag; 2 newspaper headline stretching across the top of the page

stream'line' *vt* to make streamlined

stream'lined' *adj* 1 having a surface that offers the least resistance when moving through air or water; 2 modern; 3 compact; full of frills

stream'-of-con'scious·ness *adj* (fictional writing) in which the thoughts of the characters are presented as wandering from preoccupations to random incidentals and back again, independently of what the characters say or seem to be thinking

street /strēt/ [OE *strǣt* < L (via) *strata* paved (road)] *n* 1 public road in a city or town, usu. paved and with sidewalks and buildings on both sides; 2 that part of such a road reserved for vehicles; 3 **the Street** *colloq* **a** the financial district; **b** the theater and entertainment district || *adj* 4 of or pert. to a street; 5 level with the street; 6 suitable for general wear in public || SYN *n* highway, thoroughfare, road, avenue (see *way*)

street'car' *n* electric passenger conveyance running on rails through the streets, formerly common in most cities and towns

street' name' *n* stockbroker who holds a customer's securities in his own name, as a matter of convenience, esp. in frequent trading

street'walk'er *n* prostitute who solicits on the streets

strength /streŋth'/ [OE *strengthu*] *n* 1 state or quality of being strong; force, power; 2 power of resistance to a force; toughness; 3 vehemence; 4 intensity; 5 potency; 6 military force as measured in numbers; 7 one who or that which is a support or stay; 8 **on the strength of** on the basis of || SYN robustness, power, sturdiness, toughness (see *energy*) || ANT weakness, feebleness, frailty

strength'en *vt* 1 to make strong or stronger || *vi* 2 to become stronger || **strength'en·er** *n*

stren·u·ous /ˈstrenyo͞oˈəs/ [L] *adj* marked by or requiring great exertion

strep·to- /strep'tō-/ [Gk *streptos*] *comb form* twisted

strep'to·coc'cus *n* (-coc·ci /-kok'sī/) any of a genus (*Streptococcus*) of spherical or oval bacteria, several species of which are pathogenic to man

strep'to·my'cin /-mīs'in/ [< *strepto-* + Gk *mykes* fungus] *n* antibiotic —C₁₁H₃₉N₇O₁₂— extracted from the soil microorganism *Streptomyces griseus*

stress /stres'/ [*abbr* of *distress*] *n* 1 compulsion; strain; pressure; 2 importance; emphasis; 3 *mech* a force causing deformation or change of volume; **b** ratio of such a force to the area over which it is exerted; 4 *phonet* relative emphasis with which certain syllables are pronounced || *vt* 5 to subject to stress; 6 to emphasize; 7 *phonet* to accent

-stress /-stris/ *nfem suf* [-*ster* + -*ess*] denoting a feminine agent, as *songstress*

stretch /strech'/ [OE *streccan*] *vt* 1 to draw out to full length or breadth; extend; 2 to extend, as a rope, between two points; 3 to draw out or distend forcibly; 4 to strain to the utmost; 5 to reach out, extend; 6 to make taut || *vi* 7 to spread, reach, as *the rope stretches across the street;* 8 to extend or spread the body or limbs; 9 to become stretched; 10 **stretch out** to lie down at full length || *n* 11 act or instance of stretching, or state of being stretched; 12 continuous line, space, or time; 13 either of the two long straight sides of an oval race track; 14 elasticity; 15 *slang* term of confinement in jail

stretch'er *n* 1 one who or that which stretches; 2 any of various devices for stretching; 3 canvas-covered frame or litter for carrying the disabled

strew /strōō'/ [OE *strewian*] *v* (*pp* **strewed** or **strewn**) *vt* 1 to scatter or spread loosely over a surface; 2 to cover (a surface) with something scattered

stri·ate /strī'āt/ [< *stria* furrow] *vt* to mark with furrows or stripes || **stri'**at·ed *adj*

strick·en /strik'ən/ 1 *pp* of **strike** || *adj* 2 beset or afflicted

strict /strikt'/ [L *strictus* tight, narrow] *adj* 1 exacting, rigorous; 2 exact, precise; 3 rigidly enforced or observed; 4 narrowly limited; 5 harsh, severe || **strict'ly** *adv* || **strict'ness** *n* || SYN rigid, stringent, stern, harsh, exacting, exact (see *austere*) || ANT careless, lenient, indulgent, lax

stric·ture /strik'chər/ [LL *strictura* tightening] *n* 1 adverse criticism; 2 abnormal narrowing of a passage or duct in the body || SYN censure (see *criticism*)

stride /strīd'/ [OE *strīdan*] *v* (**strode;** **strid·den** /strid'ən/) *vi* 1 to walk with long steps || *vt* 2 to pass over with one long step; 3 to walk with long steps on || *n* 4 long step; 5 striding gait; 6 **hit one's stride** to reach one's level of competence; 7 **take in one's stride** to handle with one's accustomed ease

stri·dent /strīd'ənt/ [L *stridens* (-*entis*) creaking] *adj* harsh; shrill; grating

strife /strīf'/ [OF *estrif*] *n* 1 discord; conflict; 2 contention

strike /strīk'/ [OE *strīcan*] *v* (**struck;** **struck** or **strick·en**) *vt* 1 to hit, smite; attack; 2 to give, as a blow; 3 to come into forcible contact with; 4 to lower, as a flag; 5 to take down and pack, as a tent; 6 to cause to sound, as a bell; 7 to announce by sound, as *the clock struck twelve;* 8 to cause (a match) to ignite by rubbing the head; 9 to stamp with a die, as coins; 10 to occur to; 11 to impress or affect, as with emotion; 12 to conclude (a bargain); 13 to assume, as a pose; 14 to impress, as *it strikes me funny;* 15 to find, as gold or oil; 16 to arrive at (a balance); 17 to make suddenly (blind, deaf, or dumb); 18 to walk out of (a shop, factory, etc.) in a dispute with the employer over pay or working conditions; 19 **strike down** to kill or afflict suddenly; 20 **strike it rich** to become suddenly wealthy; 21 **strike off, a** to print (a certain number of copies); **b** to remove, as a name from a list; 22 **strike out, a** to cross out; **b** *baseball* to put out by a strike-out; 23 **strike up, a** to begin to play (a tune); **b** to commence (a friendship) || *vi* 24 to deal a blow; make an attack; 25 to hit, collide; 26 to proceed, as *they struck north;* 27 to sound, as a clock; 28 to cease work in order to gain better pay or working conditions; 29 **strike home** to hit the mark; 30 **strike on** or **upon** to come unexpectedly and suddenly on; 31 **strike out** *baseball* to be put out by a strike-out || *n* 32 act or instance of striking; 33 stopping of work in order to secure better pay or working conditions; 34 discovery of ore or oil; 35 any sudden success; 36 *baseball* a unsuccessful attempt by the batter to hit the ball; **b** ball in the strike zone not hit at by the batter; 37 *bowling* knocking down of all the pins by the first ball bowled; 38 quantity of coins minted at the same time; 39 metal piece on the door jamb into which the bolt slides; 40 **on strike** engaged in a strike against an employer

strike'break'er *n* one who works in place of a worker on strike, or who furnishes such workers to an employer

strike'-out' *n baseball* out made by a batter who has received three strikes

strik'er *n* **1** one who or that which strikes; **2** a mechanism of a clock that strikes the hour; **b** clapper of such a mechanism that strikes a bell or gong; **3** employee who goes out on strike

strike' zone' *n baseball* area above home plate, usu. from the batter's shoulders to his knees

strik'ing *adj* very noticeable; remarkable ‖ **strik'ing·ly** *adv*

string /string/ [OE *streng*] *n* **1** small cord, thick thread, twine, etc., for tying and binding; **2** narrow strip of cloth used for tying, as *an apron string;* **3** tightly stretched cord whose vibrations produce musical tones in certain instruments; **4** set of things, as beads, arranged on a string; **5** series of things in or as in a line, as *a string of cars, a string of oaths;* **6** fiber of a plant; **7 strings** *pl* **a** the stringed instruments of an orchestra; **b** *colloq* conditions attached to an offer or proposal; **8 pull strings** to use influence ‖ *v* (**strung**) *vt* **9** to furnish with a string or strings; **10** to thread on a string; **11** to extend, as *to string a wire across the room;* **12** to extend in a line or series; **13** to remove the strings from, as beans; **14 string along** to hoax; **15 string up, a** to fasten by hanging up; **b** to kill by hanging ‖ *vi* **16** to form into or as into strings; **17 string along** with to follow the lead of; **18 string out** to extend or stretch

string' bean' *n* **1** any of various beans cooked and eaten in their pods; **2** *colloq* tall, skinny person

stringed' in·stru·ment *n* musical instrument in which the sound is produced by causing the strings to vibrate with a bow, a plectrum, or the fingers

strin·gent /strin'jənt/ [L *stringens* (*-entis*) tightening] *adj* **1** strict, severe, exacting; **2** tight (money market) ‖ **strin'gen·cy** *n*

string·er /string'ər/ *n* **1** heavy horizontal timber connecting uprights and supporting other members; **2** board supporting the ends of steps in a staircase; **3** *journalism* part-time correspondent covering a local area for a newspaper

string' quar·tet' *n* **1** quartet consisting of two violins, a viola, and a cello; **2** composition for such a group

string' tie' *n* very narrow straight necktie, usu. tied in a bow

string'y *adj* (**-i·er; -i·est**) **1** full of, consisting of, or like strings or fibers, as meat; **2** gluey, ropy

strip¹ /strip/ [ME *strippe*] *v* (**stripped** or **stript; strip·ping**) *vt* **1** to make naked; **2** to deprive of a covering; **3** to deprive; **4** to plunder, rob; **5** to pull off; **6** to empty out, as *to strip*

a house; **7** to break the threads of a bolt or the teeth of a gear; **8** to dispossess, as of wealth or honors ‖ *vi* **9** to strip something; **10** to remove all one's clothes; **11** to do a striptease ‖ *n* **12** *colloq* striptease

strip² [ME] *n* **1** long narrow piece, as of paper, cloth, or land; **2** airplane runway

stripe /strīp/ [MD] *n* **1** long narrow band of a different color or nature than the rest of the surface; **2** strip of braid or the like worn on a uniform to indicate rank, service, wounds, etc. ‖ *vt* **3** to mark with stripes ‖ **striped'** *adj*

strip·ling /strip'ling/ [ME] *n* youth, young lad

strip' min'ing *n* mining, esp. of coal, from the surface, after removal of the topsoil

strip'per *n* **1** one who or that which strips; **2** stripteaser

strip'tease' *n* burlesque act in which a woman slowly removes her clothes a garment at a time to music ‖ **strip'·teas'er** *n*

strive /strīv/ [OF *estriver* to quarrel] *v* (**strove; striv·en** /striv'ən/) *vi* **1** to make strenuous efforts; **2** to struggle; **3** to compete

strobe /strōb/ *n colloq* stroboscope

stro·bo·scope /strōb'ə-, strob'-/ [< Gk *strobos* a twisting + *-scope*] *n* **1** instrument for studying or observing periodic motion by rendering a moving body visible only at regular intervals; **2** *photog* a lamp that produces short bursts of light that synchronize with a camera shutter for photographing speeding objects, as a bullet in flight; **b** photograph made with such a lamp ‖ **stro·bo·scop·ic** /-skop'ik/ *adj*

strode /strōd/ *pt of* **stride**

stroke /strōk/ [< OE *strican* to strike] *n* **1** act of striking; blow; **2** striking of one body against another; **3** sudden attack of apoplexy or paralysis; **4** discharge (of lightning); **5** gently moving touch, as of the hand; **6** single complete movement of a part or mechanism, often one of a series; **7** sound of a bell or of a clock in marking the time; **8** time so marked; **9** single movement of a pen, pencil, or brush; **10** mark made by a pen, etc.; **11** movement of the arm in swimming; **12** feat, as *a stroke of genius;* **13** sudden chance happening; **14** vigorous effort; **15** *rowing* **a** complete movement of the oars or manner of moving them; **b** oarsman who sets the time; **16** beat of the heart ‖ *vt* **17** to rub gently with the hand; **18** to hit (a ball) ‖ **syn** *n* impact, hit, knock (see *blow*)

stroll /strōl/ [?] *vi* **1** to wander on foot from place to place; **2** to ramble, saunter ‖ *vt* **3** to ramble along or through ‖ *n* **4** ramble, leisurely walk

stroll'er *n* 1 one who strolls; 2 low chairlike carriage for a young child, propelled by pushing

strong /strôɳ, strɒɳ/ [OE *strang*] *adj* (**strong·er** /strôɳ'gər, strɒɳ'gər/; **strong·est** /strôɳ'gist, strɒɳ'gist/) 1 physically, mentally, or morally powerful; 2 persuasive, compelling, as proof, an argument, etc.; 3 favorable, well-endowed, as a *strong economy*; 4 resistant, durable; 5 firm, uncompromising, as *strong views*; 6 intense, concentrated (light, sound, coffee, perfume, etc.); 7 containing much alcohol, as *strong drink*; 8 *gram* inflected by change in the root vowel; 9 *phonet* **a** (vowel) made with the jaws or the lips more open than for a weak vowel; **b** (syllable) that is stressed; 10 of a specified numerical force, as *9,000 strong* ‖ *adv* 11 strongly ‖ **strong'ly** *adv* ‖ SYN *gist* adj hardy, powerful, brawny, sinewy, compact, concentrated, violent ‖ ANT *adj* weak, feeble

strong'-arm' *adj* 1 threatening the use of force and violence to gain an end ‖ *vt* 2 to use force and violence on

strong'box' *n* strongly built box for storing valuables

strong'hold' *n* 1 fortress; 2 bastion of like-minded partisans, as *the Bronx is a Democratic stronghold*

strong' man' *n* 1 man who performs feats of strength in a circus; 2 leader; good planner; 3 man who controls by force; dictator

strong'-mind'ed *adj* 1 having a vigorous mind; 2 obstinate

stron·ti·um /stron'sh(ē)əm/ [< *Strontian* parish in Scotland] *n* soft white alkaline metallic element (Sr; at.no. 38; at.wt. 87.62) resembling calcium, used in fireworks and flares

stron'ti·um 90' *n* radioactive isotope of strontium, harmful to animal life, present in the fallout of certain nuclear reactions

strop /strop'/ [OE] *n* 1 strip of leather for sharpening razors ‖ *v* (**stropped**; **strop·ping**) *vt* 2 to sharpen on or as on a strop

stro·phe /strōf'ē/ [Gk] *n* 1 rhythmic scheme in which two or more lines are repeated but not always with the same structure; 2 stanza

strove /strōv'/ *pt* of **strive**

struck /struk'/ *pt & pp* of **strike**

struc·ture /struk'chər/ [L *structura*] *n* 1 that which is built; edifice; construction; 2 manner or form of building; 3 form or arrangement of parts or elements of something constructed or of a natural organism ‖ *vt* 4 to give a structure or organization to ‖ **struc'tur·al** *adj* ‖ SYN edifice (see *building*)

stru·del /strood'əl/ [G] *n* pastry made of fruit rolled in a thin sheet of dough and baked

strug·gle /strug'əl/ [ME *strugle*] *vi* 1 to contend violently with an opponent; 2 to strive, labor ‖ *n* 3 effort or endeavor; 4 contest, strife ‖ **strug'gler** *n*

strum /strum'/ [imit] *v* (**strummed**; **strum·ming**) *vt* 1 to pluck idly at the strings of (a musical instrument); 2 to play (a tune) by strumming ‖ also *vi*

strum·pet /strump'it/ [ME] *n* harlot

strung /struɳ'/ *pt & pp* of **string**

strut¹ /strut'/ [OE *strūtian* to jut] *v* (**strut·ted**; **strut·ting**) *vi* 1 to walk stiffly with a pompous or conceited air ‖ *n* 2 strutting walk

strut² [?] *n* brace or bar to support weight or pressure

strych·nine /strik'nīn, -nin, -nēn/ [< Gk *strychnos* kind of nightshade] *n* poisonous bitter alkaloid —C₂₁H₂₂ N₂O₂— obtained chiefly from the nux vomica; used as a nerve and heart stimulant

stub /stub'/ [OE *stubb* stump] *n* 1 any short projection; 2 short remaining part, as of a cigar or pencil; 3 the part of a leaf left in a checkbook or receipt book serving as a memorandum; 4 the part of an admission ticket torn off and returned to the user ‖ *v* (**stubbed**; **stub·bing**) *vt* 5 to strike against some fixed object, as *to stub one's toe*

stub·ble /stub'əl/ [OF *stuble*] *n* 1 the stumps of grain left in the ground after mowing; 2 anything resembling stubble, as a beard of two or three days' growth

stub·born /stub'ərn/ [ME *stiborne*] *adj* 1 obstinately perverse; 2 obstinately pursued, practiced, or maintained; 3 unyielding, intractable ‖ **stub'born·ly** *adv* ‖ SYN inflexible, perverse, obstinate (see *headstrong*)

stub·by *adj* (**-bi·er; -bi·est**) 1 full of stubs; 2 bristly; 3 short and thick ‖ **stub'bi·ness** *n*

stuc·co /stuk'ō/ [It] *n* (**-coes** or **-cos**) 1 exterior finish for walls, made of cement, sand, and hydrated lime; 2 fine plaster for decorations such as cornices and moldings ‖ *vt* 3 to cover or decorate with stucco

stuck /stuk'/ 1 *pt & pp* of **stick²** ‖ *adj* 2 stuck on *slang* infatuated with

stuck'-up' *adj colloq* conceited; supercilious

stud¹ /stud'/ [OE *studu* post] *n* 1 upright timber in walls to which the laths are nailed; 2 ornamental boss or knob projecting from a surface; 3 device resembling a two-headed button and used as a fastener, esp. in shirt fronts; 4 stud bolt; 5 projecting pin serving as a support, stop, etc. ‖ *v* (**stud·ded**; **stud·ding**) *vt* 6 to furnish, set, or adorn with studs; 7 to be set thickly in, as *stars stud the sky*

stud² [OE *stōd*] *n* 1 place where horses are kept for breeding; 2 studhorse; 3 herd of horses or other animals kept for breeding; 4 **at stud** used or available for breeding

stud′ bolt′ *n* headless bolt threaded at both ends

stud′book′ *n* register giving the pedigree of thoroughbred stock, esp. of race horses

stu·dent /st(y)ōōd′ənt/ [L *studens* (*-entis*) studying] *n* 1 one enrolled for study in a school; 2 anyone who studies or investigates || *adj* 3 of or pert. to students

stud′horse′ *n* stallion kept for breeding

stud·ied /stud′ēd/ *adj* designed; premeditated; deliberate

stu·di·o /st(y)ōōd′ē·ō′/ [It = study] *n* 1 workroom of an artist; 2 place equipped to produce radio and television shows and motion pictures

stu′di·o a·part′ment *n* one-room apartment with a kitchen or kitchenette and bathroom

stu′di·o couch′ *n* backless couch convertible into a double bed

stu·di·ous *adj* 1 given to, pert. to, or characterized by study; 2 heedful, thoughtful, earnest

stud′ pok′er *n* poker game in which the players are dealt one card face down and four cards face up one at a time, with bets made at each round

stud·y /stud′ē/ [OF *estudie* < L *studium*] *n* (**-ies**) 1 application of the mind to the gaining of knowledge, as by reading or investigation; 2 particular branch of learning; 3 examination of a particular question, as *a study of childhood*; 4 written account of such an examination; 5 deep thought, reflection; 6 room set apart for study, reading, etc.; 7 *mus* piece for a special kind of practice || *v* (**-ied**) *vi* 8 to devote oneself to the acquisition of knowledge; 9 to pursue a regular course of study || *vt* 10 to acquire knowledge about; 11 to learn or memorize; 12 to investigate carefully; 13 to observe closely

stuff /stuf′/ [OF *estoffe*] *n* 1 material of which anything is made; 2 any immaterial principle or essence; 3 things and objects in general; 4 doings of a particular kind, as *cut that stuff out!*; 5 baseball spin, speed, or curve that a pitcher imparts to a ball; 6 **know one's stuff** *colloq* to know what one is doing or talking about || *vt* 7 to crowd, cram, or pack; 8 to fill by cramming; 9 to fill with specially prepared material, as a fowl with bread crumbs or a pillow with feathers; 10 to fill (the skin of a dead animal) to give it a lifelike appearance; 11 to put votes dishonestly into (a ballot box); 12 **stuff up** to stop up or plug || *vi* 13 to eat glut-

tonously || SYN *v* satiate, cloy, glut, crowd, cram

stuffed′ shirt′ *n colloq* pompous self-satisfied person

stuff′ing *n* 1 that with which a thing is stuffed; 2 preparation, as of bread crumbs, for filling poultry before roasting

stuff′ing box′ *n* device for establishing a water-tight or air-tight passage for a moving part, as a piston, through another part

stuff′y *adj* (**-i·er; -i·est**) 1 close or badly ventilated, as a room; 2 stodgy, dull; 3 rigid; old-fashioned

stul·ti·fy /stult′ifī′/ [LL *stultificare*] *v* (**-fied**) *vt* 1 to make foolish, reduce to absurdity; 2 to render futile || **stul′ti·fi·ca′tion** *n*

stum·ble /stum′bəl/ [ME] *vi* 1 to trip or fall in walking; 2 to walk in an unsteady or clumsy manner; 3 to act in a blundering fashion; 4 to fall into error or crime; 5 to come by chance || *n* 6 act of stumbling; 7 failure or blunder

stum′ble·bum′ *n slang* maladroit, clumsy person, esp. a third-rate boxer

stum′bling block′ *n* obstacle or hindrance

stump /stump′/ [ME *stumpe*] *n* 1 that part of a tree remaining in the ground after the trunk is cut off; 2 base, as of an arm, tooth, or cigar, remaining after the main part is removed; 3 political rostrum || *vt* 4 to canvass (a district) making political speeches; 5 to perplex, nonplus, baffle || *vi* 6 to walk stiffly, as if with a wooden leg; 7 to make stump speeches

stump′ speech′ *n* one of a series of political speeches made on a campaign tour

stump′y *adj* (**-i·er; -i·est**) short and thick, stubby

stun /stun′/ [OF *estoner*] *v* (**stunned; stun·ning**) *vt* 1 to make senseless by or as by a blow; 2 to confuse or daze with noise; 3 to benumb with amazement, astound

stung /stuŋ′/ *pt & pp* of **sting**

stunk /stuŋk′/ *pt & pp* of **stink**

stun′ning *adj* 1 overpowering the senses; 2 strikingly beautiful

stunt¹ /stunt′/ [OE = stupid] *vt* 1 to check the growth or development of; dwarf || *n* 2 check in growth; 3 plant or animal that has been checked in growth or development, esp. a dwarfed plant

stunt² [?] *n* 1 striking feat performed to attract attention or gain applause; 2 exhibition of skill or daring || *vi* 3 to perform a stunt or stunts

stunt′ man′ *n* in motion pictures, person who substitutes for an actor in dangerous or acrobatic scenes

stu·pe·fy /st(y)ōōp′ifī′/ [MF *stupefier*] *v* (**-fied**) *vt* 1 to dull the senses of;

benumb; **2** to astound, astonish ‖ **stu′pe·fac′tion** *n*

stu·pen·dous /st(y)ōō·pen′dəs/ [< L *stupendus*] *adj* **1** overcoming the senses by enormous size or greatness; **2** astonishing, astounding ‖ SYN enormous, prodigious, monstrous, amazing

stu·pid /st(y)ōōp′id/ [L *stupidus*] *adj* **1** benumbed; incapable of feeling; **2** slow-witted, dull; **3** foolish, inane, as *a stupid act* ‖ **stu′pid·ly** *adv* ‖ **stu·pid′i·ty** /-pid′itē/ *n* (**-ties**) ‖ SYN simple, sluggish, absurd, doltish, heavy, obtuse, senseless (see *blunt*) ‖ ANT astute, intelligent, keen

stu·por /st(y)ōōp′ər/ [L] *n* suspension or great lessening of the senses and faculties, as by drink, drugs, or illness

stur·dy /sturd′ē/ [OF *estourdi* stunned] *adj* (**-di·er; -di·est**) **1** hardy, robust; stout; **2** resolute, firm

stur·geon /sturj′ən/ [OF *esturgeon*] *n* any of a family (Acipenseridae) of large fishes of northern seas, having rows of long bony plates on the body and an elongated upper jaw; an important source of caviar and isinglass

stut·ter /stut′ər/ [ME *stutten*] *vt & vi* **1** to stammer ‖ *n* **2** stammer

St.′ Vi′tus dance′ /vīt′əs/ [*St. Vitus* 3rd-cent. saint] *n* disease of the nervous system characterized by involuntary jerky movements

sty¹ /stī′/ [OE *stig*] *n* (**sties**) pigpen

sty² /stī′/ [< ME *styany*] *n* (**sties**) small inflamed swelling like a boil on the edge of the eyelid

Styg·i·an /stij′ē·ən/ [< Gk *Stygios*] *adj* **1** pert. to the river Styx; **2** infernal, hellish; **3** gloomy, dark

style /stīl′/ [L *stylus* var of *stilus* stylus] *n* **1** stylus; **2** characteristic manner of writing or speaking; **3** mode of expression or execution in any art; **4** sort or kind, with reference to form, appearance, etc.; **5** manner of conduct or action; **6** fashion, smart design; **7** form of address, title; **8** *bot* narrowed prolongation of the ovary which, when present, bears the stigma ‖ *vt* **9** to term, name, or call; **10** to design the distinctive style of ‖ SYN *n* fashion, manner, way (see *mode, diction*)

styl′ish *adj* fashionable, following the latest style ‖ **styl′ish·ly** *adv*

styl′ist *n* **1** writer or speaker whose literary style shows high quality or individuality; **2** designer of styles, esp. of clothing and interior decoration

sty·lis′tic *adj* of or pert. to style

styl′ize *vt* to make conform to a particular style or artistic convention

sty′lo·graph′ /stīl′ə-/ *n* fountain pen fitted with a pierced conical writing point which controls the flow of ink

sty·lus /stīl′əs/ [L var of *stilus*] *n* (**-lus·es; -li** /-lī/) **1** pointed instrument for writing on wax, mimeograph stencils, etc.; **2** needle for cutting grooves in a phonograph record; **3** phonograph needle

sty·mie /stīm′ē/ [?] *n* **1** *golf* position of a ball on the putting green lying directly between the ball of an opponent and the hole ‖ *v* (**-mied; -mie·ing** or **-my·ing**) *vt* **2** to obstruct or thwart

styp·tic /stip′tik/ [Gk *styptikos* binding] *adj* **1** astringent; **2** checking bleeding

styp′tic pen′cil *n* small stick of a styptic substance, as alum, used to stop bleeding from minor cuts while shaving

Styx /stiks′/ *n* *Gk myth.* river across which Charon ferried the shades of the dead to Hades

sua·sion /swāzh′ən/ [L *suasio* (*-onis*)] *n* persuasion

suave /swäv′/ [F < L *suavis* gracious] *adj* urbane, smooth in manner ‖ **suav′i·ty** /swäv′-, swav′-/ *n* (**-ties**)

sub /sub′/ *n* **1** substitute; **2** submarine ‖ *v* (**subbed; sub·bing**) *vi* **3** to substitute

sub- /sub′-, səb-/ [L = beneath] *pref* **1** lower in position, rank, order, or degree, as *submarine, subdivision;* **2** *chem* a indicating a basic compound, as *subacetic;* **b** indicating presence in a less than normal amount, as *subcarbide*

sub·al·tern /subôlt′ərn/ [L *subalternus*] *adj* **1** of lower rank; subordinate ‖ *n* **2** person occupying a subordinate position; **3** *Brit* army lieutenant

sub·a·tom′ic *adj* of or pert. to particles contained within the atom

sub′com·mit′tee *n* subordinate committee made up of some of the members of the main committee

sub·con′scious *adj* **1** occurring in the mind without conscious perception; unconscious ‖ *n* **2** the **subconscious** the totality of subconscious mental activities

sub′con′ti·nent *n* **1** large subdivision of a continent that is geographically, politically, racially, and in other possible ways separated from it; **2** large mass of land, completely surrounded by water, that is not large enough to be designated as a continent, as Greenland ‖ **sub′con·ti·nen′tal** *adj*

sub·con′tract *n* contract granted by a contractor to another person to fulfill a part of the original contract ‖ **sub·con′trac·tor** /also sub′kəntrak′tər/ *n*

sub·cu·ta′ne·ous *adj* under the skin

sub′deb′ also **sub·deb′u·tante′** *n* young girl during the year or two preceding her debut into society

sub·di·vide′ *vt* **1** to divide into parts; **2** to divide further; **3** to divide (land) into building lots ‖ *vi* **4** to undergo division of a part ‖ **sub′di·vi′sion** *n*

sub·due /səbd(y)ōō′/ [MF *so(u)duire*

to decline < L *subducere* to withdraw] *vt* 1 to conquer, vanquish; 2 to bring under control, as by persuasion or influence; 3 to tone down or soften || **sub-dued′** *adj* || SYN control, subjugate, defeat (see *vanquish*)

subj. 1 subject; 2 subjective(ly); 3 subjunctive

sub-ject /sub′jekt, -jikt/ [L *subjectus* thrown under] *n* 1 one who owes allegience to a government, esp. to a sovereign; 2 one who or that which is submitted to experiment or treatment; 3 object of discussion or of investigation; 4 course of study; 5 theme, topic; 6 *gram* word or word group in a sentence denoting that concerning which an affirmation is made; 7 thing represented by an artist in a work of art || *adj* 8 under the power or control of another; dependent; 9 **subject to,** a exposed to the influence of; b prone to, liable to; c conditional upon || /səbjekt′/ *vt* 10 **subject to,** a to bring under the control of; b to expose or make liable to; c cause to undergo the action of || **sub-jec′tion** *n*

sub-jec′tive /səb-/ *adj* based on one's own feelings about an object thought of, and not objectively on the object itself || **sub-jec′tive-ly** *adv* || **sub′-jec-tiv′i-ty** /sub′jektiv′itē/ *n*

sub-join′ /sub-/ *vt* to add to the end, append

sub-ju-gate /sub′jəgāt′/ [LL *subjugare* (-*atus*)] *vt* to conquer, bring under subjection || **sub′ju-ga′tion** *n* || **sub′-ju-ga′tor** *n* || SYN defeat, overcome, enslave (see *vanquish*)

sub-junc-tive /səbjuŋk′tiv/ [< L *subjunctus* subjoined] *adj* 1 designating or pert. to the mood of a verb which expresses state or action as provisional, contingent, or dependent, rather than as a fact, as *were* in *if I were king* || *n* 2 subjunctive mood; 3 verb in the subjunctive

sub′lease′ *n* 1 lease granted by a lessee to another person || **sub-lease′** /sub-/ *vt* 2 to grant a sublease of; 3 to take or hold a sublease of

sub-let′ /sub-/ *v* (-let; -let-ting) *vt* 1 to sublease; 2 to subcontract

sub-li-mate /sub′limāt′/ [L *sublimare* (-*atus*)] to elevate] *vt* 1 to sublime; 2 to refine or purify; 3 to divert (physical impulses or drives) to more socially acceptable goals || *vi* 4 to sublime || /also sub′limit/ *n* 5 solid material or deposit condensed when a substance is sublimed || **sub′li-ma′-tion** *n*

sub-lime /səblīm′/ [L *sublimis* high] *adj* 1 exalted, elevated; 2 inspiring awe and reverence || *vi* 3 to pass from solid to vapor and back to solid form without becoming liquid || *vt* 4 to cause to sublime

sub-lim-i-nal /sublim′inəl/ [*sub-* + L *līmen* threshold + -*al*] *adj* below the threshold of conscious perception

sub-lim′i-ty /-lim′itē/ *n* (-ties) 1 state or quality of being sublime; 2 that which is sublime || SYN splendor, magnificence, nobility (see *grandeur*)

sub-lux-a-tion /sub′luksāsh′ən/ [NL *subluxatio* (-*onis*)] *n* partial dislocation of a joint

sub′ma-chine′ gun′ *n* light automatic firearm fired from the shoulder or the waist

sub-ma-rine′ *adj* 1 living, situated, or used beneath the surface of the sea || usu. **sub′ma-rine′** *n* 2 war vessel that operates submerged, armed with torpedoes or guided missiles

sub-merge /səbmurj′/ [L *submergere*] *vt* 1 to place under, or cover with, water or other liquid || *vi* 2 to sink under water or out of sight || **sub-mer′gence** *n*

sub-merse /səbmurs′/ [< L *submersus* submerged] *vt* to submerge || **sub-mer′sion** /-zhən, -shən/ *n*

sub-mers′i-ble *adj* 1 capable of submersion || *n* 2 submarine

sub′mi-cro-scop′ic *adj* too small to be seen with an optical microscope

sub-min′i-a-ture /sub-/ *adj* extremely small or compact (electronic equipment)

sub-mis-sion /səbmish′ən/ [L *submissio* (-*onis*) lowering] *n* 1 act or instance of submitting; 2 state of having submitted; 3 submissiveness || SYN subjection, obedience, meekness (see *patience*)

sub-mis-sive /səbmis′iv/ *adj* 1 yielding to authority; obedient; 2 humble, meek || **sub-mis′sive-ness** *n* || SYN subservient, unassertive, passive, compliant, docile || ANT independent, disobedient, unyielding

sub-mit /səbmit′/ [L *submittere* to lower] *v* (-mit-ted; -mit-ting) *vt* 1 to yield to the will of another; surrender; 2 to present for approval or decision; 3 to propose, offer as an opinion || *vi* 4 to yield or surrender; 5 to defer; acquiesce; 6 to be submissive, be obedient

sub-mul′ti-ple *n* number that is contained in another an exact number of times

sub-nor′mal *adj* below normal, esp. in intelligence or emotional response

sub-or′der *n biol* division of animals and plants comprising the group between an order and a family

sub-or′di-nate /-nit/ [ML *subordinatus*] *adj* 1 lower or inferior in rank, nature, value, power, or importance; 2 subject to another || *n* 3 subordinate person or thing || /-nāt′/ *vt* 4 to place in a lower order, make secondary; 5 to make subject or obedient || **sub-or′di-na′tion** *n*

sub-or′di-nate clause′ *n gram* clause that modifies the principal clause

sub-or′di-nat′ing (or **sub-or′di-nate**)

con·junc′tion n conjunction that introduces a subordinate clause

sub·orn /səbôrn′/ [L *subornare* to equip, adorn] vt 1 to induce (someone) to do something unlawful, as by bribery; 2 *law* to induce (a person) to give false testimony ‖ **sub′-or·na′tion** n

sub·poe·na /sə(b)pēn′ə/ [L = under penalty] n 1 written order commanding the attendance of a person in court ‖ vt 2 to serve with a subpoena

sub·ro·gate /sub′rōgāt′/ [L *subrogare* (-*atus*) to name a substitute] vt to substitute (one person, spec. a creditor) for another ‖ **sub′ro·ga′tion** n

sub ro′sa /rōz′ə/ [L = under the rose] adv privately, in strict confidence

sub·scribe /səbskrīb′/ [L *subscribere*] vt 1 to write (something) beneath or at the end of a document; 2 to bear witness to by signing; 3 to promise to pay or contribute (a certain sum) by signing one's name ‖ vi 4 to affix one's name to a document; 5 to assent or agree, give support; 6 to sign as a promise to contribute, as to a charity; 7 to obtain a subscription to a newspaper or periodical ‖ **sub·scrib′er** n

sub·script /sub′skript/ adj 1 written or printed below ‖ n 2 character or symbol written next to and slightly below another

sub·scrip·tion /səbskrip′shən/ n 1 act of subscribing; 2 contribution of money; 3 order to receive a periodical for a certain number of issues; 4 amount pledged for any object

sub·se·quent /sub′səkwənt/ [L *subsequens* (-*entis*)] adj following, succeeding ‖ **sub′se·quent·ly** adv

sub·ser·vi·ent /səbsurv′ē·ənt/ [L *subserviens* (-*entis*)] adj 1 servile; obsequious, truckling; 2 subordinate ‖ **sub·ser′vi·ence** n ‖ SYN submissive, truckling, cringing, abject

sub·side /səbsīd′/ [L *subsidere*] vi 1 to sink to a lower level or to the bottom; 2 to become less violent; grow calm, abate

sub·sid·i·ar·y /səbsid′ē·er′ē/ adj 1 auxiliary, supplementary; 2 secondary, subordinate ‖ n (-ies) 3 subsidiary person or thing; 4 company owned by another company

sub·si·dize /sub′sidīz′/ vt 1 to furnish with a subsidy; help financially; 2 to purchase the aid of, with money; to bribe

sub·si·dy [L *subsidium* aid] n (-dies) 1 grant of money by a government to a private industry or organization or to another government; 2 any gift made to aid another financially

sub·sist /səbsist′/ [L *subsistere* to remain] vi 1 to remain in existence; 2 to be supported, live

sub·sist′ence n 1 state of subsisting or existing; 2 means of livelihood, as food and clothing

sub·sist′ence al·low′ance n money paid for meals and housing in addition to the regular salary, as to employees or to members of the armed forces

sub′soil′ n bed of earth beneath the surface soil

sub·son′ic adj 1 infrasonic; 2 less than the speed of sound; 3 traveling at a speed less than the speed of sound

sub·stance /sub′stəns/ [L *substantia* essence] n 1 essential part of anything; 2 material or matter of which a thing consists; 3 solidity; firmness; 4 wealth, worth; 5 purport or meaning of a speech or writing

sub·stand′ard adj 1 below standard; 2 not good enough

sub·stan·tial /səbstansh′əl/ adj 1 pert. to or having substance; 2 solid, firm; 3 of real worth or value; 4 wealthy, prosperous; 5 real or true for the most part, as *substantial justice* ‖ **sub·stan′tial·ly** adv

sub·stan·ti·ate /-shē·āt′/ vt 1 to establish by evidence or proof; verify; 2 to give concrete form to; embody ‖ **sub·stan′ti·a′tion** n ‖ SYN confirm, establish, ratify, sustain, settle, fix ‖ DISCR To *substantiate* is to prove the truth of a charge, assertion, claim, or the like, by producing evidence, good grounds, or some such body of facts to back it. To *establish* is also to prove absolutely; that which is *established* as a fact, is beyond dispute. Solidity is the thought back of *substantiate;* foundation lies back of *establish.* To *confirm* is to *establish* that which was doubtful, as a rumor, that which was trembling in the balance, as power, that which needed authority, as an agent's right to do business for some one else, that which was uncertain, as the time of a meeting. To *sustain* is to uphold, as a decision by a higher court; to tend to prove or bear out, as the witnesses who followed him *sustained* his testimony. To *ratify* is formally to *confirm;* we *ratify* certain agreements by signature; nations *ratify* treaties. To *settle* an argument or question is to arrive at a conclusion that is final

sub·stan·ti·val /-stəntīv′əl/ adj of, pert. to, or like a substantive or noun

sub·stan·tive /sub′stəntiv/ [L *substantivus* self-existent] adj 1 existing independently; 2 essential; 3 real, permanent; 4 substantial; 5 *gram* expressing existence ‖ n 6 *gram* a noun; b word or phrase used as a noun

sub·stan·tive·ly adv 1 essentially; in essence; 2 as a substantive or noun

sub·sta′tion n 1 branch station, esp. of a post office; 2 power station where high-tension alternating current is transformed to a lower voltage, to direct current, or to a different frequency

sub·sti·tute /sub'stĭt(y)o͞ot'/ [L *substitutus*] *n* **1** one who or that which is put in the place of another; **2** cheaper or inferior article ‖ *adj* **3** functioning in place of another person or thing; **4** pert. to or involving a substitute ‖ *vt* **5** to put in the place of someone or something ‖ *vi* **6** to act as a substitute; **7** substitute for to take the place of ‖ **sub'sti·tu'tion** *n*

sub·stra'tum *n* (-ta /-tə/ or -tums) **1** under layer or stratum, as of soil or rock; **2** that which forms a groundwork or support

sub·sume /subso͞om'/ [< *sub-* + L *sumere* to take] *vt* **1** to include in some particular class or under some particular rule; **2** to cite as being covered by a principle

sub'teen' *n* person eleven or twelve years old

sub·tend /subtend'/ [L *subtendere* to stretch beneath] *vt* **1** *geom* to lie opposite to, as the chord of an arc to the arc; **2** *bot* to enfold or enclose in an axil, that is, between a leaf or branch and a stem or trunk

sub·ter·fuge /sub'tərfyo͞oj'/ [LL *subterfugium*] *n* anything, as a trick, pretext, or evasion, by which one seeks to escape from a difficulty; false excuse ‖ SYN artifice, cunning, finesse, maneuver, trick, ruse, stratagem ‖ DISCR *Artifice* is cleverly planned indirection. It wriggles out of a difficult situation by using some crafty device; it screens its real purpose while apparently effecting something else; it secures an advantage or benefit by artful contriving. It is ready and skillful, as she used every *artifice* in her power to keep the officer from the room where the prisoner lay hidden; she averted questions by *artifice*. The other words are kinds of *artifice*. A *subterfuge* is a dodge to avoid blame or get out of something through a false excuse; *subterfuge* employs evasion, as his excuses for not going were transparent *subterfuges*; he justified everything from politics to lapses from duty by miserable *subterfuges*. A *trick* is a fraudulent measure or device, sometimes elaborately planned, to deceive or get the better of somebody. *Trick* has the connotation of underhandedness, of not being aboveboard, and of being actually harmful; "a dirty trick" is a common expression. A *maneuver* is like *artifice* in that it is carefully planned, but it accomplishes its purpose by false or deceiving movements, elusiveness, or sidestepping, as by adroit *maneuvers* he succeeded in circumventing his enemies. *Stratagem* is *artifice* deeply laid, minutely worked out, and usually di-

rected toward some considerable end, as "fit for treasons, *stratagems,* and spoils." A *ruse* is a feint to draw away attention from what one is really going to do; it uses the false movement of *maneuver* with the purpose of *trick*, as he was inveigled into betraying his secret by a clever *ruse*. *Finesse* is adroit manipulation, usually subtle, exercised on that which is critical, ticklish, or requires careful handling. Diplomats sometimes need to use *finesse*. *Cunning*, which is either the quality or the act of artfulness, is a craftiness that ensnares, a wiliness that entraps, as he flattered him with low *cunning* until the trap was sprung. Sometimes these words are used innocently, playfully, or in a good sense, as a childish *trick;* a *stratagem* by which a surprise is effected in war; an *artifice* by which an invalid is enticed to follow advice; a *finesse* at cards; the *maneuvers* of an army or navy at war; the *ruse* by which a lunatic is persuaded to return to his cell

sub·ter·ra'ne·an /-tərăn'ē·ən/ [L *subterraneus*] *adj* **1** underground; **2** hidden, secret

sub'ti'tle *n* **1** secondary, usu. explanatory, title; **2** *motion pictures* descriptive title, dialogue, or translation of a dialogue, flashed on the screen between scenes or superimposed on the bottom of the screen ‖ *vt* **3** to give a subtitle to

sub·tle /sut'əl/ [OF *soutil* < L *subtilis* fine-woven] *adj* **1** thin, fine; **2** delicate, refined; **3** sly, cunning; **4** clever, ingenious; **5** acute, discerning; **6** intricate, abstruse; **7** insidious ‖ **sub'tle·ty** *n* (-ties) ‖ **sub'tly** /sut'lē/ *adv* ‖ SYN delicate, elusive, penetrating, crafty (see *wily*)

sub·tract /səbtrakt'/ [L *subtrahere* (-*tractus*) to draw from under] *vt* to withdraw, take away, as a part from the whole or one quantity from another ‖ **sub·trac'tion** *n*

sub·trac'tion sign' *n* the symbol —, indicating subtraction

sub·tra·hend /sub'trəhend'/ [L *subtrahendum*] *n* number subtracted from another

sub·trop'i·cal *adj* of or pert. to the regions bordering the tropic zone

sub·urb /sub'ərb/ [L *suburbium*] *n* town or district, usu. residential, adjacent to a larger town or city ‖ **sub·ur·ban** /səburb'ən/ *adj*

sub·ur·ban·ite /səburb'ənīt'/ *n* resident of a suburb

sub·ur'bi·a /-bē·ə/ *n* **1** the suburbs collectively; **2** the social and cultural life of the suburbs

sub·ven·tion /səbven'shən/ [LL *subventio* (-*onis*)] *n* **1** provision of help; support; **2** grant of money, as by a government in aid of research

sub·ver·sive /səbvurs'iv/ [< L *subversus* overthrown] *adj* 1 causing subversion || *n* 2 subversive person

sub·vert /səbvurt'/ [L *subvertere* to overthrow] *vt* 1 to overthrow or destroy, as a government or established institutions; 2 to undermine, as a man's principles || **sub·vert'er** *n* || **sub·ver'sion** /-zhən, -shən/ *n*

sub'way' *n* 1 underground passage; 2 underground electric railway

suc- *pref* var of **sub-**

suc·ceed /səksēd'/ [L *succedere*] *vt* 1 to take the place of, be the successor of; 2 to follow, come next after || *vi* 3 to follow and replace another; 4 to come next after something; 5 to accomplish something attempted; 6 to be successful, prosper; 7 **succeed to** to come next in the possession or tenure of; become heir to

suc·cess /səkses'/ [L *successus*] *n* 1 favorable end or result; 2 attainment of wealth and fame; 3 successful person or thing || SYN attainment, accomplishment (see *victory*)

suc·cess'ful *adj* 1 resulting in or achieving success; 2 having achieved wealth and fame || **suc·cess'ful·ly** *adv* || SYN happy, auspicious, victorious (see *lucky*)

suc·ces'sion /-shən/ *n* 1 a following in order; sequence; 2 series of persons or things following each other in order; 3 act or right of succeeding to the office, title, or possessions of another

suc·ces'sive *adj* following in succession

suc·ces'sor *n* person or thing that follows or succeeds another

suc·cinct /səksiŋkt'/ [L *succinctus*] *adj* expressed in few words; terse, concise || **suc·cinct'ly** *adv* || SYN summary, brief, concise (see *short*)

suc·cor /suk'ər/ [OF *sucurir*] *vt* 1 to help or relieve in difficulty or distress || *n* 2 relief, aid; 3 one who or that which brings aid or relief || SYN *v* comfort, aid, serve, relieve (see *help*)

suc·co·tash /suk'ətash'/ [< Narragansett] *n* green corn and beans boiled together

suc·cu·lent /suk'yələnt/ [LL *succulentus*] *adj* 1 juicy, as fruit; 2 not dry or uninteresting

suc·cumb /səkum'/ [L *succumbere*] *vi* 1 to give way; yield, submit; 2 to die

such /such'/ [OE *swilc*] *adj* 1 of that kind, similar; 2 having the particular quality or character named, as *all such things*; 3 the same as previously mentioned, as *such it remained*; 4 indicating a certain person or thing, as *on such a date*; 5 so remarkable, so great, as *he did such work that he won the prize*; 6 the same, as *such as I have always used* || *adv* 7 to such a degree, as *I have such tired feet*; 8 very, as *she has*

such beautiful eyes; 9 **such that** in such a way that || *pron* 10 such a person or thing; 11 the person or thing indicated; 12 **such as**, a of that kind; b for example

such' and such' *pron* 1 someone or something not specified || *adj* 2 not specified

suck /suk'/ [OE *sūcan*] *vt* 1 to draw (a liquid) into the mouth; 2 to suck a liquid from; 3 to apply the mouth to as in sucking, as *to suck one's thumb, to suck a lemon drop*; 4 to drink in, absorb, as *a sponge sucks up water*; 5 **suck in** *slang* a to flatten (the abdomen) by taking a deep breath; b to defraud || *vi* 6 to suck something || *n* 7 act of sucking

suck'er *n* 1 one that sucks; 2 any of various fresh-water fishes (family Catostomidae) related to the carps; 3 organ of some animals used to adhere to other bodies; 4 *colloq* person easily cheated; 5 *colloq* lollipop; 6 shoot springing from roots or from a stem near the ground

suck'er bait' *n slang* something that lures a person into a position where he may be fleeced

suck'er bet' *n slang* foolish bet which one has no chance of winning

suck·le /-əl/ [ME] *vt* 1 to nurse at the breast; 2 to rear, nourish || *vi* 3 to suck at the breast

suck'ling *n* unweaned child or animal

su·cre /sōō'krā/ [Antonio José de *Sucre* (1795–1830) South Am liberator] *n* monetary unit of Ecuador

Su·cre /sōō'krā/ *n* nominal capital of Bolivia (58,359)

su·crose /sōō'krōs/ [< F *sucre* sugar] *n* a sugar —$C_{12}H_{22}O_{11}$— found in sugar cane, sugar beets, and maple sugar

suc·tion /suk'shən/ [L *suctio* (-*onis*)] *n* 1 process or condition of sucking; 2 force that causes a substance to move to the region of least pressure, as in a suction pump

suc'tion pump' *n* pump which, by the upstroke of its piston, reduces pressure in an area which is then occupied by a fluid forced in by atmospheric pressure

Su·dan /sōōdan'/ *n* Arabic-speaking republic in NE Africa, S of Egypt and W of Ethiopia (15,600,000; 967,-500 sq.m.; cap. Khartoum) || **Su'da·nese'** /-dənēz', -dənēs'/ *adj & n* (-nese)

sud·den /sud'ən/ [MF *sodain*] *adj* 1 happening quickly or unexpectedly; 2 quickly prepared or done; hasty, abrupt; 3 **all of a sudden** suddenly, unexpectedly || **sud'den·ly** *adv*

suds /sudz/ [?] *npl* 1 soapy water; 2 froth or foam; 3 *slang* beer || **suds'y** *adj* (-i·er; -i·est)

sue /sōō/ [OF *suivir*] *vt* 1 to institute legal action against || *vi* 2 to entreat or petition, as *to sue for peace;* **3** to institute a lawsuit

suede /swād'/ [F (gants de) *Suède* (gloves of) Sweden] *n* undressed kid, used for gloves, shoes, etc.

su·et /sōō'it/ [ME *sewet*] *n* the hard fat around the kidneys and loins of mutton and beef, used in cooking and for making tallow ‖ **su'et·y** *adj*

Su'ez Ca·nal' /sōō'ez, sōō·ez'/ *n* canal in NE Egypt connecting the Mediterranean and the Red Sea

suf- *pref* var of **sub-**

suf·fer /suf'ər/ [OF *sofrir*] *vt* **1** to feel (what is painful, disagreeable, or distressing); endure with pain or distress; **2** to experience, undergo; **3** to allow, permit; **4** to tolerate ‖ *vi* **5** to experience loss, pain, distress, etc.; **6** to undergo punishment ‖ SYN endure, support, tolerate (see *allow*)

suf'fer·ance *n* toleration; passive permission implied by not forbidding or hindering

suf'fer·ing *n* **1** bearing of pain; anguish; **2** the pain borne; distress

suf·fice /səfīs'/ [L *sufficere*] *vi* **1** to be sufficient ‖ *vt* **2** to be enough for, content ‖ SYN serve, do, content (see *satisfy*)

suf·fi·cient /səfish'ənt/ [L *sufficiens* (*-entis*)] *adj* adequate, enough ‖ **suf·fi'cient·ly** *adv* ‖ **suf·fi'cien·cy** *n* (*-cies*)

suf·fix /suf'iks/ [L *suffixus* fastened] *n* **1** affix added to the end of a word, as *-ant* in *defendant;* **2** something added ‖ /also səfiks'/ *vt* **3** to add a suffix to; **4** to add as a suffix

suf·fo·cate /suf'əkāt'/ [L *suffocare* (*-atus*)] *vt* **1** to kill by stopping the breath; **2** to smother, stifle; **3** to cut the supply of air from ‖ *vi* **4** to be suffocated; **5** to suffer from lack of fresh air ‖ **suf'fo·ca'tion** *n*

suf·fra·gan /suf'rəgən/ [ML *suffraganeus* assistant] *adj* **1** assistant (bishop); **2** (diocese) subordinate to the see of an archbishop ‖ *n* **3** suffragan bishop

suf·frage /suf'rij/ [L *suffragium*] *n* **1** vote; **2** right or act of voting

suf·fra·gette /suf'rəjet'/ *n* militant woman advocate of female suffrage

suf·fuse /səfyōōz'/ [L *suffundere* (*-fusus*)] *vt* to overspread, as with a fluid or color ‖ **suf·fu'sion** /-zhən/ *n*

Su·fi /sōō'fē/ [Ar = man of wool] *n* member of a mystical Muslim sect ‖ **Su'fism** *n*

sug·ar /shŏŏg'ər/ [MF *sucre* < Ar *sakkar*] *n* **1** *chem* any of a group of carbohydrates soluble in water and having a sweet taste; **2** sweet crystalline substance —C₁₂H₂₂O₁₁— obtained from sugar cane or sugar beet; the ordinary sugar of commerce ‖ *vt* **3** to sprinkle, cover, sweeten, or mix with sugar; **4** to make agreeable ‖ *vi* **5** to form sugar crystals

sug'ar beet' *n* variety of beet (*Beta vulgaris*) with white roots from which sugar is obtained

sug'ar cane' *n* a tall grass (*Saccharum officinarum*) of tropical and subtropical regions, the chief source of sugar

sug'ar-coat' *vt* **1** to coat with sugar; **2** to make (something disagreeable) appear more pleasant

sug'ar ma'ple *n* a maple (*Acer saccharum*) of the E U.S., from the sap of which sugar is made

sug'ar·plum' *n* candy made of sugar and flavoring

sug'ar·y *adj* **1** like, made of, or containing sugar; **2** sweet; **3** honeyed; flattering

sug·gest /səg(g)jest'/ [L *suggerere* (*-gestus*)] *vt* **1** to present or introduce indirectly to the mind or thoughts; **2** to call to mind through the association of ideas; **3** to propose for consideration or acceptance ‖ SYN allude, hint, intimate, indicate

sug·ges·tion /səg(g)jes'chən/ *n* **1** act of suggesting or state of being suggested; **2** something suggested; **3** faint trace; **4** *psychol* **a** stimulation of one idea, impulse, or the like, by another; **b** insinuation of an idea into the mind by external means; **c** idea so insinuated

sug·ges'tive *adj* **1** tending to suggest; **2** suggesting something immoral or indecent; risqué

su·i·cide /sōō'isīd'/ [< L *sui* of oneself + *-cide*] *n* **1** act of intentionally taking one's own life; **2** person who commits suicide; **3** ruin of one's own interests ‖ **su'i·cid'al** *adj*

su·i gen·e·ris /sōō'ī jen'əris/ [L] *adj* **1** of his, her, its, or their own kind; **2** unique

suit /sōōt/ [OF *suite*] *n* **1** set of men's outer garments consisting of matched jacket and trousers, and optionally a vest; **2** woman's outfit consisting of a matched skirt and jacket; **3** one of the four sets of thirteen each in a deck of cards; **4** lawsuit; **5** courtship, wooing; **6** act of seeking favor or justice; petition; **7** follow suit, **a** *cards* to play a card of the suit led; **b** to follow or imitate another's actions ‖ *vt* **8** to fit, adapt; **9** to be suitable to; become; **10** to please, satisfy; **11** suit oneself to do as one pleases ‖ *vi* **12** to prove acceptable ‖ SYN conform, adapt, accommodate (see *fit²*)

suit'a·ble *adj* fitting, appropriate ‖ **suit'a·bil'i·ty** /-bil'-/ *n* ‖ SYN fit, accordant, convenient, adequate, appropriate, compatible (see *becoming*) ‖ ANT unfit, unbecoming, inconvenient, inappropriate

suit'case' *n* flat, rectangular valise

suite /swēt'/ [F] *n* **1** company of attendants; retinue; **2** connected series of rooms, as in a hotel; **3** *mus* **a** set of dances in the same or related keys, for a single instrument or for an orchestra; **b** composition consisting of a number of connected movements or parts; **4** /also sŏōt'/ set of matched furniture

suit·ed /sŏōt'ĭd/ *adj* appropriate or compatible

suit'ing *n* cloth for making suits

suit'or *n* man who courts a woman

su·ki·ya·ki /sōōk'ē·yäk'ē/ [Jap] *n* Japanese dish of beef, chicken, or pork with other ingredients, often cooked at the table

sul·fa /sulf'ə/ [< *sulfanilamide*] *adj* **1** related to sulfanilamide; **2** pert. to sulfa drugs || *n* **3** sulfa drug

sul'fa drug' *n* any of a group of drugs related to sulfanilamide

sul'fa·nil'a·mide' /-nil'ə·mīd'/ [*sulfur* + *aniline* + *ammonia* + *-ide*] *n* white crystalline drug —NH₂C₆H₄SO₂ NH₂— used to treat infections caused by streptococci, gonococci, and the like

sul·fate /-fāt/ [< *sulfur*] *n* salt or ester of sulfuric acid

sul'fide /-fīd/ *n* compound of sulfur with another element or radical

sul'fite /-fīt/ *n* salt or ester of sulfurous acid

sul·fur /sulf'ər/ [L] *n* pale-yellow nonmetallic element (S; at.no. 16; at.wt. 32.064) used in the manufacture of gunpowder, in medicine, in vulcanizing rubber, etc.

sul'fur di·ox'ide *n* colorless suffocating gas —SO₂— formed when sulfur burns, used in the manufacture of sulfuric acid, in bleaching and disinfecting, and as a preservative

sul·fu·ric /sulfyŏōr'ĭk/ *adj* of or containing sulfur

sul·fu'ric ac'id *n* dense, oily, colorless, highly acid liquid —H₂SO₄— made chiefly from sulfur dioxide and used extensively in manufacturing processes

sul·fur·ous /sul'fyŏōrəs, sulfyŏōr'əs/ *adj* **1** of, like, or containing sulfur; **2** smelling like burning sulfur

sul·fur'ous ac'id *n* very unstable acid —H₂SO₃— formed by the solution of sulfur dioxide in water and used as a bleach and a disinfectant

sulk /sulk'/ [< *sulky*] *vi* **1** to be sulky || *n* **2** also the **sulks** *pl* sulky mood, fit of sulkiness

sulk'y [OE *asolcen* lazy] *adj* (**-i·er**; **-i·est**) **1** moody, sullen, unsociable || *n* (**-ies**) **2** light two-wheeled, one-horse vehicle for one person || **sulk'i·ness** *n* || SYN *adj* ill-humored, morose, cross (see *gloomy*)

sul·len /sul'ən/ [ME *solein*] *adj* **1** morose, sulky, unsociable, ill-humored; **2** dismal, gloomy || SYN surly, splenetic, morose, grim, churlish, gloomy,

ill-humored, somber, depressing || DISCR *Sullen* describes one who is resentfully discontented and openly *ill-humored*, often to the discomfort of those about him. He is stubbornly silent and centered upon himself. The *surly* and *morose* vent their ill humor upon others in an active rather than a passive way. *Splenetic* is like *surly* and *morose* in that it describes a rooted trait rather than a passing mood. *Splenetic* people are waspish, fretful, sour, and sometimes malicious. *Grim* is applied to the aspect, visage, or nature, and connotes harshness and sternness, as a *grim* judge; or to fate, death, torture, and the like, connoting relentlessness, mercilessness; or to the sinister or ghastly, as a *grim* smile (see *gloomy*)

sul·ly /sul'ē/ [prob MF *soiller* to soil] *v* (**-lied**) *vt* **1** to tarnish or soil; **2** to defile, hurt the good name of

sul·pha /sulf'ə/ *adj & n* var of **sulfa**

sul·phur /sulf'ər/ *n* var of **sulfur**

sul·tan /sult'ən/ [Ar = king] *n* sovereign of a Muslim country || **sul·tan·a** /sultan'ə, -tän'ə/ *nfem*

sul'tan·ate' /-ĭt/ *n* office, tenure, or territory of a sultan

sul·try /sult'rē/ [< *obs sulter* var of *swelter*] *adj* (**-tri·er**; **-tri·est**) **1** intensely hot; **2** intensely hot and humid; **3** arousing sexual passion, as *a sultry blonde* || **sul'tri·ness** *n*

sum /sum'/ [L *summa* (res) the highest (thing)] *n* **1** total of two or more numbers, quantities, substances, etc.; **2** the whole; all; **3** quantity, indefinite amount, as of money; **4** summary, gist; **5** arithmetic problem; **6** **in sum** concisely put || *v* (**summed**; **sum·ming**) *vt & vi* **7** **sum up** to summarize, recapitulate

su·mac /sŏō'mak, shŏō'-/ [ML < Ar *summāq*] *n* **1** any of a genus (*Rhus*) of plants of the cashew family, including various trees, shrubs, and vines, of which certain species produce a severe skin rash; **2** dried leaves and roots of certain species, used in tanning and dyeing

Su·ma·tra /sŏōmät'rə/ *n* large island S of the Malay Peninsula, a part of Indonesia || **Su·ma'tran** *adj & n*

Su·me·ri·an /sŏōmir'ē·ən/ *n* **1** native of Sumer, an ancient country in Mesopotamia that had a highly developed civilization and flourished ab. 3300–1800 B.C.; **2** language of the Sumerians || *adj*

sum·ma cum lau·de /sum'ə kum lôd'ē/ [L = with highest praise] *adj & adv* with highest academic distinction

sum·ma·rize /sum'ərīz'/ *vt* to make or be a summary of

sum·ma·ry [L *summarium*] *n* (**-ries**) **1** brief account containing the sum or substance of a fuller account; abridgment; compendium || *adj* **2** brief, concise; **3** done without delay or ceremony; **4** *law* conducted without the delay of a formal trial ‖ **sum-mar·i·ly** /səmər′ilē, sum′ər-/ *adv*

sum·ma·tion [ML *summatio* (*-onis*)] *n* **1** act or process of finding a total; **2** recapitulation; **3** final summing up by an attorney of a case being tried in court

sum·mer /sum′ər/ [OE *sumor*] *n* **1** warmest season of the year; in the Northern Hemisphere from June 21st to September 22nd; **2** time of happiness and prosperity ‖ *vi* **3** to pass or spend the summer ‖ *vt* **4** to maintain during the summer

sum′mer·house′ *n* (**-hous·es** /-ziz/) small rustic open building for rest or shade in a park or garden

sum′mer sol′stice *n* the solstice occurring on June 21st

sum′mer·time′ *n* summer season

sum′mer·y *adj* **1** pert. to or like summer; **2** warm, cheerful; **3** lightweight (clothes)

sum′ming-up′ *n* (**summings-up**) act or instance of summing up

sum·mit /sum′it/ [OF *somet*] *n* **1** highest point, top; **2** highest state or degree; **3** highest level of government ‖ *adj* **4** taking place between heads of state

sum·mon /sum′ən/ [OF *somondre*] *vt* **1** to call by authority; **2** to command to appear at a certain time or place, as in court; **3** to send for, call, bid, invite; **4** often **summon up** to call forth, rouse ‖ **sum′mon·er** *n* ‖ SYN arraign (see *call*)

sum′mons *nsg* **1** call, request, or command to appear or to do something; **2** *law* order or notice to appear in court

su′mo (wrest′ling) /so͞om′ō/ [Jap] *n* form of Japanese wrestling participated in by men of great height and girth, in which the winner must force his opponent out of the ring or cause any part of his body except the soles of his feet to touch the floor

sump /sump′/ [MD] *n* **1** pit in which water or other liquid collects; **2** reservoir in the bottom of a machine, pump, etc., into which a fluid collects before being recirculated

sump·tu·ous /sump′cho͞o-əs/ [L *sumptuosus*] *adj* **1** lavish; costly; **2** luxurious, magnificent

sum′ to′tal *n* essence; what something adds up to

sun /sun′/ [OE *sunne*] *n* **1** central body of the solar system, an incandescent mass of gas around which the earth and the other planets revolve; **2** any self-luminous heavenly body; star; **3** anything like the sun in brightness or splendor ‖ *v* (**sunned**; **sun·ning**) *vt* **4** to expose to the sun's rays, as for warming, drying, tanning, etc. ‖ *vi* to expose oneself to the light and heat of the sun

Sun. Sunday

sun′ bath′ *n* exposure of the body to the rays of the sun to acquire a tan ‖ **sun′bathe′** *vi*

sun′beam′ *n* ray of sunlight ·

sun′burn′ *n* **1** inflammation or darkening of the skin caused by exposure to the sun ‖ *v* (**-burned** or **-burnt**) *vt* & *vi* **2** to tan or burn by exposure to the sun

sun′burst′ *n* something resembling the sun with rays issuing from a circle, as an ornament or piece of jewelry

sun·dae /sun′dē, -dā/ [perh < *Sunday*] *n* serving of ice cream covered with syrup and sometimes also with fruits, nuts, or whipped cream

Sun·day /sun′dē, -dā/ [OE *sunnandæg*] *n* first day of the week, the Christian Sabbath ‖ **Sun′days** *adv*

sun·der /sun′dər/ [OE *sundrian*] *vt* **1** to divide or rend; sever ‖ *vi* **2** to become separated, be severed

sun′di′al *n* instrument for showing the time of day by the position of the shadow cast by a gnomon on a dial

sun′dog′ *n* **1** bright spot of light near the sun caused by refraction from ice crystals in the air; **2** small or fragmentary rainbow near the horizon

sun′down′ *n* **1** sunset; **2** the time of sunset

sun·dry /sun′drē/ [OE *syndrig* separate] *adj* **1** various, several ‖ **sundries** *npl* **2** sundry items

sun′fish′ *n* (**-fish** or **-fishes**) **1** large stubby fish (*Mola mola*) found in most warm seas; **2** any of various small American fresh-water fishes (genus *Lepomis*)

sun′flow′er *n* any of various plants of the genus *Helianthus*, having flattened, showy heads with yellow ray flowers, the seeds of which are used for stock feed and yield an edible oil

sung /sung′/ *pp* of **sing**

sun′glass′es *npl* spectacles with darkened lenses to protect the eyes from the sun's glare

sunk /sungk′/ *pt* & *pp* of **sink**

sunk′en [*archaic pt* of *sink*] *adj* **1** lying beneath the surface; submerged; **2** depressed; on a lower level; **3** hollow, as *sunken cheeks*

sun′ lamp′ *n* ultraviolet-ray lamp, used therapeutically and for getting a sun tan

sun′light′ *n* light of the sun

sun′lit′ *adj* lighted by the sun

sun′ny *adj* (**-ni·er**; **-ni·est**) **1** full of sunshine; **2** bright, cheerful

sun′ny-side′ up′ *adj* (eggs) fried without being turned over

sun′rise′ *n* **1** rise of the sun above the horizon in the morning; **2** time of this

sun′set′ *n* **1** setting of the sun beyond

the horizon in the evening; **2** time of this

sun'shade' *n* **1** anything used as a protection against the sun, as an awning; **2** parasol

sun'shine' *n* **1** light or rays of the sun; **2** place where they fall; **3** brightness, cheeriness || **sun'shin'y** *adj*

sun'spot' *n* one of the dark spots visible periodically on the sun's disk, affecting the earth's magnetism

sun'stroke' *n* acute prostration, often fatal, caused by exposure to the sun or to other intense heat

sun' tan' *n* darkening of the skin caused by exposure to the rays of the sun or of a sun lamp || **sun'-tanned'** *adj*

sun'up' *n* **1** sunrise; **2** the time of sunrise

sun' vi'sor *n* flap attached at the top of the inside of an automobile windshield, that can be swung down to protect the driver's eyes from the rays of a low sun

sup /sup'/ [OF *souper*] *v* (**supped; sup-ping**) *vi* to take supper

su-per /sōōp'ər/ [< *super-*] *colloq adj* **1** excellent; **2** to an extreme or excessive degree || *n* **3** superintendent; **4** supernumerary

su-per- /sōōp'ər-, sōōp'ər-/ [L = above] *pref* **1** over, beyond; **2** exceeding; **3** greater than others of its kind; **4** above, **5** superior to

su'per·a·bun'dance *n* state of being in excess; more than enough || **su'per·a·bun'dant** *adj*

su'per·an'nu·at'ed /-an'yōō-āt'id/ [ML *superannuatus* more than a year old] *adj* **1** retired because of age; **2** too old for work or use; **3** antiquated

su-perb /sōōpurb', sə-/ [L *superbus* proud] *adj* **1** grand, stately; impressive; **2** rich, elegant

su'per·car'go *n* (**-goes** or **-gos**) agent on a merchant ship in charge of its cargo and business during a voyage

su'per·charg'er *n* device for increasing the intake of air into an internal-combustion engine to increase its power

su'per·cil'i·ous /-sil'ē-əs/ [L *supercilious* with raised eyebrows] *adj* contemptuously haughty; arrogantly disdainful of others || **SYN** contemptuous, disdainful, superior, haughty

su'per·con·duc·tiv'i·ty *n* complete or almost complete disappearance of electrical resistance in some metals and organic solids at temperatures near absolute zero || **su'per·con·duc'tive** *adj*

su'per·du'per /-dōōp'ər/ *adj colloq* great, marvelous

su'per·e'go *n* the part of the psyche that mediates between the drives of the ego and the rules laid down by society and by parental authority

su'per·er·o·ga'tion /-er'əgāsh'ən/ [< L *supererogare* to pay out more than

is expected] *n* **1** the doing of more than is required by duty; **2** superfluity

su·per·fi'cial /-fish'əl/ [LL *superficialis*] *adj* **1** pert. to or located on the surface; **2** not profound; shallow || **su·per·fi'cial·ly** *adv* || **su·per·fi'cial·i·ty** /-shē-al'-/ *n* (**-ties**)

su·per·fine' *adj* **1** very fine; of the choicest quality; **2** too refined; overnice

su·per·flu·ous /sōōpurf'lōō-əs/ [L *superfluus*] *adj* being more than is needed or wanted; excessive; needless || **su·per·flu'i·ty** *n* (**-ties**)

su·per·het'er·o·dyne' *electron adj* **1** pert. to a form of heterodyne reception in which the current is rectified, then amplified, and finally detected at audible frequencies || *n* **2** superheterodyne reception; **3** superheterodyne receiver

su·per·high' fre'quen·cy *n* radio frequency between 3,000 and 30,000 megahertz

su'per·high'way' *n* high-speed highway with separated roadways, two or more lanes in each direction, and cloverleaf intersections

su'per·hu'man *adj* **1** exceeding normal human abilities; **2** divine; supernatural

su'per·im·pose' *vt* to lay or add (something) on top of something else

su'per·in·tend' *vt* to direct or supervise || **su'per·in·tend'ence** *n*

su'per·in·tend'ent *n* **1** one who manages or supervises an institution, business, organization, school district, etc.; **2** janitor of an apartment house

su·pe·ri·or /səpir'ē·ər/ [L, *comp* of *super* above] *adj* **1** higher in place, more elevated; **2** higher in rank, dignity, or office; **3** of higher quality, intelligence, ability, etc.; **4** greater in quantity or number; **5** haughty, arrogant; **6** superior to above yielding to or making concessions to || *n* **7** one who is superior to another; **8** head of a religious order or house || **su·pe'ri·or'i·ty** /-or'-, -ōr'-/ *n* || **SYN** paramount, dominant, principal, foremost

Su·pe·ri·or, Lake *n* northernmost and largest of the Great Lakes

superl. superlative

su·per·la·tive /sōōpur'lətiv/ [LL *superlativus*] *adj* **1** surpassing all others; highest in degree; **2** *gram* designating the highest degree of comparison of adjectives and adverbs || *n* **3** highest degree of excellence; **4** superlative thing or person; **5** *gram* **a** superlative degree; **b** form in the superlative || **su·per·la·tive·ly** *adv*

su'per·man' /-man'/ *n* (**-men'/ -men'**) **1** ideal superior being conceived by Nietzsche as the result toward which evolution should tend; **2** superhuman man

su'per·mar'ket *n* large retail market

selling mostly food, in which the customers wait on themselves, place their purchases in trundle carts, and wheel them to check-out counters, where they are paid for

su·per·nat·u·ral /-ˈnætʃ.ɚ.əl/ *adj* 1 being outside of or exceeding the laws or forces of nature; 2 of or pert. to ghosts and spirits; 3 miraculous; divine ‖ **su·per·nat·u·ral·ly** *adv*

su·per·nat·u·ral·ism *n* 1 quality of being supernatural; 2 belief in supernatural intervention in the laws and forces of nature

su·per·no·va *n* (-vas or -vae /-vē/) nova which may emit 100 million times as much light as the sun

su·per·nu·mer·ar·y /< L *super* *numerum* above the number/ *adj* 1 extra, additional; 2 substitute ‖ *n* (-ies) 3 supernumerary person or thing; 4 *theat* actor with a small nonspeaking part, as one of a crowd or of a company of soldiers, etc.

su·per·pose /F *superposer*/ *vt* to lay or place above or on something

su·per·pow·er *n* one of the two or three most powerful nations of the world whose ascendancy cannot be challenged except by its peers

su·per·sat·u·rate *vt* to increase the concentration of (a solution) beyond the saturation point ‖ **su·per·sat·u·ra·tion** *n*

su·per·scribe /L *superscribere*/ *vt* to write or engrave on the outside or top of ‖ **su·per·scrip·tion** /-ˈskrɪp.ʃən/ *n*

su·per·script *adj* 1 written or printed above ‖ *n* 2 character or symbol written next to and slightly above another

su·per·sede /-ˈsēd/ /L *supersedere* to refrain/ *vt* 1 to displace or supplant; 2 to set aside, make void; 3 to remove and put another in the place of ‖ **su·per·ses·sion** *n*

su·per·son·ic *adj* 1 ultrasonic; 2 greater than the speed of sound; 3 traveling at a speed greater than the speed of sound

su·per·sti·tion /-ˈstɪʃ.ən/ /L *superstitio* (-onis)/ *n* 1 irrational fear of the unknown, the mysterious, or the supernatural; 2 belief, act, or practice or system of beliefs and practices, based not on rational thought, but on the supposed power of omens, signs, charms, etc.; 3 any belief accepted without question ‖ **su·per·sti·tious** *adj*

su·per·struc·ture *n* 1 any structure built on something else; 2 the part of a building above the basement or foundation; 3 the part of a ship built above the main deck

su·per·ton·ic *n* *mus* note next above the tonic

su·per·vene /-ˈvēn/ /L *supervenire*/ *vi* 1 to come as something extraneous or additional; 2 to ensue

su·per·vise /-ˈvīz/ /< *super-* + L *videre* (*visus*) to see/ *vt* to direct, oversee, superintend ‖ **su·per·vi·sor** *n* ‖ **su·per·vi·so·ry** *adj* ‖ **su·per·vi·sion** /-ˈvɪʒ.ən/ *n*

su·pine /sōˈpīn/ /L *supinus*/ *adj* 1 lying on the back face upward; 2 inert; passive; indifferent

supp., suppl. supplement

sup·per /ˈsʌp.ɚ/ /OF *souper*/ *n* last meal of the day, following dinner

sup·plant /səˈplænt/ /L *supplantare* to trip up/ *vt* 1 to displace or supersede; 2 to take the place of

sup·ple /ˈsʌp.əl/ /OF *souple*/ *adj* 1 easily bent; flexible; 2 lithe; 3 submissive, yielding; 4 mentally alert and adaptable ‖ SYN limber, pliant, elastic (see *flexible*)

sup·ple·ment /ˈsʌp.lə.mənt/ /L *supplementum*/ *n* 1 that which completes or adds to something already made; 2 part added to a book to complete it or correct errors; 3 special additional section of a newspaper or magazine ‖ /-ˈment/ *vt* 4 to complete by supplying what is lacking; 5 to add a supplement to ‖ **sup·ple·men·ta·ry** *adj*

sup·pli·ant /ˈsʌp.lɪ.ənt/ /MF/ *adj* 1 supplicating ‖ *n* 2 one who supplicates

sup·pli·cant /ˈsʌp.lɪ.kənt/ *adj & n* suppliant

sup·pli·cate /L *supplicare* (-atus)/ *vt* 1 to seek earnestly by prayer or humble entreaty; 2 to beseech humbly ‖ *vi* 3 to make earnest entreaty ‖ **sup·pli·ca·tion** *n*

sup·ply /səˈplī/ /MF *souplier*/ *v* (-plied) *vt* 1 to furnish, provide; 2 to meet or make up for, as *supply a need* ‖ *n* (-plies) 3 act of supplying; 4 that which is supplied; 5 amount of any article on hand; stock; 6 **supplies** *pl* necessary items for equipment and daily operations, as of a business or an army; 7 **in short supply** *colloq* hard to obtain, not readily available ‖ **sup·pli·er** *n*

sup·port /səˈpôrt, -ˈpōrt/ /L *supportare* to transport/ *vt* 1 to bear the weight of, hold up; 2 to endure, bear; 3 to encourage, help; 4 to establish the truth of, confirm; 5 to favor, back up, advocate; 6 to keep up, maintain; 7 to provide for, bear the expense of; 8 *theat* to act a subordinate part to ‖ *n* 9 act of supporting, or state of being supported; 10 one who or that which supports; 11 maintenance; 12 one who bears expenses ‖ **sup·port·a·ble** *adj* SYN *v* maintain, prop, carry, sustain, patronize, encourage, substantiate, hold, cherish, assist

sup·port·er *n* 1 one who or that which maintains or upholds; 2 elastic device used to support or bind some part of the body

sup·port lev·el *n* point in a declining

market at which a security ceases to decline because of the attractiveness of its low price

sup-pose /səpōz'/ [OF *supposer*] *vt* 1 to assume as a probability; formulate as a working hypothesis; 2 to believe, think; 3 to involve, imply; 4 to consider as a probability, as *suppose we all go*; 5 **be supposed to** be be expected to ‖ *vi* 6 to presume, think ‖ SYN think, deem, guess, conjecture, surmise

sup-posed' *adj* 1 believed or accepted as true; 2 imagined ‖ **sup-pos'ed-ly** /-idlē/ *adv*

sup-po-si-tion /sup'əzish'ən/ [L *suppositio* (-*onis*) substitution] *n* 1 act of supposing; 2 that which is supposed; conjecture, assumption ‖ SYN guess, conjecture, surmise, opinion

sup-pos-i-to-ry /səpoz'itôr'ē, -tôr'-/ [ML *suppositorium*] *n* (-*ries*) solid medicated preparation that melts at body temperature, for insertion into the rectum or vagina

sup-press /səpres'/ [L *supprimere* (-*pressus*)] *vt* 1 to subdue by force, crush; 2 to restrain, stifle; 3 to conceal; withhold knowledge of, stop the publication of; 4 *psychol* to repress, inhibit ‖ **sup-pres'sion** /-shən/ *n*

sup-pu-rate /sup'yərāt/ [L *suppurare* (-*atus*)] *vi* to form or discharge pus ‖ **sup'pu-ra'tion** *n* ‖ **sup'pu-ra'tive** *adj*

su-pra /sōō'prə/ [L] *adv* above, usu. in a text

su-pra- /sōō'prə-/ [L] *pref* above, beyond, superior to

su'pra-na'tion-al *adj* done, planned, or controlled by a group of nations

su-prem-a-cy /səprem'əsē, sōō-/ *n* 1 state of being supreme; 2 supreme power or authority ‖ SYN domination, ascendancy, mastery, victory

su-preme /səprēm', sōō-/ [L *supremus*] *adj* 1 highest in power or authority; 2 highest in degree; 3 greatest possible, utmost

Su-preme' Be'ing *n* God

Su-preme' Court' *n* 1 highest court in most states; 2 highest U.S. court

Su-preme' So'vi-et *n* legislature of the Soviet Union

supt., Supt. superintendent

sur-¹ /sur-/ [OF < L *super*] *pref* over, beyond, above

sur-² *pref* var of **sub-**

sur-cease /sursēs'/ [MF *sursis*] *n* end, discontinuance

sur'charge' *n* 1 additional or excessive charge; 2 additional or excessive load; 3 overprint on a stamp that alters its face value ‖ also **sur-charge'** *vt* 4 to add an additional charge to; 5 to print a surcharge on (a stamp)

sur'cin'gle /-sin'gəl/ [MF *surcengle*] *n* belt or strap for passing around the body of a horse to secure the saddle, blanket, etc.

sur'coat' *n* 1 coat or cloak worn over another coat or garment; 2 long loose garment worn by knights over their armor

sure /shōōr'/ [OF *seur* < L *securus* secure] *adj* 1 confident beyond doubt; positive, certain; 2 known beyond question; 3 certain to be or to happen, as *sure to succeed*; 4 certain to find or retain, as *sure of a welcome*; 5 dependable, reliable; 6 firm, steady, as *sure footing*; 7 **for sure** certainly; 8 **make sure** to be certain; 9 **sure enough** *colloq* without a doubt ‖ *adv* 10 *colloq* surely ‖ **sure'ness** *n* ‖ SYN *adj* assured, actual, positive, authentic, real

sure'-fire' *adj colloq* sure to work

sure'ly *adv* 1 certainly, doubtless; 2 firmly, safely; 3 without fail

sure' thing' *colloq n* 1 someone or something sure to win or succeed ‖ *interj* 2 most certainly!

sure-ty /shōōr'/it/ *n* (-*ties*) 1 state of being sure; 2 security against loss or damage, or as a pledge for payment of a debt, fulfillment of an obligation, etc.; 3 person who pledges himself as security or as guarantor

surf /surf'/ [< earlier *suffe*] *n* 1 waves of the sea as they break upon the shore ‖ *vi* 2 to ride a surfboard

sur-face /surf'is/ [*sur-¹* + *face*] *n* 1 exterior face of any object; 2 one of the faces of a solid; 3 exposed upper boundary of a liquid; 4 external appearance; 5 *geom* magnitude having length and breadth but no thickness ‖ *adj* 6 of or pert. to the surface; 7 superficial, not profound; 8 (mail, travel, etc.) via land and sea, not via air ‖ *vi* 9 to rise to the surface

sur'face ten'sion *n* molecular force that causes the surface of a liquid to act like an elastic membrane, tending to reduce the liquid to a form having the least possible surface area

surf'board' *n* long flat board on which one stands or lies while riding toward shore on the crest of the surf ‖ **surf'board'ing** *n*

sur-feit /surf'it/ [MF *surfait*] *n* 1 excessive indulgence in anything, as in eating; 2 excess; excessive amount; 3 morbid condition caused by excessive eating; 4 discomfort or disgust resulting from satiety ‖ *vt* 5 to feed to excess or otherwise satiate ‖ *vi* 6 to overindulge, as in eating ‖ SYN *n* glut, sate, cloy, satiate (see *satisfy*)

surge /surj'/ [L *surgere* to rise] *n* 1 large wave or billow; 2 great roll of water, swell; 3 strong forward motion; sweep or rush, as of a crowd or current of electricity or water ‖ *vi* 4 to move, rise, or swell in a surge

sur-geon /surj'ən/ [AF *surgien*] *n* physician who practices surgery

Sur·geon Gen·er·al *n* (**Surgeons General**) 1 chief medical officer of one of the armed forces; 2 head of the U.S. Bureau of Public Health

sur·ger·y /surj'ərē/ *n* (**-ies**) 1 treatment of injuries, deformities, or diseases by manual or operative procedures; 2 place or room for surgical operations

sur·gi·cal *adj* of, pert. to, or used in surgery

Su·ri·name /soor'ənäm'/ *n* Dutch-speaking republic on the NE coast of South America (400,000; 70,060 sq.m.; cap. Paramaribo)

sur·ly /sur'lē/ [< *sir* + *-ly*] *adj* (**-li·er; -li·est**) bad-tempered, uncivil, rude ‖ **sur'li·ness** *n* ‖ SYN churlish, rude, gruff, cross (see *sullen, gloomy*)

sur·mise /sur'mīz, sərmīz'/ [AF] *n* 1 conjecture, guess ‖ /sərmīz'/ *vt & vi* 2 to conjecture, guess

sur·mount' [MF *surmonter*] *vt* 1 to mount up on or pass over, as a hill; 2 to be on top of; 3 to overcome, prevail over ‖ **sur·mount'a·ble** *adj* ‖ SYN conquer, master, overcome (see *vanquish*)

sur'name' *n* 1 additional name, often descriptive, added to the Christian name, as *Charles the Bold*; 2 last or family name ‖ **sur'named'** *adj*

sur·pass' /sər-/ [MF *surpasser*] *vt* 1 to exceed; 2 to excel; 3 to transcend ‖ **sur·pass'ing** *adj*

sur·plice /surp'lis/ [AF *surpliz*] *n* loose outer linen garment with wide sleeves worn over the cassock by priests and the choir of ritualistic churches

sur·plus /surp'ləs/ [MF < ML *superplus*] *n* 1 that which remains over and above what is required; 2 excess of revenues over expenditures; 3 excess of assets over liabilities ‖ *adj* 4 forming a surplus

sur·prise /sə(r)prīz'/ [MF *surprendre* (-*pris*)] *vt* 1 to attack unexpectedly and without notice; 2 to come upon unexpectedly; 3 to strike with wonder or confusion by something unusual or unfamiliar; 4 to detect unexpectedly; 5 **surprise into** to lead (someone) without his awareness into ‖ *n* 6 act or instance of surprising; 7 that which or one who surprises ‖ **sur·pris'ing** *adj* ‖ SYN *v* amaze, dumfound, bewilder, perplex; *n* amazement, astonishment, consternation, bewilderment

sur·re·al·ism /sə-/ [F *surréalisme*] *n* movement in the arts that attempts to show the activities of the subconscious mind by means of images that frequently are without apparent order ‖ **sur·re'al·ist** *adj & n* ‖ **sur·re'al·is'tic** *adj*

sur·ren·der /sərən'dər/ [OF *surrendre* to give up] *vt* 1 to give up possession of, on compulsion or demand; 2 to give up, relinquish, as a claim or right; 3 to yield (oneself) to any instinct, emotion, or influence ‖ *vi* 4 to give oneself up ‖ *n* 5 act or instance of surrendering ‖ SYN *v* abandon, relinquish, quit, give up, yield

sur·rep·ti·tious /sur'əptish'əs/ [L *surrepticius*] *adj* 1 done or obtained in a stealthy manner; clandestine; 2 acting in a secret or stealthy way ‖ **sur·rep·ti'tious·ly** *adv* ‖ SYN furtive, sly, secret, clandestine, unauthorized ‖ ANT open, undisguised, authorized, overt

sur·rey /sur'ē/ [< *Surrey* county in England] *n* light, four-wheeled, two-seated carriage for four people

sur·ro·gate /sur'əgāt', -git/ [L *surrogatus*] *n* 1 deputy; 2 substitute; 3 court officer in some states who deals with the probating of wills and the administration of estates

sur·round' /sə-/ [AF *surrounder*] *vt* 1 to enclose on all sides, encompass ‖ *n* 2 *arch.* something that borders or surrounds a panel or opening ‖ SYN *v* encircle, encompass, compass, enclose

sur·round'ings *npl* things, conditions, or circumstances that make up an environment

sur'tax' *n* 1 extra tax in addition to the regular tax ‖ *vt* 2 to put a surtax on

sur·veil·lance /sərvāl'(y)əns/ [F] *n* close watch on a person or group, as by the police

sur·vey /sərvā'/ [AF *surveier*] *vt* 1 to look at; view broadly; 2 to inspect, examine closely, appraise; 3 to determine exactly, by geometry and trigonometry, the area, contour, dimensions, etc., of (a tract of land or the like) ‖ /usu. sur'vā/ *n* 4 act or instance of surveying ‖ SYN *n* inspection, examination, review, prospect

sur·vey'ing *n* act, business, or science of one who surveys land ‖ **sur·vey'or** *n*

sur·viv·al /sərvīv'əl/ *n* 1 act or instance of surviving; 2 any ancient use, custom, belief, etc., that survives to a later time

sur·viv'al of the fit'test *n* natural selection; the persistence of those forms of animal and plant life best adjusted to their environments

sur·vive /sərvīv'/ [MF *survivre*] *vt* 1 to outlive; 2 to live past or through (an event, state, etc.) ‖ *vi* 3 to remain alive or in existence ‖ **sur·viv'or** *n*

sus- *pref* var of **sub-**

sus·cep·ti·ble /səsep'tibəl/ [LL *susceptibilis*] *adj* 1 capable of being changed, influenced, or easily affected; 2 open, accessible, or sensitive; 3 impressionable; 4 **susceptible of** admitting, open to; 5 **susceptible to** easily affected by ‖ **sus·cep'ti·bil'i·ty** /-bil'-/ *n* (**-ties**) ‖ SYN yielding, sensitive, impressionable, receptive

sus·pect /səspekt′/ [L *suspectare*] *vt* 1 to conjecture, surmise; 2 to believe in the possible guilt of without sufficient proof; 3 to consider as questionable; doubt, mistrust ‖ *vi* 4 to have suspicion ‖ /also sus′pekt/ *adj* 5 under suspicion ‖ /sus′pekt/ *n* 6 one who is suspected

sus·pend /səspend′/ [L *suspendere*] *vt* 1 to hang from above; 2 to hold as if hanging, as dust in the air or solid particles in a liquid; 3 to stop or discontinue, as work, payment, etc.; 4 to defer, withhold action concerning; 5 to cause to be inoperative for a time, as a law; 6 to debar temporarily from some privilege, function, or office ‖ *vi* 7 to stop operations for a time; 8 to be suspended

sus·pend′ers *npl* 1 two supporting straps or bands passing over the shoulders, for holding up the trousers; 2 *Brit* garters

sus·pense /səspens′/ [ML *suspensum* suspension] *n* state of uncertainty, doubt, or anxiety; indecision

sus·pen·sion /səspen′shən/ *n* 1 act of suspending or state of being suspended; 2 contrivance by which something is suspended or hung; 3 system of springs, shock absorbers, etc., that connect the body of a vehicle to its wheels; 4 condition of a solid dispersed in very fine particles throughout a liquid ‖ SYN discontinuance, intermission, adjournment

sus·pen′sion bridge′ *n* bridge the roadway of which is hung from cables that are stretched over towers across a waterway, valley, or the like

sus·pen′sion points′ *npl* series of periods, usu. three, used to indicate the omission of one or more words

sus·pen′so·ry /-sərē/ *adj* 1 fitting or serving to suspend or suspend, as a ligament ‖ *n* (-ries) 2 *med* that which supports a part, as a bandage or truss

sus·pi·cion /səspish′ən/ [L *suspicio* (-*onis*)] *n* 1 act of suspecting or state of being suspected; 2 feeling or state of mind of one who suspects; 3 trace or hint ‖ SYN apprehension, misgiving, diffidence, jealousy (see *doubt*) ‖ ANT belief, confidence, assurance

sus·pi′cious /-shəs/ *adj* 1 causing suspicion; 2 feeling or expressing suspicion ‖ **sus·pi′cious·ly** *adv*

sus·tain /səstān′/ [OF *sustenir*] *vt* 1 to support, bear the weight of; 2 to keep up, keep going; 3 to support or keep alive; 4 to undergo, suffer; 5 to bear up under; 6 to encourage, comfort; 7 to confirm, corroborate; 8 to uphold as valid ‖ SYN support, nourish, encourage (see *substantiate*)

sus·tain′ing pro′gram *n rad & telv* program without a commercial sponsor

sus·te·nance /sust′inəns/ [AF] *n* 1 act

of sustaining; 2 means of livelihood; 3 that which sustains life; food

su·ture /sōōch′ər/ [L *sutura* seam] *n* 1 seam or stitch; 2 any seamlike junction; 3 joining of the edges of a wound, as by stitches or clamps; 4 stitch or fastening used for this

su·ze·rain /sōōz′ərin/ [F] *n* state or sovereign exercising international control over an internally autonomous state ‖ **su′ze·rain·ty** *n*

s.v. [L *sub verbo* or *voce*] under the word (used in referring to articles in dictionaries and encyclopedias)

svelte /svelt′/ [F < It *svelto*] *adj* slender, lithe

SW, S.W. southwest(ern)

Sw. 1 Sweden; 2 Swedish

swab /swob′/ [D *zwabber* swabber] *n* 1 large mop for cleaning decks, floors, etc.; 2 brush or wad on the end of a rod for cleaning the bore of a gun; 3 bit of cotton or the like attached to a handle for cleaning or applying medicine to the mouth or throat; 4 *slang* clumsy fellow ‖ *v* (swabbed; swab·bing) *vt* 5 to use a swab on ‖ **swab′ber** *n*

swad·dle /swod′əl/ [OE *swæthel*] *n* 1 long narrow strip of cloth used to wrap newborn babies ‖ *vt* 2 to wrap (a newborn baby) in swaddles

swag /swag′/ [prob < Scand] *n slang* stolen goods, booty

swage /swāj′/ [MF *souage*] *n* 1 metal-shaping tool having a groove or perforation into which the metal to be shaped is pressed or hammered ‖ *vt* 2 to shape with a swage

swag·ger /swag′ər/ [< *swag*] *vi* 1 to strut arrogantly; 2 to boast noisily ‖ *n* 3 swaggering walk or manner

swag′ger stick′ *n* short leather-covered stick, often carried by army officers

Swa·hi·li /swähē′lē/ *n* 1 a Bantu language, lingua franca in E Africa, official in Kenya and Tanzania; 2 member of certain Swahili-speaking groups

swain /swān′/ [ON *sveinn* servant] *n* 1 country youth; 2 lover

swal·low[1] /swol′ō/ [OE *swalewe*] *n* any of a widely distributed family (Hirundinidae) of small perching birds with forked tails and long pointed wings, noted for swift and graceful flight

swal·low[2] [OE *swelgan*] *vt* 1 to transfer from the mouth to the stomach by a voluntary muscular act; 2 to retract or take back; 3 to put up with, bear submissively; 4 *colloq* to accept without question; 5 to suppress, as a sigh; 6 often **swallow up** to cause to disappear; engulf ‖ *vi* 7 to perform the act of swallowing ‖ *n* 8 act of swallowing; 9 amount swallowed; 10 small amount swallowed, mere taste; 11 passage between the mouth and the stomach; gullet

swal'low-tailed' coat' *n* man's full-dress coat, having the front cut away below the waist and the back descending in two tapered skirts

swam /swam'/ *pt* of *swim*

swa·mi /swä'mē/ [Hindi = lord] *n* 1 title given to a Hindu teacher of religion; 2 seer; pundit

swamp /swomp'/ [?] *n* 1 tract of wet, spongy land || *vt* 2 to flood or drench; 3 to cause to sink by filling with water; 4 to overwhelm || *vi* 5 to be swamped || **swamp'y** *adj* (-i·er; -i·est)

swan /swän/ [OE] *n* any of several large, aquatic, gooselike birds (subfamily Anserinae) with long, graceful necks and white plumage

swan' dive' *n* fancy dive in which the diver keeps the legs straight and the arms stretched out sideways, moving them forward before hitting the water

swank /swaŋk'/ [perh < MHG *swanken* to sway] *colloq n* 1 dashing and ostentatious stylishness in dress and manner || *adj* 2 pretentious, showy || **swank'y** *adj colloq* (-i·er; -i·est)

swans'down' *n* 1 soft fine down of the swan, used in trimming, powder puffs, etc.; 2 soft thick cloth of fine wool

swan' song' [< belief that a swan sings just before death] *n* final act or utterance

swap /swop'/ [ME *swappen* to strike] *v* (swapped; swap·ping) *vt & vi* 1 to barter, trade || *n* 2 barter, trade

sward /swôrd'/ [OE *sweard* rind, skin] *n* stretch of land covered with grass; turf

swarm /swôrm'/ [OE *swearm*] *n* 1 large number of honeybees accompanied by a queen leaving one hive to establish a new one; 2 colony of bees settled in a hive; 3 great throng of people or things, esp. in motion || *vi* 4 to crowd together, move about in great numbers; 5 to be crowded or overrun; 6 to leave a hive in a body and make a new colony || *vt* 7 to throng or crowd || SYN *n* body, crowd, swarm, collection (see *herd*)

swart /swôrt'/ [OE *sweart* black] *adj* swarthy

swarth·y /swôr'thē̮, -thē/ [var of *swart*] *adj* (-i·er; -i·est) dark-skinned || **swarth'i·ness** *n*

swash'buck'ler /swosh'-/ [< *obs swash* swagger] *n* blustering, swaggering fighting man

swas·ti·ka /swost'ikə/ [Skt *svastika* good-luck charm] *n* 1 ancient crosslike ornament or symbol of good luck, shaped like four capital L's joined; 2 this figure with the L's reversed, used as the emblem of Nazism

swat /swot'/ [*dial.* var of *squat*] *v* (swat·ted; swat·ting) *vt* 1 to hit or slap || *n* 2 blow or slap || **swat'ter** *n*

swatch /swoch'/ [?] *n* piece or patch, as of cloth, used as a sample

swath /swoth', swôth'/ [OE *swæth* track, trace] *n* 1 line or row of grass or grain cut down and thrown together by the mower; 2 space cut by a mowing machine or scythe; 3 long narrow strip or row of anything; 4 **cut a swath** to make a big impression

swathe /swāth'/ [OE *swathian*] *vt* 1 to bind or wrap with a band or bandage; 2 to enclose or envelop

sway /swā'/ [ME *sweyen*] *vi* 1 to move or swing from side to side or to and fro; 2 to incline to one side; 3 to veer in opinion || *vt* 4 to cause to sway; 5 to cause to change opinion; influence; 6 to dominate, rule || *n* 7 act of swaying; 8 swaying movement; 9 controlling influence; 10 rule, dominion || SYN *v* swing, oscillate, influence (see *shake*)

sway'-backed' *adj* (horse) having an abnormally sagging back

Swa·zi·land /swä'zēland'/ *n* monarchy in SE Africa adjoining Mozambique and South Africa (515,000; 6,704 sq. m.; cap. Mbabane)

swear /swer'/ [OE *swerian*] *v* (swore; sworn) *vi* 1 to make a solemn declaration, with an appeal to God or to something held sacred as to the truth of what is affirmed; 2 to make a solemn vow; 3 to give evidence on oath; 4 to use profane language; 5 **swear at** to curse or use profane language to; 6 **swear by**, a to appeal to (God or something held sacred) in swearing; b to rely on || *vt* 7 to declare solemnly, with an appeal to God or some sacred object; 8 to vow solemnly; 9 to make a sworn affirmation of; 10 to take (an oath); 11 to administer an oath to; 12 **swear in** to induct into office by administering an oath; 13 **swear off** *colloq* to swear to give up; 14 **swear out** to procure (a warrant) under oath || SYN testify, affirm, promise, blaspheme, curse

swear'word' *n colloq* profane or obscene word

sweat /swet'/ [OE *swāt*] *v* (sweat or sweat·ed) *vi* 1 to give off moisture through the pores of the skin; 2 to give off moisture, as hay when packed closely; 3 to become covered with moisture from condensation; 4 *colloq* to work hard; 5 *colloq* to be distressed, as from fear or anxiety || *vt* 6 to cause to sweat; 7 to exude (moisture) from the pores; 8 to wet with perspiration; 9 to force out (moisture) by heat; 10 to join (metal objects) by heating and pressing together; 11 *colloq* to extract information from by insistent questioning; 12 to employ at hard labor for low wages; 13 **sweat out** to endure anxiously ‖ *n* 14 moisture given off by sweating; 15 act or process of sweating; 16 spell of sweating; 17 *colloq* hard work; 18 *colloq* state of impatience or anxiety; 19 short rapid exercise given a horse ‖ **sweat'y** *adj* (**-i·er; -i·est**)

sweat'er *n* knitted outer jacket with or without sleeves, open or closed down the front

sweat' shirt' *n* loose long-sleeved pullover worn to prevent chill while exercising or to induce sweating

sweat'shop' *n* shop employing workers at low wages for long hours under unfavorable conditions

Swed. 1 Sweden; 2 Swedish

Swede /swēd/ [MLG] *n* native or inhabitant of Sweden

Swe·den /swēd'ən/ *n* kingdom in N Europe in the Scandinavian Peninsula (7,869,000; 173,666 sq.m.; cap. Stockholm)

Swed·ish /swēd'ish/ *adj* 1 of or pert. to Sweden or the Swedes ‖ *n* 2 language of Sweden; 3 **the Swedish** *pl* the people of Sweden

sweep /swēp/ [ME *swepe*] *v* (**swept**) *vt* 1 to clean, as a floor or rug, with a broom or brush; 2 to remove or clear away, as dirt, with a broom or brush; 3 to drive, flow over, or carry along or off with force, as *the flood swept away the dam*; 4 to pass lightly over or across, as *her gown swept the floor*; 5 to scan or gaze at; traverse or range swiftly, as *to sweep the sky*; 6 to carry away, as by enthusiasm; 7 to win an overwhelming victory in, as an election; 8 to win every game, round, or hand in (a series of contests) ‖ *vi* 9 to clean with a broom or brush; 10 to pass with speed or force; 11 to move with stateliness; 12 to lie or extend in a continuous line or curve, as *the lawn sweeps down to the river* ‖ *n* 13 act of sweeping; 14 sweeping motion; 15 compass or range of something that has a sweeping motion; 16 curve or bend, as in a road; 17 well sweep; 18 *Brit* chimney sweeper; 19 continuous stretch; 20 overwhelming victory in a contest; 21 winning of all the games, rounds, or hands in a contest or series ‖ **sweep'er** *n*

sweep'ing *adj* 1 of great scope; comprehensive ‖ **sweep·ings** *npl* 2 dirt swept up; refuse

sweep'-sec'ond hand' *n* second hand mounted centrally with the other hands of a watch and reaching the edge of the dial

sweep'stake' *n* or **sweep'stakes'** *nsg & npl* 1 any gambling, race, or other contest in which the winnings come from the contributions of the participants; 2 lottery in which winning tickets are drawn by chance, the amount of the prizes being determined by the outcome of a specific race

sweet /swēt/ [OE *swēte*] *adj* 1 tasting like sugar; 2 fresh, not stale, sour, or rancid; 3 not salt, as *sweet butter*; 4 fragrant; 5 pleasing in sound; 6 pleasant, delightful; 7 easily done; 8 gentle, mild; 9 beloved, darling; 10 (wine) containing sugar, not dry; 11 **sweet on** *colloq* infatuated with ‖ *n* 12 one beloved; darling; 13 sweet dish, dessert; 14 **sweets** *pl* confectionery ‖ **sweet'ish** *adj* ‖ **sweet'ly** *adv* ‖ **sweet'ness** *n* ‖ SYN *adj* saccharine, luscious, kind, winsome

sweet'bread' *n* pancreas or thymus of an animal, esp. of a calf or lamb, used for food

sweet'bri'er *n* shrub (*Rosa elganteria*) of the rose family having aromatic leaflets, single pink flowers, and hooked thorns

sweet' corn' *n* variety of corn with sweet kernels, used as a table vegetable

sweet'en *vt* 1 to make sweet; 2 to make pleasant or agreeable; 3 to make kind or mild; 4 *colloq* to make the terms of (a business proposition, contract, etc.) more attractive ‖ *vi* 5 to become sweet ‖ **sweet'en·er** *n*

sweet'heart' *n* 1 lover; 2 one beloved; 3 *colloq* extremely kind and friendly person

sweet'heart con'tract *slang n* contract favoring the employer, sometimes made in collusion with union leaders and without the approval of the rank and file

sweet' mar'jo·ram *n* fragrant herb (*Majorana hortensis*), used for seasoning in cookery

sweet'meat' *n* confection, candy

sweet' pea' *n* annual climbing plant (*Lathyrus odoratus*) cultivated for its sweet-scented flowers

sweet' po·ta'to *n* 1 tropical American vine (*Ipomoea batatas*) with a thick sweet root used as a vegetable; 2 *colloq* ocarina

sweet' talk' *n colloq* flattery, cajolery ‖ **sweet'-talk'** *vt & vi*

sweet' tooth' *n* craving for sweets

sweet' wil'liam *n* plant (*Dianthus barbatus*) of the pink family, having flowers of many colors growing in dense, showy clusters

swell /swel/ [OE *swellan*] *v* (**swelled; swelled** or **swol·len**) *vi* 1 to expand, dilate; 2 to increase in size, volume, or force; 3 to increase in importance, value, or the like; 4 to be inflated, bulge out; 5 to be puffed up or elated ‖ *vt* 6 to cause to swell ‖ *n* 7 act of swelling or state of being swollen; 8 long continuous wave or billow; 9 gradual, sloping elevation of land; 10 *slang* a person of high society; **b** one fashionably dressed || ~ *adj slang* **11** excellent; fine; **12** well-dressed, smart; **13** elegant, stylish

swelled/ head/ *n colloq* insufferable conceit

swell/head/ *n colloq* insufferably conceited person || **swell/head/ed** *adj*

swell/ing *n* **1** lump or protuberance; **2** abnormal enlargement

swel·ter /swelt'ər/ [OE *sweltan* to die] *vi* to suffer from oppressive heat

swel/ter·ing *adj* oppressively hot; sultry

swept /swept/ *pt & pp* of **sweep**

swerve /swurv/ [OE *sweorfan* to file] *vi* **1** to turn aside from a direct course of action or movement || *vt* **2** to cause to swerve || *n* **3** act or instance of swerving

swift /swift/ [OE] *adj* **1** moving rapidly; fast, speedy; **2** prompt, quick; **3** happening quickly || *adv* **4** swiftly || *n* **5** any of a family of birds (Apodidae) allied to the hummingbirds but resembling the swallows, noted for their rapid flight || **swift/ly** *adv* || **swift/ness** *n* || SYN *adj* expeditious, rapid, quick, hasty, sudden

swig /swig/ [?] *colloq v* (**swigged**; **swig·ging**) *vt & vi* **1** to drink in deep drafts || **2** deep swallow, as of liquor

swill /swil/ [OE *swilian* to wash] *vt* **1** to drink greedily, guzzle; **2** to feed swill to (hogs) || *vi* **3** to drink greedily, guzzle || *n* **4** liquid food for swine; **5** garbage

swim /swim/ [OE *swimman*] *v* (**swam**; **swum**; **swim·ming**) *vi* **1** to move in water by moving the limbs, fins, or tail, etc.; **2** to proceed with easy graceful motions as if in water; **3** to float on the surface of water or other liquid; **4** to glide smoothly; **5** to overflow, be flooded, as *eyes swimming with tears*; **6** to be dizzy, as *his head was swimming* || *vt* **7** to pass over or through by swimming || *n* **8** act or instance of swimming; **9** **in the swim** in the main current of affairs || **swim/mer** *n*

swim/ming·ly *adv* without trouble; easily

Swin·burne, Al·ger·non Charles /al'jərnən chärlz/ swin'bərn/ *n* (1837–1909) English poet and critic

swin·dle /swin'dəl/ [< G *Schwindler* giddy-minded person] *vt* **1** to obtain money or property from by fraud or deceit || *vi* **2** to secure money fraudulently || *n* **3** act or instance of swindling; fraud, deceit || **swin/dler** *n* || SYN *v* steal, trick, cheat, defraud, delude

swine /swin/ [OE *swīn*] *n* (*pl* **swine**) **1** hog, pig; **2** coarse, vicious, or degraded person || **swin/ish** *adj*

swing /swiŋ/ [OE *swingan*] *v* (**swung**) *vi* **1** to move to and fro regularly,

as a pendulum; **2** to turn on, or as on, a hinge or axis; **3** to proceed with a loose free gait, as *the soldiers swung down the road*; **4** to move to and fro seated in a swing; **5** to move in a curve; **6** *colloq* to be hanged; **7** to be suspended freely; **8** to hit at a person or object with the hand or with something in the hand; **9** *slang* to be characterized by uninhibited freedom and gaiety || *vt* **10** to cause to swing; **11** to cause to turn in a curve; **12** *colloq* to bring about, as *to swing a deal*; **13** to move with a swinging motion, as a bat or one's fist || *n* **14** act of swinging; **15** sweep of something that swings; **16** loose, free gait; **17** seat suspended by two ropes in which to swing back and forth; **18** free scope or freedom of action; **19** course or movement of a practice, business, event, or the like; **20** rhythmic movement or lilt in poetry or music; **21** kind of jazz characterized by a smooth beat and usu. played by large bands; **22** **in full swing** *colloq* working at full capacity and speed || SYN *v* sway, oscillate, wave (see **shake**)

swing/er *n slang* person uninhibited in his pursuit of pleasure

swing/ mu/sic *n* swing **21**

swing/ shift/ *n* work shift from mid-afternoon to midnight

swipe /swip/ [prob var of *sweep*] *n* **1** *colloq* vigorous blow || *vt* **2** *colloq* to hit with force; **3** *slang* to steal

swirl /swurl/ [ME < Scand] *vi* **1** to move with a whirling motion || *vt* **2** to cause to eddy or whirl || *n* **3** whirling or eddying motion

swish /swish/ [imit] *vi* **1** to move with or make a hissing sound, as a whip swung smartly through the air; **2** to rustle || *vt* **3** to cause to swish || *n* **4** swishing sound or movement; **5** *slang* effeminate male homosexual || **swish/y** *adj* (**-i·er; -i·est**)

Swiss /swis/ [F *Suisse*] *adj* **1** of or pert. to Switzerland or its people || *n* (*pl* **Swiss**) **2** native or inhabitant of Switzerland

Swiss/ chard/ *n* chard

Swiss/ cheese/ *n* a firm pale-yellow cheese with many holes

Swiss/ steak/ *n* thick steak covered with flour and pounded and braised with tomatoes, onions, etc.

switch /swich/ [perh < LG] *n* **1** thin flexible rod used for whipping; **2** movable section of rail for directing railroad trains onto another track; **3** tress of false hair used by women in hairdressing; **4** device for making, breaking, or shifting electric circuits; **5** shift or change || *vt* **6** to whip with a switch; **7** to swing or jerk; **8** to shift to another track; **9** to make, break, or rearrange (an electrical circuit) by means of a

switch; 10 to exchange or change;
11 switch off to disconnect (an electric light or device); **12 switch on** to connect (an electric light or device) ‖ *vi* **13** to shift or change; **14** to exchange something for something else; **15** to switch a train to another track

switch'back' *n* **1** railway for going up and down a steep incline by way of zigzag tracks; **2** mountain highway with many hairpin turns; **3** roller coaster

switch'blade' (**knife'**) *n* pocketknife the blade of which is retained in the handle by a spring and is released usu. by pressing a button

switch'board' *n* **1** panel containing electric switches; **2** panel for connecting telephones

switch' hit'ter *n* baseball player who bats both left-handed and right-handed

switch'man /-mən/ *n* (**-men** /-mən/) one who operates railroad switches

switch' tow'er *n* small tower from which railroad switches and signals are controlled

Switz. Switzerland

Swit·zer·land /switz'ərlənd/ *n* German-, French-, Italian-, and Romansh-speaking republic in central Europe in the Alps (6,300,000; 15,944 sq.m.; cap. Bern)

swiv·el /swiv'əl/ [OE *swīfan* to move swiftly] *n* **1** anything that turns axially on a headed bolt or pin; **2** link in two parts either of which can rotate independently of the other ‖ *v* (**-eled** or **-elled; -el·ing** or **-el·ling**) *vt* **3** to cause to turn on, or as on, a swivel ‖ *vi* **4** to turn on, or as on, a swivel

swiv'el chair' *n* chair whose seat turns horizontally on a swivel

swiz'zle stick' /swiz'əl/ [?] *n* small rod or stick for stirring mixed alcoholic drinks

swol·len /swōl'ən/ **1** *pp* of **swell** ‖ *adj* **2** distended; enlarged

swoon /swōōn'/ [< OE *geswōgen* in a swoon] *vi* **1** to faint ‖ *n* **2** faint

swoop /swōōp'/ [OE *swāpan* to rush] *vi* **1** to sweep swiftly and suddenly through the air; pounce; **2 swoop down on** or **upon** to come down on in a sudden attack ‖ *vt* **3 swoop up** to grab or seize as with a sweeping motion ‖ *n* **4** act or instance of swooping

sword /sôrd', sōrd'/ [OE *sweord*] *n* **1** weapon consisting of a long pointed blade with one or two sharp edges, set in a hilt; **2** this weapon as the symbol of military power, war, conflict, vengeance, or violence; **3 at swords' points** ready to fight or quarrel; **4 put to the sword** to kill, slaughter

sword'fish' *n* (**-fish** or **-fishes**) large edible marine fish (*Xiphias gladius*)

having the upper jaw formed into a swordlike beak

sword'play' *n* fencing; fighting with swords

swords'man /-mən/ *n* (**-men** /-mən/) one skilled in using the sword; fencer ‖ **swords'man·ship'** *n*

swore /swôr', swōr'/ *pt* of **swear**

sworn /swôrn', swōrn'/ **1** *pp* of **swear** ‖ *adj* **2** bound by an oath

swum /swum'/ *pp* of **swim**

swung /swuŋ'/ *pt & pp* of **swing**

syb·a·rite /sib'ərīt'/ [< *Sybaris* ancient Gk city in S Italy noted for its luxury] *n* one devoted to luxury and pleasure ‖ **syb'a·rit'ic** /-rit'ik/ *adj*

syc·a·more /sik'əmôr', -mōr'/ [OF *sicomor*] *n* **1** fig tree (*Ficus sycomorus*) of the Near East; **2** a maple tree of Britain; **3** American plane tree (*Platanus occidentalis*) that sheds its outer bark

syc·o·phant /sik'əfənt/ [Gk *sykophantes* fig-shower, i.e., informer against fig smugglers] *n* flatterer; parasite; toady ‖ **syc'o·phan·cy** *n* ‖ **syc'o·phan'tic** /-fant'ik/ *adj*

syl- *pref* var of **syn-**

syl·la·bar·y /sil'əber'ē/ [see **syllable**] *n* (**-ies**) list of characters representing syllables instead of letters, used in the writing systems of some languages instead of an alphabet, as Japanese and Cherokee

syl·lab·ic /silab'ik/ *adj* of, pert. to, or consisting of a syllable or syllables

syl·lab·i·fy' /-lab'-/ *v* (**-fied**) *vt* to form or separate into syllables ‖ **syl·lab'·i·fi·ca'tion** *n*

syl·la·ble /sil'əbəl/ [< Gk *syllabē*] *n* **1** segment of speech produced by a single pulse of air expelled from the lungs, consisting of or having at its peak a vowel sound or sometimes a sonorant consonant; **2** the letters corresponding approximately to a syllable as pronounced

syl·la·bus /sil'əbəs/ [LL < Gk *sittyba* or *sillybos* parchment label of a book] *n* (**-bus·es** or **-bi** /-bī'/) abstract or outline of the main points of a subject, book, course of study, or the like

syl·lo·gism /sil'əjiz'əm/ [Gk *syllogismos*] *n* **1** logic form of reasoning consisting of a major premise, a minor premise, and a conclusion, as *all men are mortal; A is a man; therefore A is mortal;* **2** deductive reasoning ‖ **syl'lo·gis'tic** (**-ti·cal**) *adj* ‖ **syl'lo·gize'** *vi*

sylph /silf'/ [coined by the Swiss physician Paracelsus < L *sylva* forest + *nymph*] *n* **1** imaginary spirit living in the air; **2** slender, graceful young woman

syl·van /sil'vən/ [L *silvanus*] *adj* **1** of, pert. to, or inhabiting woods; **2** wooded

sym- *pref* var of **syn-**

sym·bi·o·sis /sim′bī-ōs′is, -bē-/ [Gk = a living together] *n* the living together of two dissimilar organisms, usu. to their mutual advantage ‖ **sym′bi·ot′ic** /-ot′ik/ *adj*

sym·bol /sim′bəl/ [Gk *symbolon* sign, token] *n* **1** object used to represent something else, often something abstract and immaterial, as *the cross is the symbol of Christianity;* **2** mark, character, or letter representing something else, as *H is the symbol of hydrogen;* **3** something, as a writing or image, having a special meaning apart from the usual one ‖ **sym·bol′ic** /-i-cal/ /-bol′-/ *adj* ‖ **sym·bol′i·cal·ly** *adv* ‖ SYN character, token, type (see *emblem, figure*)

sym′bol·ism *n* **1** representation by means of symbols; **2** system of symbols; **3** symbolic meaning

sym′bol·ize′ *vt* **1** to be a symbol of; **2** to represent by symbols; **3** to treat as figurative or symbolic ‖ **sym′bol·i·za′tion** *n*

sym·me·try /sim′itrē/ [Gk *symmetria*] *n* (-**tries**) **1** due proportion between the parts of a whole; balance, harmony; **2** correspondence of parts on opposite sides of an axis, center, or plane ‖ **sym·met′ri·cal** /-met′-/ *adj*

sym·pa·thet·ic /simp′əthet′ik/ [see **sympathy**] *adj* **1** characterized by, showing, or feeling sympathy; **2** congenial, harmonious; **3** pert. to that part of the nervous system carrying impulses from the brain to the organs not under voluntary control; **4** *phys* pert. to vibrations produced in a body as a result of similar vibrations in another body ‖ **sym′pa·thet′i·cal·ly** *adv* ‖ SYN kindred, harmonious, human, tender, kindly

sym·pa·thize /simp′əthīz′/ *vi* **1** to feel sympathy; **2** to be in sympathy (with someone or something); **3** to express sympathy; **4** to be in agreement or accord ‖ **sym′pa·thiz′er** *n*

sym′pa·thy [Gk *sympatheia*] *n* (-**thies**) **1** feeling of being harmoniously affected by the emotional state of another, or of sharing another's emotions; **2** feeling of compassion; **3** mutual understanding or agreement of tastes or inclinations; **4** harmony or agreement; **5** **sympathies** *pl* feeling of compassion ‖ SYN pity, commiseration, condolence, compassion, tenderness, kindness, pathos ‖ DISCR *Sympathy* is the tendency to share, or the state of sharing, the feelings of another; often, it is a mental sharing of another's trouble. *Sympathy* may also flow out for the aims, joy, or success of another; *pity, commiseration,* and *compassion* flow out only to those who are suffering. *Pity* desires to relieve and help those in trouble, but sometimes it is tinged with contempt because, per-

haps unconsciously, it regards its object as weak or inferior. *Pity* is therefore sometimes coldly received, but *sympathy* is appreciated always. *Compassion* is a combination of sorrow and *tenderness;* it is gentle and merciful toward the grief-stricken and the burdened. *Commiseration,* like *compassion,* is excited by grievous misfortunes, is deeply sympathetic and desirous to help; but *commiseration* is often felt for those in some way beyond help. The good Samaritan had *compassion* for the man who had fallen among thieves; we feel *commiseration* for the family of a man condemned to the electric chair. *Condolence* is expressed *sympathy,* often formal, and most frequently elicited by a grave or terrible happening ‖ ANT ruthlessness, inhumanity, indifference, antipathy

sym′pa·thy strike′ *n* strike by workers in support of a strike by another body of workers and not because of grievances of their own

sym·pho·ny /simf′ənē/ [Gk *symphonia* harmony] *n* (-**nies**) **1** harmony, as of sounds or colors; **2** symphony orchestra; **3** *mus* **a** elaborate instrumental piece in sonata form for a full orchestra; **b** instrumental prelude, interlude, or postlude in a vocal composition ‖ **sym·phon′ic** /-fon′-/ *adj*

sym′pho·ny or′ches·tra *n* large orchestra for performing symphonies

sym·po·si·um /simpōz′ē·əm/ [Gk *symposion* a drinking together] *n* (-**ums** or -**a** /-ə/) **1** meeting or conference for discussion of some topic; **2** collection of essays in which various writers express their views

symp·tom /simp′təm/ [Gk *symptoma* calamity, occurrence] *n* **1** sign or indication of something; **2** any change or phenomenon in the body or its functions as an evidence of disease ‖ **symp′to·mat′ic** /-mat′-/ *adj*

syn- [Gk] *pref* **1** with, together with; **2** at the same time

syn. synonym

syn·a·gog or **syn·a·gogue** /sin′əgog′, -gôg/ [Gk *synagoge* assembly] *n* Jewish house of worship

syn·a·le·fa or **syn·a·loe·fa** /sin′əlēf′ə/ [*syn-* + Gk *aleiphein* to smear] *n* fusion of two adjacent vowels into one, as *th′eagle* for *the eagle*

sync /sink/ *colloq n* **1** synchronization ‖ *vt & vi* **2** to synchronize

syn·chro·mesh /sink′rəmesh′/ [*synchronize* + *mesh*] *n* synchronized transmission gears

syn·chron·ic /sin·kron′ik/ *adj ling* **1** (phenomena) existing at a particular stage of development; **2** (study) of such phenomena

syn·chro·nism /sink′rəniz′əm/ *n* **1** sameness in time of two or more events; 2 *phys* state of being synchronous

syn′chro·nize′ [Gk *synchronizein*] *vt* 1 to assign to the same date or period of time; 2 to cause to agree in time, speed, or rate of vibration ‖ *vi* 3 to happen at the same time or at the same rate ‖ **syn′chro·ni·za′tion** *n* ‖ **syn′chro·niz′er** *n*

syn′chro·nous [Gk *synchronos*] *adj* 1 happening at the same rate; 2 occurring at the same time; 3 *phys* having the same period or rate of vibration

syn·co·pate /siŋk′əpāt′/ [LL *syncopare* (-*atus*) to shorten by syncope] *vt* 1 to contract (a word) by syncope; 2 *mus* to modify (the rhythm) by beginning a tone on an unaccented beat or after a beat has begun and continuing it into the following accented beat ‖ **syn′co·pa′tion** *n*

syn·co·pe /siŋk′əpē/ [Gk = a cutting short] *n* 1 omission of one or more sounds from the middle of a word, as in *ne′er* from *never;* 2 brief loss of consciousness from a temporary lack of circulation of blood in the brain

syn·di·cate /sin′dikit/ [MF *syndicat*] *n* 1 association of persons or corporations to promote some particular enterprise, esp. one requiring a large amount of capital; 2 company that sells articles, features, comic strips, etc., for simultaneous publication in a number of newspapers; 3 the syndicate reputed organization that controls nationwide organized crime ‖ /-kāt′/ *vt* 4 to form into a syndicate; 5 to distribute (features, comic strips, etc.) for simultaneous publication

syn·drome /sin′drōm/ [Gk = concurrence] *n* 1 pattern of symptoms that characterize a given disease or condition; 2 group of coincident states or happenings

syn·ec·do·che /sinek′dəkē/ [Gk = taking with another] *n* figure of speech in which a narrower term is used for a wider term, as *a roof* for a house; or vice versa, as *mink* for mink fur (cf. *metonymy*)

syn·er·e·sis also **syn·aer·e·sis** /siner′isis/ [Gk *synairesis*] *n* 1 the uniting into one syllable of two vowel sounds; 2 *chem* separation of the liquid component of a gel

syn·er·gism /sin′ərjiz′əm/ [Gk *synerg-* (on) working together + -ism] *n* co-operative or joint action which achieves an end which independent action could not achieve ‖ **syn′er·gis′tic** *adj*

syn·od /sin′əd/ [Gk *synodos* assembly] *n* 1 assembly or council of churches, church officials, or delegates; 2 governing body or subdivision in some churches; 3 any council

syn·o·nym /sin′ənim/ [Gk *synonymon*] *n* one of two or more words having approximately the same meaning ‖ **syn·on·y·mous** /sinon′iməs/ *adj* ‖ **syn·on′y·my** *n* (-mies)

syn·op·sis /sinop′sis/ [Gk] *n* (-ses /-sēz/) condensed statement giving a general view of something; summary or abstract ‖ **syn·op′tic** *adj*

syn·tax /sin′taks/ [Gk *syntaxis*] *n* 1 the way words are combined into grammatical sentences; 2 the rules for this ‖ **syn·tac′tic** (-ti·cal) /-tak′tik(əl)/ *adj*

syn·the·sis /sinth′isis/ [Gk] *n* (-ses /sēz′/) 1 combining of separate elements, substances, or subordinate parts into a single unified entity; 2 *chem* the uniting or building up of substances into a compound ‖ **syn′the·size′** *vt*

syn·thet·ic /sinthet′ik/ *adj* 1 pert. to or involving synthesis; 2 *chem* made by synthesis; not of natural origin; 3 artificial, not genuine; 4 (language) showing many syntactical relationships by affixes rather than by separate words ‖ **syn·thet′i·cal·ly** *adv*

syph·i·lis /sif′ilis/ [< *Syphilis* character in 16th-cent. Latin poem on the subject] *n* infectious venereal disease caused by a spirochete, *Treponema pallidum* ‖ **syph′i·lit′ic** *adj* & *n*

Syr·i·a /sir′ē·ə/ *n* Arabic-speaking republic in SW Asia at the E end of the Mediterranean (6,300,000; 71,498 sq.m.; *cap.* Damascus) ‖ **Syr′i·an** *adj* & *n*

Syr·i·ac /sir′ē·ak′/ [Gk *syriakos*] *n* form of Aramaic spoken in Syria before the Arabic conquest, now used as a liturgical language in some Eastern churches

sy·ringe /sirinj′, sir′inj/ [Gk *syrinx* (-*ingos*) pipe] *n* 1 instrument for injecting liquids into the body or withdrawing them from the body through a narrow tube, operated by a rubber bulb; 2 hypodermic syringe ‖ *vt* 3 a to inject by the use of a syringe; b to cleanse or irrigate with a syringe

syr·up /sir′əp/ [LL *syropus* < Ar *sharāb* drink] *n* 1 any of various thick, sweet liquids, made from sugar and water, molasses, maple sap, etc., often flavored, as with fruit juice; 2 liquid containing medicine, sugar, and water ‖ **syr′up·y** *adj*

sys- *pref* var of syn-

sys·tem /sist′əm/ [Gk *systema* organized whole] *n* 1 arrangement or combination of parts or elements united by some regular form of interaction or interdependence and forming an organic whole, as *the solar system, a railroad system;* 2 orderly collection of rules, principles, etc.; 3 set of coordinated doctrines; 4 orderly method of classification; 5 any specified method of procedure, as *the Gregg system of shorthand;* 6 orderliness, methodicalness; 7 living organism, as the human body, considered as a functional unit; 8 method or plan of procedure ‖ SYN order, arrangement, method, mode, rule

sys·tem·at·ic /-mat'-/ *adj* 1 of, pert. to, or characterized by a system; 2 methodical, orderly ‖ **sys'tem·at'i·cal·ly** *adv*

sys·tem·a·tize /-mə-/ *vt* to reduce to or organize according to a system; make systematic

sys·tem·ic /sistem'ik/ *adj* of or pert. to the bodily system as a whole

sys'tem·ize *vt* to systematize

sys'tems *adj* of, pert. to, or characteristic of the combination of a group of functions or operations into a unitary system

sys'tems a·nal·y·sis *n* 1 breaking up of complex problems into unambiguous elements and cause-and-effect relationships; 2 written results of this process in the precise mathematical language of the computer ‖ **sys'tems an'a·lyst** *n*

sys·to·le /sist'olē/ [Gk = placing together] *n* rhythmical contraction of the heart which, alternating with the diastole, causes the blood to circulate ‖ **sys·tol'ic** /-tol'-/ *adj*

syz·y·gy /siz'ijē/ [Gk *syzygia* yoke, pair] *n* (**-gies**) 1 either of the two points at which the moon is most nearly in line with the earth and the sun, as when it is full or new; 2 either of the two points at which any three celestial bodies have the same relationship in a gravitational system

T

T, t /tē'/ *n* (**T's** or **Ts; t's** or **ts**) 20th letter of the English alphabet

T 1 20th in order or in a series; 2 something shaped like a T; **3 to a T** perfectly; with precision

't it, as in *'twas*

-t var of **-ed,** as *slept*

t. 1 temperature; 2 tense; 3 time; 4 ton; 5 town, township; 6 transitive

Ta *chem* tantalum

tab¹ /tab'/ [?] *n* 1 small flap or tag, usu. attached to the edge of something; 2 loop for pulling or lifting; 3 *colloq* bill or check as at a restaurant; **4 keep tab(s) on** *colloq* to keep under observation ‖ *v* (**tabbed; tabbing**) *vt* 5 to designate, name

tab² *n colloq* tabloid

Ta·bas·co /təbas'kō/ [trademark] *n* very pungent sauce made from cayenne peppers

tab·by /tab'ē/ [F *tabis* < Ar *'attābi* district in Baghdad] *n* (**-bies**) 1 striped or brindled cat; 2 any domestic cat, esp. a female cat

tab·er·na·cle /tab'ərnak'əl/ [L *tabernaculum* tent] *n* 1 portable tent used as a place of worship by the Israelites in the wilderness (Ex. 26-27); 2 any place of worship; 3 *eccl* small receptacle to hold the sacred elements

tab' key' *n* tabulator

ta·ble /tāb'əl/ [OF < L *tabula* board] *n* 1 thin piece of wood, stone, metal, etc., with a flat surface; 2 article of furniture consisting of a flat slablike top supported by one or more legs; 3 the food served at a table; 4 the persons seated at a table; 5 arrangement of words, facts, figures, etc., in systematic order, esp. in columns, for reference; 6 index or summary; 7 any plane surface or level area; **8 turn the tables** to reverse an existing situation ‖ *vt* 9 to lay on a table, as cards or money; 10 a to lay aside, as a proposal or resolution; b to postpone indefinitely

tab·leau /tab'lō, tablō'/ [F = picture] *n* (**-leaux** /-lōz/ or **-leaus**) striking and lifelike representation, esp. scene in which living models pose silently and without moving

ta·ble·cloth' *n* cloth spread on a table, esp. for a meal

ta·ble d'hôte /täb'əl dōt'/ [F = host's table] *n* (**tables d'hôte**) complete meal served at a fixed price

ta'ble·hop' *v* (**-hopped; -hop·ping**) *vi* to move about from table to table, as in a night club, to visit and chat with the people seated at them

ta'ble·land' *n* plateau

ta'ble rap'ping *n* supposed communication with the spirits of the dead by raps made with a table

ta'ble·spoon' *n* large spoon for use in preparing and serving meals, holding three times as much as a teaspoon, or ½ fluid ounce ‖ **ta'ble·spoon·ful'** *n*

tab·let /tab'lit/ [MF *tablete*] *n* 1 small flat panel, esp. one intended to bear an inscription or engraving; 2 set of blank sheets of paper fastened together at one end and used to write on; 3 one of a number of thin flat pieces of wax-coated ivory, wood, etc., fastened together and used for memoranda; 4 small flat cake, as of soap, candy, or medicine

ta'ble ten'nis *n* form of tennis played on a table with small paddles and a small celluloid or plastic ball

ta'ble·ware' *n* articles put on a table for use at meals

tab·loid /tab'loid/ [*tablet* + *-oid*] *n* 1 half-size newspaper; 2 such a newspaper that concentrates on illustrations and sensational news and scandals; 3 condensed version of anything

ta·boo also **ta·bu** /təbōō', ta-/ [Polynesian] *adj* 1 set apart; made sacred or untouchable by religious custom; 2 prohibited by social custom ‖ *n* 3 religious system and practice in which certain things are made sacred and contact with them forbidden; 4 prohibition by law, convention, or prejudice ‖ *vt* 5 to place under a taboo; prohibit

tab·u·lar /tab'yələr/ [L *tabularis*] *adj* 1 of, pert. to, or arranged in tables; 2 arranged systematically by columns and rows; 3 reckoned or computed from tables; 4 flat-topped, as a mountain

tab·u·late /tab'yəlāt'/ [< L *tabulatus* boarded] *vt* to put into tabular form ‖ **tab'u·la'tion** *n*

tab'u·la'tor (or **tab' key'**) *n* typewriter key that advances the carriage a given number of spaces each time it is depressed

ta·chom·e·ter /təkom'itər/ [< Gk *tachos* speed + *-meter*] *n* 1 instrument for measuring speed; 2 instrument that measures revolutions per minute of an engine

tac·it /tas'it/ [L *tacitus* silent] *adj* 1 implied but not stated outright; 2 silent, unspoken ‖ **tac'it·ly** *adv*

tac·i·turn /tas'iturn'/ [L *taciturnus* quiet] *adj* disinclined to talk ‖ **tac'i·tur'ni·ty** *n* ‖ SYN silent, reticent, uncommunicative ‖ ANT talkative, unreserved, loquacious, communicative, garrulous

tack /tak'/ [ME] *n* 1 short sharp-pointed nail with a flat head; 2 long stitch used for basting; 3 direction of a ship in regard to the position of the sails; 4 change in a ship's direction to take advantage of side winds; 5 one of several alternating movements from port to starboard and vice versa, in order to advance against the wind; 6 course of action; 7 **on the wrong tack** following a wrong course of action ‖ *vt* 8 to fasten with tacks; 9 to fasten lightly; 10 to change the course of (a vessel) to the opposite tack; 11 **tack on** to add or append to ‖ *vi* 12 to change the course of a vessel by shifting the position of the sails

tack·le /tak'əl/ [ME *takel*] *n* 1 apparatus consisting of pulleys and ropes for raising heavy weights; 2 equipment, gear; 3 act of tackling; 4 *foot-ball* player in the line next to either end ‖ *vt* 5 to grapple with, endeavor to overcome, as a problem; 6 *football* to throw oneself on (an opponent running with the ball) in order to stop him

tack'y [?] *adj* (**-i·er; -i·est**) 1 sticky, adhesive; 2 *colloq* a shabby; b dowdy

ta·co /täk'ō/ [MexSp] *n* fried, rolled, and filled tortilla

tact /takt'/ [L *tactus* sense of touch] *n* skill in saying and doing what is most appropriate; intuitive ability to deal wisely with others ‖ SYN delicacy, adroitness, diplomacy, address

tact'ful *adj* careful to say and do the most fitting thing ‖ **tact'ful·ly** *adv*

tac·tic /tak'tik/ [Gk *taktikos* fit for ordering] *n* 1 plan or expedient; maneuvering to achieve a desired end; 2 **tactics**, a *sg* science of maneuvering military forces in battle; b *pl* the maneuvers ‖ **tac'ti·cal** *adj* ‖ **tac·ti'cian** /-tish'ən/ *n*

tac·tile /tak'til, -tīl/ [L *tactilis* tangible] *adj* 1 of or pert. to the sense of touch; 2 tangible

tact'less *adj* lacking tact; undiplomatic ‖ **tact'less·ly** *adv*

tad'pole' /tad'-/ [ME *taddepol*] *n* larval form of frogs and toads, having a long tail and breathing by means of gills

taf·fe·ta /taf'itə/ [MF *taffata* < Pers *tāftah*] *n* lustrous cloth of silk, nylon, or rayon, with a fine, plain texture

taff'rail' /taf'-/ [MD *tafereel*] *n* 1 upper part of a ship's stern; 2 rail around the deck of a ship's stern

taf·fy /taf'ē/ [var of *toffee*] *n* candy made of brown sugar or molasses and butter, often with nuts added

Taft, William Howard /hou'ərd taft'/ *n* (1857–1930) 27th president of the U.S. 1909–13, and Chief Justice of the U.S. 1921–30

tag /tag'/ [ME *tagge*] *n* 1 attached identifying card or label; 2 anything hanging or loosely attached; 3 metal binding at the end of a string or lace; 4 children's game in which one player chases the others until he touches one of them; 5 end or concluding part; 6 last words of a speech, story, scene of a play, etc.; 7 traffic ticket; 8 descriptive word or epithet; 9 *baseball* act or instance of tagging a runner ‖ *v* **tagged; tag·ging** *vt* 10 to attach a tag to; 11 to touch in the game of tag; 12 to give a traffic ticket to; 13 *baseball* to put out (a base runner) by touching him with the ball while he is off base; 14 to name, label; 15 to pick out or select (someone), as for a special assignment; 16 *colloq* to follow closely; 17 *slang* to hit hard; 18 **tag out** *baseball* to put out by tagging || *vi* **19 tag after** or **along** to follow or go along with a person or group; **20 tag up** *baseball* (of a base runner) to touch the base occupied after a fly ball is caught, before advancing

Ta·ga·log /təgä′log/ [Tagalog] *n* **1** member of one of the chief native tribes of the Philippines; **2** their language

tag′ end′ *n* final part or ending of something

tag′ line′ *n* last line of a story, play, speech, etc.

Ta·gus /täg′əs/ *n* large river flowing W through central Spain to the Atlantic at Lisbon

Ta·hi·ti /təhēt′ē/ *n* principal island of the French-ruled Society Islands in the S Pacific || **Ta·hi′tian** /-hēsh′ən, -hēt′ē·ən/ *adj* & *n*

tail /tāl′/ [OE *tægl*] *n* **1** hindmost part of an animal's body, esp. the appendage formed by the prolongation of the end of the backbone; **2** anything resembling a tail in position or shape; **3** back, last, or lesser part of anything; **4** final or concluding part; **5** luminous stream extending from the head of a comet; **6** *colloq* person assigned to follow and keep close surveillance on someone; **7** *slang* buttocks, esp. when seated; **8 tails** *pl* a swallow-tailed coat; **b** reverse of a coin; **9′ turn tail** to flee, as from a dangerous encounter || *vt* & *vi* **10** *colloq* to follow close behind

tail′board′ *n* tailgate

tail′ coat′ *n* swallow-tailed coat

tail′ end′ *n* **1** rear or end part; **2** final or concluding part

tail′gate′ *n* **1** hinged or removable board at the back of a wagon, station wagon, or truck || *vi* **2** to drive too close to the vehicle in front || *vt* **3** to drive too close to

tail′ing *n* **1** that part of a projecting stone or brick that is imbedded in a wall; **2 tailings** *pl* a refuse, waste, as washed ore; **b** gravel too large to pass through a screen

tail′light′ *n* red light at the rear of a vehicle

tai·lor /tāl′ər/ [AF *tailour*] *n* **1** one who makes, repairs, or alters outer garments || *vi* **2** to do the work of a tailor || *vt* **3** to make by tailoring; **4** to form or adapt to fit a particular purpose

tai·lor·made′ *adj* **1** made by a tailor; **2** made to order; **3** made to fit a particular purpose

tail′piece′ *n* **1** something added at the end; **2** flat piece of wood at the wider end of a violin to which the strings are attached; **3** decorative design at the bottom of a page or at the end of a chapter

tail′pipe′ *n* exhaust pipe at the rear of a vehicle

tail′race′ *n* channel carrying water away from a water wheel

tail′spin′ *n* downward spiral motion of an airplane with the tail describing circles

tail′stock′ *n* adjustable sliding part of a lathe that holds the dead center

tail′wind′ *n* wind coming from behind a vessel or aircraft

taint /tānt′/ [OF < L *tinctus* tinged] *n* **1** trace of something bad, harmful, infectious, contaminating, or corrupting || *vt* **2** to affect with a taint || SYN *n* contamination, stain, infection, spot, trace, corruption, impurity (see *blemish*)

Tai·pei /tī′pā′/ *n* capital of Taiwan (1,135,500)

Tai·wan /tī′wän′/ *n* large Chinese island off the SE coast of China (14,-700,000; 13,885 sq.m.; cap. Taipei) || **Tai·wan·ese** /tī′wənēz′, -nēs′/ *adj* & *n* (-ese)

Taj Ma·hal /täj′ məhäl′, täzh′/ [Pers *tāj* crown + Ar *mahāl* palaces] *n* white marble mausoleum, renowned for its architectural beauty, built at Agra, India by the Emperor Shah Jahan in the 17th century for his favorite wife

take /tāk′/ [OE *tacan* < Scand] *v* (**took**; **tak·en** /tāk′ən/) *vt* **1** to lay hold of, as with the hands; **2** to gain possession of; **3** to receive, accept; **4** to react to, as *he took it hard*; **5** to seize, capture; **6** to captivate, as *the hat took her fancy*; **7** to avail oneself of, as *to take a holiday*; **8** to add to food, as *I take sugar in my tea*; **9** to lead to, as *this street takes you uptown*; **10** to travel by, as *take the train*; **11** to occupy (a seat); **12** to act (a part in a play); **13** to write down; **14** to study (a specified subject); **15** to be bound by (an oath); **16** to assume (an office); **17** to assume for oneself, as credit or blame; **18** to determine by observation or examination, as someone's temperature; **19** to derive; **20** to engage or rent; **21** to buy regularly or subscribe to; **22** to carry, convey; **23** to conduct or escort; **24** to abstract, remove, steal; **25** to subtract, deduct; **26** to consume, as food or meals; **27** to inhale, as gas; **28** to expose (a photograph); **29** to submit to, endure; **30** to come upon suddenly, as *to take by surprise*; **31** to catch, be infected with; **32** to require, as *it will take two days;* **33** to perform, do, as *take exercise;* **34** to pass, clear, as *the horse took the obstacle;* **35** to experience, feel, as offense, pride, joy, etc.; **36** *gram* to be followed by (a certain construction); **37** to remove by death; **38** to quote, cite; **39** to choose, select; **40** to assume, attain, as *brass takes a high polish;* 41 *slang* to cheat, swindle; 42 **take back,** a to accept again; b to retract; 43 **take down,** a to disassemble; b to write down; 44 **take for,** a to treat or regard as, as *they took him for a fool;* b to assume (someone) to be (someone else); 45 **take in,** a to make (a garment) smaller; b to include; c to observe, watch; d to give lodging to; e to trick; 46 **take it,** a to understand; b *slang* to endure adversity; 47 **take it out on** *colloq* to vent one's wrath on; 48 **take it upon oneself** to to assume the responsibility for; 49 **take off,** a to remove; b to deduct; c *colloq* to burlesque; 50 **take on,** a to hire; b to undertake; c to acquire; d to challenge, stand up to; 51 **take out,** a to withdraw; b to apply for and get; c to act as escort to (a lady); d to buy (food) in a store or restaurant to be eaten at some other place; 52 **take over,** a to assume charge of; b *slang* to cheat, swindle; 53 **take up,** a to devote oneself to the study of; b to occupy, as space or time; c to resume || *vi* 54 to have the intended effect; 55 to take root; 56 to become (the sick); 57 to prove attractive, be acceptable; 58 **take after,** a to resemble; b to start chasing; 59 **take off,** a *colloq* to depart; b to leave the ground, as an airplane; 60 **take to,** a to fall into the habit of using; b to form a liking for; c to go to, have recourse to, as *he took to his bed, he took to his heels;* 61 **take up with** *colloq* to start going around with || *n* 62 act of taking; 63 that which is taken; 64 *slang* money taken in, receipts; 65 **on the take** *slang* looking for bribes || SYN *v* carry, seize, gain, get, withdraw, revoke, abstract, steal, deduce, charm, select, require, assume, receive, contract, capture, secure

take'-home pay' *n* amount of salary remaining after deducting the social security tax, withholding tax, and in some cases state unemployment and payroll taxes

take'off' *n* 1 act of leaving the ground, as in jumping or in beginning a flight in an aircraft or a rocket; 2 *colloq* satirical imitation, burlesque

take'o'ver *n* act of taking over

tak'er *n* 1 one that takes, receives, collects, or notes down, as *ticket taker, taker of dictation;* 2 person who accepts or buys something offered, as *there were no takers for those bargains*

tak'ing *adj* attractive, winning

talc /talk'/ [< *talcum*] *n* a hydrous mineral silicate of magnesia —H_2Mg_3 $(SiO_3)_4$— very soft and slippery to the touch, used in making talcum powder, lubricants, etc.

tal'cum pow'der /talk'əm/ [ML *talcum* < Ar *talq* mica] *n* toilet powder made of finely pulverized talc

tale /tāl'/ [OB *talu*] *n* 1 narrative, story; 2 false report or piece of gossip; 3 falsehood || SYN account, narrative, story (see *anecdote*)

tale'bear'er *n* one who spreads gossip, scandal, etc.

tal·ent /tal'ənt/ [Gk *talanton* balance, sum of money] *n* 1 ancient unit of varying value of weight and money in the Near East; 2 natural ability, skill, or aptitude; 3 superior ability fitting one for a particular business, art, or profession; 4 persons with talent collectively || SYN facility, cleverness (see *ability, genius, gift*)

tal'ent·ed *adj* having talent, gifted

tal'ent scout' *n* person who seeks out talented people, esp. for show business

tales·man /tālz'mən/ [< ML *tales* (de circumstantibus) such (of the bystanders)] *n* (-men /-mən/) person summoned to fill a vacancy on a jury

tal·is·man /tal'ismən, -iz-/ [Sp < Ar < Gk *telesma* payment] *n* 1 figure cut in metal or stone supposed to possess magical powers; 2 charm, amulet

talk /tôk'/ [ME *talken*] *vi* 1 to utter words; communicate thoughts by speaking; 2 to confer; consult; 3 to chatter, prattle; 4 to gossip; 5 to give a speech or lecture; 6 to reveal secrets or confidential information; 7 to mean something definite, as *money talks;* 8 to communicate by nonvocal means, as by signs; 9 **talk back** to answer disrespectfully; 10 **talk down to** to speak condescendingly to; 11 **talk of** to discuss || *vt* 12 to utter, express in words, discuss, as *talk business;* 13 to express oneself in (a language); 14 to affect or influence by talking, as to *talk someone to sleep;* 15 **talk away** to spend (time) in talking; 16 **talk someone into** (or **out of**) **something** to persuade someone to do (or refrain from doing) something; 17 **talk something over** to consider or discuss something || *n* 18 speech; conversation; 19 subject of gossip; 20 rumor, report; 21 meaningless speech, prattle; 22 conference; 23 informal address; 24 dialect; manner of speech || **talk'er** *n* || SYN *n* chat, colloquy, confabulation, parley, communication, conference, gossip (see *conversation*)

talk'a·tive *adj* given to talking a great deal || SYN chattering, loquacious (see *garrulous*)

talk'ie *n* motion picture with synchronized speech or sound

talk'ing-to' *n colloq* scolding

talk' show' *n* television program that

consists largely of interviews with all kinds of people

tall /tôl/ [prob < OE *getæl* swift] *adj* 1 of more than average height; 2 having a specified height, as *six feet tall*; 3 *colloq* a high-sounding, boastful; exaggerated; b considerable; excellent ‖ **tall′ish** *adj*

Tal·la·has·see /tal′əhas′ē/ *n* capital of Florida (50,000)

Tal·linn /täl′in/ *n* capital of Estonia (325,000)

tal·low /tal′ō/ [ME *talgh*] *n* the harder and less fusible fat of animals, as suet, separated from membranous tissues by melting and used for making candles, soap, etc.

tal·ly /tal′ē/ [ME *taly* < L *talea* rod] *n* (**-lies**) 1 anything upon which an account, reckoning, or score is kept; 2 reckoning, account, or score; 3 one of a series of marks for recording a number of objects; 4 the number of objects so recorded; 5 label or tag; 6 anything corresponding to something else, as a duplicate or counterpart ‖ *v* (**-lied**) *vt* 7 to mark or enter on a tally; register, record; score; 8 to count, reckon up ‖ *vi* 9 to correspond, agree

tal·ly·ho /tal′ēhō′/ [prob < F *taïaut*] *interj* 1 huntsman's cry on sighting the fox ‖ /tal′ēhō′/ *n* 2 the cry "tallyho"; 3 pleasure coach drawn by four horses

Tal·mud /tal′məd, täl′mŏŏd/ [Heb = instruction] *n* the collection of Jewish civil and canonical laws not included in the Pentateuch ‖ **Tal·mud·ic (-i·cal)** /-m(y)ŏŏd′-/ *adj* ‖ **Tal′mud·ist** *n*

tal·on /tal′ən/ [OF < LL *talo* (*-onis*) heel] *n* claw of an animal, esp. of a bird of prey

tam /tam/ */n* tam-o'-shanter

tam·a·ble or **tame·a·ble** /tām′əbəl/ [see tame] *adj* capable of being tamed

ta·ma·le /təmäl′ē/ [MexSp *tamal*] *n* Mexican dish of seasoned chopped meat and corn meal, wrapped in corn husks and steamed

tam·a·rack /tam′ərak′/ [< *Algonquian*] *n* any of several American larches, esp. a species (*Larix laricina*) of the eastern U.S.

tam·a·rind /tam′ərind/ [Sp *tamarindo* < Ar *tamr-hindī* date of India] *n* tall tropical tree (*Tamarindus indica*) having pinnate leaves and showy yellow flowers striped with red, bearing podlike fruit from which preserves and a cooling drink are made

tam·a·risk /tam′ərisk/ [LL *tamariscus*] *n* any of a large genus (*Tamarix*) of Old World tropical shrubs and small trees having feathery leaves

tam·bou·rine /tam′bərēn′/ [MF *tambourin* small drum] *n* small hand drum consisting of a hoop with a skin stretched over it and little metallic jingles on the hoop, played by shaking and striking

tame /tām/ [OE *tam*] *adj* 1 changed from a wild state; domesticated, made useful to man; 2 gentle, docile; 3 lacking in spirit, dull ‖ *vt* 4 to make tame; domesticate; 5 to subdue, make tractable; 6 to remove spirit or courage from; 7 to quiet, tone down; 8 to control, harness ‖ **tame′ly** *adv* ‖ **tame′ness** *n*

Tam·il /tam′il/ *n* 1 one of a people of Dravidian stock of S India and Ceylon; 2 language of the Tamils ‖ also *adj*

tam-o'-shan·ter /tam′əshant′ər/ [*Tam O'Shanter* hero of a poem by Robert Burns] *n* Scotch cap with a tight headband and a round flat top

tamp /tamp/ [< *obs tampion* plug] *vt* 1 to plug (a blast hole in a rock) in order to direct the force of the explosion; 2 to drive or ram down with light strokes

Tam·pa /tamp′ə/ *n* seaport in W Florida (277,767)

tam·per /tamp′ər/ [prob var of *temper*] *vi* 1 to meddle improperly; 2 **tamper with,** a to make meddlesome alterations in; b to use unfair influence with, as by bribery ‖ **tam′per·er**

tam·pon /tam′pon/ [F] *n* plug, as of cotton, inserted into a wound or cavity to stop bleeding ‖ *vt* to plug with a tampon

tan¹ /tan′/ [L *tannum* oak bark] *n* 1 tanbark; 2 yellowish brown; 3 brown color given to the skin by exposure to the sun ‖ *v* (**tanned**; **tan·ning**) *vt* 4 to convert (hides) into leather, as by treating with tannin; 5 to make brown by exposure to the sun; 6 *colloq* to beat, thrash ‖ *vi* 7 to become tanned ‖ *adj* 8 tan-colored

tan² tangent

tan·a·ger /tan′əjər/ [Tupi *tangara*] *n* any of a family (Thraupidae) of American songbirds, most of which are brightly colored

Ta·na·na·rive /tənan′ərēv′/ *n* capital of the Malagasy Republic (360,000)

tan′bark′ *n* 1 oak or other bark containing tannin, used in tanning; 2 this material, after the tannin has been exhausted, spread to make a soft surface, as in a circus ring

tan·dem /tan′dəm/ [L = finally] *adv & adj* 1 one behind the other ‖ *n* 2 pair of horses harnessed tandem; 3 tandem bicycle

tan′dem bi′cy·cle *n* bicycle for two or more persons with seats and pedals arranged tandem

Ta·ney, Rog·er /tôn′ē/ *n* (1777–1864) Chief Justice of the U.S. 1836–64

tang¹ /taŋ′/ [ME *tange* < Scand] *n* 1 the part of a knife, file, etc., that goes into the handle; 2 strong, sharp taste or flavor; **3** characteristic flavor or tinge ‖ **tang′y** *adj* (**-i·er; -i·est**)

tang² [imit] *n* **1** sharp, twanging sound ‖ *tr* **2** to cause to sound with a twanging noise ‖ *vi* **3** to twang, clang

Tan·gan·yi·ka /ˌtanˈɡənyēkˈə/ *n* former German and British territory in E Africa, now the mainland part of Tanzania

tan·gent /tanˈjənt/ [L *tangens* (*-entis*)] *adj* **1** touching; **2** *geom* touching a line or surface at a single point without intersecting ‖ *n* **3** *geom* tangent line or surface; **4** *trig* in a right triangle, ratio of the side opposite a given angle to the side adjacent to it; **5 off on a tangent** diverging suddenly from one course of action to another ‖ **tan·gen′tial** /-jenshˈəl/ *adj*

tan·ger·ine /tanˈjərēn/ [< *Tangier*, Morocco] *n* **1** small loose-skinned variety of mandarin orange with a sweet spicy flavor and dry pulp; **2** reddish yellow

tan·gi·ble /tanˈjəbəl/ [L *tangibilis*] *adj* **1** capable of being touched; **2** evident; real; existing ‖ *n* **3** tangible asset or property having a definite monetary value ‖ **tan′gi·bly** *adv* ‖ **tan′gi·bil′i·ty** /-bil′-/ *n*

Tan·gier /tanjir′/ *n* capital of former Tangier Zone (142,000)

Tan·gier′ Zone′ *n* former international zone on the African side of the Strait of Gibraltar, since 1956 part of Morocco

tan·gle /tanˈɡəl/ [ME *tangil* < Scand] *vt* **1** to knot or intertwine so as to make difficult to unravel; **2** to catch as in a snare ‖ *vi* **3** to be or become tangled; **4 tangle with** *colloq* to get involved in an altercation with ‖ *n* **5** tangled or confused mass or jumble; **6** *colloq* altercation

tan·go /tanˈɡō/ [Sp] *n* **1** ballroom dance with strongly marked rhythm and a large variety of steps; **2** the music for it ‖ *also vi*

tank /tank/ *n* **1** large receptacle or structure for holding a liquid or gas; **2** small metal container for gasoline, usu. in the rear of an automobile; **3** armored combat vehicle moving on caterpillar treads and carrying machine guns and cannon; **4** *slang* large cell for holding prisoners awaiting trial; **5** *slang* heavy drinker ‖ **tank′-ful′** *n*

tank·ard /tankˈərd/ [ME] *n* large drinking vessel, usu. with a handle and hinged lid

tank′er *n* ship or plane constructed to transport oil or other liquids

tank′ farm′ *n* collection of oil tanks in one place

tank′ town′ [< fact that trains drawn by steam engines stop only to replenish their water supply] *n* small unimportant town

tan′ner *n* one who tans hides

tan′ner·y *n* (**-ies**) place where hides are tanned

tan′nic ac′id /tanˈik/ *n* tannin

tan·nin /tanˈin/ *n* astringent acid —$C_{76}H_{52}O_{46}$— present in various substances, as tea, gallnuts, sumac, and certain barks, used in tanning leather, in dyeing, in medicine, etc.

tan·ta·lize /tantˈəlīz′/ [< *Tantalus*, son of Zeus, who was punished by being placed up to his neck in water which receded when he stooped to drink, and under fruit-laden branches which retreated when he reached up] *vt* to tease or torment by arousing expectations that will not be realized ‖ **tan′ta·liz′ing** *adj* ‖ SYN tease, torment, provoke, harass, vex, irritate, plague ‖ ANT satisfy, appease, conciliate

tan·ta·lum /tantˈələm/ [< *Tantalus*; see *tantalize*] *n* rare, heavy metallic element (**Ta;** at.no. 73; at.wt. 180.948) used, because of its high melting point and resistance to corrosion, for chemical apparatus and for surgical and dental instruments

tan·ta·mount /tantˈəmount′/ [< AF *tant amunter* to amount to so much] *adj* **tantamount to** equivalent to, the same as

tan·trum /tantˈrəm/ [?] *n* uncontrolled outburst of temper or caprice

Tan·za·ni·a /ˌtanˈzənēˈə, tanzänˈēˈə/ *n* republic in E Africa (14,900,000; 364,-943 sq.m.; cap. Dar es Salaam)

Tao·ism /touˈizəm, douˈ-/ [< Chin *tao* way] *n* Chinese religious system, whose greatest exponent, Lao-tzu, in the sixth century B.C. prescribed a life of contemplation and reason, avoidance of force, and disregard of ceremony ‖ **Tao′ist** *adj & n* ‖ **Tao·is′tic** *adj*

tap¹ /tap′/ [OE *tæppa*] *n* **1** faucet or spigot; **2** plug or stopper for closing an opening in a cask; **3** tool for cutting threads on an inner surface; **4** *elec* device for making connection with a wire; **5** connection placed on a telephone line for surreptitious listening; **6** *surg* withdrawal of fluid; **7 on tap, a** ready to be drawn as beer in a cask; **b** *colloq* readily available ‖ *v* (**tapped; tap·ping**) *vt* **8** to furnish with a spigot; **9** to pierce, as the side of a cask or the bark of a tree, in order to draw out liquid; **10** to draw liquid from; **11** to extract, remove, withdraw, as to *tap sources of information*; **12** to cut screw threads on the inner surface of; **13** to make connection with (an electric line, pipe, etc.) so as to draw off current or liquid; **14** to place a tap on (a telephone) ‖ **tap′per** *n*

tap² [ME *tappen*] *v* (**tapped; tap·ping**) *vt* **1** to strike or touch lightly; **2** to cause to strike or touch lightly, as to *tap the feet on the floor*; **3** to make or do by tapping, as *to tap a message on a pipe* ‖ *vi* **4** to strike light blows ‖ *n* **5** gentle blow or pat; **6** piece of leather or metal attached to the sole or heel of a shoe; **7** taps *pl mil* bugle call or drum signal signifying lights out

tap′ dance′ *n* dance in which the rhythm is tapped out with shoes equipped with taps or with hard soles and heels ‖ **tap′-dance′** *vi* ‖ **tap′-danc′er** *n*

tape /tāp′/ [OE *tæppe* cloth strip] *n* **1** long narrow strip of cloth used for tying, binding seams, etc.; **2** narrow strip of paper used on a printing telegraph or stock ticker; **3** line stretched across the track to mark the finish of a race; **4** tape measure; **5** magnetic tape ‖ *vt* **6** to furnish with or fasten with tape; **7** to measure with a tape measure; **8** to tape-record ‖ *vi* **9** to tape-record

tape′ car′tridge *n* cartridge 5

tape′ deck′ *n* high-fidelity component consisting of a tape recorder and tape player for attaching to a power amplifier and speaker

tape′ meas′ure *n* strip of fabric or metal, marked off in inches and feet or in metric units, for measuring

tape′ play′er *n* device for playing back tape recordings

ta·per /tāp′ər/ [OE *tapur, taper* candle wick] *n* **1** slender candle; **2** long wick impregnated with wax or tallow for lighting candles or gas lamps; **3** gradual lessening of thickness toward one end of an elongated object ‖ *vi* **4** to become smaller in size toward one end; **5 taper off** to lessen gradually ‖ *vt* **6** to cause to taper

tape′-re·cord′ *vt* to record on magnetic tape

tape′ re·cord′er *n* device for recording and reproducing on magnetic tape

tape′ re·cord′ing *n* recording on magnetic tape

tap·es·try /tap′istrē/ [MF *tapisserie*] *n* (**-tries**) **1** cloth containing handwoven pictures or designs, used for wall hangings, coverings for furniture, etc. ‖ *v* (**-tried**) *vt* **2** to hang or adorn with, or as with tapestry

tape′worm′ *n* any of several long parasitic flatworms (chiefly genus *Taenia*) which infest the intestines of man and other animals

tap·i·o·ca /tap′ē·ōk′ə/ [Port < Tupi *tipioca* cassava juice] *n* the starch prepared from cassava, used in puddings and cookery

ta·pir /tāp′ər/ [Tupi *tapira*] *n* any of a family (Tapiridae) of hoofed, herbivorous mammals, having short stout legs and a flexible snout, native to Central America, South America, and the Malay Peninsula

tap·pet /tap′it/ [< *tap*²] *n* small lever which, actuated by another piece

such as a cam, imparts motion to an arm for opening and closing valves

tap′room′ *n* barroom

tap′root′ *n* main root of certain plants, having many small branches

tap′ wa′ter *n* water directly from a faucet, that has not been specially treated or purified

tap′ wrench′ *n* wrench for holding and turning a tap to cut threads on an inner surface

tar¹ /tär′/ [OE *teru*] *n* **1** thick dark oily substance obtained by distillation of wood, coal, etc.; **2** beat or knock the tar out of to beat severely ‖ *v* (**tarred; tar·ring**) *vt* **3** to cover with or as with tar; **4 tar and feather** to punish or humiliate with a coat of tar and feathers

tar² /tär′/ [perh < *tarpaulin*] *n colloq* sailor

tar·an·tel·la /tar′əntel′ə/ [It < *Taranto*, Italy] *n* rapid whirling Italian dance or the music for it

ta·ran·tu·la /təranch′ələ/ [ML < It *tarantola*] *n* **1** large hairy spider (*Lycosa tarantula*) of southern Europe; **2** any of several similar spiders (family Theraphosidae) of the warmer regions of America, having a painful but not fatal bite

tar·boosh /tärbōōsh′/ [Ar *tarbūsh*] *n* brimless, tasseled cap, usu. red, worn by Muslim men

tar·dy /tärd′ē/ [< L *tardus* slow] *adj* (**-di·er; -di·est**) **1** moving with a slow pace or motion; **2** not prompt; late; **3** dilatory ‖ **tar′di·ness** *n* ‖ SYN dilatory, late, sluggish, (see *slow*)

tare¹ /ter′/ [MF = deficiency, waste] *n* **1** allowance for the weight of the container in determining the weight of the contents; **2** weight of a vehicle without cargo or passengers

tare² [ME] *n* **1** any of various vetches, esp. *Vicia sativa*; **2** *Bib* unidentified noxious weed (Matt. 13:25,36)

tar·get /tärg′it/ [MF *targuete*] *n* **1** mark set up to be aimed at for practice or in shooting contests; **2** anything used for this; **3** anything shot at; **4** object of attack; **5** goal; **6** butt, object of scorn or abuse ‖ also *adj*

tar′get date′ *n* date set for the commencement or completion of some endeavor

tar′get lan′guage *n* **1** foreign language being taught; **2** language into which a translation is made (opposite of *source language*)

tar·iff /tar′if/ [It *tariffa* < Ar *ta′rīfa* information] *n* **1** schedule or table of duties or customs placed on imports and/or exports; **2** such duties collectively; **3** tax or duty levied according to such a schedule; **4** any schedule of rates or charges

Tar·mac /tär′mak/ [trademark] *n* **1** bituminous binder used to surface

roads and paved areas, as in airports and parking lots; 2 tarmac area paved with this binder

tarn /tärn/ [ME *terne* < Scand] *n* small mountain lake or pool

tar·na·tion /tärnāsh'ən/ [*eternal* + damn*nation*] *n* damnation || *interj* damnation!, hell!

tar·nish /tär'ish/ [MF *ternir* (*-niss-*) to dull] *vt* 1 to discolor, dull the luster of; 2 to sully, as a good name || *vi* 3 to lose luster, discolor || *n* 4 discoloration, lack of brightness; 5 dull or discolored coating; 6 blemish, as of a reputation

ta·ro /tär'ō, ter'ō/ [Polynesian] *n* tropical plant (genus *Colocasia*), grown esp. in the islands of the Pacific for its edible root

ta·rot /tarō'/ [MF *taroto*] *n* set of 22 playing cards bearing allegorical figures, used in fortunetelling

tar'pa'per *n* heavy paper coated or impregnated with tar, used esp. for waterproofing roofs

tar·pau·lin /tärpôl'ĭn, tärp'əl-/ [< *tar*¹ + *pall*¹] *n* waterproof canvas used for covering ship's hatches, baseball infields when it rains, etc.

tar·pon /tärp'ən/ [?] *n* (*-pon* or *-pons*) large game fish (*Tarpon atlanticus*) found in the warmer waters of the Atlantic

tar·ry¹ /tar'ē/ [ME *tarye*] *v* (*-ried*) *vi* 1 to stay in a place for a time; to delay, linger; 2 to wait

tar·ry² /tär'ē/ *adj* (*-ri·er; -ri·est*) 1 covered with or like tar; 2 thievish (fingers) || **tar'ri·ness** *n*

tar·si·er /tärs'ē-ər/ *n* small nocturnal arboreal primate (genus *Tarsius*) of the East Indies, with large ears and eyes, and large disks on the ends of the toes and fingers

tart¹ /tärt/ [OE *teart*] *adj* 1 sharp to the taste, acid; 2 biting, cutting, as a remark || **tart'ly** *adv* || SYN piquant, sour, biting (see *bitter*)

tart² [MF *tarte*] *n* 1 pastry shell filled with fruit or jam and without a top crust; 2 *slang* prostitute

tar·tan /tärt'ən/ [MF *tertaine*] *n* 1 woolen cloth with a pattern of stripes crossing at right angles, worn particularly in the Scottish Highlands, where special patterns distinguish the various clans; 2 any plaid fabric

tar·tar /tärt'ər/ [Gk *tartaron*] *n* 1 a potassium salt forming a crusty deposit in wine casks; 2 brownish-yellow deposit forming on the teeth

Tar·tar /tärt'ər/ [ML *Tartarus* < Pers *Tātār*] *n* 1 member of one of the nomadic Mongol tribes of central Asia that overran Asia and much of Europe during the Middle Ages; 2 language of the Tartars; 3 also **tartar** intractable savage-tempered person; 4 **catch a tartar** to undertake something or deal with someone that

proves more troublesome than expected || also *adj*

tar'tar sauce' *n* mayonnaise dressing with chopped pickles, onions, olives, etc., added

Tar'ta·ry *n* indefinite area in E Europe and Asia that was overrun by the Tartars during the Middle Ages

task /task/, täsk/ [ML *tasca* < L *taxa* tax] *n* 1 assigned piece of work; definite job to be done; 2 arduous duty, difficult undertaking; 3 **take to task** to reprimand, call to account || SYN undertaking, toil, stint, drudgery, lesson

task' force' *n* 1 *mil* group of special units assembled to carry out a specific mission; 2 group of knowledgeable persons organized to study a special problem and present proposals for its solution

task'mas'ter *n* 1 one who assigns tasks to others and oversees their execution; 2 exacting employer or superior

Tas·ma·ni·a /tazmān'ē-ə/ *n* island S of and constituting a state of Australia

tas·sel /tas'əl/ [OF = clasp] *n* 1 hanging ornament consisting of a tuft of threads or cords; 2 anything resembling this, as a tuft of corn silk || **tas'seled** or **tas'selled** *adj*

taste /tāst/ [MF *taster*] *vt* 1 to perceive the flavor of; 2 to test the flavor of by eating or drinking a little; 3 to eat or drink a little of; 4 to have experience of || *vi* 5 to try food by the tongue or palate; 6 to have a certain flavor; 7 **taste of**, a to eat or drink a little of; b to smack of || *n* 8 sense by which flavor is perceived by the taste buds; 9 sensation or flavor so perceived; 10 act of tasting; 11 small portion tasted; sip or bit; 12 predilection; 13 faculty of nice discrimination as to what is beautiful, refined, elegant, or fitting; 14 manner or style in relation to what is refined, elegant, or fitting; 15 trace or sample || SYN *n* relish, savor, sip (see *flavor*)

taste' bud' *n* one of the end organs of the sense of taste on the tongue

taste'ful *adj* marked by or showing good taste || **taste'ful·ly** *adv* || SYN artistic, pleasing, well-chosen, dainty, elegant

taste'less *adj* 1 without flavor; flat, insipid; 2 lacking good taste

tast·y /tāst'ē/ *adj* (*-i·er; -i·est*) good-tasting, savory

tat /tat/ [< *tatting*] *v* (**tat·ted; tat·ting**) *vi* 1 to do tatting || *vt* 2 to make by tatting

Ta·tar /tät'ər/ [Pers] *n* Tartar *1 & 2* || also *adj*

tat·ter /tat'ər/ [ME < Scand] *n* 1 loose-hanging rag; 2 piece of cloth torn off; 3 **tatters** *pl* rags

tat·ter·de·mal·ion /tat'ərdimāl'yən,

-mal′-/ [tatter + ?] n ragged fellow; ragamuffin

tat′tered adj 1 ragged; 2 raggedly dressed

tat′ting [?] n 1 narrow lace made with a hand shuttle by looping and knotting thread; 2 art or process of making such lace

tat·tle /tat′əl/ [MFlem tatelen] vi 1 to talk idly; 2 to tell tales or secrets ‖ vt 3 to disclose (a secret) while chattering ‖ n 4 idle talk; gossip ‖ tat′-tler n

tat′tle-tale′ n informer, talebearer

tat·too¹ /tatoo′/ [< D taptoe = the tap (in a barroom) is shut] n 1 drum or other signal to call soldiers to quarters; 2 continuous beating, as of a drum

tat·too² [Polynesian tatau] vt 1 to produce a permanent design on (the skin) by puncturing a design on it and filling the punctures with indelible ink ‖ n 2 tattooed mark or design on the skin ‖ tat·too′er n

tau /tou′, tô′/ n nineteenth letter of the Greek alphabet T, τ

taught /tôt′/ pt & pp of teach

taunt /tônt′, tänt′/ [?] vt 1 to reproach with bitter, sarcastic, or insulting language ‖ n 2 bitter or sarcastic reproach ‖ SYN v deride, ridicule, mock, chaff, banter ‖ DISCR To taunt is to cast something in one's teeth, such as one's conduct, an unfulfilled boast, or the like, with insulting or reproachful words; taunting maddens one by sarcasm and contempt. Ridicule may connote malice and contempt, as by holding one up as a laughingstock in a humiliating way; but it often suggests good-natured fun poked thoughtlessly or teasingly. Bell was unkindly ridiculed for thinking people could talk over the newly invented telephone. Some people, naturally observant of human frailties, make the mistake of ridiculing their friends for the entertainment of others. Deride and mock suggest a hostile intention, openly contemptuous, cutting, and jeering, mock being the stronger term. Deriding is done by sneering, scornful laughter, and jeers. Mocking is accomplished by ironical words, often accompanied by defiant or atrocious imitation in action, and pretended laughter. To banter is to ridicule, especially personalities, good-humoredly or playfully; bantering usually is accepted as it is meant, save that it leaves a slight sense of wounded vanity, as they goad me until I play, and then banter me on my lack of skill. To chaff is to ridicule, either in sport or in malice, in a teasing way

tau·rine /tôr′in, -in/ [L taurinus] adj 1 of, pert. to, or resembling a bull; 2 pert. to Taurus

Tau·rus /tôr′əs/ [L < Gk tauros bull] n 1 a northern zodiacal constellation, the Bull; 2 second sign of the zodiac

taut /tôt′/ [ME togt] adj 1 stretched tight, not slack; 2 tense, strained

tau·tol·o·gy /tôtol′əjē/ [Gk tautologia] n (-gies) 1 needless repetition of an idea in different words; 2 example of this repetition, as the universal esteem of all men ‖ tau′to·log′i·cal /-əloj′-/ adj ‖ SYN n wordiness, diffuseness (see circumlocution)

tav·ern /tav′ərn/ [OF taverne < L taberna] n 1 inn; 2 saloon, bar

taw·dry /tôd′rē/ [< lace bought at the fair of St. Audrey in England] adj (-dri·er; -dri·est) gaudy; cheap and showy ‖ taw′dri·ness n ‖ SYN flashy, cheap, gaudy (see showy)

taw·ny /tôn′ē/ [AF taune tanned] adj (-ni·er; -ni·est) tan, yellow-brown ‖ taw′ni·ness n

tax /taks′/ [ML taxare to appraise, tax] n 1 charge or duty on income, property, sales, etc. levied for the support of a government; 2 heavy or oppressive burden ‖ vt 3 to impose a tax on; 4 to burden or oppress; 5 to accuse or charge ‖ tax′a·ble adj ‖ SYN n exaction, demand, tribute, contribution

tax·a′tion n 1 act of taxing or state of being taxed; 2 the tax imposed or paid

tax′ de·duc′tion n deduction from the gross amount of income before calculating the tax ‖ tax′-de·duct′i·ble adj

tax·i /taks′ē/ [< taxicab] n (-is or -ies) 1 taxicab ‖ v (-i·ing or -y·ing) vi 2 to ride in a taxi; 3 (of an airplane) to move on the surface under its own power ‖ vt 4 to cause (an airplane) to taxi

tax′i·cab′ [taximeter + cab] n automobile carrying passengers for pay, usu. provided with a taximeter

tax′i danc′er n woman who dances with patrons at a dance hall at a set fee per dance

tax′i·der′my /-durm′ē/ [< Gk taxis arrangement + derma skin] n art of preparing, stuffing, and mounting the skins of animals so as to preserve their lifelike appearance ‖ tax′i·der′mist n

tax′i·me′ter [F taximètre < G taxameter < ML taxa charge] n device for measuring the distance traveled by a cab and recording the fare

tax′ing adj oppressive; fatiguing

tax′ loss′ n sale of property at less than the cost of acquisition, so that the difference can be used as a tax deduction

tax·on·o·my /takson′əmē/ [F taxonomie] n 1 science of classification; 2 science of classification of animals or plants in established categories ‖ **tax′o·nom′ic** (-i·cal) /-onom′-/ *adj*

tax′ sale′ *n* sale of real property, usu. at auction, for nonpayment of taxes

Tay·lor, Zach·a·ry /zak′ərē tāl′ər/ *n* (1784–1850) 12th president of the U.S. 1849–50

Tb *chem* terbium

TB, T.B., t.b. [*t*ubercle *b*acillus] tuberculosis

T′-bone steak′ *n* loin steak having a T-shaped bone

tbs., tbsp. tablespoon(s)

Tc *chem* technetium

TCBM transcontinental ballistic missile

Tchai·kov·sky, Pe·ter Il·yich /il′yich chīkôf′skē, -kof′-/ *n* (1840–93) Russian composer

TDN touchdown(s)

Te *chem* tellurium

tea /tē/ [Chin (Amoy *dial.*) *t′e*] *n* 1 dried leaves of a shrub (*Thea sinensis*) of E Asia; 2 beverage prepared by steeping them in hot water; 3 any of various infusions prepared from other plants; 4 *Brit* light afternoon meal; 5 afternoon social affair, as a reception, at which tea is served

tea′ bag′ *n* small porous bag containing enough tea to make one cup

tea′ ball′ *n* small perforated metal ball in which tea leaves are placed to be immersed in boiling water

teach /tēch/ [OE *tǣcan*] *v* (taught) *vt* 1 to show or instruct how to perform some action; give instruction to; 2 to give lessons in ‖ *vi* 3 to be a teacher

teach′er *n* one who teaches, esp. as a profession

teach′ing *n* 1 act or profession of one who teaches; 2 also **teachings** *pl* something taught; doctrine ‖ SYN instruction, training, education, doctrine

teach′ing as·sis′tant or **teach′ing fel′low** *n* graduate-school student who teaches one or two undergraduate courses in return for expenses and free tuition

teach′ing hos′pi·tal *n* hospital associated with a medical school in which medical students can observe and learn from actual cases and operations

tea′cup′ *n* small cup for serving tea

tea′ dance′ *n* dance in the afternoon

teak /tēk/ [Port *teca* < Malayalam *tēkka*] *n* tall East Indian tree (*Tectona grandis*), the hard, close-grained timber of which is much used for shipbuilding and furniture

tea′ket′tle *n* covered kettle with spout and handle for heating water

teal /tēl/ [ME *tele*] *n* 1 any of several small, short-necked fresh-water ducks (chiefly genus *Anas*); 2 also **teal′ blue′** dark greenish blue

team /tēm/ [OE = progeny, set] *n* 1 two or more animals harnessed together; 2 one animal with harness and the vehicle drawn; 3 number of persons working or playing together as a unit, esp. one side in a competitive game or sport ‖ *vt* 4 to join together in a team ‖ *vi* 5 **team up** to join together in some activity

team′mate′ *n* member of the same team

team′ster *n* 1 driver of a team of horses in hauling; 2 truckdriver

team′work′ *n* work done in harmony by a group of persons for a common cause

tea′pot′ *n* vessel with a spout, handle, and cover, in which tea is made and from which it is served

tear[1] /ter′/ [OE *teran*] *v* (tore; torn) *vt* 1 to pull apart by force, rend; 2 to lacerate; scratch; 3 to produce or cause by tearing, as *to tear a hole in cloth;* 4 to wrench or sever by force or violence; 5 to disrupt, rend; 6 to distress greatly; 7 **tear down** to pull down, dismantle; 8 **tear up, a** to tear to shreds; **b** to cancel (a written contract or agreement) ‖ *vi* 9 to become torn; 10 to move with speed or violence; 11 **tear at** to grasp violently at; 12 **tear into** *colloq* to attack boldly and heedlessly ‖ *n* 13 act of tearing; 14 hole made by tearing; 15 *slang* spree ‖ SYN *v* rip, split, cleave, sunder, rive, rupture (see *break*) ‖ ANT *v* mend, weld, reunite, join

tear[2] /tir/ [OE] *n* 1 small drop of watery liquid secreted by the lachrymal gland, serving normally to moisten the eye, but overflowing the lids as the result of irritation or under emotional stress; 2 **tears** *pl* sorrow; 3 **in tears** weeping ‖ *vi* 4 to overflow with tears ‖ **tear′ful** *adj* ‖ **tear′y** *adj* (-i·er; -i·est)

tear′drop′ /tir′-/ *n* 1 a tear; 2 something shaped like a falling drop of liquid, globular at the bottom and tapering to a point at the top; 3 gem hanging on an earring

tear′gas′ /tir′-/ *n* gas which causes watering of the eyes and temporary blindness ‖ **tear′-gas′** *vt*

tear′-jerk′er /tir′-/ *n* movie, play, etc. which moves the audience to tears

tea′room′ *n* restaurant or luncheonette serving tea and light lunches

tea′ rose′ *n* variety of rose having a scent like that of tea

tear′ sheet′ /ter′/ *n* page torn from a publication and sent to the advertiser as proof that his advertisement appeared on it

tease /tēz/ [OE *tǣsan* to pull to pieces] *vt* 1 to comb or unravel, as wool or flax; 2 to raise a nap on (cloth) with teasels; 3 to annoy by petty irritations and provocations; 4 to tantalize; 5 to puff up (a hairdo) by holding the hair by the ends and combing it toward the scalp; 6 to separate the fibers of; comb or unravel, as wool or flax || *n* 7 act of teasing; 8 one who teases

tea·sel /tēz′əl/ [OE *tǣsel*] *n* 1 any of a genus (*Dipsacus*) of herbs with oblong flower heads bearing stiff hooked spines; 2 the dried flower heads of one species (*D. fullonum*) used to tease cloth; 3 any mechanical device for teasing

teas′er *n* 1 one that teases; 2 one of several borders used to frame the setting of a stage

tea′ serv′ice *n* articles used in serving tea

tea′spoon′ *n* spoon of ordinary size, as for stirring tea or coffee, holding ⅓ tablespoonful or 1⅓ fluid drams || **tea′spoon·ful′** *n*

teat /tēt/ [ME & OF *tete* < Gmc] *n* protuberance on the mammary gland through which milk passes

tea′ time′ *n* hour at which tea is served

tea′wag′on *n* light table on wheels for serving or transporting food indoors

tech. 1 technical; 2 technology

tech·ne·ti·um /teknēsh′(ē)əm/ [< Gk *technetos* artificial] *n* metallic element (**Tc**; at.no. 43; at.wt. 99) made artificially by bombarding molybdenum

tech·ni·cal /tek′nikəl/ [< Gk *techne* art] *adj* 1 relating to the mechanical arts or to any art or science; 2 having to do with the exact or mechanical part of an art or science; 3 according to strict interpretation of the rules; 4 pert. to or exhibiting technique

tech′ni·cal′i·ty /-kal′-/ *n* (-ties) 1 technical point or detail; 2 strict interpretation of a rule, as *acquitted on a technicality*

tech′ni·cal knock′out *n* termination of a boxing bout in favor of the opponent when a boxer, though not knocked out, cannot continue without risking severe injury

tech·ni·cian /teknish′ən/ *n* one skilled in the technique of a science, art, or craft

tech·nique /teknēk′/ [F] *n* 1 method of procedure in the performance of any art or any process involving special knowledge or skill; 2 technical skill

tech·no- [< Gk *techne* art] *comb form* 1 art; 2 technical, technological

tech·noc·ra·cy /teknok′rəsē/ *n* social and economic system administered by scientists and engineers || **tech′no·crat′** /-nəkrat′/ *n* || **tech′no·crat′ic** *adj*

tech·nol·o·gy /teknol′əjē/ [Gk *technologia* systematic treatment] *n* 1 science of industrial arts and manufactures; 2 applied science; 3 all the means employed by a social group

to provide for material comforts; 4 technical terminology

ted′dy bear′ /ted′ē/ [*Teddy* (Theodore) Roosevelt] *n* stuffed toy bear

Te De·um /tēdē′əm/ [L *Te Deum* (laudamus) (we praise) Thee, O God] *n* 1 ancient Christian hymn of praise or thanksgiving to God; 2 musical setting of this hymn; 3 religious service of praise or thanksgiving in which this hymn plays a part

te·di·ous /tēd′ē-əs, tēj′əs/ [< *tedium*] *adj* wearisome, tiresome; boring || SYN irksome, fatiguing || DISCR That is *fatiguing* which wearies either mind or body, or both, to the point of lassitude and exhaustion; labor or exertion prolonged for hours or beyond our strength is *fatiguing*. That is *irksome* which we must do when we want to do something else, or which we dislike, or for which we lack sympathy; hence, that which is *irksome* is not only *fatiguing* to the body but tiring to the mind. The *tedious* is more mentally than physically tiresome; that is *tedious* which is long-drawn-out, boresome, or repetitious; long waits, stories without point, monotonous routine, are *tedious* (see *slow*) || ANT stimulating, exciting, interesting, animated, stirring

te·di·um /tēd′ē-əm/ [L *taedium*] *n* state or quality of being tedious

tee[1] /tē/ [?] *n* 1 *golf* **a** small peg from which the ball is driven at the initial stroke on each hole; **b** area of turf within which such a peg must be placed || *vt* 2 to place (the ball) on a tee; 3 **tee off** *colloq* **a** to begin; **b** to anger, irritate, as *he was teed off by the delay* || *vi* 4 **tee off** to strike a ball from the tee; 5 **tee off on** *slang* to reprimand, scold

tee[2] *n* 1 the letter T; 2 something shaped like a T; 3 **to a tee** to a T

teem[1] /tēm/ [OE *tēman*] *vi* to abound, swarm || **teem′ing** *adj*

teem[2] [ME *temen* < ON *toma* to empty] *vi* to pour, to rain torrentially || **teem′ing** *adj*

-teen /-tēn′/ [OE *-tēne*] *suf* plus ten (used to form the cardinal numbers from 13 to 19)

teen′·age′ *adj* of or pert. to a person in his or her teens || **teen′·ag′er** *n*

teens′ *npl* years of one's age marked by numbers ending in *-teen*

tee·ny /tē′nē/ [blend of *tiny* and *weeny*] *adj* (-ni·er; -ni·est) *colloq* tiny

tee·ter /tēt′ər/ [var of Eng *dial. titter*] *vi* 1 to seesaw; 2 to waver || *vt* 3 to move (something) with a seesawing motion || *n* 4 seesaw

tee′ter-tot′ter /-tot′ər/ *n* 1 seesaw || *vi* 2 to seesaw

teeth /tēth/ *pl* of tooth

teethe /tēth′/ [ME *teth*] *vi* to cut one's teeth, grow teeth

tee·to′tal /tē-/ [coined < *total* by Richard Turner in a temperance speech in 1833] *adj* **1** pert. to or advocating total abstinence from intoxicating liquors; **2** *colloq* entire or total ‖ **tee·to′tal·er** or **tee·to′tal·ler** *n* ‖ **tee·to′tal·ism** *n*

Te·gu·ci·gal·pa /tegōōs′igälp′ə/ *n* capital of Honduras (170,535)

teg·u·ment /teg′yəmənt/ [L *tegumentum*] *n* integument

Te·he·ran /te′hərän′, -rän′/ *n* capital of Iran (2,317,116)

tel. **1** telephone; **2** telegram; **3** telegraph

Tel A·viv /tel′ əvēv′/ *n* largest city of Israel, seaport on the Mediterranean (395,000)

tele- [Gk = far off] *comb form* transmitted over a distance

tel′e·cast′ /tel′ə-/ [*television* + *broadcast*] *n* **1** television broadcast ‖ *v* (-cast or -casted) *vt & vi* **2** to broadcast by television

tel′e·com·mu′ni·ca′tion *n* **1** communication at a distance by electrical or electronic means; **2** often **telecommunications** *sg* science or technology of such communication

tel′e·gram′ *n* message sent by telegraph

tel′e·graph′ *n* **1** device for sending signals or messages over long distances by transmitting electrical impulses over wires or by wireless; **2** device for communicating between the bridge and the engine room on a ship ‖ *vt* **3** to send (a message) by telegraph; **4** to send a telegram to ‖ *vi* **5** to send a telegram ‖ **tel′e·graph′ic** *adj* ‖ **te·leg·ra·pher** /təleg′rəfər/ *n*

te·leg·ra·phy /təleg′rəfē/ *n* the sending of messages by telegraph

te·lem·e·ter /təlem′itər, tel′əmēt′ər/ *n* **1** instrument for measuring the distance of a point remote from the observer; **2** apparatus for transmitting and recording electrically, at a distance, the readings of another apparatus ‖ *vt* **3** to transmit and record by telemeter ‖ **te·lem′e·try** *n*

tel·e·ol·o·gy /tel′ē·ol′əjē, tēl′-/ [< Gk *telos* (*teleos*) end + -*logy*] *n* **1** doctrine that the existence of everything in nature can be explained in terms of purpose; **2** philosophical study of evidence of a coordinated creative design in nature ‖ **tel·e·o·log·i·cal** /tel′ē·ələj′ikəl, tēl′-/ *adj*

te·lep·a·thy /təlep′əthē/ *n* transmission of thought from one person to another without communication through the senses ‖ **tel·e·path·ic** /tel′əpath′ik/ *adj*

tel′e·phone′ *n* **1** instrument for transmitting sound and articulate speech over a distance ‖ *vt* **2** to send (a message) by telephone; **3** to communicate with by telephone ‖ *vi* **4** to send a message by telephone ‖ **tel′·e·phon′ic** /-fon′-/ *adj*

te·leph·o·ny /təlef′ənē/ *n* the sending of messages by telephone

tel′e·pho′to lens′ *n* lens that produces a larger image than a normal lens, as for taking pictures of distant objects

Tel′e·prompt′er [trademark] ·*n* device that enables a speaker or performer on television to read lines without seeming to do so by the unrolling of a script visible to him as he faces the camera

tel′e·scope′ *n* **1** optical instrument for making distant objects appear closer and larger ‖ *vt & vi* **2** to slide together one into another, as the tubes of a collapsible telescope or colliding railroad cars ‖ **tel′e·scop′ic** /-skōp′-/ *adj*

Tel′e·type′ [trademark] *n* **1** device whereby a text that is typed on a typewriter in a central office is simultaneously typed on distant typewriters electronically connected with the sending typewriter ‖ **tel′e·type′** *vt & vi* **2** to send by Teletype

tel′e·type′writ′er *n* device consisting of two instruments similar to electrical typewriters, located at a distance from each other but connected by wire, whereby a text that is typed on one of them is instantly reproduced on the other

tel′e·vise′ /-vīz′/ [< *television*] *vt & vi* to broadcast by television

tel′e·vi′sion /-zhən/ *n* **1** process of broadcasting images via radio-frequency waves and receiving them on sets which reproduce them on a screen; **2** set for receiving the images; **3** the business of broadcasting television shows

tel·ex /tel′eks/ [*tele-* + *exchange*] *n* service based on the use of teletypewriters ‖ also *vt*

tell /tel′/ [OE *tellan*] *v* (told) *vt* **1** to relate, narrate; **2** to utter; **3** to make known, disclose; **4** to inform (a person); **5** to order, bid; **6** to distinguish, recognize; **7** to assure with emphasis; **8 tell off,** **a** to detach for special duty; **b** to count and set apart; **c** *colloq* to rebuke ‖ *vi* **9** to give an account or report; **10** to play the informer; **11** to have a marked effect; **12 tell on,** **a** to inform on; **b** to weary; wear out

Tell, Wil·liam *n* legendary Swiss patriot who, because of his refusal to salute the hat of the Austrian governor, was forced to shoot an apple from his son's head

tell′er *n* **1** one who tells or narrates; **2** bank clerk who receives and pays money over the counter; **3** one who counts the votes in a legislative body, meeting, etc.

tell′ing *adj* **1** striking; effective; **2** revealing; meaningful ‖ **tell′ing·ly** *adv*

tell′tale′ *n* **1** talebearer, informer; **2** device that gives information or warning ‖ *adj* **3** betraying what should be kept secret

tel·lu·ri·an /teloŏr′ē·ən/ [< L *tellus*

(-uris) earth] adj 1 of or pert. to the earth || n 2 inhabitant of the earth

tel·lu·ric /teloor'ik/ adj 1 pert. to the earth; 2 pert. to tellurium

tel·lu·ri·um /-ē-əm/ n white nonmetallic element (Te; at.no. 52; at.wt. 127.60) resembling sulfur, and usu. occurring with gold or silver; used in alloys and to color glass and ceramics

tel·ly /tel'ē/ n (-lies) Brit colloq television

Tel'star' /tel'-/ [tele- + star] n one of several communications and tracking satellites orbiting the earth

Tel·u·gu /tel'ōōgōō'/ n 1 member of a Dravidian race inhabiting SE India; 2 language of the Telugus || also adj

te·mer·i·ty /təmer'itē/ [L temeritas] n foolhardiness, rashness

temp. 1 temperature; 2 temporary

tem·per /temp'ər/ [OE temprian < L temperare to regulate, proportion] vt 1 to soften, tone down; moderate; 2 to mix to a proper consistency, as clay; 3 to bring to a proper degree of toughness or hardness, as steel, by reheating after hardening || vi 4 to become tempered || n 5 degree of hardness or toughness imparted to a metal by tempering; 6 mental disposition, esp. with reference to the emotions; 7 rage, anger; 8 proneness to anger; 9 something added to another substance to change its nature; 10 keep one's temper to keep one's self-control; 11 lose one's temper to give way to rage || SYN n irritation, anger (see disposition)

tem·per·a /temp'ərə/ [It] n process of painting in which the pigments are mixed with an albuminous or gelatinous substance, esp. egg white

tem·per·a·ment /temp'(ə)rəmənt/ [L temperamentum proper proportion] n 1 disposition; characteristic mental and physical make-up of a person; 2 excessive sensitivity of feelings leading to rebellious outbursts || SYN constitution, nature (see disposition)

tem'per·a·men'tal /-ment'əl/ adj 1 arising from or pert. to temperament; 2 moody, sensitive; 3 given to rebellious outbursts

tem·per·ance /temp'(ə)rəns/ [AF < L temperantia moderation] n 1 moderation; avoidance of extremes; 2 practice of total abstinence from the use of intoxicating liquors || SYN abstinence, abstemiousness, sobriety, self-restraint || DISCR Abstinence, generally, means voluntarily refraining from something one wants to do or eat or drink; specifically, especially in the phrase "total abstinence," it means going without intoxicating liquors. Temperance, when used in reference to intoxicating liquors, though originally used of moderation, has come to mean total abstinence. In general, temperance means self-restraint and moderation in eat-

ing and drinking, in conduct, in expression, and in the taking of pleasures. Abstemiousness names the quality that evidences itself in habitual moderation; abstemious habits are temperate and self-denying. Like temperance, abstemiousness is habitual rather than occasional. Sobriety generally names a state of calm control, moderation, balance, as the sobriety of middle age; specifically, it is used as the opposite of intoxication, as from alcoholic indulgence

tem'per·ate /-it/ [L temperatus] adj 1 moderate; not inclined to eat or drink to excess; 2 calm, restrained; 3 moderate in temperature || tem'per·ate·ly adv || SYN moderate, self-controlled, calm, mild

Tem'per·ate Zone' n either of the two zones of relatively mild climate lying between the torrid and the polar zones of the earth's surface

tem'per·a·ture /-əchər/ n 1 degree or amount of heat or cold as measured by a thermometer; 2 a degree of heat of the human body; b excess of this over the normal

-tem'pered comb form having a specified disposition or temper, as sweet-tempered

tem·pest /temp'ist/ [OF tempeste] n 1 violent storm; 2 violent commotion or tumult

tem·pes·tu·ous /tempes'chōō-əs/ adj 1 stormy; 2 agitated; turbulent

tem·plate or **tem·plet** /temp'lit/ [F templet] n pattern or guide, as of wood or metal, used to indicate the shape of a piece of work

tem·ple¹ /temp'əl/ [OE tempel < L templum] n 1 edifice dedicated to the worship of a deity; 2 building for Christian public worship; 3 imposing building devoted to some special purpose, as temple of the arts; 4 synagogue; 5 Mormon church; 6 Masonic meeting place; 7 Temple either of two of the Inns of Court in London (Inner Temple and Middle Temple) occupied by law societies; 8 the Temple any of three successive edifices built in Jerusalem for the worship of Jehovah

tem·ple² [MF < L tempora] n 1 flat part of the head at each side, between the eye and the ear; 2 side-piece of pair of spectacles

tem·po /temp'ō/ [It = time] n (-pos or -pi /-pē/) 1 rate of speed at which a musical composition is rendered; 2 rate of work or activity

tem·po·ral¹ /temp'(ə)rəl/ [L temporalis] adj 1 pert. to time; 2 not eternal; transitory; 3 pert. to the present life; of this world; 4 civil; secular; 5 gram a expressing time; b pert. to tense || SYN earthly, worldly, secular, civil, mundane || ANT spiritual, heavenly, ecclesiastical

tem·po·ral² [< L tempora temples] adj

anat of, pert. to, or situated near the temples

tem·po·rar·y /temp'ərer'ē/ [L *temporarius*] *adj* not permanent; existing or continuing for a limited time only ‖ **tem'po·rar'i·ly** *adv*

tem'po·rize' [ML *temporizare* to delay] *vi* **1** to yield temporarily to current opinion or circumstances; **2** to avoid committing oneself to gain time or delay making a decision ‖ **tem'po·riz'er** *n*

tempt /tempt'/ [L *temptare* to try] *vt* **1** to try to persuade; entice, esp. to evil; **2** to allure, be inviting to; **3** to provoke or try to provoke, as fate ‖ **tempt'er** *n* ‖ **tempt'ress** *nfem* ‖ **tempt'ing** *adj*

temp·ta'tion *n* **1** act of tempting; **2** that which tempts, esp. to evil ‖ SYN allurement, attraction, beguilement, inducement

ten /ten'/ [OE *tīen*] *n* **1** one more than nine (10; X); **2** playing card with ten spots; **3** set of ten persons or things ‖ also *adj & pron*

ten·a·ble /ten'əbəl/ [F] *adj* capable of being held, maintained, or defended ‖ **ten'a·bil'i·ty** /-bil'-/ *n*

te·na·cious /tənāsh'əs/ [< L *tenax* (-*acis*)] *adj* **1** holding fast or firmly; **2** retentive (memory); **3** tough, cohesive; **4** sticky, adhesive ‖ **te·na'·cious·ly** *adv* ‖ **te·nac'i·ty** /-nas'itē/ *n* ‖ SYN cohesive, retentive, pertinacious, unyielding

ten·ant /ten'ənt/ [MF = holding] *n* **1** one who holds possession of real estate by title or right; **2** one who rents real estate from a landlord; **3** occupant ‖ *vt* **4** to hold or occupy as a tenant ‖ **ten'an·cy** *n* (-cies)

Ten' Com·mand'ments *npl* the precepts of God given to Moses on Mount Sinai (Ex. 20:1–17)

tend¹ /tend'/ [MF *tendre* < L *tendere* to stretch] *vi* **1 tend to** to be disposed or inclined to (do something); **2 tend to** or **towards** to be inclined toward (an idea, principle, state of mind, etc.)

tend² [< *attend*] *vt* **1** to care for; attend to; apply one's attention to, as *to tend bar* ‖ *vi* **2 tend to, a** to pay attention to; **b** to work at

tend·en·cy /ten'dənsē/ [ML *tendentia*] *n* (-cies) **1** aim; direction; course toward some purpose or result; **2** inclination, bent; predisposition ‖ SYN inclination, proneness, proclivity, propensity

ten·den·tious /tendensh'əs/ *adj* exhibiting a definite bias or tendency

ten·der¹ /ten'dər/ [< *tend²*] *n* **1** one who tends or takes care of a person or thing; **2** car containing coal and water attached behind a locomotive; **3** small vessel attending and supplying a larger one; **4** rowboat or launch used to land passengers from a ship

ten·der² [< *tend¹*] *vt* **1** to offer for acceptance; present ‖ *n* **2** offer or proposal for acceptance; **3** that which is tendered, as money ‖ **ten'der·er** *n*

ten·der³ [OF *tendre*] *adj* **1** (meat) easily cut or chewed; **2** weak, not hardy or tough; **3** sensitive physically, as *a tender skin*; **4** easily moved to compassion; sympathetic; **5** gentle; loving; **6** immature, youthful; **7** requiring careful handling, ticklish ‖ **ten'der·ly** *adv* ‖ **ten'der·ness** *n* ‖ SYN effeminate, soft, charitable, pitying, compassionate ‖ ANT hardy, hard-hearted, unfeeling

ten'der·foot *n* (-foots or -feet) **1** one new to the life of a ranch or mining camp; **2** novice, inexperienced person; **3** lowest rank in the Boy Scouts or Girl Scouts

ten'der·ize' *vt* to make (meat) tender ‖ **ten'der·iz'er** *n*

ten'der·loin' *n* **1** tenderest part of the loin of beef or pork; **2** strip of tender meat under the short ribs in beef or pork; **3 the Tenderloin** the district in some large cities devoted to crime, corruption, and vice

ten·don /ten'dən/ [ML *tendo* (-*onis*)] *n* tough band of inelastic fibrous tissue connecting a muscle to a bone or some other part

ten·dril /ten'dril/ [?] *n* slender twining organ of a climbing plant which attaches itself to something so as to support the plant

ten·e·ment /ten'əmənt/ [ML *tenementum*] *n* **1** dwelling house; **2** any portion of a house or building occupied as a separate dwelling; **3** run-down apartment house in a poor section of a city

ten·et /ten'it/ [L = he holds] *n* doctrine, dogma, opinion, or belief maintained as true

ten'fold' *adj* **1** having ten times as much or as many ‖ *adv* **2** ten times as much or as many

Tenn. Tennessee

Ten·nes·see /ten'isē'/ *n* state in the S central U.S. (3,924,000; 42,246 sq.mi.; cap. Nashville) ‖ **Ten'nes·see'an** *n*

ten·nis /ten'is/ [AF *tenetz* (*impv*) receive] *n* game played on a rectangular court by two or four persons who bat a ball with rackets back and forth over a net

ten'nis shoe' *n* rubber-soled sports shoe with a canvas upper

Ten·ny·son, Alfred, Lord /ten'isən/ *n* (1809–92) English poet; poet laureate 1850–92

ten·on /ten'ən/ [MF] *n* projection at the end of a timber shaped to fit into a mortise to make a joint

ten·or /ten'ər/ [OF < L = course] *n* **1** settled tendency; course; **2** general meaning or drift; purport; **3** *mus* **a** highest adult male voice, or part written for it; **b** one who sings, or an instrument which plays, such a part

|| SYN course, trend, direction, tendency, import

ten·pen·ny /tenˈpenē/ *adj* designating a nail three inches long

ten·pin' *n* 1 one of the pins used in tenpins; 2 **tenpins** *sg* bowling game played with ten wooden pins

tense¹ /tens/ [L *tensus*] *adj* 1 stretched tight; rigid; not lax; 2 severely strained, as nerves || *vt* 3 to make tense || *vi* 4 to become tense || **tense'ly** *adv* || **tense'ness** *n* || SYN *adj* rigid, strained, tight, taut, intense, rapt

tense² [MF *tens* < L *tempus* time] *n* 1 form a verb takes to indicate the time of an action or state of being; 2 time thus indicated; 3 set of the forms used in inflecting a verb to express tense

ten·sile /tensˈil/ [< *tense¹*] *adj* 1 pert. to tension; 2 capable of being stretched

ten·sion /tenshˈən/ [LL *tensio (-onis)*] *n* 1 act of stretching or straining, or state of being stretched or strained; 2 mental or emotional strain; 3 condition of strained relations; 4 stress caused by the action of a pulling force; 5 condition of a body due to such a force; 6 electromotive force; voltage

ten·sor /tensˈər, -ôr/ *n* muscle that stretches or tightens some part of the body

ten'-spot' *n* 1 playing card or die with ten pips; 2 *slang* ten-dollar bill

ten'-strike' *n* 1 tenpins strike; 2 *colloq* successful stroke or find

tent /tent/ [OF *tente*] 1 portable shelter, usu. of canvas, stretched over poles || *vt* & *vi* 2 to lodge in a tent

ten·ta·cle /tentˈəkəl/ [< L *tentare* to handle, touch] *n* 1 slender flexible appendage growing from the mouth or head of certain invertebrates, used for feeling, feeding, or grasping; ·2 feeler on the leaf of a plant

ten·ta·tive /tentˈətiv/ [ML *tentativus*] *adj* 1 made or done as an experiment or trial; provisional; 2 unsure, hesitant

tent' cat'er·pil'lar *n* any of numerous species of leaf-eating caterpillars (genus *Malacosoma*) which live gregariously in silky tentlike webs

ten'ter·hook' /tentˈər-/ [< L *tentus* stretched + *hook*] *n* 1 one of the hooked nails set on a frame for stretching cloth; 2 **on tenterhooks** in suspense or an anxious state

tenth /tenth/ *n* 1 the one next in order after the ninth; 2 one of ten equal parts; 3 *math* position of the first digit to the right of the decimal point || also *adj*

ten·u·ous /tenˈyo͞o-əs/ [< L *tenuis* thin] *adj* 1 slender, thin; 2 rare, not dense; 3 unsubstantial; 4 vague || SYN delicate, refined, subtle, slender,

weak, flimsy, fine || ANT coarse, heavy, thick

ten·ure /tenˈyər/ [AF = a holding] *n* 1 holding or possession, as of property or office; 2 period of such possession; 3 right to permanency of employment, granted to certain persons, as teachers and those in civil service

te·pee /tēˈpē/ [Siouan *tipi*] *n* cone-shaped tent of the American Indians

tep·id /tepˈid/ [L *tepidus*] *adj* lukewarm || **te·pid'i·ty** *n*

te·qui·la /təkēˈlə/ [*Tequila* district in Mexico] *n* strong liquor distilled from a Mexican plant of the genus *Agave*

ter. 1 territory; 2 terrace

ter·bi·um /turbˈē·əm/ [< *Ytterby*, Sweden] *n* rare-earth metallic element (Tb; at.no. 65; at.wt. 158.924) found in certain minerals

ter·cen·te·nar·y /tərsentˈənerˌē, turs'-əntenˈərē/ [L *ter* thrice + *centenary*] *adj* 1 comprising or including 300 years; 2 pert. to a term of 300 years or to a 300th anniversary || *n* 3 (-ies) 300th anniversary or its celebration

term /turm/ [OF *terme* < L *terminus* limit] *n* 1 fixed or limited period of time; 2 one of the periods of instruction into which the school year is divided; 3 time of a court's session; 4 word or expression used to express a definite conception, esp. in a particular field; 5 *math* a any of the members of a proportion or ratio; b any of the members of an algebraic expression connected by plus or minus signs in a binomial or polynomial quantity; 6 *logic* word or words used as subject or predicate of a proposition; 7 **terms** *pl* a conditions or stipulations; b relationship, footing; 8 **bring to terms** to force into an agreement; 9 **come to terms** to reach an agreement || *vt* 10 to name, call || SYN *n* phrase, name, expression, member, condition

ter·ma·gant /turmˈəgənt/ [OF *Tervagan* turbulent god supposedly worshipped by the Saracens] *n* 1 noisy, violent, and quarrelsome woman || *adj* 2 noisy, shrewish, quarrelsome

ter·mi·na·ble /turmˈinəbəl/ [see **terminate**] *adj* capable of being terminated

ter·mi·nal /turmˈinəl/ [L *terminalis*] *adj* 1 pert. to, placed at, or forming the end or extremity; 2 concluding, final, closing || *n* 3 one end of an electrical circuit; 4 end of a transportation line; 5 station at which trains, buses, etc., originate and terminate || **ter'·mi·nal·ly** *adv*

ter·mi·nate /turmˈināt/ [L *terminare (-atus)*] *vt* 1 to form the end of; 2 to bring to an end; stop || *vi* 3 to come to an end; 4 **terminate at** to end a scheduled run at, as a bus or train || **ter'mi·na'tion**

n ‖ SYN bound, limit, cease, end (see *close*)

ter'mi·na'tor *n* 1 one who or that which terminates; 2 line that separates the sunlit part from the dark part of a planet or the moon

ter'mi·nol'o·gy /-nol'əjē/ [< L *terminus* term + *-logy*] *n* (*-gies*) the terms peculiar to a science, art, business, or any specialized field or occupation ‖ **ter'mi·no·log'i·cal** /-nəloj'-/ *adj*

term' **in·sur'ance** *n* life insurance in effect for a stipulated length of time only and having no cash value

ter'mi·nus /-nəs/ [L = limit, end] *n* (*-ni* /-nī'/ or *-nus·es*) 1 limit or boundary; 2 end or extremity; 3 end of a railway line

ter·mite /tur'mīt/ [L *termes* (*-mitis*) woodworm] *n* any of numerous destructive, wood-eating, pale-colored social insects (order Isoptera)

tern /turn'/ [Scand] *n* any of a subfamily (Sterninae) of sea birds resembling gulls, but generally smaller and swifter in flight, and having a straight bill

Terp·sich·o·re /turpsik'ərē/ *n Gk myth.* Muse of the dance and choral song

terp·si·cho·re·an /turp'sikərē'ən, turp'-sikōr'ē·ən/ *adj* 1 pert. to dancing ‖ *n* 2 *colloq* dancer

ter·race /ter'əs/ [MF *terrasse*] *n* 1 level space or platform with sloping sides, often one of a series on a hillside; 2 flat roof of a house; 3 open paved area next to a house, often overlooking a garden; 4 short residential street ‖ *vt* 5 to form or build in a terrace or terraces

ter·ra cot·ta /ter'ə kot'ə/ [It = baked earth] *n* 1 pottery of baked clay or earth, esp. when reddish brown; 2 reddish-brown color ‖ **ter'ra-cot'ta** *adj*

ter'ra fir'ma /furm'ə/ [L] *n* solid earth; dry land

ter·rain /tərān', ter'ān/ [F = piece of ground] *n* tract of land, considered from the standpoint of its fitness for some purpose

Ter·ra·my·cin /ter'əmīs'in/ [trademark] *n* crystalline antibiotic powder —C₂₂ H₂₄N₂O₉— used chiefly to treat infections caused by staphylococci and streptococci

ter·ra·pin /ter'əpin/ [AmInd] *n* any of several North American fresh-water turtles (family Emydidae) esteemed as food

ter·raz·zo /tərraz'ō/ [It = terrace roof] *n* flooring composed of chips of broken stone and cement, polished smooth

ter·res·tri·al /tərest'rē·əl/ [< L *terrestris* earthly] *adj* 1 pert. to the earth; 2 pert. to, growing on, or living on the land or ground; 3 worldly, mundane ‖ *n* 4 inhabitant of the earth

ter·ri·ble /ter'ibəl/ [L *terribilis*] *adj* 1

inspiring fear or awe; dreadful; 2 extreme, excessive; severe; 3 of very bad quality ‖ **ter'ri·bly** *adv* ‖ SYN shocking, formidable, grim, horrible

ter·ri·er /ter'ē·ər/ [MF (*chien*) *terrier* earth (dog)] *n* any of several breeds of small, alert dogs, used originally to drive small game out of burrows

ter·rif·ic /tərif'ik/ [L *terrificus* terrifying] *adj* 1 terrifying; 2 *colloq* **a** intense; **b** very great or good

ter·ri·fy /ter'ifī'/ [LL *terrificare*] *v* (*-fied*) *vt* to fill with terror

ter·ri·to·ry /ter'itōr'ē, -tōr'-/ [L *territorium*] *n* (*-ries*) 1 tract of land; region, district; 2 entire extent of land and water under the control of one ruler or government; 3 area or sphere of action; 4 **Territory**, **a** region of the United States, not a state, with an elected legislature and a governor and other officials appointed by the President; **b** similar region in certain other countries ‖ **ter'ri·to'ri·al** *adj*

ter·ror /ter'ər/ *n* 1 extreme fear; 2 one who or that which causes extreme fear; 3 *colloq* annoying or obnoxious person or thing ‖ SYN fear, consternation, dread (see *horror*)

ter'ror·ism *n* calculated use of violence, mayhem, and murder to inspire terror ‖ **ter'ror·ist** *n* & *adj*

ter'ror·ize' *vt* 1 to intimidate by terrorism or the threat of terrorism; 2 to practice terrorism on ‖ **ter'ror·i·za'-tion** *n*

ter'ror-strick'en *adj* terrified

ter'ry (**cloth'**) /ter'ē/ [?] *n* cloth having a pile with the loops uncut

terse /turs'/ [L *tersus* polished] *adj* concise, brief, to the point ‖ **terse'ly** *adv* ‖ SYN pointed, pithy, succinct (see *short*)

ter·ti·ar·y /tur'shē·er'ē, tursh'ərē/ [L *tertiarius*] *adj* 1 third in order of time or rank ‖ *n* 2 **Tertiary** *geol* period forming the earlier parts of the Cenozoic era, marked by the appearance of mammals

tes·sel·late /tes'ilāt'/ [< L *tessella* small square block] *vt* to lay out in or inlay with small squares in a mosaic pattern ‖ **tes'sel·lat'ed** *adj*

tes·ser·act /tes'ərakt'/ [< Gk *tesseres* four + *aktis* ray] *n* four-dimensional cube

test /test'/ [MF < L *testu*(*m*) pot with a lid] *n* 1 *chem* a specific treatment of a substance to determine its nature or to detect the presence of any ingredient; **b** reagent used in this treatment; 2 any examination or trial; 3 means employed in such an examination; 4 *med* method of detecting the presence or absence of some bodily condition or disease; 5 *psychol* method of observing or measuring the reactions or qualities of an individual or group under standard conditions; 6 *educ* examination for determining what students have learned about a particular subject || *vt* 7 to subject to a test || *vi* 8 to conduct a test; 9 to undergo a test || **test′er** *n* || SYN *n* criterion, experiment, ordeal, trial

Test. Testament

tes·ta·ment /test′əmənt/ [L *testamentum*] *n* 1 will 5, esp. in the phrase *last will and testament;* 2 **Testament**, a either of the two parts of the Bible, the Old Testament and the New Testament; b book containing the New Testament

tes′ta·men′ta·ry /-ment′ərē/ *adj* 1 pert. to a will; 2 given, bequeathed, done, or appointed by will

tes·tate /test′āt/ [L *testatus*] *adj* having made and left a valid will

tes·ta·tor /testāt′ər, test′ātər/ *n* one who has made a valid will

test′ ban′ *n* international agreement not to test nuclear bombs in the atmosphere || **test′-ban′** *adj*

test′ case′ *n* case brought before a court the decision of which may be expected to set a precedent for similar future cases

tes·ti·cle /test′ikəl/ [L *testiculus*] *n* testis

tes·ti·fy /test′ifī′/ [L *testificari*] *v* (-fied) *vi* 1 to bear witness; make a formal declaration; 2 *law* to declare under oath or affirmation before a court || *vt* 3 to bear witness to; attest; 4 to be an indication of; 5 *law* to assert under oath or affirmation before a court || SYN affirm, avow, declare, support

tes·ti·mo·ni·al /test′imōn′ē̇·əl/ [LL *testimonialis*] *n* 1 written statement praising a person or thing; 2 something done or given in token of gratitude or esteem || *adj* 3 pert. to or containing a testimonial

tes′ti·mo′ny [L *testimonium*] *n* (-nies) 1 statement made to prove some fact; affirmation; 2 open profession, as of faith; 3 proof, evidence; 4 *law* declaration of a witness under oath || SYN witness, affidavit, attestation, affirmation

tes·tis /test′is/ [L] *n* (-tes /-tēz/) either of the two male genital glands in the scrotum

tes·tos·ter·one /testost′ərōn/ [< *testis* + *sterol* an alcohol] *n* the male sex hormone —$C_{19}H_{28}O_2$— also made synthetically and used in certain hormone deficiencies

test′ pi′lot *n* pilot who flies new or experimental airplanes to test their performance

test′ tube′ *n* tube of thin glass closed at one end, used in chemical and biological experiments

tes′ty [MF *testif*] *adj* (-ti·er; -ti·est) touchy, irritable || **tes′ti·ly** *adv* || SYN fretful, petulant, impatient, touchy, snappish

tet·a·nus /tet′ənəs/ [L < Gk *tetanos* spasm] *n* acute, infectious, and usu. fatal disease causing muscular spasms or rigidity, esp. in the neck and lower jaw; caused by the bacterium *Clostridium tetani*

tetched /techt/ [ME *techyd* marked] *adj* slightly mad, queer

tête-à-tête /tāt′ətāt′/ [F = head to head] *adj* 1 face to face; confidential || *n* 2 private conversation between two persons || also *adv*

teth·er /teth′ər/ [ON *tjöthr*] *n* 1 rope or chain to fasten an animal so as to limit its movements; 2 **at the end of one′s tether** at the end of one′s endurance or resources || *vt* 3 to tie or confine with a tether

tetra- or **tetr-** [Gk] *comb form* four

tet′ra·eth′yl lead′ /tet′rə-, led′/ *n* poisonous compound of lead —$(C_2H_5)_4Pb$— added to gasoline to prevent or reduce engine knock

tet′ra·he′dron *n* (-drons or -dra /-drə/) solid figure bounded by four triangular plane surfaces || **tet′ra·he′dral** *adj*

te·trarch /tē′trärk, te′-/ *n* 1 ruler or governor of a province or country in the Roman Empire; 2 one of four joint rulers || **te′trarch·ate** /-kāt′, -kit/ *n* || **te′trarch·y** *n* (-ies)

tet·ra·va·lent /tet′rəvāl′ənt, tetrav′ə-/ *adj chem* having a valence of four || **tet′ra·va′lence** *n*

te·trox′ide *n* oxide of which each molecule contains four atoms of oxygen

Teut. 1 Teuton; 2 Teutonic

Teu·ton /t(y)ōōt′ən/ [< L *Teutones* the Teutons] *n* 1 member of an ancient Germanic tribe that settled in N Europe ab. the fourth century B.C.; 2 German || also *adj*

Teu·ton′ic /-ton′ik/ *adj* 1 of or pert. to the Teutons; 2 Germanic || *n* 3 Germanic

Tex. 1 Texas; 2 Texan

Tex·as /teks′əs/ *n* state in the S U.S. (11,197,000; 267,339 sq.m.; cap. Austin) || **Tex′an** *n*

Tex′as lea′guer *n baseball* fly ball that falls safely between the infield and the outfield

text /tekst/ [ML *textus* written character] *n* 1 original words of an author, not a paraphrase or translation; 2 passage from scripture forming the subject of a sermon; 3 theme, topic; 4 main body of any piece of written or printed matter, as distinguished from notes, illustrations, etc.; 5 textbook || **tex′tu·al** /-chōō·əl/ *adj*

text′book′ *n* book used by students as a basis of instruction or study

tex·tile /teks′təl, -tīl/ [L *textilis* woven] *n* 1 any woven material; 2 material capable of being woven || also *adj*

tex·ture /teks′chər/ [L *textura*] 1 structure of a woven fabric; arrangement of threads making up a fabric; 2 manner in which the constituent parts of a substance are arranged ‖ *vt* **3** to give a particular texture to ‖ **tex′tur·al** *adj*

T′ for·ma′tion *n football* offensive formation in which the backs form a T behind the center

Th *chem* thorium

Th. Thursday

-th¹ [OE] *suf* forming abstract nouns of quality, state, etc., as *truth, stealth, wealth*

-th² [OE -(o)*tha*] *suf* forming ordinal numbers, as *sixth*

-th³ var of **-eth¹**

Thai /tī/, tä/ē̱/ *n* **1** native or inhabitant of Thailand; **2** language of the Thais ‖ also *adj*

Thai′land /-lənd/ *n* kingdom in SE Asia, formerly known as Siam (35,000,000; 198,500 sq.m.; cap. Bangkok)

thal·a·mus /thal′əməs/ [L < Gk *thalamos* chamber] *n* mass of gray matter at the base of the brain through which sensory impulses pass

tha·las·sic /thəlas′ik/ [< Gk *thalassa* sea] *adj* **1** pert. to seas or oceans; **2** pert. to bodies smaller than oceans, as seas, bays, etc.; **3** grown or found in the sea

Tha·li·a /thəlī′ə, thāl′yə/ *n Gk myth.* **1** Muse of comedy and pastoral poetry; **2** one of the Graces

thal·li·um /thal′ē·əm/ [< Gk *thallos* green shoot] *n* rare, soft bluish-white metallic element (**Tl**; at.no. 81; at. wt. 204.37), used in alloys

thal·lo·phyte /thal′əfit′/ [< Gk *thallos* young shoot + *phyton* plant] *n* plant of the phylum Thallophyta, comprising the algae, fungi, and lichens, usu. characterized by a very simple form showing no differentiation into leaves, stems, or true roots

Thames /temz′/ *n* river in S England, flowing S and E through London to the North Sea

than /than′, thən/ [OE *thanne* then, than] *conj* **1** (after an adjective or adverb in the comparative of superiority or inferiority and joining the two members of the comparison), as *he is taller than I* (or *I am*); *he writes better than he speaks;* **2** (after adjectives and adverbs expressing difference) except, but, as *it was none other than my brother; that custom does not exist anywhere else than in Spain; that task was different for me than for him;* **3** (after *barely, scarcely,* and *hardly*) when, as **as** *hardly had he rung the bell than the door opened;* **4** *colloq* (after *prefer, preferable,* and *preferably*) rather than, as *I prefer to live in the country than in the city* ‖ *prep* **5** (followed by the second member of a comparison) when or as compared with, as *he is taller than me; a friend than whom I have none more faithful*

than·a·tol·o·gy /than′ətol′əjē/ [Gk *thanatos* death + -*logy*] *n* study of death and dying

thane /thān/ [OE *thegn* servant, soldier] *n* **1** among the Anglo-Saxons, freeman attached to the service of a lord and corresponding to a knight or baron; **2** in Scotland, one holding land of the king; the chief of a clan, who became one of the king's barons

thank /thaŋk′/ [OE *thancian*] *vt* **1** to express gratitude to, acknowledge obligation to; **2 have oneself to thank** to be the cause of one's own misfortunes ‖ *n* **3 thanks** *pl* expression of gratitude; **4 thanks to** because of ‖ **thanks** *interj* **5** I thank you!

thank′ful *adj* feeling, or expressive of, gratitude

thank′less *adj* **1** ungrateful; **2** unappreciated ‖ SYN ungracious, profitless, unthankful, ungrateful

thanks′giv′ing *n* **1** act of giving thanks; **2** form of worship acknowledging divine blessing; **3** public celebration in acknowledging divine goodness

Thanks′giv′ing Day′ *n* **1** in the United States, the fourth Thursday in November, a national holiday for giving thanks to God; **2** in Canada, the second Monday in October, a national holiday for giving thanks to God

that /that′, thət/ [OE *thæt*] *adj* (**those**) **1** designating something more or less distant, as *that mountain over there;* **2** designating something already spoken of or considered as known, as *that man we were discussing;* **3** the other, or second, of two (used as a correlative of *this*) ‖ *pron* (**those**) **4** something more or less distant, as *do you see that?* **5** something already spoken of or considered as known, as *so that is what he said;* **6** the thing, the one, etc., as *that which is good;* **7** who, whom, or which, as *the book that I bought;* **8** in, for, on, or at which, as *the time that he arrived;* **9** at that, **a** nevertheless; **b** in addition; **10 that is** (to say) more exactly; **11 that's that** *colloq* the matter is finished ‖ *conj* **12** introducing a noun clause serving as object, subject, or predicate nominative of a verb, as *he said that he would come;* **13** introducing a clause of purpose, reason, or result, as *work that you may succeed;* **14** introducing an exclamation, as *Oh that you were here!* ‖ *adv* **15** to such a degree, to that extent, as *she was that angry she cried*

thatch /thach′/ [OE *thæc* roof] *n* **1** roof or covering made of straw, reeds, etc.; **2** any of various palms the leaves of which are used for thatching; **3** hair of the head ‖ *vt* **4** to cover with thatch

that's /thats′/ **1** that is; **2** that has

thaw /thô′/ [OE *thawian*] *vi* **1** to melt,

as ice or snow; **2** to become warm enough to melt ice and snow; **3** to be freed from coldness or self-restraint, become friendlier ‖ *vt* **4** to cause to thaw ‖ *n* **5** act or process of thawing; **6** weather warm enough to melt ice and snow

the /thē′, thə (before a consonant), or thē (before a vowel)/ [OE] *def art* used: **1** before a noun with particularizing force, as *the book I want;* **2** before a noun naming something well known, as a river, ocean, hotel, ship, etc.; **3** before a singular noun used generically, as *the horse is a useful animal;* **4** before an adjective used as a noun, as *the brave deserve the fair;* **5** before a noun with the meaning of "each", as *ten dollars the pound* ‖ *adv* **6** by however much, by so much, as *the sooner the better*

the- *comb form* var of **theo-**

the·a·ter also **the·a·tre** /thē′ətər/ [Gk *theatron*] *n* **1** public building or open place furnished with seats, where plays, entertainments, or motion pictures are presented; **2** place resembling a theater, as for lectures; **3** any place or locality where events occur, as *the theater of war;* **4** the theater, **a** the drama as an art form; **b** the art or business of producing, staging, writing for, or acting in theatrical productions

the′a·ter·go′er *n* person who goes regularly to the theater

the′a·ter-in-the-round′ *n* theater in which the seats are arranged around a center stage

the·at·ri·cal /thē·at′rikəl/ *adj* **1** of or pert. to the theater; **2** dramatic; **3** affectedly emotional; **4** showy, artificial ‖ *n* **5** theatricals *pl* dramatic performances, esp. by amateurs ‖ SYN *adj* melodramatic, showy, affected, extravagant ‖ ANT *adj* simple, modest, sincere, unpretentious

the·at′rics *npl* exaggerated, theatrical actions or mannerisms

thee /thē′/ [OE *thē*] *pron* **1** *archaic & poet.* objective singular of **thou; 2** thou (formerly common among the Quakers)

theft /theft′/ [OE *thēofth*] *n* act or instance of stealing

their /ther′, thər/ [ME < Scand] *adj* possessive of **they;** of or belonging to them

theirs /therz′/ *pron* that or those belonging to them

the·ism /thē′izəm/ [*the-* + *-ism*] *n* **1** belief in the existence of a god or gods; **2** monotheism ‖ **the′ist** *n & adj* ‖ **the·is′tic** *adj*

them /them′, thəm/ *pron* objective case of **they**

theme /thēm′/ [Gk *thema* proposition] *n* **1** subject or topic of a discussion, speech, essay, etc.; **2** short essay or composition on a given subject; **3** *mus* principal melodic subject of a composition or movement; **4** *gram* word stem ‖ **the·mat′ic** /-mat′ik/ *adj*

theme′ song′ *n* **1** melody identifying a dance band, a performer, or a radio or television program; **2** melody repeated in a musical performance to characterize the work or to identify one of the characters

them·selves′ *pron* **1** reflexive form of **them; 2** their normal selves, as *they are not themselves today;* **3** emphatic form of **them,** as *they themselves admit it*

then /then′/ [OE *thænne*] *conj* **1** in consequence, therefore; in that case; **2 but then** but on the other hand ‖ *adv* **3** at that time; **4** next; immediately thereafter ‖ *adj* **5** existing at that time, as *the then minister* ‖ *n* **6** that time, as *by then he was ready*

thence /thens′/ [ME *thennes*] *adv* **1** from that place or time; **2** from that source; **3** therefore

thence·forth /thens′fôrth′, -fôrth′, thens′fôrth′, -fôrth/ *adv* from that time on

the·o- [< Gk *theos*] *comb form* god

the·oc·ra·cy /thē·ok′rəsē/ *n* (-cies) **1** government by God or a deity through the medium of an organized church; **2** state with such a government ‖ **the·o·crat′ic** /thē′əkrat′ik/ *adj*

The·oc·ri·tus /thē·ok′ritəs/ *n* (third century B.C.) Greek bucolic poet

the·od·o·lite /thē·od′əlīt′/ [NL *theodolitus*] *n* surveying instrument containing a small telescope for measuring horizontal and vertical angles in determining distances and heights

the·ol·o·gy /thē·ol′əjē/ *n* (-gies) **1** study of God and of religion; **2** particular form or system of theology ‖ **the·o·lo·gian** /thē′əlōj′ən/ *n* ‖ **the·o·log′i·cal** /-loj′-/ *adj*

the·o·rem /thē′ərəm/ [Gk *theorema* spectacle] *n* **1** that which can be shown to be true and is established as a principle of law; **2** *math* a proposition to be proved; **b** general statement of mathematical relations

the·o·ret·ic (-i·cal) /thē′əret′ik(əl)/ [Gk *theoretikos*] *adj* **1** of or pert. to theory; not practical or applied; **2** hypothetical; **3** speculative ‖ **the′o·ret′i·cal·ly** *adv*

the′o·rize /thē′ərīz′/ *vi* to form theories; speculate ‖ **the′o·rist** *n*

the′o·ry [Gk *theoria* contemplation] *n* (-ries) **1** tentative statement of a supposed principle or relationship advanced to explain facts as observed; **2** hypothesis that has been largely verified by facts; **3** abstract principles of a science or art distinguished from its practice or application; **4** guess, conjecture; **5** speculative opinion

the·os·o·phy /thē·os′əfē/ [*theo-* + Gk

sophia wisdom] *n* 1 any of various systems of philosophy teaching the attainment of truth by direct contact with God, as by religious ecstasy or direct revelation; 2 system of belief embodying doctrines derived from Brahmanism and Buddhism ‖ the-os'o·phist *n* ‖ the'o·soph'ic (-i·cal) /thē'əsof'-/ *adj*

ther·a·peu·tic /ther'əpyōōt'ik/ [Gk *therapeutikos*] *adj* 1 curative, healing ‖ *n* 2 therapeutics *sg* branch of medicine dealing with the treatment and cure of disease

ther·a·pist /ther'əpist/ *n* 1 person trained in therapeutics; 2 person trained in psychological therapy; 3 person trained to rehabilitate the sick or handicapped by special exercises, baths, etc. designed to help regain physical functions

ther'a·py [Gk *therapeia* healing] *n* (-pies) 1 specific treatment; 2 cure; 3 something serving to cure or soothe, as a hobby

there /ther/ [OE *thēr*] *adv* 1 in or at that place; 2 to or toward that place; 3 at that point or stage; 4 in that manner or respect, as *you're right, there;* 5 used to draw attention to something or someone, as *there's a mess for you;* 6 used as an expletive in the position of subject of an intransitive verb and esp. of some form of the verb *to be,* with the subject following the verb, as *there was a fire last night, is there any hurry?* ‖ *interj* 7 expressing defiance, triumph, confirmation of a fear or statement, etc.; 8 expressing a desire to allay or soothe, as *there, there!* ‖ *n* 9 that place, as *I left there this morning*

there'a·bout' also there'a·bouts' *adv* near that place, time, number, degree, etc.; nearly

there'af'ter *adv* after that; afterward

there'at' *adv* 1 at that place or time; there; 2 on that account; upon that

there·by' also there'by *adv* 1 by that means; 2 connected with that; 3 near by

there'for' *adv* for this or that

there'fore' *adv* for this or that reason; consequently

there'from' *adv* from that or it

there'in' *adv* 1 in or into that place, time, or thing; 2 in that respect or particular

there'of' *adv* 1 of that or it; 2 from this or that cause or source

there'on' *adv* 1 on that or it; 2 thereupon

there's /therz/ 1 there is; 2 there has

there'to' *adv* to that, it, or that place

there'to·fore' *adv* up to that time

there'un'der *adv* under that or it

there'up·on' *adv* 1 thereon; 2 immediately after that; 3 in consequence of that

there'with' *adv* 1 with that; 2 immediately thereafter

ther·mal /thurm'əl/ [< *thermo*-] *adj* 1 pert. to heat; 2 warm, hot, as *thermal springs*

ther·mo- [Gk *thermos* hot] *comb form* heat, hot

ther'mo·cou'ple /thurm'ō-/ *n* device for converting thermal energy into electrical energy by joining two dissimilar metallic conductors kept at different temperatures; used for the accurate measurement of temperature

ther'mo·dy·nam'ics *nsg* science of the relations between heat and mechanical energy and the conversion of one into the other ‖ ther'mo·dy·nam'ic *adj*

ther·mom·e·ter /thərmom'itər/ *n* instrument for measuring temperature, as a sealed glass tube partly filled with a liquid that expands and contracts with changes in temperature

ther'mo·nu'cle·ar *adj* of, pert. to, or employing the energy released by the heat of nuclear fission

ther'mo·plas'tic *adj* 1 having or pert. to the property of becoming plastic when heated ‖ *n* 2 thermoplastic substance

Ther·mos /thurm'əs/ [trademark] *n* vacuum bottle

ther'mo·stat' *n* device for automatically regulating temperature ‖ ther'mo·stat'ic *adj*

the·sau·rus /thisôr'əs/ [L < Gk *thesauros* treasury] *n* (-ri /-rī/) 1 storehouse; treasury; 2 reference book or dictionary, esp. a dictionary of synonyms

these /thēz/ *adj & pron pl* of this

The·seus /thēs'(y)ōōs, -ē·əs/ *n* Gk myth. leading legendary hero of Attica, famed for a great number of exploits, such as slaying the Minotaur in Crete

the·sis /thēs'is/ [Gk = a putting, placing] *n* (-ses /-sēz/) 1 proposition advanced for consideration, esp. one to be maintained in argument; 2 essay; 3 dissertation entailing original research, presented by a candidate for an academic degree

Thes·pi·an /thesp'ē·ən/ [< *Thespis* ancient Gk poet] *adj* 1 of or pert. to the drama or dramatic art ‖ *n* 2 actor or actress

the·ta /thēt'ə, thāt'ə/ *n* eighth letter of the Greek alphabet θ θ

they /thā/ [ME *thei* < Scand] *pron* (3rd pers *pl nom*) 1 *pl* of he, she, or it; 2 people in general, men, as *they say she's very bright*

they'd /thād/ 1 they had; 2 they would

they'll /thāl/ 1 they will; 2 they shall

they're /ther/ they are

they've /thāv/ they have

thi·a·mine /thī'əmēn', -min/ [< Gk

theion sulfur + *amine*] *n* white crystalline compound of the vitamin-B complex —$C_{12}H_{17}ClN_4OS$— essential to the normal functioning of the nervous system, found in many foods, as peas, cereals, liver, etc.; vitamin B_1

thick /thik′/ [OE *thicce*] *adj* 1 measuring a specified distance in the smallest dimension, length and breadth being the other two, as *one inch thick;* 2 relatively extensive from one surface to its opposite; not thin; 3 of dense texture or consistency, as *thick glue;* 4 close-packed; abundant; 5 stupid, dull; 6 not clear; foggy or roiled, as *the air was thick with smoke;* 7 colloq friendly, intimate; 8 noticeable (accent); 9 indistinct (speech); 10 **a bit thick** offensively exaggerated ‖ *adv* 11 thickly; 12 **lay it on thick** to flatter excessively ‖ *n* 13 thickest, most crowded, or most active part; 14 **through thick and thin** unwaveringly; under all sorts of conditions ‖ **thick′ly** *adv* ‖ **thick′ness** *n*

thick′en *vt* 1 to make thicker ‖ *vi* 2 to become thicker; 3 to become more complex, as a plot

thick·et /thik′it/ [OE *thiccet*] *n* dense growth of underbrush, shrubbery, or small trees

thick′set′ *adj* 1 planted closely or thickly; 2 having a stout body

thick′skinned′ *adj* 1 having a thick skin; 2 insensitive to criticism

thief /thēf′/ [OE *thēof*] *n* (thieves /-vz/) one who steals, esp. furtively ‖ **thiev′ish** *adj*

thiev·er·y /thēv′ərē/ *n* (-ies) act or practice of stealing

thigh /thī′/ [OE *thēoh*] *n* the part of the leg between the hip and the knee

thigh′bone′ *n* bone extending from the pelvis to the knee

thim·ble /thim′bəl/ [OE *thȳmel*] *n* cap, as of metal or plastic, worn on the end of the finger to protect it from the needle when sewing

thin /thin′/ [OE *thynne*] *adj* (thin·ner; thin·nest) 1 small in diameter, slender; 2 having little extent between two opposite and more or less flat surfaces; of little thickness; 3 sparse, loose, or separated; 4 slight, shallow; flimsy; 5 lacking density; rarefied; 6 lacking fullness or volume, as *a thin voice;* 7 lean, slender, gaunt; 8 scanty; lacking substance; 9 lacking body or strength; 10 faint, feeble ‖ *v* (thinned; thin·ning) *vt* 11 to make thin or thinner ‖ *vi* 12 to become thinner ‖ **thin′ly** *adv* ‖ **thin′ness** *n* ‖ SYN *adj* slim, fine, slight, bony; shrill (see *lean²*)

thine /thīn′/ [OE *thīn*] *archaic & poet.* *pron* 1 that or those belonging to thee ‖ *adj* 2 (used before a vowel sound) thy

thing /thiŋ′/ [OE] *n* 1 that which is or may be made an object of thought; 2 any concrete tangible entity; 3 abstract conception or entity; 4 any object or existence not known or specifically designated; 5 episode or event; 6 particular fact, course, or affair; 7 creature, being, as *poor thing!;* 8 item, detail; 9 colloq a predilection; b phobia; 10 **the thing** that which is correct or in style, as *spearfishing is the thing;* 11 **things** *pl* a personal possessions; b articles of clothing, esp. outer garments

thing′a·ma·gig′ /-əməjig′/ also **thing′a·ma·bob′** /-bob′/ *n* colloq something, as a device or gadget, whose name is unknown or forgotten

think /thiŋk′/ [OE *thencan*] *v* (thought) *vi* 1 to meditate, ponder; reason; 2 to have an opinion or judgment; 3 **think better of** to reconsider; 4 **think fit** to consider it advisable, as *come early if you think fit;* 5 **think of,** a to remember; b to meditate about; c to turn one's thoughts toward, as *think of a number and I will tell you what it is;* d to intend to; 6 **think twice** to consider carefully ‖ *vt* 7 to form in the mind, imagine, conceive; 8 to review or examine mentally; 9 to hold as an opinion, believe; 10 to judge, consider; 11 **think of** to have (a certain opinion) of, as *this is what I think of him;* 12 **think over** to ponder carefully; 13 **think through** to reach a conclusion about after pondering; 14 **think up** to devise by thinking ‖ **think′er** *n* ‖ SYN conceive, meditate, believe, cogitate, muse

think′ tank′ *n* colloq group of experts that are organized to study and solve problems that are presented to it and place where it functions

thin′ner *n* volatile liquid added to paint, varnish, etc. to dilute it to a thinner consistency

thin′-skinned′ *adj* 1 having a thin skin; 2 sensitive, easily hurt by criticism, insult, etc.

thio- [< Gk *theion* sulfur] *comb form* containing sulfur usu. in place of oxygen

Thi·o·kol /thī′əkōl′, -kol′/ [trademark] *n* a synthetic rubber, used for gasoline hoses, sealants, etc.

thi·o·sul·fate /thī′ōsul′fāt/ *n* salt or ester of thiosulfuric acid

thi′o·sul·fu′ric ac′id *n* acid —$H_2S_2O_3$— derived from sulfuric acid by the replacement of one oxygen atom by one sulfur atom

third /thurd′/ [OE *thridda, thirda*] *n* 1 the one next in order after the second; 2 one of three equal parts; 3 *mus* interval between any tone in the diatonic scale and the tone next but one above it; 4 *auto* highest or next to the highest gear || also *adj* ||

third′·ly *adv*

third′ class′ *n* 1 least costly and least luxurious accommodations, as on a ship; 2 class of mail not exceeding one pound in weight, including books, circulars, and other printed matter not sealed against postal inspection || **third′-class′** *adj & adv*

third′ de·gree′ *n* intensive questioning, often accompanied by torture, as of a suspect by the police

third′ per′son *n gram* 1 person or thing spoken of; 2 form indicating such a person or thing

third′ rail′ *n* rail running parallel to the two rails of an electric railway, carrying the electric current

third′-rate′ *adj* of poor quality, inferior

Third′ Reich′ *n* Germany under the Nazis 1933-45

Third′ World′ *n* nonaligned African, Asian, and American nations supposedly united ideologically

thirst /thurst′/ [OE *thurst*] *n* 1 the desire for drink, as of water or liquor; 2 craving; longing or desire || *vi* 3 to be thirsty; 4 to feel a desire or craving || SYN *n* appetite, craving, lust, relish || ANT *n* indifference, antipathy, repulsion

thirst′y *adj* (-i·er; -i·est) 1 feeling thirst; 2 eager, desirous; 3 lacking moisture; parched, dry || **thirst′i·ly** *adv* || **thirst′i·ness** *n*

thir·teen /thur′tēn′/ [OE *thrēotēne*] *n* three more than ten (13; XIII) || also *adj & pron*

thir′teenth′ *n* 1 the one next in order after the twelfth; 2 one of thirteen equal parts || also *adj*

thir′ti·eth *n* 1 the one next in order after the twenty-ninth; 2 one of thirty equal parts || also *adj*

thir·ty /thurt′ē/ [OE *thrītig*] *n* (-ties) 1 three times ten (30; XXX); 2 the **thirties** *pl* a to numbers from 30 to 39; b the years from 30 to 39 in a century or a lifetime || also *adj & pron*

this /this′/ [OE] *adj* (these) 1 designating that which is near or nearer in space, time, or degree; 2 designating the person, place, or thing that is present, near, or just mentioned || *pron* (these) 3 the thing present or near; 4 the thing just mentioned or about to be mentioned

this·tle /this′əl/ [OE *thistel*] *n* 1 any of various plants of the composite family (esp. *Cirsium lanceolatum*), with prickly stem and leaves and purple, yellow, or white flowers; 2 the Scotch thistle *Onopordum acanthium*; 3 any of various similar plants

thith·er /thith′ər, thith′-/ [OE *thider*] *adv* to or toward that place; there

tho or **tho'** /thō′/ *conj & adv* var of **though**

thole /thōl′/ [ME *tholle*] *n* one of a

pair of pins set vertically in the gunwale of a boat, the pair functioning as a sort of oarlock

Thom·as /tom′əs/ *n Bib* one of the twelve apostles, who doubted the resurrection of Jesus until he had visible proof (John 20:24-29)

Tho·mism /tō′mizəm, thō′-/ *n* the theological and philosophical system of St. Thomas Aquinas

Thomp′son sub′ma·chine′ gun′ /tomp′sən/ [J. T. *Thompson* (1860-1940) Am army officer] *n* portable machine gun fired from the shoulder

thong /thôŋ′, thoŋ′/ [OE *thwong*] *n* 1 thin leather strap or string for fastening; 2 lash of a whip

Thor /thôr′/ [OE] *n Scand myth.* god of thunder and strength, for whom Thursday is named

tho·rax /thôr′aks, thōr′-/ [Gk = breastplate] *n* (-rax·es or -ra·ces /-rəsēz′/) 1 that part of the body in man and higher vertebrates between the neck and the abdomen; chest; 2 second of the three main divisions of the body of insects, between the head and the abdomen || **tho·rac′ic** /-ras′ik/ *adj*

Tho·reau, H. D. /thôr′ō, thərō′/ *n* (1817-62) U.S. naturalist and writer

tho·ri·um /thôr′ē·əm, thōr′-/ [< *Thor*] *n* rare, grayish, radioactive metallic element (Th; at.no. 90; at.wt. 232.038), parent of a series of radioactive decomposition products similar to the uranium series

thorn /thôrn′/ [OE] *n* 1 in plants, branch modified into a sharp-pointed projection; 2 any tree or shrub bearing thorns, or its wood; 3 source of trouble or annoyance; worry; 4 runic character used in the alphabets of Old English and Icelandic for the sounds /th/ and /th/ and in modern Icelandic for the sound /th/

thorn′y *adj* (-i·er; -i·est) 1 full of thorns; 2 harassing; painful; 3 full of difficulties and hardships

tho·ron /thôr′on, -ən, thōr′-/ [< *thorium*] *n* inert gaseous element (Tn; at.no. 86; at.wt. 220), a decomposition product of thorium, that has a halflife of 54.5 seconds

thor·ough /thur′ō/ [OE *thuruh*] *adj* 1 done or carried through to the end; complete; 2 utter, absolute, as *a thorough fool*; 3 accurate, exact; 4 careful, painstaking || **thor′ough·ly** *adv* || **thor′ough·ness** *n*

thor′ough·bred′ *adj* 1 (animal) of pure unmixed breed or stock; 2 highspirited, courageous; 3 accomplished, polished (person) || *n* 4 thoroughbred animal; 5 thoroughbred person; 6 **Thoroughbred** one of the breed to which all race horses belong

thor′ough·fare′ *n* 1 street, road, or passage open at both ends, esp. a public highway; **2** right of passage ‖ SYN passage, highway, street (see *way*)

thor'ough·go·ing *adj* thorough, complete, exhaustive

those /thōz'/ *adj & pron pl* of that

thou /thou'/ [OE *thū*] *pron* (2nd pers sg nom) *archaic & poet.* (used when referring to one person only) you

though /thō'/ [ON *thō*] *conj* **1** notwithstanding or in spite of the fact that; **2** even if; **3** although ‖ *adv* **4** for all that; however

thought[1] /thôt'/ [OE *thōht*] *n* **1** act or process of thinking; **2** meditation, reflection; **3** that which one thinks; **4** idea, conception; **5** capacity or function of thinking; **6** concern, care; **7** way of thinking of a period, nation, class, society, etc., as *modern thought*; **8** a thought a bit, a mite ‖ SYN cogitation, contemplation, notion, idea, judgment, imagination, reverie, study, deliberation, view, concern, solicitude ‖ ANT actuality, substance; forgetfulness, negligence, thoughtlessness

thought[2] *pt & pp* of think

thought' con·trol' *n* propaganda and rigid coercion to fix opinion and political attitudes, often exercised by a totalitarian government

thought'ful *adj* **1** given to thought; reflective; **2** careful, heedful; **3** considerate ‖ **thought'ful·ly** *adv* ‖ **thought'ful·ness** *n* ‖ SYN pensive, contemplative, attentive, mindful, considerate, kind ‖ ANT inattentive, heedless, careless, inconsiderate, unkind

thought'less *adj* **1** unthinking; heedless; **2** inconsiderate; remiss ‖ **thought'·less·ly** *adv* ‖ **thought'less·ness** *n*

thou·sand /thouz'ənd/ [OE *thūsend*] *n* ten times 100 (1000; M) ‖ also *adj*

thou'sand·fold' *adj* **1** having a thousand times as much or as many ‖ *adv* **2** a thousand times as much or as many

thou'sandth *n* **1** last one in order in a series of one thousand; **2** one of one thousand equal parts; **3** position of the third digit to the right of the decimal point ‖ also *adj*

thrall /thrôl'/ [OE *thræl* < Scand] *n* **1** slave; **2** slavery; **3** person in mental or moral bondage ‖ SYN serf, serfdom, bondage (see *slave*)

thrall'dom or **thral'dom** *n* **1** condition of servitude; **2** mental or moral bondage ‖ SYN captivity, slavery, bondage

thrash /thrash'/ [var of *thresh*] *vt* **1** to beat or flog soundly; **2** to defeat soundly; **3 thrash out** to discuss conclusively ‖ *vi* **4** to move about violently, toss around

thrash'ing *n* a whipping

thread /thred'/ [OE *thrǣd*] *n* **1** thin twisted cord of cotton, flax, or other fibrous substance; **2** filament, as of glass or metal; **3** fine line, as of mercury in a thermometer, of smoke, or of color; **4** something running through and connecting the parts of anything, as *the thread of a story*; **5** helical ridge, as on a screw, bolt, nut, or pipe ‖ *vt* **6** to put a thread through the eye of (a needle); **7** to put (beads, etc.) on a string; **8** to pass (tape, film, or cord) into or through the device on which it is to be wound; **9** to make (one's way) as through a narrow passage or crowd; **10** to cut a thread on or in (a screw, bolt, nut, or pipe)

thread'bare' *adj* **1** worn to the threads; with the nap worn off; **2** shabby; wearing threadbare clothes; **3** hackneyed, trite

threat /thret'/ [OE = oppression] *n* **1** menace; **2** declaration that harm or injury will be inflicted in retaliation for something; **3** announcement or indication of coming evil or danger

threat'en *vi* **1** to give notice of coming evil or danger; **2** to utter threats ‖ *vt* **3** to utter threats against; **4** to become a menace to; **5** to portend (something injurious or harmful)

threat'en·ing *adj* ‖ SYN menace ‖ DISCR *Threaten*, a Saxon word, is more common in familiar usage than *menace*, the Latin word for the same meaning. Large or small misfortunes may *threaten* us; only great ones *menace*. Things or persons may *threaten*; only persons, or things personified, *menace.* One boy may *threaten* in words to strike another; he *menaces* him with a whip. He may *threaten* by a gesture or a frown; he *menaces* by actual approach to accomplish his end

three /thrē'/ [OE *thrīe, thrēo*] *n* **1** sum of two and one (3; III); **2** set of three persons or things; **3** playing card with three spots ‖ also *adj & pron*

three'-deck'er *n* something having three layers or levels

three'-di·men'sion·al *adj* **1** (space) having three dimensions; **2** (photograph or moving picture) giving the illusion of depth or a third dimension

three'fold' *adj* **1** having three times as much or as many ‖ *adv* **2** three times as much or as many

three'-mile' lim'it *n* area extending into the open sea three miles beyond the coast line, over which the nation possessing the coast exercises territorial jurisdiction

three·pence /thrip'əns, threp'-, thrup'-/ *n Brit* sum of three pence

three'-phase' *adj elec* (circuit or device) through which an alternating current flows which pulsates in three phases differing by one third of a cycle

three'-ply' *adj* having three plies, layers, thicknesses, or strands

three'-quar'ter time' *n mus* meter of a composition having three quarter notes or their equivalent to each measure and a time sign of ¾

three'-ring' cir'cus *n* 1 circus in which performances take place in three adjacent rings; 2 something characterized by spectacle, noise, and confusion

three' R's' *npl* reading, 'riting, and 'rithmetic, considered the basic subjects of education

three'score' *adj* three times twenty; sixty

three'some *n* 1 group of three persons; 2 game played by three persons

three'-spot' *n* card, domino, or die with three spots

thren·o·dy /thren′ədē/ [Gk *threnoidia*] *n* (**-dies**) dirge, funeral song; lament for the dead

thresh /thresh′/ [OE *threscan*] *vt* 1 to beat out (grain) from the hull or husk; 2 to beat (heads or husks) to extract the grain; 3 **thresh out** to discuss conclusively ‖ *vi* 4 to thresh grain ‖ **thresh'er** *n*

thresh·old /thresh′ōld, -hōld/ [OE *threscold*] *n* 1 doorsill; 2 building entrance; 3 place or occasion of entering upon or beginning something; 4 *psychol* degree of intensity at which a stimulus becomes perceptible

threw /thrōō′/ *pt* of **throw**

thrice /thrīs′/ [ME *thries* < OE *thrīga*] *adv* 1 three times; 2 threefold; 3 greatly, extremely

thrift /thrift′/ [ME < Scand] *n* economical management; economy, frugality

thrift'y *adj* (**-i·er**; **-i·est**) 1 showing good management; provident; 2 prosperous; thriving ‖ **thrift'i·ly** *adv* ‖ **thrift'i·ness** *n* ‖ SYN frugal, prudent (see *economical*)

thrill /thril′/ [OE *thyrlian* to pierce] *vt* 1 to fill with a sudden keen emotion; stir deeply; 2 to cause to have a tingling sensation ‖ *vi* 3 to feel deeply or exquisitely; 4 to experience a sharp tingling or quivering sensation ‖ *n* 5 stirring, vibrating sensation; 6 wave of emotion; tremor; 7 cause of thrills ‖ **thrill'ing** *adj*

thrill'er *n colloq* exciting or suspenseful story or play

thrive /thrīv′/ [ME *thriven* < Scand] *v* (**throve** or **thrived**; **thrived** or **thriv·en** /thriv′ən/) *vi* 1 to prosper; become rich; succeed; 2 to grow vigorously, flourish ‖ **thriv'ing** *adj*

throat /thrōt′/ [OE *throtu*] *n* 1 passage between the mouth and the stomach or lungs; 2 any narrow entrance or passage

throat'y *adj* (**-i·er**; **-i·est**) (sound) produced in the throat; husky, guttural

throb /throb′/ [?] *v* (**throbbed**; **throb·bing**) *vi* 1 to beat forcefully and rapidly; pulsate, vibrate; 2 to thrill

with emotion or excitement ‖ *n* 3 act of throbbing; 4 pulsation or vibration; 5 thrill; tremulous excitement

throe /thrō′/ [ME *throwe*] *n* 1 agony, extreme pain; 2 **throes** *pl* a agony; violent struggle; b convulsion, paroxysm ‖ SYN pang, pain, paroxysm, torture, anguish

throm·bo·sis /thrombōs′is/ [Gk = curdling] *n* formation of a clot in any part of the circulatory system

throm·bus /throm′bəs/ [Gk *thrombos*] *n* (**-bi** /-bī′/) obstructive blood clot in a blood vessel or the heart

throne /thrōn′/ [Gk *thronos* raised seat] *n* 1 ceremonial chair of state of a king, bishop, or other high dignitary; 2 sovereign power, dignity, or office; 3 occupant of a throne

throng /thrông′, throng′/ [OE *gethrang*] *n* 1 crowd; 2 great number ‖ *vt* 3 to crowd into, fill ‖ *vi* 4 to crowd ‖ SYN *n* crowd, populace, mob, rabble, multitude ‖ DISCR A *crowd*, whether great or few in number, is too numerous to be comfortable in the space at its disposal; *crowds* are usually moving about, and are packed closely together. *Crowd* sometimes connotes noise, agitation, and tumult, but a *crowd* may be hushed into a silent, respectful group. A *crowd* motivated by wild excitement or inflamed to some purpose becomes a *mob*. Those who make up a *mob* may ordinarily be people of sense and standing, but the *rabble* is always the lowest and most miserable class of people. The *populace* is the common people; the term is sometimes contemptuous, connoting the ignorance and vulgarity ordinarily associated with great uneducated masses. A *throng* is characterized by vast numbers that are densely packed together and moving, but usually not so agitated or tumultuous as a *crowd*. A *multitude* names a vast assemblage

throt·tle /throt′əl/ [ME *throtel*] *vt* 1 to strangle by pressure on the windpipe; 2 to suppress or check as if by choking; 3 to reduce or stop the flow of (a fluid) in order to control the speed of an engine ‖ *n* 4 valve to control supply, as of steam or gas; 5 lever or pedal actuating this valve

through /thrōō′/ [OE *thurh*] *prep* 1 in one end or side and out the other of; 2 from beginning to end of; throughout; 3 by means of; 4 over all the steps or phases of; 5 by reason of; 6 beyond; 7 from one to the other of, as *through many hands*; 8 by way of, as *we went through Albany*; 9 within, around, as *we traveled through Spain*; 10 to and including, as *Monday through Thursday* ‖ *adv* 11 in one end or side and out the other; 12 from the beginning to the end; 13 to the end or to a conclusion; **14** all the way, as *this bus goes through to Chicago;* **15** thoroughly, as *wet through;* **16 through and through** thoroughly ‖ *adj* **17** extending from one place or surface to another, as *a through street;* **18** going the whole distance, as *a through train;* **19** finished, as *I am through;* **20** having no further association, as *he and she are through;* **21** of no further usefulness

through·out′ *adv* **1** in every part, everywhere ‖ *prep* **2** during; in every part of

through′way′ *n* limited-access toll highway

throve /thrōv′/ *pt* of **thrive**

throw /thrō′/ [OE *thrāwan* to twist] *v* (**threw; thrown**) *vt* **1** to fling or hurl, as by a motion of the wrist and arm; **2** to propel or project; **3** to hurl to the ground, as a wrestling opponent; **4** to unhorse, unseat; **5** to don (clothes) hastily or carelessly; **6** to cause to move rapidly forward, bring to bear, as troops; **7** to direct, cast, as a glance; **8** to cast (dice); **9** to make a (specified cast) with the dice; **10** *colloq* to lose intentionally; **11** to put into a specified place or condition, as *thrown into prison, thrown into confusion;* **12** *slang* to give (a party); **13** to deliver (a punch); **14** *colloq* to astonish; **15** *mach* **a** to move (a lever) into a new position; **b** to connect or disconnect by a lever; **16 throw away, a** to discard; **b** to waste; **17 throw in** *colloq* to add for good measure; **18 throw off, a** to rid oneself of; **b** to escape from (pursuers); **19 throw oneself into** to engage in wholeheartedly; **20 throw out, a** to discard; **b** *baseball* to put out (a runner) by throwing the ball to a fielder who steps on a base before the runner can reach it; **21 throw over** to desert, abandon; **22 throw up, a** to give up; **b** to recall tauntingly ‖ *vi* **23** to cast, hurl; **24 throw in with** to join in an enterprise; **25 throw up** to vomit ‖ *n* **26** act or instance of throwing; **27** distance that something may be thrown, cast, or projected ‖ SYN *v* fling, toss, hurl, propel (see *cast*)

throw′a·way′ *n* advertising circular passed out on the street, stuck in mail boxes, etc.

throw′back′ *n* **1** reversion to an earlier type; **2** example of this

thrown /thrōn′/ *pp* of **throw**

throw′ rug′ *n* scatter rug

throw′ weight′ *n* payload capacity of the launcher of a nuclear missile

thru /thrōō′/ *prep, adv & adj colloq* var of **through**

thrum /thrum′/ [imit] *v* (**thrummed; thrum·ming**) *vt* **1** to play on (a stringed instrument) idly, monotonously, or listlessly; **2** to drum on or tap, as a table ‖ *vi* **3** to thrum an in-

strument; **4** to drum or tap idly with the fingers ‖ *n* **5** act or sound of thrumming

thrush¹ /thrush′/ [OE *thrysce*] *n* **1** any of a large, nearly world-wide family (Turdidae) of small songbirds; **2** *slang* female singer

thrush² [< Scand] *n* mouth disease of infants, marked by small gray spots, caused by a fungus (*Candida albicans*)

thrust /thrust′/ [ME *thrusten* < Scand] *v* (**thrust**) *vt* **1** to push or shove with force; drive or impel; **2** to pierce; **3** to put forth boldly and insistently ‖ *vi* **4** to make a lunging motion, as with a knife; **5** to push, shove ‖ *n* **6** act or instance of thrusting; **7** push, lunge, or stab; **8** stress tending to push a part of a structure out of position; **9** forward force exerted by a propeller or gases to propel a vessel or aircraft; **10** guiding principle, import, tendency ‖ SYN *v* force, press, urge ‖ ANT *v* pull, drag, lead

thud /thud′/ [OE *thyddan*] *n* **1** dull sound, as of a blow or fall ‖ *v* (**thud·ded; thud·ding**) *vi* **2** to strike with a thud

thug /thug′/ [Hindi *thag* one of a former organization of religious assassins in India] *n* vicious criminal, ruffian, or cutthroat

Thu·le /thōōl′ē/ *n* the part of the world which the ancients regarded as farthest north, variously identified with Norway, Iceland, or the Shetland and Orkney Islands

thu·li·um /thōōl′ē·əm/ [< *Thule*] *n* rare metallic element (**Tm**; at.no. 69; at.wt. 168.934) of the rare-earth group

thumb /thum′/ [OE *thyma*] *n* **1** the shortest and thickest digit of the hand; **2 all thumbs** clumsy, awkward; **3 thumbs down** expression of disapproval; **4 thumbs up** expression of approval; **5 under the thumb of** under the influence or control of ‖ *vt* **6** to soil or wear with the thumb; **7** to turn the pages of (a book) with the thumb; **8** to solicit (a ride in a passing auto) by pointing with the thumb; **9 thumb one's nose** to show contemptuous defiance by placing the thumb on one's nose and extending the fingers

thumb′ in′dex *n* series of labels fastened along the fore edge of a book to indicate sections ‖ **thumb′-in′dex** *vt*

thumb′nail′ *n* **1** nail of the thumb ‖ *adj* **2** small or brief

thumb′screw′ *n* **1** screw that may be tightened with the thumb and finger; **2** instrument of torture for twisting and squeezing the thumb

thumb′tack′ *n* tack with a large flat head for pushing into place with the thumb

thump /thump'/ [imit] *n* 1 hard heavy blow; 2 sound of a heavy fall or blow || *vt* 3 to pound or strike with dull heavy blows || *vi* 4 to beat or fall with a thump; 5 to pound or throb, as the heart

thump'ing *adj colloq* enormous; exceptional; heavy

thun·der /thun'dər/ [OE *thunor*] *n* 1 sound accompanying a flash of lightning, due to the rapid heating of the air in the path of the electrical disturbance; 2 any loud resounding noise; 3 **steal someone's thunder** to ruin the effect of someone's efforts by anticipating them || *vi* 4 to send forth thunder; 5 to make a loud resounding noise; 6 to utter, move, or act with a thundering sound || *vt* 7 to utter in a thundering voice || **thun'der·er** *n*

thun·der·a'tion *interj* expression of surprise or annoyance

thun'der·bolt' *n* 1 flash of lightning accompanied by thunder; 2 something that strikes with sudden fury

thun'der·clap' *n* violent crash of thunder

thun'der·storm' *n* storm accompanied by lightning and thunder

thun'der·struck' *adj* overcome with amazement or consternation

Thurs. Thursday

Thurs·day /thurz'dē, -dā/ [OE *Thursdaeg* Thor's day] *n* fifth day of the week, following Wednesday || **Thurs'days** *adv*

thus /thus'/ [OE] *adv* 1 in this or that manner; 2 so, therefore, consequently; 3 to this degree or extent

thwack /thwak'/ [imit] *vt* 1 to strike with a flat object || *n* 2 blow with something flat; wack

thwart /thwôrt'/ [ME *thwert* athwart < Scand] *vt* 1 to oppose or baffle; 2 to frustrate; outwit or defeat || SYN frustrate, oppose, baffle, circumvent, foil, hinder || ANT aid, abet, promote

thy /thī'/ [var of *thine*] *adj archaic & poet.* possessive of **thou;** of or belonging to thee

thyme /tīm'/ [Gk *thymon*] *n* any of a genus (*Thymus*) of herbs of the mint family, esp. the common *T. vulgaris* with aromatic leaves used for seasoning

thy·mus (gland) /thīm'əs/ [Gk *thymos* = wart] *n* ductless gland of uncertain function, located in infants below the base of the neck, gradually wasting away until it disappears

thy·roid /thī'roid/ [Gk *thyreoeides* shield-shaped] *n* 1 cartilage forming the outer wall of the Adam's apple; 2 thyroid gland; 3 extract prepared from the thyroid glands of animals, used to treat goiter

thy'roid gland' *n* ductless gland, lying on each side of the windpipe below the pharynx, the secretions of which regulate growth and metabolism in the body

thy·self' *pron archaic & poet.* reflexive and emphatic form of **thee**

ti /tē'/ [var of *si*] *n mus* seventh tone in the diatonic scale

Ti *chem* titanium

ti·a·ra /tē-ar'ə, -är'ə, -er'ə/ [Gk = Persian headdress] *n* 1 triple crown worn by the Pope; 2 coronet or other crownlike headdress worn by women

Ti·ber /tīb'ər/ *n* river in central Italy, flowing through Rome to the Mediterranean

Ti·bet /tibet'/ *n* country in S Central Asia between India and China, under Chinese control (1,300,000; 471,660 sq.m.; cap. Lhasa) || **Ti·bet'an** *adj & n*

tib·i·a /tib'ē-ə/ [L] *n* (-ae /-ē'/ or -as) inner and larger of the two bones of the leg, extending from the knee to the ankle

tic /tik'/ [F] *n* recurring, involuntary, convulsive twitching of the muscles, as of the face

tick¹ /tik'/ [ME *tek* light touch] *n* 1 light recurring tap or click, as of a clock; 2 small mark, as a dot or check, used in checking off or in marking something for attention || *vi* 3 to emit ticks || *vt* 4 to mark off (time) in ticks, as a clock; 5 **tick off** to mark off with ticks, as items on a list

tick² [OE *ticia*] *n* any of numerous tiny bloodsucking arachnids (order Acarina) that attach themselves to the skin of various **animals**

tick³ [< Gk *theke* case] *n* 1 cloth case of a mattress or pillow; 2 ticking

tick⁴ [< *ticket*] *n* **on tick** *colloq* on credit

tick'er *n* 1 telegraphic device which automatically prints stock quotations and other market news on a paper tape; 2 *slang* heart

tick·et /tik'it/ [MF *etiquet* little note] *n* 1 certificate, usu. a small card, that entitles the holder to certain privileges, as admission or transportation; 2 label or tag attached to goods, giving their price, size, etc.; 3 list of candidates nominated by one party or group; 4 traffic or parking summons; 5 license of a ship's officer; 6 **the ticket** *colloq* just the thing || *vt* 7 to mark by a ticket or label; 8 to serve with a ticket as for illegal parking

tick'ing *n* strong closely woven cloth used for mattress and pillow covers

tick·le /tik'əl/ [ME *tikelen*] *vt* 1 to touch lightly so as to produce a tingling sensation or involuntary laughter; 2 to amuse or gratify || *vi* 3 to be affected by tickling || *n* 4 act or instance of tickling; 5 tickling sensation

tick·lish /tik'lish/ *adj* 1 sensitive to

tickling; 2 delicate to handle or achieve; 3 touchy

tick'tack'toe' /imit/ *n* game in which two players mark crosses and ciphers respectively in the nine spaces of a figure formed by two pairs of parallel lines crossed, the winner being the first to fill three spaces in a row

tick'tock' /-tok'/ [imit] *n* 1 ticking sound of a clock ‖ *vi* 2 to make a ticking sound

tid·al /tīd'əl/ [< *tide*] *adj* of, pert. to, subject to, or caused by tides

tid'al flat' *n* flat tideland

tid'al wave' *n* 1 extraordinarily large and destructive ocean wave caused by a submarine earthquake or other unusual natural cause; 2 widespread manifestation of public sentiment

tid'bit' /tid'-/ [< OE *tīd* occasion] *n* 1 small bit or choice morsel, as of food; 2 choice bit, as of gossip

tid·dly·winks /tid'lē winks'/- [dial. tiddly drunk + dial. wink winch] *n* game in which the players try to snap small plastic disks into a cup by pressing down on the edges with a larger disk

tide /tīd'/ [OE *tīd* time, hour] *n* 1 time, season, as *Eastertide;* 2 periodic rise and fall of the waters of the oceans and their inlets, due to the attraction of the moon and sun; 3 anything which rises and falls or ebbs and flows like the tide; 4 stream, current; 5 natural drift or tendency; 6 **turn the tide** to reverse the course of events ‖ *vt* 7 **tide over,** a to give temporary relief to; b to surmount, get over (a difficulty)

tide'land' *n* land covered by the tide when high and exposed when it is low

tide' pow'er *n* power produced by harnessing the rising or falling tide and used to generate electricity

tide'wa'ter *n* 1 water affected by the rise and fall of the tide; 2 land bordered by such water

ti·dings /tīd'inz/ [OE *tīdung*] *npl* news, information ‖ SYN message, news, information (see *intelligence*)

ti·dy /tīd'ē/ [ME *tidi* timely] *adj* (-di·er; -di·est) 1 trim, neat, orderly; 2 *colloq* considerable ‖ *v* (-died) often **tidy up** *vt* 3 to make tidy; put in order ‖ *vi* 4 to make things tidy ‖ *n* (-dies) 5 antimacassar ‖ **ti'di·ly** *adv* ‖ SYN *adj* cleanly, nice, neat, trim, dapper, prim

tie /tī/ [OE *tīegan*] *v* (**ty·ing**) *vt* 1 to fasten, bind, or attach by a cord or other bond; 2 to make a knot in, as a necktie, rope, or shoelace; 3 to make the same score as; 4 *mus* to unite (notes) with a tie; 5 *colloq* to unite in marriage; 6 to fasten or join; 7 to limit, restrict; 8 **tie down** to confine, curtail the freedom of; 9 **tie off** to disconnect by tying; 10 **tie up,** a to bind or fasten by tying; b to impede, bring to a stop; c to make unavailable; d to occupy completely

‖ *vi* 11 to equal the score in a contest; 12 **tie in** to be connected; 13 **tie up** to moor to a dock ‖ *n* 14 something, as a cord or ribbon, used to tie things; 15 beam or rod used to hold parts together and to receive tensile strength; 16 one of the crossbeams to which the rails of a railroad are fastened; 17 bow, knot; 18 necktie; 19 bond of kinship, affection, common interests, etc.; 20 equality of numbers, as of votes or points in a game; 21 contest resulting in a tie; 22 *mus* curved line connecting two notes to be sung or played as one

tie'back' *n* strip of fabric or metal used to hold a curtain back at about midlength

tie'-dye' *vt* to dye (a fabric) after tying it into knots so that parts of it are not reached by the dye

tie'-in' *n* 1 sale or promotion in which two or more often unrelated products are sold or advertised together; 2 connection or link

tier /tir/ [OF *tire* sequence, order] *n* one of a series of rows or ranks arranged one above or behind the other, as seats in a theater

tie'-up' *n* 1 temporary stoppage, as of traffic; 2 connection or involvement

tiff /tif/ [?] *n* 1 slight fit of anger; huff; 2 slight quarrel ‖ *vi* 3 to be in a tiff; 4 to quarrel slightly

tif·fin /tif'in/ [< *obs tiff* liquor] *n* Brit lunch

ti·ger /tīg'ər/ [OF *tigre* < Gk *tigris*] *n* 1 large Asiatic beast of prey (*Felis tigris*) having tawny fur with black stripes; 2 fierce aggressive person; 3 *colloq* added cheer given after a round of three cheers ‖ **ti'ger·ish** *adj* ‖ **ti'gress** *nfem*

ti'ger cat' *n* 1 any of various kinds of wild cats smaller than a tiger and of variegated coloring; 2 domestic cat with a striped coat like a tiger's

ti'ger lil'y *n* 1 lily (*Lilium tigrinum*) bearing orange-colored flowers spotted with black; 2 any of various similar lilies

ti'ger moth' *n* any of a family (Arctiidae) of moths having striped or spotted wings

tight /tīt/ [ME, var of *thight* solid] *adj* 1 firmly fixed; secure, as *a tight knot;* 2 built so that water or other fluid cannot go through the seams or joints; 3 fitting too closely; 4 stretched taut; 5 hard to get, scarce, as money or commodities; 6 difficult to get through, as *a tight fix;* 7 *colloq* stingy; 8 *colloq* drunk; 9 *colloq* very close or even, as *a tight race* ‖ *adv* 10 tightly; 11 firmly, steadily, as *sit tight* ‖ *n* 12 **tights** *pl* closely fitting garment for the lower part of the body and the legs, worn esp. by dancers and acrobats ‖ **tight'ly** *adv* ‖ **tight'ness** *n*

tight'en *vt* 1 to make tight ‖ *vi* 2 to become tight

tight'-fist'ed *adj* stingy

tight'-lipped' *adj* saying little or nothing

tight'rope' *n* taut rope or cable on which acrobats balance themselves while performing

tight'wad' *n colloq* stingy person

Ti·gris /tīg'ris/ *n* river flowing from Turkey through Iraq to join the Euphrates and form the Shatt-al-Arab, which empties into the Persian Gulf

til·de /til'də/ [Sp < L *titulus* title] *n* diacritic ˜, used in Spanish over *n* (as in *señor*) to indicate a palatal pronunciation, and in Portuguese and some phonetic alphabets to indicate a nasal vowel

tile /tīl'/ [OE *tigele* < L *tegula*] *n* 1 thin slab of baked clay, stone, etc., used for roofing, floors, wall decoration, hearths, etc. ‖ *vt* 2 to cover with tiles

til'ing *n* 1 tiles collectively; 2 work made of tiles

till¹ /til'/ [ME *tillen* to draw out] *n* drawer or box for money, as in a shop or bank

till² [ON *til*] *prep & conj* until

till³ [OE *tilian* to strive, acquire] *vt* 1 to prepare for seed, as by plowing; cultivate ˜; ‖ *vi* 2 to cultivate the soil

till'age /-ij/ *n* 1 act or practice of tilling land; 2 tilled land

till'er¹ *n* one who cultivates land; farmer; husbandman

till'er² [ME] *n* lever for turning the rudder of a vessel

tilt /tilt'/ [ME *tilten* to upset] *vi* 1 to lean, incline, slope; 2 to contend on horseback armed with a lance; 3 to engage in a joust or contest; 4 **tilt at windmills** to fight imaginary opponents ‖ *vt* 5 to cause to tilt ‖ *n* 6 act of tilting or state of being tilted; 7 incline; 8 joust; contest of any sort; 9 (at) **full tilt** at full speed

tim·ber /tim'bər/ [OE = building material] *n* 1 wood suitable for building; 2 growing trees; 3 wooded land; 4 single piece of wood used in or suitable for construction; 5 person with potential for better things, as *presidential timber* ‖ *interj* 6 watch out for the falling tree! (said by lumberjacks as a warning)

timb'er·land' *n* land covered with trees suitable for carpentry and building

timb'er line' *n* 1 altitude above which trees cease to grow; 2 line in the Arctic and the Antarctic at which trees cease to grow

tim'ber wolf' *n* the North American gray wolf (*Canis lupus*), formerly very common in wooded areas

tim·bre /tim'bər/ [F] *n* 1 *mus* quality of a musical sound as determined by the number and character of its overtones; 2 *phonet* characteristic quality of a sound without reference to pitch or loudness

time /tīm'/ [OE *tīma*] *n* 1 measured or measurable duration; 2 finite duration as distinguished from infinite duration; 3 period required or consumed in performing an action, as *the winner's time was 3.01;* 4 period, season, as *summertime;* 5 particular period of a day, week, etc., as *lunch time, play time;* 6 period of history, era, age, as *in the time of Caesar;* 7 moment, occasion, as *the time of death* or *birth;* 8 definite or precise moment, as *the time was twelve o'clock;* 9 period characterized by some special quality or experience, as *a good time, a hard time;* 10 period available for some purpose or event, as *time for golf;* 11 system of reckoning or measuring duration, as *solar time;* 12 occasion; occurrence of an event, as *this is the first time I saw her; three times;* 13 interval between two events, as *a long time between drinks;* 14 period allotted to do something, as *we haven't much time;* 15 *colloq* period of service, incarceration, or apprenticeship; 16 indefinite duration; lapse of time; 17 *mus* a arrangement of the rhythmic beats into equal measures included between successive bars; b metrical duration of a note or rest; c tempo; d characteristic tempo of a composition, as *waltz time;* 18 **times** *pl* a period of history; b prevailing conditions, as *hard times;* c multiplied by, as *five times two is ten;* 19 **ahead of time** early; 20 **at the same time** however; 21 **at times** occasionally; now and then; 22 **behind the times** out-of-date, obsolete; 23 **do time** *colloq* to serve a term in prison; 24 **for the time being** for now; 25 **from time to time** occasionally; now and then; 26 **in good time** punctually, or ahead of time; 27 **in no time** very quickly; 28 **in time, a** eventually; b not late; c in the correct tempo; 29 **keep time, a** to record the passing time, as a clock; b to mark the tempo; 30 **kill time** to fill waiting time with some activity; 31 **make time** to move or act rapidly; 32 **mark time, a** *mil* to move the feet as in marching without advancing; b to wait to see what happens; 33 **on time, a** at the appointed time; punctually; b in installments, as a purchase; 34 **take one's time** to move or act unhurriedly; 35 **time after time** also **time and again** repeatedly; 36 **time of one's life** *colloq* wonderful time ‖ *interj* 37 *sports* a time out!; b time's up! ‖ *vt* 38 to regulate or adjust as to time, as a clock; 39 to record the time, speed, or duration of

time' and a half' *n* rate of overtime pay equal to one and a half times the regular pay

time' bomb' *n* bomb fitted with a

mechanism that can be set to explode it at a certain time

time′card′ n card that records an employee's presence at work

time′ chart′ n 1 chart that shows in a circular series the twenty-four standard times around the world at a given time at a given place, for example, at noon at New York City; 2 chronological list of events that took place within a given period of history

time′ clock′ n clock having a mechanism for recording the time on a card or tape, as the time on and off of employees, the time in and out of a car in a parking lot, etc.

time′ ex·po′sure n photog 1 exposure made by opening and closing the shutter by hand or by some timing device; 2 picture made by such exposure || **time′-ex·po′sure** adj

time′-hon′ored adj respected or reverenced because of age or long continuance

time′ im′me·mo′ri·al n ancient time, beyond record or memory

time′keep′er n 1 timepiece; 2 one who keeps track of time, as the duration of a speed contest or the hours worked by employees

time′ kill′er n 1 person who passes the time in idle pursuits; 2 something that helps to pass the time pleasantly

time′-lapse pho·tog′ra·phy n cinematography in which exposures are made at relatively long regular intervals to be projected at normal speed, so that a slow action, as the growth of a plant or the opening of a flower bud, appears greatly accelerated

time′less adj eternal, everlasting

time′ loan′ n loan that must be paid within a specified time or by a specified date

time′ lock′ n lock with a timing device on the door of a bank vault, that cannot be opened before the time set

time′ly adj (-li·er, -li·est) 1 seasonable; opportune; well-timed || adv 2 opportunely; in good season || **time′li·ness** n || SYN adj seasonable, fortunate, favorable, opportune || ANT adj unseasonable, unlucky, inopportune

time′ of day′ n 1 time indicated by a timepiece; 2 present time; 3 true situation; state of affairs; 4 **pass the time of day** to greet or to exchange greetings

time′-out′ n 1 brief intermission from some activity; 2 sports suspension of play in order to make a substitution, etc.

time′ pay′ment n payment made periodically in equal installments, as for the purchase of expensive items

time′piece′ n clock or watch

tim·er /tīm′ər/ n 1 device for measuring, regulating, or indicating time; 2 device for closing or opening a circuit or for starting or stopping a

machine at a predetermined time; 3 device that makes and breaks the primary circuit of a spark coil to cause the spark to occur at the proper time in an internal-combustion engine

time′serv′er n one who, to serve his own ends, fits his actions to suit public opinion or those in power

time′ta′ble n 1 schedule of the times of arrival and departure of trains, buses, or planes; 2 any schedule of events planned to occur at certain times

time′work′ n work paid for by the hour or day || **time′work′er** n

time′worn′ adj showing the effects of age and use

time′ zone′ n one of the 24 segments of the globe, each approximately 15 degrees wide, the time of each being exactly one hour earlier than that of the adjoining zone to the east

tim·id /tim′id/ [L timidus] adj 1 timorous, shy; 2 faint-hearted, fearful || **ti·mid′i·ty** /timid′-/ n || SYN shrinking, diffident, fearful (see afraid)

tim·ing /tīm′iŋ/ n 1 regulation and synchronization of the various parts of a cooperative effort in order to achieve smooth performance; 2 selection of the best time to do something with maximum effect; 3 regulation of the time or the intervals of time at which a device is to act; 4 sports a control of the speed and proper movement of blows, strokes, etc., to achieve maximum effect; b act or effect of recording the elapsed time of an event

tim′ing gears′ npl gears through which the crankshaft drives the camshaft and thus controls the timing of the valves of a four-cycle internal-combustion engine

tim·or·ous /tim′ərəs/ [ML timorosus] adj 1 fearful, timid; 2 indicating or due to fear or alarm || SYN fearful, shrinking, timid (see afraid)

tim·o·thy /tim′əthē/ [Timothy Hanson, Am farmer] n coarse grass (Phleum pratense) with cylindrical flower spikes, grown for hay

tim·pa·ni /timp′ənē/ [It] npl set of kettledrums || **tim′pa·nist** n

tin /tin′/ [OE] n 1 silvery white, malleable metallic element (Sn; at.no. 50; at.wt. 118.69) used in plating and in making solder and tinfoil; 2 tin plate; 3 baking pan; 4 Brit a container made of tin plate; b tin can || v (tinned; tin·ning) vt 5 to plate with tin; 6 Brit to can

tin′ can′ n sealed can for food, made usu. of tin-plated steel

tinc·ture /tiŋk′chər/ [L tinctura dyeing] n 1 slight infusion; 2 trace, tinge; 3 pharm alcoholic solution of a nonvolatile substance || vt 4 to color slightly, tinge, tint

tinc′ture of i′o·dine n alcoholic solution of iodine used in treating cuts, insect bites, etc.

tin·der /tin′dər/ [OE *tynder*] *n* any dry inflammable material, esp. that used in kindling a fire

tin′der·box′ *n* **1** box designed to hold tinder and, usu., a flint and steel; **2** anything highly inflammable; **3** any explosive situation

tine /tīn′/ [OE *tind*] *n* projecting point or prong, as of a fork

tin′foil′ *n* tin or an alloy of tin rolled into very thin flexible sheets, used as wrapping

tinge /tinj′/ [L *tingere* to dye, color] *v* (**tinge·ing** or **ting·ing**) *vt* **1** to color slightly; **2** to give a slight flavor or touch of something else to ‖ *n* **3** slight coloration; **4** trace, flavor ‖ SYN *n* tint, stain, flavor, taste (see *color*)

tin·gle /tiŋ′gəl/ [var of *tinkle*] *vi* **1** a to feel or have a stinging or prickling sensation, as from cold or a sharp blow; **b** to cause such a sensation; **2** to tinkle ‖ *n* **3** tingling sensation; **4** tinkling ‖ **tin′gly** *adj* (**-gli·er; -gli·est**)

tin′ god′ *n* self-important person who demands and gets respect and adulation from his subordinates

tin′ hat′ *n* safety hat made of steel or aluminum

tin′horn′ *n slang* **1** inconsequential person who pretends to power and influence he does not have, esp. a cheap gambler ‖ *adj* **2** small-time; cheap

tink·er /tiŋk′ər/ [ME *tinkere* tinworker] *n* **1** mender of metal pots, pans, etc., esp. a wandering one; **2** unskilled worker; bungler ‖ *vi* **3** to work as a tinker; **4** to work clumsily and ineffectually; **5** to work experimentally and to little purpose

tin·kle /tiŋk′əl/ [< *obs tink* to clink] *vi* **1** to make slight clinking sounds, like a small bell ‖ *vt* **2** to cause to tinkle ‖ *n* **3** tinkling sound

tin·ny /tin′ē/ *adj* (**-ni·er; -ni·est**) **1** pert. to or containing tin; **2** hollow-sounding, not resonant; **3** unsubstantial, not strongly made

tin′ plate′ *n* thin sheet iron or steel coated with tin ‖ **tin′-plat′ed** *adj*

tin·sel /tins′əl/ [MF *estincelle* spark] *n* **1** thin, glittering metallic material in strips or sheets, used for showy decoration; **2** something showy but of little value

tin′smith′ *n* one who makes or repairs articles of tin or other light metals

tint /tint′/ [*obs tinct* < L *tinctus* dyed, colored] *n* **1** color, hue; **2** delicate variation of a color, esp. one mixed with white; **3** hair dye ‖ *vt* **4** to give a tint to, tinge ‖ SYN *n* tinge, hue (see *color*)

tin·tin·nab·u·la·tion /tint′inab′yəlāsh′-ən/ [L *tintinnabulum* bell] *n* tinkling, as of bells

tin′type′ *n* photograph made directly

on a sensitized plate of enameled tin or iron

ti·ny /tīn′ē/ [< *obs tine*] *adj* (**-ni·er; -ni·est**) very small, diminutive

-tion /-shən/ [L *-tio* (-*onis*)] *n suf* indicating **1** act of, as *invention*; **2** state of being, as *dejection*; **3** result or product of an act, as *plantation*

-tious /-shəs/ [L *-tiosus*] *adj suf* used to form adjectives usu. corresponding to nouns in *-tion*, as *superstitious*

tip¹ /tip′/ [ME] *n* **1** anything small or tapering; **2** small piece or part attached to the end of a thing; **3** on the tip of one's tongue, a just escaping one's memory; **b** about to be said ‖ *v* (**tipped; tip·ping**) *vt* **4** to form or put a tip on; **5** to cover the tip of; **6** tip in to glue (an insert) in a book at the inside margin of a page

tip² [ME *type* to overturn] *v* (**tipped; tip·ping**) *vt* **1** to slant or tilt; **2** tip one's hat to touch or lift one's hat in greeting; **3** tip over to overturn ‖ *vi* **4** to slant, incline; **5** also tip over to overturn ‖ *n* **6** act of tipping, or state of being tipped

tip³ [?] *n* **1** glancing blow; **2** gratuity; **3** secret or advance information; **4** useful idea; piece of advice ‖ *v* (**tipped; tip·ping**) *vt* **5** to hit or tap lightly; **6** to give a gratuity to; **7** tip off *colloq* **a** to give secret or advance information to; **b** to warn ‖ SYN gratuity, gift, fee (see *boon¹*)

tip′-off′ *n colloq* **1** hint or warning; **2** secret or advance information

tip′per *n* one who gives tips or gratuities

tip·ple /tip′əl/ [< ME *tipeler* barkeep] *vt* to drink small amounts of (alcoholic liquors) habitually ‖ also *vi* ‖ **tip′pler** *n*

tip′staff′ *n* **1** staff with metal tip, carried as a badge of office; **2** officer who carries such a staff; **3** crier or attendant in a law court

tip′ster *n* one who gives or sells tips, as on sporting events

tip·sy /tip′sē/ [< *obs tip* liquor] *adj* (**-si·er; -si·est**) **1** slightly drunk; **2** shaky; unsteady ‖ **tip′si·ness** *n*

tip′toe′ *n* **1** tip of a toe; **2** on tiptoe, a on the tips of the toes; **b** stealthily; **c** eager, expectant ‖ *v* (**-toed; -toe·ing**) *vi* **3** to walk on tiptoe; **4** to step softly or cautiously

tip′top′ *n* **1** the highest point or degree; the best of anything ‖ *adj* **2** fine, without equal ‖ *adv* **3** in a tiptop manner

ti·rade /tī′rād, tīrād′/ [F = pull] *n* long violent speech, esp. of bitter denunciation

Ti·ra·na /tirän′ə/ *n* capital of Albania (167,000)

tire¹ /tī′ər/ [ME = attire] *n* **1** band or hoop of iron fastened on the rim of a wagon wheel; **2** band of rubber, solid or inflated with air, attached to the rim of a bicycle or automobile wheel

tire² [OE *tēorian*] *vt* **1** to exhaust or wear out the strength, interest, or patience of; fatigue, make weary ‖ *vi* **2** to become tired; **3** tire of to become weary of or bored by ‖ SYN exhaust, jade, fag ‖ ANT refresh, revive

tire' chain' *n* set of chains fastened across the tread of a tire to improve traction on ice and snow

tired /tīʳd/ *adj* weary, fatigued

tire'less *adj* untiring

tire'some *adj* **1** causing fatigue; wearisome; **2** annoying ‖ SYN tedious, fatiguing, irksome, troublesome, dreary, monotonous

'tis /tiz/ *archaic & poet.* it is

tis·sue /tish'ōō/ [MF *tissu* woven] *n* **1** thin gauzelike woven fabric; **2** closely woven network or mass, as *a tissue of lies*; **3** tissue paper; **4** soft, gauzelike, absorbent paper, used for cleansing, etc.; **5** group of similar cells of an animal or plant body forming a continuous mass or layer

tis'sue pa'per *n* thin gauzelike paper used for wrapping, protecting engravings in books, etc.

tit /tit/ *n* **1** teat, nipple; **2** *slang* female breast

Ti·tan /tīt'ən/ [Gk] *n* **1** *Gk myth.* one of the fabled giants who fought against the Olympian gods and were overthrown; **2** **titan** person or thing of enormous strength, size, or influence and power

ti·tan·ic /tītan'ik/ *adj* of great size, strength, or power

ti·ta·ni·um /tītän'ē·əm/ [< *Titan*] *n* lustrous, hard light, metallic element (**Ti**; at.no. 22; at.wt. 47.90) found in small amounts in many minerals and used in metallurgy as a deoxidizer

tit' for tat' /tat'/ [var of *tip* for *tap*] *n* fair return, blow for blow

tithe /tīth'/ [< OE *teogothian* to take the tenth of] *n* **1** tenth part, esp. the tenth part of one's income given to support the church; **2** any tax or levy amounting to one tenth ‖ *vt* **3** to grant or pay a tithe of; **4** to impose a tithe on

Ti·tian /tish'ən/ [*Titian* (1477–1576) Venetian painter] *n* reddish-brown color; auburn ‖ *also adj*

tit·il·late /tit'ilāt'/ [L *titillare* (-*atus*) to tickle] *vt* to rouse pleasing excitement in ‖ **tit'il·la'tion** *n*

ti·tle /tīt'əl/ [OF < L *titulus*] *n* **1** inscription or name of a book, writing, picture, piece of music, or the like; **2** appellation indicating rank, dignity, profession, or position; **3** alleged or recognized claim or right; **4** *law* **a** legal right to property, esp. real estate; **b** document setting forth such a right; **c** means by which one has obtained a right to property; **d** division of a law or statute; **5** *sports* championship; **6** *motion pictures* subtitle ‖ *vt* **7** to entitle, give a name or title to ‖ SYN *n* appellation, caption, heading (see *name*)

ti'tled *adj* having a noble title

ti'tle page' *n* page at the beginning of a book, giving its name, author, publisher, and date

ti'tle role' *n* role or character in a play or opera for which it is named

tit'mouse' [ME *titmose*] *n* (-**mice**) any of a large family (Paridae) of small songbirds, including the chickadee

Ti·to·ism /tēt'ō·iz'əm/ *n* type of communism associated with Marshal Tito (Josip Broz), Yugoslav statesman and political leader and president since 1953, characterized by nationalistic tendencies and independence from Soviet policy

tit·ter /tit'ər/ [?] *vi* **1** to laugh in a restrained, half-suppressed way ‖ *n* **2** tittering laugh

tit·tle /tit'əl/ [ME *titel* stroke over letter < L *titulus*] *n* **1** very small particle; iota or jot; **2** mark put on a letter as a diacritic

tit'tle-tat'tle [reduplication of *tattle*] *n* **1** chatter, gossip ‖ *vi* **2** to gossip, babble

tit·u·lar /tich'ələr, tit'yə-/ [see **title**] *adj* **1** pert. to, having, or resulting from a title; **2** existing in name or title only

tiz·zy /tiz'ē/ [?] *n* (-**zies**) *colloq* state of flustered excitement

TKO, T.K.O. technical knockout

Tl *chem* thallium

Tm *chem* thulium

tn. ton

TNT, T.N.T. *n* trinitrotoluene

to /tōō', tŏŏ, tə/ [OE] *prep* expressing **1** direction toward, as *turn to the right*; **2** approach and arrival, as *come to town*; **3** as far as, until, as *rotten to the core*; *open to six o'clock*; **4** correlation, agreement, as *words set to music*; **5** comparison, ratio, as *drawn to scale*; **6** on, onto, as *a left to the jaw, tied to the pole*; **7** resulting state, as *torn to shreds*; **8** belonging or appurtenance, as *there is no point to that*; **9** consequence, as *he learned to his cost*; **10** opposition, antithesis, as *face to face*; **11** the person or thing affected by the action of an intransitive verb, as *apply to the manager, drink to his health*; **12** in addition, as *add five to five*; **13** belonging with, as *the hat to this coat*; **14** contained in, as *three to the pound*; **15** the indirect object, as *give it to me*; **16** purpose, as *we live to eat*; **17** the definition or limitation of the application of an adjective, as *fit to eat*; **18** the marker of the infinitive, as *I want to go*; **19** the substitute for an infinitive, as *go if you want to* ‖ *adv* **20** into the usual or desired position or condition, as *the door* *clanged to; the man came to;* **21** in a certain direction, as *they stood wrong end to;* **22 to and fro** moving alternately forward and backward

toad /tōd/ [OE *tādige*] *n* any of various tailless hopping amphibians (esp. family Bufonidae) resembling the frog, but with a warty skin, chiefly living on land except when breeding

toad/stool/ *n* **1** any of various umbrella-shaped fungi; **2** any poisonous umbrella-shaped mushroom

toad/y *n* (**-ies**) **1** mean flatterer; sycophant || *v* (**-ied**) *vt* **2** to be a sycophant to || *vi* **3** to be a sycophant

toast /tōst/ [MF *toster* to roast, grill] *n* **1** sliced bread browned by heat; **2** act of drinking in honor of some person or thing; **3** one who or that which is named when drinking a toast || *vt* **4** to brown by exposing to heat; **5** to warm or heat at a fire; **6** to propose or drink a toast to || *vi* **7** to become toasted; **8** to propose or drink a toast

toast/er *n* appliance for toasting bread

toast/mas/ter *n* person who announces the toasts and introduces the speakers at a banquet

to·bac·co /təbak′ō/ [Sp *tabaco* < Arawak] *n* (**-cos** or **-coes**) **1** any of a genus (*Nicotiana*) of plants native to America, esp. *N. tabacum*; **2** the dried leaves of this plant prepared in various ways for smoking, chewing, or as snuff

to·bac/co·nist /-ənist/ *n* dealer in tobacco, cigars, cigarettes, pipes, etc.

-to-be /-təbē′/ *adj comb form* soon to become, as *bride-to-be*

to·bog·gan /təbog′ən/ [CanF *tabagane* < AmInd] *n* **1** long flat-bottomed sled without runners, curving up at the front || *vi* **2** to coast on a toboggan; **3** to decline or fall rapidly

toc·sin /tok′sin/ [F] *n* **1** bell for sounding an alarm; **2** sound made by it; **3** alarm; warning

to·day /tədā′/ [OF *tō dæg*] *adv* **1** on the present day; **2** at the present time || *n* **3** the present day; **4** this present time or age

tod·dle /tod′əl/ [?] *vi* **1** to go with short uncertain steps, like a young child || *n* **2** act of toddling; **3** toddling gait || **tod/dler** *n*

tod·dy /tod′ē/ [Hindi *tārī* palm juice] *n* (**-dies**) sweetened mixture of liquor and hot water

to-do /tədōō′/ *n colloq* ado, bustle, stir

toe /tō/ [OE *tā*] *n* **1** one of the digits of the foot; **2** forepart of the foot or of anything worn on it; **3** any of various things resembling a toe; **4 on one's toes** *colloq* alert, ready; **5 step on the toes of** to interfere in the province or jurisdiction of; to offend || *v* (**toed; toe·ing**) *vt* **6** to touch, reach, or strike with the toe; **7 toe the line**

to do what is expected; follow orders || *vi* **8** to stand or walk with the toes in a given position, as *to toe out*

toe/ dance/ *n* dance on the tips of the toes || **toe/-dance/** *vi* || **toe/ danc/er** *n*

toe/hold/ *n* **1** place to support the toes, as in climbing; **2** entering wedge or opening, which enables further progress; **3** wrestling hold in which the foot is twisted

toe/nail *n* **1** nail of a toe; **2** *carp* nail driven obliquely

tof·fee /tof′ē/ [?] *n Brit* taffy

to·ga /tōg′ə/ [L] *n* loose outer garment worn by the citizens of ancient Rome

to·geth·er /tōōgeth′ər, tə-/ [OE *tōgædere*] *adv* **1** in company or association; in the same place; **2** the one with the other; mutually; **3** in combination or conjunction, as *two pieces sewn together;* **4** without intermission, uninterruptedly; **5** at the same time, simultaneously; **6** considered collectively, as *all of them together have only ten dollars;* **7 get together, a** to meet; **b** to come to agreement

to·geth/er·ness *n* feeling of close unity within a group, family, etc., from being and acting together

tog/gle switch/ /tog′əl/ [?] *n* electric switch in which a projecting knob or lever is pushed to close or open the circuit, commonly used to turn lights on and off

To·go /tōg′ō/ *n* republic in W Africa on the Gulf of Guinea (1,724,000; 21,600 sq.m.; cap. Lomé) || **To·go·lese** /tō′gōlēz′, -lēs′/ *adj & n* (**-lese**)

togs /togz′/ [< *toga*] *npl* clothes

toil /toil′/ [AF *toiler* to strive, dispute] *vi* **1** to work arduously; **2** to move laboriously || *n* **3** exhausting labor || **toil/er** *n* || SYN *n* drudgery, work, exertion (see *labor*)

toi·let /toil′it/ [F *toilette* small cloth] *n* **1** act of dressing, arranging the hair, etc.; **2** bowl-shaped bathroom fixture containing water and a means of flushing it, used for defecating and urinating; **3** bathroom

toi/let bowl/ *n* ceramic bowl of a toilet

toi/let pa/per *n* soft, absorbent paper for cleansing after defecating and urinating

toi·lette /toilet′, twä-/ [F] *n* **1** act of dressing and grooming oneself; **2** dress, costume

toi/let wa/ter *n* scented liquid milder than a perfume

toils /toilz′/ [< MF *toile* web, cloth] *npl* entanglements, snares; difficulties

To·kay /tōkā′/ [town in Hungary] *n* **1** kind of large sweet white or purple grape; **2** sweet wine made from it

to·ken /tōk′ən/ [OE *tāc(e)n*] *n* **1** sign, symbol, or indication of something else; **2** memento, keepsake; **3** coinlike piece of metal issued at a fixed price and good for special purposes, as the payment of fares; **4** sign or portent; **5** **by the same token, a** for the same reason; **b** moreover, furthermore || *adj* **6** serving as a sample; **7** minimal; perfunctory || SYN mark, sign, guarantee, evidence (see *emblem*)

to'ken·ism /-/ *n* practice of acquiescing in a minimal way with the hope of placating one's opponents

To·ky·o /tōk'ē·ō'/ *n* capital of Japan (11,047,647)

told /tōld'/ **1** *pt* & *pp* of **tell** || *adj* **2** **all told** altogether

To·le·do /təlēd'ō/ *n* **1** city in W Ohio on Lake Erie (383,818); **2** city in central Spain on the Tagus (40,700); **3** sword or blade of the finest temper, originally made in Toledo, Spain

tol·er·a·ble /tol'ərəbəl/ [see **tolerate**] *adj* **1** endurable, supportable; **2** fairly good, passable || **tol'er·a·bly** *adv*

tol·er·ance /tol'ərəns/ [see **tolerant**] *n* **1** state or condition of being tolerant; **2** allowable variation from a standard, as of weight, dimension, etc.; **3** ability or capacity to endure or resist, as noise or the effects of a drug or poison

tol'er·ant /-ənt/ [L *tolerans* (*-antis*) enduring] *adj* willing or inclined to tolerate views different from one's own, or practices one does not approve of

tol'er·ate' [L *tolerare* (*-atus*)] *vt* **1** to suffer, put up with; **2** to permit; **3** *med* to withstand the effects or action of (a drug or poison) || **tol'er·a'tion** *n* || SYN endure, stand, suffer (see *allow*)

toll[1] /tōl'/ *n* **1** fee charged for some special use, as crossing a bridge or traveling on a highway; **2** charge for a long-distance telephone call; **3** extent of loss or damage, as *the storm took a heavy toll* || SYN custom, impost, assessment, tax, due

toll[2] *n* [ME *tollen* to pull] *vt* **1** to cause (a bell) to sound with slow, regular strokes; **2** to announce by such strokes, as a knell or the hour || *vi* **3** to emit a slow, regular, ringing sound, as a bell || *n* **4** sound of a ringing bell

toll'booth' *n* booth at the entrance or exit of a toll facility for the collection of tolls

toll' bridge' *n* bridge to cross which a toll must be paid

toll' call' *n* telephone call which costs more than a local call

toll'gate' *n* gate for stopping travel to collect tolls

Tol·stoy, Leo /tol'stoi, tōl'/ *n* (1828–1910) Russian novelist

tom /tom'/ [*Tom* < *Thomas*] *n* male of certain animals, as *tom turkey*

tom·a·hawk /tom'əhôk'/ [< Algonquian] *n* hatchet used by the North American Indians as a weapon or tool

to·ma·to /təmāt'ə, -mät'ō/ [Sp *tomate* < Nahuatl] *n* (**-toes**) **1** garden plant (*Lycopersicon esculentum*) bearing a usu. red pulpy and juicy fruit, highly regarded as food; **2** the fruit; **3** *slang* attractive girl or woman

tomb /tōōm'/ [AF *tumbe*] *n* **1** grave or vault for the dead; **2** monument erected to the memory of the dead

tom'boy' /tom'-/ *n* girl with boisterous boyish ways || **tom'boy'ish** *adj*

tomb'stone' /tōōm'-/ *n* stone marking a grave

tom'cat' /tom'-/ *n* **1** male cat || *vi* **2** *slang* to go looking for women in order to indulge in sexual intercourse

Tom' Col'lins /kol'inz/ [?] *n* iced and sweetened mixed drink made with gin, soda water, and lemon or lime juice

tome /tōm'/ [Gk *tomos* piece cut off] *n* **1** large heavy book; **2** one of several volumes of a single work

tom'fool' /tom'-/ *n* foolish or silly person || **tom'fool'er·y** *n* (**-ies**)

tom'my gun' /tom'ē/ *n* Thompson submachine gun

tom'my·rot' *n* utter nonsense

to·mor·row /təmor'ō, -môr'ō/ [OE *tō morgen*] *adv* **1** on the day following today; **2** at some future time || *n* **3** the day following today; **4** the future

Tom' Thumb' *n* **1** hero of many folk tales, who was no bigger than his father's thumb; **2** person of diminutive stature

tom'-tom' [Hindi *tamtam*] *n* primitive drum, used in the Orient and by American Indians

-to·my /-təmē/ [Gk *tomia*] *comb form* **1** cutting, removal, as *appendectomy*; **2** division, as *dichotomy*

ton /tun'/ [var of *tun*] *n* **1** also **short ton** unit of weight equal to 2,000 pounds; **2** *Brit* also **long ton** unit of weight equal to 2,240 pounds; **3** metric ton; **4** unit of the internal capacity of ships, equal to 100 cubic feet; **5** unit for measuring the displacement of ships, equal to 35 cubic feet of sea water; **6** also **tons** *pl colloq* a lot, a great quantity

ton·al /tōn'əl/ [< *tone*] *adj* pert. to tones or tonality

to·nal·i·ty /tōnal'itē/ *n* (**-ties**) **1** quality of tone; **2** *mus* quality of melodic and harmonic relationship in a composition; **3** *art* relation of the shades of color in a picture or design

tone /tōn'/ [Gk *tonos* tension, tone] *n* **1** sound or the quality of a sound; **2** characteristic of a sound as determined by its pitch; **3** the voice as expressive of feeling; **4** spirit, tenor, as *the severe tone of the letter*; **5** quality and harmony of the colors of a painting; **6** hue, tint, or shade; **7** normal or healthy condition of an organ or of the body; **8** musical pitch that in some languages distinguishes one word from another; **9** *mus* a one of the larger intervals in a diatonic scale; full step; **b** fundamental sound in a musical note as distinguished from the overtones ‖ *vt* **10** to give a desired tone to; **11** to improve the physical tone of; **12 tone down** to modify or make less intense

tone′ arm′ *n* free-swinging arm of a record player that holds the pickup and permits the needle to follow the groove of the record

tone′-deaf′ *adj* unable to distinguish differences in musical pitch

tone′ lan′guage *n* language, such as Chinese and Swedish, in which meaning is distinguished by pitch in words that are otherwise identical

tone′ po′em *n* composition for symphony orchestra in a single movement, based on the deeds and thoughts of a literary figure

tong /toŋ′, tôŋ′/ [Chin *t′ang* meeting hall] *n* Chinese-American fraternal society

Ton·ga /toŋ′gə/ *n* kingdom in the S Pacific consisting of a group of small islands NE of New Zealand (87,400; 269 sq.m.; cap. Nukualofa) ‖ **Ton′gan** *adj & n*

tongs /toŋz′, tôŋz′/ [< OE *tong*] *npl* any of various devices consisting of two arms connected by a hinge, pivot, or spring, for holding or grasping objects

tongue /tuŋ′/ [OE *tunge*] *n* **1** muscular organ in the mouth of most vertebrates, used in tasting, swallowing, and in man, for speech; **2** language or dialect; **3** manner of speaking; **4** speech, talk; **5** faculty of speaking; **6** anything resembling a tongue in shape, position, or use, as the strip of leather under the lacing of a shoe, the point of a flame, a projecting rib on the edge of a board for fitting into a groove, etc.; **7** tongue of an animal used for food; **8 hold one's tongue** to remain silent; **9 on the tip of one's tongue,** a just escaping one's memory; **b** about to be said; **10 slip of the tongue** something said by mistake ‖ *vt* **11** to join (two boards) by means of a tongue-and-groove joint; **12** *mus* to modify or change (notes or tones) by the use of the tongue, as in playing the flute ‖ SYN *n* speech, vernacular (see *language*)

tongue′-and-groove′ joint′ *n* joint between two boards in which a projecting rib on the edge of one fits into a groove on the edge of the other

tongue′-lash′ing *n* severe scolding ‖ **tongue′-lash′** *vt & vi*

tongue′-tied′ *adj* **1** unable to speak clearly because the connecting membrane beneath the tongue is abnormally short; **2** silent, as from amazement or embarrassment

tongue′ twist′er *n* word or group of words difficult to pronounce because of the alternation of certain sounds, as *she sells sea shells*

ton·ic /ton′ik/ [Gk *tonikos* pert. to tone] *adj* **1** of or pert. to tones; **2** bracing mentally or physically; **3** pert. to or marked by muscular tension; **4** restoring the normal physical tone; **5** *phonet* accented; **6** *mus* pert. to the harmony built upon the keynote ‖ *n* **7** anything that invigorates or restores; **8** *mus* keynote; **9** quinine water; **10** in Eastern New England, soft drink

to·night /tənīt′/ [OE *tō niht*] *adv* **1** on or during the present or coming night ‖ *n* **2** the night of the present day

ton·nage /tun′ij/ [< *ton*] *n* **1** weight of goods carried in a ship; **2** cubic capacity of a ship; **3** entire shipping of a port or country stated in tons

ton′o·graph′ /tōn′-/ [Gk *tonos* tension + -*graph*] *n* recording device for measuring tension, as of the eyeball ‖ **to·nog·ra·phy** /tənog′rəfē/ *n*

ton·sil /tons′əl/ [L *tonsillae* tonsils] *n* oval mass of lymphoid tissue on each side of the throat near the base of the tongue

ton·sil·lec·to·my /tons′əlek′təmē/ *n* (-mies) surgical removal of the tonsils

ton·sil·li·tis /tons′əlī′tis/ *n* inflammation of the tonsils

ton·so·ri·al /tonsôr′ē·əl, -sōr′-/ [< L *tonsorius*] *adj* pert. to a barber or his trade

ton·sure /tonsh′ər/ [L *tonsura* shearing] *n* **1** act of cutting the hair or of shaving the crown of the head, as for persons entering a monastery; **2** the part of the head left bare by such shaving ‖ *vt* **3** to subject to tonsure

ton·y /tōn′ē/ [*tone* + -*y*] *adj* (-i·er; -i·est) *slang* stylish; fashionable; aristocratic

too /tōō′/ [var of *to*] *adv* **1** more than enough, as *too long;* **2** also; in addition; **3** exceedingly; **4** indeed (used in emphatic contradictions), as *you are too*

took /tōōk′/ *pt* of **take**

tool /tōōl′/ [OE *tōl*] *n* **1** any instrument or implement used in doing work, esp. one that is hand-held, as a hammer or saw; **2** machine tool; **3** anything used as a means; **4** person employed as the agent of another; cat's-paw ‖ *vt* **5** to work or shape with a tool; **6** to ornament by impressing a design with tools; **7** *colloq* to drive (a vehicle) ‖ *vi* **8** *colloq* to drive or ride in a vehicle; **9 tool up** to install machinery for the manufacture of a particular item ‖ SYN *n* apparatus, appliance, mechanism, implement

toot /tōōt′/ [LG *tuten*] *vt* **1** to cause to sound, as a horn or whistle; **2** to sound (notes) on a horn or the like ‖ *vi* **3** to sound or blow a horn or whistle; **4** to sound like a horn or whistle ‖ *n* **5** act or sound of tooting ‖ **toot′er** *n*

tooth /tōōth′/ [OE *tōth*] *n* (**teeth**) **1** one of the hard bony structures set in the jaws of most vertebrates, used for biting and chewing; **2** any projection resembling a tooth, as on a gear wheel, a comb, or a saw; **3** taste or fondness; **4 by the skin of one's teeth** barely; **5 cut one's teeth on** to do or learn at an early age; **6 in the teeth of, a** straight into; **b** in defiance of; **7 put teeth into** to make effective, as a law

tooth′ and nail′ *adv* with all one's might

toothed /tōōtht′, tōōthd′/ *adj* **1** having teeth; **2** serrate

tooth′paste *n* paste for cleaning the teeth

tooth′pick′ *n* pointed piece of wood, plastic, etc., for cleaning the spaces between the teeth

tooth′ pow′der *n* powder for cleaning the teeth

tooth′some *adj* palatable or pleasing to the taste

tooth′y /-thē, -thē/ *adj* (**-i-er; -i-est**) having or showing conspicuous teeth

top¹ /top′/ [OE] *n* **1** highest part, summit; **2** upper surface, side, or part; **3** most important person, place, or rank, as *the top of his profession*; **4** crown of the head; **5** the part of a plant above the ground, as distinguished from edible roots; **6** utmost degree, highest point or pitch; **7** lid, cover, or cap; **8** *baseball* first half of an inning; **9 blow one's top** *slang* to lose one's temper; **10 on top** victorious; dominant; **11 on top of, a** on, upon; **b** in addition to; **c** in control of ‖ *v* (**topped; top·ping**) *vt* **12** to put a top on; **13** to reach the top of; **14** to leap over the top of; **15** to be a top for; **16** to excel, be better than; **17** to cut off the upper part of, as a tree; **18 top off** to climax, wind up ‖ *vi* **19. top off with** to finish with (something exceptional); **20 top out** to reach the highest point possible after which the only way to go is down ‖ *adj* **21** highest in location, degree, price, etc.; **22** capital; first-class

top² [OE] *n* child's cone-shaped toy, with a point on which it can be made to spin

to·paz /tō′paz/ [Gk] *n* **1** a basic aluminum silicate mineral, often used as a gem, varying in color from yellow to blue and green; **2** the yellow sapphire, a valuable precious stone

top′ bill′ing *n* **1** position of a star's name at the top of a theatrical bill; **2** prominence in advertising, news, public attention, and the like

top′coat′ *n* lightweight overcoat

top′-drawer′ *adj colloq* **1** of the highest social level; **2** of the highest excellence; first-rate

to·pee also **to·pi** /tōpē′, tō′-/ [Hindi = hat] *n* sun hat made of pith

To·pe·ka /təpēk′ə/ *n* capital of Kansas (120,000)

top·er /tōp′ər/ [< *obs* top to drink] *n* heavy drinker

top′flight′ *adj* outstanding; first-rate

top′ hat′ *n* man's tall black cylindrical hat worn with formal clothes

top′-heav′y *adj* **1** too heavy or bulky at the top; likely to topple; **2** overcapitalized

to·pi·ar·y /tōp′ē·er′ē/ [L *topiarius* of gardening] *adj* **1** (shrub or tree, as a box or yew) trimmed into odd or decorative shapes; **2** of or pert. to such trimming ‖ *n* (**-ies**) **3** topiary art or work; **4** plant trimmed by this art

top·ic /top′ik/ [< Gk (ta) *Topika* Topics (title of a work by Aristotle)] *n* subject of a discussion, discourse, composition, paragraph, etc.

top′i·cal *adj* pert. to matters of current or local interest

top′ kick′ *n slang* first sergeant

top′knot′ *n* tuft of hair, feathers, wool, or ribbons worn on top of the head

top′less *adj* **1** (woman's garment) without a part covering the breasts; **2** (woman) wearing such a garment; **3** (mountain) so high that its top cannot be seen

top′mast /-mast′, -mäst′; *naut* -məst/ *n* mast next above a lower mast

top′most *adj* highest, uppermost

top′notch′ *adj colloq* first-rate

to·pog·ra·phy /təpog′rəfē/ [Gk *topographia*] *n* (**-phies**) **1** surface features of a region or locality; **2** detailed description of such features; **3** science of representing such features on a map ‖ **to·pog′ra·pher** *n* ‖ **top·o·graph·ic** (**-i·cal**) /top′əgraf′ik(əl)/ *adj*

top′per *n* **1** one who or that which tops; **2** *colloq* top hat

top′ping *n* that which is put on the top of something, esp. a sauce or garnish over food

top·ple /top′əl/ [< *obs* top to tilt] *vi* **1** to fall forward, as from being topheavy; **2** to fall over, tumble down ‖ *vt* **3** to cause to topple; **4** to overthrow, as a government

top′ round′ *n* cut of beef from inside the round

tops *colloq adj* **1** highest; best; topmost ‖ *n* **2 the tops** the best or choicest of its kind

top′sail′ /-sāl′; *naut* -səl/ *n* sail next above the lowest sail on a mast

top′-se′cret *adj* pert. to or designating information of the greatest secrecy, to be divulged only to authorized persons

top′ ser′geant n colloq first sergeant

top′side′ adv naut up on deck

top′soil′ n upper or surface layer of soil

top·sy-tur·vy /top′sĕtur′vē/ [?] adj & adv 1 upside down; 2 in a reversed position; 3 in confusion and disorder

toque /tōk/ [F] n woman's close-fitting brimless hat

tor /tôr′/ [OE torr < Celt] n rocky pinnacle

-tor /-tər/ [L] s suf one who, as administrator

To·rah /tōr′ə, tôr′ə/ [Heb = instruction, law] n 1 the Pentateuch; 2 entire body of Jewish law

torch /tôrch′/ [OF torche] n 1 light made by burning pitchy wood or grease-soaked flax, etc.; 2 any of various portable devices giving out a hot flame; 3 source of enlightenment and learning, as the torch of civilization; 4 Brit flashlight; 5 carry a torch for slang to have unrequited love for

torch′bear′er n backer; leader; crusader

torch′ song′ n slow, melancholy popular song of unrequited love || **torch′ sing′er** n

tore /tôr′, tōr′/ pt of tear

tor·e·a·dor /tôr′ē-ədôr′/ [Sp] n bullfighter

tor′e·a·dor pants′ npl women's close-fitting slacks extending below the knees

tor·ment /tôr′ment/ [L tormentum rack] n 1 extreme pain or suffering; agony; 2 that which causes pain or anguish || /tôrment′/ vt 3 to put to extreme pain of mind or body; 4 to harass, annoy || **tor·men′tor** n

torn /tôrn′, tōrn′/ pp of tear

tor·na·do /tôrnād′ō/ [Sp] n (-does or -dos) violent and destructive rotary storm accompanied by a dark funnel-shaped cloud moving rapidly along a narrow path

To·ron·to /təront′ō/ n capital of Ontario (673,000)

tor·pe·do /tôrpēd′ō/ [L = electric ray; numbness] n (-does) 1 cigar-shaped projectile, self-propelled through the water, containing explosives to blow up enemy ships; 2 any of various underwater explosive devices; 3 signal cartridge placed on a railroad track to alert the crew of a passing train that an obstacle is ahead; 4 kind of fireworks which explodes when thrown against a hard surface; 5 slang gangster specializing in murder || vt 6 to damage or sink with torpedoes

tor·pe′do boat′ n small speedy war vessel equipped with torpedo tubes

tor·pe′do-boat′ de·stroy′er n large swift torpedo boat, equipped to pursue and destroy torpedo boats and submarines

tor·pe′do tube′ n tube from which torpedoes are launched

tor·pid /tôrp′id/ [L torpidus benumbed] adj 1 sluggish, inactive; 2 dormant; 3 dull, apathetic || **tor·pid′i·ty** /-pid′-/ n || syn dormant, numb, apathetic, inert, spiritless

tor·por /tôrp′ər/ [L = numbness] n torpid state or condition

torque /tôrk′/ [L torques twisted collar or necklace] n mech 1 force that tends to produce a rotating or twisting motion; 2 moment of a twisting force

torque′ con·vert′er n fluid coupling that transmits and regulates torque, as in automatic transmissions for automobiles

torque′ wrench′ n wrench with a dial showing the amount of torque applied

tor·rent /tôr′ənt, tor′-/ [L torrens (-entis) boiling stream] n 1 swift violent stream; 2 any similar violent flow, as of words or objects || **tor·ren·tial** /tôrensh′əl, tor-/ adj

tor·rid /tor′id, tôr′-/ [L torridus parched] adj 1 dried by the sun; arid; 2 hot, burning

Tor′rid Zone′ n the part of the earth on both sides of the equator between the tropics of Cancer and Capricorn

tor·sion /tôrsh′ən/ [< LL torsus twisted] n 1 act of twisting or state of being twisted; 2 force with which a twisted rod or wire tends to return to its previous position || **tor′sion·al** adj

tor·so /tôrs′ō/ [It = stalk, trunk of statue] n (-sos or -si/-sē/) 1 trunk of the human body; 2 sculpture representing this

tort /tôrt′/ [LL tortum wrong, injustice] n law any wrong, injury, or damage, not including breach of contract, for which a civil suit can be brought

tor·til·la /tôrtē′(y)ə/ [Sp] n round, thin, unleavened Mexican cake, made from corn meal and baked on a hot stone

tor·toise /tôrt′əs/ [ME tortuce < LL tortuca] n turtle, esp. one that lives on land

tor′toise shell′ n 1 mottled brown and yellow shell of the hawksbill turtle; 2 any synthetic substance resembling it || **tor′toise-shell′** adj

tor·tu·ous /tôrch′ŏŏ-əs/ [L tortuosus] adj 1 full of twists and turns; crooked; winding; 2 devious, not straightforward || **tor′tu·ous·ly** adv

tor·ture /tôrch′ər/ [LL tortura twisting, torment] n 1 act of inflicting extreme pain; 2 agony of mind or body || vt 3 to inflict torture on; 4 to twist from a normal position; 5 to pervert, distort || **tor′tur·er** n

to·ry /tôr′ē, tōr′ē/ [Ir toiridhe highwayman] n (-ries) 1 conservative person opposed to reform or change; 2 **Tory,** a American who remained loyal to the British king during the Revolution; b *Brit* member of the political party that after 1832 has been known as the Conservative party || **Tory** *adj*

toss /tôs/, tos// [< Scand] *vt* 1 to throw or pitch with an easy motion; 2 to lift or throw up quickly, as the head; 3 to put into violent motion, cause to rise and fall, as *tossed by the waves;* 4 to agitate, disturb; 5 to throw (a coin) into the air to determine heads or tails; 6 **toss off** to consume rapidly || *vi* 7 to roll about restlessly, as when trying to fall asleep; 8 to toss a coin || *n* 9 act of tossing || SYN *v* fling, lift, throw, jerk (see *cast*)

tossed′ sal′ad *n* salad of greens, etc., with dressing, mixed together in a large bowl

toss′pot′ *n* heavy drinker, drunkard

toss′up *n* 1 *colloq* even chance or choice; 2 tossing of a coin to determine heads or tails

tot[1] /tot′/ [*abbr* of *total*] *v* (**tot·ted; tot·ting**) *vt* **tot up** to total, add

tot[2] [?] *n* little child

to·tal /tōt′əl/ [ML *totalis*] *adj* 1 whole, not divided; 2 absolute; complete || *n* 3 whole sum or amount || *v* (-**taled** or -**talled; -tal·ing** or -**tal·ling**) *vt* 4 to find the sum of, add; 5 to add up to; 6 *slang* to wreck completely; demolish || *vi* 7 **total** to add up to || **to′tal·ly** *adv* || SYN *n* aggregate, sum, whole, entirety, mass

to·tal·i·tar·i·an /tōtal′iter′ē·ən/ *adj* 1 of or pert. to a government exercising complete control over the lives of its citizens and brooking no dissent || *n* 2 adherent of such a government || **to·tal′i·tar′i·an·ism** *n*

to·tal·i·ty /tōtal′itē/ *n* (-**ties**) 1 wholeness; 2 total amount

to·tal·i·za·tor /tōt′əlizāt′ər/ *n* machine that records and totals all bets made in parimutuel betting

to′tal re·call′ *n* 1 recall of all the details of a story; 2 *colloq* recital of a story with inclusion of irrelevant details

tote /tōt/ [Afr] *vt colloq* 1 to carry, transport; 2 to haul

tote′ board′ *n colloq* totalizator

to·tem /tōt′əm/ [< Algonquian] *n* 1 animal or object conceived as the emblem of a tribe or clan; 2 carved or painted representation of this || **to·tem′ic** /-tem′ik/ *adj*

to′tem pole′ *n* post containing carved or painted totemic figures, such as those erected by the Indians of NW North America

tot·ter /tot′ər/ [ME *toteren*] *vi* 1 to shake as if about to fall; 2 to be unsteady on the feet, stagger || *n* 3 act of tottering; 4 tottering gait

tou·can /tōō′kan, tōōkän′/ [F < Port *tucano*] *n* any of a family (Rhamphastidae) of fruit-eating birds of tropical America, with enormous pointed beaks and brilliant plumage

touch /tuch′/ [OF *tochier* to knock, strike] *vt* 1 to come into contact with; 2 to extend the hand or an object so as to come into contact with; 3 to lay a hand on; 4 to have to do with; 5 to perceive by feeling; 6 to bring into contact; 7 to concern, affect; 8 to refer or relate to; 9 to reach, attain; 10 to affect the senses or feelings of; soften; 11 to affect to a slight extent; 12 to strike lightly; 13 to take a portion of, taste; 14 to impress, affect; 15 *geom* to be tangent to; 16 *slang* to apply and get money from; 17 to equal or compare with; 18 to stop at, as a ship; 19 to border on; 20 **touch up** to improve (a painting, photograph, *etc*), as by adding small strokes || *vi* 21 to be in contact; 22 **touch at** to call at (a port); 23 **touch down** (of aircraft) to land; 24 **touch on** or **upon,** a to mention briefly or in passing; b to verge on || *n* 25 act or state of touching or state of being touched; 26 sensation of touching or being touched; 27 sense of feeling; 28 manner of execution, as in painting or playing a musical instrument; 29 knack or skill; 30 distinguishing trait; 31 *slang* act of applying to and getting money from someone; 32 single stroke on a painting, drawing, or the like; 33 slight amount, dash; 34 suggestion, trace; 35 **put the touch on** *colloq* to apply to for money

touch′ and go′ *n* precarious situation || **touch′-and-go′** *adj*

touch′back′ *n football* grounding of the ball by a player behind his own goal line, provided the impetus which sent it across was given by an opponent

touch′down′ *n football* 1 act of carrying the ball to a position on or behind the opponents′ goal line; 2 the six points scored by so doing

tou·ché /tōōshā′/ [F = touched] *interj* 1 *fencing* expression indicating a hit; 2 expression indicating that a telling remark or reply has been made

touched′ *adj* 1 deeply moved; 2 a bit crazy

touch′hole′ *n* hole at the breech of old-time firearms through which the powder was ignited

touch′ing *adj* affecting; pathetic

touch′stone′ *n* 1 kind of black stone used for testing the fineness of gold and silver by rubbing; 2 any standard for testing quality

touch′ sys′tem *n* system of typing in which the typist uses all ten fingers and can strike any desired key without looking at the keyboard

touch'-type' *vt* & *vi* to typewrite using the touch system

touch'y [var of *tetchy* < *tetched*] *adj* (**-i·er**; **-i·est**) 1 supersensitive; easily offended; 2 precarious, requiring caution ‖ SYN testy, fractious, peevish, irritable

tough /tuf'/ [OE *toh*] *adj* 1 standing great strain without tearing or breaking; 2 hard to chew; 3 able to endure hardship or strain; 4 strong; firm; 5 hard to influence, stubborn; 6 difficult, hard to solve; 7 hard to bear; 8 rough, vicious ‖ *n* 9 ruffian, rowdy ‖ **tough'ness** *n*

tough'en *vt* 1 to make tough ‖ *vi* 2 to become tough

tou·pee /tōōpā', -pē'/ [F *toupet* tuft of hair] *n* small wig

tour /tōōr'/ [MF] *n* 1 long journey, esp. one covering the chief sights of a region or country; 2 circuit, as of inspection; 3 period, shift, as of work or duty; 4 extended journey from town to town, as of a band or theatrical company ‖ *vi* 5 to go on a tour ‖ *vt* 6 to go on a tour through

tour' de force' /də/ [F = feat of strength] *n* feat of unusual strength or skill of execution

tour·ist *n* 1 one who goes on a tour for rest, recreation, or sightseeing ‖ *adv* 2 tourist-class

tour·ist class' *n* least costly class of accommodations on ships and planes ‖ **tour·ist-class'** *adj* & *adv*

tour·ist trap' *n* hotel, shop, restaurant, etc., located at a place frequented by tourists, which charges them much more than natives pay for similar accommodations

tour·na·ment /tōōrn'əmənt, turn'-/ [OF *tornelement*] *n* 1 contest or series of contests between knights carrying blunt lances and swords; 2 any meeting for a trial of skill; 3 series of contests to determine a championship

tour·ney /turn'ē, tōōrn'ē/ [OF *torneier* to take part in a tourney] *n* tournament

tour·ni·quet /turn'ikit, tōōrn'-/ [F] *n* device for compressing a blood vessel to stop bleeding, as a bandage twisted tight by a stick

tour' of du'ty *n* period of service on some assignment

tou·sle /touz'əl/ [< ME *tusen* to pull] *vt* 1 to pull about roughly; 2 to disorder, dishevel

tout /tout'/ [OE *tōtian* to peep out] *colloq vi* 1 to canvass importunately, as for customers; 2 *horse racing* to be, or act as, a tout ‖ *vt* 3 to praise or recommend; boom; 4 to solicit importunately for; 5 to supply the name of (the purported winner) in a horse race, esp. for a fee ‖ *n* 6 one who solicits business importunately; 7 one who makes a living by touting horses

to·va·rich /tōvär'ish/ [Russ *tovarishch*] *n* comrade (title of address used by Russian Communists)

tow[1] /tō'/ [OE *tōgian* to drag] *vt* 1 to pull or drag by a rope or line ‖ *n* 2 act of towing or state of being towed; 3 anything towed; 4 towline; 5 **in tow**, a being towed; b in one's charge; c in one's company

tow[2] [ME] *n* the short coarse part of flax or hemp

tow·age *n* 1 act of towing; 2 charge for towing

to·ward or **to·wards** /tôrd(z)', tōrd(z)', təwôrd(z)'/ [OE *tōweardes*] *prep* 1 in the direction of; 2 with respect to, regarding; 3 near to, close to; 4 with a view to, for; contributing to

tow·el /tou'əl/ [OF *toaille*] *n* 1 cloth or absorbent paper for drying wet objects, as dishes or the body; 2 **throw in the towel** *slang* to concede defeat ‖ *v* (**-eled** or **-elled**; **-el·ing** or **-el·ling**) *vt* 3 to rub or dry with a towel

tow·el·ing or **tow·el·ling** *n* material from which towels are made

tow·er /tou'ər/ [OF *tur*] *n* 1 high structure rising above its surroundings, either standing alone or attached to a building; 2 such a structure used as a citadel or fortress; 3 anything resembling a tower ‖ *vi* 4 to rise to a great height; 5 to surpass all others

tow·er·ing *adj* 1 very high; lofty; 2 extraordinary; 3 extreme; violent

tow·er·man /-mən/ *n* (**-men** /-mən/) 1 man who works in a railroad switch tower and controls the movement of cars and trains; 2 man who works in the control tower of an airport and controls the landing and take-off of airplanes

tow·head' /tō'-/ *n* 1 head of very light-colored hair; 2 person with such hair ‖ **tow·head·ed** *adj*

tow·line' *n* line or rope used for towing

town /toun'/ [OE *tūn* enclosed place, town] *n* 1 municipality larger than a village but smaller than a city; 2 city; 3 township; 4 built-up area as contrasted with open country; 5 business center of a city; 6 **go to town** *slang* to act with speed and efficiency; 7 **on the town** on public welfare; 8 **out of town** away from one's home town or city; 9 **out on the town** *slang* making the rounds of bars and night clubs in search of entertainment; 10 **paint the town red** *slang* to carouse, make merry

town' hall' *n* public building belonging to a town, containing public offices and used for meetings of the town council, etc.

town' house' *n* 1 house in the city, not one in the country; 2 more or less pretentious house in the city; 3 row house

town′ meet′ing *n* meeting of the voters or of the citizens of a town, esp. as practiced in New England

town′ship′ *n* 1 administrative division of a county; 2 division of land six miles square, divided into 36 sections

towns′man /-mən/ *n* (-men /-mən/) 1 inhabitant of a town; 2 inhabitant of one's own town or city; 3 *New England* selectman

towns′peo′ple *npl* the people living in a town

tow′path′ /tō′-/ *n* path beside a canal or river, for use in towing boats

tox·e·mi·a /toksēm′ē·ə/ [< *toxic* + *-emia*] *n* blood poisoning caused by toxins in the bloodstream || **tox·e′mic** *adj*

tox·ic /tok′sik/ [< Gk *toxikon* (pharmakon) bow (poison), i.e., poison for arrows] *adj* 1 pert. to, affected with, or caused by toxins; 2 poisonous || **tox·ic′i·ty** /-sis′itē/ *n*

tox·i·col·o·gy *n* science of poisons, their detection, effects, and antidotes || **tox′i·col′o·gist** *n*

tox·in /tok′sin/ [see **toxic**] *n* 1 poisonous protein substance produced in animal and vegetable tissue; 2 poison produced by specific microorganisms and causing various diseases

toy /toi′/ [ME *toye* dalliance] *n* 1 child's plaything; 2 thing very small of its kind; 3 something of no real value; bauble || *vi* 4 **toy with**, a to play with; b to trifle with || *adj* 5 of the nature of a toy or plaything, as *a toy house, toy soldier*; 6 tiny; small of its kind, as *toy dog*

tr. 1 trace; 2 transitive; 3 translated; 4 translation

trace¹ /trās′/ [OF *trais pl* of *trait* act of drawing] *n* 1 either of the side straps connecting the harness with a vehicle; 2 **kick over the traces** to assert one's independence

trace² [MF *tracier*] *vt* 1 to draw or sketch; 2 to copy by following the lines of, as on transparent paper placed over the original; 3 to chart, map out; 4 to follow the history and development of; 5 to determine the source of; 6 to follow, as by tracks or vestiges; 7 to pursue one's way along, as *to trace a path* || *n* 8 mark, indication, or sign left by something that has passed away or disappeared; 9 track left by a passing person, animal, or thing; 10 mark or record made by a recording instrument; 11 barely discernible amount or indication of something || **trace′a·ble** *adj*

trac′er *n* 1 one who or that which traces; 2 one whose business is locating lost persons, packages, or property; 3 inquiry sent out for the recovery of lost letters, packages, etc.; 4 chemical added to ammunition to cause it to trail smoke and fire when fired, for the purpose of making its path visible; 5 substance, generally radioactive, whose presence or path can be traced in a biological, chemical, or physical system

trac′er bul′let *n* bullet containing a tracer

trac′er·y *n* (-ies) ornamental work of interlaced lines, as in windows or embroidery

tra·che·a /trāk′ē·ə/ [Gk *tracheia*] *n* (-ae /-ē′/) tube that conveys air from the larynx to the lungs || **tra′che·al** *adj*

tra·che·ot·o·my /-ot′əmē/ *n* (-mies) *surg* the cutting of an opening into the trachea to allow breathing when the natural opening has become closed due to disease or accident

tra·cho·ma /trəkōm′ə/ [Gk = roughness] *n* contagious inflammation of the eyelids and cornea

trac′ing *n* 1 that which is traced, as a drawing made by marking on a transparent sheet placed over the original; 2 graphic record made by a recording instrument such as a seismograph

trac′ing pa′per *n* thin transparent paper used for tracing

track /trak′/ [MF *trac*] *n* 1 mark or impression left by anything that has passed, as by the foot or a wheel; 2 beaten path; 3 set of parallel metal rails for cars or trains to run upon; 4 tread of a caterpillar tractor; 5 course laid out for racing; 6 part of a film or tape that provides the path for the recording; 7 path or line of motion; 8 sports performed on a track, as running and jumping; 9 **in one's tracks** *colloq* where one is standing at the moment; 10 **keep track of** to keep informed about; 11 **lose track of** to lose contact with; 12 **off the track** astray; 13 **on the track of** in pursuit of; 14 **on the right side of the tracks** in the wealthy part of the community; 15 **on the wrong side of the tracks** in the poor part of the community || *vt* 16 to follow the track of; 17 to observe and record with scientific instruments the passage of (a missile or spacecraft); 18 to leave a track of (mud, dirt, etc.), as on a carpet; 19 **track down** to catch by tracking || **track′er** *n*

track′age /-ij/ *n* 1 extent or amount of railroad tracks; 2 right to use the tracks of another railroad

track′ing sta′tion *n* radio or radar station whose function is to follow the flight path of and maintain contact with a rocket or satellite

track′less trol′ley *n* trolley bus

track′ meet′ *n* series of track sports, as running and jumping

track′walk′er *n* person employed to walk along railroad tracks to inspect them

tract¹ /trakt′/ [L *tractatus*] *n* short

pamphlet, usu. on some moral or religious subject

tract² [L *tractus* extent of space or time] *n* 1 expanse or area of land; 2 *anat* system of related organs, or the region in which they are situated, as *the digestive tract*

trac'ta·ble [L *tractabilis*] *adj* 1 docile; easily managed; 2 easily worked; malleable ‖ **trac'ta·bil'i·ty** /-bil'-/ *n*

trac·tion /trak'shən/ [ML *tractio* (-*onis*) drawing] *n* 1 act of drawing or pulling, or state of being drawn; 2 adhesive friction, as of a body moving over a surface; 3 *med* pulling of a muscle or limb, as by weights, for therapeutic reasons

trac·tor /trak'tər/ [ML = that which pulls] *n* 1 powerful motor-driven vehicle for pulling farm machinery, etc.; 2 short truck consisting of a powerful engine and a driver's cab, for hauling trailers

trac'tor truck' *n* tractor 2

trade /trād'/ [MLG = track, course] *n* 1 occupation, business; 2 skilled craft; 3 buying and selling; commerce; 4 persons collectively engaged in a particular business; 5 exchange, swap; 6 purchase or sale; 7 a field of business; 8 customers, clientele ‖ *vi* 9 to carry on a trade; 10 to swap; 11 to traffic; 12 to shop; 13 trade on to exploit ‖ *vt* 14 to exchange; 15 trade in to give (a used article) as part payment toward the purchase of a new one ‖ SYN *n* (see *business*); *v* sell, barter, bargain ‖ DISCR The idea of exchange underlies any buying or selling, but we buy and *sell* for a price, dispose of a thing for money. When we *barter* we exchange the goods or commodity which we have for the actual goods or commodity that the other person has. *Trade* is used of the regular interchange of goods in the general business of buying and selling; it is also used, like *barter*, of an exchange of object for object, or article for article. Farmers drive in to near-by cities to *trade*; that is, to do business on a money basis. People *trade* one piece of land for another

trade' book' *n* any book other than a textbook or a reference book

trade'-in' *n* 1 used article given as part payment on a new purchase; 2 deal involving such an article ‖ *adj* 3 (value, price, conditions, terms) of such an article or such a deal

trade'mark' *n* 1 word, symbol, or device registered and protected by law, used by a merchant or manufacturer to distinguish his goods ‖ *vt* 2 to register the trademark of

trade' name' *n* 1 name generally used for some article; 2 official name of a firm

trad'er *n* 1 one engaged in trade; 2 one who barters or exchanges goods,

as *a fur trader;* 3 vessel engaged in commerce

trade' school' *n* school where various skilled trades are taught

trades'man /-mən/ *n* (-men /-mən/) man engaged in buying and selling

trade' un'ion *n* labor union of workers in a particular craft ‖ **trade' un'ion·ist** *n*

trade' wind' *n* wind in or near the tropics that blows steadily toward the equator from an easterly direction

trad'ing post' *n* 1 station for carrying on business in a thinly settled territory, mostly by barter; 2 station on the floor of a stock exchange at which a particular stock is traded

trad'ing stamp' *n* stamp given with a purchase and exchangeable for various articles when a certain number is accumulated

tra·di·tion /trədish'ən/ [L *traditio* (-*onis*) handing down] *n* 1 the oral handing down of information, opinions, doctrines, practices, etc. through successive generations; 2 that which is so handed down

tra·di'tion·al *adj* 1 of or pert. to tradition; 2 handed down by or in accordance with tradition

tra·duce /trəd(y)ōōs'/ [L *traducere* to lead across] *vt* to defame, slander ‖ **tra·duc'er** *n*

Tra·fal·gar, Cape /trəfal'gər/ *n* cape in SW Spain at entrance to Strait of Gibraltar, scene of British naval victory over French and Spanish fleets 1805

traf·fic /traf'ik/ [It *traffico*] *n* 1 trade, commerce; 2 business done by a railway or other carrier in transporting passengers or freight; 3 movement or number of vehicles, ships, planes, etc., in or through a given area, street, airport, etc.; 4 dealings; intercourse ‖ *v* (-**ficked; -fick·ing**) *vi* 5 to carry on traffic or trade; 6 traffic in to deal in (something, usu. base or illegal) ‖ **traf'fick·er** *n*

traf'fic cir'cle *n* circle at the intersection of two or more roads, into which all traffic feeds, to expedite the passage of vehicles from one road to another

traf'fic jam' *n* congestion of automobile traffic

traf'fic light' *n* set of signal lights at an intersection to control traffic

tra·ge·di·an /trəjēd'ē·ən/ *n* 1 writer of tragedy; 2 man noted for his acting in tragedies

tra·ge'di·enne' /-en'/ *n* actress noted for her acting in tragedies

trag·e·dy /traj'idē/ [Gk *tragoidia*] *n* (-**dies**) 1 serious drama in which the protagonist is brought to catastrophe, usu. because of a tragic flaw; 2 any literary work of a similar type; 3 disastrous event, calamity

trag·ic /traj'ik/ also **trag·i·cal** [Gk *trag-*

ikos] *adj* 1 pert. to or like tragedy; 2 distressingly sad; disastrous; fatal ‖ **trag′i·cal·ly** *adv* ‖ SYN sad, mournful, catastrophic, calamitous

trag′ic flaw′ *n* defect in the character of the protagonist of a tragedy that leads to his downfall

trag′i·com′e·dy *n* (**-dies**) 1 play that combines tragic and comic scenes and does not have a fatal ending; 2 happening which has both tragic and comic elements

trail /trāl′/ [ME *trallen*] *vt* 1 to draw or drag along behind; 2 to follow by tracking; 3 *mil* to carry (a rifle) grasped near the middle by the right hand with the barrel tilted upward; 4 to follow or be behind ‖ *vi* 5 to fall or hang down, or extend behind; 6 to grow at some length, as a vine; 7 to stream behind, as sparks or smoke; 8 to lag behind, straggle; 9 to be behind in a race or contest; 10 to follow behind; 11 to go along in leisurely fashion; 12 **trail off** or **away** to dwindle, as a sound ‖ *n* 13 tracks left by a person, animal, or thing; 14 path or track through a wilderness; 15 anything drawn out in the wake of something

trail′blaz′er *n* 1 one who discovers or opens a way through or to a place; 2 one who discovers or invents a solution to a problem or leads in any undertaking

trail′er *n* 1 one who or that which trails; 2 large freight van with wheels only at the rear, attached to and drawn by a tractor truck; 3 vehicle with living accommodations designed to be drawn by an automobile; 4 *motion pictures* short film containing scenes from a forthcoming attraction

trail′ing ar·bu′tus *n* arbutus 2

train /trān′/ [MF *trainer* to draw, drag] *n* 1 something drawn or dragged behind; 2 the trailing part in certain dresses; 3 connected line of railroad cars; 4 retinue of servants; 5 company or procession of vehicles, animals, etc.; 6 line of men, vehicles, etc., for transporting the supplies of an army; 7 series of connected things, as *a train of ideas*; 8 *mach* series of connected wheels or other parts transmitting motion; 9 series or succession of things or events ‖ *vt* 10 to instruct by practice; drill; discipline; 11 to discipline or tame for use, as an animal; 12 to make fit for athletic contests or horse racing; 13 to direct the growth of, as a plant; 14 to aim or point, as a gun ‖ *vi* 15 to undergo training, as in preparation for athletic contests ‖ **train′er** *n* ‖ **train·ee′** *n* ‖ **train′ing** *n*

train′man /-mən/ *n* (**-men** /-mən/) member of a train crew subordinate to the conductor

traipse /trāps′/ [?] *vi colloq* to walk or tramp along; wander idly

trait /trāt′/ [MF] *n* distinguishing characteristic ‖ SYN feature, quality (see *characteristic*)

trai′tor /trāt′ər/ [OF *traitur*] *n* 1 one guilty of treason; 2 one who betrays a cause, a person, or a trust ‖ **trai′tress** *nfem* ‖ **trai′tor·ous** *adj*

tra·jec·to·ry /trəjek′tərē/ [< L *trajectus* cast, thrown over] *n* (**-ries**) 1 curve described by a body moving through space, esp. that of a missile or projectile; 2 *geom* curve or surface that cuts all the curves or surfaces of a given system at a fixed angle

tram /tram′/ [MFlem = shaft of a cart] *n Brit* streetcar

tram·mel /tram′əl/ [MF *tramail* fishnet] *v* (**-meled** or **-melled; -mel·ing** or **-mel·ling**) *vt* 1 to hamper, hinder, restrain ‖ *n* 2 **trammels** *pl* that which hampers; hindrance, restraint

tramp /tramp′/ [ME *trampen* to stamp] *vt* 1 to step on forcibly; 2 to travel over on foot ‖ *vi* 3 to wander on foot; 4 to walk with a heavy step; 5 to walk or march steadily ‖ *n* 6 hobo, vagrant; 7 journey on foot; hike; 8 sound of steady marching; 9 tramp steamer; 10 woman of loose morals

tram·ple /tramp′əl/ [ME *trampelen* to stamp] *vt* 1 to tread under the feet; tread heavily on ‖ *vi* 2 **trample on**, to tread heavily or roughly on; b to ride roughshod over ‖ *n* 3 act or sound of trampling

tram·po·line /tramp′əlēn/ [It *trampolino* springboard] *n* canvas sheet stretched taut, used by acrobats as a springboard for tumbling

tramp′ steam′er *n* freighter without a regular schedule which takes cargo when opportunity offers

trance /trans′, träns′/ [MF *transe*] *n* 1 state of consciousness between sleeping and waking; 2 state of deep absorption; 3 state in which a medium's body is said to be entered by the spirit of a dead person; 4 state of unconsciousness brought on by catalepsy or hypnosis; 5 daze, stupor

tran·quil /traŋk′wil/ [L *tranquillus*] *adj* 1 placid; unruffled, as *a tranquil mind;* 2 undisturbed; peaceful, as *a tranquil country place;* 3 steady, unwavering ‖ **tran′quil·ly** *adv* ‖ **tran·quil′li·ty** *n* ‖ SYN quiet, composed, serene (see *calm*)

tran′quil·ize or **tran′quil·lize** *vt* 1 to make tranquil ‖ *vi* 2 to become tranquil ‖ SYN soothe, calm, appease, allay, compose, pacify ‖ ANT arouse, irritate, excite, disturb, alarm

tran′quil·iz′er *n* drug that calms, soothes, and tranquilizes

trans- [L] *pref* across; over; beyond; through; as *trans-Mississippi*

trans·act /transakt′, -zakt′/ [L *transigere* (-*actus*) to drive through, accomplish] *vt* to conduct or manage, as business; to carry through to a conclusion ‖ **trans·ac'tor** *n*

trans·ac'tion *n* 1 act, fact, or instance of transacting; 2 that which is transacted, as a business deal; 3 **trans·ac'-tions** published report of the speeches and other proceedings of the meeting of an organization ‖ SYN action, process, proceeding, deed, business

trans·al'pine /trans-, tranz-/ *adj* 1 on the other side of the Alps, esp. from Italy; 2 passing across or through the Alps

trans·at·lan'tic /trans-, tranz-/ *adj* 1 beyond the Atlantic; 2 crossing the Atlantic

trans·ceiv·er /transē'vər/ *n* unit consisting of a radio transmitter and receiver

tran·scend /transend'/ [L *transcendere* to surmount] *vt* 1 to rise above; exceed, go beyond; 2 to excel, surpass

tran·scend'ent /-ənt/ *adj* 1 that transcends or goes beyond; 2 of surpassing excellence; supreme; 3 outside the limits of human knowledge

tran'scen·den'tal /-dent'əl/ *adj* 1 supernatural; 2 metaphysical; abstract; 3 beyond the realm of experience or of sense impressions; 4 existing not as a material object, but as a subjective ideal

tran'scen·den'tal·ism *n* any philosophy which bases knowledge on a spiritual intuition of reality beyond the realm of material experience ‖ **tran'scen·den'tal·ist** *n*

trans·con'ti·nen'tal /trans-/ *adj* extending across a continent

tran·scribe /transkrīb'/ [L *transcribere* to copy] *vt* 1 to make a written or typewritten copy of, as shorthand notes; 2 to arrange (music) for an instrument or voice other than that for which it was originally intended; 3 to write out in another language or alphabet; 4 to represent (speech sounds) in phonetic or phonemic symbols; 5 *radio & telv* to make a recording of

tran'script *n* 1 copy, esp. one written or typewritten; 2 something transcribed; 3 official copy, as of court proceedings; 4 official academic record of courses, credits, and grades of a student

tran·scrip'tion *n* 1 act of transcribing; 2 transcript; 3 recording of a radio or television program

trans·duc·er /transd(y)ōōs'ər/ *n* device, as a photoelectric cell, that receives energy in one form and retransmits it in the same or another form

tran·sept /tran'sept/ [*trans-* + L *septum* enclosure] *n* 1 the part of a cruciform church perpendicular to the nave; 2 arm of this on each side of the central aisle

trans·fer /trans'fər, transfur'/ [L *transferre*] *v* (-ferred; -fer·ring) *vt* 1 to convey, carry, or send from one person or place to another; 2 to convey (a design) from one surface to another; 3 *law* to convey to another, as a right or title ‖ *vi* 4 to proceed on a journey by changing from one conveyance to another; 5 to move from one place, situation, job, or school, to another ‖ /trans'fər/ *n* 6 act of transferring or state of being transferred; 7 one who is transferred; 8 design that is or can be transferred; 9 ticket permitting a passenger to transfer to another conveyance; 10 *law* conveyance and delivery of a right, title, property, etc. ‖ **trans·fer'-a·ble** *adj* ‖ **trans·fer'ence** *n* ‖ SYN *v* sell, give, change, move, shift, transport, transmit ‖ ANT *v* keep, retain, preserve

trans·fig'u·ra'tion /trans-/ *n* 1 act of transfiguring or state of being transfigured; 2 **the Transfiguration,** a the supernatural change in the appearance of Christ on the mount (Matt. 17:2); b the church festival on August 6 solemnizing this event

trans·fig'ure [L *transfigurare* to change in shape] *vt* 1 to change the outward form or appearance of; 2 to transform or exalt into something impressive and glorious

trans·fix' /trans-/ [L *transfigere* (-*fixus*)] *vt* 1 to pierce through as with a pointed weapon; impale; 2 to hold or render motionless, as if pierced through

trans·form' /trans-/ [L *transformare*] *vt* 1 to change the shape or appearance of; 2 to change the character, substance, or function of; 3 *math* to change the form of (a figure or expression) without changing the value; 4 *elec* to change (a current) from higher to lower voltage or vice versa

trans'for·ma'tion *n* 1 act of transforming or state of being transformed; 2 woman's wig or hairpiece

trans·form'er *n* device that raises or lowers the voltage of an electric current

trans·fuse /transfyōōz'/ [L *transfundere* (-*fusus*) to pour] *vt* 1 to transmit; impart; instill, as a desire for knowledge; 2 *med* to transfer (blood) from the blood vessels of one person or animal to those of another ‖ **trans·fu'sion** /-zhən/ *n*

trans·gress /transgres', tranz-/ [L *transgradi* (-*gressus*) to step across] *vi* 1 to break a law, rule, commandment, etc.; sin ‖ *vt* 2 to break, sin against, or violate, as a law; 3 to pass or go beyond, as a limit ‖ **trans·gres'sor** *n* ‖ **trans·gres'sion** /-shən/ *n*

tran·sient /transh'ənt/ [L *transiens* (-*entis*) going across] *adj* 1 transitory, not permanent; 2 fleeting, brief;

hasty; **3** staying temporarily, as hotel guests ‖ *n* **4** transient person, esp. a temporary lodger ‖ **tran′sience** or **tran′sien·cy** *n* ‖ SYN *adj* fleeting, passing, fugitive (see *transitory*)

tran·sis·tor /tranzĭs′tər/ [*trans-* + *re·sistor*] *n* **1** tiny electronic device, made of a semiconductor, that performs many of the functions of a vacuum tube with but a fraction of the size, power requirement, and heat; **2** radio equipped with transistors

tran·sis′tor·ize′ *vt* to equip with transistors

tran·sit /trans′ĭt/ [L *transitus* a crossing] *n* **1** passage through or over; **2** conveyance; transportation; **3** *astron* **a** passage of a celestial body across the meridian of a given place; **b** passage of a smaller body across the disk of a larger one, as of Venus across the disk of the sun; **4** *surveying* instrument for measuring horizontal angles; **5 in transit** in passage; on the way ‖ *vt* **6** *astron* to cross (a meridian, the disk of the sun, etc.)

tran·si·tion /tranzĭsh′ən, -sĭsh′-/ [L *transitio (-onis)*] *n* **1** passage from one place, period, state, or condition to another; change; **2** *mus* abrupt change from one key to another ‖ **tran·si′tion·al** *adj*

tran·si·tive /trans′ĭtĭv/ [LL *transitivus*] *adj* **1** (verb) accompanied by a direct object and that can have a passive form ‖ *n* **2** transitive verb

tran·si·to·ry /trans′ĭtôr′ē, -tōr′-/ [MF *transitoire*] *adj* of brief duration; not lasting; fleeting ‖ SYN transient, evanescent, ephemeral ‖ DISCR *Transient* and *transitory* alike describe that which is not permanent, as a *transient* feeling; the *transitory* griefs of childhood. *Transient* is used especially of things that are of momentary duration, as a *transient* glance, thought, gleam; *transitory* is applied more to those things that in their perishable nature cannot last, must pass on, as all life on earth is *transitory;* modes and fashions are *transitory.* *Ephemeral* also connotes short life, perishability, and brief duration; a fleeting dream is *ephemeral;* the word connotes a lack of substantiality as well as brevity. The flower that lasts but a day has an *ephemeral* existence; the "books of the hour," as Ruskin defines them, enjoy an *ephemeral* vogue. That is *evanescent* which fades quickly, or seems to disappear while one is looking at it, as an *evanescent* impression, vision ‖ ANT lasting, permanent, enduring, eternal

trans·late /translāt′/ [L *translatus* transferred] *vt* **1** to change from one place, state, condition, or form to another; **2** to express (writing or speech) in a different language; **3** to interpret in different words ‖ **trans·la′tor** *n*

trans·la·tion /-shən/ *n* **1** act of translating or state of being translated; **2** translated version of a writing

trans·lit·er·ate /translĭt′ərāt′, tranz-/ [*trans-* + L *lit(t)era* letter] *vt* to write (letters or words) in the characters of a different alphabet ‖ **trans·lit′er·a′tion** /-shən/ *n*

trans·lu·cent /translōōs′ənt/ [L *translucens (-entis)* shining through] *adj* allowing light to pass through but not transparent, so that objects on the other side are seen indistinctly ‖ **trans·lu′cence** *n* ‖ SYN semitransparent (see *transparent*)

trans·mi·grate /transmī′grāt, tranz-/ [L *transmigrare (-atus)*] *vi* **1** to move from one place to another; migrate; **2** to pass at death into another body, said of the soul ‖ **trans′mi·gra′tion** *n*

trans·mis·si·ble /transmĭs′ĭbəl/ [< L *transmissus* transmitted] *adj* capable of being transmitted

trans·mis·sion /transmĭsh′ən/ *n* **1** act or fact of being transmitted; **2** that which is transmitted; **3** mechanism for transmitting power from an engine to the driving axle, usu. by changing torque and speed by means of gears; **4** broadcasting by means of electromagnetic waves

trans·mit /transmĭt′/ [L *transmittere*] *v* (**-mit·ted; -mit·ting**) *vt* **1** to send, dispatch; convey; **2** to pass on (a disease); **3** to permit (radiation, heat, sound waves) to pass through; **4** to send out (radio or television signals); **5** to transfer, pass on, as a title ‖ *vi* **6** to transmit radio or television signals

trans·mit′ter *n* **1** one who or that which transmits; **2** that part of a telegraph, telephone, or broadcasting apparatus that transmits the signals

trans·mute /transmyōōt′/ [L *transmutare* to change] *vt* to change from one form, nature, substance, or class to another ‖ **trans·mut′a·ble** *adj* ‖ **trans′mu·ta′tion** /-shən/ *n*

trans·o·ce·an′ic /trans′-, tranz′-/ *adj* **1** across the ocean; **2** crossing or engaged in crossing the ocean

tran·som /trans′əm/ [ME *traunsum* < L *transtrum* cross-beam] *n* **1** horizontal crossbar in a window or over a door; **2** window above a door or another window, generally hinged to such a crossbar

trans·pa·cif′ic /trans′-/ *adj* **1** beyond the Pacific; **2** crossing the Pacific

trans·par·en·cy /transper′ənsē, -par′-/ *n* (**-cies**) **1** state or quality of being transparent; **2** picture or design done on translucent material, made visible by light shining through it; **3** photographic slide

trans·par·ent /transper′ənt, -par′-/ [L

transparens (*-entis*) appearing through] *adj* **1** allowing light to pass through so that objects can be seen distinctly; **2** sheer, diaphanous; **3** easy to understand, evident; **4** obvious, easily detected || **trans·par'ent·ly** *adv* || SYN translucent, lucent, lucid, limpid, pellucid, clear, diaphanous, luminous, lustrous, apparent, manifest, evident || DISCR That is *transparent* which allows objects to be seen clearly through it; that is *translucent* which transmits light, but does not allow objects to be seen clearly through it, though blurred shapes or indistinct forms might be visible; plain window glass is *transparent*; the stained-glass windows in churches are *translucent*. The waves of the ocean have been described as *translucent*, emphasizing their shining, partially clear quality. *Lucent* is like *translucent*; a spring-green leaf in the sunlight is *lucent*; a dewdrop in the morning light is *lucent*. *Lucid* is like *transparent*, but is oftener used in its figurative sense and employed to describe that which is transparently clear to the mind, as a *lucid* argument. *Limpid*, which means shiningly or liquidly clear, can mean either *transparent* or *translucent*; it is applied oftenest to clear streams, or, figuratively, to literary style flowing and free from obscurity || ANT cloudy, opaque, obscure, turbid

tran·spire /transpī'ər/ [< *trans-* + L *spirare* to breathe] *vi* **1** to pass off, as a vapor; escape by evaporation; **2** to emit vapor or moisture, as through the skin; **3** to become known; **4** to occur

trans·plant /transplant', -plänt'/ *vt* **1** to remove and establish in a new place, as plants or people; **2** *surg* to transfer (an organ or tissue) from one place in the body to another or from one body to another || /trans'-plant, -plänt/ *n* **3** act of planting; **4** that which is transplanted

tran·spond·er /transpon'dər/ [*transmitter* + *responder*] *n* transmitter-receiver unit, with distance-measuring equipment, that receives a signal and automatically transmits a response

trans·port /transpôrt', -pōrt'/ [L *transportare* to carry across] *vt* **1** to carry from one place to another; **2** to carry away emotionally; **3** to deport or banish, as formerly done to British convicts || /trans'pôrt, -pōrt/ *n* **4** act of transporting; **5** means of transporting, as a bus or truck; **6** ship or plane for carrying troops or supplies; **7** strong emotion; passion; rapture || SYN *v* (see *banish*); *n* (see *rapture*)

trans·por·ta·tion /trans'pərtāsh'ən/ *n* **1** act of transporting or state of being transported; **2** means of transporting;

3 cost of transport or travel; **4** the business of transporting goods and people; **5** stocks or bonds of companies engaged in the business of transportation, such as railroads, airlines, and the like

trans·pose /transpōz'/ [MF *transposer*] *vt* **1** to change the relative position, order, or sequence of; **2** *alg* to transfer (a term) from one side of an equation to the other with a change of sign; **3** *mus* to write or render (a composition) in a different key || **trans·pos'al** *n* || **trans'po·si'tion** *n*

trans·ship *v* (**-shipped; -ship·ping**) *vt* to transfer from one carrier, as a ship or truck, to another || **trans·ship'ment** *n*

tran'sub·stan'ti·a'tion [ML *transubstantio* (*-onis*)] *n* R C Ch & Orthodox Ch change of the bread and wine of the Eucharist, at consecration, into the body and blood of Christ, only the appearance of the bread and wine remaining

trans·u·ra·ni·an /trans'yŏŏrā'nē·ən, tranz'-/ **trans'u·ra'ni·um**, or **trans'u·ran'ic** /-ran'-/ *adj* (element) with a higher atomic number than uranium, or higher than 92

Trans·vaal /transväl'/ *n* province of the Republic of South Africa (6,255,-000; 110,450 sq.m.; *cap.* Pretoria)

trans·verse /transvurs', tranz-/ [L *transversus*] *adj* **1** lying or being across or crosswise || *n* **2** something transverse || **trans·verse'ly** *adv*

trans·ves·tite /tranzves'tit, trans-/ [G *Transvestit*] *n* person who wears the clothes of the opposite sex || **trans·ves'tism** *n*

trap /trap/ [OE *træppe*] *n* **1** snare, pitfall, or spring-loaded device for catching animals; **2** any means of tricking people by catching them unawares; **3** bend in a pipe for sealing a drain with water against the return of sewer gas; **4** any of various straining and separating devices; **5** device for throwing clay pigeons into the air to be shot at; **6** trap door; **7** light two-wheeled carriage; **8** *slang* mouth; **9** **traps** *pl* percussion instruments of a band || *v* (**trapped; trapping**) *vt* **10** to catch in or as in a trap; **11** to catch by trick or stratagem; **12** to hold back (gas), as by a bend in a pipe; **13** *baseball* to catch (a batted ball) just after it hits the ground || *vi* **14** to set traps for animals, esp. for their fur

trap' door' *n* hinged or sliding door, usu. mounted flush, in a ceiling, roof, or floor

tra·peze /trapēz', trə-/ [F *trapèze*] *n* swinging horizontal bar suspended from ropes, used by acrobats

trap·e·zoid /trap'izoid'/ [Gk *trapezoeides*] *n* plane figure with four sides, only two of which are parallel

trap'per *n* one who catches animals, esp. fur-bearing animals

trap'pings [ME] *npl* dress or equipment, esp. ornamental

Trap-pist /trap'ist/ [< La *Trappe* monastery in France] *n R C Ch* one of an order of monks whose austere discipline includes study, fasts, manual labor, and silence

trap'shoot'ing *n* sport of shooting clay pigeons thrown into the air from a trap

trash /trash'/ [< Scand] *n* 1 refuse or rubbish; 2 anything worthless or useless; 3 worthless person; 4 such persons collectively ‖ **trash'y** *adj* (-i•er; -i•est)

trau-ma /trôm'ə, troum'ə/ [Gk = wound] *n* (-ma•ta /-mətə/, -mas) 1 bodily injury; wound; 2 emotional shock having a lasting effect ‖ **trau-mat'ic** /-mat-/ *adj*

tra•vail /trəvāl', trav'āl, -əl/ [OF = suffering, trouble] *n* 1 pains of childbirth; 2 physical or mental agony; 3 exhausting labor or work

trav•el /trav'əl/ [special use of *travail*] *v* (-eled or -elled; -el•ing or -el•ling) *vi* 1 to pass, be transmitted; 2 to go from one place to another, make a journey; 3 *mach* to move over a fixed course; 4 *colloq* to move rapidly; 5 travel with to associate or consort with ‖ *vt* 6 to travel to or through ‖ *n* 7 act of traveling; 8 trip, journey; 9 *mach* stroke, or length of the stroke, of a moving part

trav'el a'gent *n* one whose business is to arrange trips and provide transportation and accommodations for travelers

trav'el•er or **trav'el•ler** /-ər/ *n* 1 one who or that which travels; 2 *theat* transverse curtain that opens in the center and is drawn to both sides of the stage

trav'el•er's check' *n* check sold in fixed denominations, usu. by banks, that is signed by the purchaser at the time of purchase and that must be countersigned by him in the presence of the person cashing it

trav•el•og or **trav•e•logue** /trav'əlôg', -lôg'/ *n* illustrated lecture or motion picture describing travels

trav•erse /trav'ərs, trəvurs'/ [MF *traverser*] *adj* 1 lying or being across ‖ *n* 2 act of crossing over or through; 3 crosspiece; something lying or placed across something else; 4 *mil* parapet or barrier placed transversely; 5 *ordnance* horizontal turning of a gun ‖ *vt* 6 to lay or place crosswise; 7 to cross in traveling; travel or pass over; 8 to go from one end or side to the other; 9 to turn (a gun) to the right or left ‖ *vi* 10 to turn as on a pivot; 11 to walk or move across; move back and forth

trav•es•ty /trav'istē/ [F *travesti* disguised] *n* (-ties) 1 burlesque or parody; 2 burlesque imitation or treatment of a serious literary work; 3 any absurd or grotesque imitation ‖ *v* (-tied) *vt* 4 to make a travesty of ‖ **SYN** *n* imitation, burlesque (see *parody*)

tra•vois /trəvoi'/ [CanF] *n* (*pl* -vois /-voiz/) primitive vehicle for transporting goods used by some North American Indian tribes, consisting of two poles supporting a frame and dragged along the ground by a man or an animal

trawl /trôl'/ [MD *traghel* dragnet] *n* 1 large fishing net for dragging along the sea bottom; 2 trawl line ‖ *vi* 3 to fish with a trawl ‖ *vt* 4 to catch with a trawl; 5 to drag (a line or net) in fishing

trawl'er *n* 1 one who trawls; 2 vessel used in trawling

trawl' line' *n* line attached to buoys from which many shorter lines are suspended containing baited hooks, used in sea fishing

tray /trā'/ [OE *trīg*] *n* 1 flat or shallow receptacle of wood, metal, glass, etc.; 2 shallow removable boxlike compartment, as in a trunk or drawer ‖ **tray'ful'** *n*

treach•er•ous /trech'ərəs/ *adj* 1 characterized by treachery; disloyal; 2 untrustworthy, unreliable; 3 insecure, dangerous, as footing ‖ **treach'er•ous•ly** *adv* ‖ **SYN** false, untrue, intriguing, perfidious, insidious, perjured, forsworn ‖ **ANT** true, loyal, faithful, honest

treach'er•y [MF *trecherie*] *n* (-ies) 1 treasonable or disloyal conduct; 2 betrayal of trust; treason; faithlessness

trea•cle /trēk'əl/ [OF] *n* 1 *Brit* molasses; 2 overdone sentimentality ‖ **trea'cly** *adj* (-cli•er; -cli•est)

tread /tred'/ [OE *tredan*] *v* (trod; trod or trod•den) *vi* 1 to step or walk; 2 to step, trample, as *to tread on grapes* ‖ *vt* 3 to walk on; 4 to press or crush under the feet; 5 to subdue or overcome; 6 to dance; 7 **tread the boards** to be a professional actor; 8 **tread water** to keep the head above water and the body erect by moving the legs up and down ‖ *n* 9 a walking or stepping; 10 manner or sound of stepping; 11 horizontal upper surface of a step in a stair; 12 the part of a shoe or foot that touches the ground; 13 the part of a wheel, tire, or runner that touches the road or rail; 14 raised pattern or design on the face of a tire

trea•dle /tred'əl/ [OE *tredel*] *n* 1 lever worked by the foot to operate a sewing machine, lathe, etc.; 2 platform that actuates an exit door when stepped on, as in a bus

tread'mill' *n* 1 mill kept in motion by

persons or animals walking on an endless belt; **2** any monotonous round, as of work or duty

treas. 1 treasurer; 2 treasury

trea·son /trēz′ən/ [AF *treisoun*] *n* betrayal of allegiance to one's sovereign or country, as by yielding vital secrets or aiding an enemy in time of war ‖ **trea′son·a·ble** or **trea′son·ous** *adj*

treas·ure /trezh′ər/ [OF *tresor* < Gk *thesauros*] *n* **1** accumulation of valuables, as money or jewels; **2** wealth, abundance; **3** someone or something highly prized or of great value ‖ *vt* **4** to lay by for future use; **5** to retain in the mind; **6** to value highly, cherish

treas′ur·er *n* official in charge of receiving, managing, and disbursing the money of a corporation, organization, or government

treas′ure-trove′ /-trōv′/ [AF *tresor trové* found treasure] *n* **1** something of value discovered; **2** *law* unclaimed money or valuables found hidden

treas′ur·y *n* (-ies) **1** place where wealth is stored, esp. place where public funds are kept and paid out; **2** funds of a government, company, or organization; **3** collection or storehouse of words or literary gems; **4** **Treasury** department of a government that administers the public revenues

treas′ur·y bill′ *n* obligation of the U.S. government, issued in denominations of $1000 and up, maturing in 90 days, and bearing no interest but sold at a discount

treat /trēt′/ [OF *tretier, traitier*] *vt* **1** to deal with or discuss, as a subject or topic; **2** to behave or act toward, as *to treat others kindly;* **3** to regard, consider, as *to treat it as unintentional;* **4** to cause to undergo a process for a special purpose, as *to treat something with chemicals;* **5** to entertain or pay the cost of entertainment for; **6** to deal with for some desired result, as *to treat a headache, to treat a patient* ‖ *vi* **7** to negotiate, as *to treat with the enemy;* **8** to give or pay for a treat; **9 treat of** to deal with (a subject) ‖ *n* **10** entertainment given as an expression of friendship or esteem; **11** something that affords great pleasure; **12** act of treating; **13** one's turn to treat

trea·tise /trēt′is/ [AF *tretiz*] *n* formal detailed essay on some subject

treat′ment *n* **1** act or manner of treating; **2** treating of patients, disease, or pathological conditions

trea·ty /trēt′ē/ [AF *trete*] *n* (-ties) formal agreement or contract between nations for the adjustment of differences or for the arrangement of commercial relations

tre·ble /treb′əl/ [MF < L *triplus*

triple] *adj* **1** threefold or triple; **2** *mus* of or pert. to the treble ‖ *n* **3** *mus* **a** highest vocal or instrumental part; **b** soprano singer or instrument ‖ *vt & vi* **4** to triple

tre′ble clef′ *n mus* sign that locates the G above middle C on the second line of the staff

tree /trē′/ [OE *trēo(w)*] *n* **1** any large perennial woody plant having a high main trunk; **2** anything suggestive of or resembling a tree; **3 up a tree** *colloq* **a** at a loss to know what to do; **b** in a difficult situation ‖ *vt* **4** to chase up a tree ‖ **tree′less** *adj*

tree′ frog′ *n* any of several arboreal frogs, as of the family Hylidae, with suckerlike pads on the toes

tree′ sur′geon *n* one who specializes in the repair and rehabilitation of damaged and diseased trees ‖ **tree′ sur′ger·y** *n*

tre′foil /trē′-/ [AF *trifoil*] *n* **1** any plant of the genus *Trifolium,* having leaves divided into three leaflets, as the common clover; **2** any of several other plants with similar leaves; **3** ornament or design resembling a three-lobed leaf

trek /trek′/ [D *trekken* to draw, march] *v* (**trekked; trek·king**) *vi* **1** travel or migrate, esp. in slow laborious stages ‖ *n* **2** organized migration; **3** journey, esp. by wagon

trel·lis /trel′is/ [MF *trelis*] *n* **1** lattice forming a support for vines; **2** summerhouse constructed largely of lattice

trem·ble /trem′bəl/ [MF *trembler*] *vi* **1** to shake or shudder, as with fright or cold or great excitement; **2** to quaver, as sound; **3** to quiver or vibrate ‖ *n* **4** act or fit of trembling ‖ **trem′bling·ly** *adv* ‖ SYN *v* vibrate, waver, flutter, quiver, shake

tre·men·dous /trimen′dəs/ [L *tremendus* frightful] *adj* **1** very great in size, amount, power, or effect; **2** causing awe or astonishment; **3** *colloq* fine, excellent ‖ **tre·men′dous·ly** *adv*

trem·o·lo /trem′əlō′/ [It = trembling] *n* **1** trembling or quivering effect of a tone in vocal or instrumental music; **2** device in an organ by which such an effect is produced

trem·or /trem′ər, trēm′-/ [L] *n* **1** involuntary trembling of the body or limbs; **2** vibration or shaking

trem·u·lous /trem′yələs/ [< L *tremulus*] *adj* **1** trembling, quivering, shaking; **2** timid, fearful

trench /trench′/ [OF *trenchier* to cut] *n* **1** long narrow ditch, as for drainage; **2** *mil* deep narrow ditch protected by a parapet, dug in the zone of battle ‖ *vt* **3** to dig a trench or trenches in; **4** to entrench ‖ *vi* **5 trench on** or **upon, a** to verge on; **b** to encroach on

trench·ant /trench′ənt/ [OF = cutting] adj **1** forceful and clear; sharp, as *trenchant language;* **2** vigorous, energetic, as *a trenchant policy* ‖ **trench′an·cy** n ‖ **trench′ant·ly** adv

trench coat′ n military-style raincoat having a belt and shoulder straps

trench′er·man /-mən/ [obs *trencher* wooden platter] n (-men /-mən/) hearty or heavy eater

trench′ foot′ n disease of the feet caused by prolonged exposure to cold and wet

trench′ mouth′ n infectious disease characterized by ulceration of the mucous membranes of the mouth and throat

trend /trend′/ [OE *trendan*] n **1** inclination in a certain direction; general tendency ‖ vi **2** to have a particular direction or course; **3** to have a general tendency

trend′y adj (-i·er; -i·est) stylish, up-to-date

Tren·ton /trent′ən/ n capital of New Jersey (115,100)

tre·pan /trĭpan′/ [ML *trepanum* crown saw] n **1** obs trephine; **2** tool for boring holes ‖ v (-panned; -pan·ning) vt **3** to trephine

tre·phine /trĭfīn′, -fēn′/ [obs *trafine* < L *tres fines* three ends] n **1** delicate cylindrical saw used to remove a button of bone from the skull ‖ vt **2** to operate on with a trephine

trep·i·da·tion /trep′ĭdāsh′ən/ [< L *trepidare* to tremble] n **1** trembling; vibration; **2** fear, nervous alarm; perturbation

tres·pass /tres′pəs, -pas′/ [OF *trespasser*] vi **1** to commit an offense; sin; **2** to intrude, encroach; **3** law **a** to enter unlawfully upon the property of another; **b** to commit an unlawful act with violence against the property of another ‖ n **4** act or instance of trespassing ‖ **tres′pass·er** n

tress·es /tres′iz/ [< MF *tresse* braid of hair] npl long locks of unbraided hair ‖ **tressed′** adj

tres·tle /tres′əl/ [MF *trestel* beam] n **1** frame consisting of a horizontal beam and spreading legs, as for supporting a table; **2** connected framework of timbers or steel supporting the roadway of a bridge; **3** bridge with this framework

trey /trā′/ [MF *treis* < L *tres* three] n playing card, die, or domino with three pips

tri- /trī′-/ [L & Gk] pref **1** three, threefold; **2** having three parts; **3** every third; **4** into three

tri·ad /trī′ad/ [Gk *trias* (-ados)] n **1** group of three; **2** mus chord of three tones consisting of a fundamental tone with its third and fifth higher; **3** chem trivalent element or radical

tri·age /trē′äzh, trē·äzh′/ [F sorting out] n **1** selection of those to be treated, esp. after a battle or a disaster, on the basis of their chance of recovery; **2** use of scarce resources, notably grain, where they will do the most good

tri·al /trī′əl/ [AF] n **1** act of testing or putting to proof; **2** state of being tested or tried; probation; **3** attempt or endeavor; **4** experiment; **5** hardship; suffering; **6** affliction, trouble; **7** annoying person or thing; **8** law judicial examination of a case in court ‖ SYN test, experiment, proof ‖ DISCR These words have in common the idea of trying to establish or verify something that is uncertain. *Trial* is rather generally applied to the host of things that in ordinary existence require trying. We make a *trial* of our skill to find out what degree of it we possess; we buy a radio set on *trial* to see how we like it. *Test* is narrower in its application than *trial:* a *test* is a *trial* that proves, and hence is decisive; we put a new appliance through a strict *test;* one who has proved himself loyal has stood a *test. Proof* is like *test* in that it is final; it is a definite discovery, frequently in the intellectual field, but often in the realm of practical affairs. That which is put on *trial,* to *test,* or to *proof,* has something depending on the outcome. In this respect *experiment* differs from these words, for no more may depend on a successful *experiment* than the confirmation of an opinion. The failure of an *experiment* may mean nothing. On the other hand, when *experiment* proves or demonstrates, it becomes *test* and *proof* of the greatest value

tri·al and er′ror n method of discovering the correct solution to a problem by repeated trials

tri′al bal·loon′ n statement or act intended to test public reaction to a proposed policy or course of action

tri′an·gle [L *triangulum*] n **1** plane figure bounded by three lines and having three angles; **2** any triangular object; **3** mus percussion instrument consisting of a steel rod bent in the form of a triangle, struck by a metal rod; **4** situation in which two persons are both in love with a third person ‖ **tri·an′gu·lar** adj

tri·an·gu·la·tion /trī·aŋ′gyəlāsh′ən/ n method or process of establishing the distance of a point, not readily accessible, by measuring the base line opposite to it and the angles formed by the base line and the lines running from the ends of the base line to the distant point

Tri·as·sic /trī·as′ik/ [Gk *trias* group of three] geol adj **1** designating or pert. to a period of the Mesozoic era, characterized by volcanic activity and the appearance of dinosaurs ‖ *n* 2 the Triassic period

tribe /trīb'/ [L *tribus*] *n* 1 group of aboriginal people, usu. a group of several clans under one chief; 2 group of people united by common descent, customs, and usu. under common leadership; 3 class or group of animals, plants, or things; 4 *stockbreeding* animals descended through the female line from a particular female; 5 *colloq* a group of people connected by some common occupation or trait; **b** family ‖ **trib'al** *adj* ‖ **tribes'man** /-mən/ *n* -**men** /-mən/) ‖ SYN group, class, division, clan (see *nation*)

trib·u·la·tion /trib'yəlāsh'ən/ [L *tribulatio* (-*onis*)] *n* 1 severe affliction or distress; 2 acute trial; cause of affliction ‖ SYN sorrow, affliction, trouble (see *grief*)

tri·bu·nal /trībyōōn'əl, tri-/ [L = judgment seat] *n* 1 court of justice; 2 any place of justice

trib·une[1] /trib'yōōn/ [L *tribunus*] *n* 1 *Rom hist* magistrate elected by the common people to protect their liberties; 2 one who champions the rights of the people

trib·une[2] [LL *tribuna* < L *tribunal*] *n* 1 platform for public speaking; 2 gallery, as in a church; 3 in Christian basilicas, a throne of the bishop; **b** apse where it is situated

trib·u·tar·y /trib'yəter'ē/ [L *tributarius*] *adj* 1 paying tribute or taxes to another; 2 subordinate or subject; 3 due or owed as tribute ‖ *n* (-**ies**) 4 state that pays tribute to or is under the control of another government; 5 stream or river flowing into another body of water

trib·ute /trib'yōōt/ [L *tributum*] *n* 1 stated sum of money, paid by one state or ruler to another, to obtain protection or in token of subjection; 2 any enforced payment; 3 acknowledgment of worth, service rendered, or the like

trice /trīs'/ [ME] *n* **in a trice** in an instant

tri·chi·na /trikīn'ə/ [Gk = hairy] *n* (-**nae** /-nē/) microscopic worm (*Trichinella spiralis*) parasitic in the muscles of man, swine, and other animals

trich·i·no·sis /trik'inōs'is/ *n* disease due to the presence of trichinae in the muscular tissue and intestinal tract, caused by eating infected undercooked pork

trick /trik'/ [OF *trique* deceit] *n* 1 artifice or fraud; crafty or deceitful device or action; 2 mean act; 3 sleight-of-hand feat; 4 mischievous prank; 5 peculiarity of manner; habit; 6 particular skill, knack; 7 *cards* all the cards played in one round; 8 shift or turn, as at work or duty; 9 illusion, deception; 10 dexterous feat; 11 *slang* **a** prostitute's customer; **b** instance of paid-for sexual intercourse; 12 **do** or **turn the trick** to achieve the desired result; 13 **play a trick on** to make (someone) the object of a prank ‖ *vt* 14 to cheat; 15 to deceive, beguile ‖ SYN ruse, artifice, fraud (see *subterfuge*)

tricked' out' *adj* ostentatiously dressed or decked out

trick'er·y *n* (-**ies**) 1 fraud, deception; 2 deceitful act

trick' knee' *n* condition in which the knee suddenly buckles or stiffens

trick·le /trik'əl/ [ME *triklen*] *vi* 1 to flow in a small continuous stream or run in drops; 2 to move slowly, as a crowd ‖ *n* 3 trickling flow

trick' or treat' *n* children's Halloween game in which they call on neighbors and threaten to play a trick if they do not get a treat ‖ **trick'-or-treat'** *vi*

trick'ster *n* tricky person

trick'y *adj* (-**i·er**, -**i·est**) 1 crafty, wily; given to trickery; 2 difficult to solve or do

tri'col'or /trī'-/ *n* flag of three colors arranged in equal stripes, esp. the national flag of France

tri·cy·cle /trī'sikəl/ *n* child's three-wheeled vehicle, having a single seat and operated by pedals

tri·dent /trīd'ənt/ [L *tridens* (-*dentis*) three-toothed] *n* three-pronged spear

tried /trīd'/ *adj* proved, tested, trustworthy

tri·en·ni·al /trī·en'ē·əl/ [< L *triennium* space of three years] *adj* 1 happening every three years; 2 lasting three years ‖ *n* 3 something happening every three years; 4 something lasting three years; 5 third anniversary

tri·fle /trīf'əl/ [OF *trufle* mockery] *n* 1 anything of little value or importance; 2 small amount or sum; 3 **a trifle** rather, somewhat ‖ *vi* 4 to act or talk without seriousness; 5 to dally, toy, play ‖ *vt* 6 **trifle away** to waste away (time) ‖ **tri'fler** *n*

tri'fling *adj* 1 of small value or concern; trivial; 2 frivolous

tri·fo'cals *npl* eyeglasses having lenses in three parts, one for near, one for intermediate, and one for far vision

trig /trig'/ [< Scand] *adj* 1 trim, neat; 2 in good condition; 3 active, agile

trig. 1 trigonometric(al); 2 trigonometry

trig·ger /trig'ər/ [var of *dial. tricker* < D *trekker*] *n* 1 lever which, when pulled by the finger, releases the hammer of a firearm; 2 any similar device, as for springing a trap ‖ *vt* 3 to initiate or precipitate (an action or series of actions or events)

trig'ger-hap'py *adj* ready to shoot or react at the slightest provocation

trig'ger·man' /-man'/ *n* (-**men** /-men'/)

colloq 1 gangster who fires a gun at his victim; 2 personal bodyguard of a gangster

tri·glyc·er·ide /trīglis'ərīd/ [*tri-* + *glycerol* + *-ide*] *n* ester of glycerol with fatty acids

trig·o·nom·e·try /trig'ənom'itrē/ [< Gk *trigonon* triangle + *-metry*] *n* branch of mathematics that deals with the relationships between the angles and sides of triangles, and the calculations based on them ‖ **trig'o·no·met'ric** /-nəmet'rik/ *adj*

tri·lat·er·al /trī-/ *adj* having three sides

tri·lin·gual *adj* 1 spoken or written in three languages; 2 speaking three languages

trill /tril/ [It *trillo*] *n* 1 *mus* quick alternation of two adjacent notes; 2 any similar sound, as of a bird singing or a person laughing; 3 vibration of the tongue or uvula in making certain speech sounds ‖ *vi* & *vi* 4 to speak, sing, or sound with a trill

tril·lion /tril'yən/ [F] *n* 1 *US* million million (one followed by 12 zeros); 2 *Brit* one million squared (one followed by 18 zeros) ‖ also *adj* ‖ **tril'lionth** *adj* & *n*

tril·o·gy /tril'əjē/ [Gk *trilogia*] *n* (*-gies*) series of three plays, novels, operas, etc., closely related as to theme, characters, etc., yet each complete in itself

trim /trim/ [OE *trymian* to make firm] *v* (**trimmed**; **trim·ming**) *vt* 1 to make tidy or neat by cutting or clipping; 2 to decorate or adorn; 3 to make smooth or ready for use, as lumber by planing; 4 to cut or clip (superfluous parts); 5 to balance; adjust, make even, as a load on a ship, the curtains on a stage, the capacity of a condenser; 6 *naut* to adjust (the sails) for sailing; 7 *colloq* a to beat, chastise; b to defeat; 8 to change (one's expressed opinions) for expediency; 9 to arrange a display in (a shop window) ‖ *vi* 10 to try to please two sides or parties at the same time; 11 to adjust one's views for expediency; 12 *naut* to take a certain position in the water ‖ *n* 13 order; adjustment; 14 suitable condition; 15 dress, style; 16 inside woodwork of a building around the windows, doors, etc.; 17 trimming; 18 a trimming by cutting or clipping; 19 out of trim *naut* improperly ballasted ‖ *adj* (**trim·mer; trim·mest**) 20 neat; compact; 21 in good order ‖ **trim'ly** *adv* ‖ **trim'mer** *n*

tri·mes·ter /trimest'ər/ [L *trimestris* of three months] *n* 1 period of three months; 2 one of three equal school terms (used by schools that are open the year round)

trim'ming *n* 1 adornment; added decoration; 2 *colloq* scolding; thrashing;

3 **trimmings** *pl* a parts removed by trimming; b garnishings and accessories of a dish

Trin·i·dad and To·ba·go /trin'idad' ən tōbāg'ō/ *n* English-speaking republic in the Caribbean off the NE coast of Venezuela, comprising the islands of Trinidad and Tobago; member of the British Commonwealth (1,016,000; 1980 sq.m.; cap. Port-of-Spain, on Trinidad)

Trin·i·tar·i·an /trin'iter'ē-ən/ [see **Trinity**] *adj* 1 pert. to the Trinity; 2 pert. to or believing in the doctrine of the Trinity ‖ *n* 3 believer in the doctrine of the Trinity ‖ **Trin'i·tar'i·an·ism** *n*

tri·ni·tro·tol·u·ene /trīnī'trōtol'yōō-ēn'/ *n* yellow crystalline solid —CH$_3$C$_6$H$_2$(NO$_2$)$_3$— used for blasting and as an ingredient in bombs and artillery shells

trin·i·ty /trin'itē/ [OF *trinite* < LL *trinitas*] *n* (*-ties*) 1 any group of three; triad; 2 **Trinity** union in one divine being of the three persons of the Godhead: the Father, the Son, and the Holy Ghost

trin·ket /trink'it/ [?] *n* 1 small ornament or piece of jewelry; 2 something trivial; trifle

tri·no·mi·al /trīnōm'ē-əl/ [*tri-* + L *nomen* name] *n* 1 *alg* expression composed of three terms connected by plus or minus signs; 2 *biol* name composed of three terms ‖ also *adj*

tri·o /trē'ō/ [It] *n* 1 set of three; 2 *mus* a composition for three voices or instruments; b company of three performers

tri·ox·ide /trī-/ *n* oxide containing three atoms of oxygen per molecule

tri·ox·ide of ar'se·nic *n* poisonous white powder —As$_2$O$_3$— used in rat poison, weed killers, and insecticides

trip /trip/ [MD *trippen*] *v* (**tripped; trip·ping**) *vi* 1 to run or step lively or nimbly; 2 to take short quick steps; 3 to stumble over something; 4 to make a mistake; err ‖ *vt* 5 to cause to stumble; 6 *mach* to release as by pulling a catch or trigger; 7 often **trip up**, a to cause to stumble; b to cause to blunder; c to catch in a lie, slip, or error; 8 **trip the light fantastic** to dance nimbly ‖ *n* 9 misstep or stumble; 10 mistake; 11 journey or excursion; 12 course of travel, as *the daily trip to the city*; 13 device that releases a mechanism; 14 *slang* period of aberration caused by a hallucinogen

tri·par·tite /tripär'tīt/ [< *tri-* + L *partire* to divide] *adj* 1 divided into or having three parts; 2 involving three parties

tripe /trīp/ [OF = entrails] *n* 1 lining of the stomach of the ox or other ruminant, used for food; 2 *slang* something worthless

trip' ham'mer *n* heavy hammer raised

and allowed to drop by a tripping device

triph·thong /trif'thŏŋ, -thoŋ, trip'-/ [MGk *triphthongos*] *n* combination of three sounds in a single syllable, represented in spelling by three vowels, as in *meow*, *wow* ‖ **triph·thon'gal** /-gəl/ *adj*

tri'plane' *n* early model of the airplane having three parallel wings

tri·ple /trip'əl/ [L *triplus*] *adj* 1 threefold; composed of three parts; 2 three times as great ‖ *vt* 3 to make triple ‖ *vi* 4 to become triple; 4 *baseball* to make a three-base hit ‖ *n* 5 *baseball* three-base hit ‖ **tri'ply** *adv*

trip·let /trip'lĭt/ [< *triple*] *n* 1 set or combination of three; 2 one of three children at one birth; 3 *mus* three notes sounded in the time of two notes of the same value

tri'ple threat' *n* one who is proficient in three different skills

trip·li·cate /trip'likĭt/ [L *triplicatus* tripled] *adj* 1 threefold, triple; 2 made in or consisting of three identical copies ‖ *n* 3 one of three identical things; 4 **in triplicate** in three identical copies ‖ /-kāt'/ *vt* 5 to triple; increase threefold; 6 to produce in triplicate

tri·pod /trī'pŏd/ [< *tri-* + Gk *pous* (*podos*) foot] *n* 1 three-legged stand or support, as for a camera; 2 article with three feet or legs, as a vase or stool

Trip·o·li /trip'əlē/ *n* 1 seaport and one of the capitals of Libya (213,506); 2 seaport in N. Lebanon (160,000)

trip·tych /trip'tik/ [Gk *triptychon*] *n* picture, design, or carving on three panels, generally hinged together, often used as an altar piece

trip' wire' *n* 1 wire placed close to the ground to keep people off a lawn; 2 electric wire placed close to the ground to actuate an explosive device or a warning signal

tri·reme /trī'rēm/ [L *triremis*] *n* ancient galley with three banks of oars, used as a warship

tri·sect /trīsĕkt'/ [*tri-* + L *secare* (*sectus*) to cut] *vt* to divide into three parts, esp. three equal parts

trite /trīt/ [L *tritus* worn down] *adj* lacking freshness; stale, commonplace ‖ **trite'ly** *adv* ‖ **trite'ness** *n* ‖ SYN threadbare, commonplace, vapid, stereotyped, banal ‖ ANT fresh, vivid, striking, new

trit·i·um /trit'ē·əm, trish'əm/ [< Gk *tritos* third] *n* radioactive isotope of hydrogen having an atomic weight of three

Tri·ton /trīt'ən/ *n* Gk *myth.* 1 son of Poseidon, represented as a man down to the waist and a dolphin below, and as blowing a shell trumpet; 2 any of many minor sea deities

trit·u·rate /trich'ərāt'/ [LL *triturare*

(*-atus*) to thresh] *vt* 1 to rub or grind to a powder ‖ *n* 2 triturated substance ‖ **trit'u·ra'tion** *n*

tri·umph /trī'əmf/ [L *triumphus*] *n* 1 *Rom hist* grand parade and celebration in honor of a victorious general; 2 exultation over success; 3 success; victory; conquest ‖ *vi* 4 to rejoice over success; 5 to gain a victory; be successful ‖ SYN *n* exultation, achievement (see *victory*)

tri·um·phal /trī·um'fəl/ *adj* of or pert. to victory or its celebration

tri·um·phant /trī·um'fənt/ *adj* 1 victorious; 2 exulting in victory

tri·um·vir /trī·um'vər/ [L = one of three] *n* (*-virs* or *-vi·ri* /-vərī'/) 1 *Rom hist* one man of three sharing equally public authority and rule; 2 one of three persons sharing a position of authority or the leadership of a government

tri·um'vi·rate /-rĭt, -rāt'/ *n* 1 government by triumvirs; 2 term or office of triumvirs; 3 any group or set of three

tri·va·lent /trīvāl'ənt, triv'ə-/ [< *tri-* + L *valens* (*-entis*) worth] *adj chem* having a valence of three ‖ **tri·va'lence** *n*

triv·et /triv'ĭt/ [OE *trefet*] *n* 1 three-legged stand for holding a kettle over a fire; 2 short-legged metal plate on which to set hot dishes

triv·i·a /triv'ē·ə/ [< *trivial*] *npl* things of no importance or consequence

triv·i·al /triv'ē·əl/ [L *trivialis* belonging to the crossroads, common] *adj* 1 trifling, of little worth or importance; 2 common, ordinary; 3 shallow, unscholarly ‖ **triv'i·al'i·ty** /-al'-/ *n* (*-ties*)

triv·i·um /triv'ē·əm/ [L = place where three roads meet] *n* (*-a* /-ə/) *medieval education* the first course in the liberal arts, consisting of grammar, rhetoric, and logic

-trix /-triks/ [L] *n suf* (*-trix·es* or *-tri·ces* /-trīsēz'/) (feminine form corresponding to *-tor*) one who, as *administratrix*

tro·chee /trō'kē/ [Gk *trochaios* running] *n pros* foot of two syllables, the first long or accented, and the second short or unaccented ‖ **tro·cha'ic** /-kā'-/ *adj*

trod /trŏd/ *pt & pp* of *tread*

trod·den /trŏd'ən/ *pp* of *tread*

trog·lo·dyte /trŏg'lədīt'/ [Gk *troglodytes*] *n* 1 cave dweller; cave man; 2 hermit

troi·ka /troik'ə/ [Russ] *n* 1 Russian carriage drawn by three horses abreast; 2 team of three abreast; 3 triumvirate

Tro·jan /trō'jən/ [L *Trojanus*] *adj* 1 pert. to ancient Troy or its inhabitants ‖ *n* 2 inhabitant of Troy; 3 industrious and fearless person, as *he worked like a Trojan*

Tro'jan Horse' *n* 1 *Gk myth.* huge hollow wooden horse within which Greek soldiers were concealed and which was taken inside the gates of Troy by the unwitting Trojans, leading to the conquest and destruction of the city by the Greeks; **2** any undercover group working to destroy or take over from within

Tro'jan War' *n Gk myth.* the ten-year conflict between the Greeks and the Trojans to avenge the abduction of Helen of Sparta by Paris of Troy

troll¹ /trōl/ [MF *troller* to run about] *vi* **1** to share in a round or part song; **2** to sing lustily; **3** to fish with a hook and line or a spoon-shaped lure drawn slowly through the water behind a boat ‖ *vt* **4** to sing the parts of, in succession; **5 a** to fish for by trolling; **b** to fish in by trolling ‖ *n* **6** round or part song; **7** act of trolling; **8** line used in trolling; **9** spoon-shaped lure for trolling

troll² [ON] *n Scand folklore* giant or dwarf living in caves

trol·ley /trol'ē/ [< *troll¹*] *n* **1** pulley or truck running on an overhead track and designed to carry a load suspended from it; **2** grooved wheel at the end of a **pole** forming the contact with an overhead electric wire and transmitting power to a streetcar or bus; **3** trolley car; **4 off one's trolley** *slang* insane

trol'ley bus' *n* electrically operated bus obtaining power from a pair of overhead wires through trolleys

trol'ley car' *n* electrically operated streetcar obtaining power from a circuit consisting of the tracks, an overhead wire, and a trolley

trol·lop /trol'əp/ [?] *n* **1** prostitute; **2** slattern

trom·bone /trombōn', trom'bōn/ [It] *n* long brass wind instrument with two U-shaped bends and with a slide or valves to change the pitch

troop /trōōp/ [MF *trope* flock] *n* **1** company or band of persons, animals, or things; **2** cavalry unit commanded by a captain; **3** smallest independent unit of Boy Scouts or Girl Scouts; **4 troops,** a body of soldiers; **b** soldiers collectively ‖ *vi* **5** to march; march in a body; **6** to collect or move in crowds; congregate

troop'er *n* **1** cavalryman; **2** mounted policeman; **3** state trooper

troop'ship' *n* military transport vessel

troph·ic /trof'ik, trōf'-/ [< Gk *trophikos* pert. to food] *adj* of or pert. to nutrition

troph'ic lev'el *n* energy level at which an organism sustains itself

tro·phy /trōf'ē/ [F *trophée*] *n* (-phies) **1** anything kept as a memento of a victory, as a captured flag; **2** memento of one's deeds or achievements, as *a hunting trophy*; **3** prize, award

-tro·phy /-trəfē/ [< Gk *trophe* food] *comb form* **1** nutrition; **2** growth

trop·ic /trop'ik/ [Gk *tropikos* pert. to turning] *n* **1** either of two parallels of latitude, at a distance of 23°27' north and south of the equator, marking the limits of the Torrid Zone; **2 the tropics** *pl* the region of the earth lying between these two circles ‖ *adj* **3** pert. to, characteristic of, or growing in the tropics ‖ **trop'i·cal** *adj*

trop'ic of Can'cer *n* the tropic to the N of the equator

trop'ic of Cap'ri·corn' *n* the tropic to the S of the equator

tro·pism /trō'pizm/ [< Gk *trope* turning] *n* tendency of a plant or animal to be attracted or repelled by an external stimulus

trop'o·sphere' /trop'ə-/ [< Gk *trope* change + *sphere*] *n* lowest stratum of the earth's atmosphere, below the stratosphere, and within which all weather occurs

trot /trot/ [MF *troter*] *v* (**trot·ted; trot·ting**) *vi* **1** (of a horse) to move at a pace faster than a walk, lifting the right forefoot and left hind foot and then the left forefoot and right hind foot; **2** to run at a moderate pace; **3** to hurry ‖ *vt* **4** to cause to trot; **5 trot out** *colloq* to bring out for exhibition ‖ *n* **6** gait of a trotting horse; **7** jogging gait; **8** *colloq* literal translation, used dishonestly by students

troth /trōth, trôth/ [var of *truth*] *n archaic* **plight one's troth 1** to promise to be faithful; **2** to make a promise of marriage

Trot·sky·ism /trot'skē·iz'əm/ [Leon *Trotsky* (1879–1940) Russ revolutionary] *n* form of communism advocated by Trotsky looking to immediate revolution everywhere ‖ **Trot'sky·ite'** *n*

trot'ter *n* horse trained for trotting in harness racing

trou·ba·dour /trōōb'ədôr', -dōr/ [Prov] *n* **1** one of a class of poets and singers of love songs who flourished from the 11th to the 13th century in southern France; **2** any minstrel

trou·ble /trub'əl/ [OF *trubler*] *vt* **1** to distress, worry, agitate; **2** to cause inconvenience to; annoy; **3** to stir up, agitate, as water ‖ *vi* **4** to take pains; worry ‖ *n* **5** distress, worry; annoyance; uneasiness; **6** inconvenience; exertion; pains; **7** illness, affliction; **8** misfortune; distressing occurrence; **9** civil disturbance; **10** something wrong, not working, or not working right, as *the trouble is in the wiring*; **11** cause or source of trouble ‖ SYN *v* plague, incommode; *n* calamity, misfortune, disaster, catastrophe, cataclysm, mishap, mischance, adversity ‖ DISCR *Trouble*, as here compared, is the broadest of the terms relating to situations affecting us in a negative or undesirable way: *trouble* may arise from mere perplexity, lack of gasoline, or the death of a friend. A *mishap* is a bit of ill luck. A *misfortune* is a *mishap* on a large scale. A *mishap* may be a matter of momentary regret or slight inconvenience; a *misfortune* is the beginning of a train of consequent ills. *Disaster* and *calamity* are terrible *misfortunes*, with ruin, destruction, and loss following in their wake. A *calamity* is sudden, crushing, and inevitable; a devastating earthquake is a *calamity*. A *disaster* is sudden and ruinous; it often occurs through a culpable neglect, a guilty omission, or lack of proper foresight. A great and destructive fire is a *disaster*, as is a railroad wreck, or a personal failure involving one's family in financial ruin or scandal. A *catastrophe* is an event so calamitous and disastrous as to be final or fatal. In a personal sense, a *catastrophe* would be so grave a *misfortune* that one's life or some aspect of it would cease. In dramatic literature, the dénouement of a play is called the *catastrophe* ‖ ANT *n* comfort, happiness, gratification, pleasure, triumph

trou·ble·mak·er *n* person who causes trouble and stirs up strife often out of malice

trou·ble·shoot·er or **trou·ble-shoot·er** *n* person expert in locating and eliminating trouble in mechanical equipment, personal relationships, international affairs, etc.

trou·ble·some *adj* causing trouble, vexation, or difficulty ‖ SYN annoying, wearisome, tiresome, irksome, arduous, laborious, burdensome, painful ‖ ANT pleasant, light, helpful, amusing, easy

trou·ble spot' *n* region where conflict exists or is threatening to break out

trough /trôf', trof'/ [OE *trōh*] *n* 1 long narrow receptacle, as one for holding water or food for animals; 2 channel for carrying off water, as a roof gutter; 3 any long depression, as between sea waves or between two ridges

trounce /trouns'/ [?] *vt* 1 to beat severely; 2 to defeat utterly ‖ **trounc'·ing** *n*

troupe /trōōp/ [F] *n* company of performers, esp. one that travels

troup·er *n* 1 member of a troupe; 2 veteran actor; 3 person loyal to his work or his commitments

trou·sers /trouz'ərz/ [< *obs trouse* < Gael *triubhas* breeches] *npl* outer garment covering the body from the waist to the knee or ankle and divided into two pipelike parts for the legs

trous·seau /trōō'sō, trōōsō'/ [F] *n* (-seaus or -seaux /-sōz/) bride's outfit of clothes, linens, etc.

trout /trout'/ [OE *truht* < L *tructa*] *n* (trout or trouts) any of several fresh-water game fishes of the salmon family

trou·vère /trōōver'/ [F] *n* one of a class of poets who flourished in the 11th and 12th centuries in northern France

trow·el /trou'əl/ [OF *truele*] *n* 1 any of various flat-bladed hand tools used for shaping and smoothing plastic material; 2 gardener's hand tool for digging and transplanting ‖ *v* (-eled or -elled; -el·ing or -el·ling) *vt* 3 to apply, smooth, or shape with a trowel

Troy /troi'/ *n* ancient ruined city in NW Asia Minor, besieged by the Greeks for ten years during the Trojan War

troy' weight' [< *Troyes*, France] *n* system of weights used for gold or silver, with twelve ounces to the pound, which is equal to 0.82286 pound avoirdupois

tru·ant /trōō'ənt/ [OF = beggar, vagabond] *n* 1 one who stays out of school without permission; 2 one who shirks work or duty ‖ **tru'an·cy** *n* (-cies)

tru'ant of'fi·cer *n* attendance officer, official who deals with unauthorized absences from school

truce /trōōs'/ [ME *trewes* pl of *trewe* < OE *trēow* compact, pledge] *n* 1 brief cessation, pause, respite; 2 temporary suspension of warfare by agreement; armistice

truck¹ /truk'/ [OF *troquer* to exchange] *n* 1 vegetables raised for the market; 2 *colloq* rubbish; 3 *colloq* dealings, intercourse

truck² [< *truckle*] *n* 1 motor vehicle of various sizes for transporting loads; 2 platform on wheels or barrow for carrying baggage, heavy packages, etc.; 3 set of wheels, or frame mounted on wheels, to support one end of a railroad car, etc. ‖ *vt* 4 to transport by truck ‖ *vi* 5 to carry goods on a truck; 6 to drive a truck

truck'driv·er *n* person who drives a truck

truck'er¹ *n* truckdriver

truck'er² *n* truck farmer

truck' farm' *n* farm for growing vegetables for market ‖ **truck' farm'ing** *n* ‖ **truck' farm'er** *n*

truck'ing *n* the business of transporting goods by truck

truck·le /truk'əl/ [AF *trocle* sheave] *n* 1 trundle bed ‖ *vi* 2 to submit tamely to another's will

truck'le bed' *n* trundle bed

truc·u·lent /truk'yələnt, trōōk'-/ [L *truculentus*] *adj* 1 belligerent; aggressively hostile; **2** savage, ferocious ‖ **truc′u·lence** *n* ‖ SYN ruthless, destructive, brutal, inhuman, bloodthirsty, rapacious ‖ ANT gentle, merciful, kind, tender

trudge /truj′/ [?] *vi* **1** to walk with labor or fatigue ‖ *vt* **2** to walk wearily along or over

true /trōō′/ [OE *trēowe* loyal] *adj* **1** in accord with fact or reality, not false; **2** faithful, steadfast; **3** genuine; **4** rightful, legitimate; **5** corresponding to a standard; **6** correct; exact; **7** accurately conforming to type, as *a true moth;* **8** *mach* fitting exactly in relation to other parts or components ‖ *adv* **9** in truth; **10** accurately ‖ *n* **11** condition of being accurate or in exact alignment ‖ *v* (**tru·ing** or **true·ing**) *vt* **12** to make accurate, adjust ‖ SYN *adj* just, upright, good, right, moral, pure, truthful, staunch, real, exact, legitimate, correct, authentic ‖ ANT *adj* dishonest, faithless, treacherous, bad, deceptive, counterfeit, artificial, illegitimate

true′ bill′ *n* indictment handed down by a grand jury

true′-blue′ *adj* staunchly faithful or loyal; of unyielding principles

true′ north′ *n* the direction of the north pole from any point on earth, in contrast to the magnetic pole to which compass needles point

truf·fle /truf′əl, trōō′f-/ [< MF *trufe*] *n* any of various potato-shaped edible fungi (genus *Tuber*) that grow underground

tru·ism /trōō′izəm/ [< *true*] *n* an obvious truth ‖ SYN axiom, saw, saying, precept, maxim, motto, proverb, aphorism, byword, dictum ‖ DISCR These words agree in naming the expression of a truth in terse, meaty form. The *axiom* is a truth so evident that any reasoning brought forth to prove it is superfluous. A common *axiom* in logic is, "Things equal to the same thing are equal to each other." A *precept* is a rule concerning conduct, especially moral conduct, often expressed as a command, and frequently on a lofty plane, as "My children, love one another." A *maxim* is like a *precept*, but is more often directed toward the practical side of life, as "Tell the truth and shame the devil." A *motto* condenses a slogan or truth into a few words, sometimes inspirational in character. *Adage* and *proverb* name pithy expressions in which practical truths have been garnered; both the *adage* and the *proverb* are widely known, but the *adage* gives the more ancient wisdom, the *proverb* the homelier: "It's a long lane that has no turning" is an *adage*; "The early bird gets the worm" is a *proverb*. A *saying* is habitual, current, sensible, as "There's many a slip 'twixt the cup and the lip." A *saw* is an old, worn-out, tiresome *saying*. A *truism* is self-evident, often vapid and flavorless

tru′ly *adv* **1** in agreement with truth or fact; **2** precisely; **3** sincerely; honestly; **4** in fact, indeed; **5** legitimately

Tru·man, Har·ry S. /trōō′mən/ *n* (1884–1972) 33rd president of the U.S. 1945–53

trump /trump′/ [var of *triumph*] *n* **1** *cards* card of a suit that temporarily outranks the other suits; **2** *colloq* admirable fellow; **3** **trumps** *sg cards* suit to which the trump cards belong ‖ *vt* **4** *cards* to take with a trump; **5** to outdo; **6** **trump up** to fabricate ‖ *vi* **7** to play a trump

trump′er·y [MF *tromperie*] *n* (**-ies**) **1** worthless finery; **2** trash; **3** nonsense ‖ *adj* **4** showy but worthless

trum·pet /trump′it/ [MF *trompette*] *n* **1** brass wind instrument formed of a single curved tube with a flared end; **2** trumpet-shaped horn held to the ear by persons with defective hearing; **3** cry of an elephant ‖ *vt* **4** to proclaim loudly; **5** to sound on a trumpet ‖ *vi* **6** to blow a trumpet; **7** to utter a sound like that of a trumpet ‖ **trum′pet·er** *n*

trum′pet·er swan′ *n* large North American wild swan [*Olor buccinator*] having a very loud note

trun·cate /trung′kāt/ [L *truncare* (*-atus*)] *vt* **1** to cut or lop the top or end of; **2** to cut short

trun·cheon /trunch′ən/ [MF *tronchon* piece cut off] *n* **1** policeman's club; **2** staff indicating power or authority

trun·dle /trun′dəl/ [< OE *trendel* circle, ring] *vt* **1** to cause to roll; **2** to convey in a wagon or other wheeled vehicle ‖ *vi* **3** to roll along ‖ *n* **4** low wheel, roller

trun′dle bed′ *n* low bed on casters that may be rolled under another

trunk /trungk′/ [L *truncus*] *n* **1** main upright stem of a tree; **2** body of a man or animal, not including the head and limbs; **3** elephant's proboscis; **4** large box or chest for holding or transporting personal belongings; **5** compartment in an automobile for holding the spare tire, packages, luggage, etc.; **6** main channel or artery; **7** **trunks** *pl* shorts worn by men, as for swimming or boxing ‖ *adj* **8** pert. to a trunk line

trunk′ line′ *n* major transportation or telephone line, from which tributary lines branch off

truss /trus′/ [OF *trusser*] *vt* **1** to bind, tie, or fasten; **2** to support or brace with a truss or trusses; **3** **truss up** to tie tightly and securely ‖ *n* **4** timbers or bars fastened together to form a brace or framework, as for a bridge

or roof; **5** supporting device to prevent the return of a reduced hernia
trust /trust/ [< Scand] *n* **1** confidence; faith; belief in someone's goodness and integrity; **2** expectation or hope; **3** one who or that which is relied on; **4** credit granted because of belief in one's intention and ability to pay; **5** duty or responsibility; **6** something given over to one's custody or care; **7** charge or custody; **8** *com* **a** any combination of companies designed to establish a monopoly; **b** any large commercial or industrial operation with monopolistic tendencies; **9** *law* **a** right or property held by one party for the benefit of another; **b** responsibility or guardianship of such an estate; **10** **in trust** left in the care of another || *vt* **11** to place confidence in, rely on; **12** to believe; **13** to entrust to someone's care; **14** to sell on credit; **15** to hope with confidence || **trust'ing·ly** *adv* || SYN *n* reliance, assurance, faith, credence, expectation, care, charge, custody || DISCR *Reliance* is a leaning upon something, in the confidence that it can be depended upon, as *reliance* upon his word; her son was her sole *reliance* in her old age. *Trust*, which pours forth to those who evoke it, is an assured *reliance* upon their truthfulness, honesty, and uprightness. We have *trust* in those we love; in a higher sense, we have *trust* in God. *Assurance* is *trust* plus certainty afforded by some evidence or inner persuasion; we feel the *assurance* of a life to come; we make provisions in our will with the *assurance* that they will be carried out. *Faith* is belief founded on *trust*; it may be felt toward persons or things. We may have *faith* in the power of a physician and in the efficacy of the remedy that he prescribes. Religiously, *faith* believes and trusts to such an extent that the outward conduct is governed by implicit confidence and dependence on the goodness of God (see *assurance, belief*) || ANT *n* distrust, disbelief, suspicion
trust' com'pa·ny *n* company, usu. a bank, exercising the functions of a trustee and also of a commercial bank
trus·tee' *n* **1** person to whom property, or the management of property, is entrusted; **2** member of a board administering a company, college, or other institution
trus·tee'ship *n* **1** office or function of a trustee; **2** administrative control of a trust territory
trust'ful *adj* full of trust; ready to believe in others
trust' fund' *n* money or other tangible wealth left in trust
trust'ing *adj* trustful

trust' ter·ri·to'ry *n* territory or country placed under the administration of another country by the United Nations
trust'wor'thy *adj* reliable; meriting trust and confidence
trust'y *adj* (-i·er; -i·est) **1** trustworthy, reliable || *n* (-ies) **2** convict found worthy of special privileges
truth /trooth/ [OE *trēowth*] *n* (**truths** /-ths, -thz/) **1** conformity with fact; **2** veracity; integrity; **3** correctness, accuracy; **4** something real and actual; fact; **5** truism; **6** true state or condition; **7** **in truth** in fact, actually || SYN veracity, verity, constancy, fidelity, genuineness, fact, reality, verisimilitude, right, righteousness || DISCR *Truth* is accordance with fact or actuality. When one tells the *truth*, he tells what actually happened, what he really thinks, or what he sincerely feels. *Veracity* is the quality belonging to persons who are naturally truthful; a man of *veracity* is the opposite of a habitual liar (see *reality*) || ANT falsity, falsehood, treason, faithlessness, evil, deception, artificiality
truth'ful *adj* **1** according to fact; **2** habitually telling the truth
truth' se'rum *n* drug or barbiturate administered to induce a person to speak freely and truthfully
try /trī/ [OF *trier* to select] *v* (**tried**) *vt* **1** to put to a trial or experiment; test; **2** to experiment with, as *to try a new recipe*; **3** to subject to trouble or affliction; **4** to test the strength or endurance of; **5** to attempt, endeavor; **6** *law* **a** to examine into the guilt of in court; **b** to act as judge at the trial of; **7** **try on** to put on (an article of clothing) for fit or appearance; **8** **try out** to test || *vi* **9** to endeavor; make an effort; **10** **try out for** to compete for (a position, membership in a team, etc.) || *n* (**tries**) **11** attempt; effort; test
try'ing *adj* annoying; hard to bear; difficult
try'out' *n* test or trial of fitness or qualifications, as for athletic competence or a theatrical role
try'sail' /-sāl', *naut* -səl/ *n* small, stout fore-and-aft sail, set without a boom, to keep the ship's bow to the wind in stormy weather
tryst /trist/, trist/ [OF *triste* hunting station] *n* **1** engagement to meet at a certain place and time, as between lovers; **2** meeting; **3** place of meeting
tsar /(t)sär/ [Russ] *n* czar || **tsa·ri'na** /-rēn'ə/ *nfem*
tset'se fly' /tset'sē, tsēt'-/ [< Bantu] *n* any of several small blood-sucking African flies (genus *Glossina*) that carry infections to man and animals, including sleeping sickness
T'-shirt' *n* pullover collarless shirt

with short sleeves, worn as an undershirt or as a casual outer garment

T'-square' *n* ruler having a crossbar at one end, for drawing parallel lines

tsu·na·mi /tsŏŏnäm′ē/ [Jap] *n* large wave produced by an earthquake or volcanic eruption on the ocean bed

Tu. Tuesday

Tua·reg /twä′reg/ *n* **1** member of a nomadic Berber tribe of the Sahara; **2** language of the Tuaregs

tub /tub′/ [MLG *tubbe*] *n* **1** circular open wooden container or low cask; **2** any similar receptacle, as for washing clothes; **3** bathtub; **4** slow or clumsy boat; **5** *Brit* bath in a bathtub

tu·ba /t(y)ŏŏb′ə/ [L = trumpet] *n* any of various large deep-toned brass wind instruments

tub·by /tub′ē/ *adj* (**-bi·er; -bi·est**) short and fat

tube /t(y)ŏŏb′/ [L *tubus*] *n* **1** narrow hollow cylinder of glass, metal, rubber, etc., used esp. for conducting fluids; **2** collapsible cylinder of thin metal or plastic, with a cap at one end, from which semifluid substances may be squeezed out as needed; **3** *anat* any tubelike vessel or part; **4** tubular tunnel for an underground railway; **5** *colloq* underground railroad; **6** vacuum tube; **7** inner tube; **8** the tube *colloq* television

tu·ber /t(y)ŏŏb′ər/ [L = swelling] *n* **1** thick roundish underground stem bearing small buds or eyes, as the potato; **2** *anat* knot or rounded swelling

tu·ber·cle /t(y)ŏŏb′ərkəl/ [L *tuberculum*] *n* **1** small knob or rounded lump, as on a bone, the skin, or a plant; **2** such a swelling in the tissues of a lung affected by tuberculosis

tu·ber·cu·lar /t(y)ŏŏburk′yələr/ *adj* **1** of, pert. to, or affected with tuberculosis; **2** pert. to or having tubercles

tu·ber·cu·lin /-lin/ *n* liquid made from cultures of the tuberculosis bacillus, used in diagnosing and treating tuberculosis

tu·ber·cu·lo·sis *n* infectious disease characterized by the growth of tubercles in any part of the body, esp. the lungs, caused by the bacillus *Mycobacterium tuberculosis* ‖ **tu·ber′cu·lous** *adj*

tub·ing /t(y)ŏŏb′iŋ/ *n* **1** piece of tube; **2** material in the form of tubes; **3** tubes collectively; **4** system of tubes

tu′bu·lar /-byələr/ [< L *tubulus* small tube] *adj* of, like, pert. to, or characterized by tubes

tuck /tuk′/ [OE *tūcian* to torment] *vt* **1** to gather close together or into a small compass, as clothing; **2** to fold or turn back in place neatly or tightly; **3** to make and sew folds in; **4** to cover snugly, as a child in bed; **5** to thrust or place into a small or compact space ‖ *n* **6** sewed fold

tuck′er [< *tuck*] *vt* **tucker out** *colloq* to tire

Tuc·son /tŏŏ′son, tŏŏson′/ *n* city in S Arizona (225,000)

-tude /-t(y)ŏŏd′/ [L *-tudo*] *n suf* quality or state of being, as *servitude*, *gratitude*

Tu·dor /t(y)ŏŏd′ər/ *n* **1** member of the royal house that ruled England from 1485 to 1603 ‖ *adj* **2** pert. to the Tudors or to the period of their reign

Tues. Tuesday

Tues·day /t(y)ŏŏz′dē, -dā/ [OE *Tīwesdæg* day of Tiw, god of war] *n* third day of the week, following Monday ‖ **Tues′days** *adv*

tuft /tuft′/ [MF *tofe*] *n* **1** knot or bunch of long slender parts, as hair, grass, or threads, held together at one end; **2** cluster or clump ‖ *vt* **3** to furnish with tufts; **4** to divide, as upholstery, with depressions marked by tufts or buttons

tug /tug′/ [OE *togian* to tow] *v* (**tugged; tug·ging**) *vt* **1** to pull or haul laboriously; tow ‖ *vi* **2** to use great effort in pulling; **3** to struggle, exert oneself ‖ *n* **4** act or instance of tugging; **5** any great exertion; struggle; **6** tugboat

tug′boat′ *n* small but powerful boat for towing and pushing ships and barges

tug′ of war′ *n* contest in which two teams, pulling at opposite ends of a rope, try to pull each other over a line

tu·i·tion /t(y)ŏŏ·ish′ən/ [L *tuitio* (*-onis*) guardianship] *n* **1** instruction; **2** charge for instruction

tu·lip /t(y)ŏŏl′ip/ [It *tulipano* < Turk *tülbend* turban] *n* any of a genus (*Tulipa*) of plants of the lily family, bearing brilliantly colored bell-shaped flowers

tulle /tŏŏl′/ [< *Tulle*, France] *n* delicate netlike material made of silk, nylon, etc., used chiefly for veils, scarfs, and dresses

Tul·sa /tuls′ə/ *n* city in NE Oklahoma (331,638)

tum·ble /tum′bəl/ [< OE *tumbian* to dance] *vi* **1** to fall suddenly; **2** to fall down, rolling end over end; **3** to fall precipitously, as prices; **4** to roll or toss around; **5** to execute gymnastic feats on mats, as leaps and somersaults; **6** to go or move in a disorderly fashion; **7** *colloq* to understand, become aware ‖ *vt* **8** to throw down carelessly or roughly; **9** to topple, overthrow ‖ *n* **10** act of tumbling or falling; **11** precipitous descent; **12** state of confusion or disorder; **13** interested response

tum′ble-down′ *adj* dilapidated, run-down

tum′bler *n* **1** one who performs feats of tumbling; **2** stemless drinking glass without a handle; **3** a part of a lock that must be lined up in a certain position by the key before the bolt can be moved; **4** self-righting toy

tum·ble·weed /tum′bəl′wēd/ *n* any of various weeds, common in the prairies of the U.S., which break off from the root in the fall and are blown by the wind

tum·brel or **tum·bril** /tum′brəl/ [OF *tomberel*] *n* **1** dumpcart; **2** such a cart used during the French Revolution to take the condemned to the guillotine

tu·mes·cent /t(y)ōōmes′ənt/ [L *tumescens* (-*entis*)] *adj* swelling; in a swollen state ‖ **tu·mes′cence** *n*

tu·mid /t(y)ōōm′id/ [L *tumidus*] *adj* **1** swollen; enlarged; **2** pompous (style) ‖ **tu·mid′i·ty** /-mid′-/ *n*

tum·my /tum′ē/ *n* (-**mies**) *colloq* stomach

tu·mor /t(y)ōōm′ər/ [L] *n* abnormal swelling or mass of new tissue growing independently in the body and having no physiological use

tu·mult /t(y)ōōm′əlt/ [L *tumultus*] *n* **1** uproar, commotion, as of a rioting mob; **2** any violent agitation or disturbance ‖ **tu·mul/tu·ous** /-mulch′-ōō-əs/ *adj* ‖ SYN confusion, uproar, turbulence (see *noise*)

tun /tun′/ [OE *tunne*] *n* large cask, esp. for wine

tu·na /tōōn′ə/ [AmSp] *n* (**tuna** or **tunas**) any of several large food and game fishes of the family Scombridae

tun·dra /tun′drə/ [Russ] *n* any of the large, level, treeless plains of the arctic regions

tune /t(y)ōōn′/ [< *tone*] *n* **1** sequence of musical tones forming an air or melody; **2 call the tune** to be in control; **3 change one's tune** to change one's mind; **4 in tune, a** in the proper pitch; **b** agreeing in pitch; **5 in tune with** in harmony with; **6 out of tune, a** not in the proper pitch; **b** not agreeing in pitch; **7 out of tune with** not in harmony with; **8 to the tune of** *colloq* at the price of (a specified amount) ‖ *vt* **9** to adjust (a voice or instrument) to the correct pitch; **10** to put into harmony or agreement; **11** to adjust for proper functioning; **12** *rad* to adjust (a receiver or transmitter) to a certain wavelength or frequency; **13 tune out** *rad* to eliminate (unwanted signals) by adjusting the wavelength of the receiving set; **14 tune up** to adjust (an automobile engine) ‖ *vi* **15** to be in harmony; **16 tune in** *rad* to adjust a receiving set so as to hear the program of a given station; **17 tune up** to tune the instruments of a band or orchestra

tune′ful *adj* melodious

tune′-up′ *n* tuning of an engine or motor to assure proper functioning

tung·sten /tun′stən/ [Sw = heavy stone] *n* hard, heavy grayish-white metallic element (W; at.no. 74; at.wt.

183.85), used to increase the hardness of steel for cutting tools and for electric-lamp filaments

tu·nic /t(y)ōōn′ik/ [L *tunica*] *n* **1** gownlike outer garment, with or without sleeves, worn by the ancient Greeks and Romans; **2** woman's blouse extending over the skirt to the hips; **3** *mil* coat worn as part of a uniform; **4** *anat & zool* natural covering membrane; **5** *bot* membranous covering, as an onion skin

tun′ing fork′ *n* fork-shaped piece of steel with two equal prongs, which when struck gives a fixed tone, used to tune musical instruments

Tu·nis /t(y)ōōn′is/ *n* capital of Tunisia (662,000)

Tu·ni·sia /tōōnēzh′ə, -nēsh′ə, -nizh′ə, -nish′ə/ *n* Arabic-speaking republic in N Africa on the Mediterranean opposite Sicily (5,100,000; 63,379 sq.m.; cap. Tunis) ‖ **Tu·ni′sian** *adj & n*

tun·nel /tun′əl/ [MF *tonele* tube-shaped net] *n* **1** underground passage, as one cut through a hill or under a river, or one dug by an animal; **2** any similar passage made under or through something ‖ *v* (-**neled** or -**nelled**; -**nel·ing** or -**nel·ling**) *vt* **3** to make a tunnel through or under; **4** to excavate (a passageway) ‖ *vi* **5** to make a tunnel

tun·ny /tun′ē/ [ML *tunnina*] *n* (-**nies**) tuna

Tu·pi /tōōpē′, tōō′pē/ *n* **1** member of several related Indian tribes of Brazil and Paraguay; **2** language of the Tupis ‖ also *adj*

tup·pence /tup′əns/ *n* twopence

tur·ban /turb′ən/ [< Turkish *tülbend* < Pers *dulband*] *n* **1** headdress worn by men in the Orient, chiefly Muslims, consisting of a cap around which a long cloth is wrapped; **2** any similar headdress; **3** close-fitting hat, brimless or with a very small brim, worn by women

tur·bid /turb′id/ [L *turbidus* disturbed] *adj* **1** not clear or transparent, clouded, as by stirred-up sediment; **2** thick, dense, as smoke; **3** confused, muddled ‖ **tur·bid′i·ty** /tər-bid′-/ *n*

tur·bine /turb′in, -bīn/ [F < *turbo* (-*inis*) whirl, revolution] *n* motor driven by the pressure of steam, water, air, or gases on the vanes or blades of a rotor

tur·bo- /tur′bō-/ *comb form* turbine

tur′bo·fan′ *n* **1** turbojet engine in which a propeller or fan forces low-pressure air through ducts directly into the hot turbine exhaust at the turbine-exhaust pressure; **2** airplane driven by turbofan engines

tur′bo·jet′ *n* **1** turbojet engine; **2** airplane driven by turbojet engines

tur′bo·jet en′gine *n* jet-propulsion engine in which atmospheric air is compressed for combustion by a turbine-driven compressor

tur·bo·prop' /turb'yələnt/ n 1 turboprop engine; 2 airplane driven by a turboprop engine

tur·bo·prop en'gine n jet engine with additional thrust added by a turbine-driven propeller

tur·bu·lent /turb'yələnt/ [L *turbulentus*] adj 1 disorderly; uncontrollable, riotous; 2 agitated, disturbed ‖ **tur'bu·lence** n

tu·reen /t(y)ŏŏrēn'/ [F *terrine* earthenware dish] n deep, covered dish, as for serving soup

turf /turf'/ [OE] n 1 grassy top layer of earth, including plant roots; 2 peat as used for fuel; 3 piece of sod; 4 **the turf,** a the race course; b horse racing ‖ vt 5 to cover with sod

tur·gid /tur'jid/ [L *turgidus*] adj 1 swollen, bloated; 2 bombastic, pompous ‖ **tur·gid'i·ty** /tərjid'-/ n

Tu·rin /t(y)ŏŏr'in, t(y)ŏŏrin'/ n city in NW Italy (1,025,000)

Turk /turk'/ [Gk *Tourkos*] n native or inhabitant of Turkey

Turk. 1 Turkey; 2 Turkish

Tur·ke·stan /turk'istan', -stän'/ n large region in W central Asia extending from the Caspian Sea to China; original homeland of the Turks

tur·key /turk'ē/ [< *turkey cock* guinea fowl, originally from Turkey] n 1 large wild or domesticated American fowl (family Meleagrididae); 2 *theat slang* flop; 3 **talk turkey** *colloq* to talk frankly, get down to business

Tur·key n republic in Asia Minor and SE Europe (36,300,000; 296,382 sq. m.; cap. Ankara)

tur'key buz'zard n large black-and-brown vulture (*Cathartes aura*) of Central America and South America and the southern U.S., with a featherless red head and neck

Tur'kic n branch of the Altaic language family spoken in central and SW Asia, including Turkish ‖ also *adj*

Turk'ish adj 1 of or pert. to Turkey, the Turks, or their language ‖ n 2 language of the Turks

Turk'ish bath' n bath in which one is made to perspire freely in a steam room and then is washed and rubbed down and finally given a cold shower

Turk'ish de·light' n candy consisting of cubes of flavored gelatin covered with powdered sugar

Turk'ish tow'el n towel made of cotton terry cloth

Tur·ko·man /turk'əmən/ [Pers *turkumān* one like a Turk] n (**-mans**) member of any of various nomadic Turkish tribes in Afghanistan and Turkestan

tur·mer·ic /turm'ərik/ [< ML *terra merita* excellent earth] n 1 East Indian plant (*Curcuma longa*) or its aromatic rootstock, used as a yellow dye and as a condiment, esp. in curry powder; 2 any of several other plants with colored juices

tur·moil /tur'moil/ [?] n commotion and confusion; disturbance, tumult

turn /turn'/ [OE *turnian* < L *tornare* to turn on (a lathe)] vt 1 to rotate, as a wheel; 2 to do or perform by means of a revolving motion, as *to turn handsprings;* 3 to give a circular shape to, as on a lathe; 4 to fashion gracefully, as *to turn a phrase;* 5 to change the direction, attitude, or position of, as *to turn an automobile, to turn one's attention;* 6 to upset (one's stomach); 7 to change the nature or appearance of; 8 to convert, as *to turn cream into butter;* 9 to make (milk) sour; 10 to bend or twist; 11 to repel (an attack); 12 to translate; 13 to cause to become, as *the news turned her pale;* 14 to cause to go; to send, as *to turn back the crowds;* 15 to move to the other side of, go around, as *to turn a corner;* 16 to invert, reverse, as *to turn a shirt collar;* 17 **turn back,** a to repel; b to cause to go back; 18 **turn down,** a to reject; b to lessen the intensity of; c to fold down; 19 **turn in,** a to submit; b to inform on; 20 **turn off,** a to stop the flow of (water, gas, etc.); b to extinguish (a light); c to switch off (a motor); 21 **turn on,** a to cause to flow, as water or gas; b to light (a light); c to switch on (a motor); d *slang* to arouse, excite, as *that blonde turns me on;* 22 **turn out,** a to extinguish (a light); b to produce; c to dismiss, remove from office; 23 **turn over,** a to invert; b to revolve in the mind, ponder; c to hand over; d to start (an engine); e *com* to move goods; 24 **turn up,** a to dig up; b to find; c to increase the intensity of ‖ *vi* 25 to revolve, rotate; 26 to change in direction, attitude, or position; 27 to become upset, as the stomach; 28 to whirl, reel, as the head; 29 to change one's attitude or course of action, as *they turned against me;* 30 to change in condition, nature, or appearance; 31 to become sour or rancid; 32 to become, as *he turned blue, he turned twenty;* 33 to direct the attention and efforts, as *to turn to farming;* 34 to change course, as *turn to the left;* 35 to change position by rotating; 36 to bend or curve; 37 to change one's allegiance; defect; 38 **turn back** to retrace one's steps; go back; 39 **turn in** *colloq* to go to bed; 40 **turn on,** a to hinge on, depend on; b to become hostile toward; 41 **turn off** *slang* to give up, lose interest; 42 **turn out,** a to result, eventuate; b to prove to be; c to come out, as to a meeting; 43 **turn over,** a to move or roll over; **b** to start, as an automobile engine; **44 turn to, a** to appeal to; have recourse to; **b** to change to; **45 turn up, a** to happen, develop; **b** to put in an appearance ‖ *n* **46** act of revolving, circular motion; **47** single revolution or twisting, as *a turn of the rope around the post;* **48** change of direction; **49** point where change of direction occurs; **50** bend or curve; **51** short promenade or ride, as *a turn in the park;* **52** deed or act, as *do a good turn;* **53** time for some act which one does in rotation with others, as *it is your turn;* **54** change in condition, as *a turn for the worse;* **55** period of work; shift; **56** need, occasion, as *this will not serve your turn;* **57** tendency, bent; **58** short piece or act on the stage; **59** *colloq* startling surprise or shock; **60 in turn** in proper sequence; **61 out of turn, a** out of proper sequence; **b** at an inappropriate time; **62 take turns to** alternate in order; **63 to a turn** to perfection ‖ SYN *n* inclination, bent, aptitude (see *gift)*

turn′a‧bout′ *n* **1** reversal of opinion or allegiance; **2** retaliatory action

turn′buck‧le *n* device, as a metal sleeve with ends threaded in opposite directions, so that when connected between the ends of two rods it may be turned to regulate their tension or the distance between them

turn′coat′ *n* one who forsakes his allegiance to go over to the other side

turn′ing *n* **1** angle or corner; bend, as in a road; **2** act of fashioning metal or wood on a lathe

turn′ing point′ *n* critical or decisive moment in the course of something

tur‧nip /turn′ip/ [< *turn* + *dial. nepe* turnip] *n* **1** either of two biennials (*Brassica rapa* or *B. napobrassica*) of the mustard family, having a flat or globular root which is used as a vegetable; **2** *colloq* heavy, old watch

turn′key′ *n* jailer

turn′out′ *n* **1** yield or production; **2** railroad siding; **3** passage on a one-lane road to allow automobiles and other vehicles to pass; **4** public gathering of persons, as at a meeting; **5** array, equipment

turn′o′ver *n* **1** act or result of turning over; **2** tart made semicircular or triangular by folding one half of the crust over the other half; **3** number of times in a given period that a sum invested in a business is returned for reinvestment; **4** amount of business done in a specified period; **5** movement of customers in and out of a retail establishment; **6** rate at which a stock is depleted and replaced; **7** rate at which the employees in a given establishment are replaced ‖ *adj* **8** capable of being turned over or folded down

turn′pike′ *n* **1** originally, a road barrier, turned aside upon payment of a toll; **2** toll highway; **3** highway

turn′stile′ *n* **1** gate made of four arms pivoted on the top of a post and turning to allow a person through; **2** similar device, as at the entrance to a building or subway platform, operated by a coin or token

turn′ta′ble *n* **1** rotating platform with tracks for turning locomotives and cars around; **2** rotating disk to hold the record in a phonograph

tur‧pen‧tine /turp′əntīn/ [MF *terbentine*] *n* light-colored volatile fluid distilled from the sap of various coniferous trees, used chiefly in paints and varnishes

tur‧pi‧tude /turp′it(y)ōōd′/ [L *turpitudo*] *n* baseness; shameful wickedness, depravity

turps /turps′/ *nsg colloq* turpentine

tur‧quoise /tur′k(w)oiz/ [F = Turkish (stone)] *n* **1** opaque bright-blue or greenish-blue hydrous phosphate of aluminum and copper, used as a gem; **2** color between green and blue ‖ *also adj*

tur‧ret /tur′it/ [MF *turete*] *n* **1** small tower, usu. at a corner of a large building; **2** *mil* armored revolving structure containing usu. large-caliber guns, mounted on a battleship, fortification, or tank; **3** pivoted attachment, as on a lathe or camera, holding several different tools or lenses that can be quickly rotated into place

tur‧tle /turt′əl/ [< F *tortue*] *n* **1** any of an order (Chelonia) of reptiles with horny toothless jaws, and bodies enclosed in a bony shell; **2 turn turtle** to turn over completely, capsize

tur′tle‧dove′ [OE *turtle* < L *turtur* turtledove + *dove*] *n* **1** any of several Old World wild doves (genus *Streptopelia*), esp. *S. turtur*, noted for its soft cooing; **2** any of several species of North American doves, as the mourning dove; **3** sweetheart

tur′tle‧neck′ *n* **1** high snug-fitting turnover collar usu. on a pullover sweater; **2** sweater with a turtleneck

Tus‧ca‧ny /tus′kənē/ *n* region and former grand duchy of NW Italy (cap. Florence) ‖ **Tus′can** *adj & n*

tush /tush′/ [imit] *interj* expression of contempt, reproof, or restraint

tusk /tusk′/ [OE *tusc*] *n* **1** long projecting tooth, usu. one of a pair, as in the elephant or walrus; **2** any very long tooth or toothlike part

tus‧sle /tus′əl/ [var of *tousle*] *n* **1** scuffle, wrestle; **2** hard struggle ‖ *vi* **3** to wrestle, struggle

tus‧sock /tus′ək/ [?] *n* tuft or clump of grass or the like

tut /tut′/ [?] *interj* expressing rebuke, impatience, disdain, etc.

tu‧te‧lage /t(y)ōōt′ilij/ [< L *tutela* protection] *n* **1** act of teaching or acting as guardian for someone; protection; **2** state of being under a tutor or guardian ‖ **tu′te·lar′y** /-ler′ē/ also **tu′te·lar** /-lər/ *adj*

tu·tor /t(y)ōōt′ər/ [L = guardian] *n* **1** one who instructs another; **2** private teacher, as one who takes charge of a child's education or one who coaches students ‖ *vt* **3** to act as a tutor to ‖ *vi* **4** to act as a tutor; **5** to be taught privately ‖ **tu·to′ri·al** /-tôr′ē·əl, -tōr′-/ *adj*

tut·ti-frut·ti /tōōt′ē frōōt′ē/ [It = all fruits] *n* flavoring or confection made of various kinds of preserved fruits ‖ also *adj*

tu·tu /tōō′tōō/ [F] *n* short full ballet skirt, made of many layers of sheer fabric, as tulle

tux /tuks′/ *n colloq* tuxedo

tux·e·do /tuksēd′ō/ [< *Tuxedo* Park, N.Y.] *n* man's jacket for semiformal evening wear

TV television

TVA Tennessee Valley Authority

TV′ din′ner *n* complete meal on a tray, cooked, wrapped, and quick-frozen, requiring only to be heated

twad·dle /twod′əl/ [< *dial. twattle*, var of *tattle*] *n* **1** foolish empty talk or writing ‖ *vi* **2** to utter twaddle

twain /twān′/ [OE *twegen*] *adj* & *n poet.* & *archaic* two

twang /twaŋ′/ [imit] *n* **1** sharp quick vibrating sound, like that produced by plucking a stringed instrument; **2** nasal tone in speech ‖ *vt* **3** to cause to sound with a twang; **4** to pluck (a stringed instrument) ‖ *vi* **5** to give off a twanging sound; **6** to speak with a twang ‖ **twang′y** *adj* (-i·er; -i·est)

'twas /twuz′, twoz′/ it was

tweak /twēk′/ [OE *twiccian*] *vt* **1** to pinch or twist with a jerk; twitch ‖ *n* **2** sudden sharp pull or pinch

tweed /twēd′/ [< Sc *tweel* twill] *n* **1** coarse twilled wool fabric showing two or more colors mixed in the yarn; **2** tweeds *pl* garments of tweed

Twee·dle·dum and Twee·dle·dee /twēd′-əldum′ ən twēd′əldē′/ [humorous coinage] *n* two persons, groups, or things between which there is scarcely any difference

tweed′y *adj* (-i·er; -i·est) **1** made of or like tweed; **2** wearing tweeds, esp. as a mark of informal outdoor living

'tween /twēn′/ *prep poet.* between

tweet /twēt′/ [imit] *n* **1** thin chirping note ‖ *vi* **2** to utter a tweet

tweet′er *n* small loudspeaker designed to reproduce sounds of higher acoustic frequency

tweeze /twēz′/ [F *étuis pl* of *étui* case for small instruments] *vt* to pluck, as with tweezers

tweez′ers *npl* small pincers for grasping and pulling out hairs and other tiny objects

twelfth /twelfth′/ [OE *twelfta*] *n* **1** one next in order after the eleventh;

2 one of twelve equal parts ‖ also *adj*

Twelfth′-night′ *n* the evening before Epiphany, the twelfth day after Christmas

twelve /twelv′/ [OE *twelf*] *n* **1** one more than eleven (12; XII); **2 the Twelve** *pl* the Twelve Apostles, Christ's original disciples ‖ also *adj* & *pron*

twen′ti·eth *n* **1** the one next in order after the nineteenth; **2** one of twenty equal parts ‖ also *adj*

twen·ty /twent′ē/ [OE *twentig*] *n* (-ties) **1** two times ten (20; XX); **2 the twenties** *pl* a the numbers from 20 to 29; b the years from 20 to 29 in a century or a lifetime ‖ also *adj* & *pron*

twen′ty-one′ *n* card game the winner of which is the one who draws cards adding up to 21 or the closest to it without exceeding it

'twere /twur′/ it were

twerp /twurp′/ [?] *n slang* small, despicable fellow

twice /twīs′/ [OE *twiges*] *adv* **1** two times; **2** doubly; in twofold measure or degree

twice′-told′ *adj* told over and over again; hackneyed, trite

twid·dle /twid′əl/ [?] *vt* **1** to twirl or play with idly; **2 twiddle one's thumbs** to be idle ‖ *vi* **3** to play or trifle

twig /twig′/ [OE *twigge*] *n* small branch of a tree or shrub

twi′light′ /twī′-/ [ME] *n* **1** the faint light before sunrise and esp. after sunset; **2** period between sunset and darkness; **3** end period, as of one's life; **4** darkness, gloom ‖ also *adj*

twi′light sleep′ *n* state of partial insensibility to pain induced by drugs, used esp. in childbirth

twill /twil′/ [< OE *twilīc*] *n* **1** weave of cloth that shows diagonal ribs on the surface; **2** fabric woven with such ribs ‖ *vt* **3** to weave so as to show a twill

'twill /twil′/ it will

twin /twin′/ [< OE *getwinnas* twins] *adj* **1** being one of a pair of identical or very similar things; **2** being a twin or twins ‖ *n* **3** one of two born at one birth; **4** person or thing very like another

twin- *adj comb form* consisting of or constructed with two identical parts, as *twin-engine, twin-screw*

twin′ bed′ *n* one of two single matching beds

twine /twīn′/ [OE *twīn*] *n* **1** strong cord or thread made of twisted strands ‖ *vt* **2** to twist together; **3** to make by twisting or coiling; **4** to wind; encircle; **5** to interlace ‖ *vi* **6** to twist; **7** to wind or coil

twinge /twinj′/ [OE *twengan* to pinch] *n* **1** sudden sharp pain, physical or emotional ‖ *vt* **2** to cause to have a twinge ‖ *vi* **3** to feel a twinge

twi'night' /twī'-/ *adj* baseball noting a doubleheader in which the first game starts late in the afternoon and the second after it has gotten dark

twin-kle /twiŋk'əl/ [OE *twinclian*] *vi* 1 to shine with a flickering light, as a star; 2 to sparkle or gleam; 3 (of the eyes) to flash, as with amusement; 4 to dart to and fro, as the feet in dancing ‖ *vt* 5 to cause to twinkle ‖ *n* 6 intermittent light; 7 flash or sparkle; 8 twinkling

twin'kling *n* brief moment; flash

twirl /twurl'/ [?] *vt* 1 to cause to rotate rapidly; whirl, spin ‖ *vi* 2 to rotate rapidly; 3 baseball to pitch ‖ *n* 4 quick circular motion; 5 coil, twist, curl

twirl'er *n* 1 person or thing that twirls; 2 baseball pitcher

twist /twist'/ [ME *twisten* to divide] *vt* 1 to wind (strands) together; 2 to form (a rope, twine, etc.) by this means; 3 to give a spiral form to; 4 to contort, distort; 5 to distort the meaning of; 6 to wrench or turn, as one's ankle; 7 to wind around, entwine, wreathe; 8 to revolve or rotate; 9 to remove by rotating; 10 **twist the arm of** to use intense coercion on, esp. in political matters ‖ *vi* 11 to become twisted; 12 to take a spiral form; 13 to curve, bend, wind; 14 to rotate, revolve; 15 to wind about something; 16 to become wrenched or turned; 17 to writhe or squirm; 18 to turn from a direct line ‖ *n* 19 act or manner of twisting; 20 curve or bend; 21 kink; 22 distortion; 23 spiral shape or arrangement; 24 abrupt change in the course of events; 25 twisted piece, as of lemon peel; 26 something made by winding strands together, as certain kinds of thread; 27 tobacco in a twisted roll; 28 rolled loaf of bread; 29 wrench or turn, as of a muscle; 30 onward motion combined with rotation about a line of motion; 31 torsional stress; torque

twist'er *n* colloq cyclone or tornado

twit /twit'/ [OE *ætwītan* to taunt] *v* (**twit·ted; twit·ting**) *vt* 1 to reproach, scold; 2 to taunt, tease

twitch /twich'/ [OE *twiccian* to pluck] *vt* 1 to pull with a sudden jerk ‖ *vi* 2 to move jerkily or spasmodically ‖ *n* 3 quick jerk or pull; 4 quick involuntary movement of a muscle

twit·ter /twit'ər/ [ME *twiteren*] *vi* 1 to chirp rapidly; 2 to feel nervous excitement; 3 to titter ‖ *vt* 4 to utter by chirping ‖ *n* 5 act or sound of twittering; 6 nervous trembling ‖ **twit'ter·y** *adj*

'twixt /twikst'/ *prep* betwixt

two /tōō/ [OE *twā*] *n* 1 sum of one and one (2; II); 2 set of two persons or things; 3 card or die with two

spots; 4 **in two** into two parts ‖ also *adj & pron*

two'-bit' [< *two bits*] *adj slang* cheap, inferior, of low caliber

two' bits' [< *bit³*] *n slang* a quarter, 25 cents

two'-by-four' *adj* 1 measuring two by four units, usu. inches; 2 *colloq* small; narrow; of limited space; 3 *colloq* of little account ‖ *n* 4 piece of lumber with a thickness of 1⅝ inches and a width of 3⅝ inches

two'-cy'cle *adj* (internal-combustion engine) having a cycle of two strokes, one of intake and compression and one of ignition (power) and exhaust

two'-edged' *adj* 1 having two edges; 2 effective both ways; 3 ambiguous, as *a two-edged reason*

two'-faced' *adj* 1 having two faces; 2 deceitful; treacherous

two'-fist'ed *adj* 1 strong; virile; 2 ready to use one's fists

two'fold' *adj* 1 having two times as much or as many ‖ *adv* 2 two times as much or as many

two'-hand'ed *adj* 1 having two hands; 2 used with two hands; 3 intended for use by two persons; 4 played or engaged in by two persons

two·pence /tup'əns/ *nsg* or *npl* 1 sum of two British pennies; 2 coin worth this amount

two'-phase' *adj* (circuit or device) through which an alternating current flows which pulsates in two phases differing by one quarter of a cycle

two'-piece' *adj* having two pieces or parts

two'-ply' *adj* having two plies, layers, thicknesses, or strands

two'some *n* 1 group of two persons; 2 game played by two persons

two'-step' *n* ballroom dance in 2/4 time ‖ also *vi*

two'-time' *vt slang* to be unfaithful in love to ‖ **two'-tim'er** *n*

two'-tone' *adj* having two colors

'twould /twōōd'/ it would

two'-way' *adj* 1 allowing or entailing passage or communication in two directions at the same time; 2 involving mutual responsibilities

two'-way switch' *n* one of two three-terminal switches that control a single outlet

two'-wheel'er *n* bicycle having two wheels

-ty¹ /-tē/ [OF *-te* < L *-tas* (*-tatis*)] *suf* forming abstract nouns denoting quality, state, or condition, as *piety*, *loyalty*

-ty² [OE *-tig* tens] *suf* times ten; used for numerals, as *thirty*, *forty*

ty·coon /tīkōōn'/ [Jap *taikun* great prince < Chin] *n* wealthy and powerful financier, industrialist, business man, publisher, etc.

ty·ing /tī′iŋ/ *prp* of **tie**

tyke /tīk′/ [ME] *n* 1 cur; 2 small child

Ty·ler, John /tīl′ər/ *n* (1790–1862) 10th president of the U.S. 1841–45

tym·pa·num /timp′ənəm/ [L < Gk *tympanon* kettledrum] *n* (-nums or -na /-nə/) 1 middle ear; 2 eardrum; 3 diaphragm of a telephone; 4 *arch.* triangular or semicircular surface, usually decorated, enclosed between the slanting sides of a pediment or within an arch over a window or door ‖ **tym·pan′ic** /-pan′-/ *adj*

type /tīp′/ [L *typus*] *n* 1 person or thing representative of a group because of common characteristics; 2 specimen, example; 3 form of structure common to a group or an exemplification of it; 4 model or pattern; 5 kind, class, sort; 6 *typ* a block or piece, usu. of metal, bearing on one end a letter or character in relief; **b** such pieces collectively; **c** printed character or characters ‖ *vt* 7 to typify, represent; 8 to typewrite; 9 to determine the type of, classify ‖ *vi* 10 to typewrite

-type *comb form* 1 type, as *archetype*; 2 photographic process, as *tintype*

type′cast′ *v* (-cast) *vt theat* to cast (an actor) in the same type of role that first brought him fame, and with which the public identifies him

type′face′ *n* 1 surface of printing type that makes the impression; 2 this impression; 3 style or size of the character on the type; 4 all the type of a given design of any size

type′script′ *n* typewritten manuscript

type′set′ter *n* 1 one who sets type for printing; 2 typesetting machine

type′set·ting ma·chine′ *n* keyboard machine for automatically producing type from hot metal and setting it or setting foundry type

type′write′ *v* (-wrote; -writ·ten) *vt & vi* to write on a typewriter

type′writ′er *n* 1 writing machine with a keyboard that produces characters like those in print; 2 style of type that imitates typewritten copy; 3 typist

ty·phoid /tī′foid/ [*typhus* + -*oid*] *adj* 1 pert. to or resembling typhus; 2 pert. to typhoid fever ‖ *n* 3 typhoid fever

ty′phoid fe′ver *n* acute, infectious, often fatal disease, caused by the typhoid bacillus *Salmonella typhosa* and generally acquired through infected food and drink

ty·phoon /tīfoōn′/ [Ar *tūfān* or Chin *tai fung*] *n* violent cyclonic storm of the western Pacific

ty·phus /tīf′əs/ [ML < Gk *typhos* smoke, mist] *n* acute contagious fever marked by great weakness, mental disorder, and an eruption of red spots on the body, caused by microorganisms of the genus *Rickettsia* and spread by lice and fleas

typ·i·cal /tip′ikəl/ [< Gk *typikos*] *adj* 1 symbolic; representative of a class; 2 like others of its kind; 3 representative, characteristic ‖ **typ′i·cal·ly** *adv* ‖ SYN characteristic, regular, normal ‖ ANT exceptional, irregular, rare, abnormal, unusual

typ′i·fy /tip′-/ *v* (-fied) *vt* 1 to represent, symbolize; 2 to exemplify, be a typical representative of

typ′ist /tīp′-/ *n* one who operates a typewriter

ty·po /tī′pō/ *n colloq* typographical error

ty·pog·ra·phy /tīpog′rəfē/ *n* (-phies) 1 art or process of printing from type; 2 setting up of or printing from type; 3 appearance, style, or arrangement of printed matter ‖ **ty·pog′ra·pher** *n* ‖ **ty′po·graph′i·cal** /tīp′əgraf′-/ *adj*

ty·pol·o·gy /tīpol′əjē/ *n* 1 doctrine of types; 2 study or classification of types ‖ **ty′po·log′ic** (-i·cal) /-pəloj′-/ *adj*

ty·ran·ni·cal /tiran′ikəl, tī-/ [see **tyr·rany**] *adj* cruel; harsh, oppressive; despotic ‖ **ty·ran′ni·cal·ly** *adv*

tyr′an·nize′ /tir′ə-/ *vi* 1 to exercise tyrannical control ‖ *vt* 2 to treat tyrannically

tyr′an·nous *adj* tyrannical

tyr·an·ny /tir′ənē/ [ML *tyrannia*] *n* (-nies) 1 tyrannical government or rule; 2 unbridled abuse of power or authority; 3 tyrannical act

ty·rant /tīr′ənt/ [OF *tirant* < Gk *tyrannos*] *n* 1 cruel and oppressive ruler; 2 anyone who exercises authority tyrannically; 3 absolute ruler in ancient Greece and Sicily

ty·ro /tīr′ō/ [L *tiro* recruit] *n* novice or learner; beginner

Tyr·ol /tī′rōl, tir′ōl, tirōl′/ *n* alpine region in N Italy and W Austria ‖ **Ty·ro·le·an** /tirōl′ē·ən/ also **Tyr·o·lese** /tir′əlēz′, -lēs′/ *adj & n* (-lese)

tzar /tsär′/ *n* czar ‖ **tza·ri′na** /-rēn′ə/ *nfem*

U

U, u /yoo′/ *n* (U's or Us; u's or us) 21st letter of the English alphabet

U 1 21st in order or in a series; 2 *chem* uranium; 3 something shaped like a U

U. University

U.A.R. United Arab Republic

u·biq·ui·tous /yo͞obik'witəs/ [< L *ubique* everywhere] *adj* being everywhere at the same time ‖ **u·biq'ui·ty** *n*

U'-boat' [G *U-Boot* contr. of *Unterseeboot*] *n* German submarine

U' bolt' *n* U-shaped bolt having threads and a nut at each end

u.c. *typ* upper case

ud·der /ud'ər/ [OE *ūder*] *n* milk gland having more than one teat, as in the cow

UFO unidentified flying object

u·fol·o·gy /yo͞ofol'əjē/ *n* study of unidentified flying objects ‖ **u·fol'o·gist** *n*

U·gan·da /yo͞ogan'də/ *n* republic in central Africa between the Congo and Kenya (9,600,000; 91,134 sq.m.; cap. Kampala); member of the British Commonwealth ‖ **U·gan'dan** *adj & n*

ugh /ug', o͝okh'/ *interj* expressing disgust or aversion

ug·ly /ug'lē/ [ON *uggligr* fearsome] *adj* (-li·er; -li·est) **1** displeasing to the eye; hideous; **2** morally repulsive; **3** vile, disagreeable; **4** suggesting danger or trouble; **5** quarrelsome, ill-tempered ‖ **ug'li·ness** *n*

U·gri·an /y)o͞og'rē·ən/ [< Russ *Ugri* the Ugrian people] *n* **1** member of a race including the Hungarians and related peoples of N Russia and Siberia; **2** Ugric ‖ *also adj*

U·gric /y)o͞og'rik/ *n* **1** branch of the Uralic languages that includes Hungarian and related languages of N Russia and Siberia ‖ *also adj*

UHF ultrahigh frequency

U.K. United Kingdom

u·kase /yo͞o'kās, yo͞okāz'/ [Russ *ukaz*] *n* **1** formerly, a decree of the czar of Russia, taking effect as law; **2** any official decree, esp. by an absolute authority

uke /yo͞ok'/ *n slang* ukulele

U·kraine /yo͞o'krān, yo͞okrān'/ *n* constituent republic of the Soviet Union in S Russia ‖ **U·krain'i·an** *adj & n*

u·ku·le·le /yo͞ok'əlāl'ē/ [Hawaiian = flea] *n* four-stringed instrument resembling a small guitar

U·lan Ba·tor /o͞o'län bä'tôr/ *n* capital of the Mongolian People's Republic (195,300)

ul·cer /uls'ər/ [L *ulcus* (-ceris)] *n* **1** open sore on the skin or any mucous surface of the body, often secreting pus; **2** corrupting influence ‖ **ul'cer·ous** *adj*

ul'cer·ate' *vi* **1** to become ulcerous ‖ *vt* **2** to cause ulcers in ‖ **ul'cer·a'tion** *n*

-ule /-(y)o͞ol/ [L *-ulus*] *n suf* forming diminutives, as *globule, granule*

-u·lent /-(y)ələnt/ [L *-ulentus*] *adj suf* abounding in, as *fraudulent*

ul·na /ul'nə/ [L = elbow] *n* (-nae /-nē/ or -nas) inner and larger of the two bones of the forearm ‖ **ul'nar** *adj*

-u·lous /-(y)ələs/ [L *-ulus* or *-ulosus*] *adj suf* tending to, as *bibulous*

ul·ster /ul'stər/ [< *Ulster* region of Ireland] *n* long loose overcoat

ult. ultimate(ly)

ul·te·ri·or /ultir'ē·ər/ [L = farther] *adj* **1** lying beyond; more distant; **2** beyond what is expressed or implied; hidden

ul·ti·ma /ult'imə/ [L = last] *n* last syllable of a word

ul'ti·mate /-mit/ [LL *ultimatus* having come to the end] *adj* **1** last, final; beyond which it is impossible to proceed; **2** admitting of no further discussion or analysis; fundamental; **3** highest; maximum; **4** total, final ‖ *n* **5** ultimate point ‖ **ul'ti·mate·ly** *adv* ‖ SYN elementary, primary; final (see *last*)

ul·ti·ma·tum /ult'imāt'əm/ [see **ultimate**] *n* (-tums or -ta /-tə/) final demand or offer made by a party to a dispute, the rejection of which can cause the severance of relations or open hostilities

ul·tra /ult'rə/ [L = beyond] *adj* **1** excessive, extreme ‖ *n* **2** extremist

ul·tra- *pref* **1** beyond, as *ultramarine*; **2** excessively, as *ultramodern*

ul'tra·high' fre'quen·cy *n* radio frequency between 300 and 3,000 megahertz

ul'tra·ma·rine' *adj* **1** beyond the sea; **2** of a deep-blue color

ul'tra·son'ic *adj* of, pert. to, or using vibrations with frequencies above the frequency of audible sound

ul'tra·vi'o·let *n* that part of the spectrum which lies beyond the visible range at the violet end ‖ *also adj*

u·lu·late /ul'yəlāt', yo͞ol'-/ [L *ululare* (-atus)] *vi* to wail, howl, or hoot ‖ **ul'u·la'tion** *n*

U·lys·ses /yo͞olis'ēz/ *n* Odysseus

um·ber /um'bər/ [MF *umbre* shade] *n* **1** a dark earth used as a reddish-brown pigment; **2** reddish brown ‖ *also adj*

um·bil·i·cal /umbil'ikəl/ [< L *umbilicus* navel] *adj* of or pert. to the navel

um·bil'i·cal cord' *n* tubelike structure connecting the fetus or embryo at the navel with the placenta of the mother and serving to conduct nourishment

um·bra /um'brə/ [L] *n* (-brae /-brē/) **1** shade; shadow; **2** *astron* cone of shadow cast by a planet or satellite on the side opposite the sun, in the limits of which the entire disk of the sun is invisible; **3** darkest portion of a sunspot

um·brage /um'brij/ [OF] *n* **1** offense, hurt pride, pique; **2** take umbrage

at to feel harmed by, be offended by

um·brel·la /umbrel′ə/ [It *ombrella*] *n* **1** portable device for protection against the rain and sun, consisting of a folding frame of radiating ribs covered with fabric and attached to the end of a stick or handle; **2** anything suggesting this in shape or function

um·brel′la tree′ *n* American magnolia (*Magnolia tripetala*) with large leaves so arranged as to suggest an umbrella

Um·bri·a /um′brē·ə/ *n* region in central and N Italy (795,000; 3270 sq.m; cap. Perugia)

Um′bri·an *n* **1** native or inhabitant of Umbria; **2** dialect of Umbria; **3** one of the Italic people inhabiting the ancient district of Umbria; **4** extinct Italic language of these people || also *adj*

um·laut /ŏŏm′lout/ [G] *n* **1** modification of a stressed vowel, esp. in the Germanic languages, under the influence of a following vowel (which disappears in the later stages of some languages), as German *Land, Länder,* and English *foot, feet;* **2** the mark ¨ placed over a vowel to indicate umlaut, as in German || *vt* **3** to change (a vowel) by umlaut; **4** to mark with an umlaut

um·pire /um′pi·ər/ [ME *an ompere* < *anompere* a peerless one < OF *nomper* peerless] *n* **1** person chosen to decide a controversy or question; **2** official who oversees a game to enforce the rules and decide disputes || *vt* **3** to arbitrate; **4** to act as umpire of || *vi* **5** to act as umpire

UN, U.N. United Nations

un-[1] /un-, un′-/ [OE] *pref* **1** not; the reverse of, as *unfair, unseen;* **2** lack of, as *unconcern*

un-[2] [OE *on-, and-* back, against] *pref* used **1** to express reversal or annulment, as *untwist, unfrock;* **2** with intensive effect, as *unravel, unloose*

un·a′ble *adj* **1** incapable; **2** weak, incompetent || SYN incapable, powerless, helpless || DISCR *Incapable* connotes an innate or permanent lack, as *incapable* of receiving a higher education; popularly, *incapable* is often used to suggest an inherent inability to stoop to what is bad or undesirable, as *incapable* of deceit. *Unable* means merely not able; a child is through weakness *unable* to walk; through ignorance, which may be remedied, a pupil is *unable* to do a certain problem. *Unable* may imply a permanent lack of ability, but it may also describe a merely temporary want; an idiot is both *incapable* of reasoning and *unable*

to reason; an invalid is *unable* to take, not *incapable* of taking, solid food || ANT able, capable, competent

un′a·bridged′ *adj* **1** not abridged; complete; **2** (dictionary or other book or writing) not condensed from original size

un′ac·count′a·ble *adj* **1** inexplicable; **2** not responsible || **un′ac·count′-a·bly** *adv*

un′ac·count′ed-for′ *adj* **1** unexplained; **2** missing

un′ac·cus′tomed *adj* **1** not usual or customary; **2** not accustomed, as *unaccustomed to work*

un′ad·vised′ *adj* **1** indiscreet, ill-advised; **2** without counsel or advice || **un′ad·vis′ed·ly** /-idlē/ *adv*

un′al·loyed′ *adj* **1** pure, unmixed; **2** complete, unqualified

un′-A·mer′i·can *adj* **1** not resembling or characteristic of American customs or principles; **2** lacking in loyalty to American ideals or government

u·nan·i·mous /yōōnan′iməs/ [L *unanimus*] *adj* **1** united in a single opinion, being of one mind; **2** without a dissenting voice, as *a unanimous vote* || **u′na·nim′i·ty** /-ənim′-/ *n*

un·armed′ *adj* without weapons; not armed

un′as·sail′a·ble *adj* **1** impregnable; **2** undeniable; incontrovertible

un′as·sum′ing *adj* modest, retiring

un′at·tached′ *adj* **1** free, not connected; **2** not married or engaged

un′a·vail′ing *adj* futile, ineffectual

un′a·void′a·ble *adj* that cannot be avoided; inevitable || **un′a·void′a·bly** *adv*

un′a·ware′ *adj* **1** not aware; not cognizant || *adv* **2** unawares

un′a·wares′ *adv* **1** suddenly, by surprise; **2** inadvertently

un·bal′anced *adj* unsound in mind; mentally deranged

un·bar′ *v* (-**barred; -bar·ring**) *vt* to unlock, open, as a door

un·bear′a·ble *adj* not to be endured; intolerable

un′be·com′ing *adj* **1** not attractive, as clothes or hairdo; **2** not suitable, improper, as conduct

un′be·known′ also **un′be·knownst′** *adj* without being known

un′be·lief′ *n* lack of belief, esp. in the teachings of religion || **un′be·liev′er** *n* || **un′be·liev′ing** *adj* || SYN incredulity, skepticism (see *disbelief*)

un·bend′ *v* (-**bent**) *vt* **1** to straighten; **2** to release from tension || *vi* **3** to become unbent; **4** to become less severe or stiff; relax from formality

un·bend′ing *adj* stiff, inflexible, unyielding

un·bi′ased *adj* not biased; without prejudice

un·blink′ing *adj* **1** not blinking; **2** unwavering

un·blush′ing *adj* shameless

un·bolt' *vt* 1 to open by sliding a bolt; 2 to remove the bolts from

un·born' *adj* 1 not yet born; future; 2 existing in the womb but not yet delivered

un·bos'om *vt* 1 to disclose, reveal; 2 **unbosom oneself** to disclose all of one's feelings, thoughts, etc.

un·bowed' /-boud'/ *adj* unconquered, unsubdued

un·bri'dled *adj* free, unrestrained

un·bur'den *vt* 1 to relieve (oneself, one's mind, etc.), as of an oppressive secret; 2 to throw off as being burdensome

un·called'-for' *adj* 1 not called for; 2 not needed; 3 out of place; unwarranted

un·can'ny *adj* 1 weird, unearthly; 2 inexplicably keen or acute

un·cer·e·mo'ni·ous *adj* 1 informal, without ceremony; 2 abrupt, discourteous ‖ **un'cer·e·mo'ni·ous·ly** *adv*

un·cer'tain *adj* 1 not sure, doubtful; 2 not convinced or positive; doubting; 3 lacking firmness, irresolute; 4 untrustworthy ‖ **un·cer'tain·ly** *adv* ‖ **un·cer'tain·ty** *n* (-ties) ‖ SYN variable, fitful, vague (see *precarious*)

un·chain' *vt* 1 to remove the chains from; 2 to set free, release from restraint

un·char'i·ta·ble *adj* lacking in charity; unkind

un·chart'ed *adj* unexplored; not recorded on any map

un·char'tered *adj* 1 not chartered; 2 irregular; lawless

un·chaste' *adj* 1 not chaste or virtuous; 2 bawdy; obscene

un·chris'tian *adj* 1 not Christian; 2 unworthy of a Christian or of Christian teachings

un·ci·al /unsh'(ē)əl/ [L *uncialis* inch-high] *adj* 1 designating or pert. to a variety of letters found in manuscripts from about the fourth to the ninth century, resembling modern capitals, but with more rounded shapes ‖ *n* 2 uncial letter; 3 manuscript written in uncials

un·cir'cum·cised' *adj* 1 not circumcised; 2 not Jewish

un·civ'i·lized' *adj* savage; barbarous

un·clad' *adj* naked, nude

un·clasp' *vt* 1 to undo the clasp of; 2 to release from the clasp or grasp ‖ *vi* 3 to become unclasped

un·clas'si·fied' *adj* 1 not arranged in classes according to a system; 2 available; not kept secret for security reasons

un·cle /uŋ'kəl/ [AF < L *avunculus*] *n* 1 brother of one's father or mother; 2 husband of one's aunt; 3 elderly man; 4 *slang* pawnbroker; 5 **say uncle** *slang* to concede defeat

un·clean' *adj* 1 dirty; 2 evil; morally impure; 3 *Bib* ceremonially impure

Un'cle Sam' /sam'/ [< *U.S.*] *n* personification of the U.S., represented as a tall spare man with white chin whiskers, wearing a red-white-and-blue outfit and a starred top hat

Un'cle Tom' /tom'/ [protagonist of Harriet Beecher Stowe's *Uncle Tom's Cabin* (1852)] *n contemptuous* black person who is deferential to whites

un·cloak' *vt* to expose, reveal

un·co /uŋ'kō/ [< Sc *unkow* uncouth] *Scot* and *N Eng adj* 1 strange, surprising; extraordinary; 2 weird, uncanny ‖ *adv* 3 remarkably, uncommonly; extraordinarily ‖ *n* 4 unusual person or thing; 5 stranger; 6 **uncos** *pl* news

un·com'fort·a·ble *adj* 1 not comfortable; 2 causing discomfort; 3 ill at ease

un·com·mit'ted *adj* not pledged or obliged to follow a given belief or program

un·com'mon *adj* 1 rare, unusual; 2 remarkable, exceptional ‖ **un·com'·mon·ly** *adv*

un·com·mu'ni·ca'tive *adj* not disposed to give information; reserved

un·com·pro·mis'ing *adj* unyielding; inflexible

un·con·cern' *n* lack of interest or anxiety, indifference ‖ SYN apathy, heedlessness (see *indifference*)

un·con·cerned' *adj* 1 not worried or anxious; 2 uninterested; indifferent

un·con·di'tion·al *adj* without conditions; absolute

un·con·gen'ial *adj* 1 incompatible; 2 unpleasant, unfriendly

un·con'scion·a·ble *adj* 1 not guided by conscience; unprincipled; 2 unreasonable; 3 extortionate, as *he charges unconscionable prices*

un·con'scious *adj* 1 not conscious; 2 not aware, ignorant, as *unconscious of error*; 3 not done knowingly, without conscious volition ‖ *n* 4 **the unconscious** *psychoanal* the part of the psyche of which the ego is unaware ‖ **un·con'scious·ness** *n*

un·con·sti·tu'tion·al *adj* in direct contravention of the provisions of a constitution

un·con·ven'tion·al *adj* not bound by established customs or fixed usage ‖ **un'con·ven'tion·al·ly** *adv*

un·cork' *vt* to draw the cork from

un·count'ed *adj* innumerable

un·cou'ple *vt* 1 to unfasten the coupling between; disconnect ‖ *vi* 2 to become uncoupled

un·couth /unkōōth'/ [OE *uncūth* unknown] *adj* 1 clumsy, awkward; 2 unmannerly; boorish, uncultured

un·cov'er *vt* 1 to remove a cover from; 2 to remove the hat from; 3 to disclose, reveal ‖ *vi* 4 to take off one's hat ‖ SYN divulge, reveal, expose (see *disclose*)

unc·tion /uŋk'shən/ [L *unctio* (-*onis*)] *n* 1 act of anointing, as for medical or religious reasons; 2 oil used for anointing; **3** anything soothing; **4** manner which betokens deep emotion, esp. religious fervor; **5** affected fervor; **6** extreme unction

unc·tu·ous /uŋk′chōō-əs/ [ML *unctuosus*] *adj* **1** oily, greasy; **2** excessively pious or moralistic; **3** overly suave and smug || **unc′tu·ous·ly** *adv* || **unc′-tu·ous·ness** *n*

un·cut′ *adj* **1** not shortened or condensed; **2** (pages of a book) having the edges not trimmed or slit; **3** not ground and polished, as diamonds

un·daunt′ed *adj* fearless; unsubdued; not dismayed

un·de·ceive′ *vt* to free from error or deception

un·de·cid′ed *adj* **1** not decided; **2** irresolute

un·de·ni′a·ble *adj* **1** not to be denied; **2** unquestionably good || **un·de·ni′a·bly** *adv*

un·der /un′dər/ [OE] *prep* **1** beneath or below; **2** indicated by, as *under the name of;* **3** subordinate to; **4** during the rule of; **5** less than; **6** below an average or standard of, as *under age;* **7** for less than, as *under cost;* **8** subject to the action or effect of, as *under treatment, under orders;* **9** because of, as *under the circumstances;* **10** in conformity with, as *under the law;* **11** classified beneath, as *under this heading;* **12** subject to the teaching of, as *he studied under Professor Brown* || *adj* **13** lower in position, rank, degree, or amount || *adv* **14** in or to a lower place or subordinate position; **15 to go under,** a to sink; go below the surface; b to give in; yield; c to fail

un·der- *pref* **1** situated beneath, as *undershirt;* **2** subordinate, as *undersheriff;* **3** less than the usual or standard, as *underweight, underpay*

un′der·age′ *adj* below the required or legal age

un′der·arm′ *adj* **1** pert. to the armpit; **2** underhand || *adv* **3** underhand

un′der·armed′ *adj* lacking sufficient weapons

un′der·brush′ *n* bushes, shrubs, and small trees growing beneath large trees in a forest

un·der·car′riage *n* **1** supporting framework of a vehicle; **2** landing gear of an airplane

un·der·clothes′ *npl* underwear

un′der·coat′ *n* **1** primer or paint applied under a finishing coat; **2** undercoating || *vt* **3** to apply an undercoating to

un′der·coat′ing *n* tarlike coating sprayed on the underside of an automobile to prevent rust and to dampen vibrations

un′der·cov′er *adj* **1** done or occurring in secret; **2** engaged in secret investigations

un′der·cur′rent *n* **1** current, as of air or water, below another current or

below the surface; **2** hidden trend of opinion, thought, or feeling

un′der·cut′ *n* **1** any part that is cut away below, as in sculpture or in felling trees || **un′der·cut′** *v* (-**cut′; -cut′ting**) *vt* **2** to cut away below so as to leave an overhanging part; **3** to sell or work for less than (another person)

un′der·de·vel′oped *adj* **1** not sufficiently developed; immature; **2** (photograph) not developed long enough to give sufficient contrast; **3** (nation) that has not attained the standard of living it has the potential for

un′der·dog′ *n* **1** contestant or team not expected to win; **2** person at the bottom of the social and economic heap

un′der·done′ *adj* not cooked enough

un′der·drawers′ *npl* drawers; undergarment for the lower part of the body and the legs

un·der·es′ti·mate′ *vt* & *vi* to estimate at too low a quantity, degree, power, or worth

un′der·ex·pose′ *vt* to expose (photographic film) insufficiently to light || **un′der·ex·po′sure** *n*

un·der·foot′ *adv* **1** beneath the feet; underneath; **2** in the way

un′der·gar′ment *n* garment worn next to the skin

un·der·go′ *v* (-**went; -gone**) *vt* **1** to be subjected to; experience; **2** to suffer, endure

un·der·grad′u·ate *n* **1** college student who has not yet earned his bachelor's degree || *adj* **2** a of or pert. to undergraduates; **b** of or pert. to courses leading to the bachelor's degree

un′der·ground′ *n* **1** region beneath the surface of the earth; **2** clandestine organization fighting the established government or enemy occupation forces; **3** *Brit* subway || **un′der·ground′** *adj* **4** below the surface of the earth; **5** secret; undercover || also *adv*

un′der·growth′ *n* underbrush

un′der·hand′ *adj* **1** done secretively; sly, deceitful; **2** (ball) thrown with a forward and upward swing of the arm, with the palm turned upward || also *adv*

un′der·hand′ed *adj* underhand || **un′-der·hand′ed·ly** *adv*

un·der·lie′ *v* (-**lay; -lain; -ly·ing**) *vt* **1** to lie or be beneath; **2** to be at the bottom of; serve as the basis of

un′der·line′ *vt* **1** to draw a line beneath; **2** to stress, emphasize

un′der·ling /-liŋ/ [OE] *n* person occupying a low, menial position; lowly subordinate

un′der·ly′ing *adj* **1** lying beneath; **2** basic; **3** prior in claim or right

un′der·manned′ *adj* not having enough workers, soldiers, etc., to do what is required

un'der·mine' *vt* 1 to dig under or underneath; form a tunnel under; 2 to weaken or cause t cave in by destroying the foundation, as by digging or erosion; 3 to work against secretly or insidiously; 4 to weaken, as one's health

un'der·most' *adj* lowest in place, position, or rank

un'der·neath' [OE *underneothan*] *adv & prep* 1 beneath, below || *adj* 2 lower, situated under

un'der·pass' *n* passage or road passing under a railroad, street, or highway

un'der·pin'ning *n* supporting structure beneath a wall, etc.

un'der·priv'i·leged *adj* under social and economic disadvantage because of poverty or discrimination

un'der·rate' *vt* to rate too low, underestimate

un'der·score' *vt* 1 to underline; emphasize || **un'der·score'** *n* 2 line drawn under a word

un'der·sea' *adj & adv* beneath the surface of the sea || **un'der·seas'** *adv*

un'der·sec're·tar'y *n* (-ies) subordinate secretary, spec. an official subordinate to a cabinet member or a minister

un'der·sell' *v* (-sold) *vt* 1 to sell at a lower price than; 2 to understate the value of

un'der·shirt' *n* man's undergarment for the upper part of the body

un'der·shoot' *v* (-shot) *vt* 1 to shoot or launch a projectile that falls short of (the target); 2 *aeron* to land an aircraft before reaching (the landing strip)

un'der·shot' *adj* 1 a (person) having the lower jaw protruding over the upper; b (dog) having the lower front teeth projecting in front of the upper; 2 (water wheel) operated by water flowing beneath it

un'der·side' *n* side that is underneath

un'der·signed' *adj* 1 (person or persons) whose signature is affixed at the end of a letter or document || *n* 2 the **undersigned** *sg* or *pl* the person or persons who sign a letter or document

un'der·slung' *adj* (automobile) having the supporting springs attached to the underside of the axle

un'der·staffed' *adj* not having sufficient personnel to do the work required

un'der·stand' [OE *understandan*] *v* (-stood) *vt* 1 to perceive the meaning of; 2 to interpret the significance of; perceive the motive or character of; 3 to learn, be informed of; 4 to know by experience; 5 to take as settled; 6 to believe; 7 to recognize as meant; 8 to infer; take as implied || *vi* 9 to comprehend; 10 to be made aware; 11 to know what is meant; 12 to be sympathetic || **un'der·stand'·a·ble** *adj*

un'der·stand'ing *n* 1 comprehension; 2 state of mutual tolerance; 3 mutual agreement, esp. tacit; 4 power of organizing the impressions of the senses under ideas or concepts || *adj* 5 that understands; 6 discerning; 7 sympathetic || **un'der·stand'ing·ly** *adv* || SYN *n* reason, apprehension, comprehension, discernment, judgment, perception, mind (see *intellect*)

un'der·state' *vt* 1 to tell less than the actual truth about; 2 to represent (a matter under consideration) as less important than it really is || **un'der·state'ment** *n*

un'der·stood' 1 *pt & pp* of **understand** || *adj* 2 *gram* implied but not expressed

un'der·stud'y *n* (-ies) 1 actor or actress trained and standing by to substitute for another; 2 any person ready to take another's place || *v* (-ied) *vt* 3 to act as an understudy to

un'der·take' *v* (-took; -tak·en) *vt* 1 to take upon oneself, as a task or mission; 2 to attempt; 3 to promise, guarantee

un'der·tak'er *n* one whose business it is to prepare the dead for burial and to conduct funerals

un'der·tak'ing *n* 1 the taking upon oneself of a task or responsibility; 2 task; enterprise || **un'der·tak'ing** *n* 3 business of an undertaker

un'der-the-coun'ter *adj* kept or done out of sight or surreptitiously, because of scarcity, illegality, or impropriety

un'der·tone' *n* 1 low or subdued tone; 2 underlying quality or element; undercurrent; 3 subdued color

un'der·took' *pt* of **undertake**

un'der·tow' *n* current below the surface of the water that moves in a direction opposite to the current on the surface

un'der·trick' *n* *bridge* each trick the declarer fails to win to make his contract

un'der·wa'ter *adj* existing, located, or occurring beneath the surface of the water || also *adv*

un'der·wear' *n* garments worn next to the skin under the outer clothing

un'der·went' *pt* of **undergo**

un'der·world' *n* 1 hell, Hades; 2 the world of criminals; criminals collectively; 3 region under the water; 4 opposite side of the earth

un'der·write' *v* (-wrote; -writ·ten) *vt* 1 to agree with, concur with, as a policy or decision; 2 to guarantee financially; 3 to guarantee the sale of (an issue of securities); 4 *insurance* a to insure; b to sign (a policy), assuring liability for specified losses

un'der·writ'er *n* 1 person or concern that carries on an insurance business; 2 person or concern that underwrites an issue of securities

un·der·wrote′ *pt* of **underwrite**

un·de·serv′ed·ly /-idlē/ *adv* unjustifiably; wrongly

un·de·sir′a·ble *adj* 1 not desirable; objectionable || *n* 2 undesirable person

un·dies /un′dēz/ *npl colloq* underwear for females and children

un·dis·tort′ed *adj* 1 (image) like the original; 2 (output of sound or current) that is faithful to the source

un·do′ *v* (-did; -done) *vt* 1 to make null and void; do away with the result of; 2 to erase, efface; 3 to destroy, ruin; 4 to loosen or untie; 5 to unwrap (a package)

un·do′ing *n* 1 reversal of something accomplished; 2 ruination; 3 cause of ruin

un·done′ *adj* 1 not done; 2 made of no effect; negated; 3 brought to ruin; 4 untied; loosened

un·doubt′ed *adj* certain; not to be questioned, indisputable || **un·doubt′ed·ly** /-idlē/ *adv*

un·dress′ *vt* 1 to take the clothes off (a person); 2 to take the dressing from, as a wound || *vi* 3 to take off one's clothes || also **un′dress** *n* 4 informal dress

un·dressed′ *adj* 1 not clothed; 2 not prepared for cooking, as fowl; 3 (leather) with a napped finish on the flesh side

un·due′ *adj* 1 not yet due; 2 inappropriate; improper; 3 excessive; unwarranted || **un·du′ly** *adv*

un′du·lant fe′ver /un′dyələnt, un′jə-/ *n* infectious disease causing remittent fever in man, and abortions in animals

un·du·late /un′dyəlāt, un′jə-/ [L *undulatus* waved] *vt* 1 to cause to move in waves; 2 to give a wavy shape to || *vi* 3 to move with a wavelike motion; move in waves || **un′du·la′tion** *n*

un·dy′ing *adj* deathless, immortal

un·earned in′come *n* income, such as interest and dividends, for which the recipient has not worked

un·earned in′cre·ment *n* natural increase in the value of land or property occurring without labor or expenditure on the part of the owner, as from increased demand through larger population

un·earth′ *vt* 1 to dig up from the ground; 2 to disclose, bring to light

un·earth′ly *adj* 1 weird, uncanny; 2 extreme, fantastic; 3 supernatural

un·eas′y *adj* (-i·er; -i·est) 1 not at ease in mind or body; disturbed; anxious; 2 awkward, constrained; 3 unstable, uncertain

un·em·ployed′ *adj* 1 out of work; 2 not in use, as *unemployed funds* || 3 **the unemployed** *pl* persons who are out of work || **un·em·ploy′ment** *n*

un·e′qualed or **un·e′qualled** *adj* unmatched; without parallel; unexcelled

un·e·quiv′o·cal *adj* unmistakably clear as to meaning; certain; unambiguous

un·err′ing *adj* 1 not erring; 2 accurate; unfailing; 3 undeviating

U·NES·CO /yo͞ones′kō/ *n* United Nations Educational, Scientific, and Cultural Organization

un·e′ven *adj* 1 lacking regularity of contour; not smooth or flat; 2 not uniform; irregular; 3 not level or horizontal; 4 not symmetrical; unbalanced; 5 odd (number) || **un·e′ven·ly** *adv* || **un·e′ven·ness** *n*

un·e·vent′ful *adj* lacking in noteworthy happenings; calm, quiet

un·ex·am′pled *adj* without parallel; unprecedented

un·ex·cep′tion·a·ble *adj* not open to blame or criticism; irreproachable || **un·ex·cep′tion·a·bly** *adv*

un·fail′ing *adj* 1 not failing; not likely to fall short; inexhaustible; 2 reliable, sure || **un·fail′ing·ly** *adv*

un·fair′ *adj* 1 not fair; unjust; 2 dishonest, as *unfair practices* || **un·fair′ly** *adv*

un·faith′ful *adj* 1 not faithful; 2 adulterous; 3 not accurate or exact || **un·faith′ful·ly** *adv* || **un·faith′ful·ness** *n*

un·fa·mil′iar *adj* 1 strange, unknown; 2 without knowledge, unversed, as *unfamiliar with the law* || **un′fa·mil′i·ar′i·ty** *n*

un·fas′ten *vt* 1 to detach; untie, loosen || *vi* 2 to become detached; become loose

un·fa′vor·a·ble *adj* 1 not favorable; 2 disadvantageous

un·fazed′ *adj* undisturbed, not bothered

un·feel′ing *adj* 1 not feeling; insensible; 2 callous, unsympathetic || SYN hard, insensible, apathetic, indifferent

un·feigned′ *adj* sincere, real

un·fet′tered *adj* free, without restraint

un·fin′ished *adj* 1 not finished, incomplete; 2 lacking a polished style; 3 lacking a finishing coat

un·fit′ *adj* 1 not suitable; 2 not qualified; 3 not in good health

un·fledged′ *adj* 1 (bird) without feathers; 2 immature, undeveloped

un·flinch′ing *adj* 1 not shrinking or yielding; 2 steadfast

un·fold′ *vt* 1 to open or spread out (what is folded); 2 to reveal, disclose, esp. gradually || *vi* 3 to become unfolded

un·for·get′ta·ble *adj* that cannot be forgotten; memorable

un·for′tu·nate *adj* 1 not fortunate, unlucky; 2 badly chosen, infelicitous; 3 deplorable; 4 sad || *n* 5 unfortunate person || SYN *adj* sad, calamitous, disastrous, unsuccessful

un·found′ed *adj* 1 without sound basis; 2 not established

un·fre′quent·ed *adj* not visited or traveled over by many people

un·friend′ly *adj* (-li·er; -li·est) 1 not like a friend; lacking kindness or cordiality; **2** hostile; antagonistic ‖ *adv* **3** in an unfriendly manner ‖ un·friend/li·ness *n*

un·frock/ *vt* to deprive of ecclesiastical rank or authority

un·furl/ *vt* **1** to spread or shake out from a furled state; **2** to reveal, disclose ‖ *vi* **3** to become disclosed

un·fur/nished *adj* **1** not provided or equipped; **2** not provided with furniture

un·gain·ly /ungān/lē/ [< *un·*¹ + ON *gegn* ready] *adj* **1** awkward; clumsy; uncouth ‖ *adv* **2** in an awkward manner

un·god/ly *adj* **1** wicked, sinful; **2** atheistic; **3** irreligious; **4** *colloq* outrageous; excessive ‖ un·god/li·ness *n*

un·gov/ern·a·ble *adj* **1** impossible to govern; **2** unruly, uncontrollable ‖ SYN froward, intractable, unruly, refractory

un·gra/cious *adj* **1** rude, uncivil; **2** disagreeable, unpleasant

un·grate/ful *adj* **1** lacking gratitude or appreciation; **2** distasteful; not pleasant ‖ un·grate/ful·ly *adv* ‖ un·grate/ful·ness *n*

un·grudg/ing *adj* unstinting, wholehearted ‖ un·grudg/ing·ly *adv*

un·guard/ed *adj* **1** not guarded; **2** indiscreet, careless

un·guent /uŋ/gwənt/ [L *unguentum*] *n* ointment or salve for burns, sores, etc.

un·gu·late /uŋ/gyəlit, -lāt/ [< L *ungula* claw, hoof] *adj* **1** hooflike or hoofed ‖ *n* **2** hoofed mammal

un·hand/ *vt* to let go of, release from a grasp

un·hap/py *adj* (-pi·er; -pi·est) **1** not happy; sad; **2** unfortunate; **3** inauspicious; **4** unsuitable ‖ un·hap/pi·ly *adv* ‖ un·hap/pi·ness *n*

un·health/y *adj* (-i·er; -i·est) **1** not healthy; **2** not conducive to health; unwholesome; **3** morally injurious; **4** *colloq* risky, dangerous

un·heard/ *adj* **1** not heard; **2** not given a hearing

un·heard/-of/ *adj* **1** unknown; **2** unprecedented

un·hinge/ *vt* **1** to remove from its hinges; **2** to take from its place; displace; **3** to unsettle, disorder, as the mind

un·ho/ly *adj* (-li·er; -li·est) **1** not sacred; not hallowed; **2** irreligious; **3** *colloq* dreadful, outrageous

un·hoped/-for/ *adj* not expected

un·horse/ *vt* to throw (a rider) from a horse

u·ni- /yōōn/i-, yōōn/i- [L] *comb form* one, single

U·ni·at /yōōn/ē·at/ [Russ] *n* member of an Eastern church that gives allegiance to the Roman pope, but retains Eastern rites and customs, such as a married clergy

u·ni·cam/er·al /-kam/ərəl/ [< *uni-* + L

camera chamber] *adj* (legislative body) having a single chamber

U·NI·CEF /yōōn/isef/ *n* United Nations International Children's Emergency Fund, established in 1946 to improve the health and nutrition of children throughout the world

u·ni·cel/lu·lar *adj* *biol* consisting of or having one cell only

u·ni·corn/ [LL *unicornis* one-horned] *n* mythical animal resembling a horse with one horn projecting from its forehead

u·ni·cy/cle *n* vehicle having a single wheel, usu. pedal-driven

un·i·den/ti·fied fly/ing ob/ject *n* fast-moving object, thought to be seen in the sky, whose origin and purpose are unknown and whose existence is not confirmed

u·ni·di·rec/tion·al *adj* having or moving in one direction only

u·ni·fi·ca/tion [see *unify*] *n* act or process of unifying, or state of being unified

u·ni·form/ *adj* **1** not varying in form, shape, degree, rate, kind, amount, etc.; **2** like one another; **3** unchanging ‖ *n* **4** distinctive dress of uniform design identifying the wearer as a member of an organized group ‖ u·ni·form/ly *adv* ‖ u·ni·form/i·ty *n*

U·ni·form Code/ of Mil/i·ta·ry Jus/tice *n* ordinances for the government of military personnel, in effect since 1951, when it replaced the Articles of War

u·ni·fy/ [< LL *unificare*] *v* (-fied) *vt* **1** to make (what was separated) into one entity; unite; **2** to make alike or uniform ‖ u·ni·fi/er *n*

u·ni·lat/er·al *adj* **1** having one side only; **2** pert. to or involving one side only; **3** involving or done by one party only; not reciprocal ‖ u·ni·lat/·er·al·ly *adv*

u·ni·lin/gual *adj* speaking, spoken in, or written in one language only

un·im·peach/a·ble *adj* **1** irreproachable; **2** not to be doubted as regards honesty or integrity

un·im·proved/ *adj* **1** not improved; **2** (land) in a wild state, not cleared, graded, or built upon

un·in·hib/it·ed *adj* **1** open; not restricted; **2** free of social conventions

un·in·spired/ *adj* dull; lifeless; not inspired or creative

un·in·tel/li·gent *adj* **1** deficient in intelligence; **2** devoid of intelligence

un·in/ter·est·ed *adj* having no interest; lacking concern ‖ SYN apathetic, lukewarm, unconcerned, detached, disinterested ‖ DISCR The *uninterested* person is detached and unconcerned. The *disinterested* person is unselfish and free of prejudice and acts dispassionately

un·ion /yōōn/yən/ [LL *unio* (-*onis*) unity] *n* **1** act of uniting two or more things, or state of being united; combination; **2** state of matrimony; **3** uniting of several autonomous or independent states into one nation; **4** flag or part of a flag emblematic of union, as the field of stars on the U.S. flag; **5** association of individuals or groups for some common purpose, as *postal union, credit union;* **6** labor union; **7** any of various couplings for connecting pipes or rods; **8** the **Union** the United States ‖ *adj* **9** of or pert. to a labor union ‖ SYN unity, oneness, combination, coalition, conjunction, juncture ‖ DISCR *Union* is either the act of bringing together to make one, as in the *union* of two branches to make a main stream, or the state or product resulting from such a bringing together, as the American *Union;* a labor *union. Unity* is a state of *oneness,* as *unity* of faith or sentiment; *unity* of purpose. *Unity* is used either of that which was always one, as the *unity* of the universe; or of that which has been brought together to be one, as the feeling of *unity* among all Americans, however diverse their national origin. A *combination* is a *union* for a purpose, made up of either individuals or corporations, and organized for action as a whole, as a *combination* of car dealers to insure a fixed price ‖ ANT separation, dissociation, disjunction, division

un'ion card' *n* membership card in a labor union

un'ion cat'a·logue *n* catalogue made up of the catalogues of a number of libraries, usu. in one single alphabet

un'ion·ize' *vt* **1** to organize (workers) into a labor union; **2** to cause (a shop, factory, or industry) to hire union employees only ‖ *vi* **3** to form a labor union; **4** to join a labor union ‖ **un'ion·i·za'tion** *n*

un'ion jack' *n* **1** jack or flag consisting of the union of a national flag; **2** the **Union Jack** the flag of the United Kingdom

Un'ion of So'vi·et So'cial·ist Re·pub'-lics *n* official name of the Soviet Union

un'ion shop' *n* shop or factory that employs only union labor

un'ion suit' *n* undergarment having the shirt and drawers in one piece

u'ni·pod' *n* one-legged support for a camera

u·nique /yo͞onēk'/ [F < L *unicus*] *adj* **1** being the only one of its kind; **2** unmatched; without equal; **3** rare, unusual; **4** limited to a region, class, or time, as *the unique customs of the Middle Ages* ‖ **u·nique'ly** *adv*

u·ni·son /yo͞on'isən, -zən/ [ML *unisonus* with a single sound] *n* **1** agreement, concord; **2** *mus* a s. meness of pitch; **b** sounding together of two

tones an octave apart; **3 in unison, a** all together doing the same thing; **b** in perfect harmony

u·nit /yo͞on'it/ [< *unity*] *n* **1** one person or thing; **2** single group in an association or organization made up of groups; **3** any cohesive group or entity; **4** fixed amount, quantity, distance, etc., taken as a standard of measurement; **5** *math* the least whole number; one; **6** apparatus or machine having a specific purpose

U'ni·tar'i·an /-ter'-/ [< L *unitas* unity] *n* member of a Christian denomination that believes that God is one being only, and rejects the doctrine of the Trinity ‖ also *adj* ‖ **U'ni·tar'-i·an·ism** *n*

u'ni·tar'y *adj* **1** of or pert. to units; **2** characterized by or relating to unity; **3** of the nature of or like a unit; undivided; **4** centralized (government)

u·nite /yo͞onīt'/ [L *unire* (*-itus*)] *vt* **1** to bring together; combine so as to form one; **2** to join together; **3** to join in marriage; **4** to c. use to adhere ‖ *vi* **5** to be joined together; **6** to become one; **7** to join in a common action; act in conceit ‖ SYN combine, connect, conjoin, cohere, amalgamate, coalesce, incorporate (see *combine, mix*) ‖ ANT disjoin, dissociate, separate, sunder, analyze, divide

u·nit'ed *adj* **1** joined; **2** in agreement; **3** done jointly, as *a united effort* ‖ **u·nit'ed·ly** /-idlē/ *adv*

U·nit'ed Ar'ab E·mir'ates *npl* Arabic-speaking country composed of seven sheikhdoms, located on the E coast of the Arabian Peninsula (900,000; 32,300 sq.m.; cap. Abu Dhabi)

U·nit'ed Ar'ab Re·pub'lic *n* Arabic-speaking republic formed in 1958 by the union of Egypt and Syria, but from which the latter subsequently withdrew, now comprising only Egypt

U·nit'ed King'dom *n* kingdom in NW Europe consisting of Great Britain and Northern Ireland (56,100,000; 94,279 sq.m.; cap. London)

U·nit'ed Na'tions *npl* international organization with headquarters in New York, comprising most of the nations of the world, founded in 1945 for mutual cooperation and world peace

U·nit'ed States' (**of A·mer'i·ca**) *n* republic in North America and the Hawaiian Islands of the Central Pacific, consisting of 50 states and the District of Columbia (222,000,000; 3,615,220 sq.m.; cap. Washington)

u·ni·ty /yo͞on'itē/ [OF *unite* < L *unitas*] *n* (**-ties**) **1** state of being one; **2** state of being composed of parts having connection among themselves and coherence; **3** complex whole; systematic totality; **4** harmony, agreement, uniformity; **5** *literature & art* relation of parts such as to promote a singleness of effect; **6** *math* the number one; **7** in the dramatic theory of Aristotle, one of the three limitations to the structure of a play, namely, that of time (one day), that of place (one locality), and that of action (one plot) ‖ SYN agreement, sameness, harmony (see *union*)

Univ. University; Universalist

u·ni·va·lent /yōō'nivāl'ənt, yōōniv'ələnt/ [< L *unus* one + L *valens* (*-entis*) worth] *adj chem* **1** having a valence of one; **2** having one valence ‖ **u'ni·val'ence** *n*

u'ni·valve' *n* **1** mollusk having a single one-piece shell; **2** such a shell

u·ni·ver'sal /-vurs'əl/ [L *universalis*] *adj* **1** of or pert. to the universe, or whole system of creation; **2** all-embracing, general; prevailing everywhere; **3** entire, whole; **4** used by or intended for all ‖ *n* **5** characteristic possessed by many diverse things or beings, as mother love ‖ **u'ni·ver'sal·ly** *adv* ‖ **u'ni·ver·sal'i·ty** /-vər-sal'-/ *n* ‖ SYN *adj* common, unlimited (see *general*)

U'ni·ver'sal·ist *n* member of a Christian denomination (merged in 1961 with the Unitarian denomination) that believes in the final salvation of all mankind ‖ also *adj* ‖ **U'ni·ver'sal·ism** *n*

u·ni·ver'sal joint' or **cou'pling** *n* coupling between two shafts that permits angular motion in any direction while at the same time transmitting rotary motion

u'ni·verse' /-vurs'/ [L *universum*] *n* **1** the whole system of existing things, including the earth and everything on it, outer space, and all the heavenly bodies; **2** mankind; the world

u'ni·ver·si·ty [ML *universitas*] *n* (-ties) institution of learning comprising undergraduate schools granting bachelor's degrees, one or more graduate schools granting higher degrees beyond the bachelor's degree, and professional schools granting higher degrees in medicine, law, engineering, etc.

un·just' *adv* not just; unfair ‖ **un·just'ly** *adv*

un·kempt' /-kempt'/ [var of *obs un·kembed* uncombed] *adj* **1** disheveled, messy, uncared-for; **2** slovenly, unpolished, rough

un·kind' *adj* not gentle or sympathetic; harsh ‖ **un·kind'ness** *n*

un·known' *adj* **1** not known; **2** undiscovered; not experienced ‖ *n* **3** unknown person or thing; **4** *math* a quantity of unknown value; **b** symbol representing such a quantity, frequently one of the letters *x*, *y*, and *z*

Un'known Sol'dier *n* unidentified soldier killed in battle, whose remains rest in a national shrine as a memorial to all the unidentified dead of the armed forces

un·learn'ed /-lurn'id/ *adj* **1** not edu-

cated, untaught ‖ /-lurnd'/ *adj* **2** not learned, as *an unlearned lesson*

un·leash' *vt* **1** to release from a leash; **2** to release from control, turn loose

un·less' [ME *onlesse* on less ground than] *conj* except in case that, except if

un·let'tered *adj* **1** uneducated; **2** illiterate; **3** without letters ‖ SYN uneducated, illiterate, unlearned (see *ignorant*)

un·like' *adj* **1** different, dissimilar ‖ *prep* **2** not in the manner of; **3** different from; **4** not characteristic of

un·like'ly *adj* (-li·er; -li·est) **1** not likely; **2** not apt to succeed; unpromising ‖ **un·like'li·hood'** *n*

un·lim'ber *vt* **1** to detach (a gun) from the front part of a gun carriage; **2** to make ready for use ‖ *vi* **3** to get ready for action

un·lim'it·ed *adj* **1** boundless, without limits; **2** without restrictions; unrestrained

un·list'ed *adj* **1** not listed; **2** (security) not traded on a stock exchange; **3** (name and number) not given in a telephone book

un·load' *vt* **1** to remove a load or cargo from; **2** to discharge (passengers); **3** to relieve from anything troublesome; **4** to remove the charge from (a gun); **5** to sell in large quantities; **6** to get rid of ‖ also *vi*

un·lock' *vt* **1** to unfasten, open, esp. with a key; **2** to reveal, disclose

un·looked'-for' *adj* unexpected, unforeseen

un·loose' *vt* **1** to untie, undo; **2** to set free, release; **3** to loosen

un·loos'en *vt* to loosen

un·luck'y *adj* (-i·er; -i·est) **1** having bad luck; **2** causing bad luck ‖ **un·luck'i·ly** *adv*

un·man' *v* (-manned; -man·ning) *vt* to deprive of courage, virility, or strength

un·man'ly *adj* lacking manliness; without courage; weak

un·manned' *adj* without men aboard, as an aircraft guided by remote control

un·mask' *vt* **1** to remove a mask or disguise from; **2** to expose, show the true nature of ‖ also *vi*

un·matched' *adj* **1** unequaled; **2** not matching, odd

un·mean'ing *adj* devoid of meaning

un·men'tion·a·ble *adj* **1** not fit to be mentioned ‖ *n* **2** **unmentionables** *pl* things not to be mentioned, as women's underwear

un·mer'ci·ful *adj* **1** without mercy; **2** cruel, pitiless; **3** extremely severe; unconscionable

un·mind'ful *adj* heedless, careless; inattentive

un·mis·tak'a·ble *adj* clear, obvious, incapable of being misunderstood

un·mit'i·gat'ed *adj* **1** not lessened; not softened; **2** absolute, unqualified

un·mor′al *adj* neither moral nor immoral; amoral

un·nat′u·ral *adj* 1 not natural; 2 abnormal; 3 monstrous; 4 contrary to nature; perverse

un·nec′es·sar′y *adj* not necessary; not needed; useless

un·nerve′ *vt* 1 to deprive of strength, vigor, or courage; 2 to fluster, disconcert

un·num′bered *adj* 1 not numbered; 2 not counted; 3 innumerable

un·oc′cu·pied′ *adj* 1 not inhabited; empty, vacant; 2 free; not busy

un·or′gan·ized′ *adj* 1 not organized; 2 not belonging to a labor union

un·pack′ *vt* 1 to remove the contents of (a case, trunk, etc.); 2 to take out (something) from a case, trunk, etc.

un·par′al·leled′ *adj* unequaled, unmatched, without parallel

un′per·son *n* person whose existence is completely disregarded, as if he were not alive

un·pleas′ant *adj* disagreeable; distasteful; offensive

un·pop′u·lar *adj* not approved or liked by the public ‖ **un·pop′u·lar′i·ty** *n*

un·prec′e·dent′ed *adj* 1 having no precedent; 2 unparalleled, unique ‖ **un·prec′e·dent′ed·ly** /-idlē/ *adv*

un′pre·med′i·tat′ed *adj* not planned or considered beforehand

un′pre·ten′tious *adj* modest; unostentatious; simple

un·prin′ci·pled *adj* lacking moral principles, unscrupulous

un·print′a·ble *adj* not fit to be printed because of obscenity, illegality, or bad taste

un′pro·fes′sion·al *adj* 1 not professional; 2 (conduct or action) inconsistent with professional standards or ethics

un·qual′i·fied′ *adj* 1 lacking the proper qualifications; unfit; 2 unrestricted, not limited

un·ques′tion·a·ble *adj* not to be doubted or disputed

un·ques′tioned *adj* not open to question, undisputed

un·quote′ *vi* to terminate a quotation

un·rav′el *v* (-eled or -elled; -el·ing or -el·ling) *vt* 1 to pull apart the threads of; disentangle; 2 to free from complications; solve ‖ *vi* 3 to become unraveled

un·read′ /-red′/ *adj* 1 not read; 2 having read little or nothing

un·re′al *adj* not actual; imaginary, fanciful

un·rea′son·ing *adj* thoughtless; irrational

un′re·gen′er·ate *adj* 1 not renewed spiritually; 2 unreformed; unrepentant; 3 wicked, sinful

un′re·lent′ing *adj* 1 relentless; 2 inflexible; 3 not easing or relaxing in intensity, speed, or effort

un′re·mit′ting *adj* never ceasing or relaxing; incessant; persistent

un′re·served′ *adj* 1 without restriction; unqualified; 2 outspoken, frank ‖ **un′re·serv′ed·ly** /-idlē/ *adv*

un·rest′ *n* 1 restlessness, uneasiness; 2 rebelliousness

un·ri′valed or **un·ri′valled** *adj* unequaled, without comparison, peerless

un·roll′ *vt* 1 to open or spread (something rolled up); 2 to display, reveal ‖ also *vi*

un·rul′y /-rool′ē/ [*un-¹* + *rule*] *adj* (-i·er; -i·est) 1 not submissive; 2 hard to manage, ungovernable ‖ **un·rul′i·ness** *n* ‖ SYN contumacious, intractable, refractory

un·sad′dle *vt* 1 to remove a saddle from; 2 to unhorse

un·sat′u·rat′ed *adj* 1 not saturated; 2 *chem* (compound) in which the combining power of one or more elements or radicals is not satisfied

un·sa′vor·y *adj* 1 tasteless; 2 disagreeable to taste or smell; 3 offensive, disgusting

un·say′ *v* (-said) *vt* to retract (something said)

un·scathed′ /-skāthd′/ [*un-¹* + *obs scathed* harmed] *adj* unharmed

un·scram′ble *vt* to bring to an orderly or comprehensible condition, esp. a radio or telephone message distorted by a scrambler

un·screw′ *vt* 1 to remove the screws from; 2 to unfasten by removing or loosening the screws; 3 to remove (a threaded cap or nut) by turning ‖ *vi* 4 to become unscrewed; 5 to admit of being unscrewed

un·scru′pu·lous *adj* having no scruples; unprincipled

un·sea′son·a·ble *adj* 1 not at the proper time; inappropriate to the occasion; 2 out of season

un·sea′soned *adj* green, inexperienced

un·seat′ *vt* 1 to dislodge from a seat; 2 to unhorse; 3 to remove from public office

un·seem′ly *adj* not becoming or fitting; improper, indecorous

un·seen′ *adj* 1 not seen; invisible; 2 a (text) translated without prior study; b (musical score) performed without prior practice

un·self′ish *adj* altruistic; disinterested

un·set′tle *vt* 1 to move or loosen from a fixed position; 2 to derange or disturb, as one's opinions or sense of security ‖ *vi* 3 to be disturbed

un·shack′le *vt* 1 to remove the shackles from; 2 to free from all restraint

un·sheathe′ *vt* to draw from or as if from a scabbard or sheath

un·sight′ly *adj* displeasing to the eye

un·skilled′ *adj* 1 not skilled; 2 not requiring special skill

un·snap′ *v* (-snapped; -snap·ping) *vt* to open or unfasten by opening the snaps

un′so·phis′ti·cat′ed *adj* 1 not sophisticated; 2 artless, innocent; 3 simple, not complex, as a mechanism or procedure

un·sound' *adj* 1 not sound or healthy; 2 not in good condition, as timber or finances; 3 not valid, not founded on fact; 4 light, fitful (sleep)

un·spar'ing *adj* 1 liberal, lavish; 2 harsh, unmerciful

un·speak'a·ble *adj* inexpressible; beyond description; 2 inexpressibly bad or malevolent

un·sta'ble *adj* 1 not fixed or steady; 2 liable to change; wavering; 3 not having mental stability; 4 *chem* (compound) that readily decomposes

un·stop' *v* (-stopped; -stop·ping) *vt* 1 to remove the stopper from; 2 to remove an obstruction from, as a pipe

un·stressed' *adj* (syllable or word) that is not stressed

un·strung' *adj* 1 having strings loose or missing, as a violin; 2 nervously upset; unnerved

un·stud'ied *adj* 1 not read or worked over; neglected; 2 spontaneous; natural; unaffected; 3 not informed, lacking knowledge

un·sub·stan'tial *adj* 1 insubstantial; 2 without material form or body; 3 fanciful or imaginary

un·suc·cess'ful *adj* 1 failing to achieve success; 2 failing to achieve wealth and fame

un·sung' *adj* not celebrated in song or story, not acclaimed

un·tan'gle *vt* 1 to disentangle; 2 to clear up (a confused situation)

un·ten'a·ble *adj* 1 not capable of being held, maintained, or defended, as an opinion or a fortress; 2 not fit for occupation or living

un·think'a·ble *adj* not to be considered; out of the question

un·think'ing *adj* heedless, inconsiderate

un·tie' *v* (-ty·ing) *vt* 1 to unfasten by loosening; 2 to set free from restraint ‖ *vi* 3 to become untied

un·til' /until'/ [ME *untill*] *prep* 1 up to the time of; 2 before ‖ *conj* 3 up to the time when; 4 to the degree or place that; 5 before

un·time'ly *adj* 1 not at the right moment or on the right occasion; inopportune; 2 premature ‖ *also adv*

un·tir'ing *adj* without stopping or weakening because of fatigue; indefatigable

un·to /un'tŏŏ/ [ME] *prep archaic & poet.* 1 to; 2 until

un·told' *adj* 1 not told; 2 uncounted; 3 vast, incalculable

un·touch'a·ble *adj* 1 not capable of being touched, reached, or affected ‖ *n* 2 member of the lowest caste in India, whose touch is regarded by the higher castes as defiling

un·to·ward' /-tôrd', -tôrd'/ *adj* 1 unfortunate; unfavorable; 2 improper, unseemly

un·truth' *n* 1 lack of veracity; 2 falseness; 3 lie ‖ **un·truth'ful** *adj* ‖ **un·truth'ful·ly** *adv* ‖ SYN treachery, disloyalty (see *lie*[1])

un·tu'tored *adj* having little learning; untaught

un·used /unyŏŏzd'/ *adj* 1 not in use; not put to use; 2 never having been used; 3 unused to /unyŏŏst'ŏŏ/ unaccustomed to

un·u'su·al *adj* 1 not usual, uncommon; 2 strange, remarkable

un·ut'ter·a·ble *adj* inexpressible; beyond description

un·var'nished *adj* 1 not varnished; 2 plain, without embellishment, as *the unvarnished truth*

un·veil' *vt* 1 to remove a veil from; 2 to disclose by removing or as if by removing a veil or covering from ‖ *vi* 3 to take off one's veil

un·voiced' *adj* 1 not expressed; not uttered; 2 *phonet* not voiced; voiceless

un·war'rant·ed *adj* not justified; groundless

un·war'y *adj* not wary or cautious; off one's guard

un·well' *adj* 1 not well, ailing; 2 menstruating

un·wept' *adj* not mourned for, not lamented

un·whole'some *adj* 1 unhealthy; 2 unhealthful; 3 harmful to morals

un·wield'y *adj* 1 difficult to move or manage because of size, shape, or weight; 2 awkward, clumsy

un·will'ing *adj* 1 reluctant, disinclined; 2 stubbornly opposed

un·wind' /-wīnd'/ *v* (-wound) *vt* 1 to loosen by uncoiling; 2 to untwist, disentangle ‖ *vi* 3 to become unwound; 4 *colloq* to relax; become less tense

un·wise' *adj* lacking good judgment; foolish, imprudent

un·wit'ting /-wit'iŋ/ [*un-*[1] + *wit*[1]] *adj* 1 unknowing, unaware; 2 unintentional ‖ **un·wit'ting·ly** *adv*

un·wont'ed /-wunt'id, -wônt'-, -wŏnt'-/ [*un-*[1] + *wont*] *adj* unusual, uncommon; rare

un·world'ly *adj* 1 not worldly; spiritually minded; 2 naïve; 3 unearthly ‖ **un·world'li·ness** *n*

un·wor'thy *adj* 1 lacking merit, value, soundness, etc.; 2 discreditable; 3 unworthy of, a not deserving or worthy of; b beneath the dignity of

un·wrap' *v* (-wrapped; -wrap·ping) *vt* 1 to remove the wrapping from; 2 to bring in the open ‖ *vi* 3 to become unwrapped

un·writ'ten law' *n* 1 legal code developed from customs and precedents, as the English common law; 2 **the unwritten law** a code supported by public opinion that justifies leniency to those who commit criminal acts in avenging injury to their honor

un·yoke' *vt* 1 to free or release from a yoke; 2 to separate, disconnect

un·zip′ (**-zipped; -zip·ping**) *vt* **1** to unfasten the zipper of ‖ *vi* **2** to become unzipped

up /up′/ [OE] *adv* **1** toward or in a higher place or position; **2** to or at a place thought of as higher, usu. to the north, as *up in Canada;* **3** into being or action, as *start up the engine;* **4** into notice or consideration, as *to bring up a question, the missing hat turned up;* **5** completely, in or to a finished state, as *to tear up a report;* **6** away, in a safe place, as *to store up wealth;* **7** to a higher scale, price, degree, or volume, as *potatoes have gone up, to swell up;* **8** even with in time, degree, space, amount, etc., as *to catch up;* **9** each, as *the score is three up;* **10** in an erect position; **11** out of bed, as *she gets up at seven o'clock;* **12** baseball at bat; **13** ahead in a score, as *he was one up;* **14 up against** confronted with; **15 up against** it *colloq* in difficult circumstances; **16 up and around** or **up and about** recovered from being bedridden; **17 up to, a** as far as; **b** as many as ‖ *prep* **18** to in, toward, or at a higher place, position, or rank in; **19** to, toward, or at a farther point on, as *up the road;* **20** against the direction of (the wind); **21** toward the source of (a river); **22** toward the interior of (a country or region) ‖ *adj* **23** leading, moving, or sloping toward a higher place, as *the up train, on the up grade;* **24** finished, concluded, as *his time is up;* **25** going on, as *what's up?* **26** in a higher position; **27** erect or raised; **28** aloft; **29** out of bed, as *he was already up when I arrived;* **30** erected, as a building; **31** facing upward; **32** ahead in a game, as *up two points;* **33** under consideration, as *up for reelection;* **34 up on** well informed about; **35 up to, a** capable of, competent for; **b** engaged in; **c** incumbent upon ‖ *n* **36 on the up and up** *slang* honest, sincere ‖ *v* (**upped; up·ping**) *vt* **37** to raise ‖ *vi* **38 up and** + verb *colloq* to abruptly and unexpectedly . . . , as *he up and hit me*

up- *comb form* up, as *uplands*

up′-and-com′ing *adj* enterprising, likely to succeed

up′beat′ *n* **1** *mus* unaccented beat preceding a downbeat ‖ *adj* **2** cheerful, optimistic

up·braid′ *vt* to censure, reprove severely ‖ SYN condemn, admonish, chasten (see *scold*)

up′bring′ing *n* training of the young, rearing

up′coun′try *adv* **1** to, at, or toward the interior of a region or country ‖ *n* **2** interior of a country

up·date′ *vt* to bring up to date

up·end′ *vt* **1** to place on end ‖ *vi* **2** to be upended

up′grade′ *n* **1** ascent, as in a road; **2 on the upgrade** showing improvement ‖ **up′grade′** *vt* **3** to raise the grade, rank, or value of

up·heav′al /-hēv′əl/ [< *up-* + *heave*] *n* **1** act of heaving up or state of being heaved up; **2** violent commotion or disturbance; violent change

up′hill′ *adv* **1** to a higher level or point on a slope; **2** in an upward direction ‖ **up′hill′** *adj* **3** sloping upward; **4** tiresome, difficult (task)

up·hold′ *v* (**-held**) *vt* **1** to hold up, support, keep erect; **2** to give support to, defend; **3** to maintain or confirm, as a decision ‖ **up·hold′er** *n*

up·hol·ster /up-hōl′stər/ [< *uphold*] *vt* **1** to fit out with curtains, cushions, coverings, etc., as rooms or furniture; **2** to provide with springs, stuffing, and textile covering, as a chair seat ‖ **up·hol′ster·er** *n*

up·hol′ster·y *n* (**-ies**) **1** curtains, cushions, furniture coverings, etc.; **2** business of an upholsterer

up′keep′ *n* **1** maintenance, repair; **2** means or cost of maintenance

up′land /-lənd, -land′/ *n* high ground; land elevated above other land

up·lift′ *vt* **1** to raise to a higher level socially, spiritually, or morally ‖ **up′lift′** *n* **2** act of uplifting, or state of being uplifted

up′most′ *adj* uppermost

up·on /əpon′, əpôn′/ [ME] *prep* **1** on; up and on; **2** at the moment of, as *upon arrival*

up·per /up′ər/ [< *up*] *adj* **1** higher in place, position, or rank; **2** higher in elevation, more northerly, or farther inland ‖ *n* **3** the part of a shoe above the sole; **4 on one's uppers** *colloq* in straitened circumstances

up′per case′ *n* typ capital letters used in printing ‖ **up′per-case′** *adj*

up′per-class′ *adj* of or pert. to the wealthy ruling class of society

up′per crust′ *n colloq* highest social class

up′per-cut′ *n* boxing swinging blow directed upward toward the chin

up′per hand′ *n* dominating position

up′per·most′ *adj* highest in place, rank, or authority ‖ also *adv*

Up′per Vol′ta /vōlt′ə/ *n* republic in W Africa (5,300,000; 105,870 sq.m.; *cap.* Ouagadougou)

up′pish also **up′pi·ty** /-pitē/ *adj colloq* haughty, arrogant; snobbish

up·raise′ *vt* to lift up, raise, elevate

up′right′ *adj* **1** standing erect; vertical; **2** just, righteous, honest ‖ *adv* **3** in an erect position ‖ *n* **4** something standing vertically, as a timber ‖ SYN equitable, pious, just, honest; erect

up′right pi·an′o *n* piano with a vertical rectangular case

up′ris′ing *n* rebellion or insurrection

up′roar′ [D *oproer*] *n* **1** noisy disturbance or tumult; **2** noise, din ‖ SYN hubbub, racket, commotion (see *noise*)

up·roar'i·ous *adj* **1** making or accompanied by noise or disturbance; **2** loud and boisterous; **3** causing loud laughter, very funny

up·root' *vt* **1** to pull up by, or as if by, the roots; **2** to remove, eradicate; **3** to displace violently

ups' and downs' *npl* alternate states of good and bad fortune

up·set' *v* (**-set; -set·ting**) *vt* **1** to overturn; **2** to perturb, disturb; **3** to disorder, derange; **4** to cause malfunction in (the/ stomach); **5** to defeat unexpectedly ‖ *vi* **6** to become overturned ‖ **up·set'** *n* **7** act of upsetting or state of being upset; **8** unexpected defeat ‖ SYN *v* overthrow, confuse, discompose, disquiet

up'set price' *n* the lowest price at which a seller will allow his property to be sold at auction or public sale

up'shot' *n* **1** final issue or result; end, outcome; **2** gist, essence

up'side *n* upper part or side

up'side down' *adv* **1** having the top part at the bottom; **2** in disorder ‖ **up'side-down'** *adj*

up·si·lon /yōōp'sĭlon', yōō'-/ [Gk = slender *u*] *n* twentieth letter of the Greek alphabet Υ, υ

up'stage' *adv* **1** at or toward the rear of the stage ‖ *adj* **2** pert. to the rear of the stage; **3** supercilious, haughty ‖ *vt* **4** to move or stand on a stage in such a way as to overshadow (another actor); **5** to act superciliously toward

up'stairs' *adv* **1** toward or on an upper floor; **2 kick someone upstairs** *colloq* to promote someone to a nominally higher but relatively unimportant post in order to get rid of him ‖ *adj* **3** of or on an upper floor ‖ *n* **4** upper story or stories

up·stand'ing *adj* **1** erect and tall; **2** honorable, upright, straightforward

up'start' *n* one who has suddenly risen to wealth and position, esp. if arrogant and presumptuous

up'state' *adj* **1** of or from the northern part of a state or the part farthest from the largest city ‖ *adv* **2** in or toward such a part

up'stream' *adv* against the current of a stream or river ‖ also *adj*

up'surge' *n* **1** increase, rise ‖ **up'surge'** *vi* **2** to surge up; to rise up rapidly

up'take' *n* **1** act of taking up; lifting; **2** understanding, comprehension

up' tight' or **up'tight'** *adj slang* tense, nervously apprehensive

up'-to-date' *adj* **1** up to the present time; **2** reflecting the latest styles, techniques, improvements, etc.

up'town' *n* **1** upper part of a city ‖ *adv* **2** in, at, or to this part of a city ‖ **up'town'** *adj* **3** located in or moving toward this part of a city

up'turn' *n* a turning upward, as of a trend, prices, or business

up'turned' *adj* **1** turned up; **2** upside down

up'ward /-wərd/ *adj* **1** directed from lower to higher ‖ *adv* also **up'wards 2** toward a higher place, rank, or position; **3** upward or upwards of more than

up'wind' /-wind'/ *adv & adj* in the direction from which the wind is blowing

U·ral·ic /yōōral'ik/ *n* language family that includes the Finno-Ugric and Samoyed languages ‖ also *adj*

U'ral Moun'tains /yōōr'əl/ *npl* mountain range in Russia forming the boundary between Europe and Asia

U·ra·ni·a /yōōrā'nē·ə/ *n* Gk *myth.* Muse of astronomy

u·ra·ni·um /yōōrā'nē·əm/ [< *Uranus*] *n* ductile, white, radioactive metallic element (U; at.no. 92; at.wt. 238.03), one of the heaviest elements known, producing in the course of its atomic disintegration a series of substances including radium, helium, and actinium; found chiefly in pitchblende and used in atomic and hydrogen bombs and in the production of nuclear energy

U·ra·nus /yōōr'ənəs, yōōrā'nəs/ [Gk *ouranos* heaven] *n* **1** Gk *myth.* son of Gaea (Earth) and father of the Titans and the Cyclopes; **2** planet of the solar system, appearing as a faint star to the naked eye

ur·ban /urb'ən/ [L *urbanus < urbs* city] *adj* **1** of, pert. to, or constituting a city; **2** living in a city; **3** characteristic of a city

ur·bane /urbān'/ [see **urban**] *adj* suavely courteous; polite, polished ‖ SYN suave, polished, courteous (see *polite*)

ur·ban'i·ty /-ban'-/ *n* (**-ties**) **1** politeness; refinement; **2 urbanities** *pl* amenties; courtesies ‖ SYN courtesy, civility, affability

ur'ban·ize' /-bən-/ *vt* to make or render urban ‖ **ur'ban·i·za'tion** *n*

ur'ban re·new'al *n* reconstruction of decayed and run-down city districts, often by demolition of the original buildings

ur·chin /urch'in/ [ONF *herichun* hedgehog] *n* small boy, esp. a mischievous boy

Ur·du /ŏŏr'dŏŏ/ [Hindi *urdū* (zabān) camp (language)] *n* form of Hindi having a large number of Arabic words and written in the Arabic alphabet, used by Muslims in India and one of the official languages of Pakistan

-ure [OF < L *-ura*] *n suf* denoting action, state, or result, as *fissure, juncture*

u·re·a /yōōrē'ə, yōōr'ē·ə/ [< Gk *ouron* urine] *n* **1** white soluble crystalline substance —$CO(NH_2)_2$— one of the final products of oxidation of the nitrogenous compounds of the body, found in urine; **2** synthetic powdered form of this substance, used as a fertilizer, in medicine, and in the manufacture of plastics

u·re·mi·a /yo͝orēm′ē·ə/ [Gk *ouron* urine + *-emia*] *n* poisoned condition of the blood caused by the retention of substances normally excreted in the urine

u·re·ter /yo͝orēt′ər/ [Gk *oureter*] *n* duct or tube through which urine passes from a kidney to the bladder

u·re·thra /yo͝orēth′rə/ [Gk *ourethra*] *n* (**-thrae** /-thrē/ or **-thras**) duct or canal through which the urine is discharged from the bladder and in males through which the semen is conveyed

urge /urj′/ [L *urgere*] *vt* **1** to force onward; impel, drive; **2** to seek to influence the will of; **3** to present insistently; advocate strongly and earnestly ‖ *vi* **4** to insist upon a statement, argument, etc.; persist ‖ *n* **5** impulse, desire ‖ SYN *v* encourage, promote, push (see *insist*)

ur·gent /ur′jənt/ [L *urgens* (*-entis*)] *adj* **1** pressing; calling for prompt attention; **2** insistent, importunate ‖ **ur′gent·ly** *adv* ‖ **ur′gen·cy** *n* (**-cies**)

-ur·gy /-ur′jē/ [Gk *-ourgia*] *n comb form* method of working with, fabricating, as *metallurgy*

u·ric /yo͝or′ik/ [< Gk *ouron* urine] *adj* pert. to or derived from urine

u′ric ac′id *n* white crystalline compound —$C_5H_4N_4O_3$— present in urine and found in the joints affected with gout and in kidney stones and gall stones

u·ri·nal /yo͝or′inal/ [LL = of urine] *n* **1** receptacle for urine; **2** fixture into which men and boys may urinate

u′ri·nal′y·sis /-nal′isis/ *n* (**-ses** /-sēz′/) analysis of the urine

u′ri·nar′y /-ner′ē/ *adj* pert. to urine, or to the organs that excrete it

u′ri·nate′ *vi* to pass urine ‖ **u′ri·na′-tion** *n*

u·rine /yo͝or′in/ [OF < L *urina*] *n* watery yellowish fluid secreted by the kidneys, stored in the bladder, and cast off as waste from the body

urn /urn′/ [L *urna*] *n* **1** large vase, usu. with a base or pedestal; **2** receptacle for making coffee in quantity; **3** vase for the ashes of the dead

u·rol·o·gy /yo͝orol′əjē/ *n* study and treatment of the diseases of the urinary organs ‖ **u·rol′o·gist** *n* ‖ **u′ro-log′i·cal** /yo͝o′rəloj′ikəl/ *adj*

Ur′sa Ma′jor /urs′ə/ [L] *n* the Great Bear, the most prominent of the northern constellations, containing the seven stars that form the Big Dipper

Ur′sa Mi′nor [L] *n* the Little Bear, comprising the Little Dipper, the end star of the handle being Polaris

U·ru·guay /yo͝or′əgwā′, -gui′/ *n* Spanish-speaking republic in SE South America (2,900,000; 72,173 sq.m.; cap. Montevideo)

us /us′/ [OE] *pron* objective case of *we*

U.S. United States

USA United States Army

U.S.A. 1 United States of America; **2** United States Army

us·a·ble also **use·a·ble** /yo͞oz′əbəl/ [see *use*] *adj* that can be used; fit for use

U.S.A.F., USAF United States Air Force

us·age /yo͞os′ij, yo͞oz′-/ *n* **1** act or method of using; treatment; **2** long-continued custom or practice; **3** habitual and customary manner of using language

use /yo͞oz′/ [L *usus* use] *vt* **1** to employ, put to some service; **2** to avail oneself of; **3** to expend, consume; **4** to practice or make habitual use of; **5** to treat, act, or behave toward ‖ *vi* (*pt* only) **6** used to did habitually or formerly, as *he used to drink a lot*; **7** used to be was formerly, as *he used to be rich* ‖ /yo͞os′/ *n* **8** act of using or state of being used; employment; **9** way of using; **10** right or ability to use; **11** practical worth, utility; **12** reason for employing; need; **13** custom, continued practice; **14** have no use for, **a** to have no need for; **b** to refuse to tolerate; to dislike; **15** make use of; **16** put to use to use to good purpose ‖ **us·er** /yo͞oz′ər/ *n* ‖ SYN *n* (see *utility*); *v* (see *employ*)

used /yo͞ozd′/ *adj* **1** worn; worn out; **2** secondhand; **3** used to /yo͞ost′o͞o/ accustomed to; inured to

use·ful /yo͞os′fəl/ *adj* **1** of practical use; **2** serviceable; helpful ‖ **use′-ful·ness** *n*

use·less /yo͞os′lis/ *adj* of no use, of no practical value; to no avail ‖ **use′-less·ness** *n* ‖ SYN ineffectual, futile, unavailing, bootless ‖ ANT effectual, beneficial, helpful, useful, serviceable

ush·er /ush′ər/ [AF *usser* doorkeeper] *n* **1** doorkeeper; **2** one who announces strangers or precedes persons of rank; **3** one who directs persons to seats in a church, theater, etc.; **4** bridegroom's attendant at a wedding ‖ *vt* **5** to escort, accompany; **6** usher in to introduce, cause to commence, as a new theatrical season ‖ *vi* **7** to act as an usher

ush′er·ette′ *n* female usher in a church, theater, etc.

U.S.M.C., USMC United States Marine Corps

U.S.N., USN United States Navy

USO, U.S.O. United Service Organizations

U.S.S.R., USSR Union of Soviet Socialist Republics

usu. usual(ly)

u·su·al /yōozh′ōo·əl/ [LL *usualis*] *adj*
1 common; commonplace; 2 ordinary; habitual; 3 **as usual** in the usual manner || **u′su·al·ly** *adv* || SYN accustomed, regular, wonted, prevailing, customary, normal || ANT unaccustomed, extraordinary, rare

u·surp /yōosurp′, -zurp′/ [L *usurpare*] *vt* to take possession of (power, office, etc.) unjustly or by force || also *vi* || **u·surp′er** *n* || **u′sur·pa′tion** /-ər-/ *n*

u·su·ry /yōozh′ərē/ [ML *usuria*] *n* (-ries) 1 practice of lending money at an exorbitant or unlawful rate of interest; 2 exorbitant interest || **u′su·rer** *n* || **u·su′ri·ous** /yōozhōōr′-ē·əs/ *adj*

ut /ut′, ōot′/ *n mus* syllable formerly used in solmization for *do*

Ut. Utah

U·tah /yōo′tô, -tä/ *n* state in W U.S. (1,059,000; 84,196 sq.m.; cap. Salt Lake City) || **U′tah·an** *n*

Ute /yōot′, yōot′ē/ *n* 1 member of a Shoshonean Indian tribe, now mostly found in Colorado and Utah; 2 their language

u·ten·sil /yōotens′əl/ [ML *utensilis* fit for use] *n* implement or vessel for practical work, esp. for common domestic use

u·ter·us /yōot′ərəs/ [L] *n* (-i /-ī′/) organ in a female mammal in which the embryo or fetus is carried and developed || **u′ter·ine** /-in, -īn′/ *adj*

u·til·i·tar·i·an /yōotil′iter′ē·ən/ *adj* 1 pert. to or consisting in utility; 2 stressing practical usefulness rather than style or beauty || *n* 3 adherent of utilitarianism

u·til·i·tar·i·an·ism *n* doctrine that the greatest happiness of the greatest number should be the goal of all human action and effort and that all goodness is based on usefulness

u·til·i·ty [L *utilitas*] *n* (-ties) 1 usefulness; 2 essential commodity or service supplied by a public utility; 3 **utilities** *pl* stocks or bonds of public utilities || SYN usefulness, use || DISCR *Use* is applied to the actual

employment of a thing, or the end secured by that employment, as the *use* of good materials; what is the *use* of growling? We may say we have discovered the *use* or *usefulness* of a certain thing; *usefulness*, however, is ordinarily applied to that which has actually proved its value, service, or practical quality, as the *usefulness* of the automobile to the farmer. *Utility*, though often interchangeable with *usefulness*, is a more abstract term, and is of more general connotation, as the *utility* of scientific research

u′ti·lize′ *vt* to make use of, put to use || **u′ti·li·za′tion** *n*

ut′most′ [OE *ūtemest*] *adj* 1 greatest; 2 most removed in space or time; farthest || *n* 3 extreme limit; 4 greatest possible degree, extent, or effort

U·to·pi·a /yōotōp′ē·ə/ [Gk *outopia* no place] *n* 1 imaginary island described in Sir Thomas More's *Utopia* (1516), where perfection existed in society and government; 2 **utopia**, a any conception of an ideal state; b any visionary plan || **U·to′pi·an, u·to′pi·an** *adj*

ut·ter¹ /ut′ər/ [OE *uttera* outer] *adj* 1 absolute, unqualified; 2 total, complete || **ut′ter·ly** *adv*

ut·ter² [ME *uttren*] *vt* 1 to speak, sound, make vocal; 2 to express in words

ut′ter·ance *n* 1 act or manner of uttering; 2 something uttered

ut′ter·most′ *adj & n* utmost

u·vu·la /yōov′yələ/ [L = small grape] *n* small fleshy projection in the mouth, hanging from the soft palate above the back of the tongue || **u′vu·lar** *adj*

ux·o·ri·ous /uksôr′ē·əs, ugzôr′-, -sōr′-, -zōr′-/ [< L *uxor* wife] *adj* excessively or foolishly fond of or submissive to one's wife

Uz′bek So′vi·et So′cial·ist Re·pub′lic /ōoz′bek, uz′-/ *n* constituent republic of the Soviet Union, in S central Asia (10,581,000; 158,500 sq.m.; cap. Tashkent)

V

V, v /vē′/ *n* (V's or Vs; v's or vs) 1 22nd letter of the English alphabet; 2 velocity; 3 volt

V 1 22nd in order or in a series; 2 *chem* vanadium; 3 Roman numeral 5; 4 something shaped like a V

v, v. verb

v. 1 vide; 2 versus

V., v. volume

Va. Virginia

VA, V.A. Veterans Administration

va·can·cy /vāk′ənsē/ [see **vacant**] *n* (-cies) 1 state of being vacant or empty; 2 empty or unoccupied space; 3 office or position open to applicants; 4 room or quarters offered for rent

va·cant /vāk′ənt/ [L *vacans* (-antis)* being empty] *adj* 1 empty of contents; 2 lacking thought, intelligence, or attentiveness; 3 unoccupied; 4 *law* a unused or unoccupied; b abandoned, without claimant, as an estate ‖ **va′cant·ly** *adv* ‖ SYN void, blank, disengaged (see *empty*)

va·cate /vā′kāt′/ [L *vacare* (*-atus*) to be empty] *vt* 1 to make empty; 2 to give up the possession of, as a house, office, or position; 3 to nullify, make void ‖ also *vi*

va·ca·tion /vəkāsh′ən, vā-/ *n* 1 act or instance of vacating; 2 period of interruption in work or study for rest or recreation; 3 **on vacation** enjoying such a cessation from one's usual work ‖ *vi* 4 to go on a vacation ‖ **va·ca′tion·ist** *n*

vac·ci·nate /vak′sināt′/ [see **vaccine**] *vt* to inoculate with a vaccine in order to render immune to a specific disease, esp. if done to prevent smallpox ‖ also *vi* ‖ **vac′ci·na′tion** *n*

vac·cine /vaksēn′, vak′sēn, -sin/ [< L (variola) *vaccina* cowpox] *n* 1 virus of cowpox, used in vaccinating for smallpox; 2 any modified virus used for preventive inoculation against a disease

vac·il·late /vas′ilāt′/ [L *vacillare* (*-atus*) to fluctuate, oscillate] *vi* 1 to waver in mind or opinion, be indecisive; 2 to be unsteady; stagger ‖ **vac′il·lat′ing** *adj* ‖ **vac′il·la′tion** *n* ‖ SYN waver, oscillate, undulate, vary; veer, swerve (see *fluctuate*) ‖ ANT abide, stay, adhere

va·cu·i·ty /vakyōō′itē/ [L *vacuitas*] *n* (**-ties**) 1 lack of intelligence in mind or expression; 2 inanity; 3 unoccupied space; 4 vacuum

vac·u·ous /vak′yōō·əs/ [< L *vacuus* empty] *adj* 1 empty, vacant; 2 blank, expressionless; 3 stupid, inane; 4 purposeless

vac·u·um /vak′yōō·əm, -yōōm/ [L = empty] *n* (**-ums** or **-a** /-ə/) 1 space entirely empty of matter; 2 space nearly emptied of air or containing a gas under very low pressure; 3 emptiness, void ‖ *adj* 4 pert. to, using, making, or operated by a vacuum ‖ *vt & vi* 5 to clean with a vacuum cleaner

vac′u·um bot′tle *n* bottle having a double wall the interior space of which has a vacuum for maintaining the contents at near-constant temperature

vac′u·um clean′er *n* machine for cleaning rugs, upholstery, etc., by suction

vac′u·um tube′ *n* 1 sealed glass tube containing highly rarefied gas, for observing electric discharges in gases; 2 such a tube used for producing, detecting, or amplifying electrical oscillations or for rectifying an alternating current

Va·duz /vä′dōōts, fädōōts′/ *n* capital of Liechtenstein (3,714)

vag·a·bond /vag′əbond′/ [LL *vagabundus* strolling about] *n* 1 one who roams about with no permanent

abode; 2 idle fellow; 3 tramp, vagrant

va·gar·y /vəgər′ē/ [L *vagari* to wander] *n* (**-ies**) 1 odd, erratic, unpredictable act or occurrence; 2 fanciful notion; caprice; whim

va·gi·na /vəjīn′ə/ [L = sheath] *n* (**-nae** /-nē/, **-nas**) passage leading from the uterus to the vulva in most female mammals ‖ **vag·i·nal** /vaj′inəl/ *adj*

va·grant /vā′grənt/ [ME *vagraunt*] *adj* 1 wandering from place to place; roaming; nomadic; 2 of, pert. to, or like a vagabond ‖ *n* 3 tramp, vagabond; 4 *law* person without visible means of support ‖ **va′gran·cy** *n*

vague /vāg/ [L *vagus* wandering] *adj* 1 hazy or indistinct in form, thought, expression, or nature ‖ **vague′ly** *adv* ‖ **vague′ness** *n* ‖ SYN dim, shadowy, nebulous, indistinct, obscure, loose, ill-defined, ambiguous, undetermined, indefinite (see *obscure*) ‖ ANT clear, unmistakable, absolute

vain /vān/ [OF < L *vanus* empty] *adj* 1 valueless, inconsequential; 2 useless, futile; 3 proud of small accomplishments or of personal appearance; conceited; 4 **in vain, a** to no purpose or effect; **b** profanely, irreverently ‖ **vain′ly** *adv* ‖ SYN ineffectual, fruitless, unavailing, useless, futile, bootless, profitless, vapid, trivial, idle ‖ ANT effective, powerful, sound, valid, worthy, valuable

vain′glo′ry *n* 1 boastful vanity; 2 vain pomp or show ‖ **vain′glo′ri·ous** *adj* ‖ SYN conceit, pompousness, vanity (see *pride*)

val·ance /val′əns/ [*Valence*, city in S France] *n* short curtain hung across the top of a window or used as a border, as on a canopy

vale /vāl/ [OF *val*] *n* valley

val·e·dic·to·ri·an /val′idiktôr′ē·ən, -tōr′-/ *n* student, usu. the highest ranking of the graduating class, who delivers the valedictory at commencement exercises

val′e·dic′to·ry /-tərē/ [< L *valedicere* to say farewell] *n* (**-ries**) 1 farewell address at a school or college commencement; 2 any farewell address ‖ *adj* 3 pert. to or expressing a farewell

va·lence /vāl′əns/ [L *valentia* strength] *n* *chem* combining power of an element, measured by the number of hydrogen atoms with which an atom of the element will combine or which it will replace in a chemical reaction

-va·lent /-vāl′ənt/ [L *valens* (*-entis*) worth] *adj comb form* having a (specified) valence

val·en·tine /val′əntīn′/ [St. *Valentine* 3rd-cent. Christian martyr] *n* 1 sweetheart chosen on St. Valentine's Day, February 14th; 2 gift or sentimental or burlesque card sent on this day

val·et /val′it, val′ā/ [F] *n* 1 male servant who attends to the personal wants of a man, as dressing him and taking care of his clothes; **2** hotel employee who does pressing, cleaning, laundering, etc., for guests; **3** stand or metal framework for holding coats, hats, and other hand-carried objects of a number of people

val'et park'ing n provision of drivers to park private cars and bring them back at parties, hospitals, and the like

Val·hal·la /valhal'ə/ [ON valhöll hall of the slain] n Norse myth. palace of Odin, in which the souls of heroes slain in battle dwell

val·iant /val'yənt/ [AF] adj **1** brave, courageous; **2** bravely done; marked by bravery || **val'iant·ly** adv || **val'·ian·cy** n

val·id /val'id/ [L validus strong] adj **1** based on fact; sound, well-grounded; **2** legally sufficient and binding || **va·lid'i·ty** /vəlid'/- / n

val'i·date' vt **1** to substantiate; confirm; **2** to make legally valid || **val'·i·da'tion** n

va·lise /vəlēs'/ [F] n suitcase, traveling bag

Val·kyr·ie /valkir'ē, valk'irē/ [ON valkyrja chooser of the slain] n Norse myth. one of Odin's hand-maidens who watched over the battlefields and conducted to Valhalla the souls of the favored heroes

Val·let·ta /vəlet'ə/ n capital of Malta (17,679)

val·ley /val'ē/ [OF valee] n **1** low land between hills or mountains; **2** land drained by a river; **3** any low place resembling a valley; **4** low point, as of a line on a graph; **5** depression or angle formed by the meeting of two inclined sides of a roof

val·or /val'ər/ [LL = worth] n bravery, courage || **val'or·ous** adj || SYN intrepidity, gallantry, heroism (see bravery)

val·u·a·ble /val'yōō-əbəl, -yəbəl/ [see value] adj **1** having intrinsic worth; costly; **2** dear to one, estimable, as a valuable friend; **3** of great importance or use || n **4** valuables pl costly possessions, esp. of small size, as jewels or papers

val·u·a·tion /val'yōō-āsh'ən/ n **1** act of setting a price; appraisal; **2** estimated worth or value

val·ue /val'yōō/ [fem pp of OF valoir to be worth] n **1** monetary worth; **2** relative worth or merit; **3** that which makes something desirable; **4** import, exact meaning, as of a word; **5** valuation, estimated worth; **6** mus relative duration of a note or rest; **7** math magnitude or quantity; **8** values pl traditional institutions and ideals of a social group || vt **9** to estimate the worth of, appraise; **10** to

take into account; consider the worth of; **11** to esteem highly, hold dear || SYN n preciousness, excellence, price, importance, utility, worth, desirability, signification

val'ue-ad'ded tax' n sales-type tax imposed on the value added to goods at each stage of production and distribution

val'ued adj highly appreciated, dearly prized

val'ue-less adj having no value; worthless

valve /valv/ [L valva leaf of folding door] n **1** device for stopping or controlling the movement of a fluid through a pipe or tube; **2** anat membranous fold or flap allowing flow in one direction only; **3** either of the pieces of the shell of a bivalve; **4** Brit vacuum tube; **5** device in certain wind instruments which, when depressed, changes the pitch of a tone || **val'vu·lar** adj

va·moose /vəmōōs'/ [Sp vamos let's go] vi slang to depart suddenly, decamp

vamp¹ /vamp/ [< MF avant-pie forefoot] n **1** the part of a shoe covering the toes and instep; **2** something patched up; **3** mus improvised accompaniment || vt **4** to furnish with a vamp; **5** to patch; **6** mus to improvise

vamp² [< vampire] n **1** seductive and unscrupulous adventuress who lures men on to their ruin || vt **2** to seduce, to charm into submission || vi **3** to act as a vamp

vam·pire /vam'pīər/ [F < Slavic] n **1** reanimated corpse said to suck the blood of sleeping persons; **2** one who preys on others; **3** vamp²; **4** vampire bat

vam'pire bat' n **1** any of various South American bats (genera Desmodus and Diphylla) that suck the blood of animals and man; **2** any of several other bats (esp. genus Vampyrus) erroneously believed to suck blood

van¹ /van/ [< van] n **1** vanguard; **2** front or front part, as of a moving line of people or vehicles

van² [< caravan] n **1** large covered truck for moving furniture, animals, etc.; **2** Brit railway baggage car

va·na·di·um /vənād'ē·əm/ [< Vanadis Norse goddess of love and beauty] n rare silver-white metallic element (V; at.no. 23; at.wt 50.942) chiefly used as an alloying element in steel, to which it adds strength and resistance to shock

Van Al'len belt' /al'ən/ [James Alfred Van Allen (1914–) Am physicist] n either of two regions of high-intensity radiation surrounding the earth, the outer one of which extends far into outer space

Van Bu·ren, Mar·tin /van byōōr'ən/ n

(1782–1862) 8th president of the U.S. 1837–41

Van·cou·ver /vankōōv'ər/ *n* 1 island of British Columbia, off the SW coast (210,000; 12,500 sq.m.); 2 seaport in SW British Columbia, opposite the island (385,000)

Van·dal /van'dəl/ [LL *Vandalus*] *n* 1 one of a Germanic people who, in the fifth century, sacked Rome and ravaged Gaul and Spain, finally settling down in N Africa, where they were conquered by Belisarius in 534; 2 **vandal** one who willingly destroys or injures property, esp. a work of art ‖ **van'dal·ism** *n* ‖ **van'dal·ize'** *vt*

Van' de Graaff' gen'er·a·tor /də graf'/ [R. J. *Van de Graaff* (1901–67) Am physicist] *n* electrostatic generator consisting of a sphere to which high voltages are conveyed by an endless belt and used to accelerate particles for nuclear bombardment

Van·dyke' (beard') /vandīk'/ [Anthony *Vandyke* (1599–1641), Flemish painter] *n* beard trimmed to a point

vane /vān'/ [OE *fana* flag] *n* 1 weather vane; 2 one of a number of blades projecting radially from an axis and moving a fluid or moved by a fluid, as in a pump, turbine, or windmill; 3 fixed or movable fin attached to a rocket or guided missile to provide stabilization or guidance; 4 web of a bird's feather

van'guard' [MF *avant-garde*] *n* 1 forward elements or advance guard of an army; 2 forefront or lead in a movement or activity; 3 leaders of a movement

va·nil·la /vənil'ə/ [Sp *vainilla* pod] *n* 1 any of a genus (*Vanilla*) of tropical climbing orchids, various species of which bear a pod or bean which yields a flavoring extract; 2 the extract

van·ish /van'ish/ [OF *esvanir* (-*niss*-)] *vi* 1 to disappear from sight; 2 to pass out of existence, be lost

van·i·ty /van'itē/ [OF *vanite*] *n* (-ties) 1 state or quality of being vain; 2 shallow pride; conceit; 3 worthlessness, futility; 4 vanity case ‖ SYN conceit, ostentation (see *pride*, *egotism*)

van'i·ty case' *n* small case or bag for holding a woman's cosmetics, etc.

van·quish /vaŋ'kwish/ [< OF *vencus* conquered] *vt* to conquer, subdue, defeat ‖ **van'quish·er** *n* ‖ SYN conquer, defeat, subjugate, subdue, rout, overcome, surmount, overpower, discomfit, crush, humble, beat, reduce ‖ DISCR To *overcome* is to prevail over, to get the better of, as obstacles or enemies. To *defeat* is to overthrow decisively, though perhaps only temporarily; a *defeated* army may rally in another action. To *rout* troops is not only to *defeat* them, but to force

them into disorderly, disgraceful retreat. To *conquer* is to secure more than a temporary advantage; it is to achieve a victory that is considered final, and it is accompanied by the idea of gain; a *conquering* army *defeats* its enemies and occupies their territory. To *vanquish* is to *defeat* decisively, often in a single action or combat; it has the finality of *conquer*, for which it is now chiefly a rhetorical synonym. Both *conquer* and *vanquish* may be applied figuratively to moral objects, always with the idea of struggle, as to *conquer* a vicious temper; to *vanquish* unworthy fears. To *subjugate* is to bring under a yoke, or into bondage; literally, *subjugate* applies to a people *conquered* and kept in hand by military control. Figuratively, we *subjugate* our passions or animal natures. To *subdue* is not only to *conquer* but to tame; a *subjugated* people is disciplined, but, though helpless, resistant in attitude. A *subdued* people is a cowed people. We *surmount* difficulties, obstacles, and hindrances by rising above them through force of will

van·tage /vant'ij/ [< *advantage*] *n* superior position or opportunity; advantage

van'tage point' *n* position which gives its holder an advantageous view

vap·id /vap'id/ [L *vapidus*] *adj* lacking life or spirit; flat, stale ‖ **va·pid'i·ty** /vapid'-/ *n* ‖ SYN dull, spiritless, insipid, characterless, stupid ‖ ANT effective, powerful, spirited, substantial

va·por /vāp'ər/ [L = steam] *n* 1 visible cloudlike substance floating in the air, as fog or steam; 2 *phys* gaseous form of any substance that is normally liquid or solid ‖ **va'por·ous** *adj*

va'por·ize' *vt & vi* to change into a vapor ‖ **va'por·i·za'tion** *n*

va'por·iz'er *n* device used to vaporize a liquid, as for inhaling medicinal substances

va'por lock' *n* stopping of the flow of fuel to a gasoline engine caused by bubbles in the fuel line due to overheating

va'por trail' *n* contrail

var·i·a·ble /ver'ē·əbəl, var'-/ [L *variabilis*] *adj* 1 changeable; liable to change or capable of being changed; 2 inconstant, fickle; 3 *astron* (star) changing in brightness ‖ *n* 4 something variable; 5 *math* a quantity that may assume any value or set of values; b symbol representing such a quantity ‖ **var'i·a·bil'i·ty** /-bil'-/ *n*

var·i·ance /ver'ē·əns, var'-/ *n* 1 state or quality of being variant; 2 discrepancy; 3 degree of alteration or change; 4 disagreement, dispute; 5

official permission to bypass a provision of a zoning law or ordinance; **6 at variance, a** differing; **b** in disagreement

var·i·ant /-ənt/ [L *varians* (*-antis*)] *adj* **1** differing from others of the same class; **2** changeable, variable ‖ *n* **3** something that differs from another in form, though essentially the same; **4** alternative reading of a form in a text; **5** different spelling or pronunciation of a given word

var·i·a·tion *n* **1** difference, dissimilarity; **2** act of varying; **3** variant; **4** deviation; **5** extent, degree, or rate of change; **6** *mus* repetition of a single melody with certain changes and elaborations in tune, harmony, tempo, etc. ‖ SYN deviation, diversity, vicissitude, variety ‖ ANT invariability, unchangeableness. uniformity

var·i·cel·la /var′isel′ə/ [NL, *dim.* of *variola*] *n* chicken pox

var·i·col·ored /ver′i-, var′-/ [*vari*(ous) + *colored*] *adj* having various colors

var·i·cose' veins' /ver′ikōs′, var′-/ [L *varicosus* pert. to varicose veins] *npl* abnormally swollen veins, esp. the superficial veins of the legs

var·ied /ver′ēd, var′-/ [< *vary*] *adj* **1** changed; **2** of many different sorts, diverse; **3** diversified, variegated

var·i·e·gat·ed /ver′ē·igāt′id, ver′ig-, var′-/ [LL *variegatus*] *adj* **1** varied in appearance or color; **2** spotted or streaked with various colors

va·ri·e·ty /vərī′itē/ [L *varietas*] *n* (*-ties*) **1** diversity; state of being varied; **2** class of things differing in details from the rest of a larger class to which they belong; **3** individual differing in some details from others of the same class; **4** sort, kind; **5** subspecies; **6** lack of monotony or sameness; **7** vaudeville

va·ri′e·ty store′ *n* retail store carrying a large variety of inexpensive goods

var′i·form′ /ver′i-, var′-/ *adj* having various forms

va·ri·o·la /vərī′ələ/ [ML] *n* smallpox

var·i·o·rum /ver′ē-ôr′əm, -ōr′-, var′-/ [*gen pl* of L *varius* various] *adj* **1** (edition or text) with notes of various scholars or editors; **2** (edition or text) containing different versions ‖ also *n*

var·i·ous /ver′ē·əs, var′-/ [< L *varius*] *adj* **1** different; diverse; **2** differing; **3** several; **4** having several different characteristics ‖ **var′i·ous·ly** *adv* ‖ SYN different, diverse, diversified, manifold

var·let /vär′lit/ [MF, var of *valet*] *n archaic* scoundrel, knave

var·mint /vär′mint/ [var of *vermin*] *n* **1** *dial.* vermin; **2** any small predatory animal, esp. one that preys on small game and barnyard animals; **3** despicable person

var·nish /vär′nish/ [MF *vernis*] *n* **1**

resinous matter dissolved in oil or a volatile liquid, used to give a gloss to the surface of wood or metal work; **2** polished surface; gloss; **3** superficial smoothness or polish, as of politeness ‖ *vt* **4** to apply varnish to; **5** to give a gloss to; **6** to adorn, embellish

var·si·ty /värs′itē/ [< *university*] *n* (*-ties*) **1** *Brit colloq* university; **2** *school sports* first-string team ‖ also *adj*

var·y /ver′ē, var′ē/ [L *variare*] *v* (*-ied*) *vt* **1** to alter in appearance, shape, substance, etc.; **2** to cause to be different; **3** to diversify, make different ‖ *vi* **4** to undergo a change; **5** to differ; **6** to alternate; **7 vary from** to diverge or deviate from

vas·cu·lar /vas′kvələr/ [< L *vasculum* small vessel] *adj biol* relating to or having vessels or ducts that convey fluids, as blood, lymph, or sap

vas de·fe·rens /vas′ def′ərenz′/ [L = conducting vessel] *n* (**va·sa de·fe·ren·ti·a** /vās′ə def′ərensh′ē-ə/) duct that carries the semen from the testicle to the urethra

vase /vās′, vāz′, väz′/ [F < L *vas* vessel] *n* vessel of glass, pottery, etc., usu. having a height greater than its width, used for decoration, holding flowers, etc.

vas·ec′to·my /vasek′-/ [L *vas* vessel + *-ectomy*] *n* (*-mies*) excision of a part of the vas deferens, a common method of rendering men sterile

Vas·e·line /vas′əlēn′, vas′ēlēn′/ [trademark] *n* petrolatum

vas′o·mo′tor /vas′ō-/ [< L *vas* vessel + *motor*] *adj* (nerve, drug, or other agent) that causes contraction or dilation of the walls of the blood vessels

vas·sal /vas′əl/ [MF < ML *vassallus*] *n* **1** *feudalism* one who placed himself under the protection of another and in return rendered homage and service; feudal tenant; **2** subordinate; retainer; **3** servant or slave ‖ **vas′sal·age** *n*

vast /vast′, väst′/ [L *vastus*] *adj* of great size, area, extent, quantity, or degree ‖ **vast′ly** *adv* ‖ **vast′ness** *n* ‖ SYN huge, mighty, immense (see *enormous*)

vat /vat′/ [OE *fæt*] *n* large tub, tank, or vessel for holding liquids

VAT value-added tax

Vat·i·can /vat′ikən/ [L *Vaticanus* hill in Rome] *n* **1** palace of the Pope in Vatican City; **2** government and authority of the Pope

Vat′i·can Cit′y *n* tiny independent state entirely within the city of Rome, including the Vatican and St. Peter's Church; it is ruled by the Pope and is the headquarters of the Roman Catholic Church (940; 108.7 acres)

vaude·ville /vôd′vil, vōd′-/ [F] *n* theatrical performance consisting of a series of separate acts, sketches, songs and dances, acrobats, etc.

vault[1] /vôlt′/ [MF *volter*] *vt* 1 to leap over || *vi* 2 to leap over a high barrier, esp. by aid of the hands or a pole; 3 to arrive suddenly, as by leaping, as *he vaulted into prominence* || *n* 4 act of vaulting

vault[2] [MF *voute, vaulte*] *n* 1 arched roof or ceiling; 2 arched room or hall; 3 storage space, usu. underground; 4 any subterranean chamber; 5 tomb; 6 steel room, as in a bank, in which valuables are kept; 7 anything resembling a vault || *vt* 8 to shape like a vault; 9 to provide with or cover with a vault || **vault′ed** *adj*

vaunt /vônt′, vänt′/ [MF *vanter* to boast] *vt* 1 to boast of, display boastfully || *n* 2 boast || **vaunt′ed** *adj* || **vaunt′ing·ly** *adv*

vb, vb. verb

V.C. Victoria Cross

VD, V.D. venereal disease

've have, as *they've gone*

veal /vēl′/ [AF *vel*] *n* meat of the calf

veal′ cut′let *n* slice of veal dipped in bread crumbs and broiled or fried

vec·tor /vek′tər/ [L = carrier] *n* 1 *math* **a** line having both length and direction; **b** quantity or magnitude capable of being represented by such a line; 2 organism that transmits disease

V′·E′ Day′ *n* the day of Germany's surrender to the Allies in World War II, May 8, 1945

ve·dette /vədet′/ [F] *n* 1 mounted sentinel stationed in front of the regular pickets to give the signal of danger; 2 small boat used to watch the movements of the enemy

veer /vir′/ [MF *virer*] *vt* & *vi* 1 to shift, turn, change in direction; 2 to turn away from the wind

Ve·ga /vēg′ə/ [ML < Ar *wāqi'* falling] *n* bluish-white star of the first magnitude in the constellation Lyra

veg·e·ta·ble /vej′(i)təbəl/ [ML *vegetabilis* animating] *n* 1 plant cultivated for food; 2 edible portion of such a plant; 3 any plant

veg·e·tar·i·an /vej′iter′ē·ən/ *n* 1 one who eats no meat or fish, and sometimes also nothing derived from an animal, as milk or eggs || *adj* 2 of or pert. to vegetarians; 3 (meals or food) consisting only of vegetables

veg·e·tate /vej′itāt′/ [L *vegetare* (-atus) to quicken] *vi* 1 to grow as plants do; 2 to allow mind and body to become inactive; lead a passive existence

veg′e·ta′tion *n* 1 plant life; plants in general; 2 act or process of vegetating

ve·he·ment /vē′əmənt/ [L *vehemens*

(-*entis*) violent] *adj* 1 violent, furious; 2 ardent, impassioned || **ve′he·mence** *n* || **SYN** furious, impassioned, fiery, impetuous

ve·hi·cle /vē′ikəl/ [L *vehiculum*] *n* 1 any kind of conveyance, esp. one used on land; 2 any means of transferring, conveying, or communicating; 3 *pharm* substance, usu. fluid, used as a medium for medicine; 4 liquid, such as oil, with which a colored pigment is mixed for painting || **ve·hic·u·lar** /vēhik′yələr/ *adj*

V′-eight′, V′-8′ *adj* (internal-combustion engine) having two banks of four cylinders each, inclined to each other so as to form a V

veil /vāl′/ [OF *veile*] *n* 1 thin gauzy covering for the face; 2 piece of fabric hanging from the head over the shoulders, as worn by a nun; 3 anything that covers, hides, or separates; 4 **take the veil** to become a nun || *vt* 5 to cover with or as with a veil; 6 to conceal, mask

veiled *adj* 1 wearing or having a veil; 2 covered by or as if by a veil; 3 concealed; obscure; 4 muffled, indistinct

vein /vān′/ [OF *veine*] *n* 1 particular strain, mood, or disposition, as *a vein of humor*; 2 one of the tubelike vessels that carry blood to or toward the heart; 3 branching, supporting, or conducting structure, as in a leaf or in the wing of an insect; 4 mass or stratum of ore, coal, etc., underground or embedded in a rock; 5 streak of a different color, as in wood or marble || *vt* 6 to mark as with veins; 7 to furnish with veins; 8 to spread in veinlike array || **vein′ing** *n*

ve·lar /vēl′ər/ [< L *velum* veil] *adj* 1 of or pert. to the velum, esp. the soft palate; 2 (sound) articulated with the back of the tongue against the soft palate || *n* 3 velar sound

veld or **veldt** /velt′, felt′/ [D *veld* field] *n* in S Africa, open grassy country with few or no trees

vel·lum /vel′əm/ [MF *velin* pert. to a calf] *n* 1 fine parchment made from the skin of calves, lambs, or kids; 2 writing or manuscript on vellum; 3 paper or cloth having the texture of vellum

ve·loc·i·pede /vəlos′əpēd′/ [F *velocipède* bicycle] *n* 1 light two- or three-wheeled vehicle propelled by the rider; 2 bicycle or tricycle

ve·loc·i·ty /vəlos′itē/ [L *velocitas* speed] *n* (-ties) 1 speed, swiftness of motion; 2 *phys* **a** rate of motion, as of rotation; **b** rate at which a body changes its position in space

ve·lour /vəloor′/ [F = velvet] *n* any of various fabrics having a pile like that of velvet

ve·lum /vēl′əm/ [L = veil] *n* (-la /-lə/)

1 *anat* & *biol* any membranous or veillike organ or partition; **2** soft palate

vel·vet /vel'vit/ [ML *velvetum*] *n* **1** closely woven material of silk, nylon, etc. with a short thick pile of upright cut threads; **2** soft skin on the horns of young deer; **3** anything soft like velvet; **4** *colloq* desirable condition or situation; **5** *slang* clear or easy profit ‖ **vel'vet·y** *adj*

vel'vet·een' /-tēn'/ *n* imitation velvet made of twilled cotton

vel'vet glove' *n* outwardly gentle manner disguising an inner ruthlessness

ve·nal /vēn'al/ [< L *venum* sale] *adj* open to or characterized by bribery and corruption ‖ **ve·nal'i·ty** /-nal'-/ *n* (**-ties**)

vend /vend'/ [L *vendere*] *tr* **1** to sell, esp. by hawking or peddling; **2** to sell by means of a vending machine; **3** to put forth for public consideration or debate

ven·det·ta /vendet'ə/ [It < L *vindicta* vengeance] *n* **1** private feud for revenge by bloodshed; **2** bitter rivalry

vend'ing ma·chine' *n* coin-operated machine for vending beverages, foods, cigarets, or other small articles

ven'dor *n* **1** person or agency engaged in vending: **2** vending machine

ve·neer /vənir'/ [< G *furniren* to furnish] *n* **1** thin surface of fine wood overlaying wood of poorer quality; **2** any outer layer of a different material, as brick veneer; **3** pleasing but superficial appearance ‖ *vt* **4** to face or overlay with a veneer

ven·er·a·ble /ven'ərəbəl/ [L *venerabilis*] *adj* **1** worthy of respect or reverence because of age, character, dignity, or seniority; **2** sacred by reason of religious or historic associations; **3** *R C Ch* revered (title given one who has reached the first of three degrees of sanctity)

ven·er·ate /ven'ərāt'/ [L *venerari*] *vt* to revere

ven'er·a'tion *n* **1** act of venerating; **2** state of being venerated; highest degree of respect and reverence ‖ SYN adoration, honor, reverence (see *awe*)

ve·ne·re·al /vənir'ē·əl/ [< L *Venereus* of Venus] *adj* **1** of or pert. to sexual intercouse; **2** pert. to venereal diseases

ve·ne're·al dis·ease' *n* disease transmitted by sexual intercourse

ven·er·y[1] /ven'ərē/ [< L *Venus* (-*eris*)] *n archaic* indulgence in sexual intercourse

ven'er·y[2] [< L *venari* to hunt] *n archaic* the sport of hunting

Ve·ne·tian /vənēsh'ən/ [< ML *Venetia* Venice] *adj* **1** of or pert. to Venice ‖ *n* **2** native or inhabitant of Venice

Ve·ne'tian blind' *n* window blind made of horizontal slats that are turnable

so as to admit or exclude light or air

Ven·e·zue·la /ven'izwāl'ə, -zwēl'ə/ *n* Spanish-speaking republic in N South America (10,400,000; 352,144 sq.m.; cap. Caracas) ‖ **Ven'e·zue'lan** *adj* & *n*

venge·ance /ven'jəns/ [OF] *n* **1** repayment for an injury or offense; revenge; **2 with a vengeance, a** with great fury; vehemently; **b** extremely; **c** to an excessive degree

venge'ful *adj* revengeful; vindictive

ve·ni·al /vēn'ē·əl, -yəl/ [< L *venia* pardon] *adj* not beyond forgiveness; pardonable ‖ **ve'ni·al'i·ty** /-al'-/ *n* SYN trivial, slight ‖ ANT unpardonable, inexcusable

Ven·ice /ven'is/ *n* seaport in NE Italy, built mainly on many small islands; before 1815, an independent republic and a maritime power in the Mediterranean (340,000)

ve·ni·re·man /vinī'rēmən/ [L *venire* to come + *man*] *n* (**-men** /-mən/) *n* person summoned to jury duty

ven·i·son /ven'isən, -zən/ [OF *veneison*] *n* flesh of the deer or similar animal, used for meat

ven·om /ven'əm/ [OF *venim*] *n* **1** poison secreted by certain snakes, spiders, insects, etc.; **2** malice, spite ‖ **ven'om·ous** *adj*

ve·nous /vēn'əs/ [< L *vena* vein] *adj* **1** of or pert. to veins; **2** (blood) that has lost its oxygen and become charged with carbon dioxide

vent /vent'/ [MF *f nte*] *n* **1** small opening for the passage of air, liquid, etc.; **2** outlet, passage; **3** expression, utterance, as *to give vent to one's feelings;* **4** slit in a garment ‖ *vt* **5** to provide with a vent; **6** to allow to escape, as through a vent; **7** to utter publicly; **8** to relieve by speech, as pent-up emotions

ven·ti·late /vent'ilāt'/ [L *ventilare* (-*atus*) to fan] *vt* **1** to introduce and circulate fresh air in; **2** to expose to the air; **3** to supply with an opening for the escape of air, gas, etc.; **4** to bring out (a subject) for public examination and discussion; **5** to talk openly and without reserve about (one's opinions, concerns, etc.) ‖ **ven'ti·la'tion** *n*

ven'ti·la'tor *n* contrivance for admitting fresh air and letting out foul air

ven·tral /vent'rəl/ [< L *venter* (-*tris*) belly] *adj* pert. to or situated on or near the abdomen or belly

ven·tri·cle /vent'rikəl/ [L *ventriculus* little belly] *n* either of the two lower chambers of the heart which send the blood through the arteries to the lungs and through the aorta to the whole body

ven·tril·o·quism /ventril'əkwiz'əm/ [< LL *ventriloquus* belly speaker] *n* act or art of speaking in such a manner that the voice seems to come from another person or place || **ven·tril'o·quist** n

ven·ture /vench'ər/ [< *adventure*] n 1 dangerous or daring undertaking; 2 speculative or risky business transaction || vt 3 to risk, expose to danger; 4 to chance; assume the risk of; 5 to tender at the risk of incurring criticism or refutation, as an opinion || vi 6 to dare to go

ven'ture·some also **ven'tur·ous** adj 1 daring, rash; 2 dangerous

ven·ue /ven'(y)ōō/ [MF = coming] n law 1 locality in which a crime or cause of action takes place; 2 locality in which the jury is selected and the case is tried

Ve·nus /vēn'əs/ n 1 Rom myth. goddess of love and beauty, identified with the Greek Aphrodite; 2 second planet in order of distance from the sun, the most brilliant as seen from the earth; 3 extremely beautiful woman

Ve·nu·si·an /vən(y)ōō'sē·ən, -zhən/ adj 1 of or pert. to the planet Venus || n 2 supposed inhabitant of Venus

ve·ra·cious /vərāsh'əs/ [< L *verax* (-acis)] adj truthful

ve·rac·i·ty /vəras'itē/ [ML *veracitas*] n (-ties) 1 truthfulness; 2 accuracy, exactness; 3 that which is true; truth || SYN truthfulness, accuracy (see *truth, reality*)

ve·ran·da /vəran'də/ [Port *varanda*] n open porch, usu. with a roof, attached to the outside of a house

verb /vurb'/ [L *verbum* word] n part of speech that expresses action, existence, or condition, and which combines with a subject to form a sentence

ver'bal adj 1 pert. to, consisting of, or expressed in words; 2 pert. to, derived from, or used like a verb

ver'bal·ize vt 1 to express in words; 2 to convert into a verb; 3 to make wordy || vi 4 to be wordy

ver'bal noun' n verb form used as a noun, as a gerund or infinitive

ver·ba·tim /vərbāt'im/ [ML] adv word for word || adj word-for-word

ver·bi·age /vurb'ē·ij/ n wordiness; excess or superfluity of words

ver·bose /vərbōs'/ [L *verbosus*] adj wordy, using more words than necessary || **ver·bos'i·ty** /-bos'-/ n

ver·dant /vur'dənt/ [< OF *verd* green] adj 1 covered with green vegetation; 2 green; 3 inexperienced

Ver·di, Giu·sep·pe /jōōzep'e verd'ē/ n (1813–1901) Italian composer of operas

ver·dict /vur'dikt/ [< L *verum dictum* true saying] n 1 decision; judgment; 2 finding of a jury in a trial

ver·di·gris /vur'digrēs', -gris/ [MF *vert de Grice* green of Greece] n green patina that forms on copper, brass, and bronze when exposed to air

ver·dure /vur'jər/ [MF] n 1 greenness or freshness, esp. of vegetation; 2 green vegetation

verge /vurj'/ [MF < L *virga* rod] n 1 margin, brink, extreme edge || vi 2 **verge on, a** to border on; **b** to come close to, be on the verge of || SYN n edge, brink, limit, margin (see *border*)

Ver·gil /vur'jil/ n (70–19 B.C.) Roman poet, author of the *Aeneid* || **Ver·gil'i·an** adj

ver·i·fy /ver'ifī/ [MF *verifier* < LL *verificare*] v (-fied) vt 1 to ascertain the truth or correctness of; 2 to prove the correctness or truth of; confirm; 3 to support by facts; substantiate; 4 law a to authenticate or give legal authority to; b to affirm by affidavit || **ver'i·fi·a·ble** adj || **ver'i·fi·ca'tion** n

ver·i·ly /ver'ilē/ [< *very*] adv archaic in truth; really

ver·i·si·mil'i·tude /ver'i–/ [L *verisimilitudo*] n appearance of truth; likelihood

ver·i·ta·ble /ver'itəbəl/ [MF] adj actual; genuine, real

ver·i·ty /ver'itē/ [L *veritas* truth] n (-ties) 1 something which is true or real; 2 quality or state of being true || SYN truthfulness, fact (see *reality*)

ver·mi· /vur'mi-, vur'mi-/ [L *vermis*] comb form worm

ver'mi·cel'li /-sel'ē, -chel'ē/ [It = small worms] n very thin threadlike spaghetti

ver'mi·cide' n substance that kills worms, esp. a drug for killing intestinal worms

ver'mi·form' adj like a worm in structure or shape

ver'mi·form' ap·pen'dix n small blind tube, now functionless, attached to the cecum

ver'mi·fuge' /-fyōoj'/ [*vermi-* + L *fugare* to put to flight] n any remedy or drug that expels worms or other intestinal parasites from animal bodies

ver·mil·ion /vərmil'yən/ [AF *vermillon*] n 1 brilliant red pigment, sublimed mercuric sulfide; 2 vivid red color || also adj

ver·min /vur'min/ [MF] npl 1 harmful and offensive small animals or insects, as lice and rats; 2 small predatory animals, esp. those that prey on small game and barnyard animals; 3 odious people || nsg 4 odious person

Ver·mont /vərmont'/ n state in the NE U.S. in New England (444,700; 9,609 sq.m.; cap. Montpelier) || **Ver·mont'er** n

ver·mouth /vərmōōth'/ [G *wermuth* wormwood] n a white wine flavored with herbs, roots, bark, etc. that is used as an aperitif and in mixed drinks

ver·nac·u·lar /vərnak'yələr/ [L *vernaculus* native] n 1 native speech of a place; **2** colloquial speech of a place or people, as opposed to the standard or literary language; **3** language peculiar to a business, class, or profession || also *adj* || SYN tongue, speech (see *language*)

ver·nal /vurn'əl/ [L *vernalis*] *adj* **1** of, pert. to, or occurring in the spring; **2** springlike; **3** pert. to youth

ver'nal e'qui·nox' *n* equinox occurring in the spring, around March 21

ver·ni·er /vurn'ē·ər/ [Pierre *Vernier* (1580–1637) F mathematician] *n* **1** small auxiliary scale made to slide along a main scale in order to measure fractional parts of the latter; **2** device used to increase the accuracy of the setting or reading of an instrument || also *adj*

ver·sa·tile /vurs'ətil/ [L *versatilis* revolving] *adj* **1** able to do many things well; **2** having many uses; **3** *bot & zool* turning freely, as anthers or toes || **ver'sa·til'i·ty** /-til'-/ *n*

verse /vurs'/ [OE *fers* < L *versus* turning] *n* **1** single metrical line in poetry; **2** poetry; **3** stanza; **4** numbered division of a chapter in the Bible; **5** *mus* **a** part of a song between the introduction and the chorus; **b** part of a song written for one voice

versed' /< L *versari* to be engaged in] *adj* trained, skilled; learned

ver·si·fi·ca'tion /vurs'i-/ *n* **1** art or practice of composing verses; **2** metrical structure; **3** act of versifying; **4** metrical version

ver'si·fy' /L *versificare*] *v* (-**fied**) *vi* **1** to make verses || *vt* **2** to express in verse; **3** to change (prose) into verse || **ver'si·fi'er** *n*

ver·sion /vur'zhən/ [L *versio* (-*onis*) turning] *n* **1** translation, esp. of the Bible; **2** account of an occurrence from a particular point of view; **3** adaptation of a story, play, piece of music, etc. into another medium or style; **4** variant or particular form of an object

ver·sus /vurs'əs/ [L] *prep* **1** against; **2** compared to

ver·te·bra /vurt'əbrə/ [L] *n* (-**brae** /-brē'/ or -**bras**) any of the single bones or segments composing the spinal column

ver'te·brate /-brit, -brāt'/ *adj* **1** having a backbone or spinal column || *n* **2** vertebrate animal

ver·tex /vur'teks/ [L = whirl; head] *n* (-**tex·es** or -**ti·ces** /-tisēz'/) **1** highest point; top, apex; **2** *geom* **a** point opposite to and farthest from the base; **b** point where the sides of an angle meet; **c** point in a solid common to three or more sides

ver·ti·cal /vurt'ikəl/ [L *verticalis*] *adj* **1** pert. to or situated at the apex; **2** at right angles with the horizon; upright || *n* **3** something in a vertical position || **ver'ti·cal·ly** *adv*

ver'ti·cal an'gle *n geom* one of two opposite and equal angles made by two intersecting lines

ver·ti·go /vurt'igō'/ [L] *n* (-**goes** or **ver·tig·i·nes** /vərtij'inēz'/) giddiness; extreme dizziness || **ver·tig·i·nous** /vərtij' inəs/ *adj*

verve /vurv'/ [F] *n* **1** enthusiasm; energy, vigor; **2** vivaciousness

ver·y /ver'ē/ [OF *verai* true] *adj* (-**i·er**; -**i·est**) **1** absolute; utter, as *the very truth*; **2** same, as *the very hat I wanted*; **3** even the; mere, as *the very thought frightens me*; **4** actual, as *the very act* || *adv* **5** truly, absolutely, as *the very last thing I expected*; **6** extremely

ver'y high' fre'quen·cy *n* radio frequency between 30 and 300 megahertz

ver'y low' fre'quen·cy *n* radio frequency between 3 and 30 kilohertz

ves·i·cle /ves'ikəl/ [L *vesicula* little bladder] *n* **1** *anat & zool* small bladder or sac containing fluid; **2** blister || **ve·sic·u·lar** /vəsik'yələr/ *adj*

ves·per /vesp'ər/ [L = evening] *n* **1** evening bell; **2** **vespers** *pl* evening religious services or prayers || also *adj*

Ves·puc·ci, A·me·ri·go /əmer'igo vespy(y)ōō'chē/ *n* (1451–1512) Italian explorer after whom America was named

ves·sel /ves'əl/ [AF] *n* **1** hollow receptacle or container, usu. for liquids, as a bowl or kettle; **2** ship, boat; **3** airship; **4** any tube or canal in the body through which a fluid passes

vest[1] /vest'/ [It *veste* robe] *n* **1** man's sleeveless garment, worn beneath the coat; **2** similar garment worn by a woman

vest[2] [MF *vestir* to clothe] *vt* **1** to dress in ecclesiastical vestments; **2** to clothe, as with authority or power; invest; **3** to bestow upon a person the possession or use of || *vi* **4** to be fixed; pass or take effect, as a title to property; **5** to put on vestments

ves'tal vir'gin /vest'əl/ [L *vestalis*] *n* one of the six virgin priestesses in ancient Rome who tended the sacred, perpetual fire on the altar of the temple of Vesta, goddess of the hearth

vest'ed *adj* **1** clothed, esp. in priestly vestments; **2** *law* fixed; characterized by rights consummated and established by law

vest'ed in'ter·ests *npl* persons or groups of persons who are firmly entrenched in the power structure

ves·ti·bule /vest'ibyōōl'/ [L *vestibulum*] *n* **1** small entrance hall or lobby between the outer door and the interior of a building; **2** enclosed entrance to a railway passenger car

ves·tige /vest'ij/ [L *vestigium* footprint] *n* **1** visible sign or trace of something that is gone or has ceased; **2** minute trace or amount; **3** *biol* any poorly developed or degenerate part or organ formerly well developed || **ves·tig′i·al** /-jē-əl/ *adj*

vest′ing *n* **1** irrevocable right, in the event of termination of employment before retirement, of an employee after a certain number of years of service to enjoy the full earned benefits of a pension fund to which he and his employer have contributed or to transfer pension credit from one employer to another; **2** seizure of private property by a government usu. in return for some compensation

vest′ment [ML *vestimentum*] *n* robe; garment, esp. one worn by a clergyman

vest′-pock′et *adj* **1** designed to be carried in the pocket of a vest; **2** diminutive; miniature

ves·try /ves′trē/ [ME *vestrie*] *n* (**-tries**) **1** room in a church where the clergy put on their vestments or where the sacred utensils of the service are kept; **2** in some churches, a room or building attached to a church and used as a chapel or Sunday-school room; **3** *Prot Episc Ch* elected committee that directs the affairs of a parish

ves′try·man /-mən/ *n* (**-men** /-mən/) member of a church vestry

Ve·su·vi·us /vəsōōv′ē-əs/ *n* volcano in Italy near Naples; its eruption in 79 A.D. destroyed Pompeii and Herculaneum || **Ve·su′vi·an** *adj*

vet¹ /vet′/ *n colloq* veterinarian

vet² *n colloq* veteran

vetch /vech′/ [AF *veche*] *n* any of several plants (esp. of genus *Vicia*) of the pea family, often used as fodder

vet·er·an /vet′ərən/ [L *veteranus*] *n* **1** person with long experience in a job or office; **2** soldier who has been in battle; **3** person who has served in the armed forces in time of war

Vet′er·ans Day′ *n* national holiday, celebrated on the fourth Monday of October, formerly celebrated on November 11, commemorating the signing of the Armistice that ended World War I

vet·er·i·nar·i·an /vet′əriner′ē-ən/ [< *veterinary*] *n* one who practices veterinary medicine

vet′er·i·nar′y [L *veterinarius* pert. to a beast of burden] *adj* **1** pert. to the treatment of diseases and injuries of domestic animals || *n* (**-ies**) **2** veterinarian

vet′er·i·nar·y med′i·cine *n* branch of medicine that deals with the diagnosis and treatment of diseases and injuries of domestic animals

ve·to /vēt′ō/ [L = I forbid] *n* (**-toes**) **1** act or right of preventing the enactment of a measure as law, usu. vested in the chief executive of a nation or state; **2** act or right of prohibiting something proposed or intended; **3** vote by which one of the five permanent members of the Security Council can defeat a motion on any matter that is not procedural || *vt* **4** to exercise the right of veto against; **5** to prohibit, forbid

vex /veks′/ [L *vexare* to annoy] *vt* **1** to irritate by small annoyances; **2** to grieve, distress || **vexed′** *adj* || SYN provoke, exasperate, annoy, displease, affront

vex·a′tion *n* **1** act of vexing or state of being vexed; **2** cause of vexation || **vex·a′tious** *adj* || SYN mortification, humiliation (see *chagrin*)

VHF very high frequency

vi, v.i. intransitive verb

vi·a /vī′ə, vē′ə/ [L] *prep* by way of

vi·a·ble /vī′əbəl/ [F < *vie* life] *adj* **1** capable of living; **2** (fetus) sufficiently developed to be able to live outside the uterus; **3** workable || **vi′a·bil′i·ty** /-bil′-/ *n*

vi·a·duct /vī′ədukt′/ [L *via* way + (aque)*duct*] *n* high bridge consisting of a series of arches or short spans, used to carry a roadway over a valley or ravine

vi·al /vī′əl/ [OF *viole*] *n* small stoppered bottle, usu. of glass, as for medicine

vi·and /vī′ənd/ [MF *viande*] *n* **1** article of food; **2 viands** *pl* food, fare

vi·brant /vī′brənt/ [L *vibrans* (-*antis*) quivering] *adj* **1** vibrating; **2** resonant; **3** vigorous, energetic; **4** lively, stimulating || **vi′bran·cy** *n*

vi·brate /vī′brāt/ [L *vibrare* (-*atus*) to move to and fro] *vi* **1** to swing rapidly back and forth periodically; **2** to quiver; **3** to be stirred; thrill || *vt* **4** to cause to vibrate

vi·bra′tion *n* **1** act of vibrating or state of being vibrated; **2** *phys* periodic motion to and fro, as of a stretched cord, the particles of a fluid, or an elastic solid; **3** emanation said to be sensed by certain people that forebodes good or ill || **vi·bra′tion·al** *adj*

vi′bra·tor *n* **1** one who or that which vibrates; **2** any of various devices causing vibration; **3** rubber-tipped oscillating appliance used in massaging; **4** device that rapidly closes and opens a circuit in an electric bell or buzzer; **5** electromagnetic device that converts direct current to a pulsating direct current or an alternating current || **vi′bra·to′ry** /-ətôr′ē, -ətôr′ē/ *adj*

vic·ar /vik′ər/ [AF *vicare*] *n* **1** *Ch of Eng* priest of a parish of which the tithes belong to a religious chapter or to a layman; **2** *Prot Episc Ch* a clergyman who is the head of one chapel in a large parish; **b** bishop's representative in charge of a church or mission; **3** *R C Ch* clergyman representing a bishop or the Pope; **4** deputy

vic·ar·age /-ij/ *n* office, position, benefice, or residence of a vicar

vi·car·i·ous /viker′ē·əs, vī-/ [L *vicarius* substituted] *adj* **1** delegated; **2** taking the place of another; **3** done or endured in place of another; **4** felt by imagined participation in the experience of others ‖ **vi·car′i·ous·ly** *adv*

vice[1] /vīs/ [OF < L *vitium*] *n* **1** fault, defect, blemish; **2** depraved or immoral conduct; **3** debased or immoral habit

vice[2] *n* vise

vi·ce[3] /vīs′ē/ [L] *prep* in the place of

vice- /vīs′-/ [*vice*[3]] *pref* deputy, as *vice-president*

vice′-ad′mi·ral *n* naval officer next below an admiral

vice′-con′sul *n* consular officer ranking below a consul

vice′-pres′i·dent *n* **1** officer or one of several officers ranking next below a president; **2** *U.S.* officer ranking next below the president, serving in his place in the absence, removal, death, or incapacity of the president ‖ **vice′-pres′i·den·cy** *n*

vice·re′gal *adj* pert. to a viceroy

vice′-re′gent *n* **1** deputy regent; **2** one who acts in place of a ruler or governor ‖ **vice′-re′gen·cy** *n*

vice′roy /-roi/ [MF < *vice-* + *roy* king] *n* ruler of a colony or province, acting in the name of a sovereign

vice′ squad′ *n* division of a municipal police force charged with stamping out vice, esp. prostitution

vice ver·sa /vīs′(ə) vurs′ə, vīs′ē/ [L] *adv* the relation or order of terms being reversed; conversely

Vi·chy /vish′ē/ *n* city in central France, famous for its hot springs; seat of the provisional government 1940–44 (34,000)

vi·chys·soise /vish′ēswäz′/ [F = of Vichy] *n* soup made with potatoes, leeks, and cream, usu. served cold

Vi′chy wa′ter *n* **1** effervescent mineral water from springs at Vichy, France; **2** similar natural or manufactured water

vi·cin·i·ty /visin′itē/ [L *vicinitas*] *n* (-ties) **1** nearness, closeness; **2** region about or near; neighborhood

vi·cious /vish′əs/ [*vice*[1]] *adj* **1** corrupt, depraved, immoral; **2** savage, ferocious; **3** malicious, full of spite; **4** very severe, as an ache

vi′cious cir′cle *n* situation in which the attempt to solve one problem brings on new and more difficult problems, the attempted solution of which brings back the original problem, sometimes in more aggravated form

vi·cis·si·tude /visis′it(y)ōōd′/ [L *vicissitudo*] *n* **1** change, variation; **2** vicissitudes *pl* changing or alternating circumstances or conditions of life or fortune

vic·tim /vik′tim/ [L *victima*] *n* **1** someone or something hurt or destroyed as the result of an action by another person or agency, either accidentally or by design; **2** person who is deceived or cheated

vic′tim·ize′ *vt* **1** to make a victim of; **2** to cheat or swindle ‖ **vic′tim·i·za′tion** *n*

vic·tor /vik′tər/ [L] *n* **1** conqueror; **2** winner

Vic·to·ri·a /viktôr′ē·ə -tōr′-/ *n* **1** Roman goddess of victory; **2** (1819–1901) queen of the United Kingdom 1837–1901 and empress of India 1876–1901; **3** capital of Hong Kong (675,000); **4** capital of British Columbia (60,000); **5** state in SE Australia (2,930,000; 87,884 sq.m.; cap. Melbourne)

Vic·to′ri·a Cross′ *n* highest British decoration for valor, awarded to members of the armed forces for conspicuous bravery

Vic·to′ri·an *adj* **1** pert. to Queen Victoria or to the period of her reign; **2** characteristic of the Victorians, esp. of their prudery and conventionality; **3** noting or pert. to the styles of architecture, furniture, and art prevalent in the Victorian period ‖ *n* **4** person who lived or flourished during this period

vic·to′ri·ous *adj* **1** having conquered or won; triumphant; **2** marked by or pert. to victory

vic·to·ry /vik′tərē/ [L *victoria*] *n* (-ries) **1** defeat of an enemy or antagonist; triumph; **2** gaining of superiority in any contest or struggle ‖ SYN triumph, conquest, success, achievement, advantage, mastery, supremacy ‖ DISCR The attainment of any desired object is *success*. *Success* does not necessarily imply defeating opponents or competitors; *victory* does; a *victory* is a decisive, strikingly successful winning of the day. *Conquest* is *victory* to which is added the idea of permanent *advantage* over subjugated opponents. *Triumph* is brilliant *victory* characterized by exultant joy and, often, open rejoicing

vict·ual /vit′əl/ [AF *vitaille* nourishment] *v* (-ualed or -ualled; -ual·ing or -ual·ling) *vt* **1** to supply with food ‖ *n* **2** victuals *pl* food, provisions

vi·cu·ña or **vi·cu·na** /vik(y)ōōn′(y)ə/ [Sp < Quechua] *n* **1** wild ruminant of the Andes of South America (*Lama vicugna*) related to the llama, yielding a soft fine wool; **2** fabric of this wool

vid. vide

vi·de /vī′dē/ [*impv* of L *video*] *vt impv* see (the page or place indicated)

vid·e·o /vid′ē·ō′/ [L = I see] *n* 1 that part of television having to do with the transmission and reception of the image, as distinguished from *audio;* 2 television ‖ also *adj*

vid′e·o car′tridge *n* device, containing a cassette, for recording and playing video tape directly through a television set

vid′e·o·cas·sette′ re·cord′er or **VCR** *n* device for recording television programs and playing them back through a television set

vid′e·o·disk′ *n* disk stamped with a television recording to be played back through a television set

vid′e·o home′ sys′tem or **VHS** *n* recording-playback device similar to a videocasette recorder

vid′e·o·phone′ *n* telephone apparatus or system for seeing as well as hearing the person one is talking to

vid′e·o tape′ *n* magnetic tape for the recording, playback, and broadcasting of television and motion-picture programs, generally accompanied by the associated sound ‖ **vid′e·o·tape′** *vt*

vie /vī′/ [< OF *envier* to challenge] *v* (**vy′ing**) *vi* to contend for superiority; compete

Vi·en·na /vē·en′ə/ *n* capital of Austria (1,650,000) ‖ **Vi·en·nese** /vē′ənēz′, -nēs′/ *adj & n* (-**nese**)

Vien·tiane /vyentyän′/ *n* administrative capital of Laos (165,000)

Vi·et·cong /vē′etkoṅ′/ *n* (*pl* -**cong**) 1 former North Vietnamese military and guerrilla force fighting against South Vietnam; 2 former North Vietnamese belonging to or supporting this force ‖ also *adj*

Vi·et·minh /vē′etmin′/ *n* (*pl* -**minh**) 1 Communist Vietnamese league organized to fight the Japanese and the French between 1941 and 1954; 2 Vietnamese who belonged to or supported this league ‖ also *adj*

Vi·et·nam /vē′etnäm′/ *n* country in SE Asia (51,200,000; 130,654 sq.m.; cap. Hanoi) ‖ **Vi·et′nam·ese′** /-nə-mēz′, -nəmēs′/ *adj & n* (-**ese**)

view /vyōō′/ [MF *veue* sight] *n* 1 act or instance of seeing; inspection; 2 range of sight; 3 that which is seen; spectacle, as *a splendid view;* 4 pictorial representation of something; 5 mental survey; 6 aspect; 7 outlook, prospect; 8 inclusiveness of mental perception, as *a broad view;* 9 opinion, attitude; 10 purpose, intention; 11 aim, goal; 12 **in view,** in sight; **b** under consideration; **c** as an end or goal; 13 **in view of** in consideration of; 14 **on view** displayed, exhibited; open to public inspection; 15 **with a view to,** with the aim of; **b** in the hope of ‖ *vt* 16 to see, gaze at; 17 to inspect, look at; 18 to consider

view′ cam′er·a *n* camera of usu. large size, with an extendable bellows and adjustable front, used chiefly for portraits and architectural photography

view′er *n* 1 one who views or looks on; 2 one who watches television; 3 device for facilitating viewing or examining, as photographic transparencies; 4 *colloq* viewfinder

view′find′er *n* small lens or frame on a camera through which one may see what will be included in the picture

view′ing *n* 1 the looking at and the opportunity of looking at paintings, models, etc. that have been put on view; 2 provision to view a body at a funeral parlor

view′point′ *n* 1 place from which one looks at something; 2 point of view

vi·ges·i·mal /vījes′iməl/ [L *vigesimus*] *adj* 1 twentieth; 2 progressing by twenties; 3 pert. to or based on twenty

vig·il /vij′əl/ [AF *vigile*] *n* 1 purposeful wakefulness during a time usu. devoted to sleep; 2 watchfulness; 3 period of watchfulness; 4 eve of a church festival, esp. an eve which is a fast; 5 often *vigils pl* devotions in the evening or nighttime

vig·i·lant /vij′ilənt/ [L *vigilans* (-*antis*) watching] *adj* 1 keenly watchful; 2 alert; wary ‖ **vig′i·lance** *n* ‖ SYN wakeful, circumspect, observant, watchful

vig·i·lan·te /vij′ilant′ē/ [Sp = vigilant] *n* member of an unauthorized and self-appointed group of citizens organized to maintain order and deal out summary punishment to those they consider wrongdoers

vi·gnette /vinyet′/ [F *dim.* of *vigne* vine] *n* 1 ornamental border of twisting vines, as on a title page; 2 ornamental flourishes around a capital letter in a manuscript; 3 small design decorating a blank space, as at the end of a chapter; 4 any engraving or picture that shades off gradually without definite border; 5 short gracefully elegant literary sketch ‖ *v* (-**gnett·ed;** -**gnett·ing**) *vt* 6 to make a vignette of ‖ *vi* 7 (of a lens) to leave a dark border around a photograph

vig·or /vig′ər/ [L = liveliness] *n* 1 active strength or energy; 2 vitality; intensity ‖ **vig′or·ous** *adj* ‖ SYN power, vitality, strength, health (see *energy*) ‖ ANT lassitude, apathy, weakness

Vi·king /vī′kiṅ/ [< Scand] *n* one of the Scandinavian pirates who terrorized the coasts of Europe from the eighth to the tenth centuries

vile /vīl′/ [OF *vil*] *adj* 1 mean, ignoble; 2 morally debased or depraved; 3 foul or offensive; 4 bad; of the lowest quality

vil·i·fy /vil′ifī′/ [LL *vilificare*] *vt* to traduce, slander ‖ **vil′i·fi·er** *n* ‖ **vil′·i·fi·ca′tion** *n* ‖ SYN abuse, asperse, debase, revile, slander, defame, calumniate ‖ ANT acclaim, extol, honor, praise

vil·la /vil'ə/ [L = country house, farm] *n* pretentious residence in the country or suburbs, usu. in extensive grounds

vil·lage /vil'ij/ [MF < L *villaticum*] *n* 1 small group of houses in a country district, larger than a hamlet and smaller than a town; 2 small incorporated municipality ‖ **vil'lag·er** *n*

vil·lain /vil'ən/ [MF *vilein* farm laborer] *n* 1 very wicked person; rascal; 2 evil character in a play or novel, who opposes the hero

vil'lain·ous *adj* 1 of, pert. to, or like a villain; 2 showing great depravity; viciously criminal; 3 abominable; wretched; objectionable ‖ SYN infamous, bad, detestable, heinous, vile, dishonorable ‖ ANT honorable, good, noble

vil·lain·y /vil'ənē/ *n* (-ies) 1 quality or state of being villainous; great wickedness; 2 villainous act

Vil·na /vil'nə/ *n* capital of Lithuania (295,000)

vim /vim'/ [L < *vis* force, energy] *n* vitality, spirit, vigor

vin·ai·grette /vin'əgret'/ *n* small, usu. ornamental bottle or box for holding aromatic vinegar, smelling salts, or a pungent drug

vin·ai·grette' sauce' *n* vinegar and oil sauce for use on cold meats or salads

Vin'ci, Le·o·nar'do da *n* see Leonardo da Vinci

vin·di·cate /vin'dikāt'/ [L *vindicare* (-*atus*) to lay claim to, avenge] *vt* 1 to defend successfully against denial, objection, or accusation; 2 to clear from suspicion of wrong, dishonor, or invalidity; 3 to uphold, justify ‖ **vin'di·ca·tor** *n* ‖ **vin·di·ca'tion** *n* ‖ SYN justify, clear (see *avenge; assert*)

vin·dic·tive /vindik'tiv/ [< L *vindicta* revenge] *adj* given to or prompted by revenge; vengeful

vine /vīn'/ [OF *vigne*] *n* 1 any plant that twines or climbs by tendrils or other means, or trails on the ground; 2 grapevine

vin·e·gar /vin'igər/ [OF *vinegre* = sour wine] *n* 1 sour liquid, dilute and impure acetic acid, obtained by the fermentation of cider, wine, etc. beyond the alcohol stage, used to season or preserve food; 2 sour manner or speech; 3 *colloq* high spirits

vin'e·gar·y *adj* 1 sour; like vinegar; 2 crabbed; disagreeable

vine·yard /vin'yərd/ *n* plantation of grapevines ‖ **vine'yard·ist** *n*

vin'i·cul'ture /vin'i-/ [< L *vinum* wine + *culture*] *n* cultivation of grapes for wine

vin·tage /vint'ij/ [AF] *n* 1 yearly produce of a vineyard or by a wine-producing district; 2 wine produced in a given season; 3 season of harvesting grapes and producing wine; 4 product or style of a particular year or time, as *a car of the vintage of 1930* ‖ *adj* 5 of a specific vintage; 6 of fine production from the past, as *vintage automobiles*; 7 outdated, belonging to the past

vin'tage wine' *n* superior wine from a good vintage

vin'tage year' *n* year of the production of superior wines from a given vineyard or district

vint·ner /vint'nər/ [AF *vineter*] *n* 1 wine maker; 2 wine merchant

vi·nyl /vīn'əl, vin'-/ [< L *vinum* wine + -*yl*] *chem adj* 1 containing the group CH₂ = CH— derived from ethylene ‖ *n* 2 plastic made by polymerizing compounds containing the vinyl group

vi'nyl chlo'ride *n* flammable, colorless, pleasant-smelling gas —CH₂= CHCl— used as a refrigerant and in the manufacture of plastics

vi·ol /vī'əl/ [MF *viole*] *n* medieval stringed instrument played with a bow, from which the violin was developed

vi·o·la /vē·ōl'ə, vī-/ [It] *n* stringed instrument of the violin family, slightly larger than the violin and tuned a fifth below it

vi·o·late /vī'əlāt'/ [L *violare* (-*atus*) to treat forcibly] *vt* 1 to encroach or trespass upon; 2 to profane or treat irreverently; 3 to break (a law, ordinance, treaty, agreement, promise, etc.); 4 to break in on; disturb; 5 to rape ‖ **vi'o·la·tor** *n* ‖ **vi'o·la'tion** *n* ‖ SYN abuse, desecrate, ravish, injure, transgress, deflower, pollute, defile ‖ ANT honor, respect, regard

vi·o·lence /vī'ələns/ [see **violent**] *n* 1 great strength or energy, physical or emotional, forcibly exerted or expressed; 2 profanation; outrage; desecration; 3 ravishment; 4 abuse by distortion of meaning or intent ‖ SYN intensity, fierceness, impetuosity, vehemence, eagerness, severity, rage, violation, oppression, transgression (see *compulsion*) ‖ ANT calmness, forbearance, patience, meekness, gentleness

vi·o·lent [L *violentus*] *adj* 1 marked by or acting with great physical force, esp. when unlawfully exercised, as *to lay violent hands on someone*; 2 characterized by or due to strong feeling, as *a violent dislike*; 3 resulting from the use of force; unnatural, as *a violent death*; 4 marked by intensity of any kind; extreme, as *a violent shock* ‖ **vi'o·lent·ly** *adv*

vi·o·let /vī′əlit/ [OF] n 1 any of a large genus (*Viola*) of low-growing flowering herbs having purple, white, yellow, or variegated flowers; 2 bluish purple ‖ adj 3 bluish-purple

vi′o·let ray′ n shortest ray of the visible spectrum

vi·o·lin /vī′əlin′/ [It *violino*, dim. of *viola*] n 1 smallest and highest-pitched of the family of stringed instruments played with a bow; 2 violin player ‖ **vi′o·lin′ist** n

vi·o·lon·cel·lo /vē′ələnchel′ō/ [It, dim. of *violone* bass viol] n cello ‖ **vi′o·lon·cel′list** n

V/I′P′, V.′I.′P.′ n colloq very important person

vi·per /vīp′ər/ [OE *vīpere* < L *vipera*] n 1 any of various Old World venomous snakes (family Viperidae); 2 any venomous or supposedly venomous snake; 3 malignant or treacherous person

vi·ra·go /virāg′ō, vī-/ [L = female warrior] n (-goes or -gos) quarrelsome loud-mouthed woman; shrew

vir·e·o /vir′ē·ō/ [L] n any of a family (Vireonidae) of small American insectivorous birds, chiefly olive-green or grayish in color

vir·gin /vur′jin/ [OF *virgine* < L *virgo* (-*ginis*)] n 1 person, esp. a woman, who has had no sexual intercourse; 2 **the Virgin** Mary, mother of Jesus ‖ adj 3 chaste, maidenly; 4 pure, undefiled, as *virgin snow*; 5 fresh, untouched, as *virgin soil*; 6 first done or used, as *a virgin speech, virgin wool* ‖ **vir′gin·al** adj ‖ **vir·gin′i·ty** /vərjin′-/ n

Vir·gin·ia /vərjin′yə/ n state in the central E United States (4,648,000; 40,815 sq.m.; cap. Richmond) ‖ **Vir·gin′ian** n

Vir·gin′ia creep′er n North American woody vine (*Parthenocissus quinquefolia*) having leaves divided into five or seven parts and bluish-black berries

Vir·gin′ia ham′ n ham cured in hickory smoke

Vir·gin′ia reel′ n dance in which the partners, facing each other in opposite lines, perform a series of set figures

Vir′gin Is′lands npl group of islands in the West Indies E of Puerto Rico, divided between the U.S. and Great Britain (U.S. Virgin Islands: 32,000; 133 sq.m.; cap. Charlotte Amalie)

Vir·go /vurg′ō/ [L = virgin] n 1 a northern zodiacal constellation, the Virgin; 2 sixth sign of the zodiac

vir·gule /vur′gyōōl/ [F < L *virgula* small rod] n stroke slanting to the right /, used to indicate alternatives, as *and/or*, to divide fractions, dates, or verses, as *1/5; 12/13/75*, to enclose phonemic symbols, etc.

vir·ile /vir′əl/ [L *virilis*] adj 1 characteristic of a man; manly; 2 forcefully and masterfully masculine; 3 capable of procreation ‖ **vi·ril′i·ty** /viril′-/

vi·rol·o·gy /vīrol′əjē, vi-/ [< *virus* + -*logy*] n science that deals with viruses and virus diseases ‖ **vi·rol′o·gist** n

vir·tu·al /vurch′ōō·əl/ [ML *virtualis*] adj existing in effect though not in fact or fact

vir′tu·al im′age n image formed by the apparent but not actual convergence of rays, as that seen in a plane mirror

vir′tu·al·ly adv almost; for the most part

vir·tue /vurch′ōō/ [AF *vertu* < L *virtus* strength, manliness] n 1 inherent power; efficacy; 2 admirable quality; merit; 3 moral excellence; 4 chastity; 5 **in** or **by virtue of** because of

vir·tu·o·so /vurch′ōō·ōs′ō/ [It] n (-sos or -si /-sē/) 1 connoisseur or collector of art, antiques, etc.; 2 one skilled in the technique of an art, esp. music; 3 any highly skilled or knowledgeable person ‖ **vir′tu·os′i·ty** /-os′-/ n

vir·tu·ous /vurch′ōō·əs/ adj 1 morally excellent; righteous; 2 chaste (woman)

vir·u·lent /vir′(y)ələnt/ [L *virulentus* poisonous] adj 1 highly infective; spreading rapidly; deadly; 2 poisonous, noxious; 3 bitterly hostile; malicious ‖ **vir′u·lence** n

vi·rus /vīr′əs/ [L = slime, poison] n 1 highly infective agent of disease, considerably smaller than bacteria, and able to reproduce only in the presence of living cells; 2 moral poison

vi·sa /vēz′ə/ [F] n 1 official endorsement on a passport giving the bearer permission to enter a country ‖ vt 2 to give a visa to; 3 to endorse (a passport with a visa

vis·age /viz′ij/ [OF] n 1 face or countenance; 2 appearance, aspect

vis-à-vis /vēz′əvē′/ [F] adv 1 face to face ‖ prep 2 facing; 3 with regard to; 4 in comparison with ‖ n 5 person face to face with another, as in dancing; 6 carriage in which persons sit facing each other

vis·cer·a /vis′ərə/ [L = entrails] npl the organs in the great cavities of the body

vis′cer·al adj 1 of or pert. to the viscera; 2 inner; deep-felt; earthy

vis·cid /vis′id/ [L *viscidus*] adj having a glutinous consistency; sticky ‖ **vis·cid′i·ty** /visid′-/ n

vis·cose /vis′kōs/ [L *viscosus* sticky] n gelatinous substance produced by treating cellulose with carbon disulfide, used in making rayon and cellophane

vis·cos′i·ty /-kos′-/ [< *viscous*] n 1

stickiness; **2** *phys* **a** internal frictional resistance offered by a fluid to forces causing it to flow; **b** measure of a fluid's resistance to flowing

vis·count /vī′kount′/ [AF *viscounte*] *n* nobleman ranking between an earl or count and a baron ‖ **vis′count·ess** *nfem*

vis·cous /visk′əs/ [L *viscosus* sticky] *adj* **1** glutinous; sticky; **2** *phys* having the property of viscosity

vise /vīs′/ [OF *vis* screw] *n* any of various devices having two jaws that may be drawn together to hold objects firmly, as on a workbench

vi·sé /vēz′ā, vēzā′/ [F = inspected] *n* **1** visa ‖ *vt* **2** to visa

Vish·nu /vish′nōō/ *n* second member of the Hindu trinity, called the Preserver

vis·i·bil·i·ty /viz′ibil′itē/ *n* **1** state of being visible; **2** relative ability to be seen under prevailing conditions; **3** range of vision; **4** capability for unobstructed vision

vis·i·ble /viz′ibəl/ [L *visibilis*] *adj* **1** capable of being seen; **2** apparent, evident ‖ **vis′i·bly** *adv*

Vis·i·goth /viz′igoth′/ *n* one of the western Goths that in the fifth and sixth centuries overran Europe and finally settled in Spain ‖ **Vis′i·goth′ic** *adj*

vi·sion /vizh′ən/ [L *visio* (-*onis*) sight] *n* **1** act or faculty of seeing; **2** that which is seen; **3** imaginative foresight; **4** perception of mental images, as of the fancy or imagination; **5** something seen in a dre..m or trance; **6** someone or something beautiful to behold ‖ *vt* **7** to see as in a dream

vi′sion·ar′y /-ner′-/ *adj* **1** pert. to or favorable for vision; **2** disposed to accept fancies as realities; impractical; **3** imagined, not real ‖ *n* (-ies) **4** one given to fancies or reveries; **5** impractical person ‖ SYN *adj* impracticable, fanciful, romantic, unreal, unfounded, wild, delusive (see *fanciful*)

vis·it /viz′it/ [OF *visiter*] *vt* **1** to go or come to see, as for friendship, pleasure, business, inspection, examination, etc.; **2** to stay with as a guest; **3** to afflict; **4** to avenge ‖ *vi* **5** to make a visit ‖ *n* **6** act or instance of visiting; **7** stay as a guest ‖ **vis′i·tor** *n*

vis′i·tant *n* **1** visitor; **2** migratory bird that appears for a limited period in passing through a locality

vis′i·ta′tion *n* **1** act of visiting, esp. for an official inspection; **2** special dispensation of divine favor or wrath; **3** any unusual event resembling such a dispensation; judgment; **4** **Visitation** church festival celebrated July 2 in honor of the visit of the Virgin Mary to Elizabeth the mother of John the Baptist (Luke 1:39-56)

vis′it·ing fire′man *n colloq* **1** visiting

dignitary entertained with special attention; **2** stranger who has a big time in a large city

vi·sor /vīz′ər/ [AF *viser*] *n* **1** the movable front on a knight's helmet covering the face; **2** projecting brim on the front of a cap to shade the eyes; **3** pivoted flap in an automobile that can be lowered to shield the driver's eyes from the rays of a low sun

vis·ta /vist′ə/ [It = view] *n* **1** outlook or view, usu. along a passage, street, avenue, or the like; **2** mental view of remembered or anticipated events

vis·u·al /vizh′ōōəl/ [LL *visualis*] *adj* **1** pert. to or used in seeing; **2** visible, perceptible ‖ **vis′u·al·ly** *adv*

vis′u·al·ize *vt* **1** to make a mental picture of ‖ *vi* **2** to form a mental picture ‖ **vis′u·al·i·za′tion** *n*

vi·tal /vīt′əl/ [< L *vita* life] *adj* **1** of or pert. to life; **2** supporting or essential to life; **3** indispensable, essential; **4** critically important; **5** full of life and energy; **6** fatal, as a wound or blow ‖ *n* **7** **vitals** *pl* **a** vital organs of the body; **b** essential parts of anything

vi·tal′i·ty /-tal′-/ *n* **1** life force; ability to sustain life; **2** capacity for enduring or continuing in effect; **3** mental or physical strength and vigor ‖ SYN life, endurance, strength ‖ ANT death, dissolution, lassitude

vi′tal·ize *vt* **1** to fill or endow with life; **2** to animate

vi′tal sta·tis′tics *npl* statistics concerning human beings or populations, as births, deaths, marriages, incidence of disease, etc.

vi·ta·min /vīt′əmin/ [< L *vita* life + *amine*] *n* one of a class of complex substances found in natural foods or produced synthetically lack or deficiencies of which interfere with the normal processes of animal growth or produce disease

vi′ta·min A *n* a fat-soluble alcohol found in carrots, green vegetables, and egg yolk; prevents night blindness

vi′ta·min B₁ *n* thiamin

vi′ta·min B₂ *n* riboflavin

vi′ta·min B₁₂ *n* crystallized solid —$C_{63}H_{90}N_{14}O_{14}PCo$— found in fish, milk, eggs, and liver, used in the treatment of pernicious anemia

vi′ta·min C *n* water-soluble substance —$C_6H_8O_6$— found in citrus fruits and green vegetables and produced synthetically; essential for normal metabolism and used to treat or prevent scurvy

vi′ta·min D *n* any of several antirachitic vitamins found in fish-liver oils

vi′ta·min E *n* viscous fluid, found in wheat-germ oil, that promotes fertility

vi′ta·min K *n* either of two fat-soluble

vitamins —$C_{31}H_{40}O_2$ and $C_{41}H_{56}O_2$—obtained from alfalfa and fish meal and essential for blood clotting

vi·ti·ate /vish'ē·āt'/ [L vitiare (-atus)] vt 1 to corrupt, debase, contaminate; 2 to invalidate, render ineffectual or worthless || vi'ti·a'tion n || vi'ti·at'ed adj

vit·re·ous /vit'rē·əs/ [L vitreus] adj 1 of, pert. to, or resembling glass; 2 made from or containing glass

vit're·ous hu'mor n transparent jelly-like substance filling the eyeball between the lens and the retina

vit·ri·fy /vit'rifī/ [F vitrifier < L vitrum glass] v (-fied) vt 1 to convert into glass or a glassy substance; 2 to cause to have a glassy surface || vi 3 to be converted into glass or a glassy substance || vit'ri·fied' adj

vit·ri·ol /vit'rē·ol/ [L vitreolus pert. to glass] n 1 sulfuric acid; 2 any of several metallic sulfates of characteristic colors, as blue vitriol (copper sulfate) or green vitriol (iron sulfate); 3 anything sharp or caustic, as sarcasm or vituperation

vit'ri·ol'ic /-ol'-/ adj 1 of, pert. to, like, or derived from vitriol; 2 sharp, caustic, sarcastic

vi·tu·per·ate /vīt(y)ōōp'ərāt', vi-/ [L vituperare (-atus) to blame, abuse] vt to blame abusively; berate, revile || vi·tu'per·a'tion n || vi·tu'per·a·tive /-ăt'iv, -ətiv/ adj || SYN censure, berate, abuse, revile, insult

vi·va /vē'vä, -və/ [It or Sp] interj 1 long live (someone or something)! || n 2 shout of "viva!"

vi·va·cious /vīväsh'əs, vi-/ [< L vivax (-acis) lively] adj full of spirit; lively, gay, animated || vi·vac'i·ty /-vas'-/ n || SYN spirited, sportive, merry, gay, jocose, sparkling, mirthful || ANT dull, stupid, stolid, dead, lifeless

vi·va vo·ce /vīv'ə vōs'ē/ [L = with the living voice] adv by word of mouth

vive /vēv'/ [F] interj viva!

vivi- [L] comb form living, alive

viv·id /viv'id/ [L vividus lively] adj 1 animated, lively; 2 intense, brilliant, as color or light; 3 producing lifelike images in the mind; 4 strong, clear, keen, as a vivid recollection || SYN graphic, colorful, striking, brilliant || ANT dull, flat, colorless, lifeless, prosy

viv·i·fy /viv'ifī'/ [LL vivificare] v (-fied) vt to give life to; animate || viv'i·fi·ca'tion n

vi·vip·a·rous /vīvip'ərəs/ [L viviparus] adj 1 bringing forth living young instead of eggs; 2 producing seeds that germinate on the plant

viv'i·sec'tion /viv'i-/ n dissection of the living body of an animal, as for medical research

vix·en /viks'ən/ [OE fyxen] n 1 female fox; 2 quarrelsome ill-tempered woman || vix'en·ish adj

viz. [L videlicet /videl'isit/ it is allowable to see] namely, to wit

vi·zier /vizir'/ [Ar wazīr = burden bearer] n high official in certain Muslim countries; minister of state

V/-J' Day' n the day of Japan's surrender to the Allies in World War II, September 2, 1945

VL Vulgar Latin

Vla·di·vos·tok /vlad'ivos'tok/ n seaport in E Siberia on the Sea of Japan (360,000)

vo·cab·u·lar·y /vōkab'yəler'ē/ [ML vocabularium] n (-ies) 1 list of words alphabetically arranged and defined, usu. of a particular language, book, author, branch of science, etc.; 2 list of words alphabetically arranged and translated, accompanying each lesson of a foreign language textbook or placed at the end of the book; 3 stock of words employed by a class or individual; 4 all the words of a language || SYN word list, wording (see diction)

vo·cal /vōk'əl/ [L vocalis] adj 1 pert. to, uttered with, or intended for the voice; 2 having a voice; 3 using one's voice freely, as to express a point of view; 4 pert. to or like a vowel

vo'cal cords' npl either of two pairs of fibrous tissue in the larynx, the vibration of the lower pair of which produces the voice

vo·cal·ic /vōkal'ik/ adj pert. to, resembling, consisting of, or characterized by vowels

vo'cal·ist n singer

vo'cal·ize' vt 1 to utter with the voice, make vocal; 2 to sing; 3 to change into a vowel || also vi || vo'cal·i·za'-tion n

vo·ca·tion /vōkāsh'ən/ [L vocatio (-onis) call, summons] n 1 occupation, profession; calling; 2 call to, or sense of fitness for, a particular career, esp. a call to a religious life

vo·ca'tion·al school' n school, usu. on the high-school level, preparing students for practical work in industry, agriculture, etc., rather than for liberal arts or a profession

voc·a·tive /vok'ətiv/ [< L vocare to call] n 1 grammatical case in Latin, Greek, and other highly inflected languages used to designate the person or thing being addressed or called; 2 a noun in this case; b noun in a noninflected language performing this function || also adj

vo·cif·er·ate /vōsif'ərāt', L vociferari (-atus)] vt & vi to shout, cry out noisily || vo·cif'er·a'tion n || vo·cif'er·ous adj

vod·ka /vod'kə/ [Russ] n colorless distilled liquor, originally made in Russia from fermenting potatoes, rye, or corn

vogue /vōg'/ [MF = swaying motion,

sailing/ *n* 1 prevailing fashion; 2 popularity, acceptance ‖ SYN style, fashion (see *mode*)

voice /vois'/ [AF < L *vox* (*vocis*)] *n* 1 sound proceeding from the mouth, esp. human utterances; 2 such sound considered for its quality or character, as *a gracious voice;* 3 power of utterance; speech; 4 anything suggesting or likened to speech, as *the voice of the wind;* 5 expressed choice or opinion, or the right to express a choice or opinion, as *he had no voice in the matter;* 6 impression or message conveyed, as by speech, as *the voice of conscience;* 7 singer; 8 *mus* vocal part; 9 *gram* form or function of a verb indicating whether the subject acts or is acted upon ‖ *vt* 10 to give utterance to, express; 11 *phonet* to pronounce with vibration of the vocal cords

voice/ box/ *n* larynx

voice/ coil/ *n* coil which receives sound vibrations from the diaphragm of a microphone and transmits them over wires as audio-frequency electric vibrations or which imparts vibrations to the diaphragm of a telephone receiver from the line or of a loudspeaker from a phonograph or a radio

voiced/ *adj* 1 expressed by the voice; 2 *phonet* pronounced with vibration of the vocal cords

voice/less *adj* 1 having no voice or vote; mute, silent; 2 unspoken; 3 *phonet* not voiced

voice/print/ *n* electronically produced graphic representation of a spoken word or part of a word which shows the frequency, amplitude, and rate of speaking of a voice and which may be used for purposes of identification

voice/ vote/ *n* vote decided by the apparent strength of the ayes and noes called out rather than by actual count

void /void'/ [OF *voide* empty] *adj* 1 empty; 2 vacant, unoccupied; 3 without effect, useless; 4 of no legal effect or force ‖ *n* 5 empty space; 6 vacuum ‖ *vt* 7 to discharge, evacuate, as urine; 8 to empty the contents of; 9 to render of no effect or validity; annul

voi·là /vwälä'/ [F] *interj* look!, there you are!

voile /voil'/ [F = veil] *n* thin, sheer dress material of cotton, wool, silk, etc.

vol. volume

Vo·la·pük /vōl'əpYk'/ [= world speech] *n* one of the earliest of artificial auxiliary languages, invented about 1879 by Johann Schleyer (1831–1912), G linguist

vol·a·tile /vol'ətəl/ [L *volatilis* flying] *adj* 1 fickle, changeable; 2 mercurial, explosive (temperament, person,

etc.); 3 readily and quickly evaporating ‖ vol'a·til/i·ty /-til/-/ *n*

vol'a·til·ize' *vt* & *vi* to evaporate ‖ vol'a·til·i·za'tion *n*

vol·can·ic /volkan'ik/ *adj* 1 pert. to, or discharging from, a volcano; 2 having volcanoes; 3 resembling a volcano; violent, explosive

vol·ca·no /volkān'ō/ [It < L *Vulcanus* Vulcan] *n* (-noes or -nos) 1 opening in the earth's surface from which molten rock, fire, and steam are or have been expelled; 2 hill or mountain formed from the lava and ash expelled from such an opening, usu. having a conical shape and a cuplike crater at the summit

vole /vōl'/ [< *volemouse* < ON *völlr* field] *n* any of a genus (*Microtus*) of mouselike or ratlike rodents

Vol·ga /vol'gə/ *n* river flowing SE across Russia from near Leningrad to the Caspian; longest river in Europe

vo·li·tion /vōlish'ən/ [ML *volitio* (-*onis*)] *n* 1 act or power of willing; 2 exercise of the will; 3 decision or choice made by the will ‖ SYN will, desire, inclination, wish, choice, preference, resolution ‖ DISCR In ordinary, not technical, usage, *will* and *volition* are often interchangeable, particularly in the sense of desire or inclination, as he acted according to his own *will* (or *volition*) in the matter. When a popular distinction is made, it frequently centers upon *will* as the power of willing and upon *volition* as the act or exercise of that power

vol·ley /vol'ē/ [MF *volee* flight] *n* 1 simultaneous discharge of a number of missiles or firearms; 2 missiles so discharged or hurled; 3 burst or emission of any sort; 4 *tennis* a flight of the ball before it touches the ground; b stroke that returns the ball before it touches the ground; 5 *soccer* kick given the ball before it touches the ground ‖ *vt* 6 to discharge in a volley; 7 *tennis* to return (the ball) before it touches the ground; 8 *soccer* to kick (the ball) before it rebounds ‖ *vi* 9 to be discharged in a volley

vol'ley·ball/ *n* 1 game in which two teams attempt to keep a large ball moving over a net with the hands without letting the ball touch the ground; 2 the ball used

volt /vōlt'/ [Alessandro *Volta* (1745–1827) It physicist] *n* the practical mks unit of electromotive force, being the force that moves a current of one ampere through a resistance of one ohm

volt/age /-ij/ *n* electromotive force or difference of potential expressed in volts

volt/age di·vid/er *n* resistor tapped at

intervals to provide fractional voltages

vol·ta·ic /voltā′ik/ *adj* of or pert. to
electricity or electric currents, esp.
if produced by chemical action

vol·ta′ic cell′ *n* device for producing
electrical energy by chemical action,
consisting of two electrodes of different materials in contact with an
electrolyte

Vol·taire /volter′, vōl-/ *n* (François
Marie Arouet) (1694–1778) French
philosopher and author

volte-face /volt′fäs′/ [F = turn face]
n complete turning around or reversal, as in policy

volt′me′ter *n* instrument for measuring difference of potential in volts

vol·u·ble /vol′yəbəl/ [L *volubilis*] *adj*
smooth or fluent in speech; talkative,
glib ‖ **vol′u·bil′i·ty** /-bil′-/ *n* ‖ SYN
loquacious, fluent, glib (see *garrulous*)

vol·ume /vol′yōōm, -yəm/ [L *volumen*
roll, book] *n* 1 book; 2 one of a
numbered series of books making up
a set; 3 space occupied, as measured
by cubic units; 4 degree of loudness;
5 large quantity ‖ SYN bulk, mass,
quantity, size, amount

vo·lu·mi·nous /vəlōōm′inəs/ [LL *volu-
minosus* full of folds] *adj* 1 enough
to fill a volume or many volumes; 2
great in bulk; swelling, full

vol·un·tar·y /vol′ənter′ē/ [L *voluntarius*]
adj 1 done or brought about by one's
own free will; 2 intentional, not accidental, as *voluntary manslaughter*;
3 controlled by the will, as *the voluntary muscles*; 4 able to act by one's
own free will; free; 5 *law* a acting
without compulsion; b acting without valuable consideration ‖ **vol′un·
tar′i·ly** *adv* ‖ SYN spontaneous, un-
constrained, volitional, intentional,
deliberate, gratuitous, unsolicited ‖
ANT involuntary, automatic, unintentional

vol·un·teer′ *n* 1 one who enters into
any transaction or service, esp. military service, voluntarily; 2 one who
performs a service without pay ‖
adj 3 of or pert. to volunteers; 4
performed without pay ‖ *vt* 5 to give
or offer (help, services, information,
etc.) freely and without solicitation
‖ *vi* 6 to offer one's services; 7 to
enlist as a volunteer

vo·lup·tu·ar·y /vəlup′chōō·er′ē/ [< L
voluptas pleasure] *n* (-ies) one who
is devoted to the pursuit of sensual
pleasure ‖ also *adj*

vo·lup′tu·ous *adj* 1 producing, ministering to, arising from, or devoted to
sensual pleasure; 2 arousing the sensual appetites, as *voluptuous beauty*

vo·lute /vəlōōt′/ [L *voluta*] *n* 1 spiral
scroll-shaped architectural ornament;
2 any of several mollusks with
whirled shells (family Volutidae); 3
whirl or turn, as of a spiral shell

vom·it /vom′it/ [L *vomitus*] *n* 1 matter thrown up by the stomach ‖ *vt* 2
to throw up from the stomach; spew;
3 to discharge with violence; belch
forth ‖ also *vi*

von /von′/ [G = from] *prep* used as
part of some German family names,
originally indicating origin, later as
a mark of nobility, as *Manfred von
Richthofen*

voo·doo /vōō′dōō/ [WAfr *vodu*
dēmon] *n* 1 quasi-religious rites developed in the West Indies from
African cult worship, mixed with
Christian elements and containing
magic and sorcery; 2 adherent of
voodoo; 3 object or fetish of voodoo
worship ‖ *vt* 4 to bewitch by voodoo
‖ **voo′doo·ism** *n*

vo·ra·cious /vōrāsh′əs, vō-, və-/ [< L
vorax (-*acis*) greedy] *adj* 1 greedy in
eating; ravenous; 2 greedy, insatiable, as *a voracious reader* ‖ **vo·
rac′i·ty** /-ras′-/ *n*

-vore /-vôr′, -vōr′/ [L -*vorus*] *n comb
form* eating, as *carnivore* ‖ **-vo·rous**
/-v(ə)rəs/ *adj comb form*, as *carnivorous*

vor·tex /vôr′teks/ [L = eddy] *n* (-tex·es
or -ti·ces /-tisēz′/) 1 water or air with
a rotary motion tending to suck
bodies caught in it into a vacuum at
the center; eddy or whirlpool; 2 any
violent commotion or activity that
draws into it everything in its vicinity

vo·ta·ry /vōt′ərē/ [< L *votum* vow] *n*
(-ries) 1 one consecrated by a vow to
some service; 2 one devoted to any
pursuit; 3 devoted follower

vote /vōt′/ [L *votum* vow] *n* 1 formally stated choice, opinion, or decision of one or more persons; 2
that which is so expressed; 3 right to
vote; 4 something by which a vote is
expressed, as a ballot; 5 votes collectively, as *a heavy presidential vote*
‖ *vt* 6 to declare or authorize by
vote; 7 to pronounce by general consent ‖ *vi* 8 to cast a ballot ‖ **vot′er** *n*

vo·tive /vōt′iv/ *adj* given or consecrated by a vow

vouch /vouch′/ [AF *vo(u)cher*] *vt*
vouch for to give guaranty for; attest to

vouch′er *n* 1 one who or that which
vouches; 2 evidence of payment, as
a receipt

vouch·safe′ *vt* to deign to grant; concede

vow /vou′/ [OF *vou*] *n* 1 solemn promise or pledge, esp. one made to or
before God; 2 take **vows** to enter a
religious order ‖ *vt* 3 to promise
solemnly; 4 to assert solemnly, swear
‖ *vi* 5 to make a solemn promise or
declaration; 6 to declare with emphasis ‖ SYN *n* promise, oath, pledge,
engagement

vow·el /vou′əl/ [OF *vouel*] *n* 1 vocal
sound in which there is no audible

friction or stoppage; **2** letter representing such a sound

vox po·pu·li /voks′ pop′yəlī′/ [L] *n* voice of the people

voy·age /voi′ij/ [AF < L *viaticum* provisions for a journey] *n* **1** long journey, as by ship, plane, or spacecraft; **2** travel; trip || *vi* **3** to make or take a voyage || **voy′ag·er** *n*

vo·yeur /voiyur′/ [F] *n* person who gets sexual gratification from watching sexual acts or objects || **vo·yeur′-ism** *n*

V.P., VP Vice President

vs. versus

Vt. Vermont

vt, v.t. transitive verb

Vul·can /vulk′ən/ *n* Roman god of fire and of metalworking; identified with Gk Hephaestus

vul′can·ite *n* hard rubber made by vulcanizing rubber with large amounts of sulfur, used in making combs, chemical and electrical apparatus, etc.

vul′can·ize *vt* **1** to harden (rubber) by the admixture of sulfur or a compound of sulfur and the application of heat; **2** to patch or repair (a rubber article) with crude rubber which is fused in position under heat and pressure

vul·gar /vul′gər/ [< L *vulgus* common people] *adj* **1** unrefined; in bad taste; crude, boorish; **2** of or pert. to the common people || **vul′gar·ize′** *vt* || **vul′gar·i·za′tion** *n* || SYN coarse, gross, common, base, low, boorish, underbred, vile, offensive || ANT cultivated, refined, cultured, elegant, dainty

vul·gar′i·an /-ger′ē·ən/ *n* vulgar person, esp. if rich or prominent

vul′gar·ism *n* **1** vulgar behavior; vulgarity; **2** coarse or vulgar phrase or expression || SYN vulgarity || DISCR A *vulgarism* is a phrase or expression in common but not standard usage.

It is not necessarily coarse or low, but is not always in good taste; "enthuse" and "dark-complected," for instance, are *vulgarisms* avoided by careful speakers, as is also the word "party" for "person." A *vulgarity* is an instance of grossness, coarseness, or clownishness in manners or speech; the use of profanity or unrefined expressions is a *vulgarity*

vul·gar′i·ty /-gar′-/ *n* (-ties) **1** state or quality of being vulgar or coarse; **2** vulgar act or expression || SYN (see *vulgarism*)

Vul′gar Lat′in *n* popular or spoken Latin as distinguished from literary or Classical Latin

Vul·gate /vul′gāt, -gāt/ [< L *vulgata* (editio) popular (edition)] *n* Latin translation of the Bible prepared by St. Jerome in the fourth century, the authorized version of the Roman Catholic Church

vul·ner·a·ble /vuln′ərəbəl/ [< L *vulnus* (-*eris*) wound] *adj* **1** capable of being wounded or hurt; **2** open to criticism or temptation; **3** difficult to defend, open to attack; **4** *bridge* having won one game in a rubber and liable to increased penalties || **vul′ner·a·bil′i·ty** /-bil′-/ *n* || SYN assailable, susceptible, liable

vul·pine /vul′pīn, vulp′in/ [< L *vulpes* fox] *adj* pert. to or like a fox

vul·ture /vulch′ər/ [L *vultur*] *n* **1** any member of either of two families of large carrion-eating birds of prey allied to the hawks and eagles, one family (Accipitridae) native to Europe and the other (Cathartidae) confined to America; **2** unscrupulous person who preys on others

vul·va /vul′və/ [L = covering] *n* (-vae /-vē/) external parts of the female sexual organs || **vul′var** *adj*

vy·ing /vī′iŋ/ **1** *prp* of *vie* || *adj* **2** competing

W

W, w /dub′əlyōō′/ *n* (W's or Ws; w's or ws) 23rd letter of the English alphabet

W 1 23rd in order or in a series; **2** *chem* tungsten; **3** something shaped like a W

W. Wednesday

W, w, W., w. west(ern)

W., w. watt(s)

wab·ble /wob′əl/ *vi, vt, & n* var of **wobble**

Wac, WAC /wak′/ *n* member of the Women's Army Corps

wack /wak′/ [< *wacky*] *n* slang wacky person

wack′y [?] *adj* (-i·er; -i·est) slang crazy; irrational; odd

wad /wod′/ [prob < Scand] *n* **1** small mass or ball of some soft material; **2** soft bunch of cotton, wool, etc., for stuffing or padding; **3** plug to hold a charge of powder or shot in position in a gun or a cartridge; **4** slang a roll of paper money; **b** large amount, as of money || *v* (**wad·ded**; **wad·ding**) *vt* **5** to form into a wad; **6** to insert a wad into; **7** to pad, stuff

wad′ding *n* soft material for padding, lining, or packing, or for gun or cartridge wads

wad·dle /wod′əl/ [< *wade*] *vi* **1** to walk with short steps, swaying from side to side, like a duck ‖ *n* **2** waddling gait

wade /wād′/ [OE *wadan*] *vi* **1** to walk through water, mud, snow, or other substance that hinders progress; **2** **wade through** to proceed through slowly or with difficulty, as *to wade through a tiresome book;* **3 wade in** or **into** *colloq* **a** to attack vigorously; **b** to begin with determination ‖ *vt* **4** to cross by wading

wad′er *n* **1** person or thing that wades; **2** any of several long-legged shore birds that wade in shallow water while hunting food; **3 waders** *pl* waterproof hip boots worn by fishermen and hunters

wa·di /wäd′ē/ [Ar] *n* **1** in N Africa, Arabia, etc., dry riverbed that fills with water during the rainy season; **2** stream flowing through it

Waf, WAF /waf′/ *n* member of the Women in the Air Force

wa·fer /wāf′ər/ [MD] *n* **1** thin crisp cake or biscuit; **2** thin cake of unleavened bread used in the communion service of the Roman Catholic Church; **3** any small flat disk

waf·fle /wof′əl/ [D *wafel*] *n* flat batter cake with a characteristic gridlike pattern on each side, baked in a waffle iron

waf′fle i′ron *n* device for baking waffles consisting of a pair of plates hinged so as to close over batter poured on one of them and shaped with rows of square projections

waft /wäft′, waft′/ [prob < MD *wachten* to guard] *vt* **1** to cause to float lightly along through the air; **2** to direct or send, as if through the air ‖ *vi* **3** to float or pass lightly along, as if through the air ‖ *n* **4** act of wafting; **5** something wafted, as a gust of air, a sound, or a scent

wag /wag′/ [< Scand] *v* (**wagged; wag·ging**) *vt* **1** to move from side to side or up and down ‖ *vi* **2** to move rapidly from side to side or up and down; **3** to move in idle chatter or gossip, as the tongue ‖ *n* **4** act of wagging; **5** witty person; person full of jests and tricks

wage /wāj′/ [AF = prize] *vt* **1** to engage in, carry on, as a war, conflict, or campaign ‖ *n* **2** also **wages** *pl* money paid or received for work or services, esp. if paid by the hour, day, or week; **3 wages** *sg* or *pl* recompense, requital ‖ SYN *n* hire, pay, recompense (see *salary*)

wage′-price′ freeze′ *n* legislative action to hold wages and prices at a stationary level or to control their rise within fixed limits

wa·ger /wāj′ər/ [AF *wageure*] *n* **1** that which is risked on the outcome of an uncertain event; bet; **2** term of

a wager ‖ *vt* **3** to risk or stake (something) on the outcome of some uncertain event ‖ *vi* **4** to make or offer a wager

wage′work′er *n* one who works for pay by the hour, day, or week

wag·gish /wag′ish/ *adj* **1** characteristic of or like a wag; **2** roguish, jesting

wag·gle /wag′əl/ [< *wag*] *vt* & *vi* **1** to move rapidly up and down or from side to side ‖ *n* **2** waggling motion

Wag·ner, Rich·ard /väg′nər/ *n* (1813–83) German composer ‖ **Wag·ne′ri·an** /-nir′ē·ən/ *adj* & *n*

wag·on /wag′ən/ [D *wagen*] *n* **1** four-wheeled vehicle for hauling and delivering, usu. pulled by draft animals; **2** child's toy vehicle, pulled by a long handle; **3** patrol wagon; **4 on the (water) wagon** *slang* having given up or abstaining from alcoholic beverages

waif /wāf′/ [AF = thing lost] *n* **1** homeless child; **2** stray animal

Wai·ki·ki /wī′kēkē′/ *n* beach near Honolulu

wail /wāl′/ [< Scand] *vt* **1** to mourn, lament ‖ *vi* **2** to utter high-pitched mournful cries, as in grief or pain; **3** to make mournful sounds, as the wind ‖ *n* **4** act of wailing; **5** wailing cry or sound

wain·scot /wān′skōt, -skət, -skot/ [MD *wagenschot* fine oak wood] *n* **1** wooden lining, usually paneled, of a room wall or the lower portion of it ‖ *v* (**-scot·ed** or **-scot·ted; -scot·ing** or **-scot·ting**) **2** to line (an interior wall) with wood

wain′scot·ing or **wain′scot·ting** /-skōtiŋ, -skət-, -skot-/ *n* paneling for wainscots

wain′wright′ [*obs wain* wagon + *wright*] *n* wagon maker

waist /wāst′/ [ME *wast*] *n* **1** the part of the body between the ribs and the hips; **2** slender middle part of anything; **3** the part of a garment that covers the waist; **4** blouse; **5** middle part of a ship between the forecastle and the quarter-deck

waist′band′ *n* band, as of a skirt or trousers, that encircles the waist

waist·coat /wāst′kōt′, wes′kit/ *n* Brit vest

waist′line′ *n* line around the narrowest part of the waist

wait /wāt′/ [AF *waitier*] *vi* **1** to linger or tarry, esp. when in a state of expectation, as *wait till he comes;* **2** to be ready or available, as *the taxi is waiting;* **3** to stay in abeyance, as *it can wait;* **4 wait for, a** to await in expectation; **b** to look forward to; **5 wait on, a** to act as a servant to; **b** to serve meals to; **c** to serve (a customer); **6 wait up** *colloq* to postpone going to bed; **7 wait up for** *colloq* **a** to postpone going to bed until the arrival of; **b** to pause and wait for, in walking or running ‖ *vt* **8** to cause to be deferred, as *don't wait dinner;* **9 wait one's turn** to wait until one's turn comes ‖ *n* **10** act or duration of waiting; **11** delay; **12 lie in wait** to lie in ambush

wait′er *n* **1** man who serves at table; **2** serving tray

wait′ing *n* **1** period of waiting; **2 in waiting** in attendance upon a high-ranking person, as *the queen's lady in waiting*

wait′ing list′ *n* list of persons waiting their turn, as for reservations, a job, etc.

wait′ing room′ *n* room for people to wait in, as at a bus or railroad station or a doctor's office

wait′ress *n* female waiter

waive /wāv′/ [AF *weyver* to surrender, abandon] *vt* **1** to forgo, relinquish, as a right or claim; **2** to dispense with, defer

waiv′er *n* act, or document certifying to the act, of voluntary relinquishment of a right

wake[1] /wāk′/ [ME *waken*] *v* (waked or woke; waked or wok·en) *vi* **1** to be awake; **2** to become awake; **3** often **wake up, a** to be roused from sleep; awaken; **b** to be aroused or made active ‖ *vt* **4** often **wake up, a** to rouse from sleep; awake; **b** to arouse from inactivity; make active ‖ *n* **5** vigil over a dead body prior to burial

wake[2] [< Scand] *n* **1** trail left behind some moving object, as a vessel, storm, etc.; **2 in the wake of, a** behind, following; **b** as a result of

wake′ful *adj* **1** unable to sleep; **2** watchful, vigilant ‖ **wake′ful·ness** *n*

wak·en /wāk′ən/ [OE *wæcnan*] *vt & vi* to awaken

Wal′dorf sal′ad *n* /wôl′dôrf/ [*Waldorf*-Astoria Hotel in New York City] *n* salad of celery, nuts, chopped apples, and mayonnaise

wale /wāl′/ [OE *walu*] *n* **1** ridge or mark produced on the skin by flogging; **2** ridge on the surface, as of cloth

Wales /wālz′/ *n* division of the United Kingdom in W Great Britain, joined administratively to England (2,640,-000; 8,016 sq.m.)

walk /wôk′/ [OE *wealcan* to roll] *vi* **1** to go on foot; proceed by steps at a moderate pace; **2** to take a stroll for exercise or pleasure; **3** to behave in a certain manner, as *walk proudly;* **4** baseball to go to first base on four balls; **5 walk off with, a** to steal; **b** to win easily; **6 walk out, a** to leave unceremoniously or in protest; **b** to go on strike; **7 walk out on** *colloq* to desert, abandon ‖ *vt* **8** to traverse or pass over on foot; **9** to lead, ride, or drive at a walk; **10** to accompany on a walk; **11** to move (a large and heavy object) by

a rocking motion; **12** baseball to give first base to (the batter) by pitching four balls ‖ *n* **13** act of walking; **14** one's line of work or station in life; **15** baseball granting of first base to a batter as a result of walking him; **16** sidewalk; path for walking; **17** stroll; promenade; **18** manner of walking; gait; **19** distance covered in walking

walk′a·way′ *n* easy triumph

walk′er *n* **1** person who walks a great deal; **2** device with straps and mounted on wheels or casters for supporting a baby who is learning to walk; **3** lightweight framework with handgrips used to aid cripples, invalids, and the aged to walk

walk′ie-talk′ie *n* portable radio transmitter and receiver

walk′-in′ *adj* large enough to be walked into, as *a walk-in closet*

walk′ing beam′ *n* oscillating lever pivoted on a central axis, transmitting power by means of connecting rods on each end

walk′ing pa′pers *npl colloq* notice of dismissal

walk′ing stick′ *n* **1** hand-held stick for assistance in walking or as an article of fashionable attire; **2** any of various insects (family Phasmidae) with a long slender body resembling a stick

walk′-on′ *n* small part in a play, consisting usu. of a single short appearance

walk′out′ *n* act or instance of walking out, as on strike or in protest

walk′-up′ *n* apartment building without an elevator

walk′way′ *n* passageway, esp. one connecting various parts of a ship or factory

wall /wôl′/ [OE *weall* < L *vallum* rampart] *n* **1** any of various solid upright structures serving to defend, protect, enclose, partition, support floors and roofs, hold back earth, etc.; **2** side or inside surface of any cavity, vessel, or receptacle; **3** biol organic partition or covering, as of cells or organs; **4** something suggesting a wall, as *a wall of fire;* **5 walls** pl fortifications; ramparts; **6 drive** or **push to the wall** to force into a desperate situation; ruin ‖ *vt* **7** usu. **wall in** or **off** to enclose, separate, divide, etc., with or as with a wall; **8 wall up** to seal off or close up with a wall ‖ **walled**/ *adj*

wal·la·by /wol′əbē/ [< nat. Australian] *n* (**-bies**) any of several small kangaroos

wall′board′ *n* artificial board of fiber in large sheets for making or covering walls, usu. as a substitute for plaster

wal·let /wol′it, wôl′-/ [ME *walet*] *n* flat pocketbook for carrying paper money, cards, etc.

wall'eye' [< ME *wawileghed* walleyed] *n* 1 eye with a white or whitish iris; 2 eye showing much white because of divergent strabismus; 3 large and glaring eye, as in some fishes; 4 any of various fishes with prominent eyes || **wall'eyed'** *adj*

wall'flow'er *n* 1 plant (*Cheiranthus cheiri*) with sweet-scented yellow, orange, or red flowers; 2 at a dance, one who, for lack of a partner, sits at the side of the room

Wal·loon' /woloon'/ [F *Wallon*] *n* 1 French-speaking Belgian; 2 French dialect spoken by the Walloons || also *adj*

wal·lop /wol'əp/ [AF *waloper* to gallop] *colloq vt* 1 to beat, thrash; 2 to strike vigorously; 3 to defeat soundly || *n* 4 strong blow; 5 thrill, kick

wal·low /wol'ō/ [OE *wealwian* to roll] *vi* 1 to roll about, flounder, or welter, as in mud; 2 to be immersed or to revel, as in filth or vice || *n* 3 act of wallowing; 4 place in which animals wallow

wall'pa'per *n* 1 paper for covering walls and ceilings of rooms || *vt* 2 to put wallpaper on

Wall' Street' *n* 1 street in the heart of the financial district of New York City, the main financial center of the U.S.; 2 the financial interests

wal·nut /wôl'nət/ [OE *wealh-hnutu* = foreign nut] *n* 1 edible nut of a tree of the genus *Juglans*; 2 the tree; 3 wood of this tree

Wal·pur'gis Night' /välpŏŏr'gis/ [St. Walpurgis, eighth-century G abbess] *n* the eve of May 1, when witches are said to meet and revel with the devil

wal·rus /wôl'rəs, wol'-/ [D] *n* large sea mammal (genus *Odobenus*) of the Arctic Ocean, related to the seals, and having flippers and two large tusks

waltz /wôlts'/ [< G *walzen* to revolve] *n* 1 ballroom dance in triple time or the music for it || *vi* 2 to dance a waltz; 3 *colloq* to move casually or lightly || *vt* 4 to lead in a waltz; 5 *colloq* to lead briskly

wam·pum /womp'əm, wômp'-/ *n* beads made of shells, used by North American Indians as money and as ornaments

wan /won'/ [OE *wann* dark] *adj* (**wan·ner; wan·nest**) 1 pale, colorless; 2 of a sickly hue; 3 weak, ineffective

wand /wond'/ [< Scand] *n* 1 slender rod or stick, esp. one of supposedly magic power; 2 staff of authority

wan·der /won'dər/ [OE *wandrian*] *vi* 1 to rove, ramble, roam idly about; 2 to stray, go astray; 3 to err, go wrong; 4 to be incoherent or confused; 5 to deviate, digress; 6 **wander off** to go astray, get lost || *vt* 7 to rove or roam through or over || **wan'der·er** *n* || SYN digress, deviate, diverge, stray, roam, ramble, rove || DISCR To *wander* is to move hither and thither purposelessly, as we *wandered* from field to field; or it may mean to turn away, culpably, from a proposed object, the path of right, or the control of reason, as to *wander* from the truth. To *deviate* is to turn aside from a predetermined course, rule, truth, or the like, as he *deviated* from his customary routine. To *diverge* is to go aside from the track or course previously pursued, or to go in different directions from a common point or from one another, as lines, roads, rays of light, the spokes of a wheel, or figuratively, statements or opinions. To *digress* is to leave the main theme of a speech or a writing

wan'der·lust' [G] *n* impulse to wander; love of travel

wane /wān'/ [OE *wanian*] *vi* 1 to decrease in size, power, degree, etc.; 2 (of the moon) to show a decreasing amount of illuminated surface to the earth; 3 to grow weak, fail, approach the end || *n* 4 period of waning; 5 **on the wane** declining, growing less

wan·gle /waŋ'gəl/ *colloq vt* 1 to procure or bring about by dubious, wheedling, or indirect methods || *n* 2 act or instance of wangling

Wan'kel en'gine /wäŋ'kəl, waŋ'-/ [Felix *Wankel* G engineer (1902-   )] *n* internal-combustion engine which has, instead of a piston, a rotor in the form of a rounded equilateral triangle and two ports instead of valves

want /wont', wônt'/ [ON *vant* lacking] *n* 1 state of being without; 2 lack, scarcity; 3 poverty, destitution; 4 thing needed; necessity || *vt* 5 to be without, lack; 6 to have need of; require; 7 to wish, desire; long for || *vi* 8 to be absent or lacking; 9 to be in poverty; 10 to wish; to feel inclined; 11 **want for, a** to be lacking in; **b** to have need for

want' *ad'* *n* small advertisement in a newspaper listed with others of the same category, seeking or offering employment, merchandise, housing, etc.

want'ing *adj* 1 short of; lacking || *prep* 2 lacking; without; 3 minus; less

wan·ton /wont'ən/ [ME *wantoun*] *adj* 1 acting without restraint or discipline; 2 unprovoked; uncalled-for; 3 dissolute, lewd; 4 reckless; malicious || *n* 5 immoral dissolute person, esp. a woman || **wan'ton·ly** *adv* || **wan'ton·ness** *n*

wap·i·ti /wop'itē/ [< Shawnee] *n* large American elk (*Cervus canadensis*)

war /wôr'/ [OF *werre*] *n* 1 conflict by force of arms, as between nations; 2 state or period of such conflict;

3 science or art of making war; **4** any contest or contention ‖ *v* (**warred**; **war·ring**) *vi* **5** to engage in armed conflict; **6** to fight, contend

war·ble /wôr′bəl/ [MF *werbler* to quaver] *vt* **1** to sing with quavers, runs, and trills, as a bird ‖ *vi* **2** to sing, trill, or carol ‖ *n* **3** act of warbling; **4** trill, carol

war′bler *n* **1** one who or that which warbles; **2** any of a family (Sylviidae) of small, chiefly Old World birds related to the thrushes; **3** any of a large American family (Parulidae) of small insect-eating, singing birds

war′ chest′ *n* money accumulated for a specific purpose, as a political campaign

war′ cloud′ *n* some indication of imminent war

war′ crime′ *n* inhumane treatment of enemy nationals in violation of international agreements

war′ cry′ *n* **1** name or phrase shouted in battle; **2** slogan used to unite and rally adherents and workers in a campaign or contest

ward /wôrd′/ [OE *weard* guard] *n* **1** act of guarding, as *to keep watch and ward*; **2** person, esp. a minor, placed under the protection of a court or guardian; **3** section of a hospital or prison; **4** administrative division of a town or city ‖ *vt* **5** **ward off** to repel, turn aside

-ward also **-wards** /-wərd(z)/ [OE *-weard*] *adj* & *adv suf* toward, in the direction of

war′ dance′ *n* dance of primitive peoples before going to war or to celebrate a victory

war·den /wôrd′ən/ [OF *wardein*] *n* **1** one who keeps guard; guardian; keeper; **2** head keeper of a prison; **3** churchwarden; **4** any of various officials in charge of something, as wild game, a port, etc.

ward′er *n* **1** one who watches or keeps guard; **2** guard in an English prison

ward′ heel′er *n* minor political worker in a ward who does chores for the local organization

ward′robe′ **1** tall cabinet for clothes; **2** one's stock of wearing apparel; **3 a** theatrical costumes; **b** place where they are kept

ward′room′ *n* living and dining quarters of the commissioned officers on a war vessel

ware[1] /wer′/ [OE *waru* article] *n* **1** pottery; **2 wares** *pl* manufactured articles; merchandise

ware[2] [OE *wær* heedful] *vt archaic* to beware of, as *ware hounds*

-ware /-wer′/ *comb form* specific kind of wares, as *silverware*, *hardware*

ware′house′ *n* (**-hous·es** /-hou′ziz/) *n* **1** building for storing goods in quantity, and from which they are sent to retail outlets as ordered or needed;

2 building where furniture and other household articles are stored ‖ /-houz′, -hous′/ *vt* **3** to place or store in a warehouse ‖ **ware′house′man** /-mən/ *n* (**-men** /-mən/)

war′fare′ *n* **1** open hostilities between enemies; condition of armed conflict; **2** any strife, contest, or struggle

war′head′ *n* front section of a missile, bomb, torpedo, etc., containing the explosive charge

war′-horse′ *n* **1** horse used in battle; **2** veteran of many struggles, as in war, politics, etc.

war·i·ly /wer′ilē/ *adv* in a wary manner ‖ **war′i·ness** *n*

war′like′ *adj* **1** fit for or fond of war; martial; **2** of or for war; **3** threatening war; bellicose; hostile

war′lock′ [OE *wǣrloga* deceiver] *n* **1** sorcerer; conjurer; **2** male witch

war′lord′ *n* **1** military leader in a warlike nation; **2** military leader who has seized power and is moving to seize the government

warm /wôrm′/ [OE *wearm*] *adj* **1** having, giving off, or feeling a moderate degree of heat; **2** of a comparatively high temperature; **3** serving to keep heat in, as *warm gloves*; **4** eager, ardent; **5** close, as a *warm friendship*; **6** hearty, as a *warm welcome*; **7** lively, brisk, as a *warm argument*; **8** (color) having tones of red, orange, or yellow; **9** fresh, newly made, as a *warm trail*; **10** *colloq* close to the object sought for; **11** *colloq* uncomfortable ‖ *vt* **12** to make warm ‖ *vi* **13** to become warm; **14 warm up, a** to become warm; **b** to prepare for participation in a game or contest by exercise or by making practice plays or throws, etc.; **15 warm (up)** *to colloq* to become friendlier or more receptive toward ‖ **warm′er** *n* ‖ **warm′ly** *adv*

warm′-blood′ed *adj* **1** having warm blood and constantly maintained body temperature, as mammals and birds; **2** ardent; impetuous

warmed′-o′ver *adj* **1** reheated (food); **2** repeated without fresh ideas added; stale

warm′-heart′ed *adj* kind-hearted, affectionate; sympathetic

war′mong′er /-mung′gər/ *n* one who advocates or attempts to precipitate a war

warmth /wôrmth′/ *n* **1** sensation, state, or quality of being warm; moderate heat; **2** zeal, ardor; **3** affectionate intimacy; **4** anger, irritation ‖ SYN heat, glow, fervency, animation, cordiality, geniality, excitement, life, passion, vehemence ‖ ANT coldness, indifference, insensibility, frigidity

warm′-up′ *n* act of warming up

warn /wôrn′/ [OE *wearnian*] *vt* **1** to make aware of possible danger; put on guard; **2** to advise against something; admonish; 3 to inform beforehand || SYN caution, admonish, advise, notify

warn'ing *n* 1 act of one who or that which warns; 2 that which warns or gives notice

warp /wôrp/ [OE *wearp*] *vt* 1 to bend or twist out of shape; 2 to pull (a ship) along by a rope attached to a fixed point; 3 to distort from the truth; pervert || *vi* 4 to become twisted or bent || *n* 5 bend or twist, as from a straight or flat form; 6 towline used in warping a ship; 7 *weaving* lengthwise parallel threads in a loom that are interlaced with the woof

war' paint' *n* 1 paint applied to the face and body by some primitive peoples when about to go to war; 2 *colloq* a make-up; b ceremonial dress; regalia

war'path' *n* 1 route taken by Indians going to war; 2 **on the warpath,** a engaged in war; b angered and hostile

war·rant /wor'ənt, wôr'-/ [AF *warantir* to protect] *n* 1 guarantee or security; 2 just grounds, justification; 3 *law* written authorization to make an arrest, make a search, or execute a judgment; 4 *com* a written authorization for the payment or receipt of money; b authorization issued by a corporation giving the holder the right, for a specified period, to buy its stock at a fixed price; 5 certificate of appointment of a warrant officer || *vt* 6 to guarantee; 7 to authorize; 8 to declare as certain, as *I warrant that this will happen;* 9 to justify

war'ran·tee' *n* one to whom a warranty is given

war'rant of·fi·cer *n* officer in the armed forces ranking above a noncommissioned officer but below a commissioned officer

war'ran·tor' /-tôr/ or **war'rant·er** *n* one who gives a warrant

war'ran·ty *n* (-ties) 1 *law* assurance given by one party to a contract that the subject matter of a transaction is as represented; 2 written guarantee given to the purchaser of a manufactured article that the dealer or manufacturer will repair or replace it within a specified period if found defective

war·ren /wor'ən, wôr'-/ [AF *warenne*] *n* 1 place where rabbits live and breed; 2 any building or district containing crowded living quarters

war·rior /wôr'ē·ər, wor'-, -yər/ [AF *werreìeor*] *n* 1 experienced soldier; 2 any brave fighter

War·saw /wôr'sô/ *n* capital of Poland (1,300,000)

War'saw Trea'ty Or·gan·I·za'tion also

War'saw Pact' *n* defensive organization of the communist countries of Europe (1955)

war'ship' *n* vessel designed for combat

wart /wôrt/ [OE *wearte*] *n* 1 small, usu. hard, elevation on the skin; 2 any similar growth, as on a plant stem or the skin of an animal || **wart'y** *adj* (-i·er; -i·est)

wart' hog' *n* any of a genus (*Phacochoerus*) of wild hogs of Africa, having large tusks and two pairs of warty protuberances on the face

war·y /wer'ē/ [< *ware*²] *adj* (-i·er; -i·est) 1 watchful, alert; 2 marked by caution || SYN cautious, watchful, circumspect (see *careful*)

was /wuz/, woz/, wəz/ [OE *wæs*] *pt 1st & 3rd pers sg* of **be**

wash /wosh/, wôsh/ [OE *wascan*] *vt* 1 to cleanse by means of a liquid, usu. water; 2 to remove, as dirt or stains, by the use of water; 3 to cover with water, cause water to flow against, as *the shores are washed by the breakers;* 4 to overlay with thin metal; 5 to cover with a thin coat of color; 6 to purify (a gas) by passing through a liquid; 7 *mining* to subject (ore) to the action of water in order to extract the valuable part; 8 **wash away,** a to remove by washing, as dirt; b to erode by the action of water; 9 **wash down,** a to wash completely; b to aid in swallowing (food) with a beverage; 10 **wash off** to remove by washing, as dirt; 11 **wash out,** a to wash; cleanse; b to remove by the action of water, as *the storm washed out the road* || *vi* 12 to wash oneself; 13 to wash clothes; 14 to undergo washing; 15 *colloq* to be proved valid, as *his story won't wash;* 16 to move with a flowing lapping sound; 17 **wash ashore** to be carried onto a beach by the action of wind and waves; 18 **wash away** to be removed by flowing water; 19 wash off to be removed by washing; 20 **wash out** *colloq* to be dropped, as from school; 21 **wash up** to wash one's face and hands || *n* 22 act or instance of washing; 23 quantity of clothes washed or to be washed at one time; 24 dash, sound, or action of a body of water; 25 material deposited by water; 26 disturbed air behind a moving airplane; 27 disturbed water behind a moving vessel; 28 liquid with which anything is washed, as a thin coat of color, a dentifrice, a lotion, etc.; 29 thin coating of metal; 30 area of land flooded by water; marsh || *adj* 31 able to be laundered without injury, as *wash material* || **wash'a·ble** *adj*

Wash. Washington (state and city)

wash'-and-wear' *adj* (garment) that requires no ironing after washing

wash'ba'sin *n* washbowl

wash′board′ *n* 1 board with a ribbed surface on which clothes are rubbed while being washed; 2 board about the bottom of the wall of a room; 3 board attached to the gunwale to keep out water in heavy sea

wash′bowl′ *n* large bowl in which to wash the hands and face

wash′cloth′ *n* small cloth for washing the face and body

washed′-out′ *adj* 1 faded; 2 *colloq* tired, spiritless

washed′-up′ *adj colloq* failed, done for, through

wash′er *n* 1 one who or that which washes; 2 machine for washing clothes, dishes, etc.; 3 flat ring of metal, leather, rubber, etc., used to secure the tightness of a joint, screw, or bolt

wash′er·wom′an *n* (-wom′en) woman who earns a living by washing clothes; laundress

wash′ goods′ *npl* textiles that can be washed without fading

wash′ing *n* 1 act of one who or that which washes; 2 clothes, sheets, etc., washed or to be washed; 3 matter removed by the action of water; 4 also **washings** *pl* liquid which has been used to wash something; dirty water

wash′ing ma·chine′ *n* appliance for washing clothes, etc.

wash′ing so′da *n* sodium carbonate

Wash·ing·ton /wosh′intən, wôsh′-/ *n* 1 capital of the U.S. (756,510); 2 state in the NW U.S. (3,409,000; 68,192 sq.m.; cap. Olympia) ‖ **Wash′ing·to′ni·an** /-tōn′ē-ən/ *n*

Wash′ing·ton, George *n* (1732–99) commander of the American armies in the Revolution and first president of the U.S. 1789–97

wash′out′ *n* 1 washing out of earth, rocks, etc., as from a road; 2 *colloq* failure

wash′rag′ *n* washcloth

wash′room′ *n* room in a public place having washbowls and toilets

wash′ sale′ *n* illegal sale of securities among the members of a group to give the impression of heavy transactions and exchanges of ownership that do not actually take place

wash′stand′ *n* 1 table holding a basin and a pitcher of water for washing up; 2 fixture containing a wash-basin and faucets with running water

wash′tub′ *n* tub for washing clothes, etc.

wash′y *adj* (-i·er; -i·est) 1 watery, diluted; 2 lacking strength, feeble; 3 lacking color; pallid

was·n′t /wuz′ənt, woz′-/ was not

wasp /wosp′/ [OE *wæps*] *n* 1 any of numerous insects (order Hymenoptera), typically with a slender body, a narrow waist, and a venomous sting; 2 irritable, peevish person

Wasp, WASP *n* white Anglo-Saxon Protestant, considered to be one of the dominant majority in the United States

wasp′ish *adj* peevish; irritable; irascible

was·sail /wos′əl, -āl, was′-/ [ME *was hail* be healthy < Scand] *n* 1 originally, salutation uttered when drinking someone's health; 2 merrymaking accompanied by drinking, esp. at Christmas time; 3 liquor made of ale, spices, apples, and sugar ‖ *vt* 4 to carouse; celebrate with wassail ‖ *vt* 5 to drink to the health of

Was′ser·mann test′ /wäs′ərmən/ [August von *Wassermann* (1866–1925) G bacteriologist] *n* blood test for the detection of syphilis

wast·age /wāst′ij/ [< *waste*] *n* 1 loss from use, wear and tear, etc.; 2 loss from wastefulness; 3 that which is wasted

waste /wāst′/ [AF *wast*] *vt* 1 to destroy, devastate; 2 to wear away gradually; 3 to spend or use needlessly; squander; 4 to fail to use; 5 to emaciate ‖ *vi* 6 often **waste away**, a to be consumed needlessly; b to gradually lose strength or vitality ‖ *n* 7 act or process of wasting; 8 devastated region; 9 barren unproductive land; desert; 10 surplus material of no use; refuse; 11 cloth remnants, used for wiping and packing; 12 loose soil material carried away by erosion; 13 **wastes** *pl* excrement; 14 **go to waste** to be wasted, fail to be used; 15 **lay waste** to devastate ‖ *adj* 16 desolate, desert, bare; dreary; 17 useless; sterile; 18 not used; no longer used; 19 left over; 20 rejected; thrown out; 21 used to carry off used or useless material ‖ **wast′er** *n*

waste′bas′ket *n* basket for wastepaper, trash, etc.

waste′ful *adj* 1 characterized by or causing waste; 2 spending or consuming extravagantly or uselessly ‖ **waste′ful·ness** *n* ‖ SYN extravagant, profuse, lavish, prodigal, ruinous ‖ ANT economical, frugal, careful, saving

waste′land′ *n* barren land

waste′pa′per *n* paper discarded after use

waste′ prod′ucts *npl* 1 material discarded as useless in any manufacturing process; 2 wastes excreted by the body

wast·rel /wās′trəl/ *n* wasteful person; spendthrift

watch /woch′/ [OE *wacian*] *vi* 1 to observe attentively; 2 to keep guard; 3 to be expectant; wait; 4 **watch for** to look for expectantly; 5 **watch out for** to be on the lookout for; 6 **watch over** to protect, keep from harm ‖ *vt* 7 to observe, regard; 8 to tend; guard ‖ *n* **9** close observation; **10** vigilance; **11** guard or body of guards; **12** time a guard is on duty; **13** small portable timepiece; **14** *naut* a any one of the periods into which the day is divided during which a given part of the ship's crew is on duty; **b** the section of a crew on duty during this period

watch'band' *n* bracelet or strap worn on the wrist to which a wrist watch is attached

watch'dog' *n* **1** dog for guarding property; **2** any watchful guardian

watch'er *n* **1** person who keeps watch or guard, as *car watcher*; **2** person who watches the passing scene out of curiosity or for some other motive, as *girl watcher*; **3** close observer of the internal conditions and the foreign policy of a foreign country, as *China watcher*

watch'ful *adj* alert, vigilant ‖ **watch'-ful·ly** *adv* ‖ **watch'ful·ness** *n* ‖ SYN vigilant, heedful, circumspect, observant, alert ‖ ANT inattentive, heedless, careless, unobservant

watch'mak'er *n* one who makes or repairs watches

watch'man /-mən/ *n* (-men /-mən/) *n* guard, esp. a man who guards a building at night

watch' night' *n* **1** last night of the year; **2** religious meeting held on this night

watch'tow'er *n* any tower or high platform used as a lookout

watch'word' *n* **1** password; **2** slogan, motto

wa·ter /wôt'ər, wot'-/ [OE *wæter*] *n* **1** transparent, odorless, colorless liquid —H₂O— that constitutes the rivers, lakes, oceans, and rain, freezing at 32°F or 0°C and boiling at 212°F or 100°C; **2** water with reference to its surface or relative level, as *above water, high water*; **3** any of various liquids secreted by animals, made up chiefly of water, as tears, sweat, urine, etc.; **4** any of various solutions of gases or other substances in water, as *ammonia water, lemon water*; **5** degree of brilliance of a precious stone; **6** wavy shiny pattern in fabrics or metals; **7** *com* fictitious assets giving inflated value to a stock; **8** **waters** *pl* water from a mineral spring; **9** **above water** free of financial difficulties; **10** **hold water** to be proved logical or valid; **11** **in hot water** *colloq* in trouble, as with superiors, parents, or the authorities ‖ *vt* **12** to moisten, sprinkle, or flush with water; **13** to dilute with water; **14** to flow through, irrigate, as *the Mohawk waters central New York*; **15** to produce a wavy shiny pattern on, as a fabric; **16** *com* to issue additional shares of (stock) without a corresponding increase in

assets; **17** **water down**, to soften, mitigate, as *to water down a critical report* ‖ *vi* **18** to secrete or discharge liquid matter, as the eyes or mouth; **19** to take on a supply of water, as a ship

wa'ter bed' *n* water-filled plastic mattress, notable for its resilience and elasticity

wa'ter buf'fa·lo *n* buffalo (*Bubalus bubalis*) of Asia and Africa, ofen domesticated

wa'ter chest'nut *n* aquatic plant (genus *Trapa*) bearing an edible fruit resembling a chestnut

wa'ter clos'et *n* **1** room or compartment containing a flush toilet; **2** flush toilet; **3** *dial.* privy

wa'ter col'or *n* **1** paint using water as the vehicle; **2** a painting done in water colors ‖ **wa'ter-col'or** *adj*

wa'ter-cooled' *adj* cooled by circulating water

wa'ter cool'er *n* **1** stand containing a large bottle of cooled drinking water, drawn off by a spigot; **2** drinking fountain in which the water is cooled by refrigeration

wa'ter·course' *n* **1** brook, river, or the like; **2** natural or artificial channel for water

wa'ter·cress' *n* perennial cress (*Rorippa nasturtium*) with pungent stalks and leaves, found growing in brooks and used for salad

wa'ter·fall' *n* very steep descent or fall of the water of a stream or river

wa'ter·fowl' *n* **1** bird that lives on or close to the water, esp. one that swims; **2** *pl* such birds collectively

wa'ter·front' *n* **1** land abutting on a body of water; **2** harbor section of a city

wa'ter gap' *n* cleft in a mountain or mountain range through which a stream runs

Wa'ter·gate' *n* series of events which began in 1972 with the break-in in the National Democratic Committee Headquarters in the Watergate Hotel in Washington, D.C., continued through the efforts to cover up the scandal and protect those involved in it, and terminated in 1974 with the resignation of Nixon from the presidency and the conviction of the offenders

wa'ter gauge' *n* instrument attached to a boiler, tank, etc., indicating the level of water

wa'ter glass' *n* **1** drinking glass; **2** water gauge; **3** silicate of sodium or potassium, used in preserving eggs, in fireproofing, and in fixing dyes

wa'ter ham'mer *n* hammering noise made when the flow of water in a pipe is suddenly stopped

wa'ter hole' *n* **1** pond, pool; **2** hole in the frozen surface of a body of water

wa′ter ice′ *n* frozen dessert made with sugar, fruit juices, and water

wa′ter·ing place′ *n* 1 fashionable resort noted either for mineral springs or for bathing beaches; 2 place for getting drinking water

wa′ter jack′et *n* casing through which water is circulated for cooling or for maintaining an even temperature, as around the cylinders of an internal-combustion engine

wa′ter lev′el *n* 1 surface level of a body of water; 2 water line

wa′ter lil′y *n* any of a genus (*Nymphaea*) of aquatic plants with flat floating leaves and showy flowers

wa′ter line′ *n* 1 the part of a ship's hull at water level; 2 any of several marks on the sides of a vessel showing the level at various weights of load

wa′ter·logged′ *adj* 1 soaked or filled with water, so as to be unmanageable or heavy, as a ship; 2 saturated with water, as a field

Wa′ter·loo′ *n* 1 village in Belgium, scene of Napoleon's final defeat on June 18, 1815; 2 final and decisive defeat

wa′ter main′ *n* a main pipe in a water-supply system

wa′ter·mark′ *n* 1 identifying mark or design in some papers, visible when held up to the light ‖ *vt* 2 to mark with a watermark

wa′ter·mel′on *n* 1 trailing plant (*Citrullus vulgaris*) having a large edible fruit with thick green rind and a red, sweet, juicy pulp; 2 this fruit

wa′ter moc′ca·sin *n* cottonmouth

wa′ter po′lo *n* water game played by swimmers who try to push or throw a ball across the opponent's goal

wa′ter pow′er *n* power from falling or running water, used to operate machinery, esp. to generate electricity

wa′ter·proof′ *adj* 1 impervious to water ‖ *n* 2 *Brit* waterproof garment ‖ *vt* 3 to make waterproof

wa′ter rat′ *n* 1 any of several aquatic rodents; 2 muskrat

wa′ter·shed′ *n* 1 area drained by a single river; 2 ridge dividing two drainage areas; 3 turning point in events or attitudes

wa′ter ski′ *n* short broad ski used for water-skiing

wa′ter-ski′ *vi* to be towed wearing skis by a swift motorboat

wa′ter·snake′ *n* snake that lives in or near fresh water, esp. of the genus *Natrix*

wa′ter·spout′ *n* 1 funnel-shaped cloud, usu. of fresh water, extending down to a whirling column of mist and spray from the sea or a lake; tornado over water; 2 pipe running down the side of a building for the discharge of rain water

wa′ter ta′ble *n* level below which the soil is saturated with water

wa′ter·tight′ *adj* 1 so closely or compactly made as to permit no water to pass; 2 impossible to circumvent or nullify, as a contract or plan

wa′ter tow′er *n* 1 tower containing a tank for holding water; 2 fire-fighting apparatus for throwing jets of water into the upper stories of tall buildings

wa′ter va′por *n* water in the form of vapor, esp. when below the boiling point

wa′ter wag′on *n* 1 wagon used to carry water, spec. for troops on the march; 2 **on the water wagon** *slang* having given up or abstaining from alcoholic beverages

wa′ter·way′ *n* 1 body of water used for navigation; 2 channel for vessels, as in a harbor

wa′ter wheel′ *n* 1 wheel turned by flowing or falling water, used to generate power; 2 wheel with buckets on its rim, used for raising water; 3 paddle wheel

wa′ter wings′ *npl* device which when inflated is used to keep afloat a person learning to swim

wa′ter·works′ *nsg* or *npl* 1 system for collecting, purifying, and distributing water to users in an urban area; 2 *nsg* pumping station in such a system

wa′ter·y *adj* 1 of, like, or full of water; 2 containing too much water; 3 tearful; 4 thin, diluted; 5 soggy, soaked; 6 tasteless

watt /wot′/ [James *Watt* (1736–1819) Sc inventor] *n* mks unit of power, equal to one joule per second and to the product of a current of one ampere and an electromotive force of one volt

watt′age /-ij/ *n* amount of power measured in watts

watt′-hour′ *n* unit of work equal to the power of one watt acting for one hour

watt′-hour me′ter *n* instrument that measures electric work or energy, usu. in kilowatt-hours

wat·tle /wot′əl/ [OE *watul* cover] *n* 1 framework made from pliant rods interwoven with twigs; 2 fleshy flap, as one hanging from the throat of some birds ‖ *vt* 3 to twist or interweave (twigs or rods) into a framework, fence, or the like; 4 to construct with wattles

watt′me′ter *n* 1 instrument that measures electric power in watts; 2 watt-hour meter

wave /wāv′/ [OE *wafian*] *vi* 1 to move up and down or back and forth in undulating fashion, as a flag; 2 to have undulations or curves; 3 to move some object, as the hand, up and down or back and forth, as in signaling ‖ *vt* 4 to cause to wave; 5 to brandish; 6 to give an undulating form to; **7** to beckon or signal by waving the hand or some object; **8** to express by waving, as *wave good-by* || *n* **9** act or instance of waving; **10** recurring movement, as *waves of troops attacked;* **11** curve or undulation; **12** disturbance in the surface of a liquid, as water in the form of a moving ridge; **13** signal made by waving; **14** steady increase or sweeping advance of any sentiment, condition, etc., as *a wave of emotion, a crime wave;* **15** spell of hot or cold weather; **16** *phys* a disturbance of the particles of an elastic medium by which a vibrating motion is progressively communicated from particle to particle without corresponding advance of the particles, as *sound waves;* **b** similar phenomenon in space whether occupied with a solid, liquid, or gaseous medium or not, as *light waves*

Wave, WAVE /wāv/ [Women's Appointed Volunteer Emergency Service] *n* member of the Women's Reserve of the U.S. Naval Reserve

wave′-form′ *n* graphic representation of the shape of a wave, showing variation in amplitude with respect to time

wave′ front′ *n* surface of a wave that is the locus of all points in the same phase at the same time

wave′length′ *n* distance in the advance of a wave between two successive points that are in the same phase

wave′let /-lit/ *n* ripple, small wave

wave′ mo′tion *n* characteristic motion of the elements that constitute a wave

wa·ver /wāv′ər/ [< *wave*] *vi* **1** to sway to and fro; flutter; **2** to flicker; **3** to tremble; **4** to vacillate, show indecision || *n* **5** act of wavering || **syn** tremble, shake, reel, totter (see *fluctuate*)

wav′y *adj* (-i-er; -i-est) **1** undulating; **2** having or resembling waves

wax¹ /waks/ [OE *weaxan*] *vi* **1** to increase in size, power, degree, etc.; **2** (of the moon) to show an increasing amount of illuminated surface to the earth; **3** to become gradually, as *to wax merry*

wax² [OE *weax*] *n* **1** beeswax, a solid yellowish substance secreted by bees, plastic when warm and easily melted, from which the honeycomb is built and which is used for candles, modeling, etc.; **2** any of several similar substances || *vt* **3** to rub or polish with wax || *adj* **4** pert. to, made of, or resembling wax || **wax′en** *adj*

wax′ bean′ *n* variety of string bean with rich yellow pods

wax′ myr′tle *n* any of a genus (*Myrica*) of slender, evergreen shrubs or trees growing in wet places in eastern U.S., from the waxy berries of which candles are made

wax′ pa′per *n* wrapping paper made moistureproof by a coating of paraffin

wax′wing′ *n* any of several crested birds (genus *Bombycilla*) with waxlike tips on the secondary wing feathers

wax′works′ *nsg* museum displaying wax figures, esp. life-size representations of historical characters

wax′y *adj* (-i-er; -i-est) **1** resembling wax in some way; **2** consisting of or abounding in wax; **3** *pathol* (tissue) degenerated by deposits of a waxlike protein

way /wā/ [OE *weg*] *n* **1** street, road, path, or passage; **2** room for passage, as *make way;* **3** direction or route; **4** distance, as *a long way;* **5** moving; passage, as *lead the way;* **6** manner; **7** method or means; **8** habitual course of action or mode of life; **9** aspect, feature, respect; **10** range or field of action or notice, as *in the way of business;* **11** condition, state, as *in a bad way;* **12** *naut* movement through the water; **13** ways *pl* structure of timbers on which a ship is built and down which it slides when launched; **14** by the way incidentally; **15** by way of, a passing through; **b** as a means of; **c** serving for, as *he said that by way of an apology;* **16** give way, a to yield; withdraw; **b** to break down; **17** in a way to some extent; **18** in the way being or constituting a hindrance; **19** make one's way, a to proceed; **b** to achieve success; **20** make way to clear the way; **21** out of the way, a not hindering or obstructing; **b** disposed of; **c** away from traveled routes; secluded; **22** under way in motion or progress, as a ship or project || **syn** road, street, highway, avenue, thoroughfare, driveway, passage, pathway, lane, alley || **discr** A *way* affords room for passing along; it is the general term. A *road* is a route, a *way* for getting to a place. It may be private or public; if public, it is suitable for the use of passengers, riders, and vehicles. A *street* is a *road* in a town, village, or city, with houses on one or both sides. A *highway* is a public, and often a main, *road;* it may be a main route by water as well as by land. An *avenue* is a *way* of approach, hence, a *street; avenue* usually names a *street* marked by trees, but the name is often applied to any wide *street*. A *thoroughfare* is a *way* through; it is a public *road* or *passage,* open at both ends, especially one much used

way′bill′ *n* document describing and containing shipping instructions for goods carried on a common carrier

way′far′er /-fer′ər/ n traveler, esp. on foot || **way′far′ing** adj & n

way′lay′ v (-laid) vt 1 to attack from ambush on the road; 2 to accost unexpectedly

way′-out′ adj colloq bizarre; esoteric; eccentric

way out′ n 1 means of escaping from a problem or dilemma; 2 Brit exit, as in a theater

-ways /-wāz′/ adv suf in a specified way, direction, manner, or position, as sideways

ways′ and means′ npl methods and resources for accomplishing something, esp. raising money for the government

way′side′ n 1 edge or side of a way or road; 2 **fall by the wayside**, **a** to disappear; **b** to fail; collapse, go to pieces

way′ sta′tion n small station between larger ones on a railroad

way′ train′ n train that stops at all the stations on its route

way′ward /-wərd/ [< away + -ward] adj 1 perverse; disobedient; 2 capricious, erratic || SYN willful, self-willed, obstinate (see headstrong)

w.c. Brit water closet

W.C.T.U. Women's Christian Temperance Union

we /wē/ [OE wē] pron (1st pers pl nom) 1 pl of I (used by the speaker or writer to designate himself along with others); 2 people in general; 3 used by sovereigns to mean I; 4 used by speakers and writers to denote the class of which they represent themselves as spokesmen; 5 used by editors instead of I to avoid being too personal

weak /wēk′/ [ME weike < Scand] adj 1 lacking in bodily strength and vigor; feeble; 2 lacking in strength or durability; fragile; 3 lacking in force, intensity, or potency; ineffectual; 4 lacking in strength of character; 5 faulty, defective, below standard, as weak in algebra, a weak point; 6 thin, watery; 7 gram inflected by change in the suffix; 8 phonet **a** (vowel) made with the jaws or the lips close together; **b** (syllable) that is unstressed

weak′en vt 1 to make weak or weaker || vi 2 to become weak or weaker

weak′fish′ n (-fish or -fishes) any of several edible fishes (genus Cynoscion) with a tender mouth

weak′-kneed′ adj lacking firmness; timid

weak′ling n person lacking physical or moral strength

weak′ly adj (-li·er; -li·est) 1 feeble; sickly || adv 2 in a weak manner

weak′ness n 1 state or quality of being weak; 2 fault or defect; 3 inordinate fondness || SYN languor, imbecility, infirmness, infirmity, feebleness, de-

crepitude, faintness, frailty (see debility) || ANT strength, vigor, health, force, energy

weak′ sis′ter n slang member of a group who is in need of help; weakling

weal¹ /wēl′/ [var of wale] n wale

weal² [OE wela wealth] n archaic prosperity; welfare

wealth /welth′/ [< weal²] n 1 riches, affluence, material prosperity; 2 abundance or profusion of anything; 3 econ all goods and properties that are capable of ownership and that can be bought and sold

wealth′y adj (-i·er; -i·est) having great wealth || **wealth′i·ness** n || SYN opulent, rich, affluent || ANT poor, poverty-stricken, seedy, destitute, needy, impecunious

wean /wēn/ [OE wenian] vt 1 to accustom (a child or young animal) to substitute other food for mother's milk; 2 to draw away the affections or interest of (a person or animal) from any object or habit

wean′ling n child or animal recently weaned || also adj

weap·on /wep′ən/ [OE wǣpen] n 1 any instrument for attack or defense or for armed combat; 2 any means of attacking or defending

weap′on·ry n 1 weapons collectively; 2 design and production of weapons

wear /wer′/ [OE werian] v (wore; worn) vt 1 to carry on or about the body, as a coat or sword; 2 to exhibit in one's appearance, as a frown; 3 to bear habitually or in a specified manner, as to wear a beard, to wear one's hair long; 4 to use up or consume gradually; 5 to diminish or waste gradually by rubbing, scraping, or friction; 6 to make (a hole, groove, etc.) by such action; 7 to weaken; weary; 8 **wear down**, **a** to use up by wear; **b** to exhaust; 9 **wear out**, **a** to use up by constant wear; **b** to exhaust || vi 10 to go through or endure the process of wearing; 11 to stand up under use; 12 to become gradually, as his patience wore thin; 13 **wear off** to diminish gradually in effect; 14 **wear on** to pass slowly, as time; 15 **wear out** to become used up by wear || n 16 act of wearing or state of being worn; 17 garments for particular persons or use, as men's wear, sportswear; 18 damage caused by use, as to show wear || **wear′er** n

wear′ and tear′ n damage caused by ordinary use

wear′ing adj 1 wearying; 2 causing wear; 3 to be worn, as wearing apparel

wea·ri·some /wir′ēsəm/ [< weary] adj fatiguing; tiresome; tedious

wea·ry /wir′ē/ [OE wērig] adj (-ri·er; -ri·est) 1 characteristic of, causing, or accompanied by fatigue || v (-ried) *vt* 2 to make weary ‖ *vi* 3 to become weary ‖ **wea'ri·ly** *adv* ‖ **wea'ri·ness** *n* ‖ SYN *v* worry, fag, exhaust, tire, jade ‖ ANT *v* rest, exhilarate, stimulate, refresh, invigorate

wea·sel /wēz'əl/ [OE *wesle*] *n* 1 any small carnivore (genus *Mustela*) with a pointed face and a long thin body; 2 *slang* despicable, sneaky person ‖ *vi* 3 **weasel out** *colloq* to back out in a sneaky or cowardly fashion

wea'sel words' *npl* intentionally misleading or evasive words or statements ‖ **wea'sel-word'ed** *adj*

weath·er /weth'ər/ [OE *weder*] *n* 1 state of the atmosphere as to temperature, wind, moisture, cloudiness, etc.; 2 adverse conditions in the atmosphere, as storm, cold, etc.; 3 **under the weather** *colloq* **a** indisposed; **b** suffering from a hangover; **c** tipsy; somewhat drunk ‖ *vt* 4 to alter, discolor, or injure by exposure to the weather; 5 to season, dry, or affect by exposure to the weather; 6 to come through safely, as a storm or adversity

weath'er-beat'en *adj* 1 showing the effects of exposure to the weather; 2 toughened by the weather

weath'er·board' *n* 1 clapboard; 2 side of a ship toward the wind

weath'er·bound' *adj* detained or kept indoors by threatening or stormy weather

Weath'er Bu'reau *n* division of the U.S. Department of Commerce that keeps statistics of weather reports and forecasts the weather

weath'er·cock' *n* 1 weather vane shaped like a rooster; 2 fickle person who hastens to follow the latest styles and opinions

weath'ered *adj* affected, altered, or seasoned by exposure to the weather

weath'er eye' *n* 1 sharp eye for changes in the weather; 2 keen watch for any kind of change or development

weath'er·man' /-man'/ *n* (-men /-men'/) one whose profession is forecasting the weather, keeping weather statistics, etc.

weath'er·proof' *adj* 1 capable of withstanding exposure to the weather ‖ *vt* 2 to make weatherproof ‖ **weath'·er·proof'ing** *n*

weath'er strip'ping *n* narrow strip of felt, metal, rubber, etc., placed between a door or window sash and the frame to keep out drafts ‖ **weath'·er·strip'** (-**stripped**; -**strip·ping**) *vt*

weath'er vane' *n* flat piece of variously shaped metal or wood, fastened to a spire, roof, or pole, where it turns with and shows the direction of the wind

weave /wēv'/ [OE *wefan*] *v* (**wove**; **wo·ven** or **wove**) *vt* 1 to interlace, as threads, into a texture or fabric; 2 to form, as cloth or a basket, by in-

terlacing threads or strips of some material; 3 to form by intermingling many elements, as *to weave a story*; 4 to interweave, as *to weave false-hoods into a story* ‖ *vi* 5 to work at weaving; make cloth; 6 to become interlaced ‖ *v* (**weaved**) *vt* 7 to make (one's way) by moving from side to side ‖ *vi* 8 to wind in and out, as *the car weaved through the heavy traffic* ‖ *n* 9 pattern or method of weaving cloth; 10 woven cloth; fabric ‖ **weav'er** *n*

web /web'/ [OE] *n* 1 anything woven; fabric; 2 silken tissue woven by spiders and by the larvae of certain insects; 3 anything of complicated arrangement or intricate interrelated structure, as a plan or plot; 4 skin between the digits, as in certain aquatic birds and mammals; 5 *mach* thin flat part, often perforated, connecting more solid parts; 6 network ‖ *v* (**webbed**; **web·bing**) *vt* 7 to unite or envelop with, or as with, a web; entangle ‖ **webbed'** *adj*

web'bing *n* 1 strong cloth woven in strips, used for belts, straps, supports in upholstered furniture, etc.; 2 membrane joining the digits of webfooted animals; 3 any interlaced thongs, threads, etc., as in the face of a tennis racket

web'foot' *n* (-**feet**) foot with the toes joined by a membrane ‖ **web'foot'ed** *adj*

Web·ster, Dan·iel /web'stər/ *n* (1782–1852) U.S. senator and statesman

Web'ster, No·ah *n* (1758–1843) American lexicographer

wed /wed'/ [OE *weddian* to pledge] *v* (**wed·ded** or **wed**; **wed·ding**) *vt* 1 to marry; 2 to join in marriage; 3 to attach closely ‖ *vi* 4 to contract marriage ‖ **wed'ded** *adj*

Wed. Wednesday

we'd /wēd'/ 1 we had; 2 we should; 3 we would

wed'ding *n* 1 marriage ceremony; 2 marriage anniversary or its celebration ‖ SYN nuptials (see *marriage*)

wedge /wej'/ [OE *wecg*] *n* 1 piece of wood, metal, etc., thick at one end and tapering to a thin edge, used in splitting objects apart, in raising heavy objects, etc.; 2 anything shaped like a wedge, as *a wedge of cake*; 3 anything used to divide, separate, or split ‖ *vt* 4 to force apart or raise with a wedge; 5 to force in, press in closely

Wedg'wood (ware) /wej'wood/ [Josiah *Wedgwood* (1730–95) Eng potter] *n* fine English pottery, usu. of colored clay decorated with white cameo reliefs

wed'lock' [OE *wedlāc*] *n* state of being married; matrimony ‖ SYN matrimony (see *marriage*)

Wednes·day /wenz'dā, -dā/ [OE *Wōd-*

nesdæg Woden's day] *n* fourth day of the week, following Tuesday ‖ **Wednes′days** *adv*

wee /wē′/ [ME (a litel) *we* (a little) way or bit] *adj* (**wee·er; wee·est**) **1** tiny, very small; **2** very early

weed /wēd′/ [OE *wēod*] *n* **1** unwanted plant growing wild among and injuring or crowding out cultivated plants; **2** *colloq* cigar or cigarette; **3** marihuana; **4 the weed** *colloq* tobacco ‖ *vt* **5** to root out weeds from; **6 weed out** to remove (something unwanted) ‖ also *vi*

weed′-kill′er *n* substance used to kill plants esp. weeds

weeds′ [< OE *wǣd* garment] *npl* widow's mourning garment

weed′y *adj* (**-i·er; -i·est**) **1** pert. to, like, or abounding in weeds; **2** lean, lanky, ungainly

week /wēk′/ [OE *wice*] *n* **1** period of seven consecutive days; **2** workweek

week′day′ *n* any day of the week except Sunday ‖ **week′days′** *adv*

week′end′ *n* **1** period between usu. Friday night and Monday morning ‖ *vi* **2** to spend the weekend ‖ **week′ends′** *adv*

week′ly *adj* **1** done, occurring, or appearing every week or once a week; **2** determined by the week, as *a weekly wage* ‖ *adv* **3** once a week; every week ‖ *n* (**-lies**) **4** periodical issued once a week

ween /wēn′/ [OE *wēnan* to hope] *vt* & *vi archaic* to suppose, think

weep /wēp′/ [OE *wēpan* to wail] *vi* **1** to shed tears, cry; **2** to give forth moisture; **3** to exude moisture, as soil or the stems of plants ‖ *vt* **4** to shed, as tears, moisture, etc.; **5** to weep for, lament ‖ **weep′er** *n* ‖ **weep′y** *adj* (**-i·er; -i·est**) *adj*

weep′ing wil′low *n* willow (*Salix babylonica*) with slender drooping branches

wee·vil /wēv′əl/ [OE *wifel* beetle] *n* any of numerous beetles (family Curculionidae) having the head extended into a beak with mouth parts at the end, doing much damage by feeding on dry grain, nuts, fruits, and leaves

weft /weft′/ [OE] *n* **1** woof; **2** woven fabric or garment

weigh /wā′/ [OE *wegan* to carry] *vt* **1** to determine the weight of; **2** to reflect carefully over; ponder; **3 weigh anchor** to raise a ship's anchor; **4 weigh down** to press heavily on ‖ *vi* **5** to have (a given) weight; **6** to be esteemed important; **7** to be oppressive or burdensome; **8** *naut* to raise anchor; **9 weigh in** *sports* to be weighed officially before a boxing or wrestling match

weight /wāt′/ [OE *wiht*] *n* **1** amount a person or thing weighs; **2** *phys* force that gravity exerts on a body, equal

to its mass times the acceleration of gravity; **3** system of units for expressing weights, as *apothecaries′ weight;* **4** piece of metal used as a counterbalance in determining the weight of objects on a balance; **5** heavy mass or load; **6** something oppressive, as *a weight on the mind;* **7** importance, consequence; **8** *statistics* relative importance of an object in relation to a set of objects to which it belongs; **9 carry weight** to have importance or influence; **10 pull one's weight** to do one's full share; **11 throw one's weight around** to make an offensive show of one's authority or importance ‖ *vt* **12** to add weight to; **13** to treat, as fabric, with minerals or other substances to cause it to appear stronger; **14** to burden; **15** to give statistical weight to ‖ SYN *n* ponderousness, gravity, import, moment, burden (see *encumbrance*)

weight′less *adj* not having any apparent weight because of the neutralization of the pull of gravitation ‖ **weight′less·ness** *n*

weight′ lift′ing *n* the lifting of standard weights for exercise or in athletic competition ‖ **weight′ lift′er** *n*

weight′y *adj* (**-i·er; -i·est**) **1** heavy; **2** burdensome; **3** important, significant ‖ **weight′i·ness** *n*

Wei·mar·an·er /vīm′ərän′ər, wī-, -rän′-/ [G = of Weimar] *n* German breed of large hunting dog with a smooth gray coat and a cropped tail

Wei′mar Re·pub′lic /vī′mär/ *n* the German republic of 1919–33, founded in Weimar

weir /wir′/ [OE *wer*] *n* **1** dam in a stream, esp. one which forms a millpond; **2** fence of brush or stakes set in a stream for catching fish

weird /wird′/ [OE *wyrd* fate] *adj* **1** uncanny, unearthly; **2** queer, odd, bizarre ‖ **weird′ness** *n*

weird′o /-ō/ *n slang* odd, eccentric person

welch /welch′/ *vi slang* to welsh

wel·come /welk′əm/ [ME < *Scand*] *adj* **1** gladly received; **2** permitted gladly, as *you are welcome to keep it;* **3** without obligation for a favor received, as *you're welcome* ‖ *n* **4** greeting or reception ‖ *vt* **5** to greet with kindness, receive with hospitality; **6** to accept gladly; **7** to greet in a specified way, as *he was welcomed with boos* ‖ *interj* feel welcome!

weld¹ /weld′/ [< *obs* well to boil] *vt* **1** to join, as pieces of metal, by heating to the melting point with or without pressure; **2** to unite into a harmonious whole ‖ *vi* **3** to be welded ‖ *n* **4** act of welding or state of being welded; **5** welded joint ‖ **weld′er** *n*

weld² *n* **1** Old World plant (*Reseda luteola*) yielding a yellow dye; **2** the dye

wel·fare /wel′fer′/ [well² + fare] n 1 state or condition of having good health, happiness, and prosperity; 2 official efforts to improve the living conditions of the needy; 3 aid from official sources for the needy 4 on welfare receiving financial or other aid from an official agency

wel′fare state′ n state in which the government has assumed responsibility for the welfare of its citizens

wel·kin /welk′in/ [OE wolcen cloud] n archaic & poet. sky, vault of heaven

well¹ /wel′/ [OE wella] n 1 spring or fountain; 2 hole dug or bored into the earth to obtain water, oil, gas, etc.; 3 source of steady or continuous supply; 4 enclosed sunken space resembling a well, as the well of a stair; 5 container for a liquid, as an inkwell || vi 6 to flow or gush forth, as from a well

well² [OE wel] adv (bet·ter; best) 1 in a right, just, or praiseworthy manner; 2 with good reason, as I can well spare it; 3 favorably; fortunately; prosperously; 4 to a considerable extent or degree, as well on in years; 5 thoroughly, as shake well; I know him well; 6 as well in addition; 7 as well as equally as; 8 wish someone well to wish success or prosperity for someone || adj (bet·ter; best) 9 in good health; 10 in a satisfactory state || interj 11 expressing surprise, relief, resignation, or reproof; 12 used to continue a conversation

we'll /wēl/ 1 we will; 2 we shall

well′-ap·point′ed adj excellently furnished or equipped

well′-bal′anced adj 1 properly regulated or adjusted; 2 having good judgment, sane

well′-be′ing n general health and prosperity; welfare

well′born′ adj born of good or high-ranking family

well′-bred′ adj well brought up; refined in manners; courteous

well′-cared′-for′ adj carefully watched over; kept in the best condition

well′-dis·posed′ adj friendly, receptive, sympathetic

well′-done′ adj 1 done well; 2 thoroughly cooked (meat)

well′-dressed′ adj carefully dressed; dressed in good taste

well′-fa′vored adj good-looking, pleasing in appearance

well′-fed′ adj fat from good eating

well′-fixed′ adj colloq wealthy

well′-formed′ adj having regular proportions; shapely

well′-found′ed adj based on facts or sound reasoning

well′-groomed′ adj 1 clean, neat, and well-dressed; 2 well-cared-for

well′-ground′ed adj 1 well-founded; 2 having a thorough knowledge of the basic principles of a subject

well′-heeled′ adj colloq wealthy

well′-in·formed′ adj having considerable knowledge of some subject or subjects

Wel·ling·ton /wel′intən/ n capital of New Zealand (135,000), located on North Island

Wel′ling·ton, Duke of n (Arthur Wellesley) (1769–1852) British general, conqueror of Napoleon at Waterloo

well′-in·ten′tioned adj well-meaning

well′-knit′ adj closely joined or constructed

well′-known′ adj widely known; familiar

well′-mean′ing adj having good intentions

well′-meant′ adj done with good intentions

well′-nigh′ adv very nearly, almost

well′-off′ adj 1 prosperous; 2 fortunate

well′-read′ /-red′/ adj having read considerably

well′-round′ed adj 1 having manifold knowledge, ability, and interests; 2 comprehensive; wide in scope; 3 fully developed; well-balanced

well′-spo′ken adj 1 skillfully or aptly said; 2 speaking graciously and well

well′spring′ n source of never-failing supply

well′ sweep′ n long pole which acts as a lever to raise and lower a bucket in a well

well′-thought′-of′ adj highly esteemed

well′-timed′ adj opportune; occurring at an opportune time

well′-to-do′ adj prosperous

well′-turned′ adj 1 well-formed; 2 gracefully expressed

well′-wish′er n person who extends good wishes to another or others

well′-worn′ adj worn from much use

welsh /welsh/ [?] vi slang 1 to fail to pay a gambling debt; 2 to fail to fulfill a promise or obligation; 3 welsh on, a to cheat (a person) by failing to pay a debt or meet an obligation; b to fail to pay (a debt) or fulfill (a promise or obligation)

Welsh /welsh/ [OE welisc foreign] adj 1 pert. to Wales, its people, or its language || n 2 language of Wales; 3 the Welsh pl the people of Wales || **Welsh′man** /-mən/ n (-men /-mən/) || **Welsh′wom′an** n fem (-wom′en)

Welsh′ rab′bit also **rare·bit′** n dish made of melted cheese cooked with milk, ale, beer, etc., seasoned and spread on toast

welt /welt/ [ME welte] n 1 narrow strip of leather around a shoe between the upper and the sole; 2 strip of cloth enclosing a cord, sewed on a seam to reinforce it; 3 mark raised on the skin by a blow; wale

wel·ter /weltʹər/ [ME *weltren*] *vi* **1** to roll, wallow || *n* **2** violent tossing or rolling; **3** state of turmoil and confusion

welʹter·weightʹ *n* boxer or wrestler intermediate between a lightweight and a middleweight, weighing between 135 and 147 pounds

wen /wenʹ/ [OE *wenn*] *n* benign encysted tumor of the skin filled with fatty secretions

wench /wenchʹ/ [OE *wencel* child] *n archaic* **1** young woman; **2** female servant || *vi* **3** to consort with lewd women || **wenchʹer** *n*

wend /wendʹ/ [OE *wendan* to turn] *vt* **1** to direct or continue (one's way) || *vi* **2** *archaic* to go, journey

went /wentʹ/ *pt* of **go**

wept /weptʹ/ *pt & pp* of **weep**

were /wurʹ, wərʹ/ [OE *wǣre*] **1** *2nd sg & whole pl pt ind* of **be**; **2** *pt subj* of **be**

we're /wirʹ/ we are

were·n't /wurʹənt, wurntʹ/ were not

wereʹwolfʹ /wirʹ-, wurʹ-, werʹ-/ [OE *werwulf* man wolf] *n* (**-wolves** /-vz/) *folklore* person changed or capable of being changed into a wolf but retaining human intelligence

Wes·ley, John /wesʹlē/ *n* (1703–91) English theologian, founder of the Methodist Church || **Wesʹley·an** *adj & n*

west /westʹ/ [OE] *n* **1** one of the four cardinal points of the compass, 90° to the left of north; the general direction of the setting sun; **2** the **West**, **a** the Western Hemisphere; **b** the noncommunist countries of Europe and the Americas; **c** the part of the U.S. between the Mississippi and the Pacific || *adj* **3** situated in, directed toward, or facing the west; **4** (wind) blowing from the west || *adv* **5** in or toward the west; **6** go west *colloq* **a** to die; **b** to come to naught

Westʹ Ber·linʹ *n* western sector of Berlin, associated politically and economically with West Germany (2,-250,000)

westʹboundʹ *adv* headed west

Westʹ Endʹ *n* elegant section of W London, noted for its theaters, parks, fashionable shops, and aristocratic residences

westʹer·ly *adj & adv* **1** in the direction of or moving toward the west; **2** (wind) from the west || *n* (**-lies**) **3** west wind

westʹern *adj* **1** situated in, directed toward, or facing the west; **2** **Western**, **a** of or pert. to the West; **b** Occidental || *n* **3** story, play, or movie about the American West of the 19th century || **Westʹern·er** *n*

Westʹern Hem/i·sphereʹ *n* western part of the globe: the New World, including all of America and the surrounding waters and islands

westʹern·mostʹ *adj* farthest west

westʹern om/e·let *n* omelet made with green peppers, onions, and ham

Westʹern sadʹdle *n* heavy saddle used by American cowboys, having a high pommel and back and a high horn on the pommel

Westʹern Sa·mo/a *n* independent state in the W part of Samoa (150,000; 1,097 sq.mi.; cap. Apia) || **Westʹern Sa·mo/an** *adj & n*

Westʹ Ger·man/ic *n* the subbranch of Germanic that includes English, German, Dutch, Flemish, Frisian, and Yiddish

Westʹ Ger/ma·ny *n* republic in central Europe created by the division of Germany in 1945 (57,699,000; 95,-743 sq.m.; cap. Bonn) || **Westʹ Gerʹman** *adj & n*

Westʹ In/dies *npl* the islands of the Caribbean Sea, between Florida and South America || **Westʹ In/di·an** *adj & n*

Westʹ Vir·gin/ia *n* state in the E U.S. (1,744,237; 24,181 sq.mi.; cap. Charleston) || **Westʹ Vir·gin/ian** *n*

westʹward /-wərd/ *adj & adv* toward the west || **westʹward·ly** *adj & adv*; **westʹwards** *adv*

wet /wetʹ/ [OE *wēt*] *adj* (**wet·ter; wet·test**) **1** moistened, covered, or soaked with water or other liquid; **2** not dry, as *wet paint*; **3** rainy or misty, as *wet weather*; **4** opposed to the prohibition of alcoholic beverages, as *a wet county*; **5** all wet *slang* completely wrong || *v* (**wet** or **wet·ted; wet·ting**) *vt* **6** to make wet; **7** to urinate on or in || *vi* **8** to become wet || *n* **9** water, moisture; liquid; **10** one opposed to prohibition of alcoholic beverages || **wetʹness** *n*

wetʹbackʹ *n colloq* Mexican who enters the U.S. illegally to work

wetʹ blan/ket *n* one who dampens pleasure or enthusiasm

wetʹ cellʹ *n* primary electric cell whose electrolyte is free to flow

wetʹlandsʹ *npl* land with a wet spongy soil, where the water table stands at or above the land surface for at least part of the year

wetʹ nurseʹ *n* woman employed to suckle another's child

wetʹ-nurseʹ *vt* **1** to be a wet nurse to; **2** to give excessive care to

wetʹwareʹ *n computer science* the human brain, correlating to *software* and *hardware* **4**

we've /wēvʹ/ we have

whack /(h)wakʹ/ [prob imit] *n* **1** *colloq* sharp resounding blow; **2** *slang* trial, attempt, turn; **3** out of whack *slang* not in working order || *vt* **4** *colloq* to strike with a sharp resounding blow; **5** *slang* to share; **6** **whack up** *slang* **a** to divide, share; **b** to gather, put together

whale[1] /(h)wālʹ/ [OE *hwǣl*] *n* (**whale** or **whales**) **1** any of several large sea mammals of the order Cetacea, having finlike forelimbs, no external hind limbs, and a fishlike tail, some species constituting the largest living animals; 2 *colloq* anything big or impressive, as *a whale of a story* || *vi* 3 to engage in whale fishing || **whal′ing** *n*

whale² [< *wale*] *vt* to flog or beat soundly

whale′boat′ *n* long narrow boat pointed at both ends, used formerly by whalers, now used mostly for sea rescues

whale′bone′ *n* 1 stiff springy substance found in the upper jaw of some whales; 2 small strip of this substance used to stiffen corsets

whal′er *n* 1 whaling boat; 2 person engaged in whaling

wham /(h)wam′/ [imit] *v* (**whammed**, **wham·ming**) *vt* & *vi* 1 to hit with noise and violence || *n* 2 noisy impact; 3 loud noise, as of a collision or explosion

wham′my *n* (**-mies**) *slang* 1 jinx, evil eye; 2 **put the whammy on** to jinx

wharf /(h)wôrf′/ [OE *hwearf* embankment] *n* (**wharves** /-vz/ or **wharfs**) structure built along the water's edge or projecting out into the water at which ships may be moored, loaded, or unloaded

wharf′age /-ij/ *n* 1 use of a wharf; 2 charge for this; 3 wharves collectively

what /(h)wot′/ *adj* 1 which kind of, as *what books?*; 2 whatever, as *give me what money you have*; 3 how unusual, as *what beauty!* || *pron* 4 which thing or things (requesting definition or information), as *what's wrong?; what is that?*; 5 which reason, as *for what?*; 6 the thing or things that, as *do what he wants*; 7 how much, as *I don't know what it cost*; 8 **so what?** *colloq* the matter is of no interest or importance; 9 **what have you** *colloq* and so forth; 10 **what if** suppose that; 11 **what it takes** what is needed to attain success or a desired end; 12 **what's what** *colloq* the true facts of the situation || *adv* 13 how much, as *what does it profit a man?*; 14 **what with** taking into consideration, as *what with the cold, we stayed home* || *conj* 15 **but what** *colloq* that, as *I do not believe but what he is right* || *interj* 16 indicating astonishment, dismay, indignation, etc.

what·ev′er *pron* 1 all that; anything that; 2 no matter what; 3 anything in addition, as *bananas, apples, or whatever*; 4 what || *adj* 5 of any kind, as *there is no truth whatever in it*; 6 all that; any that; no matter what kind of

what′ll /(h)wot′əl/ what will

what′not′ *n* stand of shelves for ornaments, books, etc.

what's′ 1 what is; 2 what has; 3 *colloq* what does

what′so·ev′er *pron* & *adj* emphatic whatever

wheat /(h)wēt′/ [OE *hwǣte*] *n* grain of any cereal grass of the genus *Triticum*, used as a food in the form of flour || **wheat′en** *adj*

wheat′ germ′ *n* nucleus of the wheat kernel, added to foods as a source of vitamins

whee·dle /(h)wēd′əl/ [?] *vt* 1 to get by coaxing or flattery; 2 wheedle someone into to cajole or coax someone into (doing something) || also *vi* || **whee′dler** *n*

wheel /(h)wēl′/ [OE *hwēol*] *n* 1 circular frame or disk turning on a central axis or axle, used to move vehicles, transmit power in machinery, etc.; 2 *colloq* bicycle; 3 any apparatus having a revolving disk or frame as an essential part, as *a potter's wheel*; 4 wheel used for steering an automobile or boat; 5 something resembling a wheel, as certain fireworks; 6 wheeling movement; 7 **wheels** *pl* inner workings, essential machinery, as *the wheels of state*; 8 **at the wheel**, **a** at the steering wheel; **b** in command || *vt* 9 to cause to turn, swing around, or rotate; 10 to move or convey on wheels or in a wheeled vehicle || *vi* 11 to turn on or as if on an axis; 12 to move on wheels, as a vehicle; 13 **wheel and deal** *slang* to make big deals, operate in a big way || **wheeled′** *adj*

wheel′bar′row *n* light vehicle with two handles by which it is pushed and usu. one wheel, for carrying small loads

wheel′base′ *n* distance in inches between the centers of the hubs of the front and rear wheels of an automobile

wheel′chair′ *n* mobile chair for invalids and incapacitated persons, mounted on large wheels

wheel′er-deal′er *n* one who wheels and deals

wheel′ horse′ *n* 1 horse, or one of the horses, harnessed nearest to a vehicle behind other horses; 2 reliable worker

wheel′wright′ *n* one who makes or repairs wagon and carriage wheels, or the vehicles themselves

wheeze /(h)wēz′/ [ME *whesen*] *vi* 1 to breathe noisily and with a whistling sound; 2 to make a noise like wheezing || *n* 3 wheezing sound; 4 old joke

whelk /(h)welk′/ [OE *weoloc*] *n* any of a number of large spiral-shelled marine gastropods of the family Buccinidae

whelp /(h)welp′/ [OE *hwelp*] *n* 1 the young of a dog, wolf, fox, lion, etc.; 2 worthless youth || *vt* 3 to give birth to (whelps) || also *vi*

when /(h)wenʹ/ [OE *hwenne*] *adv* **1** at or during what time, as *when are you coming?; tell me when you are coming* || *conj* **2** at the time that, as *the hour when he arrived;* **3** whenever; **4** as soon as, as *when the war is over;* **5** while on the contrary, as *he gave me ten dollars when he owed me five* || *pron* **6** what or which time, as *until when?, since when?*

whence /(h)wensʹ/ [ME *whennes*] *adv* **1** from what place, end, result, or the like || *conj* **2** from which place

when·ev·er *adv* **1** when || *conj* **2** at whatever time

where /(h)werʹ/ [OE *hwǣr*] *adv* **1** at or in what place; **2** in what respect, as *where am I wrong?; tell me where I am wrong;* **3** to what place; **4** from what place or source || *conj* **5** in, at, or to the place in, at, or to which, as *the house where I live;* **6** in a position in which, as *he did much where we expected little* || *pron* **7** what place, as *from where?;* **8** the place in which, as *this is where he lives*

where·a·bouts *adv* **1** about where || *nsg* or *npl* **2** location of a person or thing

where·as *conj* **1** considering that, it being the case that; **2** while on the contrary || *n* **3** qualifying statement, esp. one beginning with "whereas"

where·at *adv* **1** at which; **2** whereupon

where·by *adv* by which

where·fore *adv* **1** why || *conj* **2** for which reason, therefore || *n* **3** cause or reason

where·in *adv* **1** in what || *conj* **2** in which, in what

where·of *adv & conj* of what, which, or whom

where·on *adv & conj* on what or which

where·to *adv & conj* **1** to what place or end; **2** to which

where·up·on *conj* upon, at, or after which

wher·ev·er *adv* **1** where || *conj* **2** at, in, or to whatever place

where·with *adv* with which

where·with·al /-ôlʹ/ *n* means, esp. money, with which to do something

whet /(h)wetʹ/ [OE *hwettan*] *v* (**whet·ted; whet·ting**) *vt* **1** to sharpen by rubbing or grinding; **2** to stimulate, as the appetite

wheth·er /(h)wethʹər/ [OE *hwæther*] *conj* **1** used to introduce the first of two or more alternatives, having *or* or *or whether* as its correlative, as *whether he comes or stays home;* **2** if it be the case that, as *see whether they have a room*

whet·stone *n* stone for whetting edge tools

whew /hwyōōʹ/ [imit] *interj* exclamation of surprise, disgust, or dismay

whey /(h)wāʹ/ [OE *hwǣg*] *n* the thin watery part of milk, which separates from the curds when the milk is coagulated

which /(h)wichʹ/ [OE *hwilc*] *pron* **1** what one or ones (of several), as *which of these men is your friend?;* **2** introducing a subordinate clause when the antecedent is not a person; **3** the one that, as *point out which is yours* || *adj* **4** what one or ones of the, as *I do not know in which house he lives*

which·ev·er *pron & adj* **1** no matter which; **2** anyone that

whiff /(h)wifʹ/ [ME *weffe*] *n* **1** slight puff, as of air or smoke; **2** inhalation, as of tobacco smoke; **3** faint odor, trace || *vt* **4** to blow or drive in whiffs; **5** to inhale in whiffs || *vi* **6** to blow in whiffs; **7** baseball to strike out swinging

whif·fle·tree /(h)wifʹəl-/ [?] *n* pivoted bar attached crosswise to the front of a carriage or wagon to hold the traces of a harness

Whig /(h)wigʹ/ [abbr of *whiggamore* Sc supporter of Cromwell] *n* **1** Brit member of the party opposed to the Tories, known as the Liberals after 1832; **2** supporter of independence in the American Revolution; **3** member of a U.S. political party, ab. 1832–55, which was succeeded by the Republican party || also *adj*

while /(h)wīlʹ/ [OE *hwīl*] *n* **1** period of time; **2** worth one's while worth one's time and efforts || *conj* **3** during the time that; **4** as long as; **5** although; whereas || *vt* **6** usu. **while away** to pass (the time), esp. pleasantly

whi·lom /(h)wīlʹəm/ [OE *hwīlom* at times] *archaic adj* **1** former || *adv* **2** formerly

whilst /(h)wīlstʹ/ *conj* chiefly Brit while

whim /(h)wimʹ/ [?] *n* fancy, caprice, notion

whim·per /(h)wimpʹər/ [< obs *whimp* to whine] *vi* **1** to cry with a low, whining, broken voice || *vt* **2** to utter in a whimper || *n* **3** whimpering sound or cry

whim·si·cal /(h)wimʹzikəl/ *adj* **1** given to or characterized by whims or whimsy; **2** capricious, unpredictable || **whim·si·cal·i·ty** /-kalʹ-/ *n* (**-ties**)

whim·sy /(h)wimʹzē/ [?] *n* (**-sies**) **1** capricious or fanciful humor; **2** fanciful notion

whine /(h)wīnʹ/ OE *hwīnan* to whiz] *vi* **1** to utter a plaintive, nasal cry, esp. in complaint || *vt* **2** to utter with a whine || *n* **3** act or sound of whining; **4** whining complaint

whin·ny /(h)winʹē/ [imit] *v* (**-nied**) *vi* **1** to neigh || *n* (**-nies**) **2** neigh

whip /(h)wipʹ/ [MD *wippen* to shake] *v* (**whipped** or **whipt; whip·ping**) *vt* **1** to strike, as with a whip; **2** to flog, beat; **3** to flay, lash; **4** to beat into a froth, as cream; **5** colloq to defeat decisively; **6** **whip into line** to unite or drive to concerted action; **7** **whip off, a** to pull off with a jerk; **b** to turn out hurriedly, as *he whipped off* *a new story in a day;* **8 whip out** to pull or snatch out, as a gun; **9 whip up** *colloq* **a** to prepare quickly; **b** to arouse, stir up ‖ *vi* **10** to thrash or flap about; **11** to move quickly, whisk, as *the fox whipped out of sight* ‖ *n* **12** flexible rod, often tapering to a lash, used in punishment, guidance, etc.; **13** party leader in a legislative assembly, who secures attendance, enforces discipline, etc.; **14** dish composed largely of whipped eggs or cream

whip′cord′ *n* close-woven fabric with a diagonally ribbed surface

whip′ hand′ *n* dominant or controlling position

whip′lash′ *n* **1** lash of a whip; **2** injury to the neck caused by a sudden snapping of the head, as in an auto collision

whip′per-snap′per [< *whip snapper*] *n* insignificant but impertinently presumptuous person

whip-pet /(h)wip′ĭt/ [?] *n* small swift dog resembling a greyhound, used for racing

whip′ping boy′ *n* scapegoat

whip′ple-tree′ /(h)wip′əl-/ *n* whiffletree

whip-poor-will /(h)wip′ərwil′/ [imit] *n* nocturnal North American bird (*Caprimulgus vociferus*) mottled buff, brown, and black, and nesting on the ground; so called from its oft-repeated note

whip′saw′ *n* **1** narrow tapering saw set in a frame and operated by one or two persons ‖ *v* (*pp* **sawed** or **sawn**) *vt* **2** to saw with a whipsaw; **3** to get the best of (a person) in two ways at once

whir /(h)wur′/ [< Scand] *v* (**whirred; whir-ring**) *vi* **1** to fly, revolve, or move quickly with a buzzing sound ‖ *n* **2** act or sound of whirring

whirl /(h)wurl′/ [< Scand] *vi* **1** to spin, rotate, or turn around rapidly; **2** to move rapidly while revolving; **3** to travel swiftly; **4** to seem to spin around, as *my brain whirled* ‖ *vt* **5** to cause to whirl ‖ *n* **6** act of whirling; **7** whirling motion; **8** something whirling; **9** attempt, as *give it a whirl;* **10** giddy state; **11** rapid succession, as of events, parties, etc.

whirl′i-gig′ [*whirl* + *obs gig* toy top] *n* **1** anything that turns around rapidly; **2** child's toy that spins or whirls; **3** merry-go-round; **4** water beetle (family Gyrinidae) that dashes swiftly about on the surface of the water

whirl′pool′ *n* whirling eddy in water, usu. with a central depression into which floating objects are drawn

whirl′wind′ *n* **1** moving and often destructive current of air whirling around a vertical axis; **2** anything resembling a whirlwind in speed or destructiveness

whirl′y-bird′ *n colloq* helicopter

whish /(h)wish′/ [imit] *n* **1** swish, hissing sound ‖ *vi* **2** to move or rush by with a whish

whisk /(h)wisk′/ [< Scand] *vt* **1** to sweep or brush rapidly; **2** to move or carry off with a quick sweeping action ‖ *vi* **3** to move rapidly and nimbly ‖ *n* **4** act of whisking; **5** quick nimble movement

whisk′broom′ *n* short-handled hand broom for brushing clothes

whisk′er [ME] *n* **1** single hair of the beard; **2** one of the long bristly hairs growing near the mouth of a cat, rat, etc.; **3 whiskers** *pl* man's beard or any part of it ‖ **whisk′ered** *adj*

whis-key or **whis-ky** /(h)wis′kē/ [Gael *uisge* (beatha) water (of life)] *n* (**-keys** or **-kies**) strong alcoholic liquor distilled from a grain, as rye, corn, or barley

whis-per /(h)wisp′ər/ [OE *hwisprian*] *vi* **1** to speak softly or under the breath, without vibration of the vocal cords; **2** to speak furtively; gossip; plot; **3** to rustle or hiss ‖ *vt* **4** to say in a whisper; tell privately; **5** to speak to in a whisper or privately ‖ *n* **6** whispered speech; **7** whispered remark; gossip; slander; **8** hint or suggestion; **9** soft, sibilant rustling ‖ **whis′per-er** *n*

whist /(h)wist′/ [< *whisk* (cards from the table)] *n* card game for four persons, opposite pairs being partners; the forerunner of bridge

whis-tle /(h)wis′əl/ [OE *hwistlian*] *vi* **1** to make a shrill or musical sound by forcing air, steam, or the like, through a small aperture, as in a whistle, a teakettle, or between the teeth or puckered lips; **2** to go or pass with a whistling sound, as bullets or the wind; **3 whistle for** to ask vainly for ‖ *vt* **4** to utter by whistling; **5** to call or signal by whistling ‖ *n* **6** sound produced by whistling; **7** instrument to produce a whistling sound; **8 blow the whistle on** *slang* **a** to inform on; **b** to stop; **9 wet one's whistle** *colloq* to take a drink ‖ **whis′tler** *n*

whis′tle stop′ *n* **1** way station at which trains stop only if signaled to stop; **2** brief stop at a small town for a campaign speech

whit /(h)wit′/ [OE *wiht* thing, creature] *n* **not a whit** not the least bit

white /(h)wīt′/ [OE *hwīt*] *adj* **1** of the color of clean snow; reflecting all of the light rays of the spectrum without absorption; **2** of a light color, light in comparison with some darker tint or hue; **3** fair-skinned; Caucasian; **4** silvery or gray (hair); **5** pale, pallid; **6** pure; innocent; **7** favorable, harmless, as *a white witch;* **8** *slang* fair, honorable ‖ *n* **9** color of clean snow; **10** white object or substance; **11** white man, Caucasian; **12** albumen; **13** white part of an eyeball ‖ **white/ness** *n*

white/ ant/ *n* termite

white/ ar/se·nic *n* trioxide of arsenic

white/cap/ *n* wave crest shattered into foam

white/ coal/ *n* water power

white/-col/lar *adj* pert. to or designating clerical or professional workers, supervisors, etc., who do not have to wear work clothes on the job

white/ dwarf/ *n* star whose mass is concentrated into a relatively small volume, making it very dense

white/ el/e·phant *n* **1** rare Asiatic elephant with a pale skin; **2** anything difficult or costly to keep and, therefore, unwanted

white/ feath/er [sign of inferior breeding and poor fighting quality if found in a gamecock's tail] *n* **1** symbol of cowardice; **2 show the white feather** to betray cowardice

white/fish/ *n* (-fish or -fishes) **1** any of several widely distributed edible fishes (family Coregonidae) of the NE U.S.; **2** any of several other silvery fishes

white/ flag/ *n* white flag or cloth hoisted in token of truce or surrender

white/ gold/ *n* white alloy of gold and nickel, zinc, tin, or copper

white/ goods/ *npl* **1** bleached fabrics of cotton or linen; **2** household goods, as tablecloths, towels, bed sheets, curtains, etc.; **3** electrical household appliances with finish in white enamel

white/-haired boy/ *n* *colloq* favorite person

White/hall/ [street in London in which are situated the Admiralty, War Office, and other administrative offices of the British government] *n* the British government or its policies

white/ heat/ *n* **1** intense heat at which a metal glows white; **2** state of intense activity or emotion ‖ **white/-hot/** *adj*

White/ House/ *n* **1** residence in Washington of the President of the United States; **2** executive branch of the U.S. government

white/ lead/ /led/ *n* heavy white basic lead carbonate —2PbCO₃·Pb(OH)₂— used as a pigment and in putty

white/ lie/ *n* harmless lie told without evil intent, as to spare someone's feelings

white/-liv/ered *adj* cowardly

white/ meat/ *n* any light-colored meat, as the breast of chicken

white/ met/al *n* any of several whitish alloys of copper, tin, and antimony, used for making small castings, ornaments, etc.

whit/en *vt* **1** to make white ‖ *vi* **2** to become white

white/ oak/ *n* any of several American oaks, esp. *Quercus alba* of the E U.S., valued for its hard wood

white/ pa/per *n* **1** authoritative report of one of the media or other agency; **2** *Brit* official report of the House of Commons on a specific subject

white/ pine/ *n* **1** valuable lumber tree (*Pinus strobus*) of E North America; **2** any of numerous other related pines

white/ plague/ *n* pulmonary tuberculosis

White/ Sea/ *n* arm of the Arctic Ocean in NW Russia

white/ slav·er·y *n* condition of or traffic in women forced into prostitution ‖ **white/ slav/er** *n*

white/ tie/ *n* **1** man's white bow tie worn with formal evening clothes; **2** men's formal evening dress

white/wash/ *n* **1** liquid mixture, as of lime and water, used to whiten walls, fences, etc.; **2** statement or report that glosses over, minimizes, or denies faults or errors; **3** *colloq* defeat in which the loser fails to score ‖ *vt* **4** to cover with a coat of whitewash; **5** to cover up or gloss over the faults and errors of; **6** *colloq* to defeat (an opponent) in a game without allowing him to score

white/ wine/ *n* wine made from light-colored grapes or from dark grapes fermented without the skins, pulp, and seeds, which ranges in color from yellowish to amber

whith·er /(h)with/ər/ [OE *hwider*] *adv* **1** to what place, end, result, or the like ‖ *conj* **2** to which place

whit·ing /(h)wit/in/ [ME] *n* **1** any of various marine food fishes, esp. a North American species (*Merluccius bilinearis*) or a common European species (*Merlangus merlangus*); **2** powdered preparation of chalk used in whitewash, putty, silver polish, etc.

whit/ish *adj* somewhat white

whit·low /(h)wit/lō/ [< ME *whitflawe* white flaw] *n* abcess of a finger or toe on the joint nearest the nail or under the nail

Whit·man, Walt /wôlt/ (h)wit/mən/ *n* (1819–92) U.S. poet

Whit·sun·day /(h)wit/sun/dē̠, -səndā/ [< *White Sunday* perh because white robes were worn for christenings on that day] *n* Pentecost

Whit/sun·tide/ /-sən-/ *n* the week following Whitsunday

Whit·ti·er, John Green·leaf /(h)wit/-ē̠·ər/ *n* (1807–92) U.S. poet

whit·tle /(h)wit/əl/ [< ME *thwitel* knife] *vt* **1** to cut, shape, or trim (wood) with a knife; **2 whittle away** or **down** to reduce bit by bit as if by whittling ‖ *vi* **3** to whittle wood

whiz or **whizz** /(h)wiz/ *v* (**whizzed; whiz·zing**) *vi* **1** to make a humming or hissing noise as from rapid motion; **2** to move rapidly with such a sound ‖ *vt* **3** to cause to whiz ‖ *n* (**whiz·zes**) **4** whizzing sound; **5** *colloq* expert in some field

who /hōō'/ [OE *hwā*] *pron* **1** what or which person or persons, as *who did it?; I know who did it;* **2** (the person or persons) that, as *Mr. Smith, who lives here;* **3** *colloq* whom, as *who did you speak to?*

whoa /(h)wō'/ [var of *ho*] *interj* stop! (usu. said to a horse)

who·dun·it /hōōdun'it/ *n colloq* detective story, play, or film

who·ev·er *pron* **1** anyone who; whatever person or persons; **2** no matter who; **3** *emphatic* who

whole /hōl'/ [OE *hāl* healthy] *adj* **1** hale and sound; **2** not defective or broken; intact; **3** complete, entire; containing all the parts; **4** in one piece, undivided; **5** with no essential element removed, as *whole milk, whole blood;* **6** having the same parents, as *a whole brother* ‖ *n* **7** all the parts of something taken together; total; **8** unity formed from an organization of parts; **9 as a whole** taking everything into consideration; **10 on the whole** all things considered; in general ‖ SYN *adj* entire, unbroken, unimpaired, integral, perfect, hale, sound ‖ ANT *adj* incomplete, broken

whole'-heart'ed *adj* devoting all one's efforts; sincere; energetic

whole' hog' *n go* (the) **whole hog** *slang* to be very thorough in doing something

whole' note' *n mus* note taking up a whole measure in four-four time

whole' num'ber *n* any number, positive or negative, that is not a fraction or does not contain a fraction as part of it

whole'sale' *n* **1** sale of goods in large quantities, as to jobbers and retailers ‖ *adj* **2** of or engaged in selling at wholesale; **3** widespread; indiscriminate ‖ *adv* **4** on a wholesale basis ‖ *vt & vi* **5** to sell at wholesale ‖ **whole'sal'er** *n*

whole'some *adj* **1** promoting health of body or mind; **2** characteristic of or suggesting physical or moral well-being ‖ SYN healthful, salubrious, nourishing, nutritious, beneficial, salutary (see *healthy*)

who'll /hōōl'/ who will or who shall

whol·ly /hōl'ē, hōl'lē/ *adv* completely, entirely

whom /hōōm'/ *pron* objective case of **who**

whom·ev'er *pron* objective case of **whoever**

whoop /hōōp', *also* hwōōp'/ [ME *whopen*] *n* **1** loud shout, as of pursuit, attack, or triumph; **2** gasping sound characteristic of whooping

cough; **3** hooting cry, as of certain birds ‖ *vi* **4** to utter a whoop or whoops ‖ *vt* **5** to utter with a whoop or whoops

whoop-de-do /(h)wōōp'dēdōō', -dōō', (h)wōōp'-/ *n colloq* **1** merrymaking; **2** big commotion

whoop·ee /(h)wōōp'ē/, (h)wōōp'ē'/ [< *whoop*] *interj* **1** expressing exuberant joy ‖ /(h)wōōp'ē,(h)wōōp'ē/ *n* **2 make whoopee** to engage in gay and noisy hilarity

whoop'ing cough' /hōōp'iŋ, hōōp'-/ *n* infectious disease, esp. of children, characterized by spasmodic coughing followed by a long shrill inspiration

whoop'ing crane' *n* large, white, nearly extinct crane (*Grus americana*) of North America having a whooping call

whoosh /(h)wōōsh', (h)wōōsh'/ [imit] *n* **1** loud noise, as of rushing water ‖ *vi* **2** to move or surge with a whoosh

whop·per /(h)wop'ər/ [< ME *whop* to beat] *n colloq* **1** something unusually large; **2** big lie

whop'ping *colloq adj* **1** unusually large ‖ *adv* **2** very; thoroughly

whore /hōōr', hôr', hōr'/ [OE *hōre*] *n* **1** woman who engages in promiscuous sexual intercourse, esp. for pay ‖ *vi* **2** to be a whore; **3** to consort with whores

whorl /(h)wurl', (h)wôrl'/ [< ME *whorvel*] *n* **1** any circular or coiled arrangement of like parts around a central axis; **2** anything shaped like a coil; **3** one of the convolutions of a spiral shell; **4** circular ridge of a fingerprint ‖ **whorled'** *adj*

whor'tle·ber'ry /(h)wurt'əl-/ [< ME *hurtilberye*] *n* (**-ries**) **1** old-world shrub (*Vaccinium myrtillus*) bearing a small edible black berry; **2** the berry

who's /hōōz'/ **1** who is; **2** who has

whose /hōōz'/ [OE *hwæs*] *pron* **1** possessive case of **who**, a of whom, as *I do not know whose hat that is;* b the one or ones of whom, as *tell me whose this is;* **2** possessive case of **which**, as *the church, whose steeple I see from here*

who'so·ev'er *pron* whoever

why /(h)wī'/ [OE *hwī, hwȳ*] *adv* **1** for what cause, purpose, or reason, as *why did he come?; tell me why he came;* **2** *colloq* on account of which, for which, as *tell me the reason why he came* ‖ *interj* **3** indicating the speaker's interest, sympathy, indignation, surprise, etc. ‖ *n* (**whys**) **4** reason, as *the why of it*

wick /wik'/ [OE *wice*] *n* fabric, as an absorbent cotton cord, tape, or the like, that draws up liquid fuel to be burned in a lamp, candle, etc.

wick·ed /wik'id/ [< ME *wikke* evil] *adj* **1** evil in intention and practice; sinful, immoral; **2** mischievous, roguish; **3** unpleasantly severe; **4** dreadful ‖ **wick′ed·ly** adv ‖ **wick′ed·ness** n ‖ syn depraved, vicious, evil, infamous (see bad)

wick·er /wik′ər/ [< Scand] n **1** pliant twig; **2** wickerwork ‖ also adj

wick′er·work′ n **1** fabric made of plaited twigs; **2** articles made of wicker

wick·et /wik′it/ [AF wiket] n **1** small door or gate, esp. one in a larger door or gate; **2** small window, often with a grating, as in a ticket office; **3** croquet arch through which the ball must be hit; **4** cricket either of the two frames at which the ball is bowled

wid·der /wid′ər/ n diāl. widow

wide /wīd′/ [OE wīd] adj **1** of considerable extent from side to side; broad; **2** vast, spacious; **3** inclusive of mucn, comprehensive, as a wide acquaintance; **4** far from a point aimed at, as wide of the mark; **5** open, expanded, as wide eyes; **6** having a specified extent from side to side, as two feet wide ‖ adv **7** widely, far, as the news spread wide; **8** fully, to the fullest extent, as open your mouth wide; the door was open wide; **9** far from the point or purpose aimed at, as the shot went wide ‖ **wide′ly** adv ‖ **wide′ness** n

wide′-an′gle adj pert. to, noting, or made with a lens taking in a wider-than-normal view

wide′-a·wake′ adj **1** entirely awake; **2** alert, keen

wid′en vt **1** to make wider; broaden ‖ vi **2** to become wider

wide′-o′pen adj **1** fully opened; **2** lacking enforcement of laws prohibiting gambling and vice

wide′spread′ adj spread far and wide; occurring over a wide area

wid·ow /wid′ō/ [OE widuwe] n **1** woman who has lost her husband by death and has not remarried; **2** cards extra hand dealt on the table ‖ vt **3** to cause to become a widow ‖ **wid′ow·hood′** n

wid′ow·er n man whose wife has died and who has not remarried ‖ **wid′ow·er·hood′** n

wid′ow's peak′ n point in the hairline in the middle of the forehead

width /width′/ [< wide] n **1** extent from side to side; breadth; **2** piece of the full width, as of cloth

wield /wēld′/ [OE wieldan to control] vt **1** to use with the hands; handle effectively; **2** to exercise (power, control, influence, etc.)

wie·ner /wēn′ər/ [G Wiener (Wurst) Vienna (sausage)] n frankfurter

Wie·ner schnit·zel /vēn′ər shnit′səl/ [G = Vienna cutlet] n breaded and garnished veal cutlet

wife /wīf′/ [OE wīf woman] n (wives /-vz/) woman joined to a man in marriage ‖ **wife′ly** adj (-li·er; -li·est)

wig /wig′/ [< periwig] n artificial covering of hair for the head, to conceal baldness, to adorn, or to form part of official dress ‖ **wigged′** adj

wig′ging n Brit colloq scolding

wig·gle /wig′əl/ [ME wigelen to reel] vt & vi **1** to move from side to side with a jerky, shaky motion ‖ n **2** wiggling motion ‖ **wig′gly** adj (-gli·er; -gli·est)

Wight, Isle of /wīt′/ n island a few miles off the S coast of England

wig·wag /wig′wag′/ [< wiggle + wag] v (-wagged; -wag·ging) vt & vi **1** to move rapidly back and forth; **2** to signal with flags or movable lights, moved according to a code ‖ n **3** process or act of signaling by wig-wagging; **4** message so transmitted ‖ **wig′wag′ging** n

wig·wam /wig′wom/ [< Algonquian] n American Indian hut consisting of a framework of poles covered with bark or hides

wil·co /wil′kō/ [will comply] interj indicating that radio message has been received and will be complied with

wild /wīld′/ [OE wilde] adj **1** living in a natural state; untamed, not domesticated; **2** uninhabited; desolate; **3** uncultivated, as flowers; **4** savage, uncivilized; **5** violent; turbulent; **6** uncontrolled; passionate; **7** crazy, frantic; **8** unrestrained, uninhibited, as a wild party, wild youth; **9** fantastic, visionary; **10** disorderly, reckless; **11** wide of the mark, as a wild shot; **12** colloq eager, enthusiastic; **13** (playing card) having any desired value ‖ adv **14** wildly ‖ n **15** often **wilds** pl wilderness; **16 the wild** the wilderness ‖ **wild′ly** adv ‖ syn adj savage, rude, uncivilized, uncultivated, uninhabited; romantic, insane, absurd, fierce, irregular

wild′ boar′ n undomesticated European hog (Sus scrofa) from which the domestic hog is thought to be derived

wild′cat′ n **1** any of numerous species of the smaller undomesticated cats, widely spread over the world, as the North American bobcat or lynx; **2** savage, aggressive person; **3** exploratory oil or gas well; **4** very risky enterprise or business venture ‖ adj **5** highly speculative or risky, as stocks or business; **6** (strike) unauthorized by the union to which the strikers belong

wild′cat′ter n colloq **1** oil prospector; **2** promoter of risky business ventures

wil·de·beest /wil′dəbēst′/ [D = wild beast] n gnu

wil·der·ness /wil′dərnis/ [< ME wilderne desert] n **1** wild uncultivated region uninhabited by humans; **2** large, tangled, confusing mass or multitude

wild′-eyed′ adj staring in a wild manner, as from fear, insanity, or excitement

wild′fire′ *n* **1** highly inflammable substance hard to extinguish, as Greek fire, formerly used in warfare; **2 spread like wildfire** to spread rapidly and widely

wild′-goose′ chase′ *n* useless pursuit or futile attempt

wild′/life′ *n* wild animals collectively

wild′ oat′ *n* **1** any uncultivated species of oat, esp. *Avena fatua*; **2 sow one's wild oats** to lead a dissolute life in one's youth

wild′ rice′ *n* **1** a tall aquatic grass (*Zizania aquatica*) of NE North America bearing an edible grain; **2** the grain used as food

Wild′ West′ *n* frontier region of the American West before the period of pacification

wile /wīl′/ [ME *wil*] *n* **1** sly trick; crafty maneuver; **2** also **wiles** *pl* artful cunning; trickery ‖ *vt* **3** to wheedle, beguile; **4 wile away** to while away

will¹ /wil′/ [OE] *n* **1** power by which the mind decides upon and directs its energies to carry out an action; **2** control over impulse, as *a strong will*; **3** wish, desire; volition; **4** determination; purpose; **5** legal document disposing of one's property at death; **6 at will** as or when one wishes ‖ *vt* **7** to resolve or bring about by act of will; **8** to bequeath by will ‖ SYN *n* (see *volition*)

will² /wil′/ [< OE *wyllan*] *v* (**would**) *modal aux* used to express: **1** simple futurity, as *I will arrive at two o'clock*; **2** promise or determination, as *I will do it whether you approve or not*; **3** polite command, as *will you please open the door?*; **4** obligation, as *you will leave at once*; **5** probability, as *that will be John at the door*; **6** habitual inclination, as *boys will be boys*; **7** customary action, as *he will go for days without smoking*

will′-call′ *adj* (department of a store) where a purchase will be held until called for

-willed /-wild′/ *adj comb form* having a specified will, as *weak-willed*

Wil·lem·stad /wil′əmstät′/ *n* city on Curaçao, capital of the Netherlands Antilles (45,000)

will′ful or **wil′ful** *adj* **1** stubborn, obstinate; **2** intentional, deliberate ‖ **will′ful·ly** *adv* ‖ **will′ful·ness** *n* stubborn, perverse, self-willed, firm (see *headstrong*)

Wil′liam Tell′ /wil′yəm/ *n* legendary Swiss patriot forced to shoot an apple from his son's head for refusing to bow to the cap of the Duke of Austria

Wil′liam the Con′quer·or *n* (1027–87) duke of Normandy 1035–87 and king of England 1066–87

wil·lies /wil′ēz/ [?] *npl* **the willies** *slang* the jitters, great nervousness

will′ing *adj* **1** favorably disposed; ready; consenting; **2** given or done freely and gladly ‖ **will′ing·ly** *adv* ‖ **will′ing·ness** *n*

will′-o′-the-wisp′ /wil′ə-/ [= Will with a torch] *n* **1** light that flits above marshy ground, supposed to be due to combustion of gas from decaying organic matter; **2** anything that misleads one or escapes one's grasp

wil·low /wil′ō/ [OE *welig*] *n* any of a genus (*Salix*) of trees and shrubs usu. growing near water and having slender branches which are easily bent and twisted

wil′low·y *adj* lithe; slender; graceful

will′ pow′er *n* self-control; strength of will

wil·ly-nil·ly /wil′ēnil′ē/ [< *obs* will ye, nill ye whether you want to or not] *adv* **1** willingly or unwillingly ‖ *adj* **2** vacillating, irresolute

Wil·ming·ton /wil′miŋtən/ *n* **1** city in N Delaware on the Delaware River (96,000); **2** seaport in SE North Carolina (44,000)

Wil·son, Wood·row /wood′rō wils′ən/ *n* (1856–1924) 28th president of the U.S. 1913–21; Nobel peace prize 1919 ‖ **Wil·so′ni·an** /-sōn′ē·ən/ *adj*

wilt¹ /wilt′/ [*dial.* var of *obs* welk to fade] *vi* **1** to wither or droop, as a flower; **2** to lose strength; become faint or weak ‖ *vt* **3** to cause to wilt

wilt² archaic 2nd pers sg of **will²**

Wil′ton (car′pet or rug′) /wilt′ən/ [*Wilton*, England] *n* kind of carpet woven with loops cut to form a thick velvet pile

wil·y /wil′ē/ [< *wile*] *adj* (-i·er; -i·est) full of wiles; cunning, crafty ‖ **wil′i·ness** *n* ‖ SYN cunning, crafty, artful, sly, subtle, deceptive, designing, tricky, hypocritical ‖ DISCR The *cunning* man is shrewd enough to divine how to compass his ends, and clever enough to conceal the means which he has employed. His wit is directed toward covering up, outwitting, and escaping entrapment; such wit is not of a high order, being possessed by some animals, notably the foxes, a fact which has produced a synonym for *cunning*—"foxy." A child may be naturally *cunning*, but it requires an experienced person to be *crafty*. A *crafty* man may descend to graver deception than the *cunning* one; he is also more alert, and possessed of greater ability, as a *crafty* old schemer; a *crafty* politician. *Artful* persons are likely to be tricky and indirect; their purposes are ingeniously concealed under their careful words and actions. An *artful* child may deceive the most observant of adults. *Sly* connotes a smooth *cunning*; the *sly* man is more vulgar and less able, however, than the *cunning* man; he is, too, more wary and silent; a *sly* trick is mean as well as underhand. *Subtle* implies unusual mental ability; the *subtle* man has in mind more than the immediate object; his aim is worthwhile, and he attains it with skill, as a *subtle* statesman. The *wily* person ensnares and deceives others by stratagems and tricks, as a *wily* detective

wim·ble /wim′bəl/ [ME] n 1 any of several boring tools, such as a gimlet or auger ‖ vt 2 to bore with or as with a wimble

wim·ple /wimp′əl/ [OE *wimpel*] n woman's covering for the head extending over the forehead, neck, chin, and sides of the face, worn by some orders of nuns

win /win′/ [OE *winnan* to toil, fight] v (won; win·ning) vt 1 to acquire, gain, as fame or a prize; 2 to get by effort, conquest, or competition; 3 to gain the favor or affection of; 4 to reach by effort, as a point on a journey; 5 to be victorious in; 6 to persuade to marry; 7 often **win over** to prevail on, persuade ‖ vi 8 to be successful; gain a victory; 9 to finish first in a race or contest; 10 also **win out** to succeed ‖ n 11 victory in a game or contest ‖ **win′ner** n ‖ SYN v acquire, earn, achieve, attain (see *get*)

wince /wins′/ [ME *wincen* to kick] vi 1 to shrink or draw back suddenly; flinch ‖ n 2 act of wincing ‖ SYN v shrink, start (see *flinch*)

winch /winch′/ [OE *wince*] n 1 handle or crank for a revolving machine; 2 windlass turned by a crank

Win·ches·ter (ri′fle) /win′chest′ər/ [O. F. *Winchester* Am manufacturer] n repeating rifle, famous for its use on the Western frontier of the U.S.

wind[1] /wind′/ [OE] n 1 current of air; breeze; 2 gale, storm; 3 breath; ability to breathe; 4 idle words or threats; 5 wind instrument; 6 hint, intimation; 7 air bearing an animal's scent; 8 gas formed in the digestive organs; 9 **break wind** to expel gas through the anus; 10 **in the wind** about to happen; 11 **take the wind out of one's sails** to disconcert or deflate a person ‖ vt 12 to make short of breath, as by exercise

wind[2] /wind′/ [OE *windan*] v (wound) vi 1 to turn; keep changing direction; bend; 2 to twine round and round; 3 **wind up**, a to conclude, finish; b *baseball* to swing the arm in preparation for pitching the ball ‖ vt 4 to twist round and round on something, as wire on a spool or a bandage around the arm; 5 to turn, as a crank; 6 to entwine; 7 to make (one's or its way) in a winding course; 8 often **wind up**, a to coil into a ball; b to coil the spring of (a spring-operated mechanism), as

by turning a key or stem; 9 **wind up**, a to bring to a conclusion; b to settle, as one's affairs; c to excite, make tense

wind′bag′ /wind′-/ n *slang* pompous person who talks much and says little

wind′break′ /wind′-/ n hedge, row of trees, or fence serving as protection from the wind

Wind′break′er /wind′-/ [trademark] n jacket for outdoor use, with close-fitting elastic cuffs and waistband and hipband

wind′burn′ /wind′-/ n inflammation of the skin caused by exposure to the wind

wind′ cone′ /wind′/ n windsock

wind′ed /wind′-/ adj out of breath

wind′fall′ /wind′-/ n 1 something brought down by the wind, as ripe fruit, branches, or a whole tree; 2 unexpected piece of good fortune

wind′ gap′ /wind′/ n indentation in the upper part of a mountain ridge

wind′ing /wind′-/ adj 1 twining, twisting, turning ‖ n 2 coil of wire in an electrical device

wind′ing sheet′ n shroud 1

wind′ in′stru·ment /wind′/ n mus any of several musical instruments sounded by a current of air produced by blowing the breath

wind′jam′mer /wind′-/ n colloq 1 large vessel propelled by sails; 2 member of its crew

wind·lass /wind′ləs/ [ME *windelas* < Scand] n machine for hoisting by winding a rope or chain on a cylinder turned by hand or by machinery

wind′mill′ /wind′-/ n 1 mill operated by a large wind-driven wheel whose oblique vanes or sails catch the wind; 2 imaginary threat or opponent

win·dow /win′dō/ [ME *windoge* < Scand = eye of the wind] n 1 opening in the side of a building or vehicle to let in light and air, usu. fitted with glass in a movable frame; 2 sash, casement, or other framework that fills such a space; 3 windowpane; 4 anything resembling a window, as the transparent part of an envelope so that the address can be seen through it

win′dow box′ n box on a window ledge for growing plants

win′dow dress′ing n 1 decorative arrangement of goods in a shop window; 2 statement or acts intended to give a misleadingly favorable impression

win′dow en′ve·lope n envelope with a transparent panel through which the address, written on the enclosure, may be read

win′dow·pane′ n pane of glass in one compartment of a window sash

win′dow sash′ n sash[2]

win'dow seat' *n* **1** seat designed to be placed or to fit at a window; **2** seat next to the window in a bus, car, airplane, etc.

win'dow-shop' *v* (-**shopped**; -**shop·ping**) *vi* to look at displays in shop windows without entering ‖ **win'dow-shop'per** *n*

win'dow sill' *n* sill of a window

wind'pipe' /wĭnd'-/ *n* trachea

wind-row /wĭnd'rō, wĭn'-/ *n* ridge of raked hay, or row of sheaves of grain stacked in a line, for drying in the wind

wind'shield' /wĭnd'-/ *n* glass partition in front of the passenger compartment of an automobile or truck

wind'sock' /wĭnd'-/ *n* large cone-shaped bag attached to the top of a mast at an airport to show wind direction

wind'storm' /wĭnd'-/ *n* violent wind with little or no rain

wind' tun'nel /wĭnd'-/ *n* tunnellike passage through which air is forced to determine wind resistance in airplanes, automobiles, etc., the tests often being made on small-scale models

wind'up' /wīnd'-/ *n* **1** end, conclusion, **2** *baseball* preliminary motion used by pitchers to accumulate momentum in throwing the ball

wind-ward /wĭnd'wərd/ *adj & adv* **1** at or toward the side from which the wind blows ‖ *n* **2** direction from which the wind blows

Wind'ward Is'lands *npl* group of small islands in the SE West Indies, divided between Great Britain and France

Wind'ward Pas'sage *n* strait about 50 miles wide between Cuba and Haiti

wind·y /wĭnd'ē/ *adj* (-**i·er**; -**i·est**) **1** exposed to or characterized by wind; **2** resembling or consisting of wind; **3** empty, intangible; **4** verbose; bombastic ‖ **wind'i·ness** *n*

wine /wīn/ [OE *wīn* < L *vinum*] *n* **1** fermented juice of grapes, used as a drink; **2** fermented juice of other fruits or plants, such as currants or dandelions; **3** dark-reddish color ‖ *vt* **4** **wine and dine** to entertain with food and drink

wine'bib'ber /-bĭb'ər/ [< *wine* + *bib*] *n* one who drinks wine to excess

wine' cel'lar *n* **1** cellar in which wine is stored; **2** stock of wine

wine' press' *n* machine for pressing the juice from grapes

win'er·y *n* (-**ies**) establishment for making wine

Wine'sap' *n* large deep-red fall and winter apple

wine'skin' *n* skin of an animal made into a vessel for wine

wing /wĭŋ/ [< Scand] *n* **1** forelimb of a vertebrate, corresponding to the human arm, developed for flying, as in birds and bats; **2** appendage on the back of an insect, used for flying; **3** one of the main supporting surfaces of an airplane; **4** part of a building projecting from the main body of the structure; **5** either side of a stage, extending out of sight of the audience; **6** either of two forward extensions of the back of a chair; **7** either of the two sides of a combat force; **8** administrative and tactical unit of the U.S. Air Force; **9** in some sports, position or player on the extreme sides; **10** section of a political party representing a particular shade of opinion; **11** **on the wing** in flight; **12** **take wing** to fly away, take to flight; **13** **under one's wing** under one's care or protection ‖ *vt* **14** to accomplish by flying, as *the bird winged its way*; **15** to cross in flight; **16** to wound in the wing or arm ‖ *vi* **17** to fly ‖ **winged** /wĭŋd' or *poet.* wĭŋ'ĭd/ *adj*

wing'back' *n* *football* offensive back lining up beyond the end

wing' chair' *n* upholstered chair with wings

wing' col'lar *n* man's starched collar having the upper ends folded down, worn with formal clothes

wing'-ding' /-dĭng'/ *n* *slang* wild celebration or party

wing' nut' *n* nut with two projecting wings for tightening by hand

wing'span' *n* distance between the wing tips of an airplane

wing'spread' *n* distance between the tips of a pair of spread wings

wink /wĭŋk'/ [OE *wincian*] *vi* **1** to close and open quickly one or both eyelids; **2** to convey a hint or signal by a motion of an eyelid; **3** to twinkle; shine; gleam at irregular intervals; **4** **wink at** to feign ignorance of, ignore deliberately ‖ *vt* **5** to close and open (an eye or the eyes) quickly; **6** to remove by winking, as *to wink the tears away* ‖ *n* **7** act of winking; **8** instant; short interval of time; **9** gleam, sparkle

win'ning *adj* **1** victorious; **2** charming, ingratiating ‖ *n* **3** act of one who wins; **4** **winnings** *pl* that which is won; gains

Win·ni·peg /wĭn'ĭpeg'/ *n* capital of Manitoba (270,000)

win·now /wĭn'ō/ [OE *windwian* to blow] *vt* **1** to blow chaff and refuse from (grain) by a current of air; **2** to sift; separate; analyze; **3** to disperse by blowing ‖ *vi* **4** to winnow grain

win·o /wīn'ō/ *n slang* one who habitually gets drunk on cheap wine

win·some /wĭns'əm/ [OE *wynsum*] *adj* engaging; charming

win·ter /wĭnt'ər/ [OE] *n* **1** coldest season of the year; in the Northern

Hemisphere, from December 21st to March 21st; **2** time of gloom or sorrow ‖ *vi* **3** to pass or spend the winter ‖ *vt* **4** to maintain during the winter ‖ *adj* **5** of, pert. to, or characteristic of winter; **6** (fruit and vegetables) that may be kept for use during the winter; **7** (wheat) planted in the autumn and ripening in the following spring or summer

win'ter·green' *n* **1** low evergreen plant (*Gaultheria procumbens*) that bears edible red berries and whose leaves yield an aromatic oil; **2** this oil, used as a flavoring

win'ter·ize' *vt* to prepare for the cold weather of winter

win'ter sol'stice *n* the solstice occurring on December 21

win'ter-time' *n* winter season

win·try /wintʹrē/ *adj* (-tri·er; -tri·est) **1** pert. to or like winter; **2** cold, bleak

wipe /wīp/ [OE *wīpian* to rub] *vt* **1** to dry or clean by rubbing with something soft; **2** to remove by rubbing, as dirt; **3** to form (a joint, usu. between lead pipes) by spreading solder with a greased piece of leather or cloth); **4 wipe out** to destroy completely ‖ *n* **5** act of rubbing or wiping; **6** *mach* wiper; **7** sweeping blow

wip'er *n* **1** one who or that which wipes; **2** *mach* projecting cam that imparts a reciprocating motion to another part; **3** *elec* moving or sliding contact

wire /wīʹər/ [OE *wīr*] *n* **1** rod, strand, or string of ductile metal, usu. flexible and of circular cross section; **2** telephone or telegraph wire or cable; **3** telegraph; **4** telegram; **5** open telephone line; **6** finish line of a race track; **7 pull wires** to use influence in order to gain an end; **8 under the wire** just before the deadline ‖ *vt* **9** to bind, fit, or provide with wire; **10** to furnish with electric wiring; **11** *colloq* **a** to telegraph (a message); **b** to send a telegram to ‖ *vi* **12** *colloq* to telegraph

wire' en·tan'gle·ment *n* barbed-wire trap stretched along a front and designed to stop or delay an enemy advance

wire' gauge' *n* metal plate with a series of notches on its edge, used for measuring the diameter of wire

wire' glass' *n* glass strengthened by a netting of wire enclosed within it

wire'hair' or **wire'-haired' ter'ri·er** *n* fox terrier with a wiry coat

wire'less *adj* **1** (device) operated by electromagnetic waves without conducting wires ‖ *n* **2** wireless telegraphy; **3** wireless message; **4** *Brit* radio ‖ *vt* & *vi* **5** to telephone or telegraph by wireless

Wire'pho'to [trademark] *n* **1** system of transmitting photographs by wire; **2** photo so transmitted ‖ *vt* **3** wire-

photo to send (a photograph) by Wirephoto

wire'pull'ing *n* use of influence in order to gain an end

wire' re·cord'er *n* device that records sound on a steel wire ‖ **wire' re·cord'ing** *n*

wire' room' *n* illegal bookmaking establishment

wire' serv'ice *n* organization that syndicates news by wire to subscribers

wire'tap' *v* (-tapped; -tap·ping) *vt* **1** to eavesdrop on (a message or conversation) by tapping telephone or telegraph wires ‖ *vi* **2** to tap telephone or telegraph wires ‖ *n* **3** tap placed on a telephone or telegraph wire ‖ **wire'tap'per** *n* ‖ **wire'tap'ping** *n*

wir'ing *n* **1** act of installing electrical wires; **2** complete system of electrical wires, as in a building or electrical device

wir'y *adj* (-i·er; -i·est) **1** like wire; stiff; **2** lean and strong; sinewy

Wis. Wisconsin

Wis·con·sin /wiskonsʹin/ *n* state in the N central U.S. (4,417,933; 56,154 sq. m.; cap. Madison) ‖ **Wis·con'sin·ite'** *n*

wis·dom /wizʹdəm/ [OE] *n* **1** state or quality of being wise; discernment; sagacity; discretion; **2** learning, knowledge, erudition ‖ SYN care, prudence, circumspection, caution; forecast, foresight, forethought; frugality, providence ‖ DISCR *Care* is a watchful, constructive policy applied to one's affairs; it may refer to the present or the future. We plan our children's education with *care*; save for old age with *care*. *Prudence*, which considers the future, is a sane, moderate management of practical affairs. *Prudence* enjoys life as it passes, but is not caught without money for an unexpected illness, nor without an umbrella when it rains. *Providence* also considers the future, but more boldly than *prudence*; *providence* spends now for big returns to come, develops new resources, and does not neglect daily comfort nor fail to enjoy life. *Frugality* may be forced upon one by insufficient means, or it may be the fruit of a natural disposition to save. *Frugality* implies sufficiency but not abundance; it connotes a grudging expenditure for necessities (see also *knowledge*)

wis'dom tooth' *n* **1** third molar on each side of each jaw, the last tooth to appear; **2 cut one's wisdom teeth** to reach the years of discretion

wise[1] /wīz/ [OE *wīs*] *adj* **1** having the faculty of forming a true judgment; discerning; sagacious; **2** learned, erudite; **3 get wise to** *slang* to become aware of; **4 put someone wise** *slang* to make someone aware ‖ *vt*

5 wise up *slang* to make (someone) aware ‖ *vi* **6 wise up** *slang* to become aware ‖ SYN *adj* sagacious, sage, judicious, knowing, intellectual, profound, discerning, prudent, intelligent, discreet, provident, politic ‖ ANT *adj* foolish, ignorant, imprudent

wise² [OE] *n* way, manner, mode

-wise /-wiz/ *adv suf* in the manner of, as *clockwise*

wise'a'cre /-āk'ər/ [MD *wijssegger* seer] *n* one who makes pretensions to wisdom

wise'crack' *colloq n* **1** facetious or flippant remark ‖ *vi* **2** to make wisecracks ‖ **wise'crack'er** *n*

wise' guy' *n* conceited, obnoxiously cocksure person

wish /wish/ [OE *wȳscan*] *vi* **1** to desire; **2** to make a wish; **3 wish for** to long for, have a strong desire for ‖ *vt* **4** to desire, long for, crave; **5** to desire for someone else, invoke, as *wish him luck*; **6 wish something on someone** *colloq* to palm something off on someone ‖ *n* **7** strong or eager desire; **8** expression of desire; request; **9** object wished for ‖ SYN *n* longing, yearning (see *desire*)

wish'bone' *n* forked bone in front of the breastbone in most birds, often broken in making a wish

wish'ful *adj* desirous, longing ‖ **wish'ful-ly** *adv*

wish'ful think'ing *n* interpretation of events and prospects according to one's wishes rather than the real facts

wish'y-wash'y *adj* **1** watery, thin; **2** weak, irresolute

wisp /wisp/ [< ME *wips*] *n* **1** handful or small bundle, as of straw; **2** thin tuft, as of hair; **3** anything slight or delicate ‖ **wisp'y** *adj* (-i-er; -i-est)

wis-te-ri-a /wistir'ē-ə/ [Caspar *Wistar* (1761–1818) Am anatomist] *n* any of a genus (*Wisteria*) of climbing shrubs bearing showy clusters of purple, white, or pink flowers

wist'ful /wist'-/ [?] *adj* **1** wishful, longing; **2** sadly pensive ‖ **wist'ful-ly** *adv*

wit¹ /wit'/ [OE *witan* to know] *vt* to **wit** namely

wit² [OE] *n* **1** intellect; wisdom; sagacity; **2** ability to quickly perceive the incongruous and to phrase it in an unexpected and amusing way; **3** written or spoken words showing such ability; **4** person exhibiting this ability; **5 wits** *pl* mental faculties; senses; **6 at one's wit's end** at the end of one's mental resources; at a loss; **7 to keep one's wits about one** to remain alert, esp. in an emergency

witch /wich'/ [OE *wicce*] *n* **1** woman supposed to have supernatural powers from a compact with the devil or evil spirits; **2** old crone, hag

witch'craft' *n* **1** powers or practice of witches; sorcery; **2** fascination; charm

witch' doc'tor *n* in some primitive societies, man who purports to cure sickness and counteract witchcraft by magic

witch'er-y *n* (-ies) **1** fascination; compelling charm; **2** witchcraft

witch'es' Sab'bath *n* secret meeting of witches, warlocks, and sorcerers to worship the devil, characterized by orgiastic rites

witch' ha'zel [< OE *wice*] *n* **1** shrub (*Hamamelis virginiana*) having small yellow flowers; **2** extract from its bark and leaves, used as a soothing lotion

witch' hunt' *n* intensive drive to expose, root out, and punish disloyalty, subversion, and wrongdoing, accompanied by much publicity but usu. based on flimsy or doubtful evidence

witch'ing hour' *n* midnight, as a time suitable for sorcery

with /with', with'/ [OE = against] *prep* indicating: **1** accompaniment or proximity, as *come with me*; **2** association, connection, or intercourse, as *he has been with the firm for years*; **3** attitude or judgment, as *I am pleased with you*; **4** agreement or harmony, as *blue does not go with green*; **5** possession, as *a man with money*; **6** keeping, care, or guardianship, as *leave the child with me*; **7** instrument, as *slain with a dagger*; **8** manner or circumstances, as *with ease*; **9** cause, as *perish with hunger*; **10** estimation or opinion, as *it's okay with me*; **11** proportion, relation, or simultaneousness, as *the river rose higher with every minute*; **12** in spite of, as *with all his learning, he was very modest*; **13** separation or difference, as *he parted with me*; **14** antagonism, as *he fought with the enemy*

with- *pref* **1** against, as *withstand*; **2** back, as *withdraw*

with-al /withôl'/ [ME *withalle*] *adv* **1** moreover, beside; **2** nevertheless

with-draw' /with-, with-/ *v* (-drew; -drawn) *vt* **1** to remove; take back; **2** to retract ‖ *vi* **3** to retire; **4** to give up the use of an addictive drug ‖ **with-draw'al** *n*

with-draw'al symp'tom *n* mental or physical disturbance suffered by a drug addict when he is deprived of his usual amount of drug

with-drawn' *adj* shy, retiring

withe /with', with', with'/ [OE *withthe*] *n* tough, flexible twig, esp. a willow twig, used as a binding material

with-er /with'ər/ [ME] *vi* **1** to dry up, shrivel; decay ‖ *vt* **2** to cause to wither; **3** to abash

with'ers [?] *npl* highest part of the back of a horse or similar quadruped, between the shoulder blades

with·hold' /with-, with-/ v (-held) vt 1 to hold back, restrain; 2 to keep back, refrain from giving || vi 3 to refrain, hold back

with·hold'ing tax' n income tax withheld from an employee's salary and paid directly to the government by his employer

with·in' /with-, with-/ [OE withinnan] adv 1 in or into the inner part; inside; indoors || prep 2 inside of; 3 in the limits or space of; 4 not exceeding a margin of error of, as I can tell you what time it is within three minutes

with·out' /with-, with-/ [OE withūtan] adv 1 in or to the outside; externally; 2 do or go without to do without something || prep 3 at, on, or to the outside of; 4 beyond, as without question; 5 lacking, in the absence of; 6 not, as he left without saying good-by; 7 do without to dispense with, to give up || n 8 place outside

with·stand' /with-, with-/ v (-stood) vt to oppose; resist; endure

wit'less adj lacking wit; stupid; senseless

wit·ness /wit'nis/ [OE witnes] n 1 testimony, evidence; 2 person or thing that gives evidence; 3 person who gives evidence, as in court; 4 one who attests to another's signature on a document; 5 person who from actual presence knows of the occurrence of some fact or event || vt 6 to testify to; 7 to attest by signing; 8 to see or know by personal presence; 9 to be present at

wit'ness stand' or **box'** n place in a court of law occupied by a witness

-wit·ted /-wit'id/ adj comb form having such a wit or mind, as dull-witted

wit·ti·cism /wit'isiz'əm/ [< witty] n witty remark

wit'ting [ME witing] adj knowing, deliberate || **wit'ting·ly** adv

wit'ty adj (-ti·er; -ti·est) showing or marked by wit; clever; amusing || **wit'ti·ly** adv || SYN humorous, droll, clever, comical, original || ANT dull, serious, melancholy, grave, sober

wives /wivz'/ pl of wife

wiz·ard /wiz'ərd/ [ME wisard] n 1 magician, sorcerer; 2 colloq very skillful or clever person || **wiz'ard·ry** n

wiz·ened /wiz'ənd/ [< OE wisnian to wither] adj shriveled, withered

wk. 1 week; 2 work

woad /wōd'/ [< OE wād] n 1 European plant of the mustard family (Isatis tinctoria) formerly cultivated for a blue dye obtained from its leaves; 2 dye from this plant

wob·ble /wob'əl/ [LG wabbeln] vi 1 to move unsteadily from side to side; 2 to vacillate || vt 3 to cause to wobble || n 4 wobbling motion or movement || **wob'bly** adj (-bli·er; -bli·est)

Wo·den /wōd'ən/ [OE] n the chief god

of the pagan Anglo-Saxons, identified with the Norse Odin

woe /wō'/ [OE wā] n 1 sorrow; grief; misery; affliction || interj 2 exclamation of lamentation or distress || SYN n sadness, pain, calamity (see grief)

woe'be·gone' [ME wo begon] adj overwhelmed with or showing woe, as a woebegone appearance

woe'ful adj 1 sorrowful; miserable; 2 mean, paltry, wretched || **woe'ful·ly** adv

woke /wōk'/ pt of wake

wok'en pp of wake

wolf /woolf'/ [OE wulf] n (wolves /-vz/) 1 any of various carnivorous wild animals (genus Canis) of wide distribution throughout the world; 2 cruel, greedy, or destructive person; 3 colloq man who makes bold advances to many women; 4 cry wolf to raise a false alarm; 5 keep the wolf from the door to keep away want; 6 wolf in sheep's clothing evil person who hides behind an innocent exterior || vt 7 often wolf down colloq to swallow (food) voraciously || **wolf'ish** adj

wolf'hound' n any of several tall swift breeds of dog, used for hunting wolves

wolf·ram /woolf'rəm/ [G] n 1 tungsten; 2 wolframite

wolf'ram·ite' /-īt'/ n iron manganese tungstate —(Fe,Mn)WO₄— one of the chief ores of tungsten

wolfs'bane' n any of several plants of the genus (Aconitum) bearing yellow flowers

wol·ver·ine /wool'vərēn'/ [< wolf] n fierce, voracious, carnivorous mammal (Gulo luscus) of North America, related to the weasel

wolves /woolvz'/ pl of wolf

wom·an /woom'ən/ [OE wīfmann] n (wom·en /wim'in/) 1 adult female of the human race; 2 female sex; 3 female servant or attendant; 4 womanly qualities; 5 wife || **wom'an·hood'** n || **wom'an·ish** adj

wom'an·ize' vi to chase after women || **wom'an·iz'er** n

wom'an·kind' n women in general; the female sex

wom'an·ly adj like or befitting a woman; feminine || also adv || SYN gentle, sympathetic, tender (see female)

wom'an of the streets' n streetwalker

wom'an of the world' n sophisticated, experienced woman

womb /woom'/ [OE wamb] n 1 uterus; 2 anything that holds something concealed or in which something is produced

wom·bat /wom'bat/ [< nat. Australian] n any of several burrowing Australian marsupials of the family Vombatidae

wom·en /wim'in/ pl of woman

wom'en·folk' *npl* 1 womankind; 2 particular group of women

won[1] /wun'/ *pt & pp* of **win**

won[2] /wôn/ *n* monetary unit of Korea (North and South)

won·der /wun'dər/ [OE *wundor* portent] *n* 1 strange thing; cause of surprise or admiration; marvel; miracle; 2 emotion caused by something new, unusual, strange, or marvelous; astonishment || *vi* 3 to be affected with surprise or amazement; marvel; 4 to entertain doubt or curiosity; speculate || *vt* 5 to entertain doubt or curiosity about, as *I wonder what she has*

won'der drug' *n* drug, such as the antibiotics, which is noted for having dramatic curative effects on certain diseases

won'der·ful *adj* 1 exciting wonder; marvelous; astonishing; 2 very good, fine || SYN astonishing, amazing, extraordinary, prodigious, marvelous || ANT common, unimportant, ordinary

won'der·land' *n* 1 fairylike place full of imaginary wonders; 2 region of marvelous beauty, fertility, productivity, and the like

won'der·ment *n* 1 astonishment; 2 wonder; wondering

won'drous *adj* 1 marvelous; strange || *adv* 2 archaic wonderfully

wont /wunt', wônt', wônt'/ [< ME *woned*] *adj* 1 accustomed, as *he is wont to come early* || *n* 2 custom, habit || SYN *n* habitude, custom, way, practice, system

won't /wōnt'/ will not

wont·ed /wunt'id, wont'-, wônt'-/ *adj* accustomed; usual, customary

woo /wōō'/ [OE *wōgian*] *vt* 1 to court or make love to, esp. with a view to marriage; 2 to ask earnestly, coax; 3 to seek, as *to woo success* || *vi* 4 to go courting || **woo'er** *n*

wood /wōōd'/ [OE *wudu*] *n* 1 the hard part of a tree or shrub between the pith and the bark; 2 lumber or timber; 3 firewood; 4 *golf* club with a wooden head; 5 often **woods** *pl* thick growth of trees; grove or forest; 6 **out of the woods** finally out of danger or a difficult situation || *adj* 7 wooden; 8 growing or living in the woods

wood' al'co·hol' *n* methyl alcohol

wood'bine' /-bīn'/ [OE *wudubind*] *n* 1 any of several vines of the honeysuckle family, esp. a twining vine (*Lonicera caprifolium*) bearing long-tubed, sweet-scented white or purplish flowers; 2 the European species (*L. periclymenum*); 3 the Virginia creeper

wood'chuck' [Cree *wuchak*] *n* common American burrowing rodent (*Marmota monax*) about 18 inches long, heavily built, and having coarse reddish and grayish fur

wood'cock' *n* 1 small European game bird (*Scolopax rusticola*) allied to the snipe; 2 related American bird (*Philohela minor*)

wood'craft' *n* 1 knowledge of anything pert. to woods or forests, such as hunting, camping, or trapping; 2 art of making objects out of wood

wood'cut' *n* 1 engraving cut on wood; 2 print from such an engraving

wood'ed *adj* covered with woods or trees

wood'en *adj* 1 made or consisting of wood; 2 awkward, stiff; 3 dull, spiritless || **wood'en·ly** *adv*

wood'en In'di·an *n* 1 wooden statue of a standing American Indian, formerly placed in front of cigar stores; 2 *colloq* expressionless, unresponsive person

wood'en wed'ding *n* fifth wedding anniversary

wood'land /-lənd, -land'/ *n* land covered with trees or woods

wood' louse' *n* any of several small terrestrial crustaceans (genera *Oniscus*, *Armadillidium*, and others) found under old logs

wood' nymph' *n* Gk myth. any wood- or tree-inhabiting female deity

wood'peck'er *n* any of various birds (family Picidae) having strong beaks for piercing the bark of trees in search of insects

wood' pe'wee *n* small flycatcher (*Contopus virens*) of E North America, resembling the phoebe but living in the woods

wood' pulp' *n* wood fiber reduced to pulp; used in making certain kinds of paper

wood' screw' *n* metal screw with a tapering thread for driving into wood with a screwdriver

wood'shed' *n* shed for keeping firewood

woods'man /-mən/ *n* (-men /-mən/) *n* one who frequents or lives in the woods and is skilled in woodcraft

woods'y /-zē/ *adj* (-i·er; -i·est) suggesting or characteristic of the woods

wood'wind' /-wind'/ *n mus* wind instrument, usu. with a reed mouthpiece, including the oboe, English horn, bassoon, clarinet, flute, and piccolo

wood'work' *n* objects or parts made of wood, esp. the wooden finishings of a house, as stairways, moldings, etc.

wood'work'ing *n* process or art of working with or making things of wood || **wood'work'er** *n*

wood'y *adj* (-i·er; -i·est) 1 wooded; 2 pert. to woods; sylvan; 3 consisting of or containing wood; 4 pert. to, resembling, or characteristic of wood

woof /wōōf', wŏŏf'/ [OE *ōwef*] *n* 1 weaving threads carried back and forth by the shuttle, interlacing at right angles with the warp; 2 texture of a fabric or cloth

woof·er /woŏf′ər/ [< *woof* imit of dog's bark] *n* loudspeaker designed to reproduce sounds of lower acoustic frequency

wool /woŏl′/ [OE *wull*] *n* 1 the fine, often curly hair that covers the domestic sheep and certain other animals; 2 anything resembling wool in texture, as *steel wool;* 3 garment or fabric of wool; 4 woolen yarn; 5 dyed **in the wool** confirmed, thorough; 6 **pull the wool over one's eyes** to delude one

wool′en or **wool′len** *adj* 1 made of wool; 2 of or pert. to wool ‖ **wool′ens** or **wool′lens** *npl* 3 wool cloth or clothing

wool′gath′er·ing *n* indulgence in idle fancies; daydreaming

wool′grow′er *n* person who raises sheep or other animals for the production of wool ‖ **wool′grow′ing** *n*

wool′ly *adj* (**-li·er; -li·est**) 1 pert. to, like, or consisting of wool; 2 bearing or covered with wool; 3 not organized; unclear, as *woolly thinking;* 4 *colloq* rough, uncivilized, as *wild and woolly*

wool′sack′ *n* 1 cushion stuffed with wool on which the Lord Chancellor sits in the British House of Lords; 2 office of the Lord Chancellor

wooz·y /woŏz′ē, woŏz′ē/ [?] *adj* (**-i·er; -i·est**) *colloq* 1 confused, befuddled; 2 dizzy, faint

Worces′ter·shire sauce′ /woŏst′ərshər/ [*Worcestershire,* county in England] *n* pungent sauce made with soy, vinegar, spices, etc.

word /wurd′/ [OE] *n* 1 speech sound or combination of sounds, or its written representation, used to communicate a meaning; 2 saying; remark; 3 information; news; 4 command, order; 5 password, watchword; 6 affirmation, promise, as *you have my word;* 7 **words** *pl* a conversation; **b** quarrel; **c** text or lyrics of a song; 8 **eat one's words** to retract one's statement; 9 **in a word** in short; 10 **put in a (good) word for** to recommend, speak favorably of; 11 **take one at one's word** to believe someone implicitly; 12 **weigh one's words** to speak with deliberation ‖ *vt* 13 to express in words

word′-for-word′ *adj* 1 in exactly the same words; 2 literal (translation)

word′ing *n* manner in which something is expressed in words; phrasing

word′ or′der *n* order in which words must be placed to make sense in a given language

word′ square′ *n* set of words arranged in a square so that they read sequentially the same vertically as horizontally

word′stock′ *n* total body of the words of a language or dialect

Words′worth′, Wil·liam *n* (1770–1850) English poet; poet laureate 1843–50

word′y *adj* (**-i·er -i·est**) using an abundance of words; verbose

wore /wŏr′, wŏr′/ *pt* of **wear**

work /wurk′/ [OE *weorc*] *v* (**worked** or in certain meanings **wrought**) *vi* 1 to put forth physical or mental effort; labor; 2 to be employed; 3 to operate or run, as a machine; 4 to be moved through agitation, as *his features worked from emotion;* 5 to progress slowly and laboriously, as *the brick worked loose;* 6 **work on someone** to try to influence someone; 7 **work out, a** to materialize, prove feasible; **b** to amount; **c** to exercise or train; 8 **work up to** to advance to (a higher position) ‖ *vt* 9 to operate or manage, as a machine; 10 to operate, as a mine or farm, so as to produce a yield; 11 to prepare for use, manipulate, as *to work the soil;* 12 to win by labor; achieve gradually or with difficulty, as *to work one's way;* 13 to bring or move gradually or laboriously, as into a given position or situation, as *he worked the stone into position;* 14 to perform, produce, or cause, as *to work magic, work a change;* 15 to make or fashion; 16 to embroider; 17 to extract labor from, cause to labor; 18 to influence or control; 19 to ply a trade in or operate in (a district); 20 *colloq* to utilize or exploit (a person); 21 **work in** to put in slowly or indirectly; 22 **work off, a** to dispel gradually and by effort; **b** to discharge (a requirement); 23 **work out, a** to pay for with labor; **b** to secure (a solution); **c** to solve (a problem); **d** to achieve through effort; **e** to exhaust, as a mine; 24 **work over, a** to make over or revise; **b** *slang* to beat severely; 25 **work up, a** to fashion or elaborate; **b** to incite or excite ‖ *n* 26 physical or mental effort directed to some end or purpose; toil, labor; 27 occupation, employment; 28 task, undertaking; 29 product of one's work, as *a work of art, literary works;* 30 material on which work is done; 31 engineering structure; 32 structure used as a fortification; 33 workmanship; 34 *phys* effect of a force in producing displacement, equal to the product of the force and the amount of the displacement in the line of action of the force, measured in ergs, foot-pounds, joules, horsepower-hours, and watt-hours; 35 mechanical treatment that a piece of metal receives, as hammering or rolling; 36 *theol* meritorious act; 37 **works** *pl* moving parts of any machinery; 38 **works** *sg* or *pl* factory; 39 **at work** working; 40 **get the works** *slang* to be victimized; 41 **give someone the works** *slang* **a** to take outrageous advantage of someone, victimize someone; **b** to treat someone roughly; 42 **gum up the works** *slang* to spoil something, as by stupid blunders; **43 shoot the works** *slang* to go all out, stint at nothing ‖ SYN *n* toil, drudgery, employment (see *labor*)

work′a·ble *adj* **1** practicable, feasible; **2** able to be, or worth being worked

work′a·day′ [ME *werkedei* workday] *adj* everyday, commonplace, prosaic

work′bench′ *n* table at which skilled work is done

work′day′ *n* **1** day on which most people work; **2** hours of a workday during which one works

worked′-up′ *adj* overwrought

work′er *n* **1** one who or that which works; **2** sterile or infertile female insect, as a bee or ant, that does work for the colony

work′ eth′ic *n* faith in the value of work

work′ farm′ *n* farm to which juvenile offenders are committed for rehabilitation

work′horse′ *n* **1** horse used for heavy work, as hauling; **2** tireless worker

work′house′ *n* (-hous·es /-ziz/) house of correction for petty offenders

work′ing *n* **1** act of one that works ‖ *adj* **2** that works; **3** sufficient to produce results; **4** needed or used for work or practical purposes; **5** used as a guide for work

work′ing class′ *n* social class composed of wage workers, esp. if unskilled or laborers ‖ **work′ing-class′** *adj*

work′ing·man′ /-man′/ *n* (-men /-men′/) one who works for a living, esp. at manual labor

work′ing or′der *n* condition of a machine in which it functions properly

work′ing pa′pers *npl* document that must be obtained by minors to enable them to work

work′ load′ *n* amount of work assigned, as to a machine, person, or group, in a given period of time

work′man /-mən/ *n* (-men /-mən/) man employed in manual labor, skilled or unskilled ‖ SYN artist, mechanic, craftsman (see *artisan*)

work′man·like′ *adj* like a good workman; **2** skillfully or competently executed

work′man·ship′ *n* **1** quality of work done on something; **2** competence in doing or making something

work′ of art′ *n* **1** piece of creative artistic work; **2** work of a practical nature which appeals also to the sense of beauty

work′out′ *n* **1** practice session, as in a sport; **2** physical exercise

work′shop′ *n* **1** building or room where work is done; **2** seminar or study group for exchange of ideas or to teach or explore new methods of accomplishing a result

work′week′ *n* total number of normal working days or hours in a week

world /wurld′/ [OE *w(e)oruld*] *n* **1** the earth; the globe; **2** mankind, humanity; **3** heavenly body; **4** the material universe; **5** particular part of the earth, as the *New World*; **6** any separate system, state, or sphere of existence, as *the world of dreams, the literary world*; **7** the public; public opinion; **8** material affairs as opposed to spiritual; **9** the people concerned with material affairs; **10** the social habits, manners, and motives of mankind; **11** current of events; course of human affairs; **12** great number or amount; **13 for all the world** in every respect; **14 in the world, a** emphatically, as *never in the world;* **b** among all possibilities, as *how in the world did you do that?;* **15 not for all the world** by no means, not under any circumstances; **16 out of this world** *colloq* excellent; **17 think the world of** to esteem highly ‖ *adj* **18** pert. to or extending over the whole world; **19** international, as *world affairs*

World′ Bank′ *n* agency of the United Nations, established at Bretton Woods in 1944 for the purpose of guaranteeing loans to member nations for their postwar reconstruction

world′-beat′er *n* person or thing surpassing all others

World′ Court′ *n* chief judicial body of the United Nations, founded in 1945 to settle disputes among the nations of the world

world′ly *adj* (-li·er; -li·est) **1** temporal, secular, of the world; **2** devoted to the pleasures and affairs of this world ‖ **world′li·ness** *n*

world′ly-wise′ *adj* wise in the ways of the world; sophisticated

world′ pow′er *n* political entity that has world-wide influence

World′ Se′ries *n* annual series of baseball games played by the champion teams of the two major leagues

world′-shak′er *n* something of great consequence ‖ **world′-shak′ing** *adj*

World′ War′ I′ *n* the world-wide war of 1914–18

World′ War′ II′ *n* the world-wide war of 1939–45

world′-wea′ry *adj* tired of this life

world′-wide′ *adj* extending throughout the world, universal

worm /wurm′/ [OE *wyrm* worm, snake] *n* **1** any small, slender, creeping or crawling, limbless or very short-limbed animal, as earthworms, insect larvae, and certain insects; **2** any device that resembles a worm, as a rotating screw that meshes with a worm gear; **3** insignificant or contemptible person; **4 worms** *sg* any disease due to the presence of parasitic worms in the intestines or tissues ‖ *vt* **5** to get or cause by crawling or by devious or insidious means; **6** to insinuate (oneself); **7** to remove worms from || *vt* 8 to accomplish or proceed by devious methods

worm′ drive′ *n* drive mechanism operated by a worm gear

worm′-eat′en *adj* 1 gnawed or bored into by worms; 2 weakened, decayed

worm′ gear′ *n* 1 gear wheel the teeth of which engage with the threads of a rotating worm; 2 combination of this wheel and the rotating worm

worm′wood′ *n* 1 any of a genus (*Artemisia*) of plants of the composite family, esp. a bitter and aromatic species (*A. absinthium*) formerly used as a remedy for worms, now used chiefly in making absinth; 2 bitterness

worm′y *adj* (-i·er; -i·est) 1 damaged by or infested with worms; 2 mean; debased; groveling

worn /wôrn′, wōrn′/ *pp* of **wear**

worn′-out′ *adj* 1 spoiled or consumed by use; 2 tired out, exhausted

wor·ri·some /wur′ēsəm/ *adj* 1 troublesome; causing anxiety; 2 fretful

wor·ry /wur′ē/ [OE *wyrgan* to strangle] *v* (-ried) *vt* 1 to bite and shake with the teeth, as a dog does; 2 to disquiet, make uneasy; 3 to trouble, torment, harass || *vi* 4 to be anxious, fret; 5 worry along or through to manage to get by || *n* (-ries) 6 anxiety, worried state of mind; 7 cause of worry || **wor′ri·er** *n* || SYN *n* vexation, harassment, anxiety (see *care*)

worse /wurs′/ [OE *wiersa*] *adj* (*comp* of **bad**) 1 bad in a greater degree; 2 less good or well in health || *adv* 3 in a more evil or extreme manner; 4 in a less good or favorable way || *n* 5 that which is worse

wors′en *vi* 1 to become worse || *vt* 2 to make worse

wor·ship /wur′ship/ [OE *weorthscipe*] *n* 1 reverence, homage, or adoration rendered to God or a deity; 2 formal rendering of such homage, as at a church service; 3 admiration, devotion, adoration, as *hero worship*; 4 *Brit* title used in addressing or referring to certain persons of high position; preceded by *your* or *his* || *v* (-shiped or -shipped; -ship·ing or -ship·ping) *vt* 5 to adore or show honor to, as God; 6 to admire excessively, idolize || *vi* 7 to render worship; 8 to attend church in order to worship || **wor′ship·er** or **wor′ship·per** *n* || SYN *v* adore, venerate, idolize, revere, exalt, deify

wor′ship·ful *adj* 1 worthy of worship; 2 given to worship

worst /wurst′/ [OE *wursta*] *adj* (*superl* of **bad**) 1 bad, evil, or ill in the highest degree; 2 most faulty or unsatisfactory; 3 in the poorest condition; 4 least skilled or able; 5 in the worst way *colloq* very much || *vt* 6 to defeat || *adv* 7 in the worst manner; 8 in the greatest degree || *n* 9 the one that is worst; 10 at worst

under the worst conditions; 11 get the worst of to be defeated in, to come out of with a loss; 12 if worst comes to worst if the worst happens

wor·sted /wōōst′id, wur′stid/ [*Worsted*, England] *n* 1 well-twisted yarn made of long-staple wool; 2 cloth having a hard smooth surface made from it

wort /wurt′/ [OE *wyrt* root, herb] *n* unfermented malt liquid which, after fermenting, becomes beer or mash

-wort′ *n comb form* plant, vegetable, as *liverwort*

worth /wurth′/ [OE *weorth*] *n* 1 excellence or desirable qualities; merit; 2 importance; 3 value, as in money; 4 quantity that can be had for a specific sum, as *ten cents′ worth*; 5 extent of possessions; riches || *adj* 6 deserving of, meriting; 7 having the actual value of; 8 priced at; 9 possessed of, as *worth a million dollars*; 10 worth one′s while worth one′s time and efforts || SYN *n* usefulness, merit, desert, character, integrity

worth′less *adj* having no worth; useless

worth′while′ *adj* worth the time, money, or trouble expended

wor·thy /wurth′ē/ *adj* (-thi·er; -thi·est) 1 excellent; honorable; estimable; 2 worthy of deserving of, meriting || *n* (-thies) 3 person of eminence or distinction

would /wōōd′, wəd/ [< OE *wolde*, *pt* of *wyllan*] *v* (*pt* of **will**²) modal *aux* used to express: 1 determination, as *he would try it in spite of everything*; 2 future action in the past in indirect discourse, as *he said he would return*; 3 customary action in the past, as *every day he would come to call*; 4 a wish, as *would that I could go along with you!*; 5 the conclusion of a condition contrary to fact, as *if he were here, he would help me*; *if he had been here, he would have helped me*

would′-be′ *adj* 1 pretending or wishing to be; 2 intended to be

would·n′t /wōōd′ənt/ would not

wound¹ /wōōnd′/ [OE *wund*] *n* 1 injury caused by violence, esp. if the skin or other tissue is cut or broken; 2 injury to reputation or feelings || *vt* 3 to inflict a wound on || also *vi*

wound² /wound′/ *pt* & *pp* of **wind²**

wove /wōv′/ *pt* & *pp* of **weave**

wo·ven /wōv′ən/ *pp* of **weave**

wow¹ /wou′/ *interj* 1 expressing surprise or admiration || *n* 2 *slang* striking success || *vt* 3 *slang* to gain the enthusiastic admiration of

wow² [imit] *n* distortion in the pitch of a reproduced sound caused by variation in speed of the sound-reproducing system

wow·ser /wou′zər/ [?] *n Australian* objectionably puritanical person

wrack′ and ru′in /rak′/ [OB *wræc* vengeance] *n* utter destruction

wraith /rāth'/ [?] *n* ghost, specter

wran·gle /raŋ'gəl/ [ME *wranglen* to wrestle] *vi* 1 to argue or dispute noisily ‖ *vt* 2 to herd or round up (livestock) ‖ *n* 3 angry or noisy dispute ‖ **wran'gler** *n*

wrap /rap'/ [ME *wrappen*] *v* (**wrapped; wrap·ping**) *vt* 1 to roll or fold, as a blanket around a child; 2 to enfold, envelop, as a child in a blanket; 3 to do up in a package; 4 **wrapped up in** engrossed in; 5 **wrap up, a** to wrap something; **b** *colloq* to conclude, finish; **c** *slang* to damage by collision ‖ *n* 6 outer garment to be wrapped around the body; 7 **keep under wraps** to keep out of sight, to keep concealed; 8 **wraps** *pl* outer garments

wrap'per *n* 1 that in which something is wrapped; 2 woman's loose informal garment, as a bathrobe

wrap'ping *n* that in which something is wrapped

wrap'-up' *n* final report or summary

wras·tle /ras'əl/ *vi, vt, & n* dial. var of **wrestle**

wrath /rath', rāth/ [OE *wrǣththo*] *n* 1 anger, fury, rage; 2 punishment; vengeance ‖ **wrath'ful** *adj* ‖ SYN rage, passion, fury, violence (see *anger*)

wreak /rēk'/ [OE *wrecan* to avenge] *vt* 1 to inflict, as punishment, revenge, etc.; 2 to vent, as anger, rage, etc.

wreath /rēth'/ [OE *wrǣth*] *n* (**wreaths** /-thz/) 1 circular band of flowers or leaves; garland; 2 anything curled or twisted into circular or spiral form, as *a wreath of smoke*

wreathe /rēth'/ *vt* 1 to give a twisted form to; 2 to make by intertwining, as a garland; 3 to encircle as with a wreath ‖ *vt* 4 to take the form of a wreath

wreck /rek'/ [< Scand] *n* 1 act or process of destruction, ruin, or disablement by force, violence, or misuse; 2 any structure, vehicle, ship, etc., that has been thus ruined or disabled; 3 ruin or destruction of anything ‖ *vt* 4 to cause the wreck of; 5 to involve in a wreck; 6 to destroy, ruin; 7 to dismantle or raze

wreck'age /-ij/ *n* 1 act of wrecking or state of being wrecked; 2 remains of something wrecked

wreck'er *n* 1 one who wrecks; 2 person or vehicle that salvages or removes wrecks; 3 one whose business or occupation is to raze or dismantle buildings

wren /ren'/ [OE *wrenna*] *n* any of a large family (Troglodytidae) of small song birds found chiefly in the New World tropics, a few species appearing in temperate climates in North America and Europe

wrench /rench'/ [OE *wrencan* to twist] *n* 1 violent turn, pull, or twist; 2 sprain, as at a joint; 3 sudden, severe distressed feeling; pang; 4 tool for grasping and turning nuts, bolts, pipes, etc. ‖ *vt* 5 to twist, wring, or pull with effort or violence; 6 to strain or injure (a joint) by twisting; 7 to distort, pervert, as a meaning

wrest /rest'/ [OE *wrǣstan*] *vt* 1 to wrench or turn, esp. from its normal state; 2 to pull or take away by force or violence

wres·tle /res'əl/ [OE *wrǣstlian*] *vi* 1 to grapple with an opponent in a hand-to-hand struggle in an endeavor to force him to the ground; 2 to struggle; strive; contend ‖ *vt* 3 to strive with in wrestling; 4 to force or move by wrestling; 5 to throw, as an animal for branding ‖ *n* 6 act of wrestling; 7 struggle ‖ **wres'tler** *n* ‖ **wres'tling** *n*

wretch /rech'/ [OE *wrecca* outcast, exile] *n* 1 miserable or unfortunate person; 2 mean contemptible person

wretch·ed /-id/ *adj* 1 miserable; unhappy; 2 causing misery; 3 mean; happy 4 poor ‖ **wretch'ed·ly** *adv* ‖ **wretch'·ed·ness** *n*

wrig·gle /rig'əl/ [MLG *wriggelen*] *vi* 1 to move by twisting and turning; 2 to squirm; writhe; 3 **wriggle out of** to extricate oneself from (a difficult situation) by devious means ‖ *vt* 4 to cause to wriggle ‖ *n* 5 wriggling motion ‖ **wrig'gly** *adj* (**-gli·er; -gli·est**)

wrig'gler *n* mosquito larva

Wright /rīt'/ *n* **Or·ville** /ôr'vil/ (1871–1948) and **Wil·bur** /wil'bər/ (1867–1912) brothers, U.S. inventors who constructed the first airplane to fly under its own power 1903

-wright /-rīt'/ [OE *wyrhta* worker] *n comb form* one who makes or constructs something, as *shipwright, playwright*

wring /riŋ'/ [OE *wringan*] *v* (**wrung**) *vt* 1 to twist or wrench forcibly; 2 to force out by twisting or pressure, as water from wet clothes; 3 to extract by twisting; 4 to extort as if by twisting; 5 to clasp and shake vigorously (a hand in greeting); 6 to affect painfully; distress ‖ *n* 7 twist, squeeze

wring'er *n* machine with rollers that squeezes the water out of wet clothes

wrin·kle¹ /riŋk'əl/ [ME] *n* 1 slight ridge caused by folding, puckering, or rumpling; crease ‖ *vt* 2 to form a wrinkle or wrinkles in ‖ *vi* 3 to become wrinkled ‖ **wrin'kly** *adj* (**-kli·er; -kli·est**)

wrin·kle² [< OE *wrenc* trick] *n colloq* clever notion; good idea

wrist /rist'/ [OE] *n* joint between the forearm and hand

wrist'band' *n* band of a sleeve, esp. a shirt sleeve, that covers the wrist

wrist′ pin′ *n* pin serving to attach a crank wheel or other moving part to a connecting rod

wrist′ watch′ *n* watch worn on a strap on the wrist

writ /rit′/ [OE] *n law* written order in the name of a court or government, ordering or prohibiting some action

write /rīt′/ [OE *wrītan* to inscribe, write] *v* (**wrote; writ·ten**) *vt* 1 to trace (symbols representing words or sounds) on a surface with an instrument, as on paper with a pen or pencil; 2 to produce as author; compose; 3 to leave traces on, engrave, as *trouble is written on his face;* 4 to address a letter to; 5 **write down** to set down in writing; 6 **write off,** a to remove (an item, as a bad debt) from an open account; b to dismiss as worthless or lost; 7 **write out** to put into writing; 8 **write up** to write an account of ‖ *vi* 9 to form letters, as with a pen or pencil; 10 to compose; 11 to write as a profession; 12 to communicate by letter; 13 to be in good working order, as a pen or pencil

write′-in′ *n* candidate or vote for a candidate not listed on the official ballot ‖ also *adj*

write′-off′ *n* 1 cancellation from an account as a loss; 2 reduction in book value

writ′er *n* 1 one who writes; 2 one who writes as a profession

write′-up′ *n* written account or record

writhe /rīth′/ [OE *wrīthan* to twist] *vi* to squirm or twist about, as from pain or distress

writ′ing *n* 1 act of one that writes; 2 state of being written; 3 that which is written; 4 art of literary production; 5 product of literary work; 6 profession of a writer

writ·ten /rit′ən/ *pp* of **write**

wrong /rôṅ, roṅ/ [OE *wrang*] *adj* 1 deviating from what is morally right or just; 2 incorrect; mistaken; 3 unsuitable, inappropriate; amiss, out of order; 4 (side of a fabric) meant to be turned away from view ‖ *n* 5 that which is wrong; evil; 6 *law* a invasion of a legal right; b tort; 7 **in the wrong** in error, mistaken ‖ *adv* 8 in a wrong manner; 9 incorrectly; 10 **go wrong, a** to go amiss; **b** to pursue an incorrect course; **c** to wind up in an immoral state ‖ *vt* 11 to treat unjustly; injure, harm ‖ **SYN** *adj* erroneous, incorrect, false, untruthful, perverse, injurious, illegal, immoral

wrong′do′ing *n* offense against law or right; evil behavior ‖ **wrong′do′er** *n*

wrong′ful *adj* 1 evil; unjust; unfair; 2 illegal ‖ **wrong′ful·ly** *adv*

wrong′-head′ed *adj* misguided; stubbornly perverse

wrote /rōt′/ *pt* of **write**

wroth /rôth′, Brit rōth′/ [OE *wrāth*] *adj* wrathful; indignant; angry

wrought /rôt′/ 1 *pt* & *pp* of **work** ‖ *adj* 2 worked, fashioned; 3 shaped by hammering

wrought′ i′ron *n* iron of low carbon content, useful because of its toughness, ductility, and malleability ‖ **wrought′-i′ron** *adj*

wrought′-up′ *adj* perturbed, excited

wrung /ruṅ/ *pt* & *pp* of **wring**

wry /rī′/ [< OE *wrigian* to drive, bend toward] *adj* (**wri·er; wri·est**) 1 twisted, askew; 2 misdirected, perverted; 3 disdainfully ironic ‖ **wry′ly** *adv*

wry′neck′ *n* spasmodic contraction of the muscles of the neck, causing an unnatural position of the head

wt. weight

wurst /wurst′, wŏŏst′/ [G] *n* sausage

W.Va. West Virginia

Wy·an·dotte /wī′əndot′/ *n* one of an American variety of domestic fowl of medium size

Wyo. Wyoming

Wy·o·ming /wī·ō′miṅ/ *n* state in the NW U.S. (332,416; 97,914 sq.m.; cap. Cheyenne) ‖ **Wy·o′ming·ite′** *n*

X

X, x /eks′/ *n* (**X's** or **Xs; x's** or **xs**) 24th letter of the English alphabet

X 1 24th in order or in a series; 2 Roman numeral 10; 3 Christ; 4 designation of a film recommended for adults only; 5 something shaped like an X

x 1 unknown quantity; 2 times, as 6 x 5; 3 by, as 2″ x 4″ ‖ *v* (**x-ed** or **x'd; x-ing** or **x'ing**) *vt* 4 often **x out** to cross out, as by writing x's over

Xan·thip·pe /zantip′ē/ *n* wife of Socrates, notorious for her shrewishness and ill nature

x′-ax′is *n* (**-ax′es** /-ēz/) *math* axis along which the abscissa is measured and from which the ordinate is measured

X′ chro·mo·some′ *n* chromosome found in humans and most mammals, carrying genes for femaleness and occurring in pairs in females and singly in males

Xe *chem* xenon

xeno- [Gk *xenos* stranger] *comb form* alien, strange

xe·non /zen′on, zēn′-/ [Gk = strange] *n* inert gaseous element (Xe; at.no. 54; at.wt. 131.30) occurring in the atmosphere in very minute quantities

xen·o·pho'bi·a /zen'ə-/ n inordinate fear or hatred of strangers or foreigners, or of strange or foreign things ‖ **xen'o·phobe'** n ‖ **xen'o·pho'bic** adj

Xen·o·phon /zen'əfən, -fon'/ n (430?-355? B.C.) Greek general, historian, and essayist

xe·ro- [Gk xeros] comb form dry

Xer·ox /zir'oks/ [trademark] n 1 process for reproducing written or printed matter by precipitating on an electrically charged surface a resinous powder in a pattern corresponding to the original ‖ vt 2 to copy by this process

Xerx·es I /zurk'sēz/ n (519–465 B.C.) king of Persia 486–465 B.C.

xi /zī', sī'/ n fourteenth letter of the Greek alphabet Ξ, ξ

X·mas /kris'məs, eks'məs/ n Christmas

X' rat'ing n rating given to reading

matter, art, stage presentations, and esp. films, indicating that they are suitable to be seen or heard by adults only ‖ **X'-rat'ed** adj

X' ray' n 1 x-ray; 2 x-ray photograph

x'-ray' /eks'-/ n 1 radiation similar to a light ray, but of shorter wave length, capable of penetrating opaque solids; used in medical diagnosis and in the treatment of certain diseases; 2 photograph made with x-rays ‖ vt 3 to examine, photograph, or treat with x-rays ‖ adj of or pert. to x-rays

xy·lem /zīl'em, zīl'əm/ [< Gk xylon wood] n the woody tissue of plants; esp., in higher plants, the supporting and water-conducting cells of the vascular bundle

xy·lo- also **xy·l-** [Gk xylon] comb form wood

xy'lo·phone' /zīl'ə-/ n mus instrument made of parallel wooden bars of graduated length, which are struck with mallets

Y

Y, y /wī'/ n (**Y's** or **Ys; y's** or **ys**) 25th letter of the English alphabet

Y 1 25th in order or in a series; 2 chem yttrium; 3 something shaped like a Y

-y¹ /-ē/ [ME] n suf forming diminutives, as kitty, Katy

-y² [OE -ig] adj suf of, pert. to, having, characterized by, or full of, as stony, guilty, grouchy

yacht /yot'/ [< D jaght(schip) (ship) for chasing] n 1 vessel used privately for cruising, racing, etc. ‖ vi 2 to sail in a yacht ‖ **yacht'ing** n ‖ **yachts'man** /-mən/ n (-men /-mən/)

yack·e·ty-yack /yak'itēyak'/ [?] slang n 1 idle, unceasing talk ‖ vi 2 to engage in yackety-yack

yah /yä'/ interj exclamation of impatience, derision, or disgust

ya·hoo /yä'hōō, yä'-/ [Yahoo, one of a race of brutish people in Swift's Gulliver's Travels] n uncouth, ignorant, loutish person

Yah·weh /yä'we/ also **Yah'veh** /-ve/ [Heb] n modern transliteration of a Hebrew name for God, written Jehovah in the King James version of the Bible

yak /yak'/ [Tibetan gyag] n wild or domesticated long-haired ox (Poephagus grunniens) of central Asia

Yal·ta /yôl'tə/ n port on the Black Sea in the Soviet Union (48,000); site of wartime conference of Roosevelt, Churchill, and Stalin 1945

Ya·lu /yäl'ōō/ n river forming part of the North Korea-Manchuria border

and flowing about 300 miles SW to the Yellow Sea

yam /yam'/ [< Port inhame < WAfr] n 1 edible root of any of a genus (Dioscorea) of tropical vines; 2 S U.S. sweet potato

Yang·tze /yaŋ'sē/ n river rising in Tibet and flowing E through central China to the East China Sea

yank /yaŋk'/ [?] n 1 sharp jerk or pull ‖ vt 2 to jerk, pull, or pull out sharply

Yank /yaŋk'/ n slang Yankee

Yan·kee /yaŋk'ē/ [prob < D Jan Kees nickname applied by the Dutch of New York to the English colonists of Connecticut] n 1 native or inhabitant of New England; 2 native or inhabitant of the U.S.; 3 native or inhabitant of the North of the U.S. ‖ also adj

Yan'kee·dom n 1 a New England; b the North of the U.S.; 2 the United States; 3 Yankees collectively

Ya·oun·dé /yä·ōōndā'/ n capital of Cameroon (100,000)

yap /yap'/ [imit] v (**yapped; yap·ping**) vi 1 to bark or yelp; 2 slang to jabber, chatter ‖ n 3 bark or yelp; 4 slang noisy foolish talk; 5 slang mouth

yard¹ /yärd'/ [OE gyrd stick] n 1 standard unit of linear measure in most English-speaking countries, equal to three feet or 36 inches; 2 naut comparatively slender spar slung crosswise to a mast to support a sail

yard[2] [OE *geard* court] *n* **1** small piece of enclosed ground beside or around a building; **2** any outdoor space surrounded by buildings; **3** space, often enclosed, within which any work is carried on, as *a brickyard;* **4** place for making up trains, storing cars and locomotives when not in use, etc.; **5 the Yard** Scotland Yard

yard'age /-ij/ *n* measurement or the amount measured in yards

yard'arm' *n naut* either end of the yard that supports a sail

yard' goods' *npl* piece goods

yard'stick' *n* **1** graduated measuring stick 36 inches in length; **2** any standard of measurement

yar·mul·ke also **yar·mel·ke** /yär'məlkə, yä'-/ [Yiddish] *n* skullcap worn by male Jews, esp. during prayer

yarn /yärn'/ [OE *gearn*] *n* **1** any thread spun from natural or synthetic fibers, used for weaving and knitting; **2** *colloq* tale or story

yaw /yô'/ [?] *vi* **1** to turn unintentionally, fail to hold a steady course, as a vessel or plane; **2** to oscillate about a longitudinal axis in the horizontal plane, as a rocket or projectile || *n* **3** act or amount of yawing

yawl /yôl'/ [D *jol* skiff] *n* **1** two-masted fore-and-aft-rigged vessel having the smaller mast aft of the rudder post; **2** small boat of a ship

yawn /yôn'/ [OE *geonian*] *vi* **1** to open the mouth wide involuntarily while inhaling, as from drowsiness, boredom, or fatigue; **2** to gape, open wide || *n* **3** act of yawning

yaws /yôz'/ [< WInd] *nsg* contagious skin disease of the tropics, characterized by raspberrylike excrescences

y'-ax'is *n* (-ax'es /-ēz/) *math* axis along which the ordinate is measured, and from which the abscissa is measured

Yb *chem* ytterbium

Y' chro'mo·some' *n* chromosome found in most mammals and man and carrying genes for maleness, occurring singly and in males only

y-cleped or **y-clept** /ēklept'/ [< *obs. clepe* to call] *adj archaic* called, named

yd. yard(s)

yds. yards

ye[1] /yē'/ [OE *gē*] *pron archaic & poet.* you

ye[2] /thē, thə, yē/ [y represents the OE letter þ, called **thorn**] *archaic* the (used mostly in signs, as *Ye Olde Tea Shoppe*)

yea /yā'/ [OE *gēa*] *adv* **1** *archaic* **a** yes (expressing affirmation or assent); **b** indeed || *n* **2** reply of assent; **3** affirmative vote; **4** affirmative voter

yeah /ye'(ə)/ *adv colloq* yes

yean'ling /yēn'-/ [ME *yenen* to bring forth young] *n* lamb or kid; young of a sheep or goat

year /yir'/ [OE *gēar*] *n* **1** length of time required by the earth to make one complete revolution around the sun, consisting of 365 days, 5 hours, 48 minutes, and 46 seconds; **2** period of twelve months consisting of 365 or 366 days, beginning January 1 and ending December 31; **3** any period of twelve consecutive months; **4** any period out of a full year devoted to a recurring activity, as *the school year;* **5 years** *pl* **a** age; **b** old age; **c** a long time

year'book' *n* book published or revised annually, containing statistics or other currently important information

year'ling [ME] *n* **1** animal between one and two years old; **2** racehorse considered one year old, dating from January 1st of the year after the year in which it was foaled

year'long' *adj* lasting a year

year'ly *adj* **1** pert. to a year or to each year; **2** happening or coming once a year or every year; **3** lasting or continuing for a year || *adv* **4** once a year, annually || *n* (-lies) **5** yearly publication

yearn /yurn'/ [OE *giernan*] *vi* **1** to be filled with longing; **2** to be deeply moved

yearn'ing *n* deep longing

year'-round' *adj* continuing or operating throughout the year

yeast /yēst'/ [OE *gist*] *n* **1** yellowish frothy substance consisting of minute cells, causing fermentation in sugar solutions or starchy substances, used to make fermented liquors, to cause dough to rise, and in medicine; **2** froth; foam; **3** mental ferment; agitation

yeast'y *adj* (-i-er; -i-est) **1** of, resembling, or containing yeast; **2** frothy, foamy; **3** trifling, frivolous; **4** ebullient; agitated

yegg /yeg'/ [?] *n slang* thug; burglar; criminal

yell /yel'/ [OE *giellan*] *n* **1** sharp loud cry; scream; **2** characteristic shout or cheer, as *a college yell* || *vi* **3** to utter a yell || *vt* **4** to utter with a yell

yel·low /yel'ō/ [OE *geolu*] *adj* **1** of the color of ripe lemons; **2** having a yellowish skin; **3** of or pert. to the Mongoloid races; **4** *colloq* cowardly; **5** sensational (journalism or newspaper) || *n* **6** yellow color; **7** yellow pigment or dye; **8** egg yolk || *vt* **9** to make yellow || *vi* **10** to become yellow || **yel'low·ness** *n*

yel'low-bel'lied *adj slang* cowardly

yel'low fe'ver *n* acute infectious fever, chiefly of tropical America, characterized by yellowness of the skin, vomiting, etc., and transmitted by a mosquito, *Aedes aegypti*

yel'low·ish *adj* somewhat yellow

yel'low·jack'et *n* any of several social

wasps (family Vespidae) with a black abdomen spotted or banded with yellow

yel'low pag'es *npl* classified section of a telephone directory, listing businesses and services alphabetically

Yel'low Sea' *n* arm of the Pacific between N China and Korea

yel'low streak' *n colloq* cowardly element in one's make-up

yelp /yelp'/ [OE *gielpan* to boast] *n* 1 sharp quick bark or cry || *vi* 2 to utter a yelp

Yem·en /yem'ən/ *n* Arabic-speaking republic in SW Arabia (5,000,000; 75,000 sq.m.; cap. San'a) || **Yem'-en·ite'** also **Yem'e·ni** /-ənē/ *adj & n*

yen[1] /yen'/ [Jap < Chin *yüan* round, dollar] *n* (*pl* **yen**) monetary unit of Japan

yen[2] [?] *n colloq* craving, desire

yeo·man /yōm'ən/ [ME *yoman*] *n* (-men /-mən/) 1 *Brit* a formerly, freeholder ranking below the gentry; **b** small landowner or farmer; **2** *U.S. Navy* petty officer who does clerical work || *adj* **3** of or pert. to a yeoman; **4** staunch, valiant, workmanlike

yeo'man of the guard' *n* soldier of the bodyguard of the British sovereign

yeo'man·ry *n* 1 yeomen collectively; **2** *Brit* cavalry of the Territorial Army, composed of gentlemen and farmers

yes /yes'/ [OE *gese*] *adv* 1 it is so (the affirmative answer to a question); **2** furthermore; what is more; **3** expressing strong contradiction to a negative statement, as *you can't do that!; Yes I can!;* **4** expressing polite interest, as *Yes? What is it?* || *n* 5 affirmative reply || *v* (**yessed; yes·sing**) *tr* to give an affirmative reply to

yes' man' *n* one who slavishly agrees with his superior

yes·ter·day /yes'tərdē, -dā'/ [OE *geostran dæg*] *n* 1 day preceding the current day; **2** a recent day || *adv* 3 on the day before today; **4** a short time ago

yet /yet'/ [OE *gīet*] *adv* 1 now, as *don't go yet;* **2** up until a specific time, as *he has not come yet;* **3** in addition, besides, as *bigger yet;* **4** finally, eventually, as *the day will yet come;* **5** nevertheless || *conj* 6 nevertheless, however

yew /yōo'/ [OE *īw*] *n* any of several cone-bearing evergreen trees (genus *Taxus*) yielding a fine-grained wood, formerly much used for making bows

Yid·dish /yid'ish/ [G *jüdisch* Jewish] *n* language of the Ashkenazi Jews of E Europe, a High German dialect with many words from Hebrew and Slavic, written in Hebrew letters || also *adj*

yield /yēld'/ [OE *gieldan* to pay] *vt* 1 to produce, as *the land yields wheat;*

2 to give as a return for labor, money invested, etc.; **3** to concede as true, acknowledge, as *I yield the point;* **4** to give up, surrender, relinquish || *vi* **5** to give a return, produce; **6** to assent, comply; **7** to give way, submit, surrender || *n* 8 that which is yielded; **9** amount yielded; **10** income from an investment || SYN *v* afford, relinquish, surrender, produce, give, comply || ANT *v* defy, refuse, resist, endure

yield'ing *adj* 1 inclined to give way; flexible; **2** compliant; submissive

-yl [< Gk *hyle* wood, substance] *suf chem* used to designate a radical, as *ethyl*

Y.M.C.A. Young Men's Christian Association

Y.M.H.A. Young Men's Hebrew Association

yod /yōd'/ [10th letter of the Hebrew alphabet] *n ling* sound represented by the *y* of *year* or the second *i* of *William*

yo·del /yōd'əl/ [G *jodeln*] *v* (**-deled** or **-delled; -del·ing** or **-del·ling**) *vi* 1 to sing or call with sudden changes in the voice from normal to falsetto || *vt* 2 to give or render thus || *n* 3 call so given or song so sung || **yo'del·er** or **yo'del·ler** *n*

yo·ga also **Yo·ga** /yōg'ə/ [Skt = union] *n* 1 form of Hindu philosophy that enjoins withdrawal from worldly things and a concentration of thought upon spiritual things; **2** exercises designed to promote the attainment of this end

yo·gi /yōg'ē/ [Hindi] *n* one who practices yoga

yo·gurt or **yo·ghurt** /yōg'ərt/ [Turk *yoghurt*] *n* thick semiliquid food made from milk curdled by the addition of certain bacterial cultures

yoke /yōk'/ [OE *geoc*] *n* 1 wooden frame, usu. with a bow at each end, to couple together draft animals, esp. oxen, by the neck; **2** any of several similar devices, as a wooden frame made to fit a person's shoulders, for carrying buckets, etc. suspended from the ends; **3** piece of cloth cut to fit the shoulders or hips to support a gathered or plaited part, as of a skirt; **4** that which binds or connects; bond or tie; **5** mark or sign of slavery or subjection; **6** bondage, servitude || *n* (*pl* **yoke**) **7** pair of animals coupled together by a yoke || *vt* 8 to put a yoke on; **9** to join, couple, link

yo·kel /yōk'əl/ [?] *n* country bumpkin

yolk /yō(l)k/ [OE *geolca*] *n* yellow part of an egg, containing the embryo and food material to support it

Yom Kip·pur /yom kip'ər/ [Heb] *n* the Hebrew Day of Atonement, observed by 24 hours of fasting and prayer on the 10th day of the first month of the Jewish civil year

yon /yon′/ [OE *geon*] *poet. adj & adv*
1 yonder || *pron* 2 that or those
yonder

yon·der /yon′dər/ [ME] *adj* 1 situated
at a distance, but still visible || *adv*
2 at that place; there

yore /yôr′, yōr′/ [OE *gēara*] *n* of yore
poet. & literary in old time; long ago

York′shire pud′ding /yôrk′shir, -shər/
n unsweetened batter pudding baked
under beef or other meat

York′town *n* village in SE Virginia,
where the American Revolution
ended with the surrender of Cornwallis to Washington October 19,
1781

you /yōō′, yōō, yə/ [OE *ēow acc &
dat* of *gē* ye] *pron* (*2nd pers sg &
pl nom & objective*) 1 person or
persons addressed or spoken to; 2
one, anyone; a person, people generally, as *because of the noise you
can hardly hear what he is saying*

you-all /yōō-ôl′, yôl′/ *pron S U.S.*
used with plural meaning of you

you'd /yōōd′/ you had or you would

you'll /yōōl′/ you will or you shall

young /yuŋ′/ [OE *geong*] *adj* (younger /yuŋ′gər/, young-est /yuŋ′gist/) 1
being in an early period of life or
development; 2 vigorous, fresh,
strong; 3 inexperienced; 4 of or pert.
to youth; 5 of youthful appearance
|| *n* 6 young offspring; 7 **the young**
pl young people generally

young′ster *n* child or young person

Young′ Turk′ [< Turkish political
party founded in late 19th cent. to
reform and modernize Turkey] *n*
member of any political party or
movement that aggressively advocates immediate reform

your /yôr′, yər/ [OE *ēower*] *adj* possessive of **you**; of or belonging to
you

you're /yōōr′/ you are

yours /yōōrz′/ *pron* that or those belonging to you

your·self′ *pron* (-**selves** /-vz/) 1 reflexive form of **you**; 2 emphatic
form of **you**, as *go yourself*; 3 your
normal self, as *you're not yourself
today*

yours′ tru′ly *pron* 1 conventional
phrase used to end a letter, placed
just above the signature; 2 *colloq* I
or me

youse /yōōz′, yəz/ *pron illit* plural of
you

youth /yōōth′/ [OE *geoguth*] *n* (**youths**
/-ths, -thz/) *n* 1 state or quality of
being young; 2 young person, esp. a
young man; 3 period of life between
childhood and maturity; 4 early
period of anything; 5 young people
collectively

youth′ful *adj* 1 young; 2 of, pert. to,
characterized by, or befitting youth;
3 fresh; vigorous; 4 immature; not
advanced || **youth′ful·ness** *n* || SYN
fresh, childlike, young, buoyant,
vigorous || ANT old, mature, aged,
senile, withered

you've /yōōv′/ you have

yowl /youl′/ [ME *youle*] *n* 1 howl;
long yell || *vi* 2 to utter a yowl

yo-yo /yō′yō/ [*Yo-Yo* former trade-
mark] *n* toy resembling a flat spool
which may be made to spin and move
up and down a string wound around
it

yr. 1 year; 2 your

yrs. 1 years; 2 yours

Yt *chem* yttrium

yt·ter·bi·um /iturb′ē-əm/ [< *Ytterby*,
Sweden] *n* very rare metallic element (**Yb**; at.no. 70; at.wt. 173.04)
of the rare-earth group, resembling
yttrium

yt·tri·um /i′trē-əm/ [*Ytterby*, Sweden]
n rare, trivalent metallic element (**Y**,
Yt; at.no. 39; at.wt. 88.905)

Yu·ca·tán /yōō′kətan′/ *n* peninsula in
SE Mexico between the Gulf of
Mexico and the Caribbean

yuc·ca /yuk′ə/ [Sp *yuca* < Taino] *n*
any of a genus (*Yucca*) of plants of
the lily family bearing long pointed
leaves and white blossoms, found
in the warmer regions of America

Yu·go·sla·vi·a /yōōg′ōsläv′ē-ə/ *n* republic in SE Europe in the Balkans
(20,500,000; 98,767 sq.m.; cap. Bel-
grade) || **Yu′go·slav′** /-släv′, -slav′/
also **Yu·go·sla′vi·an** *adj & n*

Yu·kon /yōō′kon/ *n* river flowing NW
from NW Canada to Alaska and SW
to the Bering Sea

Yu′kon Ter′ri·to′ry *n* territory in NW
Canada (14,382; 207,076 sq.m.; cap.
Whitehorse)

yule /yōōl′/ [OE *gēol*] *n* Christmas or
the Christmas season

yule′ log′ *n* log traditionally forming
the backlog of the fire at Christmas

yule′tide′ *n* Christmas time; the holiday season

yum·my /yum′ē/ [?] *adj* (-**mi·er**; -**mi·
est**) *colloq* 1 delicious; 2 very attractive

Y.W.C.A. Young Women's Christian
Association

Y.W.H.A. Young Women's Hebrew
Association

Z

Z, z /zē′, *Brit* zed′/ *n* (**Z's** or **Zs**; **z's** or
zs) 26th and last letter of the Eng-
lish alphabet

Z 1 26th in order or in a series; 2 something shaped like a Z

Za·ire /zä·ir′/ *n* republic in central

Africa, formerly the Belgian Congo (22,500,000; 890,000 sq.m.; cap. Kinshasa) ‖ **Za·ir′e·an** or **Za·ir′i·an** *adj & n*

Zam·bi·a /zam′bē-ə/ *n* republic in S Africa (4,300,000; 290,586 sq.m.; cap. Lusaka)

za·ny /zān′ē/ [It *dial. Zanni* John] *adj* (-ni·er; -ni·est) 1 ludicrously comical; clownish ‖ *n* (-nies) 2 zany person

Zan·zi·bar /zan′zĭbär′/ *n* island off the E coast of central Africa; former British colony, now part of Tanzania

zeal /zēl′/ [Gk *zelos*] *n* ardor in a cause or in promoting some end; eager enthusiasm

zeal·ot /zel′ət/ [Gk *zelotes*] *n* excessively zealous person; fanatic

zeal·ous /zel′əs/ *adj* showing, characterized by, or full of zeal; enthusiastic ‖ **zeal′ous·ly** *adv*

ze·bra /zēb′rə/ [Port] *n* any of several horselike African wild animals (genus *Equus*) with dark stripes on a white or tawny body

ze′bra cross′ing /Brit often zeb′rə/ *n* safety crossing on a street, marked with painted white stripes

ze·bu /zēb′(y)ōō/ [F < Tibetan] *n* one of an Asiatic breed of domestic cattle (*Bos indicus*) with a large hump on the shoulders and a large dewlap

zed /zed′/ [ME < *zeta*] *n* Brit the letter Z

Zen /zen′/ [Jap] *n* Japanese sect of Buddhism that teaches enlightenment by direct intuition rather than by formal study

ze·nith /zēn′ith, Brit zen′-/ [OSp *zenit* < Ar *samt*-(ar-rās) way (of the head)] *n* 1 point of the heavens directly over the observer's head; 2 highest point; summit

zeph·yr /zef′ər/ [Gk *zephyros* west wind] *n* soft gentle breeze

Zep·pe·lin /zep′əlin/ [F. von *Zeppelin* G inventor] *n* large cigar-shaped, rigid, dirigible balloon

ze·ro /zir′ō/ [It < Ar *sifr* cipher] *n* (-ros or -roes) 1 cipher; 2 nothing; 3 point on a scale from which reckoning begins, either in a positive or negative direction; 4 lowest point ‖ *vt* 5 to adjust, as a gauge or meter, to the zero point; 6 zero in a to adjust the sight setting of (a rifle) by calibrated firing on a range ‖ *vi* 7 a, zero in on to find the exact range of (a target); b to concentrate sharply on

ze′ro grav′i·ty *n* lack of apparent weight because of the neutralization of the pull of gravitation

ze′ro hour′ *n* 1 mil time at which an attack is set to begin; 2 critical or crucial moment

ze′ro pop′u·la′tion growth′ *n* balance in the average number of births and deaths after a period of growth

zest /zest′/ [F *zeste* lemon or orange peel] *n* 1 something added to give

pleasant taste or relish; 2 keen enjoyment; 3 piquant charm ‖ **zest′ful** *adj*

ze·ta /zēt′ə, zāt′ə/ *n* sixth letter of the Greek alphabet Z, ζ

Zeus /zōōs′/ *n Gk myth.* the son of Cronus, who overthrew his father and became the supreme god; identified with the Roman Jupiter

zig·zag /zig′zag′/ [F] *n* 1 course or line the direction of which changes in sharp turns alternately from one side to the other; 2 part of such course between successive turns ‖ *adv* 3 in a zigzag course ‖ *v* (-zagged; -zag·ging) 4 to move or form in a zigzag manner

zil·lion /zil′yən/ [modeled on *million*] *n colloq* indeterminately large number

Zim·ba·bwe-Rho·de·sia /zimbä′bwe rōdēzh′ə/ *n* republic in S Africa (7,000,000; 150,685 sq.m.; cap. Salisbury)

zinc /zink′/ [G *zink*] *n* bluish-white metallic element (**Zn**; at.no. 30; at. wt. 65.37) used in making brass, bronze, German silver, and other alloys and in galvanizing

zinc′ ox′ide *n* white powder —ZnO— used chiefly as a pigment, in medicine, in making opaque glass, etc.

zing /zing′/ [imit] *n* 1 sharp shrill noise; 2 animation, verve ‖ *vi* 3 to move with a zing ‖ *vt* 4 to cause to move with a zing

zin·ni·a /zin′ē-ə, -yə/ [J. G. *Zinn* (1727–59) G botanist] *n* any of several species of a plant (genus *Zinnia*) bearing bright-colored dahlialike flowers

Zi·on /zī′ən/ [Heb *tsīyōn*] *n* 1 hill in Jerusalem, site of the Temple; 2 the Jewish people; 3 Palestine considered as the homeland of the Jews; 4 heaven

Zi′on·ism *n* movement formerly for establishing a homeland for the Jews, now for supporting the state of Israel

zip[1] /zip′/ [imit] *n* 1 sudden hissing sound, like that of a bullet in flight; 2 speed; verve, energy ‖ *v* (zipped; zip·ping) *vt & vi* 3 to move with a zip; 4 to move with great speed

zip[2] [< *zipper*] *v* (zipped; zip·ping) *vt & vi* to close and fasten with a zipper

zip′ code′ or **ZIP′ code′** [zone *improvement plan*] *n* five-digit code number written after the address on mail, designating the state, region, and locality

zip′ gun′ *n* homemade pistol usu. firing a .22-caliber bullet

zip′per [*Zipper* former trademark] *n* 1 device for closing and fastening clothing, cases, valises, etc., having a toothed track on each edge and a piece that slides along the tracks to lock or separate them ‖ *vt & vi* 2 to close and fasten with a zipper

zir·con /zur′kon/ [G] *n* native zirconium silicate —Zr₂SiO₄—, transparent varieties of which are used as gems

zir·co·ni·um /zərkōn′ē·əm/ [NL < *zircon*] *n* lustrous blackish-gray metallic element (Zr; at.no. 40; at.wt. 91.22) resembling titanium and found widely distributed in nature; useful as a constituent of various alloys and in compounds as an agency for resisting heat and acids

zith·er /zith′ər/ [G < Gk *kithara*] *n mus* instrument with about 36 strings over a flat sounding box, played in a horizontal position by plucking with a plectrum and the fingers

zlo·ty /zlô′tē/ [Pol = gold piece] *n* (-tys) monetary unit of Poland

Zn *chem* zinc

zo- var of **zoo-**

-zo·a /-zō′ə/ *pl of* **-zoon**

zo·di·ac /zōd′ē·ak′/ [Gk *zodiakos* of or pert. to animals] *n* 1 imaginary belt of constellations extending eight degrees on each side of the ecliptic, containing the paths of the sun, moon, planets, and most of the asteroids, and divided into twelve equal parts called signs, named after certain constellations but no longer coinciding with them, as the signs have shifted about twenty-five degrees behind their respective constellations because of precession; 2 figure or diagram representing this belt, used in astrology || **zo·di·a·cal** /-dī′əkəl/ *adj*

Zom·ba /zom′bə/ *n* capital of Malawi (19,616)

zom·bie /zom′bē/ [< WAfr] *n* 1 corpse animated by supernatural power; 2 drink made with rum, citrus juices, and other ingredients; 3 *slang* eccentric person; 4 *slang* exceptionally dull and stupid person

zone /zōn′/ [Gk *zone* girdle] *n* 1 any encircling belt, band, strip, or path; 2 *math* portion of the surface of a sphere included between two parallel planes which intersect the sphere; 3 any of the five sections into which the earth's surface is divided by imaginary lines parallel to the equator, and named for the prevailing temperature; 4 one of the sections into which a transportation line is divided for the purpose of determining the fare; 5 area including all post offices between two specified radial distances from a given mailing point, used in determining postal rates for parcels; 6 area distinct because of its use, natural characteristics, etc., as *a safety zone, desert zone;* 7 urban district restricted as to its use, as *a residential zone;* 8 time zone || *vt* 9 to encircle; 10 to divide into zones; 11 to specify the types of buildings that may be constructed or the use to which the land may be put in (a

given district of a city or town) || **zon′al** *adj*

Zon·i·an /zōn′ē·ən/ *n* U.S. citizen resident in the Canal Zone || also *adj*

zoo /zōō′/ [*zoo*logical garden] *n* park or other large enclosure in which living animals are kept for public exhibition

zo·o- [Gk] *comb form* animal, living being

zo′o·log′i·cal /zō′ə-/ *adj* 1 pert. to zoology; 2 pert. to animals or animal life

zo′o·log′i·cal gar′den *n* zoo

zo·ol·o·gy /zō·ol′əjē/ *n* (-gies) branch of biology dealing with animal life || **zo·ol′o·gist** *n*

zoom /zōōm′/ [imit] *vi* 1 to move quickly with a loud buzzing sound; 2 to fly an airplane upward at a steep angle suddenly and at a great speed; 3 *photog* to magnify or reduce an image suddenly by adjusting a zoom lens || *vt* 4 to cause to zoom || *n* 5 sound of zooming; 6 act or process of zooming

zoom′ lens′ *n* lens assembly with individual elements whose positions relative to each other can be quickly changed, providing focal lengths varying from those provided by relatively wide-angle lenses to those provided by telephoto lenses, without having to change lenses

-zo·on /-zō′on/ [Gk] *comb form* animal

zo·o·phyte /zō′əfīt′/ [*zoo-* + Gk *phyton* plant] *n* any animal that has the appearance of a plant, as a coral or sponge || **zo′o·phyt′ic** /-fit′-/ *adj*

zo′o·spore′ *n* freely swimming spore or reproductive cell of a flowerless plant, as in some algae and fungi

Zo·ro·as·tri·an·ism /zōr′ō·as′trē·əniz′-əm/ [< *Zoroaster* Persian religious teacher of the 6th cent. B.C.] *n* the religion of the Persian before the conversion of the majority to Mohammedanism, characterized by belief in a supreme deity and in a continuing struggle between the forces of good and evil; now professed chiefly by some Iranians and the Parsees of India || **Zo′ro·as′tri·an** *adj & n*

Zou·ave /zōō·äv′/ [F < Ar *Zwāwa* Algerian tribe] *n* 1 member of a French infantry unit originally composed of Algerians, wearing a distinctive uniform with baggy trousers; 2 member of units in other armies adopting a similar dress and drill, esp. one of the volunteer regiments in the American Civil War

zounds /zoundz′/ [contr. of *God's wounds*] *interj archaic* mild oath

Zr *chem* zirconium

zuc·chet·to /zōōket′ō/ [It] *n* skullcap worn by Roman Catholic ecclesiastics varying in color according to the rank of the wearer

zuc·chi·ni /zōōkēn′ē̠/ [It] *n* variety of
summer squash, shaped like a cucumber

Zu·lu /zōō′lōō/ *n* **1** one of a warlike
native tribe of Natal, South Africa;
2 their language ‖ also *adj*

Zu·ñi /zōō′nyē̠, sōōn′-/ [Sp < Keresan]
n **1** one of a tribe of Pueblo Indians
of New Mexico; **2** their language ‖
Zu′ñi·an *adj*

zwie·back /zwī′bak′/ [G = twice
baked] *n* kind of biscuit or roll first
baked in the form of a loaf and then
sliced and browned in the oven

zy·gote /zī′gōt, zig′ōt/ [Gk *zygotos*
yoked] *n biol* product of the union
of two gametes; fertilized ovum

zy·m- or **zy·mo-** [Gk *zyme* leaven] *comb
form* fermentation, leaven

zy·mur·gy /zī′murjē̠/ *n* branch of
chemistry dealing with fermentation,
as in winemaking

PRINCIPAL LANGUAGES OF THE WORLD

Listed are 175 languages spoken natively by at least 1 million persons. (Parentheses indicate the areas where they are *chiefly* spoken.)

The ten largest languages each have over 100 million native speakers. In descending order they are Chinese, English, Russian, Spanish, Hindi, Bengali, Arabic, Portuguese, German, and Japanese.

	Millions
Achinese (Indonesia)	2
Afrikaans (S. Africa)	5
Albanian	3
Amharic (Ethiopia)	9
Arabic	125
Armenian	4
Assamese (India)	15
Aymara (Bolivia, Peru)	1.5
Azerbaijani (USSR, Iran)	8
Balinese (Bali)	3
Baluchi (Pakistan, Iran)	3
Bambara (Mali)	1.5
Bashkir (USSR)	1
Batak (Indonesia)	2
Bemba (Zambia)	1
Bengali (Bangladesh, India)	130
Berber (N. Africa)	8
Bhili (India)	4
Bihari (India)	22
Bikol (Philippines)	2
Breton (France)	1
Buginese (Indonesia)	2
Bulgarian	9
Burmese	25
Byelorussian (USSR)	10
Cambodian (see Khmer)	
Catalan (Spain)	6
Cebuano (Philippines)	8
Chinese	1,000
Chuang (China)	6
Chuvash (USSR)	2
Congo (see Kongo)	
Czech	11
Danish	5
Dayak (Borneo)	1
Dinka (Sudan)	1
Dutch-Flemish (Netherlands, Belgium)	20
Edo (W. Africa)	1
Elik (Nigeria)	2
English	360

	Millions
Esperanto (not native)	1
Estonian	1
Ewe (E. Ghana, Togo)	2
Fang (Cameroon, Gabon)	1.5
Finnish	5
Fon (Benin)	1
French	90
Fula, Fulani (W. Africa)	10
Galician (Spain)	2
Galla (Ethiopia)	7
Ganda (Uganda)	3
Georgian (USSR)	3
German (Germany, Austria, Switzerland)	120
Gilaki (Iran)	1
Gondi (India)	2
Greek	10
Guarani (Paraguay)	3
Gujarati (India)	30
Hausa (W. and Central Africa)	20
Hebrew (Israel)	3
Hindi (India)	210
Hungarian	13
Ibibio (see Elik)	
Ibo (E. Nigeria)	10
Ijaw (W. Africa)	1
Ilocano, Iloko (Philippines)	4
Indonesian	50
Italian	60
Japanese	110
Javanese (Indonesia)	45
Kamba (Kenya)	1
Kanarese, Kannada (India)	30
Kanuri (W. and Central Africa)	2
Karen (Burma)	2
Kashmiri	3
Kazakh (USSR)	5
Khakha, Khalkha (Mongolia)	1
Khmer (Cambodia)	7
Kikongo (see Kongo)	
Kikuyu (Kenya, Tanzania)	2
Kimbunku (see Mbundu)	
Kirghiz (USSR)	2
Kituba (Congo, Zaire)	2
Kongo (Congo, Zaire)	2
Konkani (India)	2
Korean	52
Kumauni (India)	1
Kurdish	7
Kurukh (India)	1
Lao (Laos)	3
Latvian	2

	Millions		Millions
Lingala (Congo, Zaire)	2	Russian (USSR)	230
Lithuanian	3	Samar-Leyte (Philippines)	1
Luba (Congo, Zaire)	3	Sango (Central Africa)	1
Luganda (see Ganda)		Santali (India)	4
Luhya (Kenya)	1	Sepedi (see Sotho)	
Luo (Kenya)	1	Serbo-Croatian (Yugoslavia)	18
Luri (Iran)	1	Shan (Burma)	1
Macedonian (Yugoslavia)	1	Shona (S.E. Africa)	4
Madurese (Indonesia)	7	Siamese (see Thai)	
Makua (Mozambique)	2	Sidamo (Ethiopia)	4
Malagasy	3	Sindhi (India, Pakistan)	9
Malayalam (India)	25	Singhalese (Sri Lanka)	10
Malay-Indonesian	95	Slovak	4
Malinke (W. Africa)	2	Slovenian (Yugoslavia)	2
Mangbetu (Congo)	1	Somali (Somalia, Ethiopia)	5
Marathi (India)	55	Sotho (S. Africa)	4
Mayan (Mexico)	2.5	Spanish	215
Mazandarini (Iran)	1	Sukuma (Tanzania)	1
Mbundu (Angola)	3	Sundanese (Indonesia)	15
Mende (Sierra Leone)	1	Swahili (E. Africa)	20
Miao (China)	2.5	Swedish	10
Minangkabau (Indonesia)	3	Tadzhik (USSR)	2
Moldavian (Rumania)	2.5	Tagalog (Philippines)	21
Mongolian (see Khakha)		Tajiki (USSR)	3
Mordvin (USSR)	1	Tamil (India, Sri Lanka)	55
More, Mossi (Upper Volta)	3	Tatar (USSR)	6
Nahuatlan (Mexico)	1	Telugu (India)	53
Ndongo (see Mbundu)		Thai (Thailand)	30
Nepali (Nepal, India)	10	Tibetan	7
Ngala (see Lingala)		Tigrinya (Ethiopia)	4
Norwegian	4	Tiv (Nigeria)	1
Nyamwezi-Sukuma		Tswana (S. Africa)	2
(S.E. Africa)	1	Tulu (India)	1
Nyanja (Malawi, Zambia)	4	Turkish	39
Oraon (see Kurukh)		Turkoman (USSR)	2
Oriya (India)	25	Twi (Ghana)	4
Panay-Hilgaynon (Philippines)	4	Uighur (China)	4
Pedi (see Sotho)		Ukrainian (USSR)	42
Persian (Iran, Afghanistan)	25	Urdu (Pakistan, India)	60
Polish	35	Uzbek (USSR)	9
Portuguese (Portugal, Brazil)	125	Vietnamese	37
Provençal (France)	4	Visayan (Philippines)	15
Punjabi (India)	55	Welsh (Wales)	1
Pushtu (Afghanistan)	15	Wolof (Senegal)	2
Quechua (S. America)	6	Xhosa (S. Africa)	5
Rajasthani (India)	22	Yi (China)	3
Ruanda (Rwanda, Congo)	6	Yiddish	4
Rumanian	22	Yoruba (W. Nigeria)	12
Rundi (Burundi)	3	Zulu (S. Africa)	5

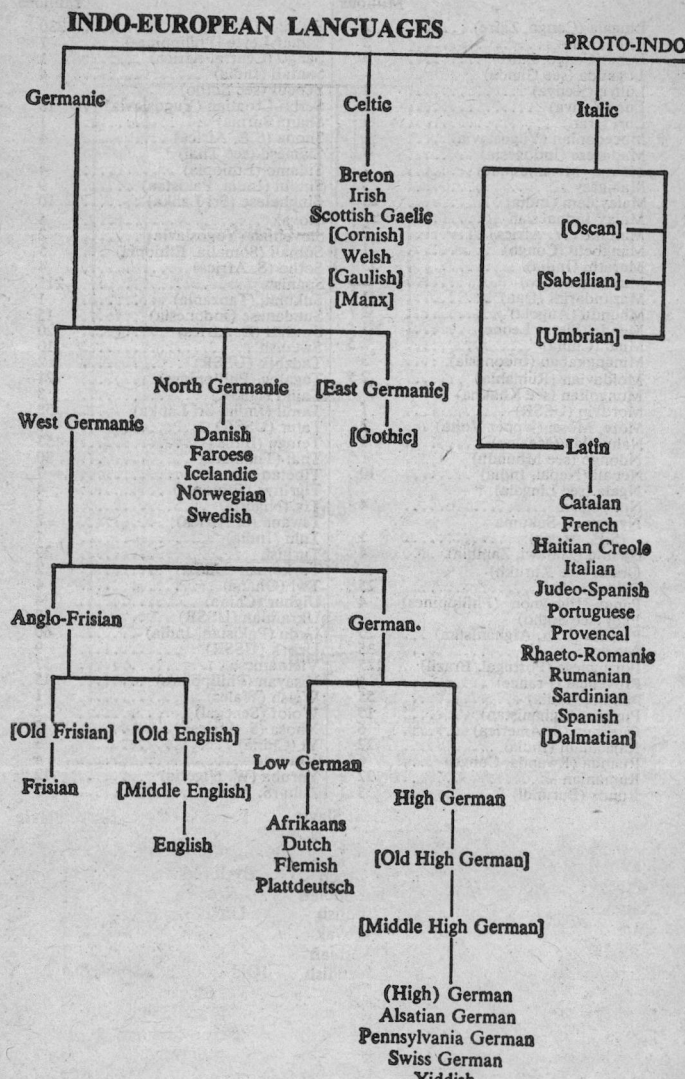

INDO-EUROPEAN LANGUAGES

PROTO-INDO-

Germanic

Celtic

Breton
Irish
Scottish Gaelic
[Cornish]
Welsh
[Gaulish]
[Manx]

Italic

[Oscan]

[Sabellian]

[Umbrian]

North Germanic **[East Germanic]**

Danish
Faroese
Icelandic
Norwegian
Swedish

[Gothic]

West Germanic

Latin

Catalan
French
Haitian Creole
Italian
Judeo-Spanish
Portuguese
Provencal
Rhaeto-Romanic
Rumanian
Sardinian
Spanish
[Dalmatian]

Anglo-Frisian

German

[Old Frisian] [Old English]

Frisian [Middle English]

English

Low German

Afrikaans
Dutch
Flemish
Plattdeutsch

High German

[Old High German]

[Middle High German]

(High) German
Alsatian German
Pennsylvania German
Swiss German
Yiddish

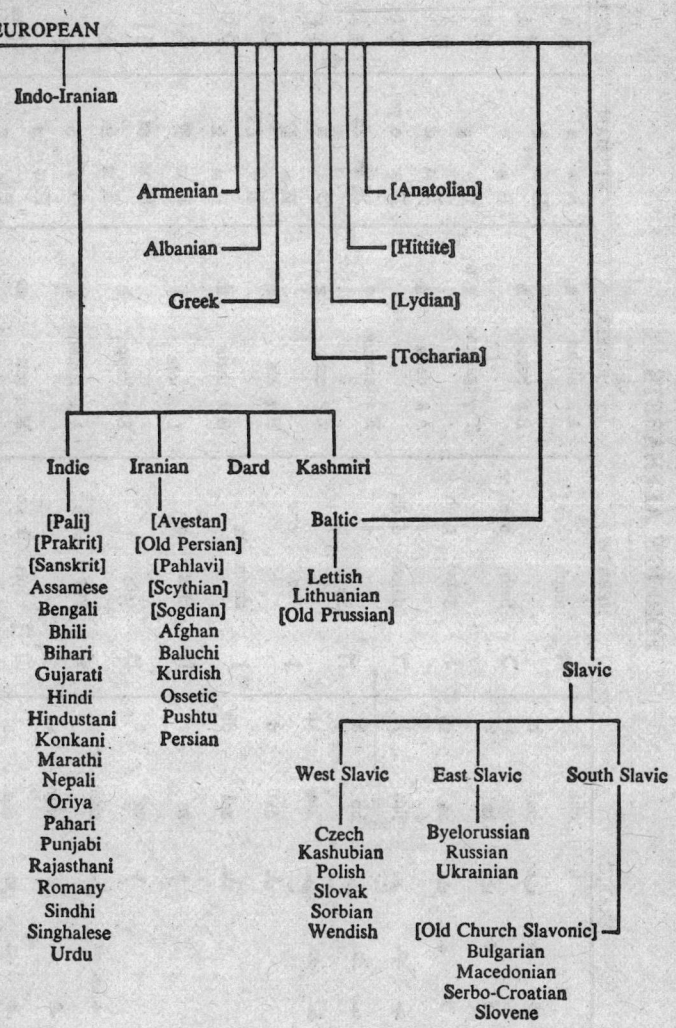

EUROPEAN

- Indo-Iranian

Armenian

Albanian

Greek

[Anatolian]

[Hittite]

[Lydian]

[Tocharian]

Indic	Iranian	Dard	Kashmiri

Baltic

[Pali]
[Prakrit]
[Sanskrit]
Assamese
Bengali
Bhili
Bihari
Gujarati
Hindi
Hindustani
Konkani
Marathi
Nepali
Oriya
Pahari
Punjabi
Rajasthani
Romany
Sindhi
Singhalese
Urdu

[Avestan]
[Old Persian]
[Pahlavi]
[Scythian]
[Sogdian]
Afghan
Baluchi
Kurdish
Ossetic
Pushtu
Persian

Lettish
Lithuanian
[Old Prussian]

Slavic

West Slavic	East Slavic	South Slavic

Czech
Kashubian
Polish
Slovak
Sorbian
Wendish

Byelorussian
Russian
Ukrainian

[Old Church Slavonic]
Bulgarian
Macedonian
Serbo-Croatian
Slovene

Brackets indicate dead languages.

FOREIGN ALPHABETS

ARABIC						HEBREW			GREEK			RUSSIAN		GERMAN	
ا	alif	؎	؍	‎ا	aleph	א	– or '	Α α	alpha	a	А а	a	Ua a	a
ب	ba	b	؎	؎	‎	beth	ב	b, bh, v	Β β	beta	b	Б б	b	Bb b	b
ت	ta	t	؏	؏	‎	gimel	ג	g, gh	Γ γ	gamma	g, n	В в	v	—	ae
ث	sa	th	؏	؏	‎	daleth	ד	d, dh	Δ δ	delta	d	Г г	g	Bb b	b
ج	jim	j	؎	؎	‎	he	ה	h	Ε ε	epsilon	e	Д д	d	Cc c	c
ح	ha	h	؎	؎	‎	vav	ו	v, w	Ζ ζ	zeta	z	Е е	e, ye	Dd d	d
خ	kha	kh	؎	؎	‎	zayin	ז	z	Η η	ēta	e, ē	Ж ж	zh	Ee e	e
د	dal	d	؎	؎	‎	cheth	ח	ḥ	Θ θ	theta	th	З з	z	Ff f	f
ذ	zal	dh	؎	؎	‎	ṭeth	ט	ṭ	Ι ι	iota	i	И и	i	Gg g	g
ر	ra	r	؎	؎	‎	yod	י	y, j, i	Κ κ	kappa	k	Й й	ĭ, ĭ	Hh h	h
ز	za	z	؎	؎	‎	kaph	כ ך	k, kh	Λ λ	lambda	l	К к	k	Ii i	i
س	sin	s	؎	؎	‎				Μ μ	mu	m	Л л	l	Jj j	j
ش	shin	sh	؎	؎	‎							М м	m	Kk k	k
ص	sad	s	؎	؎	‎							Н н	n	Ll l	l
												О о	o	Mm m	m
												П п	p		
												Р р	r		

А а	a	О о	o	Ѳ ѳ	oe

Greek			Transliteration
Ν ν nu			n
Ξ ξ xi			x
Ο ο omicron			o
Π π pi			p
Ρ ρ rho			r, rh
Σ σ ς sigma			s
Τ τ tau			t
Υ υ upsilon			y, u
Φ φ phi			ph
Χ χ chi			ch, kh
Ψ ψ psi			ps
Ω ω omega			o, ō

Russian		
С с		s
Т т		t
У у		u
Ф ф		f
Х х		kh
Ц ц		ts
Ч ч		ch
Ш ш		sh
Щ щ		shch
Ъ ъ		"
Ы ы		i, y
Ь ь		'
Э э		e
Ю ю		yu, ju
Я я		ya, ja

Hebrew			
ל	lamed		l
מ ם	mem		m
נ ן	nun		n
ס	samekh		s
ע	ayin		'
פ	pe		p, ph
צ ץ	sadi		s
ק	koph		k, q
ר	resh		r
ש	shin		sh
ש	sin		s
ת	tav		t, th

Arabic			
dad			d
ta			t
za			z
ain			'
ghain			gh
fa			f
qaf			q
kaf			k
lam			l
mim			m
nun			n
ha			h
waw			w
ya			y

The four forms of Arabic letters; when standing alone; when joined to the following letter; when joined to the preceding and the following letter; when joined to the preceding letter.

PROOFREADER'S MARKS

⊙	Insert period	*Caps.*	Caps—used in margin
⌃	Insert comma	≡	Caps—used in text
:	Insert colon	C+SC	Caps & small caps—used in margin
;	Insert semicolon	≡	Caps & small caps—used in text
?	Insert question mark	*l.c.*	Lowercase—used in margin
!	Insert exclamation mark	/	Used in text to show deletion or substitution
=/	Insert hyphen	*w.f.*	Wrong font
⌄	Insert apostrophe	⌒	Close up
⌄⌄	Insert quotation marks	⌐	Delete
⊥	Insert 1-en dash	⌐	Close up and delete
⊥	Insert 1-em dash	⊙	Correct the position
#	Insert space	⊐	Move right
ld⟩	Insert lead	⊏	Move left
shill	Insert virgule	⊓	Move up
∨	Superior	⊔	Move down
∧	Inferior	‖	Align vertically
(/)	Parentheses	—	Align horizontally
[/]	Brackets	⊐⊏	Center horizontally
⊡	Indent 1 em	⊔⊓	Center vertically
⊡⊡	Indent 2 ems	⌄	Push down space
¶	Paragraph	⌒	Use ligature
no ¶	No paragraph	*eq.#*	Equalize space—used in margin
tr	Transpose—used in margin	∨∨∨	Equalize space—used in text
∩	Transpose—used in text	*stet*	Let it stand—used in margin
sp	Spell out	....	Let it stand—used in text
ital	Italic—used in margin	⊗	Dirty or broken letter
___	Italic—used in text	*run over*	Carry over to next line
b.f.	Boldface—used in margin	*run back*	Carry back to preceding line
～	Boldface—used in text	*out, see copy*	Something omitted—see copy
s.c.	Small caps—used in margin	?/?	Question to author to delete
≡	Small caps—used in text	∧	Caret—general indicator used to mark exact position of error in text
rom.	Roman type		

1064

TYPOGRAPHICAL ERRORS

It does not appear that the earliest printers had any method of correcting errors before the form was on the press. The learned ~~The learned~~ correctors of the first two centuries of printing were not proofreaders in our sense; they were rather what we should term office editors. Their labors were chiefly to see that the proof corresponded to the copy, but that the printed page was correct in its Latinity, ~~that the words were there,~~ and that the sense was right. They cared ~~but~~ little about orthography, bad letters, or purely printers' errors, and when the text seemed to them wrong they consulted fresh authorities or altered it on their own responsibility. Good proofs, in the modern sense, were ~~impossible~~ until professional readers were employed, men who had first a printer's education, and then spent many years in the correction of proof. The orthography of English, which for the past century has undergone little change, was very fluctuating until after the publication of Johnson's Dictionary, and capitals, which have been used with considerable regularity for the past 80 years, were previously used on the miss or hit plan. The approach to regularity, so far as we have, may be attributed to the growth of a class of professional proofreaders, and it is to them that we owe the correctness of modern printing. More errors have been found in the Bible than in any other one work. For many generations it was frequently the case that Bibles were brought out stealthily, from fear of governmental interference. They were frequently printed from imperfect texts, and were often modified to meet the views of those who published them. The story is related that a certain woman in Germany, ~~who was~~ the wife of a Printer, ~~and~~ had become disgusted with the continual assertions of the superiority of man over woman which she had heard, hurried into the composing room while her husband was at supper and altered a sentence in the Bible, which he was printing, so that it read Narr, instead of Herr, thus making the verse read "And he shall be thy fool" instead of "And he shall be thy lord." The word not was omitted by Barker, the king's printer in England in 1632, in printing the seventh commandment. He was fined £3,000 on this account.

(8/?)

WEIGHTS AND MEASURES

Listed are the units of weight and measurement most commonly used in the United States. Part 1 gives U.S. and metric equivalents. Part 2 gives the conversion values by which a measurement in one unit must be multiplied to obtain the correct measurement in another unit or units. (Example: You want to convert 10 miles to feet. The conversion factor is 5280. Then 10 miles = 10 × 5280 = 52,800 feet. Or again, you want to convert 32 ounces to pounds. The conversion factor is 0.0625. Then 32 ounces = 32 × 0.0625 = 2 pounds.)

The conversion can be from one system of measurement to another, as from inches to centimeters, or from one unit to another unit of the same system of measurement, as from inches to miles.

There are U.S. and metric units of length (linear, chain, mariner's); area; volume; weight (liquid and dry avoirdupois, apothecaries', troy); angular and circular measures; temperature; time; typography; force, power, and energy; and so on.

1. EQUIVALENTS

Units	U.S. Values	Metric Values
1 acre (A.)	43,560 sq. ft.	4047 sq. m.
	4840 sq. yds.	0.4047 ha.
	160 sq. rods	
	10 sq. chains (surveyor's)	
1 agate (typography)	¹⁄₁₄ in.	
1 are	119.6 sq. yds.	100 sq. m.
	0.0247 acre	1 sq. dcm.
1 bale	500 lbs.	
1 barrel (bbl.)		
liquid	31–42 gals.	
	4.14–5.61 cu. ft.	
alcohol	50 gals.	189 liters
petroleum	42 gals.	159 liters
	5.61 cu. ft.	0.159 cu. m.
dry salt	280 lbs.	127 kg.
dry cement	376 lbs.	171 kg.
1 board foot (fbm)	144 cu. ins.	
1 bolt (of cloth)	40 yds.	36.58 m.
1 bushel (bu.)	4 pecks	35.238 liters
struck measure:	2150.42 cu. ins.	
	32 qts.	
heaped measure:	15⅛ struck measures	45.04 liters
	2747.7 cu. ins.	
1 cable length	720 ft.	219.456 m.
	120 fathoms	
1 carat (metric)	3.086 gr.	200 mg.
	0.007 oz. (avdp.)	0.2 g.
Celsius (C)	212°F (boiling pt. of water)	100°C
	32°F (freezing pt.)	0°C
centare see square meter		
1 centigram (cg.)	0.15 gr.	10 mg.
	0.0004 oz. (avdp.)	0.01 g.

Unit:	U.S. Value:	Metric Value:
1 centiliter (cl.)	0.6 cu. in.	10 ml.
	0.338 fluid oz.	0.01 liter
	0.018 pt. (dry)	
1 centimeter (cm.)	0.39 in.	10 mm.
1 century	100 yrs.	
1 chain (ch.)		
Gunter's or surveyor's	100 links	20.1168 m.
	66 ft.	
	1/10 furlong	
engineer's	100 links	30.48 m.
	100 ft.	
1 circle (revolution)	360°	
	4 quadrants	
1 cord (firewood)	128 cu. ft.	3.6 cu. m.
1 cubic centimeter (cu. cm.)	0.0610 cu. in.	1000 cu. mm
	0.0003 gal.	
1 cubic decameter (cu. dcm.)	1307.9 cu. yds.	1000 cu. m.
1 cubic decimeter (cu. dm.)	61.023 cu. ins.	1000 cu. cm.
	0.035 cu. ft.	
1 cubic foot (cu. ft.)	1728 cu. ins.	28.3 cu. dm.
	7.481 gals. (liq.)	0.0283 cu. m.
	0.0370 cu. yd.	
seawater	64 lbs.	
fresh water	62.43 lbs. at 39.2°F	
ice	56 lbs.	
1 cubic hectometer (cu. hm.)	1,307,950.6 cu. yds.	1000 cu. dcm.
1 cubic inch (cu. in.)	4.43 fluid dr.	16.387 cu. cm.
	0.554 fluid oz.	0.016 liter
	0.00058 cu. ft.	
	0.000021 cu. yd.	
1 cubic meter (cu. m.)	264.2 gals.	1,000,000 cu. cm.
	35.3147 cu. ft.	1000 cu. dm.
	1.3079 cu. yds.	
1 cubic millimeter (cu. mm.)	0.00006 cu. in.	0.001 cu. cm.
1 cubic yard (cu. yd.)	46,656 cu. ins.	765.534 liters
	201.974 gals.	0.765 cu. m.
	27 cu. ft.	
1 cubit	18 ins.	45.72 cm.
1 cup (measuring)	16 tablespoons	236.6 ml.
	14.44 cu. ins.	
	8 fluid oz.	
	0.5 pt. (liq.)	
1 day	24 hrs.	
1 decagram (decg.)	0.35 oz. (avdp.)	10 g.
1 decaliter (dcl.)	18.16 pts. (dry)	10 liters
	2.6 gals.	
	1.14 pecks	
	0.284 bushel	
1 decameter (dem.)	393.7 ins.	10 m.
	32.81 ft.	
	10.93 yds.	
1 decastere (dcs.)	13.1 cu. yds.	
1 decigram (dg.)	1.5 gr.	10 cg.
	0.0035 oz. (avdp.)	0.1 g.
1 deciliter (dl.)	6.1 cu. ins.	100 ml.
	3.38 fluid oz.	10 cl.
	0.182 pt. (dry)	
	0.106 qt. (liq.)	
1 decimeter (dm.)	3.937 ins.	100 mm.
		10 cm.
1 decistere (ds.)	3.53 cu. ft.	
1 degree (°)	60 minutes (')	

dekagram *see* decagram
dekaliter *see* decaliter
dekameter *see* decameter
dekastere *see* decastère

Unit:	U.S. Value:	Metric Value:
1 dram (dr.)		
avoirdupois (dr. avdp.)	27.34 gr.	1.772 g.
	0.0625 oz.	
apothecaries' (dr. ap.)	60 gr.	3.887 g.
	3 scruples	
	0.14 oz. (avdp.)	
Fahrenheit (F)	212° (boiling pt. of water)	100°C
	32° (freezing pt.)	0°C
1 fathom (fm.)	72 ins.	1.83 m.
	8 spans	
	6 ft.	
1 fluid dram (fl. dr.)	60 minims	3.7 ml.
	0.23 cu. in.	3.7 cu. cm.
	0.125 fluid oz.	
1 fluid ounce (fl. oz.)	8 fluid dr.	29.57 ml.
	6 teaspoons	29.57 cu. cm.
	2 tablespoons	
	1.8 cu. ins.	
	1/16 pt. (liq.)	
1 foot (ft.)	12 ins.	30.48 cm.
	0.333 yd.	0.3048 m.
1 furlong (fur.)	660 ft.	201.2 m.
	220 yds.	
	40 rods	
	10 chains (surveyor's)	
	1/8 statute mi.	
1 gallon (gal.)	231 cu. ins.	3.785 cu. cm.
	128 fluid oz.	3.785 liters
	16 cups	0.0003785 cu. m.
	8 pts.	
	4 qts.	
1 gill (gi.)	7.22 cu. ins.	118.3 ml.
	4 fluid oz.	0.118 liter
1 grain (gr.)		
avoirdupois	0.036 dr.	65 mg.
	0.0023 oz.	0.065 g.
troy	0.042 dwt.	0.065 g.
apothecaries'	0.05 scruple	65 mg.
	0.0021 oz.	0.065 g.
1 gram (g.)	15.43 gr.	1000 mg.
	0.035 oz.	100 cg.
	(avdp.)	10 dg.
1 great gross	12 gross (1728)	
1 gross	144 items	
	12 dozen	
1 hand	4 ins.	10.16 cm.
1 hectare (ha.)	2.47 acres	10,000 sq. m.
		100 ares
1 hectogram (hg.)	3.5 oz. (avdp.)	100 g.
		10 dcg.
1 hectoliter (hl.)	26.42 gals.	100 liters
	3.53 cu. ft.	10 dcl.
	2.84 bushels (dry)	
1 hectometer (hm.)	328.08 ft.	100 m.
	109.36 yds.	10 dcm.
1 hogshead	14,553 cu. ins.	
	2 bbls.	
1 hour (hr.)	60 mins.	
	0.0417 day	
1 hundredweight (cwt.)		
long	112 lbs. (avdp.)	50.80 kg.
	0.05 long ton	
short	100 lbs. (avdp.)	45.36 kg.
	0.05 short ton	
1 inch (in.)	0.083 ft.	25.40 mm.
	0.027 yd.	2.540 cm.
1 kilogram (kg.)	35.3 oz. (avdp.)	1000 g.
	32.1 oz. (troy)	10 hg.

Unit:	U.S. Value:	Metric Value:
	2.9 lbs. (troy)	
	2.2 lbs. (avdp.)	
1 kiloliter (kl.)	264.18 gals.	1000 liters
	35.3 cu. ft.	10 hl.
1 kilometer (km.)	3280.8 ft.	1000 m.
	1093.6 yds.	100 dcm.
	0.621 mi. (stat.)	10 hm.
	0.540 mi. (Brit. naut.)	
1 kilowatt (kw.)	1.341 hp.	
1 league		
land	3 mi. (stat.)	4.827 km.
nautical	3.452 mi. (stat.)	5.556 km.
	3 mi. (Brit. naut.)	
1 light-year	5,880,000,000,000 mi.	
1 link (li.)		
Gunter's or surveyor's	7.92 ins.	0.2012 m.
engineer's	1 ft.	0.3048 m.
1 liter (l.)		
liquid	33.81 fl. oz.	1000 ml.
	2.113 pts.	100 cl.
	1.057 qts.	10 dl.
	0.264 gal.	
dry	61.02 cu. ins.	1000 cu. cm.
	0.908 qt.	
1 meter (m.)	39.37 ins.	1000 mm.
	3.2808 ft.	100 cm.
	1.0936 yds.	10 dm.
	0.547 fathom	
	0.0006215 mil. (stat.)	
	0.0005396 mi. (Brit. naut.)	
1 microgram (μg.)	0.000015 gr.	0.000001 g.
1 micron (μ)	0.00004 in.	1000 nm.
		0.001 mm.
1 microsecond	0.000001 sec.	
1 mil	0.001 in.	0.0254 mm.
1 mile (mi.)		
statute (stat.)	5280 ft.	1609 m.
	1760 yds.	1.609 km.
	320 rods	
	80 chains	
	8 furlongs	
	0.8684 mi. (Brit. naut.)	
nautical (Brit. naut.)	6080 ft.	1852 m.
	2026.67 yds.	1.852 km.
	1.151 mi. (stat.)	
1 millennium	1000 yrs.	
1 milligram (mg.)	0.015 gr.	1000 μg.
		0.001 g.
1 milliliter (ml.)		
liquid	16.23 min.	
	0.27 fl. dr.	
dry	0.06 cu. in.	
	0.002 pt.	
1 millimeter (mm.)	0.04 in.	1000 μ
millimicron *see* nanometer		
1 minim (min.)		
liquid	0.0167 fluid dr.	0.062 ml.
	0.0038 cu. in.	
	0.0021 fluid oz.	
1 minute (')	60 seconds ('')	
1 month	28–31 solar days	
1 nanometer (nm.)	0.00000004 in.	0.001 μ
1 ounce (oz.)		
avoirdupois	437.5 gr.	28.349 g.
	16 dr.	
	0.9115 oz. (apoth. or troy)	
	0.0625 lb.	
apothecaries'	480 gr.	31.1 g.

Unit:	U.S. Value:	Metric Value:
	24 scruples	
	8 dr.	
	1.0971 oz. (avdp.)	
troy	480 gr.	31.1 g.
	20 dwt.	
1 parsec	3.26 light-years	
1 peck	537.6 cu. ins.	8809.7 cu. cm.
	16 pts. (dry)	8.81 liters
	8 qts. (dry)	
1 pennyweight (dwt.)		
troy	24 gr.	1.555 g.
	0.05 oz.	
1 pica	12 points	
1 pint (pt.)	⅙ in.	
liquid	128 fluid dr.	473.2 cu. cm.
	28.875 cu. ins.	0.473 liter
	16 fluid oz.	
	4 gills	
	2 cups	
dry	33.6 cu. ins.	0.550 liter
	0.5 qt.	
1 pipe	2 hogsheads	
1 point (typography)	½ pica	
	0.014 in.	
1 pound (lb.)		
avoirdupois	7000 gr.	453.6 g.
	256 dr.	0.4536 kg.
	16 oz. (avdp.)	
apothecaries'	5760 gr.	373.2 g.
	288 scruples	0.373 kg.
	96 dr.	
	13.17 oz. (avdp.)	
	12 oz. (troy)	
troy	5760 gr.	373.2 g.
	240 dwt.	0.373 kg.
	13.17 oz. (avdp.)	
	12 oz. (troy)	
	0.823 lb. (avdp.)	
	(avdp.)	
1 quadrant	90°	
	1 right angle	
1 quart (qt.)		
liquid	256 fluid dr.	0.946 liter
	57.75 cu. ins.	
	32 fluid oz.	
	4 cups	
	2 pts.	
dry	67.20 cu. ins.	1101 cu. cm.
		1.101 liters
1 quintal (q.)	220.46 lbs. (avdp.)	100,000 g.
		100 kg.
1 quire	25 sheets	
1 radian	57.296°	
1 ream	20 quires	
	500 sheets	
1 rod (rd.)	16.5 ft.	5.029 m.
	5.5 yds.	
1 scruple (apoth.)	20 gr.	1.30 g.
	0.33 dr.	
	0.0457 oz. (avdp.)	
section *see* square mile		
1 span	9 ins.	22.86 cm.
1 square (building)	100 sq. ft.	
1 square centimeter (sq. cm.)	0.16 sq. in.	100 sq. mm.
	0.0011 sq. ft.	
1 square chain (sq. ch.)	484 sq. yds.	404.7 sq. m.
	16 sq. rods	

Unit:	U.S. Value:	Metric Value:
1 square decameter (sq. dcm.)	119.6 sq. yds.	100 sq. m.
	0.025 acre	
1 square decimeter (sq. dm.)	15.5 sq. ins.	100 sq. cm.
	0.108 sq. ft.	
1 square foot (sq. ft.)	144 sq. ins.	929.03 sq. cm.
	0.111 sq. yd.	0.093 sq. m.
1 square hectometer (sq. hm.)	2.471 acres	100 sq. dcm.
1 square inch (sq. in.)	0.0069 sq. ft.	6.451 sq. cm.
	0.00077 sq. yd.	
1 square kilometer	247.1 acres	1,000,000 sq. m.
	0.3861 sq. mi. (stat.)	100 ha.
	0.2912 sq. mi. (Brit. naut.)	
1 square meter (sq. m.)	10.76 sq. ft.	1,000,000 sq. mm.
	1.1960 sq. yds.	10,000 sq. cm.
		100 sq. dm.
1 square mile (sq. mi.)	27,878,400 sq. ft.	258.89 ha.
	102,400 sq. rods	2.5889 sq. km.
	640 acres	
1 square millimeter (sq. mm.)	0.0016 sq. in.	
square pole *see* square rod		
1 square rod (sq. rd.)	625 sq. links	25.293 sq. m.
	272.25 sq. ft.	
	30.25 sq. yds.	
	0.00625 acre	
1 square yard (sq. yd.)	1296 sq. ins.	0.8361 sq. m.
	9 sq. ft.	
stere *see* cubic meter		
1 straight angle	180°	
	2 quadrants	
1 tablespoon	4 fluid dr.	14.79 ml.
	3 teaspoons	
	½ fluid oz.	
1 teaspoon	1⅓ fluid dr.	4.93 ml.
	⅓ tablespoon	
ton		
assay		29,167 mg.
		29.2 g.
freight or measurement	40 cu. ft.	
long or displacement	2240 lbs. (avdp.)	1.0160 metric tons
	20 long cwt.	
metric (mt.)	2204.6 lbs. (avdp.)	1000 kg.
		10 q.
	1.1023 short tons	
short or net	2000 lbs.	907,185 kg.
	20 short cwt.	0.9072 metric ton
1 township (tp.)	36 sq. mi.	93.2 sq. km.
1 week	7 days	
1 yard (yd.)	36 ins.	0.9144 m.
	3 ft.	
1 year		
common	365 solar days	
leap	366 solar days	

2. CONVERSIONS

Multiply:	By:	To Obtain:
acres	43,560	sq. ft.
	0.4047	hectares
	0.0015625	sq. mi.
ampere-hours	3600	coulombs
atmospheres	76.0	cm. of mercury
	33.90	ft. of water
	14.70	lbs./sq. in.

Multiply:	By:	To Obtain:
British thermal units	1054	joules
	777.5	ft.-lbs.
	252.0	gram calories
	0.0003927	horsepower-hrs.
	0.0002928	kilowatt-hrs.
B.T.U./hr.	0.2928	watts
B.T.U./min.	12.96	ft.-lbs./sec.
	0.02356	horsepower
bushels	3523.8	hectoliters
	2150.42	cu. ins.
	35.238	liters
°C + 17.78	1.8	°F
centimeters	0.3937	inches
cm-grams	980.1	cm.-dynes
chains	66	ft.
circumference	6.2832	radians
cubic centimeters	0.0610	cu. ins.
cu. feet	1728	cu. ins.
	62.43	lbs. of water
	7.481	gals. (liq.)
	0.0283	cu. m.
cu. ft./min.	62.43	lbs. water/min.
cu. ft./sec.	448.831	gals./min.
cu. inches	16.387	cu. cm.
	0.0005787	cu. ft.
cu. meters	264.2	gals. (liq.)
	35.3147	cu. ft.
	1.3079	cu. yds.
cu. yards	27	cu. ft.
	0.765	cu. m.
days	86,400	seconds
degrees/sec.	0.1667	revolutions/min.
°F — 32	0.5556	°C
faradays/sec.	96,500	amperes
feet	30.48	cm.
	0.3048	meters
	0.0001894	mi. (stat.)
	0.0001645	mi. (Brit. naut.)
ft. of water	62.43	lbs./sq. ft.
	0.4335	lbs./sq. in.
ft./min.	0.5080	cm./sec.
ft./sec.	0.6818	mi./hr.
	0.5921	knots
fluid ounces	29.573	milliliters
furlongs	660	feet
	0.125	mi.
gallons	231	cu. ins.
	8.345	lbs. of water
	8	pts.
	4	qts.
	3.785	liters
	0.003785	cu. m.
gals./min.	8.0208	cu. ft./hr.
grains	0.0648	grams
grams	980.1	dynes
	15.43	grains
	0.0353	oz. (avdp.)
	0.0022	lbs. (avdp.)
hectares	107,600	sq. ft.
	2.47	acres
hectoliters	2.838	bushels
horsepower	33,000	ft.-lbs./min.
	2545	B.T.U./hr.
	745.7	watts
	42.44	B.T.U./min.
	0.7457	kilowatts
inches	25.40	mm.

Multiply:	By:	To Obtain:
	2.540	cm.
	0.00001578	mi.
ins. of water	0.03613	lbs./sq. in.
kilograms	980,100	dynes
	2.2046	lbs. (avdp.)
kg. calories	3086	ft.-lbs.
	3.968	B.T.U.
kg. cal./min.	51.43	ft.-lbs./sec.
	0.06972	kilowatts
kilometers	3280.8	ft.
	0.621	mi.
km./hr.	0.621	mi./hr.
	0.5396	knots
kilowatts	737.6	ft.-lbs./sec.
	56.92	B.T.U./min.
	1.341	horsepower
kilowatt-hrs.	2,655,000	ft.-lbs.
	3415	B.T.U.
	1.341	horsepower-hrs.
knots	6080	ft./hr.
	1.151	stat. mi./hr.
	1	(Brit.) naut. mi./hr.
liters	61.02	cu. ins.
	2.113	pts. (liq.)
	1.057	qts. (liq.)
	0.264	gals. (liq.)
	1.816	pts. (dry)
	0.908	qts. (dry)
	0.1135	pecks
	0.0284	bushels
meters	39.37	inches
	3.2808	ft.
	1.0936	yds.
	0.0006215	mi. (stat.)
	0.0005396	mi. (Brit. naut.)
miles		
statute	5280	ft.
	1.609	km.
	0.8624	mi. (Brit. naut.)
nautical (Brit.)	6080	ft.
	1.151	mi. (stat.)
mi./hr.	1.467	ft./sec.
milligrams/liter	1	parts/million
milliliters	0.0338	fluid oz.
millimeters	0.03937	inches
ounces		
avoirdupois	28.349	grams
	0.9115	oz. (troy)
	0.0625	lbs. (avdp.)
troy	31.103	grams
	1.0971	oz. (avdp.)
pecks	8.8096	liters
pints		
liquid	473.2	cu. cm.
	28.875	cu. ins.
	0.473	liters
dry	0.550	liters
pounds		
avoirdupois	444,600	dynes
	453.6	grams
	32.17	poundals
	14.58	oz. (troy)
	1.21	lbs. (troy)
	0.4536	kg.
troy	0.373	kg.
lbs. (avdp.)/sq. in.	70.22	g./sq. cm.
	2.307	ft. of water

Multiply:	By:	To Obtain:
quarts		
liquid	57.75	cu. ins.
	32	fluid oz.
	2	pts.
	0.946	liters
dry	67.20	cu. ins.
	1.101	liters
quires	25	sheets
radians	3437.7	minutes
	57.296	degrees
reams	500	sheets
revolutions/min.	6	degrees/sec.
rods	16.5	ft.
	5.5	yds.
	5.029	meters
slugs	32.17	lbs. (mass)
square centimeters	0.155	sq. ins.
sq. feet	0.093	sq. m.
sq. inches	6.451	sq. cm.
sq. kilometers	247.1	acres
	0.3861	sq. mi.
sq. meters	10.76	sq. ft.
	1.1960	sq. yds.
sq. miles	27,878,400	sq. ft.
	640	acres
	2.5889	sq. km.
sq. yards	0.8361	sq. m.
tons		
long	2240	lbs. (avdp.)
	1.12	short tons
	1.0160	metric tons
metric	2204.6	lbs. (avdp.)
	1000	kg.
	1.1023	short tons
	0.9842	long tons
short	2000	lbs. (avdp.)
	0.9072	metric tons
	0.8929	long tons
watts	3.415	B.T.U./hr.
	0.001341	horsepower
yards	36	inches
	3	ft.
	0.9144	meters
	0.0005682	mi. (stat.)
	0.0004934	mi. (Brit. naut.)

ROMAN NUMERALS

Arabic	Roman	Arabic	Roman	Arabic	Roman
1	I	18	XVIII	900	CM
2	II	19	XIX	1,000	M
3	III	20	XX	1,111	MCXI
4	IV	29	XXIX	1,776	MDCCLXXVI
5	V	40	XL	1,977	MCMLXXVII
6	VI	41	XLI	2,000	MM
7	VII	49	XLIX, IL	3,000	MMM
8	VIII	50	L	4,000	$M\overline{V}$
9	IX	60	LX	5,000	$\overline{V}$
10	X	90	XC	6,000	$\overline{V}M$
11	XI	99	XCIX, IC	10,000	$\overline{X}$
12	XII	100	C	20,000	$\overline{XX}$
13	XIII	111	CXI	100,000	$\overline{C}$
14	XIV	200	CC	500,000	$\overline{D}$
15	XV	400	CD	1,000,000	$\overline{M}$
16	XVI	500	D		
17	XVII	600	DC		

FORMS OF ADDRESS

Listed are the fifty most common forms of address that are used in correspondence with public officials, ecclesiastical officials, and other dignitaries.

The forms of address to be used on an envelope are given before the parallels in each entry. After the parallels appear the salutations to be used in the letter itself.

In correspondence with women, use *Madam* instead of *Sir.*

alderman Honorable... || Dear...:

ambassador (American) His Excellency the American Ambassador to...*or* The Honorable..., American Ambassador to...*or* The Honorable..., The Ambassador of the United States || Sir: *or* Your Excellency:

ambassador (foreign) His Excellency the Ambassador of...*or* His Excellency..., Ambassador of... || Sir: *or* Excellency:

archbishop (Catholic) The Most Reverend..., Archbishop of...*or* The Most Reverend Archbishop... || Most Reverend Sir: *or* Your Excellency: *or* Dear Archbishop...:

assemblyman The Honorable..., Member of Assembly (*or State Assembly*) *or* Assemblyman... || Sir: *or* My Dear Sir:

associate justice The Honorable..., Associate Justice of the...*or* Mr. Justice..., The Supreme Court || Sir: *or* Dear Mr. Justice:

attorney see **lawyer**

bishop (Methodist) The Reverend Bishop... || Reverend Sir:

bishop (Protestant Episcopal) The Right Reverend..., Bishop of... || Right Reverend and Dear Sir:

bishop (Roman Catholic) The Most Reverend... || Most Reverend Sir: *or* Dear Bishop...:

brother of a religious order Brother..., (*and the initials of his order*) || Dear Brother...:

cabinet officer The Honorable..., Secretary of... || Dear Sir: *or* Dear Mr. Secretary:

cardinal His Eminence...Cardinal... || Your Eminence:

chargé d'affaires...Esq., Chargé d'Affaires || Sir: *or* Dear Sir:

chief justice of the U.S. The Chief Justice, The Supreme Court || Sir: *or* Dear Mr. Chief Justice:

clergyman (Protestant) The Reverend ...*or* (*if a doctor of divinity*) Reverend Dr....*or* Reverend..., D.D. || Dear Sir: *or* Reverend Sir:

commissioner of a government bureau The Honorable..., Commissioner of the Bureau of... || Sir: *or* Dear Sir:

congressman Honorable..., House of Representatives || Sir: *or* Dear Sir:

consul of the U.S. Mr...., Esq., American Consul at... || Dear Sir:

county executive Honorable..., Office of the Executive || Dear Sir: *or* Dear County Executive:

dean (cathedral) The Very Reverend... *or* Dean... || Very Reverend Sir:

dean of a college or university Dean ..., School of...*or* Dr...., Dean of the School of...*or* Dr...., Dean of the School of... || Dear Sir: *or* Dear Dean...:

governor of a State The Honorable the Governor of...*or* The Honorable ..., Governor of... || Sir: *or* Dear Sir:

judge The Honorable..., Chief Judge of...(*or* United States District Judge, *etc.*) || Sir:

justice see **associate justice, chief justice, judge**

lawyer Mr...., Attorney at Law *or*..., Esq. || Dear Sir:

lieutenant governor of a State The Lieutenant Governor, State of...*or* The Honorable..., Lieutenant Governor of... || Sir: *or* Dear Sir:

mayor of a city The Mayor of the City of...*or* The Honorable..., Mayor of the City of... || Sir: *or* Dear Sir:

minister (diplomatic) The Honorable ..., American Minister *or* The Honorable..., Minister of... || Sir: *or* Dear Sir:

minister (religious) see **clergyman**

monsignor The Right Reverend Monsignor... || Right Reverend Sir: *or* Dear Monsignor...:

mother superior of a sisterhood Mother..., Superior, Convent of...

or The Reverend Mother Superior, Convent of..., *(initials of the order)* ‖ Reverend Mother: *or* Dear Reverend Mother:

officers of armed services Lieutenant General..., Commanding Officer, Army of the United States ‖ Sir: *or* Dear General...: *or* Dear Admiral...: *or* Dear Mr....

patriarch (Eastern Church) His Beatitude the Patriarch of...*or* His Beatitude the Lord..., Patriarch of... ‖ Most Reverend Lord: *or* Your Beatitude:

physician (or dentist) ..., M.D. (*or* D.D.S.) ‖ Dear Sir: *or* Dear Dr....:

pope His Holiness the Pope *or* His Holiness, Pope... ‖ Your Holiness: *or* Most Holy Father:

president of a college or university ..., LL.D. (*or* Litt.D., D.Sc., *etc.*), President of... *or* Dr...., President of...*or* President..., ... College ‖ Dear President:

president of a State senate The Honorable..., President of the State Senate of... ‖ Sir:

president of the Senate of the U.S. The Honorable..., The President of the Senate of the United States *or* The Honorable..., President of the Senate ‖ Sir:

President of the United States The President, The White House *or* The President of the United States, The White House ‖ Sir: *or* Mr. President: *or* The President:

President's wife Mrs...., The White House ‖ Dear Mrs....:

priest (Roman Catholic) The Reverend ..., *(and the initials of his order if needed)* ‖ Reverend Father: *or* Dear Father:

professor at a college or university Professor..., Department of...*or* ..., Ph.D., Professor of...*or* Dr. ..., Department of... ‖ Dear Sir: *or* Dear Professor...: *or* Dear Dr. ...:

rabbi Rabbi...*or* Reverend...*or* Reverend..., D.D. *or* Dr.... ‖ Reverend Sir: *or* Dear Sir: *or* Dear Rabbi...: *or* (*if he holds a doctor's degree*) Dear Dr....: *or* Rabbi...:

representative (U.S.) see **congressman**

secretary of executive department (U.S.) see **cabinet officer**

Secretary-General of the UN His Excellency..., Secretary-General of the United Nations ‖ Excellency: *or* Dear Mr. Secretary-General:

senator (U.S.) The Honorable..., United States Senate *or* Senator..., The United States Senate ‖ Sir: *or* Dear Sir:

sister of a religious order Sister..., *(and the initials of her order)* *or* The Reverend Sister... ‖ Dear Sister...: *or* Dear Sister:

Speaker of the House of Representatives The Honorable..., Speaker of the House of Representatives ‖ Sir: *or* Dear Sir:

State representative The Honorable..., The House of Representatives, The State Capitol ‖ Sir: *or* Dear Sir:

State senator The Honorable..., The State Senate *or* Senator..., The State Capitol ‖ Sir: *or* Dear Sir:

superior of a brotherhood Brother..., *(and the initials of his order)*, Superior ‖ Dear Brother...:

Supreme Court see **chief justice, associate justice**

United Nations representative (U.S. ambassador) The Honorable..., United States Representative to the United Nations ‖ Sir: *or* My Dear Mr....:

United Nations representative (foreign ambassador) His Excellency..., Representative of...to the United Nations ‖ Excellency: *or* Sir:

Vice-President of the U.S. The Honorable..., The Vice-President of the United States *or* The Vice-President, United States Senate ‖ Sir: *or* Mr. Vice-President:

PRONUNCIATION SYMBOLS

See full Pronunciation Key (page 33a) and Guide (page 14a).

/a/

hat /hat′/, plaid /plad′/

/ä/

fa·ther /fä*th*′ər/, calm /käm′/, hearth /härth′/, ser·geant /sär′jənt/

/a, ä/

ask /ask′, äsk′/, half /haf′, häf′/, com·mand /kəmand′, -mänd′/

/ā/

fate /fāt′/, aid /ād′/, say /sā′/, gaol /jāl′/, break /brāk′/, they /*th*ā′/

/b/

bed /bed′/, rob·ber /rob′ər/

/ch/

cheep /chēp′/, much /much′/, butch·er /booch′ər/, right·eous /rīch′əs/

/d/

day /dā′/, rud·der /rud′ər/

/e/

met /met′/, says /sez′/, feath·er /fe*th*′ər/, chair /cher′/, prayer /prer′/

/ē/

she /shē′/, re·ceive /risēv′/, peo·ple /pēp′əl/, quay /kē′/, foe·tus /fēt′əs/

/ē/

shin·y /shīn′ē/, du·te·ous /d(y)oot′ē-əs/, lib·er·ty /lib′ərtē/

/ə/

or·phan /ôrf′ən/, cu·ri·ous /kyoor′ē-əs/, per·ceive /pərsēv′/

/f/

face /fās′/, muf·fin /muf′in/, phone /fōn′/, tough /tuf′/

/g/

go /gō′/, give /giv′/, ag·grieve /əgrēv′/, ex·act /igzakt′/

/h/

home /hōm′/, al·co·hol /al′kəhôl′/, who /hoo′/

/i/

fit /fit′/, se·ri·al /sir′ē-əl/, been /bin′/, wom·en /wim′in/, hymn /him′/

/i/

rag·ged /rag′id/, serv·ice /surv′is/, re·ceive /risēv′/

/ī/

time /tīm′/, night /nīt′/, tie /tī′/, aisle /īl′/, height /hīt′/, eye /ī′/

/j/

gem /jem′/, jeal·ous /jel′əs/, ver·dure /vur′jər/, ad·join /əjoin′/

/k/

come /kum′/, back /bak′/, chord /kôrd′/, ac·quit /əkwit′/

/l/

late /lāt′/, al·low /əlou′/

/m/

man /man′/, sum·mer /sum′ər/

/n/

not /not′/, man·ner /man′ər/, know /nō′/

/ŋ/

king /kiŋ′/, con·quer /koŋk′ər/, anx·i·e·ty /aŋzī′itē/

/o/

hob·by /hob′ē/, prop·er /prop′ər/, watch /woch′/

/ô/

north /nôrth′/, bought /bôt′/, warm /wôrm′/, salt /sôlt′/, saw /sô′/

/o/ or /ô/

bor·row /bor′ō, bôr′ō/, sor·ry /sor′ē, sôr′ē/, gone /gôn′, gon′/

/ō/

nose /nōz′/, owe /ō′/, sew /sō′/, though /*th*ō′/, brooch /brōch′/

PRONUNCIATION SYMBOLS *Continued*

See full Pronunciation Key (page 33a) and Guide (page 14a).

/ô/ or /ō/

pork /pôrk′, pōrk′/, coarse /kôrs′, kōrs′/, door /dôr′, dōr′/

/ô/ or /ä/

gaunt /gônt′, gänt′/, saun·ter /sônt′ər, sänt′-/, vaunt /vônt′, vänt′/

/oi/

voice /vois′/, boy /boi′/, oys·ter /oist′ər/

/o͝o/

wolf /wo͝olf′/, good /go͝od′/, should /sho͝od′/, bush /bo͝osh′/, pull /po͝ol′/

/ōō/

move /mōōv′/, tomb /tōōm′/, fruit /frōōt′/, drew /drōō′/

/ou/

bough /bou′/, sound /sound′/, cow /kou′/

/p/

pen /pen′/, sup·per /sup′ər/, stop /stop′/

/r/

rob /rob′/, art /ärt′/, car·ry /kar′ē/, rhyme /rīm′/, ca·tarrh /kətär′/

/s/

sell /sel′/, es·say /es′ā/, hiss /his′/, cent /sent′/, fa·çade /fəsäd′/

/sh/

shoe /shōō′/, o·cean /ōsh′ən/, vi·cious /vish′əs/, na·tion /nāsh′ən/

/t/

ten /ten′/, bet·ter /bet′ər/, hat /hat′/

/th/

this·tle /this′əl/, e·ther /ēth′ər/, truth /trōōth′/

/th/

this /this′/, ei·ther /ēth′ər/, smooth /smōōth′/

/u/

cup /kup′/, love /luv′/, does /duz′/, jour·ney /jurn′ē/

/v/

vest /vest′/, riv·er /riv′ər/, of /uv′/, revved /revd′/

/w/

work /wurk′/, tweed /twēd′/, queen /kwēn′/, choir /kwī′(ə)r/

/y/

yes /yes′/, on·ion /un′yən/, feud /fyōōd′/, few /fyōō′/, ewe /yōō′/

/z/

zeal /zēl′/, bus·y /biz′ē/, his /hiz′/, these /thēz′/

/zh/

az·ure /azh′ər/, gla·zier /glāzh′ər/, meas·ure /mezh′ər/, vi·sion /vizh′ən/

FOREIGN SOUNDS

/kh/

Scottish: loch /lokh′/; German: doch /dôkh′/, J. S. Bach /bäkh′/

/kh/

German: ich /ikh′/, nichts /nikhts′/, Kö·chel list·ing /kœkh′əl/

/œ/

French: feu /fœ′/, peu /pœ′/; German: schön /shœn′/, Goe·the /gœt′ə/

/Y/

French: tu /tY′/, dé·jà vu /däzhä vY′/; German: Walküre /välkY′rə/

/N/

This symbol is not a sound but indicates that the preceding symbol is a nasal. See page 35a.